THE OXFORD COMPANION TO CANADIAN LITERATURE

SECOND EDITION

GENERAL EDITORS

EUGENE BENSON & WILLIAM TOYE

TORONTO OXFORD NEW YORK

OXFORD UNIVERSITY PRESS

1997

Oxford University Press Canada
70 Wynford Drive, Don Mills, Ontario M3C 1J9
http://www.oupcan.com

Oxford New York
Athens Auckland Bangkok Calcutta
Cape Town Chennai Dar es Salaam Delhi
Florence Hong Kong Istanbul Karachi
Kuala Lumpur Madrid Melbourne Mexico City
Mumbai Nairobi Paris Singapore
Tapei Tokyo Toronto Warsaw

and associated companies in
Berlin Ibadan

Canadian Cataloguing in Publication Data

Main entry under title:

The Oxford companion to Canadian literature

2nd ed.
ISBN 0-19-541167-6

1. Canadian literature – Dictionaries. 2. Canadian literature – Bio-bibliography. I. Benson, Eugene, 1928- . II. Toye, William, 1926- .

PS8015.093 1997 C810'.3 C97-931369-4
PR9180.2.084 1997

Design: Brett Miller
Composition: IBEX Graphic Communications Inc.

1 2 3 4 – 00 99 98 97

This book is printed on permanent (acid-free) paper ∞.

Printed in Canada

Preface

Reviewing the First Edition of *The Oxford Companion to Canadian Literature* (1983), the late Robertson Davies wrote: 'It deserves something far beyond a library circulation. Buy it. Read it. Think about it.' The first of his injunctions was certainly heeded, because there are now over 14,000 copies in print.

In his Introduction to that volume, the general editor, William Toye, referred to the 'explosion of creative writing' in both English and French Canada that began in the late 1950s. This Second Edition was prepared in response to the continued extraordinary growth and diversification of Canadian literature. The First Edition contained 770 entries written by 193 contributors; the Second Edition adds 342 entries on new subjects, and there are 132 new contributors. In addition, virtually all the original entries have been modified or updated; most of the survey entries have long additions, some of them by new contributors.

Sadly, a number of contributors to the First Edition have died: Lovat Dickson, Edith Fowke, Ralph Gustafson, John Margeson, F. Hilton Page, Charles R. Steele, George Wicken, and George Woodcock. We have silently amended their entries where additions were slight; where substantial updating was called for, a second name has been credited.

The basic content and general characteristics of the First Edition, as described by William Toye in his Introduction, have been maintained, and the intention is the same—to provide a reference work for both the ordinary reader and the specialist. Also, the proportion of entries on Québécois and Acadian literatures and authors is similar. But the scope has been broadened by the many new entries, including author entries on historians, philosophers, and writers of SF, crime fiction, and children's books. We have allowed for extensive treatment of genre surveys: those on NOVELS IN ENGLISH and DRAMA IN FRENCH, for example, run to 31,000 and 17,000 words respectively; and the entry on CRITICISM IN ENGLISH is over 19,000 words. There are, of course, new entries on a selection of major titles; some of those on plays have been adapted from material in *The Oxford Companion to Canadian Theatre* (1989), which should be considered a complement to this *Companion*. As for the new subject entries, we wish to draw attention to the following:

AWARDS
CARIBBEAN-CANADIAN LITERATURE
CENSORSHIP
FANTASTIC LITERATURE AND SCIENCE FICTION IN FRENCH
FANTASTIC LITERATURE IN ENGLISH

GAY LITERATURE
ITALIAN-CANADIAN LITERATURE
LANGUAGE (English)
LANGUAGE (French)
LESBIAN LITERATURE
MULTICULTURAL WRITING IN FRENCH
SOUTHEAST ASIAN-CANADIAN LITERATURE
SOUTHERN ONTARIO GOTHIC
SPORTSWRITING IN ENGLISH

We are aware that criticism of this very comprehensive work may be directed at what it omits along with what it contains. But it is well to remember that, like the other titles in this venerable series of Oxford reference books, this volume is intended as a useful and interesting *companion* for readers of the literature, and is not in any way canonical in its approach.

One should keep in mind that names, subjects, and book titles that appear in SMALL CAPITALS have entries of their own. Cross-references are mostly to authors whose work receives more than passing comment in genre or subject entries or in regional surveys (NEWFOUNDLAND, The MARITIMES, QUEBEC [in English], ONTARIO, The PRAIRIES, and BRITISH COLUMBIA).

We are grateful for the assistance of an Advisory Board: Diana Brydon, University of Guelph; Gwendolyn Davies, Acadia University; Carole Gerson, Simon Fraser University; and Ben-Z. Shek, University of Toronto. Their advice in a number of key areas was appreciated. In his field of Québécois literature, Professor Shek's support was constant.

But of course our primary debt is to the great many writers of entries. Our contributors expended far more time in research and writing than their condensed entries, or updating of entries, might suggest. For this we are most grateful. We take pleasure in recalling the co-operation and helpfulness of our Québécois contributors. Our warmest thanks go out to all these scholars, who together produced the text for this *Companion*.

We owe much to Sally Livingston, who proofread with her usual meticulousness, while suggesting some textual improvements that were gratefully carried in. She also translated a number of entries, as did Professor Renate Benson. We thank them both, and express our appreciation to the Canada Council for providing a grant to help defray translation costs.

Others to whom we are indebted, for advice and help, include Russell Brown, Marie J. Carrière, John Robert Colombo, Terry Crowley, Tara L. Curtis, Graeme Gibson, Sherrill E. Grace, Annika Hannan, Mary Henley Rubio, Paul Hjartarson, François Lachance, Jean Levasseur, Michel Lord, Cynthia Messenger, Bruce Meyer, Penny Petrone, and David Staines.

We are grateful to many people and organizations that provided information and statistics: Penny Dickens, Executive Director, the Writers' Union of Canada; Jean Dickson, Awards Committee, Stephen Leacock Associates; R.J. Elmslie, Director, Computing and Communications Services, University of Guelph, and his staff; Nancy Fleming, Executive Director, the Book and Periodical Council of Canada; Bob Hilderley, Quarry Press; Nancy Kroeker, Executive Director, the Writers' Development Trust; Katherine Berg, Senior Advisor to the Director, and Danielle Philbert, Communications Section, the Canada Council; the Playwrights' Union of Canada; and Gord Ripley, Reference Press. Michael Ridley, Chief Librarian, University of Guelph, and his staff, and the reference staff of the Robarts Library, University of Toronto, answered numerous enquiries about titles, publication years, and authors with patience and professional expertise.

Sandra Brown, of Oxford University Press Canada, performed with skill the task of inputting entries. Jan Walker also contributed to the typing. We thank them both. We also acknowledge with gratitude a grant from the Office of the Vice President Research, Dr L.P. Milligan, University of Guelph.

Finally, at Oxford University Press Canada we wish to thank Anne Erickson, Director, Trade, Medical and Professional Division, for her blessing, and Phyllis Wilson, Managing Editor, who was always a helpful presence behind the editorial scene.

September 1997 EUGENE BENSON, WILLIAM TOYE

Advisory Board

Contributors

Maroussia Ahmed
McMaster University

Jacques Allard
Université du Quebéc à Montréal

Anne-Marie Alonzo
Université de Montréal

Geraldine Anthony

Leslie Armour
University of Ottawa

Ivor Arnold
University of Western Ontario

Stan Atherton
St Thomas University

Mary Elizabeth Aubé
York University

Irene Aubrey
National Library of Canada

John Ayre

Janet Baker
St Mary's University

Jars Balan

Douglas Barbour
University of Alberta

Caroline Bayard
McMaster University

Hélène Beauchamp
Université du Québec à Montréal

Francesca Benedict
CÉGEP de l'Abitibi-Témiscamingue

Donna Bennett
University of Toronto

Eugene Benson
University of Guelph

Katherine Berg
The Canada Council

Raymond Bertin

Diane Bessai
University of Alberta

Joseph Bonenfant
Université de Sherbrooke

Laurel Boone
Goose Lane Editions

Raoul Boudreau
Université de Moncton

Nicole Bourbonnais
Université d'Ottawa

Colin Boyd
University of Ottawa

Russell Brown
University of Toronto

Diana Brydon
University of Guelph

Roberta Buchanan
Memorial University of Newfoundland

Peter Buitenhuis
Simon Fraser University

J. M. Bumsted
University of Manitoba

William Butt
University of Western Ontario

Lorraine Camerlain
Jeu

Elspeth Cameron
University of Toronto

Marie J. Carrière

Robert Cockburn
University of New Brunswick

Andrew Cohen
The Globe and Mail

Joan Coldwell
McMaster University

Don Coles
York University

Paulette Collet
University of Toronto

John Robert Colombo

Odette Condemine
Carleton University

L. W. Conolly
Trent University

Rebecca Conolly

Nathalie Cooke
McGill University

Dennis Cooley
University of Manitoba

Jacques Cotnam
York University

Terrence Craig
Mount Allison University

Terry Crowley
University of Guelph

Burke Cullen
University of Toronto

Tara L. Curtis

Steven J. Daniell
Auburn University at Montgomery, Alabama

Frank Davey
University of Western Ontario

Gwendolyn Davies
Acadia University

Marie C. Davis
University of Winnipeg

Bernard Delpêche
University of Toronto

Patricia Demers
University of Alberta

Lawrence Dewan
Dominican College of Philosophy and Theology

Peter Dickinson
University of British Columbia

Lovat Dickson
Madeleine Dirschauer

Sandra Djwa
Simon Fraser University

Kathleen Donohue

Joyce Doolittle
University of Calgary

Max Dorsinville
McGill University

L. E. Doucette
University of Toronto

James Doyle
Wilfrid Laurier University

Dennis Duffy
University of Toronto

François Dumont
Université Laval

Klay Dyer

Leon Edel

Mary Jane Edwards
Carleton University

Sheila Egoff
University of British Columbia

Sarah Ellis

Susan Elmslie

Howard Engel

Margery Fee
University of British Columbia

Douglas Fetherling

Claude Filteau
Université de Sherbrooke

Sheila Fischman

David Flint

Louise Forsyth
University of Saskatchewan

Edith Fowke

Marian Fowler

Wynne Francis
Concordia University

Janet Friskney
Carleton University

Robert Fulford

Michelle Gadpaille

George Galt

Keith Garebian

Lise Gauvin
Université de Montréal

Gary Geddes
Concordia University

Carole Gerson
Simon Fraser University

Robert Gibbs
University of New Brunswick

Richard Giguère
Université de Sherbrooke

Susan Gingell
University of Saskatchewan

Barbara Godard
York University

Patricia Godbout
Université de Sherbrooke

Jean Cléo Godin
Université de Montréal

Noreen Golfman
Memorial University of Newfoundland

John Webster Grant
University of Toronto

Judith Skelton Grant

Michael Greenstein

Armand Guilmette
Université du Québec à Trois-Rivières

Bernadette Guilmette
Université du Québec à Trois-Rivières

Ginette Guindon
Bibliothèque de Montréal

Ralph Gustafson

Stefan Haag
Simon Fraser University

Francess G. Halpenny
University of Toronto

Kathryn Hamer
Mount Allison University

Geoff Hancock

Annika Hannan

Dick Harrison
University of Alberta

Jocelyn Harvey
The Canada Council

Ramon Hathorn
University of Guelph

David M. Hayne
University of Toronto

Annette Hayward
Queen's University

Jeffrey Heath
University of Toronto

Pierre Hébert
Université de Sherbrooke

Ajay Heble
University of Guelph

Jennifer Henderson

Allan Hepburn
University of Toronto

Rota Herzberg Lister

Paul Hjartarson
University of Alberta

Susan Holbrook

Anthony Hopkins
York University

Elizabeth Hopkins
York University

Marta Horban-Carynnyk

Chaviva Hošek

Shawn Huffman
Université du Québec à Montréal

Renée Hulan

William Humber
Seneca College

Michael Hurley
Royal Military College of Canada

Patrick Imbert
Université d'Ottawa

Christopher Innes
York University

Patricia Irwin

David Jackel

Susan Jackel
University of Alberta

JoAnne James
Calgary International Children's Festival

Kim Jernigan
University of Waterloo

Karl Jirgens
Algoma University College

Chris Johnson
University of Manitoba

Chelva Kanaganayakam
University of Toronto

J. Kieran Kealy
University of British Columbia

L. W. Keffer
Bishop's University

W. J. Keith
University of Toronto

Reinhold Kramer
University of Brandon

Joy Kuropatwa

Eva Kushner
University of Toronto

Yvan Lamonde
McGill University

M. Travis Lane
University of New Brunswick

Louis Lasnier
CÉGEP de Saint-Laurent

David Latham
York University

Laurent Lavoie
University College of Cape Breton

David Leahy
Concordia University

Maurice Lebel
Université Laval

Barbara Leckie
Carleton University

Alexander Leggatt
University of Toronto

Pierre H. Lemieux
Université d'Ottawa

John Lennox
York University

Lucie Lequin
Concordia University

Jean Levasseur
Bishop's University

Douglas Lochhead
Mount Allison University

Grant Loewen

Michel Lord
University of Toronto

Robert Lovejoy
Carleton University

Alec Lucas
McGill University

Mary Lu MacDonald

Barbara McEwen
Brock University

S. R. MacGillivray
Lakehead University

Robin Gedalof McGrath

Louis K. MacKendrick
University of Windsor

Ken MacKinnon
St Mary's University

Carrie MacMillan
Mount Allison University

Lorraine McMullen
University of Ottawa

Jay Macpherson
University of Toronto

Laurent Mailhot
Université de Montréal

Marguerite Maillet
Université de Moncton

John Margeson

Joyce Marshall

Robert K. Martin
Université de Montréal

Kerry Mason
Provincial Archives of British Columbia

C.R.P. May

Cynthia Messenger
University of Toronto

Bruce Meyer
University of Toronto

Hugo A. Meynell
University of Calgary

Jacques Michon
Université de Sherbrooke

Marianne Micros
University of Guelph

Orm Mitchell
Trent University

Guy Monette
Royal Military College of Canada

Ian Montagnes

Goldie Morgentaler

Lianne Moyes
Université de Montréal

Laura J. Murray
University of Toronto

Elaine Nardocchio
McMaster University

Elaine Kalman Naves

Pierre Nepveu
Université de Montréal

Graeme Nicholson
University of Toronto

Gerald Noonan
Wilfrid Laurier University

James Noonan
Carleton University

John North

Robert C. Nunn
Brock University

Stephanie Nutting
University of Guelph

Ed Nyman

John O'Connor
University of Toronto

Shane O'Dea
Memorial University of Newfoundland

Patrick O'Flaherty
Memorial University of Newfoundland

Jean O'Grady

Mariel O'Neill-Karch
University of Toronto

David O'Rourke
Centennial College of Applied Arts and Technology

F. Hilton Page

Donna Palmateer Pennee
University of Guelph

Ruth Panofsky

Jacques Paquin
Université du Québec à Trois-Rivières

George L. Parker
Royal Military College of Canada

Michel Parmentier
Bishop's University

Jacques Pelletier
Université du Québec à Montréal

Michael Peterman
Trent University

Penny Petrone
Lakehead University

Joseph Pivato
Athabasca University

Richard Plant
Queen's University

James Polk

Zailig Pollock
Trent University

Lisbie Rae
Brock University

Victor J. Ramraj
University of Calgary

Ann Rayner
University of British Columbia

Magdalene Redekop
University of Toronto

Keith Richardson

Pascal Riendeau
Université de Montréal

Gord Ripley
Reference Press

Yves Roberge
University of Toronto

Lucie Robert
Université du Québec à Montréal

Katherine Roberts
Queen's University

Ian Ross Robertson
University of Toronto

Linda Rogers

Constance Rooke
University of Guelph

Marilyn Rose
Brock University

Catherine Ross
University of Western Ontario

Malcolm Ross
Dalhousie University

Jennie Rubio

Mary Henley Rubio
University of Guelph

Ronald Rudin
Concordia University

Leila Ryan
McMaster University

Lori Saint-Martin
Université du Québec à Montréal

Annette Saint-Pierre

Judith Saltman
University of British Columbia

Heather Sanderson
University of British Columbia

Peter Sanger
Nova Scotia Agricultural College

Robert J. Sawyer

Stephen Scobie
University of Victoria

Howard Scott

Wendy Scott

Andrew Seaman
St Mary's University

Phyllis Senese
University of Victoria

Vincent Sharman
Nipissing University

Ben-Z. Shek
University of Toronto

Gillian Siddall
University of Guelph

Antanas Sileika
Humber College

A. I. Silver
University of Toronto

Sherry Simon
Concordia University

Antoine Sirois
Université de Sherbrooke

David Skene-Melvin

Patricia Smart
Carleton University

Cal Smiley
University of Toronto

Donald Smith
Carleton University

Shannon Smyrl

Paul Socken
University of Waterloo

Alexander Sokalski
University of Saskatchewan

Sam Solecki
University of Toronto

D. O. Spettigue
Queen's University

David Staines
University of Ottawa

Charles R. Steele

Donald Stephens
University of British Columbia

Peter Stevens
University of Windsor

Philip Stratford
Université de Montréal

J. R. (Tim) Struthers
University of Guelph

Rosemary Sullivan
University of Toronto

Fraser Sutherland

Wendy K. Sutton

Michael Tait
University of Toronto

Thomas E. Tausky
University of Western Ontario

M. Brook Taylor
Mount Saint Vincent University

Richard Teleky
York University

Jules Tessier
Université d'Ottawa

Donald F. Theall
Trent University

Sharon Thesen
Capilano College

Gerald Thomas
Memorial University of Newfoundland

Gillian Thomas
St Mary's University

Deborah Torkko

William Toye

Rhea Tregebov

Elizabeth Trott
Ryerson Polytechnic University

Claude Trottier

Claudette S. Trudeau

James H. Tully
McGill University

Marino Tuzi
Seneca College

Renate Usmiani
Mount Saint Vincent University

Pierre-Louis Vaillancourt
Université d'Ottawa

André Vanasse
Université du Québec à Montréal

Aritha van Herk
University of Calgary

Frederick Vaughan
University of Guelph

Maïr Verthuy
Concordia University

Tom Vincent
Royal Military College of Canada

Miriam Waddington

Anton Wagner

Robert S. Wallace
York University

Germaine Warkentin
University of Toronto

Jack Warwick
York University

Elizabeth Waterston
University of Guelph

Robert Weaver

Justine Whitehead

Bruce Whiteman
University of California, Los Angeles

Patricia Whitney
University of Prince Edward Island

George Wicken

Ann Wilson
University of Guelph

George Woodcock

Lorraine York
McMaster University

Alan R. Young
Acadia University

Sally Zerker
York University

Francis Zichy
University of Saskatchewan

Cynthia Zimmerman
York University

IN MEMORY OF

Robertson Davies

Margaret Laurence

Hugh MacLennan

Gabrielle Roy

Aboriginal legends and tales. Legends and tales are part of the oral traditions inherited by Canadian Native peoples from their forefathers and preserved through countless recitations. Because they are not a homogeneous people, because they speak a number of languages, practise many diverse customs, and hold many distinctive beliefs, their mythology is varied and vast.

From the beginning of the seventeenth century, when early missionaries first recorded a number of Huron and Algonkin tales in their *JESUIT RELATIONS*, Native stories have been gathered piecemeal by such interested laymen as traders, explorers, travellers, clergymen, and Native agents. Towards the end of the nineteenth century the 'doomed-culture theory'—the belief that the Native peoples would soon be extinct—prompted a more systematic effort to preserve their oral heritage. Expeditions of anthropologists, ethnologists, folklorists—and, much later, sociologists—went to live and work in specific regions among particular tribes. These trained specialists recorded the tales verbatim, transcribing them into literal translations, in simple English, with little or no attempt at literary style, in order to preserve their integrity. In many instances their publications offered the narratives in the original, with an interlinear literal English translation, thus adhering as closely as possible to the forms in which the tales were told. In their concern for scientific accuracy these specialists invariably commented on their methods of obtaining texts and translations, often even citing the names and backgrounds of their Native informants and their interpreters. Interpreting and evaluating their materials from the point of view of their academic disciplines, they produced numerous valuable scholarly studies. And, in an effort to systematize Aboriginal lore, they applied a European system of categories and classifications. To prove their pet hypotheses they exaggerated similarities to Scandinavian, Greek, and Hindu mythologies and found Jewish and Christian analogies; they also studied resemblances among the tales themselves. Though many modern scholars have deemed such comparative studies futile speculation, recurrent patterns and motifs do exist in aboriginal legends and tales and they transcend geographical and linguistic barriers: other-world journeys, heroic encounters with supernatural powers, animal wives and husbands, animal divinities, powerful magicians, guardian spirit quests; the ritual observance of animal corpses; belief in the significance of dreams, in the indwelling spirit of every created thing, inanimate and animate, in the coupling of all animate and inanimate things or beings (even colours and words), and in the magical power of numbers (4—Ojibwa; 5—Athabascans). Metamorphosis and anthropomorphism are essential and significant features. And plots may offer ancient tribal rituals (those of the shaking tent, sweat lodge, bear-walk, sun, rain and ghost dances, potlatch), purification and expiation ceremonies, as well as initiation, puberty, and mortuary rites. The vision quest—requiring fasting, prayer, deprivation, and ceremonial purity—holds a prominent place in Native legends and tales.

The culture hero or trickster-transformer figure, who brings about the origins of life as a series of transformations, is the central character in the majority of Canadian Native myths. Human or animal, he is known to the different tribes under various names. Raven, of the Pacific coast tribes, accounts for the existence of all things—the sun, moon, stars, fire, water, even the alternation of tides; for the Cree and Saulteaux, Wisakedjak (there are many phonetically similar versions of his name) is responsible for shaping the existing world; the Micmacs' Glooscap and the Ojibwa's Hare made the world ready for man; Nanabozho, son of the West Wind and great grandson of the Moon, gave the Ojibwa the necessities of life; and for the Plains people, Coyote or 'old man', who existed on earth before mankind, when humans and animals were not really distinct, is credited with putting the world in order.

At times the hero-trickster is presented in antithetical roles: as an actual creator or as a helper who might either co-operate with or thwart the creator; as a beneficent culture hero and helper of mankind or a malevolent being; as an all-wise, powerful shaman or a credulous fool; as a crafty trickster able to change himself into animal and human shapes or the butt of ridicule; as a joker or a scapegoat who often falls victim to his own and others' wiles. His adventures, whether mischievous or not, always lie in well-known localities within the territory of the band among whom the story is told. The trickster performs his altruistic services first to satisfy his own ends and only incidentally for men. A variety of animals—wolverine, badger, raccoon, mink, crow, fisher—might also be selected as trickster-transformers.

For non-Native readers preoccupied with exact chronology and factual details, Native chronicles based on oral traditions are disappointing. The constant evocation of a confusing assemblage of mythological figures, and the frequent introduction of supernatural causes and interventions, have created a hodge-podge of details concerning historical origins. Countless variations of a single tale, even within the same tribe or band, are confusing: the treatment of a story may be altered by the taste, gender, or life-circumstances of the narrator, as well as by the place and time of the telling, and even the particular audience. West Coast families have handed down their own versions of stories that often contradict the traditions of their neighbours; there is no interest in reconciling such differences. Although the Iroquois form of government inspired the praise and emulation of the American founding fathers, and their traditions are among the most systematic and coherent, their chronicles lack historical data. For example, details concerning Deganahwidah—the chief who carried out such important constitutional change as the formation of the League of the Iroquois—are often obscure and casual. The famous Ojibwa interpreter and author Peter JONES stated that the Natives' 'notions as to their origins are little better than a mass of confusion'. Many traditions, he claimed, were founded on dreams, 'which will account for the numerous absurd stories current amongst them'.

Because of their many wanderings and because the history of European-Native relations has obscured many original Native values and attitudes, much legendary lore has been debased and distorted by later generations or has entirely disappeared and been forgotten by the living. Elements of European thought and missionary teaching (Bible stories fascinated Native people) have been so assimilated into an acculturated tradition that it is difficult to separate the European accretions from authentic Native lore. According to the *Jesuit Relations* the notion of the Great Manitou in its personal sense was introduced by the Jesuits themselves; the concepts of one incorporeal god, the devil as prince of darkness, the distinction between good and evil gods and the pitting of one against the other, and the belief in future punishment or in an abode of evil spirits were all foreign to the Algonkin tribes. In modern times some tribes (with only a handful of Native elders remembering) tend to emphasize what is most recent in their collective memory, relating stories of events that took place since the advent of whites.

Native folklore, as it is commonly recorded by scholars, presents other difficulties. Language manipulation is a problem in the translation process. Since collectors have depended chiefly on Native informants or mixed-blood interpreters who were unable or unwilling to explain the full implications of words or episodes, mistranslations and misconceptions undoubtedly arose. And the more literary the English texts, the more apt they are to misinterpret the originals. For the Euro-Canadian mind—with its different conceptions of time, the supernatural, material possessions, the phenomena of nature, and humour—it is difficult to comprehend and appreciate Native mythology. Foreign to Western sensibilities are totemism, metamorphosis, and animism; a moral code that, while it prescribes right conduct, glorifies the ingenious rogue whose cleverness seems to deserve success (fools deserve to be duped); and the realistic and imaginative depictions of erotic love, procreation, and excretory processes.

For the non-Native, transcriptions of oral myths lack dramatic emphasis and highlights, subtlety, characterization, and plot motivation. Anecdotal and episodic, they tend to be a potpourri of unrelated and incomplete fragments, often very brief and almost incoherent; some are merely summaries of reports or events. To people schooled in the English literary tradition (including many Native people who understand little of the language of their ancestors), the rambling conversational manner and exaggerated action of Native myths can be tedious, their arcane subject matter and hermetic meanings frustrating.

According to Natives themselves, much of the dramatic power and fun of their mythology and folklore emerge only when their stories are told in performance in the original language. Many tales (some of which were sung) comprise the dramatic portions of ritual, festival, and ceremony—elements considered more important than plot and characterization. In print—particularly in English—they lose their dramatic force; but the Native linguistic context brings to life their pungent wit and rich vein of comic pleasantry, metaphorical skill, imagination, and psychological insight. Their humour—sometimes considered obscene by non-Natives—provides comic relief in a violent world; the variations and incongruities, which detractors find chaotic, mirror the rich diversity the people saw in nature. Indeed, there are scholars today whose knowledge of Native languages and traditions has led them to recognize an appropriateness and coherence in Aboriginal myths and folklore—in the context of the Native way of life—that had not previously been understood.

Countless Native tales have been retold and interpreted by non-Natives. Partly because of the demands of the market-place, much reshaping and editing has been effected: references to sex, procreation, and excretory matters expunged or minimized; difficult allegories and allusions either ignored or simplified; repetitions, digressions, asides, and obscurities omitted; missing links provided; loose structures tightened; a perceived 'childishness' concealed; and poor syntax and faulty grammar corrected. To be fair, these editorial revisions have often been carried out with every attempt to recreate the spirit of the Native originals, but the well-intentioned desire to extract English storytelling elements from them has sometimes led to total misrepresentations. Generally speaking, non-Native storytellers, unfamiliar with the Native mind, have failed to master Native material.

Native writers have begun to object strongly to the corrupt and intrusive writing process that non-Natives have applied to their stories, and particularly to the appropriation of their stories by non-Natives. Basil H. JOHNSON, for example, decries the misconceptions and misrepresentations surrounding Nanabush: 'To look upon stories concerning him as no more than fairy tales intended solely for the amusement of children serves only to inhibit further inquiry into, and an appreciation of, Algonquian oral traditions. It is only within the context of Ojibway perception of the world and of the individual, and of tribal customs as commemorated in oral traditions and in ritual, that Nanabush may be more fully understood.' Lenore KEESHIG-TOBIAS states emphatically that 'stories are power'; their appropriation is 'culture theft, the theft of voice'. Some—like Beth Brant, Marie Annharte Baker, and Emma LaRocque—regard the oral as *Native*, in conflict with the *written*, which they identify with the colonizer's medium, English, the language of 'the enemy'. As a result, Native writers have begun to reclaim and recover their stories, retelling the old and creating new ones as traditions and events unfold into the future. A few, like Keeshig-Tobias, have taken up storytelling seriously as a profession and an important art form. Some, however, are finding it difficult to include features from oral narratives in their written works. In Maria CAMPBELL's words: 'It was hard, we had to change from telling a story to a group of people to being alone and telling the story to the paper.'

Bibliography. There is a staggering collection of Native folklore, more from some tribes than from others. Much of it lies buried in journals of learned societies like the American Folklore Society, the Royal Society of Canada, the Canadian Institute, and the British Association Committee; in reports and bulletins of government agencies, such as the Geological Survey of Canada and the National Museum of Canada; and in monographs not readily available, as well as in manuscripts in archival and personal collections. Much of this voluminous material, however, has been gathered more in the interests of science than for literary reasons.

The first professional collector to record the myths of Canada's Native peoples in English was the American ethnologist Henry Rowe Schoolcraft (1793-1864), who worked among the Ojibwa of the Great Lakes and was probably most responsible for popularizing the Natives' oral literature. His *Algic researches, comprising inquiries respecting the mental characteristics of the North American Indians* (2 vols, New York, 1839) provided the earliest source material for compilers and editors. In 1956 Mentor L. Williams brought together Schoolcraft's *Indian legends from Algic researches, The myth of Hiawatha, Oneóta, The red race in America, and Historical and statistical information respecting . . . the Indian tribes of the United States.*

Dr Franz Boas (1858-1942), considered to be the first professional anthropologist to do field work in Canada, and other anthropologists associated with him, collecting and analysing masses of texts and tales, made significant scholarly contributions, many of which were published by American agencies such as the Smithsonian Institution, Bureau of American Ethnology: *Tsimshian texts* (Bulletin 27, 1902); *Tsimshian mythology based on texts recorded by Henry W. Tate* (1916, rpr. 1970); *Kutenai tales* (Bulletin 59, 1918), with texts collected by Alexander Chamberlain; and by Columbia University in its Contributions to Anthropology: *Kwakiutl tales* (1910, rpr. 1969), text in Kwakiutl and English; *Bella Bella Texts* (1928, rpr. 1969; *The religion of the Kwakiutl Indians* (2 vols, 1930), Part 1, Texts; Part 2, Translations. Texts collected by the Tlingit George Hunt are in *Kwakiutl tales* (New Series, 2 vols, 1935), Part 1, Translations; Part 2,

Aboriginal legends and tales: bibliography

Texts. Tales recorded by Hunt, of Fort Rupert, are in *Contributions to the ethnology of the Kwakiutl* (1969), in which Kwakiutl texts and English translations are on opposite pages. *Ojibwa texts* (2 vols, 1917), collected by William Jones, edited by Trueman Michaelson, is a publication of the American Ethnology Society. Published by the American Museum of Natural History, Publications of the Jesup North Pacific Expedition, Hunt recording, Boas editing, are *Kwakiutl texts* (Memoirs, vol. 5, 1905); *Kwakiutl texts* (Second Series, Memoirs, vol. 14, part 1, 1906); and *The Kwakiutl of Vancouver Island* (Memoirs, vol. 8, part 2, 1909). Also published for the Museum are Leonard Bloomfield, *Plains Cree texts* (1934), and John R. Swanton, *Haida texts—Masset dialect* (1908). For the American Folklore Society, Boas compiled *Bella Bella tales* (Memoirs, vol. 25, 1932) and edited *Folk-tales of Salishan and Sahaptin tribes* (Memoirs, vol. 11, 1917).

The Society also published Alexander Chamberlaine, *Tales of the Mississaugas* (vol. 2, 1889); Edward Jack, *Maliseet legends* (vol. 8, 1895); Stansbury Hagar, *Weather and the seasons in Micmac mythology* (vol. 10, 1897); James A. Teit, *Traditions of the Thompson River Indians of British Columbia* (Memoirs, vol. 6, 1898), in which Coyote is the principal character, and *Tahltan Tales* (vol. 32, 1919); W.H. Mechling, *Maliseet tales* (vol. 26, 1913); William Jones, *Ojibwa tales from the north shore of Lake Superior* (vol. 29, 1916); Frank G. Speck, *Montagnais and Naskapi: tales from the Labrador Peninsula* (vol. 38, 1925); and Douglas Leechman, *Loucheux tales* (vol. 63, 1950).

Many collections were published under the auspices of the new (1910) anthropology division of the Geological Survey of Canada. In *Some myths and tales of the Ojibwa of southeastern Ontario* (Memoir 48, no. 2, 1914) Paul Radin (1883-1959) offers fifty-five tales in English, in many of which Nenebojo (Nanabozho) plays the role of trickster. In his essay *Literary aspects of North American mythology* (Bulletin no. 16, series no. 6, 1915), Radin characterizes North American mythology as a distinctive literature and explains the variability in versions of one myth. Other Geological Survey texts are W.H. Mechling, *Malecite tales* (Memoir 49, no. 4, 1914); Frank G. Speck, *Myths and folk-lore of the Timiskaming, Algonquin and Timagimi Ojibwa* (Memoir 71, no. 9, 1915); and Marius BARBEAU, *Huron and Wyandot mythology with an appendix containing earlier published records* (Memoir 80, no. 11, 1915), in which he treats such subjects as literary style, themes, and diffusion in the Introduction. Much that has been recorded here shows the influence of European tales, riddles, and fables. Names and descriptions, as well as photographs of the Native informants, are included; English translations only are given. Published by the Canadian Institute are Father A.G. Morice, *Three Carrier myths* (Toronto, 1895), and James Cleland Hamilton, *Famous Algonquins: Algic legends* (Toronto, 1898); by the Royal Society of Canada, Charles Hill-Tout (1858-1944), *The origin of the totemism of the aborigines of British Columbia* (Ottawa, Section II, 1901); and by the National Museum of Canada, Leonard Bloomfield, *Sacred stories of the Sweet Grass Cree* (Bulletin no. 60, Anthropological Series no. 11, 1930), which includes both the original Cree and English translations; and Barbeau's *Huron-Wyandot traditional narratives in translations and native texts* (Bulletin no. 165, Anthropological Series no. 47, 1960). Since Huron-Wyandot, an Iroquoian dialect, is now extinct, the forty texts presented by Barbeau, 'chiefly for linguistic purposes', are extremely valuable. Free translations of texts appear in the first part, with original texts and English literal transcriptions in parallel columns in the second part; the Appendix contains texts with French interlinear translations taken from the *Jesuit Relations*. Barbeau's *Indian days on the western Prairies* (National Museum, Bulletin no. 163, Anthropological Series no. 46, 1960) contains narratives from the Stoney Indians of the Morley Reserve in Alberta. William Benyon of Port Simpson, B.C., Barbeau's Native assistant from 1915 to 1960, recorded *Tsimsyan myths* (National Museum, Bulletin no. 174, Anthropological Series no. 51, 1961), which includes only English translations, and Barbeau himself wrote *Haida myths; illustrated in argillite carvings* (Bulletin 127, Anthropological Series no. 32, 1953). Diamond Jenness (1886-1969), chief anthropologist of the National Museum of Canada (1926-48), was the author of a number of valuable scientific reports on the tribes of Canada, notably *The corn goddess and other tales from Indian Canada* (Bulletin no. 141, no. 39, 1956), for which he selected 'such tales as appear to possess literary merit'.

Pioneer collectors of Northeast Woodland lore are Silas T. Rand (1810-89), missionary and philologist, and Charles Leland. They produced the earliest and the two most frequently cited authentic sources: *Legends of the Micmacs* (New York and London, 1894), in which Rand offers stories of Glooscap, the central figure of northeastern Algonkin mythology; and *The Algonkin legends of New England; or myths and folklore of the Micmac,*

Passamaquoddy, and Penobscot tribes (Boston, 1884), in which Leland makes detailed comparisons with the Norse eddas and sagas.

Other early regional presentations of Native tales include Sir James David Edgar, *The white stone canoe: a legend of the Ottawas* (Toronto, 1885); Egerton Ryerson YOUNG, *Algonquin Indian tales* (1903); George E. Laidlaw, *Ojibway myths and tales* (1915); and Alfred Carmichael, *Indian legends of Vancouver Island* (1922). In Charles Clay, *Swampy Cree legends; being twenty folk tales from the annals of a primitive, mysterious, fast-disappearing Canadian race, as told to Charles Clay... by Kuskapatchees, the Smoky One* (1938), Wesukechak, the trickster hero, appears as the principal figure. (Clay notes the influence of biblical prose, the only type of literature to which the North Manitoba Swampy Cree had been exposed.) See also Alice Ravenhill, *Folklore of the Far West* (1953); James F. Sanderson, *Indian Tales of the Canadian Prairies* (1965); and Ella Elizabeth Clark, *Indian Legends from the northern Rockies* (1966). Frances Fraser's *The wind along the river* (1968) contains seventeen Blackfoot tales that include several ancient Creation myths of Old Man or Nape. *Once upon an Indian tale: authentic folk tales* (1968) by Norman H. Lerman and Helen S. Carkin is a collection of nine folktales told by Native women of the British Columbia coast and Fraser River valley. *Legends of the river people* (1976) by Norman Lerman and Betty Keller is a collection of thirty legends told by the Chilliwack people of British Columbia. See also Herbert T. Schwartz, *Windigo and other tales of the Ojibway* (1969); Marion Robertson, *Red earth; tales of the Micmac* (Nova Scotia Museum, 1969); George Bauer, *Tales from the Cree* (1973); Peter Desbarats, *What they used to tell about Indian legends from Labrador* (1969); James Stevens, *Sacred legends of the Sandy Lake Cree* (1971); Patricia Mason, *Indian tales of the Northwest* (1976), a collection of twenty-three tales from British Columbia, with an accompanying Teacher's Guide; Harold HORWOOD, *Tales of the Labrador Indians* (1981); and Howard Norman, who gathered and translated Cree Windigo tales in *Where the chill came from* (1982). Ralph Maud provides a fresh approach to a new field of study in *A guide to B.C. Indian myth and legend* (1982), which contains brief biographies of the myth collectors (Boas, Teit, Hill-Tout, Barbeau, Swanton, Jenness, and Sapir) and their Native informants, as well as evaluations of their work.

The trickster figure, in relation to Greek mythology and to psychology, is the subject of Paul Radin in *The trickster: a study in American Indian mythology* (1956; rpr. 1972). Radin bases his important study on the texts of the Winnebago trickster cycle, but he also includes summaries of the Assiniboine and Tlingit trickster myths.

Useful compilations of a general nature are Margaret Bemister, *Thirty Indian legends of Canada* (1917, rpr. 1973); Katherine Judson, *Myths and legends of British North America* (1917); Mabel Burkholder, *Before the white man came* (1923); Marius Barbeau and Grace Melvin, *The Indian speaks* (1943); Hilda Mary Hooke, *Thunder in the mountains: legends of Canada* (1947); Douglas Leechman, *Indian summer* (1949); Ella Elizabeth Clark, *Indian legends of Canada* (1960); Olive M. Fisher and Clara L. Tyner, *Totem, tipi and tumpline: stories of Canadian Indians* (1962); John S. Morgan, *When the morning stars sang together* (1974), which draws parallels between the ancient Greek and Native stories; and Herbert S. Schwartz, *Tales from the smokehouse* (1974), which includes little-known erotic tales from the Ojibwa, Mohawk, Naskapi, and other tribes.

Of the many collections that have been published in French, see *Traditions indiennes du Canada nord-ouest* (Paris, 1886; rev. ed. 1887) by Émile Petitot, which offers the Native dialect and French translation in parallel columns; *Carcajou et le sens du monde: récits Montagnais Naskapi* (1971) by Rémi Savard; *Légendes indiennes du Canada* (1967) by Claude Mélançon; *Anish-Nah-Be: contes adultes du pays Algonquin* (1971) by Bernard Assiniwi; and *Atanúkana: légendes montagnaises* (1971), collected and translated by Marie-Jeanne Basile and Gérard E. McNulty.

Scholars have presented versions of one myth and analysed them. In *Tshakabesh: récits Montagnais-Naskapi* (1971), Madeleine Lefebvre examines the versions of a Montagnais-Naskapi myth provided by four different narrators. Catherine McClellan studies eleven versions of the girl who married a bear in *The girl who married a bear: a masterpiece of oral tradition* (National Museum of Canada, 1970).

Legends recounted by Native people have been published in Native and non-Native newspapers and collected in numerous books, including: *The life and traditions of the red man* (Bangor, Maine, 1893; rpr. 1979) by Joseph Nicolar; *Legends of Vancouver* (1911, new ed. 1961) by the famous Mohawk poet Pauline JOHNSON, who adapted the legends of the Squamish tribe told to her by Chief Joseph Capilano; *Abenaki Indian legends; grammar and place names* (1932) by Henry Lorne Masta;

Tales of the Kitimat (1956) by William Gordon Robinson; *Men of Medeek* (2nd edn., 1962), as told in 1935-6 to Will Robinson by Walter Wright, a Tsimshian chief of the Kitselas band of the Middle Skeena River—this material concerns the legendary city of Tum-L-Hanna and the migration westward to Kitselas Canyon in British Columbia; *Legends of my people: the great Ojibway* (1965) by the prominent Ojibwa artist Norval Morriseau; and *Son of Raven, son of Deer* (1967), a collection of twelve tales of the Tse-Shaht people by George CLUTESI, who also wrote an apologia for his people's potlatch ceremony in *Potlatch* (1969). *Tales of Nokomis* (1970) by Patronella Johnston presents Ojibwa legend and custom within the narrative framework of children visiting their grandmother. In *Voice of the Plains Cree* (1973) Ruth M. Buck edited legends collected by the Rev. Edward AHENAKEW. *Squamish legends* (1966) was edited by Oliver N. Wells from tape-recorded interviews with Chief August Jack Khahtsahlano and Domanic Charlie. *Visitors who never left: the origins of the people of Damelahamid* (1974)—translated by Chief Kenneth B. Harris, a Tsimshian chief, in collaboration with Francis M.D. Robinson—is a collection of eight myths dealing with the origin and history of the Native peoples from the regions of the Skeena and Nass Rivers in northern British Columbia. In *Wild drums* (1972) Alex Grisdale relates tales and legends of the Plains people to Nan Shipley. See also *Tales of the Mohawks* (1975) by Alma Greene (Forbidden Voice); *Ojibway heritage* (1976), which offers ceremonies, rituals, songs, dances, prayers, and legends of the Ojibwa by Basil H. Johnston, who also published *Tales the Elders told: Ojibway legends* (1981) and *Ojibway ceremonies* (1983); *The adventures of Nanabush: Ojibway Indian stories* (1979) told by Sam Snake, Chief Elijah Yellowhead, Alder York, David Simcoe, Annie King, compiled by Emerson Coatsworth and David Coatsworth; *Kwakiutl legends* (1981) as told to Pamela Whitaker by Chief James Wallas; *Tagish Tlaagu Tagish stories* (1982), told in English by Angela Sidney; and *Where the chill came from: Windigo tales and journeys* (1982) translated from the Swampy Cree by Howard Norman.

More recent publications are *Micmac legends of Prince Edward Island* (1988) by John Joe Stark and *Earth elder stories: the Penayzitt path* (1988) by Alexander Wolfe. *Write it on your heart: the epic world of an Okanagan storyteller* (1989) contains the stories of Harry Robinson (1900-90) transcribed by Wendy Wickwire, who tried to retain their original flavour and sound, setting them typographically in lines structured to evoke the speech rhythms without attempting to polish the English. In his review of the book, Thomas KING wrote: 'In reading Robinson one is forced to read the story out loud, thereby closing the circle, the oral becoming the written becoming the oral.' See also Basil Johnston's *Tales of the Anishinaubaek* (1993) and *The Manitous, the spiritual world of the Ojibway* (1995).

See also CHILDREN'S LITERATURE IN ENGLISH 1970s TO 1996: 4.

PENNY PETRONE

Aboriginal literature

Native and Métis literature. 1. HISTORICAL BACKGROUND. The literature of the Native peoples of Canada had its origins in an oral tradition that was rooted in, and transmitted through, the social contexts of storytelling and ceremony. Storytelling included all types of myths, legends, tales, and folklore, while compositional elements of ceremony offered a wide range of songs, ritual chants, drama, poems, prayers, and orations. This spoken literature was first printed when scattered specimens were translated into French and recorded in the *JESUIT RELATIONS*. The missionaries expressed amazement at the Native people's literary faculties, Father Paul Le Jeune observing that 'metaphor is largely in use among these Peoples' (1636). Because Native peoples associate an idea with an object, with visual memory, they invariably make use of metaphors and analogies, and because they pay more attention to the implications or suggested meanings of their words —the connotative as opposed to the specific or denotative meaning—their metaphors embody an emotional force. It is this power of arousing emotion by making apt comparisons that constitutes one of the great strengths of their oratory. Oratorical skill was held in the highest esteem. Le Jeune stated that a Native leader was obeyed in proportion to his use of eloquence because his followers had no other law than his word. In his *Relation* of 1633 Le Jeune commended a Montagnais chief for a 'keenness and delicacy of rhetoric that might have come out of the schools of Aristotle or Cicero.' In his *Relation* of 1645 Father Jérôme Lalemant quotes a speech given by an Iroquois spokesman to Governor Montmagny at Quebec that illustrates the orator's style: 'Onontio, thou hast dispersed the clouds; the air is serene; the Sky shows clearly, the Sun is bright. I see no more trouble. Peace has made everything calm: my heart is at rest. I go away very happy.' Sentences are short and straightforward. Language is clear and simple. A nature image dramatizes the speaker's feelings. A poetic quality and a certain grace permeate the entire speech, while courtesy as well as a sense of dignity and a laconic reserve dominate. If the occasion warranted a long speech, however, the orator had appropriate metaphors and vocabulary, a syntax that allowed him to formulate complex relationships between ideas, as well as employing a vivid imagination and literary inventiveness.

In time numerous samples of Native eloquence in translation, from different tribal cultures across Canada, appeared in the writings of white explorers, traders, travellers, adopted captives, missionaries, and settlers. Admired chiefly for their literary value rather than for their content, they were recorded to illustrate certain stylistic qualities: 'pathos', 'caustic wit', or 'genial pleasantry'.

Translation into French and English presented many difficulties. The Native predilection for figurative and symbolic language, for allegorical meanings and allusions, contributed greatly to the problems of exact translation. The eighteenth-century English fur-trader Alexander Henry recognized this dilemma when he explained that 'The Indian manner of speech is so extravagantly figurative, that it is only for a very perfect master to follow and comprehend it entirely.' The speeches of two outstanding eighteenth-century warrior-orators—the Ottawa war-chief Pontiac (1720-69) and the Iroquois Thayendanegea, better known as Joseph Brant (1742-1807)—exemplify Native eloquence at its best. Pontiac could not write, but his recorded speeches in council outlining his vision of a separate, independent Native confederacy allied to the French inspired the revolt in 1763-4 of nearly all the tribes around Lake Superior, and as far south as the lower Mississippi. His dictated letters to British and French officials are also impressive, demonstrating the cunning of an astute warrior, a brilliant diplomat, or a wily politician as the need arose. The great orator Joseph Brant was a spokesman for the Mohawk Loyalists who moved to the Grand River (Ontario) in 1784. Besides his speeches, his extant writings consist mainly of letters to British and American military and civil authorities, and to royalty, many of them expressing his idealistic vision of an independent Native confederacy that would be a sovereign ally of the British. Written in lucid, direct, highly persuasive English, and notable for their patrician tone, they can be read in W.L. Stone's *Life of Joseph Brant* (2 vols, New York, 1838) and Charles M. Johnston's *The valley of the Six Nations* (1964). The celebrated Shawnee chief, Tecumseh (1768-1813), renowned for his military genius, also used his remarkable oratorical talents not only in his attempts to unite the Native peoples into a western confederacy but also in support of the British cause in the War of 1812. Tecumseh's famous speeches in council reveal his adroit reasoning powers as well as his keen political sense, at times combining dry sarcasm with rich metaphor.

The many treaties that emerged out of the complexities of Native-white relations over the span of three centuries also represent recorded Native literature. During treaty-making sessions, which resembled ancient councils in their drama and ceremonial formality, orators delivered highly rhetorical speeches using the ancient formulaic metaphors of chain, fire, sun, tree, road, hatchet, and pipe, and made traditional analogies to the natural world while they poured forth their embittered eloquence in defence of home and hunting ground. Western orators of the late nineteenth century—like Crowfoot, Poundmaker, Big Bear, Sweet Grass, and Misto-wa-sis—kept alive the tradition of their forefathers to persuade and lead by means of the oratory of exhortation, which contained inherited images and a strong element of didacticism and aphoristic, dignified language; their speeches can be read in A. Morris's *The treaties of Canada with the Indians*. . . (1880; rpr. 1976).

2. THE NINETEENTH CENTURY. The first signs of literary creativity in English among the Native peoples appeared as a result of organized missionary efforts to convert them. Christianized Natives, some of whom became missionaries (mostly Methodist), were encouraged to write for an international audience in order to create interest in, and possibly raise money for, their people. Since they wrote for an international audience of Christian philanthropists, they had a deliberate aim: to encourage compassion and support for the 'poor Indian', who required patience and understanding in the process of being assimilated into the blessings and benefits of European civilization. Their mainly autobiographical works present a wealth of proudly recounted historical information about tribal beliefs, ceremonies, customs, and folklore; ironically, for the modern reader, they are pervaded by deep Christian piety and biblical cadences, the Bible being the predominant literary influence in these peoples' lives. Their books comprise the first body of Canadian Native literature in English; they also offer the

first written evidence of the ideas, responses, and feelings of individuals, as opposed to the collective expressions contained in myths and legends.

The first Canadian Native to publish a book in English was George COPWAY, who was born near the mouth of the Trent River in Upper Canada and lived for a time in the Rice Lake area before moving to the USA. An Ojibwa (Mississauga) Methodist minister who later converted to Roman Catholicism, lecturer, orator, Native-rights leader, and herbal doctor, Copway wrote *The life, history, and travels of Kah-ge-ga-gah-bowh (George Copway), a young Indian chief of the Ojibwa nation, a convert to the Christian faith, and a missionary to his people for twelve years: with a sketch of the present state of the Ojibwa nation, in regard to Christianity and their future prospects. Also an appeal; with all the names of the chiefs, now living, who have been Christianized, and the missionaries now labouring among them, written by himself* (Albany, N.Y., 1847). An instant success, it was reprinted six times by the end of the year and republished in London under the title *Recollections of a forest life*. . . (1850). What is probably Copway's most famous work, described by himself as 'the first volume of Indian history written by an Indian', is *The traditional history and characteristic sketches of the Ojibwa nation* (London, 1850). Copway wrote a compelling and vigorous prose. One contemporary newspaper praised his 'biting satire', 'pungent anecdote', 'strokes of wit and humour', 'touches of pathos', and 'most poetical descriptions of nature'. His success as a writer brought him international recognition and he toured Europe as a celebrity, writing of his experiences in *Running sketches of men and places in England, France, Germany, Belgium and Scotland* (New York, 1851).

Another remarkable Native author was the Rev. Peter JONES, the son of a white surveyor and a Mississauga woman, who was born at Burlington Heights (present-day Hamilton, Ontario). Interpreter, translator, author, Native-rights leader, preacher, and the first Native Methodist minister in Canada, Jones was a prolific and indefatigable writer who played a vigorous role in the religious and secular life of his time. His autobiography, *Life and journals of Kah-Ke-Wa-Quo-Na-By (Rev. Peter Jones) Wesleyan minister* (Toronto, 1860), was published posthumously, as was his *History of the Ojibway Indians; with especial reference to their conversion to Christianity* (London, 1861; rpr. 1970). Jones was a gifted writer whose English prose is highly personal and literate, and occasionally amusing and anecdotal. He also translated several books of the Bible and many hymns. The writings of two other Native ministers reveal the lucid, correct style that many of these men attained. *Journal of the Reverend Peter Jacobs, Indian Wesleyan missionary from Rice Lake to the Hudson's Bay Territory, and returning. Commencing May, 1852. With a brief account of his life, and a short history of the Wesleyan Mission in that country* (Toronto, 1854) is a straightforward factual record of the three-month journey from Toronto to York Factory of Peter JACOBS, who was a keen observer; his diary entries are written with precision and clarity. *The diary of the Reverend Henry Budd 1870-1875* (1974), edited by Katherine Pettipas for the Manitoba Record Society Publications, offers the personal record of a former Hudson's Bay Company clerk who was a farmer, teacher, and for thirty-five years a missionary in the remote diocese of Rupert's Land. He was the first ordained Native Anglican minister in North America (1858).

Besides the missionaries, a number of other educated Natives also wrote and published. George HENRY, the author of two pamphlets, *Remarks concerning the Ojibway Indians, by one of themselves, called Maungwudaus, who has been travelling in England, France, Belgium, Ireland, and Scotland* (Leeds, 1847); and *An account of the Chippewa Indians, who have been travelling among the whites in the United States, England, Ireland, Scotland, France and Belgium* (Boston, 1848)—which, along with Peter Jones' reactions, to his visits to Britain, offer the earliest-known detailed impressions of Europeans from the Native perspective.

Francis Assikinack (1824-63)—a young Roman Catholic interpreter and school teacher on Manitoulin Island who had studied at Upper Canada College, Toronto—wrote three informative essays for the *Canadian Journal* in 1858: 'Legends and traditions of the Odahwah Indians'; 'The Odahwah Indian language'; and 'Social and warlike customs of the Odahwah Indians'. He was a competent writer—controlled and dignified, though at times stiffly pedantic.

The last half of the nineteenth century did not have the flood of literary publications that characterized the first half. However, a few missionary-sponsored journals encouraged such literary activities as story-writing, memoirs, conversion anecdotes, various expressions of ethnic pride, and letter-writing: *Petaubun (Peep of Day)*, published in Sarnia (Ontario) in 1861-2; the *Algoma Missionary News and Shingwauk Journal* (Sault Ste Marie, Ont., 1877-84); and *Na-Na-kwa; or Dawn on the northwest coast* (Kitimat, B.C., 1898-1903).

Peter Edmund Jones, son of the Rev. Peter Jones, published *The Indian* (Hagersville, Ont., 1885-6); though short-lived, it is of interest as the first Canadian periodical edited by a Native *for* Natives. The last three decades of the century produced only two books of any significance by a Native person, both histories. Peter Dooyentate Clark wrote *Origin and traditional history of the Wyandotts, and sketches of other Indian tribes of North America: true traditional stories of Tecumseh and his league, in the years 1811 and 1812* (Toronto, 1870), an attempt to present historical personages and events through a series of vividly dramatized tableaux. Louis Jackson was the author of a booklet, *Our Caughnawagas in Egypt: a narrative of what was seen and accomplished by the contingent of North American voyageurs who led the British boat expedition for the relief of Khartoum up the cataracts of the Nile* (Montreal, 1885), which gives a firsthand account, both factual and observant, of the famous Nile expedition to the Sudan in 1884-5.

The best-known Native writer before and after the turn of the century was a poet, Emily Pauline JOHNSON, author of *The white wampum* (London, 1895), *Canadian born* (1903), and *Flint and feather* (1912; rev. 1914; paperback 1972). Her collections of short fiction included *Legends of Vancouver* (1911) and *The moccasin maker* (1913) which was published posthumously.

Probably the most interesting Native author of the first decade of the twentieth century was John Brant-Sero (Ojijatekha, 1867-?), interpreter, poet, and dramatist of Hamilton, Ont. He saw himself as the historian of the Six Nations Indians, dedicated to make known his 'hitherto untold lore', and gave public concerts and lectures in Great Britain and North America. He translated 'God Save the King' into Mohawk and was the author of six articles: 'Some descendants of Joseph Brant', *Ontario Historical Society papers and records*, I (1899); 'The Six Nations Indians in the Province of Ontario, Canada', *Wentworth Historical Society, Transactions*, II (1899); 'Dekanawideh: the law-giver of the Caniengahakas', *Man* (1901); 'Indian Rights Association after government scalp', *Wilshire's Magazine* (Oct. 1903); 'View of a Mohawk Indian', *Journal of American Folklore* 58 (1905); and 'O-no-dah', *Journal of American Folklore* XXIV (1911). Brant-Sero combined a sense of the enduring past with the realities of the present; but his writing, though straightforward, is flat.

3. THE 1960s AND 1970s. In the 1960s more and more Native newspapers and periodicals sprang up across Canada to provide a forum for growing, politically conscious Native organizations. Native speakers emerged and Native oratory once again became a vigorous literary form. Idiomatic and rhetorical speeches were recorded in Native and non-Native newspapers and journals alike. Journalistic prose, in the form of reports and essays, also became popular as Native activists began to attack and criticize the dominant society. Whether in speech or essay, they reacted politically to their problems in a frank and often angry and bitter manner, and in language that is sometimes flamboyant but always direct and forceful. Concerned with the wrongs inflicted on their people, they were more interested in content than in literary style. Native-authored books—frequently written with the aid of a collaborator or amanuensis—revealed five trends: (1) a pan-Native approach that played down tribal affiliation and focused on a common Native identity, while sometimes shifting emphasis from the shared experiences of the group to the single experiences of the individual; (2) a greater diversification of literary genres; (3) inspirational writing intended to provide a sense of historical continuity and making use of ancient beliefs and values; and (4 and 5) two militant approaches: one that advocated separation from the dominant society, and another that sought an as-yet-undefined revisionist presence in society.

The statement of the Government of Canada on Indian policy (1969), the controversial 'White Paper' that recommended the abolition of special rights for Native peoples, sparked a burst of literary activity. An immediate and angry reaction to the government proposals came from the Alberta Cree, Harold Cardinal, in *The unjust society: the tragedy of Canada's Indians* (1971). He argued for the retention of special rights within the strengthened contexts of treaty and the Indian Act, and his book, which gained national prominence, has become a classic on the Native situation in Canada. Arguing a minority point of view, William Wuttunee, a Calgary Cree lawyer originally from Saskatchewan, opposed special status as a barrier to progress, and in his controversial *Ruffled feathers: Indians in Canadian society* (1971) advocated instead integration, individual development, and a radical change in the Native psyche itself. *Bulletin 201* (1970), edited and published by the Anglican Church of Canada, is a collection of the responses to the White Paper by such Native writers as Dave Courchene, the Rev. Ernest Willie, Walter Currie, Harold Sappier, and the Rev. Adam Cuthand, who wrote the Preface.

The growing self-consciousness of Native peoples in the 1970s produced more protest literature, some of it written by militant patriots and couched in strident, sloganistic language. Examples of such books are *Prison of grass: Canada from the native point of view* (1975) by Howard Adams; Harold Cardinal's *The rebirth of Canada's Indians* (1977); *Half-breed* (1973) by Maria CAMPBELL; and *We are Métis* (1980) by Duke REDBIRD.

Antitheses of such angry presentations were a number of popular histories focusing on personal experience as well as family and tribal traditions. In *The feathered U.E.L.'s* (1973), Enos T. Monture recreates some memorable occasions in the lives of the first Native United Empire Loyalists and their descendants. He combines fully dramatized scenes with dialogue and folksy entertaining anecdotes. In *A social history of the Manitoba Métis* (1974) Émile Pelletier tries to prove—in an affirmative and optimistic text, with maps and statistical tables and quotations from primary sources—that the demand for Aboriginal rights of the Métis has a strong moral and legal basis. *My tribe the Crees* (1979) by Joseph F. Dion, a treaty Cree descendant of Big Bear, traces the history of the Crees before the arrival of the white man and provides insights, from a Native perspective, into the Northwest Rebellion of 1885. This was edited by Hugh A. Dempsey, who also edited *My people the Bloods* (1979), drawn from a book-length manuscript entitled 'Indians of the Western Plains', completed in 1936 by Mike Mountain Horse (1888-1964). It is well written and of historical interest. *The ways of my grandmothers* (1980) by Beverly Hungry Wolf records the ancient ways of the Blood women as well as some personal and tribal history. Two historical books have a strong quality of prophecy and vision: *The fourth world: Indian reality* (1974) by George Manuel and Michael Posluns, in which the background of Manuel as a Shuswap from British Columbia is used to trace the struggle of Canadian Native people for recognition, and Manuel offers his vision of a fourth world where the values of special-status people are integrated with those of all peoples; and *These mountains are our sacred places* (1977) by Chief John Snow, of the Wesley band of Stoney Indians, who records the past of his people in a moving and sometimes lyrical prose.

Biography, and its allied forms, is a favourite genre of Native writers. At their best, such books—which are sometimes the result of taped interviews, collaborations, or translation—have a good-humoured, warm, flowing narrative style. *Recollections of an Assiniboine chief* (1972) by the highly articulate Dan Kennedy (Ochankugahe, 1877-1973), a Saskatchewan Assiniboine, brought together his writings of the twenties, thirties, and forties and offered primary data about his tribe's history and culture in an engaging and informative style. *Great leader of the Ojibway: Misquona-queb* (1972) by James Redsky (edited by James R. Stevens), the last of the Midewin holy men in the Lake of the Woods area of western Ontario, traced the history of the last Ojibwa war leader, Misquonaqueb. More documentary than literary, the book includes a section devoted to the Midewin Society and another containing explanations of Ojibwa customs, such as the Shaking Tent. *Guests never leave hungry: the autobiography of James Sewid, a Kwakiutl Indian* (1969) describes Sewid's successful adjustment to the culture change in British Columbia. Anahareo, who had lived with the famous Englishman turned Ojibwa, Grey Owl (Archibald Stansfeld BELANEY), and was the author of *Devil in deerskins: my life with Grey Owl* (1940; rpr. 1980), published *Grey Owl and I: a new autobiography* (1972). *First among the Hurons* by Max Gros-Louis, in collaboration with Marcel Bellier, translated from the French by Sheila Fischman, is the autobiography of a Quebec chief who played a vital role in the James Bay hydro-electric project. *No foreign land: the biography of a North American Indian* (1976) by Wilfred Pelletier (edited by Ted Poole) tells, in a straightforward manner, of Pelletier's life in two worlds—both on and off the reservation. *Buffalo days and nights* (1976), containing the memoirs of Peter Erasmus (1833-1931), the last surviving member of the Palliser Expedition of 1857-60, as told to Henry Thompson in 1920, was published by the Glenbow-Alberta Institute. It includes an introduction by Dr Irene Spry, copious footnotes, a bibliography, and an index that make it by far the most scholarly of these memoirs.

I am an Indian (1969) edited by the non-Native Kent Gooderham, was the first anthology of Native literature to be published in Canada. It offers a wide assortment of literary forms—from legends, essays, and stories, to poems by such well-known Native writers as Duke Redbird, Chief Dan George, Howard Adams, Alma Greene, Ethel Brant Monture, and George CLUTESI. *The only good Indian: essays by Canadian Indians* (1970) edited by Waubageshig (Harvey McCue) deals with aboriginal rights, red power, Native education and identity, and contains a few protest poems by Duke Redbird; a short play by

Nona Benedict; the well-known essay by Chief Dan George, 'My very good dear friends. . .'; and an extract from 'Citizens plus', often called 'The red paper', prepared by the Native Chiefs of Alberta. Two collections of essays were published by the Neewin Publishing Company Limited of The Nishnawbe Institute, Toronto, a Native educational, cultural, and research centre: *For every North American Indian who begins to disappear, I also begin to disappear* (1971) and *Who is chairman of this meeting?* (1972).

Although poetry and song constituted an integral part of the Native literary heritage—special occasions in life were celebrated with song—publications in this area lagged behind prose. In 1963, however, there appeared the interesting Sepass poems: *The songs of Y-Ail-Mihth* (1963), a cycle of fifteen sacred songs of the Chilliwack people recited by Chief Kholserten Sepass to Eloise Street, and translated into English by her mother, Mrs Sophia Street. The 1970s was a decade of productive activity in which young poets experimented with loose, irregular verse forms. The outrage against the dominant society, so evident in the social-protest poetry of the angry young Duke Redbird, among others, was balanced by an output that expressed a new affirmative spirit and often featured wit and irony. In fact *Loveshine and red wine* (1981), the collected verse of Duke Redbird, reflects both these attitudes: a mellow, loving, mature Redbird, as well as the angry young man. Chief Dan George's lyrical responses to life are enjoyable, and his vision of the divine in living things is mirrored in his prose poem 'My heart soars' (1974). In 1977 the Highway Bookshop published two collections of verse: *Wisdom of Indian poetry* and *Okanagan Indian*, by the Okanagan Ben Abel, who writes gentle lyrical verse and is most compelling when he deals with his own experiences. George Kenny, an Ontario Ojibwa, is the author of *Indians don't cry* (1977), in which the best poems are permeated with a sense of the abiding ironies of Native life. *Poems of Rita Joe* (1978) is an autobiographical sequence by the Micmac Rita JOE, detailing the experiences and values that helped her define the Native perception of life. The texts of a few of the poems offer both Micmac and English in parallel columns.

Many voices: contemporary Indian poetry (1977) was edited by two non-Natives, David Day and Marilyn BOWERING. Over thirty poets from across Canada are represented in this volume, which is marked by variety of thought, tone, topic, and treatment.

Native stage plays based chiefly on tribal ritual, legend, and ancient custom also appeared in the 1970s. The versatile Duke Redbird's *Wasawkachak* (1974) used traditional and contemporary song and dance in dramatizing the creation of humanity. *October stranger* by George Kenny was performed in Monaco at the sixth International Theatre Festival in 1977. *Ayash* by Jim Morris, a stage adaptation of an ancient Ojibwa legend, had its première in Sioux Lookout, Ont., on 18 Feb. 1983.

The best Native short-story writer of the period was Basil JOHNSON. His entertaining *Moose meat & wild rice* (1978) uses gentle irony and satire to poke fun at the pretensions and prejudices of Native and non-Native alike.

4. 1983 TO 1996. The creative output in this period has surpassed the great upsurge of literary activity in the 1970s, to which must now be added the great diversity and iconoclasm of Native writing. A younger generation of Canadian college- and university-trained writers has formed writing groups, conducted writing workshops, organized conferences discussing the difficulties of language and translation—debating the issues of the appropriation of 'voice', writing introductions and epilogues to each other's books, reviewing each other's work, and editing anthologies. Some writers, like Basil Johnston, Lenore KEESHIG-TOBIAS, Rita Joe and Jeannette ARMSTRONG are writing bilingually, using their own languages and English.

This body of new writing is distinguished by a wide range of forms. Beatrice Culleton (Métis, b. 1949) was the first Native writer to tackle the novel: *In search of April Raintree* (1983; reissued in 1984 minus a graphic rape scene). Set in Winnipeg, it is the moving account of two Métis sisters who are raised by different foster parents to develop in antithetical directions. Two years later Jeannette Armstrong published *Slash* (1985). Thomas KING wrote two well-received novels, *Medicine River* (1990), which has been made into a television film, and *Green grass, running water* (1993). Two novels by Ruby Slipperjack (b. 1942), *Honour the sun* (1987) and *Silent words* (1992), are told respectively from the point of view of a young girl and boy growing up in small isolated Native communities in northern Ontario. The award-winning Jovette MARCHESSAULT, a major figure among contemporary Quebec feminist writers, draws upon the details of her own life in her three novels translated from the French: *Like a child of the earth* (1975), which chronicles a childhood paradise on the banks of the St Lawrence; *Mother of grass*

(1980), which tells of her hardships and poverty in the slums of Montreal's inner city and ends with the death of her beloved grandmother, her comfort and mentor; and *White pebbles in the dark forests* (1990)—the last of a trilogy that traces a reconciliation between men and women, children and parents, and includes elements of myth and visionary experiences. Joan Crate's first novel, *Breathing water* (1990)—told from the point of view of a Métis cocktail waitress newly married to her former boss, a rich Greek hotel owner—demonstrates an astonishing mastery of technique. The three novellas by Jordan Wheeler (b. 1964) in *Brothers in arms* (1989)—'Hearse In Snow', 'Red Wave', and 'Exposure'—deal with the relationship between pairs of Native brothers trying to re-establish contact after years of separation and to reconnect with their ancestral past. In *Keeper'n me* (1994), Richard Wagamese, a former award-winning columnist for the *Calgary Herald*, draws upon his own life to tell of foster homes, street kids, jail, and finally recovery through the redemptive powers of his Native family and tradition.

Many Native writers experiment with the poetic form, preferring looser, and concrete, poetry over the conventional; and satire, humour, and irony over direct confrontation. Although they continue to write about the pain and abuse suffered from the cultural clash with church, state, and school during the years of 'colonization', they also write about joyful childhood memories, grandchildren, ancient beliefs, sexual love, and the beauty and rhythms of the natural and spiritual worlds. Poets such as Duke Redbird, Rita Joe, Jeannette Armstrong, Lenore Keeshig-Tobias, Marie Annharte Baker (Saulteaux, b. 1942), Beth Cuthand (Cree, b. 1949), Joan Crate, and Daniel David MOSES, are now familiar. The Plains Cree Louise Halfe, who published *Bear bones* and *Feathers* in 1994, is a new name.

The short-story form is still the choice of many writers. *Achimoona* (1985) is an interesting collection of ten short stories written as the result of a workshop conducted by Maria Campbell, who wrote the Introduction; three of the stories were written by Jordan Wheeler and one by his mother, Bernelda Wheeler (Cree/Saulteaux, b. 1937), a writer and broadcaster who has published three children's books. Thomas King uses the form with considerable skill, combining techniques from the oral tradition and mainstream literary conventions. In his collection *One good story, that one* (1993), his acute ear for dialogue and the oral English rhythms and colloquial speech of his Native characters is striking. A volume of light short stories, *Food and spirits* (1991) by Beth Brant, a Bay of Quinte Mohawk, is uneven in quality; but it contains a gem, 'Turtle Girl'—which first appeared in *CANADIAN FICTION MAGAZINE* (no. 60, 1987)—about an aged black musician and a young Native girl.

Native writers have been meeting the need for books written specifically for children, especially their own children. Among these are Bernelda Wheeler (Métis), *A friend called 'chum'* (1984), *I can't have bannock, but the beaver has a dam* (1984), and *Where did you get your moccasins?* (1986); Jeannette Armstrong, *Enwhisteekwa/walk in water* (1982) and *Neekna and chemai* (1984); Beatrice Culleton, *Spirit of the white bison* (1985), in which the mythological white bison tells the story about the decimation of the buffalo on the plains. *How the mouse got brown teeth* (1988) and *How the birch tree got its stripes* (1988) are two Cree stories translated and edited by Freda Ahenakew (Cree). In 1989 Joseph McLellan published *The birth of Nanabosho, Nanabosho dances*, and *Nanabosho steals fire*. Thomas King's *A coyote Columbus story* (1992) takes a fresh and witty look at the arrival of the European in North America from the perspective of one of the principal trickster figures of Native mythology.

Many Native writers are still choosing the autobiographical form to tell their personal stories. Following Maria Campbell's landmark classic *Halfbreed* (1973), there have been *I walk in two worlds* (1987) by Eleanor Brass; *Indian school days* (1988) by Basil H. Johnston; *I am Woman* (1988) by Lee MARACLE; and *Inside out: an autobiography by a Native Canadian* (1990) by James Tyman. *Occupied Canada: a young white man discovers his unsuspected past* (1991), co-written by Robert Calihoo and Robert Hunter, is Calihoo's life-story, and tells of degradation and desperation; it won a Governor General's Award. Beth Brant's *Writing as witness: essay and talk* (1994) is a warm, chatty discourse that ranges over a wide range of topics from Pauline Johnson and Pocahontas to Brant's parents, her children, and her lesbianism. In *Back on the rez: finding the way home* (1996) Brian Maracle, a former broadcaster and journalist for the Toronto *Globe and Mail*, who grew up as an urban non-Status Indian, writes about his first year back on the Six Nations Grand River Territory, and gives a personal account of Mohawk culture and history, as well as a description of contemporary Native life in Canada.

Oral histories are still popular. *Enough is enough: aboriginal women speak out* (1987) is a collection of stories, as told to Janet Silman, about being Native and female by a small group of women activists from the Tobique Reserve in New Brunswick who, through their struggles and demonstration marches, contributed to the passing of Bill C-31 by Parliament in June 1985, which ended over 100 years of legislated sexual discrimination against Native women. *Kôhkominawak otâcimowiniwâwa; or Our grandmothers' lives as told in their own words* (1992), edited and translated by Freda Ahenakew, records the stories of seven Cree women who grew up in northern Saskatchewan during the 1930s. *Crazy water: Native voices on addiction and recovery* (1993), by the award-winning print and broadcast journalist Brian Maracle, features notably honest and poignant interviews with Native drug dealers, alcoholics, hookers, and con-artists. Maracle, who specializes in Native issues, has said that his idea for the book was rooted in the fact 'that native wit and wisdom is largely unappreciated'. *I'll sing 'til the day I die: conversations with Tyendinaga Elders* (1995) by Beth Brant reconstructs the stories of fourteen Mohawks and gives 'the sense of orality'.

Because of the growing need for aboriginal literature texts in high schools, colleges, and universities, there has been a proliferation of anthologies. The first major anthology, *First people, first voices* (1983), edited by Penny Petrone, was distributed internationally and is in its sixth printing. *Seventh generation: contemporary Native writing* (1989), edited and compiled by Heather Hodgson, is the first anthology of poems by Native writers. It was followed by *Our bit of truth: an anthology of Canadian Native literature* (1990), edited by Agnes Grant, and *Writing the circle: Native women of western Canada* (1990) edited by Jeanne Perreault and Sylvia Vance, presenting the writings of fifty-two young, little-known First Nations women. The Preface, 'Here are Our Voices—Who will Hear'? by Emma La Rocque, a Cree-Métis professor of Native studies at the University of Manitoba, has often been quoted from. The first Native-edited anthology is *A gathering of spirit: a collection by North American Indian women* (1984; rev. 1988) by Beth Brant. According to Daniel David Moses in *Books In Canada*, 'It is Brant's sensitivity and sensibility that inform the collection and make what could be called the inadequacies of some of the contributions (inarticulateness, semi-literateness) shine more, like scars on healthy skin.' Thomas King edited the first anthology of short fiction by Native writers in Canada as guest editor of *Canadian Fiction Magazine* (no. 60, 1987). There are eighteen stories by fourteen writers, the majority of whom were unknown at the time. King also edited *All my relations: an anthology of contemporary Canadian Native writing* (1990). While many of the same authors from his previous anthology are here, King also included Ruby Slipperjack, Jordan Wheeler, Jovette Marchessault, Basil H. Johnston, and Joan Crate, among others. The introduction to *An anthology of Canadian Native literature in English* (1992), edited by Daniel David Moses and Terry Goldie (a non-Native professor at York University, Toronto), rather than interpreting the anthology, offers a dialogue between Moses and Goldie—who is ambiguous about the reasons that prompted the editorial selections. In the same year appeared *Voices: being Native in Canada*, edited by Linda Jaine (Cree) and Drew Hayden TAYLOR (Ojibwa), a collection of nineteen short stories and essays by well-known writers, including Jeannette C. Armstrong, Jordan Wheeler, Lee Maracle, Gilbert Oskaboose, and others. *Steal my rage: new Native voices* (1995), edited by Joel T. Maki, grew out of a project sponsored in 1993 by Toronto's Na-Me-Res, a Native men's residence. A collection of poetry, fiction, and non-fiction, it features 34 new Native writers from across Canada who treat a wide range of topics, including the difficulties of urban life, identity problems, difficulties with self-esteem, romantic love, spirituality, and the need for self-government.

Some books that do not fall easily into categories include *Contemporary challenges: conversations with Canadian Native authors* (1990), in which a German academic, Hartmut Lutz, interviews eighteen Native writers. *Thunder in my soul: a Mohawk woman speaks* (1993), by Patricia Monture-Angus, is a landmark collection of essays and papers by a First Nations woman scholar who addresses aboriginal people's experience with education, racism, feminism, and the reformation of the criminal justice system.

Eight writers and nineteen visual artists responded to the five-hundredth anniversary of Columbus's landfall in the Americas in *Indigena: contemporary Native perspectives* (1992), edited by Gerald McMaster (Plains Cree) and Lee-Ann Martin (Mohawk). Created specially for the Canadian Museum of Civilization exhibition *Indigena*, the book includes essays with such titles as 'From colonization to repatriation' by Gloria Cranmer Webster, '1992: the discovery of Americity' by Georges E. Sioui Wendayette, 'What more do they want?' by Loretta Todd, and a set of trickster poems by Lenore Keeshig-Tobias—all written to condemn colonialism and racism, as well as to heal the wrongs of the past. *Kelusultiek: original women's voices of Atlantic Canada* (1994) includes poems and articles by Shirley Bear, Shirley Kiju Kawi, and Mary Louise Martin, and Rita Joe's autobiography.

The most exciting literary development has taken place in drama. Tomson HIGHWAY's *The rez sisters* (1988) and its sequel *Dry lips oughta move to Kapuskasing* (1990), both of which won Dora Mavor Moore Awards, brought the Manitoba-born Cree writer international fame. Daniel David Moses and Drew Hayden Taylor are two other award-winning Native playwrights whose dramas have received acclaim. Two new and promising playwrights are Manitoba's Ian Ross and British Columbia's Joseph Dandurand.

A surprisingly large number of Native women have been writing for the theatre: Maria Campbell, Margo Kane, Shirley Cheechoo, Alanis King Odjig, Joyce J.B. Joe, Tina Mason, Monica Marx, and Yvette Nolan. Two other playwrights have gained enthusiastic recognition for their woman-centred plays. In *Princess Pocahontas and the blue spots* (1991) Monique Mojica, a stage and film actress formerly associated with Native Earth Performing Arts, combines song, verse, and docudrama in a 'revue-style feminist history of Native women in the Americas'; it is played by two women who go through what the playwright calls 'thirteen transformations, one for each moon of the lunar year'. This volume also contains Mojica's radio play *Birdwoman and the suffragettes: a story of Sacajawea*, which focuses on the Native guide for the 1805 Lewis and Clark expedition to the Pacific Coast. Like *Princess Pocahontas*, it challenges sexual and racial stereotypes.

Among the plays of Jovette Marchessault translated into English are *Night cows* (1979); *Saga of the wet hens: a play* (1983); and *Alice and Gertrude and Natalie and Renée and dear Ernest* (1983), which principally concerns four lesbian literary figures, Alice B. Toklas, Gertrude Stein, Natalie Barney, and Renée Vivien—and Hemingway. Marchessault's most recent celebration of women writers and artists is *Le voyage magnifique d'Émily Carr* (1990), which won a Governor General's Award.

A number of Native and other small presses have made much of this writing possible: Pemmican (Winnipeg, Manitoba), Theytus (Penticton, British Columbia), Fifth House (Saskatoon, Saskatchewan), Women's Press (Toronto), Seventh Generation Publishers (Toronto), Press Gang (Vancouver, B.C.), NeWest (Edmonton, Alberta), Sister Vision (Toronto), Williams-Wallace (London, Ontario), and Coteau Books (Regina, Sask.). Also contributing to the upsurge of Native self-expression are Aboriginal organizations such as the Saskatchewan Indian Federated College, Regina; the Gabriel Dumont Institute of Native Studies and Applied Research, Saskatoon; Native Earth Performing Arts Inc., Toronto; De-ba-jeh-mu-jig Theatre Group, Manitoulin Island, Ont.; and the En'owkin International School of Writing, Penticton, which publishes annually *Gatherings: the En'owkin journal of First North American people*: it is the only journal of writing by First Nations people in North America featuring a wide range of genres from the best-known Native writers to young aspiring authors being published for the first time. Funding from federal and provincial sources has also been a major force in creating this vitality. And the literary journal *Whetstone*—edited at the Department of English, University of Alberta—has published special Native issues for Spring 1985, Spring 1987, and Fall 1988. Recognizing the canon of Native literature that is being created, *CANADIAN LITERATURE* published a double issue, 'Native writers & Canadian literature' (1990), which included critical essays by non-Native academics and creative writing by Natives: poems by Joan Crate, Rita Joe, Emma Larocque, Daniel David Moses, Thomas King, Ben Abel, Wayne Keon, Bruce Chester, Frank Conibear, and a short story and an essay by Basil Johnston: 'One generation from extinction'.

Native literature in Canada: from the oral tradition to the present (1990) by Penny Petrone is the first book-length critical study of the literature of Canada's First Peoples. Although the concept of criticism as it is understood in the Western literary tradition does not exist in Aboriginal culture, several Native writers have taken up the role of literary critic, objecting to the Eurocentric literary standards and approaches used by non-Native academics, who, they claim, misinterpret the Native message. As a result they have been working hard to find new and culturally appropriate modes, both in literature and criticism. Some women writers—Jeannette Armstrong, Lee Maracle, Lenore Keeshig-Tobias, Beth Brant, Beth Cuthand, and Marie Annharte Baker—have become passionate critics of the Canadian literary establishment, and their critical essays have been appearing in newspapers, anthologies, and journals—in *Feminist studies, Books in Canada*, and *Canadian Woman Studies*. Three publications that grew out of gatherings held in Vancouver offer more of their outspoken criticism. *Telling it: women and language across cultures* (1990) celebrates the thoughts and words of women writers and artists from Canada's fractured margins, and challenges non-marginal assumptions about the nature of writing in Canada, with Jeannette Armstrong and Lee Maracle speaking on the problems of cross-cultural communications and the appropriation of voice. According to Maracle, 'If the culture in which we live cannot accommodate new thoughts, new feelings, new relationships, then we need a *cultural revolution*.' *In the feminine: women and words* (1983), edited by Ann Dybikowski et al., offers such papers as 'Transmitting our identity as Indian writers' by Beth Cuthand, 'Coming out as Indian Lesbian writers' by Beth Brant, and 'Writing from a Native woman's perspective' by Jeannette C. Armstong. *Give back: First Nations perspective on cultural practice* (1992) includes Lee Maracle's 'Oratory: coming to theory', Jeannette Armstrong's 'Racism: racial exclusivity and cultural supremacy', and two essays by the Cree cultural activist Joy Asham Fedorick, 'Decolonizing language: reflections on style' and 'Fencepost sitting and how I fell off to one side', about the appropriation by non-Aboriginal people of Native stories.

Looking at the words of our people: First Nations analysis of literature (1993), edited by Jeannette Armstrong—a ground-breaking collection of Native criticism—includes two essays by Janice Acoose, 'Halfbreed: a revisiting of Maria Campbell's text from an indigenous perspective' and 'Post halfbreed: indigenous writers as authors of their own realities'; two essays by Kateri Damm, 'Says who: colonialism, identity and defining indigenous literature' and 'Speaking Native realities in Maria Campbell's *Halfbreed* and Beatrice Culleton's *In search of April Raintree*; 'Thomas King's *Medicine River*' by Gerry William; and 'Reading tracks from a Native perspective' by Armand Garnet Ruffo.

Canada's Native writers are creating a body of new writing that has an amazing versatility, vitality, and commitment. They are questioning why they should be expected to conform to the constraints of Eurocentric critical theories; they are using the language of 'the enemy' to break from a colonized past, bending and stretching mainstream rules of genre, reinventing new ones, and redefining traditional notions of orality and literacy to enrich and extend Canada's literature. Considering the power and sacredness that traditional Aboriginal cultures attribute to the word as a force of change, the Native word—whether oral or written—will never cease contributing new perspectives and insights to the literature of Canada. PENNY PETRONE

Inuit literature. 'Eskimo' or Inuktitut as a written language did not develop in the Arctic but was introduced with Christianity in the early eighteenth century. Moravian missionaries in London were publishing the gospels in the Labrador dialect by 1813, and as Christianity spread, both the Old and New Testaments, hymnals, and the Book of Common Prayer were translated and published. A demand for non-religious literature quickly developed, and abridged classics such as *The Odyssey* and *Pilgrim's progress* were published in Inuktitut, the Inuit language. The writing systems for Inuktitut vary across Canada, from modified Roman orthographies in Labrador and in the Mackenzie district in the West to a system of shorthand called syllabics that is in use throughout the Central Arctic. In recent years most Inuit literature has been written by Inuit authors and published in both Inuktitut and English. Dozens of English/Inuktitut periodicals such as *Inuktitut*, *Inuit Today* and *Igalaaq* have flourished, and hundreds of books have been produced by commercial publishers as well as by religious, governmental, and cultural agencies.

There are two major sources of traditional Inuit poetry: Knud Rasmussen's ten-volume report *The fifth Thule expedition—the Danish ethnographical expedition to Arctic North America, 1921-24* (1928-45, 1976), and Helen Roberts' and Diamond Jenness's *Songs of the Copper Eskimos: report of the Canadian Arctic expedition 1913-18, vol. XIV* (1925). Some of the songs in these reports have been reprinted by Edmund Carpenter; *Beyond the high hills: a book of Eskimo poems* (1961) edited by Guy-Marie Rousselière; James HOUSTON's *Songs of the dream people: chants and images from the Indians and Eskimos of North America* (1972); and Charles Hofmann's *Drum dance: legends, ceremonies, dances and songs of the Eskimos* (1974). All are reliable and varied treatments of these old Eskimo poems. John Robert COLOMBO's *Poems of the Inuit* (1981) arranges and assesses the traditional poems in a format that is both accessible to popular taste and academically sound. Colombo's introduction provides a cultural context for the songs, and his notes give specific information on the works of Aua, Orpingalik, and other leading Inuit poets.

Until relatively recently Inuit legends appeared only in academic and scientific publications such as the reports of Rasmussen and

Jenness. Traditional stories were thought to be too bloody, too bawdy, and, curiously, too boring in their original form to interest the general reader. This attitude changed considerably with the development of the soapstone-carving industry in the North. Zebedee Nungak's and Eugene Arima's *Stories from Povungnituk, Québec* (1969), an English/Inuktitut collection, was the first book of genuine Inuit legends aimed at this new market. *Tales from the igloo* (1972), translated and edited by the Rev. Maurice Metayer, was followed by *How kabloonat became and other Inuit legends* (1974) by the Inuk newspaper editor Mark Kalluak, and by *Stories from Pangnirtung* (1976), illustrated by Germaine Arnaktauyok. She also illustrated *Inuit legends* (1977), which contained further stories collected by Father Metayer and edited after his death by Leoni Kappi.

Diaries and autobiographies constitute an important element of Inuit literature today. Since Lydia Campbell's *Sketches of Labrador life* (1980) was first published in the St John's, Nfld, *Evening Telegram* in 1894, Inuit have produced numerous reminiscences and excerpts from diaries for magazines and newspapers. *The autobiography of John Ayaruaq* (1969) is available only in syllabic edition, but life in the old days in the Western Arctic is described in *I, Nuligak* (1966), translated and edited by Maurice Metayer. *People from our side* (1975), by Dorothy Eber and Peter Pitseolak, documents the more recent contact culture through the very personal and humorous memoirs of one of Cape Dorset's legendary leaders. Alice French describes her education in a boarding school in Aklavik in *My name is Masak* (1977) and Minnie Aodla Freeman's *Life among the Quallunaat* (1978) reveals the pain and loneliness such experiences brought to Inuit children. Anthony Apakark Thrasher, whose father was a contemporary of Nuligak, gives a much grimmer picture of modern Inuit life in *Thrasher: skid row Eskimo* (1976). Thrasher's view of life from a Prince Albert jail is counterbalanced by the lyrical and humorous *Shadows* (1975) by the Rev. Armand Tagoona. Dorothy Eber's *Pitseolak: pictures out of my life* (1971) is an oral biography of the famous Eskimo printmaker Pitseolak Ashoona. Many more oral biographies can be found in recent catalogues from printmaking centres such as Cape Dorset, Holman Island, and Baker Lake.

Traditional Inuit did not distinguish between children's and adults' literature, believing that any good story or song had something for everyone. With the introduction of formalized schooling in the Arctic, however, numerous books in both English and Inuktitut were produced for Inuit children. Though most of these books are not easily available in southern Canada, Markoosie's *Harpoon of the hunter* (1970), the first Inuit novel, has been published in a dozen languages; and two lavishly illustrated memoirs—*Peter Pitseolak's escape from death* (1977), edited by Dorothy Eber, and Norman Ekoomiak's *An Arctic childhood* (1980)—give some idea of what is being written for Inuit children today.

Most Inuit publications now appear in bilingual or trilingual editions, have a high proportion of illustration, and include both transcribed oral material and texts from original manuscripts. Books such as *The northerners* (1974), edited by Josepi Padlayat, and *We don't live in snow houses now* (1976), edited by Susan Cowan, respond to the requirements of the literature by printing texts in English, Roman orthography, Inuktitut, syllabics, and sometimes French, all within one cover. *Paper stays put: a collection of Inuit writing* (1980), edited by Robin Gedalof, includes examples of both traditional and contemporary literature from most of the major Inuit publications of the 1960s and 1970s. More Inuit literature can be found listed in Gedalof's *An annotated bibliography of Canadian Inuit literature* (1979).

The emendation of government policies on Native language rights, the development of a standard Roman orthography, the modification of the syllabic system, and technological developments affecting the typing and printing of Inuktitut have all ensured that Eskimo-language publications will continue. At the same time the interest of publishers and readers in southern Canada suggests that Inuit literature in English will also flourish in the future. It would seem that the movement from an oral to a written literature in Northern Canada does not destroy but rather helps to preserve and develop a tradition.

ROBIN GEDALOF McGRATH

1982 to 1996. As Inuit communities gain control over education, media, and government, their first priority is to ensure the survival of traditional culture and language. Inuit writers have been active in the promotion of Inuktitut in education and communication as a means of ensuring that survival. In 1987 the Baffin Island Writers' Project was established to provide writers with access to desktop publishing technology and to organize workshops with other creative writers, especially Aboriginal authors. Two literary publications emerged from the project: the bilingual *Kivioq: Inuit Fiction Magazine* and *Titirausivut*, devoted to writing by students. Part of the inspiration for such initiatives has been a realization that the existence of reading materials in Inuktitut is crucial for the preservation of the language. The transmission through education and media of traditional oral culture, which has been disrupted by the arrival of English, would also become a priority of writing programs.

Inuit elders insist that preserving old ways and stories is a way to preserve culture, and younger generations have responded energetically with collections of traditional stories and periodicals intended primarily for Inuit audiences. As a result, contemporary Inuit poems, stories, and essays can be found dispersed across the number of serial publications that have circulated in the North, including *Inuit Today*, *Inuit Monthly*, *Inuvialuit*, *Isumavut*, *Up Here,* and *Nunavut*. *Inuktitut*, which is published by the Inuit Tapirisat of Canada, features articles, poems, and stories in Inuktitut, English, and French. Many of the authors published in these magazines were collected and reprinted in *Northern voices: Inuit writing in English* (1988) by Penny Petrone, which has helped Inuit writers to achieve wider recognition and critical attention in southern Canada. Petrone includes writers whose names are known in the North: Ruth Qanatsiaq, Sam Metcalfe, Willie Thrasher, Leah Idlout d'Argencourt, Tumasi Quissa, Susie Tiktalik, Mark Kalluak, Mary Carpenter Lyons, Martha Flaherty, Taguk Curley, Liz Semigok, and Aksaajuuq Etuangat. To date, *Canadian Inuit literature: the development of a tradition* (1984) by Robin Gedalof McGrath provides the most comprehensive study, tracing the contemporary literature back to its oral roots. McGrath shows how the oral tradition was transformed by the establishment of the Inuktitut writing system and by the growing literacy of Inuit people, arguing that the oral tradition lives on in the new written forms. As McGrath indicates, autobiography has been an important form in Inuit literature. While Them Days published Margaret Baikie's *Labrador memories* (1983), continuing its series of writing by Inuit women of Labrador, autobiographical material is increasingly represented in illustrated prose, such as Ruth Annaqtuusi Tulurialik's *Qikaaluktut: images of Inuit life* (1986), a bilingual book written with David Pelly and illustrated with the artist's colourful drawings. The best-known autobiography by an Inuit person, *Life among the Qallunaat* (1978), is no longer in print, but its author, Minnie Freeman, has collaborated with Odette Leroux and Marion Jackson on *Inuit women artists: voices from Cape Dorset* (1994); and, given the prevalence of the illustrated prose genre in Inuit literature, books on Inuit art can be considered part of contemporary literature.

Traditional stories, songs, and poems continue to appear in collections edited by both Inuit and non-Inuit. William A. Oquilluk and Laurel L. Bland's *People of Kauwerak: legends of the northern Eskimo* (1981), Lawrence Millman's *A kayak full of ghosts: Eskimo tales* (1987), and Howard Norman's *Northern tales: traditional stories of Eskimo and Indian peoples* (1990) are but a few. Agnes Nanogak, the illustrator of *Tales from the igloo* (1975), demonstrates her storytelling and editing talents in the sequel, *More tales from the igloo* (1986). Introduced by Robin McGrath, this collection contains a variety of Inuit animal-spouse, cautionary, and epic stories. Traditional literature has achieved greater visibility in the south by its inclusion in a variety of anthologies such as Agnes Grant's *Our bit of truth: an anthology of Canadian Native literature* (1990), John Robert COLOMBO's *Songs of the great land* (1989), and *An anthology of Canadian Native literature in English* (1992), edited by Daniel David MOSES and Terry Goldie. Thus, pieces in English by Martin Martin, Susan Martin, Marion Tuu'luq, Simon Arnaviapik, Anthony Apakark Thrasher, and Alootook Ipellie, as well as traditional songs in translation, have reached a wider audience. Poems by Aua, Orpingalik, Nakasuk, and other well-known Inuit poets collected by Rasmussen were reprinted in Neil Philip's *Songs are thoughts: poems of the Inuit* (1995).

Southern libraries continue to classify Inuit oral literature and traditional literature as 'children's literature', even though Inuit writers and readers have begun to distinguish between them. The Baffin Divisional Board of Education has published numerous books for children, such as Monica Ittuksardjuat's *Akumalik* (1988). Another well-known Inuit children's author, Michael Arvaarluk Kusugak, has enjoyed great success in southern Canada with his children's books, including a collaboration with Robert MUNSCH entitled *A promise is a promise* (1988). In Kusugak's *Hide and sneak* (1992) the heroine, Allashua, encounters an *Ijiraq*, a fantastic little man resembling a ptarmigan who takes her to a hiding-place where no one will find her and she must outwit him in order to escape. In *Northern Lights and soccer trails* (1993) another Inuit girl, Kataujaq, learns to cope with the death of her mother from her grandmother who teaches her that, in death, people become the Northern Lights.

Alootook Ipellie, perhaps the best-known Inuit author and artist, has been editor of *Kivioq*, as well as a long-standing contributor to other northern publications. Ipellie's first book, *Arctic dreams and nightmares* (1993), combines conventional Inuit literary forms, such as story borrowing and satire, with modern themes to reflect the two worlds experienced by Inuit people. The book consists of pen-and-ink drawings that are said to be the inspiration for the corresponding stories, all told in the first-person voice of a shaman who has recently ascended in death.

Because Inuit inhabit a circumpolar world, the literature written by Inuit people is transnational. Inuit communities in the former Soviet Union, Greenland, and Alaska share many of the patterns in literary production with Canadian Inuit. In 1988 the King Island Native community published *Ugiuvangmiut and Quliapyuit King Island tales: Eskimo history and legends from Bering Strait*, which includes texts in English and Inupiaq. Transnational vitality is evident in Lela Kiana Oman's *The epic of Qayaq: the longest story ever told by my people* (1995); *Tales of Ticasuk* (1987), collected by Emily Ivanoff Brown (Ticasuk); and *Esquimaux d'Asie: contes et récits* (1988) by K.S. Sergeeva and E.S. Rubcova. The need for publications in Inuktitut that address readers in all these areas seems evident, and the number of texts in Inuktitut has increased in recent years: *Sanaaq* (1984), a novel by Salome Nappaluk Mitiarjuk, is in Inuktitut only, while *Voices from the Eastern Arctic* (1987), a collection of writing by students between the ages of twelve and eighteen, edited by Jane Ann Shapiro, is just one of the publications in which texts appear in Inuktitut, English, and French. One of the early books to adopt this form, Zebedee Nungak's and Eugene Arima's *Stories from Povungnituk, Québec* (1969), was republished as *Inuit stories: Povungnituk* (1988), and Norman Ekoomiak's *Arctic memories* (1990) is in its second edition. The continued interest in these texts demonstrates the growing audience for Inuit literature in Canada. As Inuit communities continue to heal the damage done by colonization and to endure the transition from traditional to modern life, Inuit artists and writers voice their people's experiences as part of that healing process.

See Robin Gedalof McGrath, *Canadian Inuit literature: the development of a tradition* (1984). RENÉE HULAN

Acadian literature. In 1958 Antonine MAILLET, not yet famous, published her first novel, *Pointe-aux-Coques*. Anselme Chiasson's first ethnological study, *Chéticamp: histoire et traditions acadiennes*, appeared three years later. Since then numerous other authors have been inspired by the anecdotal history, or tried to preserve the rich oral literature, of Acadia—the name given in the seventeenth century to French Atlantic-seaboard possessions in the New World. Student protests at the Université de Moncton in 1968 revealed, or gave birth to, a group of writers who both denounced the distressing conditions endured by the Acadians and exhorted them to break out of their fear and silence. These protesters, and the collectors of ancestral traditions and values, breathed new life into Acadian literature—or, as some would say, gave it birth. This entry will not linger over works published before 1960, especially since almost none are available in bookstores or even the best libraries. Extracts from the principal works published between 1609 and 1975 have been collected in *Anthologie de textes littéraires acadiens* (1979) edited by Marguerite Maillet.

I. THE BEGINNINGS. Marc Lescarbot created the myth of the Promised Land of Acadia in his account of the first permanent French settlement in North America. In the fourth volume of his *Histoire de la Nouvelle-France* (Paris, 1609) he lauded the many beauties and natural riches of Port-Royal in picturesque style and with biblical vision, emphasizing the enthusiasm and *joie de vivre* that existed there despite inevitable hardships. Until the middle of the eighteenth century French memorialists and essayists—such as Pierre Biard, Nicolas Denys, N. Dièreville, and Louis Franquet—echoed one or the other element of Marc Lescarbot's Edenic image of Acadia. (See also Writing in NEW FRANCE: I.)

The deportation of the Acadians (1755-62) put a tragic end to the original enthusiasm of settlement, replacing it with a long century of suffering, confusion, and silence. There was no one, French or Acadian, to lament this Paradise Lost until 1847, when Henry Wadsworth Longfellow took up the theme and wrote *EVANGELINE*, which attracted the attention of America and Europe to the Acadian people, whom he praised even as he mourned their disappearance. Evangeline, the image of faithfulness unto death, would represent a song of hope to the dispersed Acadians and inspire their rallying cry. Beginning in 1867 *Le moniteur acadien* (Shediac, New Brunswick) chronicled the birth and activities of an Acadian ruling class. Young, educated Acadians in the

Maritime provinces—having become aware that their ancestors had been dispersed, disorganized, impoverished, and that they themselves had been made to feel inferior to their neighbours—held national conferences (1881, 1884, 1890), wrote in the newspapers, and gave lectures. Some (Pascal Poirier and Philéas Bourgeois) were conscious of giving birth to a truly Acadian literature. Orators and writers tried to convince their compatriots that their isolation had come to an end and that their inferior position was due entirely to the deportation. All reiterated the same thing: Acadia had had a glorious past before 1755; the deportees had been heroic; and as they themselves were no less valiant than their ancestors, their survival as a nation would be assured if they remained faithful to the traditions, language, and faith of their forefathers. During the 1930s, 1940s, and 1950s this ideology of survival through keeping faith with the past was expressed in drama (J.-B. Jégo, J. Branch), fiction ('Sabattis' Thomas Gill, A.-J. Léger, J.-A. Deveau), and poetry (F.-M. Lanteigne, N.-P. Landry). The unhappy phase of Acadian history was repeated over and over again and glorified, thus bringing the myth of Evangeline to its height.

2. 1958 TO 1979. The socio-political arena changed in 1960 when Acadian L.-J. Robichaud, who advocated 'an equal chance for all', was elected premier of New Brunswick. In literature the change in direction occurred in 1958 with the publication of Antonine Maillet's *Pointe-aux-Coques* and Ronald DESPRÉS's *Silences à nourrir de sang*; and even more so with the foundation in 1972 of the first publishing house in Acadia, Les Éditions d'Acadie. Antonine Maillet dominates Acadian literature, as much by the number of books she has published as for the fame she achieved, nationally and internationally, even before receiving the Prix Goncourt. In *La SAGOUINE* (1971) she not only universalized the complaints and demands of her people but expressed beautifully their *joie de vivre* and common sense: she forced attention onto Acadia. Her influence on Acadian literature is incontestable, as to both the content of her books (exploitation of the heritage and anecdotal history of Acadia) and their form (use of Acadian oral structure and the spoken word).

Ronald Després has been considered one of French Canada's major poets ever since the publication of *Silences à nourrir de sang*; two other collections, *Les cloisons en vertige* (1962) and *Le balcon des dieux inachevés* (1969), confirm this judgement. His *roman-sotie*, or satirical farce, *Le scalpel ininterrompu* (1962), was also well received by critics; but Acadians are generally disturbed by these books, considering them to be overly bloody and obscure. Even so, Després's works, despite their purely aesthetic and personal bent, are Acadian, if only because of his obsession with the sea. His anguish and his description of a dehumanizing society have found more than one echo in the literature of the 1970s—a decade during which young Acadian authors, beginning with the poets, resolutely committed themselves to the confrontation they felt was necessary to free their people.

2(a). *Poetry*. Raymond LeBlanc's *Cri de terre* (1973) was the first publication of Les Éditions d'Acadie. Torn between his refusal to live as a slave or colonial and his reluctance to become an exile, the poet tries to capture the sacred flame in the very roots of his country, to reinvent his homeland through the magic of words. This collection cries out against the silence that permitted injustices and oppression and warns against the Anglicization of Acadiens; at the same time it is a brotherly call to an awakening, and then a revolt, before the only hope left is in alliance between Acadia and Quebec.

Following LeBlanc, Guy Arsenault, Herménégilde CHIASSON, Calixte Duguay, and Ulysse Landry respectively showed the difficulty they had in identifying with their exploited, half-assimilated brothers—with those who had had all desire for revolt crushed out of them by fear. Since the Acadians' unacceptable position was perceived as being closely related to a problem of language, these poets—Calixte Duguay excepted—used different levels of language, the better to reach their people or to translate the reality they wished to denounce. This led them to question the possibility and the utility of poetry as a means of awakening their society. Chiasson is the most avant-garde of this group, and possibly the most pessimistic. After the publication of his first collection, *Mourir à Scoudouc* (1974), a book of great poetic force and beauty, he remained torn between his determination to denounce firmly the aberrant, brutalizing realities in Acadia and his wish to give to the very language that was suppressing his people a poetic intensity that would load his words with promises (*Rapport sur l'état de mes illusions*, 1976). Duguay, who seemed the least committed, considered his people incapable of a collective revolt and offered them songs 'to make a summer out of the cold of our winters' and dreams of a land where solidarity and liberty would replace dispersion and subjugation. The magical

Acadia of his *Les stigmates du silence* (1975) is only a dreamland in Léonard Forest's *Saisons antérieures* (1973), in which 'Bittersweet Lachigan' presents itself as 'castles of hope'. This poet, who uses such beautiful images and has such a fresh style, received the Prix France-Acadie for his second collection, *Comme en Florence* (1979).

2(b). *Theatre.* The two recurring themes of the 1970s—protest and recovery—are both treated by the few dramatists whose works have been published. Antonine Maillet excepted, Laval Goupil has attracted the most attention from critics. His first play, *Tête d'eau* (1974), which is dream-like, surrealistic, fantastic, treats universal concerns: it supports all forms of creativity by showing the kind of madness that results when the imagination has been browbeaten. In contrast, *Le Djibou* (1975) is very realistic and is rooted in a specific Acadian socio-cultural milieu. The characters—whose language is violent, raw, and vulgar—try to trap and exorcise their past and present fears. The play ends when they begin to take steps to free themselves. In a relatively short text, *Les pêcheurs déportés* (1974), Germaine Comeau brings out several problems that hinder the development of Nova Scotia Acadians. But one theme is clear: the need to break down the barriers preventing people from speaking to, and understanding, each other.

Jules Boudreau wrote the book, and Calixte Duguay the words and music, for the musical *Louis Mailloux* (created in 1975), which was so successful that the sound-track was recorded (Kapociré KC5304). Boudreau also used history as the source for his play *Cochu et le soleil* (1977): around 1783 the arrival of the Loyalists forces an Acadian family to uproot itself for the second time in less than thirty years. After watching some resist and others submit, the younger daughter decides to give up this shameful existence and chooses life in a 'real' country, that of the English. The father, proud and stubborn, consoles himself for this disgrace as he sees his elder daughter continue the fight to maintain her culture and identity. In *Sacordjeu* (1979) Claude Renaud brings back to life another moment in history, the revolt of the parishioners of Grande-Digue, New Brunswick, in 1848. This play, never performed, denounces the sector of the clergy it judges to be hypocritical and allied with the colonizers and merchants to rob 'the poor'. *Cochu et le soleil* and *Sacordjeu* are not simply retellings of history—like, for example, *Le Capitaine St-Simon*, one of Vincent Dumas's *Deux pièces acadiennes* (1979). Besides wishing to stimulate a renewal among their people, Boudreau and Renaud try to debunk the Longfellow myth of the submissive Acadian.

In addition to the few plays that have been published, a good number have been produced, some—especially those of Herménégilde Chiasson and Raymond LeBlanc—quite successfully.

2(c). *Legends, tales, stories, novels.* The publication of Anselme Chiasson's monograph *Chéticamp: histoire et traditions acadiennes* (1961), which featured popular culture, along with Antonine Maillet's *Pointe-aux-Coques*, marks the beginning of a movement that prompted several authors to turn towards the Acadian heritage, either to record it or to draw inspiration from it. This movement has grown; yet some, especially the poets, have protested or warned that another retreat into the past must not result in an unwillingness to denounce shortcomings of present times. Even so, the vast majority of the works published in the seventies deal with anecdotal history or oral literature.

Some authors transcribe and reproduce a few of the beautiful legends collected in New Brunswick and Nova Scotia (Francis Savoie, Anselme Chiasson, Catherine Jolicoeur), or publish fairy tales (Melvin Gallant, Gérald Aucoin); while others mix their own recollections with oral traditions, recreating typical Acadians from the past (Félix-E. Thibodeau, Désiré d'Eon), or tell of their own life and that of the region (Antoinette Gallant, Lina Madore). This last category includes simply written accounts, by authors who not only are not professionals but are not especially concerned with creating literary masterpieces. Louis Haché, who went from stories to novels, stands out clearly from this group. With his historical sketch of the little island of Miscou, *Charmante Miscou* (1974), followed by his novel *Adieu P'tit Chipagan* (1978), and his short stories in *Toubes jersiaises* (1980), the Acadian peninsula seems to have found its historian-storyteller, and Acadia its bard of the sea.

In *La Mariecomo* (1974) Régis Brun tells the story of the witches of the south coast of New Brunswick during the second half of the nineteenth century. These people, with their taste for gaiety and freedom, protested, by their very presence in an Acadian village, against a 'bourgeois' lifestyle dictated by clerical and national interests. Jacques SAVOIE's characters, in *Raconte-moi Massabielle* (1979), are also on the fringes of society; but the author, instead of going back into the past, treats a very topical subject, the expropriations at Kouchibouguac. *Raconte-moi* has a new tone: there are no lamentations, no violent denunciations, but instead humour, a pleasure in word-games, and above all a very modern form—it is not a book with a message. Claude LeBouthillier has published two novels set in the future: *L'Acadien reprend son pays* (1977) and *Isabelle-sur-mer* (1979). If, in 1988, the Acadian has taken peaceful possession of his paradise, it is because he has lived through, and vanquished, his fear; and if the new country solves the world crisis in the year 2000, it is because Acadians have concentrated on the best of the old and new values: love of the arts, respect for nature, and fidelity to themselves and their roots. Such an optimistic vision of the future is exceptional among Acadian authors.

2(d). *Biography, memoirs, essays.* Biography was one of the first literary forms cultivated in Acadia; the foremost examples are *Le Père Lefebvre et l'Acadie* (1898) by Pascal Poirier and *Vie de l'abbé François-Xavier Lafrance* (1913) by Philéas Bourgeois. It subsequently attracted little interest until the publication of Camille-Antonio Doucet's *Une étoile s'est levée en Acadie: Marcel-François Richard* (1973), Alexandre Savoie's *Un demi-siècle d'histoire: le Docteur A.-M. Sormany* (1976), and Éloi DeGrâce's *Mgr Stanislas Doucet* (1977). The goal is still the same: to honour the builders of Acadia. These three biographies are not necessarily more interesting than those published by Poirier and Bourgeois, but they are more complete and better documented. In the last few years, as Acadians have begun to tell their own story, their confidences or testimony have taken the form of poetry, diary, and fiction. Only Calixte Savoie has written his memoirs. Teacher, school principal, and superintendent, and then secretary and president of the Société l'Assomption (1926-62), he wrote his *Mémoires d'un nationaliste acadien* (1979) to tell the story of a life of struggle, and especially of the fight of a minority-nationalist whose compatriots obtained the most basic educational rights crumb by crumb. Whoever reads the book will better understand why some Acadian authors are so bitter and violent and also why some, like Michel Roy, see no future for Acadia except by joining with Quebec. Roy has produced the most literary essay on Acadia in *L'Acadie perdue* (1978), whose fervour and passion leave no one unmoved. While the position he takes in most of this essay may inspire doubt or despair in some minds, there are pages in his book that can arouse positive speculation about Acadia's future. MARGUERITE MAILLET

3. 1980 TO 1995. The 1980s were a turning-point in Acadian literature. If the preceding decade saw the birth of a modern literature marked by the themes of homeland and identity, the eighties saw the consolidation of a literary institution in an outpouring of works that were wide-ranging in both form and content. This was brought about, particularly, by the advent of new publishing houses in the northeast and northwest of New Brunswick and in Nova Scotia, creating literary centres outside Moncton, which had previously monopolized literary and publishing activities. Furthermore, university courses on Acadian literature developed, as did research, which brought to light indispensable tools for the compilation of all kinds of anthologies and bibliographies and, above all, made possible Marguerite Maillet's *Histoire de la littérature acadienne* (1983).

3(a). *Poetry.* As is often the case in an emergent literature, Acadian writers have favoured poetry. While only about fifteen collections by Acadian poets were published between 1970 and 1980, nearly seventy appeared between 1980 and 1995. No longer dominated by nationalistic themes, this poetry reflects the leading trends in modern (sometimes post-modern) literature: discontinuous syntax, diversity of style and content ('hétérogénéité'), narrative and minimalist prose-poetry, verbal violence, discursive extravagance, etc. If it is evident that Acadian poetry is part of a regional literature ('l'exiguïté', to use the expression of François Paré), it is no less clear that the poetry itself has abandoned its regionalist themes.

Among some thirty poets who have been published since 1980, those who have been the most prolific are also the most remarkable. Gerald Leblanc, with seven collections published since 1981, is in the front rank of Acadian poets. From *Comme un otage du quotidien* (1981) to *L'éloge du chiac* (1995), his writing is imbued with immense energy in poems of revolt or dispute; this literature accommodates, blends, and transforms the most diverse realities and influences in order to participate in the development of a modern culture. Herménégilde Chiasson's *Miniatures* (1995), the fifth of his collections since 1986, gives a modern form to a classical lyricism that is stamped with feeling and depth: the memory of Blaise Cendrars's rhythmic prose is clearly evident. Serge Patrice Thibodeau, who has published five collections since 1990, made a brilliant entry into the world of Acadian poetry with his first collection, *La septième chute* (1990), which was a finalist for the Prix

Émile Nelligan—he won the prize for *Le cycle de Praque* (1992). Choosing to take the uncommon path of spirituality and mysticism, he continues to produce a carefully constructed body of work that reveals a rare mastery. Dyane Léger (*Les anges en transit*, 1992) and Huguette Bourgeois (*Espaces libres*, 1990), among others, have effectively sounded the voice of women in Acadian poetry. Roméo Savoie (*L'eau brisée*, 1992) specializes in the interaction of poetry and painting. Fredric Gary Comeau—in his third collection, *Ravages* (1995)—has shown how young poets can quickly attain surprising formal coherence. All these writers—and others, including Maurice Raymond, Georges Bourgeois, Rose Després, Raymond Guy LeBlanc, and Rino Morin Rossignol—have given Acadian poetry a smooth and steady pace of productivity, and originality of style, in which a localized distinctiveness (*exiguïté*) and modernism intersect and blend. Finally, mention should be made of the anthology *Rêves inachevés: poésie acadienne contemporaine* (1982), edited by Fred COGSWELL and Jo-Ann Elder.

3(b). *Theatre.* Considering that of all plays produced, only a few are published, Antonine Maillet remains the most prolific playwright. She continued and ended her Acadian saga with *La contrebandière* (1981) and *Garrochés en paradis* (1986), and also wrote plays inspired by Rabelais and even Shakespeare. Moncton theatre has been sustained by (among others) Gracia Couturier, whose *Mon mari est un ange* (1988) deals humorously with the modern themes of the war of the sexes and the modern family, and Christiane St-Pierre, who treats the same themes in *Hubert: ou Comment l'homme devient rose* (1994). The theatre of Herménégilde Chiasson is marked by seriousness that often borders on tragedy: in *L'éxil d'Alexa* (1993) the issues of identity and language are a springboard for treating the greater matters of life and death.

3(c). *Legends, tales, stories, novels.* The richness of Acadian folklore continues to persuade writers to collect and publish legends and traditional folkways. Foremost among them is Anselme Chiasson, the author of six books since 1981—including *Le nain jaune et autres contes des îles de la Madeleine* (1995), an anthology of stories, legends, songs, and traditions. Similarly, Melvin Gallant added a second volume to his Acadian tales, *Ti-Jean-le-Fort* (1991).

The publication of non-traditional tales for children has flowered since 1980. Notable works are the very successful *Le tapis de Grand-Pré* (1987) by Réjean Aucoin and Jean-Claude Tremblay, and the books of Jean Péronnet, *Pépère Goquen l'hiver* (1993), and Denise Paquette, *Souris Baline et son ami Georges-Henri* (1993).

In a genre that combines fiction and factual descriptions of a way of life, Louis Haché's *Le guetteur* (1991) and other books portray the fishing villages of the Acadian peninsula at the beginning of the twentieth century. In a different vein there is the story of a voyage in India, in which the narrator employs the practice of writing fragments that explore his inner life: *Oasis* (1993) by Charles Pelletier. The development of the Acadian short story was marked by the publication of an anthology by Les Éditions d'Acadie, *Concerto pour huit voix* (1989). Individual collections by Evelyne Foëx, *Voyages sans retour . . . parfois* (1994), which borders on the fantastic, and Pol Chantraine, *Le grand bal des baleines* (1994), eleven stories depicting characters from the Magdalen Islands, have followed.

Among novels of the period, we have witnessed the great success of the Acadian saga *Crache à Pic* (1984) by Antonine Maillet. She returned to her legendary characters and hyperbolic style in an animal epic, *L'oursiade* (1990). But it is in her biographical novel *Les confessions de Jeanne de Valois* (1992) that she has really found a new mode—and has written one of her finest works. Maillet certainly continues to influence Acadian fiction. Indeed, Laurier Melanson, in three novels—*Zélika à cochon vert* (1981), *Otto de la veuve Hortense* (1982), and *Aglaé* (1983)—combines folksy characters, and racy humour and language, in a manner that recalls his illustrious predecessor. Maillet's influence is also felt in the predilection among novelists for history, and the life of our more-or-less recent forebears. This subject seems to have been the main inspiration of Jeanne Ducluzeau, as well as of Jeanine-Landry Thériault, Anne Lévesque, and Sylvain Rivière. Claude LeBouthillier's two long novels—*Le feu du mauvais temps* (1989) and *Les marées du Grand Dérangement* (1994)—in which literary quality has not quite matched the remarkable historical research underlying them, go all the way back to pre-Expulsion history. But the Acadian novel also has its modernists, like Jacques Savoie, who pursues in Quebec a double career as scenarist and novelist. His narratives are strongly multi-voiced and self-reflexive. In *Le cirque bleu* (1995) he treats the reunited family (after having written in preceding novels about the broken family). In a more profound and subtle vein, France Daigle, in her seventh novel, *1953: Chronique d'une naissance annoncée* (1995), continues an original body of writing in which fiction and commentary meet and enrich each other in the play, serious or light-hearted, of creation that is also the play of life and death. Jean Babineau's *Bloupe* (1993), his first novel, is as baroque as one could wish, with its tip of the hat to James Joyce, echoes of Réjean DUCHARME, and its combination of tenderness, humour, and despair in an endless and fragmented narrative.

3(d). *Biography, memoirs, essays.* Biographies, previously rather rare, have proliferated throughout the past fifteen years, and pioneer priests are often the subject (as they were formerly). This is the case with Fernand Arsenault and Edmour Babineau's *François-Amédée bourgeois* (1985) and *Philippe Belliveau* (1988) and Robert Pichette's *Batie sur le roc: Mgr Numa Pichette, témoin d'une époque* (1995). Starting with the biographical account, they end by revealing an entire swath of local history, or the life of an institution, or a traditional Acadian activity. Among memoirs, Alexandre J. Boudreau's *À l'assaut des défis* (1994) and Andréa Richard's *Femme après le cloître* (1995) are of special interest.

It is above all in the realm of scholarly studies and essays that the number of publications has increased remarkably. The historical essay, as always, has an important place; a notable example is *Les Acadiens de la Nouvelle Écosse, hier et aujourd'hui* (1995) by Sally Ross and J. Alphonse Deveau. However, diverse subjects are now being treated in essay form, such as women, family law, language, and the fishing industry. A notable work in ethnology is *Médecine traditionelle en Acadie* (1992) by Marielle-Cormier Boudreau, winner of the Luc LACOURCIÈRE Medal. Several out-of-print critical books have recently seen the light of day, of which the most important is *Glossaire acadien* (1993) by Pascal Poirier, edited by Pierre M. Gérin. The artists Claude Roussel, Marie-Hélène Allain, and Yvon Gallant have been the subjects of monographs. Politics and society remain preferred subjects for essayists, especially for Léon Thériault, author of *La question du pouvoir en Acadie* (1982), and Michel Doucet, who wrote *Le discours confisqué* (1995). In the sphere of reference books, besides Marguerite Maillet's *L'histoire de la littérature acadienne*, and *Bibliographie des publications d'Acadie, 1609-1990: Sources premières et sources secondes* (1992), one work is dominant. This is *L'Acadie des Maritimes* (1993), an encyclopaedia of more than 900 pages, with thirty contributors writing on all aspects of Acadian life in the Maritimes.

One can best appreciate the considerable upsurge of Acadian literature by taking into account the fact that the steady flow of publications between 1980 and 1995 represents twice the number of books published between 1604 and 1980.

RAOUL BOUDREAU

Acadian Magazine*, *The (Halifax, 1826-8). Published between July 1826 and Jan. 1828, *The Acadian Magazine; or Literary Mirror* was the most important literary journal in early-nineteenth-century Maritime Canada. It appeared monthly, printed by Jacob S. Cunnabel and edited by Beamish Murdock (1826 to mid-1827) and J. Scott Tremaine (mid-1827 to 1828). Nineteen numbers were issued; the average length of each was forty double-column pages. While it included reprints from British, American, and Upper Canadian sources, over three-quarters of the published material was locally written. Fiction and poetry were prominently featured, most of it original. There were pieces on local and North American history, a short series on travel in eastern Nova Scotia, and reviews of local literary productions. As well there were general essays on a wide variety of topics, and early issues included foreign domestic news. During the life of the journal four handsome engravings by Halifax engraver Charles W. Torbett were published; one of them depicted the recently completed Province House (1819), seat of the legislative assembly of Nova Scotia.

Very little is known about the local contributors because most published anonymously. It is suspected that Thomas Chandler HALIBURTON wrote one of the longer poems, 'Western scenes'. John Templedon wrote several pieces of fiction, James Irving several literary essays, and Joseph Hart Clinch some poetry. There is clear evidence that the contributors were not concentrated in Halifax but came from the area: Saint John, Pictou, Truro, Cape Breton, Windsor, and Annapolis Royal.

TOM VINCENT

Achard, Eugène. See CHILDREN'S LITERATURE IN FRENCH: 2, 3.

Acorn, Milton (1923-86). Born in Charlottetown, Prince Edward Island, he served in the Second World War, suffering a serious head injury. On his return to P.E.I. he eventually became a carpenter, but gave up carpentry in 1956—after privately publishing his first collection of poems, *In love and anger*—to devote himself to poetry in Montreal, where he met Irving LAYTON, Al PURDY, and other poets. *The brain's the target* and a broadsheet, *Against a league of liars*, were published in 1960. In 1962 he married Gwendolyn MacEWEN in Toronto, and when the marriage failed the following year he moved to Vancouver. Fifty-eight of his poems were printed in a special issue of *The FIDDLEHEAD* (Spring 1963), and in the same year *Jawbreakers* (1963) appeared. Throughout the sixties he became increasingly involved in political activities and many of his poems developed through public readings. At the end of the sixties he returned to Toronto. When *I've tasted my blood: poems 1956 to 1968* (1969), selected and introduced by Purdy, failed to win a Governor General's Award in 1970, a group of Toronto poets created the 'Canadian poetry award' for Acorn and named him 'The people's poet'. His next two collections were *I shout love and on shaving off his beard* (1971) and *More poems for people* (1972), which was dedicated to Dorothy LIVESAY and inspired by her *Poems for people* (1947). *The island means Minago* (1975), which won a Governor General's Award, was followed by *Jackpine sonnets* (1977), *Captain Neal MacDougal and the naked goddess* (1982), and *Dig up my heart: selected poems of Milton Acorn 1952-1983* (1983), selected by Al Purdy. Since Acorn's death, several collections edited by James Deahl have appeared: *Whiskey jack* (1986), *A stand of jackpine* (1987), *The uncollected Acorn* (1987), and *Hundred proof earth* (1988). *The Northern red oak: poems for and about Acorn*, also edited by James Deahl, appeared in 1987.

Acorn described himself as a 'believer in Dialectics'. His lifelong Marxism was the most obvious manifestation of this belief, but it found expression even in poems that seem totally unpolitical. Acorn's is a poetry of opposites, of delicacy and toughness, of 'love' and 'anger', which come together in a single dialectical vision: the delicate beauty that Acorn celebrates in humanity and nature must be defended through tough-minded, unrelenting struggle, and is the ultimate inspiration of even his most harshly aggressive works.

The poems of Acorn's early maturity, collected for the most part in the first half of *I've tasted my blood*, are generally brief and straightforward, but have a subtlety of technique that gives them a surprisingly rich resonance. A sensitive ear for the nuances of North American speech rhythms and a gift for imagery, ranging from delicately precise notation to almost surrealistic evocativeness, are joined to a fine organizing intelligence. Acorn's best lyrics are miniature dramas in which conflict and resolution find expression through the subtle interplay of rhythm and imagery. It is on the basis of some of these poems, such as 'Charlottetown harbour' or 'The island', that Acorn has come to be known as one of Canada's finest regional poets. And the argument is sometimes made that it is Acorn's regional, as opposed to his political, poems that form the real core of his achievement. But politics in the broadest sense is never absent from even the most lyrically descriptive of the regional poems. And many of the finest poems of the period (such as 'Poem for the Astronauts' or 'Words said sitting on a rock sitting on a saint', a statement of the artist's adversary role in modern society comparable in importance to A.M. KLEIN's 'Portrait of the poet as landscape') express a kind of playfully serious wit, reminiscent of the metaphysical poets, which seems unique to Acorn and has little to do with regionalism.

In the mid-sixties Acorn's poems tended to become longer and looser, the imagery less organic, speech rhythms yielding to the cruder rhythms of public exhortation and vituperation. For whatever reason—Acorn's declining health in this period may be partly to blame—the writing in this period often seems flaccid and prosaic in contrast with the tense wit and lyricism of his earlier work. However, although Acorn would never again produce work equal to the best of the poems included in *I've tasted my blood*, in many of the poems in *Jackpine sonnets*, and in the sonnet sequence *Captain MacDougal and the naked goddess*, Acorn seems to have rediscovered the real source of his strength in the 'dialectical play of argument', which he defines as the essence of the sonnet ('Tirade by way of introduction', *Jackpine sonnets*). Though not as rich in sensuous appeal as the best early work, these sonnets and sonnet-like poems show a renewed control and vitality, and contain some of Acorn's most powerful expressions of his twin themes of love and anger. In general, the posthumous collections, although serving a valuable function of filling out our sense of Acorn's career, have not added much to his reputation.

The liveliest and most illuminating introduction to Acorn remains Al Purdy's memoir in *I've tasted my blood*. For accounts of Acorn's life and work, see the essays by Francis Zichy in *Profiles in Canadian Literature* 4; and by Ed Jewinski in *Canadian Writers and their Works* 7 (1990). See also Dorothy Livesay, 'Search for a style: the poetry of Milton Acorn', *CANADIAN LITERATURE* 40 (Spring 1969).

ZAILIG POLLOCK

Adam, Graeme Mercer (1839-1912). Born in Loanhead, Midlothian, Scotland, and educated in Edinburgh, Adam came to Toronto in 1858 as manager for the Canadian book-retailing enterprise of Cunningham Geikie. Two years later he assumed control of the business—which eventually became Adam, Stevenson and Company, publishers and booksellers. Adam was at times the publisher or editor of a series of important periodicals: *The British American Magazine* (1863-4), *The Canada Bookseller* (1869-72), *The Canadian Monthly and National Review* (1872-78), *ROSE-BELFORD'S CANADIAN MONTHLY* (1879-82), and *The Canadian Educational Monthly* (1883-8). At the same time he served as a literary assistant to Goldwin SMITH and as the business manager (1880-3) for Smith's *The Bystander* (1880-90). He eventually became a major contributor to *The WEEK* (1883-96), as well as to other periodicals and newspapers. Adam left Canada for the United States in 1892, apparently succumbing to the frustrations of literary life in Canada and to the financial attractions of the American publishing industry. He spent some time in Chicago and Akron, Ohio, but lived mostly in New York, where he died.

Through his own writings and his choice of contributors to the periodicals he edited, Adam promoted a literary life for Canada. He fought for a fair copyright law to protect Canadian publishers; he paid contributors to *The Canadian Monthly*; and he offered criticism and praise for the work of Canadian authors. He also involved himself in the issues of the day, compiling the *Handbook of commercial union: a collection of papers read before the Commercial Union Club, Toronto, with speeches, letters and other documents in favour of unrestricted reciprocity with the United States* (Toronto, 1888); writing *The Canadian North-west: its history and its troubles, from the early days of the fur-trade to the era of the railway and the settler; with incidents of travel in the region, and the narrative of three insurrections* (Toronto, 1885) in response to the Riel rebellion; and preparing *Toronto, old and new* (Toronto, 1891). He contributed an 'Outline of Canadian literature' to William Henry WITHROW's *History of Canada* (Toronto, 1876); compiled *Prominent men of Canada: a collection of persons distinguished in professional and political life, and the commerce and industry of Canada* (Toronto, 1892); and wrote a series of travel pieces, including *Canada, historical and descriptive from sea to sea* (Toronto, 1888), *Illustrated Quebec* (Montreal, 1891), *Illustrated Toronto* (Montreal, 1891), and *Muskoka Illustrated* (Toronto, 1888). His *Canada's patriot statesman* (Toronto, 1891), a life of Sir John A. Macdonald, is a revision of an earlier life by Edmund Collins. He collaborated with George Dickson on the History of Upper Canada College, 1829-1892 (Toronto, 1893); and wrote a *History of Toronto and county of York, Ontario* (Toronto, 1885). Adam also helped to produce a five-volume series of school readers, the *Royal Canadian readers* (Toronto, 1887), plus *The high school English word book: a manual of orthoepy, synonymy, and derivation* (Toronto, 1887), and the *Public school history of England and Canada* (Toronto, 1886).

Adam made one venture into fiction in a collaborative effort with the poet Agnes Ethelwyn WETHERALD—*An Algonquin maiden: a romance of the early days of Upper Canada* (Montreal, 1887). An unfocused look at aristocratic life in the Upper Canada of the 1820s, this novel sought to be no more than 'breezy, lofty, wholesome and bright'—Adam's own description of good fiction.

Adam nurtured Canadian literary life in the last quarter of the ninteenth century, not with any artistic creativity but with his practical talents as an editor and publisher.

CAL SMILEY

Adams, Levi (1802-32). Probably born in the seigneury of Noyan, just east of the Richelieu River, he became an articled law clerk in the Montreal office of F.P. Bruneau in 1822 and was admitted to the bar in 1827. He and his wife Elizabeth, whom he had married in 1830, both died in June 1832; they were among the first cholera victims of that epidemic year.

Adams' long poem *Jean Baptiste: a poetic olio, and II cantos* (1825) was published under his own name in Montreal. Adhering to the *ottava rima* verse-form of Byron's *Beppo* and *Don Juan*, often at the expense of logical speech patterns, it tells, in mock-heroic tones, how the bachelor politician of the title, rejected by his true love, comes eventually to marry the willing Rosalie. It is set in contemporary Montreal, and the central 'plot' is the occasion for 160 stanzas of discursive comment on the themes of mortality, love, marriage, literature, and the law. A few short poems, signed 'L.A.', were published in *The Montreal Herald* and *The Canadian Courant* in 1825 and 1826.

Adams also wrote two amateurish short stories—'The young lieutenant; a tale' and 'The wedding', both signed 'L.A.'—which appeared in *The Canadian Magazine and Literary Repository* (June 1825). Set in Canada, though they could have taken place anywhere in the world without changes in detail, they are narrated by an omniscient third person and written in a melancholic vein after the fashion of the day.

Like many other young men of his time, Adams seems to have ceased writing for publication once he entered his chosen profession. He was unusual in that he signed his own name to his major work in a period when gentlemen published their literary productions anonymously.

Because of similarities in form and subject between *Jean Baptiste* and an earlier volume, *The charivari*, Adams' name was linked for many years to this and other anonymous works subsequently proved to have been written by George LONGMORE. A modern edition of *Jean Baptiste*, with an introduction by C.F. KLINCK, was published by the Golden Dog Press, Ottawa, in 1978.

MARY LU MacDONALD

Ahenakew, Edward (1885-1961). A Plains Cree, grandnephew of the famous Cree chief Poundmaker, he was born on the Ah-tah-ka-koops Reserve at Sandy Lake, north of Prince Albert, Saskatchewan, and attended the day school there. At the age of eleven he entered Emmanuel College Indian Boarding School, where he completed his high-school education with distinction. After two years' study at the Anglican Wycliffe College, Toronto, he completed his studies in theology at Emmanuel College in Saskatoon, graduating in 1910 with the degree of licentiate in theology. He was appointed deacon the same year and in 1912 was ordained an Anglican priest. His first mission was at Onion Lake, Saskatchewan. During the influenza outbreak of 1918, the suffering of his people affected him so deeply that he decided he could serve them better if he had a knowledge of medicine. In 1918 he was granted a three-year study leave at the University of Alberta, Edmonton, but ill health prevented him from completing his course. In 1923, while still recuperating, he collected the tales of his people from Chief Thunder Child (1849-1927) and created the stories of Old Keyam, which were published posthumously in *Voices of the Plains Cree* (1973), edited by Ruth M. Buck. He also completed *Cree trickster tales*, which appeared in *The journal of American folk-lore*, vol. 42 (Oct.-Dec. 1929). Once his health was restored he was assigned the supervision of Native missions in the huge northwestern area of the diocese. In 1932 he was named General Indian Missionary for the northern Diocese of Saskatchewan and in 1933 he was appointed honorary canon of St Alban's Cathedral, Prince Albert. Because of the shortage of men and the financial condition of the diocese, in 1935 he was once again asked to take a mission post. For more than twenty years, even past his official retirement age of seventy, he was in charge of the Fort à la Corne mission. For over thirty years he published the *Cree Monthly Guide* in syllabics. He also helped edit a 26,000 word Cree-English dictionary, which was published in 1938.

Emmanuel College (Saskatoon) awarded Ahenakew, in 1947, an honorary D.D.; he was the first Cree clergyman to receive this. Lake Ahenakew, in the Wooleston Lake area of northern Sakatchewan, was named in his honour.

PENNY PETRONE

'Ahkoond of Swat, The: a threnody'. This humorous poem by George T. Lanigan (1845-86), with its epigraph '"The Ahkoond of Swat is dead"—Press dispatch', was composed while Lanigan was working for the New York *World*. A.J.M. SMITH says in *The book of Canadian poetry* (1957) that Lanigan wrote the poem after receiving a cryptic message over the wires that the Ahkoond of Swat was dead; but J.D. Logan in *Highways of Canadian literature* (1924) quotes L.J. Burpee as saying that 'one evening, after learning the fact from the English mail just received, Lanigan announced that the Ahkoond of Swat was dead and that he was writing a poem about him.'

Lanigan was born in St Charles, Lower Canada, became interested in journalism, and founded the Montreal *Star* with Hugh Graham (later Lord Atholstan) in 1869. Later he moved to the United States, where he pursued his career in journalism and wrote *Fables: taken anywhere, anywhere out of the world, by G. Washington Aesop* (New York, 1878). He had previously published *National ballads of Canada. Imitated and trans. from the originals by Allid (pseud)* (Montreal, 1865). He died in Philadelphia.

VINCENT SHARMAN

Akenson, Donald (b. 1941). Donald Harman Akenson was born in Minneapolis, USA, and was educated at Yale University (B.A., 1962) and Harvard University (Ed.M., 1963; Ph.D., 1967). Appointed to Yale's history department in 1967, he moved three years later to Queen's University, Kingston, Ontario, where he became professor in 1974 and a fellow of the Royal Society of Canada in 1976. Akenson has won the Chalmers Prize (1986), the Grawemeyer World Order Award (1993), the Trillium Prize (1995), the University of British Columbia Medal for History (1995), and the Molson Prize (1996).

Akenson's historical writing has concentrated on the Irish, not only in their homeland but around the world. *The Irish education experiment* (1970) and *A mirror to Kathleen's face* (1975) examined the evolution of Irish schooling in the nineteenth and twentieth centuries, while *Education and enmity* (1973) looked at Northern Ireland and *The Church of Ireland* (1971) analysed ecclesiastical reform between 1800 and 1885. Having published *The United States and Ireland* (1973), Akenson turned to transnational history to explain the Irish diaspora free from past assumptions. While *The Irish in Ontario* (1984) was a localized study of one eastern-Ontario township, Akenson mustered census data and other sources to confront deeply rooted historical interpretations about the nature of Irish-Catholic and Protestant experiences in Canada and the United States, which had prevailed for two generations. This book was cited in 1990 by the Social Sciences and Humanities Research Council of Canada as one of the twenty most important social-science publications of the past half-century. Akenson extended his critique more broadly in *Being had: historians, evidence and the Irish in North America* (1985) and *Small differences* (1988). Books on the Irish in New Zealand and South Africa (1990, 1991) were followed by two award-winning volumes: *God's peoples: covenant and land in South Africa, Israel, and Ulster* (1992) and *Conor: a biography of Conor Cruise O'Brien* (2 vols., 1994).

Akenson founded *Canadian Papers in Rural History* and created Langdale Press to publish the ten volumes he edited between 1978 and 1996. Engaged as a senior editor at MCGILL-QUEEN'S UNIVERSITY PRESS in 1982, he has edited the impressive Studies in Ethnic History series. Also the author of five novels, including historical fiction, Akenson maintained in *At face value: the lives and times of Eliza McCormack/John White* (1990) that Canada's first woman member of Parliament had been a female transvestite in drag during the 1870s. A postmodern blending of history's thin tissue with fiction, this Canadian reworking of *Moll Flanders* illustrated late twentieth-century skepticism with discrete intellectual categories. TERRY CROWLEY

Alderson, Sue Ann (b. 1940). Born in New York City, she received a B.A. in English (1962) from Ohio State University and an M.A. in English literature (1967) from the University of California (Berkeley). Her first position in Canada was as an instructor at Simon Fraser University, British Columbia. She is now a professor in the Creative Writing Department, University of British Columbia, and the initiator and sole instructor in the university's Writing for Children Programme. The title of her first book, *bonnie mcsmithers you're driving me dithers* (1974), and its refrain—'and blithery-blathery out of my mind'—have now moved into the incantation chants of Canadian children's verse. The storyline reveals a kind of psychological tug-of-war between a harassed single mother and an intelligent, obstreperous child that is practically and humorously resolved. The sequels, *hurry up, bonnie* (1977) and *bonnie mcsmithers is at it again!* (1979), also feature the realistic but often light-hearted aspects of child-rearing.

A perceptive give-and-take attitude towards mother-and-daughter relationships also forms the core of Alderson's novel *The not impossible summer* (1983); set on one of the Gulf Islands off the coast of British Columbia, it began to establish Alderson as a regional writer. The past of Saltspring Island has inspired two of her finest picturebooks, *Ida and the wool smugglers* (1987) and *A ride for Martha* (1993). In the former a quick-witted little girl saves the family's lambs from sheep stealers and in the latter a group of children, identified only in the illustrations as white, Native, and black, save the life of a younger child in their care. *Sure as strawberries* (1992) has a 1930s prairie setting and the themes of bonding between the young and the old and the transmission of nature lore.

Alderson is an eclectic writer; her works vary in age interest, subject matter and in genre, from her light-hearted family story *Comet's tale* (1983) to her narrative poem *Ten Mondays for lots of boxes* (1995). However, while all her books are marked by a simplicity of idea and style, they treat seriously and sensitively child-adult relationships and the child's point of view. SHEILA EGOFF

Alford, Edna (b.1947). Born and raised in the village of Turtleford, Saskatchewan, she was educated at Adam Bowden Collegiate, Saskatoon, and awarded scholarships to attend the Saskatchewan Summer School of the Arts, where her teachers included Jack HODGINS, W.P. KINSELLA, Rudy WIEBE, and Robert KROETSCH. She majored in English at the University of Saskatchewan, and worked summers at hospitals and nursing homes for the chronically ill. These experiences inspired her early fiction. She is currently associate director of the Writing Studio at the Banff Centre for the Arts.

A meticulous and conscientious writer, she wrote her first stories during a ten-year period living in Calgary and attending summer writing schools, especially at Fort Qu'Appelle, Saskatchewan. In 1975 Alford co-founded the literary magazine *Dandelion*. In 1982 she was co-winner of the Gerald Lampert Award for best new Canadian writer. In 1988 she won the third annual $10,000 Marian ENGEL Award for her inspired, disturbing, and original fiction.

Alford's first story collection was *A sleep full of dreams* (1981). These ten stories, linked by a nurse named Arla, are set in Pine Mountain Lodge, a grim nursing home for old and terminally ill women in Calgary, where the inmates struggle to survive. Her second collection, *The garden of Eloise Loon* (1986), is finely crafted, original, and sometimes upsetting. Many of the fourteen stories are hallucinatory and fragmented, with central themes as varied as mental breakdown and the nuclear threat suggested by cruise missiles over Alberta. One story is told from the point of view of a decomposing head; in others a plague of caterpillars invades a house, and a character tries to steal the hand of a corpse from a freezer.

With Claire HARRIS, Alford edited the anthology *Kitchen talk* (1992), which uses the kitchen as a creative metaphor in the lives of women and their families from different cultural perspectives. Alford discusses her work with Alan Twigg in *Strong voices* (1988) and with Laurie Kruk in the *Wascana Review* (Spring/Fall 1991). GEOFF HANCOCK

Alianak, Hrant (b.1950). Born in Khartoum, Sudan, he came to Canada in 1967 and studied economics at McGill University, Montreal, and English at York University, Toronto. He has worked as a writer, actor, and director for stage, television, and film. His plays have been seen throughout Canada, and in the United States and England. His best work is witty and theatrically inventive, sometimes dispensing with dialogue altogether: *Mathematics* (1973, prod. 1972) recounts a day in the life of a suburban couple simply in terms of properties thrown one by one on to the stage; in *Christmas* (1974, prod. 1973) an actor traces in mime the brief career and death of a Christmas tree. Both were published in his 1975 collection *The return of the big five*, and they show that even plays without dialogue can entertain a reader through the wit of the stage directions.

In the same collection, the characters of *Western* (1973, prod. 1972) act out sex and power games in dialogue that consists mostly of one character's calling out the title of an old Western while another responds with the name of the star. Alianak's interest in film also emerges in *The violinist and the flower girl* (1982, prod. 1972), a wordless play that imitates the pathos and melodrama of a silent film. More characteristically, he draws on *film noir* in gangster plays like *Mousetown* (1982, prod. 1974); in *The blues* (1985, prod. 1975), an atmospheric piece about four losers in a New York bar in 1951, which combines self-mocking pastiche with real sadness; and in the violent, hallucinatory *Lucky strike* (1989, prod. 1978, 1996), an experimental postmodern performance piece featuring two wounded men, a girl, two guns, a bag of money, a matchbook with one match left, a lot of movement, little dialogue, and very loud music.

Alianak's sense of alienation from more recent developments in theatre is given sharp, ironic treatment in *The big hit* (1992), in which a frustrated playwright (played in the first production by Alianak himself) battles with his agent and artistic director over his insistence on wordless plays with a lot of nudity in a theatre that has become socially conscious and politically correct. Part of the joke is that in *The big hit* itself there is no nudity and dialogue carries the main weight. Though the play's central character is accused of being narrow and repetitive, and though Alianak's work can sometimes provoke the same criticism, this energetic counterblast shows that he is still a resourceful theatre artist.

ALEXANDER LEGGATT

Allan, Peter John (1825-48). Born in York, England, he was brought to New Brunswick as a child and grew up in Fredericton. He briefly attended King's College (now the University of New Brunswick), but left to take up the study of law. In 1843 he began to publish verse in *The New Brunswick Reporter*, a Fredericton newspaper published by James Hogg, a sometime poet. Allan took his poetry seriously enough to plan a volume of verse and solicit subscriptions to underwrite the cost of publication, but he died suddenly in Fredericton. It was posthumously published under the title *The poetical remains of Peter John Allan* (London, 1853). Allan was influenced by the aesthetic principles of the Romantic movement, particularly with reference to perceiving ideal truths within the sensuality of nature. Not surprisingly, he was fascinated by the potential of human imagination and the range of perception it offered to human awareness. These aesthetic interests brought an intellectual toughness to his verse that prevented the overflow of emotion and controlled the sentimentality and banal moralizing that are so noticeable in the poetry of other local poets. In his nature poetry especially, a distinctive quality of tone and mood emerges from the interplay of intellectual perception and emotional sensitivity that looks forward to the early poetry of Charles G.D. ROBERTS and Bliss CARMAN.

TOM VINCENT

Allan, Ted (1916-95). Born Allan Herman in Montreal, Quebec, he left high school to supplement the family income, working first in the family gift store, then as a hardware clerk in Westmount. At eighteen, a dedicated Young Communist, he became Montreal correspondent for the *Toronto Daily Worker*. He served in the International Brigades in the Spanish Civil War and as a political commissar in Dr Norman Bethune's blood-transfusion unit. In 1939 he married Kate Schwartz, by whom he had a son and a daughter. Resident in London, England, for almost three decades, he later lived in Toronto and Los Angeles.

Allan's best-known book was *The scalpel, the sword: the story of Doctor Norman Bethune* (1952, with Sydney Gordon; rev. 1971). A heroic biography (one million copies in print in nineteen languages), it is enthusiastically vivid about Bethune's personality, medical innovations, and revolutionary commitment. Acknowledging the flaws in his obsessive and mercurial temperament, it nevertheless occasionally sees Bethune's earlier life—including its self-indulgent phases and his sad and stormy relationship with his wife Frances—as too prophetic of his later humanitarian dedication, in Spain and China, to fundamental political and social change. A film version, *Bethune: The Making of a Hero*, screenplay by Allan, was released in 1990.

Allan's novel of the Spanish Civil War, *This time a better earth* (1939), centres on Bob Curtis, a twenty-one-year-old Canadian volunteer in the International Brigades. Characters who are courageous, compassionate, and socialist, and compelling evocations of love, loyalty, and battle, are rendered sparely, without ideological sentimentality. Allan's science-fiction novel *Quest for Pajaro* (1970) was published under the pseudonym 'Edward Maxwell'. A children's book *Willie the squowse* (1977), with its half-squirrel, half-mouse hero, provided the opportunity for a parable about how two families wrongly value money and mistakenly equate financial success with happiness. His novel *Love is a long shot* (1984) won the Stephen LEACOCK Award for Humour.

Allan's plays were produced in Toronto, Paris, London, Rome, East Berlin, and Los Angeles. *Double image* (1957), which ran for five years in Paris under the title *Gog et Magog*, is a murder mystery complicated by the hero's impersonating his twin—to the confusion of the police, his wife, and the audience. In *My sister's keeper* (1976) Allan establishes that Sarah, who desperately seeks emotional comfort from her brother Robert, suffers not insanity but an extreme sensitivity and a profound need for love. An authentic relationship between them is prevented by Robert's 'sanity'—his psychological refusal to risk genuine or generous emotion. Allan wrote the original stage treatment for Joan Littlewood's 1964 *Oh, what a lovely war!* The actor Sean Connery directed his *I've seen you cut lemons* (unpublished) when it opened in London, England, in 1969.

Allan retained in his writing an obvious left-wing orientation and a disgust with tyranny. But perhaps more significant thematically was his repeated exploration of the possibility of positive transformation through acceptance of another person, or of a principle unconnected with the isolated ego.

Allan's short stories appeared in many magazines, including *The New Yorker* and *Harper's*; a number were published in the collection *Don't you know anybody else?* (1985). He also wrote several dozen radio and television dramas (and acted in many) for CBC, BBC, ITV, and films for major studios. He wrote the original screenplay for the film *Lies my father told me* (1976) and co-authored (with John Cassavetes) the script for the 1984 movie *Love Streams*.

ANTHONY HOPKINS

Allen, Grant (1848-99). Although born on Wolfe Island near Kingston, Canada West (Ontario), he owed little as a writer to his country of origin. Educated privately, and in France and England, Allen completed his formal education at Merton College, Oxford (1867-71). From 1873 to 1876 he taught at a newly founded school for black students in Jamaica and when it failed he returned to England, where he wrote many unpublished articles on scientific subjects; published at his own expense *Physiological aesthetics* (London, 1877); and tried his hand at journalism in London. The book, which had no commercial success, did bring him to the attention of a few editors, including Leslie Stephen of the *Cornhill Magazine*, and Allen began to earn 'a modest—a very modest—and precarious income'. A second book, *The colour sense: its origin and development; an essay in comparative psychology* (London, 1879), attracted the notice of Alfred Wallace, Charles Darwin, and Herbert Spencer. But Allen had no success until 1880, when he began writing magazine fiction. His first collection was *Strange stories* (London, 1884); his first novel, *Philistia* (London, 1884), like many of the earlier magazine pieces, appeared under a pseudonym. From this time on, Allen's production of fiction was enormous: more than forty novels and collections of stories (along with thirty works of non-fiction). As a fiction writer Allen, who had the good journalist's sense of contemporary intellectual movements, presented advanced social ideas in an accessible form, such as questions of class and other social issues in *The British barbarians. A Hilltop novel* (London, 1895), and feminism and women's rights in *The woman who did. A Hilltop novel* (London, 1895). ('Hilltop' was Allen's house at Hindhead, Surrey, the highest spot in south-eastern England.) Joseph Conrad equated Allen's popular fiction with that of Marie Corelli and Hall Caine, saying: 'There are no lasting qualities in their work.' In one small way, however, Allen assured himself of some lasting recognition: *An African millionaire: episodes in the life of the illustrious Colonel Clay* (London, 1897) introduces a character whom Frederic Dannay (half of 'Ellery Queen') described as 'the first great thief of short mystery fiction', anticipating by two years E.W. Hornung's much better-known A.J. Raffles.

Though Allen's work was known and discussed in Canada, and some of it appeared in *The Canadian Monthly and National Review*, it had no significant effect on Canadian literature and very little of it reflects his Canadian origins. Some titles have been reprinted, among them: *Physiological aesthetics* (New York, 1977), *The British barbarians* (New York, 1975), *Charles Darwin* (Philadelphia, 1973), *The evolution of the idea of God* (New York, 1977), and *An African millionaire* (New York, 1980), which has a useful introduction by Norman Donaldson that sketches Allen's career and comments on his place in the history of detective fiction. DAVID JACKEL

Allen, Lillian. See CARIBBEAN-CANADIAN LITERATURE.

Allen, Ralph (1913-66). Born in Winnipeg, Manitoba, and educated in Ontario and Saskatchewan, he was the son of a CPR railway agent. At sixteen he became sports writer for the Winnipeg *Tribune*, moving to the Toronto *Globe* in 1938. During the Second World War he served as a gunner in the Royal Canadian Artillery, becoming a war correspondent for the Toronto *Globe and Mail* in 1943 and subsequently receiving the OBE for his coverage of the Allied landings in Sicily, Italy, and Normandy. In 1946 Allen moved to *Maclean's*, becoming editor of that magazine in 1940. In 1964 he joined the *Toronto Star* as managing editor, a position he held when he died.

Acclaimed for his high editorial standards, Allen is perhaps most remembered for his journalistic craft and his fierce tutelage of those under his supervision, such as Pierre BERTON, Peter Gzowski, June CALLWOOD, and Christina McCALL. He was most proud, however, of his literary productions. Of his five published novels, three portray wartime experience. *Home made banners* (1946) deals with Canadian soldiers who served overseas in the Second World War, and particularly the resentment of active soldiers (typically pressed into service in a cause not of their choosing) towards the conscientious-objector 'zombies' allowed to remain at home. *The high white forest* (1964) is set during the Battle of the Bulge (1944), and *Ask the name of the lion* (1962) portrays the Congo during the struggle for independence, depicting a group of fugitives forced to flee when an isolated hospital is attacked by a detachment of marauding Congolese solders. Allen also wrote *The chartered libertine* (1954), a satire about the conflict between private-broadcast interests and the publicly owned Canadian Broadcasting Corporation; *Peace River country* (1958), the story of the flight of a mother and her two children from Saskatchewan to an assumed refuge in the unspoiled Northwest; and *Ordeal by fire: 1915-1945* (1961), a volume in the Doubleday Canadian History Series. A collection of Allen's newspaper and magazine articles, *The man from Oxbow: the best of Ralph Allen* (1967), was edited by Christina McCall-Newman. See also James Macgowan, 'Looking back on a legend', *Ryerson Review of Journalism* (March 1992). MARILYN ROSE

Alline, Henry (1748-84). Born in Newport, Rhode Island, he received some formal schooling before his family immigrated in 1760 to Nova Scotia as part of the influx of New Englanders into the Annapolis Valley after the expulsion of the Acadians, taking up land in the future township of Falmouth. He remained on his father's farm until 1776, assisting in its operation and privately pursuing theological studies through the books that were available to him. His conversion came in Mar. 1775, and a year later, as political rebellion erupted in New England, Alline dedicated himself to raising the spiritual consciousness of Nova Scotia (which then included present-day New Brunswick) by preaching the gospel of Christ's salvation and the transcendence of God's grace. Preaching throughout the area until his death, Alline almost single-handedly precipitated a revival of faith that ultimately laid the foundation of the Baptist movement in the Maritimes. His followers were called the 'New Lights' and, although Alline himself avoided institutionalizing his faith, the 'New Lights' established themselves as 'churches' in various parts of Nova Scotia.

As part of his evangelical activities Alline sought to broaden his influence in the 1780s through the written word. He published three sermons and two theological treatises: *Sermon preached to, and at the request, of a religious society of young men* (Halifax, 1782), *A sermon on a day of thanksgiving* (Halifax, 1782), *A sermon preached on the 19th of Feb. 1783 at Fort-Midway* (Halifax, 1783), *Two mites on some of the most important and much disputed points of divinity* (Halifax, 1781), and *The anti-traditionalist* (Halifax, 1783). The theological views presented in his sermons and treatises are not particularly original and not always logically coherent. Alline was influenced by the writings of the English theologian William Law, and found the pietistical bent of Law's theology, together with its mysticism and asceticism, particularly attractive. At the same time, however, he also asserted the need for enthusiastic evangelism, demanding a personal commitment to the active proclamation of the gospel of salvation. His view of God's love was Universalist and Arminian in nature: God's love was extended to all men, and those who had received this truth must actively participate in extending it to others. Alline was strongly attacked for his theological views; his chief detractor was Jonathan Scott, a Calvinistic Congregationalist minister, who refuted Alline's theology in *A brief view of the religious tenets and sentiments . . . of Mr. Henry Alline* (Halifax, 1784).

In addition to his sermons and theological works, Alline published two volumes of hymns: *Hymns and spiritual songs* [I] (Halifax, 1782) and *Hymns and spiritual songs* [II] (Boston, 1786). These hymns, which generally follow the simple verse-forms established by Isaac Watts and other English hymnists of the late-seventeenth and early-eighteenth centuries, deal with aspects of Christian life, particularly with the glory of salvation and the agony of man's sinfulness. The 1786 edition, written during a lengthy illness just prior to Alline's death, may be viewed as a kind of spiritual autobiography describing the emotional ups and downs of his spiritual condition. Ironically, Alline was travelling to Boston to publish this work when he died at North Hampton, New Hampshire. His *Life and journal* (Boston, 1806) was published posthumously.

See M. Armstrong, 'The literature of the great awakening' in *The great awakening in Nova Scotia* (1948) and 'Henry Alline's "Hymns and spiritual songs"', *Dalhousie Review* XXXIV (1955); J.M. Bumsted, *Henry Alline* (1971); and Thomas B. Vincent, 'Alline and Bailey', *CANADIAN LITERATURE* 68-69 (Spring/Summer 1976). TOM VINCENT

Alonzo, Anne-Marie (b. 1952). An Arab, born in Egypt into a Catholic family with ancestors from Palestine, Syria and Malta, Alonzo grew up in a multilingual environment, learning to speak French, Italian, English, Arabic, and German. In 1963, she immigrated to Canada with her parents and settled in the Montreal area where, in 1966, an automobile accident left her permanently quadriplegic. She nevertheless acquired a Ph.D. from the Université de Montréal and became a leading literary figure in Quebec, creating the publishing firm Trois, which co-launched a mainly postmodernist literary journal of the same name and now also publishes audio-cassette readings of literary texts. She initiated the Trois literary festival of poetry and theatre, held every summer in the town of Laval. She was made a Member of the Order of Canada in 1997.

Alonzo is mainly known for some twenty books. Several were an innovative collaboration with other writers—*French conversation* (1986), with Alain Laframboise, a deconstructionist view of Renaissance painting; photographers—*Seul le désir*, with Marie-Christine Simard, in *La Nouvelle BARRE DU JOUR* (1987), in which the narrator seeks through a sequence of fragmented photographs to identify a woman; or a translator—*Esmal*, with an Egyptian hieroglyphic version by Nihal Mazloum, in *La Nouvelle Barre du Jour* (1987). Many of these take the form of theory/fictions, narratives, or letters; Alonzo prefers, nevertheless, to consider herself a poet, because of the care with which she sculpts each text.

Immobility, and Alonzo's determination to overcome it through the power of the word, have been a central concept from her first book, *Geste* (1979), in which she recounts her accident and its aftermath, through to *Galia qu'elle nommait amour* (1992) which relates past passion. Alonzo is a modern-day Scheherezade, and her art is more powerful than any constraint. With *Margie Gillis: la danse des marches* (1993), which also involves photography, Alonzo moved beyond the theme of immobility, of the inert body, to celebrate the mobility she participated in thanks to the dancer—a page was turned.

Alonzo's themes are wide-ranging, including mythical visions of an Egypt she barely knows that evoke all the colour and sensuality of the Middle East and much of its cruelty (*Bleus de mine*, 1985); biblical events (*Le livre des ruptures*, 1988); images of female love, for her mother, her lover, her friends (*Droite et de profil*, 1984; *Écoute, Sultane*, 1987). Her work is also characterized by its theoretical emphasis, its intertextuality, its efforts to erase the limits of the written word and to penetrate other forms of art. Alonzo has been awarded the Prix Émile-Nelligan, the first non-native Quebecker to be so honoured.

The Winter 1994 issue of *VOIX ET IMAGES* published a substantial dossier on Anne-Marie Alonzo, edited by Lucie Lequin and Maïr Verthuy. MAÏR VERTHUY

Alphabet (1960-71). First published in Sept. 1960, this adventurous little magazine from London, Ontario, was edited and distributed, and often typeset and printed, by its founder, James REANEY, whose interest in the theories of Northrop FRYE was given special prominence in the quotation that frequently headed the table of contents: 'There is such a thing as the iconography of the imagination.' Each issue was dedicated to an archetypal image or myth—for example, Narcissus (1), Icarus (4), and Horoscope (5). In content, viewpoint, and visual appearance, *Alphabet* changed considerably in the course of its nineteen issues. In the beginning it featured writers who were comfortable within traditional typographic conventions, and it contained few graphics. Later issues bristled with typographic collages, hand-drawn poems, and charts, as Reaney welcomed to *Alphabet* such unconventional writers as bill BISSETT, David W. Harris, bp NICHOL, and George BOWERING, as well as the London painters Jack Chambers and Greg Curnoe. It had an ever-expanding range of editorial curiosity: from myth and literature, it grew to include discussions of concrete poetry, popular music, Ojibwa art, cinema, sound poetry, and performance art. *Alphabet* became a place where the writing of the 1950s could interact with that of the 1960s, where early British Columbia concrete poets like bissett and Judith Copithorne could reach an eastern audience, and where the young Margaret ATWOOD could mature as both poet and reviewer. The nineteenth and final issue appeared in June 1971—seven issues short of Reaney's original hope of one issue for each letter of the alphabet. FRANK DAVEY

Altham: a tale of the sea (London, 1849). Perhaps the most interesting early Canadian novel because it is solidly and straightforwardly written, and because the plot is compelling enough to sustain interest, *Altham* was published in a two-volume edition in London, England, by Saunders and Otley. The first two-thirds of the work had appeared in *BARKER'S CANADIAN MONTHLY MAGAZINE* (Kingston) between Oct. 1846 and Apr. 1847, when *Barker's* ceased publication.

The author, John Swete Cummins, was born in Cork, Ireland, in 1811. He immigrated to Canada in 1836 as agent for Lord Mountcashel and lived on his employer's property near Delaware, Upper Canada, and at Amherst Island, near Kingston (Ontario). He was active in the militia in 1837, and in later years became a militia lieutenant-colonel, as well as chairman of the Midland District Council. In the late 1850s he was resident in the Eastern Townships of Quebec, employed by the British American Land Company. The date and place of his death are presently unknown. (The entry on Cummins in Morgan's *Bibliotheca Canadensis* confuses him with John S. Cummings, a prominent Kingstonian.)

Set in the period of the Napoleonic Wars, about a third of *Altham* takes place in Ireland, about a third at sea, and the remainder at various places in North America, including Halifax, Montreal, and an island in the Gulf of St Lawrence. The young hero, James Annesley, initially the friendless and persecuted bastard son of an Irish lord, eventually becomes a naval hero, marries the daughter of Sir Isaac Brock, and is proved to be the legitimate heir to his father's title and fortune. Noble, manly, and loyal at the beginning, he is the same at the end, despite his many trials. The other continuing plot thread is the story of Amos Bushe, a law student who befriends Jemmy. The male characters—heroes and villains alike—are all men of action, and it is through their actions rather than their words that we know them. The females are passive and long-suffering. The young ones are almost interchangeable objects of male adoration; only the two mature women are at all developed as individuals. Good, bad, and mixed characters belong to the middle and lower classes; but the rich, the adult nobility, and the naval hierarchy are villainous oppressors. The author claims to have eschewed scenic description; however, there are vivid accounts of naval battles, especially that of the *Chesapeake* and the *Shannon*, and of a hurricane survived at sea.

See M.L. MacDonald, 'The *Chesapeake* and the *Shannon* approach the canon', in *Canadian Poetry*, no. 30 (Spring/Summer 1992).

MARY LU MacDONALD

Amy, William Lacy. See NOVELS IN ENGLISH 1920 TO 1940: I

Anansi, House of. A small Toronto publishing house that was instrumental in shaping Canada's sense of literary identity after Expo 67. Founded by novelist Dave GODFREY and poet Dennis LEE that same year, Anansi was named for an African spider god, a trickster and tale-spinner, after Godfrey's CUSO stay in Ghana. The mandate was at once literary and political: modernism in art, a concerned social conscience, Canadian nationalism in all things. Some of the early titles, such as a manual for American draft-dodgers in Canada, brought the firm instant notoriety as a haven for radical hippies. More durable publishing choices included books now considered Canadian classics, by such writers as Margaret ATWOOD (*The circle game*, *SURVIVAL*), Michael ONDAATJE (*The collected works of Billy the Kid*, *Coming through slaughter*), Northrop FRYE (*The bush garden*), and George GRANT (*Technology and empire*).

The house became a mecca for unpublished talent, with anthologies of new poets sharing the catalogue with important collections by P.K. PAGE, Al PURDY, Paulette JILES, George BOWERING, bill BISSETT, and Dennis Lee. A 'spiderline series' of first novels introduced Matt COHEN and Peter SUCH, and first-time fiction by Graeme GIBSON, Chris SCOTT, and Ray SMITH confirmed Anansi's penchant for experimental prose with a surrealist bent. Anansi pioneered writing in translation from the Quebec of the Quiet Revolution: Roch CARRIER's *La Guerre, yes sir!*, one of the house's best-sellers, initiated a distinguished tradition that brought Hubert AQUIN, Jacques FERRON, Jacques POULIN, and Jacques BRAULT to English Canada. By the early 1970s, the original founders had moved on. Jim Polk and Ann Wall stayed to continue the house's traditions with poetry by Erin MOURÉ, John THOMPSON, Don Domanski, Christopher DEWDNEY, and Kristjana GUNNARS; fiction by Helen WEINZWEIG, Marian ENGEL, and David WILLIAMS, and non-fiction emphasizing pioneer women, Canadian social issues (acid rain, nuclear waste), and literary criticism. The press was able to stabilize its cash-flow by expanding the market to the USA and Britain, but at home Anansi's Canada-first stance was no longer news and many of its star writers had moved on to other venues. The major Toronto publishers were beginning to realize that quality Canadian writing could sell, as readers grew more sophisticated and CanLit courses multiplied in the universities. On some level the Anansi revolution had been won. In 1988, the last book published by the 'old' Anansi, Erin Mouré's *Furious*, won the Governor General's Award for poetry. In August 1989, owner Ann Wall sold the house to Stoddart Publishing, one of the country's most successful Canadian-owned trade publishers. Today, the Anansi name lives on as the literary imprint for its commercial parent company, with the suave Stoddart parabola replacing the horned spider-god logo of 1967. Editors Martha Sharpe and Michael Byron Davis continue to welcome poets, quality fiction writers, Quebec novels in translation, and unorthodox political commentary (John Ralston SAUL's *The unconscious civilization*).

In retrospect, what Anansi pegged as 'Canadian' in 1967 may seem to reflect many of the international modernist trends of the day. Black comedy, magic realism, concrete poetry, stream of consciousness, myth and fantasy were valued over naturalism; notes from underground men and women were preferred to the more traditional Canadian themes of angst on the farm or the call of the wild. The Anansi aesthetic looked for a cultural identity through literature—an odd perspective now, perhaps, in the age of postmodernism, but a goal that opened some windows and identified some major authors. JAMES POLK

Anciens Canadiens*, *Les (Quebec, 1863). A historical romance of the Seven Years' War by Philippe-Joseph AUBERT DE GASPÉ. In April 1757 two students at the Jesuit College in Quebec City, their studies completed, are about to sail for Europe and enter the French and English armies. One, Jules d'Haberville, is the son of a French-Canadian *seigneur*; the other, Archibald Cameron of Locheil, is the son of a Scot killed at Culloden. When war breaks out the two friends find themselves back in Canada as officers in the opposing forces. Arché is compelled by his superior to burn the farms on the South Shore, including the d'Haberville manor, where he had often been a guest. Subsequently he saves Jules' life, and after the war assists the ruined d'Haberville family, with whom he returns to live, although Jules' sister Blanche refuses to marry him.

The novel falls into three parts. The first six chapters recount in detail the slow journey from Quebec City to Saint-Jean-Port-Joli, in the company of a talkative family servant, José Dubé, who regales his masters with folksongs, legends, and anecdotes about the region; he makes particular reference to the murderess Marie-Josephte Corriveau, who was hanged in 1763. (See *The* GOLDEN DOG.) On the way, Arché rescues a local resident, Dumais, who is stranded on an ice floe. Chapters 7 to 11 describe life at the d'Haberville manor-house, including the May Day and Saint-Jean Baptiste Day festivities. The two friends also hear the life story of a genteel misanthrope, M. d'Egmont, whose shattered career resembles that of Aubert de Gaspé himself. The final seven chapters recount episodes of the Conquest, among them Arché's capture by Natives and his rescue by the grateful Dumais.

Although Aubert de Gaspé probably contributed at least one chapter to his son's novel *L'INFLUENCE D'UN LIVRE* (Québec, 1837), *Les anciens Canadiens* was the septuagenarian's first published work. It is crammed with his personal and family reminiscences, and with countless details of popular customs and daily life at the end of the French régime. Aubert de Gaspé's relatives served as models for the characters of the novel, and life in the d'Haberville manor is essentially that of the author's family, filtered through the memory of a lifetime reader of Sir Walter Scott. As a *seigneur*, Aubert de Gaspé regretted the abolition of seigneurial tenure in 1854 and attempted in his novel—which he called a pot-pourri of memories—a nostalgic reconstruction of seigneurial society in its ideal form; in it he also urged the need for greater integration with the English-speaking population. Rambling and at times repetitive, this early example of oral history affords an intimate and charming introduction to the cultural heritage and political disillusionment of French-Canadian landowners in mid-nineteenth-century Quebec. It is typical of the retrospective and compensatory writing of members of the professional and seigneurial classes after the abortive Rebellion of 1837.

The novel was first translated into English by Georgiana M. Pennée in 1864; in 1890 Charles G.D. ROBERTS published a new translation under the title *The Canadians of old* (it was reissued in 1905 as *Cameron of Lochiel*). His version is available in the New Canadian Library (1974), with an Introduction by Clara THOMAS and an Appendix containing Aubert de Gaspé's notes to the original French edition.

The best English-language articles on the novel are by James S. Tassie in Robert L. McDougall, ed., *Our living tradition: second and third series* (1959), and by Ben-Zion Shek in *Keeping Canada together* (1978), edited by Norman Penner. DAVID M. HAYNE

Anderson, Patrick (1915-79). Born in Ashtead, Surrey, England, he was educated at Oxford University, where he was president of the Union, and at Columbia University, where he held a Commonwealth Fellowship (1938-40). He then came to Montreal, where he taught for six years at a private school, Selwyn House. In Apr. 1941 he edited—with his wife, Peggy Doernbach—a poetry newsletter called *The Andersons*. This was followed by the more political, but equally short-lived, *The victory broadsheet* and *En masse*. But it was as founder and leading editor of *PREVIEW* that Anderson rose to local prominence and established his reputation in Canadian letters. After becoming a Canadian citizen in 1945, he made a year-long trip to England in 1947 (when he was divorced), and then returned to teach at McGill University (1948-50), before departing for teaching assignments at the University of Malaya (1950-2) and finally at Dudley Training and Trent Park colleges in England.

In addition to being the dynamic force behind *Preview*, Anderson acted as an important catalyst in the development of Canadian poetry by disseminating contemporary techniques that influenced poets such as P.K. PAGE, A.M. KLEIN, and, to a lesser extent, F.R. SCOTT. Although the early poetry in Anderson's *A tent for April* (1945), *The white centre* (1946), and *The colour as naked* (1953)—noticeably indebted to W.H. Auden, T.S. Eliot, and Dylan Thomas—is frequently too wordy, it is metaphorically rich, permeated with Marxist and Freudian symbols, and offers a striking combination of technical sophistication and an immigrant's fresh wonder at a new country and its winter. A prominent motif in this poetry is the child and his perceptions of, and encounters with, experience. Anderson's later poetry, collected in *A visiting distance—poems: new, revised, and selected*

(1976) and *Return to Canada: selected poems* (1977)—reflects his usual competence and verbal facility, but lacks somewhat the passion of earlier years.

After he left Canada, Anderson gained a literary reputation in England for his autobiographical works, *Snake wine: a Singapore episode* (1955), *Search me: the black country, Canada and Spain* (1957), and *The character ball* (1963); and for his travel books, *First steps in Greece* (1958), *Dolphin days* (1963), *The smile of Apollo: a literary companion to Greek travel* (1964), *Over the Alps* (1969), and *Foxed!* (1972). He also wrote a children's book, *Finding out about the Athenians* (1961), and edited, with Alistair Sutherland, *Eros: an anthology of male friendship* (1961).

Christopher Xerxes Ringrose provides an illuminating discussion of Anderson's poetry in 'Patrick Anderson and the critics', *CANADIAN LITERATURE* 43 (Winter 1970). See also Seymour MAYNE, 'A conversation with Patrick Anderson', *Inscape* 11 (Fall 1974).

DAVID O'ROURKE

Anderson-Dargatz, Gail. See NOVELS IN ENGLISH 1983 TO 1996: OTHER NOVELS 2(a).

Angéline de Montbrun (Quebec, 1884). This novel by Marie-Louise-Félicité ANGERS (pseud. 'Laure Conan'), Quebec's first woman novelist, was published in serial form in *La Revue canadienne*, Montréal, from June 1881 to Aug. 1882, and as a book in 1884. The beautiful and intelligent eighteen-year-old Angéline —who lives with her father, Charles de Montbrun, on their idyllic small estate 'Valriant' on the North Shore of the St Lawrence River—is courted by Maurice Darville, brother of her former convent classmate, the coquettish Mina. In the first part of the novel—composed of letters exchanged among Angéline, Maurice, Mina, and M. de Montbrun—we witness the growing love between Angéline and Maurice, and share her joy in her adored father and her cherished fiancé. Suddenly, in a few pages of impersonal narrative, the situation changes: M. de Montbrun dies as a result of an accident while hunting; Angéline suffers a disfigurement (caused by a facial tumour in the early editions; by an operation, necessitated by a fall, in the later ones), and becomes convinced that Maurice's ardour has cooled. Proud and independent, Angéline returns his engagement ring and decides to live alone. The final section is made up of Angéline's diary, in which the entries recount her anguished solitude, and her determination to devote herself to the service of the humble inhabitants of the district.

For the novel's publication as a book, under the pseudonym 'Laure Conan', Abbé Henri-Raymond CASGRAIN wrote a preface, which contained biographical material about the author that Angers insisted must be deleted. In Casgrain's slightly altered 'study', he praised the novel as an edifying portrait of Christian resignation. Recent critics, however—particularly Sister Jean de l'Immaculée (Suzanne Blais), in her doctoral thesis submitted to the Université d'Ottawa, and Roger Le Moine in two articles published in the *Revue de l'Université d'Ottawa* in 1966—have shown that *Angéline de Montbrun* is really a transposed account of the author's disappointed love for the surveyor and member of Parliament, Pierre-Alexis Tremblay. Others have noted the incestuous overtones in Angéline's excessive devotion to her father, even after the latter's death. Recent critics have also stressed the masochism of Angéline's isolation and self-chastisement, for it is by no means certain that Maurice has ceased to love her. Thus this century-old novel has become a focal-point of contemporary Quebec criticism as scholars attempt to identify and unravel the psychological, autobiographical, and psychoanalytical elements in its composition—although all are united in praising its author's elegantly sober style.

An English translation, with a useful introduction, by Yves Brunelle appeared in 1974.

See Patricia Smart, *Writing in the father's house: the emergence of the feminine in the Quebec literary tradition* (1991), 20-61.

DAVID M. HAYNE

Angers, Marie-Louise-Félicité (1845-1924). Quebec's first woman novelist, who used the pseudonym 'Laure Conan', was born at La Malbaie (Murray Bay), Quebec. The daughter of a blacksmith, she was educated there and at the Ursuline Convent in Quebec City. She fell in love with a surveyor and politician, Pierre-Alexis Tremblay (1827-79), and this unrequited attachment, which lasted from 1862 to 1867, seems to have affected her whole existence, leading to a rather solitary life and furnishing a theme—frustrated love and the anguish attending it—that reappears in her fiction. Thereafter, except for the years 1893 to 1898 spent at the Monastery of the Precious Blood in St-Hyacinthe, she lived most of her life in semi-retirement at La Malbaie, reading voraciously, particularly in pious works, and writing articles and books as a means of earning a living. She died at the Hôtel-Dieu in Quebec City.

Félicité Angers's first published work was a novelette entitled *Un amour vrai*; it was serialized in *La Revue de Montréal* in 1878-9 and later published, with an unauthorized change of title, as *Larmes d'amour* (Montréal, 1899). Thérèse Raynol is deeply in love with a young Scottish Protestant, Francis Douglas, but vows not to marry him until he becomes a Roman Catholic. Her death is eventually the instrument of his conversion. The author here introduces both the theme (an impossible love) and the narrative technique (a combination of epistolary and diary forms) that constitute the originality of Angers's early fiction. A similar frustrated love affair, again reminiscent of her own passion for P.-A. Tremblay, forms the basis of her best-known novel, *ANGÉLINE DE MONTBRUN* (Québec, 1884). In her next novel, *À l'oeuvre et à l'épreuve* (Québec, 1891)—translated as *The master-motive: a tale of the days of Champlain* (1909)—Angers again treated aspects of her disappointed love affair, although with greater detachment. Drawing on the historical works of François-Xavier GARNEAU and Abbé Jean-Baptiste-Antoine Ferland, and utilizing the *JESUIT RELATIONS* for the years 1636 to 1649, she set about reconstructing the climate of mystical heroism that characterized the missionary period of New France, modelling her hero on the Jesuit martyr Father Charles Garnier. Instead of fulfilling his parents' hope that he will marry Gisèle Méliande, an orphan girl they have raised, Garneau is ordained priest in 1635 and sent to the Canadian mission in Huronia, to die a martyr in the Iroquois onslaught of 1649. Gisèle lives on with the Garnier parents until their death, and then enters a Carmelite convent. As Angers had little information about Garnier's life, she concentrated on the mental and emotional states of her characters.

During her residence at the Monastery of the Precious Blood, Angers was greatly influenced by her friend Mother Catherine-Aurélie Caouette, founder of the Institute of the Precious Blood, who urged her to take a more positive view of her life; her subsequent fiction was therefore less autobiographical. In *L'oublié* (1900) she returned to the heroic days of New France to recount the life of Lambert Closse, garrison sergeant-major of Ville-Marie (Montreal), who was killed by marauding Iroquois in 1662. Closse had helped rescue some French prisoners taken by the Iroquois; among them was a young girl, Elisabeth Moyen, who, after saving Closse's life, became his bride. Once again the novelist concerned herself with the psychological motivation of her characters and the spiritual climate of the time, rather than with the chronicle of events, which she nevertheless recounted with respect for historical accuracy. Awarded a small prize by the French Academy in 1903, *L'oublié* was unsuccessfully adapted by its author as a five-act play entitled *Aux jours de Maisonneuve* (1920).

During the last half-dozen years of her life the elderly Angers completed three less-important works of fiction. Her short novel *L'obscure souffrance* (1919)—which incorporated an early (1883) fragment, 'À travers les ronces'—is the imaginary journal of the daughter of an alcoholic father, whom she saves by her devotion. In *La vaine foi* (1921) a worldly and indifferent woman re-examines her faith when she is courted by a Protestant. *La sève immortelle* (1925)—Anger's third historical novel, written on her deathbed—is set in 1760: a French officer, Jean Le Gardeur de Tilly, decides to stay in Canada to help build a new French-Canadian society instead of returning to France with his French fiancée. Anger's last novel thus anticipates the transition from patriotic historical fiction to the nationalistic regional novels that would be dominant in Quebec until the Second World War.

In addition to her fiction, Angers published numerous patriotic or moralizing works, such as her dialogue *Si les Canadiennes le voulaient* (Québec, 1886), in which she urged women to use their influence in the family to raise the standard of public life. She also wrote more than fifty articles on religious and moral subjects for the periodical *La Voix du Précieux Sang*, which she edited from 1894 to 1898, and published a widely read biography (1903) of Mother Elizabeth Seton (1774-1821), the founder in 1809 of the American branch of the Sisters of Charity.

Félicité Angers, whose work is distinguished by its psychological depth and its elegantly sober style, is one of nineteenth-century Quebec's most original writers. The modern reader will find all her fiction conveniently presented and annotated in a three-volume edition prepared by Roger Le Moine and published by Fides in the 'Collection du Nénuphar' (1974-5). DAVID M. HAYNE

Anne of Green Gables (1908). This enduring children's classic by Lucy Maud MONTGOMERY—perhaps the best-selling book by a Canadian author—was written in 1904-5 and rejected by five firms before it was published by L.C. Page of Boston in 1908; it has never been out of print since then. Montgomery called it a 'juvenilish story, ostensibly for girls', but it has proved very popular in several media with people of all ages, who have responded to Montgomery's wry humour, her deflating of stuffiness, her affectionate descriptions of the Prince Edward Island countryside, and her remarkably loquacious heroine. Based in part on a Barnardo child, Ellen Macneill—she was adopted by relatives of Montgomery who were expecting a boy and received a girl—it is about the quest of the orphan Anne Shirley for acceptance both by the elderly brother and sister Matthew and Marilla, who adopt her, and by her community. Convinced that her red hair is a liability, Anne is consoled by her love of nature and her friendship with Diana; her rivalry with Gilbert Blythe ends with her winning a college scholarship, which she declines after Matthew's death in order to stay on the farm at Avonlea (Cavendish) with Marilla. One of the first portraits in Canadian fiction of the artist as a young girl, Anne's transformation from ugly duckling to comely maiden leads to a compromise between the private world of her imagination and the genteel, practical world around her. Mark Twain called Anne 'the dearest, and most lovable child in fiction since the immortal Alice', while generations of women, including Alice MUNRO, Jane URQUHART, and Marian ENGEL's fictional heroine Sarah Porlock in *No clouds of glory*, reread the puce-coloured Anne books and applauded Anne's determination to succeed on her own terms in a man's world.

The first Canadian edition was issued by The RYERSON PRESS in 1943. *Anne* and its seven sequels have sold millions of copies in over fifteen languages; Anne is almost a cult among Japanese readers. There were film versions of *Anne of Green Gables* in 1919 and 1934, two different dramatic versions in 1937 by Alice Chadwicke and Wilbur Braun, and a film version of *Anne of Windy Poplars* in 1940. An adaptation by Mavor MOORE, Donald Harron, and Norman Campbell became the longest-running Canadian stage musical, with annual performances since 1965 at the Charlottetown Confederation Centre, and successful tours across Canada and to New York, London, and Japan. The novel was adapted for television in Britain and Japan. In 1974 Anne appeared on a Canadian stamp. The Canadian television films of *Anne of Green Gables* (1985) and its sequel *Anne of Avonlea* (1987), which incorporates *Anne of Avonlea*, *Anne of the Island*, and *Anne of Windy Poplars*, have been shown around the world. Craft shops on PEI sell under licence Anne dolls, soap, posters, and other merchandise associated with the red-haired heroine. One can browse the World Wide Web for information on Montgomery's books, her life and houses, and her literary clubs.

Anne of Green Gables is in the NEW CANADIAN LIBRARY with an Afterword by Margaret ATWOOD. See Elizabeth Waterston, *Kindling spirit: L.M. Montgomery's 'Anne of Green Gables'* (1993). GEORGE L. PARKER

Anthologies in English: Poetry. Selections and retrospective surveys of Canadian poetry have played the predominant role in establishing a literary tradition. In the nineteenth century particularly they provided showcases for authors whose work was overshadowed in the mass-market publications that featured popular British and American writers. Edward Hartley DEWART addressed this problem when he compiled the first Canadian anthology, *Selections from Canadian poets with occasional critical and biographical notes and an introductory essay on Canadian poetry* (Montreal, 1864). Dewart knew the importance of a recognizable literary tradition, stating in his introduction that 'A national literature is an essential element in the formation of a national character.' His view of poetry as 'the medium by which the emotions of beauty, joy, admiration, reverence, harmony, or tenderness kindled in the poet-soul, in communion with Nature and God, is conveyed to the souls of others' was reflected in much of the conventional poetry of nineteenth-century Canada. Dewart singled out Charles SANGSTER, followed by Alexander McLACHLAN, as the best of a group of poets that included Charles HEAVYSEGE, William KIRBY, Thomas D'Arcy McGEE, and Susanna MOODIE.

The first major post-Confederation anthology is William Douw LIGHTHALL's *Songs of the great dominion: voices from the forests and waters, the settlements and cities of Canada* (London, 1889). It demonstrates the spirit and flavour of Canadian life—the athletic virility of snowshoeing and moose-hunting, the joyous traditions of barn bees and winter carnivals, the romantic heritage of warriors and voyageurs, and the awesome geography of waterfalls and buffalo plains. Presenting a new generation of poets, Lighthall recognized a renaissance characterized by a tone of 'exultation and confidence' that superseded the 'apologetic and depressed' tone of the pre-Confederation poets. Here Charles G.D. ROBERTS replaces Sangster as the foremost poet, followed by Isabella Valancy CRAWFORD. The anthologist's foresight contrasts with the conventional notion of writers labouring long without recognition: shortly after their first or second books were published, Sangster, Roberts, and

Crawford were heralded as the best in the country.

Other early anthologies range from the superficial *Canadian birthday book, with selections for every day in the year from Canadian writers in English and French* (Toronto, 1887), edited by 'Seranus' (Susie Frances HARRISON) and limited to brief extracts from poems, to the overly moralizing *Treasury of Canadian verse: with brief biographical notes* (1900) edited by Theodore Harding Rand. While *Poems of wild life* (London, 1888), edited by Charles G.D. Roberts, includes only a few Canadian poems, *A Victorian anthology: 1837-1885* (Boston, 1885), edited by E.C. Stedman, includes a large Canadian section of 140 pages. *Later Canadian poems* (Toronto, 1893), edited by J.E. Wetherell, is devoted to the young post-Confederation poets.

Edward S. CASWELL's *Canadian singers and their songs* (1902; rev. 1919, 1925) introduced each poet's selection of verse with an autographed portrait. This popular format was emulated by John Garvin with his influential *Canadian poets and poetry* (1916; rev. 1926). The focus on poets as public figures gave way to two opposing trends: one was led by Lawrence Burpee, who compiled specialized anthologies showcasing a subject, a genre, or an ethnic group, as in *Flowers from a Canadian garden* (1909), *Songs of French Canada* (1909), *A century of Canadian sonnets* (1910), and *Humour of the North* (1912); and the other was represented by *The Oxford book of Canadian verse* (1913), edited by Wilfred CAMPBELL. Wishing to document both the origins and directions of the Canadian literary tradition, the manager of the Oxford University Press in Canada, S.B. Gundy, called in John D. Logan to help make the anthology more comprehensive.

War anthologies were too plentiful to be considered an extension of the interest in specialized anthologies. As is suggested in an early title, *Poems and songs on the South African War: an anthology from England, Africa, Australia, United States, but chiefly Canada* (edited by J.D. Barthwick in 1901), Canadians derived a greater proportion of their identity from foreign wars than did citizens of other countries. Other war anthologies are Carrie Ellen Holman, ed., *In the day of battle: poems of the Great War* (1916); George Herbert Clarke, ed., *A treasury of war poetry* (1917; rev. 1919); John Garvin, ed., *Canadian poems of the Great War* (1918); and J.E. Wetherell, ed., *The Great War in verse and prose* (1919)—recommended for use in schools.

In response to the nationalist pride that followed the war, anthologists during the 1920s demonstrate the confidence that Canadian literature should be studied in schools and performed on stage. Albert Durrant Watson and Lorne PIERCE edited *Our Canadian literature: representative prose and verse* (1922; rev. 1923), while Bliss CARMAN and Lorne Pierce edited *Our Canadian literature: representative verse, English and French* (1922; rev. by V.B. Rhodenizer and retitled *Canadian poetry in English*, 1954). Other anthologies of the twenties were E.K. and Eleanor Hammond Broadus, eds, *A book of Canadian prose and verse* (1923; rev. 1934); A.M. Stephen, ed., *The voice of Canada: a selection of prose and verse* (1926) and *The golden treasury of Canadian verse* (1928); John Murray Gibbon, ed., *Canadian Folksongs (old and new)* (1927; rev. 1949); and W.R. Mackenzie, ed., *Ballads and sea songs from Nova Scotia* (1928).

The anthologies of the 1930s showcase social verse by and about farmers, miners, and sealers. Examples include *An anthology of Y.C. verse: a volume of selections from the verse contributed by the Young Co-operators and published in the Western Producer from 1932 to 1936* (1937); *Rhymes of the miner: an anthology of Canadian mining verse* (1937), edited by Eugene Louis Chicanot; and *Songs sung by old time sealers of many years ago* (1935) edited by James Murphy. But in retrospect the anthology that dominates the populist decade is the élitist *NEW PROVINCES: POEMS OF SEVERAL AUTHORS* (1936), edited by A.J.M. SMITH and F.R. SCOTT as a self-conscious manifesto for a poetry reflecting the cosmopolitan modernism of 'contemporary English and American verse'. However, the impact of this anthology was not felt until the 1940s, when anthologists grew determined to establish a central historic tradition in Canadian literature. Ralph GUSTAFSON's modest *Penguin anthology of Canadian poetry* (1942) was followed by the decade's most important anthology: *The book of Canadian poetry: a critical and historical anthology* (1943; rev. 1948, 1957), an important work of scholarship edited by A.J.M. Smith in which he polarizes Canadian poetry, placing it in either a native or cosmopolitan tradition. The drift towards a continentalist mentality was further demonstrated by John SUTHERLAND's rebellious alternative anthology *Other Canadians: an anthology of the new poetry in Canada 1940-1946* (1947). Sutherland blamed Smith's omission of several young poets on the ideological argument over which cosmopolitan writers should be imitated. Sutherland preferred such American models as Williams and Moore to the British and American expatriates Auden and Eliot, whom Smith preferred.

Several of Sutherland's young poets emerged to dominate the literary scene of the 1950s. Louis DUDEK and Irving LAYTON edited *Canadian Poems 1850-1952* (1952) and Raymond SOUSTER edited *Poets '56: the younger English Canadians* (1956). *Cerberus* (1952) was an anthology that featured the poetry of all three. But the sudden prevalence of student anthologies in the fifties demonstrates the effort to cultivate still newer and younger voices. Earle BIRNEY edited *New Voices: Canadian university writing of 1956* (1956) and Anthony Frisch edited *First flowering: a selection of prose and poetry by the youth of Canada* (1956). John Robert COLOMBO began his career as an anthologist when still a student by editing *Rubato: new poems by young Canadian poets* (1958), *Jargon, 1958/59 by students of the University of Toronto* (1959), and *The Varsity chapbook* (1959); Leslie Kaye edited its companion *The McGill chapbook* (1959). Outside the trends of the decade are *Canadian anthology* (1955; rev. 1966, 1974), a teaching anthology edited by Carl KLINCK and R.E. Watters, and *The blasted pine: an anthology of satire, invective and disrespectful verse chiefly by Canadian writers* (1957; rev. 1967), edited by F.R. Scott and A.J.M. Smith.

The expansion of the universities and the revival of national pride during the 1960s were reflected in the number of anthologies designed for advanced studies. General surveys had to be supplemented with specialized surveys of historical periods. Malcolm Ross selected poetry by Roberts, Carman, Lampman, and D.C. Scott for his *Poets of the confederation* (1960) and Milton Wilson selected poetry by PRATT, F.R. Scott, Smith, LIVESAY, and KLEIN for his *Poets between the wars* (1967) and work by ten newer poets for his *Poetry of mid-century: 1940-1960* (1964). These NEW CANADIAN LIBRARY surveys of historical periods were completed with Eli MANDEL's *Poets of contemporary Canada, 1960-1970* (1972), featuring the work of ten young poets, and David Sinclair's *Nineteenth-century narrative poems* (1972), featuring one poem each by GOLDSMITH, HOWE, Sangster, Kirby, and McLachlan. Smith's *Oxford book of Canadian verse* (1960) is entirely unlike Campbell's 1913 predecessor, not only in the fact that it presents a chronological sampling of poets writing in both English and French. Smith's *Modern Canadian verse in English and French* (1967) is a modern supplement to his *Oxford book* and provides a wider range than Louis Dudek's *Modern Canadian anthology* (1965). A discerning and colourfully presented selection for children is *The wind has wings: poems from Canada* (1968; rev. 1984) edited by Mary Alice Downie and Barbara Robertson and beautifully illustrated by Elizabeth Cleaver.

Experimental, regional, and ethnic anthologies dominated the literary scene throughout the 1970s. The national consciousness that emerged with the 1967 Centennial celebrations inevitably led to the recognition of local distinctions, the preservation of racial and cultural heritages, and explorations of alternatives to the newly identified traditions. With the historic periods and central canon now established, anthologists turned their attention to trends of the future, to the experimental approaches of the avant-garde. *New wave Canada: the new explosion in Canadian poetry* (1966) was an influential Canadian anthology of work inspired by the American Black Mountain school, whose followers lived on the West Coast. Its editor, Raymond Souster, joined Douglas LOCHHEAD to edit the optimistic *Made in Canada: new poems for the seventies* (1970). Jack LUDWIG and Andy Wainwright introduced with equal optimism fourteen writers in *Soundings: new Canadian poets* (1970). John Robert Colombo's *New directions in Canadian poetry* (1971) included some interesting critical commentary, and Al PURDY's *Storm warning* (1971) included self-conscious manifestos by thirty new poets; Purdy followed this by presenting a second group of new poets in *Storm warning 2* (1976). A mature anthology of self-confident avant-garde writers was *Where? the other Canadian poetry* (1974) edited by Eldon Garnet. bp NICHOL edited the first Canadian anthology of concrete poetry, *The cosmic chef* (1970), a box containing the work of 52 poets ranging from Earle Birney and Margaret AVISON to Nichol and bill BISSETT. The best introduction to sound poetry was Steve McCAFFERY's and bp Nichol's *Sound poetry: a catalogue* (1978), which included critical introductions to the texts of performances by the participants at the International Festival of Sound Poetry held in Toronto in 1978. In other genres, Robert WEAVER edited *Poems for voices* (1970), a collection of six radio verse-dramas by Al Purdy, Margaret ATWOOD, John NEWLOVE, Phyllis GOTLIEB, Tom MARSHALL, and Alden NOWLAN; and Michael ONDAATJE edited *The long poem anthology* (1979) featuring experimental narratives by ten poets. Sharon THESEN edited *The new long poem anthology* (1991), with thirteen poets adding brief commentaries on their poems. After the experimental had matured from the margins to the mainstream, anthologies of new poetry were designed not to upset but to update the establishment. Dennis LEE's *The new Canadian poets 1970-1985* (1985) is a canonical textbook of poets who published their first book since 1970. Patrick LANE and Lorna CROZIER's *Breathing fire: Canada's new poets* (1995) is a further updating, though it risks a touch of Purdy's earlier storm warnings.

The regional is the second industry that began its predominance in the 1970s. From the East Coast came *Voices underground: poems from Newfoundland writers* (1972) edited by Harold HORWOOD; *Baffles of wind and tide: a selection of Newfoundland writers* (1974), and *The blasty bough: a selection of Newfoundland writing* (1976), both edited by Clyde Rose. Robert Cockburn and Robert GIBBS edited *Ninety seasons: modern poems from the Maritimes* (1974) and Donald Cameron edited *Voices down east: a collection of new writing from the Atlantic provinces* (1974). Elaine Crocker, Eric Norman, and Michael Nowlan edited the larger *Choice Atlantic writing of Newfoundland and the Maritimes* (1990), a survey of poets and songwriters ranging from traditional folk songs and Joseph HOWE's colonial poetry to Rita JOE and Rita MacNeil. To represent the English subculture of Montreal, David SOLWAY edited *Four Montreal poets* (1972) and Endre Farkas and Ken Norris edited *Montreal English poetry of the seventies* (1977). Farkas later edited a more comprehensive collection, *The other language: English poetry of Montreal* (1989), ranging from F.R. Scott to Erin MOURÉ. Ontario anthologies include Colin Morton's *Capital poets: an Ottawa anthology* (1989), with work by ten poets who actually write little about the capital, where they reside, and *Voices from Niagara* (1987), edited by Peter and Brenda Baltensperger. Laurence Ricou edited *Twelve prairie poets* (1976); Ken MITCHELL selected prose and poetry for *Horizon: writings of the Canadian prairies* (1977); and Dennis Cooley introduced fifty-one poets in *Draft: an anthology of prairie poetry* (1981), and later selected eighteen poets for *Inscriptions: a prairie poetry anthology* (1992). Daniel Lenoski edited *A/long prairie lines: an anthology of long prairie poems* (1989), wherein the drought, the Depression, and death remain the pervasive trinity. *Heading out: the new Saskatchewan poets* (1986), edited by Don Kerr and Anne SZUMIGALSKI, is complemented by *A sudden radiance: Saskatchewan poetry* (1987) edited by Lorna Crozier and Gary Hyland. John W. Chalmers edited *The Alberta Diamond Jubilee anthology: a collection from Alberta's best writers* (1980). J. Michael YATES edited *Contemporary poetry of British Columbia* (1970) and Gary GEDDES edited *Skookum Wawa: writings of the Canadian Northwest* (1975). Allan Safarik's *Vancouver poets* (1986) features poems about Vancouver as well as by Vancouver poets, while Tom WAYMAN and Calvin Wharton's *East of the main: an anthology of poems from east Vancouver* (1989) conveys the cultural experience of the lively east-end urban West Coast life.

The poetry of French Canada in translation (1970) was edited by John GLASSCO, who, with F.R. Scott, contributed many of the translations. Scott translated all eleven poets presented in his beautifully printed *Poems of French Canada* (1977). Philip Stratford edited *Voices from Quebec: an anthology of translations* (1977). The most active translator was Fred COGSWELL, who edited four anthologies: *One hundred poems of modern Quebec* (1971), *A second hundred poems of modern Quebec* (1971), *The poetry of modern Quebec* (1976), and (with Jo-Anne Elder) *Unfinished dreams: contemporary poetry of Acadie* (1990), which shifts from the religious, patriotic, and conformist characteristics of traditional modernist Acadian literature to the postmodernist Acadian renaissance since the 1960s. To commemorate Cogswell's work as a publisher of more than 300 FIDDLEHEAD POETRY BOOKS, Gregory Cook edited *Scroll* (1980), featuring fifty poets whom Cogswell had published.

The responsibility for reflecting Canada's multicultural heritage had long been left to one man: Watson KIRKCONNELL. Among his many volumes of translation, his *Canadian overtones: an anthology of Canadian poetry written in Icelandic, Swedish, Hungarian, Italian, Greek, and Ukrainian* (1935) best showed his own diversity as well as Canada's. The proliferation since 1970 of editors of, and translators for, ethnic anthologies reflects widespread interest in preserving our heritage. J. Michael Yates edited *Volvox: poetry from the unofficial languages of Canada in English translations* (1971); Tomi Nishimura edited *Maple: poetry by Japanese-Canadians with English translations* (1975); Harold Head edited *Canada in us now: the first anthology of Black poetry and prose in Canada* (1976); Pier Giorgio DI CICCO edited *Roman candles: an anthology of poems by seventeen Italo-Canadian poets* (1978); and Caroline Morgan DiGiovanni edited *Italian Canadian voices: an anthology of poetry and prose (1946-1983)* (1984). William and Christine Mowat edited *Native peoples in Canadian literature* (1975), Marilyn BOWERING and David Day edited *Many voices: an anthology of contemporary Canadian Indian poetry* (1977), and John Robert Colombo edited *Songs of the Indians* in two volumes (1983) and *Poems of the Inuit* (1981). Harry Loewen edited *Mennonite images*

(1980), Jars Balan and Yuri Klynovy edited poetry and fiction in *Yarmarok: Ukrainian writing in Canada since the Second World War* (1987), and Cyril Dabydeen edited Caribbean-born poets in *A shapely fire: changing the literary landscape* (1987).

While the ideological trends begun in the 1970s changed the literary landscape, anthologists in the 1980s attempted to consolidate the canon. Scholarly textbooks offering critical introductions to a chronology of poets include the two-volume, well-annotated *Anthology of Canadian literature in English* (1982, 1983), edited by Russell Brown and Donna Bennett, which presents fifty poets (from ODELL to Mouré); the two-volume *Canadian poetry* (1982), containing forty-six poets (from Sangster to Nichol), edited by Jack David and Robert Lecker, who also edited *The new Canadian anthology: poetry and short fiction* (1988), which includes thirty-four poets (from Crawford to Roo BORSON). Canadian poetry of the twentieth century was given substantial treatment in three editions of *15 Canadian poets* (1970), edited by Gary Geddes, which was followed by *15 Canadian poets + 5* (1978) and *15 Canadian poets × 2* (1988). All these anthologists demonstrated faith in a traditional canon. *The new Oxford book of Canadian verse in English* (1982), edited by Margaret Atwood, typified this post-Centennial confidence. In her introduction Atwood speaks wittily of cultural nationalism, regionalism, and feminism as no longer controversial issues in a mature country. While she apologizes for ignoring the experiments of the concrete poets, she is as concerned about future trends as she is about the roots of our past. She is loyal to the cause of preserving traditional favourites, cautious in her predictions of success for the most promising new talents, and determined in her concern that women poets receive a fair share in representing the Canadian literary tradition.

However, by the 1990s this tradition was fractured to the point that Atwood's selection came to appear reactionary to some critics for giving too little attention to issues of genre and gender, of race and region. What had begun in the 1970s as an effort to preserve our heritage as a multicultural mosaic became a commitment to redress the absence of other voices in the 1990s, when anthologies were frequently designed as revisionist and subversive assaults on the traditional canon, presenting alternative subcultures or histories based on race and gender.

The first anthology devoted to what she called the 'female ghetto' was Dorothy Livesay's *40 women poets of Canada* (1972). In *Poetry by Canadian women* (1989) Rosemary SULLIVAN presented a chronological selection beginning with Margaret Blennerhasset's 1824 poems. *Sudden miracles* (1991), edited by Rhea TREGEBOV, included introductions by Roo Borson, Susan Glickman, Claire HARRIS, Beth HARVOR, Paulette JILES, Anne MICHAELS, Erin Mouré, and Bronwen WALLACE to their own work. *The girl wants to* (1993), edited by Lynn Crosbie, explores—through poetry, prose, art, and comics—radical modes of inscribing female desire. A previously silenced subculture was foregrounded in Makeda Silvera's *Pearls of passion: a treasury of lesbian erotica* (1994), presenting twenty-five lesbian poets and prose writers. Other previously marginalized groups include Asian, African, and Native women. Diane McGifford and Judith Kearns edited *Shakti's words: an anthology of South Asian Canadian women's poetry* (1993). In *Daughters of the sun, women of the moon: poetry by Black Canadian women* (1991), edited by Ann Wallace, ten Canadian poets deal with their 'experience of racism, sexism, class disparity, and alienation'.

Since appearing in biennial issues of *Whetstone* (1985-9) and in the annual *Gatherings: the En'owkin journal of First North Americans* (1990-), Native writers are at last well represented in many anthologies. The following include both poetry and prose: *Seventh generation: contemporary Native writing* (1989) edited by Heather Hodgson; *Writing the circle: Native women of western Canada* (1990) edited by Jeanne Perrault and Sylvia Vane; *Our bit of truth: an anthology of Canadian Native literature* (1990) edited by Agnes Grant; *An anthology of Canadian Native literature in English* (1992) edited by Daniel David MOSES and Terry Goldie, a chronological arrangement from traditional oral songs to nineteenth and twentieth-century writers; *The colour of resistance: an anthology of writing by aboriginal women* (1993) edited by Connie Fife; *Into the moon: heart, mind, body, soul* (1996) edited by Lenore KEESHIG-TOBIAS; and *Let the drums be your heart: new Native voices* (1996) edited by Joel T. Maki.

Anthologies of black writing also have dramatically increased in number. *Voices: Canadian writers of African descent* (1992) and *Fiery spirits: a collection of short fiction and poetry by Canadian writers of African descent* (1994) were both edited by Ayanna Black. With its title referring to what escaped slaves kept in sight, as they travelled north, *Eyeing the North Star: directions in African-Canadian literature* (1997), edited by George Elliott CLARKE, presents

Dionne BRAND, Claire Harris, Olive Senior, and other poets of African and Caribbean descent who published between 1971 and 1997.

It is ironic that the interest of the 1990s in subcultures—derived from the international concern with race, class, and gender—raises issues that are problematic for a post-colonial Canadian culture whose subversive effort once was to establish a native literary community no longer dependent on a foreign centre. We are returned to the native-cosmopolitan debate of the 1930s and 1940s, as the literary concerns of the 1970s and 1980s have been replaced by the international postmodernist concerns of the 1990s. However, the very nature of our post-colonial literary tradition may place us in a better position than other countries to refashion the canon in future anthologies without subsuming the marginalized in a homogenizing mainstream.

In fact, the refashioning of the canon through the integration of other voices began with the origins of our literature in the eighteenth and nineteenth centuries. *Early long poems on Canada* (1993), edited by D.M.R. Bentley, represents the scholarly editing of fourteen long poems that demonstrate a colonial community of poets already working within a literary tradition, as Sangster was influenced by Adam KIDD's *The Huron chief* (1830) and Crawford was influenced by McLachlan's *The emigrant* (1861). New scholarship led to the revision of the texts of Sangster and Crawford by Frank Tierney and Glenn Clever for *Nineteenth-century narrative poems* (1988) which was first edited by David Sinclair in 1972. Similarly, Malcolm Ross's 1960 *Confederation poets* (1960) has been superseded by two anthologies: Bryan N.S. Gooch and Maureen Niwa's *The emergence of the muse: major Canadian poets from Crawford to Pratt* (1993) adds PICKTHALL, Crawford, Campbell, and Pratt to Ross's four poets. More ambitious is Carole Gerson and Gwendolyn Davies' *Canadian poetry: from the beginnings through the First World War* (1994) starting with Robert HAYMAN and Henry Kelsey from the seventeenth century and introducing many previously neglected women, Native, and working-class poets of the eighteenth and nineteenth centuries. The application of ideological principles to the literature of our present age promises a flexible and inclusive canon, one that reflects a dynamic culture. Canadian anthologies play an important role in the development of our literature, for they not only represent changing fashions but also anticipate the reputations of new writers, thereby continuing to determine our literary tradition. DAVID LATHAM

Short fiction. 1. HISTORICAL AND HISTORIC ANTHOLOGIES. The most fundamental and common principle for arranging short-fiction anthologies has been the historical basis, introduced by Desmond PACEY in *A book of Canadian stories* (1947; rev. 1950, 1952, 1962), and repeated in Robert WEAVER's *Canadian short stories* (1960), Giose Rimanelli and Roberto Ruberto's *Modern Canadian stories* (1966), Alec Lucas's *Great Canadian short stories* (1971), Wayne Grady's *The Penguin book of Canadian short stories* (1980), Rosemary SULLIVAN's *Stories by Canadian women* (1984), Margaret ATWOOD and Robert Weaver's *The Oxford book of Canadian short stories in English* (1986) and their *The new Oxford book of Canadian short stories in English* (1995), W.H. New's *Canadian short fiction: from myth to modern* (1986) and its successor, *Canadian short fiction* (1997), Miriam WADDINGTON's *Canadian Jewish short stories* (1990), as well as J.R. (Tim) Struthers' two-volume *The possibilities of story* (1992). Other anthologies—from Raymond KNISTER's conscientiously edited *Canadian short stories* (1928), the first anthology of its kind, to John METCALF's scrupulously chosen *Making it new: contemporary Canadian stories* (1982) and *The new story writers* (1992)—are historical in a different sense: they reflect Canadian short-story writing over a specific period. W.H. New, however, in the introductions to his anthologies and through his selections, impresses upon us the importance not only of arranging texts but also of reading them with various concerns in mind: thematic repetition and/or variation, historical breadth and/or focus, along with aesthetic diversity and aesthetic enjoyment.

Raymond Knister's *Canadian short stories* marked, in his words, 'the outset of a new era'—or, seen from a different vantage point, the termination of an earlier era. It summed up one man's view of the achievements made in the short-story form during the preceding four decades, and contained works by seventeen writers, including Morley CALLAGHAN, Norman DUNCAN, Stephen LEACOCK, Thomas Murtha, Gilbert PARKER, Charles G.D. ROBERTS, Duncan Campbell SCOTT, Edward William THOMSON, and two women, Marjorie PICKTHALL and Mazo DE LA ROCHE. Knister's introduction, selections, and extensive critical apparatus continue to be of value. Yet research by Lorraine McMullen and Sandra Campbell for *Pioneering women: short stories by Canadian women, beginnings to 1880*

(1993), *Aspiring women: short stories by Canadian women, 1880-1900* (1993), and *New women: short stories by Canadian women, 1900-1920* (1991) reclaims the work of a large number of women writers, up to and including Knister's time, and invites readers to review the early history of short fiction in Canada. The period preceding Knister's is also represented in David Arnason's *Nineteenth century Canadian stories* (1976), in Carole Gerson and Kathy Mezei's *The prose of life: sketches from Victorian Canada* (1981), and in R.G. Moyles' *'Improved by cultivation': an anthology of English-Canadian prose to 1914* (1994), which exhibits five kinds of short fiction: travel and exploration narratives, memoirs and descriptive sketches, satirical and humorous sketches, animal stories, and short stories. The decade immediately following that of Knister's anthology is represented in Donna Phillips' *Voices of discord: Canadian short stories from the 1930s* (1979).

Robert Weaver's 1960 volume, *Canadian short stories*—in Oxford's World's Classics series—opens with selections by Edward William Thomson, Charles G.D. Roberts, Duncan Campbell Scott, and Stephen Leacock, proceeds to stories by Ethel WILSON, Raymond Knister, and Morley Callaghan, and closes with early works by writers such as Mavis GALLANT and Alice MUNRO. This was reprinted (1966) in an Oxford paperback series, and was followed by Weaver's *Canadian short stories: second series* (1968), which opens with stories by Callaghan and Wilson, then concentrates on works from the 1950s and 1960s by Gallant and Munro and other writers of their generation, such as Hugh HOOD. John Metcalf's *Sixteen by twelve: short stories by Canadian writers* (1970) and *The narrative voice: short stories and reflections by Canadian authors* (1972) give evidence of the growing activity in the short-story form at the end of the 1960s and the beginning of the 1970s. Metcalf's 1982 anthology, *Making it new*, containing stories with authors' commentaries, and his *Writers in aspic* (1988), an anthology of stories and assorted critical essays, including a fascinating study of Alice Munro's 'Walker Brothers cowboy' (written by Metcalf under the pseudonym James A. Maitland), present judicious selections from Canada's premier short-story writers in the 1980s. John Metcalf and J.R. (Tim) Struthers' *Canadian classics: an anthology of short stories* (1993) and their companion volume, *How stories mean* (1993), take stock of creative achievements in, as well as critical thinking about, the short-story form by Mavis Gallant, Norman LEVINE, Hugh Hood, Alice Munro, and other writers, including Metcalf, who emerged soon after them. Metcalf's 1992 volume, *The new story writers*, and a number of selections in Tim Inkster and John Metcalf's *The Porcupine's Quill reader* (1996) call attention to a subsequent and ever-expanding generation of short-story writers including Douglas GLOVER, Diane SCHOEMPERLEN, Steven HEIGHTON, and Caroline Adderson.

In the almost exactly forty years from the publication of Knister's *Canadian short stories* through to the celebration of Canada's Centennial, only a few short-fiction anthologies appeared. The most important was Pacey's *A book of Canadian stories*; his selections and lengthy critical introduction provided readers with a good sense of the historical development of short fiction in Canada. Although his approach remained substantially the same from the first edition to the last, the final edition reflected the advance made in Canadian short-story writing during the 1950s. For the final edition of *A book of Canadian stories*, Pacey narrowed his selections of earlier work and added stories by ten writers whose reputations were currently rising, such as Ernest BUCKLER, Henry KREISEL, Mordecai RICHLER, Alice Munro, and Alden NOWLAN. In the interim he had also replaced Morley Callaghan's 'Father and son' with 'The blue kimono'. Other anthologies in this period were Robert Weaver and Helen James's *Canadian short stories* (1952), selected from stories read on CBC Radio; William McConnell's *Klanak Islands: a collection of short stories* (1959), which included work by Henry Kreisel, Robert HARLOW, Jane RULE, McConnell, and four other writers; Robert Weaver's *Canadian short stories* (1960) and his *Ten for Wednesday Night* (1961), another selection from stories read on CBC Radio; and Giose Rimanelli and Roberto Ruberto's fine *Modern Canadian stories* (1966)—a rare instance, at least for its time, of an anthology designed according to several principles. Rimanelli and Ruberto's collection adheres to a loosely historical structure overall, shifts thematically about midway from stories with an international outlook to ones with a stronger Canadian viewpoint, and concludes by acknowledging the recent emergence of more poetic conceptions of form and style in the short story.

In the fifteen years immediately after Canada's Centennial—starting in 1968 with the publication of Robert Weaver's *Canadian short stories: second series* and Norman Levine's *Canadian winter's tales*, a collection of nine stories by Malcolm LOWRY, Brian MOORE, Morley Callaghan, Hugh Hood, Margaret

LAURENCE, Mavis Gallant, Mordecai Richler, Levine, and Ethel Wilson—scores of short-fiction anthologies began to be published, a rapid development that paralleled exciting advances in all aspects of Canadian writing and publishing. Many of these anthologies appealed to the growing audiences for Canadian learning materials in high schools, colleges, and universities that energetic editors like Weaver, Metcalf, and Rudy WIEBE strove hard to cultivate. Among the very best anthologies were Metcalf's 1972 volume, *The narrative voice*, Clark BLAISE and John Metcalf's *Here & now: best Canadian stories* (1977), and Metcalf's 1982 volume, *Making it new*. Fourteen exceptional writers are represented in Blaise and Metcalf's *Here & now: best Canadian stories*, including Levine, Gallant, Laurence, Hood, Rule, Munro, Austin CLARKE, Leon ROOKE, Audrey THOMAS, Dave GODFREY, Metcalf, Russell Banks, Blaise, and Ray SMITH. However, works by only seven of these authors (Thomas, Munro, Laurence, Godfrey, Hood, Levine, and Blaise) appear among the twenty-four selections in Ivon Owen and Morris Wolfe's *The best modern Canadian short stories* (1978), and works by only three (Munro, Gallant, and Laurence) are included among the twenty-six selections in John Stevens' mistitled *Best Canadian short stories* (1981).

Many of these titles are examples of the 'contemporary voices' type of anthology, a category that, by 1982, included Tony Kilgallin's textbook, *The Canadian short story* (1971), Donald Stephens' *Contemporary voices: the short story in Canada* (1972), George BOWERING's *Fiction of contemporary Canada* (1980), Terence Byrnes' *Matinées daily* (1981), Wayne Grady's *The Penguin book of modern Canadian short stories* (1982), and two more anthologies edited by Robert Weaver, *Canadian short stories: third series* (1978) and *Small wonders: new stories by twelve distinguished Canadian authors* (1982). Other examples since 1982 included Weaver's *Canadian short stories: fourth series* (1985) and *Canadian short stories: fifth series* (1991), Rosemary SULLIVAN's *More stories by Canadian women* (1987), Linda HUTCHEON and Marion Richmond's *Other solitudes: Canadian multicultural fictions* (1990), Thomas KING's *All my relations: an anthology of contemporary Canadian Native fiction* (1990), and George Bowering and Linda Hutcheon's *Likely stories: a postmodern sampler* (1992).

Two strikingly different series begun in 1971 by OBERON PRESS and COACH HOUSE PRESS offered numerous other instances of the 'contemporary voices' type of anthology. The first volume in the mainly conservative or modernist Oberon Press series was David HELWIG and Tom MARSHALL's wittily entitled *Fourteen stories high: best Canadian stories of 71* (1971). Successive volumes were edited by Helwig and Joan Harcourt under the titles *72: new Canadian stories*, *73: new Canadian stories*, and so forth until 1977, when John Metcalf (having replaced Helwig as co-editor of the series the preceding year) felt that Canadian short-story writing had finally reached a height at which a Canadian anthology could dare to emulate *The best American short stories*. The new series title, *Best Canadian stories*, was then introduced, though these volumes were shorter than their American counterparts. Stories by W.P. KINSELLA, W.D. VALGARDSON, Elisabeth HARVOR, Jack HODGINS, Elizabeth SPENCER, Kent THOMPSON, Judith Penner, and Ann COPELAND comprised Harcourt and Metcalf's benchmark *77: Best Canadian stories*. The 1978, 1979, and 1980 volumes were co-edited by Metcalf and Clark Blaise; the 1981 and 1982 editions by Metcalf and Leon ROOKE. At the end of 1982, Metcalf and Rooke resigned to edit *The New Press anthology*, which published short fiction and ran for two years, 1984 and 1985; they then moved on to edit *The Macmillan anthology*, which published new Canadian writing in a range of genres, including short fiction, poetry, memoirs, and criticism, and ran for two years, 1988 and 1989, under Metcalf and Rooke, and for a third year, 1990, under Metcalf and Kent Thompson.

In 1983 the editorship of *Best Canadian stories* reverted to David Helwig—first in collaboration with Sandra Martin, from 1983 to 1986, and then with Maggie Helwig, from 1987 to 1994. The 1995 volume was edited by David Helwig alone, twenty-five years after he first helped to lay the groundwork for this series, and in 1996 the editorship passed to Douglas Glover, who had co-edited Oberon's *Coming attractions* series from 1991 to 1995. The mainly experimental or postmodernist Coach House Press series originated with George Bowering's anthology *The story so far* (1971) and continued under a policy of rotating editorship, with volumes edited by Matt COHEN (1973), David Young (1974), Steve McCAFFERY and bp NICHOL (1976), and Douglas BARBOUR (1978); in 1979 a bilingual selection of Québécois fiction was chosen by Nicole BROSSARD. The most frequently anthologized writers in the Oberon series, up to 1982, were Munro, Spencer, and Thompson—five times each in the first twelve volumes. bp Nichol's fiction appeared in all five anglophone volumes of Coach House's *The story so far*; George Bowering, Matt Cohen, Daphne MARLATT, Steve McCaffery, and David Young were represented in three volumes apiece. Relatively few writers—Margaret Atwood, Clark Blaise, George Bowering, Matt Cohen, Jack Hodgins, Greg HOLLINGSHEAD, W.P. Kinsella, David McFADDEN, Alden Nowlan, Stephen SCOBIE, and Kent Thompson—were anthologized in both the Oberon series and the Coach House series over the relatively few years in which the two series co-existed.

Commencing in 1989, an important new annual showcase for Canadian short fiction was inaugurated: *The Journey Prize anthology*, a selection of the best short fiction by Canada's new writers from Canadian literary magazines. The final choices for the anthology have been made each year by an editorial board headed by a distinguished writer; Alistair MacLEOD, Leon Rooke, Jane URQUHART, Sandra BIRDSELL, Guy VANDERHAEGHE, Douglas Glover, M.G. VASSANJI, and Olive Senior have already served.

2. REGIONAL AND COTERIE ANTHOLOGIES. Although Pacey's *A book of Canadian stories* contained a sizeable representation of stories from the Atlantic provinces, and although McConnell's *Klanak Islands* consisted of stories by writers living in the westernmost provinces, the regional anthology *per se* became popular only in the 1970s, beginning with Rudy Wiebe's *Stories from Western Canada* (1972), Kent Thompson's *Stories from Atlantic Canada* (1973), Andreas SCHROEDER and Rudy Wiebe's *Stories from Pacific and Arctic Canada* (1974), and Germaine Warkentin's *Stories from Ontario* (1974). The most interesting of these anthologies, in terms of imaginative structure, is Warkentin's, which uses Stephen Leacock's 'The marine excursion of the Knights of Pythias' as the prologue to sections entitled 'In the clearings' (an echo of the title of Susanna MOODIE's book of descriptive sketches *Life in the clearings*), '"Is this the way to Sunshine?"' (a line from Alice Munro's story 'Walker Brothers cowboy', included in the anthology), 'Men and women' (the title of a short-story collection by Hugh GARNER), and 'Where the myth touches us' (the title of a Hugh Hood story, included in the anthology), then concludes with Dave GODFREY's 'Out in Chinguacousy' as the epilogue.

These anthologies were followed by Rudy Wiebe and Aritha VAN HERK's *More stories from Western Canada* (1980), Muriel Whitaker's *Stories from the Canadian North* (1980), and, in many cases, more localized anthologies of stories, chiefly representing the western provinces, such as David Carpenter's *Wild rose country: stories from Alberta* (1977)—though George Peabody's *Best Maritime short stories* (1988) was a notable exception from the Atlantic provinces. Additional anthologies of Western Canadian stories, all from increasingly influential small presses in Western Canada, included: Robert KROETSCH's *Sundogs: stories from Saskatchewan* (1980); Joan Parr's *Manitoba stories* (1981); Ron Smith and Stephen Guppy's *Rainshadow: stories from Vancouver Island* (1982); Leah Flater, Aritha van Herk, and Rudy Wiebe's *West of fiction* (1983); Caroline Heath's *Double bond: an anthology of prairie women's fiction* (1984); Fred Stenson's *Alberta bound: thirty stories by Alberta writers* (1986); Allan Forrie, Patrick O'Rourke, and Glen Sorestad's *The last map is the heart: Western Canadian fiction* (1989); Kristjana GUNNARS' *Unexpected fictions: new Icelandic Canadian writing* (1989); Aritha van Herk's *Alberta rebound: thirty more stories by Alberta writers* (1990); and Wayne Tefs, Geoffrey Ursell, and Aritha van Herk's *Due West: 30 great stories from Alberta, Saskatchewan and Manitoba* (1996).

Francophone writing from Quebec was recognized by Philip Stratford in his anthology of translations *Stories from Québec* (1974)—and subsequently by Richard Teleky's *The Oxford book of French-Canadian short stories* (1983), Matt Cohen and Wayne Grady's *Intimate strangers: new stories from Quebec* (1986), Geoff Hancock's *Invisible fictions: contemporary stories from Quebec* (1987), Beverley Daurio and Luise von Flotow's *Ink and strawberries: an anthology of Quebec women's fiction* (1988), and Matt Cohen and Wayne Grady's *The Quebec anthology: 1830-1990* (1996). Anglophone writing from the same province went relatively unnoticed until Douglas Daymond and Leslie Monkman's *Stories of Quebec* (1980) and Steve Luxton's *Saturday night at the Forum* (1981)—followed by P. Scott Lawrence's *Souvenirs: new English fiction from Quebec* (1987) and Linda Leith's *Telling differences: new English fiction from Quebec* (1988). Even more localized were anthologies of short fiction from a specific city, such as Joan Parr's *Winnipeg stories* (1974), Morris Wolfe and Douglas Daymond's *Toronto short stories* (1977), Hugh Hood and Peter O'Brien's *Fatal recurrences: new fiction in English from Montreal* (1984), Carole Gerson's *Vancouver short stories* (1985), David WATMOUGH's *Vancouver fiction* (1985), Cary Fagan and Robert MacDonald's *Streets of attitude: Toronto stories* (1990), and Barry CALLAGHAN's *This ain't no healing town: Toronto stories* (1995).

The coterie anthology was represented by a number of small-press books, such as Rudy

Wiebe's *Getting here* (1977), a collection of seven stories by seven women, and by anthologies of stories reprinted from single magazines, such as *Stories to read again* (1965), selected by H. Gordon Green from the *Family Herald*, and *Fiddlehead greens: stories from The Fiddlehead* (1979), selected by Roger Ploude and Michael Taylor, and by special issues of various literary magazines.

3. OTHER ANTHOLOGIES. A different type of anthology—Michael ONDAATJE's *Personal fictions: stories by Munro, Wiebe, Thomas, & Blaise* (1977), for example—included several contributions by each writer, thereby providing some sense of the range of each author chosen. Clarke, Irwin's *New Canadian writing, 1968* and *New Canadian writing, 1969* offered selections of stories by three writers in each volume: David Lewis Stein, Clark Blaise, and Dave Godfrey in 1968; John Metcalf, D.O. Spettigue, and C.J. Newman in 1969. Oberon Press's *First impressions* (1980), *Second impressions* (1981), and *Third impressions* (1982), which contained Metcalf's selections from the work of nine newer writers, were also anthologies of this kind. Annually for the next fifteen years, with the guidance of various editors, this idea has been continued by Oberon under the inviting series title *Coming attractions*.

Certain anthologists have concentrated on particular subgenres of short fiction as a principle of selection. George Bowering's *Great Canadian sports stories* (1979) is one such volume, as are Muriel Whitaker's *Great Canadian animal stories* (1978), *Great Canadian adventure stories* (1979), and *The best Canadian animal stories: classic tales by master storytellers* (1997). Douglas Daymond and Leslie Monkman's anthology *On middle ground* (1987) provides a valuable introduction to the novella form as practised by Malcolm Lowry, Ethel Wilson, Mavis Gallant, Audrey Thomas, John Metcalf, Clark Blaise, and Keath FRASER. At the other end of the spectrum, Kent Thompson's *Open windows: Canadian short short stories* (1988) and Kristina Russelo's *Snapshots: the new Canadian fiction* (1992) afford various illustrations of the form Thompson terms 'postcard stories'. Of specialized interest are John Robert COLOMBO and Michael Richardson's *Not to be taken at night: thirteen classic tales of mystery and the supernatural* (1981), Michael Richardson's *Maddened by mystery: a casebook of Canadian detective fiction* (1982), Greg Ioannou and Lynne Missen's *Shivers: an anthology of Canadian ghost stories* (1989), and Alberto MANGUEL's *The Oxford book of Canadian ghost stories* (1990) and *Canadian mystery stories* (1991).

A number of anthologies emphasize fiction's aesthetic potential rather than its representational dimension. They provide a salutary alternative to some basic premises of the many historical and regional anthologies that have exerted the most influence up to the present time. Anthologies in this category are George Bowering's *The story so far*, *Great Canadian sports stories*, *Fiction of contemporary Canada*, and Bowering and Hutcheon's *Likely stories*, as well as Geoff Hancock's *Magic realism* (1980), Hancock's two-volume anthology of fables, fantasies, and metafiction, *Illusion one* and *Illusion two* (1983), and his *Moving off the map: from 'story' to 'fiction'* (1986), *Singularities: fragments, parafictions, prose poems—new directions in fiction and physics* (1990), and *Fire beneath the cauldron* (1991), along with W.H. New's *Canadian short fiction* and J.R. (Tim) Struthers' *The possibilities of story*. Such volumes might well represent the future of anthologies of Canadian short fiction in English.

The changing cultural politics and the changing conceptions during the three decades following Canada's Centennial are perhaps most fully reflected in an anthology that stands as a counterpart, or a complement, to Rimanelli and Ruberto's 1966 volume, *Modern Canadian stories*: Michael Ondaatje's broadly and imaginatively conceived *From ink lake: Canadian stories* (1990). Ondaatje's selections powerfully signal the development—during an era of what Frank DAVEY, in an essay reproduced in Ajay Heble, Donna Palmateer Pennee, and J.R. (Tim) Struthers' *New contexts of Canadian criticism* (1997), terms 'post-national arguments'—of a more international, more multicultural, yet in some respects more regional, more local outlook. Ondaatje frames his anthology, very interestingly, with particularly chosen works by Alistair MacLeod, Gabrielle ROY, and Wallace Stegner at the opening and by Alice Munro, Stephen Leacock, and, again, Alistair MacLeod at the closing. For a new generation of readers, the contents of *From ink lake* challenge, blur, and perhaps dissolve various widely accepted conceptions of boundaries—of cultural identity, geopolitics, language, literary reality, and genre.

J.R. (TIM) STRUTHERS

General. Probably the most significant anthologies of Canadian literature are the general anthologies of prose and poetry that seek to define the past and/or the present of the literature as a whole. The first group of these, appearing between the wars, included Albert Durrant Watson and Lorne PIERCE's *Our*

Canadian literature: representative prose & verse (1922; 2nd edn 1923), Edmund Kemper Broadus and Eleanor Hammond Broadus's *A book of Canadian prose and verse* (1923; 2nd edn 1934), A.M. Stephen's *The voice of Canada: a selection of prose and verse* (1926), William K.F. Kendrick's *Canadian stories in verse and prose* (1932; 2nd ed. 1936), and Ralph GUSTAFSON's *Canadian accent: a collection of stories and poems by contemporary writers from Canada* (1944). More comprehensive and scholarly anthologies followed, beginning with Carl F. KLINCK and Reginald E. Watters' pioneer teaching volume *Canadian anthology*, editions of which were published in 1955, 1966, and 1974. H. Gordon Green and Guy Sylvestre's bilingual *A century of Canadian literature/Un siècle de littérature canadienne* was published in 1967, in honour of Canada's Centennial, and was succeeded by a flurry of major anthologies during the 1970s, most of them intended for classroom use: Mordecai RICHLER's *Canadian writing today* (1970), which was dedicated to Morley CALLAGHAN; Robert WEAVER and William Toye's *The Oxford anthology of Canadian literature* (1973; 2nd edn 1981); a four-volume series, under the general editorship of Mary Jane Edwards, entitled *The evolution of Canadian literature in English* (1973), to which was added Paul Denham and Mary Jane Edwards' one-volume *Canadian literature in the 70's* (1980); Desmond PACEY's *Selections from major Canadian writers: poetry and creative prose in English* (1974); Catherine M. McLay's *Canadian literature: the beginnings to the 20th century* (1974); and Douglas Daymond and Leslie Monkman's two-volume *Literature in Canada* (1978). The 1980s produced the first comprehensively annotated anthology, Russell Brown and Donna Bennett's two-volume *An anthology of Canadian literature in English* (1982, 1983).

The impulse of Canadians to compile anthologies is closely tied to a desire to articulate the Canadian identity, or to establish a framework within which questions about it can be intelligently discussed. This tendency has found significant expression in a number of national anthologies consisting principally —and often exclusively—of prose: Malcolm Ross's *A book of Canadian essays* (1954), William Toye's *A book of Canada* (1962), Al PURDY's *The new Romans: candid Canadian opinions of the U.S.* (1968), Andy Wainwright's *Notes for a native land: a new encounter with Canada* (1969), Alan Dawe's *Profile of a nation: Canadian themes and styles* (1969), William KILBOURN's *Canada: a guide to the peaceable kingdom* (1970), and William H. New's *Modern Canadian essays* (1976). Two interesting anthologies, which offer unique portraits of Canada's imaginative and intellectual life, grew out of periodicals: Robert Weaver's *The first five years: a selection from The Tamarack Review* (1962) and J.L. Granatstein and Peter STEVENS' *Forum: Canadian life and letters 1920-70: selections from The Canadian Forum* (1972).

The desire to articulate a specific part of the Canadian identity—a region or an ethnic group—produced numerous anthologies. The first major regional anthologies of prose and poetry were W.G. Hardy's *The Alberta Golden Jubilee anthology* (1955), Carlyle King's *Saskatchewan harvest: a Golden Jubilee selection of song and story* (1955), Reginald E. Watters' *British Columbia: a centennial anthology* (1958), Will R. BIRD and Alec Lucas's *Atlantic anthology* (1959), and John Patrick Gillese's *Chinook arch: a centennial anthology of Alberta writing* (1967). Subsequent examples include: Peter Neary and Patrick O'Flaherty's *By great waters: a Newfoundland and Labrador anthology* (1974); Gary GEDDES's *Skookum wawa: writings of the Canadian Northwest* (1975); Jack HODGINS' *The frontier experience* (1975) and *The West Coast experience* (1976); *East of Canada: an Atlantic anthology* (1976), edited by Raymond Fraser, Clyde Rose, and Jim Stewart; Ken MITCHELL's *Horizon: writings of the Canadian prairie* (1977); Philip Stratford and Michael Thomas's *Voices from Québec: an anthology of translations* (1977); and John W. Chalmers' *The Alberta Diamond Jubilee anthology* (1980). Notable ethnic anthologies of prose and poetry are Harold Head's *Canada in us now* (1976), the first anthology of black poetry and prose in Canada; Robin Gedalof's *Paper stays put: a collection of Inuit writing* (1980); and Gerri Sinclair and Morris Wolfe's *The spice box: an anthology of Jewish Canadian writing* (1981).

Alternatively, anthologies may be constructed according to an individual theme, as in the delightful *Peter Gzowski's spring tonic* (1979), or an individual image, as in Peter Carver's series *Air* (1977), *Earth* (1977), *Fire* (1978), and *Water* (1978).

At their best, what these anthologies achieve is not so much a definition of part of, or the whole of, Canadian *life* as a representation of a verbal universe: Canadian *writing*. Indeed, certain anthologists follow this premise strictly and produce works selected entirely according to literary distinctions. A.J.M. SMITH's two-volume *The book of Canadian prose* (1965, 1973) showcases a wide range of addresses, letters, essays, sketches, portions of historical or autobiographical writing, excerpts from novels, and short stories. John Robert COLOMBO's *Other Canadas: an anthology of science fiction and fantasy*

(1979) celebrates individual subgenres that encompass both prose and poetry.

The general anthologies, then, possess much the same patterns as do anthologies of poetry or short fiction. An occasional anthology, such as Robert KROETSCH's *Creation: Robert Kroetsch; James Bacque; Pierre Gravel* (1970), is formally inventive. A few anthologies, such as Morris Wolfe's *Aurora: new Canadian writing 1978*, *Aurora: new Canadian writing 1979*, and *Aurora: new Canadian writing 1980*, reflect the leading edges of Canadian literature. But, on the whole, general anthologies are more conservative and traditional than various highly individual and innovative anthologies of poetry or short fiction.

1982 TO 1997. The two-volume *An anthology of Canadian literature in English* (1982, 1983), co-edited by Russell Brown and Donna Bennett, was followed, in 1990, by a much-revised version, in one volume, co-edited by Brown, Bennett, and Nathalie Cooke and containing numerous intriguing additions, substitutions, and deletions to the selection of authors and works in the original edition. From one perspective, this new volume could be seen as a last brave, impossible gesture towards trying to represent Canadian literature as, or within, a single dynamic mythic construct imagined in different ways in the highly influential critical writing of Northrop FRYE, D.G. JONES, Margaret ATWOOD, Eli MANDEL, and Robert Kroetsch. From another perspective, the particular additions to, and deletions from, the new volume could be seen as a response to growing challenges, in the last fifteen years and more, to the idea of a national canon, challenges made in the name of gender, sexual difference, class, ethnicity, race, religious background, language, and/or region.

The authors added to the 1990 edition of *An anthology of Canadian literature in English* include one born in the late eighteenth century, Anna Brownell Jameson; three born in the mid-to-late nineteenth, Sara Jeannette DUNCAN, Pauline JOHNSON, and Marjorie PICKTHALL; and ten born in the twentieth: Timothy FINDLEY, Joy KOGAWA, Fred WAH, Sandra BIRDSELL, Paulette JILES, Bronwen WALLACE, Lorna CROZIER, David Adams RICHARDS, Rohinton MISTRY, and Dionne BRAND. In this fifteen-year period each of these writers found advocates among those who read and admired them and, significantly, would find further advocates through republication in this and other anthologies. But as in the figure of speech synecdoche, in which a part is seen as standing for a whole, these individual writers, as distinguished as they may be in terms of their individual artistic talents, acquired considerably more importance in the broader political terms that were at this time gaining such a stronghold in (some would say a stranglehold on) many academic if not all artistic circles. For, willingly or unwillingly from the artists' own viewpoints, such figures acquired a sizeable proportion of their significance on account of the constituencies—and the ideologies—that such figures were considered to represent.

It is the politics of recognition, then, to echo the title of an essay by Charles TAYLOR reproduced by co-editors Ajay Heble, Donna Palmateer Pennee, and J.R. (Tim) Struthers in *New contexts of Canadian criticism* (1997)—the politics of a particular kind of recognition rather than what might be described as the aesthetics of quite a different kind of recognition—that has dominated much anthology-making in Canada in recent years. Some signposts of this trend include Penny Petrone's *First people, first voices* (1983), Lorris Elliott's *Other voices: writings by Blacks in Canada* (1985), Cyril Dabydeen's *A shapely fire: changing the literary landscape* (1987), Petrone's *Northern voices: Inuit writing in English* (1988), Jeanne Perreault and Sylvia Vance's *Writing the circle: Native women of Western Canada* (1990), Bennett Lee and Jim Wong-Chu's *Many-mouthed birds: contemporary writing by Chinese Canadians* (1991), Makeda Silvera's *Piece of my heart: a lesbian of colour anthology* (1991), George Elliott CLARKE's two-volume *Fire on the water: an anthology of Black Nova Scotian writing* (1991, 1992), Edna ALFORD and Claire HARRIS's *Kitchen talk: contemporary women's prose and poetry* (1992), Diane McGifford's *The geography of voice: Canadian literature of the South Asian diaspora* (1992), Daniel David MOSES and Terry Goldie's *An anthology of Canadian Native literature in English* (1992), Smaro Kamboureli's *Making a difference: Canadian multicultural literature* (1996), and Clarke's *Eyeing the north star: directions in African-Canadian literature* (1997). A clearly dissenting voice, or dissenting chorus of voices—including eminent older writers such as James REANEY, Hugh HOOD, Leon ROOKE, John METCALF, Clark BLAISE, and Ray SMITH, along with distinguished younger male and female writers, all published by The PORCUPINE'S QUILL and individually and collectively making the case for a renewed Art for Art's sake—is strongly sounded by Tim Inkster and John Metcalf's anthology of fiction, photographs, and brief memoirs, *The Porcupine's Quill reader* (1996).

Of course the possibility remains, as Beth Brant points out in an essay on Native writing reproduced in *New contexts of Canadian criticism*, of connecting different factions (like fictions) in a new entity, a new community, as myriad bright threads can be sewn together to create a single magnificent weaving. The opportunity remains—as celebrated in *Telling it: women and language across cultures* (1990), published under the editorship of a collective consisting of Sky LEE, Lee MARACLE, Daphne MARLATT, and Betsy WARLAND, with an introduction by Marlatt and, very importantly I think, containing both critical and creative work—of writing in ways that powerfully communicate not only from, but also between, different positions, connecting them without diminishing them.

J.R. (TIM) STRUTHERS

Anthologies in French. 1. THE PIONEERS. The first great anthology was James Huston's *Le Répertoire national; ou, Receuil de littérature canadienne* (4 vols, 1848-50), for which Huston (1820-54) culled newspapers and periodicals published in Quebec between 1777 and 1850, with the help of fellow members of the Institut Canadien. It contains mainly poems, short stories, and the texts of lectures. His total exclusion of politics makes the selection somewhat bland and unrepresentative, but it was only recently superseded as a survey of literature before 1850. The anthology acknowledges Native culture by including a war hymn in translation. Huston's substantial preface, the first and finest of Quebec's many nineteenth-century literary manifestos, briefly surveys the difficult years after the Conquest and describes the enormous disincentives to the writer in French Canada (harsh criticism, lack of outlets, the oblivion of mainly newspaper publication); but he is heartened by signs of a growing enthusiasm for literature, by the appearance of libraries, and by signs that the literature is rising above its early obsession with politics, breaking its ties with Europe, and achieving individuality.

Mgr Camille Roy (1870-1943) founded the academic study of Canadian literature and produced as teaching tools a manual of literary history and, to accompany it, *Morceaux choisis d'auteurs canadiens* (1934). He has been criticized for his benign paternalism and for praising indiscriminately, while imposing a conservative, patriotic pattern on Canadian writing; but his anthology is a substantial and judicious selection of texts, including 215 pieces by 82 authors, with poetry and history given greatest prominence. Notable are essays by the art historian Olivier Maurault, the criticism of Marcel DUGAS, and the early prose of Alain GRANDBOIS. The 1948 edition includes ten pages of Roy's own definition of the 'terroiriste' vocation of Canadian literature: 'L'écrivain qui n'est pas fortement enraciné au sol de son pays, ou dans son histoire . . . court risque d'être un rêveur, un joueur de flûte, ou d'être inutile à sa patrie.'

2. POETRY. Jules Fournier's *Anthologie des poètes canadiens* (1920), which appeared two years after his death, was completed and prefaced by his friend and fellow journalist Olivar Asselin (1874-1937), who shared Fournier's view that there was no such thing as a national literature—that is, works of genuine literary merit—in French Canada. Asselin placed poetry higher than the other genres in French Canada and detected a considerable progress between 1800 and 1920. An anthology of poets, not of poems, it offers as wide a cross-section of writers as possible. A third edition, in which twenty-six poets disappeared and fifteen new ones were added to give a total of 71, appeared in 1933, with the original preface. With laudably high standards, Asselin recognized in a handful of poets 'un souci de propreté' and acknowledged that French Canada came close to having great poets in Émile NELLIGAN, Paul MORIN, René CHOPIN, and Albert LOZEAU.

For years Guy Sylvestre's *Anthologie de la poésie canadienne française* (1942) fulfilled the need for comprehensive selection. It appeared in five subsequent editions between 1958 and 1971 and was revised yet again as *Anthologie de la poésie québécoise* in 1974. No benign paternalism here either: Sylvestre was scrupulous in his insistence on intrinsic poetic worth, and half a dozen of the countless nineteenth-century poets find favour. Sylvestre's stylish, concise introduction, based on an intimate acquaintance with Canadian and French poetry, has lost none of its value as a brief general survey that covers more than a century of writing in Quebec.

John Hare showed much more indulgence than Sylvestre in his treatment of early writers in his *Anthologie de la poésie québécoise du XIXe siècle 1790-1890* (1979). This is a fine piece of scholarship—richly annotated—in an accessible form. Hare paid an indirect tribute to James Huston, time and again culling his examples from *Le répertoire national* and giving prominence to the poets of the 1830s—notably J.-G. Barthe—who were inspired by the liberal and patriotic spirit of those troubled years. Sadly, too few of the examples quoted can claim to be poetry.

Anthologies in French 2

Jeanne Paul-Crouzet compiled her *Poésie au Canada* (Paris, 1946) to present Canadians to the French in the post-war period of euphoria, following the Fournier/Asselin anthology very closely. Twenty-four poets represented a century of writing in four equal periods of roughly twenty-five years, and the principal poets were treated to a lengthy, meticulous literary analysis in the French manner. Her strictures on imitation were harsh, but she noted tactfully that it could create 'une divergence entre l'instinct profond et la forme poétique dans une littérature naissante.' *Tradition du Québec/The Quebec tradition* (1946) was an anthology of poetry and prose selected by the painstaking chronicler of Canadian letters Séraphin Marion; French texts were accompanied by Watson KIRKCONNELL's translations.

A number of short anthologies prepared by poets attempted the hazardous task of choosing the best from a year's production. Eli MANDEL and Jean-Guy PILON compiled *Poetry 62/Poésie 62* (1961) and Jacques GODBOUT and John Robert COLOMBO *Poetry 64/Poésie 64* (1964). Pilon offered to students—both as a textbook and as a source of words and images—his *Poèmes 70* (1970), an attractive collection of verse (in French only) by thirty-three poets, selected from works published in 1969; it was followed by *Poèmes 71* (1972). This worthwhile tradition was taken up more economically by journals—*La Nouvelle BARRE DU JOUR*, for example, publishing *Poésie 1980* (Issue 92-93) and *Poésie 1981* (Issue 100-101).

Like Pilon, Guy ROBERT saw his *Littérature du Québec: poésie actuelle* (1970), an augmented edition of a 1964 publication, as an inspiration to the young creative writers of the CEGEP generation, inviting them to draw from it breath for their demonstrations and meaning for their action. Robert's choice of poets was safe but astute. More than just an anthology, this book contained valuable comments by poets on their work and methods, particularly impressive being Paul CHAMBERLAND's powerful essays, and an interview with Alain Grandbois.

The most enjoyable anthologies of verse to handle and to use were A.J.M. SMITH's *Oxford book of Canadian verse: in English and French* (1960) and the equally attractive *Modern Canadian verse: in English and French* (1967), including poets from PRATT and Morin to BROCHU and ONDAATJE. Smith's experience as a teacher, his taste and accumulated wisdom as a critic, and his poet's flair made these two books richly authoritative. Jacques Cotnam's inexpensive, uncluttered *Poètes du Québec* (1969) offered a balanced and representative sample. Later in this field of anthologies of poetry was that of Laurent Mailhot and Pierre Nepveu, discussed below in section 7.

3. DOCUMENTARY HISTORY. As well as serving to establish the literary corpus, anthologies were frequently used to give a community a sense of their roots. The pioneers in this field—Michel BRUNET, Guy FRÉGAULT, and Marcel TRUDEL—published their two-volume *Histoire du Canada par les textes* (1963), which did valuable service. The selections were long and carefully chosen, each prefaced by a lengthy historical comment; sources and bibliographical notes, together with the index, made this work a mine of indispensable and reliable material. Classiques Canadiens included a short volume entitled *Éloquence indienne* (1968). The books in this series—a kind of anthology in itself—made available, for the period of the French régime, selected texts by Cartier, Biard, Champlain, Lescarbot, Sagard, Brébeuf, Le Jeune, MARIE DE L'INCARNATION, Marguerite Bourgeoys, Talon, Frontenac, Charlevoix, and Élisabeth Bégon, whose names provided the titles for their respective volumes. (See also Writing in NEW FRANCE.) Cameron Nish's *Le régime français 1534-1760* (1966) offered Canadians of all origins the opportunity to discover in the texts of the Jesuit missionaries and other founders of New France a common heritage. A somewhat similar volume, *La nouvelle France* (1976), was edited by a team led by Michel Allard. Both these anthologies—drawing on letter reports and official texts, and including many extracts that are rather brief—gave a picture largely of public life; they failed to convey a sense of the day-to-day life of the population. *La civilisation de la Nouvelle-France d'après les témoins* (1963) by Claude Francis and Sibylle Sinval, comprising first-hand accounts of the mission to New France, again from obvious sources, frequently distorted the texts by selecting passages that stress excessively the role played by the Church in founding New France; but it was attractively presented. Ostensibly just another anthology of historical documents, *Québec: hier et aujourd'hui* (1967), prepared by a McGill University team led by Laurier LaPierre, provided valuable materials for an intellectual history of Quebec. Its three sections—each containing an introduction, bibliography, and questions for further study—covered intellectual and artistic life (32 authors), social and economic activity (28 authors), and politics (18 authors). This valuable collection was further enhanced with

illustrations and a glossary. André Renaud's *Recueil de textes littéraires canadiens-français* (1968)—a companion volume to Roger Duhamel's *Manuel de littérature canadienne-française* (1967)—is dated, but the section on nineteenth-century essayists is still original and exciting. The second section, 'Une naissance laborieuse' (1840-1900), has extracts from Arthur Buies, Hector Fabre, Oscar Dunn, and the collector of short stories Faucher de Saint-Maurice. Eighty-seven authors represent a century and a half of writing in this useful teaching text. Centennial year (1967) also saw the publication of an anthology of journalism, *Un siècle de reportage*, and Jacques Hébert's *Ah! mes aïeux! chronique de la vie sociale et politique des Canadiens français de 1867, tirée des journaux de l'époque*. Reine Malouin's *La poésie il y a cent ans* appeared in 1968. A voluminous and very diverse anthology edited by Gérard Boismenu, Laurent Mailhot, and Jacques Rouillard, *Le Québec en textes* (1980), subtitled 'tour d'horizon de la réalité québécoise de 1940 à 1980', gave space to extensive quotations from texts, and has the valuable advantage of drawing where possible on periodical and journalistic sources.

4. OTHER SPECIALIST ANTHOLOGIES. Adrien Thério's *L'humour au Canada français* (1968) included some decidedly dubious examples (pastiches of Canadian authors, for example, a genre now totally out of fashion), but succeeded better with selections drawing on the resources of the music-hall and popular entertainment. Laurent Mailhot and Doris-Michel Montpetit co-edited an exceptionally valuable anthology, *Monologues québécois, 1890-1980* (1980), which brought belated recognition to many raconteurs who have delighted audiences in this mode of entertainment characteristic of Quebec's oral and family culture. The difficulties of producing such an anthology led regrettably to the omission of poets such as Claude GAUVREAU, Claude PÉLOQUIN, and Raoul DUGUAY—showmen principally remembered for the public performance of their work, in what Péloquin used to call 'shows de la parole'—but this book illustrated nearly a century of Quebec popular theatre, cabaret and music-hall, supplying valuable visual and biographical documentation. The texts constitute a priceless record of the evolution of the spoken language in Quebec, allowing us to relive the profound shared emotion of theatre or music-hall when packed houses fell under the spell of Les Cyniques, Gratien GÉLINAS, Raymond Lévesque, Yvon Deschamps, Clémence Desrochers, and Marc Favreau ('Sol').

Gilles MARCOTTE's *Présence de la critique* (1966) serves both as a panorama of Quebec criticism and as a very useful collection of literary essays and book reviews. Arranged chronologically by critic, with several examples from each, running from René Garneau to André Brochu, it contained particularly valuable essays by René Garneau, Jean LE MOYNE, Jeanne Lapointe, a brief and incisive statement on Pierre Baillargeon from Maurice Blain, and the impressive early writing of Brochu. Four essays by Pierre de Grandpré were included, but a fuller selection from this fine critic is available in his own *Dix ans de vie littéraire au Canada français* (1966). Breaking new ground were Étienne-F. Duval's *Anthologie thématique du théâtre québécois au XIXe siècle* (1978), reflecting faithfully the nationalist and moralistic aims of nineteenth-century Quebec writing, and of interest to the social historian as well as the student of literature; Guildo Rousseau's illuminating anthology of prefaces to novels, *Préfaces des romans québécois du XIXe siècle* (1970), witnessing to the artistic diffidence of almost all the novelists of the period; and Daniel Latouche and Diane Poliquin-Bourassa, *Le manuel de la parole: manifestes québécois, t.1: 1760-1890* (1977), an indispensable guide to the growing national and political self-awareness and self-articulation of French Canada expressed in political, social, and literary manifestos. This last compilation should be read alongside a special number of *Études françaises* (16/3-4, 1980) that covers the whole development of a peculiarly Québécois form of pamphleteering. In addition to the Duval anthology, Quebec theatre was also anthologized in Jan Doat's *Anthologie du théâtre québécois, 1606-1970* (1973), a collection of scenes from (mostly) contemporary plays (1945-70). Victor-Lévy BEAULIEU performed a curious but valuable service in recuperating many specimens of the ephemeral and often disturbingly unwholesome writing of the last century in his *Manuel de la petite littérature du Québec* (1974), which contains samples of temperance tracts, biographies of 'enfants martyrs', parish histories, and pulp literature and novelettes in which, he says, is to be found 'une imagerie fondamentale, un inconscient collectif qui cherchait à se libérer.' *Le choc des langues au Québec, 1760-1970* (1972), compiled by G. Bouthillier and J. Meynaud, was a sourcebook, anthology, and crusading pamphlet; an introduction and chronology are followed by 700 dense pages culled from the record of two hundred years of impassioned debate on the French language in Quebec. The sources are varied—speeches, parliamentary debates, travellers' journals—but much of the material is drawn from the press.

One-author anthologies were Gérard BESSETTE's *Anthologie d'Albert Laberge* (1963); Adrien Thério's judicious selections from the work of Bishop Bourget in *Ignace Bourget, écrivain* (1975); and Laurent Mailhot's *Anthologie d'Arthur Buies* (1978), which follows a special number of *Études françaises* (VI, 3, 1970), presented by G.-A. Vachon, that contains a considerable biographical and critical apparatus on Buies (1840-1901), along with a selection from his writings. Mailhot included copious extracts from Buies's journals; his social, historical, and political comment; his fascinating travel writing, particularly on the Saguenay and the lower St Lawrence; and ended with an ingenious dictionary of observations and aphorisms. Buies dazzles by his boldness, wit, and intelligence, and gives us the first real and early apprehension of the vast strangeness of North America. This is anthologizing at its best.

Until the 1980s the French presence outside Quebec was only just beginning to receive attention in anthologies. Roger Motut produced in *Racines* (1979), a volume in the Alberta Heritage collection, an anthology of French writing on western Canada, much of it by immigrants or travellers, including Georges BUGNET, Marie LE FRANC and Maurice CONSTANTIN-WEYER. (See FOREIGN WRITERS ON CANADA IN FRENCH.) *Anthologie de textes littéraires acadiens, 1606-1975* appeared in Moncton in 1979. (See ACADIAN LITERATURE.) Gaétan Vallières presented 250 texts in *L'Ontario français par les documents* (1980)—a good example of the valiant work being done on French Ontario at the Université d'Ottawa.

5. TRANSLATIONS. John Robert Colombo followed his and Jacques Godbout's anthology of 1964 with *How do I love thee: sixty poets of Canada (and Québec) select and introduce their favourite poems from their own work* (1970), ten of the poets represented being French Canadian. John GLASSCO's *The poetry of French Canada in translation* (1970), 47 poets translated by several hands, goes back even to pre-Conquest times. One must take issue with Glassco's contention, stated in his introduction, that Quebec poets 'seem too often preoccupied by political and national ideas', as the reverse is, surprisingly, the case; but he is on safer ground when he deplores the effects of 'the dead hand of surrealism'. Fred COGSWELL continued to enhance his reputation as a translator with *One hundred poems of modern Quebec* (1970) and a second hundred in 1971. But the most outstanding endeavour in the translation of Canadian poetry remains the bilingual quarterly *Ellipse* (1969-). Short fiction and some non-fiction in translation from the French appear in the anthologies edited by William KILBOURN, Robert WEAVER, Mordecai RICHLER, and Wayne Grady, described in ANTHOLOGIES IN ENGLISH. The most enjoyable of these is certainly William Kilbourn's *Canada: a guide to the peaceable kingdom* (1970), which contains a selection of some of the finest writing on Canada, including Kilbourn's own perceptive introduction on the 'alternative to insanity' Canada offers. The Quebec writers represented are Pierre Trudeau, Pierre Trottier, Anne HÉBERT, Jean Le Moyne, Claude Ryan, René Lévesque, Fernand DUMONT, André Laurendeau, and Jean ÉTHIER-BLAIS in a sensitive and moving personal portrait of Paul-Émile Borduas. A historical anthology of short stories is *The Oxford book of French-Canadian short stories* (1983) edited by Richard Teleky.

6. SPREADING THE WORD. Anthologies produced outside Quebec are growing proof of the wide interest in French-Canadian writing. Some of the anthologies already referred to fall into this category—those of Jeanne Paul-Crozet, A.J.M. Smith, and Roger Motut. Laure Rièse published her *L'âme de la poésie canadienne-française* in Toronto in 1955. Gérard Tougas edited the attractive *Littérature canadienne-française contemporaine* (1969), giving separate sections to the novel, poetry, essays, and theatre; the twenty-eight authors covered are represented by short but meaningful selections, each carefully and helpfully annotated. Alain Bosquet's *La poésie canadienne* (Paris, 1962) reappeared as *Poésie du Québec* (1968). The compiler was criticized for his rather fulsome introduction, but his poet's flair in assembling the collection is undeniable. Serge Brindeau's ambitious compendium *Poésie contemporaine de langue française depuis 1945* (Paris, 1973), covering French poetry from Montreal to Beirut, from Martinique to Madagascar, gives nearly 100 pages and one of its five sections to Quebec poetry, surveyed by Jacques Rancourt. He wisely chooses to give considerable space to a few poets—Gauvreau, BROSSARD, Péloquin, Duguay, MIRON, GIGUÈRE, PILON, MORENCY, PARADIS, and OUELLETTE—and emphasizes vigorous prophetic utterance and neo-symbolist lyricism rather than arcane experiment. *Littérature de langue française hors de France* (Paris, 1976) was prepared by the Fédération internationale de professeurs de français, again covering the

whole of the francophone world in what it calls an 'anthologie didactique'. A special number of *Les Lettres nouvelles* (Dec. 1966-Jan. 1967) presented Canadian writers of the 1960s to the French public, 22 of the 30 authors included being French Canadian, and the review *Europe* (1969) followed a survey of the arts in Quebec with an anthology of recent prose and verse. Auguste Viatte, doyen of French studies, has followed his *Histoire littéraire de l'Amérique française* (Paris, 1954), and the best available general survey of the history and current extent of the influence of French language and culture in the world, *La francophonie* (Paris, 1969), with an *Anthologie littéraire de l'Amérique francophone* (1971). Eighty-seven Québécois authors, half of them poets, occupy half the book, the rest being given to writers from Louisiana and the Caribbean. The cut-off date of 1960, however, excluded the brilliant literary explosion that followed, so that theatre, the latecomer, is understandably the poor relation, represented only by Paul TOUPIN and Jacques LANGUIRAND. Ambitiously attempting 'un échantillonnage complet', this book is marked by scrupulous scholarship, but it reflects the natural preference of a foreign anthologist for local colour and the exciting theme of survival. An anthology compiled by Michel Le Bel and Jean-Marcel Paquette, *Le Québec par ses textes littéraires, 1534-1976* (1979), is a Franco-Québécois production aimed particularly at a French readership—an attractive book, with photographs and some striking pen-and-ink sketches. The socio-historical approach is stressed, and historical documents and brief explanations culled from sociologists complement the literary selections. The weakness lies in the extreme brevity of the texts: lifted out of context, a 350-word passage from AQUIN's difficult and daring *PROCHAIN ÉPISODE* ceases to be part of a web of multiple reference and becomes a crude political statement. On the other hand, this anthology is the first to do justice to Quebec's oral culture by including extracts from eleven dramatists and fourteen singers and monologuists. In addition to anthologies in English translation, the following have appeared for other language groups: N.I. Vannilova, *Littérature canadienne de langue française, 1945-1965* (Moscow, 1969); Constantin Bida, *Poésie du Québec contemporain* (1968), a bilingual Ukrainian edition; Wolfram Burghardt, *Poésie/Québec, de Saint-Denys Garneau à nos jours* (1972), another bilingual French/Ukrainian collection; and Eva Kushner, *Oda a szent löring folyóhoz Québec mai francia kilteszete* (Budapest, 1978) in Hungarian.

7. THE CULMINATION OF THE ART. Alongside the best of the anthologies discussed here must be set two anthologies that represent the culmination of a long process of selection and reflection: a four-volume set from Gilles Marcotte and his team and a one-volume poetry anthology, again a collective venture, edited by the experienced anthologist Laurent Mailhot and the poet Pierre Nepveu. Marcotte's *Anthologie de la littérature québécoise* comes in four periods, each entrusted to a specialist or pair of specialists: Léopold Leblanc, *Écrits de la nouvelle France, 1534-1760* (1978); *René Dionne, La patrie littéraire, 1760-1895* (1978); Gilles Marcotte and François Hébert, *Vaisseau d'or et croix du chemin, 1895-1935* (1979); and René Dionne and Gabrielle Poulin, *L'age de l'interrogation, 1937-1952* (1980). This priceless library fulfils all the functions of the anthology—didactic, celebratory, publicist, and evaluative. Over the whole reigns the benign presence of Marcotte, an urbane, gentle critic, at ease in his vast acquaintance with the literature of his people. His general introduction in the first volume is superb. The anthology starts with no preconceptions, adopts a liberal definition of literary writing, and avoids exclusive principles, though the first volume classifies texts under exploration, mission, description, and civilization. No genre is left out; sermon, poem, history, travel tale, literary criticism, novel, political speech, private diary, letters—all are here. Erudition and annotation, though not skimped, have been kept to a strict minimum: 'place aux textes' sums up the anthologists' policy. The reader's enthusiasm is even more compellingly aroused by *La poésie québécoise des origines à nos jours* (1980) edited by Laurent Mailhot and Pierre Nepveu. Over 170 poets are featured and almost all are represented by their portraits—some by an illustration that evokes their imaginative world or by a reproduction of the title page of one of their books. There is an extensive bibliography, an authoritative and well-focused preface, and an uncluttered presentation of the texts on the page. The poets given the most space, in descending order, are P.-M. LAPOINTE, Miron, SAINT-DENYS-GARNEAU, NELLIGAN, BRAULT, CHAMBERLAND, Hébert, GIGUÈRE, Grandbois, LASNIER, Gauvreau, Ouellette, HÉNAULT, Lozeau, and Brossard; but it is refreshing to see two poets of the turn-of-the-century among them, and one poet representing the 1970s; the emphasis here is clearly on the *automatistes*—Lapointe, Miron, Giguère, Gauvreau, and Hénault in particular—but the selection is not otherwise tendentious. The compilers have made bold

decisions about contemporary poets: almost the last third of all the texts are from poets still alive and active, and generous space is given to poets such as Roger des Roches, Nicole Brossard, and François CHARRON. If the prize goes to this anthology over all others, it is not because poetry ultimately anthologizes best of all the genres but because it is in its poetry that Quebec has been most original and audacious, most truly itself; has come nearest to breaking the solitude that masks its authentic self and keeps it from us; and has found the voice that most faithfully articulates the song and the story of a people and a land.

C.R.P. MAY

1980 to 1996. 1. POETRY. In the 1980s Yolande Grisé and Jeanne d'Arc Lortie, in collaboration with Pierre Savard and Paul Wyczynski, began an anthology of truly vast proportions. *Les textes poétiques du Canada français 1606-1867* was, and is intended to be, an exhaustive, chronologically grouped repertory of all the rhymed verse ('pièces rimées') produced between the time Marc Lescarbot set foot on the shores of New France and the birth of Confederation. Of the twelve projected volumes, nine have been published over the last decade and the three remaining volumes are scheduled to appear—along with a supplement—by the year 2000. In total, some three thousand poems, including transcriptions of early songs, will have been painstakingly dated and reproduced. Unfortunately, after the first two volumes the practice of annotating the works was abandoned, doubtless owing to temporal and material constraints.

The *Anthologie de la littérature québécoise* (1978-80) by Gilles MARCOTTE has remained unmatched in richness and erudition. The handsome 1994 reprint by Hexagone does justice to the contents of the much-admired four-volume collection. Jean Royer's *Le Québec en poésie*, first published by Gallimard in 1985 (rpr. 1995), belongs to the series 'Folio junior en poésie', aimed at young European readers. This trim, didactically oriented volume is comprehensive yet concise, featuring a well-balanced sampling of nineteenth- and twentieth-century poets (Jacques Cartier is included, but more as a curiosity). It includes a useful annotated biobibliography in which Royer briefly encapsulates the distinguishing characteristics of each poet's work. Royer's *La poésie québécoise contemporaine* (1987, rpr. 1995) highlights the surrealists (dubbed 'poètes surréalisants') such as Gilles HÉNAULT, Isabelle Legris, Claude GAUVREAU, Paul-Marie LAPOINTE, Roland GIGUÈRE, as well as their precursors, Alain GRANDBOIS, SAINT-DENYS-GARNEAU, Rina LASNIER, and Anne HÉBERT.

However, Pierre Nepveu's and Laurent Mailhot's *La poésie québécoise des origines à nos jours* (1980) is still unparalleled for its compact presentation and high-calibre evaluative scholarship. Revisions in the 1986 paperback edition eliminated the work of several early poets as well as the cultural-history appendix. Gone too are portraits of the authors, the space saved being used to update more contemporary poets like France THÉORET. Until very recently regarded as a poor substitute for poetry by the literary institution, the art of songwriting in Quebec has at last gained the respect and legitimacy it deserves, thanks to the efforts of Roger Chamberland and André Gaulin and their work, *La chanson québécoise. De la Bolduc à aujourd'hui* (1994). The *Anthologie du Noroît 1971-1996* presents, as its title indicates, a selection of poems by authors affiliated with Le Noroît. This anniversary anthology is edited by Hélène Dorion, Paul Bélanger, and Claude Prud'Homme and presents mainly Québécois poets in alphabetical order—a format that unfortunately affords little contextualization of the poems or authors. *Poètes québécois* (1993), compiled by Louise Blouin and Bernard Pozier, follows a similar publisher-specific alphabetical format. In this instance the selection is made from the catalogue of Les Écrits des Forges dating back to 1971, and for this reason is fairly restrictive. The seven-hundred-page swan-song of *La Nouvelle BARRE DU JOUR—Fin. Vingt-cinq ans de littérature* (1990)—marks the end of twenty-five years of publishing for the review/publisher. It includes many important contemporary poets, such as Louise Dupré, Normand de Bellefeuille, and Nicole BROSSARD.

Lucien FRANCOEUR's less traditional anthology, *Vingt-cinq poètes québécois 1968-1978* (1989), casts a nostalgic look on the countercultural 'psychédélisme' and euphoria of the 1970s, while paying effusive homage to Gaston MIRON, Patrick Straram, and Denis VANIER. In 1985 Antonio D'ALFONSO edited a bilingual text, *Voix off: dix poètes anglophones du Québec* (1985).

In the field of women's poetry, worthy of note are *80 voix au féminin. Anthologie Arcade 1981-1996* (1996) edited by Claudine Bertrand and Louise Cotnoir; the *Anthologie de la poésie des femmes au Québec* (1991) compiled by Nicole Brossard and Lisette Girouard; and the anthology in English, *Ink and strawberries, an anthology of Quebec women's writing* (1988), edited by Beverley Daurio and Luise von

Flotow. The first, described by Christiane Lahaie as a 'livre kaléidoscope', chronologically presents several different genres and covers such contemporary women writers as Anne-Marie ALONZO, Anne Dandurand, and Louise Warren. The anthology by Brossard and Girouard is, quite simply, impressive. The editors scrupulously trace the development of women writers in Quebec by grouping them in different 'generations'; there is an informative introduction, an index, and a comprehensive bibliography. While it includes well-known writers such as Rina Lasnier, Michèle LALONDE, Madeleine GAGNON, Denise DESAUTELS, and Brossard, there are some surprises—Fernande Saint-Martin, Eva Kushner, and Pauline Julien, for example. Daurio's and von Flotow's volume is one of the rare anthologies of Québécois poets to appear in English in the last decade. Consistent with much recent writing by Quebec women writers, the extracts fall into a vague classification, somewhere between prose-poetry and short stories. Contributors include Suzanne Jacob, Madeleine OUELLETTE-MICHALSKA, Marie-Claire BLAIS, Claire Dé, Anne Dandurand, and Lori Saint-Martin. The selection is colourful, but the notes on contributors are regrettably scant.

2. FRENCH-CANADIAN ANTHOLOGIES FROM OUTSIDE QUEBEC. In the growing field of Franco-Ontarian studies two anthologies deserve mention: the four-volume, hard-cover set *Anthologie de textes littéraires franco-ontariens* (1982) edited by the indefatigable anthologist Yolande Grisé, and the *Anthologie de la poésie franco-ontarienne* (1991) by another well-known researcher and bibliographer, René Dionne. Grisé's anthology is intended primarily for teachers and school-age children. Dionne presents verse by forty-two different authors and focuses on the two most productive periods of the region's literary history: the end of the nineteenth century, with Benjamin Sulte, William Chapman, and Jules Tremblay, and the 1970s, a time of incredible effervescence among such younger poets as Patrice Desbiens and Robert Yergeau.

J.R. Leveille's *Anthologie de la poésie franco-manitobaine* (1990) is the first anthology of its kind, with more than thirty-five poets and two hundred poems covering two centuries of poetry. It also boasts a complete collection of Louis Riel's poetic writings. In 1992 a group of francophone writers and artists in Saskatchewan founded a literary review, *Ruelle*, edited by Lynne Carigan. Unfortunately only the first issue, which functions as an anthology, seems to be available.

In the Maritimes at least four new Acadian anthologies have been published since the mid-1980s. Henri-Dominique Paratte edited the bilingual *Poésie acadienne contemporaine/ Acadian poetry now* (1985), and two celebrated poets—an Acadian, Gérald Leblanc, and a Québécois, Claude BEAUSOLEIL—edited the authoritative *La poésie acadienne 1948-1988* (1988). Beausoleil also wrote the preface to *Les cents lignes de notre américanité* (1984), which showcased poems by Acadian and Québécois poets, including Herménégilde CHIASSON, Raymond Leblanc, Dyane Léger, Gérald Leblanc, Rose Després, France Daigle, Yolande VILLEMAIRE, and Claude Beausoleil. In an effort to identify and consolidate a specifically Acadian body of literature, Marguerite Maillet, Gérard LeBlanc, and Bernard Émont compiled a pioneering work, *Anthologie de textes littéraires acadiens 1606-1975* (1992).

3. URBAN ANTHOLOGIES. Montreal has inspired at least two celebratory anthologies: *Montréal en prose, 1892-1992* by Nathalie Fredette, and *Montréal est une ville de poèmes vous savez* (1992) compiled by Claude Beausoleil. In *Québec. Des écrivains dans la ville* (1995), a slick coffee-table anthology co-ordinated by the Musée du Québec, Gilles Pellerin guides the reader through beautiful glossy photographs and four centuries of history and literature.

4. TEACHING MANUALS, ESSAYS, AND DOCUMENTARY HISTORY. *Littérature québécoise contemporaine* (1982), edited by Patrick Coppens, has been superseded by *Littérature et société québécoise. Histoire, méthode et textes* (1991) edited by Marie-Claude Leclercq and Claude Lizé. The strong focus on college-level instruction still distinguishes this latter work from more recent offerings. Although it has the distinct feature of embracing francophone literature inside and outside Quebec, *Anthologie critique: littérature canadienne-française et québécoise* (1992) by Michel Erman, a professor at the Université de Bourgogne, France, has been criticized for the text's under-representation of women writers and its rather puzzling bibliographical inadequacies. Heinz Weinmann's and Roger Chamberland's *Littérature québécoise. Des origines à nos jours. Textes et méthodes* (1996), designed for use by college students in Quebec, strikes an attractive balance between a classical anthology and a textbook. Literary excerpts, organized into five historical periods, are punctuated by vivid representations of cultural artefacts. The *Anthologie de la littérature québécoise* (1996), edited by Michel Laurin, is structured along the same line. More specific in scope are the authoritative *Écrivains québécois*

contemporains depuis 1950 (1989), edited by Lise Gauvin and Gaston Miron,and Luc Bouvier's and Max Roy's *La littérature québécoise du XXe siècle*, (1996). The Gauvin/Miron anthology, designed to acquaint a European readership with contemporary Québécois authors, includes more than eighty different poets, novelists, playwrights, and essayists. Two notable features of this work are the introduction, which provides a substantive overview, and the series of bibliographies, which include primary and secondary literature and the names and addresses of cultural and literary journals and of all major publishers.

La vie littéraire au Québec (1991, 1992, 1996) is an invaluable three-volume reference work (three more volumes are planned). Compiled by a team of researchers led by Maurice Lemire and Denis Saint-Jacques, this meticulous tool empirically analyses the processes by which early literary texts acquired legitimacy within Québécois society. *'Cité libre': une anthologie* (1991) was edited by the noted historian Yvan Lamonde, in collaboration with Gérard Pelletier. Laurent Mailhot compiled the lengthy *Essais québécois 1837-1983* (1984), and also worked with Gérard Boismenu and Jacques Rouillard to produce *Le Québec en textes. Anthologie 1940-1985* (1986). Robert Hébert's *L'Amérique française devant l'opinion étrangère* (1989) provides a different vantage point, as does Lori Saint-Martin's two-volume anthology of women's literary criticism, *L'autre lecture. La critique au féminin et les textes québécois* (1992, 1994).

5. OTHER SPECIALIST ANTHOLOGIES. *Les meilleurs romans québécois du XIXe siècle* (1996), edited by Gilles Dorion, is a fine anthology of the most representative novels of the period. The novels, reprinted in their entirety and with individual prefaces, are bound in two dense volumes of over a thousand pages each. Volume one presents the prose of Philippe Aubert de Gaspé (fils), Joseph Doutre, Eugène L'Écuyer, Patrice LACOMBE, Georges Boucher de Boucherville, and Pierre-Joseph-Olivier Chauveau. Volume two includes the work of Antoine GÉRIN-LAJOIE, Philippe AUBERT DE GASPÉ (père), Napoléon BOURASSA, Joseph MARMETTE, and Laure Conan (Felicité ANGERS).

In the field of Québécois and French-Canadian drama, an area where anthologies are typically scarce, the Centre d'essai des auteurs dramatiques has published a lively anthology, *Le Centre d'essai des auteurs dramatiques. 20 ans* (1985). To celebrate its twentieth anniversary the Centre commissioned twenty playwrights to produce a short piece (seven or eight pages in length) on the theme of 'twenty years'. The result is a diverse collection, with established playwrights like Michel TREMBLAY, Michel GARNEAU, and Antonine MAILLET rubbing shoulders with a more recent generation that includes Michel Marc BOUCHARD, Claude Poissant, and Gilbert Turp.

Regionally specific anthologies include Fulvio Caccia's and Antonio d'Alfonso's *Quêtes. Textes d'auteurs italo-québécois* (1983), and David Lonergan's *Paroles de l'est. Anthologie de la littérature de l'est du Québec* (1993). Anthologists such as Claude Beausoleil and Axel Maugey have also been branching out into the literature of other countries: in 1989 Beausoleil published *La poésie mexicaine*, followed by *La poésie suisse romande* (1993); Maugey edited *Incertitudes. Anthologie de la poésie roumaine* (1992). With five anthologies and eight of his own works published between 1988 and 1996, Claude Beausoleil is one of the the most prolific anthologists of poetry in Quebec. Not only has he translated Mexican poetry into French, he has also translated Quebec poetry into Spanish. His *El recital de Los Angeles*, a selection of Émile Nelligan's poetry, was published by the Mexican publisher El Tucan in 1991. He has also edited and re-edited the works of Louis FRÉCHETTE in *La légende d'un peuple* (1989, 1991, 1992). Another one-author anthology is Laurent's Mailhot's *Anthologie* (1994), devoted to Arthur Buies.

6. THE CULMINATION OF THE ART. In this period three separate approaches have predominated in the field of anthologizing. The first, grounded in a meticulous empiricism, stems from a desire to contextualize and disseminate texts that are largely unpublished or hard to find. The second produces anniversary anthologies, often reprinting texts affiliated with a certain review or publishing house within a specific framework. The third approach benefits from the groundwork laid down by the first two, but corresponds more closely to a traditional model of the genre; it seeks to present only the most representative works by the most significant authors in a given field. It is interesting to note that some of the most acclaimed anthologies coming out of Quebec—those by Marcotte, Nepveu, Mailhot, Gauvin, Miron, Brossard, and Girouard—are the ones in which the 'archaeological' and evaluative traditions are seamlessly blended. STEPHANIE NUTTING

Short stories. Despite the large number of stories published in periodicals, there are relatively few anthologies of French-Canadian stories. The first is James Huston's *Légendes canadiennes* (Paris, 1853). This was followed by Abbé H.-R. CASGRAIN's popular manual of the same title (Québec, 1861) and at the turn of the century by Honoré BEAUGRAND's *La Chasse-galerie. Légendes canadiennes* (1900) and E.-Z. Massicotte's *Conteurs canadiens-français du XIXe siècle* (1902). Collections focusing on nineteenth-century material include Guy Boulizon's *Contes et récits d'autrefois* (1961) and John Hare's *Contes et nouvelles du Canada français, 1778-1859* (1971). Anthologies of more recent work are even rarer. Adrien Thério's *Conteurs canadiens-français* (1965, rev. 1970) includes work by twenty-eight writers and in Gérard BESSETTE's *De Québec à Saint-Boniface* (1968) sixteen authors are represented—the majority of them contemporaries. The issues of *ÉCRITS DU CANADA FRANÇAIS* (1954-) also provide a wealth of short stories.

Four anthologies of stories in English translation are Philip Stratford, ed., *Stories from Quebec* (1974); Richard Teleky, ed., *The Oxford book of French-Canadian short stories* (1983); Matt COHEN and Wayne Grady, eds, *Intimate strangers: New stories from Quebec* (1986); and Geoff Hancock, ed., *Invisible fictions: contemporary stories from Quebec* (1980). Although there are too many anthologies to mention them all, we may note in particular the thematic series (including the fantastic, science fiction, adventure, romance, etc.) of volumes entitled *Dix contes et nouvelles par dix auteurs québécois*, a series published in the 1980s by Éditions Quinze and edited first by André MAJOR and then by André Carpentier. With Matt Cohen, the latter published *Voix parallèles/Parallel voices* (1993), a unique bilingual volume produced by two publishers (XYZ and Quarry Press), in which ten authors from French Canada and ten from English Canada translate one another; thus Margaret ATWOOD translates Monique PROULX and vice versa, Jean Pierre Girard and Steven HEIGHTON translate each other, and so on. André Vanasse, for his part, in 1985 launched the series 'Nouvelles fraîches' at the Université du Québec à Montréal, which each year helps young authors to become known. This phenomenon underlines the fact that the short story is one of the most popular genres among students of literature in Quebec.

Generally speaking, academics are becoming increasingly interested in short stories from Quebec. For some time there have been many entries in the *Dictionnaire des oeuvres littéraires du Québec* (vols 1-5 edited by Maurice Lemire; vol. 6 edited by Gilles Dorion). The Archives des lettres canadiennes at the Université d'Ottawa has published *La nouvelle* (1996). PHILIP STRATFORD/MICHEL LORD

Anvil Press (1988-). It was founded in Vancouver, British Columbia, by Brian Kaufman and Dennis E. Bolen to publish the quarterly *sub-TERRAIN*, an independent literary journal devoted to the work of new and emerging writers, photographers, and artists. By 1991 the press had begun to publish pamphlets, broadsides, playscripts, poems, and fiction without CANADA COUNCIL assistance. In 1992 it acquired from Pulp Press the sponsorship of the International 3-Day Novel Writing Contest: this notorious literary marathon has been held every Labour Day weekend since its inception in 1981. Anvil's best-known title, *Stupid crimes* (1990), is by co-publisher Dennis E. Bolen; a gritty account of a parole officer's life, it has been reprinted with an international commercial publisher and film rights have been sold. GEOFF HANCOCK

Appel de la race, L'. See Lionel-Adolphe GROULX.

Apprenticeship of Duddy Kravitz, The (1959). Although Mordecai RICHLER was only twenty-eight when his fourth novel was published in Britain and the USA, the book established him as a major novelist. This breakthrough work shows him as an early user of the 'black comedy' that subequently emerged, in the 1960s, as the most prominent new feature of English-language fiction. It also marks, as George WOODCOCK suggested, a new stage in Canadian writing: its appearance in 1959, along with Sheila WATSON's *The double hook*, prepared the ground for the extraordinary flowering of Canadian fiction that took place in the 1960s and 1970s. However, the importance of Richler's novel was not immediately apparent: its early critical reception was mixed, with some reviewers and readers expressing reservations or finding it morally offensive. Despite this, and the fact that the novel was not published in Canada until 1969, and though many critics now find some of Richler's later fiction more satisfying, *The apprenticeship of Duddy Kravitz* remains Richler's best-known book. In print since its original publication (a new edition of the novel was published in the NEW CANADIAN LIBRARY in 1989), and translated into several languages, including French, German, and Hebrew, it has been made into a highly successful film (1974) and has long been a staple on secondary-school reading lists.

Apprenticeship of Duddy Kravitz

A loosely episodic study of a young hustler on his way up, *Duddy Kravitz* is part of Richler's larger exploration of his home territory—the Jewish ghetto around St Urbain Street in Montreal—begun in *Son of a smaller hero* (1955), extended in *The street* (1969), and continued in parts of *St. Urbain's Horseman* (1971) and *Joshua then and now* (1980). The influence of Budd Schulberg's *What makes Sammy run?* (1941) on *Duddy Kravitz* has frequently been noted (Richler's novel even contains an allusion to Sammy Glick); the impact of James T. Farrell is visible as well. However, in contrast to Farrell, who described brutalized city-life in his Studs Lonigan trilogy, Richler resists the dark and potentially tragic dimensions of his material. *Duddy Kravitz* is prevented from becoming either a parable of environmental determinism or an illustration of the moral bankruptcy of unrestrained ambition by its exuberance and sometimes broad comedy, as in set-pieces such as the tale of the bizarre movie produced by Duddy's questionable film company (Dudley Kane Productions), which he has created to film bar mitzvahs for the socially ambitious.

Because of the way Duddy embodies so much attractive energy, early critical debate focused on how readers ought to judge his moral failures. The problems inherent in this question were addressed in John Ferns' 1974 essay (see below), which argues that there is no single answer because the novel creates 'an oscillating pattern of sympathetic and judicial response'. In a lecture given in 1978 Richler suggested that the difficulty of judging Duddy was comparable to that of judging one of the late nineteenth-century American 'robber barons': while they were morally reprehensible, they were nevertheless agents of change, and therefore made things happen.

Just as Richler's *Son of a smaller hero* dramatized the need for the artist to escape the limitations of the Montreal ghetto, the opening pages of *Duddy Kravitz*, which locate Duddy as a student at Fletcher's Field High, imply that more important than graduating high school successfully is the need to graduate from the ghetto itself. This opening passage also mentions Fletcher's Field's 'most celebrated former student, Jerry Dingleman, the Boy Wonder'. A legendary presence in the novel, he is an already-successful hustler against whom Duddy can measure himself; it gives Duddy special delight when he eventually outdoes him.

While Duddy in pursuit of his goals is contemptuous of, and willing to manipulate, most of the people with whom he comes into contact, he is also eager for approval, especially that of his own family. Told by his grandfather that 'A man without land is a nobody', he spends the novel trying to acquire the land that will make him a somebody—betraying those individuals around him who had thought they could depend on him—only to find that his grandfather disapproves of his ultimate success. At the end of the novel Duddy finds victory emptier than he had anticipated, but the reader senses that he is not without achievement. Among other things, he has contributed a new example of escape to the mythology of the ghetto and has disrupted a world that had too often been static.

John Ferns presents a balanced view of the novel and its protagonist in 'Sympathy and judgement in Mordecai Richler's *The apprenticeship of Duddy Kravitz*', *Journal of Canadian Fiction* 3 (1974). Victor J. Ramraj's *Mordecai Richler* (1983) contains a good overview of the book in the context of Richler's larger body of work. George Woodcock wrote *Introducing Mordecai Richler's 'The apprenticeship of Duddy Kravitz': a reader's guide* (1990), aimed at undergraduates. RUSSELL BROWN

April, Jean-Pierre. See FANTASTIC LITERATURE AND SCIENCE FICTION IN FRENCH.

Aquin, Hubert (1929-77). Born in Montreal's east end, near Parc Lafontaine, he did his pre-university studies at l'École Olier (the same elementary school attended by Émile NELLIGAN), l'Externat Saint-Croix, and Collège Sainte-Marie. In 1951 he completed a licentiate in philosophy at the Université de Montréal. After three years' study at the Institut d'études politiques in Paris (1951-4), he returned to Montreal, where he worked as a producer at Radio-Canada (1955-9) and spent four years as a scriptwriter and film director for the National Film Board (1959-63). In 1960, while working as a stock-broker at the Montreal Stock Exchange, he joined the Rassemblement pour l'Indépendance nationale (RIN), in which he held executive positions from 1963 to 1968. In 1964 he disappeared for a time from public view, after stating in a press release that he was joining an underground terrorist movement; he was arrested in July 1964 while in possession of a stolen car and an automatic pistol and transferred from Montreal Prison to the Albert Prévost Psychiatric Institute, where he spent four months awaiting trial for illegal possession of a firearm. During this period he wrote his first and most famous novel, *PROCHAIN ÉPISODE* (1965). Acquitted in Dec.

1965, Aquin had become a literary sensation, described by establishment literary critic Jean-Éthier Blais as the 'great writer' Quebec had been waiting for throughout its history.

The years following were characterized by a series of dramatic incidents that indicated Aquin's inability to compromise with any established structure, professional or political. In 1966 he was expelled from Switzerland, by his own account because of RCMP influence on the Swiss government. In 1968 he publicly broke with the RIN when it merged with René Lévesque's Mouvement Souveraineté-Association to form the Parti Québécois, describing the merger as 'suicidal' for the Quebec independence movement. In 1969 he became the first Quebec writer to refuse a Governor General's Award (offered to him for *Trou de mémoire*) on political grounds. In 1971 he left the editorial board of *LIBERTÉ* magazine, accusing his co-directors of dependence on CANADA COUNCIL support and of consequent silence in the face of the federal government's role in the 1970 October Crisis. In 1972 he was awarded the Prix David. In 1976, after eighteen months as literary director of Éditions La Presse, he resigned publicly, accusing the editor and director of *La Presse*, Roger LEMELIN, of 'colonizing Quebec from within'. On 15 Mar. 1977 Aquin took a pistol left to him in his father's will the preceding year, placed it to his temple, and shot himself. His suicide was accompanied by a message to the public stating that his death was a free and positive choice: 'I have lived intensely, and now it is over.' He had consciously made his life a publicly acted-out myth that was meant to be seen as an incarnation of modern Quebec's contradictions.

It is of course Aquin's writings—political articles and essays, television plays and films, as well as the novels—that account for his importance; and his inability to write after 1974 appears to be the only valid explanation of his suicide. Yet Aquin was constantly wary of being trapped as an artist in a role that would be a mere compensation for the economic and political power that he claimed history had denied him as a Québécois. The three novels he published after *Prochain épisode*—*Trou de mémoire* (1968), *L'antiphonaire* (1969), and *Neige noire* (1974)—were attempts to make the novel into a 'total' art-form, based on a process of co-creation shared by author and reader, that would integrate not only all the arts but the cognitive processes of modern science and the mythic and ritual dimensions of religious experience. The literary influences he most often mentioned were Joyce's *Ulysses* and the work of Vladimir Nabokov, as well as the detective novels he loved, whose 'whodunit' form may have influenced the often sadistic and teasing relationship his novels establish with the reader.

In *Trou de mémoire*, translated by Alan Brown as *Blackout* (1974), the main character is a revolutionary pharmacist-writer who, after murdering his English-Canadian lover, writes in a vain attempt to fill with words the absence created by her death—an absence that becomes a metaphor for Quebec's tormented historical silence and its ambivalent relationship with English Canada. A series of doubles, mirror images, and contradictory narrative viewpoints develop an analogy between Quebec and the colonized nations of the Third World. The other side of a historical 'rape' that goes back to the Conquest is shown as a need for violence that will seemingly explode the Quebec male into manhood. The novel itself is presented as a historical 'event', a revolutionary and blasphemous act that will destroy the old order and permit the birth of a culture.

In *L'antiphonaire*, translated by Alan Brown as *The antiphonary* (1973), Aquin moved away from Quebec history and politics to a broader canvas. The novel traces the decline of Christine Forestier, a medical student married to an epileptic, who attempts unsuccessfully to complete her thesis on sixteenth-century medicine and to take control of her life. It is constructed as an exchange of voices that establishes a contrapuntal relationship between twentieth-century Montreal and San Francisco and Europe in the sixteenth century, which is seen as the period of schism between religion and rationalism, science and culture; its central metaphor is an epileptic crisis. Christine's early identification with Paracelsus, whom she sees as a symbol of unity, gives way to a series of images in which the rape and violence in her own life reveal her as the double not of Paracelsus but of a fictional sixteenth-century victim of rape and violence. Her suicide, an escape into mystical passivity, appears now—like the suicides of the male protagonists of *Trou de mémoire*—as a literary foreshadowing of Aquin's own death.

In 1971 Aquin published *Point de fuite*, a collection of essays and letters preceded by a foreword in which he describes himself as isolated, aging, and out of tune with the new generation of Quebec students and intellectuals. In 1974, however, he published *Neige noire* (translated by Sheila Fischman as *Hamlet's twin*, 1979), perhaps his greatest novel. An 'unfinishable' film scenario, and a modern reply to Hamlet, it attempts to integrate the temporal and the sacred in a philosophical meditation on time that counterpoints a violent and erotic detective-type plot. *Neige noire* was Aquin's final statement, his ultimate attempt to create the 'total novel': Aquin saw as the particular domain of literature an integration of the visual potency of film, the mobility of musical structure, and a mythical evolution.

See Patricia Smart, *Hubert Aquin agent double* (1973); Françoise Iqbal, *Hubert Aquin romancier* (1978); René Lapierre, *L'imaginaire captif: Hubert Aquin* (1981); and Anthony Purdy, ed., *Writing Quebec: selected essays by Hubert Aquin* (1988).

See also ESSAYS IN FRENCH: 7, and NOVELS IN FRENCH 1960 TO 1982: 2.

PATRICIA SMART

Arcadian adventures with the idle rich (1914). Along with *SUNSHINE SKETCHES OF A LITTLE TOWN*, *Arcadian adventures* is one of Stephen LEACOCK's best and most popular books. It was published two years after *Sunshine sketches*, and, as numerous parallels between the two books in overall structure and detail indicate, it was intended as a companion-piece. It portrays the full flowering in a large American city (based in fact on Montreal) of the seeds of corrupt materialism already detected in small-town Mariposa. In its bitter satire of the 'conspicuous consumption' of the 'idle rich', it shows the influence of *Theory of the leisure class* by Thorstein Veblen, Leacock's teacher at the University of Chicago. Unlike *Sunshine sketches, Arcadian adventures* shows sympathy not for those it satirizes but only for their hapless victims. There are few memorable characters; the inhabitants of Plutoria Street are presented primarily as hypocritical and dangerous embodiments of corrupt institutions or forces, such as the church, politics, finance, and education. However, what the book lacks in charm and affection it makes up for in intensity; as it proceeds it becomes progressively darker until in its final chapter, 'The Great Fight', there is a foreshadowing of the tyranny and violence that were to grip the world in the 1920s and 1930s. It is in the NEW CANADIAN LIBRARY.

ZAILIG POLLOCK

Archambault, Gilles (b. 1933). Born in Montreal, Quebec, he completed studies at the Collège Sainte-Marie in 1955 and received his B.A. from the Université de Montréal in 1957. The following year he went to work for Radio Canada to present reviews of his two favourite topics—literature and jazz. Although Archambault interrupted his radio career to pursue writing after the publication of his first novel, *Une suprême discrétion* (1963), he has continued to write reviews and humorous commentary on current events for radio, print media, and recently the Internet.

While references to jazz and blues permeate his fiction, Archambault's expertise lies in his treatment of serious issues through the eyes of deeply conflicted protagonists. In *La fuite immobile* (1974)—translated by David Lobdell as *Standing flight* (1986)—writer and journalist Julien struggles with class distinctions as he moves from a blue-collar upbringing into a professional environment, reluctant to leave his tavern friends, yet unable to curse in front of them without sounding affected. Archambault treats even basic questions of life and death on this personal level. At the end of *Le voyageur distrait* (1981), Michel faces the possibility of a friend's suicide, and wonders whether it might not be the best outcome for her.

Archambault's sensitive portrayals have earned him the Prix Anathase-David in 1981 for his combined works, and a Governor's General's Award in 1987 for his short-story collection *L'obsédante obèse et autres agressions*.

STEVEN J. DANIELL

Ardizzi, Maria. See ITALIAN-CANADIAN LITERATURE.

Armstrong, Jeannette (b. 1948). A member of the Okanagan nation, she was born on the Penticton Indian Reserve, British Columbia, and attended the reserve's elementary school and the Penticton Senior Secondary School. In 1975 she received a Diploma in Fine Arts from Okanagan College and in 1978 a Bachelor of Fine Arts degree from the University of Victoria. A fluent speaker of the Okanagan language, she has also studied under a number of Okanagan elders and is co-founder and director of Penticton's En'owkin International School of Writing, the first credit-giving creative-writing school in Canada operated for and by Native people. Her poetry collection *Breath tracks* (1991)—divided into four sections: 'From the landscape of Grandmother' 'History lesson', 'Fire madness' and 'Wind woman'—is innovative in form, with free verse and concrete poems reflecting personal experiences and social and political concerns intensely and compassionately, but without sentimentality. Her poetry has appeared in anthologies and many journals.

Her novel *Slash* (1985), now in its sixth printing, is the story of an Okanagan Native youth's search for truth and meaning in his life as he grows into manhood during the turbulent sixties and seventies. Non-Natives criticized Armstrong's disruptive style, lack of character development and time perspective, but Native critic Lee MARACLE has praised it for not being a European piece of literature: 'It is Native literature from beginning to end' (*Fuse*, July 1988). Another Native critic, Lenore KEESHIG-TOBIAS, referred to it as 'emergence literature, a stage in the evolution of Native literature as a written art form. It is a process of learning decolonization' (*Fuse*, March/April 1988).

Armstrong has also written two children's books: *Enwhisteetkwa-walk-in-water* (1982) and *Neekna and chemai* (1983). *The Native creative process* (1991) is a collaborative discourse between Armstrong and the distinguished Native architect Douglas Cardinal. Armstrong edited a collection of essays, *Looking at the words of our people: First Nations analysis of literature* (1993), in which she says in an Editor's Note that 'First Nations Literature, as a facet of cultural practise contains symbolic significance and relevance that is an integral part of the deconstruction-construction of colonialism and the reconstruction of a new order of culturalism and relationship beyond colonial thought and practise.' She helped edit *We get our living like milk from the land* (1993), a historical overview of the Okanagan Nation from the Creation story to the present.

PENNY PETRONE

As for me and my house (1941). Sinclair ROSS's first novel is widely recognized as a Canadian classic and is in fact the most critically appraised of Canadian novels, having generated more than fifty critical articles and book chapters since its publication. The story portrays Philip Bentley, a clergyman whose ministry has brought him to a small prairie town during the Depression, as an ineffectual minister and frustrated artist caught up in a vocation to which he may never have been suited. This view of Philip and his discontents is tempered, however, by the reader's awareness that the story is being told through the diary entries of his wife, a woman who once dreamed of being a concert musician and chafes at the duties and expectations surrounding the role of a minister's wife. Mrs Bentley can indeed be suspected of exaggerating Philip's artistic talent, and his disaffection for the ministry, in order to justify her own desire to have him leave it—especially given the various schemes and manipulative acts in which she engages during the year-long period she records. At the same time, however, there is poignancy in Ross's portrayal of Mrs Bentley's attempts to maintain and transform a difficult marriage under trying circumstances, and a degree of apparent admiration in the text for her stalwart resistance to the conformist demands of the ironically named town of 'Horizon'.

The novel has been read traditionally as a novel of social realism notable for its accurate portrayal of the experience of Depression life on the Prairies—the ceaseless winds, ubiquitous dust, meagre harvests, grinding poverty, and throttled hope that marked that time and place. It has also been praised for its psychological realism, its powerful rendition of the effects of physical isolation and spiritual aridity on the human soul, and its success in using the diary form as a symbol, in effect, of Mrs Bentley's strategies for managing her feelings of impotence and alienation.

In recent years *As for me and my house* has proved amenable to a wide variety of new critical approaches. Beginning in the 1970s, with renewed theoretical interest in narrativity, much attention has been paid to the structure of the novel and particularly to the question of Mrs Bentley's reliability as a narrator. Contemporary approaches to the novel, from such varied perspectives as reader-response theory, feminism, semiotics, ethics, and new historicism, have proved fruitful and testify to the protean achievement that this novel represents. The novel is in the NEW CANADIAN LIBRARY with an Afterword by Robert KROETSCH.

See David Stouck, ed., *Sinclair Ross's As for me and my house: five decades of criticism* (1992), as well as John Moss, ed., *From the heart of the heartland: the fictions of Sinclair Ross* (1992). Lorna CROZIER's *A saving grace: the collected poems of Mrs. Bentley* (1996), a collection of poetry written in Mrs Bentley's imagined voice, is a contemporary gloss on Ross's text that reflects the perspective of an accomplished western-Canadian poet.

MARILYN ROSE

Asselin, Olivar. See ANTHOLOGIES IN FRENCH: 2.

Assikinack, Francis. See ABORIGINAL LITERATURE: 2.

À toi, pour toujours, ta Marie-Lou (1971). Michel TREMBLAY's play was first produced in French on 29 April 1971 at the Théâtre de quat'sous, directed by André Brassard. The English translation, *Forever yours, Marie-Lou* (1975), by Bill Glassco and John Van Burek, premièred in November 1972 at Tarragon Theatre, Toronto.

Tremblay considers this 'string quartet for four voices' his best play. Within the cycle of *Les* BELLES-SOEURS, it is at once the most sophisticated in dramatic structure and the most vitriolic in its attack on the family ('I want to put a bomb in the family cell'). It works on three levels: as a universal statement on the difficulties of communication between members of a family; as an indictment of socio-economic and clerical pressures that have degraded the family in Quebec; and as a political allegory, the parents representing the past, one daughter (Manon) the status quo, the other (Carmen) liberation. The main subject of the play, the monstrous family—impotent, frustrated, and unable to communicate—is common in the 'nouveau théâtre québécois' and is a reaction against the Church-imposed idealized family life of earlier literature.

A highly theatrical work, *À toi, pour toujours, ta Marie-Lou* consists of two interwoven dialogues, one between Léopold and Marie-Lou, the parents, the other between Manon and Carmen. The parents' dialogue occurs just before a fatal 'accident', in which Léopold crashes the car against a cement wall, killing them both; the daughters' dialogue is set ten years after that event. The entire play occurs in one location, the kitchen of the parents' home; however, only the daughters actually occupy this space, centre-stage. The parents, now dead, are given symbolic locales representing their favourite spots: Léopold to one side, in front of a tavern table, Marie-Lou to the other, in front of the television. To underline the absence of communication, all four characters remain static, speaking straight to the audience.

The play is composed along musical lines ('it is a purely aural thing for me,' says Tremblay), creating a strong sense of unity and harmony, in spite of the harshness of the theme and language. Tremblay conveys the desperate state of the marriage of Léopold and Marie-Lou through heavy irony and a number of repeated key words: 'renvoyer' (vomit), 'péter' (fart), 'cracher' (spit), and 'merde' (shit). Marie-Lou's aversion to both sex and her husband is aptly suggested by such words as 'cochonnerie' (swinishness) and 'écoeurant' (disgusting). Léopold himself is caught in the 'engrenage' (cogwheels) of a monotonous job, and fears the onset of madness, which runs in his family. Suicide is his solution. The two daughters react in opposite ways to their parents' death. Manon remains in the house, her life patterned after her mother's prayerful resignation; Carmen moves out and becomes a sexually liberated singer of cowboy songs on the Main. Both women reappear in subsequent plays: Carmen as the central martyr figure in *Sainte Carmen de la Main*, Manon as the religious fanatic in *Damnée Manon, sacrée Sandra*.

See *Le monde de Michel Tremblay* (1993), edited by Gilbert David and Pierre Lavoie.

RENATE USMIANI

'At the Mermaid Inn'. This column—conducted by the poets Wilfred CAMPBELL, Archibald LAMPMAN, and Duncan Campbell SCOTT—appeared in the Toronto *Globe* every Saturday (with one exception) from 6 Feb. 1892 to 1 July 1893 and dealt with such wide-ranging concerns as literature, painting, history, politics, and religion. Each contributor was paid three dollars a week. The column argued vigorously for the promotion of Canadian literature: Campbell points to the need for an association of Canadian authors; Lampman calls for the establishment of 'a really good literary magazine'; Lampman and Scott bemoan the high tax on books and call for its removal; and Scott suggests the promotion of Canadian literature at the Chicago Exhibition of 1893. 'At the Mermaid Inn' also served as a forum for the development of the aesthetic values that were implicit in its contributors' poetry. Campbell, whose work approaches the decadent in 'How one winter came in the lake region' and 'The were-wolves', discusses the 'beauties and vastness of glory in the darkness'. Lampman, who had received considerable critical praise for such sonnets as 'The largest life' and 'The modern politician', writes extensively about the sonnet form. Scott, who explored Christian themes in 'The forsaken' and 'On the way to the mission', demands that poetry serve a moral purpose and calls nature 'a setting for man's life'.

The column was the object of controversy on 27 Feb. 1892 when Campbell observed that 'much of the earlier part of the Old Testament, such as the stories of Jonah, have all been proved to belong to the class of literature called mythic. The story of the cross itself is one of the most remarkable myths in the history of humanity . . .' The sensibilities of the *Globe*'s readers were offended by these observations, and the following Monday the paper was obliged 'to condemn and repudiate' the poet's views and 'to express regret that the columns of the *Globe* should have been used to circulate them'.

Selections from the column, edited by Arthur S. BOURINOT, appear in *At the Mermaid Inn, conducted by A. Lampman, W.W. Campbell, Duncan C. Scott* (1958). The entire run of the column has been reprinted, with an introduction by Barrie Davies, in *At the Mermaid Inn: Wilfred Campbell, Archibald Lampman, Duncan Campbell Scott in the* Globe *1892-3* (1979). GEORGE WICKEN

Atwood, Margaret (b. 1939). Margaret Eleanor Atwood was born in Ottawa, Ontario, and moved with her family to Sault Ste Marie in 1945, and to Toronto a year later. The daughter of an entomologist who specialized in forest insects, she came to know intimately the bush country of northern Ontario and Quebec. She graduated from Victoria College, University of Toronto, in 1961 and received an A.M. degree from Radcliffe College, Cambridge, in 1962. She studied at Harvard University in 1962-3 and 1965-7. In the early part of her career she taught at the University of British Columbia, Vancouver; Sir George Williams University, Montreal; the University of Alberta, Edmonton, and York University, Toronto. She was writer-in-residence at the University of Toronto (1972-3), Macquarie University, Australia (1987), Trinity University, Texas (1989); Honorary Chair, the University of Alabama (1985); and Berg Chair, New York University (1986). In the early 1970s she worked as an editor for the House of ANANSI, and was a member of the board; she served as president of the WRITERS' UNION OF CANADA in 1981-2 and President of PEN, Canadian Centre, from 1984 to 1986.

Atwood published books include: (POETRY) *Double Persephone* (pamphlet, 1961; *The circle game* (1966), *The animals in that country* (1968), *The JOURNALS OF SUSANNA MOODIE* (1970), *Procedures for underground* (1970), *Power politics* (1971), *You are happy* (1974), *Selected poems* (1976), *Two-headed poems* (1978), *True stories* (1981), *Interlunar* (1984), *Selected poems II: poems selected and new 1976-86* (1986), *Selected poems 1966-84* (1990), *Morning in the burned house* (1995); (NOVELS) *The edible woman* (1969), *Surfacing* (1972), *Lady oracle* (1976), *Life before man* (1979), *Bodily harm* (1981); *The HANDMAID'S TALE* (1985), *Cat's eye* (1988), *The robber bride* (1993), *Alias Grace* (1996); (SHORT FICTION) *Dancing girls* (1977), *Murder in the dark* (1983), *Bluebeard's egg* (1983), *Wilderness tips* (1991), *Good bones* (1992); (CRITICISM) *SURVIVAL: A THEMATIC GUIDE TO CANADIAN LITERATURE* (1972), *Second words: selected critical prose* (1982), *Strange things: the malevolent north in Canadian literature* (1995); (HISTORY) *Days of the rebels: 1815-1840* (1977); (CHILDREN'S BOOKS) *Up in the tree* (1978), *Anna's pet* (with Joyce Barkhouse, 1980), *For the birds* (1990), *Princess Prunella and the purple peanut* (1995). She is the editor of *The new Oxford book of Canadian verse in English* (1982), *The Oxford book of Canadian short stories in English* (with Robert WEAVER, 1986, 2nd edn, 1995), *The Canlit foodbook* (1987), and *The best American short stories* (with Shannon Ravenel, 1989). She has published a number of art and small-press editions of her work and has written several television and radio scripts.

Atwood has received numerous awards and honours, including the Governor General's Award (for *The circle game* and *The handmaid's tale*); the Molson Prize (1981); a Guggenheim Fellowship Award (1981); Companion of the Order of Canada (1981); the *Los Angeles Times* Fiction Award (1986); *Ms.* Magazine Woman of the Year (1986); short-listed for the Booker Prize (1987, 1989, 1996); Commonwealth Literary Prize, Regional Winner (1987, 1994); Fellow of the Royal Society of Canada (1987); Foreign Honorary Member, American Academy of Arts and Sciences (1988); Centennial Medal, Harvard University (1990); Government of France's Chevalier dans l'Ordre des Arts et des Lettres (1994); *Sunday Times* Award for Literary Excellence (1994); Trillium Award for Excellence in Ontario Writing (1992, 1994, 1996); the Giller Prize for Fiction (1996); the Medal of Honor, National Arts Club, New York (1997). She has received honorary degrees from over ten universities. A writer of international prominence, Margaret Atwood is as well known in the USA, Europe, and Australia as she is in Canada. Her work has been translated into over thirty languages.

From the time of her first publication in 1961 Atwood has demonstrated remarkable artistic control of her poetic material. Each book has a thematic unity and can be seen to elaborate a central preoccupation of her work: the role of mythology, both personal and cultural, in the individual life. Like Northrop FRYE, she is fascinated by the conventions that lie behind everyday reality, by the mythological substructures of modern culture.

In her poetry Atwood continually startles the reader with her imagery, which unfolds in a terse, elliptical style. The game of 'Ring-around-the-rosie', alluded to in the title of her first major collection, *The circle game*, is one of ritual exclusion in which the known is circumscribed by a garrison of bodies that keeps out the threatening unknown world. For Atwood the essential human impulse is to reduce an irrational and threatening environment to a closed circle of orthodoxy. Thus the writer's responsibility is to expose the conventions (psychological, linguistic, mythic) by which we invent convenient versions of ourselves. She sees modern man as being prey to continual invasions of fear and paranoia from the subliminal mind, yet committed to an anachronistic belief in civilized order that is patently contradicted by the barbarism of the twentieth century. The rational mind must be integrated with the dark side of the psyche that has been repressed by humanistic ideas of order. To enter the wilderness of the self, then, is one of Atwood's major concerns. In *The journals of Susanna Moodie* a nineteenth-century Canadian pioneer becomes the archetypal colonial entering the unknown wilderness of the New World. Imprisoned within the outmoded conventions of the Victorian world that she carries in her head, she retreats into her own circle game—projecting nostalgic Victorian preconceptions onto an alien landscape, while remaining ignorant of the challenges of her new environment. (For Atwood, as for Frye, such a garrison mentality once characterized the Canadian sensibility.) Moodie's last meditations are from underground. *Procedures for underground* explores the same themes in a different context. The title poem is indebted to West Coast Native mythology for its motifs. Entering the mirror-world of the psyche, the poet becomes a shaman whose visions are threatening to her tribe. From the 'underland' she sees the world as an ambiguous landscape of violence and death—the landscape we enter in many other poems in the book.

In the brief, aphoristic poems of *Power politics*, Atwood exposes, with the same scalpel-like precision, the sadistic deceptions implicit in the myth of romantic love. Lovers are predatory, even cannibalistic; relationships are a sophisticated form of consumption: love is power politics. Each individual seeks the security of role reinforcement from the other and remains trapped in an essential solipsism, committed only to his or her own needy appetite. How, the poet asks, are we to escape this locked dance? *You are happy*, which represents an expansion of these themes, includes the brilliant sequence of 'Circe/Mud' poems in which the story of Odysseus arriving in Aiaia is retold from the perspective of Circe. Her experience represents the extortion of women, who must be entirely passive—malleable as clay to male desire. With these two books Atwood became a major voice in the feminist debate over personal relationships.

The themes of Atwood's later poetry also include the world of modern politics and the domestic world of mother and child. In *Two-headed poems* she returns to a concern that first emerged in *Survival*: the complexities of being Canadian. The title poem is an elegy for a nation divided between two cultures: not only in the 'two-headed' national persona—represented by a 'leader' who speaks duplicitously in two languages—but in the ensuing debate, which 'is not a debate/but a duet/with two deaf singers'. An antidote to this public cynicism appears in poems that create potent myths for the child, offering a private magic, and in a treatment of nature that reveals its benevolence in the cyclical renewal of life. In *True stories* Atwood's political concerns are transferred to an international context. We live in a fragile security, cocooned from the global realities of famine, political terrorism, and war: our willed ignorance of such evils is a form of collusion. In a peculiarly Canadian way Atwood is a staunch moralist, essentially demanding that modern man reinvent himself. Her work challenges us to become human. *Interlunar* contains the remarkable 'Snake poems', a sequence reminiscent in its eloquent lyricism of D.H.Lawrence's 'The snake', and demonstrates Atwood's total control of her voice and material. *Morning in the burned house* was published after a poetic silence of twelve years. As Atwood explains: 'Poetry is something that happens to you at irregular intervals and with no guarantees it will happen again. . . . All you can do is wait.' There is no diminution in her power. The poems encompass various moods from playful to sombre; some draw on mythic, historical, and literary figures such as Sekhmet, Helen of Troy, and King Lear, while others are intensely intimate, particularly the elegiac series of meditations on the death of the poet's father. The book is the work of a mature poet coursing back through memory, searching for the values of compassion and forgiveness.

The impulse to write poetry and fiction coincided in Atwood's career. She had already written a novel and short stories when she submitted *The edible woman* to publishers in 1965. It was eventually published in 1969. Atwood explained that, for her, the novel is a 'social vehicle' that 'reflects society'. In each of her first five novels, the main character is a woman living a professional life in a modern consumer society (a consumer research analyst, a commercial artist, a novelist, an anthropologist, a 'life-styles' journalist) who is forced to engage in a radical process of reassessment when the props supporting her carefully constructed version of herself are knocked out from under her. After experiencing a mental breakdown Marian, the narrator of *The edible woman*, exorcises the menace of a predatory sexist society by baking an 'edible woman' cake and ritualistically offering it to her man in place of herself. In *Lady oracle* the narrator, Joan, lives her life as if it were a trashy and melodramatic script, one of the Costume Gothics she writes. When neurotic relationships and her invented personas (she has at least three identities) become too confusing, she decides to simulate her own death; but whether this escape into normalcy is successful is left ambiguous. *The edible woman* is in the NEW CANADIAN LIBRARY, with an Afterword by Linda HUTCHEON. *Life before man* is the story of a love triangle; but in an anaesthetized, plastic world—the puritanical world of WASP Toronto—the characters can't seem to transcend clichés of feeling. The most fascinating aspect of the novel is the backdrop—Lesje, one of the main characters, works at the Royal Ontario Museum, and prehistoric dinosaurs walk like phantoms through the pages of the novel. Atwood's implicit question is: Have we earned the right to call ourselves human?

Atwood's most complex early novels are *Surfacing* and *Bodily harm*. In *Surfacing* the unnamed narrator searches the wilderness of northern Quebec for her father, a botanist, who has been reported missing. Trying to re-establish contact with her past, she must re-evaluate all her cultural assumptions. In this retreat into the wilderness, which is both a literal and a psychological place, Atwood is challenging Western ways of seeing, particularly of relating to nature. The modern compulsion is to treat nature as raw material, to explain and master it in accordance with the technological myth of progress. By showing her protagonist moving through a ritual preparation that corresponds to the stages of shamanistic initiation, Atwood attempts to recover a primitive, mystical participation in nature, in which the heroine must recreate herself. In *Bodily harm* the heroine flees from a constricting consumer society and a broken relationship to another alien territory—the politically complex environment of a Caribbean island. Confronted with its stark realities, she comes to acknowledge her narcissistic entrapment in a culture where feelings are invented, packaged, and merchandised. *Surfacing* is in the New Canadian Library, with an Afterword by Marie-Claire BLAIS.

With *The handmaid's tale* Atwood achieved immediate international recognition for her portrait of a futuristic American society in the throes of a fundamentalist dictatorship where women, forced into servitude as handmaids, are commandeered into producing babies for the governing elite. The book demonstrates Atwood at her most intellectually fierce, understanding how an epidemic of infertility in the Western democracies as a consequence of chemical pollution could be used by right-wing fundamentalists to impose their own repressive theocratic rule. With *Cat's eye*, Atwood turned back to a more private world, chronicling the return of a middle-aged painter, Elaine Risley, to Toronto for a retrospective of her work. Risley's re-entry into the world of her childhood allows Atwood to examine the betrayals and cruelties of adolescent females with a sympathy and a humour that combine the lyrical intensity of her poetry with the social vision of her fiction. For many critics this is one of her finest novels. *The robber bride* develops this strength. Playing on the title of the sadistic Grimm's fairy tale 'The Robber Bridegroom', the novel explores the friendship between three women who are united in part by their involvement with a common nemesis, a charismatic and manipulative woman called Zenia who, thought dead, surfaces again to subvert their peace. Each woman experiences her life in retrospect, unfolding back to the encounter with Zenia, who has robbed her of the significant male in her life. The book becomes a meditation on how we concoct versions of ourselves, and elaborates Atwood's fascination with illusion, camouflage, and deception. Shrewdly understanding the narrative and dramatic potential of psychological projection, Atwood creates characters who, because wounded, have been vulnerable to another's con-artistry of the mind. Atwood's most recent novel, *Alias Grace*, represents a departure. Her first foray into historical fiction, it is based on an actual murder case in Upper Canada in 1843. The heroine, thirty-two year old Grace Marks, is sixteen years into a life sentence in Kingston Penitentiary for her involvement in the murder of her employer, Thomas Kinnear, and his housekeeper/mistress, for which her supposed accomplice, fellow servant James McDermott, was hanged. Grace claims to have no memory of the murders, and, under the auspices of a group of Kingston reformers and Spiritualists, Dr Simon Jordan, a pioneer in the new science of mental illness, has been brought to Canada to determine

Grace's innocence or guilt. Atwood had been fascinated by the Grace Marks story since reading Susanna Moodie's inaccurate account of the murder in *Life in the clearings* (1853) in her high-school reader. In 1974 she wrote a CBC play, *The servant girl*, based on the story. Twenty years later she had a vision of Grace in a prison yard, and began the novel. It is carefully crafted, interweaving two nineteenth-century female artefacts—the keepsake album and the patchwork quilt—as structural motifs. By using the new science of psychology as backdrop to her novel, and threading it with quotations from Tennyson, Browning, Poe, Dickinson, and others, as well as popular ballads and newspaper clippings of the time, Atwood vividly conjures up nineteenth-century fears and fantasies about 'the female murderess'. The novel becomes a meditation on the nature of identity, memory, and the unconscious in a fascinating exploration of the distortion of male/female relationships, and again demonstrates Atwood's gift for richly textured, imaginative fiction with a social range that is rare among contemporary novelists.

As a prose stylist Atwood also demonstrates a mastery of the short-story form, which allows for interesting technical experiments with point of view, dialogue, and epigrammatic style. In *Dancing girls* the characters—like the protagonists of her novels—are psychologically complex individuals trapped by paranoia and radical alienation. Two stories are representative. 'Polarities' is a study of madness, both inside and outside mental institutions, in which a clinically insane student proves to have a deeper understanding of the general psychosis of modern society than the so-called sane protagonist. 'The grave of the famous poet' is one of Atwood's most compassionate fictional studies of the failure of relationships. With acerbic irony she penetrates beneath the level of clichéd passion to expose love as an addictive habit. *Murder in the dark: short fiction and prose poems* takes a new direction. The main subject is writing itself: what is the writer's plot against the reader? The title piece describes writing as a treacherous parlour game in which the writer is the murderer, the reader her victim, and, by the rules of the game, the writer must lie. The price the writer exacts from herself justifies her sinister assumption of authority: 'If you decide to enter the page, take a knife and some matches,' because the journey is horrifying: 'You can become lost in the page forever.' The last section of the book explores the varieties of darkness beneath the page where the writer enters a limbo between sanity and madness. In these witty experimental pieces, as in all her work, Atwood has designs on our psyches—we are to be instructed through the underdarkness so that we can become saner and more resilient. Her collection *Bluebeard's egg* contains several avowedly autobiographical stories, including 'Significant moments in the life of my mother', and 'Unearthing suite', compassionate and tender accounts of family life that demonstrate the great gap between Atwood's own childhood experience and the gothic world that is often her fictional subject; while *Wilderness tips* contains the story 'Isis in Darkness', a thinly disguised tribute to Gwendolyn MacEWEN, her friend and contemporary poet. *Good bones* is a much more playful book, parodying traditional forms such as the parable, monologue, mini-romance, mini-biography, and reconstructed fairy-tale. But beneath its satiric humour, the vignettes offer serious meditations on a theme that has long fascinated Atwood: human evolution and our hubristic arrogance in the face of the natural world. As she remarked in an interview with Graeme GIBSON: 'Does anyone ever achieve it [being human]? If you define human beings as necessarily flawed, then anybody can be one. But if you define them as something potentially better, then it's always something that is just our of reach.' *Murder in the dark* and *Good bones* are both in the New Canadian Library, with Afterwords, respectively, by Steven HEIGHTON and Rosemary SULLIVAN.

Atwood has published much informal literary criticism, beginning with *Survival*. *The new Oxford book of Canadian verse in English*, for which she wrote a brilliant introductory overview of Canadian poetry, was published in the same year as *Second words: selected critical prose*. These book reviews, lectures, critical articles, and meditations on poetics represent Atwood's early interest in aesthetic questions of style and technique, in the importance of nationalism to the Canadian writer, and her growing involvement with human-rights issues. While her style as a critic is witty and colloquial, Atwood is demanding when it comes to formal concerns.

See *Margaret Atwood: conversations* (1990), edited by Earl G. Ingersoll and, for a full bibliography of books about Atwood, *Margaret Atwood: the writer's official site* on the Web page, compiled by O.W. Toad.

See also CRITICISM IN ENGLISH: 5(d), NOVELS IN ENGLISH 1960 TO 1982: 2, and POETRY IN ENGLISH 1950 TO 1982: 2.

ROSEMARY SULLIVAN

Aubert de Gaspé, Philippe-Joseph (1786-1871). Born in Quebec City, he was the scion of an old and aristocratic Quebec family. His childhood was spent at the ancestral manor-house at Saint-Jean-Port-Joli on the south shore of the St Lawrence River, and in Quebec City. From 1798 to 1806 he completed his classical secondary course at the Petit Séminaire de Québec—latterly while living with a Church of England clergyman—and then studied law under the chief justice of Lower Canada, Jonathan Sewell. Admitted to the bar in Aug. 1811, he married later that year Susanne Allison (by whom he had thirteen children), and practised law in Quebec City. In 1816 he was named sheriff of the town; but, heavily in debt to the Crown, he was removed from office in 1822 and retired to Saint-Jean-Port-Joli. He was imprisoned for debt from 1838 to 1841 and released by a special act of Parliament. In the meantime his journalist son Philippe-Ignace-François Aubert de Gaspé (1814-41) had written, with his father's help, the first French-Canadian novel, *L'INFLUENCE D'UN LIVRE* (Québec, 1837), and had died in Halifax.

After his release Aubert de Gaspé spent his summers on his estate and the winters in Quebec City, participating in the social and literary life of the capital. He belonged to the 'Club des anciens' that met daily in Charles Hamel's shop, and he frequented Octave CRÉMAZIE's bookstore, which in the late 1850s became the meeting-place of the writers of the MOUVEMENT LITTÉRAIRE DE QUÉBEC. In 1862 Aubert de Gaspé, then in his mid-seventies, published in *Les SOIRÉES CANADIENNES* passages of a historical romance, *Les ANCIENS CANADIENS*. With the encouragement and assistance of Abbé Henri-Raymond CASGRAIN it became a novel that, when it was published in 1863, was an immediate success.

Three years later Aubert de Gaspé published his *Mémoires* (Québec, 1866), for which the seventy-nine-year-old author gathered hundreds of anecdotes and reminiscences that form a fascinating social history of Quebec in the last years of the eighteenth century and the first quarter of the nineteenth. This has been translated and annotated by Jane Brierly in *A man of sentiment: the memoirs of Philippe-Joseph Aubert de Gaspé 1786-1871* (1988). A further collection of posthumous fragments, *Divers*, appeared in 1893.

A few days after Aubert de Gaspé died in Quebec City on 29 Jan. 1871, Abbé Casgrain began publishing in *Le Courrier du Canada* an enthusiastic biography of his elderly friend. The modern reader will find the essential biographical information in an article by Luc LACOURCIÈRE in the *DICTIONARY OF CANADIAN BIOGRAPHY*, vol. X. DAVID M. HAYNE

Aubin, Napoléon (1812-90). Aimé-Nicolas Aubin was born of French Protestant parents near Geneva during its annexation to France; he adopted the name 'Napoléon' soon after immigrating first to New Orleans (1829), then to Lower Canada (Jan. 1835). Primarily a journalist, he wrote first for *La Minerve* in Montreal and *L'Ami du peuple* in Quebec City before founding his own newspaper, *Le Fantasque*, there in 1837. Most or all of each issue was written by Aubin himself, and his brilliant, humorous attacks on public figures and policies opposed to French-Canadian interests were widely influential. They led, however, to frequent difficulties with the authorities and, on one occasion (Jan.-Feb. 1839), to his imprisonment for sedition. Even before *Le Fantasque*'s demise in 1845 Aubin had founded *Le Castor* (1843). He subsequently founded *Le Canadien indépendant* (1849); the bilingual *Sentinelle du peuple* (1850); *La Tribune* (1863); and the political review *Les Veillées du père Bonsens* (two series, 1865 and 1873). He also edited, at various times, *Le Canadien* and *Le Pays*, and contributed to several other newspapers.

All of Aubin's non-journalistic production appeared between 1834 and 1839. This consisted of some 17 poems and 9 short stories. The poems express, in tones directly reminiscent of the French Romantic poet Pierre-Jean de Béranger, Aubin's firm patriotism ('Les Français aux Canadiens', 'L'amour de la patrie', 'Les Français en Canada') and the pervasive romanticism then current in France ('À Jenny', 'Quarante ans', 'Tristesse', etc). The personal and melancholy qualities of much of his lyric verse are directly modelled upon the works of Lamartine and Hugo, who were both practically unknown in Canada before Aubin. With his friend and early collaborator in journalism, Philippe Aubert de Gaspé *fils*, he was also a pioneer in introducing the short story to French-Canadian readers. Aubin's 9 stories all appeared in newspapers, and they exhibit a remarkable variety of styles and themes. The longest, and generally considered the best of them, is 'Mon voyage à la lune', a satire on customs and conditions in Lower Canada. 'Une chanson—un songe—un baiser' skilfully exploits a Canadian voyageur legend, infusing it with romantic pathos. Still others, such as 'Une entrée dans le monde' and 'Monsieur Desnotes', are more conventional in subject and form.

Aubin's political stance, as evidenced in his journalism, was that of a *rouge*, turning more and more towards L.-J. Papineau after an initial period of distrust, and espousing the latter's arguments for annexation to the USA well after Confederation. His European education and wide interests gave him great advantage in his combative journalism, and are attested to in his pamphlets *La chimie agricole mise à la portée de tout le monde* (Québec, 1847), *Cours de chimie* (Québec, 1850), and *Manifeste adressé au peuple du Canada par le comité constitutionnel de la réforme et du progrès* (Québec, 1847); in his active membership in cultural and scientific organizations; in his public lectures; and finally in his establishment (1839) of an active theatrical group, 'Les amateurs typographes', whose influence would continue for a generation.

Aubin is the subject of an excellent monograph by J.-P. Tremblay, *À la recherche de Napoléon Aubin* (1969), in which Tremblay disproves the previously accepted attribution of the anonymous novel *Le rebelle* (1842) to Aubin. L. E. DOUCETTE

Aude. Pseudonym of Claudette Charbonneau-Tissot. See FANTASTIC LITERATURE AND SCIENCE FICTION IN FRENCH.

Audet, **Noël** (b. 1938). Born in Maria (Bonaventure) in the Gaspé area of Quebec, he was educated at the Collège Bourget (B.A., 1959), Université Laval (Licence ès Lettres, 1962), and the Sorbonne, Paris (Ph. D., 1965; thesis on Paul Valéry). He then became a professor of literature at the Université du Québec à Montréal. His literary career began with *Figures parallèles* (1963), a collection of poems in which, as in *La tête barbare* (1968), he questions language and its forms in an intellectual Quebec deeply involved in the *JOUAL* debate. After more than a decade of silence, his collection of short stories examining the real and not-so-real lives of the inhabitants of Gaspé, *Quand la voile faseille* (1980), was highly praised. In the first of his five novels, *Ah, l'amour l'amour* (1981), the reader follows a couple, destined soon to separate, in a journey through the Gaspé. Inspired by a trip to the coast of Gaspésie in 1944 taken by one of André Breton's characters, Élisa, this novel once again afforded Audet the opportunity to tell legends and humorous stories from his native Gaspésie, and to establish a symbiotic relationship between nature and his characters. Much less poetic and intimate, *La parade* (1984) concentrates on the economical, political, and amorous problems of four more-than-average Montrealers in the critical 1968-72 period. Never far from the surface, language comes back to haunt this book through Toto-lebègue, a secondary character who opens and closes the novel. He attains the ability to speak properly after the death of his mother, for which he is partly responsible. *L'ombre de l'épervier* (1988) gave Audet a wider readership. Structured around three generations of Gaspesians (Pauline, the mother, Catherine, her daughter, and Martin, Pauline's out-of-wedlock son), this saga carries the reader through the entire twentieth century, in a shrewd mixture of reality and fiction. In *L'eau blanche* (1992), still sustained by his own region's myths and traditions, Audet tells the story of two men, one white and one Native, neither of whom is ever entirely right nor entirely wrong in their motives, and their quest for Quebec's Far North. *Frontières ou tableaux d'Amérique* (1995) is a series of seven strolls through North and South America by a universal mother from different times and different countries.

Although he freely uses humour in his first novels, Audet progressively became more philosophical and serious in his study of the human condition. In a powerful and polemic essay, *Écrire de la fiction au Québec* (1990), he proposed, among other original and controversial ideas, the establishment of a linguistic norm for Quebec writing, purged of anglicisms and enriched by *québécismes*.

See Réginald Martel, anim., *Entrevue avec Noël Audet* (video recording, Université de Montréal, 1985).

See also NOVELS IN FRENCH 1982 TO 1996. JEAN LEVASSEUR

Avison, **Margaret** (b. 1918). Born in Galt, Ontario, the daughter of a Methodist minister, she grew up in Calgary. She studied at Victoria College, University of Toronto, graduating with a B.A. in English in 1940. Her first published poem, 'Gatineau', had appeared the previous year in *The CANADIAN FORUM*. She worked for the educational book publisher W.J. Gage and then for the Canadian Institute of International Affairs as an editor in the Information Service until the end of the war. While working as a librarian at the University of Toronto, she published *A history of Ontario* (1951), a textbook for use at the high-school level. Between 1955 and 1957, and with the aid of a Guggenheim Fellowship, she attended schools of creative writing at the universities of Indiana and Chicago. She returned to the University of Toronto to do graduate work from 1963 to 1966, and then taught at the university's Scarborough College. In 1968 she began work as a social worker for the Presbyterian Church Mission, Evangel Hall, in Toronto. From 1973 she worked in the archive division of the Canadian Broadcasting Corporation and, after 1978, with the Mustard Seed Mission in Toronto.

Avison has published six collections of poetry. *Winter sun* (1960), which won a Governor General's Award, is intensely metaphysical, concerned with problems of belief and moral knowledge. The title refers to the soul's weather; the peculiarly beautiful but desolate light of a winter sun is a metaphor for the poet's state on the edge of imminent revelation: 'Light, the discovering light, is a beginning/where many stillnesses/yearn' ('Prelude'). Stylistically difficult, sometimes excessively introspective, the poems are concerned with seeing. The controlling image is the 'optic heart' ('Snow'), which must venture on a quest for spiritual understanding. The American poet Cid Corman, in a commentary on *Winter sun*, spoke of the poet's protective coloration, as if Avison were hiding behind language ('Response', *Origin: featuring Margaret Avison*, 4 Jan. 1962). In Avison's second collection, *The dumbfounding* (1966), the language and imagery are less inward. The title poem records the experience of a religious vision that confirmed the poet's commitment to the Christian faith, which was to direct her future work: 'what before was *Possibility* is now *God*' ('Strong yellow, for reading aloud'). These two collections have been published together in the Modern Canadian Poets series: *Winter sun/The dumbfounding: poems 1940-66* (1982). Profoundly affected by the Hungarian uprising of 1956, Avison undertook to prepare English versions of eight poems for *The plough and the pen: writings from Hungary 1930-1956* (1963), edited by Ilona Duczynska and Karl Polanyi, a book that helped to bring international recognition to some of the most notable twentieth-century Hungarian poets.

Avison's third collection, *Sunblue* (1978), is the product of a profound religious conviction. Many of the poems are based on biblical myths and are increasingly orthodox in tone and vocabulary. However, Avison resists writing didactic poetry, and—like Gerard Manley Hopkins, with whom she is often compared—explores her Christian vision in poems about nature, where the natural world is used metaphorically to locate spiritual realities.

Avison is not a prolific writer. Her fifth book of poems, *No time* (1989), which also won a Governor General's Award, appeared after a silence of eleven years. It is a personal book about death and the loss of friends, in particular the poet b.p. NICHOL and a childhood friend, Josephine Grimshaw, who is the subject of the most eloquent sequence in the book, 'The Jo Poems'. All Avison's skill is evident: the play of rhythm and enjambment, the syntactical complexity and metaphysical imagery in the tradition of seventeenth-century poets like Donne and Herbert; and yet the poems are astonishingly direct. One feels the personal cost to Avison as she mourns these friends 'clear now of time and unforgettable'. There are no false consolations here in her struggle to find a spiritual affirmation in the face of death's brutal finality: 'Dying is fall/of leaf, or day./A body sculptures desuetude,/outguttering. And yet, it will,/in time, know everlasting awe.' Few Canadian poets can match Avison in the sophistication and beauty of her linguistic and imagistic gifts, and even the reader who does not share her religious belief will find in her poetry a profound and imaginative perception of reality.

Margaret Avison: selected poems (1991) contains selections from her previous volumes as well as a number of new and previously uncollected poems; it also includes her 'adaptations' of poems by the Hungarian poets Gyula Illyes and Ferenc Juhasz, from the literal translations by Ilona Duczynska. Avison's latest book, *A kind of perseverance* (1993), contains two lectures delivered at the annual Pascal Lectures on Christianity and the University, at the University of Waterloo, Ontario; they record the journey, in her words 'often unfocused', that finally led to her Christian conversion.

For further reading on Avison, see Ernest Redekop, *Margaret Avison* (1970), in the Studies in Canadian Literature series, and a collection of reminiscences and critical essays, *'Lighting up the terrain': the poetry of Margaret Avison* (1987) edited by David Kent.

ROSEMARY SULLIVAN

Awards. Until the nineteen-twenties there were few Canadian literary prizes, though the lack was alleviated to some extent by the awarding to Canadians of foreign prizes. In 1925 the Dodd-Mead Prize was given to Martha OSTENSO's *Wild Geese*, and in 1927 Mazo DE LA ROCHE won the Atlantic Monthly Prize for *JALNA*. These American awards were announced 'triumphantly' in the *Canadian Bookman* and *The CANADIAN FORUM*, and helped contribute to a mood of literary nationalism and optimism that persisted until the stock-market crash of 1929.

Awards

Publishers and literary associations gradually began to favour the establishment of literary prizes as a device for 'making literature hum' (and, consequently, for selling books and subscriptions). In 1922 the Province of Quebec established a $5000 annual fund for literary prizes, and the CANADIAN AUTHORS' ASSOCIATION (CAA) lobbied the Government of Ontario to create similar awards. In 1926 the first Lorne Pierce Gold Medal was awarded by the Royal Society of Canada to Charles G.D. ROBERTS. A decade later the CAA persuaded Lord Tweedsmuir to establish the annual GOVERNOR GENERAL'S LITERARY AWARDS (GGA). Now, sixty years later, there is a range of Canadian literary prizes that is broad by any standard, though proliferation is a fairly recent phenomenon—beginning in the 1970s with an explosion of literary activity and unparalleled expansion in the book trade.

An overview of Canadian literary prizes necessarily begins with those of particular national and international importance. These awards are long-established, or richly endowed, or both. Launched by the CAA in 1937, the Governor General's Literary Awards have evolved into Canada's premier literary prizes. In 1959 the CANADA COUNCIL took over partial responsibility for the awards, creating matching categories for works in French. Prizes of $10,000 and a specially bound copy of the winning book are presented annually for works in several genres in English and in French. The $10,000 Journey Prize was established in 1988 through the generosity of American novelist James Michener, who directed that all Canadian royalties from his novel *Journey* (published by McCLELLAND & STEWART) be used in support of developing Canadian writers. The Lorne Pierce Medal of the Royal Society of Canada is awarded every two years for an achievement 'of special significance and conspicuous merit in imaginative or critical literature' written in either English or French, and preferably dealing with a Canadian subject. The award commemorates Lorne PIERCE, editor of The RYERSON PRESS for more than forty years. The W.H. Smith/*Books in Canada* First Novel Award was instituted in 1977, becoming the Chapters/*Books in Canada* Award in 1996; the value of the prize is $5000. Michael ONDAATJE was the first co-winner and Keath FRASER won it in 1996. The $100,000 Prix Gilles-Corbeil is Canada's largest literary prize. Established in 1990, it is awarded every three years to a French-language writer in recognition of his or her entire literary output. The Giller Prize awards $25,000 annually to the author of the best Canadian full-length novel or collection of short stories published in English. Named in honour of the late literary journalist Doris Giller, it was founded by her husband Jack Rabinovitch in 1994. The CBC/*Saturday Night* Literary Awards were established in 1979. Formerly called the CBC Radio Literary Competition, the awards were enlarged in 1994 and given in conjunction with *Saturday Night* magazine: $10,000 prizes are awarded in each of three categories: fiction, poetry, and personal essay. The Canada Council's Molson Prize acknowledges Canadian citizens whose contributions have enriched the cultural or intellectual heritage of Canada. Two prizes of $50,000 are awarded annually, one for outstanding achievement in the arts, the other in humanities or social sciences. Winners have included Morley CALLAGHAN, Robertson DAVIES, Margaret ATWOOD, Alice MUNRO, Michel TREMBLAY, and Mavis GALLANT.

The Stephen LEACOCK Memorial Medal was established in 1946. It is accompanied by a cash award of $5000, and is presented to the author of what is judged to be the best book of humour published in Canada during the previous year. The Philips Information Systems Literary Prize is awarded annually in October in conjunction with the International Festival of Authors at HARBOURFRONT CENTRE, Toronto. It honours a general contribution to Canadian literature and is open to authors, editors, and journalists. The award is a cash prize of $5000 and the latest-model Philips word-processor or personal computer. Winners have included Margaret Atwood, Michael Ondaatje, and Douglas FETHERLING. Barbara GOWDY, Edna ALFORD, and Joan BARFOOT have been winners of the $10,000 Marian ENGEL Award, established in 1986 to honour outstanding women writers. Among the several author-of-the-year awards is the Canadian Booksellers' Association prize, first given in 1972. Originally known as the Canadian Booksellers' Association Book Award, it recognizes a Canadian author for a body of work and contribution to Canadian literature. Winners have included Carol SHIELDS, Michael Ondaatje, and Farley MOWAT. The Prix Esso du Cercle du Livre de France provides an annual $5000 award for a French-language work by a Canadian author. The Canadian Authors' Association Literary Awards were established in 1975 'to honour writing that achieves literary excellence without sacrificing popular appeal'. Winners in four categories (fiction, non-fiction, poetry, and drama) receive prizes of $5000 and silver medals.

Prizes for children's literature are especially numerous in Canada. Since 1987 the Governor General's Awards for Children's Literature (formerly named the Canada Council Prizes for Children's Literature) have provided $10,000 annual prizes for children's writers and illustrators. The Silver Birch Awards were established in 1963 by the Ontario Library Association. Each year more than 15,000 Ontario schoolchildren vote to select winners in fiction and non-fiction categories. Winners have included Carol Matas, Laurie McGaw, and Kit PEARSON. The Ruth Schwartz Children's Book Award was established in 1975 in memory of a Toronto bookseller; the $2000 prize is awarded annually to the writer or creative source of an outstanding work of Canadian children's literature, and a jury of children chooses the winner. The IODE Book Award has been presented since 1975 to encourage the publication of books for children between the ages of six and twelve years; it carries a prize of $1000 and an inscribed scroll. The Young Adult Canadian Book Award was established by the Saskatchewan Library Association in 1981. Winners have included Susan Reynolds, Janet LUNN, and Monica HUGHES. Established in 1987, the Sheila A. Egoff Children's Prize (British Columbia Book Prizes) annually awards $1000 to an author or illustrator, or both. The Vicky Metcalf Award ($2000) is presented by the Canadian Authors' Association to an author for a body of work (more than three books) 'inspirational to Canadian youth'. The Canadian Library Association's Book of the Year for Children is awarded annually, the prize a sterling gilt medal 'suitably engraved'. Winners have included Kevin MAJOR, Kit Pearson, and Brian DOYLE. The Geoffrey Bilson Award for Historical Fiction was established in 1988 in memory of children's author Geoffrey Bilson, and is administered by the Canadian Children's Book Centre. The $1000 award is made for an 'outstanding work of historical fiction for young people'. Mr. Christie's Book Award was first presented in 1989; winners are awarded cash prizes of $7500 each. The $500 Ann Connor Brimer Award is presented annually by the Nova Scotia Library Association for 'an outstanding contribution to children's literature by an author residing in Atlantic Canada'. The R. Ross Annett Award for Children's Literature is presented annually by the Writers Guild of Alberta. Established in 1993, the Joyce Barkhouse Award is awarded annually by the Writers' Federation of Nova Scotia.

In addition to the prestigious Governor General's Awards for Poetry, there are other important prizes for poets. The bp NICHOL Chap-Book Award, established in 1986, offers a prize of $1,000 for the best poetry chapbook in English published in Canada during the previous year. The annual Pat LOWTHER Memorial Award is presented by The LEAGUE OF CANADIAN POETS for a book of poetry by a Canadian woman. It carries a $1000 prize. Winners have included Lorna CROZIER and Beth Goobie. Also sponsored by the League is the Gerald Lampert Memorial Award: a prize of $1000 for the first book of poetry by a Canadian poet published in the preceding year. The Archibald LAMPMAN Poetry Award, established in 1986 by Ottawa Independent Writers, is awarded to the author of the 'best collection of English language poetry produced by a writer in the Ottawa area'. The Milton ACORN Memorial People's Poetry Award was established in 1987 as an alternative prize to the GGA, and its value fluctuates from year to year according to the amount of donations received; winners have included Marty Gervais and Louise Halfe. In 1991 the family of poet Gwendolyn MacEWEN presented the first Gwendolyn MacEwen Memorial Award to Eddy Yanofsky. The $1000 prize is given annually to a Canadian poet publishing work for the first time in a literary magazine. The $5000 Prix Émile NELLIGAN is awarded annually for a book of poetry by a Quebec writer.

Prizes given for fiction include the Ethel WILSON Fiction Prize, one of annual B.C. Book Prizes; winners have included George McWHIRTER, Keath Fraser, and Audrey THOMAS. The Arthur Ellis Awards were established in 1984 to honour the authors of 'outstanding works in the genre of crime writing in Canada'. Recipients are awarded the 'Arthur', a wooden figure hanging from a gibbet, along with cash prizes as sponsorship allows. The Foundation Awards for Fiction, formerly known as the McClelland & Stewart Awards, are presented annually by the National Magazine Awards Foundation. The biennial Howard O'HAGAN Award for Short Fiction is sponsored by the Writers Guild of Alberta; winners have included Cecilia Frey and W.P. KINSELLA. Established—at first with tongue in cheek—by Mordecai RICHLER, the Prix Parizeau was awarded for the first time in 1996, providing $3000 for 'the best work of fiction by an ethnic Quebecer'. The Canadian Science Fiction and Fantasy Awards (Aurora Awards) are presented annually for both French and English-language science fiction.

Awards

The Thomas RADDALL Atlantic Fiction Award of $2000 is given each year to a resident of Atlantic Canada by the Writers Federation of Nova Sotia.

Awards for drama include the Canadian Children's Play Award, established in 1982, honouring outstanding creators of plays for school-age children; a total of $16,000 is divided among the winner and runners-up. The Dora Mavor Moore Awards were established in 1981 to acknowledge 'outstanding achievement in the theatre season of metropolitan Toronto'. The $24,000 Floyd S. Chalmers Canadian Play Award is presented each year by the Ontario Arts Council for 'the most outstanding Canadian play produced by any theatre organization in Canada'.

Several awards honour literary translators and critics. The John GLASSCO Translation Prize is presented each year by the Literary Translators Association of Canada for a translator's first work in book-length literary translation into French or English. The prize honours the memory of one of Canada's notable writers and translators, and is intended to encourage new practitioners of literary translation. To encourage the study of Canadian literature, *Essays on Canadian Writing* established the George Wicken Prize in 1985. A $200 award is given to the student who submits the best critical essay on any aspect of Canadian literature. The Nathan COHEN Award is presented annually by the Canadian Theatre Critics Association to 'critics residing or working in Canada'. Under the aegis of the Canada Council, the $10,000 Japan-Canada Prize is awarded annually for books translated into English or French from the Japanese.

Many local and regional prizes are awarded across Canada, and the following are representative. The Prix Molson was established in 1983. Jointly sponsored by the Union des écrivains québécois and the Académie canadienne-francaise, it provides a $5000 prize to the author of a French-language novel appearing during the previous year. Since 1988 QSPELL Awards of $2000 each have been presented in the categories of poetry, fiction, and non-fiction for books of outstanding literary excellence published by Quebec authors. The City of Montreal and the Salon du Livre de Montréal jointly sponsor the annual Prix du Livre de Montréal, which provides an award of $10,000 for the author of a book published during the preceding year. Winners must be residents of Montreal. In British Columbia, the B.C. Book Prizes (established 1986) are given annually for fiction, non-fiction, poetry, children's literature, and publishing excellence. Winners receive cash awards of $1000 each.

The Manitoba Book of the Year is intended to honour and draw public attention to the high quality of Manitoba writing. The award of $2500 was created by booksellers Paul and Holly McNally in 1988. The City of Toronto Book Awards were established in 1973 by Toronto City Council to honour authors of 'books of literary excellence that are evocative of the city'. The annual Trillium Book Award provides a $12,000 prize for the best 'Ontario-authored' book. In Newfoundland, prizes are awarded for poetry and fiction in the annual Newfoundland and Labrador Arts and Letters Competition. The annual Saskatchewan Writers Guild Literary Awards were first presented in 1971. They are given to recognize excellence in work by Saskatchewan writers in six categories: drama, humour, short fiction, poetry, non-fiction, and children's literature.

A time-honoured and prevalent class of Canadian literary awards is that of the magazine or festival contest. Journals have long used the lure of prizes to attract attention, subscriptions, and new talent. The Pottersfield Portfolio Compact Fiction/Short Poem Competition is typical. Writers pay an entry fee that entitles them to a one-year subscription to the magazine, and winners receive $100 each. The annual *Fiddlehead* Writing Contest awards prizes of $300 for best poem and best story, which are subsequently published in *The* FIDDLEHEAD. The *Prism International* Short Fiction Contest awards $3000 annually. *Arc* sponsors an annual Poem of the Year contest, with prizes totalling $2250 and an entry fee of $12.00. Again, all entrants receive a subscription to the magazine. *The Claremont Review*, *CONTEMPORARY VERSE II*, *PRAIRIE FIRE*, *filling station*, and *sub-Terrain* hold similar events. The *NeWest Review* puts a spin on awards for new writers with its Late Bloomers Writing Contest: prizes are given for unpublished fiction by writers over the age of forty. Since 1977 ANVIL PRESS has sponsored an annual Three-Day Novel Writing Contest. Entrants pay a $25.00 fee, and work feverishly over the end-of-summer holiday weekend. The Eden Mills Writing Contest for New Writers awards prizes for short fiction, poetry, and drama, with a $5.00 entry fee. The WRITERS' UNION OF CANADA sponsors a Short Prose Competition for Developing Writers, with prizes of $2500 and $1000. The entry fee is $25.00. Entrants in *Books in Canada*'s annual Student Writing Awards competition can win up to $500.

Untypically, *Books in Canada* does not demand an entry fee.

Finally, there are a number of Canadian prizes that reach beyond the borders of the nation. The Canada-Australia Literary Prize was established in 1976 to familiarize Australians and Canadians with each others' writers. It is presented each year, alternately to an English-language Canadian writer and an Australian writer, and recognizes a writer's entire work. Open to poets, fiction writers, and playwrights, the value of the prize is $3000, presented in the country making the award. The Canada-French Community of Belgium Literary Prize was created in 1971 to promote Canadian and Belgian French-language literature. It is awarded in alternate years to a writer from the French community of Belgium and to a Canadian writer. The Prix France-Québec Jean HAMELIN was established by the Association des écrivains de langue française in 1965. It is given annually to a French-language writer for a body of work; winners travel to Paris to receive an award of 2000 francs. The $2500 Canada-Switzerland Literary Prize is awarded yearly by the Canada Council and the Swiss Fondation Pro Helvetia to a Canadian or Swiss writer for a work of poetry, fiction, drama, or non-fiction.

GORD RIPLEY

Awful disclosures of Maria Monk (New York, 1836). In Oct. 1835 the *American Protestant Vindicator*, a New York newspaper supported by the Rev. W.C. Brownlee and the Rev. George Bourne, both of whom had recently published works of anti-Catholic propaganda, announced that a young woman was preparing the story of her life as a nun in the Hôtel-Dieu Nunnery in Montreal; the story, *Awful disclosures of Maria Monk, as exhibited in a narrative of her sufferings during a residence of five years as a novice, and two years as a Black Nun, in the Hotel Dieu Nunnery at Montreal*, appeared in Jan. 1836. It describes the travails of Monk, a young woman born a Protestant in St John's, Lower Canada (Quebec), who, after attending convent schools, converts to Roman Catholicism and becomes a nun of the Hôtel-Dieu. There she learns, among other things, that nuns are forced to 'live in the practice of criminal intercourse with the priests' and that the offspring from these unions are killed after being baptized, their corpses thrown into lime-pits in the convent's cellar. At last, finding herself pregnant by 'Father Phelan', Monk escapes to the United States to save her child and rediscover her Protestant faith.

Awful disclosures caused a sensation. Thousands of copies were sold, and it became a topic of discussion in newspapers in the United States and Canada. Although many believed its revelations, others—especially both Roman Catholics and Protestants in Montreal—denied their veracity. An affidavit, attributed to a woman said to be her mother, claimed that Maria Monk, subject to 'occasional mental derangement', had been taken advantage of by 'designing men' to make 'scandalous accusations against the priests and nuns of Montreal'. The 'designing men'—George Bourne; Theodore Dwight, to whom Monk was supposed to have dictated her story; William K. Hoyt[e], who allegedly brought her from Montreal; and the Rev. John J. Slocum, who became her legal guardian—were each said by contemporary sources to be the real author of *Awful disclosures*. The resemblances between it and other nuns' stories typical of the anticonventual strain in Gothic fiction were noticed. A second edition (New York, 1836) contained as appendices 'Reception of the first editions'; 'Sequel of her narrative'; 'Review of the case'; a supplement 'Giving more particulars of the nunnery and grounds'; and 'Plan of the nunnery'. *Further disclosures by Maria Monk concerning the Hotel Dieu Nunnery of Montreal* (New York, 1837) included Slocum's *Reply to the priest's book*, his attempt to refute the *Awful exposure of the atrocious plot formed by certain individuals, against the clergy and nuns of Lower Canada through the intervention of Maria Monk* . . . (New York, 1836).

The 'Maria Monk affair', however, soon ran into trouble. When the Hôtel-Dieu Nunnery was inspected and found to be unlike Monk's description of it, even Protestant believers began to doubt her narrative. Her supporters quarrelled among themselves. In May 1837 Monk and Slocum charged in a court case that Harper Brothers had 'wrongfully possessed' stereotyped plates of a work called 'The Hotel Dieu Nunnery Unveiled', 'pretended to take out another copyright of the work under the name 'Awful Disclosures, . . . in Massachusetts, . . . published a large number of impressions . . . and had large profits'. The judge dismissed the complaint, but advised the two litigants to sue the Harpers for damages. Since there was no suit, and since no copy of *Awful disclosures* that names the Harpers as publishers apparently survives, their role in Maria Monk's story remains unclear. After the court case Monk, possibly pregnant for a second time, left Slocum and disappeared. She is supposed to have died in prison in 1849, after being arrested as a pickpocket.

Awful disclosures nevertheless remains interesting. Its motifs of subterranean passages, imprisoned nuns, and secret murders link it to the Gothic novel and show how suitable this type of fiction was for anti-Catholic literature. Its origin in New York City reveals how strong anti-Catholic feeling was among certain American Protestants in the 1830s, and how easily it was projected onto what they perceived as the exotic, mysterious setting of French-Canadian, Roman Catholic Quebec. The story's popularity in England suggests that it also became part of the anti-Catholic literature and feeling there. In *Lectures on the present position of Catholics in England* (1851), John Henry Newman analyses the role the 'very wicked, very mischievous' Maria Monk and her 'Awful Disclosures' played for English Protestants; he also notes that since 1836, 'from 200,000 to 250,000 copies' of 'the calumny' had been put into circulation in America and England. In the twentieth century, editions, translations, and commentaries emphasize the continued fascination of this sensational but essentially sorry tale that is now read not only as an anti-Catholic tract but as an example of the 'cultural anxiety' felt in the United States in the nineteenth century by Protestant men about the spiritual reliability of Protestant women.

The contemporary response to *Awful disclosures* is conveyed in such newspapers as *The New York Herald* (1836 ff.). In *Maria Monk's daughter: an autobiography* (New York, 1874), Mrs L. St John Eckel (Lizzie Harper), claiming to be Monk's daughter, includes an extract from the court's judgement in the copyright case (pp. 171-3). A modern reprint of *Awful disclosures* (Hamden, Conn.: Archon Books, 1962) contains an introduction by Ray Allan Billington—largely based on his essay 'Maria Monk and her influence', *Catholic Historical Review*, XXII (Oct. 1936)—in which he calls the book 'the most influential single work of anti-Catholic propaganda in America's history'. See also Ralph Thompson, 'The Maria Monk affair', *The Colophon* 17, 6 (1934); B. Dufebvre (Emile Castonguay), 'Le "roman" de Maria Monk', *La Revue de l'Université Laval*, VIII (fév. 1954); and Susan M. Griffin, 'Awful disclosures: women's evidence in the escaped nun's tale', *PMLA* 3,1 (1996).

MARY JANE EDWARDS

B

Babiuk, Andrii. See UKRAINIAN-CANADIAN LITERATURE.

Backwoods of Canada, The (London, 1836). Catharine Parr TRAILL's first 'Canadian' book is composed of eighteen letters to family and friends in Suffolk, England. Beginning with the departure of Thomas and Catharine Traill from Scotland in July 1832, the letters follow their progress through the spring of 1835, by which time, with the help of Catharine's brother Samuel Strickland, they were comfortably settled in their own log house on the shore of Lake Katchewanook, near present-day Lakefield, Ontario. The manuscript letters were sent to England, likely to Catharine's sister Agnes Strickland, and were recommended for publication by Charles Knight, who at that time was the publishing supervisor for the Society of Useful Knowledge. Knight hastily included the book in the Society's popular series The Library of Entertaining Knowledge, under the title *The backwoods of Canada: being letters from the wife of an emigrant officer, illustrative of the domestic economy of British America.* Traill made some late additions to her manuscript at Knight's request and it appeared in print in two parts in January 1836, a mere seven months after Knight had received it.

The book not only provides a record of the Traills' adventures and adjustments as settlers but also dispenses useful information and practical advice for the womenfolk of British families contemplating 'a home amid our Canadian wilds'. The letters are of an optimistic and reassuring cast, drawing deeply upon Traill's fund of Christian patience and her faith in British character. Throughout, she is cheerful, uncomplaining, curious, adaptive, and practical. Unlike her sister Susanna MOODIE—who in *ROUGHING IT IN THE BUSH* (1852) emphasized her personal emotions and candid reactions to bush life and dwelt upon the felt loss of her English home—Traill concentrates on what stimulates her curiosity and interest. Acknowledging that she has little aptitude for imaginative flights, and believing that in the Upper Canadian backwoods, 'Fancy would starve for lack of marvellous food,' she attends instead to the settlers, the Native people she meets, domestic details characteristic of backwoods life, and the flora and fauna she discovers in the woods around her. 'Habit reconciles us to many things that at first were distasteful,' she writes. Her adaptive attitude, her eye for the picturesque, and her commitment to objectivity (as she saw it) contribute to one of the best-written records of settlement experience and the early British presence in Upper Canada. If she is selective in her documentation, that strategy is but a part of the insistently positive and pragmatic outlook that was one of her strengths as both a pioneer and a writer.

See the NEW CANADIAN LIBRARY edition (1989) with an Afterword by D.M.R. Bentley; Carl Ballstadt, 'Catharine Parr Traill' in *Canadian writers and their works*, fiction series, vol. 1 (1983). A scholarly edition of *The backwoods of Canada*, edited by Michael Peterman, was published by the CENTRE FOR EDITING EARLY CANADIAN TEXTS in 1997.

MICHAEL PETERMAN

Bacque, James (b. 1929). Born in Toronto and educated at Upper Canada College and the University of Toronto, he worked as an assistant editor on *Saturday Night*, as editor of *Canadian Packaging and Canadian Homes*, and as trade editor for the MACMILLAN COMPANY OF CANADA (1961-8). He was a co-founder of New Press, Toronto, in 1969. Until recently, Bacque was best known for three modestly successful novels. *The lonely ones* (1969), reprinted in paperback as *Big lonely* (1971), depicts a painter who becomes involved in the activities of a separatist cell in Quebec in the 1960s. In *A man of talent* (1972), a bright young man, who is dean of arts at a university, becomes caught up in a conflict between student radicals and the university administration. *The Queen comes to Minnicog* (1979) portrays a fictional visit of the Queen of England to a small Georgian Bay town, employing to humorous effect stock rural types, farcical situations, and dialogue heavily dependent on malapropisms.

More recently Bacque has become known for his non-fiction, notably the controversial *Other losses: an investigation into the mass deaths of German prisoners at the hands of the French and Americans after World War II* (1989), and *Just Raoul: adventures in the French resistance* (1991).

MARILYN ROSE

Bailey, Alfred Goldsworthy (b. 1905). Born in Quebec City, he received his early schooling there, then completed a B.A. at the University of New Brunswick in 1927; he took his M.A. and Ph.D. (1934) at the University of Toronto, combining studies in history, anthropology, archaeology, and art. On a Royal Society fellowship he completed his formal education at the London School of Economics. In 1935 he became assistant director and associate curator of the New Brunswick Museum, and in 1937 professor of history at the University of New Brunswick, where he remained head of the department for more than thirty years. Now Professor Emeritus at UNB, he held there the positions of dean of arts (1946-64), honorary librarian (1946-70), and vice-president academic (1965-70). He was made a Fellow of the Royal Society of Canada in 1951 and an Officer of the Order of Canada in 1978.

Bailey's career as a poet began with *Songs of the Saguenay* (1927) and *Tao* (1930), traditional verse in the style of the Canadian romantics. When he met such writers as Robert FINCH and Earle BIRNEY in Toronto, he began experimenting with new forms. As teacher and poet in Fredericton—where he helped to establish a poetry club and a magazine, *The FIDDLEHEAD*—he strongly influenced such younger writers as Fred COGSWELL and Robert GIBBS. His mature work appeared in *Border River* (1952), *Thanks for a drowned island* (1973), and *Miramichi lightning: the collected poems of Alfred Bailey* (1981). Bailey's concerns in these books are personal, social, and intellectual, stemming from his background and his close involvement with the culture of his own community. His central themes are the impingement of one culture on another, the aspirations of explorers and settlers, and the difficulties of maintaining continuity and purpose. His style is compact and elliptical; sometimes playful, sometimes difficult.

Bailey's doctoral thesis, *The conflict of European and eastern Algonkian cultures, 1504-1700: a study in Canadian civilization* (1937; 2nd edn 1969), is now recognized as seminal in its field. As an editor of the *Literary history of Canada* (1965), he contributed the chapter 'Overture to nationhood'. His *Culture and nationality: essays by A.G. Bailey* (1972) contains the important 'Creative moments in the culture of the Maritime Provinces'. Noteworthy appraisals of Bailey's poetry are Albert MORITZ's 'Faith, hope and charity', a review article in *Books in Canada* (Aug./Sept. 1982) and M. Travis LANE's 'A sense of the medium: the poetry of A.G. Bailey' in *Canadian Poetry* 19 (Fall/Winter 1986). Travis Lane's 'An interview with A.G. Bailey' appeared in *Studies in Canadian Literature* 11:2 (1986).

ROBERT GIBBS

Bailey, Jacob (1731-1808). Born in Rowley, Massachusetts, he graduated from Harvard in 1755. After a brief career as a school teacher and Congregationalist minister, he converted to the Church of England. Ordained priest in 1760, and appointed to a frontier parish at Pawnalborough, Maine (then part of Massachusetts), he was resented by the largely Congregationalist community. As America slid towards open defiance of British authority, resentment of Bailey and the state-supported Church he represented sharpened. From 1774 on he was frequently harassed and assaulted. In 1779 he was permitted to depart as a Loyalist refugee for Nova Scotia, where he served as parish priest at Cornwallis (1779-82) and at Annapolis Royal (1782-1808).

Bailey left a voluminous amount of correspondence, journals, sermons, moral commentaries, histories, expository prose 'descriptions', fiction, and poetry. William S. Bartlet published selections from the journals and correspondence in *The frontier missionary* (Boston, 1853), but most of his work was never published. His most interesting works of non-fiction are his sermons—written in a clear, simple style, their tone amiable and intelligent—and his geographical 'descriptions', which are designed for the average intelligent reader: one is on Maine in the 1760s; the other describes Nova Scotia in the 1780s and employs a journey motif.

Bailey's fiction consists mainly of two incomplete novels—interesting attempts to integrate form and intention in the early North American novel. 'The flower of the wilderness' is a mixture of narrative, letter, and dialogue, set in frontier New England. A later and more coherent work structurally is 'Serena' (*c.* 1786-90), an epistolary novel about a Nova Scotian Loyalist girl who is captured and carried back to New England by rebel privateers.

Bailey's most sustained literary achievement lay in poetry. The best poem from his American period is 'Farewell to Kennebec' (1779), a valedictory lamenting his exile from Maine. The finest practitioner of Hudibrastic verse satire after Samuel Butler himself, Bailey produced a large number of verse satires. 'Character of a trimmer' (1779-80) attacks political fence-sitters as well as rebels, but much of its sharpness is lost in its dual focus. In 'America' (1780-4), an incomplete poem designed to present the Loyalist view of the causes of the Revolution, Bailey's satiric verse becomes a trenchant and incisive instrument for clarifying and articulating his fears, frustrations, and moral indignation. After the war Bailey turned his attention to social and political concerns pertinent to the emerging post-war society of Nova Scotia. His most ambitious poem, 'The adventures of Jack Ramble, the Methodist preacher' (*c.* 1785-late 1790s), incomplete in over 9200 lines, attacks evangelical itinerant preachers as purveyors of irrationality and immorality and as promoters of disrespect for all forms of order; it also deplores the increase of religious dissenters that undermined the strength of the Established Church, which together with government ensured the stability and order of society.

See R.P. Baker, 'The poetry of Jacob Bailey', *New England Quarterly* II (1929); Thomas B. Vincent, 'Alline and Bailey', *CANADIAN LITERATURE* 68-69 (Spring/Summer 1976); T.B. Vincent, ed., *Narrative verse satire in Maritimes Canada 1779-1814* (1978); and Thomas B. Vincent, 'The poetic development of Jacob Bailey', *Early American Literature* XIV (1979).

TOM VINCENT

Baillargeon, Pierre. See ESSAYS IN FRENCH: 5 and NOVELS IN FRENCH 1940 TO 1952:2.

Baird, Irene (1901-81). Born in England, Irene Todd came with her parents to British Columbia in 1919 and pursued a career as a reporter for the *Vancouver Sun* and the *Daily Province*. She later married John Baird. In 1942 she joined the National Film Board and worked primarily in publicity and public relations. At her retirement from the federal civil service she was chief of information for the Department of Indian Affairs and Northern Development.

Baird's first novel, *John* (1937), restrained in style and precise in plotting, is a study of John Dorey, a Scot who has created a ten-acre haven for himself on Vancouver Island. Despite its love interest and a feud with a neighbour who is cruel to animals, the novel centres on the description and revelation of Dorey's character. *Waste heritage* (1939), her second novel, is an unacknowledged classic of Canadian literature. Initially received as a stylistically imperfect but powerful and honest portrayal of the predicament and rage of the chronically unemployed in the Depression, it later came to be admired only for its accurate depiction of events based on the trek to Victoria by

1,000 unemployed after the forcible expulsion of the 'sit-downers' from the Vancouver Post Office in 1938. These views neglect the thematic consistency through which Baird creates a vision of an entire society straining under tensions that can lead only to fruitless destruction. Both major and minor characters are repeatedly caught between a frustrated rage that demands radical economic and social reform and a desperate loyalty to the mythology of capitalist democracy. The inevitable conclusion is government betrayal of the men's attempts at mass action to gain jobs and dignity, the arrest of the twenty-three-year-old hero Matt Striker, and the death of his companion Eddy, whose ideal of economic and social security has narrowed to a simple-minded obsession—getting a new pair of shoes. In her third novel, *He rides the sky* (1941), Baird chronicles, through his letters home to Victoria, the emotions and experiences of a young man who trains as a pilot with the RAF in 1938 and is lost in battle in 1940. Though the letters aim at creating a sense of spontaneity, their stylistic cohesiveness and painstaking detail render them artificial in tone and content. Also artificial is the persistently brash, enthusiastic naïvety of the hero, Peter O'Halloran. *Climate of power* (1971), Baird's last novel, is based on her experience of federal bureaucracy and her knowledge of the Arctic. Centring on the imminent retirement of George McKenna, it begins as an apparently mildly cynical examination of bureaucratic tactical politics and develops into a psychologically competent and carefully plotted study of the disintegration of McKenna's position and personality under the pressures of his young wife's infidelity and an accidental opportunity for murder. Underlying the plot are government's sincere but muddled attempts to improve Inuit culture—though in fact they destroy it.

See Roger Leslie Hyman, 'Wasted heritage and *Waste heritage*: the critical disregard of an important Canadian novel', *Journal of Canadian Studies* 17, no. 4 (Winter 1982/83).

ANTHONY HOPKINS

Baker, Nancy. See NOVELS IN ENGLISH 1983 TO 1996: OTHER NOVELS 4.

Baksh, Ishmael.. See CARIBBEAN-CANADIAN LITERATURE.

Balconville (1980). David FENNARIO's third published play was commissioned by Montreal's Centaur Theatre, where it was first produced (as a bilingual play) on 2 Jan. 1979. Also performed that same year in Toronto and Ottawa and later at London's Old Vic, it was generally acclaimed by the critics, receiving the 1979 Chalmers Award.

The action takes place in Pointe-Saint-Charles, Montreal, where the author grew up; the situations and characters are reminiscent of those described in his journal, *Without a parachute* (1972). Balconville is the name one of the characters ironically gives the working-class district where the balconies provide a dubious refuge from the stuffy exiguous apartments. Four of the characters are French Canadians, four are anglophones. The bilingual Bolduc (making only a brief appearance, of doubtful dramatic value, in the second act) is a corrupt politician, a mere tool of exploiters whose presence is felt throughout the play as loud-speakers blare out Bolduc's empty election promises.

Balconville has virtually no plot, the second act being almost a repetition of the first—though the situation has worsened for most of the characters. Paquette has lost his job, Tom's attempt at escaping from his environment has ended in failure, and Diane has decided to leave school to become a waitress.

On the balconies where they spend their summers, people are both observers and observed. Privacy is impossible, but paradoxically, because they are so close, they feel desperately lonely. True communication is non-existent; the play is one long quarrel from beginning to end. If there are moments of tenderness, their signs are usually misinterpreted. Prejudice, the language barrier, and the generation gap are obvious obstacles to communication, but the real obstacle is bitterness. For the people of *Balconville* life is a vicious circle from which there is no escape. When they have work, they hate what they are doing; those who have no work do not look for employment because they know they would find only menial, poor-paying jobs. Irène, the strongest character, realizes that they must help themselves, but she receives little support from those around her. Unable to face reality, they escape into cheap dreams.

In the last lines of the play the four English-speaking characters ask, 'What are we going to do?', which is echoed by the francophones' question, 'Qu'est-ce qu'on va faire?'. French and English are finally united in a mutual despair. Those final words, however, are addressed to the audience.

Selected criticism of *Balconville* is included in *Canadian drama and the critics* (rev. ed. 1995), edited by L.W. Conolly.

PAULETTE COLLET

Ballantyne, R.M. (1825-94). Robert Michael Ballantyne was born in Edinburgh, Scotland, to a family of printers and publishers brought down in the financial ruin of Sir Walter Scott, and received only two years of formal schooling before joining the Hudson's Bay Company at the age of sixteen. He served as a clerk at Fort Garry, Norway House, and York Factory from 1841 to 1845, when he was transferred to the Lower St Lawrence district, taking charge of posts at Île-Jérémie and Sept-Iles and wintering at Tadoussac before sailing home in May 1847.

His first book, *Hudson Bay; or Every-day life in the wilds of North America, during six years' residence in the territories of the Hon. Hudson Bay Company* (Edinburgh, 1848), was assembled from his journals and letters saved by his mother. With *Snowflakes and sunbeams; or, The young fur traders. A tale of the far North* (London, 1856) and *Ungava; a tale of Exquimaux-land* (London, 1858), he began a long and celebrated career as a writer of adventure stories for boys. While his most popular books included *The coral island* (London, 1858) and *Martin Rattler; or A boy's adventures in the forests of Brazil* (London, 1858), Ballantyne continued to exploit his experiences in the Northwest, setting more than twenty of his 120 books in the New World. In addition to boys' books such as *Away in the wilderness* (London, 1863), *The buffalo runners: a tale of the Red River* (London, 1891), and *The giant of the North* (London, 1882), he wrote fiction for a general audience, such as *The Red Man's revenge; a tale of the Red River flood* (London, 1880).

In Ballantyne's tales the Northwest—interchangeable with the wilds of Brazil or the high seas—is a conveniently exotic wilderness to try the daring of the heroes. In spite of his first-hand experience, his New World settings never exhibit any vivid particularity, and whatever the Company clerk must have learned about Canada's Native peoples never emerges through the romancer's stereotyped noble savages and heathen devils. See Eric Quayle, *Ballantyne the brave* (1967), and Eric Quayle, *R.M. Ballantyne: a bibliography of first editions* (1968). DICK HARRISON

Ballem, John (b. 1925). Born in New Glasgow, Nova Scotia, he was educated at Dalhousie University (B.A., 1946; M.A. 1948; LL.B. 1949) and Harvard Law School, where he took a post-graduate LL.M. (1950). In 1944-5 he was a pilot with the Royal Navy Fleet Air Arm; an assistant professor of law at the University of British Columbia, 1950-2; worked in the oil industry for a decade; and entered private law practice in Calgary in 1962. Ballem is an acknowledged legal authority on oil and gas and winner of the Petroleum Law Foundation Prize in 1973. In 1993 he was awarded an honorary doctor of laws degree by the University of Calgary for his contributions to the legal profession and to the community.

As a regional writer Ballem's major work is his 'Oilpatch trilogy' consisting of *Oilpatch empire* (1985), *Death spiral* (1989), and *The barons* (1991), which treat of the vortex of oil, business, politics, power, and sex in Canada's oilpatch, a country that Ballem knows better than any other Canadian writer. In his thrillers Ballem has also used his intimate knowledge of Alberta politics and the oil business, notably in *The devil's lighter* (1973), set in the Canadian Arctic; *The dirty scenario* (1974), set in Ottawa, in which an energy crisis affecting Canada and the USA is used by the CIA to foster an annexationist plot; *The Judas conspiracy* (1976), re-published as *Alberta alone* (1981), in which Alberta separates from Canada; and *The moon pool* (1978), set in the Beaufort Sea, where Inuit terrorists attempt to seize an oil rig. Ballem has also written two crime novels set in the Caribbean: *Sacrifice play* (1981) and *The Marigot run* (1984).

Ballem's most important book, an internationally recognized authoritative text, is *The oil and gas lease in Canada* (1973; 2nd edn, 1985). DAVID SKENE-MELVIN

Barbeau, Jean (b. 1945). Born in Saint-Romuald, near Quebec City, he studied at the Collège de Lévis and Université Laval. From 1966 to 1969 he experimented in various creative and collective forms of drama (all unpublished) that were put on in the Collège de Lévis, at the Théâtre Estoc in Quebec City, and at Université Laval: *Caïn et Babel*, *La Geôle*, *Et caetera* (which reached the finals of the Dominion Drama Festival in 1968), *Les temps tranquilles*, and *Le frame all-dress*. 'To write drama is to limit it, to turn it away from its basic purpose,' Barbeau has said: he therefore sketches and improvises and refuses to be an 'author'. He became one in spite of himself, however, in *Le chemin de Lacroix* (1971), produced by the Théâtre quotidien de Québec (of which Barbeau was a founder and resident playwright) in 1970, which presents the 'stations' and 'passion' of a young employed workman at a police station. Lacroix is a victim of circumstances; nevertheless Barbeau refuses to allow him to fulfil the expectations of the audience by radicalizing him at the play's end. *Ben-Ur* (1971) presents another victim—Benoît-Urbain—who searches in comic strips for the ritual, the formulas, and the gestures of the hero. The two-character *Goglu* (1971) and the monologue *Solange* (1974) express in a simple manner intense and pathetic solitude.

0-71 is a kind of historical fresco; it is also a number (unlucky?) in bingo and 1971, year zero, when everything in Quebec was beginning all over again. *Le chant du sink* (1973) and *Le théâtre de la maintenance* (1979) still owe something to the revue and to the initiation ceremony (to both theatre and life—which to Barbeau are one and the same thing). In *0-71* and several other published pieces—*Tripez-vous, vous?, Lésés boys, Boursaille, L'herbe à puces*—Barbeau yields to situation comedy, or verbal comedy, that is a little facile, verbose, confusing. On the other hand *Manon Lastcall* and *Joualez-moi d'amour* (published together in 1972) are clearer and more lively. Manon is a waitress who has become a guide in the provincial museum, where she converts the curator to masterpieces of the flesh. In the second play the Parisian Julie and her Quebec lover Jules are able to embrace only in JOUAL. Here, as in *Le chemin de Lacroix*, vulgarity is healthy and dramatically necessary; the author plays rapidly and effectively on the various levels of language and society.

Most of Barbeau's plays have had successful runs in Montreal and elsewhere in Quebec, and in Toronto and Paris. *Citrouille* (1975) places a normal, rather banal but sympathetic young man in a situation customarily reserved for women: he is held captive, violated, and humiliated by three young feminists. The sex-role reversal provides a highly dramatic situation and the play, written and performed with good humour, is an amusing and effective critique of phallocratism. In *Le jardin de la maison blanche* (1979) Barbeau attacks the values of contemporary North American society through five invalids who are stereotypical to the point of caricature: another phallocrat, a feminine woman, an unemployed worker, a Black, and a young girl so naive as to be almost a fool. All of them cling to life by means of electronic life-support systems and their ideological delusions. *Une marquise de Sade et un lézard nommé King-Kong* (1979) centres on Hercule, a very minor civil servant, who prefers to dwell in a childish fantasy rather than confront reality. The other characters, also powerless socially and economically, are doubly alienated. For them, any form of art is merely one more illusion, an opaque veil, a prison that makes them restless and frantic. The 'moonshiner' in *Émile et une nuit* (1979) is more fortunate. Happily he is able to use literature, from *The thousand and one nights* (hence the title of the play) to the poems of SAINT-DENYS-GARNEAU, to prevent a young man from committing suicide in the subway. For Émile, the wise man, 'words are the keys', just as music can be for the gypsy, Étienne. Though Barbeau has abandoned *joual* for a more normal French, the problems that language and communication create remain at the core of his dramatic work.

Barbeau's language is more relaxed, less hard, broken, and tragic than that of Michel TREMBLAY. His themes, structure, and style approach rather those of the experimental companies Les P'tits Enfants Laliberté and Le Grand Cirque Ordinaire (whose *T'es pas tannée, Jeanne d'Arc?* influenced *Ben-Ur*). His characters are naive young provincials. Dispossessed, bittersweet, given to moods of violence or calm, they still love life, dreaming, and joking. Barbeau believes that 'all the great québécois tragedies will be humorous ones because our greatest misfortune occurred in 1763 and nothing worse awaits us.' Unfortunately, since about 1980 this prolific dramatist, having moved from the sphere of theatre to that of popular entertainment, has limited his production more and more to slapstick comedies. LAURENT MAILHOT

Barbeau, Marius (1883-1969). Born at Sainte-Marie-de-la-Beauce, Quebec, Charles-Marius Barbeau was the scion of a family whose beginnings in Canada can be traced to the 1660s, although his perfect bilingualism may have been influenced by an Irish paternal grandmother. Beginning formal studies in 1895, he completed his B.A. at the college of Saint-Anne-de-la-Pocatière in 1903. He studied law at Université Laval and he was admitted to the bar in 1907. Concurrently he won a Rhodes Scholarship and in 1910 was awarded the B.Sc. degree and diploma in anthropology by Oxford University for his thesis 'The totemic systems of the North Western tribes of North America'. During vacations in this period he also studied in Paris at the Sorbonne and the École d'Anthropologie. On his return to Canada in 1911 he was appointed as an anthropologist to the National Museum of Canada (then the Museum Branch of the Geological Survey of Canada), where he remained until his retirement in 1949, though he acted as a consultant for another fifteen years.

After meeting the influential American anthropologist Franz Boas in 1913, Barbeau added the traditional culture and folklore of

French Canadians to his scholarly interests. He gave these interests tangible form in his role as associate editor of the *Journal of American Folklore*. From 1916 to 1950 he was responsible for ten Canadian issues, the contents of which remain the major body of published French-Canadian folklore *collectanea*; these include eight series of 'Contes populaires canadiens', many of which he had collected. He was president of the American Folklore Society in 1918. Barbeau's major interest, however, was folksong, and his prolific field collections gave the National Museum a corpus of over 10,000 songs, including some 7,000 French-Canadian, 3,000 Native, 1,500 English, and 195 Eskimo songs. He founded the Canadian Folk Music Society in 1956 as a branch of the International Folk Music Council, continuing as president until 1963 and as honorary president until his death.

Barbeau was made a member of the Royal Society of Canada in 1916, and was later awarded its Gold Medal. He was co-founder, with Lawrence J. Burpee, of the Société historique du Canada, and won the Prix David in 1925, 1929, and 1945. He received honorary degrees from the universities of Laval, Oxford, and the Sorbonne; was made an honorary fellow of Oriel College, Oxford, in 1941; was awarded the Médaille Parizeau by the Association canadienne-française pour l'avancement des sciences in 1946; and in 1967 was one of the first Canadians to be named a Companion of the Order of Canada.

Barbeau was the founder of modern folklore studies in Canada. Apart from the pioneering work of Ernest Gagnon, whose *Chansons populaires du Canada* (1865) was long perceived as the definitive work on French-Canadian folksong, Barbeau was the first to undertake a methodical exploration of the traditions of French Canada. Early in his career he gathered about him a team of collectors, including E.-Z. Massicotte, Adélard Lambert, Frère Archange Godbout, and J.-Thomas Leblanc, whose materials formed the basis of the immense collections of the National Museum. Later he inspired a new generation of scholars: among them François Brassard, Madeleine Doyon, Carmen Roy, Félix-Antoine SAVARD, and Luc LACOURCIÈRE.

Barbeau's recognition of the need for a scholarly base for folklore studies was realized in 1944 with the creation of a chair of folklore at Université Laval occupied by Luc Lacourcière, whom Barbeau had introduced to the subject in the 1930s. Lacourcière, as director of the Archives de Folklore, was able to call upon Barbeau's immense experience both as a teacher (he was made a professor in the Faculté des Lettres at Laval in 1945) and as an editor of the prestigious series, *Les Archives de Folklore*. In 1947 Barbeau was honoured with the dedication of volume II of the series as a 'Hommage à Marius Barbeau'.

The range of Barbeau's research was vast. His insatiable curiosity led him to study the whole domain of the folklorist—clothing, foodways, housing, furniture, weapons, domestic utensils, games, formulas, customs and beliefs, folk art and imagery, tales, legends, anecdotes, song and music. He was a prolific, indeed a compulsive, publisher of his research. He authored some 600 journal and newspaper articles, over 100 books and brochures, and collaborated on another sixty. Among his many scholarly publications on Native culture, the most eminent include *Huron and Wyandot mythology with an appendix containing earlier published records* (1915); *Totem poles on the Gitksan, Upper Skeena River, British Columbia* (1929); *Totem poles* (2 vols, 1950-1); *Haida myths illustrated in argillite carvings* (1953); *Haida carvers in argellite* (1957); and *Huron-Wyandot traditional narratives in translation and native texts* (1960). His scholarly writings on Indian lore are major documents of Native ethnography. Barbeau used his knowledge of Native culture in two novels: *The downfall of Temlaham* (1928) and *Mountain Cloud* (1944).

Barbeau's work on traditional French folksongs represents the single most important corpus of French-Canadian folksongs ever published: *Folk songs of French Canada* (1925, with Edward Sapir); *Chansons populaires du vieux Québec* (1935); *Le romancéro du Canada* (1937), his major scholarly contribution to Canadian folksong studies; *Alouette! Nouveau recueil de chansons populaires avec mélodies, choisies dans le Répertoire du Musée National du Canada* (1946); *Le rossignol y chante* (1962); and the series 'Chants populaires du Canada', which he edited in collaboration with E.-Z. Massicotte (*Journal of American Folklore*, 1919).

Barbeau also edited several volumes of tales, legends, and other folklore studies aimed at both the general public and scholars: *Au coeur de Québec* (1934), which includes legends, history, and artisans; *Grand'mère raconte* (1935), ten folktales; and *Quebec where ancient France lingers* (1936), with important studies on traditional artisans, and its French edition, *Québec ou survit l'ancienne France* (1937). *Maîtres artisans de chez nous* (1942) also deals with folk artists and artisans. *L'arbre des rêves* (1948)—with its English edition, *The tree of dreams* (1955)—is a collection of legends presented in a somewhat literary manner; while the twelve volumes of *Les contes du grand'père sept-heures* (1950-3) were written for children; some of these stories were adapted by Michael Hornyansky and published in *The golden phoenix and other French-Canadian fairy tales* (1958).

Barbeau's love of art was not restricted to the traditional. He was instrumental in fostering appreciation of several Canadian artists including Emily CARR, whom he visited in 1927, and in works such as *Cornelius Krieghoff, pioneer painter of North America* (1934) and *Painters of Quebec* (1946). He also wrote a number of short monographs on Krieghoff.

The 'Hommage à Marius Barbeau' (*Les Archives de Folklore*, vol. II, 1947) contains a 'Bio-bibliographie de Marius Barbeau' prepared by Clarisse Cardin, which is an indispensable guide to Barbeau's scholarly career; an unpublished manuscript prepared by the National Museum in 1969 added well over 200 items to this bibliography.

GERALD THOMAS

Barbour, Douglas (b. 1940). Born in Winnipeg, Manitoba, he studied briefly at McGill University before completing his B.A. in English (1962) at Acadia University and his M.A. (1964) at Dalhousie; he received a Ph.D. (1976) from Queen's University with a thesis on science-fiction literature. Since 1969 he has taught Canadian literature and creative writing at the University of Alberta. Barbour has served as editor of *Quarry* (1966-8), as a member of the editorial boards of *White Pelican* (1971-6) and *NeWest Press* (1980-), as poetry editor for *The CANADIAN FORUM* (1978-80), and as co-chairman (with Stephen SCOBIE) of the LEAGUE OF CANADIAN POETS (1972-4). In 1980 he co-founded Longspoon Press, Edmonton, with Stephen Scobie and Shirley Neuman; it ceased publishing in 1986.

In Barbour's first poetry collections—*A poem as long as the highway* (1971), *Land fall* (1971), and *White* (1973)—he uses a free-flowing lyrical style and vibrant images to capture the nuances of western landscapes, while at the same time introducing ideographic characters into some poems. This device he carried further in *Songbook* (1973) and *He & she &* (1974), which link Barbour with bp NICHOL and bill BISSET, for they show an interest in defying the confines of natural speech in order to accommodate a vast range of sound, tone, and spoken music. This interest is also demonstrated in Barbour's sound-poetry performances with Scobie, 'Re:Sounding', which they began in 1977. Barbour even employs sound poetry in the long narrative poem *Visions of my grandfather* (1976). It is less evident, however, in *Shorelines* (1979), *Stargazing* (1980), and *The harbingers* (1984), a sequence of nineteen poems that explore the archetypal significance of the three white horses of death found in dreams, mythology, and folklore. *Visible visions: the selected poems of Douglas Barbour* (1984)—which won the Stephan Stephansson Award for Poetry, given by the Alberta Writers' Guild—is a generous sampling from his eight earlier books, highlighting his sense of humour and his ability to find joy in the commonplace. The selection also shows how he developed and expanded his interest in language, and subsequent experiments in typography, layout, space, and sound. *Story for a Saskatchewan night* (1990) is a ten-year selection of poems, which are displayed in a wide variety of forms; open space is important, as is a resistance to closure, common in so-called 'prairie anecdotal poetry'.

Barbour edited *The story so far 5* (1978), *Inscriptions: a prairie poetry anthology* (1992), and *Beyond 'Tish'* (1991); and co-edited with Scobie an anthology of Canadian comic poetry, *The maple laugh forever* (1981), and with Marni Stanley *Write right: poetry by Canadian women* (1982). Barbour has also written for ECW PRESS studies of three poets and their works: Daphne MARLATT (1991), bp Nichol (1991), and John NEWLOVE (1991); and for Twayne Publishers *Michael Ondaatje* (1993).

BRUCE MEYER/GEOFF HANCOCK

Barfoot, Joan (b. 1946). Born and raised in Owen Sound, Ontario, Barfoot studied English at the University of Western Ontario, graduating in 1969. A reporter/editor for the *London Free Press*, she divides her time between journalism and writing fiction, and lives in London, Ontario.

Barfoot has published six novels. *Abra* (1978), which won the W.H. Smith/*Books in Canada* First Novel Award; *Dancing in the dark* (1982); *Duet for three* (1985); *Family news* (1989); *Plain Jane* (1992); and *Charlotte and Claudia keeping in touch* (1994). Her novels focus on the domestic lives of women. She is interested in the emotional injuries inflicted by family, and explores female madness as a response to the position of women within Canadian society.

Barfoot's first novels feature women who must escape suburban domesticity in order to rediscover themselves. In *Abra* the title character abandons her comfortable lifestyle (including husband, children, and pet) to live in isolation in a northern-Ontario cabin. *Dancing in the dark* tells the story of Edna, a housewife isolated in the suburbs, who has spent two decades keeping herself, her home, and her husband in perfect condition. But she is driven mad by the knowledge of her husband's affair with his secretary: this, and the desperate act it inspires, introduces the possibility of reinventing herself. Barfoot's next two novels present a slightly more optimistic view of the family. *Duet for three* details the precarious relationship between eighty-year-old Aggie and her daughter June, and explores the powerful, complex, painful bond that unites mother and daughter. *Family news* focuses on Susannah, and her reconciliations with blood relatives and chosen family. Each chapter is introduced by sensational newspaper clippings, but Susannah's stories quietly highlight Barfoot's conviction that the ordinary can be compelling. *Plain Jane* is a dark comedy which introduces Jane Smith, a quiet, lonely librarian prone to elaborate fantasy, and possibly madness. Jane's pen-pal relationship with a wife-murdering convict provides the basis for an extended fantasy of suburban love. *Charlotte and Claudia keeping in touch* celebrates female friendship: it is the story of two very different women who have been friends for fifty years, and the point of view alternates between the two women, each of whom has interesting things to say about love, sexuality, and aging.

In 1992 Barfoot received the Marian ENGEL Award, presented to a woman writer in mid-career. JUSTINE WHITEHEAD

Barker's Canadian Monthly Magazine (May 1846-April 1847). Of the many pre-Confederation periodicals, this was the first whose contents were written entirely in Canada. The owner, editor, and publisher was Edward John Barker, born near London, England, in 1799. He had practised medicine in England before he immigrated to Canada in 1832, settling in Kingston, Ontario, where he edited newspapers owned by others before he began his own *British Whig* in 1834. The contents of *Barker's Magazine* varied in form, style, and quality. In addition to poetry and fiction, there were serious political articles and political satire, biographies of Canadian politicians, and reviews of books by Canadians or about Canada. Barker had announced that the magazine would be politically independent, and this seems to have been the case, since it was criticized by Tories for being Reform and by Reformers for being Tory. The two biographies—of John Beverly Robinson and Christopher Hageman—were certainly not hagiographic and, with one exception, the book reviews were savage. There was a greal deal of competent poetry, though only the verse satire is interesting today, and some quite remarkable fiction: notably the first two-thirds of J.S. Cummins' novel *ALTHAM* and a series of 'Legends of the early settlements' by 'Cinna'. Many years later Henry Scadding identified 'Cinna' as W.B. Wells, a lawyer who was born in Augusta Township, Upper Canada, in 1809. Since the attribution, made in Wells' lifetime, was not contradicted, and since what we know of 'Cinna' tallies with what we know of Wells, we can assume that he was the author of the two biographies, two articles, and several poems both long and short, as well as the following 'legends': 'Tula; or, the Ojibwa's leap'; 'Maroon Hensey'; and 'De Soulis; the runner of the woods'. They are somewhat romantic in tone, but the two articles, 'Deer stalking on the south branch' and 'A bear hunt', describe pioneer life with vigour and immediacy. Although Barker had hoped that the low price of 10 shillings per annum would bring him a thousand subscribers, there were only 400. Reluctantly, he discontinued his magazine with vol. 1, no. 12, at the end of the first year. MARY LU MacDONALD

Barometer rising (1941). Hugh MacLENNAN's first published novel was his first attempt to base his fiction securely on familiar and national ground. In an introduction to the NEW CANADIAN LIBRARY edition (1958), Hugo McPherson writes that it 'ushered in the most productive period in the nation's writing, and it introduced a novelist who was to lead his contemporaries in a most absorbing quest.' This quest was for a new relevance in fiction that would examine the Canadian consciousness.

The protagonist of this tightly structured novel—it takes place over eight days towards the end of 1917—is Neil Macrae. He returns incognito to Halifax from the First World War in the hope of clearing himself of a false accusation of insubordination, laid by Colonel Wain, a representative of the old colonial order who happens to be his hated uncle and the father of his former sweetheart Penelope, who has another suitor, Angus Murray, though she remains faithful to Neil. (McPherson points to the outline of the Perseus legend visible in the novel; George WOODCOCK, in his essay 'A nation's odyssey', sees MacLennan using the Homeric epic as a source.) The tight, melodramatic plot unfolds against a compelling backdrop of wartime Halifax that permits frequent views of the harbour and the shipping within. At the moment the *Imo* emerges from behind Richmond Bluff, all the characters seem to be inevitably arranged so that, after its fatal collision with the French munitions ship *Mont Blanc* and the frightful aftermath, all the threads of the plot explode in a dénouement. MacLennan shows superlative skill in conveying the effects of the ships' explosions, which were both researched and recollected (he witnessed them as a boy). The crisis (representing the death of the old Canada), and the response as his characters survive and attempt to bring about a kind of rebirth after the catacylsm, form a parable of Canadian self-realization that is firmly rooted in actual and vividly reconstructed historical events. MacLennan is less successful when he represents the unfolding of national consciousness by means of unconvincing reflections, by Neil and others, that relate panorama to felt nationalism. The overt didacticism of *Barometer rising*, however, is more than offset by its formal precision, imaginative power, and literary craftsmanship. With his first published novel, MacLennan produced a minor classic of Canadian fiction.

Barometer rising is in the New Canadian Library with an Afterword by Alistair MacLEOD.

D.O. SPETTIGUE

Barr, Robert (1850-1912). Born in Glasgow, Scotland, he was taken by his family in 1854 to Wallacetown, Canada West (Ontario); after several moves the family settled in Windsor. Barr attended area schools and then obtained a temporary teaching certificate and taught until 1873, when he entered the Toronto Normal School to obtain a permanent licence. In 1875, after teaching in Wallaceburg and Walkerville, he became principal of Windsor Central School. In 1876 he married Eva Bennett and gave up teaching to become a reporter for the *Detroit Free Press*. Barr's success with the *Free Press*, evident from his quick rise to exchange editor by 1881, culminated in his move to London, England, to establish an English weekly edition. In 1892, with Jerome K. Jerome, he founded *The Idler*, an illustrated magazine for men, and became a well-known and well-travelled journalist and writer, counting among his friends and acquaintances Stephen Crane, George Gissing, Henry James, Joseph Conrad, and Arthur Conan Doyle. Well known on both sides of the Atlantic, Barr was featured in a number of magazine articles of the day, and in 1900 was awarded an honorary M.A. by the University of Michigan. He died at his home, Hillhead, in Woldingham, Surrey.

Barr's literary career began with his submissions in the form of ironic correspondence and humorous squibs—under the pen name 'Luke Sharp'—to the Bothwell, Ontario, *Advance*, and to the satiric Toronto periodical *GRIP*. But he was not able to make much headway as a writer until he caught the attention of the editor of the *Detroit Free Press*, William E. Quinby, with his sketch 'A dangerous journey', and was invited to be a reporter. His first collection of sketches and short stories, *Strange happenings* (London, 1883), was followed by fourteen others, three of which were published posthumously. Probably the most notable of these collections is *The triumphs of Eugène Valmont* (1906), which, in catering to the contemporary vogue of the detective story, introduced the delightful Valmont, seen by recent critics as a precursor to, and possibly a model for, Agatha Christie's Hercule Poirot. Barr was at his best as a writer of short fiction, particularly the detective story. His ear for crisp, functional dialogue, his eye for social and national nuances, his ability to outline a situation, and his faculty for constructing, then quickly and credibly resolving, a mystery, make these stories and sketches entertaining reading. The Eugène Valmont stories are still included in anthologies. See the *Selected Stories of Robert Barr* (1977), edited by John Parr.

Barr also wrote twenty novels that cover the literary range from historical romance to socio-political realism, but today only four are of interest: his first novel, *In the midst of alarms* (London, 1894; rpr. 1973), *The measure of the rule* (1907; rpr. 1973), *The mutable many* (New York, 1896), and *The victors* (1901). The first two make full and direct use of Barr's Canadian experience. *In the midst of alarms* is set in 1866 at the scene of the Battle of Ridgeway, a Fenian incursion into Canada. Barr well portrays the largely farcical battle and provides an accompanying message about the futility of war, and a comic description of a revival meeting. Similarly *The measure of the rule*, making use of Barr's Toronto Normal School experiences in 1873, contains some trenchant material on the education of both students and teachers, and on the social realities of Toronto boarding houses of the day; there are also penetrating portraits of identifiable historical figures. But the latter part of the novel—treating the hero's career as a struggling artist in Paris and an eventual reunion with his beloved—is merely sentimental romance.

The lasting impression of a typical Barr novel is of individual portions that are in themselves well done but that relate adventitiously to the whole. First and foremost a commercial writer who was more discerning than most, Barr exploited a popular formula for the writing of fiction. Arnold Bennet wrote in his *Journals* that Barr was 'an admirable specimen of the man of talent who makes of letters an honest trade', though he had not much, 'if any at all, feeling for literature'.

In addition, Barr completed *The O'Ruddy* (1903), a novel left unfinished by Stephen Crane at his death; collaborated with S. Lewis-Ransome to write a play, *The conspiracy* (London, n.d.); and wrote a travel book, *The unchanging east* (1900).

See Louis K. MacKendrick's introduction to the 1973 reprint of *The measure of the rule*, and John Parr, 'The measure of Robert Barr', *Journal of Canadian Fiction*, vol. III, no. 2 (1974).

S.R. MacGILLIVRAY

Barre du jour, La (1965-90). Founded by Nicole BROSSARD, Marcel Saint-Pierre, Roger Soublière, and Jan Stafford, this Montreal periodical was initially committed to the development of a strong Québécois literature by documenting previously unpublished or unavailable texts from the nineteenth century—such as the correspondence of Albert LOZEAU (fév. 1966), unpublished poems by SAINT-DENYS-GARNEAU (Sept.-Oct. 1969), an inaccessible play, *L'anglomanie* (July-Dec. 1965) and a previously unpublished play, *Les républicains français* (Summer 1970), by Louis-Joseph QUESNEL; by publishing avant-garde literary modes and young authors who rejected the more conventional expectations of their contemporaries (Aug.-Sept. 1968); and by supporting the concept of literary transgression, its politics, and stylistic consequences (Fall 1973). The magazine also noticed new methodological approaches to literature, such as the impact of structuralist theories on contemporary criticism (Spring-Summer 1973) and contemporary, as opposed to avant-garde, writers: the issue of May 1968 was devoted to Roland GIGUÈRE and that of Oct. 1970 to Gaston MIRON. In addition, para-literary and unconventional literary modes—such as cartoons, and their impact on literature—were featured in the issues of Winter and Spring 1975, and of Feb. 1977 and Feb. 1982.

After Nicole Brossard left *La Barre du jour* in 1975 to devote herself to the feminist monthly *Têtes de Pioche*, the magazine underwent a number of editorial changes and became in Sept. 1977 *La Nouvelle Barre du jour*. Brossard returned to it in that same year—remaining until 1990—and gave it a feminist impulse, making it a highly visible focus for women's writings. *La Barre du jour*'s subsequent involvement with both avant-garde and feminist writings stemmed from a literary perception that was linked to major transformations in the image women have of themselves and to the role women have been given in the modern world.

During the last decade of its existence *La Nouvelle Barre du jour* went through several phases. In 1984 the editorial board changed and this was followed by changes in policy. The new editors decided to publish the journal sixteen times per year, and between April 1985 and April 1987 they actually published fifty-one issues. But the journal began to lose energy and only twenty-three issues were published between 1987 and 1990, when the journal ceased publication. Of particular interest to students of Québécois literature is the *Index général* in two volumes, the first (1985) covering 1965 to 1985; the second (1990) covering 1985 to 1990.

CAROLINE BAYARD/FRANCESCA BENEDICT

Barrette, Jacquéline. See DRAMA IN FRENCH 1948 TO 1981: 4.

Barrington, E. See Lily Adams BECK.

Barthe, Ulric. See NOVELS IN FRENCH 1900 TO 1920.

Barton, John. See GAY LITERATURE: POETRY.

Basile, Jean (b. 1932). Jean Basile-Bezroudnoff was born in Paris of Russian parents and came to Quebec as a young man. He worked as a journalist on *Le Devoir* in Montreal starting in 1962—as editor of the weekly Arts and Letters section, as a critic of popular music (writing under the pseudonym 'Penelope'), and later as the television critic. He left *Le Devoir* in 1969 to collaborate on the underground monthly magazine *Mainmise*, which he co-founded—an exciting avant-garde expression of the Quebec counter-culture that enjoyed a remarkable commercial success. Since 1973 Basile has written on the media for various Quebec magazines.

Basile's first novel, *Lorenzo* (1963), and *Journal poétique* (1965) are restrained yet lyrical questionings of emotion. *Joli tambour* (1966), a historical play that explores the relationship between hangman and criminal in New France, has been performed only in English, in Toronto, as *The drummer-boy*.

With the trilogy initiated by *La jument des Mongols* (1964) Basile found his voice as a writer of the 1960s generation in Quebec. Despite their exotic titles, *La jument, Le grand Khan* (1967), and *Les voyages d'Irkoutsk* (1970) are about Quebec, and specifically about the personal and collective manifestations of underground culture in Montreal—paralleling Leonard COHEN's and Réjean DUCHARME's contemporary emphasis on Montreal as an 'American' city, though Basile's Montreal is more of a protagonist than in most fictions of the period. Each novel is narrated by one member of a trio—Jonathan, Jérémie, and Judith—and each narrative is a relentless flow of fantasy, humour, and reflection. Basile's writing becomes increasingly dazzling and dense as he enters the world of drug experimentation. As Basile later said of himself: 'There was my life before LSD and my life after. . . . Drugs were, and remain for me, a tool of knowledge, not an object of consumption.' Likewise, in *Les voyages* the personal quests of the characters embody an overall view of the cultural turbulence of the time; it has since acquired a serious documentary value, in addition to its interest as fiction.

Basile's second collection of poetry, *Iconostase pour Pier Paolo Pasolini: discours poétique sur les gays, le féminisme et les nouveaux mâles* (1983), was little remarked on and is a strange, eclectic work. His next novel, *Le piano-trompette* (1983), is another rich, fantastic account of Montreal. Set in a hallucinatory, apocalyptic Arctic future, the narrative centres on a Monsieur Barnabé, whose ethno-linguistic differences and anxieties are quite reminiscent of Basile/Bezroudnoff's relationship to his adoptive culture. For as much as he loved Montreal, Basile consistently experienced himself as an outsider—perhaps this is why he became such an important counter-cultural guru. Having initially tried to assimilate to Québécois culture, Basile increasingly saw his role as a 'métèque' as being important ('métèque' is a historically pejorative reference to a 'foreigner' and was counter-discursively appropriated by some Quebec writers during the 1980s). As he put it: 'The more I express my complex roots, the more I am of use to Québécois literature.'

See also *Adieu—je pars pour Vazma!: tragi-farce d'après des recits de Tchekhov* (1987), and *Keepsake 1* (1992).

SHERRY SIMON/DAVID LEAHY

Bates, Walter (1760-1842). Born in Stamford, Connecticut, he immigrated to Saint John, New Brunswick, as a Loyalist with the Spring Fleet of 1783, settling at Kingston in King's County, where he was sheriff for many years. He wrote *The mysterious stranger* (New Haven, 1817), a popular account of 'Henry Moon' (Henry More Smith), a notorious horse thief who was incarcerated in Bates' prison for a time before being pardoned and then went to the United States, where he continued his criminal activities. It was also published in England under the title *Companion for Caraboo: a narrative of the conduct and adventures of Henry Frederic Moon, alias Henry Frederic More Smith, alias William Newman . . . now under sentence of imprisonment, in Connecticut . . . containing an account of his unparalleled artifices, impostures, mechanical ingenuity, &c. &c. displayed during and subsequently to his confinement in one of His Majesty's gaols in the province of New Brunswick . . . with an introductory description of New Brunswick; and a postscript, containing some account of Caraboo, the late female imposter, at Bristol* (London, 1817)—covering the 'dreadful doings' of Smith since the appearance of the first edition. (Many other editions followed.) Bates describes, not without some admiration, the exploits of his 'hero', but explains that his book was written 'to prevent future mischiefs'. Written in a quaint, unsophisticated style, *The mysterious stranger* is an intriguing oddity in early Canadian literature and provides an insight into the rough-and-ready conditions of prisons in the early nineteenth century. Bates also wrote a history of the church at Kingston, posthumously published by W.O. Raymond in *Kingston and the Loyalists of the 'Spring fleet' of A.D. 1783, with reminiscences of early days in Connecticut: a narrative. By Walter Bates, Esq., sometime high sheriff of the county of King's. To which is appended a diary written by Sarah Frost on her voyage to St. John, N.B., with the Loyalists of 1783* (Saint John, 1889). In this work he provides an authentic picture of the Connecticut Loyalists, their sufferings at the hands of the American revolutionists, and their subsequent hardships when they were forced to confront the Canadian wilderness.

DOUGLAS LOCHHEAD

Batten, Jack (b. 1932). Born in Montreal, Quebec, he graduated from the University of Toronto and Osgoode Hall Law School and practised law from 1959 to 1963, when he turned his attention to magazine-writing and then book-writing. He has published more than thirty books on popular subjects. He writes with ease and insight, and at length, in books devoted to sports (swimming, golf, hockey, champions, jogging, squash, basketball), law (profiles of jurists, studies of trials), biographies (lawyers, hockey personalities, businessmen, swimmers), and mystery fiction. In the latter field are the fast-moving novels about the Toronto criminal lawyer and jazz buff named simply Crang: *Crang plays the ace* (1987), *Straight, no chaser* (1989), *Blood count* (1991), and *Riviera blues* (1990). Batten is the editor of *Bloody York: tales of mayhem, murder and mystery in Toronto* (1996).

JOHN ROBERT COLOMBO

Bauer, Nancy. See Writing in the MARITIMES: 5

Bauer, Walter (1904-76). Born in Merseburg, Germany, he graduated from the teacher's college there and was a widely published author when the Nazis came to power and banned his books. Disillusioned with German attitudes, both during and after the Second World War, he immigrated in 1952 to Toronto, where he found work as a dishwasher. He attended the University of Toronto and taught in the German department from 1958 until his retirement a few months before his death. He published more than seventy books in West Germany—novels, story collections, biographies, poetry, essays, and children's books. In the last years of his life he wrote in English.

Henry BEISSEL translated two collections of Bauer's lyrical poetry, *The price of morning* (1968) and *A different sun* (1976). Beissel arranged the tribute to Bauer in *The TAMARACK REVIEW* 77-8 (Summer 1979), which includes seven translations from the German and eight original English poems. In much of his poetry Bauer explored the experience of the immigrant who in the New World craves the Old ('He lives now / On a huge new continent, / But he pines away / For a country that / No longer exists') and is ambivalent about his fate: 'A sun without depth, without shame, without guilt, without shadows.'

JOHN ROBERT COLOMBO

Beardsley, Charles E. See *The VICTIMS OF TYRANNY.*

Beauchemin, Nérée (1850-1931). Born at Yamachiche, Quebec, he attended the Séminaire de Nicolet and studied medicine at the Université Laval, graduating in 1874. Early in life he showed his gift for poetry in work clearly influenced by the romanticism of that era. His first poem, 'Les petits pèlerins', was published in *L'Opinion publique* in 1871. He was the author of two poetry collections—*Les floraisons matutinales* (Trois-Rivières, 1897) and *Patrie intime* (1928)—and approximately 100 more poems appeared in magazines. Beauchemin also wrote close to 200 unpublished fragments of prose and correspondence, and over 600 variations of poems that he had chosen to publish. All are accounted for in the critical edition *Nérée Beauchemin, son oeuvre* (3 vols, 1973-4) edited by Armand Guilmette.

One of the most important regionalists in Quebec's literary history, Beauchemin was above all a poet of transition between two great literary movements: the patriotic school of Quebec and the literary school of Montreal. Like FRÉCHETTE and CRÉMAZIE, he was at first heavily influenced by Romanticism. He relied on the basic themes of his era—nature, homeland, religion—but thanks to a refined sensibility, and a more subtle artistry than that of his predecessors, his work gradually transcended the traditional flamboyant style. Though he is usually considered a poet of the nineteenth century, his best book appeared in the twentieth. He wrote for himself, secretly, in his country-doctor's office, tossing finished poems into a drawer with no thought of publication. Finally a friend persuaded him to publish *Patrie intime* and it was acclaimed by critics. It consists of short poems written in a spare style in which each word seems stamped with a special status. Beauchemin's poetic voice is muted and, despite Romantic accents, his poetry is subdued, showing delicate colours and many shades and modulations. He sought to create beauty out of the things around him: the simplicity of objects, a hand's skill, the patina of time—all are shown through homely things such as a cupboard, a chest, a glass-fronted cabinet, etc. Beauchemin said in his notes that he preferred slight, insignificant subjects so that the craftsmanship of execution would appear more striking. This attitude to art—a fierce desire to polish its form—helped to set him apart from the mainstream. The famous 'Cloche de Louisbourg' has been anthologized most frequently; yet other poems from *Les floraisons*—such as 'Hantise', 'Mirage', 'L'idylle dorée', and 'Rayons d'octobre'—are also important.

Besides the critical edition mentioned above, see also *Choix de poésies de Nérée Beauchemin* (1950) edited by Clément MARCHAND, who wrote *Nérée Beauchemin* (1957); and Armand Guilmette, 'Nérée Beauchemin, poète de la conciliation', *Cahiers de l'Académie canadienne-française*, vol. 14 (1972).

ARMAND GUILMETTE

Beauchemin, Yves (b. 1941). Born in Noranda, Quebec, he attended elementary school in Clova, Abitibi, before moving to Joliette, where he completed his 'cours classique' at the Séminaire. In 1965 he obtained his Licence ès lettres from the Université de Montréal. After teaching for a while and working for the Bibliothèque générale of the Université de Montréal, he worked for the book publisher Holt, Rinehart and Winston from 1967 to 1969, when he went to Radio-Québec.

Beauchemin published many articles in newspapers and magazines, such as *Sept Jours* and *Digest Éclair*, before writing his first novel, *L'enfirouapé* (1974). A satirical and imaginative blend of realism and fantasy that recalls the events of the October Crisis in 1970, it was well received by the critics. A naïve young man who has been manoeuvred into prison by an unscrupulous politician seeks revenge for all the humiliations he has suffered in his life: he decides to organize the kidnapping of the politician, but he and those who join him must also kidnap an English-speaking businessman in order to compel the government to pay $500,000 ransom and to release thirteen political prisoners. An enraged would-be poet shoots the businessman for insulting his captors in English, and after various episodes—some hilarious—the terrorists decide to crash the plane taking them to sanctuary in Cuba on the crowd of policemen and politicians below. *Le matou* (1981) is a fast-paced story of fantasy and adventure. Florent Boisonneault, little thinking his action will disrupt his whole life, helps a man knocked senseless by a bronze quotation mark that has fallen from a sign. He soon receives, however, a bizarre invitation from a witness to the accident—Egon Ratablavasky—who insists on meeting him. Later, little by little, Ratablavasky reveals his mysterious, diabolical plans. Warmly received in both Canada and France, this extraordinary novel was considered one of the best ever written in Quebec and its author one of the most gifted storytellers to emerge in recent years in French-language literature.

Beauchemin has since published two novels, *Juliette Pomerleau* (1989) and *Le second violon* (1996); an autobiographical book, *Du sommet d'un arbre* (1986), which includes extracts from his diary; and three books for children: *Finalement . . . les enfants* (1991), *Une histoire à faire japper* (1991), and *Antoine et Alfred* (1992).

See also NOVELS IN FRENCH 1960 TO 1982: 3. JACQUES COTNAM

Beaugrand, Honoré (1848-1906). Born at Lanoraie, Quebec, he spent four years at the Collège de Joliette before entering the Montreal Military School. At seventeen he enlisted in the Emperor Maximilian's army and served in the Mexican War (1865-7). After two years in France, where he was exposed to liberal, radical, and anticlerical philosophies, he moved to the United States in 1869 and pursued a career as a journalist and newspaper publisher in Fall River, Massachusetts; St Louis, Missouri; Boston, Mass.; and Ottawa, Ontario. In 1879 he founded *La Patrie*, a reformist newspaper, in Montreal; he was mayor of that city in 1885 and 1886, after which he abandoned politics. In 1887 he published the *Daily News*, which he soon left to travel in Europe and elsewhere. His 'Lettres de voyage' appeared often in the columns of *La Patrie*. Beaugrand retired at the age of forty-nine, after handing over *La Patrie* to J.-I. Tarte, and devoted himself until his death in Westmount to travel and folklore.

Beaugrand's novel *Jeanne-la-Fileuse: épisode de l'émigration franco-canadienne aux États-Unis* (Fall River, Mass., 1878, and Montreal, 1888) was as much a political pamphlet as a novel, aimed at justifying immigration to the United States at a period when many French Canadians associated this with a poverty-ridden and degenerate section of society.

Following his involvement with the first Canadian Folklore Society, a branch of the American Folklore Society, which was founded in Montreal in 1892, Beaugrand published, in 1900, *La chasse-galerie: légendes canadiennes* and *La chasse-galerie and other Canadian stories*. His *New studies of Canadian folk lore* (1904) includes an article on traditional French-Canadian beliefs; a translation of 'Macloune', a tale that had appeared earlier in *La chasse-galerie*; a lengthy study of Native picture writing; and 'Legend of the North Pacific', in which Beaugrand suggests, somewhat romantically, that all the indigenous dwellers of America are descendants of the Japanese Ainus. Beaugrand's writing is very literary, but he remains nonetheless one of the pioneers of folklore studies in French Canada.

Beaugrand's travelogues, which he had contributed to *La Patrie*, were published in *Letters de voyage—France—Italie—Sicile—Malte—Tunisie—Algérie—Espagne* (Montréal, 1889); in 1890, also in Montreal, he published a second volume, *Six mois dans les Montagnes Rocheuses—Colorado—Utah—Nouveau-Mexique*. Beaugrand had earlier published a highly appreciated book entitled *Le vieux Montréal, 1611-1803—Album historique, chronologique et topographique de la ville de Montréal depuis sa fondation* (Montréal, 1884). GERALD THOMAS

Beaulieu, Germaine. See LESBIAN LITERATURE.

Beaulieu, Jocelyne. See DRAMA IN FRENCH 1948 TO 1991: 4.

Beaulieu, Michel (1941-85). Born in Montreal, he was educated at the Collège Jean-de-Brébeuf and the Université de Montréal. There he edited the student newspaper, *Le Quartier Latin*, and directed the student press. He helped found Éditions Estérel in 1965, and the short-lived *Quoi* in 1967. In the 1970s he was a member of the Centre d'essai des auteurs dramatiques; helped to found *Jeu*, the experimental theatre journal, in 1975; and was president of the association of literary translators. His sustained contribution at a high level of personal commitment and artistic integrity to the best of Quebec's avant-garde was recognized by the award of the Prix de la revue *Études françaises* in 1973, the year that his first retrospective collection of poems, *Variables*, was published.

In poetry alone Beaulieu's listed titles number some thirty items, ranging from the 250 pages of *Desseins* (1980), collected poems from 1961 to 1966, to the literary spoof *Le 'Flying Dutchman'* (1977). *Visages* (1981) is an extensive collection of poems written in 1977 that is described as fifth and last in the cycle *Lettre des saisons*, another example of Beaulieu's desire to gather his production retrospectively into larger units. Several of his titles—*Desseins, Variables, Anecdotes* (1977), and *Visages*—point to the tension in his work between the fragment and the totality. Beaulieu wrote series of brief poems, usually ten to twenty lines, though the links were not made explicit: any unity is a unity of voice—a quiet, private, personal voice, but one that strains insistently to be heard. His poetry is one of anguish, doubt, and shame patiently borne and painstakingly verbalized, though words are rarely his salvation: they provoke constant questionings and uncertainties. The poetry is occasionally playful—he puns and makes recondite literary allusions and takes mischievous liberties with syntax—but it is never light-hearted. In the tight-knotted universe of Beaulieu ('noeud' is a key word in his writing), nothing is easy.

Beaulieu's novel *La représentation* (1972; new edn, 1980) is the monologue—constantly interrupted by asides in different type—of a timid, rather violent man coming to terms with the liberated woman and free love. It draws an analogy between the clumsiness, and scope for misunderstanding, of sexual communication with another person and the problem of self-expression in Quebec.

The bulimia that took hold of Beaulieu in 1977 did not end until the publication of *Kaléidoscope; ou Les aléas du corps grave* (1985) in the year of his premature death. The rest of his work confirms that, for him, birth—even political birth, which he tackled in *Le cercle de justice* (1977)—remained forever impossible. Also emphasized in Beaulieu's work is everyday life, which is balanced by the importance, for the poet, of writing to someone, to the second person singular. No doubt it is this grounding in everyday life, and connection to the other, that prevented his work from sinking into the lassitude and fatigue that seemed to lie in constant wait for him. In *Kaléidoscope*—which in 1985 earned the Prix de Poésie Gatien-Lapointe (later renamed the Prix de la Fondation des Forges)—the *you* has become the poet speaking to himself. But the poetic line is so close to prose that the reader continually feels challenged by that voice, which seems so close and familiar, despite the detachment it proclaims. Recently anthologies and retrospectives have begun to make available Beaulieu's poems that were published in limited editions (*Vu*, 1989; *Indicatif présent et autres poèmes*, 1993; *Fuseaux*, 1996). The republication of his books, which has barely begun, will allow us to judge better the importance and quality of his work.

C.R.P. MAY/JACQUES PAQUIN

Beaulieu, Victor-Lévy (b. 1945). Born in Saint-Jean-de-Dieu, near Rimouski, Quebec, he added Victor to his given name for Victor Hugo, whose creative force and mythopoeic imagination he sought to emulate (*Pour saluer Victor Hugo*, 1971). Largely self-taught, he is among the most prolific of Quebec writers (forty-one titles to the present). His controversial literary output includes novels, plays, biographies, polemical essays, literary journalism, anthologies, and long-running television series (*Race de monde*, 1978-81, *L'héritage*, 1987-9)—though he has scant regard for traditional literary categories, using a variety of playful terms to characterize his works, 'cantique', 'oratorio', 'comédie', 'plagiaire', 'pèlerinage'. His critical study *Jack Kerouac: essai-poulet* (1972)—translated by Sheila Fischman as *Jack Kerouac: a chicken-essay* (1975) —explores the links between writing, criticism, appetite, and consumption. Some of Beaulieu's excellent journalism (largely from

Le Devoir and *L'Illettré*, 1970, the latter co-founded by him, Jean-Claude GERMAIN, and J.-M. Poupart), along with rare autobiographical writing, appeared as *Entre la sainteté et le terrorisme* (1984)—in which he attacked André LANGEVIN, whose work he considered too derivative, Eurocentric, and alienated from its roots. His own intention has been to repatriate Quebec culture and to save it from 'une déliquescence bondieusarde', a tacky piety. He sees himself as coming from 'le Québec d'en bas', meaning not simply from the South Shore but from Quebec's large sub-culture. His considerable achievement is in creating convincing portraits of characters on the fringes of normality and psychological viability; he does this with an air of acceptance and even approval that makes them not unsympathetic. The influence of others who have explored through literature the shadowlands of derangement and alienation—such as Jack Kerouac, Malcolm LOWRY, and Réjean DUCHARME—is clear. The title and themes of *Don Quichotte de la démanche* (1974), which play on physical and mental deformity, sum up this aspect of his work. It won a Governor General's Award and was translated by Sheila Fischman as *Don Quixote in Nighttown* (1978).

Beaulieu has constantly been in the forefront of Quebec's literary development. He worked at Jacques Hébert's Éditions du Jour (1969-73), before helping to found Éditions de l'Aurore and then opening a bookstore and publishing from it between 1976 and 1984 his own Éditions VLB. The quality of the books produced, his own among them, set new standards in Quebec publishing. Beaulieu's predilection for the work of Hugo was evident in the recurrent use of grotesque or architecturally fantastic pictorial material from the poet's pen and ink sketches, with the whale a recurrent figure. Beaulieu has written a lengthy study of whale-obsessed Herman Melville (*Monsieur Melville*, 3 vols, 1978) and this interest is echoed in his use of whaling in the St Lawrence as the backdrop to some of his fiction (*Blanche forcée*, 1975; *Sagamo Job J*, 1977; *Una*, 1980). His copious use of illustration favours early engravings, with the emphasis on exploration, the morbid, and the fantastical—evisceration of whales is a frequent visual theme. He works hard to hold in balance his or his characters' tenuous grasp of a consensual reality, constantly threatened with annihilation. His panicky sense of things tending to fall apart, and the challenge this presents to the creative artist to sum it all up, lead to exclamations such as: 'Oh, bouillonnement de la vie fragmentée!' Beaulieu's cross-media, non-linear approach is his method of presenting this exploded vision. Supremely through words and writing and through a protracted voyage of self-discovery, extrovert rather than introspective, his characters attempt to construct reality through transcendental meditation, Buddhism, interpersonal relations, the search for roots, or the renewal of history. One of the cycles of his fiction is entitled 'Voyageries'.

Beaulieu's biographical portrait of his friend and mentor Jacques FERRON (*Docteur Ferron*, 1991)—his crowning achievement to the present—is called a 'pèlerinage', a brilliant dialogue in which the author frantically seeks his subject in the scattered locations of his personal itinerary. It combines biography with autobiography, anthology, literary criticism (not all of it eulogistic), and an ambitious critique of Quebec stereotypes and pet assumptions in the Ferron manner. Ferron fed the younger Beaulieu's voracious appetite for reading, and was the source of many of the parish histories, pages from Quebec's pathetic martyrology, temperance tracts, and such-like that Beaulieu put into his *Anthologie de la petite littérature du Québec* (1974). Ferron provided Beaulieu with Pierre Leroy's fantastical life-story as Zouave, visionary, and educational reformer, which Beaulieu turned into a highly fictionalized biography: *Moi Pierre Leroy, prophète, martyr et un peu fêlé du chaudron* (1982). Ferron also inspired *Ma Corriveau, suivi de La sorcellerie en finale sexuée* (1976), Beaulieu's one venture into Quebec folklore and the literary transposition of a classical patois, as opposed to urban slang. Beaulieu makes his own distinctive contribution to Quebec's principal literary challenge—the forging of an authentic literary idiom from the colourful, inventive forms of Quebec popular speech—by the use of theatre and television, dialogue novels, first-person inner monologue, and copious use of direct speech or indirect free style. Reading Beaulieu's work as profoundly autobiographical, however, fails to take account of his projections of aspects of his personality in characters who fantasize, invent to deceive and mislead, or whose grasp of reality and memory is unreliable. What does come across very strongly is his love for his daughters (Julie and Mélanie illustrated his novel *Una*); his love of words; his inordinate admiration for prophet-polymaths such as Melville, Cervantes, Hugo, Ferron; his abiding concern with man ('être puissant et complexe'); and his fight for the arts in Quebec. (His novel *N'évoque plus que le désenchantement de ta ténèbre, mon si pauvre Abel*, 1976, contains a central episode in which Abel, Beaulieu's projection of himself as writer, pleads the cause of the artist with the late Premier Robert Bourassa.) Beaulieu believes that the ability to fictionalize one's experience, and to create and perpetuate myth, is an essential feature of a healthy culture.

See Gérard BESSETTE, *Trois romanciers québécois* (1973); Gabrielle Poulin, *Romans du paysage: 1968-1979* (1980); *Québec français* (45, 1982); *VOIX ET IMAGES* III, 2 (1977); *Études françaises* (1983/1); and Ben-Z. Shek, *French-Canadian and Québécois novels* (1991).

See also NOVELS IN FRENCH 1960 TO 1982: 3(a). C.R.P. MAY

Beausoleil, Claude (b. 1948). Born in Montreal, Beausoleil has had an extremely prolific career as poet, critic, essayist, and translator. He received a B.A. at Collège Sainte-Marie (Université de Montréal), a Bac. Spécialisé in literary studies and an M.A. from the Université du Québec à Montréal, and a Ph.D. in literary studies from Sherbrooke University. He studied Spanish at Cuernavaca, Mexico, art history at the Université de Montréal, and semiotics at Urbino, Italy. Since 1973 he has been professor of Quebec literature at Collège Édouard-Montpetit (Longueuil). He has published over forty books. His essays (*Les livres parlent*, 1984; *Extase et déchirure*, 1987) affirm the originality of Quebec literature and attempt to define its connections with different American and European cultures. Beausoleil's poetry, which has been translated into eight languages, includes the collections *Intrusion ralentie* (1972); *Journal mobile* (1974); *Promenade modern style* (1975); *Sens interdit* (1976); *La surface du paysage* (1979); *Au milieu du corps l'attraction s'insinue*, awarded the Prix Émile-NELLIGAN (1980); *Dans la matière rêvant comme une émeute* (1982); *Le livre du voyage* (1983); *Une certaine fin de siècle*: I (1983) and II (1991); *Concrete city: selected poems 1972-82* (1983), a bilingual edition containing poems translated by Ray Chamberlain from eight collections; *Il y a des nuits que nous habitons tous* (1986); *Grand hôtel des étrangers* (1988); *Fureur de Mexico* (1992); and *Montréal est une ville de poèmes vous savez* (1992). Beausoleil's highly experimental work of the 1970s developed a poetics of dislocation and prized multiplicity of meaning. The big city, especially Montreal, has been painstakingly inscribed in his work from the 1980s onward, which is characterized by an intense self-questioning of his identity as a Québécois poet. He defines the central paradox of his identity as a tear through the stomach of language ('déchirure centrale au ventre du langage'), for the language of America is not his own, even though America's culture informs his sense of self. In 1989 the lieutenant-governor of Quebec and the Office de la langue française awarded Beausoleil the Ordre des francophones d'Amérique. He has compiled anthologies of Acadian and Mexican poetry, is editor of the review *Lèvres urbaines*, and has collaborated on other journals, including *Estuaire*, *Jungle*, and *Europe*.

SUSAN ELMSLIE

Beautiful Joe (Philadelphia, 1894). Subtitled *An autobiography* and narrated by a dog, this novel for children by Marshall SAUNDERS was designed to arouse for dogs the kind of sympathy stirred for horses by *Black Beauty* (1877; first American publication 1890). Joe's life story moves from puppy days, when his ears and tail were cruelly cropped by his first brutal owner, to happy times with kind Miss Laura and the Morris family. Joe prevents a burglary, takes a train-ride to a well-run farm, visits an ill-run one, and witnesses a fire in which the members of a performing troupe of animals perish. Readers of *Beautiful Joe* learn of the pleasures and responsibilities of raising dogs, cats, canaries, parrots, snakes, goldfish, and rabbits. They also see the life experiences of foxes, bears, sheep, cattle, and horses, all from a fellow-animal's point of view. This novel shared with the much finer contemporary animal stories of Charles G.D. ROBERTS and Ernest Thompson SETON a sympathy for animals and a recognition of cruel streaks in both animal and human life. But *Beautiful Joe* is unashamedly sentimental and didactic: Joe supports the views of Miss Laura and her friends on temperance, mannerliness, and worship, and exploits the reader's sympathy by indulging in sensitivities that seem inappropriate in an animal. In a revised version (1927) violence was softened and colloquialism reduced; but the quick succession of exciting incidents and the sense of a likeable voice continued to make this 'fine tale of an ugly dog' a world-wide best-seller.

The centenary of *Beautiful Joe* was marked by a reprinting of the first edition (Owen Sound, 1994). ELIZABETH WATERSTON

Beaven, James. See PHILOSOPHY IN CANADA: *3*.

Beck, Lily Adams (d. 1931). The daughter of the British admiral John Moresby, she spent many years in the Orient, travelling in India, Ceylon, China, Java, Burma, Japan, and Tibet, until 1919, when she came to Canada and settled in Victoria, British Columbia. Here she became known as a proponent of Oriental customs and philosophy. Beck did not begin to publish her work until 1919, but between then and 1931, when she died in Kyoto, Japan, she produced more than thirty books. Those published under her own name tended to be stories rooted in Oriental philosophy and traditions; but in 1925 it was revealed that Beck, to the surprise of the general public, was simultaneously producing historical romances under the pseudonym E. Barrington. One of these novels, *The divine lady: a romance of Nelson and Emma Hamilton* (1924), became a popular silent film, and another, *The duel of the queens: a romance of Mary, Queen of Scots* (1930), was a great popular success both as a book and as a serialized magazine offering. In addition, she wrote three novels under the pseudonym Louis Moresby.

Beck was the author of *The ninth vibration, and other stories* (1922), *The key of dreams* (1922), *The perfume of the rainbow, and other stories* (1923), *The treasure of Ho* (1924), *The way of stars* (1925), *Dreams and delights* (1926), *The splendour of Asia* (1926), *The house of fulfilment* (1927), *The way of power* (1928), *The story of Oriental philosophy* (1928), *The garden of vision* (1929), *The openers of the gate* (1930), *The joyous story of Astrid* (1931), *The graces* (1934), and *Dream tea* (1934).

As E. Barrington she wrote *The ladies* (1922), *The chaste Diana* (1923), *The gallants* (1924), *Glorious Apollo* (1925), *The exquisite Perdita* (1926), *The thunderer* (1927), *The empress of hearts* (1928), *The laughing queen* (1929), *The Irish beauties* (1931), *Anne Boleyn* (1932), *The great romantic* (1933), and *The crowned lovers* (1935).

As Louis Moresby she wrote *The glory of Egypt* (1926), *Rubies* (1927), and *Captain Java* (1928). MARILYN ROSE

Bedard, Michael (b. 1949). Born in Toronto, Ontario, he was educated at the University of Toronto (B.A., 1971). He worked for a time in the university library, than as a pressman in a small print shop, publishing his first books, both collections of original fairy tales: *Woodsedge* (1979) and *Pipe and pearls* (1980). They began his interest in the form and style of the fairy tale because they were followed by another original tale, *The lightning bolt* (1989), and two retellings, *The tinder box* (1990) and *The nightingale* (1991). The fairy tale's influence on his novels *A darker magic* (1987), *Redwork* (1990), and *Painted devil* (1994) expressed itself primarily in the clarity of Bedard's images and settings and in his mingling of fantasy and realism. The important influence of William Blake's and Jacob Boehme's visionary writings, of Emily Dickinson's and George MacDonald's mysticism, and of the Brontës' Romanticism and Gothicism is reflected in Bedard's novels in several ways: he sees eternity folded in with time; he sees dream and reality as interrelated; he sees the imagination as the catalyst for good and evil. Both *A darker magic* and *Painted devil* combine realism, horror, and mystery in their examination of a young girl's chilling encounter with darkness as it is embodied in Professor Mephisto, a magician, whose spell is broken only by the movement of the potential victim from a state of passive observation to a state of creative action and resistance. The technically impressive *Redwork*, Bedard's most mature work and winner of a Governor General's Award, uses Blake's visionary poetry and the second stage in alchemy—redwork—as guiding metaphors of artistic activity, involving, among other things, reconnection with one's youth as a means towards self-enlightenment. Bedard's general subject matter is lower-middle-class life, early adolescence, and the special relationship between the old and the young. He remains preoccupied with the allure of the dark and the necessity for imaginative engagement with the world. MARIE C. DAVIS

Bégon, Élisabeth. See Writing in NEW FRANCE: 4.

Beissel, Henry (b. 1929). Born in Cologne, Germany, he studied philosophy at the universities of Cologne and London before coming to Canada in 1951. He received his M.A. in English (1960) from the University of Toronto, and then taught at the University of Alberta, Edmonton, and at Concordia University, Montreal, as professor of English. Beissel's concern for human aspirations in the face of civilization's march towards self-destruction, experienced personally in Europe during the Second World War, first found expression in his editorship of the controversial political and literary journal *Edge*, which moved with him from its inception in Edmonton in 1963 to its final year in Montreal in 1969. In 1980-1 he was president of the LEAGUE OF CANADIAN POETS.

Beissel's strong conviction about the necessity to ground one's life in the pursuit of artistic truth is apparent in *New wings for Icarus* (1966), a long poem in four parts. His first book of shorter poems was *Face on the dark* (1970), though this volume still demonstrates an emphasis on making larger poetic statements, as it also contains parts of longer uncompleted poems. *The salt I taste* (1975) is taken up principally with the title poem, meditations in long form on the bitterness of life, the image of the sea echoing through the sequence as a symbol of life's continuance in the face of the erosion of life. He has also written 'an epic poem about Canada in twelve cantos', *Cantos North* (1980). Other volumes of poetry are *Season of blood* (1984) and *Poems new and selected* (1987).

Beissel's plays have often focused on Canadian themes and cultures, especially in *Inook and the sun* (1973), a play for young people about the Inuit, first staged at the Stratford Festival in 1973. He has also written a play for marionettes, *Skinflint* (1969), and another play about Native American peoples, *Under Coyote's eye: a play about Ishi* (1979), as well as *Goya* (1978), which he describes as a dramatic 'exploration of the creative imagination'. Beissel edited a collection of Canadian one-act plays, *Cues and entrances* (1977; 2nd edn 1993), and was joint-editor (with Jill Bennett) of a tribute to Irving LAYTON, *Raging like a fire* (1993).

Beissel's interest in international culture, notably poetry, is exemplified by his translations of the German-Canadian poet Walter BAUER, collected in two volumes, *The price of morning* (1968) and *A different sun* (1976). He has also translated poems from the German by Peter Huchel, and from the Spanish by Pablo Neruda. PETER STEVENS

Belaney, Archibald Stansfeld (1888-1938). When Grey Owl—the famous trapper, writer, and lecturer—died suddenly in his fiftieth year in Saskatchewan, few were aware that he had no Amerindian blood but was in fact an Englishman named Archibald Stansfeld Belaney. Two elderly maiden ladies of extreme gentility and unquestionable veracity, living in Hastings, England, confirmed that Grey Owl was their nephew Archie, whom they had brought up, and who had gone to Canada as soon as he left school. When the full story of his life became known, the character that surfaced was far more interesting than the Thoreau-like naturalist and writer who occasionally emerged from the Canadian woods to give lectures and assist in the promotion of his books.

Archie Belaney was born in Hastings, the son of George Belaney, a Victorian 'remittance man' who led a wandering life of adventure and dissipation in America. Brought up in a household of women, the boy created for himself an image of his missing father as a doughty fighter in the Wild West. He believed that his mother, who visited him briefly two or three times in his boyhood, was an Apache. The published history of Hastings Grammar School records that he read and dreamt of North America's Native peoples; this is supported by the numerous drawings he made of Amerindians and animals in the margins of the books he left behind when he went to Canada.

Belaney immigrated to Canada in 1906 and became a guide and packer in northern Ontario. Within a year he joined a band of Ojibwa who summered on Bear Island in Lake Temagami. In 1910 he married an Ojibwa girl, Angele Eguana, and quickly came under the influence of the band, which was then barely spoilt by any contact with civilization. Belaney lived and hunted with these Ojibwa and, by his own account, went through a ceremony of adoption and was given the name Grey Owl. But in 1912 he left the band and moved to Biscostasing, the headquarters of the Mississauga Reserve. He served in the First World War and was wounded. While recovering in England in 1917 he married Constance Holmes, a childhood sweetheart. The marriage was brief, for he soon returned to Canada, taking up again his life as trapper and guide in the Mississauga River country. Sickened by his war experiences, he turned again to Canada's Native peoples, and resumed his Grey Owl identity, though he was still known to whites as Belaney.

His meeting in 1926 with Anahareo, an Iroquois girl with whom he had an eight-year passionate though stormy love affair, was the turning-point of his life. Anahareo's horror of his bloody trade as a trapper made him aware of what he was doing, and ultimately resulted in his fame. She persuaded him to save and bring into their cabin two baby beaver, whose mother had drowned in one of his traps. These infant creatures—pathetic relics of what then seemed, because of overtrapping, to be a vanishing species—adopted Grey Owl and Anahareo as their parents. Their affectionate behaviour and childlike ways made Grey Owl vow never to take the life of another beaver. He and Anahareo went to Cabano, in northern Quebec, to find a sanctuary for the beavers and to found a colony for the preservation of the species. (Their heroic journey is unforgettably described in Grey Owl's best-known book, *Pilgrims of the wild*.) The couple and their charges were discovered by the Canadian government in 1930. Grey Owl was appointed an Honorary Park Warden and a home was built for him and his beaver at Lake Ajawaan in Prince Albert National Park, Saskatchewan.

While at Cabano, Grey Owl had turned to writing to support his adopted 'family', as his sole income was a monthly war pension of fifteen dollars. His first published piece, 'The falls of silence', appeared under the name of A.S. Belaney in *Country Life*, the famous English sporting and social magazine. Its theme was the silence of the great north woods, 'the most silent country on the face of the globe, in which man moves observed only by animals whose senses are trained to hair-trigger delicacy'. With a further series of articles on animal lore, contributed to *Forest & Outdoors* in the next few years under the name of Grey Owl, he became well known in naturalist circles in Canada and the USA.

In the last eight years of his life Grey Owl wrote four books. In *The men of the last frontier* (1931) he recreated vividly and simply life as it was lived when he first came under the tutelage of the Ojibwa and listened to their legends. *Pilgrims of the wild* (1934), which was published in England by Lovat Dickson Limited, established his fame as a writer. *The adventures of Sajo and her beaver people* (1935) was an attempt at fiction for children. Although this story of a Native boy's attempt to find his lost beaver pet has a number of stock city characters that weaken its impact, it was enormously popular. *Tales of an empty cabin* (1936), which shows Grey Owl the writer at his best, is an impressive collection of sketches of men and animals in a forest world; it is full of humour and close, affectionate observation. All four books are a lament for a lost frontier.

In 1935-6 and 1937-8 Grey Owl made two highly successful lecture tours of the United States and Britain, ending with a lecture to the royal family at Buckingham Palace. Those who listened to him, and watched the half-dozen films a cameraman employed by the Canadian government had made of him, saw something that would possibly never be seen again: man and animal living together in perfect harmony. Undeterred by the camera, the beavers came and went about their business, pushing open the door of Grey Owl's cabin and advancing with armfuls of sticks and mud to repair the structure of their house (built against an inner wall of the cabin but with an underwater outlet in the lake); or disporting themselves like so many water-nymphs around his canoe, inviting him to play. At the height of the Depression, Grey Owl's simple message touched something in the hearts of his audience. 'You are tired with years of civilization. I come to offer you what. . . ? A single green leaf.' *The Times* of London called him 'A Canadian Thoreau'. Though known as a naturalist and environmentalist in his own time, Grey Owl was really an unsurpassed observer of animal behaviour and recorder of wilderness life.

His grave is beside his cabin on Lake Ajawaan in Prince Albert National Park. The cross that was first raised over it bore the name Archibald Stansfeld Belaney. A few years later the Canadian government replaced this with a stone, bearing the name Grey Owl and the dates of his birth and death, and restored his cabin, which is frequently visited. After his death Angele Eguana, his Ojibwa wife, represented by John G. Diefenbaker, established that she had been truly married to him—she shrugged away his infidelity saying, 'he liked to go travel in the Indian way'. Although she had not seen him for many years, she was awarded the wife's share of his quite substantial estate.

Anahareo has written a revealing memoir of their life together: *Devil in deerskins* (1972). *The green leaf* (1938), edited by Lovat DICKSON, is an account of the controversy prompted by the revelation of Grey Owl's English origin. It includes some of Grey Owl's letters to his publisher, and a record of his last days. See also Lovat Dickson's biography, *Wilderness man* (1973), Donald B. Smith, *From the land of shadows: the making of Grey Owl* (1990), and Armand Garnet Ruffo, *Grey Owl: the mystery of Archie Belaney* (1997).

LOVAT DICKSON

Belle bête*, *La (1959). The first novel by Marie-Claire BLAIS, which was published to mingled astonishment and acclaim when she was only twenty—and was translated by Merloyd Lawrence as *Mad shadows* (1960; NCL, with an Afterword by Daphne MARLATT)—remains, despite some youthful crudities of structure, an important work, both as a brilliant introduction to the vision of a dazzling new writer and as a link between the social novelists of the 1940s and such later experimental Quebec writers as Hubert AQUIN and Réjean DUCHARME. Striking in its macabre intensity, its denial of pure realism, and in the boldness of its imagery and sheer headlong force, the novel presents characters less as individualized human beings than as raw essences—embodiments of evil, narcissism, jealousy, and greed. The setting is as stripped as the characters, almost featureless—a country house, a lake, a train, a faraway city. Against this background, which resembles a painted stage set more than any known landscape, the characters (all of them rootless and all obsessed—a frivolous mother, a beautiful imbecile boy, a jealous sister, a blind youth) move with the strict and inexorable fluidity of dance, enacting a nightmare ritual of envy, murder, betrayal, and disfigurement. The American critic Edmund Wilson, who pronounced Marie-Claire Blais a genius, called the book 'a tragic fairytale', but it is more precisely a hallucinatory moral fable—an examination of pure evil in a society torn from its roots. JOYCE MARSHALL

Belles-soeurs*, *Les (1968). A major turning-point in the recent history of Québécois theatre, this play by Michel TREMBLAY was written in 1965, but was turned down by many groups—including the Dominion Drama Festival—before being given a public reading by the Centre d'essai des auteurs dramatiques on 4 Mar. 1968. It was first performed by Montreal's Théâtre du Rideau Vert on 28 Aug. 1968. Many people were shocked by its use of *JOUAL*, and by its frank depiction of an ugly reality; some critics thought it too peculiar—regional and parochial—to be exported beyond the linguistic boundaries of its setting. But success soon made it a 'classic'. It was performed in France and other European countries; the English-language première took place at the St Lawrence Centre, Toronto, on 31 Mar. 1973, and was followed by many productions in other Canadian cities and in the USA. First published in French in 1968, it was translated into English by Bill Glassco and John Van Burek and published in 1974. *The guid sisters* (1988), a Scottish dialect translation by Martin Bowman and William Findlay, had a decisive impact on cultural life in Scotland, where it was seen as an example to follow with local translations of other foreign plays. In 1983, for the play's fifteenth anniversary, the Nouvelle Compagnie Théâtrale presented a new production, directed by André Brassard, which stressed more clearly the absurd, quasi-surrealistic dimension of the play. In a new translation by van Burek and Glassco, *Les belles-soeurs* (rev. ed. 1992) was part of the 1991 season of the Stratford Festival, Ontario.

Les belles-soeurs is almost plotless. A poor woman, Germaine Lauzon, wins a million trading stamps and, realizing 'it's gonna take forever to paste all those stamps', decides to give 'a stamp-pasting party' for fifteen women—neighbours, sisters, friends, but only one literal sister-in-law. The women, however, steal the stamps and the play ends in an uproar, with Germaine crying over her lost stamps and happiness, and the other women standing at attention singing 'O Canada'. The stamp-pasting party is a vehicle for the women to voice their social and sexual deprivations; in so doing they realize how symbolic and short-lived their dreams of a better life are, how useless their revolt. Though it frequently provokes laughter, this pessimistic drama is justly perceived as a realistic depiction of the working class in Montreal, or of the condition of women—figures of Quebec's destiny—simmering in revolt.

A true (and perhaps necessary) metaphor for national alienation, *Les belles-soeurs* remains a landmark as a formally innovative play. The choruses and monologues that structure it express collective solitudes; and its diction, *joual*—which is used poetically, not realistically—is the language of visceral, spontaneous, and apparently disordered lamentation.

See *Le monde de Michel Tremblay* (1993) edited by Gilbert David and Pierre Lavoie.

JEAN CLÉO GODIN

Benoît, Jacques. See FANTASTIC LITERATURE AND SCIENCE FICTION IN FRENCH and NOVELS IN FRENCH 1960 TO 1982: 3(e).

Beresford-Howe, Constance (b. 1922). Born in Montreal and educated at McGill University and Brown University, Rhode Island, USA (Ph.D., 1950), she taught English literature and creative writing at McGill and at Ryerson Polytechnical Institute, Toronto, retiring in 1988. While living in Montreal she wrote four novels that explore the emotional lives of young women. *The unreasoning heart* (1946) is the story of a homeless adolescent girl who wins a place in the family of a prosperous Montreal widow. *Of this day's journey* (1947) is about a young graduate of McGill and Radcliffe lecturing at a college in a small American town, who has an affair with the college president. *The invisible gate* (1949), set in Montreal at the end of the Second World War, focuses on the romance of a high-spirited young woman whose suitor proves to be unworthy of her. *My Lady Greensleeves* (1955) is a historical romance set in sixteenth-century England and based on a documented Elizabethan lawsuit. While these early novels are slight and predictable in plot, they are notable for the development of a fluid and natural prose style, suitable to Beresford-Howe's realist agenda.

After settling in Toronto in 1971, Beresford-Howe wrote the first of three critically acknowledged and popular novels that portray the day-to-day lives of contemporary women. *The book of Eve* (1973), the most successful, portrays a spirited middle-class woman who suddenly, at the age of sixty five, decides to leave her ailing and demanding husband, trading comfort and social respectability for the freedom to live as she pleases. A successful stage adaptation of this novel, *Eve*, by Larry FINEBERG, starred Jessica Tandy and premièred at the Stratford Festival in 1976. In *A population of one* (1976) a thirty-year-old virgin leaves her sheltered family life in Toronto to take up a teaching position in Montreal, where she sets out to lose her virginity and learns that casual love affairs are neither as easy to come by nor as desirable as she had thought. *The marriage bed* (1981) describes a few weeks in the life of a twenty-four-year-old woman who has two pre-school children, is eight months pregnant, and has been left by her lawyer husband, yet cheerfully continues to affirm the values, and indeed the pleasures, of domesticity and motherhood. The novels are successful on the whole, partly because of the wry humour and admirable resilience that characterize each protagonist, and partly because the novels challenge largely uncontested ideas of their time concerning women and female identity—the assumption, for example, that women must succour even ungrateful spouses, or that sexual promiscuity will be fulfilling, or that women must always feel dissatisfied when staying at home to raise children. *A population of one* and *The marriage bed* have been made into films by the Canadian Broadcasting Corporation.

Irony and the courage to carry on, in spite of life's unalterable exigencies, also characterize Beresford-Howe's later fiction. Each is intelligent and entertaining, though none achieve the fullness of character that marked her earlier, more affecting novels. *Night studies* (1985), in which she departed from her usual single protagonist, delineates the often-humorous intersection of the lives of fourteen hapless characters at Simcoe College, a dismal utilitarian Toronto institution whose concentric corridors are explicitly Dantean. *Prospero's daughter* (1988) differs as well, in its English manor-house setting (wherein a celebrated and inflated Canadian expatriate successfully manipulates his bland yet mysterious daughter into a conventional marriage), and in its elaborate use of British historical and cultural detail. *A serious widow* (1991) returns to more familiar territory, portraying an initially incompetent and impoverished Toronto widow who moves towards independence and self-realization, partially through amusing real-life encounters and partially through fanciful conversations with such virtual cronies as Canadian novelist Ethel WILSON and Britain's Prince Charles, both of whom she construes as wise eccentrics.

See Fergus Cronin, 'Showing the hands: a profile of Constance Beresford-Howe', *CANADIAN FORUM* (October 1985), and Andrea O'Reilly, 'Feminizing feminism: Constance Beresford-Howe and the quest for female freedom', *Canadian Woman Studies/Les Cahiers de la Femme* 8, no. 3 (1987). MARILYN ROSE

Bergen, David. See NOVELS IN ENGLISH 1983 TO 1996: OTHER NOVELS 2(b).

Berger, Carl (b. 1939). Born in The Pas, Manitoba, he was educated at the University of Manitoba (B.A., 1961), and the University of Toronto (M.A., 1962; Ph.D., 1967), where he studied under Maurice CARELESS. He was appointed there in 1964 and is professor of history. Berger's inquiries into intellectual history have deepened the understanding of the Canadian past and pointed towards new sophistication in historiography. *The sense of power: studies in the ideas of Canadian imperialism, 1867-1914* (1970) appeared at a time when Canadians were fiercely debating American influence and argued that British imperialism had evolved in Canada as a form of Canadian nationalism. Free from previous preoccupations that had infested former inquiries when the subject was hotly contested in the political arena, Berger's work added a new dimension to historical scholarship in revealing the complicated roles that ideas play in history.

Turning next to the output of his colleagues, Berger wrote the landmark *The writing of Canadian history: aspects of English-Canadian historical writing since 1900* (1976; 2nd edn 1986), the first in-depth analysis of how earlier historians had understood the past. Evoking the principal themes that had governed intellectual output while analysing the country's major historians, Berger cast a mirror on an academic discipline that had been little prone to introspection. His book received a Governor General's Award. In *Science, God, and nature in Victorian Canada* (1983) he examined the intricate interplay between scientific inquiry and religion; but in *Honour and the search for influence: a history of the Royal Society of Canada* (1996) he went on to portray the difficulties that intellectuals have in fulfilling ideals. Among Berger's doctoral students have been some significant historians of the succeeding generation—including Gerald Friesen, Doug Owram, and Marlene Shore.

TERRY CROWLEY

Bergeron, Léandre (b. 1933). He was born in Saint-Lupicin, Manitoba, and graduated from Collège Saint-Boniface (B.A., 1954).

Teaching French and then obtaining a B.Ed. from the University of Manitoba in 1956, he taught high school from 1957 to 1958. Winning a French government scholarship, Bergeron studied at the Université Aix-Marseille, where he obtained a doctorate (D. l'U., 1961) for a thesis on French poet Paul Valéry that was published in 1963. Appointed assistant professor in 1961 at the Collège Militaire Royale, Kingston, he moved to Sir George Williams College (now Concordia University), Montreal, in 1964, retiring in 1975 to McWatters (near Rouyn), Quebec, to raise sheep.

During the turbulent years of the Quiet Revolution in Quebec, Bergeron became associated with the group publishing the leftist journal *PARTI PRIS* as well as with the Mouvement de libération populaire and the Parti socialiste du Québec. Interested in furthering the expression of alternative viewpoints in print, he helped found a series of small publishing concerns—Diffusion Québec, Éditions de l'Aurore, and Éditions Québécoises—that published his best-selling *Petit manuel d'histoire du Québec* (1970). Part socialistic polemic and part potted history, Bergeron's irreverent account of the province's past paraded anticlericalism and decried Quebec's social and political leaders based on rhetorical class analysis. Historians condemned the account, but the public loved the book's audacity. A translation appeared as *The history of Quebec: a patriote's handbook* (various editions, 1971-80), and Bergeron followed up in the wake of the October 1970 FLQ crisis with *Pour une révolution au Québec* (1972). After producing a phonograph record in 1971, mounting dramatic performances in Quebec and France, and publishing a play on Quebec's history (1974), Bergeron devoted part of his retirement to *Dictionnaire de la langue québécoise* (1980). Another instant popular success in celebrating Quebec French, a language that had for too long been derided by an imperialistic snobbishness once also characteristic of English, the book was attacked by linguists as vociferously as historians had attacked the history. Bergeron snubbed all by publishing *Petit manuel de l'accouchement à la maison* (1982), which also aroused enormous controversy.

TERRY CROWLEY

Bernard, Harry (1898-1979). Born in London, England, he studied in Paris, then in St Alban's, Vermont, and from 1911 to 1918 at the Séminaire de Saint-Hyacinthe, Quebec, where he received his B.A. After a short stay in Lowell, Massachusetts, he registered in 1919 at the Université de Montréal, where he obtained his 'licence ès lettres'. Parliamentary correspondent for *Le Droit* in Ottawa from 1919 to 1923, he then became director of *Le Courrier de Saint-Hyacinthe* and was associated with that paper until 1970. In 1933-4 Bernard was also director of *L'Action nationale*. For over fifty years a contributor to many newspapers, he received the Prix David three times (1924, 1926, and 1932) and the Prix d'Action intellectuelle six times. In 1943 he was elected to the Royal Society of Canada; he received its Silver Medal in 1959 and the Prix Olivar Asselin in 1961. He died in Saint-Hyacinthe.

Apart from numerous articles in newspapers (sometimes written under the pseudonym 'L'Illettré') and reviews, Bernard published more than a dozen books, but he is mainly remembered for his fiction, which gave him a place in the history of literary regionalism and the psychological novel in French Canada. In *L'homme tombé* (1924)—a rarity for the time in being set in a city (Saint-Hyacinthe)—Dr Étienne Normand marries, despite his mother's warnings, a working-class girl. He soon realizes his error as Alberte succumbs easily to the frivolous temptations of the city and begins to neglect her duties as wife and mother, but Normand is powerless to change her. The artificial characters in this didactic novel simply echo the ideologies of the day in Quebec: élitism, suspicion of the city and its deceptive pleasures, the necessity for a wife to be submissive to her husband. (Jules-Ernest Larivière reworked the characters in a novel called *L'associée silencieuse*, 1925, in which he tried to correct Bernard's portrait of Saint-Hyacinthe, showing that a working-class girl could very easily marry a man from a higher social class and be a worthy helpmate.) Bernard also used this theme of the city as the place of man's degradation in *La maison vide* (1925). The virtues of the land and the 'call of the race' were promoted in *La terre vivante* (1925) and *La ferme des pins* (1930). (In *La ferme*, unusually, it is an anglophone peasant from the Eastern Townships who feels the 'call of the race', and that his children are threatened with assimilation.) These novels, whose cardboard characters are simply mouthpieces for an agricultural ideology, were part of the flourishing Quebec regional literature of the 1920s. *Juana, mon aimée* (1931) shows improvement in technique and in psychological verisimilitude. The narrator, Raymond Chatel, a journalist whose career in Ottawa and Montreal is interrupted when he is obliged to take a health cure in Saskatchewan, tells how he came to know and love

Juana, and to lose her as a result of a misunderstanding. He likes the West, and says: 'If, instead of emigrating to the south, our excess population had moved immediately in the direction of the West, we would today be masters of the Prairies.' In *Dolorès* (1932), which is often reminiscent of *Juana, mon aimée*, Bernard not only describes the pretty *paysage* of the Mont-Laurier region but gives an in-depth psychological analysis of his characters. His last novel, *Les jours sont longs* (1951), is similar in theme and technique to the previous two but is more successful and more convincing.

La dame blanche (1927) is a collection of fourteen stories, with an edifying tone, that were inspired by French-Canadian legends or historical events. The first nine, along with 'Montcalm se Fâche', were published under that title in 1935. Bernard's *Essais littéraires* (1929)—which examines the work of Robert de ROQUEBRUNE, Émile CODERRE, Blanche Lamontagne, Jules Fournier, and Louis Dantin (Eugène SEERS)—was well received at the time but does not engage the present-day reader's attention.

For his doctoral thesis presented at the Université de Montréal, *Le roman regionaliste aux États-Unis, 1913-1940* (1949), Bernard drew up an inventory of some 3000 American novels in which he sought to demonstrate the links between regionalism and literary nationalism. Bernard also wrote a children's book. *ABC de petit naturaliste canadien* (1935), and *Passages et routes d'eau en Haute Mauricie* (1953).

JACQUES COTNAM

Bernier, Hector. See NOVELS IN FRENCH 1900 TO 1920.

Bernier, Jovette-Alice (1900-81). Born in Saint-Fabien, Quebec, she was educated at École Normale des Ursulines, Rimouski, and taught from 1917 to 1923. Her first volume of poetry, *Roulades* (1924), drew little attention; but *Comme l'oiseau* (1926)—in which the poet dared to say 'Je' and to confess the deep deception of her love, her suffering, her remorse, and nostalgia—was more successful. In *Tout n'est pas dit*—first published in 1928, then destroyed, and published again in an enlarged edition in 1929, with a preface by Louis Dantin (Eugène SEERS)—she used a variety of structures and metrical rhythms to convey her will to live fully and to taste the sensual pleasures of life, even though love was often deceptive and left painful memories. *Les masques déchirés* (1932), in which the poet, no longer able to endure hypocrisy and social convention, attempts to reveal her true self, acknowledges her happiness in having known love and in having suffered from it. The last section is composed of poems from *Roulades* and *Comme l'oiseau*. In *Mon deuil en rouge* (1945), which includes poems dating from 1933, Bernier continued to expose the wounds of love and to relate her sorrow and disillusion, while questioning, sometimes with irony, the human condition.

On vend le bonheur (1931), a collection of articles, tales, reflections on life, and memories of childhood, was not much appreciated by the critics. Bernier's first novel, *La chair décevante* (1931; rpr. 1982), however, was widely discussed and its morality questioned by critics who found its title too provocative. A melodrama, it tells the story of a young woman who had been abandoned by her lover and left with his child. This far-fetched tale, with its improbable episodes and clichés—mistaken identity, threat of incest, sudden death, a murder trial and acquittal, and the heroine's eventual madness—was considered daring and shocking in the Quebec of the thirties. Although Bernier kept writing for newspapers, magazines, and radio broadcasts, she published no book between 1945 and 1969. The undoubtedly autobiographical *Non monsieur* (1969), which tells of an unfortunate love between a young schoolteacher and a Métis ladies' man named Noc, takes up again the theme of the difficulties of an independent girl in pursuit of happiness.

JACQUES COTNAM

Bersianik, Louky (b. 1930). Born Lucille Durand in Montreal, Quebec, she studied French literature at the Université de Montréal and then at the Sorbonne and the Centre d'études de radio et de télévision, Paris, where she lived for five years. She has worked as a writer and researcher for radio, television, and cinema, and taught creative writing at Concordia University, Montreal, and the Université du Québec à Montréal. Her first published writings were stories for children. She has since also published poetry, novels, essays, and songs.

Using the name Louky Bersianik, she published *L'EUGUÉLIONNE* (1976), a groundbreaking feminist novel combining allegory and parable, and parody, that became an immediate best-seller. It is the story of a 'sister [Euguélionne] from another planet' who has come to Earth in search of the 'male of her species'. The Euguélionne (from the Greek *euaggeion*, meaning 'gospel' or good news) is a female Christ figure who discovers the bizarre state of relations between the sexes in our world, and in the process demystifies and deconstructs, satirizes and lampoons, the mythologies and conventions of human male-female relations. *Firewords/Les terribles vivantes* (1986) is a National Film Board film, directed by Dorothy Todd Hénaut, based on this novel.

After publishing *L'Euguélionne*, Bersianik spent a year on the island of Crete writing another novel, *Le pique-nique sur l'Acropole* (1979), a feminist rewriting of Plato's *Symposium*. She has also published poetry and prose-poems on feminist themes in the collections *La page de garde* (1978), *Maternative* (1980), *Au beau milieu de moi* (1983), *Axes et eau* (1984), and *Kerameikos* (1987). Her essay *La agénésies du vieux monde* (1982), on feminist theory, was republished in *La main tranchante du symbole* (1990) with some twenty texts on feminist themes written between 1980 and 1990. It has been translated by Mirande Hay and Lise Weil as 'Agenesias of the Old World', *Trivia* 7 (Summer 1985). *Permafrost* (1997) is the first novel in a cycle entitled *Les inenfances de Sylvanie Penn*.

Bersianik is fond of coining words (often drawing from science or mythology), as is evident in some of her titles: *agénésies*, meaning the absence of an origin, *inenfances*, unchildhood.

See Jennifer Waelti-Waters, 'The food of love: Plato's banquet and Bersianik's picnic', *Atlantis* 6, no. 1 (1981). HOWARD SCOTT

Berthiaume, André. See FANTASTIC LITERATURE AND SCIENCE FICTION IN FRENCH.

Berton, Pierre (b. 1920). Pierre Francis de Marigny Berton was born in Dawson City, the Yukon, and was educated at the University of British Columbia (B.A., 1941). In 1942 he became city editor of the Vancouver *News-Herald*. He then served in the army, rising to captain/instructor at the Royal Military College, Kingston. After the war he was a feature writer for the Vancouver *Sun*, joined *Maclean's* in 1947, and was its managing editor from 1952 to 1958, when he left to become a columnist and associate editor of the Toronto *Star*. In 1959 he was awarded the J.V. McAree Memorial Award for the best daily newspaper column in Canada. Devoting his time increasingly to radio and television work, Berton left the *Star* in 1962 to return to *Maclean's* for a year and to work for his own TV program, 'The Pierre Berton Show', which ran until 1973. For over twenty-five years he was a regular panelist on CBC's 'Front Page Challenge'. He holds two ACTRA awards, one for integrity and outspokenness in broadcasting and a second for public-affairs broadcasting. He has been awarded a number of honorary degrees, is a Companion of the Order of Canada (1986), chairman of the Heritage Canada Foundation, and a former Chair of the WRITERS' UNION OF CANADA (1987-8).

The colour and excitement of Berton's spirited historical narratives and his passionate nationalism have done much to stir up interest in Canadian history. Berton received a Governor General's Award for *The mysterious North* (1956)—a graphic description of the Canadian North and an appraisal of its potentialities—and for *Klondike: the life and death of the last great goldrush* (1958; rev. 1972; American title *Klondike fever*), considered by many to be Berton's finest work, in which he dramatically recreated the gaudy personalities who, from 1896 to 1903, were attracted to the Klondike by the lust for gold. Berton's Yukon background gave this book a notable degree of immediacy and enthusiasm. For young readers he wrote *The golden trail: the story of the Klondike rush* (1954), reprinted as *Stampede for gold* (1955). He also wrote and narrated the National Film Board documentary *City of gold*, winner of the Grand Prix (Cannes). He returned to the North in *The arctic grail: the quest for the North-West Passage and the North Pole 1818-1909* (1989).

The history of the Canadian Pacific Railway is portrayed in two volumes: *The national dream, the great railway, 1871-1881* (1970) and *The last spike, the great railway, 1881-1885* (1971). The national dream, written as a heroic epic, and often criticized for being exaggerated and overly imaginative, described the bitterness, intrigues, scandals, and personal animosities among politicians, surveyors, and railway contractors. While Berton's political interpretation identifies the good of the country with central-Canadian manufacturing and industrial interests, he provides new and captivating anecdotes and human-interest stories in describing the landscape and the politicians, financiers, eccentrics, and ordinary people who struggled against handicaps of geography and economy to build the railway. The more subdued *The last spike* won Berton his third Governor General's Award. *The impossible railway* (1972) is a single-volume edition published for the American market; *The great railway illustrated* (1972) is another one-volume abridgement.

The invasion of Canada, 1812-1813 (1980), *Flames across the border, 1813-1814* (1981), and *Vimy* (1986) offer vivid descriptions of battle scenes and exact and extensive details of military history; many anecdotes reveal the ironies and tragedies of wartime. Berton is at his best depicting the experiences of rank-

and-file soldiers and civilians who happen into the fighting—though his portrayal of soldiers, politicians, Natives, and frontiersmen is somewhat romantic. He believes that the most lasting impact of the 'absurd' war of 1812-14 are the myths created by Canadians to justify their separateness from the USA.

Aware of the impact of mass media on the Canadian consciousness, Berton, in *Hollywood's Canada: the Americanization of our national image* (1975), expresses his outrage in an angry, often comical and entertaining diatribe against the American film industry's treatment of Canada as the American West transplanted. In *Why we act like Canadians: a personal exploration of our national character* (1982), a series of fictional letters to an American friend, Berton dispels American myths about Canada and explains that history, climate, and geography have given Canadians a unique lifestyle and sense of independence. *My country: the remarkable past* (1976) and *The wild frontier: more tales from the remarkable past* (1978) are, respectively, collections of eighteen and seven short biographies of bizarre Canadians and their exploits. In *The Dionne years: a thirties melodrama* (1977) Berton focuses on the public phenomenon surrounding the Dionne family, maintaining that the quintuplets were a symbol of hope in the Depression, a period he examines in *The great Depression* (1990).

Berton's early writing was dominated by his journalistic interest in public opinion and his concern for contemporary social problems and issues. *The royal family; the story of the British monarchy from Victoria to Elizabeth* (1954) contains gossipy and often humorous character sketches. Five books are products of his entertaining *Star* newspaper columns: *Just add water and stir* (1959)—awarded the LEACOCK Medal for Humour; *Adventures of a columnist* (1960); *Fast fast fast relief* (1962); *The big sell: an introduction to the black art of door-to-door salesmanship and other techniques* (1963); and *My war with the 20th century* (1965), an adaptation of *The big sell* published for the American market. The Anglican Church commissioned the agnostic Berton to write *The comfortable pew* (1965), a critique of the church's public image that attacks the complacency of clergy and laity in the face of rapid social change. *The smug minority* (1968) somewhat tediously condemns the Canadian Establishment, identified by Berton as an inbred Liberal/Conservative, Protestant/Catholic/capitalistic minority that is reluctant to invest in education or the betterment of society.

Berton has written many books in McCLELLAND & STEWART's Adventures in Canadian History Series, including *Before the Gold Rush* (1993), *The battle of Lake Erie* (1994), and *Attack on Montreal* (1995). *The secret world of Og* (1961; rpr. 1974) is an exuberant adventure fantasy for children. Berton is co-author, with his wife Janet, of the *Centennial food guide* (1966)—reissued in 1974 as the *Canadian food guide*. Among his other books are *Historic headlines; a century of Canadian news drama* (1967) and *Drifting home* (1973), a chronicle of the Berton family's holiday adventure on a northern river.

See *Starting out, 1920-1947* (1987), Berton's accounts of his early life, and *My times: living with history, 1947-1995* (1995).

See also HISTORICAL WRITING IN ENGLISH: 7.

DAVID FLINT

Bessette, Arsène. See NOVELS IN FRENCH 1900 TO 1920.

Bessette, Gérard (b.1920). Born on a farm near Sainte-Anne-de-Sabrevois, Quebec, he spent his early childhood in the village of Saint-Alexandre before moving to Montreal in 1930. He was educated at the Sainte-Croix day school, the École Normale Jacques-Cartier, and the Université de Montréal, obtaining a master's degree in 1946 and a doctorate in 1950. He taught at the University of Saskatchewan (1946-9), Duquesne University, Pittsburgh (1951-8), the Collège Militaire Royale, Kingston (1958-60), and Queen's University (1960-79). In 1979 he began to devote his time entirely to writing. He has contributed to various periodicals and received several awards: the Prix du Concours Littéraire from the Province of Quebec in 1947; two Governor General's Awards; and the Prix David in 1980. He became a member of the Royal Society of Canada in 1966.

Bessette began his career as a creative writer with the publication of *Poèmes temporels* (1954) and as a literary critic with *Les images en poésie canadienne-française* (1960). Later psychocritical studies—of Émile NELLIGAN, Anne HÉBERT, Yves THÉRIAULT, and Gabrielle ROY in *Une littérature en ébullition* (1968), of Victor-Lévy BEAULIEU, André LANGEVIN, and Roy in *Trois romanciers québécois* (1973)—reveal a psychoanalytical approach to the study of literature that is Freudian in nature. Bessette also compiled anthologies: *Anthologie d'Albert Laberge* (1962), which helped to introduce Quebec's first naturalist writer (q.v.); *De Québec à Saint-Boniface (récits et nouvelles du Canada-français* (1968); and *Histoire de la littérature canadienne-française* (1968) in collaboration with Lucien Geslin and Charles Parent.

During his father's fatal illness (1957-9) Bessette turned to novel-writing. *La bagarre* (1958) and *Les pédagogues* (1961) are realistic and traditional, his narrators objective and omniscient. *La bagarre* examines three aspects of French Canada and describes the problems that confront students—three types of student, three failures. Jules Lebeuf, who hopes to become a writer and goes out with a waitress who hardly interests him, eventually opts for trade-unionism; Sillery, a homosexual, chooses exile and the study of anthropology and colonialism; the American Weston plans the study of French Canadians for his thesis but abandons his project in favour of journalism. *La bagarre* was translated by Mark Lebel as *The brawl* (1976). *Les pédagogues* satirizes the narrow-minded atmosphere in a school whose director is a doctrinaire conformist; Sarto Pellerin can neither change his environment nor prevent the abuse inflicted by the clerical authorities. His failure is echoed in *Le libraire* (1960), a witty satire on book censorship in the Duplessis era. Hervé Jodoin, after losing his job as college proctor, becomes a cynical, depressed country librarian, but once again breaks the rules and loses his job for having sold a censored book to a student. This novel, which attacks the hypocrisy of a situation that could be saved only by a 'quiet revolution', was translated by Glen Shortliffe as *Not for every eye* (1962). *Le libraire* prepared the ground for *L'INCUBATION* (1965), in which the student-professor-bookseller of the first novels is a repressed librarian no longer belligerent but dismayed by the disintegration he sees in human relationships. The narrative, related by the librarian, takes the form of a long, unpunctuated stream of ideas and emotions. It won a Governor General's Award and was translated as *Incubation* (1967) by Shortliffe.

La commensale (1975), which was written before *L'incubation* but not published until much later, pursues further the type of satire found in *La bagarre* and *Le libraire*. Directed at urban small businesses, it portrays harshly and ironically the manias of the autistic protagonist, Chayer, an accountant or bookkeeper—a product of the repressive Duplessis era, like Jodoin the bookseller—who decides to oppose his boss. Formerly timid and compliant, these men come to life in a spirit of revolt—becoming devious, calculating, and sly—just as the Quiet Revolution dawns.

In 1954, in 'Les douze meilleurs romans français du XIXe siècle' (*Nouvelle Revue canadienne, III*), Bessette revealed his principles as a novelist: the supremacy of persons; physical surroundings presented in human terms; believable characters; the development of passions outlined; individual feelings analysed; the interactions between social behaviour and inner response described; and the avoidance of bombast and excess. He seemed to dread the 'novel of the unconscious', the 'apparent break with tradition', the 'preference for the abnormal, the strange, the unconscious', and the 'contempt for established critical methods, disparaged since the rise of Surrealism'. After Bessette wrote *La commensale*, however, his writing underwent a profound change: as he persisted with the introspective novel, while also trying to incorporate his understanding of psychology, his work evolved from a positivist rationalism into an exploration of the unconscious. He eliminated conventional punctuation, the better to convey a stream of consciousness, and invented new words, including composites made up of unexpected, vivid juxtapositions of nouns, adjectives, and verbs. To the simple parentheses and hyphens that replaced normal punctuation in *L'incubation*, Bessette added double parentheses in *Le cycle* (1971) to indicate the emergence of a character's unconsciousness; dashes frame physical observations and sensations; and single parentheses surround hallucinations of the preconscious. In *Le cycle* three generations of the same family—seven members presented through seven interior monologues—are reunited by the death of their relative, which offers an occasion for them to consider his life and ruminate on their own problems and ruling passions. *Le cycle* won a Governor General's Award.

Les anthropoides (1977) conducts the reader to the source of the interior monologue: to the birth of consciousness and speech, and to the beginnings of the individual and the species. A novel of origins, it is both an epic and a personal myth, and concerns the solitude of a young 'speaker'—an ancestor and son of heroes who is preparing for his test: to tell the history of the primitive horde. The book ends with a great battle among various opposing hordes, one horde winning with the help of another.

Le semestre (1979), an autobiographical novel, is about a university professor, Omer Marin, on the verge of retirement. He reflects on his youth, his career, his loves, his adventures with a young female student (much as Bernard Malamud does in *A new life*), and analyses the work of another author, Gilbert LA ROQUE. A novel-essay, *Le semestre* is similar to *Mes romans et moi* (1979), in the first half of which Bessette recounts the first ten years of his life and in the second half analyses his novels. Both *Le semestre* and Bessette's second novel, *Les pédagogues*, have academic settings and criticize the educational system, the first dealing with a professor who looks forward to the end of his teaching life and the second with the failure of a young teacher at the start of his career. Bessette returned to Marin in the novel *Les dires d'Omer Marin* (1985).

La garden-party de Christophine (1980), a collection of all Bessette's short stories, belongs to his 'assessment' period. One of these stories, 'Romance', is of particular interest for its subject matter and style; it uses a concise, biblical verse form and violent imagery in evoking the agony of an unemployed man who commits suicide after assessing his miserable life.

With their disregard for conventional punctuation, Bessette's narratives present different variations on the interior monologue—exploring the many levels of the unconscious, and the link between the world of the emotions and the world of the senses. Together the novels compose a uniform picture of heroes who are in some way enclosed or trapped by circumstances—they observe, reflect, and question themselves from behind counters, desks, and windows, or within streetcars, automobiles, cubicles, caves, or labryinthine basements. They struggle to break the barriers that surround them and escape to find their place in the outside world.

Bessette's novels show not only the Québécois 'choirboy' in the process of becoming a Freudian, but that the ego can emerge in spite of a condition of orphanhood—the orphanhood of liberation. Bessette has made a major contribution to the exploration of the inner life of Québécois.

See Patricia Smart, 'Relire *l'Incubation*', *Études françaises*, VI, 2 (mai 1970); J.-J. Hamm, ed., *Lectures de Gérard Bessette* (1982); Alain Piette, *Gérard Bessette:L'Incubation et ses figures* (1983); Réjean Robidoux, *La création de Gérard Bessette* (1987); André Vanasse, 'Gérard Bessette: biographie fictive et fiction de la biographie' in *Pére vaincu, la Méduse et les fils castrés, psychocritiques d'oeuvres québécoises contemporaines* (1990).

See NOVELS IN FRENCH 1940 TO 1959:3; 1960 TO 1982: 1, 2, 3. LOUIS LASNIER

Bibaud, Michel (1782-1857). He was a farmer's son, born in the Côte-des-Neiges suburb of Montreal, who did not begin classical college studies until the late age of nineteen. After graduation he supported himself and his family as a teacher, free-lance translator, and journalist. Neither by birth, marriage, nor occupation was he a member of any élite group in Quebec society. From 1817 to 1819 he owned and edited a newspaper, *L'Aurore*, and, after selling it, acted as editor of *Le Spectateur canadien*, *Le Courrier du Bas-Canada*, and *La Minerve*. He also owned and edited the periodicals *La Bibliothèque canadienne* (1825-30), *L'Observateur* (1830-1), *Le Magasin du Bas-Canada* (1832), and *L'Encyclopédie canadienne* (1842-3). *La Bibliothèque canadien* was the first French-language periodical to last more than a year. Bibaud's *Épîtres, satires, chansons, épigrammes et autres pièces de vers* (1830), which collected verse printed in newspapers over many years before its publication, was the first volume of poetry to be published in French Canada. In 1837 Bibaud published the first serious attempt at Quebec history, *Histoire du Canada, sous la domination française*, using unpublished letters and reminiscences. A second volume, *Histoire du Canada et des Canadiens, sous la domination anglaise*, appeared in 1844, the year in which he was employed as a translator for the new Geological Survey of Canada. He remained in that post until suffering a stroke in 1856. Bibaud was also the author of two arithmetic textbooks and edited Gabriel Franchère's *Relation d'un voyage à la côte du nord-ouest de l'Amérique septentrionale* (1820).

As a poet Bibaud followed eighteenth-century models, though his subject matter was contemporary. The periodicals reveal an editor, with broad interests and an understanding of many languages, who felt that it was his mission to instruct his fellow citizens both in practical science and in their national history and culture. The periodicals also reflect his interest in Aboriginal peoples in an anthropological, rather than a stereotypical, sense. His historical writing is didactic, strictly chronological, and inclined to give as much weight to small details as to major events. Clerical critics found the histories to be anti-Catholic, and political activists rejected Bibaud's acceptance of the status quo. The two volumes of his *Histoire* were almost immediately superceded by François-Xavier GARNEAU's history.

Michel Bibaud was intensely proud of his French language and his Canadian nationality. The titles of his histories, with *Canadiens* as the focus and the colonial powers as peripheral players, are representative of his attitude. He thought of French Canada as a national entity, not as a geographically delimited place called Lower Canada. As a man of letters he had little interest in power struggles—unless he perceived that the identity, language, and achievements of the French Canadian people were threatened. MARY LU MacDONALD

Bidwell, Barnabas. See ESSAYS IN ENGLISH: 1.

Biography and memoirs in English. At their best, biography and autobiography are forms that encourage a high development of literary art; but they are also genres in which amateurs, with neither art nor craftsmanship, are most likely to indulge because they think their own experiences are worth recording, or because they believe the same of other people's careers. The result is that, though at least 2,000 biographies, and autobiographies of various kinds (memoirs, journals, etc.) were published in English by Canadians until the early 1980s, a very high proportion tell of uninteresting lives (with perhaps here and there a sudden illumination for the social historian) in uninteresting ways. The account that follows—which excludes books discussed elsewhere under the headings EXPLORATION LITERATURE IN ENGLISH and PIONEER MEMOIRS—is inevitably selective.

1. COLLECTIONS AND SERIES. The most impressive works of Canadian biography in English before and after the turn of the century, when there were still relatively few full-scale biographies of well-known Canadians, appeared in biographical collections. Henry J. Morgan was a pioneer in this field with his *Bibliotheca canadensis* (Toronto, 1867), which contained short lives of pre-Confederation writers; he followed this, three decades later, with his *Canadian men and women of the time: a handbook of Canadian biography* (Toronto, 1898). The idea of a series of biographical volumes developed just after the turn of the century with the Makers of Canada series, published in Toronto by George Morang and edited by Duncan Campbell SCOTT and Pelham Edgar. Its twenty volumes (1903-8) varied in quality; only a few, such as Scott's *John Graves Simcoe* (1905) and Adam Shortt's *Lord Sydenham* (1908), were well researched and written. Thirteen volumes in the 32-volume Chronicles of Canada series (1914-16) are centred on single historical figures, but the emphasis is on history rather than biography. After the First World War, Lorne PIERCE launched the Makers of Canadian Literature series, of which eleven volumes were published between 1923 and 1926, with a twelfth (*Arthur Stringer: son of the North* by Victor Lauriston) appearing long afterwards, in 1941. They were only marginally biographical: a brief life of the writer was accompanied by a critical appraisal, a selection of his work, and a check-list of his writings. Biographical compilations, revealing an increasing degree of scholarly effort and accuracy, have continued to the present. W. Stewart Wallace's *Dictionary of Canadian biography* (1926) has been a standard work since its first appearance and has been revised several times, most recently in 1978 by W.A. McKay; this edition includes Canadians who died before 1976. All earlier biographical compilations are overshadowed by the *DICTIONARY OF CANADIAN BIOGRAPHY*, published under the auspices of the University of Toronto Press and the press of Université Laval. Between 1967 and the end of 1982, seven volumes appeared in a series that has no equal in Canadian biographical scholarship for exactitude, concision, and clarity. Other reference books whose entries are wholly or largely biographical include *Canadian writers/Écrivains canadiens: a biographical dictionary* (1964), edited by Guy Sylvestre, Brandon Conron, and Carl F. KLINCK, and Norah Story's *Oxford Companion to Canadian history and literature* (1967), with its *Supplement* (1973) edited by William Toye.

Two short-lived biographical series appeared in the early 1970s. The first, established to supplement Wallace's *Dictionary of Canadian biography*, was composed of John L.H. Henderson's *John Strachan* (1969), Bruce Hodgins' *John Sandfield Macdonald* (1970), and J.M. Bumsted's *Henry Alline* (1971). The second, the Canadian Lives series of brief biographies launched by the Oxford University Press, combined good scholarship with clear writing and was directed to a general readership. It included Dorothy Blakey Smith's *James Douglas* (1971), Hartwell Bowsfield's *Louis Riel* (1971), David Flint's *William Lyon Mackenzie* (1971), Donald Swainson's *John A. Macdonald* (1971), and George WOODCOCK's *Amor de Cosmos* (1975).

2. BIOGRAPHIES. Notable biographies of prominent figures in Canada's early history were such anglophone approaches to New France as W.D. LeSueur's *Count Frontenac* (1906) and W.J. ECCLES' much richer *Frontenac, the courtier governor* (1959); E.B. Osler's *La Salle* (1967) and John Upton Terrell's *La Salle: the life and times of an explorer* (1968); and several books on Champlain, from Ralph Flenley's *Samuel Champlain: founder of New France* (1924) to Morris Bishop's *Champlain: the life of fortitude* (1963).

Aspects of Upper Canadian and Ontarian life and history were reflected in a non-scholarly manner in such biographies as Mary Agnes Fitzgibbon's *A veteran of 1812: the life of James Fitzgibbon* (1894); W.S. Wallace's skeptical *The story of Laura Secord: a study in historical evidence* (1932); W. Kaye Lamb's *The hero of Upper Canada* (1962), a life of Sir Isaac Brock; Jessie

Beattie's *Black Moses: the real Uncle Tom* (1951), about Josiah Henson (1789-1883); Molly Gillen's account of the Duke of Kent's liaison with Mme St Laurent, *The prince and the lady* (1970); and Frederick C. Hamil's *Lake Erie baron: the story of Colonel Thomas Talbot* (1955).

A feature of recent western biography was the appearance of well-documented lives of Native leaders, such as William Fraser's *Big Bear, Indian patriot* (1966), Norman Sluman's *Poundmaker* (1967), and Hugh Dempsey's *Crowfoot, chief of the Blackfoot* (1972). The life of the fur traders—their travels and conflicts—produced many good biographical or largely biographical works. Among the most valuable were John Morgan GRAY's *Lord Selkirk of Red River* (1963), Harold A. INNIS's *Peter Pond: fur trader and adventurer* (1930), A.S. Morton's *Sir George Simpson; overseas governor of the HBC* (1944), Marjorie Wilkins Campbell's *McGillivray: lord of the Northwest* (1962), J.G. MacGregor's *Peter Fidler: Canada's forgotten surveyor* (1966), *Cuthbert Grant of Grantown* (1963) by Margaret Arnett Macleod and W.L. MORTON, and Jean Murray Cole's *Exile in the wilderness* (1979), the life of Chief Factor Archibald Macdonald. One of the classic works on an architect of white settlement beyond the Rockies was Walter N. Sage's *Sir James Douglas and British Columbia* (1930); Derek Pethick's *James Douglas: servant of two empires* (1969) is well researched, if somewhat adulatory. Other aspects of far-western life were represented in William Rodney's *Kootenai Brown, his life and times* (1969) and David R. Williams' *'The man for a new country': Sir Matthrew Baillie Begbie* (1977).

The largest single group of Canadian biographies treated political leaders, though definitive lives of these people have in many cases not appeared until quite recently. Joseph Pope, John A. Macdonald's private secretary, wrote with insight on Canada's first prime minister in *Memoirs of the Right Honourable Sir John Alexander Macdonald* (1894), but his book is mainly of interest today for its documentary material. The first adequate biography—and the last to date—was D.G. CREIGHTON's *John A. Macdonald* (2 vols, 1952, 1955). Two substantial books on Wilfrid Laurier appeared during the 1920s: O.D. Skelton's *Life and letters of Sir Wilfrid Laurier* (1921) and John Stephen Willison's *Sir Wilfrid Laurier* (1926); but the most perceptive study of Laurier's personality is probably Joseph Schull's *Laurier: the first Canadian* (1963). Schull also produced the first complete biography of Laurier's predecessor as Liberal leader in his two-volume *Edward Blake* (1975-6).

Among Macdonald's associates, D'Arcy McGEE, doubtless because of the dramatic way he died, has received most biographical attention, beginning with Fennings Taylor's *The Hon. D'Arcy McGee: a sketch of his life and death* (1868), and continuing through Alexander Brady's *Thomas D'Arcy McGee* (1925), Josephine Phelan's *The ardent exile* (1951), and Thomas P. Slattery's *The assassination of D'Arcy McGee* (1968). Other notable biographies of nineteenth-century political figures include G.E. Fenety's *Life and times of the Hon. Joseph Howe: the great Nova Scotian and ex-lieutenant governor, with brief references to some of his contemporaries* (Saint John, 1896). Charles Biggar's *Sir Oliver Mowat* (1905), O.D. Skelton's *Life and times of Sir Alexander Tilloch Galt* (1920), William Kennedy's *Lord Elgin* (1926), Chester New's *Lord Durham, a biography* (1926), John Stephen Willison's *Sir George Parkin* (1929), George P. deT. Glazebrook's *Sir Charles Bagot in Canada* (1929), Ronald Stewart Longley's *Sir Francis Hincks* (1943), J.M.S. Careless's *Brown of the Globe* (2 vols, 1959, 1963), Dale Thompson's *Alexander Mackenzie: clear grit* (1960), and Alistair Sweeny's *George-Étienne Cartier* (1976).

Moving into the area of public affairs, one finds certain figures in the Canadian past who, because of the dramatic or enigmatic quality of their lives, have attracted more attention than others who were perhaps historically more important. A small literature has centred on William Lyon MACKENZIE, beginning with the two-volume *The life and times of William Lyon Mackenzie* (Toronto, 1862) by Charles Lindsey, a useful and conscientious presentation of incidents and documents, though not an unbiased biography, the author being Mackenzie's son-in-law. This literature continues through William KILBOURN's *The firebrand: William Lyon Mackenzie and the rebellion in Upper Canada* (1956) and William Dawson LeSueur's *William Lyon Mackenzie* (1979). This last is a biographical curiosity, for it was written half a century before it was published; suppressed at the insistence of Mackenzie's descendants, it became celebrated *in absentia*, and on publication turned out to be a very dull biography.

A third figure to attract attention in the 1960s and 1870s was Louis Riel. Among the biographies of him are E.B. Osler's rather superficial *The man who had to hang: Louis Riel* (1961), George F. Stanley's *Louis Riel* (1963), and Thomas Flanagan's study of Riel's religious experiences, *Louis 'David' Riel: prophet of a new world* (1979). Riel's principal associate is the subject of George Woodcock's biography, *Gabriel Dumont* (1975).

Among twentieth-century politicians there is a similar disproportion, as in earlier generations, between the attention given to the more dramatic figures and that given to the dull and worthy. William Lyon Mackenzie King, who had a hand in the suppression of LeSueur's biography of his grandfather, had enough prime-ministerial eccentricities to make him the subject of far more books than any other Canadian political leader. These include Reginald Hardy's *Mackenzie King of Canada* (1949); Bruce HUTCHISON's *The incredible Canadian* (1952); *The age of Mackenzie King* (1955; 2nd edn 1976) by M.S. Ferns and Bernard Ostry; Robert MacGregor Dawson's *William Lyon Mackenzie King: a political biography* (1958)—a projected two-volume work whose second part, *Mackenzie King: the lonely heights* (1963), was written by M. Blair Neatby after Dawson's death; F.A. McGregor's *The rise and fall of Mackenzie King: 1911-1919* (1962); C.P. Stacey's bizarrely revelatory volume, *A very double life: the private world of Mackenzie King* (1976); J.L. Granatstein's *Mackenzie King: his life and world* (1977); and Joyce Esberey's psycho-biographical study, *Knight of the holy spirit* (1980). Already there had been many books on Pierre Elliott Trudeau, the best by far of the period being Richard GWYN's *The northern magus* (1980). Gwyn had already written *Smallwood: the unlikely revolutionary* (1968). Still the best of the studies of John Diefenbaker is Peter C. NEWMAN's *Renegade in power: the Diefenbaker years* (1963). J.S. Woodsworth, the first leader of the CCF, has been the subject of two excellent books: by his daughter, Grace MacInnis, *J.S. Woodsworth: a man to remember* (1953), and by Kenneth McNaught, *A prophet in politics: a biography of J.S. Woodsworth* (1959). Other notable books on twentieth-century Canadian political figures include Margaret Prang's *N.W. Rowell: Ontario nationalist* (1976); Roger Graham's *Arthur Meighen* (3 vols, 1960-5); Dale Thompson's *Louis St. Laurent* (1967); Geoffrey Stevens' *Stanfield* (1973); John English's *Borden: his life and world* (1977); Robert Bothwell's *Pearson: his life and world* (1978); *C.D. Howe: a biography* (1979) by William Kilbourn and Robert Bothwell; and Claude Bissell's *The young Vincent Massey* (1981).

Books on Canadian writers tend to fall into three categories, none of which is unadulterated literary biography. There are general studies, like those in the Canadian Writers and Studies in Canadian Literature series, launched in the later 1960s, which included biographical sections but were mainly concerned with critical discussion. Some of these books—for example, George BOWERING's *Al Purdy* (1970) and Stephen SCOBIE's *Leonard Cohen* (1978)—offered especially interesting biographical insights that have a close bearing on the writers' works; but in general they fell outside the field of true biography, following a long-established Canadian tradition of combining the biographical and the critical. Early books of this kind were James Cappon's *Roberts and the influence of his time* (1905), Francis Blake Crofton's *Haliburton: the man and the writer* (1889), Theodore Arnold Haultain's *Goldwin Smith: his life and opinions* (1913), V.L.O. Chittick's *Thomas Chandler Haliburton: a study in provincial Toryism* (1924), Lorne PIERCE's *William Kirby: the portrait of a Tory loyalist* (1929), James Cappon's *Bliss Carman and the literary currents and influences of his time* (1930), Ralph L. Curry's *Stephen Leacock: humorist and humanist* (1959), and *Edwin J. Pratt: the man and his poetry* (1947) by Carl F. KLINCK and Henry C. Wells.

Another type of literary biography tends to find reinforcement in areas outside the actual writing life of the subject. For example, William McCulloch's *Life of Thomas McCulloch* (1920) put far more emphasis on the founding of the Pictou Academy than it did on McCULLOCH's earlier role as the pioneer of satirical fiction in Canada. Norman Shrive's excellent *Charles Mair: literary nationalist* (1965) had added interest because of MAIR's place in the history of Upper Canadian nationalism. Clara THOMAS's sensitive life of Anna Jameson, *Love and work enough* (1967), was mainly appealing as a study of a very intelligent woman, caught up in the difficulties of an unhappy Victorian marriage, who attempts to come to terms with a colonial society. W.H. Graham's *The tiger of Canada West* (1962) saw William Dunlop as an eccentric phenomenon of colonial society as much as it considered his intermittent literary career. And Lovat DICKSON's *Wilderness man: the strange story of Grey Owl* (1973) was a well-researched biography that corrected the gaps and errors in Dickson's earlier *Half-breed: the story of Grey Owl* (1939), which was heavily influenced by the tales Archie BELANEY told of his past.

Literary biographies that centred on the relation between writers' lives and their work were few and of varying quality. Books like Elsie May Pomeroy's *Sir Charles G.D. Roberts: a biography* (1943) and C.F. Klinck's *Robert Service* (1976) tended to be informative but uncritical. David R. Beasley's *The Canadian Don Quixote: the life and works of Major John Richardson, Canada's first novelist* (1977) is an admirable reconstruction of RICHARDSON's rather turbulent life and eccentric behaviour, including his assiduous attempts to make a career for himself as a writer. But again, the literary nature of his actual writings is virtually unexamined. Douglas Day's *Malcolm Lowry* (1973) and Elspeth Cameron's *Hugh MacLennan: a writer's life* (1981), however, tackled with insight the central problems of the sources of creativity.

Canadians have written biographies of a number of foreign writers. These include Phyllis GROSSKURTH's two fine works, *John Addington Symonds* (1964) and *Havelock Ellis* (1980), Douglas FETHERLING's *The five lives of Ben Hecht* (1978), Paul Delany's *D.H. Lawrence's nightmare* (1979), Lovat Dickson's *H.G. Wells: his turbulent life and times* (1969; rpr. 1971), and George Woodcock's *The crystal spirit: a study of George Orwell* (1966), winner of a Governor General's Award.

Moving into other specialized fields, books on artists tended to mingle sketchy biographical details with criticism or description in heavily illustrated volumes. However, a few good lives of painters were written, including Donald Buchanan's *James Wilson Morrice* (1937), Moncrieff Williamson's *Robert Harris, 1849-1919* (1971), Maria TIPPETT's *Emily Carr* (1979), and Russell Harper's *Krieghoff* (1979). Terry Reksten's *Rattenbury* (1978) is a biography of the architect who put his stamp on Victoria, B.C., with his Parliament Buildings and Empress Hotel; but much of the book is devoted to his personal life, his murder in England, and its aftermath. The world of science in Canada was represented by Dora Hood's life of the discoverer of Peking Man, *Davidson Black* (1964), and Charles O. O'Brien's *Sir William Dawson: a life in science and religion* (1971). Medicine was treated in Lloyd Stevenson's *Sir Frederick Banting* (1946) and Iris Noble's *The doctor who dared: William Osler* (1959). Medicine and politics were both represented by two notable books on Norman Bethune: *The scalpel and the sword* (1952) by Ted ALLAN and Sydney Gordon and *Bethune* (1973) by Roderick Stewart; business by Michael BLISS's distinguished biography *A Canadian millionaire: the life and business times of Sir Joseph Flavelle, Bart. 1858-1939* (1978); journalism by Murray Donnelly's *Dafoe of the Free Press* (1969); and education by Clara Thomas's *Ryerson of Upper Canada* (1969), which was preceded by C.B. Sisson's *Egerton Ryerson: his life and letters* (2 vols, 1937-47).

The life of crime found its way early into Canadian biography with a curious work by Walter BATES, *The mysterious stranger* (1817), a life of the horse thief Henry Moon. A good latter-day example of this genre was Thomas Patrick KELLEY's *The black Donnellys* (1954).

3. MEMOIRS. One of the earliest Canadian writers of autobiography was the novelist Major John Richardson, who lived an eventful life and felt the urge to describe and justify it. The military experience of his teens led to *The War of 1812* (Brockville, 1842); his involvement in Upper Canadian politics to *Eight years in Canada* (Montreal, 1847). Both these books reflect Richardson's strong sense of having lived in the midst of stirring historic events. Memoirs of writers in the first half of the twentieth century featured a notable mediocrity that must be linked to the relative unoriginality of their other works. Goldwin SMITH's posthumously published *Reminiscences* (1910) has a special interest because of his position in Canadian public life. Laura Goodman SALVERSON's *Confessions of an immigrant's daughter* (1939) gives a clear picture of youth among Canadian Icelanders; and Frederick NIVEN's *Coloured spectacles* (1938) is a sensitive evocation of a varied life. But imaginatively meagre are such autobiographies as Ernest Thompson SETON's *Trail of an artist naturalist* (1940), Nellie McCLUNG's *Clearing in the West* (1935) and *The stream runs fast* (1945), Robert SERVICE's *Ploughman of the moon* (1945) and *Harper of heaven* (1948), and Mazo DE LA ROCHE's *Ringing the changes* (1957). Since the mid-1960s, however, Canadian writers were inclined to write their autobiographies not as mere narratives of their lives but as creative works that extended the perimeters of their art. Often they selected a comparatively short period, which for one reason or another seemed to project the very essence of their lives, and this enabled them to achieve a luminous concentration of insight. Such works included Margaret LAURENCE's *The prophet's camel bell* (1963); Morley CALLAGHAN's *That summer in Paris* (1963); John GLASSCO's *Memoirs of Montparnasse* (1970)—though this is now known to have a fictional construction; and Dorothy LIVESAY's *A Winnipeg childhood* (1973), later expanded in *Beginnings* (1988). Livesay experimented in another direction—producing a collage of documents and memories—in *Left hand right hand* (1977), her account of political involvement in the 1930s. Mordecai RICHLER's *The street* (1969), perhaps his unacknowledged best book—a collection of half-fictional sketches and half-autobiographical stories—is on the verge between invention and recollection. James M. GRAY, in *The winter years* (1966) and *The boy from Winnipeg* (1970), saw his life against the background of prairie social events, and thus

combined history and biography. Norman LEVINE in *Canada made me* (1958) used a journey home to tell his life story, and Earle BIRNEY's *Spreading time* (1980) tended to concentrate on the feuding politics of the Canadian literary world. More conventional accounts, in the sense that they are straightforwardly autobiographical, were Patrick ANDERSON's *Search me* (1957) and Hugh GARNER's characteristically irascible *One damn thing after another* (1973). Reminiscences of the writer as publisher were eloquently conveyed by Lovat DICKSON, who became a director of Macmillan of London, in *The ante-room* (1959, rpr. 1975) and *The house of words* (1963, rpr. 1976), and by John Morgan Gray, longtime head of MACMILLAN OF CANADA, in *Fun tomorrow: learning to be a publisher and much else* (1978).

All these memoirs have their share of imaginativeness, with sometimes more than touches of sheer invention. But fact was inextricably mingled with fiction in Frederick Philip GROVE's *In search of myself* (1946), a novel masquerading as autobiography. The mysteries behind Grove's life for a time made him perhaps the most discussed of Canadian writers. Desmond PACEY's *Frederick Philip Grove* (1945) was followed by books with the same title by Douglas Spettigue in 1969 and Margaret Stobie in 1973. It was Spettigue, in his *FPG: the European years* (1973), who showed, by splendid detective work, that Grove's account of his pre-Canadian years was almost wholly fictional, and that he was in fact a minor German writer, Felix Paul Greve, who had vanished from his own country after serving a term of imprisonment for fraud.

Some of the most interesting autobiographical documents were journals or narratives snatched from the past long after the death of their writers. One of these was *The reminiscences of Doctor John Sebastian Helmcken* (1975) edited by Dorothy Blakey Smith. Helmcken (1824-1920) was a prominent early resident of Victoria, B.C.—the son-in-law of the 'Father of British Columbia', Sir James Douglas—who was not only a surgeon but a member of the legislative assembly of Vancouver Island and British Columbia. The most moving journal from the past is Edgar Christian's diary of starvation in the Arctic, originally published as *Unflinching: a diary of tragic adventure* (1937) and reissued as *Death in the barren ground* (1979), edited by George Whalley, who described the end of Christian and his cousin John Hornby in *The legend of John Hornby* (1962). There have been reminiscences by scholars, like *My windows on the streets of the world* (1923) by James Mavor (1854-1925), a political scientist at the University of Toronto who had strong ties with Russia; John Kenneth Galbraith's *The Scotch* (1964), telling of his youth in Ontario's Glengarry County; and Kathleen Coburn's fascinating *In pursuit of Coleridge* (1977), which is both a biographical search and a personal memoir. Coburn (1905-91) was a well-known professor of English at Victoria College, University of Toronto, and a Coleridge scholar, editor of the Coleridge Notebooks. Some painters produced lively autobiographies: for example, Charles Comfort's *Artists at work* (1956), A.Y. Jackson's *A painter's country* (1958), and Emily CARR's inimitable series: *Klee Wyck* (1941), *The book of Small* (1942), *The House of All Sorts* (1944), and *Growing pains* (1946), crowned by the posthumous publication of her journals, *Hundreds and thousands* (1966). Recollections by newspapermen almost always provide an interesting inside-outside look at public life. In this category were Bruce HUTCHISON's *The far side of the street* (1976), Wilfrid Eggleston's *While I still remember* (1969), Grattan O'Leary's *Recollections of people, press and politics* (1977), and James F. Minifie's engagingly ironic *Expatriate* (1976). Many autobiographies by Canadian political leaders, ghost-written by academics, were generally of scant literary merit—though not Joey Smallwood's *I chose Canada* (1973), the text of which bears the unmistakable stamp of his personality; it was perhaps the best memoir of its time by a Canadian politician. There were illuminating and sophisticated accounts of observations and experiences by several civil servants who had less-prominent roles to play in Canadian public life. Among such books were the posthumously published *Public servant: the memoirs of Sir Joseph Pope* (1960), edited by his son Maurice Pope; Vincent Massey's *What's past is prologue* (1963); and Arnold Heeney's *The things that are Caesar's* (1972). But the classic memoir of a Canadian civil servant and diplomat was presented in the three beautifully written volumes of Charles RITCHIE's journals: *The siren years* (1974), *An appetite for life* (1977), and *Diplomatic passport* (1981). *The siren years*, which won a Governor General's Award, provided the first evidence that from the rich experience of a Canadian public servant, literature could be created.

GEORGE WOODCOCK

1983 to 1996. In Canada, as in most of the English-speaking world, the reading and writing of biography, autobiography, and their allied forms are increasingly popular pastimes. In the past three decades literary theorists have challenged the notion that any form of life writing can recreate the 'true' story of a life. Biography and particularly autobiography are viewed by some merely as vehicles for the author's self-expression. But these claims have not heralded the end of biography and autobiography. The debate on the one hand may have given us biographies and memoirs of greater authenticity and honesty, and on the other may have enhanced interest in these works by calling attention to the nature of subjectivity, the respective roles of author and reader, and the influence of cultural context on the reading and writing of all texts.

The current interest in social history has produced a shift in focus away from 'major' figures onto the more 'minor' ones who help us understand culture and society. Feminist writers and readers have also had some success in introducing more female subjects and calling attention to issues of race and class in life-writing. Regional presses and the growing audience in Canada for biography and memoirs have also led to an apparently steady increase in works published in this area. Although previous scholars have made estimates of numbers of works produced, the variety of sources, idiosyncracies of cataloguing, and questionable validity of merely counting volumes obscure any meaningful discussion of this issue. Suffice it to say that the numbers published since 1900 are in the thousands. Giving thought to all the volumes that have appeared since 1980 was a daunting task. Our choice of titles is by its nature idiosyncratic, but we have used the general criteria of overall quality and the degree to which books will interest the general reader.

1. BIOGRAPHY. Biographies of figures who lived prior to the twentieth century have been few since 1980. For the early settlement period, Joe Armstrong's *Champlain* (1987) and William Godfrey's *Pursuit of profit and preferment in colonial North America: John Bradstreet's quest* (1982) are worthy of mention. James Beck's two-volume *Joseph Howe* (1982, 1983) suffers from a lack of sources about the Conservative reformer's personal life, but is informative on nineteenth-century society. Brian Young's *George Étienne Cartier; Montreal bourgeois* (1981) is a brief, but solid, source on Cartier, while D.J. Hall's two-volume exploration of the life of Clifford Sifton (1981, 1985) displays the man, warts and all. Viscount Byng, controversial governor general in the 1920s, is well served in Jeffery Williams' *Byng of Vimy* (1983), which won a Governor General's Award.

One of the few modern biographies to deal with an explorer is William Hunt's *Stef: a biography of Vilhjalmur Stefansson, Canadian arctic explorer* (1986). Religious figures are at times akin to explorers, as is demonstrated by Stephen Endicott's *James Endicott: rebel out of China* (1980), David Mulhall's *Will to power: the missionary career of Father Morice* (1986), and Ronald Rompkey's *Grenfell of Labrador: a biography* (1991).

Western biographers continue to produce solid biographies of First Nations leaders, notably Hugh Dempsey's *Red Crow: warrior chief* (1980), *Big Bear: the end of freedom* (1984), and *The gentle persuader: a biography of James Gladstone, Indian senator* (1986). Donald Smith's *Sacred Feathers: the Reverend Peter Jones (Kahkewaquonaby) and the Mississauga Indians* (1987) brings to light a First Nations figure (q.v.) who advocated land and education rights for his people in early Upper Canada. David Raine's *Pitseolak: a Canadian tragedy* (1980) is a personal account of the death of a young Inuit man caught between two cultures.

Doris Pennington's *Agnes Macphail, reformer: Canada's first female M.P.* (1989) and Mary Hallett's and Marilyn Davis's *Firing the heather: the life and times of Nellie McClung* (1993) enhance our understanding of women and Canadian politics. Of more general interest is June CALLWOOD's *Emma* (1984), the story of a Doukhobor woman who was both fashion writer and a Russian spy.

In terms of more 'traditional', but still relatively unknown, political history, Robin Fisher's *Duff Pattullo of British Columbia* (1991) fills a gap in this area for British Columbia. Moving eastward, Susan Mann Trofimenkoff's *Stanley Knowles: the man from Winnipeg North Centre* (1982) is an affectionate biography of the legendary parliamentarian. Cameron Smith's *Unfinished journey: the Lewis family* (1989) and Judy Steed's *Ed Broadbent: the pursuit of power* (1989) shed light on the politics of the left in Canada. Jamie Swift's *Odd man out: the life and times of Eric Kierans* (1988) portrays the Liberal Kierans as economist, politician, and businessman. Margaret Conrad's *George Nowlan: Maritime Conservative in national politics* (1986) is well researched.

As was the case when George WOODCOCK compiled his survey of Canadian biography for the First Edition of this *Companion*, a significant number of Canadian biographies focus on the lives of Canada's prime ministers. Some, like Peter Waite's *The man from Halifax: Sir John Thompson, prime minister* (1985), focus on the political fortunes of those who rise to such prominence; others take more diverse orientations. Laurier LaPierre, for example, is affectionate and uncritical in his *Sir Wilfrid Laurier and the romance of Canada* (1996), while Joy Esbery's *Knight of the Holy Spirit: a study of William Lyon Mackenzie King* (1980) delves into the personal, with its psychoanalytic orientation, to produce a book that is oddly entertaining and advances scholarship on King. John English's two-volume biography of Lester B. Pearson—*Shadow of heaven: the life of Lester Pearson 1897-1948* (1989); *The worldly years: the life of Lester Pearson 1949-1972* (1992)—and Denis Smith's *Rogue Tory: the life and legend of John G. Diefenbaker* (1995) are examples of a more balanced and thorough approach.

Among recent prime ministers, most biographies have been written about Pierre Trudeau. The best of these is Christina McCALL's and Stephen Clarkson's two-volume *Trudeau and our times: 1. The magnificent obsession* (1990; Governor General's Award); *2. The heroic delusion* (1994), which was preceded by Richard GWYN's less comprehensive but still useful *The northern magus: Pierre Elliott Trudeau and Canadians* (1980). John Sawatsky's *Mulroney: the politics of ambition* (1991) is the most comprehensive biography of the former prime minister published to date. Informative, but less challenging of their subjects and their material, are Warner Troyer's *200 days: Joe Clark in power* (1980), Jack Cahill's *John Turner: the long run* (1984), Murray Dobbin's *The politics of Kim Campbell: from school trustee to prime minister* (1993), Robert Fife's *Kim Campbell: the making of a politician* (1993), and Lawrence Martin's *Chrétien* (1995). In the service of Canadian political history Michael BLISS wrote biographical studies of important prime ministers for *Right Honourable Men* (1994).

In the related areas of diplomacy and public affairs are Claude Bissell's biography of the first Canadian governor general, *The young Vincent Massey* (1981) and *The imperial Canadian: Vincent Massey in office* (1986), Brian McKenna's and Susan Purcell's *Drapeau* (1981), and Donald Horton's *André Laurendeau: French-Canadian nationalist* (1992). J.L. GRANATSTEIN's *A man of influence: Norman A. Robertson and Canadian statecraft 1929-1968* (1981) is a guidebook to the bureaucracy and foreign policy of the period.

As the title of Peter C. NEWMAN's *The establishment man: a portrait of power* (1982) suggests, the distance separating the worlds of Canadian politics and business is often very small. Two other books that underline the same point are H.B. Timothy's *The Galts: vol. 2, A Canadian odyssey* (1984) and Michael Marrus's *Mr. Sam: the life of Samuel Bronfman* (1981). More strictly about business are Kelly Russell's *Pattison: portrait of a capitalist superstar* (1986), Joy Santink's *Timothy Eaton and the rise of his department store* (1990), Anne Kingston's *The edible man: Dave Nichol, president's choice and the making of popular taste* (1994), and Paul Waldie's saga of the feuding McCains of New Brunswick, *House divided* (1996).

Also closely allied with politics are the worlds of journalism and the media. Of interest here are Jock Carroll's *The life and times of Greg Clark: Canada's favourite storyteller* (1981), Barbara Freeman's *Kit's kingdom: the journalism of Kathleen Blake Coleman* (1989), and Scott Young's *Gordon Sinclair: a life—and then some* (1987). Linda Frum's *Barbara Frum* (1996) is a daughter's controversial account of an important and beloved figure in Canadian radio and television broadcasting.

Although not as well known to many Canadians, intellectual and academic figures continue to figure prominently in Canadian biography. Clifford Holland's *William Dawson Lesueur, 1840-1917, a Canadian man of letters: the sage of Ottawa* (1993), Douglas Francis's *Frank Underhill: intellectual provocateur* (1986), Stanley Frost's *The man in the ivory tower: F. Cyril James of McGill* (1991), and William Christian's *George Grant: a biography* (1993) chronicle the lives of those who have shaped, and in some ways continue to shape, Canada's intellectual environment. Philip Marchand's *Marshall McLuhan: the medium and the messenger* (1989) successfully treats the life of a Canadian known internationally for his theories on the influential role of the media in modern life.

In the more particular disciplines of science and medicine are Howard Lewis's *Something hidden: a biography of Wilder Penfield* (1983), Michael Bliss's *Banting: a biography* (1984), Christine King's *E.W.R. Steacie and science in Canada* (1989), and Susan Sheets-Pyenson's *John William Dawson: faith, hope and science* (1996). From the social sciences comes Laurence Nowry's *Marius Barbeau: man of mania* (1995), which recounts the life of the multitalented ethnologist, folklorist, and writer (q.v.) who had a lifelong career at the National Museum.

Biographical writing about Canadian visual artists is not extensive, and tends to concentrate on those working in established traditions and to rely heavily on criticism and illustration. Jean Blodgett's *Kenojuak* (1985) combines brief biography and autobiography with illustrations of the work of the Inuit artist. Terrence Heath's *Uprooted: the life and art of Ernest Lindner* (1983) and Patricia Morley's *Kurelek: a biography* (1986) concentrate on painters who lived and worked mainly in western Canada. Peter Varley's *Frederick H. Varley* (1983) is an appreciation of the painter as artist and father. David Silcox's *Painting place: a biography of David B. Milne* (1996) is the long-anticipated, thorough study of this artist's life and work and, like Mark Cheetham's *Alex Colville: the observer observed* (1994), is well illustrated in colour. Ann Davis's *Somewhere waiting: the life and art of Christiane Pflug* (1991) has fewer illustrations, but is a compelling and disturbing account of a young artist who took her own life.

While the biography of a musician often suffers at the hands of music criticism, this is not the case with Sheila Jane Eastman's and Timothy McGel's *Barbara Pentland* (1983), which informs without being too academic, or with Ezra Schabas's readable, though narrowly focused, *Sir Ernest MacMillan: the importance of being Canadian* (1994). The jazz world comes to life in Gene Lees' *Oscar Peterson: the will to swing* (1990), about the internationally famous Canadian musician, while Mark Miller's *Jazz in Canada; fourteen lives* (1982) is about lesser-known figures important to jazz in this country.

Of interest to theatre buffs are Keith Garebian's *William Hutt: a theatre portrait* (1988) and Paula Sperdakos' *Dora Mavor Moore: pioneer of the Canadian theatre* (1995). Turning to builders of another sort, Edith IGLAUER's *Seven Stones: a portrait of Arthur E. Erickson, architect* (1981) and Anthony Barrett's *Francis Rattenbury and British Columbia: architecture and challenge in the imperial age* (1983) explore the world of Canadian architecture.

Perhaps the single largest group of Canadian biographies to appear since 1980 treats figures from the world of Canadian letters past and present. Ira Nadel, in his *Biography: fiction, fact and form* (1984), the only Canadian critical work devoted solely to literary biography, points out that the record of an individual's life is a literary process as well as a historical product. This point of view is particularly obvious when the subject of the work is a writer and the biographer attempts to explain the artistic process. Since 1980 there has been a gradual movement in literary biography towards Nadel's concept that the value of biography derives as much from appraisal and presentation as from the accumulation and accuracy of facts. The ECW PRESS series has been valuable in this respect; while the biographies are brief, the subjects include such literary figures as Alice MUNRO, Dorothy LIVESAY, Irving LAYTON, Leonard COHEN, Northrop FRYE, Timothy FINDLEY, and Stephen LEACOCK.

In many ways this was a coming-of-age period for Canadian literary biography. In works on pre-twentieth century authors, women subjects are particularly well represented. (All the subjects of the following literary biographies have entries.) Lorraine McMullen's *An odd attempt in a woman; the literary life of Frances Brooke* (1993) recounts the life of Canada's first novelist, and Elizabeth McNeil Galvin's *Isabella Valancy Crawford; we scarcely knew her* (1994) reveals an author whose prose and poems gave her a posthumous reputation. Indeed, the lives of late nineteenth- and early twentieth-century writers attracted a number of notable Canadian biographers after 1980, including Betty Keller, whose *Pauline: a biography of Pauline Johnson* (1981) was followed by *Black Wolf: the life of E.T. Seton* (1984); Marian Fowler with *Redney* (1983), an intriguing glimpse into the life of journalist, novelist, and world traveller Sara Jeannette DUNCAN; John Adams with *Sir Charles god damn: the life of Sir Charles G.D. Roberts* (1986); and Joan GIVNER with the aptly sub-titled *Mazo de la Roche: the hidden life* (1995). Continuing their ongoing exploration of the journals and archives of Prince Edward Island's famous writer, Mary Rubio and Elizabeth Waterston co-authored *Writing a life: L.M. Montgomery* (1995). Representative of books focusing on literary lives from the middle years of the century are Usher Caplan's *Like one that dreamed: a portrait of A.M. Klein* (1982), David Pitt's two-volume *E.J. Pratt* (1984, 1987), Sandra Djwa's *The politics of the imagination: a life of F.R. Scott* (1987), Paul Stuewe's *The storms below: the turbulent life and times of Hugh Garner* (1988), Gordon Bowker's *Pursued by furies: a life of Malcolm Lowry* (1993), and Patricia Morley's *As though life mattered: Leo Kennedy's story* (1994). Judith Skelton Grant's *Robertson Davies: man of myth* (1984) portrays the author at the peak of his career, while Mary McAlpine's *The other side of silence: a life of Ethel Wilson* (1988) and Ira Nadel's *Various positions: a life of Leonard Cohen* (1996) are affectionate portraits. James King's *The life of Margaret Laurence* was published in the summer of 1997.

Two literary biographers have distinguished themselves with five books between them: Elspeth Cameron with *Hugh MacLennan: a writer's life* (1981), *Irving Layton: a portrait* (1985), and *Earle Birney: a life* (1994); and Rosemary SULLIVAN with *By heart: Elizabeth Smart, a life* (1991) and *Shadow maker: the life of*

Gwendolyn MacEwen (1995), which won a Governor General's Award. *Shadow maker* is particularly interesting in that it illuminates not only the life and art of MacEWEN, but the intimate and often undiscussed interaction that takes place between the biographer and her subject.

Canadian literature owes much to the quality of its critics, and Northrop Frye has been the subject of several biographies, the most noteworthy and comprehensive being John Ayre's *Northrop Frye* (1989). Laura Groening's appropriately subtitled *E.K. Brown: a study in conflict* (1993) does similar service for her subject (q.v.). Perhaps more of a cultural critic and book-reviewer was William Arthur DEACON: he and his times are well served in Clara THOMAS's and John Lennox's *William Arthur Deacon: a Canadian literary life* (1982).

Biographers whose subjects are not authors tend to be less introspective about the nature of their task, though this does not preclude respect and empathy, as shown by Jack BATTEN's *Robinette: the dean of Canada's lawyers* (1984) and Carolyn Swayze's *Hard choices: a life of Tom Berger* (1987).

Biographies of sports figures have proliferated since 1980. They are difficult to categorize, not only because of their numbers, but because many of them appear to be exercises in marketing, or at least in promotion of their subjects. Escaping some of these problems are Stephen Brunt's *Mean business: the creation of Sean O'Sullivan* (1987) and Scott Young's *Neil and me* (1985; updated 1997).

Increasingly among the best Canadian biographers are scholars of non-Canadian subjects. Literary biographies, again, are predominant. They include Michael Millgate's *The life and work of Thomas Hardy* (1985), Joan Givner's *Katherine Anne Porter: a life* (1982), and Robert Calder's *Willie: the life of Somerset Maugham* (1989), which won a Governor General's Award and does renewed justice to Maugham's personal life. Michael COREN's *Gilbert: the man who was G.K. Chesterton* (1990) and *The invisible man: the life and liberties of H.G. Wells* (1993) are shorter, frankly opinionated works. James King has made a noteworthy contribution with subjects from both literature and art: *William Cowper: a biography* (1986), *Interior landscapes: the life of Paul Nash* (1987), *The last modern: a life of Herbert Read* (1990), *William Blake: his life* (1991), and *Virginia Woolf* (1994). Phyllis GROSSKURTH added to her reputation as a biographer with *Havelock Ellis: a biography* (1980), *Melanie Klein: her world and her work* (1986), *The secret ring: Freud's inner circle and the politics of psychoanalysis* (1991), and *Byron: the flawed angel* (1997). Other notable projects are Jack Chambers' two-volume *Milestones: the music and times of Miles Davis* (1983-1985), Marian Fowler's group biography *Below the peacock fan: first ladies of the Raj* (1987), Alan Walker's memorable three-volume biography of Franz Liszt (1983-96), and Deborah Gorham's *Vera Brittain: a feminist life* (1996). Closer to journalism is Farley MOWAT's *Virunga: the passion of Dian Fossey* (1987), which weaves a biographical narrative around excerpts from Fossey's journals.

2. MEMOIR/AUTOBIOGRAPHY. Proving the acuity of the late Robertson DAVIES' observation that good autobiographies are largely the product of fine writing, Canadian literary figures have continued the tradition of considering their life experiences as fuel for their creative fires, with Gabrielle ROY's spiritual reminiscences *Enchantment and sorrow* (1987), P.K. PAGE's engaging *Brazilian journal* (1987), and Margaret LAURENCE's celebratory *Dance on the earth* (1989)—all of which are likely to attract both scholarly and popular attention for years to come. Other writers took the opportunity to advance ongoing and evolving autobiographical projects. Dorothy Livesay, for instance, followed the political remembrances of *Right hand left hand* (1977) with the more openly confessional self-portrait *Journey with my selves* (1991), and George Woodcock's autobiographical series—*Letter to the past* (1982), *Beyond the blue mountains* (1987), and *Walking through the valley* (1994)—continued as a testament to the multifacetedness of the human personality. This trend towards serial autobiography was picked up by Douglas FETHERLING, whose 1960s reminiscence *Travels by night* (1994) was followed by the candid though somewhat quaint *Way down deep in the belly of the beast: a memoir of the seventies* (1996). Important single-volume memoirs appeared as well, including Austin CLARKE's *Growing up stupid under the Union Jack* (1980), Al PURDY's *Reaching for the Beaufort Sea* (1993), and *The tightrope walker: autobiographical writings of Anne Wilkinson* (1992), edited by Joan Coldwell—an intimate self-portrait of the Toronto poet (q.v.) as well as a kind of social history.

Maria TIPPETT's *Becoming myself: a memoir* (1996) is an interesting, unpretentious account of her life—as an adopted child and as an ambitious, hardworking cultural historian—up to the publication of her biography of Emily Carr in 1979. Mary Meigs is probably less well known as a painter than for her work in film, but her *Lily Briscoe, a self-portrait: an autobiography* (1982) and *The Medusa head*

(1983) speak eloquently of her lifelong devotion to her art and her struggle for acceptance as a lesbian.

The autobiographical form also gave writers the opportunity to promote or provoke a vital rethinking of the stability of the boundaries separating autobiography from other literary genres. Such personal explorations as Michael ONDAATJE's *Running in the family* (1982), Daphne MARLATT's poetic *How hug a stone* (1983), Clark BLAISE's *Resident alien* (1986), and Aritha VAN HERK's *Places far from Ellesmere—a geografictione: explorations on the site* (1990) fuse the traditional life story with, respectively, elements of fiction, feminist politics, social history, travel writing, and literary theory and criticism.

The life stories of four luminaries of the performing arts are recounted in their interesting memoirs: contralto Maureen Forrester's *Out of character* (1986), dancer Karen Kain's *Karen Kain* (1994), and actors Hume Cronyn's *A terrible liar* (1991) and William Hutt's *William Hutt* (1995). Canada as a geographic and cultural place figures prominently in both their professional successes and their personal lives.

Shifting attention to politics and the media opens the floodgates to a large number of books that are predominantly—but not entirely—open to being considered self-serving and superficial. The end of the Trudeau years produced a shelfload of interpretations and reinterpretations from such notable Grit insiders as James Jerome (*Mr. Speaker*, 1985), Eugene Whelan (*Whelan*, 1986), Keith Davey (*The rainmaker: a passion for politics*, 1986), and J.W. Pickersgill (*Seeing Canada whole*, 1994). Trudeau himself opened what appears to be a political serial with *Memoirs* (1993), a nostalgic counterpoint to the more current reflections shaping Jean Chrétien's *Straight from the heart* (1985) and Sheila Copps' *Nobody's baby* (1986). Longtime Tories Jack Horner (*My own brand*, 1980), Heath Macquarrie (*Red Tory blues*, 1992), high-profile strategist Hugh Segal (*No surrender: reflections of a happy warrior in the Tory crusade*, 1996), and ex-prime minister Kim Campbell (*Time and chance: the political memoirs of Canada's first woman prime minister*, 1996) added their partisan voices to this mix, as did such ostensibly Left-oriented politicians as Mike Harcourt (*Mike Harcourt: a measure of defiance*, 1996), and Bob Rae (*From protest to power*, 1996). For the latter three writers in particular, remembering the recent political past seemed little more than an invitation for self-justification rather than insightful reflections on the experiences of a political life lived large.

In those infrequent instances when readable prose and reasonable modesty found their way into political memoirs, sheer bulk proved daunting to all but the most intrepid reader: both high-ranking diplomat Hugh Keenleyside's highly polished *Memoirs* (1981, 1982) and Paul Martin's *A very public life* (1983, 1985), though insightful and subdued, are two-volume affairs that are sometimes tedious. More accessible in terms of length and style are David Lewis's posthumously published *The good fight* (1981), an occasionally touching account of socialist politics as it transformed Canada's mid-century, and Ellen Fairclough's discreet *Saturday's child: memoirs of Canada's first female Cabinet minister* (1995), a reflection on the power of quiet persuasion to effect change in the Diefenbaker government. Also of some interest are Escott Reid's *Radical mandarin* (1989), the acerbic Eugene FORSEY's *Life on the fringe* (1990), and from the urbane Charles RITCHIE, more 'undiplomatic diaries', *Diplomatic passport* (1981), *Storm signals* (1983), and his family memoir *My grandfather's house* (1987).

Rarely hesitant to appear in the public eye, members of Canada's media and journalistic community were equally active and, at times, equally open to charges of self-promotion. Familiar faces adorn many covers, with longtime broadcasters Knowlton Nash (*History on the run*, 1984) and Harvey Kirck (*Nobody calls me Mr. Kirck*, 1985) penning reflections on their experiences in front of, and behind, the cameras of Canadian television. The press corps is represented with memoirs from Stuart Keate (*Paper boy*, 1980), Charles Lynch (*You can't print that!*, 1983), Peter Worthington (*Looking for trouble*, 1984), and the late Marjorie Nichols, whose *Mark my words: the memoirs of a very political reporter* (1992, with Jane O'Hara) is a tough and touching book from one of Canada's premier political commentators. Picking up the autobiographical threads introduced in his *Drifting home* (1973), Pierre BERTON continued in the more traditional serial style with *Starting out* (1987) and *My times* (1995). Physical and spiritual journeys proved fertile autobiographical ground for established media figures like Bronwyn Drainie (*My Jerusalem*, 1994) and Mordecai RICHLER (*This year in Jerusalem*, 1994), as well as for relative newcomer Jan Wong (*Red China blues*, 1996). Recent additions to this field include Scott Young's *A writer's life* (1994), Doris Anderson's feminist *Rebel daughter* (1996), and Mel Hurtig's heartfelt though uneven *At twilight in the country: memoirs of a Canadian nationalist* (1996).

Other Canadian autobiographies cover a diverse field. Notable books to emerge from boardrooms in Canada and abroad include entrepreneur Garth Drabinsky's *Closer to the sun* (1995, with Marq de Villiers), newspaper mogul Conrad Black's *A life in progress* (1993), and Christopher Ondaatje's *The man-eater of Punanai: a journey of discovery to the jungles of old Ceylon* (1992), though the latter succeeds in keeping revelations of corporate posturing to a minimum. Life in similarly high-profile and profitable professions is recounted in Edward Greenspan's self-titled legal memoir (1987) and John Clyne's *Jack of all trades* (1985), as well as in the memoirs of various Canadian athletes, from Wayne Gretzky (*Gretzky*, 1990, with Rick Reilly) to downhill-skiers Steve Podborski (*Podborski!*, 1987) and Ken Read (*White circus*, 1987), to Jim Nelford's intriguing glimpse at *Seasons in a golfer's life* (1984). High-jump innovator Debbie Brill's *Jump* (1986) and Ken Dryden's *The game* (1983) offer interesting and articulate counterpoints to contemporary stories of professional sporting lives.

The game of war is represented in autobiography as well, and Jeffry Brock's *With many voices* (1981), following his course from sea cadet to the Second World War, is one of the most outspoken of these. *But this is our war* (1981) by Grace Craig is told from the civilian perspective and is excellent on the effects of the First World War on Canadian society. The memoirs of generals tend to be more ponderous, as in those of Howard Graham (1987) and Jean Allard (1988); and although Lewis Mackenzie avoids this problem in *Peacekeeper: the road to Sarajevo* (1993), his political views are never far from the surface.

Further removed from the public eye, the academic life is positioned centre stage in Albert Trueman's *A second view of things* (1982) and historian C.P. STACEY's *A date with history* (1983), while Robert Ogle's *North/south calling* (1987) and minister/peace activist Lois Wilson's *Turning the world upside down* (1989) focus on ecumenism. The late Sean O'Sullivan's *Both my houses* (1986) spans the worlds of politician and priest, and Tara Singh Bains' *The four quarters of the night* (1995, with Hugh Johnston) points to the driving force of religious faith in the life of an immigrant Sikh.

Emerging as major contributors to the memoir market in terms of both quantity and quality, women have contributed a number of notable autobiographies, including Alice A. Chown's *The stairway* (1988), Sylvia FRASER's *My father's house* (1988), and Marnie Jackson's *The mother zone* (1992). The exploration of a life of abuse, which is the theme of Fraser's autobiography, has been echoed eloquently by others, including Elly Danica's *Don't* (1988) and *Beyond don't: dreaming past the dark* (1996), and Liza Potvin's *White lies: for my mother* (1992). Of interest also are Makeda Silvera's *Silenced* (1983), a group memoir of Caribbean domestic workers, and Eva Brewster's poignant *Vanished in darkness: an Auschwitz memoir* (1986). Lee MARACLE's *Bobbie Lee, Indian rebel* (1990)—the reissue, with epilogue, of an earlier work—parts with the conventions of good writing but tells a powerful tale of a formative period in the life of a Native-rights activist, while Evelyn Lau's *Runaway: diary of a street kid* (1989) is a vivid account of Lau's determination to write about life on the street.

An important extension of autobiographical writing in Canada has been the increased interest in the form as a separate and distinct field of literary research and criticism, as well as writing. See the critical and theoretical approaches presented in the collections edited by Marlene Kadar: *Essays in life-writing* (1989), *Essays on life writing: from genre to critical practice* (1992), and *Reading life writing: an anthology* (1993); as well as *Reflections: autobiography and Canadian literature* (1988) edited by K.P. Stich, a collection of papers arising from a scholarly symposium on life-writing.

Feminist theorists and critics are of vital importance in exploring the theory and practice of autobiographical writing. At the forefront of this movement has been Helen M. Buss, whose *Canadian women's autobiography in English: an introductory guide for researchers and teachers* (1991) and *Mapping our selves: Canadian women's autobiography in English* (1993) are notable for the depth and clarity with which they cover vast theoretical and primary terrains.

3. COLLECTIONS AND SERIES. The *DICTIONARY OF CANADIAN BIOGRAPHY*, published simultaneously in English and French and edited by Ramsay COOK and Jean HAMELIN, remains in a class by itself, both in terms of its consistently high level of scholarship and its readable narrative style. Eschewing the scholarly in favour of the accessible, the Canadian Biography series of the *ECW Press* provides brief illustrated biographies of Canadians from all walks of life who have had a major impact on the Canadian scene. To date the series includes approximately twenty biographies of major Canadian novelists and poets, as well as others on cultural figures as diverse as Wayne Gretzky (1993), David Cronenberg

(1994), and Big Bear (1995). The American *Dictionary of literary biography* has six volumes dedicated to Canadian writers: before 1890 (one volume), 1890-1920 (one), 1920-59 (two), and since 1960 (two). Biographies of five premiers of Ontario are included in the University of Toronto Press's now-defunct Ontario Historical Studies series; the discontinued Canadian Composers Series was also from the same press. Carleton University Press's Women's Experience Series has published nine volumes, four of which are biographies of Canadian women. Although not strictly in print, the Canadian Institute for Historical Microreproductions, established in 1978, continues as a valuable source for pre-1900 biographical texts.

LEILA RYAN/KLAY DYER

Biography and memoirs in French. BIOGRAPHIES 1. 1671 TO 1900. It was only in the 1850s that biographies began to appear with any frequency in French Canada, and it was Father Étienne-Michel Faillon (1799-1870) who gave biographical writing its initial impetus. From 1852 to 1860 this French Sulpician—who visited the Canadian missions of his community in 1849, 1854, and 1857, staying in Montreal for five years on his last visit—wrote four biographies, totalling more than 2,500 pages, on Madame d'Youville (Ville-Marie, 1852), Marguerite Bourgeoys (Ville-Marie, 1853), Jeanne Mance (2 vols, Ville-Marie, 1854), and Jeanne Le Ber (Ville-Marie, 1860), which appeared in an abridged English translation the following year as *The Christian heroine of Canada; or Life of Miss Le Ber* (Montréal, 1861). These works are really hagiographies describing the many virtues of the great founders of the French-Canadian religious orders with a view to encouraging others to adopt a religious vocation and in order to promote in Rome the beatification of these heroines of New France, a necessary first step in their subsequent canonization. They were written in response to requests from the religious communities themselves, who paid the printing costs and sold and distributed them with great zeal, for each religious order presumably wanted to be the first to have its founder recognized officially by the Pope. The biographies are generally well documented, but the supernatural world and interventions from the Great Beyond play an important role.

The works of Father Faillon, as Serge Gagnon has shown in *Le Québec et ses historiens de 1840 à 1920* (Québec, 1978), are proof of the spectacular ascendancy of clericalism in French Canada during the second half of the nineteenth century. 'The historical story', he affirms, 'is the first step in the consecration of clerical power through recourse to history.' He elaborates: 'hagiography in the 19th century is an exceptional manifestation of the clergy's will to power.' Progressively assuming the national leadership from the 1840s on—that is, following the defeat of the Rebellion of 1837, which had put an end to the political aspirations of an often liberal-minded bourgeoisie—the clergy undertook the formulation of a collective memory. It was a conservative one, in keeping with its providentialist conception of history and inevitably reflecting its own concerns and values. To a conquered people anxious about its future, the clergy offered the refuge of a religion, preaching the supremacy of spiritual and moral values. At the same time, responding to French Canadians' natural instinct for self-preservation, it laid the foundation of a nationalist ideology and maintained it by extolling a system of protective values centred on upholding traditions, the French language, and the Catholic religion, and respect for the Church and the family. In teaching people to distrust change, the clergy quite naturally overvalued the past—the period of New France in particular—extolling the merits of agricultural and rural life to the detriment of industrial and urban life. In this context, history and literature were asked to take on a didactic function. Abbé CASGRAIN's *Histoire de la Mère Marie de l'Incarnation* (Québec, 1864) suggests that Canada was discovered in response to a plan of divine Providence—namely that of hastening the conversion of the Native populations—and that MARIE DE L'INCARNATION participated in this plan: as a simple instrument in the hand of God, she made it her sacred duty to obey blindly His holy will. Endowed with a romantic temperament, Casgrain likes to evoke the marvellous and the supernatural; he speaks of the ecstasies and visions of Marie de l'Incarnation, even of the apparition of a deceased nun, as incontestable facts. His biography had a very great success.

A large number of edifying and patriotic biographies were published in the nineteenth century. With very few exceptions, most of the national heroes who were their subjects lived in the epic times of New France. Narcisse-Eutrope Dionne, who in his well-documented *Jacques Cartier* (Québec, 1889) had painted the discoverer of Canada as a devoted Christian more interested in giving new souls to God and new land to his king than in becoming rich, presented another great Catholic hero in his first volume of *Samuel de Champlain, fondateur de Québec et père de la Nouvelle-France: histoire de sa vie et de ses voyages* (2 vols, Québec, 1891, 1906). Even more virtuous than Cartier, Champlain had no personal ambition save that of converting as many Natives as possible to the only true religion. Casgrain, in his *Champlain, sa vie et son caractère* (Québec, 1898), also insisted on Champlain's strong faith in God and on his qualities as a missionary. Both H.J.J.B. Chouinard in his *Paul de Chomedey, sieur de Maisonneuve, fondateur de Montréal* (Québec, 1882) and Father P. Rousseau in his *Histoire de la vie de M. Paul de Chomedy, sieur de Maisonneuve, fondateur et premier gouverneur de Villemarie 1640-1676* (Montréal, 1886) recognized in their hero a man guided by the hand of God—like Mgr de Laval, whose exceptional qualities and numerous virtues, both as a priest and as an administrator, were praised by Abbé Auguste-Honoré Gosselin in his *Vie de Monseigneur de Laval, premier évêque de Québec et apôtre du Canada, 1622-1708* (2 vols, Québec, 1890). Indeed, this example of hagiography was intended to promote the case of Laval for canonization. Henri Lorin's *Le Comte de Frontenac; étude sur le Canada français à la fin du XVIII*[e] *siècle* (Paris, 1895) was much more critical of the bishop's conduct and of his policies. While Father Félix Martin, a former missionary, was satisfied simply to relate Montcalm's glorious military career in his well-documented *De Montcalm; ou Les dernières années de la colonie française (1756-1760)* (Paris, 1867), Casgrain in his *Guerre du Canada, 1756-1760: Montcalm et Lévis* (2 vols, Québec, 1891; Tours, 1899), showing his bias against an impious France that had abandoned Canada and her children, was hostile to Montcalm; only Lévis appeared to be a bona fide hero.

Some families have been fortunate enough to generate heroes worthy of being remembered forever by their compatriots and descendants. A famous family, the Le Moynes of Longueuil, was the subject of *Les Macchabées de la Nouvelle France* (Québec, 1878) by Joseph MARMETTE, who portrayed the courage and patriotism of these men as a constant source of inspiration to French Canadians. Other edifying biographies of families are *Histoire des grandes familles françaises du Canada* (Montréal, 1867) by Abbé François Daniel; *Les Normands au Canada* (1634-1668) (Evreux, 1892) by Abbé Auguste-Honoré Gosselin; and *Nicolas Le Roy et ses descendants* (Québec, 1897) by Joseph-Edmond Roy. Not to be forgotten on the subject of pious and courageous ancestors are *Le premier colon de Lévis, Guillaume Couture* (Lévis, 1884) by Joseph-Edmond Roy; and Abbé Georges Dugas's *La première canadienne du Nord-Ouest; ou Biographie de Marie-Anne Gaboury* (Montréal, 1883), a portrait of the ideal French-Canadian wife of the time: obedient to her husband, entirely devoted to her children, pious, hard-working, and supportive of the priest in his mission.

By the last two decades of the nineteenth century, ultramontane clergy and laymen had succeeded in imposing their reactionary views and conservative values on all spheres of French-Canadian society. Biographies of bishops, priests, missionaries, founders and members of religious communities were therefore very much in favour in French Canada. Such works, often on clerics who today rest in obscurity, are too numerous and undistinctive to mention here.

Many biographies paying tribute to politicians, educators, businessmen, and men of the law were published in the last quarter of the nineteenth century. Quite flattering to their subjects in many cases, and supplying information that is sometimes inaccurate, they were often written by a friend or a devoted admirer. A very popular pattern for such books is first a sketchy physical description of the subject, then an enumeration of his many moral and intellectual qualities, followed by a discourse on his patriotism and sense of duty; finally, the biographer proposes his subject to the admiration of his compatriots. One could list here *Philémon Wright* (Montréal, 1871) by Joseph Tassé; *L'Honorable Sir G.E. Cartier, ministre de la milice* (Québec, 1873) by Louis-Philippe Turcotte; *Biographies canadiennes* (Québec, 1875) by Abbé Casgrain; *Biographies et portraits* (Montréal, 1876) by Laurent-Olivier David; *Les Canadiens de l'Ouest* (2 vols, Montréal, 1878) by Joseph Tassé; *La vie de Joseph-François Perrault, surnommé le père de l'éducation du peuple canadien* (Québec, 1878) by Philippe Baby Casgrain, a well-documented book; *Histoire de Joseph Montferrand* (Montréal, 1884; rev. 1889) by Benjamin Sulte; *L'Honorable Joseph-Adolphe Chapleau. Sa biographie, suivie de ses principaux discours* (Montréal, 1887) edited by A. de Bonneterre; *Biographie, discours, conférences, etc. de l'Honorable Honoré Mercier* (Montréal, 1890) by Joseph-Octave Pelland; *Mes contemporains* (Montréal, 1894) and *Les deux Papineau* (Montréal, 1896) by Laurent-Olivier David.

Biographies devoted to writers are fewer in number. Here the pattern is usually to provide brief biographical information, followed by a summary of the writer's main works and themes and a moral judgement on the quality and patriotic values of these works. Casgrain is the leading biographer in this category with his *François-Xavier Garneau* (Québec, 1866) and *Philippe Aubert de Gaspé* (Québec, 1871) and an 87-page 'Notice biographique' on Octave CRÉMAZIE preceding the poet's *Oeuvres complètes* (Montréal, 1886). In *Nos hommes de lettres* (Montréal, 1873) Louis-Michel Darveau gave fourteen short 'esquisses biographiques', while Pierre-Joseph Oliver CHAUVEAU wrote the interesting *François-Xavier Garneau. Sa vie et ses oeuvres* (Montréal, 1883).

Albani (Québec, 1874), Napoléon Legendre's book on the famous French-Canadian opera singer Marie Louise Cécile Lajeunesse, better known as Emma Albani—written shortly after her Covent Garden début—is the only biography in its category.

2. 1900 TO 1920. Berthe Jetté's *Vie de la vénérable mère d'Youville, fondatrice des Soeurs de la Charité de Montréal, suivie d'un historique de son Institut* (1900), the first biography written by a woman, shows the tradition of hagiography being perpetuated into the twentieth century, and the supernatural and the number of miracles playing an even greater role than in the works of Father Faillon. Further evidence of that tradition can be found in *Une fleur mystique de la Nouvelle-France. Vie de la mère Marie-Catherine de Saint-Augustin, religieuse de l'Hôtel-Dieu de Précieux-Sang de Québec, 1632-1668* (1907) by Father Léonidas Hudon, and in *Le Frère Didace Pelletier, Récollet* (1910) by Abbé Odoric-Marie Jouve—not to mention Narcisse-Eutrope Gagnon's biographies of several priests and nuns.

The history of New France remained much in favour. Jetté's and Hudon's heroines were from that period and so were the following historical figures: *Louis Jolliet, découvreur du Mississipi et du pays des Illinois* (1902, 1913, 1926) by Ernest Amédée Gagnon; *Frontenac et ses amis* (1902) by Ernest Myrand; *Jean Talon, intendant de la Nouvelle France, 1665-1672* (1904) by Thomas Chapais; and *Le Marquis de Montcalm (1712-1759)* (1911) by Thomas Chapais, a biased work in praise of Montcalm.

In *Laurier et son temps* (1905) Laurent-Olivier David testifies to his friendship with, and admiration for, the first French-Canadian prime minister, then at the height of his popularity. When Laurier died in 1919, David published *Laurier, sa vie, ses oeuvres* (1919), a revised and enlarged version of the earlier work. One year later, Alfred Duclos De Celles gave David's former title to a book of his own: *Laurier et son temps* (1920). This historian was already well known for having edited *Discours de Sir Wilfrid Laurier* (3 vols, 1909-20) and for writing a successful trilogy: *Papineau, 1786-1871* (1905; English trans., 1904; new trans., 1905), *Lafontaine et son temps* (1907), and *Cartier et son temps* (1907). These three books bear witness to French Canadians' growing interest in their political history and political leaders. In *Athlètes canadiens-français: recueil des exploits de force, d'endurance, d'agilité, des athlètes et des sportmen de notre race, depuis le XVIIIe siècle. Biographie, portraits, anecdotes, records* (1909), Édouard-Zotique Massicotte proposed more modest heroes for his compatriots to admire.

3. 1929 TO 1940. During these two decades New France remained an attraction and a field of scholarly interest for historians and biographers. Two new biographies of Jeanne Mance appeared in 1934, one by Pierre Benoît and the other by Marie-Claire Daveluy, whose book was honoured by the Académie française. While novelist Maurice CONSTANTIN-WEYER mixed fiction with reality in his *Champlain* (1931), Robert Rumilly's approach to the life of Marguerite Bourgeoys (1936) was that of a pious historian. Three years after *La grande aventure de Le Moyne d'Iberville* (1934) by Pierre Daviault, Father Louis-Marie Le Jeune published his well-documented *Le Chevalier Pierre Le Moyne, sieur d'Iberville* (1937). Le Jeune's reputation as a serious scholar had already been established by his *Dictionnaire général de biographie* (2 vols, 1931). There was an increased interest in the lives of explorers, pioneers, and adventurers. Besides the books written on d'Iberville, there were *Cavalier de La Salle* (1927) by Constantin-Weyer; *La Vérendrye, découvreur canadien* (1933) by Robert Rumilly; *Un pioneer canadien, Pierre Boucher* (1927) by Séraphin Marion; and *Pierre Radisson, roi des coureurs de bois* (1933) by Donatien Frémont.

As in the previous periods, religious figures were the subject of many biographies between 1920 and 1940, but for the most part the interpretation of historical facts and documents took precedence over the mere narration of virtues, miracles, visions, and supernatural interventions. Such biographies included *Le Curé Labelle. Sa vie et son oeuvre* (1930) by Abbé Elie-Joseph Auclair; *Mgr Taché et la naissance du Manitoba* (1930) by Donatien Frémont; *Mgr Provencher et son temps* (1935) by the same author; and *Mgr Laflèche et son temps* (1936) by Robert Rumilly. Only two hagiographies seem to have been published: *La vie de mère Marie-Rose* (1928) by Abbé Joseph-Marie Mélançon and *Kateri Tekakwitha* (1934) by Robert Rumilly.

Bearing witness to the rise of French-Canadian nationalist fervour in the 1930s are the biographies of charismatic leaders: *Sir Wilfrid Laurier* (1931) and *Mercier* (1936) by Robert Rumilly; *Olivar Asselin* (1938) by Hermas Bastien; and *L'abbé Lionel Groulx* (1939) by André Laurendeau. Rumilly's *Chefs de file* (1934) treats a number of such figures.

Books on writers include *Louis Fréchette* (1924) by Henri d'Arles; *Antoine Gérin-Lajoie: la résurrection d'un patriote canadien* (1925) by Léon Gérin; *François-Xavier Garneau* (1926) by Gustave Lanctôt; *La vie aventureuse d'Arthur Buies* (1933) by Raymond Douville, a study of the prolific journalist; and a second book on Louis FRÉCHETTE: *Un romantique canadien* (1934) by Marcel DUGAS.

4. 1941 TO 1960. Biographies of heroes of New France and religious figures continued to predominate in this period. There were no less than three books on Marguerite Bourgeoys: by Albert Jammet (1942), Yvon Charron (1950), and Marie-Anne Goulthier-Landreville (1958). Thanks to Maurice Constantin-Weyer, Pierre Benoît, and Sister Allard, *La Vérendrye* (1941), *Maisonneuve* (1960), and *Jeanne Mance* (1960) remained in the limelight, while Esther Lefebvre and Father Léon Pouliot respectively made two other less-celebrated figures better known to historians and the public in general with *Marie Morin, premier historien de Ville-Marie* (1960) and *François-Xavier de Charlevoix* (1957).

Biographers were by now adopting a more critical and objective approach to their subjects, re-evaluating their predecessors' pious statements and conclusions and their patriotic bias in the light of a scientific and methodical analysis of facts and documents. Hence the undeniable value of the scholarly research undertaken by a new generation of historians, such as Guy FRÉGAULT, Marcel TRUDEL, Father Léon Pouliot, and Brother Philippe Sylvain. After *Iberville, le conquérant* (1944), Guy Frégault wrote *François Bigot, administrateur français* (2 vols, 1948) and *Le grand marquis, Pierre Rigaud de Vaudreuil et la Louisiane* (1952). In that book he attempted to rehabilitate Vaudreuil, who had previously often been decried by French-Canadian historians. Marcel Trudel, who would become a renowned historian of New France, published the well-documented *Chiniquy* (1955), on the scandal-ridden priest turned Presbyterian minister. That same year Father Pouliot produced the first volume of his monumental *Mgr Bourget et son temps* (5 vols, 1955-77), on the Bishop of Montreal (1799-1885), and Frère Philippe Sylvain published his *La vie et l'oeuvre de Henry de Courcy* (1955), on the historian. Many other books on priests (and missionaries) were published during these two decades by Fathers Antoine Bernard, Romain Légaré, and Gaston Carrière.

Albert Faucher introduced the world of finance and economics to French-Canadian biography with *Alphonse Desjardins, pionnier de la coopération d'épargne et de crédit en Amérique* (1950). Donatien Frémont wrote a book on *Les secrétaires de Riel: Louis Schmidt, Henry Jackson, Philippe Garnot* (1953). Raymond Tanghe, in *Laurier, artisan de l'unité canadienne* (1960), introduced a theme that was to be much debated in the years to come. The ever-productive Robert Rumilly wrote *Henri Bourassa. La vie publique d'un grand Canadien* (1953).

Rumilly's *Le Frère Marie Victorin et son temps* (1949) is a study of the writer and botanist (q.v.). Written on the eve of the Quiet Revolution, two other books on writers were devoted to well-known 'journalistes de combat': *Jules Fournier: journaliste de combat* (1955) by Adrien Thério and *Arthur Buies* (1957) by Léopold Lamontagne.

La vie et l'oeuvre du Frère Luc (1944) by Gérard Morrisset turned the attention of readers to the arts. *La Bolduc* (1959) by Pierre Benoît paid homage to a very popular French-Canadian singer.

5. 1961 TO 1981. For the most part biographies written in these two decades reflect the new spirit of Quebec, which called into question traditional values. They were seldom written by clergy and many were by women.

Though biographers and historians continued to favour the times of New France, they certainly did not confine themselves to that period. Besides *Dans le nid d'aiglons, la colombe. Vie de Jeanne Le Ber, la recluse* (1963) and *Paul de Chomedey, sieur de Maisonneuve* (1967) by Léo-Paul DESROSIERS, and *Les La Vérendrye et le poste de l'Ouest* (1969) by Antoine Champagne, several books were written on people of lesser fame, such as *La Gallissonnière et le Canada* (1962) by Roland Lamontagne, *Messire Pierre Boucher, seigneur de Boucherville* (1967) by Estelle Mitchell, *Claude-Thomas Dupuy, intendant de la Nouvelle-France* (1969) by Jean-Claude Dubé, and *François-Étienne Cugnet, entrepreneurs et entreprises en Nouvelle-France* (1975) by Cameron Nish. Two books were written on the Marquis de Denonville by T. Falmagne (1965) and Jean Leclerc (1976).

In books on subsequent periods in the history of French Canada, attention continued to be focused on politicians and, to a lesser extent, on religious figures of the time:

Camilien Houde, le p'tit gars de Ste-Marie (1961) by H. La Roque; *La vie orageuse d'Olivar Asselin* (1962) by Marcel-André Gagnon, who also published *Olivar Asselin toujours vivant* (1974); *L'histoire bouleversante de Mgr Charbonneau* (1962) by Renaude Lapointe; *Lord Durham* (1963) by Roger Viau; *L'imprévisible Monsieur Houde* (1964) by Charles Renaud; *Henri Bourassa* (1966) by Cameron Nish; *Un bourgeois d'une époque révolue: Victor Morin, notaire* (1967) by Renée Morin; *Hector-Louis Langevin, un père de la Confédération canadienne* (1969) by Andreé Désilets; *Joseph-Charles Taché* (1971) by Evelyne Bossé; *Maurice Duplessis et son temps* (2 vols, 1973) by Robert Rumilly; *Étienne Parent* (1975) by Jean-Charles Falardeau; *Papineau et son temps* (2 vols, 1977) by Robert Rumilly; *Le curé Labelle: le colonisateur, le politicien, la légende* (1979) by Robert Lévesque and Robert Miguier; *Louis-François Laflèche, deuxième évêque de Trois-Rivières* (1979) by Nive Voisine; *Jean-Jacqus Lartigue, premier évêque de Montréal* (1980) by Gilles Chaussé; *La vie studieuse et obstinée de Denis-Benjamin Viger* (1980) by Gérard Parizeau. *Papineau: un être divisé* (1960) and *Julie Papineau, un cas de mélancolie et d'éducation janséniste* (1961) by Fernard Ouellet are two socio-psychological studies of the well-known family.

Several books were devoted to Canadian politicians who won fame in the sixties and the seventies: *Le vrai visage de Jean Drapeau* (1962) by L. Patenaude; *Les trois vies de Pearson* (1968) by J.R. Beal and J.M. Poliquin; *Le phénomène Trudeau* (1972) by Jean Pellerin; *René Lévesque, tel quel* (1973) by François Aubin and *René Lévesque, portrait d'un Québécois* (1973) by Jean Provencher; and *Daniel Johnson* (1980) by Pierre Godin.

The large number of studies of Quebec's writers who published in this period shows the high degree of scholarly interest that had developed in French-Canadian literature. Few, if any, of these books could be classified as biographies, but most supply much useful information about the lives of the authors whose works they analyse and criticize—particularly those in the series 'Écrivains canadiens d'aujourd'hui' (Éditions Fides) and Vie des lettres québécoises (Les Presses de l'Université Laval). The former collection includes *Germaine Guèvremont* (1963) by Rita Gauthier-Leclerc; *Anne Hébert* (1965) by Pierre Pagé; *Léo-Paul Desrosiers* (1966) by Julia Richer; *Émile Nelligan* (1967) by Paul Wyzynski; *Félix-Antoine Savard* (1968) by André Major; *Robert Élie* (1968) by Marc Gagnon; *Gabrielle Roy* (1970) by François Ricard; *Ringuet* (1970) by Jean Panneton; *Marcel Dubé* (1970) by Maximilien Laroche; and *Robert Charbonneau* (1972) by Madeleine Ducrocq-Poirier. The more scholarly second collection includes *Le ciel et l'enfer d'Arthur Buies* (1965) by Marcel-A. Gagnon; *Joseph Marmette (1844-1895): sa vie, son oeuvre* (1968) by Roger Le Moine; and *À la recherche de Napoléon Aubin* (1969) by Jean-Paul Tremblay.

Other interesting biographies (all on writers who have entries in this *Companion*) are: *Alain Grandbois* (1968) by Jacques BRAULT; *Jean-Charles Harvey et son oeuvre romanesque* (1969) by Guildo Rousseau; *Jean-Charles Harvey, précurseur de la Révolution tranquille* (1970) by Marcel-Aimé Gagnon; *Jacques Ferron malgré lui* (1970) by Jean Marcel; *Visages de Gabrielle Roy. L'oeuvre et l'écrivain* (1973) by Marc Gagné; *Marie Le Franc, deux patries, deux exils* (1976) by Paulette Collet; *Robert Choquette, romancier et dramaturge de la radio et de la T.V.* (1977) by Renée Legris; *Antoine Gérin-Lajoie, homme de lettres* (1978) by René Dionne; *Lionel Groulx* (1978) by Georges-Émile Giguère; *Claude Gauvreau, poète et mythocrate* (1979) by Jacques Marchand; and *Marie Le Franc. Au-delà du personnage* (1981) by Madeleine Ducrocq-Poirier. Of special interest are *Pour saluer Victor Hugo* (1971), *Jack Kerouac* (1972), and *Monsieur Melville* (1978) by Victor-Lévy BEAULIEU—biographical essays that tell as much, if not more, about the author than about his subjects.

Several books on French-Canadian artists published since the beginning of the sixties offer a mixture of biographical information and comments on their works: Guy ROBERT's *Pellan, sa vie et son oeuvre* (1963) and *Borduas* (1972); Hugues de Jouvancourt's *Suzor-Côté* (1967), *Marc-Aurèle Fortin* (1968), and *Clarence Gagnon* (1970); François-Marc Gagnon's *Paul-Émile Borduas* (1978); Jean ÉTHIER-BLAIS's *Autour de Borduas* (1979); and Jean-Pierre Duquette's *Fernand Leduc* (1980).

6. MEMOIRS. BEGINNINGS TO 1900. Philippe AUBERT DE GASPÉ's *Mémoires* (Ottawa, 1866) is the best-known work in this genre published in French Canada in the last century. (It was translated and annotated by Jane Brierly as *A man of sentiment: the memoirs of Philippe-Joseph-Aubert de Gaspé, 1786-1871*, 1988.) These loosely structured recollections can be considered a by-product of his *Les ANCIENS CANADIENS* (1863), for they convey some anecdotes and legends that were to have appeared in that novel. With great charm, simplicity, and good nature, Aubert de Gaspé tells about his life (1786-1871), people he met, and events he witnessed. A real storyteller, he wanders from one subject to another, letting one

memory bring forth another and giving a nostalgic account of life in Quebec at the beginning of the nineteenth century.

Notes d'un condamné politique (Montréal, 1864), by François-Xavier Prieur, gives an interesting, though rather poorly written, account of the author's participation in the 1837 Rebellion and of his exile in Australia. It also describes the penitentiary system in New South Wales. Published the same year, *Mémoires sur les moeurs, coutumes et religions des sauvages de l'Amérique septentrionale* (Paris, 1864) by Nicolas Perrot (1643-1717) supplies still-useful information on wars with the Native peoples, habits, and ways of life. Perrot, a fur trader, also offers advice to Intendant Michel Bégon on the government of the colony. He draws attention to his personal contribution in establishing good relations between the French and the Amerindians, but regrets that his advice was not followed more often. Published more than a hundred years after the death of Louis Franquet (1697-1768), his *Voyages et mémoires sur le Canada* (Québec, 1889) is a valuable source of information on life in New France in the years preceding the Conquest. A conscientious observer, Franquet, who was inspector of fortifications in New France in 1750-2, is considered most reliable by historians. Pierre de Sales Laterrière (1747-1815) intended to bring special moments of his eventful life to light in his private diary, *Mémoires de Pierre de Sales Laterrière et de ses traverses* (Québec, 1873), which Abbé Henri-Raymond Casgrain revealed in 1870, but the book seems to owe as much to fiction as to reality; he arrived in Canada in 1766 claiming to have studied medicine in France (he did some medical studies in Montreal), practised medicine for a time and then became manager of the Forges de Saint-Maurice, was overtly pro-American against the British, and in 1779 was jailed for three years as a traitor.

In *Souvenirs d'un demi-siècle* (Montréal, 1885) Joseph-Guillaume Barthe (1818-93) recalls the years of his childhood and gives word-portraits of some of the political figures of his time, such as Vollières de Saint-Réal, Étienne Parent, Jacques Viger, and Louis-Joseph Papineau. *Cinquante ans dans l'Église de Rome* (Montréal, 1885) by Charles Chiniquy (1809-99) is probably the most successful book of memoirs to appear in French Canada in the nineteenth century. By 1898 it had been reprinted seventy times and had been translated into eight languages. It tells of the author's conversion to Protestantism after spending most of his life in the Catholic Church. Wishing to justify himself and to project his image as a saintly man, Chiniquy jumps at every opportunity to attack his former Church and to denounce not only the priests and their school system but also the sacrament of penance, the Eucharist, and the Virgin Mary. Needless to say, the book scandalized people. In *Le 38e fauteuil; ou Souvenirs parlementaires* (Montréal, 1891), Joseph Tassé (1848-1893), a member of the Conservative party and a deputy minister in Ottawa from 1878 to 1887, recalls some great moments of Canadian political life between 1867 and 1887 and makes lively comments on politicians he has known.

7. 1900 TO 1940. Louis FRÉCHETTE's *Mémoires*, which appeared for the most part in *Le Monde illustré* from May to Nov. 1900, were edited by George A. Klinck and published as a book in 1961. Mainly known as a poet, Fréchette obviously enjoys telling anecdotes about his youth and about his compatriots and their way of life; he proves himself to be a talented storyteller with a good sense of humour. Most memoirs published between 1900 and 1940 seem to have been written by politicians. In his *Souvenirs politiques* (2 vols, 1909), Charles Langelier tells of the beginning of the Liberal party in French Canada. Although his testimony is obviously far from impartial, it provides many anecdotes and very useful information on political life between 1878 and 1896. Other interesting political memoirs are Armand Lavergne's *Trente ans de vie nationale* (1934), which covers the period from 1880 to the eve of the First World War (a second volume was to have been written), and Philippe-Auguste Choquette's *Un demi-siècle de vie politique* (1936), on the years from 1880 to 1930. *Quatre-vingts ans de souvenirs* (1939), by Mme Frédéric-Liguori Beique, daughter of Louis-Antoine Dessaulles, also deals mainly with politics.

8. 1941 TO 1960. Edouard Montpetit's well-written *Souvenirs* (3 vols, 1944-55) tells of his career as a renowned professor of political science and a lecturer of international reputation, and is particularly interesting on the foundation of the Université de Montréal and the intellectual life in Quebec in the author's day; it also gives personal views of some of the political issues of the time. In *Testament de mon enfance* (1952; *Testament of my childhood*, 1964), which mixes autobiography with fiction, Robert de ROQUEBRUNE describes the vanished world of his childhood in the family manor of Saint-Ours, at L'Assomption. This elegantly written book, often anthologized, was acclaimed by most critics, in both France

and Canada, and was awarded the Prix Duvernay. Two further memoirs followed: *Quartier Saint Louis* (1966) and *Cherchant mes souvenirs* (1968).

Father Émile Legault's *Confidences* (1955) is largely devoted to the establishment in 1937 and the history of Les Compagnons de Saint-Laurent, the theatre company of which he was the guiding spirit and that gave scope to French-language theatre in Quebec until its dissolution in 1952. Mgr Olivier Maurault's *Confidences* (1959), which he first read on Radio-Canada, is disappointing in comparison, though Maurault, who was rector of the Université de Montréal from 1939 to 1955, had many anecdotes and memories worth telling. His *Confidences* often repeats commonplaces and is finally rather superficial.

9. 1960 TO 1980. Since 1960 politicians seem to have occupied the first place among authors of memoirs in Quebec—not surprisingly, considering the importance of politics in modern Quebec society. Although tainted with political bias and a tendency towards self-justification, these memoirs supply first-hand information about behind-the-scenes events and tactics and bring to light the personalities of both important and lesser contemporary political figures. Worthy of mention are *Mémoires* (1960) by Télesphore-Damien Bouchard; *Mémoires* (1966) by Antonio Barrette; *Les mémoires du sénateur Raoul Dandurand* (1967); *Mémoires politiques* (1969) by René Chaloult; *Une femme chez les hommes* (1971) by Thérèse F. Casgrain (translated by Joyce MARSHALL as *A woman in a man's world: memoirs*, 1972); and *Mémoires, choses vues... entendues... vécues... en politique de 1906 à 1958* (1972) by Lionel Bertrand.

As priest, historian, teacher, lecturer, and prolific writer, Father Lionel GROULX played an influential role in the socio-cultural, intellectual, and political life of Quebec; the four volumes of *Mes mémoires* (1970-4) are of great interest in giving a well-rounded picture of his personality, his work, and his times. Highlights are his description in Volume II of the Action française movement, the controversy that surrounded the publication of *L'appel de la race* (1922), and his portraits of Harry BERNARD and Léo-Paul Desrosiers among others; the account in the third volume (1926 to 1939) of his stay in France and sketches of Armand Lavergne, Maurice Duplessis, and Jean-Charles HARVEY; and, in the last volume (1940-67), Groulx's reflections on the Quiet Revolution and his advice to French Canadians on the years to come.

In *Sous le soleil de la pitié* (1965) by Jean-Paul Desbiens, the author of the famous *Insolences du Frère Untel* (1960) recalls the often difficult times of his first teaching experiences. In *Confidences* (1965), Ringuet (Philippe PANNETON) recounts a few of his memories through a series of well-chosen anecdotes, without any nostalgia for days gone by. With much humour he invites the romantic eulogists of the past to contemplate abandoning their modern comforts in favour of their grandparents' style of life.

In her remarkable *DANS UN GANT DE FER* (1965) and *La joue droite* (1966), Claire MARTIN remembers the traumatic years of her youth and offers a very critical judgement on the French-Canadian society of yesteryear and of its religious/moral values.

Journal et souvenirs (2 vols, 1973, 1975) by Félix-Antoine SAVARD offers a good idea of the author's intellectual life between 1961 and 1964 and conveys his reflections on social and political changes in these first years of the Quiet Revolution.

Other memoirs of interest are Albert Tessier's *Souvenirs en vrac* (1975); Alfred Laliberté's *Mes souvenirs*; Théodore Dupont's *Mes mémoires* (1980); *Une symphonie inachevée* (1972), by Quebec's famous conductor Wilfrid Pelletier; *Une mémoire déchirée* (1978) by Thérèse Renaud, a member of the Automatiste movement and one of those who signed the *REFUS GLOBAL* in 1948; and *Mes romans et moi* (1979) by Gérard BESSETTE.

10. 1980 TO 1996. BIOGRAPHY. A fair number of biographies dealing with the most diverse subjects have been published in French Canada in recent years. The decline in the number of religiously oriented biographies is obvious, although André-Marie Cimichella (1985) and Henri Béchard (1993) each devoted a book to Kateri Tekakwitha, Fleurette Tremblay proposed as a model the life of Sister Rose-Yvonne Tremblay in *Voici que je viens* (1989), Gérard Mercier that of Gérard Raymond in *Un défi aux jeunes* (1992), and Céline Langelier that of Jeanne Le Ber in *La récluse de Montréal* (1996). Much more prominent are biographies of important figures in Canadian history, which continue to be regularly published by scholars. Whereas Louis-Martin Tard tells about the glorious actions of characters as different as *Pierre Le Moyne d'Iberville. Le conquérant des mers* (1994) and *Chomedey de Maisonneuve. Le pionnier de Montréal* (1994), Daniel Poliquin allows us to discover the adventurous life of *Samuel Hearne. Le marcheur de l'Arctique* (1994), in a well-documented book on life in the Great

North, and customs and traditions of the Native peoples in the eighteenth century. Yvan Lamonde and Brian Young show genuine interest in famous French-Canadian political figures: *Louis-Antoine Dessaulles: un seigneur libéral et anticlérical* (1994) in the case of the former, and *Georges-Étienne Cartier, bourgeois montréalais* (1982) in the case of the latter. Responding to the expectations of the general public curious to know more intimately those who have shaped the history of contemporary Quebec, Bernard L. Vigod wrote *La carrière politique de Louis-Alexandre Taschereau* (1996), whose subject became premier of Quebec in 1921, while Jean-Guy Genest underscores the important contribution of *Adélard Godbout* (1996) to the birth of modern Quebec. Particularly well received by the public were Jean-François Lisée's 1994 two-volume book on Robert Bourassa, published under the titles *Le tricheur. Robert Bourassa et les Québécois, 1990-1991*, and *Le naufrageur. Robert Bourassa et les Québécois (1991-1992)*, as well as *René Lévesque. Un enfant du siècle* (1994); there was also Pierre Godin's *René Lévesque. Héros malgré lui* (1996). An equally important contribution was that of Denis Monière who, in *André Laurendeau et le destin d'un peuple* (1983), retraces the intellectual and political path of a man whose thought has had a great influence on the evolution of nationalism in Quebec. Although the two following books are translations—which in itself is revealing—mention should be made of *Brian Mulroney* (1984) by Rae Murphy, Robert Chodos, and Nick Auf der Maur and of Christina MCCALL's and Stephen Clarkson's two-volume *Trudeau: l'homme, l'utopie, l'histoire* (1990) and *Trudeau: l'illusion héroique* (1995).

On several occasions biographers have tried to satisfy the public's avowed interest in actors and popular singers, or those who made the front page, such as Dr Henry Morgentaler, who was the subject of Sylvie Halpern's *Morgentaler, l'obstiné* (1992). Among performers' biographies were Micheline La France's *Denise Pelletier, ou la folie du théâtre* (1979); Pierre Day's *Une histoire de la Bolduc* (1992), about a popular singer; and Jacques Bertin's *Félix Leclerc. Le roi heureux* (1988). In the two volumes of *La ferveur et le doute* (1995, 1996), Anne-Marie Sicotte reveals the major events that marked the exceptional life and career of her grandfather Gratien GÉLINAS, actor, playwright, and founder of La Comédie-Canadienne. Another important name in the history of Quebec theatre is the subject of Hélène Jasmin-Bélisle's *Le Père Émile Legault et ses Compagnons de Saint Laurent* (1986).

In *Micheline Lanctôt. La vie d'une héroïne* (1995), *Judith Jasmin. De feu et de flamme* (1992), and *Marie Gérin-Lajoie. De mère en fille, la cause des femmes* (1985), Denise Pérusse, Colette Beauchamp, and Helène Pelletier-Baillargeon respectively bring to life three outstanding women who are revealed as much by their actions as by their commitment to progress in Quebec society. This was also the case with *Adrien Pouliot. Un homme en avance sur son temps* (1986) by Danielle Ouellet.

Whether they be biographies in the literal sense of the word—such as Paul Wyczynski's excellent *Émile Nelligan, 1879-1941* (1987) or François Ricard's monumental *Vie* (1996) of Gabrielle ROY—or more general works devoted to the writer and his or her works, the life of Quebec writers has remained a field of interest. Among such books containing important biographical information were *Louis-Joseph Béliveau et la vie littéraire de son temps* (1985) by Paul Wyczynski; *Hertel: l'homme et l'oeuvre* (1986) by Jean Tétreau; *Au temps de Philippe Aubert de Gaspé* (1987) by Jacques Castonguay; *Charles ab der Halden. Portrait d'un inconnu* (1993) by Marie-Andrée Beauder; *Laure Conan. La romancière aux rubans* (1994) by Louise Simard, who attempts to discover the intimate secret of the author of *ANGÉLINE DE MONTBRUN*; *De Saint-Denys Garneau, l'enfant piégé* (1994) by Antoine Prévost; *L'homme sans rivages. Portrait d'Alain Grandbois* (1994) by Denise Pérusse and *Livres et pays d'Alain Grandbois* (1995) by Nicole Deschamps and Jean Cléo Godin. Fascinating and of special interest is Gordon Sheppard and Andrée Yanacapoulo's book *Signé Hubert Aquin. Enquête sur le suicide d'un écrivain* (1985), a book in which they reconstitute the circumstances of this drama and the events that followed.

MEMOIRS. To the same extent as biographies, memoirs illustrate the important role of politics in Quebec life. Paul Michaud in *Au temps de l'Index. Mémoires d'un éditeur, 1949-1961* (1996), Gérard Filion in *Fais ce que peux. En guise de mémoire* (1989), and Jean-Paul Desbiens in *Journal d'un homme farouche, 1983-1992* (1993) confirm this fact. It is not surprising that politicians are usually anxious to take a stand for their fellow citizens and for posterity when they wish to explain their vision of Canada's and Quebec's future, or to justify their personal political actions. It is thus that René Lévesque in *Attendez que je me rappelle* (1986), having rapidly summarized Quebec political life from Maurice Duplessis's years as premier to the rise of the Quiet Revolution, recounts how he became a political figure. As a privileged witness to the major political moments of the Quiet Revolution, Claude Morin relates his memories in *Mes premiers ministres: Lesage, Johnson, Bertrand, Bourassa et Lévesque* (1991) and in *Les choses comme elles étaient* (1994). If they have documentary value, these works, as a whole, have little value as literature.

If it is true, as shown by Pierre Hébert and Marilyn Baszczynski in *Le Journal intime au Québec* (1988), that Quebec writers have long been uncomfortable writing about themselves, this is certainly no longer the case. Not only are they indeed now inclined to insert obvious autobiographical references in their fiction—and even in their critical works, as shown by André BROCHU's *La visée critique: essais autobiographiques et littéraires* (1988)—but in recent years they have published extracts from their personal diaries and their correspondence, or written their autobiographies. The publications of Jean-Louis Major's critical edition of the *Journal* (1989) of Henriette Dessaulles and of Bernard Beugnot's critical edition of the *Journal 1948-1971* (1992) of Hubert AQUIN were posthumous; but such is not the case for the *Journal* (5 vols, 1986-8) of Jean-Pierre Guay, nor for *Du sommet d'un arbre* (1986) by Yves BEAUCHEMIN, in which he combines autobiographical chapters about his childhood and adolescence with pages from his diary, which reveal the music lover, the novelist, the reader of Balzac, and a militant for the cause of separatism. In *Fragments d'une enfance* (1989) and in *Le seuil des vingt ans* (1992), where he recalls certain events that marked his youth at Sturgeon Falls and Sudbury, Ontario, from 1925 to 1946, Jean ÉTHIER-BLAIS brings to life an important period of his life in a milieu where French-speaking people were a minority. It is, however, the magnificent autobiography by Gabrielle Roy, *La détresse et l'enchantement* (1984), that is really exemplary in the present category.

See Yvan Lamonde, *Je me souviens: la littérature personnelle au Québec (1860-1980)* (1983); Françoise Van Roey-Roux, *La littérature intime du Québec* (1983); and Pierre Hébert, with the collaboration of Marilyn Baszczynsi, *Le journal intime au Québec* (1988).

JACQUES COTNAM

Bird, Will R. (1891-1984). William Richard Bird was born in East Mapleton, Nova Scotia, and educated at Amherst Academy. After service overseas in the First World War, he became a free-lance writer and subsequently an information officer for the Nova Scotia government. The author of twenty-seven books, he is best known for his historical romances. Only three of his novels—*Maid of the marshes* (1935), *So much to record* (1951), and *The misadventures of Rufus Burdy* (1975)—have twentieth-century settings. His eight historical novels are all set in the raw atmosphere of eighteenth-century Nova Scotia. Portraying mainly humble folk, they require little psychological analysis but are attractive for their evocation of colourful incidents, characters, and settings. Bird's best work, *Here stays good Yorkshire* (1945), introduces the rough-hewn Crabtree family, settlers in the Chignecto region in the troubled times of the American Revolution. *Tristram's salvation* (1957) and *Despite the distance* (1961) make the Crabtree saga a trilogy. Two other novels are derived from Bird's Yorkshire-settlement heritage: *Judgment glen* (1947) and *The shy Yorkshireman* (1955). *The passionate pilgrim* (1949) is another Chignecto novel, set during the time of the Acadian expulsion. *To love and to cherish* (1953) portrays the founding of Shelburne by the Loyalists, and *An Earl must have a wife* (1969) is a lurid account of the life of a famous colonial administrator, J.F.W. DesBarres (1722-1824).

Bird's short stories have been collected in *Private Timothy Fergus Clancy* (1930), *Sunrise for Peter, and other stories* (1946), and *Angel Cove* (1972). As well, Bird edited, with Alec Lucas, *Atlantic anthology* (1959), a collection of writings by Maritime authors. Two memoirs, *And we go on* (1930) and *Ghosts have warm hands* (1968), are expressions of Bird's experiences in the First World War; *Thirteen years after: the story of the old front revisited* (1932) and *The communication trench* (1933) are compilations of his journalistic analyses of the war. *The two Jacks* (1954) deals with an episode from the Second World War, and *No retreating footsteps: the story of the North Nova Scotia Highlanders* (1954) and *The North Shore (New Brunswick) Regiment* (1963) are regimental histories. Two other histories, *A century at Chignecto: the key to old Acadia* (1928) and *Done at Grand Pré* (1955), treat Chignecto and Acadia before 1780. *This is Nova Scotia* (1950), *Off-trail in Nova Scotia* (1956), and *These are the Maritimes* (1959) are travel books.

KEN MacKINNON

Birdsell, Sandra (b. 1942). She was born Sandra Bartlette in Hamiota and raised in Morris, Manitoba, and lived for many years in Winnipeg. She is now an instructor in the Department of English, Capilano College, North Vancouver.

Birdsell began writing stories in the mid-1970s. The guidance of Robert KROETSCH in the late 1970s proved to be vital to her development as a writer. Her first collection of stories, *Night travellers* (1982), is based on the fictional town of Agassiz. It won the Gerald Lampert Memorial Award. *Ladies of the house* (1984), a second collection, is linked to her first through interrelated storylines about the fictional Lafrenière family. A French translation appeared as *Agassiz: nouvelles* (1990) and in 1987 Birdsell's two collections were reissued by Turnstone Press as *Agassiz stories*. The title of the American edition of these same stories, *Agassiz: a novel in stories* (1991), aptly suggests that her work defies easy categorization. Like Alice MUNRO and Margaret LAURENCE, Birdsell writes of women's lives in rural Canada, but her work is much darker, and her refusal to disguise or underplay hopelessness has prompted some critics to liken her fiction to that of American writers Raymond Carver and Bobbie Ann Mason.

Birdsell's two novels brought her further recognition and more awards: *The missing child* (1989) won the W.H. Smith-*Books in Canada* First Novel Award, and *The chrome suite* (1992) won the McNally Robinson Award for Manitoba Book of the Year. Like her short-story collections, Birdsell's novels are preoccupied with generations of women whose problems go largely unresolved. Her fiction is not without humour, and while the sexual oppression of women is a dominant concern, erotic love also finds its place. When, however, Birdsell confronts what is horrific in women's lives, she does so without flinching. In *The missing child*, a complex novel that experiments with narrative structure and conventions of storytelling, the rape and murder of young girls is one of the central, devastating themes. *The chrome suite* adheres more closely to realist traditions and is also less disturbing, though it has its share of break-ups, deep disappointments, and death.

Birdsell published two books in 1997: *The two-headed calf*, a collection of stories, and *The town that floated away*, a children's book.

Articles on Birdsell appear in *Contemporary Manitoba writers* (1900), edited by Kenneth James Hughes; in *Canadian women writing fiction* (1993), an American publication edited by Mickey Pearlman; and *The guises of Canadian diversity: new European perspectives* (1995), a Dutch publication edited by Serge Jaumain and Marc Maufort. See also Dallas Harrison's 'Sandra Birdsell: an annotated bibliography', *Essays on Canadian writing*, no. 48 (1992-3).

CYNTHIA MESSENGER

Birney, Earle (1904-95). Alfred Earle Birney was born in Calgary, Alberta, then part of the Northwest Territories, and spent his early life as an only child on an isolated farm near Lacombe. His family moved to Banff in 1911 and, following his father's service in the Great War, moved in 1916 to a fruit-farm near Creston, British Columbia. After high-school graduation Birney worked as a bank clerk, a farm labourer, and as a government labourer in the nearby national parks, before enrolling in chemistry at the University of British Columbia in 1922. During his second year he became interested in English literature and was appointed associate editor of the campus newspaper, *The Ubyssey*. He became editor-in-chief in 1925 and graduated in Honours English in 1926. After receiving his M.A. from the University of Toronto in 1927, he did further graduate work at the University of California at Berkeley, and accepted a lectureship at the University of Utah in 1930. In 1932-3 he completed doctoral course work at the University of Toronto and became a party organizer for the Trotskyist branch of the Communist Party. After returning to Utah to teach for one more year, Birney received a fellowship to the University of London, England, where he studied Old and Middle English and completed his dissertation, entitled 'Chaucer's Irony', worked for the Independent Labour Party, and travelled to Norway to interview Leon Trotsky.

On receiving his Ph.D. in 1938 Birney accepted a junior faculty position at the University of Toronto and undertook the literary editorship (1936-40) of *The CANADIAN FORUM*. He began writing poetry seriously at this time, and shortly after enlisting for officer training in the Canadian Army published his first collection, *David* (1942), which won a Governor General's Award. After serving overseas as a personnel selection officer, in 1946 he became supervisor of the International Service of the Canadian Broadcasting Corporation. His second poetry collection, *Now is time* (1945), also won a Governor General's Award. From Sept. 1946 to June 1948 he was editor of *The Canadian Poetry Magazine*. From 1948 to 1965 he was professor of medieval literature at the University of British Columbia, where he established Canada's first department of creative writing.

Although he began writing poetry relatively late in life, Birney became a marvellously resourceful and innovative writer. The Audenesque qualities of his first two collections, repeated in *The strait of Anian* (1948), were followed by the ingeniously varied styles of the verse-play *Trial of a city* (1952). In his next collection, *Ice cod bell or stone* (1962), Birney unveiled a precise new free verse, a colloquial first-person viewpoint, and a strong interest in visual or 'concrete' poetry; in its poems set in Latin America he presented the first of the world-travel poetry by which he would be widely known throughout the next two decades. *Near False Creek mouth* (1964), with its innovative, contrapuntally structured title poem, also contains impressively vivid travel meditations set in South America and the Far East. Throughout the 1960s and 1970s Birney's concern to expand the technical resources of his poetry was reflected in various kinds of hand-drawn poems, typewriter-concrete poems, and chant-poems that appeared in *Pnomes, jukollages & other stunzas* (1969), *Rag and bone shop* (1971), *What's so big about green* (1973), *The rugging and the moving times* (1976), *Alphbeings and other seasyours* (1976), and *Fall by fury* (1978); and in the substitution of space for conventional punctuation marks that characterizes these books and the retrospective gatherings *Selected poems* (1966), *The poems of Earle Birney* (1969), *Collected poems* (1975), and *Ghost in the wheels: selected poems* (1977). In this later work Birney repudiated the humanistic themes of his first three books to envision a vast, indifferent cosmos in whose 'mammoth corridors' human energy is little more than a glorious absurdity. *Last makings* (1991) is a volume of new and selected poems. Overall, Birney's poetry is marked by extraordinary technical virtuosity, playfulness, and openness to experimentation. Most important are his long poems 'David', 'The damnation of Vancouver', and 'November walk near False Creek mouth', which reflect both his resourcefulness as a craftsman and his profound empathy with human limitation.

Birney's prose—of less interest than his poetry—includes the comic war novel *Turvey* (1949; NCL, with an Afterword by Al PURDY); the novel *Down the long table* (1955), which depicts the Trotskyist scene in which Birney worked in the 1930s; *Big bird in the bush* (1978), a collection of stories and sketches; and the semi-autobiographical non-fiction works *The creative writer* (1966), *The cow jumped over the moon* (1972), and *Spreading time: Book I, 1940-1949* (1980).

International publication of Birney's work includes a pirated edition of *Turvey* called *The Kootenay Highlander* (London, 1960); three selections of his poems: *Memory no servant* (Trumansburg, N.Y., 1968), *The bear on the Delhi road* (London, 1973), and *The mammoth corridors* (Okemos, Mich., 1980); and his two editions of work by Malcolm LOWRY: *Selected poems* (San Francisco, 1962) and *Lunar caustic* (London, 1968). Birney also edited the anthology *Twentieth-century Canadian poetry* (1953).

Considerable critical attention has been focused on Birney's writings. See Peter Noel-Bentley, 'Earle Birney: an annotated bibliography' in Robert Lecker and Jack David, eds, *The annotated bibliography of Canada's major authors* 4 (1983); and Elspeth Cameron, *Earle Birney: a life* (1994).

See also POETRY IN ENGLISH 1900 TO 1950: 4; 1950 TO 1982: 2. FRANK DAVEY

Bishop, Elizabeth. See FOREIGN WRITERS ON CANADA IN ENGLISH: 2.

bissett, bill (b. 1939). Although he was born in Halifax, Nova Scotia, and now lives in London, Ontario, bill bissett is mostly associated with Vancouver and the West Coast, where he was the defining figure of the Vancouver cultural scene in the 1960s. He embodied then, and to a great extent now, the vision and idealism of the so-called 'hippy' movement. His open espousal of drug use frequently led him into legal trouble, and his books have also been the focus for charges of obscenity, in the face of which he was able to rally impressive statements of support from the cultural community.

bissett's first book of poems, *we sleep inside each other all* (1966), were followed by a steady stream of collections over a period of thirty years, many published by his own *BLEW OINTMENT* magazine, and in recent years by TALONBOOKS. Among many titles, one may mention *awake in the red desert* (1968), *pomes for yoshi* (1972, rpr. 1977), *MEDICINE my mouths on fire* (1974), *Sailor* (1978), *Seagull on Yonge Street* (1983), *Canada gees mate for life* (1985), *Animal uproar* (1987), *Hard 2 beleev* (1990), *Th last photo uv th human soul* (1993), and *Th influenza uv logik* (1995). There have been two volumes of selected poems: *nobody owns th earth* (1971) and *Selected poems: beyond even faithful legends* (1980). As a visual artist bisset has also produced paintings, drawings, and collages.

bissett has been a tireless experimenter in the forms of poetry, exploring visual and sound poems, chants, collages, short lyrics and extended narratives, and poems of vision and social satire. The most obvious and obtrusive aspect of his style is his unconventional spelling and orthography: he believes that 'correct' spelling symbolizes social and political oppression. But one soon becomes accustomed to bissett's spelling, which quickly built up its own, loosely phonetic conventions. The importance of the orthography is chiefly visual; bissett sees each poem as a composition on the page, with line divisions determined more by visual than by rhythmic criteria. The visual and oral elements of his work are thus separate; but the oral is important, as his readings demonstrate—especially the chants, based on Native chanting as much as on the tradition of sound poetry, and conveying a mesmeric, meditative effect that provides one of the foundations of his vision.

This vision can be divided into the Blakean categories of 'innocence' and 'experience'. Although his evocations of an ideal state of being—attained through communion with nature, drugs, sex, and the free expression of the personality unhampered by social restraints—may seem romantic, naive, or simplistic, they are expressed with a singular intensity, and often transcend the banal images and the unsophisticated ideas. At his best, bissett writes with remarkable subtlety and quiet irony. In narrative poems such as 'Killer whale' or 'Th emergency ward', the gentle humour and ironic distance show a fine control of nuance and tone. One of his finest sequences is *Pomes for Yoshi*, in which a series of love lyrics is juxtaposed to an increasingly weird and nightmarish story of bisset's troubles in the house he lives in; yet the long closing narrative, one of his most devastating accounts of the 'straight' world, ends with the humanistic assertion that 'its / beautiful / to feel so many / peopul around me'.

What is remarkable about bissett's later work, in the eighties and into the nineties, is its consistency. This might be seen as a criticism. Yet that very consistency, given the changing social and political milieu of these decades, is in itself a remarkable accomplishment. bissett may be the last surviving hippy, the last poet in Canada who can still write 'far out' and get away with it. He has refused to become obsolete. STEPHEN SCOBIE

Bissoondath, Neil (b. 1955). Born in Arima, Trinidad, West Indies, he had his high-school education at St Mary's College before leaving for Canada in 1973. He completed a B.A. degree in French (1977) at York University, Toronto, and worked as a teacher until 1985. He now lives in Montreal.

In 1985 Bissoondath published his first volume of short stories, *Digging up the mountains*. A novel set in the Caribbean, *A casual brutality*, followed in 1988, and another short-story collection, *On the eve of uncertain tomorrows*, appeared in 1990. The next novel, *The innocence of age*, was published in 1992. In *Selling illusions: the cult of multiculturalism in Canada* (1994), a critique of multiculturalism in Canada, the author comments: 'One makes a life, puts down roots, and from this feeling of belonging comes the wish to be as fully part of the country as possible.' This sentence encapsulates a whole attitude to migration, a way of negotiating the binaries of centre and margin, a resistance to hyphenated identities, that informs all his work. It is also reminiscent of the work of Bissoondath's uncle, V.S. Naipaul, and demonstrates that the parallels between them critics often draw attention to are not far-fetched. In both writers there is no naïve nostalgia, no simplistic denunciation of the West; instead there is a rigorous examination of what it means to be a migrant, of living in a world characterized by ambivalence and indeterminacy.

Although much of his fiction is set in the Caribbean, Bissoondath is not committed to exploring his East Indian background or the particular circumstances that inform exile in the Caribbean. As fiction writer, essayist, and cultural critic, he casts his net wide and is as comfortable dealing with the imaginary island of Casaquemada (in *A casual brutality*) as he is in portraying a Japanese girl trying to make a living in Toronto (in *On the eve of uncertain tomorrows*). The excitement and controversy caused by *Selling illusions* has established Bissoondath as a major essayist and cultural critic, but he is at his best as a writer of fiction—*The innocence of age* is a notable work, written with insight, humour, and commitment.

See Anthony Boxill, 'Women and migration in some short stories of Bharati Mukherjee and Neil Bissoondath', *Literary Half-Yearly* (July 1991); Penny Van Toorn, 'Positioning Neil Bissoondath: post-colonial, multicultural and national formations', *New Literatures Review* (Summer 1994).

CHELVA KANAGANAYAKAM

Blais, Marie-Claire (b. 1939). Born in Quebec City, she left school at fifteen to work in a shoe factory. Later she took courses in French literature at Université Laval, where she was encouraged in her writing by Jeanne Lapointe and the Rev. Georges-Henri Lévesque. In 1962—after the publication, when she was only twenty, of her first novel, *La* BELLE BÊTE, and of *Tête blanche*—she was awarded a Guggenheim Fellowship (sponsored by Edmund Wilson).

Since the appearance in 1959 of *La belle bête*—translated by Merloyd Lawrence as *Mad shadows* (1960; NCL, with an Afterword by Daphne MARLATT)—Blais has experimented in book after book with language, method, and form, using stream-of-consciousness, the crudest of street-talk, lyric symbolism, and various blends of the real and the surreal to depict her own particular world, in which evil exists as a monstrous force, relationships are doomed from the start or truncated, and children are destroyed by those around them or by the mere fact of growing up. Parents, except in some of the later works, are callous or depraved, nuns sadistic, priests venal or rascally or at least half mad. The featureless landscape of the early novels became fuller, more recognizable, but always tinged with the phantasmagoric and with Blais's particular vision of rampant evil and of innocence betrayed. The style is always impelling—at times stripped and subtle, at other times lyrical, incantatory, rhapsodic, or brutally forceful.

Une saison dans la vie d'Emmanuel (1965)—translated by Derek Coltman as *A season in the life of Emmanuel* (1966; NCL, with an Afterword by Nicole BROSSARD)—ranks with *La belle bête* and the three Pauline Archange novels (see below) as her most significant and characteristic works. In this powerful and tragic novel, Blais makes a statement about the rural Quebec society of the time by reducing it to its bleak and brutish essence. The sixteen children of an exhausted mother and an illiterate farmer-father live a life deprived of grace, beauty, and hope—even of such solaces as pictures and books. All their desires and strivings for something more are in succession stifled, brutalized, or corrupted by the rigidity of their society and the indifference or viciousness of those who should look after them. To one daughter life in a brothel seems a refuge, providing an ease and comfort she can never hope to find elsewhere; to the most gifted son, who had wanted to be a writer, death from tuberculosis comes as a welcome release from an existence that can offer him nothing. Over the series of frustrations, deprivations, and mutilations that mark the first months in the life of Emmanuel broods the figure of the grandmother, the one source of warmth for the children, to the youngest of whom she appears chiefly as a sturdy pair of feet that dominate the room. It is this strong if limited embodiment of the old virtues who offers at the end a sort of summation: 'You get used to everything, you'll see'—a message less of hope than of blind animal endurance. This novel was awarded the Prix France-Canada and the Prix Medicis of France.

In Blais's three semi-autobiographical novels about a girl growing up in Quebec—*Les manuscrits de Pauline Archange* (1968), winner of a Governor General's Award; *Vivre! Vivre!* (1969); and *Les apparences* (1970)—the first two of which were translated by Derek Coltman and published in a single volume as *The manuscripts of Pauline Archange* (1969) and the third by David Lobdell as *Dürer's angel* (1976)—a more robust central figure, the young Pauline, fights, often savagely, to maintain her integrity in a milieu in which parents, even though at times pitiable, are enemies, and friendships are curtailed by death or become distorted. Even the priest, if not as depraved as most of Blais's priests, is in his own words 'diseased with pity' and rendered powerless by the very force of his compassion. There is great vitality in these books in the character of Pauline Archange herself, in her determination to live as a free individual despite the flaws in her upbringing and education, and in the sense, for the first time in Blais's work, of a layered and complex society.

Three smaller novels—*Tête blanche* (1960), translated by Charles Fullman with the same title (1961); *L'insoumise* (1966), translated by David Lobdell as *The fugitive* (1978); and *David Sterne* (1967), translated by David Lobdell with the same title (1973)—deal with boys or young men who are all thwarted rebels, at odds with society and their own nature. *Le loup* (1972)—translated by Sheila Fischman as *The wolf* (1974)—uses a wider canvas to take a more profound and complicated look into human emotions. The homosexual youth who is the central character, though he is drawn again and again to relationships of the most mutually destructive sort—to 'souls', in his own words, 'who were only wounded but whom I left dying'—comes to feel finally that 'love given unstintingly, even if it is given very badly, is not wasted.' *Une liaison parisienne* (1975)—translated by Sheila Fischman as *A literary affair* (1979)—is a relatively slight novel satirizing Québécois's romanticizing of the French literary scene: a young writer obtains a grant to work in Paris, where he is entranced and absorbed by, but finally escapes, a highly sophisticated, corrupt, and corrupting family of French intellectuals. *Un joualonais, sa joualonie* (1973) is also satirical in intent; this time the target is those Quebec writers who use *JOUAL* as a literary and political device. While the intellectuals debate the matter, two young members of the class they sentimentalize die wretched, almost disregarded deaths—one in a wild street demonstration (which Blais describes in a magnificent set-piece of surrealistic writing), the other despairingly, in a flophouse, of malnutrition. This novel was published in France as *À coeur joual* in 1974 and translated by Ralph Manheim—unfortunately with considerable misunderstanding of Québécois idiom, especially street idiom—as *St Lawrence blues* (1974). *Les nuits de l'underground* (1978)—translated by Ray Ellenwood as *Nights in the underground* (1979)—is a study of the lesbian as outcast, combining vivid street-talk in both French and English with long, sinuous, looping sentences to trace the sometimes tragicomic, often tragic lives of a group that frequents a tawdry lesbian bar in Montreal. *Le sourd dans la ville* (1979)—which won a Governor General's Award and was translated by Carol Dunlop as *Deaf to the city* (1980)—returns to the underside of Montreal, this time a rundown hotel. As the life of petty corruption and small hopes goes on around them, two condemned people—a boy with a brain tumour who longs to live and a wealthy woman devastated by the desertion of her husband—contemplate one another, unable to communicate, each hoping to read in the other's eyes some answer to their own and the world's pain. There is almost no dialogue, just a prolonged anguished contemplation described in lengthy twining sentences that shift from character to character, from present to past, often within a phrase. *Visions d'Anna* (1982), translated by Sheila Fischman as *Anna's world* (1984), poses the same question—why should one live?—but provides for two of the characters at least a partial answer. Two young women who have withdrawn from a world of barbarism and indifference—one into petty crime, the other into complete nullity—become reconciled to their mothers and, through this, to the need to go on living. The style is a sort of third-person stream-of-consciousness, the sentences as long and dense as in Blais's two preceding novels, linking character and character, present and past, memory and hallucination, present despair and future dread. *Pierre, la guerre du printemps* (1984)—translated by David Lobdell and Philip Stratford as *Pierre* (1991)—is the account of a disillusioned well-to-do young man who becomes involved with bikers, drugs, and vice of various sorts, but finds that there is no answer to his world-weariness there either. *L'ange de la solitude* (1989)—translated as *The angel of solitude* by Laura Hodes (1993)—is a study of eight lesbians who attempt to found an ideal society. *Soifs* (1995), which won Marie-Claire Blais her third Governor General's Award, has been described as a tropical storm. In a series of long, undulating, swooping sentences run into a single paragraph, which swing from past to present, from reality to fantasy, from character to character, Blais offers a picture of the world at the turning of this century.

Parcours d'un écrivain: notes américaines (1993) is a collection of articles contributed to *Le Devoir* in 1963 while she was spending a year in Cambridge, Massachusetts, with a Guggenheim Fellowship. It has been translated by Linda Gaboriau as *American notebooks: a writer's journey* (1996).

Marie-Claire Blais has also published two collections of poetry, *Pays voilés* (1963) and *Existences* (1967), and four plays: *L'exécution* (1968), translated by David Lobdell as *The execution* (1976); *Fièvre et autres textes dramatiques* (1974); *Océan suivi de murmures* (1977); and *L'île* (1989), translated by David Lobdell as *The island, a drama* (1991). Two minor novellas—*Le jour est noir* (1962), a study of a group of children who see their parents' death as a betrayal, and *Les voyageurs sacrés* (1969), the story of a marital triangle in which disloyalty to a marriage is equated with disloyalty to childhood—have been translated by Derek Coltman and published in a single volume as *The day is dark and Three travelers* (1967).

Marie-Claire Blais's fiction is analysed by J. Raymond Brazeau in *An outline of contemporary French-Canadian literature* (1972) and, more philosophically, by Philip Stratford in a study in the Canadian Writers and Their Works series (1970). *Marie-Claire Blais: le monde perturbé des jeunes dans l'oeuvre* (1973), a critical study by Thérèse Fabi, includes 'Le fin d'un enfance', a brief autobiographical sketch by Blais, who contributed the preface to *Illustrations to two novels by Marie-Claire Blais* (1977), a collection of drawings by Mary Meigs illustrating *The manuscripts of Pauline Archange* and *St Lawrence Blues*. See also Françoise Laurent, *Oeuvre romanesque de Marie-Claire Blais* (1986).

JOYCE MARSHALL

Blaise, Clark (b. 1940). Born in Fargo, North Dakota, of a French-Canadian father and an English-Canadian mother, he passed his childhood and youth—the frequent subjects of his fiction—in various places, the American South and the Canadian Prairies among them. Educated at Denison University and the University of Iowa's Writer's Workshop (whose program he now directs), he has taught at various universities in Canada and the USA.

Blaise's fiction—the short stories in *A North American education* (1973), *Tribal justice*

(1974), *Resident alien* (1986), *Man and his world* (1992), and the novels *Lunar attractions* (1979) and *Lusts* (1983)—deals compassionately with the outcast and the victimized. At times appearing as connected short stories, at times as novels, his fiction generally deals with lengthy, episodic narratives replete with social and cultural detail. *I had a father: a post-modern autobiography* (1992) blends memoir and fictional sketch to re-present the mysterious presence that is at the centre of Blaise's fiction: the magnetic, neglectful, mercurial, larger-than-life father. Often marked by bizarre violence and displacement, his narratives convey the plight of the perennial outsider—a Canadian in the South, a backwoods boy in Canada. His heroes are always found at crossroads.

Days and nights in Calcutta (1977), written in collaboration with the noted writer Bharati Mukherjee, his wife, deals with their lengthy stay in India. Comprised of separate accounts, it provides an interesting and unusual dual vision as Blaise seeks to accommodate himself to conditions that his wife accepts more matter-of-factly, but not uncritically. He has also written *The sorrow and the terror: the haunting legacy of the Air India tragedy* (1987), a journalistic study of a terrorist bombing.

See Barry Cameron, *Clark Blaise and his works* (1984); Robert Lecker, *On the line: readings in the short fiction of Clark Blaise, John Metcalf, and Hugh Hood* (1982); and Robert Lecker, *An other I: the fictions of Clark Blaise* (1988). DENNIS DUFFY

Blake, William Hume (1861-1924). Born in Toronto, the grandson of the Liberal politician Edward Blake, he was educated at the University of Toronto and admitted to the bar in 1885. He published two books of essays—*Brown waters and other sketches* (1915, rpr. 1925 with a preface by Vincent Massey) and *In a fishing country* (1922)—that are similar in structure, containing essays on fishing, camping, weather, the survival of legends and witchcraft, and portraits of *habitant* families. In both collections Blake expresses his love of the Laurentian wilderness and admiration for its Native and French-Canadian inhabitants who lived close to nature. *A fisherman's creed* (1923) is an essay on the importance of the intellect in the elaboration of an individual religious faith. Blake's translations of Louis HÉMON's *MARIA CHAPDELAINE* (1921) and Adjutor Rivard's *Chez nous* (1924) brought to English-speaking readers two of the most traditional portraits of *habitant* life. Blake's essays and translations are clear evidence of his knowledge of French and of his sympathetic interest in French-Canadian rural life. They also provide an implicit indication of the image of French Canada—that of simple peasantry, traditional rural values, large families, and unswerving religious faith—that was current in much of English Canada in Blake's time. KATHRYN HAMER

Blaser, Robin (b. 1925). Born in Denver, Colorado, USA, he was educated at the University of California, Berkeley (B.A., 1952; M.A., 1955; M.L.S., 1956) and, after terms as a librarian at Harvard University and San Francisco State University, he immigrated in 1966 to Vancouver, British Columbia, to teach in the Department of English at Simon Fraser University, first as University Lecturer, then as Professor of English (1972-85)—he is now Professor Emeritus. Considered a member of the so-called San Francisco Renaissance of poets and artists active in the 1950s and early 1960s, Blaser published *The moth poem* and *Les chimères* in 1964, each a series of linked poems that examine facets of an experience, image, or phenomenon. (The 'serial' poem is a form also associated with the work of other San Francisco poets such as Jack Spicer and Robert Duncan.) Blaser has been a significant influence on the West Coast poetry scene as teacher, poet, and editor. Additional collections of poetry since his arrival in Canada include *Image-nations 1-12* (1974), *Image-nations 13 & 14 &* (1975), *Syntax* (1983), *Pell mell* (1988), and his collected poems, *The holy forest* (1993), which includes all Blaser's previous work in addition to new work, notably an ongoing series entitled 'The great companions'. It was nominated for a Governor General's Award. Blaser has edited, in addition to *The collected books of Jack Spicer* (1975), George BOWERING's *Particular accidents: selected poems* (1980) and *Infinite worlds: the poetry of Louis Dudek* (1988).

At an international conference held in Vancouver in June 1994 *The holy forest* was launched and fifty papers were presented on the conference subject, 'The recovery of the public world: a conference in honour of Robin Blaser's poetry and poetics'. Following the conference, a Festschrift was published by *The Capilano Review* 17-18 (Fall 1995), edited by Robert Sherrin. Selected papers from the conference are in *Sulfur* 37 (Fall 1995), edited by Clayton Eshelman. SHARON THESEN

Blewett, George. See PHILOSOPHY IN CANADA: 4.

Blew Ointment (1963-78). The first issue of this unconventionally political literary magazine, edited and published in Vancouver by poet bill BISSETT, appeared in October 1963. The magazine was characterized by its editor's personal spelling conventions, and by his view of the artist as oppressed by state and corporate 'fascism'. Five volumes, with varying numbers per volume, were published until 1968. Subsequent issues were released as unnumbered 'speshuls': notably 'Fascist Court' (1970), 'Occupation Issue' (1970), 'Oil Slick Speshul' (1971), 'Open Picture Book nd the News' (1972), 'What isnt Tantrik Speshul' (1973), and 'End of th World Speshul Anthology' (1978). All issues were produced in crude mimeograph. Most were printed on variously sized and coloured paper and bound together with random newspaper clippings, and occasionally with one-of-a-kind drawings, so that individual copies of issues differed considerably in appearance. The content made it both a community newsletter of the arts, documenting work-in-progress by Vancouver writers and graphic artists, and a national literary magazine. As Margaret ATWOOD reported in 1969: 'It can print poetry so awful you have to be high to appreciate it and poems so good they create their own high.' Contributors constituted a cross-section of Canadian poetry, and included Atwood, bissett, Margaret AVISON, Colleen Thibaudeau, Gwendolyn MacEWEN, Earle BIRNEY, Michael ONDAATJE, George BOWERING, bp NICHOL, Al PURDY, Dennis LEE, John Robert COLOMBO, and John NEWLOVE.

Blew Ointment Press, founded by bissett in 1967, published books in a similarly unusual mimeographed format, but confined itself mostly to writers of the 1960s Vancouver counterculture. In the mid-1980s bissett sold Blew Ointment Press to musicians David and Maureen Lee of London, Ontario, who briefly continued the press as Nightwood Editions, before in turn selling its backlist, in 1992, to Pulp Press of Vancouver.

FRANK DAVEY

Bliss, Michael (b. 1941). He was born in Leamington, Ontario, and educated at a District High School and at the University of Toronto (B.A., 1962; M.A., 1966; Ph.D., 1972), where he received an appointment in the department of history and is now professor of history. A Fellow of the Royal Society of Canada, he was appointed, in 1994, a senior fellow at Massey College, University of Toronto.

A pivotal historian in moving historiography away from a concentration on past politics, Bliss has written numerous books of social history that are firmly rooted in his knowledge as a scholar and an academic as well as being highly readable and illuminating. He first wrote a business history, *A living profit: studies in the social history of Canadian business 1833-1911* (1974). He followed this with a monumental biography that masterfully evoked the worlds of retailing, food processing, high finance, and supply during the First World War, *A Canadian millionaire: the life and business times of Sir Joseph Flavelle, Bart* (1978), which won several awards, including the University of British Columbia Medal for Biography and the City of Toronto Book Award. The latter award was also given to Bliss's *The discovery of insulin* (1982), a model for writing scientific history engagingly (it was published internationally and has been translated into Japanese and French). One of the key figures in the discovery of insulin was the subject of *Banting: a biography* (1984). *Plague: a story of smallpox in Montreal* (1991) combined Bliss's social and medical knowledge in a dramatic examination of the last major outbreak in 1886 of smallpox in the Western world. Concerned in the early 1990s about the fragmentation in Canadian historical scholarship as it sought new vistas in untold directions, Bliss turned to national political history in an account of the country's prime ministers since Confederation, *Right Honourable men: the descent of Canadian politics from Macdonald to Mulroney* (1994), which is a lively and occasionally scathing examination of federal politics.

TERRY CROWLEY

Blodgett, E.D.. See CRITICISM IN ENGLISH: 5(c), 5(h) and POETRY IN ENGLISH 1983 TO 1996: 2.

Blondal, Patricia. See NOVELS IN ENGLISH: 1940 TO 1960.

Boas, Franz. See ABORIGINAL LEGENDS AND TALES: BIBLIOGRAPHY.

Boatman, The (1957). This collection by Jay MACPHERSON, one of the landmarks of modern Canadian poetry, is an intricate sequence of epigrammatic poems that is a colloquial and familiar retelling of myths. Carefully constructed from biblical and classical allusions—their strict metres recalling ballads, nursery rhymes, and hymns—the poems are organized in six parts. (A model would be William Blake's *For the sexes: the gates of paradise* or *The crystal cabinet*.) While employing simple language, charming wit, and playful humour, they are richly metaphorical, recording the struggle from a fallen vision to an anagogic vision, where the imagination is resurrected by love. The first section, 'Poor child' (reminiscent of Blake), describes the archetypal human state as fallen: man longs to return to the security of the insatiate womb. The poet, symbolically orphaned, struggles wistfully to recover the third eye's fading vision. 'O earth return' (the title is from Blake's *Songs of experience*) describes the earth as a fallen woman (Northrop FRYE's fallen nature in female form): Eve, Sibylla, Sheba. In 'The ploughman in darkness' (also from Blake), man lives in an atrophied darkness, struggling against the failure of love. The fourth section, 'The sleepers', describes corresponding male figures: the shepherd (Endymion), Adonis, Adam—portraits of man in the fallen garden of the world. Blake's theory that the human psyche must progress through three stages of vision, from innocence and experience to a higher innocence, provides an informing structure, implying that the world could be renewed if only the imagination could ignite the will. The fifth section, 'The boatman', reworks the motif of Noah and his ark. These poems—in which the ark speaks to Noah, as each poem speaks to its maker, or the creature to its creator—struggle towards a vision of man in his anagogic phase as creator. The sixth and final section is 'The fisherman: a book of riddles', and the last poem, 'The fisherman', is a portrait of man egotistically claiming the world as his idea until God intervenes and the creature realizes his 'creatureliness'. With the golden hook of love, fallen man catches the fish of wisdom.

The poet seems withdrawn into a mythological world that reflects the real world as in a glass globe, as though the mythological structures represented a delicate and poignant defence against a deeply personal anguish. What intrigues the reader is the voice of the poet trying to will her own renewal.

The boatman, which received a Governor General's Award, was reissued in 1968 with sixteen new poems, and this collection, along with Macpherson's second book, *Welcoming disaster* (1974), was republished in 1981 under the title *Poems twice told*, which includes drawings by the author. ROSEMARY SULLIVAN

Bociurkiw, Marusya. See LESBIAN LITERATURE.

Bodsworth, Fred (b. 1918). Born and educated in Port Burwell, Ontario, he worked as a reporter there and in St Thomas, Ontario, before joining the *Toronto Star* in 1943. After the war his free-lance journalism gained him a position with *Maclean's*, where he worked until 1955. As a journalist he has travelled widely and written on many subjects, but he is best known for his articles on nature. He has led birding tours to many parts of the world, and his ornithological expertise informs much of his periodical writing as well as his novels.

Bodsworth's first novel, *The last of the curlews* (1954; NCL 1963), portrays the extinction of the Eskimo curlew. Following in realistic detail a lonely male's seasonal migration and doomed search for a mate, the book expresses deep sorrow and pessimism about man's interference with nature. *The strange one* (1959), published in the United States as *The mating call*, tells a similar but much more optimistic story of two geese that is complemented by a parallel plot involving people. A Hebridean-born biologist's romance with a Cree woman in the James Bay area is set against the mating of a Canada goose with a Hebridean barnacle goose that had been windswept across the Atlantic. Just as the barnacle goose resists his instincts in order to stay with his new mate, so the biologist takes a lesson from nature and remains with his lover. The plot is complicated by white racism, which drove the educated Cree woman back to her people and which the couple must combat together.

In *The atonement of Ashley Morden* (1964) an RCAF bombardier's sense of his war guilt drives him to become an altruistic scientist. Afraid that his research will be redirected into germ warfare by the Canadian military establishment, he tries to destroy his work and flees to the North to live with a German girl whose father had fled the Nazis. An anti-war book that is topical in its treatment of military distortion of medical research, it too employs birds to convey a didactic parallel with nature. *The sparrow's fall* (1967) explores nature's crueller side. A missionary's preaching is seen to have had a near-fatal influence on a young Ojibwa couple whose survival in the bush depends on the killing of animals: Christian concepts imported into the North seem out of place in the elemental struggles of people so close to the land. The two Ojibwas move towards a more practical philosophy based on the obvious lessons of nature.

Bodsworth's novels are sparely written and fast-paced, reflecting the care and authentic detail of an experienced journalist as well as his strong commitment to the preservation of nature, particularly in the Canadian North, and his belief that nature shows man the way to live. His interweaving of nature with human characters—exaggerated though some of them are—is done with much skill.

Bodsworth is also the author of *The pacific coast* (1970), a history of British Columbia, and a contributor to *Wilderness Canada* (1970).

TERRENCE CRAIG

Boileau, Chantale. See DRAMA IN FRENCH 1981 TO 1996: 3.

Boissonneault, Diane. See NOVELS IN FRENCH 1983 TO 1996: 2.

Bök, Christian. See POETRY IN ENGLISH 1983-1996: 3.

Bolt, Carol (b. 1941). Carol Johnson was born in Winnipeg, grew up in British Columbia, and spent a year in Britain and Israel after graduating from the University of British Columbia in 1961. On her return to Canada, she and a few friends started a small theatre in Montreal, where she began writing children's plays. When it closed, she moved to Toronto in 1964 and married David Bolt.

In the late sixties and early seventies Bolt developed her scripts through the COLLECTIVE CREATION process with George Luscombe's Toronto Workshop Productions and Paul Thompson's Theatre Passe Muraille. Her early plays for adults—*Buffalo jump* (1972), *Gabe* (1973), and *Red Emma* (1974), all developed collectively—offered a political reinterpretation of historical events, but Bolt rejects the 'documentary' label for them because of their theatricality. Essentially their dramatic strength lies in their colourful characters and their 'montage' of swiftly changing scenes, while idealism, heroism, and comic parody shade their historical actuality and political messages. While *Buffalo jump* explores the conflict between 'Red Evans' and Prime Minister R.B. Bennett during the 1935 unemployed workers' trek to Ottawa, and *Gabe* studies the relevance of Louis Riel and Gabriel Dumont to their modern descendants, *Red Emma* examines the nature of revolutionary commitment in the person of Emma Goldman, turn-of-the-century Russian-born American anarchist who had a colourful life before she died in Toronto in 1940. Emma's belief in women's emancipation signals a change in Bolt's work at this time. In *Shelter* (1975), a satirical rendition of the involvement of five Saskatchewan women with the contemporary political process, her earlier emphasis on myth and heroism gives way to more naturalistic presentation and rounded character development.

Although her work since *Shelter* continued to be influenced by the unusual juxtapositions and comic characterization learned from Luscombe and the Theatre Passe Muraille, Bolt preferred to write independently, concentrating on 'trying to make the form of a play more powerful'. Her most successful play, *One night stand* (1977), started from the formal challenge of creating a thriller with a small cast: a casual encounter between boy and girl moves from situation comedy to a terrifying psychological exposé. Bolt's adaptation of *One night stand* as a television film won three Canadian Film Awards in 1978. *Escape entertainment* (1981), about making and reviewing Canadian films, pushed the absurdist juxtaposition of art and nature even further. Its exaggerated comic characters; its multi-dimensional use of film, set, and soundstage; its stripping away of verbal clichés; and its pervasive conflict between romantic visions and real-life experiences—were all characteristics of Bolt's work up to that point. 'Love or money', premièred at the Blythe Summer Festival in 1981, has not been published.

In addition to her plays for adults, Bolt has written several innovative children's scripts: *My best friend is twelve feet high* (1972), *Cyclone Jack* (1972), *Tangleflags* (1974), *Maurice* (1974), and *Finding Bumble* (1975). She has since written widely for radio and television, to which areas she turned almost exclusively in the 1980s and 1990s.

See Sandra Souchotte, Introduction to *Playwrights in profile: Carol Bolt* (1976).

ELIZABETH HOPKINS

Bonheur d'occasion (1945). This first novel by Gabrielle ROY was the first Canadian work to win a major French literary prize (the Prix Fémina); it has been translated into nine languages. In a flawed English translation by Hanna Josephson, *The tin flute* (1947), it won a Governor General's Award. A poetic, compassionate, and authentic portrayal of a Montreal slum family whose fortunes rise ironically—unique in French-language fiction for its sweep, its masterful characterization, and its creative unity—it has been seen as a progenitor of the protest literature that would explode in Quebec in the 1960s.

When Roy returned from Europe in the spring of 1939 to settle in an area of Montreal where poverty and wealth rub shoulders, she was struck both by this tension and by the paradox that the war was bringing relative prosperity to the slum dwellers. *Bonheur d'occasion* deftly interweaves these thematic pulls and contradictions. It is set in Saint-Henri, criss-crossed by railway lines, bounded by the Lachine Canal and hemmed in by factories, with the elevated and prosperous Westmount to the north and the dump village of Pointe-Saint-Charles to the south. The action focuses on Florentine's search for security and love and on the trials of the Lacasse family. As in other Quebec novels of the period, the family is in a state of disintegration: at the end, pregnant Florentine marries Emmanuel, who, like Florentine's father and brother, goes off to war; one brother gets a job in a munitions factory, one dies of leukemia, and a sister decides to become a nun. Deeply rooted in a historical period and sharply questioning the value of a social system that 'solves' its crises through war, the novel develops characterization and action with a minimum of authorial intervention. Roy captures, more extensively than Ringuet (Philippe PANNETON) had done earlier, several levels of popular speech, including *JOUAL*, thus anticipating the interest of many sixties' writers in this facet of Quebec life.

The original Pascal edition of the novel, in two volumes, was succeeded in 1965 by the somewhat reworked text published by Beauchemin. (For a discussion of the changes, see R. Robidoux and A. Renaud, *Le roman canadien-français du vingtième siècle*, 1966, and Ben-Z. Shek, *Social realism in the French-Canadian novel*, 1977.) *The tin flute* was reissued in the NEW CANADIAN LIBRARY in 1958; a new and not entirely successful English translation by Alan Brown, retaining the title, appeared in 1980 (NCL, 1981). A feature film, *The tin flute*, directed by Claude Fournier, was released in 1983.

Critical attention to this work has since been constant, and includes a number of polemical articles. *Études littéraires*, vol. 17 (hiver 1984) published a special issue ('Gabrielle Roy: hommage') a year after the author's death, containing texts by Ben-Z. Shek and Carole Melançon on *Bonheur*. . ., and a bibliographical study by Richard Chadbourne. Patrick Coleman's *The limits of sympathy: Gabrielle Roy's 'The tin flute'* (1993) is a highly intelligent study of the novel's narrative techniques for English-language readers. Claude Romney and Estelle Dansereau's *Portes de communications! études discursives et stylistiques de l'oeuvre de Gabrielle Roy* (1995) has articles on *Bonheur*. . . by Madeleine Frédéric and Andrew Gann. The authoritative biography by François Ricard, *Gabrielle Roy: une vie* (1996), treats the gestation and publication of Roy's best-known book, while *Colloque international 'Gabrielle Roy'* (1996), edited by André Fauchon, a collection of papers marking the 50th anniversary of the publication of *Bonheur* . . . , includes studies on the novel by Ben-Z. Shek and Richard Chadbourne. BEN-Z. SHEK

Boraks-Nemetz, Lillian. See CHILDREN'S LITERATURE IN ENGLISH 1970s TO 1996: 1(c).

Borduas, Paul-Émile. See ESSAYS IN FRENCH: 5 and *REFUS GLOBAL*.

Borson, Roo (b. 1952). Born in Berkeley, California, she majored in religious studies at the University of California at Santa Barbara, and at Goddard College, Vermont (B.A., 1973). In 1974 she moved to Vancouver, where she worked as a library assistant at the Vancouver Public Library while studying creative writing with Robert BRINGHURST at the University of British Columbia (M.F.A., 1977). She has lived in Toronto since 1977, working in a physics laboratory with her partner, physicist and poet Kim Maltman. With Maltman, and Andy Patton, she formed in 1992 a collaborative writing group, Pain-not-bread, a pun on the facts surrounding the death of French critic Roland Barthes—originator of the notion of the death of the author—who was killed by a bread truck. Borson was the youngest poet to be included in *The new Oxford book of Canadian verse* (1985) edited by Margaret ATWOOD, and her work signalled a revival in Canadian lyric poetry.

Borson's poems are characterized by deft, delicate descriptions and sensuous images of birds, flowers, rain, and sky; her precise, hauntingly beautiful images articulate and define the meaning of her existence. Her spiritual leanings have been compared to the 'inscape' of Gerard Manley Hopkins, and to the spirituality of Denise Levertov and Margaret AVISON. The early collections *Landfall* (1977) and *Rain* (1980) contain warm and deceptively simple poems; the latter uses images of rain, water, and flowing away to suggest the loss of mortality. *In the smoky light of the fields* (1980) time, relationships, and mortality are considered, as the narrator tries to build meaning out of fragments; through loss she finally comes to an acceptance of her life.

Night walk (1981) and *A sad device* (1983) earned Borson recognition as one of the major poets to emerge in the 1980s. The latter collection recalled her family and childhood;

there is also a sense of loss, coupled with a spiritual quest. She warned that in a mechanical world, love can be a dismantled mechanism. 'I think my heart is a sad device/like a can opener.' In *The whole night, coming home* (1984) relations between men and women are described against the 'feminine' landscapes of California vineyards and gardens. Borson's great strength was revealed in the second section, 'Folklore', a triumphant series of prose-poems about decay and disintegration. *The transparence of November/snow* (1985, with Kim Maltman) is a sad book, with many cold images—moon, night, wind, snow—relating to the nature of death and defeat. *Intent: or the weight of the world* (1989) is a loose collection, with several weak poems. After *Night walks: selected poems* (1994) was published some critics wondered if she could develop her lyrics any further; the collection traces her development from melancholy to moments of warmth, grace, and joy. *Water memory* (1996) not only confirmed her talent, but celebrated moments of intense happiness; this book of love poems is exuberant and beautiful.

See Don McKay, 'Sunsets like an armful of pink flamingoes', *BRICK* 15 (Spring 1982), and Tim Lilburn, 'This, that, and the other thing', *Brick* 42/43 (Spring 1992); 'A conversation with Roo Borson' by Robert Billings, *Waves*, vol. 12, 2/3 (1984); and 'Interview' by Daniel Lewis, *Arc* (Spring 1989).

GEOFF HANCOCK

Bosco, Monique (b. 1927). Born in Vienna, Austria, she received her early education in France and came to Canada in 1948, receiving her M.A. from the Université de Montréal in 1951 and her Ph.D. in 1953 with a thesis on 'L'isolement dans le roman canadien-français'. She worked for many years as a freelance journalist until she became in 1963 a professor in the French department of the Université de Montréal and one of the pioneers of modern Québécois studies.

Bosco's novels all treat basically the same themes—de/racination, the alienated female body, solitude and bitterness—but increase in their intensity of lamentation and rage from the lyrical *Un amour maladroit* (1961) and *Les infusoires* (1965) to *La femme de Loth* (1970), winner of a Governor General's Award and translated by John GLASSCO as *Lot's wife* (1975). This novel is a strong and bitter jeremiad, the lament of a rejected woman who has not yet broken through her fascination with a man-god. *New Medea* (1974) takes this rage to an even higher pitch, not quite succeeding in making convincing either Medea or her enormous act, but inspiring respect for the strength of her obsession. *Charles Lévy M.D.* (1977), despite the banality of its title and the familiarity of the situation it depicts (it is the monologue of a dying man), is a compassionate and subtle work, the confession of a weak man who is bound to his wife and convention through some fundamental lack of energy.

The subsequent novels, *Portrait de Zeus peinte par Minerve* (1982) and *Sara Sage* (1986), return to the appropriation of tragic classical and biblical myths, but are more developed structurally and linguistically. In *Portrait de Zeus* the poetic-prose style of recurrent waves of words and phrases combines with the anachronistic mixing of mythological and historical figures, literatures, and modern referents to create a moving and engaging demystification of patriarchal values. *Sara Sage* appropriates the biblical story of Sarah, resets it in France during the Second World War, and presents it from a first-person perspective in a lyrical, biblical style that nevertheless parodically expresses profound rage at male-dominant gender values.

Bosco turned to the short-story form in the late 1980s and 1990s, publishing the highly thematic collections *Boomerang* (1987), *Clichés* (1988), *Remémoration* (1991), and *Éphémères* (1993). She also published the novel *Le jeu des sept familles* (1995). The stories are, in general, more atmospheric than plot-oriented and often present highly interiorized but engaging characters. In *Éphémères* the characters are more static than in most of the preceding collections, perhaps because of a reliance on mythological allusions. In *Le jeu de sept familles* the condensed fluidity of its characters' perspectives during a family reunion—half of them are bourgeois Québécois and the others are working-class Italo-Canadians—is reminiscent of Virginia Woolf's ability to create a complex sense of collective and individual psychologies.

Jéricho (1971), a collection of verse, and *Schabbat 70-77* (1978), *Babel-Opéra* (1989), and *Miserere 77-90* (1991)—all short, complex prose-poems—share many of the same gender issues and moral themes, as well as the same forceful precision and grace of language, as Bosco's fiction. Given such a rich corpus, it was appropriate that she received the 1996 Prix Athanase-David in recognition of her life's work.

See Gloria Escomel, 'Monique Bosco ou le miroir brisé', *La NOUVELLE BARRE DU JOUR* 65 (1978). See also 'Dossier: Monique Bosco',

VOIX ET IMAGES (printemps 1984), which includes a bibliography.

SHERRY SIMON/DAVID LEAHY

Bouchard, Louise Anne. See NOVELS IN FRENCH 1983 TO 1996: 6, 7.

Bouchard, Michel Marc (b.1958). Born in the Lac Saint-Jean region of Quebec, which has provided the background for several of his plays, he exhibited an artistic bent at an early age, writing a novel and organizing a tour for his theatre sketches. In the late 1970s, while he was studying in Matane (Gaspésie) for a career in tourism, he directed and produced his plays *Mortadelle*, *Angelus*, and *Dans les bras de Morphée Tanguay*. The last of these provided the ideas for his later 'Tanguay' series, which borrowed elements from Greek mythology to explore emotional development.

Realizing that his future lay in the theatre, Bouchard studied drama at the Université d'Ottawa, and on completion of his B.A. he worked as an actor for the Atelier du Centre national des Arts, and served variously as producer, author, actor, vice-president for several Franco-Ontarian theatre companies, including the Théâtre du Nouvel Ontario, Théâtre-Action, and Théâtre de la Vieille 17. From 1988 to 1990 he was artistic director of the Théâtre du Trillium, Ottawa, and taught briefly at the Université d'Ottawa. He has produced summer theatre in Roberval, Quebec, and was author in residence at the Théâtre du Nouveau Monde, Montreal, for the 1994-5 season.

Bouchard has been successful in all these capacities, but his reputation rests on his achievements as a playwright. He first came to critical attention in Quebec with *La contre-nature de Chrysippe Tanguay, écologiste* (1984; translated by James Magruder as *The counter nature of Chrysippe Tanguay, ecologist*, 1987), a psychodrama focusing on the experience of a homosexual couple, Louis/Chrysippe and Jean/Laios, who want their own child. A psychological and symbolical drama, *La poupée de Pélopia* (1984), followed (translated by Gideon Schein as Pelopia's doll, 1986), dealing with rape and incest within the family of a famous doll-maker pretending to respectability. Critics and public alike acclaimed his *Les feluettes; ou La répétition d'un drame romantique* (1987; translated by Linda Gaboriau as *Lilies; or The revival of a romantic drama*, 1990), which marked the beginning of his national and international career. Mixing estheticism and coarseness, this baroque drama—a play within a play, in which male and female roles are taken by male prisoners—re-enacts in 1952 a series of passionate and tragic episodes occurring in 1912 that disrupted or ended the lives of those involved. Truth emerges from a tale of homosexual love, and from fantasy bordering on madness. It was filmed as *Lilies* (1996), directed by John Greyson, with Bouchard's French scenario translated/adapted by Linda Gaboriau.

Of Bouchard's next plays, two have received particular recognition. *Les muses orphelines* (1989; version for France 'translated' under the same title by Noelle Renaude, 1992; translated by Linda Gaboriau as *The orphan muses*, 1993) centres on the destiny and neuroses of three sisters and a brother as these are revealed during a contrived reunion many years after they have been abandoned by their mother and have lost their father. *L'histoire de l'oie* (1991; translated by Linda Gaboriau as *The tale of teeka*, 1992, and into many European languages) was written initially as a play for children. Set once more in rural Quebec in the 1950s, it examines the relationship between a boy, physically abused by his parents, and the goose who is his sole friend. During the play's international tours it reached audiences of all ages through its subtle and imaginative approach to the seemingly insoluble problem of violence engendering violence.

Bouchard's plays—all of which have been produced (although not all published)—generally undergo substantive reworking before and after their appearance. *Le voyage du couronnement* (produced in 1995)—which includes political allegory, along with several storylines dealing with corruption and sacrifice, impossible love, and cowardice—is undergoing major change. Nevertheless, the emphasis on highly theatrical structure and the use of different levels of language are trademarks. There are also recurrent patterns of homosexuality and victim/torturer relationships. Bouchard's characters are often marginalized and tormented, and self-contradictory: they struggle to distinguish between reality and fiction. And while the plots of his neoromantic dramas veer towards the melodramatic, there are no simplistic solutions. Though there are unexpected touches of humour, the subjects appear sombre.

Bouchard has also published *Du haut de ses vingt ans* (1985), in which an actress reconsiders an earlier suicide role; *Rock pour un faux bourdon* (1987), a musical alternating drama and comedy; and *Les grandes chaleurs* (1993; translated by Bill Glassco as *Heat wave*, 1996), a comedy of love between two generations.

Unpublished but produced in the 1980s and 1990s are *Les porteurs d'eau*, a drama; *Cyrano de Bergerac dans un parc*, an adaptation; and *Soirée bénéfice pour ceux qui ne seront pas là en l'an 2000*, a black science-fiction comedy (a reading); and several comedies: *La visite*, *L'amour à l'agenda*, and *Les papillons de nuit*. Bouchard's plays have garnered many prizes, and he has been a finalist three times for a Governor General's Award.

See Mariel O'Neill-Karch, *Théâtre franco-ontarien, espaces ludiques* (1992); *Jeu* 49 (1988), featuring articles on *Les feluettes*; André Dion, 'Tout plein d'émotions: interview', *Lettres québecoises*, no. 53 (printemps 1989). See also DRAMA IN FRENCH 1981 to 1996: 2.

BARBARA MCEWEN

Boucher, Denise (b.1935). Born in Victoriaville, Quebec, she obtained her teaching certificate from the École normale Marguerite-Bourgeois, Sherbrooke, in 1953, and taught at the primary and secondary level in Victoriaville from then until 1961. At the same time she studied diction and dramatic art at the Conservatoire Lasalle and created a series of programs on introductions to music and poetry for the local radio station. She then moved to Montreal, where she continued as a broadcaster while also pursuing a career in journalism, contributing to newspapers and magazines.

Boucher's first book, *Retailles: complaintes politiques* (1977), written with Madeleine GAGNON, combines poetic and ironic prose in an oral style, and portrays the authors' subjective and intellectual feminist convictions. In *Cyprine: essai collage pour être une femme* (1978)—passages of prose, tender and indignant poetry, brief essays, and quotations—she reiterates her views on the trials and joys of women as new roles develop for both sexes in modern society.

Boucher's first play, *Les FÉES ONT SOIF* (1978; translated by Alan Brown as *The fairies are thirsty*, 1982), brought major success and controversy. Produced over the opposition of the Greater Montreal Arts Council, which was accused of censorship, it is essentially a series of monologues for three voices. Three women appear on stage: the living statue of the Virgin Mary in a plaster cast; Mary, the submissive wife and mother; and Mary Magdalene, the sinner—both contemporary characters. Each is an aspect of the archetypal Holy Virgin, and together they rebel against the roles imposed upon them by the Church and patriarchal society, and express their readiness for love and dialogue.

After this 'succès de scandale', Boucher undertook other types of writing with *Lettres d'Italie* (1987), *Paris Polaroid et autres voyages* (1990), and *Grandeur nature* (1993). In the first, in the form of letters written to some twenty friends in the Montreal artistic milieu and to family members (read on Radio-Canada during her travels), the author reflects on her pilgrimage throughout Sicily and mainland Italy. *Paris Polaroid et autres voyages* consists of poems, strongly coloured but not overwhelmed by the places visited—Paris, Brussels, Spain, Italy, Quebec. Her poems in *Grandeur nature*, with paintings and drawings by French artist Thierry Delaroyère, cover their wanderings during a year in the countryside near Chartres.

Boucher has written the texts of prize-winning songs, notably for Louise Forestier and Pauline Julien (music by Gerry Boulet), that earned respectively the 'Félix' in 1977, and the Charles Cros prize in 1985.

Boucher continues to give readings, and lectures on women and writing in Canadian, American, and European universities. Her newest play, *Les Divines* (1996), in which seven daughters reunite in a ritual wake for an idealized mother, reaffirms indirectly her continuing feminist preoccupations.

See Elaine R. Hopkins, 'Feminism and a female trinity in Denise Boucher's "Les Fées ont Soif"', *American Review of Canadian Studies*, XIV (1984). Le Collectif 'L'Autre Parole', *Cahier*, no. 1 (1979), features articles on *Les fées ont soif*.

BARBARA MCEWEN

Boucher, Pierre. See Writing in NEW FRANCE: 2.

Boucher, Yvon. See DRAMA IN FRENCH 1948 TO 1981: 3.

Bouchette, Robert-Errol. See NOVELS IN FRENCH 1900 TO 1920.

Boudreau, Jules. See ACADIAN LITERATURE: 2(b).

Boult, Jean-Claude. See NOVELS IN FRENCH 1983 TO 1996: 4.

Bourassa, Napoléon (1827-1916). Better known today as the father of Henri Bourassa, the influential politician and founder of *Le Devoir*, Napoléon Bourassa was an important figure in the cultural life of late nineteenth-century French Montreal. Abandoning legal studies, he trained as an artist under Théophile Hamel before studying in Europe. After his return he painted, taught, and gave public lectures on art; portraiture and ecclesiastical art appear to have been his specialties. In 1872 he moved from the mural decoration of churches to the actual architectural design of these buildings, combining both activities for the remainder of his active life.

Bourassa published four books between 1866 and 1889: one novel and three collections of lectures and essays on art, travel, and French-Canadian social ideals. A fifth volume, containing unpublished letters, edited by his daughter Adine, appeared in 1929. While president of the editorial board of *La Revue canadienne*, he wrote his historical novel *Jacques et Marie* for serial publication in that periodical during 1865-6. The novel was published in book form in 1866, and continues to be read and studied as an example of the attitudes dominating late nineteenth-century French-Canadian culture. The story is set against the background of the Acadian deportation and the battles for New France. The two lovers of the title are separated through a combination of misunderstanding, jealousy, and political events. After many trials they are reunited in the Quebec village of L'Acadie (Bourassa's birthplace), where they marry and live happily ever after. As historical myth-making their story neatly unites the Acadian experience with the history of Quebec.

Napoléon Bourassa is considered today to have been, both in his art and in his writing, the central figure in the formulation and articulation of artistic theory in late nineteenth-century Quebec. The attitudes that underlay his theories were those of a devout, conservative, ultramontane Catholic, and were thus entirely acceptable to the majority of Québécois who, in that period, held the same views.

A modern edition of *Jacques et Marie*, with an introduction by Roger LeMoine, was published by Fides in 1976.

MARY LU MacDONALD

Bourget, Elizabeth. See DRAMA IN FRENCH 1948 TO 1981: 4.

Bourguignon, Stéphane. See NOVELS IN FRENCH 1983 TO 1996: 5.

Bourinot, Arthur Stanley (1893-1969). Son of the historian Sir John Bourinot, he was born in Ottawa and educated at the University of Toronto. From 1915 to 1919 he served in the First World War, the last two years as a prisoner of war. He completed his legal training at Osgoode Hall, Toronto, and was called to the bar in 1920. He then practised law in Ottawa until his retirement in 1959.

With the encouragement of Sir Andrew MACPHAIL, Bourinot began to publish poems while still an undergraduate. His first books—*Laurentian lyrics and other poems* (1915), *Poems* (1921), *Lyrics from the hills* (1923), *Pattering feet: a book of childhood verses* (1925), *Ottawa lyrics and verses for children* (1929), and *Selected poems (1915-1935)* (1935)—are the work of a deft versifier enthralled with the beauty of nature, the major subject of both his poems and his paintings. More conservative than Duncan Campbell SCOTT, his close friend and mentor, Bourinot at first seldom engaged in formal experimentation. *Under the sun* (1939), which won a Governor General's Award, reveals a new versatility in its terse rhythms and free verse, and in its frank poems about the Depression and the coming war. The Second World War brought out Bourinot's ability as a war poet, displayed in *Canada at Dieppe* (1942) and *True harvest* (1945). After the publication of his *Collected poems* (1947) he produced more than a dozen books and chapbooks of poetry, the last being *Watcher of men: selected poems (1947-66)* (1966). His later work consisted largely of nature lyrics and contemplative poems: he was also a skilful narrative poet, often selecting themes from Canadian history.

An active member of the Canadian literary community, Bourinot edited the *Canadian Poetry Magazine* (1948-54 and 1966-8) and *Canadian Author and Bookman* (1953-4, associated editor 1957-60). His critical articles, in which he advocated simplicity, clarity, and 'reasonable experiment', were collected in *The quick and the dead: views and reviews on poetry* (1955). *Five Canadian poets* (1954, rev. 1956) contains essays on Duncan Campbell Scott, Archibald LAMPMAN, William E. Marshall, Charles SANGSTER, and George Frederick CAMERON. As well, Bourinot compiled and edited *Edward William Thomson (1849-1924): a bibliography, with notes and some letters* (1955); *Archibald Lampman's letters to Edward William Thomson (1890-98)* (1956); *The letters of Edward William Thomson to Archibald Lampman (1891-97)* (1957); *At the Mermaid Inn, conducted by A. Lampman, W.W. Campbell, Duncan C. Scott* (1958), selections from the column (q.v.) in the *Globe*; *Some letters of Duncan Campbell Scott, Archibald Lampman and others* (1959); and *More letters of Duncan Campbell Scott (2nd series)* (1960). He collaborated with Marius BARBEAU in *Come a singing!* (1947), a collection of folk songs illustrated by Arthur Lismer.

CAROLE GERSON

Bourne, George. See FOREIGN WRITERS ON CANADA IN ENGLISH: 2

Bouthillette, Jean. See ESSAYS IN FRENCH: 7.

Bowen, Gail (b. 1942). Born Gail Bartholomew in Toronto, she learned to read by age three from tombstones in Prospect Cemetery, a facility that was extremely useful when she was struck by polio two years later. She was educated at the University of Toronto (B.A.), University of Waterloo (M.A.), and the University of Saskatchewan, where she almost completed a Ph.D. After a series of extension-course teaching contracts in small-town locations across Saskatchewan and a ten-year sessional stint with the Saskatchewan Federated Indian College, University of Regina, she was granted tenure in the English department of the university in 1986, one year before the publication of *1919; the love letters of George and Adelaide*, a novella written in collaboration with Ron Marken.

While she has had three plays produced at Regina's Globe Theatre—*Dancing in poppies* (in 1993), an adaptation of *1919; Beauty and the beast* (in 1993); and *The tree* (in 1994)—Bowen has received widespread acclaim for her detective series featuring Joanne Kilbourn, a fictional character who has much in common with her creator. Both are teachers at Saskatchewan universities, sometime TV panelists, and each has several children and a politically connected husband. The five books of the series (*Deadly appearances*, 1990; *Murder at the Mendel*, 1991; *The wandering soul murders*, 1992; *A colder kind of death*, 1994, winner of a Crime Writers of Canada Arthur Ellis Award; and *A killing spring*, 1996) offer challenging puzzles and motives with a fair sprinkling of clues. But it is the added elements of the books with which her readers empathize: complex family interactions alongside everyday domestic details, prairie urban life and work, the ever-present prairie weather, and the often uneasy presence of the Aboriginal peoples. JOHN NORTH

Bowering, George (b. 1935). Born and raised in the Okanagan Valley of British Columbia, he was an RCAF aerial photographer after finishing high school (1954-7). He then enrolled at the University of British Columbia and received a B.A. in history (1960) and an M.A. in English (1963). At UBC, after an academic grounding in the English poets, he read William Carlos Williams and was electrified to discover that poetry could employ speech models and very simple words. Along with fellow students Frank DAVEY and Lionel KEARNS, he became influenced by the writing and theories of the American poets Robert Duncan, Robert Creeley, and Charles Olson—who were associated with Black Mountain College in North Carolina—particularly when Duncan visited Vancouver in 1961 and Creeley became a visiting professor (and Bowering's M.A. thesis adviser) at UBC. In 1961 Bowering—with Frank Davey, Fred WAH, and others—founded the controversial little magazine *TISH*. By 1963 he had acquired not only an M.A. but a sophisticated poetics. He then taught at the University of Calgary; did further graduate studies at the University of Western Ontario; taught at Sir George Williams (now Concordia) University in Montreal; founded another little magazine, *Imago* (1964-74); and became contributing editor for Davey's *OPEN LETTER*. He now teaches at Simon Fraser University.

A prolific writer, Bowering has published almost 50 books of many kinds since his first poetry collection, *Sticks and stones* (with a preface by Creeley), appeared in 1963 as a Tishbook. Among the poetry collections that followed were *Points on the grid* (1964); *The man in yellow boots* (1965); *The silver wire* (1966); *Baseball* (1967); *Two police poems* (1968); *Rocky Mountain foot* (1968) and *The gangs of Kosmos* (1969), which together won a Governor General's Award; *Sitting in Mexico* (1970); *Touch: selected poems 1960-1970* (1971); *Selected poems: particular accidents* (1980); and *Smoking mirror* (1982), which contains lyrics from the 1970s. Bowering also wrote long, book-length poems, including *George Vancouver* (1970) and *Autobiology* (1972), which were included in *The catch* (1976), and *Allophanes* (1976); his long poems have also been collected in *West window* (1982). *Kerrisdale elegies* (1984) gained wide critical notice as a long serial poem.

Bowering's prose fiction includes short stories—collected in *Flycatcher & other stories* (1974), *Protective footwear: stories and fables* (1978), and *A place to die* (1983); a novella, *Concentric circles* (1977); and several novels, including *A mirror on the floor* (1967) and *Burning water* (1980), a metalingual narrative about George Vancouver's search for the Northwest Passage, which won a Governor General's Award. The fiction—including *Caprice* (1987), a spoof on the Western and its gendered roles—becomes increasingly parodic and metafictional. Another Western, *Shoot!*, appeared in 1994.

Bowering prizes spare language and minute attention to phrasing in his poetry. The hesitations at the end of his (usually) short lines register the tensions between wanting to move on, restlessly, with the speed of the moment, and wanting to observe the moment so he will not betray, by sliding past it, the exact word he is on the verge of finding. He distrusts adjectives and metaphors and forms of premeditated writing, preferring to work as close as possible to the immediate and personal. The early poetry focuses on things, but (particularly when he took up the long poem in the late sixties) Bowering gradually concentrated on voicing his responses.

His prose has taken him in quite different directions. Wary of realism, he composed such prose fiction as *A short sad book* (1977) with an intense desire to invent and subvert. This writing, largely inspired by Gertrude Stein, displays his wit and his outrageous manipulations of the novel's conventions. Bowering has come more and more to think of writing as playing with the conventions of language and literature.

In both his poetry and his prose fiction he observes the two chief features of postmodernism. He takes in his poetry a phenomenological position that attempts to respond to the flow of consciousness at the moment of occurrence; and in his prose fiction he assumes a semiotic position that goes out of its way to stress the artificial structures and practices of art.

Bowering's critical publications include a monograph on Al PURDY (1970), *A way with words* (1982), *The mask in place: essays on fiction in North America* (1983), and *Errata* (1988). His criticism is often shrewd, particularly in its discussion of poetics. When Bowering chooses sides, however, he tends to overrate authors who share his assumptions and to depreciate others, his curiosity sometimes succumbing to advocacy.

Two interesting interviews with Bowering are in Donald Cameron, *Conversations with Canadian novelists*, vol. 2 (1973); and in Caroline Bayard and Jack David, *Outposts/Avant-postes* (1978). See also Frank Davey, 'George Bowering', *From there to here* (1974); Ken Norris, 'The poetry of George Bowering', in Jack David, ed., *Brave new wave* (1978); Ellen Quigley, '*Tish*: Bowering's infield position', *Studies in Canadian literature* (1980); Robin BLASER, 'George Bowering's plain song', in George Bowering, *Selected poems: particular accidents* (1980); and Frank Stewart, 'Wonderfully conscious poetry', *BRICK* 14 (Winter 1982). See also Eva-Marie Kröller, *George Bowering: bright circles of colour* (1992); John Harris's monograph *George Bowering* (1992), in the ECW series, and Roy Miki's *A record of writing: an annotated and illustrated bibliography of George Bowering* (1989). DENNIS COOLEY

Bowering, Marilyn (b. 1949). Born in Winnipeg, Manitoba, raised and educated in Victoria, British Columbia, where she graduated from the University of Victoria (B.A., 1971; M.A., 1973), Bowering has spent time in Spain, Greece, Scotland, France, and Eastern Canada, where she did work towards a Ph.D. in Canadian literature (University of New Brunswick) in 1976. She has made her living as a writer, editor, and teacher, principally in the Department of Creative Writing, the University of Victoria, and won the gold and silver medals (1978, 1989) from the National Magazine Awards, and the *MALAHAT REVIEW* Long Poem Prize (1994).

Bowering's collections of poetry include *The liberation of Newfoundland* (1973), *One who became lost* (1976), *The killing room* (1977), *Sleeping with lambs* (1980), *Giving back diamonds* (1982), *The Sunday before winter: new and selected poems* (1984, runner-up for a Governor General's Award), *Anyone can see I love you* (1987), *Grandfather was a soldier* (1987), *Calling all the world* (1989), *Love as it is* (1993), *Autobiography* (1996), and the chapbooks *Third/child/Zian* (1978), *The book of glass* (1979), and *Interior castle* (1994).

Her works of fiction are *The visitors have all returned* (1979), in which prose poems combine to form an experimental and compelling novel about the relationship of two lovers, and *To all appearances a lady* (1989). If titles are revealing, *To all appearances a lady*, a novel about the Anglo-Chinese colonization of the West Coast of Canada, is probably quintessential Bowering. It describes an inscrutable femininity, which dissembles as it tells.

Bowering has also written several radio dramas for the British and Canadian Broadcasting Corporations. *Temple of the stars*, a play for children, was produced in Victoria in 1996.

Bowering has a scholarly fascination with history and biography: research often provides the architecture of her creative writing. An enigmatic, archetypically feminine writer, she presents different personae, but her own voice prevails, even though it is at one moment Marilyn Monroe and the next a credible dog orbiting the earth. It is not surprising that her work has often been dramatized on radio, stage, and television, despite the somewhat cerebral nature of her writing. Raised a charismatic Christian and educated in mythology, Bowering has made magic play a large part in her poetry and fiction.

LINDA ROGERS

Bowman, Louise Morey. See Writing in English in QUEBEC: 2.

Brady, John (b. 1955). Born in Dublin, Ireland, he attended Trinity College there and graduated in sociology. He came to Canada in 1975 and after a stint as an elementary school teacher is now a full-time writer living in Bradford, Ontario.

Brady's writing is rooted in his upbringing. Brady uses the crime novel to probe the socio-economic and political tensions troubling Ireland. With Inspector Matt Minogue of the Criminal Investigation Department of the Dublin detachment of the Garda, the Irish national police force, as his 'Everyman', Brady skilfully dissects Irish society and mores in a series of novels that rank as some of the best writing in the genre being published anywhere. His début was *A stone of the heart* (1988), in which gunmen from the North, on the run, kill a Garda officer and Minogue is drawn into Irish-American gun-running. Winner of an Arthur Ellis Award, it transcends the formulaic pattern of the mystery as Brady explores the problems and moral ambiguities faced by the Irish at the end of a century that has seen their society riven, and holds up to the light the professional ethnicity of Irish Americans who express a nostalgic philosophy that rings hollow in its falseness. Brady followed this with *Unholy ground* (1989) in which Minogue duels with British Intelligence in the no man's land of 'The Irish Question'. *Kaddish in Dublin* (1990) is a *tour de force*: the body of the son of a prominent Dublin Jewish family washed up on a beach leads Minogue into political intrigue surrounding ultra-nationalists who would resurrect the 'Troubles'. In *All souls* (1993), Minogue's investigation into the twelve-year-old murder of a young Canadian tourist in County Clare reveals the strains that tourism as an industry is bringing to a conservative and economically depressed land. *The good life* (1994) is a much more traditional thriller in which Minogue outwits Dublin's underworld, although it is not without its sociological insights. DAVID SKENE-MELVIN

Braithwaite, Max. See HUMOUR AND SATIRE IN ENGLISH.

Brand, Dionne (b. 1953). Born in Trinidad, she immigrated to Canada in 1970, and holds a B.A. degree from the University of Toronto (1975) and an M.A. from the Ontario Institute for Studies in Education (1989). A radical social activist, she has worked with black and feminist community groups since then and was a founding member and editor of *Our Lives*, the first black women's newspaper in Canada. Politicized by the Black Power movement of the 1970s, Brand worked as an information officer in Grenada with CUSO in 1983, when the United States invaded that country. That same year she came out as a lesbian. She has said that she attempts to balance writing and political activism in her life, and the body of creative work she has produced to date attests to that determination.

Brand's publications include five books of poetry: *Earth magic* (1978), a book of poetry for children; *Primitive offensive* (1982); *Winter epigrams and epigrams to Ernesto Cardenal in defense of Claudia* (1983); *Chronicles of the hostile sun* (1984); and *No language is neutral* (1990), which was nominated for a Governor General's Award. She has also produced a collection of short stories, *San Souci and other stories* (1988), and a novel, *In another place, not here* (1996), as well as two collections of essays, *Rivers have sources, trees have roots: speaking of racism* (1986), co-edited with Kisantha Sri Bhaggiyadatta; and *Bread out of stone* (1994). She has also contributed to several National Film Board documentaries: *Older stronger wiser* (1989), *Sisters in the struggle* (1991), *Long time comin'* (1993), and *Listening for something: Adrienne Rich and Dionne Brand in conversation* (1996). Her work is featured, along with that of Claire HARRIS and M. Nourbese PHILIP, in *Grammar of dissent: poetry and prose by Claire Harris, M. Nourbese Philip and Dionne Brand* (1994) edited by Carol Morrell.

Brand's work is centrally concerned with issues of race, gender, and cultural politics, and is fiercely polemical in tone. She attacks colonization and the 'tyranny of mapping' that is its instrument, exposes racism in Canada as less visible but no less vitriolic than that of the United States, and lambastes the belittling and silencing of women, particularly lesbian women, by male establishments of all kinds. In celebrating struggle and encouraging resistance, Brand frequently employs what might be called 'unruly language', a counter-discourse that, guerilla-like, challenges standard English, which she associates with imperial power. Dialect, direct address, repetition, street slang, and political rhetoric are tools through which she attempts to write the disenfranchised into visibility, and hence into the discourse of power.

See Teresa Zackodnik, '"I am blackening in my way": identity and place in Dionne Brand's *No language is neutral*', *Essays on Canadian Writing* 57 (1995). MARILYN ROSE

Brandt, Di (b. 1952). Born in Winkler, Manitoba, she grew up in Reinland, a Mennonite farming village. Her extensive post-secondary training includes a B.Th. (1972) from the Canadian Mennonite Bible College, an honours B.A. (1975) from the University of Manitoba, an M.A. in English (1976) from the University of Toronto, and a Ph.D. in English (1993) from the University of Manitoba. She taught English at the University of Winnipeg from 1986 to 1995 and served a term as Writer-in-Residence at the University of Alberta in 1995-6. Her awards include the CANADIAN AUTHORS' ASSOCIATION National Poetry Award (1996) and the McNally Robinson Award for Manitoba Book of the Year (1990).

Brandt's work has secured her an important place in a growing school of Canadian feminist writers, which includes Daphne MARLATT, Libby Scheier, and Betsy WARLAND. To date, Brandt has published four volumes of poetry: *questions i asked my mother* (1987); *Agnes in the sky* (1990); *mother, not mother* (1992); and *Jerusalem, beloved* (1995). Place, whether it is the prairies or Jerusalem, is Brandt's muse, inspiring her to write poems about family, politics, and eroticism with a vitality that has attracted a large readership. One of her central themes is the relationship between mothers and daughters. Brandt is also interested in Mennonite narratives, and her work is deeply imbued with her struggle to reconcile the values of her Mennonite upbringing with her stance as a feminist.

Brandt has also published a volume of literary criticism, *Wild mother dancing: maternal narrative in Canadian literature* (1993), based on her doctoral dissertation, and a collection of what she refers to as 'creative essays', *Dancing naked: narrative strategies for writing across centuries* (1996). Both her poetry and her criticism are informed by the work of feminist theorists such as Adrienne Rich, Héléne Cixous, Julia Kristeva, and Luce Irigaray.

CYNTHIA MESSENGER

Brant, Beth. See ABORIGINAL LITERATURE: 4 and LESBIAN LITERATURE.

Brant, Joseph. See ABORIGINAL LITERATURE: 1.

Brant-Sero, John. See ABORIGINAL LITERATURE: 2.

Brault, Jacques (b. 1933). Born in Montreal, he studied philosophy there as well as in Paris and Poitiers. He teaches in the Institut des Sciences Médiévales and the Faculté des Lettres of the Université de Montréal.

In the poems collected in *Mémoire* (1965) —including moving recollections of Brault's father and his brother Gilles, who died and was buried in Sicily—memory blends with eulogy, introspection, and learning. The poet faces the 'daily grape-shot' of the city streets; says 'Grief is the bread of my homeland.' He characterizes the land as having been 'born in the orphanage of the snow' and its people as 'half-rebels . . . the only Negroes to have beautiful white beliefs . . . savages in neckties', 'knees knocking and hands gnarled from crawling about in shame'. The same salutary mockery—which links Brault with Gaston MIRON—appears again in *La poésie ce matin* (1971). Here he speaks of 'we the sub-human, the valourless', but out of the 'long fatigue of the ages' arises forbearance. Fragmented, 'dazed' Quebec is the only land to love; its unrivalled poverty must be accepted. These first two collections—marked by an immediate, painful awareness of the state of things—were followed by two books that broke new ground. In *Poèmes des quatre côtés* (1975) Brault offers 'nontranslations' of the Nordic silence and solitude of the American poet John Haines; the 'spiral rhythms' of Gwendolyn MacEWEN; the ironic dread and chilly sensuality of Margaret ATWOOD; and the fascinating pure lyricism of e.e. cummings. This work is more an 'exercise in self-criticism' than the development of a new theory. Rather than erecting false barriers between the different poets, Brault captures the spirit of a fraternity of craftsmen, of poets who reinvent language and who cannot be strangers because they are members of the same brotherhood.

In *L'en dessous l'admirable* (1975) Brault explores the world of the individual: 'I, thin skin of identity.' The peripatetic poet both contemplates and feels the 'suffering of the age', recreating it in the 'naked song of the inexpressible'. Brault's poetry entirely rejects formalism and sterile convention and thrives on simplicity and direct speech; it is concerned with what is seen and felt, dreamed and encountered. Free in both form and content, it expresses honestly his belief that 'Poetry and freedom are synonymous dreams.' *L'en dessous l'admirable* has been translated by Gertrude Sanderson as *Within the mystery* (1986).

For some fifteen years the poetry of Brault has shown a constant deepening interest in what may be termed 'quotidian metaphysics'. There are three collections: *Moments fragiles* (1983) alternates three sequences—'Vertiges bref', 'Leçons de solitude', and 'Presque silence'—among others, to evoke the frailty of existence. *Il n'y a plus de chemin* (1990) depicts the solitude of the vagrant for whom it is important 'to eke out a kind of life, a kind of agony'. *Au petit matin* (1993), written in collaboration with—or in interaction with—Robert Melançon, is a collection of Haikai-renga, of Japanese inspiration, 'free in rhythm, voluntarily playful, linked together'. In a few lines each renga states the essential about a sensation, about a fragment of reality, about fraternal regard.

Four more recent important works show the rich facets of Brault's poetic skill. *Agonie* (1984)—which won a Governor General's Award—is a novel that represents itself as autobiography but is, in fact, a long and fervent commentary on a poem by Giuseppe Ungaretti and presents a slow drift into 'the condition of the *clochard*'. *La poussière du chemin* (1989) is a collection of twenty-seven essays where literary erudition and extended meditation shine equally. The intellectual progress simplifies the complex and makes the simplest matter complex. *Ô saison, ô châteaux* (1991) is a collection of seventeen articles, personal in character, that blend indiscriminately the highest thoughts and the most trivial events of life, all of which reveal the essential character of poetry. The repeated address to his readers, 'très chers', conveys an intimate tone that is moving. *Au fond du jardin* (1996), subtitled 'accompaniments', consists of fifty-five prose pieces as well as intense 'miniature' essays that are loaded with elementary truths.

In addition to his studies of Alain GRANDBOIS and SAINT-DENYS-GARNEAU, mention should be made of Brault's anthology of poems by the French Symbolist poet Jules Laforgue, *Que la vie est quotidienne* (1993)—whose writings are a kind of embroidery of Brault's own work to that time, and of his future work.

Brault has also written important prose, expressing himself as a poet in his criticism. In *Alain Grandbois* (Paris, 1968) he refers to the poet's 'unbridled delight in language', his insatiable desire to dwell in the world; in a 1966 article 'Mon ami Nelligan', included in *Chemin faisant* (1975), he sees poetry that 'shelters us from sorrow' in the work of NELLIGAN; in Saint-Denys-Garneau (whose *Oeuvres* Brault edited with Benoît Lacroix, 1971) he sees a poet whose language and everything else was taken from him, a fate 'we Québécois know well'. Brault writes most eloquently in *Miron le magnifique* (1969) of Gaston Miron's struggles, tenacity, love, and 'historic hope'. *Chemin faisant* is a collection of essays from various sources accompanied by reflective comments that trace the development of Brault's thought. A work of evaluation and intense scrutiny, without being pedantic, it is written in the style of Barthes, cultivating the pleasure of reading, writing, and reflection.

For the theatre Brault has written *Trois partitions* (1972), short plays that demonstrate his care in rendering the complexities of love, death, happiness, and sorrow in simple terms and situations. He has also published *Nouvelles* (1963), three stories that introduce characters—part real, part fictional—who are all striving for life's good fortune. *Trois fois passera* (1981) employs both poetry and prose. The poet speaks, in short phrases and a concise style, of the hardships of life and of his joy in writing. He reflects on a profession that leaves him dissatisfied, wavering between the need to speak and the temptation to remain silent. However, the prose writer, 'lover of writing', always wins out. No poet better illustrates the indestructible link between living and writing, between writing and dying.

Éditions du Noroît has published an audio cassette of poems read by Brault, with music by Violaine Corradi (Productions transversales, 1994). Brault's writings have been translated into many languages and have received numerous awards, among them the Prix Duvernay, the Prix Alain Grandbois, the Prix David, a Governor General's Award, and the $100,000 Prix Gilles-Corbeil, awarded for his entire literary output.

See the special number of *VOIX ET IMAGES* 35 (1987); an important article by Claude Lévesque on *Agonie* in *Le proche et le lointain* (1994), pp. 11-78, and an interview with Brault, pp. 79-92; Patrick Coleman, *American Review of Canadian Studies* (Spring 1991), pp. 29-44; and Joseph Melançon, in *Le roman québécois* (1992), pp. 75-88.

JOSEPH BONENFANT

Breakwater Books. Newfoundland's first commercial publisher is, with the theatrical company CODCO, one of the most visible results of the development of cultural awareness in the province after the Smallwood era. The successful publication, by four professors at Memorial University, of *Baffles of wind and tide* (1973), an anthology of Newfoundland and writing, made it apparent that there was a need to provide an outlet for the literature of Newfoundland. One of the professors, Clyde Rose, left Memorial to direct the new company, named Breakwater, which he formed in partnership with colleagues: Richard Buehler,

Pat Byrne, Tom Dawe, and Al Pittman. Clyde Rose, as president, has been the dominant figure. Breakwater's initial publications focused on the school market, but it soon branched out into general, and children's, literature, achieving a notable success with a collection of Ray GUY's columns, *That far greater bay* (1977), which won the Leacock Medal for Humour, and with *Down by Jim Long's stage*, an award-winning children's book by Al Pittman and Pam Hall. There have followed series on the culture of Newfoundland and Atlantic Canada, on folklore and folklife, on the poetry and history of Newfoundland, along with art books, fiction, and books for the educational market—some of which are marketed internationally, in English and in translation. SHANE O'DEA

Brett, G.S. (1879-1944). George Sidney Brett was born in Wales of English parents, was head boy at Kingswood, Wesley's great school at Bath, England, and an Exhibitioner at Christ Church, Oxford, taking a first in 'Greats' in 1902. After teaching philosophy and English in India, where he published *Representative English poems* and *The philosophy of Gassendi*, he came in 1908 to Trinity College, Toronto, as lecturer in classics and librarian. From 1927 he was head of the department of philosophy at the University of Toronto. He was not only a trusted administrator but an outstanding teacher whose lectures were lightened by memorable phrases and quiet humour. A check-list of his writings contains 126 entries.

The philosophy of Gassendi (1908) is a tribute to a long-neglected French priest, humanist scholar, scientist, philosopher, and contemporary of Descartes. Later Brett was attracted to the similarly inclusive philosophy of George Santayana. In 'The achievement of Santayana' (*University of Toronto Quarterly*, IX, Oct. 1939) he applauds Santayana's assertion that science, philosophy, and literature have each a part to play in increasing 'the wealth of the world in its spiritual dimension'. In 'Parallel paths in philosophy and literature', a paper read before the English Association in 1929, Brett expressed his alarm at the commercialism of contemporary publishing that threatened the integrity of both philosophy and literature. *The government of man: an introduction to ethics and politics* (1919; 2nd edn. 1921) relates the historical development of moral and political ideas to the social and religious conditions that constitute their setting. Within its limits it foreshadows in miniature Brett's great contribution to scholarship: his three-volume *History of psychology* (1912-21). Brett's psychology was broader in range, and more philosophical in content, than that of today; but this important work gave full scope to Brett's vast learning. The result is a uniquely comprehensive portrayal of the diversities, development, and continuity of the human spirit.

Brett remains a continuing presence in Canadian literature. The novelist Phyllis Brett Young—author of *Psyche* (1959) and *The Torontonians* (1960)—was his daughter. In Morley CALLAGHAN's *The Varsity story* (1948) Brett makes a brief appearance as 'a man with an orderly mind'. Hugh HOOD in *Reservoir ravine* (1979) relates an imaginary conversation between Brett and a newly appointed young lecturer in philosophy; while Ernest BUCKLER, in his essay 'The best place to be' (*Whirligig*, 1977), draws, from his own experience as a graduate student under Brett, a splendidly lifelike sketch that is a gracious and fitting tribute. F. HILTON PAGE

Brewster, Elizabeth (b. 1922). Born at Chipman, New Brunswick, she enjoyed a rural childhood in various parts of her native province. Between 1942 and 1946 she attended the University of New Brunswick, where she got to know a number of writers who eventually launched *The FIDDLEHEAD*; some of her poems appeared in early issues. After graduating with first-class honours in English and Greek, she studied at Radcliffe College (A.M. 1947), and at King's College, London. On returning to Canada she took a Bachelor of Library Science degree at the University of Toronto, and in 1962 obtained her Ph.D. from Indiana University. For many years she worked as a librarian and cataloguer in New Brunswick (where she was associate librarian of the Legislative Library) and in Ontario, Alberta, and British Columbia. She also lectured at the University of Victoria and taught creative writing at the University of Alberta. From 1972 until her retirement in 1990 she was on the English faculty of the University of Saskatchewan.

The subject of Brewster's doctoral dissertation, George Crabbe, has been a palpable influence on her poetry. One of her earlier descriptive poems, 'Lillooet: a Canadian village' (1954), reproduces her early memories in rhymed couplets that are looser than Crabbe's but share his interest in ordinary lives and maintain a similarly sharp, committed attitude to her subject. Many early poems interpret her rural upbringing and embody a curious tension between the intensely personal and the deliberately objective. They frequently draw upon biographical experience, discovering a form in memory and in the very process of writing. Old conventions are used in an original, revivifying way; and although nostalgia and reminiscence are frequently the inspiration behind her poetry, the poems themselves are remarkable for a tough honesty. Some of these early poems first appeared in small limited editions; the best of them were collected in *Passage of summer* (1969).

Later volumes include *Sunrise north* (1972), *In search of Eros* (1974), *Poems* (1977), *The way home* and *Digging in* (both 1982), *Selected poems* (1985), *Entertaining angels* (1988), *Spring again* (1990), and *Wheel of change* (1993). Brewster's poems are generally short, and are written for the most part in so-called free verse, but with a careful control of rhythm and cadence. Certain themes recur—an undeveloped love affair, memories of dead parents and relatives, analysis of a doubtful faith—and there are frequent references to her work in libraries, her apartment overlooking a city, her frank reappraisals of an uneventful but satisfying life. Her poems are mainly about what she sees and feels in everyday situations, and she has a remarkable capacity to universalize her own modest experiences. Her unostentatious straightforwardness is not always suited to mythological subjects, which she treats in *In search of Eros*, but she can sometimes domesticate the great myths with acuteness and economy. Hers is the poetry of understatement, containing lines that rarely haunt the memory but impress during the process of reading by their sensitivity and delicate rightness. Her verse is valuable for its documentary accuracy as well as for its elegance and quiet grace.

Brewster has also published two novels. *The sisters* (1974) is concerned with a girl growing up in the Maritimes, living for a short time at Lillooet and attending the University of New Brunswick; it has the feel of autobiography and is structured by the reminiscences of the main characters. *Junction* (1983) is an intelligent and curiously absorbing romance about time-travel in early twentieth-century Canada. Brewster's short stories, collected in *It's easy to fall on the ice* (1977) and *Visitations* (1987), are about women who are mostly timid and lonely. Once again, situations recur—work in a library, attempted suicide, conversion to Catholicism. None is especially eventful; the ordinariness suggests autobiography rather than fictional 'making'. But these stories are finely crafted, and Brewster's intelligence and sensitivity are evident throughout. Although poetry is Brewster's chief means of expression, the thematic connections between her verse and prose give an impressive solidity to her work, and she has also published an autobiographical miscellany of prose and verse, *Invention of truth* (1991).

Studies of Brewster's poetry include Desmond PACEY's 'The poetry of Elizabeth Brewster' in *Ariel* 4 (July 1973) and Robert GIBBS' 'From a different country' in CANADIAN LITERATURE 62 (Autumn 1974). See also 'Elizabeth Brewster' by Fred COGSWELL in *Dictionary of literary biography* 60 (1987). Brewster's own useful account of her principles and practices as a poet, 'Chronology of summer', appeared in the *Humanities Association Bulletin* 21 (Winter 1970).

See also POETRY IN ENGLISH 1950 TO 1982:1.

W.J. KEITH

Breyfogle, William Arthur. See NATURE WRITING IN ENGLISH: 4.

Brick (1997-). *Brick* magazine originated under the influence of James REANEY's Alphabet Press in London, Ontario. Two small presses, Nairn Publishing House and Applegarth Follies, were founded in 1971. Nairn struggled with a few titles before passing along its custodianship to poet Stan Dragland, who reactivated it in 1979 as *Brick/Nairn*. Meanwhile, Applegarth Follies began with large ambitions that did not materialize. The first item to appear was the magazine *Applegarth's Folly* (1973), named for a pioneer settler in the London area. The publication was irregular, with issues appearing up to two and a half years apart. Applegarth Press would not apply for grants, did not receive any other funding, and eventually discontinued. Dragland became associated with the enterprise when he was asked to become review editor of *Applegarth's Folly*. The second issue contained a review section that seemed too large to be contained in the magazine, so this split off in 1977 and became *Brick: A Journal of Reviews*. The thrice-annual magazine was eccentric, even quirky, with its reviews of Canadian small-press titles usually overlooked by larger review magazines, as well as reviews of books long out of print.

By 1978 the publishing house had folded. Dragland and Jean McKay published 24 issues of *Brick* from London until 1985, including several special issues; no. 5 featured Colleen Thibaudeau; no. 8 James Reaney's play *King Whistle*, with commentary on the Stratford railworkers' strike of 1933; no. 12 a sampler with index; no. 22 the writings of naturalist Kit Chubb; no. 23 bp NICHOL; and no. 24 included an index.

With Issue 25 the editorship passed to Linda SPALDING, with contributing editors Michael ONDAATJE and Daphne MARLATT and a new location in Toronto. After no. 33 the magazine changed its subtitle to 'A Literary Journal'. As a journal of literary and political ideas it is considered one of the best in the English-speaking world. In 1993 Esta Spalding, Linda's daughter, joined the magazine to become assistant editor. The magazine expanded its publishing program to include outstanding literary and personal essays and articles by internationally known novelists and poets, with thoughts on their work and the creative work of others, alongside interviews, excerpts, 'found pieces' (such as memos from the Duke of Wellington, obituaries, and other unusual and unconventional writings), the occasional poem, and belles-lettres from some of the world's major authors. But the magazine's focus is on Canadian writing within a world context. Many of the contributors have had an association with COACH HOUSE PRESS, where the magazine is laid out.

Because *Brick* has subscribers world-wide, an amusing feature has been photos from distant places of such people as a Masai warrior and a New Zealand sheep-herder reading the magazine. *The Brick reader* (1991), edited by Linda Spalding and Ondaatje, features numerous genres; royalties from the book were donated to International PEN. GEOFF HANCOCK

Bridle, Augustus. See NOVELS IN ENGLISH 1920 TO 1940.

Bringhurst, Robert (b.1946). Born in Los Angeles, California, and raised in Utah, Montana, and Wyoming, he moved with his parents to Alberta, Canada, in 1952; but since the 1970s he has lived in British Columbia. He has studied widely in a variety of disciplines: architecture, physics, and linguistics (at the Massachusetts Institute of Technology); philosophy and oriental languages (at the University of Utah); Arabic language and Islamic history (at the Defense Language Institute, Monterey, California). Bringhurst has a B.A. in comparative literatures (1973) from Indiana University and an M.F.A. in poetry (1975) from the University of British Columbia. He began learning Haida, with the further intention, 'no matter how preposterous and impossible it might be—to learn all the words and all the grammars of the world.' A cultural historian, he is as much at ease with Aztec theology as with modern French poets. Our literary culture, he insists, is enriched by our knowledge of the past.

Bringhurst's poems are complex, but tend to fall into four main patterns. First are the dramatic monologues spoken by characters as diverse as Moses, Jacob, and Petrarch. A second group of poems is erudite and difficult, though not obscure, with elusive, often enigmatic references to pre-Socratic philosophers, Egyptian pharoahs, and primitive South American gods. A third group includes haunting poems with strong individual images, precise, often stark diction, and controlled lines. Much of his poetry in the 1980s—including 'The blue roofs of Japan: a score for interpenetrating voices', which won the 1985 CBC Poetry Prize and was published as a book in 1986, 'New World suite #3', and 'Lyall island variations'—has been written for polyphonic performance by multiple voices. He has published more than a dozen books of poetry since 1972, including *Bergschrund* (1975), *Tzuhalem's mountain* (1982), *The beauty of the weapons: selected poems 1972-82* (1982), *Pieces of map, pieces of music* (1986, which includes an autobiographical 'meditation' and an interview on his working methods), *Conversations with a toad* (1987), and *The calling: selected poems 1970-1995* (1995), which make abundantly clear Bringhurst's masterful use of images, rhythm, and sound to illuminate his erudite subjects.

Many of Bringhurst's long poems—such as *Cadastre* (1973), *Deuteronomy* (1974), *Jacob singing* (1977), *The stonecutter's horses* (1977), and *Tzuhalem's mountain: a sonata in three movements* (1983)—appear in limited fine editions, often on handmade paper in chapbooks designed by himself.

In prose Bringhurst has published a number of books on Aboriginal and European cultural history. These include *The raven steals the light* (1984), an extraordinary cycle of ten illustrated Trickster stories from Haida mythology, written in collaboration with Haida sculptor and artist Bill Reid; and a study of Haida art and culture, *The black canoe* (1991).

An authority on letterforms, limited editions, antiquarian books, and book design, he published a monograph, *Shovels, shoes, and the slow rotation of letters: a feuilleton in honour of John Dreyfuss* (1986); *The elements of typographic style* (1992); and he edited *The form of the book: essays on the morality of good design* (1996), a tribute to Swiss modernist typographer Jan Tschichold.

With Doris Shadbolt, Geoffrey James, and Russell Keziere, Bringhurst edited *Visions: contemporary art in Canada* (1983), a major work on Canadian visual art since 1945. He wrote the text for an exhibition of B.C. literary and small-press publishing, *Ocean, paper, stone* (1984), a catalogue important for establishing the primacy of B.C. as a centre for creative writing since the 1950s.

See Peter Sanger, 'Poor man's art: on the poetry of Robert Bringhurst', *The Antigonish Review* 85/86 (Spring/Summer 1991).

GEOFF HANCOCK

British Columbia, Writing in. Unless one counts the journals of exploration and discovery produced by Cook, Vancouver, Mackenzie, Thompson, and Fraser, the literature of British Columbia may be said to be barely a century old. The journals are important culturally and, along with travel writings such as Milton's and Cheadle's *The North-West passage by land...* (London, 1865) and Morley Roberts' *Western avenues* (1887), provided a foretaste of what was to come when the educated imagination confronted an advanced primitive culture and an untamed and elemental terrain. Simon Fraser declared in 1808 that he had never seen anything like the country around Hell's Gate: 'It is so wild that I cannot find words to describe our situation at times.' David Thompson wrote in his journal in the Rockies that he felt 'a new world' was opening up before him.

The central struggle since that time has been to find the forms of expression that would make it possible to describe and interpret life in this intensely dramatic and infinitely various segment of the Canadian West. Emily CARR, who of course stands squarely in the centre of this search for appropriate artistic forms, said of her region: 'It is different. The spirit is different. Everyone knows that the moment we go from the Old Country to the New .... Misty landscapes and gentle cows do not express Western Canada, even the cows know that.' This difference is recorded not only in her remarkable paintings, but also in her writings, particularly *Klee Wyck* (1941). Roderick HAIG-BROWN, one of our finest essayists and nature authors, is another modern writer who revealed much about British Columbia in such books as *A river never sleeps* (1946) and *Measure of the year* (1950), as did George WOODCOCK, whose many books in several genres include *Ravens and prophets: an account of journeys in British Columbia, Alberta and southern Alaska* (1952) and *Peoples of the coast: the Indians of the Pacific Northwest* (1977).

The fiction of British Columbia coincides with the beginning of the twentieth century, with works as diverse as Morley Roberts' *The prey of the strongest* (1906), M. Allerdale GRAINGER's *Woodsmen of the west* (1908), Bertrand W. Sinclair's *Poor man's rock* (1920), and Frederick NIVEN's *Wild honey* (1927). As one might expect from such titles, these works celebrate the frontier virtues of courage and self-reliance in the face of severe hardships; they also make considerable use of the techniques of realism/naturalism to document the particulars of language, place, and social relations. Howard O'HAGAN's *Tay John* (1939) was the most important work of fiction to come out of British Columbia before the Second World War. It is not only a brilliantly written and conceived mythic novel, which attempts to analyse the forces transforming the Canadian wilderness in the name of so-called progress, but is also a work so self-reflexive, so overtly conscious of the limits of the fictive act, that it can be called Canada's first serious work of metafiction. O'Hagan's treatment of the collision of cultures laid the foundations for such future myth-makers as Sheila WATSON, Robert HARLOW, Rudy WIEBE, Robert KROETSCH, and Jack HODGINS.

If *Tay John* ushered British Columbia fiction into the modern period, the bulk of post-war fiction continued along more traditional lines, moving from popular romance to more sophisticated studies of character and society. Among the best works of this period are Ethel WILSON's *Hetty Dorval* (1947), Hubert EVANS' *Mist on the river* (1954), and Earle BIRNEY's *Down the long table* (1955). Ethel Wilson went on to publish five more books before her death and to earn a high reputation as a stylist and exquisite ironist. Sheila Watson, however, dominated the postwar period of fiction, much as the mythical Coyote dominates the remote community of *The double hook* (1959). This novel, which is both moral fable and symbolist poem, represented a technical breakthrough of the calibre of *Tay John*. Although she owed a debt to French fiction and to Faulkner's *As I lay dying*, Watson did for prose what Ezra Pound did for poetry, paring it to the bone. Her spare, subtle, and evocative examination of the nature of human community was like nothing else in Canadian fiction.

The bountiful harvest of prose writers since 1960 includes such names as Jane RULE, Audrey THOMAS, George RYGA, Joy KOGAWA, Paul St Pierre, Robert Harlow, George BOWERING, Leon ROOKE, Dave GODFREY, J. Michael YATES, Gladys Hindmarch, W.C. VALGARDSON, John MILLS, John Peter, Alan Fry, Jan Drabek, and Jack Hodgins, some of whom were from abroad or elsewhere in Canada;

following close on the heels of these gifted writers were lesser-known figures like Derk WYNAND, Beverley Mitchell, Ron Smith, Steve Guppy, Theresa Kishkan, and Sonia Birch-Jones.

If any one writer may be said to have dominated this period, it was Jack Hodgins. In contrast to the spareness and economy of Watson, Hodgins pushed fiction once more towards its epic beginnings with *The invention of the world* (1977). In this expansive novel, which draws inspiration and example from new fiction in Spanish from Central and South America, Hodgins followed in the myth-making tradition of O'Hagan and Watson, examining the tacky realities of life in British Columbia against a background of Utopian dreams. A witty and exuberant collage of lists, interviews, tall tales, improbable happenings, and epic desires, *The invention of the world* remains a permanent landmark in British Columbia fiction.

In 1946 Roderick Haig-Brown published his best-known children's book, *Starbuck valley winter*, and Catherine Anthony CLARK became Canada's first serious writer of fantasy for children. In *The golden pine cone* (1950) and other books set in British Columbia she made imaginative use of myths and legends of the Native peoples. The possibilities of magic and enchantment in the B.C. forest were also seen by Ruth NICHOLS, who introduced herself as a remarkable fantasist with *A walk out of the world* (1969), written when she was only eighteen. It begins in an unidentified city resembling Vancouver and moves into the forest and thence into an 'Other World'. A third well-known writer for children from the West Coast is Christie HARRIS, whose novel *Raven's cry* (1966) treats the white man's impact on the Haida. A notable use of Native material by a Native author was *Son of raven, son of deer: fables of the Tseshaht* (1967) by George CLUTESI.

Although the bulk of British Columbia poetry has been written since 1960, Earle Birney, Dorothy LIVESAY, and P.K. PAGE may be said to have provided essential models for the new generation. Birney's narrative poem 'David' and his Pacific meditations clearly prepared the ground for the poets who would gather around the poetry newsletter *TISH* in the early sixties. On one level *Tish* functioned as a vehicle for 'killing' the literary forefathers by declaring new, and foreign, allegiances; on the other it unconsciously confirmed many of the lessons implicit in Birney's poetry, particularly what Frank DAVEY called the *Tish* preference for 'localism of taste'. In fact poems such as Birney's 'Near False Creek Mouth' are deeply rooted in the particulars of language and place; and his verse drama 'The damnation of Vancouver' (published in 1952 as *Trial of a city*), though free-wheeling and mythic, reveals an obvious delight in both the history and the varieties of speech, particularly the vernacular, to be found in Vancouver. Among the poets of British Columbia who owed a debt to Birney, especially in his incarnations as philosopher and raconteur, were Patrick LANE, Peter Trower, Lionel KEARNS, Pat LOWTHER, Robin SKELTON, Florence McNEIL, George Bowering, and Davey himself.

In the work of Dorothy Livesay the new poets found encouragement to explore both their emotional lives and their political condition. Livesay pioneered the documentation in poetry of private agony and public malaise. Her lyrics and narratives, such as 'The outrider' and 'Call my people home', about the evacuation of Japanese-Canadians from the West Coast during the Second World War, anticipated the impassioned and socially committed work of Pat Lowther, Tom WAYMAN, and bill BISSETT, as well as the documentary concerns of Daphne MARLATT's *Steveston* (1974).

P.K. Page's poetry is characterized by wit, elegance, and impersonality. The finely wrought formal poems in *Cry Ararat!* (1967), which rely on surprising imagery and cross-fertilization of metaphor, tend more towards ambiguity and artifice than towards simplicity and directness of statement. This formalism, combined with a touch of mysticism, made her example very attractive to a number of poets in British Columbia, including Phyllis WEBB, Robin Skelton, Susan MUSGRAVE and, to a lesser degree, Robert BRINGHURST.

Of course homegrown influences never explain the full range and variety of what is happening at any given moment in the history of a nation's or a region's poetry. British Columbia poets were looking outward as well. The *Tish* group—which included Davey, Bowering, and Fred WAH—looked mainly towards the United States, to Charles Olson, Robert Creeley, and Robert Duncan, all of whom visited Vancouver in the early 1960s. The American poets emphasized the importance of biology, place, and history on the moment of creation: breath and speech rhythms, particularity, private and collective thought—elements that deepened Canadian poetry in general but which, in the hands of many young poets, too often translated into an obsessive preoccupation with process.

The arrival of J. Michael YATES in Vancouver provided another pervasive influence:

Surrealism seen though an American filter. Yates started SONO NIS PRESS and published several of his own books, including *The Great Bear Lake meditations* (1970). This surrealistic rendering of northern landscapes had something of the shock of Lawren Harris's Cubist paintings of the Arctic and did not fail to leave its mark on many young writers associated with the creative-writing program at UBC, including Derk Wynand, Andreas SCHROEDER, and George McWHIRTER.

British Columbia poetry between the 1960s and 1990s was too diverse to categorize accurately. Three of the strongest voices of the period are Phyllis Webb, as seen in her *Selected poems* (1982); Pat Lowther, whose *A stone diary* (1975) appeared just after her untimely death; and Patrick Lane, whose work progressed from the narrowly anecdotal to the grace and maturity of vision in *Old mother* (1982). These poets seem to stand beyond influences and to have been perfecting forms that emphasize the inclusiveness of poetry as a medium of expression; they also reaffirm the great oral tradition of poetry. Other singular voices to celebrate were Robin BLASER, bill bissett, Alexander Hutchison, Helene Rosenthal, Robert Bringhurst, Jon Furberg, George Woodcock, Norbert Ruebsaat, Allan Safarick, Kevin Roberts, and Paul Belserene.

Anthologies give evidence of the large number of British Columbia poets. *Skookum Wawa: writings of the Canadian Northwest* (1975), edited by Gary GEDDES, includes more than forty poets. *New: West Coast* (1977), edited by Fred Candelaria, boasts seventy-two contemporary B.C. poets; and *Western windows* (1977) contains forty-four. Jim Brown and David Phillips declared in their important early anthology *West Coast seen* (1969) that the poetry scene was 'essentially open, undefined', and the writers 'not provincial or limited by borders'. Perhaps the existence of such powerful natural and political boundaries as the Pacific Ocean, the Rockies, Alaska, and the 49th parallel helped make B.C. poets both more parochial and more international than their counterparts elsewhere in Canada. Certainly the great influx of poets from beyond these boundaries resulted in a constantly changing literary mosaic.

Poetry and fiction in British Columbia benefited from the stabilizing and energizing effects of indigenous magazines and publishing houses. No longer was it necessary to write pan-Canadian poems or stories in order to achieve acceptance or publication in Toronto. Outlets and audiences existed in B.C. for local writers, however regional or eclectic their work might be. In addition to TALONBOOKS, the important literary presses were Sono Nis, Oolichan, Pulp, Intermedia, Caledonia Writing Series, Blackfish, HARBOUR PUBLISHING, and BLEW OINTMENT. Among the vigorous literary magazines were *Capilano Review*, *Event*, *The MALAHAT REVIEW*, *Prism International*, *West Coast Review*, *BC Monthly*, *Island*, *Georgia Straight*, *Raincoast Chronicles*, and *NMFG*.

Until the 1960s very little writing for the theatre appeared in B.C. Poets such as George Woodcock, Earle Birney, and Dorothy Livesay made occasional excursions into theatrical forms, writing scripts for CBC radio, some of which were produced on stage. But a new interest in theatre was generated by the appearance of George RYGA's one-act play *Indian* on CBC television in 1962. Ryga moved to Summerland, B.C., from Alberta, where he wrote the controversial *The ECSTASY OF RITA JOE* (1970) and *Captives of the faceless drummer* (1971). His presence, along with encouragement for the arts in the form of government assistance, led to the establishment of new theatres and the emergence of a number of new writers. At the same time, Talonbooks began to publish playscripts, quickly becoming Canada's major publisher of new plays. By the 1970s there was a tremendous amount of activity in drama, mostly centred in Vancouver. Herschel Hardin wrote several plays, the most interesting of which was *Esker Mike and his wife Agaluk* (1973); Cam Hubert (Anne Cameron) wrote scripts for several media, including the successful 'Dreamspeaker'; Lawrence Russell, Margaret HOLLINGSWORTH, Paul Ledoux, Steve Petch, Sherman Snukal, and Bryan WADE made their presence known in theatre circles. New plays continued to emerge and find production or workshopping at the Arts Club Theatre, West Coast Theatre, Vancouver Playhouse, and Vancouver East Cultural Centre, where Tamanhous Theatre Company provided guidance and inspiration to a new generation of playwrights. GARY GEDDES

1982 to 1996. How soon after moving to British Columbia can a writer be considered a 'B.C. writer'? Since immigration—from both inside and outside Canada—has become the dominant social trend in the province, the boundaries of B.C.'s literary space are difficult to draw. In the past decade, Robert KROETSCH, Lorna CROZIER, and Elizabeth BREWSTER have moved to B.C. from the Prairies, a region with which they have all been strongly identified as writers. Are they now B.C. writers, or will they have to write 'about' B.C. to claim to be 'in' or 'from' that place? Does the fact that Vancouverite Anita Rau Badani's *Tamarind Mem* (1996) describes life in India before emigration mean that hers is not a B.C. novel? How do Marilyn Dumont's Métis blood and long residence in Vancouver merge to identify or locate her as a writer?

Issues of origins, indigenousness, and definitions of place permeate B.C. writing since 1982. In the fifteen years since critic Gary GEDDES stated that unless one counted the European narratives of late eighteenth- and early nineteenth-century exploration, writing did not begin in British Columbia until a century ago, these accounts of exploration and discovery have come to be considered by literary scholars as equivalent to, perhaps indistinguishable from, imaginative literature. In addition, B.C. writers have used these narratives as rich sources of form, quotation, plot, character, and metaphor. In *Convergences* (1984) Lionel KEARNS arranges his responses —critical and poetic—to Captain Cook's journal in parallel columns beside selections from the journal. A multi-vocal, collage approach and revisions of earlier narratives also inform the most significant recent B.C. fiction. Audrey THOMAS quotes exploration narrative and fragments chronology in *Intertidal life* (1984). Daphne MARLATT combines fictions and documentary in *Ana Historic* (1988), as ground-breaking a novel of origins and lost history as Jack HODGINS' *The invention of the world* (1977), which Geddes accurately identified as a foundation text for B.C. Hodgins abandons the postmodern, encyclopedic form of *Invention* in his latest novel *The Macken charm* (1995), a much more succinct reconsideration of what it means to belong to the Comox Valley, his birthplace on Vancouver Island.

The coast continues to inform much of the province's fiction, no doubt because that is where the population is concentrated: some significant fiction writers describing that landscape include Anne Cameron (her most recent novel being *The whole fam damily*, 1995), Linda Svendsen (*Marine life*, 1992), Carol Windley (*Visible light*, 1993), Gladys Hindmarch (*The watery part of the world*, 1988), and Jane RULE (*After the fire*, 1989). Despite being non-fiction, two other coastal narratives that should be noted are Edith IGLAUER's *Fishing with John* (1988), and Joan Skogan's *Voyages: at sea with strangers* (1992). The interior has been the site of fictional inspiration for such writers as Paul St Pierre in *Smith and other events: stories of the Chilcotin* (1983), George BOWERING in *Caprice* (1987), and Robert HARLOW in *The saxophone winter* (1988). Keith MAILLARD and Keath FRASER continue to publish fiction, while Bill Richardson and Tom Henry have been creating a B.C. genre of rural whimsy.

Notions of origins and definitions of place have traditionally been treated in non-Aboriginal B.C. writing through invocation of First Nations narratives and iconography. Fortunately there has been a recent, long-overdue proliferation of published First Nations writing, which is reaching a wide audience. Native writers whose understanding of belonging to a place, of calling B.C. home, stems from a tradition predating European contact in the province. Jeannette ARMSTRONG, Joanne Dumont, Brian Maracle, Lee MARACLE, Eden Robinson, and Gregory Scofield, for example, have in the past decade become established as significant voices. Many of these writers, however, resist being labelled as 'First Nations' writers, preferring that their work be considered simply as writing.

Joy KOGAWA has followed her novel of Asian-Canadian disenfranchisement, *Obasan* (1981), with *Itsuka* (1992), a more overtly political revision of *Obasan* that uses the same principal character; her latest novel, *The rain ascends* (1995), concerns forms of oppression other than racism. The province's increasing awareness of its Pacific Rim heritage owes a great deal to the work of novelists Denise Chong (*The concubine's children*, 1994), Wayson Choy (*The jade peony*, 1995), Larissa Lai (*When fox is a thousand*, 1995), and Sky LEE (*Disappearing Moon Cafe*, 1990). In many of these works, personal histories enmesh with those of the province, or regions in the province, a development that suggests just how many British Columbias there are, depending on the perspectives of race, gender, landscape, and time.

Over the past fifteen years B.C. lost some of the major figures of the generation that established a literary culture in the province. George WOODCOCK was still writing enthusiastic criticism of B.C. poetry shortly before his death. Dorothy LIVESAY is remembered as much for her long career of political activism as for her poetry, while Earle BIRNEY, as founder of the UBC Creative Writing program in 1959 and mentor of many younger writers, was responsible for much of the development of the province's writing, as well as having written some of the region's best poetry. Charles LILLARD devoted his writing life as much to recovering nearly-forgotten writing about the B.C. coast as to his poetry: his final collection, *Shadow weather* (1996), is both intensely local and among his best work.

The theatre has suffered in B.C. over the past decade and a half, for three main reasons: funding cuts from government agencies; competition from an explosion of sophisticated, well-marketed entertainment from outside the province, particularly in Vancouver; and a decline in the left-leaning political energy that fuelled much experimental and protest theatre in the 1960s and 1970s. Established B.C. playwrights John GRAY, Morris PANYCH, and Judith THOMPSON continue to write for production both in Vancouver and outside the province. Joan McLEOD has won acclaim for many of her plays, which incorporate regional material, since moving to B.C.: *Amigo's blue guitar*, for instance, won the 1991 Governor General's Award for Drama. Her latest play, 2000 (1997), was the Vancouver Playhouse's only Canadian production over the 1996-7 season, suggesting that established theatres are wary of producing locally written scripts. The 'B.C.' element in drama generally resides in smaller regional theatres, where playwrights including Frank Moher and Kevin Roberts, with scripts using local, usually historical subjects, command enthusiastic audiences in mid-Vancouver Island theatres. It is in these smaller centres that the vitality that once permeated theatre in the province's urban areas is now generally concentrated.

Poetry still resists easy categorization. Phyllis WEBB and P.K. PAGE, among the founders of B.C. poetry, remain among its strongest voices, while bill BISSETT's latest collection, *th influenza uv logik* (1995), continues his witty, political tradition. Robert BRINGHURST has moved from polyphonic poetry to another oral form: he has been translating Haida cycles of ritual narratives, which he calls 'a major classical literature'. Other familiar established poets active in B.C. include Doug Beardsley, Robin BLASER, George Bowering, Patrick LANE, Florence McNEIL, George McWHIRTER, Daphne Marlatt, Susan MUSGRAVE, Al PURDY, Stephen SCOBIE, Robin SKELTON, Sharon THESEN, Peter Trower, and Fred WAH. Among emerging poetic voices are Grant Buday, Bill Gaston, Zoe Landale, Evelyn Lau, Ron Smith, and Sherri-D Wilson.

The breadth of the province's writing reflects the international gaze that has been turned on B.C., and that B.C. has turned on the world in the decade since Expo 86, the event that was supposed to make Vancouver a 'world-class' city. Three B.C. novelists have become commercially successful in a manner unprecedented a decade or two ago: William GIBSON is credited with creating the cyberfiction genre with *Neuromancer* (1984) and *Mona Lisa overdrive* (1988), Doug COUPLAND with inventing a term—Generation X—that has been adopted globally as an expression of *fin-de-siècle* despair among young Western adults, and Nick Bantock with redefining the book as physical object in his Griffin and Sabine trilogy. Mystery writers such as William DEVERELL, Laurence GOUGH, and L.R. WRIGHT are marketed far outside the province. The province has begun to be represented internationally by film-makers who identify themselves as regional B.C. writers, notably Sandy Wilson (*My American Cousin*, 1989) and Peggy Thompson (*The Lotus Eaters*, 1993).

Amidst this wealth of literary activity, the significant and puzzling absence is a full-length critical study of British Columbia writing: treatment of the province's literature, considered as a whole, is rare even in periodicals. Until recently a thriving element of the province's culture, anthologies of British Columbia writing have disappeared in the 1980s and 1990s: in their place are many anthologies from specific places—regions, cities, and even neighbourhoods: for example, northern B.C., the Okanagan, the Strait of Georgia, the Fraser Valley, and the downtown eastside of Vancouver. These anthologies are generally published by writing collectives or small, local presses, not by the larger firms based in Vancouver, such as DOUGLAS & MacINTYRE. The lack of both critical attention and anthologies specifically devoted to the province suggests that the phrase 'writing in British Columbia' describes something much looser and more elusive than a cohesive, recognizable literature.

See Allan Pritchard's two-part article 'West of the great divide: a view of the literature of British Columbia', *CANADIAN LITERATURE* 94 (1982) and 'West of the great divide: man and nature in the literature of British Columbia', *Canadian Literature* 102 (1984); George Bowering, 'Home away: a thematic study of some British Columbia novels', *B.C. Studies* 62 (1984); W.H. New, 'A piece of the continent, a part of the main: some comments on B.C. literature', *B.C. Studies* 67 (1985); Laurie Ricou, 'Dumb talk: echoes of the indigenous voice in the literature of British Columbia', *B.C. Studies* 65 (1985) and 'The writing of British Columbia writing', *B.C. Studies* 100 (1993-4); and Allan Pritchard, 'The shapes of history in British Columbia writing', *B.C. Studies* 93 (1992).

ANN RAYNER

Brochu, André (b. 1942). Born in Saint-Eustache, Quebec, he studied at the Université de Montréal, obtained his doctorate in Paris under Jean-Pierre Richard, and has since taught in the French department at the Université de Montréal. In the course of publishing eight significant critical works and numerous articles, essays, and reviews, he became one of the founders of modern Québécois studies, on a par with Gilles MARCOTTE, though his literary efforts, until recently, have had a more chequered history.

His *Privilèges de l'ombre* (1961) and *Délit contre délit* (1965) revealed Brochu as an excellent young poet. He was one of the founders of *PARTI PRIS*, and his critical writings covering the 1960s—collected in *L'instance critique* (1974)—were directed against the moralistic approach of earlier Quebec critics and devoted to a 'life project' of representing the specificity of Quebec literature through a systematic thematic study of the literary heritage. This included an emphasis on the continuities of Québécois literature, a position markedly different from that of a number of contemporaries who ignored the works of the past, and privileged contemporary works. Brochu's doctoral thesis on Victor Hugo, *Hugo-amour/crime/révolution* (1974), represents his longstanding conviction that Québécois critics must come to terms with the literature of France.

Brochu is, above all, a brilliant critic. In *La littérature et le reste* (1980), an engrossing epistolary exchange with the critic Marcotte, Brochu showed his ever-present interest in the more formal approaches of contemporary French critics, although he never adopted their methods. This is further demonstrated in several subsequent texts. For instance, *L'évasion tragique. Essai sur les romans d'André Langevin* (1985), like his several articles on Gabrielle ROY's *oeuvre* from the late 1970s through the mid-1980s, addresses André LANGEVIN's novels with the kind of intertextual precision formerly reserved for major European authors. *La visée critique. Essais autobiographiques et littéraires* (1988) consists of autobiographical, contextual, theoretical, and critical pieces. Not all four of these levels are successfully integrated in these close readings, but the collection reveals much about Brochu's lifelong struggle to reconcile his childhood fascination with an inspirational figure like Sartre, his related desire to write a literary masterwork, and his consequent bouts of manic-depressiveness when he failed to achieve the excellence he sought. Brochu's more recent critical works, as well as an interview in *VOIX ET IMAGES* (printemps 1995), frequently discuss the tentative viability of both nationalist literary projects and political projects. This is especially true of *La grande langue. Éloge de l'anglais* (1993), a polemic about the decline of Québécois linguistic and political nationalism.

Brochu's first novel, *Adéodat I*, which he himself has characterized as 'foolish', appeared in 1973, and was followed by a long hiatus. Cured in 1988 of manic-depression by lithium treatment, he recommenced regular publication: four volumes of poetry, *Les matins nus, le vent* (1989), *Dans les chances de l'air* (1990), *Particulièrement la vie change* (1990), and *Delà* (1994); two novellas, *La Croix du Nord* (1991; Governor General's Award) and *Fièvres blanches* (1994); a collection of stories, *L'esprit ailleurs* (1992); and three novels, *La vie aux trousses* (1993; Prix du *Journal de Montréal*), *Les épervières* (1996), and *Adèle intime* (1996). Brochu's poetry is not very innovative and is sometimes too grandiloquent, but its seriousness, and its command of metaphor and metonymy, especially in its invocations of natural elements, are often impressive and attractively passionate. His fiction is much more innovative and complex, as when *La vie aux trousses* twins anxieties about a collective Québécois identity with anxieties about masculinity. Critical works by Brochu include *Le singulier pluriel* (1992) and *Tableau du poème. La poèsie québécoise des années quatre-vingt* (1994).

See 'Dossier: Andre Brochu', *Voix et images* (printemps 1995), which includes a bibliography. SHERRY SIMON/DAVID LEAHY

Brooke, Frances (1720s-89). The daughter of an Anglican clergyman in Claypole, England, Frances Moore was born there and grew up in rural Lincolnshire and in Peterborough. About 1748 she moved to London, where she became a distinguished woman of letters. In 1755-6, shortly after her marriage to the Rev. John Brooke, she used the pseudonym 'Mary Singleton, Spinster' to edit *The Old Maid*, a weekly periodical; although she wrote most of it herself, others—including John Boyle and the Earl of Cork and Orrery—contributed. In 1756, after David Garrick refused to produce her tragedy *Virginia* because there had already 'been two so lately on the same subject', it was published along with some 'Odes, Pastorals, and Translations', the last from the Italian of Battista Guarini. In 1760 she published her translation of Marie-Jeanne Riccoboni's extremely popular epistolary novel of 1759, *Letters from Juliet Lady Catesby, to her friend Lady Henrietta Campley*.

Frances Brooke's own first epistolary novel, *The history of Lady Julia Mandeville* (London, 1763), a sentimental work ending with the deaths of the two chief characters, includes a plea for Great Britain's keeping the newly conquered French colony of Canada, 'an acquisition beyond our most sanguine hopes'. Shortly after it appeared, Brooke—seen off by Samuel Johnson, among others—left for 'this Canada'. Accompanied by her only son, she went to join her husband, who had been in Quebec since 1760 as chaplain to the Garrison. The family returned permanently to England late in 1768.

Brooke's second epistolary novel, *The history of Emily Montague* (4 vols, London, 1769; NCL), comprises 228 letters. Despite its English provenance and several features that make it an integral part of the tradition of late eighteenth-century European fiction, it is deservedly called the first Canadian novel, being set mostly in Canada in the 1760s. Ed. Rivers, the chief male character who eventually marries Emily Montague, arrives in Quebec in June 1766, during the 'interregnum of government' between the departure of Gov. James Murray and the arrival of the next governor, Guy Carleton, to whom the novel is dedicated. Besides Rivers, a retired English army officer who plans to settle in Canada, the chief correspondent is Arabella Fermor, the clever 'coquet' who is Emily's best friend. The letters, which describe many aspects of Canada, are particularly detailed on the manners and customs of the Québécois and the Native peoples, and on the 'sublime' scenery of places like Montmorency Falls. They also deal with such subjects as taxation and freedom of worship in the Thirteen Colonies, and explore with sense and sensibility English-French relations in Canada. Partly because of this political content, Brooke worried that it would not be 'so popular a book by much' as *Lady Julia Mandeville*. In fact *Emily Montague* was well reviewed in the leading periodicals of the day and was reprinted several times during the eighteenth century in both London and Dublin. It was translated into Dutch and three times into French, and was imitated at least once by the anonymous author of *All's right at last* (1774), a novel sometimes wrongly attributed to Brooke.

Brooke continued to have an active writing career in England. Her translation of Nicholas-Étienne Framéry's epistolary novel *Mémoires de M. de Marquis de S. Forlaix* (1770) was published in 1770; her translation of Claude-François-Xavier Millot's *Élémens de l'histoire d'Angleterre* (1769) in 1771. Her third and last novel, *The excursion* (1777), criticized David Garrick's management of the Drury Lane Theatre, particularly his refusal to put new works upon the stage. (Garrick by then had rejected not only *Virginia* but an opera by Brooke.) In the novel's second edition (1785) she apologized for, and omitted, much of her criticism of the great actor-manager. She also wrote a preface for this 'new edition' in which she praised Samuel Richardson's 'divine writings' as an 'illustrious example' of her 'assertion' that the contemporary novel in England 'displayed the standard of moral truth, and breathed the spirit of purest virtue'. In the 1780s Brooke, having gained experience in the theatre through her involvement in the management of the King's Theatre, Haymarket, had three dramatic works staged and subsequently published: *The siege of Sinope: a tragedy* (1781) and two comic operas, *Rosina* (1783) and *Marian* (1788). Brooke died while visiting her son, a rural clergyman, and was buried in Sleaford, Lincolnshire. *The history of Charles Mandeville*, a sequel to *Lady Julia Mandeville* that has been wrongly attributed to her, appeared in 1790.

For much of the nineteenth century Brooke's works—except for *Rosina*, which was still produced and published—were largely forgotten. In the twentieth century, however, she has gained increasing recognition as an eighteenth-century feminist and as the author of Canada's first novel. *An odd attempt in a woman: the literary life of Frances Brooke* by Lorraine McMullen, who has also written articles and dictionary entries on this author, appeared in 1983. A scholarly edition of *Emily Montague*, prepared by Mary Jane Edwards, was issued in 1985 in the CENTRE FOR EDITING EARLY CANADIAN TEXTS series. These publications have helped encourage a re-evaluation of Brooke's achievements, particularly in her Canadian novel.

MARY JANE EDWARDS

Brooker, Bertram (1888-1955). Born in Croydon, Surrey, England, Bertram Richard Brooker came to Canada with his parents in 1905 and settled in Portage-la-Prairie, Manitoba, where he and his father found work with the Grand Trunk Pacific Railway. He worked at various jobs there, and in Winnipeg, before moving to Toronto in 1921 and embarking on a career in advertising.

A man of many talents and boundless energy, Brooker gained recognition as a painter, illustrator, editor, columnist, novelist, poet, dramatist, and musician. In all his activities he was an innovator and a catalyst. Best known today as a pioneer of abstract painting in Canada—his best-known painting is probably the geometric *Sounds Assembling* (1928)—and as a member of the Canadian Group of Painters, he received nation-wide recognition as a novelist in 1937 when *Think of the earth* (1936) won the newly established Governor General's Award for Fiction. A character study of an itinerant labourer who believes he is destined to commit an act of unmitigated evil that will ultimately lead to the salvation of humanity, this novel is perhaps best understood in the context of Brooker's conception of the spiritual and of 'consciousness', which was informed by theosophical writings, including Richard M. BUCKE's *Cosmic consciousness: a study of the evolution of the human mind* (1901). Brooker wrote two other novels, both of which explore spiritual issues. *The tangled miracle: a Mortimer Hood mystery* (1936), published under the pseudonym 'Huxley Herne', is a murder mystery about a missing cult leader whose disciples believe he has ascended to heaven. *The robber: a tale of the time of the Herods* (1949) is a study of Barrabas set in Palestine in the year prior to the crucifixion of Christ; it was adapted for radio and broadcast by the Canadian Broadcasting Corporation in 1950 and in 1951.

The breadth of Brooker's interests is apparent in both 'The seven arts', a syndicated column he wrote for the Southam newspaper chain from 1928 to 1930, and in *The yearbook of the arts in Canada 1928-1929* (1929), which he designed, edited, and introduced, and for which he wrote an article on Canadian sculpture. Plans to make the yearbook an annual survey collapsed with the onset of the Depression, but Brooker managed a second volume, *Yearbook of the arts in Canada* (1936). These two volumes, and 'The seven arts' columns, constitute a valuable resource for the study of Canadian culture in the 1920s and 1930s. Victoria Evans examines the columns in 'Bertram Brooker's theory of an art as evinced in his "The seven arts" columns and early abstractions', *The Journal of Canadian Art History* 9.1 (1986). Dennis Reid has published a monograph, *Bertram Brooker* (1973), in the Canadian Artist Monograph series.

Brooker's achievements as a poet were recognized with the publication of *Sounds assembling: the poetry of Bertram Brooker* (1980), a selection edited by Birk Sproxton. This collection of poems, most of which were unpublished in his lifetime, reveal not only Brooker's fascination with the spiritual and his ability to discover it in everyday life, but his willingness to experiment with form and line, his eye for detail, and his love of music. The volume also includes a number of Brooker's statements on poetry, painting, and the arts generally.

Brooker's activities as a dramatist are less well known. Two of his plays, *Within: a drama of mind in revolt* and *The dragon: a parable of illusion and disillusion*, were produced in Herman VOADEN's Play Workshop in 1935 and 1936. Voaden himself described these two one-act plays as 'milestones in Canadian expressionistic theatre writing'. Both plays were published in the journal *Canadian Drama* 11.1 (1985), with an introduction by Sherrill Grace. Grace offers a more detailed analysis in '"The living soul of man": Bertram Brooker and expressionist theatre', *Theatre History in Canada* 6.1 (1985). Some of Brooker's other plays were staged at the Arts and Letters Club, Toronto, where he was a member and where he first exhibited his abstract paintings.

Under the pseudonym 'Richard Surrey', Brooker published three books on advertising: *Subconscious selling* (1923), *Layout technique in advertising* (1929), and *Copy technique in advertising* (1930). PAUL HJARTARSON

Brossard, Jacques. See FANTASTIC LITERATURE AND SCIENCE FICTION IN FRENCH.

Brossard, Nicole (b. 1943). Born in Montreal and educated at the Collège Marguerite Bourgeoys and the Université de Montréal, she was active in the avant-garde Quebec poetry movements of the middle sixties as founding editor of *La* BARRE DU JOUR. Her first book of poems, *Aube à la saison* (1965)—which stayed within the boundaries of traditional syntax and semantics—shows traces of the influence of the preceding generation of poets; Brossard's metrical structures and use of metaphor are reminiscent of the work of Fernand OUELLETTE and Paul-Marie LAPOINTE in particular. But the irony and eroticism of her subsequent collections—*Mordre en sa chair* (1966), *L'écho bouge beau* (1968), *Suite logique* (1970), and *Le centre blanc* (1970)—exhibit a determination to throw readers off balance by challenging normal expectations about punctuation, spacing, and typography. Transgression, according to Brossard, is the assertion of a subject whose desire realigns power relations, the rules of syntax, logic, and narrative. She pursued her experiments in fiction: *Un livre* (1970), *Sold-out: étreinte/illustration* (1973), and *French kiss: étreinte/exploration* (1974), which extended the possibilities of the *nouveau roman* (delineated in France by Robbe-Grillet, Sarraute, and Butor) into self-reflexive meditations on language and identity. In the

Quebec of the seventies writing became an act of subversion to overthrow logic and mimetic modes: this included playing with grammatical constructions, especially pronouns, the introduction of blanks, gaps, ruptures, and occasionally—as in *Sold-out*—the use of frames to confound the distinctions between text and comic strip, poem and film. Brossard's rejection of convention extends to genre, as is evident in her preference for the term 'text' (from Roland Barthes)—meaning process and production, a system of unfinalizable differences—over the closure of 'poem' and 'novel'. In 1978 Hexagone published a collection of her poetry, *Le centre blanc: poèmes 1965-75*, that included all her previous collections with *La partie pour le tout* (1975) and some new poems. Brossard won a Governor General's Award for *Mécanique jongleuse suivi de masculin grammaticale* (1974).

From 1974 feminism gave a new dimension to Brossard's writing. Between 1976 and 1979 she worked on the editorial collective of the feminist monthly *Les Têtes de pioche;* made *Some American Feminists* (1976), about feminist theory, for the National Film Board; and introduced feminist theory and writing into the renamed *Nouvelle Barre du jour.* 'L'écrivaine', her contribution to the collective play *La nef des sorcières* (1976), and the publication in 1977 of *L'amèr; ou Le chapitre effrité* (subtitled *Fiction theory*), signalled both her realization of women's need to emerge from the silence imposed on them by the patriarchal society and her determination to voice their censored and repressed desire. In *L'amèr*'s hybrid text—novel and manifesto, fiction and theory—Brossard exposes the contradictions of the mother under patriarchy, when women are limited to the role of symbolic mother, and contrasts these with the different possibilities for relations between women figured in the embrace of three generations of women, a feminine plural inscribing women into the trajectory of history. The poems of *Amantes* (1980) and the fiction *Le sens apparent* (1980) continue this theoretical speculation into the 'surfaces of sense' and posit an association of the writing/reading process with sexual pleasure. For Brossard, the production of meaning from a lesbian perspective ceased to hinge on a relation between a subject and an object, between a writer/reader and a text/interpretation, to become an interactive process between subjects. *Picture theory* (1982), Brossard's major fiction to date, continues and expands on these questions in a complex text that interweaves fiction (five women interact on a Utopian lesbian island) with a theoretical investigation (problems of representation and language are analysed in a vast conceptual apparatus that draws on the ideas of Wittgenstein, Stein, Wittig, Joyce, and others). In a 'mathematics of the imaginary', influenced by contemporary science, Brossard offers a model of the text as process of transformation to articulate a new (feminist-lesbian) inflection of the 'real'. These ideas are further elaborated in the collection of feminist theoretical essays *La lettre aérienne* (1985), which focuses on the problem of representation for women, and in Brossard's contribution to the collective *La théorie, un dimanche* (1988). Fiction is the way to fight the hegemonic patriarchal fictions framing reality and constraining women. The possibilities for a different and lesbian economy of desire are also developed in essays included in *Double impression: poèmes et textes 1967-1984* (1984), winner of a second Governor General's Award; in the erotic prose poems in *Sous la langue/Under tongue* (1987) and *La nuit verte du parc labyrinthe* (1992). Questions of representation and narrative are also pursued in *Journal intime* (1984), a diary that rejects both the conventional temporal sequence and confessional form of the genre to expose how a life is constructed within socio-linguistic conventions. A life in writing is the focus of *Domaine d'écriture* (1985). Concerns with the constitution of subjectivity are addressed in poetic texts such as *Installations (avec et sans pronoms)* (1989); *À tout regard* (1989); and *Langues obscures* (1992), which explores the adventures of the subjective pronoun 'I'.

Brossard's work on language and social codes extends to translation as both a textual practice and a metaphor for transformation. English-French translations of texts by poet Daphne MARLATT in *Mauve* (1986) and *Jeu de lettres/Character* (1985) were followed by homolinguistic translation in the book of poetry *L'aviva* (1985) and, more extensively, in *Le désert mauve* (1987), a novel about a translator's work. The most popular of Brossard's works, it examines the interpretative processes one makes in transferring a text into a different cultural milieu and considers the ethics of such a transformation. Continuing her games with repetition and constraints, Brossard's novel *Baroque d'aube* (1995) returns to her *Aube à la saison* of thirty years earlier, revising its eroticism. The vertiginous, perspectival play between the character Brossard, an 'English' novelist, and the author Brossard, a Québécoise, stages Brossard's continuing interest in the shifting boundary between 'art' and 'life', and in fiction as virtual reality offering manifold potentialities for transformation. It was translated as *Baroque at dawn* (1997) by Patricia Claxton. In 1991 Brossard was awarded Toronto's Harbourfront Festival Prize and the Athanase-David Prize of the Government of Quebec for the entire body of her work.

Brossard's interest in new and experimental approaches was also reflected in her editing of *Les stratégies du réel/The story so far* (1979), an anthology of avant-garde Québécois writings published bilingually by COACH HOUSE PRESS, and of feminist projects such as the *Anthologie de la poésie des femmes au Québec* (1991, with Lisette Girouard) and those of her own publishing house, L'Intégrale éditrice, founded in 1982.

Coach House published numerous works by Brossard in translation, including *A book* (1976) and *Daydream mechanics* (1980), Larry Shouldice tr.; *Turn of a pang* (1976) and *French kiss* (1986), Patricia Claxton tr.; *These our mothers; or The disintegrating chapter* (1983), Barbara Godard tr.; *Surfaces of sense* (1989), Fiona Strachan tr.; and *Mauve desert* (1990), Susanne de Lotbinière-Harwood tr., who also translated *Under tongue* (1987). Other books by Brossard in translation are *Aerial letter* (1988), Marlene Wildman tr.; and *Lovhers* (1986) and *Picture theory*, Barbara Godard tr. A trilingual edition—French/English/Spanish—of the title text of *La nuit verte du Parc Labyrinthe* (1992) included an English translation by Lou Nelson. Brossard's work has also been translated into German and Italian.

A bibliography and a list of critical articles on Brossard can be found in Issue 118-119 of *La Barre du jour* (nov. 1982). See also Louise Dupré, *Stratégies du vertige* (1989) and Barbara Godard, *Nicole Brossard*, in *Profiles in Canadian Literature*, series 6 (1986).

CAROLINE BAYARD/BARBARA GODARD

Brouillet, Chrystine. See NOVELS IN FRENCH 1983 TO 1996: 1, 6.

Brown, Audrey Alexandra (b. 1904). Born and raised in Nanaimo, British Columbia, she is the last important representative of romantic poetry in Canada, deeply indebted to the English Romantic poets, especially Keats. Her five volumes of verse—*A dryad in Nanaimo* (1931; enlarged with eleven new poems, 1934), *The tree of resurrection and other poems* (1937), *Challenge to time and death* (1943), *V-E day* (1946), and *All fools' day* (1948)—reveal little artistic development. Her finest poem, 'Laodamia', which appeared in her first volume, epitomizes her poetic world: her attraction to a legendary past, her love of colourful descriptions, her musical cadences, as well as a derivative dimension that leads to ornate and frequently undisciplined verse.

The log of a lame duck (1938) is Brown's prose diary of her ten-month treatment for rheumatic illness at Queen Alexandra Solarium on Malahat Beach. In *Poetry and life* (1941), an address originally delivered to the CANADIAN AUTHORS' ASSOCIATION in Vancouver on 24 Aug. 1941, she defined her poetic creed: 'Poetry is to life what sunlight is to a stained-glass window. In poetry the mind of the poet strikes through life, revealing its pattern and colour. . . . Poetry is life transfused and irradiated.' In 1944 Brown received the Royal Society's Lorne PIERCE Medal 'for distinguished contributions to Canadian literature'.

DAVID STAINES

Brown, E.K. (1905-51). Edward Killoran Brown was born in Toronto, Ontario, and educated at the universities of Toronto (B.A., 1926) and Paris, from which he received in 1935 a Docteur-ès-Lettres for a major thesis on Edith Wharton and a minor one on Matthew Arnold's prose. From 1929 to 1941 he taught English at the University of Toronto, except for two years when he served as chairman of the English department at the University of Manitoba (1935-7). He was chairman of English at Cornell University from 1941 to 1944, when he moved to the University of Chicago, where he remained until his death. The Royal Society of Canada awarded him its Lorne PIERCE Medal posthumously.

Brown published many articles and reviews dealing with British and American writers—he wrote over fifty for the *CANADIAN FORUM*, of which he was an associate editor from 1930 to 1933—translations of Louis Cazamian's *Carlyle* (1932) and Balzac's *Père Goriot* (1946), editions of Arnold (*Representative essays*, 1936; *Four essays on life and letters*, 1947) and of Dickens' *David Copperfield* (1950), and an anthology (*Victorian poetry*, 1942). He was the author of *Matthew Arnold–a study in conflict* (1948); *Rhythm in the novel* (1950; rpr. 1978), the published version of the Alexander Lectures given at the University of Toronto in 1949 and a valuable study of technique in the novels, with special reference to E.M. Forster; and *Willa Cather: a critical biography* (1953; rpr. 1980), which was completed for publication by his friend and colleague Leon EDEL and has not been superseded.

Northrop FRYE called Brown 'the first critic to bring Canadian literature into its proper context'. That context was one in which a national interest was not vitiated by the excesses of nationalism, and in which a cosmopolitan outlook never succumbed to the pressures of colonialism. From 1932 to 1941 Brown was one of the editors of the *University of Toronto Quarterly* and was instrumental in establishing its annual 'Letters in Canada' reviews. From 1936 to 1950 his judicious and perceptive articles on Canadian poetry exemplified his dedication to what he described as 'the raising of aesthetic and intellectual standards in Canada'. The early assessments—'The contemporary situation in Canadian literature' (1938) and 'The development of poetry in Canada, 1880-1940' (1941)—show Brown preparing himself for *On Canadian poetry* (1943; rpr. 1973), which incorporated the two articles and appeared in the same year as A.J.M. SMITH's *Book of Canadian poetry*. These two works established the standards of excellence and many of the subsequent directions of Canadian criticism.

As a 'critical essay', *On Canadian poetry*—which received a Governor General's Award and was resissued the following year in a revised and expanded version—was an advance on the tradition of mere historical enquiry. Brown's purpose in this lucid and cogently argued book was to show the difficulties of the Canadian writer in a colonial, materialistic, and puritanical society; to define the tradition of Canadian poetry by discovering what work 'remains alive and in some degree at least, formative'; and to describe and assess the poetry of those who were in Brown's view the 'masters': LAMPMAN, D.C. SCOTT, and PRATT. Brown insisted that 'careful interpretation, conducted with insight and a measure of sympathy, must precede judgment'. In his revaluation of earlier writers he stressed the merits of Lampman and Scott and the limitations of ROBERTS and CARMAN. This revaluation was continued (with Scott's assistance) in Brown's edition of *At the Long Sault and other new poems by Archibald Lampman* (1943) and in the posthumously published *Selected poems of Duncan Campbell Scott* (1951), with a memoir by Brown.

Brown's emphasis on interpretation sometimes led him to be over-cautious in evaluating younger poets; his comments on the Canadian scene are occasionally too sweeping (perhaps betraying a central-Canadian perspective) to do justice to the diversity of the Canadian experience: his assertion that a great literature is produced by a 'mature and adequate society' but that it is 'not in the province of a student of letters to say how a society becomes mature and adequate' seems an abrogation of part of the critical function. Nevertheless Brown's stature as a major critic is assured.

In *Responses and evaluations: essays on Canada* (NCL, 1977) David Staines gathered a valuable selection of Brown's essays, including his annual surveys for the *Quarterly*; Staines' introduction is the best commentary on Brown's achievement. Staines' bibliographical article in *CANADIAN LITERATURE* 83 (Winter 1979) should be consulted. See also Robert L. McDougall, ed., *The poet and the critic: a literary correspondence between D.C.Scott and E.K.Brown* (1983) and Laura Groening, *E.K.Brown: a study in conflict* (1993).

See also CRITICISM IN ENGLISH: 3.

DAVID JACKEL

Bruce, Charles (1906-71). Charles Tory Bruce was born of Scottish ancestry in Port Shoreham, Nova Scotia, and graduated from Mount Allison University in 1927. Joining the Canadian Press in Halifax, he became one of the original and most active members of the Song Fishermen, a group of regional poets that included Andrew Merkel, Robert NORWOOD, Kenneth LESLIE, Bliss CARMAN, and Charles G.D. ROBERTS. He later became a war correspondent and superintendent of the Canadian Press in London (England), and in 1945 was appointed general superintendent of the Canadian Press in Toronto.

Bruce's first collection of verse, *Wild apples* (1927), introduced the concrete images, musical rhythms, and fascination with the sea that are characteristic of his later work. It was followed by *Tomorrow's tide* (1932), a collection of personal and descriptive lyrics; *Personal note* (1941), 'a statement of belief' in the midst of war about the spirit 'of mankind at its best'; and *Grey ship moving* (1945), a series of poems affirming the values of kinship and regional identity, especially in wartime. In the narrative poem *The flowing summer* (1947), an Ontario boy visiting Nova Scotian grandparents awakens to a sense of the land, the sea, and the traditions that are part of his heritage. These influences are further explored in *The Mulgrave Road* (1951), a collection that won a Governor General's Award for its finely crafted poems integrating landscape, mood, and a sense of the 'salt in the blood'.

A close relationship among the environment, tradition, and community values informs *The Channel Shore* (1954), Bruce's lyrical chronicle of three generations of family life in coastal Nova Scotia between 1919 and 1946. Similar in theme and in the skilful handling of time is *The township of time* (1959), a sequence of interrelated stories set along the Channel Shore between 1786 and 1950. Bruce's interest in family chronicles found further expression in *News and the Southams* (1968), a history of the Southam newspaper empire in Canada. However, it is the careful craftsmanship and vivid evocation of life in Bruce's creative writing that have continued to win for his work the respect of critics from William Arthur DEACON to John Moss.

See J.A. Wainwright, *Charles Bruce: a literary biography* (1988). GWENDOLYN DAVIES

Bruce, Harry (b. 1934). Born in Toronto, he was educated at Mount Allison University, New Brunswick (B.A., 1955). He grew up in Toronto as the son of the poet, novelist, and newspaperman Charles BRUCE, who wrote about Nova Scotia long after leaving it. The son attended the father's old university and entered the father's profession, moving from newspaper reporting in Ottawa and Toronto to *Maclean's*; in the 1960s he was successively managing editor of *Saturday Night*, editor of *The Canadian*, and columnist for the *Star Weekly*. In 1971 he moved with his family to Halifax, where he became an impassioned advocate for the Maritimes and a essayist of great charm and perception. His move outside the usual confines of journalism had begun with a series of personal essays written under a pseudonym for the Toronto *Star* and then published as *The short happy walks of Max Macpherson* (1968), in which he transformed grimy beer parlours and back alleys into places of mystery and nostalgic beauty. Later, established in Nova Scotia, he published a stream of pieces that made his reclaimed region and his own life into one subject.

Bruce's essays can be read as an enactment of the romance of Canadian regional longing, the struggle of a central Canadian to reclaim parental roots in Nova Scotia. The best of these appeared in two collections, *Each moment as it flies* (1984) and *Movin' east* (1985). An original work, *Down home: notes of a Maritime son* (1988), is perhaps his best and best-received book. One persistent theme of his writing emerged in a 1980 essay offering advice to the young: 'Nurture your sense of wonder' because 'time moves slowly for a while, like a snowball on a mountainside, but then it tumbles faster and faster and, in a speeding avalanche, thunders to its end.' Bruce established a parallel career as a biographer of business leaders with books about the entrepreneur R.A. Jodrey, the supermarket tycoon Frank Sobey, and the corporate lawyer Frank M. Covert. In 1992 he published *Maud: a life of L.M. Montgomery*.

ROBERT FULFORD

Brun, Régis. See ACADIAN LITERATURE: 2(c).

Brunet, Michel (1917-85). Born in Montreal, Quebec, he was first educated at the Université de Montréal. Between earning his B.A. (1939) and his M.A. (1947) he taught school; he then obtained his Ph.D. in history (1949) from Clark University, Massachusetts, and was appointed to the history department of the Université de Montréal, where he was chair of the department from 1959 to 1968.

The prolific publicist of the Montreal school of history after the Second World War, Brunet drew on the ideas of the other two founders of the school, Guy FRÉGAULT and Maurice SÉGUIN. In his most thorough historical work, *Les Canadiens après la conquête* (1969)—which won a Governor General's Award and the 1970 France-Québec prize—Brunet attempted to show how the normally developing colony of New France had become the truncated colony of Quebec through the British conquest. The transfer from one empire to another weakened economic structures and imperilled an entrepreneurial middle class, whose wealth in furs had rested on links to France. The conquest had decapitated Quebec society and led to the themes of messianism, agriculturalism, and anti-statism that Brunet identified as pervasive for nearly two centuries in French-Canadian history.

While Brunet's interpretation reached near-orthodoxy in Quebec nationalist circles—and even became incorporated, in part, into the program of the Parti Québécois—Brunet's other historical works constantly juxtaposed the two nations within a federal state, a concept popular in French Canada during the 1960s. A fine essayist, Brunet sought in books such as *Canadians et Canadiens* (1954) and *Québec, Canada anglais: deux itinéraires, un affrontement* (1968) to expose the conflicts between presumptuous majority and conscious minority. Jean Lamarre analyses the thought of the Montreal school of history in *Le devenir de la nation québécois* (1993).

TERRY CROWLEY

Bryce, George. See HISTORICAL WRITING IN ENGLISH: 4.

Buchan, John. See FANTASTIC LITERATURE IN ENGLISH: 1 and FOREIGN WRITERS ON CANADA IN ENGLISH: 1.

Bucke, Richard Maurice (1837-1902). Born in Methwold, England, he was raised on a farm near London, Upper Canada (Ontario). Self-educated until he entered McGill University, he graduated in medicine in 1862 with the prize-winning dissertation. He studied abroad and practised in Sarnia and London (Ontario) before being appointed in 1877 superintendent of the Asylum for the Insane in London, a position he held until his death. Bucke pursued two different careers: as the originator of occupational therapy, he was a world-renowned alienist, professor of mental and nervous diseases at the future University of Western Ontario, and president of both the American Medico-Psychological Association and the Psychological Section of the British Medical Association; and, as a mystic and an idolator of Walt Whitman, he was the famous poet's editor, official biographer, and literary executor. Whitman visited Bucke in London twice, the first time in the summer of 1880 when he travelled to Montreal and Quebec City, a trip that was recorded in *Walt Whitman's diary in Canada with extracts from other of his diaries and literary note-books* (1904).

One night in the spring of 1872, after reading Whitman's poetry, Bucke experienced a mystical illumination—an epiphany in which he saw that the cosmos promises man fulfilment in happiness, love, and immortality. He elaborated on this Utopian vision in *Man's moral nature: an essay* (New York, 1879). The thesis of this book—that if the world is steadily improving, then the most advanced example of a superior moral nature must be embodied in a contemporary—was exemplified in his next work, *Walt Whitman* (Philadelphia, 1883), the first biographical study of the poet, whom Bucke saw as a paragon of moral nature. This *collecteana* of reminiscences, conversations, travels in Canada, bibliographical details, and a philosophical exegesis of the poetry incorporates revisions made by Whitman himself, some of which were directed at modifying Bucke's idolatrous tone.

Bucke wrote Whitman several letters—the last one written six days before the poet's death in 1892—about his theory of 'cosmic consciousness' (the omniscient, intuitional mind that transcends self-consciousness), seeking confirmation of nineteen points of cosmic consciousness that he suspected Whitman must have experienced. But on this subject Whitman never replied. Out of Bucke's theories grew his most ambitious and enduring work, *Cosmic consciousness: a study of the evolution of the human mind* (Philadelphia, 1901), a major contribution to the field of mysticism that remains in print. The book presents fourteen case-studies documenting evidence of mystical illuminations shared by Homer, Christ, Shakespeare, Blake, and Whitman, and concludes with a millennial vision of a world revolutionized by aerial navigation, of work revolutionized by socialism, and of souls revolutionized by cosmic consciousness. William James called it 'an addition to psychology of first-rate importance' and praised Bucke as 'a benefactor of us all'.

Bucke edited several posthumous volumes of Whitman's writings, including *The wound dresser. A series of letters written from the hospitals of Washington during the War of Rebellion by Walt Whitman* (Boston, 1898), and was one of the editors of the *Complete writings of Walt Whitman* (10 vols, 1902).

Artem Lozynsky's *Richard Maurice Bucke, medical mystic* (1977) is both a critical biography and an edition of Bucke's letters to Whitman and his friends. See also *Richard Maurice Bucke: a catalogue based upon the collections of the University of Western Ontario Libraries* (1978) edited by Mary Ann Jameson.

S.E. Short has evaluated Bucke's medical achievement in *Victorian lunacy: Richard M. Bucke and the practice of late nineteenth-century psychiatry* (1987), and Peter Rechnitzer has written a popular biography, *Journey to cosmic consciousness: the life of Dr. R.M. Bucke* (1993). Colm Feore and Rip Torn starred as Bucke and Whitman in *Beautiful dreamers* (1990), a feature film about Bucke's life, directed by John Harrison. DAVID LATHAM

Buckler, Ernest (1908-84). Born in Dalhousie West, Nova Scotia, he was educated at Dalhousie University and the University of Toronto. After a brief career in an actuarial office in Toronto, he returned to the family farm near Bridgetown, N.S., where he lived in semi-retirement.

During the forties and fifties Buckler's short stories appeared in *Esquire, Saturday Night, Maclean's,* and *The Atlantic Advocate.* Many of them dramatized rural family relationships in an Annapolis Valley setting. Their characters and events were similar to those in *The MOUNTAIN AND THE VALLEY* (1952), Buckler's first novel and best-known publication. Described by Claude Bissell in the introduction to the NEW CANADIAN LIBRARY edition (1961) as 'a magnificent paean to the wonder and innocence of youth', it is a portrait of the potential artist. David Canaan, a precocious and over-sensitive child, is the gifted member of a family of sturdy, earthy, sensitive but largely inarticulate people. Their farm, the focus for David of all love, beauty, and security, is continually threatened by time and change. On the mountain that has symbolized his goal he achieves a momentary vision of the unity he has failed to recreate in his writing, then dies. Enclosed by his overprotective family, by the valley, and by his own supersensitive ego, David is another of the many portraits of the unfulfilled artist in Canada. The novel was reissued in the New Canadian Library with an Afterword by Robert GIBBS.

In Buckler's second novel, *The cruelest month* (1963), Paul Creed is a recluse who seasonally 'rents people'—renting out his rural retreat at Endlaw to city sophisticates and inviting his visitors to play dangerous intellectual parlour games in which they strip each other's personalities bare. The emotions released lead to unexpected rearrangements before, in the tradition of pastoral comedy, relations are re-established on a surer footing. Paul, too, needs rearranging; like David Canaan he is inwardly scarred. When a purifying forest fire helps the others to face themselves, and Paul—with Letty, his illiterate housekeeper—is brought close to death, he sees the terror of his withdrawn life and symbolically embraces Letty. *The cruelest month* confirmed Buckler's sense of the primacy of the intuitive over the intellectual, and his concern with the nature of perception.

Ox bells and fireflies (1968) is Buckler's most genial book. In the tradition of the descriptive sketch and rural reminiscence, it recreates the country childhood (based partly on his own) of a simpler era. Its strength is in the affectionate details and whimsical anecdotes that one expects of the genre; but Buckler's intensity of descriptive simile—all phenomena are both exactly themselves and imaginatively something else—emphasizes the subjectivity of perception. The prose in *Ox bells*, and in *The mountain and the valley*, moves toward those moments of unity when, as Buckler says, inside and outside become one. In these passages his prose has a prelapsarian freshness that, if sometimes strained, still impresses with its emotional and visual accuracy.

In the sense that he looked to moments of unified being—where the conscious and unconscious selves are united with each other, with others, and with the external environment—as the essence of existence, Buckler was a romantic writer. He was also, however, a realist, aware of how rare, fleeting, and fragile such moments are. At its best his prose effects a unity between the rural setting and the individual attuned to it. In *Window on the sea* (1973) Buckler's descriptive commentary effectively complements photographs by Hans Weber. His fondness for word-play is shown not very happily in *Whirligig* (1977), a selection of light sketches, interspersed with comic and satiric verse, that did not enhance the author's reputation.

A selection of reviews and early Buckler criticism is contained in *Ernest Buckler* (1972) edited by Gregory Cook. See also Alan R. Young, *Ernest Buckler* (1976), Robert Chambers, *Sinclair Ross and Ernest Buckler* (1978), and Claude Bissell, *Ernest Buckley remembered* (1989). D.O. SPETTIGUE

Budd, Henry. See ABORIGINAL LITERATURE: 2.

Buell, John (b. 1927). Born in Montreal, he was educated at the Université de Montréal, where he received a Ph.D. with a thesis on form and craft in Shakespeare. He is Professor Emeritus of the Communication Studies faculty at the Loyola campus of Concordia University. The author of five suspense novels of unusual skill, he is often misunderstood as a purely 'escapist' writer of thrillers and crime novels. He is really somewhere between Graham Greene and Raymond Chandler in his mode, for his central theme is the mystery of good and evil in a decaying world. In his first novel, *The pyx* (1959), filmed by Harvey Hart in 1973, the vulnerability and self-knowledge of Elizabeth Lucy, a high-class call girl and drug addict, operate as counterpoints to the destructive Montreal underworld—especially the demonic setting of Keerson's Black Mass rituals. Although not entirely successful, this slim work skilfully blends Eliabeth's outer world of action and her inner world of dream, nightmare, and illusion. Elizabeth despairs of the 'huge nothingness of evil confronting her', and, without benediction, she falls victim to Keerson's criminal agents. In *Four days* (1962), ostensibly a chronicle of a young boy's fatal idealization of his criminal elder brother, reality is so perverted that life ultimately becomes an ambush. The tension in this book is far less contrived than that in *The pyx*, and the pacing is as expert as the probing of the young protagonist's innocence and paranoia.

Buell's most disciplined novels are *The Shrewsdale exit* (1972), *Playground* (1976), and *A lot to make up for* (1990). In the first, the theme of unachieved retribution is worked out with relentless clarity as Joe Grant fails to obtain revenge against three motorcycle thugs who have murdered his wife and young daughter. *Playground* is an interior drama of a man trapped in a wilderness after a plane-crash. Buell tells this slow-moving, single-character story without mythicizing his protagonist or slipping into a philosophic essay on survival. *A lot to make up for* is quietly unspectacular, and is in the tradition of George Simenon as it follows two young people in trouble. Stan Hagan, once addicted to drugs and booze, turns up in Ashton, a small Canadian town, looking for Adele Symons, who has taken their baby girl (born addicted) and left him in order to make a new life for herself. Stan has a lot to make up for, and so has Adele, who is victimized anew in the town where she seeks refuge; but with the help of some benevolent townspeople the two find absolution for their past errors and a new direction for themselves.

All of Buell's novels combine ordinariness, grim humour, and suspense. Life in them is a crucible for the protagonists who, nevertheless, come to learn something true about existence.

See Keith Garebian, 'The authority of the writer: an interview with John Buell', *Journal of Canadian Studies*, vol. 12, no. 2 (Spring 1977). KEITH GAREBIAN

Bugnet, Georges (1879-1981). Born at Chalon-sur-Saône, Burgundy, France, he spent some time in a seminary; though he never became a priest, his deep faith reveals itself in his writing. After working briefly in France as a journalist, he immigrated to Canada in 1905 and settled north of Edmonton. For fifty years he worked on the land, writing to while away the winter hours and to supplement the meagre earnings farming brought him. He published his first two novels under the pseudonym 'Henri Doutremont'. *Le lys de sang* (1923) is a far-fetched adventure story set in Africa. In *Nipsya* (1924) a young Métisse has to make a choice between the white and Native ways of life; she compromises by marrying a man who is half-Native and by becoming a Christian. This novel at first passed unnoticed in French, but in an excellent translation (1929) by Contance Davies-Woodrow it was acclaimed by English-speaking readers. In *La forêt* (1935), Bugnet's masterpiece, the Bourgoins, a young French immigrant couple, are doomed, because instead of trying to live in harmony with nature, they struggle against it or mistrust it. Nature becomes a true protagonist, and Bugnet conveys its pervading, awesome presence in powerful yet restrained language. It was translated by David Carpenter as *The forest* (1976). *Siraf: étranges révélations; ce qu'on pense de nous par-delà la lune* (1934) is a philosophical dialogue between two spirits who condemn humans' materialism and pride. *Les voix de la solitude* (1935) contains a fine short story, 'Le pin du maskeg', and philosophical poems in which the author celebrates the glory of night from which light is born. This poetry, interesting for the ideas rather than for the form, was republished in *Poèmes* (1978), with an excellent introduction by Jean-Marcel Duciaume. The posthumous *Albertaines* (1990) consists of twenty pieces (short stories, plays, essays) chosen by Bugnet, which had been published in various periodicals and newspapers in the thirties and forties. Some of the author's views on literature, politics, and religion may seem somewhat conservative, but the anthology illustrates his deep attachment to Canada—he never returned to France—and his empathy with nature. Long before ecology became a common concern, Bugnet, who was also a distinguished horticulturist, chastised his fellow creatures for abusing the environment. Indeed, the primary theme of his *Journal, 1954-1971* (1984) is not his reading or his correspondence, but the weather and the effect it will have on his garden.

See David C. Carpenter, 'Georges Bugnet: an introduction', *Journal of Canadian Fiction*, I, 4 (Fall 1972) and 'A Canadian *Fête mobile*: interview with Georges Bugnet', *Journal of Canadian Fiction*, II, 2 (Spring 1973); and Jean Papen, *Georges Bugnet, homme de lettres canadien* (1985). PAULETTE COLLET

Buies, Arthur. See ANTHOLOGIES IN FRENCH: 4 and ESSAYS IN FRENCH: 2.

Bullock, Michael (b. 1918). Michael Hale Bullock was born in London, England. When he was ten months old his mother died, a trauma that influenced his creative work. He was educated at Stowe School, Buckinghamshire (one of his teachers was T.H. White, author of *The once and future king*), and at the Hornsey College of Art. He developed an early interest in languages and became an outstanding translator from German, French, and Italian. He came to Vancouver, British Columbia, as a Commonwealth Fellow in 1968, and in 1969 became a faculty member of the Department of Creative Writing at the University of British Columbia, remaining until his retirement in 1983. Always a prolific writer, he produced over a dozen volumes of poetry and fiction in the following decade.

A poet and painter, Bullock is also an important West Coast writer, developing the tradition of exploring landscape as inner and outer world that links image and mythic consciousness. Critic Jack Stewart sees Bullock's development in four main phases. In his first collection, *Transmutations* (1938), which appeared under the pseudonym 'Michael Hale', he began his experiments with automatism or freeflowing imagery. This beginning included influences from imagism, surrealism, and Orientalism. His second phase was marked by a personal amalgam of expressionism, surrealism, and immersion in nature. His work expanded considerably in *Sunday is a day of incest* (1960), *Poems of solitude* (with Jerome Ch'en, 1961/70), *World without beginning amen* (1963/73), and *Zwei Stimmen in meinum Mund/Two voices in my mouth* (1967). After he arrived in Canada, Bullock—together with J. Michael YATES and Andreas SCHROEDER—was central in the development of a short-lived wave of 'West Coast surrealists' in B.C., which resulted in, among other things, Schroeder's *Contemporary literature in translation* and *CANADIAN FICTION MAGAZINE*, of which Bullock has been a member of the editorial board since its inception.

In his third and most successful phase, Bullock explored the possibilities of short fiction and prose poetry in a series of brilliant short pieces collected in *A savage darkness* (1969), *Sixteen stories as they happened* (1969), and *Green beginning, black ending* (1971). He is a master of the fragment, the fable, the nightmare, and the enigma. Everything in his fiction is fluid and changable. Many of his pieces, however strange, are autobiographical at their source and deal with Bullock's concerns with evil, power, war, ecology, and immortality.

The loose format of these collections became more developed and structured in *Randolph Cranstone and the pursuing river* (1975; UK title *Randolph Cranstone and the glass thimble*, 1977). In this important collection of linked short stories, dreamlike sequences unfold with their own fantastic logic, yet remain entirely convincing as the main character tries to achieve aesthetic distance in his life, though he is forever chased by a torrent of words that causes everything about him to become transformed. Bullock's fourth phase refines his original techniques and themes in a prodigious outpouring of poetry and short fiction. From 1978 to 1996 he published a dozen collections of poetry as well as six volumes of short fiction, and the interconnected fables and fictions, *Randolph Cranstone and the veil of Maya* (1986) and *The story of Noire* (1987). Many of the poems were inspired by his family home in London, England, or his adopted home, Vancouver. Others use river and water imagery to symbolize creativity, depth, mirrors, and whatever is mysterious or unconscious. Bullock might be studied as a magic realist or fabulist; equally, he could be approached as a mystic or transcendental poet.

Because surrealism has had only a minor impact in English Canada, Bullock's work is generally self-published, or confined to such small presses as Third Eye, London, Ontario; Ekstasis Editions, Victoria, B.C.; or Rainbird Press, Vancouver. In his long association with *Canadian Fiction Magazine* he has contributed stories, prose-poems, and essays on the prose-poem and surrealism in fiction.

In addition to his own prolific output, sometimes two or three titles a year, Bullock—who was director of the translation program in creative writing at UBC—has translated over 150 books and plays from German, French, and Italian. In 1978 he won the CANADA COUNCIL Translation Prize for Michel TREMBLAY's *Stories for late night drinkers* (*Contes pour buveurs attardés*). His own poems and stories have been translated into many European and Oriental languages.

In celebration of his fifty years of publishing, Bullock was the subject of a critical appreciation by Jack Stewart, *The incandescent word: the poetic vision of Michael Bullock* (1990), published on his seventieth birthday. Bullock discusses his work with Andrew Parkin in 'An interview with Michael Bullock', *Canadian Fiction Magazine* 50/51 (1984). Critical articles on Bullock's writing include Jack Stewart, 'Image and mood: recent poems by Michael Bullock', *CANADIAN LITERATURE* 115 (Fall 1987), and Peter Loeffler, 'The poet as alchemist: five thoughts on Michael Bullock', *Canadian Fiction Magazine* 84 (1993).

GEOFF HANCOCK

Burnard, Bonnie (b. 1945). Born in Saskatchewan, now living in Ontario, Burnard is a respected reviewer, past fiction editor of *GRAIN* (1982-86), and editor of the short-fiction anthologies *The old dance* (1986) and *Stag line: stories by men* (1995). Her stories are collected in *Women of influence* (1988), winner of the Commonwealth Award for Best First Book, and in *Casino and other stories* (1994), the 1994 Saskatchewan Book of the Year and finalist for the first Giller Prize. Her first collection catalogues the intimate retrospections occasioned by deaths of siblings, parents, marriages, past relationships and past selves, bringing to the surface regrets and denials but also tentative self-awareness and quiet self-assertion. Her second collection is thematically more diverse and more loosely and meditatively structured; most of the stories are orchestrated by emotional and psychological revelations rather than by plot or event, by healing encounters between lovers old and new, and by the loss of innocence for young and middle-aged characters alike. If Burnard's stories are concerned with any one thing, it is love in its many forms, especially its loss, treated gently, openly, with respect, and with wonder at the ordinary heroism of emotional survival.

DONNA PALMATEER PENNEE

Burwell, Adam Hood (1790-1849). Probably the best lyric poet Canada produced in the early nineteenth century, he was born of Loyalist parents near Fort Erie, Upper Canada (Ontario). He was raised on the family farm in Welland County and moved to the Talbot Settlement about 1817. The details of his education have not been documented, but he was ordained deacon in 1827 and in 1828 priest of the Church of England. His first appointment was in Lennoxville, Lower Canada (Quebec), and while there he was married in Troy, N.Y., to a parishioner, Sarah Barnard. He served a joint pastorate at Nicolet, Trois-Rivières, and Rivière-du-Loup, and then moved to Hull as a missionary in 1832. By 1836 he had been expelled from the Anglican priesthood for doctrinal irregularity. He spent the remainder of his life in Kingston as a minister of the Catholic Apostolic Church ('Irvingite').

Burwell's earliest published poetry appeared in Upper Canadian newspapers from 1816, under the pseudonym 'Erieus'. A number of poems appeared in *The Scribbler* between 1821 and 1823 and in *The Canadian Review and Literary and Historical Journal* in 1825. For one year (Sept. 1830-Sept. 1831) Burwell edited a religious weekly, *The Christian Sentinel*, in which a number of his works, literary and theological, appeared both under his own name and under several pseudonyms. His Irvingite beliefs resulted in two tracts published in 1835, and a spate of tracts and long poems published just before his death, some of which appeared in *The LITERARY GARLAND*.

Much of Burwell's early poetry is inspired either by nature or by love. Using a variety of forms, he is at his best when he escapes from the jogging rhythms of end-stopped lines; sometimes he achieves an almost mystic intensity. Of greatest interest today are the poems that describe specific Canadian scenes and events, such as 'The Battle of Lundy's Lane', 'Talbot Road', 'Farewell to the shores of Erie', and 'Journal of a day's journey in Upper Canada'. The last poem in particular has several arresting scenes. Burwell's late poetry combines his life-long feeling for nature with his theological convictions—in it nature becomes a vehicle of revelation.

The poems of Adam Hood Burwell, pioneer poet of Upper Canada (1963), edited by C.F. KLINCK, is available from the University of Western Ontario Library. See also M.L. MacDonald, '"New poems" of Adam Hood Burwell', *Canadian Poetry*, no. 18 (Spring/Summer 1986).

MARY LU MacDONALD

Bush, Catherine. See NOVELS IN ENGLISH 1983 TO 1993: OTHER NOVELS 3.

Butala, Sharon (b. 1940). Sharon Le Blanc was born, the second oldest of five girls, near the northern village of Nipawin, Saskatchewan. When she was thirteen her family moved to Saskatoon. She was educated at St Mary's Roman Catholic school, and obtained a B.A. in English and Art at the University of Saskatchewan. After a decade in the workforce she obtained a B.Ed. as an educational psychologist, specializing in teaching children with learning disabilities. She taught boys' vocational classes at the YMCA in Halifax, Nova Scotia. After her first marriage of fourteen years ended in 1975, she married Peter Butala and now lives on an isolated cattle ranch in southwest Saskatchewan.

Frequently describing the landscape's natural beauty, and evoking the geographical, Aboriginal, and historical past, Butala's writing often affirms the experience and validates the dreams of middle-aged women, especially farm and country women. Her characters are troubled by loneliness, strained marriages, remorse for the past, and unresolved relationships, which push them to a crisis point. Yet Butala's vision is not one of despair. Many of her stories utilize parallel plot lines, a technique learned from Alice MUNRO. The real time of the story is offset by memories or dreams; the spiritual side of life often appears in the ordinary; and the past and present are sometimes reconciled. Her fiction is also shaped by the landscape, weather, and by regional issues that enhance the dimensions of her characters.

Butala's best work is found in her short stories. Her first collection, *Queen of the headaches* (1985), nominated for a Governor General's Award, contains fourteen stories about ordinary men and women who suffer moral anxiety, and especially the struggles, joys, and regrets of broken or stifling family circumstances. Many of the protagonists are stubborn farm wives with a strong work ethic who believe in responsibility and self-reliance. In the title story, a woman with a headache finds solace in her pain as her family of overachievers find success in their various careers. The idea of succumbing to a physical illness also appears in Butala's *Fever* (1990). These sixteen highly emotional stories are mostly about middle-aged prairie people stoically wrestling with the bewildering complexities of their lives. The stories are linked by themes of illness, depression, or life-threatening physical ailments that are in turn connected to mid-life crises such as infidelity, guilt, and attempts to make sense of an unlived life. In the title story a woman has an affair while her husband lies in hospital with a fever. In the best story, 'The prize', a man deals with self-doubt and insecurity after winning a major literary award.

Butala's first novel, *Country of the heart* (1984), was nominated for the W.H. Smith/*Books in Canada* First Novel Award. Her second, third, and fifth novels—*The gates of the sun* (1986), *Luna* (1988), and *The fourth archangel* (1992)—form a loosely linked trilogy. *The gates of the sun* is a traditional novel of education; it describes the life of Andrew Simpson from childhood to old age and death. His picaresque life is set against a mini-history of Saskatchewan, especially farm politics, the natural cycles of the moon and seasons, and the wind and grasslands, with the sun as a motif in Andrew's spiritual education. *Luna* is about women. Butala describes wives, daughters, sisters, daughters, matriarchs, their lives, dreams, aspirations, and isolation. She expertly contrasts the women's world indoors (and their inner world) with the outdoor world of ranchers and their struggles with weather and animals. For her women the traditions of home, family, and hard work are the surest means of finding happiness.

Butala wrote her fourth novel, *Upstream: 'le pays d'en haut'* (1991), to reclaim her father's lost French-Canadian heritage. Possibly her most autobiographical novel, it uses the device of a diary to link past and present, language and culture, Saskatchewan and Quebec, in the story of Chloe coming to terms with her estranged father in one of the province's dwindling francophone villages. With *The fourth archangel* Butala created one of the finest portraits of a small Canadian town. A millennial elegy for the passing of rural life, and a deep lament for the lost wild grasslands that farming has destroyed, the novel describes the plight of the small western town of Ordeal and the turmoil of its inhabitants. A futuristic Depression—with bad weather, financial insecurity, creditors, and bankers—is set against a backdrop of history, memory, and dream.

Butala wrote the introduction to Todd Korol's photography book *Harvest* (1992), which includes a history of Saskatchewan harvesting, the economics of wheat farming, and the changing community structure of the Prairies. She has also written six plays, which have all been workshopped or produced in her home town, in Saskatoon, and Vancouver, but remain unpublished.

Butala's spiritual views were expressed in *The perfection of the morning* (1994). Subtitled 'An apprenticeship in nature', these essays reflect on her move from a city to an isolated ranch. *Coyote's morning cry* (1995) comprises twenty brief essays on subjects as varied as old age, meditation, dreams, morals, the awe-inspiring beauty of ancient petroglyphs, and 'the chorus of coyotes on a frosty morning'.

GEOFF HANCOCK

Butler, Audrey. See LESBIAN LITERATURE.

Butler, Juan (1942-81). Born in London, England, the son of an English father and a Spanish mother, he came to Canada with his family in 1942 and grew up in Toronto. He dropped out of school after Grade 10, travelled extensively in Europe and Morocco, than returned to Canada at the end of the sixties to reside at various times in Toronto and Montreal. In 1981 he hanged himself in a Toronto psychiatric hospital.

Butler's three novels—*Cabbagetown diary: a documentary* (1970), *The garbageman* (1972), and *Canadian heating oil* (1974)—are impassioned indictments of a squalid world that robs man of dignity. Michael Armstrong Taylor, the young diarist of *Cabbagetown diary*, is an immigrant bartender whose callous eyes witness the stupidity and hypocrisy of his low-class associates and his high-class customers. Written from his slum apartment in downtown Toronto, the entries begin in July and end in October of one year—the length of an affair Michael abruptly ends when his girlfriend becomes pregnant: 'Somebody had to show her how to make out in this world.' The first-person narrator of *The garbageman* is an insane writer from Toronto. Incapable of love yet anxious for human contact, he commits murders in France and Spain. An inmate of the mental institution where his story ends summarizes the novel's theme: 'Life killing itself because of its lack of pride in itself.' The first-person narrator of

Canadian heating oil, set in a timeless surrealistic universe, is 'I St. John, the Eagle, the evangelist whom Christ loved the most', who believes himself destined to bestow dignity on people through love. He falls in love with Miss Pat, who is a black woman, a Chinese woman, an Indian princess, and Joan of Arc. The narrator becomes Jean Brébeuf, achieving salvation in a martyrdom of love. The artist-as-martyr theme became a sad prophecy of Butler's final years, when his psychological suffering offered him no peace.

In 'The Happy Gang rides again' (*Northern Journey* 3, 1973) Butler attacks the Group of Seven and the London school of painters: 'A culture must be based on a feeling, not of geography, but of national community.'

DAVID STAINES

Butler, Samuel. See FOREIGN WRITERS ON CANADA IN ENGLISH: 1 and 'O God! O Montreal!'.

Butler, William Francis. See FOREIGN WRITERS ON CANADA IN ENGLISH: 1, PRAIRIE WRITING, and TRAVEL LITERATURE IN ENGLISH.

By Grand Central Station I sat down and wept (1945). This novel by Elizabeth SMART was begun in 1940 while the author was living at a writers' colony in Big Sur, California, and was completed in 1941 at Pender Harbour, British Columbia, where she was awaiting the birth of her first child. It was published in an edition of two thousand copies by James Meary Tambimuttu of Editions Poetry, London, the imprint of his famous journal, *Poetry London*. A mass-paperback edition came out in England in 1966, and the first North American edition in 1977. Since then it has been recognized as a classic. In her Foreword to the paperback edition Brigid Brophy calls it one of the 'half a dozen masterpieces of poetic prose in the world . . . *By Grand Central Station* is one of the most shelled, skinned, nerve-exposed books ever written.'

A love story written in the form of a rhapsodic prose-poem, it is quintessentially lyrical: sounding antiphonally throughout are rhythms, images, and refrains that echo the Song of Solomon. It takes its title from a play on the opening of Psalm 137 ('By the rivers of Babylon, there we sat down, yea, we wept, when we remembered Zion.') Set in North America in the early years of the Second World War, it is a type of interior monologue where all attention is focused on the narrator's intense and obsessive passion for a married man. There are few external events beyond a car journey through the western United States, the narrator's ultimate return alone to the west coast of Canada to have her child, and a failed reunion of the lovers at Grand Central Station in New York.

The book is haunting because Smart moves the story into a mythological key. Behind the narrator's voice one hears the echoes of other passionate heroines from Homer's Helen, to Virgil's Dido, and Emily Brontë's Catherine. The story does not hide its autobiographical origins because one of Smart's themes is the interpenetration of life and literature—it is not simply that the narrator lives her life as myth, but that the myths themselves have been rendered quotidian, and Dido walks living onto the book's stage. Smart crafted a new form of lyric prose to tell her archetypal story. The erotic passion the narrator records with dazzling metaphoric exuberance infuses even the landscape with a kind of animistic intensity; few readers forget the famous sentence: 'Under the waterfall he surprised me bathing and gave me what I could no more refuse than the earth can refuse the rain.' The book seduces the reader into identifying with its record of a hopelessly addictive, life-engrossing passion, yet there is considerable humour. *By Grand Central Station I sat down and wept* turned Smart into a cult figure—she has been called a forerunner of Jack Kerouac's Beat Generation, a pioneer espousing freedom from moral convention.

The novel has been translated into numerous languages, including Danish, French, German, Italian, Spanish, and Swedish.

ROSEMARY SULLIVAN

C

Cailloux, André. See CHILDREN'S DRAMA IN FRENCH.

Calef, George. See NATURE WRITING IN ENGLISH: 2.

Call, Frank Oliver. See POETRY IN ENGLISH 1900 TO 1950: 2(b), Writing in English in QUEBEC: 2, and GAY LITERATURE: POETRY.

Callaghan, Barry (b. 1937). The son of Morley CALLAGHAN, he was born in Toronto, Ontario, and educated at St Michael's College, University of Toronto (B.A., 1960; M.A., 1962), which he left in 1965 before completing his doctoral dissertation. He worked as a part-time reporter for CBC television news (1958-62) and gave weekly book reviews on the CBC radio program 'Audio' (1964-6). From Sept. 1966 to Mar. 1971 Callaghan was literary editor of the Toronto *Telegram*, for which he wrote essays and book reviews that were noted for their insight and controversial candour. After seven months as a host for the CBC-TV program 'The Public Eye', he became host and documentary producer for the public-affairs program 'Weekend' (Nov. 1969-Feb. 1972); in this capacity he made some twenty short films on political trouble-spots and taped interviews with international figures such as Golda Meir and King Hussein. He has also produced and directed a number of documentaries (he was imprisoned in South Africa in 1976 during the filming of *The white lager*). As a journalist Callaghan has received four national magazine awards, including the Gold Medal from the University of Western Ontario in 1979. Since 1965 he has taught contemporary literature at Atkinson College, York University, Toronto, where in 1972 he founded the literary magazine *EXILE*, and in 1976 EXILE EDITIONS, which now has a backlist of more than 160 titles.

Callaghan's *The Hogg poems and drawings* (1978) is a sequence detailing the protagonist's semi-religious quest to Jerusalem in order to liberate himself from the stifling conventions of Hogtown (Toronto). Finding passion, history, and even absurdity at the end of his pilgrimage, he makes a descent into the underworld of the Toronto subway, emerging with a new awareness of his identity and an acceptance of his roots. Although not all poems are of the same order, 'Judas Priest'—with its street wisdom, vernacular rhythm, and complex rhymes—is exceptionally fine. A second volume of his poems, *Seven last words*, appeared in 1983. The sensuality, aloneness, and distrust of the 'thought-police' (any person or establishment that would identify the non-conformists with the criminal) that are apparent in the *Hogg poems* are also motifs in *The Black Queen stories* (1982), a collection of fourteen highly polished tales that range from vivid portraits of gamblers and gays to subtle explorations of their relationships. Callaghan's ear for the spoken word is most acute in 'The Cohen in Cowan' and 'Poodles John'. His use of symbolism is sophisticated—the outcome of a story is often foreshadowed in the opening paragraphs. Evident throughout is Callaghan's compassion for his characters, despite their idiosyncrasies and occasional outrageousness. Eight of these stories appeared in *Punch*, and two—'Crow Jane's blues' and 'A drawn blind'—were reprinted in *The Punch book of short stories* (1980 and 1981 respectively).

Callaghan is also a skilled memoirist in his introduction to *Shapes and sounds: poems of W.W.E. Ross* (1968) and in his recollections of Edmund Wilson in *Exile* I, no. 2 (1972). In the fall of 1997 he published a memoir of his father, *Barrel-house kings*. His translations of the French poet Robert Marteau—*Atlante* (1979) and *Treatise on white and tincture* (1979)—are marked by sensitivity and intelligence. Two more translations—*Interlude* by Marteau and *Singing at the whirlpool* by Miodrag Pavlovic—were published in 1982.

DAVID O'ROURKE

Callaghan's career as a polymath creator continued in the 1990s: journalist, poet, translator, editor, critic, novelist, short-story writer, publisher, and professor. He won an ACTRA award for best host of a TV show, 'Enterprise', in 1984; shared the Harbourfront Phillips Information System Literary Prize with Margaret ATWOOD in 1986; and won a Toronto Arts Award in 1993.

Though Callaghan often complains about being ignored by Canadians, his fiction and poetry are widely anthologized abroad. His poetry collection *Stone blind love* (1987) is a moving sequence inspired by the death of his mother. His first novel, *The way the angel spreads her wings* (1989), is a profound and complex work in Joycean prose about a war photographer searching for a woman he loved and lost. His second novel, *When things get worst* (1993), is a compelling story of a strange woman who maintains her connection to the land in a farm community where most farmers have severed their ties. The stories collected in *A kiss is still a kiss* (1995) are linked by images of blindness, war, cemeteries, and decay. One story, 'Because Y is a crooked letter', is a remake of an award-winning article, 'A motiveless malignancy', which described a vicious act of vandalism that destroyed his home and art collection.

Callaghan has edited a variety of collections by several Canadian writers: *Singing at the whirlpool: the poems of Miodrag Pavlovic* (1983), *Wells of light: selected poems by Fernand Ouellette* (1988), *The poetry of Gwendolyn MacEwen* (1994, with Margaret ATWOOD), and *The Austin Clarke reader* (1996). Among his anthologies are *Lords of winter and of love: Canadian love poems* (1984); *Canadian travellers in Italy* (1989); and a three-volume anthology celebrating his highly regarded literary magazine *Exile*: *Exile's exiles: portraits by John Reeves* (1992), and *Fifteen years in Exile* (2 vols, 1992). *This ain't no healing town: Toronto stories* (1995) focuses on new immigrants to the city.

GEOFF HANCOCK

Callaghan, **Morley** (1903-90). Born in Toronto, where he lived all his life, Morley Edward Callaghan was educated at St Michael's College, University of Toronto, from which he graduated in 1925, and at Osgoode Hall. He was called to the bar in 1928 but never practised law. As a student he had worked during summer vacations as a cub reporter on the *Toronto Daily Star* during Ernest Hemingway's short period there, and the American novelist had shown an interest in his stories, encouraging Callaghan to pursue writing instead of law. Hemingway demonstrated the solidity of his interest by taking some of Callaghan's stories to France, where they were published in expatriate literary magazines; while in the United States, stories that Callaghan himself had sent out were accepted by *American Caravan* and noticed by F. Scott Fitzgerald, who showed them to his New York publisher, Scribner's. In 1928 Scribner's published Callaghan's first novel, *Strange fugitive*, and a year later his first volume of short stories, *A native argosy*. In the same year, 1929, Callaghan went to Paris, where he encountered Hemingway again, became friendly with James Joyce and Fitzgerald, and was ironically observed by the young John GLASSCO (see his *Memoirs of Montparnasse*). This Parisian interlude became the subject of one of Callaghan's most appealing books, *That summer in Paris* (1963).

While Callaghan devoted most of his creative energy to fiction—both novels and short stories—for a brief period, in 1939, he turned to drama and wrote two plays, 'Turn home again' and 'Just ask for George', which was produced in New York in 1940; 'Turn home again', as 'Going home', was staged in 1949 in Toronto, where another play, 'To tell the truth', was performed the following year. The response to these productions, however, did not encourage Callaghan to continue as a playwright. During the Second World War, when he was writing comparatively little, Callaghan turned to radio as a means of livelihood, serving as chair of the CBC Forum program 'Of things to come'; he was intermittently involved in CBC programs until his death. He made a single foray into juvenile literature with *Luke Baldwin's vow* (1948); and in *The Varsity story* (1948) he described in a hybrid form, part fiction and part history, the growth of the University of Toronto.

Callaghan's career as a writer of fiction follows a strikingly uneven graph of productivity and silence. There is an early cluster of six novels written in the late 1920s and early-to-middle 1930s, from *Strange fugitive* (1928) to *MORE JOY IN HEAVEN* (1937; NCL, with an Afterword by Margaret AVISON). To this period also belong most of Callaghan's stories—collected in *A native argosy* (1929) and *Now that April's here* (1936), and brought together in *Morley Callaghan's stories* (1959)—and his Paris-printed novella, *No man's meat* (1931). There is a long interval from the end of the 1930s to the early 1950s before *The LOVED AND THE LOST* (1951), and after that almost a decade before the publication in fast succession of two other novels, *The many colored coat* (1960) and *A passion in Rome* (1961). There was a further long interval before Callaghan's late novels appeared—again in close succession: *A fine and private place* (1975), *Close to the sun again* (1977), *The enchanted pimp* (1978), *A time for Judas* (1983), *Our lady of the snow* (1985), and *A wild old man on the road* (1988).

Callaghan's three early novels—*Strange fugitive*, *It's never over* (1930), and *A broken journey* (1932)—are gauche and tentative in manner, implausible and melodramatic in plot. They are novels of consequences, in which the characters' acts shape their generally unhappy fates. *Strange fugitive* is a kind of Rake's Progress, whose central character graduates from a bullying lumberyard foreman into a bootlegger who dies under the sawed-off shotgun of his rivals. *It's never over* traces how the tangled emotions of the people close to a man about to be hanged for murder take them near to a second murder situation. *A broken journey* uses the rivalry between a mother and daughter to illuminate the problems of innocence and infidelity and the destructive aspects of love. In none of these novels did Callaghan really find himself as a writer: the influence of both Hemingway and Fitzgerald is intermittently evident. There is a quite striking contrast between the uncertain forms and feelings of these early novels and the laconic sureness of the early short stories in which, in the same period, Callaghan was so empathetically tracing the vagaries of human behaviour.

A sudden sureness of tone appeared in Callaghan's fourth novel, *Such is my beloved* (1934; NCL, with an Afterword by Milton Wilson), and continued through *They shall inherit the earth* (1935; NCL, with an Afterword by Ray Ellenwood) and *More joy in heaven*, which have an economy of form and a lucidity of expression and feeling that make them the best of Callaghan's works, and perhaps the best novels written in Canada during the 1930s. They were written after Callaghan had come under the influence of the French philosopher and theologian Jacques Maritain, then teaching in Toronto, and they show the way in which ideas can influence form. They are moralist novels that bear a generic resemblance to the *récits* (or novellas) of French writers like Gide and Camus. Set in the Depression era, whose physical rigours their characters suffer, they avoid the political conclusions that so many novels of the era sought and offer the moral predicaments of their characters as routes to spiritual ends—which, however, they see only 'through a glass, darkly'.

Callaghan's next three novels—*The loved and the lost*, *The many colored coat*, and *A passion in Rome*—are all attempts to combine the moral searchings of the earlier novels with more ambitious formal structures, so that what emerges is an unhappy compromise between the simple economy of the moralistic novella and the more decorated complexity of the classic realist novel. What Callaghan once again shows, now in a negative rather than a positive way, is that, with his special talent for the shorter and more concise forms of fiction, he is not really equipped for the construction of larger fiction: in each of these three novels the attempt to adjust leads to a softening of style and a straining of credibility. The unity of conception and the force of moral passion that distinguished the novels of the 1930s are evident in neither *The loved and the lost* nor *A passion in Rome*; and *A many colored coat* is a moral tale that would have made an excellent novella but was laboured into an over-long and over-written full-length novel.

A fine and private place may well be Callaghan's least effective novel, for it is the story of an unappreciated novelist that clearly has personal implications and is used to present a flattering self-analysis and a contemptuous dismissal of the characters who are blind to the worth of the novelist and clearly represent Callaghan's critics. Callaghan redeemed his record, however, with *Close to the sun again*, in which he returned successfully to the terse novella form of his best period, evading the temptations of realism in favour of moral symbolism as he writes a strange story of how the will to power develops in men when their personal defeats dominate them and destroy their natural impulses.

Edmund Wilson once said (in *O Canada*, 1965) that Callaghan 'is perhaps the most unjustly neglected novelist in the English-speaking world.' The record of honours paid him does not now bear this out: the Governor General's Award for *The loved and the lost*; the Lorne PIERCE Medal of the Royal Society of Canada in 1960; the Canada Council Medal in 1966; the Molson Prize and the Royal Bank Award in 1970; and in 1982 his appointment as a Companion of the Order of Canada.

Of Callaghan's late fiction, *The enchanted pimp* is combined with his novella of the thirties, *No man's meat*, and they provide a contrast in settings: downtown Toronto for the first and Muskoka cottage country for the second. The most admirable of the last novels is *A time for Judas*, which is narrated by the fictitious Philo of Crete, secretary to Pontius Pilate and a friend of Judas, who is redeemed. It is a daring, imaginative novel. *Our lady of the snows* is an expanded version of *The enchanted pimp*, and *A wild man on the road*, a novella, is thinly veiled autobiography set in the twenties in Toronto, Paris, and Rome. Barry CALLAGHAN edited *The lost and found stories of Morley Callaghan* (1985), which contains twenty-six of his father's stories that had never appeared in book form, and in 1997 published a biography of his father, *Barrelhouse kings*.

See Patricia Morley, *Morley Callaghan* (1978); David Staines, editor, *The Callaghan symposium* (1981); and Judith Kendle, 'Morley Callaghan: an annotated bibliography' in Robert Lecker and Jack David, eds, *The annotated bibliography of Canada's major authors* (1985). GEORGE WOODCOCK

Callwood, June (b. 1924). Born in Chatham, Ontario, she became a journalist whose pieces can be found in many magazines and newspapers from the 1950s onward, especially in *Maclean's* and the *Globe and Mail*. She has written many books on a variety of subjects, including *Love, fear, hate and anger* (1964); *Portrait of Canada* (1981), a history; and *Emotions: what they are and how they affect us* (1986). As Callwood's writing career sharpened her awareness of social injustice she became a civil libertarian and social activist who helped to bring social issues, such as homelessness among youth and drug addiction, into the public consciousness. A good example of her social activism may be seen in *The right to have enough money: a straightforward guide to the disability income system in Canada* (1990). She has also written on AIDS-related issues—for example, *Jim: a life with AIDS* (1988) and *Trial without end: a shocking story of women and AIDS* (1995)—and in 1987-8 she founded Casey House, a home for terminally ill AIDS patients.

Callwood has also addressed women's issues, either in the form of general treatises on certain areas of concern to women, such as *The law is not for women* (1976), with Marvin Zuker, or in such case studies as *The sleepwalker* (1990), documenting a specific criminal case. She has written a biography of a woman spy, *Emma: Canada's unlikely spy* (1984), and ghost-written numerous memoirs of American celebrities.

The recipient of more than a dozen honorary degrees, Callwood has been on the executive of Amnesty International, Canada (1983), Chair of the WRITERS' UNION OF CANADA (1979-80), and a Bencher of the Law Society of Upper Canada (1987-91). She was appointed an Officer of the Order of Canada in 1986 and an Officer of the Order of Ontario in 1988. STEFAN HAAG

Cameron, Anne. See LESBIAN LITERATURE.

Cameron, George Frederick (1854-85). Born in New Glasgow, Nova Scotia, he moved with his family to Boston in 1869 and in 1872 entered Boston University to study law. Later he worked with a law firm there. His early interest was in the classics and he is said to have read most of Virgil and Cicero in the original before he was fourteen. While articling in law he contributed poems and essays to several Boston newspapers. In 1882 he entered Queen's University, Kingston, Ontario, and was named the prize poet in 1883, when he was made editor of the Kingston *News*, a position he held until his death. In 1887 his brother, Charles L. Cameron, edited and published a selection of Cameron's poems under the title *Lyrics on freedom, love and death* (Kingston, 1887). Cameron's poetry was unlike other Canadian verse of the time: there is little effort to write about 'Canadian' subjects such as nature and patriotism. It reflects Cameron's strong interest in classical culture, and his wide political concerns in poems sympathetic to the independence of Cuba and in praise of the democratic aspirations of the United States. His poems are clouded, however, by a prevailing pessimism. Cameron also wrote the libretto for *Leo, the Royal cadet. An entirely new and original miliary opera in four acts* (Kingston, 1889), with music by Oscar F. Telgmann; it was performed in Kingston, Toronto, and elsewhere in Ontario in 1889.

DOUGLAS LOCHHEAD

Campbell, Maria (b. 1940). This Métis writer was born on a trapline in northwestern Saskatchewan, the eldest of eight children; she was raised in a road-allowance community and attended a one-room elementary country school in northern Saskatchewan. When her mother died, Campbell at twelve years of age had to leave school to look after the other children. She left home at fifteen and went to Vancouver. In her twenties she returned to the Prairies, where she was a community worker, activist, and organizer. With the help of a collective she wrote *Many laws* (1969), explaining the laws that confront aboriginal people when they move to the city.

Campbell's memoir *Half-breed* (1973; rpr. 1983) is a daring account of a strong-willed woman who overcame poverty, alcoholism, drug addiction, sexual abuse, and prostitution by the age of thirty-three because 'I had a whole lot of stuff inside me that I had to write to find out who I was, to heal myself.' It rises above the level of confessional biography because Campbell views her life in the larger context of a distinct Métis culture. She gives a mythic dimension to the story of her people, and a powerfully distinctive voice to a people with few illusions and even fewer realizable hopes, who had been ignored for too long. On school and university course-lists across the country, *Half-breed* became a watershed publication for the Aboriginal peoples of Canada and established Campbell as 'the Mother of us all', in the words of Daniel David MOSES.

Campbell has also written three children's books: *People of the buffalo* (1975), *Little badger and the fire spirit* (1977), and *Riel's people* (1978).

She translated *Stories of the road-allowance people* (1995) from Cree-Mitchif, spoken by the Métis people, to the oral English spoken by the Métis. Campbell likes to explore theatre as a way of bringing her messages to Canadians, and has written four plays collectively. *Jessica*, written in collaboration with Linda Griffiths, portrays a young Métis woman's transformations from innocence to despair to self-discovery. It opened in 1986 at the Theatre Passe Muraille, Toronto, winning the Dora Mavor Moore Award for outstanding new play, and also played at the Quinzanne International Festival in Quebec City, when it was judged the Best Canadian Production. In 1989 it was published, along with the story of its turbulent creation, under the title *The book of Jessica: a theatrical transformation*. Campbell also wrote the script for *The red dress* (1977), a National Film Board film. From 1984 to 1994 she produced thirty-four community documentaries, four of which appeared on television.

Campbell has received two honorary doctorates: from the University of Regina (1995) and from York University, Toronto (1995). In 1996 she won a National Aboriginal Achievement Award. PENNY PETRONE

Campbell, Wilfred (1860-1918). An Anglican clergyman's son, William Wilfred Campbell was born in Newmarket, Canada West (not in Berlin/Kitchener, in 1858, as has been supposed). Upon completing high school in Owen Sound (Ontario), he taught for a year in a country school at Zion, near Wiarton. He enrolled at University College, University of Toronto, in 1880 but transferred to Wycliffe, the university's Anglican divinity school, in 1882. The following year he transferred again, this time to the Episcopal Theological School in Cambridge, Massachusetts. Ordained in 1886, Campbell served parishes in West Claremont, New Hampshire; St Stephen, New Brunswick; and Southampton, Ont., before resigning from the ministry in 1891. For the rest of his life he worked in the Ottawa civil service, holding positions in such areas as the Department of Railways and Canals, the Department of the Secretary of State, the Department of Militia and Defence, the Privy Council Office, and the Public Archives. He died of pneumonia on 1 Jan. 1918.

In the late nineteenth century the encroachment of science upon religion and higher criticism of the Bible were subjects of considerable debate in Canadian intellectual circles. The poetry of Wilfred Campbell—who is sometimes included among the CONFEDERATION POETS—to a large extent is the chronicle of a sensitive man's struggle to find meaning in an age of shifting values. His first book, *Snowflakes and sunbeams* (St Stephen, N.B., 1888; rpr. 1974) is concerned chiefly with nature, and the influence of the English Romantics is apparent in almost every poem. A Wordsworthian celebration of memory dominates 'Midwinter night's dream', and the beauty of nature is glorified in his best-known and most-anthologized poem, 'Indian summer'.

In *Lake lyrics and other poems* (Saint John, N.B., 1889) nature is perceived less as a manifestation of God's presence on earth than as a spiritual force in itself. 'Vapor and blue', 'On the ledge', and particularly 'To Thunder Cape' show the poet striving to touch the spirit in nature. In seeking to align his energy with that of nature, Campbell does not emulate the American transcendentalists but looks instead to the work of Bliss CARMAN. Carman's 'Low tide on Grand Pré', written in 1886, serves as a model of transcendental experience for Campbell in 'August evening on the beach, Lake Huron' (*c*. 1889). Campbell's most significant nature poetry is stark and horrifying in its imagery. In 'The winter lakes' (*Lake lyrics*) the poet casts off the conventional nineteenth-century pose of being transported by nature's beauty and probes instead a profound sense of doubt in the face of a landscape unrelieved by hope. Similarly, in 'How one winter came in the lake region' in *The dread voyage* (Toronto, 1893) he paints a bleak portrait of a world untouched by God's grace. Campbell's best dramatic poems also arise from settings that are stark and threatening. In 'Lazarus' (*Lake lyrics*) the protagonist questions God's authority and embarks on a dangerous mission to wrest a suffering man from the horrors of hell; and in 'Unabsolved' (*The dread voyage*) a coward's unassuageable guilt is mirrored in the bleak, frozen vastness of the Arctic. In winter lakes and landscapes Campbell found a metaphor for his despair over the religious doubt of the age.

After the turn of the century Campbell, for whom the monarchy and Empire provided a reassuring link between past and present, expressed his imperialist philosophy in verse. 'Victoria (Jubilee Ode, A.D. 1897)', in *Beyond the hills of dream* (Boston, 1899), celebrates Queen Victoria's Diamond Jubilee, and the elegiac 'Victoria', in *The poems of Wilfred Campbell*—also published under the title *The collected poems of Wilfred Campbell* (both 1905)—laments her death. Campbell's final book, *Sagas of vaster Britain: poems of the race, the Empire and the divinity of man* (1914), argues for the imperialist cause at a time when the

Empire was going to war. His commitment to imperialism is also reflected in the two anthologies of poetry he edited: *The Oxford book of Canadian verse* (1913; rpr. 1976) and *Poems of loyalty by British and Canadian authors* (1913). Campbell saw in imperialism's idealism and continuity the potential for meaningful action in an age of uncertainty and flux.

A prolific writer, Campbell also wrote poetic drama, fiction, travel books, and newspaper columns. His poetic dramas, *Mordred and Hildebrand. A book of tragedies* (Ottawa, 1895) and *Poetical tragedies* (1908), offer somewhat convoluted plots and stilted Elizabethan dialogue. His two novels, *Ian of the Orcades; or The armourer of Girnigoe* (1906) and *A beautiful rebel: a romance of Upper Canada in 1812* (1909), are similarly exaggerated in plot and diction. *The beauty, history, romance and mystery of the Canadian lake region* (1910) is a travel book exploring the region where Campbell set many of his poems. Campbell provided the text for T. Mower Martin's collection of paintings, *Canada* (1907), and collaborated with George Bryce on the two-volume work *The Scotsman in Canada* (1911). As a newspaper columnist, Campbell joined his fellow poets Archibald LAMPMAN and Duncan Campbell SCOTT to write the column 'AT THE MERMAID INN' for the Toronto *Globe* (1892-3). For the Ottawa *Evening Journal* Campbell wrote another column, 'Life and letters' (1903-5).

As a Romantic, a transcendentalist, and particularly as an imperialist, Wilfred Campbell was not held in high regard by the generation of Canadian poets who succeeded him, though his literary executor, W.J. Sykes, published *The poetical works of Wilfred Campbell* (1923) and Carl F. KLINCK wrote a fine biography of the poet, *Wilfred Campbell: a study in late provincial Victorianism* (1942; rpr. 1977). In some ways modernism defined itself in contrast to the very poetical and political values Campbell had come to represent, and his work remained virtually ignored until the 1970s, when there was a revival of critical interest in his poetry. Two selections have been published in recent years: *Selected poems* (1976) edited by Klinck and *Vapour and blue: Souster selects Campbell* (1978) edited by Raymond SOUSTER.

See George Wicken, 'William Wilfred Campbell (1858-1918): an annotated bibliography', *Essays on Canadian Writing* 9 (Winter 1977/78), and his critical study in *Canadian writers and their works: poetry series: volume 2* (1983) edited by Robert Lecker, Jack David, and Ellen Quigley; and Laurel Boone, ed. *William Wilfred Campbell: selected poetry and essays* (1987). GEORGE WICKEN

Canada Council for the Arts, The. The 1951 report of the Royal Commission on National Development in the Arts, Letters and Sciences—popularly known as the Massey Commission Report after its Chair, Vincent Massey—recommended to Parliament the creation of the Canada Council in order 'to foster and promote the study and enjoyment of, and the production in, the arts, humanities and social sciences.' Passage of The Canada Council Act by Parliament followed on 28 March 1957, with initial funding from an Endowment Fund of $100 million derived from the death duties of Nova Scotia industrialists Sir James Dunn and Izaak Walton Killam. In 1966 a parliamentary grant of $16.9 million was approved, which grew annually to represent in the early 1990s ninety per cent of the Council's budget. In the first year of operation, 1957-8, the Council dispensed grants and awards in the value of $1.4 million; in 1995-6 the Council distributed more than $84 million as follows: Dance ($10,075,000); Music ($14,847,760); Theatre ($14,889,000); Visual Arts ($5,447,250); Media Arts ($4,310,190); Writing and Publishing ($12,212,703); Touring Office ($4,021,324); Explorations Program—for innovative projects ($10,104,923); Arts Awards Service ($48,980); Art Bank ($48,980); Public Lending Right—payment to writers for the use of their books in Canadian libraries ($6,077,961). Research in the humanities and social sciences was founded by the Council until 1978, when the Social Sciences and Humanities Research Council of Canada was established. Heavy cuts in funding between 1992 and 1997 led to widespread protest; but there are now hopeful signs that more secure and equitable funding will be restored.

When the Council celebrated its fortieth birthday in 1997, writers, artists, and publishers throughout Canada praised it for so effectively and imaginatively carrying out its mandate—at arm's length from government. See also GOVERNOR GENERAL'S LITERARY AWARDS.

EUGENE BENSON

Canadian Authors' Association. It was established in 1921 to fight proposed copyright legislation that threatened to discriminate against Canadian writers. Its founders—Stephen LEACOCK, Pelham Edgar, B.K. SANDWELL, and John Murray Gibbon, who became its first president—anticipated a binational literary association. Pilloried by F.R. SCOTT in his famous satirical poem 'The Canadian Authors Meet' (1927), the CAA, as it soon became known, worked to develop a sense of cultural and literary solidarity among writers throughout Canada. The Association, composed of local branches across Canada, convened annually in the spring; it included a self-governing French Section that lasted until 1936, when planning for the Société des Ecrivains Canadiens (est. 1938) began. The CAA grew quickly to 750 members in its second year. Since then, its membership has remained constant and today numbers 775. In the early 1920s it lobbied successfully for changes in copyright legislation and kept its members informed in the pages of the *Canadian Bookman* (1921-2), edited by Sandwell, and successively in the *Authors' Bulletin* (1922-33), the *Canadian Author* (1933-40), the *Canadian Author and Bookman* (1940-92), and the *Canadian Author* (1992-). In an attempt to make Canadians more aware of the writers and books of their country, the CAA sponsored the first Canada Book Week in November 1921, which took place annually until 1957, and there were other literary initiatives. The poetry chapbooks of the different branches, privately printed in the late 1920s and early 1930s, culminated in the founding of *Canadian Poetry Magazine* (1936), which eventually merged with the *Canadian Author and Bookman* in 1968. The CAA was also responsible for the establishment in 1937 of the GOVERNOR GENERAL'S LITERARY AWARDS, whose administration by the CAA under a specially appointed Awards Board (est. 1944) lasted until 1959, when it was assumed by the CANADA COUNCIL. In 1946 the Awards Board was entrusted with the adjudication of the new Stephen Leacock Medal for Humour, which it administered until 1960, when responsibility for the award passed to the Stephen Leacock Society.

In 1946 the Association also undertook the preparation of a standard book contract, and secured from the federal government special income-tax provisions for writers. Since 1963 the CAA has administered the Vicky Metcalf Award (now $10,000), given in recognition of a significant body of work written for children; and, since 1979, the Vicky Metcalf Short Story Award, currently worth $3000. Beginning in 1975 the Association instituted the CAA Literary Awards (including a Silver Medal and a cash prize, presently $5000) in each of four fields: prose fiction, prose non-fiction, poetry, and drama. Since 1983 it has administered the Okanagan Short Story Award ($125), given quarterly, and the Student Creative Writing Prize ($500) for poetry, fiction, and essays or articles by full-time students at the high-school, college, or university level. Other awards are the Air Canada Award, and the Allen Sangster Memorial Award for long and distinguished service to the Association. Lyn Harrington's *Syllables of recorded time: the story of the Canadian Authors' Association 1921-1981*, was published in 1981. See also the WRITERS' UNION OF CANADA and the LEAGUE OF CANADIAN POETS.

JOHN LENNOX

Canadian Fiction Magazine (1971-). Beginning as a student publication in the Creative Writing Department at the University of British Columbia, *CFM* grew into an independent national journal. Since its first gestetnered issue it has fostered a national and international awareness of contemporary Canadian short fiction in both English and French, and in translation from the unofficial languages of Canada. The first editor was R.W. Stedingh (1971-4), and since 1975 it has been edited by Geoff Hancock, who will become editor emeritus at the end of 1997 while continuing to work on the magazine. In 1991 the magazine entered into partnership with QUARRY PRESS, Kingston; it became owner of the publication in 1996. Generous support from the Ontario Arts Council and the CANADA COUNCIL (up to $50,000 annually) enabled the magazine to continue publication for nearly three decades, until financial restraints led to a reformatting of the publication as a biannual anthology.

Many of the finest Canadian writers of short stories served their apprenticeship in the pages of *CFM*. It has published entire issues devoted to single authors (Robert HARROW, Jane RULE, Leon ROOKE, Mavis GALLANT); and *Canadian writers at work* (1987), edited by Geoff Hancock, is a selection of interviews.

Among some ambitious 300-page issues were 'Writers from Ontario', 'A decade of Quebec fiction', 'Latin American writers in Canada', and the fifteenth- and twentieth-anniversary issues. The *Silver anniversary anthology* of 1997, over 400 pages, includes many distinguished Canadian short-story writers, and some who rose from obscurity to international prominence during the magazine's first twenty-five years. GEOFF HANCOCK

Canadian Forum, The (1920). This 'independent journal of opinion and the arts', as its masthead proclaims, sprang from *The Rebel*, a periodical that had been started at the University of Toronto by students and professors—one of whom, Barker FAIRLEY, became the first literary editor of the *Forum*. While it has generally been on the left side of the political spectrum—its writers on political and social issues have included F.H. Underhill, Eugene FORSEY, and F. R. SCOTT—it has always complied with its editorial stance of being an independent forum for ideas and opinions, while also devoting space to poetry, fiction, and book reviews.

Canadian Forum has survived in spite of several economic crises, notably in the 1930s when it ceased publication for a few months, and then in the early 1970s. One further crisis in 1983 resulted in its displacement from Toronto when a new editorial board, based in Ottawa—the current place of publication—took over.

Because the *Forum* published the first work of many Canadian poets as well as new work by established writers, the monthly has been highly regarded by members of the Canadian literary community. In the early 1970s it started a policy of giving a double-page spread to new work by a different poet, and this has continued to the present. Among its editors and literary editors have been such writers and critics as Earle BIRNEY, Northrop FRYE, Milton Wilson, Peter STEVENS, and Tom MARSHALL. The present editor is Duncan Cameron.

See J.L. GRANATSTEIN and Peter Stevens, eds, *Forum: Canadian life and letters from 1920-70: selections from 'The Canadian Forum'* (1972).

PETER STEVENS

Canadian Literary Magazine*, *The (1833). An early cultural periodical, it was issued monthly between April and June 1833 in York (Toronto), Upper Canada. Its editor was John Kent, 'a gentleman recently arrived from England', its printer Thomas Dalton, and its publisher George Gurnett. Before the first number appeared on 6 Apr. 1833, Gurnett included in his newspaper, *The Courier of Upper Canada*, a prospectus and several advertisements about the 'Journal'. They announced its contents as articles on such subjects as the 'U.E. Loyalists' and 'News of the Literary World', invited contributions from 'provincial authors', and promised 64 pages and a 'lithograph engraving' in each number. The April issue had all these features; its 20 items included an introductory editorial, a description of Niagara Falls, three poems and a tale by Susanna MOODIE, a 'prize poem' by Henry Scadding, a review of a recently published sermon on the cholera epidemic of 1832 by Archdeacon George Jehoshaphat Mountain, and a sketch of the late Sir Walter Scott, accompanied by a lithograph 'engraved in Upper Canada . . . on Canadian Stone, and from thence, by means of a Canadian press, transferred to Canadian paper'. The succeeding two issues contained items by William 'Tiger' Dunlop and W.F. HAWLEY, and more poems by Moodie. The magazine, distributed in both Upper and Lower Canada, was well reviewed by newspapers in both provinces. Still, it ceased publication after the third issue—perhaps because its editor miscalculated the financial resources of the recently arrived well-educated English immigrants towards whom it was at least partly aimed. Nevertheless it was significant. As one of the first cultural periodicals in Upper Canada it provided an early Canadian outlet for the works of its new settlers. For example, Moodie's 'Oh can you leave your native land: a Canadian song', which appeared in the April issue, was the first 'Canadian' poem that she published. Furthermore, even though the magazine did not survive, its formula of mixing several types of articles on various subjects and encouraging local authors was similar to that used a few years later by the first really successful Canadian periodical, *The LITERARY GARLAND*.

The Canadian Literary Magazine is included in Tom Vincent's *Index to pre-1900 Canadian cultural and literary magazines*, which was issued as a CD-ROM in 1993. The periodical has been reproduced as a microfiche by the Canadian Institute for Historical Microreproductions.

MARY JANE EDWARDS

Canadian Literature (1959-). The first quarterly devoted entirely to the criticism and discussion of Canadian writing, it was founded by George WOODCOCK and published at the University of British Columbia. The introductory editorial of the first issue declared that 'it will not adopt a narrowly academic approach, nor will it try to restrict its pages to any school of criticism or class of writers.' This policy led to a wide variety of critical approaches, and to contributions not only from the most distinguished Canadian critics, but also from important writers in other fields, notably fiction and poetry. The same policy was continued by W.H. New, who took over the editorship when Woodcock resigned in 1977 after producing 73 issues. With Laurie Ricou and Eva-Marie Kröller as associate editors, New edited the journal until 1995, producing 72 issues. Kröller succeeded New in 1995, with Laurie Ricou, Margery Fee, and Iain Higgins as associate editors.

In 1995 the magazine underwent its first major design change: a narrower trim, one-colour covers, and more pages to accommodate a focus on such thematic subjects as post-colonialism, poetics, cultural history, postmodernism, literary censorship, and multiculturalism—as well as the much larger number of books published. The magazine also announced its intention to continue publishing some forty poems a year as part of its tradition as an 'in-between' literary periodical.

Essays from the magazine have been collected in a number of anthologies. *A choice of critics: selections from 'Canadian Literature'* (1966) and *The Sixties: Canadian writers and writing of the decade* (1969) are general selections. More specialized are *Malcolm Lowry: the man and his work* (1971); *Wyndham Lewis in Canada* (1971); *Poets and critics: essays from 'Canadian Literature' 1966-74* (1974); *Colony and Confederation* (1974); and *The Canadian novel in the twentieth century: essays from 'Canadian Literature'* (1975). All these volumes were edited by Woodcock, who wrote the introductions to them, except for *Colony and Confederation*, which was introduced by Roy DANIELLS. Other *Canadian Literature* anthologies are *Dramatists in Canada: selected essays* (1972), edited and introduced by W.H. New, and *Writers of the Prairies* (1973), edited and introduced by D.G. Stephens, who for a period was associate editor of the journal.

GEORGE WOODCOCK/GEOFF HANCOCK

Canadian Mercury*, *The (1928-9). This was 'A Monthly Journal of Literature and Opinion', published in Montreal, that was national in outlook and international in standards; it offered the reader serious poetry, fiction, commentary, and criticism. Seven issues appeared between Dec. 1928 and June 1929, when it collapsed with the stock market. Among its founding editors were F.R. SCOTT and Leo KENNEDY, who were members of the so-called MONTREAL GROUP, which introduced literary Modernism to Canada. In spirit, at least, *The Canadian Mercury* was an outlet for the writers who, as students at McGill University, had established the *Literary Supplement* (1924-5) to the *McGill Daily*, a student newspaper, and then its offshoot the *McGILL FORTNIGHTLY REVIEW* (1925-7). Other contributors to *The Canadian Mercury* were A.J.M. SMITH, A.M. KLEIN, John GLASSCO, and Leon EDEL (who in 1984 remembered it fondly, describing it as 'a kind of Quebec counterpart to the *Canadian Forum*').

JOHN ROBERT COLOMBO

Cape, Judith. Pseudonym of P.K. PAGE.

Cappon, James (1854-1939). Born in Dundee, Scotland, and educated at the University of Glasgow, he taught literature for two years at Geneva and then at Glasgow, where he wrote his first critical study, *Victor Hugo* (1885). In 1888 he became professor of English language and literature at Queen's University, Kingston, Ontario, and edited, and contributed articles frequently to, *Queen's Quarterly*. He was appointed the first dean of arts in 1906 and was elected to the Royal Society of Canada in 1917. His series of letters, collected as *Britain's title in South Africa* (1901), defended Britain's stand in the South African War.

Cappon's pamphlet *Charles G.D. Roberts and the influence of his times* (1905) was a milestone in Canadian literary criticism in placing a Canadian poet in his context. In it Cappon gives an overview of modern literary trends and traces in ROBERTS' work the Romantic influences of the early nature poetry through to the Pre-Raphaelite influences in the later poetry from the New York period, concluding with a carefully argued criticism of what he terms the lack of ethical centre that mars Roberts' work as a whole. This pamphlet was expanded to *Charles G.D. Roberts* (1925), a volume in the Makers of Canadian Literature series. Cappon wrote two other critical studies: *Bliss Carman and the literary currents and influences of his time* (1930) and *What classical education means* (n.d.). Cappon's critical writing is distinguished by its engagingly familiar yet scholarly style.

See also CRITICISM IN ENGLISH: 2.

JANET BAKER

Cardinal, Harold. See ABORIGINAL LITERATURE: 3.

Careless, J.M.S. (b. 1919). James Maurice Stockford Careless was born in Toronto, Ontario, and educated at the University of Toronto schools, the University of Toronto (B.A., 1940), and Harvard University (A.M., 1941; Ph.D., 1950). He joined the history department at the University of Toronto in 1945; on his retirement in 1984 he was appointed University Professor Emeritus. He was made an Officer of the Order of Canada in 1981 and named to the Order of Ontario in 1987.

After publishing *Canada: a story of challenge* (1953) which received a Governor General's Award, Careless proceeded to suggest new lines for historical inquiry, including the ways in which metropolis and hinterland had interacted in Canada's past. The concluding volume of *Brown of the Globe* (1959, 1963), where he convincingly demonstrated that the origins of nineteenth-century Canadian liberalism owed much to British antecedents, won a second Governor General's Award. In *The union of the Canadas, 1841-1857* (1967) Careless disentangled a complicated period fraught with conflicts. Developing an idea first expressed by Ramsay COOK, he maintained in an influential article in 1969 that excessive attention to the federal state had obscured more 'limited identities' through which Canadians had defined themselves. In advocating the intellectual pursuit of such concepts as region, class, and ethnicity, Careless opened the floodgates to a multiplicity of new historical approaches. Later he devoted himself to developing a sense of place in *Toronto to 1918* (1984), which won the City of Toronto Book Award, and *Frontier and metropolis* (1989).

Active in a variety of heritage organizations and chair of the Multicultural History Society of Ontario (1976-88), the Historic Sites and Monuments Board of Canada (1980-85), and the Ontario Historical Studies Series (1982-93), Careless has also published *Ontario: a celebration of heritage* (2 vols, 1991, 1992) and *Canada: a celebration of heritage* (2 vols, 1994, 1995). His essays are collected in *Careless at work* (1990) and his historical scholarship is examined in *Old Ontario* (1990), edited by D. Keane and C. Read. As adept at the podium as in print, and despite having had part of one arm amputated, Maurice Careless reminded audiences that while they might consider his name unfortunate for someone who headed Toronto's history department (1959-67), one of his predecessors had been George Wrong.

TERRY CROWLEY

Caribbean-Canadian literature in English. As recently as the 1960s, Caribbean-Canadian writing was not a recognized component of Canadian literature; and if it were, it would have comprised just one name, Austin CLARKE. Today it is: its long bibliography includes Neil BISSOONDATH, Dionne BRAND, Claire HARRIS, M. Nourbese PHILIP, Sonny LADOO, and Sam Selvon (1923-94), who immigrated to Canada in 1978, after twenty-eight years in the UK, to which he had immigrated from his native Trinidad in 1950—and numerous others discussed below. Their writing inevitably is *immigrant writing*, absorbed with the immigrant experience of adjusting to life in a new land, complicated by the writers' status in Canada and their colonial and post-colonial history as African or Chinese or Indian or Portuguese diasporans in the Caribbean. The writing is not homogeneous; the writers have identifiable distinctness, emanating from their intellectual and emotional individuality as well as from the historical and cultural particularities of their pockets of the complex Caribbean community.

For instance, to come from Clarke's, Brand's, or Philip's angry protest-writing, about their harsh experiences as members of racial minorities in Canada, to the poetry and fiction of Cyril Dabydeen is to be made quickly aware of Dabydeen's emphasis on the integrative rather than the confrontational. Though he is aware of the immigrant's plight in a country that he acknowledges 'still is a xenophobic place', his poems in *Coastland: new and selected poems 1973-1987* (1989) and his novels and stories (invariably preoccupied with socio-cultural and socio-historical issues) remain receptive to the possibilities of incorporating differences within himself. His novel *Dark swirl* (1989), set in the primordial, riverine region of Guyana that the distinguished Guyanese novelist Wilson Harris mythologizes, portrays the colonizer and colonized as an antithetical yet complementary binary.

Dabydeen differs from his fellow Guyanese-Canadians Arnold Itwaru and Sasenarine Persaud. Itwaru's poems—in his early volumes *Shattered songs* (1982) and *Entombed survivors* (1987)—are evocations of the immigrant's loneliness. Like Bissoondath's stories, Itwaru's poetry often omits specifics of place, time, or situation, and addresses feelings that are derived from immigrants' experiences but are not exclusive to them. Historical specificities, however, are much in evidence in *Shanti* (1988), a novel that, like Ladoo's *No pain like this body* (1972), is a portrait of the harsh existence of rural Indo-Caribbeans in the colonial period. Itwaru's *Closed entrances: Canadian culture and imperialism* (1994) is a polemical study of racial biases in Canada. Persaud's novels and poems are less about his experiences as an immigrant than about his life in Guyana. In his novel *Demerara telepathy* (1988) and *Between the dash and the comma* (1989), a collection of poems, he exhibits more than any other West Indian poet his acute consciousness of his Indian cultural heritage. His second novel, *The ghost of Bellow's man* (1992), examines a young writer's vocational insecurities against a backdrop of political corruption in Guyana after independence.

Other writers who made their mark in the 1980s include Lillian Allen, a member of the Toronto group *de dub* poets. *Rhythm an' hardtimes* (1982), a collection of *dub* poems with a feminist perspective, using the Jamaican vernacular in a way that recalls the Jamaican poet and short-story writer Louise Bennett. Two poets from Alberta are Nigel Darbasie, whose *Last crossing* (1988) examines class and ethnic conflicts on the Canadian prairie towns, and Brian Chan, whose *Thief with leaf* (1988) and *Fabula rasa* (1994) turn inward to themes of ephemerality, spirituality, and creativity. Ishmael Baksh's *Black light* (1988), the first West Indian example of the 'academic novel', is set in Memorial University, Newfoundland, with flashbacks to the Trinidadian-Canadian protagonist's early life in the Caribbean.

The 1990s saw the appearance of several new talents. Ramabai Espinet's *Nuclear seasons* (1991) is a collection of poems that examines from a feminist perspective the plight of the culturally dispossessed and the economically disadvantaged, in both Canada and Trinidad. She has published several books for children, including *The princess of Spadina: a tale of Toronto* (1992). The better stories in Shani Mootoo's first collection, *Out on main Street* (1993), are about characters coming to grips with their multiple cultural perspectives and identities—national, racial, and sexual. Her protagonists are not overly disturbed by their lack of self-identification; in fact they revel in their cultural fluidity and develop an ironic perception of the absurdity of cultural narrowness and exclusivity. Mootoo's first novel, *Cereus blooms at night* (1996), employs magic realism to explore the social and psychological experiences of several generations of an Indo-Caribbean family living on a fictional Caribbean island. H. Nigel Thomas's *Spirits of the dark* (1993), a first novel, is a Bildungsroman set in St Vincent that confronts issues of religious, racial, and—what is exceptional in Caribbean fiction—sexual identity and orientation. His collection of stories, *How loud can the village cock crow* (1995), draws on folklore in depicting various facets of island life. Kwame Dawes' poems in his first collection, *Progeny in air* (1994), treat growing up in Jamaica of the 1970s; his first novel, *Bivouac* (1997), explores how an artist in Jamaica copes with dislocation and impermanence. Rabindranath Maharaj's collection of stories in *The interloper* (1995) and his novel *Homer in flight* (1997) depict the ambivalence of recent immigrants caught between their old and new homes.

Many others writers have published the occasional poems, plays, or stories in Canadian and Caribbean little magazines and chapbooks, or in the anthologies devoted primarily to Caribbean-Canadian writing: Harold Head's *Canada in us now* (1976), Lorris Elliott's *Other voices* (1985), Cyril Dabydeen's *A shapely fire: changing the literary landscape* (1987), Ann Wallace's *Daughters of the sun, women of the moon: poetry by Black Canadian women* (1991), Ayanna Black's *Voices: 16 Canadian writers of African descent* (1992) and *Fiery spirits: a collection of short fiction and poetry by Canadian writers of African descent* (1994), and George Elliott CLARKE's *Fire on the water: an anthology of Black Nova Scotia writing* (2 vols, 1991, 1992) and *Eyeing the North Star: directions in African-Canadian literature* (1997).

See also MULTICULTURAL WRITING IN FRENCH. VICTOR J. RAMRAJ

Carleton Library. A paperback reprint series aimed at the secondary and post-secondary school markets but also endeavouring to appeal to the general reader, the Carleton Library was launched on 25 May 1963, a co-operative venture between Carleton University's Institute of Canadian Studies and McCLELLAND & STEWART. The series' original objective was to make available inexpensive editions of texts in Canadian history and the social sciences. To date volumes in the fields of history, politics, economics, sociology, geography, law, anthropology, business science, and media studies have appeared.

The Carleton Library is guided by a general editor, an associate editor, and an editorial board drawn from a variety of disciplines. MACMILLAN COMPANY OF CANADA and then Gage briefly took over as publisher in 1979 and 1980, producing about ten volumes before Carleton University Press assumed the responsibility. Since 1981 CUP has added some sixty titles, bringing the complete series to over 185 volumes, which are now distributed by Oxford University Press Canada.

JANET FRISKNEY

Carman, Bliss (1861-1929). William Bliss Carman, a first cousin of Charles G.D. ROBERTS and a distant relation of Ralph Waldo Emerson, was born in Fredericton, New Brunswick, and educated at the University of New Brunswick. He spent an unhappy year at Oxford and Edinburgh in 1882-3, and then tried various professions in Fredericton before attending Harvard University in 1886-8, where he met Richard Hovey (1864-1900), who later coauthored several books of poetry with Carman. At Harvard he attended the lectures of Josiah Royce and George Santayana, whose anti-materialistic philosophies he found congenial. He became a literary journalist in New York, first with a religious weekly, *The Independent*, and later in Boston, where he worked for *The Atlantic Monthly*, *The Chap-book*, and the Boston *Transcript*. On these and other periodicals, he helped

Canadian writers into print. In 1896 he met Mary Perry King, who became his lifelong patron and companion, and after 1908 he settled near the Kings in Connecticut. Although not a political activist, Carman during the First World War was a member of the Vigilantes, who supported American entry into the conflict on the Allied side. In 1921, terribly impoverished and recovering from a near-fatal bout of tuberculosis, he undertook the first of several strenuous poetry-reading tours across Canada, and was acclaimed as an unofficial poet laureate. He renewed his connection with the Maritimes with membership in The Song Fishermen, an informal group centred in Halifax and composed of local writers such as J.D. Logan and Charles BRUCE and ex-Maritimers such as Carman and Robert NORWOOD. He was elected a corresponding member of the Royal Society of Canada in 1925 and received the Lorne PIERCE Medal for distinguished service to literature in 1928 and honorary degrees from the Universities of New Brunswick and McGill; he was awarded posthumously the medal of the Poetry Society of America. Carman died in New Canaan, Connecticut, USA, following a reading tour, and his ashes were buried in Fredericton.

Like his cousin Charles G.D. Roberts, Carman was a poet of the Maritime landscape, a blend of forest, field, and sea that he employed both realistically and symbolically. He was the first Canadian poet to transform the external world into an interior, psychic landscape that delineated his characteristic moods—yearning, loss of love, melancholy, grief, and, on occasion, rapture. His particular sensibility was nurtured by Wordsworthian 'pantheism' and Emersonian transcendentalism, both of which emphasized humanity's oneness with the universe. He borrowed the Pre-Raphaelites' fondness for associating colours and emotions. He was attracted to contemporary *fin-de-siècle* Romanticism, which rejected the scientific rationalism of the age and sought reality in a visionary dream world whose symbols were drawn from art and nature. Having drifted from the Anglican faith, Carman recognized Nature as the source of his creative power and spiritual consolation. His poetry celebrates the 'kinship' he felt with all living things, and his work, particularly up to 1910, records his quest for a philosophical system to underpin his emotional experiences. Josiah Royce, Richard Hovey, and Mary Perry King provided Carman with the means of combatting his own melancholy with optimistic philosophies that would integrate the universe of art and the world of human experience.

A mystical vision in 1886 sustained Carman in his earliest volumes: *Low tide on Grand Pré: a book of lyrics* (New York, 1893), *Behind the arras: a book of the unseen* (Boston, Toronto, 1895), and *Ballads of lost haven: a book of the sea* (Boston, 1897). This experience is at the centre of his finest poem, 'Low tide on Grand Pré', in which the grieving speaker recaptures the timelessness and ecstasy of what may have been a past love affair. In these volumes Carman's voice, elegiac and gentle, observes the fragility of life, the passing of time, and the coming of death. In his collaboration with Hovey on *Songs from Vagabondia* (Boston, 1895; rpr. 1972, 1992), Carman found another 'voice', that of the literary vagrant whose back-to-nature heartiness and optimism had wide appeal and helped to initiate a revolt against the 'genteel tradition' that characterized much American poetry of the time. Hovey helped Carman to see how exaltation of the physical could lead to spiritual insights. The sequels include *More songs from Vagabondia* (Boston, 1896; rpr. 1972) and *Last songs from Vagabondia* (1901; rpr. 1972); and Carman by himself wrote *Echoes from Vagabondia* (1912). Turning to classical themes in the carefully organized *Sappho: one hundred lyrics* (1904), Carman produced several flawless and timeless songs, some of which are 'translations' and 'restorations' of Sappho while others are Carman's original poems. The figure of Pan, the goat-god, traditionally associated with poetry and with the fusion of the earthly and the divine, becomes Carman's organizing symbol in the five volumes issued between 1902 and 1905 and reprinted as *The pipes of Pan: containing 'From the book of myths,' 'From the green book of the bards,' 'Songs of the sea children,' 'Songs from a northern garden,' 'From the book of valentines'* (1906). His intention was to trace the religious and philosophical evolution of man through Pan's music.

Carman's search for a more substantial philosophy was aided by Hovey's wife, who introduced him to François Delsarte's theories of aesthetics in the teaching of dramatic expression through the co-ordination of the voice with bodily gestures and—in the United States—with gymnastics. Delsarte's complex interrelationships between the human faculties and sensations was called Unitrinianism. This became Carman's criterion for judging art; as he wrote, 'art approaches perfection in proportion as it charms our senses, convinces our intelligence, and elates or moves our spirit in something like equal degree. And a similar three-fold manner of thinking is my only criterion in the conduct of life. . . .' Thus Carman merged this philosophy with Mary Perry King's and his own notions about personality—which they drew from the Greek concepts of Truth, Beauty, and the Good—into a system in which a balance was achieved between the physical, the emotional, and the mental. In collaboration with Mrs King, Carman expounded these theories in a book of essays, *The making of personality* (1908); and in two dramas, *Daughters of dawn: a lyrical pageant or series of historical scenes for presentation with music and dancing* (1913) and *Earth deities, and other rhythmic masques* (1914). Occasionally his poems illustrating this theory are didactic. His later poetry retains the same subjects and themes, but the mystical and visionary characteristics are less prominent, and his language and rhythms are closer to colloquial speech; too often the sound is more important than the sense. After 1914 Carman's popularity was due to poems like the semi-religious 'Vestigia'; the ballad 'The ships of St. John'; 'The eavesdropper' and 'A northern vigil', with their haunted atmospheres; and his own elegy 'The grave-tree'. His later volumes include *April airs* (1916); *Later poems* (1921); and *Ballads and lyrics* (1923); *Far horizons* (1925); *Wild garden* (1929); and *Sanctuary* (1929).

In more than fifty volumes of poetry, Carman showed great versatility with musical cadences, and with poetic forms ranging from lyrics and dramatic monologues to meditations. Often accused of verbosity, he admitted his 'prolixity' and his problems in editing repetitive passages and trite language. Despite the early praise he received from poets such as Ezra Pound and Wallace Stevens, modernist poets and critics in Canada, particularly the MONTREAL GROUP, spent half a century torpedoing most of Carman's oeuvre. However, since the 1970s he has received more positive reappraisals. Contemporary poets such as Al PURDY, D.G. JONES, and Elizabeth BREWSTER have come to Carman's rescue, and recent critics have found much to admire in his poems.

Carman's essays include *The kinship of nature* (1903); *The friendship of art* (1904); *The poetry of life: Longfellow, Emerson, Swinburne* (1905), reprinted by R. West in 1973; *Address to the graduating class 1911 of the Unitrinian school of personal harmonizing* (1911); *James Whitcomb Riley* (1917; rpr. 1976); and *Talks on poetry and life; being a series of five lectures delivered before the University of Toronto, December 1925* (1926), transcribed by Blanche Hume. He edited *The world's best poetry* (10 vols, 1904; rpr. 1975); *The Oxford book of American verse* (1927; rpr. 1976); and *Our Canadian literature; representative verse, English and French* (1922), edited with Lorne PIERCE, then revised by V.B. Rhodenizer as *Canadian poetry in English* (1954; rpr. 1976).

Carman's poetry in print includes a selection in *Poets of the Confederation* (1960, NCL) edited and introduced by Malcolm Ross; *The poems of Bliss Carman* (1976, NCL) introduced by John Robert Sorfleet; and *Canadian poetry from the beginnings through the First World War* (1994, NCL) edited and with an afterword by Carole Gerson and Gwendolyn Davies.

See H.D.C. Lee, *Bliss Carman: a study in Canadian poetry* (1912); Odell Shepard, *Bliss Carman* (1923); James CAPPON, *Bliss Carman and the literary currents and influences of his time* (1930); Malcolm Ross, 'A symbolic approach to Carman', *Canadian Bookman*, 14 (Dec. 1932); Desmond PACEY, 'Bliss Carman' in *Ten Canadian poets* (1958); Donald Stephens, *Bliss Carman* (1966); John Robert Sorfleet, 'Transcendentalist, mystic, evolutionary idealist: Bliss Carman 1886-1894', in *Colony and confederation* (1974) edited by George WOODCOCK; Malcolm Ross, '"A strange aesthetic ferment"', *CANADIAN LITERATURE* 68-69 (Spring-Summer 1976); Robert GIBBS, 'Voice and persona in Carman and Roberts' in *Atlantic provinces literature colloquium papers* (1977) edited by Kenneth MacKinnon; D.M.R. Bentley, 'Pan and the Confederation Poets', *Canadian Literature* 81 (Summer 1979); *Letters of Bliss Carman* (1982) edited by H. Pearson Gundy; Terry Whalen, 'Bliss Carman', in *Canadian writers and their work: poetry series: volume two* (1983) edited by Robert Lecker, Jack David, and Ellen Quigley; Tracy Ware, 'The integrity of Carman's *Low tide on Grand Pré*', *Canadian Poetry* 14 (Spring/Summer 1984); D.M.R. Bentley, 'Threefold in wonder: Bliss Carman's *Sappho: one hundred lyrics*', *Canadian Poetry* 17 (Fall/Winter 1985); Barrie Davies, 'English poetry in New Brunswick 1880-1940', in *A literary and linguistic history of New Brunswick* (1985) edited and with an introduction by Reavley Gair; Mary McGillivray, 'Colour out of silence: a study of the poetry of Bliss Carman' (1985), Ph.D. dissertation, Queen's University, Kingston, Ontario; Muriel Miller, *Bliss Carman: quest and revolt* (1985); Malcolm Ross, *Bliss Carman and the poetry of mystery: a defense of the personal fallacy* (1985), reprinted in his *The impossible sum of our traditions* (1986); *Bliss Carman: a reappraisal* (1990) edited and with an introduction by Gerald Lynch; C. Nelson-McDermott, 'Passionate beauty: Carman's *Sappho poems*', *Canadian Poetry* 27 (1990); Gwendolyn Davies, 'The Song Fishermen: a regional poetry celebration', in *Studies in Maritime literary history*

(1991); and Thomas Vincent, 'Bliss Carman's "Low tides"', *Canadian Literature* 129 (Summer 1991). GEORGE L. PARKER

Caron, Jean-François. See DRAMA IN FRENCH 1981 TO 1996: 8.

Caron, Louis (b. 1942). Born in Sorel, Quebec, Caron worked at several occupations—broadcasting, public relations, and journalism—before publishing a selection of short stories and poems, *L'illusionniste suivi de Le guetteur* (1973). The first president of the Union des Écrivains du Québec and the author of many radio and television plays for Radio-Canada, Caron since 1976 has devoted his time completely to writing.

L'emmitouflé (Paris, 1977) won the French Prix Hermès and the Prix France-Canada. Certain changes made by the author appeared in the English translation by David Toby Homel (*The draft-dodger*, 1980); and a definitive French version soon followed (Seuil, 1982). Caron convincingly recreates the atmosphere of the 1917 Conscription Crisis and offers a point of view rarely heard or accepted in English Canada; namely, a sympathetic portrayal of a French Canadian refusing to fight in a war he does not believe in. The juxtaposition of the elderly Nazaire's experiences with those of his nephew Jean-François, a Franco-American conscientious objector to the Vietnam War, provides an ideological continuity within the francophone community: the nephew's recollections of events in his grandfather's life enable the reader to understand Nazaire's flight from the law and his subsequent alienation. Caron's talents as a storyteller were confirmed in *Bonhomme sept-heures* (1978), whose title is the Québécois equivalent of 'the bogeyman'. The imaginary world of children contrasts with the horror of the 1955 flooding of Nicolet; on a symbolic level the author alludes to death itself and the death of childhood in all of us.

Le canard de bois (1981), the first volume of a trilogy entitled 'Les Fils de la liberté', won the Prix France-Québec and was successfully adapted for television. Once again a parallel storyline contrasts two different generations of the same family. Hyacinthe Bellerose, a humble villager from Port Saint-François, finds himself inexorably drawn into the Rebellion of 1837-8 and is ultimately exiled for his part in the uprising. On another level we meet the rebellious fifteen-year-old Bruno Bellerose, who receives from his father's dying hands in 1935 a symbol of his link with previous generations: a duck carved from wood by his ancestor, Hyacinthe. *La corne de brume* (1982) describes Hyacinthe's exile in Australia and his return to Sorel fifty years later. The main focus of the plot, however, is Tim Bellerose, the Irish orphan adopted by Hyacinthe and left behind in the care of a Métisse, Marie-Moitié. Now a grown man, Tim bridles at the injustices committed against the Métis in 1855, and his obsessive anger at the English lumber companies' economic exploitation of French-Canadian lumberjacks ultimately leads to his drowning. The third volume of the trilogy, *Le coup de poing* (1990), plunges the reader into a recreation of the FLQ crisis of October 1970, where fictional characters replace those of history. As frustrated by injustice as was his outspoken relative, Hyacinthe, in 1837, Jean-Michel Bellerose is swept up in the tumultuous events following the kidnapping and killing of Pierre Laporte. He is pursued by the authorities, a result of his anger at the impact of the War Measures Act on his compatriots, and of his love for the land of his ancestors.

Caron's storytelling skills in this trilogy recall both Jacques FERRON and Roch CARRIER, while his concern for the common man, swept along despite himself by historical events, reminds us of SAVARD's epic *MENAUD MAÎTRE-DRAVEUR* (1937). In the tradition of DESROSIERS's *Les engagés du grand portage* (1939), Caron's saga of the Bellerose family brings to life colourful characters, and their milieu, with vividness and authenticity.

In *La tuque et le béret* (1992)—the first of a second series, 'Les Chemins du nord'—Félix Métivier's slowly evolving friendship with a visiting French painter, the young Henri Ramier, enables Caron to recall the dangerous way of life of the Quebec lumberjack at the turn of the century. In *Le bouleau et l'épinette* (1993), set in 1937-8, the middle-aged Ramier falls in love with the Amerindian Martha Bélanger who, like Métivier, reveals to the Frenchman the beauty and mysteries of the northern forest. In both these novels Caron speaks not only to his compatriots, but also to his wide French readership.

In 1984 the Montreal branch of the Société Saint-Jean-Baptiste awarded Caron the Prix Ludger-Duvernay for his writings, and in 1995 Caron's peers welcomed him to the Académie des lettres du Québec.

See also NOVELS IN FRENCH 1960 TO 1982: 3(c); 1981 TO 1996.

RAMON HATHORN

Carpentier, André. See FANTASTIC LITERATURE AND SCIENCE FICTION IN FRENCH.

Carr, Emily (1871-1945). Born in Victoria, British Columbia, she studied painting at the California School of Design in San Francisco (1891-3), in England (1899-1904), and Paris (1910-11); two of her paintings were hung in the prestigious Salon d'Automne in Paris in 1911. In the summer of 1898 she made the first of many trips to Native villages, travelling by steamer up the west coast of Vancouver Island to Ucluelet. Here the seed of what was to be a lifelong interest in West Coast Native people and culture germinated. In the summer of 1912 she made a highly productive trip to the remote Skeena River region and the Queen Charlotte Islands. In these Native villages Carr gathered a wealth of images and impressions that would be a recurring focus of varying intensity throughout her career as a painter. The bold colours and aggressive brush strokes that characterized her work when she returned from Europe, and her 'new' way of looking at things, were not well received by local people, who were unprepared for any deviation from the English landscape tradition. After 1913 she painted less and turned to other means of supporting herself, including running an apartment house, called Hill House, on her father's property in Victoria; raising sheepdogs; and making pottery. A turning-point came in 1927 when Carr received an invitation to be part of the National Gallery exhibition 'Canadian West Coast Art, Native and Modern' and travelled to Ottawa and Toronto, where she was greatly influenced by meeting with Lawren Harris and other Group of Seven artists. She revisited the Skeena River region and the Queen Charlottes in 1928, but a year later she abandoned her Native themes and concentrated on the British Columbia forests, which held a particular mystery for her.

From her many trips to Native communities and the remote regions of British Columbia, Carr drew creative inspiration for powerful paintings—huge, pulsating skies bursting with light and energy and intense sculptural forests—and for the journals and notes that she later used for her published sketches and stories. She began keeping a journal in 1927, recording ideas, themes, or impressions that could be reworked in paint. Always a good story-teller, she enrolled in a short-story correspondence course in 1926 and in another course at Victoria College in the summer of 1934. He first attempts at creative writing were aided by the constructive criticism of three 'literary' friends: Flora Burns, Ruth Humphrey, and Margaret Clay. After 1937, when Carr was often confined to bed as a result of several strokes and heart attacks, she turned seriously to writing. In 1940 some of her Native stories were read on the Canadian Broadcasting Corporation—first by Dr Garnet Sedgewick, head of the English Department at the University of British Columbia, and then by Ira Dilworth, a regional director of the CBC in Vancouver. With Dilworth's encouragement and assistance, she completed her first book, *Klee Wyck* (1941)—the title, meaning 'laughing one', is the name the Nuu-chah-nulth people gave her. This series of short stories, which won a Governor General's Award, describes with perception, warmth, wit, and originality aspects of British Columbia life, based on her visits to Native villages. The next year *The book of Small* (1942) was published. Like all Carr's books, it is autobiographical: describing her family life and nineteenth-century Victoria from the point of view of Emily Carr the child (nicknamed 'Small'). Her writing style —simple, clear, direct, gently humorous, and carefully pruned of all but essential elements, like her painting—was now clearly established. A few months after the publication of *The House of All Sorts* (1944), which describes entertainingly her period as a landlady and raiser of bobtail sheepdogs, she died. Her autobiography, *Growing pains*—written between 1939 and 1944 and which, by her request, was to be published posthumously—appeared in 1946. This engaging account of her life highlights particularly her art-school days in San Francisco and London.

Other posthumous books followed. *Pause: a sketch book* (1953) centres on Carr's 15-month convalescence in the East Anglia Sanatorium in Suffolk, England (1903-4). These humorous and sometimes poignant reminiscences of the people and events in the sanatorium, written thirty years later, are supplemented by drawings and doggerel verse. *The heart of a peacock* (1953) is a selection of stories and previously unpublished prose sketches edited by Ira Dilworth, whom she had made her literary trustee. Selections from Carr's journals, composed between 1927 and 1941, were combined in *Hundreds and thousands: the journals of Emily Carr* (1966) which, in recording her joys, challenges, disappointments, and her constant search for the means to understand and express the world around her, is marked by the vivid descriptions and touching honesty of her very personal style. *An address* (1955), with an introduction by Ira Dilworth, contains a memorable speech Carr gave on 4 Mar. 1930 before the Victoria Women's Canadian Club, which was celebrating her first exhibition in her native city. See also *Fresh seeing: two addresses by Emily Carr* (1972), with a preface by Doris Shadbolt and an introduction to the 1930 speech by Ira Dilworth. *Klee Wyck*, *The book of Small*, *The House of All Sorts*, *Growing pains*, *The heart of a peacock*, and *Hundreds and thousands* are all available in paperback and have been translated into several languages. *The Emily Carr omnibus* (1993) contains all Carr's previously published works, with an introduction by Doris Shadbolt.

Emily Carr's careers as both painter and writer are described in Maria TIPPETT, *Emily Carr: a biography* (1979); Doris Shadbolt, *The art of Emily Carr* (1979); Edythe Hembroff-Schleicher, *Emily Carr: the untold story* (1978); and Paula Blanchard, *The life of Emily Carr* (1987). Doris Shadbolt reassesses her earlier biography in *Emily Carr* (1990). Kerry Mason (Dodd) and Michael Breuer present excerpts from Carr's previously unpublished journals and letters together with photographs of her sketching locations in *Sunlight in the shadows: the landscape of Emily Carr* (1984). Letters from Carr are edited by Doreen Walker in *Dear Nan: letters of Emily Carr, Nan Cheney and Humphrey Toms* (1990).

More than a dozen fine exhibition catalogues have been produced (by Doris Shadbolt, Ian Thom, Christopher Varley, Ruth Appelhof, and others). A play, *The magnificent voyage of Emily Carr* (1992), was written by Jovette MARCHESSAULT, translated by Linda Gaboriau, and has been produced. Carr has also sparked the creation of poetry and documentary films. Her life, her writing, and her painting continue to stimulate much scholarly reasearch. World-wide, several Ph.D. dissertations and countless M.A. theses, as well as many articles, have focused on this remarkable woman. KERRY MASON

Carrier, Roch (b. 1937). Born in Sainte-Justine-de-Dorchester, a small village in the Beauce region of Quebec, Carrier studied at the Université de Montréal and the Sorbonne, Paris, where he wrote a doctoral thesis on the poetry of Blaise Cendrars. He has been secretary-general of the Théâtre du Nouveau Monde, Montreal, taught at the Collège Militaire St-Jean, and served a term, ending in 1997, as director of The CANADA COUNCIL. He is also a successful lecturer in both French and English; in the fall of 1982 he gave a series of lectures on Quebec literature in six west-coast American universities. He received the Prix de la Province du Quebec in 1964 for *Jolis deuils* and the Grand Prix de la Ville de Montréal in 1981.

With Michel TREMBLAY, Carrier is one of the most widely read Québécois authors in English Canada as well as in Quebec. Both authors express a humorous, ironic, sometimes sentimental view of Quebec life (rural for Carrier, urban for Tremblay), often adopting the viewpoint of childhood. Though certain themes recur in Carrier's work (nostalgia for Quebec's rural past, the reality of the dream world, a diffuse nationalism), it is much more varied, more ambitious than Tremblay's. Carrier has moved through different narrative styles to develop his themes; some have been more successful than others.

Carrier's earliest publications were poems and short stories. His first book was *Jolis deuils* (1964), a collections of fantastic and allegorical tales. A series of three novels followed: *La guerre, yes sir!* (1968; trans. 1970); *Floralie, où es-tu?* (1969; *Floralie, where are you?*, 1971); and *Il est par là le soleil* (1970; *Is it the sun, Philibert?*, 1972). *La guerre* is still Carrier's best-known and most popular work. It is a post-colonial, decolonizing work that dramatizes the linguistic and social violence of individuals and village life within the context of the Conscription Crisis of the Second World War. Carrier combines extreme bitterness against Les Anglais (who are uncomprehending and wooden British stereotypes) with the depiction of a warm and solid village life. The more dream-like *Floralie* goes back thirty years before this event to the wedding night of the parents of *La guerre*'s central character, combining a comic tale of religion and sex with nightmare. *Il est par là le soleil* is the dark story of a French-Canadian village boy confronting the horrors and corruption of work in Montreal.

One of the most important of Carrier's subsequent novels is *Le deux-millième étage* (1973; *They won't demolish me!*, 1974). It is one of the few with an urban setting. This was followed by *Le jardin des délices* (1975; *The garden of delights*, 1978). One of his most successful works, it is a rather Rabelesian, parodic story of the attempt by an unscrupulous profiteer to exploit the desires and credulity of a small town—but also a bitter exposé of the pettiness of those who would allow themselves to be exploited.

Il n'y a pas de pays sans grand-père (1979; *No country without grandfathers*, 1981) and *Les fleurs vivent-elles ailleurs que sur la terre* (1980) are both extended fables whose meaning finally refers to the activity of the writer. The first—which is more a statement of Carrier's literary and ideological affiliations than an original story—is a kind of twentieth-century re-write of

SAVARD's *MENAUD, MAÎTRE-DRAVEUR*. *Les fleurs* tells of how a very ordinary man's life was changed after his body was imprinted with rays from outer space: now he, like the writer, must 'tell and retell and retell' the story of his link with the beyond. *La dame qui avait des chaînes aux chevilles* (1981) is Carrier's most ambitious novel to date. A long, dense story of a woman's dream for revenge, it is harsh, bare, and intense. The strength of the novel, though, is severely prejudiced by the nature of the husband's unlikely crime—abandoning his baby in a snow-storm. Carrier's next novel, *De l'amour dans la feraille* (1984; *Heartbreaks along the road*, 1987), like *La dame*, received mixed reviews. It is a powerful political satire of life in Quebec under Premier Maurice Duplessis. Carrier's fiction since *De l'amour* includes two collections of stories, *La fleur et autres personnages* (1985) and *Prières d'un enfant très très sage* (1988), and the novels *L'homme dans le placard* (1991), *Fin* (1992), and *Petit homme tornade* (1996).

Les enfants du bonhomme dans la lune (1979) was translated as *The hockey sweater and other stories* (1979). The famous title story inspired *The sweater*, an animated short subject by Sheldon Cohen produced by the National Film Board. Carrier has continued to publish work directed to young people, such as *Les voyageurs de l'arc-en-ciel* (1980); *Le plus long circuit* (1993); *The longest home run*, 1993) is quickly becoming, like 'The hockey sweater', a children's classic.

Carrier has made stage adaptations of *La guerre, yes sir!* (1970)—an English translation was successfully produced at the Stratford Festival in 1972—and *Floralie* (1973); he has written several other plays, including *La céleste bicyclette* (1980), which, as *The celestial bicycle*, was produced in English at the Tarragon Theatre, Toronto, in 1982. Other plays include *Le cirque noir* (1982) and *L'ours et le kangourou* (1986).

The English translations of Carrier's work have been made by Sheila Fischman. In spite of the abundance of his diverse literary production over the last quarter-century, critical attention to the French editions of Carrier's books has slowly declined, presumably because of his federalist sympathies.

See Margot Northey, 'Sportive grotesque', *CANADIAN LITERATURE* 70 (Autumn 1976). See also DRAMA IN FRENCH 1948 TO 1981:3 and NOVELS IN FRENCH 1960 TO 1982: 3(b).

SHERRY SIMON/DAVID LEAHY

Carson, Anne (b. 1950). Born in Toronto, Ontario, and educated at the University of Toronto (B.A., 1974; M.A. 1975; Ph.D., 1980), she was professor of classics at the University of Calgary (1979-80), at Princeton University (1980-7), and at Emory University, Atlanta, Georgia, from 1987 to 1988, when she became professor of classics at McGill University, Montreal, Quebec.

A poet and essayist as well as a classical scholar, Carson uses the mixed genre, modernist fragment, and journal entry in an intensely personal quest to understand the nature and complexities of romantic love, family bonds, the self, and love of God. Her work—which has been championed by American writers Susan Sontag, Annie Dillard, and Guy Davenport—has appeared widely in the United States in leading literary journals such as *Grand Street*, and in *The New Yorker*, and her work has been reprinted in *The best American poetry 1990* and *The best American essays 1991*, and, in Canada, in a *Journey prize anthology*. Four books indicate the unusual range of Carson's writing: *Eros the bittersweet: an essay* (1986), a reading of Sappho that focuses on the meaning of erotic desire and its relation to pleasure and pain, a process that the English word 'bittersweet' inverts; *Short talks* (1992), a collection of prose poems that were later included in *Plainwater: essays and poetry* (1995); and *Glass, irony and God: essays and poetry* (1995).

For Carson, essays and poems may be written in either prose or verse. Her writing shows a wide range of influences: the Greek texts she has spent her life studying; experimental writers, including Gertrude Stein and Italo Calvino; European surrealism; the Catholic mystics; and Chinese poetry. Dense with literary and cultural allusions, her work creates a timeless space in which Carson's own spiritual and emotional concerns can exist along with the trials of Emily Brontë (in 'The glass essay', a long poem about a failed love affair) or Bashō's retreats from the world, which gloss her own pilgrimage through Spain in the rhapsodic 'Kinds of water: an essay on the road to Compostela'. At heart an experimental religious writer, with a rich knowledge of the Christian mystic tradition as well as an interest in Eastern religions, metaphysics in general, and psychoanalysis, Carson addresses both worship and doubt, and the difficulties of living in a world of divine immanence. Her sympathies are for marginal figures—outsiders, *isolatos*, lovers, pilgrims, penitents, the ill, and the old. Whether she is recreating some of the violent contradictions in ancient Judaism in the powerful poem 'Book of Isaiah', or recounting her own dislocation during a trip to Rome in 'The fall of Rome:

a traveller's guide', Carson remains a lapidary stylist, writing lyrical and reflective narratives of the pain of daily existence.

In 1996 Carson won the Lannan Literary Award, a $50,000 prize given by the Lannan Foundation, Los Angeles (the only other Canadian to win this award was Alice MUNRO). That a writer of Carson's importance should be almost unknown in her own country attests to the eccentricities of contemporary Canadian literary culture.

See Mary DI MICHELE, 'Interview', *MATRIX* 49 (1996). RICHARD TELEKY

Cartier, Jacques. See Writing in NEW FRANCE: 1.

Casgrain, Henri-Raymond (1831-1904). Born at Rivière-Ouelle, Lower Canada (Quebec), he was educated in Quebec City and ordained a priest in 1856. With Hubert LaRUE, Antoine GÉRIN-LAJOIE, and Joseph-Charles TACHÉ he was actively involved in the renascence of French-Canadian letters as co-founder of the MOUVEMENT LITTÉRAIRE DU QUÉBEC and of the periodicals *Les SOIRÉES CANADIENNES* (1861) and *Le FOYER CANADIEN* (1863). Casgrain devoted his entire life to history and literature and was one of the most prolific writers of the nineteenth century, sometimes using the pseudonyms 'Placide Lépine' and 'Eugène de Rives'. He benefited greatly from his lengthy visits to Paris, where his work at the Bibliothèque Nationale, and the associations he formed, helped to attract attention in the French intellectual community to Canada and its history. A founding member of the Royal Society of Canada (1882), he was its president in 1889.

Casgrain is best known as a historian, and he endeavoured to continue the work of F.-X. GARNEAU and J.B.A. Ferland. But he began his writing career with *Legendes canadiennes* (Québec, 1861), in which he retold French-Canadian folktales. He also wrote two books of poems, *À ma soeur Rosalie* (Québec, 1860) and *Les miettes: distractions poétiques* (Québec, 1869), of which fifty copies were printed; a work of literary criticism, *Chauveau* (Québec, 1872); *Silhouettes canadiennes* (Québec, 1872), a collection of literary profiles written in collaboration with J.-E.-E. MARMETTE and published under the pseudonym 'Placide Lépine'; and a series of eight biographies entitled *Biographies canadiennes* (Québec, 1875) on such figures as Champlain, Francis Parkman, his friend F.-X. Garneau, Antoine Gérin-Lajoie, and Philippe AUBERT DE GASPÉ. Casgrain's historical works are *Histoire de la Mère Marie de l'Incarnation* (Québec, 1864); *Histoire de l'Hôtel-Dieu de Québec* (Québec, 1878); *Une paroisse canadienne au XVIIe siècle* (Québec, 1880); *Un pèlerinage au pays d'Evangeline* (Québec, 1887); *La Société des Filles du Coeur de Marie, d'après ses annales* (Paris, 1889); the two-volume *Montcalm et Lévis* (Québec, 1891); *Une seconde Acadie; l'Île Saint-Jean—île du Prince Edward sous le régime français* (Québec, 1894); *L'Asile du Bon-Pasteur de Québec, d'après les annales de cet institut* (Québec, 1896); and *Les Sulpiciens et les Prêtres des Missions Etrangères en Acadie 1676-1762* (Québec, 1891). Casgrain also published the twelve-volume *Collection des manuscrits du maréchal de Lévis* (Québec and Montréal, 1889-95), in addition to leaving a massive correspondence with both foreign and Canadian authors. *Wolfe and Montcalm* (1905), a posthumous study written in English, is in the Chronicles of Canada series.

As a historian Casgrain was chiefly interested in heroic figures, striking portraits, and dramatic epochs. He preferred Lévis to Montcalm and considered *Montcalm et Lévis* to be his best work. Acadia fascinated him, as did the history of the early missionaries and clergy. Of an enthusiastic and romantic temperament, he nevertheless rid himself of the defects in style that had marred his early writings—an excessive use of figurative language, florid descriptions, and lack of taste—for his major works, which are marked by versatility, vigour, liveliness, controlled feeling, and fine composition—traits that contributed to Casgrain's gaining not only public acclaim but also the affection of the readers of his time.

Casgrain lived long enough to see publication of the three volumes of his *Oeuvres complètes* (Québec, 1873-5). He also collaborated on the publication of the *Oeuvres complètes* (1878-82) of Octave CRÉMAZIE.

MAURICE LEBEL

Caspar, Claudia. See NOVELS IN ENGLISH 1983 TO 1996: OTHER NOVELS 2(a).

Caswell, Edward (1861-1938). The son of a Methodist New Connexion missionary, he was born in Goderich, Canada West (Ontario). After working for a Lucknow newspaper, he joined the Methodist Book and Publishing House in 1881, two years into the lengthy tenure of the Rev. William Briggs as Book Steward. Working with men like E.H. DEWART and William WITHROW, Caswell rose steadily within the ranks. In 1892 he was appointed manager of the book-publishing operation and became a force in the editing of manuscripts and in communications with authors. His time as manager coincided with the emergence of the firm's commitment to Canadian nationalism and its increasing promotion of Canadian literature. Caswell did much of the editorial work and prepared many of the letters that William Briggs signed; he was influential in the publication of works by Catharine Parr TRAILL, Nellie McCLUNG, Robert SERVICE, William Wilfred CAMPBELL, Charles G.D. ROBERTS, and Isabella Valancy CRAWFORD. Though he left the MBPH in 1908 for a better-paying position as assistant librarian and secretary-treasurer of the Toronto Public Library, his commitment to promoting and developing Canadian literature continued until his death. During these years he was co-publisher with Willet Haigt of editions of John RICHARDSON's *WACOUSTA* and *The war of 1812* and William Dunlop's *Recollections of the war of 1812*; the editor of the first Canadian edition (1929) of Traill's *The backwoods of Canada*; an essayist and active promoter of Canadian writing; a leading figure in Toronto arts organizations, debating societies, and the Canadian Club; and the editor of his own collection, *Canadian singers and their songs* (1902).

See Michael Peterman and Janet Friskney, '"Booming" the Canuck book, Edward Caswell and the promotion of Canadian writing', *Journal of Canadian Studies*, 30 (Fall 1995); Janet Friskney, 'Beyond the shadow of William Briggs, Part II', *Papers of the Bibliographical Society*, 35 (Fall 1997).

MICHAEL PETERMAN

Cather, Willa. See FOREIGN WRITERS ON CANADA IN ENGLISH: 2.

CEECT. See CENTRE FOR EDITING EARLY CANADIAN TEXTS.

Censorship. Although censorship in Canada of books, plays, films, and television has been relatively benign, it has been based primarily on moral or religious grounds, and only rarely on political ones. In 1694 Bishop Saint-Vallier's suppression of Molière's *Tartuffe*, and the excommunication of the lead actor for blasphemy, foreshadowed the frequently diverging views of religious authorities and the civil courts from Confederation to the present.

The advent in the 1880s of touring theatrical companies, and the rapid growth of theatres, introduced Canadian audiences to values and opinions that frequently clashed with those of the local community. Sarah Bernhardt's first visit to Montreal in 1880 sparked controversy as Bishop Fabre urged Catholics to avoid attending *Adrienne Lecouvreur* because of its adulterous theme, and asked city council to cancel her two performances on Christmas Day. Bernhardt returned to Montreal in 1905, offering her most recent Paris success, *La sorcière*, with its anti-clerical interpretation of the Spanish Inquisition. This provoked two pastoral letters by Archbishop Bruchési—whose episcopate was characterized by his preoccupation with the moral authority of the Church in the midst of the rapidly changing society of French Quebec—and one by the Archbishop of Quebec who, after Bernhardt's departure, insisted that Catholics refrain from attending Quebec City's Auditorium until a censorship committee was established some weeks later to approve choices of repertory. Bruchési's continuing campaign against immorality on the stage in the next few years culminated in the appointment of Montreal's first theatre censor, Jean-Paul Filion, in July 1913.

In Toronto during the same period, the Protestant clergy of several denominations kept a watchful eye on theatrical events. In 1898 the Methodist Church of English Canada formally forbade attendance at plays, though its stand softened dramatically by 1914. The Reverend John Coburn, a prominent Methodist, spearheaded the creation of the Committee of Forty, whose aim was to clean up the city's theatres and presentations of dubious morality. In December 1913 William Banks was appointed theatre censor by the Police Commission. His refusal to suppress Legrand Howland's *Deborah*, portraying an unmarried mother, was contested unsuccessfully in court by Coburn. The following year, however, Banks refused to allow the production of Bernard Shaw's *The shewing-up of Blanco Posnet* because of 'blasphemy, profanity and language of the lowest type'. In 1926 the censor, H.M. Wodson, ordered cuts made in the script of Hastings' *Scotch mist*, but allowed the play to be performed, despite the objections of many clerics who described it as 'an apology for adultery'.

Writers of fiction also came under the watchful eye of Archbishop Bruchési. In 1904 he condemned Rodolphe GIRARD's novel *MARIE CALUMET*, whose protagonist is an earthy, irreverent, and somewhat anti-clerical housekeeper living in a country parish. The author was dismissed from his position as a reporter at *La Presse*. Although Girard won a judgement in 1912 for libel against *La Vérité*, a conservative Catholic paper that supported the Archbishop's denunciation of his novel, Girard's reputation as a writer was undermined by this controversy. Five years later, Albert LABERGE read a short story to members of the ÉCOLE LITTÉRAIRE DE MONTRÉAL, which was published soon after. An allusion to masturbation was described by Bruchési in a vigorous public denunciation as 'ignoble pornography'; Laberge subsequently published this excerpt as a chapter in his novel, *La SCOUINE*, which he read only to close friends in private because he feared further controversy—and published at his own expense. The condemnation of Jean-Charles HARVEY's *Les demi-civilisés* in 1934 provides the most striking example of religious and political censorship of a fictional work. In this novel of social criticism, Harvey—a former Jesuit and reporter with *La Presse* and *La Patrie*, and editor at *Le Soleil*—condemned the control of Quebec's economy by English businesses, the exploitation of the working class, as well as the power of the Quebec clergy in all spheres, and particularly the Church's betrayal of the spirit of the Gospel message. Swift retribution followed. Cardinal Villeneuve officially placed Harvey's novel on the Index, expressly forbidding the ownership, purchase, sale, or reading of this book. Fired immediately by *Le Soleil*, Harvey publicly withdrew his novel from circulation. Promised the directorship of the Legislative Library by the government in power, he was appointed instead to the Department of Statistics, because of the Cardinal's interference. Three years later, on the election of Maurice Duplessis, he was fired from his civil-service post.

Political censorship in Canada as a whole has been relatively rare and directed primarily at plays. In 1933 *Eight men speak*, produced collectively by the Workers' Experimental Theatre of Toronto, protested against the imprisonment of eight members of the Communist Party of Canada and the alleged attempted murder in prison of Party leader Tim Buck. The Toronto Police's 'Red Squad' closed the play after its first and only performance. In 1936 Vancouver police and city authorities threatened to revoke the licence of the Ukrainian Labour Temple for performing Clifford Odets' *Waiting for Lefty*. In 1970 Pierre Vallières wrote his autobiographical essay *Les nègres blancs d'Amérique* while in prison on charges of sedition. The book was confiscated and an edition printed in France was refused entry to Canada. In 1971 George RYGA's *Captives of the faceless drummer*, with its explicit analogies to the FLQ crisis, aroused controversy when the board of the Vancouver Playhouse refused to allow its performance, which finally took place at the Vancouver Art Gallery in April of the same year.

Obscenity in books and theatrical performances is an offence under Section 163 of the Criminal Code, while Section 167 refers to Immoral Theatre Performances, which include strip shows, and more recently, lap-dancing. Sexuality on stage has attracted the attention of both police and politicians, particularly since the Second World War. In 1953 Vancouver police arrested five actors on stage during a performance of *Tobacco Road*; subsequent legal wrangling caused the Everyman Theatre Group to fold. The Vancouver Playhouse Theatre withdrew a planned performance of *Hair* in 1969 when the city's Licensing Inspector threatened to cancel its licence for allowing nude scenes on stage; in the same year Michael McClure's *The beard* was closed by the Vancouver morality squad, management and actors being fined for presenting 'an obscene performance'. Toronto police authorities, however, allowed full nudity in a 1970 production of *Hair* on condition that the lights be dimmed, and in 1983 they tolerated the nude review *Oh! Calcutta!* Changing sexual mores and official tolerance characterized the 1970s; in Montreal, religious attitudes were equally evolving. Denise BOUCHER's *Les FÉES ONT SOIF* (1978), a feminist critique of the cult of the Virgin Mary, provoked indignation among conservative Catholics. However, in 1980 the Supreme Court of Canada refused to hear charges of blasphemy brought by them against the play.

Obscenity in books imported into Canada comes under the purview of the federal government—which, since 1867, has given customs officers broad powers to prevent certain foreign publications from entering the country. The Department of National Revenue banned *Ulysses* in 1923, and three books by the American novelist James Farrell in the 1940s; by 1949 the list of banned books contained more than 500 titles, including those of such prominent writers as Faulkner, Maupassant, Steinbeck, and D.H.Lawrence. In 1989 a temporary embargo was placed by customs on Salman Rushdie's *The Satanic verses*. In the 1980s and 1990s customs routinely targeted gay literature—which, if judged by customs officers to be obscene, was either destroyed or returned to the shipper. The 1994 challenge to the control of customs officials over imported books by the Little Sister's bookstore of Vancouver was partially upheld by Justice Smith; his suggestion that the administration of the

Customs Act be improved will see an appeal carried forward to the British Columbia Court of appeal and ultimately to the Supreme Court of Canada.

In recent years the censorship of books has become extremely complex. School officials, parents, and frequently religious groups have brought about the banning of a wide range of titles and authors—including Margaret ATWOOD, Alice MUNRO, Margaret LAURENCE, and Hugh MacLENNAN, whose writings have been removed from school reading lists. And childrens' literature is not exempt from scrutiny: Robert MUNSCH's *Giant, or waiting for the Thursday Boat* (1989), for example, has been banned from some primary schools for depicting violence, the giant in the story threatening to pound God 'until he looks like apple sauce.' If criminals write books describing their crimes, Ontario's Bill 210 will prevent them from having access to royalties; a committee of provincial officials, the Uniform Law Conference, has been asked to draft similar legislation that might be adopted by other provinces. 'Libel chill' and 'political correctness' have become significant factors in the writing or accepting of a manuscript for publication, while the concept of 'appropriation of voice' (authors writing about a culture or race different from their own) has led at least one Canadian publisher (Women's Press) to refuse to publish manuscripts 'in which the protagonist's experience in the world is substantially removed from that of the writer.' In response to the growing threat of censorship, the Book and Periodical Council of Canada in 1996 published a guide for teachers, librarians, and booksellers: *When the censor comes*. Finally, the technological phenomenon of the Internet, which provides unfettered access to information of all kinds, will provide governments and courts, both in Canada and elsewhere, with new challenges in the field of censorship.

See Peter Birdsall and Delores Broten, *Mind war: book censorship in English Canada* (1978); *Freedom to read week 1997* (1997; published by the Book and Periodical Council of Canada); Ramon Hathorn, 'Censorship', *The Oxford companion to Canadian theatre* (1989); L.W. Conolly, 'Censorship (Canada)', *Encyclopedia of post-colonial literatures in English* (1994); and Ramon Hathorn, *Our lady of the snows. Sarah Bernhardt in Canada* (1996).

RAMON HATHORN

Centre for Editing Early Canadian Texts. A project begun at Carleton University, Ottawa, in 1979, whose objective has been to prepare and publish scholarly editions of major works of early Canadian prose that were either out of print or available only in corrupt editions. The General Editor of the CEECT is Mary Jane Edwards, Carleton University, who is assisted by an editorial board and a team of distinguished advisers; the project has received long-term funding from the Social Sciences and Humanities Research Council of Canada and from Carleton University.

The text of each scholarly edition in the CEECT series is established only after the history of the composition and first publication of the work has been researched and the various versions analysed and compared. Each edition has an editorial introduction with a separate section on the text and accompanying scholarly apparatus. In the case of Thomas Chandler HALIBURTON's *The clockmaker series one, two, and three*, edited by George L. Parker and published in 1995, this apparatus includes illustrations, explanatory notes, bibliographical description of copy-texts, a list of published versions of the text, emendations in copy-texts, line-end hyphenated compounds in copy-texts, line-end hyphenated compounds in the CEECT edition, historical collation, and a reproduction of the advertisement for the first edition.

Ten works in the series have been published to date (1996): Frances BROOKE, *The history of Emily Montague*, edited by Mary Jane Edwards (1985); Catharine Parr TRAILL, *Canadian Crusoes*, edited by Rupert Scheider (1986); James DE MILLE, *A strange manuscript found in a copper cylinder*, edited by Malcolm Parks (1986); John RICHARDSON, *WACOUSTA*, edited by Douglas R. Cronk (1987); Susanna MOODIE, *ROUGHING IT IN THE BUSH*, edited by Carl Ballstadt (1988); Rosanna LEPROHON, *Antoinette De Mirecourt*, edited by John C. Stockdale (1989); Thomas McCULLOCH, *The Mephibosheth Stepsure letters*, edited by Gwendolyn Davies (1990); Julia Catherine Beckwith HART, *ST. URSULA'S CONVENT*, edited by Douglas G. LOCHHEAD (1991); John Richardson, *The Canadian brothers*, edited by Donald Stephens (1992); and Haliburton's *The clockmaker*, described above. Other volumes are forthcoming.

EUGENE BENSON

Chamberland, Paul (b. 1939). Born in Longueuil, Quebec, he was educated at the Séminaire St-Croix and the Collège St-Laurent. Later he studied philosophy at the Université de Montréal and in 1963 was one of the founding members of *PARTI PRIS*. He also worked on a doctoral thesis at the Sorbonne under the supervision of Roland Barthes. In an act of revolutionary zeal during the turmoil of the 1968 student uprising in Paris, he deliberately destroyed the completed version of his thesis.

From his first collection of poems, *Génèses* (1962), to his most recent works, Chamberland has pursued specific themes. Fire—viewed not only as the supreme generator, an element that unites spirit and matter, but also as a man-made creation capable of producing a nuclear holocaust—is a central image and symbol. Since this work, which features the forge, hammer, and anvil of revolt, it is evident that both social and political explosions are at the core of his concerns. With *L'afficheur hurle* (1964)—a poem that is a cry, a howl, a shout of dereliction—and *L'inavouable* (1968), the poem becomes an angry, aggressive act of rupture, confirming Chamberland's statement that 'poetry is subversive or it is not poetry' (*parti pris* Feb. 1966, p. 59). The subversion here is twofold: as a political statement the poem upholds the right of the Québécois people to self-determination and an egalitarian society; as a text it rejects aestheticism, formal perfection, and good taste. 'I am proud to write badly,' he affirms in *L'afficheur hurle*. Yet for all of Chamberland's rejection of the canons of standard French, of poetic humanism, he never really adopted *JOUAL* as a mode of expression.

The reading of Karl Marx and Frantz Fannon seems to have played a formative role in Chamberland's early years (1963-8). But in the 1980s his ideological trajectory moved from a revolutionary Marxist viewpoint, centred on the necessity of armed struggle, to a more spiritual vision. Indeed, one notices in his writings of the seventies an element of social justice and balance that implies inner peace and personal change. Other changes—the shifts of focus from Quebec to the planet Earth, and from nationalistic values to Utopian aspirations, appearing as early as 1972 in *Éclats de la pierre noire d'où jaillit ma vie*—were emphasized by his participation in the counter-culture magazine *Hobo Québec* during the 1970s and were developed in *Demain les dieux naîtront* (1974), *Le Prince de Sexamour* (1976), *Extrême survivance, extrême poésie* (1978), *Terre souveraine* (1980), and *L'enfant doré* (1981). Love as the motivating force capable of generating global changes is first defined as a bond uniting man and woman; next it is viewed from a homosexual perspective; then it is expressed as love of children, of the fragile and the innocent, before being turned into a sentiment that encompasses all humanity. Yet all of these volumes anticipate an apocalypse, an unavoidable millennium, the imminence of man-made destruction as well as the promise of a new age.

Stylistically Chamberland's poems move from conventional typographic texts, organized in lines and stanzas, to montages of calligraphic poems strewn with newspaper clippings, photographs, quotations, rock-singers' lyrics, philosophers' thoughts, and news items. The attempt to fuse diverse elements has been viewed as a reflection of their author's apocalyptic consciousness.

L'afficheur hurle is Chamberland's most frequently translated text. Malcolm Reid published a translation in *The shouting sign painters* (1972) and C.P. May translated extracts in *Ellipse* 8-9 (1971) under the title 'The poster-hanger howls'. Larry Shouldice translated other poems in *Ellipse* 17 (1975). One of Chamberland's most famous critical essays, a political and critical commentary on the situation of Quebec poetry in the 1950s and 1960s, was translated by Larry Shouldice as 'Founding the territory' and appeared in *Contemporary Quebec criticism* (1979).

Like many writers of the generation of the Quiet Revolution, Chamberland published numerous articles in periodicals such as *Les Herbes Rouges*, *Estuaire*, LIBERTÉ, including (as in the case of Gaston MIRON) some rewritings. He also ventured into other forms of communication, as in his 'book on tape' *Lointaine terre d'amour* (1992), and he collaborated on the making of movies, participated in the organization of a 'Nuit de la poésie', and the Premier festival de l'Archipel des poètes francophones, in 1991.

Like many intellectuals, particularly poets, Chamberland is sensitive to the precarious nature of contemporary life, which he represented in a number of short texts/poems gathered under the title *Aléatoire instantané et midsummer 82* (1983). That same year he published *Un partis pris anthropologique*, focusing on the major issues of the Quiet Revolution (ideology, definition of the term 'nation', autonomy, separation), and *Le recommencement du monde: méditations sur le processus apocalyptique*, which centres on issues of humanity and civilization, and on the end of the world. With books of poems such as *Compagnons chercheurs* (1984), *Phoenix intégral suivi de Après Auschwitz. Poèmes (1975-1987)* (1988)—which is influenced by Lyotard's and Adorno's idea that after Auschwitz the world as we knew it changed—the text of his speech to the Union des Écrivains québécois was also published: *Mise à distance de toute technologie* (1984). His essay *Ouverture pour un livre de morale. L'incest et le génocide* (1985) anticipates his analysis of contemporary society in *Un livre de morale: essais sur le nihilisme contemporain* (1989), which addresses the question from an ethical point of view. But Chamberland never loses sight of the question of Quebec nationalism, as can be seen in his essay 'L'indépendance est pour 1993' (first printed in *The Massachusetts Review*, Spring 1990, and reprinted in *Les grands textes indépendantistes* [1992]' co-edited by Gaston Miron and Andrée Ferrretti), where he analyses the connections between ethics and politics centred on the notion of cultural identity.

Chamberland was awarded the Prix Édouard-Maurick (Île Maurice) in 1991, which coincided with the publication of *Le multiple événement terrestre, Géogrammes 1*. He currently teaches at the Université du Quebec à Montréal.

See Richard Giguère, 'Chamberland, poète anthrope', *Lettres québécoises* 23 (automne 1981).

CAROLINE BAYARD/FRANCESCA BENEDICT

Champagne, Dominic. See DRAMA IN FRENCH 1981 TO 1996: 8.

Champlain, Samuel de. See Writing in NEW FRANCE: 1.

Chan, Brian. See CARIBBEAN-CANADIAN LITERATURE.

Chapman, William (1850-1917). Born in Saint-François-de-la-Beauce, Canada East (Quebec), he studied at the Collège de Lévis and enrolled in the law school of Université Laval but never completed his courses. He became a businessman, an insurance broker, and then a journalist with *La Patrie* in 1883, and with *La Minerve* from 1884 to 1889; he also wrote for *La Vérité* and *Courrier du Canada*.

Chapman wrote six books of poetry: *Les Québecqoises* (Québec, 1876), *Les feuilles d'érable* (Montréal, 1890), *À propos de la guerre hispano-américaine* (Québec, 1898), *Les aspirations* (Paris, 1904), *Les rayons du nord* (Paris, 1910), and *Les fleurs de givre* (1912). A belated romantic of the Quebec school, he was inspired both by his compatriots Octave CRÉMAZIE and Louis FRÉCHETTE and by Hugo, Gautier, Lamartine, François Coppée, and Longfellow—some of whose poems he translated. Preferring occasional verse to religious or love poetry, he never strove to perfect his craft: his thought lacks sustained elevation and his ponderous, wordy stanzas—chiefly alexandrines—are rarely lyrical or tender. He began with patriotic verses addressed to France, but gradually became fervently inspired by the landscapes of his native land: his best descriptions are of open spaces and of nature seen as violent and savage. Among his best poems are 'Janvier', 'La forêt vierge', 'Le lac dans les bois', 'Coucher de soleil', 'Le laboureur', 'La Beauce', 'L'Île d'Orléans', 'Le Saguenay', and 'Le Saint-Laurent'.

Chapman's prose works, apart from his many magazine articles, include *Mines d'or de la Beauce* (Lévis, 1881); *Guide et souvenir de la St. Jean-Baptiste, Montréal* (Montréal, 1884); and two bitter attacks on the work of Louis Fréchette: *Le lauréat manqué—critique des oeuvres de M. Louis Fréchette* (Québec, 1894) and *Deux copains: réplique à Mm. Fréchette et Sauvalle* (Québec, 1894). Truculent, easily offended, irascible and violent, often narrow-minded and petty in his critical writing, Chapman was given to a polemical, flashy, and gradiloquent style that lacked taste and critical judgement.

MAURICE LEBEL

Charbonneau, Jean (1875-1960). Born in Montreal, the son of a carpenter, he was educated at the Collège Sainte-Marie and studied law at Université Laval. He later practised law and then pursued other activities. One of the founders of L'ÉCOLE LITTÉRAIRE DE MONTRÉAL, he is chiefly remembered for his poetry, but he was also the author of an important work on philosophy. The theatre was Charbonneau's first and persistent love and he wrote at least three (unpublished) plays: 'Zopyre' (1904), 'Les Emmurés' (1910), and 'La Mort de Tristan et d'Iseut' (n.d.). He published his first poem in *Le Samedi* under the pseudonym 'Delagny' (he later appeared as an actor under the same name). His first poetry collection, *Les blessures* (Paris, 1912), was attacked by the Catholic weekly *La Vérité* as a threat to Christian belief, though its rather formal stanzas constitute chiefly a recall to classicism. The wounds of the title are ascribed in part to an 'unknown evil', but the main thrust of the often poignant stanzas is against the breach between past and present. *Les blessures* was followed by similar volumes: *L'âge de sang* (Paris, 1921), in which Charbonneau juxtaposes the hopes of civilization against the blood of the First World War, and *Les prédestinés* (1923), concerned with the idea and images of America and thought to be his best work. *L'ombre dans le miroir* (1925) speaks of the fountain of youth, and *La flamme ardente* (1928), perhaps his most metaphysical collection, is concerned with the discovery of the invisible world and the structure of visible nature. Charbonneau also published two other volumes of poems: *Tel qu'en sa solitude* (1940) and *Sur la borne pensive et L'ecrin de Pandore* (Paris, 1952). *Solitude*'s title suggests its theme, while *Pandore* is a long mythological poem that fills the second half of a volume whose other contents are varied. There are many unpublished poems in the archives at the Université d'Ottawa, as well as the manuscript of a novel, 'Tentative d'évasion', and a collection of prose writings, 'À l'ombre de l'oasis'.

Charbonneau's affiliations were strongly classical. In *L'École littéraire de Montréal* (1935) he recalls the literary movement as a revolt against the undisciplined romanticism that he and many of his friends thought to be widespread in both France and Quebec. He sought a poetry less personal and more knowledgeable, and his inspiration was the Parnassian movement in France, which insisted on strict forms.

In *Des influences françaises au Canada* (3 vols, 1916-20)—for which he was made a laureate of the Académie française in 1922—Charbonneau deals at length with the state of philosophy in France and then with the situation in Canada, and attempts to associate philosophical tendencies and climates with social trends. He argues that there is a continuing tradition in Western civilization, which French thought had lost track of, that persists best, perhaps, in Quebec. His philosophy has a Stoic tinge to it, though he appreciated Nietzsche and kept up with all the currents of European thought on visits to France. LESLIE ARMOUR

Charbonneau, Robert (1911-67). Born in Montreal, he began his studies at the École Saint-Stanislas (1919-25) and continued at the Collège Sainte-Marie (1925-33), working during summer vacations as a labourer for the Canadian Pacific Railway. In 1933 he joined the Young Canada Movement. After a year of studies at the Université de Montréal, he received a diploma in journalism (1934). With Paul Beaulieu he founded *La* RELÈVE (1934-40), a literary review influenced by Jacques Maritain's neo-Thomism and E. Mounier's Personalism. During this period of the Depression the review proposed a humanistic transformation of the individual rather than social revolution.

To earn a living Charbonneau first worked as a journalist on *La Patrie* (1934-7), *Le Droit* (1937-8), and *Le Canada* (1938-42). In 1940 he founded, with Claude Hurtubise, Les Éditions de l'Arbre, which republished literary works that were prohibited in Occupied France and young French-Canadian writers such as Roger LEMELIN, Jean-Jules RICHARD, and Yves THÉRIAULT. An affiliation with *La Relève* produced *La Nouvelle Relève* (1941-8). From here on Charbonneau divided his time between editing and writing. While convalescing from pleurisy in 1936 he had begun work on his first novel, *Ils posséderont la terre* (1941; new edition 1970), for which he was awarded the Prix David. This work launched a series of psychological novels that were popular with the intellectuals of the forties and fifties. In an essay entitled *Connaissance du personnage* (1944), Charbonneau made known his aesthetic and philosophical positions, explaining that a novel's role was not to reflect an era or a society, but to emphasize man's spiritual quest, his search for identity. He developed this theme in such novels as *Fontile* (1945) and *Les désirs et les jours* (1948), which describe interior conflicts and the personal dramas of characters in search of an authenticity that eludes them. Their refusal to make a choice, their fear of action, their paralysis of will—making existence impossible—are typical concerns of the psychological novel about 'la vie intérieure', whose passive, forever inward-looking heroes cannot respond to worldly conventions.

Apart from his activities as editor and well-known writer (he received the Prix Duvernay for *Fontile* in 1945), Charbonneau helped found and direct the Académie canadienne-française (1944). As president of the Société des éditeurs (1945-8) he was a staunch supporter of French-Canadian literature, which he defended in a series of articles—later published in *La France et nous* (1947; new edition 1993)—that placed him in opposition to certain French intellectuals. He also published a poetry collection, *Petits poèmes retrouvés* (1945).

Les Éditions de l'Arbre and *La Nouvelle Relève* were forced to terminate in 1948. After fourteen years of intense activity, Charbonneau suddenly saw himself cut off from his usual literary functions. In 1949 he returned to his former post as journalist at *La Presse*, and from 1950 he performed numerous editorial and managerial functions for Radio-Canada. For many years his writing was confined to radio scripts: a drama entitled 'Précieuse Élizabeth' in 1949; adaptations of his last two novels in 1951; and eighteen radio talks or lectures on French-Canadian novelists, published as *Romanciers canadiens* (1972). He returned to fiction with the short story

Aucun chemin n'est sûr (1959, 1990) and a novel, *Aucune créature* (1961), which reintroduced the romantic universe of the troubled hero. In *Chronique de l'âge amer* (1967) Charbonneau abandoned the psychological novel in favour of a thinly veiled semi-autobiographical narrative that recreated the literary generation between 1934 and 1936. Unfortunately, he could not follow up on these disguised memoirs. In the midst of full activity, after having been named president of the Société des écrivains (1966). Charbonneau was fatally stricken by a heart attack.

See Jean-Charles Falardeau, *Notre société et son roman* (1972); Madeleine Ducrocq-Poirier, *Robert Charbonneau* (1972); André Belleau, *Le romancier fictif: essai sur la représentation de l'écrivain dans le roman québécois* (1980); Jacques Michon, 'Robert Charbonneau parmi nous', *Écrits du Canada français*, 57 (1986); Pierre Vuillemin-Salducci, *Robert Charbonneau, le doute et le secret* (1990); and Jacques Michon, ed., *Éditeurs transatlantiques* (1991).

JACQUES MICHON

Charbonneau-Tissot, Claudette (pseudonym, Aude). See FANTASTIC LITERATURE AND SCIENCE FICTION IN FRENCH.

Charlebois, Jean (b. 1945). Born in Baie-Saint-Paul, he studied literature at the Université de Montréal. He works as an editor, translator, proofreader, researcher—and as a very productive poet.

Popèmes absolument circonstances incontrôlables (1972), *Tête de bouc* (1973), and *Tendresses* (1975) represent Charlebois's first phase and are marked by humour and whimsy, puns and buffoonery, a bantering and provocative tone. Nevertheless the author's sensitivity and a tender quality emerge, giving the love theme —inspired primarily by Paul Éluard—an important place in his work. *Hanches neige* (1977) is a pivotal book, composed of a script, a photo-romance, a lampoon, a fictional interview with the author, and theatre dialogues, whose appearance on the page—a skilful assembly of quotations, photographs, advertising slogans, proverbs, and distortions of famous poems—is remarkably original. Here Charlebois's sense of parody and raillery is at its peak. In *Conduite intérieure* (1978) and *Plaine lune suivi de Corps fou* (1980) the sensuality in the language of love is accompanied by reflections on death, and the lighthearted tone of the first collections is replaced by a serious, pensive voice, increasingly aware of the uncertainties of life and love. Youthful bragging gives way to sober, adult reflection. The engaging tone and liveliness of the first collections endure, however, making Charlebois one of the foremost exponents of the new lyricism in Quebec poetry.

Since 1980 Charlebois has published seven books of poetry, including *Présent!* (1984), *Tâche de naissance* (1986), *Corps cible* (1988), *Confidentielles* (1990), *Coeurps* (1994), and *De moins en moins l'amour de plus en plus* (1996).

See Claude BEAUSOLEIL, 'Lire aujourd'hui. En d'autres textes', *Hobo/Québec* (avril-juin 1977); André-G. Bourassa, 'Poèmes de veille, poèmes du temps', *Le Droit*, 24 février 1979; Richard Giguère, 'Poésie', *University of Toronto Quarterly* (Summer 1978); and Jean Royer, 'Les chemins de la tendresse', *Le Devoir*, 20 décembre 1980.

RICHARD GIGUÈRE

Charlesworth, Hector (1872-1945). Born in Hamilton, Ontario, he was trained as an accountant but instead became a renowned figure in Toronto journalism and a notable force in the arts. As a drama critic he survives only as a brief portrait in a Robertson DAVIES' novel, *World of wonders* (1975), where his bearded resemblance to Edward VII is noted; but his criticism of the Group of Seven gave him a peculiar place in Canadian art history. Though he admired many of their paintings, he criticized them often enough ('the hot mush school') to become, in the 1920s, the new movement's most notorious enemy; for the Group he was a convenient symbol of Establishment rigidity, 'Old Hec' to A.Y. Jackson. Charlesworth put down his journalistic roots as a reporter and editor on the Toronto *Mail and Empire*, but his career flourished at *Saturday Night*, then a national weekly—first as a contributor, then associate editor (1910-25), finally editor (1925-32). Aside from the twentieth-century volume in *A cyclopaedia of Canadian biography* (1919) and his collected essays in *The Canadian scene* (1927), he left three superb volumes of anecdotal memoirs —*Candid chronicles* (1925), *More candid chronicles* (1928), and *I'm telling you* (1937)—describing everything from famous murders he covered in his youth to the plagiarism suit against H. G. Wells that a Toronto woman pursued, relentlessly but unsuccessfully, for many years. In 1932 R.B. Bennett's Conservative government brought Charlesworth to Ottawa as chairman of the Canadian Radio Broadcasting Commission, the foundation-stone of public broadcasting, but he was dismissed after Mackenzie King and the Liberals were elected in 1935. He retreated to Toronto and a twilight career as freelance music reviewer. He died a critic's death in Toronto on 30

December 1945: a heart attack killed him after he received a telephone call from Duke Ellington angrily objecting to Charlesworth's *Globe and Mail* review ('jungle music à la Harlem') of an Ellington concert.

ROBERT FULFORD

Charlevoix, Pierre-François-Xavier de. See Writing in NEW FRANCE: 1.

Charron, François (b. 1952). Born in Longueuil, Quebec, he began writing poetry in his teens; in 1975 he became interested in painting and has had several exhibitions. A member of the editorial board of *Chroniques*, he was also a co-founder of *Stratégies* and a contributor to *Dérives* and *La BARRE DU JOUR*. His closest literary ties, however, have been with the modernist writers associated with the publishing house and periodical *Les Herbes rouges*. Charron has received a number of awards, including the Prix Nelligan for his poetry collection *Blessures* (1978), the Canada-Belgium Literary Prize for his overall contribution to literature (1982), the Grand Prix de Poésie de la Fondation Les Forges (1990), the Prix Air-Canada (1991), the Grand Prix de Poésie du *Journal de Montréal* (1992), and he has been nominated four times for a Governor General's Award. A prolific writer (over thirty published works since 1972), Charron is a leader of the Quebec literary avant-garde. From a Marxist-Leninist approach, much influenced by *PARTI PRIS* and the first writings of Paul CHAMBERLAND, Charron has developed towards the more intimate one of *Toute parole m'éblouira* (1982), in which the couple supersedes the collectivity as the new hope for survival. Charron manifests his desire to subvert any norm or 'doxa' in writing that is constantly renewed by means of breaking down language and submitting it to multiple experiments—a 'theoretical fiction' that removes all boundaries that separate theory of art and literature, poetry, history, ideology, subjectivism, political slogans, *JOUAL*, parody, and lyricism.

Charron's collections—*Dix-huit assauts* (1972), *Au 'sujet' de la poésie* (1972), *Projet d'écriture pour l'été 76* (1973), *Littérature/obscénités* (1974), and *Pirouette par hasard poésie* (1975)—either disparage traditional writings or make parodic assaults on earlier conventional writers; while *Enthousiasme* (1976) and *Propagande* (1977) call for both textual and political subversion. But *La traversée/le regard* (1973), *Persister et se maintenir dans les vertiges de la terre qui demeurent sans fin* (1974), *Du commencement à la fin* (1977), and *Feu* (1978) contain a lyricism that celebrates physical interaction in the loves and life of an artist who pictures himself as a 'sexed subject' and moves through an ever-changing historical reality that can be neither annexed by any institution (such as the family or the nation) nor mythicized. *Le temps échappé des yeux* (1979), *D'ou viennent les tableaux?* (1980), and *1980* (1981) explore poetically art theory, painters, and poets, seeking openness, extremism, and intensity. An intertextual dialogue (with Borduas's manifesto *REFUS GLOBAL*) launches *Peinture automatiste précédé de Qui parle dans la théorie?* (1979), in which Charron rediscovers both the relevance of the historical dimension of artistic creation and its autonomy *vis-à-vis* any norm or creed—automatism being the very expression of the artist's freedom.

The dialectic of creation and ideology inherent in *Refus global* is essential to Charron and reappears in *La passion d'autonomie: littérature et nationalisme* (1982), in which he attacks the nationalistic writings of his predecessors. Works such as *Blessures* and *Mystère* (1981) show a feminine dimension that perceives the act of writing as a possible substitute for the Mother as opposed to the 'Law of the Father'. The astonishing lyricism of the period between 1980 and 1995, the simplification and 'readability' of style, a contemplation of the sublime and concern with metaphysics and religion have steered Charron's work away from the formalist project of his earlier writing into what some critics consider postmodernism—a change that is signalled in 'Irrévérence. À propos de la modernité de gauche et du retournement à soi', published in *Qui a peur de l'écrivain* (1984).

Toute parole m'éblouira (1982), and the poetic journal *Je suis ce que je suis* (1983), signal a revival of individuality, while language continues to precede meaning and dictate the real—ideas also pursued in the prose piece on the 'mal du siècle', 'L'invention du réel', *Possibles* 10.1 (1985). The sensual poetic prose of *François* (1984) begins to posit desire as a founding motivator of writing, as the intimate text of *La chambre des miracles* (1986) unveils both a searching for and decentring of the speaking subject, as well as a quest for an evanescent origin. Such tensions pertaining to the writing 'I', and the essential ambiguity of language, figure in *La vie n'a pas de sens* (1985) and the autobiographical *Le fait de vivre ou d'avoir vécu* (1986). Faced always by the quotidian, the arbitrary, and the mediated, Charron turns to metaphysics in *La fragilité des choses* (1987), *Le monde comme obstacle* (1988), and *La beauté pourrit sans douleur, suivi de La très précieuse qualité du vide* (1989). Along with *La beauté des visages ne pèse pas sur la terre* (1990), these texts seek to go beyond the opposition of inner and outer, real and imaginary, while *L'intraduisible amour* (1991) tackles, in Charron's familiar aphoristic style, the notions of memory, discontinuity, love, desire, and transcendence, even recalling the poetry of his famous predecessor SAINT-DENYS-GARNEAU. The complexity of Charron's thinking arises from a quest for the absolute, always undertaken in the light of concrete reality, in a style that continues to blend wonder, revolt, irony, and passion in the prose-poems of *Pour les amants* (1992), *Clair génie du vent* (1994), and *Le passé ne dure que cinq secondes* (1996). An ethical dimension—a concern with the 'other'—pervades his recent work. In 1994 Charron republished *La vie n'a pas de sens, suivi de La chambre des miracles*, and *La fragilité des choses*. Selections from his poems have appeared in English in *Ellipse* 44 (1990) and in Bruce Whiteman's and Francis Farley-Chevrier's *After ten thousand years of desire* (1995).

Charron's entire work reflects an obsession with unity. Again and again it reconsiders the interaction between the creating subject and his place in history, using a diversity of expression that continually evolves against all norms and constraints.

For Charron's personal thoughts on literature and his own work, see 'La croyance', *Moebius* 67 (1996). For interviews see Gérald Gaudet, 'Vivre de sa plume au Québec', *Lettres québécoises* 47 (automne 1987) and Pierre Ouellette and Jacques Pelletier, 'Entretient avec François Charron', *Foldaan* 5 (1984). For critical essays on Charron's work from the 1970s to the 1990s, and an extended bibliography, see the special issue on Charron in *VOIX ET IMAGES* 16.3 (printemps 1991).

MAROUSSIA AHMED/MARIE J. CARRIÈRE

Châtillon, Pierre. See NOVELS IN FRENCH 1960 TO 1982: 3(f).

Chaurette, Normand (b.1954). A native of Montréal, he obtained his B.A. in literature at the Université de Montréal in 1976. He then interrupted his formal education to enhance his musical knowledge in Europe, returning in 1979 to the Université de Montréal, where he presented his master's thesis in 1981. During this period he also lectured in linguistics at the Université du Québec à Trois-Rivières. He has written many texts for radio, a number of scenarios, articles of theatre criticism, and translations—notably of Shakespeare, Schiller, and Strindberg—that have been staged in Quebec from 1989 to 1995. He is a skilled amateur musician, with his expertise extending from sacred music to the romantics and opera. An editor at Éditions Leméac, Montreal, from 1984 to 1988, he has since devoted himself to creative writing.

Best known as a virtuoso dramatist with a penchant for the unusual and the metaphysical, Chaurette is the author of eight plays and a short novel, which have earned him an international reputation. Their subjects vary greatly, and the plots are secondary to the role of structure, but all the works are characterized by Chaurette's passion for language, form, and music. While psychological realism of character and event is lacking, it is the richly allusive texts that hold one's interest.

His first play, *Rêve d'une nuit d'hôpital* (1980), originated as a radio script that won the fourth Radio-Canada competition for drama. Taking the title from Émile NELLIGAN's poem, Chaurette created a dream-like vision of the poet's madness and tragic destiny, interspersing dialogue with music and Nelligan's poetry. The play also reveals the distinctive features that will recur throughout Chaurette's works: the interplay of reality and the imaginary, and non-linear drama unfolding as flashback without apparent logical order, despite specific chronology.

Provincetown playhouse, juillet 1919, j'avais 19 ans (1981; translated by William Boulet as *Provincetown playhouse, July 1919, I was 19*, 1986), is based on the destruction by fire in 1977 of the Provincetown Playhouse-on-the Wharf. A play within a play, it takes place at several levels simultaneously in the mind of a thirty-eight-year-old playwright, interned for madness, whose career was interrupted abruptly by a death/murder nineteen years earlier. In nineteen tableaux—evoking youth, homosexual love and beauty—Chaurette constructs an ambiguous and lyrical drama on the theme of the artist in society.

In *Fêtes d'automne* (1982), and *La société de Métis* (1983), reality is barely present. The genesis of *Fêtes d'automne* is found in the brief writings of Danielle Sarréra, a seventeen-year-old who committed suicide in 1949—before her texts were published in 1966. Choosing the form of the Requiem Mass to mark dramatic progression, Chaurette writes of mystical passion leading to fulfilment beyond death, drawing on the fictional journal of a schoolgirl portrayed as a mythical figure. *La société de Métis* is closer to ironic comedy: the imaginary individuals, in portraits hanging in a small village museum, make far-fetched attempts at finding a guarantee of eternity. Chaurette's most enigmatic exercise in style, again without a plot in the conventional sense, is *Fragments d'une lettre d'adieu lus par des géologues* (1986; translated by Linda Gaboriau as *Fragments of a farewell letter read by geologists*, 1989). A commission of inquiry is held into the mysterious death of a geologist who led an expedition to Cambodia. The search has metaphysical overtones, the fragments revealed are tantalizing, but nothing is resolved. The language—by turns technical, amusing, disquieting—constitutes a dialogue of the deaf.

The primarily literary nature of Chaurette's theatrical writing places additional demands on staged production: in *Les reines* (1991; translated by Linda Gaboriau as *The queens*, 1992) the oratorical language is both a lyrical score for six women's voices and a dramatic text. With specific historical and literary references, Shakespearian rhythm without imitation, ironic humour with feminist implications, Chaurette debates the atemporal nature of power. In *Je vous écris du Caire* (1996), Chaurette—taking artistic liberties with chronology, opera, and Verdi—fuses the composer's music with a reflection on the theme of the duality of man/artist in society. *Le passage de l'Indiana* (1996), which won a Governor General's Award, is a poignant suspense drama about literary plagiarism, and creative and personal obsessions.

Schumann's music provides the title and leitmotif of Chaurette's novel *Scènes d'enfants* (1988), which parallels his dramatic work in the elegant text and masterly construction of an ambiguous development of long-hidden memories. It was nominated for a Governor General's Award (as was *Fragments d'une lettre d'adieu lus par des géologues*).

See Jean-Cléo Godin, 'Deux dramaturges de l'avenir?', *Études littéraires*, vol. 8, no. 3 (hiver 1985); Marta Dickman, 'Le triomphe de la beauté', *Jeu* 64 (1992); and Alexandre Lazaridès, 'Je vous écris du Caire', *Jeu* 68 (1993). See also DRAMA IN FRENCH: 1981 TO 1996:2.

BARBARA McEWEN

Chauveau, Pierre-Joseph-Olivier (1820-90). The precocious son of a Quebec City merchant, he attended the Petit Séminaire de Québec and at seventeen began to study law under Judge Hamel; he opened his own law office, after being admitted to the bar, at twenty-one and received the degree of doctor of laws from McGill University in 1857. At twenty-four he was elected to the Quebec House of Assembly. He was solicitor general in the Hincks-Morin ministry (1851), provincial secretary and Queen's Counsel (1853), minister of education (1866-7), and the first prime minister of the new province of Quebec (1867-73). In 1873 he resigned to join the Senate, where he was made Speaker. He resigned four years later and was named sheriff of Montreal district (1877-90). Chauvin founded in 1857 the Écoles normales in Montreal and Quebec, along with the *Journal de l'instruction publique* and its English counterpart, the *Journal of Education*. He was dean of the law faculty at Université Laval, Montreal, from 1884 to 1890. In 1848 he married Marie Louise Flore Masse and they had eight children.

Lawyer, administrator, politician, lecturer and orator, university professor, poet, novelist, biographer, historian, and bibliophile (his personal library was extensive), Chauveau was deeply involved in the intellectual life of his time. His most interesting publication is *Charles Guérin: roman des moeurs canadiennes* (Montréal, 1853), the fifth novel to appear in French Canada and one of the best novels of the nineteenth century. Plainly showing the influence of Chateaubriand, Balzac, and Hugo, it is a slight love story that unfolds over three years (1830-3) and ends, unexpectedly and inexplicably, in the epilogue, at the Battle of Saint-Eustache in Dec. 1837. The novel has many defects, among them an insipid style that was fashionable at the time and much holding-forth on philosophy, politics, and socio-economics (though some of these observations still have force today). It is impressive, however, for its rich and precise vocabulary, for its use in dialogue of popular speech (employed here for the first time in French-Canadian fiction), and for its portrayal of the society of the day and its customs, with the occasional introduction of lively characters. Among Chauveau's other books are *Souvenirs et légendes* (Québec, 1877), a collection of poetry, and *François-Xavier Garneau: sa vie et ses oeuvres* (Montréal, 1883).

MAURICE LEBEL

Chevalier, Henri-Émile (1828-79). Born at Châtillon-sur-Seine, France, he was imprisoned as the result of an article in which he attacked the government of Napoleon III. When freed, the republican journalist went to New York, where for a year he worked for the *Courrier des États-Unis*. In 1852 he arrived in Montreal. He immediately took an active part in the intellectual life of the city and contributed articles to *Le Pays* and *La Patrie*. He was one of the founders of *La Ruche littéraire*, a monthly periodical in which he published as serials his first novels: *La Huronne des Lorettes*

(1854) and *L'Île de Sable* (1854); the latter was published in Paris under the more titillating title *39 hommes pour une femme: épisode de la colonisation du Canada* (1862), and translated as *Legends of the Sea: 39 men for one woman* (New York, 1862). Here, the heroine, disguised as a man, is left on Sable Island with thirty-nine men, most of them mutineers; is kidnapped by a deaf mute, none other than her own father; and after five years of horrendous experiences is reunited with her love, only to die in childbirth shortly afterwards. The plot of *L'Île de Sable* is a measure of those of Chevalier's other novels. In 1860 he returned to France, where he wrote for various newspapers and continued to work on a series of novels—some thirty with the general title 'Drames de l'Amérique du Nord'. Though Chevalier was a great admirer of François-Xavier GARNEAU, his books about Canada have little to do with history. Such titles as *Les mystères de Montréal* (Montréal, 1855), *Le pirate du Saint-Laurent* (Montréal, 1859), and *Le chasseur noir* (Paris, 1877) indicate his subject matter. One of his most interesting novels is *La fille des Indiens rouges* (Paris, 1866), the first part of which takes place in Labrador and Greenland, among the Inuit, in the fifteenth century. Toronto is the setting for *L'enfer et le paradis de l'autre monde* (Paris, 1866). In this work Chevalier discusses, with political overtones, some of the problems Canada had to face in the 1850s: free trade, the deficit, immigration. Perhaps the chief value of his novels lies in the wealth of information they provide, the author being as erudite as he was prolific. As his peripatetic characters move from east to west, Chevalier, who had read every book available, describes landscape, geology, local customs. Professor David Hayne considers him 'le roi du roman feuilleton au Canada' (the king of Canadian serial romance).

Beatrice Corrigan's article 'Henri-Émile Chevalier and his novels of North-America' (*Romantic Review*, XXXV, 3, 1994) contains a complete bibliography of Chevalier's Canadian works. See also Paulette Collet, 'Il y à 150 ans: l'Ouest selon Henri-Émile Chevalier', *Après dix ans: les actes du onzième colloque du Centre d'études francophones de l'Ouest*, Institut de recherche de la Faculté Saint-Jean (Edmonton, 1992). PAULETTE COLLET

Chiasson, Herménégilde (b. 1946). Born in St-Simon, New Brunswick, he studied fine art at the University of Moncton, Mount Allison University, New York University, and the Sorbonne, where he obtained his doctorate in aesthetics. For many years Chiasson was a director of Radio-Canada, Moncton; he now pursues a many-faceted career as cinematographer, poet, visual artist, dramaturge, essayist, and professor. He is a Chevalier dans l'Ordre des Arts and Lettres (France) and a member of the Ordre des francophones d'Amérique.

With Guy Arsenault, the author of *L'Acadie Rock* (1973), and Raymond Guy LeBlanc, author of *Cri de terre* (1972), Chiasson was one of those who, with his collection *Mourir à Scoudouc* (1974), initiated the new Acadian poetry. It received a favourable reception in Québécois reviews, where its modern structure—a mix of poetic prose and long-lined poetry, rhythmically like that of Cendrars—was noted. The theme of a humiliated Acadia was apparent, sometimes veiled in a dreamlike or distanced atmosphere.

Rapport sur l'état de mes illusions (1976) is a book of anti-poetry, very different from Chiasson's first volume, in which the black humour leaves no doubt about its underlying feelings of anguish. There followed a period of poetic silence when Chiasson mounted exhibitions of paintings and photography, wrote numerous stage and radio plays, and directed several movies, all relating to Acadia.

Chiasson returned eagerly to poetry with four collections: *Prophéties* (1986), *Existences* (1991), *Vous* (1992, Prix France-Acadie), and *Vermeer (toutes les photos du film)* (1992). His solid training in the visual arts is obvious in all his collections, not only in the omnipresent illustrations, photographs, and drawings but also in the verbal transposition of pictorial and cinematographic images. The collection *Miniatures* (1995) received the Prix des Terrasses Saint-Sulpice (sponsored by the journal *Estuaire*) in 1995; it again adopts a structure very similar to that of *Existences*, where a series of texts, contained on a single page, are inspired (as in *Miniatures*) by personal objects that then become the generating force of what the author calls 'a kind of autobiographical essay'.

In his poetry as well as in other pieces like *Pierre, Hélène et Michael*, an unpublished play produced in 1990, and *L'exile d'Alexa* (1993), Chiasson has developed Acadian themes, such as the journey and the search for identity, and made them universal.

A committed writer and the most prolific and remarkable of the new generation of Acadian artists, Chiasson has expressed in a number of statements, most unpublished, the position of those Acadians who pursue their art in Acadia versus those who choose to do so in Montreal, suggesting that the latter group cannot live and thrive in Acadia.

RAOUL BOUDREAU

Child, Philip (1898-1978). Son of a major figure in Ontario's steel industry, Philip Albert Child attended schools in Germany and Switzerland. He was a student at Trinity College, University of Toronto, in 1917, when he enlisted in the army and served as an artillery officer during the First World War, an experience that marked his life. Returning to Trinity in 1919, he earned a B.A. in 1921 and proceeded to an affiliated B.A. at Christ's College, Cambridge, in the same year, and a Harvard M.A. in 1923. A lectureship at Trinity followed. In 1926 he married Gertrude Potts and had two children. There followed a Harvard doctorate, jobs as a journalist and settlement-house worker, teaching at the University of British Columbia, and sustained work as a writer of fiction, until his return to Trinity in 1942. Eventually Chancellor's Professor of English there, Child was president of the CANADIAN AUTHORS' ASSOCIATION in 1946.

Alongside the surface realism of Child's fiction rests his preoccupation with the visionary, the nightmarish, and the fabular as escape from the terrors of the everyday. Thus *The village of souls* (1933), set in New France, is in many ways a post-war novel. The hero, Jornay, struggles amid a modernist wasteland in his search for a ground of being. Torn between two women, Aboriginal (Anne) and European (Lys), Jornay unites himself with wilderness Canada when Lys dies of smallpox. In the manner of adventure fiction, his endurance is tested during a visionary experience with his dead love. The novel concludes with a journey to the Mississippi alongside his living one.

God's sparrows (1937; NCL 1978) deals overtly with the Great War (as does the later narrative poem of 1965, *The wood of the nightingale*). Combining the family saga with the war novel, featuring its hero's reconciliation with a dead cousin through a dream, *God's sparrows* leaves David Thatcher (whose American-Canadian ancestry resembles Child's) shattered at the end. *The wood of the nightingale*, in blank verse, stresses character doubling and the blending of opposites within a universe of death, concluding with a message of reconciliation—which was read aloud at Child's funeral service.

Blow wind, come rack (1954)—written under the pseudonym 'John Wentworth'—thrusts an academic into the violent world of the spy thriller. *Day of wrath* (1945) offers a grim account of a Jew's fate under Hitler. *Mr. Ames against time* (1949) pits an old man against time in his efforts to save his son from a frame-up for murder; it won both the Ryerson Fiction Award and a Governor General's Award. *The Victorian house* (1951), a long poem, funnels the break-up of Anglo-Canadian cultural values through its narrator's recollections of a property that he finally refuses to sell.

Modernist in its themes of disintegration, Child's work is often old-fashioned in style. His fiction's concern with the adaptation of the European newcomer to the Canadian wilderness (*The village of souls*) and with the loss of social coherence (*God's sparrows*, *The Victorian house*) reflects major cultural preoccupations in the southern Ontario of its time.

DENNIS DUFFY

Children's drama in English. Since the founding in 1953 of the first professional company performing for young people, Holiday Theatre of Vancouver, hundreds of scripts have been created or commissioned by many such other groups across Canada; they began to be published, however, only in 1972. While some writers have created plays of great power and joy that transcend severe limitations of place, time, and human resources, producers have often been required to realize the stage potential of seemingly prosaic material. Most scripts have been written for specific theatre companies or occasions and are one-act plays, about 45 minutes long, tailored to fit between two bells in a school schedule. Weekend, holiday, or subscription-series presentations feature full-length plays intended for family audiences, plays such as *Anne of Green Gables*, a musical by Norman Campbell, adapted by Donald Harron from the 1908 novel by L.M. MONTGOMERY, which opened the Charlottetown Festival in 1965; and *The mystery of the Oak Island treasure* (1985) by Jim Betts, commissioned by Toronto's Young People's Theatre. The Stratford Festival has also presented plays for young people. They include James REANEY's *Colours in the dark* (1969), produced in 1967; Henry BEISSEL's *Inook and the sun* (1974), produced in 1973, which borrows from both Japanese Bunraku puppet tradition and Inuit culture to create a strong poetic evocation of a young boy's quest for adulthood; and the 1994 production of *Alice through the looking-glass*, adapted by James Reaney, repeated in 1996. His *Names and nicknames* (1973) is a good example of the many scripts developed for a specific company with close collaboration between a director and a writer. Directed by John Hirsch and Robert Sherrin, it was produced at the Manitoba Theatre Centre in 1963. Using choral speech, improvisation, and mime, and creating its 'scenery' with bodies and voices alone, it deploys an eclectic and unconventional array of lists, objects, rituals, rites of passage—characteristic of Reaney's theatre pieces in general—and a list of names taken from an old speller that belonged to Reaney's father. The poet's craft evokes the clear conflict between good and evil and the deep feelings associated with names.

Some playwrights for children's theatre, having learned their craft through the creation of short scripts, later wrote successful full-length plays for adult audiences. Rex DEVERELL wrote shows for both children and adult audiences for Regina's Globe Theatre, which was founded in 1966 by Ken and Sue Kramer to produce and tour the plays—containing elements of audience participation—of British producer and playwright Brian Way. Deverell used participation in *Shortshrift* (1973), whose political overtones were evident in the children's efforts to help the actors 'rebuild' the town hall in opposition to an impersonal government bureaucracy, while his *Sarah's play* (1975) uses a 'computer' into which the audience feeds data by whispering words from their seats in a circle on the floor. Deverell's plays, frequently set in Saskatchewan but successfully performed elsewhere, also include *The Copetown City kite crisis* (1973), *The Shinbone general store caper* (1977), *Melody meets the bag lady* (1984), and *Switching places* (1994). Playwrights who have written for both adult and young audiences include Carol BOLT—*My best friend is twelve feet high* (1972), *Cyclone Jack* (1972), and *Icetime* (1988); Michael COOK—*The fisherman's revenge* (1985); Clem Martini—*Swimmers* (1989); Sharon POLLOCK—*Prairie dragons* (1989); and Morris PANYCH, whose provocative plays for adolescents address such issues as AIDS, sexuality, drug and alcohol abuse, and teenage alienation. These plays—which include *Life science*, *2B wut UR*, and *The cost of living*—were published in the anthology *Other schools of thought* (1994).

Plays based on Canadian history make up a significant part of the theatre for young audiences' repertoire. Alberta Theatre Projects of Calgary was founded in 1972 to 'bring history to life' in a historic log cabin: the Canmore Opera House. Plays developed for ATP include Paddy Campbell's historical revue *Under the arch* (1976), with music by William Skolnik; Gloria Sawai's *Neighbor* (1981), in which a pioneer farmer's wife goes mad through loneliness; and Jan Truss's *A very small rebellion* (1978), about Louis Riel, and *The judgement of Clifford Sifton* (1979), about British immigration to 'the last, best west', the prairies. Three scripts about local history, developed for Ottawa's Great Canadian Theatre Company, were published in the anthology *Playmakers: adventures in Canadian drama* (1980): *The secret of the golden fiddle* by Robin Mathews; *The curse of the viking grave*, Mathew's adaptation of Farley MOWAT's novel of the same name; and *Shantymen of Cache Creek*, Arthur Milner's adaptation of Bill Freeman's 1975 novel of the same name. Other popular history plays include Len PETERSON's *Billy Bishop and the red baron* (1974), about the Canadian air ace of the First World War; Rick McNair's *Dr Barnardo's pioneers* (1984), about British orphans indentured as servants to Canadian households and farms in the nineteenth century; W.O. MITCHELL's *The day Jake made her rain* (produced in 1984) in which Depression prairie farmers' delicate balance of hope and despair is manipulated by an amateur rainmaker; and Paula Wing's *Naomi's road* (1994)—adapted from Joy KOGAWA's adaptation of her novel *Obasan*—about the Canadian government's imposed relocation of a young Japanese girl and her family. The legends, myths, and contemporary concerns of aboriginal peoples, at one time researched and rewritten by white people, are now more frequently and authentically represented by First Nations' playwrights such as Drew Hayden TAYLOR, whose prize-winning play *Toronto at dreamer's rock* (1990) mixes past, present, and future in a fantasy about a teenage boy's discovery and acceptance of his Native roots.

A significant trend since the early 1970s has been to commission and perform plays about contemporary problems that confront young people. A leader in this field is Green Thumb Theatre for Young People, Vancouver, founded in 1972 by Dennis Foon and Jane Howard Baker. The company has encouraged many writers whose plays explore contemporary issues in a format that is easily accessible to young people. Peggy Thompson's play *The bittersweet kid* (1984) is about coping with diabetes. The anthology *Not so dumb: four plays for young people* (1993) by John Lazarus, includes *Schoolyard games*, which exposes bullies; *Not so dumb*, which compassionately examines problems of the mentally challenged; *Night light*, which probes fears of the dark; and *Secrets*, which tells hard truths about teenage dating and malicious gossip. Colin Thomas's *One thousand cranes* (1989), dealing with questions and fears of nuclear war, won a Chalmers Award in 1984, and his play about divorce, *Two weeks, twice a year* (1994), has toured widely. Various theatrical conventions enhance these plays and reduce the danger of didacticism, as when the 'monster' in Lazarus's

Night light is seen by the protagonist and the audience, but not by other stage characters. Foon's *New Canadian kid* (1982), which explores the experiences of an immigrant child, is based on interviews with hundreds of children in the Vancouver area. The isolation of the immigrant is uniquely portrayed by having all the residents speak in gibberish, while the newcomer is the only one who speaks English. This script broke new ground for Green Thumb, becoming its signature piece and leading to national and international tours. Foon's other plays for young people include *Skin* (1988), *Liars* (1988), and *War* (1995). Other successful issue-based scripts are Ruth Smillie's *Teenage Moms* (1993) and those published in an anthology of three plays for high schools, *Wanna play?* (1994), which includes Shirley Barrie's *Carrying the calf*, Banuta Rubess's and Beverley Cooper's *Thin ice*, and Anna Fuerstenberg's *Blind dates*. Duval Lang, co-founder of Calgary's Quest Theatre, works closely with playwrights to develop new plays for school tours. One long-time associate is JoAnne James, whose poignant and funny scripts about everyday problems of growing up—such as losing your best friend (*Moving day*), repairing friendships lost through cruel acts and angry arguments (*The echo box*), and the effect of peer pressure upon friendship (*Willa and Sam*)—have been produced in other parts of Canada and in the USA. These plays have been published in *Three quest plays for children* (1966).

Direct input from young people themselves has led to both scripted plays by adult writers and the dramatization of young people's stories by a team of players, directors, composers, and designers. For Green Thumb, Campbell Smith worked with teenagers to create, write, and direct *Juve* (1980), a rock musical with monologues, songs, and scenes based on autobiographical material, and Irene Watts wrote *Tomorrow will be better* (1980), using the ideas, stories, and poems of British Columbia children. *Feeling yes, feeling no*, first produced in workshop in 1982, is a play about sexual abuse, researched from actual cases and developed collectively by Dennis Foon, Fran Gebhard, Judith Mastai, Wendy Van Reisen,and Brian Torpe. Because of the sensitive nature of the subject matter, actors presented material in single classrooms and the 'performance' included a lengthy feed-back time for informal talks with children. The project was widely produced, but was too expensive for many venues. It reached a wider public when it was sensitively filmed by the National Film Board and released along with teachers' guides.

Although few plays are published that have not been professionally produced, some excellent plays have been performed but not published. *Comet in Moominland*, adapted by Graham Whitehead for Manitoba Theatre for Young People under the leadership of Leslee Silverman, and produced in 1990, is an example of a script that is so closely identified with its original production that publishing the script is considered secondary to its significance as a remarkably original piece of theatre. Elizabeth Gorrie has created many evocative theatre pieces to suit the special demands of Kaleidescope Theatre in Victoria.

Quest Theatre produced *Summerplay* and *Winterplay* in 1988, both performed by adults but written by children. Art work, poetry, and stories about the seasons were solicited from children through the schools—locally for 'Summerplay' and nationally for 'Winterplay', which was the only work for young people in the cultural component of the 1988 Winter Olympic Games in Calgary.

In the some twenty years since plays for the young began to be published regularly, a body of work has emerged that reflects both the concerns of Canadian children and the variety of theatrical styles used in production. However, more scripts of lasting literary merit would raise the power and prestige of this fragile field, heavily dependent upon education budgets, government grants, and parents' disposable incomes for their children's entertainment.

See Joyce Doolittle and Zina Barnieh, *A mirror of our dreams; children and the theatre in Canada* (1979), with a chapter on theatre for children in Quebec by Hélène Beauchamp. The catalogues of the Playwrights Union of Canada are the best sources of information about published scripts for children and young people.

JOYCE DOOLITTLE/JOANNE JAMES

Children's drama in French. Theatre for young people is a very recent development in Quebec. In the 1950s and early 1960s adult theatre companies in Montreal—such as Les Compagnons de Saint-Laurent, Le Théâtre-Club, Les Apprentis-Sorciers, and Les Saltimbanques—took special pains to produce plays that would delight young audiences. Actors and producers, however, were faced with a serious problem: the lack of scripts for such productions. Theatre companies, therefore, tried to interest authors of children's literature in writing for the theatre.

In 1960 Le Théâtre-Club of Montreal succeeded in acquiring and producing a play by

Luan Asslani, *Les trois désirs de Coquelicot* (1973). Inspired by the popularity in children's theatre of fairy tales—especially those of Charles Perrault—Asslani created, in *Les trois désirs*, a young hero whose battles with elves and fairies teach him to have a sense of generosity towards others. The first company to devote itself entirely to productions for young audiences was Le Théâtre pour Enfants de Québec (1965-70) of Quebec City. Ably directed by Pauline Geoffrion, it resolutely adopted a policy favouring the creation of original plays for children, and produced works by Monique Corriveau, Roland LePage, Patrick Mainville, and Pierre MORENCY—the only one of these authors to publish his plays for children. Morency's *Tournebire et le malin Frigo* (1978) was typical of this company's productions, which encouraged audience participation in games featuring robots, or heroes of 'soft' science-fiction adventures that usually occurred in mysterious laboratories inhabited by absent-minded professors.

Between 1970 and 1980 the number of children's plays written both by collectives and by individual authors increased greatly, though not many have been published. When André Cailloux—whose plays are published by Éditions Leméac—assumed the artistic direction of the youth section of Montreal's Théâtre du Rideau Vert, 'Manteau d'Arlequin 5-15', in 1970, he elected to produce his own plays. *Frizelis et Gros Guillaume* (1973) and *Frizelis et la Fée Doduche* (1973) both take place in a land called Milieu, the realm of Frizelis, king of elves. This kingdom—in which the woodcutter, Gros Guillaume, and his wife Charlotte continually become mired or lost—is coveted by the greedy Fée Doduche. Magic objects appear and disappear; characters become instantly and mysteriously transformed; voyages are made into space and time; and all these activities are punctuated by the verbal participation of the children in the audience. Magic is also featured in Cailloux's *François et l'oiseau du Brésil; ou La comédie des erreurs* (1977), in which identity-changes and tricks of illusion play a central part. Although these three plays are light and highly entertaining, they tend to confuse credulous youngsters who cannot always distinguish—especially in the theatre—between the real and the imaginary. Cailloux turned to educational subjects—pollution, respect for the past, astronomy, geography—for two more plays: *L'Île-au-Sorcier* (1974), a folkloric tale in which the young hero is led by the fabulous Raccoon and Renaak to discover a magic bracelet that controls the weather; and *Tombé des étoiles* (1977), which—less felicitously—adopts the situations and style of the 'police thriller'. In these two plays the author attempts, with only partial success, to combine an exciting plot with serious content.

Treatment of serious themes is characteristic of the development of young people's drama from 1973 to the 1980s. Contemporary playwrights strove consciously to write plays that would establish links between the spectacle on the stage and the experience of the children in the audience. Marie-Francine Hébert, long associated with Montreal's Le Théâtre de la Marmaille, wrote *Cé tellement 'cute' des enfants* (1980), a pioneering play in which children playing in back-alleys on a school holiday fail to conform wholly to their elders' idealized view of them: using a language so frank and realistic that it amounts to a social document and a political statement, the children set up an infernal racket of disputes and misunderstandings. Altogether different from Hébert's previous play—the poetic and gently amusing *Une ligne blanche au jambon* (1974)—*Cé tellement 'cute'* is a landmark of the 'new children's theatre', which, since 1975, concentrated on reflecting the realities that children and adolescents know and recognize: this is real theatre for real audiences. *Un jeu d'enfants* (1980), created by Montreal's Théâtre du Quartier, is about a group of children who are unhappy because they have no playground, and portrays their reactions to having their schoolyard turned into a parking lot. The child-characters in *On est capable* (1981), by Louis-Dominique Lavigne, manoeuvre bravely through a world of fears and taboos; written in a poetic realist style, the play encourages youngsters to recognize their own talents and strengths and urges them to dare, to hope, and to have confidence. *On n'est pas des enfants d'école* by Gilles Gauthier in collaboration with Le Théâtre de la Marmaille, stresses the fact that school is not the only place to learn, and that it can be a centre for sharing and belonging. *Histoire de Julie qui avait une ombre de garçon* (1982), by Denis Chouinard and Nicole-Marie Rhéault, tells of a touching encounter in the park between Julie, a tomboy, and the clownish but gentle François, who are both the butts of their uncomprehending parents.

Regarde pour voir (1981), a creation of Montreal's Théâtre de l'Oeil, is a puppet play designed to make this mode of expression accessible to children: within the framework of preparations being made by Lise and Jocelyn for their own neighbourhood puppet-show, it describes the history of puppetry, shows how puppets can be made from second-hand materials, and presents sketches showing examples of what can be achieved. Puppets are also used in *La couleur chant un pays* (1981), by Diane Bouchard *et al.*, which introduces the audience to the history of Quebec painting. Characters created by Quebec artists are brought to life through puppets and masks that are faithful to the period and style of each artist represented.

For very young children—ages three to six—Suzanne Lebeau wrote a very fine poetic piece that used sound and rhythm to great advantage: *Une lune entre deux maisons* (1980) employs a flashback method to show the gradual shedding of fears and growth of friendship between two very dissimilar persons, Plume and Taciturne.

Since 1950 authors have left behind the conventions of the fairy tale and television and built new themes and structures, styles and forms, suited to young audiences. Children's drama in Quebec has evolved into a specific genre, worthy of appreciation and analysis.

See the *Répertoire des textes* (1981) of Le Centre d'Essai des Auteurs dramatiques; Hélène Beauchamp, 'L'histoire et les conditions du théâtre pour enfants au Québec 1950-1980' (Université de Sherbrooke thesis, 1982); Hélène Beauchamp, *Le théâtre à la p'tite école* (1980), a study for the Ministry of Cultural Affairs for Quebec.

HÉLÈNE BEAUCHAMP

1980 to 1996. Children's drama in Quebec in this period developed at an even more rapid pace than in the 1970s, becoming more heterogeneous and complex in the process. Performances of plays written for children were numerous and varied, as authors expanded a corpus that was previously rather limited, and almost all major texts were published. Certain playwrights (Jasmine Dubé, Louis-Dominique Lavigne, Suzanne Lebeau) have succeeded, both in terms of the quality and the quantity of their texts, in creating an actual *oeuvre* of children's drama.

Several factors characterize the development of theatre for young people since 1980. First, specialists now agree on the expression used to refer to this type of drama: drama or theatre for young audiences (*théâtre jeunes publics*). In addition, children's drama in Quebec now consists of two different practices that developed independently of each other: theatre for children (aged five to twelve) as distinguished from theatre for adolescents, which developed somewhat later. Two texts were particularly important in the recent evolution of children's drama in general. The first, *Les enfants n'ont pas de sexe?* (1981), was performed by the Théâtre de Carton company. This play, adapted from a German text, presents an initiation into sexuality, and was performed more than a hundred times in ten years. The second play, Louis-Dominique Lavigne's *Où est-ce qu'elle est ma gang?* (1984), created by the Théâtre Petit à Petit company in 1982, set the tone for adolescent drama of this period. Addressed specifically to teenagers, this play resolutely adopts their perspective, emphasizing their activities and their frustrations in relation to authority.

Although didactic theatre, 'which aims to instruct spectators while privileging a progressive point of view', according to critic Hélène Beauchamp, has not dominated children's drama since 1982, several important plays of this type were written in this period. Suzanne Lebeau's *Les petits pouvoirs* (1983) questions everyday powers negotiated between parents and children. Jasmine Dubé's *Bouches décousues* (1985) consists of a simple story, urging children to speak up, especially those who have been victims of sexual harassment. In a didactic but poetic style, Marie-Francine Hébert's *Oui ou non* (1988) also depicts the prevention of various forms of aggression. This play presents numerous possible situations that encourage children to respond affirmatively to their own desires and negatively when they feel threatened. A much less didactic play, Michel-Marc BOUCHARD's *L'histoire de l'oie* (1993), treats the question of violence inflicted on children by means of a beautiful but serious story in which a young boy constructs his own imaginary world to escape the physical abuse he has suffered.

Drama for adolescents, which frequently features a high-school setting, has dealt well with several subjects of direct concern to this age group. Alain Fournier's *Circuit fermé* (1987) addresses the problem of juvenile prostitution frankly. Written in a language that closely approximates that of its teenage audience, and punctuated with rock songs, this realistic text, while harsh, leaves room for hope. In *Tiens tes rêves* (1988), Sylvie Provost *et al.* describe the intimate universe of adolescents experiencing their first sexual relationship. The amorous bond between two teenagers develops in parallel to the passionate Harlequin romance novel that the young girl is reading, creating a humorous contrast between the fictitious stereotypical romance and the actual sexual reality of adolescents. Finally, Lavigne's *Le sous-sol des anges* (1991) and Yves Masson's *L'ange gardien* (1992) both tackle the delicate problem of teenage suicide directly and intelligently.

Playwrights have published texts in the 1990s to which young audiences are less accustomed. René-Daniel DUBOIS's *Julie* (1996), for example, depicts the initiation quest of a young eight-year-old girl who experiments with cigarettes and alcohol to 'taste' the adult world. Adroitly avoiding the enumeration of repeated sordid details, Suzanne Lebeau recounts in *Salvador* (1996) the story of a South American writer who remembers his poverty-stricken childhood. Michelle Allen's *Zoé perd son temps* (1996), a puppet play that oscillates between science fiction and the marvellous, is a delightful fable about time that incites young children to think while being entertained. In *L'épreuve du merveilleux* (1996) Michel Garneau constructs a universe for adolescents that is very different from their secondary-school world—the play is structured around a meeting with Montaigne's ghost. Here both culture and imagination are emphasized.

Since 1982 children's and adolescents' drama in Quebec has continued to evolve along much the same lines as in the 1970s, but it has also charted much new territory. The result is evident: drama for young audiences now consists of a significant number of rich and diversified texts.

See Hélène Beauchamp, *Le théâtre pour enfants au Québec* (1985) and *Cahiers de théâtre*, nos. 46 (1988) and 76 (1996).

PASCAL RIENDEAU

Children's literature in English: To the 1970s. The growing awakening in early Victorian England to the imaginative and intellectual possibilities of literature for children was slow to develop in Canadian writing. This is not surprising in a country whose scattered population was essentially non-literate and composed mainly of recent immigrants and exiles, explorers, and visitors. Among the earliest publications for children was *The SNOW DROP; or, Juvenile magazine* (Montreal, 1847-53), which could have been published in London, with its moral and religious tales, indifferent verse, and historical and natural-history anecdotes that pointed a lesson—though its six-year duration suggests that it was well received. Catharine Parr TRAILL's *Canadian Crusoes: a tale of the Rice Lake Plains* (London, 1852)—reprinted as *Lost in the backwoods: a tale of the Canadian forest* (London, 1882)—reveals two characteristics that were to become constants in our best literature for children: a love of the vast though dangerous land and of its animal inhabitants, and (Margaret ATWOOD's survival theory notwithstanding) a determination to come to terms with the land, exuberantly and successfully—not only in forest, but on plain, sea, tundra, and ice. Traill's account of three young people lost in the Ontario wilderness, north of what is now Cobourg, is not the work of a genuine storyteller—her Christian moralizing takes over what plot there is—but *Canadian Crusoes*, like its English predecessor, was based on a true event and can now be seen to have a genuinely Canadian sensibility in its portrayal of the Canadian landscape and of children's participation in it.

It was left to a temporary resident, R.M. BALLANTYNE, to see, and use successfully, the possibilities of Canadian subject-matter in strengthening the fairly new British tradition of adventure stories for boys. His gift for creating strong plots and spirited protagonists, for gripping narrative and lively descriptive detail—beginning with *The young fur traders* (London, 1856)—would make him one of the leading practitioners of the genre in the nineteenth century. Ballantyne's interest in only the external features of character and incident was shared by countless other writers of outdoor adventures who followed him, including James DE MILLE, the author of numerous children's books, including *B.O.W.C.; a book for boys* (Boston, 1869), and other books about the B.O.W.C. ('Brethren of the White Cross'). Surprisingly for its time in Canada, this is a school story; but most of the action takes place outside the school, sailing and adventuring on the Bay of Fundy in Nova Scotia. That Canadian writers of boys' books in this period were not interested in individualizing their characters is also apparent in the works of James Macdonald OXLEY, the author of twenty books for boys, including *Up among the ice-floes* (Philadelphia, 1890), *Fife and drum at Louisbourg* (Boston, 1899), and *L'Hasa at last* (London, 1902), an unusual tale about an expedition to the Forbidden City. The Rev. Egerton Ryerson YOUNG was a direct heir of Catharine Parr Traill in his frank use of the outdoor adventure story to inculcate Christian precepts in *Three boys in the wild north land, summer* (Toronto, 1896) and its sequel *Winter adventures of three boys in the great lone land* (London, 1899). Norman DUNCAN carried outdoor adventure to the sea, writing in *The adventures of Billy Topsail* (1906) a popular story about young Billy's travails and adventures in and on the waters off

Newfoundland, and his acceptance by the crew of a deep-fishing vessel. Billy's adventures were included in school readers until the 1930s. Ernest Thompson SETON's *TWO LITTLE SAVAGES: being the adventures of two boys who lived as Indians and what they learned* (1906)—based on his boyhood play near Lindsay, Ontario, and in Toronto's Don Valley—is the most enduring and the finest of these outdoor adventure stories, bringing together Seton's knowledge as a naturalist, his competence as a writer for the young, and his skill as an artist (his marginal drawings are an integral part of the book).

Books about animals have been a Canadian speciality, and in this period one such book became a best-seller and is still read today. *BEAUTIFUL JOE: an autobiography* (Philadelphia, 1894) by Marshall SAUNDERS resembles in form and purpose Anna Sewell's *Black Beauty* (1877), but it is about a homely dog (rather than a handsome horse) whose powers of speech are frequently devoted to moralizing. A new and comparatively realistic trend in fictionalizing animal behaviour was initiated by two other Canadian writers. Ernest Thompson Seton showed true originality in his *WILD ANIMALS I HAVE KNOWN* (New York, 1898), in which he created a new genre, the animal biography—a genuine native product that eventually influenced the animal story around the world. Charles G.D. ROBERTS—who had previously published *Earth's enigmas: a book of animal and nature life* (Boston, 1896)—used the same approach in *The kindred of the wild* (1902). The stories in the Seton and Roberts books are of course fictional; but, unlike previous animal stories, they are so closely based on knowledge and observation of wild animals in their own environments as to be almost documentaries. Seton's stories are written in the matter-of-fact style of a professional naturalist, while Roberts' stories—based on his boyhood experiences in the woods of New Brunswick—are the somewhat romantic tales of a literary artist. Both authors used the form of the animal biography to relate the thoughts and emotions of their subjects, as well as their instincts (and both have been criticized for the anthropomorphism of their stories). Their fascinating detailed descriptions, and their ability to arouse emotions in their readers, have kept *Wild animals* and *Kindred of the wild* very much alive as children's books. Seton and Roberts followed these early publications with many others in the same vein.

In the turn-of-the-century period, two Canadian authors had great success with domestic fiction that was both sentimental and informed with Christian uplift, like most children's books of this period. *GLENGARRY SCHOOL DAYS* (1902) by Ralph Connor (Charles William GORDON) was written for adults, but its youthful characters, schoolhouse scenes, and descriptions of pioneer activities in which children were involved quickly captured the interest of the young. Connor's sentimental look backwards to pioneer days in Glengarry Country, Ontario, gave him ample opportunity for some gentle proselytizing, but this never quite detracts from the force of his narrative skill or his ability to arouse emotion. *Glengarry school days* remains in print and can still be read with pleasure. This cannot be said of Nellie McCLUNG's *Sowing seeds in Danny* (1908), whose heroine, twelve-year-old Pearlie Watson, is closely related to the pious and sacrificial Elsie Dinsmore. Yet McClung shared with Connor an ability to write vividly about a particular setting, in this case the small-town and farm life of Manitoba.

L.M. MONTGOMERY wrote the most famous of all Canadian children's books, *ANNE OF GREEN GABLES* (1908). Montgomery certainly belongs to the 'sweetness and light' school of Saunders, Connor, and McClung, but in the whole stream of Edwardian books for children—filled with the unbearable goodness of Little Lord Fauntleroy, Elsie Dinsmore, Pollyanna, Rebecca of Sunnybrook Farm, and others—Anne sounded an original and refreshing note. Owing to pressures exerted by her publisher, Montgomery turned out many books of sticky sweetness that are best forgotten; but even these contain effective lyrical passages on the natural beauty of Prince Edward Island, and cast a humorous look at adult behaviour. Her Emily books—*Emily of New Moon* (1923), *Emily climbs* (1925), and *Emily's quest* (1927)—which appear to be largely autobiographical, are outstanding examples of realistic domestic novels for the young that are surprising for the period in not ignoring such manifestations of the adult world as the broken family, closet skeletons, family feuds, tensions, and the rigid standards of period and place. Montgomery had a sharp ear for dialogue; and though her books are not strongly plotted, she manages to keep reader interest to the very end. True to her period, and to the canons of children's literature of the time, Montgomery was a moralist; but unlike most of her contemporaries, she was not doctrinaire.

In many ways the early period summarized above represents a high plateau of Canadian children's literature: its originality, popularity, and lasting appeal have been equalled only in recent times. Indeed, the next few decades were marked by a paucity of titles published, and of talent. One notable exception was *The adventures of Sajo and her beaver people* (1935) by Archibald Stansfeld BELANEY, who lived and wrote under the Native alias Grey Owl. Unlike the animal biographies of Seton and Roberts, which are played out almost completely in the animal world, Grey Owl projected a strong emotional link between a Native child and her pet beavers. It is also strongly plotted with a forest fire, two Native children lost in a big city, a group of loving, helpful adults, and the reunion of two beaver pups—a piece of sentiment in a strong Canadian environment.

The period from the 1940s to the 1970s belongs chiefly to three writers of the outdoor/survival story: Roderick HAIG-BROWN, Farley MOWAT, and James HOUSTON, who brought the genre into the modern age. Haig-Brown's *Starbuck Valley winter* (1946) and its sequel *Saltwater summer* (1948) broke new ground in their portrayal of a capable but sensitive teenager at home in the British Columbia wilderness and on its coastal waters. Mowat's settings range from the Arctic in *Lost in the Barrens* (1956), in which his skills as a naturalist and conservationist form the background for a story of adventurous friendship between two boys, a white boy and a Native, to Newfoundland in *The black joke* (1962), a tale of high adventure involving sea-going boys. His *The dog who wouldn't be* (1957) and *Owls in the family* (1961) brought both humour and a warm feeling for family life that were sadly lacking in children's books of this period: both can be considered Canadian classics. Houston's great contribution has been to produce an extensive body of work rooted in Inuit life. Several of his books, such as *Tikta'Liktak* (1965) and *The white archer* (1967), have only Inuit characters; the ways of the white man do not intrude on Inuit ways. Houston also used the traditional theme of friendship between an Inuit boy and a white boy, in which both protagonists come to appreciate the other's culture, in *Frozen fire* (1977) and other novels.

The 1960s, which brought so many changes to children's literature—especially the emphasis on harsh realism that emanated from the United States—were marked in Canada by the interest in, and respect for, the legends of the various Native and Inuit groups. Early Native collections were virtually non-existent, Pauline's JOHNSON's *Legends of Vancouver* (1911) being the only example. A white writer, Cyrus Macmillan, produced *Canadian wonder tales* (1918) and *Canadian fairy tales* (1922)—reprinted in one volume in 1974 as *Canadian wonder tales*. In retrospect it can be seen that the question of how indigenous tales were to be told (or retold), especially for children, was not to be easily answered. However, although Johnson was half Mohawk, she published the legends told to her in halting English by a West Coast Native chief. Macmillan cast his tales in the style of the romantic European fairy tale. Non-Natives in the 1960s undertook to give meaning, brevity, and coherence to what appeared to them to be a large, unwieldy, fragmented, rough-hewn body of anecdotal material. Frances Fraser's *The bear who stole the Chinook* (1959, Blackfoot), Robert Ayre's *Sketco the Raven* (1961, West Coast), Christie HARRIS's *Once upon a totem* (1963, West Coast), Kathleen Hill's *Glooscap and his magic* (1963, Micmac), and Dorothy Reid's *Tales of Nanabozho* (1963, Ojibwa) were among the story collections that resulted. This trend of non-Native retellers as the collectors and interpreters of Native myth and legend continued into the 1970s with Christie Harris's popular re-creation of the legendary *Mouse Woman in Mouse Woman and the vanished princesses* (1976) and its sequels. But what proved to be the highlight of the active period of the 1960s was a linked collected of Aesop-like fables by the Nootka, George CLUTESI. His *Son of Raven, Son of Deer: fables of the Tse-shaht People* (1967) served the primary purpose of the oral tradition: to transmit the manners and mores of a society to the next generation. Only a few collections of Inuit legends were published. However, some major legends were simply and dramatically retold by the white writer Ronald Melzak in *The day Tuk became a hunter* (1967) and *Raven, creator of the world* (1970). Books presenting a single illustrated legend greatly outnumbered collections of legends and folktales. This trend began with the happy combination of William Toye as reteller and the collage artist Elizabeth Cleaver as illustrator, who conveyed the visual excitement in what have become some of the best-known Native legends: *The mountain goats of Temlaham* (1969), *How summer came to Canada* (1969), *The loon's necklace* (1977), and *The fire stealer* (1979). James Houston wrote and illustrated an Inuit legend, *Kiviok's magic journey* (1973).

Canadian historical fiction forms a considerable part of the total body of publications. Early Native life—that is, in times before recorded history—inspired Edith Lambert

Sharp's *Nkwala* (1958) and Roderick Haig-Brown's *The whale people* (1962). Both describe West Coast Native life and are concerned with the theme of responsibility: that of a boy towards his tribe. Both writers were steeped in anthropological research; but they managed to show, as a natural part of their stories, what early Native societies were like. The prolific John Hayes wrote about many of the significant events in Canadian history, but often blandly, and to the detriment of the fictional component of the story. Still, such titles as *A land divided* (1951, the expulsion of the Acadians), *The steel ribbon* (1967, the building of the CPR), and *Flaming prairie* (1965, the Northwest Rebellion of 1885), all complete with young heroes, gave some life to the pages of history. During the 1950s and 1960s the Great Stories of Canada series presented fictionalized accounts of many colourful events, such as Pierre BERTON's *The golden trail: the story of the Klondike rush* (1954); and colourful figures, such as Luella Creighton's *Tecumseh: the story of the Shawnee chief* (1965).

The best fantasies for children have been bred in Great Britain, the land of romantic and bloody history and of myth, legend, and poetry. Apart from its Native legends, Canadian literature lacks most of the components that make up the stuff of fantasy, which has traditionally been a literature of place: there has to be a place to go to, or even to come from. Our two early important fantasists wisely used the Canadian terrain for their 'other worlds', and even managed to make a virtue of its vastness and anonymity. Catherine Anthony CLARK set her six fantasies in, on, and around the towns, mountains, valleys, lakes and rivers of British Columbia. In her first book, *The golden pine cone* (1950; reprinted in 1994) her children are shown to be as at home in their natural environment as in a quasi-magical world peopled with beings indigenous to the landscape, such as a Lake Snake, a Rock Puck, an Ice Maiden, and Native spirits. In *The one-winged dragon* (1955) Clark introduced a Chinese dragon as well as a Chinese father and his daughter and was thus the first fantasist to indicate the strong presence of the Chinese in British Columbia. All her plots followed a similar pattern—sensible, practical boy and a girl go on a quest for a selfless reason. The children, although they may be orphaned or bereft of one parent, are in no way the ultra-sensitive, even tortured protagonists of both current fantasy and realistic fiction. With *A walk out of the world* (1969) and *The marrow of the world* (1972) Ruth NICHOLS introduced epic fantasy (that is, the great battle between good and evil) into a then-sparse genre and gave it Canadian settings—Vancouver and the Prairies in the former and the rugged lake country around Georgian Bay in the latter. As an heir and afficionado of the great English fantasists C.S. Lewis and J.R.R. Tolkien, Nichols successfully moved English-type legendary and folklore beings into her Canadian settings.

1970s to 1996. 1. REALISTIC FICTION. Canadian children's literature began with realistic fiction and it continues, as in other countries, to be the staple genre, chiefly because it encompasses such varied sub-genres: outdoor survival stories, stories of child and family life, mysteries, animal stories, and other less classifiable groupings that can simply be called light realism. Within these categories several definite trends can be discerned. There is continued strength and variety in the outdoor survival story; works that endeavour to show the growing diversity of cultures within Canada have become numerous; and young-adult novels (here defined by the age of the protagonist) appear to take precedence, in numbers published, over novels for ages nine to twelve.

1(a) *Outdoor survival stories*. Ninety per cent of Canadians live in urban areas, yet our vast wilderness and the spaces beyond our cities and towns continue to influence the Canadian literary imagination. Writers of the 1980s brought new dimensions to the outdoor survival story, demonstrating its extraordinary flexibility as a vehicle for reflecting current ideas about the young and their problems. They broadened the simple ingredients of the traditional outdoor survival story to include elements of social realism, mysticism, and the strong portrayal of character, often revealed through the convention of rites of passage. They committed themselves to the reasonable belief that the interior life of their protagonists is just as important as the exterior space they inhabit, if not more so. They have also tended to use the wilderness more as a haven or a place of healing than as a direct physical challenge to survival. Although their heroes and heroines do face and overcome physical dangers, tests of courage are no longer the crux of the story, as in the past. In Monica HUGHES' *Hunter in the dark* (1982), set in an Alberta wilderness, the 'hunter' is death—pursuing a young teenager who knows he is dying of leukemia but still fights for survival. An Alberta wilderness is also the setting for Jan Truss's *Jasmin* (1982), which joins the few books of wilderness life with a girl as the chief character. Jasmin (one of seven in a very poor family) is a very modern heroine. Having too much responsibility at home, she runs away to find a haven in an unstructured environment—and she is only in Grade 6. To date the most unusual outdoor survival story is Tim WYNNE-JONES's *The maestro* (1995), which oddly but brilliantly combines family abuse, northern Ontario bush survival, and the last days of a world-famous, eccentric Canadian pianist (a thinly disguised Glenn Gould). Monica Hughes' *Log jam* (1987) and Marilyn Halvorson's *Nobody said it would be easy* (1987) are simpler in concept and plot than the three titles previously mentioned, but they add to the evidence that stories involving physical courage, skills, inventiveness, and daring outside the security net of urban living also encompass emotional survival and healing. It is interesting that the authors of these new survival stories make a greater use of imagery and metaphor than do the modern fantasists.

1(b). *Stories of child and family life.* Jean LITTLE is Canada's most notable writer of family stories: her books have been translated into at least seven languages. In more than twenty books she has been concerned with the universal problems of childhood: the need for friendship and acceptance, disabilities, and such other psychological issues as dealing with the death of a parent or a sibling. Her popularity lies in her sincerity, empathy with the young, and an ability to write with both simplicity and emotion—from her earliest books such as *Mine for keeps* (1962), about a child with cerebral palsy, to her more symbolic *Momma's going to buy you a mocking bird* (1984) in which an eleven-year-old must find out 'how it is going to be' in his life after his father dies. Little has also been one of the first writers to use the often anonymous urban setting rather than the more specifically defined regional ones. Urban settings, deeply emotional problems, and a minimalist style are the hallmarks of Sarah ELLIS in such books as *The baby project* (1986; *The family project* in its American edition), *Pick-up sticks* (1991), and *Out of the blue* (1994). They provide a very modern look at child and family life with realistic dialogue and considerable wit. With his *Angel Square* (1984) Brian DOYLE showed himself to be a regional novelist and a storyteller rather than a problem-solver for the young in conceiving a multi-layered book with a strong plot, and providing a sensitive and humorous look at family life towards the end of the Second World War. Its Ottawa setting is continued and expanded in his later works for young adults. Alberta during the depression of the 1930s would seem to be a strange setting for Cora Taylor's *Summer of the mad monk* (1994) whose young protagonist, blessed with a taste for reading and a strong imagination, persuades himself that the town blacksmith is really Rasputin of former Tsarist Russia. In strong contrast, Toronto's wealthy Rosedale area and cottage life in northern Ontario are the settings for Kit PEARSON's the 'Guests of War' trilogy: *The sky is falling* (1989), *Looking at the moon* (1991), and *The lights go on again* (1994). The time is the Second World War and the springboard for the plot is the arrival in Canada of two 'war guests', a ten-year-old girl and a five-year-old boy, taken in by a wealthy widow and her spinster daughter. These are stories of adjustment—to wealth after the strictures of an English lower-middle-class life and to Canada itself. On the whole, Canadian realistic fiction tends to be serious; but there are a few writers who see the light-hearted and comic aspects in child and family life, such as Betty Waterton with her *Quincy Rumple* series, beginning in 1984, Ellen Schwartz with *Starshine* (1987), and Ken Roberts with *Pop bottles* (1987) and *Hiccup champion of the world* (1988). Such books are not mere pieces of froth; they frequently flesh out the realities of child and family life with the absurdities, even the slapstick, that are part of most functional families. With his collection of short stories, *Some of the kinder planets* (1994), Tim Wynne-Jones took humour a step further and invested the ordinary lives of children with a kind of wacky surrealism.

1(c). *Cultural diversity.* Friendships between white teenage boys and Natives (Amerindian or Inuit) have often formed the basic plot in early Canadian children's literature. Farley Mowat and James Houston continued this tradition from the late 1950s to the 1980s in works in which rather easy-going friendships were mostly played out in short-lived survival crises and the different cultures did not heavily impinge upon one another. Recent examples of ethnic mix are now more often set (as in life itself) in urban or semi-urban environments and have harsher components: acceptance, respect, and friendship do not come easily; though the children live next door to one another, attend the same schools, and play in the same streets, the time of adjustment will last for a lifetime, not just through an isolated adventure. Among the earliest sensitive immigration stories are Jean Little's *From Anna* (1972) and *Listen for the singing* (1977), both of which incorporate the author's experience with a disability as well as with prejudice, here against a German immigrant family in Toronto just before and after the outbreak of the Second World War. Sarah Ellis's *Next-door neighbours* (1989) is also multi-faceted: it deals with intolerance towards another race while portraying a happy and lively family of Canadian children in the 1950s in Vancouver who meet prejudice for the first time. There is little doubt that the books with an autobiographical component are the most compelling, the most painful to read, and possibly have the greatest chance of actually changing attitudes—the purpose of most of these books, especially those of the 1990s. Such books often also give the greatest literary experience because of their ring of authenticity. Bernice Culleton's *In search of April Raintree* (1983; with a shortened version published as *April Raintree* in 1984) is based on the early lives of two young Métis sisters in Manitoba. Joy KOGAWA's *Naomi's road* (1986) is also a memoir-novel, the result of the author's experience as a Japanese-Canadian child interned during the Second World War in the interior of British Columbia. *My name is Seepeetza* (1992), by Shirley Stirling, is a semi-autobiographical recollection by a Native girl at a residential school in British Columbia where her name is changed to Nancy. Like Kogawa's book, this story of a forced loss of identity is told quietly from a child's point of view and without bitterness. Personal experience certainly lends both emotion and credibility to Lillian Boraks-Nemetz's *The old brown suitcase* (1994) and *Tell no one who you are: the hidden childhood of Regine Miller* (1994), as told to Walter Buchignani. Both convey the terror and loneliness of Jewish children who barely escaped the Holocaust. That the effects of the Holocaust are still with us is shown in Sharon Kirsh's *Fitting in* (1995) in which a Jewish child of the 1960s first learns of the persecution of her people in Nazi Germany. The flexibility of the ethnic or immigrant story can be seen in Sharon Gibson Palermo's *Chestnuts for the brave* (1991) in which a 1960s Italian family in Halifax finds that the adults must adjust to Canadian ways in order to give their daughter the new life they had planned for her. It is a realistic look at the problems of teenage immigrants.

Recent political events abroad have brought many more immigrants of diverse backgrounds to Canada. Although the literature centring on them will always lag a bit, there are enough recent publications to show that immigrant children and their well-being in this country are a concern of both writers and publishers. Ann Alma's *Skateway to freedom* (1993) tells of the tribulations of a family both before they flee East Germany in 1989 and when they start life anew in Calgary. The child here, a promising figure skater, is reminiscent of Lyn Cook's protagonist in *The bells on Finland Street* (1950) in which an immigrant Ukrainian child wants to 'skate for Canada'. One can only ask if a child has to be especially talented to be accepted as a peer. With the appearance of a Croatian child in *The onlyhouse* (1995) by Teresa Toten, it can be deduced that writers and publishers wish to keep up with the newest of immigrants. *There goes the neighbourhood* (1995) by Valerie Lupini is also up-to-date in its view of wealthy immigrant Chinese families in Vancouver who build monster houses and cut down trees on their property in the interests of the Chinese beliefs in *feng-shui*. The Chinese, who have figured in children's literature at least since the nineteenth century, have their own spokesperson in Paul YEE. His *The curses of third uncle* (1986), set in Vancouver's Chinatown of 1909, combines a mystery, the harsh life of girls left without a father, the daring journey of a fourteen-year-old girl into the interior of British Columbia, and the Chinese community's link with the fall of the Manchu Empire in China. His *Tales from Gold Mountain: stories of the Chinese in the New World* (1989) is, as its subtitle suggests, a group of short stories based on the mostly bitter immigrant experiences that blend historical fact, realism, and legendary motifs, and recount the daily hardships and emotional lives of the nineteenth-century Chinese immigrants on the Pacific coast. There is little doubt, given the increasing Canadian ethnic mix, that such books will increase in numbers. It is unfortunate that—whether for dramatic tension or in the interests of realism—Canadian young people are so often seen, at least at first, as antagonistic to newcomers from an alien culture.

1(d). *The young-adult novel.* If the 'young-adult novel' is defined by the age of the protagonist alone, then most Canadian fiction for the young, especially of the earlier days, falls into this category. Certainly modern writers prefer to write about adolescents rather than children. Perhaps they cannot cope with the restrictions still placed on children, or they feel that childhood has been eroded in our society, or that writing novels for teens gives more scope for exploring emotions—clearly of more interest to recent writers than developing plot. Many novels for teens grow out of a strong sense of regionalism. Kevin MAJOR was one of the earliest writers for this age group to combine a knowledge and love of a region (Newfoundland) with empathy for the universal problems of the young. His themes range from the accidental death of parents in *Hold fast* (1978) to a generally troubled teenager in *Far from shore* (1980) to a metaphor of teenage life in *Thirty-six exposures* (1984) and an imaginary relationship with an American rock star in *Dear Bruce Springsteen* (1987). His concern with the problems of the teenage male is more than matched by Diana Wieler with *Bad boy* (1989), which raised the then-daring topic of homosexuality. Marilyn Halvorson's *Cowboys don't cry* (1984) and *Let it go* (1985) and Mary-Ellen Lang Collura's *Winners* (1984) also have male teenage protagonists in a state of raw anger in situations caused by either the death of a parent or parental desertion. Brian Doyle's *Up to low* (1982) is unusual in young adult literature in that its teenage narrator is not the person with the problem. The result is a wider look at the human condition than the usual highly introspective teenage novel provides, as it includes a succession of comical adult characters and macabre events. Doyle has the ability to create memorable youthful characters such as Tommy (also of *Angel Square*) and Spud Sweetgrass of the novel of that title (1992) and of *Spud in winter* (1995). Both are set in Ottawa, both contain a plot, and both have a kind of sweetness that is far from saccharine—an unusual characteristic. William Bell's young-adult novels focus on current issues. He first came to notice with *Forbidden City* (1990), the story of a Canadian teenager who becomes involved in the horrific events of Tiananmen Square in Beijing. In his *Speak to the earth* (1994) the dramatic tension comes from an effort to save the old-growth forests on Vancouver Island. The short-story form has rather surprisingly leapt into prominence with Martha Brooks' two collections, *Paradise Café and other stories* (1988) and *Traveling on into the light* (1994) in which we hear the voices of Manitoba young people as they observe the adult world around them. Budge Wilson's *The leaving* (1992) presents a series of linked stories of Nova Scotian life in the recent past, somewhat in the mode of Alice MUNRO's *Lives of girls and women*, as they feature relationships between sisters and between mothers and daughters. Sarah Ellis's *Back of beyond* (1996) brings touches of the supernatural and witty dialogue into the lives of adolescents to highlight their concerns.

2. HISTORICAL FICTION. In its pure definition a work of historical fiction evokes a period that is beyond the memory of those living. Such novels are also 'rendered historical by the introduction of dates, personages, or events to which identification can readily be given' (Alfred T. Sheppard, *The art & practice of historical fiction*, 1930, p.3). It is obvious that what is historical to a child is not so to any adult over the age of fifty—the Great Depression of the 1930s and the Second World War are two examples. Moreover, there is the theory that all realistic fiction eventually becomes historical simply through the passage of time. However, two main streams of historical fiction for young people can be identified: books that provide background on a great event of history and those that provide a small slice of social history—both types sharing youthful protagonists. Most writers of the seventies and eighties were interested only in social history. Among the varied topics chosen were strike action and unions. These form the core of Bill Freeman's *Shantymen of Cache Lake* (1975) and *Trouble at Lachine Mill* (1983), Marsha Hewitt's and Claire Mackay's *One proud summer* (1981), and Geoffrey Bilson's *Goodbye Sarah* (1982)—ranging in time periods from the 1870s to the Valleyfield strike in Quebec in 1939. Many other writers of social life have concentrated on immigrant and pioneer experiences, and their books vary as greatly as Canada's vast regions. The United Empire Loyalists are well represented in Mary Alice Downie's and John Downie's *Honor bound* (1971), John Hayes' *On Loyalist trails* (1971), and Mary Beacock Fryer's *Escape: adventures of a Loyalist family* (1976). In all these books (and others) the pros and cons of the American War of Independence are treated from the Loyalist side only, and it is the flight to Canada and the pioneer experience that is the focus of each tale. The Prairies, of course, are a natural background for the detailing of immigrant life. The title of Barbara SMUCKER's *Days of terror* (1979) refers to the persecution of the Mennonites in the days of the Russian Revolution and the escape of a family to a new home. Exodus and arrival, a journey from hardship and injustice to the promise of freedom and success in the New World, is the great North American theme. Smucker's *Underground to Canada* (1977) is about the slave trade in the United States and the underground railroad to Canada, simply but poignantly detailed. However, most of our pioneer historical fiction is a rather simple record of both hardships and joys in a new country. In Celia Barker Lottridge's *Ticket to Curlew* (1992), a young boy who emigrates with his father from Iowa to find a better life

in Canada quickly falls in love with the Saskatchewan prairie. Cecil Freeman Beeler's *The girl in the well* (1991), and its sequel, *No room in the well* (1993), are richer novels combining harsh prairie life with warm family values and a heroine who has too much responsibility for her age. Ontario farm life is contrasted with the bustling routine of a Toronto hotel in the 1830s in Marianne Brandis's trilogy *The tinderbox* (1982), *The quarter-pie window* (1985), and *The sign of the scales* (1990)—lengthy, leisurely, but page-turning novels with a spirited heroine. Her latest novel, *Rebellion* (1996), can be considered traditional historical fiction in its detailed depictions of the events that led to and culminated in William Lyon MACKENZIE's doomed effort to reform the government of Upper Canada in 1837. Most writers look to Canada's past for inspiration, but a few have found it in the European past. Karleen Bradford's *There will be wolves* (1992) and *Shadows on a sword* (1996) display both the disasters and the pageantry of the first two Crusades. Carol Matas, perhaps better known for her books set in Denmark in the Second World War, such as *Lisa* (1987), turned to medieval France in *The burning time* (1994) to expose the terrible position of women healers accused of witchcraft. It seems safe to conjecture that the new historical fiction has put life into what the young have often considered the dry bones of history.

3. FANTASY. Janet LUNN with *Double Spell* (1968; American title *Twin spell*) was the first Canadian writer of fantasy to use an urban setting (here Toronto), and the first to adopt a relatively new concept of fantasy, which almost reverses that of the past. Fantasists no longer (or at least rarely) take young readers to an 'Other World', a secondary reality, but rather unleash the forces of magic and the supernatural into the real world. Thus reality and fantasy exist side by side. Such stories can be read to focus on believability (the supernatural is a part of everyday life) or on psychological causes (the stress and distress put upon the protagonists caused them to imagine strange events or to act beyond their normal behaviour). In either case, modern fantasy tends to be played out entirely in the real world, with the possibility of strange events being left to the reader to think about. That this is the trend in Canada can be seen in Joan CLARK's *Wild man of the woods* (1985), Welwyn Wilton Katz's *False face* (1987) and *Come like shadows* (1993), Michael BEDARD's *A darker magic* (1987) and its sequel *Painted devil* (1994), Monica Hughes' *Castle Tourmandyne* (1995), and Margaret Buffie's *Who is Frances Rain?* (1987) and *The dark garden* (1995). Although varied in themes and plots, all the above titles share a strong realistic component and a deep psychological one. Kit Pearson's *Awake and dreaming* (1996) partially fits the new concept of fantasy in its psychological aspects, but is best described as a ghost story, a genre that subtly differs from fantasy. Of all types of fantasy, past-time fantasy—stories in which the characters travel into the past from their own time—can still be considered conventional fantasy in that whatever talisman or spur (generally unhappiness) propels them into the past, they return refreshed and healed as a result of their experiences. Janet Lunn's introverted heroine in *The root cellar* (1981) returns from her involvement in the American Civil War to an appreciation of her noisy and loving extended Canadian family. Cora Taylor's *The doll* (1987) and Kit Pearson's *A handful of time* (1987), although very different in plot, skilfully combine fantasy and social and family history through emotional crises; Canada's pioneer prairie past in the former and Ontario of the 1930s in the latter. In *White jade tiger* (1993) by Julie Lawson, a Chinese-Canadian girl opens a door into the 1880s in British Columbia, in a search for a magical amulet, and into the lives of the Chinese who helped to build the Canadian Pacific Railway. O.R. Melling takes modern teenagers back into Ireland's violent mythology and history in *The Druid's tune* (1983), *The singing stone* (1986), and *The hunter's moon* (1993).

4. NATIVE LEGENDS. In the 1980s Native Canadians protested against what they described as the appropriation of stories and voice in the retelling by non-Natives of the tales of Amerindians. Lenore KEESHIG-TOBIAS stated that 'stories are power', and that their appropriation is 'culture theft, the theft of voice'. Others regarded the oral as Native and the written as belonging to 'the enemy', the colonizer. And Basil H. JOHNSTON objected to the misrepresentation of Nanabush (Nanabozho) in the popular stories about him because the characterization omitted a world of Ojibwa perceptions, oral traditions, and rituals. Stories of the Rama Ojibwa elders in *The adventures of Nanabush: Ojibway Indian stories* (1979), recorded and compiled by Emerson and David Coatsworth, meld the inflections of various elders into a confiding voice that seems to belong to a single storyteller. Johnston, an Ojibwa ethnologist at the Royal Ontario Museum, has also made use of the living Native oral tradition in *Tales the elders told: Ojibway legends* (1981). The Native

artist Bill Reid and the poet Robert BRINGHURST have combined their talents to retell some of the Raven legends in *The Raven steals the light* (1984) in a lyrical but also somewhat bawdy style that is open to young readers who have some knowledge of the legends and culture of West Coast Native peoples. As with the retelling and publishing of folklore in general, the trend is towards the single illustrated tale, such as *How Turtle set the animals free* (1991), developed by the Okanagan Tribal Council. (See also ABORIGINAL LEGENDS AND TALES.)

5. OTHER GENRES. Science fiction, popular with many children, has become almost a one-person monopoly by Monica Hughes. She has also achieved an international reputation with her futuristic works, as well as with her realistic fiction and fantasy. Her Isis trilogy—*The keeper of the Isis light* (1980), *The guardian of Isis* (1981), and *The Isis pedlar* (1982)—have echoes of Canadian pioneer experience, as well as highly original plots as space settlers adjust to a strange environment. *The golden Aquarians* (1994), which also takes place on a far-flung planet, has an environmental focus.

Modern verse has been dominated by Dennis LEE, whose *Alligator pie* (1974) has become a Canadian classic. It was quickly followed by *Nicholas Knock* (1974), *Garbage delight* (1977), and *Jelly belly* (1983). His aim has been to give Canadian children a sense of their own particular time and space—a feat that cannot be accomplished in writing from other countries, no matter how excellent it is. His verses chiefly take their mode from the English nursery rhymes and from the childhood poems of Robert Louis Stevenson and A.A. Milne, but always with a Lee twist and often with a Canadian reference. His verses are also often interspersed with brief lyrical poems. Other versifiers have followed Lee: Lois Simmie with *Auntie's knitting a baby* (1984); Sheree Fitch with *Toes in my nose* (1987), *There were monkeys in my kitchen* (1992), and *Mabel Murple* (1995); Robert Heidbreder with *Don't eat spiders* (1985) and *Eenie meenie Manitoba* (1996). Two anthologies—*The new wind has wings* (1984) compiled by Mary Alice Downie and Barbara Robertson and *Till all the stars have fallen* (1989) compiled by David Booth—offer a variety of Canadian poems, chiefly drawn from poems written for adults but deemed (quite rightly) appealing to the young. The poems in Booth's *Images of nature: Canadian poets and the Group of Seven* (1995) range from traditional Inuit songs to a poem by Leonard COHEN. Linda Granfield tells the background story of the writing of the famous Canadian war poem by John McCRAE in *In Flanders Fields* (1995).

History came alive with the publication of *The story of Canada* (1992) by Janet Lunn and Christopher Moore, a splendid amalgam of fact and storytelling. An equally appealing and unusual look at history is found in *A pioneer story: the daily life of a Canadian family in 1846* (1994) by Barbara Greenwood. This compendium of facts, fiction, recipes, activities, and pictures is presented from a child's point of view. Jean Little has ventured into the area of semi-autobiography with a partly fictionalized story of her own life in *Little by Little* (1987) and *Stars come out within* (1990) and of semi-biography with *His banner over me* (1995), the story of her missionary parents, particularly her mother.

In general, information books have increased in quantity and quality. Much of this is owing to the editors of *Owl*, a popular and long-lasting nature magazine. The single illustrated tale dominates the general as well as the Canadian publishing scene of folk and fairy tales. But Eva Martin's *Canadian fairy tales* (1984), is the only major and comparatively recent *collection* of tales with a Canadian ambience. Its stated purpose was to retell some of the stories 'collected by folklorists in the early twentieth century from second or third generations of settlers who in their retelling of the stories retained the original theme motifs, and adapted the stories to suit their new environment.' Since the 1970s the fastest-growing and most vital genre of children's-book publishing has been the picturebook. A great many writers, and gifted illustrators, keep the scene lively for the pre-school child, while many illustrators are eagerly sought outside Canada and Canadian publishers have little difficulty in achieving co-publication in another country. Some Canadian writers and illustrators have built up a considerable body of work: Sue Ann Alderson, Jan Andrews, Ann Blades, Lazlo Gal, Ted Harrison, Robert Munsch, Ian Wallace, Betty Waterton, to name but a few. Others have swung into prominence very quickly: Phoebe Gilman, Nan Gregory, Sharon Jenning, Michael Kusugak, Tim Wynne-Jones, and many others. All in all, there is little doubt that the picturebook is alive and well and living in Canada and is making excursions to other countries.

Canadian children's books have become more sophisticated, more distinguished, more popular, and those published after the 1970s have become less parochial. But while they have joined international trends, the best are still distinctively Canadian.

See Sheila Egoff and Judith Saltman, *The republic of childhood: a critical guide to Canadian children's literature in English* (1990), Irma McDonough, *Canadian books for young people* (1980), Judith Saltman, *Modern Canadian children's books* (1987), and Elizabeth Waterston, *Children's literature in Canada* (1992).

See also CHILDREN'S DRAMA IN ENGLISH.

SHEILA EGOFF

Children's literature in French. 1. THE NINETEENTH CENTURY. Canadian children's literature in French does not have a long tradition. Nineteenth-century examples include mostly books that were read by children though not specially written for them—Claude Potvin's enlarged edition of *Le Canada français et sa littérature de jeunesse* (1982) mentions the 16-page *William, ou l'imprudent corrigé; petite histoire dédiée à l'enfance, suivi de La mendiante* (Québec, 1840), author unknown, containing two didactic stories of which one teaches a lesson in obedience and the other a lesson in generosity. One early book that was popular because of its subject matter was *L'enfant perdu et retrouvé; ou Pierre Cholet* (Montréal, 1887; rpr. 1978), by Jean-Baptiste Proulx, an adventure story about three kidnapped children who are sold as cabin-boys to a sea captain; only the eldest survives to tell of his adventures, which eventually bring him back to Canada.

Several books were devoted to tales and legends rooted in the past and were enjoyed by children because of the familiar background and speech patterns (more easily understood than such books imported from France): *Contes populaires* (Ottawa, 1867; rpr. 1912) by Paul Stevens, *Légendes canadiennes* (Québec, 1861; rpr. 1876) by Henri-Raymond CASGRAIN, *Le tomahahk et l'épée* (Québec, 1877) by Joseph MARMETTE, *La terre paternelle* (Montreal, 1846; rpr. 1924) by Patrice LACOMBE, and *Une de perdue, deux de trouvées* (2 vols, Montréal, 1874; rpr. 1956) by Pierre-Georges Boucher de Boucherville. These books were often distributed as school prizes by the Département de l'Instruction Publique (Quebec). The policy of circulating books in the schools began in 1876 and continued through the early part of the twentieth century in the hope that a sound basis for the development of children's literature could be established.

2. 1900 TO 1939. *À l'oeuvre et à l'épreuve* (Québec, 1891) by Laure Conan (Félicité ANGERS), the romanticized story of the Jesuit martyr Charles Garnier, was widely read by young people well into the 1940s; but another book of hers was even more popular with children and young people, *L'oublié* (1900; rpr. 1964), a novel about Lambert Closse, who participated in the founding of Ville-Marie. Over the years Félicité Angers wrote articles on Canadian personalities and collected several of them in *Silhouettes canadiennes* (1917; rpr. 1922), which she dedicated to the French-speaking school children of Ontario.

The preface of *Contes et légendes* (1915), by Adèle Bourgeoys Lacerte, states that it represents 'a completely new genre in Canada, where no one, until now, had made the effort to write particularly for children.' Four years later, *Récits laurentiens* (1919; rpr. 1964) by Frère MARIE-VICTORIN (Conrad Kirouac) was dedicated to 'la vaillante jeunesse du pays d'érable'. It was translated by James Ferres as *The chopping bee and other Laurentian stories* (1925).

One of the important events in the first stages of the development of French-Canadian literature for children took place in 1920, when Arthur Saint-Pierre, managing editor of the magazine *L'Oiseau bleu* (published by the Société St-Jean-Baptiste), asked Marie-Claire Daveluy to contribute a pioneer story in which the principal characters were children. Her story, about two French orphans who settle in New France, was serialized in *L'Oiseau bleu*; published in book form as *Les aventures de Perrine et de Charlot* (1923), it received the Prix David and was reprinted several times. Although Daveluy also wrote modern fairy tales, she is best known for her series of historical novels on the early French settlers. Other budding writers of the period, like Marie-Louise d'Auteuil (*Mémoires d'une souris canadienne*, 1932; rpr. 1945), contributed to the output and success of L'Oiseau bleu, which ceased publication in 1940.

Three other well-known authors who began to write in the 1920s were Maxine, Eugène Achard, and Claude Melançon. Maxine—the pseudonym of Marie-Caroline Alexandra Taschereau-Fortier—was a prolific author of rather fanciful historical novels and short biographies of well-known figures (*Le marin de Saint-Malo, Jacques Cartier*, 1946). She is best, and fondly, remembered for her novel *Le petit page de Frontenac* (1930; rpr. 1963). Eugène Achard, who emigrated from France, had a writing career that extended over forty years, beginning in 1921 with *Aux quatre coins des routes canadiennes* and ending with *Sur les sentiers de la Côte Nord* (1960). He wrote some seventy books, including retellings of traditional tales (*L'oiseau vert et la princesse fortunée*, 1956) and biographies (*Les grands noms de l'histoire canadienne*, 1940), but mostly fiction (*Sous les plis du drapeau blanc*, 1935) and collections of modern fairy tales with a Canadian or Quebec setting (*Les contes de la claire fontaine*, 1943). During this period there were several books on the natural sciences, fostered by the creation of the Cercle des jeunes naturalistes and nurtured by one of its founders, Frère Marie-Victorin: *ABC du petit naturaliste canadien* (9 vols, 1935) by Harry BERNARD, *A travers les champs et les bois* (1931) by Louis-Jean Gagnon, *Les confidences de la nature* (1936) by Adolphe Brassard, *Nos animaux domestiques* (1933) by Odette Oligny, and *Oiseaux de mon pays* (1939; rpr. 1970) by Alice Duchesnay. The trend was continued in the 1940s by Marcelle Gauvreau, who wrote *Plantes curieuses de mon pays* (1943), and by Claude Melançon, who wrote several books, including one on the birds of Quebec (*Charmants voisins*, 1940; rpr. 1964) and one on Canadian animals (*Mon alphabet des animaux*, 1944). Melançon's books are something of a landmark in Canadian children's-book publishing in French. Besides the two books cited above, he wrote his popular *Légendes indiennes du Canada* (1967) and several other informational books on a variety of subjects; for example, *Mon alphabet des villes du Québec* (1944) and *Les poissons de nos eaux* (1936). His first publication, *Par terre et par eau* (1928), an adventure story of two kidnapped children, is overwhelmed by a geography lesson on Quebec. Although informative, it is tedious, and children today would find it difficult to read and to identify themselves with the hero and heroine, who act beyond their years. In many books the child was pictured as a model child—obviously a reflection of the feelings adults entertained about children. There were few novels portraying children in the home or in their daily lives, but two books that show how children were taught to behave are *Autour de la maison* (1916) and *La plus belle chose du monde* (1937; rpr. 1961) by Michelle Le Normand (pseudonym of Marie-Antoinette Desrosiers).

3. 1940 TO 1970. During the Second World War few French children's books were available in Quebec and publishers attempted to fill the gap. The ever-popular genre of fairy tales and legends was represented by Achard's *Les deux bossus de l'île d'Orléans et autres contes* (1944); two collections by Marius BARBEAU, *Les contes du grand-père sept-heures* (1950-3) in twelve paperback volumes—some of these stories were adapted and translated by Michael Hornyansky in *The golden phoenix and other French-Canadian fairy tales* (1958; rpr. 1980)—and *Les rêves des chasseurs* (1942); and Félix LECLERC's successful trilogy of fables and poems *Adagio* (1943; rpr. 1976), *Allegro* (1944; rpr. 1976), and *Andante* (1944; rpr. 1975). Guy Boulizon (who emigrated from France) and Ambroise Lafortune wrote adventure stories in which some of the principal characters were Boy Scouts. A typical book by Lafortune, who was himself a Scout leader, is *Le secret de la rivière perdue* (1946). Boulizon's *Prisonniers des cavernes* (1950) was rewritten and published in 1979 as *Alexandre et les prisonniers des cavernes*. A few other notable books of this period were Claude Aubry's *La vengeance des hommes de bonne volonté* (1944), reprinted twice under the title *Le loup de Noël*, and Andrée MAILLET's picturebook *Ristontac* (1945), illustrated by Robert Lapalme, and *Le marquiset têtu et le mulot réprobateur* (1944).

For some years after the war, it became evident that interest in children's books was on the wane, and there was good reason for this: sameness and mediocrity ruled in the themes and treatment of historical novels and the many books of folk and fairy tales, history, and biography. Changes were necessary in order to reflect new societal attitudes, and to provide children with a greater number of books that responded to their needs and interests. In the late fifties four writers began to bring some distinction to the field: Paule DAVELUY, Yves THÉRIAULT, Claudine Vallerand, and Monique Corriveau—Daveluy with *L'été enchanté* (1958—translated by Munroe Stearns as *Summer in Ville-Marie*, 1962), Thériault with *Alerte au camp 29* (1959), Vallerand (under the pseudonym 'Maman Fonfon') with *Chante et joue* (1957), and Corriveau with *Le secret de Vanille* (1959; rpr. 1981) and *Le Wapiti* (1964; *The Wapiti*, 1968), a captivating romance of seventeenth-century New France that offers not only a marvellous adventure story but genuine insight into the lives of both the Natives and the French in Canada's earliest days. Corriveau was able to develop atmosphere that becomes an essential component of the story, as in *Les saisons de la mer* (1975), about an Irish family in Newfoundland in the 1920s. Another interesting writer who began to be published in this period is Suzanne Martel, whose *Quatre Montréalais en l'an 3000* (1963)—reprinted under the title *Surréal 3000* (1980) and translated as *The city underground* (1982)—shows her lively ability to introduce humour even in her inventive science-fiction novels, of which *Nos amis robots* (1981) is the most recent. Claude Aubry's *Agouhanna* (1974; rpr. 1981), written in a simple, even poetic manner, is another novel of the period that has worn well. Informational books on a variety of subjects—such as *Chevalier du Roi; vie de saint Ignace de Loyola* (1956) by Beatrice Clément—were not as appealing to young readers as were the mystery and adventure stories.

Between 1965 and 1970 a slump occurred in children's literature: books were no longer given as school prizes, and French and Belgian imports increased. Retail trade declined, while textbook publishing increased to keep up with the demands brought about by the changes in the newly laicized educational system. Between 1965 and 1968 only about 80 trade titles appeared, and in 1969 and 1970 fewer than 10—a mere trifle compared to the 1,000 children's books that were being published annually in France.

4. 1971 TO 1982. The founding in 1971 of Communication-Jeunesse in Quebec inspired authors, illustrators, publishers, booksellers, librarians, and teachers to work together, and this organization became a key factor in the promotion of children's-book publishing in the province. Working within the whole socio-cultural and political context of 1976, the year the Parti Québécois came to power, Communication-Jeunesse has since been developing the need for a specifically Quebec children's literature.

Several writers responded to this need. Bertrand Gauthier wrotes inventive, droll stories filled with puns. *Hébert Luée* (1980), in which the two main characters search for a circus in Montreal, offers a critical view of contemporary society without being preachy; it was illustrated with colourful, often outlandish pictures, by Marie-Louise Gay, who has also written and illustrated a counting book, *De zéro à minuit* (1981). Ginette Anfousse has written and illustrated a series of books about a little girl and her toy anteater, all of which were translated into English and published by NC Press. The first two—*La cachette* (English title, *Hide and seek*) and *Mon ami Pichou* (English title, *My friend Pichou*)—were published in 1976; all the titles in the series were reprinted and may well become classics. A charming fantasy, in which three children go on a search for time, is *Le voyage à la recherche du temps* (1981) by Lucie Ledoux, illustrated in black and white by Phillippe Béha.

In 1974 Fides inaugurated its series 'Du Goéland', whose titles include *Le garçon au cerf-volant* (1974) by Monique Corriveau; *Le ru d'Ikoué* (1963; rpr. 1977) by Yves Thériault; *Le chat de l'Oratoire* (1978) by Bernadette Renaud; and *Chansons pur un ordinateur* (1980) by Francine Loranger. Les Éditions Héritage, which publishes the magazine *Hibou* (an adaptation of the English-language magazine *Owl*), launched several series of children's books, among them 'Pour lire avec toi', designed for young readers in the post-picturebook transitional phase. Fantasy and reality intermingle in three books belonging to this series: *Fend-le-vent et le visiteur mystérieux* (1980) by Serge Wilson; *Émilie la baignoire à pattes* (1976) by Bernadette Renaud; and *Alfred dans le métro* (1980), written and illustrated by Cécile Gagnon. *La révolte de la courtepointe* (1979) by Bernadette Renaud also combines the real and the fantastic. The Héritage series 'Katimavik' includes Suzanne Martel's *Pi-Oui* (1974)—which was translated into English as *Peewee*—and *Contes de mon pays* (1980) by Germain Lemieux. The series 'Jeunesse Pop', published by Les Éditions Paulines, includes Louis Landry's *Glausgab créateur du monde* (1981) and *Glausgab le protecteur* (1981), two novels that create a new mythological hero, an Algonquin who lands in France in the late fifteenth century and is invited by the French court to tell his story. The joint title of the two books is *La véritable histoire du Grand Manitou Algonquin*.

Young francophone readers have been introduced to good texts from English Canada by a series called 'Deux solitudes—jeunesse', published by Les Éditions Pierre Tisseyre. Among its titles are stories about growing up—*La promesse de Luke Baldwin* (1980) by Morley CALLAGHAN, translated by Michelle Tisseyre (*Luke Baldwin's vow*) and *Je t'attends à Peggy's Cove* (1982) by Brian DOYLE, translated by Claude Aubry (*You can pick me up at Peggy's Cove*); about handicapped children—*Écoute l'oiseau chantera* (1980) by Jean LITTLE, translated by Paule Daveluy (*Listen for the singing*); about animals—*Deux grands ducs dans la famille* (1980) by Farley MOWAT, translated by Paule Daveluy (*Owls in the family*); about Mennonites in Russia who eventually settled in Manitoba—*Jours de terreur* (1981) by Barbara SMUCKER, translated by Paule Daveluy (*Days of terror*); and about the North—*L'archer blanc* (1978) by James HOUSTON (*The white archer*).

See Louise Lemieux, *Pleins feux sur la littérature de jeunesse au Canada français* (1972) and Claude Potvin, *Le Canada français et sa litérature de jeunesse* (1982). IRENE E. AUBREY

1980s to 1996. The 1980s saw a considerable expansion in the production of books for children and young people, which has increased to the point of becoming in many cases more profitable than publishing for adults. A number of publishers either specialize in books for youth or devote a significant part of their production to them. In addition to the novels it published, Québec-Amérique Jeunesse created the series 'Contes pour tous' based on the scenarios of films produced by Rock Demers. Les Éditions du Raton Laveur published picturebooks on both serious and entertaining themes. A passion for books led the veterinarian Michel Quintin to establish a publishing house specializing in informational books as well as stories and novels about animals and nature in general.

Cécile Gagnon, founder of the Association des Écrivains Québécois pour la Jeunesse (AEQJ), published several books in the 1980s, including the excellent novel *Châteaux de sable* (1988) and an anthology of Quebec tales and legends, *Mille ans de contes* (1996), which has been very useful for parents, teachers, librarians, and all those who tell stories to children. Gilles Gauthier's series 'Babouche' (1988-90) and 'Marcus' (1991-6) proved that novels continuing over several volumes can be of high quality and sustained interest. The same is true of Raymond Plante's popular 'Raisins' series, which began to appear in 1986 with *Le dernier des raisins*, about sixteen-year-old François Gougeon and his girlfriend, the beautiful Anik. All Quebec knows the story of François—Plante was the first Québécois writer to treat frankly the dawning of sexuality in young people. Susanne Julien's historical novel *Enfants de la Rébellion* (1989) was a lively and feeling account of the Patriotes of 1837-8. *Aller-retour* (1986) and *Le don* (1987)—which won a Governor General's Award (GGA)—by David Schinkel and Yves Beauchesne are two of the great successes of these authors who wrote as a team and won many literary prizes; tragically, the premature death of Beauchesne put an end to their collaboration. Robert Soulières, an author and editor well known to young people, had a hit with his novel *Casse-tête chinois* (1985), thanks to its outlandish humour.

Science fiction and fantasy are very popular genres with young Québécois. Among the most interesting titles of the last few years are *Ludovic* (1983) and *Le cercle de Khaleb* (1991) by Daniel Sernine, *Le domaine des sans yeux* (1989) and *Le rêve couleur d'orange* (1996) by Jacques Lazure, *L'ombre et le cheval* (1992) by Esther Rochon, the 'Inactifs' series by Dennis Côté, and *Le jour-de-trop* (1993) by Joël Champetier.

New provincial regulations for the development of cultural enterprises, assistance programs for publishers, and mobilization on the part of those involved in the field all contributed to the explosion of young people's literature in the 1980s. The first university program devoted specifically to young people's literature was established in 1985 at the Université du Québec à Montréal.

Communication-Jeunesse promoted reading through its 'Livromanie' and 'Livromagie' clubs, which found great success among young people. Activities centred on books grew exponentially, including those led by publishers who used them as promotional tools. The numbers of authors' tours increased and opportunities to meet authors became popular events at book fairs and elsewhere.

In the 1990s an industry was consolidated that is now viable and prosperous. All markets are catered to, and the competition is broad and healthy. Most universities offer courses or certificates in literature for young people. Numerous conferences are held, and the media regularly provide coverage of young people's literature. In 1995 the 'Explorations' series published by Québec-Amérique Jeunesse devoted itself to works aimed at assisting in the choice and analysis of young people's books, as well as in the organization of activities around them—incontestable proof of the abundance and richness of the field. Similarly, the presence of Québécois young people's literature on the international scene is an undeniable mark of its vitality: for example, Éditions Chouette's famous 'Caillou' series has been translated in numerous countries and has sold hundreds of thousands of copies. The same is true of some very popular novels published by Éditions La Courte Échelle, which has had many of its titles translated into various languages. The 'Plus' series published by Hurtubise HMH presents works by francophone authors from around the world aimed at immersion classes, courses in French as a second language, and remedial reading, as well as adult literacy programs. The active publishing program of Éditions Héritage has been extended by three new series: 'Alli-bi', thrillers translated from English; 'En plein coeur', novelized biographies of Quebec personalities; and the lovely 'Carrousel', short texts for beginning readers. Québec-Amérique Jeunesse, well aware that the boundary between books for young people and those for adults is becoming increasingly narrow, has introduced 'Titan +', a series for older teenagers. A new publishing house, Les 400 Coups, has distinguished itself with 'Billochet', a particularly interesting series presenting Quebec legends in elegant picture books. The 'Conquêtes' series published by Éditions Pierre Tisseyre includes three collections of poetry for children: *Des mots pour rêver* (1990), *Le souffle du poème* (1993), and *De Villon à Vigneault* (1994).

Ginette Anfousse has continued her 'Rosalie' series, begun in 1987, and written an excellent novel for teenagers, *Un terrible secret* (1991). Yves BEAUCHEMIN has told of the unusual friendship between a rat and a little boy in *Antoine et Alfred* (1992). Linda Brousseau has made readers cry with her touching *Marélie de la mer* (1993), while Denis Côté has given them the shivers with his novels, notably *Aux portes de l'horreur* (1994). Dominique Demers has had great success with her 'Marie-Lune' trilogy, beginning in 1992 with *Un hiver de tourmente*. Sylvie Desrosiers won the 12-17 prize (Brive, France/Montréal) for *Le long silence* (1995). Christine Duchesne continues to write superb love stories filled with fantasy, especially with *Victor* (1992, GGA), *La 42e soeur de Bébert* (1993), and *La bergère de chevaux* (1995). In *Zamboni* (1990) by François Gravel, the delightful operator of an ice-cleaning machine invites a nine-year-old to sit beside him, and the strange machine encourages dreaming. In the course of his trips on the Zamboni the boy learns to deal with his family problems, and even resolve them. In *Deux heures et demie avant Jasmine* (1991, GGA) Gravel recounts the minutes that separate an adolescent boy from 'l'heure' when Jasmine will come to share with him her 'first time'; and he evokes our sympathy for an introvert with a stammer in *Guillaume* (1995). Québec/Amérique Jeunesse has garnered several literary prizes through its writers, notably Michèle Martineau, with her unforgettable novel *La route de Chlifa* (1992, GGA), the story of Karim, who relives a sad period of his past in Lebanon; Jean Lemieux with his exciting adventure story, *Le trésor de Brion* (1995); and Gilles Tibo with *Noémie: Le secret de Madame Lumbago* (1996, GGA). Sonia Sarfati also won a Governor General's Award for *Comme une peau de chagrin* (1995), a novel about the experience of an anorexic girl.

Worth mentioning is the 'Cyrus' series, published by Québec/Amérique Jeunesse, which found unexpected success with its treatment of encyclopaedia-style information in the form of short stories. Finally, the series 'Deux Solitudes, Jeunesse' continues to excel in its choice of English-Canadian novels in translation, specifically *Un monde hors du temps* (1985) by Barbara SMUCKER, *Maman va t'acheter un moqueur* (1986) by Jean LITTLE, *Le ciel croule* by Kit PEARSON, *Shan Da et la cité interdite* (1991) by William Bell, and *Le grand désert blanc* (1994) by James HOUSTON.

At the end of the twentieth century some fifteen Quebec publishers are producing about two hundred books for young people every year. Three of them alone (Héritage, Pierre Tisseyre, and Courte Échelle) account for half the total. There are also a few courageous houses outside Quebec that publish children's books in French; in Ontario, Annick Press, the Centre Franco-Ontarien de Ressources Pédagogiques, Vermillon, Scholastic, Tundra, and Prise de Parole; Éditions d'Acadie in New Brunswick; and Éditions des Plaines et du Blé in Manitoba.

See Louise Lemieux, *Pleins feux sur la littérature de jeunesse au Canada français* (1972); Claude Potvin, *Le Canada français et sa littérature de jeunesse* (1982); and Edith Madore, *La littérature pour la jeunesse au Québec* (1994).

GINETTE GUINDON

Chiniquy, Charles. See BIOGRAPHY AND MEMOIRS IN FRENCH: 6.

Chislett, Anne (b. 1942). Born in St John's, Newfoundland, she studied at Memorial University and the University of British Columbia. With her husband, James Roy, she founded in 1975 the Blyth Festival, in southwestern Ontario, and retired from teaching high-school English and drama in 1980 to become a full-time playwright.

Most of Chislett's work has been successfully produced at the Blyth Festival, including her adaptation of Harry J. Boyle's 1964 novel *A summer burning* (1977); *The tomorrow box* (1980); *Quiet in the land* (1983); *Another season's promise*, co-authored with Keith Roulston (1988); *Yankee notions* (1992), and her adaptation of Ralph Connor's 1902 *GLENGARRY SCHOOL DAYS* (produced in 1994). Chislett has also written plays for young audiences, including *The gift* (1989) and *Flippin'in* (1995).

The principal recurring theme in Chislett's plays is the concept of change, with older generations often pitted against the young. For example, in *Quiet in the land* (Chalmers Play Award, 1982; Governor General's Award, 1983) a rebellious Amish teenager comes into conflict with family traditions and religious conventions. A similar conflict is seen in *Another season's promise*, though in this play the younger generation (embodied by a farmer's city-dwelling son) is eager to return to a more traditional way of life that is being threatened by encroaching urbanization and capitalist values. Drawing upon the conflict between rural and urban life as a dramatic framework, Chislett delves into more political territory in *The tomorrow box*, where the changing role and value of women in society is examined from differing perspectives. The layered, cycloramic structure of *Yankee notions*, which deals with the aftermath of the 1837 Upper Canada rebellion, is evidence of Chislett's flexibility as a playwright. Conventional dramatic structure, comedic undertones, and sensitive characterization are the hallmarks of all these plays. She has also written for radio, television, and film. REBECCA CONOLLY

Chittick, V.L.O. See CRITICISM IN ENGLISH 2.

Choquette, Ernest (1862-1941). Born at Beloeil, Canada East (Quebec), he took his classical course at the Collège de Saint-Hyacinthe and studied medicine in Montreal. He received his medical degree in 1886, and practised in Saint-Hilaire for the rest of his life. He was elected mayor of the village several times and in 1910 was appointed to the Quebec legislative council. He died in Montreal.

Choquette is the author of three novels, a collection of short stories, and two plays adapted from his fiction. *Les Ribaud: une idylle de 37* (Montréal, 1898) reflects renewed popular interest in the Rebellion of 1837 after the publication in the 1880s of two conflicting accounts, Charles-Auguste-Maximilien Globensky's *La Rébellion de 1837 à Saint-Eustache* and Laurent-Olivier David's *Les Patriotes de 1837-1838*. In Choquette's novel a sexagenarian Patriote, Dr Ribaud, whose father died fighting the English at Waterloo and whose son has been killed in a duel with an English officer, is furious when his daughter Madeleine falls in love with an English captain, Percival Smith. Despite the doctor's machinations, Percival's high-mindedness during the Rebellion, Madeleine's innocent passion, and the parish priest's wise counsel combine to ensure the triumph of love over bigoted nationalism—an unusual outcome for the period. With the assistance of a French critic, Charles ab der Halden, the novel was adapted as a play and performed in Jan. 1903 at the Théâtre National in Montreal under the title *Madeleine*, enjoying considerable success.

Choquette's second novel, *Claude Paysan* (Montréal, 1899), was first published as a serial in *La Patrie*; an abridged version later appeared in France. It recounts the silent love of the *habitant* Claude Drioux for a summer visitor from the city, Fernande Tissot, and his lonely wait each winter for her return. When she dies of tuberculosis, Claude disappears, and his body is later recovered from the river. Here again Choquette's primary theme is love, although the original edition also contains substantial descriptions of rural life.

The following year Choquette brought out, under the title *Carabinades* (Montréal, 1900), a lively collection of twenty-six anecdotes and stories drawn from his years as a medical student (*carabin*) and general practitioner. His last novel, *La terre* (1916), composed some years before its publication, is a didactic work setting forth the thesis that the French-Canadian population can hope to survive only by remaining agricultural and avoiding competition with English-speaking Canadians. Old Beaumont has two sons, Lucas and Yves: the former takes over the family farm, the latter becomes a skilled chemist, but finds his career constantly blocked by English rivals. Discouraged, Yves goes off to fight in the Transvaal, while his older brother falls into alcoholism, neglects his land, and even commits a murder. When Yves returns from South Africa he takes charge of the farm, having learned from the Boers to value agriculture and to resist assimilation. *La terre*, adapted for the stage in 1927 under the title *La bouée*, thus fitted into the regionalist pattern that was dominant in Quebec fiction in the early years of this century—although it assumed a hereditary incapacity for commerce and industry among French Canadians, a view not usually expressed in such fiction.

Choquette is a secondary Quebec novelist, but his books show some thematic originality, and his fictional technique improved steadily over the dozen years during which he wrote his novels and stories.

The only recent articles devoted to Choquette's novels are those found in the *Dictionnaire des oeuvres littéraires du Québec*, vols I and II (1978, 1980). DAVID M. HAYNE

Choquette, Robert (b. 1905). Born in Manchester, New Hampshire, of parents who had emigrated from Quebec, he spent his early youth in Lewiston, Maine. Following his mother's death in 1913 his father returned with his family to Montreal, where he opened a medical practice. Robert Choquette studied at the Collège Notre-Dame, the Collège Saint-Laurent, and Loyola College. After a short period as a reporter with the *Gazette*, he became secretary and librarian at the École des Beaux-Arts in Montreal (1928-31), at the same time becoming literary editor of *La Revue moderne*. In the early 1930s he began his long career as a writer for radio and, later, television.

Choquette's first poetry was written at Loyola College where, influenced by the

English and French Romantics, he composed some fifty poems that were published under the title *À travers les vents* (1925). Conventional for the most part, they reveal a gift for epic and a feeling for the sweep and grandeur of North America that won for the young poet the Prix David in 1926. A lyric-epic poem, *Metropolitan Museum* (1931), astonished critics by its breadth of vision: a panorama of the history of art, from ancient to modern times, that evokes the realities of science, mechanization, and urban life in the great American cities. In 1932 Choquette was again awarded the Prix David, both for this work and for the manuscript of a poetry collection, *Poésies nouvelles* (1933), that recalls the themes and style of his previous books. *Suite marine* (1953), a long poem in twelve cantos begun in 1934, marked the summit of both his poetic art and the lyric-epic vein. It won the Prix de l'Académie française in 1954 and the Prix David in 1956. *Oeuvres poétiques* (1956), assembled by the author, includes revisions of the first three collections, a reprinting of *Suite marine*, and 'Vers inédits'. A French edition of *Metropolitan Museum*, containing a preface by André Maurois, was published in 1963.

Choquette also wrote *La pension Leblanc* (1927; rpr. 1976), a novel that attempts to portray village life in the realistic manner of Flaubert. *Les Velder* (1941) and *Elise Velder* (1958; rpr. 1973) are adaptations of scripts written for radio. *Le curé de village* (1936) is composed of extracts from Quebec's first radio serial (CKAC, 1935-8); related to the regionalist novels of the 1930s, it became a model for many later serials. Other works by Choquette include *Le fabuliste La Fontaine à Montréal* (1935), a series of fifteen fables originally presented in the form of radio plays; a play, *Sous le règne d'Augusta* (1974); *Le sorcier d'Anticosti et autres légendes* (1975); and *Moi, Petruchka* (1980).

During his long career Choquette has written innumerable scripts for radio and television (sketches and dramatic serials, plays, cultural programs), only a few of which have been published. The best-known of the radio and television plays, *La pension Velder* (1938-42 and 1957-61) and *Métropole* (1943-56), use satire and caricature to create an amusing social portrait of Montreal. After leaving the airwaves at the start of the 1960s, Choquette lived in Paris in 1962-3, and visited Italy and Greece, returning to Ottawa to accept the post of associate commissioner of the Centennial Commission (1963-4). His diplomatic career began when he was Canadian consul-general in Bordeaux, France, from 1964 to 1968. He next served as Canadian ambassador to Argentina, Uruguay, and Paraguay from 1968 to 1970 and was director-general of Information Canada in Quebec (1971-3). He has since held various honorary posts and continued his work as writer. He was named Companion of the Order of Canada in 1969.

Representative selections of Choquette's poetry and prose can be found in *Robert Choquette* (1959) edited by André Melançon; *Poèmes choisis* (1970); and *Le choix de Robert Choquette* (1981). For critical studies of his work, see *Robert Choquette, romancier et dramaturge de la radio-télévision* (1977) by Renée Legris; *Le comique et l'humour à la radio québécoise, 1930-1970* (1976) by Pierre Pagé and Renée Legris; *Paragraphes* (1931) by Alfred DESROCHERS; and *Poètes de l'Amérique française* (1934) by Louis Dantin (Eugène SEERS).

RICHARD GIGUÈRE

Chouinard, Ernest. See NOVELS IN FRENCH 1900 TO 1920.

Choy, Wayson. See NOVELS IN ENGLISH 1983 TO 1996: OTHER NOVELS 2(b).

Choyce, Lesley (b. 1951). Born in Riverside, New Jersey, a graduate of Rutgers University, Montclair State College, and City University of New York, he settled in 1978 at Lawrencetown Beach, Nova Scotia, where he established Pottersfield Press (1979-). A man of great spirit and many talents, he teaches part-time at Dalhousie University, surfs (year-round) in the North Atlantic, hosts a syndicated TV talk show in Halifax, and publishes books. Between 1977 and 1997 he found time to write or compile more than forty of his own books. His first collection of lyrical poems was *Re-inventing the wheel* (1980). His short stories, written in a variety of modes, are collected in *Dance the rocks ashore* (1997). He has written a dozen young-adult novels, including *Dark end of dream street* (1994). *The trapdoor to heaven* (1996) is an ingenious science-fiction novel. *The second season of Jonas MacPherson* (1989) portrays the emotional life of an aging fisherman, and *The republic of nothing* (1994) is an ambitious coming-of-age novel. *Transcendental anarchy* (1993) is the title of a memoir. Choyce has also written a history, *Nova Scotia: shaped by the sea* (1996), and co-edited with John Bell *Visions from the edge: an anthology of Atlantic Canadian science fiction and fantasy* (1981). With a group called the Surf Poets, this protean talent has released a poetry-music album titled *Long lost planet*.

JOHN ROBERT COLOMBO

Christie, Robert. See HISTORICAL WRITING IN ENGLISH: 2.

Chronicles of Canada. See BIOGRAPHY AND MEMOIRS IN ENGLISH: 1.

Cité libre. See LITERARY MAGAZINES IN QUEBEC: 3.

CIV/n (1953-5). A Montreal little magazine nominally edited by Aileen Collins, it was heavily influenced by the editorial ideas of Louis DUDEK and Irving LAYTON, in whose home editorial meetings were held. The name was contributed by Dudek from a line about civilization in an Ezra Pound letter: 'CIV/n not a one man job.' The seven issues carried both poems and reviews, the latter nearly all by Dudek and Layton. Poets who contributed were mostly Canadian and included, as well as Dudek and Layton, Anne WILKINSON, Phyllis WEBB, Miriam WADDINGTON, Raymond SOUSTER, A.J.M. SMITH, Eli MANDEL, D.G. JONES, and Robert Currie.

The seven issues have been reprinted in *CIV/n: a literary magazine of the 50's* (1983) edited by Aileen Collins, with the assistance of Simon Dardick. FRANK DAVEY

Clark, Catherine Anthony (1892-1977). Born in London, England, Catherine Smith immigrated to Canada in 1914. In 1919 she married Leonard Clark and settled in the Kootenay Mountains of British Columbia, where she raised her family and wrote part time, not publishing her first book until she was fifty-eight. *The golden pine cone* (1950) chronicles the adventures of two children who abandon the security of their families and journey to the mysterious world of fantasy (called by Clark the 'inner world') to rescue their dog and to return a magical pine cone to its rightful owner. This plot reappears in various guises in all of Clark's subsequent fantasies. *The sun horse* (1950), *The one-winged dragon* (1955), *The silver man* (1959), *The diamond feather* (1962), and *The hunter and the medicine man* (1966) are all quests set within the Kootenay wilderness so familiar to Clark.

Fortunately it is not Clark's plots that define her importance in Canadian children's literature, but the uniqueness of her fantasy world and the moral values it embodies. Her 'inner world' is not the never-never land of traditional fantasies but the quasi-magical world of Native lore, a world inhabited not by giants, ogres, and fairy godmothers, but by the Glass-Witch, the Flame-lighter Woman, and other figures drawn from Aboriginal legends. In her Kootenay wilderness the natural and supernatural merge; there is no rigorous distinction between the real and the unreal.

Similarly, Native legends influence Clark's presentation of moral values. Her fantasies present no absolute goodness or evil; rather, individuals are judged as either selfish or selfless. The true hero and heroine are judged not for their courage but for their ability to give to others; their identity is defined in terms of the community. All Clark's fantasies preach a common doctrine: humanity survives by acting, by confronting chaos, and by caring for each other. Her heroes and heroines do not discover magical treasures; rather, they find their place in society.

Clark's tales are clearly both formulaic and predictable and her prose is uneven. Nor does her approach to fantasy allow the imaginative flourishes so often associated with the genre. And yet, the re-publication of *The golden pine cone* in 1994, with an introduction by Sheila Egoff and Judith Saltman, and a renewed interest in Clark by feminist critics, suggest that there is a place for her unique approach to fantasy: a merging of traditional elements of fantasy and Native folklore that may well have provided the prototype for a distinctly Canadian fantasy.

See two essays in *CANADIAN LITERATURE*: Joan Selby, 'The creation of fantasy: the fiction of Catherine Anthony Clark', Issue 11 (Winter 1962), and J. Kieran Kealy, 'The flamelighter woman: Catherine Anthony Clark's fantasies', Issue 78 (Autumn 1978).

J. KIERAN KEALY

Clark, Joan (b. 1934). Born Joan MacDonald in Liverpool, Nova Scotia, she studied drama at Acadia University and education at the University of Alberta, and spent several years teaching. She married Jack Clark, an engineer with the Royal Canadian Air Force, and went with him to Winisk, Hudson Bay, later the inspiration for her novel *The victory of Geraldine Gull*. She lived for twenty years in Alberta, was President of the Writers' Guild of Alberta, and editor (with Edna ALFORD) of *Dandelion*, Alberta's first literary magazine. She moved to St John's, Newfoundland, and served as president of the Writers' Alliance of Newfoundland and Labrador.

Although Clark made her name initially as a children's writer, she started by publishing adult short fiction and poetry in literary magazines. Her first three books were children's stories: *Girl of the Rockies* (1968), *Thomasina and the trout tree* (1971), and *The hand of Robin Squires* (1977), which was translated into Swedish, Danish, and French (*Deux solitudes*). Her first adult book was a collection of short stories, *From a high thin wire* (1982), focusing on problems of adolescence and motherhood and the struggle for self-realization. Then came three more children's books: *The leopard and the lily* (1984), a poignant fable in the manner of Oscar Wilde, and a pair of coming-of-age stories, *Wild man of the woods* (1985) and *The moons of Madeleine* (1987), written from a male and then a female perspective. A second book of short stories, *Swimming toward the light* (1990), was followed by two novels for adults, *The victory of Geraldine Gull* (1988) and *Eiriksdottir: a tale of dreams and luck* (1994). *Eiriksdottir* shared the same historical material about the Vikings as her children's book *The dream carvers* (1995).

The places where Clark has lived have strongly influenced her fiction: a mining town in Nova Scotia; Alberta and the Rockies; and Newfoundland and the Viking site at L'Anse aux Meadows. She does not shrink from taboo subjects in her stories, such as an incestuous attraction ('Her father's daughter'), or bodily functions (urination in 'Passage by water'). A fascination with violence has disturbed some of her readers—the gruesome severing of the hero's hand in *The hand of Robin Squires*, for example, or Freydis's satisfaction in splitting the skulls of her fellow Vikings and watching the blood spurt in *Eiriksdottir.* Clark portrays strong female characters, like the rebellious and ungovernable Ojibway Geraldine Gull, who commits terrorist acts against whites. Yet Clark can also write passages of delicate poetic beauty, as in her lyrical description of the moths in her story 'Luna moths'.

The quality of Joan Clark's writing has been recognized by several literary awards: the Marian ENGEL Award; the Canadian Authors' Association Award for *The victory of Geraldine Gull*; and for *The dream carvers* the Mr Christie Award for best Canadian children's book and the Geoffrey Bilson Award for historical fiction for young people.

ROBERTA BUCHANAN

Clark, **Sally** (b.1953). Born in Vancouver, she moved to Toronto in 1973 to study fine arts and theatre at York University, where she wrote a short story about a professor's middle-aged wife who disappears while the couple are on vacation. This became her first full-length play, *Lost souls and missing persons* (1985), a comedy that premièred at Theatre Passe Muraille in 1984. In 1984 Toronto's Buddies in Bad Times Theatre produced her one-act *Ten ways to abuse an old woman* (1990). Her biggest success was *Moo* (1989), which premièred at Alberta Theatre Project's 1988 festival of new plays. The production of *Moo* by the Factory Theatre, Toronto, won the 1989 Chalmers Canadian Play Award. Dramatized in two acts comprising forty-seven small scenes, it is the story of an eccentric, feisty woman and her romantic obsession with Harry, an exciting cad. Though her genteel family are appalled, chasing her evasive lover all over the world allows Moo an adventurous and highly unconventional life. Extremely funny in Act One, the play turns dark in Act Two when Moo is institutionalized by the family and abandoned. Harry finds her and the play concludes with a stunning finale.

The Canadian Stage's 1989 production of Clark's *The trial of Judith K* (1991)—an earlier version was produced in 1985—was nominated for a Dora Award and for a 1991 Governor General's Award. In 1989 Toronto's Tarragon Theatre mounted *Jehanne of the witches* (1993), a dramatization of the story of Saint Joan and her friendship with Gilles de Rais. In 1991 Toronto's Theatre Plus mounted *Life without instruction* (1994), a revenge comedy based on the true story and real trial of Artemisia Gentileschi, the seventeenth-century Italian painter who charged her teacher with rape.

In 1993 Clark was a co-writer of the collective *Sleeproom* and directed several short films, including a version of *Ten ways to abuse an old woman*, which won the Special Prix du Jury at the Henry Langlois Short Film Festival. Her next stage play, *Saint Frances of Hollywood* (produced in 1994), bears clear thematic and stylistic connections to her other plays. Based on the life of the glamorous Paramount movie star of the 1930s Frances Farmer, Clark's play rejects a linear structure, employing instead a series of short scenes. Again, the play is a dramatization of a true story and the protagonist is an extraordinary woman in a power struggle with a society that has no place for her. Clark's characters are wilful heroines, and not simply victims: in their inevitable defeat they exhibit an admirable vitality: hence Farmer's 'sainthood'. Plays that incorporate more of farce and the outrageous than the heart-breaking and familiar, Clark's comedies—viewed from a distance—are tragedies. *Wasps* (produced in 1996), a 'drawing-room comedy for distempered times', is a frenetic social satire of manners.

CYNTHIA ZIMMERMAN

Clarke, Austin (b. 1934). Born and educated in Barbados, Austin Chesterfield Clarke became a schoolteacher there before moving to Canada in 1955 to study at the University of Toronto. In 1959-60 he worked as a reporter in Timmins and Kirkland Lake, Ontario, before joining the CBC and eventually becoming a freelance broadcaster. Between 1968 and 1974 he taught creative writing and was writer-in-residence at Yale, Brandeis, Williams, and Duke universities and at the University of Texas. In 1974-5 he served as cultural attaché to the Barbadian embassy in Washington, then spent a year as general manager of the Caribbean Broadcasting Corporation and adviser to the prime minister of Barbados. Returning to Canada, he served as writer-in-residence at Concordia University, Montreal, in 1976-7. An acknowledged spokesman for the black community in Toronto, Clarke served on the Metro Toronto Library Board from 1973 to 1976, and subsequently on the Ontario Board of Censors and the Canadian Immigration and Refugee Board. He won the Cuban literary prize, the Casa de las Americas, in 1980.

Clarke's first two works of fiction deal with life in Barbados. *Survivors of the crossing* (1964) and *Amongst thistles and thorns* (1965)—the latter a collection of short stories—present Barbados as economically bleak and impoverished, full of desperate people struggling for survival. For the ambitious individual, escape to North America is the only chance for prosperity. *The meeting point* (1967), the first novel in Clarke's trilogy about the lives of Caribbean immigrants in Toronto, explores what that chance means in human terms. Introducing a group of West Indian immigrants, it presents the underside of wealthy Toronto by revealing the racist exploitation of Blacks. *Storm of fortune* (1971) and *The bigger light* (1975) chart their slow and eventful adaptation to Canadian social values and conventions. These novels are filled with bitterness and sadness, lightened by the indomitable humour and spirit of Clarke's characters, the most successful of whom renounces his hard-earned material success in Canada to investigate Black Power pride in the United States —a move that seems to imply the impossibility of his finding a meaningful life in Canada. While exposing racial hypocrisy in Canada, Clarke describes both white and black sides with fairness and perspicuity. These novels—which say as much about Canada in general as about the concerns of Blacks in Toronto and Barbados in particular—are enriched by Clarke's mastery of dialogue, realism, and psychologically subtle and astute characterizations. His second collection of short stories, *When he was free and young and he used to wear silks* (1971), further elaborates the theme of Blacks struggling to make good in Canada. *When women rule* (1985) continues this theme with eight more stories—mordant still lifes of immigrant dreams failed, and of characters caught in the cracks of Canada's floor. *Nine men who laughed* (1986) collects nine stories of such characters, including some from earlier collections. *In this city* (1992) contains eight new stories about life in Toronto, and shows the development of Clarke's style as he plays the nuances of language more skilfully and subtly than before. *There are no elders* (1993) maintains this theme, but has a broader base of material for eight more stories. Throughout his writing, which is about white and black Canadians at 'the meeting point', Clarke moves back and forth between 'Wessindian' and Anglo-Canadian English; but while the Caribbean dialect may be amusing at times, Clarke's themes are stringently tragic, as his characters and their language are swamped by a Puritan white Canada. The novel *The prime minister* (1977), an exposé of political corruption in a developing nation that grew out of Clarke's experiences as a civil servant in Barbados, expresses his cynical view of the upper class there, even though this novel is deliberately vague in its tropical setting. *The origin of waves* (1997) begins with the reunion, after almost fifty years, of two Barbadians who meet in a Toronto blizzard and proceed to exchange memories for hours on end in a bar. A rich and vibrant novel grows out of their irrepressible recollections, a narrative thread that reaches far into the past, and the cumulative life histories of the two men.

The first volume of Clarke's autobiography, *Growing up stupid under the Union Jack* (1980), continues this trend towards universality. Although Clarke concentrates on his own childhood in Barbados, allusions to the larger framework of British colonialism expand his topic as he demonstrates what the British Empire meant to its non-white population. The novel *Proud empires* (1986) fictionalizes this same material, with a stronger cynicism concerning island politics, and a stronger tone about the frigidity of white Canadian life supplanting the *joie de vivre* of the Caribbean peoples.

Clarke has also written *A passage back home* (1994), a personal memoir of the late Trinidadian writer Sam Selvon in the form of a series of anecdotal sketches that are as much about

Clarke as about Selvon. A pamphlet, *The confessed bewilderment of Dr. Martin Luther King: and the idea of non-violence as a political tactic*, was published in 1968. In 1992 Harper Collins published Clarke's *Public enemies: police violence and black youth* in the Point of View Series. This pamphlet, written after the 4 May 1992 protest demonstration in Toronto, examines racial confrontations in that city with a blunt clarity, ending with the statement that white Canadians must accept Canadians of colour: 'We live here. I live here. I ain't going nowhere.'

A sympathetic biography has been written by Stella Algoo-Baksh, *Austin C. Clarke* (1994); and a perceptive critical study of Clarke's fiction is provided by Lloyd W. Brown in *El Dorado and Paradise* (1989).

TERRENCE CRAIG

Clarke, George Elliott (b. 1960). Born in Windsor Plains, Nova Scotia, he grew up in Halifax and was educated at the University of Waterloo (B.A., 1984), Dalhousie University (M.A., 1989), and Queen's University (Ph.D., 1993). Clarke is a tireless political and cultural activist who was instrumental in establishing a Creative Writing Collective at the University of Waterloo, worked as a social worker in the Annapolis Valley for a time, served as parliamentary aide to New Democratic Member of Parliament Howard McCurdy while completing the Ph.D. program at Queen's, and writes an arts and cultural affairs column for the Halifax *Chronicle Herald*. Devoting much time to public speaking on topics related to African-Canadian experience and writing, he is currently Professor of English and Canadian Studies at Duke University, North Carolina.

A seventh-generation Canadian and descendant of Black Loyalists who settled in Nova Scotia in 1783, Clarke has coined the term 'Africadian' to describe the Black Nova Scotian experience that is central to his poetry. Drawing upon abundant memories of childhood visits to his maternal grandparents' home in Three Mile Plains, N.S., his poetry celebrates the richness of life encountered in even the poorest rural Black communities in his youth—the familiarity with biblical stories, phrasing, and cadences, the emphasis on oral narrative, the vivacity of an everyday language enriched by metaphor, and above all the presence of music, from spirituals to jazz and the blues.

Clarke's poetry is animated by a powerful and convincing sense of racial injustice, as is especially apparent in his first collection of poems, *Saltwater spirituals and deeper blues* (1983). He prefers, however, to move beyond the simple contours of protest poetry to record the beauty as well as the pain that marks the Africadian experience. Convinced of the power of myth, and the epic scope available to twentieth-century poets in the form of the lyric sequence, he combines the elegance of certain European literary forms and traditions with the spikiness of local and popular idiom in his attempt to bring Black Nova Scotian experience to life. His most accomplished work, *Whylah Falls* (1990), which depicts what Clark calls 'a place where the death of poetry has not yet occurred', is a *tour de force* in this regard. Mingling blank verse, traditional poetic forms (such as the aubade, distich, and idyll), prose poems, journalistic snippets, recipes, old photographs borrowed from Nova Scotian archives, and a lush language that is simultaneously arcane and richly contemporary, the cycle recreates African-Canadian life in a fictional village in Jarvis County, N.S., in the 1930s, as an educated Black poet returns to woo his beloved Shelley—a woman whose practicality and rootedness resist and deflate some of his more romantic illusions, and force his re-connection with life lived in the lee, as it were, of comfortable mainstream notions of life, love, and conveniently distant violence.

Lush dreams, blue exile: fugitive poems 1978-1993 (1994) includes a number of tightly constructed political poems, such as 'To Liu Chan, near Nanking' and 'November 22, 1963', but primarily features Africadian poems in praise of landscape and elucidation of ancestry that are marked by the bounteous language, insistent rhythms, and lively allusiveness that characterize Clarke's poetry at its best.

The play *Whylah Falls*—with a musical score by Joe Sealy, sung by jazz musician Jackie Richardson—was produced by the Eastern Front Theatre, Dartmouth, N.S., in January 1997. See George Elliott Clarke, 'Discovering Whylah Falls', *Quarry* 40 (1991).

Clarke edited *Fire on the water: an anthology of Black Nova Scotian writing* (2 vols, 1991, 1992) and *Eyeing the North Star: directions in African-Canadian literature* (1997).

MARILYN ROSE

Cloutier, Cécile (b. 1930). Born in Quebec City, Quebec, she studied literature and aesthetics at Université Laval, where she obtained a Licence-ès-lettres and a Diplôme d'études supérieures, and then in France, where she studied literature, classics, philosophy, and psychology. She obtained a Doctorat de l'Université in aesthetics (1962) from the Sorbonne. Interested in languages, she has studied Greek, Latin, Spanish, German, Polish, Sanskrit, Inuktituk, and Chinese, in addition to French and English. In the early 1960s she taught French and Quebec literature and aesthetics in Quebec City and at the Université d'Ottawa. Since 1966 she has been Professor of French at the University of Toronto. She is married to Jerzy Wojciechowski and has two daughters.

As a poet, literary critic, and essayist, Cloutier was influenced by the social history and culture of Quebec: she is usually considered to be a member of the Hexagone generation of poets, though she rarely refers to Quebec explicitly in her poetry. The unique qualities of Cloutier's restrained personal style of poetry have remained constant, and her creative practice has matured through her twelve volumes of poetry: *Mains de sable* (1960), *Cuivre et soies* (1964), *Cannelles et craies* (1969), *Paupières* (1970), *Câblogrammes* (1972), *Chaleuils* (1978), *Près* (1983), *L'échangeur* (1985), *Lampées* (1990), *Périhélie* (1990), *Ancres d'encre* (1993, Médaille de la Société des poètes français), and *Ostraka* (1994). *Paupières* and *Câblogrammes* mainly contain the same pieces, though they are ordered differently. *Chaleuils* was translated by Alexandre Amprimoz as *Springtime of spoken words* (1979). Cloutier published a retrospective volume in 1986: *L'écouté: poèmes 1960-1983*, for which she received a Governor General's Award.

Cloutier's poetry has been written within a set of vital tensions between sensation, memory, and spiritual revelation: the world for her is highly charged with energy, proffering signs to those who are able to listen to, and hear, the sounds of its infinite silences. Cloutier sees the poem as a window, a fleeting vision of forces usually hidden in the universe. Carefully wrought language is the means by which these forces can be revealed. Her short, elliptical poems are a search for the essential word, a shift to a site of origin for things and words, where names have evocative, creative, and erotic power. Discrete personal pronouns situate the poet's voice and experience. Her images, most frequently drawn from the world of nature, but transmuted to take on hard, metal-like qualities, are carefully chosen to pass beyond the contingencies of material reality.

Cloutier's first theoretical formulation on poetry was given in an address in 1958, published in 1959 as 'Propos sur la poésie' and republished under the title 'Cum' in *Paupières* and in *L'écouté*. In her critical and theoretical publications she has provided strong support for the study of Quebec poetry. She founded the Centre de recherches en poésie québécoise d'aujourd'hui and other associations; co-founded such journals as *Émourie*, *Incidences*, and *Vécrire*; organized a number of colloquia; and has co-edited the proceedings and other important volumes: *Opuscula aesthetica nostra, essais sur l'esthétique* (1984), *Solitude rompue [en hommage à David M. Hayne]* (1986), and *La poésie de l'Hexagone* (1990).

Cloutier's one-act play *Utinam!*—produced in Montreal, Quebec City, Paris, New York, Toronto, and on Radio-Canada—was published in *La* BARRE DU JOUR (mai-août 1977) and translated by Josée M. LeBlond as *Room of one's own* (1978). Her children's book, *La girafe* (1984), was illustrated by Mireille Levert.

See *Livres et auteurs québécois* (1964, 1970, 1971, 1979), *Poetry Windsor Poésie* (1976), *La poésie de l'Hexagone* (1990), and *Anthologie de la poésie des femmes au Québec* (1991).

LOUISE FORSYTH

Clutesi, George (1905-88). Born at Port Alberni, British Columbia, Clutesi was among the first Native writers to record in a popular way, and to interpret from a Native perspective, the culture of the indigenous peoples, notably that of the Nootka nation of the Pacific Northwest Coast. Clutesi worked as a fisherman and a pile-driver for more than twenty years. During convalescence from a back injury he began to teach the traditional ways. Emily CARR was impressed with his drawings and in 1945 bequeathed her artist's materials to him. Clutesi subsequently worked for CBC Radio and ran an art shop before his death in Victoria, B.C. He is the author of two illustrated books of traditional lore that proved to be popular and to have special appeal for young readers: *Son of Raven, son of Deer: fables of the Tse-shaht People* (1967) and *Potlatch* (1969).

JOHN ROBERT COLOMBO

Coach House Press. Synonymous for most of its life with fine-crafted books and adventurous editorial policies, this publishing house was founded in Toronto in 1965 by Stan Bevington, with the editorial assistance of Wayne Clifford. Clifford was succeeded as editor in 1966 by Victor COLEMAN, who by 1973 had built Coach House into one of the three largest publishers in Canada of new literary titles. Coleman resigned in 1974 because of his disagreement with Bevington's decision to adopt and develop computer typesetting and book-design technology. Between 1974 and 1988 the Coach House list was edited by a collective, initially consisting of Bevington; writers bp NICHOL, Michael ONDAATJE, Frank DAVEY, and David Young; graphic artist Rick/Simon (who left the press in 1979); and lawyer Linda Davey. Other editors in this period included Martin KINCH, Val Frith, art-historian Dennis Reid, novelist Sarah Sheard, drama critic Robert Wallace, and poets David McFADDEN and Christopher DEWDNEY. The press's early years, under Coleman's editorship, were characterized by hand-set type, multi-coloured offset printing, fortuitous collaborations between author and designer, and titles by open-form writers from both the USA and Canada. These included Ondaatje, George Bowering, Bill Hutton, Nichol, David Rosenberg, David McFadden, Joe ROSENBLATT, Daphne MARLATT, Matt COHEN, Allen Ginsberg, and Robert Creeley. In many ways Coach House represented here a continuation of CONTACT PRESS, extending Contact's welcome to new poets and supporting most of the writers of the Contact Press anthology *New wave Canada: the new explosion in Canadian poetry* (1966), edited by Raymond SOUSTER. In the 1974-88 period the interests of the press diversified to include the work of previously established writers like D.G. JONES, Phyllis WEBB, Louis DUDEK, Eli MANDEL, Sheila WATSON, John MARLYN, Dorothy LIVESAY, Gwendolyn MacEWEN, and Robert KROETSCH; numerous first books, including those of Paul QUARRINGTON, Gail SCOTT, Lola Lemire Tostevin, Sharon THESEN, and Anne MICHAELS; textbooks such as Ondaatje's *The long poem anthology* (1979) and Bowering's *Fiction of contemporary Canada* (1980), plays by Kinch, George F. WALKER, and Ann-Marie MacDONALD; various titles on the history of Canadian photography and architecture; and a Quebec translation series that included titles by Victor-Lévy BEAULIEU, Jacques FERRON, Nicole BROSSARD, and Claude GAUVREAU. The press became the first Canadian literary press to use computer technology to simulate the appearance of hand-printed pages and to attempt on-demand publishing.

In 1987-8 Bevington's decision to withdraw from publishing in order to focus on his commercial printing business led to a crisis that saw several editors leave and others, notably David Young and Sarah Sheard, attempt to reorganize Coach House as a more mainstream and profitable enterprise. A limited company was formed to acquire the press from Bevington, with its board of directors including business people unfamiliar with Canadian small-press publishing. The death of bp Nichol in 1988 robbed the board of its strongest advocate of innovative writing and activist publishing. Because of the generous federal and provincial subsidies available to Ontario publishers in the early 1990s, however, the new Coach House grew rapidly, with its titles now commercially designed and printed, its distribution contracted to McCLELLAND & STEWART, and most of its editorial work performed by employees rather than by its unpaid volunteer editors. The latter had little contact with the press's directors and little or no influence on their business decisions. Among the most active of the editors in this period were writers Alberto MANGUEL, Lynn Crosbie, Susan SWAN, Michael Redhill, and Jason SHERMAN. In the fall of 1996, after federal subsidies to publishing had been cut by up to 60 per cent, and an Ontario loan guarantee program for publishers was cancelled, the Directors voted to dissolve the press and return all copyrights to its authors. In January 1997, however, Bevington announced the birth of Coach House Press Books, whose publications will appear both as expensive handmade limited-edition volumes and as on-line tests on the Internet.

See Victor Coleman, *The day they stole the Coach House Press* (1993). FRANK DAVEY

Coburn, Kathleen. See BIOGRAPHY AND MEMOIRS IN ENGLISH: 3.

Cocke, Emmanuel. See FANTASTIC LITERATURE AND SCIENCE FICTION IN FRENCH.

Coderre, Émile (1893-1970). Coderre, who wrote under the pseudonym 'Jean Narrache', was born in Montreal and orphaned at an early age. He was educated at the Séminaire de Nicolet (1904-12) and received his licentiate's degree in pharmacology from the Université de Montréal in 1919. He assumed the management of a pharmacy in one of Montreal's poorer districts, where he came to know the most impoverished victims of the Depression. He was editor-in-chief of the *Pharmacien* (1939-42), secretary of the Collège des pharmaciens (1945-61), and professor of pharmaceutical legislation at the Université de Montréal (1953-61).

A brief association with the ÉCOLE LITTÉRAIRE DE MONTRÉAL in 1912-13 awakened Coderre's serious interest in literature, and between 1922 and 1963 he published five books of poetry and two of prose. *Les signes sur le sable* (1922) is a collection of poetry largely inspired by the Romantics and Symbolists; the only poems that stand out from the others are those of the vagabond-poet reminiscent of Villon, Jean Richepin, or Jehan Rictus (for example, 'La chanson des gueux'). Stirred by the Depression, Coderre published *Quand j'parl' tout seul* (1932) and *J'parl' pour parler*. . . (1939) under the pseudonym 'Jean Narrache' ('j'en arrache': I have a hard time making ends meet). Conveying the same sense of humour and suggesting the same sad smile of many a 'Jean Narrache' during the Depression and after, these books were an instant success and gained Coderre a large following in the press and on radio. The two collections are based on acute observation of the habits and conditions of the poor, while at the same time analysing the bourgeois class, often most harshly. Here the poet of the destitute found a suitable formula: a sincere tone mixed generously with grinding humour, irony, and even sarcasm, in a language later to be known as *JOUAL*. *Bonjour, les gars!* (1948) is composed mainly of 'revamped verses' taken from the preceding collections, offering only eight new pieces. However, it is enriched by an interesting biographical introduction. *J'parle tout seul quand Jean Narrache* (1961) is a collection of previously published and unpublished verse. *Histoires du Canada* . . . (1937) recounts in prose some 'revamped lives' (Columbus, Cartier, Maisonneuve, Laviolette, La Vérendrye). In treating the history of Canada and alluding to both historical and contemporary events and politicians, it contains a strong dose of social criticism. *Jean Narrache chez le diable* (1963) presents a series of dialogues with the devil, examining such topics as politics and separatism, journalism and radio, art and literature. None of the books of prose, however, possess the humour, the critical scope, or the sting of the poetry of the thirties.

In 1932 Coderre began writing humorous sketches, dramatic series, plays, and short stories for radio and theatre, most of which are unpublished. Starting in the 1940s, he produced his best-known works; here, in monologue form, he gave both recollections and commentaries on current events: 'Rêveries de Jean Narrache' (1940-41, 1946, 1947-8), 'Jean Narracheries' (1944), 'Le vagabond qui chante' (1941-5, 1947-8), 'Les souvenirs de Jean Narrache' (1947), and 'Zigzags à travers mes souvenirs' (1956). The humour of these radio scripts lies in a distinctive mixture of wisdom, melancholy, and lightheartedness that, for the author, are the only attitudes that resist the ravages of time.

For discussions of Coderre's work, see Jacques Blais, *De l'ordre et de l'aventure: la poésie au Québec de 1934 à 1944* (1975); Richard Giguère, 'Quand j'parl' tout seul' and 'J'parl' pour parler . . .' in *Dictionnaire des oeuvres littéraires du Québec* (1980); and Pierre Pagé and Renée Legris, *Le comique et l'humour à la radio québécoise, 1930-1970* (1979).

RICHARD GIGUÈRE

Cody, Hiram Alfred (1872-1948). Born in Cody's, New Brunswick, on the Canaan River north of Saint John, and educated at the Saint John Grammar School and King's College, Windsor, Nova Scotia, he was ordained in 1898 as an Anglican clergyman. During his career as a priest he served a number of parishes in his native province—he became rector of St James Church, Saint John, in 1910—and as far afield as the Yukon. Cody's first book was a biography of Bishop Bompas, *An apostle of the North* (1908). He went on to write twenty-three novels, published between 1910 and 1937, among them *The frontiersman: a tale of the Yukon* (1910), *The fourth watch* (1911), *The long patrol; a tale of the Mounted Police* (1912), *The king's arrow: a tale of United Empire Loyalists* (1922), and *The trail of the Golden Horn* (1923).

Although Cody's fiction owes much to the boy's-adventure-tale tradition of R.M. BALLANTYNE and Frederick Marryat, it attempted to reach beyond an all-male readership by providing both a 'romantic interest' and a Christian message. His novels are imbued with the 'muscular Christianity' that emerged in the latter part of the nineteenth century and flourished sporadically until the 1930s. In *The unknown wrestler* (1918), for example, the accomplished fighter who wins the respect of a tough rural community eventually reveals himself as their new Anglican minister. Cody's fiction typically owes more to his literary ancestors than to his own immediate observations and experiences. Despite his familiarity with the North, his Yukon tales never really go beyond well-worn stereotypical scenes and events.

GILLIAN THOMAS

Cogswell, Fred (b. 1917). Frederick William Cogswell was born in East Centreville, New Brunswick, where he grew up. After serving in the Canadian Army (1940-5), he completed a B.A. at the University of New Brunswick in 1949 and an M.A. in 1950. After earning a Ph.D. from Edinburgh University in 1952, he returned to the University of New Brunswick to teach in the Department of English, where he remained until his retirement, and his appointment as Professor Emeritus, in 1983. Editor of *The* FIDDLEHEAD from 1952 to 1967, he inaugurated Fiddlehead Books, a publishing enterprise involving more than 300 titles, which he continued until 1981. (See FIDDLEHEAD POETRY BOOKS.)

Cogswell's poems—characterized by compression, wit, the use of a wide variety of both traditional and modern forms, and a gentle, ironic view of the world—appear in twenty-four volumes: *The stunted strong* (1954), *The haloed tree* (1956), *Descent from Eden* (1959), *Lost dimension* (1960), *Star-People* (1968), *Immortal plowman* (1969), *In praise of chastity* (1970), *The chains of Liliput* (1971), *The house without a door* (1973), *Light bird of life: selected poems* (1974), *Against perspective* (1977), *A long apprenticeship: the collected poems of Fred Cogswell* (1980), *Fred Cogswell: selected poems* (1983, edited with a preface by Antonio D'ALFONSO), *Pearls* (1983), *Meditations: fifty sestinas* (1986), *An edge of life* (1987), *The best notes merge* (1988), *Black and white tapestry* (1989), *Watching the eagle* (1991), *When the right light shines* (1992), *In praise of old music* (1992), *As I see it* (1994), *In my own growing* (1995), and *The trouble with light* (1995). Cogswell's strengths as a craftsman are evident in his six books of translations: *The testament of Cresseid* (1957), *One hundred poems of modern Quebec* (1970), *A second hundred poems of modern Quebec* (1971), *Confrontations* by Gatien LAPOINTE (1973), *The poetry of modern Quebec* (1976), *The complete poems of Émile Nelligan* (1983), and *Unfinished dreams: contemporary poetry of Acadie* (1990), with Jo Anne Elder. Cogswell's criticism includes four articles in *The literary history of Canada* (1965, 2nd edn 1976): 'Newfoundland (1715-1880)', 'The Maritime Provinces (1720-1815)', 'Haliburton', and 'Literary activity in the Maritime Provinces (1815-1880)'. He has also written two monographs in the ECW PRESS series: *Sir Charles G.D. Roberts* (1983) and *Charles Mair* (1988).

As critic, editor, publisher, and poet, Cogswell has maintained a broadly tolerant and humane stance, a disregard of fashion, and a wide eclecticism of taste. He has been particularly encouraging to young and unknown writers. In 1980 the Writers' Federation of Nova Scotia honoured him with *Scroll*, a collection of poems in tribute by forty-nine Canadian poets. He was made a member of the Order of Canada in 1981.

ROBERT GIBBS

Cohen, Leonard (b. 1934). Born in Montreal, Quebec, he grew up in its affluent Westmount district and attended McGill University. Shortly after graduating he published his first book of poetry, *Let us compare mythologies* (1956). In the next few years he attempted graduate study at Columbia University, worked in his family's clothing business, and wrote an unpublished novel, 'Ballet of lepers'. After publishing a second book of poetry, *The spice-box of earth* (1961), and spending some time in England, he published a novel, *The favorite game* (1963). Since then he has lived intermittently on the Greek island of Hydra, and in New York, Montreal, and California. In the 1960s he published the poetry collections *Flowers for Hitler* (1964) and *Parasites of heaven* (1966); a second novel, *Beautiful losers* (1966); *Selected poems* (1968), for which he declined a Governor General's Award; and began a successful career as a popular composer-singer. Later books of poetry include *The energy of slaves* (1972), *Death of a lady's man* (1978), and *Book of mercy* (1984). His song albums include *Songs of Leonard Cohen* (1968), *Songs from a room* (1969), *Songs of love and hate* (1971), *Live songs* (1973), *New skins for the old ceremony* (1974), *The best of Leonard Cohen* (1975), *Death of a ladies' man* (1977), *Recent songs* (1979), *Various positions* (1985), *I'm your man* (1988), and *The future* (1992). Both *The favourite game* and *Beautiful losers* are in the NEW CANADIAN LIBRARY.

Throughout the sixties Cohen's poetry and fiction were extremely popular, particularly with high-school and college readers. The appeal of his poetry was based chiefly on a traditional and recognizably 'poetic' prosody, suggestive imagery that subjective readers could easily project themselves into, and a theme of moral non-responsibility. George WOODCOCK argued that Cohen was usually conservative in poetic craft and escapist in theme. The poetry of his first two books draws heavily on Greek and Hassidic mythologies—not to reveal them as alive in the present but to convert the present into the sepulchral figures of mythology. Cohen's language here is highly decorative, reminiscent of the early Yeats. While the poems of his third book, *Flowers for Hitler*, adventure into both satire and experimental verse forms, those of the fourth, *Parasites of heaven*, return to the conventional and dispassionate measures of the earlier volumes.

A consistent theme in his books—the importance of reducing life to ceremony, of escaping from life by transmuting its slippery actualities into the reliable simplicities of myth and art—is developed most clearly in Cohen's novels. It is the lesson by which Breavman 'comes of age' in *The favorite game.*

In *Beautiful losers* it is the lesson 'I' must learn from 'F', and includes not only the transmuting of object and event but the self-reduction of personal identity into the anonymity of sainthood. The loser triumphs by escaping the desire to win. A clear extension of this belief appears in *The energy of slaves*, a collection of fragments, failed poems, and anti-poems. On the surface its directness and self-deprecating cynicism appear to mark a repudiation of the earlier poetry; in fact, it represents a logical step in the saintly self-abnegation Cohen has always advocated: master becomes slave, poetic craftsman becomes his own beautiful loser—'only a scribbler' in his words. Once again Cohen is working towards a kind of martyrdom. This opposition between decadent craftsman and beautiful loser reappears in *Death of a lady's man*, which juxtaposes texts exemplifying a quest for beauty and sardonic commentaries. Here Cohen manages, simultaneously and with equal weight, to affirm his visions of ceremony and to deconstruct them. Thus the book becomes both his most traditional and most postmodern work.

See Michael ONDAATJE, *Leonard Cohen* (1970), Stephen SCOBIE, *Leonard Cohen* (1978), Linda HUTCHEON, *Leonard Cohen and his works* (1989), and Ira Bruce Nadel, *Various positions: a life of Leonard Cohen* (1996).

See also POETRY IN ENGLISH 1950 TO 1982: 1. FRANK DAVEY

Cohen, Matt (b. 1942). Born in Kingston, Ontario, he moved with his family to Ottawa, where he attended grade school and high school. Though his parents were Jewish, he has recorded that his upbringing was not religious. He went on to the University of Toronto (B.A., 1964; M.A., 1965). His postgraduate degree was in political theory, for which he prepared a thesis on Albert Camus. In 1967-7 he lectured in the department of religion at McMaster University, Hamilton. The following year he took up full-time writing, though at intervals since then he has returned to the academic ambience as writer-in-residence. Cohen has worked in a variety of literary genres. For a period he was fiction editor for COACH HOUSE PRESS, and prepared the second volume of its *The story so far* (1972). He has written fiction that verges on ironic poetry in *Peach Melba* (1974); and two books for children, *Too bad, Galahad* (1972) and *Leaves of Louise* (1977). But it is as a writer of novels and short stories that he has found his real literary vocation.

Korsoniloff (1969) was followed shortly afterwards by a fantasy novella, *Johnny Crackle sings* (1971). These are both tales of inner alienation, of divisions within the consciousness that can end only in permanent loss and that hold the characters on the edge of madness. In *Korsoniloff* a schizoid teacher of philosophy tells the separate but inter-intrusive lives of the cold and analytical 'I' and the ineffectually passionate and amoral Korsoniloff, who seeks truths that would destroy him. *Johnny Crackle sings*—a freer fantasy that lacks the clinical verisimilitude of *Korsoniloff*—is the tale of a country boy ruined by an ambition to become a big-time folk singer. In its exploration of drug-created states of mind it moves constantly on the edge of surrealism, and has the kind of self-consciousness that shows a writer still searching for his appropriate form. While this novel was being written Cohen was already working on the stories included in *Columbus and the fat lady* (1972), which established the territory he would occupy in his later novels. *Night flights* (1978) includes some stories from *Columbus* and offers the same mixture of rural fantasy in stories that prefigure the larger novels and somewhat symbolic tales that explore the verges of psychological breakdown in a similar way to Cohen's earlier, smaller novels. *The expatriate* (1982) and *Café le dog* (1983) are later collections of his stories.

The five novels published between 1974 and 1981—*The disinherited* (1974), *Wooden hunters* (1975), *The colours of war* (1977), *The sweet second summer of Kitty Malone* (1979), and *Flowers of darkness* (1981)—are at first glance more conventional than Cohen's earlier books, but they can be linked with the more obviously experimental novels because they work less by linear chronology than by a constant interpenetration of past and present. There is a disturbing sense of the provisional in the lives of all their characters, and ominous transitions that do not always turn out to be disastrous. All these novels—except for *Wooden hunters*, which takes place among deprived Natives and washed-up whites on an island resembling one of the Queen Charlottes in British Columbia—are set, or end, in the fictional Salem, in a southern-Ontario countryside, where the once-prosperous farming economy established by Loyalists and British immigrants is fast disintegrating. *The disinherited* is a chronicle novel that develops the theme of agrarian decline through the changes in the lives of a pioneering family. *The colours of war* seems at first to be a futurist novel as it describes a journey across a Canada riven by civil war; but the hero's journey through the future, and his destination in the heart of the Ontario countryside, which Cohen has made his special terrain, represents a flight into the protective past. *The sweet second summer of Kitty Malone* centres on two drunken, ugly, life-worn people and their eventual happiness, and gains its effect by inverting the pattern of the customary romance. *Flowers of darkness*, which shows the destruction by the consequences of his own hypocrisy of a demonic preacher, reads in many ways like a genial parody of William Faulkner, to whose Yoknapatawpha County Cohen's creation of his own country of the imagination has been compared.

GEORGE WOODCOCK

The Spanish doctor (1984), Cohen's most commercial novel, is set in medieval Spain, a time of anti-Jewish pogroms. The main character, Avram Halevi (who came to Cohen in a dream), becomes a wandering Jew, a stranger and an outsider, moving east, not west, through the Renaissance medical centres, and eventually into the heart of Russia (where Cohen's ancestral roots lie). Critical reception was mixed; some considered the book a sentimental and improbable swashbuckler, others chastised Cohen for deserting his talent. But most agreed that the historical background was impressively researched. *Nadine* (1986) describes a woman's attempt to reconstruct herself physically and psychologically after throwing herself on a terrorist's grenade in front of a Jerusalem hotel. Born of Jewish parents during the German occupation of Paris, she was left in the care of her aunts while her parents tried to flee. *Emotional arithmetic* (1990) tells the harrowing story of a reunion of three survivors of a Nazi internment camp in France. A virtuoso performance, it began with Cohen wondering what it must have been like to have been on a train destined for Auschwitz. Here Cohen explores 'love and hate, time passed and time remaining, injuries suffered, and revenge meted out.' The novel is linked to *Nadine*—Jakob Bronski, one of the three survivors, is Nadine's father. *Freud: the Paris notebooks* (1991) is a slim, complex, somewhat mystifying three-part novella about expatriates. A humorous sendup of the myth of Sigmund Freud, the main character is not the famous doctor but a fictional nephew whose life parallels that of the real Freud. *The bookseller* (1993) explores notions of obsessive love and revenge. A *roman à clef* set in Toronto's Annex (near the University of Toronto) in the 1970s, this fast-paced thriller has several strong scenes set in used-book stores, a pool hall, and seedy Yonge Street hotels that provide a subtle and poignant subtext of Toronto as a city of bleak subcultures. *Last seen* (1996), Cohen's most autobiographical novel, is about a writer, Alec, who copes with the death of his younger brother, Harold, from lung cancer. It is narrated from the points of view of both the dying Harold and the grieving Alec. Unable to follow him into the grave, Alec finds healing in a fantasy about a club of Elvis Presley impersonators.

Living on water (1988) is a collection of deeply moving, poetically acute stories that include as subject matter cancer, infidelity, alchoholism, decay, and dread; they reveal a luminosity within the central characters, even at the moment of death. *Lives of the mind slaves* (1994) features often humorous stories of lonely, middle-class Jewish male intellectuals who despair over life's unfairness; every opportunity for success meets with even greater failure.

Cohen edited the experimental fiction anthology *The story so far: 2* (1973), and, with David Young, *The dream class anthology: writings from Toronto high schools* (1983). His translations include *Intimate strangers: new stories from Quebec* (1986, with Wayne Grady), and *The secret voice* (1990) by Gaetan Brulotte.

Cohen's literary manuscripts are in the Mills Memorial Library, McMaster University. See Geoff Hancock, 'An interview with Matt Cohen', CANADIAN FICTION MAGAZINE 52 (1985); and CANADIAN LITERATURE 130 (1991), for an interview with George WOODCOCK.

GEOFF HANCOCK

Cohen, Nathan (1923-71). Born in Sydney, Nova Scotia, he attended Mount Allison University from 1939 to 1942, acting and directing for the Mount Allison Players and writing for the *Argosy Weekly*. His columns in the *Argosy* (which he edited in 1942) already revealed Cohen's self-confident and often controversial views on politics, theatre, and the arts. After obtaining his B.A. in English, he wrote for and edited the labour *Glace Bay Gazette* in Nova Scotia from 1944 to 1945. In Toronto he began to attract attention with his theatre reviews for the *Canadian Jewish Weekly* and *Wochenblatt* in 1946. He was the CBC's Toronto drama critic from 1948 to 1958, gaining national exposure on the programs 'Across the Footlights' and 'CJBC Views the Shows'. Besides editing his own publication, *The Critic*, from 1950 to 1953, and working as a CBC Television story editor from 1956 to 1958, Cohen chaired the CBC TV series 'Fighting Words' (also aired on CBC Radio) from 1953 to 1962, and appeared as theatre critic on the radio series 'Critically Speaking'. His weekly theatre column appeared in the Toronto *Telegram* in 1957-8. From 1959 until his death he was the drama critic of the *Toronto Star*.

In his twenty-five years as a Toronto and national theatre critic, Cohen helped to guide the transformation of indigenous Canadian theatre from an amateur activity to fully professional status, and in his often controversial *Toronto Star* columns he made Canadian theatre a matter of national interest. Cohen saw the critic as the conscience of the theatre and demanded the highest standards of play production and dramatic writing, often infuriating actors and directors with his devastating reviews. He insisted that theatre be a vital art form and not merely a social diversion. Cohen repeatedly called for the writing and production of Canadian plays, while demanding that Canadian theatres meet international professional production standards—an attitude that frequently caused unprecedented animosity in the theatre community. Philip Stratford, in the *CANADIAN FORUM* (Feb. 1960), declared that 'the Cohen mystique consists in bringing ultra-Broadway standards to bear on a sub-Broadway product, and the result is always dispiriting, often ludicrous.'

Cohen's life and critical work are surveyed in Wayne E. Edmonstone's *Nathan Cohen: the making of a critic* (1977). His colourful personality and impact on Canadian theatre and culture were dramatized in Rick SALUTIN's *Nathan Cohen: a review*, which was produced by Theatre Passe Muraille, Toronto, and published by the *Canadian Theatre Review* in 1981. See also Allan Gould, 'A critical assessment of the theatre criticism of Nathan Cohen', Ph.D. thesis, York University, 1977.

ANTON WAGNER

Colas et Colinette; ou Le bailli dupé (1812). An operetta by Joseph QUESNEL, it was the first composed in North America and the first dramatic text in French to be composed, performed, and published in Canada.

First performed on 14 Jan. 1790 by Le Théâtre de société, an amateur troupe the author had helped found, the work was well received. The anonymous reviewer for the *Montreal Gazette/Gazette de Montréal* praised its tight structure, consistency of character portrayal, and above all the impeccably 'moral' resolution of the plot. A modern spectator might be less impressed by its static depiction of character and the predictability of its plot. The setting is quaintly pastoral, an unidentified village in France, and only the description of costumes and set suggests that the time is roughly contemporary with that of its composition—the late 1780s, according to a note appended to the published text. The plot involves an attempt by an aging village bailiff (unnamed) to win by bribery, ruse, or violence the hand of young Colinette, who loves Colas and hopes to marry him. Colinette's ingenuity, along with the wise integrity of her protector, the village squire Dolmont, are more than a match for the Bailiff, and the two title characters wind up happily with each other. The five characters lack depth or subtlety: the Bailiff is unscrupulous cynicism personified; Dolmont is the very exemplar of a humane seigneur; Colinette is pretty, loyal, and resourceful, while Colas and L'Épine, the only two peasant characters (Colinette has been raised by Dolmont) are simpletons whose rustic speech is a sure and easy source of humour in the play.

Quesnel had hit upon a dramatic form and an innocuous theme most apposite for French Canada at the time. Yet it is a mistake to see this work as a mere anachronistic copy of a continental model. Precisely this type of musically enhanced entertainment was in vogue in France in the 1780s, and Quesnel found a responsive audience for his operetta in Montreal.

When *Colas et Colinette* was revived in Quebec City in 1805, and again in 1807, it proved to have lost none of its appeal. The printer John Neilson decided to publish it, with the author's approval and assistance. But the difficulty of reproducing the musical score proved insurmountable and the work did not appear until 1812, without music and bearing the imprint '1808'. It was included in James Huston's *Répertoire national* (1848), was reprinted in its original form in 1968, and published in English in 1974. *Colas et Colinette* was successfully recorded for Radio-Canada in 1968, in a sparkling version reconstituted by Godfrey Ridout, and has since been performed in Ottawa, Hamilton, and Milan (Italy).

See L.E. Doucette, *Theatre in French Canada, 1606-1867* (1984).

L.E. DOUCETTE

Coleman, Victor (b. 1944). Born in Toronto, he grew up there and in Montreal and was a high-school drop-out. Living on Toronto's Ward's Island in 1965, he founded the magazine *Island* and Island Press, which helped to shift the avant-garde poetry centre from Vancouver to Toronto. He entered book publishing as a production assistant for the Oxford University Press, Toronto (1966-7), and in 1967 joined COACH HOUSE PRESS, where for nearly a decade he served as the major Coach House editor: his catholic tastes were reflected in the work of the new Canadian writers and the American poets published by Coach House. After discontinuing *Island* and Island Press, he founded the Coach House literary magazine *Is*. For two years Coleman was director of the Nightingale Arts Council, operating in Toronto as A Space, which sponsored literary readings and performance art. He has also worked as editor and writer for the Association of Non-Profit Artist-Run Centres and published *Retrospective 4: documents of artist-run centres in Canada* (1981). At present he is director of the National Film Theatre, Kingston, Ontario.

An important figure in Canadian avant-garde or postmodernist verse, Coleman believes poetic form to be the natural extension of content. Though influenced by many American poets—including Jack Spicer, Charles Olson, and Robert Creeley—he has developed his own distinctive voice. His poems are usually short reflections that eschew any formal structure. His early volumes—*From Erik Satie's notes to the music* (1965), *One/eye/love* (1967), *Light verse* (1969), *Old friends' ghosts: poems 1963-68* (1970), *Back east* (1971), and *Some plays: on words* (1971)—are filled with idiosyncratic verses condensed almost to the point of impenetrability. Yet the poems are always playful and challenging: intoxicated with the limitless possibilities of imagery and thought existing as inseparable entities, they demand to be seen as moments of intuition or discovery. Later volumes—*America* (1972), *Parking lots* (1972), *Strange love* (1974), *Speech sucks* (1974), and *Traffic at both ends* (1978)—continue, sometimes at greater length, his experiments to shape language to its maximum force. Letting sound and movement create the form of poetry, Coleman rarely uses any tense other than the present, preferring to have all subjects exist simultaneously in the ear and the mind. Though some poems suffer from his tendency to play linguistic games for their own sake, more often his rejection of formal structures makes his verse a linguistic exploration and an intellectual discovery.

With *Corrections* (1985), Coleman continued to open his poetry to the influences and explorations of recent currents in literary theory. The collection is a self-conscious and at times frustratingly disrespectful rewriting of six of the poet's first nine books of poetry. Shaped by a strategy that allows Coleman to foreground concerns both old (sex and the physicality of being) and new (theories of chaos and flux), the book implicates both the poet and his written word in the instability and relentlessly personal processes of creating poetry itself.

Although a tenacious interest in things theoretical continued to shape to varying degrees such later collections as *Honeymoon suite* (1990), *Waiting for Alice* (1993), and the selected poems of *Lapsed W.A.S.P.* (1994), the fundamentals of Coleman's poetry remain for the most part unchanged.

Coleman is the author of *The day they stole the Coach House Press* (1993).

DAVID STAINES

Coles, Don (b. 1928). Born in Woodstock, Ontario, he graduated from the University of Toronto, gained a further degree (M.A., 1953) at Cambridge University, and spent a decade travelling around Europe, an experience that profoundly influenced the content and tone of his subsequent poetry. Since returning to Canada in 1965, he has taught humanities and creative writing at York University.

His poetry collections are *Sometimes all over* (1975); *Anniversaries* (1979); *The Prinzhorn collection* (1982); *Landslides: selected poems, 1975-1985* (1986), including a selection of new poems; *K. in love* (1987), a poem-sequence based on the love-letters of Franz Kafka; *Little bird* (1991), an extended verse-letter addressed to his dead father; *Forests of the medieval world* (1993), which won him a Governor General's award; and *Someone has stayed in Stockholm* (1994), a selection published in England.

Coles served a long and rigorous poetic apprenticeship, moving from what he calls 'ornate stuff' to a crisp and chaste diction that can accommodate vernacular speech-rhythms and subtle intellectual distinctions. While most of his verse is technically 'free', it is carefully controlled by a fine ear for rhythm, cadence, and sonority. His poems may be conveniently divided into two main groups. Many are devoted to the 'changeless, ordinary things' of everyday life (the satisfaction and anguish of love, the tensions of marriage, the ever-fluctuating relations between parents and children, our manifold human responses to 'the catastrophe of time'). Others represent a detached, resigned, yet profound brooding on the cultural monuments of the past.

Unlike most of his Canadian contemporaries, Coles remains aloof from narrowly nationalistic concerns, and insists on maintaining links with European culture. He expects his readers to be conversant with the main traditions of Western civilization—his poems are full of references to such figures as

Tolstoy, Ibsen, Kafka, Mann, Rilke, and Munch. At the same time, he consistently emphasizes the need for verbal clarity. A poem, he argues, 'should offer a comprehensive and usable piece of content', while employing a language 'accessible to serious readers'. W.J. KEITH

Collective creations in English. A collective creation is the product of a cohesive theatre group's exploration of a given topic through research and the improvisation of scenes and characters. These improvisations are criticized and reworked until a basic shape for a play emerges under the guidance of a director. However, as Paul Thompson, the major proponent of collective theatre in English Canada, emphasized: 'the actor is more than a puppet. . . . He's got his observations and he's quite as capable as anybody else of making a statement.' Although a rough script might record the main shape of the play for stage-management purposes, most collective creations do not exist in written form at all. Only the most successful productions might be scripted for publication: for example, Rick SALUTIN's *1837: the farmers' revolt* (1975, prod. 1973), *The farm show* (1976, prod. 1972), and Linda Griffiths' and Paul Thompson's *Maggie and Pierre* (1980, prod. 1979)—all productions of Theatre Passe Muraille, Toronto.

Often associated with words like 'alternate', 'documentary', 'agit-prop', and 'populist', collective creation began in France in the early 1960s with Roger Planchon and came to Canada via Thompson, who joined Theatre Passe Muraille and became its artistic director in 1972. Since then the collective method has had an important and widespread influence on Canadian theatre. Collective companies sprang up from Newfoundland to British Columbia and, in the post-1967 years, created plays with national and regional Canadian subjects where none had existed. The number of collective companies has declined, but the subjects of collective plays have broadened, and the rather loose 'collage' format of early collective creations has developed into a more coherent narrative structure. The great appeal of a collective creation lies in the actors' sense of commitment and immediacy, while its main weakness is a tendency to be predictable in attitudes and theatrical devices.

A quite different, but equally important, way in which collective creation influenced Canadian drama was in its emphasis on workshop development of a playwright's new work. The initial script was improvised upon by actors, sometimes vetted by an audience, before the playwright tackled the final version of the play, incorporating what he or she learned from the collective workshop. Many successful plays grew out of this process: Carol BOLT's *Buffalo jump* (1972) was collectively workshopped with Theatre Passe Muraille in 1972; Ken GASS's *Hurray for Johnny Canuck!* (1975) was the result of Toronto's Factory Theatre Lab's treatment in 1974; and Rex DEVERELL's *Medicare!* (1981) was a collaboration with Regina's Globe Theatre in 1980.

Toronto's Theatre Passe Muraille has been the major theatre collective in Canada, with over thirty collective creations to its credit, including *Doukhobours* (1972, prod. 1971), *I love you, Baby Blue* (1977, prod. 1975), *The west show* (1975, prod. 1976), and *Les maudits anglais* (1984, prod. 1978). It directly and individually influenced most of the collectives in Canada throughout the 1970s. The Mummers Troupe of Newfoundland with *They club seals, don't they?* (prod. 1978), Saskatoon's 25th Street House with *Paper wheat* (1978, prod. 1977), Edmonton's Theatre Network with *Hard hats and stolen hearts* (prod. 1977) and its Catalyst Theatre's *Stand up for your rights* (prod. 1980)—all followed Theatre Passe Muraille's pattern of critical examination of social issues in an episodic framework. However, Passe Muraille's political and social emphasis was less influential on West Coast collectives like Vancouver's Tamahnous Theatre. Founded in 1971 to explore the psycho-dramatic theories of Grotowski and Artaud, it was a tightly knit collective headed by Larry Lillo. However, when shaping its collective creations, it made majority decisions rather than deferring to a director, as Passe Muraille did; and it was more interested in exploring psychological than social problems in over twenty collective creations, including *The shaman's cure* (prod. 1975), *Deep thought* (prod. 1976), and *Vertical dreams* (prod. 1979). The collective approach was abandoned in 1984 when Morris Panych became artistic director.

See Robert Wallace and Cynthia Zimmerman, eds, *The work: conversations with English-Canadian playwrights* (1982); Alan Filewod, *Collective encounters* (1987); and Diane Bessai, *Playwrights of collective creation* (1992).

ELIZABETH HOPKINS

Collective creations in Quebec. In the strict sense of a form of dramatic writing shared by all the actors, collective creation was one of the main currents in Quebec theatre between 1965 and 1980. The critic Fernand Villemure, who counted '415 collective creations produced in Quebec between 1965 and 1974', cites as the first a work entitled *L'homme approximatif*, performed at the Séminaire Saint-Antoine de Trois-Rivières in 1965. Le Théâtre universitaire of Université Laval ('Les Treize') was one of the first groups to devote itself to collective creation, beginning in 1968. Villemure's figures show a clear increase in this trend, beginning in 1970: 'There were 35 different creations in 1970, then 60 in 1971, 92 in 1972, and 113 in 1973.' Since 1975, however, the movement has slowed down and collective creations almost completed disappeared after 1980.

Two companies in particular left their mark on the 1970s: Le Grand Cirque Ordinaire and Le Théâtre Euh!. Founded in 1969, the first of these had a remarkable success with *T'es pas tannée, Jeanne d'Arc?*, which played in Montreal and on tour from 1969 to 1973, and contributed more than any other show to the development of collective creation. *La famille transparente* (1970), *T'en rappelles-tu, Pibrac?* (1971), *L'opéra des pauvres* (1973), and *La tragédie américaine de l'enfant prodigue* ('rock opera', 1975) also made Le Grand Cirque Ordinaire the most influential and most imitated group in Quebec until its dissolution in 1977. Théâtre Euh!, which defined itself as an 'agit-prop' group, performed mainly in Quebec City between 1970 and 1975. It gave 436 shows in all, generally in the street, or in cafeterias or other public places. Since 1971, the mode of operation of Théâtre de l'Eskabel in Montreal was to consider production as a joint effort, but the script was generally signed. This model may be compared with the activity of playwright Michel GARNEAU who, for several years, defined himself as a 'one-man collective'—an author who based his writing on suggestions from an actors' collective. Between 1969 and 1971, Jean-Claude GERMAIN worked in a similar way, presenting, among other plays, *Les enfants de Chénier dans un autre grand spectacle d'adieu* in 1969, *Si Aurore m'était contée deux fois* in 1970, and *Mise à mort d'la Miss des Miss* in 1970.

After 1974 Le Théâtre Parminou in Victoriaville—stemming from Théâtre Euh!—became unquestionably the most active group in the area, putting on shows with Marxist-Leninist ideological leanings and according to demands from various unions or social groups. Other groups marked by their social commitment were Les Gens d'en bas in Rimouski, Le Théâtre de quartier and Le Théâtre a l'ouvrage in Montreal, and Le Théâtre de Carton in Longueuil. After 1973, a number of children's theatre companies devoted themselves (though not exclusively) to collective creation: they included La Marmaille (now Théâtre des deux mondes), La Grosse Valise, Le Théâtre de l'oeil, and Le Théâtre de Carton.

In the 1980s, the trend was to emphasize shared ideology and the collective operation of the group rather than joint writing. Thus were born several 'women's collectives', the best known of which, Le Théâtre expérimental des femmes, started with collective creations but rapidly went on to produce signed works. The Théâtre expérimental de Montréal, also dedicated at first to collective creation, has become the Nouveau Theatre expérimental de Montréal. In 1978 it created the Ligue nationale d'improvisation and, after 1980, devoted most of its time to Jean-Pierre Ronfard's *Vie et mort du roi boiteux* (produced between July 1981 and June 1982)—which was first a collective project entitled 'Shakespeare Follies'—and to other signed plays. Few companies in the 1990s produce collective creations.

See Michel Vaïs, 'Auteur/création collective: mythe et réalité', *Jeu* 4; Fernand Villemure, 'Aspects de la création collective au Québec', *Jeu* 4; and articles by Gérald Sigouin in *Jeu* 3 and *Jeu* 4. JEAN CLÉO GODIN

Collin, W.E. See *The WHITE SAVANNAHS*.

Colombo, John Robert (b. 1936). Born in Kitchener, Ontario, he studied at the University of Toronto and while there organized poetry readings at The Bohemian Embassy and edited *The Varsity Chapbook* (1959). In the more than three decades since he graduated—as in-house editor for various publishers, an associate editor of *The TAMARACK REVIEW*, teacher of creative writing, essayist and book-reviewer, editor and anthologist, translator and poet, and most importantly as the man who collects Canadian quotations and much else—he has become a national figure: John Robert Colombo, Man of Letters.

In the mid-sixties Colombo co-edited *Poetry 64/Poésie 64* (1963) with Jacques GODBOUT, an anthology of some of the most important new poets of his generation, and published his first book of 'found poetry', or what he also terms 'redeemed prose', *The Mackenzie poems* (1966). He never looked back, but became more and more the 'Master Gatherer' Robin SKELTON named him in an early review. And, although he earned artistic and critical recognition as a poet, he has gained mass popularity by becoming the pack-rat of Canadian culture and history.

Probably Canada's best-known maker of 'found poetry', Colombo created in *The Mackenzie poems*, *John Toronto: new poems by Dr. Strachan* (1966), *The great wall of China* (1966), and *The great San Francisco earthquake and fire* (1971), pure examples of the genre. *Abracadabra* (1967) reveals a writer of larger ambitions, one who seeks the poem where previous texts and life collide. *Neo poems* (1970) is a paradigmatic example of his generous and open poetics, as are such later collections as *Off earth* (1987) and *Luna Park* (1994). Even when his poems do not contain clearly found prose, they still insist that almost everything we know or imagine depends upon some previous 'text'. A richly ironic, devious, and witty imagination drives these books (the first is dedicated to the great Dada collagist Kurt Schwitters). In 'A Found Introduction' to the 'Found Poetry' section of *Open poetry* (1973) edited by Ronald Gross, Colombo says found poetry can teach us to 'respond aesthetically to the universe around us, not just to those separate parts of the world called works of art. It is possible to act as if the universe itself were an immense piece of art, a collage perhaps.' Some of his books are rather slight, but others, like *The sad truths* (1974), mix found texts with various kinds of commentary on privileged subtexts to reveal the traces of previous writing on our lives. Perhaps Colombo's most provocative book is *The great cities of antiquity* (1979), a collection of found poems in a dizzying variety of modes, based on entries in the famous Eleventh Edition of the *Encyclopedia Britannica*. It is Colombo's most extreme collage, a veritable textbook on the many formal experiments of modern and postmodern poetry. Colombo's mastery of his chosen art is clearly demonstrated in his *Selected poems* (1982).

Collage, of course, is the great art of juxtaposition, and Colombo is a master of witty parataxis, as the whole of *Translations from the English: found poems* (1974) demonstrates. Basically the same impulse that led to the notes and commentaries of that book led to his vast collection *Colombo's Canadian quotations* (1974), the first of many mass-market books that have followed in the decades since. A critic can fit this reference work into Colombo's creative *oeuvre* with no trouble, for although Colombo has not 'redeemed' its prose, he has organized it so that the whole emerges as a massive *trouvé* designed to show us what has been said of and in Canada throughout its history. Later versions—*The dictionary of Canadian quotations* (1991) and *Colombo's all-time great Canadian quotations* (1994)—are larger and cover a wider and more contemporary range, but they follow the basic paradigm of the original. Some later reference works—*Colombo's Canadian references* (1976), *Colombo's book of Canada* (1978), *Colombo's names and nicknames* (1979), *Colombo's Canadiana quiz book* (1983), *Canadian literary landmarks* (1984), and *999 Questions about Canada* (1989)—while not quite so audaciously successful, are manifestations of the same impulse to gather and collate various leaves of the world's book.

Colombo's abiding interest in the weird and mysterious in Canadian folklore and experience has led to numerous compilations, including *Windigo: an anthology of fact and fantastic fiction* (1982), and its companion volume *The mystery of the shaking tent* (1993)—relating to two cultural phenomena of Algonkian-speaking peoples: respectively, the evil spirit of possession and cannibalism, and a sacred rite—and *Mysterious Canada* (1988), *Extraordinary experiences* (1989), *UFOs over Canada* (1991), *Strange stories* (1994), *Ghosts galore!* (1994), *Ghost stories of Ontario* (1995), and *Haunted Toronto* (1996).

Many of Colombo's other compilations—such as *Colombo's little book of Canadian proverbs, graffitti, limericks & other vital matters* (1975), *Colombo's Hollywood* (1979), *René Lévesque buys Canada savings bonds* (1983), *The little blue book of Canadian UFOs* (1993), and *666 Canadian jokes* (1996)—are slapstick-comedy versions of the more serious reference books, but they spring from the same impulse to collect the texts of ordinary life and frame them aesthetically. One of Colombo's most delightful books, *Mostly monsters* (1977), is both comic compilation and witty found poetry. It is a collage of the pop mythology of the past century in which pulp fiction, films, radio shows, comic strips, and much else are ransacked to create a vision of our dreams of good, nightmares of evil, and of our ambiguous awareness that real power lies somewhere between and cannot easily be identified or found on the 'right' side.

Displaying as an editor the same wide-ranging curiosity that activates his poetry, Colombo has edited several anthologies of verse, including *How do I love thee: sixty poets of Canada (and Québec) select and introduce their favorite poems from their work* (1970), *Rhymes and reasons: nine Canadian poets discuss their work* (1971), and *The poets of Canada* (1978); a number of anthologies dedicated to the fantastic, beginning with *Other Canadas: an anthology of science fiction and fantasy* (1979), and including *Year of light* (1982); and some anthologies of translations, including *Balkan range: a Bulgarian reader* (with Nikola Roussanoff, 1976), *Poems of the Inuit* (1981), *Some Hungarian poets* (with George Jonas, 1995), and his own *Selected translations* (1982).

If the impression left by all these titles, and too many others to list, is one of indefatigable energy and unstoppable enthusiasm, that is in fact what Colombo's poetic is all about. Douglas FETHERLING's 'The literary politics of John Robert Colombo', *Saturday Night* (May 1974), and Jean Mallinson's 'John Robert Colombo: a documentary poet as visionary', *Essays on Canadian Writing* (Fall 1976), offer further insights into this protean literary force. See also the entries on Colombo in Richard Kostelanetz, *Dictionary of the avant-gardes* (1993) and Thomas Riggs, ed., *Contemporary poets* (6th ed., 1996).

DOUGLAS BARBOUR

Combustion (1957-60). Raymond SOUSTER's fourth little magazine (following *Direction*, 1943-6; *Enterprise*, 1948; and *CONTACT*, 1952-4), *Combustion* was probably begun to help replace the American magazine *Origin*, recently suspended by its editor, Souster's friend Cid Corman, who wrote weekly to Souster during the *Combustion* years suggesting subscribers and contributors and offering manuscripts that might otherwise have been published in *Origin*.

Combustion was mimeographed in editions of 100 to 125 copies. Initially its content was balanced between Canadian and international material; but in the later issues international work predominated, including generous selections by American writers previously published in *Origin*: Robert Creeley, Gary Snyder, Robert Duncan, Fielding Dawson, and Louis Zukofsky. *Combustion* made a significant contribution to American literature, and a modest one to Canadian writing by keeping it informed of international accomplishments. Souster published fourteen issues, the last appearing in Aug. 1960, eight months before Corman's launching of the second series of *Origin*.

See Frank DAVEY, *Louis Dudek and Raymond Souster* (1980). FRANK DAVEY

Conan, Laure. Pseudonym of Marie-Louise-Félicité ANGERS.

Cone, Tom. See DRAMA IN ENGLISH 1953 TO 1981.

Confederation poets. Since the publication of Malcolm Ross's influential anthology *Poets of the Confederation* (1960)—with selections from the poetry of Charles G.D. ROBERTS, Bliss CARMAN, Archibald LAMPMAN, and Duncan Campbell SCOTT—the term 'Confederation poets' has been generally taken to refer to these four writers, although others—such as William Wilfred CAMPBELL, George Frederick CAMERON, and Isabella Valancy CRAWFORD—are sometimes included under this term. Malcolm Ross's retrospective application of the term 'Confederation poets' is a good example of canon-making along national lines, in a cultural moment inspired by the founding of the Canada Council (1957), and the establishment of the NEW CANADIAN LIBRARY, with Ross himself as general editor (*Poets of the Confederation* was the first anthology in the series). As Hans Hauge puts it, Ross 'is beginning to construct a national literature and he does so by providing it with a past, that is to say, by projecting the project of a Canadian national literature into the past' ('The invention of national literatures', in *Literary responses to Arctic Canada*, ed. Jørn Carlsen, 1993).

Publishing their first volumes of verse in the 1880s and 1890s, Roberts, Lampman, Carman, and Scott were among the first really good poets writing in the recently formed Dominion of Canada. There are several good reasons, both biographical and literary, for grouping them together. All were close contemporaries born in the early 1860s. Roberts and Carman were cousins; Roberts briefly edited *The WEEK*, in which Carman published his first poem. Lampman was encouraged in his poetic efforts by his reading of Roberts' *Orion and other poems* (Philadelphia, 1880). Lampman and Scott were close friends; with Wilfred Campbell they began the column 'AT THE MERMAID INN' in the Toronto *Globe*, in 1892; after Lampman died, Scott published a memorial edition of his poems in 1900. All four poets drew much of their inspiration from Canadian nature, but they were also trained in the classics and were cosmopolitan in their literary interests. All were serious craftsmen who assimilated their borrowings from English and American writing in a personal mode of expression, treating the important subjects and themes of their day, often in a Canadian setting. They have been aptly called the first distinctly Canadian school of writers. FRANCIS ZICHY

Connor, Ralph. Pseudonym of Charles William GORDON.

Constantin-Weyer, Maurice (1881-1961). Born in Bourbonne-les-Bains, France, he had to interrupt his science studies at the

Sorbonne for lack of funds. He immigrated to Canada in 1903 and settled in Saint-Claude, Manitoba, where he raised cattle and became a jack-of-all-trades. In 1914, after an unsuccessful marriage to a Métisse, he returned to France to fight in the war and was gravely wounded. Contrary to what was long believed, he never returned to Canada. He spent the rest of his long life, mostly in Paris and Vichy, working as a newspaper editor, writing numerous articles, and about fifty books: novels, biographies, essays on a variety of subjects, translations, and even a play about Shakespeare, *Le grand Will* (Paris, 1945). In 1932 he received the Légion d'honneur.

Some fifteen books by Constantin-Weyer have Canadian content and are grouped under the title 'L'épopée canadienne'. In his first novel, *Vers l'ouest* (Paris, 1921), translated as *Towards the West* (1931)—the love story of two Métis set against the background of the war between the Sioux and the Métis—Louis Riel's father plays a minor role. *La bourrasque* (Paris, 1926)—the translation of which was called *The half-breed* (1930) in the USA and *A martyr's folly* (1930) in Canada—is a highly fictionalized treatment of Louis Riel's stormy career. Both works are marred by the extravagant liberties the author takes with history, especially in *La bourrasque*, where Riel becomes a grotesque figure. Constantin-Weyer was attacked by some writers for caricaturing the Métis (see Donatien Frémont, *Sur le ranch de Constantin-Weyer*, 1932), yet he was not devoid of sympathy for them, as *Napoléon* (Paris, 1931), the story of a Métis, shows. His best-known work, *Un homme se penche sur son passé* (Paris, 1928)—translated by Slater-Brown as *A man scans his past* (1929)—won him the Prix Goncourt and fame. The plot, partly autobiographical, is a variation on the love triangle, and the characters are rather superficial; but the critics praised 'the atmosphere of the Prairies and the Forests, of the Great North and Cold . . . in this poem of Action' (Robert Garric). Also well received were his essay *Manitoba* (Paris, 1924); *Cinq éclats de silex* (Paris, 1927), which is subtitled 'novel' but is rather a collection of five separate stories; and *Clairière: récits du Canada* (Paris, 1929), another essay about Manitoba—translated by Conrad Elphinestone as *Forest wild* (London, 1932)—in which Constantin-Weyer, a keen observer of fauna and flora, poignantly depicts what he calls the 'rhythm of Life and Death'. His admiration for physical strength and moral courage is evident in his biographies of great men: *Cavelier de la Salle* (Paris, 1927)—translated as *The French adventurer: the life and exploits of La Salle* (1931); *Champlain* (Paris, 1931); *La Vérendrye* (Paris, 1941); and *Autour de l'épopée canadienne* (Paris, 1941), a series of sketches of the builders of New France. *Une corde sur l'abîme* (Paris, 1937), *Un sourire dans la tempête* (Paris, 1934), and *Telle qu'elle était en son vivant* (Paris, 1936)—which was reissued under the title *La loi du Nord* (Paris, 1947) and made into a successful film, *La piste du Nord*, by Jacques Feyder—show men pitched against the North and against each other. Even in the novels of Constantin-Weyer that take place in France, memories of Canada are often present. Of the francophones who have written novels about western Canada, he is certainly the most prolific, and Roger Motut considers him to be the best painter of the western landscape.

See Marguerite Constantin-Fortin, *Une femme se penche sur son passé* (Paris, 1939); Roger Motut, *Maurice Constantin-Weyer, écrivain de l'Ouest et du Grand Nord* (1982); and *Cahiers franco-canadiens de l'Ouest*, numéro spécial: Maurice Constantin-Weyer, I, 1 (printemps 1989). PAULETTE COLLET

Contact (1952-4). The third little magazine founded by Raymond SOUSTER, following *Direction* (1943-6) and *Enterprise* (1948), it was begun in Jan. 1952 in open discontent with the policies of John SUTHERLAND's *NORTHERN REVIEW*. Souster's two principal advisers in this project were Louis DUDEK, who hoped it could be a 'workshop' for young Canadians, and the American poet and editor Cid Corman, who advocated high standards, even to the exclusion of Canadian contributors. For the most part Souster steered a middle course, although publishing many more American and international writers than Dudek liked. *Contact* was thus the first Canadian magazine to publish American poets of the Black Mountain school—among them Charles Olson, Robert Creeley, Paul Blackburn, Denise Levertov, and Vincent Ferrini. It led eventually to Souster's arranging public readings for both Olson and Creeley in Toronto, in his Contact Poetry Readings of 1959-62. Published in mimeograph format, *Contact* continued for ten issues until Mar. 1954. Despite its American and European contributors (among the latter were Octavio Paz, Jean Cocteau, Hugh McDiarmid, Jacques Prévert, and George Seferis), it never attracted more than fifty subscribers.

See Frank DAVEY, *Louis Dudek and Raymond Souster* (1980) and Ken Norris, 'The significance of *Contact* and *CIV/n*' in *CIV/n: a literary magazine of the 50's* (1983), edited by Aileen Collins, with the assistance of Simon Dardick. FRANK DAVEY

Contact Press (1952-67). Raymond SOUSTER's small mimeographed magazines *Direction* (1943), *Enterprise* (1948), *CONTACT* (1952-4), and Aileen Collins' *CIV/n* (1953-5) (which advocated the new poetry of the 1950s, especially the Black Mountain poets, Cid Corman and Ezra Pound) evolved into Canada's first major small press. With the guidance of Louis DUDEK and Souster—and, after 1959, with the financial support of Peter Miller—the press kept alive the tradition of artistic independent publishing that had begun with the *McGILL FORTNIGHTLY REVIEW*.

The first title from Contact Press was *Cerberus* (1952). Perhaps fittingly, the title reference to the three-headed dog of myth, and guardian of the underworld, linked Irving LAYTON, Dudek, and Souster. The Contact Poetry Readings (1957-62), held in Toronto and organized by Souster, brought in such readers as Charles Olsen, Robert Creeley, and Louis Zukowsky, and were well attended by up to a hundred patrons. *Contact* published early work by Eli MANDEL, Al PURDY, Milton ACORN, Gwendolyn MacEWEN, R.G. EVERSON, George BOWERING, Gerry Gilbert, Eldon GRIER, Robert HOGG, Daphne Buckle (MARLATT), Frank DAVEY, George JONAS, D.G. JONES, David McFADDEN, Fred WAH, Phyllis WEBB, and, in its final year of operation, twenty-seven-year-old Margaret ATWOOD (*The circle game*, 1966; the circles on the cover were done by Atwood with red stick-on dots from a stationary store). Dudek's decision not to reprint the book led in part to the formation of the House of *ANANSI*, which carried *The circle game* in its backlist.

When Peter Miller withdrew financial support for family reasons, the press was discontinued. The last title published by Contact Press, *New Wave Canada: the new explosion in Canadian poetry* (1966), edited by Souster, and assisted in his editorial choices by Victor COLEMAN, was a symbolic passing of the torch to the newly formed COACH HOUSE PRESS. With poetry by George Bowering, Daphne Marlatt, bp Nichol, Frank Davey, and David McFadden, the book was not an anthology of the past, but a prophecy of the future. By then the literary model of writer-editors and writer-publishers was established for other small presses, along with an enlarged perspective and important subsequent trends in Canadian literature.

See Louis Dudek and Michael Gnarowski, *The making of modern poetry in Canada* (1967); Frank Davey, *Louis Dudek & Raymond Souster* (1980); and Ken Norris, *The little magazine in Canada, 1925-80* (1984). GEOFF HANCOCK

Contemporary Verse (1941-52). One of the leading Canadian poetry magazines of the 1940s and early 1950s, it was founded by Alan Crawley; at various times he was assisted by Dorothy LIVESAY, Anne MARRIOTT, Doris Ferne, and Floris Clarke McLaren. The first issue was published from North Vancouver in Sept. 1941; later the journal was edited from Victoria. *Contemporary Verse* played an important role at a time when there were few literary magazines in Canada. Crawley sought to maintain a high standard of writing, while keeping his pages open to poets of many inclinations. The criteria he announced in one of his editorials were that the work he published must be 'serious in thought and expression and contemporary in theme, treatment, and technique'. The more than 120 poets that appeared included virtually every important name in that vital era in the development of a Canadian tradition in poetry, as well as new talents; a number of the best modern Canadian poets were first published in his magazine. Thirty-nine issues had appeared by the time Crawley felt he had completed his task and ceased publication at the end of 1952.

See *Alan Crawley and 'Contemporary Verse'* (1976) edited by Joan McCullagh, with a reminiscent introduction by Dorothy Livesay. GEORGE WOODCOCK

Contemporary Verse II (1975-). It was established by Dorothy LIVESAY—who had given editorial assistance to *CONTEMPORARY VERSE*—as a periodical devoted exclusively to contemporary Canadian poetry and poetry criticism. Published three times a year from the University of Manitoba, it surveys Canadian poetry as well as special topics of interest, such as spiritual poetry, the politics of language, and the writers of individual provinces. In 1986 the magazine was redesigned and individual editors were replaced by a collective. GEOFF HANCOCK

Contes du pays incertain (1962). The most important work of Jacques FERRON, and winner of a Governor General's Award, it is a collection of legends, fables, and tales that illustrate the 'indépendantiste' notion that the 'uncertain country' has become an essential political and literary myth in Quebec, opposing and contradicting the 'two solitudes' myth created by Hugh MacLENNAN. Ferron claims that French Canada will remain an uncertain and absurd country as long as its territorial imagination extends from St John's to Victoria, from 'one pond to another'. *Contes du pays incertain* established Ferron as the most gifted *conteur* of Quebec. His imagination excelled in the use of fable, irony, and allegory.

These tales were inspired by Ferron's contact with storytellers in the Gaspé. Their themes identify the problems of an 'uncertain people': the breaking down of the myth that the land and the *revanche des berceaux* were means of survival; the slavery of the city-dweller victimized by capitalism; the corruption of politicians; the complicity of the Church with the politically powerful and the wealthy; the hypocrisy of writers like SAINT-DENYS-GARNEAU, who described their personal anguish instead of helping to construct a national literature; the desirability of Native peoples and Québécois working together towards common goals of territorial and cultural recognition. In 'Mélie et le boeuf', the most striking tale, a depressed and sickly mother of thirteen (the typical mother of Québécois 'anti-terroir' literature) becomes emotionally close to her favourite calf, which eventually becomes an English-speaking bull that excites all the cows in the country. In 'Le paysagiste' Ferron explores one of his most positive recurring themes: the need to be close to nature in order to achieve personal and collective awareness.

Contes du pays incertain was republished in 1968 with *Contes anglais et autres* and *Contes inédits*. A selection of these stories, many of them from the first collection, was translated by Betty Bednarski and published in English under the title *Tales from an uncertain country* (1972).

See Jean-Pierre Boucher, *Les contes de Jacques Ferron* (1974); Gérard BESSETTE, '"Mélie et le boeuf" de Jacques Ferron', *Modern Fiction Studies*, vol. XXII, 3 (1976); Mary Ziroff, *A study guide to Jacques Ferron's 'Tales from the uncertain country'* (1977); Donald Smith, 'Jacques Ferron ou la géographie d'un pay certain', *Journal of Canadian Fiction* 25-6 (1979). See also *BRICK* 16 (Fall 1982) and *VOIX ET IMAGES* 8 (Spring 1983), special issues on Ferron. DONALD SMITH

Cook, Michael (1933-94). Born in London, England, Cook attended various schools until he was fifteen. In 1949 he joined the British Army, serving for the next twelve years in Europe and the Far East and rising to the rank of sergeant. Some of his time was spent devising theatrical entertainment for the troops. After leaving the army, he worked briefly in a ball-bearing factory and in 1962 he entered Nottingham University College of Education, where he trained as a teacher. In the mid-1960s he arrived in Newfoundland and soon afterwards was employed as a drama specialist in Memorial University's Extension Service. Subsequently he joined the university's English department and in 1979 was promoted to associate professor. He was active in Newfoundland as a promoter of theatre, a critic, director, actor, and, after 1970, as a playwright. He retired from his teaching position in 1993.

Cook's first published play, *Colour the flesh the colour of dust* (1972), is a historical drama set in St John's, Newfoundland, in 1762. It is strongly influenced by Bertolt Brecht, and Cook later described it, somewhat too harshly, as 'a lousily structured play'. The radio drama *Tiln* (1973) perhaps showed too plainly the influence of Samuel Beckett. *The head, guts and sound bone dance* (1974) is an effort to evoke the antiquated attitudes of oldtime Newfoundlanders as a bizarre contrast to the contemporary lifestyle on the island. It features—for perhaps the first time in Canadian theatre—the splitting and gutting of codfish on stage. *Jacob's wake* (1975) is an ambitious and occasionally powerful depiction of the disintegration of a Newfoundland outport family. *Quiller* (1975) and *Terese's creed*, which is included in *Tiln & other plays* (1976), are one-act plays, the latter a monologue in which Cook explores the inner life of outport characters. *Quiller*—a pathetic, sometimes tender, sometimes funny monologue by an outcast living on the fringe of a Newfoundland outport—is probably Cook's finest work. *The fisherman's revenge* (1976) treats the relationship between merchant and fisherman in comic fashion. *On the rim of the curve* (1977) is an attempt to dramatize the final days on earth of the Beothuks, Newfoundland's Aboriginal people. *The Gayden chronicles* (1977) is a three-act play exploring the life of a rebel in the British navy who was hanged in St John's in 1812. The Newfoundland setting here is of no importance, which suggests that Cook may have been trying to give his work more general appeal. In 1980, however, he published the first chapter of a novel set in a Newfoundland outport (in *Aurora: new Canadian writing*, edited by Morris Wolfe); and his fascination with Newfoundland endured to the end of his life. Much of his writing, including numerous radio plays, remains unpublished.

Cook's plays celebrate the elemental and instinctive; they are harangues—assaults upon the audience's sense of decorum, and even upon intellect. Cook wrote: 'I've always had a deep distrust in my own head of intellectual responses.' One critic suggested that he was one of the 'rebarbarizers of civilized culture'. His plays achieve few subtle effects, yet they are daring, passionate, and full of movement. 'My plays', he wrote, 'are about real people, with blood and guts and sinews. The language is of the people, remembered and cherished with love.' Cook wrote a provocative comment on art and life in an exhibition catalogue of the painter Gerald Squires called *The Newfoundland landscape 1988-1993* (1993). There is an essay by him on Newfoundland theatre in *Proceedings of the workshop on Newfoundland theatre research* (1993), edited by Denyse Lynde, Helen Peters, and Richard Buehler.

Cook's plays have been collected in *Tiln & other plays* and *Three plays* (1977). He discussed his own life and work in *Canadian Theatre Review*, I (1974) and XVI (1977); in *Canadian Drama*, II (1976); and in Geraldine Anthony, ed. *Stage voices* (1978). *The head, guts and sound bone dance* is included in *Major plays of the Canadian theatre 1934-1984*, edited by Richard Perkins (1984); *Jacob's wake* is in *Modern Canadian plays* (1985), edited by Jerry Wasserman.

PATRICK O'FLAHERTY

Cook, Ramsay (b. 1931). Born in Alameda, Saskatchewan, he attended schools there and in Manitoba, and the University of Manitoba (B.A., 1954); Queen's University, Kingston, Ontario, where he worked under A.R.M. Lower (M.A., 1955); and the University of Toronto, working under Donald CREIGHTON (Ph.D., 1960). Cook was appointed to the history department of the University of Toronto in 1958, but moved to York University, Toronto, as professor of history a decade later, retiring in 1996. He is a Fellow of the Royal Society of Canada (1968) and an Officer of the Order of Canada (1986).

After publishing *The politics of John W. Dafoe and the Free Press* (1963), Cook turned his back on the prevailing paradigms in the discipline so as to explore Canadian pluralism. A fine essayist who emerged as one of the principal interpreters of French-Canadian thought, he combined an interest in ideas with his knowledge of events and personalities. As the struggle of French Canadians to express themselves during the Quiet Revolution brought consternation to many confused English Canadians, Cook's explanations made sense of recent developments by linking them to history. Fascinated by Canadian nationalism in both its majority and minority expressions, he succeeded in revealing a variety of guises assumed by the French-Canadian sphinx in collections of essays such as *Canada and the French-Canadian question* (1966) and *The Maple Leaf forever* (1971) and the series of articles in *French Canadian nationalism* (1969). Committed to the federal state, Cook wrote *Canada: a modern study* (1964) and delineated the interplay of *Provincial autonomy, minority rights and the compact theory, 1867-1921* (1969). In *Canada 1896-1921: a nation transformed* (1974) in The Canadian Centenary Series, co-authored with Robert Craig Brown, the country's two solitudes disappeared into an account that was magisterial in its sweep about the Laurier-Borden years, a critical juncture in Canadian history.

Deepening an interest in cultural history, Cook provided a series of portraits of unconventional intellectuals in *The regenerators: social criticism in late Victorian English Canada* (1985), which won a Governor General's Award. Essays appearing under the title *Canada, Quebec and the uses of nationalism* (1986; 2nd edn 1995) updated established themes, but also examined English-Canadian nationalism and cultural expression searchingly. As evidence of his range, he wrote a long introduction to the reissue of H.P. Biggar's translation of *The voyages of Jacques Cartier* (1993). He has been editor of McCLELLAND & STEWART's Canadian Centenary Series and is now General Editor of the *DICTIONARY OF CANADIAN BIOGRAPHY*. Among Cook's doctoral students have been Michael BLISS, David Bercuson, and Franca Iacovetta.

TERRY CROWLEY

Cooper, Douglas. See NOVELS IN ENGLISH 1983 TO 1996: OTHER NOVELS 2(b).

Copeland, Ann (b. 1932), pseudonym of Virginia Ann Furtwangler (née Walsh). Born in Connecticut, USA, Copeland was educated in Catholic schools and in New Rochelle College before entering the Ursuline order of nuns as Sister John Bernard. She attended the Catholic University of America and Cornell University, where she completed a Ph.D. in English literature, and has taught English and music in the United States and Canada. She left the Ursuline order after thirteen years, married, and moved in 1971 with her husband and two sons (one of whom was adopted) to Sackville, New Brunswick, where she began to write fiction. Her short stories have been published in numerous journals and anthologies and collected in *At peace* (1978), *The back room* (1979), *Earthen vessels* (1984), *The golden thread* (1989), nominated for a Governor

General's Award, and *Strange bodies on a stranger shore* (1994).

Copeland's style is precise, understated, and often ironic. She frequently uses a central metaphor to create resonance among the images in her stories, such as the golden thread of Ariadne, which was used by Theseus to negotiate the labyrinth and which in the story and book of the same name suggests the delicate relations of faith, obedience, and friendship needed to negotiate the labyrinth of cloistered life in the time of Vatican II, the era in which Copeland sets many of her stories. She draws upon her experiences as a nun, a mother, and a teacher in convent schools and, later, at Dorchester Penitentiary. A key concept is commitment, uniting disparate experiences from a nun's vows to marriage vows, motherhood, education, and incarceration. Many of the stories in *At peace* are published in revised form in *The golden thread*, refocused on Sister Claire Delaney, who is also the central character of the stories in *Strange bodies on a stranger shore*. These are more amibitious structurally, blending past and present, as Claire negotiates middle age and her memories of her former life as a nun.

Copeland has discussed her work in *Books in Canada* 21.2 (March 1992).

HEATHER SANDERSON

Copway, George (Kahgegagahbowh, Standing Firm, 1818-69). An Ojibwa born and raised near the mouth of the Trent River in the Rice Lake area of Upper Canada (Ontario), he was converted to Christianity at the age of twelve. In 1834 he began mission work as a teacher and interpreter with the American Methodist Episcopal Church among the Ojibwa on the south shore of Lake Superior. He spent the winters of 1835 and 1836 in La Pointe, Wisconsin, where he helped the Rev. Sherman Hall translate the Acts of the Apostles and the Gospel of St Luke into Ojibwa. In 1836 he was sent to the Ebenezer Manual Labour School in Illinois, graduating in the fall of 1839. While on a visit to Rice Lake in the summer of 1840, he married a white woman, Elizabeth Howell, whom he had met at the Credit River Mission. They immediately left for the American West, where they spent two years in the Upper Mississippi missions, at first in the Sioux and Ojibwa war zone, and later at Fond du Lac, at the head of Lake Superior away from the battlefields. In late 1842 they returned to Canada. Accepted as a preacher by the Wesleyan Methodist Canadian Conference, Copway left early in 1843 on a three-month missionary tour of Upper Canada with the Rev. William Ryerson. The next year he was sent to the Saugeen Mission on Lake Huron; he transferred in 1844 to Rice Lake, returning in 1845 to the Saugeen. The same year he was elected vice-president of the Grand Council of the Methodist Ojibwa of Canada West. Less than a year later the Saugeen band, and later the Rice Lake band, accused Copway of embezzlement. He spent a few months in prison and was expelled from the Methodist Conference. When he was released he moved back to the United States, where he became a literary celebrity and popular public speaker. Early in 1847 his autobiography appeared: *The life, history and travels of Kah-ge-ga-gah-bowh (George Copway), a young Indian chief of the Ojibwa Nation, a convert to the Christian Faith, and a Missionary to his people for twelve years*. A memoir of a childhood spent in the traditional migratory way, it provides a unique picture of what it was like to grow up as a nineteenth-century woodland Ojibwa. So successful was the book, the first written by a Canadian Native, that it went through six editions by the end of the year and was republished in 1851 as *Recollections of a forest life*. By the late 1840s Copway had become a passionate advocate of Native rights. He toured the United States, delivering addresses from South Carolina to Massachusetts, pleading for support for his scheme to set aside a large tract of land on the northeastern shore of the Missouri River as a permanent country for Natives of all tribes, to be known as Kahgega (Ever to be). In 1850 he published his most famous work, *The traditional history and characteristic sketches of the Ojibwa nation*, later published in the United States as *Indian life and Indian history by an Indian author. . .* (Boston, 1860). (A facsimile edition of the 1850 original was published by Coles in 1972, and a modern edition appeared in 1978.) In it he praised the lyricism and bountiful vocabulary of the Ojibwa language and Ojibwa orators: 'Our orators have filled the forests with the music of their voices, loud as the roar of a water fall, yet soft and moving as the gentle murmur of a mountain stream.' He expressed the hope 'to awaken in the American heart a deeper feeling for the race of red men'. The book's success brought him international recognition and an invitation to speak at an important Peace Conference in Frankfurt, Germany. He recorded his experiences in *Running sketches of men and places in England, France, Germany, Belgium and Scotland* (1851).

In 1851 Copway launched his weekly newspaper, *Copway's American Indian*, in New York City to raise support for the implementation of his scheme. Although his vision appealed to many prominent Americans, the United States government was bent on its 'Indian removal' policy. The time was not ripe for Copway's vision and the paper survived for only three months (10 July to 4 October 1851). He enjoyed the praise and friendship of such prominent literary figures as James Fenimore Cooper, Washington Irving, Henry Wadsworth Longfellow, Henry Rowe Schoolcraft, and Francis Parkman. But by late 1851 Copway had become a beleaguered individual, plagued by poverty, conflicting loyalties, and the desertion of many of his admirers. Parkman, for one, began to suspect Copway's sincerity and to resent his continuing requests 'for pecuniary aid'. Disillusioned and frustrated, but still enterprising and even hopeful, Copway remained in the United States for at least another sixteen years, trying to earn a living as a lecturer. When that career failed, the once-celebrated writer and lecturer was forced to take a job as a Union Army recruiter. In the summer of 1868 he appeared, without his family, at the Algonkian-Iroquois mission at Lac-des-Deux-Montagnes, northwest of Montreal. At first he was accepted enthusiastically by both tribes because of his success as a herbal doctor. But he became involved in a dispute between the Sulpicians, who claimed ownership of the reserve, and the Iroquois, who were threatening to convert to Methodism in protest. When a Methodist preacher arrived, Copway persuaded most of the Algonkians not to attend his service. He himself had converted to Roman Catholicism, but on the night before his first communion he suddenly died.

The writings of Canada's first Native author have been challenged for their authorship and reliability. In 1850, an epic poem, *The Ojibway conquest*, was published under his name. But in 1898 Julius Taylor Clark—of Topeka, Kansas—confessed that he himself had written the poem in order to help Copway's fund-raising efforts, and had allowed Copway to publish it. No one can be certain whether or not Copway's educated wife collaborated in the writing of his books. George Harvey Genzmer, an American critic of the time, described Copway's writing style as 'an amalgam of Washington Irving, St Luke and elements derived from Methodist exhorters'. Copway's truth is in his understanding of his own history in the spirit of Aboriginal oral traditions. PENNY PETRONE

Corbeil, Carole. See NOVELS IN ENGLISH 1983 TO 1996: OTHER NOVELS 2(a).

Coren, Michael (b. 1959). He was born in Walthamstow, Essex, England, and studied politics at the University of Nottingham (B.A., 1980) and then journalism at City University, London. He worked as a reporter for the *New Statesman* and as a commentator for BBC Radio before moving to Canada in 1987. He became a jack-of-all-writing-trades in Toronto, reviewing books, writing articles, contributing columns, hosting a weekly evening talk show on CFRB Radio, etc. As a public personality his speciality is the expression of acerbic comment and sometimes polemical opinion on the issues and personalities of the day. Of some literary interest are his biographies of British writers G.K. Chesterton (1988), H.G. Wells (1993), C.S. Lewis (1994), and Conan Doyle (1995). There are two collections of his journalism: *Aesthete: the Frank diaries of Michael Coren* (1993) consists of satiric contributions to *Frank* magazine; *Setting it right* (1996) is a gathering of newspaper and magazine columns. 'If the pen is mightier then the sword', he once asked, 'why isn't it a felony to carry a ball-point in your jacket pocket?' JOHN ROBERT COLOMBO

Corriveau, Monique. Pseudonym of Monique Chouinard. See CHILDREN'S LITERATURE IN FRENCH: 3.

Costain, Thomas B. (1885-1965). Thomas Bertram Costain was born in Brantford, Ontario, and educated there. He began his journalistic career as a reporter for the Brantford *Expositor* and then worked in Guelph and for the Maclean-Hunter publications in Toronto. He became editor of *Maclean's* in 1914 and held that post until 1920, when he immigrated to the United States (he later became an American citizen) to be an associate editor of the *Saturday Evening Post*. In 1934 he became eastern story editor for Twentieth-Century Fox, and from 1939 to 1946 was advisory editor for Doubleday in New York. In this period he began to write historical fiction, and his first novel, *For my great folly* (1942), was a bestseller. This was followed by *Ride with me* (1944). In 1946 he began to devote his full time to writing fiction.

Costain's novels remain entertaining specimens of the historical-romance/adventure mode of popular fiction, and range in subject-matter from the Cathay of Kubla Khan, to Napoleon's Europe, to New France. Fast-paced, exciting, stocked with easily understood characters, both fictional and historical, and employing complex, coincidence-packed plots, his works sold in the millions. *The black rose* (1945), for example, topped the two-million mark in all editions and was made into a Hollywood spectacle film. Other novels include *The moneyman* (1947), *The silver chalice* (1952), *The tontine* (1955), *Below the salt* (1955), and *The darkness and the dawn* (1959). Costain's novels with Canadian settings are *High towers* (1949), a treatment of the Le Moyne family of New France that ranges from Hudson Bay to New Orleans; and *Son of a hundred kings* (1950), the rags-to-riches story of an orphaned immigrant boy in a Canadian small town in the 1890s. Costain also wrote a popular history of New France: *The white and the gold: the French régime in Canada* (1954).

Costain's career follows in some respects a pattern set by Gilbert PARKER and others, in which small-town Canadians made their way in the great metropolitan centres on the strength of their gifts as writers of popular fiction and romance. His books sold nearly 12 million copies. His success as a popular writer was recognized by academe when he was given an honorary doctorate by the University of Western Ontario. DENNIS DUFFY

Coulter, John (1888-1980). Born in Belfast, Ireland, he attended the School of Art and School of Technology there and then won a scholarship to the University of Manchester. He returned to Belfast in 1912 and moved to Dublin in 1917, chiefly to be close to the leaders of the Irish literary renaissance and to the Abbey Theatre. Unable to establish his own theatre in Belfast, he moved to London to write and do freelance work for the BBC, for which he worked until 1936. During those years he edited the *Ulster Review* in 1924, and wrote for John Middleton Murry's *The Adelphi*, becoming managing editor (1927-30) when Murry reorganized it and renamed it *The New Adelphi* in 1927. In London Coulter met Olive Clare Primrose, a Canadian writer whom he married in 1936 after settling in Toronto. Coulter published the story of their courtship in *Prologue to a marriage: letters and diaries of John Coulter and Olive Clare Primrose* (1979), a tribute to their happy life together until her death in 1971. They had two daughters: Primrose, a writer, and Clare, a well-known actress.

Besides writing for journals, magazines, and radio in both Canada and Britain, and working for three years (1938-41) in New York for CBS radio, Coulter published plays, librettos, poetry, a novel, a biography, and his memoirs. His early plays, reflecting his Irish background in setting and theme, are noteworthy for their local colour; but their lack of an element of surprise or dramatic reversal detracts from their overall effect. *The house in the quiet glen* (1937), which won several prizes at the Dominion Drama Festival in 1937, is a one-act comedy about an Irish girl whose parents arrange to marry her to a widower, not knowing she has designs on the widower's son. Another short folk drama, *Father Brady's new pig* (later retitled *Pigs*, then *Clogherbann Fair*—unpublished), concerns the struggle between a parish priest and his housekeeper over the purchase of a sow. Both a radio and a stage play, and the first play Coulter wrote in Canada, it was first produced by the Arts and Letters Club in Toronto in 1937. *The family portrait* (1937) is a full-length comedy—written for the Abbey Theatre, though not produced there—about the reactions of a Belfast family to its playwrighting son and his successful play, which mirrors their own lives. *The drums are out* (1971) treats a more serious theme: the effect of the Irish civil war on Protestants and Catholics alike. Set in Belfast in the early 1920s, it focuses on a family whose father is a policeman and whose daughter is secretly married to a member of the Irish Republican Army. It premièred at the Abbey Theatre on 12 July 1948, and played for five weeks to full houses. These plays of Coulter's, while reflecting life in Northern Ireland, do not have the genuine Irish dialogue that O'Casey gave to his Dublin plays; with the exception of *The drums are out*, they also fail to develop the potential of their characters' situations. *The family portrait* was refused by the Abbey because Coulter could not rewrite the final scenes to the satisfaction of the director Lennox Robinson. Nevertheless it had a successful production by the Group Theatre in Belfast in 1948 and, under the title *The sponger*, was presented on CBC television in 1956.

Coulter became fascinated with the Métis leader Louis Riel and wrote a RIEL TRILOGY. In 1949 he completed *Riel* (1962; rev. 1975), a wide-ranging dramatization of events in Riel's life between the Red River Rebellion of 1870 and his hanging in 1885. According to the author's note, it was 'designed for presentation in the Elizabethan manner'—a far-sighted step to take four years before the construction of Stratford's revolutionary thrust stage. In 1975 *Riel* received a production worthy of that design at the National Ars Centre, directed by Jean Gascon, with Albert Millaire as Riel. *The trial of Louis Riel* (1968), a courtroom drama and a much more limited play, uses transcripts from the trial and includes some French dialogue. Since its first production in Regina, where Riel was hanged, this play has become an annual attraction there. *The crime of Louis Riel* (1976)—a revised version of *Riel* for theatre groups unable to meet the technical demands of the original, it combines the expansiveness of *Riel* with the intensity of *The trial of Louis Riel Riel*—won the Dominion Drama Festival's regional prize for best Canadian play of 1967. (See Riel Trilogy.) Earlier Coulter had written another courtroom drama on Canadian history, *The trial of Joseph Howe* (unpublished), produced on CBC radio in 1942. Based on the 1835 libel suit brought against HOWE as publisher of *The Novascotian*, it dramatizes the trial and its 'not guilty' verdict to show the importance of freedom of the press.

Coulter wrote three opera librettos, all for the Canadian composer Healey Willan. *Transit through fire* (1942), a short verse-drama, concentrates on the bitter reflections of a young soldier on leave, and of his wife, about their society before the Second World War. This, and *Deirdre of the sorrows* (1944)—a retelling in verse and prose of the ancient Irish story of the foundling girl whose lovers are fated to die—were the first two Canadian operas commissioned and broadcast by the Canadian Broadcasting Corporation. Coulter's first published play, *Conochar* (1917), is about the same legend. *Deirdre* (1965), a slightly revised version of the 1944 work, was first staged in 1965 at the MacMillan Theatre, Toronto, and was also the first Canadian opera to be produced, in 1967, by the Canadian Opera Company, at Toronto's O'Keefe Centre.

Coulter's *The blossoming thorn* (1946)—a collection of light, lyrical, romantic, elegiac, and sometimes humorous poems that are superior to the verse in his three librettos—is his alternative to what he considered to be the over-intellectual and unemotional qualities in modern poetry. His one novel, *Turf smoke: a fable of two countries* (1945)—an adaptation of an unpublished play, *Holy Manhattan*—tells of an Irish immigrant in New York who is unable to adapt to the American way of life but finally realizes he cannot return to Ireland either. Coulter also wrote *Churchill* (1945), which he called a 'dramatic biography'—a short journalistic account based on the sources he used for an unpublished 'living-newspaper' play, *Mr Churchill of England*.

In later life Coulter continued to write and revise plays for the stage and for radio. One of these, *François Bigot: a rediscovery in dramatic form of the fall of Quebec* (1978), was revised from a version broadcast on CBC radio in 1970. Two unpublished radio presentations further indicate Coulter's interest in, and sympathy for, French Canada: *A tale of old Québec in 1670*, broadcast on BBC radio in 1935 and on CBS in 1940. Other unpublished scripts are *Oblomov*, adapted from the Russian novel of Goncharov, which has been translated into several languages and was produced on CBC television in 1962; *Sleep, my pretty one*, a verse-play about a woman who cannot accept her stepmother, produced at Toronto's Centre Stage in 1961; *A capful of pennies* (also titled *This glittering dust*), about the off-stage life of the famous British actor Edmund Kean, produced in Toronto on stage and on CBC radio in 1967; and *God's Ulsterman*, a sequence of two plays (*Dark days of ancient hate and Red hand*) about the injustice committed by Cromwell in Ireland and its legacy in strife-torn Belfast, both produced on CBC radio in 1974. Coulter spent his last years writing his memoirs, *In my day* (1980), a long account of his life, career, and of people he knew in Canada and abroad. It was published the year he died in a signed limited edition of 93 copies—one for each year of the author's life.

Coulter was active in the cultural life of Canada in other ways. In 1944 he was among the artists who presented a brief to the Turgeon Committee of the House of Commons, which was responsible for the formation of the Massey Commission, and thus the CANADA COUNCIL; and in 1952 he persuaded his friend Tyrone Guthrie to come to Canada to direct the first production of the Stratford Festival. Coulter was also a founder of the Canadian Arts Council, now the Canadian Conference of the Arts. Near the end of his life he received an honorary doctorate from York University and an honorary life membership in the Association for Canadian Theatre History, now the Association for Canadian Theatre Research. For both his eightieth and ninetieth birthdays the CBC produced special radio and television tributes to him.

Coulter was never totally at home in Canada. His preference for non-Canadian subjects, and in his Canadian plays for historical subjects with formal dialogue rather than contemporary topics and a Canadian idiom, suggests that he was not completely in touch with Canadian life. In fact his Irish plays were not Irish enough for the Irish, nor were his Canadian plays Canadian enough for Canada. Nevertheless Coulter showed younger writers that they must write from their own roots, and that Canadian history could be interesting on stage.

The Mills Memorial Library of McMaster University has a collection of Coulter's literary essays and plays; many of his out-of-print and unpublished works can be found in the Metropolitan Toronto Central Library. His reflections on radio drama, which he wrote throughout his career, are in a slim booklet, *Radio drama is not theatre* (1937). He also wrote two accounts of his writing career in an introduction to *The drums are out*, and in a chapter of *Stage voices* (1978), edited by Geraldine Anthony, who has also written the only book on Coulter for the Twayne World Authors series (1976). JAMES NOONAN

Coupland, Douglas (b. 1961). Born a Canadian citizen on a Canadian NATO base in Baden-Sollingen, Germany, he shortly afterward was brought by his family to West Vancouver, British Columbia, where he still lives. Both a sculptor and novelist, Coupland graduated in 1984 from the studio sculpture program at Vancouver's Emily Carr Institute for Art and Design, furthering his studies in Japan and Italy, before holding a solo sculptural installation at the Vancouver Art Gallery in 1987. However, it is on the basis of the near overnight success of his avant-garde first novel, *Generation X: tales for an accelerated culture* (1991), that Coupland has gained prominence. Three more novels—which continue his experiments in the literary avant-garde, expand the range and targets of his satire, and reaffirm his fundamentally ironic vision of contemporary culture—have consolidated his place in both learned and popular circles.

By its very title, *Generation X* became identified with the subculture of the late baby boomers, whose condition 'X' was the result of having been born too late to enjoy the post-war spoils of their forebears but too soon after their early boomer confrères to be recognized as chronic have-nots. The novel's narrator-protagonist and two companions make their protest by opting out of mainstream North American society and maintaining an existential vigil while trading stories from the sidelines of the desert retirement community of Palm Springs, California. From such a setting—at once awesome and cliché-ridden—Coupland launches a grand satire in which the foibles and banality of a middle-class, consumer-driven culture are pitted against this more minimalist, thoughtful, if agonizingly self-ironic young threesome. Among Coupland's chief satiric devices are inventive marginalized glossings of his mottos and neologisms (such as McJobs), and his elaborate metaphors and similes that yoke together, often in hyphenated form, strands of observed pedestrian life that instantly take on a comically pejorative incongruity.

Shampoo planet (1992) continues in the vein of satire with a street-smart twenty-year-old narrator-protagonist whose sense of irony is sharp enough to set him above the risible lifestyle of his Galiano Island hippie mother and the locals of his declining hometown of Lancaster, Washington, but is not quite sufficient to grant him a revelation of the transparency of his own wholesale belief in the future, good grooming, and corporate success. In short, he too emerges as an object of irony in his own account of what is objectionably ironic. *Life after God* (1994) moves out of comic satire and offers instead an elegaic confession from the viewpoint of a middle-aged Vancouverite travelling into the British Columbia interior. Images from the countryside's natural splendour provide points of departure for the narrator's nostalgic reminiscences of his childhood 'paradise lost' and of his generation's loss of God. Such a loss he attributes to his generation's ironic cast of mind, 'an irony that scorched everything it touched' and which arguably amounted to the 'price paid for the loss of God'.

Marking another radical shift in narrative strategies, *Microserfs* (1995) consists of an on-line diary of computer entries and incoming e-mail from the 'screen' of an erstwhile 'Microsoft' employee, Daniel Underhill. Thin on plot but thick with buzzwords, codewords, doodle pages, and idiosyncratic ramblings and rants, *Microserfs* critiques the malaise of high-tech corporate 'serfs' by juxtaposing the paralysing drudgery of Underhill's mechanistic work-world as a computer coder with the redemptive randomness of life itself. *Polaroids from the dead* (1996) collapses the border between fiction and history while sharpening the dialectic in our time between the iconographic and iconoclastic with a series of 'mini-stories' illustrated throughout with full-page photographs taken from the annals of 'the early 1990s'. These stories bring full circle Coupland's central theme of the acceleration of history in the information age by serving as both mementoes for, and post-mortems on, recent select newsmaking events that so quickly become dated snapshots.

Coupland is a frequent contributor to the *New York Times*, the *New Republic*, *Wired*, and *Art Forum*. BURKE CULLEN

Crath, Paul. See UKRAINIAN-CANADIAN LITERATURE.

Crawford, Isabella Valancy (1850-87). Born in Dublin of an educated and cultured family, she came to Canada in 1858, living first in Paisley, Canada West (Ontario), where her father, Dr Stephen Dennis Crawford, was the first doctor. She moved with her family to Lakefield, staying initially in the house of Robert Strickland, nephew of Mrs MOODIE and Mrs TRAILL; then to Peterborough, where Dr Crawford died in 1875 and Isabella's only surviving sister died in 1876; and finally to Toronto, remaining there with her mother in poverty until her death from heart failure. The Crawford family history is a record of hardships that included the childhood deaths of all of the twelve or thirteen Crawford children except Isabella Valancy, Emma Naomi, and Stephen Walter; the family's frequent moves and progressive impoverishment; and the disgrace of Dr Crawford's trial and conviction for misappropriation of public funds while he was township treasurer in Paisley. This event—accounts of which Eric Parker has uncovered in the *Paisley Advocate* (1865, 1866, and 1867)—provides a hitherto unsuspected explanation for the Crawford family's later reputation for being proud and keeping to themselves.

Although Isabella Valancy Crawford wrote a great many short stories and novelettes, largely for the American magazine market, her literary reputation is based on her poems, particularly her narrative poems. She published only one book in her lifetime, *Old Spookses' Pass, Malcolm's Katie, and other poems* (Toronto, 1884), 1,000 copies of which James Bain & Son produced at the author's expense. Despite generally favourable reviews in the English and Canadian publications to which she sent this 224-page volume, only fifty copies were sold. No definitive and complete edition of her poetry exists (many poems that appeared in newspapers have been uncollected). But it has been published in five volumes: *Old Spookses' Pass* (1884), reissued in 1886 and 1898, which Crawford herself declared was as 'decorated with press errors as a Zulu chief is laden with beads'; John Garvin's cavalierly edited *The collected poems of Isabella Valancy Crawford* (1905), with an introduction by Ethelwyn WETHERALD, reprinted in 1972 in a facsimile edition, along with a new introduction by James REANEY; Katherine Hale's selected anthology *Isabella Valancy Crawford* (1923), reproducing the editorial 'improvements' of John Garvin (Hale's husband) that he made for the 1905 edition; *Hugh and Ion* (1977), Glenn Clever's edition of the incomplete but nonetheless powerful narrative poem found by Dorothy LIVESAY buried among the four boxes of Crawford manuscripts and materials in the Lorne PIERCE Collection at Queen's University; and D.M.R. Bentley's scholarly edition, *Malcolm's Katie: a love story* (1987).

Crawford's prose, generally considered to be the bread-and-butter writing by which she earned her precarious living, is even less accessible. Much of it is in manuscript form in the Lorne Pierce Collection, and probably much more is still hidden in unindexed nineteenth-century magazines. Some, however, has been published in *Selected stories of Isabella Valancy Crawford* (1975) and *Fairy tales of Isabella Valancy Crawford* (1977), both edited by Penny Petrone, and *The Halton boys: a story for boys* (1979) edited by Frank M. Tierney. The fiction displays a skilful and energetic use of literary conventions made popular by Dickens, such as twins and doubles, mysterious childhood disappearances, stony-hearted fathers, sacrificial daughters, wills and lost inheritances, recognition scenes, and, to quote one of her titles, 'A kingly restitution'.

With her own life filled with tribulation, Crawford chose to make the dialogue of hope and despair, and the purgatorial role of suffering, the central themes of much of her work, including the narrative poems 'Malcolm's Katie' and *Hugh and Ion*. Written in blank verse, interspersed with lyrics of various metrical forms, they are early milestones in Canada's tradition of narrative poetry. In 'Malcolm's Katie' Crawford adapted to the setting of pioneer Canada the domestic idyll as she learned it from Tennyson. Striking and new, however, is Crawford's location of Max and Katie's conventional love story within a context of Native legends—Indian Summer and the battle of the North and South Winds. In *Hugh and Ion*, an incomplete poem written near the end of Crawford's life, two friends who have fled the noxious city—probably contemporary Toronto—for purification in the primal wilderness, carry on a sustained dialogue, Hugh arguing for hope, light, and redemption and Ion pointing out despair, darkness, and intractable human perversity. 'Old Spookses' Pass' is a dialect poem, set in the Rocky Mountains, concerning a dream vision of a midnight cattle stampede towards a black abyss that is stilled by a whirling lariat; 'The helot' makes use of the Spartans' practice of intoxicating their helots in order to teach their own children not to drink, as the starting-point for a highly incantory and hypnotic poem that ends in Bacchic possession and death; and 'Gisli the

Chieftain' fuses mythic elements, such as the Russian spring goddess Lada and the Icelandic Brynhild, into a narrative of love, betrayal, murder, and reconciliation. These poems follow a pattern of depicting the world as a battleground of opposites—light and dark, good and evil—reconciled by sacrificial love.

Recognition of Isabella Valancy Crawford's extraordinary mythopoeic power, and her structural use of images, came first in James Reaney's lecture 'Isabella Valancy Crawford' in *Our living tradition* (series 3, 1959). Although knowledge about Crawford's short and elusive life will always be fragmentary, since so many gaps remain in the evidence, two biographies summarize what is known about Crawford: Dorothy Familoe's *Isabella Valancy Crawford: the life and the legends* (1983) and Elizabeth McNeill Galvin's *Isabella Valancy Crawford: we scarcely knew her* (1994). See also *The Isabella Valancy Crawford symposium* (1979), a collection of papers delivered at the University of Ottawa in 1977, and Lynne Suo's 'Annotated bibliography on Isabella Valancy Crawford' in *Essays in Canadian Writing* 11 (Spring 1977). CATHERINE ROSS

Crawley, Alan. See *CONTEMPORARY VERSE*.

Creeps (1972). A long one-act play about the lives of men afflicted with cerebral palsy; its author, David FREEMAN, was born with the same handicap. Director Bill Glassco encouraged him to develop 'The world of can't', an article Freeman had written for *Maclean's* in 1964 about workshops for CP victims, and the resulting play was produced by Toronto's Factory Theatre Lab on 5 Feb. 1971. Directed by Glassco, it was immediately hailed by critics and audiences. T.E. Kalem, writing in *Time* of a 1973 USA production, called the play 'powerful, harrowing, grimly humorous and altogether absorbing.'

The play's locale is the men's washroom of a workshop where five residents, all suffering from cerebral palsy, argue about their lives and their mindless work routine (folding boxes, sanding blocks). The slight plot turns on the efforts of Tom, a would-be painter, to persuade Jim, a potential writer, to leave the shelter for the outside world (as Freeman had done). The power of the play lies in its searing probing of the stricken men as they escape from their supervisor to the washroom, and from an outside world that treats them as objects of pity or ridicule.

The language of the play is brutal and obscene. The contrast between the condition of these spastics and their constant talk of sex might be disturbing, but the play is surprisingly funny—Freeman has a good ear for humour. *Creeps* is not a balanced view of society's treatment of the handicapped, but Freeman's aim is to shock his audience into greater awareness of the common humanity that links the healthy and the disabled, and to suggest that freedom is essential to the health of body and mind.

Creeps won the 1971 Chalmers Play Award and the 1973 New York Drama Desk Award for Outstanding New Playwright. It is included in *The Penguin book of modern Canadian drama* (1984), edited by Richard Plant.

Selected criticism of *Creeps* is included in *Canadian drama and the critics* (rev. ed. 1995), edited by L.W. Conolly.

EUGENE BENSON

Creighton, D.G. (1902-79). Donald Grant Creighton was born in Toronto and educated at the University of Toronto. He never lived for long away from his birthplace and its vicinity, except for a brief period at Oxford University, from which he returned in 1927 to teach in the department of history at Toronto. He remained there, acting as chairman from 1954 to 1959; he was made University Professor of History in 1968, and when he died he was a Fellow of Massey College.

Though Creighton was a natural writer to a degree few historians attain, his literary inclinations never diminished his zest for teaching; and in other respects he was a dedicated participant in the academic community, active in the Royal Society of Canada, to which he was elected in 1946 and whose Tyrrell Medal he won in 1951, and in the Canadian Historical Association, of which he was president in 1956-7. He twice won a Governor General's Award, in 1952 and 1955, for the two volumes of his biography of Sir John A. Macdonald; he was one of the first winners of the Molson Prize (in 1964); and in 1967 he became a Companion of the Order of Canada. He was advisory editor for the eighteen volumes of histories in the Canadian Centenary Series.

Creighton was never merely an academic historian, for he placed a high value on literary style, writing in a craftsmanly prose and deliberately making his books accessible to a large public outside the universities. He wrote with great strength of opinion, so that his historical narratives are coloured by his conservative and nationalistic political attitudes. He always remained at heart an Upper Canadian, distrustful of the aspirations of Quebec and unwilling to give importance to the regional differences between central and western Canada. He disputed freely with the liberal historians who, in his younger days, represented the dominant trend in his own discipline in Canada. But his controversial stance had its positive aspects, for he thought daringly, designed his books on a dramatic scale, and created some enduring Canadian myths. Like the Greeks, who assigned history to its muse Clio, Creighton regarded his discipline as a creative art.

Perhaps the most important formative influence on Creighton was that of Harold INNIS, who wrote as an economist but contributed much to our understanding of Canadian history through books like *The fur trade in Canada* (1930) and *The cod fisheries* (1940), in which he showed that Canada had an economic history before it had a political one. Creighton adopted and considerably adapted Innis's ideas, expressing them, in their changed forms, in an attractively fluent prose that contrasted with the gnarled and obscure manner in which his mentor wrote. (Later Creighton paid his intellectual debt by writing a tribute, *Harold Adams Innis: portrait of a scholar*, 1957.) Creighton's first book, *The commercial empire of the St. Lawrence: 1760-1850* (1937)—reprinted in 1956 as *The empire of the St. Lawrence*—showed how the fur-trading system of the St Lawrence and the Great Lakes created an east-west pattern of transport, occupation, and development that became an enduring historical factor, countering the geographical lines of the continent that run from north to south. *British North America in Confederation* (1939), a more specialized and limited book, was concerned with the balance of financial and economic powers in 1867, the year of Confederation.

In his third book, *Dominion of the North: a history of Canada* (1944), Creighton developed on a much larger time-scale the insights projected in *The empire of the St. Lawrence*. Since he saw the process of early Canadian development as dependent on a single urge—that of fur-trading and consequent exploration—lasting almost a century to the eve of Confederation, he tended to have a highly unified view of the history of Canada. He was not a regionalist, impressed by the historical differences between the various parts of Canada; nor was he a continentalist, impressed by the geographical urge that pointed towards a coalescence between Canada and the United States. *Dominion of the North* showed that he was an early Canadian nationalist, and he remained one to the end of his life. It demonstrated Creighton's conviction that Canada had its own manifest destiny, defined by the old trade routes that went east to west from Montreal to the Pacific, the routes that railways and highways would later follow. *Dominion of the North* was at once brilliantly polemical and impeccably researched; the combination of information and imagination resulted in a grand mythic view of Canadian history that the rest of Creighton's works developed.

A myth requires a hero. The idea of Canada as a nation emerged in the movement towards Confederation that followed the decline of the fur traders, and Creighton saw the personification of that idea in Sir John A. Macdonald, the Dominion's founding prime minister, whose first adequate biography he wrote. The first volume, *John A. Macdonald: the young politician* (1952), takes Macdonald's career to the high point of Confederation; the second and final volume, *John A. Macdonald: the old chieftain* (1955), deals with the years of power and decline. Most political biographies submerge the man in the events, but in these two books Creighton sustained the biographical intent and produced a vital—if perhaps excessively heroic—portrait of Macdonald.

After the rather pedestrian *Story of Canada* (1959), Creighton's next book showed him still deeply involved in Macdonald's period. *The road to Confederation: the emergence of Canada, 1863-67* (1964) is an account of how British North Americans, from Nova Scotia to Upper Canada, recognized that unity was the best way to solve their common economic problems, and perhaps the only way to protect themselves from the political danger posed by an America resurgent at the end of the Civil War.

Nationalistic myths, like any other, are subject to erosion by events, and by 1970, when Creighton published *Canada's first century, 1867-1967*, he was considerably less confident about Canada's destiny than in his earlier books. He recognized that the north-south pull was stronger than he had thought, and that Canada's historic east-west ties were strained by the cultural and economic invasion from the United States. He also saw the trend to provincial autonomy and the rise of Quebec separatism as elements weakening the Canadian political structure. He was unable to admit that stronger regions might build a new kind of confederalism, and as a result he felt a weakening confidence regarding the future of his country.

This pessimistic mood was further developed in his last major work, *The forked road:*

Canada 1939-1957 (1976), in which Mackenzie King is cast—in contrast to John A. Macdonald—as the betrayer of Canada's future, the politician who sold the past to continentalism. The element of gloom does not lessen the power of these later and less hopeful books. Indeed, it provides the element of shadow that is perhaps necessary for a great myth.

Among Creighton's lesser works are *Towards the discovery of Canada* (1972), a collection of memoirs, essays, and speeches; *Canada: the heroic beginnings* (1974), a pictorial history that revives some of his earlier confidence in Canada's destiny; and *Takeover* (1978), his only adventure into imaginative writing—a highly ambiguous novel about Canadian-American relations that reinforces one's feeling that Creighton in the end saw his early vision of Canada ending, like so many myths of great adventure, in negation.

No account of Creighton is complete without reference to the obliquity of his influence. He has rarely been popular among other historians. But to imaginative writers—poets and novelists—he has offered a pattern within which they could shape their intuitions about Canadian life. On writers whose deep sense of history was modified by their awareness of place—like Hugh MacLENNAN, Margaret LAURENCE, Margaret ATWOOD, and Al PURDY—his glancing effect was evident.

See J.M.S. CARELESS, 'Donald Creighton and Canadian history: some reflections', in J.S. Moir, ed. *Character and circumstance: essays in honour of Donald Grant Creighton* (1970); Carl BERGER, *The writing of Canadian history: aspects of English-Canadian historical writings, 1900-1970* (1976); George WOODCOCK, 'Literary echoes', in *Books in Canada* (Mar. 1980).

See also HISTORICAL WRITING IN ENGLISH: 7. GEORGE WOODCOCK

Crémazie, Octave (1827-79). Claude-Joseph-Olivier Crémazie, called Octave by his mother, was born in Quebec City and studied at the Petit Séminaire from 1836 to 1843. In Jan. 1844 he opened a bookstore in Quebec that sold, along with books, a variety of imported goods and became within a decade an important business establishment. Crémazie was an active member of the Institut canadien de Québec, founded in 1847 to promote French cultural activities and to ensure the preservation of the French language. His first verse was published in 1849; by 1858 he was being called the national bard. When his bookstore became bankrupt in Nov. 1862, owing to some questionable financial transactions, he left for France, changed his name to 'Jules Fontaine', and for sixteen years lived mostly in Paris, subsisting on a small allowance sent by his brothers. He died in Le Havre.

Two patriotic poems brought fame to Crémazie: 'Le vieux soldat canadien' (1855), celebrating the arrival in 1855 of *La Capricieuse*, the first French naval ship to visit Quebec in almost a century, and 'Le Drapeau de Carillon' (1858), marking the centenary of Montcalm's victory at Fort Carillon (Fort Ticonderoga). Québécois were deeply moved by Crémazie's stanzas expressing their undying attachment to the land, the language, and the traditions of their ancestors. Both poems include a song in the manner of Béranger; set to music, their popularity lasted for many years.

Following a visit to Paris in 1856, Crémazie began to explore traditional themes in a series of lyric poems: death and faith in 'Les Morts'; tragedy striking at humble folk in 'La fiancée du marin'; the exotic lure of Spain, Italy, and the Orient in 'Les Mille-Îles'; and the courage of the Canadian logger in 'Le Chant des voyageurs'. Attracted later by the concept and realism of Gautier's 'La comédie de la mort', and seeking to give leadership to the emerging literary movement, Crémazie conceived a lengthy narrative poem in three parts, 'Promenade de trois morts', of which only Part I was completed.

Crémazie ceased to write verse when he went into exile at the age of thirty-five. From France he corresponded regularly with his family and occasionally with friends. Of special interest are his letters to Abbé Henri-Raymond CASGRAIN, in which the poet presents his views on many questions relating to literature. During the Franco-Prussian war, Crémazie wrote a diary that gives, besides an account of life in Paris during the siege, a further insight into the opinions and character of the writer.

Most of Crémazie's poems were first published in *Le Journal de Québec*; 'Promenade de trois morts' appeared in *Les SOIRÉES CANADIENNES* (1862). *La littérature canadienne de 1850 à 1860* (vol. II, 1864) reprinted 25 of Crémazie's poems. The *Oeuvres complètes* (Montréal, 1882) presented 24 poems, the 'Journal du siège de Paris', and 46 letters. The modern critical edition of Crémazie's complete works is in two volumes: *Oeuvres I—poésies* (1972) and *Oeuvres II—prose* (1976).

Some biographical and critical writings dealing with Crémazie are: H.-R. Casgrain's 'Notice biographique' in the 1882 *Oeuvres complètes*; O. Condemine's introductions to *Oeuvres I—poésies* and *Oeuvres II—prose*; S.

Marion, 'Octave Crémazie', in *Les lettres canadiennes d'autrefois*, V (1946); and several studies in *Crémazie et Nelligan, recueil d'études* (1981), edited by Réjean Robidoux and Paul Wyczynski. ODETTE CONDEMINE

Criticism in English. 1. THE NINETEENTH CENTURY. Written chiefly in the form of the instructive essay, early criticism tended to be corrective in function, addressing writers as much as readers about the need for a practical literature that would further the establishment of the Canadian community while maintaining the values, standards, and aesthetics of nineteenth-century Britain. Most critics were predisposed to admire or call for a literature of an idealized reality portraying Canadian experience and affirming Protestant morality. The inhibiting or distorting effect of American and British dominance of the culture, and of its publishing industry, were the subject of recurring commentary, beginning with Susanna MOODIE's introduction to *Mark Hurdlestone* (London, 1853). Sir Daniel Wilson, in his review article in *The Canadian Journal of Industry, Science and Art* (Jan. 1858), commented on the difficulties that arose for writers who saw the settler's Canada in terms of either European myths or indigenous Amerindian lore. Edward H. DEWART compiled *Selections from Canadian poets* (Montreal, 1864; rpr. 1973), the first anthology of Canadian poetry, in the belief that 'A national literature is an essential element in the formation of national character.' In his introductory essay he wrote unequivocally that 'the growth of an indigenous literature' had been stunted by 'our colonial position'. While admitting the 'crudity and imperfection' of Canadian poetry of the time, he nevertheless found much 'true poetry'—in the work of SANGSTER, McLACHLAN, and others. The twenty-five years that elapsed between this pioneer work and William Douw LIGHTHALL's *Songs of the great Dominion* (London, 1889; rpr. 1971) saw many changes: a political identity for Canada; a spirit not only of patriotism but of enthusiasm and hopefulness; and a great increase in the number of what Dewart would have called 'true poets'. In his introduction to the anthology, which was compiled mainly for a British readership, Lighthall pointed to the contrast between the 'apologetic and depressed' verse of Dewart's anthology and the new poetry in his collection, which was not only 'more confident, but far better'. His book's organization ('The new nationality', 'The Indian', 'Settlement life', 'The spirit of Canadian history', 'Places', 'Seasons', etc.) is an early attempt to offer unifying myths and themes that grew out of a vision of a unified culture in which the individual was entirely subordinate. This viewpoint shaped and coloured the critical approach to Canadian literature for many decades.

Archibald LAMPMAN's 'Two Canadian poets: a lecture' (on ROBERTS and CAMERON), delivered in 1891 (*University of Toronto Quarterly* 13, no. 4, July 1944), expressed the view that the character of Canada was to be found in a literature based on local experience. Although the idea of the 'local' was by Lampman's time associated more with a regional than a national milieu (as opposed to the earlier colonial/imperial distinction), Lampman saw another important geographical opposition: the rural versus the urban. Since English-Canadian poetry treated the former exclusively (the latter, according to Lampman, was the realm of fiction), he saw poetry as offering the most promise for a strongly Canadian literature. In the late nineteenth century, however, the older vision of Canadian writing—as a shadowy imitation of British, or occasionally of American literature—largely continued, particularly among writers and critics whose viewpoint was imperial or continental. John G. Bourinot, in *Our intellectual strength and weakness* (Montreal, 1893; rpr. 1973), expanded on earlier ideas about Canadian literature mentioned in his *Intellectual development of the Canadian people* (Toronto, 1881), seeing English-Canadian writing as inferior to both French-Canadian and American—principally because it lacked a strong national identity, which he thought should be developed by creating an imperialistic and bicultural literature.

Most Canadian criticism written between 1820 and 1920 did not appear in book form, or appeared only as hard-to-find contributions to books, and is not readily available today. A selection of early critical pieces can be found in *The search for English-Canadian literature* (1975) edited by Carl Ballstadt. See also the journalism of Wilfred CAMPBELL, Lampman, and Duncan Campbell SCOTT that appeared in '*AT THE MERMAID INN*' (the Toronto *Globe*, 1892-3), reprinted in *At the Mermaid Inn* (1979) edited by Barrie Davies; and the essays of Charles G.D. ROBERTS collected in *Selected poetry and critical prose* (1974) edited by W.J. Keith.

2. THE EARLY TWENTIETH CENTURY. The first extended critical study in Canadian letters is James CAPPON's *Roberts and the influences of his time* (1905; later expanded as a book in the Makers of Canadian Literature series,

Charles G.D. Roberts, 1925). Cappon faulted Roberts for creating a pale aesthetic pastoralism instead of focusing on everyday rural life, realistically centred on man and his community, that would by its familiarity produce a national poetry. Cappon was the first critic to identify a characteristically Canadian poetic form—a nature poetry of detailed description that he contrasted with the then-popular neoclassical idyll. He also gave voice to the growing populist movement by calling for a more democratic, less aristocratic, literature; yet he wanted one that, unlike the 'erotic' aestheticism in contemporary American and British poetry, retained an ethical centre. Although his *Bliss Carman* (1930) is less impressive, Cappon's use of texts was exceptional for his period in Canadian studies: he looked at lines not just for their metrics but for their thematic and tonal aspects. Even though Cappon seemed to have rejected modernist literature, his analyses anticipated those of the 'New Critics' who emerged following the Imagist movement.

During the next fifteen years criticism appeared in the form of surveys, as well as in prefatory statements in several anthologies: Archibald MacMurchy's *Handbook of Canadian literature* (1906); Lawrence Burpee's *A little book of Canadian essays* (1909), which consisted of individual appreciations of several authors; T.G. MARQUIS's *English-Canadian literature* (1914)—originally published as vol. 12 of *Canada and its provinces* (1914; rpr. 1973); John Garvin's *Canadian poets and poetry* (1916; rpr. 1926), an anthology in which selections from appreciative reviews preceded each writer's work. And Pelham Edgar wrote a chapter on 'English-Canadian literature' in *The Cambridge history of English literature* (1916). Most of these discussions were little more than lists, with biographies and plot summaries attached, affirming the existence of Canadian literature. (An important exception was Arthur STRINGER's preface to his own book of poetry, *Open water*, 1914, which contained a very early—and striking—statement on modernism.) Only Edgar's introductory essay, written for a British audience, was evaluative, albeit apologetic; in it he noted again the problems of a colonial literature—the product of 'a young country born into the old age of the world'—and the need to view such literature tolerantly because of its youth. He also saw Canada's literature as principally British in origin and sensibilities.

In contrast, Ray Palmer Baker's *A history of English Canadian literature to the Confederation: its relation to the literature of Great Britain and the United States* (1920), written for an American readership, considered the literature to be more American in its antecedents than British, and assumed that it was old enough to merit serious book-length examination. However. like Edgar, Baker concluded that Canadian literature was an extension of the literature of another country and that its real identity was yet to emerge. Duncan Campbell Scott, in his essay 'Poetry and progress' (1922; rpr. in S.L. Dragland, ed., *Duncan Campbell Scott: a book of criticism*, 1974), also emphasized this sense of evolutionary process, seeing Canadian literature as maintaining a fixed ethical viewpoint, while changing in technique and topic. Also in 1922, Albert Watson and Lorne PIERCE brought out the anthology *Our Canadian literature*, in which they perceived a search for identity to be the overriding preoccupation in Canadian writing. They saw Canadian literature, at its best, as having universal appeal, a moral tone, and such national characteristics as a sense of historical and political continuity, a communitarian spirit, and an awareness of the 'vastness of our spaces'.

Odell Shepard's *Bliss Carman* (1923) exemplified the hostility towards modernism that was prevalent in Canadian criticism at the time. (Compare Roberts' 'A note on modernism', *Open house*, 1931.) Neither a cultural biography nor a detailed analysis of Carman's life or work, it was nevertheless a good example of impressionistic criticism. In contrast were V.L.O. Chittick's and John Logan's studies of Thomas Chandler HALIBURTON, both of which appeared in 1924; no less Victorian in approach, these works grew out of the tradition of historical criticism. Chittick's biography—written for an American audience and the more scholarly of the two—discussed the contradictory sides of Haliburton's philosophy, aiming to give insights into the man. Logan, more interested in the literature, sought to establish both Haliburton's cultural heritage and the contemporary contexts. This book was an early example of thesis criticism—in this case, that Haliburton presented throughout his fiction a systematic argument for economic and cultural unity among all peoples of British origin. Logan also wrote, with Daniel French, *Highways of Canadian literature* (1924), in which origins, backgrounds, and influences formed the substance not only of analyses of individual writers, but also of the discussions of literary movements and genres in Canadian writing. Taking a progressive and idealistic view, Logan and French concluded that Canadian literature was still in its adolescence. *Highways* also attempted to assess Canadian critics up to 1924—particularly Archibald MacMECHAN, whose *Headwaters of Canadian literature* came out in the same year (NEW CANADIAN LIBRARY, 1974). Logan and French disliked MacMechan's approach (although, in its historical orientation, it was not unlike their own): MacMechan judged Canadian writing by external standards and found it prosaic and imitative, lacking inventiveness and realism, outmoded in content, and too popular in its aims. MacMechan was also an extreme nationalist in his designation of 'Canadian' authors: MOODIE and CRAWFORD were among the writers excluded from his consideration.

Lionel Stevenson's *Appraisals of Canadian literature* (1926) was an important watershed in Canadian criticism. Stevenson, who later became known for his cultural criticism documenting the impact of Darwinism and other new modes of thought on late-Victorian English writers, attempted not only to confirm the existence of Canadian literature (as had many critics before him), but also to define it in a more systematic way. In this seminal work he discussed the mythopoeic quality of Canadian writing ('In Canada the modern mind is placed in circumstances approximating those of the primitive mythmakers'), and suggested that Canadians' 'sympathy with nature is practically an inbred trait', leading them to respond 'to those features of religion, myth, or philosophy that retain some meaning as interpretations of Ancient Earth and man's relationship to her.' Like Northrop FRYE after him, Stevenson thought that Canadians, remaining attached to the European sources of their civilization, attempted to shut out the New World wilderness. He was the first critic to detect a central cultural pattern in Canadian literature.

In *The poetry of Archibald Lampman* (1927) Norman Guthrie saw Canadian poetry, exemplified by the work of Lampman, as meditative, not lyric—a poetry in which the poet merges with the landscape, and human values and relationships become abstract. Published in the same year, O.J. Stevenson's *A people's best* (1927) is of interest today as an example of a blending of criticism with the popular Canadian form of the sketch, while Lorne Pierce's *An outline of Canadian literature* (1927) continued his critical assessment of Canadian literature that extended over a number of books and into his editorial influence at the RYERSON PRESS. Similar in viewpoint to his *Our Canadian literature*, the new book was more overtly nationalistic, calling for protection against assimilation. It also depicted Canada as searching not just for identity but for a yet-to-be realized destiny. Canada's literature, Pierce thought, was generally dependent on surface realism and moral epigram.

A.J.M. SMITH, in 'Wanted—Canadian criticism' (*CANADIAN FORUM*, April 1928), called for a modern criticism to guide Canadian writers into twentieth-century art. He saw Canadian critics as using moral, not aesthetic, criteria and supporting writers who used clichéd themes and trite Canadian images to produce a false, romantic ideal of Canada. Smith believed that Canada's adolescence was over, and that its 'adult' writing should therefore be realistic and not exclude irony, cynicism, and a liberal viewpoint. This article was the formal declaration of a split between those critics who supported modernist sensibilities and those who adhered to nationalistic goals.

3. TOWARDS MODERNISM. By the end of the twenties the notion of 'realism' had changed from an earlier 'idealized realism' to a new social realism, a depiction of everyday life that pointed to the problems of society, if not to solutions. Frederick Philip GROVE, in *It needs to be said* (1929), a collection of essays on literature, provided a good statement of Canadian social realism in calling for a literature that, while adopting universal concerns, focused on regional actualities. In the decade to follow, historians, writers, and literary critics alike tended to seek a new vision of Canada by looking at small details (the mundane specifics of fur trading, the everyday life of farm and factory, the particulars of individual texts) in order to discover the larger patterns of Canadian culture that had been ignored by their predecessors. These writers were responding to a need in the Depression for a revision of previous concepts of Canadian identity. V.B. Rhodenizer's survey *A handbook of Canadian literature* (1930) called for more realism and supported regionalism tempered with a national consciousness. E.K. BROWN, in his first extended article on Canadian writing, 'The immediate present in Canadian literature' (*Sewanee Review* 41, 1933), is in accord with A.J.M. Smith about the lack of a vital Canadian criticism. Brown specifically attacked the jingoism that had become popular following the Great War; he also enunciated the Canadian writer's economic difficulties and lack of a perceptive Canadian audience, and saw the necessary role of the writer in such a culture as being that of rebel.

W.E. Collin, in *The* WHITE SAVANNAHS (1936; rpr. 1975), the first book of modernist criticism in Canada, discussed the work of Lampman, PICKTHALL, PRATT, LIVESAY, F.R. SCOTT, KLEIN, Smith, and KENNEDY. Explicating texts rather than discussing influences and contexts, Collin found a central image in the work of each writer, and argued that Canadian literature as a whole was evolving into a literature of redemption. His central Canadian images—landscape, dream, the garden in the wilderness and the accompanying Eden myth, epic heroism of real men, stoic puritanism, exile, martyrdom, faith, and redemption—were ones that writers and critics have continued to use and discuss. Doctrinaire in many ways, and stronger on contemporary writers than on earlier ones, *The white savannahs* extended an important concept in Canadian criticism: the notion of mythic renewal.

E.K. Brown's *On Canadian poetry* (1943; rev. 1944; rpr. 1973) was the second modern book-length study of Canadian literature. Although a historical survey, it utilized close textual readings to present assessments of individual poets (Lampman, D.C. Scott, and Pratt) and of Canadian poetry in general, and also provided a social and cultural commentary on Canada. For Brown, the isolation of the individual was a condition of the nineteenth-century poet cut off from his cultural roots and the literary mainstream, as well of the young post-war (i.e. Great War) poets at odds with their own society and outsiders to any other. Brown related the old complaints of a lack of audience, publishers, and critics in Canada to the psychological restrictions on the Canadian writer—the result of a colonial spirit, the lack of a national crisis, practical frontier attitudes, puritanism (by which Brown meant a Calvinistic materialism), and regionalism. These points were reiterated in his other essays on Canadian literature (collected in *Responses and evaluations*, 1977, edited by David Staines). Brown's type of cultural criticism, in which society and writing were viewed as inseparable, remained the single most-used approach to literary analysis in Canada.

A.J.M. Smith's essays of the 1940s, included in *Toward a view of Canadian letters: selected critical essays 1928-1971* (1973) and in *On poetry and poets* (NCL, 1977), were written from the activist perspective that Brown had prescribed. In 'Canadian anthologies, new and old' (1942), Smith condemned critical and literary writing that was unthinkingly nationalistic, romantic, or complacent, and supported work that was intense, intellectual, and universal in theme and concern. Smith's introduction to the First Edition of his influential *The book of Canadian poetry* (1943) was not only the most extensive statement of his view of Canadian literature, but the source of a lengthy critical debate between John SUTHERLAND and himself, in which Northrop Frye and Milton Wilson, among others, played intermittent roles, and that marked the two major directions modernist writing took in Canada following the Great War. In that essay Smith divided Canadian poetry into two groups that cut across period, movement, and location. The first, a 'cosmopolitan' poetry, focuses on universal elements of life and on world-wide advances, utilizes man-centred perspectives, and deals with 'the civilizing culture of ideas'; its opposite, 'native' poetry, which is emotional and unintellectual, is concerned with individual awareness, with unique and specific events or locales, and with providing a realistic description of environment. Smith saw the cosmopolitan stream as superior to that of native poetry, which he viewed as subject to nationalistic rhetoric or romantic sentimentalism. Underlying this evaluative aspect of Smith's categories was another critical assumption: he believed that the search for identity that preoccupied Canadian critics and writers was not only fruitless but trivial. Nationalism, and a national sense of self, were unimportant in the modern, global environment—in which Smith saw Canadian writers helping to define not so much Canada, but Canada's place in a new international age. Northrop Frye, in a contemporary review of Smith's anthology ('Canada and its poetry', reprinted in *The bush garden*, 1971), avoided dealing directly with Smith's categories (though he later suggested that every Canadian writer struggled with both the cosmopolitan and native urges). He stated that there were definable characteristics of Canadian poetry, and that a *national* writing was preferable to the 'creative schizophrenia' of a colonial one, which included both a large imperial vision and a cramped provincial or regional perspective. In this review Frye noted for the first time that what he found central in Canadian poetry was 'the evocation of stark terror' in the face of the 'frightening loneliness of the huge land', sometimes combined with a tenacious 'refusal to be bullied by space and time, [and] an affirmation of the supremacy of intelligence and humanity over stupid power.' (In the frequent references made to this observation by later critics, the notion of terror tended to be cited without

Frye's qualifications about the conquering abilities of the mind and heart.) Like E.K. Brown, Frye found in Canadian literature the image of an isolated man; but for Frye, the picture of man in epic struggle against a native reality rivaled any mere cosmopolitan vision.

Another important response to Smith's divisions was John Sutherland's defence of the second stream of modernism that developed in Canada: a militant realism. In his introduction to *Other Canadians* (1947)—an anthology edited by Sutherland to focus attention on those writers he felt Smith had overlooked—he identified socially aware poets with Smith's 'native' tradition, and—like Brown and several other observers of early modern culture—linked 'native' with nationalistic; for Sutherland 'cosmopolitan' concealed a colonial attitude that was inappropriate to the indigenous Canadian experience. The conflict that developed between Smith and Sutherland over this issue is of some importance in the development of Canadian literature and its criticism: Smith enunciated the neoclassical aspect of modernism, with its accompanying standards and judicial criticism, while Sutherland favoured an egalitarian modernism, colloquial in style and diction and concerned more with social revolution than with literary innovation. However, the two viewpoints were not entirely dissimilar. While the 'realists' engaged in substantial social activism and (in the statements of Dorothy Livesay, Sutherland, and Louis DUDEK) developed the beginnings of a Marxist criticism, they never supported for long the extremes of social and literary change advocated by such groups in other English-speaking cultures; with the possible exception of Livesay, their proletarianism often resembled middle-class liberalism or humanitarianism. Smith, while resisting the perennial call to describe a coherent national literature, strove like his predecessors to give the populace a literature and criticism that Canadian readers could identify as their own. See also Smith's introduction to *The Oxford book of Canadian verse* (1960) and his anthologies of Canadian criticism: *Masks of fiction* (NCL, 1961) and *Masks of poetry* (NCL, 1962); as well as *John Sutherland: essays, controversies, and poems* (1973) edited by Miriam WADDINGTON; and *The making of modern poetry in Canada* (1967), edited by Louis Dudek and Michael Gnarowski, a useful anthology that features critical articles from the 1940s.

4. POST-WAR CRITICISM. Another important critic to establish himself in the forties was Desmond PACEY. In *Frederick Philip Grove* (1945) he made biographical consideration secondary to critical evaluation; he judged GROVE by standards similar to the Aristotelian ones Grove himself articulated, though Pacey also delineated Grove's cultural, historical, and literary contexts. In discussing Grove as a failed but worthy novelist—the best that Canada had yet offered—and as a better essayist than fiction writer, Pacey established his own standards for Canadian fiction. He thought writing should be both regional and universal, but should originate in real experience. Pratt and Grove came nearest to fulfilling his ideal, for they depicted real Canadian ways of life, dealt with significant social issues, portrayed man's true humanity in crises, and saw the special relationship Canadians had with nature. Pacey's survey *Creative writing in Canada* (1952; rev. 1961) became a standard text on Canadian literature. *Ten Canadian poets* (1958), also an influential book, was a particularly good example of Pacey's critical technique. Although he agreed with New Critics about the value of close textual reading, his own analyses often tended to develop from his overview rather than from the dynamics of the texts themselves. His articles were collected in *Essays in Canadian criticism: 1938-1968* (1969).

Edwin J. Pratt: the man and his poetry (1947) expressed the general feeling among literary critics of the forties that Pratt was the father of modernism in Canada and the country's most exemplary poet; but it was unusual for combining a historical-biographical essay on Pratt by Carl KLINCK with a comparative study by Henry Wells of nine poems as paralleled to nine works from world literature. Condemning the sentimental romanticism of early twentieth-century Canadian poetry, Klinck saw Pratt as shifting the focus in Canadian poetry from nature to humanity, and thereby discovering a new content, new myths, and new structures for Canadian writing. Wells employed comparative criticism to distinguish those features of Pratt's writing that were unique to him or to Canada from those that were universal. Both Klinck and Wells attempted objective criticism; but W.P. Percival's subjective biographical survey of the following year, *Leading Canadian poets* (1948), once again took up the task of discovering the qualities of 'good poetry' in Canadian writing.

Though the ideal of scientific, unbiased literary analysis had influenced American and British criticism since the nineteenth century, it played a relatively small role in Canadian criticism prior to the fifties. Before then, most criticism developed out of a kind of romantic idealism and had a messianic or missionary nature, designed to convert the ignorant and restore misguided believers to the right path. By the end of the Second World Ward few critics valued criticism written before 1936; many rejected the perspectives, values, and techniques of even the best writing prior to the late twenties. This sense of being distinct from, and discontinuous with, writing and criticism of the nineteenth and early twentieth centuries led critics to reassess the past; they tended either to reshape it in order to find the hidden origins of the modern movements that had previously been misperceived as typical of Canadian romanticism, or to approach early texts as sources from which to develop social or historical theses on given periods. Edward MCCOURT's *The Canadian West in fiction* (1949, rev. 1970) was the first book to construct a regional literary history in order to discover the origins of modern western literature. Although he used literary standards of judgement, McCourt did not limit himself to works of literature, but developed an overview of western writing that traced its characteristic factual, unornamental, succinct style to accounts by fur traders, explorers, missionaries, and Mounties, and its romance formulas to preconceived notions from the east, found in the dime novel. McCourt approached writers as diverse as Ralph Connor (Charles William GORDON), Nellie MCCLUNG, Sinclair ROSS, and Margaret LAURENCE from a socio-historical viewpoint, seeing in their work the evolution of a western culture and values based on mobility that retarded tradition.

The most important criticism of the fifties was done by critics who had established themselves in the previous decade: Desmond Pacey, who published both books and essays; and A.J.M. Smith and Northrop Frye, who published articles and reviews. (Frye's contribution was particularly felt after 1950, when he took over from E.K. Brown the summary reviews of the year's poetry for *The University of Toronto Quarterly*'s annual 'Letters in Canada'.) Of the critical books published in this decade a number were collections, frequently of essays that had originally been created for oral presentation—lectures, broadcast scripts, or papers from conferences. Books such as *Canadian writers* (1951) by Arthur Phelps—a series of lectures on individual English- and French-Canadian authors—reflected the often casual and simplified nature of their original oral presentation. *Writing in Canada* (1956), edited by George Whalley, consisted of speeches and discussions from the Canadian Writers' Conference at Queen's University in July 1955, the first meeting of its kind in Canada, which brought together creative writers, critics, and publishers. It was essentially a declaration that Canadian writers need no longer be isolated from one another. *Our living tradition* (1957), edited by Claude Bissell, was the first of a series of five volumes (published until 1965; subsequent volumes were edited by Robert L. McDougall) made up of lectures given at the Institute of Canadian Studies, Carleton University. Reflecting the Institute's program of interdisciplinary cultural history, the lectures generally were conservative in technique and in their goal of establishing the real continuities we share with our cultural past. Of particular interest in the series are Smith's essay on D.C. Scott, Earle BIRNEY's on E.J. Pratt and his critics, both in Volume II, and James REANEY's on Isabella Valancy Crawford in Volume III. *The culture of contemporary Canada* (1957), edited by Julian Park, was a collection of essays directed at Americans. In it Millar MacLure's 'Literary scholarship' argued that Canadian literary history tended to be chauvinistic and that Canadian criticism was influenced by the British tradition of impressionistic interpretations and comprehensive commentaries rather than by the bibliographic and annotative criticism that had prevailed in Europe and America. *Our sense of identity* (1954), edited by Malcolm Ross, was a collection of literary and other essays, and prose selections, that Ross hoped could clarify some of the confusion about the Canadian identity. In his Introduction he saw Canada as a nation characterized not by compromise but by irony, and Canadians as a 'bifocal people' who perceived themselves as being 'at once inside and outside' with 'no simple reconciliation'—a situation that produced a strong need to orient oneself in space and time. By bringing together the shared perspectives of literary and social critics, historians, and creative writers, Ross suggested that the goals of cultural definition would be best served by an interdisciplinary approach, which in fact has continued to influence criticism in Canada. Wilfrid Eggleston's *The frontier and Canadian letters* (1957), a history of Canadian writing from its pre-Confederation beginnings (not, as is often mistakenly assumed, a study of western-Canadian literature), was the most extensive application to Canadian writing of the widely disseminated 'frontier thesis' formulated by American historian Frederick Jackson Turner, who saw in America's development a progressive and evolutionary movement from frontier culture to an established native one. R.E. Rashley's

Poetry in Canada: the first three steps (1958), while dependent on some of the assumptions about assimilation popularized by this thesis, pointed to a literary evaluation in Canada marked by a break with aristocratic British values. This book has been seen as the first piece of Canadian Marxist criticism.

In *The arts in Canada* (1958), another anthology of essays edited by Malcolm Ross, Claude Bissell, writing on the novel, pointed out that contemporary Canadian fiction began with the 'contemplative realism' of Grove and CALLAGHAN, which examined people in their social environment and illuminated rather than resolved their problems. He said that this type of fiction dominated the Canadian novel until the 1950s, when formal experiments finally started with Ethel WILSON's fiction, and when a comic vision began to appear in the novels of Earle Birney and Robertson DAVIES. In a discussion of poetry, Northrop Frye returned to Smith's dichotomy, arguing that the cosmopolitan and native urges did not constitute a true division between writers but were 'centifrugal' and 'centripetal' impulses to be found within each poet. He distinguished between contemporary Canadian poets who sought to unify humanity and nature by finding a central myth (the academic mythopoeic poets) and writers for whom the depiction of reality was more important (F. R. Scott, SOUSTER, Dudek, and LAYTON).

The recurrent concern over whether or not there was an evolving Canadian literature that showed marked improvement over its precursers—given new prominence after the Smith-Sutherland debate—continued to play an important role in fifties' criticism. Milton Wilson in '*Other Canadians* and After' (*TAMARACK REVIEW*, 9, Autumn 1958), instead of finding a progressive development of a native Canadian literature, saw a tradition of a colonial or 'permanent tourist' (a phrase borrowed from a P.K. PAGE poem) mentality. Thus neither Smith's nor Sutherland's use of the terms 'cosmopolitan', 'native', and 'colonial' had much value for Wilson. Since Canadian poets had always borrowed forms from other cultures, he thought that, instead of bemoaning the British colonialism of the *PREVIEW* group or the American colonization of the *FIRST STATEMENT* writers, critics needed to respect a traditional native literature that drew its substance from its own culture and only its structures from abroad. Wilson located Canada's uniqueness in its ahistorical condition, in which its sense of time was foreshortened and its sense of space made discontinuous (resulting in a transcontinental 'hopping regionalism')—a state of flux that brought to Canadian writing a tradition of 'the inclusive, the self-sustaining, even the encyclopedic'.

Louis Dudek, whose work as an editor has had a wide influence, published a number of his short critical pieces in the fifties. The most important of these on Canadian literature may be found in his *Selected essays and criticism* (1978). (A second collection of his essays is in a special issue of *OPEN LETTER*, 4th series, nos. 8-9, 1981.) Although often a polemicist and social commentator as much as a literary critic, Dudek saw the chief critical act as that of relating the text to reality, to the experience of the external world, not to theory or ideology. He identified two large schools of Canadian criticism: the historical or social realists, and the mytho-symbological critics, who do not realize that symbols should correspond directly to experience.

James Reaney's article 'The Canadian poet's predicament' (*University of Toronto Quarterly* 26, April 1957) expressed a growing sense among Canadian writers and critics of the fifties that they must remain in Canada, no longer choosing expatriation or extended periods of education abroad but absorbing and transforming the wealth of culture both outside and inside Canada. In 'The Canadian imagination', a succinct statement in a special Canadian issue of *Poetry*, Chicago (94, June 1959), Reaney saw the early poets as using the 'wilderness and frontier not as fact but as symbols of something undeveloped in the human imagination—as a rich but brooding hostile monster.' In the work of Pratt and the writers who followed him the environment remained seductively evil, but now it could be humanized through myth-making. The two most influential figures for contemporary Canadian writers, according to Reaney, were Pratt, because he introduced the image of humanity capable of struggling against the landscape and what it symbolized, and Frye, because his first two books gave Canadian poets a handbook of 'maps' and designs for poems, as well as an example of precision and organization.

John Sutherland became one of the first critics to identify a major shift affecting Canadian literature and criticism in 'The past decade in Canadian poetry' (*NORTHERN REVIEW*, Dec.-Jan. 1950-1), where he argued that the activist poetry of the forties, based on the notion of class oppression, was being replaced by a religious sort of poetry grounded in the universal guilt of each individual. In a 1954 essay, 'Refining fire: the meaning and use of poetry', A.J.M. Smith similarly assigned a spiritualizing function to literature. Rejecting the ephemeral goal of objective realism as a literary method and that of social amelioration as an end, he opted for a poet who would be an 'uncoverer of the hidden secrets', revealing the decay caused by mechanization and secularization and—through the recovery of myth and spiritual responsibility—restoring the individual 'to grace or society to civilization'. (Smith elsewhere suggested—in 1955, and again in 1960—that Canadians were particularly well suited to producing this kind of literature because they possessed an 'eclectic detachment' that enabled them to utilize a variety of forms and ideas from other cultures. This concept, picked up by Milton Wilson and others, may also be seen as underlying Frye's theories of education and Marshall McLUHAN's notion of the global village.) There was, then, the growing sense of a sacred dimension to literature in which the writer, sometimes in the role of seer, sometimes of sacrificial victim, produced gnostic writing that required critics to play the part of priests who would initiate the reader into the literary mysteries. The emergence of Northrop Frye as a critic of world reputation—following the publication in 1957 of his theoretical magnum opus, *Anatomy of criticism*, with its account of literature as descending from sacred texts such as myth and the Bible—may be seen as part of this new vision.

Among Frye's ideas on the nature of Canadian literature and society was his suggestion that Canada has a dualist culture, in which the pull towards the primitive and the mysterious wa always countered by a pull towards civilization and objective knowledge. He also suggested that in an environment like that of Canada—a railway-created 'nation of stops', with an east-west orientation and a people divided by language and virtually surrounded by wilderness—narrative, not lyric, was the more natural poetic form. (See in particular 'The narrative tradition in English-Canadian poetry', 1946, and 'Preface to an uncollected anthology', 1956, in *The bush garden*.) Frye's most extended piece of Canadian criticism, the Conclusion to the *Literary history of Canada* (1965), contained some of his best-known statements, including his view of Canadian culture as having been shaped by a garrison mentality that arose from the settlers' tendency to shut out the wilderness while attempting to maintain the ways of the Old World, and his idea of Canada's having an 'imaginative continuum' that Canadian writers could draw on as they faced new threats to their identity.

Frye's idea that literature develops from cultural milieu, and national identity from literature, was formulated during a period of great cultural stress and change for Canada. Most of the criticism of the fifties was in effect a catalogue of national literary traits and often took the form of manifesto. The 1951 *Report* of the Massey Commission—in itself a piece of literary and cultural criticism—had profound effects, both direct and indirect, on literary studies. It concluded that national identity and unique ways of life were strongly affected by the cultural environment and that, following the Second World War, Canada was more endangered by American mass culture than by any political or economic takeover. Harold INNIS's investigations into the nature of communications and mass media, and Marshall McLuhan's declaration of the end of distinct nations and the emergence of a global village, provided, like Frye's theories, large patterns of social structure and spoke to the fears and sense of loss felt by many Canadians. Historians and other social commentators lamented the encroachment of populist taste, specialized technological education, and mass cultural forms on Canada's more classical, more general forms of learning and on its conservatism in the arts and in society. Literary critics and writers, however, found themselves in a more complicated position: because Canadian literature had, since the 1920s, been in rebellion against its old order, defining genuine Canadian literary values did not involve affirming a traditional standard but choosing one of several recently emergent modern standards. In a 1961 article, 'Canadian literature in the fifties', Desmond Pacey outlined three modern traditions he saw developing: that of the mythopoeic writers, whose work he often disliked because he saw it as literature on literature; that of the urban realists, whose vision he tended to affirm; and that of the rural or regional poets, whose work he also valued.

5. 1960s TO THE EARLY 1980s. (a). The volume of Canadian literary criticism increased substantially in this period, partly because Canadian literature became a recognized field of academic study in the late sixties. Several reprint series (especially McCLELLAND & STEWART's New Canadian Library, under the general editorship of Malcolm Ross) made accessible previously unavailable works, many of them bearing introductions that were important contributions to criticism. With the founding by George WOODCOCK in 1959 of

CANADIAN LITERATURE at the University of British Columbia, the outlet for critical essays on Canadian writing increased dramatically. This was followed in the seventies by other critical journals, including *The Journal of Canadian Fiction* (1972-), *Essays on Canadian Writing* (1974-), *Studies in Canadian Literature* (1976-), *Canadian Poetry: Studies Documents and Reviews* (1977-), and *The Journal of Canadian Poetry* (1978-). (See LITERARY MAGAZINES IN ENGLISH: 3, 4.) A number of magazines produced special issues on the work of some of the leading writers (e.g., *Journal of Canadian Studies* on Hugh MacLENNAN; *Canadian Drama* on Robertson Davies; *Essays on Canadian Writing* on HOOD, BIRNEY, and Reaney; *DESCANT* on LEE; *Journal of Canadian Fiction* on Laurence; *Open letter* on KROETSCH), and several of these were republished as books. Three series of small-format critical studies—chiefly aimed at student readers seeking introductions to individual writers—were founded in 1969; Canadian Writers, under the general editorship of Dave GODFREY; Canadian Writers and Their Work, under the general editorship of William FRENCH; and Studies in Canadian Literature, under the editorship of Gary GEDDES and Hugh McPherson. Books in the Canadian Writers series were very short (around 15,000 words each) and, for that reason, often superficial; but as part of the New Canadian Library they were widely distributed and some of them (such as ONDAATJE on Leonard COHEN, Davies on LEACOCK, and Milton Wilson on Pratt) provided commentaries of lasting interest. Canadian Writers and Their Work produced only a few studies of English-Canadian writers, but their format was less rigid and their space less constricted; of particular interest was Eli MANDEL's introductory study of Layton. The Studies in Canadian Literature series, which aimed at more sophisticated readers and frequently broke new ground, first appeared as small paperbacks of 35,000 words and up, but later shifted to full-sized book format. Among its most notable studies were *Frederick Philip Grove* by Douglas Spettigue; *Hugh MacLennan* by George Woodcock; *Sinclair Ross & Ernest Buckler* by Robert Chambers; *E.J. Pratt: the evolutionary vision* by Sandra Djwa; and *Louis Dudek & Raymond Souster* by Frank DAVEY. Two other series were Profiles in Canadian Literature (eight vols, 1980-91), edited by Jeffrey Heath, and Canadian Writers and Their Works (twelve vols, 1982-96), edited by Jack David, Robert Lecker, and Ellen Quigley. The extensive American-based Twayne World Authors' series has included full-length studies of Canadian authors, usually by Canadian critics, since its inception in 1966. Two somewhat different series were Critical Views on Canadian Writers (begun in 1969 under the general editorship of Michael Gnarowski; no new volumes after 1976), collections of reviews and critical essays on individual writers; and the Reappraisals series, which published the proceedings of conferences on established Canadian writers held at the University of Ottawa, including important volumes on Crawford, D.C. Scott, Grove, Pratt, Lampman, and Klein.

5(b). Other occasional monographs (such as Glenn Clever's *On E.J. Pratt*, 1977, and Grazia Merler's *Mavis Gallant: narrative patterns and devices*, 1978), and several full-scale critical books dealing with single authors appeared in the late 1960s and 1970s. Margaret ATWOOD had the most—and often the most critically sophisticated—attention devoted to her; in addition to Sherrill Grace's study *Violent duality* (1980) and Frank Davey's *Margaret Atwood: feminist poetics* (1983), there were two collections of previously unpublished critical essays; *The art of Margaret Atwood: essays in criticism* (1981), edited by Arnold and Cathy Davidson, and *Margaret Atwood: language, text and system* (1983), edited by Sherill Grace and Lorraine Weir, as well as a special Atwood issue of *The MALAHAT REVIEW* (no. 41, 1977). Clara THOMAS—a prolific critic, producing handbooks such as *Canadian novelists, 1920-1945* (1946) and *Our nature—our voices* (1972)—expanded her Canadian Writers study of Margaret Laurence into *The Manawaka world of Margaret Laurence* (1975), while Patricia Morley, another critic who published widely, paired authors in two studies, *The immoral moralists: Hugh MacLennan and Leonard Cohen* (1972) and *The comedians: Hugh Hood and Rudy Wiebe* (1977). W.J. Keith wrote a full-length study of Rudy WIEBE's novels, *Epic fiction* (1981), and edited a collection of essays on the author, *A voice in the land* (1981). Karen Mulhallen, Donna Bennett, and Russell Brown edited *Tasks of passion* (1982), an innovative collection of work about and by Dennis Lee. More specialized approaches to authors included Gretl Fischer's *In search of Jerusalem: religion and ethics in the writings of A.M. Klein* (1975) and Patricia Monk's *The smaller infinity: the Jungian self in the novels of Robertson Davies* (1982). (Davies' work was also the subject of a collection of essays by various hands: *Studies in Robertson Davies' Deptford trilogy*, 1980, edited by Robert Lawrence and Samuel Macey.)

Among the literary biographies of this period were Norman Shrive's *Charles Mair: literary nationalist* (1965), a revisionist work written to balance the conflict between old, admiring literary values and critical-historical ones, and to portray the effects of post-Confederation nationalism on literary writing; two biographies of Stephen Leacock—by Ralph Curry (1959) and David Legate (1970); and Clara Thomas's *Love and work enough: the life of Anna Jameson* (1967). Of special note were three works: *F.P.G.: the European years* (1973), in which D.O. Spettigue, who had begun his research on Grove for his Studies in Canadian Literature monograph, revealed Grove's true identity and background; *Like one that dreamed: a portrait of A.M. Klein* (1982) by Usher Caplan, which shed new light on Klein's breakdown and lapse into silence; and Elspeth Cameron's *Hugh MacLennan: a writer's life* (1982), a thorough treatment of MacLennan's career. *The embroidered tent: five gentlewomen in early Canada* (1982) by Marian Fowler included short but valuable critical biographies of Catherine Parr TRAILL, Susanna Moodie, and Anna Jameson among others.

Two of the most important literary studies of this period were reference books: the *Literary history of Canada* (1965; expanded and revised 1976), edited by Carl F. KLINCK and others, and Norah Story's *The Oxford companion to Canadian history and literature* (1967). These two books gave Canadians new and easily available access to discussions of Canadian literature and to the events and individuals who had shaped it. The *Literary history* dealt not just with literature proper, but with Canadian writing in general, discussed by scholars in separate essays organized by period, place, and genre. While many of its chapters tended to be more annotated bibliography than essay, several were useful for the non-specialist, particularly those on specific genres—and Northrop Frye's Conclusion. Story's book is especially valuable for its dictionary-style format, giving easy access to information about both writers and their work and about Canadian history. (A *Supplement*, edited by William Toye, appeared in 1973.)

5(c). By the late 1950s international or comparative criticism became important in Canada. Canadian comparative critics saw in their literature qualities that were not only distinct from those of Britain and the United States but similar to those of other countries that opposed being absorbed into a 'superstate' yet were not actively able to fend off cultural assaults from the increasingly American-dominated media. R.E. Watters, for example, in an essay that influenced later critics, 'A quest for national identity' (*Proceedings of the IIIrd Congress of the International Comparative Literature Association*, 1962), outlined this vision of Canadian literature by describing differences in plot structures of British, American, and Canadian fiction. He saw British fiction as often dealing with an individual's rebellion against the class structure, which tended to be resolved by his or her assimilation, according to merit, into a ranking class; the American form, on the other hands, dealt with the encroachment upon an individual's liberty of 'an entangling net of circumstances' from which he or she could only flee and begin a new life. In contrast to both, the Canadian narrative featured an individual who neither rebelled nor fled but, through an ability to 'absorb and transform' infringements upon the sense of self, was able 'to maintain his own separate identity within the social complex'. This essay marked the beginning of discussions of patterns of action rather than literary traits. John P. Matthews' *Tradition in exile* (1962), which compared Australian and Canadian poetry, also expressed this new spirit of internationalism.

Ronald SUTHERLAND, in his two collections of essays—*Second image* (1971) and *The new hero* (1977)—compared, by content analysis alone, the literatures of Quebec and English Canada. Sutherland found 'no fundamental differences between the two major ethnic groups of Canada' as he traced, through their literatures, parallels in the relationship of English and French Canadians to the land and to their conception of 'Divine Order'; he believed their writings had been strongly affected by differing forms of puritanism, but that both cultures had now achieved a healthier, guilt-free vision that showed up in the more positive depictions of heroes and events in recent works.

Among those critics who sought to locate English-Canadian literature in larger or alternate English-language traditions, W.H. New in *Among worlds: an introduction to modern Commonwealth and South African fiction* (1975) treated it as one facet of Commonwealth literature. (A similar treatment occurred in the periodicals *Journal of Commonwealth Literature* and *World Literature Written in English*.) In addition, there was renewed interest in what was now often referred to as 'Canadian-American relations'. Marcia Kline in *Beyond the land itself: views of nature in Canada and the United States* (1970) contrasted attitudes to nature in nineteenth-century Canadian and American literature; although this monograph was somewhat superficial, especially in its acceptance of the frontier thesis as descriptive of Canadian settlement, it offered sound observations about differing attitudes in the two cultures and paired works interestingly for comparison. The proceedings of two conferences on western literature—*The westering experience in American literature* (1977) edited by Merrill Lewis and L.L. Lee, and *Crossing frontiers* (1979), edited by Dick Harrison—contained several papers that made connections between Canadian and American responses to the West. The former dealt chiefly with American works, but contained several essays on Canadian or comparative topics, including 'Problems in comparing Canadian and American western fiction' by Harrison. The latter volume, in which comparative questions were central, contained essays by Kroetsch, Mandel, and the American critic Leslie Fiedler, plus responses and summations by Sandra Djwa, Rosemary SULLIVAN, Henry KREISEL, and others. There was also a special issue of *Essays on Canadian Writing* (No. 22, 1981) on 'Canadian-American literary relations'.

This new interest in comparative work resulted both in a special issue of *Mosaic* (vol. 14, no.2, 1982), 'Beyond nationalism: the Canadian literary scene in global perspective', and in the wide-ranging and critically sophisticated essays by E.D. Blodgett collected in *Configuration: essays on the Canadian literatures* (1982). Blodgett made comparisons between Canadian writers and those from world literature, and between English-speaking and other Canadian writers (from both French and other ethnic groups). His 'The Canadian literatures as a literary problem' provided a history and evaluation of the studies done in comparative criticism. Another valuable overview was David M. Hayne's 'Comparative Canadian literature: past history, present state, future needs' in the journal *Canadian Review of Comparative Literature* 3 (1976).

5(d). Canadian criticism—unlike that of the United States, Britain, and Europe—lends itself to classification by goals rather than by methodology. Although it assimilated a number of critical techniques and values—such as modernist aesthetics, formalist analysis, and comparativist procedures—these innovations remained secondary to a larger, usually cultural, orientation. Since 1960, however, several writers influenced by Frye's criticism have been grouped together as 'thematic' critics because their criticism was based on the idea that literature has controlling archetypes of myths. Their critical writings were variously attacked as non-literary, in that they emphasized content over style and form; as too literary, in that they treated works as if they exist hermetically, outside historical contexts; or simply as too generalizing and reductive. Of these critics, Eli Mandel was the most literary and wide-ranging. In *Criticism: the silent-speaking words* (1966), he was the first Canadian critic to suggest that the advent of new literary forms (what is now called post-modern literature) necessitated corresponding innovations in critical methodology. He rejected American 'New Criticism' and traditional Canadian criticism, which he saw as chiefly concerned with environmental determinism. He called instead for a 'savage criticism'—a type of 'phenomenological criticism' that would enable the critic to 'participate' in the work, rather than evaluate or explain it. Mandel's own criticism, however, as well as being phenomenological, was also archetypal. He also showed an interest in language and silence, and in the relationship of the dream to the text. His best essays (collected in *Another time*, 1977) were more meditations than analyses and are valuable not for the answers they supply but for the questions they ask.

The other major 'thematicists'—D.G. JONES, Margaret Atwood, and John Moss—were more interested in developing a thesis about national identity than in participating in literary analysis. (Atwood's early critical writings were also strongly nationalistic.) Their criticism blended Frye's mythic or archetypal analysis with his concept of a 'thematic' criticism. Historically oriented, Jones, Atwood, and Moss sought to discover a central vision that was the common mode of perception in Canadian writers, and, by extension, in the Canadian people; and they tended to read a body of texts as one would a medieval allegory or a difficult modernist lyric—uncovering controlling 'myths' or conceptual frameworks expressed in narrative form.

Jones' highly prescriptive book *Butterfly on rock: a study of themes and images in Canadian literature* (1970), which developed from his 1965 *Canadian Literature* essay 'The sleeping giant', tried to amend the notion that Canadians lived with 'a sense of exile, of being estranged from the land and divided within', by finding, along with numerous images supporting this idea, others suggesting that this alienation was not permanent—that Canadians could create a 'vital community'. Jones detected in early Canadian literature a recurrent Adam archetype, with Adam more imprisoned by the garden than protected from the wilderness beyond. (In the course of his argument, he recast this archetype into the sleeping giant, Noah, and Job—all of whom he collectively calls the 'major man'.) Like W.E. Collin before him, Jones uncovered in Canadian literature a progress towards redemption, finding in contemporary Canadian writing an Adam who escaped from his self-imprisoned garrison and came to terms with the wilderness. *Butterfly on rock* has many of the strengths and weaknesses of thesis criticism. Its first chapters are particularly dazzling, summoning an array of images to support the presence of the Adam archetype. But Jones so fragmented the texts he used that some critics rejected the study on principle, and the general reader may be wary of unseen distortions. Such free movements among texts (necessary to Jones' type of criticism, and also characteristic of the work of Frye, Mandel, and Atwood) requires a reader's absolute faith in the critic's judgement, especially when it leads to cultural generalizations. Jones' essay 'Myth, Frye and the Canadian writer' (*Canadian Literature* 55, Winter 1973) serves as a conclusion to *Butterfly on rock*.

The brevity and casual style of Margaret Atwood's *SURVIVAL: A THEMATIC GUIDE TO CANADIAN LITERATURE* (1972; rpr. 1996)—originally conceived as a manual for secondary-school teachers, and eventually becoming a handbook for the general reader—gave it a currency that made it the most influential work of Canadian criticism in the 1970s. While dominated by an evaluative, nationalistic argument, it has an underlying conceptual model that echoes Frye's garrison thesis: for Atwood, Canadian were not only alienated from their environment but—having long existed in a colonial relationship, first to England and then to America—obsessed with an image of themselves as victims. Beneath *Survival*'s insistent attempt to prove that Canadians were implicated in their own victimization (a concept not really new or startling) lies a witty guide to the themes and images in Canadian literature. (Despite its deliberately selective range of material, *Survival* examined the same subjects that Lighthall and those who followed him considered typical of Canadian writing: Natives, explorers, Calvinists, settlers, immigrants, wilderness, nature, and death.) Though its notions seem to have been absorbed into the popular consciousness, critical reaction was not simply mixed but polarized, with the majority of academic critics rejecting it, finding its argument more rhetorical than cogent.

Atwood's significant contribution lay in her notion that the important images, archetypes, and genres in Canadian literature are tied to concepts of monsters, ghosts, and the Gothic. (Mandel, in his essays 'Atwood Gothic' and 'Criticism as ghost story', was the first to notice the pervasive link between Atwood and the Gothic; he suggested that *Survival* should be read as a ghost story.) In *Second words* (1982), a collection of her short critical pieces, Atwood reprinted her 1977 lecture 'Canadian monsters: some aspects of the supernatural in Canadian fiction', which (like *Survival*) tended to become a catalogue—in this case, of supernatural elements in Canadian fiction. The assumptions that underlie the Gothic and its sister genres, the mystery and the horror story, were indeed the real sources of Atwood's conceptual framework: given a seemingly frightening setting filled with threatening father-figures, the protagonist (whether a fictional character or a real writer, a woman, or simply a Canadian) must find some flaw in the environment though which a true reality can be penetrated where he/she will become part of the environment, at one with it, and able to control it. In other words, Atwood too has a redemptive vision—or at least a redemptive hope. (The topic of the Gothic in Canadian literature was further developed by Margot Northey in *The haunted wilderness: Gothic and grotesque in Canadian fiction*, 1976, which, while lacking a well-defined concept of Gothic literature, was the first study of Canadian writing to focus on genre.)

John Moss, the most prolific of the thematic critics, began his work with *Patterns of isolation* (1974), another book built around the image of the Canadian as exiled individual. Moss's thesis—which distinguished four types of cultural exile: garrison, frontier, colonial, and immigrant—was primarily an attempt to apply to the concept of isolation the stages of the American 'frontier thesis'. Here Moss looked not so much for literary images or themes as for underlying discussions of the 'Canadian experience', concluding that novels are an index for the developing national identity, and then devoted over two-thirds of the remainder of his study to discussing fiction that did not fit into his categories. This contradiction, and Moss's equivocations, stemmed, on the one hand, from his attempt at a 'thematic' criticism, that quickly became social commentary (reading literature in order to read a culture); and, on the other, from his honesty, which forced him to include works that argued against his thesis. Although repudiating thematic criticism in the introduction to his *Sex and violence in the Canadian novel* (1977), Moss proceeded to examine the literature thematically, in a not very persuasive counterpart to Leslie Fiedler's *Love and death in the American novel*. Moss's strength in his first two books—and in his later handbook, *A reader's guide to the Canadian novel* (1981)—lay in his encyclopaedic knowledge of Canadian fiction, and in his ability to give the general reader critical access to the problems and content of the books he discusses. Moss has published three volumes of collected essays, entitled as a group The Canadian Novel: *Here and now* (1978), *Modern times* (1982), and *Beginnings* (1986).

Warren Tallman's collection of essays, gathered in *Open Letter*, 3rd series, no. 6 (1977), reprinted three important essays on Canadian literature, including 'Wolf in the snow' (1960), which has been seen as one of the earliest examples of 'thematic' criticism. Tallman, like Frye, found in several Canadian novels an individual isolated because of landscape, but viewed this as a North American condition. Anticipating Jones, Tallman discerned images of a new relationship forming between people and their environment, in which 'the gods come back—snow gods, wind gods, wolf gods—but life gods too.'

Under the methods of the thematic critics lay four rather divergent goals: to indulge in nationalistic polemic; to continue to formulate theories about national identity; to show that literature is regionally or locally defined; and to see writing in literary rather than sociological terms. The debate about thematics obscured the fact that the issues raised by these types of criticism—nationalistic, national, regional, and formalist—were generally the most important in Canada in the 1960s and 1970s.

5(e). Prominent in the 1960s and 1970s was nationalistic criticism that called for social action, or for a change in the way one perceived Canadian literature and experience. Dennis LEE's important essay 'Cadence, country, silence: writing in a colonial space' (*Open Letter* 2, no. 6, Fall 1973, and elsewhere) stated that because American and British influences shaped the language in Canada and thereby determined conceptualization, he was deprived of both a culture and a truly native language to call his own. Writing in Canada, which had always been concerned with the colonial condition, had hitherto been forced to take an external perspective. Therefore to establish a 'Canadian' language, and thus a literature and national identity, Lee felt he had to fall silent for a time, until he could define words in terms of Canadian experience; only then could he reject the alien values inherent in the old definitions. Lee believed that there was a 'press of meaning'—a culturally indigenous energy that he called 'cadence'—whose local nature gave actuality to one's word. In *Savage fields: an essay in literature and cosmology* (1977), and in his article written in response to reviews, 'Reading *Savage fields*' (*Canadian Journal of Political and Social Theory* 3, no. 2, Spring-Summer 1979), he continued to discuss the difficulties of writing in a colonized state. Although over three-quarters of *Savage fields* discussed two works by Canadian authors (Ondaatje's *Billy the kid* and Cohen's *Beautiful losers*), Lee nevertheless moved beyond his nationalistic position, extending his concerns to the problems of creating literature in a complex environment. He found their source in a modern value system that treated the concepts of nature and civilization as dualities—in which nature and the efforts of humanity were pitted against each other. Lee did not suggest that this 'liberal' dualism came only from outside the Canadian tradition, or that it should be replaced by any conceptual unity, but opted for a different duality: 'earth' (or energy) and 'world' (or consciousness), which exist not as separate entities but as contraries that are in dynamic tension and offer new ways of seeing the same things. While Lee's ideas were abstract and sometimes obscure, his sense that Canadians must redefine their world was shared by a number of contemporary Canadian critics.

A different kind of nationalistic stand was taken by Robin Mathews in *Canadian literature: surrender of revolution* (1978) and elsewhere. Seen by some commentators as more Marxist-reactionary than nationalist, Mathews—like Lee—struggled against modernity, which he saw as embodied in American 'liberal anarchist individualism'. He divided English Canada into two social groups: the exploiters, who prefer foreign dominance; and the community builders, who uphold the values of 'communal, responsible Christian conservation'. What was important in Mathews' criticism was his attempt to begin an analysis of the relation of class structure to literature, a form of Marxist-influenced criticism little seen in Canada. Unfortunately Mathews too often tended to look at writers simply for evidence of their right-mindedness on certain key issues, examining works from different periods primarily for support of what he considered necessary attitudes and beliefs, and equating good writing with moral righteousness. Mathews' criticism was basically concerned with identifying those writers who ought to be excluded from the real 'Canadian literary tradition'; among the many he rejected were Frye, Atwood, Lee, and Mandel.

Mathews' ideas on 'revolution' were more clearly stated in 'Developing a language of struggle: Canadian literature and literary criticism', in Paul Cappon's collection of essays calling for a Marxist literature and criticism in Canada: *In our own house: social perspectives on Canadian literature* (1978). In this article Mathews proposed a class analysis of past literature that would expose 'the forces of exploitation, of oppression' that have governed Canada, and called for an anti-establishment literature that would see 'ordinary' Canadians as heroic. Cappon and his contributors thought of literary criticism as a form of sociology that should make a prescriptive analysis based on the standards of an extreme social realism and a set of approved social beliefs. An example of the problems arising from this type of criticism of Canadian literature can be seen in the Mathews-influenced book by Keith Richardson, *Poetry and the colonized mind: Tish* (1976). Although Richardson limited himself to what was essentially a regional examination, he ignored the fact that Canadian regions have a natural affinity for north-south rather than east-west alliances. Condemning this West Coast school of poets and critics as betraying the 'Canadian tradition'—which, for Richardson, was apparently that of Ontario—he failed to deal with the complexities of east-west, north-south dynamics.

5(f). Of the writers who continued to search for a national identity, George Woodcock, in his essays and review articles (in various journals, particularly *Canadian Literature*) contributed more to our notions of what constitutes Canada and Canadian writing than most writers of organized book-length theses. His discussions of Canadian writers and their work were collected in several books, including *Odysseus ever returning: essays on Canadian writers and their writings* (NCL, 1970) and *The world of Canadian writing: critiques & recollections* (1980). Although Woodcock sometimes linked writers to large myths and believed that certain myths, such as the story of Odysseus, were particularly appropriate to Canadian writing, he generally used them as devices to structure his essays rather than as keys to underlying unity in the Canadian imagination. Writing in the belletristic tradition, he rarely focused on a single work; instead he tended to examine a writer's corpus—fitting the author into the Canadian tradition and explaining the work in terms of the larger contexts of European and British writing. His essays provided both particular insights and general evaluations, and his personal sympathy lay first with the writer and then with the general reader—never with the academic specialist.

Some of the essays of W.H. New, Woodcock's successor as editor of *Canadian Literature*, collected in *Articulating West: essays on purpose and form in modern Canadian literature* (1972). In his introduction, New argued that avoiding definitive statements, or the 'sentencing' of one's new environment out of existence, was characteristic of Canadian writing and a result of Canadian duality that he described as the ordering 'East' and the undefined frontier 'West'. Canada has a shifting 'West' that is vulnerable to its inhabitants' need to find a new language to describe their experience. But once the 'West' is articulated, it becomes another 'East' and loses its essence. The frontiersman's choice was paradoxical: he might either remain invisible in his new surroundings by refusing to speak or, finding words, he might lose his new-found land. The essays and review-articles in *Articulating West*, which tend to look at a single book and trace a particular image or pattern in relation to the writer's larger work, deal with the problems of ordering reality through language.

One of the most important anthologies of Canadian criticism was Eli Mandel's *Contexts of Canadian criticism* (1971). Mandel brought together the disciplines of history, philosophy, and literary theory in essays by E.K. Brown, W.L. MORTON, H.A.Innis, William KILBOURN, F.H. Underhill, and George GRANT, and of such theoreticians as Northrop Frye, Marshall McLuhan, and Francis SPARSHOTT. There are also important critical articles, including overviews by Frye and Milton Wilson; two 1960 essays, 'Ethos and epic: aspects of contemporary Canadian poetry' by Paul West, and 'Wolf in the snow' by Warren Tallman; and three essays on special topics: 'The Dodo and the *Cruising auk*', Robert L. McDougall's 1963 article on class in Canadian literature; Henry Kreisel's discussion of regional psychology, 'The prairie: a state of mind' (1968); and Dorothy Livesay's attempt to define a native Canadian literary form, 'The documentary poem: a Canadian genre' (1969). This collection placed Canadian literary criticism within the larger context of post-war cultural criticism in Canada.

There were two other collections of essays on Canadian literature and its place in the national identity. *The Canadian imagination: dimensions of a literary culture* (1977), edited by David Staines, was another attempt to define Canada to an American audience and included essays by Atwood, Peter Buitenhuis, Douglas Bush, Frye, McLuhan, and Woodcock. *The arts in Canada: the last fifty years* (1980), edited by W.J. Keith and B.-Z. Shek—originally the fiftieth-anniversary issue of *The University of Toronto Quarterly*—included agreeably personal essays by Frye, Hugh MacLENNAN, Robertson Davies, Ralph GUSTAFSON, and Woodcock.

Another attempt to define a Canadian tradition could be found in Tom MARSHALL's *Harsh and lovely land: the major Canadian poets & the making of a Canadian tradition* (1979). While Marshall's rather derivative book was composed of brief essays (mostly appreciations of individual poets) that identified some characteristic features of each writer's work (Ondaatje's 'violence', MacEWEN's 'arcane knowledge'), its striking neglect of western writing, such as that of the *Tish* group and the prairie poets, led to a distorted view of Canadian poetry as a progressive evolution that culminated in the work of central-Canadian poets of the 1960s and after.

Two other books that continued the tradition of evaluative criticism in Canada were D.J. Dooley's *Moral vision in the Canadian novel* (1979) and Wilfred Cude's *A due sense of differences: an evaluative approach to Canadian literature* (1980). Dooley invoked evaluative standards that derived from late nineteenth- and early twentieth-century realism as well as from the longstanding Canadian critical tradition of desiring a literature that is moral, pragmatic, and realistic. Cude, asserting that he would restore evaluation to a criticism now dominated by a search for patterns and contexts, suggested that critical consensus was the main criterion for establishing that book's classic status; he examined *AS FOR ME AND MY HOUSE*, *FIFTH BUSINESS*, *Lady Oracle*, and *St. Urbain's horseman* as 'classics'. (The issue of what constituted a 'classic' was central to the 1978 Calgary conference on the Canadian novel, the proceedings of which were published in *Taking stock* [1982], edited by Charles Steele; the conclusions of the conference—especially its lists of 'classic' books—became the subject of prolonged debate.) A contrasting approach to Cude's and Dooley's is that of Robert Lecker in *On the line: readings in the short fiction of Clark Blaise, John Metcalf, and Hugh Hood* (1982). Lecker seeks to capture the 'unnameable, elusive quality' of the experience of reading, working partly in the meditative or phenomenological tradition of Mandel and George Bowering, but adding very close textual readings in order to convey the 'feel' of an individual story.

5(g). Edward McCOURT's ground-breaking study of regional literature, *The Canadian West in fiction* (1949), had no immediate successors; however, by the time of its revised publication in 1970, regionalism had become an important critical topic. Since then there have been several regional studies, with the Prairie West receiving the most attention. Henry Kreisel's 1968 essay, 'The prairie: a state of mind', in which he discussed 'the impact of the landscape upon the mind', gave new impetus to consideration of the West as a literary region, as did a series of multi-disciplinary conferences on the Prairies. After the late 1960s four critics—Laurence Ricou, Dick Harrison, Eli Mandel, and Robert Kroetsch—made extensive statements about the nature of western, or prairie, literature and two full-length studies appeared: Ricou's *Vertical man/horizontal world: man and landscape in Canadian prairie fiction* (1973) and Harrison's *Unnamed country: the struggle for a Canadian prairie fiction* (1977), both of which were concerned with the relationship between environment and literature. Ricou viewed the prairie landscape as 'obsessing' its writers and producing a psychology in which man sees himself as 'vertical' or objective, devoted to life and industry, in relation to the 'horizontal' land, associated with meaninglessness and death. In this psychological reading of literature in the West, in which anxiety about individual identity is strongly affected by a growing knowledge of what the prairie is, Ricou emphasized the importance of the experience of place but did not ignore the fact that individual temperament ultimately controls a writer's vision. Harrison, like McCourt, treated the entire spectrum of western writing in his attempt to show how writers adapted to their environment—throwing off inherited cultural structures and old ways of seeing for new and appropriate indigenous ones—and created, in the last generation, not only a true prairie literature but one that moved away from a social to a psychological realism. In many ways Harrison's book was a conclusion to McCourt's, for McCourt announced that there was a nascent western literature and Harrison declared its maturity.

Both Mandel and Kroetsch developed theories about the West's relation to the literary imagination. In *Another time* Mandel included three important essays on the meaning of the West as a literary region—'Images of prairie man', 'Romance and realism in western-Canadian fiction', and 'Writing west'—in which he suggested (following Frye) that environment was the literary construct of the mind, as opposed to the more common thesis of regional critics that environment shaped literatures. Thus to Mandel, unlike Harrison, the notion of 'prairie' was nothing more than 'a mental construct, a region of the human mind, a myth'. Mandel believed that the central prairie myth was one in which an innocent sees the world anew and names his surroundings. The critical ideas of Kroetsch—expressed in essays collected in *Open Letter* (5th series, no. 4, 1973), and in lectures and published interviews—became very influential. He originally felt that prairie writers, in what was still a newly settled environment, had to name the as-yet-undefined features of their experience and find myths to give life meaning in the vast and empty prairie landscape. In 'The fear of women in prairie fiction: an erotics of space' (1970), Kroetsch attempted to establish a grammar of western experience by describing opposing pairs—horse/house, man/woman, movement/stability—that defined the narrative structures of the region. In his 1974 essay 'Unhiding the hidden', he modified his earlier views, suggesting that, before naming, Canadian writers must 'un-name' their environment. Like Lee in 'Cadence, country, silence', Kroetsch believed that languages contain concealed alien experiences; because of this, writers should subvert or demythologize 'the systems that threaten to define them.' Kroetsch's later criticism used a structuralist framework.

Other regional literatures were the subject of less extensive study. Patrick O'Flaherty's *The rock observed: studies in the literature of Newfoundland* (1979) emphasized Newfoundland history as well as the 'relentless pressures of geography' that produced 'a race apart'. Like McCourt and Harrison, O'Flaherty provided useful examinations of early non-literary writing, finding it in the origins of the imaginative consciousness that eventually resulted in the work of E.J. Pratt and Margaret DULEY, and in the emerging writers of the province. In *Gardens, covenants, exiles: loyalism in the literature of Upper Canada/Ontario* (1982) Dennis Duffy wrote a regional account that emphasized history rather than landscape. Like D.J. Jones, Duffy also saw 'the garden' as the primary Canadian myth: because of their experience, Canadians developed a sense of Canada as the lost garden and its inhabitants as fallen exiled Adams. Duffy, however, did not make any pleas for changing or coming to terms with the condition he described. Lorraine McMullen edited *Twentieth-century essays on Confederation literature* (1976), a collection that was largely regional (Upper Canada/Ontario) as well as historical, and one that contained important articles by critics such as D.C. SCOTT, Smith, Pelham Edgar, F.W. Watt, Elizabeth Waterston, and James Polk.

While there was a general feeling among Canadian critics that British Columbia had a separate regional character, there were no critical or historical studies of the literature of the province, though there were several anthologies of B.C. writing, some of which contained statements about its regional nature. However, a fair amount of commentary existed on the *TISH* movement. C.H. Gervais collected a number of essays and interviews in *The writing life: historical and critical views of the Tish movement* (1978); and there was the earlier *Poetry and the colonized mind: Tish* by Keith Richardson. Several of the *Tish* writers were themselves critics, and their criticism was distinctive enough to qualify as a West Coast school, especially in the essays of its leading practitioners, George BOWERING and Frank Davey. This criticism was implicitly regional in that these critics had a distinctive aesthetic and set of critical concerns and tended to give their sympathetic attention most often to West Coast authors and other writers who responded to similar postmodern and phenomenological strains in poetry and criticism. Both Bowering and Davey were prolific essayists and reviewers. Like Tallman's essays, those of Bowering in *A way with words* (1982) and *The mask in place: essays on fiction in North America* (1982) utilized poetic techniques—word-play, associative leaps, dramatizations of the movements of the mind, a juxtaposition of subjective and objective responses—that were the consequence of his assuming that the essence of a poem or novel could not easily be expressed in discursive prose and must therefore be approached indirectly in an evocative fashion. Though Bowering's arguments were occasionally oblique and his style and tone unorthodox, several of his essays—such as 'The poems of Fred WAH' and 'That fool of a fear: notes on *A jest of God*'—succeeded in conveying the spirit of contemporary writing better than more traditional approaches. Davey's *From there to here: a guide to English-Canadian literature since 1960* (1974) deliberately resisted generalizations (especially of the 'thematic' kind) by providing sixty separate discussions of the writers covered. In *Surviving the paraphrase and other essays* (1983), Davey attempted to break free of the linear argument featured in the traditional critical essay. In his book *Margaret Atwood: feminist poetic* (1983) he dealt with another emerging strain of critical theory—feminist criticism—by discussing Atwood's work in terms of two grids, language and pattern, and discovered in her writing an ongoing quarrel with patriarchal inheritance and its formalist rules. Davey's essay 'Surviving the paraphrase', originally published in *Canadian Literature* 70 (Autumn, 1976), was important because it called for an end to 'thematic' discussions. It suggested that it was time Canadian critics set aside questions of nationality or identity and began to emulate the close reading of the formalist or New Critical school, and to approach literature through generic criticism, phenomenological criticism (by which he seemed to mean the 'criticism of consciousness', that deriving from the work of George Poulet), and 'archetypal' criticism (an application of Frye's theory of modes from *The anatomy of criticism*). In 'Critic, culture, text: beyond thematics' (*Essays on Canadian Writing* 11, 1978), Russell Brown analysed Davey's essay and other recent Canadian criticism, and suggested some of the implications of the advent of structuralist criticism. He argued that 'thematics' could still be useful when combined with newer critical theories.

6. THE EIGHTIES AND THE NINETIES. (a) An explosion of critical studies took place in the 1980s—both in response to the boom in the production and study of Canadian texts in the 1960s and after, and as a result of the great increase in literary criticism being published internationally throughout the academic world. Thus a brief survey of Canadian criticism of the last fifteen years cannot do justice to even the best and most useful recent critical texts. From the early eighties to the present, Canadian criticism was generally marked by the taking over of newer critical methodologies; by structural changes resulting from changing Canadian demographics, culture, and institutions; and by continuing debates over the nature and importance of national identity. This was a period in which canon formation and reformation became important to critics within Canada and in which a strong critical interest in Canadian writing was established abroad.

Undoubtedly Canadian criticism was most influenced methodologically by theories generally grouped together under the term poststructuralism. Two books published in 1982, E.D. Blodgett's *Configuration: essays on the Canadian literatures* (see below) and *Labyrinths of voice: conversations with Robert Kroetsch*, by Robert Kroetsch, Shirley Neuman, and Robert Wilson, marked the beginning of a number of explicitly poststructural volumes, shaped by the writings of such French theorists as Derrida, Barthes, Foucault, and Bakhtin. Although the subtitle of *Labyrinths of voice* suggests a book-long interview, it is in fact highly scripted, laying out not only the basic precepts of poststructuralist theory but also Kroetsch's poststructural approach to Canadian writing, which he developed in his critical essays of the 1970s and 1980s, collected as *The lovely treachery of words* (1989). Blodgett and Kroetsch, along with Linda HUTCHEON in the essays she published in the 1980s, several of which are collected in *The Canadian postmodern: a study of contemporary English-Canadian fiction* (1988), have also helped to mould the emerging Canadian canon. *Future indicative—literary theory and Canadian literature* (1987), edited by John Moss, is a 1985 conference proceedings that introduced poststructuralist practice more generally into Canadian criticism: it brings together statements by George Bowering, Robert Kroetsch, Barbara Godard, Heather Murray, Terry Goldie, Shirley Neuman, Sherrill Grace, Linda Hutcheon, and Stephen SCOBIE, many of whom became Canada's most prominent poststructuralist critics. Other books closely associated with this approach are Stephen Scobie's *Signature event cantext* (1989), Aritha VAN HERK's *In visible ink: crypto-frictions* (1991), Smaro Kamboureli's *The edge of genre: the contemporary Canadian long poem* (1991), Winfried Siemerling's *Discoveries of the other: alterity in the works of Leonard Cohen, Hubert Aquin, Michael Ondaatje, and Nicole Brossard* (1994), and Pamela Banting's *Body Inc: a theory of translation poetics* (1995). The University of Toronto Press's Theory/Culture series, under the general editorship of Linda Hutcheon and Paul Perron, has been particularly important in fostering poststructuralist criticism in Canada. Canadian poststructuralism has also been influenced by Hutcheon's writing (see below), particularly by her theory of historiographic metafiction as a characteristic postmodern form. Most criticism written in Canada today has either absorbed some of the tenets of poststructuralism or is (in a few cases) consciously written against this theory.

A second theoretical context that has played an important role in shaping Canadian criticism since the beginning of the 1990s is postcolonialism. While some of its practitioners are by no means hostile to poststructuralist or other contemporary theories, they emphasize the importance of Canada's history as a former colony (and often as a country that then became dominated, in colonial-like fashion, by the culture of the USA), and focus on strategies that authors and critics have devised to counter the distorting influence of a distant imperial centre. The postcolonial model has also been adopted by critics who use it as way of delineating the subnational concerns of regions and minority subgroups. In Canada, Diana Brydon and Stephen Slemon helped connect international theories of postcolonialism with those that locate Canada and its writing in the post- Second World War environment of decolonization. Donna Bennett's essay 'English Canada's postcolonial complexities' (*Essays on Canadian writing*, 51-52, Winter 1993-Spring 1994) gives an extended survey of the development and implications of this approach in Canada. Brydon and Australian Helen Tiffin have written *Decolonising fictions* (1993), a study of the postcolonial literatures of Canada, Australia, and the West Indies. Margaret Turner's *Imagining culture: New World narrative and the writing of Canada* (1995) argues that Canadian literature creates a metaphorical landscape reflecting the doubled nature of experience—the formation of a settlement culture and the encounter with an unmapped environment. Also of importance are special issues of *Essays on Canadian writing*, 'Testing the limits: postcolonial theories and Canadian literatures' (no.56, 1995), edited by Brydon, and of *Canadian Literature*, 'Postcolonial identities' (no. 149, 1996), edited by Eva-Marie Kröller *et al.*

The use of other contemporary methodologies in Canadian criticism during this period can be seen in studies such as Laurie Ricou's *Everyday magic: child languages in Canadian literature* (1987), a linguistic and structuralist approach to Canadian writing; Rosmarin Heidenreich's *The postwar novel in Canada: narrative patterns and reader response* (1989); Stan Dragland's *Floating voice: Duncan Campbell Scott and the literature of Treaty 9* (1994), a study that unites postcolonial theory with a New Historical and cultural-studies approach to early Canadian writing; and Sonia Mycak's *In search of the split subject: psychoanalysis, phenomenology, and the novels of Margaret Atwood* (1996).

6(b). One reason why postcolonial theory has been particularly important in Canada is the nature of the demographic change that has taken place since the Second World War. Although Canada has always had a history of immigration and ethnic variety, the massive displacement after the war and the worldwide decolonization that followed have altered, and continue to alter, not only the ethnic and racial makeup of the country, but also the way in which immigrants are accepted into Canadian culture and the degree to which they seek to be assimilated. The distinct qualities of the writing of both new and of older immigrant groups has become an important critical topic. Immigrant writing is not a completely new topic for literary criticism—consider, for example, the chapter 'Failed sacrifices: the reluctant immigrant' in Margaret Atwood's *Survival* (see above), and 'The Ethnic Voice in Canadian Writing', the watershed discussion of ethnic fiction in Eli Mandel's *Another time* (see above)—but by the 1980s it became a central focus in the study of Canadian literature. Two book-length works indicate the change that took place in the critical community. *Identifications: ethnicity and the writer in Canada* (1982), edited by Jars Balan, the proceedings of a conference held at the University of Alberta in 1979, discussed two subjects that have become central to the study of subculture writing in Canada: the existence of distinct subculture literatures (which, for this conference, were those of the Ukrainian, Icelandic, and Yiddish communities); and the relationship between a larger Canadian culture and the identity of the 'hyphenated Canadian'. Blodgett's *Configuration* (see above) is the first book-length critical study to suggest that the Canadian exists as plural literatures, neither the writing of a single English-speaking community nor simply the product of a bicultural nation clearly descended from Britain and France.

The writing of Canada's 'other' cultures first became visible through the creation of subgroup literary anthologies, and then through the publication of critical surveys and single-author studies. These works often suggest that immigrant literary works tend to focus on a doubled identity, one stemming from their country of origin and another from the nature of a Canadian existence. Good examples of critical overviews of individual groups are *The old world and the new: literary perspectives of German-speaking Canadians* (1984) edited by Walter E. Riedel; *Contrasts: comparative essays on Italian-Canadian writing* (1985) edited by Joseph Pivato; George Bisztray's *Hungarian-Canadian literature* (1987); and Michael Greenstein's *Third solitudes: tradition and discontinuity in Jewish-Canadian literature* (1989). Also of interest are Hallvard Dahlie's *Varieties of exile: the Canadian experience* (1986); Joseph Pivato's *Echo: essays on other literatures*, 1994; Irving Massey's *Identity and community: reflections on English,*

Yiddish, and French literature in Canada (1994); and Frank Birbalsingh's *Novels and the nation: essays in Canadian literature* (1995)—all of which attend to the issues of inherited identity, immigrant experience, and the possibility of national culture.

The legal enshrining of multiculturalism in the 1982 Constitution Act, the Charter of Rights and Freedoms, and the 1988 Multiculturalism Act is reflected in the emergence of critical discussions, broadly postcolonial in orientation, in which the immigrant or ethnic condition is seen as the product of widespread discrimination. The essays collected in the conference proceedings *Literatures of lesser diffusion* (1990), edited by Joseph Pivato *et al.*, focus on the way in which minority writing in Canada has been treated by the literary establishment. Arnold Itwaru's *The invention of Canada: literary text and the immigrant imaginary* (1990) and Arun Mukherjee's *Towards an aesthetic of opposition: essays on literature, criticism and cultural imperialism* (1988; revised and expanded as *Oppositional aesthetics: readings from a hyphenated space*, 1994) argue that Canada has been imperialistic towards its immigrants and ethnic minorities, particularly those who differ in tradition or colour from the British norm out of which Canadian identity has thus far been formed. See also *Writing ethnicity: cross-cultural consciousness in Canadian and Québécois literature* (1996), edited by Winfried Siemerling, for a variety of critical approaches to this and larger questions of plurality within Canada. *New contexts of Canadian criticism* (1997), edited by Ajay Heble, Donna Palmateer Pennee, and J.R. (Tim) Struthers, is described as a 'sequel' to Eli Mandel's 1971 publication and examines topics relating to the current literary landscape with essays by M. Nourbese PHILIP, Frank Davey, Beth Brant, Arun Mukherjee, Thomas KING, W. H. New, Basil H. JOHNSTON, Robert Kroetsch, Linda Hutcheon, and others.

The primary orientation of multiculturalism changed from its inception in the late 1970s—moving from an emphasis on ways of maintaining the distinctiveness of ethnic cultural identities, invisible within the context of those of British or French origin, to policies dealing with the needs of visible groups, and to anti-racism efforts more social than cultural in nature. In the last ten years some members of Canada's subgroups have come to view multiculturalism negatively, either as itself destructive of group individuality, or as a barrier that separates minorities from the dominant majority culture. Itwaru and others—including Neil BISSOONDATH, in *Selling illusions: the cult of multiculturalism in Canada* (1994), and some of the writers interviewed in *Other solitudes: Canadian multicultural fictions* (1990) edited by Linda Hutcheon and Marion Richmond—take an anti-multicultural stand, though for very different reasons.

Terrence Craig looked at the history of *Racial attitudes in English Canadian fiction, 1905-1980* (1987), and other critics preferred to use the category of 'race' rather than that of 'ethnicity' in considering questions of subgroup marginalization. Some individuals identify certain groups as sharing common concerns, if not identities, because of the way their skin colour sets them off from Canadians of European descent. *The other woman: women of colour in contemporary Canadian literature* (1995), a collection of critical essays and interviews with writers edited by Makeda Silvera, is a good example of this approach. However, although race and colour have played significant roles in critical discussions of Canadian cultural, social, and political experience, few book-length critical works have focused on the literary aspects of these subjects.

6(c). Several recent studies have focused on the literatures of First Nations peoples. These critical studies began in Canada with Leslie Monkman's *A Native heritage: images of the Indian in English-Canadian literature* (1981) and Penny Petrone's *Native literature in Canada: from the oral tradition to the present* (1990). Other recent volumes of importance include the collections *The Native in literature* (1987) edited by Thomas King, Cheryl Calver, and Helen Hoy; *Native writers and Canadian writing* (1990) edited by W.H. New; and a collection of essays by Native critics, *Looking at the words of our people: First Nations analysis of literature* (1993) edited by Jeannette ARMSTRONG. Terry Goldie's *Fear and temptation: the image of the indigene in Canadian, Australian, and New Zealand literatures* (1989), which is comparative, poststructuralist, and postcolonial, is an analysis (influenced by Edward Said's critique of 'orientalism') of the colonial ideology embedded in the depictions of Native people found in the literatures of the dominant groups.

6(d). Canadian criticism has also been influenced by a new emphasis on gender as a determining factor in literary writing. While there have so far been no book-length studies focusing on gay or masculinist approaches to Canadian writing, there has been an extensive critical literature concerned with women writers or with feminism and literary issues. The volume prepared by Barbara Godard, *Gynocritics: La gynocritique* (1987), combines an extensive bibliography of Canadian feminist theory and criticism with the proceedings of York University's 1981 Dialogue conference, an important early conference on Canadian feminist criticism. The proceedings of a second important early conference, 'Women and Words' (Vancouver, 1983), is collected as *In the feminine: women and words* (1985). These two books—along with the wide-ranging critical collection *A mazing space* (1986), edited by Shirley Neuman and Smaro Kamboureli—formed the ground of contemporary Canadian feminist criticism. Other important studies focusing on gender and the construction of the feminine in Canadian writing include the American critic Lorna Irvine's *Sub/version* (1986), the Australian scholar Coral Ann Howells' *Private and fictional words—Canadian women novelists of the 1970s and 1980s* (1987), Susan Rudy Dorscht's *Women, reading, Kroetsch: telling the difference* (1991), and Helen Buss's *Mapping our selves: Canadian women's autobiography in English* (1993). *Collaboration in the feminine: writings on women and culture from 'Tessera'* (1994), edited by Barbara Godard, is a collection of feminist theory, political writing, and criticism from the Canadian feminist journal Godard helped to establish. Clara Thomas, one of the founders of Canadian literary study and a pioneer in her concern for women's writing, collected a number of her essays in *All my sisters: essays on the work of Canadian women writers* (1994).

6(e). While region has long been a factor in Canadian criticism, it has become of renewed importance in the contemporary era. The Prairie West has been the focus of such studies as Dennis Cooley's *The vernacular muse* (1987); Carol Fairbanks's *Prairie women: images in American and Canadian fiction* (1986); *Writing Saskatchewan: 20 critical essays* (1989) edited by Kenneth G. Probert; and Arnold Davidson's *Coyote country: fictions of the Canadian West* (1994). Gwen Davies has made significant contributions to an understanding of the literature of Atlantic Canada in her *Studies in Maritime literary history* (1991) and her *Myth and milieu: Atlantic literature and culture, 1918-1939* (1993), as has Janice KULYK KEEFER in *Under eastern eyes: a critical reading of Maritime fiction* (1987). Ontario has been treated in the publication of W.J. Keith's *Literary images of Ontario* (1992). Writing from British Columbia has received special emphasis in George Bowering's writing (see below) and in the accounts of the *TISH* movement in *Beyond 'Tish'* (1991), edited by Douglas BARBOUR, and elsewhere. The increasing sense of a rift between the cultures of English Canada and Quebec seems to have reduced interest in English-language studies of French-Canadian writing; but, as can be seen throughout this entry, bicultural studies comparing anglophone and francophone writing continue to be written. See Philip Stratford's *All the polarities: comparative studies in contemporary Canadian novels in French and English* (1986); Caroline Bayard's study of the relationship between concrete poetry and word-based postmodernist writing, *The new poetics in Canada and Québec: from concretism to post-modernism* (1989); Sylvia Söderlind's *Margin/alias: language and colonization in Canadian and Québécois fiction* (1991), which employs a postcolonial frame; and Winfried Siemerling's poststructuralist study *Discoveries of the other: alterity in the works of Leonard Cohen, Hubert Aquin, Michael Ondaatje, and Nicole Brossard* (1994).

6(f). Canadian critics have not limited themselves to studies dealing with Canadian writers alone. As already seen in Terry Goldie's *Fear and temptation*, critics have found useful the placing of Canadian writing in the context of works by writers of other nationalities. Other critics who have compared Canadian literature to the writing of the antipodes are W.H. New in *Dreams of speech and violence—the art of the short story in Canada and New Zealand* (1987) and Graham Huggan in *Territorial disputes: maps and mapping strategies in contemporary Canadian and Australian fiction* (1994). Studies concerned with American comparisons include Stan Fogel's *A tale of two countries: contemporary fiction in Canada and the United States* (1984); Sherrill Grace's *Regression and apocalypse: studies in North American literary expressionism* (1989); and the collection *Context North American: Canadian/U.S. relations* (1994) edited by Camille La Brossière. T.D. MacLulich looked at the dual influence of Britain and the United States on Canadian writing in *Between Europe and America: the Canadian tradition in fiction* (1988). In *New World regionalism: literature in the Americas*, David Jordan examines the larger relationship of literary tradition throughout the Americas; while the collection *Cultural difference and the literary text: pluralism and the limits of authenticity in North American literatures* (1996), edited by Winfried Siemerling and Karen Schwenk, places Canadian writing within the context of a cultural-studies approach to North American literature. Europe has not been entirely forgotten as a context in this period: see, for example, *Biography and autobiography: essays on Irish and Canadian history and literature* (1993) edited by James Noonan. Asia provides a comparative context in the collection *Nature and identity in Canadian and Japanese literature* (1988), edited by Kinya Tsuruta and Theodore Goossen.

6(g). The growth of international interest in Canadian writing has prompted Canadian critics to provide introductions to Canadian literature intended primarily for readers outside of Canada. In particular Arnold Davidson edited *Studies on Canadian literature: introductory and critical essays* (1990), a valuable collection intended for scholars in the Modern Language Association, and W.J. Keith introduced British and European readers to Canadian literature in his *Canadian literature in English* (1985), a volume in Longmans' Literature in English series. At the same time, international study of Canadian literature has become significant. In part as a response to the attention given it in the seminal book of postcolonial theory, Bill Ashcroft, Gareth Griffiths, and Helen Tiffin's *The empire writes back: theory and practice in post-colonial literatures* (1989), scholars in countries around the world have begun to study, teach, confer, and write extensively on Canadian literature. Among the many volumes by international scholars looking at Canadian writing, either alone or in relation to another literature or in the context of larger topics, of particular recent note are *The great prairie fact and literary imagination* (1989) by the American scholar Robert Tacker; *Framing truths: parodic structures in contemporary English-Canadian historical novels* (1992) by the German scholar Martin Kuester; *Reverberations: explorations in the Canadian short story* (1993) by Simone Vauthier, a French scholar who has organized important conferences at her university, the University of Strasbourg; and *Outsider notes* (1996), a feminist examination of Canadian literature with respect to gender, class, race, and ideology by Lynette Hunter, who, although born in Canada, has spent her life in England and teaches at the University of Leeds. Margaret Laurence, Joy KOGAWA and, particularly, Margaret Atwood have been of great interest to international critics, especially those focusing on women writers. It should, however, be noted here that American critics have sometimes treated Canadian writers, especially Atwood, as if they were part of the larger American culture. For example, see King-Kok Cheung's *Articulate silences: Hisaye Yamamota, Maxine Hong Kingston, Joy Kogawa* (1993); Molly Hite's *The other side of the story: structures and strategies of contemporary feminist narratives* (1989); Julian Fleenor's *The female Gothic* (1983); and Maggie Humm's *Border traffic: strategies of contemporary women writers* (1991).

6(h). While Atwood's writings have of course received attention in Canadian critical commentary, her work has dominated the critical discourse of international critics considering Canadian writers—for whom Atwood is primarily a feminist writer. A good example of the contrasting approaches to Atwood on the two sides of the Canadian-American border are the essays in the MLA collection *Approaches to teaching Atwood's 'The Handmaid's Tale' and other works* (1996), edited by Sharon Wilson, Thomas Friedman, and Shannon Hengen: the Canadian critics in this volume focus on national traits in Atwood's writing, but those same features are associated, by American academics, with gender. A number of collections of essays on Atwood's work by both Canadian and international critics have been published abroad, including the 1994 British volume *Margaret Atwood: writing and subjectivity*, edited by Colin Nicholson; and the American collections *Margaret Atwood: vision and forms* (1988), edited by Kathryn Van Spanckeren and Jan Garden Castro, and *Critical essays on Margaret Atwood* (1988), edited by Judith McCombs—whose *Margaret Atwood: a reader's guide* (1991), a voluminous annotated bibliography of Atwood's work and its criticism, is a scholarly landmark. In Canada, Sherrill Grace and Lorraine Weir edited *Margaret Atwood: language, text, system* (1983), and Lorraine York gathered the essays in *Various Atwoods: essays on the later poems, short fiction, and novels* (1995). The first full-length studies of Atwood's work, Sherrill Grace's *Violent duality: a study of Margaret Atwood* (1980) and Frank Davey's poststructuralist approach to Atwood and to feminist writing, *Margaret Atwood: a feminist poetics* (1983), have now been supplemented by a number of volumes from scholars around the world writing in several languages. The American scholar Sharon Wilson has provided a particularly thorough study of folklore and fairy-tale motifs in Atwood's writing in *Margaret Atwood's fairy tale sexual politics* (1993).

Other writers than Atwood have received extended attention during this period. Alice Munro has been the subject of several books, including the essay collections *Probable fictions: Alice Munro's narrative acts*, edited by Louis K. MacKendrick (1983), and *The art of Alice Munro: saying the unsayable*, edited by Judith Miller (1984). Full-length studies include Magdalene Redekop's engaging study, *Mothers and other clowns: the stories of Alice Munro* (1992); Ajay Heble's theoretically informed *The tumble of reason: Alice Munro's discourse of absence* (1994); *Controlling the uncontrollable—*

the fiction of Alice Munro (1989) by the American scholar Ildiko de Papp Carrington; and James Carscallen's enlightening analyses of informing patterns in *The other country: patterns in the writing of Alice Munro* (1993).

Margaret Laurence has also garnered considerable critical attention, including the essay collections *A place to stand on: essays by and about Margaret Laurence* (1983) edited by George Woodcock; *Crossing the river: essays in honour of Margaret Laurence* (1988) edited by Kristjana GUNNARS; *Margaret Laurence: an appreciation* (1988) edited by Christl Verduyn; *Critical approaches to the fiction of Margaret Laurence* (1990) edited by Colin Nicholson; Helen Buss's *Mother/daughter relationships: Manakawa works of Margaret Laurence* (1985); *Margaret Laurence: the long journey home* (1991), Patricia Morley's expansion of her earlier book for Twayne; and Fiona Sparrow's treatment of Laurence's early African writing, *Into Africa with Margaret Laurence* (1992). All provide a variety of approaches to Laurence's writings.

In general, the full-length critical study of a single author has been a prominent form during this period. Other notable works on single authors include Christl Verduyn's *Lifelines: Marian Engel's writings* (1995); Lorraine York's *Front lines: the fiction of Timothy Findley* (1991); Philip Kokatailo's *John Glassco's richer world: 'Memoirs of Montparnasse'* (1988); Jan Bartley's *Invocations: the poetry and prose of Gwendolyn MacEwen*; Andrew Stubbs' *Myth, origins, magic: a study of form in Eli Mandel's poetry* (1993); Stephen Scobie's *bp Nichol: what history teaches* (1984); a collection of essays on Michael ONDAATJE's writing, *Spider blues* (1985), edited by Sam Solecki; Solecki's own analysis, *Prague blues: the fiction of Josef Škvorecký* (1990); Leslie Mundwiler's *Michael Ondaatje: word, image, imagination* (1984); Ada Craniford's *Fiction and fact in Mordecai Richler's novels* (1992); George Bowering's *Sheila Watson and 'The double hook'* (1985); W.J. Keith's *Epic fiction: the art of Rudy Wiebe* (1981); Penny Van Toorn's *Rudy Wiebe and the historicity of the word* (1995); and *On coasts of eternity: Jack Hodgins' fictional universe* (1996) edited by J.R. (Tim) Struthers.

Publishers' series have also played an important role in introducing individual writers and their works. Several Canadian writers have now appeared in the World Author series that the American publisher Twayne directs chiefly towards undergraduates. In the multi-volume series Canadian Writers and Their Works, ECW PRESS has published extended and informed introductions to a wide range of writers as well as publishing a series of short books that introduce undergraduates to individual canonical texts. Dundurn Press has published eight volumes in a series entitled Profiles of Canadian Writers; Tecumseh Press has started a series of annotated texts, beginning with LEACOCK's *SUNSHINE SKETCHES OF A LITTLE TOWN* and DUNCAN's *The imperialist*; McClelland & Stewart's NEW CANADIAN LIBRARY continues republishing Canadian books (the books in the present series no longer have critical introductions but Afterwords that function as appreciations); and the University of Ottawa's Reappraisal series has contributed a number of books of conference proceedings dealing with individual writers, as well as with special critical topics.

Biographies of Canadian writers have become more important during this period, a period that has generally been an age of biography throughout the English-speaking world. (See BIOGRAPHY AND MEMOIRS IN ENGLISH.) Notable biographers and their subjects include Elspeth Cameron (Hugh MacLENNAN, Irving Layton; Earle Birney), Sandra Djwa (F.R. Scott), Judith Skelton Grant (Robertson Davies), Ira Nagel (Leonard Cohen), David Pitt (E.J. Pratt), Rosemary Sullivan (Elizabeth SMART, Gwendolyn MacEWEN), and James King (Margaret Laurence). Memoirs of interest include Timothy FINDLEY's *Inside memory: pages from a writer's notebook* (1990), Margaret Laurence's *Dance on the earth* (1989), and Robert Kroetsch's *A likely story: the writing life* (1995).

A number of writers published volumes of their own critical, autobiographical, and occasional essays in this period. Of particular note are Margaret Atwood's *Second words: selected critical prose* (1982); Louis Dudek's two volumes of essays, *In defence of art: critical essays and reviews* (1988) and *Paradise: essays on myth, art and reality* (1992); Hugh HOOD's *Unsupported assertions: essays* (1991); Eli Mandel's critical essays in *The family romance* (1986); Miriam WADDINGTON's *Apartment seven—essays selected and new* (1989); and Bronwen WALLACE's *Arguments with the world* (1992). During this period, George Bowering published two volumes of his non-fiction prose, essays that are difficult to categorize ranging from meditation to criticism: *Craft slices* (1985) and *Imaginary hand* (1988). A third book, *Errata* (1988), is a series of brief *aperçus* that move close to prose poems.

As well, several important collections of letters have appeared, including *Dear Marian, dear Hugh: the MacLennan-Engel correspondence* (1995), edited by Chrystl Verduyn, and Erin MOURÉ's and Bronwen Wallace's exchange in *Two women talking: correspondence, 1985-87*

(1993). The increasing attention critics are paying to life-writing makes the three collections of Al PURDY's correspondence—*The Bukowski/Purdy letters, 1964-1974* (1983) edited by Seamus Cooney; *The Purdy-Woodcock letters* (1988) edited by George Galt; and *Margaret Laurence—Al Purdy: a friendship in letters* (1993) edited by John Lennox—of particular interest because for each correspondence Purdy seems to assume a different persona.

6(i). Canadian critics continued to focus on genre. As we have seen, critical considerations of fiction have been plentiful during this period. Other important studies of fiction are David Williams' *Confessional fictions: a portrait of the artist in the Canadian novel* (1991), Karen Smythe's *Figuring grief: Gallant, Munro, and the poetics of elegy* (1992), and Glenn Deer's *Postmodern Canadian fiction and the rhetoric of authority* (1994). During this period John Moss completed *Present tense* (1985), the last of his four-volume collection of essays on the Canadian novel.

Poetry has had less attention, although D.M.R. Bentley, through his journal *Canadian Poetry* and in his two major studies—*The gay]grey moose: essays on the ecologies and mythologies of Canadian poetry, 1690-1990* (1992) and *Mimic fires: accounts of early long poems on Canada* (1994)—maintained a critical engagement with Canadian poetry, as has Kamboureli in her volume on the contemporary long poem (see above). Other critics (see throughout) have also considered poetry by looking at individual poets. For other critical approaches to genre, see also David Ketterer's *Canadian science fiction and fantasy* (1992), and *Out of this world: Canadian science fiction and fantasy literature* (1995), compiled by Andrea Paradis.

6(j). Early Canadian literature has also been an area of critical activity. Besides Bentley's work and Stan Dragland's book on D.C. Scott, critical and biographical studies of single authors include Lorraine McMullen's *An odd attempt in a woman: the literary life of Frances Brooke* (1983); Marian Fowler's *Redney: a life of Sara Jeannette Duncan* (1983); Muriel Miller's *Bliss Carman: quest and revolt* (1985); John Coldwell's *Sir Charles god damn: the life of Charles G.D. Roberts* (1986); Misao Dean's *A different point of view: Sara Jeannette Duncan* (1991); Paul Hjartarson, ed., *A stranger to my time: essays by and about Frederick Philip Grove* (1986); a collection on John RICHARDSON, *Recovering Canada's first novelist* (1984), edited by Catherine Sheldrick Ross; John Hurley's *The borders of nightmare: the fiction of John Richardson* (1992); and Dennis Duffy's *A world under sentence: John Richardson and the interior* (1996).

The topic of gender is also important to studies of earlier writing. Of particular significance are three titles. *Rediscovering our foremothers: nineteenth-century Canadian women writers* (1990), edited by Lorraine McMullen, is an early conference proceedings on this subject. Elizabeth Thompson's *The pioneer woman: a Canadian character type* (1991) deals with the fiction and non-fiction of Catharine Parr TRAILL, and the portrayal of pioneer women in the works of Sara Jeannette Duncan, Ralph Connor (Charles W. GORDON), and Margaret Laurence. Carrie MacMillan, Lorraine McMullen, and Elizabeth Waterson's *Silenced sextet: six nineteenth-century Canadian women novelists* (1992) looks at the writing of Rosanna Mullins LEPROHON, May Agnes FLEMING, Margaret Murray ROBERTSON, Susie Frances HARRISON, Margaret Marshall SAUNDERS, and Joanna E. WOOD.

Broader considerations of early writing include James Doyle's two volumes dealing with Canada and America—*North of America: images of Canada in the literature of the United States, 1775-1900* (1983) and his biography *The fin de siècle spirit: Walter Blackburn Harte and the American/Canadian literary milieu of the 1890s* (1995), in which Harte's career is measured against that of Bliss Carman. Carole Gerson's useful and insightful study *A purer taste: the writing and reading of fiction in English in nineteenth-century Canada* (1989) provides a sense of the ways in which Canadian first read fiction. Scholarly collections of letters have helped to increase our understanding of nineteenth-century Canadian writers and their writing. Carl Ballstadt, Elizabeth Hopkins, and Michael Peterman have edited three important volumes: Susanna Moodie's *Letters of a lifetime* (1985); *Letters of love and duty: the correspondence of Susanna and John Moodie* (1993); and *Bless you in my heart: selected correspondence of Catharine Parr Traill* (1996). Also of interest is *The poet and the critic: a literary correspondence between D.C. Scott and E.K. Brown* (1983) edited by Robert L. McDougall.

Three important books serve as bridges between criticism of the past and that of the present: the conference proceedings, *Prefaces and literary manifestoes* (1990), edited by E.D. Blodgett and A.G. Purdy, in collaboration with S. Tötösy de Zepetnek; and the two-volume republication of early statements on literature, covering the years 1752 to 1983, *Towards a Canadian literature: essays, editorials and manifestos* (1984, 1985), edited by Douglas M. Daymond and Leslie G. Monkman.

6(k). The concept of literary 'period' in Canadian writing is just beginning to receive intense consideration by Canadian scholars. Although the question of whether Canada ever had a 'modernism' has previously been debated, and although critics have examined individual writers as modernists, Brian Trehearne's study *Aestheticism and the Canadian modernists* (1989) and Sherrill Grace's consideration of the role of symbolism in North America modernism (see above) take the question beyond speculative argument or implicit assumption. Trehearne and Grace both trace Canadian writers' relationships to particular European traditions. Like Trahearne's and Grace's books, Glenn Willmott's *McLuhan, or modernism in reverse* (1996) also places Canadian thinking within a larger context. (See Willmott's article 'The nature of modernism in [Sheila Watson's] *Deep hollow creek*', *Canadian Literature*, no. 146.) The question of postmodernism has had even more attention. Linda Hutcheon's book on Canadian postmodernism and her related study, *Splitting images: contemporary Canadian ironies* (1991), as well as works by Frank Davey, Glenn Deer, Caroline Bayard, and others have established a strong basis for defining Canadian postmodernism.

6(l). One of the oldest debates in Canadian criticism, the existence of a coherent national literature and identity, has continued in this period, despite the popularity of theories that emphasize fragmentation over wholeness, and despite the intensified emphasis on subgroup and regional identities. Late works were published by several of the figures who helped frame the construction of Canadian identity that was so important to 1960s criticism. Carl F. Klinck's memoir *Giving Canada a literary history* (1991) is an account of the production of the landmark *Literary history of Canada*. Northrop Frye—whose Conclusion to the *Literary history* and whose early essays on Canadian writing (collected in *The bush garden*) shaped this literary nationalist dialogue—published his later essays on the topic in *Divisions on a ground: essays on Canadian culture* (1985). There he suggested that Canada was now moving into a post-national era. In 1986 Malcolm Ross, another influential important early voice and shaper of the canon, brought together his essays in *The impossible sum of our traditions*.

Though her work is also informed by structuralist methodology, Gaile McGregor, in *The Wacousta syndrome: explorations in the Canadian langscape* (1985), continues the Frye tradition in her attempt to detect large patterns of the collective Canadian consciousness through thematic comparisons of literary works, identifying types and narratives as manifestations of national traits. (Margaret Atwood, in *Strange things: the malevolent North in Canadian literature*, 1995, also continues Frye's approach, looking at the effect on Canadian writing of narratives and myths concerning the North.) Russell Brown takes another approach to theme and its relation to nation. In his essays, and in *Borderlines and borderlands in English Canada: the written line* (1990), he argues that narrative patterns and concepts do not carry specific meanings but are rather building blocks that writers and readers use to shape their own construction of the culture around them; thus, while no individual work employs a theme in the same way as another, certain themes are particularly useful to national (and subnational) groups of writers and readers. Connecting Canadian poets to tradition, landscape, and intellectual history, D.M.R. Bentley's *The gay]grey moose*, a thoughtful and widely informed work, also shows that the discovery of overarching patterns does not preclude sensitivity to the uniqueness of individual texts. And despite their poststructuralist sympathies, a sense of large national patterns runs through Kroetsch's *The lovely treachery of words* (1989) and Hutcheon's *Splitting images* (1991). The most recent attempt to read a coherent set of Canadian values in Canadian literary works may be seen in the comparative study *Nationalism and literature: the politics of culture in Canada and the United States* (1997) by the American scholar Sarah M. Corse, who, like Gaile McGregor, is a sociologist.

The possibility of discussing a coherent Canadian literary tradition and analysing works in that context continued to be assumed by many critics, such as William New, in his *History of Canadian literature* (1989), and W.J. Keith, whose wide-ranging discussions of Canadian writers—grounded in mid-century British 'practical criticism'—may be found in *A sense of style: studies in the art of fiction in English-speaking Canada* (1989) and *An independent stance: essays on English-Canadian criticism and fiction* (1991).

At the same time, anti-nationalist voices—often grounded in deconstructive theory and shaped by social subgroup and regional identities—have made themselves strongly heard. John METCALF, whose sensibilities derive from a British sense of modernism and who has cast himself in the role of cultural gadfly, published two essay collections that attack what he perceives as unexamined pieties about the Canadian literary tradition. In *What is a Canadian literature?* (1988) and *Freedom from culture: selected essays, 1982-1992* (1993), Metcalf argues against government funding for the arts, and against the idea that Canadian writing has unique characteristics, other than its tradition of funding. As suggested previously, many critics arguing from a postcolonial position also distrust unitary versions of Canadian identity, or seek to redefine Canadian characteristics as those traits common to the immigrant experience. Various westerners, many of whom were frequently associated with the journal *Open Letter*, have also taken an anti-nationalist position. Their strongest spokesman has been Frank Davey, whose *Post-national arguments: the politics of the anglophone-Canadian novel since 1967* (1993) contends that the reading of national identity out of fiction at any time in the last thirty years has been a misreading, because Canadian novels are both transnational and skeptical about effective social structures at a national level. Robert Lecker has played an ambivalent role in this debate. Perceived as an anti-nationalist when he argued that the Canadian canon needed deconstructing (in an essay originally published in *Critical Inquiry* 16, Spring 1990, with a response by Davey that produced an ongoing critical debate between the two), Lecker subsequently supplemented that essay with others in a volume called *Making it real: the canonization of English-Canadian literature* (1995), in which he argues for the value of having a canon, and calls for a development of a Canadian criticism in which critics could once again play the role of public intellectuals. *Canadian canons: essays in literary value* (1991), edited by Lecker, provides a larger and valuable context for this discussion.

6(m). A few critics have focused on the relationship between literature and other arts. See, in particular, Lorraine York's *'The other side of dailiness': photography in the works of Alice Munro, Timothy Findley, Michael Ondaatje, and Margaret Laurence* (1988); David Williams' *Confessional fictions* (mentioned above); and Linda Hutcheon's *Double-talking: essays on verbal and visual ironies in contemporary Canadian art and literature* (1992).

6(n). Criticism as its own subject has become an important topic: a discourse that not only shapes both the canon and the reader's understanding of Canadian literature, but has also influenced large patterns of thought. W.J. Keith in *An independent stance* defends and demonstrates the efficacy of employing British practical criticism to any effort to understand Canadian culture and literature. Frank Davey has published two books whose primary focus is on criticism. In many of the essays that constitute *Reading Canadian reading* (1988), he looks retrospectively at his own critical writing and its reception, and at the publishing environment, as contexts for understanding contemporary Canadian writing and criticism, while in *Canadian literary power* he examines the role of criticism in its shaping perceptions not only of literary writing but of the larger culture as well. Robert Lecker in *Making it real* is concerned with the responsibilities of the critic as a maker of the canon and as an influence on the larger national community. The collection *100 years of critical solitudes: Canadian and Québécois criticism from the 1880s to the 1980s* (1992), edited by Caroline Bayard, looks at the history of various critical approaches in Canadian criticism. Individual critics have also been treated in extended studies. See, for example, the following biographical studies: *William Arthur Deacon: a Canadian literary life* (1982) by Clara Thomas and John Lennox (1982); Laura Groening's volume on E.K. BROWN, *A study in conflict* (1994) and John Ayres' *Northrop Frye: a biography* (1989). Several of the book-length discussions and collections of essays on Northrop Frye's criticism—such as *Centre and labyrinth: essays in honour of Northrop Frye* (1983), edited by Eleanor Cook *et al.*, and *The legacy of Northrop Frye* (1991), edited by Alvin A. Lee and Robert D. Denham—include discussions of his influence on Canadian writing and criticism.

6(o). Although not criticism as such, the history, institutional structure, and sociology of publishing have concerned literary scholars. Carl Spadoni and Judy Donnelly's *A bibliography of McClelland and Stewart imprints, 1909-1985* (1994) provides a record of the contributions of this publishing house to the development of Canadian literature. Of related interest are Ken Norris's *The little magazine in Canada, 1925-80* (1984), a survey of the role of little magazines in the development of modernism and postmodernism in Canadian poetry, and Maria TIPPETT's *Making culture: English-Canadian institutions and the arts before the Massey Commission* (1991). Perhaps the most extensive effort to record the interrelationships of literature, publishing, and criticism is a project of the University of Alberta's Research Institute for Comparative Literature. In the 1980s, under the leadership of E.D. Blodgett and A.G. Purdy, a series of colloquia (the proceedings of which were subsequently published) attempted to document the history of the literary institutions of

Canada: see above, *Literatures of lesser diffusion* and *Prefaces and literary manifestoes*.

DONNA BENNETT

Criticism in French. The beginning of genuine French literary criticism in Canada coincides with the dawn of the twentieth century. It took more than a hundred years of patient development for French-Canadian society to acquire a fledgling literary establishment, complete with its first critic, Camille Roy (1870-1943). Roy's many publications constitute the inaugural manifestations of a genre that we understand today as literary criticism.

1. THE NINETEENTH CENTURY. Clerical criticism—a non-critical criticism, a kind of historic impressionism, at once serious but often too kind, always polite and ceremonious and, while concerned about the collective future, more anxious to set incorrect terms and texts straight than to consider drab or threadbare expression—dominated almost the entire century, leaving not much room for current aesthetic preoccupations. This was the period when Québécois called themselves Canadiens, when the Church loomed all-powerful, and when Canadiens were busy reinstating (after the English Conquest of 1760) history and reality.

Camille Roy was preceded by several sporadic chroniclers such as Valentin Jautard (?-1785?), who was known as the 'spectateur tranquille' of *La Gazette de Montréal* (1778); by gifted dilettantes, of whom André-Romuald Cherrier (1821-63) is an example; and by talented promoters, such as Henri-Raymond CASGRAIN. The latter, a Catholic priest and a polymath by taste and interest, was the great animator of the MOUVEMENT LITTÉRAIRE DE QUÉBEC around 1860, and one of the founding fathers of the francophone literary establishment. At his instigation criticism, along with other productions, blossomed following the discovery of a collective destiny that had been forged in the crucible of a feverishly active press (mainly periodical and retrospective). Casgrain set the tone right up to the ultramontane excesses at the close of the century: literature was to be Catholic, conservative, and 'clericaliste'. Accordingly criticism was a kind of national service, obliging in tone and content. Objective criticism was no more possible than were realistic and naturalistic works of fiction. Other typical and historical consequences of this context—criticism's lack of continuity, its superficial nature, and its mosaic quality—were all due to the medium used: chronicles are not syntheses. Above all, criticism's development depended upon the growth and spread of fiction.

Against this background it is not surprising that Monseigneur Camille Roy emerged as the 'father of French-Canadian criticism'. A doctor of philosophy and former student at the Sorbonne and the Institut Catholique de Paris, he was very prolific, producing some twenty works, one being dedicated to his forerunner, Casgrain. Roy's *Manuel d'histoire de la littérature canadienne-française* (1918) remained unchallenged long after his death. In this charitable, painstakingly dedicated work, Roy relayed the best of Casgrain, practising a style of critical discourse that rarely strayed from mere compilation. Nevertheless Roy did not forget his French masters Brunetière, Faguet, and Lanson, as is readily apparent in his collected lectures, *La critique littéraire au XIXe siècle, de Mme de Stael à Emile Faguet* (1918).

2. 1934 TO 1962. The heritage of clerical criticism continued to define the horizon into the 1930s—until the inevitable economic crisis that followed industrialization and urbanization gave birth to a new and modern attitude. Signs of change, however, were already visible in the twenties; and even prior to that (1914) in the writing of the defrocked Louis Dantin (Eugène SEERS) in his Boston refuge, and Marcel DUGAS in Paris, leader of the 'exotistes' (historical enemies of the regionalists)—both defenders of aesthetic values who were thus seen as undermining the clericalist message and its chauvinistic reduction.

But especially important to the new look of the thirties was the group of young intellectuals self-acclaimed as 'La Relève' (literally 'the relief crew'); *La RELÈVE* was also the name of their monthly periodical dedicated to philosophy, religion, and literature. This journal began publishing in 1934, the same year that saw publication of the famous novel *Les demi-civilisés* by Jean-Charles HARVEY, who is also remembered as an essayist and critic (*Pages de critique*, 1926). Among *La Relève's* founders were Robert CHARBONNEAU, who later became director of the 'Service des textes' for Radio-Canada; and Jean LE MOYNE, later chief editor of the literary section of *Le Canada*. Other important critics were Guy Sylvestre (b. 1918), founder of the periodical *Les Gants du ciel* (1943-6), who went on to become national librarian; and Roger Duhamel (b. 1916), Queen's Printer from 1960 to 1969. Many of these writers, whether from *La Relève* or other periodicals, were formed by the famous 'ratio studiorum' of the Collèges Jean-de-Brébeuf and Sainte-

Marie in Montreal: as students of the Jesuits they did not exactly follow Camille Roy, but instead were influenced by Emmanuel Mounier (1905-50) and his Parisian review *Esprit* (1932)—and by Maritain, Péguy, Mauriac, and Bernanos. This background helps to explain the group's critical distance and uncompromising attitude: as if from a tower, they had a point of view that foreshortened the regionalist scene below, where so many of their elders—and even some contemporary writers—still roamed, combat-weary. They rose above the fighting by means of the attention they gave to the individual quest apparent in the new writers and their works. *La Relève*'s gifted poet of free verse, Hector de SAINT-DENYS-GARNEAU, was an exemplary figure for the group in that his poetry reflected the Catholic, metaphysical, Bernanosian, and Mauriacian restlessness that tended to inflect traditional clerical discourse. But above all this group dedicated itself to studies of modern forms of writing. And even though the first issue of *La Relève* appeared on 15 Mar. 1934—Annunciation Day—the work of the journal secularized theology. All these characteristics left an imprint on works of imagination by members of the group, as well as on their criticism of contemporary literature, which in their view was mainly French. Some of these writers went beyond reviews and published essays, such as Charbonneau with *Connaissance du personnage* (1944) and the posthumous *Romanciers canadiens* (1972). *La Relève*—rebaptized *La Nouvelle Relève* in 1941 —lasted until 1948, by which time the people involved with it were so firmly established in the various media (they were influential for twenty years to come) that the journal was no longer needed.

After being founded in 1950, *Cité libre*—obviously conserving *La Relève*'s main reference points but shedding its literary pretensions—carried on the task of renewal. Its humanist and universalist writers attacked both nationalism and clericalism and set their sights on the political arena, as is shown in the careers of two members of its editorial board: Gérard Pelletier, who became a cabinet minister, and Pierre Elliott Trudeau, later prime minister. More important still were those who were fervent enemies of ecclesiastical power —the automatiste painters and poets who signed the *REFUS GLOBAL* (1948) of Paul-Émile Borduas (1905-60). The *Relève* group quickly engaged in a dialogue with these surrealist writers, asking for an 'ordre nouveau'—while keeping their faith and despising anarchy. But the automatistes' influence was long-lasting, especially among some writers published by Gaston MIRON's Éditions de l'Hexagone (1953-), and among the founders of *LIBERTÉ*.

Meanwhile academic circles kept their distance from reviews and journals. Camille Roy, founder of Quebec studies ('Études canadiennes') at Université Laval, had no important disciples. In the 1940s important studies on nineteenth- and twentieth-century writing were carried out at the Université d'Ottawa, where Séraphin Marion (b. 1896) produced *Les lettres canadiennes d'autrefois* (9 vols, 1939-58) and David Hayne (b. 1921) 'The historical novel and French Canada' (doctoral thesis, 1945). Serious research continued with Auguste Viatte's *Histoire de la littérature française des origines à 1950* (1954); Samuel Baillargeon's *Littérature canadienne-française* (1957); and Gérard BESSETTE's *Les images en poésie canadienne-française* (1960).

As the 1960s were ushered in, literary criticism progressively addressed modern concerns, particularly aesthetic ones, though it was still somewhat dependent on religious and primalistic traditions, and still trying to come to terms with forties' novels of social realism by such writers as Ringuet (Philippe PANNETON), Gabrielle ROY, and Roger LEMELIN. Periodical criticism, so often confined to biographical or moral considerations, was directed towards sociological analysis, necessary to the understanding of realistic fiction. Notable among these sociological 'amateurs' was Guy Sylvestre, author of *Panorama des lettres canadiennes-françaises* (1964). The young (25-year-old) friend of *La Relève*'s elders, Gilles MARCOTTE, began writing for *Le Devoir* in 1950, giving precise attention to the literary text, its narrative structure, and its social aim or value. Like the contributions of Pierre de Grandpré (b. 1920), such criticism was not highly specialized, and the scope was bounded mainly by writing elsewhere.

At this time, when television was being introduced in Canada (1952), Quebec criticism was refined and about to mature: while still maintaining its clerical connection (though casting aside the consecrating or polemical tone), it was becoming secularized, more demanding, modern. This period, however, produced no definitive synthesis or thorough work: critics were still questioning the mere fact of Quebec literature, as had been the practice since the nineteenth century. They were somewhat awed by the emergence of Quebec's 'parole' and by the media structure. Riveted to the moment in Quebec, and only slightly moved by theory, they were nevertheless well informed on current events in France and elsewhere.

3. 1962 TO 1982. In considering this phase, several social and historical facts should be recalled: the atmosphere of the sixties in particular; widespread political reforms; left-wing nationalism; the rise of unions; changing moral values; and finally the new liberalism of a society that invested more in the state than in the Church—which was gradually being abandoned by great masses of the population and by so many of its own priests. In these years of 'quiet revolution', the well-worn path of clerical and traditional discourse faded from view. This period is described in the title of Gérard Bessette's *Une littérature en ébullition* (1968), containing essays on Claude-Henri GRIGNON, Anne HÉBERT, Émile NELLIGAN, Gabrielle Roy, and Yves THÉRIAULT.

The predominant 'amateurs' decided to give the critical edifice a thorough house-cleaning, sorting out their articles and preserving only the best. Jean Le Moyne's *Convergences* (1961) was a true flower of *La Relève*'s philosophical, religious, and literary ideas. Other important critical works of the period were Pierre de Grandpré's *Dix ans de vie littéraire au Canada français* (1966); Maurice Blain's *Approximations* (1967); Gilles Marcotte's *Une littérature qui se fait* (1962); and Jean ÉTHIER-BLAIS's *Signets* (vols 1 and 2, 1967; vol. 3, 1973). A few critics remained true to tradition, despite the excitement, as Roger Duhamel illustrated in *Aux sources du romantisme français* (1964); but in general the cry was 'Let's take stock!' Marcotte's *Présence de la critique* (1966), an anthology of representative articles from 1941 to 1965, gave the last word to André BROCHU: Marcotte appointed him the new generation's spokesman. Brochu's *La littérature par elle-même* (1962) was unquestionably a reliable guide for the era, with its autarkical title so like that of Marcotte (*Une littérature qui se fait*). In his introduction, Brochu made an appeal to history and to a 'devenir concret', opposing Marx and Sartre on the one hand and St Thomas Aquinas on the other. This young critic also called for coherence and commitment to end the reign of 'amateurs'. His appeal bore fruit in 1963, with the appearance of *PARTI PRIS*, a literary and political periodical that set the tone for an entire new generation of writers and critics. 'Laïcité', 'indépendance', and 'socialisme' were the word-wedges that broke up old roads and routines and pointed the way towards another *Refus global* instead of another *Relève*. When *parti pris* expired in 1968, most of its literary contributors were integrated into the academic structure, where they frequently followed the new French criticism. As critical works by 'amateurs' declined, university criticism came into being.

Obviously academics had been preparing the ground beforehand. A group of scholars, working under the guidance of Paul Wyczynski, had been busy at the Centre de recherche en civilisation canadienne-française, Université d'Ottawa, whence came many basic studies, among them the series *Archives des lettres canadiennes* (4 vols, 1961, 1963, 1965, 1975), which provided new and pertinent data on literary history. Those who remained unsure about the existence of Quebec literature found many of their doubts removed by the depth and quality of these studies. In addition, works coming out of Université Laval were proving to be fundamental: for example, a special issue ('Littérature et société canadienne-française') of Jean-Charles Falardeau and Fernand DUMONT's journal *Recherches sociographiques* (1964) constituted what can now be viewed as a cultural event. Meanwhile at the Université de Montréal, Ernest Gagnon (1905-78), author of *L'homme d'ici* (1952), *Albert Le Grand* (1916-76), and younger professors such as Laurent Mailhot (b. 1931), Réginald Hamel (b. 1931), André Brochu, and others continue to define Quebec studies.

Another example of the scholarly vitality of the sixties is to be found in the rise of basic journals: *Livres et auteurs canadiens* (changed to '*québécois*' in 1969) founded in 1961; *Études françaises* (Université de Montréal) in 1963; *VOIX ET IMAGES* (Université du Québec à Montréal) in 1967; and *Études littéraires* (Laval) in 1968. Finally, manuals and literary histories became numerous: *Histoire de la littérature canadienne-française* (1960) by Gérard Tougas; *Manuel de littérature canadienne-française* (1967) by Roger Duhamel; *Histoire de la littérature canadienne-française par les textes* (1968) by Gérard Bessette, Lucien Gélin, and Charles Parent, and Pierre de Grandpré's *Histoire de la littérature française du Québec* (4 vols, 1967-9). One should also mention the many essays and monographs appearing during this period. Their number was proportional to the widespread social evolution that characterized Quebec society, and to the increased subsidies granted by the CANADA COUNCIL after 1957. The number of critical essays doubled from 1961 to 1965, tripled from then to 1970, and hovered near fifty or so in 1980—an expansion that reflected the giant strides made in the production of works of the Quebec imagination: Quebec songs increased tenfold, becoming a veritable repertoire of popular poetry; works by novelists doubled in number—and so on.

Literary criticism in the 1960s, contained within a French-oriented range, thus appeared diversified: hermeneutical and structuralist tools were being widely used in the reading of Quebec's nationalistic representation—the only remaining thread of a time-honoured tradition. Such approaches were generally maintained during the seventies—a decade that saw, however, the gradual attenuation of the nationalist point of view. The *parti pris* generation laid claim to French literature, publishing many essays on French authors: *Henri Bosco: une poétique du mystère* (1968) by Jean-Cléo Godin; *Albert Camus; ou L'imagination du désert* (1968) by Laurent Mailhot; *Flaubert; ou L'architecture du vide* (1972) by Jean-Pierre Duquette; *Hugo, amour, crime, révolution* (1974) by André Brochu; *Mallarmé, grammaire générative des contes indiens* (1975) by Guy Leflèche; and *Zola, le chiffre du texte* (1978) by Jacques Allard. These works obviously raised several questions. What were these critics, also read for their studies in Quebec literature, out to prove? Were they simply asserting their claim to 'universal' literature? Were they seeking a larger audience? Were they dissatisfied with the confines of a 'village voice'? Were they staking their claim on literature of the 'motherland'? Or, more ambitious still, were they giving form and substance to a Quebec discourse on 'other' literature?

Another remarkable feature of this period is to be found in the publication of anthologies and many useful reference works, including those of the 'companion' sort: *Dictionnaire des oeuvres littéraires du Québec* (3 vols, 1979, 1980, 1982) by Maurice Lemire; *Dictionnaire pratique des auteurs québécois* (1967) by Réginald Hamel, John Hare, and Paul Wyczynski; *Anthologie de la littérature québécoise* (4 vols, 1978-80) by Gilles Marcotte et al.; *Théâtre québécois* (2 vols, 1970, 1980) by Jean-Cléo Godin and Laurent Mailhot; *La littérature québécoise* (1974; rpr. 1997) by Laurent Mailhot; *La poésie québécoise des origines à nos jours* (1980) by Mailhot and Pierre Nepveu; and the periodical *Histoire littéraire du Québec et du Canada français* edited by René Dionne.

Important general studies on poetry included *Les mots à l'écoute* (1979) by Pierre Nepveu, on Fernand OUELLETTE, Gaston MIRON, and Paul-Marie LAPOINTE, and *Poésie des frontières—études comparées des poésies canadienne et québécois* (1979) by Clément Moisan. Similar work appeared on the novel, such as *Le roman à l'imparfait* (1976) by Gilles Marcotte and *Le romancier fictif* (1980) by André Belleau. Publications of criticism became almost too numerous. In 1978—an exceptional year—there appeared a hundred essays of diverse kinds. On criticism itself, the most important was *La littérature et le reste* (1980) by André Brochu and Gilles Marcotte, an epistolary volume by two authors who were representative of a historical shift in Quebec criticism from a rather journalistic level to scholarly standing, in which the historical, sociological, psychoanalytical (pioneered by Gérard Bessette), and semiotic fields predominated up to 1980.

4. BIBLIOGRAPHY. The titles that follow are a selection of important critical writings not mentioned above: Jean-Charles Falardeau, *Notre société et son roman* (1967) and *Imaginaire social et littérature* (1974); Gérard Bessette, *Trois romanciers québécois* (1973) containing studies of Victor-Lévy BEAULIEU, André LANGEVIN, and Gabrielle Roy; André Brochu, *L'instance critique 1961-1973* (1974); D.M. Hayne, *Bibliographie analytique de la critique littéraire au Québec* (1981); Ben-Zion Shek, *Social realism in the French-Canadian novel* (1977); Jacques Allard, 'Les lettres québécoises depuis 1930', *University of Toronto Quarterly*, vol. 50, no. 1 (1980); and Ben-Z. Shek, *French-Canadian and Québécois novels* (1991) in Oxford's Perspectives on Canadian Culture series. See also *Contemporary Quebec criticism* (1979) edited and translated by Larry Shouldice.

5. 1983 TO 1996. Critical writing in this period has confirmed the trends remarked on, along with the sovereignty of a literature that is now strong in every genre, of which criticism is not the least. In the great many critical works and essays that have been published, one first notices the end of structuralism and the return of historical criticism; the increase in critical editions of individual works, and in feminist criticism; and the evolution of the scholarly critic (though journalistic reviewing of a high order continues). Towards the end of the century one wonders if context has become more important than text (which is sometimes treated as merely a 'product'), and if criticism has become more important than creation. This alarming possibility would have been most agreeable to Camille Roy and our clerical tradition!

6. BIBLIOGRAPHY. See David M. Hayne, *Bibliographie analytique de la critique littéraire au Québec* (1981); Patricia Smart, *Écrire dans la maison du père: l'émergence du féminin dans la tradition littéraire du Québec* (1988); Jacques Allard, *Traverses/De la critique littéraire au Québec* (1991); Annette Hayward and Agnès Witfield, eds, *La critique littéraire québécoise* (1992); Lori

Saint-Martin, *L'autre lecture* (1992); Claude Duchet and Stéphanie Vachon, eds, *La recherche littéraire. Objets et méthodes* (1993); Nicole Fortin, *Une littérature inventée: littérature québécoise et critique universitaire* (1994); and Joseph Melançon, *Le discours de l'université sur la littérature québécoise* (1996).

JACQUES ALLARD

Crozier, Lorna (b. 1941). Born and raised in Swift Current, Saskatchewan, Crozier earned a B.A. from the University of Saskatchewan in 1969. She married a high-school chemistry teacher, completed a teaching certificate and returned to Swift Current. Under her married name, Uher, she taught high-school English. Her first poem was published in *GRAIN* in 1974. She then published two collections of poetry—*Inside is the sky* (1976) and *Crow's black joy* (1978)—before joining the poet Patrick LANE in 1978 and completing an M.A. in English at the University of Alberta —her thesis being a collection of poems, *Humans and other beasts* (1980). *No longer two people* (1979), containing poems by both Uher and Lane, announced their creative and personal partnership and functioned as a turning-point in Crozier's feminist poetics.

Between 1977 and 1982 Crozier taught at the Saskatchewan Summer School of the Arts, and co-edited an anthology of Saskatchewan poetry with Gary Hyland (*A sudden radiance*, 1987)—indications of her commitment to that region's writing community. But just as Crozier's reputation as a Prairie poet was firmly established, she began to move around the country so that Lane, and later she herself, could take up positions as writers in residence. They eventually settled in Saanichton, British Columbia, in 1991, when Crozier took up a full-time faculty position in the Creative Writing Department of the University of Victoria. In 1995 she and Patrick Lane edited a collection of poetry by young writers called *Breathing fire*.

The weather (1981) was a watershed publication for Crozier. Dedicated to her family, whose name she 'reclaimed' and used for this and subsequent collections, it extended the range and tone of Crozier's poetry and displayed her increasing control and versatility. Most notably, although there were glimmers of a characteristically anecdotal voice in *Humans and other beasts* (as in 'This one's for you'), what Dennis LEE calls the 'literate vernacular' established itself more fully here, as in such poems as 'Spring Storm 1916'. *The garden going on without us* (1985), new and selected poems, and her subsequent collection, *Angels of flesh, angels of silence* (1989), were nominated for a Governor General's Award—which she won for *Inventing the hawk* (1992). Crozier's *Everything arrives at the light* (1995) includes a sequence of ghazals (a form of Oriental lyric poetry) that had been published in a chapbook, *Eyewitness* (1993). *A saving grace: the collected poems of Mrs. Bentley* (1966) is an imaginative and moving evocation of the narrator of Sinclair ROSS's *As for me and my house.*

There is an apparent paradox at the heart of Crozier's *oeuvre*: although seemingly grounded in daily life, it increasingly gestures towards a world of myth and magic that lies both within and beyond that everyday world. Its central images (bread, hands, light, prairie, and sky), and figures (messenger angel, snake, horse, child, and fisherman), appear at the intersection of these two planes, in garden and prairie settings that are more figurative than earthly. In an ongoing project of feminist remythification, Crozier challenges inherited myths by allowing a silent female character to tell her side of the story. For example, 'On the seventh day' (*Inventing the hawk*) retells the Creation story from the engagingly down-to-earth perspective of God's wife and combines humour with a distinctly feminist frame of reference (crucial to Crozier's aesthetic, and perhaps most apparent in *No longer two people*). Bitingly funny, as in 'the sex lives of vegetables' (a series animating garden vegetables in *The garden going on without us*) and 'the penis poems' (in *Angels of flesh*), politically engaged (as in the challenge to Pinochet's regime in the Chilean sequence), and evocatively personal (as in the elegiac poems for the speaker's father in *Inventing the hawk*), Crozier's poetry has been praised for its range of voice, tone, and subject matter, and above all for its craftsmanship, humour, and accessibility.

There is an interesting commentary by Crozier on her own poetics, 'Searching for the poem', in *Waves* 14.1-2 (1985): 82-3.

NATHALIE COOKE

Culleton, Beatrice. See ABORIGINAL LITERATURE: 4. and NOVELS IN ENGLISH 1983 TO 1996.

Cummins, John Swete. See *ALTHAM: A TALE OF THE SEA*.

Cumyn, Alan. See NOVELS IN ENGLISH 1983 TO 1996: OTHER NOVELS 2(b).

Curtis, Herb. See Writing in the MARITIMES: 5.

Curtis, Wayne. See Writing in the MARITIMES: 5.

Curwood, James Oliver. See FOREIGN WRITERS ON CANADA IN ENGLISH: 2.

Curzon, Sarah Anne (1833-98). Born in Birmingham, England, the daughter of an affluent manufacturer, George Phillips Vincent, she received a private education and contributed prose and verse to various family periodicals during her childhood and youth. She married Robert Curzon of Norfolk in 1858 and immigrated with him to Toronto in 1862. Her Canadian literary career included contributions of verse, essays, and fiction to the *Canadian Monthly*, the *Dominion Illustrated*, *GRIP*, *The WEEK*, *Evangelical Churchman*, and the *Canadian Magazine*. She also published women's-suffrage articles in British and American newspapers, and was a founding member in Nov. 1876 of the Toronto Women's Literary Club, which was based on the model of the American Society for the Advancement of Women. After her husband's death in 1878, she supported herself as a freelance journalist. In 1881 she was appointed associate editor of the *Canada Citizen*, the first Canadian prohibitionist paper, writing a regular column on women's suffrage. She is best known for her verse drama *Laura Secord, the heroine of 1812* (1887), a sentimental paean to Laura Secord's heroism in the War of 1812. Curzon's only other play, *The sweet girl graduate* (published in the periodical *Grip-Sack* in 1882), deals with the topical issue of women's higher education; it contributed to the passing of an Order-in-Council on 2 Oct. 1884 admitting women to University College, Toronto.

Laura Secord and *The sweet girl graduate* are reprinted in *Women pioneers*, vol. 2 of *Canada's lost plays* (1979), edited by Anton Wagner.

ROTA HERZBERG LISTER

D

Dabydeen, Cyril. See CARIBBEAN-CANADIAN LITERATURE.

Daigle, France. See ACADIAN LITERATURE: 3(c).

Daigle, Jean. See DRAMA IN FRENCH 1948 TO 1981: 4.

D'Alfonso, Antonio (b. 1953). Born in Montreal, Quebec, to parents from Molise, Italy, he obtained a B.A. and an M.S. in Communication Studies at Loyola College and the Université de Montréal. He has published books in both French and English, is a literary critic for both French and English magazines across Canada, and is a theorist of ethnic literature. He also is a publisher and an editor, having founded GUERNICA EDITIONS in 1978. His iconoclasm and commitment to new ways of seeing reality are evident in his creative and critical texts.

In *The other shore* (1986) and *Panick love* (1992)—collections of poetry that were first published in French—D'Alfonso explores the problems of living in several cultural environments, suggesting that change and contradiction embody ethnic subjectivity. In *The other shore*, a darkly passionate poetic figure meditates on the effects of cultural dislocation, questioning the success of immigration, and balances his admiration for Italy with a criticism of its social divisions. Intense personal experience is interwoven with an ethnic community's anxiety and yearning. In *Panick love* the eroticism and treachery of love are connected to the poet's view of the beauty and inaccessibility of Parisian society and to his own ambivalence towards Italian and Québécois cultures. Dream, passion, delirium, and alienation commingle, creating a world in which illusion is inseparable from reality. Both collections present a tortured and ongoing journey to self-discovery, unfulfilled sexual desire, and an open-ended life process. These motifs recur in the novel *Fabrizio's passion* (1995), which was also first published in French. Its realistic portrayal of an Italian family in Montreal is imbued with nightmarish elements that capture the problems of immigration and assimilation. D'Alfonso's books, which have a postmodern quality and defy standard expectations about closure, play with various forms that cut across genres, transgress aesthetic boundaries, and generate multiple, interconnecting themes.

This multi-faceted mode of writing is itself emblematic of the complexities of ethnicity. As D'Alfonso states in his critical work *In italics: in defense of ethnicity* (1996), minority writing is not about defining territory but about cultural processes that inform social reality and Canadian literary production.

MARINO TUZI

Dalpé, Jean-Marc (b. 1957). Born in Ottawa, Ontario, he studied theatre in the 1970s at the Université d'Ottawa and at the Conservatoire d'art dramatique (Quebec City). While he was a student he acted in and directed shows produced in and around Montreal and Quebec City. In September 1979 he participated in the creation of a Rockland/Ottawa-based French-language theatre company, La Vieille 17. The co-founders of this Franco-Ontarian troupe were Robert Bellefeuille, Roch Castonguay, Lise Roy, and Dalpé. They all directed and acted in the early productions, including *Protégera nos foyers . . .* (unpublished), *J'ai au creux des mains une chanson* (unpublished), and a very popular evening of poetry and dramatic situations entitled *Les murs de nos villages* (1980). This show was co-written by Dalpé with Robert Bellefeuille, Hélène Bernier, Anne-Marie Cadieux, Roch Castonguay, Vivianne Rochon, and Lise Roy. It was produced by La Vieille 17 in Montreal and Ottawa several times between 1979 and 1981.

In 1981 Dalpé moved to Sudbury as artist-in-residence with the Théâtre du Nouvel Ontario. Once again he participated at all levels in all the productions, including three plays that toured francophone communities across Ontario: *Hawkesbury blues* (1982), *1932, La ville du nickel* (1984)—both were co-written with Brigitte Haentjens—and *Les Rogers* (1985), written in collaboration with Robert Bellefeuille and Robert Marinier. These plays were published in Sudbury by Les Éditions Prise de Parole, which from its inception in the 1970s played a particularly important role in the recognition of young Franco-Ontarian dramatists, publishing the plays of André Paiement in the 1970s and, throughout the 1980s, the works of Dalpé.

In 1987 Dalpé was appointed writer-in-residence at the Université d'Ottawa. In 1988 he was awarded a Governor General's Award for his powerful play *Le chien* (1987), which, like those that followed, is situated in northern Ontario, where the language of the rural working-class characters contains English words, regional expressions, and turns of phrase. Dalpé's language bears a surface resemblance to the JOUAL used by Michel TREMBLAY's urban, working-class characters, but Dalpé's remains distinctly Franco-Ontarian. On the other hand, his drama's use of such universal themes as hate, violence, bitterness, frustration, misery, and hoplessness touched a wide range of audiences when playing in Ontario, Quebec, and Manitoba. In 1988 the Théâtre du Nouvel Ontario and the Centre National des Arts co-produced *Le chien* throughout Quebec and Ontario. In 1989 it was also presented in Limoges, France, as part of the Festival international des Francophones. The English version, also called *Le chien*, was produced by Toronto's Factory Theatre in 1988.

In 1994 Dalpé's *Eddy* (1994) was produced in Montreal by the Nouvelle Compagnie Théâtrale; the English version, entitled *The ring*, translated by Robert Dickson, was performed at the Festival Theatre in Stratford, Ontario. Small-time boxers, ex-boxers, and boxing coaches are its colourful characters, who never give up hope of fame, fortune, and social acceptance. For *Lucky lady* (1995), which premièred in French at Montreal's Théâtre d'Aujourd'hui in 1996, Dalpé switched from boxing to horse racing and from rural Ontario to an industrial setting near Montreal. In these two plays, as in *Le chien*, he has created a complex network of memorable working-class characters who lead unfulfilled lives, but who never give up their struggle for something better.

ELAINE NARDOCCHIO

Daniells, Roy (1902-79). Born in London, England, he came with his family in 1910 to Victoria, British Columbia He became a school teacher, went on to the University of British Columbia, and then to the University of Toronto for graduate studies. He taught English at Victoria College, Toronto; at the University of Manitoba; and at UBC, where he became head of the English department in 1948. He retired in 1974. As a scholar he was chiefly interested in seventeenth-century English poetry: he published his major work, *Milton, mannerism and baroque*, in 1963. Throughout his career he wrote critical articles on, and reviews of, Canadian literature that showed his continuing concern for the development of an authentic Canadian voice. He received the Lorne PIERCE Medal in 1970 and was made a Companion of the Order of Canada in 1971.

As a poet Daniells used traditional forms, particularly sonnet sequences linked by a common persona or an underlying theme, such as a quest or journey. Technical skill, scrupulous phrasing, and a highly accomplished arrangement of effects, including dislocation and surprise, are always evident. Clearly attracted by the new 'metaphysical' poets of the 1920s and 1930s, Daniells drew upon symbol and myth for ironic and witty counterpoint to images from contemporary life. His scholarly work on seventeenth-century poets influenced his technique, as well as his religious and philosophical thought. Two sonnet sequences make up the major part of *Deeper into the forest* (1948). The 'Anthony' sequence centres on an ironic character, at the time of the Spanish Civil War, whose skepticism, rash impulses, and desire for action reflect that period's longing for belief and a sure cause. The twenty-one sonnets of the 'Forest' sequence are linked by the image of an emblematic forest drawn from folklore and legend, both frightening and enchanted. *The chequered shade* (1963) is also chiefly a collection of sonnets, arranged in three series. The first represents a pilgrimage across Europe by a travelling poet-humanist who is both vitally alive to landscape and works of art, and aware of the cruelties and triumphs of the past; the second group is a rewriting of Bible stories, psalms (some reminiscent of A.M. KLEIN's psalms of Abraham and David), and parables in which contemporary images and colloquial speech reflect the doubts and tensions of an individual seeking a lost faith. The third series, bringing the seeker back to Canada, asks insistently: What must the artist, the poet, do in this land and in this age?

Daniells also wrote *Alexander Mackenzie and the North West* (1969), a well-crafted biography for young people.

A brief autobiographical piece of unusual interest, 'Plymouth brother', was published posthumously in *CANADIAN LITERATURE* 90 (Autumn 1981). JOHN MARGESON

Danis, Daniel (b.1961). Born in Hull, Quebec, he resides in the Saguenay region. After studying theatre intermittently, he freelanced as producer and actor, simultaneously developing his artistic talents as sculptor and dramatist. The author of three staged plays, he has a budding international career, and has been hailed by critics as a distinctive new voice in Quebec drama.

A version of his first play, *Le gâchis*, was presented in reading format in 1991; a second version, *Statues de rien*, offered another perspective on the highly allusive text, and was given a reading later that year. It is the third version, *Celle-là* (1993), which received a Governor General's Award, and was singled out in competition ('Cartes Blanches'—Théâtre Ouvert, Paris) and by France Culture. It recounts elliptically a sordid tale of frustration and solitude, a struggle between the unquenchable thirst for life and the impulse towards death. The characters—the Mother (Celle-là), the Old Man, and the Son—irrevocably separated, draw on fragments of memory in soliloquies giving three versions of a drama that has already taken place. Juxtaposed, the fragments form a coherent theatrical poem of striking images.

Danis's second play, *Cendres de cailloux* (1992; translated by Linda Gaboriau as *Stone and ashes*, 1995; Governor General's Award, 1996), uses many of the same theatrical techniques: communication is between the characters and the public, for the solitude of each character cannot be altered. Four monologues interweave in a quartet, replaying a drama that ended before the curtain went up. The monologues tell a harrowing tale of suffering in a world of senseless and repeated tragedy. Although the play is non-linear and without psychological explanation, the characters are vivid, and the images form a coherent and powerfully lyrical poem. It was well launched before publication as a winning play in an international competition in Maubeuge (France), and was read at the Festival of Avignon (La Chartreuse) in the summer of 1992. It was also staged in Limoges during the Festival International des Francophonies en Limousin.

Danis's poetic images accumulate further in his third play, *Les nuages de terre* (unpublished), the first part of a projected trilogy, to be called *Le souffle de l'imparadis*. A fable, as yet incomplete, about an adolescent couple seeking to love freely, but fated to meet death, it was staged in 1994 at the Festival in Limoges as a Quebec/Ivory Coast co-production; and in Montreal in 1995 at the Festival des Amériques.

See Patricia Belzil, '*Celle-là*', *Jeu* 66 (1993); and Patricia Belzil, 'Le rituel de la vie', *Jeu* 70 (1994). See also DRAMA IN FRENCH: 1981 TO 1996: 2. BARBARA McEWEN

Dans un gant de fer (1965). This first of two books of memoirs by Claire MARTIN is both the record of a wretched childhood and a clear and devastating account of a society too long oppressed by the prohibitions and taboos of a crushing monolithism. The entire account is dominated by the menacing presence of the all-powerful father, who establishes a reign of terror and a complete lack of freedom in a home that is a microcosm of the oppressive climate of Quebec between the wars. The narrative moves from the ill-treatment and deprivations suffered at home to the injustices and insults endured in a convent; but hovering over everything is the spectre of the tyrannical father, or in other words the Law descending from a coercive religion. Those few nuns who manage to show kindness or real competence are swiftly undermined by ignorance and stupidity; at home the gentle mother is completely dominated. The only oasis of tenderness in this arid desert of meanness is provided by visits to the maternal grandparents, whose kindness and warmth are in striking contrast to the general atmosphere of hatred and denial, and help the reader to understand the author's opening declaration: 'I have forgiven everything.' This unvarnished autobiographical account of an unhappy childhood, filled with abuse and humiliations, has the structure, objectivity, and saving humour of a fine novel. Remarkably it is without bitterness or recriminations.

Dans un gant de fer, and its sequel *La joue droite* (1966), were translated by Philip Stratford as *In an iron glove* (1968) and *The right cheek* (1975). NICOLE BOURBONNAIS

Dantin, Louis. Pseudonym of Eugène SEERS.

Daoust, Jean-Paul. See GAY LITERATURE.

Darbasie, Nigel. See CARIBBEAN-CANADIAN LITERATURE.

Daveluy, Paule (b. 1919). Paule Cloutier was born in Ville-Marie in northwestern Quebec. She received her formal education with the Commission des écoles catholiques de Montréal and the Pensionnat Mont-Royal and pursued further studies in social work at the Institut Notre-Dame-du-Bon-Conseil and in creative writing at the Université de Montréal. She married André Daveluy in 1944 and is the mother of six children. One of the few Quebec authors who write successful fiction for young people, Daveluy has long been active not only as a writer of children's books but also in promoting children's literature and related cultural material. She was one of the founders of Communication-Jeunesse (1970) and the Association canadienne pour l'avancement de la littérature de jeunesse (1977), and for twelve years was employed with the publishing firm Éditions Pierre Tisseyre as a translator and director of a series in translation, Deux Solitudes—Jeunesse. She successfully coordinated, and presided over, a symposium on children's book publishing in Quebec and, with Guy Boulizon, collated the texts in *Création culturelle pour la jeunesse et identité québécoise; textes de la rencontre de 1972, Communication-Jeunesse* (1973).

Among Daveluy's themes are first love and its joy and sorrows, friendship, family life, and the relevance of natural beauty in our daily lives. Daveluy reflects sensitivity, humour, a zest for life, and a sound understanding of young people's behaviour. Her books contain colourful descriptions of the regions that she knows and loves—for example, Montreal and its environs, Témiscamingue, and the Gaspé. Her first novel *L'été enchanté; roman* (1958)—translated by Munroe Stearns as *Summer in Ville-Marie* (1962)—takes place in the 1930s and revolves around a sixteen-year-old girl, Rosanne Fontaine, and her experience with first love. With the success of this novel, which won two awards, Daveluy undertook to write a quartet in which she would describe her heroine in each of the four seasons. *L'été enchanté* was followed by *Drôle d'automne; roman pour adolescentes* (1961) and *Cet hiver-là; roman* (1967). Éditions Fides published, in two volumes, a revised condensed version of the three novels, plus the unpublished text of a fourth, *Cher printemps*, under the title *Une année du tonnerre* (1977). In 1996 all four novels were reissued as a series under the overall title *Rosanne*. The heroine's personality undergoes positive changes as she develops new friendships and becomes more aware of her responsibilities at home and at work. She gains in inner strength and knowledge of herself and, in the end, finds true love. *Un cop, un mur, deux garçons: roman* (1983) is set in the Antilles and develops the theme of friendship between two boys—one, a native of the region, and the other from Quebec—and acceptance of a disability.

Daveluy has also written, in diary form, two novels about Sylvette Forest, who learns to share in family life and accept her father's remarriage: *Sylvette et les adultes; roman pour adolescentes* (1962; rpr. 1992) and its sequel, *Sylvette sous la tente bleue; roman* (1964; rpr. 1993). Although well structured and accurately portraying tourist life in the Gaspé area, these two novels were not as popular as the earlier books about Rosanne Fontaine. *Cinq filles compliquées; nouvelles* (1965, 1980) is composed of five short stories that are rich in details of human behaviour as they describe five girls and their attempts to overcome their problems. *Pas encore seize ans . . .* (1982) is another collection of short stories that faithfully depict young people learning to cope with the pressures and challenges of today's society, while . . . *et la vie par devant* (1984) is a collection of fifteen stories about problems that young adults can identify with. Daveluy is also the author of several novels for adult readers, including *Chérie Martin* (1957) and *Les Guinois: chroniques de la maison heureuse* (1957), both of which met with limited success.

A gifted translator from English to French, Daveluy has translated books by Jean LITTLE, Janet LUNN, L.M. MONTGOMERY, Farley MOWAT, and Barbara SMUCKER. Now retired, Daveluy received in 1986, for her contribution to Canadian children's literature, the Claude Aubry Award from the International Board on Books for Young People (IBBY).

IRENE E. AUBREY

Davey, Frank (b. 1940). Born in Vancouver and brought up in Abbotsford, British Columbia, he attended, in the early 1960s, the University of British Columbia, where he was one of the founding editors of the influential (and, in some circles, notorious) poetry newsletter *TISH*, whose first nineteen issues he later brought together in one volume (1975). After doing graduate work at the University of Southern California (Ph.D. 1968, with a thesis on Black Mountain poetics), Davey taught in Montreal, Toronto, and London, Ontario, where he is now the Carl F. KLINCK professor of Canadian Literature at the University of Western Ontario.

Davey's early books of poetry include *D-Day and after* (1963), *Bridge force* (1965), and *The scarred hull* (1966); work from this period was collected in *L'an trentiesme: selected poems 1961-1970* (1972). Perhaps the most important period of Davey's writing as a poet occurred in the early 1970s. Such books as *Weeds* (1970), *King of swords* (1972), *Arcana* (1973), and *The Clallam* (1974) formed the basis for a second selection, *Selected poems: the arches* (1980), edited with an important introduction by bp NICHOL. In the 1980s Davey published *Capitalistic affection* (1982), *Edward and Patricia* (1984), *The Louis Riel organ and piano company* (1985), and *The Abbotsford guide to India* (1986). Since then, he has been less prolific as a poet—though *Popular narratives* (1991) is an important collection.

Davey's poetry has been balanced between public and private themes, the public poems dealing with Canadian history, and the private poems with family relationships. bp Nichol suggested that 'notions of responsibility & duty within a context of trust, & of how that trust is realized or betrayed' form a link between the two. Stylistically, the early Davey was concerned with adapting Charles Olson's poetics into a Canadian context, while the later Davey has focused on what he himself has called 'the validity of fact': a strong distrust of metaphor is evident in both his poetry and his criticism. Indeed, in recent years his poetry and criticism have drawn even closer together, and both could be subsumed under the general heading of 'cultural studies'.

The historical poems (such as those on shipwrecks) reject the idea that the 'documentary' can confine itself to objective facts; rather, these facts fuel the poet's intense anger at the incompetence and arrogance of ships' captains, and at the imperialist habit of mind they represent. The more personal poems analyse the sterility of relationships based on false ideals of chivalric or imperialistic culture. *King of swords* and *Arcana* subject the material of the Arthurian legends to a ruthlessly contemporary criticism: 'the death of Arthur continues' in Belfast and in the suburbs of Vancouver.

Davey's later poetry approaches 'the validity of fact' in the form of long, seemingly prosaic anecdotes. However, it has always been characterized by tightness of form and control of language; beneath the apparent blandness of books like *Edward and Patricia* lies a fiercely ironic intelligence. Similarly, *The Abbotsford guide to India* is at one and the same time a travel book, a parody of a travel book, and a brilliant poetic commentary on post-colonialism. Among Davey's finest works is the poem/essay 'Dead in France' (from *Popular narratives*), which moves flawlessly back and forth between history (the story of Héloise and Abelard), cultural studies (the popular reception of a French film on Camille Claudel), and personal emotion (the poet's grief for the death of his friend bp Nichol).

Davey has often been seen as a 'poet's poet', employing his precise craftsmanship and theoretical intelligence within an esoteric set of intellectual concerns defined by *Tish* and *OPEN LETTER*. But his poetry is by no means inaccessible, and its emotional force could well speak to a much wider audience. In recent years he has reached out to that audience, not only in his poetry but also in his critical work.

Davey has written extensively on Canadian literature, with monographs on Earle BIRNEY, Louis DUDEK, Raymond SOUSTER, and Margaret ATWOOD, among other writers. His sometimes polemical positions are exemplified in *From there to here: a guide to Canadian literature since 1960* (1974), and in the vastly influential essay 'Surviving the paraphrase' (1976), later collected in a volume of the same title (1983). He subjected much of his own early work to a critical re-evaluation in *Reading Canadian reading* (1988). More recent collections include *Post-national arguments: the politics of the Anglophone-Canadian novel since 1967* (1993) and *Canadian literary power* (1994). Increasingly, however, Davey has reached out beyond the strict confines of academic literary criticism to the broader field of cultural studies, where (as suggested above) his critical and poetic concerns often converge. He attracted wide attention with *Reading 'Kim' Right* (1993), an incisive account of the cultural images defining public perception of Prime Minister Kim Campbell. More controversial was *Karla's Web* (1994), on the Homolka murder case. Always provocative, often uncomfortable, Davey's criticism is among the most individual and influential ever written in Canada. STEPHEN SCOBIE

Davies, Robertson (1913-95). William Robertson Davies was born in Thamesville, Ontario, where he lived for five years. The newspaper interests of his father, W. Rupert Davies, later Senator, took the family to Renfrew, and then to Kingston. He attended Upper Canada College, Toronto, Queen's University, Kingston, and Balliol College, Oxford, where he took his B. Litt. in 1938. He then joined the Old Vic Company for two seasons of acting bit parts, teaching theatre history in its school, and doing literary work for Tyrone Guthrie, the director. In 1940 he married Brenda Mathews, who had been a stage manager with the Old Vic. They had three daughters. Returning to Canada, Davies became literary editor of *Saturday Night* in Toronto from 1940 to 1942, then editor of the *Peterborough Examiner* (a paper his father owned), and in 1946 owner (with his two brothers). Until 1960 he threw his considerable 'leisure' energies into theatre, writing and directing plays for the 'Little Theatre' and for several professional companies. He served on the board of the Stratford Festival from 1953 to 1971. When he moved to Toronto in 1963 as Master of Massey College, University of Toronto, he ceased to edit the *Examiner*, although he maintained an active interest in the paper until it was sold in 1968. At the university he taught in the English department and the Drama Centre until he retired in 1981. His many books encompass not only plays and the novels that have won him international renown, but criticism, *belles-lettres*, stories, and speeches. He was awarded the Stephen LEACOCK Medal for humour (for *Leaven of malice*), the Lorne PIERCE Medal (1961), a Governor General's Award (for *The manticore*), and the Molson Prize (1988). He was made FRSC (1967), a Companion of the Order of Canada (1972), an honorary member of the American Academy and Institute of Arts and Letters (1980)—the first Canadian to be so honoured—and in 1986 Honorary Fellow of Balliol College. Among his many honorary degrees are a D. Litt. from Oxford (1991), and another from the University of Wales (1995).

Davies had a distinctive career as a journalist. He made the *Examiner* one of the most frequently quoted papers in Canada. His weekly Saturday column of urbane and witty comment on the Canadian scene, written under the pseudonym Samuel Marchbanks for the *Examiner* and for several other papers between 1943 and 1953, yielded four books. *The diary of Samuel Marchbanks* (1947) and *The table talk of Samuel Marchbanks* (1949) both capture Davies' early voice. *Marchbanks' almanack* (1967) includes the exuberant 1949-50 letters when the column was called 'The correspondence of Samuel Marchbanks' and more typical entries from the column's final years. *The papers of Samuel Marchbanks* (1985) gathers the earlier books into a 'scholarly edition', with explanatory notes by Marchbanks' old academic friend and look-alike, Robertson Davies. *A voice from the attic* (1960) includes a few of the review articles Davies wrote for *Saturday Night* during his second stint as its literary editor from 1953 to 1959, but the bulk of the book is fresh material. This volume (with its handy index) offered an invaluable introduction to Davies' idiosyncratic cast of mind, since many of the books and ideas discussed were favourites. In *A voice*, Davies argued that Canada needed intelligent, literate, general (as opposed to professional) readers as a stimulus to writers and as the basis of civilized life. *The enthusiasms of Robertson Davies* (1979; rev. 1990)—reprinting samples of Davies' journalism from *Saturday Night* in the forties, through his *Toronto Star* column, 'A writer's diary' (1959-62), and his many freelance articles—gives a good sense of the quality and range of his journalism. *The well-tempered critic: one man's view of theatre and letters in Canada* (1981) presents Davies' astute commentary on two aspects of Canadian culture.

Davies played an important part in the development of Canadian drama. His fine Oxford thesis, published as *Shakespeare's boy actors* (1939), considered the capacities of boys and what they might be trained to do. He selected appropriate scenes and gave useful advice on acting them in the frequently reprinted *Shakespeare for young players: a junior course* (1942). Later he wrote *A masque of Aesop* (1952) and *A masque for Mr Punch* (1963) for the boys of the Preparatory School of Upper Canada College, and he composed the libretto of *Dr. Canon's cure*, which was first performed by the Canadian Children's Opera Chorus in 1982.

But it was the lively, topical plays of the forties and fifties that made Davies Canada's most important playwright for a time. A recurrent theme is Canada's failure to see art as essential to its development into a civilized nation. *Overlaid* (1948), which was reprinted in his one-act collection, *Eros at breakfast and other plays* (1949), along with the title play, *Hope deferred*, *The voice of the people*, and *At the gate of the righteous*, is deservedly his most frequently performed play. In it the life-enhancing force of art meets temporary defeat at the hands of respectability as 'Pop' relinquishes a cultural spree in New York to his daughter's yearning for a solid granite family tombstone. The full-length *Fortune, my foe* (1949) and *At my heart's core* (1950) reveal Davies effectively manipulating his broader theatrical resources.

Three plays are associated with the Crest Theatre, Toronto. *A jig for the Gypsy* (1954) got its first production there, as did the specially commissioned *Hunting Stuart* the following year. *General confession*, also commissioned, was completed in 1958 but never produced. *Hunting Stuart* and *General confession* were published along with the earlier *King phoenix* in *Hunting Stuart and other plays* (1972). In the Crest plays, art, magic, imagination, and love triumph. The highly theatrical Jungian play *General confession* is particularly wise in its depiction of the human condition. In it, the aged Casanova summons the spirits of Voltaire, the Ideal Beloved, and Cagliostro, and with them acts out key incidents in his life. The play ends with a trial in which the spirits accuse, defend, and try Casanova and through which he gains self-acceptance.

The emergence of a number of talented Canadian playwrights and his own reputation as a novelist obscured Davies' later theatrical activities. His adaptation of his novel *Leaven of malice*—titled *Love and libel* for its staging in 1960 and renamed *Leaven of malice* when he adapted it afresh for productions in 1973 and 1975—was published in *Canadian Drama* 7, no. 2 (1981). The 1974 television play *Brothers in the black art*, inspired by tales Davies' father told about his early experience as a printer, was published in 1981. *Question time* (1975)—a Jungian play in which Canada's prime minister undergoes an identity crisis that has national implications—appeared in print soon after it was produced. *Pontiac and the green man*, written for the University of Toronto's sesquicentennial in 1977, has not been published. Nor has Elliott Hayes' dramatization of *World of wonders*, which had a successful run at the Stratford Festival in 1992. *Jezebel*, the oratorio for which Davies created a lively libretto, was performed in 1993. And his opera *The golden ass* is to be given its première by the Canadian Opera Company in its 1998-9 season.

Neither his journalism nor his drama is as important as the fiction that in the 1970s won Davies international recognition. Earlier he wrote *Tempest-tost* (1951), *Leaven of malice* (1954), and *A mixture of frailties* (1958), novels linked by their setting in the university town of Salterton (inspired by Kingston, Ontario) and by the recurrence of several characters. They have rightly been called satiric romances, for their plots are romantic and their omniscient narrator observes the foibles of small-town Ontario sharply. But these novels are also nicely constructed comedies of manners. *Tempest-tost*, the slightest of the three, pursues the various stages of the local Little Theatre's production of *The tempest* and contains Davies' first examination of a crisis of middle age. In *Leaven of malice*, a false engagement notice in Salterton's *Evening Bellman* initiates a series of reactions that bring about the unmasking of the malicious prankster and the publication of a genuine engagement notice. *A mixture of frailties*, conceptually the most adventurous of the three, explores the transformation of an amateur into a professional, internationally acclaimed singer and articulates Davies' deepest convictions about the nature of art.

Davies' reading of the works of C.G. Jung in the fifties and sixties had a strong impact on his writing. Where earlier he had turned away from images and ideas that rose unbidden in dream and vision, he now opened himself to them. He came to see the writer as giving shape to the archetypal material rising from the unconscious. As a result he ceased to write novels that were essentially comedies of manners, and in the Deptford trilogy—*FIFTH BUSINESS* (1970), *The manticore* (1972), and *World of wonders* (1975)—wrote fictional autobiography or 'confession', in which the underlying presence of the archetypes is palpable. (Confession is one of the four categories of prose fiction Northrop FRYE defines in his 'Theory of genres', the Fourth Essay in his *Anatomy of criticism*.) This was a particularly happy shift for Davies, since theoretical and intellectual interests (always an aspect of his writing) are as central to confession as presentation of character. In *Fifth business*, the master-work of the trilogy, Dunstan Ramsay tells the story of his life as a memoir to be read after his death. He can thus speak frankly as he tells how ducking a stone-laden snowball resulted in his lifelong fascination with saints and his brush with the devil. In *The manticore*, the story of Boy Staunton, thrower of the fateful snowball, is revealed indirectly as his son, the eminent lawyer David Staunton, undergoes a Jungian analysis. David tells his (and his father's) story, in a series of notebooks as he enters, experiences, and finishes treatment. In *World of wonders* Davies supplies yet another context for his first-person narrative. As historian, creating a 'document' on a great man, Dunstan provides a verbatim record of Magnus recounting, over a series of lunches and dinners, the surprising life that began prematurely as a result of his mother's being hit by the snowball. Magnus reveals himself broadly knowledgeable about carnivals, vaudeville, travelling theatre companies, mechanical toys, and the nineteenth-century illusions of Robert Houdin.

The Cornish trilogy confirmed and expanded Davies' international reputation. Inventive technically, sweeping in conception and substantial in length, *The* REBEL ANGELS (1981), *What's bred in the bone* (1985), and *The lyre of Orpheus* (1988) reveal Davies, as he moved into his seventies, writing at the top of his bent. In these three books he considered the character and the underpinnings of the culture that had sustained him, and celebrated Canada's cultural coming of age with stories that present Canadians as full participants in Western civilization. The story of *The rebel angels* is unfolded by two narrators—Maria Magdalena Theotoky, a graduate student, and Simon Darcourt, a middle-aged priest and professor—and takes as its subject the nature of a university. In the remaining books of the trilogy Davies shifted his form once again, writing novels that have glints of romance and strong interests in art and in opera. In *What's bred in the bone*—which functions as the trilogy's fulcrum—the angel of biography sets going a record of the life of the artist and collector Francis Cornish and, from time to time, discusses it with Francis's daimon from the chilly perspective of eternity. The record reveals how a boy born in Blairlogie, Ontario (which draws on Davies' painful recollections of Renfrew) became a master painter in the manner of the Renaissance, and it explores the subtle relationships between art, deception and truth. *The lyre of Orpheus* is told omnisciently, but is centred, as was *The rebel angels*, in the perceptions of Maria Magdalena Theotoky and Simon Darcourt. As in *What's bred in the bone*, there is comment on events from the spirit world—this time by E.T.A. Hoffmann in Limbo. *Lyre* presents two intertwined stories—one concerning the creation and production of an opera from fragments left by Hoffmann, and the other about the researching and writing of the biography of Francis Cornish. Davies' ninth novel, *Lyre* not only rounds the Cornish trilogy to a conclusion but gathers, restates, and expands many of the themes and ideas of the Salterton and Deptford trilogies.

Had Davies lived to write its third volume, the linked series that began with *Murther and walking spirits* (1991) and *The cunning man* (1994) might well have been called his Canadian trilogy, for the two completed books explore the roots of contemporary Canada. *Murther and walking spirits* is told by a ghost who finds himself growing and coming to a fresh understanding of himself after death. He watches and learns and changes as events unfold in time present and as a series of films acquaints him with the lives of his forebears—lives that shaped his own in fundamental ways. These forebears were based on Davies' own, and, in his view, are characteristic of Canada's immigrants in that they were forced to leave lands they loved and to make their way in a place where life was limited and hard. Although *Murther* contains several of Davies' most vivid scenes, it is the least successful of his mature novels, largely because the ancestral sections attempt far too much. *The cunning man*, his last fictional venture, is a 'confession'. It tells the story of a doctor who chooses to treat both body and soul.

Characteristically, Davies placed this life in the larger scheme of things through references to myth and to classical texts, here primarily Sir Thomas Browne's *Religio medici* and Robert Burton's *The anatomy of melancholy*. As in *Fifth business*, the story is concerned with the making of a saint and, as in *The rebel angels* and *Murther and walking spirits*, with a murder. *The cunning man* also explores Toronto's cultural life from the 1930s to the 1970s—particularly as manifested in participants in the Hart House Theatre and in key (recognizable) musicians.

Davies wrote, or collaborated in the writing of, many other books. He contributed most of the three volumes commemorating the Stratford Festival's crucial first three years: *Renown at Stratford: a record of the Stratford Shakespeare Festival in Canada, 1953* (1953, with Tyrone Guthrie and Grant Macdonald), *Twice have the trumpets sounded: a record of the Stratford Shakespeare Festival in Canada, 1954* (1954, with

Tyrone Guthrie and Grant Macdonald), and *Thrice the brinded cat hath mew'd: a record of the Stratford Shakespeare Festival in Canada, 1955* (1955, with Tyrone Guthrie, Boyd Neel, and Tanya Moiseiwitsch). He wrote a short critical study, *Stephen Leacock* (1970), and edited *Feast of Stephen: an anthology of the less familiar writings of Stephen Leacock* (1970) and *The Penguin Stephen Leacock* (1981). With Michael R. Booth, Richard Southern, Frederick Marker, and Lise-Lone Marker he prepared *The Revels history of drama in English. Volume VI: 1750-1880* (1975). Some of Davies' speeches have been published in *One half of Robertson Davies: provocative pronouncements on a wide range of topics* (1977), including the valuable 'Jung and the theatre' and 'Masks of evil'; in *The mirror of nature* (1982); in *Reading and writing* (1993); and in *The merry heart* (1996). *High spirits* (1982) collects the eighteen ghost stories Davies wrote for Massey College from 1963 to 1980. *Conversations with Robertson Davies* (1989) gathers some of the interviews he granted between 1963 and 1988.

A high point in the criticism of Davies' work is W. J. Keith's balanced, insightful chapter in his *A sense of style: studies in the art of fiction in English-speaking Canada* (1989). Four collections of articles give a good feel for the range of comment Davies' writing has attracted: *Journal of Canadian Studies* 12, no. 1 (Feb. 1977); *Studies in Robertson Davies' Deptford trilogy* (1980); *Canadian Drama* 7, no. 2 (1981); and *Robertson Davies: an appreciation* (1991). Three book-length studies delve into particular aspects of his writing: Patricia Monk's *The smaller infinity: the Jungian self in the novels of Robertson Davies* (1982), Susan Stone-Blackburn's *Robertson Davies, playwright: a search for the self on the Canadian stage* (1985), and Dave Little's *Catching the wind in a net: the religious vision of Robertson Davies* (1996). Volume 3 of *The annotated bibliography of Canada's major authors* (1982) provides an extensive list of writings on and by Davies to the end of 1980. Judith Skelton Grant's *Robertson Davies: man of myth* (1994), which draws on a long series of interviews with Davies, is a comprehensive biography.

Davies' novels and many of his other books are available from Penguin Books. Simon and Pierre has reprinted *At my heart's core & Overlaid*; *Fortune, my foe & Eros at breakfast*; and *Hunting Stuart & The voice of the people*. *The papers of Samuel Marchbanks* has been brought out by Stoddart and *Conversations with Robertson Davies* by General Publishing.

See also NOVELS IN ENGLISH 1960 TO 1982: 2. JUDITH SKELTON GRANT

Davin, Nicholas Flood (1843-1901). Born Nicholas Francis Davin in Kilfinane, Ireland, he spent six years of his youth as an ironmonger's apprentice before going to London in 1865 to read law at the Middle Temple, supporting himself through shorthand reporting in the House of Commons press gallery. Called to the bar in 1868, he continued an active career in journalism, serving as correspondent to London and Dublin papers during the Franco-Prussian war, and then becoming editor of the *Belfast Times*. In 1872 he brought his combined talents in law and journalism to Toronto, where he joined the editorial staff of George Brown's *Globe*; he later switched to the opposition *Mail*, which accorded more closely with his Conservative sympathies. Davin won public acclaim as a lecturer, and his celebrated address, *British versus American civilization* (Toronto, 1873), was published as the second in a series of pamphlets put out by the Canada First group. In 1874 he was called to the Canadian bar and made his legal reputation in Canada with his defence of the man accused of murdering George Brown in 1880.

After rendering valuable services to the Conservative cause in politics, Davin moved in 1883 to Regina, the capital of the Northwest Territories, to establish the *Regina Leader*. His coverage of the Riel rebellion and trial once again brought Davin's name into national prominence, restoring his hopes for a political career. From 1887 to 1900 he sat in the House of Commons as Conservative member for Assiniboia. His increasing identification with regional aspirations and the interests of the Territories complicated his political life, however, and prevented him from acceding to government measures with the unquestioning loyalty that might have brought him the cabinet post he ardently desired.

Davin's pamphlet and periodical production was considerable. It included long articles on John Stuart Mill, Disraeli, 'Ireland and the Empire', 'Culture and practical power', and many others on political and cultural topics, as well as an edited pamphlet promoting immigration to the Northwest, *Homes for millions* (Toronto, 1891). A play, *The fair grit; or, The advantages of coalition* (Toronto, 1876), is a political satire. *The Irishman in Canada* (Toronto, 1877) is a 700-page study cataloguing the contributions of Irish immigrants to Canadian political, economic, and cultural life.

Declaring 'the cultivation of taste and imagination as important as the raising of grain', Davin published three slim volumes of verse as 'a step towards the creation of a

Canadian literature'. *Album verses and other poems* (Ottawa, 1882) was published privately; an enlarged and revised version appeared as *Eos: a prairie dream, and other poems* (Ottawa, 1884). Enlarged and revised once more, *Eos: an epic of the dawn and other poems* (Regina, 1889) was offered to the public as 'the first purely literary work printed and published in the North-West Territories'. Notoriously ambitious in his other endeavours, Davin was uncharacteristically (but realistically) modest about his poetic powers. In the long title poem Eos, goddess of the dawn, takes the narrator on an aerial trip across the Old World to the New, enabling Davin to combine descriptive passages with commentary on new versus old forms of civic life. American-style democracy he deplores, but the 'young Dominion . . . /gives large promise of the mightier day'. 'The critics' in the same volume is an engaging mixture of satire and honest self-appraisal.

Davin's powers as critic and supporter of literature led him to urge parliament in 1890 to enlarge its library's appropriations for literary publications, citing Archibald LAMPMAN's work as that of 'a genuine poet'. In 1893, during a tariff debate, Davin argued successfully for the removal of duty on university texts. Won over to the cause of women's independence by his long association with the poet, story-writer, and journalist Kate Simpson-Hayes ('Mary Markwell'), by whom he had two children, Davin moved in Parliament on 8 May 1895 that women be given the vote, a measure that was not granted federally until 1918.

C.B. Koester has written a full and reliable biography in *Mr. Davin, M.P.* (1980), while Davin's life in western Canada has been made the subject of a play by Ken MITCHELL: *Davin: the politician* (1979).

SUSAN JACKEL

Dawes, Kwame. See CARIBBEAN-CANADIAN LITERATURE.

Day, Frank Parker (1881-1950). Born in Shubenacadie, Nova Scotia, and educated at Pictou Academy and Mount Allison University, he attended Oxford University as New Brunswick's second Rhodes Scholar and later studied at the University of Berlin. From 1909 to 1912 he was a professor of English at the University of New Brunswick. He then moved to the United States and taught English at the Institute of Technology, Swarthmore, and from 1929 to 1933 was president of Union College, Schenectady, N.Y. In the First World War he served in the Canadian army and was instrumental in recruiting and training the 185th Infantry Battalion, the Cape Breton Highlanders; he was promoted to the rank of colonel at Amiens and was commanding officer of the 25th Overseas Battalion.

In middle life Day became a writer, the author of three novels and a work of non-fiction. *River of strangers* (1926) is an imaginative account of life on the Churchill River. There is no evidence, however, that he ever visited the North. In his best-known novel, *Rockbound* (1928; rpr. 1973)—a realistic account of life in a primitive south-shore fishing community of Nova Scotia in the decade preceding the Great War—the passions of ambition, greed, and jealousy are exposed. Day depicts the narrow, harsh, and primitive life of the Rockbound Island fishermen and their families against the hostile and often violent background of the Atlantic. In *John Paul's rock* (1932) the central character is a Micmac who has run from the white man's law to live in isolation among the many lakes and barrens of inland Nova Scotia. In his solitude John Paul attempts to come to terms with God through the folklore of Glooscap, the God of the Micmacs, and the morality of his Micmac background. For Day, God was 'the sum total of all human idealism, aesthetic and moral desires, and the craving for perfection'. In his *Autobiography of a fisherman* (1927) he demonstrates his deep knowledge of inland fishing and his close familiarity with nature: 'Nature always wins or takes her revenge because we refuse to face the fact that we are animals—fine animals to be sure—in a world of nature.'

DOUGLAS LOCHHEAD

Deacon, William Arthur (1890-1977). Born in Pembroke, Ontario, he was raised in Stanstead, Quebec, where he lived until he was seventeen. He was educated at Stanstead College and Victoria College, University of Toronto, which he left at the end of his second year. In 1918 he earned the degree of LL.B. at the University of Manitoba and later joined the Pitblado law firm in Winnipeg. Meanwhile, Deacon had developed an intense enthusiasm for literature and had undergone years of rigorous self-training in writing, publishing essays and reviews in Canadian and American periodicals. His conversion to Theosophy in 1917, his appointment in 1921 as assistant literary editor of the *Manitoba Free Press*, and his charter membership the same year in the Winnipeg Branch of the CANADIAN AUTHORS' ASSOCIATION, were crucial in convincing him of his literary vocation. In 1922 he left Winnipeg and went to Toronto where, on the recommendation of B.K. SANDWELL, he was hired as literary editor of the magazine *Saturday Night*.

Deacon's six years with *Saturday Night* (1922-8)—which coincided with, and reflected, a period of buoyant Canadian nationalism—were stimulated by his enthusiastic commitment to the encouragement of Canadian writers, and to the building of a reading public for their work. His plain, direct style as a reviewer (he was most at ease with fiction, biography, and history), and his special literary sections, speedily attracted and held a community of readers, while his column 'Saved from the wastebasket', containing book news and writers' gossip, served as an informal literary forum.

During these years Deacon's essays and reviews continued to appear in several international publications, including H.L. Mencken's *American Mercury*, the *Saturday Review of Literature*, and the *International Book Review*. Encouraged by Lorne PIERCE of the RYERSON PRESS, he published two essay collections: *Pens and pirates* (1923), composed of humorous and whimsical pieces on a wide range of topics, and *Poteen* (1926), containing essays on national themes and a lengthy critical discussion of Canadian literature. Deacon also wrote an appreciative monograph, *Peter McArthur* (1924), for Pierce's Makers of Canadian Literature series, and *The FOUR JAMESES* (1927), a comic celebration of four of Canada's best bad poets—the work for which he is best remembered. All his writing in this decade was marked by an intense Canadian cultural nationalism, and considerable wit.

Dismissed from *Saturday Night* in April 1928, after a series of disagreements over the editor Hector CHARLESWORTH's rigorous editorial policies, Deacon began syndicating book reviews in newspapers across Canada. Within a few months he was working almost exclusively for Toronto's *Mail and Empire*. With Wilfred Reeves he edited *Open house* (1931), a collection of essays by members of the Toronto Writers' Club that addressed controversial political and social subjects. Under the stresses of the 1930s Deacon's interests, and his journalistic capacities, broadened remarkably into the fields of national and world affairs. He became active in the Couchiching Conferences on International Affairs (est. 1932). The intensity of his concerns for world peace and for Canada's future was articulated in the impassioned rhetoric of *My vision of Canada* (1933), in which Deacon imagined a romantic, Utopian national destiny. His *Literary map of Canada* (1936) was a handsome four-colour poster featuring writers and places significant to Canadian literature. His pamphlet attacking censorship, *Sh-h-h . . . here comes the censor* (1940), was his last independent publication. When the *Mail and Empire* was sold to the *Globe* in 1936, Deacon became literary editor of the new *Globe and Mail*, a position he held until 1960.

Always active in the Toronto Branch of the Canadian Authors' Association, and for some time its president, Deacon became national president of the CAA in 1946. He formed committees that produced a standard book contract; secured from the federal government special income-tax provisions for Canadian writers; and engaged Earle BIRNEY as editor of the *Canadian Poetry Magazine*. He had been active in establishing the GOVERNOR GENERAL's LITERARY AWARDS under the aegis of the CAA in 1937 and served as chairman of the Awards Board from 1944 to 1949. However, his hope that after the Second World War the CAA would be completely rebuilt by the strength and energies of young upcoming writers proved elusive. The old constituency was resistant to change, and the young were impatient. By the 1950s Deacon was himself experiencing the fatigue of more than thirty years of full-time reviewing. Inevitably, attention shifted to younger critics.

Throughout his career Deacon maintained a voluminous correspondence with Canadian writers such as E.J. PRATT, Raymond KNISTER, and Grey Owl (Archibald Stansfeld BELANEY) in the 1920s and 1930s; Hugh MacLENNAN, Gabrielle ROY, and Roger LEMELIN in the 1940s; and Thomas RADDALL, Peter NEWMAN, Scott Young, and June CALLWOOD in the 1950s and 1960s. Deacon's extensive papers, housed in the Thomas Fisher Rare Book Library of the University of Toronto, bear impressive testimony to his unstinting encouragement of Canadian writers, and to their eager and grateful response.

Deacon retired from the *Globe and Mail* in Jan. 1961, but continued his news and gossip column, 'The fly leaf', until 1963. He contracted with Doubleday for a two-volume history of his life and times in Canadian literature, but poor health prevented its completion.

See Clara THOMAS and John Lennox, *William Arthur Deacon: a Canadian literary life* (1982), and John Lennox and Michèle Lacombe, eds, *Dear Bill: The correspondence of William Arthur Deacon* (1988).

JOHN LENNOX

Decter, Ann. See LESBIAN LITERATURE.

De Grandmont, Éloi (1921-70). Born in Baie du Febvre, Quebec, he attended classical college in Nicolet and studied art at L'École des Beaux-Arts de Montréal, the Sorbonne, and L'École du Louvre. He worked as a journalist and theatre critic for several Montreal papers, including *Notre Temps*, which he founded in 1954. He also wrote numerous short stories and radio dramas for Radio-Canada, and hosted a series of variety and talk shows on radio. Between 1951 and 1954 he served as secretary general of the Théâtre du Nouveau Monde. Shortly before his death he became a professor at the Université de Montréal's École de Traduction.

De Grandmont wrote the first play by a Canadian to be presented by the Théâtre du Nouveau Monde: *La fontaine de Paris* (1953), a one-act farce of little consequence that was produced as a radio play in 1952 and 1953 and was the basis for a ballet televised by Radio-Canada in 1954. His three-act drama *Un fils à tuer* (1950) was not particularly well received when it was first performed in Montreal in 1949, but it has since obtained some critical recognition for its elegant style, classical structure, and socio-political connotations. The action takes place in New France and revolves around a bitter father-son conflict of wills—between a stern, intolerant, and unsympathetic man who believes strongly in his patriotic duty to the land and a young idealist who would seek adventure in France but is killed as a deserter by his father. It is typical of a number of plays written and produced in Quebec after the Second World War in that it vehemently defends the notion of individual freedom of thought and action and sanctions the concept of a pluralistic society. Unusual, however, is the hero's longing to seek his fortune in France and not, as others would, in North America.

A macabre one-act drama, *Le temps des fêtes* (1952), was published with *La fontaine de Paris*, as well as in the collection of De Grandmont's *Théâtre I* (1968).

Of De Grandmont's several translations and adaptations, his 1968 French version of *Pygmalion* was the most popular and controversial: his Professor Higgins attempts to teach standard French to a young woman who speaks JOUAL. De Grandmont's collaborative works include a lively and successful musical comedy, *Doux temps des amours*, written with Louis-Georges Carrier and produced in 1964, and a pictorial history of the Théâtre du Nouveau Monde, *Dix ans du Théâtre du Nouveau Monde* (1961), of which he was one of the founders.

Although De Grandmont is now considered to be of minor importance as a poet, his poetry was well received when first published in the collections *Le voyage d'Arlequin* (1946), *La jeune fille constellée* (1948), *Premiers secrets* (1951), *Plaisirs* (1953), *Chardon à Foulon* (1963), and *Une saison en chanson* (1963).

De Grandmont was a man of letters whose numerous publications include discussions of Émile NELLIGAN in (*Poèmes choisis*, 1966) and Alfred Pellan (*Ciquante dessins d'Alfred Pellan*, 1946), and three books on his travels in Europe: *Voyageurs ou touristes* (1970), *Je n'aurais jamais cru* (1971), and *Vernousser* (1971).

See Laurent Mailhot, 'Deux saisons dans la vie de la Nouvelle France: un fils (ou un père) à tuer' in Jean-Cléo Godin and Laurent Mailhot, eds, *Théâtre québécois* (1970).

ELAINE NARDOCCHIO

de Grandpré, Pierre. See ANTHOLOGIES IN FRENCH: 4.

De Koninck, Charles (1906-65). Born and educated in Belgium, he completed his docteur en philosophie at the Université de Louvain in 1934. From that year until his death he was professor of natural philosophy at Université Laval, Quebec City, serving as dean of the faculty of philosophy from 1939 to 1956, and again from 1964. He lectured widely, and from 1957 to 1963 was visiting professor at the University of Notre Dame, Indiana. He died in Rome while accompanying Maurice Cardinal Roy of Quebec to the Second Vatican Council in the role of theological expert to the Cardinal—the only layman who held such a position on that occasion.

De Koninck published extensively on philosophical and theological topics, writing in both English and French with admirable lucidity. A primary feature of his scholarly interest was an insistence on the unity of the philosophical spirit, whether manifesting itself in the heights of metaphysics or on such questions as why dogs run in a certain way. He deplored the divorce of philosophy and science as resulting in the impoverishment of both. He also sought to distinguish the doctrines of perennial validity—particularly those contained in Aristotle's *Physics* (for example, on the nature of time)—from what is no longer tenable. In *The hollow universe* (1960), De Koninck's Whidden lectures given at McMaster University in 1959, he moved progressively through considerations of mathematics, physics, and biology in order to bring to light the distinction (in all these domains) between the work of the calculative mind and the contemplative mind.

De Koninck was anything but an ivory-tower thinker. Highly adept at communicating his philosophical seriousness, he attracted as dean at Laval students from all over North America who became disciples in the best sense. That seriousness showed itself, in a rather polemical setting, after the publication of his *De la primauté du bien commun contre les personnalistes; Le principe de l'ordre nouveau* (1943). This book contains two quite distinct essays. 'Le principe de l'ordre nouveau' is an ironic reference to Marxism, radicalism, and nihilism. It was the other essay that provoked injured outcries. De Koninck was troubled by the teachings of certain Thomist philosophers (he names Mortimer Adler and Walter Farrell) who, in their opposition to totalitarianism, tended to set up an either/or situation as between 'person' and 'society'. He sought to reshape the discussion. Instead of asking, Is the person better than society? he asked, Is the proper good of the person better than his common good? De Koninck affirmed the primacy of the common good (cf. his later 'In defence of Saint Thomas', *Laval Théologique et philosophique*, vol. 1, no. 2, 1945). Father I. Th. Eschmann, O.P., of the Pontifical Institute of Mediaeval Studies, Toronto, took this essay to be an attack on Jacques Maritain (it can hardly be denied that Maritain was seen, even by De Koninck, as to some extent open to its criticism). Eschmann's 'In defence of Jacques Maritain' accused De Koninck of proposing a new and entirely unacceptable interpretation of St Thomas by means of quite amateurish methods of interpretation. Eschmann's paper had at least the effect of provoking De Koninck into a fuller presentation of his (as it seems to us) quite invulnerable position with 'In defence of Saint Thomas', the tone of which is at times harsh, though its philosophizing is painstaking.

De Koninck was quite vocal in the controversies of the early 1960s in Quebec concerning public schools with no religious affiliation ('non-confessional' schools). In *Tout homme est mon prochain* (1964)—reprints of letters to editors, etc.—we read his beautifully clear defence of freedom of conscience for non-believers as well as believers: he knew how to express the grounds of tolerance. This is public controversy at its best.

A bibliography of De Koninck's writings can be found in *Mélanges à la mémoire de Charles De Koninck* (1968) published by Les Presses de l'Université Laval.

LAWRENCE DEWAN

De Lamirande, Claire. See NOVELS IN FRENCH 1960 TO 1982: 3(g).

Delaney, Marshall. Pseudonym of Robert FULFORD.

de la Roche, Mazo (1879-1961). She was born Maisie Roche in Newmarket, Ontario (though she invented a Toronto birthplace for herself), to lower middle-class parents who moved frequently in an unsuccessful search of economic betterment, at times encamped within large households, at times on their own. Educated at various public schools, for a brief time an art student, de la Roche, in the manner of the Brontë children, began early to immerse herself in a world of fantastic invention that took the form of what she called 'the Play'. The entry into the family, when she was sixteen, of her younger cousin and lifelong companion, Caroline Clement, further enriched this activity. A fantasy narrative enacted daily by the two adolescents, and continued into old age, the Play nourished the writer's imagination ever after.

Having published a short story in the *Atlantic Monthly* in 1915, de la Roche was more than halfway through her life before the appearance of her first book-length work, *Explorers of the dawn* (1922), a collection of stories about three boys set in the never-neverland of Edwardian domesticity. *Possession* (1923) continues the search for a workable setting, as its opening idyll yields to the grim realism of the life she knew from her family's unsuccessful venture into fruit farming near Bronte, Ontario. *Delight* (1926; NCL, 1961) presented de la Roche's readers with her first memorable protagonist, Delight Mainprize, a passionate misfit harassed by her stodgy neighbours. It draws heavily upon the time her family spent in Acton, Ontario. Both *Delight* and her later novel *Growth of a man* (1938), based on the life of her successful lumberman cousin H.R. MacMillan, represent convincingly life in a rural slum. Had her literary biography closed here, de la Roche would have earned herself a minor niche alongside a rural realist/romanticist like Martha OSTENSO: she might have been viewed as a precursor of Alice MUNRO.

In 1927, however, in her late forties—when most writers are set in their ways and the course of their career is established—de la Roche entered a long period of fame with the publication of *JALNA*, a novel about the Whiteoaks family, whose existence was centered on a house called 'Jalna', an amalgam of several grand houses that the writer had observed in the neighbourhood of Clarkson, Ontario. (The Play had provided many of its characters and situations.) *Jalna* won the

Atlantic Monthly's highly publicized first-novel prize, and de la Roche was duly fêted and lauded—and prodded to produce more stories about the Whiteoaks family.

De la Roche had not planned on producing serial fiction. Her time-frame in *Jalna* was too articulated to make such an enterprise a simple one. Nonetheless, encouraged mightily by publishers who knew a gold-mine when they saw it, she wrote fifteen sequels that moved either backward or forward in time from the opening centre. After her death, Robertson DAVIES called the series 'the most protracted single feat of literary invention in the brief history of Canada's literature'. The titles are *Jalna* (1927), *Whiteoaks of Jalna* (1929), *Finch's fortune* (1931), *The master of Jalna* (1933), *Young Renny* (1935), *Whiteoak harvest* (1936), *Whiteoak heritage* (1940), *Wakefield's course* (1941), *The building of Jalna* (1944), *Return to Jalna* (1946), *Mary Wakefield* (1949), *Renny's daughter* (1951), *Whiteoak brothers* (1953), *Variable winds at Jalna* (1954), *Centenary at Jalna* (1958), and *Morning at Jalna* (1960). By 1966 the series had sold 11 million copies, nine million of them in hardback, with translations in nine languages. A dramatized version of the first two novels (*Whiteoaks*) played successfully in London from 1936 to 1939, and the film *Jalna* appeared in 1935. The many fan letters among the de la Roche papers (Fisher Library, University of Toronto) testify to readers' acute interest in the Whiteoaks, especially in Europe during the Second World War. Various radio versions of the series appeared over the years. A 1972 CBC television production was a failure; yet a 1994 version on a French public channel, starring the famous film actress Danielle Darrieux as Gran, proved wildly popular and was televised on Radio-Canada.

The series supported an opulent lifestyle for de la Roche that made possible shifts between English country houses and Ontario mansions, until the Toronto area was chosen for a final settlement in 1939. In 1931 de la Roche and Caroline Clement adopted two English children, a boy and a girl.

Jalna and its successors concern themselves first of all with a house and an estate governed by Adeline Whiteoak (Gran), a vital, high-spirited, tyrannical Upper Canadian version of Victoria Regina. She and her grandson Renny, an Ontario Heathcliff, do not so much govern Jalna as power it. Their tempestuousness and anti-intellectualism are offset by the troubled Finch (named after the Toronto academic and poet Robert FINCH), the artistic brother whose temperament most resembles his creator's; his financial sacrifice saves Jalna at a crucial point. The many characters share an inexhaustible interest in each other's doings and passions, particularly the latter. Often quarrelsome, they remain loyal to each other. Credibility necessitated the death of Gran; the need for new material introduced a less-interesting generation (because less known to the author); and imagination waned, along with de la Roche's life. Still, an Upper Canadian myth of creation and decline articulates itself. The series epitomizes the colonial mentality in its unswerving allegiance to British institutions and mores, and conveys the Loyalist myth of a Canada redeemed by its British allegiance—and the myth of a humane, harmless gentry—though the author does not flinch from observing the ebbing of the material foundations for that cultural stance. Renny fights in the Second World War with a British regiment; an anachronistic Britain presents the Whiteoaks with their most memorable sights; New York is where the shysters come from. By the series' conclusion, burgeoning modernity, American in origin, with television as its primary exemplar, has irrevocably altered the culture surrounding the property. Yet Jalna, the house, remains the great good place. The series is a soap-opera in its narrative structure, but it is nonetheless ideologically weighted. Only within imperial-colonial arrangements could the obsessions about family and the often unconventional vitality sustaining the Whiteoaks be possible. Whether or not Jalna's Ontario ever existed is of less interest than the tightness with which de la Roche entwined strong colonial and familial values.

Fact and fiction combine in de la Roche's dateless autobiography, *Ringing the changes* (1957), where she highlights her United Empire Loyalist ancestry. Other works include children's and animal stories (*Beside a Norman tower*, 1934; *The very house*, 1937; *The sacred bullock and other stories of animals*, 1939; *The song of Lambert*, 1955; *Bill and Coo*, 1958). Despite its title, *Portrait of a dog* (1930) also deals with the daily life of its owners. Novels dealing with tensions between individuals and their social environment are *The two saplings* (1942) and *A boy in the house* (1952); *Lark ascending* (1932) is a romance set in Sicily; *Quebec, historic seaport* (1945) concentrates on the romantic aspects of the Old Régime and post-Conquest Quebec. Three of her one-act plays—*Low life* (1925), *Come true* (1927), and *The return of the emigrant* (1929)—were performed at Hart House Theatre, University of Toronto; they are included in *Low life and other plays* (1929).

Douglas Daymond has collected some of her periodical fiction in *Selected stories of Mazo de la Roche* (1979).

The life and work of de la Roche have attracted much critical interest since her death. See Ronald Hambleton, *Mazo de la Roche of Jalna* (1966); George Hendrick, *Mazo de la Roche* (1970); Douglas Daymond, 'Whiteoak chronicles: a reassessment', *CANADIAN LITERATURE* 66 (1975); Dennis Duffy, *Gardens, covenants, exiles: loyalism in the literature of Upper Canada/Ontario* (1982); Ruth Panofsky, '"Go my own way?": the publication of Mazo de la Roche's *Jalna*', *Epilogue* IX, no. 1 (1994); Daniel L. Bratton, *Thirty-two short views of Mazo de la Roche. a biographical essay* (1996). Joan GIVNER's *Mazo de la Roche: the hidden life* (1989) boldly uses the fiction to illuminate many previously unrecorded details of the author's life.

DENNIS DUFFY

de Lint, Charles (b. 1951). Born in Bussum, The Netherlands, and brought to Canada four months later, he grew up in a number of cities in Ontario and abroad; but from the age of eleven he has lived in the vicinity of Ottawa, Ontario. Through the late 1970s and early eighties he worked in a record store through the week and played with a Celtic band on weekends, all the while writing his urban fantasies, about the operation of magic in modern society, which have become his stock-in-trade. He sold three novels in 1983 and since then has been a full-time writer, having published some forty books between 1984 and 1997 for a North American readership. He published three horror novels as Samuel M. Key. Among his major urban fantasies are *Moonheart: a romance* (1984) and *Trader* (1996). Many of his novels are set in Ottawa, but some take place in the fictional city of Newford. His short stories, characterized by Celtic lyricism and character analysis, appear in his collections *Dreams underfoot* (1993) and *The ivory and the horn* (1995).

JOHN ROBERT COLOMBO

Delisle, Jeanne-Mance. See DRAMA IN FRENCH 1948 TO 1981: 4.

Delta (1957-66). Edited, printed, and published by Louis DUDEK in 26 issues between Oct. 1957 and Oct. 1966, *Delta* offered not only poems, mostly by younger Canadian writers, but quotations from Dudek's personal readings in politics, science, and sociology, and occasionally poems, essays, and reviews by Dudek himself. Overall it reflected Dudek's conviction that poetry was an essential part of intellectual life, inseparable from the chief issues of its time. Although clearly a vehicle for his personal views of literature, *Delta* was used generously by Dudek to assist younger writers and to welcome new developments. Issue 16 (Nov. 1961) published 'Njarit', an early typewriter-concrete poem by Earle BIRNEY; issue 19 (Oct. 1962) was devoted to Vancouver poetry, largely from the *TISH* group, and included examples of Lionel KEARNS' 'stacked verse'.

See Frank Davey, *Louis Dudek and Raymond Souster* (1980).

FRANK DAVEY

Demers, Jérôme (1774-1853). Born at Saint-Nicholas, near Quebec City, Quebec, he was educated at the Séminaire de Québec, where philosophy had been taught since 1665, and the Collège des Sulpiciens, Montreal. Ordained a priest in 1798, he became in 1800, and remained until 1842, a professor of philosophy and science at the Séminaire de Québec. Demers was the author of the first work of philosophy published in Canada, *Compendium philosophicae ad usum studiosae juventutis* (Québec, 1835). This work, the greater part of it in Latin, was actually his philosophy courses, which he had been improving constantly since the beginning of the century. Marked by the philosophical controversy that had just ended when the book appeared, it covers the three traditional areas of philosophy—logic, metaphysics, and ethics—with the addition of several pages in French on proofs of revealed religion. Eclectic in nature, it clearly reflects the difficulty experienced at the time by those who sought to find a 'Catholic' philosophy to oppose Descartes and the ideas of the Enlightenment. Demers could not follow Descartes on the question of the origin of ideas or on the criteria of certainty; he could not support knowledge on the authority of evidence (Descartes) or on the evidence of authority (common sense and traditionalism). In refuting the ideas of the Enlightenment and the French Revolution, which asserted the sovereign power of the people, the *Compendium* opposes the idea of the divine origin of political power and counters 'systems' of atheism with lengthy proofs of the existence of God.

Though Demers left many manuscripts and much correspondence, he published only the *Compendium*, which was used by several generations of students in the five classical colleges in Lower Canada.

See also PHILOSOPHY IN CANADA: I.

YVAN LAMONDE

***Demi-civilisés*, *Les*.** See Jean-Charles HARVEY.

De Mille, James (1833-80). Born in Saint John, New Brunswick, he was educated at Horton Academy and Acadia College in Wolfville. In 1850-1 he and his brother Elisha toured Britain and Europe; Italy made a lasting impression on James. After obtaining his M.A. from Brown University, Providence, Rhode Island, he worked briefly in Cincinnati, Ohio, but returned to Saint John, where he conducted a bookstore from 1857 to 1861 and in the latter year acted as unofficial editor of *The Christian Watchman* in place of his brother Elisha. In 1858 he married Elizabeth Ann Pryor, the daughter of the first president of Acadia; he taught classics at Acadia from 1861 to 1865. He then taught history, rhetoric, and literature at Dalhousie College, Halifax, until his death.

De Mille was one of North America's most popular novelists in the last quarter of the nineteenth century. His intricate plots, his deft handling of comedy and suspense, and his gift for dialogue—the raciest and slangiest since T.C. HALIBURTON's Clockmaker stories—contributed to this popularity. In his haste to publish—possibly to pay off debts associated with his bookstore—De Mille padded excessively and occasionally left his plots with crude endings; yet his books reflected his own delight in linguistic puzzles and puns and his hatred of sham and humbug. Indeed, his 'potboilers' (as he called them) were often parodies of Victorian fictional realism through the use of narrative techniques now associated with postmodernist novels. He wrote historical romances, 'international' novels of manners and adventure, and sensational novels of mystery and ratiocination. His archetypal situation is a voyage, for pleasure or escape, by a group of men and women. Before the dénouement the protagonist becomes increasingly obsessed, even temporarily insane, and each novel centres on one or more poetic scenes evoking terror.

De Mille's first two novels reveal his interest in early Christianity: *The martyr of the catacombs; a tale of ancient Rome* (New York, 1865; rpr. 1970) is a children's story, while *Helena's household; a tale of Rome in the first century* (New York, 1867) is the first of his works to demonstrate his doubts about Christian doctrine in its contrasts between Nero's court and Helena's Christian home. This questioning of traditional religious beliefs and contemporary values became an important motif underlying the surface humour and irony of his fiction. His first hit, *The dodge club; or, Italy in MDCCCLIX* (New York, 1869; rpr. 1981), a series of comic sketches about American tourists in war-torn Italy, spoofs national traits and flatters De Mille's American readers with the first of his gallery of sharp-witted Yankees. The same setting reappears in *The American baron; a novel* (New York, 1872) and in *The babes in the wood; a tragic comedy; a tale of the Italian Revolution of 1848* (New York, 1875). *The lady of the ice; a novel* (New York, 1870; rpr. 1973), a first-person narrative about the foibles of two British garrison officers at Quebec, contains a satiric explanation of the Fenian takeover of the United States and an Irish parody of Homer's *Iliad*. *A comedy of terrors* (New York, 1872) has a spectacular balloon escape from Paris during the Franco-Prussian war. De Mille's imitations of the mysteries popularized by Poe, Dickens, and Wilkie Collins—*Cord and creese; a novel* (New York, 1869), *The cryptogram; a novel* (New York, 1871; rpr. 1973), and *The living link; a novel* (New York, 1874)—are exciting, carefully convoluted stories of secret codes and assumed identities. The simpler plot of *The lily and the cross; a tale of Acadia* (Boston, 1874) deals with the rescue of a French woman from Louisbourg by an American-raised Frenchman; as De Mille's only historical romance with a Maritime setting, it anticipates Charles G.D. ROBERTS' treatment of similar themes.

A strange manuscript found in a copper cylinder (New York, 1888; NCL 1969; CEECT 1986) is the most complex and philosophical nineteenth-century Canadian novel. Possibly written in the 1860s, it was published posthumously to cash in on the fashion for fantasy travels to imaginary societies—and anonymously, to protect its copyright. Adam More, a practical British seaman, narrates his experiences among the Kosekin of Antarctica, and his story is framed by the commentary of several gentlemen on a pleasure cruise who discover the manuscript. In the tradition of Thomas More's *Utopia*, Swift's *Gulliver's travels*, and Poe's *Narrative of Arthur Gordon Pym*, De Mille organizes his double-edged satire around the Kosekins' worship of poverty, darkness, and death to present a mirror reflection of European values; but what first appears as superior to them is ultimately revealed as far worse.

One of the first Canadians to write for boys, De Mille avoided the overt didacticism commonly found in children's literature of the time. The Brethren of the White Cross series, drawing on the author's boyhood pranks around the Minas Basin, includes *The*

'B.O.W.C.' (Boston, 1869), *The boys of Grand Pré school* (Boston, 1870), *Lost in the fog* (Boston, 1870), *Fire in the woods* (Boston, 1872), *Picked up adrift* (Boston, 1872), and *The treasure of the seas* (Boston, 1873). The Young Dodge Club series, which includes *Among the brigands* (Boston, 1871), *The seven hills* (Boston, 1873), and *The winged lion; or, stories of Venice* (New York, 1877), recounts the European adventures of four teenaged boys. Other works by De Mille include the famous comic poem 'Sweet maiden of Passamaquoddy'; a religious monograph, *The early English church* (Halifax, 1877); a textbook containing a defence of 'humorous' and 'pathetic' literature, *The elements of rhetoric* (New York, 1877); and the posthumously published threnody, *Behind the veil; a poem* (Halifax, 1893) edited by Archibald MacMECHAN, which deals with a mystic quest for a lost love and culminates in the discovery of divine love.

See Douglas E. MacLeod, 'A critical biography of James De Mille' (M.A. thesis, Dalhousie University, 1968); Minerva Tracy, 'James De Mille', *DICTIONARY OF CANADIAN BIOGRAPHY*, vol. 10 (1972); Crawford Kilian, 'The cheerful inferno of James De Mille', *Journal of Canadian Fiction* 2 (*Summer* 1973); W.R. Kime, 'The American antecedents of James De Mille's *A strange manuscript found in a copper cylinder*', *Dalhousie Review* 55 (Summer 1975); M.G. Parks, 'Strange to strangers only', *CANADIAN LITERATURE* 70 (Autumn 1976); Patricia Monk, 'James De Mille as mystic: a reconsideration of *Behind the veil*', *Canadian Poetry* 3 (1978); George WOODCOCK, 'De Mille and the Utopian vision', and Kenneth J. Hughes, 'A strange manuscript: sources, satire, a positive Utopia', both in *The Canadian novel, vol. II: beginnings* (1980) edited by John Moss; 'Kosekin country' in *Dictionary of imaginary places* (1980) edited by Alberto MANGUEL and Gianni Guadelupi; Gwendolyn Davies, '*The Dodge Club* and the tradition of nineteenth-century American travel literature', introduction to *The Dodge club: or, Italy in MDCCCIX*, Maritime Literature Series 3 (1981); Carole Gerson, 'Three writers of Victorian Canada', in *Canadian writers and their work: fiction series: volume one* (1983) edited by Robert Lecker, Jack David, and Ellen Quigley; Camille La Bossière, 'The mysterious end of James De Mille's unfinished strange manuscript', *Essays on Canadian writing* 27 (1983-84); Richard Cavell, 'Bakhtin reads De Mille: Canadian literature, post-modernism, and the theory of dialogism', in *Future indicative literary theory and Canadian literature* (1987) edited and with an introduction by John Moss; Bruce F. MacDonald, '*Helena's household*: James De Mille's heretical text', *Canadian Literature* 128 (1991); and Patricia Monk, *The gilded beaver: an introduction to the life and work of James De Mille* (1991). See the critical edition of *A strange manuscript found in a copper cylinder* (1986), CENTRE FOR EDITING EARLY CANADIAN TEXTS, edited and with an introduction by Malcolm G. Parks. GEORGE L. PARKER

de Montigny, Louvigny. See DRAMA IN FRENCH 1900 TO 1948.

Denison, Merrill (1893-1975). Playwright, journalist, raconteur, broadcaster, historian, summer-resort owner (at Bon Echo, Ontario), conservationist, and man of many other interests and abilities, Denison was born in Detroit, Michigan, of a Canadian mother and an American father. His early training was in architecture at the universities of Toronto and Pennsylvania, but he soon turned to writing as his profession. Denison's output in many literary forms was prodigious; its quality, however, ranged from the first-rate to the embarrassing.

Denison's major contribution to Canadian letters was as a playwright. Throughout the 1920s he was at the forefront of Canada's Little Theatre movement as designer, actor, and playwright for Toronto's Hart House Theatre. Denison published some of his best work, in which he established himself as a kind of backwoods Sean O'Casey, in *The unheroic North: four Canadian plays* (1923), containing *Brothers in arms*, *The weather breeder*, *From their own place*, and *MARSH HAY*. Set in the backwoods of northern Ontario, the plays gently satirize the eccentricities and pretensions of backwoods people, astutely capturing their environment and the ironies of their various predicaments. Only *Marsh hay*, a full-length play, takes on a sombre note, aiming to illuminate what Denison saw as the tragic futility of his characters' lives. In all four plays Denison was in full command of structure and dialogue. *The prize winner* (1928) is an effective one-act comedy dealing with a down-at-heel carnival road show; and *Balm*, published in *Canadian plays from Hart House*, vol.1 (1926), is a perfectly constructed and perceptive short piece on the foibles of old age. *On Christmas night* (1934) is a predictable and wholly unoriginal nativity play.

Denison made a significant contribution to radio drama (then in its infancy), though his achievement in this medium is less memorable than his stage plays. *Henry Hudson and other plays* (1931) contains six romantic historical radio dramas: 'Henry Hudson', 'Pierre Radisson', 'Montcalm', 'Seven Oaks', 'Laura Secord', and 'Alexander Mackenzie'. All were broadcast on CNRM, Montreal, in 1931, directed by Tyrone Guthrie. *An American father talks to his son* (1939)—broadcast on CBS radio and sponsored by the Council Against Intolerance in America—is a well-intentioned but trite apology for the principles of American democracy. *Haven of the spirit* (1939) and *The U.S. vs. Susan B. Anthony* (1941) openly espouse the same principles but artistically are much more satisfying because they begin to recognize the complexities of their subject: religious and political prejudice.

As a historian of Canadian commerce, Denison wrote *Harvest triumphant: the story of Massey-Harris, a footnote to Canadian history* (1948), *The barley and the stream: the Molson story* (1955), and *Canada's first bank: a history of the Bank of Montreal* (2 vols, 1966, 1967). Based on original documents in company archives and engagingly written, these studies suffer from a lack of rigorous objectivity (the books invariably being commissioned by the company concerned) and scholarly discipline, a jaunty style often taking precedence over historical substance.

In addition to his histories and plays, Denison wrote *Boobs in the woods; sixteen sketches by one of them* (1927), a collection of more-or-less satirical essays dealing mostly with his experience as a resort owner at Bon Echo; *Canada, our Dominion neighbor* (1944), a pamphlet intended for uninformed American readers; and *Klondike Mike: an Alaskan odyssey* (1945), a best-seller about the Canadian folk hero Michael 'Mike' Mahoney. Denison also wrote some witty sketches of prominent Canadian figures to accompany Jack McLaren's caricatures in *Twelve caricatures cut in linoleum* (1932), for which E.J. PRATT wrote the foreword.

Denison's first wife, Muriel, was the author of the successful 'Susannah' series of children's books. *Mugwump Canadian: the Merrill Denison story* (1973) by Dick MacDonald is a skimpy biography padded by lengthy excerpts from Denison. The Denison archives are housed at Queen's University, Ontario.

L.W. CONOLLY

de Pasquale, Dominique. See DRAMA IN FRENCH 1948 TO 1981: 3.

Derome, Gilles. See DRAMA IN FRENCH 1948 TO 1981: 2.

Desautels, Denise (b. 1945) A native of Montreal, she attended the Collège Basile-Moreau and the Université de Montréal (M.A., 1980). Since 1977 she has taught literature at the Sorel-Tracy CÉGEP.

The poems in her first collection, *Comme miroir en feuilles* (1975), were illustrated by Léon Bellefleur's drawings. Les Éditions du Noroît, Desautels' publisher, is known for its editorial policy of bringing together the graphic and literary arts, and Desautels has come to centre her writing on a dialogue with the graphic arts: drawings, photographs, installations, 'objects', paintings, and watercolours by various artists. In *Leçons de Venise* (1990), for example, the text is inspired by Michel Goulet's installations, while in *Le saut de l'ange* (1992) 'objects' by Martha Townsend constitute the point of departure for the texts. Desautels's books draw on the contributions of many other artists, including Lucie Laporte, Francine Simonin, Raymonde April, Irène F. Whitmore, Jocelyne Alloucherie, Ariane Thézé, and Betty Goodwin.

But the attraction to other art forms is not the only significant aspect of this writing. Attentive to the place of form in literature, Desautels also draws on feminist poetics, in her case oriented less towards protest than towards the exploration of intimism, particularly around the figures of the mother and father. In a book of letters written in collaboration with Anne-Marie ALONZO (*Lettres à Cassandre*, 1994), she discusses the motivation for her 'archaeology of the intimate'.

Numerous prizes attest to the importance that critics have attached to Desautels's already considerable body of work: in 1990 the poetry prize of the *Journal de Montréal*; in 1991 the Fondation Les Forges prize; in 1993 a Governor General's Award for *Le saut de l'ange*; the prize of the journal *Estuaire*; and Radio-Québec's Signet d'Or.

See *Lettres québécoises* 74 (été 1994) and Louise Dupré, 'Denise Desautels: la pensée du jour', *Études françaises* 29, 3 (hiver 1994), 41-50.

FRANÇOIS DUMONT

Desbiens, Jean-Paul. See *JOUAL*.

Descant (1971-). It began as a literary supplement to the Newsletter of the Graduate English Association, University of Toronto. In 1974 the magazine left the university, and under the editorship of Karen Mulhallen it became one of Canada's major literary quarterlies for poetry, fiction, interviews, visual arts, sculpture, photographs, and even music —always distinguished by fine production values, often in collaboration with printer Tim Inkster and The PORCUPINE'S QUILL. The magazine has long had an interest in international authors, and published special issues on Greece, Australia and New Zealand, India, and China. It also published a special issue on Dennis LEE (no. 39, 1982), which was simultaneously released as a hard-cover book, and on composer R. Murray Schafer, 'The labyrinth and the thread' (no. 73, 1991). *View from the North: travel writing* (1984) had a joint imprint: *Descant*/The Porcupine's Quill. In the 1980s the editorial board turned its attention to theme issues, such as 'Comedy and the Sporting Life', 'Memory Work/Dreams', 'Male Desire', 'Blood Relations', etc., as well as annual anthologies. It celebrated its 25th anniversary with a deluxe anthology, *The 'Descant' reader* (1995). An index to issues 1-50 appears in no. 58 (Fall 1989).

GEOFF HANCOCK

Desmarchais, Rex (1908-74). Born in Montreal, Quebec, and educated at Mont Saint-Louis and the Collège Sainte-Marie, he first worked for Albert Lévesque at the Librairie de l'Action française. He then began to contribute to newspapers such as *L'Ordre*, *Le Devoir*, and *Le Canada*. Later, while employed by the Montreal Catholic School Board, he wrote for *L'École canadienne*. In 1948 he became editor-in-chief of that journal and in 1955 its director. He published many articles in various magazines, reviews, and newspapers under more than a dozen pseudonyms.

In 1932 Desmarchais published 'Altitudes', a short story, in *Almanach de la langue française*, and *L'initiatrice*, a psychological novel, said to be largely autobiographical, that was much influenced by Maurice Barrès. It is a melodrama about a man's love for the rather standoffish Violaine. After her death at the age of twenty-two he learns that she was illegitimate and wished to sacrifice her love in atonement for her mother's sin; her death teaches him the true value of life. *Le feu intérieur* (1933), the story of a mismatched couple, also deals with an unfortunate love. *Tentatives*, published in *Les oeuvres d'aujourd'hui* (1937), is a collection of five essays that harshly criticize contemporary French-Canadian society and values. Desmarchais encouraged young people to put aside political and religious verbiage and to discover their own values and the taste of an authentic intellectual life. *Pour la vie française au Canada* (1938) and *La France immortelle* (1941) are also critical of his milieu, but Desmarchais's ideas regarding change were vague.

Bête de proie (1942), a philosophical novella, was followed by *La Chesnaie* (1942), a novel that is less interesting as literature than for going against the literary current of the time by publicly expressing not only a nationalist viewpoint but a right-wing ideology. By means of a rather incredible plot and characters that are little more than puppets, it tells the story of Hugues Larocque, whose ambition is to become the French-Canadian Salazar, believing that only a dictator can put Quebec back on the road to its destiny as an independent, French-speaking, Catholic country in North America. Democracy would be restored only after an educated élite were in position to govern in accordance with Larocque's ideas for an 'integral nationalism', bordering on fascism. Larocque urged his compatriots to capture control of their economy (then in the hands of anglophones) by developing its agriculture, arts, and crafts. This novel shocked many readers for its revolutionary ideas and for advocating the use of violence to overthrow the government. Perhaps it is no coincidence that it was reissued in 1971.

JACQUES COTNAM

Després, Ronald (b. 1935). Born in Moncton, New Brunswick, he studied at King George School and at St-Joseph, L'Assomption, and Ste-Anne colleges. Between the ages of seven and twenty he gave piano recitals on radio and television; and during a brief stay in Paris, while writing sketches for the Moncton paper *Évangéline*, he studied music and philosophy. On his return to Canada he spent a year as a journalist and then became a translator in the House of Commons, Ottawa, where he inaugurated a new system of translation and interpretation and assisted in a training program for translators.

Després's first collection of poems, *Silences à nourrir de sang* (1958), was published by Éditions d'Orphée at the author's expense. Though the themes are conventional—love, the sea, rain, dreams—the poems are profoundly moving for their lyricism and delicate melodiousness, reminiscent of Paul Verlaine and Paul Éluard. Quite different is *Les cloisons en vertige* (1962), which depicts a cloistered, impenetrable world from which the poet struggles to break free; anguish reigns here, and only the sea is capable of bringing a furtive hope as fragile as shifting sand. The compound words, alliteration, and assonance of these poems recall the style of Jules Laforgue. *Le scalpel ininterrompu* (1962), modelled on a medieval farce, uses a sadism similar to that of Edgar Allan Poe to attack modern science for being the ruination of mankind and to cry out against the misery of living in a cold, impassive, masochistic, and mechanistic world. *Le balcon des dieux inachevés* (1968), a compact collection of delicate lyrical poems celebrating human individuality and the power of imagination, deals with love, work, the macabre, youth, and spring.

LAURENT LAVOIE

DesRochers, Alfred (1901-78). Born in Saint-Élie d'Orford, near Sherbrooke, Quebec, he studied at the Collège Séraphique de Trois-Rivières (1918-21) and joined the staff of *La Tribune*, Sherbrooke, in 1925. Except for the interruptions of founding and managing the weekly *L'Étoile de l'Est* (1927-8) in Coaticook, Que., military service in the Canadian army (1942-4), and work as a parliamentary translator in Ottawa (1944-5), DesRochers was employed by the Sherbrooke weekly until 1950 as translator, sports editor, and advertising director. From 1953 to 1956 he worked for the Canadian Press as a translator. He went into semi-retirement after the death of his wife in 1964.

While working for *La Tribune* DesRochers became known as a poet. He met other young writers (Jovette BERNIER and Éva Senécal, among others) and founded the Société des Écrivains de l'Est, a literary movement that flourished in the late twenties and early thirties. The interests of this Sherbrooke group went beyond the Eastern Townships region, since DesRochers organized meetings that attracted writers from Montreal, Trois-Rivières, Quebec City, and even from New England. His reputation as a poet grew with the publication of *L'offrande aux vierges folles* (1928), a collection that shows the influence of the Romantics, Baudelaire, and the Parnassians. The poet's own voice became evident in *À l'ombre de l'Orford* (1929), which included the famous prefatory 'Je suis un fils déchu'; two parts of the 'Cycle des bois et des champs', sonnets inspired by life in lumber camps and on farms; and three long poems, notably 'Hymne au vent du nord'. This collection confirmed DesRochers's technical excellence and his pre-eminent place as a poet of the rural scene and of the call of the North, of freedom and adventure. *À l'ombre de l'Orford* won the Prix David of the Province of Quebec in 1932.

During the forties and fifties DesRochers's only published collection was the third edition of *À l'ombre de l'Orford* (1948), which included the thirteen sonnets of the 'Cycle du village' and the poem 'Ma patrie'. In the sixties he produced two collections: *Le retour de Titus* (1963), fifty 'stances royales' inspired by the love of the Roman emperor Titus for Bérénice, composed during the thirties, and *Élégies pour l'épouse en-allée* (1967), a series of forty-nine elegiac sonnets written after the death of his wife. In 1977, with the poet's co-operation, Romain Legaré gathered together the previously published collections and the unfinished thematic series of the 1930s and 1940s under the collective title *Oeuvres poétiques* (2 vols, 1977). While not including the entire corpus of DesRochers's poetry, the two volumes contain some 6000 poems written over a 45-year period (1922-67).

DesRochers's critical writings were overlooked until well into the sixties. And yet *Paragraphes. Interviews littéraires* (1931)—thirteen articles in the form of imaginary interviews with books (not their authors), and criticisms of writers of the 1930s like Jovette Bernier, J.-C. HARVEY, Alice Lemieux, Robert CHOQUETTE, Simone Routier, and Éva Senécal—was well received. In this work, as well as in other articles and essays that appeared in various publications, DesRochers revealed himself as a critic of the highest order. He had an innovative perception of both old and contemporary Quebec writers, doubling as theoretician and relentless defender of traditional verse.

Towards the end of his life DesRochers received awards and distinctions that recognized the quality of his writing and his position as one of the major Quebec literary figures between the wars: the Prix Duvernay in 1964, a doctorate *honoris causa* from the Université de Sherbrooke in 1976, and he was made an Officer of the Order of Canada in 1978, three months before he died.

See Richard Giguère, 'Alfred DesRochers, *Oeuvres poétiques I et II*', *Livres et auteurs québécois 1977* (1978); *À l'ombre de l'Orford précédé de L'offrande aux vierges folles* (1993); Jacques Pelletier, 'Alfred DesRochers, critique', *VOIX ET IMAGES du pays VII* (1973); and Jack Warwick, 'Alfred DesRochers: reluctant regionalist', *Queen's Quarterly* (Winter 1965).

RICHARD GIGUÈRE

Desrosiers, Léo-Paul (1896-1967). Born in Berthier-en-Haut, Quebec, he studied law at the Université de Montréal and was associated with *L'Action française*. He worked as Ottawa parliamentary correspondent for *Le Devoir* before abandoning journalism to devote himself more fully to writing. He was employed as French editor of the *Proceedings and orders of the House of Commons* from 1928 until 1941, when he became librarian of the Montreal Municipal Library, from which he retired in 1953.

Desrosiers's first work, *Âmes et paysages* (1922), a volume of conventional anecdotal tales, early displayed his mastery of language and description. *Nord-Sud* (1931), a novel for which Desrosiers was honoured by the Académie française, records the exodus in the 1840s of young Québécois from a birthplace no longer able to nurture all its sons, and the ensuing tragedies when gold fever and the hope of a better life lured many—including the main character, Vincent Douaire—to California. A loosely knit, often rambling plot serves mainly to provide a framework for vivid evocations of the Quebec rural experience and the traditional occupations of farmer, *voyageur*, lumberman, and *colon*. In his most important historical novel, *Les engagés du Grand Portage* (1938)—winner of the Prix David and translated by Christina van Oordt as *The making of Nicolas Montour* (1978)—an earlier, more colourful era of Canadian history is dramatically captured as Nicolas Montour, an unscrupulous *voyageur*, climbs to the upper echelons of the North West Company in the highly competitive fur trade of the early 1800s. The harsh environment forms a backdrop to the realities of bitter personal rivalries. Narrated in an epic present tense, this novel is enhanced by a descriptive power that Desrosiers was to consolidate in later work. He shifted towards a more idyllic portrayal of the strengths of his province's 'grass-roots' with *Les opiniâtres* (1941), a tale of the trials of day-to-day living in New France under the threat of Amerindian marauders, and with *Sources* (1942), in which Nicole de Rencontre stout-heartedly renounces twentieth-century urban comforts for the solitary and often emotionally crushing world of the land. *L'ampoule d'or* (1951)—whose theme is the inevitability of suffering and the harsh consolations of Holy Scripture—is the tale of a passionate young woman twice denied human love and saved from despair by a sense of the indestructiblity of a love for God. Theme, plot, and setting (a Gaspé village) are overshadowed by a text that is intensely poetic, in both feeling and imagery. Continuous narrative, verging on 'stream-of-consciousness', enables Desrosiers to capture the inner thoughts and emotions of his troubled heroine. Achieving a psychological impact that is typical of much French and French-Canadian fiction of the 1960s and 1970s, *L'ampoule d'or* is regarded as a modest masterpiece. Desrosiers chose not to develop the admirable technique it displays but to pursue its underlying spiritual philosophy in a more ambitious trilogy (1958-60): *Vous qui passez (Vous qui passez; Les angoisses et les tourments; Rafales sur les cimes)*. Centred on the tribulations of Romain Heurfils, a Quebec engineer, it evokes the mores of contemporary middle-class society but collapses by the middle of the second volume under the weight of excessive metaphysical discussion.

Desrosiers published a second collection of stories, *Le livre des mystères* (1936). His historical bent was expressed in several works of non-fiction: *L'accalmie* (1937), a portrait of Lord Durham; *Commencements* (1939), a preliminary for a major work on the role of the Iroquois in French-Canadian history; *Iroquoisie 1534-1646* (1947); and religious biographies of Marguerite Bourgeoys in *Les dialogues de Marthe et de Marie* (1957), and Jeanne le Ber in *Dans le nid d'aiglons, la colombe: vie de Jeanne le Ber, la recluse* (1963).

See Julia Richer, *Léo-Paul Desrosiers* (1966); Michelle Gélinas, *Léo-Paul Desrosiers ou le récit ambigu* (1973); and 'Léo-Paul Desrosiers' in Claude Pelletier, ed., *Dossiers de presse sur les écrivains québécois*, Bibliothèque du séminaire de Sherbrooke, Québec, no. 34 (1986).

IVOR ARNOLD

Deverell, Rex (b. 1941). Born in Toronto and raised in Orillia, Ontario, he graduated from McMaster University with a B.A. in Arts in 1963, and in Divinity in 1966 (submitting his first play, *The invitation*, as a thesis); in 1967 he earned a Master's degree from Union Theological Seminary, New York City. He now lives in Toronto.

During three years as a Baptist pastor in St Thomas, Ontario, Deverell wrote several plays that were produced at church conferences. In 1970 he and Ernest Schwarz adapted *The brothers* for Toronto's Studio Lab Theatre, which also produced his first children's play, *Sam and the tigers* in 1971. Later that year Deverell and his actor wife Rita began a long association with Regina's Globe Theatre (1975-90), which toured several of his plays for children, including *Shortshrift* (1972), *The Copetown City kite crisis* (1974), and *The Shinbone General Store caper* (1977). Set in small prairie towns, these plays frequently involve audience participation, although this is usually secondary to Deverell's playful treatment of serious social issues. In 1996 *Belonging* won the Chalmers Award for Plays for Young Audiences. Appointed writer-in-residence at the Globe in 1975, Deverell soon turned to adult plays with *Boiler room suite* (1978), which received numerous productions across Canada. Here fantasy brightens the lives of two homeless outcasts who, with compassion and humour, expose flaws in the powerful institutions that had failed them. In *Drift* (1981) and *Righteousness* (1983) action centres on an artist/prophet figure who recognizes that he has fallen short. In *Beyond Batoche* (1985), published also in *Deverell of the Globe* (1989), a playwright writing a documentary exposes the screens through which people filter history, especially that relating to Louis Riel. This play drew on Deverell's experience in writing a radio documentary, one of more than thirty radio and television scripts he has written for the CBC. Deverell's documentaries rely heavily on primary source material, with the addition of song and of invented scenes. *Medicare!* (1981) investigates the Saskatchewan doctors' strike of 1962, while *Black powder: Estevan 1931* (1982) deals with riots arising from a miners' strike.

Deverell has written most of his more than thirty plays specifically for the Globe's theatre-in-the-round, which encourages episodic structure and cinematic techniques. Underlying his work is a strong spiritual conviction expressed as the need for communal effort. His sympathy for the underdog is ultimately optimistic, as he gives the audience power to effect change. LISBIE RAE

Deverell, William (b. 1937). Born in Regina, Saskatchewan, and raised there and in Saskatoon, where his father was a newspaper editor, Deverell worked his way through law school at the University of Saskatchewan as a reporter, graduating in 1963, and moved to Vancouver, British Columbia, to establish a law practice specializing in civil-liberties cases. After the success of his novel *Needles* (1979), he gradually withdrew from the legal profession and is currently a full-time writer living on North Pender Island, B.C.

Deverell attempted both indigenous crime novels and international thrillers; of the latter novels—*High crimes* (1981), *Mecca* (1983), with its main character a Canadian poet named Jacques Sawchuk), and *Platinum blues* (1988)—the least said the better. *Needles* owes more of its success to publicity hype than to its content, which is sensationalist in the extreme, while *The dance of Shiva* (1984), set in and around Vancouver, is a contrived and grossly biased piece of liberal humanist propaganda.

With *Mindfield* (1989), however, Deverell found a topic that suited his philosophy. It is one of three novels based on the disgraceful practice of Dr Ewen Cameron at McGill University, Montreal, who developed brainwashing techniques for the CIA. (See also Anne Collins' *In the sleep room; the story of the CIA brainwashing experiments in Canada*, 1988; Timothy FINDLEY's *The telling of lies*, 1986; and Elizabeth Nickson's *The monkey puzzle tree*, 1994. Trevor Cole's play, *Just a thought*, is also based on the subject.)

Deverell returned to Vancouver as the setting for *Kill all the lawyers* (1994), a mystery novel that feminists are likely to view as a mere wimp's sexist fantasy.

Deverell's *Street legal: the betrayal* (1995) is a prequel to his long-running TV series 'Street Legal'. Set in Toronto in 1980, it is a spin-off in which a killer stalks the city.

Deverell has also written a non-fiction account of his unsuccessful defence of Robert Frisbee against a charge of murder, *Fatal cruise* (1991). DAVID SKENE-MELVIN

Dewart, Edward Hartley (1828-1903). Born in Stradone, County Cavan, Ireland, Dewart was six years old when his parents settled in Dummer Township, Upper Canada (Ontario). He attended local schools and the provincial Normal School, entered the Methodist ministry in 1851, and was ordained in 1855. In 1879 he received a D.D. from Victoria University, Toronto. He held various posts in Canada East (Quebec) and West (Ontario) until 1869, when he became editor of the *Christian Guardian*, Toronto, remaining in that position until 1894. Dewart compiled the first and last collection of Canadian poetry prior to Confederation, *Selections from Canadian poets; with occasional critical and biographical notes, and an introductory essay on Canadian poetry* (Montreal, 1864). He attempted to preserve poetry that he feared would be lost. In his introductory essay he attributed the lack of acceptance for Canadian poetry to a general preference among the educated for poems inspired by the romantic past of the countries in which they were born, and argued for the role of poetry in building a national spirit. Dewart marked out 'a future bright with promise' as the alternative inspiration for Canadian poets.

Dewart also published a book of original verse, *Songs of life* (Toronto, 1869); a collection of essays and verse, *Essays for the times: studies of eminent men and important living questions* (Toronto, 1898); and numerous pamphlets on religious subjects. CAL SMILEY

Dewdney, Christopher (b. 1951). Born in London, Ontario, into a family of scientists and artists, he received his education through local public schools, the Beal Art Annex in London, and his father, Selwyn, who was an anthropologist, ethno-archaeologist, writer, and teacher. Christopher Dewdney's poetic vision is partly inspired by the geology of the coves of the oxbow lakes in southwestern Ontario. He moved to Toronto in 1980.

Dewdney has been writer-in-residence at Trent University (1990) and the University of Western Ontario (1991). Appointed in 1993 Fellow to the McLuhan Program in Culture and Technology (University of Toronto), he was poetry editor at COACH HOUSE PRESS, and teaches creative writing at York University, Toronto. He appears in Ron Mann's film *Poetry in motion* (1982), and his text 'Hand in glove with an old hat' was staged in 1982 at the Theatre Centre in Toronto. In 1996 he was invited to read at the prestigious International Poetry Festival in Rotterdam, The Netherlands.

Dewdney's poetry, published in journals across North America and in Britain, features a unique scientific idiom and oscillates between science and myth, reason and intuition, the empirical and the surrealistic, in its quest for the 'secular grail'—or a scientific explanation of the mystery of being. His early writing, collected in *Predators of the adoration* (1983), nominated for a Governor General's Award, spins out of a vortex of the transitory and the infinite as perspectives onto the natural history and palaeozoic geology of southwestern Ontario. Featuring postmodern form and a Romantic influence, Dewdney's subsequent collections of poetry—including *The immaculate perception* (1986) and *The radiant inventory* (1988), both nominated for a Governor General's Award—explore linguistics, neurophysiology, and the topology of human consciousness as they contemplate the self. *Demon pond* (1995) returns to postmodern concerns with conceptual paradoxes and multiple meanings in language, which are aligned with the Barthesian notion of finding pleasure in the open or unfixed meaning of the text. Dewdney's prose work, *The secular grail* (1993), explores the cityscape from a McLuhanist perspective, and offers an interdisciplinary response to technoculture, cyberspace, information synthesis, and the medium of language as extensions of human cognitive processes.

See Eli MANDEL, *The family romance* (1986); Stan Dragland, *Bees of the invisible: essays in contemporary English-Canadian writing* (1989); and Karl Jirgens, *Canadian writers and their works*, vol. 12 (1996). See also POETRY IN ENGLISH 1950 TO 1982: 3. KARL JIRGENS

Di Cicco, Pier Giorgio (b. 1949). Born in Arezzo, Italy, he was brought by his parents to Montreal in 1952 and lived briefly in Toronto before his family moved to Baltimore, where Di Cicco received his early education. He returned to Canada in 1968 to attend high school and then the University of Toronto, where he studied creative writing under F.W. Watt and received a B.A. in English (1972) and a B.Ed. in 1973. He worked as an assistant editor for *Books in Canada* and became involved with several literary journals, including *Waves*, *Poetry Toronto*, DESCANT, *Argomenti Canadesi* (Rome), and *Italia-America* (San Francisco). He received a Master of Divinity degree in 1990 and is now a Brother in the Order of St Augustine.

Di Cicco's first collection of poetry, *We are the light turning*, was published in 1975; but his writing did not come to public attention until it was anthologized in Al PURDY's *Storm warning II* (1976). Thereafter his poems appeared in a great many literary magazines in Canada and abroad. Writing with originality and honesty about a wide range of interests—from the Italo-Canadian experience to neo-surrealism—and employing a variety of forms, including surrealism and 'deep images' (images in which the vehicle tends to be both archetypal and subconscious), Di Cicco has been a prolific poet: *The sad facts* (1977), *The circular dark* (1977), *Dancing in the house of cards* (1977), *A burning patience* (1978), *Dolce-Amaro* (1979), *The tough romance* (1979), *A straw hat for everything* (1981), *Flying deeper into the century* (1982), *Dark to light: reasons for humanness* (1983), *Women we never see again* (1984), *Post-sixties nocturne* (1985), *Virgin science* (1986), and *The city of hurried dreams: poems 1977-1983* (1993). Di Cicco edited *Roman candles: an anthology of seventeen Italo-Canadian poets* (1978). BRUCE MEYER

Dickson, Lovat (1902-87). Horatio (Rache) Lovat Dickson was born in New South Wales, Australia, the son of a mining engineer, and was taken to South Africa at the age of seven. He attended school in England from 1913 to 1917 before coming to Canada. He worked at various jobs, travelling widely, and founded and edited a weekly newspaper at the Blue Diamond Mine in Alberta. In 1923 he enrolled at the University of Alberta, graduated with distinction in 1927, winning the Governor General's Gold Medal, and stayed on to lecture for a year. (During the Second World War Dickson wrote a romantic novel, *Out of the west land*, 1944, based in part on his arrival in Canada as a youth and on his life as a student in Alberta.) He then accepted the offer of a wealthy Canadian, who had bought the *Fortnightly Review*, to edit that periodical and thus entered the London publishing world. (He also edited *The Review of Reviews* from 1931 to 1934.) In 1932 he started his own publishing firm, Lovat Dickson Limited, and in 1933 launched *Lovat Dickson's Magazine* to establish his imprint in the literary world. One of his first publishing successes was *Pilgrims of the wild* (1935); he made its author, Grey Owl (Archibald Stansfeld BELANEY), a celebrity in England by arranging two highly successful lecture tours for him in 1936-7 and 1937-8. In 1938 Dickson sold his publishing list to Peter Davies and joined the Macmillan Company as assistant editor of general books, working under the editor, Harold Macmillan. He became chief editor, and then a director of the firm in 1941; when he retired in 1967 he moved with his wife Marguerite to Toronto. He was an Officer of the Order of Canada and a Fellow of the Royal Society of Canada.

Dickson's lifelong devotion to writing and writers, which led him into publishing, sustained another career as a biographer. Unlike many editors, Dickson was a born writer, with the literary skill to master a variety of subjects and present them in a graceful narrative. The subject with whom he was most identified as a biographer was Grey Owl, who became his friend. In 1938, shortly after Grey Owl's death, Dickson published *A green leaf: a tribute to Grey Owl*, which includes an affectionate account of Grey Owl's two visits to England, press commentaries, and Grey Owl's letters. *Half-breed: the story of Grey Owl* (1939), a somewhat romantic portrait, with lyrical descriptions of Grey Owl's Canadian wilderness, is based partly on anecdotes told by Grey Owl to the author; it was coloured by the desire to defend him against the charge of being an impostor. It was superseded by *Wilderness man: the strange story of Grey Owl* (1973; rpr. 1975), the product of assiduous research and greater objectivity, in which a complex and well-rounded Grey Owl emerges. Dickson's other biographies are *Richard Hillary* (1950), about the author of a classic war memoir, *The last enemy*, who was disfigured in the Second World War and was later killed in action at twenty-three; *H.G. Wells: his turbulent life and times* (1969; rpr. 1971), a study of the author, with an emphasis on his works, that was written with the permission of two of Wells's sons and the encouragement of Rebecca West; and *Radclyffe Hall and the well of loneliness: a Sapphic chronicle* (1975), a biography of the lesbian novelist that Dickson was asked to write by her companion, Una Troubridge.

Dickson's flair for relating both the influential events and the atmosphere of a life (in this case his own) is evident in two volumes of memoirs: *The ante room* (1959; rpr. 1975), and *The house of words* (1973; rpr. 1976), which takes him into his early years with Macmillan's.

The museum makers: the story of the Royal Ontario Museum (1986), Dickson's last work, is a readable, informative, concise history of this great museum. WILLIAM TOYE

Dictionary of Canadian biography/Dictionnaire biographique du Canada. The largest sustained historical research project ever undertaken in Canada and one of the country's most important reference works, the *DCB/DBC* has been planned chronologically, according to the death dates of the persons included. Thus the volumes so far published, I (1966)-XIII (1994), present individuals who died between the years 1001 and 1910. An index volume for I-XII has been published. The decision to arrange volumes chronologically has meant that persons related in their lives, or living through much the same events, are also associated in print; the volumes therefore make a substantial contribution to the social history of a developing Canada as well as to biography. The 500-to-600 biographies in each volume, arranged alphabetically, are based as far as possible on documentary sources and are prepared by hundreds of contributors in Canada, the United States, Great Britain, France, and Australia. The *DCB/DBC* has a staff of professional editors, with graduate training usually in history, who are based at the University of Toronto and Université Laval and who work under the direction of a general editor (from 1989, Ramsay COOK) and a directeur général adjoint (from 1973, Jean Hamelin). Each volume appears in two editions published simultaneously, one in English (published by the UNIVERSITY OF TORONTO PRESS) and one in French (published by Les Presses de l'Université Laval).

The project came into being as a result of a bequest by a Toronto businessman, James Nicholson (1861-1952), which made provision for the use of the income from the residue and bulk of his estate by the University of Toronto to create a dictionary of national biography for Canada, modelled on the *Dictionary of national biography* of Great Britain. The bequest became available in 1959, the University having meanwhile entrusted the publication to the University of Toronto Press. Dr George W. Brown was the first general editor, and before he died in 1963 he established the tradition of wide discussion with the scholarly community and with research institutions such as libraries and archives that has been a notable aspect of the DCB/DBC. In March 1961 arrangements were completed with Université Laval and its press for a French edition. The DCB/DBC quickly became a bilingual, bicultural project in which there is full and daily collaboration between its two offices in all aspects of planning, writing, and editing, and in maintaining a high level of translation as contributions, written in either English or French, are translated into the other language. The second general editor, Dr David Hayne (1965-9), was particularly concerned with the methodologies of translation and bibliography to be followed. Marcel Trudel was directeur général adjoint of the DCB/DBC in its founding years (1961-5) and was succeeded for 1965-71 by André Vachon. The general editor from 1969 to 1989 was Francess G. Halpenny, who had been associated with the project from its beginning in her capacity as Editor, then Managing Editor, of University of Toronto Press. Together she and Jean Hamelin brought to the DCB/DBC a wide acquaintance with scholars across Canada writing in English and in French.

By 1972 the financial needs of the project had gone well beyond the capacities of the Nicholson bequest and special subventions from the CANADA COUNCIL, the Centennial Commission, and Quebec's Ministère des Affaires culturelles. In 1973 and 1974 the DCB/DBC, with an enlarged staff, received increased funds from the Canada Council, and during the late seventies and eighties it had grants from the Social Sciences and Humanities Research Council, with further help from various government bodies. Since 1989 reductions in its grants have meant a significant loss of staff and concern for maintenance of the publication program; special aid has come from the two sponsoring universities, the government of Ontario, and some private funding.

The project has received special citations of merit from the Royal Society of Canada, the Canadian Historical Association, the Association for Canadian Studies, and was awarded the University of British Columbia Medal for Biography (for vol. VIII).

The DCB/DBC is in several senses a 'public' project. Maintained by public funds, it is public in the visibility of its activities; in its reliance on numerous consultants, contributors, and institutions; in reaching out to general readers as well as scholars; and in its very subject: the people of Canada from east to west, from south to north.

FRANCESS G. HALPENNY

di Michele, Mary (b. 1949). Born in Lanciano, Italy, she came to Canada at the age of six. She completed a B.A. in English at the University of Toronto (1972), and an M.A. in English and creative writing at the University of Windsor (1974). In Toronto she became part of a literary circle—including Pier Giorgio DI CICCO, Roo BORSON, and Bronwen WALLACE—that supported and inspired her work. Concentrating on her writing, di Michele gained some income through work as a freelance writer and editor (*Toronto Life*, *Poetry Toronto*); writer-in-residence positions (in and around Toronto; as well as in Regina, 1987-8, Montreal, 1990; and Rome, 1991); writing workshops (throughout Ontario and in Banff, Alberta, 1990); and from several CANADA COUNCIL grants. Since 1991 she has been a member of the English department at Concordia University, Montreal.

Di Michele's collections of poetry include *Tree of August* (1978); *Bread and chocolate* (1980), printed together with a sequence of poems by Bronwen Wallace; *Mimosa and other poems* (1981), of which the title poem won first prize in the 1980 CBC Literary Competition; *Necessary sugar* (1984); *Immune to gravity* (1986), a finalist for the Ontario Trillium Award; *Luminous emergencies* (1990), which contains a sequence of Chilean poems based on a 1987 tour with poets Patrick LANE, Lorna CROZIER, and Gary GEDDES; and *Stranger in you* (1995), new and selected poems. She has also written a novel, *Under my skin* (1994), and edited an anthology of poetry, *Anything is possible* (1984). Vivid images and metaphysical intensity characterize di Michele's lyrical poems. The early works explore the poet's Italian-Canadian heritage, her family, and her coming of age. An independent young girl's ambivalence towards patriarchal authority, as characterized by the father figure, is the basis of many poems and central to 'Mimosa', a sequence of monologues spoken by a father and his two daughters. Even in her earliest work, the poet's awareness of the power dynamics inherent in the confessional act transforms personal lyrics into self-conscious meditations on the writer's craft. In her later work she increasingly situates herself within larger contexts of her literary legacies (as in 'My Hart Crane' and 'Rilke Sentiero'), and of her political responsibilities as a feminist poet (see especially the Chilean poems in *Luminous emergencies*).

There is a detailed article on di Michele's work by Michael Morgan Holmes in *Canadian writers and their works*, vol. II (1995).

NATHALIE COOKE

Diviners, The (1974). Winner of a Governor General's Award, Margaret LAURENCE's last novel is also the culmination of her Manawaka cycle and is linked to earlier ones by the inclusion of characters such as Stacey MacAindra of *The fire-dwellers*, events such as the fiery death of Piquette Tonnerre, and objects such as Hagar Shipley's plaid pin from *The STONE ANGEL*.

As in the earlier novels, the main character is a woman, but unlike the others Morag Gunn grows up in the poorest section of town, looked down upon by most of the townspeople. Orphaned young, she is cared for by the garbage-collector Christie Logan and his obese wife. In the eyes of the Manawakans only the Métis are lower on the social scale; it is with Jules Tonnerre, a Métis, later to be father of her child, that Morag forms a life-long bond.

Like the protagonists of the three previous Manawaka novels, Morag leaves the town as soon as she can, only to find that she carries it always in her head. The narrative traces her life from childhood poverty to work as a local journalist, through her years at university, early marriage to and divorce from a professor of English, her career as a successful novelist, the birth of her daughter, life as a single mother in Vancouver and England, and her eventual return to claim Canada as her homeland. Some aspects of this loosely parallel Laurence's own life-story; the resemblance is clearest in the setting of the present where, like Laurence, Morag is writing a novel in her cabin on the banks of Ontario's Otonabee River. In an interesting example of self-reflexivity, the last words of the book imply that Morag's novel is in fact *The diviners*.

The present action of the novel covers the events of one summer, narrated in the opening section of each chapter and the whole of the final chapter. In the present, Morag completes a novel, worries over and comes to a new understanding with her eighteen-year old daughter, and visits the dying Jules. Morag strives to distinguish fact from fiction, myth from reality, only to discover the paradox that such dualities co-exist. The river that seems to flow both ways as the wind blows against its current provides a metaphor for this paradox, for the simultaneous backward flow of memory and forward flow of time.

Among the novel's large and varied cast of characters, Christie Logan is the most original creation. He is a natural poet and storyteller whose knowledge of society from analysis of its garbage leads to his socialist philosophy and uninhibited, often very funny, social commentary. Scavenging serves as a correlative for the writer's hoarding of seemingly irrelevant material picked up in unlikely places. Water-divining is, as the title suggests, the key metaphor in the novel's exploration of the nature of writing. To Laurence, the art of writing is a gift of grace, a mystery as impossible to fathom as is the power to locate underground water.

The novel incorporates a range of styles, from the racily colloquial to the lyrical, the latter especially evident in the nature descriptions that give a mystical tone to this deeply spiritual novel.

Susan J. Warwick's book-length analysis of the novel is entitled *River of now and then* (1992); a bibliography of the many articles on the novel is found in Hildegard Kuester's *The crafting of chaos* (1994). The selected correspondence of Margaret Laurence and Al PURDY, *A friendship in letters* (1993), edited by John Lennox, provides insight into some of the difficulties Laurence faced in writing the novel. A film version of *The diviners* (1992) was directed by Anne Wheeler.

JOAN COLDWELL

Dobbs, Kildare (b. 1923). He was born in Merrut, India, and educated at St Columba's College, Rathfarnum, Ireland, and Jesus College, Cambridge, from which he graduated in 1947. During the Second World War he served in the Royal Navy, first as an able seaman and later as a sub-lieutenant, before going into the commandos. After the war he took a teaching diploma at London University before going in 1947 to what was then Tanganyika, where he served as a magistrate. He taught high school in Venice, Ontario, after immigrating to Canada in 1952. Thereafter he worked in Toronto as a book editor for nearly ten years with the MACMILLAN COMPANY. It was at this time that he began writing and broadcasting radio scripts for the Canadian Broadcasting Corporation. These ranged from short talks and reviews to an impressive exploration of Joyce's *Finnegans Wake*. Through the 1960s and 1970s, he was a regular contributor to the CBC's literary program *Anthology*, produced for most of that time by ROBERT WEAVER, with whom, in 1956 he became one of the founding editors of the influential *TAMARACK REVIEW*. From 1965 to 1967 he served as managing editor of *Saturday Night*. In 1968 he became a literary columnist for the *Toronto Star*. Now a free-lance journalist, he is particularly known as a travel writer.

In the previous entry George WOODCOCK called Dobbs's first book, *Running to paradise* (1962; rpr. 1974), which won a Governor General's Award, 'a work of embroidered autobiography', and complimented the book's urbanity and wit, which he contrasted with the prevailing 'laboured Leacockian tradition of Canadian humour'. With photographer Peter Varley, Dobbs produced *Canada* (1964; rev. 1969), a celebration of the beauties of the country. In 1968 he put together a collection of wise and quirky literary essays, *Reading the time*, taken from his CBC and newspaper writings, in which he invited the reader to 'see the house of mirrors [contemporary society] for what it is'.

In quite another mood Dobbs produced, with the English artist Ronald Searle, *The great fur opera* (1970), a history of the Hudson's Bay Company that manages to be both good history and good fun (surely the closest a Canadian has come to touching Sellar's and Yeatman's celebrated *1066 and all that*). In *Pride and fall* (1981) Dobbs turned to fiction, looking back to his African experiences and hewing stories that touch many levels of the passion and ironies of colonial life.

Widely travelled, Dobbs has not only written about his travels (*Anatolian suite*, 1989, *Ribbon of highway*, 1992), but has edited an anthology of travel writing by a selection of Canadian writers: *Away from home* (1985). *Ribbon of highway*, a journey across Canada by Greyhound bus, draws the country together the way the railways once did. Always fascinated by the ways of the rich, Dobbs has written articles in the *Financial Post*, which have been collected in a volume called *Smiles and chukkas* (1995), in which he explores the curiosities of affluence with wisdom and humour. At a time when most writers his age are slowing down, Dobbs tried something new: his first volume of poetry, *The eleventh hour: poems for the third millennium* (1997).

Because of his outspoken tongue, his intelligence, and his inability to suffer fools, Dobbs has, in the parlance of the times, been marginalized. Nevertheless, over the past twenty years he has come to the aid of many of the best-known cultural leaders, by making them more eloquent in their speeches.

HOWARD ENGEL

Domanski, Don. See Writing in the MARITIMES: 5.

Donaldson, Jeffrey. See POETRY IN ENGLISH 1983 to 1996: 3.

Donnell, David (b. 1939). Born in St Mary's, Ontario, he was largely self-educated through his own reading and research in Montreal. Donnell moved to Toronto in 1958 and worked at a variety of jobs before publishing his first book, *Poems* (1961), about which Eli MANDEL cited their 'rich and sombre music'. During this early period in Toronto, Donnell read his poems at the Thursday Night readings at the Bohemian Embassy, where Margaret ATWOOD, Gwendolyn MacEWEN, Milton ACORN, and other poets began to establish their reputations. With John Robert COLOMBO, he printed Atwood's first book, *Double Persephone* (1961), and then abruptly stopped writing between 1963 and 1974.

The Donnell who re-emerged with *The blue sky: poems 1974 to 1977* (illustrated by Joe ROSENBLATT) can best be described as a 'spiritual surrealist' who examines the relationships of his life from an oblique perspective, as in the title poem 'The blue sky' or in the playfully moving 'Letter to the mountains', where he mixes the ironic and the deeply spiritual. Donnell continued his growth and exploration of the ironic, set against a backdrop of high culture, contemporary thought, and twentieth-century history from an urban perspective, in *Dangerous crossings* (1980). In 'A poem about Poland', where 'the obvious comes in and sits down at our table', or 'Making it in the city', Donnell presents the first inklings of a major theme that evolves in his work over the next several volumes: the contextualization of the individual within the psychological, moral, and imaginative fabric of the contemporary urban experience.

Settlements (1983), for which Donnell won a Governor General's Award, is a compilation of work from his previous two volumes with some reworkings (e.g. 'A poem about Poland') and new material, containing poems such as 'Strachan Avenue', which blend Donnell's love for the urban landscapes of Toronto with his flair and passion for nostalgia. In *Water Street days* (1989) he examines his familial past and his childhood in St Mary's; the poems are simultaneously confessional and openly narrative in the voice of the ironic, self-critical raconteur. By contrast, *China blues* (1992) is a far more general book. As in its predecessor volumes, Donnell offers poems about the city and about the subtle tensions and ironies of contemporary urban life; but the voice here is that of a narrator who is determined to find and mine stories from the realities of overlooked daily existence and the strange twists of perception that inhabit those moments.

Donnell's fascination with prose fiction, evident in the final sections of *China blues* and *Water Street days*, becomes an important feature in *Dancing in the dark* (1996), which concludes with a series of stories focused on the protagonist Tom Garrone—an Everyman for the nineties, a young urbanite searching for his identity in the labyrinthine world of contemporary pop culture and 'alternative lifestyles'. In many respects he is a 'Hemingway' of the present era, a character in search of verity and understanding who cannot disconnect himself from his milieu. In *The blue Ontario Hemingway boat race* (1985) Donnell fictionalized the factual material he had gathered in *Hemingway in Toronto: a post-modern tribute* (1982). In both cases, Donnell strove not only to follow Hemingway through the events of the author's days in Toronto after the First World War, but to get inside his character's mind and look at the world through the erudite vision of a figure totally immersed in the culture of his age. BRUCE MEYER

Donovan, Rita. See NOVELS IN ENGLISH 1983 TO 1996: OTHER NOVELS 2(a).

Dooley, D. See CRITICISM IN ENGLISH: 5(f).

Double hook, The. See Sheila WATSON.

Doucet, Louis-Joseph. See POETRY IN FRENCH: 3.

Dougall, Lily (1858-1923). Born in Montreal and educated in New York, and at the University of Edinburgh and St Andrew's University, Scotland, she lived in Montreal from 1897 to 1903. By 1911 she had moved permanently to Cumnor, England, becoming the centre of a group dedicated to religious thought. Her first novel, *Beggars all*, appeared in 1892, and in all she published ten novels, one volume of short stories, and eight books of religious philosophy. Four of Dougall's novels have Canadian settings. *What necessity knows* (London, 1893) deals with British immigrants and religious conflict in eastern Quebec, and focuses on rural Canada's challenge to imported hierarchies in terms of religion, class, and gender. In *The madonna of a day: a study* (New York, 1895), the heroine finds her attitudes and values are challenged when she experiences life in a mining camp in British Columbia. *The mermaid: a love tale* (New York, 1895), set on Prince Edward Island and the Magdalens, is about a doctor who is profoundly affected by a child murder he had witnessed in his youth. *The Zeit-Geist* (London, 1895) is the story of a young man's conversion from a life of dissolution to spirituality through non-dogmatic religious thought.

Dougall's fiction is characterized by popular melodramatic conventions of her time such as coincidence, disguise, hidden identity, and thwarted love, but is noteworthy for its constant exploration of religious and philosophical themes, based on her own thorough knowledge of contemporary religious theories and sects, and for its portrayal of intelligent and spirited young women who are independent, morally reflective, and naturally drawn to the idea of egalitarian marriage.

Dougall was the first editor of *The World Wide* (Montreal), a journal of contemporary thought. After 1908 she turned to writing religious tracts, the first of which, published anonymously, was the essay *Pro Christo et ecclesia* (1900).

See Lorraine McMullen, 'Lily Dougall: the religious vision of a Canadian novelist', *Studies in Religious Sciences* 16, no. 1 (Winter 1987). MARILYN ROSE

Douglas, Gilean. See NATURE WRITING IN ENGLISH: 5.

Douglas, Marion. See LESBIAN LITERATURE.

Douglas & McIntyre. Co-founded in Vancouver, British Columbia, in 1971 by Jim Douglas and Scott McIntyre, it has grown from its inaugural two titles into Canada's fifth-largest Canadian-owned trade house and the largest Canadian-owned English-language publishing house headquartered outside Toronto. Still based in Vancouver, with Scott McIntyre its president, it is something of a Canadian success story, having maintained a strong presence in British Columbia while expanding a national base in Toronto and an international export market that accounts for a fifth of its sales. There are three publishing divisions. The adult division's strengths include Canadian fiction, with an emphasis on Chinese-Canadian and Native authors, as well as French-Canadian literature in translation. Some notable works are Sky LEE's *Disappearing moon cafe* (1991), Bill Richardson's *Bachelor brothers' bed and breakfast* (1993), Wayson Choy's *The jade peony* (1995), and Monique PROULX's *The sex of the stars* (1996). Its strengths in non-fiction include Native studies, art and architecture, history, social/

environmental issues, transportation, biography, and food and wine. In 1993 the firm launched a new division out of Vancouver, Greystone Books, focusing on natural history, natural science, environmental issues, guidebooks, sports, and the prairie interests of its newly acquired Western Producer Books. The company's children's division, based in Toronto and overseen by Patsy Aldana, conjoins the well-established Groundwood books with Douglas & McIntyre's own titles. Along with its own publications, the firm also acts as representative and distributor for a number of national and international publishers. Currently it publishes seventy-five new titles and fifty reprints a year, having produced since its inception over 1500 books.

BURKE CULLEN

Doyle, Brian (b. 1935). Born in Ottawa, Ontario, and educated there at Carleton University (Bachelor of Journalism, 1957; B.A., 1959), he became a high-school teacher and the author of outstanding fiction for young people. From his earliest novel, *Hey, Dad* (1978), to his darkest, *Uncle Ronald* (1996), Doyle's subject matter has been the city of Ottawa and the Gatineau hills, their streets and schools, topography, history, and eccentric residents. Doyle is known for his robust humour, his sensitivity to the rhythm and sound of words, his psychological penetration of young adulthood, and his detailed renderings of Irish-Canadian home life. His nine young-adult novels are populated by wildly comic caricatures and first-person (usually young male) narrators who distinctively combine strength and sensitivity: they are as comfortable reading poetry as playing hockey. His young adults are deliberately unprotected from the realities of sickness and death (*Up to low*, 1982), runaway fathers (*You can pick me up at Peggy's Cove*, 1979), racial and ethnic prejudice (*Angel Square*, 1984; *Spud Sweetgrass*, 1992), and wife and child abuse (*Uncle Ronald*, 1996). But they are also affected by the spirit of optimism about human nature that permeates Doyle's fiction. Indeed, Doyle's imagination tends to lead him to extremes: a kind of Dickensian comedy and sentimentality sit side by side with tragedy, with little revealed of the ground in between. This dramatic tendency is underscored by his technique: he structures his work in scenes, and even gives to places the dramatic presence and influence of well-realized characters. His narrators speak in a fluid, conversational style that catches the voices of other characters in a manner reminiscent of James Joyce's interior monologues. Both *Up to low* and *Easy Avenue* (1988) won the Canadian Library Association's Book of the Year Award. In 1991 Doyle won the Vicki Metcalf Award for his body of work, and *Covered bridge* (1990) won the Mr. Christie's Book Award.

MARIE C. DAVIS

Doyle, Mike (b. 1928), who has also written under the name of Charles Doyle, was born in England of Irish parents. He lived in New Zealand from 1951 to 1966 and it was there that he first published his poetry. In 1967 he was a Visiting Fellow in American Studies at Yale University and decided to stay in North America. The next year he became a professor of English at the University of Victoria. While there he edited a poetry magazine, *Tuatara*, which he ran from 1969 to 1974.

Doyle's poetry has always shown a concern for place, at times taking on the focus of locality that is at the centre of the poetry of William Carlos Williams—for whom, he says, he has a great deal of affection and respect. He edited *William Carlos Williams: the critical heritage* (1980) and in 1982 published a critical study, *William Carlos Williams and the American poem*. For many years Doyle was actively involved in the publication of *The William Carlos Williams Newsletter*. Doyle's own poetry has gone through several developments since his arrival in Canada, from the imagistic notations of *Preparing for the ark* (1973) through to more formally constructed poems in *Stonedancer* (1976). His straightforward approach appeared more succinctly in *A steady hand* (1982) and in the chapbooks *The urge to raise hats* (1989) and *Separate fidelities* (1991). In succeeding years he has sharpened his linguistic responses, still keeping his concern for place and the relation of art and life, assuming a steadfastly honest and direct expression, often underpinned with clear-eyed irony and a deft satirical touch. His poetry shows a keen response to the work of other artists from a whole range of countries. See *Intimate absences: selected poems 1954-1992* (1993).

Doyle has written two books about New Zealand authors, *H.A.K. Mason* (1970) and *James Baxter* (1976), as well as a critical survey, *Aspects of New Zealand poetry* (1967).

He has written other volumes about literary figures, including *Richard Aldington: a biography* (1989); he is the Canadian correspondent for the society devoted to the study of Aldington and edited *Richard Aldington: reappraisals* (1990). In 1985 he edited a book of essays about the work of Wallace Stevens.

PETER STEVENS

Dragland, Stan. See NOVELS IN ENGLISH 1960 TO 1982: OTHER TALENTS, OTHER WORKS: 4.

Drama in English. The beginnings to 1953. 1. EIGHTEENTH AND NINETEENTH CENTURIES. Although several garrison and amateur groups were performing plays in the Maritimes in the late eighteenth century, no Canadian drama emerged, well-known English plays being the standard repertoire. Two dull verse dramas—George Cockings' *The conquest of Canada; or, The siege of Quebec* (London, 1766), and Robert Rogers' *Ponteach; or, The savages of America* (London, 1766)—are Canadian only by virtue of their subject matter and their authors' brief sojourns in Canada. In the nineteenth century the situation began to change rapidly. An indigenous dramatic literature developed despite the domination of Canadian theatre by foreign touring stars and companies throughout the century. A prominent genre was verse drama, most of which lacked theatrical vitality and literary originality. Eliza Lanesford Cushing published poetic plays on historical and biblical themes in *The LITERARY GARLAND* in the late 1830s and early 1840s. Charles HEAVYSEGE's *Saul* (Montreal, 1857), although admired by Hawthorne and Longfellow, is turgid, as is his later *Count Filippo; or, The unequal marriage* (Montreal, 1860). *The enamorado* (Summerside, Prince Edward Island, 1879) and *De Roberval* (Saint John, 1888) by John HUNTER-DUVAR are undistinguished blank-verse history plays. Charles MAIR's ponderous *Tecumseh* (Toronto, 1886) was widely acclaimed in its time; but, like Sarah Ann CURZON's *Laura Secord; or, The heroine of 1812* (Toronto, 1887), it is marked more by patriotic excess than by literary or theatrical quality. Two historical verse dramas by Wilfred CAMPBELL were published in one volume as *Mordred and Hildebrand* (Ottawa, 1895), appearing again, with *Daulac and morning* (Ottawa, 1897), in *Poetical tragedies of Wilfred Campbell* (Toronto, 1908). Political and social satire was a livelier and far more stageworthy dramatic genre than verse drama. Many satires were published anonymously in such periodicals as *GRIP* and the *Canadian Illustrated News*; others appeared as independent publications, though still sometimes anonymously, as was the case with *The female consistory of Brockville* (Brockville, 1856) by 'Caroli Candidus', an imperfect but sharp attack on hypocrisy in the Presbyterian Church, and two interesting political sketches by 'Sam Scribble': *Dolorsolatio* (Montreal, 1865) and *The king of the beavers* (Montreal, 1865). Nicholas Flood DAVIN's *The fair Grit; or, The advantages of coalition* (Toronto, 1876) is one of the best nineteenth-century political satires, but it did not meet with the stage success of William Henry Fuller's *H.M.S. Parliament; or, The lady who loved a government clerk* (Ottawa, 1880), an attack on Sir John A. Macdonald and his National Policy that was performed in many Canadian cities in 1880. Sarah Ann Curzon ridiculed sexual discrimination in *The sweet girl graduate* (first published in *Grip-Sack*, volume 1, 1882). *Ptarmigan; or, A Canadian carnival* (Hamilton, 1895), by Jean Newton McIlwraith, is a less adroit satire on the annexation issue. Parodies and burlesques were other lively and popular nineteenth-century genres. John Wilson Bengough's *Bunthorne abroad; or, The lass that loved a pirate* (Toronto, 1833) is a parody of Gilbert and Sullivan operettas; and two burlesques by George Broughall, *The 90th on active service; or, Campaigning in the North West* (Winnipeg, 1885) and *The tearful and tragical tale of the tricky troubadour; or, The truant tracked* (Winnipeg, 1886) were performed at Winnipeg's Princess Opera House in 1885 and 1886. The masques, comic operettas, fantasies, and burlesques of Fredrick Dixon were well received as private theatricals in Government House, Ottawa, in the 1870s.

2. THE TWENTIETH CENTURY. The first half of the century, like the nineteenth, produced a wide variety of dramatic forms. *A runaway couple* (1910), *The man who went* (1918), and other dramatic comedies and melodramas by W.A. Tremayne, were popular in both Canada and the United States and are wholly conventional. Equally conventional are the morality plays of Ida Potter, such as *Wanted—a chauffeur* (1928), a temperance play performed at the Manitoba Provincial Temperance Convention in May 1928. Many plays written for children (see CHILDREN'S DRAMA IN ENGLISH) betray similar moral and didactic purposes. Didacticism is the hallmark too of workers' plays of the 1930s, some of which are printed in *'Eight men speak' and other plays from the Canadian workers' theatre* (1976), edited by Richard Wright and Robin Endres. Though there is a raw dramatic force in these political plays, they suffer inevitably from plot predictability and unsubtle language and characterization. Greater skills are evident in radio drama, a genre that attracted many playwrights (and listeners) in the 1930s and 1940s. Merrill DENISON's *Henry Hudson and other plays* (1931) contains six unsophisticated examples of radio drama; more mature are the

plays of Lister Sinclair in *'A play on words' and other radio plays* (1948). Thousands of radio playscripts are now housed in a unique archive at Montreal's Concordia University.

The development of stage plays in the early years was encouraged by several related factors: the decline in foreign touring companies because of increased costs and the popularity of movies; the establishment of competitions, like the Earl Grey Musical and Dramatic Competition (1907-11) and the Dominion Drama Festival (1932-70); and the rise of the Little Theatre movement, led by groups such as the Arts and Letters Players of Toronto, formed in 1905. Also important was the work of theatre critics and essayists. Essays like Fred Jacob's 'Waiting for a dramatist' (*Canadian Magazine*, vol. 43, 1914), Vincent Massey's 'The prospects of a Canadian drama' (*Queen's Quarterly*, vol. 30, 1922), Merrill Denison's 'Nationalism and Drama' (*Yearbook of the arts in Canada 1928-1929*, Bertram BROOKER ed., 1929), and Herman VOADEN's introduction to *Six Canadian plays* (1930)—though differing in arguments and conclusions—provided an intelligent critical context for playwrights and prospective playwrights. Other writers—among them B.K. SANDWELL, Arthur Phelps, John COULTER, and Hector CHARLESWORTH—contributed to the critical discussion of Canadian drama. Charlesworth's theatre reminiscences are collected in two of his books: *Candid chronicles: leaves from the notebook of a Canadian journalist* (1925) and *More candid chronicles: further leaves from the notebook of a Canadian journalist* (1928). Some essayists were also important playwrights: Denison, Voaden, and Coulter, for example. Other notable playwrights of the period are Gwen Pharis RINGWOOD, Elsie Park Gowan, and Mazo DE LA ROCHE. de La Roche's *'Low Life' and other plays* (1929) contains three one-act plays—*Low life*, *Come true*, and *The return of the emigrant*—each well constructed and showing a keen sense of comedy and irony. *Whiteoaks* (1936) is a full-length dramatization of her novel *Whiteoaks of Jalna* (1929). Elsie Park Gowan wrote radio plays, children's plays, and one-act comedies.

The one-act play was, in fact, the major form of early twentieth-century Canadian drama—scores being published and many more performed in amateur theatre community theatres throughout the country. One-act plays dominated the several drama anthologies published in Canada from the 1920s to the 1950s. Collectively these anthologies reveal the strengths and weaknesses of Canadian drama during this period. Fred Jacob's *One third of a bill* (1925) contains five one-acts: *Autumn blooming*, *The clever one*, *And they meet again*, *Man's world*, and *The basket*, all performed in Ontario in the 1920s. With the exception of *The basket*, they are lightly satirical and witty middle-class comedies—reminiscent of the plays of Noël Coward, but lacking their elegance and substance. *The basket* is a rather heavy-handed mystery drama. Volume one of *Canadian plays from Hart House* (1926), edited by Vincent Massey, includes Merrill Denison's *Brothers in arms*, *The weather breeder*, and *Balm*, as well as five other plays produced at Hart House: Duncan Campbell SCOTT's *Pierre*, a domestic melodrama set in a Quebec village; Marian Osborne's *The point of view*, an amusing domestic comedy owing something to Shaw's *Heartbreak House*; Henry Borsook's black comedy *Three weddings of a hunchback*; Isabel MacKay's psychological drama *The second lie*; and Britton Cooke's melodrama *The translation of John Snaith*. Other short plays by Scott are published in *The poems of Duncan Campbell Scott* (1926). Isabel MacKay wrote two well-constructed three-act plays: *Two too many* (1927) and *Goblin gold* (1933). Volume two of *Canadian plays from Hart House Theatre* (1927) contains three full-length plays: Carroll Aikins' *The god of gods*, a refreshingly unsentimental view of Native customs; L.A. MacKay's *The freedom of Jean Guichet*, a tragi-comedy ruined by a melodramatic ending; and Leslie Reid's toothless comedy about the chauvinism of an English MP, *Trespassers*. There are nineteen plays in *One-act plays by Canadian authors* (1926), none showing much genuine dramatic imagination. *Six Canadian plays* (1930), edited by Herman Voaden, contains the best plays submitted to a competition organized by Voaden at Toronto's Central High School of Commerce in 1929-30. Two are worthy of note: T.M. Morrow's *Manitou portage*, for its interesting central character, an arrogant and bullying lumberjack, and its partly expressionistic form; and Jessie Middleton's adroitly handled domestic drama *Lake Doré*. Nathaniel Benson's *Three plays for patriots* (1930) has two simplistic history plays: *The paths of glory* (in praise of General Brock) and *The patriot* (in praise of William Lyon MACKENZIE), and a more interesting work, *The leather medal*, a bitter attack on political patronage. There are eight forgettable plays in Hilda Mary Hooke's *One-act plays from Canadian history* (1942), and another undistinguished history play, *General Wolfe*, by Raymond Card, in *Curtain rising: seven one-act plays* (1958) edited by W.S. Milne. Milne's volume also includes five comedies (by Merrill

Denison, Milne, Virginia Knight, Elsie Park Gowan, and Robertson DAVIES) and a serious drama about the clash of Western and traditional cultures in Japan, *Protest*, by Norman Williams.

Catering mainly for audiences of middle-class tastes and expectations, and having to rely almost exclusively on amateur companies for productions of their plays, Canadian playwrights in the first half of the twentieth century, with only isolated exceptions, opted for traditional forms and unprovocative subject matter. Many achieved technical competence; many wrote stageworthy plays. Missing, however, was the incentive to surpass the ordinary. Eventually some measure of that incentive was provided by the spread of professional theatre in Canada, spurred by the founding of the Stratford Festival in 1953, and government's acceptance of a responsibility to fund the arts, ratified by the formation of The CANADA COUNCIL in 1957.

L.W. CONOLLY

1953 to 1981. During the Second World War, except for a surprisingly steady flow of New York productions touring to Toronto and Montreal, theatrical entertainment in Canadian cities was in support of the war effort, in productions that included both civilians and armed forces on stage and radio in such shows as Ritzin' the Blitz, The Armory Show, Merry-Go-Round, and Meet the Navy. These productions, and some of their performers, found their way into a developing theatre scene. The immediate post-war years were enlivened by the renewal of various amateur activities at the local and Dominion Drama Festival levels, by the establishment of university drama programs, and by the founding of nearly two dozen professionally oriented companies. Among them were Dora Mavor Moore's New Play Society, Toronto, which produced 47 new Canadian scripts between 1946 and 1956; the Canadian Repertory Theatre in Ottawa; Kingston's International Players; Calgary's Workshop 47; and Sidney Risk's Everyman Theatre in Vancouver; as well as several summer-stock ventures, such as the Straw Hat Players in Ontario. The movement to found professional theatres had its immediate culmination in the establishment of the Jupiter Theatre, Toronto, in 1951; the touring Canadian Players in 1953; the Stratford Shakespearean Festival in 1953; and the Crest Theatre, Toronto, in 1954. The changing theatrical climate meant that the current works of the period's leading playwright, Robertson DAVIES—*A jig for the gypsy* (1954) and *Hunting Stuart* (1955; pub. 1972)—were performed by Toronto's professional Crest Theatre instead of by one of several local Little Theatres. Yet making a living as a playwright was not easy at the time, as Davies often remarked. His biting, satirical view of a philistine Canada was hardly endearing, despite the Shavian wit and eloquence with which it was expressed.

Before and during this period the main outlet for Canadian playwrights was provided by radio drama, produced by the Canadian Broadcasting Corporation. The most prolific radio dramatist, Lister Sinclair (b. 1921), had a notable stage success in the 1950s with *The blood is strong* (1948; Jupiter Theatre, 1953; CBC radio, 1957)—about a nineteenth-century Scots immigrant family in Cape Breton, Nova Scotia. W.O. MITCHELL was another writer who made stage adaptations of his radio dramas, none of which has been as critically successful as his novel *WHO HAS SEEN THE WIND*. In *The devil's instrument* (broadcast in 1949) he allowed an excellent idea—the revolt of a Hutterite youth against his religion—to remain underdeveloped; he displayed a light dry humour in the often-produced *The black bonspiel of Wullie MacCrimmon* (broadcast in 1951), in which Wullie competes against the devil, an avid curler. (These are among the five plays in *Dramatic W.O. Mitchell*, 1982.) The poet Earle BIRNEY turned his gifts to radio drama in the verse play *Trial of a city* (1952), a witty indictment of Vancouver for despoiling Buttle Creek; it was later adapted for the stage under its original title *The damnation of Vancouver* (prod. 1957). A more popular radio drama of the period was Patricia Joudry's *Teach me how to cry* (1955), a sentimental and psychologically naïve play about small-town prejudice. Broadcast in 1953 and staged by the Crest Theatre in 1955, it won a Dominion Drama Festival Award but was not a success when produced in New York and London; it became a film, *The restless years*. John Reeves, owing a debt to Dylan Thomas's *Under Milkwood*, wrote *A beach of strangers: an excursion* (1961), a lyrical prose drama for radio that was critical of Canadian puritanism. John COULTER, whose Irish plays were popular in amateur theatre, also wrote for radio; he gained his greatest success (stage 1950, radio 1951, TV 1961) with *Riel* (1962), an emotionally charged portrait of the martyred Métis leader, which drew attention to the use of a Canadian as a heroic figure. (Coulter followed this with two other plays about Riel: *The trial of Louis Riel*, 1968; and *The crime of Louis Riel*, 1976.) Also in 1962 Len PETERSON's Inuit tragedy *The great hunger* (1967), which had been staged in 1960 by the Arts Theatre, Toronto, was aired on the CBC. Almost two decades earlier Peterson had begun writing for radio with the slightly avant-garde *Burlap bags* (1972; CBC 1946), which pictured an alienated post-war world—the title comes from characters wearing bags to shield them from reality. These two modestly successful plays represent the highest achievement of this prolific author.

The 1960s witnessed the appearance of what came to be called 'regional theatres': loosely defined, the term might apply to the Vancouver Playhouse (1962); the Neptune Theatre, Halifax (1963); the Citadel Theatre, Edmonton (1965); the Globe Theatre, Regina (1966); the National Arts Centre, Ottawa (1969); Theatre New Brunswick, Fredericton (1964); Theatre Calgary (1968); Centaur Theatre, Montreal (1969); Toronto Arts Productions/St Lawrence Centre, Toronto (1970); and Theatre London (1971). Based to varying degrees on the model established by the Manitoba Theatre Centre, Winnipeg (1958), these theatres offered audience-development programs in each locale, maintained high production standards, and employed artists from across the country. Although most of their plays were chosen from an international repertoire, the regionals added to the momentum fostered by a decade of public funding of the arts, which combined with the nationalist spirit surrounding the Canadian Centennial to create increased opportunities even for Canadian playwrights. With the presence of large, well-equipped, and well-financed theatres, and the period's affinity for history, it is not surprising in hindsight to see the emergence of a body of broadly conceived history plays throughout the 1960s and 1970s. As the popularity of John Coulter's *Riel* had foretold, Canadian individuals and events became a focus after the late 1960s in a body of history plays. In Newfoundland, Michael COOK used early Canadian history in a somewhat Brechtian way to comment on present-day social and political injustices. In his major plays, *Colour the flesh the colour of dust* (1972), *The Gayden chronicles* (*Canadian Theatre Review* 13, 1977), and *On the rim of the curve* (1977), for all their richness in themes and language, dramatic effectiveness is muted by a diffused focus. Cook's less historical plays, which included *The head, guts and sound bone dance* (1974), *Quiller* (1975), and *Tiln* (1973), among others, comment philosophically on present-day Newfoundland life. Other Canadian history plays worth mentioning include John Thomas McDonough's *Charbonneau and le Chef* (1968), James Nichol's *Sainte-Marie among the Hurons* (1977), Ron Chudley's *After Abraham* (1978), and Alden NOWLAN's and Walter Learning's *The dollar woman* (1981). At the same time the lure of foreign history drew Canadian writers: Munro Scott to a Chinese folk tale in the engaging *Wu-feng* (1971); Stewart Boston to Queen Elizabeth I in *Councillor extraordinary* (1972); and Michael Bawtree to aristocratic Russia for his dull *Last of the Tsars* (1973).

Centennial year, 1967, saw the production of many new Canadian plays, but three have gained special significance. John HERBERT's *FORTUNE AND MEN'S EYES* (1967; 2nd edn 1974) graphically depicted the violent, homosexually exploitative world of Canadian prisons, implying that the brutally homophobic outside world of the time was little better. Although given a workshop production at the Stratford Festival in 1965, this controversial play did not receive a full commercial staging until Feb. 1967 in New York; it was filmed in Montreal in 1971. George RYGA captured national attention with *The ECSTASY OF RITA JOE* (1970), a provocative dramatization of a Native woman's destruction by an urban white society. The play's use of music, and an episodic structure that demanded a lyrical, non-realistic staging, suggested new possibilities for Canadian dramatists. Ryga's concern for social and political issues shaped his next plays, at least two of which—the 'hippie' *Grass and wild strawberries* (contained in *The ecstasy of Rita Joe and other plays*, 1971) and *Captives of the faceless drummer* (1971), about anarchists kidnapping a Canadian diplomat—became embroiled in heated controversy. The third Centennial-year title was *Colours in the dark* (1969), staged by the Stratford Festival and the first of James REANEY's innovative dramas to receive a major professional performance. In previous amateur productions of his early plays—*The killdeer* (1962; rev. 1972), *The Easter egg* (1972), and *Listen to the wind* (1972)—Reaney evolved an improvisational drama based on fragmented, often melodramatic plots and with mythopoeic echoes resonating between a dialogue rich in imagery and the physical presence of characters, actions, and objects. In the 1970s Reaney added to his reputation with the Donnelly trilogy—*Sticks and stones* (1974), *The St. Nicholas Hotel* (1976), and *Handcuffs* (1977)—which carried episodes of Ontario history into universal myth.

Ann Henry's *Lulu Street* (1972), about the 1919 Winnipeg strike, was performed in 1967 at the Manitoba Theatre Centre. British

Columbia's Beverly SIMONS wrote *Crabdance* (1969), in which she used absurdist techniques to depict the stresses of modern life on her middle-aged heroine, Sadie Goldman. In the same year Herschel Hardin saw his Inuit drama *Esker Mike and his wife, Agiluk* published in the *Drama Review* (14, no. 1, 1969); it was published in book form in 1973.

The late 1960s and early 1970s witnessed the growth of many small professional theatres that were dedicated to Canadian plays. There was a concentration of them in Toronto: Theatre Passe Muraille (1968), Factory Theatre Lab (1970), Toronto Free Theatre (1971), and the Tarragon Theatre (1971). Scattered across the rest of the country were others, such as the Mummers Troupe (1972) and Codco (1973) in St John's, Newfoundland; 25th Street Theatre (1971) in Saskatoon; Alberta Theatre Projects (1972) in Calgary; Theatre Network (1975) in Edmonton; and Tamahnous (1971) in Vancouver. The range of tough political satire and grand silliness of both CODCO and the Mummers Troupe, as well as plays by other Newfoundland collectives, are now available in *The plays of CODCO* (1992) and *Stars in the sky morning* (1996); but even with Helen Peters' skilled editing, these printed versions give only a glimpse of the articulate improvisations these companies offer on stage. One might also mention Festival Lennoxville (Quebec), founded in 1971 as a summer theatre for the production of Canadian plays. The 1970s also saw the establishment in Toronto of Playwrights' Co-op (1972)—now Playwrights Canada—which is the main source for scripts in Canada; and of its West Coast equivalent, the New Play Centre (1970), which not only published scripts but produced them. TALONBOOKS, founded in 1967, maintains a vigorous program of publishing leading Canadian plays in handsome editions.

Some of the new theatres produced 'documentary dramas' evolved from a COLLECTIVE CREATION process in which acting companies improvised around an idea or historical event. Toronto Workshop Productions had introduced a related, and influential, style of performance when the theatre was founded by George Luscombe, a disciple of England's Joan Littlewood, in 1959. Actors playing multiple roles, rapid changes of time and place, and a vignette structure are characteristics of a form that finds its strength in topicality, polemicism, and an inventive presentational acting style rather than deep probing of a subject. Among the best of such productions were *The FARM SHOW* (1976) by Theatre Passe Muraille and *Paper wheat* (*Canadian Theatre Review* 17, 1978) by Saskatoon's 25th Street Theatre. The collective process sometimes involved a playwright: Rudy WIEBE's *Far as the eye can see* (1977) and Rick SALUTIN's *1837: the farmers' revolt* (1975) were both scripted with Theatre Passe Muraille. Salutin's very popular *Les Canadiens* (1977) also showed characteristics of documentary drama and collective creation, but offered a more thorough analysis of its subject: Quebec history.

Conventional realism was another major form chosen by playwrights throughout the 1970s. David FREEMAN began his association with the Tarragon Theatre with a successful production of *Creeps* (1972)—set in the washroom of a sheltered workshop for the cerebral palsied—which is a lacerating comedy revealing the metaphorical 'lower depths' that trap the physically or psychologically handicapped. His next play, *Battering ram* (1972), showed the multi-levelled interdependence among a crippled youth, a young woman, and her mother; but his third play, *You're gonna be alright, Jamie Boy* (1974), rarely rose above a TV sitcom level. David FRENCH entered the 1970s with as much force as Freeman, and has shown more staying power. *Leaving home* (1972), and its sequel *Of the fields, lately* (1973), detail the psychological tensions in a Newfoundland-born family, the Mercers, forced to move to Toronto. A realistic poolroom drama, *One crack out* (1975), followed these emotionally powerful plays; but French then developed the humorous bent that gave so much life to his early work. *Jitters* (1980), about the opening of a new Canadian play, is a clever comedy of manners satirizing Canadian theatre in particular and Canadian foibles in general.

Since then French has added to his MERCER PLAYS a very popular bitter-sweet courtship drama, *Salt-water moon* (1985), and a loose-jointed, critical reflection on Newfoundland's entry into Confederation, *1949* (1989). William Fruet's *Wedding in white* (1973) and Tom WALMSLEY's drug-culture sex and violence in *The workingman* (1976), *The Jones boy* (1978), and *Something red* (1980) were also part of 1970s realism. On the Prairies Rex DEVERELL used a realistic mode for *Boiler room suite* (1978)—first produced at the Globe, Regina—in which an old wino couple find joy in each other's company; as did Joanna GLASS in her slightly clichéd portrayal of a *ménage à-rois* in *Artichoke* (1979). Glass found great success in both the United States and Canada with *Play memory* (1990) and *To Grandmother's house we go* (1981). The Centaur Theatre, Montreal, was the first theatrical home of David FENNARIO, who followed the success of his *On the job* (1976) and *Nothing to lose* (1977)—short, realistic plays about the plight of exploited workers—with his award-winning *BALCONVILLE* (1980). In this play, as in the two earlier works, Fennario lightened what might otherwise have been a sombre, even didactic play about the oppressed poor of Montreal with generous amounts of comedy, much of it derived from the clash of languages and attitudes among French- and English-speaking tenement dwellers. Robert Nunn has offered a convincing argument that the naturalism of the *Balconville* staging ran counter to its Marxist leanings, suggesting that Fennario would have been better served by less realism. Fennario has since left Centaur to work with a specific community orientation, as he did for *Joe Beef* (1991), produced by the Blackrock Centre, Montreal.

Among the many works (stage, radio, TV) by Sharon POLLOCK, one of Canada's most distinguished dramatists, *Generations* (1981), in which different generations of a prairie family clash over a homestead inheritance, was almost unique among her works in its wholly realistic convention. Her other plays depend on imaginative rearrangings of historical detail and disruptions of realistic illusion that force audiences to concentrate on issues inherent in the events portrayed. *Walsh* (1972), first produced by Theatre Calgary, uses an episodic structure to present the injustice the famous officer felt duty-bound to commit against Sitting Bull. In *The Komagata Maru incident* (1978) Pollock indicted Canada's racist handling of a 1914 shipload of Sikh immigrants by giving the action a side-show atmosphere. *One tiger to a hill* (1981) dramatizes the complex tensions in a prison hostage-taking. In *Blood relations* (1981) Pollock skilfully employed a play-within-a-play device and juxtaposed different time-frames to create a tantalizing ambiguity about Lizzie Borden's guilt in the famous murders, allowing us to see a range of forces controlling her destiny. It won the first Governor General's Award for published drama. *Doc* (1986), which won Pollock a second Governor General's Award, draws to some extent on her own family history in exploring questions ranging from the metaphysical to the political and psychological. Another inventive layering of realities on stage presents a tale of a renowned doctor obsessed with helping people while he allows his wife to commit suicide and robs his daughter of his love. In *The making of warriors* (1991), Pollock mixes several subjective and objective voices/characters to interweave three stories (about abolitionist Sarah Moore Grimke, Native activist Anna Mae Aquash, and a woman who witnesses Anna Mae's murder) in a moving, urgent call to action that was broadcast on CBC radio. *Getting it straight* (1992) has met with a mixed reception; in it Eme, a middle-aged escapee from a schizophrenic ward, hardly mad at all, rails, rages, and contemplates the perilous state of women, men, and the world. It is a *tour de force* for a performer and ends in glorious ambiguity on an image of a net spun of women's hands and Rapunzel's hair, which encircles the globe—and with the repeated questions: 'What would it spell?/what would it spell?/ what would it spell?'

The powerful feminism of Pollock's work is a reminder of the large contribution made by women in Canadian theatre, from major creative forces earlier in the century—such as Dora Mavor Moore, Elizabeth Sterling Haynes, Gwen RINGWOOD, Elsie Park Gowan, and Catherine Cissie Brickenden—through to Patricia Joudry, Ann Henry, Beverly Simons, and others in the 1950s and 1960s. This legacy lamentably remains uncelebrated, but the late 1960s and 1970s saw a marked increase in the recognized presence of women as creators of drama, ranging from skilled, conventional works to the most inventive and daring. Carol BOLT, one of the founders of the Playwrights Union of Canada, attracted attention for her documentary satire *Buffalo jump* (1972), about farm and labour unrest on the Prairies in the 1930s, and for her episodic portrait of the feminist/anarchist Emma Goldman in *Red Emma* (1974). *One night stand* (1977), a tightly crafted psychological thriller, revealed the horror awaiting a young woman who brings a pick-up home. However, *Escape entertainment* (1981) somewhat misfired as light satire, as did the filmic *Desperadoes* (prod. 1997). Erika RITTER was also in this company with *Automatic pilot* (1980), an adroitly written comedy that is her most important play to date. In it we are introduced to the central character, a stand-up comedienne/writer, exploited by the masculine world around her; she in turn exploits the psychological and identity turmoil she and the males must face. In the 1970s Margaret HOLLINGSWORTH, too, launched her career as one of Canada's leading playwrights. *Alli Alli oh* (1977) was first staged by Redlight Productions, Toronto, one of Canada's earliest feminist companies, and is a companion piece to *Islands* (1985). *Ever loving* (1981) offers critical vignettes of the lives of three war-brides in Canada; later plays, such as *War babies* (1985) and *In confidence* (1995), challenges the boundaries of realistic illusion in a way that allows the expression of profound relationships between women.

In addition to the boundaries crossed by feminist writers, by James Reaney's idiosyncratic genius, and by the innovations of documentary drama and the collective-creation method, the national preference for traditional modes was disturbed in many other ways. To some extent conventional English-Canadian drama was challenged by Québécois works staged in translation, notably Michel TREMBLAY's multi-layered and forceful plays throughout the 1970s; and later by translations of plays by Denis BOUCHER, Jovette MARCHESSAULT, Antonine MAILLET, and others. Among disruptive plays in English, Michael HOLLINGSWORTH's *Clear light* (1973), which ran afoul of the censor, and *Strawberry fields* (1973) were mildly bizarre, but unconventional enough to foreshadow the innovative approach that led to the founding in 1976 of the multimedia VideoCabaret with the Hummer Sisters. Starting in 1985, VideoCab staged the first of eight (so far) episodes of *The village of small huts* (1994), which chronicles Canadian history in wildly satirical caricatures. Lawrence Russell used surrealism in his short plays *Penetration* (1972) and *The mystery of the pig killer's daughter* (1975). Nor can one ignore the very successful adaptations of Michael ONDAATJE's *Collected works of Billy the Kid*, which remains unpublished as a stage piece, but has had some thirty different stagings (not all authorized) since the first one in 1971. The anti-fascist *Hurray for Johnny Canuck!* (Toronto, 1975) by Ken Gass has a cartoon-like quality derived from the Johnny Canuck comic books. Gass's controversial *Winter offensive* (1978) dramatizes a kinky sex party for Nazi officers hosted by Mrs Adolf Eichmann. Bryan Wade also showed a fascination with Nazi dreams of sex and power in his Hitler/Eva Braun play, *Blitzkreig* (1974). Many of Wade's short plays—including *Lifeguard* (1976), *Alias* (1974), and *Aliens* (1975)—display imaginative qualities reminiscent of early Sam Shepard, but they have not been followed by anything substantial. Hrant ALIANAK experimented with a range of satirical, non-realistic modes, and there were hints of unconventionality in the early works of Larry FINEBERG. But Fineberg received a Stratford Festival production of his adaptation of a novel by Constance BERESFORD-HOWE, *Eve* (1977), which is undistinguished, but allows an actress a star turn; his treatment of Euripides' *Medea* (1978) limits the scope of the original. George WALKER's 'cartoon' *Bagdad saloon* (1973), *Zastrozzi* (1977), and *Theatre of the film noir* (1981) possess entertaining theatricality spoofing traditional dramatic and film conventions. At the same time they express a sense of perceived modern-day chaos and decay, and celebrate the ability of the disadvantaged to survive in such circumstances. One of the most inventive plays of the early eighties was *Tamara* (1989). A script by John Krizanc, staged by Richard Rose and the Necessary Angel Theatre Company, *Tamara* allowed audience members to follow individual actors throughout the old mansion where it was staged in Toronto in 1981—'spying', as it were, on the political and amorous intrigues unfolding simultaneously in the many rooms. A form of 'environmental drama', hence difficult to capture in a traditional script, *Tamara* requires an analytical method as unconventional as the performance itself. The same group also brought to the stage Krizanc's complex, but more conventional, *Prague* (1987), which is set in that city and like *Tamara* explores artistic responsibility and creativity in different political systems. *Newhouse* (1989) is an environmental piece by Richard Rose, joined by D.D. Kugler, that interweaves a narrative about the sexually promiscuous son of a cabinet minister with that of a Canadian prime minister. The PM has banned unauthorized sex because his country is under a plague of a sexually transmitted disease, which, ironically, he discovers he has contracted from an extramarital affair. The play consciously drew on *Oedipus tyrannus*, Molière's *Don Juan*, and Diderot's *Rameau's nephew*, but was wholly twentieth century in its multimedia staging in a Toronto hockey arena, where the audience could follow the action that swirled about the *platea* and at stations around the periphery or was projected live on giant video-screens.

In addition to the fact that Canadian playwrights tended to favour short plays, one of the notable characteristics of the past thirty years was that very few dramatists had more than one or two considerable titles to their credit. The well-known novelist Timothy FINDLEY wrote *Can you see me yet?* (1977), a philosophical anti-war play set in an insane asylum. Jim Garrard, one of the founders of Theatre Passe Muraille, wrote the often-produced *Cold comfort* (1981), an obliquely humorous Gothic tale that speaks metaphorically of spiritual starvation and sexual sterility in Canada. American-born Sheldon ROSEN in *Ned and Jack* (1978) brought together the flamboyant Jack Barrymore and a quiet Ned Sheldon to discover themselves as they dealt with Ned's imminent death. In *Memoir* (1978) John MURRELL created a dramatically uncompelling yet successful theatrical vehicle for an actress playing the aged Sarah Bernhardt dictating her memoirs to her secretary, and in *Waiting for the parade* (1980) he evoked nostalgia to link vignettes from the lives of five women in a Canadian city during the Second World War.

Canadian dramatists in this period fell prey to economic cutbacks in the theatre, which encouraged small-cast plays. One-person shows, like the immensely popular and often perceptive *Billy Bishop goes to war* (1981) by John GRAY, became prevalent. *Billy Bishop* also exemplified a trend in Canadian theatre towards musical drama: here the script is punctuated with songs and piano accompaniment. Other popular works in this genre are Gray's *18 wheels* (1987) and *Rock and roll* (*Canadian Theatre Review* 35, Summer 1982) and Ken MITCHELL's *Cruel tears* (1976), a trucker's *Othello*. Mitchell was an active playwright with *Davin: the politician* (1979) and *The shipbuilder* (*Canadian Theatre Review* 21, Winter 1979) among his two-dozen titles. *Herringbone* (*Three plays by Tom Cone*, 1976) is a one-man show by American-born Tom Cone, in which an old vaudevillian soft-shoes through the story of his life. Cone's *Star gazing* (1978) received a Stratford Festival Third Stage production in 1978, but the weak script takes us on a familiar journey where characters discover commonplace truths about themselves. Paul Thompson and Linda Griffiths, in the very popular *Maggie and Pierre* (1980), utilized the topicality of Pierre Trudeau's notorious marriage and the novelty of Griffiths' playing all three roles in the cast to hide a very thin script. Such concessions to the commercial viability of theatres undoubtedly will continue to influence Canadian drama. Situation comedies, such as the inferior *Westmount* (1980) by Richard Ouzounian, began to proliferate. Fortunately one effect of this was that playwrights with more serious intentions, such as Allan Stratton—author of the subtle, insightful *Rexy!* (1981), about Mackenzie King—could earn a living from the commercial success of frothy, entertaining pieces like his *Nurse Jane goes to Hawaii* (1980).

1982 to 1996. By the end of the 1970s a new generation of dramatists joined the existing theatre and expanded its artistic base, audience, issues, and theatrical forms. The nationalist focus began giving way to a greater concern for situating Canadian art in an international context, new technologies were shaping the possibilities of the stage, and financial self-sufficiency was becoming a predominant indicator of theatrical success. The negative aspect of these developments was that the affluent 1980s and reactionary conservativeness of the 1990s brought major cuts to public funding for the arts at a time when the costs of mounting shows were climbing. The period fostered a climate of restraint that extended beyond the financial level to the artistic level as globalization in the arts—as demonstrated by such shows as *The phantom of the opera* and *Miss Saigon*—led to an unwelcome homogeneity: mega-musicials like these are mounted in exactly the same way in Toronto, London, New York, and Tokyo. Despite these serious problems, which led to the demise of many companies and caused established companies to avoid risks, artists responded with amazing resourcefulness and imagination, staging some two hundred Canadian plays annually, with some of them published by The Playwrights Union of Canada, TALON BOOKS, COACH HOUSE PRESS, Blizzard Publishing, and other small houses. Variety characterized the overall scene in the late 1980s and the 1990s, when many types of drama, from the experimental to the traditional, co-existed within a range of theatre structures, both professional and amateur, from a production centred on a single person to large corporate hierarchies and co-operative or collective ventures. Several communities developed Colway-style plays, such as the Ontario village of Eramosa's *Spirit of shivaree* (1996) and Blyth's *Many hands* (prod. 1993), both scripted by Dale Hamilton, and *Ka'ma'-mo'pi cik/The gathering* (*Canadian Theatre Review*, 1997) in Fort Qu'Appelle, Saskatchewan, scripted in Cree and English by Rachael Van Fossen and Darryl Wildcat. These huge undertakings involved hundreds of local people and addressed crucial local issues. Interventionist projects, such as Catalyst's early 1980s *Stand up for your rights* and Augusto Boal-inspired theatre of the oppressed, lived (not always in harmony) alongside Theatresports, dinner theatre, fringe-theatre festivals, mega-musicals, and commercial vehicles. Unfortunately cuts in funding for the publishing industry in the 1990s threatened to reduce the number of plays published.

Playwrights who had established a name for themselves through the 1970s, such as Sharon POLLOCK, were given opportunities to extend their bodies of work in this period. George WALKER's layered comedies grew to include *Theatre of the film noir* (1981) and the last of the Power plays, *The art of war* (1984), in which an even more dissipated, inept Tyrone M. Power continued his well-meaning but ineffectual war against the powerful and stylish philistines. *Criminals in love* (1984), *Better living* (1986), *Love and anger* (1990), and *Escape from happiness* (1992) took Walker's gifts for eloquent wit and incisive criticism to the probing of serious problems facing the urban working-class. He also scored an enormous hit with *Nothing sacred* (1988), adapted from Turgenev's *Fathers and sons*. John MURRELL's early career was located more in Alberta than elsewhere, but he entered the realm of those commanding broad attention with the international success of *Memoir* (1978). His *Farther west* (1986) is a heavily metaphorical tale of a prostitute doomed to be driven ever farther west until her violent death at the hands of her lover. Murrell's propensity to explore large philosophical questions—creativity, war, human nature, passion, in allusive action and language but with greater irony than in *Farther west*—was evident in *New world* (1986), *October* (1988), and *Democracy* (1992). Judith THOMPSON's career was launched by *The crackwalker* (1981), a compassionate handling of the devastation visited on emotionally dynamic young people living under economic, social, and mental handicaps. Her subsequent plays drew on powerful imagery that takes audiences into the terrifying experiences of the subconscious. *White biting dog* (1984), *I am yours* (1989), and *Lion in the streets* (1992) are her best-known full-length plays. But she has written a number of potent shorter scripts such as *Pink* (1989), an intense monologue in which a young white girl tells of her Black nanny; and *Tornado* (1989), the title of which gives a sense of what both the audience and the central character, who suffers from epilepsy, experience.

Francophone plays in translation continued to entertain and enlighten anglophone audiences—and to influence anglophone theatre, and even some playwrights. Michel TREMBLAY's popularity in English Canada never waned as each new play was produced in translation. Other francophone dramatists whose plays were well received in English included Michel Marc BOUCHARD, Normand CHAURETTE, Jean-Marc DALPÉ, René-Daniel DUBOIS, and Jovette MARCHESSAULT. (See DRAMA IN FRENCH: 1981 TO 1996.)

That Canada consists of many different cultures has been increasingly acknowledged in recent theatre. Among the most potent expressions have been the plays of First Nations artists. Native characters appeared in plays by non-Natives beginning in 1606, when Marc Lescarbot's *Le Théâtre de Neptune* was first performed. In modern times they appear in works as various as Robertson DAVIES' *Pontiac and the green man* (prod. 1975), Michael COOK's *On the rim of the curve* (1977), Len PETERSON's one-acter *Almighty Voice* (1974), and George RYGA's *Indian* (1971) and *The ecstasy of Rita Joe* (1970). *Alanienouidet*, created by Marianne Ackerman and Robert Lepage, combined Cree, English, and French in a play about the English actor Edmund Kean's visit to Quebec, and a Native tribe there, in 1826. Ackerman's work with her theatre company, 1774, is aimed at creating a drama that brings together different cultures through texts utilizing more than one language—as in *L'affaire Tartuffe/The garrison officers rehearse Molière* (1994). But Native portraits in non-Native works have generally come to be seen as flawed—even in Ryga's plays, though they did much to raise non-Native awareness of serious injustices towards Native peoples. One of the most revealing theatrical encounters between non-Native and Native artists is recorded in *The book of Jessica: a theatrical transformation* (1989). With Paul Thompson as director, Linda Griffiths and Maria CAMPBELL set about creating *Jessica: a transformation* (1989), based on Campbell's *Halfbreed* (1973), about the horrifying life of the Métis Jessica before she achieves health and self-discovery. It received several awards, including a Dora for Outstanding New Play in 1986. The passionate disagreements that existed throughout and after the creative period of the joint playwrights are documented in *The book of Jessica*. The heated discussions throw light on such issues as intent, identity formation, appropriation, and personal tension that are inherent in the cultural interface.

One of the most prominent names among Native playwrights is Tomson HIGHWAY. His huge success with *The rez sisters* (1988), which traces the humorous and terrible experiences of a group of Native women who travel to Toronto for a gigantic bingo game, was followed by the equally successful *Dry Lips oughta move to Kapuskasing* (1990), which shows the devastating impact of white society on Natives before leading the audience to an image of hope for the future. The play's graphic exuberance and gritty reality were a shock to some audiences in its remount for the upscale Royal Alexandra Theatre, Toronto. Native dramaturgy has tended to use a range of deconstructivist strategies to neutralize the power of commonly held impressions. Daniel David MOSES' *Almighty Voice and his wife*

(1992) juxtaposes a first act containing the ironic romance of Almighty Voice and his wife—he is hunted down and killed by the Royal Canadian Mounted Police—against a vicious burlesque of medicine-/minstrel-show caricatures of Natives. A somewhat similar caricaturing exists in *Princess Pocahontas and the blue spots* (1990) by Monique Mojica, who exposes the abuse and exploitation of Native women throughout the history of the Americas. Other notable playwrights from Native communities include Drew Hayden TAYLOR, Shirley Cheechoo, and Margot Kane, all of whom have written plays that have made a significant impact on the theatre scene.

The work of other minority cultures has also found its way to the Canadian stage, although the impact of the individual pieces, however powerful, has often been constrained by their presentation in marginalized venues. *Gens du silence* (1982), by Marco MICONE, reveals the explosive tensions in an immigrant family, and is, like *Addolorata* (1984), another of Micone's plays that come out of an Italian, French, and English background in cosmopolitan Montreal. Maristella Roca provided a somewhat similar voice in Toronto in his *Clutching the heat* (1990) and other plays. As well as *Bhanumati Ka Pitara*, in Hindustani, Montreal-based Rahul Varma wrote and staged works in English, often with his Teesri Duniya group, which was founded in 1981: *No man's land* (1994), *Isolated incident* (written with Stephen Orlov, 1989), exploring the police shooting of a black youth in Montreal, and *Land where the trees talk* (1990), produced at Montreal's Centaur Theatre. Argentina-born Guillermo Verdecchia's *Fronteras Americanas/American borders* (1993) dramatizes the struggle of Latin Americans living in two cultures. Verdecchia was also the co-author with Daniel Brooks of *The Noam Chomsky lectures* (1991), a hilarious metatheatrical 'explication' inspired by Chomsky's ideas on 'thought control' and 'the manufacture of consent'. The psychological and political ties experienced by a young Cuban-born playwright returned home from Canada for a week are at the centre of René Aloma's *A little something to ease the pain* (1981). The experiences of Canadians of East Asian background are reflected in a number of plays. Rick Shiomi uses a Japanese-Canadian detective in *Yellow fever* (1984) to parody Asian private-eye stereotypes as well as to draw attention to racism; it was successfully produced in Los Angeles, Vancouver, and Toronto. *The tale of a mask* by Terry Watada presents a taut fusion of Japanese with Western theatre techniques to recount the tragic events that befall a Japanese-born woman, her son, and husband amid the tensions created by their immigration to Canada.

Montreal's Black Theatre Workshop (founded 1968), Toronto's Black Theatre Canada (1973) and Theatre Fountainhead (1974), Winnipeg's Caribbean Theatre, and Kwacha (1984) in Saint John, New Brunswick, provided forums for such black writers as Jeff Henry, Hector Bunyan, Linda Ghan, Walter Borden, and Ricardo Keens-Douglas. Their plays remain unpublished, but George Seremba's *Come good rain* (1993)—a performance piece in which he dramatizes his harrowing experience of being tortured, shot, and left for dead in Uganda—has fortunately been published. Djanet Sears' *Afrika solo* (1990) is another text that records the virtuoso performance abilities of a black artist who in this case—using song, dub, and storytelling techniques—chronicles a young black woman's voyage of self-discovery. Andrew Moodie's *Riot* (1995) offers a raw, critical, exuberant depiction of young black urban life in Toronto, where it had its first production; that city will be replaced by the cities of its subsequent productions.

Knotty urban life, but this time white and in Edmonton, was the focus of Brad FRASER's very successful *Unidentified human remains and the true nature of love* (1990). Its exhilarating mix of open sexuality, drug culture, and the horror of a serial killer were only part of the reason this play drew so much attention. Expressed in a language and from reference points central to an electronic generation, *Human remains* was seen to draw a new audience to a theatre Fraser claimed had become moribund. While his *The ugly man* (1993) was not as well received, *Poor super man* (1995) was almost as successful as *Human remains*. Equally outspoken, witty, and critical, this play draws on comic-book lore and the vulnerability of Superman to show a group of young people —a transsexual with AIDS, his lover, an apparently straight couple, and an acerbic writer—who are dealing with a world that is cynical and devoid of superheroes. Fraser is among a young generation of dramatists that includes Daniel Brooks, Sally CLARK, Maureen Hunter, Wendy LILL, Bryden MacDonald, Daniel MacIvor, Joan MacLEOD, John Mighton, and Jason SHERMAN. These are talented and skilled dramatists whose work augurs well for the future of Canadian theatre.

Bibliography. The extensive compiling of bibliographic tools for the study of Canadian drama in English is a relatively recent activity that developed during the 1970s. The following titles will provide a fundamental body of resources.

REFERENCE. John Ball and Richard Plant, eds, *Bibliography of theatre history in Canada: the beginnings through 1984* (1993). This large volume supersedes Ball and Plant, eds, *A bibliography of Canadian theatre history 1583-1975* (1976) and their *Supplement 1975-76* (1979). Eugene Benson and L.W. Conolly, eds, *The Oxford companion to Canadian theatre* (1989); P.B. O'Neill, 'A checklist of Canadian dramatic materials to 1967, Part I: A to K', *Canadian Drama/L'Art dramatique canadien* 8, no. 2 (1982); P.B. O'Neill, 'A checklist of Canadian dramatic materials to 1967, Part II: L to Z', *Canadian Drama/L'Art dramatique canadien* 9, no. 2 (1983); P.B. O'Neill, 'Unpublished Canadian plays copyrighted 1921-1937', *Canadian Drama/L'Art dramatique canadien* 4, no. 1 (1978); Playwrights Union of Canada, *Catalogue of plays* (annual or biennial compilation); Anton Wagner, gen. ed., *The Brock bibliography of published Canadian plays in English 1766-1978* (1980).

GENERAL. Geraldine Anthony, ed., *Stage voices* (1978); Eugene Benson and L.W. Conolly, *English-Canadian theatre* (1987); Diane Bessai, *Playwrights of collective creation* (1993); Per Brask, ed., *Contemporary issues in Canadian drama* (1995); Per Brask and William Morgan, eds, *Aboriginal voices* (1992); Chris Brookes, *A public nuisance: a history of the Mummers Troupe* (1988); Neil Carson, *Harlequin hogtown: George Luscombe and Toronto Workshop Productions* (1995); L.W. Conolly, ed., *Canadian drama and the critics*, rev. ed. (1995); L.W. Conolly, ed., *Theatrical touring and funding in North America* (1982); *L'École: le premier quart de siècle de l'École Nationale de Théâtre du Canada/The School: the first quarter century of the National Theatre School of Canada* (1985), edited by Jean-Louis Roux, Michel Garneau, and Tom HENDRY; Murray D. Edwards, *A stage in our past* (1968); Chad Evans, *Frontier theatre* (1983); Alan Filewod, *Collective encounters* (1987); Kathleen Foreman and Clem Martini, *Something like a drug: an 'unauthorized' oral history of theatresports* (1995); Nora Alice Frick, *Image in the mind: CBC radio drama, 1944-1954* (1987); Albert-Reiner Glaap, with Rolf Althof, eds, *On-stage and off-stage: English Canadian drama in discourse* (1996); Franklin Graham, *Histrionic Montreal* (1897; 2nd ed. 1902); Yvonne Hodkinson, *Female parts: the art and politics of women playwrights* (1991); Denis W. Johnston, *Up the mainstream: the rise of Toronto's alternative theatres* (1991); Robert Lecker, ed., *Canadian canons: essays in literary value* (1991); Betty Lee, *Love and whisky* (1973); George Mann, *Theatre Lethbridge: a history of theatrical production in Lethbridge, Alberta (1885-1988)* (1993); Mary Jane Miller, *Turn up the contrast: Canadian television drama since 1952* (1987); Rita Much, ed., *Women on the Canadian stage: the legacy of Hrotsvit* (1992); William H. New, ed., *Dramatists in Canada* (1972); Don Rubin, series ed., *Canada on stage: CTR yearbook* (1974 to 1982); Don Rubin, ed., *Canadian Theatre history: selected readings* (1996); Judith Rudakoff and Rita Much, eds, *Fair play: 12 women speak, conversations with Canadian playwrights* (1990); Toby Gordon Ryan, *Stage left: Canadian theatre in the thirties* (1981); Ann Saddlemyer, ed., *Early stages: essays on the theatre in Ontario, 1800-1914* (1990); Ann Saddlemyer and Richard Plant, eds, *Later stages: essays in Ontario theatre from the First World War to the 1970s* (1997); Mary E. Smith, *Too soon the curtain fell* (1981); Mary E. Smith, 'English drama in New Brunswick', in *A literary and linguistic history of New Brunswick* (1985); E. Ross Stuart, *The history of prairie theatre* (1984); Renate Usmiani, *Second stage: the alternative theatre movement in Canada* (1983); Anton Wagner, ed., *Contemporary Canadian theatre* (1985); Robert Wallace and Cynthia Zimmerman, eds, *The work: conversations with English-Canadian playwrights* (1982); Robert Wallace, *Producing marginality* (1990); Cynthia Zimmerman, *Playwriting women: female voices in English Canada* (1994).

PERIODICALS. *Canadian Drama/L'Art dramatique canadien*, which was begun in 1975 and was conflated with *Essays in Theatre* under the latter title in 1991; *Canadian Theatre Review* (1975-); *Theatre Research in Canada/Recherche Théâtrale au Canada* (formerly *Theatre History in Canada/Histoire du Théâtre au Canada* (1979-). Articles appear occasionally in periodicals such as *CANADIAN LITERATURE*, *Journal of Canadian Studies*, *Books in Canada*, and a range of other journals. The *University of Toronto Quarterly* publishes an annual survey of drama publications in its 'Letters in Canada' issue.

ANTHOLOGIES. Henry BEISSEL, ed., *Cues and entrances: ten Canadian one-act plays* (1977); Eugene Benson, ed., *Encounter: Canadian drama in four media* (1973); Diane Bessai, ed., *Prairie performance: a collection of short plays* (1980); Diane Bessai and Don Kerr, eds, *NeWest plays by women* (1987); Diane Bessai and Don Kerr, eds, *Showing West: three prairie docu-dramas* (1982); Constance Brissenden, ed., *The Factory Lab anthology* (1974); Constance Brissenden, ed., *Now in paperback: Canadian playwrights of the 1970s* (1973); Constance Brissenden, ed., *West Coast plays* (1975); Canadian Authors' Association, *One-act plays by Canadian authors*

(1926); Dave Carley, ed., *Take five* (1991); Neil Carson, ed., *New Canadian drama—1* (1980); Joyce Doolittle, ed., *Heroines: three plays* (1992); Leonard E. Doucette, ed. and trans., *The drama of our past: major plays from nineteenth-century Quebec* (1997); Alan Filewod, ed., *The best of Canadian Theatre Review* (1992); Howard Fink and John Jackson, eds, *All the bright company: radio drama produced by Andrew Allan* (1987); Ann Jansen, ed., *Airborne* (1991); Rolf Kalman, ed., *A collection of Canadian plays* (5 vols, 1972-8); Denyse Lynde, ed., *Voices from the landwash: selected plays from Newfoundland and Labrador* (1995); Vincent Massey, ed., *Canadian plays from Hart House Theatre* (2 vols, 1926-7); Rita Much, ed., *New Canadian drama —6* (1993); P.B. O'Neill, ed., *New Canadian drama—2* (1981); Richard Perkyns, ed., *Major plays of the Canadian theatre 1934-1984* (1984); Helen Peters, ed., *The plays of CODCO* (1992); Helen Peters, ed., *Stars in the sky morning: collective plays of Newfoundland and Labrador* (1996); Richard Plant, ed., *The Penguin book of modern Canadian drama* (1984); Playwrights' Co-op, *Five Canadian plays* (1978); Playwrights Union of Canada, *Four new comedies* (1987); Playwrights Union of Canada, *Six Canadian plays* (1992); Playwrights Union of Canada, *New works* (1987); Aviva Ravel, ed., *Canadian mosaic* (1995); Gordon Ralph, ed., *Boneman: an anthology of Canadian plays* (1995); Stanley Richards, ed., *Canada on stage* (1960); Denis Salter, ed., *New Canadian drama—3* (1984); John Stevens, ed., *Ten Canadian short plays* (1975); Madeline Thompson, ed., *Women write for the theatre* (4 vols, 1976); Herman VOADEN, ed., *Six Canadian plays* (1930); Anton Wagner and Richard Plant, eds, *Canada's lost plays, volume one: The nineteenth century* (1978); Anton Wagner, ed., *Canada's lost plays, volume two: Women pioneers* (1979); Anton Wagner, ed., *Canada's lost plays, volume three: The developing mosiac* (1980); Anton Wagner, ed., *Canada's lost plays, volume four: Colonial Quebec: French-Canadian drama, 1606 to 1966* (1982); Robert Wallace, ed., *Making out: plays by gay men* (1992); Robert Wallace, ed., *Quebec voices* (1986); Jerry Wasserman, ed., *Modern Canadian plays*, 3rd edn (2 vols, 1993-4); Jerry Wasserman, ed., *Twenty years at play. A New Play Centre anthology* (1990); Marian M. Wilson, ed., *Popular performance plays of Canada* (2 vols, 1976); Richard Wright and Robin Endres, eds, *Eight men speak and other plays from the Canadian Workers' Theatre* (1976).

RICHARD PLANT

Drama in English: collective creations. See COLLECTIVE CREATIONS IN ENGLISH.

Drama in French. The beginnings to 1900. The first play written in French in North America was Marc Lescarbot's fanciful *Théâtre de Neptune en la Nouvelle-France*, performed at Port Royal in Nov. 1606 to celebrate the return of the colony's leaders from an expedition. Published in his *Muses de la Nouvelle-France* (Paris, 1609), the short text belongs more validly to French than Canadian literature, yet it contains a serious attempt to reproduce a New World setting, with its four 'Indian' roles and its scattering of words from Native languages. The play is of the type known as a *réception*, long practised in France, composed to celebrate the visit or return of an important personage. This is the only genre to have taken root in New France, and two other surviving dramatic texts belong to it: the anonymous *Réception de monseigneur le vicomte d'Argenson* (Québec, 1890), performed in 1658, which is remarkable for its use of Amerindian languages; and a *Réception de monseigneur de Saint-Vallier* published in *Mgr de Saint-Vallier et l'Hôpital Général de Québec* (Québec, 1882), written in verse by the Jesuit P.-J. de La Chasse and performed in Quebec in 1727.

By 1650 there had also developed a tradition of staging, at least sporadically, plays by major French authors, in particular those of Pierre Corneille. But all such 'profane' performances ceased as a result of the conflict in 1694 between Governor Frontenac and Bishop Saint-Vallier over the former's intention to present Molière's controversial *Tartuffe*. The Bishop bought off Frontenac on this occasion, and succeeded in prohibiting all public theatre thereafter. Rare are the references to dramatic performances for the rest of the French régime.

Soon after the Treaty of Paris (1763) occasional performances are again reported. The British garrison often took the lead in presenting plays in French, favouring Molière's works. Theatre returned to the schools as well, and a manuscript text from 1780, entitled *L'éducation négligée*, suggests a nascent native dramaturgy. By the end of the decade, French-born Joseph QUESNEL, a resident of Montreal since 1779, had written *COLAS ET COLINETTE; OU LE BAILLI DUPÉ*, the first operetta composed in the New World; performed in 1790, it was published in Quebec in 1812 (with the imprint '1808'). But to the Catholic Church public theatre was suspect, so that any attempts at establishing a permanent stage were discouraged.

From the nineteenth century some 150 plays by 75 known authors survive, the vast majority of them composed after 1875. Apart from a series of anonymous political satires in dramatic form—never intended for performance and generally referred to as 'Les comédies du statu quo', written in 1834, and republished by N.-E. Dionne in *Les trois comédies du statu quo* (Québec, 1909)—the first play published (it was never performed) by a native French Canadian was *Griphon; ou La vengeance d'un valet* (Québec, 1837) by Pierre PETITCLAIR. The 1830s also saw the performance and publication of plays by French immigrants, notably *Valentine; ou La Nina canadienne* (Montréal, 1836) by H.-P. LEBLANC DE MARCONNAY. But Lord Durham's observation that French Canada seemed, in 1839, incapable of maintaining a national stage was indeed valid. And despite the number of plays written before the 1890s, no real native dramatic tradition arose, if one excludes unplayable political satires. In 1842 a second play by Petitclair, *La donation*, was performed with some success and revived several times before its publication in 1848, making of it the first text by a native dramatist to receive both honours. A. GÉRIN-LAJOIE, while still a student, wrote and had performed, in 1844, the patriotic tragedy *Le jeune Latour*, which was successful enough to be published four times that same year. His formula (but not its verse form) was to prove the most popular one for generations: historical drama with strong nationalistic appeal, such as L.-H. FRÉCHETTE's *Félix Poutré* (Montréal, 1871), which was performed with great success in 1862, and his *Papineau* (1880), both of which attempted to rehabilitate the heroes of 1837-8. Extracts from many of these nationalistic plays have been included by E.-F. Duval in his *Anthologie thématique du théâtre québécois au xixe siècle* (1978). New France was the setting for a dozen historical plays, from the immensely popular adaptations of P.-J. AUBERT DE GASPÉ's *Les ANCIENS CANADIENS* (Québec, 1863) (the first of which, by Camille Caisse, was performed in Montreal in 1865 and published, in a somewhat different version, in 1894), to J.-L. Archambault's *Jacques Cartier; ou Canada vengé* (Montréal, 1879), and J. MARMETTE's *L'intendant Bigot* (Montréal, 1872). Patriotic sentiment with more immediate application was the theme of *Si les Canadiennes le voulaient!* (Québec, 1886) by Laure Conan (Félicité ANGERS), P. LEMAY's *Rouge et bleu* (Québec, 1891), and of two works occasioned by the Métis rebellions: *Riel* by C. Bayer and E. Parage, and another play of the same title by E. Paquin, both published in Montreal in 1886. At the same time the increasingly frequent tours by professional companies from Paris, so long and so bitterly contested by the Church (see *L'église et le théâtre au Québec*, 1979, by J. Laflamme and R. Tourangeau), began to influence playwrights after 1870. Evidence of this influence can be seen in the polished light theatre of F.-G. MARCHAND, whose *Les faux brillants* (Montréal, 1885) was adapted and revived with modest success in 1977; in the situation comedies of the prolific Régis Roy—*Consultations gratuites* (Montréal, 1896) and *Nous divorçons* (Montréal, 1897); and the 30-odd adaptations of foreign works by the lawyer J.G.W. McGown (1847-1914). Soon the clergy took to composing or adapting plays for purposes of propaganda, such as the anonymous *Soirées de village* (Montréal, 1860) and *Stanislas de Kostka* (Montréal, 1878) by H.-A. Verreau; for campaigns against drunkenness, as in *L'hôte à Valiquet, ou Le fricot sinistre* (Montréal, 1881), by J.-B. Proulx; or in favour of internal colonization, as in *Les pionniers du lac Nominingue; ou Les avantages de la colonisation* (Montreal, 1883), also by Proulx.

In the 1890s the first professional troupes were established in Montreal, playing a mixture of adaptations and indigenous plays — influenced by the light-comedy tradition of boulevard theatre in France—in the first permanent theatres for francophones. That decade represents the most active period in the history of French-Canadian theatre before the twentieth century. Its flowering proved to be brief; but for a moment, before the advent of cinema, it appeared that Durham's remarks would finally lose their truth. This is the subject of a monograph by J.-M. Larrue, *Le théâtre à Montréal à la fin du xixe siècle* (1981).

See L.E. Doucette, *Theatre in French Canada: laying the foundations, 1606-1867* (1984).

L.E. DOUCETTE

1900 to 1948 (drama and theatre). While theatrical activity in French dates back a long time in Quebec, with sporadic activity elsewhere in the country, most theatrical activity in Montreal around the turn of the century has been estimated as more than 85% English. Changes in this situation, beginning in the 1890s, produced a radical turn-around in the first decade of the twentieth century. This dynamic period saw the establishment in Montreal of francophone theatres; the emergence of companies of professional actors, directors, designers, and technicians from Quebec and France; the development of public taste for theatre; the production of a range of plays, amateur and professional, for sophisticated and popular audiences; tours to Quebec City; and the emergence of theatre criticism. Over the next years and decades francophone theatre also took place in Ottawa-Hull, Quebec City (Théâtre Jacques Cartier de Saint-Roch and L'Auditorium) and other cities throughout Quebec, and in Manitoba, Ontario, and New Brunswick. During the first half of the twentieth century, theatre expanded and evolved, particularly during the first decade of the century and the 1930s. Radio stations and networks created a new demand for plays, serials, and adaptations in French.

While no great works of dramatic literature were written and produced in the first half of the century, E.-F. Duval estimates in *Le jeu de l'histoire et de la société dans le théâtre québécois, 1900-1950* (1981) that 193 Quebec authors wrote more than 813 plays. Duval's anthology demonstrates that almost all the plays written during this period, many of which are unpublished, were on historical subjects. With the exception of the war years, when dramatic production declined significantly, Guy Beaulne's data (in *Répertoire du théâtre de langue française au Canada*, 1966, unpublished manuscript at the Université de Montréal) appear to show that an average of six to seven original stage plays were produced each year. There was an average of sixteen original radio scripts per year in the 1930s, thirty-five in the 1940s, along with an uncounted number, possibly in the thousands, of modest and grandiose pageants, produced throughout Quebec during the first half-century. A few dramatists showed originality in subject, style, or dramatic technique. Despite efforts by many theatre people during the first half of the twentieth century to encourage the creation of what was then called French-Canadian drama, the vast majority of productions were plays from France or translations from the USA. Many dramatists and their plays were first catalogued by Édouard G. Rinfret in the four-volume *Le théâtre canadien d'expression française* (1975, 1976, 1977, 1978). Considerable information on dramatists and their works, on theatres, theatre people, theatrical activity, and conditions affecting theatre and drama can be found in special issues of *L'annuaire théâtral* (founded 1985), *Cahiers de la Société d'Histoire du Théâtre du Québec*, and *Theatre History (Research) in Canada/Histoire (Recherche) du théâtre au Canada* (founded 1976).

Throughout the period the Church influenced in a significant way the nature of literary and theatrical production, and the constraints surrounding their various manifestations. Whereas drama and theatre were used and strongly supported by the clergy for educational and commemorative purposes, its representatives exercised surveillance on all forms of writing, theatre, and the emerging medium of movies (which had close ties and also competed with theatre). As Jean Laflamme and Rémi Tourangeau discuss in *L'Église et le théâtre au Québec* (1979), the popular taste for film, which came to Quebec in 1902, and for commercial theatre of all kinds, led to renewed opposition around 1907 by the Church to commercial public entertainment. However, urbanization favoured the development of theatre and cinema and diminished the ability of the clergy to apply strict codes of censorship. Along with clerical control, writers, actors, and all in the theatre community had to cope with difficult financial pressures.

Until the last decade of the nineteenth century, all theatres in Montreal had English owners. André-G. Bourassa and Jean-Marc Larrue have shown in *Les nuits de la 'Main': cent ans de spectacles sur le boulevard Saint-Laurent 1891-1991* (1993) and Larrue's *Le monument inattendu: Le Monument-National, 1893-1993* (1993) that francophone theatre in Canada finally obtained a home, in real and symbolic terms, in 1894 when the first French theatre, the Monument National, was constructed under the auspices of the Société Saint-Jean-Baptiste. The founding at the Monument National of an amateur theatre company, Les Soirées de famille (1898-1901), with the sanction of the Church, marked the beginning of regular theatrical activity in French in Montreal. Les Soirées presented a new play each week drawn from the repertory of popular French theatre and melodrama. With the exception of a few touring shows, the Soirées represent the first time women and men appeared together on the public stage in Quebec.

The first permanent francophone professional company, Le Théâtre National Français (1900-17), was founded by Julien Daoust. His original play, *La passion*, created collaboratively with Germain Beaulieu in 1901, was presented with great success at the Monument National. The well-known and respected Paul Cazeneuve became artistic director of the Théâtre National in 1901. Comedies, melodramas, operettas, revues, and vaudeville were performed at the National. Other companies followed, such as Les Nouveautés (1902-8), which tried to appeal to an élite audience by presenting the latest Paris hits. More than twenty professional companies were established during the pre-1914 period. Their first objective was necessarily commercial success. Nevertheless, efforts were also made at the Théâtre National to encourage Canadian dramatists by organizing contests and producing original plays. Of the thousands of plays produced there, about fifty were by Quebec writers: W.A. Baker, Germain Beaulieu, Jean CHARBONNEAU, Ernest CHOQUETTE, Rodolphe GIRARD, Louis Guyon, Madeleine Huguenin, and Régis Roy. The most gifted dramatist of the period, Louvigny de Montigny, whose *Les boules de neige* was presented at the Monument-National in 1903, wrote of the almost insurmountable difficulties encountered by Canadian dramatists in the early twentieth century. The subject matter of de Montigny's plays is drawn from Quebec legend and contemporary society. *Les boules de neige* (1903), for example, is a satire on hypocrisy in the Montreal bourgeoisie. Most of the plays performed at the Théâtre National were chosen from the contemporary commercial French repertoire, with increasing use made of the technological innovation occurring on American stages. Throughout the first half of the twentieth century there was much innovation and experimentation in design and staging techniques in Montreal. During the same period there was awareness among francophone leaders of the need for training in language and acting skills. The Conservatoire d'art dramatique was founded in 1907.

Information on this first period of professional theatre in Montreal is found in Palmieri (Joseph Archambault), *Mes souvenirs de théâtre* (1944); Robert Prévost, *Que sont-ils devenus?* (1939); and Geo. Robert, *L'annuaire théâtral* (1909). Information on theatre in Quebec City during the same period is found in Christian Beaucage, *Le théâtre à Québec au début du XXe siècle: une époque flamboyante!* (1996) and André Duval, *Place Jacques-Cartier ou quarante ans de théâtre français à Québec, 1871-1911* (1984).

The theatrical revues offered by early professional theatres were modelled originally on French café-concert pieces but soon developed unique and highly appreciated linguistic, spectacular, and comic qualities of their own in works commenting on local events. Some of these revues enjoyed enormous popular success and launched the career of a number of Quebec actors: Jules Ferland, Jean Narrache (Émile CODERRE), Gratien GÉLINAS, Raymond Lévesque, and Doris Lussier. Some of the flavour of these original comic sketches can be found in *Monologues québécois, 1890-1980* (1980), edited by Laurent Mailhot and Doris-Michel Montpetit. In the first decade of the century, revues such as Julien Daoust's *Ohé Ohé Françoise* and *La belle montréalaise* enjoyed great notoriety. They provided a fertile theatre environment for burlesque theatre, which began to emerge in the second decade. Burlesque, with its origins in the USA, dominated the Quebec stage between 1930 and 1950. As Chantal Hébert shows in *Le burlesque au Québec, un divertissement populaire* (1981) and *Le burlesque québécois et américain* (1989), the many Quebec burlesque players, who began by imitating American routines in English, soon created a body of original material in French. The voices of Quebec burlesque artists can be heard in Gilles Latulippe's and Phil Laframboise's *Olivier: un livre-témoignage orchestré* (1985), homage to the great comic artist and burlesque creator Olivier Guimond.

In the early twentieth century, theatrical productions outside Montreal were mounted by amateur or touring professional companies or were produced by college and convent teachers and students for educational purposes, frequently to mark a special event. A strict segregation of the sexes in these college productions, and in most amateur productions, was observed until the 1930s. Many amateur groups were active throughout the first half of the century and were so widespread that when the Dominion Drama Festival was founded in 1933, Little Theatre companies throughout Canada were able to offer performances in French of sound quality. Particularly noteworthy was Le Cercle Molière, founded in 1925 in St Boniface, which is still the centre of theatre activity in francophone Manitoba. No Canadian plays were offered by Le Cercle Molière during the first half of the century. Annette Saint-Pierre provides documentation on Manitoba theatre in *Le rideau se lève au Manitoba* (1980), as do the voices in *Chapeau bas: réminiscences de la vie théâtrale et musicale du Manitoba français* (1980).

College theatre entered an important new phase in Quebec during the 1930s. Gustave Lamarche, who taught at the Collège de Joliette, sought to recapture the spirit of medieval religious drama and to follow the French example of Henri Ghéon and Paul Claudel in his grandiose poetic spectacles. He discussed his objectives in *Le théâtre québécois dans notre littérature* (1973). Lamarche is the author of more than fifty plays, the best known of which is *Jonathas* (1935). He and his students took his productions on tour throughout the province until 1947. Two shows that achieved celebrity, *La défaite de l'enfer* (first produced in

1938) and *Notre-Dame-de-la-Couronne* (produced in 1947), were staged in Montreal in the open air with casts of hundreds and spectators numbering perhaps over 100,000. A similar spectacle, *Mystère de la messe*, was staged on the Plains of Abraham, Quebec City, in 1938 by Émile Legault and Les Compagnons de Saint-Laurent. Rina LASNIER also wrote plays inspired by religion and history, frequently featuring famous female personnages from sacred or secular history. Best known of her religious spectacles is *Notre-Dame-du-pain*, written for the 1947 Eucharistic Congress held in Ottawa.

Along with these religious spectacles, there were throughout Quebec many grandiose secular spectacles, usually presented to celebrate a historical moment, such as the tricentenary of Quebec City (1908), a dramatic celebration that lasted thirteen days and in which Sir Wilfrid Laurier and the Prince of Wales both appeared in costume. Another grandiose tricentennial celebration was that of Trois-Rivières (1934), written by Laurent Tremblay, who created twenty-five such pageants between 1938 and 1963.

Legault's inspiration in founding his soon-to-be famous Compagnons in 1937 was, like that of Lamarche, strongly religious. However, unlike Lamarche, Legault quickly moved away from grandiose spectacle to a complete renewal in Quebec of theatrical technique following the example of French director Jacques Copeau, as has been discussed by Hélène Jasmin-Belisle in *Le père Émile Legault et ses Compagnons de Saint-Laurent: Une petite histoire* (1986). For the first time in college theatre, men and women performed together, a development that considerably expanded the available dramatic repertory. Legault's first priority was the quality of theatrical performance, ahead of an uplifting moral message or quick commercial success. He introduced a new international repertory to Quebec audiences; encouraged a new generation of young Quebec dramatists, such as Félix LECLERC (although Les Compagnons rarely chose to produce original drama); and above all he trained as people of the theatre a new generation of women and men, many of whom remained on the professional stage in Quebec and established its most famous companies, including the Théâtre du Nouveau Monde founded in 1951.

In the area of popular professional drama was the unique phenomenon of *Aurore l'enfant martyre* by Léon Petitjean and Henri Rollin, published for the first time by Alonzo Le Blanc in 1982 as *Aurore, l'enfant martyre: histoire et représentation de la pièce*. Taking its story from the sensational trial of a woman who abused and killed her stepchild, *Aurore* enjoyed great success as a touring show with more than 6,000 productions between 1921 and 1951, at which time a French film was made of it. It is difficult today to understand public acceptance of this scandalous and horrifying show. Nevertheless, the company of Petitjean and Rollin consistently attracted sell-out crowds to its 'comedy', subsequently modified to a melodrama.

During the 1930s a minor revival of commercial repertory theatre occurred, particularly at Le Stella (1930-5), under Fred Barry and Albert Duquesne. Le Stella was the only permanent francophone professional company of the decade. The first Canadian play created there was Yvette Mercier-Gouin's *Cocktail* (1935), which was also toured to Quebec City and Ottawa, and was repeated in Montreal. The Montreal Repertory Theatre did some plays in French during the 1930s. The only professional company of the 1940s was Pierre Dagenais's company L'Équipe, founded in 1942. It is represented in fictional form in Françoise LORANGER's novel *Mathieu* (1949).

The revue, which was popular in Quebec from the turn of the century, enjoyed renewed popularity in the 1930s in the new medium of radio, where many of Quebec's best-known writers discovered, for the first time in Quebec, the possibility of earning a living through their creative abilities. In addition to humorous sketches, these writers produced dramatizations of Quebec works; for example, Henri Letondal, *La famille Gauthier* (in 1935); Robert CHOQUETTE, *Le curé de village* (in 1935); Henry Deyglun, *Vie de famille* (in 1938); and Claude-Henri GRIGNON, *Un homme et son péché* (in 1939). Young writers such as Jovette Bernier, Robert CHARBONNEAU, Pierre Dagenais, Jean Dèsprez, Léo-Paul DESROSIERS, Germaine GUÈVREMONT, Anne HÉBERT, Rina Lasnier, Félix Leclerc, Françoise Loranger, Yvette Mercier-Gouin, and Medjé Vézina all wrote works for radio. Radio-Canada's drama productions allowed writers to learn their trade and to reach a larger audience than ever before. The audience was large and faithful. As Renée Legris and Pierre Pagé have shown in several publications, radio drama played a decisive role in preparing the socio-cultural terrain that produced great change in Quebec after the Second World War, including a radical change in the status of women.

One of the most famous radio sketches was Gratien Gélinas' 'Fridolinons', with its subject-matter and language drawn from the lives of recognizable Quebec people. It was first broadcast by CKAC in 1937 and ran weekly until 1941. In 1938 Gélinas also turned his humorous radio sketches into a live revue, *Fridolinades*, which was staged annually at the Monument-National until 1946. Gélinas wrote the material, played the main role, served as master of ceremonies, and supervized the technical aspects, to which he attached great importance. One of the 1946 sketches, 'Le retour du conscrit', was the starting point for Gélinas's famous *TIT-COQ* first performed at the Monument-National in 1948.

See also Georges Bellerive, *Nos auteurs dramatiques, anciens et contemporains. Répertoire analytique* (1933); Jean Béraud, *350 ans de théâtre au Canada français* (1958); Jean Hamelin, *Le renouveau du théâtre au Canada français* (1962); Pierre Pagé, Renée Legris, Louise Blouin, *Répertoire des oeuvres de la littérature radiophonique québécoise, 1930-1970* (1975); *Le théâtre canadien-français*, Archives des Lettres canadiennes, V (1976); Joyce Cunningham, 'L'ancien théâtre Stella', *Jeu* 6 (1977); Pierre Lavoie, 'Québec/bilan tranquille d'une révolution théâtrale', *Jeu* 6 (1977); Léon H. Bélanger, *Les Ouimetoscopes: Léo-Ernest Ouimet et les débuts du cinéma québécois* (1978); Claudette Suzanne Trudeau, *Le théâtre canadien-français à Montréal, 1867-1914: Historique, dramaturgie, idéologie* (Ph.D. thesis, Toronto, 1980); Renée Legris, *Dictionnaire des auteurs de radio-feuilleton québécois* (1982); 'Le théâtre', *Revue d'histoire littéraire du Québec et du Canada français*, 5 (1984); Renée Legris, Jean-Marc Larrue, André-G. Bourassa, Gilbert David, *Le théâtre au Québec, 1825-1980* (1988); Rémi Tourangeau, *Fêtes et spectacles du Québec. Région du Saguenay-Lac Saint Jean* (1993). LOUISE FORSYTH

1948 to 1981. 1. 1948-59: THE BEGINNINGS OF A POPULAR FRENCH-CANADIAN DRAMA: GÉLINAS TO DUBÉ. The contemporary drama of Quebec may be dated from the first performance of Gratien GÉLINAS's play *TIT-COQ* (1950) at the Théâtre Monument National in Montreal in 1948. Presenting a genuine French-Canadian hero, the 'little rooster' of the title who searches in vain for love and a family, and written in the popular spoken French of the day, it showed Québécois that someone close to their own experience could be portrayed convincingly on the stage. In spite of the enormous influence on French-Canadian theatre of Père Émile Legault's Les Compagnons de Saint-Laurent, this company performed only one Canadian play during its entire career (1937-52): Félix LECLERC's *Maluron* (unpublished) in 1947. With the arrival of Gélinas and Leclerc, the emphasis on classical and religious drama in Quebec theatre was gradually broadened to include plays about ordinary Québécois.

Gélinas did not produce another play of his own until 1959, *Bousille et les justes* (1960), which was followed by *Hier, les enfants dansaient* (1968) in 1966. His influence was principally as a man of the theatre rather than as a playwright, especially with his founding of the Comédie Canadienne in 1958 for the production of Canadian plays. Leclerc, on the other hand, continued to write for the stage such works as *Dialogues d'hommes et de bêtes* (1949), *Théâtre de village* (1951), *Le p'tit bonheur* (1959; rpr. 1966), and *Sonnez les matines* (1959). They evoke the world of working-class rural Quebec in moving and often ironic tones, but the possibilities of the situations described are rarely developed beyond the level of sketches ('saynettes', Leclerc calls them).

Many playwrights who were published in the 1950s had made careers in fields other than drama, and some did not develop this craft sufficiently to leave a lasting mark on French-Canadian theatre. Prominent among them was Paul TOUPIN, primarily an essayist and academic, who published three plays—*Le choix* (1950), *Brutus* (1952), and *Chacun son amour* (1953)—and then a volume of collected plays, *Théâtre* (1961). Though carefully structured and written in a precise, almost classical, style, none of them relate specifically to the people of Quebec. The best is *Brutus*, which treats in a psychologically probing and carefully structured manner the relationship between Brutus and Caesar and the former's remorse after betraying his friend. Jacques FERRON—a medical doctor who also wrote novels, short stories, and essays—published several plays with a variety of themes and moods, from *L'ogre* (1949), a clever and light-hearted farce on the struggle for survival, to a historical and nationalist drama, *Les grands soleils* (1958), on the French-Canadian Patriotes (led by Jean-Olivier Chenier) in the Rebellion of 1837-8. Ferron later published several of his plays in two volumes, *Théâtre I* (1968) and *Théâtre II* (1975). Éloi DE GRANDMONT, better known as a poet and art critic, wrote one notable play, *Un fils à tuer* (1950), set in Quebec in the seventeenth century, which deals in a somewhat stark and elemental way with the struggle between the forces of order and freedom as represented by a harsh father and the determined son whom he kills. This and two other plays, *La fontaine de Paris* and *Le temps des fêtes* (1952), were published in his *Théâtre I* (1968). Robert ÉLIE, better known as a novelist and critic, published one of several plays, *L'étrangère*, in the first issue of *Les ÉCRITS DU CANADA FRANÇAIS* in 1954, a periodical that for many years was one of the few publishers of plays in Quebec and continues to publish French-Canadian plays regularly. A sombre treatment of the solitude of the individual, *L'étrangère* was too discursive and intellectual to win Élie popularity as a dramatist, although it was produced on television by Radio-Canada in 1964. Jacques LANGUIRAND's best-known play, *Les grands départs* (1958), was published during this period. Other plays by him produced in the 1950s but published later—*Les insolites* (1962; best Canadian play in the Dominion Drama Festival, 1957), *Le gibet* (1960), *Les violons de l'automne* (1962)—established his reputation as an experimental dramatist who used techniques of the Theatre of the Absurd to express his ironic but basically optimistic view of man's fate. Both *Les grands départs* and *Klondyke* (1971), a fantasy with music by Gabriel Charpentier, are symbolic treatments of the situation of Québécois—showing respectively the difficulty and the need for a spirit of adventure and determination in affirming their identity. *Les grands départs* was translated by Albert Bermel as *The departures* and published in *Gambit* 5 (1966).

Anne HÉBERT also wrote plays in the 1950s before establishing her reputation as a novelist. One of these, *La mercière assassinée*, was published in *Les écrits du Canada français* (vol. 4, 1958); it is a police drama enriched by her poetic imagination and sense of humour. But her poetry was not able to rescue *Le temps sauvage* (1963) and *Les invités au procès* (both published with *La mercière assassinée* under the title *Le temps sauvage* in 1967)—allegorical plays that are weighed down by complicated plots and excessive symbolism. André LANGEVIN wrote a political satire on Quebec politics, *L'oeil du peuple* (1958), which won first prize in a contest sponsored by the Théâtre du Nouveau Monde, where it was produced in 1957. Though very funny in parts, the satire is too obvious and extreme and the play was not well received by Montreal audiences. André Laurendeau, who was more at home in journalism and politics, made a contribution to the theatre with *La vertu des chattes*, published in *Les écrits du Canada français* (vol. 5, 1959), and two other plays in the same periodical: *Deux femmes terribles* (vol. 11, 1961) and *Marie-Emma* (vol. 15, 1963); the three were republished in *Théâtre* (1970). Realistic, humorous, and literate, Laurendeau's plays deal seriously with human relationships, but they lack theatrical immediacy and are overly discursive.

The most important dramatist to emerge in these years was Marcel DUBÉ, who was to dominate the Montreal stage in the 1960s and remains the most published and accomplished French-Canadian dramatist even today. In the 1950s he began to make his mark as a dramatist with three plays (among his most popular) set in the east end of Montreal: *Zone* (1955), about a group of young smugglers; *Un SIMPLE SOLDAT* (1958), which portrays a ne'er-do-well who cannot adjust to civilian life after the Second World War; and *Le temps des lilas* (1958), a Chekhov-inspired play about lonely, disillusioned people in a Montreal boarding-house.

2. 1960-8: THE AGE OF DUBÉ. This second phase is marked by the predominance of Marcel DUBÉ's plays on stage, on television, and in print. With the exception of Françoise LORANGER, no other dramatist wrote a large body of work in these years, although several had one or two significant plays published. In keeping with the higher standard of living of many Québécois, Dubé's plays now reflected the plight of middle-class characters and their difficult relationships in *Florence* (1960), *Octobre* (1964), *Virginie* (1968), *Bilan* (1968), *Les beaux dimanches* (1968), *Pauvre amour* (1969), and what many consider his masterpiece, *Au retour des oies blanches* (1969), which resembles *Oedipus the king* in plot and structure but has a distinctively Quebec setting. Like many of his plays in this period, *Au retour* is an attempt to create a tragedy out of contemporary Quebec experience. Though all these plays are marred at times by melodrama, their humanist vision and poetic prose have made several of them classics of French-Canadian drama. In the 1970s Dubé published some plays that were written and produced in the fifties and sixties and that show the same destruction of human relationships in a world of so-called progress: *Le naufragé* (1971), *Un matin comme les autres* (1971), *Entre midi et soir* (1971), *Paradis perdu* (1972), *La cellule* (1973), and *Manuel* (1973). In the mid-1970s a more mellow mood permeated such plays as *L'été s'appelle Julie* (1975), and the comedies *L'impromptu du Québec; ou Le testament* (1974) and *Dites-le avec des fleurs* (1976). Dubé then returned to his tragic view of life in a somewhat static treatment of recent developments in Quebec, *Le reformiste; ou L'honneur des hommes* (1977).

If Dubé can be compared to Chekhov, Loranger is more akin to Strindberg. She shows the same preoccupation with family relationships as Dubé, but at a more elemental and violent level. Her treatment of the family is seen in her early plays: *Une maison . . . un jour* (1965), which probes the relationships of three generations of a family; *Encore 5 minutes* (1967), dealing with unhappy love and marriage; and the television play *Un cri qui vient de loin* (1966), which shows a happy resolution to marital problems after considerable pain. At the end of this period Loranger turned to political and social problems and adopted a different style—a more Brechtian one that sometimes involved the audience. *Double jeu* (1969) attempts to adapt the 'living theatre' to the Quebec stage and invites audience participation; *Le chemin du roy* (1969), anticipating Rick SALUTIN's *Les Canadiens*, depicts the struggle between Quebec and Ottawa in the form of a hockey game presided over by President de Gaulle on his famous visit to Canada in 1967. An even more nationalist play is *Médium saignant* (1970), which pits the two sides in the struggle for language rights in Quebec against one another at a municipal meeting. The heated reaction of supporters of both positions to the initial production at the Comédie Canadienne in 1970 was repeated when a revised version was presented at Montreal's Place des Arts in 1976; it opened there eleven days before the Parti Québécois's victory brought René Lévesque to power.

One dramatist who broke even earlier from realism in the theatre was Gilles Derome, who combines somewhat uneasily elements of both Pirandello and Brecht in his two published plays: *Qui est Dupressin?* (*Écrits du Canada français*, vol. 14, 1972), a farce about a search for identity set in a mental hospital, and *La maison des oiseaux* (1973), a tragedy about the difficulty of living with oneself and with others. In the same volume of *Les écrits du Canada français*, Eugène Cloutier's *Le dernier beatnik* explored rather verbosely the tensions and rivalries in a contemporary love triangle. The novelist Marie-Claire BLAIS wrote a macabre work, *L'éxécution* (1968), about boys in a residential school who murder one of their fellow students. While demonstrating the author's deftness in examining the evil and distortions of life, the play too often substitutes discussion for dramatic action.

Few French-Canadian dramatists in these years looked to the past for their material. One who did was novelist and folklorist Félix-Antoine SAVARD. His *La folle* (1960), written in free verse, was based on an Acadian legend of loss and recovery, and *La dalle-des-morts* (1965), set on the island of Montreal in 1830, glorifies the exploits of the *coureurs-de-bois* who went to their deaths while keeping alive the spirit of adventure that Savard considered necessary for the survival of French Canadians. Though his style is poetic and elegant and filled with noble sentiments, too many of his characters are one-dimensional. Also elegantly written, though less patriotic, was Jean BASILE's *Joli tambour* (1966). Set in mid-eighteenth-century Quebec, it is the story of a young man appointed public executioner to avoid punishment for a crime of which he was unjustly convicted. (As *The drummer-boy* it was produced in Toronto in 1968.) Jean-Louis Roux, better known as an actor and director than a playwright, wrote a historical drama, *Bois-brûlés* (1967), which he labelled an epic documentary on the rise and fall of Louis Riel, but little attention is given to the portrayal or development of character. It includes music by Gabriel Charpentier.

The beginnings of a truly avant-garde theatre in Quebec were seen in Jean Morin's *Vive l'empereur* (1966), Jacques Duchesne's *Le quadrillé* (1968), and Roger Dumas's *Les millionaires* (1967) and *Les comédiens* (1969). Often absurdist in style and showing the theatre reflecting consciously on itself, these plays were not widely produced in Quebec but they helped prepare the way for writers who would take this style for granted in the 1970s. Morin's play and those of Dumas were also important because they appeared in the first issues of a series called 'Théâtre vivant' published by Holt, Rinehart and Winston, which was a serious attempt to publish more French-Canadian drama. It was soon taken over by the Montreal publishing firm Leméac, whose two collections 'Théâtre Canadien' (later changed to 'Théâtre Leméac') in 1968 and 'Répertoire Québécois' in 1969 marked a new era in Quebec drama. One of the last plays in the 'Théâtre vivant' series was *Les BELLES-SOEURS* (1968), the first published play by Michel TREMBLAY, who soon became the dominant figure in what might be called the coming-of-age of Québécois drama.

3. 1969-76: MICHEL TREMBLAY AND THE USE OF *JOUAL*. Tremblay was the single most important dramatist in Quebec in the 1970s. His plays led the way to acceptance in the theatre of *JOUAL*, the vernacular used by many urbanized Québécois. *Les BELLES-SOEURS*—whose production in Montreal in 1968 began the assault of *joual* on the theatre and the heated debate about its validity—is about lower-class women living in the east end of Montreal who speak the fractured, vital

language that could be heard on the streets there. It revealed not only Tremblay's ability to present convincingly Québécois women, but also his sense of rhythmic dialogue and musical structure: the women speak both as individuals and as a chorus. *Les belles-soeurs* became the first of a series of plays based on the lives of characters living for the most part in the same section of Montreal, many of whom appear in several plays. The plays of this period, all published by Leméac, were: *En pièces détachées* and *La Duchesse de Langeais* (jointly published in 1970), *À TOI POUR TOUJOURS, TA MARIE-LOU* (1971), *Demain matin, Montréal m'attend* (1972), *Hosanna* (1973), *Bonjour, là, bonjour* (1974), *Les héros de mon enfance* (1976), *Sainte Carmen de la Main* (1976), *Damnée Manon, Sacrée Sandra* and *Surprise! Surprise!* (published together in 1977). *À toi pour toujours, ta Marie-Lou*, perhaps Tremblay's finest play in this period, offers a harrowing picture of a Quebec family whose two daughters, Carmen and Manon, ten years after the violent death of their parents, reflect on the quality of life in their home and the lasting effects it has had on them. The role of musical structure in Tremblay's work is seen to advantage here as the girls' conversation is intertwined with the bickering of their parents in the past. The two plays that bear the names of Carmen and Manon involve transvestitism. Here, and in two plays about homosexuality, *La Duchesse de Langeais* and *Hosanna*, the central figures and their fate become symbolic of the Québécois themselves, whom Tremblay sees as having been forced to betray their true identity and to put on a disguise that is foreign to them.

After the Parti Québécois victory in 1976, Tremblay felt that much of the political message of his plays had been heard; he even allowed his plays to be produced in English in Quebec. The direction of his drama changed, as is shown in *L'impromptu d'Outremont* (1980), which takes as its subject the concerns of middle-class women, and in *Les anciennes odeurs* (1981), in which he explores a homosexual relationship more directly and psychologically than in *Hosanna* and *La Duchesse de Langeais* and without their political overtones. Most of Tremblay's plays are available in English translation and have been produced in English, in and outside Quebec.

Robert GURIK—who came to prominence about the same time as Tremblay, although some of his plays were published earlier—combined a Brechtian style of propagandist theatre with social concerns that were both 'indépendantiste' and international. While ingenious and clever, the satire in his plays was often too obvious and heavy-handed. Thus his *Hamlet, prince du Québec* (1968) used Shakespeare's play as a model to depict the struggle between federalists and separatists. *Les tas de sièges* (1971) is a series of three one-act plays, each concerned with issues raised during the October Crisis of 1970. *Le procès de Jean-Baptiste M.* (1972) is about one man's fruitless protest against the conformity demanded by a consumer society that prevailed both in Quebec and throughout the Western world. Gurik's wider concern was evident also in *Le pendu* (1970), a somewhat bitter comment on how a society treats those who would be its saviours; in *À coeur ouvert* (1969), a depiction of an Orwellian world in which man's inhumanity to man is shown by the allegory of a heart bank that is manipulated by whatever group is in power; in *Api 2967* (1971), a futurist play that shows the fruitless efforts of Adam and Eve characters to restore humanity to a world dominated by technology; and in *La palissade* (1971), a more hopeful play about the possibility of love and humanity. In Gurik's subsequent plays, specific people or events were used to throw light on injustice in various parts of the world: *Lénine* (1975) deals with the failure of workers in today's world to achieve the goals of the Russian leader, *Le champion* (1977) is on the failure of the boxer Mohammed Ali to gain respect for his people, and *La baie des Jacques* (1978) is on the emptiness of workers' lives that are exploited for the benefit of their employers. Many of Gurik's plays finish inconclusively and open-endedly, presumably so that the audience will be moved to action by the scenes they have witnessed.

An even more aggressive political stance was taken by Dominique de Pasquale in his *On n'est pas sorti du bois* (1972), a fast-paced musical that depicts Québécois as primitives who refuse to submit to the annihilation of their race, chanting, 'We will not go to our burial . . .' and inviting the audience to join in. A similar stridency characterized de Pasquale's *Oui chef!* and *L'arme au poing ou larme à l'oeil*, which were published in one volume in 1973.

The most imaginative and satirical *joual* dramatist was Jean-Claude GERMAIN, who combined seriousness and good humour in his treatment of Quebec's past and present. As a founder in 1969 of Le Théâtre du Même Nom, and of a theatre group that performed there—Les Enfants de Chenier and then (in 1971) Les P'tits Enfants Laliberté—he had a base from which to produce his plays. *Diguidi, diguidi, ha! ha! ha!* (1970) is a biting commentary on the conflicts and oppressions that have existed in Quebec family life, while his later satire *Mamours et conjugats* (1979), a history of marital relations in *la belle province*, is subtitled 'Scènes de la vie amoureuse québécoise'. *Si les Sansoucis s'en soucient, ces Sancoucis-ci s'en soucierent-ils? Bien parler c'est se respecter!* (1972) is a farce on the serious theme of the complicity of Québécois with their English oppressors. *Le roi des mises à bas prix* (1972) takes up the fate of one member of the Sansoucis family who has accepted unquestioningly the worst aspects of North American culture. Germain's later plays include what he called a trilogy on the theatre, which became another metaphor for Quebec life and history: *Les hauts et les bas d'la vie d'une diva: Sarah Ménard par eux-mêmes* (1976) looks at Quebec through the character of a would-be opera singer; *Un pays dont la devise est je m'oublie* (1976), whose title changes Quebec's motto from 'Je me souviens', uses two travelling actors to re-enact with comic flair unpleasant and decisive moments in Quebec's history; and *L'école des rêves* (1979) focuses on the joys and sorrows of itinerant actors in Quebec, in the forties and fifties, who become symbols of the Québécois themselves. (*Un pays...* was performed with great success in French in Toronto in 1982.) In *Les faux brillants de Félix-Gabriel Marchand* (1977) Germain revised a comedy first published in 1885 by Marchand, who became the premier of Quebec in 1897.

One of the most inventive *joual* dramatists has been Jean BARBEAU, whose characters express great alienation and disenchantment with society. Two short plays, *Goglu* (1971) and *Solange* (1974), show this poignantly, as does *Ben-Ur* (1971), whose title is a 'pop' version of the anti-hero's name, Joseph Benoît Urbain Théberge, and a nickname that labels him for life. Like Barbeau's later *Le jardin de la maison blanche* (1979), the play is an indictment of the superficiality of many aspects of North American society. The main character in *Le Chemin de Lacroix* (1971), besides undergoing his own 'passion' of injustice in scenes announced like the Catholic Stations of the Cross, is mocked by a friend from France who corrects his *joual* and urges him to speak proper French. A lighter but still satirical approach to *joual* is taken in two plays published together in 1972: *Manon Lastcall*, which presents a seductive museum guide who describes paintings in *joual*, and *Joualez-moi d'amour*, in which a couple can make love only if they speak *joual*. With less emphasis on *joual* in his later plays, Barbeau continued to look at the alienated in *Citrouille* (1975), a somewhat violent treatment of women who take out their anger by violating a man; in *Une brosse* (1975), in which two unemployed Quebec workers turn to drinking, violence, and murder; in *Une marquise de Sade et un lézard nommé King Kong* (1979), in which the characters are alienated from both life and art; and in the more hopeful *Émile et une nuit* (1979), in which literature and music give meaning to the lives of two alienated characters.

An outspoken theoretician for *joual* in the theatre has been Victor-Lévy BEAULIEU, who said in an interview in 1974: 'The true counter-culture in Quebec at the level of language is created in *joual*.' A case for this is made in *En attendant Trudot* (1974), in which the central character, Ti-Bé, a symbol of the repressed Québécois, revolts against the emptiness of his life and realizes he must create his own identity. The same is found in *Ma Corriveau* (1976), a retelling of a Quebec legend, which insists on the necessity of Québécois's having their own legends and a language in which to tell them. *Cérémonial pour l'assassinat d'un ministre* (1978), subtitled 'oratorio' and written in poetic prose, makes a case for the use of violence by the would-be liberators of a society, and includes the obvious reference to the murderers of Pierre Laporte.

One of the most talented and popular of Québécois dramatists to emerge in this period was Michel GARNEAU, who excelled in both poetic language and musical structure. He wrote light comedy in *Sur le matelas* (1974); a symphonic statement on the plight of Québécois women of different generations in *Quatre à quatre* (1974)—translated as *Four to four* (1978) by Christian Bédard and Keith Turnbull and published in *A collection of Canadian plays, Volume 5* (1978), edited by Rolf Kalman; a memory play, *Strauss et Pesant (et Rosa)* (1974), portraying moral, religious, and political corruption in the days of Duplessis; and an impressionistic poetic drama on the life of Emily Dickinson in a Quebec setting, *Émilie ne sera plus jamais cueillie par l'anémone* (1981). Garneau also wrote two successful adaptations for the stage: *Gilgamesh* (1976), and *Macbeth* (1978).

During this prolific period, some established writers were able to have plays published that had been written or produced some years earlier. Yves THÉRIAULT, who had written radio and television plays for Radio-Canada, went beyond the immediate concerns of many French-Canadian playwrights to deal with the elemental forces of life in a family, or a community, in plays whose settings are often indefinite: *Le marcheur* (1968) takes place 'in a country kitchen', *Frédange*

(1970) 'somewhere in the world', *Les terres neuves* (1970) 'in the mountains'. *Le marcheur* shows how the oppression of a tyrannical father stifles his children's need to develop and grow until they finally rebel. *Frédange* is filled with foreboding as a husband returns to his wife after abandoning her for six years, only to submit to the command of his paralysed mother that he, and not the shepherd his wife has taken, must leave. *Les terres neuves* shows a poor and unhappy people from a miserable village on their way to a new village; as they approach this 'promised land' they meet its inhabitants leaving for the place they have deserted.

Guy Dufresne—another dramatist who has written much for radio and television—deals with the French-Canadian experience more directly than Thériault, and looks at it from a broader perspective than many of the *joual* dramatists. *Le cri de l'engoulevent* (1969)—translated by Philip London and Laurence Berard as *The cry of the whippoorwill* (1972)—is a realistic drama in which a strong-minded Quebec farmer refuses to make a deal to sell his land to an American, and as a result loses both his money and his daughter to the American. First produced in 1960, it can be seen as underlining both the necessity for Quebec to accept the ways of the new and open industrial society, and also the difficulties and dangers this entails. Dufresne's *Les traitants* (1969), based on an inquest in New France into the sale of intoxicating beverages to Natives in 1665, is overburdened by research and depicts rather statically a shameful episode in Canadian history. Sections of two of Dufresne's popular TV series have been published: *Cap-aux-Sorciers* (1969), a legend about a navy captain, his daughter, and three granddaughters, and *Ce maudit Lardier* (1975), a drama of conflict between shipbuilders and fur traders in New France in 1737 taken from the first season of his téléroman 'Les forges de Saint-Maurice'. Dufresne's ability to write in *joual* is evident in *Docile* (1972), a slight comedy about a pianist who reads people's fortunes in their toes and thighs.

The plays of Claude JASMIN deal with pressing social and political problems in realistic settings and situations, but they are sometimes melodramatic. The hero is often a young man seeking to save himself or his society. An early television play, *Blues pour un homme averti* (1964), presents a young man searching for his father as he tries to make up for a wasted life in the underworld of a big city. *Tuez le veau gras* (1970), also written for TV, dramatizes the story of a young intellectual who compromises himself by failing to set up a union for workers in a town's biggest plant. The irony suggested by the title ('Kill the fatted calf') is most evident in the final scene when he leaves, discouraged and physically beaten, to take up a teaching post at a small college: the contrast between his reception and that of the prodigal son in the Bible becomes clear. In a similar style, and in the discouraging mood suggested by the title, *C'est toujours la même histoire* (1972) deals with the failure and eventual suicide of a young American who plans to set up a youth centre in the Laurentians but meets opposition from the townspeople and his girlfriend's father. *Le veau dort* (1979)—written in a more impersonal, Brechtian style in ten tableaux—is a sweeping condemnation of injustices throughout the course of history; the title refers to the golden calf that men have too often worshipped. It won the Dominion Drama Festival award for the best Canadian play in 1965.

Two popular Quebec dramatists who are out of the mainstream of the *joual* writers were published during this period: Roch CARRIER and Roland Lepage. Primarily a novelist and storyteller who is concerned with recreating aspects of Quebec's recent past or 'Dark Ages', Carrier adapted some of his fiction for the stage. His best-known play, *La guerre, yes sir!* (1970), based on his novel of the same title (1968), takes place in a rural Quebec community in 1942 and shows the misunderstanding and violence that arise when the body of a French-Canadian killed in the war is accompanied to his home by a group of non-French-speaking English-Canadian soldiers. In 1972 it became the first Quebec play to be produced (in translation) at the Stratford Festival in Ontario. *Floralie* (1974), an adaptation of Carrier's novel *Floralie, où es-tu?* (1969), treats a rural Quebec community some thirty years earlier and explores the religious and cultural traditions that shaped the French-Canadian characters of *La guerre, yes sir!* The action takes place immediately before and after the wedding of Floralie and Anthyme, the parents of the boy whose body was brought home in the earlier play, and includes an elaborate fantasy, not always successful, in which the Seven Deadly Sins are personified. Carrier's first work for the stage alone is *La céleste bicyclette* (1980), a monologue written for the gifted actor and director Albert Millaire. A richly poetic play, it is set in the psychiatric ward of a hospital where an actor, confined with his bicycle, imagines himself cycling in the skies and philosophizes on many aspects of life to show

how unlimited is the human spirit. As *The celestial bicycle* it was performed in English by Millaire at the Tarragon Theatre, Toronto, in 1982. Roland Lepage's best-known play, *Le temps d'une vie* (1974)—translated by Sheila Fischman as *In a lifetime* (1978)—is set in Quebec's Abitibi region. Using several characters to portray the life of a long-suffering woman from the turn of the century until her death in the 1970s, it is an effective, if at times tedious, evocation of the lot of many Québécois women. Besides playing in many parts of Quebec, it toured France and Belgium and won the Chalmers Award for its production in English at Toronto's Tarragon Theatre in 1978. *La complainte des hivers rouges* (1974) is yet another Quebec play about the Patriotes of 1837-8, written after the Liberal Party's victory in Quebec in 1973 to remind Québécois of the need to work for independence; although it contains much elevated and heroic language, it suffers at times from a certain heaviness and melodrama. *La pétaudière* (1974), a musical satire on Quebec's language law, Bill 22, is lighter in tone. Lepage has also written *Icare* (1979), a mythological fantasy for children.

Antonine MAILLET's plays are remarkable for their use of a language that is a survival of sixteenth-century France brought to Acadia from central France, somewhat coarsened but still spoken in some regions of New Brunswick among the poor—Maillet's heroines and heroes. *Les crasseux* (1968) is a comedy that contrasts their lives with those of the rich in a small village and shows how, after years of subservience, the poor manage by determination and shrewdness to take over their wealthy neighbours' land. *La SAGOUINE* (1971) makes a central character out of a charwoman who appeared in *Les crasseux* as a spy for the poor. Maillet continued her saga of Acadian characters. In *Gapi et Sullivan* (1973), expanded and republished as *Gapi* (1976), the husband of La Sagouine, who is now dead, becomes the central figure. *Évangéline deusse* (1975) transplants a modern *EVANGELINE* figure of eighty to a park in Montreal, where she displays the same indomitability of spirit as her namesake. Maillet has adapted several of her novels for the stage: *Emmanuel à Joseph à Dâvit* (1975), not yet published in dramatic form; *Les cordes-de-bois* (1977), dramatized as *La veuve enragée* (1977); and *Mariaagelas* (1973), dramatized as *La contrabandière* (1981). *La joyeuse criée*, monologues spoken by characters from the world of *La Sagouine*, starred Viola Léger and premièred in Moncton and Montreal in 1982; it was performed in Toronto by Léger in Mar. 1983. *Le bourgeois gentleman* (1978) is a witty but obvious adaptation of the Molière play to a Montreal setting, where a *nouveau-riche* Québécois wants to move from Rosemount to Westmount.

Three dramatists stand out among the avant-garde writers for the stage in this period: Yves Sauvageau, Yvon Boucher, and Claude GAUVREAU. Sauvageau's *Wouf wouf!* (1970) is completely non-linear in its conception of time, and a violent rejection of the realistic theatre. Much of the dialogue is incomprehensible on the rational level; by the end, several characters are reduced to adding the words 'wouf-wouf' to anything they say. An absurdist reaction to the frustrations of the human spirit in a dehumanized world, the play is at times confusing and repetitious, but its lively theatricality made it very popular with Montreal audiences, and influenced writers and theatre groups in the 1970s. Boucher's *L'ouroboros* (1973), also reacting against the realistic tradition, is a more abstract work, reflecting self-consciously on the relation between theatre and reality. The characters, who meet outside a theatre to discuss the play they have just seen, are identified only by numbers and engage in a sometimes brilliant critique of the *raison d'être* of theatre itself. Boucher prefaces the text with an attack on, and letters from, Quebec publishers who rejected the play because they couldn't categorize it. Gauvreau—who, like Sauvageau, took his own life—extended the boundaries of theatre with two plays in particular: *La charge de l'orignal épormyable*, a sympathetic portrayal of a patient in a mental hospital, and *Les oranges sont verts*, in which language is often forced into new forms to suggest a breaking of the bonds that limit body and spirit. Both plays, after important presentations at the Théâtre du Nouveau Monde in 1972 and 1974 respectively, were published posthumously with other plays in the 1500-page *Oeuvres créatrices complètes* (1971) of Gauvreau.

English readers can discover the work of some of the younger playwrights of this period in translations of seven Québécois plays included in *A collection of Canadian plays, Volume 5* (1978), edited by Rolf Kalman, which shows how dramatic technique had become even more innovative in Quebec since the early Tremblay plays, so that a more open, non-realistic, at times musically structured type of drama became the norm. Besides Michel Garneau's choric *Quatre à quatre*, already mentioned, one of the most moving plays in the volume is *Encore un peu* (1974) by Serge Mercier (translated by Allan van Meer as *A little bit left*), a tender story of an elderly married couple waiting for their days to end. Two of the plays have been published in English—Rénald Tremblay's *La céleste Greta* (translated by Allan van Meer as *Greta the divine*), a sprawling panoramic look at unpleasant aspects of French Canada's history up to 1760, and Serge Sirois's *Dodo, l'enfant do* (translated by John van Burek as *Dodo*), which shows the breakdown of a modern working-class Québécois family. Claude Roussin's *Une job* (1975) (translated by Allan van Meer as *Looking for a job*) is a comic fantasy on the political situation in Quebec shortly before and after the War Measures Act that paints a bleak picture of Quebec's will to self-determination; while André Simard's *En attendant Gaudreault* (1976), translated by Henry BEISSEL and Arlette Francière as *Waiting for Gaudreault*, is a more realistic and compact treatment of the plight of workers whose jobs are at the mercy of a heartless foreman. Finally, Louis-Dominique Lavigne's *As-tu peur des voleurs?* (1977), translated by Henry Beissel as *Are you afraid of thieves?*, is a highly orchestrated comedy about three couples that comes close to sound poetry and music, and emphasizes how far theatrical invention has progressed since Tremblay. The strong comic element in the Québécois volume of Kalman's anthology, even when serious themes are being treated, anticipates the final section of this survey.

4. 1977–81: WIDER PERSPECTIVES AND WOMEN WRITERS. From the late seventies on, in the work of Québécois playwrights, there was a shift in mood and subject beyond the political situation in Quebec, and an emphasis on comedy for its own sake—perhaps owing to the satisfaction many dramatists felt at the election of the Parti Québécois in Nov. 1976. Michel Tremblay typified the reactions of several of these playwrights when he said that this event realized much of what he had been writing about regarding a Québécois identity; as a result he allowed his plays to be performed in English in Quebec. (They had already been performed in English in other parts of Canada.) Besides a shift in Tremblay's own work, as seen in *L'impromptu d'Outremont* (1980), the change was epitomized by Louis Saia, who spoke of his collaborations with Claude Meunier: 'Ours is a "théâtre social" about Québécois who are not identified with Québécois problems. We are not concerned, as writers, with a Québec identity.' Their play, *Appelez-mois Stéphane* (1981), involves middle-class characters who are amateur actors in a drama class that brings out both comic and poignant aspects of their lives as individuals. Saia, with Louise Roy, wrote the comedy *Une amie d'enfance* (1980) and the one-woman show *Bachelor* (1981). Saia and Meunier, along with five other writers, wrote sketches for *Broue* (as yet unpublished), a hilarious comedy with three male actors playing multiple roles as they depict a day in the life of a Montreal tavern. *Broue* travelled throughout Quebec after its opening in 1979 and, with sold-out performances in English as *Brew* at Montreal's Centaur Theatre in 1982, began a tour of English Canada; it became one of the most-performed plays in Canadian theatre history. This lighter mood is seen in other collaborations, such as André Boulanger's and Sylvie Prégent's *Eh! qu'mon chum est platte!* (1979).

A shift from the preoccupation with Quebec's problems was also evident among those writing serious drama, even when Quebec's past is the setting. Jean Daigle's *Le débâcle* (1979) is set in a farm kitchen near Quebec City in 1931, though this sometimes melodramatic play is basically the Phaedra story carefully adapted to its new environment. In Daigle's *Le jugement dernier* (1979) an old man, Alphonse, reviews incidents in his life from 1923 to 1979; the décor is described as 'the skull of Alphonse at the moment of death'. Like *Le débâcle*, this is a personal and pessimistic story with universal rather than local significance.

The most ambitious work to be produced and published in Quebec in this period was the six-play epic by Jean-Pierre RONFARD, *Vie et mort du roi boiteux* (2 vols, 1981). Director, playwright, actor, and drama teacher, Ronfard brought to Canada a wide theatrical experience gained in Algeria, Greece, Portugal, and Austria when he became the first director of the French section of the National Theatre School in 1960. After directing many plays in Montreal, he wrote *Vie et mort du roi boiteux* with, and for his own, Nouveau Théâtre Expérimental de Montréal, where it was performed in 1981 and 1982 before playing in Lennoxville, Ottawa, and Hull. Written as six interconnected plays, it involves 25 actors playing 150 roles in a production that lasts fifteen hours, including intermissions for lunch and dinner. Subtitled 'a gory and grotesque epic', the play embodies a world of its own that reaches from Montreal to the land of Azerbaijan; juxtaposes past and present, cultured French and *joual*; presents a conflict over centuries between two warring families—the Roberges and the Ragones; includes such diverse figures as God, Moses, Aristotle, Joan of Arc, Brecht, Mata-Hari,

Einstein, and comic-book characters; and draws on the cultures of both East and West, including the Bible and Shakespeare.

Another important development in modern French-Canadian theatre has been the emergence of women playwrights, supported by Montreal-based women's theatre groups such as Le Théâtre des Cuisines, formed in 1974, and Le Théâtre Expérimental des Femmes, established in 1979, and by women's publishing companies such as Les Éditions du Remue-Ménage (the word means 'stirring up') and Les Éditions de la Pleine Lune. Some of their plays are propagandist statements for women's rights or grievances; others present women's problems without calling for action, or give a woman's perspective on life itself. (A number of them are COLLECTIVE CREATIONS.) Because of their authors' determination to be heard, the plays were often produced quickly and roughly, and while they had an evident sincerity and a sense of urgency, they sometimes suffered from a lack of structure and dramatic form. Such was the case of *La nef des sorcières* (1976). Seen by many as the beginning of a truly feminine force in Quebec theatre, it was a collage of six monologues written by different women, the best-known writer being Marie-Claire BLAIS. There was little attempt to tie together these individual statements about modern women, and the work can hardly be described as a play. *Môman travaille pas, a trop d'ouvrage* (1976), a collective work by the Théâtre des Cuisines, was a strong propaganda piece that insisted on the right of women working in the home to a salary. More unified than *La nef des sorcières*, it was written in a documentary style that appealed directly to the audience in song and argument. Denise BOUCHER's *Les FÉES ONT SOIF* (1978) became a *succès de scandale* because of the attack it made on the ideal image of womanhood fostered by the cult of the Virgin Mary. The play was picketed in Montreal by religious groups, and an injunction was brought against the distribution of the book for alleged blasphemy and profanity. Though a strong affirmation that women in Quebec had been repressed politically and sexually by this religious image, the play suffers from being somewhat simplistic and too blatantly iconoclastic.

Jovette MARCHESSAULT's *La SAGA DES POULES MOUILLÉES* (1981) is a statement of the need for a women's culture written in the form of a mythic meeting of four famous French-Canadian women writers of the nineteenth and twentieth centuries: Laure Conan (Félicité ANGERS), Germaine GUÈVREMONT, Anne HÉBERT, and Gabrielle ROY. Translated by Linda Gaboriau as *The saga of wet hens*, the play was presented in English at Toronto's Tarragon Theatre in 1982. Jocelyne Beaulieu's *J'ai beaucoup changé depuis*. . . (1981) combines realism and fantasy to make a moving statement about a woman's right to her own identity. The heroine, called simply 'F'—F as in *folle* and *femme*, as the author explains in the subtitle—is aided by a sympathetic woman psychiatrist who uses the approach of R.D. Laing to help her recover her sanity, overcome her past, and begin a new life.

Jacqueline Barrette anticipated those women dramatists who explore the problems not only of women but of women in relationships, often in a family setting and in society. Her *Ça-dit-qu'essa-à-dire* (1972), like *La nef des sorcières*, is a series of monologues on many topics illustrating the routine and often wearisome life of the Québécois. Though sometimes poetic and poignant, and interspersed with music, the work is not shaped into a drama. *Bonne fête papa* (1973) is an effective and disturbing treatment of the tensions and sexual frustrations in a middle-class Montreal family. Elizabeth Bourget examined the relationships of two young unmarried couples in *Bernadette et Juliette; ou La vie c'est comme la vaiselle, c'est toujours à recommencer* (1979). The promise shown in this first play was more fully realized in *Bonne fête, maman* (1982), a popular comedy about the problems of a middle-aged woman who decides that life with her taxi-driver husband is not enough after her children have left home. Louisette Dussault's one-woman show *Moman* (1981) is also a serio-comic play about the problems of a mother; in this case the bus journey from Montreal to Nicolet, of a mother with her three-year-old twin daughters, becomes the occasion, filled with humour and tenderness, for a rejection of the mother's traditional role as a policewoman. France Vézina, who has also published poetry, wrote a fanciful poetic drama, *L'hippocanthrope* (1979), about the stifling nature of family relationships in which the free form and imaginative dialogue become a paradigm for the freedom the characters seek.

Two women playwrights explored dark aspects of life in rural Quebec. Jeanne-Mance Delisle's *Un réel, ben beau, ben triste* (1980) is a tragic study of incest in a small Abitibi village in the 1960s. Marie LABERGE's *C'était avant la guerre à l'Anse à Gilles* (1981), set in 1936 in the village of the title, also concerns the exploitation of women; at the end of the play the heroine, explicitly rejecting the example of Marie Chapdelaine, decides to leave the limiting world of her native village, and the man who loves her, to seek her fortune in the city. A more ambitious work is Laberge's *Ils étaient venus pour . . .* (1981), a Brechtian play on the rise and fall (from 1902 to 1927) of the village of Van-Jolbert, which dies when the mill-owner closes down its only industry. Though fragmented and not specific enough, it reflects sensitivity for the workers and their families, and throws light on the human dimension of social problems.

Two other women playwrights celebrated life without emphasizing a particular problem. Louise MAHEUX-FORCIER is a prize-winning novelist who has published several plays. *Her Neige et palmiers* (1974), written for television, is a lyric memory play about a woman who rejoices that she has kept the child she had planned to abort; while *Un arbre chargé d'oiseaux* (1976)—which has appeared on television in France, Switzerland, and Belgium, as well as Canada—combines mystery, romance, and fantasy in the tale of a woman real-estate agent who learns of life, love, and death from an old lady whose home is for sale. *Un parc en automne* (1982), Maheux-Forcier's first stage play, is filled with poetry and nostalgia as two former lovers find each other in a retirement home. Finally, *Ma p'tite vache a mal aux pattes* (1981) by Jocelyne Goyette exemplified several features of Quebec drama of this period: comedy, theatricality, the one-person format, a woman's perspective, assured use of a distinctively Québécois French, and attention to daily life as opposed to social or political concerns. As in other recent plays, there was a certain roughness here that came from lack of experience in dramatizing this story of a day in the life of a young mother-lover-actress.

JAMES NOONAN

1981 to 1996. INTRODUCTION. During the 1960s and 1970s—a period of strong self-affirmation in Quebec—most playwrights, following the lead of Gratien GÉLINAS and Marcel DUBÉ rather than international currents, were preoccupied with dramatizing local issues related to language, culture, and interpersonal relations in plays with mostly linear plots; though some, like Michel TREMBLAY, added formal concerns. The eighties brought about several important changes, including an emphasis on the so-called *nouvelle dramaturgie*, as well as on imagistic drama: revolutionary ways of conceiving both verbal communication and pictorial space. New voices appearing in the nineties reflect their destabilized social base through 'carnavalesque' happenings.

1. A NEW MATURITY. During the 1980s and 1990s, many established dramatists continued to write for the theatre. Some, like Marcel Dubé, were unable to match their past achievements. Others, like Gratien Gélinas with *La passion de Narcisse Mondoux* (1987), enjoyed popular and critical success. Jean BARBEAU's comedies *Les gars* (1984) and *Le grand Poucet* (1985) were directed to summer audiences. Victor-Lévy BEAULIEU has a wider range, as shown in three of his most recent works: the historical recreation *Sophie et Léon* (1992), the dark drama *La nuit de la grande citrouille* (1993), and *Le bonheur total* (1995), a farce. Antonine MAILLET's unforgettable Acadian characters' literary roots were emphasized as the author used several forms of intertextuality to create a rich world where modern audiences are confronted by figures from the past. Typical of this vein are *Les drôlatiques, horrifiques et épouvantables aventures de Panurge, ami de Pantagruel* (1983) and *La Fontaine ou la comédie des animaux* (1995). Michel GARNEAU's *Les guerriers* (1989), translated by Linda Gaboriau as *The warriors*, is a topical, highly cynical play showing two men attempting to find a slogan for the Canadian armed forces. Garneau's *Héliotropes* (1994), savaged by the critics, deserved a better fate. Jeanne-Mance Delisle's *Un oiseau vivant dans la gueule* (1987), winner of a Governor General's Award—translated into English by Yves Saint-Pierre as *A live bird in its jaws* (1992)—is a poetic staging of the creative forces at work. Jean-Pierre Ronfard's experimental work is exemplified by the publication of *Cinq études* (1994), a compilation of short plays presented between 1986 and 1993 at the Nouveau Théâtre Expérimental, Montreal. These are exceptionally successful scenic representations of theoretical questions and dramaturgical realities such as objects, voice, body, lighting, and rhythm, in scenes sometimes reminiscent of Beckett.

The most prolific dramatist in this group is Marie LABERGE with at least a dozen published plays. In *Deux tangos pour toute une vie* (1985) a frustrated wife seeks change through a symbolic redecoration of the conjugal bedroom and an extramarital tango. When she realizes that the next tango will inevitably be danced with her husband, she hangs the room in grey—a colour that reappears in the title of *L'homme gris* (1986), an important play about spousal abuse and a father-daughter relationship gone sour; it was translated by Rina Fratticelli. With *Oublier* (1987), which was also mounted for television, Laberge presents a meeting between four adult sisters faced with an elderly mother suffering from Alzheimer's disease, a problem three of them have attempted in various ways to forget. These are well-made plays, dealing with important questions. The death of a mother is the basis of *Les divines* (1996) by Denise BOUCHER, whose female protagonists, beginning with the thirsty *fées* of the seventies, have becomes goddesses of the nineties. This return to the stage by the author of the 'scandalous' *Les FÉES ONT SOIF* (1978) is a disappointing mix of bourgeois realism and myth, culminating in the ritualistic burial by the sisters of seven clay figures representing their former selves.

Other mature writers—such as Anne HÉBERT, Marie-Claire BLAIS, Roch CARRIER, and Réjean DUCHARME, whose main works are in other areas—also published plays in this period. By far the most important is Réjean Ducharme's *HA! ha! . . .* (1982), an astonishing metatheatrical work whose derision extends from the title to the characters, caught in destructive, repetitive games.

2. *NOUVELLE DRAMATURGIE.* Metatheatrical devices abound in the plays of writers belonging to the postmodern current frequently called *la nouvelle dramaturgie.* Characterized to varying degrees by fragmentation, dialogic monologues, simultaneous action, the creation of possible worlds, internationalism, homosexuality—all of these dramatic texts propose a new construction of reality where the text, with its explicit literary qualities, its intertextuality, its frequent use of *mise en abyme* (play within a play), dominates the multiple stage languages. The three major playwrights of this postmodern period are Normand CHAURETTE, Michel Marc BOUCHARD, and René-Daniel DUBOIS.

Normand Chaurette's *Provincetown playhouse, juillet 1919, j'avais 19 ans* (1981), an *hommage* to his American predecessors, is essentially a hymn to the enduring power of theatre. Charles Charles, interned in an asylum since the murder of a child at the end of the first and only performance of his presciently named play, 'The Immolation of Beauty', spends his days writing his memoirs and especially reliving/replaying the events that unfolded nineteen years previously in Provincetown, on 19 July 1919, the day of his nineteenth birthday. The play within the play is a reflection of the drama unfolding within the troubled mind of the protagonist, who constantly relives his version of the events following the discovery of his lover in the arms of another. It was translated into English by William Boulet and published in *Quebec voices: three plays* (1986), edited by Robert Wallace. Multiple tellings of a single happening characterize Chaurette's *Fragments d'une lettre d'adieu lus par des géologues* (1986), translated into English by Linda Gaboriau as *Fragments of a farewell letter read by geologists* (produced but not published), in which six men and one woman, belonging to different ethnic and professional groups, give their own version of what happened during the last days of a geologist who died in Cambodia. Each of them—geologist, engineer, doctor, etc.—describes the events in highly technical language, creating a hallucinatory spell where prolonged silences are as important as words in creating this profound dialogic drama. Chaurette's *Les reines* (1991) was the first Quebec play ever to be mounted in Paris by the Comédie-Française. (6 May-20 June 1997). Translated into English by Linda Gaboriau as *The queens* (1992), the action of this play is set in London on 20 January 1493, as Gloucester plots to assassinate the dying King Edward's children during a violent snowstorm. Six women, all of whom covet the throne of England, meet in the Tower to cry, rage, laugh, reminisce, mock—and to die. The author dedicates his play 'to the queens who live in each of us, who slumber, and who sometimes awake with a start, demanding the impossible, the absolute, the infinite.' Chaurette's *Le passage de l'Indiana* (1996)—which premièred at the Avignon Festival and won a Governor General's Award—tells a troubled tale about literary plagiarism, editorial practice, and the creative process itself.

A second major dramatist of this period, Michel Marc Bouchard, explores many dark areas of the human psyche. In *La contre-nature de Chrysippe Tanguay, écologiste* (1983), part of a trilogy, Bouchard, through transposed mythological figures, presents a very contemporary situation: the adoption of a child by a homosexual couple, one of whom is called Laios, a direct reference to the story of Oedipus. Through Diane, a representative of the adoption agency, Bouchard introduces a series of female figures who, chorus-like, both interpret and provoke the action. *Les feluettes* (1987), translated by Linda Gaboriau as *Lilies; or The revival of a romantic drama* (1990), appeared in October 1996 as a feature film bearing the English title. In a wonderfully complex structure, Simon, wrongly convicted of a long-ago murder, has prepared—along with other prisoners, victims of the justice system—a reconstruction of events leading to the death of his lover Vallier, designed to be played before a bishop who, as a youth, had held an as yet unspecified role in the tragic events. This metatheatrical structure is rendered even more interesting because immediately before the death of Vallier, he and his schoolmates were rehearsing Gabriele d'Annunzio's *Martyr of Saint Sebastian*, excerpts from which punctuate the play, allowing the young men access to poetic means to express their illicit love. At the heart of *Les muses orphelines* (1989)—translated into English by Linda Gaboriau as *The orphan muses* (1993), and adapted into metropolitan French by Noëlle Renaude—is a dysfunctional family, suffering as the result of a mother's abandonment. Bouchard won a Governor General's Award for a children's play with universal appeal: *L'histoire de l'oie* (1991). It is a moving, intimate, subtle, and dark drama about a battered child who is able, as an adult, to analyse and help the audience visualize, through the aid of a puppet, how brutality is transmitted from one generation to another. It was translated into English by Linda Gaboriau as *The tale of Teeka* (1992).

The third dramatist to make an enduring mark as the creator of an inventive, complex universe is René-Daniel Dubois, whose *26 bis, impasse du colonel Foisy* (1982), a play in which Madame (played by a male actor), an exiled narcissistic princess, relates for the hundreth time, and with countless digressions, her various affairs with lovers like Tadzio, whose name evokes Venice, Thomas Mann, and death. She expresses her regret that in the modern world, among other things, hearts are no longer broken, only leases. Past and present blend through numerous intertextual references and metatheatrical devices that foreground the artificial character of all representation. *Ne blâmez jamais les bédouins* (1984)—translated by Martin Kevan as *Don't blame the bedouins*, and published in *Quebec voices: three plays*—is both a metaphor of the human condition and a poetic and dramaturgical *tour de force*. Dubois creates a polyphonic tale of an opera singer, tied to railway tracks; of a near-sighted monster poised to attack her; of a potential saviour perched on a high cliff overlooking the tracks; and of two high-speed, nuclear-powered trains hurtling towards each other on the same tracks. Playing all the parts himself, Dubois leads us into a world where time and space have been replaced by pure verbal energy. But Dubois's best-known work is *Being at home with Claude* (1986), which was translated by Linda Gaboriau and produced as a major motion picture in 1991. The apparently simple structure of a police interrogation quickly gives way to a complex webbing of city streets and park alleys, and especially of the ways of the human heart. Though the protagonist has murdered his lover, we discover that it is for the most profoundly disturbing of reasons: because their love was perfect. We are reminded of Anouilh's Antigone, who refuses to go on living, fearing that becoming adult will force her to compromise her ideals.

Other dramatists in the 1980s and 1990s have staged works in a similar vein. In René Gingras's *Le facteur réalité* (1985), video sequences alternate with scenes in a Pirandellian deconstruction, using Hubert AQUIN's complex works as a *mise en abyme*. In Normand Canac-Marquis's *Le syndrome de Cézanne* (1988), the reference to Cézanne in the title is related to a way of seeing reality not as a unified, objective whole, but as a variety of subjective points of view. Since several persons 'observe' the same event—a fatal traffic accident—there are no comforting answers in this open-ended play. Téo Spychalski's *Un bal nommé Balzac* (1989)—an imaginative reworking of Balzac's *La peau de chagrin*, featuring music by Rossini and visual effects based on Géricault's painting 'The Raft of the Medusa'—underlines forcibly renewed interest in classical works. In a similar vein, Anne Legault's play *O'Neill* (1990) shows the American dramatist, as he is writing *Long day's journey into night*, coming to grips with his demons, including, in scenes reminiscent of Michel Tremblay's *Le vrai monde?* (1987), the relationship between the members of his family and their 'fictional' counterparts. Alain Fournier's *Petit-Tchaïkovski; ou La liquéfaction de la lumière* (1990) is a play/opera score about the creation of an opera based partly on the life and sordid death of the Quebec composer, Claude Vivier, a man obsessed by his unhappy, loveless childhood in an orphanage. *Billy Strauss* (1991) by Lise Vaillancourt also deals with the creative process with 'fictional' characters becoming 'real' and vice versa, in a series of cinema-like tableaux. A new voice, that of Daniel DANIS, created a sensation with *Cendres de cailloux* (1992), translated by Linda Gaboriau as *Stone and ashes* (1995), in which four characters appear to tell their tragic story through an interweaving of their savagely lyrical, often surrealist narrations. Michèle Magny resurrects another tragedy, that of Russian poet Marina Tsvetaeva (1892-1941), in *Marina T., le dernier rose aux joues* (1994), through fictional dialogues as well as extracts from the diary and correspondence of this woman whose suicide signified her refusal to submit to further purges, exiles, and compromises. Death is once again a player in Carole

Fréchette's Governor General's Award-winning *Les quatre morts de Marie* (1995), translated by John MURRELL as *The four lives of Marie* (not yet published). The life-and-death dialectic, underscored by the title, is the subtext of the various plot sequences where we meet the child with the polished shoes, the idealistic adolescent, the narcoleptic adult, and finally the mature Marie who no longer recognizes herself as she sits in the last scene, adrift at sea in a rowboat, awaiting the final solution. In Larry Tremblay's *The dragonfly of Chicoutimi* (1995), Gaston Talbot desires, more than anything else, to blend in with his surroundings, to be like others; to be like the English-speaking Other. In a wonderfully dense monologue, delivered entirely in English but based partly on French syntax, Gaston slowly reveals the source of his linguistic transfer in a childhood game gone wrong, when his friend Pierre gave him orders in English; through a series of contradictions/lies; and a drawn-out dream containing a comparison between himself and a cubist Picasso painting that culminates in his transformation into a mother-devouring dragonfly—underlining the link between mother and the rejected mother-tongue.

3. DIVIDED SELVES. Michel Tremblay's inventive dramatic forms continue to dominate this period, renewing his own theatre and influencing younger dramatists. *Albertine en cinq temps* (1984) projects five states of a troubled character who—at ages 30, 40, 50, 60, and 70—conducts a dialogue with her sister Madeleine and specially with her various selves, rejecting some of her past, horrified at what the future holds—all of this because a basic need, love and affection, has not been met. We discover some of Madeleine's secrets in *Le vrai monde?* a scenic figuration of the dramatist's technique. Finally, in *La maison suspendue* (1990) three generations meet on the front porch of the old family house, which is suspended in space, since it overlooks a lake, but especially in time, since the late grandparents are in fact younger than their grandson Jean-Marc and his lover, who are the most recent proprietors.

Divided selves and ghostly figures have proliferated in recent dramas, both in and outside Quebec. Marie Laberge's *Jocelyne Trudelle trouvée morte dans ses larmes* (1983) features a young woman unconscious after a suicide attempt, represented by both the prone body and a persona, invisible to the other characters, who witnesses their gestures and hears their words. In Chantale Boileau's *La mort de Blanche* (1994) the two main characters are double: the sombre, frustrated Blanche 1, mirrored by the sensual Blanche 2, the woman who could have been. Blanche's daughter Joanne, aged 40, lives in Greece with a heavy secret that Joanne, aged 12, tries to bury under mounds of paper : books, proverbs and a secret diary. Written in the mode of an ancient Greek tragedy, it is a very contemporary drama because of the fragmentation of both character and plot. Even more astonishing is the avant-garde work of Denis Marleau and his Théâtre Ubu, active in Montreal since 1980. In *Les maîtres anciens* (produced in 1995), his as yet unpublished adaptation of *Alte Meister* (1985), an Austrian novel by Thomas Bernhard, Marleau chose to have two identically dressed characters play each of the two main characters and, on occasion, to have all four speaking together in what can only be compared to musical orchestration, one instrument playing the same melody, another in counterpoint—very much as in several of Tremblay's musically structured plays.

Ontario's French-speaking dramatists have also been in tune with the inherent rythms of the divided self. In Robert Marinier's *L'inconception* (1984), for example, after Pierre is confronted in a park by the naked Marc, who claims to be his as yet unconceived son, Pierre and his wife Claire are fragmented into selves of different ages, revealing in a series of tonal changes the consequences of this unusual situation to the spectator. One of the characters of Jean-Marc DALPÉ's Governor General's Award-winning *Le chien* (1987)—translated into English by the author and Maureen Labonté, and adapted into metropolitan French by Eugène Durif—is the ghostly figure of the grandfather come to speak to his grandson Jay. Layers of meaning are uncovered through conjoined monologues, and disparate dialogues featuring the estranged father, the frustrated mother, the pregnant stepsister, and the barking dog—whose differing relations to time and space are figured scenically by a raised stage surrounding a pit that serves to modulate their voices into a tragic unison. In Dalpé's next play, *Eddy* (1994), translated into English by Robert Dickson (produced but not published), the failed boxer protagonist is haunted by two ghosts: of his elder brother just before the miner's death in Sudbury, and of this same brother before the young Eddy's departure from Sudbury for a chance at the big time in Montreal. Finally, in all of Michel Ouellette's published plays, ghostly figures play a prominent role: *Corbeaux en exil* (1992); *French town* (1994), which won a Governor General's Award; and *Le bateleur* (1995).

4. IMAGISTIC DRAMA. Divided selves frequently appear in the work of two of Quebec's most imaginative creators, Robert Lepage, and Gilles Maheu of the Montreal company Carbone 14, both of whom are known for their image-based theatre. Lepage's magical, provocative work is also characterized by its multilingual, international style, a fitting counterpoint to the visual icons that owe as much to scientific experiments as to theatrical tradition. Since the creation, in 1984, of *Circulations*—an exciting mix of dance, music, and sound effects based on a map of the northeastern United States and a set of language-learning tapes—Lepage has become a major international figure and won countless awards. His most notable successes, created with a troupe collectively called Théâtre Repère, include *La trilogie du dragon/The dragon's trilogy* (developed between 1985 and 1987)—performed in French, English and Chinese—which is a grand epic tale whose action spans Canada, from Quebec City's Chinatown in 1915, to Toronto in the 1940s and Vancouver in 1985, and whose characters' lives intersect in the way East meets West, through myth, war, or travel. The point of departure for this vast fresco was a simple pair of shoes that led the company, through countless hours of improvisation, to what became *The dragon's trilogy*. And the shoes? To suggest the horrors of war, for example, some of the characters don ice-skates and, in a rythmic, military style, march around a large sand-box, then stamp on and demolish a pair of children's shoes. Another of Théâtre Repère's trademarks is the metamorphosis of an object through a change in the actor's position. A string of tiny Christmas lights, representing a piece of modern art in a Vancouver gallery, becomes, as an actor stands on a chair with arms outstretched, the whole of Vancouver as seen from a passing plane, a magical trick that consistently delights audiences who are forced to change their perception of a simple object. The central image of Repère's next spectacle, *Les plaques techtoniques/Tectonic plates* (developed in 1988-90), is perpetual movement, and its themes are separation and reconciliation, be they geographic or personal. An inground pool becomes the Atlantic Ocean or, in a dazzlingly simple scene, the addition of a few folding chairs in the water transforms it into a Venetian lagoon. In 1992 Toronto filmmaker Peter Mettler produced a cinematographic version of this play. Several of Lepage's grand illusions have been one-man shows, including *Les aiguilles et l'opium/Needles and opium* (produced in 1991), an exploration of drugs through the music of Miles Davis and the poetry of Jean Cocteau, conducted while suspended, sometimes upside-down, before a white backdrop, serving as either a screen or a trampoline, and *Elsineur/Elsinore* (produced in 1995-6) in which Lepage played all the parts of Shakespeare's *Hamlet*. With members of a newly constituted company called *Ex machina*, Robert Lepage has created his most ambitious spectacle yet, *Les sept branches de la rivière Ota/The seven streams of the River Ota* (developed in 1994-6), an epic masterpiece ranging in space and in time from war-torn Czechoslovakia to modern-day Hiroshima, the unifying image being the camera, one used by an American GI to record life in post-war Hiroshima and the other by Jana, whose childhood escape from the Nazis in a magician's suitcase is a partial explanation for her subsequent interest in the magic of the photographer's dark room. One of the most creative scenes shows one character being photographed wearing a kimono and both photographer and subject changing under our very eyes, passing from one time and place to another in an enchanting sequence, showing how art can/does transform reality. Lepage's creations are difficult to date, and impossible to fix, since all have been presented as works in progress, sometimes growing from three hours in length to six, and back to three again. The highly visual nature of these spectacles is such that publication is not an option, a notable exception being an English version of *Polygraphe/Polygraph*, translated by Gyllian Raby, which appeared in the *CTR Anthology* (1993). A 1992 National Film Board video-recording called *Breaking a leg : Robert Lepage and the echo project* shows the imagistic creator at work. Lepage also wrote and directed *Le confessional* (1995), a feature film, as well as a film version of *Polygraph* (1996).

Using a dramatic language combining theatre and dance, Gilles Maheu and Carbone 14 have created spectacles whose minimal scripts remain unpublished, presenting Maheu's obsession with the individual versus the collective, expressed through a dream-like world based on classical themes and universal symbols made manifest through kaleidoscopic images and intensely emotional kinesthetic poetry. Major shows include *L'homme rouge*, created in 1982; *Le dortoir*, whose 1988 National Arts Centre production was filmed for television; *Chair, peau et os*, an adaptation of Heiner Müller's *Paysage sous surveillance* that was recorded for television in 1991 at the Festival des Amériques; and *Les âmes mortes*, first produced in 1996. Carbone 14 has helped to redefine theatrical language, weaving several artistic disciplines, such as acrobatics, dance, song, and voice, into a seamless whole.

5. FEMINIST DRAMA. In 1992 Pol Pelletier—one of the co-founders, in 1979, with Louise Laprade and Nicole Lecavalier, of Montreal's *Théâtre expérimental des femmes*—created *Joie*, a vibrant spectacle, part monologue, part dance, part song, celebrating the rise and subsequent fall of openly feminist dramatic productions. The monologue is multi-voiced, and contains significant fragments of earlier productions, mounted in such a way as to re-energize audiences and to rekindle the joy of theatre, of the body, of a woman's body, the joy of life. Among the works cited in *Joie* are Pol Pelletier's own *La lumière blanche* (1981), *Marie-Antoine, Opus 1* (1988), by Lise Vaillancourt, and Jovette MARCHESSAULT's *La terre est trop courte, Violette Leduc* (1982). All of these productions were highly innovative in their development of new ways of expression, using symbolism and literary references in both text and *mise en scène* to create new images of women no longer necessarily categorized as 'nun, witch or playmate'.

Several of Marchessault's subsequent plays are scenic transpositions of historical female artists: Gertrude Stein and Alice B. Toklas in *Alice et Gertrude, Nathalie et Renée et ce cher Ernest* (1984), Anaïs Nin in *Anaïs, dans la queue de la comète* (1985), and Emily Carr in *Le voyage magnifique d'Émily Carr* (1990), winner of a Governor General's Award. Other plays, such as *Le lion de Bangor* (1993), use fictional characters to create a similar atmosphere, one where lesbian love is linked to the creative experience through a richly baroque style whose purpose is to reach the soul. Female homosexuality is also a major theme of *Caryopse; ou Le monde entier* (1989) by Laurence Tardi, in which a female author invents a character who has difficulty in assuming her lesbianism. There will finally be a fusion of both, thus realizing the image of the caryopsis, 'a one-seeded indehiscent fruit having the pericarp fused to the seed-coat as in wheat and maize' (*Shorter Oxford Dictionary*).

In a more realistic vein, Catherine Caron, Brigitte Haentjens, and Sylvie Trudel created a sensation in Ontario with *Strip* (1983), playing to audiences both in French and in Robert Dickson's English translation. Blending humour, metatheatrical devices, and a great deal of skin, *Strip*, a chilling exposé of the woman as sexual object and the man as voyeur, was the first Franco-Ontarian play with an overtly feminist agenda. Plays by other women writers are less explicitly feminist, such as Maryse Pelletier's *Duo pour voix obstinées* (1985), translated into English by Louise Ringuet as *Duo for obstinate voices* (1990), and *La rupture des eaux* (1989); and Hélène Pedneault's *La déposition* (1988), translated into English by Linda Gaboriau as *Evidence to the contrary*, and published in the CTR *Anthology* (1995).

6. TRANSCULTURAL DRAMA. During the eighties and nineties, Quebec culture has been enriched by the contributions of ethnic minorities, though audience acceptance has not always kept pace with demographic changes. The most visible of this growing group of dramatists is Marco MICONE who—in plays such as *Les gens du silence* (1982), translated by Maurizia Binda as *Voiceless people* (1991), and *Déjà l'agonie* (1988), translated by Jill MacDougall as *Beyond the ruins* (produced but not yet published)—has chronicled the joys and agonies of recent immigrants caught between two founding cultures. The case of Alberto Kurapel is somewhat different, since he is an exile rather than an immigrant, hoping one day to return to Chile. In plays such as *Colmenas en la sombra ou l'espoir de l'arrière-garde* (1994) and *La bruta interférence* (1995), where French and Spanish are intertwined and where postmodernism meets ancient South American gods, Kurapel uses performance theatre to underline the perennial quality of ancestral wisdom. Finally, a young author of Lebanese origin, Wajdi Mouawad, has used war-ravaged Beirut as a backdrop in *Journée de noces chez les Cro-magnons*, as yet unpublished in French but translated by Shelley Tepperman as *Wedding day at the Cro-Magnons* (1996). It presents an understandably dysfunctional family whose reaction to the devastation around them is expressed in grim fantasy, repetitive structures, and black humour—theatre of the absurd in response to an absurd situation. A version of this play in Arabic was produced in Tunis in 1996.

7. HISTORICAL DRAMA. The nineties have seen a resurgence of the historical play, based on subjects borrowed from early European history to the October Crisis of 1970. Patrick Leroux's *Le beau prince d'Orange* (1994), for example, draws a broad picture, with Brechtian overtones, of the complicated political machinations of England and France during the tumultuous reign of William of Orange. Also in the epic style is André RICARD's exploration of the Rebellion of 1837, an ambitious project, though in the central panel of his trilogy, *Le tréteau des apatrides; ou La veillée en armes* (1995), ideology sometimes

overcomes theatricality. Such is not the case with Marthe Mercure's *Tu faisais comme un appel* (1991), translated by Maureen Labonté as *Blood sisters* (produced but not published), a moving docudrama reliving the traumatic experiences in a Quebec orphanage of four of the so-called 'enfants de Duplessis', normal children who were treated as mentally ill and denied schooling so that the institution could receive government funding. This is by far the most successful of these historical plays. Finally, the October Crisis inspired some mediocre plays, including two 1992 productions, Anne Legault's *Conte d'hiver 70* and Dominic Champagne's *La cité interdite*.

8. NEW VOICES. A wildly successful cabaret style smorgasbord of show-stopping numbers, *Cabaret neiges noires* (1994), showcased the talents of a number of writers of the new generation or 'la relève', including Dominic Champagne and Jean-François Caron. Anarchy and delirium connect in this loosely structured 'carnavalesque' entertainment, a grab-bag of film clips, jokes, songs, manifestos, and scenes, with a nod to Les Joyeux Troubadours, the Quebec equivalent of The Happy Gang (the popular half-hour CBC radio program, 1937-59). Echoes of Mallarmé, Brecht, Beckett, Ionesco, Martin Luther King, and the theatre of the absurd abound in this cry of a generation. 'I have a dream,' shout the cynical, drug-ridden characters, though it is evident that few of them believe it possible to come together to listen to words of light and hope.

Dominic Champagne had earlier made his mark with *La répétition* (1990), translated by Shelley Tepperman as *Playing bare* (1993), a metatheatrical play featuring an ageing actress who has lost faith in herself as well as in the characters she portrays. She makes one last stab at linking theatre and life by attempting to produce a version of *Waiting for Godot*, using genuine tramps in the two leading roles; but, as in the case of Beckett's characters, what she hopes for does not materialize.

Metatheatre was also Jean-François Caron's springboard to prominence. *J'écrirai bientôt une pièce sur les nègres* (1990) plunges into the depth of Quebec society's malaise, reminding people about past ambition and present cowardice. Three levels of reality function simultaneously: *réalité*, *théâtre*, and *roman*. A fourth level is the inner space occupied by the character Bastarache, a creation of the fictional author, Danny. In Caron's *Saganash* (1995), Garou, the main character, is an angry young man whose unfulfilled dreams of political independence cause him to lash out at his brother's bourgeois aspirations before seeking a better life in the Far North. Other Quebec voices belonging to this generation are those of Gilbert Dupuis, *Mon oncle Marcel qui vague vague près du métro Berri* (1991), winner of a Governor General's Award; Claude Poissant, *Si tu meurs, je te tue* (1993); Michel Monty, *Accidents de parcours* (1993); Yvan Bienvenue, *Histoires à mourir d'amour* (1994) and *Règlement de contes* (1995); and François Archambault, *Cul sec* (1996).

New French voices are also being heard outside Quebec, notably in Ontario where the Ottawa-based company La Catapulte has succeeded, with little more than a forked stick and an elastic band, in attaining its objective: the creation of vibrant spectacles that challenge dramaturgical tradition. In *Implosions* (1996), Patrick Leroux, the company's artistic director and resident author, has grouped three plays in which impetuous, self-destructive, sado-masochistic, flirtatious characters exchange strange, morbid, and violent anecdotes in the presence of a slim, Giacometti-like cow, a leather-clad dominatrix muse, and an unorthodox pope who inhabit the psyches of a lost generation. Leroux and other young authors are profiled in a special issue of *Jeu* 77 (1995): *Relève, héritage et renouveau*.

CONCLUSION. The focus of recent Quebec and French-Canadian theatre has shifted from nationalist themes to self-consciously literary writing, and to the creation of images whose ambiguities nourish an increasingly sophisticated public, able to relate to a crisis in the Australian desert and to the Provincetown Playhouse as easily as to life on the streets of Montreal. The image and the text are in a symbiotic relationship in this new dramaturgy, imagistic theatre projecting objects, light, and movement to an audience that is called upon to create meaning, or text, while text-based plays rely on imagery and pictorially inspired fragmentation to produce similar results. A play is therefore no longer conceived of as a mirror of reality, an objective reproduction that everyone perceives in the same manner, but rather as a complex system capable of evoking numerous subjective responses. Quebec playwrights of the 1990s have completed their 'rattrapage', or catching-up, and are now fully attuned to the important currents in international dramaturgy.

MARIEL O'NEILL-KARCH

Bibliography. In English, articles and book reviews on French-Canadian drama may be found in *Dramatists in Canada: selected essays* (1972), edited by W.H. New; in *Stage* *voices* (1978), edited by Geraldine Anthony; and in the periodicals *Canadian Drama/L'Art dramatique canadien*, *Canadian Theatre Review*, *Essays in Theatre/Études théâtrales*, *Theatre History in Canada/Histoire du théâtre au Canada*, *Theatre Research in Canada/Recherches théâtrales au Canada*, CANADIAN LITERATURE, *Queen's Quarterly*, and the *University of Toronto Quarterly*. Mavor MOORE's introduction to Gratien Gélinas in *Four Canadian playwrights* (1973) has a brief overview, as do *Marcel Dubé and French-Canadian drama* (1970) by Edwin C. Hamblet. See also *French-Canadian theatre* (1986) by Jonathan Weiss, and *Essays on modern Quebec theatre* (1995), edited by Joseph I. Donohoe and Jonathan Weiss. Studies in English on individual dramatists are *Gratien Gélinas* (1974) and *Michel Tremblay* (1982), both by Renate Usmiani.

Useful studies in French on modern Quebec theatre are *350 ans de théâtre au Canada français* (1958) by Jean Béraud; *Le renouveau du théâtre au Canada français* (1961) and *Le théâtre au Canada français* (1964) by Jean Hamelin; *Le théâtre québécois I: introduction à dix dramaturges contemporains* (1970) and *Le théâtre québécois II: nouveau auteurs, autres spectacles* (1980) by Jean-Cléo Godin and Laurent Mailhot; *Dictionnaire critique du théâtre québécois* (1972) by Alain Pontaut; *Le renouveau du théâtre québécois* (1973) by Michel Belair; *Un théâtre en effervescence: critiques et chroniques 1965-72* (1975) by Martial Dassylva; *Le théâtre canadien d'expression française: répertoire analytique des origines à nos jours* (4 vols, 1976, 1977, 1978) by Edouard-G. Rinfret; *Le théâtre canadien français* (1976), vol. 5 in the series Archives des Lettres canadiennes, a large work by many authors that includes a good bibliography and dates of first productions of plays by John Hare; *Le théâtre québécois; instrument de contestation sociale et politique* (1976) by Jacques Cotnam; *Le fou et ses doubles: figures de la dramaturgie québécoise* (1978) by Pierre Gobin; *L'église et le théâtre au Québec* (1979) by Jean Laflamme and Rémi Tourangeau; *Le théâtre et l'état au Québec: essai* (1981) by Adrien Gruslin; *Pour suivre le théâtre au Québec: les ressources documentaires* (1985) by Pierre Lavoie; *Le théâtre du Nouvel-Ontario, 20 ans* (1991) compiled by Guy Gaudreau; *Sociocritique de la traduction: théâtre et altérité au Québec, 1968-1988* (1991) by Annie Brisset; *Veilleurs de nuit* (4 vols, 1989-92), an annual collection of reviews: *Théâtre franco-ontarien, espaces ludiques* (1992) by Mariel O'Neill-Karch; *Le théâtre Repère: du ludique au poétique dans le théâtre de recherche* (1993) by Irène Roy; *Le nouveau théâtre expérimental* (1995), conceived by Jean-Pierre RONFARD and Claudine Raymond. Volumes III-VI of the *Dictionnaire des oeuvres littéraires du Québec* contain analyses of individual plays of this period, as well as bibliographical material. The annual *Livres et auteurs canadiens* (1960-8), which became *Livres et auteurs québécois* (1969-82), has a bibliography and reviews of published plays of the period. *Nord* 4-5 (1973) is a special issue entitled 'Le théâtre au Québec 1950-1972', which includes 'Bibliographie du théâtre québécois de 1935 à nos jours' by Jean Du Berger. *Lettres québécoises*, published quarterly since 1976, regularly reviews plays. See also *Jeu* (1976-) and *L'annuaire théâtral* (1986-), periodicals devoted to the theatre, and a special issue of *Tangence* (1994), 'Un théâtre de passage'.

The anthology *Monologues québécois, 1890-1980* (1980), co-edited by Laurent Mailhot and Doris-Michel Montpetit, illustrates nearly a century of Quebec theatre, cabaret, and music-hall, and provides a valuable record of the evolution of the spoken language of Quebec. JAMES NOONAN

Drama in French: collective creations. See COLLECTIVE CREATIONS IN QUEBEC.

Drew, Wayland. See FANTASTIC LITERATURE IN ENGLISH: 1 and NOVELS IN ENGLISH 1960 TO 1984: 4.

Drummond, William Henry (1854-1907). Born at Currawn House, near Mohill, County Leitrim, Ireland, he immigrated with his parents to Montreal at the age of ten. He attended Montreal High School, McGill University (in 1878), and Bishop's University, Lennoxville, where he received an M.D. degree in 1884. He practised medicine in Montreal and died of a stroke in Cobalt, Ontario, after going there to help control a smallpox outbreak at a mine owned by his brothers. He is buried in Mount Royal Cemetery, Montreal.

Drummond's distinctive dialect verse, most of it amusing and most of it dealing with French-Canadian *habitant* life, was Canada's most popular poetry at the turn of the century. (His non-dialect verse never achieved great popularity.) His wife, Mary Isobel Harvey, helped collate scattered poems from correspondence and newspaper columns for Drummond's first collection, *The habitant and other French-Canadian poems* (New York, 1897), with an introduction by Louis FRÉCHETTE. Its popularity led to the publication of five other collections: two narrative poems in one volume, *Phil-o-Rum's canoe and Madeleine Verchères* (New York and London, 1898); *Johnnie Courteau, and other poems* (1901); *The voyageur and other poems* (1905); *The great fight* (1908), a posthumous collection containing a biographical sketch of Drummond by his wife; and *The poetical works of William Henry Drummond* (1912), again with an introduction by Fréchette. A selection of Drummond's poems was published in 1926 by McCLELLAND & STEWART.

Although Drummond professed to let his rustic Québécois 'tell their own stories in their own way' (Preface to *The habitant*), he deliberately shaped his own mixture of French and English to provide animation, sentiment, and humour. Many anglophone readers in Canada, the United States, and England delighted in what they felt was a realistic insight into the voice and attitudes of the *habitant*. Nonetheless, as the *Montreal Star* (whose editor had been a friend of the poet) noted at the time of his death, Drummond's medical practice had been mostly in Montreal, and his country experience 'was not among the French-Canadians but among the Highland Scotch'. Drummond actually modelled the mischievous five-year-old in 'Leetle Bateese' and the wan mystic child in 'The last portage' on his own sons; and the title place of 'Little Lac Grenier' was his own favourite fishing spot. His exposure to the variety of broken English used by French-Canadian woodsmen and farmers occurred at Bord-à-Plouffe, where Drummond worked for six summers, from the age of fifteen, as a telegrapher. In his later poetry, however, the distinctive language of his *habitant* characters is more accurate as a measure of Drummond's artistic achievement than of Québécois utterance. Fréchette's introductory comments, though they express a general approval of Drummond's 'daring experiment', eventually praise only the poet's personal cultivation of his material 'with tools and means of his own invention'. That point is made more strongly in some observations at the time by the French-language press: 'This very special language is confined to a particular group in our population' and 'this bastard idiom . . . has the attraction of the comedy of travesty' (translated from *La Patrie*, 15 Dec. 1901). *Le Journal de Françoise* referred to 'the bizarre language that he had created initially' (2 Nov. 1907, in translation). Critics agreed with Fréchette, however, in concluding that Drummond's *habitant* poems expressed a friendly spirit.

The autobiographical base of Drummond's work is documented by the poet's wife in an unpublished biography in the Osler Library, McGill University. Drummond's distinctive use of language is discussed most fully by R.E. Rashley in 'W.H. Drummond and the dilemma of style', *Dalhousie Review* (vol. xxviii, no. 4, Jan. 1949). Rashley credits Drummond with a 'freshened, renewed language, a genuine discovery', and implies what a later critic, Louis DUDEK, stated more strongly when he said that Drummond unconsciously 'loosened the straitjacket of literary puritanism and made it possible to free language for the expression of real life and human character' ('Literature in English', *Selected essays and criticism*, 1978). GERALD NOONAN

Dubé, Marcel (b. 1910). Born in Montreal, he attended the Jesuit Collège Sainte-Marie and the Université de Montréal. He also spent six months in the Canadian army, attended theatre schools in Paris in 1953-4, and was a scenarist at the National Film Board in 1956-7. Primarily a playwright for stage and television, Dubé has also written poetry, essays, short stories, a novel, radio scripts, art criticism, popular biography, adaptations and translations of plays written in English, and topical articles for such journals as *Perspectives*, *Le Magazine Maclean*, and *Cité libre*.

The most published and successful dramatist in Quebec before Michel TREMBLAY, Dubé is possibly the best Canadian dramatist in English or French. His pre-eminence results from a highly poetic prose style, acute sensitivity to nuances of feeling and emotion, a classic sense of dramatic structure, and a tragic vision of life applied to contemporary situations in Quebec society. His stage and television plays are concerned with humanity's search for an invariably fleeting or unattainable happiness; the fragility of human relationships; and the emptiness of modern urban life. However, his work is often marred by sentimentality and melodrama. Dubé has been influenced by Jean Anouilh and by the realists of the modern American theatre, especially Arthur Miller, whose *Death of a salesman* he adapted for French television. He uses the distinctive speech of French Canadians, but unlike many other contemporary Quebec dramatists, he rarely attempts to reproduce *JOUAL*. More than thirty of Dubé's plays have been published to date. They may be divided into three groups: those in the first, written for the most part between 1951 and 1959, deal with the lower classes, often in the east end of Montreal where Dubé grew up; the second group consists of plays (1959-72) about the emptiness and disillusionment of Quebec middle-class life; and the last shows Dubé's departure into comedy, musical comedy, ballet, satire, and a return to tragedy.

Though Dubé's first stage play, the one-act *Le bal triste* (unpublished), was produced in 1950, he came to prominence with the successful production of *Zone* (1955), judged the best Canadian play at the Dominion Drama Festival. It is a realistic, if sometimes sentimental, story of a teenage gang of smugglers whose lives are restricted by the area or 'zone' in which they live. An English adaptation of the play (1982) was made by Aviva Ravel. *Le naufragé* (1971) and *De l'autre côté du mur* (1973) have many resemblances to *Zone* in theme and style. The latter was published with five other short plays written between 1959 and 1972 (*Rendez-vous du lendemain*, *Le visiteur*, *L'aiguillage*, *Le père idéal*, and *Les frères ennemis*). *Un simple soldat* (1958) depicts the dissolute and disheartening life of Joseph Latour, who, unable after the Second World War to adjust to civilian life and the demands of his father and stepmother, returns to the army to serve in the Korean War, in which he is killed. Its theme and popularity recall GÉLINAS's *TIT-COQ*. *Le temps des lilas* (1958), a sad and moving play about a group of people in a Montreal boarding-house, is reminiscent of Chekhov (Dubé's favourite playwright) in its sensitive portrayal of the disillusionment of the characters and the final quiet resignation of an old couple. An English translation by James Noonan entitled *Time of the lilacs* was published in *Canadian Drama/L'Art dramatique canadien* 16, 2 (1990). Other plays in this first group are *Paradis perdu*, published with *L'échéance du vendredi* (1972), *La cellule* (1973), and *Médée* (1973).

Florence (1958), a transitional work, shows Dubé's shift in interest to middle-class characters; it heralds the mature work of his second period, which includes *Bilan* (1968)—the title means 'balance sheet'—about the human cost of financial success; *Les beaux dimanches* (1968), about the desperate efforts of four wealthy and unhappy couples to divert themselves in the course of one Sunday (this title was later adopted by Radio-Canada for its popular Sunday-night showcase of dramatic and musical entertainment); and *Un matin comme les autres* (1971), about the infidelities of two couples. *Au retour des oies blanches* (1969), translated by Jean Remple as *The white geese* (1972) and considered by many to be Dubé's finest play, portrays an upper-class family in Quebec City and their gradual discovery of the truth about their relationships. Its plot, structure, and emotional impact, which resemble those of *Oedipus the king*, make it Dubé's closest approach to classical tragedy. Lesser plays from this same period are *Pauvre amour* (1969), *Le coup de l'étrier* (1970), *Avant de t'en aller* (1970), *Octobre* (1964), *Virginie* (1974), *Entre midi et soir* (1971), and *Manuel* (1973).

Though Dubé was not prolific during the 1970s and 1980s, partly because of poor health and frequent hospitalization, the third category of his writing, from 1973 on (but anticipated by earlier works), offers relief from an unrelenting tragic vision. Some of these plays —such as *Hold-up!* (1969), a 'photo-roman'— were written in collaboration with Louis-Georges Carrier, who directed many of Dubé's dramas. *Jérémie* (1973) is a brief scenario for a ballet presented in 1973 by Les Ballets Jazz Contemporains at Sir George Williams University, Montreal; the published version contains an English translation by Jean Remple. *Dites-le avec des fleurs* (1976), a comedy with songs, written in collaboration with the playwright Jean BARBEAU, is a satire on communal marriage and on the unsatisfactory quality of life in a commune. *L'impromptu de Québec; ou Le testament* (1974) was Dubé's first full-fledged comedy—written, as were several of his more recent plays, for the Théâtre de Marjolaine in Eastman, Quebec, a summer playhouse near Dubé's residence at Cherry River in the Eastern Townships. The mellow play *L'été s'appelle Julie* (1975) suggests that in his later works Dubé offers, as a bulwark against an unstable and dehumanizing world, integration within the individual of the forces of beauty and nature—symbolized by Julie. Dubé returned briefly to tragedy with *Le réformiste; ou L'honneur des hommes* (1977), which comments on facets of modern Quebec life: the revised educational system, the decline of family life, unionism, corrupt work practices, political power, and loss of faith. Though interesting to read, the play is verbose and relatively static on stage. To celebrate its twentieth anniversary, Montreal's influential CEAD (Centre d'essai des auteurs dramatiques) invited twenty Québécois dramatists to submit a one-act play. Dubé's contribution, *Le trou* (1986), is a bar-room discussion about street excavations whose tone is reminiscent of the whimsical darkness of Giraudoux and the absurd humour of Ionesco. Dube's most recently published play, which he himself produced, reverts to the more lighthearted, satirical tone of this last period of his work. *L'Amérique à sec* (1986) involves the shenanigans of a king of bootlegging, based on and dedicated to a real-life French-Canadian, Conrad Labelle, in the days of prohibition in the United States. Set and premièred in June 1986 in Saint-Jean-sur-Richelieu, near the Quebec-New York border where some of the events took place, it is light and farcical in approach, with a nationalistic flavour.

Two recent works show Dubé's interest in art and dramatic biography. One is *Jean Paul Lemieux et le livre* (1988; rev. 1993), a handsomely illustrated commentary on the work of the French-Canadian painter and his illustrations for four separate books—which are reproduced. *Andrée Lachapelle: entre ciel et terre* (1995) is a biographical portrait of the admired actress and friend of Dubé for forty-two years, who acted in many of his plays. The book is part of a series entitled 'Collection Portraits d'artistes'.

Dubé has written two major television series, 'La côte de sable' and 'De 9 à 5'. From the latter series on the life of white-collar workers in Montreal a number of dramas were developed and brought together on Radio-Canada under the title 'Le monde de Marcel Dubé'. The Montreal firm Leméac—directed by Marcel's brother Yves until his death in 1991—which publishes more plays than any other Quebec publisher, has published most of Dubé's plays and a volume of his poetry, *Poèmes de sable* (1974), which recalls the themes of many of his plays: loneliness, suffering, beauty, nature, love, and death. Simple, direct, and lyrical, the poems are not innovative in style or technique. Dubé has published two volumes of non-dramatic prose—essays on literary figures, speeches, and letters—under the titles *Textes et documents* (1968) and *La tragédie est un acte de foi* (1973). He has also gathered together in one short volume some of his previously published work—poems, essays, and excerpts from five plays—under the title *Le choix de Marcel Dubé dans l'oeuvre de Marcel Dubé* (1986) in a series called 'Collection le Choix de. . .'.

No longer the prolific playwright he once was, Dubé remains one of the most admired writers in Canada. His status has been confirmed by many honours and awards including President of the Federation of Canadian Authors and Artists in 1959, the Saint-Jean-Baptiste Society's Prix Victor-Morin in 1966, Quebec's Prix David in 1973, the Canada Council Molson Prize in 1984, and the medal of the Académie canadienne-francaise in 1987. He is a Fellow of both the Académie and the Royal Society of Canada.

See Edwin C. Hamblet, *Marcel Dubé and French-Canadian drama* (1970), which places Dubé and his work in the context of modern theatre in Quebec, as well as Paulette Collet's analysis in *Profiles in Canadian literature*, vol. 4 (1982). Maximilien Laroche's *Marcel Dubé* (1970) and Jean-Cléo Godin's chapter on Dubé in *Le théâtre québécois* (1970), by Godin and Laurent Mailhot, are useful studies in French. Two volumes of newspaper articles, reviews, essays, and interviews on Dubé's work have appeared: *Marcel Dubé: dossier de presse, 1953-1980* (1981) and *Marcel Dubé II: dossier de press, 1965-1987* (1988). Journal articles are listed in the *Dictionnaire des auteurs de langue française en Amérique du nord* (1989).

Claude Roussel produced a film on Dubé in 1970 and Prisma Productions made a video recording, *L'identité des siens* (1981), containing iconographic material as well as archival footage of some of his plays.

JAMES NOONAN

Dubé, Rodolphe (1905-85). The poet, novelist, essayist, and philosopher who wrote under the pseudonym 'François Hertel' was born in Rivière-Ouelle, Quebec. He was a student at Sainte-Anne-de-la-Pocatière and at the Séminaire de Trois-Rivières before entering the Jesuit Order at the age of twenty. A licentiate in theology and philosophy, he received a doctorate from Rome and was ordained priest in 1938. He taught subsequently at the Collège Jean-de-Brébeuf, Montreal, and at the Collège de Sudbury (Ontario), where he founded the newspaper *L'Ami du peuple*. Becoming a secular priest in 1943, he wrote for various Montreal periodicals and was editor for two years of the review *Amérique française*. In 1946, when he was shaken by a crisis of faith, he left the Jesuit Order; at his request he was permitted a gradual return to secular life. While he was admired by young people as an intellectual, a spiritual guide, and a daring innovator, the ex-Jesuit was considered dangerous by a certain élite. Stifled by orthodox religion and Quebec's cultural stagnation, he left Montreal for Paris in 1947 and remained in France after 1949. He founded and edited the art review *Rythmes et couleurs*; a review of the occult, *Radiesthésie Magazine*; and ran the publishing house La Diaspora française, which published most of his books.

A dozen collections published between 1934 and 1967 have given Hertel's poetry a respectable place in anthologies of Quebec literature. His poems are both sweet and bitter, lyrical, ironic, vindictive, and at times choleric. *Poèmes d'hier et d'aujourd'hui* (1967) represents all these veins in about a hundred poems; both descriptive and philosophical, they are always speculative. This selection retains the meditative and romantic texts of the first collections, as well as the religious poems of the forties; the traditional verse of *Les voix de mon rêve* (1934), as well as the free verse and lyrical prose-poems of *Axe et parallaxes* (1941) and *Strophes et catastrophes* (1943). These collections must be considered within the context of the spiritual preoccupations of poetry during the war. However, while certain poets like Alain GRANDBOIS and Simone Routier returned from Europe, and others increasingly favoured taking root in Quebec, Hertel went into exile. So did his poetry: it became either philosophical or religious and metaphysical. The poems written after the war, and in the fifties and sixties—collected in *Cosmos* (1945), *Quatorze* (1948), *Mes naufrages* (1951), *Jeux de mer et de soleil* (1951), *Poèmes européens* (1964), and *Poèmes perdus et retrouvés* (1966)—return to a classical verse style and a more intimate voice. All anthologies of Quebec poetry cite the poems of *Mes naufrages* as the most painful and personal of the poet's work.

Hertel the philosopher surfaces throughout his work, but most particularly in five or six books in which he developed his key ideas. In *Pour un ordre personnaliste* (1942) he confronted the major movements of his era: the atheistic existentialism of Sartre, the Christian existentialism of Gabriel Marcel, and the 'personnalisme' of Emmanuel Mounier. To Hertel, philosophy represented the spirit of seeking rather than a system, and he rejected all dogmatism. *Journal philosophique et littéraire* (1961), *Méditation théologique* (1964), and *Vers une sagesse* (1966) show a thinker in quest of an original explanation of the universe, of matter, spirit, and time. Although theology may appear subordinate to his philosophy, it nevertheless constitutes its epistemological basis. Even after the crisis of 1946, the central figure of God is omnipresent in his poetry, novels, and essays. From the *Journal d'Anatole Laplante* (1947) to *Mystère cosmique et condition humaine* (1975), the apostate progressively erases the idea of a personal God; but the abstract conception remains.

Hertel's essays are concerned with social and political matters as well as with aesthetics and the philosophy of language: he never hesitated to become involved in contemporary issues. In *Leur inquiétude* (1936) he was preoccupied with the restlessness of youth in the thirties and, following in the footsteps of Jacques Maritain, denounced mechanization, the death of the individual, and the myth of rationalism. Hertel faced squarely the problems of that critical period: bilingualism and the economic handicap of French Canadians. Anti-capitalist, he upheld social corporatism and a form of 'personnalisme' (a moral and social philosophy) anchored in Quebec society. Taking a stand based on the nationalistic ideology of Lionel GROULX, he was in favour of a Laurentian state, independent of the rest of Canada. And yet he did not accept Quebec society as it was (see the virulent poem 'Au pays du Québec' of 1939). He continued to defend the nationalist position in *Nous ferons l'avenir* (1945), *Du séparatisme québécois* (1963), and *Cent ans d'injustice* (1967). In *Du métalangage* (1968) the hierarchy of spiritual values is taken up again—as the essayist expresses his allegiance to a spiritual vision of the world and to a culture that is essentially humanistic.

Hertel's novels—*Le beau risque* (1939), *Anatole Laplante, curieux homme* (1944), *Journal d'Anatole Laplante* (1947), and *Louis Préfontaine, apostat* (1967)—are almost forgotten today. Still, the portraits and characterizations in these novels are rich and varied, and Hertel's satires lash out at the intellectual and bourgeois milieux of the times. The short-story collections—*Six femmes, un homme* (1949) and *Jérémie et Barrabas* (1959)—reveal a storyteller whose technique is better in short narratives than in novels. Occasionally working in the genres of theatre, travel, and personal accounts of his adventures, Hertel also wrote *Un canadien errant* (1953), *Afrique* (1955), *Claudine et les éceuils suivi de La folle* (1953), *La morte* (1965), *Souvenirs, historiettes, réflexions* (1972), and *Nouveaux souvenirs, nouvelles réflexions* (1973).

Writing of Hertel in 1973, a critic asserted that it was time to 'break the silence that threatens to obscure a body of work of great value to us.' And yet this silence still remains to be broken. Beyond friends and old disciples who are still living, and a few critics and literary historians, not many know the work of François Hertel, who has received little recognition of any kind in Quebec.

See Jean ÉTHIER-BLAIS, 'François Hertel—le train sifflera deux fois' in *Signets II* (1967); Robert Giroux, 'François Hertel, le surhomme noyé', in *Présence francophone* (no. 6, printemps 1973); Jean Tétreau, 'François Hertel, une pensée, un style, un art de vivre' in *Livres et auteurs canadiens 1966* (1967); Gilles Thérien, 'François Hertel, curieux homme' in *VOIX ET IMAGES*, vol. 2, no. 1 (sept. 1976); and Jean Tétreau, *Hertel: l'homme et l'oeuvre* (1986).

RICHARD GIGUÈRE

Dubois, René-Daniel (b. 1955). Born and raised in Montreal, he has constructed a complex and original theatrical universe. His entrance on the Quebec theatre scene was sensational; since 1980 fourteen of Dubois's plays have been performed, nine of which have been published. *Panique à Longueuil* (1980), is a Dantesque and philosophical comedy, whereas *Adieu, docteur Münch . . .* (1982) is a disconcerting play featuring fourteen roles, all of which were originally played by the author. *26 bis, impasse du Colonel Foisy* (1983) is a play written for a fictitious Russian princess (whose role is to be played by a male actor), who discusses her love life, the theatre, and, above all, her conflicts with the author of the play. Other published plays include *Ne blâmez jamais les Bédouins* (1984); *Being at home with Claude* (1986); *Le printemps, monsieur Deslauriers* (1987), a rather realistic family drama focusing on Philippe Deslauriers, a character noted for his excessive behaviour; *Le troisième fils du Professeur Yourolov* (1990); *. . . Et Laura ne répondait rien* (1991), which highlights the reconstitution of fabrication of memories; and *Julie* (1996), a fable that Dubois wrote for children and then adapted for the stage.

There are two written version of *Ne blâmez jamais les Bédouins*, an experimental text that uses clichés ironically. Only the second version was performed (in 1984, and in 1995). In the latter version, the author himself played all twenty-five roles, pushing the deconstruction of the theatrical character to the limit. One scene, where an Italian opera singer, tied to railway tracks as two speeding trains approach from either direction, elicited the comment from the author, a former separatist: 'It pretty well sums up life in Quebec these days.' *Being at home with Claude*, Dubois's first realistic play, was his greatest popular success. The story of a man who murders his lover in a deliberate act of passion, the play consists of the uncoerced confession of the murderer, with the centenary of the Canadian Confederation as its background. The expression of a sublime and frenzied homosexual love is at the heart of this text. It was filmed in 1991 under the direction of Jean Beaudin. *Le troisième fils du Professeur Yourolov*, Dubois's most obviously postmodern play, confuses places and events, questions the search for truth, and explores the characters' identity and sexuality.

See Jean Cléo Godin, 'Deux dramaturges de l'avenir?', *Études littéraires* 18, no. 3 (1985); Alvina Ruprecht, 'Les voix scéniques de René-Daniel Dubois', *Canadian Drama* 12, no. 2 (1986); Lucie Robert, 'Les jeunes loups', *VOIX ET IMAGES* 36 (1987); Dominique Lafon, 'René-Daniel Dubois, de la polyphonie comme masque ou porte-voix', *Théâtre/Public* 117 (1994); and Hélène Laliberté, 'Espaces et territoires dans *Being at home with Claude* de René-Daniel Dubois', *L'annuaire théâtral* 21 (1997). PASCAL RIENDEAU

Ducharme, Réjean (b. 1941). Born in Saint-Félix-de-Valois, Quebec, he pursued various studies, always abandoning them, preferring to earn a living from small jobs, such as office clerk. He now lives in Montreal. He has been neither seen in public nor interviewed since Sept. 1966, when he stated in a brief interview with Gerald GODIN in *Le Magazine Maclean*: 'I don't want my face to be known. I don't want people to link me and my novel. . . . My novel is public, but I'm not.' The last statement alluded to his first novel, *L'avalée des avalés* (1966), which won immediate renown for being published by the distinguished Parisian firm of Gallimard (after having been rejected by a Montreal publisher). His anonymity raised many rumours about his identity and made him a kind of celebrity. *L'avalée des avalés*—which won a Governor General's Award and was translated by Barbara Bray as *The swallower swallowed* (1968)—is one of the high points of modern French-Canadian fiction. Its half-Jewish, half-Catholic heroine, Bérénice Einberg, who transfers her love for the neglectful mother she adores to her brother, becomes manipulative (like her quarrelling parents) and callous to protect herself, choosing to hate whatever she cannot fully possess: she decides to 'swallow' the world in order not to be swallowed up by it. Her pain is brilliantly portrayed in farcical/comic terms as she rejects all traditional values and invents an anti-social and incomprehensible language, 'le bérénicien', to replace normal language that for her is based on illusion.

Ducharme's novels have been described by critic Gilles MARCOTTE as 'both the apotheosis and the negation of the novel'. The author practises a kind of literary terrorism, building elaborate word-plays that simultaneously provoke interpretation and confound meaning. His protagonists are fiercely individualistic adolescents, determined to survive on their own terms in a world they find hypocritical. Their quests for infinite knowledge and love, which are tragically defeated by the limits of reality, are marvellously poetic, semantically evocative, and farcical in tone—Ducharme assaults the Western cultural heritage with humour or 'niaiserie' (silliness). His inventory of languages (biblical, mythological, literary, scientific, Marxist, nationalist, counter-cultural) declares all language both false and impotent to capture the complexity of reality: 'There are tons of words. But nothing to say. There are tons of things. But nothing to do.' In spite of this pessimism, the joy of his language expands and explodes in all directions.

Le nez qui voque (1967) is the journal of a

sixteen-year old boy who has made a suicide pact with his fourteen-year old girlfriend rather than allow the compromises of adult life and sexuality to separate them. As the pun in the title suggests, this novel is about equivocation and ambiguity; it is also about the pleasure and hypocrisy of growing up, and about the tragedy of attempting to cling to absolute purity and truth. *L'océantume* (1968) is the most lyrical and least cynical of Ducharme's novels. *La fille de Christophe Colomb* (1969), a mock epic written in determinedly ridiculous verse, is Ducharme's most radical attack on traditional literary structure and meaning. The wandering around the world of Columbus's modern daughter Colombe in a vain search for friendship is the pretext for a condemnation of civilization and of literature's pretense of transmitting meaning. In *L'hiver de force* (1973) and *Les enfantômes* (1976), Ducharme's protagonists are somewhat older and more sophisticated but no less uncompromising than their predecessors. In *L'hiver de force*, André Ferron and his sister Nicole make their living as proof-readers but are 'drop-outs' from society, determined to do literally nothing. The novel has the same vitality and poetry as Ducharme's earlier works, but is more realistic in its satire of the political and cultural milieu of 1970s Montreal. *Les enfantômes*, the story of Vincent Falardeau, his wife Alberta, and his sister Fériée, is—like the other novels—a baroque journey evoking the dreams, joys, and anguish of insatiable child-adults united against the world.

Ducharme has written four plays, but has forbidden publication of the first two, *Le Cid maghané* and *Le marquis qui perdit*, produced in 1968 and 1970 respectively. *Inès Pérée et Inat Tendu* (1976) and *HA! ha!...* (1982)—which won a Governor General's Award—treat the same themes as the novels, and like them display a savage joy in deconstructing language. Turning to film, Ducharme collaborated with Francis Manckiewicz on the very successful *Les bons débarras* (1979) and *Les beaux souvenirs* (1981), whose innocently cruel young heroines are familiar figures to readers of the novels. Ducharme has also composed lyrics for the popular singer Robert Charlebois and, under the name Roch Plante, has exhibited sculptures and paintings created from found objects.

After an amazing silence of some fifteen years that one feared was definitive, Ducharme surprised everyone with the novels *Dévadé* (1990) and *Va savoir* (1994). Bottom, the main character in *Dévadé*, is a social outcast so cut off from the mainstream that he finds himself welcome and at home in two contrary worlds: that of the Patronne, a cultured upper-class woman, a well-read follower of Buddhist philosophy since an accident that left her an invalid, for whom he serves as a chauffeur; and that of his city friends Juba Caïne, Bruno, and Nicole, who unwind and get high on drugs, sex, and booze. Moving back and forth between these worlds, Bottom attempts to combine their respective ethics and adapt them to his own use. *Dévadé*'s slender narrative framework is repeated in *Va savoir*, which is equally concerned with creating an atmosphere in which emotion and affection emerge in a sumptuous writing style—though the novel is more fragmented. Its main components are sporadic letters between the narrator, Rémi, and his wife, who is travelling around the world (with her husband's former mistress) in an effort to regain her mental equilibrium; various encounters, touched with humour and love, between Rémi and his rural neighbours; detailed descriptions of the renovation of a ruined chalet into which the hero has just moved; and an intense friendship with a little girl, Fanie, that gives rise to some dazzling passages.

See Gerald Godin, 'Gallimard publie un Québécois de 24 ans, inconnu' (the only existing interview with Ducharme) in *Le Magazine Maclean* (Sept. 1966), and Michel VAN SCHENDEL, 'Ducharme l'inquiétant' in *Littérature canadienne-française* (conferences J.-A. de Sève 1-10, 1969); and 'Avez-vous relu Ducharme?', a special issue of *Études françaises*, vol. 11, 3/4 (oct. 1975). To the many subsequent articles on Ducharme have been added several books and theses, including *Paysages de Réjean Ducharme* (1992), edited by Pierre-Louis Vaillancourt, and Hélène Amrit's *Les stratégies paratextuelles dans l'oeuvre de Réjean Ducharme* (Annales littéraires de l'Université de Besançon, 1995).

PATRICIA SMART/
PIERRE-LOUIS VAILLANCOURT

Dudek, Louis (b. 1918). Born in the east end of Montreal, of Polish immigrant parents, he attended McGill University and after graduating in 1940 worked as an advertising copywriter and freelance journalist. In 1943 he moved to New York and began graduate studies in journalism and history at Columbia University; shortly afterwards he changed his major from journalism to literature. On completion of his doctoral course work, he accepted an English appointment at City College, New York; he became acquainted with writers Paul Blackburn, Cid Corman, and Herbert Gold, and began a correspondence with Ezra Pound. In 1951 Dudek returned to Montreal, where he lectured at McGill in modern poetry, Canadian literature, the art of poetry, and European literature, until his retirement in 1982.

Dudek began his career as a poet in the 1936-40 period, publishing social-protest verse in the *McGill Daily*. In 1943 he joined John SUTHERLAND and Irving LAYTON in editing *FIRST STATEMENT*, which Sutherland had founded in 1942, and throughout his New York years Dudek contributed to it and to its successor, *NORTHERN REVIEW*. On his return to Canada he became immediately a major force in Canadian small-press publishing and influenced the development of Canadian poetry. Instructed by the editorial activities of Americans such as Pound and Corman, he was convinced of the necessity for poets to take their means of publication out of the hands of commercial publishers and into their own. In 1952-4 he was instrumental in shaping the editorial direction of Raymond SOUSTER's little magazine *CONTACT*. In 1952, together with Souster and Layton, he founded CONTACT PRESS, which, between 1952 and 1967, published early books by most of the major poets of the sixties and early seventies. In 1956 he began another publishing venture, the McGill Poetry Series, in which he published first poetry books by McGill students, beginning with Leonard COHEN's *Let us compare mythologies* (1956). Despite its name, the series was mostly financed and edited by Dudek. In 1957 he began *DELTA*, a personal literary magazine in which he attempted to promote further the urbane, realistic kind of writing his earlier editorial activities had encouraged. He terminated *Delta* in 1966; but the next year he co-founded, with Glen Siebrasse and Michael Gnarowski, the small press Delta Canada. On its dissolution in 1970 he co-founded, with Aileen Collins, yet another small press, D.C. Books.

Dudek's poetry collections are *East of the city* (1946), *Twenty-four poems* (1952), *The searching image* (1952), *Europe* (1955), *The transparent sea* (1956), *En Mexico* (1958), *Laughing stalks* (1958), *Atlantis* (1967), *Collected poetry* (1971), *Selected poems* (1979), *Poems from Atlantis* (1980), *Cross-section* (1980), *Continuation I* (1981), and *Continuation II* (1990). His selected poems were published as *Infinite worlds* (1988). His early poems are mostly short lyrics that proceed from incidental observation and description towards a concluding insight or philosophical statement. Employing few metaphors or elaborate images, the descriptions are direct and realistic. Although many of the scenes are from ghetto and working-class life, and many of the sentiments are Marxist, a definite pessimism about human accomplishment pervades these poems. Optimism is usually reserved for nature's powers—'the soon-rampant seed', 'the great orchestrating principle of gravity'.

With the publication of *Europe* and *En Mexico*, Dudek moved from short, incidentally related lyrics to book-length meditations with prose-like rhythms and a didactic tone. Unlike the lyrics, they interweave the general and particular so that their relationship is obscured; some passages seem to be illustrated sermons, while others offer flashes of inspiration gained from particulars. Dudek has remarked in his one book of literary theory (*The first person in literature*, 1967) that, because of our 'anarchically subjective' age, the egoist as writer must become a 'great moralist'. In *Europe*, *En Mexico*, and *Atlantis* Dudek attempts to be the morally responsible egoist, to make his self universal, to come to terms with 'the dichotomy of the self and the not-self, the I-myself and the mankind-to-which-I-belong'; but he is still pessimistic about humanity's ability to reform and save itself. Joy, beauty, and eternity are certain residents only of nature. At the end of *Atlantis*, when the poet finally gains a vision of the lost continent, its 'palaces, and domes' are a North Atlantic iceberg—'a piece of eternity', 'a carved silent coffin', that promises only 'darkness' and 'infinite night'.

Dudek is also the author of *Epigrams* (1975) and *Literature and the press* (1960), a revision of his Ph.D. thesis, which is a history of printing, printed media, and their relation to literature. In collaboration with Irving Layton he compiled *Canadian poems: 1850-1952* (1952), and in collaboration with Michael Gnarowski *The making of modern poetry in Canada* (1967), an extremely useful anthology of documents relating to the development of Canadian poetry since 1910. Dudek was also the editor of *Poetry of our time* (1965), an introduction to twentieth-century poetry, including Canadian poetry. Most of his essays on Canadian literature were included in *Selected essays and criticism* (1978), which was followed by three further prose collections: *Technology and culture* (1979), *Texts and essays* (1981), a special issue of the magazine *OPEN LETTER*, which also contains photostats of manuscript pages from *Europe* and *Atlantis*, and *In defence of art* (1988). Dudek's correspondence with Ezra Pound during the 1950s was published as *D/k: some letters of Ezra Pound* (1974).

See Frank DAVEY, *Louis Dudek and Raymond Souster* (1980); Susan Stromberg, *Louis Dudek* (1983); and Terry Goldie, 'Louis Dudek', Jack David, and Ellen Quigley, eds, *Canadian writers and their works*, Poetry Series 5 (1984).

See also POETRY IN ENGLISH 1950 TO 1982: 1.

FRANK DAVEY

Dufresne, Guy. See DRAMA IN FRENCH 1948 TO 1981: 3.

Dugas, Marcel (1883-1947). Born at St-Jacques-de-Lachigan, Quebec, he studied law at Université Laval in Montreal and worked as a journalist, chiefly covering the theatre. From 1910 to 1914 he lived in Paris, studying literature at the Sorbonne. The war forced him to leave Europe, but he returned in 1920 and remained in Paris—working for the Canadian Archives and frequenting the cafés and literary salons—until his final departure in 1940. *Pots de fer* (1941) is a moving account of his last days in occupied France. Dugas was associated, over the years, with three artistic and literary movements in Montreal—Le Soc (1910), La Tribudes Casoars, which amalgamated with L'Arche (1916-17), and *Le NIGOG* (1918)—and, in Ottawa, with Le Groupe des Sept (1943-6).

Dugas's writing is eminently poetic, although he published only one poetry collection, *Salve alma parens* (1941). Reviews that he wrote for *Le Nationaliste* were published under the pseudonym 'Marcel Henry' in *Le théatre de Montréal, propos d'un Huron canadien* (1911). His prose falls into two categories: critical essays and poetic essays. He worshipped Verlaine, Péguy, and Le Cardonnel, enthusiastically praising all three authors in *Feux de Bengale à Verlaine glorieux* (1915) and *Versions: Louis Le Cardonnel. Charles Péguy* (1917). A frequent reviewer of his compatriots' works, he usually selected those of his friends; thus, Léo-Pol Morin, Alain GRANDBOIS, François Hertel (Rodolphe DUBÉ), SAINT-DENYS-GARNEAU, and Simone Routier-Drouin were 'approached with affection and a desire to understand them, to mark their passage and pay tribute to their qualities' (*Approches*, 1942). Friends from the early days had received similar kind-hearted attention in *Apologies: M. Albert Lozeau, M. Paul Morin, M. Guy Delahaye, M. Robert La Roque de Roquebrune, M. René Chopin* (1919). These five studies were reprinted in *Littérature canadienne: aperçus* (1929), along with essays on the work of Jean-Aubert LORANGER, Jean Nolin, Robert CHOQUETTE, and Pierre Dupuy. Dugas's criticism, which is sometimes quite biased, is often more beautifully written and more skilful than the works under study. However, in *Un romantique canadien: Louis Fréchette, 1839-1908* (Paris, 1934; Montréal, 1946), he was somewhat hard on Louis FRÉCHETTE, calling him 'this bourgeois playing at being a revolutionary' and a mere artisan, 'the brutality of whose sentiments is only rarely saved by his expression'. Only with effort could he begin to like the author of *La légende d'un peuple*, whose tastes and ideas were so remote from his own. But when studying his friends' texts he searched his soul; while speaking of them he was concerned with himself. In his poetic essays Dugas cultivated emotion with a growing obsession, sharing his troubled or disturbed inner states. He venerated in *Phèdre* 'the sad renewal of hearts that recover the illusion of loving' (*Psyché au cinéma*, 1916), because Phèdre tried to submit to fate instead of running from it, and, though a skeptic, to bring about a return to 'benevolent illusion' (*Cordes anciennes*, 1933). Other works by Dugas are *Confins* (1921) and *Nocturnes* (1936), both published under pseudonyms—although *Confins* was later published under his own name as *Flacons à la mer. Proses* (1923).

As an aesthete infatuated with ornate language and long, unbroken, harmonious sentences, Dugas bridged in a unique manner the gap between his fragile universe and the outside world. With him one truly enters into what Roland Barthes calls 'the pleasure of the text', and willingly subscribes to the judgement of Philippe PANNETON that Dugas is 'the greatest of our prose writers for the richness of his language'.

BERNADETTE GUILMETTE

Duguay, Calixte. See ACADIAN LITERATURE: 2(a).

Duguay, Raoul (b. 1939). Born in Val d'Or, Quebec, he was the seventh of eleven children. When his fiddler father Armand Duguay died, Raoul was only five and was sent first to an orphanage, then to his Acadian grandparents, who raised him in New Brunswick. As a teenager he was sent to the seminary at Amos, Quebec, where he developed an interest in music. At nineteen he left the seminary and studied philosophy at the Université de Montréal, while teaching aesthetics at Collège Sainte-Croix and media techniques at the Université du Québec à Montreal.

In the early and middle sixties Duguay began to publish poems in *LIBERTÉ*, *Passe-partout*, and *Les Écrits du Canada français*; he also became involved with the young Marxist and separatist ideologues who gravitated around *PARTI PRIS*. In a number of articles published in *parti pris*, Duguay articulated indépendantiste and Marxist positions—from which he stood aloof in the early 1970s. His articles on a sound theory, phonetics, and the physical and spiritual properties of the spoken word, published in *Quoi* in 1967, demonstrate a strong commitment to the politics of sound as distinct from the politics of countries and territorial boundaries. From this point on, the aural properties of speech appear to be a central concern: how to use sound vibrations, how to turn the mantric qualities of words to a specific purpose, and how to reach a wide public.

Duguay's first collections of poetry, *Ruts* (1966; 2nd edn 1974) and *Or le cycle de sang dure donc* (1967; 2nd edn 1975) won him more lasting attention. As erotic writings they celebrate a lover's body and sexual pleasure, but they also reveal a penchant for syncopated rhythms, linguistic break-ups, and non-semantic sound patterns. From 1968 to 1971 Duguay dedicated himself to the performance of his own poetic and musical shows. He founded the Infonie group, realizing what he called 'a harmony between music and poetry, a synthesis of the two'; creating something for both the ear and the eye; and exploring the physical dimension of a poem in the context of an audience's presence and response. With the Infonie group Duguay travelled across Canada; he also performed alone on the Bobino stage in Paris. During this time he became acquainted with the German composer Karlheinz Stockhausen and studied his musical theories. The early 1970s saw the culminating point of Duguay's creative energies: out of his performing experiments with L'Infonie came *Le manifeste de l'Infonie* (1970) and *Lapokalipsô* (1971). Both volumes exemplify Duguay's theory of sound, as well as the multi-media aspects of his performances. All poems are phonetically written: some call for 99 typewriters, others for a variety of instruments and sounds—wind, waterfalls, and various languages.

Duguay—who also likes to use the reverse spelling of his name, Luoar Yaugud—dedicated himself, after 1972, almost entirely to the performing arts and the recording of his music. Performing for him did not imply moving away from writing (though it did mean publishing less), but he aimed at 'bringing what had previously been looked upon as mysterious and esoteric to a wide audience. My voice is my most natural instrument and I want to give it to everybody (*toulmonde*). I shall sing my poems as some eat an apple.'

Although he devotes the major part of his creative energy to music, Duguay has written a children's book, *Les saisons* (1981), and *Kebec à la porte: poèmes politiques, 1967-1993* (1993).

See Christiane L'Heureux, *Raoul Duguay ou Le poète à la voix d'or* (1970); chapter VII of Clément Moisan, *Poésie des frontières* (1979); and an interview with Duguay in Caroline Bayard and Jack David, *Out-posts/Avant-postes* (1978). CAROLINE BAYARD

Duley, Margaret (1894-1968). Born in St John's, Newfoundland, the daughter of a well-to-do jeweller, she was educated at the local Methodist College and in 1913 enrolled in the London Academy of Music and Dramatic Art in London, England. From 1918 until she began serious writing in the 1930s her life was occupied with travel, reading, partying with the St John's élite, and local feminist agitation. She never married. In the Depression years her father's business declined and Duley began writing fiction, apparently to make money. During the Second World War she helped to run a hostel for allied servicemen in St John's; and for a brief period afterwards she did public-relations work with the Newfoundland division of the Canadian Red Cross. In her late years she suffered from Parkinson's disease.

Duley grew up amid the snobbery and comforts of the St John's East merchant class. She knew the Newfoundland outports only from a distance, from the perspective of an occasional summer visitor; yet it was to the outports that she turned for inspiration for her first novel, *The eyes of the gull* (1936), where outharbour existence is depicted as unremittingly stifling, condemning the heroine, Isabel Pyke, to a deprived and horrid round of loveless days. Real love is seen as something attainable only in the world of culture and sophistication outside Newfoundland. This is Duley's most snobbish novel. Yet it is more carefully plotted and often more moving than the later books. *Cold pastoral* (1939) takes a similar outport heroine out of her native cove, now evoked in all its squalour and coarseness, and brings her to the greater world of St John's and, ultimately, London. Urban values are espoused until the end of the book, when she feels a sudden twinge of affection for her own 'bit of earth' in Newfoundland. This is the beginning of a reconciliation that is the theme of *Highway to valour* (1941), Duley's third and final novel with a Newfoundland setting. Her new heroine, after living through a number of grim episodes in a country that terrifies and dominates her, at length turns her face in acceptance 'towards the cold sea that was her heritage.' These books show a progressive deepening in the author's understanding of the nature of life in Newfoundland; they appear to be stages in an odyssey of discovery and acceptance. As Duley developed as a novelist, she saw Newfoundland with an increasing intensity and clarity, but never fully overcame a distaste for the jagged landscapes and stormy seas of her uncomfortable home. Nevertheless she portrayed Newfoundland with rare truthfulness and vividness.

These three books dramatize encounters between a heroine and the inappropriate 'masculine' environment in which she had to function. The theme—women in pursuit of love—is examined with shrewd insight and, on occasion, humour. If we consider all four of Duley's novels, adding *Novelty on earth* (1942)—published in England as *Green afternoon* (1944) and in Sweden as *Så stred Sara* (1946)—in which the Newfoundland setting is of no importance, we can see a theme emerging in her work that engrosses her even more than her connection with her homeland: she is struggling to define a feminist sensibility. Duley's independent womanhood is reflected in all her books. She appears to have been torn between her desire to comment on the external world and her wish to explore the nature of her feminine sensitivity towards it, and towards men. In *Novelty on earth* the setting is unimportant as Duley minutely chronicles a love affair between a twice-widowed woman and a married man. At the end her heroine rejects her lover because she 'couldn't be a squaw-woman and give him what he wanted.' We have a free modern woman before us. Duley thus transcended her provincial concerns to make a larger statement.

Duley also wrote *The caribou hut: the story of a Newfoundland hostel* (1949), a little book with much astute commentary on Newfoundland. She contributed a foreword to R.B. Job's *John Job's family* (1953). Her mother, Mrs T.J. Duley, published a pamphlet, *A pair of grey socks; facts and fancies* (*c.* 1916), that contains 'Verses' by Margaret Duley.

There is an article by Duley in the *Atlantic Guardian* (July 1956) in which she discusses her novels in the context of Newfoundland writing. Margot Duley Morrow has written a biographical sketch of her in a reprint of *Highway to valour* (1977). Alison Feder's *Margaret Duley: Newfoundland novelist, a biographical and critical study* (1983) is valuable as biography but weak as criticism. *The eyes of the gull* and *Novelty on earth* are treated in Joan Strong's *Acts of brief authority: a critical assessment of selected twentieth-century Newfoundland novels* (1994). PATRICK O'FLAHERTY

Duliani, Mario. See ITALIAN-CANADIAN LITERATURE.

Dumont, Fernand (1927-97). Born in Montmorency, near Quebec City, he was educated at Université Laval (B. ès A., 1949; M.en Sc., 1953; D. en Théol., 1987) and at the Sorbonne, Paris (D. en Soc., 1964). Having been appointed at Laval as head of the faculties of theology and sociology, and director of the Institute supérieur des sciences humaines, he was appointed Professeur titulaire de Sociologie. Dumont was president (1979-90) of the Institut québécois de recherche sur la culture, which sponsors and co-ordinates research projects aimed at safeguarding the national heritage.

Dumont's attitude as a writer and teacher through the years of rapid change in Quebec has been described by the epithet 'conscience vigilante', prompted by the title of his collection of essays *La vigile du Québec* (1971). Dumont was, for Quebec, what his fellow sociologists called 'un définisseur de la situation'; he exhibited a serene lucidity as he confidently grappled with the problems thrown up by the contemporary cultural revolution.

The desire to 'define the situation' and to see clearly the process by which a society elaborates its culture—its 'mental tools'—can be traced in Dumont's teaching, and in three colloquia organized by the review *Recherches sociographiques* (of which he was co-director), the proceedings of which appear in *Situation de la recherche sur le Canada français* (1962), *Littérature et société canadiennes-français* (1964), and *Le pouvoir dans la société canadienne-français* (1966).

Chantiers: essais sur la pratique des sciences de l'homme (1973) contains essays, all previously published (1958-70), that are powerful theoretical studies, chiefly on the role of ideology in the elaboration of cultural identity. Typical of Dumont's mode of scholarly examination is an early essay, 'L'étude systématique d'une société globale', which surveys previous attempts at a structural analysis of Quebec society (by Trudeau, BRUNET, *et al.*) and points to the need for a new analytical approach that takes into account Quebec's distinctive development. *Les idéologies*, a powerful single essay that proposes an analysis of the concept and function of ideology in the social sciences, was published in Paris in 1974. Dumont's first sociological work, a study (written with Yves Martin) of the region of Saint-Jérôme just north of Montreal, *L'analyse des structures sociales régionalies* (1963), examines the effect on traditional life in this town of the opening of the Laurentian autoroute, which both by-passed it and gave its inhabitants rapid access to the city. Leaving field-work behind in his later essays—*Pour la conversion de la pensée chrétienne* (1964), *Le lieu de l'homme* (1967), and *La dialectique de l'objet économique* (Paris, 1970)—Dumont looked at the ways in which culture conceptualizes experience, allowing members of a society to stand away from it and recognize the unfamiliar. He saw conformism as the sclerosis of the symbolical framework with which experience is processed. The portrait that emerges, of a society ill-equipped to adapt, suggests Quebec—though the essays proceed with a minimum of reference to concrete situations and are fed by the widest, most eclectic erudition. Dumont's thoughts on the transformation of the anachronistic concept of a Christian culture in Quebec were reflected in the report of the Commission d'étude sur les laïcs et l'Église, which he headed: *Pour la conversion de la pensée chrétienne* (1971). *L'anthropologie en l'absence de l'homme* (Paris, 1981) attempted an ambitious synthesis of the social sciences and sought to revitalize anthropology. His last books were *L'institution de la théologie* (1987) and *Le sort de la culture* (1987).

Dumont's definition of an ideology as 'la *justification* d'une définition de la situation d'un groupe en vue le l'action' allowed him to see both the sociologist and the writer as concerned with the same collective vision. Through his limpid, orderly poetry—*L'ange du matin* (1952) and *Parler de septembre* (1970) —Dumont fitted his own definition of both the sociologist and the writer: 'Un homme [qui], en pensant aux autres, ose tenter de définir son univers d'existence.'

See Michael A. Weinstein, *Culture critique: Fernand Dumont and new Quebec sociology* (1985). C.R.P. MAY

Duncan, Norman (1871-1916). Born in North Norwich Township, Oxford County, Ontario, Norman McLean Duncan attended the University of Toronto (1891-4), where he knew W.L. Mackenzie King, but did not graduate. Soon afterwards he began a career as a journalist in the United States. In the summer of 1900 he went to Newfoundland to write articles for *McClure's Magazine*, a journal that specialized in geographical adventure. He returned to Newfoundland for other summer visits between 1901 and 1906, and again in 1910, forming a strong attachment to the Manuel family of Exploits Island in Notre Dame Bay. In an appreciation of Duncan, Wilfred GRENFELL noted that he had been 'a guest aboard our little hospital vessel' along the Labrador coast. Duncan also travelled farther afield, to the Near East and to Australia. From 1902 to 1908 he taught English and rhetoric at Washington and Jefferson College in Washington, Pennsylvania, and at the University of Kansas. During his last years drinking became a serious problem to him. He died suddenly, on a golf course, in Fredonia, New York.

Duncan was a prolific and popular author. His writings have been neglected by recent critics, perhaps because his defects—occasional sentimentality, a flowery, rhetorical style, and a liking for melodrama—are so apparent, and his subject matter is often so remote from ordinary North American experience. Yet his faults do not much detract from his considerable achievement. Like his contemporary Jack London, Duncan went for literary inspiration to northern frontiers and to the lives of forgotten people. His spirit was democratic, his writings affirmations of the imaginative possibilities inherent in common life. His first book, *The soul of the street: correlated stories of the New York Syrian quarter* (1900), is a collection revealing his familiarity with the legends and lives of Syrian immigrants and showing his compassion and his interest in out-of-the-way modes of life. His experiences in Newfoundland stirred him deeply and provided material for ten works of fiction, much of it written for a juvenile audience: *The way of the sea* (1903; rpr. 1970, 1982), *Doctor Luke of the Labrador* (1904), *The adventures of Billy Topsail: a story for boys* (1906), *The cruise of the Shining Light* (1907), *Every man for himself* (1908), *Billy Topsail & Company: a story for boys* (1910), *The best of a bad job: a hearty tale of the sea* (1912), *Billy Topsail, M.D.: a tale of adventure with Doctor Luke of the Labrador* (1916), *Battles royal down north* (1918), and *Harbor tales down north* (1918). His collection of essays on Newfoundland, *Dr. Grenfell's parish: the deep sea fishermen* (1905), expresses his admiration for Grenfell, who was undoubtedly the model for Dr Luke in his most popular novel. Of these works the most important is *The way of the sea*, a book of stories that explore the outharbour life of Newfoundland with profound understanding and sympathy. His response to the ocean is striking. Andrew

MacPHAIL said in an unpublished essay that Duncan wrote of the sea 'as one might write of the sky and the land, who had looked upon the heavens and the earth for the first time with his bodily eyes.'

Nothing else Duncan experienced seems to have fired his imagination so strongly as Newfoundland. Yet he wrote eight other books. *The mother* (1905) is a touching novel that probably expresses his grief over the death of his own mother in 1904. A similar domestic novel, *The suitable child* (1909), describes a boy's rejection by his family. *Going down from Jerusalem; the narrative of a sentimental traveller* (1909) is an account of his travels in Palestine, Syria, and Egypt that aims at conjuring up the lives of camel drivers rather than describing monuments. *Finding his soul* (1913) is a fictional representation of this journey. *Higgins: a man's Christian* (1990) is an account of Francis Edmund Higgins' missionary work among Minnesota lumberjacks, a subject that Duncan again treated in the novel *The measure of a man; a tale of the big woods* (1911). *The bird-store man: an old-fashioned story* (1914) is another book for children. *Australian byways: the narrative of a sentimental traveler* (1915) describes travels in Australasia in 1912-13.

Duncan was capable of sustained passages of exquisite, resonant prose. Writing about Newfoundland—the 'frayed edge' of North America where he found obscure inhabitants of a hidden world of adventure—he created an unwitting epic of outport life in stories showing the stamp of genius. John Coldwell Adams, in his Introduction to *Selected stories of Norman Duncan* (1988), writes that 'a little more time and effort' on Duncan's part might have put his stories 'in the front ranks'.

See an article by Virginia Ryan in *Newfoundland Studies*, vol. 5, no. 1, and Elizabeth Russell Miller, *The frayed edge: Norman Duncan's Newfoundland* (1992).

PATRICK O'FLAHERTY

Duncan, Sara Jeannette (1861-1922). The daughter of a Scottish father and an Ulster Protestant mother, she was born and raised in Brantford, Canada West (Ontario). She attended the Toronto Normal School, but soon abandoned teaching for journalism. A high-spirited trip to the 1884 New Orleans Cotton Exposition as a freelance correspondent was followed by such substantial jobs as editorial writer and book reviewer for the Washington *Post* (1885-6), columnist for the Toronto *Globe* (1886-7), and finally columnist for the *Montreal Star* (1887-8). She also wrote extensively during this period for *The WEEK*. In Sept. 1888 she set off with a fellow journalist, Lily Lewis, on an ambitious round-the-world tour. In Calcutta she met Everard Cotes, a museum official and subsequently a journalist. She married him in Dec. 1890 and lived with him in Calcutta and Simla (then the summer administrative capital of India) for most of the next three decades, though she spent large stretches of time alone in London. In the mid-1890s she wrote editorials for the *Indian Daily News*, a newspaper her husband edited. Early personal and professional fulfilment appear to have been followed by unhappiness in India and a nostalgic affection for Canada. The last few years of her life were spent in England, where she died.

Duncan's journalism comments with intelligence, vigour, and wit on an astonishing variety of Canadian social, political, and cultural questions. Her remarks on literary issues display a shrewd understanding of contemporary controversies. Throughout her career Duncan was keenly aware of developments in fiction—she even sought out personal contact with William Dean Howells, E.M. Forster, and Henry James. (She knew Howells in Washington and Paris and entertained Forster in India; she sent James her novel *His honour and a lady*, which he acknowledged tardily and with elaborate, distancing graciousness, describing it as 'extraordinarily keen and delicate and able', before criticizing it gently but astutely.) Her first book, *A social departure: how Orthodocia and I went round the world by ourselves* (London and New York, 1890), is an edited version of her globe-trotting news paper articles, unified by the invention of a naïve young Englishwoman as the narrator's companion. It has many lively episodes (particularly those dealing with Japan, a country Duncan found delightful), but is overlong and uneven. The more inventive and polished *An American girl in London* (London and New York, 1891)—like its predecessor a collection of light sketches, which are here presented as a novel—concerns the adventures of a Chicago baking-powder heiress who is eagerly sought after by predatory Englishmen. Both books were very favourably reviewed and appear to represent the height of Duncan's commercial success. In *A voyage of consolation* (London and New York, 1898) the heroine of *An American girl* ventures onto the Continent, and the recently discovered *Two girls on a barge* (London and New York, 1891) chronicles the self-conscious exploits of another unconventional heroine.

Duncan takes her emancipated female protagonist much more seriously in *A daughter of to-day* (London and New York, 1894; rpt. 1988, with an introduction by Misao Dean), a novel that ends with the heroine's suicide. This ambitious work, set in the artist quarters of Paris and London, has admirable scenes but suffers from pretentiousness and an ultimate plunge into melodrama. Duncan's first outstanding literary achievement is *The simple adventures of a memsahib* (London and New York, 1893; rpr. 1986, with an introduction by Thomas E. Tausky), an account of a conventional young Englishwoman's entry into Anglo-Indian society as narrated by a sophisticated veteran 'memsahib'. A subtle tragicomedy, it reveals that in the years since Duncan's first sight of India, she had immeasurably deepened her understanding of the Anglo-Indian character. Two very slight works—*Vernon's aunt* (London, 1894; New York, 1895), and a juvenile, *The story of Sonny Sahib* (London, 1894; New York, 1895)—were followed by *His honour, and a lady* (London and New York, 1896), her first serious study of Indian politics. In this impressive work Duncan interweaves the fates of two women: the emancipated protagonist she so often portrayed, and a more conventional heroine. Her considerable powers of social observation are at their best in this novel, which also has a stylistic lightness and grace she was never quite able to recapture. *The path of a star* (American title, *Hilda: a story of Calcutta*; London and New York, 1899), like *A daughter of to-day*, has an artist protagonist—an actress this time—and strongly melodramatic elements. It widens the focus of Duncan's story of Calcutta society, taking in the religious, theatrical, and commercial communities as well as the civil servants; but it is flawed by a ponderous pseudo-Jamesian prose style.

It was not until 1902 that Duncan made North America a major setting for her fiction, in *Those delightful Americans* (1902), a light but entertaining story about a young English matron's discovery of American high society. Duncan's most Canadian novels—*The imperialist* (1904) and *Cousin Cinderella; or, A Canadian girl in London* (1908; rpr. 1994, with an introduction by Misao Dean)—are also her best. She wrote in a letter that, for patriotic reasons, she was 'trying very hard to make [*The imperialist*] my best book.' It is a witty though balanced and sympathetic portrait of Brantford (called Elgin), a community in which 'nothing compared with religion but politics, and nothing compared with politics but religion' as sources of interest, and where a certain leading citizen was 'no more disposed to an extravagant opinion than to wear one side whisker longer than the other.' Advena Murchison, the novel's passionate, independent, and intellectual heroine, is the finest example of an autobiographical character type Duncan had depicted in several previous novels; the elder Murchisons are affectionate portraits of Duncan's own parents. The narrative ingeniously alternates parallel plots involving severe challenges to idealistic impulses in politics and love. Though Duncan insisted that 'my book offers only a picture of life and opinion, and attempts no argument', the title character's struggle to convert his stubbornly pragmatic fellow-townsmen to the imperialist faith is presented sympathetically. *The imperialist* has been reprinted in the NEW CANADIAN LIBRARY, with an Afterword by Janette Turner HOSPITAL; and by Tecumseh Press, edited by Thomas E. Tausky (1988; 2nd ed. 1996). *Cousin Cinderella*, an account of the efforts made by a Canadian brother and sister to gain social recognition for themselves and their country in London, is Duncan's most subtle and accomplished version of the international theme. Like *The imperialist*, it centres on an emerging sense of national consciousness and a struggle against lingering colonialism. As the narrator remarks in *The imperialist*, 'We are here at the making of a nation.'

Duncan's final two Indian novels, *Set in authority* (1906, rpr. 1996, edited by Germaine Warkentin) and *The burnt offering* (1909; rpr. 1979), deal with imperialism on another front: the challenge to British rule created by the rise of militant Indian nationalism. Both books show increased sympathy towards the Indian character, and venture upon daring interracial subjects, though melodrama prevails in the end. *The consort* (1912; rpr. 1979), about British politics, is far less penetrating than its Canadian and Indian counterparts. Duncan's final novels—*His royal happiness* (1914), *Title clear* (1922), and *The gold cure* (1924)—rework the international theme in uninspired ways. In her final decade Duncan made dogged, but sadly unimpressive, efforts to become a successful playwright.

Duncan also wrote two autobiographical works. *On the other side of the latch* (American title, *The crow's nest*, 1901) describes, with both evasion and sincere emotion, a bout with tuberculosis after Duncan and her husband moved to Simla; it also contains perceptive, often acid, analyses of Simla's social conventions. In a lighter vein, the recently discovered autobiographical work *Two in a flat* (1908) contains interesting information about Duncan's sojourns in Kensington. Simla is the setting for 'An impossible ideal', the most impressive work in Duncan's short-story collection *The pool in the desert* (1903; rpr. 1984, with an introduction by Rosemary SULLIVAN). The title story's theme is the stultifying effect of a conformist society on the development of an artist.

The 1996 Tausky edition of *The imperialist*, already mentioned, also contains ten essays, five reprinted and five commissioned, along with notes, reviews, and Duncan's letters about the novel. Nearly thirty articles have been written in the same number of years about *The imperialist*. Tausky wrote the first full-length critical study, *Sara Jeannette Duncan: novelist of empire* (1980), and edited a selection of Duncan's journalism (1978). Misao Dean's *A different point of view: Sara Jeannette Duncan* (1991) is a another critical study. Marian Fowler's *Redney: a life of Sara Jeannette Duncan* (1983) contains important new information, and a lively portrait of the author.

THOMAS E. TAUSKY

Dunlop, William 'Tiger'. See NATURE WRITING IN ENGLISH: 1 and Writing in ONTARIO: 1.

Duplessis, Marie-Andrée Regnard. See Writing in NEW FRANCE: 2.

Dupuis-Déris, François. See NOVELS IN FRENCH 1983 TO 1996: 5.

Durkin, Douglas Leader (1884-1968). Raised on a farm in Ontario, he left with his family to homestead in the Swan River area of Manitoba, travelling beyond the railway with a 'prairie schooner' drawn by oxen. After studying philosophy and English at the University of Manitoba (B.A., 1908), he was a high-school principal in Carman, Manitoba, then taught for four years at Brandon College. He was with the English department of the University of Manitoba (1915-22), though on leave of absence from 1920 to 1922, before leaving Canada, probably in 1921, for New York, where Martha OSTENSO joined him. For three years he gave a course on 'The technique of the novel' at Columbia University. It is now thought that the novels published under Ostenso's name were co-authored by Durkin, although *Wild geese* is considered to be primarily Ostenso's work. In 1931 Durkin and Ostenso moved to Gull Lake, Minnesota; they married in 1945 and moved to Seattle in 1963. Writing both under his own name and under the pseudonym 'Conrad North', Durkin published poetry, novels, short stories, and serial novels, and co-authored a screenplay.

His novel *The magpie* (1923; rpr. 1974), which can be associated with the tradition of prairie realism, is set in Winnipeg and environs: it opens in July 1919, the year of the Winnipeg General Strike. Its hero, nicknamed 'The magpie', has just returned from fighting in the Great War and has resumed working at the grain exchange, where his honesty is seen as something of an amusing quirk. Characters differ about whether post-war society should re-establish pre-war conditions or look to new aims. The hero's initial desire for reform abates and then reasserts itself; he is finally driven temporarily to madness when his work and his marriage both fail. Regarded as a valuable depiction of post-First-World-War conditions, *The magpie* contributed to the movement towards realism, particularly urban realism, in Canadian fiction.

Durkin's other novels are *The heart of Cherry McBain* (1919), a sentimental romance set in the Swan River area, and *The Lobstick Trail: a romance of Northern Manitoba* (1921), set in The Pas and environs, in which characters appreciate the land primarily either as a home or for the exploitation of its resources. *Mr Gumble sits up* (1930) is a novel of black humour in which Mr Gumble awakens to find himself in his coffin and discovers that his fellow villagers, having mistaken him for dead, have settled his accounts and are no longer willing to acknowledge him. He leaves his village, meets a series of weird characters, and has inordinately strange adventures. Durkin also published *The fighting men of Canada* (1918), a collection of poems in which war is seen as marking the threshold of a new era.

For further discussion of *The magpie*, see Peter E. Rider's introduction to the 1974 reprint in the Social History of Canada series, and David Arnason's unpublished Ph.D. thesis, 'The development of prairie realism' (University of New Brunswick, 1980).

JOY KUROPATWA

Dussault, Louisette. See DRAMA IN FRENCH 1948 TO 1981: 4.

E

Eaton, Arthur Wentworth Hamilton (1849-1937). Born in Kentville, Nova Scotia, he attended Acadia College, Wolfville, before completing his studies in Massachusetts at Newton Theological Seminary and Harvard University. He was ordained in the Protestant Episcopal Church in 1885 and served a year in parish work in Boston. He then moved to New York, where he was head of the English department at the Cutler School until 1907. After his retirement from teaching, Eaton lived in Boston as a clergyman and littérateur while researching and writing historical accounts of his native province.

Eaton's poetry, with its evocative glimpses of the French and Indian era in Acadian history, first appeared in *Acadian legends and lyrics* (London, 1889) and was reviewed as belonging to a Longfellow tradition. Apart from the historic glamour and musical emphasis of Eaton's verse, it is an independent, not a derivative, creation. The lyrics are simple, sensuous, and frankly nostalgic rather than passionate. A few poems from this first volume reappear in *Acadian ballads and DeSoto's last dream* (1905). The 'ballads' masterfully evoke a full pageant of history, from the earliest times of the French régime to the coming of the Planters, the refugee fleet of John Howe, and the Loyalists; however, they tend to deal with the pictorial surface of powdered wigs and dress swords rather than with how the immigrants felt. Eaton's *Poems of the Christian year* (1905) contains sturdy religious verses remarkable for their restrained yet hopeful feeling, if not for novelty of expression. *The lotus of the Nile and other poems* (1907) completes the early cycle of poetry books, and *Acadian ballads and lyrics in many moods* (1930) brought together his best work.

Eaton co-authored with C.L. Betts *Tales of a garrison town* (New York, 1892), a volume of moral and satirical sketches of Halifax society. His best literary effort in later life was his biography, *The famous Mather Byles, the noted Boston Tory preacher, poet and wit, 1707-1788* (1914), a memorable portrait of the elder Byles portrayed against the anxious literary and intellectual background of Revolutionary Boston; it is supplemented with an account of the lives of Byles' children, including Mather Byles the younger, a Loyalist cleric who lived in Halifax and Saint John.

Eaton's *History of King's County, Nova Scotia* (1910) was his most impressive single historical work. It was followed by other studies of eighteenth-century Nova Scotia and the New England origins of its settlers that appeared in periodicals, notably *Americana*, between 1913 and 1915. KEN MacKINNON

Eaton, Edith Maud (1865-1914). She was born in England, daughter of an English-educated Chinese mother, Grace Trefusius, and an English father, Edward Eaton. At the age of seven she immigrated with her family to Montreal. A stenographer, then a freelance writer for local newspapers, she moved in about 1900 to the West Coast, thereafter living in Los Angeles, San Francisco, and Seattle, with trips east to Montreal and Boston. Making the acquaintance of the Chinese communities, Eaton—using the pseudonym Sui Sin Far—wrote articles and stories effectively criticizing social and political prejudice against Chinese immigrants and Eurasians. Her stories were collected in *Mrs. Spring Fragrance* (1908). She may be considered the first North American of Chinese extraction to write realistically and convincingly of the difficulties and prejudices encountered by the Chinese in North America. On her death the Chinese community of Montreal erected a monument in her honour.

See Lorraine McMullen, 'Double colonization: femininity and ethnicity in the writings of Edith Eaton', in *Geoffrey Davis*, ed., *Crisis and creativity in the new literatures in English Canada* (1990). LORRAINE McMULLEN

Eccles, W.J. (b.1917). Willam John Eccles was born in Thirsk, Yorkshire, England, and came to Canada in 1928. He served in the RCAF/RAF (1941-5) before attending MacDonald College and McGill University (B.A., 1949; M.A., 1951; Ph.D., 1955), and the Sorbonne, Paris (1951-2). After teaching at the universities of Manitoba and Alberta, he joined the history department of the University of Toronto as professor in 1963, retiring in 1983. The foremost anglo-Canadian historian of the French regime in Canada, Eccles succeeded in breaking the grip on the anglophone imagination held by American romantic historian Francis Parkman. Inconoclasm, sometimes to the point of contrariness, and the ability to relate and describe vividly distant events and societies, brought attention to Eccles' writing.

The publication of *Frontenac: the courtier governor* (1959), his revised doctoral dissertation, and the only modern biography in English of the famous governor of New France, met with acclaim because Eccles managed in lucid prose to overturn conventional portraits on every major interpretative point. *Canada under Louis XIV, 1663-1701* (1964) is one of the best titles in The Canadian Centenary Series. *Canada during the French regime* (1968) comprises the E.R. Adair Memorial Lectures given at McGill University in 1967. *The Canadian frontier 1534-1760* (1969; rev. 1983)—in the Histories of the American Frontier Series—discusses the fur trade, imperial expansion, and military operations, with particular attention paid to the respective roles of merchants and Natives. *France in America* (1972; rev. ed. 1990)—in the New American Nation Series—is a compressed history of New France, the result of further research. The twelve important essays in *Essays on New France* (1987), written over twenty-five years, are preceded by an interesting memoir of Eccles' career as a scholar. Included is a critique of the once-acclaimed *The fur trade in Canada* (1930) by Harold INNIS, revealing its weaknesses.

TERRY CROWLEY

École littéraire de Montréal. This was a literary society founded in 1895 by Jean CHARBONNEAU and a few young friends who shared a concern for the state of the French language in Quebec, and whose literary tastes ran to the Parnassian and decadent verse of France and Belgium that appeared in Montreal journals such as *Le Monde illustré* and *Le Samedi*. Meeting at first only among themselves, the members engaged in dictionary study; took turns giving talks, largely on literature, but also on education, science and more general matters; and criticized one another's writing. The École presented itself to the public at a literary evening in December 1898. The response was enthusiastic, and several other evenings followed over the next two years—most, like the first, at the Château de Ramezay. This first period in the history of the École culminated in the publication in 1900 of *Les soirées du Château de Ramezay*, a collective volume of writings by the École's members.

After 1900 activity was spasmodic. The École was split for a time by rivalry; it was often kept going by only three or four members, but survived nonetheless until 1925 and beyond. The years 1907-12 were a second productive period. Some names associated with it are those of Charbonneau, who wrote a history of the École in 1935, Albert LABERGE, Charles GILL, and Albert LOZEAU. The periodical *Le Terroir* (ten numbers in 1909) marked a switch to more traditional regionalist themes. In the 1920s, when the group's fortunes again revived, Ringuet (Philippe PANNETON), C.-H. GRIGNON, and J.-A. LORANGER appeared as members, and *Les soirées de l'École littéraire*, similar to the 1900 *Soirées*, was published in 1925.

The École littéraire de Montréal had more versifiers than poets among its members, and its value was more institutional than poetic: it stimulated literary activity, heightened public awareness of literature and, in particular, promoted the poetry of Quebec. In the program of its first public evening, the École acknowledged tradition by honouring the sixty-year-old Louis FRÉCHETTE; but it also paid tribute to modernity, at an evening in 1899, by providing an opportunity for readings by Émile NELLIGAN, the École's best-known, though certainly not most representative, member. The institutional aspect of the École's activity can be explored in the minutes of its meetings, which were published, together with selected correspondence and press coverage, by Réginald Hamel in 1974.

MARTA HORBAN-CARYNNYK/C.R.P. MAY

Écrits du Canada français*, *Les (1954-). Founded in Montreal by a group of writers and intellectuals—including Jean-Louis Gagnon (the acknowledged founder), Claude Hurtubise, Robert ÉLIE, Gilles MARCOTTE, Gerard Pelletier, Paul TOUPIN, and Pierre Elliott Trudeau—this journal began with a statement of intent specifying that it would be a 'collection d'oeuvres libres', meaning that no particular thematic or critical point of view was sought and that it would encourage the propagation of French-Canadian literature of all genres. It has since published many of the leading novelists, poets, playwrights, and historians of Quebec—with occasional reproductions of 'textes anciens' by Louis Riel, Marc Lescarbot, and others. The *Écrits* began as an annual publication: but since 1960 the rate of publication has varied from one to three issues per year (with no publications in the years 1956, 1975, and 1977). Notwithstanding its apparent conservative thrust, it has built a solid intellectual reputation and is the most enduring journal of its kind in French Canada.

CLAUDETTE S. TRUDEAU

Ecstasy of Rita Joe*, *The (1970). A landmark in modern Canadian theatre, George RYGA's drama was one of the first Canadian plays to win international recognition. Following the 1967 Vancouver Playhouse première, it was restaged in Ottawa two years later as the first English-language production at the National Arts Centre. It was performed in London, England, at the Hampstead Theatre Club; at the Kennedy Centre, Washington; and won an award for the best new production at the Edinburgh Fringe Festival in 1973. It also achieved considerable popularity as a 1971 ballet by the Royal Winnipeg Ballet (choreographed by Norbert Vesak), both in Canada and Latin America.

Like much of Ryga's dramatic work, *Ecstasy* presents politics through a psychological perspective. Based on newspaper reports about the deaths of Native girls in Vancouver, it deals with a highly charged issue: the exploitation and degradation of the Amerindian by a supposedly liberal white society. The play presents the history of one such victim—from her childhood on a reserve, through her repeated arrests, to her murder by a gang of rapists—but the chronological sequence is fragmented. On a multiple set, past merges with present in episodic scenes framed by a recurrent courtroom trial. Given eight hours to find character witnesses, Rita Joe searches memories for an identity. A love of nature and family ties on the reserve—berry picking, a lacrosse game, her father's refusal to sell her to a white man whose child had died, her maternal protectiveness towards her sister—are set against the city, where the cement makes her feet hurt. A job in a tire store leads to sexual harassment, the only setting for love is a graveyard. Indicted for vagrancy, shoplifting, drunkenness, assault, and prostitution, Rita Joe receives no help from the uncomprehending or paternalistic white figures who are responsible for aiding the Natives through religion (the Priest), education (the Teacher), or social services (the Indian Centre). Traditional values in the person of her father are too passive to offer a solution. Radicalism, represented by her lover who is killed by the rapists, seems equally powerless. The inherent injustice of the system is embodied in the legal process itself, and through the trial-format, the society that sits in judgement is itself put on trial.

The brevity and dislocation of the episodes, and the juxtaposition of lyricism and brutality, mirror the protagonist's thought processes. The structural impression of a labyrinth, explicitly echoed in the setting, and the circular patterning of repeated actions, represent the *status quo* that imprisons Rita Joe. Social reality, transposed into psychological terms, demonstrates the effect of political oppression on the non-conforming individual in a way that the audience can share emotionally. At the same time, the conventional liberal response is ruled out as self-indulgent romanticism through the figure of a singer, whose ballad rendering of the action is exposed as insensitive cliché. The interior nature of the drama and the repetitive trial sequences, in which all Rita Joe's court appearances merge into a composite image, universalize the action. The protagonist not only represents the plight of Native women in general, but (in intention at least) of many other Native people exploited by the system. This archetypal quality gives the play considerable power.

See Christopher Innes, *Politics and the playwright: George Ryga* (1985).

CHRISTOPHER INNES

ECW Press. It was founded in Toronto by Robert Lecker and Jack David in 1977, after David had begun in 1974 publishing the journal *Essays on Canadian writing* (also referred to as ECW); Lecker joined him a year later. ECW Press publishes a wide range of works, including poetry, dictionaries, cumulated indexes, scholarly texts, and trade books. Titles such as *Hidden Montreal: the unique guidebook to Montreal's sights, sounds, and tastes* and *Christian poetry in Canada* suggest the eclecticism of ECW's roster. ECW Press is perhaps best known for three indispensable scholarly reference projects: *The annotated bibliography of Canada's major authors*, the *Canadian writers and their works* series, and *Canadian fiction studies*, which are among the most widely read ECW publications. Inaugurated in the early 1990s was a set of slim, one-volume biographies on Canadian writers, including Leonard COHEN, Timothy FINDLEY, and Alice MUNRO. American writers will also be featured in this expanding series. Unable to rely on shrinking public funding, ECW Press is seeking a more diversified audience and is distributing its publications to a growing American market. Books that are expensive to produce, such as the art book *After geometry: the abstract art of Claude Tousignant* (1995), are subsidized by trade books on subjects such as health and nutrition.

CYNTHIA MESSENGER

Edel, Leon (1907-97). The son of immigrant parents, he was born in Pittsburgh, Pennsylvania, and raised in Yorkton, Saskatchewan. Edel attended McGill University where, with A.J.M. SMITH and F.R. SCOTT, he became a founding member of the *McGILL FORTNIGHTLY REVIEW* (1925-7). He graduated with a B.A. (1927) and an M.A. (1928); his thesis was an early study of the experimental novel and Henry James, whose unpublished plays were the subject of his D.Litt. thesis at the Sorbonne (1932). In France, Edel held a three-year province of Quebec scholarship and sent back 'Montparnasse letters'—redolent of modern music, the new art, and Paris—that were published in the *CANADIAN MERCURY*. He worked as a journalist for the *Montreal Star* (1927-9); the *Montreal Herald* (1932-34); Agence Havas, New York (1934-8); Canadian Press, N.Y. bureau (1939-41); *PM* (1942-3); and contributed reviews to the *Canadian Forum* from 1930 to 1935. From 1937 to 1939, under a Guggenheim Fellowship, he edited James's plays in Paris. He was drafted into the US Army in 1943 and served overseas as a French linguist until 1946. In 1947 Edel wrote *James Joyce: the last journey* and, after the death of E.K. BROWN, the second half of Brown's *Willa Cather: a critical biography* (1953). In 1953 he was appointed associate professor of English at New York University and from 1966 to 1973 was the first Henry James Professor of English and American letters. From 1971 until 1978 he was Citizens Professor of English at the University of Hawaii. A member of the American Academy of Arts and Letters and a Fellow of the Royal Society of Literature in Great Britain, Edel received numerous awards, including both the Pulitzer Prize for biography and the National Book Award for non-fiction in 1963.

In 1953 Edel published the first volume of his biography of Henry James, *The untried years*. The subsequent volumes were published over the next twenty years: *The conquest of London* (1962), *The middle years* (1962), *The treacherous years* (1969), and *The master* (1972). He later issued a two-volume edition (1977) and a one-volume edition (1985). Edel's biography of James—widely recognized as one of the best biographies of our time—demonstrates the application of theories put forward in 1956 in his Alexander lectures, delivered at the University of Toronto in 1955-6, and first published as *Literary biography* (1957); they were later revised and remain in print as *Writing lives: principia biographica* (1984). Edel also edited James's most important works, among them: *The complete plays* (1949), *The ghostly tales* (1949, rev. 1970), the compiled *Bibliography* (1957, 1972), *The complete tales* (1962-4), the ten-volume Bodley Head edition of selected novels (1967-74), four volumes of letters (1974-84), the two-volume *Complete criticism* (1984), and *Selected letters* (1987).

Among Edel's other publications are *The psychological novel 1900-50* (1955), *Henry David Thoreau* (1969), *Bloomsbury: a house of lions* (1979), and *Stuff of sleep and dream: experiments in literary psychology* (1982), which applies psychoanalytic theory to the writings of Thoreau, Joyce, Eliot, and Woolf. He also edited the three volumes of the Edmund Wilson papers (1975-86).

Edel maintained a lifelong friendship with his fellow students at McGill who, along with him, were associated with what is called the MONTREAL GROUP and became well-known writers. (Edel's 1984 Pratt Lecture at Memorial University, St John's, was published in 1986 as *Memories of the Montreal group*.) He wrote occasional essays on Smith, Scott, Leo KENNEDY, and A.M. KLEIN. For the semi-fictional recollections of his friend John GLASSCO (a fellow expatriate in the 1920s), *Memoirs of Montparnasse* (1970), he wrote a warmly nostalgic introduction. After Glassco's death Edel published 'John Glassco (1909-1981) and his erotic muse' in *CANADIAN LITERATURE* 93 (Summer 1982). He also wrote an introduction to the 1975 reissue of Kennedy's *The shrouding* (1933) and contributed papers to the conferences honouring A.M. Klein (*The Klein symposium*, 1974), Smith ('The worldly muse of A.J.M. Smith', *University of Toronto Quarterly*, Spring 1978), Morley CALLAGHAN (*The Callaghan symposium*, 1980), and Scott ('The young warrior in the twenties', *On F.R. Scott: essays*. . ., 1983). Following Smith's death, Edel's memorial address, 'Arthur and Jeannie: in memoriam'—read at Michigan State University on 11 Apr. 1981—was published in *The TAMARACK REVIEW* 83/84 (Winter 1982). In 1989 Edel gave the first annual Frank Scott Memorial Lecture at McGill: 'Frank Scott and the Canadian literary renaissance' (*Fontanus* III, 1990).

SANDRA DJWA

Edwards, Caterina (b. 1948). Born in Wellingford, England, she immigrated to Canada in 1956 with her English father and Italian mother and grew up in Calgary, Alberta, with many summers spent in Venice, Italy. Her education includes a B.A. (1970) and M.A. (1973) from the University of Alberta, where she worked under Rudy WIEBE and Sheila WATSON. She has taught creative writing in Edmonton. Some early short stories appeared under her married name, Caterina Lo Verso. She became the most important Italian-Canadian writer in western Canada with the publication of her novel *The lion's mouth* (1982), the coming-of-age story of an Italian immigrant woman, and one of the first Canadian novels to combine ethnicity with feminist questions. It is also a novel about the woman artist, for Bianca is not only trying to find her place between the culture of Italy and the geography of Canada but is also learning how to become a writer. The clear, elegant prose of Edwards' fiction is evident in her powerful drama *Terra straniera*, staged in 1986 at the Edmonton Fringe Festival, and published as *Homeground* (1990); it is the first play to deal with the Italian immigrant experience on the Prairies. Her two novellas in one volume, *Whiter shade of pale, Becoming Emma* (1992) have a more complex style, and explore questions of ethnic identity for men and women in western Canada. Her short stories have appeared in many literary magazines and anthologies, in Canada and abroad, and have been translated into Italian. Edwards edited, with Kay Stewart, an anthology of women's life-writing, *Eating apples* (1994).

See C. Dino Minni and Anna Foschi Ciampolini, eds, *Writers in transition* (1990); and Joseph Pivato, 'Oral roots of Italian-Canadian writing' and 'Voices of women' in his *Echo: essays on other literatures* (1994).

JOSEPH PIVATO

Élie, Robert (1915-73). Born in Pointe Saint-Charles, Quebec, a working-class neighbourhood in Montreal, he was educated at the Collège Sainte-Marie and spent one year at the Université de Montréal and at McGill University respectively. With Robert CHARBONNEAU, Jean LE MOYNE, and SAINT-DENYS-GARNEAU among others, he was one of the founders in 1934 of the cultural magazine *La RELÈVE*, writing art criticism for it from 1935 to 1940 and for its successor *La Nouvelle Relève*. He wrote art and drama criticism for *Le Canada* in 1940-1, and for *La Presse*, then did public-relations work for the CBC before becoming director of L'École des Beaux-Arts in 1958. In the 1960s he occupied various government positions related to the arts in both Quebec and Ottawa, and was the first cultural attaché for the Delegation générale du Québec in Paris.

Essayist, novelist, and dramatist, Élie has been called 'one of the first complete intellectuals' in Quebec letters. As a critic he is best known for his numerous articles on the painter Paul-Émile Borduas and on Saint-Denys-Garneau. With Jean Le Moyne he edited both Saint-Denys-Garneau's *Poésies complète* (1949) and his *Journal* (1945), and wrote the preface to the first.

Élie's best-known novel, *La fin des songes* (1950), is an existential examination of solitude and a devoted search for values. It was awarded the Prix David and translated into English by Irene Coffin as *Farewell my dreams* (1954). It has also recently been reprinted (1995) with a critical introduction by Blandine Campion. It is the story of two school companions, Marcel and Bernard, who in their thirties come to question the authenticity of their values and emotions. The first commits suicide, the second, more combative, draws from the failure of his friend the strength to commit himself to life. The writing is graceful and sensual in conveying the nuances of despair. Still Élie's most popular work, this novel was well received when it appeared, though literary historians are less unanimous than they once were about the extent to which it is the seminal novel about 'la Grande Noirceur'. *Il suffit d'un jour* (1957) treats a larger canvas: a village in the process of moving from traditional to modern life, and the pettiness and self-interest that inform people's lives. Elisabeth, the moral centre of the story, is an adolescent who has discovered the need to break with hypocrisy and move courageously towards life. This novel is not as intense as the first and not as carefully dedicated to the analysis of emotion.

Élie's *Oeuvres* (1970) contains two previously unpublished novels, *Les naufragés* and *Elisabeth*, as well as five short stories. Containing also his collected essays and plays, the *Oeuvres* is a valuable document in the history of an important generation in Quebec letters.

SHERRY SIMON/DAVID LEAHY

Elliott, George (1923-96). Born in London, Ontario, he spent his early childhood there, then moved with his family to Toronto, where he received his education and lived for a good part of his adult life. His father, T.R. Elliott, was a newspaperman and the author of *Hugh Laval: a romance of the up country* (1927). As a young man George Elliott took a position for a year during the Second World War as editor of the local newspaper in Strathroy, a small town near London. The landscape, folklore, and ritual there coalesced with impressions Elliott had formed as a boy during summers on the farm owned by his mother's father in Bruce County, Ontario. The result—a magical world developed deftly and hauntingly by Elliott at intervals over nearly twenty years following his residency in Strathroy—was his first book, *The kissing man* (1962), a cycle of linked stories admired both by writers such as James REANEY and Alice MUNRO and by critics such as Clara THOMAS and Dennis Duffy.

In 1948 Elliott joined MacLaren Advertising, Toronto, as a junior copy writer and in subsequent decades rose to the rank of vice-president. His business career at MacLaren's included a ten-year stint as a political adviser. Following a year as senior adviser in the Office of the Prime Minister in Ottawa, Elliott served as minister-counsellor for public affairs in the Canadian Embassy, Washington, then as manager of marketing services for the Export Development Corporation. His experiences and observations, during these and later years, of vastly different landscapes, folklore, and rituals provided material for *The bittersweet man* (1994), a second volume of short stories—urban, urbane, and powerfully ironic. This selection contains stories written during the three decades after his first book along with several new stories written once he settled, for the last time, near Quebec City on the Île d'Orléans.

In what proved to be his final years, Elliott wrote and published the story cycle *Crazy water boys* (1995), a third volume consisting of twenty-five very short, fiercely comic, and poignant stories set mainly in a fictitious semi-retirement home for elderly men somewhere in the Laurentian hills. An allegory of Canadian life in the last part of the twentieth century (as *The kissing man* can be seen as an allegory of Canadian life in the first part of the twentieth century), *Crazy water boys* begins with a memory of Expo 67 and ends, if it ends at all, sometime in the future.

In the mid-1980s Elliott researched and wrote *God's big acre: life in 401 country* (1986), a volume of semi-fictional sketches about rural life, with photography by John Reeves. In the mid-1990s, just before his death, Elliott completed a fourth, as yet unpublished collection of stories that gathers together additional work written during the same period as the selections in *The bittersweet man* and other new stories. J.R. (TIM) STRUTHERS

Ellipse. See TRANSLATIONS: FRENCH TO ENGLISH: 1.

Ellis, Sarah (b. 1952). Born in Vancouver, British Columbia, she was educated at the University of British Columbia (B.A. Honours, 1973; Master in Library Science, 1975), and at the Centre for the Study of Children's Literature, Simmons College, Boston (M.A., 1980). She has written four novels for young readers—*The baby project* (1986), *Next-door neighbours* (1989), *Pick-up sticks* (1991, winner of a Governor General's Award), and *Out of the blue* (1994)—and a collection of short stories: *Back of beyond* (1996). Ellis won a Vicky Metcalf Award for the body of her work.

The baby project, which won a Sheila A. Egoff Award, develops a theme common to all Ellis's fiction—that of the adolescent girl coming to terms with family change. Critics praised her sensitive and humorous portrayal of its protagonist, 11-year-old Jessica, and her reaction to her family's new baby. In *Next-door neighbour*, Ellis explored something she had not encountered in her own reading as a child: the shy female protagonist. Her depiction of 12-year-old Peggy is based on Ellis's own experience as the self-conscious daughter of a clergyman. *Pick-up sticks* was inspired by a radio broadcast in which a homeless woman recounted the series of bad breaks that forced her on to the street. *Out of the blue* concerns the feelings of a twelve-year-old girl who discovers that her mother had another daughter she gave up for adoption many years earlier. The stories in *Back of beyond* contain elements of the supernatural, and demonstrate Ellis's ability to develop such familiar themes as divorce and family violence with freshness and subtlety. KATHLEEN DONOHUE

Emblem Books (1954-62). Publication of this short-lived series of poetry booklets was begun in 1954 in Toronto by Jay MACPHERSON with her own collection *O earth return* and Daryl HINE's *Five poems* (1955). Although Macpherson's intention was to publish only these two brief works for private circulation by their authors, she agreed to publish a further booklet by Dorothy LIVESAY. The press's name was inspired by the emblems (originally linocuts by Macpherson, but redrawn for publication by Laurence Hyde) that appeared on the covers of the first two booklets. The Livesay selection, *New poems* (1955), bore a similar design drawn by Hyde and was edited by Milton Wilson.

Although still not interested in becoming a publisher, Macpherson undertook as *ad hoc* projects three more titles in the next few years: Heather SPEARS' *Asylum poems* (1958), Violet Anderson's *The ledge* (1958), and Dorothy Roberts' *In star and stalk* (1959). Like the earlier titles, each was professionally mimeographed, then hand-assembled by Macpherson. These would have been the final publications in the series had not Macpherson made contact in 1960 with Robert Rosewarne of Ottawa, who owned a manual letterpress and wished to attempt fine literary printing. A brief collaboration resulted in Emblem's two most attractive titles, each containing colour graphics by Rosewarne: Alden

NOWLAN's *Wind in a rocky country* (1960) and Al PURDY's *The blur in between* (1962).

FRANK DAVEY

***Emily Montague*, *The history of*.** See Frances BROOKE.

Engel, Howard (b. 1931). He was born in Toronto and raised in St Catharines, Ontario, whose characteristics have taken root in the fictional community of Grantham in his mystery novels. Engel graduated from McMaster University in 1955, and from the Ontario College of Education in 1956, and married Marian Passmore (the novelist Marian ENGEL) in 1962. He became a producer of literary and cultural programs for CBC Radio and TV. As a writer of crime fiction, he helped found the Crime Writers Association of Canada.

Engel is credited with creating the first truly Canadian private investigator in the figure of Benny Cooperman, a dishevelled Jewish bachelor in his early thirties who lives in Grantham, eats chopped-egg sandwiches, pays weekly visits to his parents, and stumbles upon clues and culprits in a comical way that have led some reviewers to see Cooperman as a blend of Philip Marlowe and Woody Allen. The Cooperman novels are *The suicide murders* (1980), *The ransom game* (1981), *Murder on location* (1982), *Murder sees the light* (1984), *A city called July* (1986), *A victim must be found* (1988), *Dead and buried* (1990), *There was an old woman* (1993), and *Getting away with murder* (1995). Actor Saul Rubinek played the 'gumshoe' in two CBC-TV specials based on the first and fourth novels. *Murder in Montparnasse* (1992) is set in Paris in the 1920s and features a Toronto newspaper correspondent named Mike Ward. Engel has also written a witty and interesting social history, *Lord high executioner: an unashamed look at hangmen, headsmen, and their kind* (1996).

JOHN ROBERT COLOMBO

Engel, Marian (1933-85). Marian Passmore was born in Toronto and educated at McMaster and McGill universities. At McGill in the 1950s she had Hugh MacLENNAN as her M.A. thesis adviser, and this association led to a correspondence that lasted until shortly before her death; it has been published (with most of the letters beginning 'Dear Marian') as *Dear Marian, Dear Hugh: the MacLennan-Engel correspondence* (1995) edited by Christl Verduyn. In 1960 Engel received a Rotary Foundation Scholarship that enabled her to study French literature at Aix-en-Provence, France. She lived for several years in France and in the Levant, where she taught for a while in Cyprus. She returned to Canada in 1964, married Howard ENGEL, from whom she was later divorced, and made Toronto her home. She was very active in the movement to give Canadian writers a collective voice in their relations with publishers and governments and was elected the first chairperson of the WRITERS' UNION OF CANADA.

Of Engel's eleven works of fiction, *Adventure at Moon Bay Towers* (1974) and *My name is not Odessa Yarker* (1977) are children's books. *Inside the easter egg* (1975) and the posthumous *The tattooed woman* (1985) are collections of short stories. The remaining seven fictions are novels: *No clouds of glory!* (1968), which was reissued in 1974 as *Sara Bastard's notebook*; *The Honeyman festival* (1970); *Monodromos* (1973), reissued in 1975 as *One way street; Joanne* (1975); *Bear* (1976); *The glassy sea* (1978); and *Lunatic villas* (1981), published in England as *The year of the child*.

Engel's novels are strongly concerned with the situation of women in society; yet they are not feminist so much as novels reflecting on the human condition from the point of view of women, with a woman in each case as the central character, and often as the narrator. They are simply formed, deftly patterned, and clearly written, and with one exception they are short books. In these respects they resemble much modern French fiction, and there seems no doubt that Engel's study of French literature considerably influenced the form of her writing. Her economy of structure appears at its best in her second novel, *The Honeyman festival*: a brief work in which the unities of time and place are strictly followed, since the plot occurs in a single house on a single night—yet through incident and memory, it presents the tapestry of the heroine's whole life.

Engel's novels can be seen as presenting a gallery of feminine roles in contemporary Western society. *No clouds of glory*—her most irascible book—presents the woman as academic, challenging men in the career world, but also challenging women who take a more traditionally feminine role. *The Honeyman festival* presents a kind of quintessential earth-mother who has passed through a romantic period as actress and film director's lover to enter—loaded with her memories—maternity and marriage. *Monodromos* is Engel's most elaborate novel in a structural sense, heavily decorated with background detail of life in Cyprus that satisfies sociological curiosity rather than one's aesthetic feelings; for this reason it is perhaps the least sharply drawn of all her works. Here the woman is a divorced wife suddenly caught in a spin of insecurity, and moving back—through a surrogate sisterhood with her former husband—towards a renewed individuality. *Joanne* is a novel of less substance than the others; originally written in diary form to be read over CBC Radio, it concerns the woman as wife and mother finding her way to stability through the ruins of a failing marriage. There are no successful marriages in Engel's world.

Bear, which won a Governor General's Award and gained, as well, something of a *succès de scandale* for its daring plot of a woman enamoured of a pet bear, is really a fable rather than a novel in the ordinary sense, and presents the woman as a personification of humanity recognizing and uniting with its animal nature. It has been reprinted in the NEW CANADIAN LIBRARY with an Afterword by Aritha VAN HERK. *The glassy sea* presents the woman as nun, re-entering the world and returning with new experience to the life of religious observance and service. If *Bear* shows humanity's need to recognize oneness with the natural world, *The glassy sea* shows how the spiritual life can give meaning to the brutal chaos of existence. It is perhaps Engel's best novel, beautifully concise and exemplary in the way every word tells and adds. The compassion, lyricism, and resonance of prose that underlie all Engel's novels are here brought together in their most powerful expression. *Lunatic villas*, however, can best be described (in the sense Graham Greene used the word) as an 'entertainment' rather than a novel. The story of the adventures of a haphazardly united family led by a single parent, it is a vacation into farce, whereas Engel's talent is for *la comédie humaine*.

Though Engel had an unusual gift for imaginative and truthful characterization, her prose style, with its excellent simplicity and perfect pitch, may well have been her prime virtue as a writer.

See *Room of One's Own* (1984), a special issue on Marian Engel; and NOVELS IN ENGLISH 1960 TO 1982: 3. GEORGE WOODCOCK

***English patient*, The** (1992). Michael ONDAATJE's best-known novel secured his international reputation by being named co-winner of the Booker Prize. It also won a Governor General's Award (his third). Though not, strictly speaking, a sequel to *In the skin of a lion* (1987), it features two of its characters, Hana Lewis and the thief David Caravaggio, and refers to two others, Clara and Patrick Lewis; the latter's death in wartime France is described near the end. It also resembles its predecessor by organizing its plot around a mystery story—the identity of the eponymous 'English patient'—and by being structured around two counterpointed and interwoven narratives. One is set in the novel's present, a Tuscan villa in the closing days of the Second World War; the other, a few years earlier in Cairo and the deserts of North Africa. The latter is particularly memorable for poetic descriptions of the desert landscape. In the former, Hana nurses a mysterious, severely burned pilot, meets the wounded Caravaggio, and has a love affair with the sapper Kirpal Singh, who is working in the area defusing bombs. In the temporally earlier narrative we see the patient, 'probably a Hungarian named Almasy', as a member of expeditions mapping the desert. More importantly, he is shown to be involved in an adulterous love affair (almost an Ondaatje signature) with Katherine Clifton, the beautiful English wife of one of his colleagues. Her death as a result of a plane crash, deliberately caused by her husband, indirectly sets in motion the events that later lead to the patient's presence in a villa forty miles north of Florence.

The English patient continues the engagement with history that was evident in its predecessor. But where *In the skin of a lion*, influenced by John Berger's socio-political fiction, focused on immigrants and working-class life in 1920s Toronto, its successor is more engaged, though not quite convincingly or in any depth, with issues such as nationalism, race, and colonialism. Particularly in the scenes involving Singh, the novel reminds one of 'the Empire writes back' school. The sensuous lyricism of the prose, tell-tale images, the understated, monotoned narrative voice, and temporally discontinuous structure relate *The English patient* to Ondaatje's earlier work; but it surprises by the extent of its quotations, allusions, and references to the works of other artists. Homer, Herodotus, Piero della Francesca, Michelangelo, James Fenimore Cooper, and Kipling provide a complex and sometimes obtrusive set of references that act as an indirect commentary on the two narratives. The use of della Francesca is particularly apt, however, because some of the novel's set-pieces, though beautifully composed and evocatively described, have a curiously static quality.

The English patient was adapted as a film—directed by Anthony Minghella and released in 1996—that won an Academy Award as Best Picture. SAM SOLECKI

Epps, Bernard. See Writing in English in QUEBEC: 3 and NOVELS IN ENGLISH: OTHER TALENTS, OTHER WORKS: 6(c).

Escomel, Gloria. See LESBIAN LITERATURE.

Eskimo literature. See ABORIGINAL LITERATURE: INUIT LITERATURE.

Espinet, Ramabai. See CARIBBEAN-CANADIAN LITERATURE.

Essays in English. In Canadian literature the informal essay (as opposed to literary CRITICISM and other technical essays) is not merely one of those odds-and-ends of writing that defy categorization elsewhere; it is a genre in its own right that holds a central place. Essayists are to be found in every region of Canada; and since almost all of them began by writing for local newspapers and journals, their works provide an index to the tastes, attitudes, and values of the educated élite in Canada, which they helped form for their time.

1. THE NINETEENTH CENTURY. The informal essay continued the tradition that was already well established in England by such works as the *Table talk* and *Round table essays* of William Hazlitt. The common association of the informal essay with conversation is significant, because its best examples display the same skills as those of the gifted conversationalist: allusions drawn from a mind well furnished with the best that has been thought and said; illustration by anecdote (usually humorous or moral); an acute eye for contemporary events (whether social, political, or economic); and a penchant for recollecting past events and for strong opinions—all expressed with a personal flair that depends largely on spontaneity. Indeed, a number of Canadian essays were speeches that were later committed to print, like Joseph HOWE's *Poems and essays* (Halifax, 1874).

Because of the genre's highly idiosyncratic nature examples differ widely, depending on the particular interest and emphasis of the writer. Early essayists range from newspaper economists (Barnabas Bidwell, *The prompter*, Kingston, 1821), to Montreal military officers (John H. Willis, *Scraps and sketches; or The album of a literary lounger*, Montreal, 1831), to Newfoundland Anglican ministers (Philip TOCQUE, *Wandering thoughts; or, Solitary hours*, London, 1846; and *Kaleidoscope echoes; being historical, philosophical, scientific, and theological sketches, from the miscellaneous writing of Philip Tocque, edited by his daughter, Annie S. W. Tocque*, Toronto, 1895). Some, like Tocque and Bidwell, were serious and didactic and paid little attention to literary embellishment. They sought the moral improvement of Canadian society (both men passionately espoused temperance, for example). More typically, others aimed to edify the reader subtly by describing what Willis called 'those occurrences which sometimes jut out from the commonplace. . . . One of those luminous specks in the monotonous gloom of existence . . . that shed a brightened glow of sublimity on the purer attributes of our existence.' Willis's prose is highly florid and his romanticism extremely sentimental, yet he maintained that his was 'the romance of reality'. His reflections and melodramatic anecdotes are usually stimulated by a 'ramble' through nature. In Canada, however, this well-established pastime of the Victorian English gentleman began, almost from the outset, to take on new meaning. Not only were local social and historical patterns (*voyageurs*, Canadian military battles, and monuments) unlike those of England, but the climate struck such impressive extremes that reflections on Nature began to alter. Not surprisingly, many essays took a specific season (especially winter) as their point of departure, and some collections were arranged so that they concluded at a dramatic point in the yearly cycle. Thus John Fraser in *Canadian pen and ink sketches* (Montreal, 1890) offers among his more patriotic historical reminiscences a series of six 'Summer morning walks' around Montreal; and Alexander Rae Garvie in *Thistledown: miscellanies in prose and verse* (Toronto, 1875) concludes his series of essays with 'Autumnal tints'. Some collections, like Robert Jackson MacGeorge's *Tales, sketches and lyrics* (Toronto, 1895), mixed informal essays with poetry and short stories.

By the end of the nineteenth century two main types of informal essay had emerged, both of which can be traced right back to the contradictory impulses found in Catharine Parr TRAILL's collection of letters, *The BACKWOODS OF CANADA* (London, 1836). One was a conservative inclination to preserve the cultural accomplishments of an educated élite; the other was a gradual and increasingly sympathetic exploration of the natural environment encountered by the immigrants. The first impulse found expression in the 'sketch', characteristic of the British gentry of the time, in which Nature produced sublime moods and elevated thoughts. Essayists such as Fraser and MacGeorge attempted to accomplish in words what the artist conveyed in sketching: a brief, personal impression, conventionally but creatively executed. The structure of these essays tended to reflect the 'disorder' of conversation—like the authors on their walks, they rambled—but they were written by educated men who interspersed lines of poetry, or quoted from Shakespeare, the Bible, or the English Romantic poets where appropriate. The second type of essay was more down to earth, offering what Bidwell called 'the philosophy of common life': proverbial sayings, moral poetry, and homespun wisdom garnered more from experience than from books. Here Nature was a source of information to those who studied her. Plainly didactic, such essays arranged material logically rather than through spontaneous association. Anecdotes tended to be humorous accounts of the doings of ordinary folk, as in Bruce Munro's *Groans and grins of one who survived* (Toronto, 1889).

2. THE EARLY TWENTIETH CENTURY. Right up to the middle of the twentieth century the highly civilized 'sketch' continued—the work of men (never women) who gloried in a classical education and were confident that most of the problems of the present could be resolved by applying moral lessons from history and humanist values from literature. Some were decidedly intellectual in approach, following in the tradition set by Howe. The essays in Sir Andrew MacPHAIL's *Essays in Puritanism* (1905), *Essays in politics* (1909), and *Essays in fallacy* (1910), many of which were first published in his *UNIVERSITY MAGAZINE*, were outstanding examples of the well-informed mind reflecting deeply on such issues as puritanism, the arts, Canada's national duty to England, religion, and women's role in society. With more urbanity, Toronto classics professor Maurice Hutton applied Greek thought to modern life in *Many minds* (1927), *All the rivers run into the sea* (1928), and *The sisters Jest and Earnest* (1930). John Charles Robertson (with *Mixed company*, 1939) and Gilbert Norwood (with *Spoken in jest*, 1938), also classics professors, followed suit. In a lesser way Martin Burrell in *Betwixt heaven and Charing Cross* (1928) and *Crumbs are also bread* (1934) extolled the pleasure and virtue of reading; Edmund Broadus in *Saturday and Sunday* (1935) shared Burwell's erudite idealism; and Herbert Leslie Stewart in *From a library window: reflections of a radio commentator* (1940) offered social, historical, political, and philosophical observations.

Perhaps because of his deep attachment to the England he knew as a child, Cecil Francis Lloyd—in *Sunlight and shadow* (1928) and *Malvern essays* (1930)—wrote in a more sentimental and Victorian manner than any of his contemporaries. Others sought to awaken the reader's soul to the eternal verities through descriptive rhapsodies aimed at an elaborate re-creation of mood. A minor essayist in this vein was Arthur John Lockhart, a Canadian expatriate living in Maine, who wrote *The papers of Pastor Felix* (1903). But he was greatly overshadowed by two Maritimers: Archibald MacMECHAN, professor of literature at Dalhousie University, Halifax, and the poet Bliss CARMAN. Both were idealists, and as a result of common assumptions in their classical education they took for granted a coherent world view. MacMechan espoused the absolute values of Christian idealism and negated those of liberal empiricism. He proclaimed his ideas through edifying romantic fantasy in *The porter of Bagdad and other fantasies* (1901), and in reflections on the 'decency principle' of Victorian morality in his miscellaneous collection of essays *The life of a little college* (1914), drawing his ideals from the ethical concerns expressed in mid-Victorian poetry and prose. Carman, however, found no difficulty in accepting liberal empiricism, while finding in Nature a source of inspiration and in Emerson's theory of transcendentalism a compelling version of idealism. His continual search for a philosophic basis for his emotional experiences led him to apply François Delsarte's theories of calisthenics to spiritual ends. It was this odd use of theoretical principles to harmonize the physical and emotional aspects of life, and thereby to achieve mystical heights, that led Stephen LEACOCK to comment: 'The vague and hysterical desire to "uplift" one's self merely for exaltation's sake is about as effective an engine of moral progress as the effort to lift one's self in the air by a terrific hitching up of the breeches' ('The devil and the deep sea: a discussion of modern morality', 1910, in *The social criticism of Stephen Leacock*, 1973, edited by Alan Bowker). Carman presented his theories in numerous books of essays: *The kinship of Nature* (1903), *The friendship of art* (1904), *The poetry of life* (1905), *The making of personality* (1908), and *Talks on poetry and life: being a series of five lectures delivered before the University of Toronto in December 1925* (1926). Neither MacMechan nor Carman was less idealistic than their intellectual contemporaries; but they considered that the direct Wordsworthian experience of Nature would imprint the soul with the best values. For literary allusions they turned more often to Romantic poetry, with its rhythmic mysticism, than to the edifying prose works favoured by other intellectual idealists.

It was inevitable that the mores of a post-industrial society should undermine such a coherent world view, especially since Canada was situated next to the United States, where a utilitarian and materialistic ethic was finding expression in the rising social sciences. Several essayists with a keen eye for contemporary events noted the threat to Victorian idealism and treated it in a variety of ways. One of the first was Goldwin SMITH's secretary, Arnold Haultain (1857-1941), who noted in his *Two country walks in Canada* (1903)—later reprinted as *Of walks and walking tours* (1914)—'The race for success in life is now a scramble. Once the ignoble [uneducated] were handicapped; now all are scratched.' Working for the great continentalist, Haultain was well situated to observe and record, often in detailed statistics, the real state of economic affairs. Nonetheless, Haultain 'in ruminations ... as rambling as my walk', and with liberal quotations from poetry, sought a '"Tête-à-tête" with the Infinite', and argued that more reverence should be shown for classical tongues.

Many essayists downplayed these social and economic changes because their experience was rooted directly in nature or in small rural communities. Their essays touched little upon the effects of urban industrialization. Rather they combined the 'jubilee of the soul', found in the florid romantic essayists of the nineteenth century, with observations on 'rural economy' that were also influenced by their predecessors. Outstanding in this early twentieth-century group is William Hume BLAKE, who in *Brown waters* (1915) combined vigorous descriptive passages with homespun philosophy about outdoor life among the *habitants* of the Laurentians. Blake, like Isaak Walton, found in fishing a perfect paradigm for the contemplative man: reverence for created nature, practical wisdom obtained after long and careful observation of it, and a tendency for thought to arise from deep within, like the salmon to the hook. The effect is 'Edenic', as in Frederick Philip GROVE's mystical encounters with snow in *Over prairie trails* (1922), which describes a sparkling fairyland. But Grove—whose descriptions of the trips he made between Falmouth and Gladstone, Manitoba, are rooted in precise observations—encompassed both rhapsodic and grim experiences of the prairie. In this he was not unlike Blake, for whom nature was no idealized Eden of the nineteenth century. As his title suggests, Blake loved the muddy 'brown waters' more than the shimmering blue. Or, as this preference was expressed by a prolific and popular essayist from the Ontario village of Ekfrid, Peter McARTHUR (author of *In pastures green*, 1915; *The red cow and her friends*, 1919; *The affable stranger*, 1920; *Around home*, 1925; *Familiar fields*, 1925; and *Friendly acres*, 1927): 'I like to keep my feet on the earth—in good Canadian mud—even when indulging the wildest flights of imagination.' McArthur was the first to use the animal anecdote as a vehicle for his 'philosophy of common life'. His essays offer more social observation than Blake's and more humour, and indeed are almost perfectly balanced in their mix of classical allusion, quotations from poetry (some from Canadian poets), and the use of history in recollecting and honouring the efforts of Canadian pioneers. The essays of Newton McTavish are in a similar vein, though somewhat more whimsical and charming: *Thrown in* (1923); later expanded into *Newton McTavish's Canada: selected essays of Newton McTavish* (1963) edited by Ellen Stafford. Two women essayists of this period tended to handle the informal essay personally, emphasizing literary style. For both Nina Jamieson in *The cattle in the stall* (1932) and Emily CARR in *Klee Wyck* (1941), and the collections of sketches that followed, reverence for life and recollections of childhood were central. At the other extreme, in the tradition of earlier historical and political writers like John Fraser, some informal essayists sought primarily to preserve the past through personal recollections of public rather than domestic events. Hector CHARLESWORTH in *Candid chronicles* (1925) and *More candid chronicles* (1928) wrote in a manner that resembled what he called 'vivacious conversation' about politicians and other public figures, deriving his information from recollections of men he knew.

3. THE MID-TWENTIETH CENTURY. This period marked the high point of the informal essay. Two world wars and Canada's developing autonomy stimulated a sense of national identity that transcended the regional associations of earlier essayists. Journals that enjoyed national circulation found a wider and roughly homogeneous audience, united at least by their hopes for Canada. This new perspective was anticipated as early as the mid-twenties by William Arthur DEACON in *Pens and pirates* (1923) and *Poteen* (1926), and by B.K. SANDWELL (1876-1954) in *The privacity agent and other modest proposals* (1928) and *The diversions of Duchesstown and other essays* (published posthumously, 1955). Both men had found an outlet for their informal essays in *Saturday Night*, Toronto, of which Deacon was editor from 1922 to 1928 and Sandwell from 1932 to 1951. Although they occasionally wrote skittishly, like Leacock, their pieces were informed by the seriousness of defining Canada's identity, assessing the nation's cultural achievements, and stimulating national

prowess. On the whole such essays tended to look back nostalgically on 'the good old days', preferring the way things were—when intimate small communities rather than large metropolitan centres were dominant—to the way things are. Sandwell pinpointed this as a recurring strain when he wrote that '*laudator temporis acti*'. 'Things are not what they were' was an enduring aspect of the informal essay. A similar nostalgia informs *Leaves from Lantern Lane* (1936) and *More leaves from Lantern Lane* (1937) by the liberal Christian feminist Nellie McCLUNG. These collections contain the best of her syndicated newspaper pieces: anecdotes, sketches, and reflections—often humorous and usually moral—on a wide range of topics drawn from ordinary life in the tradition of Bruce Munro (see 1 above).

Four essayists who brought out their first collections near the end of the 1950s, and continued to publish for several years afterwards, wrote in the best tradition of the informal essay. Two of them, Robertson DAVIES and Hugh MacLENNAN, practised their craft as intellectuals and humanists. The other two, Roderick HAIG-BROWN and Kenneth McNeil WELLS, continued the more rural tradition through social observation and the cultivation of a close relationship to nature. For his columns in the *Peterborough Examiner* Davies developed a curmudgeonly narrator, Samuel Marchbanks, whose social observations reflected a concern for the arts, a distaste for the bourgeois predilections of Canadians, a belief in humanist ideals, and an insatiable interest in eclectic literacy and philosophical works. Davies collected the best of these humorous columns in *The diary of Samuel Marchbanks* (1947), *The table talk of Samuel Marchbanks* (1949), and *Marchbanks' almanac* (1967). On a more serious level Davies addressed his essays in *A voice from the attic* (1960) to the 'clerisy', by which he meant those who enjoy reading books.

Hugh MacLennan, in a wide range of essays collected from the many journalistic pieces he wrote for American and Canadian publications, chiefly *The Montrealer*, drew on his classical education for standards and attitudes that echoed those of earlier classicists like MacMechan and Hutton. But despite his idealism, MacLennan was no ivory-tower theorist. Political and social observation on a national scale were combined with a wry wit and a deep appreciation of nature to produce essays that 'rambled' towards philosophical, aesthetic, or nationalistic conclusions in *Cross-country* (1949), *Thirty and three* (1954)—both winners of a Governor General's Award—*Scotchman's return* (1960), and *The other side of Hugh MacLennan* (1978). Whereas Davies followed in the path of Leacock and Sandwell, MacLennan amplified and refined the approach of Deacon. Both essayists espoused humanist values in what they observed to be an increasingly materialistic world, and defended traditional modes of education as a means of perpetuating sound values. Similarly, the Scottish immigrant J.B. McGeachy, in *A touch of McGeachy* (1962), combined classical humanism with independent social and political observation in essays for *The Financial Post*, and William T. Allison amused himself in his time off from teaching by writing human-interest editorials for the *Winnipeg Herald Tribune*, where he was literary editor for more than twenty years. His essays were collected in *This for remembrance* (published posthumously, 1949).

Roderick Haig-Brown—a naturalist who settled a farm at Campbell River, Vancouver Island, British Columbia, and later became a magistrate and judge of the juvenile court there—developed the 'Edenic' tradition of Blake. For Haig-Brown, too, fishing was a passion that transcended its practical purpose in *Fisherman's spring* (1951) and *Fisherman's summer* (1959). His first collection of essays, *The measure of the year* (1950), has as its goal the close observation of the seasonal cycle to 'take the measure of each year' and thereby acquire a deeper wisdom than that of any city-dweller. His profound rapport with nature, however, did not induce him to reject books, for reading as a pastime, once the day's chores are done, enhances man's grasp of life's purpose and meaning. But it is nature's patterns that most inform man, and Haig-Brown, like McArthur, used animal anecdotes to illustrate the supremacy of instinct over mere book-learning.

The animal anecdote and the down-to-earth philosophy of common life is best illustrated by Kenneth Wells' popular Medonte essays in *The owl pen* (1947), *By Moonstone Creek* (1949), *Up Medonte way* (1951), and *By Jumping Cat Bridge* (1956). His often humorous accounts of 'pioneering' in an explicitly 'Edenic' setting extol folk wisdom at the expense of modern science. Wells undercuts the potential sentimentality of his anecdotes and descriptions with a sharp eye for realistic detail.

4. Shifts in political, social, and moral values, as well as developments away from the traditional classical education that had nurtured earlier essayists, spawned a new breed of informal essayist in the 1960s. Kildare DOBBS,

in the preface to his second collection, *Reading the time* (1968), expresses this intellectual and cultural shift. Culture, he maintains, is no longer a 'fixed body of experience passed on from generation to generation'; hence there can be no fixed point of view. The common body of knowledge has become so vast that no one mind can encompass it. In addition, contemporary man is a 'nomad' moving literally or figuratively through a world he can never comprehensively interpret. 'I am like a man running for a trolley-car,' Dobbs says, trying to make a pattern out of the blur of sense impressions that bombard him. Hence the essayist is qualified to 'read the time' not by his well-stocked mind, but by his admission of ignorance. The resulting tone is deeply ironic. Dobb's earlier collection, *Running to paradise* (1962), which received a Governor General's Award, consists of reminiscences of an uprooted, alienated, and cosmopolitan life.

The political and cultural observations in Robert FULFORD's *Crisis at the Victory Burlesk* (1968) reflect an equally ironic view of the modern world. Fulford experiments technically, using a notebook style or fractured sentences to reflect his sense that the decorum of the gentlemanly essay must somehow adjust to mirror the disintegration of a coherent world view. Pithy and insightful, his pieces include much material that would earlier have been thought inappropriate for this genre: for example, Pop art, strippers, and moonshots as viewed on television. In fact, like the classical humanists and the 'Edenic' essayists who preceded him, Fulford expresses deep misgivings about the advancements of technology and science. Like Deacon and MacLennan, he turns to a nurturing of the indigenous arts as an antidote. The fracturing of one view into many is actually dramatized by the minor essayist Harry BRUCE, whose Hyde-like persona, Max MacPherson, contemplates Toronto in a sequence of 'walks' (*The short, happy walks of Max MacPherson*, 1968) that seem like parodies of the 'rambles' of the nineteenth-century essayists.

That superlative ironist Mordecai RICHLER wrote his informal essays (*Hunting tigers under glass*, 1968; *Shovelling trouble*, 1972; *Notes on an endangered species and others*, 1974; and *The great comic book heroes and other essays*, 1978) to goad his fellow-Canadians out of materialistic complacency and into thoughtful, creative living. Like Fulford, he included studies of the sub-culture (comic books, movies, and James Bond thrillers) as worthy of philosophical reflection. The essays of Naim KATTAN in *Reality and theatre* (1972), translated by Alan Brown, are cosmopolitan like Richler's, but uniquely so. The sense of alienation that results in irony for Dobbs, Fulford, Bruce, and Richler is exaggerated in Kattan because of an extraordinary cosmopolitan upbringing—part Arab, part Jewish—that allows him to express profound irony through personal reflection. Like the more intellectual essayists who preceded him, Kattan draws on an impressive background of reading and tries to place himself not simply in nature but in more than one perception of Nature.

The appeal of, and the readership for, the informal essay—especially the rural 'Edenic' type—has been greatly reduced by increasing materialism, urbanization, mobility, and pluralism. The essayist needs the sense of an audience with a background and ideas like his own. Nonetheless the predominant characteristics of the genre—its flexibility, and the freedom it offers for idiosyncratic expression—may very well ensure its continuance.

See also HISTORICAL WRITING IN ENGLISH: 5. ELSPETH CAMERON

1982 to 1996. Increasingly in this period, essayists articulated a vision of cultural pluralism, replacing assumptions about a singular national identity with a recognition of the multiple voices and experiences that make up Canadian culture and society. However, familiar anxieties concerning the definition of a national identity persisted, often as a function of uncertainties surrounding the power and influence of a world economy. The essayist's project to explore the relationship of the subjective individual to the objective world was influenced, at this time, by concerns with language itself and its role in the construction of the individual within political, cultural, and environmental communities.

The informal essay was often used for philosophical reflection on the condition of the essayist's culture and society. Such essays were often apprehensive about the rapid proliferation of technology and its unquestioned status in a global capitalist economy. The six essays in George GRANT's *Technology and justice* (1986) extend his arguments about the implications of a 'technological' society, and examine how language is used to naturalize a commitment to progress at the expense of traditional values. While Grant's writing emphasized the continued, if obscured, relevance of such values, the essays, aphorisms, and prose meditations in poet Christopher DEWDNEY's *The secular grail* (1993) suggest the need to seek new patterns of meaning. Dewdney draws together a dizzying range of knowledge, scientific and otherwise, in unique juxtapositions to produce a 'codebook ... for understanding the nature of the massive perceptual and technological revolution we are presently undergoing'. The essays of humanist John Ralston SAUL, such as those collected in *The unconscious civilization* (1995) and *The doubter's companion: a dictionary of aggressive common sense* (1994), advocate doubt 'as a positive force' to expose and critique the hegemony of a 'corporatist' culture. In different ways, the cultural politics of Brian FAWCETT, *Unusual circumstances, interesting times and other impolite interventions* (1991), and playwright Rick SALUTIN, *Living in a dark age* (1991), turned the alienation of the informal essay of the 1960s into a determined interrogation of the passivity and materialism of Canadian society.

The reflections on life and literature in George WOODCOCK's *Powers of observation: familiar essays* (1989) self-consciously recall the tradition of the English occasional essay as they 'combine brevity of form with breadth of reference and speculation'. Also suggestive of the traditional genre are David Adams RICHARDS' personal meditations on national and regional identity, collected in *A lad from Brantford* (1994).

Rudy WIEBE, in *Playing dead* (1989), and John Moss, in *Enduring dreams* (1994), extend the tradition of the nature essay into the Arctic region, where the search for self becomes a mediation between physical and imaginative landscapes, as the essays explore the connections among language, story, and place. Gary Saunders' reflections in *Alder music* (1989) are more reminiscent of the nature writings of Roderick HAIG-BROWN.

Many authors chose the informal essay to comment on social issues and literary subjects, as well as to reflect on their own writing and place in the Canadian literary community. Margaret ATWOOD's *Second words: selected critical prose* (1982) expresses the author's concerns with nationalism, feminism, and human rights. Mordecai RICHLER continued to court controversy and debate in two collections, *Broadsides: reviews and opinions* (1990) and *Oh Canada! Oh Quebec!: requiem for a divided country* (1992). Poet Dionne BRAND's *Bread out of stone* (1994) is a challenging social criticism written out of personal experience.

A conception of the essay as 'antigenre'—characterized, as Carl Klaus has suggested, by its 'freedom from any governing aspect of form' and by its emphasis on the process of writing—became significant for those authors who, influenced by post-structuralism, struggled with the articulation of authentic subjectivity through dominant and systematized forms of expression. Aritha VAN HERK, in *A frozen tongue* (1992) and *In visible ink* (1991), and Robert KROETSCH, in *The lovely treachery of words* (1989), challenged the boundaries of genre and identity to explore the writer's relationship to language, text, reader, and self. Gail SCOTT's use of the essay in *Spaces like stairs* (1989) facilitates a feminist emphasis on 'writing-as-change'. Other authors who have collected their literary and autobiographical essays include George BOWERING, *Imagining hands* (1988); David Carpenter, *Writing home: selected essays* (1994); Miriam WADDINGTON, *Apartment seven: essays new and selected* (1989); Phyllis WEBB, *Nothing but brush strokes: selected prose* (1995); and Adele WISEMAN, *Memoirs of a book-molesting childhood and other essays* (1987).

Cultural journalism continued to be the primary outlet for essayists in Canada. The literary journal *BRICK* is notable for its commitment to the informal essay, and many examples are collected in the *Brick reader* (1991), edited by Linda SPALDING and Michael ONDAATJE. Pieces from magazines including *Saturday Night*, *This Magazine*, *The Idler*, and *CANADIAN FORUM* are collected in the three volumes of *Best Canadian essays* (1989 and 1990, Douglas FETHERLING, ed.; 1991, George Galt, ed.). The volumes are an important index to essayists in Canada, and include work by Harry BRUCE, Sharon BUTALA, Robert FULFORD, Maggie Helwig, Michael IGNATIEFF, and Joyce Nelson.

Two general anthologies appeared in this period. *Far and wide: essays from Canada* (1995), edited by Sean Armstrong, collected contemporary essays organized by theme and genre. *The Canadian essay* (1991), edited by Gerald Lynch and David Rampton, provided a historical perspective on the form in Canada. While the genre continues to be neglected in academic study, anthologies point to a strong tradition of the informal essay as an important record of the cultural and social issues affecting Canadian communities.

See Chris Anderson, ed., *Literary nonfictions: theory, criticism, pedagogy* (1989); and Graham Good, *The observing self: rediscovering the essay* (1988). SHANNON SMYRL

Essays in French. At each stage in its history French-Canadian writing has produced spokesmen who have attempted to characterize the spirit of the nation. Priests from CASGRAIN to GROULX, historians from F.-X GARNEAU to Michel BRUNET, politicians from Papineau to René Lévesque, poets from FRÉCHETTE to CHAMBERLAND, journalists from Parent to Laurendeau, literary critics from James Huston to Jacques GODBOUT, have sought to articulate the experience of being French in North America. Each in his own way, and through his own specialism, has expressed a Québécois vision of the world—inevitably coloured by personality, and by religious and political persuasion. Alongside this tradition occasional sharp-shooters have sniped at the consensus: Arthur Buies, Olivar Asselin, François Hertel (Rodolphe DUBÉ), Paul-Émile Borduas, Gilles LeClerc, Jean-Paul Desbiens, Pierre Vallières, and Jacques FERRON. Yet another spirit has permitted rare individuals to adopt a detached, serene viewpoint, giving us the powerful reflections of Abraham-Edmond de Nevers, Félix-Antoine SAVARD, Ernest Gagnon, Fernand DUMONT, Pierre VADEBONCOEUR, Jacques BRAULT, Fernand OUELLETTE, and Jean Bouthillette.

1. SALVAGING THE PAST. James Huston (1820-54), in the preface to his *Répertoire national* (1848), wrote the first essay on the nature and function of literature in Quebec, sympathizing eloquently with those who sought to publish poetry or essays in the teeth of only a scattering of critical comment, a total lack of outlets for creative writing, and many discouragements. Henri-Raymond Casgrain stamped Quebec culture with the patriotic, messianic character it would conserve for a century; but he was the first to give his essays and travelogues a personal voice and an individual ring. See his *Oeuvres complètes* (4 vols, 3rd ed, 1895-6).

2. THE PRESS AS NATIONAL VOICE. In his short-lived anti-clerical journal *La Lanterne* (1868-9), Arthur Buies (1840-1901) inveighed against censorship and obscurantism in Quebec in limpid, caustic prose that he had learned as a journalist in Paris. His later essays were collected in *Chroniques: humeurs et caprices* (Québec, 1873), reprinted as *Chroniques: voyages etc* (Québec, 1875); *Petites chroniques pour 1877* (Québec, 1878); and *Chroniques canadiennes: humeurs et caprices* (Québec, 1884)—in which Buies sang his ardent love of science and literature and described Canada with poetry and precision. His writing is informed by a vision of freedom and intelligence, a model of humanity that he never tired of propounding. Nineteenth-century prose is made impersonal and, with the exception of the writings of Buies, is short on specifics because of its didacticism, euphemization, and moralizing. This is true of the essays and sermons of Bishop Ignace Bourget (1799-1885), published in *Fioretti viscovili* (Montréal, 1872); of Bishop Louis-François Laflèche (1818-98), anthologized in the 'Classiques canadiens' series (1970); and of Jules-Paul Tardivel (1851-1905), the Kentucky-born author of *POUR LA PATRIE* and an ardent convert to Quebec patriotism. His writings are anthologized in *Classiques canadiens* (1969). Grandiose rhetoric and moral abstractions prevented these writers from ever indulging in confidences or entertaining doubts. Though Abraham-Edmond de Nevers (Edmond Boisvert) left Quebec for Paris, he made in his *L'avenir du peuple canadien-français* (Paris, 1896) a plea for the arts, the sciences, and a modern industrial economy.

At the beginning of the twentieth century good journalism set the pace. Henri Bourassa (1868-1952) in *Le Devoir*, Olivar Asselin (1874-1937) with *Le Nationaliste,* and Jules Fournier (1884-1918), who founded *L'Action* in 1911, set new standards and engaged in impassioned polemical exchanges. Bourassa orchestrated an anti-Empire, nationalist opposition to Wilfrid Laurier, while Asselin took a balanced view of the conscription crisis of 1917. Fournier, who died of Spanish influenza at thirty-four, was described by Asselin as 'one of the sharpest minds and noblest hearts French Canada has ever known'. His essays were collected in *Mon encrier* (2 vols, 1922; rpr. 1965), but he also left his acerbic *Souvenirs de prison* (*Écrits du Canada français*, VII), written after a spell in jail for libelling Lomer Gouin.

3. THE AGE OF DEBATE. While writers like Adjutor Rivard (1868-1945), in slightly syrupy sketches of country life—*Chez nous* (1914) and *Chez nos gens* (1918), combined in *Chez nous* (1919)—were perpetuating Canada's regionalist tradition, a spirited national debate was proceeding on the French language in Canada and on the nature and existence of French-Canadian literature. (Fournier and Asselin had found few signs of a true French-Canadian culture worthy of the name.) Louis Dantin (Eugène SEERS) argued convincingly, and with admirable objectivity, the prodigious talent of his tragic young friend Émile NELLIGAN in the edition he prepared of Nelligan's poems. Marcel DUGAS wrote equally judicious literary criticism—notably in *Un romantique canadien: Louis Fréchette, 1839-1908* (Paris, 1934; Montréal, 1946). Dugas also wrote brief, delicate prose-poems—exquisite essays to which he gave the title *Flacons à la mer* (1923). The language debate was carried on by Henri Bourassa, Jules-Paul Tardivel, Adjutor Rivard, and Lionel Groulx, while Albert Pelletier and Victor Barbeau, in essays of great force and perception that bring the two themes of language and literature together, lift the

discussion to a high plane. The debate can be followed in *Le choc des langues au Québec, 1760-1970* (1972), compiled by G. Bouthillier and J. Meynaud, where the principal texts are anthologized.

The intellectual life of French Canada was also enormously enhanced by the progress made in the 1920s by men of science. Frère MARIE-VICTORIN, a botanist and member of the Christian Brothers, wrote charming vignettes of life in the Laurentians in his *Recit laurentiens* (1919), translated by James Ferres as *The chopping bee and other Laurentian stories* (1925). Filled with minute observation and prodigious knowledge, they are suffused with Christian mysticism. In 1920 the Université de Montréal became autonomous, and the first secretary and director of its Social Science School, Edouard Montpetit (1881-1955), wrote *Souvenirs* (1944), which encapsulates his philosophy of life. Inspired by Barrès, he celebrates the value to the nation of village and river 'poeticized by toil'. He defends the French language, linchpin of French-Canadian resistance and a bulwark for all Canadians against a certain mindless Americanization.

Having basically humanist intentions, all these writers deserve to be mentioned here because they contributed to the refinement of the definition of the Québécois identity, 'a human type incarnate' (Groulx) in the face of the challenge from Ottawa or from the rest of North American culture.

4. THE ANXIOUS THIRTIES. An upsurge of nationalist feeling in the 1930s responded to the growing encroachment of American capital in Canada. François Hertel (Rodolphe DUBÉ) summed up the mood of the time in *Leur inquiétude* (1936)—inspired by *Notre inquiétude* of Daniel-Rops—which with heavy erudition traces the history of philosophical anxiety. Hertel sees Barrès, Mauriac, and Gide as the recent analysts of this state of mind and lists compassionately the causes of mental disarray among young Catholics in French Canada: the dehumanizing influence of the machine age; Americanization, particularly through the growing importance of money; the economic inferiority of Quebec within Confederation; the fears of the francophone minorities outside Quebec; the arid, ritualistic character of Quebec Catholicism; and the anguish peculiar to young French Canadians politically alienated within their own province. He looks to a renewed Catholic spirituality, along the lines advocated by Jacques Maritain, to counter the demoralization of young French Canadians. Jean LE MOYNE, friend of the poet SAINT-DENYS-GARNEAU, shares his heightened spirituality while also mirroring the climate of the time in the memorable essays collected in *Convergences* (1961). Another notable writer of the 1930s, Félix-Antoine Savard, published his reflections in *Journal et souvenirs* (2 vols, 1973, 1975) and *Carnet du soir intérieur* (2 vols, 1978, 1979). His political testament (*Le Devoir*, 6, I, 1978, p. 5) reads very much like the writing of Hertel over forty years earlier: this essay has the same mixture of anxiety and hope, though Savard comes down firmly in favour of reconciliation within a federal framework.

5. CUTTING THE CORD. Pierre VADEBONCOEUR—in his vital essay on independence of mind in Quebec, *La ligne du risque* (1963)—saw no evidence of real originality in Quebec, no real 'sages inquiétants'. The one exception he admits to is Paul-Émile Borduas (1905-1960). *REFUS GLOBAL* (1948), largely the work of Borduas, is a pitiless history of the fear, anguish, and servility that maintained the spiritual and intellectual blockade of Quebec; it called for the release of psychic energy through a new openness to the transcendent forces of modern art. In his other writings—edited by Guy ROBERT in *Borduas* (1972)—Borduas describes his teaching methods and the gradual ostracism that his originality cost him. Pierre Baillargeon (1916-67) shares Borduas's ruthless independence of thought in *Le scandale est nécéssaire* (1962), which is spiced with wicked humour. Believing that the scandal of Quebec was that Québécois had been damned for non-use of their intelligence, he looked to the prestigious culture of France for salvation. Gilles Leclerc swears by Pascal and Spengler in his brilliant and massive critique of Québécois obscurantism entitled *Journal d'un inquisiteur* (1960; 1974). If these twelve chapters—written in an abstract, highly metaphorical, and aphoristic prose—were more concise and more analytical, and had clearer emphases, they would comprise the most impressive series of essays written in Quebec. The *Journal* is a painful critique of the oppression by a hierarchical power, with a monopoly on thought and expression, of a conquered people who have never seen any other solution than patience. The argument is punctuated with refrains that epitomize Leclerc's thought, such as 'la société québécoise manque de contradicteurs'. Leclerc would not give much for the chances of Socrates, Jesus, or Dante had they been born in his province. Other sardonic moralists, who are not common in Quebec, are Félix LECLERC, author of *Le calepin d'un flâneur*

(1961), and Jean SIMARD, whose *Répertoire* (1961) and *Nouveau répertoire* (1965) draw on European moralists, on Simard's experience of small-town parochialism, and on his life as an art teacher.

In an issue of *Études littéraires*—vol. 5, no. 1 (1972) devoted to the essay—Robert Vigneault traces what he calls 'la naissance d'une pensée' in the Quebec essay. Drawing on the writings of men like Jean Le Moyne, Ernest Gagnon, Pierre TROTTIER, and Pierre Vadeboncoeur, he illustrates the way in which Quebec thought—and particularly French-Canadians' reflections on their own personality expressed in their culture—has gradually freed itself from the grips of stifling orthodoxy. The effort this liberation called for can, incidentally, be felt as it betrays itself in the tetchiness and bitter humour of men like Jean Simard and Jean Le Moyne. This emancipation can be traced back to the intellectual vandalism of the 'école automatiste' and the breath of fresh air introduced by the writings of Borduas.

In *L'homme d'ici* (1963), containing influential essays of the 1950s, Father Ernest Gagnon (1905-78) combined insights derived from the teaching of the Church and his experience as an anthropologist. Pierre Elliott Trudeau's collection of essays *Le fédéralisme et la société canadienne-française* (1967)—published in English as *Federalism and the French Canadians* (1968)—shows him and his fellow contributors to *Cité libre* taking up the struggle of intellectual emancipation in the 1950s. Pierre Vadeboncoeur, one of the team that founded *Cité libre* in 1950, shares the independence of mind and the passionate objectivity of his fellow writers. The path he followed, of radical socialist thought and militant trade unionism, from the days of opposition to Maurice Duplessis to public support for the principles and objectives of the Parti Québécois, can be clearly traced in his collections of essays: *La ligne du risque* (1963; 1969), *L'autorité du peuple* (1965), *Lettres et colères* (1969), *La dernière heure et la première* (1970), *Indépendances* (1972), *Un génocide en douce* (1976), *Chaque jour, l'indépendance* (1978) and—the most eloquent of all—*Les deux royaumes* (1978), which contemplates with the clear vision of a child and the sombre realism of advancing years the prospect of a dispiritualized world.

6. BROADENING THE MIND. Other writers of the 1960s who made an important contribution to the essay were Fernand Dumont, Jacques Grand'maison, Pierre Trottier, André Laurendeau, and Gaston MIRON. Dumont offers us calm and lucid reflections on rapid cultural change in his native province in impressive essays contained in *Le lieu de l'homme* (1967) and *La vigile du Québec* (1971). *Une foi ensouchée dans ce pays* (1979), by Jacques Grand'maison, is the meditation of a priest on Christian commitment to direct political action—as a parliamentary candidate. It is a complete reversal of the author's previous position and a departure from his more specifically theological writing. Pierre Trottier, a career diplomat who spent many years in posts abroad, presents himself as an Oedipus returned from exile in *Mon Babel* (1963) and *Un pays baroque* (1979). With elegant clarity and playful detachment he explores, through the medium of universal myth, Quebec's spiritual odyssey and his own. One of French Canada's chief spokesmen and intellectual leaders was André Laurendeau (1912-68), whose life of action as editor of *L'Action nationale* in the 1930s, leader of the 'bloc populaire' in the 1940s, editor of *Le Devoir* in the 1950s, and co-chairman of the Royal Commission on Bilingualism and Biculturalism, gave his writings a sense of urgency and realism. All his moods—from biting sarcasm and polemical anger to serene meditation—can be caught in *Ces choses qui nous arrivent: chronique des années 1961-1966* (1970)—a selection, prefaced by Fernand Dumont, of the editorials Laurendeau wrote for *Le Magazine Maclean*. Gaston Miron's *L'homme rapaillé* (1970) contains essays of 1957 to 1965—eloquent statements of his commitment to poetry as social therapy and a sharp analysis of Quebec's triple alienation: economic, political, and psychological.

Naim KATTAN's reflections on art, politics, language, and religion in *Le réel et le théâtral* (1970)—translated by Alan Brown as *Reality and theatre* (1972)—contrast his native Iraq with Western civilization and values. Jean ÉTHIER-BLAIS—principally a literary critic and university teacher who has published poetry, short stories, and a novel—contributed for many years a regular personal essay to *Le Devoir* and produced a *Dictionnaire de moi-même* (1976), a series of intimate moral reflections in the pure *belles-lettres* tradition—reflections provoked by words such as *amour, bonheur, désir,* and *exil.* Louis-Marcel Raymond gave us, just before his death, his much-admired *Géographies* (1971), containing memories of youth and portraits of friends mingled with descriptive writing. Gérard Robitaille, an expatriate painter living in Paris, describes his quest for self in *Un Huron à la recherche de l'art* (1967); it contains an enthusiastic preface by Henry Miller, for whom he once acted as secretary. A few months spent in France in 1962 were decisive in the development of Pierre Vallières, author of *Nègres blancs d'Amérique* (1968)—translated by Joan Pinkham as *White niggers of America* (1971). Half autobiography and half political pamphlet, this influential book offers glowing portraits of Vallières's friends Jacques Ferron, Gaston Miron, and Charles Gagnon; a graphic description of 'la petite misère' in Quebec; and develops the 'colonial' explanation of Quebec's underdevelopment. Vallières's later essay, *L'urgence de choisir* (1971)—translated by Penelope Williams as *Choose!* (1972)—shows the former extremist re-evaluating political violence and opting for the democratic process and the program of the Parti Québécois.

7. THE ANGUISH OF LUCIDITY. The Quebec essay finds its culmination in writing of fearsome intelligence and clarity published since 1968. Almost without exception the essayists of the 1970s-80s write out of an 'indicible malaise' (Bouthillette), 'silence and anguish' (Brault), 'a sense of shame, servitude and danger' (Chamberland). To write in our time, says Fernand Ouellette, means: 'ne pas détourner la tête d'un temps invivable'. *Point de fuite* (1971) and *Blocs erratiques* (1977) are collections of texts broadcast by Hubert AQUIN or published in journals, principally *Quartier latin* and *LIBERTÉ*. *Blocs erratiques*, overshadowed by Aquin's suicide, underlines the sense of headlong flight, or vertigo, of a taste for nothingness. The Aquin who is familiar from his novels—brilliant, witty, enigmatic, the most frighteningly clever of Quebec's writers—appears in 'Essai crucimorphe': Montreal's Place Ville-Marie, a 42-storey commercial complex with a cruciform plan, becomes a symbol of the ambiguities, the humiliating palliatives, the non-being of Quebec's colonial status. Aquin's most important essay in *Blocs erratiques*, however, is his long reply to Pierre Trudeau: 'La fatigue culturelle du Canada français', a reasoned defence of a tenable nationalist stance.

Disturbingly lucid too is Jean Bouthillette's concise, incisive *Le Canadian français et son double* (1972). French Canadians, he finds, are at every turn on the losing side in the history of Canadian duality; though he concludes by pointing to the French-Canadian instinct for freedom. Bouthillette's essay is a triptych: the first two phases are profoundly negative—demonstrating how prolonged denial of identity destroys the personality and leads to the destruction of self-respect, the internalizing of shame and self-disgust; but the third phase demonstrates the eventual desperate affirmation of hope and freedom.

Jacques BRAULT's collected essays are reprinted with valuable marginal comments in *Chemin faisant* (1975), in which studies of his favourite poets (for example his excellent 'MIRON le magnifique'), essays on criticism, poetry, politics, literature, and language in Quebec, and on 'le délire innommable' of Oct. 1970, appear between short personal statements expressing his open-ended commitment to the process of writing and rewriting himself. *Le réformiste* (1977) is a collection of essays by Jacques Godbout, who expresses his commitment to peaceful change, to the power of literature and the democratic process to transform society, while also warning that the euphoria in Quebec in the 1960s, and the Québécois's sense of 'Notre libération' (the best of the essays), may be nothing more than pipe-dreams. Jacques Ferron is one of the father-figures and 'maîtres à penser' of contemporary Quebec. Tirelessly—in book reviews, letters to the press, and newspaper articles—he made his benign and original presence felt. *Du fond de mon arrière-cuisine* (1973) and *Escarmouches* (2 vols, 1975) contain the best of Ferron's ephemera. His genial erudition, his memory for the fine detail of recent history (his and other people's), his eye for the significance of the apparently trivial, give his texts their specificity; their tone is princely, full of spice and mischief. Ferron tries to put the record straight in the fields of medicine, culture, and public affairs, and we excuse him his injustices, so charmed are we by the way he thinks as well as by the way he writes.

The last two essayists are poets whose prose is charged with mystery and grandeur. Paul Chamberland identifies with 'Terre Québec'—with its anger, despair and bitterness, its determination and its hope—though few of his newspaper essays have been republished. In *Terre souveraine* (1980) he develops the 1960s notion of 'appartenance' (belonging) and asks how the Quebec community can be given reality. Though Chamberland is under no illusions about the precariousness of Quebec's future, nor about the size of the opposition, seen chiefly as a capitalist conspiracy and the power of the trans-nationals, he believes in the possibility of a Utopia—a revitalized democracy, a parish without priests—in which the soul-power of the individual can be mobilized to realize the community's true potential. Chamberland's Utopianism is all the more admirable when one considers the traumas he suffered, chronicled in *Éclats de la pierre noire d'où jaillit ma vie* (1972).

Fernand Ouellette relates a similar oscillation between despair and Utopia—or between ecstasy and gloom—in *Les actes retrouvés* (1970). Here, with an impressive blend of self-awareness and intuition, he retraces the steps by which he discovered himself through poetry, and in the process revealed his compatriots to themselves. This collection of essays contains the oft-quoted 'La dualité des langues', in which Ouellette describes the painful discovery of his linguistic impoverishment caused by his belonging to a bilingual culture. Three other such volumes followed: *Depuis Novalis* (1973), *Journal dénoué* (1974; Prix de la revue *Études françaises*), and *Écrire en notre temps* (1979). The latter contains 'Divagations sur l'essaie', a groping definition of the essayist as 'un être de la divagation et de l'espace ludique' in which the freedom of the essay makes accessible surprising and luminous insights.

The modern Quebec essay is creative, serious, and exploratory—though frequently dogmatic and ideological. Often abstract and highly conceptual, impassioned and lyrical, it is also frequently exciting, offering, at its best, words of destiny. C.R.P. MAY

1980 to 1995. Since the end of the 1970s the essay has enjoyed a remarkable expansion in quantity as well as in terms of thematic diversification and multiplicity of methodological approaches. It at once bears witness to the many-faceted changes undergone by Quebec society and serves as an instrument of sociocultural mutation. Quebec essayists analyse Québécois from all angles, expressing their aspirations, their disappointments and frustrations; values and institutions are questioned. Not surprisingly, the national question is a recurrent theme, and the essay is often used for militant purposes, as in *Un parti pris révolutionnaire* (1983), a collection of articles by Pierre Maheu. Feminists also use the essay as one the most convenient avenues for communicating their points of view and demands. Of particular interest in this regard are *L'histoire des femmes au Québec* (1982), by the group named Collectif Clio; and *La théorie, un dimanche* (1988) by Louky BERSIANIK, Nicole BROSSARD, Louise Cotnoir, Louise Dupré, Gail SCOTT, and France THÉORET.

During this period the number of essays that focus on literature and literary criticism has increased considerably. They are generally the work of university professors. Numerous books, collections of articles and special issues of journals, conference proceedings, and *Festschrifts* have enriched the discussion of literature and its genres. While literary critics and historians in Quebec have not limited themselves to the study of Quebec literary works, as François Ricard's *La littérature contre elle-même* (1985) makes obvious, they have nonetheless channelled the greatest part of their energy into analysing the national production.

Several books appeared on the subject of the essay itself, defining it as a form and describing its practice in Quebec. These include *L'essai et la prose d'idées au Québec* (1985), edited by Paul Wyczynski, François Gallays, and Sylvain Simard, a book that offers an excellent bibliography of essays published in Quebec from the origins to 1980; *Un projet de liberté: l'essai littéraire au Québec 1970-1990* (1993) by Janusz Przychodzen; *L'essai: unicité du genre, pluralité des textes* (1994) by Yolaine Tremblay; and *L'écriture de l'essai* (1994) by Robert Vigneault. Laurent Mailhot, in collaboration with Benoît Melançon, edited the anthology *Essais québécois, 1837-1983* (1984).

Janusz Przychodzen divides the essay into three categories. The first two are the socio-political essay, represented by Fernand DUMONT, Marcel Rioux, Jacques GODBOUT, and Pierre VADEBONCOEUR; and the personal essay, represented by Hubert AQUIN, Jacques FERRON, Fernand OUELLETTE, Jacques BRAULT, Paul CHAMBERLAND, and Gilles ARCHAMBAULT. His third category recognizes the important contributions made to the genre by feminist writers of this period. It includes Louky Bersianik, Madeleine GAGNON, France Théoret, and Madeleine OUELLETTE-MICHALSKA. The following inventory will be limited to the treatment of essays published as books and relating to French-Canadian literature. Collections of essays written by single authors, such as those of Jacques Godbout and Gilles Archambault, are usually mentioned in the entry under their name.

Several collections of essays are organized, entirely or partly, around the practice of literary criticism. These include *Surprendre les voix: essais* (1986) by André Belleau; *La visée critique: essais autobiographiques et littéraires* (1988) by André BROCHU; *Entrée en matière(s)* (1988) by Guy Cloutier; *Littérature et circonstances* (1989) by Gilles MARCOTTE; *Parcours* (1990) by Robert Giroux; *Traverses* by Jacques Allard; *Ouvrir le livre* (1992) by Laurent Mailhot; *Pensées, passions et proses* (1992) by Jean Marcel; *Le proche et le lointain: lectures d'oeuvres littéraires et d'autres phénomènes* (1994) by Claude Lévesque; and *Sas* (1994) by André Gervais. This practice, and the meaning of literature, are also discussed in the form of a partly fictional correspondence between André Brochu and Gilles Marcotte in *La littérature et le reste*

(1980), and between Hugues Corriveau and Normand de Bellefeuille in *À double sens* (1986).

Literary critics and historians—such as Maurice Lemire, who edited *L'institution littéraire* (1986), and Lucie Robert in *L'institution littéraire au Québec* (1989)—have brought to light the multiple facets of the literary institution and its development. Several essays in *Critique et littérature québécoise* (1992), edited by Annette Hayward and Agnès Whitfield, also deal with that subject. The literary institution is seriously questionned by Nicole Fortin in *Une littérature inventée: littérature québécoise et critique universitaire (1965-1975)* (1994) and by Bruno Roy in *Enseigner la littérature au Québec* (1994). It became the subject of a well-publicized controversy between Jean Larose, author of *La souveraineté rampante* (1994), and Jacques Pelletier, author of *Les habits neufs de la droite culturelle: les néo-conservateurs et la nostalgie de la culture d'ancien régime* (1994).

Essayists have pursued research on literary theory and published very interesting books on the subject. Georges-André Vachon, for instance, proposes a theory of art and writing in *Esthétique pour Patricia* (1980), while Pierre Ouellet studies the limits of 'littérarité' in *Chutes: la littérature et ses fins* (1990). Also worth mentioning are *Oeuvre de chair, de l'âme et du corps* (1990) and *Le sens: de la transcendance à l'immanence ou pour une science subjective* (1994) by Jean-Marc Lemelin, *Du stéréotype à la littérature* (1994) by Daniel Castillo Durante, *La recherche littéraire: objets et méthodes* (1994) edited by Claude Duchet and Stéphane Vachon, *Grimoire de l'art, grimoire de l'être* (1995) by Louis Francoeur and Marie Francoeur, and *La discursivité* (1995) edited by Lucie Bourassa.

The practice of reading is a focal point for a number of essay collections, among them *Livre et lecture au Québec (1800-1850)* (1988) edited by Claude Galarneau and Maurice Lemire; *À l'écoute de la lecture* (1993) by Claude Gervais; *La lecture et ses traditions* (1994) edited by Joseph Mélançon, Nicole Fortin and Georges Desmeules; and *L'acte de lecture* (1994) edited by Denis Saint-Jacques.

Essay collections on literature written from a feminist perspective include *Féminité, subversion, écriture* (1983) edited by Suzanne Lamy and Irène Pagès; *Quand je lis je m'invente* (1984) by Suzanne Lamy; *Féminins singuliers: pratiques d'écriture: Brossard, Théoret* (1986) by Renée-Berthe Drapeau; *Writing in the feminine: feminism and experimental writing in Quebec* (1990), in which Karen Gould analyses works by Brossard, Bersianik, Gagnon, and Théoret; *Women's writing and the literary institution/L'écriture au féminin et l'institution littéraire* (1992) by Claudine Potvin and Janice Williamson; and *La passion au féminin* (1994) edited by Claudine Bertrand and Josée Bonneville. Lori Saint-Martin edited two volumes of feminist criticism of women's writing: *L'autre lecture: la critique au féminin et les textes québécois* (I, 1992; II, 1994). Benoît Melançon and Pierre Popovic edited *Les femmes de lettres: écriture féminine ou spécificité générique?* (1995). Gabrielle Pascal edited a volume of essays, *Le roman québécois au féminin (1980-1995)* (1995). Special mention must be made of Patricia Smart's *Écrire dans la maison du père* (1988), which offers a stimulating rereading of canonical novels such as Conan's *ANGÉLINE DE MONTBRUN*, Ringuet's *TRENTE ARPENTS*, Félix-Antoine SAVARD's *MENAUD, MAÎTRE-DRAVEUR*, Louis HÉMON's *MARIA CHAPDELAINE*, Claude-Henri GRIGNON's *Un homme et son péché*, Germaine GUÈVREMONT's *Le survenant*, Gabrielle ROY's *BONHEUR D'OCCASION*, and Hubert Aquin's *Neige noire*. Other chapters are devoted to the poetry of SAINT-DENYS-GARNEAU and Anne HÉBERT, to the study of violence to women in the modern Quebec novel, and to an analysis of France Théoret's works. This study received a Governor General's Award.

Of the critical essays that have appeared on the major literary genres, the novel has undoubtedly received the lion's share. André Belleau studies the representation of the writer in the Quebec novel in *Le romancier fictif* (1980) and Patrick Imbert offers an interesting reading of several well-known novels in *Roman québécois contemporain et cliché* (1983). Janine Boynard-Frot's *Un matriarcat en procès* (1983) and Bernard Proulx's *Le roman du territoire* (1990) propose a new approach to the novel of the land. Denise Lemieux in *Une culture de la nostalgie: l'enfant dans le roman québécois des origines à nos jours* (1984), Agnès Whitfield in *Le je(u) illocutoire: forme et contestation dans le nouveau roman québécois* (1987), Marie-Claude Waymel in *Dissidence idéologique et dissonance romanesque: le roman québécois de 1900 à 1920* (1980), and Janet Paterson in *Moments postmodernes dans le roman québécois* (1990) also explore new grounds. Valuable contributions to research on the genre are collected in *Le roman contemporain au Québec (1960-1985)* (1992) edited by François Gallays, Sylvain Simard, and Robert Vigneault; *Le roman québécois depuis 1960: méthodes et analyses* (1992) edited by Louis Millot and Lintvelt Jaap; and *L'âge de la parole: romans et récits québécois des années 80* (1992) edited by Lise Gauvin and Franca Marcato-Falzoni. The short story has also received much attention recently, as shown, for example, in *La nouvelle: écriture(s) et lecture(s)*, edited by Agnès Whitfield and Jacques Cotnam, which contains a useful bibliography.

In *Les livres parlent* (1984) Claude BEAUSOLEIL offers a short introduction to Acadian poetry and analyses the works of some Quebec poets. In *Exil, révolte et dissidence: étude comparée des poésies québécoise et canadienne (1925-1955)* (1984), Richard Giguère offers a rare study and comparison of Québécois and Canadian poetry. Different aspects of theatre as genre and spectacle are studied in Jean-Marc Larrue's *Le théâtre à Montréal à la fin du XIXe siècle* (1981). Burlesque is the subject of Chantal Hébert's *Le burlesque québécois et américain* (1989).

Research on 'littérature intime'—letters, diaries, and certain forms of memoir—has aroused much interest. Françoise Van Roey-Roux studies this genre and its subgenres in *La littérature intime du Québec* (1983); in collaboration with Marilyn Bazcynski, Pierre Hébert analyses the structure, evolution, and reception of the diary in *Le journal intime au Québec* (1988). Fiction in diary form is inventoried and analysed in Valerie Raoul's *Distinctly narcissistic: diary fiction in Quebec* (1994).

As shown by *Les anges de Machiavel: essai sur le roman d'espionnage* (1994) by Paul Bleton and *Écrits sur le roman d'espionnage* (1994) by Norbert Spehner, literary forms long considered marginal have become the subject of increased interest. The publisher Nuit Blanche has created a series, 'Études paralittéraires', for the study of, in particular, the fantastic, science fiction, and the spy novel.

In *Destin littéraire du Québec* (1982) Gérard Tougas affirmed that Quebec literature had attained its autonomy and had established its own canons, different from those of France. This explained for him the limited diffusion of Quebec literary works in that country and the difference in the critical reception that some of these books have at home and elsewhere in the French-speaking world. In *La francophonie à l'estomac* (1995) Hédi Bouraoui denounces the hegemony of France's literary institution in the French-speaking world. Sylvain Simard's *Mythe et reflet de la France: l'image du Canada en France* (1988) stresses the unchanging character of that image from 1850 to 1914. The relations between Quebec and the United States have also been treated in *Les rapports culturels entre le Québec et les États-Unis* (1984) edited by Claude Savary, and *Le mythe américain dans les fictions de l'Amérique, de Washington Irving à Jacques Poulin* (1994).

Ideologies have been a fertile area for recent research. A ground-breaking work in this field is *Idéologies au Canada français (1940-1976)* (1981) edited by Fernand Dumont, Jean HAMELIN, and Jean-Paul Montmigny. Also noteworthy are *Imaginaire social et représentations collectives* (1982) edited by Fernand Dumont and Yves Martin, and *Histoire des idées au Québec* (1983) edited by Georges Vincenthier. Marie-Andrée Beaudet looks at the sociocultural aspects of literary production in *Langue et littérature au Québec, 1895-1914* (1991).

The question of nationalism and of its influence on literary works continued to find expression in books, such as *Lecture politique du roman québécois contemporain* (1984) by Jacques Pelletier; *Une société, un récit: discours culturel au Québec (1967-1976)* (1989) by Micheline Cambron; *Le roman québécois de 1944 à 1965: symptômes du colonialisme et signes de libération* (1991) by Maurice Arguin; *Margin/alias: language and colonization in Canadian and Québécois fiction* (1991) by Sylvia Söderlind; and *Le poids de l'histoire: littérature, idéologies, société du Québec moderne* (1995) by Jacques Pelletier. The related questions of cultural identity and ideology, and of their respective representations in literary forms, are discussed in *Le roman québécois de 1960 à 1975: idéologie et représentation littéraire* (1989) by Josef Kwaterko, and in *Le voleur de parcours: identité et cosmopolitisme dans la littérature québécoise contemporaine* (1989) by Simon Harel. Having looked at Quebec identity in a continental perspective, Jean-François Chassay wrote *L'ambiguïté américaine: le roman québécois face aux États-Unis* (1995). Marc Angenot takes up the question of Quebec ethnic identity in *Les idéologies du ressentiment* (1996), which gave rise to several heated responses.

The received notion of the traditional conservatism of pre-Quiet Revolution Quebec is brought into question in a number of essays. Marcel Fournier shows in *L'entrée dans la modernité: science, culture et société au Québec* (1986) that the first manifestations of modernity appeared in the mid-nineteenth century, and he analyses the contribution made to this development over the following century by Édouard Montpetit, MARIE-VICTORIN, Georges-Henri Lévesque, Paul-Émile Borduas, and Jean-Charles Falardeau. *Genèse de la société québécoise* (1994) by Fernand Dumont and *Poétique de la modernité* (1994) by Claude Filteau also show the emergence of the modern before the Second World War. The essays in *L'avènement de la modernité culturelle au Québec* (1986), edited by Yvan Lamonde and Esther Trépanier, focus on aspects of this question in literature and other creative arts.

The intertwining of cultural identity and literary expression is taken up by a number of authors who have created a substantial body of work on regional French-Canadian writing. *Les autres littératures d'expression française en Amérique du Nord* (1987), edited by Jules Tessier and Pierre-Louis Vaillancourt, is a collection of essays on this subject; while René Dionne defines the notion itself in *La littérature régionale aux confins de l'histoire et de la géographie* (1993). In *Frontières et manipulations génériques dans la littérature canadienne francophone* (1992) and *La problèmatique de l'identité dans la littérature francophone du Canada et d'ailleurs* (1994), edited by Lucie Hotte, several essays raise the essential question of the quest for identity. Evelyne Voldeng takes a look at a folk hero in *Les mémoires de Ti-Jean: espace intercontinental du héros des contes franco-ontariens* (1994). Edited by Jacques Cotnam, Yves Frenette, and Agnès Whitfield, *La francophonie ontarienne: bilan et perspectives* (1994) collects a diversity of essays, including one on Franco-Ontarian literature by François Paré. This critic has made a major contribution to the study of minority literatures in *Les littératures de l'exiguïté* (1992), which received a Governor General's Award. In *Théories de la fragilité* (1994) Paré studies a series of Canadian authors from across the country. Another important contribution to research on Franco-Ontarian literature is Mariel O'Neill-Karch's *Théâtre franco-ontarien: espaces ludiques* (1992). Acadia has also been the object of critical attention, notably in *Langues et littératures au Nouveau-Brunswick* (1986), edited by Robert Whalen and Henri-Dominique Paratte. Alain Masson has collected a number of articles and reviews on Acadian literature in *Lectures acadiennes* (1994). Francophone literature of the Canadian West is the topic of Robert Viau's *L'Ouest littéraire: visions d'ici et d'ailleurs* (1992). Another important aspect of literary history is studied in Diane Boudreau's *Histoire de la littérature amérindienne au Québec* (1992). Some of Marius BARBEAU's work on Amerindian literature has recently been translated for the first time into French in *Mythologie huronne et wyandotte* (1994), edited by Pierre Beaucage.

Finally, given Quebec's geographical position on the anglophone North American continent, it is not surprising that translation has been the subject of essays. In this regard, works of interest are *Les traducteurs dans l'histoire* (1995) edited by Jean Delisle and Judith Woodsworth; *La sirène et la pendule: attirance et esthétique en traduction littéraire* (1995) by Louis Jolicoeur; and *Le trafic des langues: traduction et culture dans la littérature québécoise* (1994) by Sherry Simon.

JACQUES COTNAM/MARY ELIZABETH AUBÉ

Estuaire. See LITERARY MAGAZINES IN QUEBEC: 4.

Éthier-Blais, Jean (1925-95). Born in Sudbury, Ontario, he studied literature at the Université de Montréal from 1946 to 1948. He then took courses at the École normale supérieure and the École pratique des hautes études in Paris, France. After receiving an Adenauer scholarship, he spent a year in Munich. From 1953 to 1960 he held a post at the Canadian embassy in Paris and then in Warsaw. In 1960 he was appointed professor of French literature at Carleton University, Ottawa, Ontario. Two years later he went to McGill University, Montreal, Quebec.

From 1961 Éthier-Blais regularly contributed articles to the literary section of *Le Devoir*. Many of his elegantly styled and interesting chronicles—in which he freely expressed his views on both French and French-Canadian literature, on the arts and humanities in general, and on politics—were reprinted in three volumes entitled *Signets* (2 vols 1967; 1 vol. 1973). On 7 April 1965 he gave an important lecture on the works of Paul MORIN, Marcel DUGAS, and François Hertel (Rodolphe DUBÉ) that was published in 1969 as *Exiles*. It is informative not only about those writers but also about Éthier-Blais himself, who had much in common with them. *Dictionnaire de moi-même* (1976) tells more about himself and his tastes and dislikes. He became a member of the French-Canadian Academy in 1971. In his inaugural address, published in 1973 with Olivar Asselin's *L'oeuvre de l'abbé Groulx*, he paid a moving tribute to Abbé Lionel GLOULX, whose disciple he was proud to be. He wrote much later *Le siècle de l'abbé Groulx* (1993). Keenly interested in Paul-Émile Borduas, the subject of his Ph.D. thesis (Laval, 1971), he wrote on Borduas and his group in *Ozias Leduc et Paul-Émile Borduas* (1973, with François Gagnon and Georges-André Vachon) and *Autour de Borduas* (1977).

Éthier-Blais wrote four novels: *Mater Europa* (1968); *Les pays étrangers* (1982), which recreates the life of certain Montreal intellectual circles in 1947-8; *Entre toutes les femmes* (1989); and *Minuit, Chrétiens* (1994). His collections of stories include *Le manteau de Ruben Dario* (1974), *Le désert blanc* (1986), and *Le Christ de Brionde* (1990). His collections of poems are *Asies* (1969) and *Petits poèmes presque en prose* (1978), in which the dominant themes are departure, memories, and times past; *Le prince Dieu* (1984), more prose poems; and *Les mères* (1993). He also wrote three memoirs: *Voyage d'hiver* (1986), *Fragments d'une enfance* (1989), and *Le seuil des 20 ans* (1992).

Éthier-Blais was one of Quebec's most cultured and well-read *hommes de lettres*. Literature was his life, and his knowledge encompassed the world. His roots seemed to be mostly in France, however, and in that respect he bore witness sometimes to a search for identity that has been experienced by many of Quebec's writers and intellectuals. Though his style seemed slightly affected and even pedantic to some readers, he was nevertheless one of the best francophone writers outside France. Whether one agreed or disagreed with his views and judgements, they left no one indifferent. JACQUES COTNAM

Étienne, Gérard (b. 1936). Born in Haiti, and persecuted for his political ideas by the Duvalier regime, he came to Canada in 1969 and is professor of linguistics at the Université de Moncton, New Brunswick. Étienne's first novel, *Le Nègre crucifié* (1974), was a best-seller, and has been translated into English as *A shapely fire* (1987) and into German. Considered a canonic example of Caribbean literature, it was the first novel to deal with all the forms of political cynicism and even cannibalism associated with Papa Doc Duvalier. The narrator forgets his own existence in a Haitian jail to analyse the situation of political prisoners and the depression and torture inflicted on them. Rejecting resignation or suicide, he creates a form of ancestral language to build a strong resistance and a new hope for himself and his comrades. Étienne's second novel, *Un ambassadeur macoute à Montréal* (1979), fantasizes about a new version of the Papa Doc regime, which Étienne moves to Montreal. Étienne's other novels—*Une femme muette* (1883) and *La reine soleil levée* (1987)—describe the complexities of social adaptation.

BERNARD DELPÊCHE

Euguélionne, L' (1976). Louky BERSIANIK's novel was a landmark work of Quebec feminist writing when it was first published (she acknowledges Simone de Beauvoir and Kate Millett in the opening) and became an immediate bestseller. It has been re-published twice in the original French (1978, 1985) and twice in English translation (1982, 1996), translated by G. Danis and Howard Scott respectively. The book chronicles the adventures of the Euguélionne ('the bearer of good news', from the same Greek roots as 'evangelist', plus a feminized ending that makes the character a lioness), a sister from another planet, who comes to our world in search of the 'male of her species'. As the name suggests, the book is a kind of anti-Bible, offering an original blend of allegory, documentary, parable, parody, and poetry in chapter and verse. The first of three sections—corresponding to, and parodying, the Old and New Testaments and Revelation—deals with the Euguélionne's arrival on Earth and her introduction to human culture through allegorical tales told by the women she meets. In the second section, she provides a wickedly witty and devastating portrait of the situation of women on this planet. In the third section she emerges from a visit to the 'Great National Storehouse of Preserved Words', where she has studied the writings of men, and tells the women of earth to rebel. 'To resist is good,' she proclaims, 'to transgress is better.' The Euguélionne denounces sexism in language and literature and the discourses of the Western philosophical tradition, and satirically demolishes Freudian and Lacanian psychology. She urges women to seize language and shape it to their needs, and to write themselves into history. HOWARD SCOTT

Evangeline: A tale of Acadie (1847). This lengthy narrative poem by Henry Wadsworth Longfellow is based on a tale of hearsay (which the poet heard from a friend of Hawthorne, who had it from an Acadian woman). It is told against the historical background of the British expulsion in 1755 of the French-speaking Acadians from their lands along the shores of the Bay of Fundy—*le grand dérangement* (as the Acadians still call it), which had to do with the end of a 150-year struggle between France and England for possession of what is now Nova Scotia. *Evangeline* tells the story of an Acadian girl who is separated from her betrothed at the time of the expulsion and wanders in search of him throughout the American Midwest and the Atlantic states, only to find him years later on his deathbed. After he dies in her arms, Evangeline too dies, released from a life of exile and steadfast loyalty that has received no reward on earth. For background Longfellow drew on the work of the French historian and encyclopaedist, the Abbé Raynal, and on Thomas Chandler HALIBURTON's *An historical and statistical account of Nova Scotia* (Halifax, 1829). In his choice of hexameters, and in the characterization of his heroine, Longfellow was influenced by Goethe's *Hermann und Dorothea* (1797), a heartfelt depiction of a young woman's expulsion from her native soil. One of the most famous works in the English language, *Evangeline* appeared in some 270 editions and 130 translations between 1847 and 1947, including a notable translation into French by Pamphile LE MAY (Québec, 1865). FRANCIS ZICHY

Evans, Allen Roy (1885-1965). Born in Napanee, Ontario, he grew up on a Manitoba farm, received a B.A. from the University of Manitoba and an M.A. from the University of Chicago, and did further graduate work at Columbia University, New York. Evans taught English in British Columbia high schools and by 1937 had organized an advisory and marketing service for writers in Vancouver. In addition to writing short stories for Canadian, American, and British magazines, he published one slim volume of poetry and four novels.

Bitter-sweet (1933) is a series of prosaic narrative and expository poems about commonplace misfortunes, revealing Evans as a competent versifier with a bitter but sentimental concern for the wronged and underprivileged. *Reindeer trek* (1935), a fictionalized account of the drive (1929-34) of 3,000 Russian reindeer from Alaska to the Mackenzie delta, effectively sustains the suspense of a journey into the unknown, though characterization is slight and incidents are often implausible. It enjoyed wide popularity both in England, as *Meat: a tale of the reindeer trek (1929-35)* (1935), and when translated into several European languages. *All in a twilight* (1944) is a psychological novel of pioneering narrated from the points of view of a prairie farmer and his wife, an eastern school teacher. In presenting the human costs of pioneer success, Evans carried on the realism of Frederick Philip GROVE, but without the same depth or intensity. In *Northward Ho!* (1947) a young delinquent is brought painfully but swiftly to maturity by the hardships of helping to build the Alaska Highway. The novel is weakened by the contrived resolution of obvious moral conflicts, and by the author's evident lack of familiarity with his setting. *Dream out of dust: a tale of the Canadian Prairies* (1956) is a clear, cold account of a twenty-seven-year domestic war between a tyrannical prairie farmer and his young wife, who longs for something more. DICK HARRISON

Evans, Hubert (1892-1986). Hubert Reginald Evans was born in Vankleek Hill, Ontario, and grew up in Galt. By 1910 he was a journalist in Toronto; he also worked for a time in British Columbia. In 1915 he joined the Canadian army and was wounded at Ypres in 1916. After the war Evans moved to British Columbia, finally settling on the coast. Married in 1920, he supported himself and his family not only as a freelance writer but also as a fisherman, fisheries officer, logger, and beachcomber—activities that greatly influenced his literary subjects and brought him into contact with local Natives, for whom he expressed a strong sympathy in his writing. Evans wrote magazine serials; radio plays; short fiction, some of which was collected in *Forest friends* (1926) and *The silent call* (1930); and three novels. *The new front line* (1927) addresses the basic choices facing a soldier after the Great War; *Mist on the river* (1954; NCL 1973), his best-known book, illustrates analogous choices facing Canada's Native peoples in their attempts to balance their heritage against an encroaching white society. Evans gave his Native characters strong, frequently anguished voices to express their often conflicting ideals of freedom and responsibility. *O time in your flight* (1979), an autobiographical novel, recounts the poignant, sometimes comic, clash between a young Ontario boy and his parents, which finally confirms his belief that his freedom and future lie in far-off British Columbia.

Evans also published four novels for young readers: *Derry, airedale of the frontier* (1928), *Derry's partner* (1929), *Derry of Totem Creek* (1930), *Mountain dog* (1956) [*Son of the Salmon People* (1981)]; and a biography of explorer David Thompson, *North to the unknown river* (1949). In later life Evans published two books of poetry, *Whittlings* (1976), which included most of the pamphlet *Bits and pieces* (1974), and *Endings* (1981). *Mostly coast people: the collected poetry of Hubert Evans* was published in 1982.

See Alan Twigg, *Hubert Evans: the first ninety-three years* (1984); Margaret LAURENCE, 'In tribute: Hubert Evans', *Quill & Quire*, vol. 52, Sept. 1986; and George WOODCOCK, 'Hubert Evans', *CANADIAN LITERATURE* 111 (Winter 1986). KEITH RICHARDSON

Evanturel, Eudore. See POETRY IN FRENCH: 2.

Everson, R.G. (1903-92). Born in Oshawa, Ontario, Ronald Gilmour Everson attended Victoria College, University of Toronto, and Osgoode Hall Law School. After practising law for several years, he took up public-relations work until his retirement in 1963. Everson started writing poetry in the late twenties, publishing then, and during the thirties and forties, in magazines in Canada and the United States. His first book, *Three dozen poems* (1957), initiated a series of volumes of carefully crafted descriptive and reflective verse: *A lattice for Momos* (1958), *Blind man's holiday* (1963), *Four poems* (1963), *Wrestle with an angel* (1965), *Incident on Côte des Neiges and other poems* (1966), *Raby Head* (1967), *The dark is not so dark* (1969), *Selected poems 1920/1970* (1970), *Indian summer* (1976), and *Carnival* (1978).

Rooted in the Ontario and Quebec landscapes he knew, Everson's poetry remained fundamentally the same throughout his career: short and gentle delineations of a horizon, a human being, or a limited action. His vision of life was direct and uncomplicated, his tone matter-of-fact and understanding. Everson was a patient and loving observer of the human condition. Especially in *Indian summer* and *Carnival* he sometimes showed personal discomfort with the contemporary world; more often he was simply content to depict, to find a sudden analogy that captured a person or an incident. Though they abound in allusions to literary and historical personages, the poems seek to calm the reader by establishing a natural affinity and bond between the observing poet and the reader, who comes to see the scenes through the poet's understanding eyes.

Recognized throughout his career as a fine though at times uneven lyric poet, Everson moved in his two final collections, *Everson at eighty* (1983) and *Poems about me* (1990), towards a style of poetry that allowed him the opportunity to balance his concern for a deeply personal present with a sense of greater distance from which to consider a past recollected. DAVID STAINES

Exile (1971-). Founded by Barry CALLAGHAN with the support of Harry Crowe, Dean of Atkinson College, York University, Toronto, the magazine was begun with the intention of making it 'one of the two best literary magazines in the world' (the name of the other, according to Callaghan, remains open for speculation). Callaghan brought with him many of the writers whose work he had supported during his tenure as editor of the *Toronto Telegram* book page: Marie-Claire BLAIS, Yehuda Amichai, Jerzy Kosinski, his father Morley CALLAGHAN, and Irish poet John Montague, to name a few.

As a finely produced literary quarterly that has always sought to emphasize artistic content, from poems and short stories to avant-garde art work, *Exile* has consistently resisted the temptation to pad its pages with what Callaghan has termed 'factual filler', such as critical reviews, essays, and articles, and has focused on introducing leading-edge work by an array of international as well as Canadian writers. Among those Canadians who have found support and a forum in the pages of *Exile* have been Seán VIRGO, David DONNELL, Diane Keating, Jane URQUHART, and David WEVILL. Callaghan has often declared his loyalty to those whose work he believes in with the phrase 'once an Exile, always an Exile'. *Exile* also holds a place of prominence in Canadian letters as a forum for international work, having published Seamus Heaney, Joyce Carol Oates, and such Eastern European authors as Imants Ziedonis and Miodrag Pavlovic. BRUCE MEYER

Exile Editions. Founded by Barry CALLAGHAN in 1976 as a book-publishing extension of the magazine *EXILE*, it has published books by authors such as Sean VIRGO, Diane Keating, Richard OUTRAM, Robert ZEND, and Michel BEAULIEU; David WEVILL's *Other name for the heart: new and selected poems, 1964-1984* (1985), *The poetry of Gwendolyn MacEwan* (two volumes, 1993), edited by Callaghan and Margaret ATWOOD, and *The selected poems of Frank Prewett* (1987) edited by Callaghan and Bruce Meyer. Almost alone among Canadian publishers, it has published a broad range of books of poetry from languages other than French—Serbian, Latvian, Ukrainian, Russian, Italian, Spanish, German, Croatian, Swedish, and Finnish—so that for a small press it is no longer small, having well over 150 titles in print. This broad range, and the literary depth of its publications, reflect the extensive background and broad interests of Callaghan.

BRUCE MEYER

Exploration literature in English. 1. INTRODUCTION. The early English-speaking explorers of Canada were assiduous writers. From the beginning their superiors—whether mercantile or military—required detailed reports on the new land, and many of the explorers' letters and documents describe their attempts to preserve these precious records while they travelled, and to continue to write them despite great deprivation and physical suffering. To 'write down every occurrence', to describe 'everything as it is', was a duty that eighteenth-century rationalism not only applauded but considered a serious philosophical task. Yet the explorers of Canada—men of the factual world, with a great deal to attend to and little time for the imaginative life—felt they had literary skills sufficient only for 'a plain unvarnished tale and unadorned language; all matter of fact', in the words of John McDonald of Garth. Nevertheless, the texts that record their experiences—fur-trade journals, diaries, letters, scientific reports, autobiographies, and treatises—form the earliest record in English-Canadian culture of the confrontation between the rationalist component of the European imagination and a vast and sensuous network of river valleys, lakes, and heights of land that invited far more in the way of interpretation than a strictly descriptive account.

The most interesting and imaginative literary phase of such writing is intimately associated with the exploration of the West and North, after they had been penetrated by the French (see Writing in NEW FRANCE), and with the great period of the fur trade. Its typical published expression has been the personal journal, mingling adventurous narrative and scientific description. The European audience for such writings was a large and well-informed one: readers abroad were as likely to have perused Hearne and Mackenzie and Henry on Canada as they were to have read their fellow explorers on other unknown lands. Many of these writings—for example, those recording purely maritime exploration and the search for a Northwest Passage—are hard to associate with our imaginative literature because they really belong to the colonial history of England. In this entry 'exploration literature' will be defined as those texts produced by an observer who is describing and interpreting for the first time Canadian regions unknown to his own culture and that he experiences as a sojourner rather than a settler. These interpretations, which naturally reflect the bias of the writer's culture, became a part of the accumulating body of explanation that entered into, and shaped, the emerging consciousness of the new English-Canadian culture and assumed an imaginative role in our literary heritage.

Exploration writing is often classed with 'quest' literature; but quests tend to have a mythic shape and a predetermined goal. In exploration writing such a goal is usually announced and may even be achieved (the crossing of the Barrens, the mapping of the Northwest, even the 'ruining' of a trading territory), but the shape of the adventure itself is not predetermined; literally anything may befall the observer, and his obligation is less to mould the account of it according to narrative conventions (though that, of course, sometimes happens, as in Alexander Henry's famous account of the massacre at Fort Michilimackinac) than to observe and record exactly what occurred, usually on a day-to-day basis. Thus there is a definite displacement of the mythic values of the quest onto a scientific and mercantile ethos that insists on the primary value of the strictly factual account. There is a firm rejection of everything 'poetic': all subjective, metaphorical, and visionary perspectives are treated with embarrassment or brisk skepticism; and familiar literary devices such as structural patterning, irony, and verbal play are almost entirely absent. (Ironically, many Hudson's Bay Company men came to Canada as 'writers', which in the terminology of the fur trade simply meant 'accountant'.) In a country without a genuine native idiom, this evasion of the intimidating example of polished literary models produced a genuinely new form of discourse. While saturated with empirical values both scientific and historical, it was closely linked with autobiography and the first-person narrative, and indirectly produced some myth-making elements of a new literature. The chronicle form, and the factual language and open-ended vision of these early writers, contributed to what Northrop FRYE calls the 'documentary tradition' in English-Canadian literature.

The explorer is uniquely a man of one book; the record of his experiences thus becomes a kind of heroic testimony, and was so perceived by his fellows. The man in the field—whether fur trader or scientific explorer—kept a daily log: a chronicle of events, natural observations, and astronomical measurements. This log he wrote up as often as he could into a journal that, if he were a fur trader, constituted his report to his masters. This might be copied out for him by a clerk before it was sent 'home'; and, indeed, by the early nineteenth century such records formed an important means of communication in the emerging culture of the fur trade and among scientific men in London. At the end of his posting the explorer looked forward to consulting his journals (as Samuel Hearne did) and turning them into a narrative that might gain him literary renown.

2. THE EXPLORER-WRITERS. Canadian exploration writing in English emerges late in the seventeenth century from contexts provided by both the personal narrative in Richard Hakluyt's *Voyages* (1582) and the elements of folktale and legend in the popular 'traveller's tale'. It is immediately and definitively transformed, however, by the more

everyday structure of the ship's log. The journals kept by Henry Kelsey (c. 1667-1724), during his years with the newly founded Hudson's Bay Company, clearly illustrate both these influences. *The Kelsey papers* (1929), edited by A.G. Doughty and Chester Martin, include his journal of a youthful journey (1690-2) into the interior, with a prologue by Kelsey in doggerel verse clearly shaped by popular narrative traditions:

Now Reader Read for I am well assur'd
Thou dost not know the hardships I endur'd
In this same desert where Ever yt I have been
Nor will thou believe without yt thou had seen
The emynent Dangers that did often me
attend . . .

This tale in verse is a skilfully told story of which the skeptical and audacious teller is the hero, and its time-honoured form contrasts awesomely with the novelty of the experience; for this youthful Englishman, solitary except for his Cree companions, was the first white man to see the Prairies. In the prose journals Kelsey does not lose his feeling for the shape of experience, as we see when in 1697 he notes 'ye end of a Tedious winter and tragical journal'; but the practical need for a day-to-day record displaces the desire to tell a tale of adventure.

Throughout the early eighteenth century the Hudson's Bay Company hugged the coast, reluctant to send men to the interior as long the Natives could be persuaded to bring their furs to the Bayside posts. But Company factors kept post journals, and James Isham (c. 1716-61) of Churchill went beyond this kind of record to compile in 1743 his *Observations on Hudson's Bay . . .* (1949), edited by E.E. Rich, in which we see at close quarters life in this 'disconsolate part of the world', and, more important, hear the very voice of an eighteenth-century fur trader. Writing in the leisure of a sickbed, Isham describes Cree life and customs, assembles facts of natural history, and editorializes mildly on Company policy. He elsewhere says of a later piece of writing, 'as such is wrote but in a bad Style, I hope it will be Excusable'; but Isham's prose style is the meat of his *Observations*, for he writes as an unselfconscious monologist. The 'dialogues' Isham included to illustrate Native language have the same vividness: 'Friend come I want to trade,' says the Native; 'Presently i am Eating,' responds the trader. 'Make haste its flood I want to be gone,' pleads the Native; 'Presently presently,' says the trader. Andrew Graham (*c.* 1734-1815) strove over many years to compile a systematic account of the Bay area, its fauna, and the life and trading habits of white men and First Nations. Ill-educated and no scientist, Graham nevertheless collected data, from about 1770 onward, with an eye to the needs of the Royal Society and systematized his findings, with the elegance and comprehensiveness of an Enlightenment intellectual addressing his peers, in the ten manuscript volumes published as *Observations on Hudson's Bay 1767-91* (1969) edited by Glyndwr Williams. The same desire to synthesize appears in Edward Umfreville's *The present state of Hudson's Bay . . .* (London, 1770; W. Stewart Wallace ed., 1954), but Umfreville (b. 1755, *fl.* 1771-89) was bitterly angry at the Company, his former employers. Despite his insistence that his style is plain and his tale a true one, the objective goal of the treatise is persistently distorted by the passionate language of polemic. The book's real vindication comes from such chilling passages as Umfreville's terse and melancholy account of the wilderness ordeal of John Farrant, James Tomson, and James Ross during the winter of 1772.

It was Anthony Henday's journey to the interior in 1754-5 and Matthew Cocking's of 1772-3 that produced the model on which most exploration writing about the land itself was to be developed: the daily journal written in the field, with its emphasis on landscape description and ethnography. Both men wrote brief and inexpressive chronicles of the events that befell them, yet even here the individuality of the observer makes itself felt. Travelling on horseback, Anthony Henday (*fl.* 1750-62) notes without much comment a considerable range of natural and human detail; he is at ease with his Native companions and always mentions their dancing and drumming appreciatively. And he confirms his masters' suspicions that the interior is already occupied by the 'French pedlars'. Henday's journal is noteworthy for its account of his meeting with the far-distant, still mysterious Blackfoot, to which 'Equestrian Natives' he, and later Cocking, give the respect due real nobility. By the time Matthew Cocking (1743-99) travelled inland, Quebec was in the hands of the English, and Scots traders were soon to command the interior. Cocking's journal suggests a better picture than Henday's of the domestic life of an exploring group. 'A Male child born. Hungry times,' he notes briefly, reminding us of the groups of women and children who were an important part of exploration culture and, by Daniel Harmon's time, posed a major responsibility for the great trading companies.

Of these shorter narratives, the most outstanding is that of the 22-year-old Peter Fidler (1769-1822), who went to live alone with the Chipewyans (Dene) in 1791-2 in order to learn their language (he ended up dreaming in it). Lonely, hungry, and for a time without trousers, he drifted with the Natives, recording his adventures, the habits of his hosts, and the usual scientific observations in a stream-of-consciousness narrative that is both uninhibited and succinct. Despite the remarkable adversity he suffered, he concludes: 'Upon the whole this has been rather an agreeable winter than otherwise.' Fidler's journal recounts one winter in the life of a young man. Peter Pond's vivid, phonetically spelled narrative, of which only a portion now exists, was begun about 1800, and attempts to sum up an entire adventurous life, of which the major achievement was the discovery in 1778 of Methy Portage, a feat that unlocked the rich Athabasca region to the fur trade. Pond (1740-*c.* 1807) left behind him in the West a legacy of controversy—David Thompson was to describe him scathingly as 'of a violent temper and unprincipled character'—but his narrative (written after a careful study of the travel writing of Baron Lahontan and Jonathan Carver) is full of shrewd humour and rich in human observation. His knowledge of the genre in which he was writing gave Pond a skeptical perspective on the obligation of verisimilitude. As he writes pungently: 'It would Sound two much Like a travelers Storey to Say What I Realey Beleve from What I have Sean.' But in his narrative we see an early attempt at turning the explorer's chronicle of his journey to a larger task: the explanation of a life.

Five notable narratives of important explorations—by Hearne, Henry, Mackenzie, Thompson, and Franklin—share this desire for a more general reading of nature and human experience. These volumes are linked as well by the explorers' portrayal of a common world that, though still unexplored at its periphery, by now had evolved its own society, customs, and history. (Captain John Franklin in 1819 encountered Dene who claimed that as children they had 'travelled with Mr. Hearne'.) Each volume had its origin in a chronicle of daily events, made by a man constantly on the move, and in a detailed record of natural astronomical observations; and each transformed the log-book—a difficult task for an unreflective man like Mackenzie, one of whose letters depicts the writer's block he developed as he tried to turn observed fact into explanatory account.

Samuel Hearne (1745-92) was a Hudson's Bay Company man with naval training who, in 1770-2, on the instructions of his masters, travelled on foot from Fort Prince of Wales to the mouth of the Coppermine River on the Arctic Ocean. Alone except for a constantly changing band of Chipewyan (Dene) companions directed by the Native 'captain' or trading-leader Matonabbee, Hearne drifted as the Natives' hunting habits determined. His goal was to find the sea and certain legendary deposits of copper; theirs was to conduct a massacre of their hereditary enemies, the Copper Inuit. Hearne's *Journey from Prince of Wales's Fort in Hudson's Bay to the Northern Ocean* . . . (London, 1795; Richard Glover ed., 1958) is the first great classic of Canadian exploration, in which Hearne transcended the limitations of Henday and Cocking to produce the archetype of such travel journals. A straightforward account of events as they transpired, the *Journey* nevertheless rises constantly to the challenge of generalization, as Hearne attempts both to report on, and to interpret, the meaning of the changing landscape and the Native life he experienced with such intimacy. Hearne's scientific exploration of this utterly unknown territory (he himself did not yet know its relationship to the Western Sea) was subject to criticism in its day and to ceaseless revision since; but it remains of the first importance. Equally interesting is his picture of human life in the Barrens. Hearne's persona is that of the ideal travelling companion: unassertive, resourceful, capable of great endurance, a comprehensive observer not easily repelled by the unexpected. His richly detailed account of Cree and Chipewyan life is nevertheless a rationalist one, drawn in the eighteenth-century conviction that 'the proper study of mankind is man', as the portrayal of Matonabbee in the character of 'noble savage' suggests. Hearne is urbane, judicious, and often deeply concerned; but he never sees the Native from the inside because of his conviction that his companions, however fascinating, are essentially 'void of common understanding'. This duality leads to an unusual juxtaposition in Hearne's anguished account of the massacre at Bloody Fall, near the mouth of the Copper Mine River; here the rigorously exact description of the empirical observer is coupled with the personal response of a man whose only language of feeling is that of the Age of Sensibility.

Alexander Henry the Elder (1739-1824) represents the entrepreneurial spirit of the Scots and Americans who flooded the Northwest after the fall of Quebec. His *Travels and adventures in Canada and in the Indian territories*. . . (New York, 1809) covers fifteen years of trading and exploration around the Sault and on the Prairies from 1760 to 1776, and it too focuses on a famous massacre (which Henry barely escaped) at Fort Michilimackinac in 1763. It relates in the first part a classic captivity narrative, the centrepiece of which is a brilliant recounting of the massacre, seen entirely from Henry's own point of view. Here the characteristic first-person stance of exploration narrative is even more dramatically restricted by Henry's stress on the helpless narrator's limited knowledge of his situation. The result is a Gothic atmosphere of tension and mystery. In Part Two, Henry is no longer the victim but the genial master of his situation ('despair is not made for man,' he observes at one moment of considerable adversity), and he reverts to pure chronicle in describing his penetration north to Cumberland House and west towards the buffalo-hunting Natives of the plains. Henry's book is of greater ethnographic than geographical value, and it is his very interest in Native life that reveals why, as a work of literature, his *Travels and adventures* divides itself so sharply between the conventions of Gothic and chronicle. When his Native 'brother' warns him in Chippewa (Ojibwa, a tongue he speaks) of the impending massacre, Henry misunderstands because the man's language is so 'extravagantly figurative'. To Henry, the 'occasions of speech' for a white man are 'the records of history, the pursuits of science, the disquisitions of philosophy'. Thus, for him, language cannot lead beyond the data of experience to the intensity of metaphor, which suggests why he took convenient refuge in the Gothic mode to shape the tense experience of captivity, and calmly dropped it to revert to chronicle in describing his travels in the West.

Like Henry, Sir Alexander Mackenzie (1763-1820) of the North West Company was an entrepreneur, but one on a heroic scale. Grasping at once the nature of the interior as a mercantile problem, he made two brief, hard-driving journeys of immense importance. The first, in 1789, was down the river bearing his name to the Arctic Ocean; the second—an expedition of great daring and rapidity—took him from Fort Chipewyan and across the Rockies to Bella Coola on the Pacific coast in 1793. He was thus the first white man to cross the continent of North America. His *Voyages . . . through the continent of North America* (London, 1801) gained him immediate fame, and a knighthood. Mackenzie, clearly recognizing that his *Voyages* could constitute an interpretation, a 'reading' of the vast territory he had crossed, prefaced the daily chronicle of his two journeys with an invaluable systematic history of the fur trade (probably from the hand of his cousin, Roderick McKenzie). The *Voyages* concludes with a 'short geographical view' in which Mackenzie attempts an organized account of the whole of British North America, seen as a geographical and economic entity. He thus built, on the foundation of the field journal, an empirical basis for the first cohesive image of the Canada that exists today. The magnitude of this vision contrasts poignantly with the severe repression in Mackenzie's writing of every level of language beyond the factual. The *Voyages* was revised by the hand of an infamous English literary hack, William Combe. A comparison of the manuscript of Mackenzie's Arctic narrative with Combe's doctored version shows that behind the latter's imperial polish and near-Augustan prose lies a much more terse, unemotive, and often rough turn of phrase. Mackenzie's genius as an explorer in the field lay in the fact that he never stopped to reflect. His narrative (whether in his own rough words, as in the journey to the Arctic, or in Combe's more polished working-up of the crossing of the Rockies) is characterized by an acute tension between the drama of real events surrounding him and his men, and the compression and terseness with which he reports what transpired. Though Mackenzie is a painstaking observer of externals, his trader's eye always measuring and counting, the heroic scale of his exploration clearly depended on the ruthless elimination of other kinds of insight. Against this severe restriction of emotional range is balanced his attempt to portray a single economic significance for territories whose extreme boundaries were still unknown—a visionary insight, given the power in later Canadian culture of economic themes and mercantile values.

It was the imagination and aggressiveness of such Nor'Westers that drew to their ranks David Thompson (1770-1857), who in 1797 left the Hudson's Bay Company, where he had been an apprentice and trader since 1784, to become astronomer and surveyor for its rival—and 'the greatest practical land geographer who ever lived', according to J.B. Tyrrell. In a series of journeys between 1798 and 1812, sometimes accompanied by his part-Native wife and young family, he mapped an area of the West stretching from Fort William to the interior of what is now British

Columbia. David Thompson's *Narrative of his explorations in western North America 1784-1812* (1916: Richard Glover ed., 1962) was compiled in his old age (1845-50) from nearly four-dozen manuscript volumes of field journals, and, though unfinished, reveals the remarkable powers of synthesis that made possible his great systematization of these landforms. Thompson's aim from the beginning seems to have been to impose an autobiographical scheme on the chronicle form of the log, yet make the result a vehicle for wide-ranging though subtle analysis. Thus his rugged but expressive narrative takes us from his youth at York Factory to the moment when at last he 'goes down' to Montreal, with a family to educate and his precious researches in hand. In the course of his chronicle he draws his experiences into large-scale patterns, interpreting phenomena that can be understood only in juxtaposition: the world of the Nahathaway (Cree) and Peigan, the geographical coherence of the Prairies, the challenges and conflicts of exploration on the edge of a fur-trade war. His vision is diametrically opposed to Mackenzie's: Thompson exemplifies the organic and mythopoeic preoccupations of nineteenth-century Romanticism as clearly as Mackenzie represents those of Utilitarianism. Thompson describes himself at one point as 'a solitary traveller unknown to the world'; and reading him we are in the company of an intensely private sensibility that is also very open to the impress of experience. Less aware than Thoreau of the metaphoric complexity in the image of the journal, Thompson nevertheless resembles him in his willingness to unfold almost endlessly the imaginative richness of observed fact, whether in describing the bedevilling northern mosquito, the implications of a river system, or the mythopoeic significance of the exploitation of the beaver.

Finally there is the *Narrative of a journey to the shores of the Polar Sea . . .* (London, 1823) in which Captain John Franklin (1786-1847) described the adventures of the British naval expedition under his command, which in 1819-22 returned so disastrously and with such drama to the Barrens that Hearne had visited fifty years earlier. Franklin's *Narrative* strives for an entirely objective effect, yet it is the most intensely dramatic of all these books. Inadequately prepared, ill-advised, surrounded by suspicious and quarrelling traders, this British naval officer found himself in command of a group often at odds with itself, on a journey that escaped complete tragedy almost by accident. These tensions are vividly expressed in Franklin's need to justify the decisions he took, which leads to an anxious emphasis on the stance of the veracious chronicler; he incorporates into his text long excerpts from the detailed journals of the three other officers of his expedition, men of widely varying temperament and perspectives. The result is not the customary single first-person narrative but a corporate journal replete with unstated ironies that reveal themselves when, with the aid of other documents, we learn of the sexual jealousies, murder, cannibalism, and internal dissension that dogged the group's nonetheless heroic endeavours. Franklin portrays the fur-trade culture with absolute courtesy, yet growing hostility. The conflicts of Hudson's Bay men and Nor'Westers, soon to be resolved in the 1821 union of the two companies, are as disastrous for his enterprise as the conflicts among his own men; but even more important is his despair at what he terms the superstition, apprehensiveness, and irresponsibility of *voyageur* customs, and at the larger mystery of Native life, which he must master in order to retain his command. There is a terrible irony in the moment at Fort Enterprise when the filthy, ragged, and starving officers are at last fed, cleansed, and clothed by the rescuing Chipewyan, and the face of the Northwest discloses itself unasked: 'The Indians set about every thing with an activity that amazed us. Indeed, contrasted with our emaciated figures and extreme debility, their frames appeared to us gigantic, and their strength supernatural.' Franklin's death on another Arctic expedition thirty years later resulted in a mystery that gripped the European imagination for two decades. Of that tragic undertaking there is no narrative—only fragments of evidence to be pieced together slowly by others.

These great explorations by Hearne, Henry, Mackenzie, Thompson, and Franklin were matched in grandeur by the brief but epic journey in 1808 down the near-impassable Fraser Canyon by Simon Fraser (1776-1862). But Fraser has a different significance: he sought both to surpass Sir Alexander Mackenzie as an explorer and to write a journal that would bring him equal fame. The latter he could not do (lacking either Mackenzie's doggedness or the aid of a William Combe), but his extant log—a detailed, factual, and gripping record of one of the most hazardous and, ironically, least profitable of all expeditions of discovery—is perhaps the more interesting for its simplicity. Fraser marks a turning-point in our account because he was strongly aware of his participation in a great tradition of exploration that had ideals of achievement and a conventional form of expression. Furthermore, he was among the first of the explorers to attempt self-consciously to ensure the continuance of a wilderness world that, although thinly populated, had densely wrought links of culture and custom in which Cree and Chipewyan, Scots entrepreneur and Orkney boatman, Métis *voyageur* and Loyalist soldier, lived together. The kinds of settlement envisioned in this world did not extend much past the trading-posts Fraser sought to establish; but as Mackenzie had already surmised, the trading-post was one way of imposing order on territories it seemed inconceivable to manage by any other system.

The intellectual life of the explorers and fur traders was not barren. Some were scientists (albeit self-educated) who eagerly purchased new books in their fields and often read more widely. In 1799 Peter Fidler ordered from England Mrs Radcliffe's *The mysteries of Udolpho* and John Gay's *Fables*, as well as Buffon's *Natural history*. About the same time David Thompson sent for *Paradise Lost* and Johnson's *The rambler*, and John Bird was reading Lucan, Tasso, Pope, and Akenside. The North West Company in particular provided books for its men; F.-W. Wentzel was eventually to describe its Athabaska post as 'formerly the delight and school of the North'. The journal of Daniel Harmon (1778-1843)—published in *Sixteen years in the Indian country: the journal of Daniel William Harmon 1800-1816* (1957), edited by W. Kaye Lamb—is not a travel journal (he explored very little) but a true diary that reflects this intellectual atmosphere. It reveals the inner life of a devout and decorous man of modest culture, living on the borderline between unexplored frontier and nascent community. Harmon was a devoted family man, a passionate gardener, and an assiduous correspondent with gentlemen of the company living at nearby posts. He had a genius for friendship, and the many evenings he spent smoking and talking with fellow traders, who made difficult journeys to join him, remind us of the deepening and solidifying texture of life on the frontier as old kinds of exploration began to give way to new. The heroic scale of the solitary ordeal, however, persisted. Even farther west, Peter Skene Ogden (1794-1854) was to make the rapacious forays below the forty-ninth parallel that briefly linked the learned science of discovery with the scorched-earth policy pursued here in the 'Snake Country' by the Hudson's Bay Company in its intense rivalry with American interests. Ogden's *Snake-Country journals* (1950, 1961, 1971) have some of the terseness of Mackenzie's and Fraser's writings; but their range and detail make them a valuable, if disturbing, portrait of a man of relentless drive, superior organizing ability, and great cunning.

For all these men, great and small, the journal was the primary, the essential, form of utterance, as is pathetically demonstrated by the story of Benjamin Frobisher (1782-1819), a Nor' Wester whose conflicts with certain Hudson's Bay men led to his injury and jailing at York Factory in 1819. Though deprived of pen and ink by his captors, Frobisher attempted to keep a journal throughout his ordeal. Escaping with two companions, he set out across a thousand miles of wilderness to reach safety, though he was starving, half clothed, and often raving from the effects of concussion. He persisted in writing his account of their suffering; when his half-burned body was recovered not far from a trading-post, the pencilled fragments of his journal were at his side.

By the second quarter of the nineteenth century, however, the narrative journal was increasingly displaced by purely scientific description and anecdotal history, though sometimes light was cast on the imaginative life of exploration, as in the *Character book* (1832) of Hudson's Bay Governor Sir George Simpson (1792-1860), which contains superlatively venomous portrayals of individuals and types from trading-post life. The explorer as such was giving way to travellers like J.J. Bigsby (1792-1881), author of *The shoe and canoe* (London, 1850), and exploration was producing its own historiography in three works by Alexander Ross (1783-1856) in which he described the life of the fur trade, and exploration, during the first half of the nineteenth century.

In the late 1850s the expeditions of John Palliser (1817-87) and Henry Youle Hind (1823-1908) were crisscrossing the West—in the words of Hind 'to ascertain the practicability of establishing an emigrant route between Lake Superior and Selkirk settlement.' The hegemony of the Hudson's Bay Company was soon to be broken and the trader to give way to what Palliser called 'the agriculturalist'. Hind's *Narrative of the Canadian Red River exploring expedition of 1857 . . .* (London, 1860) reflects this moment of transition very sharply: the detailed physiographic and ethnographic reportage of the age of exploration is mingled with interviews with the pioneer farmers of the Selkirk Settlement and repeated analyses of the settlement potential of the land; and both are fused in the sanguine voice of a professorial, didactic narrator.

The major development in the study of exploration writing over the past decade has been the recapturing, through a careful study of oral tradition, of Native narratives of contact with early explorers. Robin McGrath has studied Inuit narratives of the massacre witnessed by Hearne; John S. Long has collected narratives of early encounters between Europeans and the Cree of western James Bay; and Wendy Wickwire has worked on Nlaka' pamux narratives of Native contact with the exploring party of Simon Fraser. The increasing respect with which the oral structure of Native documentary traditions is regarded indicates that these studies represent a new wave that will soon begin to readjust the historiographic and literary balance between the Natives of Canada and their conquerors.

3. THE INFLUENCE OF THESE WRITINGS. The imaginative role of exploration literature in Canadian writing is increasingly better understood, for these texts hold the same place in our literary heritage as theological treatises and captivity narratives do in early American literature. Initially a subject for historical study, the explorers have emerged as writers in their own right with the proliferation of scholarly editions of their journals in the twentieth century. Poets like John NEWLOVE and Don GUTTERIDGE have treated the men themselves as mythic figures; or, like George BOWERING and Mordecai RICHLER, have used them to ironize the very notion of myth. But few of the exploration narratives, save perhaps Hearne's, are securely situated in the evolving canon of Canadian literature. Yet with the evolution of the character of that literature—deeply committed to close observation, to local and individual circumstance, and to an ambiguous borderline between 'document' and 'literary work'—we increasingly see links between the imaginations of the explorers and of our contemporary writers, links that suggest how much both are the product of the practical, mercantile, and scientific culture of middle-class men in the Romantic age. Twentieth-century Canadian writing reflects some of the same deep inhibitions about language and metaphor, and shows the same abiding trust in the primacy of the document. The image of the log book or journal abounds, if not as a direct inheritance from the explorers, then as the result of a similar habit of mind that is reflected also in literary analysis, which often employs the image of 'mapmaking' as a term of critical discourse. The map itself has become a central metaphor of Canadian writing, as we can see in the hilarious map made of television sets in Thomas KING's *Green grass, running water* (1993), or the 'great maps of art' in Michael ONDAATJE's *The ENGLISH PATIENT* (1992). And the explorer himself remains a powerful image, as the immense popularity of Stan Rogers' song 'North West Passage' makes clear. Exploration discourse makes its modern appearance in the enthusiasm for autobiographical first-person novels and stories, in the poet's fascination with the image of the 'field note' or scientific observation (Robert KROETSCH, Christopher DEWDNEY), in the way novelist Timothy FINDLEY's narrators struggle to unearth from some infinitely detailed but somehow unyielding documentary account the real significance of 'everything as it is', or in Rudy WIEBE's attempt, as in *A discovery of strangers* (1994), to enter completely into the point of view of the world the explorers met with. It appears in the persistence with which English-Canadian writers adopt the metaphor of exploration to describe the very act of writing itself, a persistence that underlines the perceptiveness of Don Gutteridge when he calls the explorers 'our first philosophers'. Finally, in her poem 'The Discovery' Gwendolyn MacEWEN reminds us that

when you see the land naked, look again
(burn your maps, that is not what I mean),
I mean the moment when it seems most plain
is the moment when you must begin again.

4. BIBLIOGRAPHY. Titles and sources of works not cited above follow: Matthew Cocking, *Journal 1772-73* edited by Lawrence J. Burpee in *Transactions of the Royal Society of Canada* (hereafter *TRSC*), Sec. II, 1908; Peter Fidler, *Journal of a journey with the Chepawyans or Northern Indians, to the Slave Lake, & to the east & west of the Slave River, in 1791 & 2* in *Journals of Samuel Hearne and Philip Turnor* (1934) edited by J.B. Tyrrell; Simon Fraser, *Letters and journals 1806-1808* (1960) edited by W. Kaye Lamb; Benjamin Frobisher: Samuel Hull Wilcocke, *The death of Benjamin Frobisher* (1819) in L.R. Masson, ed., *Les bourgeois de la compagnie du Nord-ouest*, II (1889-90); Anthony Henday, *Journal 1754-55*, edited by Lawrence J. Burpee, in *TRSC*, Sec. II, 1907; John S. Long, 'Narratives of early encounters between Europeans and the Cree of western James Bay', *Ontario History* 80 (1988), 227-45; Sir Alexander Mackenzie, *Journals and letters* (1970) edited by W. Kaye Lamb; John McDonald of Garth, 'Autobiographical notes,

1791-1816' (in Masson, vol. II; see Frobisher above); Robin McGrath, 'Samuel Hearne and the Inuit Oral Tradition', *Studies in Canadian Literature* 18, 2 (1993), 94-107; John Palliser, *The papers of the Palliser expedition 1857-1860* (1968) edited by Irene Spry; Peter Pond, *Narrative* in Charles M. Gates ed., *Five fur traders of the Northwest* (2nd edn, 1965); Alexander Ross, *Adventures of the first settlers on the Oregon or Columbia River* (London, 1849), *The fur hunters of the Far West* (1855; Kenneth A. Spaulding ed., 1956), *The Red River Settlement: its rise, progress, and present state* (1856; intro. W.L. MORTON, 1972); Sir George Simpson, *The 'character book' of Governor George Simpson, 1832* in Glyndwr Williams, ed., *Hudson's Bay miscellany 1670-1870* (1975); Willard-Ferdinand Wentzel, *Letters to the Hon. Roderic McKenzie 1807-1824* (in Masson, vol. l; see Frobisher above); and Wendy Wickwire, 'To see ourselves as the other's other: Nlaka' pamux contact narratives', *Canadian Historical Review* 75, 1 (1994), 1-20.

See also Germaine Warkentin, ed., *Canadian exploration literature: an anthology* (1993).

GERMAINE WARKENTIN

F

Fackenheim, Emil (b. 1916). Born in Halle, Germany, he came to maturity just as the Nazis were securing their hold on the country. After a period of pro-Jewish activity in Berlin, he was interned in a concentration camp in 1938, but managed to escape Germany for Great Britain in 1939, and came to Canada in 1940. He took a doctorate in medieval philosophy at the University of Toronto, and became a professor there, focusing on metaphysics and especially Hegel, at the same time serving as a rabbi in Toronto's Holy Blossom Temple. After his retirement in 1981 he moved with his family to Jerusalem.

In his teaching and writings Fackenheim treated the classic German philosophers, Kant, Schelling, and Hegel, as the culmination of the modern tradition of philosophy, and also as giving the intellectualized expression of Christianity. This interpretation appears in *The religious dimension in Hegel's thought* (1967) as well as in numerous articles and reviews of the 1950s and 1960s, some of which appeared in the 1996 collection *The God within*. The Hegel book treats Hegel's entire *oeuvre*, not just his *Philosophy of religion*, and it is more receptive to Hegel's claims than are the majority of scholarly commentaries, even today. Instead of deflating Hegel's dialectical and speculative thought, Fackenheim emphasizes Hegel's success in mediating historical with logical thinking, surmounting Kant's division between the speculative and the practical, reconciling empiricism with rationalism, uniting moral with political thought, and overreaching the gulf that divides the religious from the secular. But Fackenheim shows that this philosophical success was predicated upon Hegel's conviction that, with the coming of Christ and the Spirit, all existence had been redeemed. Though he treats it with respect, Fackenheim cannot endorse this conviction. And in most of the articles and reviews from that period, he shows the resistance offered by historical reality to the Christian idealism of the classic German thinkers.

Fackenheim's challenge to that tradition had in part a specifically Jewish cast, and he made this element particularly clear and graphic in his 1973 book *Encounters between Judaism and modern philosophy*, in which he grapples not only with Kant and Hegel, but with broader currents as well—empiricism and existentialism, for instance—from the point of view of Jewish thought. And Jewish themes predominate in his later work. From the time of the Six-Day War in 1967, Fackenheim worried about the precarious position of the State of Israel, and his speeches and writings of the 1970s provoked great interest and controversy. He formulated what he called 'the 614th commandment'—that Jews are commanded to survive as Jews, forbidden 'to hand Hitler posthumous victories'; papers from this period appear in the 1978 collection *The Jewish return into history*. Fackenheim's thought became even more burdened by the memory of the Nazi Holocaust in which six million Jews perished, along with other enemies of the Nazi regime. He began to speak and write more and more about Auschwitz, and in 1982 he published *To mend the world: foundations of post-Holocaust Jewish thought* (as it is called in later editions), the work that he regarded as his *magnum opus*. Its painful accounts reveal not only the world of horror in Auschwitz, but also the resistance offered there by faithful Jews, whose witness constitutes the true foundation of future Jewish thought. GRAEME NICHOLSON

Fagan, Cary. See NOVELS IN ENGLISH 1983 to 1996.

Faillon, Étienne-Michel. See BIOGRAPHY AND MEMOIRS IN FRENCH: 1.

Fairley, Barker (1887-1986). Scholar, painter, poet, and teacher, he was born in Barnsley, Yorkshire, the second son of the headmaster of an elementary school. He won a county scholarship to Leeds University, graduating in 1907 with first-class honours in modern languages, with distinction in German. This led to his appointment the same year as Lektor in English literature at the ancient German university of Jena, where he obtained his Ph.D. An accidental meeting in his boarding house at Jena with a Canadian professor, who was scouting Europe for academic staff for the newly founded University of Alberta, resulted in his being offered a lectureship in German there. Five years later, in 1915, he was appointed associate professor of German at the University of Toronto.

In Toronto the painter J.E.H. MacDonald recognized in this shy young man of his own age an intellectual restlessness and dissatisfaction with the oppressive traditions of late Victorianism, and introduced him to the little group of artists—A.Y. Jackson, Arthur Lismer, Fred Varley, and others—who a few years later were to form the Group of Seven. Fairley became a close friend of the Group, and an early collector and champion of their paintings. (His collection may be seen in the Barker Fairley Lounge of the Faculty Club, University of Toronto.) At the same time he came under the influence of a lively figure on campus, Professor Sam Hooke of Victoria College, the editor of an undergraduate paper, *The Rebel*, whose views were very much those Fairley had inherited: a dissatisfaction with the social order and a conviction that it could be remedied. In 1914 Fairley had married Margaret Keeling, the daughter of the headmaster of Yorkshire's leading grammar school. She shared and reinforced his radical sympathies, and in Toronto *The Rebel* provided an opportunity to express their opinions. Fairley contributed poems, critical articles, and reviews to it, gradually assuming an influential position in shaping its policy. It was he who suggested that *The Rebel* should 'go to the country' with a new title: *The* CANADIAN FORUM. This was in 1920, the year the Group of Seven was officially formed. Fairley linked the two events.

His scholarly and literary work was chiefly associated with Goethe, though his first published book was a biography of C.M. Doughty (1927), author of *Travels in Arabia deserta*. In 1932 Fairley accepted the Simon Professorship of German Language and Literature at Manchester University. He knew at once that he had made a mistake. The familiar company of friends and artists had vanished and he was face-to-face with blighted industrial England in the depth of the Great Depression. In 1936 he returned, thankfully, to the University of Toronto as head of the German department and set to work on the books that were to win him wide recognition as a German scholar. The first of these, *A study of Goethe* (1947), elicited an enthusiastic letter from Thomas Mann, and drew favourable notices in England, as did *Goethe's 'Faust': six essays* (1953). *Heinrich Heine: an interpretation* followed in 1954 and *Wilhelm Raabe: an introduction to his novels* in 1961. Fairley's *Goethe as revealed in his poetry* (1963) and his authoritative translation of Goethe's *Faust* (1970) completed his canon on Goethe. Rodney Symington edited *Fairley's Selected essays on German literature* (1984).

Painting had always been Fairley's passion and consolation. After his retirement from teaching in 1956, he turned for a time mostly to landscapes—as in *Georgian Bay sketches* (1957)—but he also did many portraits, quickly executed, generally in a single sitting. In the 1970s the demand for his work accelerated sharply—exhibitions were sold out at high prices even before they opened. (See *Barker Fairley portraits*, 1981, edited by Gary Michael Dault.) Fairley was also a poet of some note; his publications in this area include *Poems of 1922, or soon after* (1972), *Poems* (1977), and *Wild geese and other poems* (1984).

Margaret Fairley—who edited *The selected writings of William Lyon* MACKENZIE (1960)—died in 1968. In 1978 Barker Fairley married Nan Purdy, who was the subject of some of his best late paintings. LOVAT DICKSON

Falcon, Pierre (1783-1876). Born at Elbow Fort, Manitoba, the son of Pierre Falcon, a Québécois employed by the North West

Company, and a Cree, he was baptized in 1798 at L'Acadie, Quebec, where he lived with relatives and learned to read and write. In 1806 he returned to Red River to work for the North West Company and in 1812 he married Marie, the sister of Cuthbert Grant Jr, a Métis clerk in the Company; they had seven children. After the union in 1821 of the North West Company and the Hudson's Bay Company, Falcon remained in service until 1825. With other Métis he joined Grant, founder of Grantown (Saint-François-Xavier), and became a farmer and buffalo hunter; he was made a Justice of the Peace in 1855 and died there.

Falcon's literary significance is as a folk poet who interpreted local incidents in lively, mocking songs for which, in two cases, he also composed melodies. He was present at Seven Oaks (1816) when Grant led some Métis and Amerindians in a skirmish in which Governor Robert Semple and twenty other people of the Red River Settlement (established by the Hudson's Bay Company) were killed. His 'La chanson de la grenouillère' ('Chant de verité'), describing the confrontation at Seven Oaks, is a rousing song composed to celebrate the Métis 'victory' and ends with a stanza saying that it had been composed by 'Pierre Falcon, poète du canton'. It marked the birth of popular writing in French-speaking Manitoba. A related song, 'Le Lord Selkirk au Fort William' or 'La danse des Bois-Brûles', parodies the ball held at Fort William by Selkirk after he had taken the Nor'Westers' headquarters in retaliation for Seven Oaks. The vigorous tempi of both songs must have set the toes tapping or the oars swinging of all who were associated with the 'Pays d'en haut'.

Another famous ballad, 'Le Général Dickson', is a sardonic account of the departure from Grantown in 1837 of an American adventurer who styled himself 'Liberator of the Indian Nations'. Falcon composed 'Les tribulations d'un roi malheureux' in his old age, during the Red River Rebellion of 1870, after a party of Métis, sent by Louis Riel, prevented Governor William McDougall from reaching Red River and his 'kingdom', the Northwest Territories. 'Le dieu du Libéral' expresses the bitter feelings of the Métis when Dr J.C. Schultz, who had opposed Riel in 1869 and been imprisoned by him, ran for Liberal member of Parliament in 1871. These three songs are very different in composition and style from the first two, even allowing for the fact that they used borrowed melodies ('Dans tous les cantons', 'Un Canadien errant', and 'Cadet Rousselle' respectively): it is thought that the pastor of Saint-François-Xavier, Father Émile Dugas, may have had a hand in polishing them.

'The buffalo hunter's song'—known only in English translations that are presumed to be based on verses by Falcon—raises to six the number of songs by 'Pierre le rimeur', the Bard of the Plains ('Le barde des plaines'). He doubtless composed other songs but they have been lost, or entered the realm of oral literature.

Lake Falcon in Manitoba was probably named after this popular poet of Red River.

See Margaret Complin, 'Pierre Falcon's "Chanson de la grenouillère"', *Transactions of the Royal Canadian Society* (Sec. III, 1929, p. 39); Margaret Arnett Macleod, 'Songs of the Insurrection', *The Beaver: a magazine of the North* (Spring 1957), 'Dickson, the liberator', *The Beaver* (Summer 1956), and *Songs of old Manitoba* (1960); and Annette Saint-Pierre, *Au pays des Bois-Brûles* (1977), published by the Collège universitaire de Saint-Boniface, Saint-Boniface, Manitoba.

ANNETTE SAINT-PIERRE

Faludy, George (b. 1910). Born in Budapest, Hungary, he was educated at universities in Berlin, Vienna, Graz, and Paris. He served in the Hungary army, 1933-4, and was charged with anti-Nazi activities. In 1938 he immigrated to Paris and then to Morocco, where he was among those European intellectuals invited by President Roosevelt to enter the United States, which he did in 1941. He was appointed honorary secretary of the Free Hungary Movement and enlisted in the American army, serving in the South Pacific.

Invited to return to Hungary in 1945, he settled in Budapest, where he worked as a journalist for five years until his arrest as a conspirator and American spy. He was imprisoned for six months in the cellar of the secret-police headquarters in Budapest, then served three years of a twenty-five-year sentence at the forced-labour camp at Recsk (1950-3).

During the 1956 Revolution, he escaped from Hungary and settled in London, England, where he served as editor-in-chief of the *Hungarian Literary Gazette* (1957-61) and honorary secretary of PEN's Centre for Writers in Exile (1959-64). He joined a circle of friends in Toronto in 1967 and became a Canadian citizen in 1976. An occasional lecturer at North American universities, he was made a Doctor of Letters (*honoris causa*) by the University of Toronto in 1978.

Arthur Koestler once wrote: 'There is no doubt in my mind that Faludy belongs to the handful of contemporary Hungarian poets of international stature; and that among that handful he is *primus inter pares*.' Faludy rocketed to fame with *Ballads of Villon* (Budapest, 1937), which is, despite its title, a collection of original poems written in the manner of the French troubadour. Expressing disdain for authority, and doing so with intense musicality and technical invention, he captivated a generation of readers. But not everyone was charmed: the Nazis burnt the eleventh edition in 1943 and the Communists confiscated the fifteenth edition in 1947. Forty years would elapse before another book of Faludy's poetry would be published in Hungary.

Faludy published a dozen books in Hungarian between 1937 and 1980, the year his *Collected poems* appeared in New York. Four books of his prose have appeared in English: *My happy days in hell* (London, 1962; New York, 1963; Toronto, 1985), a meticulously observed and harrowing account of his three years at Recsk; *Karton* (London, 1966; a.k.a. *City of splintered gods*, New York, 1966), a historical novel set in Roman times; *Erasmus of Rotterdam* (London, 1970; New York, 1971), a sympathetic biography and study of humanism in action; *Notes from the rainforest* (Toronto, 1988)—a meditation, in the British Columbia interior, on human nature and inhumane society.

Three collections of his poetry were published in Canada: *East and West* (1978), *Learn this poem of mine by heart* (1983), both compiled and largely translated by John Robert COLOMBO; and *Selected poems: 1933-80* (1985), compiled and largely translated by Robin SKELTON. The music of the original poems hardly survives the act of translation, but offsetting this loss are such strong features as the sense of locale (Budapest, Morocco, London, Philadelphia, Toronto, etc.); the feeling that love, though deep, is doomed; the belief that art ennobles and endures; the conviction that Eastern European is sadistic and the Western world masochistic; the detestation of consummerism; the abhorrence of autocratic authority—this may take the form of invective (as in 'Ode to Stalin on his seventieth birthday') or extreme playfulness (like the last lines of 'Characteristics of G.F.', in which the poet boasts: 'He bowed down too soon, rose up too late. / Yet he had neither fears nor inhibitions / When attacking a Monster State.').

Invited to return to Hungary once again, he did so in 1989, and was immediately hailed as a long-lost hero. Old books were returned to print; new poetry collections were issued, including the following Hungarian texts: *Body and soul* (1988), *200 sonnets* (1990), *100 sonnets* (1995), and the 848-page collection *Poems* (1995). Reviewers and critics have judged the poems in these volumes to be among the poet's finest and strongest works. Faludy lives in Budapest, though he has retained his Canadian citizenship, and has emerged as the leading poet of post-Communist Hungary. On 23 Oct. 1994 he was awarded the Kossuth Prize, the country's highest honour.

JOHN ROBERT COLOMBO

Fantastic literature and science fiction in French. At the end of the twentieth century, the aesthetics of the fantastic and science fiction have become firmly established in Quebec. This was not always the case, though the tradition is a long one if we consider that narrative writing in Quebec was born under the influence of the first Quebec novel, by Philippe Aubert de Gaspé fils, *L'INFLUENCE D'UN LIVRE* (1837), which used two models: the English Gothic genre and the Quebec tradition of the diabolical folk tale. Thus from the beginning fantastic literature in Quebec was pulled in two directions. An early form of science fiction made its first appearance two years later: Napoléon AUBIN's 'Mon voyage à la lune', a satire on conditions in Lower Canada published in 1839 in his own newspaper, *Le Fantasque*. These were humble beginnings and were not widely imitated. Nevertheless, throughout the nineteenth century many writers—including Joseph-Charles TACHÉ, Louis FRÉCHETTE, and Honoré BEAUGRAND—applied themselves to the fantastic folk tale. And towards the end of the century the publication of Jules-Paul Tardivel's *POUR LA PATRIE* (1895), a separatist novel set in the 1940s, marked a minor advance as an example of science fiction.

A short list of SF works punctuates the twentieth century before the 1960s: *Similia similibus; ou La guerre au Canada* (1916) by Ulric Barthe; *Les aventures extraordinaires de deux Canayens* (1918) by Jules Jéhin; *La cité dans les fers* (1926) by Ubald Paquin; *Erres boréales* (1944) by Florent Laurin; *Défricheurs de Hammada* (1953) by Guy René de Plour (Laurin and Plour were pseudonyms used by Armand Grenier); and *Eutopia: Le monde qu'on attend* (1946) by Jean Berthos. In 1944, amid all these more or less SF titles, Yves THÉRIAULT's first book, the weird and fantastic *Contes pour un homme seul*, was published.

Starting in the 1960s, SF and fantastic literature advanced more rapidly, for Quebeckers literally took over these not-strictly-realistic genres. The most dynamic elements in the field were specialized magazines. The earliest of these, *Solaris*, was created in 1974 by Norbert Spehner. Published under the title *Requiem* until 1979, this magazine aimed to serve as a meeting-place for readers of fantastic literature and SF. This specialized milieu grew with the establishment in 1979 of the annual Congrès Boréal and the magazine *Imagine*. . ., founded by, among others, Jean-Marc Gouanvic and Esther Rochon and devoted exclusively to SF. Many other fanzines were created as well (*Blanc Citron*, *Énergie pure*, *Pandore*, *Pilône*, etc.) and were crowned in 1984 by *L'année de la science-fiction et du fantastique québécois*, a magazine that sought to compile an inventory of each year's production; and by the establishment of the Grand Prix de la science-fiction et du fantastique québécois (GPSFFQ).

Before this ferment of activity, publication of novels and story collections in the fantastic and SF genres was limited. Furthermore, few of these texts were specifically identifiable as fantastic or SF in the strict sense; most were hybrids. Jacques FERRON, for instance, whose imaginative world was often close to the tradition of the oral tale, portrayed the devil in *La charette* (1968) and *La chaise du maréchal-ferrant* (1972), but only to produce a thoroughly ironic tale, as in most of his *Contes* (1968). The same is true of his *L'amélanchier* (1970), where Tinamer recounts marvellous adventures reminiscent of those in *Alice in Wonderland*. Yves Thériault, in his first collection of stories, *Si la bombe m'était contée* (1962), offers the first post-disaster texts, which in a sense found their continuation in Jean Tétreau's *Les nomades* (1967), which recounts the hazards of life on earth after a nuclear disaster. In his short-fiction collection *Volupté de l'amour et de la mort* (1969) Tétreau tackles the fantastic genre, basing his stories on forms of magic related to sorcery and divination (the title story) and to an ancient Japanese pictorial technique ('Le décret impérial').

Claude Mathieu appears to have been influenced by magic realism in *La mort exquise* (1965), a collection of short fiction in which, in the title story, a scientist is swallowed by the plant he is studying under a magnifying glass yet remains alive in the midst of a death that he finds delightful. In 'Le Pélerin de Bithynie' another scholar, this time a professor, finds the ancient traces of an imperial Roman who is revealed as himself. At the moment of this extraordinary discovery, the goddess Cybèle, whom he has vowed to worship, comes to find him. The man exults as he walks into the sea to his death.

With Michel TREMBLAY the discourse becomes decidedly fantastic. Few people remember that he began writing fiction in the fantastic vein, first in 1966, with *Contes pour buveurs attardés* (*Stories for late-night drinkers*, 1977), and then in 1969 with the half-fantastic, half-SF novel *La cité dans l'oeuf*. In fact some of his *contes*, including 'L'oeil de l'idole' and 'Le Warugoth-Shala', echo the novel. Revealingly, Tremblay includes a representation of the city of Montreal, which François Laplante leaves through his contemplation of a glass egg that mysteriously transports him to a planet inhabited by gods in decline who tear one another to pieces. If one were looking for influences, one might say that this first style of Tremblay's is close to that of H.P. Lovecraft or the Belgian Jean Ray. Later his style becomes more personal. One recalls, in *La grosse femme d'à côté est enceinte* (1978)—*The fat woman next door is pregnant* (1981)—the apparitions of Duplessis, a living-dead cat, and the three women, Fates of a kind, in rocking chairs on a balcony on the Plateau Mont-Royal.

Jacques Benoit works in an entirely different register and is a special case in the literature of Quebec. In 1967 he published a peculiar novel, *Jos Carbone*, set in a bizarre and primitive world. Then between 1970 and 1981 he produced three astonishing works. In *Patience et Firlipon* (1970), subtitled 'a love story', he parodies science fiction in a novel set in the near future: in 1978, in a Montreal where dorsal propellers allow people to fly, Patience is carried off by Firlipon, who attempts to seduce her in mid-air; at the end, as in a fairy tale, they dream of having many children. In *Les princes* (1973) Benoit takes on a sub-genre related to SF that few if any French-Canadian writers before him had tried: what in English is known as fantasy. But *Les princes* is far from the canonical works in this genre (such as Robert E. Howard's *Conan*), with their muscle-bound heroes battling creatures with malevolent powers. Rather, Benoit is concerned with creating a world, a City, of blue men and of talking dogs that are at war with the men; no magical powers, gods or sorcerers, but a world of violence and division. *Gisèle et le serpent* (1981) is a humorous, parodic, and fantastic novel in which the narrator, an extremely rational doctor, is amazed by the surrealistic marvels he has witnessed.

Benoit's cast of mind blends humour and fantasy, a tendency that is unusual in Quebec's corpus of fantastic literature, but it has found a few followers, among them Emmanuel

Cocke. The 1970s were steeped in psychedelic lore as young hippies travelled all over the world, many of them on drugs. It is not surprising, therefore, to find that this produced a kind of embryonic postmodernism. Thus in *Va voir au ciel si j'y suis* (1971) Cocke places Jésus Tanné in the year 2058 and makes him a revolutionary who overturns the established order and brings happiness and immortality to the earth. Here we have a kind of upside-down Bible, a mythic reversal of which the Quebec corpus offers a number of examples. In *L'emmanuscrit de la mère morte* (1972) Cocke imagines a kind of God/Devil, Dieuble, under the influence of drugs and alcohol, who indulges in sexual orgies of all sorts before bringing the world to an end and creating a new one. This is accomplished in a joyous narrative chaos, as if the period itself—with all its political, cultural, and social upheavals—had a disruptive effect on the movement of the story.

This phenomenon of textual disruption is equally evident in the books of André Berthiaume, Louis-Philippe Hébert, Jacques Brossard, and Claudette Charbonneau-Tissot (Aude)—all of whom began to publish in the fantastic and SF genres in the 1970s. In *Contretemps* (1971) and *Le mot pour vivre* (1978) Berthiaume's fantastic is discreet. His writing reflects the conjunction of a number of tendencies that freely blend in his narrative discourse. Apparently surrealistic (one thinks of André Pieyre de Maniargues's *Musée noir*) because of the organizing principle of the writing, which appears automatic and verging on delirium, Berthiaume's work is not canonical, for the discourse rarely if ever conforms to the traditional logic of the fantastic genre. One might also say that there is a touch of Marcel Aymé (the Aymé of *Passe muraille*) in Berthiaume. Thus in 'Le fugitif' a prisoner leaves the walls of his prison by escaping his own body. No doubt it is in this way—juggling possible and impossible crossing places—that Berthiaume came to develop his aesthetic of 'border incidents', a concept that must have found receptive readers, for in addition to the GPSFFQ he was awarded the Prix Adrienne-Choquette for *Incidents de frontière* (1984).

The characters of Louis-Philippe Hébert (in *Récits des temps ordinaires*, 1972; *La manufacture de machines*, 1976; *Manuscrit trouvé dans une valise*, 1979) are caught in a world that seems to make no sense whatever but in fact is secretly regulated like a machine. The individuality of Hébert's work lies in the way he constructs his stories, which have less to do with narrative than with description. The description of actions, events, thought(s) all seem to originate with a maniacal describer, who ends up producing effects of radical strangeness.

In the same decade Jacques Brossard was cheerfully blending SF and the fantastic. From the stories of *Le métamorfaux* (1974) to the immense fresco of *L'oiseau de feu*, four (of five) volumes of which appeared between 1989 and 1995, Brossard demonstrated an exuberant imagination sustained by a dazzling style. (He received the GPSFFQ in 1989.) But his SF is not easy. In *Le métamorfaux* he offers seven markedly dreamlike and political stories, with characters who are trapped between dream and reality; it is usually withdrawal into the dream world that makes it possible to find some meaning in life, or at least consolation. This framework falls apart in the title story, 'Le métamorfaux', which reminds us that Brossard is a professor of law who takes great pleasure in playing with legal rules and with the characters who are supposed to apply them: twelve people testify in front of an extremely bizarre judge, and all of them, including the judge, make the most incredible statements. In his great work of fiction, *L'oiseau de feu*, we have a genuine hero, Adakhan, a Périphérien from Manokhsor who rebels and tries to liberate his people from the hold of the Centraliens. The book suggests a political metaphor for the struggle of Quebec within Canada. What Brossard's work treats is the metamorphosis of reality through a character who ventures slowly into what we might call the labyrinth of the real in order to provoke a revolution.

With Aude (the pseudonym of Claudette Charbonneau-Tissot), who began publishing in the same year as Brossard, the stories are conceived from quite a different perspective. From the start, with *Contes pour hydrocéphales adultes* (1974), her work has been permeated with a form of the fantastic that is close to psychopathological tragedy. Aude sees writing as a place for the liberation of fantasies of all sorts, and a place of total narrative freedom. Thus the narrators often enter deformed worlds that are in fact materialized by their own creative power. In the title story of the collection *La contrainte* (1976), this process is actually demonstrated as the female narrator enters her fiction. In Aude's world, neither the real nor the unreal is a happy space, but for women the imaginary is always preferable to the everyday banality that must be escaped at all costs because it is intolerable. In her novel *L'assembleur* (1985) it is a boy who, with the help of his mother—and above all a computer—battles a father who has mistreated the two of them. What dominates her work in general, and seems to lie at the centre of her fantastic vision, is the fragile figure of woman. This motif is eloquently illustrated in the story 'Fêlures' (*Blanc de brume*, 1987), in which a female artist attempts to contruct herself as an artist/artwork, but in the end disintegrates.

Curiously, Esther Rochon too began publishing in volume in 1974. *En hommage aux araignées* (reissued in 1987 under the title *L'étranger sous la ville*) at first seems intended for young readers; but in fact the novel is the first fragment of what was to become the Vrénalik cycle, the two other fragments being *L'épuisement du soleil* (1985) and *L'espace du diamant* (1990). She has also published two story collections (*Le traversier*, 1987; *Le piège a souvenir*, 1991) and three novels: *Coquillage* (1986) and two belonging to another cycle ('Chroniques infernales'), *Lame* (1995) and *Aboli* (1996). The career of this co-founder of the magazine *Imagine*. . . has turned out well; she has won the GPSFFQ three times: in 1986 for *L'Épuisement du soleil*; in 1987 for *Coquillage*; and in 1991 for *L'espace du diamant*. Her first major series, the Vrénalik cycle, gradually sketches the contours of an imaginary world with its own history, geography, gods, myths, fears, and hopes. At the same time a collective image is created of the history of a people, the Asvens, living on the archipelago ofVrénalik. They are a people with an imposing past that has been destroyed, ravaged, in recent centuries. Thus the cycle takes the form of an exploration, a quest in which cyclical characters—such as Anar Vranengel in *En hommage aux araignées*, Taïm Sutherland, Vranengel, and 'the Dreamer' in *L'épuisement de soleil*, and Strénid together with Vranengel and Sutherland in *L'espace du diamant*—endeavour to reverse the disastrous order of things, abolish the old paralysing myths, in order to regain hope and the good life. Rochon also uses a form of story that is almost philosophical, a tendency that is likely related to her interest in Buddhism and reappears in stories such as 'Le traversier' and 'Le labyrinthe' (1987), where thought alone seems to be active, whereas in novels such as *Coquillage* and *Lame* eroticism is given free play.

In Quebec's SF community Élisabeth Vonarburg also stands in the first rank. She has published a remarkable series of SF works, including the story collections *L'oeil de la nuit* (1980), *Janus* (1984), and *Ailleurs et au Japon* (1990); and the novels *Le silence de la cité* (1981), *Chroniques du Pays des Mères* (1992), *Les voyageurs malgré eux* (1994), and *Les rêves de la mer. Tyranaïel—1* (1996). Her work has been published in France as well as Quebec, and in translation in English Canada and the United States (*The silent city* was published in 1988), and the quality of her writing and her imagination is consistent. She has earned a series of distinctions throughout her career, including the Grand Prix de la SF française for her novel *Le silence de la cité*, as well as the GPSFFQ, the Aurora prize for best novel (Canada), and the special prize awarded by the jury for the Philip K. Dick Award (USA) for *Chroniques du Pays des Mères* in 1993. The latter novel appeared simultaneously in French and English in Quebec, English Canada, and the US, though with different titles (*The Maerlande chronicles* in Canada and *In the Mothers' land* in the USA). Vonarburg tackles themes closely tied to the difficulties created by the double and the possibility of transformations in appearance (some characters are endowed with the power to change sex at will). Thus in *Le silence de la cité* earthlings have taken refuge in subterranean Cities where the last survivors are dying; yet a geneticist is attempting to revitalize the human race. He creates Élisa, who possesses the faculty of almost instantaneous autoregeneration, an astonishing empathic capacity, and a power of total metamorphosis. She can be male or female as she wishes. After various adventures, Élisa decides to use the City to create children who will go and spread the genes for change on the Outside. Two themes, among others, are the reality of dreams and the voyage into Space achieved through the technology of the Bridge.

Towards the end of the 1970s several other important authors made their appearance in the field of fantastic literature and SF: André Carpentier, Daniel Sernine, and Jean-Pierre April. No doubt one of the most active representatives outside the circle of magazines specializing in SF and the fantastic, Carpentier played a major role in gaining recognition for these literary genres at the beginning of the 1980s, editing, with Marie José Thériault, an issue of *La BARRE DU JOUR* (no. 89, April 1980) on fantastic literature. He was determined to do justice to fantastic literature and SF by publishing two collections, *Dix contes et nouvelles par dix auteurs québécois* (1983) and *Dix nouvelles de science-fiction* (1985). His work in these genres can be found in three collections—*Rue Saint-Denis* (1988), *Du pain des oiseaux* (1982; translated as *Bread and birds*, 1993), *Carnet sur la fin possible d'un monde* (1992)—and one novel, *L'aigle volera à travers le soleil* (1988). In the latter, a man is possessed by an ancient sorceress who gets the better of all the characters. In Carpentier's stories he sometimes likes to mix genres. Thus in 'La mappemonde venue du ciel' (*Rue Saint-Denis*), which combines the fantastic and SF genres, the earth's double appears above the earth, and touching this double makes reality vanish altogether. In 'Le Fatala de Casius Sahbid' (*Rue Saint-Denis*) a magic/evil object, a cable, kills a detective. The originality of Carpentier's style is probably most evident in 'La bouquinerie d'Outre-Temps' (*Rue Saint-Denis*), 'Le vol de Ti-Oiseau' (*Du pain des oiseaux*), and 'Le "Aum" de la ville' (*Carnet sur la fin possible d'un monde*). 'La bouquinerie . . .' perfectly illustrates the power of desire over reality. Luc Guindon, a historiographer living in Montreal in 1978, unconsciously wishes to (re)become his own grandfather, Lucien Guindon, a visionary and author of science-fiction novels published between 1878 and 1899. In 'Le vol de Ti-Oiseau' the organizing principle of the fantastic discourse revolves around an Aboriginal shaman living in northern Quebec who takes advantage of a moment of hatred in the mind of Ti-Oiseau, bedridden in a hospital in the south, to kill Drien, the man who wanted to kill Ti-Oiseau. No doubt Carpentier's strangest text is 'Le "Aum" de la ville', in which Montreal island begins to move, almost destroying itself in apocalyptic fashion, then tears itself from the earth and takes flight, eventually returning to earth in the Lower St Lawrence where a new genesis can begin. In the work of Carpentier reality and more than reality, the everyday world and the world of dreams, desire, and fantasy, the possible and the impossible, all appear in diverse and fragmented ways.

In the SF books of Jean-Pierre April practically everything is turned fundamentally upside down in the worlds he creates, which often recall those of Philip K. Dick. He has published three collections of SF stories—*La machine à explorer la fiction* (1980), *TéléToTaliTé* (1984), and *Chocs baroques* (1991)—and three SF novels: *Le nord électrique* (1985), *Berlin-Bangkok* (1989), and *Les voyages thanatologiques de Yan Malter* (1995). The problematic of his work consists in the effort to show not only that the real is often no more than a simulacrum, but also that powerful, more or less hidden, institutional authorities attempt to impose this simulacrum as if it were reality! April's SF could be characterized as virulent social criticism. In *Le nord électrique*, set in an imaginary Quebec in a near future, an enormous truck has been built that is supposed to go to Mars one day. Finally we understand that it is the theatre troupe Total Theatre that has arranged and manipulated everything to produce the ultimate spectacle—History produced on the stage: but this mad performance conceals the fact that the truck that was supposed to travel to Mars is a failure. Behind the novel's sub-plots lies a critique of the hypocrisy of people in charge. In April's work, reality turns into nightmare. This is what we see in 'Canadian dream' (*TéléToTaliTé*), where it is Canada that is represented, or rather de-represented: a shaman from Cameroon maintains that Jacques Cartier invented Canada; in the end, while a Canadian flies over the Gulf of St Lawrence, reality is replaced by emptiness. In 'Le vol de la ville' (*La machine à explorer la fiction*, 1980) it is not a matter of denying reality but of literally detaching it from the earth and propelling it into space, somewhat as in Carpentier's 'Le "Aum" de la ville'. Extraterrestrials have ended up on earth with their spaceship and become integrated in Moréal [*sic*] at the beginning of the third millennium. One day they decide to leave, but the mayor refuses to let them and lashes the whole island to the spaceship, which is powerful enough to rip it away from the earth. Moréal—Quebec space—becomes a cosmic city that makes a long voyage, connecting with the constellations. April exploits the earthly elsewhere in *Berlin-Bangkok*, which pursues the author's parody of the real. In a reunited Germany of the twenty-first century a man named Axel, who is depressed, is in search of the ideal woman, whom he finds through a marriage agency. DES (drugs with specific effects) and NTR (new reproductive techniques) come together in Axel's adventures, which, as always with April, are incredible. But there is an even more fundamental tendency in his work towards the representation of mindspace. This is what we might call the Yan Malter cycle, which began with the story 'Coma-70' and 'Coma-90' (*La machine à explorer la fiction*) and later in 'Coma-123, automatexte' (*Chocs baroques*), and finally in the novel *Les voyages thanatologiques de Yan Malter*, which is set somewhere between the years 2094 and 2194. April likes to create extreme parodies of the real, of the world of consciousness and unconsciousness, of life as well as death. This is what happens in the 'cycle', where Yan Malter (Myself, the Other) literally plays the double, the alter ego, of Jean (Yan)-Pierre April, who is also represented in the character of Jan Tepernic, whose name contains an anagram of the verb 'répéter'. In these works everything goes in circles, everything repeats itself, recreates and doubles itself between life and death, one's self and the other.

Daniel Sernine is the most prolific author in the whole field of fantastic literature and SF in Quebec. His work is not simple, but it is much more traditional, in forms much more 'classic', than the work of other Quebec writers in this genre. The author of some thirty works of fiction, either fantastic or SF—for young people as well as adults—Sernine began in 1979 with the collections of fantastic stories in *Les contes de l'ombre* and *Légendes du vieux manoir*, *Quand vient la nuit* (1983), *Nuits blêmes* (1990), and *Sur la scène des siècles* (1995), which won the GPSFFQ; and a novel, *Manuscrit trouvé dans une secrétaire* (1994). In the early 1980s he embarked on a parallel, complementary career in SF: three story collections, *Le vieil homme et l'espace* (1981), *Boulevard des Étoiles* (1991), and *Boulevard des Étoiles 2* (1991, GPSFFQ) and two novels, *Les méandres du temps* (1983) and *Chronoreg* (1992). At the start of his career he stayed close to the canonical models of fantastic literature. This remained true through 1983, when *Quand vient la nuit*, with its panoply of werewolves, demons, evil objects, and cursed books, set in a world reminiscent of the old Lower Canada, marked the end of the canonical phase. His style began to change with *Nuits blêmes*, set in contemporary Montreal. In his first collection of SF stories, *Le vieil homme et l'espace*, Sernine exploits space adventure ('space opera'), which is further refined in what was to become his Carnaval cycle (*Boulevard des Étoiles 1 and 2*). More than space, however, what interests Sernine is time, which he makes the principal theme of his two long novels, *Les méandres du temps* and *Chronoreg*. But if the former is imbued with the desire for peace, the latter is anchored in violence and war. In *Les méandres*, as the earth faces annihilation by conflicting nuclear powers, an organization of ancient Earthlings living on the planet Erymède, which they have colonized, take it upon themselves to see that peace is maintained. By contrast, in *Chronoreg* (the title refers to a powerful drug that makes it possible to travel back in time), Quebec has become sovereign in the twenty-first century, but is at war with Canada over Labrador. Combined with all this are the figures of love and death, and of homosexual desire, as if Sernine had written this entire part of his work to arrive at a representation of an amorous phantasm touched by both the possible and the impossible.

Only a handful of authors have been mentioned here, but there are a good thirty more—including François Barcelo, René Beaulieu, Michel Bélil, Bertrand Bergeron, Evelyne Bernard, Guy Bouchard, Denys Chabot, Pierre Chatillon, Joël Champetier, Agnès Guitard, Pierre Karch, Carmen Marois, Yves Meynard, Stanley Péan, Gilles Pellerin, Annick Perrot-Bishop, Négovan Rajik, Jacques Renaud, Jean-François Somcynsky (Somain), Jean-Louis Trudel, and Marie José Thériault. There are also dozens of anthologies, and publications of other kinds that relate to the history of the genre for the past twenty years. See Maurice Émond, *Anthologie de la nouvelle et du conte fantastiques québécois au XXe siècle* (1987); Michel Lord, *Anthologie de la science-fiction québécoise contemporaine* (1988); Aurélien Boivin, Maurice Émond, and Michel Lord, *Bibliographie analytique de la science-fiction et du fantastique québécois (1960-1985)* (1992); Élisabeth Vonarburg and Jane Brierley, *Tesseracts* (1996); and Aurélien Boivin, *Les meilleurs contes fantastiques Québécois du XXe siècle* (1997). MICHEL LORD

Fantastic literature in English. This is the term for 'the literature of the fantastic', which refers specifically to three literary genres: science fiction, fantasy fiction, and weird fiction. These three genres of fantastic literature (FL) may be more distinct in theory than in practice, yet they represent different traditions of narration, rhetoric, and storytelling.

Science fiction (SF) is writing that is realistic and deals with reasonable change that follows upon the introduction of a scientific discovery or a technological invention or application; it is quite often set in the future. Fantasy fiction (FF) is writing that seems closer to myth, legend, and folklore than to mimetic realism, often depicting heroic action that takes place in a world quite unlike our own and set in the dim and distant past or in some bright new parallel world or universe. Weird fiction (WF)—sometimes described as 'occult fiction', 'supernatural fiction', 'horror fiction', 'dark fantasy', sometimes even 'magical realism'—takes place in the present, in a realistic world much like our own, except that some element or agent of a non-scientific nature interferes with the laws of cause and effect.

Writers of FL tend to specialize, though some have contributed to all three genres. Brian MOORE, a mainstream novelist committed to psychological realism, is a case in point. *Catholics* (1972) is set in the immediate future (hence it is SF); *The great Victorian collection* (1975) deals with a 'wild talent' that transforms the present world (so it is FF); *Cold heaven* (1983) deals with the terror of a dead man who refuses to die (thus it is WF).

Fantastic literature was slow to take root in early Canada, although fanciful and fantastic elements abound in the earliest journals kept by explorers. In the sixteenth century, for instance, Samuel de Champlain took delight in describing the sea creature Gougou and the rite of the Shaking Tent, much to the dismay of the skeptical-minded colonist and lawyer Marc Lescarbot. For the next two hundred years the literary annals of New France were enriched with references to the *loup garou* (werewolf), Jean-Pierre Lavallée (sorcerer), and La Corriveau (infamous witch).

In the nineteenth century English pioneer settlers like Susanna MOODIE deliberately refrained from speculating about the 'heart' of the deep woods in their published works, yet in their private correspondence they toyed with spiritualism and the notion of possession. In the twentieth century the country's half-hearted commitment to scientific research and development resulted in a downgrading of FF and WF in the popular mind without a compensating upgrading of SF. Despite such baleful influences, there are interesting literary works to consider from the past, as well as important and internationally recognized imaginative writers in the present who have responded to the Canadian environment and temperament in fantastic ways. What follows is a joint chronological consideration of English-language FF and WF, followed by a discussion of SF.

1. FANTASTIC FICTION AND WEIRD FICTION. The earliest fantastic tales were recited in the thirteen languages of the Aboriginal populations. Only later were the traditional stories retold in French and English translation. These Native tales assume the presence of tricksters, shape-shifters, culture heroes, shamans, witches, oracular shaking tents, malevolent windigos, benevolent thunderbirds, dwarfs, giants, and transformations. By all accounts, the elders were electrifying storytellers.

From the sixteenth to the nineteenth centuries, explorers, colonists, and settlers from France, Britain, and other countries established notable regional traditions of storytelling, often fantastic in nature, and these included the *habitant* legends of Quebec (which influenced the province's characteristic *contes*), the supernatural folklore of the Ottawa Valley, the 'tall tales' characteristic of the Prairies and the West, the urban legends of the second half of the twentieth century, and the fancies and fantasies that centre on the North Pole.

The quintessential Canadian contribution to the world of FF is the so-called animal story. The drama of a wild animal in a natural setting, written to satisfy the often-opposed demands of naturalist and *littérateur*, owes its existence to Sir Charles G.D. ROBERTS and its popularity to Ernest Thompson SETON. Roberts wrote the earliest realistic story of this type, 'Do seek their meat from God', published in *Harper's Monthly* (Dec. 1892) and collected in *Earth's enigmas* (1896). But the vogue for the genre was sparked by the success of *Wild animals I have known* (1898), which Seton wrote and illustrated. In these stories, the animals do not talk, although quite often human qualities other than speech are ascribed to them—rudimentary reasoning, sympathetic feelings, etc. At the turn of the century, animal stories appealed to 'armchair naturalists'; today their attraction is largely to young readers.

Roberts was interested in history and prehistory and went on to write *In the morning of time* (1919), a series of linked stories about the dawn of time and the romance of cavemen and cavewomen. The narrative poet E.J. PRATT was attracted to an even earlier period for the setting of 'The great feud: a dream of a Pleiocene Armageddon' in *Titans and other epics of the Pleiocene* (1926). The Canadian woods at the turn of the century form the dramatic backdrop for six of the compelling tales of horror and terror penned by Algernon Blackwood, the well-known English author who spent two formative years (1890-2) in Toronto and Muskoka. In stories like 'A haunted island' in *The empty house* (1906) and 'The wendigo' in *The lost valley* (1910), the fauna and flora of the backwoods are seen to be effectively alien and hostile to nature and humanity—a counter-convention to the 'animal story'.

Journalist and historian John Charles Dent (1841-88) turned his attention to fiction in *The Gerrard Street mystery and other weird tales* (1888), and elements of supernatural horror quicken the poetry and the stories of Duncan Campbell SCOTT in *In the village of Viger* (1896) and *The witching of Elspie* (1923). In his office in Rideau Hall, Ottawa, Governor General Lord Tweedsmuir (John Buchan) dictated to his secretary the text of a novel about metaphysical menace. It was to be his final work of fiction, appearing posthumously as *Sick Heart River* (1941). Set in the Arctic, it describes 'a thing beyond humanity and beyond time' and tells the story of a dying man's sacrifice to save an entire people.

The contributions of Canadian story writers to American pulp magazines have yet to be surveyed, but among the most energetic and enthusiastic contributors of fantastic adventure stories to such publications were H. Bedford-Jones (1887-1949) and Thomas P. KELLEY, both natives of Ontario. The earliest fantastic novel of literary stature is *Tay John* (1939) written by Howard O'HAGAN. Combining elements of fantasy and realism, the author relates the tale of the miraculous birth, life, and death in modern times of a culture hero in terms of the mind-set of the Tsimshian people of the West Coast. Hagan's writing may be described as 'mythopoeic'. That word also applies to the poetry and prose of Gwendolyn MacEWEN. The Celt-like appeal and shamanistic power of MacEwen's imagination, her mesmerizing lyricism, and her fascination with magic and magicians are apparent in the poems in *The armies of the moon* and the fables in *Noman* (both 1972), to name but two collections of her high fantasy. Wayland Drew interbraids three timelines, not to mention shamanism and modernism, in his novel *Wabeno feast* (1973). He went on to write the Erthring Cycle, which consists of three environmentally minded fantasy adventure novels: *The memoirs of Alcheringia* (1984), *The Gaian experiment* (1985), and *Master of Norriya* (1986).

Fantastic elements appear in the fictions of numerous contemporary mainstream writers, including Margaret ATWOOD, Robertson DAVIES, Timothy FINDLEY, Pauline GEDGE, Jack HODGINS, Janet Turner HOSPITAL, Thomas KING, Rohinton MISTRY, Brian MOORE, Leon ROOKE, Jane URQUHART, and Sheila WATSON. For instance, Davies, while Master of Massey College, told eighteen 'spooky stories' about ghosts to be encountered in the study halls and corridors of that institution, intending them to 'stave off the Rational Rickets'; they are collected in *High spirits* (1982). Another example: Findley's *Not wanted on the voyage* (1984) is a vigorous, outlandish, inventive reworking of the biblical account of Noah. Yet the most familiar fantasy written by a Canadian remains W.P. KINSELLA's baseball novel *Shoeless Joe* (1982), which began as the title story in *Shoeless Joe Jackson comes to Iowa* (1980). Memorably filmed in 1989 as *Field of dreams*, it popularized the catchphrase: 'If you build it, he will come.'

Canadian high fantasy reached a pinnacle in Guy Gavriel KAY's trilogy 'The Fionavar tapestry': *The summer tree* (1984), *The wandering fire* (1986), and *The darkest road* (1986). Kay has been called 'the Canadian Tolkien' for his accomplished storytelling. His prose is by turns eloquent, magical, imaginative, intelligent, and romantic. In this extended work, five students of the University of Toronto 'cross' into the finely realized 'first world' of Fionavar, where they join in an epic struggle of endangered good against radical evil.

In 1979 an Ottawa bookstore called the House of Speculative Fiction opened, and among the writers were Gordon Derevanchuk, Galad Elflandsson, Charles DE LINT, Charles R. Saunders, and bibliographer and anthologist John Bell. (This Ottawa group hosted the tenth World Fantasy Convention in October 1984.) De Lint is its most prolific member. His specialty is urban fantasy and the operation of modern magic. *Moonheart: a romance* (1984) combines Celtic motifs and native worlds both real and imaginary. *Mulengro: a Romany tale* (1985) is set among the gypsies of Canada.

In Toronto in the 1980s a group of writers of FL dubbed themselves the Bunch of Seven, which grew to include nine members—Tanya Huff, Marnie Hughes, Louise Hypher, Shirley Meier, Terri Neal, Fiona Pattan, S.M. Stirling, Mike Wallis, and Karen Wehrstein—who write for magazines or have published books. Three members—Stirling, Meier, and Wehrstein—have collaborated on writing 'shared worlds'. Tanya Huff writes 'crossover' novels that combine elements of detective fiction, fantasy, and horror. She has written with great vigour about vampires and werewolves that plague private investigator Vicki Nelson and the Toronto area in such novels as *Blood price* (1991), *Blood trail* (1992), *Blood lines* (1993), *Blood pact* (1993), and *Blood debt* (1997).

Other notable individual FL works and their authors are *The night inside* (1993) by Nancy Baker; *A planet of eccentrics* (1990) by Ven Begamudré; *The pyx* (1959; filmed in 1973) by John BUELL; *A rose red city* (1987) by Dave Duncan; *Fang the gnome* (1988) by Michael Coney; *Chips & gravy* (1991) by William Gough; *The woman who is the midnight wind* (1987) by Terence M. GREEN; *Near death* (1994) by Nancy Kilpatrick; *Mysterium* (1992) by Eric McCormack; *Extreme denial* (1996) by David Morrell; *Song of the pearl* (1976) by Ruth NICHOLS; *The sun and the moon* (1944, expanded 1974) by P.K. PAGE; *The siege* (1985) by Graham Petrie; *The initiate brother* (1991) by Sean Russell; *Into the dark lands* (1991) by Michelle Sagara; *Princes of Sandastre* (1990) by Anthony Swithin; and *Fastyngange* (1988) by Tim WYNNE-JONES. Hélène Holden's novel *Snow* (1990) turns a blizzard into something of a demon. Kate Pullinger wrote the highly regarded vampire novel *Where does kissing end?* (1992). Also effective are Matthew Hart's dark fantasy *Into the purple duchy* (1995), in which the German battleship *Bismarck* is pursued up the St Lawrence River by the *Hood*, and Susie Moloney's *Bastion Falls* (1995).

Robert Charles Wilson has published a series of notable novels of fantasy, elegant in style, that verge on speculation. They include *A hidden place* (1986), *Memory wire* (1987), *Gypsies* (1989), *The divide* (1990), *Bridge of years* (1991), *The harvest* (1992), and *Mysterium* (1994). Garfield Reeves-Stevens is the author of supernatural thriller-chillers including *Bloodshift* (1981), *Dreamland* (1986), *Children of the shroud* (1987), *Nighteyes* (1989), and *Dark matter* (1990). Michael Slade is the pseudonym of two Vancouver lawyers, Jay Clarke and John Banks, authors of hard-core crime-horror novels that involve the Royal Canadian Mounted Police: *Headhunter* (1984), *Ghoul* (1987), *Cutthroat* (1992), and *Ripper* (1994). Well-known children's books include Pierre BERTON's *The secret world of Og* (1962) and Mordecai RICHLER's series *Jacob Two-Two meets the Hooded Fang* (1975), *Jacob Two-Two and the dinosaur* (1987), and *Jacob Two-Two's first spy case* (1995).

The varied nature of Canadian FF and WF flowered in the absence of commercial constraints on the imaginations of writers. ('Competition creates resemblance,' Marshall McLUHAN once remarked.) Their very individuality flows from the realization that no strong demarcation exists between the country's mainstream writers and its fantasy writers, between established writers and new writers, between given forms or norms and innovative styles.

There are six specialized anthologies of FF and WF: *Not to be taken at night: thirteen classic Canadian tales of mystery and the supernatural* (1981) edited by John Robert COLOMBO with Michael Richardson; *The windigo: an anthology of fact and fantastic fiction* (1982; enlarged edition, 1997) edited by Colombo; *13 Canadian ghost stories* (1988) edited by Ted Stone; *Shivers: an anthology of Canadian ghost stories* (1989) edited by Greg Ioannou and Lynne Missen; *The Oxford book of Canadian ghost stories* (1990) edited by Alberto MANGUEL (who intriguingly noted that some stories show that 'the ghostly presence is an absence'). There is also the ongoing anthology series titled Northern Frights. Edited by Don Hutchison, it offers original and reprint stories and poems of terror, horror, and dark fantasy. Collections appeared in 1992, 1994, 1995, and 1997. Peripherally relevant is Margot Northey's scholarly study *The haunted wilderness: the gothic and grotesque in Canadian fiction* (1976). For a serious and informed overview, with bibliographies, see 'Blood on the snow: a survey of Candian horror fiction' by Don Hutchison and Peter Halasz in *The Scream Factory*, Issue 18 (1996).

2. SCIENCE FICTION. SF is an internationally popular genre that has been slow to find a mass readership in Canada; the readership that does exist shows hardly any preference for Canadian SF over the more readily available American SF. At least until the 1980s, Canadian contributors were less influenced by earlier and contemporary Canadian writers than they were by the genre's conventions and American practitioners. In the last decade or so, new writers have begun to particularize the references and localize the settings to reflect life in Canada in the past, present, and future. The new generation's interest lies in writing fiction that is influenced by the conventions of genre SF but is not limited to them; they are creating new notions of 'other Canadas'.

Canadian SF began with a bang with the crashlanding of an early astronaut from France in New France in Cyrano de Bergerac's two-volume fantastic satire (1656, 1661), translated by Richard Aldington as *Voyages to the moon and the sun* (1962). It continued with the eruption of a volcano at the North Pole in Jules Verne's *Les aventures du Capitaine Hatteras* (1866), But the first work of literary quality and interest to be written by a Canadian is a utopian satire set in Antarctica (rather than at the somewhat closer North Pole). This is James DE MILLE's *A strange manuscript found in a copper cylinder* (1888). An engrossing novel, published serially and anonymously before it appeared posthumously as a book, it is a satire on society's values, human nature, and science. The narrator, Adam More, discovers the 'lost world' of the Kosekin, a race of human beings whose values are the inverse of normal values: they revere darkness, poverty, weakness, and death. Serious, inventive, and readable, the novel combines the fantastic with a serious debate about social values and human behaviour.

De Mille's lead was followed by Grant ALLEN (stories in *The face and the mask*, 1894) and Robert BARR (*Strange stories*, 1884), expatriate writers who lived abroad and wrote stories and novels that were published in London and New York for a progressive readership concerned with science and social change. At home, Stephen LEACOCK satirized all sorts of literary conventions, including early utopian romances and pre-genre SF in *The iron man and the tin woman, with other such futurities* (1929) and *Afternoons in Utopia: tales of the new time* (1932). But the most amazing achievement of all is the well-realized satire *Consider her ways* (1947) by the prairie novelist Frederick Philip GROVE (apparently conceived as early as 1892-8 and first drafted in 1919-20). The novel follows the trek of a colony of 10,000 telepathic worker-ants who leave their colony in Venezuela and cross the North American continent. They survive winter in the poetry section of the New York Public Library, where they continue to marvel at the absurdities of mankind. It is an audacious work, one that has yet to find a fully appreciative readership.

The spirit of early Canadian SF was primarily satirical. Between the Great Depression and the Second World War, it changed, flourishing as 'scientific adventure' in the 1930s and 1940s. Swashbuckling stories of invention and discovery were contributed to pulp magazines by such residents and expatriates as H. Bedford-Jones, John L. Chapman, Leslie A. Croutch, Chester D. Cuthbert, Francis Flagg, Nils Helmer Frome, Thomas P. Kelley, R.T.M. Scott, and Cyril G. Wates. Bylines of some of these men—there were no women among them—appeared in the so-called CanPulps, large-format magazines that were printed on low-quality paper in Canada to replace the American pulps that were embargoed during the war years. Their counterpart in the world of comic books was the Canadian Whites.

A.E. VAN VOGT (b. 1912) bears one of the great names of the so-called Golden Age of SF. Born in Manitoba, he taught himself to write in the Winnipeg Public Library. In Ottawa and Toronto he wrote some 600,000 words of SF before leaving for Los Angeles in 1944. During this period he completed the powerful story 'Black Destroyer' (1939), which was inspired by Seton's *The biography of a grizzly* (1900), and *Slan* (serial publication, 1940; 1946; rev. 1951), a classic adventure novel about a persecuted telepathic mutant. In the United States Vogt wrote an enormous number of stories and novels—often space-operas, with overtones of *noir*—to realize his aim 'to glorify man and his future'.

The 1950s are a lost decade for native SF, except for Earle BIRNEY's *Trial of a city* (1952), a comic verse-play about the destruction of Vancouver set in the near future—it was originally titled *The damnation of Vancouver*, but no publisher of the day would issue it under that title—and Ralph ALLEN's *The chartered libertine* (1954), a novel about the Canadian Broadcasting Corporation's being attacked by tycoons and rabble-rousers, which seemed outlandish at the time but was prophetic in hindsight.

The 1960s are notable in that they witnessed the emergence of Phyllis GOTLIEB, nationally appreciated as a poet but internationally prized as the writer of psychologically probing SF stories and novels. Her fiction often dramatizes the crises faced by telepathic beings and sentient animals. The novel *Sunburst* (1964) describes the life of a disturbed youngster who possesses psychic abilities. Gotlieb's body of work is interesting and impressive, though often demanding and difficult, particularly the novels in the GalFed and StarCats series. Her well-crafted stories, first published in popular SF magazines, are reprinted in *Son of the morning and other stories* (1983) and *Blue apes* (1995). For more than a decade, Gotlieb was the sole SF writer in Canada who enjoyed an international readership. At home her fiction has yet to receive the recognition and respect it deserves. The surprising appearance in Toronto in 1968 of Judith MERRIL, the doyenne of SF editors, transformed the national scene. She brought with her not only her professional contacts but also her own library of 5,000 books and magazines, which in 1968 became the basis of the Spaced Out Library.

Another surprising appearance was that of Richard ROHMER as a fiction-writer. A prominent attorney, royal commissioner, and retired brigadier general in the Canadian armed forces, Rohmer turned his hand to commercial fiction and produced a string of fast-moving, near-future thrillers. Beginning with *Ultimatum* (1973), they dramatize the consequences of political, social, economic, and ecological disasters. For some of his villains he looked no further than the White House and American corporate interests.

Yet another surprise was the sudden emergence as a novelist of Edward Llewellyn, pen name of Edward Llewellyn-Thomas (1917-84), engineer, physician, and associate dean of medicine at the University of Toronto. Between retirement and his death, he completed six fast-moving novels that meld ideas and action and complex characterization: *The Douglas convolution* (1979), *The bright companion* (1980), *Prelude to chaos* (1983), *Salvage and destroy* (1984), *Fugitive in transit* (1985), and *Word-bringer* (1986).

Two views of Montreal's future are found in novels published one year apart. *The underdogs* (1979) is a work of satire that is truly prophetic. Written by documentary-film writer William WEINTRAUB, it depicts the plight of the English-speaking population on Montreal Island twenty years after Quebec's separation and the formation of the independent Republic of Quebec, an ideological dictatorship backed by Russian loans and supported by handouts from Senegal. An Anglo Liberation Front, formed in response to the government's Linguistic Purity Laws, advocates the partition of the Island of Montreal to create 'Angloland' to preserve the English-speaking ethnic enclave. Linguistically disadvantaged Anglos are reduced to tending the hydroponic gardens located in the city's Sun Life Building in Dominion Square. Two years after the publication of the novel, the Sun Life Assurance Company abandoned its landmark head-office building, moving its corporate headquarters to Toronto. A different fate for Montreal was envisioned by Hugh MacLENNAN in *Voices in time* (1980). An atomic holocaust has reduced the city to ruins by A.D. 2030—the disintegration of society led to atomic destruction. Human vanity was the cause of it all, apparent at the time of the October Crisis of 1970.

Spider ROBINSON is well known as an SF personality who writes with a sense of the wonder of words, and often finds in communal life a proper response to the disintegrating effects of technology. He is identified with the Star books: *Stardance* (1978), *Starseed* (1991), and *Starmind* (1994).

The most widely acclaimed SF novel written by a Canadian is Margaret ATWOOD's *The HANDMAID'S TALE* (1985), which was honoured with the first Arthur C. Clarke Award and filmed by director Volker Schlöndorff (1990). Her novel is set in the Boston area in the near future, following the founding of the repressive Republic of Gilead, and it examines the ways in which the rights of women have been denied and their status reduced to that of serfs. The novel's highly imaginative dénouement is set on the campus of the fictitious University of Denay in the High Arctic in A.D. 2195, long after the fall of Gilead. Atwood has also made good use of SF themes and insights in many of her poems and stories.

The work of three Toronto-based writers is particularly rewarding and marks the beginning of the use of Canadian settings in major ways. Terence M. GREEN, who handles fantastic themes with at least as much ease as scientific ones, gives the latter a police-procedural twist in the novel *Barking dogs* (1988) and its sequel *Blue limbo* (1997), both set in Toronto in the near future. Robert J. SAWYER acquired an international following for a series of novels, written in rapid sequence, influenced by genre SF: the computer aboard the starship in his *Golden fleece* (1990) owes something to HAL 9000 of the film *2001: A Space Odyssey*. Sawyer rewrote modern intellectual history from the perspective of dinosaurs in his 'Quintaglio Trilogy', and he then moved from technical concerns to ethical considerations in the Nebula-winning *The terminal experiment* (1995). The special talent of Andrew Weiner, as shown repeatedly in his collection *Distant signals and other stories* (1989), lies in conveying the social and psychological dislocations of the *fin-de-siècle*.

Monica HUGHES, an immensely prolific novelist, is deservedly popular for her SF for young readers, an undertaking that got underway in earnest with *Keeper of the Isis light* (1980), the first of three such novels. Other titles of interest are *Invitation to the game* (1990) and *The golden aquarians* (1994). Crawford Kilian is an able novelist who began writing disaster novels, then moved to SF, and finally advanced to FF. The evolution may be traced from *Icequake* (1979) through *The fall of the republic* (1987) to *Greenmagic* (1992). Candas Jane Dorsey is active in the SF field as editor, poet, and fiction-writer. Her spirited work recalls that of the British experimental writer J.G. Ballard, especially her *Machine sex and other stories* (1988) and the novel *Black wine* (1997).

In the 1980s and 1990s the notion of cyberspace came into its own, and the originator of the term, William GIBSON, published a series of bestselling novels (often characterized as 'cyberpunk'), notably the so-called 'Sprawl Trilogy': *Neuromancer* (1984), *Count Zero* (1986), and *Mona Lisa overdrive* (1988)—set in a sprawling megalopolis called 'the Boston Atlanta Metropolitan Axis'. The Biologist Richard Dawkins has posited the existence of the 'meme', the intellectual equivalent of the biological gene. Gibson's particular genius is the creation of 'memes'—ideas with wings—that pervade the new international techno-culture. His 'memes' appear in Japan in his widely translated novel *Idoru* (1996).

Fantastic fiction in Canada generally awaits scholars, critics, and reviewers who, like Edmund Wilson, can make or break reputations. Still, notable critical contributions have been made by David Ketterer, Darko Suvin, Robert M. Philmus, Marc Angenot, Peter Fitting, Douglas BARBOUR, expatriates Douglas Hill and John Clute, and the late Susan Wood. In lieu of criticial commentary, anthologies are important in SF. John Robert Colombo compiled the first anthology, *Other Canadas:*

an anthology of science fiction and fantasy (1979), which discusses the Polar World theme and the National Disaster scenario. It reprints forty stories and poems and offers a select bibliography, as well as two major critical articles: the first academic treatment of SF (David Ketterer's 'Canadian science fiction: a survey') and the first for FF (Margaret Atwood's 'Canadian monsters: some aspects of the supernatural in Canadian fiction'). Atwood's article, reprinted in her collection *Second words* (1982), was expanded in her Clarendon Lectures, published as *Strange things: the malevolent North in Canadian literature* (1995). Other anthologies of importance are *Visions from the edge: an anthology of Atlantic Canadian science fiction* (1981) edited by John Bell and Lesley CHOYCE; *Friendly aliens: thirteen stories of the fantastic set in Canada by foreign authors* (1981) edited by Colombo; *Ark of ice: Canadian futurefiction* (1992) edited by Lesley Choyce; and *Northern stars: the anthology of Canadian science fiction* (1994) edited by David G. Hartwell and Glenn Grant.

Tesseracts is the general title of a series of paperback anthologies of original and reprint stories and poems—what Ezra Pound called 'active anthologies'. Judith Merril edited the first in 1985; Phyllis Gotlieb and Douglas Barbour the second in 1987; Jane Dorsey and Jerry Truscott the third in 1990; Lorna Toolis and Michael Skeet the fourth in 1992; Robert Runté and Yves Meynard the fifth in 1996; and Robert J. Sawyer and Carolyn Clink the sixth in 1997. Elisabeth Vonarburg and Jane Brierley published *Tesseracts Q* (French SF in English translation) in 1996. *On spec: the Canadian magazine of speculative writing* has appeared three times a year from Edmonton, Alberta, since spring 1989.

The Canadian Science Fiction and Fantasy Association sponsors the Aurora Awards, 'people's choice' prizes presented annually at the national 'Canvention'. In May 1995 the National Library of Canada mounted the exhibition 'Out of This World' based on the holdings of the Merril Collection. Issued to accompany the exhibit was the anthology *Out of this world: Canadian science fiction & fantasy literature* (1995) compiled by Andrea Paradis. It includes almost thirty essays, articles, and memoirs that, in their entirety, suggest the belated maturity of fantastic literature in Canada.

The single study of the field—which traces themes and discusses authors, and their works in both English and French—is *Canadian science fiction and fantasy* (1992) by David Ketterer. JOHN ROBERT COLOMBO

Farm Show, The (1976). The definitive example of the work of Toronto's Theatre Passe Muraille, this COLLECTIVE CREATION was first performed in a barn near Clinton, Ontario, in Aug. 1972, directed by Paul Thompson. After several weeks of immersion in the life of the farming community, the company created a series of monologues, sketches, songs, and visual images reflecting the vibrant yet vulnerable qualities of the community. In the tradition of Sunday School and Christmas concerts, skits at celebrations, parades and other festivities, *The farm show* spoke of and to a specific community—in its own patterns of speech and gesture—yet also succeeded in appealing to audiences throughout Canada and abroad, and it fused regionalism and nationalism in a powerful and exemplary fashion. Intensely theatrical, though not technically complex, it directly influenced companies such as the Mummers Troupe (Newfoundland) and 25th St Theatre (Saskatoon), as well as the work of playwrights John GRAY, Linda Griffiths, and Hrant ALIANAK. *The farm show* was also influential in encouraging the participation of actors in script development, and in drawing attention to unconventional performance venues and non-traditional theatre audiences.

Versions of the play were performed on CBC radio (1972) and television (1975). Michael ONDAATJE's film, *The Clinton special* (1974), chronicled the 1973 tour. In 1985 the play returned to the Clinton area, where it was produced (with all but two of the original company) as part of Goderich Township's sesquicentennial celebrations. In the summer of 1996 it was recreated in a different form by the 4th Line Collective near Millbrook, Ontario.

The published text (1976) was prepared by Ted Johns, a native of the Clinton community, whose conversations with Thompson in 1972 gave rise to the idea of the play. Selected criticism of *The farm show* is included in *Canadian drama and the critics* (rev. ed. 1995), edited by L.W. Conolly. ROBERT C. NUNN

Fawcett, Brian (b. 1944). Born and raised in Prince George, British Columbia, he moved to Vancouver and studied at Simon Fraser University, where he attended workshops with composer R. Murray Schafer. He published two literary magazines, *Iron*, and *NMFG* (*No Money From the Government*), and wrote seven books of poetry, including *Five books of a Northmanual* (1967), *Friends* (1971), *Permanent relationships* (1975), and *Creatures of state* (1977), which he has withdrawn from print. The poems presaged his later writing: even in early work such as *Aggressive transport: two narrative revisions, 1975-82* (1982), he asked rhetorically if a poet could be a social critic. Was it possible to change the world with the private act of poetry?

Fawcett subsequently abandoned poetry. He became a community organizer and planner with the Greater Vancouver Regional District. He later worked for eight years as an English teacher in a maximum-security prison outreach program; taught sociology at York University, Toronto; then worked as a contributing editor for *Books in Canada*, and contributed to various papers and magazines as a literary journalist.

Fawcett's strong social conscience is not at first apparent in *My career with the Leafs and other stories* (1982). These nostalgic vignettes include the narrator's charming account of a writer slipping into the starting lineup of the Toronto Maple Leafs. His tone darkens in the nineteen stories of *Capital tales* (1984). All revolve around the connotations of the word 'capital'; some are comic, some grotesque, some violent and disturbing. Many of the stories are quasi-autobiographical accounts of a boy whose illusions about life and love in a capitalistic society are painfully peeled away. The collection concludes with a comic dialogue between the narrator and a flatulent Thomas Carlyle about the nature of capitalism. The collection also indicates the new direction Fawcett would take: the postmodern author often discourses with the reader about the writing of the tales, and announces 'that the job of literature is to keep the world going.' *The secret journal of Alexander MacKenzie* (1986) uses magic-realist devices to look at the demeaning spirit of capitalism. Narrated by self-proclaimed local historian Don Benson, the stories explore the conflicts between multinational corporations and small towns; the contradictions of fiction and history; and myth versus contemporary reality. The title story is a masterpiece: the eighteenth-century explorer, who was the first to reach the Pacific by land, discovers shamanism, hallucinogenic plants, and a talking bear in a consideration of such issues as how the past weighs on the present, social breakdown, and the threat of corporate culture.

A trilogy of controversial and provocative books—*Cambodia: a book for people who find television too slow* (1986), *Public eye: an investigation into the disappearance of the world* (1990), and *Gender wars: a novel and some conversation about sex and gender* (1994)—show Fawcett's search for a deeper understanding of McLuhan's concept of the global village, cultural homogenization, and the manipulation of memory by media. All three titles ask: where is civilization going? All address the problem of middle-aged writers and Canadian nationalism; all balance the twin demands of analysis and imagination. The books combine text and subtext as a break from conventional structures stuck in the past, with flamboyant typefaces and computer-page layouts. These devices allow Fawcett to hold contradictory opinions, to be ambivalent, and to express conflicting emotions.

Fawcett's *Unusual circumstances, interesting times, and other impolite interventions* (1991) is a collection of revised newspaper and magazine articles on the arts and crucial issues facing the Western world. Fawcett has also written an amusing gardening book, *The compact garden: discovering the pleasures of planting (a socialist garden book)* (1992). GEOFF HANCOCK

Fées ont soif, Les (1978). Denise BOUCHER's feminist play, first produced by the Théâtre du Nouveau Monde on 18 Nov. 1978, directed by Jean-Luc Bastien, provoked a public outcry that earned it a place in Quebec's theatrical history. Because of the play's provocative subject matter the Montreal Arts Council refused to provide a production grant, and the ensuing controversy guaranteed the play's immediate success. While members of various religious groups—few of whom knew very much about the play—prayed at the theatre's doors, audiences flocked to this ritual of feminist liberation in large numbers. Subsequent attempts to suppress the production were unsuccessful, but the published text was temporarily banned by a Quebec Superior Court judge. Legal attacks on the play came to an end when the Supreme Court refused to hear charges of blasphemy in Feb. 1980.

The play is marked by evocative poetry and harsh realism. Assembled on the stage are three symbolic figures of feminine alienation: the Virgin, the Mother, and the Prostitute. They meet to proclaim their individual liberation as preparation for the liberation of Woman. Especially explosive is the depiction of the Virgin Mary, demythologized, laying claim to her status as a woman. Decrying the fact that her sexuality has been negated by the sublimation of her virginity, she drops, before the audience's eyes, the shackles that have made her a statue.

Through its exorcising incarnation of the Virgin, the play gave feminist demands a high profile in the theatre. At each corner of an obviously alienated triangle, three women finally 'pulled down their statues'.

LORRAINE CAMERLAIN

Fennario, David (b.1947). Born David Wiper, he assumed the name 'Fennario', which a girlfriend gave him from a Bob Dylan song. He was raised in Pointe-Saint-Charles, a working-class district of Montreal, where most of his plays are set; he now lives in nearby Verdun. He left school at sixteen, worked at odd jobs, and was part of the hippie generation of the late sixties, spending time in Montreal, Toronto, and New York. At Dawson College, Montreal, as a mature student he read widely, and became (and remains) a convinced Marxist.

His first published work, *Without a parachute* (1974)—translated into French by Gilles Hénault as *Sans parachute* (1977)—is an honest, straightforward, somewhat rambling record of his life and reflections as a blue-collar worker from Dec. 1969 to May 1971. It caught the interest of Maurice Podbrey, artistic director of Montreal's Centaur Theatre, who asked Fennario to write a play for Centaur and to become playwright-in-residence there, a position he held for several years. Fennario covered some of the same subject matter in another prose work, *Blue Mondays* (1984), based on further stories from his journals for the late 1960s; this volume is interspersed with collected poems by David Adams and illustrations by Sheila Salmela.

Fennario's career as a playwright was launched at the Centaur in 1975 with a production of *On the job* (1976), a one-act play about workers on Christmas Eve in the shipping room of a Montreal dress factory. Realistic, earthy, honest, and humorous, it depicts the plight of workers performing mindless jobs and finally rebelling against their employers. This same concern for the worker is shown in a longer one-act play, *Nothing to lose* (1977), translated into French by Robert Guy Scully as *À l'ouvrage* (1979), and produced in 1976 at the Centaur. Here Fennario introduces a character who plays himself, but Jerry Nines is not a convincing character and represents a self-indulgent tendency in Fennario's work that detracts from his often powerful dramatic statements. This tendency is also evident in his next play, *Toronto* (produced in Montreal in 1978 but unpublished), in which Jerry Nines is casting for the Toronto production of a play called *Nothing to lose*—and in two unpublished stage adaptations based on Fennario's journal: *Without a parachute*, performed in Toronto in 1978; and *Changes*, performed in Ottawa in 1980. The autobiographical dimension of his work continued in *Banana boots: Balconville in Belfast* (where *Balconville* was performed in 1981), a one-man play presented in both Toronto and Montreal in 1994, in which Fennario was both the subject and the laid-back performer.

BALCONVILLE (1980), Fennario's most successful and accomplished play, had its première at the Centaur in 1979, directed by Guy Sprung. Set among the balconies of the tenement houses of Pointe-Saint-Charles where eight characters, English and French, live out the dog days of one summer, it is considered the first bilingual Canadian play and shows a genuine understanding and concern for the working poor who struggle to survive and fight for their dignity, often humorously, in a depressing social situation; it also shows that their suffering goes deeper than the English-French conflict. The play has toured Canada, was performed at the Old Vic Theatre in London, and in 1979 received the Chalmers Award for the best Canadian play produced in the Toronto area that year. It was produced on CBC television in 1985, and revived at the Centaur in 1992, directed by Paul Thompson. Fennario's next work, produced at the Centaur in both the spring and fall of 1983, was *Moving*, a portrayal of the conflicts of a working-class, largely anglophone family, that surface when the family moves (as Fennario did) from Pointe-Saint-Charles to Verdun.

Disillusioned by the lack of empathy with his cause in mainstream theatre, Fennario formed his own company in Verdun, the Black Rock Community Group, which presented the first two of a trilogy of history plays, all directed by Simon Malbogat. The first of the trilogy was *Joe Beef (A history of Pointe Saint Charles)* presented in Verdun in 1984 and in Toronto in 1986. This musical drama is a comical and at times hard-hitting satire on the captains of industry who have exploited the workers throughout Canadian history. These same captains of industry, as well as various political leaders, are the targets of the second play in the trilogy, *Doctor Thomas Neill Cream (Mystery at McGill)* (1993), presented as *Doctor Neill Cream* by the Mixed Theatre Company in Toronto in 1988. The capitalist villains, many of whom were seen in *Joe Beef*, are shown as being more guilty of crimes against the working class of Montreal than the backstreet abortionist and brothel keeper Dr Cream. The third play in the trilogy, *The murder of Susan Parr*, marked the return of Fennario to the Centaur in 1989, following the closing of his theatre group in Verdun. Cast in the form of a murder mystery, the play presents a graphic picture of modern-day Pointe-Saint-Charles, where the condition of the working poor has barely improved since the nineteenth-century setting of the previous two plays.

The controversial *The death of René Lévesque*, produced at the Centaur in 1991, was an incomplete portrait of the former Parti Québécois leader, focusing on his betrayal of the working classes, a constant theme in Fennario's work. His next play at the Centaur was the one-act *Gargoyles*—his contribution to an evening of three short plays by himself and other playwrights, with the collective title *Mainly Montreal*—which premièred in January 1997. Described as 'an entertaining look at the history of Montreal', it continues his focus on his native city and the role of anglophone workers in its history. Most of Fennario's work has been a crusade to remind others of that place and those people.

There is a long interview with Fennario in *The work: conversations with English-Canadian playwrights* (1982), edited by Robert Wallace and Cynthia Zimmerman. See also Michael Benazon, 'From Griffintown to Verdun: a study of place in the work of Fennario', in *MATRIX*, 19 (1984), and *Ecrivains anglo-québécois II: dossiers de presse: David Fennario, 1972-1985* (1986), compiled by Claude Pelletier.

JAMES NOONAN

Ferguson, Trevor. See NOVELS IN ENGLISH 1983 to 1996: OTHER NOVELS: 1(b).

Ferron, Jacques (1921-85). Born in Louiseville, Quebec, he was educated at College Brébeuf, Trois-Rivières, and at Université Laval, where he graduated in medicine. Disheartened, while studying at Brébeuf, by the élitism of the French-Canadian upper class, he found himself turning more and more towards socialism. At the same time, discussions with Franco-Ontarians and Franco-Manitobans led him to think that Québécois alone had the opportunity to survive as a strong French-speaking nation in North America. While completing his medical studies he married Madeleine Therrien, a Communist who provided a new approach to class problems. Divorced and remarried, he spent one year in the army, where he became convinced that Canada and Quebec were incompatible solitudes, two nations that should be independent from each other. He first practised medicine on the Gaspé Peninsula, where he met several storytellers who became some of his most cherished characters. After eleven years as a general practitioner in working-class Montreal, he specialized briefly in caring for the mentally retarded before moving to Longueuil, where he practised as a family doctor. Ferron was well known for his political and social activities. In 1949 he was arrested for participating in a demonstration against NATO. In 1954 he was elected president of the Canadian Peace Congress. The following year he ran unsuccessfully as a candidate for the 'Parti social démocratique', claiming that Quebec socialism was controlled by English Canadians. In 1963 he founded the Rhinoceros Party, a nonsense federalist party whose motto was 'From one pond to another'. After the murder of Pierre Laporte during the 1970 October Crisis, the FLQ requested that Ferron be the government negotiator. This was accepted by the Bourassa government, and Ferron played a key role in the surrender of the Rose brothers and François Simard.

Ferron's first literary works were primarily plays concerned with metaphysical and social problems in which Quebec was almost never referred to directly. Reminiscent of Molière, Marivaux, and Labiche, they lacked originality. *Le licou* (1947) satirizes the classical notion of romantic and eternal love. *L'ogre* (1949) denounces the corruption of politics and religion. *Le dodu; ou Le prix du bonheur* (1956), *Tante Élise; ou Le prix de l'amour* (1956), *Le cheval de Don Juan* (1957), and *Cazou; ou Le prix de la virginité* (1963) all ridicule the rituals and conventions of love: seductions, fashion, marriages based on convenience and money.

In his next plays Ferron's unique talents as a writer appeared for the first time. Entertaining, ironical, and symbolic, his plays were also imaginative, whimsical, and humorous—they recalled the magic of a 'conteur'. *L'Américaine; ou Le triomphe de l'amitié* (1958) is a social allegory in which an educated and uneducated Québécois become friends and symbolically steal the purse of the all-American beauty Biouti Rose. *Les grands soleils* (1958), Ferron's most important play, replaces the established political and religious myths of Dollard des Ormeaux and Saint-Jean Baptiste by the memory of the Patriotes. *Le tête du roi* (1963) juxtaposes two historical events: the decapitation, by the FLQ in 1963, of the statue of General Wolfe on the Plains of Abraham and the Métis uprisings of 1870 and 1885.

Ferron's first novel, *La barbe de François Hertel* (1951), is an ironical and imaginative work that mocks the philosophical and sophistic mind of François Hertel (Rodolphe DUBÉ). In 1962 Ferron published his first major work, *CONTE DU PAYS INCERTAIN*, which won a Governor General's Award. Using legends, fables, and tales to illustrate Quebec's uncertain future, Ferron portrayed the land, formerly seen as a haven for survival, as being in an advanced state of decay; life in the city, however, offered no viable alternative, for the tillers of the land found slavery as members of the exploited working class in the city. *Contes du pays incertain* was republished in 1968 with *Contes anglais et autres* and *Contes inédits*. A selection of these stories, many of them from the first collection, was translated by Betty Bednarski and published as *Tales from the uncertain country* (1972). *Cotnoir* (1962), a novel that stylistically resembles a tale, presents one of Ferron's favourite themes: the necessity for a doctor to be both close to the people and a champion of freedom—which, in Quebec, implies political independence. It was translated by Pierre Cloutier as *Doctor Cotnoir* (1973). *La nuit* (1965) tells the story of François Ménard, a materialistic and bourgeois Québécois who, having lost contact with his heritage, gradually discovers a social order based on equality and historical awareness. It was translated by Ray Ellenwood as *Quince jam* (1977). *Papa Boss* (1966; republished with minor changes in 1972) describes the possession of an anonymous working-class woman by a capitalist angel, Papa Boss. *La charrette* (1968) depicts a doctor who, like François Ménard, liberates himself from social 'deconditioning' (unawareness) and endeavours to help the 'cart-people' (workers) victimized by the diabolical boss, Bélial. It was translated by Ray Ellenwood as *The cart* (1981). The young narrator of *L'amélanchier* (1970) is initiated by her father into the 'good side of things': family and national history as indispensable tools for growing up, and the pressing need for the preservation of the flora, fauna, and historical landmarks of Quebec. It was translated by Raymond Chamberlain as *The juneberry tree* (1975). *Le salut de l'Irlande* (1970), which argued that the salvation of Quebec and Ireland are closely linked, also tells the story of a young person who comes to realize that colonial and liberal ideologies, along with urban speculation, represent the real danger for Québécois eager to preserve their identity in a healthy environment. In *Les roses sauvages* (1971)—translated by Betty Bednarski as *Wild roses* (1976)—the businessman Baron learns the message of 'salvation' too late and joins the socially insane described in the short text, *Lettre d'amour*, which follows *Les roses sauvages*. Baron's daughter, however, will not be destroyed by ambition. Like Tinamer in *L'amélanchier* and Connie in *Le salut de l'Irlande*, she has understood the tale of survival; she will become a psychiatrist in order to help people like Rosaire Gélineau (*Rosaire*, 1981), whose mental illness is brought on by a society that discourages small craftsmen and thrives on assembly lines and seasonal unemployment. These Montreal novels are works of awareness and apprenticeship, quite obvious products of the 1960s, when Quebec was seen by most writers as a 'stupid and defenceless' suburb (*L'amélanchier*) of the USA, and when the FLQ warned that the homeland must be redeemed. For Ferron, violence was at once a threat, a warning, and a temptation.

Le ciel de Québec (1969)—Ferron's longest, most complex, and perhaps only true novel—cleverly intertwines four main stories centred in Quebec City in 1937-8 (the centennial of the Patriote rebellion): representatives of the Church involve themselves in politics, politicians display their skill in the use of patronage, Québécois reveal their feelings of exile in the West, the Métis are torn between staying on the Prairies and living in Quebec. Several digressions develop other themes: 1837; the English in Quebec; the role of Québécois writers in the elaboration of Quebec nationalism and identity. In *Le Saint-Élias* (1972), another historical novel, the launching of a ship in 1896 parallels the launching, by Dr Fauteux, of the ideals of the Patriotes. A decisive battle ensues between the supporters of the zealous monarchist Monseigneur Laflèche and the devoted and patriotic Doctor Fauteux. It was translated by Pierre Cloutier as *The Saint Elias* (1975). In *La chaise du maréchal ferrant* (1972) Ferron returned to the Gaspé, and through legend and folklore showed the devastating effects of ambition and money on an old Quebec family torn apart by the 'capitalist devil' and an amazing flying machine, the blacksmith's chair. The tale is humorously linked to the treachery of the 'federalist villain', Mackenzie King, and the 'provincial villain', Duplessis. Ferron's imaginative approach to history, inspired by Anthony Hamilton and Tallemant des Réaux and central to most of his works, is best illustrated in *Historiettes* (1969), a collection of tales or anecdotes in which historical and political figures are freely transformed into literary characters.

Most of Ferron's later novels display the same characteristics as *Contes du pays incertain*: condensed plot; legend; parable; imaginative and fabulous atmosphere; animation of the animal and plant worlds; a surrealistic and fantastic vision; fantasy as seen through the eyes of a child; irony, satire, and word-play. His tales, novels, and plays evoke both Lewis Carroll (*L'amélanchier* is a witty transposition of *Alice in Wonderland*) and *The thousand and one nights*. Ferron's father, who was a lawyer and political organizer, is a key antagonist in many of his novels. Ferron even claimed that he wanted to be a writer in order to denounce his conservative, élitist, and corrupt father; not surprisingly, biographical references were scattered throughout his works. There are also obvious links between Ferron's education and his writing. The tyranny and prejudices of religious communities encountered in his school life constituted one of his major themes.

Les confitures de coings (1972) is composed of new versions (all with minor changes) of the novels *Papa Boss*, *La nuit* (given the new title 'Les confitures de coings'), as well as 'La créance', an autobiographical tale dealing with social injustices in Louiseville, and 'Appendice aux *Confitures des coings* ou Le congédiement de Frank Archibald Campbell', an imaginative interpretation of *Les confitures de coings* combined with autobiographical insights and revelations. *Gaspé-Mattempa* (1980) is a tale that recreates Ferron's sojourn in the Gaspé.

Ferron's social and political ideas had considerable influence on modern Quebec society. His thirty-odd works form a coherent system in which their predominant themes—justice; social concepts of love; the physical and psychological effects of capitalism; the doctor's role in society; religious excesses; the creation of new myths related to Quebec history and politics; Quebec and foreign writers in relation to Ferron's view of the world—are articulated in an original and aesthetically pleasing setting. Ferron is in fact several writers in one: a 'conteur', a fabulist, a symbolist, and a creator of myths. As, also, a literary geographer, historian, botanist, and folklorist of the 'uncertain country', he, more than any other Quebec writer, turned real people and real situations into literary beings and fictional places.

Du fond de mon arrière-cuisine (1973) and *Escarmouches, la longue passe* (1975) give an excellent sampling of Ferron's innumerable articles dealing with history, medicine, literature, and politics that originally appeared in various journals and newspapers. Several books have been written on Ferron: Jean-Pierre Boucher, *Jacques Ferron au pays des amélanchiers* (1973) and *Les 'Contes' de Jacques Ferron* (1974); Jacques De Roussan, *Jacques Ferron* (1971); Jean Marcel, *Jacques Ferron malgré lui* (1970); Yves Taschereau, *La médicine dans l'oeuvre de Jacques Ferron* (1975); Pierre L'Hérault, *Jacques Ferron, cartographe de l'imaginaire* (1980); and Pierre Cantin, *Jacques Ferron, polygraphe* (1984). Special issues of *Études françaises* (1976) and *VOIX ET IMAGES* (printemps 1983) are devoted to Ferron. See also *Jacques Ferron: les lettres aux journaux* (1985), edited by Pierre Cantin, Marie Ferron, and Paul Lewis; and Donald Smith, 'Jacques Ferron: the marvellous folly of writing', *Voices of deliverance: interviews with Quebec and Acadian writers* (1986), translated by Larry Shouldice.

See also ESSAYS IN FRENCH: 7 and NOVELS IN FRENCH 1960 TO 1982: 2.

DONALD SMITH

Ferron, Madeleine (b. 1922). Born in Trois-Rivières, Quebec, a year after her brother Jacques FERRON, she spent her youth in Louiseville before attending secondary school with the Soeurs de Sainte-Anne in Lachine. She took courses in the Faculté des lettres at Université de Montréal (1942) and later studied ethnography at Université Laval (1960). In 1945 she married Robert Cliche, with whom she published two historical and ethnographical essays: *Quand le peuple fait la loi* (1972) and *Les Beaucerons ces insoumis* (1974).

Ferron has published five collections of short stories—*Coeur de sucre* (1966), *Le chemin des dames* (1977), *Histoires édifiantes* (1981), *Un amour singulier* (1987), and *Le grand théâtre* (1989)—and three novels: *La fin des loups-garous* (1966), *Le baron écarlate* (1971), and *Sur le chemin Craig* (1983). She has also written a history of her mother's family, the Carons: *Adrienne* (1993).

What is striking about this list, with its three genres, is the persistence of a thematic pattern that is always closely linked to her native region (the St-Maurice area) and her adopted home (the Beauce)—places that are metonyms for the Quebec to which Madeleine Ferron is no less attached, albeit more discreetly, than her brother. Also like her brother, but in a more traditional fashion, she has, as she reveals in the 'Preamble' to *Histoires édifiantes*, 'an ethnographer's concerns [and a] constant need . . . to have stories told to me.' The origins of this urge can be traced to the family itself, for she admits to feeling 'nostalgic for the endless stories that [her] father would tell [them]'. In her collections she has gathered no fewer than 75 stories that show a clear evolution as the writing becomes more and more assured and the attention focuses increasingly on women's lives. In this context it is interesting to note that her career as a short-story writer began with a tale in which young people try to have a good time at a sugar-house ('Coeur de sucre') and ends with one in which an elderly woman struggles to remember isolated moments of her past ('Parapluie rose avec une bordure mauve', *Le grand théâtre*). Between these two texts Ferron worked a vast range of themes, but all revolve around love of life and respect for nature in all its senses. This does not preclude the presence of love, hate, joy, death, madness, stupidity, loyalty, violence, and betrayal. But what always emerges from this writing, which focuses on the details of existence in order to show both its great and petty aspects, is a kind of disturbed serenity and a questioning of values both old and new, for in Ferron's fictional universe good and evil can be hiding anywhere.

From the beginning of her career in narrative, her work has had a touch of the *terroir*, the idealized vision of Quebec's rural past; but Ferron has tried not to identify herself with this genre by creating a kind of anti-*terroir*, presenting characters who cheerfully go against traditional rules of social behaviour. Thus in *La fin des loups-garous* and several of the stories in *Coeur de sucre*, illicit love, madness, and bizarre behaviour are common themes. The role and discourse of the curé are openly criticized on several occasions. The collection *Le chemin des dames* presents the lives of women rich and poor, French- and English-speaking, whose existential journey is not always orthodox ('La tricheuse', 'La Rolls-Royce de madame Clark'). In *Histoires édifiantes* the focus is on characters who have suffered some reversal in their personal lives, whether as a result of their own foolishness or of social injustice, and who have either recovered from it or lost themselves. Beginning with *Le chemin des dames*, the mainly (though not exclusively) feminine discourse continues in *Un amour singulier* and *Le grand théâtre*, which almost always feature a female narrator talking about the joys and pain she feels or has been a witness to. In a sense, the novel *Le baron écarlate*, though written some years earlier, belongs to the same category of feminine discourse, since in it a female narrator tells of her life with an adoptive father, as extravagant as he is good, who nevertheless keeps her in a state of happy submission. In the end the narrator shakes off her golden chains.

Like a watermark just beneath the surface of her work, there is always a hint that—in the guise of attention to the minor details of life—Madeleine Ferron is also tracing the history and intellectual life of Quebec, from the origins of French Canada through the nineteenth century (with *Sur le chemin Craig*, a fictional history of the Beauce region) to the middle and end of the twentieth century. She is still driven by a hunger for justice and truth, attention to nature, and, ultimately, humanism.

MICHEL LORD

Fetherling, Douglas (b. 1949). Born in Wheeling, West Virginia, USA, he came to Canada in 1966-7. He became associated with the newly founded House of ANANSI and began to establish himself as a poet and writer. Essentially an autodidact, Fetherling has written poetry, fiction, cultural history, art and film criticism, Canadian history, and memoirs. Most of his adult life has been spent in Toronto—with a stint in Kingston, Ontario, at the end of the 1980s and the beginning of the 1990s, when he was associated with the Kingston *Whig-Standard* as Literary Editor, and then passed a year as writer-in-residence at Queen's University. In 1990 he became the owner and editor of *Canadian Notes & Queries*, which he transformed into a larger magazine of literary history, reviews, and bibliography—much broader in focus than its eponymous British counterpart. Fetherling has been an active 'man about letters', and his contributions to Canadian literature were recognized in 1995 when he won the Harbourfront Festival Prize.

As a poet, he fits into none of the obvious contemporary Canadian categories. His work is personal without being overtly emotional, witty at times, and often focused on social and political themes. He has himself described his poetry as 'a tool to see if I could register my experience in an accurate manner that might be accessible to others', and the precision of that statement is also characteristic of his poems. His work is most easily found in two selected volumes: *Variorum: new poems and old 1965-1985* (1985) and *Selected poems* (1994). Fetherling has a natural affinity for small-press and private-press publishing, and a number of collections have been issued in limited editions or by alternate publishers. He has published one novel, a political piece called *The file on Arthur Moss* (1994).

Fetherling has been deeply interested in the history, especially the cultural history, of Canada, and this abiding obsession and affection has resulted in several important books, such as *The gold crusades: a social history of gold rushes, 1849-1929* (1988). His interest in printing and publishing resulted in two books on Canadian newspaper history, *The rise of the Canadian newspaper* (1990) and *A little bit of thunder: the strange inner life of the Kingston Whig-Standard* (1992). He has edited two collections of documents, one on Canadian art and another on Canadian film, and some of his film criticism, much of it written for *The CANADIAN FORUM*, was collected in *The crowded darkness* (1988). Fetherling is a reflective and attractively idiosyncratic travel writer, and has published two books in this genre: *Year of the horse: a journey through Russia and China* (1991) and *The other China: journeys around Taiwan* (1995).

Among all his publications, Fetherling's most accomplished, and certainly his most moving, book is *Travels by night: a memoir of the sixties* (1994), a deeply personal and wonderfully realized account of his childhood and early manhood. *Way down deep in the belly of the beast: a memoir of the seventies* (1996), the second in what will eventually be a trilogy of autobiographical books, might better be described as a memoir of his twenties in Toronto; it focuses on the friends, acquaintances, and others in the cultural world he inhabited.

In *Catalogus* (1991), Fetherling provided a charming and anecdotal bibliography of his books to that year. BRUCE WHITEMAN

Fiamengo, Maria (b. 1926). Born in Vancouver, British Columbia, of Yugoslavian parents from Dalmatia, she was educated at the University of British Columbia and received an M.A. in creative writing, under thesis director Earle BIRNEY, for her book of poems *The ikon: measured work* (1961). For many years she taught in the English department at UBC. Her poems are reprinted in such major anthologies as Dorothy LIVESAY's *Forty women poets of Canada* (1973), *Skookum Wawa: writings of the Canadian Northwest* (1975), *The Penguin book of Canadian verse* (1984), and *Words we call home: creative writing at UBC* (1990).

Fiamengo's other poetry collections—*Quality of halves* (1958), *Overheard at the oracle* (1969), *Silt of iron* (1971), and *In praise of old women* (1976), some poems of which were reprinted in *North of the cold star* (1978) and *Patience after compline* (1989)—are reflective, intellectual, humorous, and passionate. In addition to writing about political repression and social injustice, she is especially effective in dealing with the oppression of women by themselves. Her poem 'In praise of old women' criticizes aging North American women who attend beauty salons in order to remain attractive to men. Her ironic wit keeps her matter-of-fact imagery—which often draws upon her Slavic origins—from becoming forced and her poems from becoming mere tracts or polemics. Fiamengo's later poems continue her interest in Canadian ancestry, especially the strengths of immigrant women, and include meditations on nature, Norman Bethune, the RCMP, and a favourite target: American academics in Canadian universities, against whom she wages a constant guerilla action. *White linen remembered* (1996) continues her faith in language and love of words. Still a strong Canadian nationalist, feminist, and socialist, Fiamengo in this volume continues writing poems that have a loving, lyrical intensity grounded in sociopolitical realities, childhood memories, and elegies for intimate friends. The collection examines the essence of mortality and the power of art to heal and sustain the human spirit; she sings of 'the perfection/that comes at dark.' GEOFF HANCOCK

Fiddlehead, The. A literary magazine published continuously at the University of New Brunswick since 1945. Founded as a poetry magazine by Alfred BAILEY and Desmond PACEY with a group of student writers, and modelled on *PREVIEW* and *FIRST STATEMENT*, it served until 1953 as a purely local magazine. Fred COGSWELL, who became chief editor in that year and held the job until 1967, expanded the magazine to include writers from across, and outside, Canada, and to print stories and reviews as well as poems. The magazine has followed a widely eclectic policy, which has allowed it to publish many young and relatively unknown writers. A number of these—such as Al PURDY, Milton ACORN, Jay MACPHERSON, Elizabeth BREWSTER, and Alden NOWLAN—became well established. Kent THOMPSON, Robert GIBBS, Roger Ploude, Peter Thomas, Donald Conway, and Michael Taylor were the magazine's editors from 1967 to 1991. Don McKAY and Bill Gaston are now joint editors.

See *Fiddlehead gold: fifty years of the Fiddlehead* (1995) edited by Sabine Campbell, Roger Ploude, and Demetres Tryphonopoulos.

ROBERT GIBBS

Fiddlehead Poetry Books/Goose Lane Editions. One of Canada's earliest small presses, Fiddlehead Poetry Books Series was an important outlet for Canadian poets from 1954 until 1982. Writers first published by Fiddlehead include Roo BORSON (*Landfall*, 1977), Don GUTTERIDGE (*Death at Quebec*, 1971), Joy KOGAWA (*The splintered moon*, 1967), Alden NOWLAN (*The rose and the puritan*, 1958), and Robert Hawkes (*First time death*, 1979). Fiddlehead also published early work by M. Travis LANE, Norman LEVINE, Dorothy LIVESAY, and Al PURDY. The driving force behind Fiddlehead Books for twenty-five of its twenty-nine years was Fred COGSWELL, who took on editing and publishing duties when the University of New Brunswick withdrew its support in 1958. During his editorship he published 307 books, many of them financed out of his own pocket. His self-declared policy of eclectic publication, internationalism (only one-fifth of the writers published by Cogswell had connections with Atlantic Canada), and avoidance of coteries, and the sheer number of titles he produced (forty-four in 1973 alone) earned Cogswell a national reputation as a mentor of young writers.

Peter Thomas, who ran the company from 1981 to 1988, reduced the number of titles published and, under the name of Goose Lane Editions, added prose to its list. Goose Lane has introduced major changes in production, marketing, and book design, and increased representation by regional authors. It now issues about fifteen books a year—many of them noteworthy for good design—on art, crafts, cookery, folklore, regional history, and biography, as well as poetry and fiction. Goose Lane also acts as a distributor for other Maritime small-press and academic publications.

WENDY SCOTT

Fidler, Peter. See EXPLORATION LITERATURE IN ENGLISH: 2.

Fife, Connie. See LESBIAN LITERATURE.

Fifth business (1970). The first novel in the Deptford trilogy by Robertson DAVIES, it established him as one of Canada's leading writers of fiction. The story has a double focus. As the 'autobiography' of the schoolmaster Dunstan Ramsay it narrates key events in his life: his ducking of a fateful snowball, his boyhood love for the saintly Mary Dempster, his experiences in the First World War, his researches as a hagiographer, and his encounters with the business magnate Boy Staunton, the magician Magnus Eisengrim, and the fantastically ugly Liesl Naegeli. While Ramsay figures as hero in his own story, he plays quite a different part in the lives of Mary Dempster, her son Paul, Leola Cruikshank, and Boy Staunton: he is 'fifth business'—playing a subsidiary but essental role in the drama of their lives and bringing the action to an appropriate conclusion.

Gordon Roper's '*Fifth business* and "That old fantastical duke of dark corners, C.G. Jung"' in the *Journal of Canadian Fiction* 1, no. 1 (Winter 1972) first drew critical attention to Davies' rich absorption of Jung's ideas. Ramsay's gradual achievement of self-knowledge can be compared to Jung's 'individuation', and characters and situations encountered along the way to Jungian archetypes. For Jung, coming to terms with oneself involves retrieving and facing the contents of the unconscious—which contains archetypes to which he gave appropriate names. He called a man's unconscious notion of woman the Anima; those elements rejected from the conscious personality the Shadow; the characters inherited in the collective unconscious memory, shared by all people, the Magus or Magician, the Devil, the Wise Old Man—and so on. One achieves self-mastery by recognizing that the unconscious may distort one's view of other people and by reclaiming the archetype that has been projected on another person. In *Fifth business* the archetypes are not only projections that must be recognized and recovered but elements in a story that has a fairy-tale or mythic quality. At one level we are persuaded to accept a romantic world where figures like a saint (Mary Dempster), and Magus (Magnus Eisengrim), and a Wise Old Man (Padré Blazon) act out their archetypcal roles unrestrained by prosaic reality.

Fifth business was published simultaneously in Canada, the United States, and England, and has been translated into sixteen languages. It is available as a Penguin paperback.

JUDITH SKELTON GRANT

Finch, Robert (1900-95). Robert Duer Claydon Finch was born at Freeport, Long Island, New York. He studied at University College, University of Toronto, and at the Sorbonne in Paris, and in 1928 joined the staff of the Department of French, University College, Toronto, where he was a full professor from 1952 until his retirement in 1968. Finch was also been a well-known poet, and a painter and harpsichordist of considerable reputation. His masque, 'A century has roots', was presented for the centenary of University College in 1953. His distinguished career as a scholar, particularly of seventeenth- and eighteenth-century French poetry, came to fruition in *The sixth sense: a study of individualism in French poetry 1686-1760* (1966) and in an anthology, *French individualist poetry* (1971), which he edited with E. Joliat. He received the Lorne PIERCE Gold Medal in 1968, and was elected to the Royal Society of Canada in 1963.

Finch was one of six poets included in the anthology *NEW PROVINCES* (1936). From the beginning he was primarily a lyric poet. In *Poems* (1946), which received a Governor General's Award, his skill with language and form gave his wit full scope in epigrams and satiric portraits. Like other poets reacting against the confessional poetry of the Romantic era, Finch treated emotional experience with reticence and allusiveness. *The strength of the hills* (1948) contains many emblematic and allegorical poems, and features a sonnet sequence on mountains that develops moral and religious themes. Other poems include exact and vivid re-creations of places and seasons, and a series on the transforming power of snow that uses images of beauty rather than the stereotyped symbol of a hostile force.

Although two volumes published in 1961, *Acis in Oxford* (first privately printed in 1959) and *Dover Beach revisited*, contain a number of brief lyrics in Finch's characteristic voice, they revealed new interests and a considerable extension of range. *Acis in Oxford* (winner of a Governor General's Award) includes three poems linked by associations with an Oxford college, its gardens, a public park, and the river, that also draw easily on long traditions of myth and culture. The problem of faith is central to *Dover Beach revisited*, which begins with a reconsideration of Arnold's famous poem by eleven speakers who, though loosely associated with the poem's provenance, are themselves timeless. A second section, 'The place revisited', consists of nine vigorous blank-verse poems about 'Operation Dynamo', the battle of Dunkirk.

Silverthorn bush (1966) has greater variety of form, subject, and image than any previous volume. Finch ranges widely through Chinese calligraphy, ancient and modern Tibet, early Canadian history, and the Western literary tradition; but, wearing his learning lightly, he also records the small experiences of ordinary life on a road, in a train, in a shop. *Variations and theme* (1980) consists of reflections on the nature of poetry, evocative miniatures of particular times and places, witty epigrams, hints of the experience of old age and memory. The title poem—fourteen variations, with a final section in rhyming couplets—concerns the moments of illumination offered by the senses and the imagination: past experience enters the present, but each experience also opens towards the future, towards an infinity beyond guessing.

The seven parts of *Has and is and other poems* (1981) reflect Finch's characteristic diversity. Urbane, elegant, and vigorous, the poems evince ease of manner and control of tone throughout. The last poem, 'The arbiter', brings together art, poetry, and life as a single entity, a unified conception. Later collections are *Twelve for Christmas* (1982), twelve rondeaux on poets, *The Grand Duke of Moscow's favourite solo* (1983), *Double tuning* (1984), *For the back of a likeness* (1986), and *Sail-boat and lake* (1988). JOHN MARGESON

Findley, Timothy (b. 1930). Born in Toronto, Ontario, he attended St Andrew's College, Rosedale Public School, and Jarvis Collegiate until, at the age of sixteen, he finished with formal schooling. His ambition was to dance; a fused disc brought this career to an end, so the young Findley turned to acting—an alternative means of formulating what he has called 'the perfect gesture' in art. For some years he pursued a theatrical career; he participated in Ontario's Stratford Festival's première season in 1953. The National Film Board profile *Timothy Findley: anatomy of a writer* (1992) includes a fascinating sequence of Alec Guinness coaching the young actor on the speaking of Shakespearean lines. Guinness then sponsored Findley's further studies at the London Central School of Speech and Drama, and Findley toured extensively in Thornton Wilder's play *The matchmaker*. Wilder became an important mentor, largely through the intercession of the actress Ruth Gordon, for whom Findley wrote his first short story, 'About Effie' (published in Issue One of *The* TAMARACK REVIEW, Autumn 1956, and reprinted in the short-story collection *Dinner along the Amazon*, 1984). Though Findley shortly thereafter turned his attention to the writing of fiction, he never left the theatrical world behind. In the 1970s he wrote many scripts for CBC television and radio, sometimes in collaboration with his companion William Whitehead. He has written plays (*Can you see me yet?*, 1976, *Sir John A.—Himself!*, 1978, and *The stillborn lover*, 1993) and his theatrical sensibility extends into his fiction: he is a master of the dramatic scene and tableau. It was as a novelist, however, that Findley found 'the perfect gesture'—invariably a political one.

His first novel, *The last of the crazy people* (1967), about a lonely young boy, trapped in a repressive household, who kills his mother, father, and aunt as a way of silencing their pain, was largely dismissed by Canadian critics. Noting echoes of the 'Southern Gothic' of American writers like Carson McCullers and Flannery O'Connor, they pronounced the novel derivative, non-'Canadian'. In the 1990s, however, critics returned to his first novel, finding in it the seeds of his later fiction's concerns with madness as social construct and the fascistic intolerance of 'deviance'.

Findley once described himself as a 'dedicated anti-fascist writer and thinker', and, in his second novel, *The butterfly plague* (1969), he explicitly locates his critique in the historico-political frame of Nazi ideology. Moving between the poles of Hollywood and Germany

—between film's rage for 'perfection' and Hitler's—Findley produced a haunting parable whose surrealist method cannot obscure its historical referents. But again, Canadian critics barely acknowledged its existence; and even after Findley's coming into prominence in the late 1970s, they tended to remain critical of *The butterfly plague*, which they saw as a sprawling, oppressively symbolic work. In 1986, sharing some of that disaffection, Findley issued a revised version of the novel (commenting on his publisher's pressuring him to 'explain' symbols like the ever-present butterflies).

After the publication of his third novel, *The WARS* (1977), Findley would never need again to make his artistic presence known to Canadians. (This novel has also gained an international audience, having been translated into French, German, Dutch, Norwegian, and Spanish.) It won a Governor General's Award, was the basis of a film (directed by Robin Phillips, 1983), and has continued to be the most frequently written-about and taught of Findley's works. This tale of a young Canadian soldier of the Great War revisits some by-now recognizably 'Findleyan' concerns (defiance of authoritarian ideologies, the punishing of 'deviance'—homosexuality), and it returns to the sparer style of *The last of the crazy people*. But it also meditates, in a more self-conscious way, on language and texts as constructions; a researcher-narrator leads readers through a conundrum: how should an act of defiance of authority, like Robert Ross's attempt to set horses free on the battlefield, be 'read'?

Findley continued to muse upon this concern with language and texts as constructions in *Famous last words* (1981) by having two reader figures, Freyberg and Quinn, offer competing 'readings' of the memoirs of fascist sympathizer Hugh Selwyn Mauberley (Ezra Pound's persona in his poem of that name), transcribed with a silver pencil on the walls of rooms of a hotel in the Tyrol while he was a prisoner. It recounts sensational events in the thirties and early forties, and many of the characters are historical figures: the Duke and Duchess of Windsor, Queen Mary, von Ribbentrop, Rudolf Hess, Charles Lindbergh, Sir Harry Oakes, and Pound himself, described as Mauberley's 'surrogate father'. But lest readers feel too lulled by the notion of history-as-text, Findley rudely undercuts the aestheticism of Quinn, the sympathetic reader, with the objections of Freyberg, who reminds him that Mauberley 'walked with Mussolini . . . sat down with von Ribbentrop . . . wrote Fascist garbage.' Findley's text now seems to interrogate the writer's craft itself as ideological project: if a writer creates worlds reminiscent of, but other than, the experiential world, then is there a dangerous potential for that creativity to ally itself with another dream of world-making: fascism?

Like *The wars*, Findley's fifth novel, *Not wanted on the voyage* (1984), was received with acclaim. His intertextual study of fascism returns, but this time the intertexts reach back to Genesis and to medieval miracle plays. A spirited retelling of the story of Noah, the novel reconfigures the Ark as harbinger of the Holocaust; like the horses in the hold of Robert Ross's troop ship in *The wars*, the humans and animals grouped in this ship's hold are 'not wanted on the voyage'—they are potential victims of a 'final solution'. By comparison with the critical success of *Not wanted on the voyage*, the reception of *The telling of lies* (1986) was cool. Findley here adopts a first-person narrative mode, which he had usually employed in short stories. Another departure was in his engaging the mystery story as a means of meditating on institutional 'lies', and the counter-lies or defiances, that he had conceptualized in previous fictions. In this novel, however, the counter-lies participate in the very economy of deception that they are supposedly set in opposition to. In keeping the identity of the killer of drugs magnate Calder Maddox a secret, Vanessa Van Horne acknowledges that she has started to play the same game as her enemies, the CIA and global capitalism.

In many ways Findley's *Headhunter* (1993) and *The piano man's daughter* (1995) form a duet on the theme of socially constructed notions of madness. In its dark, futuristic investigation of abuses of power at the 'Parkin Institute of Psychiatric Research', *Headhunter* is Findley's most sombre novel, in which a ring of pederasts is uncovered that preys on children pandered to them by Rupert Kurtz, the power-obsessed psychiatrist-in-chief. (The novel incorporates an intertextual reading of Conrad's *Heart of darkness*, set in contemporary Rosedale, Toronto.) In many ways *The piano man's daughter* is an antidote to the despair of *Headhunter*. The madness of Lily Kilworth (the piano man's daughter and the protagonist) is both uncontrollable and strangely beautiful and healing. She is a rewriting of the 'mad' seer—the Cassandra—of the previous novel, the librarian Lilah Kemp. And Lily's son Charlie (another Marlow-type seeker), in his quest for the identity of his father, is searching, like so many of Findley's other male figures, for a way of being male that will not align him with the paternal authoritarianism of fascistic ideologies. His comments frame the events of the novel which take place between the turn of the twentieth century and the end of the Second World War—which is also the background of *You went away: a novella* (1996). The setting here, however, is Air Force bases in Barrie and Trenton, Ontario, and it is a novella only in the sense that the plot is less complex than that of Findley's other novels—though the characters (husband, wife, son, lover) and situations are treated with the same patience and insight.

Inside memory: pages from a writer's workbook (1990) is a charming memoir. Findley discusses the writing of short stories (from his second collection, *Stones*, 1988) and masculinity as construction in an interview in *CANADIAN LITERATURE* 148 (Spring 1996). See recent re-readings of Findley's novels by Barbara Gabriel, 'Staging monstrosity: genre, life-writing, and Timothy Findley's *The last of the crazy people*', *Essays on Canadian Writing* 54 (Winter 1994) and 'Performing the bent text: fascism and the regulation of sexualities in Timothy Findley's *The butterfly plague*', *English Studies in Canada* 21:2 (June 1995). See also Donna P. Pennee, *Moral metafiction* (1991), Lorraine York, *Front lines* (1991), and Carol Roberts, *Timothy Findley: stories from a life* (1994). LORRAINE YORK

Fineberg, Larry (b.1945). Born in Montreal and educated at McGill University, and Emerson College, Massachusetts, he began his theatrical career as an assistant director in New York and London. As a playwright he has explored a variety of styles. The macabre comic fantasy of *Hope* (1972), inspired by the drawings of Edward Gorey, contrasts with the gentler fantasy of the children's musical *Waterfall* (1974, prod. 1973). *Montreal* (1982, prod. 1981) presents a somewhat diffuse satire on corruption that, despite its local references, could really be set anywhere. The characters of *Tickle me* (1990)—a rich woman who is two-and-a-half centuries old, and a brilliant young man who has found a cure for AIDS—have a mythic quality. The cure involves the blood of gay men, and works only for heterosexuals; but the play is too sketchy to explore the symbolic power of this idea fully.

Fineberg's most characteristic and successful work explores the bleakness of family life, sometimes with unbroken realism, sometimes with a mixture of realism and fantasy. *Death* (1972) is an austere one-act play that shows the despair of a dying old man, and the emptiness of the lives that surround him, in a series of short scenes full of sternly economical dialogue. *Stonehenge trilogy* (1972), revised as *Stonehenge* (1978), includes some grimly witty social satire in its presentation of scenes in the life of a middle-class Jewish community. *Devotion* (1987, prod. 1985) shows a tense family gathering in the wake of the mother's suicide; as relationships break and regroup, the mother herself, still on stage, contributes caustic asides. The play's bleakness is relieved by occasional gentleness and dour, low-key humour.

Eve (1977, prod. 1976), Fineberg's stage adaptation of Constance BERESFORD-HOWE's *The book of Eve*, won the Chalmers Award for Best Canadian Play.

ALEXANDER LEGGATT

Finnigan, Joan (b. 1925). Born in Ottawa, Ontario, she attended Queen's University, Kingston (B.A., 1967), and now lives north of Kingston on Hambly Lake. Her early poetry, from *Through the glass, darkly* (1957) to *It was warm and sunny when we set out* (1970), concentrated on personal relationships and was sometimes confessional in tone, with an elegaic note of loss; though *Entrance to the greenhouse* (1968) is a series of haiku-like lyrics, focusing on her response to the quick upsurge of life in nature. This movement in her poetry is gathered in a collection, *In the brown cottage on Loughborough Lake* (1970) with photographs by Erik Christensen, that underlines the poet's feelings about nature in relation to a 'limbo all summer long' as she reflects on the death of love.

Finnigan wrote the script for a National Film Board movie, *The best damn fiddler from Calabogie to Kaladar* (1968), for which she won a Genie Award. From that time on, her writing showed an increased interest in localities throughout the Ottawa Valley, and the people living in them. She turned to prose to recount tall tales, local legends, and oral histories, as well as straightforward historical accounts, starting with *I come from the Valley* (1976), and the latest of which are *Witches ghosts & loups-garous: scary tales from Canada's Ottawa Valley* (1993) and *Dancing at the crossroads* (1995).

Finnigan's *Wintering over* (1992) contains four long poems arising from her interests in the settlers in the Ottawa Valley. Other poems continue her fascination with voice and character, and some are dramatic monologues: the title poem has been presented on stage at the Canadian Museum of Civilization and been performed in many schools throughout the Ottawa Valley. The verse-drama contained in this volume, 'Songs from both sides of the river', was commissioned by the National Arts Centre, Ottawa, and staged there in 1987.

PETER STEVENS

First Statement (1942-5). Founded in Montreal in Sept. 1942 by John SUTHERLAND—and his sister Betty, Robert Simpson, Keith MacLellan, and Audrey Aikman—*First Statement* was Sutherland's response to a rejection of his creative writing by the recently founded *PREVIEW*. Intended as a fortnightly, but appearing irregularly, the magazine averaged 8-to-10 mimeographed pages for its first fifteen issues, with a core circulation of 75. In Issue 5 it incorporated *The Western Free-lance* and its Vancouver editor, Geoffrey Ashe, and made claims to being national. By 1943 Simpson and MacLellan had dropped from the board, and were replaced by Irving LAYTON and Louis DUDEK, with Sutherland still editor-in-chief; a shift from eclecticism to a poetry that articulated the local and everyday experience in plain language, and from a North American perspective, now became more pronounced. Unlike its frequent editorial target, *Preview*—known for the wit, technical sophistication, and cosmopolitan concerns of its slightly older and more established contributors—*First Statement* disavowed any poetry that seemed 'colonial', favouring work that was influenced by American models, such as Ezra Pound and William Carlos Williams, over what were considered to be *Preview*'s British influences: W.H. Auden, T.S. Eliot, and Dylan Thomas. With the acquisition of a printing press, *First Statement* improved in appearance with vol. 2, no. 1 (Aug. 1943). It became an irregular monthly with more than double the number of pages and—in addition to the usual poetry, short stories, and criticism—offered book reviews. Because of financial constraints it became a bi-monthly in Oct.-Nov. 1944 and averaged 35 pages per issue.

In 1945 First Statement Press launched the important New Writers chapbook series with Layton's first collection, *Here and now*, which was followed later in the year by Patrick ANDERSON's *A tent for April* and Miriam WADDINGTON's *Green world*. In late 1945, after 33 issues, *First Statement* merged with *Preview* to become *NORTHERN REVIEW* with Sutherland as managing editor. He maintained control of First Statement Press, publishing Raymond SOUSTER's *When we are young* (1946); *Other Canadians: an anthology of the new poetry in Canada, 1940-46* (1947), edited by Sutherland and compiled in reaction to A.J.M. SMITH's first anthology, *The book of Canadian poetry* (1943); Layton's *Now is the place* (1948); Anne WILKINSON's *Counterpoint to sleep* (1951); and Kay Smith's *Footnote to the Lord's Prayer* (1951).

See Neil H. Fisher, *'First Statement': an assessment and an index* (1974), and Ken Norris, *The little magazine in Canada 1925-80* (1984).

DAVID O'ROURKE

Fischman, Sheila. See TRANSLATIONS: FRENCH TO ENGLISH: 3.

Fleming, May Agnes (1840-80). Born in Saint John, New Brunswick, Mary Agnes Early became one of the first Canadians to pursue a highly successful career as a writer of popular fiction. She published her first story, 'The last of the Mountjoys', in the New York *Mercury* in 1857, while she was still attending the Convent of the Sacred Heart in Saint John. From then on for the next decade, often as 'Cousin May Carleton', she sold short stories and serialized novels to such newspapers as the Boston Pilot, the New York *Mercury* and *Metropolitan Record*, and the Saint John *Western Recorder*. From 1868 to 1871 Early, now May Agnes Fleming—she had married William John Fleming, a machinist, in Saint John in 1865—wrote exclusively for the *Philadelphia Saturday Night*. After their first appearance in these periodicals, her works were usually republished, often with a different title, in volume form; sometimes they were dramatized. From 1872 until her death Fleming benefited from an arrangement that allowed her stories to appear simultaneously in the New York *Weekly* and the London *Journal*, and then be republished in book form by G.W. Carleton of New York and Low of London. The *Weekly* paid $100 per instalment and the *Journal* £12; she received a 15-per-cent royalty from Carleton. Since her annual output was at least one novel that ran to about 30 instalments, she became a wealthy woman. In 1875 Fleming moved—with her husband, from whom she later separated, and her four children—to Brooklyn; she died there of Bright's disease at age thirty-nine. Her popularity was such that her stories, frequently retitled, were regularly republished for more than thirty years after her death.

In her novels Fleming was able to achieve a balance between the domestic and the exotic that accounts chiefly for their appeal to her largely urban, middle-class, married women readers. Much of the action of her later stories took place in New York City; but her settings also included London and Paris, large estates in the USA and Great Britain, and—because French Canada provided an exotic locale for American readers—Montreal and the villages of Quebec. Her protagonists were often relatively poor working women, such as seamstresses and teachers, and her plots usually centred on marrying them to apparently good, prosperous men, preferably with connections to the British aristocracy. Complications arose from the greed and inexperience of the women, who often chose weak husbands, and the evil nature of the men. Fleming's books allowed her readers not only to live out in fantasy their most romantic dreams and bizarre impulses, but to reassure themselves that, however humble and humdrum their lives might seem, true nobility lay not in external appearances but in internal reality and eternal truths.

Among Fleming's novels are *La Masque; or, The midnight queen* (1863); *A mad marriage* (1875); and *Kate Danton; or, Captain Danton's daughters* (1876). 'A checklist of the works of May Agnes Fleming', compiled by Lorraine McMullen and published in the *Papers of the Bibliographical Society of Canada* (vol. 28, 1989) provides the most complete record available of Fleming's fiction. Her novels have been reproduced on microfiche by the Canadian Institute for Historical Microreproductions. The best analysis of her achievements is Lorraine McMullen's 'May Agnes Fleming: "I did nothing but write"' in *Silenced sextet: six nineteenth-century Canadian women novelists* (1992), by Carrie MacMillan, Lorraine McMullen, and Elizabeth Waterston.

MARY JANE EDWARDS

Flood, Cynthia (b. 1940). Born in Toronto, Ontario, she was educated at the University of Toronto (B.A., 1961) and the University of California, Berkeley (M.A., 1962). She worked in publishing in the USA and Canada before moving in 1969 to Vancouver, British Columbia, where she teaches at Langara College and is an activist in feminist and leftist politics. Her stories are collected in *The animals in their elements* (1987) and *My father took a cake to France* (1992), the title story of which won the 1990 Journey Prize. She also won the 1993 Western Magazine Award for Fiction.

Flood writes stories that deftly, and often shockingly, expose the emotional and psychological undercurrents of intergenerational lives; ordinary events resonate with devastating and scarring import when they are recognized as the source of old and new psychic wounds. Her narrative voices never judge the issues or people represented; rather, with honesty, irony, and sometimes bitter regret, her fiction's surface ordinariness gives way to mysteries and secrets otherwise obscured or repressed. Her stories often loosely parallel her own life as a student, married to (and divorced from) Maurice J. Flood, who had been an American conscientious objector, and as a writer, teacher, and political and social activist working through the inheritances of being the daughter of Canadian historian Donald G. CREIGHTON and novelist and children's writer Luella Creighton.

DONNA PALMATEER PENNEE

Folklore in English. The term 'folklore' refers both to the material handed on in tradition, whether by word of mouth or by custom and practice, and to the study of that material. Until recently most Canadian publications have emphasized the material rather than its study. Of primary concern to folklorists are books that present folklore as it actually circulated among the folk, rather than those that present it in a more literary form, as interpreted by the author.

For this *Companion* it is appropriate to emphasize the oral aspects of folklore: what may be termed oral literature or the verbal arts, of which the most important are folksongs and folktales. Folklore's customs and beliefs, however, were the first of its aspects to be reported in the writings of the early missionaries, explorers, and travellers. The journals of Henry Kelsey, David Thompson, Paul KANE, and John Franklin all included information on the beliefs and customs of the Native peoples. More relevant to folklore in English were such memoirs by travellers and settlers as Anna Jameson's *Winter studies and summer rambles in Canada* (London, 1838), Catherine Parr TRAILL's *The BACKWOODS OF CANADA* (London, 1836), John C. Geikie's *George Stanley; or, Life in the woods* (London, 1844), and Susanna MOODIE's *ROUGHING IT IN THE BUSH; or, Life in Canada* (London, 1852), which provided early accounts of pioneer customs. However, the first direct collecting of Anglo-Canadian folklore did not occur until the present century. In 1918 *Canadian Folklore* appeared, a reprint from the *Journal of American Folk-lore* with articles by Marius BARBEAU, F.W. Waugh, W.J. and Katherine K. Wintemberg, et al. Until recently most collectors have looked for songs rather than for other genres. The first major collector of folksongs was W. Roy Mackenzie, who tracked down traditional singers in his native Nova Scotia and gave a fascinating account of them in *The quest of the ballad* (1919). His later *Ballads and sea songs from Nova Scotia* (1928) is an important and still highly regarded collection, both for its early texts and for Mackenzie's careful documenting of each song's background.

Mackenzie's successor, Helen Creighton, began her collecting in 1929 and over the next half-century published a series of books: *Songs and ballads from Nova Scotia* (1932); *Traditional songs from Nova Scotia* (1950) with Doreen Senior; *Gaelic songs in Nova Scotia* (1964) with Calum MacLeod; *Maritime folk songs* (1962); and *Folksongs from southern New Brunswick* (1971).

Another important Nova Scotia collection was that of Carrie Grover, who spent her childhood in Canada, later moved to the United States, and there recorded the songs of her mother and father in an undated manuscript entitled *A heritage of songs* (1973).

When Newfoundland entered Confederation in 1949, it enriched Canada's folklore enormously. The earliest published collection of the island's songs appears to be James Murphy's *Songs and ballads of Newfoundland, ancient and modern* (1902). Later Murphy published several other booklets, as did other local bards like John Burke; and Gerald S. Doyle, a St John's merchant and folksong enthusiast, popularized many of the island's native songs through his series of pamphlets, *The old-time songs and poetry of Newfoundland* (1927, 1940, 1955, 1966, 1978). The first systematic collecting started in 1920, when Elisabeth Bristol Greenleaf began noting the songs around Sally's Cove, where she was serving as a Grenfell Mission teacher. Nine years later she and a musician, Grace Yarrow Mansfield, returned to spend a fruitful summer as the Vassar College Folklore Expedition; this resulted in the first major Newfoundland collection, *Ballads and sea songs of Newfoundland* (1933). The Vassar women included songs of both British and North American origin; but when Maud Karpeles, of the English Folk Dance and Song Society, visited the island in the summers of 1929 and 1930, she concentrated on the old British songs. Some of these she published with piano accompaniments in 1934, and the bulk of her collection appeared in 1971 as *Folk songs from Newfoundland.*

Between 1951 and 1961 Kenneth Peacock made six summer field-trips to the island for the National Museum, and the result was his massive three-volume *Songs of the Newfoundland outports* (1965). The same year MacEdward Leach, of the University of Pennsylvania, published the findings of a summer trip, sponsored by the National Museum, in *Folk ballads and songs of the lower Labrador Coast.*

Those books all included more old British songs than native Newfoundland ones, but two later songbooks return to the pattern of the early pamphleteers by concentrating on local songs: *The ballads of Johnny Burke: a short anthology* (1974), assembled by Paul Mercer, and *Hauling rope & gaff: songs and poetry in the history of the Newfoundland seal fishery* (1978), compiled by Shannon Ryan and Larry Small. Students at Memorial University, St John's, also published two useful song references: *A regional discography of Newfoundland and Labrador 1904-1972* (1975) by Michael Taft, and *Newfoundland songs and ballads in print 1942-1974: a title and first-line index* (1979) by Paul Mercer. In 1985 Genevieve Lehr published *Come and I will sing you: A Newfoundland songbook*, showing the continuance of the song tradition.

New England scholars were the first to collect in New Brunswick. Phillips Barry, Fannie H. Eckstorm, and Mary W. Smyth included forty Canadian songs in *British ballads from Maine* (1929). Local interest developed in 1947 when Lord Beaverbrook asked Louise Manny to collect the songs of his native Miramichi. Some twenty years later Manny and her music editor, James Reginald Wilson, produced *Songs of Miramichi* (1968).

Another New England folklorist, Edward D. Ives of the University of Maine, has worked extensively in the Canadian Maritimes. He published 'Twenty-one folksongs from Prince Edward Island' in *Northeast Folklore* (vol. 5, 1963) and pioneered the detailed study of local songwriters with three important volumes: *Larry Gorman: the man who made the songs* (1964), *Lawrence Doyle: the farmer-poet of Prince Edward Island* (1971), and *Joe Scott: the woodsman-songmaker* (1978).

Some smaller Maritime publications include *Folk songs of Prince Edward Island* (1973) by Christopher Gledhill, *Folksongs from Prince Edward Island* (1973) by Randall and Dorothy Dibblee, and *Songs & stories from Deep Cove, Cape Breton, as remembered by Amby Thomas* (1979) edited by Ron MacEachern.

Little was known of Ontario songs until the 1950s, when Edith FOWKE began her search in the Peterborough region and later extended it to the Ottawa Valley and Glengarry County. She was fortunate in discovering many fine traditional singers, and published some of their songs in two volumes: *Traditional singers and songs from Ontario* (1965), which emphasized old Irish and British ballads, and *Lumbering songs from the northern woods* (1969), which was the first Canadian book to concentrate on the songs of a particular occupation. In 1984 she brought out *A family heritage: the story and songs of LaRena Clark*, describing a remarkable singer with an extensive repertoire.

West of Ontario very few Anglo-Canadian songs have been reported. Margaret Arnett McLeod published *Songs of old Manitoba* (1960), which is notable for its interesting Métis ballads, including some by the famous songwriter Pierre FALCON; and Barbara Cass-Beggs produced two small pamphlets: *Eight songs of Saskatchewan* (1963) and *Seven Métis songs of Saskatchewan* (1967). So far no book has recorded Alberta songs, but in British Columbia, Philip Thomas has published *Songs of the Pacific Northwest* (1979), compiled partly from archives and partly from his own collecting. It emphasizes songs that illustrate aspects of British Columbia's history, and Thomas has provided extensive background notes.

Supplementary to those regional collections, Edith Fowke and Richard Johnston published two general anthologies with piano accompaniments as *Folk songs of Canada* (1954) and *More folk songs of Canada* (1967); Edith Fowke and Alan Mills brought out *Canada's story in song* (1960), stressing the relationship between songs and history; it was revised and enlarged as *Singing our history* (1984). Fowke also published *The Penguin book of Canadian folk songs* (1973), and *Sea songs and ballads from nineteenth-century Nova Scotia* (1981), two manuscripts of early Canadian folksongs.

While songs dominated the field until recently, some general folklore books appeared in the first half of this century. In 1931 two scholars pursuing graduate degrees published collections covering Nova Scotia tales, customs, and superstitions: for his Masters degree at the University of Pennsylvania, Arthur Huff Fauset reported on the Black community in *Folklore from Nova Scotia*, while Mary L. Fraser, a Catholic nun, published her doctoral dissertation as *Folklore of Nova Scotia*. Twenty years later two more general collections appeared—this time, coincidentally, both devoted to areas originally settled by Germans: Helen Creighton's *Folklore of Lunenburg County, Nova Scotia* (1950) and W.J. Wintemberg's *Folklore of Waterloo County, Ontario* (1950).

In contrast to the many folksong collections, very few Anglo-Canadian folktales have appeared. Both Mary Fraser and Arthur Fauset included some tales in their theses; Herbert Halpert published 'Tall tales and other yarns from Calgary, Alberta' in the *California Folklore Quarterly* (vol. 4:1, 1945); and Helen Creighton and Edward D. Ives presented 'Eight folktales from Miramichi as told by Wilmot MacDonald' in *Northeast Folklore* (vol. 4, 1962). C.I.N. MacLeod published *Stories from Nova Scotia* (1974), translations of Gaelic tales he had collected in Cape Breton; and Margaret MacDonell and John Shaw also presented English translations of *Luirean Eachainn Nill: folktales from Cape Breton*; Carol Spray brought out *Will o' the wisp: folktales and legends of New Brunswick* (1979); and Gerald Thomas published *The tall tale and Phillipe d'Alcripe, an analysis of the talltale genre with an annotated translation* (1977). In 1986 Edith Fowke published *Folktales told in Canada*, followed by *Legends told in Canada* in 1988.

More numerous are various books based partly on folktales but adapted by the authors: for example, the Maritime series by Archibald M. MacMECHAN, beginning with *Old province tales* (1924), and by William C. Borrett, beginning with *Tales told under the old town clock* (1942). There were also two undated volumes: *The treasury of Newfoundland stories* by L.W. Janes and *Newfoundland wit, humour, and folklore* by H.N. Reader. F.H. MacArthur told *Tales of Prince Edward Island* (1966); John D. Robins retold the tales he had heard in northern Ontario as *Logging with Paul Bunyan* (1957); and Robert E. Gard produced a prairie collection, *Johnny Chinook: tall tales and true from the Canadian West* (1967), based on material collected by the Alberta Folklore and Local History Project.

The French-Canadian heritage of folktales has been much richer than the Anglo-Canadian, and several authors have published their versions of these tales in English. Early samples appeared in Philippe-Joseph AUBERT DE GASPÉ's *Les ANCIENS CANADIENS* of 1863 (translated by Sir Charles G.D. ROBERTS as *The Canadians of old*, 1890), W.L. Greenough's *Canadian folklife and folk lore* (New York, 1897), J.M. LeMoine's *The legends of the St. Lawrence* (Québec, 1898), and Honoré BEAUGRAND's *La chasse-galerie and other Canadian stories* (Montréal, 1900). These were followed by Paul A.W. Wallace's *Baptiste Larocque: legends of French Canada* (1923), Edward C. Woodley's *Legends of French Canada* (1931), Natalie S. Carlson's *The talking cat and other stories of French Canada* (1952), Hazel Boswell's *Legends of Québec from the land of the Golden Dog* (1966), Claude Aubry's *The magic fiddler and other legends of French Canada* (1968) translated by Alice Kane, and Mary Alice Downie's *The witch of the North: folktales of French Canada* (1975). Perhaps most interesting in this group are two by Marius Barbeau: *The tree of dreams*

(1955) and *The golden phoenix and other French-Canadian fairy tales* (1958), the latter retold by Michael Hornyansky. Nearly all these books are based on traditional material adapted by the authors. In *Folktales of French Canada* (1980) Edith Fowke gives more literal translations in an attempt to come closer to the style of the original French narrators.

The folklife and customs depicted in various nineteenth-century narratives continue to form an important part of the multitudinous volumes of local history and personal reminiscences pouring from Canadian presses. There are far too many to survey here, but among the best are John McDougall's *Rural life in Canada* (1913), Edwin C. Guillet's *Early life in Upper Canada* (1933), Charles W. Dunn's *Highland settler: a portrait of the Scottish Gael in Nova Scotia* (1953), John Kenneth Galbraith's *The Scotch* (1964), and Barry Broadfoot's *The pioneer years, 1893-1914: memories of pioneers who opened the West* (1976). Similarly, some books describing Canada's occupations contain valuable folklore: for example, George S. Thompson's *Up to date; or, The life of a lumberman* (Peterborough, Ont., 1895), George Allan England's *Vikings of the ice: being the log of a tenderfoot on the great Newfoundland seal hunt* (1924), J.W. Grant MacEwan's *Blazing the old cattle trail* (1962), and Victor Butler's *The little Nord Easter: reminiscences of a Placentia bayman* (1975) edited by Wilfred W. Wareham.

In the second part of the twentieth century the more varied types of folklore began to receive greater attention. Helen Creighton supplemented her folksong collections with two interesting books: *Bluenose ghosts* (1957), dealing with poltergeists, forerunners, buried treasure, haunted houses, and phantom ships; and *Bluenose magic: popular beliefs and superstitions in Nova Scotia* (1968). Richard S. Lambert assembled the same kind of material from a wider area in *Exploring the supernatural: the weird in Canadian folklore* (1955), and Sterling Ramsay produced a smaller book dealing with the supernatural in *Folklore Prince Edward Island* (1976). Three more books on the supernatural appeared in 1991: *Strange terrain: the fairy world in Newfoundland* by Barbara Rieti; *The good people: new studies in fairy lore* by Peter Narvaez; and *Fables, fairies & folklore of Newfoundland* by Alice Lannon and Michael McCarthy.

Children's lore is still relatively undocumented. Some early reports appeared in a Canadian issue of the *Journal of American Folklore* (vol. 31:1, 1918), and half a century later Edith Fowke published *Sally go round the sun: 300 songs, rhymes, and games of Canadian children* (1969), *Ring around the moon: 200 songs, tongue twisters, riddles and rhymes of Canadian children* (1977), and *Red Rover, Red Rover* (1988), a collection of playground games. The first detailed study of one type of children's lore is Robert C. Cosbey's *All in together, girls: skipping songs from Regina, Saskatchewan* (1980).

Of increasing interest to folklorists is the very broad genre of folk art and material culture. Many of the relevant books to date are general rather than specifically folkloristic. As with folklife and customs, books containing *some* information are practically unlimited, but a list of a few important publications in this field will indicate its range: *'Keep me warm one night': early handweaving in eastern Canada* (1975) by Harold B. and Dorothy K. Burnham; *Quilts & other bed coverings in the Canadian tradition* (1979) by Ruth McKendry; *'Twas ever thus: a selection of eastern Canadian folk art* (1979) by Ralph Price; *Contextual studies of material culture* (1978) edited by David Zimmerly; *The ancestral roof: domestic architecture of Upper Canada* (1963) by Marion MacRae and Anthony Adamson; *The heritage of Upper Canadian furniture* (1978) by Howard Pain; and *Canadian folk art: old ways in a new land* (1983) by Michael Bird.

When folklore gained recognition as an academic discipline, the emphasis shifted from collecting to studying folk materials to see what they revealed about the people from whom they came. The development of a folklore department at Memorial University, St John's, prompted a number of scholarly publications, including two important books. Herbert Halpert and George Story edited *Christmas mumming in Newfoundland: essays in anthropology, folklore, and history* (1969), which studied the mumming tradition in widely scattered areas of the island and Labrador and provided insights into the rural communities and their folk customs. In 1982 G.M. Story, W.J. Kirwin, and J.D.A. Widdowson published their massive 700-page *Dictionary of Newfoundland English*, which was twenty years in the making. Another unusual sociological work was John D.A. Widdowson's *If you don't be good: verbal social control in Newfoundland* (1977).

In the 1970s an increasing body of scholars produced numerous papers, some of which were incorporated in books such as *Folklore and oral history: papers from the second annual meeting of the Canadian aural/oral history association at St. John's, Newfoundland, October 3-5, 1975* (1978) edited by Neil V. Rosenberg, and *Canadian folklore perspectives* (1978) edited by Kenneth S. Goldstein. Goldstein and Rosenberg also edited *Folklore studies in honour of*

Herbert Halpert: a festschrift (1980), which contained half-a-dozen articles on Canadian topics. Other studies appeared in three Canadian folklore periodicals: *Canadian Folk Music Journal* (1973-), *Culture & Tradition* (1976-), and *Canadian Folklore Canadien* (1979-), as well as in various American and British journals.

Postgraduate students from Memorial University have begun to publish their research on a wide variety of topics. A series of books came out in 1979: *On sloping ground: reminiscences of outport life in Notre Dame Bay, Newfoundland* by Audrey M. Tizzard; *More than 50%: women's life in a Newfoundland outport 1900-1950* by Hilda C. Murray; *Textile traditions of eastern Newfoundland* by Gerald L. Pocius; *Skill and status: traditional expertise within a rural Canadian family* by Laurel Doucette; *'Bloody decks and a bumper crop': the rhetoric of sealing counter-protest* by Cynthia Lamson; and *Folk music in a Newfoundland outport* by Gordon S.A. Cox.

While Newfoundland scholars were turning out these many specialized publications, two Toronto folklorists produced three more general books. Edith Fowke's *Folklore of Canada* (1976) was the first anthology to give a cross-section of the nation's varied traditions drawn from authentic sources. Carole Henderson Carpenter's *Many voices: a study of folklore activities in Canada and their role in Canadian culture* (1979) gave the first comprehensive account of the history and development of Canadian folklore studies. Later Fowke and Carpenter published *A bibliography of Canadian folklore in English* (1981), listing books, articles, periodicals, films, and records dealing with the different genres of Canadian folklore; in 1985 they published *Explorations in Canadian folklore*, selected articles on different aspects of Canadian folklore.

In 1982 Herbert Halpert published *A folklore sampler from the Maritimes*, an excellent anthology of tales, 'dites', proverbs, childlore, unusual Christmas customs, and children's marching chants, made particularly important by Dr Halpert's introduction, notes, 'Bibliographic essay on the folktale in English', and the extensive bibliography.

Two important biographical books are Helen Creighton's *A life in folklore* (1975) and Lawrence Nowry's *Marius Barbeau: man of mana* (1995). EDITH FOWKE

Folklore in French. There are two distinct groups of French-speaking Canadians: Québécois and Acadians. The former settled originally in the valley of the St Lawrence, while the latter occupied what is today Nova Scotia and New Brunswick. While both colonies were founded early in the seventeenth century, historical factors made Quebec the only province with a francophone majority; the dispersal of the Acadians in 1755 led to the creation of many little 'Acadies', with the chief concentration today in New Brunswick and with smaller groups scattered throughout Nova Scotia and Prince Edward Island, on the Gaspé peninsula and the Magdalen Islands, and in western Newfoundland. Following the cession to England of Acadia (1713) and Quebec (1763), when English was used to impose British rule (there were few French schools), oral tradition was the major binding force that helped French-speaking Canadians maintain their identity.

Awareness of the value of tradition became evident in Quebec in the 1860s with the publication of Joseph-Charles TACHÉ's *Forestiers et voyageurs, étude de moeurs* (Québec, 1863) and Philippe AUBERT DE GASPÉ's *Les ANCIENS CANADIENS* (Québec, 1864). Although these writers were of a literary rather than a folkloristic bent, they depicted with considerable understanding and sensitivity the life and legends of the lumbermen and seigneurial and peasant ways respectively. The first genuine folklore work to appear in Canada was Ernest Gagnon's *Chansons populaires du Canada* (Montréal, 1865), in which Gagnon noted the melodies of 100 songs and provided data on his sources. There was very little activity in the field for the rest of the century, although a number of literary figures published material that made use of folklore in *Les SOIRÉES CANADIENNES* (5 vols, Québec, 1861-5), *Le FOYER CANADIEN* (8 vols, Québec, 1863-6), and *Les nouvelles soirées canadiennes* (7 vols, Montréal, 1882-6).

It was not until Marius BARBEAU became interested in French folklore after 1914 that significant strides were made in the field. Supported by the National Museum of Canada, Barbeau collected extensively in many parts of Quebec, and attracted others—such as E.Z. Massicotte, an especially fine collector of folksongs; Evelyn Bolduc; Gustave Lanctôt; and Adélard Lambert—all of whom collected traditional songs and narratives. Much that they collected was published in eight French issues, edited by Barbeau, of the *Journal of American Folklore* (between 1916 and 1950), where it still remains one of the most substantial bodies of Canadian French folklore yet published. It should be added that although the major sections of the French numbers of the *JAF* covered narratives and songs, two issues (vol. 32: 1, 1919 and vol. 33:

4, 1920) dealt with children's folklore and traditional beliefs respectively, both of which are due to Massicotte. The publication of such material was, in Canada, innovative.

Barbeau's contributions are listed elsewhere, but mention should be made of his *Romancéro du Canada* (1937). He drew to him another group of followers in the late 1930s. One of these, Joseph-Thomas Leblanc, collected some 1,200 Acadian folksongs through the medium of his newspaper, *L'Evangéline* (Moncton, N.B.); François Brassard made a large collection of songs in the Saguenay region and in northern Ontario. But by far the most important recruit to Canadian folklore studies made by Barbeau was Luc LACOURCIÈRE, who in 1944 began teaching folklore at Université Laval and organized the Archives de Folklore there. Almost at once he began publishing a series of works under the imprint of the Archives. The first four volumes (1946, 1947, 1948, 1950) were collections of articles and studies on a broad range of folklore topics, and constituted the first elements of what became a major scholarly folklore series in Canada, French or English. Many subsequent publications in the series were dissertations, and volumes 5 and 6, Soeur Marie-Ursule's *La civilisation traditionnelle des Lavalois* (1951), was a model of the precise ethnographic documentation undertaken by Lacourcière's students.

Volume 7 of the Archives de Folklore series was Russell Scott Young's *Vieilles chansons de Nouvelle-France* (1956); this was followed by Nora Dawson's study of the material culture of a Quebec community, *La vie traditionnelle à Saint-Pierre (Île d'Orléans)* (1960). Volume 9 of the series, James E. La Follette's *Étude linguistique de quatre contes folkloriques du Canada français* (1969), underlined the interest folklore can offer to other disciplines; and volume 10, Germain Lemieux's *Placide-Eustache. Sources et parallèles du conte-type 938* (1970), was the first scholarly study devoted uniquely to the folknarrative tradition. Reflecting Lacourcière's interest in the comparative study of folktales are three superb analyses of the distribution and variation of Canadian versions of international folktale types and legends: Catherine Jolicoeur's *Le vaisseau fantôme. Légende étiologique* (vol. 11, 1970), Hélène Bernier's *La fille aux mains coupées (conte-type 706)* (vol. 12, 1971), and Nancy Schmitz's *La mensongère (conte-type 710)* (vol. 14, 1972). In a somewhat different vein Antonine MAILLET earned her doctorate with *Rabelais et les traditions populaires en Acadie* (vol. 13, 1971), an illuminating study of the similarities between the folklore of Maillet's native Acadie and the traditional content of the famous Renaissance author's works. Volume 15 in the series was Georges Gauthier-Larouche's *Évolution de la maison rurale traditionnelle dans la région de Québec* (1974), while volume 16 presented an important collection of Acadian folksongs collected by Dominique Gauthier, *Chansons de Shippagan* (1975). The next seven volumes were the work of Lacourcière's long-time collaborator, Conrad Laforte. The first volume, *Poétiques de la chanson traditionnelle française* (vol. 17, 1976, revised edition, vol. 26, 1993), describes the rationale and methodology adopted by Laforte. It was followed by *Le catalogue de la chanson folklorique française: I, Chansons en laisse* (vol. 18, 1977), *II, Chansons strophiques* (vol. 20, 1981), *III, Chansons en forme de dialogue* (vol. 21, 1982), *IV, Chansons énumératives* (vol. 19, 1979), *V, Chansons brèves (les enfantines)* (vol. 22, 1987), and *VI, Chansons sur des timbres* (vol. 23, 1983). The Catalogue will remain an essential research tool for generations to come, and a monument to Québécois folklore scholarship. Subsequent studies in the series include Denise Rodrigue's comparative study *Le cycle de Pâques au Québec et dans l'ouest de la France* (vol. 24, 1983) and Jean-Pierre Pichette's *L'observance des conseils du maître. Monographie internationale du conte type A.T. 910B* (vol. 25, 1991). This was the last dissertation supervised by Lacourcière before his death in 1989, and is a classic demonstration of his method; the series is currently in abeyance.

Mélanges en l'honneur de Luc Lacourcière: folklore français d'Amérique (1978), edited by Jean-Claude Dupont, contains numerous articles and tributes to Lacourcière from former students, colleagues, and friends, as well as a bibliography and list of theses and dissertations directed by him. Lacourcière's major contribution to folklore scholarship in Canada, and indeed internationally, is the still unpublished *Catalogue raisonné du conte populaire français en Amérique du nord*; it will be as important to folktale scholarship as Conrad Laforte's work is to folksong studies in French.

Among the contributors to Lacourcière's *Mélanges* was Carmen Roy, who took over folklore studies at the National Museum (now the Canadian Museum of Civilization) from Marius Barbeau, and whose *Littérature orale en Gaspésie* (1955, 1962) is one of the best folklore works to have appeared under the Museum's imprint. Following new directions in national policy, Carmen Roy became in 1970 the first head of the reorganized Folklore Division of the National Museum of Man, its new mandate reflected in its new title: The Canadian Centre for Folk Culture Studies/Le Centre canadien d'études sur la culture traditionnnelle. Previously, the Museum had supported folklore collecting chiefly among francophone eastern-Canadian and Native peoples; it now took on a multicultural mandate, evident in the titles of the Mercury Series published by the Museum. A number of scholars working in French traditions were nonetheless encouraged, and their works published. These include Jean-Claude Dupont's *Le monde fantastique de la Beauce québécoise* (1972); Lise Boily-Blanchette's *Le fournil: un rite saisonnier* (1976), and, in a non-series Museum publication, Lise Boily and Jean-François Blanchette's *Les fours à pain au Québec* (1976); Paul Carpentier's *Les croix de chemin: au-delà du signe* (1981), a major study of roadside crosses in Quebec; Carmel Bégin's *La musique traditionnelle pour violon: Jean Carignan* (1981) and her *La musique traditionnelle pour accordéon diatonique: Philippe Bruneau* (1983); and, edited by Madeleine Lemieux-Pépin, *P'tit train va loin: histoires de vie de trois cheminots* (1985). Modest in format and variable in quality, the series nonetheless contains useful and otherwise unpublished materials.

Another contributor to the Lacourcière *Mélanges* was Frère Anselme Chiasson, a pioneer collector of Acadian folklore whose four series of *Chansons d'Acadie* (1942, 1945, 1948, and 1972), with Frère Daniel Boudreau, were followed by *Chéticamp: histoire et traditions acadiennes* (1961; with supplement, 1990), *Les légendes des Îles de la Madeleine* (1969), and *Les Îles de la Madeleine: vie matérielle et sociale de l'an premier* (1981). *En r'montant la tradition* (1982), edited by Ronald Labelle and Lauraine Léger, was an *hommage* to Chiasson that included many useful and interesting essays on aspects of Acadian culture. Chiasson edited in 1985 *L'histoire des tapis 'hookés' de Chéticamp et leurs artisans*, followed by *Le diable Frigolet et 24 autres contes des Îles de la Madeleine* (1991) and *Contes de Chéticamp* (1994). He was also the driving force in establishing folklore at the Centre d'études acadiennes, Université de Moncton, where considerable research has been undertaken in recent years.

Jean-Claude Dupont, who edited Lacourcière's *Mélanges* and who succeeded him at Laval, has been one of Quebec's most prolific folklore scholars. A specialist in material culture and folk art and artisans, his works include *Le pain d'habitant* (1974), *Le sucre du pays* (1975), and *Le fromage de l'Île d'Orléans* (1977), volumes 1-3 of a series entitled Traditions du geste et de la parole; and *L'artisan forgeron* (1979). Dupont has also published works of both popular and scholarly appeal on folk narratives, including *Le légendaire de la Beauce* (1974) and *Contes de bûcherons* (1976). Much of his early research was undertaken in Acadia, as his important volumes *Héritage d'Acadie* (1977) and *Histoire populaire de l'Acadie* (1979) attest.

In addition to Lacourcière's collecting in Acadia, several Acadian folklorists were taught or influenced by him. Among these are Lauraine Léger, whose *Les sanctions populaires en Acadie* (1978) is an innovative study, and Catherine Jolicoeur, whose *Les plus belles légendes acadiennes* (1981) is a work of popular appeal stemming from her vast research into Acadian legends. Léger also produced a critical edition of André-Thaddée Bourque's *Chez les anciens Acadiens: causeries du grand-père Antoine* (1994). Georges Arsenault's *Complaintes acadiennes de l'Île-du-Prince Édouard* (1980) is an important study of the tradition of locally composed songs and the first scholarly study of the French folklore of Prince Edward Island; though modest in format, his *Courir la chandeleur* (1982) is a fascinating exploration of Candlemas traditions on the island. Also important is his *Par un dimanche au soir: Léah Maddix, chanteuse et conteuse acadienne* (1993). A valuable description of Acadian foodways appears in Marielle Boudreau and Melvin Gallant's *La cuisine traditionnelle en Acadie* (1975), and in keeping with a willingness to explore less commonly trod paths, the Équipe Héritage d'Herbage's 'Es-tu bâdré de tes vivres?', *Médecine traditionnelle en Acadie* (1979), is an uncommon insight into traditional Acadian perceptions of health. The same topic was considerably developed by Marielle Cormier-Boudreau in her *Médecine traditionnelle en Acadie, enquête ethnographique* (1992). Ronald Labelle's work in local history has had significant impact in Acadia, most notably through his *Au Village-du-bois, mémoires d'une communauté acadienne* (1985), but also in 'La vie acadienne à Chezzetcook' (vol. 22 of the *Cahiers de la Société historique acadienne*, 1991). Labelle also edited *La fleur du rosier—Acadian folksongs/chansons folkloriques d'Acadie, recueillies par Helen Creighton* (1988). Other notable Acadian folklorists include Charlotte Cormier, who has authored several articles on Acadian folksong as well as the volume-with-records *Écoutez tous, petits et grands, chansons de Pré-d'en Haut* (1978), and Alain Doucet, whose modest survey *La littérature orale de la baie Sainte-Marie* (1965, 1977), published posthumously, is unique in its description of Acadian folklore of southwest

Nova Scotia. Melvin Gallant, author of several popular collections of tales, also published *Ti-Jean-le-Fort: contes acadiens* (1991). As in Quebec, Acadian folklorists have been increasingly productive since the 1970s, and this in turn has fostered a growing number of popular works on folkloristic subjects.

Germain Lemieux, a student of Lacourcière, has devoted much of his life to the collection and study of Franco-Ontarian folklore. His early publications, between the late 1940s and early 1960s, are collections of Franco-Ontarian folktales and folksongs with popular appeal. In 1972 he founded in Sudbury the Centre franco-ontarien de folklore, and in 1973 introduced, with his useful and informative *Les jongleurs du billochet*, which examined the storytelling contexts and some of the storytellers themselves, the folktale series 'Les Vieux m'ont conté' (vol. 1, 1973; vol. 32, 1991). The 32 volumes (which also include Franco-Manitoban and Quebec tales) were followed by a thematic index to this huge collection (vol. 33, 1993), which presents the story repertoires of most of his informants; the series is unusual in that it provides not only a folkloristic transcription of all the tales, but also a normalized version of each, thereby attempting to appeal not only to the scholar but also to the artistic and general public. In 1993 a substantial volume edited by Jean-Pierre Pichette, entitled *L'oeuvre de Germain Lemieux, S.J. Bilan de l'ethnologie en Ontario français*, paid tribute to Lemieux's achievements.

West of Ontario one of the few important folklore studies of French traditions is Marcien Ferland's *Chansons à répondre du Manitoba* (1979). Perhaps the smallest French minority in Canada is that of Newfoundland. Confined to the Port-au-Port peninsula/Bay St George area and including both Acadian and metropolitan French settlers who established themselves there during the nineteenth century, it has been researched by Gerald Thomas, who founded the Centre d'études franco-terreneuviennes in 1975, at Memorial University, with the encouragement of Luc Lacourcière. The Centre has a large and unique archive of recordings and studies of Franco-Newfoundland folklore; articles by Thomas, his students Geraldine Barter and Gary Butler, have appeared in *Culture & Tradition*, a joint publication of folklore students at Memorial and Laval universities, and *Canadian Folklore canadien*, published by the Folklore Studies Association of Canada. Thomas's *Les deux traditions: le conte populaire chez les Franco-Terreneuviens* (1983) examines the repertoire, performance style, and aesthetics of his subjects. *The two traditions: The art of storytelling amongst French Newfoundlanders*, his English translation and revision of the book, appeared in 1993. Gary Butler's *Saying isn't believing* (1990) discusses supernatural beliefs as they emerge in the conversations and stories of the inhabitants of a small Franco-Newfoundland village.

One of the most dynamic figures of the second half of the twentieth century in Québécois folklore studies was Robert-Lionel SÉGUIN. Trained at Laval, the Sorbonne, and Strasbourg, in 1971 Séguin founded the Centre de documentation en civilisation traditionnelle at the Université du Québec à Trois-Rivières. Specializing in folklife and material culture, Séguin was both scholar and popularizer, as his bibliography in the *Mélanges* edited by René Bouchard, *La vie quotidienne au Québec. Histoire, métiers, techniques et traditions* (1983), attests. Representative works include *L'équipement de ferme canadienne aux XVIIe et XVIIIe siècles* (1959), *La civilisation traditionnelle de l' 'habitant' aux 17e et 18e siècles* (1967), *La vie libertiné en Nouvelle-France au XVIIe siècle* (1972), and *L'équipement aratoire et horticole en Nouvelle-France et au Québec du XVIIe au XIXe siècles* (2 vols, 1989). Séguin also founded and edited the *Revue d'Ethnologie du Québec* (12 vols, 1975-1980), and the series 'Les Archives d'ethnologie du Québec' beginning in 1976.

The explosion of folklore publications in Quebec in the 1970s continued throughout the 1980s, which saw the birth of two new major series: 'Mémoires d'Homme', published by Les Editions Quinze, Montreal, edited by Laval-trained Jean-Pierre Pichette, and 'Ethnologie de l'Amérique française', published by Les Presses de l'Université Laval, for the Centre d'études sur la langue, les arts et les traditions populaires des francophones en Amérique du Nord (CELAT), which had been founded at Laval as an interdisciplinary research centre. While both series stress the scholarly aspects of their topics, both also emphasize, through format and presentation, the popular appeal of traditional culture, reflecting a long-standing concern with issues of Québécois identity.

In the former series the first volume, Conrad Laforte's *Menteries drôles et merveilleuses. Contes traditionnels du Saguenay* (1978), includes an essay by editor Pichette outlining the transcription protocol adopted for the presentation of originally oral texts, a protocol that opted for the normalizing of the oral text rather than (as was the case for Germain Lemieux and Gerald Thomas's work) the less accessible folkloristic transcription. This volume was followed by Clément Legaré's *La bête à sept têtes et autres contes de la Mauricie* (1980), with, for Canadian folkloristics, a ground-breaking semiotic study of one of the tales; Gérald E. Aucoin's *L'oiseau de vérité et autres contes des pêcheurs acadiens de l'île du Cap-Breton* (1980); a further volume by Clément Legaré, *Pierre la Fêve et autres contes de la Mauricie* (1982), with a complementary semiotic study; Bertrand Bergeron's *Les barbes-bleues. Contes et récits du Lac Saint-Jean* (1980); and Philémon Desjardins and Gilles Lamontagne's *Le corbeau du Mont-de-la-Jeunesse. Contes et légendes de Rimouski* (1984). Breaking with the narrative stress of other volumes is Donald Deschênes's *C'était la plus jolie des filles* (1982), which presents, with a careful musical analysis, the song repertoire of a female singer from the Gaspé.

More wide-ranging in scope is the 'Ethnologie de l'Amérique française' series, which is ambitious both in format—attractive, colourful—and in content. The first volume, edited by Jean-Claude Dupont and Jacques Mathieu, *Les métiers du cuir* (1981), consists of a comprehensive series of essays, carefully documented, on all aspects of traditional leather-working. Pierre Lessard's *Les petites images dévotes* (1981) explores religious iconography, following the innovative research of Jean Simard. Conrad Laforte's *Survivances médiévales dans la chanson folklorique* (1981) explores an aspect of folksong hitherto neglected. Madeleine Béland's *Chansons de voyageurs, coureurs de bois et forestiers* (1982) examines, for its historical content and significance, the song tradition of early pioneers. Marcel Moussette's *Le chauffage domestique au Canada* (1983) brings the same descriptive rigour to the study of home heating as characterized his earlier work (such as the 1979 *La pêche sur le Saint-Laurent. Répertoire des méthodes et des engins de capture*). Marc Gagné and Monique Paulin's *Chantons la chanson* (1985) brings an interdisciplinary, 'textological' approach to bear on a collection of songs, jigs, and reels; Simonne Voyer's *La danse traditionnelle dans l'est du Canada* (1986) is the first major study of traditional dance produced by a French-Canadian folklorist. Marie-Aimée Cliche's *Les pratiques de dévotion en Nouvelle-France* (1988), Bernard Audet's *Avoir feu et lieu dans l'île d'Oréans au XVIIe siècle* (1990), and Anne-Marie Desdouits's *Le monde de l'enfance. Traditions du Pays de Caux et du Québec* (1990), all illustrate the comparative, historical, and material-cultural perspectives that have characterized the Laval school.

Quebec folklorists have found a ready audience; beyond the major series noted above, books of both scholarly and popular appeal, and of varying quality, have been published by numerous Québécois and other publishing houses. The series Connaissance (Leméac, Ottawa), in addition to works by R.-L. Séguin, Jean-Claude Dupont, Lauraine Léger, and Georges Arsenault, also includes Benoît Lacroix's *Folklore de la mer et religion* (1980), Maurice Carrier and Monique Vachon's two-volume *Chansons politiques du Québec* (vol. 1, 1977, vol. 2, 1979), Jean-Philippe Gagnon's *Rites et croyances de la naissance à Charlevoix* (1978), and Madeleine Doyon-Ferland's *Jeux, rythmes et divertissements traditionnels* (1980), a collection of articles and notes—on generally neglected topics—assembled by Andrée Paradis, a long-time researcher with Lacourcière at Laval. The collection Ethnologie (in the series 'Cahiers du Québec', Hurtubise HMH), directed by Jean-Claude Dupont, includes Conrad Laforte's *La chanson folklorique et les écrivains du XIXe siècle en France et au Québec* (1973), John R. Porter and Léopold Désy's *Calvaires et croix de chemins du Québec* (1973), the collaborative *Habitation rurale au Québec* (1978), edited by Jean-Claude Dupont, and Jean Simard's impressive *Un patrimoine méprisé. La religion populaire des Québécois* (1979). Recent major works include Jeanne Pomerleau's *Métiers ambulants d'autrefois* (1990), *Arts et métiers de nos ancêtres* (1994), *Coureurs de bois (La traite des fourrures)* (1994), and Michel Lessard's *Objets anciens du Québec. La vie domestique* (1994).

The variety and breadth of folklore publications in French Canada are more than adequate testimony both to the scholarly penchants of the majority of French-Canadian folklorists, and to the evident appeal of such works to the general public. To date, however, only one work has attempted to provide an illustrated sampling of French folklore from across Canada: Jean-Claude Dupont and Jacques Mathieu's *Héritage de la francophonie canadienne: traditions orales* (1986).

GERALD THOMAS

Foran, Charles (b. 1960). Born in Toronto, Ontario, he received his B.A. (1983) from the University of Toronto, then moved to University College, Dublin, where he received his M.A. in Irish literature in 1985. Returning to North America, he settled for three years in Amenia, New York. Working at various forms of employment during these years, he also began to write and publish short fiction. Following two years during which he worked as a literature teacher in Beijing, China, he returned to Canada in 1990.

With the appearance of *Sketches in winter: a Beijing postscript* (1992), Foran established himself among the first rank of Canadian travel writers. An account of his experiences during the late 1980s, the book is a sensitive and deeply personal glimpse at the lives of the people of Beijing in the wake of the Tiananmen Square demonstrations. Like all gifted travel writers, Foran favours an elegant, uncluttered prose style that emphasizes the description of observed detail, the nuances and intimacies layered in conversations overheard, and the rare curiosity of those to whom the whole world appears as a foreign land.

Foran continued his unique combination of travelogue and memoir in *The last house of Ulster: a family in Belfast* (1995). Nominated for a Governor General's Award and winner of the 1995 QSPELL Award, the book deals with the unromantic, often arduous demands of daily life for the middle-class Catholic McNally family in whose Belfast home Foran spent much time over a period of years. Although purposefully selective and incomplete in that Protestant and southern Irish visions of Northern Ireland are all but omitted, the book is nonetheless an instance of history written from the inside out, a personal view of a country that focuses on the workings of hearth, home, and family pub rather than the machineries of distant and distancing parliaments. And Foran's journey is ultimately a voyage of self-discovery, as he learns from the McNallys about himself as a parent and as a human being. 'Travel is always', he observes, 'as much about where you go inside your head as where your feet take you.'

Foran has also published two successful novels. In *Kitchen music* (1994) he evokes life in rural Ireland as a richly textured backdrop for the entwined stories of two Canadians on journeys of personal reconciliation. Revealing a penchant for minimalist dialogue that skilfully skirts the stereotypic renderings of dialect fiction, he explores how each of these characters—one a recent arrival from Vietnam, the other an established Torontonian of Irish descent—attempts to make meaningful connections with the past through individual and diverse passions that often seem to border on obsession. Foran's *Butterfly lovers* (1996) locates his main character in the immediate aftermath of what one Chinese character refers to simply as 'the Turmoil', the 1989 massacre of hundreds of pro-democracy protesters. Accepting a teaching post in Beijing, the book's Montreal narrator, David LeClair, experiences first-hand the paranoia and terror that grip the culture and spirit of the city and hold sway over the lives and minds of its inhabitants. The novel meditates on the demands and exigencies of democracy and the conflicting responsibilities of citizens in both Canada and China.

Prior to spending the 1997-8 academic year in Hong Kong, Foran published an autobiographical essay, 'Can't think for the racket: music and writing', in *BRICK* 56 (Spring 1997). DAVID STAINES

Ford, R.A.D. (b. 1915). Robert Arthur Douglas Ford was born in Ottawa and educated at the University of Western Ontario, London, where he studied English literature and history. He did graduate work in history at Cornell University and this led to a brief appointment in the history department there (1938-40). He then joined the Canadian Department of External Affairs and pursued a diplomatic career, during which he held various positions at the ambassadorial level in different countries. In 1968 he was appointed Canadian ambassador to the USSR, and in 1971 was made dean of the diplomatic corps in Moscow. His long diplomatic career is the subject of his memoirs, *Our man in Moscow: reflections on the Soviet Union from Stalin to Brezhnev* (1989). The literary side of his career, particularly in its relation to his interest in Russian literature, is contained in another prose work, *A Moscow literary memoir: among the great artists of Russia from 1946 to 1980* (1995). Since his retirement he has been living in Randan, France.

Ford's first volume of poetry, *A window on the North* (1956), won a Governor General's Award. As the title suggests, much of this collection concentrates on northernness, climatic extremes often being used as a metaphor for the violent extremes in contemporary life. The poems generally offer a cold and bleak attitude to life, though this atmosphere is tempered by love poems and some meditative reminiscences of warmer places and times. This volume also includes translations of the work of modern Russian poets. Ford has always had a continuing interest in translation; he has said that his versions are more like 'imitations' than literal translations. Other translated renderings appear in *The solitary city* (1969), but not just from the Russian: there are versions of Brazilian, Serbo-Croat, and French works. Ford's own poems have continued to express a distanced bleakness, the studied objectivity and control of language emphasized by his frequent use of formal metrical structures. Even his later work—as in *Holes in space* (1979, *Needle in the eye* (1983), and *Dostoyevsky and other poems* (1989)—retain arid and objective tones, with some simplification of language and form.

Ford's poetic career is summarized in *Coming from afar: selected poems 1940-1989* (1990), in which the final section is devoted to his translations from various languages.

PETER STEVENS

Foreign writers on Canada in English. This article is a survey of literary works—mostly fiction—that have Canada as a setting, written by British, American, and post-colonial anglophone writers whose involvement with Canada was brief or vicarious. On the whole, British authors have had an interest in Canada as a frontier setting for adventure fiction. Americans, finding sufficient inspiration from their own frontiers, have been more interested in the exotic elements of early Canadian history and French Canada. Though few foreign writers rose higher than romance or adventure in writing about the country, a chronicle of their 'Canadian' books is of historical interest in revealing the appeal of Canada for creative writers of other nations, and the kinds of images of Canada propagated by their books, some of which were very widely read. (See also Writing in NEW FRANCE; EXPLORATION LITERATURE; TRAVEL LITERATURE; FOREIGN WRITERS ON CANADA IN FRENCH.)

1. BRITISH WRITERS. The earliest British literary responses to Canada were in verse. *Englands honour revived* (London, 1628) by Martin Parker (d. 1656?) is a crudely written broadside ballad celebrating the temporary capture of Quebec from the French in 1628. The same year saw the publication of *Quodlibets, lately come over from New Britaniola, old Newfound-land* (London, 1628) by Robert HAYMAN, a former governor of the Bristol merchants' plantation at Conception Bay. This miscellaneous collection of 'epigrams . . . both morall and divine', also containing 'bad unripe Rimes' in praise of Newfoundland, was the work of a sincere propagandist who had no pretensions as a poet ('You feare the *Winters* cold, sharp, piercing ayre./They love it best, that have once wintered there.') *Liberty asserted* (London, 1704) by John Dennis (1657-1734) introduced Canada to the London stage. Set in New France in the seventeenth century and described as 'a Satyr upon the government of the French', the play depicts the struggle between the French under Frontenac and their allies the Hurons, and the English and their allies the Iroquois, in 'a vast Tract of Land in Northern America, on the Back of New England and New York'.

The British conquest of Quebec inspired a number of literary tributes. Thomas Paine (1737-1809) was still a loyal Englishman when he wrote 'The death of General Wolfe' (1759), a brief poetic celebration of patriotism and heroism. *Quebec: a poetical essay in imitation of the Miltonic stile* (1760) by 'J. Patrick', was a more ambitious exploitation of the Conquest, complete with explanatory footnotes possibly reflecting a firsthand knowledge of the setting. In James Belsham's Latin ode *Canadia* (London, 1760), Montcalm is saluted as a valiant foe, but the poem as a whole is a stilted celebration of English military glory. This is the main interest also of a long poem by George Cockings (d. 1802), a British colonial official who lived until 1776 in Boston, where he wrote *War: an heroic poem, from the taking of Minorca, by the French; to the reduction of the Havannah, by the Earle of Albermarle* (Boston, 1762), a Miltonic imitation that includes detailed accounts of the captures of Louisbourg and Quebec. Cockings gives more concentrated attention to the New World in *The conquest of Canada; or, The siege of Québec. An historical tragedy of five acts* (Albany, 1773). The most ambitious poetic celebration of the British victory in Canada is Henry Murphy's *The conquest of Quebec* (Dublin, 1790), an eight-book epic, modelled on *Paradise lost*, that includes episodes in heaven confirming the justice of the victory and a hand-to-hand duel between Wolfe and Montcalm.

With the defeat of the French, and the beginnings of English settlement and the economic development of Canada, a less bellicose image of the colonies began to appear, catering to the eighteenth-century fondness for 'prospect' poetry and fiction. The earliest and the most artistically significant of the post-Conquest literary travelogues on Canada is Frances BROOKE's epistolary romance *The history of Emily Montague* (London, 1769). Other 'prospects' of post-Conquest Canada are George Cartwright's *Labrador: a poetical epistle* (London, 1792), which makes the barren northland appear like a Scottish tourist resort; J. Mackay's *Quebec hill; or Canadian scenery* (London, 1797); and Cornwall Bayley's *Canada: a descriptive poem* (Quebec, 1806). The popular Irish poet Thomas Moore (1779-1852) visited Canada in 1804 and wrote his famous 'Canadian boat song', along with other pieces reflecting his responses to Canadian scenery.

Foreign writers on Canada in English 1

By the third decade of the nineteenth century, various writers had expressed their conceptions of Canada in novels of immigrant experience, or wilderness adventure—or a combination of the two. The most distinguished fictional representation of immigrant experience is *Bogle Corbet* (London, 1831) by John GALT. A lively adventure novel is the anonymous *The Canadian girl; or The pirate of the lakes* (London, 1838), set in 'one of the sublime wildernesses of Upper Canada' and involving mysterious encounters, fervent love scenes, languishing beauties, noble savages, and startling revelations. The earliest and best-known example that combines adventure and immigration propaganda is *The settlers in Canada* (London, 1844), by Captain Frederick Marryat (1792-1848), who visited Canada in 1838. In this novel episodes of hunting and Indian fighting are interspersed in a chronicle of house building and land cultivation in the Bay of Quinte region of Canada West (Ontario), as the author strives to assert the virtues of a genteel English society transplanted to North America.

Like Marryat, the prolific Mayne Reid (1818-83), whose prime source of fiction material was the American West, addressed his one Canadian novel, *The young voyageurs; or The boy hunters in the North* (London, 1854), to juvenile readers. Another author of adventure stories for young people was R.M. BALLANTYNE, some of whose works extol the heroic qualities of Britain's empire in North America and the men who created and sustained it through the fur trade and exploration. William Henry Giles Kingston (1814-80), the secretary of a colonization society, wrote novels glorifying the Empire and promoting immigration that were set in Canada as well as in Australia and New Zealand. His Canadian novels are *The log house: a tale of Canada* (London [1864]), possibly inspired by *Bogle Corbet* (to which one of the characters admiringly refers); *Snow-shoes and canoes; or, The early days of a fur-trader in the Hudson's Bay territory* (London, 1876), which includes an idealized representation of the Red River Settlement; and *The frontier fort; or, Stirring times in the North-west Territory* (London, 1879).

Sir William Francis Butler (1838-1910), explorer, adventurer, and author of many books of travel—including the classic *The great lone land; a narrative of travel and adventure in the Northwest of America* (London, 1872)—wrote one novel set in Canada, *Red Cloud, the solitary Sioux* (London, 1882). Written for English boys, it provides many vivid scenes of travel, hunting, and fighting on the Canadian Prairies in an episodic tale about the tragic but stoical title character. Another literary exploitation of the northern frontier, noteworthy for the identity of its authors if not for its artistic merit, is *The frozen deep* (1857), a three-act melodrama written for amateur performance by Charles Dickens and Wilkie Collins. Based on the Franklin expedition and set in England, the Arctic, and Newfoundland, the play is a rather bombastic tribute to heroism and self-sacrifice.

Unlike writers of travel narratives, who were frequently attracted to Montreal and Quebec with their exotic francophone culture, British novelists and poets of the nineteenth century confined their attention largely to contemporary and historical narratives of pioneering and adventure in the wilderness. But one writer who treated contemporary Canadian city life was Samuel Butler (1835-1902), author of *Erewhon* and many other works, who spent parts of 1874 and 1875 in Canada in a futile attempt to retrieve money he had invested in speculative companies. His 28-line free-verse poem 'A psalm of Montreal' (1878), with its well-known refrain 'O GOD! O MONTREAL!', denounces the aesthetic insensitivity of colonial society and reflects Butler's general feelings of disgust with Canada.

Nineteenth-century British writers were surprisingly indifferent to the epic conflict between France and England that ended in British supremacy in North America. Among noteworthy exceptions is G.A. Henty (1832-1902), the prolific romancer and exponent of imperialism for British schoolboys, whose *With Wolfe in Canada; or, The winning of a continent* (London, 1887,) is an account of the Seven Years' War as seen through the eyes of a young British soldier. Sir Arthur Conan Doyle (1859-1930), in *The refugees: a tale of two continents* (London, 1893), adapted formulas from Alexandre Dumas and James Fenimore Cooper to recount a tale of Huguenot refugees exiled to Canada after the revocation of the Edict of Nantes in 1685. The many romantic novels of Sir Arthur Quiller-Couch (1863-1944) include *Fort Amity: a story of French Canadian life in the time of Wolfe and Montcalm* (London, 1906), which celebrates strenuous life in the wilderness and the virtues of masculine loyalty and honour. Neither of these novels was based on first-hand acquaintance with Canada: Doyle did not visit North America until 1894, and Quiller-Couch never did make the trip.

Another noteworthy historical novel of the late nineteenth century, dealing with a different region and period, is *Under the great seal*

(London, 1893) by Joseph Hatton (1841-1907). Set in Newfoundland 'in the youngest days of the oldest British colony', this is a melodramatic but gripping fictionalization of a little-known episode of maritime history when the British fishing fleet, under royal orders, attempted to abolish year-round settlements on the Newfoundland coast. The character, individual and social, of rural Maritimers in the mid-nineteenth century provides the point of departure for *The master* (1895) by the English novelist and playwright Israel Zangwill (1864-1926). In this long ironic *Bildungsroman*, a young would-be painter flees his Nova Scotia backwoods home to find social and economic conflict, and eventually a barren artistic success, in England.

By the early twentieth century the most popular form of literary exploitation of Canada by British writers was the outdoor romance of adventure and love set in the Arctic, the northwestern Prairies, or the forest wilderness. Heavily influenced by the conventions of the American western romance, and by the popular Klondike tales of Jack London, these stories also celebrated the glories of the British Empire and idealized the resourceful, self-reliant colonial adventurer, as opposed to his effete stay-at-home countryman. Many of the writers of these northwest romances were themselves adventurers in the outposts of empire. They include Roger Pocock (1865-1941), who worked on the Lake Superior section of the Canadian Pacific Railway in 1883, served in the Northwest Mounted Police (1884-6), and was the author of *Tales of western life, Lake Superior, and the Canadian Prairies* (Ottawa, 1888), and an autobiographical work, *The frontiersman* (1903). Among the Canadian novels of Ridgewell Cullum (1867-1943) are *The hound from the North* (1904) and *The triumph of John Kars* (1917), set in Manitoba and the Yukon. John Mackie (1862-1939) wrote *The rising of the red man: a romance of the Louis Riel rebellion* (1905). The most prolific writer of this kind of fiction was Harold Bindloss (1866-1946), whose output included at least thirty novels set in Canada, beginning with *Alton of Somasco* (1906), through *Lorimer of the Northwest* (1909), and *Vane of the timberlands* (1911).

In 1897 Rudyard Kipling paid tribute to Canada's aspirations for sovereignty within imperial federation in his brief poem 'Our lady of the snows'; after visiting Canada in 1907, he included a series of impressionistic, allusive lyrics inspired by his experiences of the Prairies and northern forests in his *Letters to the family (notes on a recent trip to Canada)* (Toronto, 1908). Mrs Humphry Ward (1851-1920) turned her attention to the Dominion in *Canadian born* (1910), a fictionalization of her trip across Canada by rail, which contains some provocative comments on Canadian-British relations and Canada's prospects in the twentieth century.

The Gothic novelist Algernon Blackwood (1869-1951) spent ten years wandering through Canada and the United States and used Canadian settings in a number of short stories, including 'A haunted island' (1906), 'Skeleton Lake' (1906), 'The wendigo' (1910), and several pieces in *The wolves of God and other fey stories* (1921). Blackwood's suspenseful tales of loneliness, madness, terror, and death make effective use of the northern forest and of French-Canadian and Native folklore to establish a mysterious, other-worldly atmosphere. A comparable atmosphere pervades *Sick Heart River* (1941), one of the two posthumously published novels by the famous Scottish novelist John Buchan (1875-1940), who as Lord Tweedsmuir was governor-general of Canada from 1935 until his death. In the story of a dying man who seeks in the northern wilderness a climax to his life of action and duty, Buchan develops a moral theme of Christian salvation and a psychological theme involving alienation, madness, and a descent into the ambiguous depths of the self.

The more straightforward plot-oriented novel of northern adventure has continued to appeal to British writers. Hammond Innes's *Campbell's kingdom* (1952) involves love, oil drilling, and intrigue in the Canadian Rockies; his *The land God gave to Cain: a novel of the Labrador* (1958) is about the search for gold in the Arctic; Nicholas Monsarrat sets his rather pretentious mystery, *The time before this* (1963), in the Quebec north; Alistair Maclean's thriller, *Athabaska* (1980), takes place in Alaska and Alberta.

A variation on the northern adventure novel is the science-fiction or futuristic fantasy narrative, in which the Arctic becomes associated with a post-atomic holocaust era, or with extra-terrestrial visitors. John Wyndham's *The chrysalids* (1955) is set in a post-holocaust Labrador, depicted as a land of forests, farms, and villages where intellectually superior mutants struggle to escape a reactionary, repressive society.

Since the Second World War a few British writers have produced more realistic novels about modern Canadian urban life. Margaret Bullard, wife of an eminent physicist who was a visiting professor at the University of Toronto in the late 1940s, wrote *Wedlock's the devil* (1951), an acerbic satire of the academic community in 'New Glasgow' (Toronto) and of the social environment of Toronto's Wychwood Park district, where the Bullards lived. An even more unfriendly, but artistically impressive, response to urban Canada was expressed by the writer and painter Wyndham Lewis in *Self condemned* (1954), in which a British exile during the war finds reflections of his own, and the world's, cultural disorientation and spiritual malaise in the cheerless streets of 'Momaco' (an amalgam of Montreal and Toronto). Simon Gray, who studied at Dalhousie University, Halifax, before returning to his native England to pursue a career as a playwright, wrote *Colmain* (1963), a satirical novel about the lieutenant governor of a fictitious Canadian province (obviously Nova Scotia), where the narrowness of society is reflected in petty political conflicts and dull social routine. Another of Gray's novels, *Simple people* (1965), aims its satire in two directions, with the story of a naive Canadian student at Cambridge who is exploited by decadent British acquaintances.

An ambitious modern British literary use of Canada is *Goldeneye* (1981), a novel by Malcolm Macdonald that tells the story of forty years in the life of a Scottish woman who immigrates to Saskatchewan. But Macdonald, a historical novelist who specializes in works set in Victorian England, seems to be one of very few British writers of recent decades to turn to Canada for literary material. (With the Europeanization of post-modern Britain, perhaps the Commonwealth countries have been displaced as sources of imaginative inspiration.) Dick Francis, the well-known author of mystery novels that usually involve a horse-racing milieu, sets *The edge* (1989) on the transcontinental train between Toronto and Vancouver to develop an entertaining pastiche of train-travel nostalgia, local colour (including a red-coated Mountie), an ironic conjunction of dramatized and real murder mysteries—and, of course, horse racing. Another best-selling British novelist, John Le Carré, creates in *The night messenger* (1993) a globe-trotting secret agent investigating international drug and gun-running organizations, who briefly touches down at a mining town in northern Quebec. Canada has thus become one of a series of exotic settings—along with the Caribbean, South America, and Switzerland—for glamorous James Bond-like travelogue adventures.

2. AMERICAN WRITERS. The earliest imaginative exploitation of Canada by a republican American writer is probably a work by Hugh Henry Brackenridge (1748-1816), *The death of General Montgomery in the storming of the city of Quebec* (Philadelphia, 1777), a pompous closet tragedy in verse that glorifies the life and death of the American leader and casts distasteful glances at the snowbound setting and untrustworthy inhabitants of Canada. The failure of the American campaign of 1775-6, together with Protestant hostility to French Roman Catholicism, persistent recollections of French and Native depredations throughout the eighteenth century, and republican antagonism to British imperialism, all contributed to a longstanding antipathy that is reflected in much of the imaginative use of Canada by Americans. At the same time, however, many American writers recognized Canadians as pioneers like themselves, engaged in the struggle for survival against the wilderness. This ambivalence between hostility and sympathy is reflected in *The history of Maria Kittle* (Hartford, 1797) by Ann Eliza Bleecker (1752-83), a novel that recreates the terror of a French and Indian attack on an American settlement and the winter march into captivity in Canada, while presenting the people of Montreal as reasonably kind and civilized.

From the earliest years of literary activity in the United States, the imaginative response to Canada emphasized a romantic recreation of the epic wars and internecine struggles of New France before the Conquest. John Greenleaf Whittier (1807-92) used Canadian settings and historical incidents in several poems, including 'St John' (1841), a retelling of the rivalry between two feudal chieftains, Charles d'Aulnay and Charles de La Tour; 'The ranger' (1856), about the French and Indian wars; and 'The bay of Seven Islands' (1856), a melodrama of tragic love. The New York poetaster Alfred B. Street (1811-81) wrote a long jingling narrative poem, *Frontenac* (London, 1849), in which the governor of New France is mixed up in a complex plot of miscegenation and romance.

The widespread nineteenth-century American suspicion of French Roman Catholicism is reflected in a number of novels. George Bourne (1780-1845), who lived in Quebec in 1825-8, wrote *Lorette. The history of Louise, daughter of a Canadian nun. Exhibiting the interior of female convents* (New York, 1833), a conglomeration of hackneyed Gothic devices such as lecherous priests, mad nuns, and mysterious dungeons. The same formula is exploited in the notorious *AWFUL DISCLOSURES OF MARIA MONK*... (New York, 1836). The Gothic image of French Canada appears at an even more debased level in Benjamin Barker's *Cecilia; or, The white nun of the wilderness: a romance of love and intrigue* (Boston, 1845), and in Justin Jones's *Jessie Manton; or, The novice of Sacre-Coeur. A tale of the Canadian invasion* (Boston, 1848).

These calumnies against the Church in French Canada prompted Maryland Catholic novelist James McSherry (1819-69) to write *Père Jean; or, The Jesuit missionary: a tale of the North American Indians* (Baltimore, 1847), which idealizes the story of the seventeenth-century priest Isaac Jogues. Further opposition to the anti-French, anti-Catholic romance tradition was provided by American writings dealing with the Acadian expulsion. Catherine A. Williams (1781-1872), of Rhode Island, expressed her sympathy for the Acadians in *The neutral French; or, The Acadians of Nova Scotia* (Providence, 1841), a novel in which a group of exiles gradually become defiant revolutionaries in the American mould. Nathaniel Hawthorne (1804-64) presented a briefer and more moderate version of the expulsion in 'The Acadian exiles', part of his collection of historical fictionalizations for children, *The whole history of Grandfather's chair* (Boston, 1841). But the most famous version of the Acadian story is Henry Wadsworth Longfellow's narrative poem *EVANGELINE: a tale of Acadie* (1847). Although marred by an awkward verse form and by excessive sentimentality, it is a suggestive myth of North American history that dramatizes the obliteration of an Edenic ideal by the ruthless realities of progress.

Nineteenth-century American authors did not neglect English Canada. Jesse Walker (1810-52) wrote *Fort Niagara* and *Queenston* (both published in Buffalo, 1845; both subtitled 'A tale of the Niagara frontier')—two didactic fictionalized tourist guides that portray, through a series of dialogues, the border region of Canada West (Ontario). Owen Duffy's *Walter Warren; or, The adventurer of the northern wilds* (New York, 1854) is also set in Canada West, where the young American hero struggles through adversity to fortune, first in Hamilton and subsequently in the Lake Superior region. John B. Coppinger's *The renegade: a tale of real life* (New York, 1855) involves two young Americans who pursue truth among the Native people north of Lake Ontario. P. Hamilton Myers (1812-78) combined rousing adventure with the complex political issues of the Rebellion of 1837-8 in *The prisoner of the border: a tale of 1838* (New York, 1857).

Other regions of British North America were occasionally exploited by nineteenth-century American writers. Robert Traill Spence Lowell (1816-91), brother of James Russell Lowell and grandfather of the twentieth-century poet Robert Lowell, served for a time as an Episcopalian priest in Newfoundland and wrote *The new priest in Conception Bay* (Boston, 1858), in which he convincingly represented the dialect and customs of outport fishermen; but the novel is marred by a lurid plot and by the author's anti-Catholicism. Mary L. Savage wrote *Miramichi* (Boston, 1858), another partisan religious novel, in which New England Methodists attempt to bring the 'New Light' to the New Brunswick backwoods.

After the Civil War, American literary exploitations of Canada began to reflect various new influences from the changing cultural atmosphere of the United States. William Dean Howells (1837-1920), chief exponent of the realist movement in American fiction, wrote *Their wedding journey* (Boston, 1872), a travelogue novel that uses the popular tourist regions of the St Lawrence as background for the leisurely experiences and reflections of two middle-class American tourists. *A chance acquaintance* (Boston, 1873) involves one of Howells' favourite themes, the contrast between New England and the West, as personified by two tourists in Quebec whose respective reactions to Canada reveal their personal and regional prejudices. Howells also uses Canadian settings in *The quality of mercy* (New York, 1892), involving a defaulting American businessman who flees to Canada and finds in the hostile winter landscape of the Saguenay a reflection of his own moral and spiritual disintegration.

Another important literary traveller of this period was the poet Walt Whitman (1819-92), whose *Diary in Canada* (written in 1880 but not published until 1904) is an impressionistic and often lyrical evocation of the pastoral landscape and picturesque inhabitants of southwestern Ontario and the St Lawrence country. It was written after he had visited Dr Richard Maurice BUCKE in London, Ontario, and then travelled to Montreal and Quebec City.

Various 'local-colour' authors of the late nineteenth century wrote tourist fiction set in Canada. The midwestern novelist Alice French (1850-1934), who wrote as 'Octave Thanet', used a Saguenay setting for a long story included in her *Knitters in the sun* (Boston, 1887): 'The ogre of Ha-Ha Bay' presents the sordid lives of a group of French-Canadian villagers as seen through the disillusioned eyes of two American tourists. Robert Grant (1852-1940), a Boston jurist and author of many novels of social criticism, began his writing career with *Jack in the bush; or, A summer on a salmon river* (Boston, 1888), a book for boys that celebrates Americanism and the manly life through an episodic narrative of fishing adventures in the Restigouche (Quebec/New Brunswick) region. S. Weir Mitchell (1829-1914), a Philadelphia physician, wrote a more mature 'fishing romance' set in the same region, *When all the woods are green* (New York, 1894), a tale of leisurely outdoor amusement and conversation involving a group of American tourists. *The lady of the flag-flowers* (Chicago, 1899), by the minor poet Florence Wilkinson, is an ambitious but melodramatic novel involving a young American man who comes to Canada under the influence of Tolstoy's idealism, and whose intrusion into the primitive world of the Quebec backwoods results in the moral ruin and murder of a young Métis woman. The clergyman Henry Van Dyke (1852-1933) wrote many local-colour tales based on his vacations in the Quebec backwoods, focusing on a stereotyped image of the cheerful and primitive French Canadian; they were collected in *The ruling passion: tales of nature and human nature* (New York, 1901) and other volumes.

Historical novels about early Canada continued to appear throughout the nineteenth century, thanks partly to the continuing influence of the fiction of James Fenimore Cooper. Interest in New France was further inspired by the multi-volume history by the Boston historian Francis Parkman (1823-91), *France and England in North America*, which appeared between 1851 and 1892. Charles Hall's *Twice taken: an historical romance of the maritime British provinces* (Boston, 1867) uses the battle for Louisbourg as background for a lurid tale involving a sinister Jesuit priest. Edward P. Tenney (1835-1916) wrote *Constance of Acadia* (Boston, 1886), a retelling of the d'Aulnay-La Tour rivalry. W.H.H. Murray (1840-1904) was the author of *Mamelons and Ungava: a legend of the Saguenay* (Boston, 1890), a pretentiously poetic adventure novel inspired by Cooper's Leatherstocking tales. Mary Hartwell Catherwood (1847-1902), an Ohio-born writer, adapted information from Parkman to a series of romances that exalted American-style individualism and feminism in *The romance of Dollard* (New York, 1889), *The story of Tonty* (Chicago, 1890), and *The lady of Fort St. John* (Boston, 1892).

After 1900 the most prominent image of Canada in American literature was that of the northern frontier, an image encouraged by American involvement in the Klondike gold rush and effectively expounded by California writer Jack London. In many short stories—collected in *The son of the wolf* (1900), *Children of the frost* (1902), and other volumes—as well as in his famous novels *The call of the wild* (1903) and *White Fang* (1906), etc., London used his experiences of the Klondike to develop his naturalist theories about the universal struggle for survival, and the need for altruism in the efforts to establish human society above the animalistic level. London's suggestive image of the North was soon debased into mechanical formulas by Michigan-born James Oliver Curwood (1878-1927). In many novels—including *The danger trail* (1910), *God's country—and the woman* (1915), *The country beyond* (1922), etc.—Curwood glorified adventure, romantic love, and simplistic notions of courage in what he called 'God's country', roughly identifiable with the northern Prairie Provinces and southern portions of the Northwest Territories.

The immense popularity of the northern forest romances of Curwood prompted Sinclair Lewis to write one of his cynical satires in *Mantrap* (1926), involving a Babbit-type American businessman who goes on vacation to northern Manitoba in search of the primitive life in the great outdoors and encounters mosquitoes, fatigue, picayune quarrels with his companions, and, at the end of the trail, a village settlement no different from the 'main-street' society he left behind.

Curwood also applied his formulas to early Canadian history in his series of romances set in New France, including *The black hunter* (1926), *The Plains of Abraham* (1928), and *The crippled lady of Peribonka* (1929). Curwood's images of New France have been perpetuated in a continuing profusion of American popular romances, such as Benedict Fitzpatrick's *Donjon of demons* (1931), the story of Father Brébeuf as seen by a Catholic writer; Grace Stone's *The cold journey* (1934), a retelling of the seventeenth-century French and Indian attack on Deerfield, Mass., and the subsequent forced march to Canada; and Muriel Elwood's *Heritage of the river: an historical novel of early Montreal* (1945), a chronicle of settlement and adventure. Amid these and many other book-club ephemera, one work stands out: Willa Cather's *Shadows on the rock* (1931). In this sombre but optimistic novel of Quebec between 1689 and 1698, the city on the rock

rock becomes, like the mesas of the author's native Southwest, a symbol of primeval isolation where Old World immigrants attempt to create a new social and cultural order based on an ideal vision of European traditions.

Although the 'north woods' adventure continues to appeal to American writers and readers, Cather's novel could be seen as marking the beginning of a more serious literary exploitation of Canada. Film-maker Robert Flaherty's *The captain's chair* (1938), a suggestive quest novel reminiscent of Joseph Conrad's *Heart of darkness*, follows the Arctic experiences of a romantic young adventurer in his search for an enigmatic sea captain. Flaherty's *The white master* (1939), involving the Hudson's Bay Company in Labrador, is a study of the effects of the North on the white man. Similar uses of Labrador are evident in the semi-fictional autobiographical narratives of Elliott Merrick, whose *True north* (1933) and *Frost and fire* (1939) present adventure and self-discovery in a tradition that echoes Francis Parkman's *The Oregon trail.*

Besides his well-known memoir of growing up in a pioneer Saskatchewan community, *Wolf willow* (1963), Iowa-born Wallace Stegner wrote *On a darkling plain* (1940), a novel about an invalid veteran of the Great War who seeks isolation in a Saskatchewan homestead, but eventually learns the value of human community during the 1917-18 influenza epidemic. Stegner's *The big rock candy mountain* (1943) traces the life of an itinerant American whose restless pursuit of the American dream takes him all over the Middle West and into Saskatchewan, where he finds that his illusive visions are reduced to dirt farming and whisky smuggling.

William E. Barrett, author of several novels involving Catholic themes, set *The empty shrine* (1958) on the Île-d'Orléans, where an American writer learns about reverence and imaginative experience while investigating an alleged miraculous vision. Grace Metalious (of *Peyton Place* fame) set the early scenes of *No Adam in Eden* (1963) in Quebec, then traced the sex-pervaded life of her French-Canadian heroine through twenty years in New Hampshire. Similarly, Michael Rubin begins his novel *In a cold country* (1971) on the Quebec side of the St Lawrence River, and then focuses his narrative on the search for identity in the United States of a half-Italian, half-French-Canadian drifter for whom Canada becomes associated with grotesque childhood memories.

Frederick G. Walsh, a Massachusetts-born professor of drama, wrote the two-act play *The trial of Louis Riel* (1965; not to be confused with the work of the same name by Irish-Canadian playwright John COULTER). Riel's religious fanaticism and his conflict with the Canadian authorities are articulately presented, but the oversimplification of the Canadian political situation reflects the playwright's interest in making Riel a frontier hero on the American model. John Porter's *Winterkill* (1967), about an American family who open a resort hotel in northern Ontario during the Depression, also presents a rather oversimplified view of Canada, through the egocentric eyes of American characters.

Margaret Craven, a California writer, achieved popular success with *I heard the owl call my name* (1967), a novel about a fatally ill Anglican priest working among the Native people on the northwest coast of British Columbia. The Massachusetts-born poet Elizabeth Bishop spent a few childhood years and many summers in Nova Scotia. Her memories of early experiences, as well as her fascination with the rough contours of the northeast coast, are reflected in poems such as 'The map', 'Large bad picture' (describing a painting by a great-uncle of 'some northerly harbor of Labrador'), 'Cape Breton', and 'First death in Nova Scotia' (all included in her *Complete poems*, 1969).

Detroit artist and popular culture historian Gerald Dumas pays tribute to his German-Canadian grandparents, and expresses his nostalgia for boyhood summers spent in southwestern Ontario, in a long elegiac poem, *An afternoon in Waterloo Park* (1972). New Jersey novelist John Birmingham recounts the drug-taking, hitchhiking, party-crashing adventures of two American youths in British Columbia at the height of the hippie phenomenon in *The Vancouver split* (1973), an exuberant but morally conscientious novel probably influenced by the works of J.D. Salinger and Jack Kerouac. California writer Ishmael Reed looks at the fugitive slave tradition in *Flight to Canada* (1976), a wildly unpredictable comic novel in which nineteenth- and twentieth-century history is deliberately confused, and in which Canada emerges as the disillusioning anti-climax to the American quest for freedom.

Mark Helprin, author of acclaimed 'magic realist' novels, including *A soldier of the great war* (1991) and *Memoir from the antproof case* (1995), has included Canada at least once in the wide-ranging settings of his fiction. His short story 'Passchendaele' (published in the *New Yorker*, 1982) is set in ranching country within the mountains of British Columbia and involves a man too young for the First World War and too old for the Second, whose meditations on the famous Canadian battle of 1917 are commingled with the disappointments and romantic yearnings of his present and past. Like much of Helprin's fiction, the story relates male-oriented, strenuous physical experiences to dark and enigmatic dream visions, unfulfilled sexual longings, and pseudo-historical fantasies.

The title story of Deborah Eisenberg's *Transactions in a foreign currency* (1986) explores the sexual yearnings, self-discovery, and disillusionment of a neurotic woman narrator who follows a divorced male American drifter from New York to Montreal. In Montreal she begins to discover her own self-sufficiency as she learns to navigate the strange city and to use the odd-looking Canadian money. But she also deliberately complicates the sexual and economic confusions of her life, revealing that her new individualism is not securely established.

James Michener recreates the stereotypes of Curwood in *Journey: a quest for Canadian gold* (1988). Apparently salvaged from the excess research for the author's popular epic *Alaska*, *Journey* uses a narrative of an overland trek to the Klondike as an occasion for a great deal of encyclopaedic information about the region and for an episodic plot illustrating nothing more complex than the 'courage that men and women can exhibit when dealing with adversity.'

A more sophisticated use of the Canadian North is featured in Kathryn Davis' novel *Labrador* (1988), which traces the childhood and young adulthood of a woman growing up in a dysfunctional New Hampshire family in mid-century. Her detachment from her parents and her obsession with her older sister are commingled with dreams of a vague northern wilderness where her legendary grandfather went years before. The grandfather shows up and takes her to the real Canadian North, but the Labrador sequence seems a continuation of her dream-like quest for personal fulfilment.

A better-known novelist of New Hampshire, John Irving, author of *The world according to Garp* and several other best-selling novels, began living part-time in Canada in the 1980s. The narrator of his *A prayer for Owen Meany* (1989) moves to Canada as a Vietnam war protester in the 1960s, but the brief interpolated episodes in Toronto are overshadowed by the sprawling main narrative, a nostalgic tale of childhood, youth, irony, and tragedy in New Hampshire. In its use of coincidence and the working out of bizarre destinies, the novel bears more than a passing resemblance to *FIFTH BUSINESS* by Robertson DAVIES, a novelist for whom Irving has expressed much admiration. Irving's *A son of the circus* (1994) has as its central character an Indian-born immigrant to Canada, but almost the entire novel is set in India.

A short story by North Dakota novelist Larry Woiwode, 'Black winter' (in *Silent passengers*, 1993), involves a Canadian university professor, forcibly retired from his teaching position in the United States, who returns home to Winnipeg and ends up managing a repair shop to supplement his dwindling income. Set at the time of the Gulf War, the story uses the bleakness of the Canadian winter, the personal anxiety of the protagonist, and the imaginative evocation of Kuwaiti oil fires, mirrored in a destructive fire in the repair shop, to suggest the degenerating political and ecological state of the world.

William T. Vollman's *Fathers and crows* (1992) is the second volume of an ongoing series of novels entitled *Seven dreams: a book of North American landscapes*. A 900-page retelling of the history of the Catholic missions in seventeenth-century New France, *Fathers and crows* features detailed recreations of such personages as Champlain, Brébeuf, and the Micmac chieftain Membertou, as well as various fictional Natives and Europeans. Vollman's illustrations, glossaries, and digressions, unlike Michener's encyclopaedic techniques in *Journey*, create impressions simultaneously of Homeric immensity and Joycean parody.

E. Annie Proulx's *The shipping news* (1993) is more modestly conceived, but boasts both a Pulitzer prize and best-seller status. This novel is an account of a few years in the life of 'Quoyle', an American of Newfoundland ancestry who immigrates to the island at age thirty-six to turn his life around after many personal and professional failures. Proulx combines feminist ideology, ethnic humour, Gothic mystery, and pervasive resurrection imagery to establish the ostensibly dying outport society of Newfoundland as an alternative to the death and corruption that pervade American urban life.

3. POST-COLONIAL WRITERS. English-speaking writers of present and former Commonwealth countries, apart from those who have immigrated to Canada, have tended to be indifferent to this country, but there have been a few exceptions. The Anglo-Australian poet Douglas Sladen (1856-1947) travelled across Canada in 1889 and, besides producing an autobiographical account of his experiences,

wrote *Lester the loyalist: a romance of the founding of Canada* (Tokyo, 1890), a book-length narrative poem written in the hexameters of *Evangeline* that attempts to show the Anglo-American refugees of the Revolution as tragic victims, like Longfellow's Acadians. Australian poet Francis Webb includes in his *Leichhardt in theatre* (1952) a lengthy but apparently unfinished poem, 'A view of Montreal', in which the nineteenth-century explorer of Australia, Ludwig Leichhardt, is implicitly compared to Jacques Cartier. The poem focuses on images of human suffering and elemental conflict associated with primitive landscapes and modern city scenes.

Australian-born, London-based novelist James Aldridge has used widely diverse geographical settings, including Canada, in *The hunter* (1950). Set in the wilderness and a frontier village on the north shore of Lake Huron, and focusing on the experiences of an aging woodsman, the novel portrays the gradual disappearance of an older way of life, while demonstrating a sensitive awareness of the conflict between natural ecology and human needs.

Arthur Nortje (1942-70), a South African poet, spent two years in Canada before his early death in England. The posthumous *Dead roots* (1971) includes about twenty brief lyrics inspired by Canada, emphasizing the paradoxical feelings of strangeness and familiarity experienced by the immigrant, the blight of industrialism in the midst of fertile landscapes, and the shoddy atmosphere of Toronto inner-city life.

See also *Friendly aliens: thirteen stories of the fantastic set in Canada by foreign authors* (1981) edited by John Robert COLOMBO; James Doyle, *North of America: images of Canada in the literature of the United States, 1775-1900* (1983); R.G. Moyles and Doug Owram, *Imperial dreams and colonial realities: British views of Canada, 1880-1914* (1988); and *The wild is always there: Canada through the eyes of foreign writers* (1993) and *The very richness of that past: Canada through the eyes of foreign writers, vol. 2* (1995), edited by Greg GATENBY.

JAMES DOYLE

Foreign writers on Canada in French. Already in the second book of La Fontaine's *Fables* (1678) there is a reference to the magnificent structures built by beavers 'close to the north pole' ('Discours à Madame de la Sablière'). The infamous dismissal of New France by Voltaire as 'quelques arpents de neige' in *Candide* (1759) is only too well known. His short story 'L'ingénu' (1767) is a variation on the 'bon sauvage' theme. The pertinent comments of a young Huron, newly arrived in France via England, bring out the hypocrisy and prejudices of French society. Voltaire had no doubt found his inspiration in the works of Gabriel Sagard and of Baron Lahontan (see Writing in NEW FRANCE, 1).

It was not until the eighteenth century, however, that a Frenchman actually wrote *in* Canada, because after 1760 communications between the two countries were restricted. Joseph QUESNEL, who came to Canada by chance in 1779, married and settled in Montreal, where he took an active part in theatrical life. In 1789 he composed *COLAS ET COLINETTE; OU LE BAILLI DUPÉ* (Québec, 1808), the first comic opera to be performed in North America, and he also wrote poetry and plays. Joseph Mermet (1775-1828) arrived in Canada with a Swiss regiment to fight the Americans and was stationed in Kingston from 1813 to 1816. His epic poems, of which 'La victoire de Châteauguay' is the best known, relate the events of 1812. But Canada, both east and west, was to be a source of inspiration to novelists rather than poets. Baron Philippe Régis de Trobriand (1816-97), who became an officer in the American army, spent a few weeks in Canada in 1841, and wrote the second work of fiction to be published in Quebec, *Le rebelle* (1842; first published in *Le Courrier des États-Unis*, 1841), a melodramatic short story set against the background of the 1837 Rebellion. The prolific Henri-Émile CHEVALIER spent nine active years in Montreal, where some of his numerous adventure novels with a Canadian setting were published in *La Ruche littéraire*, of which he was a founder. Xavier Marmier (1802-92), an erudite and indefatigable globe-trotter, came to Canada in 1849. He wrote one epistolary novel as a result of his trip, *Gazida* (Paris, 1860), but with its summary characters and preposterous plot, it is interesting only as a repertory of Aboriginal customs and legends. Canada is frequently mentioned in the books and articles Marmier wrote about his travels in North America. (See Jean Ménard, *Xavier Marmier et le Canada*, 1967.)

Jules Verne (1828-1905), who remains the greatest French writer of science fiction, spent '192 hours' on the North American continent in 1867. Apart from Niagara Falls, he saw little of Canada. What he knew of the country and its history he found in books. *Le pays des fourrures* (Paris, 1873), translated by N. D'Anvers as *The fur country; twenty degrees latitude north* (New York, 1873), is the unlikely adventure of a Hudson's Bay Company agent who establishes a new trading post on what he believes to be an island. When the snows melt, he discovers that the island is really an iceberg. *Famille-sans-nom* (Paris, 1889), Verne's only historical novel, has as background the Rebellion of 1837-8, the author's sympathy lying wholly with the Patriotes; but the work is marred by its melodramatic style and situations. (See Bruno-André Lahalle, *Jules Verne et le Québec [1837-1889]*, 1979.) Léon de Tinseau came to Canada several times, and on his first trip in 1890 crossed the country from east to west. Canadians and Canada play a part in several of his sentimental and rather melodramatic novels, which were once very popular but have now sunk into oblivion. *Faut-il aimer* (Paris, 1892) is a love story set in the West. *Sur les deux rives* (Paris, 1909) tells of the hardships suffered by a family of ruined French aristocrats who attempt to settle in northern Quebec: only the young son is able to adjust. 'Eugène Diraison-Seylor' (pseudonym of Eugène Diraison, 1873-1916) was forced to resign from the French army because of the scandal caused by his *Maritimes* (Paris, 1900), in which he denigrated some identifiable officials. He thought of settling in Canada and in 1907 came to Montreal, but not finding there the freedom he expected, he soon returned to France. He contributed articles to *La Patrie* and wrote one vitriolic novel, *Le pays des petites filles* (Paris, 1909), in which he depicts Montreal women as coquettes and the Church as an obstacle to progress. Conversely, Georges Lechartier (1868-1955), who came to Canada on several lecture tours, tells a Corneillian story of sacrifice. In *L'irréductible force* (Paris, 1906; first published in *Le Correspondant* in 1905), a Montrealer renounces her love for a Frenchman to remain faithful to her alcoholic husband. André Siegfried (1875-1959), a French Protestant, visited Canada three times as a young scholar of political science—the last time during the election of 1904. He wrote a witty and illuminating study of the nation at the time, especially about differing attitudes of francophones and anglophones: *Le Canada, les deux races: problèmes politiques contemporains* (Paris, 1906), translated as *The race question in Canada* (1907; ed. Frank H. Underhill, 1966) is a masterpiece in both content and form. Marie LE FRANC, who was to become one of the most prolific of the French authors to find inspiration in Canada, arrived in Montreal in 1906. No other writer has been able to capture the atmosphere and beauty of the Laurentians with as much sensitivity. *Grand-Louis l'innocent* (1925), set partly in Canada, partly in her native Brittany, won her the Prix Fémina. Louis HÉMON wrote the most widely read of Quebec land novels, the world-famous *MARIA CHAPDELAINE* (1916; first published in *Le Temps*, 1914).

At the turn of the century a number of francophones were attracted to the West by government brochures promising them rapid wealth. Some of these settlers were writers. They did not become rich, but if it were not for them the West would cut a much poorer figure in Canadian francophone literature. A few of these city dwellers turned farmers recorded their experiences in journals that were later published because of their historical rather than their literary value. Such is *Un héros malgré lui* (1986) by Marcel Durieux (1889-1976), who was born in Belgium and lived in Alberta for a time. *Soupe maigre et tasse de thé* (1994) describes in detail the suffering and deprivations of a young married woman, Christine de la Salmonière (1873-1931), who tries to adapt to the harsh conditions in Sainte-Rose-du-Lac, Manitoba, at the end of the nineteenth century. Her bourgeois upbringing did not prepare her to face hardships, and her efforts end in dismal failure. The ordeals endured by new settlers are also the subject of a bitter novel, *La Pointe-aux-Rats* (Paris, 1907), by 'Georges Forestier' (the pseudonym of Georges Schaeffer, 1874-1915), who aims at demystifying the West, advertised as a land of milk and honey. The mood is lighter in his *Dans l'Ouest canadien* (Paris, 1915), a posthumous volume of short stories, both humorous and moving, which have the West as a background. Joseph-Émile Poirier (1875-1935), a Breton poet, was inspired by the Northwest Rebellion in Saskatchewan. *Les arpents de neige* (Paris, 1909)—later reissued under the title *Tempête sur le fleuve* (Paris, 1931)—was better received than Maurice CONSTANTIN-WEYER's *La bourrasque* (1926) on the same subject. Though Poirier never visited Canada, his work rings true, and the battle scenes are particularly convincing. Constantin-Weyer, one of the greatest and most prolific writers who came to Canada, spent ten years in the West, where some fifteen of his fifty books are set. Among these, his most famous novel, *Un homme se penche sur son passé* (Paris, 1928), won the coveted Prix Goncourt. Georges BUGNET arrived in the West in 1905 and never returned to France. For fifty years he farmed in Alberta, spending his few leisure hours writing. His most successful novels are *Nipsya* (1924) and *La forêt* (1935). Louis-Frédéric ROUQUETTE, in his three novels about the Northwest, describes the fight of man, and occasionally of woman, against the mercilessness of nature and of fellow creatures. Victor Forbin (1869-1947), an ardent globe-trotter, wrote *La fée des neiges* (Paris, 1926), the only Inuit novel by a Frenchman; the half-Inuit heroine attempts to join her mother's tribe, but finds its ways incompatible with her philosophy of life. Forbin's *Rose Beaulieu, Canadienne* (Paris, 1931) is a somewhat moralistic novel about a French-Canadian woman from the West who resists the temptation of fame and adulterous love to lead a life of abnegation. What is unusual about this work is that instead of the typical scenario—Frenchman comes to Canada and conquers the elements—we have a Canadian woman going to France and overcoming the seductions of a corrupt society. Forbin also wrote three essays about Canada: *17000 km de film au Canada* (Paris, 1928), which describes his trip from the Atlantic to the Pacific; *Les justiciers du pôle* (Paris, 1933), about police work in the Arctic; and *La grande passion d'un petit peuple* (Paris, 1935), the story of the Acadians. Maurice Genevoix (1890-1980), a member of the French Academy, spent four months in Canada in 1939, travelling from east to west. In *Canada* (Paris, 1944) he vividly described his journey and the people he met. His two novels—*Laframboise et Bellehumeur* (Paris, 1944), the story of two Quebec trappers who curse their life in the forest, and yet cannot resist its call when autumn returns, and *Eva Charlebois* (Paris, 1944), whose heroine, exiled in the West, longs for her native Quebec—are two of the best Canadian novels written by Frenchmen, thanks to Genevoix's feeling for nature. Pierre Hamp (1876-1962), whose novels about manual work are grouped under the title 'La peine des hommes', spent one year in 1947 teaching at the École d'Hôtellerie of Saint-Paul-l'Érmite. In *Hormisdas le Canadien* (Paris, 1952) he describes the tragic changes brought to a farming community when, in 1944, a munitions factory is built in the village.

Canada has been a large source of inspiration for several French writers in recent times, no doubt due to the more frequent cultural exchanges between Quebec and France. The most talented and prolific of these writers is Bernard Clavel (b. 1923), a highly popular author in France and a Prix Goncourt winner. Since he has visited Quebec many times, he knows the province better than most French writers and stayed from 1977 to 1979; he is also married to a Quebec novelist, Josette Pratte. In *Les compagnons du Nouveau-Monde* (Paris, 1981), which takes place in the seventeenth century, the carpenter Bisontin-la-Vertu and the young woman he loves attempt to start a new life in Quebec. But Bisontin soon discovers that New France, ruled by the iron-fisted Jesuits for whom he works, is no place for non-conformists. Instead of a new life, Bisontin and Jarnigoine, returning home to France, find death in a shipwreck (masterfully described). In the 1980s Clavel completed a series of novels that take place in the Lac Témiscamingue region and are grouped under the title 'Le Royaume du Nord'. We witness the painful birth and development of Saint-Georges d'Harricana, on the Harricana River (*Harricana*, Paris, 1983), which flows into James Bay; the arrival of newcomers attracted by the lure of gold and the promise of easy money (*L'or de la terre*, Paris, 1984); the adventures and misfortunes of those who try to make an honest living from the land (*Miséréré*, Paris, 1985); a flight from the police through the frozen wilderness (*Amarok*, Paris, 1987); and the dogged battle of an old farmer who chooses to remain alone in a parish all others have left (*L'angélus du soir*, Paris, 1988). In the last volume of the series, *Maudits sauvages* (Paris, 1989), Clavel turns to the plight of the Natives whose way of life has been destroyed by the building of the James Bay dam. Though his characters are not exempt from human failings, he has created a world in which courage, honour, and unflagging loyalty are real. But the success of his books is due chiefly to his style, which, like his subject, is of epic stature. 'Herculean', 'Promethean' are adjectives that have been used to describe his novels. Clavel has also written three novellas in which Canada plays an important part: *L'Iroquoise* (Paris, 1979), which takes place partly in the United States in the 1940s; *La bourrelle* (Paris, 1980), set in seventeenth-century Quebec; and *L'homme du Labrador* (Paris, 1982), where the characters dream of a mythical North. *Le lapin de lune* (1982), a touching, lyrical novel by Alain Gerber (b. 1943), also takes place in a mythical land which, though it is never mentioned by name, must be Quebec. Where else would one find such hard winters, an Aboriginal heroine, characters called Brouillette, and a place named Sainte-Adèle? *Angélique à Québec* (Paris, 1980) belongs to the immensely popular Angélique series by writers Anne Golon (b. 1925) and Serge Golon (1905-72). Though Serge had been dead for eight years when the novel, which takes place in seventeenth-century New France, was published, it appeared under both names, doubtless for commercial reasons. That Quebec should be chosen as the setting for this 1980 popular novel, of more historical than literary value, shows the interest the French were taking at the time in their former colony. Though Michel Desgranges (b. 1942), a Parisian journalist, never visited Canada, he suggests quite successfully the atmosphere of the Prairies in his novel *Manitoba* (Paris, 1981). Originally inspired by Riel and the Métis Rebellion, the work is nonetheless a product of the author's imagination, and should not be regarded as a historical novel.

See Paulette Collet, 'Portrait de l'immigrant français dans l'Ouest et l'Est canadiens selon les romanciers français', *L'Ouest canadien et l'Amérique française, les actes du huitième colloque du Centre d'études franco-canadiennes de l'Ouest*' (1990), Université de Régina; Sherry Simon, 'Espaces incertains de la culture' and Pierre L'Hérault, 'Pour une cartographie de l'hétérogène: dérives identitaires des années 1980' in *Fictions de l'identitaire au Québec* (1991).

See also MULTICULTURAL WRITING IN FRENCH.

PAULETTE COLLET

Forsey, Eugene (1904-91). Born in Grand Bank, Newfoundland, he attended McGill University, Montreal, and Oxford University, where, as a Rhodes scholar, he studied philosophy, economics, and politics. Forsey was rooted on the left of the Canadian political landscape and several times ran unsuccessfully for public office under the banner of the Canadian Commonwealth Federation (CCF). He was among those who helped frame the Regina Manifesto (1933), the founding document of the CCF. In addition to teaching as a sessional lecturer at McGill, Carleton University, Ottawa, and Queen's University, Kingston, Forsey was director of research for the Canadian Congress of Labour (CCL) for fourteen years. From 1956 to 1966 he served as director of research for the CCL's successor, the Canadian Labour Congress, and from 1966 to 1969 he was director of special projects. In 1970 he was summoned to the Senate, where he remained for eight years; and he was sworn to the Privy Council in 1985. The recipient of many honorary degrees, Forsey was made a Companion of the Order of Canada in 1989.

Forsey's early publications focused on labour and social issues. In 1926 he published *National problems of Canada: the economic and social aspects of the Nova Scotia coal industry*. Other studies included *The royal power of dissolution of Parliament in the British Commonwealth* (1943; rpr. 1968), his most important scholarly work, and *Our present discontents* (1968). *Freedom and order* (1974) is a collection of twenty-four essays on Canadian constitutional matters, and *How Canadians govern themselves* (1979; 2nd edn, 1988) is an informative and lucid booklet. *Trade unions in Canada* (1982) is an exhaustive history of the trade-union movement. His final work, *A life on the fringe: the memoirs of Eugene Forsey* (1990), portrays Forsey at his eclectic best. He reveals with candour how he left Canada for Oxford a Meighen Conservative only to return a committed socialist, and how he managed to maintain that improbable balancing act throughout the rest of his long life. Critic Robert FULFORD called *A life on the fringe* 'an astonishing guided tour of our entire political horizon over three generations'. It was nominated for a Governor General's Award.

Forsey was a passionate defender of what he called 'Macdonald's Constitution'—that is, the British North America Act of 1867. Deeply read in every aspect of the Constitution, he resisted the attempts of politicians, editorial writers, and constitutional experts who sought to interpret it in order to accommodate the ambitions of provincial leaders. He became well known to newspaper readers for his many 'Letters to the Editor', which severely but elegantly addressed errors on constitutional points.

The best brief overview of Forsey's constitutionalism is Donald CREIGHTON, 'Eugene Albert Forsey: an introduction', in the above-mentioned *Freedom and order.*

FREDERICK VAUGHAN

Fortune and men's eyes (1967). This prison drama by John HERBERT was first workshopped at the Stratford Festival in Oct. 1965, but was not produced because its subject and language were judged to be unsuitable for Stratford audiences. It premièred in a full production at the Actors Playhouse, New York, on 23 Feb. 1967; the first full professional Canadian production took place only in 1975 at Toronto's Phoenix Theatre and won the Chalmers Award as best Canadian play of the Toronto season.

While *Fortune and men's eyes* draws upon Herbert's openly professed homosexuality and his experiences in a Canadian reformatory on a charge of gross indecency (a charge he has always denied), its primary theme is human relationships and how denial of love can warp young lives. The play is about the 'education' of a new inmate, Smitty, whose 'teachers' are his fellow inmates: Rocky, a pimp and homosexual (who professes to hate homosexual behaviour); Queenie, a transvestite; and Mona, an eighteen-year-old boy, the victim of repeated gang rapes. In the course of the play Smitty is raped by Rocky, taught the politics and power structure of prison life by Queenie, and offered a redemptive love by the Christlike Mona. Mona's 'quality of mercy' speech from *The merchant of Venice* trial scene, and the references to Shakespeare's sonnet 29 ('When in disgrace with fortune and men's eyes /. . . Haply I think on thee . . .'), are balanced against the raw and obscene language of the other characters. The hope implied by the Shakespearean allusions is undercut, however, by the brutal whipping of Mona by the prison guards, and by the progressive moral degeneration of Smitty. At the play's close he has given himself over to violence and a criminal future. Although its subjects—homosexual gang rapes, physical abuse—are unpalatable, Herbert's play is leavened by humour and raw energy. Queenie's Christmas drag routine is a comic theatrical *tour de force*, and all the characters are compelling in their rage to survive.

Fortune and men's eyes quickly became internationally famous—in its first ten years it was performed in more than 100 countries in some forty languages. It led to the founding of the Fortune Society, which seeks to bring about prison reform. There was a film adaptation (1971), directed by Harvey Hart.

Selected criticism of the play is included in *Canadian drama and the critics* (rev. ed. 1995), edited by L.W. Conolly. EUGENE BENSON

Foster, Cecil. See NOVELS IN ENGLISH 1983 TO 1996: OTHER NOVELS 3.

Four Horsemen, The. This sound-poetry performance group began in 1970 when, after a joint reading by bp NICHOL and Steve MCCAFFERY, Rafael Barreto-Rivera proposed that they should get together, with Paul Dutton, and 'jam'. They quickly became the premier sound-poetry ensemble in Canada, and by the late 1970s had attained an international reputation. After Nichol's tragic and untimely death in 1988, the group's activities tapered off, although they occasionally performed together as simply 'The Horsemen'. Their example encouraged several other Canadian groups, such as Owen Sound, First Draft, and Re:Sounding.

The Four Horsemen worked within the traditions of sound poetry established by such early-twentieth-century pioneers as Hugo Ball and Kurt Schwitters. They stressed the *sound* of language as the primary material of their work, using such techniques as chant, repetition, and counterpoint. They developed flexible notational systems to permit a more precise interaction of the four voices. Sometimes the effect was to emphasize meaning in new ways, but often their work tended towards a diminution or 'abstraction' of the semantic content, a celebration of pure vocal sound. Their later performances became more theatrical, laying greater stress on the physicality of the performing body on stage. They set a standard of inventiveness, energy, and exuberant delight in language that continues to challenge all poets, whether or not they are working at the same edge of experimentation.

No form of publication can ever be an adequate substitute for a live performance of the Four Horsemen. They made several recordings—*CaNADAda* (1973), *Live in the West* (1977), and *Bootleg* (1981)—and they appear briefly in Ron Mann's film *Poetry in Motion* (1982; available as CD-ROM, 1992). *The prose tattoo* (1982) is an important collection of their collaborative texts, while *Horse d'oeuvres* (1975) contains separate pieces by each individual member. STEPHEN SCOBIE

Four Jameses, The (1927). This famous literary satire by William Arthur DEACON consists of biographical and critical appreciations of four real-life but mercifully obscure Canadian poetasters whose only connection was their common Christian name, their lack of talent, and the mock-admiration they aroused in Deacon, a prominent literary journalist of the day. Of the four, three wrote their doggerel about rural Ontario: James Gay (who called himself the poet laureate of Canada), James McIntyre (author of the dreadful 'Ode on the mammoth cheese'), and James MacRae (less inherently offensive than the others, but still a poet whose rhymes make the fillings in one's teeth ache). The fourth James was James Gillis of Cape Breton, who was ambidextrous, being equally ungifted in prose. *The four Jameses*, which appeared in a revised edition in 1953 and was reprinted again in 1974, is distinguished both by Deacon's use of quotations to enhance the reputations of his subjects, and by the straightness of his face while doing so. DOUGLAS FETHERLING

Fournier, Claude. See NOVELS IN FRENCH 1983 TO 1996: 7.

Fournier, Jules. See ESSAYS IN FRENCH: 2.

Fournier, Roger. See NOVELS IN FRENCH 1960 TO 1982: 3(b).

Fowke, Edith (1913-96). Edith Fulton was born in Lumsden, Saskatchewan, and educated at the provincial university (B.A., 1933; M.A., 1937). She married Franklin Fowke in 1938. In the late 1940s she began recording immigrant and lumbering ballads in central Ontario, and this interest and activity broadened until she became one of Canada's leading folklorists, dedicated to revealing 'the hidden submerged culture lying in the shadow of the official civilization about which historians write'. From 1950 to 1972 she hosted such CBC radio programs as 'Folksong Time' and 'Folklore and Folk Music'. She joined the English Department of York University, Toronto, in 1971 to teach courses in folklore; became a full professor in 1977; and retired as Professor Emerita in 1984. Fowke received many honours, including honorary doctorates from four Canadian universities, and was a Companion of the Order of Canada.

Among Fowke's more than twenty publications were many on folksongs, including *Folksongs of Canada* (1954, with Richard Johnston), *Traditional singers and songs from Ontario* (1965), *Lumbering songs from the northern woods* (1970), *The Penguin book of Canadian folk songs* (1973), and *Sea songs and ballads from nineteenth-century Nova Scotia* (1982). On non-musical folklore she collected the chants and rhymes of children for the popular *Sally go round the sun* (1969), *Ring around the moon* (1972), and *Red rover! red rover!: children's games played in Canada* (1988). Her folklore collections include *Folklore of Canada* (1976), *Folktales of French Canada* (1979), *Tales told in Canada* (1986), and *Legends told in Canada* (1988, rpr. 1994). Fowke's *Canadian folklore* (1988), in Oxford's Perspectives on Canadian Culture series, is a brief but valuable and wide-ranging survey of the subject.

WILLIAM TOYE

Foyer canadien, Le. A monthly literary magazine published in Quebec City from 1863 to 1866, it owed its origin to a disagreement in Oct. 1862 among the editors of its predecessor, *Les SOIRÉES CANADIENNES* (1861-5). As a result, three editors—Abbé Henri-Raymond CASGRAIN, Dr Hubert LaRUE, and Antoine GÉRIN-LAJOIE—withdrew from the *Soirées*; together with three new colleagues—Abbé Jean-Baptiste-Antoine Ferland, Louis-Joseph-Cyprien Fiset, and Joseph-Octave CRÉMAZIE—they founded *Le Foyer canadien*. (Although Crémazie signed the prospectus, he left Quebec a few days later for a bankrupt's exile in France.) The intention of the new periodical was to encourage the publication of original French-Canadian writing, but some French material was also included.

At first the magazine enjoyed great success, having more than 2,000 subscribers. It published biographies, fiction, poems, travel accounts, and folklore, and its contributors included several members of the MOUVEMENT LITTÉRAIRE DE QUÉBEC: Philippe AUBERT DE GASPÉ, Pierre-Joseph-Olivier CHAUVEAU, Alfred GARNEAU, Pamphile LEMAY, and Adolphe-Basile Routhier. During its first three years *Le Foyer* published several long works that extended over many issues. To meet competition from the continuing *Soirées canadiennes*, and from the new Montreal monthly *La Revue canadienne* (1864-1922), the magazine was reorganized in 1866 to include more current features. Nevertheless the death in Jan. 1865 of the senior editor, Abbé Ferland, coupled with the departure later that year for the new capital, Ottawa, of both Gérin-Lajoie and the *Foyer's* printer, Georges Desbarats, doomed the magazine. Its final issue appeared in Dec. 1866; its disappearance, followed in Feb. 1867 by the belated publication of the last 1865 issue of *Les Soirées canadiennes*, marked the break-up of the Mouvement littéraire de Québec.

Le Foyer canadien gave a powerful impetus to French-Canadian literature in the 1860s, both by the number and importance of its contributors and by the volume of publication it achieved: in addition to receiving the monthly 32-page numbers, subscribers were entitled to bonus volumes offered at reduced prices or gratis. For the first time French-Canadian writing became available to a wider audience at reasonable prices.

See Réjean Robidoux, '*Les Soirées canadiennes et Le Foyer canadien* dans le mouvement littéraire de 1860', in Réjean Robidoux, *Fonder une littérature nationale: notes d'histoire littéraire* (1994), 11-133.

DAVID M. HAYNE

Francoeur, Lucien (b. 1948). Born in Montreal, as a teenager he often ran away—not only in Montreal, but to New York and Toronto—and experimented with drugs. In 1968 he rejoined his family in New Orleans, where he finished high school. Returning to Montreal to study literature, he discovered the Hexagone poets, the Herbes Rouges group, psychedelics, LSD, and rock poetry. He founded a rock group (Aut'chose), edited a collection of poetry for Hexagone, and contributed to journals including *L'Hexagone*, *Hobo-Québec*, *La BARRE DU JOUR*, and *Le Devoir*. He received an M.A. from the Université du Québec à Trois-Rivières and since 1983 has taught at the Rosemont CEGEP in Montreal.

Francoeur's first collection of poetry, *Mini-brixes réactés* (1972), combines lyricism with a vocabulary that draws on the world of psychedelics, rock, American English, and JOUAL, and shows a predilection for technical, even hermetic, language. This collection propelled Francoeur to the forefront of Quebec's counter-culture.

Other early collections, such as *Suzanne le chacha et moi* (1975), present repeated, desperate appeals to the lost woman, and use a language in which vulgarity vies with verbal violence. *Les néons las* (1978) marks a return to a more controlled writing—quotations from authors of the American counter-culture making way for French literary culture—but the approach remains the same: the poet sees the text as the stage on which he himself is the spectacle, and this desire for self-display is so extreme that it leads to valuing masturbation, which Francoeur extends to his conception of poetry. For this writing, all that matters are the images and the shock they produce in the reader—connections between the lines are of little importance.

From 1974 to 1980 Francoeur gave in to the temptation of the stage, and the more immediate success he found with his group, Aut'chose. The publication of *Rockers sanctifiés* (1982), for which he was awarded the Prix Émile-Nelligan, enabled him to bring together the various styles he had explored until that time to create a book/object, with original typography recalling the handwritten manuscripts of sacred books. Its aim was to raise sexual impulses to a spiritual level in creating an entirely new myth, a religion in which writing becomes a kind of delirium that raises the poet to the rank of the gods. Presenting himself as a new initiate, a shaman, a 'mutant noir', Francoeur placed his effort under the patronage of Rimbaud's *Illuminations*. More recently, *Exit pour nomades* (1985; revised 1991) and *Si Rimbaud pouvait me lire....* (1987) continue in the direction of Francoeur's earlier collections, composed in a style described as 'reptilian', and exploring the most subterranean reaches of the American space. In 1989 Francoeur edited an anthology, *Vingt-cinq poètes québécois 1968-1978*.

JACQUES PAQUIN

Franklin, John. See EXPLORATION LITERATURE IN ENGLISH: 2.

Franquet, Louis. See BIOGRAPHY AND MEMOIRS IN FRENCH: 6 and Writing in NEW FRANCE: 1.

Fraser, Brad (b. 1959). Born and raised in Edmonton, Alberta, he writes unconventional, often controversial, plays that recall traditions of horror, black comedy, and farce, dramatizing such issues as love, violence, identity, and homosexuality. His early plays include *Mutants* (produced in 1980), *Wolfboy* (prod. 1981), *Chainsaw love* (prod. 1982), *Rude noises (for a blank generation)* (prod. 1982), and *Young art* (prod. 1987). Fraser is perhaps best known for *Unidentified human remains and the true nature of love* (1990), first produced by Alberta Theatre Projects, Calgary, in 1989, and by Crow's Theatre Group at the Poor Alex, Toronto. The play had a phenomenal success: it has been produced in Japan, Britain, and Mexico, and throughout North America. Fraser received a Genie Award for Best Adapted Screenplay for the 1993 feature film of the play, directed by Denys Arcand. Both romance and murder mystery, *Unidentified human remains* moves with disturbing ease between the serious and the comic, and has been compared to Dostoevsky's *The devils*, as well as to the works of David Lynch and Joe Orton. Seven characters search for and avoid love and sex in Edmonton, in a world of tension, insecurity, and violence. The characters—including a psychic prostitute, an anorexic book reviewer, a gay waiter, and a secret serial killer—circle each other, unable or unwilling to communicate meaningfully except on an answering machine.

Later theatre pieces by Fraser are *The ugly man* (1993), the musical *Outrageous* (1994), and *Poor super man* (1995). He has won numerous awards, including the 1991 Floyd S. Chalmers Award and the *London Evening Standard*'s Most Promising Play Award for *Unidentified human remains*, and the Alberta Writers' Guild Award.

JENNIE RUBIO

Fraser, Keath (b. 1944). Born in Vancouver, British Columbia, where he lives, he was educated at the University of British Columbia (B.A., 1966; M.A., 1969) and at the University of London (Ph.D., 1973). He has travelled widely in Asia, Europe, and Australia, and his travel experiences, especially in India and Cambodia, are prominent in his fiction. After teaching for five years at the University of Calgary, Fraser abandoned his career as a tenured English professor to write full time.

Fraser's work evokes the uniqueness of prosperous Vancouver as a slightly decadent place. Linked to Asia by the geographical fault lines of the Pacific Rim, the city becomes a metaphor: we are all connected, a tremor in one part of the world affects another part. He describes the West Coast with such eloquent prose that it borders on the exotic. He is one of the most gifted of the new generation of fiction writers; his startling imagery, rich ideas, textured language, and astonishing range of characters (especially new immigrants to Canada: he suggests that we are all foreigners to each other) are remarkable.

Fraser's impressive début collection of eight stories, *Taking cover* (1982), is about love, loss, and the uses and abuses of language—one story is appropriately titled 'Roget's thesaurus'. In 'This is what you were born for' a character suddenly struck deaf can only communicate through handwriting. The title story consists of instructions, in every cliché and banality imaginable, to people who enter a bomb shelter after a nuclear war has begun. Ironically, these dense stories about the inability to communicate are vivid and memorable.

Much of Fraser's fiction is preoccupied with the secret lives of ordinary characters who have lost any promise of a bright future. Often their lives are shattered by sudden and inexplicable violence. The seven stories and three novellas in *Foreign affairs* (1986) form a powerful interconnected collection of perceptive portraits. Two of the most eloquent and disturbing are 'The history of Cambodia' and 'Foreign affairs'. The former is about a female newspaper correspondent held prisoner by the Khmer Rouge for five years around the ruined temples of Angkor Wat. Telling a story of horror, violence, and atrocity, the dying woman is sustained by childhood memories of Vancouver. In 'Foreign affairs' a promising diplomat has his career cut short by multiple sclerosis; the story stands comparison with Margaret LAURENCE's *The STONE ANGEL* in its use of its broken thought patterns and shattered dreams.

The four interconnected novellas of Fraser's highly original 600-page architectonic novel *Popular anatomy* (1995)—written over a ten-year period—are a brave attempt to challenge the nature of storytelling. The novel is an x-ray of contemporary society as seen from a global perspective, with Vancouver as the fulcrum for the flow of characters. Part one, 'Against nature', tells the story of Dwight Irving, a travel agent who dislikes travel; on a rare trip to settle a dispute against a hotel that had scammed a group of tourists, he is imprisoned in a Latin American jail and slowly succumbs to the loss of his business and the decay of his body; part two, 'The life of a tuxedo', is a long soliloquy delivered by Dwight's foster child, an East Indian punk rocker in Vancouver who smuggles refugees; part three, 'Bones', is about Dwight's roommate, an unhappy chiropractor, Bartlett Day, who buys skeletons of slaughtered people in Uganda, Cambodia, and Peru to sell to medical schools; part four is a science-fiction memoir written chronologically backwards from 2091 to 1886 by a former mayor of Vancouver and details incidents of racism and intolerance. Overlong and unwieldy, and not always coherent, the novel strives for a tension between multiple perspectives rather than dramatic conflict. *Popular anatomy* won the Chapters/*Books in Canada* First Novel Award. His most recent publication is a collection of ten stories, *Telling my love lies* (1997).

Fraser has published two anthologies of travel writing: *Bad trips* (1991) and *Worst journeys: the Picador book of travel* (1992). The difficulties and satisfaction of his twenty-five year friendship with Sinclair ROSS are described in *As for me and my body: a memoir of Sinclair Ross* (1997). See 'Some random jottings on Keath Fraser', *CANADIAN FICTION MAGAZINE* 65. For Fraser's views on the metaphysics of narration, see 'Notes towards a supreme fiction', *CANADIAN LITERATURE* 100.

GEOFF HANCOCK

Fraser, Simon. See EXPLORATION LITERATURE IN ENGLISH: 2.

Fraser, Sylvia (b. 1935). Sylvia Meyers was born and raised in a working-class district of Hamilton, Ontario. Her mother was a church and community worker and president of a temperance group; her father an inspector for a steel company. She has described her early life as 'gothic' and 'emotionally disturbed'. Educated at the University of Western Ontario, she obtained a B.A. in English and Philosophy in 1957. She became a successful journalist, with five years as a feature writer for the *Star Weekly* before she began writing fiction. Fraser has won many awards for her writing, notably the Women's Press Club Award in 1967 and 1968, and the President's Medal, University of Western Ontario, in 1969.

Fraser's early fictions have been re-framed in postmodernist readings by the publication of her moving and disturbing autobiographical account of a sexually abusive father in *My father's house: a memoir of incest and healing* (1987). The incest, from her earliest childhood until her teens, led to a split personality. Her stark, yet often lyrical book is written in two typefaces—italic for the crime and boldface for recovered memories—that give a sense of both the secrecy of incest, within the family and even the community, and the split that takes place within the child and later young adult who uncovers the mystery of her life, and finally her personal and family healing. She also describes the emotional beginning and end of her long marriage. Fraser's first non-fiction work became a rallying point in the growing community of women who have recalled the abuse they suffered.

The book of strange: a journey (1992; published in the U.K. and in paperback as *The quest for the fourth monkey*) continues her effort to explore her incestuous past and that of other family members through 'strange' things that happened to her, including 'out of body' experiences. She describes her personal journey and her speculations about the mystical side of life: telepathy, premonition, coincidence, prophetic dreams, reincarnation, and death. The impressively researched book is also a comprehensive study of particle physics, paranormal phenomena, the occult, and what she describes as the split in Western society between mysticism and materialism. 'The fourth monkey' refers to a Victorian knick-knack of china monkeys covering their eyes, ears, and mouth. The fourth monkey covers its genitals and was often removed from the group; Fraser uses this image to refer to sexual repression.

Fraser's early fictions, which frequently explored tormented sexual encounters, are now seen as symbolically representing Fraser's life. Her autobiographical first novel, *Pandora* (1972), with lyrical line drawings by Harold Town, is a backward look from an adult viewpoint at an imaginative journey in the life and mind of seven-year-old, Pandora, who was raised to hate Germans and fear authority; she has a submissive mother and a cruel father with a hook for a hand. *Pandora* is in the NEW CANADIAN LIBRARY.

The candy factory (1975) is a powerful and lusty mystery novel. The factory of the title is both setting and metaphor for society and the fundamental theme of male/female relationships. The lives of several characters are examined, including a scatological tramp who lives in an abandoned drainage system and an elderly spinster who occupies a loft. *A casual affair: a modern fairytale* (1978) is an ingenious, sometimes flatly written novel about a failed love affair; fairy tales comment on and explain the characters —a beautiful blonde artist and a handsome diplomat. Fraser's occasionally overwritten and steamy novel *The Emperor's virgin* (1980) is about a vestal virgin in A.D. 81-96 who is buried alive by a king for breaking her vow of chastity. The painstakingly detailed research suggests parallels between ancient Rome and modern North America, especially in corruption and the loss of interest in traditional religion paralleled by interest in Eastern religions and the occult, ideas further developed in her later non-fiction. In her fast-paced and well-researched modern-day historical novel, *Berlin solstice* (1984), set against the rise and fall of the Third Reich, Fraser follows a group of characters from various classes. More importantly for Fraser, who is of German ancestry, the writing of this novel led her to realize what happened to her in her own life—she has said that Nazism represented her father the abuser, and that the collaborators represented her collaboration in her father's crime.

The ancestral suitcase (1996) fictionalizes ideas from *The book of strange*. Nora Locke experiences many coincidences following the death of her mother. A suitcase in the attic and a fall downstairs transport her back to Victorian England before the First World War to unravel intrigue, passion, and murder in her family past. The heroine ponders 'the impossible possibilities' of synchronicity, karma, and reincarnation in this entertaining adventure.

See Lorna Irvine, 'Assembly line stories: pastiche in Sylvia Fraser's *The candy factory*', *CANADIAN LITERATURE* 89 (1981); and an interview with Alan Twigg in *Strong voices* (1988). GEOFF HANCOCK

Fraser, William Alexander (1859-1933). Born in River John, Nova Scotia, he was educated in New York and Boston. After many years as an engineer in the oil districts of western Ontario, Burma, India, and western Canada, he began his writing career with stories published in the *Detroit Free Press*. Most of his writing life was spent in Georgetown, Ont., and Toronto, where he died. Fraser made a substantial reputation as a writer of popular fiction, using the various locales in which he had lived in short stories and novels: the Far East in story collections such as *The eye of a god: and other tales of East and West* (New York, 1899) and *The Sa'Zada tales* (1905); the Canadian West in *Mooswa and others of the boundaries* (New York, 1900) and *The blood lilies* (1903); Ontario in *The lone furrow* (1907); and New York State in *Thoroughbreds* (1902), about horse-racing, a favourite subject. He created a literary curiosity (recalling Kipling's *Jungle Book*) in *Mooswa*, which employs a large cast of animals who converse intelligently, have their own laws, and discipline each other; but the western forest setting and animal characteristics are carefully observed. Fraser, who also treated such issues as drug-taking and drug-trafficking in his fiction (*The lone furrow*, 1907, *Bulldog Carney*, 1919), wrote with a strong air of moral didacticism, though he was not always supportive of formal law-enforcement agencies, such as the Royal Canadian Mounted Police, which he satirized in *Bulldog Carney*. *The lone furrow* is perhaps his best novel. Set in western Ontario and Montreal, it uses intrigues and motifs of murder fiction, and demonstrates a not entirely conventional concern with moral and religious issues.

CHARLES R. STEELE

Fréchette, Carole. See DRAMA IN FRENCH 1981 TO 1996: 2.

Fréchette, Louis (1839-1908). Born at Hadlow Cove near Lévis, Quebec, a seventh-generation Canadian, he was educated under self-employed schoolmasters, at the college of the Brothers of the Christian Schools in Lévis, and at three different classical secondary colleges, from two of which he was expelled, presumably for neglecting his studies. Graduating from the college of Nicolet in 1859, he began to study law at the newly established (1852) Université Laval the following year.

While a law student Fréchette composed his first play, *Félix Poutré*, in 1862. The next year he published, at his own expense, a collection of his verse, *Mes loisirs*, the first volume of lyric poetry to appear in Quebec. The influence of the French Romantics Lamartine and Hugo was apparent in Fréchette's choice of amorous and nostalgic themes and in his experimentation with some forty different stanza forms.

In 1864 Fréchette opened an unsuccessful law office in Lévis, where he and his brother Edmond founded two short-lived Liberal newspapers. In June 1866, discouraged by these experiences and by the prospect of a Conservative Confederation, he moved to Chicago—where another brother, Achille, had a law practice—and remained there until 1871, working for the Illinois Central Railroad, founding more newspapers, visiting New Orleans, and writing poetry and plays, most of which were destroyed in the Chicago fire of 1871. The only major work to survive from this period was a violent verse attack on George-Étienne Cartier and the authors of the 1867 Confederation, published in Quebec newspapers in 1867-8 under the title *La voix d'un exilé*; two pamphlet editions were published in Chicago in 1868 (18 pages) and 1869 (46 pages).

Returning to Lévis in 1871, Fréchette was soon embroiled in an exchange of articles with a former friend, Adolphe-Basile Routhier, who in his *Causeries du dimanche* (Montréal, 1871) had criticized Fréchette's poetry and politics. Fréchette ran unsuccessfully in the provincial election of 1871 and in the federal election of 1872; but from 1874 to 1878 he sat in the House of Commons as a Liberal member for Lévis. Although he was not re-elected, his economic future was assured by his marriage in 1876 to Emma Beaudry, the daughter of a Montreal financier.

Fréchette's third book of poetry, *Pêle-mêle* (Montréal, 1877), was well received: its 64 poems included ten reprinted from *Mes loisirs* and seventeen sonnets, a form that was becoming popular in Quebec in the 1870s. Two years later, at the suggestion of a correspondent in France, Fréchette hurriedly assembled a new volume of verse under the double title *Les fleurs boréales. Les oiseaux de neige* (Québec, 1879) and entered it in the annual competition of the Académie française. On 5 Aug. 1880, at the annual public session of the Académie in Paris, Fréchette received a Prix Montyon of 2,500 francs. On his return to Canada he was fêted at a huge public banquet on 17 Nov. and was henceforth considered the unofficial poet laureate of French Canada. In the summer of 1880 he had also brought out two plays, *Papineau* and *Le retour de l'exilé*; the latter was later shown to be largely borrowed from a French novel, *La bastide rouge* (Paris, 1853) by Élie Berthet. Furthermore Fréchette was soon the centre of controversy again over his publication of an anti-monarchical brochure entitled *Petite histoire des rois de France* (Montréal, 1883) and other provocative articles in the Montreal Liberal newspaper *La Patrie*.

During the 1880s Fréchette composed a number of long historical poems for his major work, *La légende d'un peuple* (Paris, 1887), which he completed during a summer spent in Britanny in 1887. Modelled on Victor Hugo's *La légende des siècles*, this was a collection of 47 tableaux arranged in three chronological sequences covering the seventeenth, eighteenth, and nineteenth centuries of Quebec's history. Despite its lack of unity and the unevenness of its execution, this was Fréchette's greatest achievement; its grandiose conception and its stirring passages make it the most important volume of poetry published in nineteenth-century Quebec.

Three years later Fréchette issued his last verse collection, *Feuilles volantes* (Québec, 1890), and thereafter wrote chiefly in prose.

He published in rapid succession an amusing collection of portraits of eccentric Quebec characters (*Originaux et détraqués: douze types québécois*, Montréal, 1892); a series of letters criticizing classical secondary education (*À propos d'éducation*, Montréal, 1893); an exchange of articles (1894) on the subject of his supposed plagiarisms, with his former disciple William CHAPMAN; a collection of *Mémoires intimes* that appeared serially in *Le Monde illustré* (May-Nov. 1900); a volume of romantic short stories published in both English and French under the titles *Christmas in French Canada* (Toronto, 1899) and *La Noël au Canada* (Toronto, 1900); and an introduction for William Henry DRUMMOND's *The habitant and other French-Canadian poems* (New York, 1897). The sexagenarian poet was now laden with honours: he was Chevalier de la Légion d'honneur, a Companion of the Order of St Michael and St George, an honorary doctor of four universities, President of the Royal Society of Canada, and Honorary President of the ÉCOLE LITTÉRAIRE DE MONTRÉAL. Since 1889 he had also held the largely honorary appointment of Clerk of the Legislative Council of Quebec.

In declining health, Fréchette set about a definitive three-volume edition of his works, which would include his unpublished verse play 'Veronica' (1903), another example of 'collaboration' with a French author, Maurice de Pradel. The collected edition, under the title *Poésies choisies*, appeared a few months after Fréchette's death from a stroke on 31 May 1908. The modest attendance at his funeral demonstrated the transience of public favour: the intellectual climate had changed since 1890, and the once-revered Romantic poet had become a distant echo of a forgotten literary school.

More detailed information about individual works by Fréchette will be found in the appropriate articles of the *Dictionnaire des oeuvres littéraires du Québec, I: des origines à 1900* (1978). A short study of his poetry by David M. Hayne is included in Robert L. McDougall, ed., *Canada's past and present: a dialogue* (Our Living Tradition, fifth series, 1965). See also *Satires et polémiques*, (2 vols, 1993), a critical edition of Fréchette's satirical and polemical writings by Jacques Blais in collaboration with Luc Bouvier and Guy Champagne. DAVID M. HAYNE

Freeman, David (b.1947). Born in Toronto, a victim of cerebral palsy caused by brain damage at birth, he attended Toronto's Sunnyview School for the Handicapped until he was seventeen and began writing short stories and poetry there. An article by him, 'The world of can't'—an indictment of sheltered workshops like the one Freeman had attended—was published in *Maclean's* in 1964. The CBC commissioned him to write a play based on it and he did; but the producer, who thought Freeman's script would make unpleasant viewing on the national network, turned it down. In 1966 Freeman enrolled at McMaster University, graduating with a B.A. in political science in 1971. By that time he had shown his script to Bill Glassco, who encouraged him to rewrite it. Glassco directed *CREEPS* (1972), a long one-act play, at the Factory Theatre Lab in Toronto early in 1971. It was an instant success. Set in the men's washroom of a workshop for CP victims, *Creeps* dramatizes, not without humour, the anger and inner rebellion these victims feel towards a society that looks down on them and will not let them forget that they are different. Later in 1971 Glassco made *Creeps* the opening play at his new Tarragon Theatre in Toronto. It won the first Chalmers Award for the outstanding Canadian play produced in the Toronto area, and a New York production won Freeman a New York Critics Drama Desk Award for the outstanding new playwright of the 1973-4 season; it also played for two years in Los Angeles, where it won three Los Angeles Critics' Circle Awards. In 1981 it made a successful seven-week tour of Britain, and won an Edinburgh Fringe Award.

Freeman's next play was *Battering ram* (1972), a longer and more complexly structured work than *Creeps*. The central character, Virgil, is a cripple who is taken into the home of a middle-aged woman and her nubile daughter. In portraying the mutual exploitation of the emotions and sexual needs of all three characters, it shows Freeman's ability to go beyond the concerns of the handicapped to explore explosive situations between the sexes.

With *You're gonna be alright, Jamie boy* (1974) Freeman moved away from the world of the physically handicapped. Jamie Dinsdale returns home from the Clarke Institute of Psychiatry in Toronto to realize painfully how his family—father, mother, daughter, and son-in-law—are addicted to television and derive their life values from it. Structured as a situation comedy, it reflects the dehumanizing qualities of TV-centred lives. His next play was *Flytrap* (1980), produced at Montreal's Saidye Bronfman Centre in 1976; it is about a husband and wife, with a floundering marriage, who invite a young man to live with them. Though Freeman attempted a more sophisticated humour here than in his previous plays,

Flytrap is often merely shallow, its situational possibilities undeveloped, and its easy resolution unconvincing. Two of his plays have been produced in French in Montreal, *Creeps* (*Les Touts-Croches*) at Salle Fred Barry in 1981, and *Battering Ram* (*Le Bélier*) at Théâtre d'Aujourd'hui in 1984.

Freeman has not had a new play on stage for some years, but he has continued to write plays. Among these are *Scar*, about a post-holocaust future; and *Year of the Soul*, produced on CBC radio in the Quebec Heroes and Anti-Heroes series in 1982, about Brother André, the miracle-worker of St Joseph's Oratory in Montreal.

In 1975 Freeman moved to Montreal, where he still resides. He continues to defend the rights of the disabled, and in 1995 spoke out publicly against euthanasia in the case of Robert Latimer, the Saskatchewan farmer who ended the life of his severely handicapped daughter.

Freeman has written an interesting account of his career as a playwright in *Stage voices* (1978), edited with an introduction and bibliography by Geraldine Anthony. See also Mary Elizabeth Smith, 'Freeman's *Creeps* and *Battering ram*: Variations on a Theme', *Canadian Drama*, 4 (1978). *Creeps* may be found in two major anthologies, *The Penguin book of modern Canadian drama* (1984), edited by Richard Plant, and *Modern Canadian plays* (1993), 3rd edn, vol. 1, edited by Jerry Wasserman.

JAMES NOONAN

Frégault, Guy (1918-77). Born in Montreal, he was educated at the Université de Montréal (B.A., 1938; L. ès L., 1940) and Loyola University, Chicago (Ph.D., 1949). He was a member of the history department at the Université de Montréal from 1942 to 1959, becoming its director in 1946, and he chaired the University of Ottawa's history department from 1959 to 1961. He was Quebec's deputy minister of cultural affairs from 1961 to 1968 and from 1970 to 1975.

As a historian and writer Frégault had a vigorous intellect and was a fine stylist. His initial publications revealed the impress of the polemical writings of Lionel GROULX, but his graduate work attuned him to more rigorous international standards of historical scholarship that emphasized research into contemporary sources, leading him to make new interpretations in areas never before explored in depth. His books include *La civilisation de la Nouvelle-France: 1713-1744* (1944), *François Bigot* (1948), *Le grand marquis: Pierre de Rigaud de Vaudreuil et la Louisiane* (1952), *La société canadienne sous le régime français* (1954), *Pierre Le Moyne d'Iberville* (1968), and *Le XVIIIe siècle canadien* (1968). Not afraid to expose the corruption of French administrators such as François Bigot, Quebec's last Intendant, Frégault portrayed New France as a vibrant colonial society intent on expansion to the west and south, a colony fully capable of independence by the time Britain deported the Acadians in 1755 and 1758 and Quebec fell under British rule in 1760. Through his work the conquest became the subject of intense historiographical controversy—particularly with the publication of *La guerre de la conquête* (1955), in which he declared that 'the framework of the Canadian community, destroyed in the crisis, was never properly rebuilt.' A translation of this important book by Margaret M. Cameron, *Canada: the war of the conquest*, was published in 1969.

Frégault's memoirs, *Chronique des années perdues*, appeared in 1976.

TERRY CROWLEY

French, David (b. 1939). Born in Coley's Point, Newfoundland, he moved with his family to Toronto in 1945. French was an indifferent student, whose life was changed when a teacher in grade eight told him—as a disciplinary measure—to read a book: on completing *Tom Sawyer* he decided to become a writer. He began with short stories and poems, many of which were published in the United Church magazine, *The Canadian Boy*. After graduating from Toronto's Oakwood Collegiate in 1958 he studied acting, first in Toronto and then at the Pasadena Playhouse in California. In 1960 he returned to Toronto and worked as an actor in CBC television drama. Two years later he sold a one-act play, 'Beckons the dark river' (unpublished), to the Canadian Broadcasting Corporation for the network series Shoestring Theatre. About this time he gave up acting and wrote several radio and television scripts for the CBC, and some short stories. In 1971 he took a job in the post office so that he could have time to write a novel, *A company of strangers* (unpublished). He then wrote *Leaving home*, whose success started him on a career as a playwright. French still lives in Toronto but spends the summers writing at his cottage on the north shore of Prince Edward Island.

Leaving home (1972) was produced at the Tarragon Theatre, Toronto, in 1972 under the direction of Bill Glassco, who directed the first production of all French's plays (except his adaptation of Ostrovsky's *The forest*). The subject came from French's own experience: the breakup of a Newfoundland family, the Mercers, who have settled in Toronto. In the course of the play Jacob, the carpenter father, is forced to face his insecurities and his need for his children when both sons, Ben and Billy, decide to leave at the same time. The play's mixture of pathos and comedy, its convincing and lovable characters, and distinctively Canadian flavour, made it one of the most popular and widely produced Canadian plays. A sequel, *Of the fields, lately* (1973; 1975)—which had a similar success—resumes the story of the Mercer family. Ben returns from Saskatchewan hoping for a reconciliation with his father; finding that the hostilities between them cannot be resolved, he leaves again. A memory device (similar to that of Tennessee Williams in *The glass menagerie*) frames the main action. This play is more low-key than *Leaving home*; death and separation, and the difficulty and pain of human relationships, are treated more subtly, at times poetically. It won the Chalmers Award for 1973 and confirmed French as one of the few Canadian playwrights able to support himself by playwrighting alone. Both plays were produced on CBC television.

In *One crack out* (1975), produced in 1975, French explores the world of gamblers, pool sharks, pimps, prostitutes, and strippers, capturing their distinctive, often brutal jargon and the precarious nature of their lives. Though there are some genuinely comic and satiric scenes, they are not always well integrated with the main action.

Jitters (1980) is set in a Canadian theatre like the Tarragon and portrays a group—author, director, actors, stage people—before, during, and after the opening night of a new play. As they await a prospective New York producer (who fails to arrive) the play becomes a perceptive commentary on the hopes and insecurities of the Canadian theatre community. It is at once satiric, sad, sophisticated, and even farcical—the French work that is most pervaded by comedy. It has had widespread success on the stage including the South Coast Repertory Theatre in Costa Mesa, California, in 1986 and the National Arts Centre in 1991.

The riddle of the world (unpublished), which premièred in Toronto in 1981, was a disappointment. Ron, whose girlfriend leaves him to join an ashram in India, tries many things—psychotherapy, casual sex, and finally mysticism—to cope with his loss. The play deals with the struggle between the flesh and the spirit, but its fast-paced comedy is often at odds with its serious intentions.

French returned to the Mercer family in *Salt-water moon* (1985) and *1949* (1989), two very different plays in construction and theatrical success. *Salt-water moon* premièred at the Tarragon in October 1984 and, after a very successful run there, transferred to the Bayview Playhouse in November. It is a two-character play in one act that shows the courtship of Jacob and Mary in 1926 in the place where French was born, Coley's Point, Newfoundland. The romance, warm humour, and rich tapestry of the play includes references to characters met or mentioned in the earlier MERCER PLAYS, giving an authentic picture of Newfoundland life before Confederation. It won the Dora Mavor Moore Award for Outstanding New Play in 1984, the Canadian Authors' Association Award for Drama in 1986, and the *Hollywood Drama-Logue* Critics Award in 1987.

1949, a co-production of the CentreStage Company, Toronto, and the Manitoba Theatre Centre, opened in Toronto in 1988. Written in two acts and four scenes, it features fourteen characters including several only mentioned in the earlier Mercer plays. It is set on the three days preceding the referendum that would make Newfoundland a province of Canada, and brings together at their Toronto home—with the warmth and humour characteristic of the other Mercer plays—several Newfoundlanders with often bitterly opposed views on the fate of the province.

French's next play was a mystery thriller, *The silver dagger* (1993), a co-production of the CentreStage Company, Toronto, and the National Arts Centre produced in 1993. But the genre does not mesh easily with French's comic send-up of it, and the play left audiences laughing but confused.

French worked closely with Donna Orwin, a scholar of Russian literature, in successfully preparing a transltaion of Chekhov's *The seagull* (1978), which was produced at Tarragon in 1977 and on Broadway in 1992. In 1987 his adaptation of Alexander Ostrovsky's *The forest* (unpublished), based on Russian scholar Samuel Cioran's translation of the play, received a major production at the St Lawrence Centre, Toronto, directed by Guy Sprung. His first three plays have all been produced off-Broadway and *Of the fields, lately* had a brief run on Broadway. *Jitters* was scheduled for a Broadway opening on 14 April 1981, but it was cancelled. (See James Noonan, 'The comedy of David French and the rocky road to Broadway' in *Thalia: studies in literary humor*, vol. 3, no. 2, 1980-81.)

French gives an account of his background and the process of composing *Leaving home* in

Geraldine Anthony, ed., *Stage voices* (1978), which also contains an introduction and bibliography. See also Robert Wallace and Cynthia Zimmerman, eds., *The work: conversations with English-Canadian playwrights* (1982), and Anne Nothof, 'David French and the theatre of speech', *Canadian Drama* 13 (1987).

JAMES NOONAN

French, William (b. 1926). Born in London, Ontario, he graduated from the University of Western Ontario in 1948, when he joined the Toronto *Globe and Mail* as a general reporter. In 1954 he held a Nieman Fellowship to Harvard, and in 1960, with the retirement of William Arthur DEACON, he became the *Globe*'s literary editor. From 1971 until his retirement in 1988, he wrote a perceptive, influential, and often witty literary column in the *Globe* devoted to serious book reviews and publishing news. He won the President's Medal of the University of Western Ontario for the best general-magazine article (1965) and National Newspaper Awards for critical writing (1978, 1979). From 1955 to 1983 he was an instructor in journalism at Ryerson Polytechnical Institute and a CBC radio journalist; in 1991 he was awarded an honorary D.Litt. from the University of Western Ontario. He is anthologized in *The flamboyant Canadian* (1964) and *Vision 2020* (1970), and is the author of *A most unlikely village: a history of Forest Hill* (1964).

GEOFF HANCOCK

Friesen, Patrick (b. 1946). Born in Steinbach, Manitoba, a town southeast of Winnipeg, he graduated from the University of Manitoba with a B.A. in English (1969). His first poetry collections, *the lands i am* (1976) and *bluebottle* (1978), featuring terse, spare poems reflecting the prairie landscape they often describe, contain many of the themes, motifs, and images that have continued to resonate throughout his work. His poetry frequently explores the meaning and legacy of his Mennonite heritage. *The shunning* (1980), a powerful and multi-voiced book-length poem about two brothers and the struggle between individual faith and authoritarian community, is his fullest treatment of Mennonite culture. Later successfully adapted for the stage (1985) and for CBC radio (1990), it also examines the passage of time and the relationship between spirit and flesh, two dominant concerns of Friesen's poetry. Peter Neufeld, the shunned brother in the poem, recognizes that 'memories can kill'.

In Friesen's works, however, remembering is healing as well as painful. Resurrecting the past in the present is central to *Unearthly horses* (1984), a collection of poems that dramatizes how 'it's the living/that harrow the dead and rehearse their lives.' Ghosts of the past plunge the poet into a vital examination of grief, love, tradition, and family. In particular, Friesen deals with his troubled relationship with his father; a sequence of nine elegiac 'pa poems' exhibits various ranges of feeling—in turn angry, confused, and tender. In *Flicker and hawk* (1987) and *You don't get to be a saint* (1992), Friesen continues to examine the human condition in poems that wrestle with death, silence, and the 'several sides to love', while developing a longer line influenced by biblical prosody. These poems struggle with the inadequacy of language to 'speak once more about the flesh and spirit/the red heart and the blue wind'. *Blasphemer's wheel* (1994) is a collection of new and selected poems.

Friesen's restless desire to live and write equally in both the spiritual and carnal realms of experience has led him into collaborative work with dancers (*Handful of rain*, 1991), actors (*The raft*, 1992), and composers (*Madrugada*, 1995). He has also directed and produced several films and videos on several artists through the Manitoba Department of Education, including *Patrick Lane* (1984), *The spirit of Assessippi: Don Proch* (1984), and *Together as one: a dance collaboration* (1991).

COLIN BOYD

Frobisher, Benjamin. See EXPLORATION LITERATURE IN ENGLISH: 2.

Frutkin, Mark. See NOVELS IN ENGLISH 1983 TO 1996.

Frye, Alan. See NOVELS IN ENGLISH 1960 TO 1982: OTHER TALENTS, OTHER WORKS: 2.

Frye, Northrop (1912-91). Herman Northrop Frye was born in Sherbrooke, Quebec. He began his education at home, where his mother taught him to read and play the piano by the age of three, and continued in primary and high schools in Moncton, New Brunswick—where, after leaving school, he took a course in a business college. In 1929 he enrolled in Victoria College, University of Toronto, from which he graduated in 1933, standing first in the Honours course in Philosophy and English. He went on to study theology at Emmanuel College, Toronto, and in 1936 was ordained to the ministry of the United Church, serving briefly as a preacher in Saskatchewan. Realizing that his real vocation lay in the academic twilight world that embraced both teaching and writing, shortly afterwards he went to Merton College, Oxford, receiving his M.A. there in 1940. Already, in 1939, he had started teaching as a lecturer in English at Victoria College; he became a professor in 1947, chair of the English department in 1952, and principal of Victoria College in 1959. He retired from that rank at the end of 1966, and in 1967 became the first University Professor of English at the University of Toronto. In 1978 he was appointed chancellor of Victoria University, Toronto.

Apart from the books that will be discussed below, Frye's extra-academic activities included editorship of the CANADIAN FORUM (1948-52) and membership on the Canadian Radio-Television and Telecommunications Commission (1968-77). He was supervisory editor of the textbook series Uses of the Imagination, published by Harcourt, Brace, Jovanovitch, New York.

Frye's achievements as teacher, scholar, and writer earned him many honours, including more than thirty honorary doctorates from universities in Canada and the United States. He became a Fellow of the Royal Society in 1951, Companion of the Order of Canada in 1972, and president of the Modern Language Association in 1976. He received the Royal Society's Lorne PIERCE Medal in 1958, the Molson Prize in 1971, and the Royal Bank Award in 1978.

Frye's interests led him to combine several roles in a single career. An academic, he sought to sustain a scholarly community that would play an active role in the national intellectual life. His activities as a university teacher and administrator, as well as many of his essays and lectures, were devoted to that end; and though from childhood he cherished the ambition to be a writer, he never considered leaving the university to pursue an independent literary career. His books, however broad their influence and repute, were always written within a framework of academic preoccupations.

Yet Frye played his part in the development of a Canadian tradition of public as well as academic criticism. As early as 1936 he began to contribute critical articles to the *Canadian Forum*, and when he was editor of that journal he encouraged the new poets who began to emerge in Canada during the later 1960s by publishing their works. He also began in 1950 to write each year the section on Canadian poetry in English for the *University of Toronto Quarterly*'s annual critical roundup, 'Letters in Canada'. His surveys of current verse continued from 1950 to 1960, and in writing them Frye contributed more than any other critic to establishing the criteria by which Canadian writing might be judged.

Frye's chronicles in 'Letters in Canada' form the core of *The bush garden: essays on the Canadian imagination* (1971), in which he collected what he had written, over a quarter of a century, on Canadian literature and its creators. With its penetrating but endlessly patient judgements on individual writers, and its development of seminal attitudes to the function of a writer in a society emerging from colonialism, *The bush garden* helps to explain the influence Frye wielded, not only on academic and public critics alike but also, in a much more direct way, on Canadian poets. Among other items, *The bush garden* includes the 'Conclusion' that Frye wrote for the first edition of the *Literary history of Canada* (1975), in which he traced the liberation of Canadian culture from the 'garrison mentality' of colonial days. Frye was one of the editors of the *Literary history*, and to its second edition (1976) he wrote a further 'Conclusion', reflecting on the later richness of Canadian literary production and commenting that, despite the accompanying 'misery, injustice and savagery' in the world, what may 'matter more, eventually, is what man can create in the face of the chaos he also creates'. *Divisions on a ground: essays on Canadian culture* (1982) is a collection of writings and addresses on subjects of particular Canadian interest.

Frye was one of Canada's most significant critics, for not only was he the pioneer of systematic criticism in Canada, but his writings had a scope that extended far beyond the purviews of a national literature. His work—apart from the critiques of Canadian writings—can be divided into two distinct categories. On one side, in his books of general relevance, he proceeds from an awareness of the essential universality of intellectual pursuits to develop theories of the function of criticism, of the character of literary genres, and of the nature of the myths that inspire the culture of Western man. The earliest of his works of major stature is *Fearful symmetry: a study of William Blake* (1947), his first book, which goes far beyond studying Blake himself to examine in depth the role of myth and symbol in the various literary genres. In *Anatomy of criticism* (1957) Frye analyses the principles and techniques of criticism, isolating its various modes: the historical, the ethical, the archetypal or mythopoeic, and the rhetorical or classificatory. It is an impressive structure of prose and thought that often seems to stand in splendid independence of the literature that is its nominal reason for existence, and to develop in practice Oscar Wilde's concept of criticism as a creative art. *The great code: the Bible and literature* (1982) and *Words with power* (1990) bring together all that Frye learned—not only from literature, but also from his study of the anthropologist James Frazer, the psychologist Carl Jung, and the King James Bible—to consider how much the Bible itself may be considered a work of literature and how far it has been the source of Western literature as we know it. In these two volumes, which Frye clearly regarded as the destination of his career, he plays somewhat cavalierly with the role of earlier mythological traditions, from the Homeric to the Ovidian. (See also RELIGION AND THEOLOGY.)

These four works are without doubt Frye's masterpieces, monumentally self-contained and self-consistent in their systematization of literary and cultural history. His other books reflect the essential division between Frye the writer and Frye the teacher, since they are mainly collections of lectures and articles, gathered in such ways as to illuminate rather unevenly certain common themes. Four volumes are concerned with great English poets: *T.S. Eliot* (1963); *The return of Eden; five essays on Milton's epics* (1965); *A natural perspective: the development of Shakespearean comedy and romance* (1965); and *Fools of time: studies in Shakespearean tragedy* (1967). *A study of English romanticism* (1968) returns to the period, and to many concerns, of *Fearful symmetry*. The other more miscellaneous collections, published over the past quarter-of-a-century, include *Culture and the national will* (1957), *By liberal things* (1960), *The well-tempered critic* (1963), *The educated imagination* (1963), *Fables of identity: studies in poetic mythology* (1963), *The modern century* (1967), *The stubborn structure: essays on criticism and society* (1970), *The critical path: an essay on the social context of literary criticism* (1971), *The secular scripture: a study of the structure of romance* (1976), *Spiritus mundi: essays on literature, myth and society* (1976), and *Creation and recreation* (1980). Frye won a Governor General's Award for *Northrop Frye on Shakespeare* (1986).

See the interesting two-volume publication of the letters between Frye and his wife-to-be: *The correspondence of Northrop Frye & Helen Kemp, 1932-1939* (2 vols, 1996) edited by Robert Denham.

Apart from articles in periodicals, the significant studies of Frye are *Northrop Frye in modern criticism: selected papers from the English Institute* (1966) edited by Murray Krieger; Ronald Bates, *Northrop Frye* (1972) in the Canadian Writers Series; A.C. Hamilton, *Northrop Frye: anatomy of his criticism* (1990); and Alvin H. Lee and Robert D. Denham, *The legacy of Northrop Frye* (1994). See also John Ayre, *Northrop Frye: a biography* (1989).

See also CRITICISM IN ENGLISH: 2, 3, and 4.

GEORGE WOODCOCK

Fulford, Robert (b. 1932). Born in Ottawa, Ontario, he is descended from several generations of Canadian newspapermen and began his journalistic career as a teenager with the Toronto *Globe and Mail*. Later he moved to the *Toronto Star*, where he wrote a daily or weekly column on cultural questions for almost twenty years. He has also been on the staffs of several Canadian magazines, including *Maclean's*, but is most thoroughly identified with *Saturday Night*, which he edited from 1968 to 1987. Although mainly a periodical writer, he has also published books reflecting the politics that lie at the heart of his work and his transition from reporter to literary observer to social critic. *This was Expo* (1968), a work of almost instant reporting, nonetheless betrays a deep concern with the role of ideas in the national spectacle. *Crisis at the Victory Burlesk: culture, politics, and other diversion*, published the same year, is mainly a collection of representative *Star* columns about popular culture in the broadest sense. In *Marshall Delaney at the movies: the contemporary world as seen on film* (1974), he publicly revealed the identity behind the 'Marshall Delaney' pseudonym he used for cinema reviews in *Saturday Night*. Although he has continued to range widely over cultural matters—*An introduction to the arts in Canada* (1977) was an overview for students and New Canadians—after 1970 he became more concerned with the supposed failure of liberal ideology in society generally, as evidenced in *The Fulford file* (1980), an olio of his *Saturday Night* editorials. The transition, which followed his all-too-brief embrace of a more nationalistic viewpoint, also suggested a reversion to the natural concerns of a writer shaped by the cultural environment of the 1950s—with its agonized debate on psychoanalysis, Communism, sexual repression, and the application of those topics to virtually every other subject. By the 1990s Fulford had more or less abandoned several of his early public interests, particularly fine art and jazz, gaining a new reputation as a cogent political commentator, public scold, and wit, as, for example, in his popular weekly column in the *Globe and Mail* (a return full-circle to his first home). His two most recent books have been the most substantial. These are *Best seat in the house: memoirs of a lucky man* (1988), at once the liveliest and most elegant Canadian journalist's memoirs since those of Sir John Willison or Hector CHARLESWORTH several generations earlier, and *Accidental city: the transformation of Toronto* (1995), an affectionate but anti-nostalgic study of politics, development, and culture in the metropolis with which he is associated so thoroughly. Fulford appears as a character in several works of fiction and non-fiction, including Douglas FETHERLING's *Way down deep in the belly of the beast* (1996).

DOUGLAS FETHERLING

G

Gagnon, Ernest. See ESSAYS IN FRENCH: 5.

Gagnon, Madeleine (b. 1938). She was born in the Matapedia valley, at Amqui—'where the waters play', in the language of her Huron ancestors. A piano student from the age of seven, she entered the Conservatoire de musique de Québec at sixteen, but already writing called her, and she studied literature while continuing her musical studies until the age of twenty-one. She obtained a B.A. in literature at the Université Saint-Joseph du Nouveau-Brunswick (1959), an M.A. in philosophy from the Université de Montréal (1961), and a Ph.D. in literature from the Université d'Aix-en-Provence (1968). She taught literature at the Université du Québec à Montréal from 1969 to 1982 and was later guest professor and writer-in-residence at the Université de Montréal, the Université du Québec à Montréal, and the Université du Québec à Rimouski. She contributed to numerous periodicals, including *Chroniques* (which she founded with Patrick Straram), *LIBERTÉ*, *La Nouvelle BARRE DU JOUR*, *Possibles*, *Dérives*, *Estuaire*, *Urgences*, and *Actuels*, and in 1969 published her first book, *Les morts-vivants*, a collection of short stories. A poet as well as a writer of short stories, novels, 'fiction-essays', and stories for children, Gagnon is notable for an approach to writing that takes into account the debates and struggles of her time. She was a pioneer of feminist thought and writing in Quebec, drawing on both high and popular culture. Her early works—*Pour les femmes et tous les autres* (1974, poetry), *Poélitique* (1975, poetry), *La venue à l'écriture* (1977, fiction-essay, with Hélène Cixous and Annie Leclerc), *Retailles* (1977, fiction-essay, with Denise BOUCHER), *Antre* (1978, poetry), *Lueur: roman archéologique* (1979, fiction-essay), and *Au coeur de la lettre* (1981, poetry)—show the influence of Marxist, psychoanalytical, nationalist, and feminist thought. *Autographie 1* and *2*, subtitled *Fictions* (1982) and *Toute écriture est amour* (1989) are collections of her most significant works. In texts linking the theoretical and the fictional she creates a new form of discourse, 'fiction-essay', that combines fictional passages, an intimate voice, reflections on writing, autobiography and the everyday life, prose and poetry, and different levels of language. Two collections of her poetry have received awards: *Journal de Montréal*'s grand prize for *Les fleurs du catalpa* (1986), and a Governor General's Award for *Chant pour un Québec lointain* (1991). Gagnon's latest publications are *La terre est remplie de langage* (1993, poetry), *Les cathédrales sauvages* (1994, novella), and *Le vent majeur* (1995, novel).

RAYMOND BERTIN

Gallant, Mavis (b. 1922). Born Mavis de Trafford Young in Montreal, she attended seventeen different schools there and in the eastern United States. She left Canada for Europe in 1950, after a short period working for the National Film Board and as a writer for the Montreal *Standard*, and after a brief marriage to John Gallant. Since then, living in Paris, she has been remarkably dedicated to imaginative writing, maintaining a long connection with *The New Yorker*; most of her short stories have appeared there, the first in the issue of 1 Sept. 1951. Made a Companion of the Order of Canada in 1993, she is an Honorary Member of the American Academy and Institute of Arts and Letters, and a Fellow of the Royal Society of Literature. In 1983-4 she was writer-in-residence at the University of Toronto, which awarded her an honorary doctorate in 1994, one of her many honorary degrees. In 1993 she was given a tribute at the International Festival of Authors, HARBOURFRONT, Toronto. She was awarded the Molson Prize in 1997.

Gallant has published two novels, *Green water, green sky* (1959) and *A fairly good time* (1970); and eleven collections of shorter fiction: *The other Paris* (1956); *My heart is broken* (1964; Eng. title *An unmarried man's summer*, 1964); *The Pegnitz junction: a novella and five short stories* (1973); *The end of the world and other stories* (NCL, 1973), selected and edited by Robert WEAVER; *From the Fifteenth District: a novella and eight short stories* (1979); *Home truths: selected Canadian stories* (1981), which won a Governor General's Award; *Overhead in a balloon: stories of Paris* (1985); *In transit* (1988); *Across the bridge* (1993; NCL, 1997, with an Afterword by Robertson DAVIES); *The Moslem wife and other stories* (NCL, 1994), selected and with an Afterword by Mordecai RICHLER; and *The selected stories* (1996). Her novels and story collections are all in paperback. Many of these collections have been published in French, and some in German, Spanish, and Dutch. Gallant occasionally writes trenchant book reviews for the *New York Times*, the *New York Review of Books*, and *The Times Literary Supplement*, and eleven are included in *Paris notebooks: essays and reviews* (1986).

Gallant's talents have always been best deployed in shorter fiction. The first of her two novels, *Green water, green sky*, is no longer than many novellas, and this story of the moral destruction of a girl by her foolish, protective mother is so episodic in structure that it reads rather like a cycle of related short stories. The second novel, *A fairly good time*, is longer and much more closely knit, using with great skill a variety of devices—journals, letters, interior monologues, recollective flashbacks—to illuminate the central story of the failure of a marriage between a Canadian girl and a member of a stuffy French family.

The difficulty of entering an alien culture is a theme that runs through many of Gallant's stories. Frequently they are about Anglo-Saxons—British as well as Canadians—leading empty and often spiteful lives in France or Italy. *The Pegnitz junction* deals with the alienation of a whole people, the post-1945 Germans, not from their native land but from the past they seek desperately to forget. Even in *Home truths*, a collection of her Canadian stories, Canadians are shown as 'foreigners' not merely when they are abroad. Perhaps the most impressive cycle in that collection, the Linnet Muir stories, concerns the failure of a young returning Montrealer to find her bearings even in the city where she was born and spent her childhood. It is perilous to generalize about well over 100 stories that show a great variety of situation, characterization, and approach; but most concern people who have built up a protection from the world, and who in the end have been made to realize how precarious such defences are, and how hiding from life has only increased their vulnerability. Gallant's stories are witty and often humorous in their manner of expression, yet pathetic in their ultimate effect; detached and sharp in viewpoint—at times seeming to verge on callousness—they are nevertheless so involving that the final emotion is always nearer compassion than contempt. At times Gallant's writing seems satirical, but she is not a true satirist, for the satirist writes in the hope that mankind can be reformed. Gallant seems to conclude, sadly, that the people she writes of cannot be changed.

Many of Gallant's stories have highly complex structures involving the interplay of varying points of view. Some of them, like the novella 'The Pegnitz junction', move beyond ordinary mental connections into psychic areas where conversation and even recollections are replaced by strange telepathic awarenesses. Here, and in 'The four seasons', which opens *From the Fifteenth District*, the handling of incident, and the way the visible and audible outer world cuts away from the inner world and back again, reminds one of Gallant's early training in the cutting-room of the National Film Board. But if the handling of impressions in such stories has a cinematic quality, there is a distinctly dramatic feeling in the juxtaposition of scenes and in the strength of dialogue (whether spoken or understood). Gallant writes a clear, supple prose, and the verbal texture of her writing is impeccable—never a wrongly chosen word. She has such a fine eye for detail—settings, appearances, mannerisms, ways of speaking—and such a sense of the appropriate relationships of those details, that her stories always have a remarkably visual quality that makes the words seem like a translucent veil. Thus in many of her stories she achieves an extraordinary double effect: the scene is clearly observed, as concrete as a painting, and yet one is always moving through it into the characters' states of mind, which are so convincing because they are related constantly to the physical here-and-now.

Among the recent collections, *Across the bridge* includes some memorable stories about Canadians: '1933', 'The chosen husband', 'From cloud to cloud', 'Florida'—about the

Carette sisters—and 'The Fenton child'. *The selected stories* (American title: *The complete stories*) is a monumental collection, containing fifty-two stories selected by Gallant herself. Her Preface may well become a classic capsule memoir of the childhood and early writing years of a literary artist—who, here, describes the impulse to write as 'a jolt that unbolts the door between perception and imagination and leaves it ajar for life, or that fuses memory and language and waking dreams.'

Gallant's play *What is to be done?* (1984)—bearing the title of Lenin's pamphlet—takes place in Montreal between 1942 and 1945, and is an ironic and vivid treatment of one strain of left-wing thinking while the war on fascism in Europe continued. Produced at the Tarragon Theatre, Toronto, in November 1982 (and later televised), it was well received. Gallant's non-fiction writings have been scanty, but some of them are memorable. They include her account of experiences and observations during the abortive revolutionary situation in France during 1968, 'The events in May: a Paris notebook' (*New Yorker*, 14 Sept., 21 Sept., 1968), in which she gives a rare personal assessment of the country she has so long inhabited, and her long introduction to *The affair of Gabriel Russier* (1971), an account of the ordeal of a thirty-year-old French schoolteacher who had a love affair with an adolescent student—both are included in *Paris notebooks*.

Because of her self-created exile and her custom of publishing her stories mainly in a single American magazine, Gallant's excellence was recognized slowly in her native country. In the first edition of the *Literary history of Canada* (1965) the titles of her books were unmentioned; not until 1973 did a Canadian publisher become interested in issuing a collection of her stories. Canadian critics were equally slow in recognizing Gallant: Peter STEVENS' 1973 essay 'Perils of compassion' (*CANADIAN LITERATURE* 56) was an almost isolated study until, in 1978, *CANADIAN FICTION MAGAZINE* devoted its entire Issue 28 to a symposium on Gallant. See also Grazia Merla, *Mavis Gallant: narrative patterns and devices* (1978); Neil K. Besner, *The light of imagination: Mavis Gallant's fiction* (1988); and Janice KULYK KEEFER, *Reading Mavis Gallant* (1989).

GEORGE WOODCOCK/WILLIAM TOYE

Galt, John (1779-1839). Born in Irvine, Ayrshire, Scotland, he combined business and literary careers before coming to Canada. By 1820 he had travelled through Europe and had worked as a political lobbyist, first for the promoters of a Glasgow-Edinburgh Canal and then for the United Empire Loyalists who sought redress for losses during the War of 1812. In 1820 Galt suggested a way to satisfy UEL claimants: the Canada Company, organized to raise funds by purchasing Crown lands and selling them to immigrants, hired him as secretary and sent him to Upper Canada (Ontario) in 1825. Meanwhile he was adding to his work as biographer, dramatist, and historian a series of novels that rivalled Walter Scott's in popularity, writing eleven between 1820 and 1825.

Galt's *Autobiography* (London, 1833), and to a lesser extent his *Literary life and miscellanies* (London, 1834), present vivid details of his Canadian experiences: dashing travels with 'Tiger' Dunlop, political clashes with Bishop Strachan and Governor Maitland, the ritualistic founding of Guelph, explorations from York to Penetanguishene, then to Goderich by boat. There are also sharp speculations about the future of the colony. (The city of Galt, now Cambridge, was named after him.) Traces of these ideas and experiences appear also in fictional form in *Lawrie Todd; or, The settlers in the woods* (London, 1830), a novel set partly in upstate New York, and in the third volume of *Bogle Corbet; or, The emigrants* (London, 1831); both novels were published during the period of reversal and imprisonment that followed Galt's return to Britain in 1829.

Bogle Corbet and *Lawrie Todd* are rightly seen as a pair—not so much because they deal with the same experience (immigration) at the same time (around 1825), and in roughly the same place (north and south of Lake Ontario), as because they discriminate carefully between group settlement and independent settlement. The Scot-turned-Canadian, Bogle Corbet, is more genteel, more inhibited and dour, and more rigid in opinions than is *Lawrie Todd*, the revolutionary Scot turned successful American. Of the two books, *Lawrie Todd* was more popular, partly because of its more varied descriptions of bush and river, roads and settlements. But *Bogle Corbet*, with its unheroic protagonist, his shrewish wife, inefficient co-workers, burdensome dependants, bad luck, and uninspiring setting, opens an important line of Canadian fiction: that of counter-romance, made palatable by the play of pawky humour, and by subtlety and staunch honesty of reportage.

Journal articles by Galt generalized on New World themes and scenes: five items in *Blackwood's*, 1829-30, and three in *Fraser's*, 1832. Longer treatment included *The Canadas*

(Edinburgh, 1832), a collaboration with Andrew Picken, and *Forty years in America* (London, 1833), Galt's edition of the autobiography of Grant Thorburn, the real-life prototype of Lawrie Todd. By the time Galt died, his three sons—John, Thomas, and Alexander Tilloch Galt—had returned to Canada, where they would contribute to political, judicial, and financial development.

Many of Galt's Scottish novels have been reissued, and the Canadian section of *Bogle Corbet* was republished in a NEW CANADIAN LIBRARY edition (1977) edited by Elizabeth Waterston. The standard biography is Ian Gordon's *John Galt: the life of a writer* (1972); critical studies appear in all histories of Scottish literature, most recently in F.R. Hart's *The Scottish novel* (1978). See also the collection of essays *John Galt, 1779-1979* (1979) edited by C.A. Whatley; *John Galt, romancier écossais*, by Henri Gibault (Grenoble, 1979); and *John Galt: reappraisals* (Guelph, 1985) edited by Elizabeth Waterston.

ELIZABETH WATERSTON

Gammon, Carolyn. See LESBIAN LITERATURE.

Garneau, Alfred. See POETRY IN FRENCH: 2.

Garneau, François-Xavier (1809-66). Born at Quebec, the eldest in a relatively poor family, he showed considerable intellectual promise as a child but received little formal education beyond age fourteen. While training as a notary, Garneau benefited from the generosity and encouragement of his employers and patrons, Joseph-François Perrault and Archibald Campbell, whose private libraries and tutoring helped him to become well- but self-taught in the French, English, and Latin classics and in history. The limitations of self-tuition would mark many of his works.

Although trained as a notary, Garneau rarely practised his profession. In 1828 he travelled in the northeastern United States and Upper Canada, and in 1831 set sail for England for a brief stay. He remained, however, in London until 1833 as secretary to Denis-Benjamin Viger, the House of Assembly delegate to the Colonial Office. Garneau's nationalist leanings were intensified during the years abroad. In London he met leading British liberals and through them met many European nationalist refugees resident in London. On two trips to France he experienced at first hand the heady liberalism of the July Monarchy. (See his *Voyage en Angleterre et en France dans les années 1831, 1832, et 1833*, Québec, 1855; rpr. 1968.) It is not surprising that, on his return to Quebec, he became actively involved in the Patriote cause and formed close, lasting friendships with the movement's leading members. Garneau was increasingly drawn to journalism in the 1830s but, having married in 1835, was unable to support a family with his writing. From 1837 to 1842 he worked as a bank clerk and performed only a few notarial duties. Through the influence of Étienne Parent, Garneau became the French translator to the Legislative Assembly of the Province of Canada, and in 1844 he was made clerk of the City of Quebec, a position he held until ill health forced him to resign just before his death.

Garneau's literary reputation rests largely on the monumental and influential *Histoire du Canada depuis sa découverte jusqu'à nos jours* (3 vols, Québec, 1845-8; 9 vols, Montréal, 1944-6), which he began writing in 1840. Taking the story to 1791, this masterwork established Garneau as the 'historien national' of French Canada, and until the 1940s was not surpassed. Written from an essentially secular, liberal, and nationalist viewpoint, the *Histoire* drew a hostile clerical reaction until revised in 1859, but inspired succeeding generations of poets, novelists, historians, journalists, and politicians with its vivid images and heroic account of a small nation struggling against all odds to survive and prosper.

Garneau's poetry—at once original and imitative, conventional and unique—barely survived his lifetime. While many of his poems were modelled on the metaphors and images of eighteenth-century French classicism—poems such as 'Les oiseaux blancs', 'L'hiver', 'Le dernier Huron', and 'Le vieux chêne'—many more were inspired by the Romanticism of the 1830s. The strength of his poetry lies in its appeal to the glories of a heroic French-Canadian past, and in its call for a national struggle to survive, which Garneau effected through emotional evocations of the landscape and by explicitly linking the aspirations of his people with those of the great nationalist struggles in the Europe of his day. The secular liberal sentiments that suffuse his poetry explain why most of it was virtually ignored until the 1960s, with the resurgence of nationalism in Quebec and the celebrations of the centennial of Garneau's death.

None of Garneau's writing is remembered for its mastery of style, form, or phrase. As vibrant examples of an important current in the intellectual life of Quebec in the 1830s and 1840s, however, the poetry, and the *Histoire du Canada*, have now received the attention they deserve: Garneau the 'historien national' has survived and Garneau the poet has been rediscovered.

See 'François-Xavier Garneau' in the DICTIONARY OF CANADIAN BIOGRAPHY, vol. IX (1976), and a series of articles in *Archives des lettres canadiennes*, vol. 4: *La poésie canadienne-française* (1969).

See also HISTORICAL WRITING IN FRENCH.

PHYLLIS SENESE

Garneau, Hector de Saint-Denys. See SAINT-DENYS-GARNEAU, Hector de.

Garneau, Jacques. See NOVELS IN FRENCH 1960 TO 1982: 3(f).

Garneau, Michel (b. 1939). Radio announcer, poet, singer, and writer-celebrity—at one and the same time romantic, popular, and modern—he is a 'jack-of-all-arts', a one-man-band and a one-man-show. After writing historical fantasies such as 'Who's afraid of General Wolfe?' (unpublished), he turned to producing slim volumes of poetry—*Langage*, *Moments*, and *Elégie au génocide des Nasopodes* (all 1974)—and then, in 1977, he published a collection of major poems, *Les petits chevals amoureux*. His 'Cousine des écureuils' is a warm and thoughtful tribute to the American poet Emily Dickinson, like his play *Émilie ne sera plus jamais cueillie par l'anémone* (1981).

Garneau's dramatic works are as improbable as they are arresting. From *La chanson d'amour de cul* (1971) to *L'usage du coeur dans le domaine réel* (1974), a mind and body seem to be searching for each other. The language of these plays, which is elaborate—occasionally archaic and scholarly—appears natural because it is extremely precise. Other plays—even *Les célébrations suivi de Adidou Adidouce* (1977), which won a Governor General's Award, declined by Garneau—are too talkative and a little bit loose. *Quatre à quatre* (1974), about a generation of women, and *Strauss et Pesant (et Rosa)* (1974), about the clerico-constabulary and misogynistic Duplessisism, are Garneau's strongest plays, along with his magnificent adaptations of *Macbeth* (1978) and *The tempest* (1982), rendered in Quebec French. Garneau is well known in both Canada and France, especially for *Quatre à quatre*.

Garneau has made other translations and adaptations ('tradaptations') in archaic and popular Québécois French—for example *Coriolan* (1989). He was particularly successful in his presentation of *Célestine là-bas près des tanneries au bord de la rivière* (1991). First performed in Ottawa at the National Arts Centre in 1990, it is based on the prose dialogue of the first Spanish novel—perhaps the first European novel—by Fernando de Rojas, which appeared under the title *La Celestina; tragicomedia de Calixto y Melibea* (1501).

Garneau has been professor of improvisation (since 1972), writer-in-residence, and *animateur* of writing workshops at the National Theatre School, and at Lionel-Groulx Community College. *Petitpetant et le monde* (1982) is a fable about identity, solidarity, and fidelity, and *De la poussière d'étoiles dans les os* (1991) is a collection of four declamatory exercises in the nature of theses, argument, and journalism—one a poorly handled post-Referendum (verbal) boxing match.

Garneau remains more faithful to himself on the oral level—the song and the tale, and in researching the language of his poetry, as for example in *Le Phénix de neige* (1992). His *Poésies complètes, 1955-1987* was published in 1988.

See Claude Des Landes, *Michel Garneau, écrivain public* (1987). LAURENT MAILHOT

Garneau, Sylvain (1930-53). Born in Montreal, he spent his childhood near Sainte-Dorothée sur la Rivière-des-Prairies, Quebec, and attended the Collège Stanislas. When he was sixteen he began to publish his first poems in *Le Jour*, *Notre Temps*, and *Amérique française*. In 1948 he joined the Merchant Marine and travelled briefly through Denmark, Poland, Italy, Spain, and Portugal. After his return to Montreal, Garneau worked on construction and then as a journalist for *La Presse* and as a broadcaster for CKVM and Radio-Canada. He died accidentally after wounding himself fatally with his own rifle.

His first poetry collection, *Objets trouvés* (1951), contained a preface by Alain GRANDBOIS and appeared in an edition of 500 copies paid for by his parents. A second collection, *Les trouble-fête* (1952)—also 500 copies—was illustrated by Pierre Garneau. It was fitting that Grandbois should write the preface to the first collection of a young poet whose work was animated by a spirit of freedom and a yearning for wide open spaces. Although he seems to regret that Garneau 'writes his poetry with periods, commas, rhymes, and with great classical agitation', Grandbois characterizes it as 'tender, light, merry, casual, and filled with love, admiration, and a comprehension of Nature that is staggering'. The complete works were collected in *Objets retrouvés* (1965), edited with an introduction and notes by Guy ROBERT, which includes a long narrative poem, 'La bleue', that is filled with memories of childhood, of outdoor games and pastimes, and with Garneau's love of nature, play, fantasy, and fun. Garneau's prose, which is rhythmical and precise and has exceptional clarity and soothing fluidity, also shows his gift for 'suggestive wizardry' (Baudelaire), especially in 'Le serpent et la pêche' and 'Les vacances de Sébastien'.

Garneau was unique among Québécois writers in writing with apparently effortless spontaneity and unselfconsciousness. He had a skilful command of traditional verse forms and was equally at home in dealing with fear, despair, and delight. Above all he is Quebec's poet of childhood, which he represents in the image of the castle: 'O châteaux lumineux! la fête à chaque étage/Les enfants dans la chambre, et la bûche au foyer'. He shows the lyricism of adolescent wanderlust, of escape; and in the multiplicity of his sudden flights and returns, his lightning changes, he resembles Rimbaud. He was always fascinated by the unknown, an obsession that seemed to foreshadows his unexpected and tragic end.

Garneau's verse was swept into oblivion by the surge of nationalist poetry, with its themes of homeland and alienation, that began to dominate the field after his death, until this gave way to the revolutionary poetry of the late sixties and the formalist seventies. It does not belong to his historical scuffle but to its own post-war era, well before the end of the Duplessis régime. His poetry is not militant before its time, nor does it reflect the Québécois alienation that was so darkly portrayed by NELLIGAN and SAINT-DENYS-GARNEAU. Since 1953 no one else has attempted to write in a similar style.

Amérique française (1954) includes interesting studies of Garneau's work by Marcel DUBÉ and Angèle Dupuis. An innovative and important analysis by Jean-Cléo Godin, 'La voix retrouvée de Sylvain Garneau', appeared in *VOIX ET IMAGES du pays II* (1969). See also *Ellipse* 55 (1996), a special issue devoted to Garneau and John THOMPSON, where, in a heartfelt *hommage* to his young brother, Michel GARNEAU provides important insights on the main perspectives of Sylvain's all-too-unknown work. JOSEPH BONENFANT

Garner, Hugh (1913-79). In his autobiography *One damn thing after another* (1973) Garner described his birthplace—Batley, Yorkshire—as 'a typical English industrial-town working-class house of the type I recognized in D.H. Lawrence's *Sons and lovers* and later saw in such movies as *Room at the top* and *Saturday night and Sunday morning*.' In 1919 his father, who had worked briefly in Ontario before the First World War, moved his family to Toronto, settling in Cabbagetown, an east-central downtown area that Garner later described as 'a sociological phenomenon, the largest Anglo-Saxon slum in North America'. The father deserted his family, and Hugh Garner, a brother, and two stepsisters were brought up by their hardworking mother. Garner attended public school and a technical high school, and after graduation was briefly a copy boy on the *Toronto Star*. In 1933, one of the worst years of the Depression, he went on the road, stooking wheat in Saskatchewan, working for 20¢ a day in a relief camp in Kamloops, British Columbia, and being jailed as a vagrant in West Virginia. This itinerant life came to an end when he enlisted in the Abraham Lincoln Brigade to fight for the Loyalists in the Spanish Civil War. During the Second World War he served on a corvette in the Canadian navy.

After the war Garner set out to make his living as a writer. His first published novel, *Storm below* (1949), which drew on his wartime naval experience for its background, has been described by the critic Hugo McPherson as 'an unheroic but oddly warming record of an encounter of nature, fate and man during six days at sea in 1943.' In 1950 a butchered version of Garner's earlier novel *Cabbagetown* appeared in paperback. When the complete text was finally published in 1968, this story of the painful and sometimes melodramatic coming-of-age of Ken Tilling and his friends, with its description of working-class life in Toronto in the 1930s, was seen to be one of the major social novels written by a Canadian. Garner's other novels include *The silence on the shore* (1962), a multi-character study set in a Toronto rooming house; *A nice place to visit* (1970), in which an ageing writer-journalist investigates a sensational criminal case in a small town not far from Toronto; and a novel that began as a television play (never shown) for the Canadian Broadcasting Corporation, *The intruders* (1976), about trendy members of the middle class who have moved into the former Cabbagetown slum area. In the 1970s Garner wrote three police novels, all set in Toronto, about Inspector Walter McDumont: *The sin sniper* (1970), *Death in Don Mills* (1975), and *Murder has your number* (1978). A fourth novel about Inspector McDumont, *Don't deal with five deuces*, left unfinished when Garner died, was completed by Paul Stuewe and published in 1992.

As a working writer with a family to support, Garner found it necessary to turn his hand to a great many literary and quasi-literary activities. He wrote journalism for newspapers and magazines; appeared frequently on radio and television panel shows; and had a genius for discovering the maximum number of markets for his short stories, including radio and television dramatizations. He took pride in some of his novels (he thought that *The silence on the shore* had been unjustly neglected) and particularly in the best of his short stories, of which he published more than fifty in his lifetime; he won a Governor General's Award for *Hugh Garner's best stories* (1963). In his most successful fiction he was 'the loser's advocate . . . Garner's people are life's outsiders, and this is consistent because he himself is an outsider . . .' (Robert FULFORD). To the end of his life Garner's spirit never really left Toronto's Cabbagetown, and it seems fitting that in 1982 the Hugh Garner Co-operative, a housing development, was built on Cabbagetown's Ontario Street, a few blocks north of the place where the Garners first lived in Toronto. *Cabbagetown* is available in a paperback edition. See Doug FETHERING, *Hugh Garner* (1972), and Paul Stuewe, *Hugh Garner and his work* (1984). Stuewe has also written a biography, *The storms below: the turbulent life and times of Hugh Garner* (1988).

See also NOVELS IN ENGLISH 1960 TO 1982: OTHER TALENTS, OTHER WORKS: 6(a).

ROBERT WEAVER

Gass, Ken. See DRAMA IN ENGLISH 1953 TO 1981.

Gatenby, Greg (b. 1950). Born in Toronto, educated at York University, a former editor at McCLELLAND & STEWART, he joined Toronto's Harbourfront Centre in 1975 as its literary co-ordinator. In 1980 Gatenby became its artistic director, organizer of the weekly HARBOURFRONT READING SERIES, and founder of the annual Harbourfront International Festival of Authors. The festival has become the world's largest literary venue, each fall sponsoring readings, interviews, and talks by the world's leading poets, fiction writers, essayists, biographers, genre writers, and translators. Gatenby has received numerous awards for his work in furthering the cause of serious international writing, including the City of Toronto Arts Award, Honorary Membership in the LEAGUE OF CANADIAN POETS, and the Jack Award for the promotion of Canadian books, named in honour of Jack McCLELLAND.

Gatenby is also a noted editor and proficient poet. He is the sensitive compiler of *Whale sound: an anthology of poems about whales and dolphins* (1977) and its succesor, *Whales: a celebration* (1983), which includes prose, art, and music. He combined literary nationalism with cosmopolitanism in two collections that bear the subtitle 'Canada through the eyes of foreign writers': *The wild is always there* (1993) and *The very richness of that past* (1995). Canada's scenery, society, and spirit are caught in the public and private words from the pens of dozens of sojourning writers ranging from Charles Dickens to Ernest Hemingway.

Gatenby's achievement as a poet is the least noted of his endeavours, despite the fact that in at least one interview he has stated that he sees himself as a poet who works as an artistic director rather than as an artistic director who writes poetry. Two slight collections of occasional poems, *Rondeaus for Erica* (1976) and *Adrienne's blessing* (1976), were followed by two notable collections, *The salmon country* (1978) and *Growing still: poems* (1981). Gatenby's poetry, always witty, is sometimes gruff and outspoken. 'Academic report on Literature III' is an extended comparison of Canadian writing with the stock market: 'Major U.S. indicators continue to oustrip Canadian futures . . . the interest rate in academic continued to decline. . . .' Amid the gruff lines there are surprisingly graceful passages, as in the poem 'Screen Siren', which recounts the chance encounter in New York City with a favourite movie star, Quebec actress Carole Laure: 'I made her / hear my love for dolphins, talked of books still to come— / any nonsense to protract her present, to let me / repose fluid kite tail dancing and happy.'

JOHN ROBERT COLOMBO

Gauvreau, Claude (1925-71). Born in Montreal, he attended the Collège Ste-Marie, then studied philosophy at the Université de Montréal. He made his literary début at the age of thirteen, when he wrote and produced a play, *Ma vacation*. During the forties he became friendly with the painter Paul-Émile Borduas, through whom he acquainted himself with Dadaism, Surrealism, Automatism, and the artists, journalists, and essayists who gravitated towards this important figure of the Montreal artistic community. These associations were to have a lasting effect on Gauvreau's aesthetic choices and his personal growth as a writer. He not only co-signed Borduas's famous manifesto, *REFUS GLOBAL*, but also articulated the theoretical aspects of Automatism for the general public. A constant defender of modern art after 1948, he never hesitated to engage in polemics, against both conservative art critics and ecclesiastical authorities (who looked upon non-figurative painting as an attack against the traditional virtues upheld by the Church and good Christian families).

From 1944 on Gauvreau wrote poetry that was not published until much later. A series of poems, 'Entrailles', did not appear until 1956 in the play *Sur fil métamorphose*. *Étal mixte* (1968) was composed in 1950. *Brochuges*, however, which he worked on during the summer of 1954, was published in 1956. These poems subvert average expectations: their word order is irretrievably broken; syntactical structures appear in disarray; phonic sounds, free of semantic charge, ultimately turn a shattered textual fabric into oneiric screams and howls.

While continuing to compose poems, Gauvreau also wrote numerous plays and had some of them produced in Montreal theatres: *Bien-être* in 1947, and *La jeune fille et la lune* and *Les grappes lucides* in 1959. His plays were never popular with audiences, and a number of directors commented bitterly on the insurmountable difficulties they posed. Jean Gascon, after reading Gauvreau's first long play *L'asile de la pureté*, written in 1953, declared that it was 'unproduceable'—a comment possibly inspired by its strong Surrealist and Automatiste leanings. Yet three decades later this play can be seen to summarize Gauvreau's preoccupation with suicide, unrequited love, and polemical fights; and offers surprising glimpses of his view of himself and his contemporaries. The premature obituary of the hero by one of his foes appears to fit both Gauvreau's destiny and self-image: 'He was a polemicist, lover, pornographer, man of letters, prophet, journalist, anarchist, wrestler, libertine, epic author.' Gauvreau also wrote plays for radio: *Le coureur de Marathon*, composed in the early 1950s, which won him the Canadian Radio Award in 1957; *Magruhilne et la vie*, written in 1952 and produced in 1969 at Studio d'Essai; and *L'oreille de Van Gogh*, which displays Gauvreau's obsessions, as well as those of the painter, by repeatedly using images associated with Van Gogh's anguish: mutilations, ear, mirror, knife, and bat.

Gauvreau's dramatic works, as well as his poetry, represent a search for new meanings as well as new forms. Often conveniently and superficially dismissed as esoteric or hermetic, they nevertheless paved the way for later poetic developments, such as those of Raoul DUGUAY, Claude PÉLOQUIN, and Denis Vanier in the late sixties, and the experiments of the young writers who were associate with *La* BARRE DU JOUR in the seventies. All of Gauvreau's texts reveal a need to peel off the various linguistic layers held tight by grammar, syntax, and semantics.

Prone to intense fits of depression, for which he underwent psychiatric internments, Gauvreau committed suicide in 1971. Then, ironically, he captured public attention. In 1972 the Théâtre du Nouveau Monde produced *Les oranges sont vertes* (1977) and two years later *La charge de l'orignal épormyable* (1977). Large audiences finally discovered Gauvreau's theatre and his violent, masochistic, surreal metaphors. *Les oranges sont vertes*, written between 1958 and 1970, has been regarded by many as his testament and the cornerstone of his aesthetic convictions. Its main character, Yvirnig, a young writer and art critic who sinks slowly into madness after the suicide of his lover, is kicked to death by other jealous artists. Hallucinations, automatic word-associations, erotic digressions, hymns to free love, and tirades against censorship lead towards the writer's inevitable destruction.

Gauvreau's fame has increased with the passage of time, so that he is now seen as one of Quebec's most celebrated writers; even political activist Jacques FERRON wrote about him, expressing admiration for Gauvreau's pride and uncompromising sense of poetry and creativity.

Gauvreau's major works—*Étal mixte*, *La charge de l'orignal épormyable*, and *Les oranges sont vert*—have been republished and are still played in spite of their surrealistic dimension. His novel *Beauté baroque* (written in 1952 but published only in 1977) inspired Jean Salvy's play of the same name. Gauvreau's *Correspondance* (1993) with Jean-Claude Dussault, dating from December 1949 to May 1950, affords a glimpse into the author's mind at a time when Quebec was preparing for the Quiet Revolution and when Gauvreau was discovering what he termed his 'images poétiques, rythmiques, mémorantes, tranfigurantes et exploréennes'.

The entrails (1981) contains translations of some of Gauvreau's early poems by Ray Ellenwood, who also translated a surrealist play, *The good life*, and three brief surrealistic dramatic sketches in EXILE—vol. 1, no. 2 (1972) and vol. 3, no. 2 (1976) respectively. Gauvreau's *Oeuvres créatrices complètes* (1971; 2nd edn 1977) was published by Éditions Parti Pris. Janous St-Denis, a friend of Gauvreau's, wrote a memoir, *Claude Gauvreau, le cygne* (1978). Jacques Marchand's *Claude Gauvreau, poète et mythocrate* (1979) provides readers with a detailed critical and scholarly examination of the texts, along with the most complete bibliography. André Bourassa has offered useful insights into Gauvreau's aesthetic objectives in 'Claude Gauvreau', *Surréalisme et littérature québécoise* (1977) and 'Gauvreau et le critique baroque', *VOIX ET IMAGES*, III, no. 1 (sept. 1977). Gilles Lapointe has published some short texts on Automatism and painting by Gauvreau in *Écrits sur l'art* (1996).

CAROLINE BAYARD/FRANCESCA BENEDICT

Gay literature. 1. FICTION AND NON-FICTION. A current of homoeroticism, or what American critic Eve Kosofsky Sedgwick has called 'male homosocial desire', has been present in Canadian fiction at least since John RICHARDSON's *WACOUSTA* (1832): the note of Gothic terror throughout that novel is induced as much by the unknown nature of same-sex relationships as it is by the unknowable in nature itself. Indeed, *Wacousta* might be seen to inaugurate something of a 'counter-syndrome' in Canadian fiction, a triangular paradigm where, in texts as diverse as M.A. GRAINGER's *Woodsmen of the West* (1908), GROVE's *Settlers of the marsh* (1925), O'HAGAN's *Tay John* (1939), BUCKLER's *The mountain and the valley* (1952), MacLENNAN's *The watch that ends the night* (1959), and COHEN's *Beautiful losers* (1966), male characters displace their love for each other—and their nation—on to women whom they symbolically shame, or else on to a mythically feminized landscape. Patricia Smart has deduced a similar structuring of gender relations in early Quebec fiction, including such well-known novels of the land as HÉMON's *MARIA CHAPDELAINE* (1916), GRIGNON's *Un homme et son péché* (1933), SAVARD's *MENAUD: MAÎTRE DRAVEUR* (1937), and *TRENTE ARPENTS* (1938) by Ringuet (Philippe PANNETON). Like Cohen, Hubert AQUIN gives such a homoerotic triangle a postmodern sexually explicit twist in *Trou de mémoire* (1968).

It may seem odd to classify Sinclair ROSS's *AS FOR ME AND MY HOUSE* (1941) as gay fiction, but in writing 'across gender'—that is, in telling his story from Mrs Bentley's point of view—Ross is also in some senses writing about his own sexuality, a narrative technique that Sedgwick has discussed in connection with Willa Cather, with whom Ross is often compared. If *As for me and my house* can be seen as a closeted tale of homosexual martyrdom, then *Sawbones memorial* (1974) represents a textual coming-out of sorts, an attempt to integrate more fully a self-identified gay character (Benny Fox) into his fiction. André Béland's *Orage sur mon corps* (1944) shares with Ross's first novel a diary construction reminiscent of works by André Gide. Yet, whereas Mrs Bentley is circumspect in her private disclosures, Béland's Julien Sanche is passionately forthcoming in relating the tempestuous desires of his body, first for Céline, then for Octave.

Robert K. Martin has demonstrated that Gide's confessional style also influenced Scott SYMONS, whose account of Hugh Anderson's pederastic tour through Montreal in *Place d'Armes* (1967) earned him the opprobrium of the English-Canadian literary community, as well as the unwanted attention of the Royal Canadian Mounted Police. Like Hugh, York Mackenzie, the protagonist of Symons' *Helmet of flesh* (1986), fancies himself a fugitive from his own culture, a sexual adventurer who has travelled to another city (Marrakech this time) to 'look orgasm in the eye'. That both Hugh and York require the services of stereotypically folkloric 'foreign' youths (French-Canadian hustlers, Moroccan boys) in order to accomplish this task goes without scrutiny. Montreal's underground, including occasional glimpses of its gay bars, surfaces as well in 'The teeth of a lion', a chapter in Patrick ANDERSON's *The character ball* (1963); and, even more prominently, in Jean BASILE's *Le Grand Khan* (1967), the second instalment of his 'Les Mongols' trilogy.

The same year that *Place d'Armes* appeared Timothy FINDLEY published his first novel, *The last of the crazy people* (1967), in which the weight of family secrets—madness, homosexuality—produces a tragic climax worthy of Tennessee Williams or Carson McCullers. Throughout his subsequent novels Findley's depiction of sex, regardless of the genders involved, is often violent and disturbing: rape, sado-masochism, or paedophilia turn up in *The butterfly plague* (1969; 1986), *The WARS* (1977), *Famous last words* (1981), and *Headhunter* (1993). But Findley's fiction is less concerned with celebrating homosexual difference than with critiquing normative masculinities and especially the institution of 'compulsory heterosexuality'. Moreover, given the example of Lucy, the cross-dressing angel in *Not wanted on the voyage* (1984), camp is frequently the idiom of Findley's critique.

The discourse of camp—exaggerating the arbitrary divisions between surface and depth, artifice and reality—likewise fuels the writing of John GLASSCO. His coyness about the composition of, and the events recorded in, *Memoirs of Montparnasse* (1970; 2nd edn, 1995) can be explained in terms of a camp aesthetic, what Philip Core, in the subtitle to his encyclopaedic study *Camp* (1984), calls 'the lie that tells the truth'. Appropriately, Core illustrated

The temple of pederasty (1970), a work of Japanese pornography dating from the seventeenth century that Glassco substantially revised.

The Swinburnian notion, exploited to great effect by Glassco, that great writers are essentially bisexual, at once male and female, finds resonance in the work of Michel Conte. In his autobiographical novel *Nu . . . comme dans nuages* (1980), he argues that designations such as heterosexual or homosexual are self-limiting, since ultimately every individual is a category unto him- or herself. This would certainly seem to apply to Davey Bryant, a character whose various misadventures have been chronicled by David WATMOUGH in more than ten novels. Bryant is very much Watmough's *alter ego*, his fictional persona—someone who, like the author, just happens to be a gay man, an English immigrant, and a writer. A recurring gay character of an altogether different kind is Geoffrey Chadwick, the amoral, closeted Westmount lawyer featured in three linked mysteries by Edward PHILLIPS: *Sunday's child* (1981), *Buried on Sunday* (1986), and *Sunday's best* (1990). Chadwick bears little resemblance to Zero Macnoo, the harried HIV-positive protagonist coping with the demands of ex-lovers, eccentric family members, and dying friends in Peter McGehee's *Boys like us* (1991) and *Sweetheart* (1992).

McGehee's two earlier story collections—*Beyond happiness* (1985) and *The I.Q. zoo* (1991)—point to a rich tradition of gay short fiction in this country: from the mini-*romans-à-clef* that make up Scott Watson's *Stories* (1974) and *Platonic love* (1981), to the exquisitely realized domestic dramas of Dayv James-French's *Victims of gravity* (1990). The theme of home and homelessness runs throughout Patrick ROSCOE's *Birthmarks* (1990), with characters neither reaching Oz nor waking up in Kansas. Richard Teleky's epigrammatic 'Notes on parking', from *Goodnight sweetheart and other stories* (1993), is a subtle anatomy of the rituals of cruising. André Martin's *Crimes passionels* (1994) uses text and image to explore the unmapped terrain between pain and pleasure, abuse and gratification. Dennis Denisoff's *Queeries: an anthology of gay male prose* (1993) provides a much-needed introduction to some recent trends in English-Canadian gay short fiction. Finally, Shyam Selvadurai's *Funny boy* (1994) and Derek McCormack's *Dark rides* (1996) are similar in that each is subtitled 'a novel in stories'. Both texts are essentially coming-out narratives, but McCormack's eponymous protagonist has more in common with the calculating and world-weary Jared McCaverty of Will Aitken's *Terre Haute* (1989) than with Selvadurai's basically naïve Arjie.

Canadian gay men have also been at the forefront of experiments in the genre of creative non-fiction. Stan Persky's *Buddy's: meditations on desire* (1989) and *Then we take Berlin: stories from the other side of Europe* (1995) combine elements of travelogue, memoir, and philosophy to yield a hybrid literary form especially suited to the vicissitudes of homosexual desire. The figure of Roland Barthes looms large in both books. *Buddy's* is styled explicitly as an 'homage' to the French critic and Barthes's belief that the body is also a text to be written informs the central axiom of *Then we take Berlin*: 'Desire is the body's first epistemology.' Georges Bataille, Maurice Blanchot, and Arthur Rimbaud, among others, likewise serve as guides in Paul CHAMBERLAND's *Marcher dans Outremont ou ailleurs* (1987), his 'imaginary biography' of a Montreal neighbourhood and its male inhabitants. This mixing of cultural criticism and life-writing, and the suffusing of each with a decidedly gay sensibility, also informs the best of the late Jay Scott's brilliant film reviews for Toronto's *Globe and Mail*, which were collected in *Midnight matinées* (1985) and *Great Scott!* (1994), in the Introduction to which Robert FULFORD wrote: 'He became the first prominent journalist in Canada to absorb and project the self-confidence created by the gay liberation movement.'

Travel—already a familiar metaphor of gay self-exile in the work of Anderson, Symons, and Persky—surfaces as a recurring theme in several novels published in the 1980s and 1990s. In Guy Ménard's *L'accent aigu* (1983), for example, a young Québécois falls in love while studying in Paris; in André Martin's *Darlinghurst heroes* (1993) a gay Montrealer treks through Australia; in Patrick Roscoe's *The lost oasis* (1993) a Canadian living with his lover in Spain searches for his missing father in North Africa; and in Dennis Denisoff's *Dog years* (1991) the HIV-positive narrator drifts from Vancouver to Kiev and back again. Denisoff's text is also noteworthy for its post-AIDS apocalypticism—a tone characteristic of the work of younger Canadian gay writers who have never known sex without the association of death. One thinks of Lawrence Braithwaite's *Wigger* (1995), or Michel Butler's *L'homme de mon lit* (1992) and François Brunet's *L'acte de folie* (1993)—two Quebec novels that stand in sharp contrast to the social realism of Michel TREMBLAY's *Le coeur découvert* (1986) and *Le coeur éclaté* (1993). The various postures affected by the characters in these novels attest to the heterogeneity of queer identities, just as the texts themselves prove that contemporary gay fiction in Canada will continue to resist the narrow confines of that label.

2. DRAMA. One could argue that gay drama in Canada actually began elsewhere. John HERBERT's *FORTUNE AND MEN'S EYES* (1967) opened to great acclaim off-Broadway in 1967 and was subsequently performed around the world, but did not receive a full-scale Canadian production until 1975. Set in a prison, Herbert's play questions the rigid gender roles imposed on men in our society, demonstrating how sex becomes an instrument of power: new inmate Smitty learns from Rocky what it means to rape, from Mona what it means to be raped. That Smitty by the end of the play displaces Rocky as the cell's 'old man' indicates how well he has absorbed the brutal lessons of masculine identity formation. Only Queenie—who resurfaces in *Pearl divers*, one of four gay-themed short plays included in Herbert's *Some angry summer songs* (1976)—circumvents these prescribed social norms, largely through his climactic drag performance.

English-Canadian gay theatre began in the 1970s mostly with a group of men associated with Toronto's Factory Theatre Lab and the Toronto Free Theatre. John Palmer's *A touch of God in the golden age* (1972) and *The end* (1971), Tom HENDRY's *How are things with the walking wounded?* (1972) and *The missionary position* (1972), Larry FINEBERG's *Hope* (1972), Michael HOLLINGSWORTH's *Strawberry fields* (1973) and *Clear light* (1973), Louis Del Grande's *So who's Goldberg?* (1972), and Ken Gass's *The boy bishop* (1976) all premièred at one or another of these spaces. The plays—although frequently daring in subject matter, staging, and dialogue—are for the most part pre-Stonewall in sentiment, focusing on doomed or disintegrating relationships and recycling familiar psychological clichés about homosexual experience.

Gay theatre in Quebec during the same period centred primarily on the work of Michel Tremblay. In *La Duchesse de Langeais* (1970) Tremblay introduced audiences to the first of his gay/transvestite protagonists. The Duchess and, even more famously, Hosanna (in the 1973 play of the same name), in their respective imitations of female Hollywood icons, are meant to represent Quebec's own cultural cross-dressing as a French-speaking minority in anglophone North America. These characters, and others like them, resurface throughout Tremblay's '*BELLES-SOEURS* cycle' of plays, most notably in *Demain matin, Montréal m'attend* (1972), *Sainte-Carmen de la Main* (1976), and *Damnée Manon, sacrée Sandra* (1977). It was only with *Les anciennes odeurs* (1981) that Tremblay abandoned the allegorical baggage attached to most of his earlier gay characters and set about dissecting the past and present emotional ties between two former male lovers. *Messe solennelle pour une pleine lune d'été* (1996), although generally panned by critics, features a moving portrait of an older gay couple.

Tremblay has influenced a whole generation of gay male playwrights in Quebec who came of age—and came out—in the politically volatile 1970s, men like Normand CHAURETTE, Michel-Marc BOUCHARD, René-Daniel DUBOIS, and Robert Lepage. What the work of each of these men shares, in addition to an unprecedented eroticization of the male body on stage, is a postmodernist penchant for self-reflexivity. In Chaurette's *Provincetown Playhouse, juillet 1919, j'avais 19 ans* (1981), Bouchard's *La contre-nature de Chrysippe Tanguay, écologiste* (1984), Dubois's *26 bis, impasse du Colonel Foisy* (1982), and Lepage's *Le polygraphe* (1993), characters' internal desires become externalized, projected outward onto the performative apparatus of theatre itself. This 'repetition' or 're-playing' of romantic conventions and conceits within an explicitly homoerotic context achieves its apotheosis in Bouchard's *Les feluettes* (1987), which contains not one but two plays-within-a-play. Among the more popular gay plays produced in Quebec during this period, only Dubois's *Being at home with Claude* (1986), which deals with a young male hustler's murder of his separatist boyfriend, employs the basic techniques of dramatic realism. The play was turned into a successful 1991 film by Jean Beaudin. Bouchard's *Les feluettes* and Lepage's *Le polygraphe* have likewise been adapted for the screen.

Cree playwright Tomson HIGHWAY, in his mixing of sex and religion, has also benefited from Tremblay's example. In *The Rez sisters* (1988) and *Dry lips oughta move to Kapuskasing* (1990) Highway celebrates life on 'the rez' with a gay sensibility in much the same way that Tremblay glorifies 'la Main'. This aesthetic of local colour extends as well to the gay urban demi-monde of Edmonton depicted in Brad FRASER's plays. *Unidentified human remains and the true nature of love* (1990) and *Poor super man* (1995) are almost cinematic in their rapid-fire montage of scenes and use of overlapping dialogue; it is somewhat surprising, therefore, that Denys Arcand's 1994 film of the former, based on Fraser's own script, was so unsuccessful.

Perhaps the single most important development in English-Canadian gay theatre in the 1980s was the establishment of Toronto's Buddies in Bad Times Theatre, which has served as a showcase for the work of its co-founder and former artistic director, Sky GILBERT, and as a testing ground for new talent. Gilbert was both remarkably prolific and wildly uneven in his theatrical output, with his plays tending to fall into one of two categories. *Drag queens on trial*, *Drag queens in outer space*, and *Suzie Goo: private secretary*, collected in *Painted, tainted, sainted: four plays* (1996), are essentially parodic spectacles; *Pasolini/Pelosi*, *My night with Tennessee*, and *More Divine: a performance for Roland Barthes*, all from *This unknown flesh: a selection of plays* (1995), lean towards historiographic meditation. Other playwrights to have had their work produced by Buddies include David Demchuk, Harry Rintoul, Daniel MacIvor, and Robin Fulford, whose *Steel kiss* (1991) offers a searing indictment of homophobia by recreating a High Park gay-bashing from the perpetrators' perspective. Gilbert, Demchuk, Rintoul, and MacIvor have all had their work anthologized in *Making out: plays by gay men* (1992), an important collection edited by Robert Wallace.

The work of Gordon Armstrong and Colin Thomas deserves special mention because of the subtle lyricism and surprising humour each playwright has brought to the dramatization of AIDS. In *Blue dragons* (1992), *The plague of the gorgeous* (1996), and the posthumously produced (1996) *Sex in heaven*, Armstrong moves from memory play to satire to romantic fantasy in charting his characters' different experiences of grief, anger, forgiveness, and reconciliation. Thomas's episodic *Flesh and blood* (1991) is an uncompromising portrait of two brothers' complicated relationship; in his *Sex is my religion* (1995) a Christian mother and her HIV-positive son recite the other's monologue. These plays, together with recent cross-Canada productions of Bryden MacDonald's *Whale riding weather* (1994), Jim Bartley's *Stephen & Mr. Wilde* (1993), and Timothy Findley's *The stillborn lover* (1993), point to the vibrancy and diversity of gay drama in this country. PETER DICKINSON

3. POETRY. Gay male poetry may be said to constitute itself in the now famous shift identified by Michel Foucault from actions to identity. In this point of view, poems by men in honour of boys, in the tradition of the Greek Anthology, do not constitute gay poetry, since Greek pederasty did not (arguably) establish identity. By the late nineteenth century, however, the boundary between homosexual acts and gay identity was increasingly permeable, and the erotic boy-love poem provided a traditional form on which to draw. The decadents of English poetry, or the virile celebrations of Whitman's 'comrade love', found no immediate echo in Canadian poetry and would have to await further influences from Europe, particularly the image of the dead soldier/comrade of the Great War, most famously represented in the poems of Wilfred Owen.

Acanthus and wild grape (1920) by Frank Oliver Call (1878–1956) may be called the first book of gay poetry in Canada. A professor of French at Bishop's College, Lennoxville, Quebec, Call was well aware of continental developments, and able to work out a link between classical and modern strains in the celebration of the male body. Call's work, constructed as the title suggests around a fundamental division that might be termed Apollonian and Dionysian, locates a tension between formal poetry, represented by the series of sonnets that opens the volume, and free verse. A poem such as 'Hidden treasure' is under the spell of Whitman and at the same time more restrained than anything by the American poet, in invocation of the 'sun-browned boy with the wondering eyes' with whom he may recapture 'the treasure . . . hid in the shallows below'. 'To a Greek statue' celebrates the 'beautiful body', 'slender and white', that is the dream of the 'northern sunlight', the call of the body. This motif of the desire of the northern mind for the physical south becomes one of the enduring structures of gay male writing in Canada.

Although Call continued to write his subtle poems of desire, a generation would pass before Canadian gay poetry became modern, and it took the effort of a newcomer to Canada, Patrick ANDERSON, to accomplish this revolution. He co-edited the literary journal *PREVIEW*, which was an essential voice for new Canadian writing in the 1940s. His first volume of poetry, *A tent for April* (1945), begins forcefully with the erotic 'Drinker', a celebration of fellatio as 'a column of pure love' that 'bursts its melting flower'. The poem 'Rink' juxtaposes the speaker's desire, largely unfulfilled, and the structures of bourgeois society that send the hockey-playing boys 'towards the female goal'. Anderson's left-wing politics and his increasingly open sexuality, along with his British birth, left him on the margins of Canadian literature. A poem such as 'Night out' demonstrates his debt to American poet Hart Crane; it is a modernist poem of gay male desire in the homosocial world of the tavern. He edited, with Alistair Sutherland, *Eros: an anthology of male friendship* (1961).

The density of modernist language seemed an impediment, as well as a reticence, to the emerging gay poets of the 1960s and 1970s. E.A. Lacey's work epitomizes this period in his volumes *Forms of loss* (1965) and *Path of snow* (1974). Like his predecessor Call, but in a very different manner, Lacey identifies Canada with a moral and cultural landscape of snow, which causes him to flee to what is portrayed as the open sexuality of Latin America. Lacey leaves behind what he calls, in the 'Invocation' to his birthplace—Lindsay, Ontario—'the house of cold'. Perhaps most striking are Lacey's psycho-autobiographies, such as 'The closet', with its account of a dark menacing father and the dream with the voice that says, 'You are not a man.' Multilingual and erudite, Lacey is a successor to Gide and Verlaine as well as Whitman.

The various liberation movements of the 1960s made possible a sexual directness and frankness that had been impossible in North America only a few years earlier. Small presses and journals published outside the limits of conventional publishers. *The Body Politic* (1971-87), a Toronto-based periodical of politics and culture, created a sense of national community, bringing to a large audience work initiated by Canada's gay poet and publisher Ian Young. Young's *Year of the quiet sun* (1969) reflects the new openness about sex and captures a world of multiple encounters with strangers. The longing for the ideal inherited from the tradition is juxtaposed against the reality of sexual desire and danger. The poems are precise in their evocation of experience and cool and ironic in tone. The minimalism of the *haiku* is joined to the celebration of the young male body, as in 'A cricket': 'the silhouette of his chest/beneath the shirt,/the thin curves/of his thin, boy's body.'

The radical politics of liberation that affected gay male poetry in English in the 1960s and 1970s had no real parallel in French writing in Quebec. Much of the political energy that elsewhere was channelled into sexual politics went instead into nationalism, which often seemed to require the assumption of a virile heterosexuality. Just as lesbian writers came to distance themselves from the dominantly male world of Quebec nationalism, so too several important Québécois male writers shifted from political concerns to a more generalized and eroticized sexual utopianism. The most important of these writers, Paul Chamberland, also acted as a link between the new French erotics of language, as represented most significantly by Roland Barthes's poetics of *jouissance*, and Quebec nationalism. Barthes made his mark in English Canada as well, of course, especially in Stan Persky's *Buddy's: meditations on desire* (1989) but his influence in Quebec was vital, particularly in the development of a new feminism around *La* BARRE DU JOUR. Chamberland associates his dream of a free Québec with a liberation of desire, most pointedly in his adoration of the child, as in *Le prince de sexamour* (1976).

The other great successor of Barthes in Quebec is poet André ROY, whose *Les passions du samedi* (1979) captures gay male life of the 1970s, before AIDS, but also shifts from a concern with homosexuality as a subject to one with homosexuality as style. Roy's later volume, *Action writing* (1985), continues in the Barthes tradition with an emphasis on an erotic transgression of language, typically dense and obsessive, circling around meaning, renouncing mere representation. More public in his work, Jean-Paul Daoust creates performance poetry meant to be declaimed, even as the words swirl across the page, gathering fragments of culture. Daoust's world is sexual, brazen, and hot, as in his evocation of Montreal as a drag queen and vamp, 'Parfois Montréal se maquille les yeux'. This Quebec is equally at home in New York, far from the haunted dreams of a NELLIGAN, whose incarceration is widely taken to indicate his homosexuality and who can still function as an icon of the gay man in Quebec, destroyed by his culture and its assimilation into English.

During the 1970s Daryl HINE, a more established poet, continued to write in a largely allusive and highly formal manner, brilliantly using his formal control for a long autobiographical poem *In & Out*, first published privately in 1975. It captures a 1950s world of sexual repression, the combined pressures of religion and psychiatry that drive him 'in' and the ultimate rejection of those pressures that have led in fact to death in his own coming 'out'. The poem's tone shifts from the tragic to the campily comic, rejecting the 'cure', and depicting the connections between High Church or Roman aestheticism and an arch homosexual style, as in the narrator's response to the church: 'My dear, the decor!/with its gilding and plaster and paint/like the icing on top of a cake.' Hine's look back to an earlier time can allow for a mock-heroic of gay self-awareness.

By the 1980s and 1990s new theoretical understandings of identity made the universals of early gay work seem naïve. At the same time the pressures of AIDS meant an increased sense of threat; the idyllic encounter with the brown boy, as in Lacey, now seems troubling in terms both of disease transmission and politics. The gay poet of these years often finds it necessary to locate the idyll of love in a world of state hostility. Although a major figure on the Canadian poetry scene for some time, bill BISSETT continued his verbal play but brought to it a new sense of urgency. In 'ther ar shadows', from *what we have* (1988), bissett brings together the destruction of the environment and a call for a recovered tenderness of love between men; and similarly in 'basicalee i trust treez' from *inkorrect thots* (1992) the world of the forest conceals the violence of gay-bashing. Michael Lynch, activist and professor, published his *These waves of dying friends* (1989) two years before his own death from AIDS. Lynch's activism underlies these poems, intercut with scenes of tenderness and affection. Lynch resists the temptation to regret earlier freedoms, instead making pleasure and resistance one, as in 'Yellow kitchen gloves', based on a demonstration in front of the US Supreme Court. He calls for dead friends: 'We want you back//We want you all beside us on these steps,/this other dancefloor, gloved fists in the air.'

John Barton's *Great men* (1990) takes the reader through the 'courage' that has made possible gay love through history, celebrating a tradition of resistance essential to self-awareness. In the brilliant and evocative 'Au Garage, Montréal' he recognizes that even in the disco there is the power of transgression, the celebration of 'wayward flesh'. Barton ends his collection with a powerful call: 'refuse like us/to live as if we have never been.' Toronto writer Ian Iqbal Rashid reminds us that the body is social as well as personal. His *Black markets, white boyfriends* (1991) insists that 'My beauty is branded into the colour of my skin.' Rashid's work evokes the doubleness of subjectivity, in a poem such as 'The perils of pedagogy', in which desire for a culture and desire for a man seem dangerously entangled.

Finally, Douglas LePAN, who was born the year before Patrick Anderson, surprised his readers with the publication of *Far voyages* (1990), made up of two groups of love poems to a young man (who died in 1985 at the age of thirty-seven) that remarkably balance deep feeling, discreet eroticism, and LePan's gift for memorable imagery. The poem 'Dead of night' ends: 'If you were to leave me, how could/I ever find the strength to go on?/Or even the strength of that last act/of love—and grief and homage—/to distance your image and free it in air?'

ROBERT K. MARTIN

Geddes, Gary (b. 1940). Born in Vancouver, British Columbia, he was raised on the Prairies and the West Coast. He attended the University of British Columbia and the University of Toronto, where he obtained a Ph.D. (1975). He has taught at the University of Victoria and is now a member of the English department at Concordia University, Montreal.

Geddes's early collections of verse—*Poems* (1971), *Rivers inlet* (1971), *Snakeroot* 1973), and *Letter of the master of horse* (1973)—reveal a sharp eye for physical detail, a keen and uncompromising intellect, and a poetic sensibility that balances subjectivity and objectivity, the personal and the impersonal, and criticism and compassion. The lyric sequence of *Rivers inlet* moves from external descriptions to internal parallels, the British Columbia coastal landscape becoming a map of the poet's ancestry that explains the relationship of the past to the present. Another long suite of poems, *War and other measures* (1976), marks a new development in Geddes's writing. Paul Joseph Chartier died on 18 May 1966 in the men's washroom of the House of Commons when a bomb he was carrying accidentally exploded. Through the mind of Chartier the poetic sequence mirrors the society that resorts to violence and destruction, so that *War and other measures* becomes a scathing portrait and an impassioned indictment, a fable of contemporary Canada. Its violence and insanity surface again in *The acid test* (1981), though the setting expands to include the entire world: political tyranny, the arms race, and environmental ravage are but a few of its themes that reflect the absurd inhumanity of man. As controlled and disciplined as Geddes's earliest verse, *The acid test* has a passionate power that derives from the intensity of his commitment and intelligence. This volume, which also contains a revised version of *Letter of the master of horse*, won the national poetry prize given by the CANADIAN AUTHORS' ASSOCIATION.

Although there has been a growing tendency for critics to label him a political poet, Geddes is a writer whose interest in such ideologically charged geographies as Latin America, China, and Hong Kong is fuelled as much by questions about aesthetics and the crucibles in which art and politics intermingle as by narrowly topical politics.

Representative of the catholicity of Geddes's inquiries is his much-acclaimed 1984 collection *The terracotta army*, a blending of twenty-six poems and as many calligraphic characters inspired by the 1974 chance discovery in China of 8000 life-size terracotta soldiers and horses from 300 B.C. Individually sculptured by the potter Lao Bi on the order of the emperor Ch'in Shi Huang, the terracotta army was intended to serve as an imperial bodyguard for Huang in the afterlife. In Geddes's poems this silent massing of figures becomes much more: an egotistical challenge to mortality, a symbol of status and tyrannical will, and an embodiment of the relation between art and the often sterile structures of power that inform the daily lives of citizens of worlds past and present. Threaded throughout the poems are meditations on the passion and fears of the men who 'create' the statues and their stories: the potter Bi, the tyrant Huang, the calligrapher Shuai Lizhi, and the poet Geddes. *The terracotta army* received the Americas Best Book Award in the 1985 Commonwealth Poetry Competition and has been broadcast several times on both CBC and BBC radio.

Geddes published two books in 1986: one of verse, *Changes of state*, and his first, somewhat pedestrian, collection of short fiction, *The unsettling of the west*. The next year saw publication of a consistently strong collection, *Hong Kong poems* (1987), which again reveals his ability to balance the immensity of historical events (in this case the experiences of two Canadian battalions during the Pacific campaign) with the idiosyncrasies and sufferings of individuals on both 'sides' of the tragic encounter. The collection was awarded the 1987 Writers Choice Award and the National Magazine Gold Award.

Geddes turned to the worlds of Latin America for his next project, a co-operative, bilingual collection of poems undertaken with the Chilean poet Gonzalo Millan. Titled *No easy exit/Salida dificil* (1989), it is a record of his experiences and reflections during a troubling reading tour of Chile in 1987, and is a powerful though uneven testimony to those who resist and triumph over political oppression. As with so much of Geddes's poetry, the poems in *No easy exit* are never political in the narrow, polemical sense. As the title suggests, there are no easy solutions offered in these poems, no single answer to the myriad personal, political, and historical problems that weigh heavily on the art and, more importantly, on the daily routines of the people the writer encounters. Geddes's work in this collection, as well as in *Companeros: an anthology of writings about Latin America*, which he co-edited in 1990, were acknowledged in 1995, when he received the prestigious Gabriela Mistral Prize for his writing about, and ongoing contribution to, Chilean culture.

An indefatigable writer, Geddes followed *No easy exit* with a book of new and selected poems, *Light of burning towers* (1990), and two collections of new poetry: *Girl by the water* (1994) and *The perfect cold warrior* (1995). The latter volume again reveals his cosmopolitan vision, juxtaposing epigraphs by Czeslaw Milosz, Louise Gluck, and Adrienne Rich with three distinct groupings of poems that speak through disparate voices: The Drive, a sequence of intense first-person narratives about growing up poor in Vancouver's Commercial Drive area; a section of poems set in and about Palestine, including the award-winning 'What does a house want?', which recounts the demolition of Palestinian houses by the Israeli army; and Norwegian Rabbit, a section with the self-explanatory subtitle 'The Trotsky poems'. Many of these poems reappeared in *Active trading: selected poems, 1970-1995* (1996).

Complementing Geddes's profile as a poet has been his work as an anthologist and editor. He has edited important anthologies: *Twentieth-century poetry and poetics* (1969, 1985, 1996); *15 Canadian poets* (with Phyllis Bruce, 1970; rev. and enlarged as *15 Canadian poets plus 5*, 1978; rev. and further enlarged as *15 Canadian poets X 2*, 1988); *The art of short fiction* (1993); *Skookum wawa: writings of the Canadian Northwest* (1975); *Divided we stand* (1977), reflections from distinguished Canadians on their country after the victory of the Parti Québécois; a collection of works by new poets, *The inner ear* (1983); and a book of travel essays and memoirs, *Chinada: memoirs of the Gang of Seven* (1983). With Hugo McPherson he was general editor of Copp Clark's Studies in Canadian Literature series. His critical study *Conrad's later novels* (1980) is based on his Ph.D. dissertation. In collaboration with Theatre Passe Muraille, Toronto, Geddes wrote *Les maudits anglais*, a bilingual political farce about French-English relations in Canada. It was produced in 1978 and 1983.

DAVID STAINES

Gedge, Pauline (b.1945). Born in Auckland, New Zealand, she spent part of her life in Oxfordshire, England, before moving to Alberta. This midwestern writer made a startling début in 1977 with the best-selling *Child of the morning*, the first of five novels about ancient Egypt. Set in the time of Thothmes I and II, it focuses on a female Pharaoh inspired by the historically androgynous figure of Hatshepsut. This was followed by *The twelfth transforming* (1985; rpr. 1996), *Scroll of Saqqara* (1990), *House of dreams* (1994), and its sequel *House of illusions* (1996). Gedge's other historical novels are *The eagle and the raven* (1978; rpr. 1996), a long work that is partly about the warrior-queen Boudicca (Boadicea), set in Celtic Britain and in Rome; *Stargate* (1982), a fantasy about the early years of the history of the universe when each solar system was ruled by a sun-lord; and *The covenant* (1992), a Gothic mystery.

Gedge's novels are scrupulously researched and as historically accurate as any recognized historiographic text. While her writing is considered 'popular' in North America (less so in Europe, where her Egyptian novels interest Egyptologists) because of their straightforward, structurally uncomplicated style, her narratives are passionate, convincing, and written with exquisite detail that includes vivid descriptions of landscapes, architecture, and people. Gedge's novels are provocative interpretations of the past that fascinate and delight her very large international readership.

TARA L. CURTIS

Gélinas, Gratien (b. 1909). Born in Saint-Tite-de-Champlain, near Trois-Rivières, Quebec, he moved with his family shortly afterwards to Montreal. He was educated at the juniorate of the Blessed Sacrament Fathers in Terrebonne, and at the Collège de Montréal, where he completed the program in classical studies and was active in the school's dramatic society. Forced to leave school in 1929 because of the Depression, he worked in a Montreal department store and then as an accountant with an insurance firm, taking evening courses at the École des hautes études commerciales. But he continued his involvement in theatre by founding the Troupe des Anciens du Collège de Montréal, and by acting with the Montreal Repertory Theatre in both English and French and on radio. In 1935 he married Simone Lalonde, with whom he had six children. After her death he married the distinguished French-Canadian actress Huguette Oligny in 1973. They live in the village of Oka, near Montreal.

The first important figure in the modern Quebec theatre, Gélinas acted in 1934 in the first Radio-Canada serial, *Le curé de village* (1936), by Robert CHOQUETTE. The following year he showed his talent as a monologist in a series of sketches he performed in a satirical revue entitled *Télévise-moi-ça*. These shows prepared him for a radio series of his own in which he played a simple, sensitive, Chaplinesque character named Fridolin, a role he played on radio from 1937 to 1941. It was at this time that he decided to become a full-time writer and actor. In 1938 he began an annual stage revue, *Fridolinons*, based on the same character, at the Théâtre Monument National. It played annually until 1946, with a retrospective revue in 1956. *Les Fridolinades*, drawn from the revues, was produced at the National Arts Centre, Ottawa, in 1987 and in Toronto in 1989. These revues were later published in four volumes as *Les Fridolinades 1945 et 1946* (1980); *Les Fridolinades 1943 et 1944* (1981); *Les Fridolinades 1941 et 1942* (1981); and *Les Fridolinades 1938, 1939 et 1940* (1988)—with useful introductory material by Laurent Mailhot.

Two of the skits and monologues from *Fridolinons*—*Le départ du conscrit* and *Le retour du conscrit*—became the basis of his first full-length play, *TIT-COQ* (1994). The opening night of *Tit-Coq*, at the Monument National on 22 May 1948, was a landmark in the history of popular theatre in Quebec. The play ran for over 500 performances and made Gélinas the best-known and best-loved actor and playwright in the province.

His next play, *Bousille et les justes* (1960, 1981, 1987), was not produced until 1959, but Gélinas was busy in other theatrical activities. In 1954 he wrote and starred in a weekly comedy on Radio-Canada television, *Les quat'fers en l'air.* In 1956 he played leading roles in Stratford, Ontario, productions of *Henry V* and *The merry wives of Windsor*, and was named vice-president of the Greater Montreal Arts Council, a post he held until 1963. In 1958 he founded in Montreal the Comédie-Canadienne, which was both a theatrical company and a theatre. That same year Gélinas was elected president of the Canadian Theatre Centre, and in 1960 he was one of the founders of the National Theatre School in Montreal. In 1964 he wrote and performed in a satirical revue at the Comédie-Canadienne called *Le diable à quatre* (unpublished).

Gélinas played the leading role in *Bousille et les justes*, portraying a simple-minded and honest man victimized by the intrigues of relatives wanting to avoid a family scandal. A type of modern morality play, it is straightforward and tightly structured, raising the issue of moral honesty versus family pride, and satirizing some traditional religious practices in

Quebec, and their failure to sensitize people to moral concerns. It has been performed in many parts of Canada in an English translation, *Bousille and the just* (1961), by Kenneth Johnstone and Joffre Miville-Dechêne; and in 1996 it was successfully revived with more than 100 performances.

Gélinas's third play, *Hier, les enfants dansaient* (1968; 1988), which was published in an English translation by Mavor Moore as *Yesterday the children were dancing* (1967), is about a family divided by the issues of federalism and separatism in Quebec. However topical the play—it was first produced in 1966 at the Comédie-Canadienne, and in 1967 in English at the Charlottetown Festival—Gélinas insists: 'This isn't a political manifesto, it's a love story.' Still, it is a powerful presentation of the political issues that divide Québécois, though the family drama is at times sentimental. Both *Yesterday* and *Bousille* have been presented on CBC television.

Another long gap preceded *La passion de Narcisse Mondoux* (1987), which was translated into English by Linda Gaboriau as *The passion of Narcisse Mondoux* (1992). A two-character play, it is the story of a retired plumber who seizes the opportunity to woo the well-off woman he has loved for forty years, Laurencienne Robichaud, after her husband's death. Unapologetically romantic and sentimental, and a success wherever it has been performed, the play starred Gélinas and his wife Huguette Oligny, and was directed by Yvette Brind'Amour. It premièred at Toronto's French theatre, Le Théâtre du P'tit Bonheur, in the fall of 1986, and in January 1987 moved to Montreal's Théâtre du Rideau Vert. In 1988 it opened in English at the Piggery Theatre in North Hatley, Quebec, where English and French performances alternated. It travelled successfully across Canada in English and French, and to parts of the United States, including a five-week run off-Broadway in 1989, always with Gélinas and Oligny performing.

Gélinas expanded his involvement in the cultural life of Canada when he assumed chairmanship of the Canadian Film Development Corporation in 1969—a crucial time for the film industry in Canada. Under Gélinas's direction this agency supported several important Canadian feature films, such as *The apprenticeship of Duddy Kravitz*, *Outrageous*, *Why shoot the teacher?*, and *Who has seen the wind*. Though he took the post for one or two years, he stayed on until 1977. In 1986 he co-chaired, with Paul Siren, a task force on the status of the artist, appointed by then Minister of Communications Marcel Masse. The results of their work are in *The status of the artist: report of the task force* (1986) with its thirty-seven recommendations.

Gélinas has received honorary doctorates from twelve Canadian universities as well as the Grand Prize of the Society of Dramatic Authors, the Victor Morin Theatre Award from the Société Saint-Jean Baptiste, and the Toronto Drama Bench Award for his distinguished contribution to Canadian theatre. In 1990 Gélinas was one of the first winners of the National Theatre School's new Gascon-Thomas Award, he was promoted to Companion of the Order of Canada, and the Montreal newspaper *La Presse* named him Personality of the Year. In 1992 a gala performance—including film clips, sketches, readings, and tributes to his 52 years in show business—laid the financial basis for a Gratien Gélinas Fund to support emerging playwrights. In 1981, Prisma Productions, Montreal, produced a thirty-minute video-recording, *La gagnant*, profiling Gratien Gélinas as a winner and showing exerpts from his plays. For his theatre activities over almost seventy years and his dramatic works—which prepared the way for later playwrights in giving an authentic and memorable picture of Quebec life—Gélinas remains an influential figure in the cultural life of Quebec and the whole of Canada.

See Renate Usmiani, *Gratien Gélinas* (1977), in the Profiles in Canadian Drama series; an appendix contains a translation of Gélinas's 1949 address, 'A national and popular theatre'. His 'Credo of the Comédie-Canadienne' is in *Queen's Quarterly*, LXVI (Spring 1959). Mavor MOORE has written a short introduction to Gélinas and Quebec theatre in *Four Canadian playwrights* (1973).

Important articles on individual plays appear in volumes III and IV of the *Dictionnaire des oeuvres littéraires du Québec*, and newspaper articles on Gélinas and his plays are reproduced in *Dossier de presse, 1940-1980* (1981). A long discussion between him and Victor-Lévy Beaulieu, based on radio interviews on Radio-Canada, may be found in *Gratien, Tit-Coq, Fridolin, Bousille et les autres: entretien* (1993). An important and well-documented two-volume biography, *Gratien Gélinas: la ferveur et le doute* by Anne-Marie Sicotte, one of his granddaughters (another is the famous Mitsou), appeared in 1995-6.

JAMES NOONAN

Generals die in bed. See Charles Yale HARRISON.

Gérin-Lajoie, Antoine (1824-82). Born in Yamachiche, Lower Canada (Quebec), into a large farming family, he attended local schools before entering the Collège de Nicolet in 1837. By the time he graduated he had already acquired a certain reputation, writing the well-known folksong 'Un Canadien errant' (1847), dedicated to the exiled leaders of the Rebellion of 1837-8, and a verse play in three acts, *Le jeune Latour* (Montréal, 1844), the first tragedy written and published in Canada. In this play, which relies heavily on the since-disproved account in Michel BIBAUD's *Histoire du Canada sous la domination française* (Montréal, 1837, 1843), Claude de La Tour seeks possession for England in 1629 of the fort at Cape Sable, last outpost of the French in Canada after the successful raids of the Kirke brothers. His son 'Roger' is commander of the fort, and is resolved to retain it for France. Despite its static character, immature psychological analysis, and obvious reliance upon Corneille for its style and tone, the warm patriotism of this work struck a responsive chord in contemporary Quebec: witness its publication in full in three Canadian newspapers (1844). It was subsequently reprinted in both editions of James Huston's *Répertoire national* (1848-50, 1893), and most recently by Réédition Québec (1968).

After studying law, Gérin-Lajoie went on to a varied career as a civil servant, copyist, translator, and eventually as parliamentary librarian in Toronto, Quebec, and, after 1865, in Ottawa. Despite these occupations, his lively interest in literature, politics, and journalism continued. He is the author of a *Résumé impartial de la discussion Papineau-Nelson sur les événements de Saint-Denis en 1837* (Montréal, 1848); of a handbook to the Canadian political system of the time, *Catéchisme politique; ou Les éléments du droit public et constitutionnel du Canada, mis à la portée du peuple* (Montréal, 1851); and of a useful constitutional history, *Dix ans au Canada, de 1840 à 1850: histoire de l'établissement du gouvernement responsable* (Québec, 1891), published posthumously, as were his *Mémoires*, which were edited by H.-R. CASGRAIN and published in the second volume of Casgrain's own *Oeuvres complètes* (Montréal, 1885) and separately the following year.

Gérin-Lajoie was among the founders of the two most important literary reviews of the period, *Les SOIRÉES CANADIENNES* (1861-5) and *Le FOYER CANADIEN* (1863-6), to both of which he contributed frequently, and in which his most important literary works, the two *JEAN RIVARD* novels, were first published: *Jean Rivard, le défricheur* in *Les Soirées canadiennes* (vol. II, 1862), and its sequel *Jean Rivard, économiste* in *Le Foyer canadien* (vol. II, 1864).

Gérin-Lajoie maintained close contact with most of the intellectuals and writers of his time, helping to found the Institut Canadien in 1844, becoming president of its Montreal branch the following year, and at the same time serving as secretary to the fledgling Société Saint-Jean-Baptiste. A pioneer in theatre, he was one of the most influential French-Canadian authors of his age. His son, Léon Gérin, wrote the first biography of him, *Antoine Gérin-Lajoie: La résurrection d'un patriote canadien* (1925), an unrevealing work. He is the subject, however, of an excellent modern study by René Dionne, *Antoine Gérin-Lajoie, homme de lettres* (1978). See also Robert Major, *Jean Rivard ou l'art de reussir* (1991).

L.E.DOUCETTE

Germain, Jean-Claude (b. 1939). Primarily a journalist and drama critic, he founded in Montreal, in 1969, Le Théâtre du Même Nom, or TMN, an anagram mocking the very formal and heavily subsidized Théâtre du Nouveau Monde (TNM). Originally acting as secretary for TMN, which set out to produce collaborative works, Germain increasingly became involved in scriptwriting. He worked at first with theatrical clichés and myths and then proceeded from *Si Aurore m'était contée deux fois*, which is anti-melodrama and against the 'boulevard' style associated with Guitry, to the sham western *Rodéo et Juliette*, and *Don Quickshot*—all unpublished plays of the early 1970s. Rather than ignore or repudiate theatrical tradition, Germain subverted it—though not without a certain affection. Frequently carried away by his own verbal agility and eloquence and his Rabelaisian wit, he occasionally seems more of a raconteur than a playwright or performer.

Germain's most successful works are the still unpublished *Dédé mesure*, about a fashion designer, the women's 'boss'; *Les hauts et les bas d'la vie d'une diva: Sarah Ménard par eux-mêmes* (1976), about an opera singer who briefly believes herself to be Sarah Bernhardt; and *Un pays dont la devise est je m'oublie* (1976), about the history of French Canada in the form of a reply to Lord Durham. Germain has also found it equally interesting and amusing to revive, in an adapted 1977 version, *Les faux brillants* (1885), a comedy by Félix-Gabriel MARCHAND, a dramatist (and Liberal premier of Quebec) in the late nineteenth century.

Like other popular and committed writers, such as Jean BARBEAU and Michel GARNEAU, Germain has had difficulty in leaving the theatrical mainstream of the 1980s. Still in fine form, he has turned into a storyteller and a popularizer of history (for radio), and an *animateur*, a guest in great demand (on television), and a witness to, and actor of, public life. He is a past vice-president of the Conseil des arts et des lettres du Québec.

See also DRAMA IN FRENCH 1948 TO 1981: 3. LAURENT MAILHOT

Gervais, Marty (b. 1946). Charles Henry ('Marty') Gervais was born in Windsor, Ontario, and received his B.A. (1971) from the University of Guelph and his M.A. (1972) from the University of Windsor before embarking on a career as a journalist with the *Globe and Mail*, Toronto, Canadian Press, and the *Windsor Star*, where he has been entertainment editor, religion editor, and book editor. His work as a journalist led to the publication of *Seeds in the wilderness: profiles of world religious leaders* (1994), which collected articles on, and interviews with, figures such as Pope John Paul II, Bishop Desmond Tutu, and Mother Teresa.

In 1969, encouraged by James REANEY, with whom he co-authored the play *Baldoon* (1976), Gervais founded the literary publishing house Black Moss Press (1969-), which published the early books of David DONNELL, M.T. KELLY, and John B. Lee. As a historian of Essex County and the Windsor area who has worked on Reaney's principle that lively history and literary material can be found in any region of Canada, Gervais has produced several notable histories of the area including *The rumrunners* (1980), which chronicled the illicit liquor trade of the Prohibition era in Detroit, and the documentary drama *The fighting parson* (1983), about the Prohibition crusades of the tragic and fated Reverend J.O.L. Spracklin, whose zeal against alcohol led to murder. As a literary critic, Gervais produced *The writing life: historical and critical views of the TISH movement* (1976), reflecting an interest in the Black Mountain overtones and stylistics that he supported in his early poetry.

Gervais has undergone several phases and changes in his poetry, which has seen a transformation from the satirical voice of the early volumes—*Sister Saint Anne* (1968), *Something* (1969), *Other marriage vows* (1969), *A sympathy orchestra* (1970), *Bittersweet* (1972), *The believable body* (1979), and *Public fantasy: The Maggie T poems* (1983), a thinly veiled satire on Margaret Trudeau—to the serious interim volumes *Poems for American daughters* (1976) and *Into a blue morning* (1982). In his introduction to *Into a blue morning*, Al PURDY noted that Gervais was a 'man pushing against his limitations, trying to shove the barriers in his mind a little farther ahead; snatching spare moments from being a husband and father and wage-earner to write poems'. What may have proved to be a barrier to Gervais, in his mid-career, became the strength and substance of his more recent work in *Autobiographies* (1989) and *Tearing into a summer day: prose poems* (1996), where he writes about his life and family with joyful and enthusiastic celebration, and reverence for the beauties and revelations that daily life offers him. For Gervais, the personal is invested with the same qualities as the sacred, a carry-over from his renewed spirituality, his interest in St Martin de Porras, his travels and self-discoveries in South America, and his profound interest in American poet and monk Thomas Merton and the monastery in Gethsemane, Kentucky.

Letters from the equator (1986) and *Playing God* (1994) show Gervais in his fullest and most exquisite expression of humane spirituality. For him, especialy in *Autobiographies*, the act of making a poem or telling a story is an act of faith, so that observances of the commonplace become moments of transcendent epiphany and insight, rather than merely journalistic jottings or diaries. BRUCE MEYER

GGA. See GOVERNOR GENERAL'S LITERARY AWARDS.

Gibbs, Robert (b. 1930). Born in Saint John, New Brunswick, he was educated at the University of New Brunswick and at Cambridge University, receiving his Ph.D. from UNB, where he taught English until his retirement. He has long been associated with *The FIDDLEHEAD* and the Maritime Writers' Workshop.

Since a selection of his verse was included in Fred COGSWELL's *Five New Brunswick poets* (1962), Gibbs has brought out seven books of poetry: *The road from here* (1968), *Earth charms heard so early* (1970), *A dog in a dream* (1971), *A kind of wakefulness* (1973), *All this night long* (1978), *The tongue still dances: poems new and selected* (1985), and *Earth aches* (1991). *A space to play in* (1981) is a selection of his poems published in pamphlet form by the LEAGUE OF CANADIAN POETS. Gibbs' poems contain sensual and witty descriptions of human and non-human landscapes, subtle insights into relationships, a sophisticated understanding of the workings of the mind, the mutterings of dream, and the interworkings of conscience, the subconscious, grief, and nostalgia. His rhythms give a sense of sustaining—and detaining—energy; his language combines the melodic with the colloquial.

Gibbs also writes highly effective prose fiction. In his collection of short stories, *I've always felt sorry for decimals* (1978), he recreates, through the mind of the same observant and imaginative child, a provincial society just now fading into history: New Brunswick in the late 1930s and early 1940s. Gibbs' child narrator combines the role of author/creator with that of the innocent rememberer of things past, a 'petit Marcel', through whose purer, simpler eyes an adult world of anxiety and dread is faintly hinted. Two other stories, 'I always knew there was a Lord' (*Stories from Atlantic Canada*, 1972) and 'O think of the home over there' (*Journal of Canadian Fiction*, 1975) are also narrated by a child. Gibbs' fantasy novel *A mouthorgan for angels* (1984) has been described by Martin Waxman (*Quill and Quire*, October 1984) as an 'intricate dream sequence, part fairy tale, part Oz, part Alice in Wonderland, and part Huck Finn'. In both his poetry and fiction Gibbs shows a delicate ear for the nuances of Maritime speech and decorum, and a gentle savouring humour.

Gibbs has edited two anthologies: *Ninety seasons: modern poems from the Maritimes* (1974, with Robert Cockburn) and *Reflections on a hill behind a town* (1980). He contributed 'English poetry in New Brunswick 1940-1982' to *A literary and linguistic history of New Brunswick* (1986), and with Sandra Djwa and David Savage compiled the annotations to *E.J. Pratt: The complete poems* (1989). The literary executor of Alden NOWLAN's estate since 1983, Gibbs wrote the bio-critical introduction to *The Nowlan Papers* (1992).

Gibbs' poetry has been discussed by Susan Rudy Dorscht in 'A space to play in: or telling the (w)hole story: the recent poetry of Robert Gibbs', *CANADIAN LITERATURE* (Spring 1988), and by M. Travis LANE in 'Roads around about here', *Humanities Association Bulletin* (Fall 1972). *I've always felt sorry for decimals* was well reviewed by Edna Barker (*Canadian Book Review Annual*, 1978), Marian ENGEL (*Globe and Mail*, 7 Oct. 1978), and Alden Nowlan (Saint John *Telegraph Journal*, 2 Dec. 1978).

M. TRAVIS LANE

Gibson, Graeme (b. 1934). Born in London in the southern Ontario he would so ably chronicle, explore, and interrogate, Gibson attended Upper Canada College and the University of Western Ontario. He was a galvanizing force in Canadian cultural politics from the early 1970s, serving as a much-respected chairman of The WRITERS' UNION OF CANADA and of The WRITERS' DEVELOPMENT TRUST, and as president of Canadian PEN. Widely travelled and frequently conducting bird-watching expeditions into the Amazon and Cuba, he resides in Toronto with Margaret ATWOOD, with whom he has a daughter, Jess.

Gibson's first novel, *Five legs* (1969), voices with poetic impact concerns that are prominent in his subsequent fiction: personal and cultural paralysis, death in all its guises, omnivorous *morts-vivants* locked in a modern *danse macabre*, blocked creativity, the grieving process, and father-son entanglements. Ingeniously refracted through the opposing yet complementary sensibilities of its two main characters, this 'stream-of-consciousness' novel details a winter journey through the stricken heart of WASP Ontario. Occasioned by the funeral of a student, Martin Baillie, who succumbed to the same repressive, conventional and puritanical forces that have warped the life of his professor, Dr Crackell, the trip pits a harried Crackell against his unwanted travelling companion, Felix Oswald, Baillie's roommate and best friend. Felix—equally tormented, crippled and haunted, feeling cornered by the deadening pressures of conformity and respectability deforming Crackell—manages a temporary escape. Hailed at the time as avant-garde and a stylistic tour-de-force, the experimental *Five legs* was the impressive first novel published by the House of ANANSI.

Communion (1971) continues and darkens the fractured, feverish story of self-mocking Felix Oswald, deepening the themes of cultural malaise, of maiming, of strangled articulateness and psychological survival. Though seeking refuge in a flight to the northern wilds, Felix, an obsessive veterinarian's assistant, is unable to evolve beyond a futile identity with animal victims and entrapment in his own neuroses; the sick husky he befriends is run down by Felix's own car, choosing to be a victim—like Baillie, the hit-and-run casualty of *Five Legs*, and Felix himself, who perishes in a southern border-crossing when it was nightmarishly set ablaze by American street kids. *Communion* plunges readers into a labyrinthine lower-world of monsters and grotesques, predators and victims. As in all Gibson's fiction, characters overlap, coalesce, and reduplicate one another, giving rise to an eerie sense of doubleness, of mirrors mirroring mirrors—the hallmark of SOUTHERN ONTARIO GOTHIC. Such writing, emerging out of a region of Canada Gibson perceives as a kind of mythological country, is one of the subjects discussed in the lively *Eleven Canadian novelists* (1973), of which Gibson is the intuitive interviewer, editor, and photographer. Though he has not received the critical attention he deserves, here as elsewhere Gibson emerges as a writer's writer, respected by colleagues like Alice MUNRO, Timothy FINDLEY, Marian ENGEL, Matt COHEN, and Margaret LAURENCE.

Perpetual motion (1982), widely regarded as Gibson's best and most accessible novel, churns up nineteenth-century rural Ontario in a rich, gothic outpouring of eccentric characters colliding around fictional Mad River. Robert Fraser, a technology-intoxicated inventor of overbearing rationality, fatally obsessed with power, control, and dynastic grandeur, violently pursues perfection through a perpetual-motion machine that promises triumph over the elements. Yet he brings destruction not only on his family but also on the vibrant natural world he wars against. Again, Gibson structures this marvellous epic, enlivened by local colour and folklore, around parallel characters and doubles, especially 'the man of reason' and 'the wild man'. It is in the NEW CANADIAN LIBRARY with an Afterword by Ramsay COOK.

As with his first two linked novels, the powerful, moving *Gentleman Death* (1993) complements *Perpetual motion*, with which it shares a like-named protagonist. Set mainly in Toronto in the late 1980s, it presents an engaging portrayal of 56-year-old novelist Robert Fraser as he encounters death the leveller, and painfully yet resolutely—and not without humour and moments of serenity—comes to terms with his own ageing and mortality, his grief, and his frustrated creativity. The latter stem from a series of unsettling losses: of parents, a brother, friends, wilderness areas and entire ecosystems, of a recognizable Canada dismantled during the Mulroney regime. Slowly and honestly, adapting to and absorbing myriad private and collective losses, Fraser perseveres, keeping what is genuine, socially committed, and 'wild' in himself and in the dance of life and death.

See also NOVELS IN ENGLISH 1960 TO 1982: OTHER TALENTS, OTHER WORKS: 1.

MICHAEL HURLEY

Gibson, Margaret (b. 1948). Born and raised in Toronto, Ontario, where she still lives, her formal education ending with grade ten, she has suffered from mental illness for most of her life. She was hospitalized for the first time at fifteen and for several years thereafter was a voluntary mute. Perhaps the most important friendship of her life was that with Craig Russell, the talented female impersonator who played a leading role in the Canadian film *Outrageous* (adapted from Gibson's story 'Making it'). In 1971 she made an unfortunate marriage that ended in divorce in 1974. Also in 1974 her story 'Ada' appeared in the annual OBERON anthology *New Canadian stories*; it was later produced by CBC-TV, from a script written by Gibson and Claude Jutra. Her first collection of stories, *The butterfly ward* (1976), whose first edition bore the name Gilboord (her married name), was a critical success and a recipient of the City of Toronto Award. Gibson's second collection, *Considering her condition* (1978), was somewhat less successful; its title is that of a story in *The butterfly ward. Sweet poison* (1993) is a collection of seven confessional stories about abused women who find refuge in various kinds of oblivion, even madness. The title story in *The fear room* (1996) is partly told from the standpoint of a boy of two-and-a-half years who had been beaten by his mother's boyfriend; other stories treat obsession, memory, and mental illness. Gibson's first novel, *Opium dreams* (1997), eloquently and lyrically describes the lives of Maggie (who had suffered from mental illness) and her father, a victim of Alzheimer's disease whose mind has been reduced to jumbled memories.

Mental illness is Gibson's central theme. Often her protagonists are shown 'functioning' outside institutions, disguising themselves, walking 'the fine line between reality and fantasy'; but reality—which cannot simply be equated with normalcy or its opposite—is the hideousness of the world, from which the narrator tries to avert her gaze, as well as those rare moments of innocence when delight takes over. Although in both perceptions of reality Gibson's beautiful losers are more 'real' than her normal people, madness is no escape. 'Sometimes it can be beautiful inside this space', but more often it feels like being damned. Violence is everywhere—much of it directed against women. But there is also tenderness, especially for small children and for others who suffer alongside Gibson's protagonists. And there is sometimes a lovely gallantry in all the pain.

Gibson's style has a fine authenticity, lapsing very occasionally into cliché. She uses run-on sentences as well as unconventional punctuation, and her stories are often interestingly structured. Among the best are 'Ada',

'Making it', 'Considering her condition', 'Brian Tattoo', 'Still life', 'Sweet poison', and 'The fear room'. CONSTANCE ROOKE

Gibson, William (b. 1948). Born in Conway, South Carolina, USA, he visited Toronto in 1967 and remained in Canada to avoid being drafted into the US army. He married a teacher and settled in Vancouver, where he earned a B.A. (1977) from the University of British Columbia. During his studies Gibson began writing science-fiction short stories which he published in numerous SF journals and magazines. His first novel, *Neuromancer* (1984), was an immediate success: it was the first novel to win, in the same year, three prestigious SF awards: the Hugo, the Nebula, and the Philip K. Dick. It was also the first volume of his 'Cyberspace' trilogy, the others being *Count Zero* (1986) and *Mona Lisa overdrive* (1988). In his fiction Gibson situates our contemporary relation to a high-tech environment in an SF context in order to push the implications of that relationship to their extremes. His stories and novels focus in general less on plot than on creating vivid descriptions of techno-scenarios, although in *Virtual light* (1993) character is important, and the techno-scenarios serve to move its plot along rather than merely to indulge Gibson's descriptive powers.

Idoru (1996) is probably Gibson's most interesting and enjoyable novel from a literary standpoint, and the most wide-ranging in the territory it covers—Japan, Hong Kong (Kowloon), and Russia (the underworld of Moscow)—as well as in the characters and situations it embraces and in its mordant satire of present Western mores, translated into the early twenty-first century, which is filled with high technology. An *idoru* is a transient pop star in Japan, and one of the novel's events (a satire on celebrity) is the engagement of Rez, the lead singer in a Japanese group, to an *idoru* named Rel Toei—who turns out to have been created by a computer. In a 1996 interview Gibson said: 'I don't [i.e., no longer] feel like I'm being chased by technological change. I just sort of surf along on its spume.'

Gibson wrote the script for the film *Johnny Mnemonic* (1995), based on his short story of the same title. STEFAN HAAG

Gidlow, Elsa. See LESBIAN LITERATURE.

Giguère, Roland (b. 1929). Born in Montreal, he trained as a printer at the École des Arts Graphiques there and at the École Estienne in Paris. In 1949 he founded Éditions Erta in Montreal, which published books of poems and prints by Québécois writers and artists until 1978. During his stays in France, from 1954 to 1963, he participated in the activities of the Phases group and associated with the Surrealists and André Breton. Giguère's production as a printer has been uninterrupted, and his work is frequently exhibited in Canada and abroad.

Forever inspired by the purest spirit of Surrealism, from which it never deviated, Giguère's poetry exemplifies a centred yet constantly evolving mode of writing. His care for form and structure as a poet, reminiscent of his discipline as a printer, is at the service of an ever-springing flow of dream-like imagery whose power derives from an authentic inner exploration of the individual and collective unconscious. His first collections of poems—*Faire naître* (1949), *Trois pas* (1950), *Les nuits abat-jour* (1950), *Images apprivoisées* (1953), *Les armes blanches* (1954), and *Le défaut des ruines est d'avoir des habitants* (1957)—display an acute sense of the prevalent political and cultural oppression under the Duplessis regime. Giguère's is one of the strongest voices of rebellion; but for him revolt and the search for freedom are not simply a reaction against historically limited circumstances but more fundamentally a continuous struggle against the very roots of oppression in civilization. Reconciliation occurs in his poetry, as in *Adorable femme des neiges* (1959), but only by virtue of a momentary and precarious balance. All the books cited, as well as *Pouvoir du noir* (1966) and *Naturellement* (1968), were collected first in *L'âge de la parole: poèmes 1949-1960* (1965) and in *La main au feu, 1949-1968* (1973). His subsequent works—*Abécédaire* (1975), *J'imagine* (1976), and *Forêt vierge folle* (1978)—carry on the same devotion to the essence of Surrealism: an unflinching faith in the subversive power of the imagination, the only weapon upon which people can rely, provided they do not give up the struggle. *Temps et lieux* (1988) exemplifies Giguère's dual dedication to art and poetry, even while acknowledging the latter's fall into a subterranean mode of existence. *Mirror and letters to an escapee* (1977) is a collection of some of his poems translated by Sheila Fischman.

Giguère won the Prix France-Canada and the Grand Prix Littéraire de la ville de Montréal in 1966. *La main au feu* won a Governor General's Award, which Giguère declined. Special issues of *La BARRE DU JOUR* 11-12 13 (déc. 1967-mai 1968) and of *VOIX ET IMAGES* 9/2 (1984) were devoted to his work.

MICHEL PARMENTIER

Gilbert, **Sky** (b. 1952). Born Schyler Lee Gilbert in Norwich, Connecticut, and raised in Buffalo, New York, he graduated from York University, Toronto, with a B.F.A. in 1977, influenced strongly by the avant garde work of Robert Benedetti. He left graduate studies at the University of Toronto to found Buddies in Bad Times Theatre with Matt Walsh and Gerrard Ciccoritti. Under Gilbert's long and productive leadership (1979-97), Buddies developed a mandate to encourage innovative and gay or lesbian artists, creating a space for alternative theatre that challenged mainstream assumptions about both gender and staging. Programs such as Rhubarb! (a festival of new plays), 4-Play (featuring gay and lesbian artists), and seed shows nurture emerging artists and companies. In 1994 Buddies acquired a permanent home in the former Toronto Workshop Productions theatre, making it the largest gay and lesbian theatre in North America. After the success of early plays such as the 1980s *Lana Turner has collapsed*, about poet Frank O'Hara, Gilbert wrote, directed and/or acted in several colourful, extravagantly theatrical plays such as *Drag queens on trial* (1985) that treated gender issues with farcical and joyful irreverence. He has published two collections of plays, *This unknown flesh* (1995) and *Painted, tainted, sainted* (1996), as well as individual works, such as *The dressing gown* (1989) and *Play murder* (1995). His second film, *My addiction*, was screened at a festival in San Francisco in 1994. Honours include Dora Awards for *The whore's revenge* (1990) and *Suzie Goo* (1992), Chalmers nominations for *Play murder* and *The dressing gown*, and the Pauline McGibbon Award for Directing (1995). An outspoken gay activist with a flamboyant alter ego, 'Jane', Gilbert frequently rouses the ire of conservative factions in government and the press, completing through his life-style the process of confrontation seen in his plays. In 1997 Gilbert resigned his post as Artistic Director of Buddies to concentrate on writing.

LISBIE RAE

Gill, **Charles-Ignace-Adélard** (1871-1918). Born in Sorel, Quebec, Charles Gill was educated at the Collège Sainte-Marie, the Séminaire de Nicolet, and the Collège de Saint-Laurent. Primarily an artist, he studied painting in Montreal and, with Jean Léon Gérôme, in Paris, where he spent two periods in the early 1890s. After his return to Montreal, he painted and taught drawing at the École Normale Jacques-Cartier. While living in Paris, Gill met a number of writers, including Alphonse Allais and Paul Verlaine, and began devoting his energies to literature in addition to painting. Several periodicals in Quebec published his poems, as well as his literary and art criticism. Gill joined the ÉCOLE LITTÉRAIRE DE MONTRÉAL in 1896 and became one of its most prominent members. He married Gaétane de Montreuil (1867-1951), a prolific pioneer of women's journalism in Quebec.

Besides his shorter poems, Gill also conceived a more ambitious poetic project, a Dantesque epic allegory of the St Lawrence River. His long poem *Le Cap Éternité*, the only part of this epic ever to come out, was published posthumously, together with a collection of the shorter poems, in *Le Cap Éternité: poème suivi des Étoiles filantes* (1919). The preface, by his close friend Albert LOZEAU, is a good introduction to this belated Romantic. Lozeau sees Gill as 'la figure la plus caractéristique de la littérature canadienne-française contemporaine', because of his admiration for Hugo and Lamartine, whose *Jocelyn* inspired him, and his misty idealism and escapism. The fragment of Gill's epic, set on the Saguenay River, is a felicitous depiction in verse of the beauty, mystery, and grandeur of the Canadian landscape.

Gill's *Correspondance* (1969) was edited by Réginald Hamel. Besides a few letters to his mother, it consists largely of his lively correspondence, from 1910 to 1918, with Louis-Joseph Doucet. Full of valuable biographical detail, it provides a vivid portrait of Gill. Also of value is the brief portrait by Gill's friend, Father Olivier Maurault, written and published serially in 1919 and brought out as a booklet in 1950.

C.R.P. MAY/MARTA HORBAN-CARYNNYK

Girard, **Rodolphe** (1879-1956). Joseph-Octave-Louis-Rodolphe Girard was born in Trois-Rivières, Quebec, and attended the École Sainte-Ursule there until the family moved to Montreal in 1891. He then studied at the Académie commerciale catholique de Montréal (1891-4) and the Collège de Montréal (1894-8). While still a student he composed his first novel, *Florence* (1900), which was inspired by the Rebellion of 1837-8. Having become a reporter for *La Patrie* in 1899 and for *La Presse* the following year, Girard married Regina Lefaivre in 1901. The next year he published *Mosaique*, a collection of short stories and plays: five of his plays would be performed in Montreal between 1902 and 1912, and two others at a later date. When his best-known novel, *MARIE CALUMET* (1904), was published and denounced by the Archbishop of Montreal, he was dismissed by *La Presse* and joined the staff of Ottawa's *Le Temps*. In 1905 he became a junior clerk in the Secretary of State's office and three years later was appointed a translator for the House of Commons. His third novel, *Rédemption* (1906), which includes the saving of a 'fallen woman', gives a true account of the life of the fishermen of Paspébiac around 1892. This was followed by *L'Algonquine* (1910), about the love of a Frenchman for an Algonquin girl in seventeenth-century New France and containing detailed descriptions of Algonquin life. In the meantime Girard had been elected president of the Institut canadien-français in Ottawa (1907) and had founded the Ottawa branch of the world-wide Alliance française (1908). After his wife died in 1911, he married Cécile Archambault the following year. During the First World War Girard served in the Canadian Forestry Corps, becoming a lieutenant-colonel and being twice decorated. He was a prolific contributor to newspapers and magazines, publishing over 400 short stories and reminiscences until long after his retirement in 1941. He is remembered today chiefly for the irreverent *Marie Calumet*; but in his time he was recognized as a leading promoter of French cultural organizations, a popular dramaticist, a military figure, and as a gifted public speaker.

See André Vanasse, '*Marie Calumet*', *Dictionnaire des oeuvres littéraires du Québec*, II (1980).

MADELEINE DIRSCHAUER

Giroux, André. See NOVELS IN FRENCH 1940 TO 1959: 2.

Givner, Joan (b. 1936). Born Joan Mary Parker Short in Manchester, England, Givner took an honours degree in English at the University of London in 1958, married David Givner in 1965, and returned to London for a Ph.D. (1972), following teaching and graduate study in the USA. In 1972 she resumed teaching in the English department of the University of Regina, where she remained till taking early retirement in 1995 and moving to British Columbia to write full time. Between 1984 and 1992 she edited the *Wascana Review*.

Balancing her responsibilities as researcher, professor, and mother (she has two daughters), Givner began to publish short stories in 1981, all the while maintaining a vigorous output of scholarly articles and conference papers. Her first book was *Katherine Anne Porter: a life* (1982; rev. 1991), which established her as a feminist biographer. *Katherine Anne Porter: conversations* (1987) is a collection of interviews edited and introduced by Givner.

Givner embraced a Canadian subject in *Mazo de la Roche: the hidden life* (1989), a serious examination of DE LA ROCHE's work and life with her cousin, life-companion, and amanuensis, Caroline Clement. De la Roche's books, although immensely popular, were typically regarded as eccentric at best and risible at worst by the intelligentsia (Dorothy LIVESAY being a significant exception). Givner argues that her writings provide an essential transition from the nineteenth-century foremothers Susanna MOODIE and Catharine Parr TRAILL (both of whom were still living when de la Roche was born), to Margaret ATWOOD and Margaret LAURENCE, who were publishing at the time of de la Roche's death in 1961. Givner communicates her fascination with de la Roche's multiple ambivalences—'sexual, national, racial, and religious'—and with the necessity to 'inscribe her own female desire obliquely' within the conventions of the novel. In 1992 Givner's play *Mazo and Caroline* was presented at the Saskatchewan Playwrights' Centre.

Givner's first collection of short fiction, *Tentacles of unreason* (1985), is pleasing apprentice work that shows her exploration of the notion of 'fictional fictions' and 'fictions of autobiography', finding the female presence in the 'intertext between the two'. For example, in the title story of her second collection, *Unfortunate incidents* (1988), a literary biographer at work on the life of 'Rachel de la Warr', meets Rachel's adopted daughter Aimée, in a sophisticated reminder of de la Roche and her adopted daughter Esmée. The stories in *Scenes from provincial life* (1991) demonstrate a similar wilful assault on the sort of androcentric criticism that finds women's writing merely autobiographical.

Givner turned her life-writing talents on her own experience with *The self-portrait of a literary biographer* (1993), focusing on her grammar-school beginnings and her growth into her own writing, incidently presenting a brilliant depiction of the pettiness, appalling cosiness, and sheer meanness of the underclass way of English life. In 1996 Givner returned to short fiction with *In the garden of Henry James*.

A Room of One's Own (December 1992), edited by Cristina Gheorge, is devoted to Joan Givner's work.

PATRICIA WHITNEY

Glass, Joanna (b. 1936). Born Joan Ruth McClelland in Saskatoon, Saskatchewan, she developed an interest in theatre as a high-school student. After graduation in 1955 she performed with the Saskatoon Community Players while working as an ad writer and broadcaster at a local radio station. She soon moved to Calgary to join Betty Mitchell's Workshop 14, supporting herself as a television continuity writer. Her lead role in Maxwell Anderson's *Anne of the thousand days*, the Calgary entry in the 1957 Dominion Drama Festival, won her a scholarship from the Alberta Cultural Activities Branch to study acting for the summer at the Pasadena Playhouse, California. She next enrolled in Warner Brothers Drama School, but soon left for New York. There she met physicist Alexander Glass, whom she married in 1959; they divorced in 1976. After thirty years of residence in the United States (latterly, Guilford, Connecticut) she now makes her home in Toronto.

In the early 1960s Glass acted at Yale, where her husband was a student, but after her three children were in school she turned to writing. In 1966 she completed an early version of the play that was eventually to become *Artichoke*. A second work, *Santacqua*, was accepted at the Herbert Berghof Studio, New York, for workshop production in Dec. 1969. Further workshops of her plays were conducted soon after: *Artichoke* at the Long Wharf Theatre, New Haven, Conn., in Nov. 1970, and the one-act plays *Trying* and *Jewish Strawberries* in 1971 at the Hilberry Theatre, Wayne State University, Michigan.

Glass's breakthrough as a professional dramatist came in Nov. 1972 with the production of the companion one-act pieces *Canadian Gothic* and *American modern* (published jointly in 1977) at the off-Broadway Manhattan Theatre Club, with a revival the following spring. Set in a small prairie city and a New York suburb respectively (and usually produced together), the one is a sombre study of a failing struggle against emotional repression, the other a tragicomic sketch of eccentric accommodation to marriage breakdown. The first of many Canadian productions followed in Nov. 1973 at the Pleiades Theatre, Calgary, under the direction of Ken Dyba. *Canadian Gothic* appeared in *Best short plays of 1978* (1980) and in *Prairie performance* (1980), edited by Diane Bessai.

Glass's full-length play *Artichoke* (1979), a comedy with a Saskatchewan farm setting, was premièred at the Long Wharf Theatre, New Haven, Conn., in Oct. 1975, starring Colleen Dewhurst; Bill Glassco mounted the first Canadian production at Tarragon Theatre, Toronto, in Oct. 1976. Glass's witty dialogue and sharp-eyed view of western-Canadian rural society enliven this play about a middle-aged wife who astonishes her family by deciding to take a lover for the summer. Glass developed a similar theme in her first novel, *Reflections on a mountain summer* (1974). Set alternately in the Canadian Rockies and Grosse Point, Mich., it combines the author's perceptions of Canadian and American personality and her response to the traumas of modern living. It was serialized as a 10-part program for the BBC in 1975.

Glass's next two plays premièred on Broadway, New York: *To grandmother's house we go* (1981), starring Eva Le Gallienne, in Jan. 1981; and *Play memory* (1984), directed by Harold Prince, in Apr. 1984. Although the latter earned a Tony nomination, critical response to both plays was lukewarm. The former, in a contemporary American setting, reverses the usual generational conflict in its comic-ironic exploration of the question 'Is there life after children?' *Play memory*, set in the Saskatoon of the playwright's youth, is a largely autobiographical study of the decline of a proudly unrepentant alcoholic as recollected years later by his daughter, and has its origins in a short story, 'At the King Edward Hotel', written in 1975 and published in *Winter's tales* 22 (1976); its first dramatic version, entitled *The last chalice*, was commissioned by the Manitoba Theatre Centre for its twentieth-anniversary season in 1977. Glass was awarded a Guggenheim Fellowship in 1981 for the extensive revision of the play, which had its Canadian première at the 25th Street Theatre, Saskatoon, in Jan. 1986, directed by Tom Bentley-Fisher. A Canadian edition of the play is published in *NeWest plays by women* (1987), edited by Diane Bessai and Don Kerr.

In 1985 Glass was awarded a Rockefeller grant to work at the Yale Repertory Theatre, New Haven, on a play-in-progress, *Towering babble*. The same year she published her second novel, *Woman wanted*, a type of play-novel that skilfully integrates and expands thematic, narrative, and dramatic features of her plays. Since 1987 Glass has been more closely associated with Canadian theatre. As playwright-in-residence at the Canadian Stage Company, Toronto (1987-8) she completed a new prairie comedy, *Yesteryear*, premièred at the St Lawrence Centre in Jan. 1989. The Canadian première of *If we are women* (1994), a co-production of the Canadian Stage Company and Vancouver Playhouse, opened at the St Lawrence Centre, Toronto, in Jan. 1994, directed by Susan Cox; the American première took place the previous July at Williamstown Theatre Festival, Williamstown, Mass., directed by

Austin Pendleton. Whereas in *Yesteryear* Glass explores a light side to the Saskatoon of her youth, in *If we are women* she forwards the lives of *Play memory*'s mother and daughter into the contemporary setting of a Connecticut beach house. The four women of this play—two widowed grandmothers, a divorced daughter, and an ebullient granddaughter—having determined to make their own choices, exchange the stories, regrets, angers, and hopes of their lives. Once more the playwright's unflagging gift for character delineation through vigorous patterns of speech, in both monologue and dialogue, serves her well.

The University of Calgary has published an inventory of its Glass holdings with a biocritical essay by Diane Bessai: see *The Joanna M. Glass papers* (1985), edited by Jean F. Tener and Apollonia Steele. For an interview with Glass, see *Fair play: 12 women speak: conversations with Canadian playwrights* (1990) by Judith Rudakoff and Rita Much. For useful references to Glass's early work see John Parr, 'Reflections of Joanna Glass', *Journal of Canadian Fiction*, 20 (1977); Hetty Clews, 'Kindred points: the twin worlds of Joanna M. Glass', *Atlantis* (Autumn 1978); and *Canada's playwrights: a biographical guide* (1980), edited by Don Rubin and Alison Cranmer-Byng.

DIANE BESSAI

Glassco, John (1909–81). Born in Montreal of a merchant family, John Glassco, known to his friends as Buffy, was educated at Selwyn House, Bishop's College School, and Lower Canada College. He entered McGill University in 1925 but left in 1928 without graduating. Defying his father's displeasure, he preferred to complete his education in sensibility in Paris. He stayed in France for three years, frequenting expatriate and artistic circles, living often in deep poverty, and finally contracting tuberculosis, which forced him to return to Montreal for treatment. His account of this early part of his life, *Memoirs of Montparnasse* (1970), was immediately recognized as one of the finest Canadian autobiographies when it was published forty years later. (He says in a prefatory note that he wrote all but the first three chapters while in hospital in 1932–3 before and after a critical operation. Patricia Whitney, in doing research for a literary biography of Glassco, discovered in the National Archives the text of all but the first chapter, which had been published in *This Quarter* in 1929, handwritten with a ballpoint pen in six scribblers dated 1964.) It is a remarkably vivid account of what it was like to be young in the Paris of the late Third Republic, still recognizably the city of Verlaine and Baudelaire, even the city of Balzac. Glassco profited by the opportunity to meet, and had the sharp eye and clear memory to characterize, such writers as George Moore (whose *Confessions*, he said, were a model for the *Memoirs*), James Joyce, Ford Madox Ford, André Breton, Robert McAlmon, Gertrude Stein ('a rhomboidal woman'), and a score of others. All is recorded with a glittering freshness of prose that gives the book a sense of complete contemporaneity with the scene and its inhabitants; in addition, the controlled ordering of happenings, and the vitality of the dialogue, lend the flavour of fiction to the narrative. Indeed, in the introduction to the Second Edition of the *Memoirs* (1995), edited by Michael Gnarowski, we read that Glassco himself thought of it—privately, not publicly—as fiction. In a letter of 1968 to his friend the American writer Kay Boyle, whom he knew in Paris in 1928, he wrote: 'It's really fiction. I was trying to re-create the atmosphere and spirit of Paris of those days as it was for *me*. The way George Moore and Casanova did for the worlds of *their* youth'—who, he wrote in another letter the next year, did not feel 'tied to historical truth; they were . . . liars and produced works of art by *invention*. Who cares about their lies now?' The Second Edition throws an interesting new light on the *Memoirs*, with its Critical Introduction by Gnarowski, notes on the text, and brief accounts of people and places.

In 1935, having survived the removal of a lung, Glassco retired to Foster, in the Eastern Townships of Quebec, and immersed himself in the local life, running the rural mail route, founding the Foster Horse Show in 1951, and acting as mayor of Foster from 1952 to 1954. During his later decades he divided his time between Montreal and Foster.

Glassco once remarked that he was 'as much a novelist, anthologist, translator and pornographer' as he was a poet or a fine memoirist. His earlier publication, a surrealist poem called 'Conan's Fig', appeared in *transition* in 1928, and he first became known to Canadians as a poet through *The deficit made flesh* (1958). His later books of verse are *A point of sky* (1964); *Selected poems* (1971), which won a Governor General's Award; and the long satiric-parodic poem *Montreal* (1973). His prose works, besides *Memoirs of Montparnasse*, are the three novellas in *The fatal woman* (1974), or appeared under a variety of *noms-de-plume*. 'A season in limbo' by 'Silas M. Gooch', a fictional treatment of a later stay in hospital, appeared in *The* TAMARACK REVIEW 23 (1962). Other pseudonymous works are largely exercises in mannered pornography: *Contes en crinoline* (1930) by 'Jean de Saint-Luc'; *The English governess* (1960) by 'Miles Underwood'; *The temple of pederasty* (1970) 'after Ihara Saikaku'; and *Fetish girl* (1972) by 'Sylvia Beyer'. *The English governess* was eventually published under Glassco's name as *Harriet Marwood, governess* (1976). 'I came'—he wrote in the *Memoirs*—'under the renewed influence of Huysmans, Pater, Villiers, Barbey d'Aurevilly and others of the so-called Decadents, and decided to write books utterly divorced from reality, stories where nothing happened.' This meant, as Edmund Wilson said in *Axel's Castle*, 'cultivating one's fantasies, encouraging one's private manias, ultimately preferring one's absurdest chimeras to the most astonishing contemporary realities.' Following this direction, Glassco wrote not only the pseudonymous novels and novellas listed above, but also completed *Under the hill* (1959), Aubrey Beardsley's unfinished erotic story of Venus and Tannhäuser.

As a poet John Glassco is in the classic tradition; his combination of the bucolic and elegiac modes links him to the Augustans as well as to the decadent writers of the 1890s, while also owing much to his familiarity with the poetry of both France and Quebec. Indeed, his excellent translations of the poems of SAINT-DENYS-GARNEAU, and other Quebec writers, should be considered a part of his poetic *oeuvre*, for he achieved the rare feat of writing fine English poetry while translating from the French. His translations can be found in *The poetry of French Canada in translation* (1970), which he edited, and in the *Complete poems of Hector de Saint-Denys-Garneau* (1962), whose *Journal* he also translated (1962).

Glassco's poems—unlike his prose—are largely concerned with the simple actualities of life in the Eastern Townships ('no way of living but a mode of life', as he described it). His rural poems are full of images of derelict farmhouses and decaying roads that peter out in the bush; but reflections on the human condition are never far away from the descriptions of the countryside, so that the life of the land and the lives of people are woven together. In such poems, whose sensitivity towards the natural world strangely balances the deliberate artificiality of his fiction, Glassco combines a true joy in beauty with a sense of the pathetic in human existence—a sense of loss stirred by his reading of history and literature and his experience of a rural Quebec that time had passed over and left neglected. But not all Glassco's poems are bucolic. Some provide a link with his prose by moving into the mythology of literature and history: 'The death of Don Quixote' and 'Brummel at Calais' show Glassco as a master of echoes, and of parody and pastiche in the best sense; they evoke the philosophy of the nineteenth-century dandy and decadent (Brummel, Baudelaire, Wilde) that is also evident in his prose writings.

Glassco compiled the anthology *English poetry in Quebec* (1965), which grew out of a poetry conference held at Foster in 1963. In addition to translating poetry, he also translated three novels from French Canada: *Lot's wife* (*La femme de Loth*, 1975) by Monique BOSCO, *Creature of the chase* (*Un dieu chasseur*, 1979) by Jean-Yves Soucy, and *Fear's folly* (*Les demi-civilisés*, 1982) by Jean-Charles HARVEY.

See two articles in CANADIAN LITERATURE—Charles Murdoch, 'Essential Glassco' (Issue 65, Summer 1975), and Leon EDEL, 'John Glassco (1909-1981) and his erotic muse' (Issue 93, Summer 1982)—and *Ellipse* 14/15 (1974), which is devoted to the poetry of Glassco and Alain GRANDBOIS. See also *Canadian Poetry*, no. 13, Fall/Winter 1983, an issue devoted to Glassco, and Philip Kokotailo, *John Glassco's richer world: Memoirs of Montparnasse* (1988).

GEORGE WOODCOCK/WILLIAM TOYE

Glengarry school days (1902). A collection of loosely interrelated sketches by Charles William GORDON, who used the pseudonym 'Ralph Connor', *Glengarry school days: a story of early days in Glengarry*, is memorable for its depiction of typical one-room-schoolhouse events—a spelling bee, the annual examination, a game of shinny—drawn from Gordon's childood memories of Glengarry, Ontario's easternmost county, in the 1860s.

In the opening sketches we meet Archie Munro, teacher at the 'Twentieth' school, a man who daily conquers the physical pain of an old injury, and is an uplifting example of self-mastery. The teachers who succeed him—a brutal bully, several weaklings, and a cynical occasional drunk—fail to stir the students to do their best academically and morally. But the last teacher, John Craven, gradually becomes a worthy successor to Munro under the influence of the book's powerful inculcator of moral values, the Presbyterian minister's wife, Mrs Murray. Her example, and that of Mrs Finch, gently civilize and inspire boys and men alike.

Glengarry school days has been reprinted frequently over the years, in both Canada and the United States, and is available in the NEW CANADIAN LIBRARY (1993).

JUDITH SKELTON GRANT

Glover, Douglas (b. 1948). He was born in Simcoe, Ontario, and raised on a tobacco farm in Waterford, Ontario. He studied at York University, Toronto (B.A., 1969), and the University of Edinburgh (M. Litt., 1971), then taught for a year at the University of New Brunswick. He worked as a reporter on several Canadian newspapers. Between jobs, he lived in Scotland and the USA. He obtained a Master of Fine Arts degree at the Iowa Writers' Workshop in 1982. In 1988 he made a four-city tour of the Soviet Union at the invitation of the Soviet Writers' Union. He has been writer-in-residence at numerous universities in the USA, and has taught creative writing at workshops across Canada.

In 1986 four of Glover's stories appeared in *First fictions*, Faber & Faber's prestigious anthology (U.K.). His stories have also appeared in *Best Canadian stories* in 1985, 1987, and 1988, and in *The Journey Prize anthology* (1990). Between 1991 and 1995 he co-edited the Oberon annual anthology of emerging authors, *Coming attractions*; he is the editor of the 1996 and 1997 *Best Canadian short stories*.

As a short-story writer, Glover has astonishing virtuosity and superb language skills. His first collection, *The mad river* (1981), includes seven stories in a variety of settings ranging from contemporary Greece to ancient Rome. Exploring notions of good and evil, Glover has each of his characters come face to face with a moment of destiny. The stories in *Dog attempts to drown man in Saskatoon* (1985) are set apart from those of other writers of his generation by the sheer joy of craftsmanship. The title story, about a man and his marital separation, becomes a postmodern metafiction of confused identities. *A guide to animal behaviour* (1991) shows even greater breadth of imagination in its eleven stories. Glover's penetrating insight, inventiveness, and quick mood changes explore the ephemeral nature of the self, often in danger of disintegrating in the reality of human suffering. His character studies include gay women, a seventeenth-century missionary artist, and a mentally ill homeless man who lives in a box on the street.

Glover's first novel, *Precious* (1984), was a finalist for the W.H. Smith/*Books in Canada* First Novel Award. His second, *The south will rise at noon* (1988), is an unconvincing, though often entertaining comic novel set in Florida about a drug addict and anti-intellectual drifter on the set of a Hollywood film epic about the Civil War. *The life and times of Captain N.* (1993) is a triumph of energetic and visual prose. Glover's short-story experiments with historical settings, the dislocated sense of self, and the emphasis on myth over reason all appear in this dark, funny, violent, historical novel that teems with twentieth-century anxieties. Set on the Niagara frontier in the later years (1779-80) of the American Revolution, Glover uses a variety of voices to tell the story of Captain Hendrick Nellis, his son Oskar, and Mary Hunsraker, a German immigrant girl kidnapped by the Mississauga Amerindians who embraces their life-style, eventually becoming a medicine woman. The shifting narratives, dreamlike visions, and different voices eventually merge as one to capture brilliantly different ways of looking at the world, one's place in it, and especially the conflict between European and Native viewpoints.

See Louis K. MacKendrick, 'The fictions of Douglas Glover: a preliminary survey', *CANADIAN FICTION MAGAZINE* 65 (1989).

GEOFF HANCOCK

Godbout, Jacques (b. 1933). Born in Montreal, Quebec, he studied under the Jesuits at Collège Brébeuf. After obtaining an M.A. in French literature from the Université de Montréal in 1954 (with a thesis on Arthur Rimbaud), he taught from 1954 to 1957 at the University College of Addis Ababa, Ethiopia, returning to Montreal to work as film director and script writer for the National Film Board, where he remained. In 1960 he was one of the founders of *LIBERTÉ*, a literary review that he edited for a time. He was also a founder of the Mouvement laïque de langue française in 1962, and in 1977 of the Quebec writers' union, of which he was the first president.

Godbout's three volumes of poetry—*Carton-pâte* (1956), *Les pavés secs* (1958), and *C'est la chaude loi des hommes* (1960), all of which are collected with a radio essay in *Souvenirs shop* (1985)—introduce the reader to an ironic world where global anxiety in the age of the atomic bomb makes love difficult. The tension between the private and public domains and the use of irony and intellectual pyrotechnics to control and mask emotion are characteristics of both his poetry and his fiction. As Godbout himself has often stated, the evolution of his novels, from *L'aquarium* (1962) to *Le temps des Galarneau* (1993), consciously parallels the evolution of Quebec society on the level of language, ideology, and myth. He has been a perceptive reader of the tensions and directions of Quebec, from 'Américanité' through *JOUAL* and feminism to the post-Referendum split in the Quebec psyche.

Godbout's first novel, *L'aquarium*, has no precise location in time or space, but is narrated with a clearly allegorical motif, recording the perceptions of a group of passive foreigners in a Third World country on the brink of revolution. Clearly inspired by the author's African experience, it can also be seen as a symbolic interpretation of Quebec on the verge of the Quiet Revolution. It was awarded the Prix France-Canada. *Le couteau sur la table* (1965)—translated by Penny Williams as *Knife on the table* (1968)—continues the allegory of *L'aquarium*, recounting the outer and inner journeys through Canada and the United States of a nameless Québécois narrator as he seeks to link his identity with the garish artificiality of Disneyland décors and the repressed puritanical atmosphere of the CPR towns of western Canada. These journeys lead finally to a break with his English-Canadian mistress, Patricia, and to a suggestion that Quebec's identity may perhaps be achieved only through violence. Godbout claimed that the novel was conceived as a love story, but changed direction when the FLQ bombings began in 1963.

SALUT GALARNEAU! (1967)—translated by Alan Brown as *Hail Galarneau!* (1970)—is Godbout's most successful novel, largely because of the irrepressible humour and humanity of its central character, who provides a satiric and immensely funny view of Quebec's economic and language problems and its domination by an America that it loves. It received a Governor General's Award. *D'Amour, P.Q.* (1972) looks at the then-controversial question of *joual* and its relation to classical French. The novel consists of three versions of a novel written by Thomas D'Amour, a priggish intellectual whose language and themes bear little relation to Quebec reality. He takes his manuscript to two secretaries, who speak respectively a literary and a vulgar version of Quebec working-class French. The secretaries succeed in transforming D'Amour's novel, in dominating his life, and in getting him into bed, where the final version of the novel is produced. In *L'île au dragon* (1976)—translated as *Dragon Island* (1979) by David Ellis—the central images are of global pollution and destruction that threaten the mind as well as the planet, and of a Quebec that is slowly succumbing to the vulgarities of the American way of life. Michel Beauparlant, a writer and a modern version of Saint Michael the Archangel, confronts his dragon in the form of William T. Shaheen, Jr, an American capitalist who has bought the island Beauparlant lives on in order to use it as a site for atomic waste.

After five years of silence, due to the 'static' of the 1980 referendum period, Godbout returned to the literary scene in 1981 with *Les têtes à Papineau*, a breezy analysis of Quebec's cultural duality that tells the story of a two-headed monster, Charles-François Papineau. Charles is conservative, anglophile, and somewhat melancholy; François is a man of action, French in his tastes, and full of *joie de vivre*. The two finally agree to an operation by an English-Canadian surgeon, who joins the left lobe of Charles's brain to the right lobe of François's. Unfortunately, the doctor's computers fail to locate the French-speaking ability in the left side of François's brain and the operation produces a one-headed English-speaker who signs himself Charles F. Papineau. Although it is one of the funniest Quebec novels of the period, as a comment on the struggle between René Lévesque and Pierre Trudeau for Quebec's allegiance it is very pessimistic.

Une histoire américaine (1986)—translated as *An American story* by Yves Saint-Pierre (1988)—refocuses attention on the pervasiveness of American culture, and on the marginalization of the French language in North America in the aftermath of the 1980 Referendum. Godbout employs parallel narratives—a lengthy written despositon in journal style by Gregory Francoeur (son of an Irish tennis star and a Québécois Larousse salesman), and a third-person narrative that fills in the missing information. While this is Godbout's most serious novel since *Le couteau sur la table*, it also revisits many themes, including the search for happiness, the reconciliation of First and Third World realities, and the threat of apocalypse. Godbout's wry humour returns in *Le temps des Galarneau*, a sequel to *Salut Galarneau!*. After release from a psychiatric hospital, François goes from job to job (including one in a library, which he loses for reading too much) before becoming a security guard at a shopping mall. The mall comes to symbolize the merging of media and human realities, as when customers mistake a real robbery for the filming of a Hollywood-style action scene. Despite a relatively 'normal' life (for a Galarneau), including *mariage blanc* to a Cambodian refugee, François ultimately decides that he belongs in a sunnier climate; he steals a collection of ancient eastern erotica to pay for his new life in French Guiana.

Although more recognized as a novelist, much of Godbout's best work appears in his essays and film documentaries. While his themes do not change, he is able to probe them more deeply. The social and political relevance of artists (of all varieties) in a consumer-driven society is central to the essay collection *Le réformiste* (1975), the journal *Écrivain de province* (1991), and the documentaries *Les dieux* (1960), *Paul-Émile Borduas* (1962), and *Deux épisodes dans la vie d'Hubert Aquin* (1977). The dangers of a society saturated by market and media are themes in the essay collections *Le murmure marchand* (1984) and *L'écran du bonheur* (1990). Finally, the role of a French-speaking society in North America, as well as its share in the 'American dream', are examined in the documentaries *Alias Will James* (1988), *Le mouton noir* (1992), and *Le sort de l'Amérique* (1966).

See André Smith, *L'univers romanesque de Jacques Godbout* (1976), and Jacques Pelletier, *Le roman national: essais: néo-nationalisme et roman québécois contemporain* (1991), and Valéry Raoul, *Distinctly narcissistic* (1993).

See also NOVELS IN FRENCH 1960 TO 1982: 1, 3.

PATRICIA SMART/STEVEN J. DANIELL

Godfrey, Dave (b. 1938). Born in Winnipeg, Manitoba, he spent most of his early years in rural Ontario. After brief attendance at the University of Toronto, he did undergraduate and graduate work in the USA, receiving a B.A. (1960) from the University of Iowa, an M.A. (1961) from Stanford University, an M.F.A. (1963) in creative writing from the University of Iowa, and a Ph.D. in English (1967) from Iowa. Under the auspices of the Canadian University Service Overseas (CUSO), Godfrey served as acting head of the English department of Adisadel College, Cape Coast, Ghana, from 1963 to 1965. On returning to Canada from Iowa in 1966 he taught English at Trinity College, University of Toronto; was writer-in-residence at its Erindale College (1973-4); joined the creative-writing program of York University, Toronto, in 1977; and in 1978 was named chair of the creative-writing department of the University of Victoria, where he currently teaches.

Godfrey has been a major force in Canadian publishing and a strong advocate of nationalist policies. With Dennis LEE he co-founded the important literary press, House of ANANSI, in 1967. In 1969, hoping that a broad spectrum of Canadian titles might have a larger cultural impact than the purely literary, he joined with James BACQUE and Roy McSkimming to found another Toronto publishing house, New Press. He worked as general editor of McCLELLAND & STEWART's Canadian Writers series from 1968 to 1972 and was fiction editor of *The CANADIAN FORUM* in 1971-2. In 1973 he joined the editorial board of the *Journal of Canadian Fiction*, became founding director of the Association for the Export of Canadian Books; and, having separated himself from both House of Anansi and New Press, founded PRESS PORCÉPIC in 1973, a literary press that he and his wife Ellen GODFREY continued to operate until the early 1990s, when it merged with Beach Holme Publishing. He co-edited with the nationalist economist Mel Watkins *Gordon to Watkins to you, documentary: the battle for control of our economy* (1970), and with Robert FULFORD and Abraham Rotstein he co-edited *Read Canadian; a book about Canadian books* (1972), a polemical appeal for more action to promote Canadian book publication. Since the late 1970s Godfrey has devoted himself to the cultural implications of microcomputer technology, and has argued that the decentralization of data-banks and computer communications is essential for both the regional and national well-being of Canadian art and literature. With Douglas Parkhill he co-edited *Gutenberg two* (1979), a pioneering investigation of the social and political meaning of new electronic technologies; and with Ernest Chang he co-authored *The Telidon book* (1981), a guide to the technological requirements and social implications of videotext and electronic publishing. In the 1980s he founded a software development company, Softwords, in order to investigate a shift from print to electronic text distribution. He co-authored with Sharon Sterling *The elements of CAL* [computer-assisted learning] (1982), and co-edited with Jack Brahan *Computer-aided learning using the NATAL language* (1984).

As significant and valuable as his teaching and publishing activities have been, Godfrey's fiction—first published in Issue 19 of *The TAMARACK REVIEW* (1961): 'River Two Blind Jacks'—has been an even greater accomplishment. *Death goes better with Coca-Cola* (1967), his first collection of stories, is noteworthy for its subtle techniques of juxtaposed narratives and its symbolic use of the kitsch of American popular culture to depict the greed and latent violence of twentieth-century man. His only novel, *The new ancestors* (1970), which won a Governor General's Award, juxtaposes four different temporal perspectives of the same events to create an Einsteinian vision of relative values. Although this novel is set in Ghana, its principal content is its depiction of human experience as relative, non-linear, and atemporal.

Godfrey moved even further from conventional realism in *I Ching Kanada* (1976) and *Dark must yield* (1978), a collection of fifteen stories. *I Ching Kanada*—a prose meditation that takes the hexagrams of the traditional *I Ching* as its starting-point—is composed in images, often merely noun phrases: each meditation focuses on culture, showing how culture, born of mother and hearth, grows to become country. *Dark must yield* offers stories that blend different voices and blur expected distinctions between story and essay, story and autobiography. Their effect resides not in narrative or characterization but in the inferences a reader can draw from the juxtapositions and contrasts of voice; these stories insist that the ultimate ground of political sovereignty lies in individual consciousness.

See Calvin L. Smiley, 'Godrey's progess', *CANADIAN LITERATURE* 75 (Winter 1977), and Alan Twigg, 'Dave Godfrey: "I'm quite hopeful about the demise of some areas of publishing"', *Quill & Quill* 47 (April 1981).

See also NOVELS IN ENGLISH 1960 TO 1982: 3.

FRANK DAVEY

Godfrey, Ellen (b. 1942). Ellen Swartz was born in Chicago and received a B.A. from Stanford University, California, where she met Dave GODFREY, whom she married. They live in Victoria, British Columbia, where she is President of Softwords Research International, a computer software firm. Through Beach Holme Publishers, successor to PRESS PORCÉPIC, which she helped found in 1976, she published the first *Tesseracts* anthology (edited by Judith MERRIL, 1985). Dave and Ellen Godfrey were also principals in the founding of House of ANANSI press in Toronto in 1967.

A champion of genre fiction, Ellen Godfrey has written four mystery novels. *Murder among the well to do* (1976) and *The case of the cold murderer* (1978) feature Rebecca Rosenthal, a dauntless Jewish widow who in her early seventies solves family-related murders in Toronto and environs with vigour and a certain valiant élan. While somewhat forced at times and overly dependent on the mechanics of the 'locked room' syndrome, these novels are interesting for their portrayal of a gallant, aged detective figure who does yoga for fitness and mental health, shops for expensive clothes when stressed, and observes those younger with mordant wit—as well as for the somewhat acerbic portrayal in the second novel of the start-up of a small publishing house in Toronto in the early 1970s. *Murder behind locked doors* (1988), a classic puzzler in which an executive is cleverly murdered in a locked computer room, and *Georgia disappeared* (1992), involving the murder of a friend in a client firm, feature Jane Tregar, a corporate headhunter in the computer software industry. These novels are notable for their realistic treatment of Canadian corporate life and competitiveness, as well as for their depiction of the insecurities and costs associated with life at the executive level for single urban career women who fear they may lose the very jobs they have sacrificed so much to attain.

Godfrey has also written *By reason of doubt: the Belshaw case* (1982), which won an Edgar award from the Mystery Writers of America and is the non-fiction account of the murder of Betty Belshaw (wife of world-renowned University of British Columbia anthropology professor Cyril Belshaw), who disappeared in Paris and was found dead in the Swiss Alps.

MARILYN ROSE

Godin, Gérald (1938-94). Born in Trois-Rivières, Quebec, he dropped out of school to work as a proof-reader for the newspaper *Le Nouvelliste*. Later he was employed as a reporter for *Le Nouveau Journal* in Montreal and as a researcher for the Radio-Canada daily news-commentary program *Aujourd'hui*. An early contributor to *PARTI PRIS*, he was for a time editor of the magazine and director of Les Éditions Parti Pris. In the Parti Québécois sweep of 1976 he was elected to the Quebec National Assembly in Robert Bourassa's old riding of Mercier. Re-elected in 1981, he became Minister of Cultural Communities and Immigration with responsibility for all aspects, except education, of Bill 101, Quebec's language law.

As well as contributing satirical short stories and polemical articles to *parti pris*, Godin published eight volumes of poetry: *Chansons très naïves* (1960), *Poèmes et cantos* (1962), *Nouveaux poèmes* (1963), *Les cantouques* (1967), *Libertés surveillées* (1975), *Soirs sans atout* (1986), translated by Judith Cowan as *Evenings at loose ends* (1991), *Ils ne demandent qu'à brûler: poèmes 1960-1986* (1987), and *Les botterlots: poésie* (1993). Like other writers of the *parti pris* group, he made considerable use of *JOUAL*, calling this 'a sort of literary sit-in'—a way of using what he saw as the degradation of the French language in Canada as an instrument of revolution. Most of his poetry, however, is personal rather than political in the narrow sense. There are ironic or wrily tender love poems, mocking glances at some of his fellow-revolutionaries and at the contradictions in his own mental processes, much gaiety and exuberance, and a sheer delight in words; his rage on behalf of such victims of social injustice as lumberjacks and city slum-dwellers is never brutal. A true poet with a marvellous sense of language and its possibilities, Godin was unique among younger French-Canadian writers for his balance and good humour.

Godin also published a novel, *Ange exterminé* (1991)—translated by Judith Cowan as *Exterminated angel* (1992)—a bogus detective story with political overtones, set in Montreal of the 1970s, that is also a high-spirited romp full of jokes and word-plays but in no way equal to the poetry. In *Traces pour une autobiographie: écrits et parlés I and II* (1994) André Gervais has used Godin's own words—in articles and interviews—to provide a loose history of his personal and political life. Particularly moving and honest are Godin's discussion of the brain cancer from which he suffered during his last years.

English translations of some of Godin's poems were published in *Ellipse* 1 and 45 and in John GLASSCO's *The poetry of French Canada in translation* (1970). Malcolm Reid's discussion of Godin as poet and political thinker in *The shouting signpainters* (1972) includes English renderings of two poems.

JOYCE MARSHALL

Golden Dog, The (1877). William KIRBY's historical romance, set in New France in 1748, first appeared in the United States (Rouses Point, New York, 1877) without copyright and was pirated a year later by a New York publisher. An 'authorized' edition, with corrections and changes by Kirby and some cutting by the publisher, appeared in Boston in 1896 and was reprinted frequently; its title was *The Golden Dog (Le Chien d'or): a romance of the days of Louis Quinze in Quebec.*

The plot's romantic entanglements involve the passion of the hotheaded seigneur and army officer Le Gardeur de Repentigny for the faithless Angélique, who is bent on seducing the corrupt Intendant Bigot and thus becoming the most powerful woman in the colony. Another affair involves the love of Le Gardeur's virtuous sister Amélie for Pierre Philibert, son of the honest proprietor of the 'Golden Dog' trading firm. A chronicle in the tradition of Scott and Dumas *père*, Kirby's novel includes ambition, greed, deception, passion, and murder within a Gothic setting, and in a New France that here seems more European than North American. Rather than the New World forest Gothic of John RICHARDSON's *WACOUSTA* (1832), *The Golden Dog* features the castellated Gothic of the Old, with aristocratic villains, a witch, and a mysterious female locked within a château's vault. It is a historical romance of its time: the setting is idealized, the dialogue high-flown, the sentiments inflated, the plot fraught with coincidence. Yet even in the abridged form in which it was formerly read in the NEW CANADIAN LIBRARY—it is now available in the NCL complete, with an Afterword by James REANEY, and is forthcoming from the CENTRE FOR EDITING EARLY CANADIAN TEXTS series—the tale held interest as a sweeping account of human perversity that exemplified a cultural strategy for enfolding Quebec's history within that of anglophone Canada.

A visit to Quebec City in the summer of 1865 prompted Kirby to begin the novel, which he took pains to research. James Le Moine's *Maple leaves* (7 vols, 1863-1906)—compilations of history, legend, and oral traditions—provided Kirby with much of the historical background that he altered to suit his story. The historical Angélique Péan, wife of the adjutant and mistress of Bigot, suggested Kirby's temptress. The criminal known as 'La Corriveau', hanged in 1763 for murdering her husband, becomes a professional poisoner in Kirby. Both killer and victim, Le Gardeur and the *bourgeois* Philibert, were historical figures. The title comes from a stone bas-relief that appeared on the front of Philibert's house: a dog with a bone in its paws sits above the motto that Kirby translates as: 'I am a dog that gnaws his bone,/I couch and gnaw it all alone—/A time will come, which is not yet,/When I'll bite him by whom I'm bit!' The stonework can still be found on a post office that now commands the corner of Côte de la Montagne and rue Buade. It was probably put there long before Philibert's time, and may be a copy of a French original; for Kirby its promise of retribution conveniently epitomized the fate that overtakes all in his story.

Kirby's sense of Canadian history was a thoroughly colonial one. His Loyalist ancestry and his allegiance prompted him to figure a Canada in which the triumph of British institutions actually preserved post-Conquest Quebec from the excesses of the *ancien régime* in New France. The Victorian tendency to blame the French Revolution on the immorality of the governing class is here played out upon a New World stage. According to Kirby's Epilogue, the two Canadas shared a virtue in common—loyalty: betrayed by its former imperial masters (European corruption versus colonial innocence is a motif here), Quebec remained loyal to the Empire during both the American Revolution and the War of 1812. This moral foundation, in Kirby's view, at once united Canada and validated anglophone hegemony.

DENNIS DUFFY

Goldsmith, Oliver (1794-1861). Born in Saint Andrews, New Brunswick, he grew up in the Annapolis Valley and subsequently worked for the commissariat of the British army in Halifax (1810-33), Saint John (1833-44), Hong Kong (1844-8), and Newfoundland (1848-53). He retired to England and died at his sister's home in Liverpool.

Goldsmith's literary career was brief and limited: his narrative poem *The rising village* was published in London in 1825 and reprinted in Saint John in 1834 with some revisions and a few additional short lyrics; an *Autobiography*, found in family papers, was edited by W.E. Myatt and published in 1943, new edition 1985. The narrative of *The rising village* describes the stages of growth in frontier life: the first building, the coming of other settlers, the addition of communal institutions and occupations that shape village life, and the emotional conflicts that come with social interaction and that form the folk history of the settlement.

Goldsmith has been acclaimed as the first native-born poet to publish a volume of verse, but a biographical curiosity has attracted more attention than the poem: the fact that he was the grandnephew of the popular Irish novelist, dramatist, and poet Oliver Goldsmith, author of *The vicar of Wakefield* (1766) and *The deserted village* (1770). The obsession of commentators with this relationship, which the author himself promoted, has tended to deflect critical attention from the poem itself. Contemporary British reviewers were generally disappointed with *The rising village* in comparison with *The deserted village*; Canadian reviewers, flattered and delighted by the connection, tended to be over-complimentary to the younger Goldsmith. In both cases the shadow of the elder Goldsmith distorted appreciation of the inherent intention and value of the Canadian poem. Recent critical readings have also been plagued by the Goldsmith connection, but have generally interpreted the meaning of the poem in terms of its apparent relationship to the social and political development of colonial Nova Scotia in the 1820s and 1830s. This approach, however, tends to exaggerate the intellectual complexity of the poem by implicitly giving an allegorical or ironic intention to what is ostensibly a straightforward expository narrative. Such readings do not take into account the fact that the poem, originally published in London, was designed for a British audience for whom veiled allegorical or ironic subtleties would mean nothing. Both British and colonial readers would have grasped that the central subject of the poem was the settlement and civilizing of a wilderness area, that the heart of this experience lay in nurturing right human values (virtue) in a physical environment that was ill-suited and even hostile to their sustenance, and that the virtue invested in communal life was always vulnerable to corruption, not only from external circumstances but from internal weakness as well. Striving for civilized life while recognizing its essential vulnerability was elemental to appreciating the drama of colonial experience and is, not surprisingly, a deep-rooted theme in colonial Canadian literature.

Gerald Lynch has edited a modern reprint of *The rising village* (1989). See also K.J. Hughes, 'Oliver Goldsmith's "The rising village"', *Canadian Poetry* 1 (1977); W.J. Keith, 'The Rising Village again', *Canadian Poetry* 3 (1978); and G. Lynch, 'Oliver Goldsmith's *The rising village*: controlling nature', *Canadian Poetry* 7 (1980).

TOM VINCENT

Goose Lane Editions. See FIDDLEHEAD POETRY BOOKS.

Gordon, Alison (b. 1943). She was born in New York City, the daughter of pioneering socialist and international-relations expert King Gordon and granddaughter of the well-known novelist Charles GORDON (Ralph Connor). She attended Queen's University (Kingston, Ontario) from 1960 to 1965, leaving without a degree, and spend many years working for CBC radio and television as a program assistant, producer, and host. In 1979 she joined the *Toronto Star* as a sportswriter. Her experiences covering the Toronto Blue Jays between 1979 and 1983 are recounted in her first book, *Foul balls: five years in the American League* (1984), a perceptive work that reveals the author's passionate knowledge of baseball and much about the Jays during their formative years. Gordon has also written a series of mystery novels featuring sportswriter and amateur sleuth Kate Henry. In the first of these, *The dead pull hitter* (1988), Henry investigates murder, drugs, and blackmail surrounding the fictional Toronto Titans in the heat of a pennant race. It has been followed by three other baseball novels: *Safe at home* (1990), *Night game* (1992), and *Striking out* (1995). While Gordon's novels lack the intricate plots of classic whodunits, they skilfully evoke the sometimes clashing worlds of journalism and baseball. COLIN BOYD

Gordon, Charles William (1860-1937). Canada's first best-selling author, who published under the pseudonym 'Ralph Connor', was born in Glengarry County, Canada West (now Ontario), the son of the Presbyterian minister Daniel Gordon and Mary Robertson. In 1883 he completed a B.A. in classics and English at the University of Toronto. After graduating from Knox College in 1887, he spent a year at the University of Edinburgh, was ordained in the Presbyterian ministry in 1890, and became Doctor of Divinity in 1906. At a loss after his mother's death in 1890, he found his feet during nearly four years as a missionary to the miners, lumbermen, and ranchers around Banff, Alberta, and spent another year in Scotland raising money for church missions in western Canada. In 1894 he accepted a call from the west-end mission in Winnipeg, which became St Stephen's Church the following year and was his charge until he retired in 1924. In 1899 he married Helen Skinner King, daughter of the Rev. John M. King; they had one son and six daughters. As president of the Social Service Council of Manitoba, he was a prominent advocate of temperance in the years before the Great War. He accompanied the 43rd Cameron Highlanders to war in 1915 as their chaplain (some 350 of them were from his own congregation); he then became senior Protestant chaplain to the Canadian forces. In 1917 he was sent on a lecture tour to present the Allied view of the war to Americans. From 1920 to 1922 he chaired the highly successful Manitoba Joint Council of Industry, which mediated labour disputes after the Winnipeg General Strike of 1919. Generously unsectarian in his views, as moderator of the Presbyterian Church in 1921-2 he helped move the Presbyterians towards union with the Methodists and Congregationalists: this was realized in 1925 by the creation of the United Church of Canada.

Seeking support for the church's western missions, Gordon wrote several fictional sketches drawing on his missionary experience for the Toronto-based Presbyterian magazine *The Westminster*. They so delighted editor and readers that he was asked for more, and again more. The series was collected as *Black Rock: a tale of the Selkirks* (Toronto, 1898); its immediate success in Canada and the United States established him as an author. The pattern thus set—a serial run in *The Westminster*, followed by a book for the Christmas market—persisted through the publication in 1912 of *Corporal Cameron of the North West Mounted Police: a tale of the Macleod Trail*. Gordon had intended to use 'Cannor' (the middle syllables of Brit. *Can. Nor.* West Mission) as his pseudonym, but the telegraph operator who forwarded the name to *The Westminster* changed it to 'Connor'.

In Gordon's stories principle always wins through in the end. And although he often refers to God and Providence, his religion is human-centred, dependent on the ability of the individual to master his will. For Gordon, 'good' means acting in the interests of family and community; 'evil' is, at base, a selfish disregard of others. To live fruitful lives individuals must find the will to control their personal desires (for wealth, alcohol, violence) and withstand temptations to act selfishly. Often his characters endure physical pain silently and continue to remain effective in the role assigned to them in the community: self-control and self-abnegation are their chief virtues. However, Gordon's action-packed plots also allow ample opportunity for the display of physical courage, as much a part of a Connor hero as the more-important moral courage. Like many earlier Victorian writers, Gordon deliberately stirred his readers' softer emotions with scenes of pathos; like them, he appeared to find these morally valuable. Tapping a broad audience that read gospel fiction like Charles M. Sheldon's popular *In his steps: 'What would Jesus do?'* (1897), Connor wrote for the many readers who liked their fiction to combine adventure, lively characterization, and Christian uplift.

Gordon's popularity as a writer peaked early. His publishers sold five million copies of his first three books—*Black Rock, The sky pilot: a tale of the foothills* (Toronto, 1899), and *The man from Glengarry: a tale of the Ottawa* (1901); while the quarter-million first printing of his minor classic *GLENGARRY SCHOOL DAYS: a story of early days in Glengarry* (1902) was followed by immediate reprintings in Canada, the United States, and Britain. *Gwen's canyon* (Toronto, 1899: chapters 11 to 13 of *The sky pilot*) and *Gwen: an idyll of the canyon* (New York, 1899 and 1904: chapters 9 to 13) were also popular. Though his later novels sold well, their sales never achieved the heady heights of those early volumes.

In *Black Rock* and *The sky pilot* Gordon discovered the subject that focused his energies as a novelist until the Great War (and in two later books): the frontier. This provided colourful figures—cowboys, ranchers, shantymen, who were involved in drinking, gambling, and fighting. He typically confronts them with a civilizing agent—a minister (a 'sky pilot'), a doctor, schoolmaster, policeman, or good woman—who returns them to the structures and controls of civilization. The anarchy that is brought within bounds is both within and without, and each story climaxes in both self-mastery and the creation of a stable, caring community. The battle is bodied forth at least once in each story in a game or contest demanding skill, courage, and principle. The description of the football game between Varsity and McGill in *The prospector: a tale of the Crow's Nest Pass* (1904) is a fine example of Gordon's vigorous handling of such contests. In 1908 Gordon also wrote *The life of James Robertson: missionary superintendent in Western Canada*, a biography (almost a hagiography) of the man who challenged him to go to the western mission field. The superintendent hovers in the background of a number of Gordon's books, including *The doctor: a tale of the Rockies* (1906). Of the remaining western books—*The pilot at Swan Creek and other stories* (1905), *The foreigner: a tale of Saskatchewan* (1909), *Corporal Cameron*, its lacklustre sequel *The patrol of the Sun Dance Trail* (1914), and *The Gaspards of Pine Croft: a romance of the Windermere* (1923)—only *The foreigner* has any distinction. Powerfully portraying the sordid boarding-house life of Slavic immigrants on the outskirts of Winnipeg in the 1880s, it then follows a lad to a farm in Saskatchewan, where he gradually substitutes a 'Canadian' (orderly, socially responsible, abstemious, patient, tolerant) for an 'Old World' (disorderly, exploitative, drunken, violent, wildly passionate) conception of manhood.

Gordon's three remaining frontier books are set in the East and draw on his experience as a young boy in Glengarry, the easternmost county in Ontario, and on his parents' earlier experience ministering to pioneers. *The man from Glengarry* traces the development of Ranald Macdonald into a man of self-control and principle whose energies are thrown into the struggle to civilize the West and make it part of Canada. It describes such pioneer rituals as a sugaring-off, a wake, and a logging bee, and like Gordon's other frontier stories, makes lively use of the dialect of his French-Canadian, Irish, and Scots characters. *Glengarry school days* is about the teaching of self-mastery, while the later and slighter *Torches through the bush* (1934) focuses on a Presbyterian revival in the early 1860s. Gordon's mother appears in all three Glengarry books, disguised as the saintly Mrs Murray; and judging by his portrait of her in *Postscript to adventure: the autobiography of Ralph Connor* (1938; revised and introduced by Gordon's son, J. King Gordon), she is the informing spirit behind many other idealized women in his early books.

The Great War redirected Gordon's energies. Fearing that the fight for freedom might be lost because of the apathy he found at home when on leave, he wrote *The major* (1917) to stimulate afresh the enthusiasm that carried men overseas in 1914. (The second chapter of *The major* appeared separately as *A fight for freedom* in 1917.) But his most emotionally powerful war book is *The sky pilot in no man's land* (1919). It begins with a vivid description of the beauty of a young, fit male body as the novel's young padré, Barry Dunbar, dives nude from a rock during a camping trip. The meaning of this scene becomes clear during the book's keynote sermon, in which Dunbar, taking as his text Romans 12:1, tells a battalion of soldiers that their role is to offer clean, fit bodies as a sacrifice to God. The overplotted *Treading the wine press* (1925), concerning Canadian naval actions during the war, is much less effective.

Several novels sprang from Gordon's involvement in industrial disputes and from his concern with the moral issues raised by the stock-market crash in 1929. *To him that hath: a novel of the West today* (1921) articulates the positions of labour and management during a strike, but fails to resolve the problems it raises. Three novels concerned with the stock market, either alone or in combination with labour problems—*The arm of gold* (1932), *The girl from Glengarry* (1933), and *The gay crusader* (1936)—combine oversimplified economics with potboiler romance.

Historical novels were likewise not Gordon's strength. Though more interesting than his industrial or economic novels, they sink under the weight of historical explanation and detail. *The runner: a romance of the Niagaras* (1929) examines crosscurrents in the American, Indian, and Canadian scene before and during the War of 1812 as they affected Upper Canada, with Tecumseh and General Brock as central figures. Brock reappears in *The rock and the river: a romance of Quebec* (1931), which explores attitudes and events in Lower Canada in the same period, while *The rebel Loyalist* (1935) is concerned with Loyalist activities during the American War of Independence.

Gordon published several books and stories that amplify incidents in the life of Christ. These are *The angel and the star* (1908), *The dawn by Galilee: a story of the Christ* (1909), *The recall of love* (1910), *The friendly four and other stories* (1926), and *He dwelt among us* (1936). *Christian hope* (n.d.) is a sermon on that subject, while the pamphlet *The colporteur* (n.d.) is noteworthy for its critical attitude towards the Catholic Church in Quebec—a surprising departure from Gordon's generally liberal position towards churches other than his own.

Gordon's writing has attracted critical interest for his views on religion, imperialism, women, labour, and Canada's Native peoples. It has been seen on the whole, in its efforts to define English Canada's identity, as rising above the 'sentimentality and triteness' that mar some of the individual novels. See, for example, *A social gospel for millions: the religious bestsellers of Charles Sheldon, Charles Gordon, and Harold Bell Wright* (1988) by John P. Ferré; 'Blessed are the peacemakers: the labour question in Canadian social gospel fiction', *Journal of Canadian Studies* 10, no. 3 (Aug. 1975), by M.Vipond; and 'Ralph Connor and the Canadian identity' by J. Lee Thompson and John H. Thompson in *Queen's Quarterly* 79 (Summer 1972). The short biography *Charles William Gordon* (1981) by Keith Wilson is authoritative. *Charles W. Gordon ('Ralph Connor') and his works* (1988) by John Lennox provides a useful overview.

The man from Glengarry (1993, Afterword by Alison Gordon) and *Glengarry school days* (1993, Afterword by John Lennox) are both available in the NEW CANADIAN LIBRARY. In the United States, Lightyear Press has kept *Black Rock*, *The doctor*, *The major*, *The man from Glengarry*, *The sky pilot*, and *The sky pilot in no man's land* on its list since 1976. In the same year Amereon Ltd added *The sky pilot* and *The sky pilot in no man's land* to its list. And in 1988 Sunrise Books published *Black Rock* and *The sky pilot* as *Jim Craig's battle for Black Rock* and *Thomas Skyler: foothills preacher*, both edited by Michael R. Phillips and both still in print.

JUDITH SKELTON GRANT

Gotlieb, Phyllis (b. 1926). Born in Toronto, Phyllis Fay Gotlieb (née Bloom) received her B.A. and M.A. from the University of Toronto. Her poetry, verse-dramas, short stories, and novels (mostly science fiction) demonstrate a strong interest in family relationships, historical roots, and the cultural implications of biological or technological possibilities. She contributed a paper, 'Hasidic influences in the work of A.M. KLEIN', to *The A.M. Klein Symposium* (1974) edited by Seymour MAYNE.

Gotlieb's chapbook *Who knows one* (1961) was followed by the collection *Within the Zodiac* (1964), which reprinted some of the earlier poems and announced Gotlieb's developed style: musicality, colloquialism, relish for detail, and affirmation of her Jewish heritage. *Ordinary, moving* (1969) was a Governor General's Award nominee. The title sequence, which ends the book, is constructed from folk verse, game songs, and jump-rope ditties; its locale is the school play-yard of all time and space, in any galaxy; its subject the human child, fortunate, suffering; it ends, as does the children's game, with '*and begin again*'. Louis Martz ('New books in review', *The Yale Review* LIX, 4 June 1970) called it a 'celebration and a lament for all the world's children, ourselves'.

Doctor Umlaut's earthly kingdom (1974) includes not only shorter poems (of which the elegy 'Jennie Gotlieb Bardikoff' is perhaps the most touching), but also most of the verse-drama commissioned by the CBC: 'Doctor Umlaut's earthly kingdom' (1966), 'Silent movie days' (1971), and 'Garden varieties' (1972), a 'miracle' play on the Creation and Noah's flood, with nuances of the music hall, Don Marquis, and Thornton Wilder. Another verse-drama, 'The contract', is included in the collected poetry, *The works* (1978), which does not, however, include a later verse-drama, also commissioned by the CBC: 'God on trial before Rabbi Ovadia' (1976). Good articles on Gotlieb's poetry are the Martz essay mentioned above and Douglas BARBOUR's 'A cornucopia of poems' in *The TAMARACK REVIEW* 76 (1979).

Gotlieb's novels are as richly moving as her poetry. *Why should I have all the grief?* (1969) portrays an Auschwitz survivor coping with a painful return to the contingencies of ordinary family life, while recalling and re-understanding his own father. (The best reviews are Janis RAPOPORT's 'The grief is shared', *The TAMARACK REVIEW* 54 (1970), and Anne Montagnes' 'Gotlieb's misery', *Saturday Night* 84 (May 1969).

Gotlieb's other novels, and her short stories, are science fiction. Both *Sunburst* (1964) and *O Master Caliban!* (1976) have been published internationally and translated into several languages. *Sunburst* deals with the problems for family and community of handling juvenile delinquents genetically cursed with telekinetic and telepathic powers. *O Master Caliban!* explores 'Dahlgren's world' of genetic mutation and semi-human machines in terms of the problems of adolescence and maturation. In *A judgement of dragons* (1980), a pair of telepathic cat Candides become educated in the ways of the past and present worlds (beginning with the ancestral village of the hero of *Why should I have all the grief?*). *Emperor, swords, pentacles* (1982) and *The kingdom of the cats* (1985) continue the cat saga. 'Dahlgren's world' is revisited in *Heart of red iron* (1989). A first collection of short stories, *Son of the morning and other stories*, appeared in 1983.

Ethical concern and an interest in psychology and the effects on culture of environmental contingency fuel Gotlieb's plots, but her novels, like her poetry, are primarily memorable for the colour and charm of their personae: the avuncular Montaigne-quoting goat and the huge red cats in *A judgment of dragons*, the floating genius-enfant-terrible in *O Master Caliban!* Her imagery is as magical as that of Chagall or Tchelitchew, and combines the fantastic and the mundane with Dickensian vigour. Gotlieb's primary effect is an expression of joy in the created universe. See also FANTASTIC LITERATURE IN ENGLISH: 2.

M. TRAVIS LANE

Goto, Hiromi. See NOVELS IN ENGLISH 1983 TO 1996.

Gough, Laurence (b. 1944). He lives in the Point Grey area of Vancouver and is at the front rank of the ever-growing coterie of crime writers resident in British Columbia. Canadians don't believe in lawmen as entrepreneurs, or in the hard-boiled private eye; they don't believe in privatizing justice. Hence, Canadian crime writers have tended towards the *roman policier*, the novel with the professional public eye, as exemplified by Gough's Vancouver police officers Jack Willows and Claire Parker. Gough won two Arthur Ellis Awards from the Crime Writers of Canada for *The goldfish bowl* (1987) and *Hot shots* (1989). Between these two novels he published *Death on a #8 hook* (1988; American title *Silent knives*). Other titles are *Serious crimes* (1990); *Accidental deaths* (1991); *Fall down easy* (1992); *Killers* (1993), in which a prominent marine biologist is found afloat in the killer whale pool at the Vancouver civic aquarium; *Heartbreaker* (1995), with the detectives pitted against a pretty-boy petty thief and a beach-bunny with some very nasty friends; and *Memory Lane* (1996), in which the partners race to prevent a death, while an ex-convict develops a relationship with the girlfriend of a dead former fellow inmate. Gough has also written one out-of-series international thriller, *Sandstorm* (1990), set in Egypt.

DAVID SKENE-MELVIN

Goupil, Laval. See ACADIAN LITERATURE: 2(b).

Governor General's Literary Awards. In 1937, with the approval of the Governor General, Lord Tweedsmuir (the novelist John Buchan), the CANADIAN AUTHORS' ASSOCIATION launched the Governor General's Literary Awards, which have evolved into Canada's premier awards. The first prizes were awarded in the spring of 1937 for two books published in 1936. Subsequently prizes were awarded for the best books of fiction, non-fiction, poetry, or drama published by a Canadian writer in the previous year. Only books in English (or translated from French) were eligible. The CAA's National Executive took on the judging themselves; but in 1944 an autonomous standing committee of judges from across Canada was set up, known as the Governor General's Awards Board. The awards were usually presented at an Awards Dinner, the finale of the CAA annual convention, which was held in the spring in various cities across the country. The prize consisted of a bronze medal, but in 1942 silver medals began to be awarded. In 1951 the Association of Canadian Magazine Publishers donated $250 to accompany each medal. During the early period three changes were made in the award categories. In 1942 the drama category was dropped, and non-fiction was split into two categories: creative and academic. In 1949 an award for juveniles was added.

In 1959 The CANADA COUNCIL (created in 1957) agreed to administer the awards and to provide at least six prizes of $1,000 each for awards in both French and English in poetry or drama, fiction, and non-fiction. It also agreed to pay the costs for winners attending the presentation ceremony, and to host a dinner following the Governor General's reception. By 1971, it had assumed the entire responsibility for organizing the French- and English-language juries, which were composed of experienced writers, scholars, and literary critics. The awards board was reorganized into two nine-person juries (one for French works and one for English) divided into three sub-committees—one each for fiction, non-fiction, and poetry and drama. In 1981 a separate category for drama was inaugurated to recognize the best published play in English and in French of the year. In 1987, the Canada Council Prizes for Children's Literature (text and illustration) and Translation (English to French and French to English) were integrated into the awards. There are currently fourteen Governor General's Literary Awards, seven in English and seven in French, in the following categories: fiction, poetry, drama, non-fiction, children's literature text, illustrations, and translation (French to English and English to French). There is a separate jury for each category.

The value of the prizes was increased in 1966 to $2,500, in 1975 to $5,000, and in 1989 to $10,000. Since 1964 winners have received a copy of their award-winning book specially bound by Pierre Ouvrard, master bookbinder, of Saint-Paul-de-l'Île-aux-Noix, Quebec.

In 1980, with the agreement of Governor General Edward Schreyer, the Council decided to move the presentation of the awards outside Government House and to hold ceremonies in different cities. At the same time, the better to publicize the prizes and the work of Canadian writers, it began publishing the names of finalists in all the categories in the weeks preceding the presentation. In 1990, to increase opportunities for publishers and booksellers to promote the finalists and winning books, the Council began to make substantial changes to submission procedures and the timing of the announcement of the awards. In 1992, the Council began presenting the awards in November to coincide with the major book-buying season. This meant that if publication took place before 30 September, books could receive an award in the year they were published; books published after that date would be considered in the following year. Also in 1992, the National Library of Canada initiated an annual gala reading by inviting the award-winners to read from their works at the National Library in Ottawa the day after the ceremony.

Since 1988 the Bank of Montreal has contributed to the awards by sponsoring various promotional activities and hosting a dinner after the ceremony in honour of the winners in the presence of the Governor General.

A list of winners to 1996 follows:

1936

Bertram BROOKER. *Think of the earth.* Fiction.

T.B. Robertson. *T.B.R.—newspaper pieces.* Non-fiction.

1937

Laura G. SALVERSON. *The dark weaver.* Fiction.

E.J. PRATT. *The fables of the goats.* Poetry.

Stephen LEACOCK. *My discovery of the West.* Non-fiction.

1938

Gwethalyn GRAHAM. *Swiss sonata.* Fiction.

Kenneth LESLIE. *By stubborn stars.* Poetry.

John Murray Gibbon. *Canadian mosaic.* Non-fiction.

1939

Franklin Davey McDowell. *The Champlain Road.* Fiction.

Arthur S. BOURINOT. *Under the sun.* Poetry.

Laura G. SALVERSON. *Confessions of an immigrant's daughter.* Non-fiction.

1940

Ringuet (Philippe PANNETON). *Thirty acres.* Fiction.

E.J.PRATT. *Brébeuf and his brethren.* Poetry.

J.F.C. Wright. *Slava Bohu.* Non-fiction.

1941

Alan SULLIVAN. *Three came to Ville Marie.* Fiction.

Anne MARRIOTT. *Calling adventurers.* Poetry.

Emily CARR. *Klee Wyck.* Non-fiction.

1942

G. Herbert Sallans. *Little man.* Fiction.

Earle BIRNEY. *David and other poems.* Poetry.

Bruce HUTCHISON. *The unknown country.* Non-fiction.

Edgar McInnes. *The unguarded frontier.* Non-fiction.

1943

Thomas H. RADDALL. *The pied piper of Dipper Creek.* Fiction.

A.J.M. SMITH. *News of the phoenix.* Poetry.

John D. Robins. *The incomplete anglers.* Non-fiction.

E.K. BROWN. *On Canadian poetry.* Non-fiction.

1944

Gwethalyn GRAHAM. *Earth and high heaven.* Fiction.

Dorothy LIVESAY. *Day and night.* Poetry.

Dorothy Duncan. *Partner in three worlds.* Non-fiction.

Edgar McInnes. *The war: fourth year.* Non-fiction.

1945

Hugh MacLENNAN. *TWO SOLITUDES.* Fiction.

Earle BIRNEY. *Now is time.* Poetry.

Evelyn M. Richardson. *We keep a light.* Non-fiction.
Ross Munro. *Gauntlet to Overlord.* Non-fiction.

1946
Winifred Bambrick. *Continental revue.* Fiction.
Robert FINCH. *Poems.* Poetry.
Frederick Philip GROVE. *In search of myself.* Non-fiction.
A.R.M. Lower. *Colony to nation.* Non-fiction.

1947
Gabrielle ROY. *The tin flute.* Fiction.
Dorothy LIVESAY. *Poems for people.* Poetry.
William Sclater. *Haida.* Non-fiction.
R. MacGregor Dawson. *The Government of Canada.* Non-fiction.

1948
Hugh MacLENNAN. *The precipice.* Fiction.
A.M. KLEIN. *The rocking chair and other poems.* Poetry.
Thomas H. RADDALL. *Halifax: warden of the north.* Non-fiction.
C.P. STACEY. *The Canadian Army, 1939-1945.* Non-fiction.

1949
Philip CHILD. *Mr. Ames against time.* Fiction.
James REANEY. *The red heart.* Poetry.
Hugh MacLENNAN. *Cross-country.* Non-fiction.
R. MacGregor Dawson. *Democratic government in Canada.* Non-fiction.
R.S. Lambert. *Franklin of the Arctic.* Juvenile.

1950
Germaine GUÈVREMONT. *The outlander.* Fiction.
James Wreford Watson. *Of time and the lover.* Poetry.
Marjorie Wilkins Campbell. *The Saskatchewan.* Non-fiction.
W.L. MORTON. *The Progressive Party in Canada.* Non-fiction.
Donalda Dickie. *The great adventure.* Juvenile.

1951
Morley CALLAGHAN. *The LOVED AND THE LOST.* Fiction.
Charles BRUCE. *The Mulgrave Road.* Poetry.
Josephine Phelan. *The ardent exile.* Non-fiction.
Frank MacKinnon. *The Government of Prince Edward Island.* Non-fiction.
John F. Hayes. *A land divided.* Juvenile.

1952
David WALKER. *The pillar.* Fiction.
E.J. PRATT. *Towards the last spike.* Poetry.
Bruce HUTCHISON. *The incredible Canadian.* Non-fiction.
Donald G. CREIGHTON. *John A. Macdonald: the young politician.* Non-fiction.
Marie McPhedran. *Cargoes on the Great Lakes.* Juvenile.

1953
David WALKER. *Digby.* Fiction.
Douglas LePAN. *The net and the sword.* Poetry.
N.J. Berrill. *Sex and the nature of things.* Non-fiction.
J.M.S. CARELESS. *Canada: a story of challenge.* Non-fiction.
John F. Hayes. *Rebels ride at night.* Juvenile.

1954
Igor Gouzenko. *The fall of a titan.* Fiction.
P.K. PAGE. *The metal and the flower.* Poetry.
Hugh MacLENNAN. *Thirty and three.* Non-fiction.
A.R.M. Lower. *This most famous stream.* Non-fiction.
Marjorie Wilkins Campbell. *The Nor'westers.* Juvenile.

1955
Lionel Shapiro. *The sixth of June.* Fiction.
Wilfred WATSON. *Friday's child.* Poetry.
N.J. Berrill. *Man's emerging mind.* Non-fiction.
Donald G. CREIGHTON. *John A. Macdonald: the old chieftain.* Non-fiction.
Kerry Wood. *The map-maker.* Juvenile.

1956
Adele WISEMAN. *The sacrifice.* Fiction.
Robert A.D. FORD. *A window on the north.* Poetry.
Pierre BERTON. *The mysterious North.* Non-fiction.
Joseph Lister Rutledge. *Century of conflict.* Non-fiction.
Farley MOWAT. *Lost in the barrens.* Juvenile.

1957
Gabrielle ROY. *Street of riches.* Fiction.
Jay MACPHERSON. *The BOATMAN.* Poetry.
Bruce HUTCHISON. *Canada: tomorrow's giant.* Non-fiction.
Thomas H. RADDALL. *The path of destiny.* Non-fiction.
Kerry Wood. *The great chief.* Juvenile.

1958
Colin McDougall. *Execution.* Fiction.
James REANEY. *A suit of nettles.* Poetry.
Pierre BERTON. *Klondike.* Non-fiction.
Joyce Hemlow. *The history of Fanny Burney.* Non-fiction.
Edith L. Sharp. *Nkwala.* Juvenile.

Governor General's Literary Awards

1959
Hugh MacLENNAN. *The watch that ends the night.* Fiction.
Irving LAYTON. *A red carpet for the sun.* Poetry.
André Giroux. *Malgré tout, la joie.* Fiction.
Félix-Antoine SAVARD. *Le barachois.* Non-fiction.

1960
Brian MOORE. *The luck of Ginger Coffey.* Fiction.
Frank Underhill. *In search of Canadian liberalism.* Non-fiction.
Margaret AVISON. *Winter sun.* Poetry.
Paul Toupin. *Souvenirs pour demain.* Non-fiction.
Anne HÉBERT. *Poèmes.* Poetry.

1961
Malcolm LOWRY. *Hear us oh Lord from heaven thy dwelling place.* Fiction.
T.A. Goudge. *The ascent of life.* Non-fiction.
Robert FINCH. *Acis in Oxford.* Poetry.
Yves THÉRIAULT. *Ashini.* Fiction.
Jean LE MOYNE. *Convergences.* Non-fiction.

1962
Kildare DOBBS. *Running to paradise.* Fiction and autobiographical writing.
Marshall McLUHAN. *The Gutenberg galaxy.* Non-fiction.
James REANEY. *Twelve letters to a small town and The killdeer and other plays.* Poetry and drama.
Jacques FERRON. *CONTES DU PAYS INCERTAIN.* Fiction.
Gilles MARCOTTE. *Une littérature qui se fait.* Non-fiction.
Jacques LANGUIRAND. *Les insolites et les violins de l'automne.* Drama.

1963
Hugh GARNER. *Hugh Garner's best stories.* Fiction.
J.M.S. CARELESS. *Brown of The Globe.* Non-fiction.
Gatien LAPOINTE. *Ode au Saint-Laurent.* Poetry.
Gustave Lanctot. *Histoire du Canada.* Non-fiction.

1964
Douglas LePAN. *The deserter.* Fiction.
Phyllis GROSSKURTH. *John Addington Symonds.* Non-fiction.
Raymond SOUSTER. *The colour of the times.* Poetry.
Jean-Paul Pinsonneault. *Les terres sèches.* Fiction.
Réjean Robidoux. *Roger Martin du Gard et la religion.* Non-fiction.
Pierre PERRAULT. *Au coeur de la rose.* Poetry.

1965
Alfred PURDY. *The cariboo horses.* Poetry.
James Eayrs. *In defence of Canada.* Non-fiction.
Gilles VIGNEAULT. *Quand les bateaux s'en vont.* Poetry.
Gérard BESSETTE. *L'INCUBATION.* Fiction.
André S.Vachon. *Le temps et l'espace dans l'oeuvre de Paul Claudel.* Non-fiction.

1966
Margaret LAURENCE. *A jest of God.* Fiction.
George WOODCOCK. *The crystal spirit: a study of George Orwell.* Non-fiction.
Margaret ATWOOD. *The circle game.* Poetry.
Claire MARTIN. *La joue droite.* Fiction.
Marcel TRUDEL. *Histoire de la Nouvelle-France*: vol. II., *Le comptoir, 1604-1627.* Non-fiction.
Réjean DUCHARME. *L'avalée des avalés.* Poetry and theatre.

1967
Eli MANDEL. *An idiot joy.* Poetry.
Alden A. NOWLAN. *Bread, wine and salt.* Poetry.
Norah Story. *The Oxford companion to Canadian history and literature.* Non-fiction.
Jacques GODBOUT. *SALUT GALARNEAU!* Fiction.
Robert-Lionel SÉGUIN. *La civilisation traditionelle de 'l'habitant' aux XVIIe et XVIIIe siècles.* Non-fiction.
Françoise LORANGER. *Encore cinq minutes.* Drama.

1968
Alice MUNRO. *Dance of the happy shades.* Fiction.
Mordecai RICHLER. *Cocksure and Hunting tigers under glass.* Fiction and essays.
Leonard COHEN. *Selected poems 1956-68* (declined).
Hubert AQUIN. *Trou de mémoire.* Fiction (declined).
Marie-Claire BLAIS. *Les manuscrits de Pauline Archange.* Fiction.
Fernand DUMONT. *Le lieu de l'homme.* Non-fiction.

1969
Robert KROETSCH. *The studhorse man.* Fiction.
George BOWERING. *Rocky Mountain foot* and *The gangs of Kosmos.* Poetry.
Gwendolyn MacEWEN. *The shadow-maker.* Poetry.
Louise MAHEUX-FORCIER. *Une forêt pour Zoé.* Fiction.

Jean-Guy PILON. *Comme eau retenue*. Poetry.
Michel BRUNET. *Les Canadiens après la conquête*. Non-fiction.

1970
Dave GODFREY. *The new ancestors*. Fiction.
Michael ONDAATJE. *The collected works of Billy the Kid*. Prose and Poetry.
bp NICHOL. *Still water, The true eventual story of Billy the Kid, Beach head, The cosmic chef: an evening of concrete*. Poetry.
Monique BOSCO. *La femme de Loth*. Fiction.
Jacques BRAULT. *Quand nous serons heureux*. Drama.
Fernand OUELLETTE. *Les actes retrouvés*. Non-fiction (declined).

1971
Mordecai RICHLER. *St Urbain's horseman*. Fiction.
John GLASSCO. *Selected poems*. Poetry.
Pierre BERTON. *The last spike*. Non-fiction.
Gérard BESSETTE. *Le cycle*. Fiction.
Paul-Marie LAPOINTE. *Le réel absolu*. Poetry.
Gérald Fortin. *La fin d'un règne*. Non-fiction.

1972
Robertson DAVIES. *The manticore*. Fiction.
Dennis LEE. *Civil elegies*. Poetry.
John NEWLOVE. *Lies*. Poetry.
Antonine MAILLET. *Don l'Orignal*. Fiction.
Gilles HÉNAULT. *Signaux pour les voyants*. Poetry.
Jean Hamelin and Yves Roby. *Histoire économique du Québec 1851-1896*. Non-fiction.

1973
Rudy WIEBE. *The temptations of Big Bear*. Fiction.
Miriam Mandel. *Lions at her face*. Poetry.
Michael Bell. *Painters in a new land*. Non-fiction.
Réjean DUCHARME. *L'hiver de force*. Fiction.
Albert Faucher. *Québec en Amérique au dix-neuvième siècle*. Non-fiction.
Roland GIGUÈRE. *La main au feu*. Special Award (declined).

1974
Margaret LAURENCE. *The DIVINERS*. Fiction.
Ralph GUSTAFSON. *Fire on stone: a collection of poetry*. Poetry.
Charles RITCHIE. *The siren years*. Non-fiction.
Victor-Lévy BEAULIEU. *Don Quichotte de la démanche*. Fiction.
Nicole BROSSARD. *Mécanique jongleuse suivi de Masculin grammaticale*. Poetry.
Louise Déchêne. *Habitants et marchands de Montréal au dix-septième siècle*. Non-fiction.

1975
Brian MOORE. *The great Victorian collection*. Fiction.
Milton ACORN. *The island means Minago*. Poetry.
Anthony Adamson, Marion MacRae. *Hallowed walls*. Non-fiction.
Anne HÉBERT. *Les enfants du sabbat*. Fiction.
Pierre PERRAULT. *Chouennes*. Poetry.
Louis-Edmond Hamelin. *Nordicité canadienne*. Non-fiction.

1976
Marian ENGEL. *Bear*. Fiction.
Joe ROSENBLATT. *Top soil*. Poetry.
Carl BERGER. *The writing of Canadian history*. Non-fiction.
André MAJOR. *Les rescapés*. Fiction.
Alphonse Piché. *Poèmes 1946-68*. Poetry.
Fernand OUELLET. *Le Bas Canada 1791-1840 changements structureux et crise*. Non-fiction.

1977
Timothy FINDLEY. *The WARS*. Fiction.
D.G. JONES. *Under the thunder the flowers light up the earth*. Poetry and drama.
Frank SCOTT. *Essays on the Constitution*. Non-fiction.
Gabrielle ROY. *Ces enfants de ma vie*. Fiction.
Michel GARNEAU. *Les célébrations suivie de Adidou Adidouce*. Poetry and drama (declined).
Denis Monière. *Le développement des idéologies au Québec des origines à nos jours*. Non-fiction.

1978
Alice MUNRO. *Who do you think you are?* Fiction.
Patrick LANE. *Poems new and selected*. Poetry.
Roger Caron. *Go boy*. Non-fiction.
Jacques POULIN. *Les grandes marées*. Fiction.
Gilbert LANGEVIN. *Mon refuge est un volcan*. Poetry.
François-Marc Gagnon. *Paul-Émile Borduas*. Non-fiction.

1979
Jack HODGINS. *The resurrection of Joseph Bourne*. Fiction.
Michael ONDAATJE. *There's a trick with a knife I'm learning to do*. Poetry.
Maria Tippett. *Emily Carr*. Non-fiction.
Marie-Claire BLAIS. *Le sourd dans la ville*. Fiction.
Robert Melançon. *Peinture aveugle*. Poetry.
D. Clift and S. McLeod Arnopoulos. *Le fait anglais au Québec*. Non-fiction.

1980
George BOWERING. *Burning water*. Fiction.

Stephen SCOBIE. *McAlmon's Chinese opera.* Poetry.
Jeffrey Simpson. *Discipline of power.* Non-fiction.
Pierre Turgeon. *La première personne.* Fiction.
Michel VAN SCHENDEL. *De l'oeil et de l'écoute.* Poetry.
Maurice Champagne-Gilbert. *La famille et l'homme à délivrer du pouvoir.* Non-fiction.

1981
Mavis GALLANT. *Home truths.* Fiction.
F.R. SCOTT. *The collected poems of F.R. Scott.* Poetry.
George Calef. *Caribou and the barren-lands.* Non-fiction.
Sharon POLLOCK. *Blood relations and other plays.* Drama.
Denys Chabot. *La province lunaire.* Fiction.
Michel BEAULIEU. *Visages.* Poetry.
Madeleine OUELLETTE-MICHALSKA. *L'échappée des discours de l'oeil.* Non-fiction.
Marie LABERGE. *C'était avant la guerre à l'Anse à Gilles.* Drama.

1982
Guy VANDERHAEGHE. *Man descending.* Fiction.
Phyllis WEBB. *The vision tree: selected poems.* Poetry.
Christopher MOORE. *Louisbourg portraits: life in an eighteenth-century garrison town.* Non-fiction.
John GRAY. *Billy Bishop goes to war, a play by John Gray with Eric Peterson.* Drama.
Roger Fournier. *Le cercle des arènes.* Fiction.
Michel Savard. *Forages.* Poetry.
Maurice Lagueux. *Le Marxisme des années soixante: une saison dans l'histoire de la pensée critique.* Non-fiction.
Réjean DUCHARME. *HA ha! . . .* Drama.

1983
Leon ROOKE. *Shakespeare's dog.* Fiction.
David DONNELL. *Settlements.* Poetry.
Anne CHISLETT. *Quiet in the land.* Drama.
Jeffery Williams. *Byng of Vimy: General and Governor General.* Non-fiction.
Suzanne Jacob. *Laura Laur.* Fiction.
Suzanne PARADIS. *Un goût de sel.* Poetry.
René Gingras. *Syncope.* Drama.
Maurice Cusson. *Le contrôle social du crime.* Non-fiction.

1984
Josef SKVORECKY. *The engineer of human souls.* Fiction.
Paulette JILES. *Celestial navigation.* Poetry.
Judith THOMPSON. *White biting dog.* Drama.
Sandra GWYN. *The private capital: ambition and love in the age of Macdonald and Laurier.* Non-fiction.
Jacques BRAULT. *Agonie.* Fiction.
Nicole BROSSARD. *Double impression.* Poetry.
René-Daniel DUBOIS. *Ne blâmez jamais les Bédouins.* Drama.
Jean Hamelin and Nicole Gagnon. *Le XXe siècle: histoire du catholicisme québécois.* Non-fiction.

1985
Margaret ATWOOD. *The HANDMAID'S TALE.* Fiction.
Fred WAH. *Waiting for Saskatchewan.* Poetry.
George F. WALKER. *Criminals in love.* Drama.
Ramsay COOK. *The regenerators: social criticism in late Victorian English Canada.* Non-fiction.
Fernand OUELLETTE. *Lucie; ou Un midi en novembre.* Fiction.
André ROY. *Action writing.* Poetry.
Maryse Pelletier. *Duo pour voix obstinées.* Drama.
François Ricard. *La littérature contre elle-même.* Non-fiction.

1986
Alice MUNRO. *The progress of love.* Fiction.
Al PURDY. *The collected poems of Al Purdy.* Poetry.
Sharon POLLOCK. *Doc.* Drama.
Northrop FRYE. *Northrop Frye on Shakespeare.* Non-fiction.
Yvon RIVARD. *Les silences du corbeau.* Fiction.
Cécile CLOUTIER. *L'écouté.* Poetry.
Anne Legault. *La visite des sauvages.* Drama.
Régine ROBIN. *Le réalisme socialiste: une esthétique impossible.* Non-fiction.

1987
M.T. KELLY. *A dream like mine.* Fiction.
Gwendolyn MacEWEN. *Afterworlds.* Poetry.
John Krizanc. *Prague.* Drama.
Michael IGNATIEFF. *The Russian album.* Non-fiction.
Morgan Nyberg. *Galahad Schwartz and the cockroach army.* Juvenile (text).
Marie-Louise Gay. *Rainy day magic.* Juvenile (illust.).
Patricia Claxton. *Enchantment and sorrow: the autobiography of Gabrielle Roy.* Trans. (Fr.-Eng.).
Gilles ARCHAMBAULT. *L'obsédante obèse et autres agressions.* Fiction.
Fernand OUELLETTE. *Les heures.* Poetry.
Jeanne-Mance Delisle. *Un oiseau vivant dans la gueule.* Drama.
Jean Larose. *La petite noirceur.* Non-fiction.
David Schinkel and Yves Beauchesne. *Le Don.* Juvenile (text).
Darcia Labrosse. *Venir au monde.* Juvenile (illust.).

Ivan Steenhout and Christiane Teasdale. *L'homme qui se croyait aimé; ou La vie secrète d'un premier ministre* by Heather Robertson. Trans. (Eng.-Fr.).

1988

David Adams RICHARDS. *Nights below Station Street*. Fiction.

Erin MOURÉ. *Furious*. Poetry.

George F. WALKER. *Nothing sacred*. Drama.

Anne Collins. *In the sleep room*. Non-fiction.

Welwyn Wilton KATZ. *The third magic*. Juvenile (text).

Kim LaFave. *Amos's sweater*. Juvenile (illust.).

Philip Stratford. *Second chance* by Diane Hébert. Trans. (Fr.-Eng.).

Jacques Folch-Ribas. *Le silence; ou Le parfait bonheur*. Fiction.

Marcel Labine. *Papiers d'épidémie*. Poetry.

Jean-Marc DALPÉ. *Le chien*. Drama.

Patricia Smart. *Écrire dans la maison du père*. Non-fiction.

Michèle Marineau. *Cassiopée; ou L'été polonais*. Juvenile (text).

Philippe Béha. *Les jeux de pic-mots*. Juvenile (illust.).

Didier Holtzwarth. *Nucléus* by Robert Bothwell. Trans. (Eng.-Fr.).

1989

Paul QUARRINGTON. *Whale music*. Fiction.

Heather SPEARS. *The word for sand*. Poetry.

Judith THOMPSON. *The other side of the dark*. Drama.

Robert Calder. *Willie: the life of W. Somerset Maugham*. Non-fiction.

Diana Wieler. *Bad boy*. Juvenile (text).

Robin Muller. *The magic paintbrush*. Juvenile (illust.).

Wayne Grady. *On the eighth day* by Antonine MAILLET. Trans. (Fr.-Eng.).

Louis Hamelin. *La rage*. Fiction.

Pierre Desruisseaux. *Monème*. Poetry.

Michel GARNEAU. *Mademoiselle Rouge*. Drama.

Lise Noël. *L'intolérance: une problématique générale*. Non-fiction.

Charles Montpetit. *Temps mort*. Juvenile (text).

Stéphane Poulin. *Benjamin et la saga des oreillers*. Juvenile (illust.).

Jean Antonin Billard. *Les âges de l'amour* by Dorothy LIVESAY. Trans. (Eng.-Fr.).

1990

Nino RICCI. *Lives of the saints*. Fiction.

Margaret AVISON. *No time*. Poetry.

Ann-Marie MacDONALD. *Goodnight Desdemona (Good morning Juliet)*. Drama.

Stephen Clarkson and Christina McCALL. *Trudeau and our times*. Non-fiction.

Michael BEDARD. *Redwork*. Juvenile (text).

Paul Morin. *The orphan boy*. Juvenile (illust.).

Jane Brierley. *Yellow-Wolf and other tales of the Saint Lawrence* by Philippe-Joseph AUBERT DE GASPÉ. Trans. (Fr.-Eng.).

Gérald Tougas. *La mauvaise foi*. Fiction.

Jean-Paul Daoust. *Les cendres bleues*. Poetry.

Jovette MARCHESSAULT. *Le voyage magnifique d'Émily Carr*. Drama.

Jean-François Lisée. *Dans l'oeil de l'aigle*. Non-fiction.

Christiane Duchesne. *La vraie histoire du chien de Clara Vic*. Juvenile (text).

Pierre Pratt. *Les fantaisies de l'oncle Henri*. Juvenile (illust.).

Charlotte and Robert Melançon. *Le second rouleau* by A.M. KLEIN. Trans. (Eng.-Fr.).

1991

Rohinton MISTRY. *Such a long journey*. Fiction.

Don McKAY. *Night field*. Poetry.

Joan MacLEOD. *Amigo's blue guitar*. Drama.

Robert Hunter and Robert Calihoo. *Occupied Canada: a young white man discovers his unsuspected past*. Non-fiction.

Sarah ELLIS. *Pick-up sticks*. Juvenile (text).

Joanne Fitzgerald. *Doctor Kiss says yes*. Juvenile (illust.).

Albert W. Halsall. *A dictionary of literary devices: gradus, A-Z by Bernard Dupriez*. Trans. (Fr.-Eng.)

André BROCHU. *La croix du nord*. Fiction.

Madeleine GAGNON. *Chant pour un Québec lointain*. Poetry.

Gilbert Dupuis. *Mon oncle Marcel qui vague vague près du métro Berri*. Drama.

Bernard Arcand. *Le jaguar et le tamanoir*. Non-fiction.

François Gravel. *Deux heures et demie avant Jasmine*. Juvenile (text).

Sheldon Cohen. *Un champion*. Juvenile (illust.).

Jean-Paul Sainte-Marie and Brigitte Chabert Hacikyan. *Les enfants d'Aataentsic: l'histoire du peuple Huron* by Bruce G. Trigger. Trans. (Eng.-Fr.).

1992

Michael ONDAATJE. *The ENGLISH PATIENT*. Fiction.

Lorna CROZIER. *Inventing the hawk*. Poetry.

John Mighton. *Possible worlds and a short history of night*. Drama.

Maggie Siggins. *Revenge of the land: a century of greed, tragedy and murder on a Saskatchewan farm*. Non-fiction.

Julie JOHNSTON. *Hero of lesser causes*. Juvenile (text).

Ron Lightburn. *Waiting for the whales.* Juvenile (illust.).
Fred A. Reed. *Imagining the Middle East* by Thierry Hentsch. Trans. (Fr.-Eng.).
Anne HÉBERT. *L'enfant chargé de songes.* Fiction.
Gilles Cyr. *Andromède attendra.* Poetry.
Louis-Dominique Lavigne. *Les petits orteils.* Drama.
Pierre Turgeon. *La Radissonie: le pays de la baie James.* Non-fiction.
Christiane Duchesne. *Victor.* Juvenile (text).
Gilles Tibo. *Simon et la ville de carton.* Juvenile (illust.).
Jean Papineau. *La mémoire postmoderne: essai sur l'art canadien contemporain* by Mark A. Cheetham. Trans. (Eng.-Fr.).

1993
Carol SHIELDS. *The stone diaries.* Fiction.
Don COLES. *Forests of the medieval world.* Poetry.
Guillermo Verdecchia. *Fronteras Americanas.* Drama.
Karen Connelly. *Touch the dragon.* Non-fiction.
Tim WYNNE-JONES. *Some of the kinder planets.* Juvenile (text).
Mireille Levert. *Sleep tight, Mrs Ming.* Juvenile (illust.).
D.G. JONES. *Categorics one, two & three* by Normand de Bellefeuille. Trans. (Fr.-Eng.).
Nancy HUSTON. *Cantique des plaines.* Fiction.
Denise DESAUTELS. *Le saut de l'ange.* Poetry.
Daniel DANIS. *Cella-là.* Drama.
François Paré. *Les littératures de l'exiguïté.* Non-fiction.
Michèle Marineau. *La route de Chlifa.* Juvenile (text).
Stéphane Jorisch. *Le monde selon Jean de . . .* Juvenile (illust.).
Marie José Thériault. *L'oeuvre du Gallois* by Robert Walshe. Trans. (Eng.-Fr.).

1994
Rudy WIEBE. *A discovery of strangers.* Fiction.
Robert Hilles. *Cantos from a small room.* Poetry.
Morris PANYCH. *The ends of the earth.* Drama.
John A. Livingston. *Rogue primate.* Non-fiction.
Julie JOHNSTON. *Adam and Eve and Pinch-me.* Juvenile (text).
Murray Kimber. *Josepha: a prairie boy's story.* Juvenile (illust.).
Donald Winkler. *The lyric generation: the life and times of the baby boomers* by François Ricard. Trans. (Fr.-Eng.).
Robert Lalonde. *Le petit aigle à tête blanche.* Fiction.
Fulvio Caccia. *Aknos.* Poetry.
Michel Ouellette. *French Town.* Drama.
Chantal Saint-Jarre. *Du sida.* Non-fiction.
Suzanne Martel. *Une belle journée pour mourir.* Juvenile (text).
Pierre Pratt. *Mon chien est un éléphant.* Juvenile (illust.).
Jude Des Chênes. *Le mythe du sauvage* by Olive Patricia Dickason. Trans. (Eng.-Fr.).

1995
Greg HOLLINGSHEAD. *The roaring girl.* Fiction.
Anne SZUMIGALSKI. *Voice.* Poetry.
Jason SHERMAN. *Three in the back, two in the head.* Drama.
Rosemary SULLIVAN. *Shadow maker: the life of Gwendolyn MacEwen.* Non-fiction.
Tim WYNNE-JONES. *The maestro.* Juvenile (text).
Ludmilla Zeman. *The last quest of Gilgamesh.* Juvenile (illust.).
David Homel. *Why must a black writer write about sex?* by Dany LAFERRIÈRE. Trans. (Fr.-Eng.).
Nicole Houde. *Les oiseaux de Saint-John Perse.* Fiction.
Émile Martel. *Pour orchestre et poète seul.* Poetry.
Carol Fréchette. *Les quatre morts de Marie.* Drama.
Yvan Lamonde. *Louis-Antoine Dessaulles: un seigneur libéral et anticlérical.* Non-fiction.
Sonia Sarfati. *Comme une peau de chagrin.* Juvenile (text).
Annouchka Gravel Galouchko. *Sho et les dragons d'eau.* Juvenile (illust.).
Hervé Juste. *Entre l'ordre et la liberté* by Gérald Bernier. Trans. (Eng.-Fr.).

1996
Guy VANDERHAEGHE. *The Englishman's boy.* Fiction.
E.D. Blodgett. *Apostrophes: woman at a piano.* Poetry.
Colleen Wagner. *The monument.* Drama.
John Ralston SAUL. *The unconscious civilization.* Non-fiction.
Paul Yee. *Ghost train.* Juvenile (text).
Eric Beddows. *The rooster's gift.* Juvenile (illust.).
Linda Gaboriau. *Stone and ashes* by Daniel DANIS. Trans. (Fr.-Eng.).
Marie-Claire BLAIS. *Soifs.* Fiction.
Serge Patrice Thibodeau. *Le quatuor de l'errance followed by La traversée du désert.* Poetry.
Normand CHAURETTE. *Le passage de l'Indiana.* Drama.
Michel Freitag. *Le naufrage de l'université—et autres essais d'épistémologie politique.* Non-fiction.
Gilles Tibo. *Noémie—le secret de Madame Lumbago.* Juvenile (text).

The French-language jury gave no award for juvenile illustration.

Christiane Teasdale. *Systèmes de survie—dialogue sur les fondements moraux du commerce et de la politique.* by Jane Jacobs. Trans. (Eng.-Fr.).

JOCELYN HARVEY, KATHERINE BERG

Govier, Katherine (b. 1948). Born in Edmonton, Alberta, she has lived in Toronto, Ontario, since 1971. She studied at the University of Alberta (B.A., 1970) and York University, Toronto (M.A., 1972), and taught creative writing at York University from 1982 to 1986. She was a Visiting Fellow at Leeds University, England, in 1986-7. She was a founder of the Writers in Electronic Residence program, an initiative of the WRITERS' DEVELOPMENT TRUST, a program that links professional writers and students via telecommunications. She has been prominent in PEN, of which she is currently Canadian President.

Govier has published short stories widely in both Canadian and U.K. magazines, and there have been numerous awards and fellowships in recognition of these and her books. She has published *Random descent* (1979, novel); *Going through the motions* (1982, novel); *Fables of Brunswick Avenue* (1985, short stories); *Between men* (1987, novel); *Before and after* (1989, short stories); *Hearts of flame* (1991, novel); *The immaculate conception photography gallery* (1994, short stories); *Without a guide* (1994, travel anthology); and *Angel walk* (1996, novel). Of the early books, it was the short stories in *Fables* that deservedly won most notice: clear-eyed glances into the lives of young women (and here and there a young man) making it, not always by choice, on their own in Toronto's lower Annex in the early 1980s. *Random descent* is a generational story, altogether admirable in its detail but ponderous in movement; *Going through the motions* is better paced, shedding some of *Random descent*'s careful canvas en route. Many interesting developments are noticeable in the books that follow, but *Angel walk* is Govier's finest work. The story portrays a young Canadian woman arriving in pre-Second World War Britain, picking up, almost casually at first, an interest in photography, credibly meeting a few of London's *illuminati* (most usefully, the ex-Maritimer press lord, Lord Beaverbrook), and then, without hurry, flowering into a rich and several-dimensioned life as apprentice and ultimately internationally celebrated photographer, and the decades-long lover of a much older, consistently selfish, and minor painter. The presentation of this relationship—a complex and minutely-reported-upon affair that by sheer intelligence escapes every one of a thousand clichés—is a total triumph.

DON COLES

Gowdy, Barbara (b. 1950). She was born and raised in Windsor, Ontario, and educated in Toronto schools. Her Irish father mounted trade shows for corporations, and she moved frequently. She studied theatre arts at York University. Her first marriage ended in divorce. Active in literary publishing from 1974 to 1979, she worked in publishing at Lester & Orpen Dennys, eventually becoming managing editor. She also worked for a short time at Harlequin Books, editing the mystery line, and later was a reporter on the TVOntario literary program *Imprint*.

Gowdy has been called the most fearless black humourist in Canada. In her insistence that we can only find grace and redemption in accepting our bodies as they are, even if deformed, she has been compared to photographer Diane Arbus and American short-story writer Flannery O'Connor. Her work has an obsession with the body, the freaky, the extreme, the grotesque. In stories that are metaphors for spiritual crises, she reveals how spirit transcends the body. Her writing is innovative and unique, her language precise, her material unusual, and often funny.

Gowdy's first collection of poems and stories was *The rabbit and the hare* (1982). She then spent a year in the U.K. researching her historical novel *Through the green valley* (1988), a lyrical story of a poor Irish boy and his three sisters swept up in a war that eventually brings them to America. With her second novel, *Falling angels* (1989), Gowdy began to explore her major concerns, the metamorphosis of the flesh, and tolerance within the family. A black comic study of a dysfunctional urban family, the novel was translated into six languages and adapted for film. In it a father forces his family to spend a vacation in a bomb shelter, while three adolescent girls come to terms with their bodies, their family, and their lives. One chapter, the short story 'Disneyland', was selected by Margaret ATWOOD for *Best American Short Stories: 1989*.

The eight startling, sometimes amusing, stories in *We so seldom look on love* (1992) feature such subjects as necrophilia, exhibitionism, transvestism, Siamese twins with warring heads, a woman with two sets of reproductive organs, and a woman with an extra pair of legs. The stories, based on fact, are written with convincing detail in spare and elegant language, the characters sympathetically portrayed. The title story about necrophilia was successfully adapted as a prize-winning feature film, *Kissed,* directed by Lynne Stopkewich.

Gowdy's third and most daring novel, *Mister Sandman* (1995)—nominated for the Trillium Award and a Governor General's Award—explores preconceptions of what constitutes a happy family. The parents, unknown to each other, are closet homosexuals. Other characters include an obese sister, a speechless autistic dwarf, and an 'idiot savant' to whom the others confess their anxieties, as if at prayer. One character, Hen Bowden, has been called one of the greatest comic creations in Canadian literature. Because Gowdy sees tolerance as a form of love, the centre of this daring and witty novel has a visionary calm. GEOFF HANCOCK

Goyette, Jocelyne. See DRAMA IN FRENCH 1948 TO 1981: 4.

Grady, Wayne. See NATURE WRITING IN ENGLISH: 3, 5, 6.

Graham, Andrew. See EXPLORATION LITERATURE IN ENGLISH: 2.

Graham, Gwethalyn (1913-65). Gwethalyn Graham Erichsen-Brown was born in Toronto. She attended Rosedale Public School and Havergal College there; the Pensionnat des Allières in Lausanne, Switzerland; and Smith College, Massachusetts. A novelist and journalist, she most often dealt with the need for justice, tolerance, and international understanding. Her first novel, *Swiss sonata* (1938), which won a Governor General's Award, explores the interwoven stories of twenty-seven residents at a Swiss boarding school on the eve of the Second World War. Although somewhat awkward because of its many characters and implausible time frame (all events take place during a single day), it represents a timely appeal for international empathy and understanding.

Graham's second and stronger novel, *Earth and high heaven* (1944; NCL 1960), also won a Governor General's Award. Set in Montreal during the Second World War, it is the story of Erica Drake, a journalist from an affluent Westmount family, who falls in love with a Jewish lawyer. The novel focuses on the blatant anti-Semitism of her socially prominent family, especially her father, and is an unsparing portrait of upper-class anti-Semitism in Canada during the war. The novel, which draws upon Graham's own experience in wishing to marry a Jewish-Canadian lawyer to whom her father was unalterably opposed, was a popular and critical success in Canada and abroad and was translated into nine languages. While somewhat dated and frequently awkward in its use of excessively expository dialogue, the novel is nonetheless notable for the sharpness of its deeply felt attack on covert racism in Canada.

As a journalist Graham was a frequent contributor to the magazines *Maclean's* and *Saturday Night*, particularly on topics related to immigration, refugee policy, and human rights. *Dear enemy: a dialogue on French and English Canada* (1963), which Graham wrote in collaboration with Solange Chaput-Rolland, is an exchange of letters exploring the conflicts between English and French Canadians. At her death she was at work on a novel about English-Canadian and Québécois relations. MARILYN ROSE

Graham, Ron (b. 1948). Born in Ottawa, Ontario, he grew up in Montreal, Quebec, and was educated at McGill University (B.A., 1968) and the Institute of Canadian Studies, Carleton University (M.A., 1971). His first book was a short novel, *Naughts and crosses* (1980), a surrealistic murder story set in Montreal during the October Crisis of 1970. He was associate producer of a much-admired TV series, *The Canadian establishment*, which led to his first appearance as a national journalist with a 1980 *Saturday Night* article about the making of the series. For the next seven years he was closely identified with that magazine, where his prize-winning articles won him a reputation for resourceful reporting, excellent storytelling, and the ability to make unexpected leaps of insight in order to explain how his subjects fit into Canadian society. He wrote a much-quoted article speculating on Jean Chrétien's chances of becoming prime minister and later served as literary amanuensis for Chrétien's autobiography, *Straight from the heart* (1985). The following year he published *One-eyed kings: promise and illusion in Canadian politics* (1986), a well-reviewed book on recent politics, much of it based on his magazine profiles of Joe Clark, John Turner, and others. Pursuing his own deepest interests, he next turned to the condition of religion in Canada and wrote the remarkably broad-ranging and original *God's dominion: a sceptic's quest* (1990), in which he discerned patterns of faith in religious communities as different as the Tibetan Buddhists of Halifax and the Sikhs of British Columbia. The persistent Canadian constitutional crisis encouraged him to explore, in *The French quarter*

(1992; French translation, 1995) his own ancestral francophone connections, reaching back to Zacherie Cloutier, a master carpenter who crossed the Atlantic in 1634. More recently he wrote *All the king's horses: politics among the ruins* (1995), another account of national politics; and biographical essays on two painters, Paterson Ewen (1996) and Tim Zuck (1997), for catalogues of their work.

ROBERT FULFORD

Grain (1973-). Published by the Saskatchewan Writers Guild, *Grain*'s first issue appeared in June 1973 under Ken MITCHELL's editorship. It was produced bi-annually until 1976 and tri-annually until 1981, when it became a quarterly. Throughout its history *Grain* has been overseen by an editor, a group of associate editors, and an advisory board. Since the first issue it has been edited by Caroline Heath (1973-9), E.F. Dyck (1980-3), Brenda Riches (1984-8), Mick Burrs (1988-1990), Geoffrey Ursell (1990-3), Elizabeth Philips (1993-4), and J. Jill Robinson (1996-). Don Kerr, Anne SZUMIGALSKI, and Judith Smith shared the primary editorship for the first two issues of 1980.

Believing in the early 1970s that the endeavours of Saskatchewan and prairie writers were little recognized by literary periodicals in eastern Canada and British Columbia, the Saskatchewan Writers Guild set out to produce one that, while open to submissions nationally and internationally, would provide a forum for Saskatchewan and prairie writing. At its inception *Grain*'s creators determined to pay its contributors and to comment on all submissions. Short stories and poems characterized its content during the 1970s. Dyck opted to add drama, novel excerpts, poem-sequences, songs, and essays to the mix. During the 1980s visual art and editorial commentaries were included. Since 1989 an annual writing contest has been held. Writers who have appeared frequently in *Grain* include Les Arnold, John V. Hicks, Gary Hyland, Anne Szumigalski, Rhea TREGEBOV, Lorna CROZIER, Derk WYNAND, and Lyn Lifshin. The University of Saskatchewan holds *Grain*'s archives.

JANET FRISKNEY

Grain. See Robert STEAD.

Grainger, Martin Allerdale (1874-1941). Born in London, England, he spent most of his childhood in Australia, where his father, Henry Allerdale Grainger, was agent general for South Australia. In 1893 he won a scholarship to Cambridge University, England, where he excelled in mathematics. Upon graduating in 1896 he spent several adventurous years in northern British Columbia, then fought in the Boer War; he returned to British Columbia, trying his hand at placer-mining, logging, and some journalism. In 1908, while in England, he wrote *Woodsmen of the West* (1908) to raise enough money on which to marry. In 1910 he began his career in the British Columbia forest industry, first as secretary of the Royal Commission on Forestry (writing most of the report that led to the establishment of the B.C. Forest Service) and rose to the position of chief forester in 1917. From 1920 until his death he devoted his energies to his private lumbering businesses.

Woodsmen of the West, which is in the NEW CANADIAN LIBRARY, was based on Grainger's letters to his future wife. Less a novel than a sequence of realistic, dramatized personal observations, it is recounted by a first-person narrator who retains the author's name and identity. Enthralled by the challenge of a frontier environment and intrigued by the individualism and initiative of the western logger, Mart recounts incidents illustrating the character type he most frequently encountered: men who were enterprising yet foolhardy, pragmatically shrewd yet financially naive, physically fearless yet emotionally undisciplined. The rather spare plot centres on Mart's conflicts with his boss, Carter, who personifies the raw spirit of free enterprise. Despite his personal distaste for the man, Mart remains in his employ, held by his fascination with Carter's ruthless and single-minded exploitation of both the land and his men. Carter emerges as a villain in his relations with human beings, but as a hero in his determination to conquer both an inhospitable environment and the vagaries of the anonymous world of big business. Grainger's detailed descriptions of the unromantic life of the West Coast handlogger, and of the climate and terrain of northern British Columbia, make *Woodsmen of the West* one of the best examples of early-Canadian literary realism.

CAROLE GERSON

Granatstein, J.L. (b. 1939). Jack Lawrence Granatstein was born in Toronto, Ontario, and educated at the Royal Military College, Kingston (B.A., 1961), the University of Toronto (M.A., 1962), and Duke University, North Carolina (Ph.D., 1966). He was a historian in the Directorate of History, National Defence Headquarters, Ottawa, from 1964 to 1966, when he became professor of history at York University, Toronto; in 1995 he was appointed Distinguished Research Professor of History Emeritus. He was made an Officer of the Order of Canada in 1997.

The most prolific historian of twentieth-century Canada, Granatstein supplanted, in his many books, the themes of an earlier generation of historians who had been interested in the emergence of the country from colony to nation, from a British world to American influence. Political and military history, and occasionally foreign affairs, have been Granatstein's principal interests in his more than three dozen books and one dozen edited volumes. Asking the right questions, prodigious in research to discern the answers, and able to communicate, Granatstein altered one's understanding of Canada's history. The top brass and the political and military experiences of the Second World War have fascinated him: *Canada's war: the politics of the Mackenzie King government* (1975), *Broken promises: a history of conscription in Canada* (1977), *Bloody victory: Canadians and the D-Day campaign 1944* (1984), and *The generals: the Canadian Army's senior commanders in the Second World War* (1993). He also wrote *War and peacekeeping* (1991) and co-authored *Mutual hostages: Canadians and Japanese during the Second World War* (1990). The movement of Canada away from Britain and closer to the USA was explained with dispassion and balance, supported with sound evidence culled from North American and British archives, in *American dollars—Canadian prosperity* (1978), *For better or for worse: Canada and the United States to the 1990s* (1991), and *Yankee go home? Canadians and anti-Americans* (1996). But Granatstein did not ignore the importance of individuals, writing *Mackenzie King: his life and world* (1977), *The Ottawa men: the civil service mandarins 1935-1957* (1982), and a study of one of the mandarins, *A man of influence: Norman Robertson and Canadian statecraft 1929-68* (1981). Other Granatstein publications include a criticism of universities, *The great brain robbery* (1984), and *Sacred trust? Brian Mulroney and the Conservatives in power* (1986), which were both polemical, while in *Canada 1957-1967* (1986), written for The Canadian Centenary Series, Granatstein entered the arena of cultural history. With David J. Bercuson he wrote the *Dictionary of Canadian military history* (1992). TERRY CROWLEY

Grandbois, Alain (1900-75). Born in Saint-Casimir de Portneuf, Quebec, he studied law at Université Laval but, though admitted to the bar in 1925, never practised. A considerable inheritance allowed him to travel abroad almost continuously between 1918 and 1938. Based in Paris—where he met fellow-expatriates Ernest Hemingway, Blaise Cendrars, and Jules Supervielle—he travelled extensively in Europe, Africa, India, Russia, China, and Japan. After his return to Canada he wrote steadily, earning his living by giving many radio talks on his travels, lecturing, and writing articles, as well as working as bibliographer at the Bibliothèque Saint-Sulpice. In 1944 he was co-founder, with Victor Barbeau, of L'Académie canadienne-française, a group he never lost touch with. (In this period he translated Merrill DENISON's *The barley and the stream: the Molson story*, 1955, under the title *Au pied du courant*, 1955.) Grandbois returned to France in 1955, and in 1956 took up residence in Mont Rolland, north of Montreal. In 1960-1 he travelled in France and Italy on a CANADA COUNCIL fellowship and then settled in Quebec City, where he worked for the Musée de la Province de Québec. He was three times awarded the Prix David; he also received the Prix Duvernay, the Lorne PIERCE Medal, and an honorary doctorate from Université Laval.

Grandbois was justly renowned as a poet. In 1934 a casual acquaintance published seven of his poems in Hankow (China). These, with minor variants, were included in *Les îles de la nuit* (1944); this was followed by *Rivages de l'homme* (1948) and *L'étoile pourpre* (1957). His poems are admired for the sonorous harmonies and exotic colours of their language and for their impelling, incantatory rhetoric. The poet writes as a solitary figure in a harsh and implacable universe. His themes are love, the fleeting years, mortality.

Grandbois's prose writings, close in theme to his poetry, reflect his love of travel, and include biographies of explorers who, on their journeys in search of earth's 'éblouissants secrets' (dazzling secrets), courted danger and death. *Né à Québec: Louis Jolliet* (Paris, 1933; Montreal, 1949, 1969), was reissued in a critical edition (1994) edited by E. Côté and Jean Cléo Godin; an English translation by Evelyn Brown, *Born in Quebec*, was published in 1964, and *Les voyages de Marco Polo* was published in 1942. *Avant le chaos* (1945), a collection of short stories (republished in 1964 with four additional tales), recalls the cosmopolitan world from Paris to Djibouti, Canton to Cannes—a world irrevocably destroyed by the 'chaos' of the Second World War. In a tone of elegant detachment and suppressed passion, Grandbois describes the sights, sounds, and ambience of exotic milieux, conveying the ugliness and violence lurking behind scenes of spectacular beauty, and the alienation and loss, exile and displacement, passion and regret that underlie charm and graciousness. His astringent evocations of human emotion are subtle and resonant. A critical edition, edited by G. Bouchard and H. Deschamps, was published in 1991. Personal reflections by Grandbois on the interwar years, written for the French network of the Canadian Broadcasting Corporation in 1951, have been published in *Visages du monde: images et souvenirs de l'entre-deux guerres* (1971), edited by Léopold Leblanc; a critical edition, edited by Jean Cléo Godin, was published in 1990.

An anthology of Grandbois's verse and prose, *Alain Grandbois* (Paris, 1968), ably presented by Jacques BRAULT, contains three poems previously unpublished. A bilingual collection of his poetry, *Selected poems* (1964), contains translations by Peter Miller with the French originals. Grandbois's influence on post-war poetry in French Canada has been acknowledged by the poets of the fifties and sixties: by Jean-Guy PILON and Gaston MIRON in the review *Amérique française* in 1954; in a special number of *LIBERTÉ* (1960); and by the publication of Grandbois's collected *Poèmes* (1963). A new edition of *Poèmes* (1979) includes fourteen additional poems—confirming Grandbois's astonishing consistency of theme, vocabulary, and tone—which had already been presented by Jacques Blais in his *Présence d'Alain Grandbois* (1975). Blais's essay is a tasteful and detailed biography of the poet's early years, merging into a study of his work and a brief survey of critical responses to it, and a full bibliography. Blais has also acknowledged, and skilfully demonstrated, Grandbois's role in the modernization of poetry in Quebec in *De l'ordre et de l'aventure* (1975). More unpublished poems appeared in *Délivrance du jour et autres inédits* (1980), the main title referring to a collection of poems planned as early as 1948. A critical edition of Grandbois's complete poetry, *Alain Grandbois: poésie: I, II* (1980), was edited by M. Saint-Amour and J.-A. Stanton.

See also S. Dallard, *L'univers poétique d'Alain Grandbois* (1975); M. Greffard, *Alain Grandbois* (1975); and *Ellipse* 14/15 (1974), devoted to Grandbois and John GLASSCO; Nicole Deschamps and Jean Cléo Godin, 'Alain Grandbois, lecteur du monde', *Études françaises*, 30/2 (automne 1994); Deschamps and Godin, *Livres et pays d'Alain Grandbois* (1995); Y. Bolduc, *L'étoile mythique* (1994); M. Fortin, *Histoire d'une célébration* (1994); and D. Pérusse, *L'homme sans rivages* (1994). C.R.P. MAY

Grand'maison, Jacques. See ESSAYS IN FRENCH: 6.

Grant, George (1918-88). George Parkin Grant was born in Toronto and educated at Upper Canada College; Queen's University, Kingston; and Oxford University, where he was a Rhodes Scholar. His paternal grandfather, George Monro Grant (author of *OCEAN TO OCEAN*), had been a principal of Queen's, and his paternal grandfather, Sir George Parkin—who, like his father, had been a principal of Upper Canada College—had headed the Rhodes Trust. From 1947 to 1960 George Grant taught philosophy at Dalhousie University, Halifax, becoming head of the department; he was then chairman of the department of religion at McMaster University, Hamilton, Ontario, until 1980, when he returned to Dalhousie as Killam Professor.

Grant's writings have occupied a major place in Canadian intellectual life since the appearance of *Philosophy in the mass age* (1959). His influence has been significant in literature, political theory, and religious thinking, though he has remained outside the bounds of most professional philosophers. Christianity had always been central to his thought. He was influenced for a time by Hegel; but his strongest philosophical inclinations were generally Platonic. Both Simone Weil and Martin Heidegger influenced his later thought. *Philosophy in the mass age* (following a small work, *The Empire, yes or no?*, 1945) sought to establish the importance of the Judaeo-Christian tradition as a major element in the understanding of human freedom and the transcendence of nature, while seeking to retain the relevance of the classical notion of a natural order that sets limits to human behaviour. *Lament for a nation: the defeat of Canadian nationalism* (1965; 2nd edn, with a new introduction by the author, 1970; CARLETON LIBRARY) exercised a wide influence on proponents of Canadian economic nationalism, with its thesis that Canada had been destroyed as a viable nation by the ideology of American liberalism backed by technology and corporate capitalism. Grant's nostalgia for the values expounded by John G. Diefenbaker (Conservative prime minister of Canada from 1957 to 1963) suggests a strong conservative strand in his thought. Grant described his break with the New Democratic Party, which occurred when the party supported the official (Liberal) Opposition in a vote critical of Diefenbaker's position on the stationing of American nuclear missiles in Canada. Grant's conservatism was of the sort that figures in Canadian politics as 'red Toryism', having little to do with the support of 'free enterprise' but emphasizing social responsibility, the duties of the strong to the weak, and the sense of continuing community. The theses in *Lament for a nation* were extended somewhat in *Technology and empire* (1969), essays that clearly associated Grant's thought with that of Leo Strauss and Jacques Ellul.

Grant's writings emphasize tradition and are a severe critique of the notion that the primary meaning of human life is to be found in history that exemplifies continuous progress. His CBC Massey Lectures, published as *Time as history* (1969) and focusing on an examination of Nietzsche, insist that there are eternal values, and that basic Christian notions soundly limit what can be done to, and with, human beings. In *English-speaking justice* (1974) Grant returned to criticizing liberal ideology with a cutting analysis of the philosophy of John Rawls, and of other recent forms of the social-contract theory. While Grant's philosophical interests changed and developed considerably over the years, the centre of his political thought continued, to the end of his life, to reflect clearly his original Platonism, with its insistence on stability rather than change, eternal values rather than temporal pleasures, and community rather than individuality.

Grant's work continues to draw attention. See Joan E. O'Donovan, *George Grant and the twilight of justice* (1984); William Christian, *George Grant: a biography* (1993), which includes a general overview of his thought; and *George Grant: selected letters* (1996) edited by William Christian. A variety of responses to Grant have been collected in *George Grant and the legacy of lament for a nation* (1990) edited by Peter Emberley. They supplement an earlier collection, *George Grant in process* (1978), edited by Larry Schmidt.

LESLIE ARMOUR, ELIZABETH TROTT

Grant, George Monro. See *OCEAN TO OCEAN*.

Graphic Publishers (1925-32). Founded by Henry C. Miller, an Ottawa printer, and incorporated on 6 July 1926 with Miller as president, The Graphic Publishers, also referred to as Graphic Press, was an Ottawa-based publisher that sought, in the words of its founder, 'to handle nothing but Canadian books by Canadians and for Canadians'. Graphic's first book was Madge MacBETH's *The land of afternoon* (1926), a satire on social and political life in Ottawa, published under the pseudonym 'Gilbert Knox'. The book was an instant success and launched the press. The directors included Lawrence J. Burpee, a prolific author, who was a founder of the Canadian Historical Association and Canadian secretary to the International Joint Commission. Graphic Publishers chose as its trademark a thunderbird device adapted by Alan B. Beddoe from representations of the thunderbird in Northwest Coast First Nations cultures. Although in its seven years Graphic was seldom free from financial difficulties or infighting, it published no less than eighty-three titles under various imprints before it succumbed to the Depression. Other imprints included Ariston Publishers, Canadian Biographies Limited, Carillon Book Club of Canada, Laurentian Press Syndicate, and two vanity presses, Ru-Mi-Lou Books and Overbrook Press.

Graphic's publications included fiction, poetry, plays, essays, history, and criticism. Madge Macbeth's other titles included the feminist satire *Shackles* (1926). Another early success for the press was Frederick Philip GROVE's *A search for America* (1927), which underwent two printings and was also issued as a Carillon Book Club title. In 1929 Grove joined Graphic as head of its subsidiary, Ariston Publishers Limited. Other well-known Canadian authors published by the press included William Arthur DEACON, Merrill DENISON, and Watson KIRKCONNELL. Raymond KNISTER won first prize in The Graphic Publishers' Canadian Novel contest for his manuscript *My star predominant*; however, the press failed before the book could be printed. (It was subsequently published by the RYERSON PRESS.) In 'Graphic Publishers and the bibliographer', *Papers of the Bibliographic Society of Canada 18* (1979), David B. Kotin provides a brief history of the press and a checklist of its publications.

PAUL HJARTARSON

Gravel, François. See CHILDREN'S LITERATURE IN FRENCH 1980s TO 1996.

Gray, James H. (b. 1906). He grew up and was educated in Winnipeg during its boom years. After a succession of jobs at the Winnipeg Grain Exchange and with stockbrokers, he was forced to go on relief during the Depression. He took to writing articles, and as a result was engaged in 1935 as a reporter on the *Winnipeg Free Press*, becoming an editorial writer in 1941, and Ottawa correspondent in 1946. From 1947 to 1955 he edited the *Farm and Ranch Review*, and from 1955 to 1958 the *Western Oil Examiner*. He fought against domination of oil exploration by American multinationals, eventually moving to the Home Oil Company in Calgary to promote an all-Canadian pipeline to Montreal.

After his early retirement in 1963, Gray began to write the vivid, unconventional social histories of the Prairies that made him one of Canada's leading popular historians. Three books are chiefly autobiographical: *The boy from Winnipeg* (1970) captures the atmosphere of childhood; *The winter years* (1966) describes how the Prairies survived the Depression with such expedients as food vouchers and 'boondoggling' work projects; and *Troublemaker!* (1978), which tells of Gray's career as a journalist and the causes that engaged him, from the politics of the oil patch to the marketing of western grain.

Other works, drawing on oral history and personal knowledge as well as archival sources, investigate aspects of daily life on the Prairies that had until then received scant documentation. *Men against the desert* (1967) celebrates the success of the Dominion Experimental Farms and the Prairie Farm Rehabilitation Administration in helping farmers to combat the drought, dust, and insect infestations of the thirties. *Red lights on the Prairies* (1971) is a history of prostitution in prairie towns before the Depression, grimly revealing the lack of social amenities in early settlements. *Booze* (1972), on the tradition of heavy drinking on the Prairies, throws cold water on the received liberal view that prohibition was a disaster, and argues that life improved when the bars were closed. *Bacchanalia revisited* (1982), pursuing the theme in the modern era, adequately reveals its attitude in the subtitle *Western Canada's boozy skid to social disaster*. Gray has also written *The roar of the twenties* (1975); *Boomtime* (1979), a lavishly illustrated record of immigration up to the First World War; *A brand of its own* (1985), a history of the Calgary Stampede; and *Talk to my lawyer!* (1987), an anecdotal history of the Calgary bar.

Bucking the trend to social and oral history that he himself had pioneered, Gray turned to academic political history and biography in his *R.B. Bennett: the Calgary years* (1991). Though this was useful and well-researched, Gray is likely to be remembered chiefly for his more personal and evocative works. Engagingly written, often without footnotes, they have been honoured with a number of awards, and have been a potent means (along with prizes sponsored by Gray) of disseminating knowledge of western Canada's history to a wider public. JEAN O'GRADY

Gray, John (b. 1946). Born in Ottawa, Ontario, he was raised in Truro, Nova Scotia, and attended Mount Allison University (B.A., 1968) and the University of British Columbia (M.A., 1972). Active in Vancouver theatre, Gray founded Tamahnous Theatre. In the mid-1970s he moved to Toronto and became involved with Theatre Passe Muraille, composing music for a number of productions including Rick SALUTIN's *1837: the farmers' revolt* (1976) and *The false messiah* (1982), and Herschel Hardin's *The great wave of civilization* (1976). These early theatrical endeavours led to the aspect of Gray's career for which he is most recognized: his work as a playwright committed to forging a uniquely Canadian sense of the musical. Gray has also written a novel, *Dazzled* (1984), the satiric tale of marital breakdown in which the protagonist, Willard, sets aside his idealism and enters the world of business.

Gray's first musical to gain national attention was *18 wheels* (1987), which premièred at Theatre Passe Muraille in 1977 and was produced across Canada. Portraying Canadian truckers influenced by Country and Western music from the USA, Gray established in this early piece his recurrent interest in defining Canadian identity in the face of an array of international influences.

Billy Bishop goes to war, written in collaboration with Eric Peterson (and winner, in 1982, of a Governor General's Award) is a work for two performers. In the original production, Peterson played Billy Bishop, with Gray providing musical accompaniment as the Piano Player: it was well acted, well produced, and popular. In many ways the play is a coming-of-age story in which Bishop recounts incidents from his life, and in the process performs a range of characters. The question haunting the end of *Billy Bishop*—'Makes you wonder what it was all for?'—could usefully serve as the question raised by *Rock and roll* (1982). This semi-autobiographical piece dramatizes the reunion of a rock band, the Monarchs, in the fictionalized locale of Mushaboom, Nova Scotia. Here, using rock and roll (which developed in Canada with heavy debts to influences from the USA), Gray seems to suggest that Canadian appropriation of artistic forms leads to a vital, uniquely Canadian expression of local culture.

Both plays deal with the experiences of ageing protagonists, for whom authentic identity seems to be associated with past glories; and, in some sense, they deal also with memory and identity. In *Don Messer's Jubilee* (1985) Gray tackled issues of national nostalgia. In 1969 the

Canadian Broadcasting Corporation cancelled this popular Canadian TV show featuring Messer, a fiddler, to make way for programming aimed at a younger audience who were culturally predisposed to the musical genres that Gray had used in *Rock and roll*. In writing *Don Messer's Jubilee*, Gray sought to immerse himself in the local musical idioms of the Maritimes and recover a part of Canadian musical heritage that was disowned by the CBC's cancellation of Messer's long-running show.

Local boy makes good: three musicals by John Gray (1987) contains *18 wheels*, *Rock and roll*, and *Don Messer's Jubilee*. See Robert Wallace and Cynthia Zimmerman, eds, *The work* (1982).

ANN WILSON

Gray, John Morgan (1907-78). Born in Toronto, publisher and author John Gray was educated at Lakefield College and Upper Canada College and the University of Toronto, where he did not take his degree. Following a year as an assistant master at Lakefield, an introduction to Hugh Eayrs, the unpredictable but brilliant president of the MACMILLAN COMPANY OF CANADA—whose exasperating qualities and mannerisms are drawn with a novelist's skill in Gray's memoirs, *Fun tomorrow* (1978)—procured him a job as an educational representative. The years of crossing and recrossing the continent in the Depression gave Gray a knowledge of book publishing, and of people in hard times. This was to serve him well when, after four years' active service in Europe—during which he rose to become GSO(2) in the Intelligence Corps of the First Canadian Army in Holland—he returned somewhat reluctantly to publishing.

Hugh Eayrs died in 1940, and the appointment of a successor had been postponed by Macmillan of London until the war ended. Gray was appointed in 1946, first as manager and within a year as president, with full powers of acquisition and of forming company policy. He retired from the company in 1973. His boisterous sense of fun and gift for caricature and for puncturing pomposity—qualities that had hampered his early career—hid, as it turned out, executive abilities that put him among the leaders of postwar Canadian publishing. This was a propitious time to take charge of a Canadian publishing company. The long servitude of the industry to its British and American overlords, which had made many publishers no more than importing agencies, was about to be transformed. Given full powers and resources, limited only by British Exchange Control restrictions, Gray was provided with an opportunity to become not only a leader but, by virtue of his partnership in a world-wide publishing organization, a spokesman for the trade. Gray was one of several young veterans—like Jack McCLELLAND of McCLELLAND & STEWART and Marsh JEANNERET, later to join the UNIVERSITY OF TORONTO PRESS—who had returned to civilian life with new ideas and boundless energy that would serve the Canadian publishing industry. Established and influential figures, like Lorne PIERCE of the RYERSON PRESS who had worked with Gray on joint educational enterprises, were supportive. Youthful successors were now at the helm of a number of houses. With the Massey Report (1951) pointing the way, and the CANADA COUNCIL (1957) providing both publishers and authors with the backing they needed, the Canadian publishing industry was about to mature.

Gray's part in this period of growth in Canadian publishing can be traced in the numerous papers he gave at publishing conferences and in public addresses. The experience and achievements of the fifties and sixties are summed up in an article he contributed to *CANADIAN LITERATURE* 33 (Spring 1967). Master of a simple, unadorned style with humorous undertones, he had always wanted to be a writer. His chief interest was in Canadian history, and his *Lord Selkirk of Red River* (1963), which was awarded the University of British Columbia medal for the best biography of the year, shows what Canadian writing lost to Canadian publishing when he opted for a career as a publisher.

Gray had the gift of subordinating his own ambition to the concerns of his writers. Many leading Canadian authors joined the Macmillan list, and the evidence of how well Gray served them as editor is preserved in the correspondence in the Macmillan archives, now at McMaster University.

Fun tomorrow, published a few weeks after Gray's death from cancer, was to have been the first volume of a two-volume memoir. A delightful and amusing impression of a Canadian upbringing, and of his first faltering steps in publishing, the book ends at the point where he took over command of the Macmillan Company of Canada.

In 1932 Gray married Antoinette Lalonde, the heroine of *Fun tomorrow*. He was appointed an Officer of the Order of Canada in 1975. The recipient of many honorary degrees from Canadian universities, he was a (founding) member of the Board of Governors of York University from 1960 to 1970.

LOVAT DICKSON

Green, Terence M. (b. 1947). A science-fiction and fantasy writer, Terence Michael Green was born in Toronto, Ontario, where he has taught English at East York Collegiate Institute since 1968. He has a B.A. (1967) in English and a B.Ed. (1973) from the University of Toronto, and an M.A. (1972) in Anglo-Irish studies from University College, Dublin.

His first publication in Canada was the story 'Of children in the foliage' in *Aurora: New Canadian Writing 1979*; his first in the USA was the story 'Till death do us part' in the December 1981 issue of *Magazine of Fantasy & Science Fiction*. He has had three other stories published in that magazine, and three more in *Isaac Asimov's Science Fiction Magazine* (including a collaboration with Toronto's Andrew Weiner in the June 1988 issue).

Green is the author of a trio of increasingly accomplished novels. *Barking dogs* (1988) expands his short story of the same name in *Magazine of Fantasy & Science Fiction* (May 1984): it is a tale of vigilantism and psychological breakdown in a future Toronto, in which perfect, portable lie detectors—'barking dogs'—change both interpersonal relationships and criminal justice. The anthology *Ark of ice* (1992) edited by Leslie CHOYCE, contains a sequel novelette entitled 'Blue limbo', which was later developed and published as *Blue limbo* (1997). *Children of the rainbow* (1992) displaces a variety of characters through time, with the author undertaking to combine the *Mutiny on the bounty* story, the anti-nuclear protests of Greenpeace, and an Inca religious revival. At its best moments the book is both satiric and moving. Green's third novel, the slim *Shadow of Ashland* (1996), is again an expansion of a short story, in this case 'Ashland, Kentucky' (first published in *Isaac Asimov's Science Fiction Magazine*, Nov. 1985). About a son's search for his dying mother's brother who had disappeared decades ago, it is highly autobiographical, with real relatives of Green appearing under their own names.

'Barking dogs' and 'Ashland, Kentucky', plus eight other stories by Green, are collected in *The woman who is the midnight wind* (1987). ROBERT J. SAWYER

Gregory, Claudius Jabez. See NOVELS IN ENGLISH 1920 TO 1940: 1.

Grenfell, Wilfred Thomason (1865-1940). Born at Parkgate, Cheshire, England, he attended Marlborough College in Wiltshire. In 1883 he entered medical school in the London Hospital, and in 1888 was entered as a member of the Royal College of Surgeons and the Royal College of Physicians. While a medical student he wandered one evening into a meeting conducted by the American preacher D.L. Moody and came away 'feeling that I had crossed the Rubicon'. Determining on a life of service, in 1888 he started work with the medical section of the Nation Mission to Deep Sea Fishermen, serving in the North Atlantic from Iceland to the Bay of Biscay and becoming an expert sailor. In 1892 he travelled to Newfoundland to assess the need for medical services in the northern regions of the colony. He returned the following year with two doctors and two nurses and established at Battle Harbour the first hospital of what would be called the Labrador Medical Mission. His life thereafter was devoted to the advancement of his medical work in Newfoundland and Labrador. In 1912 the International Grenfell Association was formed to coordinate and promote Grenfell's activities. Grenfell also experimented with ways to improve the Newfoundland economy, emphasizing self-help, home industries, co-operatives, and a diversified approach to the development of resources. He was the recipient of many honours, including an honorary M.D. from Oxford University in 1907; he was knighted in 1927.

Grenfell was a brilliant publicist, and his numerous speeches, magazine articles, and books were part of his favourite activity of promoting and financing his mission. His books are somewhat repetitive and opinionated, but they are not without a certain liveliness and power, and their number reflects his popularity as a writer and the fame that came to surround him. His cocksure, dominant personality, and the sheer drama of his life on a perilous, bleak coastline, hold our interest. The books fall into three main categories. First, there are his factual, scientific, and promotional accounts of Labrador: *Vikings of today; or, Life and medical work among the fishermen of Labrador* (London, 1895); *Labrador: the country and the people* (1909), a symposium to which he contributed ten of sixteen chapters; *Labrador's fight for economic freedom* (1929); and *The romance of Labrador* (1934), an eloquent statement of his love for his adopted homeland.

The second kind of book by Grenfell is the Labrador storybook—true tales of the people and of his experiences among them. The best is *Adrift on an ice-pan* (1909)—first published as *A voyage on a pan of ice* (1908)—a hair-raising account of a brush with death that first brought Grenfell's name to the attention of the world. It can still be read with genuine pleasure, for Grenfell had real gifts as a story teller. A recent reprint (1992) has an introduction by Ronald Rompkey. Other books in this category are *The harvest of the sea: a tale of both sides of the Atlantic* (1905), *Off the rocks: stories of the deep-sea fisherfolk of Labrador* (1906), *Down to the sea: yarns from the Labrador* (1910), *Down north on the Labrador* (1911), *Tales of the Labrador* (1916), *Labrador days: tales of the sea toilers* (1919), *Northern neighbours: stories of the Labrador people* (1923), *That Christmas in Peace Haven and Three Eyes* (1923), and *Deeds of daring* (1934).

A third group of books by Grenfell comprises his religious and autobiographical works. Though born an Anglican, Grenfell had been brought to something close to an evangelical conversion by Moody, and his religion was an untroubled, wholehearted commitment to a life of Christian action. He wrote many books displaying an unshakeable and simple faith: *A man's faith* (1908); *A man's helpers* (1910); *What life means to me* (1910); *What will you do with Jesus Christ* (1910); *What the church means to me: a frank confession and a friendly estimate by an insider* (1911); *Shall a man live again? A vital assurance of faith in immortality* (1912); *What can Jesus Christ do with me* (1912); *The adventure of life: being the William Belden Noble Lectures for 1911* (1912); *On immortality* (1912); *The attractive way* (1913); *The prize of life* (1914); *A Labrador doctor: the autobiography of Wilfred Thomason Grenfell* (1919), expanded in 1932 under a new title, *Forty years for Labrador*; *Yourself and your body* (1924); *Religion in everyday life* (1926); *What Christ means to me* (1926); *Labrador looks at the Orient: notes of travel in the Near and the Far East* (1928); *The fishermen's saint* (1930); and *A Labrador logbook* (1938).

Labrador looks at the Orient and *A Labrador logbook* are in some ways his most engaging books, revealing Grenfell's idiosyncratic opinions and the extent of his miscellaneous reading.

Still useful is J. Lennox Kerr's *Wilfred Grenfell: his life and work* (1959). Pierre BERTON has a fine chapter on Grenfell in *The wild frontier* (1978). See Ronald Rompkey, *Grenfell of Labrador: a biography* (1991).

PATRICK O'FLAHERTY

Grey, Francis William (1860-1939). Born in England, he was the son of the Hon. Jane Stuart and Admiral the Hon. George Grey, grandson of Charles, the second Earl Grey, prime minister of England when the Reform Bill of 1831 was passed, and first cousin of the fourth Earl Grey, governor general of Canada from 1904 to 1911. It is not known when he came to North America, but he was teaching at Manhattan College, New York, in 1885 when he married Jessie, daughter of Jessie Chisolm and Charles Octave Rolland, seigneur of Ste Marie de Monnoir in the Richelieu district; at this time he had probably converted to Roman Catholicism. From 1903 to 1904 he taught English literature and elocution at the University of Ottawa, from which he received in 1908 the degree of Doctor of Letters for his 'many literary productions . . . in both prose and verse'. In 1905 he joined the Dominion Archives in a clerical position that was made permanent in 1908, and in 1912 he was appointed translator. He resigned in 1913 on a pension of $500 a year. In later years Grey lived in Edinburgh, Scotland, where he died. His wife predeceased him in 1928. At the time of his death Grey was heir presumptive to the fifth Earl Grey. In 1963 his great-grandson succeeded to the title.

Grey is best remembered for his novel *The curé of St. Philippe: a story of French-Canadian politics* (London, 1899), a realistic and entertaining portrait of a small Quebec community, based on the Rolland seigneury, at the end of the nineteenth century. Wide-ranging in theme and characterization in the tradition of the nineteenth-century English novel, it incorporates the religious and political interests evident in Grey's later plays and essays. The establishment of a new parish in the Richelieu district, and events surrounding the 1896 federal election—in which, for the first time in Quebec, the Rouges (Liberals) overcame the Bleus (Conservatives)—provide the central issues. English- and French-speaking Catholics and Protestants, clergymen, landowners, and local politicians all become involved. Religion, romance, and business intrigues are interwoven with English-French relations, the clergy's role in the community, and political corruption. An intrusive narrator—citing numerous literary figures (of whom Carlyle is the favourite) and maintaining a low-key and lightly humorous tone—fills in the background and comments on the issues. This light, ironic tone, along with the novel's accurate portrayal of the intricacies of the political and religious issues of late nineteenth-century Quebec, recommend the novel to us today.

Grey's plays are historical and religious. *Sixteen ninety: a series of historical tableaux* (1904) concerns intrigues against Frontenac, newly appointed governor of Canada. Grey later published *Four plays* (1931), containing *Bishop and king*, which deals with the execution of Blessed Oliver Plunkett by Charles II as a result of wrongful accusation; *The bridegroom cometh*, a one-act play about the parable of the wise and foolish virgins; *The valiant woman*, demonstrating the truth of Isaiah's prophecy, 'Every age shall shew/a valiant woman'; and *Love's pilgrimage*, which tells of a pilgrim in the time of Christ. All are didactic, none memorable.

Grey also published a collection of poetry, *Love crucified and other sacred verse* (Ottawa, 1902). His poetry and essays—dealing with religious, literary, historical, and educational topics—appeared in a variety of Canadian, American, and British publications, including the *UNIVERSITY MAGAZINE*, *Fortnightly Review*, *Westminster Review*, *American Catholic Quarterly*, and *University of Ottawa Review*.

See Rupert Schieder's introduction to the NEW CANADIAN LIBRARY edition (1970) of *The curé of St. Philippe*.

LORRAINE McMULLEN

Grey Owl. See Archibald Stansfield BELANEY.

Grier, **Eldon** (b. 1917). Born in London, England, of Canadian parents (his father was a captain in the Canadian army), he was raised in Montreal and began his professional career as a painter. In 1945 he went to Mexico to study fresco painting with Alfredo Zalce, and was later apprenticed to Diego Rivera as a plasterer. On his return to Montreal he became a teacher under Arthur Lismer at the Montreal Museum of Fine Arts.

In his middle thirties Grier developed tuberculosis, recovered, married his second wife (painter Sylvia Tait), and began to write poetry. Between 1955 and 1965 he travelled extensively in Europe—he began to write poetry while living in Spain—and spent a number of winters in Mexico. His poetry collections include *A morning from scraps* (1955), *The year of the sun: poems* (1956), *The ring of ice* (1957), *Manzanillo & other poems* (1958), *A friction of lights* (1963), *Pictures on the skin* (1967), *The women of Quebec* (1969), *Selected poems: 1955-1970* (1971), and *The assassination of colour* (1978).

Like much writing begun in maturity, his early collections contain no false starts or stumblings: Grier seemed to find his voice immediately. His poems are the product of critical intelligence and a highly visual imagination. He writes in the tradition of Modernism, displaying a remarkable linguistic virtuosity. Pleasure in language is the centre of his aesthetic experience—'Is there a single word which doesn't respond/like a servant torn from sleep?'—and his reflective poems are infused with the colloquial. He is fascinated by formal control and his poems play with line shifts, rhyme, and complicated stanzaic shapes. Some poems are surreal collages of images that push through bizarre juxtapositions to new insights. With a temperament that is urbane yet energetic, Grier earned his urbanity through a lifetime of visiting foreign parts. He has written many travel poems, of which those on Mexico are exceptionally powerful. The enormous impact of painting on his work is evident, not only in the numerous poems to painters and sculptors (Morandi, Marini, Picasso, Modigliani, Morrice, Giacometti) but in the frequency with which he approaches a poem like a still life: a 'ceramic' of images, light and colour. Many of Grier's poems are anecdotal, focusing on an emotionally fraught moment in which a character is deftly portrayed in a phrase or two, although he shares a modern cynicism—we have 'survived the relevance of our survival'—and acknowledges the 'tragic angularity' of the world. Grier in his poetry is committed to a belief in the will's capacity to reassert human values: tenderness, simplicity, beauty. Reading his work one encounters a sensibility of deep generosity and compassion; a writer committed to new explorations of creativity as an antidote to the modern temptation to nostalgia: 'we must die with conviction of regret.'

Grier currently lives in Vancouver. In 1997 he was made a 'Life Member' of the LEAGUE OF CANADIAN POETS in recognition of his contribution to Canadian poetry.

ROSEMARY SULLIVAN

Grignon, **Claude-Henri** (1894-1976), who used the pseudonym 'Valdombre', was born in Sainte-Adèle, Quebec. After being educated partly at the Collège Saint-Laurent, Montreal, and partly at home, he moved to Montreal and became a civil servant. From 1916 to 1939 he wrote articles for various newspapers, but returned to the Laurentians in 1936 and started a second career as a radio writer. He was elected mayor of Sainte-Adèle (1941-51) and became prefect of Terrebonne county. A member of the ÉCOLE LITTÉRAIRE DE MONTRÉAL since 1928, he received the Prix David in 1935 and was elected to the Royal Society of Canada in 1961.

As a journalist Grignon was a well-known polemicist and an earnest nationalist, having worked with such prominent figures as Olivar Asselin. He collected some of his numerous book reviews and critical articles on literature in *Ombres et clameurs: regards sur la littérature canadienne* (1933). From 1936 to 1943 he singlehandedly published a notorious and widely read periodical, *Les pamphlets de Valdombre*, which discloses his rather conservative political and literary ideas and conveys the ideal of a French-Canadian literature based on regionalism.

Grignon's first novel, *Le secret de Lindbergh* (1928), celebrates Colonel Charles Lindbergh's successful flight over the Atlantic in 1927. It conveys the writer's enthusiasm, especially in many epic and lyrical descriptions, but contains an undue amount of moralizing. This was followed by the important novel *Un homme et son péché* (1933), which has been reprinted many times, is still in print, and was translated by Yves Brunelle as *The woman and the miser* (1978). Its plot was the basis of a highly successful radio series (1939-65), a well-known television serial (1956-70), and two motion pictures, shot in 1948 and 1950. *Un homme et son péché* represents, within a sociological perspective, the consequences of the economic crisis of the thirties, symbolized by the selfish miser Séraphin Poudrier, and male domination of women, symbolized by the cruel treatment and ensuing death of Séraphin's wife. Its strength lies in its realistic style and in the portrayal of the sado-masochistic relationship of the lustful husband and the submissive wife. The dramatized series expanded the novel into a larger picture of rural life in Quebec. Grignon's *Précisions sur 'Un homme et son péché'* (1936)—a bitter reply to his detractors, who saw only the sordid aspects of his novel—explains how his book was based on actual events and real characters and scolds his contemporaries for their lack of imagination and their failure to write good 'regional' novels.

Le déserteur et autres récits de la terre (1934; rpr. 1976) is a collection of six short stories that reveals Grignon's knack for creating interesting characters and for depicting popular customs; but the book is weakened by constant attempts to demonstrate the advantages of rural over city life.

Grignon's polemical writings are the subject of Jean-Pierre Bonneville's *De Valdombre à André Gide* (1948). Analyses of his works by Renée Legris, Alonzo LeBlanc, Gilles Dorion, and Maurice Lemire have been published in the *Dictionnaire des oeuvres littéraires du Québec*, t. II (1980). Antoine Sirois's and Yvette Francoli's 1986 critical edition of *Un homme et son péché* contains the most extensive study of Grignon's celebrated novel.

LUCIE ROBERT

Grip (1873-94). A comic and satirical weekly, it was published in Toronto between May 1873 and December 1894 and was initiated by cartoonist John Wilson Bengough, with the financial support of publisher-bookseller Andrew Scott Irving. Beginning as a five-page weekly, of which two pages were advertisements, it eventually increased to eight pages. Bengough continued as editor and chief illustrator with the exception of one year, beginning in 1892, when John Phillips Thompson took over; the weekly was then suspended for a year, after which Bengough resumed the editorship.

With its humorous and satirical cartoons and writings on politics—local, provincial, and national—and on religion, literature, and society, *Grip* became Canada's *Punch*. It also published satiric verses; witty pseudonymous letters, such as those from 'Tabitha Twitter'; a series of 'Characters' instituted in 1880; columns such as 'Pen, Pencil, and Press' on writers and writing; and essays of social satire entitled 'Dyspeptic Papers'. While sometimes deriding aspects of the women's movement, *Grip* published Sarah Anne CURZON's blank-verse comedy *The sweet girl graduate* (1882), in which, although women are forbidden entry to university, a cross-dressing young woman graduates with top honours. Later issues of the paper included prose sketches.

Although purporting to be politically independent, *Grip* usually supported the Whig or reformist view. Its ridicule, through cartoons, of Sir John A. Macdonald and the Pacific Scandal, in its first years of publication, helped establish its popularity. In fact, so successful were these early satirical cartoons that in 1875 Bengough published *The Grip cartoons .... May 1873 to May 1874*. Although he remained *Grip*'s main illustrator, sometimes providing illustrations under pseudonyms, other illustrators in later years included Charles W. Jeffreys, Tom Thomson, Arthur Lismer, J.E.H. MacDonald, and Arthur Lismer. Writers often used pseudonyms. Jessie Kerr Lawson, for example, a prolific journalist and novelist, wrote for *Grip* as the Irish Barney O'Shea, the Scottish Hugh Airlie, the black Washington White, and as J.K. and J.K.Lawson—sometimes contributing two or three items to the same issue under more than one pseudonym. Stephen LEACOCK was a contributor in the paper's final year.

LORRAINE McMULLEN

Grohovaz, Gianni. See ITALIAN-CANADIAN LITERATURE.

Grosskurth, Phyllis (b. 1924). Born Phyllis Langstaff in Toronto, Ontario, Grosskurth was educated there at St Clement's School and the University of Toronto (B.A., 1946), and at the University of Ottawa (M.A., 1960) and the University of London (Ph.D., 1962). Like that of many outstanding Canadian women academics of her generation, her career has combined child rearing, a return to academe for further study, and eventually the establishment of a distinguished career as teacher, scholar, and writer. In 1965 Grosskurth joined the English department of the University of Toronto, of which she is now Professor Emeritus, and where she was appointed to the Humanities and Psychoanalytic Thought program in 1986. She has received fellowships and awards from the Canada Council and from the Guggenheim, Rockefeller, Laidlaw, and Killam foundations. In 1965 she won the University of British Columbia award for biography.

Grosskurth's dissertation for her Ph.D. was on 'The literary criticism of John Addington Symonds'; within two years she had published *John Addington Symonds: a biography* (1964), for which she received a Governor General's Award. (It was published in the United States as *The woeful Victorian: a biography of John Addington Symonds.*) Grosskurth returned to Symonds in her edition of *The memoirs of John Addington Symonds* (1984). Symonds' circle included Leslie Stephen, about whom she published a monograph, *Leslie Stephen* (1968), one of the Writers and Their Work series sponsored by the British Council. Grosskurth has also written two other brief monographs, *Gabrielle Roy* (1969) and *Margaret Mead: a life of controversy* (1989), among countless articles, reviews, and journalistic pieces that have appeared internationally. Her principal works, however, are dense, carefully researched and argued, indeed monumental biographcal studies of three titans of psychoanalytic thought.

In *Havelock Ellis: a biography* (1980) Grosskurth explored the life and writings of the famous Victorian sexologist, and makes clear that Ellis's first important work, *Sexual inversion*, included parts of two pamphlets by Symonds, a homosexual, that strove to eradicate cruel prejudices towards, and misinformation about, homosexuality (the two authors originally planned to collaborate). For *Melanie Klein: her world and her work* (1986), the first biography of Klein, Grosskurth was obliged not only to master Klein's theories, and her contribution to psychoanalytic practice, but also to grasp her central role in the British psychoanalytic school. The author of *The psychoanalysis of children*, Klein emerges in Grosskurth's view as *the* figure in child psychoanalysis, far eclipsing Anna Freud in theoretical vision and practice. Nicholas Wright's play *Mrs. Klein*, which opened in London in 1988 and in New York in 1995, is based on Grosskurth's biography.

The secret ring: Freud's inner circle and the politics of psychoanalysis (1991) is a portrait of Freud's 'secret committee', which included, among others, Sandor Ferenczi, the great Hungarian who both encouraged and analysed Melanie Klein; Karl Abraham, whose analysand she was in Berlin; and Ernest Jones. Grosskurth's position is that the 'subtext of psychoanalytic history is the story of how Freud manipulated and influenced his followers and successors', binding them to him in a secret society, and privileging each with the gift of a ring, making Freud indeed the 'ringmaster'. Yet for all Freud's undoubted power, the secret circle petered out in the 1920s amid acrimonious disputes. Grosskurth associates Freud with the tradition of nineteenth-century Romanticism, as if he saw himself as a Wagnerian hero. In *Byron: the flawed angel* (1997) she has portrayed perhaps the greatest Romantic, returning to a life in literature with a portrait of a man who, like Freud, 'undid the values of the Enlightenment'.

PATRICIA WHITNEY

Groulx, Lionel-Adolphe (1878-1967). Born in Vaudreuil, Quebec, Groulx was ordained a priest in 1903 and completed a doctorate in theology in Rome five years later. His appointment in 1915 to the chair of Canadian history at Université Laval (Montreal) launched him on a lifetime career of writing, speaking, and lecturing, during the course of which he became a major intellectual figure in Quebec. Topics such as the linguistic rights of French-Canadian minorities, their role within Confederation, the importance to them of a 'homeland', and the essential differences between the two 'races' of Canada caused Groulx to be praised by some, denounced by others (including Louis Saint-Laurent and *Time*), and to be widely read. When he died, the Quebec government proclaimed a day of national mourning and honoured him with a state funeral.

Groulx's efforts to promote a 'national consciousness' among his compatriots led to controversy: at the height of the Conscription Crisis of 1917, his course on the origins of Confederation, which harshly criticized the founding fathers, brought demands from the university administration for an oath of loyalty to the Crown. As editor from 1921 to 1928 of a monthly review, *L'Action française* (still being published under the title *L'Action nationale*), Groulx the polemicist remained in the vanguard of French-Canadian nationalism. Each year a particular theme was treated in depth, his 1925 attack on bilingualism and his 1927 re-evaluation of Confederation on its sixtieth anniversary being the most provocative.

As a historian Groulx was intensely interested in the French presence in North America and the lessons it could draw from the past in order to survive as a culturally autonomous group within the Canadian political reality. The following titles reflect this facet of his interpretation of history: *La confédération canadienne, ses origines* (1918), *La naissance d'une race* (1919), *Notre maître le passé* (three volumes: 1924, 1936, 1944), *Histoire du Canada français depuis la découverte* (4 vols, 1950-2), *Notre grande aventure* (1958), and *Chemins de l'avenir* (1964). At age 68 Groulx founded the Institut d'histoire de l'Amérique française; and one year later, in 1947, a scholarly journal, the *Revue d'histoire de l'Amérique française*, which still appears regularly and is highly respected. Even after his retirement, Groulx continued to write prolifically; his *Constantes de vie* (1967), urging his compatriots to continue, like their forefathers before them, to nurture their North American and French heritages, appeared on the very day of his death, at age 89. The four-volume *Mes mémoires* (1970-4), edited by his niece, Mme Juliette Rémillard, was published posthumously.

His reputation as an essayist and pamphleteer is widely acknowledged, but Groulx the fiction-writer is relatively unknown in English Canada. In *Les rapaillages* (1916) he evokes memories of childhood and the countryside in a series of *contes* written in a bucolic vein. In the expanded 1935 edition one sketch, 'Comment j'ai quitté la politique', stands out: describing a village school election between the *rouges* and the *bleus* in 1890, Groulx demonstrates a surprising skill as storyteller, and a whimsical sense of humour that reminds us of Stephen LEACOCK and Roch CARRIER.

Groulx also wrote two novels under the pseudonym Alonié de Lestres: *L'appel de la race* (1922), which became a *cause célèbre* upon publication, and *Au Cap Blomidon* (1932). One of the rare Québécois novels to be set in Ontario, *L'appel de la race* (titled *Le coin de fer* before publication) reflects the tensions aroused in the French-Canadian community by Ontario's Regulation Seventeen (1912), which limited French instruction in francophone schools to one hour per day. The protagonist, Jules de Lantagnac, is an Ottawa lawyer who has become anglicized by his McGill education, his marriage to an anglophone, and the social demands of his profession. His wife, Maud Fletcher—an Anglican who converted to Catholicism in order to marry him and is 'dominated by ethnic pride' and staunchly British in sentiment and loyalty—reflects the Anglo-Saxon stereotype popular in French Canada around the First World War. As the Regulation is being hotly debated, Lantagnac undergoes a psychological crisis that leads him, despite consequent social ostracism, to become a spokesman in the House of Commons for his Franco-Ontarian compatriots. Maud, who is innately anti-French, decides to separate from him, and the family is split irrevocably—two teenaged children siding with the mother and two with the father. For its apparently racist arguments and vocabulary *L'appel de la race* seems shocking; but its language and rhetoric are quite restrained, compared to the bitter and frequently specious arguments for eliminating French as the language of instruction in Franco-Ontarian schools that appeared in the Ontario press of the period. The novel portrays Parliament as an 'arena where two races and two civilizations confront and oppose each other', and the bonds of intermarriage as strained by 'two warring souls or spirits', each seeking constantly to dominate. The long and bitter debate within the French-Canadian community over the author's rejection of 'interracial marriage' is well documented in Bruno Lafleur's introduction to the 1957 edition.

Groulx's second novel, *Au Cap Blomidon* (1932), aroused little controversy and much praise. Jean Bérubé, a young Laurentian farmer of Acadian descent, inherits his uncle's fortune on condition that he try to regain ownership of the ancestral homestead in Nova Scotia. Working as farm manager for a Scot (Hugh Finlay, the present owner of the Bérubé property), Jean eventually gains title to the land, fulfilling Groulx's dream of Acadian re-settlement by the scattered descendants of the eighteenth-century deportees. (*La ferme des pins*, 1930, by Harry BERNARD, which described the repossession of the Eastern Townships through francophone colonization, may have been a model for the plot.)

See Susan Mann Trofimenkoff's *Variations on a nationalist theme* (1973), which offers a broad selection of excerpts from Groulx's writings in English translation; Georges-Émile Giguère's biography *Lionel Groulx*

(1978); Jean-Pierre Gaboury, *Le nationalisme de Lionel Groulx: aspects idéologiques* (1970); and Susan Mann Trofimenkoff, *Action française: French Canadian nationalism in the twenties* (1975). See also Esther Delisle, *Le traître et le juif* (1992; English translation, *The traitor and the Jew*, 1993).

See also NOVELS IN FRENCH 1920 TO 1940: 3 and HISTORICAL WRITING IN FRENCH.

RAMON HATHORN

Grove, Frederick Philip (1879-1948). Born Felix Paul Greve in Radomno, Prussia, he was raised in Hamburg where his parents, Carl Edward and Bertha (Reichentrog) Greve, settled in 1881. He attended the Lutheran parish school at St Pauli, and later the classical Gymnasium in preparation for university. Family life apparently was not happy; his parents divorced.

Early in Felix's first university year, at Bonn, his mother died and his life became unsettled. He lived extravagantly, borrowing large sums on various pretexts, mostly from a well-to-do fellow student named Herman Kilian. Greve left Bonn without graduating and spent a *Wanderjahr* in Italy. In 1902 he resumed his studies, this time at Munich, but again failed to complete his degree. That same year his first two books were privately published—*Wanderungen* (poems) and *Helena and Damon* (a verse-drama)—and he was associated briefly with the Stefan George group of young neo-Romantic poets. To earn a precarious living, he began translating English authors into German, and he wrote some impressionistic criticism, mostly on Oscar Wilde. Moving to Berlin, Greve formed a liaison with Elsa Ploetz, wife of an architect; the two spent the winter of 1902-3 in Italy, again largely on money borrowed from Kilian under false pretences. On his return to Germany in 1903 Felix was charged by Kilian with fraud and spent a year in prison. Immediately on his release in June 1904 he travelled to Paris to meet André Gide, to whom he had previously written and whose works he was then translating. Gide's record of this first meeting—published as 'Conversation avec un Allemand' in his *Oeuvres complètes* (1935)—portrays an elegant young man who, while confessing to compulsive mendacity (he was frank about his imprisonment), seemed at the same time to be soliciting some sort of encouragement from Gide. For the next five years—living with Elsa, first on the French coast at Étaples and later in Berlin—Greve worked feverishly to pay off his debts, translating, from English to German, Wilde, Pater, Dowson, Browning, Wells, Meredith, Swift, and the pseudonymous Junius letters, which appeared in a London journal in 1969-72; and Gide, Murger, Flaubert, Balzac, and LeSage from the French. His translations of Cervantes, supposedly from the Spanish, apparently used English models, as did his major project, a translation of the *Thousand and one nights*, which remained popular in Germany for half a century. Greve's original works from this period included at least one play, some pamphlets and articles on Oscar Wilde, a few poems and reviews, and two novels: *Fanny Essler* (1905) and *Maurermeister Ihles Haus* (1906).

Despite this great productivity, Greve's effort to free himself from debt and make a living by his pen failed. The competition was too keen, the rewards too small, the pressures overwhelming. Greve was in financial difficulties when, late in 1909, he faked his suicide and fled to the USA, where he was subsequently joined by Elsa. According to Elsa's autobiography, Greve attempted to farm in Kentucky for almost two years, when he abandoned her. He probably spent the next year as an itinerant labourer in the USA and Canada, a life he graphically described in *Search for America* (1927; NCL, with an Afterword by W.H. New). Under the name Fred Grove he then became a schoolteacher in Manitoba, initially at Haskett and Winkler in German-speaking Mennonite districts. In 1914 he married Catherine Wiens (1892-1972). Their only daughter, Phyllis May, born in 1915, died in 1927. A son, Leonard Grove, was born in 1930. After teaching in several Manitoba communities, Grove retired in 1923 to devote himself to writing.

Grove had begun writing again by 1915, at first long philosophical poems and then, in 1919, prose. His first book in English, *Over prairie trails* (1922; NCL, with an Afterword by Patrick LANE), grew directly out of his weekend commutings in 1917, when he had taught at Gladstone, Manitoba, and Catherine had a small school in the bush some 35 miles north. Though not entirely free of Grove's rather pedantic amateur scientific observations, *Over prairie trails* is for many readers his most engaging and confident book. Along with *The turn of the year* (1923), it attracted critical attention for its loving descriptions of nature sustained by the narrative of his almost epic weekend struggles through fog and winter storms to reach home and the longed-for 'domestic island'.

This initial success confirmed Grove's commitment to writing and to Canada: his application for citizenship virtually coincided with the acceptance of *Over prairie trails* by MCCLELLAND AND STEWART in 1920. His first Canadian novel, *Settlers of the marsh* (1925; NCL, with an Afterword by Kristjana GUNNARS)—begun in German but completed in English—was considered too frank for public taste in the 1920s and did not sell well. It has gradually won recognition, however, as one of the first works of prairie realism. A measure of financial success came with publication of the partly autobiographical *Search for America*—one of the most compelling of many North American quasi-novels that record the suffering and disillusionment, as well as the idealism, of the immigrant—and of the naturalistic novel *Our daily bread* (1928). Three cross-country tours under Canadian Club auspices in 1928 and 1929 brought Grove to prominence, and at the end of 1929 he moved to Ottawa as president of Ariston Press, a subsidiary of GRAPHIC PUBLISHERS. Selected addresses were published as *It needs to be said* (1929).

The Graphic venture was not successful. Grove believed that the true circumstances of the company, and the fact that he had no real control, had been concealed from him. (The experience was to bear fruit in *The master of the mill*, in which Sam Clark makes a similar discovery.) Grove left Ottawa after a year, bought a farm near Simcoe, Ontario, and tried raising dairy cattle. In the deepening economic depression of the thirties the attempt failed. Forced to sell most of his land, Grove lived in near-poverty for a decade, supported by his wife's private teaching. After *The yoke of life* (1930) and *Fruits of the earth* (1933; NCL, with an Afterword by Rudy WIEBE) there were no books published until *Two generations* (1939). Subtitled *A story of present-day Ontario*, this novel drew on Grove's dairying experience, but the triumph of Phil and Alice Patterson revealed a new buoyancy.

Grove's last years brought belated recognition and the publication of his most thoughtful works: *The master of the mill* (1944), Grove's second Ontario novel, which records the growth of monopoly capitalism in the story of the Clark dynasty; *In search of myself* (1946), a fictionalized autobiography; and *Consider her ways* (1947), a sometimes pedantic, often humorous, surprisingly human, satire in which a colony of ants undertakes a study of mankind.

Grove had been awarded the Lorne Pierce Medal in 1934; in 1941 he was elected FRSC. *Frederick Philip Grove*, a study of his life and work by Desmond PACEY, was published in 1945. In 1947 Grove received a Governor General's Award for *In search of myself*.

Following Pacey, early critics tended to read Grove in the light of the supposed autobiography that described a luxurious Swedish childhood and had him frequenting artistic circles and leading a dilettante life in Europe before being overtaken by unexpected poverty, wandering in America for twenty years, and re-emerging in Canada as a teacher, cosmopolitan author, and near-prophet. Some readers almost revered him: in A.L. Phelps's words, 'He was the man.' Others were offended by Grove's superior tone, and pointed to his stilted language. For still others these qualities were appropriate to the level of high tragedy on which Grove wrote: his novels of prairie pioneering drew such epithets as 'tragedy' and 'stark realism'—aspects of Grove's writing that still hold the attention of readers, particularly in high schools and universities.

Grove's novels abound in detail that is often maddeningly trivial but cumulatively effective in creating a sense of character in relation to milieu. This characteristic, rather than their larger purposes—what he called 'the tragic interpretation of life'—led critics to label Grove a 'naturalist' or 'realist'. Most of the novels portray dynamic, creative, but limited pioneer figures whose possessions turn to ashes with the alienation of family and community. In the two set in the Big Grassy Marsh district near Lake Manitoba, the young Swede Niels Lindstedt in *Settlers of the marsh* becomes a successful pioneer only to be ruined by a disastrous marriage, while *The yoke of life* (once described as 'a Canadian *Jude the obscure*') records the early idealism, disillusionment, and suicide of Len Sterner. In Grove's two prairie novels the patriarch John Elliot of *Our daily bread* escapes being cared for by his unsympathetic children by returning to the abandoned homestead to die; *Fruits of the earth* chronicles Abe Spalding's rise to power and the resultant alienation of his family. Though in Grove's German novels the protagonists were young women, many of the Canadian protagonists—John Elliot, Abe Spalding, Sam Clark, Ralph Patterson, and the narrator of *In search of myself*—are older men whose failures may be predetermined but who nevertheless are driven to try to understand. In their recurrent phrase 'I am I', character is seen as fate: these men are what they are, and at their best they are heroic and universal. Facing death, or watching their achievements slip away from them, they challenge the illusion of human progress, question the values of society, and ask where mankind has failed. Projecting himself in them, Grove transcended his own failures. In the emotional confrontations of *Settlers of the marsh* and *The yoke of life*, in the balanced complexities of *The master of the mill*, even in the allegorical *Consider her ways*, Grove wrestled with manifestations of his own psyche that may account for much in his work that earlier critics found unconvincing—such as the unexpectedly romantic elements that sometimes appear, like the unicorn Len Sterner fancies he sees in the Manitoba bush in *The yoke of life*.

No extended critical work has been done on Grove's poetry or short stories. The *Wanderungen* poems have yet to be published in translation. There are a few unpublished lyrics and fragments in German; most of the poetry in English remains in typescript. Excerpts from the memorial 'Ode' for his daughter were published in the *CANADIAN FORUM* (1930, 1932). Many of the short stories were first published in a series in the Winnipeg *Tribune* (1926-7)—some of these were closely related to, or excerpted from, the material of the western novels. While a few deserve attention—and 'Snow', first published in *Queen's Quarterly* (Spring, 1932), has been much anthologized—Grove was seldom happy in the shorter form.

Ronald SUTHERLAND's *Frederick Philip Grove* (NCL, 1969) attempted to place Grove's work in the international context of literary naturalism, while D.O. Spettigue's *Frederick Philip Grove* (1969) deflected Grove criticism towards biography. Scrutinizing Grove's past in order to date the Grove canon, Spettigue could find no foundation for either the European childhood or the American years as Grove had described them, and this insight led to a period of research and the publication by Spettigue of *FPG: the European years* (1973), which revealed Grove as Greve, and Grove's autobiography *In search of myself* as a curious blend of fiction and distorted fact. Margaret Stobie's *Frederick Philip Grove* (1973) examined critically the teacher/author as he had appeared to his Manitoba contemporaries. Despite gaps, these books—together with the *Letters* (1976) edited by Pacey (which includes the German correspondence)—made it possible at last to relate Grove/Greve the man to the writings, both late and early. This advantage, combined with advances in literary criticism in Canada, led to more psychologically oriented studies that viewed the characters of Grove's Canadian novels as aspects of the author's personality, and the protagonists of Greve's German novels as precursors. A feminist interest is apparent in both the German and Canadian novels.

Grove's contribution to the literature of his adopted country—as an early realist and something of a feminist; and as a perceptive social critic, and a cosmopolitan, if idiosyncratic, literary critic—was considerable. Grove never wrote down to his readers, and never was a 'popular' writer, but his critical influence was indirect and largely exemplary. Apart from Pacey's 1945 study and the support of such discerning friends as A.L. Phelps, Watson KIRKCONNELL, Barker FAIRLEY, and W.J. Alexander, recognition of his achievement had to await the expansion of Canadian literary studies in the 1960s. Beginning with *Over prairie trails* in 1957, four of his books are now available in the NEW CANADIAN LIBRARY. In 1963 the Grove papers were purchased from his widow by the University of Manitoba. The Grove canon was expanded with the publication of a selection of the short stories, *Tales from the margin* (1971), and *The letters of Frederick Philip Grove* (1971), both edited by Desmond Pacey. In 1976 the first of his German works was published in English: *The master mason's house*, translated by Paul Gubbins and edited by A.W. Riley and D.O. Spettigue. Unpublished manuscripts remain in the Grove Collection. See also Paul I. Hjartarson, ed., *A stranger to my time: essays by and about Frederick Philip Grove* (1986), and Paul I. Hjartarson and D.O. Spettigue, eds, *Baroness Elsa* (1992).

In 1939, while he was writing *The master of the mill*, Grove amused himself by writing a lively novella for boys called *The adventure of Leonard Broadus*, for which he drew upon his young son, himself, his family life, and the Ontario setting in which he was living. It was published in twelve instalments in *The Golden Boy*, a United Church journal, beginning in April 1940; and was republished in *Canadian Children's Literature: A Journal of Criticism and Review*, no. 27/28 (1982), with two articles, and a note on the manuscript, by Mary Rubio. See also D.O. Spettigue, 'Felix, Elsa, André Gide and others: some unpublished letters of F.P. Grove', *CANADIAN LITERATURE* 134 (1992).

See also CRITICISM IN ENGLISH: 3

D.O. SPETTIGUE

Guernica Editions. Founded in Montreal, Quebec, by Antonio D'ALFONSO in 1978, Guernica Editions has been committed to giving voice to issues and questions about ethnicity, identity, and the politics of ethnicity and gender, both French and English. The press has published the work of well-known Québécois writers, such as Gaston MIRON,

Claude BEAUSOLEIL, Nicole BROSSARD, Anne Dandurand, and Hélène Rioux, both in French and in English translation. At the same time writers of other cultural heritages, especially writers of Italian origin, have been published, including Marco Fraticelli, Filippo Salvatore, Marco MICONE, Fulvio Caccia, Mary MELFI, Pasquale Verdicchio, and Penny Petrone. Literary and cultural critics—such as Joseph Pivato, Francesco Loriggio, Enoch Padolsky, Sneja Ganew, and D'Alfonso—have examined the significance of identity and ethnicity, and of minority writing in Canada.

MARINO TUZI

Guèvremont, Germaine (1893-1968). Germaine Grignon, a cousin of Claude-Henri GRIGNON, was born in Saint-Jérôme, Quebec, and educated there and in Lachine and Toronto. She married Hyacinthe Guèvremont in 1916 and moved to Sorel, Quebec, where she started her career as a journalist on the staff of *Le Courrier de Sorel* (1928-35); after she moved to Montreal in 1935 she worked for the Montreal *Gazette*. A member of the Société des Écrivains canadiens, she was elected to the Académie canadienne-française (1949) and to the Royal Society of Canada (1961). For her first novel, *Le survenant* (1945), she received the Prix Duvernay (1945), the Prix David (1947), and the Prix Olivier-de-Serres, Paris (1947).

Guèvremont's first book, *En pleine terre* (1942)—a collection of three short stories and fourteen rural sketches (an extra story was added in the 1955 edition)—deals with life in the Sorel islands, in what is called the Chenal du Moine. Featuring the colourful language of the region's inhabitants and both realistic and impressionistic descriptions recording the simple life of a rural family, it received only mild attention. With the publication of *Le survenant* in Quebec (1945) and Paris (1947), Guèvremont became well known. Her second novel, *Marie-Didace* (1947), was to form part of a trilogy. (The third segment was never completed, though one chapter, 'Le plomb dans l'aile', was published in the *Cahiers de l'Académie canadienne-française* in 1959.) Both novels concern the Beauchemin family and depict the disintegrating rural world in a spare, highly realistic manner. *Le survenant* recounts the sudden intrusion of a stranger into a tight family circle and the consequences upon the social organization of the community. *Marie-Didace* deals with the extinction of the male line of the family represented by the birth of Marie-Didace. (In what we know of the third part, Marie-Didace is about to leave the Chenal du Moine during the economic crisis of the thirties to look for work in Sorel.) Both novels were translated into English and published together as *The outlanders* (Toronto, 1950), which won a Governor General's Award, and *Monk's reach* (London, 1950). The story of the Beauchemin family also had great success when it was dramatized as a radio series (1952-4) and serialized for television (1954-60).

The most important studies of Germaine Guèvremont's works are by Rita Leclerc, *Germaine Guèvremont* (1963), Jean-Pierre Duquette, *Germaine Guèvremont, une route, une maison* (1973), and Pierre Girouard, *Germaine Guèvremont et son oeuvre cachée* (1984). See also Yvan G. Cloutier's 1989 critical edition of *Le survenant*.

LUCIE ROBERT

Gunnars, Kristjana (b. 1948). Born in Reykjavik, Iceland, Gunnars has lived in Canada since 1969. She holds a B.A. from Oregon State University, an M.A. from the University of Regina, and is completing a Ph.D. from the University of Manitoba. She divides her time between writing and teaching at the University of Alberta.

Gunnars has published seven books of poetry—*Settlement poems, I and II* (1980, 1981), *One-eyed moon maps* (1981), *Wake-pick poems* (1982), *The night workers of Ragnarok* (1985), *Carnival of longing* (1989), and *Exiles among you* (1996)—and two books of short fiction: *The axe's edge* (1983) and *The guest house* (1992). Her publications also include three novels: *The prowler* (1989), which won the McNally Robinson Award for Manitoba Book of the Year, *The substance of forgetting* (1992), and *The rose garden* (1996). *Zero hour* (1991), a compact and poetic account of Gunnars' grief over her father's death, was nominated for a Governor General's Award.

Postmodern theories of literature and storytelling are often explored in her fiction, and all her writing probes the ambiguities of meaning, the problems and process of memory, and the character of truth and reality. Gunnars is known primarily as a poet, but she struggles against the boundaries of genre. In fact, classification of her work into distinct genres (novel/poem/autobiography) is not entirely convincing. Gunnars' books of poetry are collections of poem cycles—carefully arranged groups of poems relating to the same topic; and her novels are really prose-poems, written in a stark, elliptical language with a rich layering of images.

The prowler, which has 167 chapters, most shorter than one page, tells the story of a nameless girl growing up in Iceland, Denmark, and North America, struggling with an identity crisis brought on by internal and external repression. *The substance of forgetting* is about a woman living alone in the Okanagan Valley who has embarked on the process of recreating her world and herself. Although Gunnars turned here to a Canadian setting, her concerns have remained the same—*The substance of forgetting* is another exploration of the themes of memory and belonging. *The rose garden* was published as non-fiction but is in fact an amalgam of memoir, theory, and fiction, outlining the personal and scholarly insights gleaned by a Canadian literary scholar during a study leave in Germany.

Gunnars has edited, among other books, *Unexpected fictions: new Icelandic Canadian writing* (1989). JUSTINE WHITEHEAD

Gurik, Robert (b. 1932). Born in Paris of Hungarian parents, he came to Canada in 1950, and in 1957 received his professional engineer's certification from the Institut Polytechnique de Montréal. While working as an engineer in and around Montreal, he had his first plays—*Le chant du poète* (1963), *Les portes* (1965), and *Api or not Api* (1966)—produced by little theatres and in regional competitions of the Dominion Drama Festival. In 1967 *Le pendu* (1967) was judged the best play and the best Canadian play at the Dominion Drama Festival finals held in Newfoundland. A co-founder of the Centre d'essai des auteurs dramatiques, Gurik had four more plays produced in Montreal—*Les louis d'or* (1967), *Api 2967* (1967), *Hamlet, prince du Québec* (1968), and *À coeur ouvert* (1969)—and a public reading in 1965 of *Hello police*, written in collaboration with Jean-Pierre Morin and later published as *Allo . . . police!* (1974), before leaving engineering work in 1972 to devote himself to the theatre. He then wrote and produced radio and TV dramas and several full-length plays, including *Le procès de Jean-Baptiste M.* (1972), *Le tabernacle à trois étages* (1973), and *La baie des Jacques* (1978). Some of his one-act plays were collected in *Les tas de siègee* (1971) and *Sept courtes pièces* (1974).

Api 2967, *Le pendu*, and *Le procès de Jean Baptiste M.* have been particularly popular both in Quebec and abroad and were translated into English: *Api 2967* (1974) by Marc F. Gélinas; *The hanged man* (1972) by Philip London and Laurence Bérard; and *The trial of Jean-Baptiste M.* (1974) by Alan Van Meer. These three plays illustrate Gurik's preoccupation with runaway technology and consumerism, authoritarian regimes, the hardships of the poor, and the naïvety of those who either refuse to accept the status quo or actively try to change it. *Api 2967* is a clever and amusing play set in a futuristic world of test-tube babies, food in capsule form, long but sterile and perfectly controlled life, television monitors watching everyone, and dictionaries from which words describing such outmoded concepts as love and passion have been removed. Only the two main characters, the professor and his female research assistant, resist the system and discover and enjoy some hitherto unknown and forbidden pleasures before they perish. The hero of *Le pendu*, Yonel, is a poor young beggar and former miner who is apparently, but not really, blind. With his father's help he devises a money-making scheme: he will pretend to plan to hang himself and then try to sell a piece of 'hangman's rope'—a popular, if somewhat macabre good-luck charm. At first he makes money and seems to help luckless members of his entourage; but when they learn that the hanging is not to occur and that he means to establish organizations to help the world's poor, they force him to hang himself. The play ends with a chorus, sung by a group of children playing in the background, telling how nothing has improved in the village since Yonel's death.

Gurik's plays not only criticize those who would impose their will on society; they also offer little hope for those who conform to, and profit from, the consumer society, as in *Le procès de Jean Baptiste M.*: the name, which evokes 'Monsieur tout le monde' and Quebec's patron saint, John the Baptist, suggests a Québécois Everyman, in this case one hoping to get and keep a steady job. Though handicapped by lack of education and an unwarranted prison record, he is finally hired by a big industrial firm in Montreal, but his efficiency and inventiveness create unrest and jealousies and he is eventually fired. Frustrated by the injustice, he shoots and kills several of his former bosses. The events leading up to the shooting alternate with scenes of Jean-Baptiste's grotesque trial in which witness, judge, and jury are played by the same group of unfeeling and hysterical individuals. In the end Jean-Baptiste is convicted of both the murder and the more serious crime, in the jury's eyes, of disobeying society's laws, thereby interfering with orderly production and consumption.

Many of Gurik's plays point to the sociopolitical situation in Quebec: in *Hamlet, prince du Québec*, Shakespeare's characters wear the masks of institutions and of people who have been involved in the modern Quebec nationalist movement; *J'écoute* and *Face à face* (*Les tas de sièges*) and *Le trou* (*Sept courtes pièces*) allude to the October Crisis of 1970; in *Le tabernacle à trois étages* and *Playball* (*Sept courtes pièces*) the playing of the Canadian national anthem lends a special nationalistic flavour to the action; *La baie des Jacques* is coloured by two songs about the road to independence and the need for change; and *Le champion* (1977) contains references to a Quiet Revolution slogan, 'Maîtres chez nous'. But Quebec society is not Gurik's only target. *La baie des Jacques* also attacks Palestine and Bengal, and *La palissade* (1971—with *Api 2967*) shows filmed scenes of violence and unrest in the USA, France, Germany, Yugoslavia, and South America. His most recent play is *20 ans*, published in *20 ans* (1985), a collection celebrating the twentieth anniversary of the Centre d'essai des auteurs dramatiques, Montreal. In this three-act mini-drama, Gurik bitterly denounces what he perceives as a lack of organization, commitment, and creativity in Quebec's theatrical world.

The socio-political aspects of Gurik's theatre are as obvious as his use of such Brechtian devices as slogans, songs, news bulletins, suspended animation, and grotesque make-up. Though some critics praise his determination to criticize society and his efforts to force the audience to make judgements, perhaps even to initiate change, others decry the didactic elements of his work, his thin plots, superficial characters, and a use of language that is too clever to make any lasting effect on Quebec dramaturgy. Nevertheless Gurik was one of the most prolific and most produced Quebec playwrights in the 1960s and1970s. He will no doubt continue to be applauded for reminding his audience of the threat posed to individual and collective freedom by modern technology, giant corporations, powerful institutions, and of the importance of defending the concept of a pluralistic and humanitarian society.

Gurik has published two novels: *Spirales* (1966), a stream-of-consciousness description of one man's feelings of isolation and eventual nervous breakdown; and *Jeune délinquant* (1980), about the struggles of a group of juvenile delinquents, some of whom reform. Based on a script Gurik wrote as a five-part TV series for Radio-Canada, *Jeune délinquant* is less like a novel than a dialogue interspersed with extensive stage directions.

Gurik seemed to move away from theatre during the 1980s and 1990s and towards other media, specifically film and television. He has written, both alone and in collaboration, a number of film and television scripts, including the successful *La pépinière* (1984-5). His scripts remain unpublished.

In 1991 Gurik published *Être ou ne pas être*. Throughout the six short stories in this collection the author explores themes of being and appearance, action versus passivity, political intrigue transposed within the realm of the persona, and the place of theatre in everyday life. These themes are in fact germane to all of Gurik's work, as is, to a lesser extent, a Hamlet subtext that resonates throughout the collection.

See H. Beauchamps-Rank, 'Pour un réel théâtral objectif—le théâtre de Robert Gurik', *VOIX ET IMAGES* 8 (1974); R. Bérubé, '*Le Cid* et *Hamlet*: Corneille et Shakespeare lus par Ducharme et Gurik', *Voix et images* 1:1 (1975); B. Andrès, 'Sur notre scène: des enfants au pouvoir', *Voix et images* 2:3 (1977); Jean-Cléo Godin and Laurent Mailhot, 'Le procès de (Jean-Baptiste) Gurik, ingénieur', *Théâtre Québécois* II (1980); J. Weiss, 'The contemporary theatre and its public in Quebec', *Quebec Studies* 1:1 (1983); M. Colombo, *Il teatro sociale de Robert Gurik* (1984); S. Grace, 'The expressionist legacy in the Canadian theatre', *CANADIAN LITERATURE* 118 (1988); P. Hébert, 'Eloge de la fiction', *Voix et images* 17:3 (1992).

ELAINE NARDOCCHIO/SHAUN HUFFMAN

Gustafson, Ralph (1909-95). Ralph Barker Gustafson was born in Lime Ridge, in the Eastern Townships of Quebec, to a Swedish father and an English mother. After graduating in 1929 from Bishop's University he stayed on to do an M.A., writing a thesis on Keats and Shelley, before going to Keble College, Oxford. He took a second B.A. at Oxford in 1933, and after a short period of teaching at a private school in Brockville, Ontario, he went back to England, where he published his first two collections of poetry. With the approach of war Gustafson returned to Canada, and then moved on to New York City, where he spent the war years working for the British Information Services. After the war he continued to live in New York, where he freelanced as a writer and music critic. In 1958 he married Elizabeth Renninger, the 'Betty' of many dedications, and in 1963 he accepted an offer to return to Bishop's University as a professor of English and poet in residence. He and his wife moved to North Hatley, where he spent the remainder of his life. He retired from teaching in 1979.

The two books of Gustafson's English years, *The golden chalice* (1935) and a verse play,

Alfred the Great (1937), show the strong influence of Gerard Manley Hopkins, and are largely conventional apprentice work. Two privately issued limited-edition chapbooks, *Epithalamium in time of war* (1941) and *Lyrics unromantic* (1942), preceded his first important book of poems, *Flight into darkness* (1944), which was widely praised and demonstrated a sharp increase of poetic powers. It is evident that he underwent a considerable interior evolution at this time, for his next book did not appear until 1960. He was, however, writing short fiction (later collected in two volumes, *The brazen tower*, 1974, and *The vivid air*, 1980) as well as an unpublished novel entitled 'No music in the nightingale'. But his transformation as a poet is clearly observable in *Rivers among rocks* (1960), which was the first of his books to be published in Canada, and in some ways the real beginning of his accomplishments. *Rocky Mountain poems* (1960) is the first of many works to reflect Gustafson's long-lasting passion for travel.

In *Sift in a hourglass* (1966) and *Ixion's wheel* (1969) the language of Gustafson's poetry becomes increasingly simplified and colloquial, to its great benefit, though it remains highly allusive. His command of cultural reference is always impressive, and a close reading inevitably discovers the influence of music in his formal procedures. *Selected poems* (1972) was followed by *Fire on stone* (1974), which won a GOVERNOR GENERAL'S AWARD. Although already sixty-five years old at that time, Gustafson was not only entering on the most productive twenty years of his career, he was also only at the mid-point in his development as a poet. *Gradations of grandeur* (1982) is a book-length work, and *Directives of autumn* (1984) is the first of four final collections that contain some of Gustafson's most moving and accomplished poetry. *Configurations at midnight* (1992) is a poetic autobiography. Two versions of a reworked selected poems appeared in the 1980s, *The moment is all: selected poems 1944-83* (1983) and *At the ocean's verge* (1984), which was published in the United States. The *Collected poems* appeared initially in two volumes in 1987, to which a third volume was added in 1994. *Visions fugitive* (1996) was published posthumously.

Gustafson was the editor of one of the first critical anthologies of Canadian poetry, the *Anthology of Canadian poetry (English)* (1942), which he compiled for Penguin Books during the war. Out of this came the larger and largely rethought *Penguin book of Canadian verse* (1958), which was several times revised and reissued. Like A.J.M. SMITH's anthology of the following year, Gustafson's 1942 book was the result of an intelligent and well-informed reading of the whole history of Canadian poetry, and it contributed to the formation of a canon of good and great poets that has had a long and important influence. *A little anthology of Canadian poets* (1943) was compiled as one of the New Directions Poets of the Month series, and *Canadian accent* (1944) contained poetry and prose.

Gustafson wrote a number of literary essays over the years, collected and published as *Plummets and other partialities* (1986). His affectionate memoir of various Eastern Townships poets, including F.O. Call, with whom he studied at Bishop's, is noteworthy. His correspondence with poet W.W.E. ROSS, edited by Bruce Whiteman and published in 1984 as *A literary friendship*, documents the editing of the anthologies and contains much insightful criticism. His light verse, collected in *The celestial corkscrew and other strategies* (1979), also contains much literary and social criticism obliquely rendered.

The poetry is identifiably Modernist in tone and form, and the influence of Ezra Pound and Wallace Stevens is evident in his mature work, with the waning of Hopkins' influence. Gustafson had close ties to John SUTHERLAND and the group of poets who published in *FIRST STATEMENT* and *NORTHERN REVIEW*, without being the same kind of poet as DUDEK or LAYTON, who were both friends; but he also felt akin to poets like Robert FINCH, Robert FORD, and others whose formal affinities were more conservative than those of the *First Statement* group. Gustafson's poetry ultimately stands somewhat apart from the recognized strains of Modernist and postmodern Canadian poetry, perhaps because of his long residence outside the country.

Wendy Keitner's *Ralph Gustafson* (1979) and Dermot McCarthy's *The poetics of place: the poetry of Ralph Gustafson* (1991) comprise the major critical responses to Gustafson's work to date. *Journal of Eastern Townships Studies* 9 (Fall 1996) is a special Gustafson issue.

BRUCE WHITEMAN

Guthrie, Norman. See CRITICISM IN ENGLISH: 2.

Gutteridge, Don (b. 1937). Donald George Gutteridge was born in the village of Point Edward, Lambton County, Ontario, and graduated in English from the University of Western Ontario. After teaching high school for seven years, he joined the department of English at Western, where he is now professor emeritus in the Faculty of Education. He has written many articles on educational methodology and a textbook, *Language and expression: a modern approach* (1970).

Gutteridge won the President's Medal of the University of Western Ontario for *Death at Quebec* (1971), a poetry collection of monologues by historical figures (including the Jesuits in Huronia) and village poems. This work came between *The village within: poems towards a biography* (1970) and *Saying grace: an elegy* (1972), both of which show his inclination to stitch together his own life with that of his village and country. His talent for mythologizing history—for fusing his poetic spirit with the spirit of historical figures, somewhat in the manners of ATWOOD, PURDY, and ONDAATJE—shows best in *Riel: a poem for voices* (1968), the beginning of a tetralogy about Natives and explorers entitled *Dreams and visions; the land*. Much of *Riel* is a documentary collage in which letters, newspaper and diary entries, political proclamations, and posters are mixed with long-lined monologues and welded into a single metaphor. In *Coppermine: the quest for North* (1973) Samuel Hearne's journals are the source for a horrific, sometimes surreal, Canadian version of the El Dorado myth. *Borderlands* (1975) uses violence, irony, and a skilful interplay of voices to re-create John Jewitt's two-year enslavement by the Nootka. More political is *Tecumseh* (1976), with its theme of genocide, but Gutteridge does not capture fully his main character's personality.

Gutteridge passed to personal themes in a new series of works entitled *Time is the metaphor*, written in a demotic style and beginning with the comic and sometimes poignant novel *Bus-ride* (1974), set in a small Ontario town in March 1939, which focuses on a Junior B hockey player bewildered by the process of growing up. In *The true history of Lambton County* (1977), a long poem with multiple voices, the poet assembles an album of his own history and childhood memories that are droll, romantic, and tragic. *All in good time* (1981), a small-scale comic novel, takes up some of the characters from *Bus-ride* at a later period, and, using sports, politics, and sex, tells a touching and ironic story of a people on the edge of winter and war. *God's geography* (1982), a collection of poems that juxtapose village memories and childhood with later experience and world events, shows that *Time is the metaphor* forms a narrative of the past from which the poet evolved. The novels *St. Vitus dance* (1987) and *Shaman's ground* (1988), subtitled Volumes One and Two of *Lily's story*, explore with conviction and humour the impact of historical events on the individual fortunes of the protagonist, Lily Fairchild, and the evolving communities of Point Edward and Sarnia between 1840 and 1922. *How the world began* (1991) concludes *Time is the metaphor* and provides a foundation for earlier books in the series through a fictional representation of Lambton County pioneers buffeted by the War of 1812. *The exiled heart (selected narratives 1968-1982)* (1986) documents exploration and exile in poems and journal entries from five earlier collections. A profound shift to the personal, with a focus on intense and immediate aspects of experience, marks Gutteridge's recent poetry and fiction. In *Love in the wintertime* (1990) and *Flute music in the cello's belly* (1997) richly allusive poems celebrate connection in family, friendship, and creativity. The paired novels *Summer idyll* (1993) and *Winter's descent* (1996) recreate with precision and evocative physicality the worlds of absence and discovery that mark a boy's transition from childhood to adolescence in the fatherless years of the Second World War in southwestern Ontario.

See Don Gutteridge, 'Riel: historic man or literary symbol', *Bulletin de l'association des humanités* (automne 1970) and 'Teaching the Canadian mythology: a poet's view', *Journal of Canadian Studies* (Feb. 1973); Keith Garebian, 'Don Gutteridge's mythic tetralogy', *CANADIAN LITERATURE* 87 (Winter 1980); R.G. Moyles' review article on *The exiled heart*, *The Journal of Canadian Poetry* 3 (1986); and Ron Jenkins, 'Growing up in Canada', *Canadian Literature* 146 (Fall 1995) STAN ATHERTON

Guy, Ray (b. 1939). Raymond Guy was born in Come By Chance, Newfoundland, and spent his childhood in nearby Arnold's Cove; he was educated there, did a final year of high school on Bell Island, then a major mining town, and went on to Memorial University of Newfoundland ('one of the most sickening experiences of my life') and Ryerson Polytechnical Institute in Toronto. He graduated from Ryerson in 1963 with a diploma in journalism and began writing for the St John's *Evening Telegram*, first as a reporter and latterly as a daily columnist.

It was in the *Telegram*, which he quit in 1973 but to which he returned sporadically in subsequent years, that Guy wrote his best-known pieces—brilliant, scorching attacks on the faltering Liberal administration of Premier J.R. Smallwood and nostalgic items on his own early years in Arnold's Cove, termed by Guy 'Juvenile outharbour delights'. These latter columns have a charm and warmth that set them apart from Guy's other work. Watching Smallwood operate appears to have permanently soured him on politics, but he continued to write mordantly and fearlessly on the subject. He has become more and more outspoken, and his *Telegram* columns in 1995-6 featured bitter, though not undeserved, assaults on the Roman Catholic Church.

Guy has lived on his wits in St John's: as a journalist, freelance columnist, radio and TV commentator, a principal actor (Jack, the crotchety boarder) in the local CBC-TV series 'Up at Ours' (1978-80), and dramatist (none of his three stage plays have been published). He has written a lot on gardening, a favourite pursuit. His columns have been collected in: *You may know them as sea urchins, Ma'am* (1975; six printings by 1978; rev. ed. 1985)—the joke is that sea urchins are sometimes called whore's eggs in Newfoundland; *That far greater bay* (1976; rev. ed. 1985)—the bay is Placentia Bay, the location of Arnold's Cove; *Beneficial vapors* (1981); *This dear and fine country* (1985)—the country is Newfoundland; and *Ray Guy's best* (1987), a selection from his *Atlantic Insight* columns. *An heroine for our time* (1983) is a book for children. He has written the texts for two books of photographs by Sherman Hines: *Outhouses of the East* (1978) and *Newfoundland.Labrador* (1984).

Guy is one of the best-known and most widely admired Newfoundland writers. He has, however, published few items longer than 600-1000-word newspaper columns. An exception is 'When Jannies visited: remembering an outport Christmas', which is in *Far and wide: essays from Canada* (1995), edited by Sean Armstrong, reprinted from *Canadian Geographic* (Nov-Dec., 1993). Guy won the LEACOCK Medal for Humour in 1977.

PATRICK O'FLAHERTY

Gwyn, Richard (b. 1934). He was born in Bury St Edmunds, England, raised in China and India, and educated at Stonyhurst College and the Royal Military Academy, Sandhurst. He immigrated to Canada in 1954; four years later he married the writer Sandra Fraser. He worked as a journalist with United Press International, Thomson Newspapers, Maclean-Hunter Business Publications, *Time*, and the Canadian Broadcasting Corporation; subsequently he served as assistant to federal minister Eric Kierans and as a divisional director in the federal Department of Communications. From 1973 to the present he has been a nationally syndicated columnist for the *Toronto Star*, based in Ottawa (1973-85), London (1986-92), and Toronto (from 1992), and has received several awards, including the National Newspaper Award twice. All Gwyn's best-selling books are informed about Canadian political matters, concerned with social issues, abreast of developments in philosophical thought, and are serious contributions to their subjects. Their sense of nationalism is tempered by a pragmatism in keeping with the times. Gwyn's first book was *The shape of scandal: a study of a government in crisis* (1965), an examination of the Lucien Rivard affair, concerning a convicted drug smuggler whose escape from prison created a scandal for the Liberal government, with charges of bribery, the appointment of a Royal Commission, and the resignation of the minister of justice. This was followed by *Smallwood: the unlikely revolutionary* (1968; rev. ed., 1972); *The northern magus: Pierre Elliott Trudeau and Canadians* (1980), *The 49th paradox: Canada in North America* (1985); and *Nationalism without walls: the unbearable lightness of being Canadian* (1995; rev. ed., 1996). He has received numerous awards, including a 1985 National Magazine Award jointly with Sandra GWYN.

JOHN ROBERT COLOMBO

Gwyn, Sandra (b. 1935). Born Alexandra Fraser in St John's, Newfoundland, she graduated from Dalhousie University, Halifax (B.A., 1955) and three years later married the journalist Richard GWYN. She has served as an information officer with the National Gallery of Canada, as an editor of *Canadian Art*, and as a freelance writer and researcher for *Time*, *Maclean's*, the Canadian Broadcasting Corporation, the Royal Commission on the Status of Women, and the Federal Task Force on Information. She worked as Ottawa editor of *Saturday Night* (1975-80), and then as contributing editor (1980-7). While living in Ottawa she did considerable research at the National Archives to write two remarkable historical studies that are rich in social and personal detail. *The private capital: ambition and love in the age of Macdonald and Laurier* (1984) won a Governor General's Award and was dramatized by CBC-TV and shown in Jan. 1990. Its successor, *Tapestry of war: a private view of Canadians in the Great War* (1992), was written with passion and compassion. Gwyn has received other awards, and shared a 1985 National Magazine Award jointly with Richard Gwyn. ROBERT JOHN COLOMBO

H

Hass, Maara. See UKRAINIAN-CANADIAN LITERATURE.

Haché, Louis. See ACADIAN LITERATURE 2(c).

Haig-Brown, Roderick (1908-76). Born in Lansing, Sussex, England, Roderick Langmore Haig-Brown was educated at Charterhouse, where his grandfather had been headmaster. He left school and immigrated to Washington State in 1926. In 1927 he moved to British Columbia, where he worked as a logger, trapper—he shot cougars now and again for bounty money—fisherman, tourist guide, and occasionally as a boxer at the odd smoker for $25. He went to England in 1929 and wrote his first novel there; but homesick for B.C., he returned in 1931. In 1934 he married Ann Elmore of Seattle and they raised four children. Appointed magistrate in the village of Campbell River on Vancouver Island in 1934, he served as a provincial court judge for thirty-three years, retiring the year before his death. During the Second World War he was a captain, then major, in the Canadian army, and was briefly on loan to the RCMP. Haig-Brown was director of the National and Provincial Parks Association of Canada, a member of the International Pacific Salmon Commission, served on three federal electoral boundaries commissions, and was chancellor of the University of Victoria. He also fought publicly, and often with little support, against hydro and industrial development in B.C. for harming the natural environment. His home, 'Above Tide', on a twenty-acre farm near Campbell River, is now a Heritage House.

Haig-Brown wrote twenty-five books—including adult novels, essay collections, and children's books—but he is best known as a nature writer, specializing in fishing and natural history. An outdoorsman who was also one of the finest prose stylists in Canada, he was skilled at observing creatures in natural settings, especially 'the strangeness and beauty of the fish, their often visible remoteness, their ease in another world, the mystery of their movements and habits and whims.' He wrote the first item in the first issue of *CANADIAN LITERATURE*, about the writer in isolation.

His first publications were *Silver: the life story of an Atlantic salmon* (1931), written when he was twenty-three; *Pool and rapid: the story of a river* (1932); *Panther* (1934; American title, *Ki-yu: story of a panther*); *The western angler* (1939), which describes the Pacific salmon and western trout and established Haig-Brown as a fishing authority; and *Timber* (1942), a novel about unionizing a lumber camp (English ed. *The tall trees fall*, 1943). *Return to the river* (1941) is about a Chinook salmon in the Columbia river. These were followed by some of his best books: *A river never sleeps* (1946); *Starbuck Valley winter* (1946), which won the Canadian Library Association Award for best juvenile fiction; its sequel, *Saltwater summer* (1948), winner of a Governor General's Award for best juvenile fiction; and *Measure of the year* (1950), an evocative book of essays describing the cycle of Haig-Brown's year as writer, magistrate, fisherman, and community leader. He then began his best-known work, a tetralogy: *Fisherman's spring* (1951), *Fisherman's winter* (1954), *Fisherman's summer* (1959), and *Fisherman's fall* (1964). *Winter* is perhaps the best, combining satisfying descriptive writing with practical information for anglers, as he describes a three-month fishing trip to Chile and Argentina in 1950. *Summer*, a collection of angling adventures, stresses conservation. *Spring*, which is about the essence of sport angling and the fisherman's relationship to the fish, the river, and the natural world, best captures the quiet philosophy of Walton's *Compleat angler*. *Fall*, Haig-Brown's favourite angling season, gives an excellent account of the migratory cycles of the Pacific salmon and steelhead trout. In the remarkable final chapter he takes to scuba diving in his river and identifies himself too strongly with the fish to catch and kill them. This is probably his last important book.

Other works include *Mounted police patrol* (1954), a juvenile; *On the highest hill* (1955), a novel; *Captain of the Discovery* (1959), a biography of Captain George Vancouver; *The farthest shores* (1960), a history of B.C. that began as a series of radio dramatizations; *The living land* (1961), an account of the natural resources of B.C.; *The whale people* (1962), a children's book portraying the life and hunting methods of the Nootka who went out in canoes to hunt whales; *Fur and gold* (1962), a history of Sir James Douglas and the Hudson's Bay Company in B.C.; and *A primer of fly fishing* (1964). His last works include two factual monographs for Fisheries and Oceans

Canada: *Canada's Pacific salmon* (1967, begun in 1956), and *The salmon* (1974), which was part of Canada's presentation at the Law of the Sea Conference, Geneva, and was illustrated with Native prints. *Bright waters, bright fish* (1980), published posthumously, is an examination of sport fishing as a social and economic resource. Haig-Brown's daughter, Valerie, edited a three-volume collection, *The world of Haig-Brown*, made up of *Woods and river tales* (1980), mostly unpublished stories dating from the 1930s and 1950s; *The master and his fish* (1981); and *Writings and reflections* (1982), drawing on Haig-Brown's papers in the archives of the University of British Columbia. GEOFF HANCOCK

Hailey, Arthur. See NOVELS IN ENGLISH 1960 TO 1982: OTHER TALENTS, OTHER WORKS: 7.

Haliburton, T.C. (1796-1865). Born in Windsor, Nova Scotia, of New England stock—his father's family were Rhode Islanders and his mother's were Loyalists from Connecticut—Thomas Chandler Haliburton was educated at King's College and was called to the bar in 1820. He practised law in Annapolis Royal, representing that constituency in the provincial assembly from 1826 to 1829, when he was appointed a judge of the Inferior Court of Common Pleas. He was promoted to the Supreme Court of Nova Scotia in 1841. In 1856 he retired and went to live in England, where he held a seat in the House of Commons from 1859 until just before his death in Isleworth, Middlesex.

During his life and ever since, Haliburton has been the subject of many controversies, namely his apparent transformation from a political moderate to an inflexible Tory, his love-hate for Nova Scotia, his ambivalence towards the United States, and disagreements over his place in the Canadian tradition of humour and satire, as well as over the significance of his political vision. In the 1820s, for instance, he advocated the removal of legal disabilities against Roman Catholics; a provincial grant to Pictou Academy, Pictou, N.S., which had been founded by the Presbyterian minister, the Rev. Thomas McCULLOCH; and a system of common schools—all of which his party regarded as radical and progressive measures. In fact, he was always a Tory; he emphasized the British heritage and envisaged Nova Scotia—and all of British North America—flourishing under a monarchical system, governed by an educated élite, and guided by a state church. He argued that the British North American colonies would prosper within the empire, and he encouraged agricultural and industrial advances and the exploitation of natural resources. When Haliburton was elevated to the bench in 1829, a political maverick was removed from the assembly, and it was widely believed that he had sacrificed his views for the sake of advancement. In the 1840s, when his fellow Nova Scotians rejected government by the predominantly Loyalist, Anglican 'family compact' in favour of a more democratic system of responsible government, Haliburton could hardly contain his contempt for them behind good-humoured satire. His disappointment undoubtedly contributed to his decision to forsake Nova Scotia and go 'home' to England to pursue his literary and political ambitions. Yet the tensions created by his praise and criticism of Nova Scotia resulted in his most enduring work.

His first literary effort, the historical pamphlet *A general description of Nova Scotia, illustrated by a new and correct map* (Halifax, 1823), appeared anonymously. Encouraged by the interest in local history, and hoping to raise the status of Nova Scotia in the eyes of the world, Haliburton enlarged it into *An historical and statistical account of Nova-Scotia* (2 vols, Halifax, 1829). From the emphasis in this account on romantic highlights like the expulsion of the Acadians, Henry Wadsworth Longfellow drew background for *EVANGELINE* (1847). Although Haliburton's access to documents was limited, his history, which ends in 1763, was one of the major pieces of historical writing in nineteenth-century Canada. (See also HISTORICAL WRITING IN ENGLISH: 1.)

This book, which brought him little acclaim, did not allow him to criticize contemporary events, so Haliburton turned to satiric sketches, contributing—with his friends, who included the reformer Joseph HOWE and journalist Beamish Murdoch—to 'The Club' papers (1828-31) in *The Novascotian*. The literary influences on Haliburton's humour have been attributed to Thomas McCulloch's 'Letters of Mephibosheth Stepsure' in *The Acadian Recorder* (Halifax) in 1821-3 and to Seba Smith's *Life and writings of Major Jack Downing; of Downingville, away down east in the state of Maine* (Boston, 1833). Most of his fictions involve a journey into a new country and a first-person narrator (a mouthpiece for Haliburton), who investigates the new society. At times he uses several narrators or 'voices' in order to milk humour from the clash of perspectives between his characters, the author, and the reader. In 1835-6 he wrote 21 sketches entitled 'Recollections of Nova Scotia' for *The Novascotian*, and they proved so popular that Haliburton enlarged them into *The clockmaker; or The sayings and doings of Samuel Slick, of Slickville* (first series, Halifax, 1836). His satiric purpose was to show that actions, not complaints, were the only way to improve local conditions, and each sketch—composed mainly of dialogue—begins with an entertaining incident and ends with a pithy moral observation. He drew on his own experiences as a judge to send his fictional squire around Nova Scotia in company with Sam Slick, the brash Yankee clock pedlar whose aggressive salesmanship is a compound of 'soft sawder' and 'human natur'. Haliburton deliberately presents Slick with many inconsistencies, especially with regard to his ideals and actions, which on one level convey Haliburton's own ambivalent attitudes towards Maritimers and, in later books, towards the British, and on another level represents Haliburton's reservations about the directions of American society. Thus Slick praises American commercial know-how and attacks Nova Scotian apathy, yet he is suspicious of American demagoguery and praises Nova Scotia's natural resources and its hardy inhabitants. But readers could ignore Haliburton's message because Slick's energetic high spirits and his Yankee dialect—an unceasing flow of homely aphorisms and epigrams—charmed audiences everywhere: Slick, the archetypal swaggering and sharp American trader, became one of the most popular comic figures of the century and turned the first series of *The Clockmaker* into the first Canadian best-seller.

On an extended trip to Britain in 1838-9 Haliburton was lionized, and through the efforts of his English publisher Richard Bentley, now forgiven for pirating *The clockmaker*, he made the acquaintance of writers such as Theodore Hook, R.H. Barham, and Frances Trollope. This trip changed the direction of his literary career, for he undertook the re-invention of the British North American colonies. While the first *Clockmaker* series was directed at a Nova Scotia audience, Haliburton next addressed British readers in two sequels: *The clockmaker; or, The sayings and doings of Samuel Slick, of Slickville, second series* (London, Halifax, 1838) and *The clockmaker; or, The sayings and doings of Samuel Slick, of Slickville, third series* (London, 1840). He now believed that Nova Scotia's economic problems and the political troubles that erupted in the 1837-8 Rebellions in Upper and Lower Canada could not be solved by the provinces themselves but only by changes in Colonial Office policy, and he introduced scenes in which North Americans and British personages clashed. He also enlarged the role of Slick's Episcopal minister, the Rev. Hopewell, to articulate a conservative American vision.

With his reputation as an expert on North American affairs, Haliburton pursued the contrasts between North America and England in later books, in which he parodied the travel books on North America by such writers as Harriet Martineau, whose liberal sentiments he attacked. Exploiting the new transatlantic steamship services, he wrote *The letterbag of the Great Western; or, Life in a steamer* (London, Halifax, 1840), a series of letters from Canadian, American, and English travellers to their friends at home in which Haliburton poked fun at national characteristics. Slick reappears in *The attaché; or, Sam Slick in England: First series* (2 vols, London, 1843) and *Second series* (2 vols, London, 1844) as a member of the American legation at the Court of St James's, to point out the follies and stupidities of the English; but the satire is less effective here because of Haliburton's ignorance of English life.

Haliburton's finest picture of Nova Scotia, *The old judge; or, Life in a colony* (2 vols, London, 1849), is a sympathetic, rich canvas delineating vice-regal rituals, country picnics, and village court trials. It is the first literary collection of folklore, legends, and ghost tales, of which 'The Witch of Inky Dell' is one of the most evocative stories in nineteenth-century Canada. Haliburton uses three narrators to give coherence to the loosely structured sketches and stories: the British traveller who opens the story; the Windsor judge, Barclay, who guides the visitor and explains the details of colonial life to him; and Stephen Richardson, a vigorous and enterprising farmer who acts as master of ceremonies at an inn where a group of friends entertain each other with stories.

In *Sam Slick's wise saws and modern instances; or, What he said, did, or invented* (2 vols, London, 1853), Slick returns to Nova Scotia as an agent sent by the President to study the fisheries. The Sam Slick series ends with its sequel, *Nature and human nature* (2 vols, London, 1855). Haliburton edited two anthologies, *American humour: traits of American humour, by native authors* (3 vols, London, 1852) and *The Americans at home; or, Byeways, backwoods and prairies* (3 vols, London, 1855). His final book of prose sketches, *The season-ticket* (London, 1860), employs a railway setting for dialogues between the British narrator and his fellow

British and American travellers. A principal topic is the need for improved communications for Britain's colonial empire.

After the 1837-8 Rebellions in the Canadas, Haliburton's hardening Tory attitudes caused a rift with Howe and frequently marred the artistry of his books. His savage attacks on Lord Durham's *Report* (1838) in *The bubbles of Canada* (London, 1839), and in a series of letters to the London *Times*—reprinted as *A reply to the report of the Earl of Durham* (London, 1840)—arose from Haliburton's anger at the British abandonment of British North America and his contempt for the liberals and reformers who were gaining influence in British affairs. He was opposed to a union of the Maritime Provinces and the Canadas because he believed it would lead to independence and even annexation to the United States, and he attacked responsible government because he thought it would lead to mob rule and party factions. Even after the British North American provinces had achieved responsible government, Haliburton argued against it in *The English in America* (2 vols, London, 1851), which was republished as *Rule and misrule of the English in America* (2 vols, New York, 1851). This work traces the origins of American democracy from its beginnings in Massachusetts, and is Haliburton's most extended criticism of the ideals and institutions of the United States, as well as an attack on two centuries of British 'misrule' on the American continent. However, in *An address on the present condition, resources and prospects of British North America* (London, 1857) he grudgingly accepted the notion of a colonial federation, although he preferred an imperial federation in which the colonies would be represented at Westminster.

Haliburton was long recognized as one of the founders of American humour, although he is hardly mentioned in twentieth-century American studies of humour. He is rightly regarded as the last and best in the Loyalist Tory satiric tradition of Canada. He was the first Canadian writer to use roads, railways, and steamships as literary devices. He was also the first fiction writer to employ regional dialects, and the first to create dialogue that is colloquial and racy. Above all, he gave Nova Scotians an imaginative and mythic map based on their roots in the Old and New Worlds, which gave them a vital sense of identity and community.

Editions of Haliburton's works include *Sam Slick* (1923, rpr. 1981) edited by Ray Palmer Baker; the NEW CANADIAN LIBRARY edition of *The clockmaker*, 1st series (1958), with an introduction by R.L. McDougall, which was replaced with a new edition (1993), and an Afterword by McDougall; the Tecumseh Press edition of *Recollections of Nova Scotia: The clockmaker; or The sayings and doings of Samuel Slick, of Slickville (First series, numbers 1-21)* (1984), edited and with an introduction by Bruce Nesbitt; the CEECT edition of *The clockmaker, series one, two, and three* (1985), edited and with an introduction by George L. Parker; *The old judge* (1968), edited by R.E. Watters; *The Sam Slick anthology* (1969), selected and introduced by R.E. Watters, with 'A note on the speech of Sam Slick' by W.S. Avis; *The letter bag of the Great Western; or, Life in a steamer* (1973); *The season ticket* (1978); *A reply to the report of the Earl of Durham* (1976), introduced by A.G. BAILEY; *The old judge; or, Life in a colony* (1978), edited by M.G. Parks; and *The English in America* (1983). In 1983 the Mermaid Theatre of Wolfville, Nova Scotia, presented a musical version of *Sam Slick, the clockmaker*, by Paul Ledoux and Al MacDonald. In 1996 Acadia University hosted a Thomas Chandler Haliburton Bi-Centenary Conference to celebrate the two-hundredth anniversary of Haliburton's birth.

See Ray Palmer Baker, 'Haliburton and the Loyalist tradition in the development of American humour', in *A history of English-Canadian literature to the confederation* (1920); V.L.O. Chittick, *Thomas Chandler Haliburton: a study in provincial Toryism* (1924); R.L. McDougall, 'Thomas Chandler Haliburton', in *Our living tradition* (2nd and 3rd series, 1959); Fred COGSWELL, 'Haliburton', in the *Literary history of Canada* (1965; 2nd edn, 1976); Milton Wilson, 'Haliburton's tales', *The English Quarterly* 6 (Winter 1973); Stanley E. McMullin, 'The decline of American moral vision: a study of *The clockmaker* in relation to *Rule and misrule of the English in America*', *The American Review of Canadian Studies*, 4:2 (Autumn 1974); R.A. Davies, ed., *On Thomas Chandler Haliburton: selected criticism* (1979); H.R. PERCY, *Thomas Chandler Haliburton* (1980); Beverly Rasporich, 'The new Eden dream: the source of Canadian humour: McCulloch, Haliburton, and Leacock', *Studies in Canadian Literature*, 7 (1982); Katherine Morrison, 'In Haliburton's Nova Scotia: "The old judge or life in a colony"', *CANADIAN LITERATURE* 101 (Summer 1984); *The Thomas Chandler Haliburton symposium* (1985), edited by Frank M. Tierney; *The letters of Thomas Chandler Haliburton* (1988), edited by Richard A. Davies; Stanley E. McMullin, 'Thomas Chandler Haliburton,' in *Canadian writers and their works: fiction series: volume two* (1989), edited by Robert Lecker, Jack David, and Ellen Quigley; Gwendolyn Davies, 'The Club papers: Haliburton's literary apprenticeship,' in *Studies in Maritime literary history, 1760-1930* (1991); Matthew Laird, 'Nativist American humor', *Canadian Review of American Studies* 23 (no. 4, 1993); and George Elliott CLARKE, 'White niggers, black slaves: slavery, race and class in T.C. Haliburton's *The clockmaker*', *Nova Scotia Historical Quarterly* 14 (June 1994).

GEORGE L. PARKER

Hambleton, Ronald. See POETRY IN ENGLISH 1900 TO 1950: 5.

Hamelin, Jean (b. 1931). Born in St-Narcisse-de-Champlain, Quebec, Hamelin studied at the collège classique in Trois-Rivières, Université Laval (L.ès L., 1954), and received the *diplôme* from the École pratique des Hautes Études, Paris, France. The thesis he prepared there was published as *Économie et société en Nouvelle-France* (1960). Appointed to Laval's Institute of History in 1957, he was elected Fellow of the Royal Society in 1973.

Hamelin altered the nature of Canadian history by adopting methods forged by the *Annales* historians in France, who had revolutionized historical scholarship. Engaging in intricate historical reconstruction in his first book rather than merely accepting what colonial administrators had said, he analysed the social and economic structures that had governed people's lives during the French regime. The British conquest of 1760, Hamelin concluded, had not been the trauma portrayed by Montreal historians because export profits had flowed largely towards the mother country, and New France had not had a sufficiently entrepreneurial middle class to have been decapitated.

While this approach was extended by other historians, notably by Fernand OUELLET and McGill historian Louise Duchêne in her study of seventeenth-century Montreal, Hamelin helped to make history intellectual inquiry rather than nationalist crusade. 'Our generation no longer believes in a national historian who embodies the destiny of a people,' he wrote in introducing *Histoire du Québec* (1976), 'nor in the official doctrines declaimed on holidays. We are the sons of Questioning.' During a long career at Laval, Hamelin produced a variety of political, economic, labour, intellectual, and religious studies of Quebec's history. His *Histoire économique du Québec, 1851-1896* (1971), co-written with Yves Roby, won a Governor General's Award, and he served as directeur général adjoint of the *DICTIONARY OF CANADIAN BIOGRAPHY/DICTIONNAIRE BIOGRAPHIQUE DU CANADA*. Co-author of *Canada: unity in diversity* (1967), a survey history that was a landmark in according French Canada prominence in the country's history, Hamelin also wrote with Nicole Gagnon a two-volume *Histoire du catholicisme québécoise: le XXe siècle* (1984), which brought him a second Governor General's Award.

TERRY CROWLEY

Hamelin, Louis. See NOVELS IN FRENCH 1983 TO 1996: 5.

Handmaid's tale, The (1985). This novel by Margaret ATWOOD is in the tradition of dystopian fiction. Using a quotation from Jonathan Swift's *A modest proposal* as an epigraph, Atwood signals that she is writing satire and not science fiction. The novel is set in the near future in the United States, in a location that is recognizably Cambridge, Massachusetts. A bloody *coup d'état* has installed a neo-Puritan dictatorship whose governing class, the 'Commanders of the Faithful', has established a fundamentalist theocracy that calls itself Gilead.

Atwood's premise is that this might happen were certain trends, evident in the mid-1980s, pushed to their logical conclusion: the rise of right-wing fundamentalism as a political force in the USA, the decline in the Caucasian birth-rate in North America and northern Europe, and the rise in infertility in the first world as a consequence of chemical pollution, excessive levels of radiation, sexually transmitted diseases, and other factors. Threatened by an epidemic of infertility, the government of Gilead has made abortion, birth control, and homosexuality crimes punishable by hanging. In this nightmare society, woman's highest purpose is only to breed—fertile women, commandeered into producing babies for the state, are forced into a harem-like seclusion, while the rich and powerful male élite practise polygamy. The regime creates an 'instant pool' of women by declaring second marriages and non-marital liaisons adulterous. Such women are arrested as morally unfit and confined to 'Rachael and Leah Re-education Centers' where they must service Gilead as surrogate breeders or handmaids. Genesis 30, verses 1-3, provides the state's theological justification for this control of women. Jacob's wife Rachael, unable to conceive, used the services of her handmaid, Bilhah, as a surrogate: 'Go in unto her; and she shall bear upon my knees, that I may also have children by her.'

To create this world, Atwood drew on her own knowledge of fundamentalism: from her reading of the Bible to her deep knowledge of American history and particularly of the seventeenth-century witch burnings of her own Puritan ancestors, to her travels in Iran and Afghanistan and her interest in military tactics. Politically astute, the novel provides a disturbing and thoroughly convincing portrait of how a totalitarian system functions: how such a regime might grow out of the failure of modern democracies to deal with environmental pollution, biological weaponry, etc., by perverting the public nostalgia for 'traditional values'. As she explains: 'There was little that was truly original or indigenous to Gilead; its genius was its synthesis.'

The story is narrated as a chilling personal account by a handmaid called Offred. An Afterword closes the novel: 'Historical Notes on The Handmaid's Tale', parodying an academic conference, is a partial transcript from the Twelfth Symposium on Gilead Studies, from the year 2195, in which a Native American anthropologist, discoursing on the document that is Atwood's novel, looks back on this obscure moment in history, explains the various stages of the Gilead regime, and hypothesizes about the characters' fates.

When it was published the novel was not considered far-fetched, but rather a disturbingly prophetic analysis of the consequences of religious fundamentalism pushed to extremes. Atwood's brilliance was to locate her totalitarian dystopia not is some remote country, but within a Western democracy. *The handmaid's tale* made the *New York Times*' best-seller list, won many accolades, including the *Los Angeles Times* Fiction Prize and a Governor General's Award, and was shortlisted for the British Booker Prize. In 1990 it was released as a film, directed by Volker Schlorndorf, with a screenplay by Harold Pinter.

ROSEMARY SULLIVAN

Harbourfront Reading Series. Created following a 1972 election promise by the Liberal Party to return two kilometres of Toronto's waterfront to public usage, the Reading Series has played an integral role in a government-sponsored arts scene that has also included concerts, galleries and space for arts workshops in the Queen's Quay West area at the foot of the city. Initially founded by Don Cullen as an attempt to revive the Bohemian Embassy readings of the 1960s, and managed for a short period by John Robert COLOMBO, the Series management eventually was taken over in April 1974 by Greg GATENBY, who has since served as the Artistic Director of the program. Originally devoted to readings of poetry, the regular Tuesday night gatherings were expanded to include all genres of the creative written word.

In 1976 Gatenby decided to invite for readings every living Canadian writer born before 1920, and initiated a program of recording his readers, creating an invaluable sound archive for future generations. Through the urgings of Susan MUSGRAVE, Gatenby invited English poet and novelist George MacBeth to read in 1978—the first non-Canadian to take the stage in the Series, which soon expanded to include such international authors such as John Cheever and Joyce Carol Oates. The overwhelming response to these and other international authors during the late 1970s proved that Torontonians would support a program that featured readings on an international level.

After visiting several of the large European literary festivals, and realizing that no North American city had an international literary festival, Gatenby initiated the first Harbourfront International Festival of Authors in October 1980, inviting twenty-four authors from around the world, one of whom was the Polish writer Czeslaw Milosz, who was awarded the Nobel Prize just as the Festival got under way. The resulting publicity brought international attention to the Festival. Though it has been renamed at various times in honour of corporate sponsors, the International Festival remains an annual autumn event that attracts writers from around the globe, not only as a meeting-place but as a forum where writers can take aesthetic chances and gauge immediate audience response to new work.

The Reading Series has presented over 2500 authors from more than ninety countries and has broken the traditional London/New York axis of publishing and literary focus, to place Toronto in a frontline position as a centre of literary activity.

BRUCE MEYER

Harbour Publishing. One of British Columbia's major publishing houses, it was founded in 1974 by Howard White. He had had great success with a community newspaper, the *Peninsula Voice*, and with an annual journal of oral history, *Raincoast Chronicles* (1972-); in Harbour's first year *Raincoast Chronicles first five*, a hardcover book, began its sale of 40,000 copies. Books on a wide variety of subjects have followed, all emphasizing a West Coast sensibility and West Coast authors. Among its literary authors are Anne Cameron, Hubert EVANS, Edith IGLAUER, Patrick LANE, Susan MUSGRAVE, and Tom WAYMAN. Though not associated with the West Coast, Al PURDY has had several books published by Harbour. It also distributes Nightwood Editions (formerly Blew Ointment Press) and The Caitlan Press.

GEOFF HANCOCK

Hardy, René. See HISTORICAL WRITING IN FRENCH 1980-1996.

Hardy, W.G. See NOVELS IN ENGLISH 1920 TO 1940: 2.

Harlow, Robert (b. 1923). Born in Prince Rupert, British Columbia, he was moved in 1926 with his family to Prince George, where his father was a roadmaster with the CNR. After graduating from high school in 1941, Harlow joined the RCAF at age nineteen and was discharged as a Flying Officer, DFC, in 1945. He earned a B.A. (1948) from the University of British Columbia, where he was a member of one of Earle BIRNEY's first creative-writing workshops, and was the first Canadian to attend Paul Engle's Writers' Workshop at the University of Iowa, where he received an M.F.A. in 1950. Harlow joined the Canadian Broadcasting Corporation as a public-affairs producer and in 1953, with Robert WEAVER, was instrumental in planning and inaugurating the literary program 'Anthology'. His story 'The sound of the horn' appeared in the collection *Klanak Islands* (1959). He was appointed director of radio, B.C. region, for the CBC in 1955. In 1959 he joined with Birney and others to found the literary magazine *Prism International*. In 1965 he was appointed founding head of the newly accredited Department of Creative Writing at UBC, a position he held until 1977. A sophisticated writer, with a careful sense of style, he is a major influence on a generation of B.C. and Canadian writers.

Harlow likes 'big books' that span space, time, and generations of British Columbians. His taste runs to rich prose, and his characters operate on a full canvas. He often calls attention to the artifice of fiction: his narrative voice frequently appears as a counterpoint or subtext. The influence of William Faulkner might be detected in his regional concentration, grotesque characters, and sudden frenzied violence. The use of interlocking novellas is inspired by contemporary European fiction, especially that of Gunter Grass's *The tin drum*.

Harlow's first three novels—*Royal Murdoch* (1962), *A gift of echoes* (1965), and *Scann* (1972)—form a trilogy about the fictional town of Linden, B.C., modelled on Prince George. Connected by the maturing of relationsips among generations, they feature grotesque characters, lavish metaphors, and sudden bursts of violence. *Royal Murdoch*, the most traditional, tells the story of an old man, Royal Murdoch, who gathers his friends and family about him to witness his final days. The plot draws upon his reflections on past personalities and antagonisms, especially the tension between his wife and his Amerindian mistress, who represent civilized and natural woman. *A gift of echoes* concentrates more on commentary than on plot as the protagonist, John Grandy, contemplates the passage of time and sees that the 'structure of his history was dismembered'. The metaphysical aspect of the novel, which makes it at times seem aimless, is offset by melodramatic action: bouts with alcohol, accidents, fights, and the destruction of a lumber mill by fire. *Scann*, Harlow's major novel, interlocks five novellas about Amory Scann, editor of the Linden newspaper. Supposedly writing a special issue about the fiftieth anniversary of the town, he actually writes about his faltering marriage, his Second World War experiences, an epidemic, and chronicles the saga of trapper Linden and settler Thrain, two men central to the history of the town. Their epic struggle in the wilderness against a wolverine (modelled on a story in Howard O'HAGAN's *Wilderness men*, 1958) is one of the great set-pieces in western-Canadian fiction. The novel concludes with Scann's burning of the manuscript he has written, which constitutes the book itself. A complex and richly orchestrated work, its clarity is achieved by an omniscient narrator who comments on the various stories and unifies them.

Making arrangements (1978), a comic novel about horse-racing, portrays a group of hangers-on in a cheap Vancouver hotel attempting to raise enough money for a once-in-a-lifetime bet on a horse-race. Another complex work that is composed of several novellas, it involves drugs, the kidnapping of an industrialist, and pay-TV sex. Less philosophical than *Scann*, it includes among its characters a legless narrator, a detective with prostate trouble, a cab driver, and a prostitute; racetrack and off-track-betting slang in its dialogue; and concludes with a new reading of the chariot race in the *Iliad* as described by modern track-wise punters. *Paul Nolan* (1983) describes a few days in the restless life of the forty-nine-year-old main character who is driven by sexual conquest, but is without morality and love. With complex time shifts, Harlow expertly traces the emotional contours of a failed marriage, affinity with a homosexual friend, and Nolan's failure as a parent. Engaging feminist concerns, the novel is also a condemnation of a phallocentric male ego. Harlow makes good use of Vancouver as setting and texture. The device of diaries and letters explores the problem of limitations, the search for identity by a nation, and meaning in life and death. *Felice: a travelogue* (1985) resulted from a trip to Poland. Harlow carries on with the concerns of a woman and the theme of national identity in the story of Felice Gentry, who breaks away from domestic responsibilities when she discovers she has a cancerous tumour. A trip to Europe to help regain her emotional balance takes her to Poland at a time of political turmoil associated with Lech Walesa and the Solidarity movement. She discovers her conscience and sense of history at the death camp of Auschwitz, and a murder-suicide at the camp and a beating by secret police teach her the horrors of the modern world. The novel, sometimes predictably, explores the theme of liberation—from her past, from her female roles, and Poland's liberation from Soviet oppresion. Harlow explores adolescent sexuality in *The saxophone winter* (1988). Set in 1938, in the mythical small town of Long River, B.C., it is the perceptive and compassionate story of five months in the life of fourteen-year-old Christopher Waterton and his first romance with a thirteen-year-old. The boy's passion is for big-band jazz; like Joseph ŠKVORECKÝ's alter ego, Danny, he dreams of finding freedom as a jazz musician and his parents, with difficulty, buy him an alto saxophone for Christmas. Harlow's protagonist learns of scandal and injustice in a novel that begins with a fire and ends with a flood.

Harlow's critical essays appear in *Margaret Laurence* (1977), edited by W.H. New; *Ernest Buckler* (1972), edited by G. Cook; and *Critical essays on Wallace Stegner* (1982), edited by Anthony Arthur. See also Harlow's 'A Letter: some notes on time, perspectives, and genres', *CANADIAN FICTION MAGAZINE* 30/31 (1979), and his essay, 'Felice: the Polish beginning', *CANADIAN LITERATURE* 120 (Spring 1989). Issue 19 of *Canadian Fiction Magazine* (Autumn 1975) is devoted to Harlow and contains an interview on the writing of *Scann*. See also Louis K. MacKendrick, 'Harlow's arrangements', *Essays on Canadian Writing* 16 (1979-80). GEOFF HANCOCK

Harmon, Daniel. See EXPLORATION LITERATURE IN ENGLISH: 2.

Harou, Lise. See LESBIAN LITERATURE.

Harris, Christie (b. 1907). She was born in New Jersey, USA, and moved as a small child to British Columbia. Married to an immigration officer, she became the mother of five children, and lives in Vancouver. In the 1960s she established a reputation as a writer of children's books. Her early works—*Cariboo trail* (1957), *West with the white chiefs* (1965), and *Forbidden frontier* (1968)—though carefully researched, are dramatically effective only in isolated sections. Three realistic novels—*You have to draw the line somewhere* (1964), *Confessions of a toe-hanger* (1967), and *Let X be excitement* (1969)—are based on experiences with her children; but while containing effective moments, they are without a strong spirit of imagination.

Harris's major contribution is her presentation, in fantasies and other stories, of Northwest Coast Native material and her retellings of Native legends and folktales, beginning with *Once upon a totem* (1963). She has written historical fiction in *Raven's cry* (1966), a well-researched but weakly fictionalized account of the tragic treatment of the Haida by traders, missionaries, and government officials; a crime novel in *Mystery at the edge of two worlds* (1978), about the theft of Native artefacts; fantasies, based partly upon Native folk material, in *Secret in the Stlalakum wild* (1972) and *Sky man on the totem pole?* (1975), which borders on science fiction; and retellings of Native folktales and legends in *Once more upon a totem* (1973), *Mouse woman and the vanished princesses* (1976), *Mouse woman and the mischief-makers* (1977), *Mouse woman and the muddle-heads* (1979), *The trouble with princesses* (1980), and *The trouble with adventuring* (1982). Harris's stories create a link with another culture and age and ask us to see ourselves in a significantly 'other' way. Her creative powers are most fully realized in attempting to provide the reader with the Native world-view, for Harris goes beyond simply retelling legends and tales to reinvent them so that readers are encouraged to examine their own culture in an entirely different context.

See Harris's autobiographical remarks, 'In tune with tomorrow', in *CANADIAN LITERATURE* 78 (Fall 1978). ROBERT LOVEJOY

Harris, Claire (b. 1937). Born in Trinidad, she was educated at the National University of Ireland and the University of the West

Indies before immigrating to Canada in 1966. She taught at the secondary-school level in Calgary, Alberta, until her recent retirement. She began to write for publication in 1975 while on study leave in Lagos, where she was encouraged by Nigerian poet John Pepper Clark, and has produced six collections of poetry: *Fables from the women's quarters* (1984), which won the Commonwealth Award for Poetry for the Americas Region; *Translation into fiction* (1984); *Travelling to find a remedy* (1986); *The conception of winter* (1989); *Drawing down a daughter* (1992); and *Dipped in shadows* (1996). She has co-edited (with Edna ALFORD) *Kitchen talk* (1992), a collection of poetry and prose by women writers, and served as poetry editor of *Dandelion* (1981-9); she was also co-founder and managing editor of *blue buffalo* (1984-7).

Many of Harris's longer poems bear witness to injustice, and experiments with typography and page arrangement draw attention to the voices of those who cannot speak for themselves. In 'Where the sky is a pitiful tent' each page is divided horizontally, a contrapuntal arrangement through which a poetic narrative of terrorism in Guatemala is underscored by the real-life documentary testimony of Rigoberta Manchu, a victim of that regime. 'Nude on a pale staircase' portrays the colonization of women by male-dominated social institutions, including Western systems of aesthetic representation. Closer to home, Harris censures Canadians who tolerate evil in the form of social injustice, as in the poem 'Policeman cleared in jaywalking case', which documents public indifference to a real-life incident in which a black Albertan schoolgirl was arrested and strip-searched for an alleged misdemeanour.

In her shorter poems Harris often writes of Caribbean women exiled from their African roots by British colonial policy in the West Indies. While mourning the irrecoverable loss of her own African heritage, since all experience for her must be mediated through the English language in which she was educated, she insists nonetheless on the power of the African-Canadian poet to use English as an instrument for inscribing 'A Black reading' (to quote the title of another of her poems) upon the 'white space' that is North America's idea of itself. Indeed, Harris's faith in the power of lyric poetry and standard English (although she employs dialect at times), along with her humanist tendency to speak in terms of general truths and shared values, sets her somewhat apart from the more radical poetics of other African-Canadian writers such as M. Nourbese PHILIP and Dionne BRAND—though clearly she is no less committed to matters of social redress.

Harris has also written a number of poems that are personal in tone and portray friendship, and maternal and erotic love. *Drawing down a daughter* is an ambitious book-length narrative in which a woman addresses her unborn child in poetry and prose, through a vibrant collage of stories, songs, recipes, and historical details that signify the richness of the heritage into which the child will be born.

See Lynette Hunter, 'After modernism; alternative voices in the writings of Dionne Brand, Claire Harris and Marlene Philip', *University of Toronto Quarterly*, 62 (1992-93), as well as *Grammar of dissent* (1994), edited by Carol Morrell and featuring poetry and prose by Harris, Brand, and Philip.

MARILYN ROSE

Harris, John Norman. See MYSTERY AND CRIME.

Harrison, Charles Yale (1898-1954). Born in Philadelphia, Pennsylvania, he left school in grade four—over a dispute, it is said, with a teacher about *The merchant of Venice*—and at sixteen was working for the *Montreal Star*. Soon after the outset of the Great War he enlisted in the Royal Montreal Regiment and was a machine-gunner in Belgium and France; he was wounded at Amiens in 1918. He returned to Montreal and worked as a theatre manager, a real-estate salesman, and newspaper reporter before moving to New York, where he worked as a public-relations consultant, radio commentator, and writer.

Harrison's contribution to Canadian literature was a powerful war novel based on his experiences with his Canadian regiment: *Generals die in bed*, which was published in England and the USA in 1930, and reprinted in 1975 with an introduction by Robert F. Nielsen. Parts had appeared in magazines—some German—by 1928, the year before publication of Erich Maria Remarque's *All quiet on the Western Front*, Ernest Hemingway's *A farewell to arms*, and Robert Graves' *Goodbye to all that*. (Neilsen suggests that Remarque may have been influenced by these extracts while writing his novel.) Ford Madox Ford praised *Generals* and it was translated into Spanish, French, and Russian. Beginning in Montreal, the setting quickly changes to Europe and trench warfare, moving briefly (and terrifyingly) to no-man's land, behind the trenches, and to London. The narrator, an eighteen-year-old Canadian soldier, relates his experiences in a deceptively simple style, describing explicitly and objectively the relentless horrors of trench warfare. Fighting is not romanticized, compassion for the soldier's plight is not restricted by nationality, and war is depicted as a brutalizing process. The narrator concludes that the enemies are 'the lice, some of our officers and Death'. Neilsen compares the memorable scene in which the narrator kills a soldier at close range and has difficulty in removing the bayonet from the body to a similar scene in Remarque's novel. *Generals die in bed* is characterized by its strength and simplicity of diction, unifying motifs, cutting irony, and black humour.

Harrison's other novels are *A child is born* (1931), about impoverished lives in the waterfront district of Red Hook, New York; *There are victories* (1933), partly set in Montreal; *Meet me on the barricades* (1938), about a musician who is drawn into the Spanish Civil War, which combines a realistic prose narrative with a surreal play-like sequence; and *Nobody's fool* (1948), about a hoodwinking scheme that is recounted by a New York public-relations executive. Harrison also wrote the pamphlet *Next please!* (1927), the foreword to which is signed by John Dos Passos, among others, about a case similar to that of Saccho and Vanzetti; *Clarence Darrow* (1931), the first book-length biography of the famous lawyer; and *Thank God for my heart attack* (1949), a reassuring account of his cardiac problem.

For further discussion of *Generals die in bed*, see Robert F. Nielsen's unpublished thesis, 'A barely perceptible limp: the First World War in Canadian fiction' (University of Guelph, 1971). See also John Moss, *A reader's guide to the Canadian novel* (1981). JOY KUROPATWA

Harrison, Dick. See CRITICISM IN ENGLISH: 5(g).

Harrison, Susie Frances (1859-1935). Susie Frances Riley, who often used the pseudonym 'Seranus', was born in Toronto and educated there at a private school for girls, and for two years in Montreal. While living in the province of Quebec she developed a keen interest in French-Canadian culture that would become evident in her writing. In 1879 she married John W.F. Harrison, a professional musician; they had two children. After living in Ottawa until 1887, she made Toronto her permanent home. There she became well known as a professional pianist and vocalist, an authority on French-Canadian folksongs, and was principal of the Rosedale Branch of the Toronto Conservatory of Music for twenty years. Beginning to write when she was sixteen, she contributed literary and musical reviews (some of these appearing under the name 'Gilbert King'), articles, essays, short stories, and poetry to Canadian, British, and American newspapers and literary magazines. She was a regular correspondent for the Detroit *Free Press* and the Toronto *Globe*, and was editor of *The* WEEK for nine months.

Her first book, *Crowded out! and other sketches* (Ottawa, 1886), is a collection of stories, most of which attempt to capture particular characteristics of Canadians. The title story depicts, with psychological intensity, the frustrations of a Canadian writer who tries in London, England, to publish works with Canadian content. There are several stories whose haunted, disturbed characters, first-person narratives, and weird events show the influence of Edgar Allan Poe. Many of the stories contain French-Canadian characters and settings, the specialty of 'Seranus'. Harrison wrote two novels: *The forest of Bourg-Marie* (London, 1898), a mythic study of the disintegration of French-Canadian society as the younger generation leave their native land and tradition for the wealth of the United States, and *Ringfield* (1914), a melodrama in which an idealistic Methodist minister is corrupted by a bohemian French-Canadian actress and her English poet-lover. While the French-Canadian setting is used effectively in the early novel to heighten its mythic qualities, it is a mere backdrop for the romantic plot in the later work.

Harrison was best known in her day as a poet. Her most ambitious poetry collection is *Pine, rose and fleur de lis* (Toronto, 1891), a collection of lyrical verse organized in sections that include a long travel sequence, 'Down the river', consisting mostly of villanelles, a form appropriate to its subject—a fancy-free boat ride through French Canada; a monody on Isabella Valancy CRAWFORD; several poems on England ('From the pine to the rose'); and a miscellany of nature and love poetry. (Several of the poems have accompanying musical notation.) Conventional in language and form, these poems are of interest mainly for their subject matter: the celebration of the people and landscape of Canada and the point of view of Canadians. Her other poetry collections—most of them privately published—are short (twenty pages maximum): *Song of welcome in honor of His Excellency, the Marquis of Lansdowne, Governor-General of Canada* (Ottawa, 1883), *In northern skies, and other poems* (1912),

Songs of love and labour (1925?), *Later poems and new villanelles* (1928), *Penelope and other poems* (n.d.), and *Four ballads and a play* (1933)—in which the play, *A phantom born of song*, is a one-act melodrama set in a northern mining camp. Harrison also published *The Canadian birthday book* (Toronto, 1887), a blank diary whose right-hand pages contain excerpts from English- and French-Canadian poetry.

In the late nineteenth century Harrison enjoyed a favourable critical reception in Canada, and her work was reviewed not only in Canada but in England and the United States—in *The Week*, the *Canadian Magazine*, *Literary World*, *London Spectator*, *Saturday Review*, and *Critic*—where she was praised for her knowledge of French Canada, her 'new world conceits', and her gift of song. She is significant as a minor poet and novelist who, as a member of the Confederation generation, attempted to identify and express a distinct Canadian voice and character.

CARRIE MacMILLAN

Hart, Julia Catherine (1796-1867) Julia Catherine Beckwith was born in Fredericton, New Brunswick, of New England and French ancestry, and gathered many stories and travel impressions on her childhood visits to relatives in Quebec and Nova Scotia. A number of these were incorporated into her first novel, *ST. URSULA'S CONVENT; or, The nun of Canada* (Kingston, 1824), the first novel published in British North America written by a native-born author. In 1820 she moved from Fredericton to Kingston, Upper Canada, where she lived with her aunt, the mother of Quebec historian Abbé Ferland. Between 1822 and 1824 she married George Henry Hart; conducted a girls' boarding school in Kingston; and moved to the United States with her husband. In 1831 the Harts settled in Fredericton, where George Hart held a position in the Crown Lands office. Mrs Hart remained in her native city for the rest of her life, contributing short fiction to the *New Brunswick Reporter and Fredericton Advertiser* and working on an unpublished two-volume novel, *Edith; or, The doom*. In all her writing she revealed a heightened romantic sensibility and a strict adherence to the conventions of popular fiction. *St. Ursula's Convent* is therefore typical in introducing shipwrecks, kidnappers, exchanged babies, and a false priest into a sentimental story of Quebec seigneurial and convent life. A less sensational novel is *Tonnewonte; or The adopted son of America* (Watertown, N.Y., 1824-5), a two-volume romance published in three different editions in the United States after the Harts had moved there in 1824. Set in France and in upper-state New York, *Tonnewonte* appealed to American patriotic feelings by contrasting the democratic opportunities and naturalness of American life with the chaos and class-consciousness of France during the Napoleonic era. Like *St. Ursula's Convent*, it also reflected Mrs Hart's interest in incorporating North American history and landscape into her fiction. This interest was extended into her writing of *Edith; or, The doom*, which focuses on a family curse and its expiation during the time of the American Revolution. In her preface to *St. Ursula's Convent* Mrs Hart noted that the 'dawn of literary illumination' had not yet come to British North America. For the rest of her life she saw her fiction as part of a process of literary awakening, and as an encouragement to 'others of real and intrinsic merit' to write.

GWENDOLYN DAVIES

Hart, Matthew. See NOVELS IN ENGLISH 1983 TO 1996: OTHER NOVELS: 2(b).

Hartog, Diana. See NOVELS IN ENGLISH 1983 TO 1996: OTHER NOVELS: 1(b).

Harvey, Jean-Charles (1891-1967). Born at La Malbaie (Murray Bay), Quebec, Harvey took the traditional 'cours classique' at the Petit Séminaire de Chicoutimi (1905-8), then spent several years as a Jesuit scholastic (1908-15). A reporter with *La Presse* (1915) and *La Patrie* (1916-18), he was subsequently hired by La Machine agricole nationale in Montmagny to handle the firm's public relations. In 1922 he moved to *Le Soleil* in Quebec City, acting as editor-in-chief from 1927 until Apr. 1934, when he was relieved of this position the day after the Archbishop of Quebec condemned his novel *Les demi-civilisés*. Premier Taschereau appointed Harvey director of the Office of Statistics for Quebec, but after Maurice Duplessis's election in Aug. 1936 he was fired a second time. For nine years Harvey published his own weekly newspaper, *Le Jour* (1937-46). After the war he lectured widely, worked as a radio commentator (with CBC International and CKAC), and edited two papers, *Le Petit Journal* and *Le Photo Journal* (1953-66). Interested for a time in Marxist theory, he became a staunch anti-Communist by the late 1940s. Later, during the unsettled 1960s, Harvey defended both federalism and bilingualism and spoke out against separatism—warning his anglophone friends, however, that Québécois would need constitutional changes guaranteeing the survival of their language and culture if they were to realize their full potential as North American francophones within a federalist state.

Harvey's writing career paralleled that of journalist and public commentator. Author of three novels—*Marcel Faure* (1922), *Les demi-civilisés* (1934; 2nd edn 1962), and *Le paradis de sable* (1953)—he also wrote three collections of short stories: *L'homme qui va* (1926), *Sébastien Pierre* (1935), and *Des bois . . . des champs . . . des bêtes* (1965), as well as a volume of poetry, *La fille du silence* (1958). Among his six volumes of essays are *Pages de critique* (1926), *Art et combat* (1937), *Les grenouilles demandent un roi* (1942; Eng. trans., *The eternal struggle*, 1943), and *Pourquoi je suis anti-séparatiste* (1962). Harvey was awarded the medal of the Officier de l'Académie française in 1928 and the Prix David in 1929.

In *Marcel Faure* Harvey criticized the conservatism of Quebec's business and clerical élite and denounced the widespread exploitation of the working class. By introducing a radically new, technically oriented education for his workers, Faure sets up a steel company owned and operated by French Canadians that competes successfully with Anglo-American businesses and transforms a tiny village on the St Lawrence River into a thriving community.

Harvey's best-known novel, *Les demi-civilisés*, marks a turning-point in the liberation of Quebec fiction from unrealistic and socially irrelevant depictions of life and morality. Here he condemns the control of Quebec's economy by the English community and, more significantly, scathingly denounces the power of the Quebec clergy in all spheres, attacking in particular their betrayal of the spirit of the Gospel message. Through the sexual liaison of Max Hubert and Dorothée Meunier, and the free-thinking ideas of their revolutionary magazine, Harvey criticizes the lack of intellectual and moral freedom in Quebec during the 1920s. His anti-clericalism is harshly expressed through Hermann Lillois, who wonders what Christ would think of 'the triple alliance of capital, civil power and the Church' that keeps his people in fear and 'servile silence'. This attack on the political, economic, and religious *status quo* brought a swift public condemnation of the book by Cardinal Villeneuve, and Harvey was for many years a pariah; but he is now recognized in Quebec as a defender of intellectual, moral, and artistic freedom. *Les demi-civilisés* was first translated as *Sackcloth for banner* (1938). A superior translation, *Fear's folly* (1982), was made by John GLASSCO.

Two major studies of Harvey's works are Guildo Rousseau's *Jean-Charles Harvey et son oeuvre romanesque* (1969) and Marcel-Aimé Gagnon's *Jean-Charles Harvey, précurseur de la révolution tranquille* (1970). See also John O'Connor's long introduction to *Fear's folly*.

RAMON HATHORN

Harvey, Moses (1820-1901). An Irishman of Scottish descent, Harvey was born in Armagh and educated in Belfast, where he was ordained as a minister in the Presbyterian church in 1844. In 1852 he became pastor of St Andrew's Free Presbyterian Church in St John's, Newfoundland, and was soon prominent as a lecturer on biblical and scientific subjects. In 1878 he retired from the active ministry, apparently because his voice failed him, and dedicated himself to the profession of letters. In 1891 he was awarded an honorary LL.D. by McGill University. He committed suicide in St John's.

Harvey was a writer of wide interests, great industry and enthusiasm, and impressive ability. A Victorian polymath and optimist, he ranged in subject matter over history, science, poetry, religion, and contemporary society. A belief in progress was his *idée fixe*. He declared his faith that 'We are now on the topmost billow of this mighty tide of progress' in his early publication *The characteristic features of the present age, and the prospects of the coming era: a lecture delivered to the Mechanics' Institutions of Workington and Maryport* (1849). His literary life was preoccupied with reiterating this theme. There is little that is lighthearted or imaginative in his writing, although it should be noted that his 'Chronicles of Punch Bowl' in the *Maritime Monthly* of 1873 and 1874 are an early attempt to fictionalize a Newfoundland outport. But he is usually a serious propounder of some beneficial notion, a supplier of information, an educator, or a propagandist. His earnestness is displayed in his first book of general interest, *Lectures, literary and biographical* (Edinburgh, 1864), a miscellany of rambling essays on literature and science that showed his grasp of current ideas. One of the papers in the book, 'Human progress—Is it real?', was later expanded into a work portentously entitled *Where are we and whither tending? Three lectures on the reality and worth of human progress* (Boston, 1886).

In the late 1860s Harvey started applying his principles to his adopted country and began what might be described as a massive publicity campaign on behalf of the colony. In periodical articles, newspaper columns, speeches, encyclopaedia entries, and books, he indefatigably brought the potential of Newfoundland to the attention of outsiders. The most relentless, and possibly the most gifted, of a generation of literary boosters of Newfoundland, he wrote: *This Newfoundland of ours: a lecture* (St John's, 1878); *Across Newfoundland with the governor; a visit to our mining region; and This Newfoundland of ours. Being a series of papers on the natural resources and future prospects of the colony* (St John's, 1879); *Newfoundland; the oldest British colony, its history, its present condition, and its prospects in the future* (London, 1883); *Hand-book of Newfoundland: containing an account of its agricultural and mineral lands, its forests, and other natural resources* (Boston, 1886); *Newfoundland as it is in 1894: a hand-book and tourist's guide* (St John's and London, 1894); *Newfoundland in 1897; being Queen Victoria's diamond jubilee year and the four hundredth anniversary of the discovery of the island by John Cabot* (London, 1897); and *Newfoundland in 1900; a treatise of the geography, natural resources and history of the island, embracing an account of recent and present large material movements* (New York and St John's, 1900). This last book was reissued in 1902 as *Newfoundland at the beginning of the 20th century, a treatise of history and development* (it was characteristic of Harvey to recycle material under different titles). The most important of these works was *Newfoundland; the oldest British colony*, which was evidently written in collaboration with the English novelist and journalist Joseph Hatton (1841-1907). There was an American edition (1883) and two years later it appeared in an abridged version for Newfoundland schools. Harvey's numerous publications, with their burning message about the country's resources, possibly had incalculable effects upon generations of Newfoundland writers.

In addition to the works listed, Harvey wrote four theological tracts: *Thoughts on the poetry and literature of the Bible* (St John's, 1853); *The testimony of Nineveh to the veracity of the Bible* (St John's, 1854); *Lectures on the harmony of science and Revelation* (Halifax and St John's, 1856); and *Lectures on Egypt and its monuments, as illustrative of Scripture* (St John's, 1857). He also edited the 1873 edition of W.E. Cormack's *Narrative of a journey across the island of Newfoundland* (St John's).

PATRICK O'FLAHERTY

Harvey, Pauline. See NOVELS IN FRENCH 1983 TO 1996: 1, 6.

Harvor, Elisabeth (b. 1936). Born Erica Elisabeth Arendt Deichmann in Saint John, New Brunswick, she started nurse's training in 1954 at Saint John General Hospital but left nine months before graduation, married Stig Harvor in 1957 and, after a year-and-a-half in Europe, settled with him in Ottawa. They had two sons and were divorced in 1977. In 1983 she enrolled at Concordia University; after a qualifying year in lieu of a B.A., she obtained an M.A. in 1986. She has taught in various creative-writing programs and has been writer-in-residence at the Ottawa Public Library (summer 1993), Carleton University, the University of New Brunswick, and Concordia University, Montreal. She has published three volumes of short fiction: *Women and children* (1973), which was reprinted with slight revisions as *Our lady of all the distances* (1991); *If only we could drive like this forever* (1988); and *Let me be the one* (1996). She has also published a selection of poetry, *Fortress of chairs* (1992), which won the Gerald Lampert Memorial Award.

Harvor writes of women—women in marriage and out of marriage, as mothers, as student nurses—with a style that is at once subtle and wry, shrewd and ironic. By a deft and vivid use of detail and with a detached but not uncompassionate eye for human nature and its foibles and credulities, she is able to give overtones and undertones to even the simplest and lightest events and material.

JOYCE MARSHALL

Hatton, Joseph. See FOREIGN WRITERS ON CANADA IN ENGLISH: 1.

Haultain, Arnold. See ESSAYS IN ENGLISH: 2.

Hawley, William Fitz (1804?-55). Born in Lacolle, Lower Canada (Quebec), he lived at various times in both Quebec and Montreal. At his death in Laprairie he was registrar of No. 1 Division of the County of Huntingdon. He began to publish poetry in Canadian newspapers and periodicals in 1826, and his continuing appearances therein made him well known and admired as a native Canadian writer. Some of his early verse was collected in *Quebec, the harp, and other poems* (Montreal, 1829). The long poem 'Quebec' describes the grandeur of the city's site and history; 'The harp', which won a prize from the Quebec Society for the Encouragement of the Arts and Sciences, displays a thorough knowledge of classical mythology; 'The triumph of envy' is a thinly veiled account of the effects of slander in an unnamed garrison city; other shorter poems deal with familiar human scenes and emotions.

Hawley also published *The unknown; or, Lays of the forest* (Montreal, 1831), a short novel interspersed with narrative poems. The first English-Canadian fiction to be set in New France—in this case Trois-Rivières in 1633—it is about the rescue of a French maiden captured by Natives, and has enough suspense to make the reader impatient of the tedious but competent interpolations: four long poems with Greek, Persian, and Roman settings, the supposed work of the novel's hero. The preface points out that this structure derives from Thomas Moore's *Lalla Rookh* (1817), a prose story in which the hero narrates four oriental tales in verse. Hawley's hero, 'the Unknown', whose real name is never given, is a young Frenchman who attempts to win the Natives to a more settled life by adopting their ways and gaining their confidence. The Natives, however, are too wise to agree to his plan and in the end he settles for marriage to the maiden in whose rescue he has been instrumental. Both 'the Unknown' and the girl's father, M. de Lauzon, are instructed in New World survival by Piscaret, an Algonquin chief—a 'noble savage' for whose character Hawley owes much to Chateaubriand. The three female protagonists are one-dimensional; but the males, both European and Native, are somewhat complex. Both scenery and action are realistically described.

Two other books, *The legend of Niagara* and *History of the Canadas*, were announced in 1830 and 1837 respectively but never appeared. Hawley collected a great number of five-shilling subscriptions for the latter; in 1840, when the subscribers began to demand either the book or a refund, he was still promising that it would be published shortly.

MARY LU MacDONALD

Hayes, John. See CHILDREN'S LITERATURE IN ENGLISH: TO THE 1970s.

Hayman, Robert (1575-1629). Reared in Devon, England, he was a graduate of Exeter College, Oxford, and a student at Lincoln's Inn, London. During his stay at Lincoln's Inn, 'his geny being well known to be poetical', he became acquainted with Michael Drayton, Ben Jonson, George Withers, and other poets. Around 1618 he became governor of the Bristol merchant's plantation at Bristol's Hope in Conception Bay, Newfoundland. His initial visit to the colony was for fifteen months; he returned in successive summers until around 1628. In an address to Charles I in 1628 Hayman admitted that the commodities so far received from Newfoundland 'are in their particulars base, and meane'; yet, he added, 'they honestly imploye many people'. He proposed that Charles rename the island Britaniola. Hayman died while on an expedition up the Oyapock River in South America.

Hayman was the author of *Quodlibets, lately come over from New Britaniola, old Newfoundland. Epigrams and other small parcels, both morall and divine. The first foure bookes being the authors owne: the rest translated out of that excellent epigrammatist, Mr. Iohn Owen, and other rare authors: With two epistles of that excellently wittie doctor, Francis Rablais: translated out of his French at large. All of them composed and done at Harbor-Grace in Britaniola, anciently called Newfoundland* (London, 1628). The first book of English poetry to be written in what is now Canada, it contains much uncritical praise of the climate and resources of Newfoundland. In this respect Hayman is to linked with such propagandists for settlement in Newfoundland as Richard Whitbourne and William Vaughan. As poetry, *Quodlibets* (i.e. 'What you will') is rough, homely verse, with here and there a touch of irony or a compelling phrase. Hayman knew his book consisted of 'bad unripe Rimes', but he apparently published it to make a point about the literary potential of the new colony: 'For if I now growne dull and aged, could doe somewhat, what will not sharper, younger, freer inventions performe there?' He was thus a conscious pioneer—not just as a colonist, but also as a poet.

PATRICK O'FLAHERTY

Hearne, Samuel. See EXPLORATION LITERATURE IN ENGLISH: 2.

Heavysege, Charles (1816-76). His birthplace has been given as Huddersfield, England, but in letters to the London critic Charles Lanman, Heavysege claims only that his 'ancestors on the paternal side' were from Yorkshire, and that Bayard Taylor's article in the *Atlantic Monthly* (Oct. 1865), which gave Liverpool as his birthplace, was 'generally correct'. He immigrated to Canada in 1853 and settled in Montreal, where he was employed as a woodcarver in a cabinet works. He later became a journalist on the staff of the *Transcript* and the *Daily Witness*. There is some mystery about Heavysege's life: during his lifetime he asserted that one of his ancestors was connected with nobility; after his death several collections of his papers, including one in the McCord Museum, were riffled and personal information removed. A number of his shorter poems have also disappeared.

There are two versions of Heavysege's first dramatic poem, *The revolt of Tartarus*, a six-book epic in blank verse. The first version, bearing his name, was published in London and Liverpool in 1852; the second, considerably edited, appeared anonymously in Montreal in 1855. His successive poems and dramas draw from the Bible, Shakespeare, Byron's *Cain* and 'Hebrew melodies', and the popular dramas *Saul* and *Filippo* by Vittorio Alfieri. Heavysege's protagonists are typically romantic rebels ruled by a dominant passion: Saul is proud, Jephthah rash, and Jezebel concupiscent. However, each is placed within the old Shakespearean world of order and universal degree where spiritual revolt is inevitably followed by punishment.

In *Saul: a drama in three parts* (Montreal, 1857), Saul's character is developed to show a growing hubris that ultimately becomes satanic. Coventry Patmore, in an unsigned review in the *British North American*, praised it as 'indubitably the best poem ever written out of Great Britain'. Much of Heavysege's subsequent literary effort was dedicated to the rewriting of *Saul*, his best work: a second edition was published in London and Montreal in 1859, a third in Boston in 1859. This third edition was reprinted by John Lovell in 1876; in 1967 it was reprinted in *Saul and selected poems*, with an introduction and review of criticism by Sandra Djwa.

The verbal wit and sustained eroticism of the tragicomedy *Count Filippo; or The unequal marriage* (Montreal, 1860; rpr. 1973) made the drama unpalatable to Victorian Canada. In *Jephthah's daughter* (Montreal, London, 1865) Heavysege turns to the Bible for its saga of the great but rash Israelite leader who sacrifices his daughter to keep his vow to God. Heavysege also wrote a number of shorter poems, many of which are now unavailable. Copies of his *Sonnets* (Montreal, 1855), 'The owl', a poem of twenty-five stanzas, and the 'Ode', read at the Shakespeare Tercentenary in Montreal on 23 Apr. 1864, have not been found.

Heavysege included some sonnets in *Jephthah's daughter*, four of which are reprinted in *Saul and selected poems*. An undistinguished excerpt from the 'Ode' was published in the *New Dominion Monthly* of 1876. 'The dark huntsman' was published in the *Canadian Monthly and National Review* (Aug. 1876) with the mistaken assertion that the poem was written just before his death; an earlier version had been published by the Witness press of Montreal in 1864. 'Jezebel'—a poem that appeared in the *New Dominion Monthly* (Jan. 1868) and was reprinted by Golden Dog Press, Ottawa, in 1972—contains a description of the death of Jezebel, her bones licked by dogs, that has a macabre vitality. Heavysege also published a novel, *The advocate* (Montreal, 1865; rpr. 1973), a potboiler of unassimilated Gothic elements.

Overvalued during his lifetime by critics wishing to assert the existence of a Canadian literature, Heavysege has been undervalued since his death, largely because of the wave of revisionist criticism in the 1920s that dismissed him as British rather than Canadian, partly because much of his work is closet drama, and also because his surname encourages easy satire. Robertson DAVIES in *Leaven of Malice* puns on the 'heavy' aspects of *Saul* and wittily dubs his fictional critic, Solly Bridgetower, as the Heavysege man in 'Amcan'. Yet Heavysege was an exemplar to the early poets Charles SANGSTER, Charles G.D. ROBERTS, and W.D. LIGHTHALL and was admired by the moderns W.W.E. ROSS and A.J.M. SMITH. It is his presentation of nature—the backdrop to the sacrifice of Jephthah's daughter—on which Northrop FRYE leans heavily in his highly influential critical thesis on the existence of cruel nature in Canadian poetry ('The Narrative Tradition in English-Canadian Poetry', 1946). This interpretation is doubtful, however, as Heavysege borrows his description of nature from Tennyson's *Morte d'Arthur.* George WOODCOCK, writing on Heavysege in *Canadian writers and their works* (1988), develops much of his interpretation from the Introduction and summary of criticism appended to Djwa's edition of Heavysege. He characterizes him as a 'good bad poet', agrees that Heavysege has a 'natural power and obsessive preoccupation with the conflict between human and divine justice', and accepts her judgement regarding his placement as a major poet in relation to his time. A re-reading of *Jephthah's daughter* by Sister M.L. McKenzie argues that while Heavysege follows traditional biblical patterns, these are undermined by Jephthah's 'divided consciousness', by the presentation of a strong mother, and by their daughter's 'ambivalent reaction to her plight' (*Canadian Poetry*, 1989). To the modern reader, Heavysege offers passages of genuine poetic vigour and psychological insight. Handicapped by limitations in his literary background and by the lack of a supportive Canadian culture, his considerable achievements in his best works, *Saul* and *Jephthah's Daughter*, are all the more impressive. He is the major figure in the Canadian literary world up to 1870.

See also Writing in QUEBEC: 2.

SANDRA DJWA

Hébert, Anne (b. 1916). Born at Sainte-Catherine-de-Fossambault, Quebec, she spent her childhood and adolescence in Quebec City and since the mid-1950s has been living in Paris, making frequent visits to Canada. For her distinguished poetry and fiction she was awarded two Governor General's Awards (in 1960 and 1975), the Molson Prize in 1967, the Academie française award in 1976, and in 1982 the Prix Fémina for her novel *Les fous de Bassan.*

Anne Hébert's father, Maurice Hébert, who was a provincial civil servant and an exacting literary critic, encouraged his daughter to write and had a distinct influence on the rigour of her style. Another considerable influence, this time on the content of her writing, was that of her cousin, Hector de SAINT-DENYS-GARNEAU. A privileged witness to the development of his poetry, Hébert assimilated some of his major symbols (hand, heart, bone, the word, etc.), while modifying them considerably. His death in 1943 shattered all Hébert's tranquil notions, and her own writing was henceforth marked by revolt. Beginning with the short story 'Le torrent' (written in 1945), her characters would be rebellious, in open revolt against their fate as Québécois.

Hébert's first collection of relatively traditional poems, *Les songes en équilibre* (1942), which won the Prix David, depicts a mournful existence steeped in dream. However, overly cautious publishers would delay until 1950 the appearance of her collection of short stories *Le torrent*; the title story, about repression, has a powerful explosive charge that was, for informed readers, a symbolic depiction of the French Canadian's inner deprivation. (*Le torrent* was reissued with four new stories in 1963.)

Meanwhile Hébert was working on a collection of poems, *Le tombeau des rois* (1953), in which harsh revolt is given a highly personal expression and an ultimately liberating outcome. The title poem, a classic of modern Québécois literature, is an exploration of the unconscious filled with symbols: a bird (the poet), kings (the voices of the past), jewels and flowers (the allurements of the dead), water (dread), closed chambers (tombs), bones (death), and light (an awakening). Here liberation is as much psychological as poetic and consists in mentally expelling the figures of dead kings—those master-images, with civil as well as religious significance, that for so long dominated the colonized, clericalized minds of the Québécois.

A similar liberation appeared in the rather static novel *Les chambres de bois* (1958). Catherine marries Michael, whose life is dominated by dreams. He forces his young wife to live shut away in their Parisian rooms, then leads her to the gates of death. Catherine revolts, and in the last part of the novel we see her in a situation of light and love.

In 1954 Hébert began a new cycle of poems inspired by light, the sun, the world, and the word: *Mystère de la parole*, which was published in Paris in 1960, along with a new edition of *Le tombeau des rois*, under the title *Poèmes* (winner of a Governor General's Award). Thus Hébert's poetic trajectory was complete: from writing about solitary, anguished dreams, she had arrived at a form of expression that was both opulent and committed to the real world. *Oeuvre poétique* (1993) contains all of Hebert's poetry to date, excepting only *Les songes en équilibre.*

Anne Hébert's plays—*Le temps sauvage*, *La mercière assassinée*, and *Les invités au procès*, published in a single volume under the title *Le temps sauvage* (1967)—transpose into dramatic terms her progression from dream to language. In *Le temps sauvage*, her major play, she describes the progress of Quebec from rural and silent to urban and dynamic. The central character, Agnès, would like to keep her children 'outside of time', in her own silent, maternal night; the children grow impatient, force destiny, and in the end Agnès agrees to live in a world of speech and communication. The three plays have been translated by Eugene Benson and Renate Benson in the journal *Canadian Drama/L'Art dramatique canadien*, vol. 9, no.1 (1983), vol. 10, no. 2 (1984), and vol. 14, no.2 (1988). In 1990 Hébert published a second volume containing two plays—*La cage* and *L'île de la demoiselle*. In both plays the central character is a wronged woman and the historical circumstances relate to Quebec history.

Hébert next commenced work on a novel-cycle that begins in the nineteenth century and gradually moves into recent times. *KAMOURASKA* (1970), her most important and best-known novel, was based on an actual murder committed in nineteenth-century Quebec. *Les enfants du sabbat* (1975), set in the 1930s and 1940s, is a story of sorcery based on rigorous research into ancient and local witchcraft. The central character, Julie, and her brother Joseph are the children of parents who live on the fringes of society and engage in secret practices in the countryside outside Quebec City. Hébert uses the technique of flashback, but with a twist: Sister Julie of the Trinity, who is gifted with vision into the past, mentally leaves her convent and is literally transported to her birthplace in her parents' shanty. The main action is set in the convent, where the nuns and Church authorities are increasingly scandalized by the peculiar behaviour of Sister Julie, the daughter of a sorcerer, who is dedicated to sorcery through an initiatory rape by her father. She is submitted to divine exorcism, without result. Even worse, she finds herself mysteriously pregnant and gives birth to a baby that the authorities leave to die in the snow. However, the rebellious Julie runs away from the convent to join a waiting lover. The third novel in this cycle, *Héloïse* (1980), is no less astonishing. Here the action is set in modern Paris and the author uses the devices of fantasy and somnambulism to show how a young man, Bernard, succumbs to the lure of death and the past as embodied in a dead woman who has become a vampire named Héloïse and wanders day and night through the Paris Métro sucking people's blood. In *Les fous de Bassan* (1982) Hébert skilfully blends the voices of the wind, the sea, and the birds ('les fous de Bassan') with those of six narrators who try to reconstruct the dark events that occurred one August night in 1936 in the little English-speaking village of Griffin Creek in the Gaspé, when two lovely young girls, Nora and Olivia, were raped and murdered on the beach.

In *Le premier jardin* (1988), the central character, Flora Fantanges, who has made her career as an actor in France, returns to her native Quebec City in the summer of 1976 to play the role of Winnie in Samuel Beckett's *Oh les beaux jours* (*Happy days*). Overwhelmed by memories, she relives her dispossesed childhood (the first garden), the scenes and street names of the city reminding her not only of her own past but of the historical exploitation of women in the past. In *L'enfant chargé de songes* (1992) the central character, Julien Vallières, while travelling to Paris in 1946, relives memories focused on his mother and his lover. A letter announcing the birth of his child returns him to Quebec, possessed of greater insight and understanding. *Aurélien, Clara, Mademoiselle et le lieutenant anglais* (1995) is a slight piece, a 'récit'. Although its protagonist, Clara, is only fifteen, she too takes stock of the past as she prepares to enter into marriage with the English lieutenant. But as is so often the case when Hébert contrasts reality and dream, Clara's wedding night pales in comparison with her idealized vision of it.

The astonishing violence of her plots, the rigour of her vocabulary, the sureness of her craft, and her intense dramatic sense have brought Anne Hébert an enviable reputation as a novelist that extends beyond her native Quebec to an international readership.

Hébert's fiction has been translated as *Kamouraska* (Norman Shapiro, 1974), *The silent rooms* (Kathy Mezei, 1975), *Children of the black sabbath* (Carol Dunlop-Hébert, 1978), *Héloïse* (Sheila Fischman, 1982), *In the shadow of the wind* (Fischman, 1983), and *The first garden* (Fischman, 1991). *The torrent* (1967) was translated by Gwendolyn Moore. Hébert's poems have been translated into English by Alan Brown (*Poems*, 1975). F.R. SCOTT, Peter Miller, and John GLASSCO. *Dialogues sur la tradition à propos du 'Tombeau des rois'* (1970), with a preface by Northrop FRYE, is an exchange of letters between Hébert and Scott about his translation of her important poem that first appeared in *The TAMARACK REVIEW* 24 (Summer 1962).

See Pierre Lemieux, *Entre songe et parole: structure du Tombeau des rois d'Anne Hébert* (1978); Delbert W. Russell, *Anne Hébert* (1983); Maurice Émond, *La femme à la fenêtre* (1984); Lucille Roy, *Entre la lumière et l'ombre: l'univers poétique d'Anne Hébert* (1984); Janet M. Paterson, *Anne Hébert: architexture romanesque* (1985); and France Nazair Garant, *Ève et le cheval de grève: contribution à l'étude de l'imaginaire d'Anne Hébert* (1988).

See also NOVELS IN FRENCH 1940 TO 1959: 5; 1960 TO 1982:3(e).

PIERRE H. LEMIEUX

Hébert, Louis-Philippe. See FANTASTIC LITERATURE AND SCIENCE FICTION IN FRENCH.

Hébert, Marie-Francine. See CHILDREN'S DRAMA IN FRENCH.

Heighton, Steven (b. 1961). Born in Toronto, Ontario, he grew up in northern Ontario, and has lived in several places in western Canada, and in Red Lake, Japan. He attended Queen's University, Kingston (B.A., 1985; M.A., 1986). Inspired by Victor COLEMAN's creative-writing class at Queen's, he turned his attention to highly poetic prose. He was editor of *Quarry* magazine (1991-4). One of the most talented writers to emerge in the 1990s, in 1989 he won the Air Canada Award and in 1990 the Gerald Lampert Award for poetry. He also came first in the 1991 *Prism International* short-fiction contest; won a gold medal for fiction at the 1992 National Magazine Awards; had two stories in the *Journey Prize anthology*; and was a finalist for a Governor General's Award in 1995.

The centre section of Heighton's first collection of poems, *Stalin's carnival* (1989), is presented as translations of poems written by the Russian dictator. One long sequence in *The ecstacy of skeptics: poems* (1994) explores the Apollonian and Dionysian poles of experience, using theories of the left and right brain hemispheres (some critics felt the work was a self-conscious striving to be profound). Heighton's first collection of stories, *Flight paths of the emperor* (1992), explores the intersection of Japanese and Western cultures and the theme of change and turmoil. *On earth as it is* (1995) is made up of eleven stories in the forms of elegies, confessions, and memories that range from Kingston to Kathmandu; in the novella 'Translation of April', the narrator recalls moods of, and moments with, a deceased lover.

Foreign ghosts (1989) is made up of poetic journal entries of a trip to Japan written in the style of Basho's *Narrow road to the deep north*. In *The admen move on Lhasa: writing and culture in a virtual world* (1996), an extended essay, Heighton expresses his dislike of corporate culture, advertising, and tourism, offering the Tibetan city of Lhasa as an ideal of 'art'; though the argument is sketchy, the prose is elegant and poetic. GEOFF HANCOCK

Helprin, Mark. See FOREIGN WRITERS ON CANADA IN ENGLISH: 2.

Helwig, David (b. 1938). Born in Toronto, Ontario, he lived there, then in Hamilton and Niagara-on-the-Lake before attending the University of Toronto and doing graduate work (1960-2) at the University of Liverpool, England. He then taught at Queen's University, Kingston, Ontario (1962-74). He has also taught at the penitentiary near Kingston, an experience that led to his non-fiction work *A book about Billie* (1972), created from taped interviews with a habitual offender and revealing the author's fascination with criminal cleverness and cunning. Helwig gave up teaching in 1974 to become the literary manager of CBC-TV (until 1980); since than he has devoted himself to writing full-time.

Helwig's first collection of poems, *Figures in a landscape* (1967), delineated with clarity and directness ordinary domestic events, as well as artistic figures such as Canaletto, Matisse, Gordon Craig, and Bunyan. Many of the poems were reprinted in *The sign of the gunman* (1969)—the title sequence indicating how his work had begun to turn to darker, violent themes. *The best name of silence* (1972) has poems, many narratives, and dramatic monologues whose characters struggle with spiritual crises involving risk and danger. The narrative poems in *Atlantic crossings* (1974) focus on four travellers making the ocean journey, meditating on the paradoxes of human behaviour and the struggle between evil and violence and decency, elaborating on the polarities of morality and intelligence, opposed to creative inventiveness or even madness. These conflicts surface in the opening poem of *A book of the hours* (1979), based on the relationship between the scholar Thomas Bullfinch and his ward. *Catchpenny poems* (1983) are poems arising from nineteenth-century prints, and *The beloved* (1992) traces the interconnected lives of David and Goliath, Saul and Jonathon, and Absalom and Bathsheba.

Helwig has lately been concentrating more on fiction, though his first collection of short stories, *The streets of summer*, was published in 1969. He has continued writing novels with a wide range of themes, sometimes detailing ordinary lives, sometimes moving into political and historical arenas. His interest in the domestic and the ordinary is at the centre of his sequence of four novels set in Kingston: *The glass knight* (1976), *Jennifer* (1979), *It is always summer* (1982), and *A sound like laughter* (1983). In 1993 he published a collection of short prose pieces, *Blueberry cliffs*, that are poetic 'takes' on relationships and the people involved in them; some of these ideas and characters reappear in his ambitious novel *Just say the words* (1994).

For twenty-five years Helwig co-edited a series of short-story anthologies for OBERON PRESS. He has also edited several books of readings in the area of the social and political concerns of culture, including *The human elements* (1978) and *Love and money: the politics of culture* (1980). PETER STEVENS

Hémon, Louis (1880-1913). Born in Brest, France, he moved to Paris with his family when he was still young. His father, Félix Hémon, was a university instructor and France's inspector-general of public education. Louis took courses in oriental languages at the Sorbonne and received a law degree. After finishing his military service at Chartres (1901-2), he went to England (1903) and made London his home for eight years. In England, he honed his writing skills as correspondent for a French sports magazine (*Le Vélo*, later renamed *L'Auto*); he also won that magazine's literary contest in 1904 and 1906. During that period he married Lydia O'Kelly, with whom he had a daughter, Lydia Kathleen. Leaving both wife and daughter with her family in England, he set sail for Canada in 1911.

Hémon spent short periods in Quebec City and Montreal—he worked briefly as a bilingual stenographer for a Montreal insurance company—and then went north, living at Péribonka in the Lac Saint-Jean area, working on the farm of Samuel Bédard. It was there that he wrote his now-famous *MARIA CHAPDELAINE: récit du Canada français*. After sending the manuscript to France, he set out for western Canada, but was killed in a train mishap at Chapleau, Ontario, at the age of thirty-three.

Maria Chapdelaine appeared in serial form in *Le Temps* (Jan.-Feb. 1914) but was not published in book form in Canada until 1916. Criticized by some French Canadians for the unromantic view it presented of life among the *habitants*, it was nevertheless quickly recognized as an important work of fiction and has achieved the status of a classic. An English translation by William Hume BLAKE, with the subtitle *A tale of the Lake St. John country*, was published in 1921 and remains the standard one.

Hémon wrote other novels. They are *Colin-Maillard* (1924), translated by Arthur Richmond as *Blind man's buff* (1924); *Battling Malone, pugiliste*, (1925), translated by W.A. Bradley as *Battling Malone and other stories* (1925); and *Monsieur Ripois and nemesis* (1925), translated by W.A. Bradley, the French text *Monsieur Ripois et la némésis* appearing in 1950. A collection of short stories, *La belle que voilà* (1923), was translated by W.A. Bradley as *My fair lady* (1923). All his works were published posthumously. A new edition of *Maria Chapdelaine* (Boréal Express, 1980), edited by Nicole Deschamps, is faithful to the original manuscript submitted by Hémon, and eliminates the many stylistic changes that had been effected by previous editors.

Hémon's fascinating life and death have been the subject of much speculation. Since the 1970s he has been presented to the public as a rebel. Jacques FERRON, in his introduction to *Colin-Maillard* (1972), sees him rejecting the values of an oppressively colonial France, seeking new vistas in England and Canada, and finally taking his own life at Chapleau. In *Le mythe de Maria Chapdelaine* (1980) Nicole Deschamps portrays Hémon as a social reformer whose novel does not seek to glorify colonized Québécois, but to awaken in them a sense of their own plight. Deschamps previously edited *Louis Hémon, lettres à sa famille* (1968). Alfred Ayotte and Victor Tremblay point out in *L'aventure Louis Hémon* (1974) that Hémon's birthdate, 12 Oct., is the anniversary of Columbus's discovery of America, which is presumably a reference to Hémon's 'discovery' of a North American culture virtually unknown to Europeans of the period. All that may be said with certainty about this extraordinary man is that his life and work provoked French Canadians to scrutinize their own culture in a way they had never done before. For this reason alone, if for no other, Canadians may claim Hémon as their own. PAUL SOCKEN

Hénault, Gilles (b. 1920). Born at St-Majorique, Quebec, and educated in Montreal, he quit school early owing to financial circumstances and subsequently educated himself through voracious reading. He trained as a journalist with *Le Jour* (1939), *Le Canada* (1940-2), and *La Presse* (1942-4). He then worked with the news service of Radio-Canada (1945-6) and the radio station CKAC (1946-7). A union organizer and publicist in Montreal and Sudbury from 1949 to 1956, he resumed his journalistic career in 1957, working as a freelance writer for Radio-Canada till 1959, when he became head of the arts and letters section at *Le Devoir*; in 1951 he was a commentator on international affairs at *Le Nouveau Journal*. In 1952-3 he worked as a writer for the Royal Commission on Bilingualism and Biculturalism. He taught improvisation at the École Nationale de Théâtre in 1964 and was an interviewer for Radio-Canada in 1965. Appointed director of the Museum of Contemporary Art in Montreal in 1966, he held that position until 1971, when he became an adviser on museum affairs with the Department of Cultural Affairs of Quebec. From 1973 he worked as a freelance writer and translated several books; he was writer-in-residence at the Université d'Ottawa in 1974-5 and conducted writing workshops at the Université du Québec à Montréal in 1976 and 1977.

Hénault was co-founder with Éloi DE GRANDMONT, in 1946, of 'Les Cahiers de la file indienne', a series in which his first collection of poems, *Théâtre en plein air*, was published that year. He was already preparing the way for a new era in Quebec poetry that explored a cosmic dimension, that searched for an elemental centre from which liberation could spring forth, trusting in the power of words to re-create the world, and employing surrealistic images—all of which were to be essential preoccupations of the new generation of poets. However, despite his association with the Montreal writers and painters known as Les Automatistes, and the influence exerted by Surrealism at the time, Hénault resisted the 'automatic' mode of writing: his poetry preserved a clarity and intelligibility that it was never to lose. Indeed, reason and irony remained his chosen weapons against oppression. Although actively involved in social issues, he did not write overtly militant poetry; rather he believed that poetry and life are, and should be kept in, a dialectical, complementary relationship. He expressed this view in 'La poésie et la vie', his contribution to *La poésie et nous* (1958), a collection of essays by Michel VAN SCHENDEL, Jacques BRAULT, Wilfred Lemoine, Yves PRÉFONTAINE, and Hénault. His second volume of poems, *Totems* (1953), revives a mythical Aboriginal presence, images of a wild virgin land to be reclaimed. The imagery embodies the theme of a call for new beginnings that was taken up by most subsequent Quebec writing. It is, however, in his preoccupation with the autonomy of words that Hénault is the precursor of modernity in Quebec poetry: his poems attempt to create a world of language rather than to use language to describe any particular perception of the world. This preoccupation, already present in his first books, is amplified in *Voyages au pays de mémoire* (1959) and *Sémaphore* (1962); the latter was awarded the Prix du Grand Jury des Lettres and the second prize in the Concours littéraire du Québec. Hénault's poetry reveals a constant struggle with language: the need to express truly the self and its environment drives him to fight linguistic and literary conventions to the point of wishing to produce a 'naked scream'; simultaneously he is tempted by a purely self-referential use of language. These conflicting forces are nevertheless subordinated to the pervasive desire to create a poetry that is a 'signal'—a rallying point for potential seekers of a new reality. This is suggested by the title of *Signaux pour les voyants* (1972), in which his previous work was collected; it also contains 'L'invention de la roue' (1941), four 'Allégories' (1941), and 'Dix poèmes de dissidence'. *Signaux* won a Governor General's Award, a timely recognition of Hénault's work as a significant turning-point. After a long period of silence, Hérault published *À l'inconnue nue* in 1984, a series of poems exploring and celebrating the erotic body in meditations that feed on numerous quotations from, and allusions to, other poets. *À l'écoute de l'écoumène* (1991) is a seven-part heterogeneous collection of texts in which intimations of ecological collapse and a sense of doom and futility predominate. In 1993 Hénault received the Athanase-David prize in recognition of his entire work.

English translations of Hénault's poems are available in *Hénault—seven poems, from Le Théâtre en plein air and Totems* (1955); in *The poetry of French Canada in translation* (1970) edited by John GLASSCO; and in *Ellipse* 18 (1976).

See H. Corriveau, *Gilles Hénault: lecture de Sémaphore* (1978) and the special issue of *VOIX ET IMAGES* 61 (1995).

MICHEL PARMENTIER

Henday, Anthony. See EXPLORATION LITERATURE IN ENGLISH: 2.

Hendry, Tom (b. 1929). When Hendry started his practice as a chartered accountant in Winnipeg in 1955 he was also writing short stories for the Canadian Broadcasting Corporation and acting in television and radio productions. His first play, *Do you remember?* (unpublished), originally produced by CBC Winnipeg in 1954, was directed by John Hirsch for the Rainbow Stage in the summer of 1957. That same year Hirsch and Hendry co-founded Theatre 77, which, in 1958, merged with the Winnipeg Little Theatre and became the Manitoba Theatre Centre. Giving up accounting in 1960 to work in theatre full time, Hendry was the first manager/producer of Winnipeg's Rainbow Stage, while also serving as administrator of the Manitoba Theatre Centre. The Centre produced his plays *Trapped* (unpublished) in 1961 and *All about us* (unpublished) in 1964. A Brechtian musical revue co-written with Len PETERSON and Alan Lang, *All About us* toured the country before becoming CTV's first dramatic production. From 1964 to 1969 Hendry was secretary-general of the Canadian Theatre Centre. He served as literary manager for the Stratford Festival for two years, co-founded in 1971 Playwrights Co-op and Toronto Free Theatre, and in 1974 co-founded (with Douglas Riske) the Banff Playwrights Colony (which workshopped a number of his unpublished plays) and the Banff Playwriting Department. He directed the Banff programs for three years. His three-year association with the CBC as a writer for *King of Kensington* ended in 1979. From 1972 to 1982 he was alternately treasurer and chair of Playwrights Canada (now Playwrights Union of Canada) and president of Toronto Free Theatre. He was also chair of the federal task force on the National Arts Centre and the principal writer of its report, 'Accent on access/ favoriser l'accessibilité'(1986). Since 1983 he has been associated with the Toronto Arts Council as treasurer and policy director and, as of 1994, director of research and analysis. For several years he has been a regular commentator on the arts and social issues for CBC Radio's national 'Infotape' service.

The 1967 award of the Centennial Medal was followed by other awards acknowledging his important and continuing contribution to Canadian theatre: in 1977 the Queen Elizabeth Jubilee Medal, in 1982 the Toronto Drama Bench Award and, in 1995, appointment to the Order of Canada.

Hendry's *Fifteen miles of broken glass* (1972), produced by CBC-TV in 1967 and CBC-Radio in 1968, was adapted for the stage in 1969; as such it won Hendry the 1970 Ontario Lieutenant-Governor's Medal. In the play the central character, Alec McNabb, is a passionately committed air cadet who despairs when the Second World War ends three months before he comes of age. Some people were outraged by Hendry's musical *Gravediggers of 1942* (1973)—with music by Steven Jack—which contrasts the facts of the Dieppe disaster with the youthful enthusiasm of a group of kids trying to raise money for War Bonds. But this play, like *Fifteen miles*, points out how naïvely courageous Canadians were, and how much they wanted to be a part of the war effort. In both works the idealistic and romantic yearning to participate in a great conflict is set against the harsh realities the young characters must later face.

Satyricon (unpublished, produced in 1969) —called by the author a 'disposable opera'— was the first big-budget Canadian theatre piece performed at the Stratford Festival (Avon Theatre). It is a satire on middle-class values and vulgarity based on the satirical romance by Nero's arbiter of elegance, Petronius. Hendry's songs, set to music by Stanley Silverman, became the basis for Richard Foreman's off-Broadway production *Doctor Selavy's magic theatre* (unpublished, produced in 1972), the United Artists recording of which is now a collector's item. Hendry's next major work, *How are things with the walking wounded?* (1972), set in Montreal during Expo 67, opens with Willy, an affluent English-Canadian businessman, hosting a party for his young French-Canadian lover, René, in celebration of their two-year relationship. Much to his dismay Willy discovers that his fortune is not enough to keep René, and he is left to rearrange his alliances.

Hendry's *Byron* (unpublished, produced in 1976), based on Harriet Beecher Stowe's *Lady Byron vindicated* (1870), with music by Steven Jack, and *Hogtown: Toronto the Good* (unpublished, produced in 1981), with music by Paul Hoffert, both present imagined meetings and struggles between historic figures. In *Byron* Stowe, a friend of Lady Byron in real life, visits Lord Byron in Italy and, with puritanical zeal, rails against his aristocratic humanitarian stance. She demands from him heroic action. The central characters in *Hogtown* are taken from local history: vice-busting Toronto mayor William Howland and the madam of a brothel, Belle Howard. In spite of a structurally complex script and an ambitious attempt to mount a full-scale musical, *Hogtown* was poorly produced (by Toronto Truck Theatre) and closed early. Although *Hogtown* presented its material lightheartedly, at its core was an important issue: the legislation of civic morality. The use of serious subject matter, plus the inclusion of a musical score that is intended to widen the work's popular appeal, are characteristic of Hendry's plays.

In the 1980s Hendry continued his work as cultural critic, administrator, and playwright. Based on tapes by contributors, in 1985 he and Michel GARNEAU co-authored *The school/L'école*, an appreciation of the National Theatre School. In 1986 he wrote the children's play *East of the sun and west of the moon* (unpublished), a narrative dance drama with music by Steven Jack, which toured for two years; and, in 1994, *Not in my back yard* (unpublished), an examination of inter-generational conflict in the context of a struggling group home for street kids. *Cultural capital: the care and feeding of Toronto's artistic assets* (1985) is one of a number of studies of municipal/arts community relations that Hendry has written.

See Robert Wallace and Cynthia Zimmerman, *The work: conversations with English-Canadian playwrights* (1982).

CYNTHIA ZIMMERMAN

Hennepin, **Louis**. See Writing in NEW FRANCE: 1.

Henry, **Alexander**, the Elder. See EXPLORATION LITERATURE IN ENGLISH: 2.

Henry, **George** (Maungwudaus, 1811-after 1855). Born at the 40 Mile Creek in the Credit River area to Mesquacosy and Tubinaniqua (the mother of Peter JONES), Henry was an Ojibwa who converted to Christianity in 1824 and became one of the most promising Native candidates for the Methodist ministry. Along with Peter Jones, John Sunday, and Peter JACOBS, he was considered one of the foremost members of the Methodist Church in Canada, devoting fifteen years to the conversion of his people to Christianity, travelling long distances, teaching, interpreting, preaching, and enjoying great respect among his own people and his Methodist superiors. In the late 1830s he helped James Evans write an Ojibwa hymn book and regularly sent letters to the *Christian Guardian*, the Methodist newspaper. In 1840 he suddenly left the ministry. For the next three years he worked as the government interpreter at the St Clair Mission; and in 1843, to his half-brother Peter Jones's horror, he organized a dance troupe to tour the United States and Europe. Wherever they stopped, they were entertained and honoured as celebrities by royalty and high society alike. Henry's reminiscences and impressions of his experiences overseas appeared in three pamphlets: *Remarks concerning the Ojibway Indians, by one of themselves, called Maungwudaus, who has been travelling in England, France, Belgium, Ireland, and Scotland*, (Leeds, 1847) includes a short account of the tour as well as a few comments regarding Native religion and customs and several testimonials. *An account of the Chippewa Indians, who have been travelling among the whites in the United States, England, Ireland, Scotland, France and Belgium* (Boston, 1848) is his most detailed literary effort, recording his impressions of persons and places in London, Paris, Dublin, Edinburgh, and Glasgow, as well as shrewd comments on the contemporary scene and amusing anecdotes. *An account of the North American Indians* (Leicester, 1848) includes a very brief description of his tour written by himself. His perceptive and amusing impressions, however, are the first of few Native testimonials regarding Europeans that survive. Henry's wife and their three children born overseas all died during the tour. An advertisement in the Toronto *Globe*, on 22 April 1851, announced an 'illustrated lecture on their manners and customs' to be given by the celebrated Maungwudaus, as well as the appearance of 'three of his sons and an Ottaway Female ... in their *Original Costume* ornamented with coloured Porcupine Quills, their caps made of Golden Eagle's Feathers, and their necklaces of Grizzly Bear's Claws'. Another advertisement, this time in the *Harrisburg Morning Herald*, 11 May 1854, announced his appearance in that city. His last-known letter (in the Henry Schoolcraft Collection, Library of Congress, Washington, D.C.) is dated 23 Sept. 1855. Henry then disappeared from documentary evidence.

PENNY PETRONE

Henry, Walter (1791-1860). Born in Donegal, Ireland, he became a surgeon in the British army. In 1827 he was posted to Canada with the 66th Regiment and remained there until his death. He was well known in the medical world of his time; internationally because he had been an observer at Napoleon's autopsy, and in Canada because of his advanced views on hygiene and the treatment of cholera. He held the important post of Inspector-General of Military Hospitals before he retired in 1855 to Belleville, Canada West (Ontario).

Henry was also a well-known literary figure in Canada. His memoir in two volumes, *Trifles from my port-folio; or Recollections of scenes and small adventures during twenty-nine years' military service in the Peninsular War and invasion of France, the East Indies, campaign in Nepaul, St. Helena during the detention and until the death of Napoleon, and Upper and Lower Canada*, printed by William Neilson at Quebec in 1839, sold three times as many copies as John RICHARDSON's *Canadian brothers* when it appeared the following year. The memoir was widely reviewed and praised. In 1843, revised and considerably extended, and retitled *Events of a military life*, the work was published in London by William Pickering, again receiving extensive laudatory notices. Henry was an associate member of the Quebec Literary and Historical Society when he did not reside in that city, and one of its active officers when his regiment was stationed there. He wrote frequently for the New York *Albion*, using the pseudonyms 'Miles' and 'Piscator'. As 'Miles' he wrote commentaries on British North American politics, and as 'Piscator' he described his fishing adventures—fishing being his lifetime hobby.

Trifles from my port-folio includes ten very mediocre poems, and *Events of a military life* ends with a conventional short story set in New France about 1640, recounting the love of a noble young Frenchman for a beautiful Native maiden whom he finally marries. But the value of these volumes is in the autobiography: the maturing of a very young officer through the peninsular campaigns, where the savagery of war is mixed with amorous adventures; the campaigns in India, a country he disliked intensely; the intrigues at St Helena; a depressing return to his native Ireland; and the final posting to Canada. From his account of Canadian events in the decade before the Rebellion of 1837-8, he does not appear to have been sympathetic to either Papineau or Mackenzie or their cause.

Henry's two memoirs are solidly rooted in the custom of his age, when many army officers published autobiographical accounts of their adventures. They are more interesting and better written than many of the genre. His fellow citizens were proud of his attainments, and frequently referred to the honour he brought to Canada by residing there.

MARY LU MacDONALD

Hensley, Sophie (1866-1946). Born in Bridgetown, Nova Scotia, and educated privately in England and France, Sophie Almon came under the literary influence of Charles G.D. ROBERTS when he moved to Windsor, Nova Scotia, in 1885. Roberts endorsed her contributions to periodicals such as *The WEEK* and the *Dominion Illustrated Monthly* and encouraged the publication of *Poems* (1889). Two poems written in this period appeared in Douglas Staden's *Younger American poets* (1891).

Several years after her marriage in 1889, Hensley moved to New York. There she lectured on social issues, participated actively in groups such as the New York Mothers' Club and the Society for the Study of Life, contributed to periodicals such as the *Youth's Companion*, *Arena*, and *Everybody's Magazine*, and acted as Associate Editor of *Health: A Home Magazine Devoted to Physical Culture*. The poems in *A woman's love letters* (1895) challenged society's idealization of women and urged sexual equality. The theme of equality also informed the novella *Love & Company (Limited)*, published in New York in 1897 under the pseudonym 'John Wernbery and Another'. This was attributed to Hensley in her own lifetime, but *A semi-detached house* (Montreal, 1900), sometimes credited to Hensley, now appears to be by Montreal writer J. Try-Davies (see Carole Gerson, *Canadian Notes & Queries*, no. 39).

Although she collaborated with her husband in 1900 on a musical play, *Princess Mignon*, Hensley became increasingly engaged by feminist and child-welfare causes. Her 1906 collection of poems, *The heart of a woman*, explored issues surrounding children, motherhood, and passionate love. The essays of *Women and the race* (1907, 1911), published under the pseudonym 'Gordon Hart', argued for women's physical fitness, dress reform, informed sex education, and financial independence for women within marriage and motherhood. These ideas were further advanced in Hensley's more outspoken book *Love and the woman of tomorrow* (1913), which attacked social hypocrisy, including denying women the vote and ostracizing single mothers. *Out of silence* (n.d.) reinforced the latter theme by exposing the anguish of 'a fallen woman' denied the felicity of motherhood and the compassion of church and state. *The way of a woman, and other poems* (1928) consolidated themes of nature, love, and war.

A frequent visitor to her summer place at Barton, Nova Scotia, Hensley lived on Jersey from 1937 to 1940. She returned to her childhood home, Windsor, in 1943. A maternal feminist and an unabashed celebrant of women's sensuality in her poetry, she was what she herself would have called 'A Woman of Tomorrow'.

GWENDOLYN DAVIES

Herbert, John (b. 1926). Born John Herbert Brundage, he was educated in Toronto until age seventeen, when he went to work, first in the advertising department of Eaton's. Following a six-month sentence in the Guelph reformatory in 1946—the outcome of being harassed by local toughs and accused by them of homosexuality at a time when it was illegal—he worked at a variety of jobs. In 1955 he began to study ballet and theatre in Toronto, and during the 1960s he served successively as artistic director for three Toronto theatre companies, including his own Garret Theatre Studio. Dancer, playwright, director, designer, stage manager and novelist, he has also held appointments in theatre at universities and was associate editor of an arts newspaper, *Onion*.

Of Herbert's published dramas, the most famous is *FORTUNE AND MEN'S EYES* (1967; 2nd edn 1974), Set in a Canadian reformatory, it explicitly derives from, but does not duplicate, his own crucial experience of incarceration. It was given a workshop at the Stratford Festival in 1965 and received its first commercial production at the Actors' Playhouse, New York, in Feb. 1967; the film adaptation (1971) was directed by Harvey Hart.

Omphale and the hero (1974) is reminiscent of, but does not imitate, the style and technique of Tennessee Williams. Melodramatic in situation and dialogue, it calls for expressionism in its set design and in the character's personalities; but it is also implicitly allegorical, offering the audience an opportunity to equate the characters and their predicaments with cultural, political, economic, and moral circumstances in Canada. In a town on the border between two French- and English-speaking provinces a drifter, Mac, and a prostitute, Antoinette, become lovers out of loneliness and the need for comfort. Partly because of greed, partly under pressure from the mayor and policeman, Mac deserts Antoinette for a rich Italian widow.

Four short plays published together as *Some angry summer songs* (1976)—*Pearl divers*, *Beer room*, *Close friends*, and *The dinosaurs*—also deal with varieties of relationship and betrayal, further exploring the frequent emphasis in Herbert's work on the desperate need people have for human contact, the desperate measures they will take to achieve it, and the even more despairing retreats they will often ultimately choose in favour of personal security and safety. ANTHONY HOPKINS

Herbert, **Sarah** (1824-46) and **Mary Eliza** (1829-72). Sarah and Mary Eliza Herbert were half-sisters born in Ireland and Halifax, Nova Scotia, respectively. Raised and educated in a staunch temperance and Methodist environment, both women devoted much of their energy to Sabbath School, Temperance Society, and Benevolent Society activities in Halifax.

Sarah Herbert conducted a school in 1843-4 and from 1844 to 1845 acted as editor of a temperance newspaper, *The Olive Branch*. Between 1840 and 1846 her religious and domestic poetry appeared in regional publications under the pseudonym 'Sarah'. Appealing to pious and conventional tastes, her verse established her literary reputation in the Maritimes and created an audience for her two fictional works. *Agnes Maitland* (Halifax, 1843), a fluently written but didactic tale, won a temperance award from *The Olive Branch* for its dramatization of a self-indulgent woman's descent into alcoholism. Its serialized successor, 'The history of a Halifax belle' (*The olive branch*, 1844), was even more relentless in denouncing 'the serpent coils of the pernicious habit', and reinforced the impression that Sarah's interest in fiction lay in its utilitarian rather than its aesthetic possibilities. Her early death from tuberculosis captured the public imagination, and for many years afterward her sister Mary Eliza's literary reputation was overshadowed by the memory of 'the gifted authoress' Miss Herbert.

By 1851, however, Mary Eliza Herbert had established her name by publishing occasional verse and by founding a women's literary periodical, *The Mayflower; or, Ladies' Acadian Newspaper*. Always supportive of regional writing, this journal became an outlet for Mary Eliza's poetry and prose, written in a romantic and commemorative vein. It also published her first long fiction, *Emily Linwood; or The bow of promise* (1851) and *Ambrose Mandeville* (1852), two novellas about the devout woman of educated heart who was to be a convention in all Mary Eliza's narratives. After the collapse of *The Mayflower* in 1852 because of poor economic conditions and competition from American journals, Mary Eliza contributed poems and prose-sketches to *The Novascotian*, *The Provincial Wesleyan*, and the Halifax *Morning Sun*, and collected some of her poems and occasional pieces in *The Aeolian harp; or Miscellaneous poems* (Halifax, 1857) and *Flowers by the wayside: a miscellany of prose and verse* (Halifax, 1865). *The Aeolian harp*, also containing poetry by the deceased Sarah, became a popular gift book in the Maritimes and did much to enhance the reputation of the sisters as writers of genteel verse.

Of Mary Eliza's three fictions published soon after the demise of *The Mayflower*, *Belinda Dalton; or Scenes in the life of a Halifax belle* (Halifax, 1859) best illustrates the author's potential for developing lively confrontation, local colour, and domestic detail. While less emphatic in its treatment of the marriage theme than *Lucy Cameron*, an unpublished novel, *Belinda Dalton* reveals Mary Eliza's insight into the financial vulnerability of women in Victorian society. Unfortunately she tended to sacrifice social analysis and in-depth characterization to the conventions of popular moral fiction *Woman as she should be; or Agnes Wiltshire* (Halifax, 1861) and *The young men's choice* (Halifax, 1869) suffered from the same didacticism and sentimentality found in her earlier novels. In the last years of her life, Mary Eliza occasionally published excerpts from a manuscript entitled *A woman's thoughts on passages of Scripture* and continued to make regular contributions in prose and verse to regional publications. Much respected locally for her lyric poetry and sentimental fiction, she represented the last of a coterie of Nova Scotian Methodists who, between the 1840s and the 1870s, made Halifax and *The Provincial Wesleyan* centres of church literary activity.

GWENDOLYN DAVIES

Herbin, **John Frederic** (1860-1923). Born in Windsor, Nova Scotia, of a Huguenot father and an Acadian mother, he graduated from Acadia University in 1890 following earlier training as a watchmaker and goldsmith. Dedicated to awakening an interest in Acadian history, especially the 1755 Expulsion, he was instrumental in the years 1908-20 in creating the Grand Pré National Historic Site. This sense of advocacy for Acadian recognition also informed his *Grand-Pré: a sketch of the occupation of the shores of the basin of Minas* (1898)—reworked into *The history of Grand Pré* (*c.* 1907) and *The land of Evangeline* (*c.* 1921); two novels, *The heir to Grand Pré* (1907) and *Jen of the marshes* (1921); and three volumes of poems: *Canada and other poems* (1891), *The marshlands* (1893), and *Trail of the tide* (1899). In all his work Herbin portrayed Grand Pré as the spiritual heartland of the Acadians and rewrote the Evangeline myth made popular by Longfellow's 1847 poem. 'The returned Acadian', renamed 'Evangeline's return' by the Dominion and Atlantic Railway when is was adopted for tourism purposes, became Herbin's signature poem in regional publications. Yet a number of the descriptive poems of the marshlands around Grand Pré rivalled those of Charles G.D. ROBERTS and Bliss CARMAN, both of whom joined Archibald LAMPMAN in praising Herbin's facility with the sonnet form. For Herbin, however, the ultimate accolade was that he succeeded in his 'mission' to preserve 'the memory of my people, the terribly wronged Acadians'. In 1996 Herbin's manuscripts and papers were deposited at Acadia University. GWENDOLYN DAVIES

Here and Now. See LITERARY MAGAZINES IN ENGLISH: 3.

Herron, Shaun. See MYSTERY AND CRIME.

Hertel, François. Pseudonym of Rodolphe DUBÉ.

Hexagone, Les Éditions de l'. See Gaston MIRON and POETRY IN FRENCH: 5.

Hickman, Albert (1877-1957). Born in Dorchester, New Brunswick, into a shipbuilding family, William Albert Hickman grew up in Pictou, Nova Scotia, and graduated in 1899 from Harvard University, where he was a noted sculler. Working out of Saint John as New Brunswick Commissioner, he prepared *A handbook of New Brunswick* (1900). Experiments conducted at Pictou led Hickman after 1906 to become preoccupied with the development and promotion of advanced speedboat technology. His success as a marine engineer prompted him, after the First World War, to relocate his engineering firm in New England.

Hickman was also a writer of fiction, including the novel *The sacrifice of the Shannon* (1903), a highly readable blend of adventure, humour, and romance. The story is narrated in a breezy and slightly ingenuous vein by an Englishman of rank and cosmopolitan experience whose background is gradually linked with the milieu of his Pictou ship-owning employers. The novelist successfully combines sporting sketches of the Nova Scotia yachting élite with epic tales of ice-breakers in the dangerous pack-ice of the Gulf of St Lawrence.

Hickman contributed stories and marine-sport articles to *The Century*, *The American Magazine*, and other U.S. publications. *An unofficial love story* (1909), a novelette of manners set in Saint John, again casts the well-to-do Englishman in Canada as something of an innocent abroad. In 1909 and 1910 Hickman published, as a series in *The Century* rather than as a single volume, two other novelettes: 'The A-flat major Polonaise' and 'Compensated', which share a Pictou setting, a number of characters, and similar combinations of humour, sport, and adventure. All three novelettes, together with four short stories, were collected in his *Canadian nights* (1914).

KEN MacKINNON

Hiebert, Paul. See *SARAH BINKS*.

Highway, Tomson (b. 1951). Born on a trapline in northern Manitoba, he spoke only Cree until at age six he was separated from his family (of twelve children) to attend a Roman Catholic boarding school in The Pas, and when he was fifteen a high school in Winnipeg. A gifted pianist, he studied with William Aide at the University of Manitoba, spending a year in London, England, before graduating from the University of Western Ontario in London, Ontario, in 1976 with a B.Mus. (Hon) and a B.A. in English. While at Western, Highway worked with, and was influenced by, James REANEY.

But Highway then rejected what he termed 'the white man's game', and worked with various Native organizations across Canada for seven years. In 1985 he wrote and directed 'A ridiculous spectacle in one act' with De-Ba-Jeh-Mu-Jig Theatre on Manitoulin Island, Ontario. This Native theatre company also workshopped *The rez sisters* (1988), which catapulted Highway to national recognition when it was produced in Toronto by Act IV Theatre Company and Native Earth Performing Arts. Touring across Canada and to the Edinburgh Festival, *The Rez sisters* won a Dora Award in 1987, and was nominated for Chalmers and Governor General's Awards; in 1993 it was produced in New York and translated into French. Irreverent, exuberant, touching, and broadly humorous, the play features a Trickster figure, Nanabush, as a positive healing force who effects magical transformation in the lives of seven women on a reserve (the Rez) as they make an epic journey to the

Biggest Bingo in the World. The cultural collision between Native and non-Native societies is given a darker, more violent treatment in the second play in a projected Rez series, *Dry Lips oughta move to Kapuskasing* (1990), which focuses on seven eccentric men on the reserve. Following its première, co-produced by Theatre Passe Muraille and Native Earth, *Dry Lips* transferred to the Royal Alexandra Theatre, Toronto, for an unprecedented run in a commercial theatre; it received the Chalmers Award and was a finalist for a Governor General's Award in 1989. Between 1986 and 1992 Highway was Artistic Director of Native Earth Performing Arts, nurturing other Native playwrights such as Daniel David MOSES and Monique Mojica, as well as staging his own plays. *Aria* is a series of 22 monologues about Native womanhood first performed in Toronto in 1987. *New song . . . new dance* (performed 1988) preceeded *The sage, the dancer, and the fool* (performed 1989), about a young Native man's day in Toronto (played by three actors symbolizing the three nouns of the title). In 1993 Centaur Theatre, Montreal, premiered *Annie and the Old One*. Highway writes music for film and television, directs, acts occasionally, and has completed a screenplay, 'Kiss of the Fur Queen', and a musical, 'Rose'. He was given an Hon.D.Litt. by the University of Winnipeg in 1993 and became a Member of the Order of Canada in 1994.

LISBIE RAE

Hilles, Robert (b. 1951). Born in Kenora, Ontario, he was educated at the University of Calgary (B.A. in psychology and English, 1976; M.Sc. in educational psychology and computer-assisted instruction, 1978). For ten years he was managing editor of the literary magazine *Dandelion*; he also founded a supplement, *blue buffalo*. Since 1983 he has been a professor of computer programming at the DeVry Institute of Technology, Calgary.

Hilles won a Governor General's Award for his poetry collection *Cantos from a small room* (1993), moving meditative poems about losing a loved one to cancer. His other collections include *Look the lovely animal speaks* (1980), simple, restrained poems about his childhood and his father; *The surprise element* (1981); *An angel in the works* (1983), which questions love and its limits; *Outlasting the landscape* (1989), lyrical meditations on his daughter, sleep, dreams, family, and time; *Finding the lights on* (1991); *A breath at a time* (1992); and *Nothing vanishes* (1996). *Raising of voices* (1993) is a harrowing novel that portrays a family enduring madness and alcoholism in northern Ontario. *Near morning* (1995) is a collection of short stories and *Kissing the smoke* (1996) is a family memoir, focusing on Hilles' grandfather and father, and an extended meditation on work.

GEOFF HANCOCK

Hill-Tout, Charles. See ABORIGINAL LEGENDS AND TALES: BIBLIOGRAPHY.

Hind, Henry Yule. See EXPLORATION LITERATURE IN ENGLISH: 2.

Hine, Daryl (b. 1936). Born in Vancouver, British Columbia, he studied classics and philosophy at McGill University, Montreal (1954-8). In 1958 he received a Canada Foundation-Rockefeller fellowship and travelled to Europe, living in France until 1962. Between 1963 and 1967 he completed his M.A. and Ph.D. degrees in comparative literature at the University of Chicago; the subject of his dissertation was the Latin poetry of the sixteenth-century Scottish humanist George Buchanan. In 1967 he joined the English department at Chicago, and from 1968 to 1978 he edited the prestigious magazine *Poetry*. He has been the recipient of a Guggenheim Fellowship (1980), an American Academy Award (1982), and a MacArthur Foundation Fellowship (1986).

Hine is the author of twelve books of poetry: *Five poems* (1955); *The carnal and the crane* (1957); *The devil's picture book* (1961); *The wooden horse* (1965); *Minutes* (1968); *In and out: a confessional poem* (privately printed, 1975; reprinted 1989); *Resident alien* (1975); *Daylight saving* (1978); *Selected poems* (1980); *Academic festival overtures* (1985); *Arrondissements* (1988); and *Postscripts* (1991).

Hine's poetic gift was recognized early. He published his first poems in *CONTEMPORARY VERSE* at the age of fifteen, and *The carnal and the crane* at the age of twenty-one. Northrop FRYE described the experience of reading its long, meditative lines as being 'like watching heavy traffic at night: a brilliant series of phrases moves across a mysteriously dark background.' *Selected poems* presents an admirable cross-section of themes and styles. From the beginning Hine's poetry has been remarkable for its formal control. His poems are complex, intellectual, and technically sophisticated. He delights in traditional forms, experimenting with villanelles, satires, sestinas, and metrical patterns such as iambic pentameter with complicated rhyme schemes. Yet his tone and themes are modern, his voice is intensely personal, and he creates startling colloquial metaphors. The tension between his extraordinary technical mastery and an anguished exploration of the chaos of personal life—as in 'Aftermath'—lends some of his poetry considerable power.

Hine's training as a classical scholar has provided him with his major themes: a repeated strategy in his poetry is to reinterpret classical mythology in the light of contemporary experience. Occasionally his baroque language seems to be a defence, and the poems fall into preciousness and a debilitating overrefinement; the poet's control seems almost a neurotic strategy against an unidentified potential chaos. Most of Hine's poetry, however, is remarkable for the wit, candour, and intelligence with which he explores the range of emotions from lust to love. Hine's two book-length poems—*Academic festival overtures*, written in a modern adaptation of Homeric style, and *In and out*—are both moving autobiographical reminiscences of student life, with its homoerotic love affairs; but it is the technical *tour de force* that impresses. *Postscripts*, dedicated to the Canadian poet Virgil Burnett, is reflective, and at times amusingly cynical, as in the opening lines of '"THE FIRST" . . . snowflake that signals/The beginning of the winter/Glistens on the window/Like some early symptom/of a fatal illness.' But the power and beauty of the poems gives a dignity to this quality of resignation to human littleness—'all our wisdom is unwillingness'—that seems Hine's poetic signature.

Hine has also written a novel, *The prince of darkness and co.* (1961), constructed as an elaborate parody of mythology. Its hero, British poet Philip Sparrow, author of *A guide to witchcraft*, lives on an island called Xanadu. The climax of the book occurs on Midsummer Night in an adolescent orgy of sacrifice. Hine's purpose is to contrast those who play intellectually with the 'powers of darkness' and those for whom such forces are real. He has also written several plays, including *Defunctive music* (1961), *The death of Seneca* (1968), and, for radio, *Alcestis* (1972). He wrote a travelogue, *Polish subtitles: impressions from a journey* (1962)—after living briefly in Warsaw to edit English subtitles for a Polish film—and has published three translations from the Greek: *The Homeric hymns and the battle of the frogs and the mice* (1972), *Idylls and epigrams* (1982) by Theocritus, and *Ovid's heroines: a verse translation of the Heroides* (1991).

ROSEMARY SULLIVAN

Historical writing in English. Virtually all historians who have written about Canada could agree that history is a branch of literature. How often that agreement has been translated into works of literature is, however, another matter. Historians in the past were perhaps more willing than modern scholars to pay lip service to the literary conventions of their time. But there has probably never been a 'Golden Age' of Canadian historical writing as literature, since many of the historical genres in this country have not supported literary pretensions. In recent years, as social-science conceptualization and methodologies have become increasingly prevalent among historians in the academy, one of the basic if often unspoken questions revolves around the extent to which historical writing needs to be bound by literary assumptions about style, structure, and scope. To comment today that a historian 'writes well' no longer implies that he or she seeks to emulate the writer of imaginative literature, in either the conventional or postmodern sense—though the compliment might simply mean 'writes clearly', which is an accomplishment in itself. Most academic history has a very small audience and does not seek to reach the perhaps mythical 'general' reader. Historians, nevertheless, have produced and continue to produce a substantial proportion of the books, and a good number of best-sellers, published in this country.

1. PROMOTIONAL HISTORY. The first historical writings about Canada were, understandably, not deliberately intended as history at all, but utilized accounts of the past as part of a larger purpose of publicizing the merits and progress of infant settlements abroad, often publicizing the author in the process. In such early works the historical material was typically interspersed with information about geography, climate, flora, and fauna. The tone was enthusiastic, and the emphasis was on both past progress and future promise. Naturally enough, literary merit was not a principal concern of these authors, although the best and most successful of them appreciated that a work well constructed and well written was more likely to be read than one that lacked such qualities. But the focus on the presentation of information often detracted from the flow. These promotional works were usually ill-organized and digressive, depending on the personal knowledge and particular intention of the author. Perhaps the two most stylish of these early histories are John Stewart's *An account of Prince Edward Island* (London, 1806), and Thomas Chandler HALIBURTON's *An historical and statistical account of Nova Scotia* (2 vols, Halifax, 1829). Stewart (1758?-1834), a Scots-born office-holder resident

many years on the island, produced his account 'to make the Colony better known among those who are interested in its prosperity; or on whose judgment and determinations its future prospects depend'. Like most colonial publicists, Stewart had an axe to grind. He declared that 'any disappointment which has been experienced in regard to its colonization and settlement, is fairly to be charged to the neglect of those into whose hands, the property of the lands unfortunately fell, and not to any defect in the climate or soil', without noting that he acted as spokesman for the group to whom lack of progress might fairly be attributed. In any case the result was a coherent account of early development, told by one who had participated in many of the key events, and whose account was so persuasive that it provided until very recently the basic foundations of subsequent historical interpretations of the early British period on the island.

Haliburton's history of Nova Scotia was a later and more ambitious production than Stewart's. The research and writing occupied the author's spare time for many years, and its publication was intended both to gain applause and to demonstrate to the world how far the province had progressed. Unfortunately, here as elsewhere in Haliburton's historical output—he wrote several later histories on North American topics—there is less evidence of the stylist than of the compiler. Haliburton stayed too close to his limited sources to free his pen, and a broader sweep (especially in the second volume) is much impeded by statistical clutter. Nevertheless, Haliburton intended his history in part as a contribution to Nova Scotia's literary culture, and there are flashes of the skills he later revealed in fictional works that often dealt amusingly with historical incidents.

2. THE COMPILING TRADITION. If the promotional aspects of early writing on Canadian history did not always discourage literary standards, the tendency towards compilation certainly did. The problems facing the historians of a newly settled wilderness were many. None had any training for his task, most wrote their histories in moments snatched from a busy life, and all faced substantial problems of documentation and evidence. Many pioneer historians spent long hours collecting documents, usually laboriously copying them out by hand. Almost without exception they were not certain how best to employ them. Moreover, the collection of documents was seen as essential chiefly because there were so few secondary writings to rely on. The documents provided enormous problems of voice and perspective. Unlike later generations of professional scholars emulating the Germanic tradition, however, the early historians did not consider objectivity based on the documentary record as a positive ideal; rather they often hid behind the documents out of a sense of insecurity. This latter strategy was certainly true for William Smith Jr (1769-1846), whose two-volume *History of Canada* appeared in 1826, eleven years after it had been printed in Quebec 'for the author'. It took many years to convince him to publish, so afraid was he of offending someone. Smith was able to marshal French secondary sources to deal with the history of French Canada before the Conquest. His volume dealing with New France, while scarcely original or insightful, had considerable charm. But as he got beyond the French literature and was forced to come to terms with the recent historical record and the part played in it by his father, who had been chief justice of Quebec, he attempted to fend off criticism by paraphrasing and eventually merely reprinting *in extenso* the documents he had collected by using his access to government offices. Many other historians adopted a similar approach, especially to the more recent past, and such multi-volume works of men like William Kingsford (1819-98) and Robert Christie (1788-1856) are little more than undigested compilations; Kingsford's *The history of Canada* (10 vols, London, 1887-98) and Christie's *A history of the late province of Lower Canada* . . . (vols 1-5, Quebec, 1848-54; vol. 6, Montreal, 1855) were compiled almost verbatim from secondary material and the public documentary record. This scissors-and-paste approach stood very much in the way of good writing. History based almost exclusively on the official record is likely to be both dull in content and lacking in graceful exposition.

3. THE PARTICIPANT HISTORIANS. While the documentary record often got in the way of the pioneer historians, a few managed to be both well informed and possessed of a distinctive voice. Most of the colonies of British North America were young, and many had witnessed their development, often by participating in what were perceived as the central events of the time. Almost every colony had its participant chroniclers, who relied less on the documents than on their own memories, writing as memoirists as much as historians. Such writers could offer a narrative viewpoint, while their recollections often extended beyond the administrative, military, and political details of the official record. They

were without exception males. From a literary standpoint early participant histories are by far the most attractive and accessible of Canadian historical productions. Perhaps the most ambitious and satisfying of such work is an informal trilogy by the fur trader Alexander Ross (1783-1856) that began with *Adventures of the first settlers on the Oregon or Columbia River* (London, 1849), continued with *The fur hunters of the Far West* (2 vols, London, 1855), and culminated with *The Red River Settlement: its rise, progress and present state* (London, 1856). Ross's last work—as its title suggests—was partly promotional. Unlike John Stewart, however, Ross had some literary models culled from a lifetime of reading. He also had a topic with both chronological and geographical sweep and a potential theme—the conflict and tension between the indigenous cultures of the West and of European civilization—that lent itself to literary development. Moreover, the early West provided both picturesque settings and fascinating personalities that the author was fully prepared to exploit. Although he denied in his Preface a 'claim either to the ornaments of diction, or to the embellishments of imagination', the reader soon discovers that the text belies the author's diffidence. Ross faced consciously one of the major structural problems of the historian: that of keeping the narrative moving while providing analysis of topics that extended beyond the chronological bounds of the story. He resolved this difficulty by constructing a narrative framework that allowed occasional digressions to discuss key topics in detail. Ross's masterpiece, *The Red River Settlement*, has been unjustly neglected, largely because on the surface it deals with an isolated colony that—despite the author's best efforts—retained an image of being essentially barbaric. But his thematic emphasis on the conflict between 'savagery' and civilization, his eye for telling detail of character and circumstance, the propelling narrative told in plain style, all make it a major literary achievement—and at least arguably the most successful historical work produced by a Canadian on a Canadian theme before the twentieth century.

The participant historian always enjoyed a major literary advantage over the academic historian because his involvement in the events he chronicled could lead to an immediacy of style and provide a strong narrative voice. The participant tradition has not died, of course. It lives on in numerous memoirs that constitute an important part of Canada's annual publication output. Few modern practitioners of participant history have been more successful than James H. GRAY. In a series of works, beginning with *The winter years* (1966), Gray has employed his own history as an entry point into the exploration of larger themes in Canada's past. *The winter years* deals with the Depression period on the Prairies, and Gray's personal recollections of life as an unemployed relief recipient play a central role in his account of one of the most devastating eras in Canadian history.

4. THE SKILLED AMATEUR. By the later years of the nineteenth century, the historical study of Canada was changing in nature, particularly owing to an increasing awareness that it required a discipline beyond the occasional dabblings of those interested in the subject. Not until 1892, however, when G.M. Wrong (1860-1948) became a lecturer at the University of Toronto, was anyone appointed to a university post in Canada specifically as a historian, and the growth of Canadian history in the academy was a slow and gradual one. But even before Wrong's appointment, a new sophistication had begun emerging. The Rev. George Bryce (1844-1931), founder of Manitoba College, was responsible for organizing the Manitoba Historical Society (1875) and the Manitoba Historical and Scientific Society (1879), both devoted to a more systematic study of the past. In a sense his *Manitoba: its infancy, growth and present condition* (London, 1882), though it concentrated on the period before 1820, was written in the tradition of promotional history, but in other respects it was quite different. Bryce obtained access to the extensive papers of the Selkirk family in Scotland, and whatever his original intention, the book turned into a careful and sympathetic biography of Lord Selkirk, the creator of Manitoba. The events Bryce treated lent themselves to stirring narrative, while underlying his writing was the old theme of the conflict between barbarism and civilization, updated by use of new documentary evidence. Bryce never allowed himself to be overwhelmed by his research, however, and the result is a book that can still be enjoyed. In his later studies of the early settlers of Manitoba, as well as in his pioneering *A short history of the Canadian people* (London, 1887, rev. 1914), Bryce attempted to get beyond political and constitutional development to an understanding of Canadian society and its dynamics.

Goldwin SMITH was a major influence on historical study in Canada. Having served as Regius Professor of History at Oxford from 1858 to 1866, he settled in Toronto in 1871 and spent the remainder of his long life there. Despite his academic background, Smith in Canada operated mainly as a publicist and journalist. Nevertheless he published late in life full-length histories of the United States and Great Britain, and one major volume on a Canadian topic, *Canada and the Canadian question* (London, 1891), in which he undertook to survey the history of Canada as the 'presentation of a case and of a problem'. The use of evidence was plainly selective, but the work has a certain sweep and clear perspective, as well as an abundance of the snide remarks for which Smith is now usually remembered. Noting the problems of providing unity to so complex a topic as the historical development of a federal Canada, he opined that 'to impart anything like liveliness to a discussion of the British North America Act one must have the touch of Voltaire.' Smith was no Voltaire, but he offered a lively presentation of the Dominion's past, designed to demonstrate that Confederation was an artificial political solution that was contrary to geography, race, language, and commercial interest. However much Smith's polemic ran against the main current of Canadian historical writing—which was nationalistic in design—it was a *tour de force*, a brilliant personal exposition of one version of Canadian development.

Unlike Goldwin Smith, the civil servant William Dawson LeSueur (1840-1917) lacked any formal credentials as a historian. Nevertheless he adhered far more closely than Smith to the developing Germanic canons of scholarship, which emphasized accuracy based upon exhaustive research in the contemporary record. In common with Smith, however, LeSueur took issue with the standard interpretations of Canadian history of his time (and later), particularly in his study of William Lyon MACKENZIE, which, though completed in 1908, remained unpublished for forty years because of successful efforts by the subject's family (notably Prime Minister Mackenzie King) to suppress its appearance in print. It was eventually published in the CARLETON LIBRARY as *William Lyon Mackenzie: a reinterpretation* (1979), edited and with an introduction by A. B. McKillop. LeSueur wrote well. He had a splendid topic and a consistent if iconoclastic perspective. His study disputed vigorously the common views of Mackenzie as heroic popular reformer and of his enemies—the 'Family Compact'—as hopeless oligarchs who governed contrary to the popular will. Apart from its historiographical importance, LeSueur's book stands out for its literary merits: the prose is always lucid, often clever.

One other author in the transitional period from amateur to professional history can be mentioned. Sir Andrew MACPHAIL, a native of Prince Edward Island, used his skills as a journalist to finance a medical education. A professor of medicine at McGill University for thirty years, he is usually remembered today as a journal editor, critic, and literary doyen. But Macphail turned his dynamic prose style to history on several occasions. His study *The medical services* (1925), the inaugural volume of the series *The official history of the Canadian forces in the Great War*, remains a classic analysis of the non-combative aspects of modern warfare, written in Macphail's usual clear and assertive style. In *The master's wife* (1939), published posthumously, Macphail wrote a historical work that was quite experimental, combining personal memoir, biography, historical detail, and novelistic techniques in a moving evocation of life in his native province. Macphail also produced an account of Prince Edward Island for Shortt and Doughty's series *Canada and its provinces* (23 vols, 1913-17). Most of these volumes, like those in the *Chronicles of Canada* series, edited by G.M. Wrong and H.H. Langton (32 vols, 1914-16), were written by amateur historians like Macphail.

A few gifted amateurs continued to find success after the professionalization of history. Winthrop Pickard Bell (1884-1965), for example, published in 1961 *The 'foreign Protestants' and the settlement of Nova Scotia: the history of a piece of arrested colonial policy in the eighteenth century*.

5. THE ESSAY. This is a greatly neglected and undervalued genre within Canadian historical writing. Differing substantially from the monographic article, which represents the vast bulk of the scholarly output of academics, the essay seeks to involve the wider public in historical questions, combining erudition with a lively style and lucid argument. Most good historical essayists have sought less to advance new research than to place existing findings in a larger and more accessible context. Both Goldwin Smith and Andrew Macphail wrote superb essays on historical topics as part of their journalistic activities. Some historians have since turned occasionally to the essay—of which the two most successful Canadian practitioners are Frank Underhill and Ramsay COOK.

Frank H. Underhill (1889-1971) was professor of history at the University of Toronto from 1927 to 1955. A founder of the League for Social Reconstruction and the CCF in the 1930s who later moved to the Liberal party, he was for most of his lifetime the gadfly of the historical profession in Canada. He has been often taken to task for the extent of his involvement in affairs of the day, and for his tendency to devote himself to relating history to contemporary affairs, rather than concentrating on pure scholarship in books and monographs. Much of his best work appeared as essays and reviews in *The CANADIAN FORUM*, a journal with which he was intimately associated for many years. Underhill's essays, most readily available in a collected volume, *In search of Canadian liberalism* (1960), are characterized by their iconoclasm and trenchant wit, often bordering on sarcasm. He greatly admired the 'graceful style, the lightness of touch, . . . the subtle irony' of the *Manchester Guardian*, but recognized that 'the secret of a good style is to have something to say.' Underhill always did, although often his impatience to deliver his message detracted from the grace of his performance. Underhill's essays sometimes now seem dated (the risk one runs in remaining too close to the editorial page); but they are still models worth emulating by the committed historian

Ramsay Cook, retired professor of history at York University, Toronto—whose writings are more conventionally within the academic tradition than Underhill's—has also enjoyed remarkable success as an essayist. Cook's central themes are the politics of contemporary Canada placed in historical perspective, and especially the presentation of the culture of French Canada to the anglophone audience. Cook's essays tend to be more consciously erudite than Underhill's, studded with references drawn from wide reading. His best work often deals with the exposition and criticism of the writings of other historians. Historiographic issues are not the easiest ones to present to a lay audience, but such essays demonstrate Cook's skill at placing historical writing in the larger context of Canadian social, intellectual, cultural, and political developments. Cook occasionally oversimplifies, but he never condescends. His style is lucid, his tone reasonable, his arguments sensible. The essays in his *Canada and the French-Canadian question* (1966) show him at his best.

6. POPULAR HISTORY. As accessibility to the lay audience has become less important to most Canadian academic historians, the best-selling authors of historical writing in Canada have come from outside the universities. Undoubtedly the most successful of the modern-day popular historians is Pierre BERTON. His first historical writings were about the Canadian North, a region in which he had grown up. In one sense these works are participant history, Berton himself confessing: 'My whole life has been conditioned by the Klondike; it hangs behind me like a theatrical backdrop, it haunts my dreams and my memories.' *The golden trail* (1954) was followed by *The mysterious North* (1956) and *Klondike* (1958), a book many still regard as Berton's major literary achievement. Berton has written many other best-selling histories, including *The national dream: the great railway, 1871-1881* (1970) and *The last spike: the great railway, 1881-1885* (1971). The enormous research that went into these books is presented—to their advantage or disadvantage, according to one's point of view—with the aid of novelistic techniques in description and dialogue. The continued success in the Canadian bookstores of titles by Berton—and by Peter C. NEWMAN, Barry Broadfoot and his oral histories, Heather Robertson, and others—attests to the continued importance of Canadian history as a branch of popular literature.

7. ACADEMIC HISTORY. Few professional historians in Canada have ever thought of themselves primarily as literary stylists. One of the founders of academic history in Canada who did achieve a reputation for his writing was George MacKinnon Wrong, for many years head of the history department at the University of Toronto. Although he was an anglophile, Wrong's most highly regarded books dealt with the early interaction between British and French in Canada, a subject previously mined on the grand scale by the renowned American historical writer Francis Parkman. Especially admired among Wrong's works for the style of its presentation was *A Canadian manor and its seigneurs* (1908), a microstudy of one seigneury taken over by a Scottish family after the Conquest and based on its papers. Wrong also wrote of British and French on a larger canvas, including *The fall of Canada: a chapter in the history of the Seven Years' War* (1914) and *The rise and fall of New France* (2 vols, 1928); but such works suffered from inevitable comparison with similar studies by Parkman.

A Canadian historian of a later generation with a conscious commitment to history as literature was Donald CREIGHTON. *The commercial empire of the St Lawrence* (1937, rpr. 1956 as *The empire of the St Lawrence*) was designed as a three-act drama, with the St Lawrence River as the major protagonist. Here, as elsewhere in his writing, Creighton presented nature as something possessed of special animation, around which people and events revolved. Although he insisted that he wrote his books instinctively and 'not in conscious accordance with any literary principles', he was obviously steeped in imaginative literature (especially the realist and naturalist schools of the late nineteenth and early twentieth centuries), seeking to translate its forms into historical terms. He was one of the few Canadian historians who ever wrote a novel. In his two-volume biography of John A. Macdonald—*John A. Macdonald: the young politician* (1952) and *John A. Macdonald: the old chieftain* (1955)—Creighton attempted to recreate an age imaginatively, through the eyes of his protagonist. He described in vivid detail such disparate matters as weather conditions and his subject's internal thought processes, based on a complete command of the historical evidence, but also on total authorial identification with Macdonald. For Creighton, personalities often metamorphosed into ideas or forces, and setting was painted with loving detail. The result was both heroic and romantic. Like many Canadian historians of his generation within the academy, Creighton's main emphasis was upon nation-building.

A number of developments within Canadian historiography have militated against the perpetuation of the heroic narrative about the construction of the nation. Within the academy Canadian history has parallelled the changes in Canada itself, in political-constitutional as well as in cultural terms. Younger historians of Canada began asking new questions about race, class, ethnicity, and gender that emerged out of the political turmoil of the late 1960s. They began redressing the glaring neglect in traditional histories of Native peoples, women, the working class, and racial minorities. Such revisionism had international roots, but Canadian scholars gave it a distinctive cast. Requiring new methodologies and theories more akin to the social sciences than the humanities, the new research and writing in Canadian economic and social history asked implicitly whether the old paradigm of heroic nation-building was flexible enough to provide a framework for new insights. By 1970 it was becoming increasingly clear that it was not, although textbooks continued to focus on the nation and the problems of nationhood.

By the early 1970s the writing of Canadian history within the academy had altered as substantially as the milieu in which it was being written. Academic history became more specialized, and increasingly moved away from élitist biography and traditional narrative in favour of social and economic history that preferred analysis to narrative and groups of people to individual personalities. Historians became indifferent to such large and nebulous topics as the national character or national identity, preferring instead to examine historical development from a more limited perspective, whether regional or topical. Like the nation itself, which was increasingly becoming divided into regions and provinces split over a variety of ideological issues, Canadian history studies had experienced both fissure and diffusion.

A distinct shift has taken place away from the earlier formative periods of Canadian development (usually labelled 'preConfederation' in the national paradigm) in favour of more modern periods, particularly in the twentieth century. Canadian historians have seen their interaction with, and influence upon, the Canadian public vastly alter. Before the 1960s they were among the intellectual and cultural leaders of their generation, well-known names among university scholars. In recent years, however, the public has been exposed less and less to formal history in the educational system, at the same time as the profession has moved away from the heroic and progressive view of the past. Recent historical writing, instead, often documents a racist and sexist past of exploitation and disadvantage. In the process, Canadian history in the academy has become increasingly alienated from its larger audience, partly because of its negative view of the past, partly because of its non-narrative techniques of presentation. Postmodernism, with its deep suspicion of the objectivity of either the researcher or the research, with its denial of all-encompassing stories, will further widen the gulf as it becomes increasingly accepted by historians in Canada. Hovering above a mutual lament —of historians for the loss of their influence, and of the public for the loss of its heroes and familiar narrative lines—is the historian's constant search for historical truth, or at least factual clarification and illumination, which is always undergoing change. Whether there are ways of re-establishing the reading public's earlier interest in the serious writing of history remains to be seen.

See also entries on Don AKENSON, Carl BERGER, Michael BLISS, Maurice CARELESS, W.J. ECCLES, Eugene FORSEY, J.L. GRANATSTEIN, Christina McCALL, Hilda NEATBY, Joy PARR, and C.P. STACEY.

J.M. BUMSTED

Historical writing in French. It was only after the Conquest that the first printing press came to Canada. In Quebec, newspapers soon appeared that could both create and satisfy a demand for home-grown literary production in the form of verse, essays, reminiscences, and historical sketches. The latter stimulated an effort to find and preserve historical documents, and notable collections were made by the poet-editor-essayist Jacques Viger (1787-1858), as well as by the Literary and Historical Society of Quebec, founded in 1824. Out of this literary and historical interest emerged the *Histoire du Canada* of Michel BIBAUD, which was published in three volumes with the subtitles *Sous la domination française* (Montréal, 1837; rev. 1843) and *Sous la domination anglaise* (2 vols, Montréal, 1844, 1878). A pioneering work, especially in its treatment of the post-Conquest period, Bibaud's history did not win popularity because, in a time of militant French-Canadian nationalism, he wrote from a conservative and loyalist point of view.

Better able to express the aspirations of the time was François-Xavier GARNEAU, whose *Histoire du Canada depuis sa découverte jusqu'à nos jours* (3 vols, 1845-8) is still considered the first great masterpiece of French-Canadian literature. Journalist, clerk, notary, essayist, and poet, Garneau had been associated with the Lower Canadian reform movement during the 1830s, and his work expressed its nationalism as well as much of its ambivalence about reform and religion. While he made some criticisms of the clergy of New France, he considered Catholicism an essential element of French-Canadian nationality; and while he praised the idea of liberty, his goal was essentially to promote a conservative nationalism: 'the conservation of our religion, our language, and our laws.'

Garneau wrote shortly after the failure of the 1837-8 rebellions, after the publication of Lord Durham's remark that French Canadians had 'no history, and no literature', and after the imposition of a political régime that threatened the whole national future of French Canada. Garneau's writings were a rallying call and a vindication of the demands of French Canadians that their nationality be respected. Though he made a careful study of available documents, he was inspired by his 'profound and heartfelt sympathy' with the national cause. His history, therefore, is full of heroic deeds by which 'a people of farmers, hunters, and soldiers' opened up the greater part of a vast continent, pushing back its frontiers and marking it with the character of French civilization. His quintessential Canadians are military heroes like Iberville, or adventurous explorers and empire-builders like La Vérendrye: such men had forged a past to which French Canadians must still be true. Led now by political spokesmen rather than by soldiers, they must yet adhere to the traditions bequeathed by their history: 'Our traditions are a source of strength for us; let us not turn away from them.'

For a French Canada asserting its nationalism, Garneau's romantic portrayal of history was profoundly inspiring. But in mid-nineteenth-century Quebec, clerical influence was becoming more and more powerful, and it was necessary to go beyond Garneau to emphasize the historical role of Catholicism. This was done by the Abbé Jean-Baptiste-Antoine Ferland, in his *Cours d'histoire du Canada* (2 vols, 1861-5). Ferland wrote, as he said in his introduction, as a 'French Canadian by birth and a Catholic above all'. His history of New France tells especially of the progress of religion; his heroes are Christians first and foremost, his quintessential Canadians the Jesuit martyrs. Ferland had worked long in the French archives—and his history was solidly researched—but he wrote with a good deal of creative imagination, like the other historians of his century. These were men of broad literary interests, often writers of essays, poetry, novels, or even plays, as well as history. While they went to the sources for their 'facts', they exerted their literary talents to weave them into a living narrative and to give them general sense or significance. For a century after Garneau, that sense was nationalist and Catholic. History and religious nationalism, in fact, were scarcely separable in the late nineteenth century. 'O Canada', exclaimed A.B. Routhier (1839-1920), in a poem that would be set to music and become the national anthem, 'your arm . . . holds high the cross, your history is an epic of the most brilliant exploits' (*Les échos*, Québec, 1882). History taught French Canadians their national duties, their God-given mission to live out the life of a Catholic people—an agricultural life close to nature and its Creator. With minor variations, these basic convictions inspired most French-Canadian historical writing till the Second World War. Given that so much history was written by clerics—who wrote almost half the articles in the leading historical journal as late as 1950—this was hardly surprising.

Clerical historians were prominent outside Quebec. For example, Prairie settlement had involved a tremendous effort by colonizing missionaries, some of whom wrote significant western histories to justify and maintain a French-Catholic presence in the region. Thus,

Adrien-Gabriel Morice (1859-1938) stressed the efforts of the western clergy to promote French-Canadian settlement and secure French-Catholic rights—not only in his *Histoire de l'Église catholique dans l'Ouest canadien, du lac Supérieur au Pacifique* (3 vols, 1912); *History of the Catholic Church in Western Canada, from Lake Superior to the Pacific* (2 vols, 1910)—but even in his general western histories. French Canadians, he wrote in *Aux sources de l'histoire manitobaine* (1907), must remain true to a past whose very meaning was the expansion of conservative and clerical values. 'The parish spire must, in the West as everywhere else, be the rallying point for all those who would remain faithful to the past of our race.'

This sort of history seemed appropriate in a period when most French Canadians lived on farms, close to the parish church and under the guidance of lay and clerical notables. But turn-of-the-century industrialization soon changed that: by 1920 the majority of Québécois lived in towns and cities, and a history that taught them that they had an agricultural vocation seemed increasingly inconsistent with the world around them. A literature that assumed the leadership of the traditional élite would soon become embattled as social and political influence passed from French-Canadian lawyers, priests, notaries, and even members of Parliament to English-speaking factory-owners, bankers, and managers.

The many publications of the Abbé (later Canon) Lionel GROULX expressed the anxieties of French-Canadian nationalism in the first half of the twentieth century as powerfully as Garneau had expressed its early aspirations in the 1840s. Groulx aimed to inspire French Canadians at a time when industry was transforming their province, turning the long-settled *habitant* into a poor, urban worker, rootless and insecure, his language tainted with anglicisms. Groulx also responded negatively to the imposition of conscription during two world wars, to the abolition of French in Manitoba and Ontario schools, and to a massive immigration that threatened to drown French Canada in a sea of aliens.

History, he felt, could inspire French Canadians with a will to resist, with pride, and with a determination to assert themselves. 'To be proud,' he wrote in his 1937 collection of essays, *Notre maître le passé*, 'our young people need only to know who they are. The sons of those great Frenchmen who created the masterpiece which was New France need not search elsewhere than in their own past to find reason for self-respect.' True, there was tragedy as well as glory in the past—particularly in the Conquest, which subjected French Canada to foreign domination that was perpetuated by Confederation, as well as by the anglophone grip on Quebec's economic life. Still, those who were true to the greatness of their history would strive for their nation's emancipation. Great steps had already been taken: religious freedom, political liberties, and even provincial autonomy had already been won, thanks largely to the efforts of great men, heroes who expressed and even embodied the aspirations of their race. Without such men, Groulx wrote in his *Histoire du Canada français depuis la découverte* (4 vols, 1950-2), 'nothing great is accomplished in history.' That was why Groulx celebrated the heroes of the past, both as historian and as nationalist organizer and pamphleteer, and looked for a modern hero to lead French Canada into the future.

Groulx himself helped lead French-Canadian history into the future, not only by his work in inspiring later generations of nationalist historians but more importantly, perhaps, by his promotion of scholarly research through the founding of the Institut d'histoire de l'Amérique française in 1946, by his work between 1947 and 1967 as editor of the *Revue d'Histoire de l'Amérique française* (which, under him, became French Canada's leading forum for historical research), and by his help in establishing a professional history department at the Université de Montréal. Indeed, it was only after the Second World War that French-Canadian universities established regular history departments; men who had obtained their Ph.D.s abroad returned to run them, bringing new scholarly values and interests.

The new professional historians, armed with their secular training and accustomed to living in big cities, were no longer satisfied with the old rural and religious ideals. If Groulx had seen the modern world of business, commerce, and industry as something alien to French Canada and her traditions, his successors at Montreal looked on it as a normal part of any society's development. They began, therefore, to look for a business class in French Canada's past. Following up on an idea first suggested by his colleague Maurice SÉGUIN, Guy FRÉGAULT began to portray a New France that was commercially oriented and business-directed. If French Canadians had not followed through from such beginnings, it was because the Conquest had ruined their business class by forcing it to operate within the alien structures of British mercantilism, a context in which British merchants had an unbeatable advantage. Developed by Frégault in his 1955 masterpiece *La guerre de la conquête* (translated by Margaret Cameron as *Canada: the war of the Conquest*, 1969), this interpretation was pursued, and its long-term consequences for French-Canadian history were explored, by another Université de Montréal professor, Michel BRUNET, first in some remarkably influential essays contained in his collection *La présence anglaise et les Canadiens* (1958), and later in *Les Canadiens après la conquête* (1969; Governor General's Award).

An analytical concern about social classes and economic history had thus entered Quebec's literature. At first it coexisted with older concerns. Frégault and Brunet, for example, were both much influenced by Groulx's nationalism. Again, while both believed in 'scientific' history, in a very rigorous and critical examination of documents, and in the importance of economics, they did not abandon all literary values. Frégault in particular was much admired for his fine narrative style. Personalities and great figures played an important part in much of his work, from *Iberville le conquérant* (1944) on, and Frégault, especially in his early career, was able to derive a Groulx-like inspiration from national history. 'Oh history of ours!' he exclaimed in one rapturous outburst, 'It is through our history that French Canada has best expressed itself, best explained itself, best affirmed itself. . . . History remains our great strength.'

Such preoccupations were foreign to Marcel TRUDEL, who came to Université Laval in 1947—like Brunet and Frégault with an American Ph.D. Trudel specifically repudiated the idea that present-day or ideological preoccupations might concern the historian. 'I'm content,' he said, 'to find the past.' Nor was the past to be found in great intuitive interpretations presented in a colourful and poetic style. History had for too long been 'comfortably ensconced in the chair of rhetoric.' It must confine itself more to a minute analysis of documents and facts. Trudel's own *Histoire de la Nouvelle-France*, which covers the period down to 1663 in three volumes—*Les vaines tentatives, 1524-1603* (1963), *Le comptoir, 1604-1627* (1966; Governor General's Award), and *La seigneurie des Cent-Associés, 1627-1663*, part I (1979)—is a remarkable example of this rigorous and painstaking approach to history.

As the age of the professional historian advanced, history seemed less and less concerned with the literary, more and more with the 'scientific'. The great books of the 1960s and 1970s provoked excitement not by rhetoric so much as by the originality of their research techniques and the new problems they explored. Thus the appearance in 1966 of the *Histoire économique et sociale du Québec, 1760-1850* (*Economic and social history of Québec: 1760-1850*, CARLETON LIBRARY, 1980), by Fernand OUELLET, shook the whole Canadian historical community because of the tools of analysis (particularly quantitative) that it employed, the new types of evidence it considered, and the extraordinarily comprehensive way in which it examined and related the economic, social, ideological, and political elements of history. French-Canadian nationalism itself, which had inspired historians from Garneau to Frégault and Brunet, was seen by Ouellet as merely the product of certain economic and social circumstances present in early nineteenth-century Quebec.

But if Ouellet's work was exciting in its scope, approach, methods, and conclusions it was not the sort of colourful narrative that one could easily read. The price-curve of wheat at Quebec, the volume of timber exported, crop yields and population density—these now assumed more importance than the character and heroic deeds of great men. Was history, then, no longer part of literature? Were numbers, graphs, population movements, and notarial inventories to replace colour, personality, and style? Were *structures* and *conjonctures* to push aside character and circumstance?

Certainly non-literary elements had permanently entered historical writing. Economic preoccupations would now be central, and with them an increased use of quantification, or other complex and highly technical methods. As nationality ceased to be the only criterion by which historians identified human groups, social class drew more and more attention. Marxian analysis appeared, and with it, too often, a sort of socio-economic jargon that added nothing to the clarity of scholars' expositions. In modern Quebec, working-class life and union organization were given particular attention for the first time—but farmers, settlers, and lumbermen were also studied, as investigators exercised their ingenuity to find new sorts of evidence about the daily life and culture of the nameless ordinary people. Cultural phenomena at all levels were analysed as functions of social and economic structures, ideologies and intellectual currents as expressions of class interest and outlook. In all this, the character and actions of outstanding individuals had little significance. In the monumental *Habitants et marchands de Montréal au XVIIe siècle* (1974; Governor General's Award) by Louise Dechêne (b. 1932), population, landholding, business structures, social classes, property, religion are all carefully counted, defined, calculated, and put together to form a whole society; but narrative—the account of individual actions—is not part of the edifice.

Yet history-as-literature still flourished. Outside the university the Martinique-born Robert Rumilly (1897-1983) produced an immense body of published work. His 41-volume *Histoire de la province de Québec* (1940-63), his lives and times of great personalities, his *Compagnie du Nord-Ouest* (1980), and many other publications—are written with epic verve, a passionate style, a love for men who are larger than life and for great needs and human drama. Thus Rumilly carried on the old historical tradition.

Academic historians did not entirely depart from this tradition. Biographies were still being written—of businessmen and labour leaders, churchmen and politicians. Moreover, once the economic, social, and ideological structures had been identified, it was still necessary to come back to events. In *Le Bas-Canada, 1791-1840* (1976; GGA)—of which a badly abridged English version, *Lower Canada, 1791-1840*, appeared in 1980—Fernand Ouellet, while adding to his earlier quantitative demonstration, focused as well on individual politicians, churchmen, and administrators, showing how their personalities acted together with economic and social pressures to produce those actions that traditionalists would have recognized as 'history'.

Books that weave the various strands of history into coherent and meaningful accounts—general syntheses—will always be wanted. The great success of the *Histoire du Québec contemporain: de la Confédération à la crise, 1867-1929* (1979; *Quebec: a history, 1867-1929*, 1983, translated by Robert Chados), by Paul-André Linteau, René Durocher, and Jean-Claude Robert, illustrated this point, as did Robert's briefer and more general *Du Canada français au Québec libre* (1975), which was written for a French readership to explain the historical background of current developments in Quebec. Both interpret, and put into the context of a coherent and readable synthesis, the results of recent specialized research. However, the *Histoire*—fuller, more detailed, and richer from the scholarly point of view—raised a final consideration. It integrated so much material that its authors could not use a unified narrative, but resorted to both a thematic and chronological structure. The collaborative nature of the work also deprived it, in some measure, of the unity and personality that are usually associated with works of literature. As so many types and levels of experience are now being studied (only one of them having to do with individual action), it seems that it will no longer be possible to integrate them as a single narrative, marked by the mind of a single author, except in the briefest of surveys. If this is the case, history as literature may refer in future to nothing more than a certain clarity, perhaps elegance, of style.

See also *Quebec and its historians* (1983) by Serge Gagnon, translated by Yves Brunelle.

A.I. SILVER

1980 to 1996. Until the 1970s most French-language historical writing tended to focus on the pre-Confederation period and concentrate on a people who could be defined by their common language and religion—French-speaking Catholics who had long lived outside the mainstream of developments across the Western world. Accordingly, they were commonly depicted as primitive farmers who were at some considerable distance from the more vital sectors of the economy and lived under the close supervision of the Catholic Church.

This general orientation was maintained by historians who were otherwise at odds with one another, owing to their very different political perspectives. Post-Second World War historians associated with the Université de Montréal—such as Maurice SÉGUIN, Guy FRÉGAULT, and Michel BRUNET—viewed the marginality of Québécois as a legacy of their conquest at the hands of the British in the eighteenth century, while historians with connections to Université Laval—such as Marcel TRUDEL, Jean HAMELIN, and Fernand OUELLET—concentrated on the responsibility of francophones for their second-class economic status. Both groups of historians, however, recognized what made Québécois distinctive, such as their ties to Catholicism, and more specifically what made them weaker, both politically and economically, than their anglophone neighbours.

This depiction of Québécois as a weak and economically marginal people was consistent with the more general self-image they had of themselves before the Quiet Revolution. It was then, in the 1960s, that the Quebec government became a force to be reckoned with, Catholicism lost most of its influence, and francophones came to wield more power in both federal politics and the business world. Accordingly, by the 1970s, when a new generation of historians was beginning to make its presence felt, the traditional portrayal of francophones no longer rang true for a people who now viewed themselves as profoundly modern.

This new generation of historians—which included Paul-André Linteau, Jean-Claude Robert, René Hardy, and Normand Séguin, to name only a few—was born during the 1940s and attended university during the 1960s. By the end of that decade these historians were beginning to occupy positions in Quebec universities, which were growing rapidly as part of the Quiet Revolution. The large number of articles and monographs that have since been published concentrated on the history of Quebec since the middle of the nineteenth century—depicting a society that had long been profoundly modern and in which the Catholic Church wielded relatively little influence.

The orientation of this new generation of historians was evident, for example, in significant monographs that focused on the urban nature of Quebec society. Linteau's *Maisonneuve ou comment les promoteurs fabriquent une ville* (1981) pointed to the role of francophone land-developers in the Montreal suburb of Maisonneuve, in the process drawing attention to the central role of Quebec's linguistic majority in the city's economic life. In a similar manner, Serge Courville, in his *Entre ville et campagne* (1990), found evidence of urban life even in the more rural sections of the province. In the same spirit, Courville, along with Jean-Claude Robert and Normand Séguin, argued that in Quebec the 'nineteenth century was above all else one that saw the rise of the city and the village' (*Atlas historique du Québec: le pays laurentien au 19e siècle, les morphologies de base*, 1995).

To reinforce this depiction of francophones as having long been a modern people, historians have also been eager to reinterpret the legacy of Catholicism. René Hardy, for instance, in examining Quebec involvement in the papal army of the late 1860s, found that support for the Zouaves did not come spontaneously from the population, but rather had been cultivated by the clergy (*Les Zouaves*, 1980). This view of the clergy as a slightly sinister force was also evident in Normand Séguin's *La conquête du sol* (1977), which pointed to the role of the Church in manipulating the early settlers of the Saguenay region.

In the hands of still other historians, the Church emerged as a relatively ineffectual institution that could not prevent Québécois from being moulded by the major forces shaping the history of the Western world. For example, Jacques Rouillard—who has played a central role in tracing the history of Quebec's trade unions—has insisted that the province's Catholic unions were only incidentally linked to the Church and were more fundamentally moulded by 'the way in which Quebec belonged to the North American continent' (*Histoire du syndicalisme au Québec*, 1989).

Recent Quebec historical writing has also pointed to the strength of liberalism, and most emphatically to the ideology of the modern world, in spite of the opposition of clerical leaders. Quebec's liberal legacy has been celebrated, for instance, in the anthology *Combats libéraux* (1995), edited by Yvan Lamonde. The clearest expression of the central role of liberalism in Quebec, however, was provided by Fernande Roy, who observed that 'Liberal ideas were circulating in Quebec society in the eighteenth century, they took root over the course of the nineteenth century, and they have dominated the twentieth century' (*Histoire des idéologies au Québec aux XIXe et XXe siècles*, 1993).

These various trends in recent Quebec historical writing provided the underpinning for Paul-André Linteau, Jean-Claude Robert, and René Durocher's two-volume *Histoire du Québec contemporain* (HQC; 2 vols, 1979–86; rev. 1989). While previous syntheses had concentrated on Quebec's pre-industrial history, the authors of HQC dealt exclusively with the period since Confederation. Moreover, while earlier overviews had frequently dwelled on the distinctiveness of francophone Québécois, Linteau, Durocher, and Robert constructed a history of the territory of Quebec, in the process reflecting Québécois's newfound identification with their province in the aftermath of the Quiet Revolution. While this territorial approach led the authors to give considerable attention to non-francophone Québécois, the emphasis was still on the modern character of the francophone majority. Reflecting the findings of the historians of their generation, the authors of HQC emphasized the importance of urban and industrial activity, noted the important role that francophones played in the economy, marginalized the hold of Catholicism over the population, and pointed to the strength of liberalism. While some historians have dissented from the perspective advanced in HQC, most have tried, over the past twenty years, to depict Québécois as a people who have long been modern.

RONALD RUDIN

Hivert-Carthew, Annick. See NOVELS IN FRENCH 1983 TO 1996: 1, 6.

Hodgins, Jack (b. 1938). He grew up in the logging and farming settlement of Merville on Vancouver Island and studied creative writing under Earle BIRNEY at the University of British Columbia, from which he received a B.Ed. in 1961. On graduation he returned to Vancouver Island to teach high school in Nanaimo. In the seventies Hodgins travelled to Ireland and Japan and served as writer-in-residence at Simon Fraser University (1977) and at the University of Ottawa (1979-80 and 1981-83). Since 1983 he has lived in Victoria, B.C., where he teaches in the Creative Writing Department of the University of Victoria.

Vancouver Island, particularly the Comox Valley where Hodgins was born, has been the setting for most of his books. His first major work was the short-story collection *Spit Delaney's island* (1976; NCL, with an Afterword by Robert BRINGHURST), which introduced the recurrent theme that imagination can redeem or transcend the physical. The stories focus either on unhappy characters, limited by their belief that they can 'know' only what they see, or on dreamers, like Spit Delaney himself, who are notable for their shocking, unconventional behaviour. Structurally unremarkable, the stories feature eccentric characterizations and a pervasive fusion of realism and parable. This collection was quickly followed by two immensely good-humoured and formally innovative novels, *The invention of the world* (1977: NCL, with an Afterword by George McWHIRTER) and *The resurrection of Joseph Bourne* (1979; NCL), which won a Governor General's Award, and the collection of stories *The Barclay family theatre* (1981). Figuring in all these books are the seven daughters of the Barclay family, together with their husbands and children, who first appeared in a story in *Spit Delaney's island* ('Other people's troubles'). Because of inconsistent characterization, however, the interconnections between the books occur more in mood, setting, and theme than in the family's history.

The invention of the world and *The resurrection of Joseph Bourne* remain the most successful of Hodgins' books. Here he achieves a remarkable structural and linguistic adventurousness that parallels the adventurousness of the main characters: Maggie Kyle (daughter of Christina Barclay) and the poet Joseph Bourne. In *The invention of the world* larger-than-life characters—an evangelist who has beguiled an Irish village into coming to Vancouver Island to serve him at his personal colony, an old woman who has spent her life combing the island with donkey and manure-spreader in an unsuccessful search for her birthplace, loggers whose Bunyanesque loves and brawls culminate in an epic wedding that is both feast and battle—are presented in a style that moves easily from fable to interior monologue to epic list. In *The resurrection of Joseph Bourne* Hodgins' contention that the human spirit can 'invent' the world is manifested in the surprising changes brought about in Port Annie, an isolated Vancouver Island community, by a tidal wave that bears both a Peruvian ship and an ostensibly magical young woman of quintessential grace and beauty. Consciously defying the tradition of 'modern novels' in which 'believers were always made to look like fools', Hodgins creates an extravagant, life-affirming book that encompasses parody, romance, mystery, biblical allegory, and backwoods humour. *The Barclay family theatre* illuminates the background of his various Barclay characters, and extends, often in discontinuous narratives, Hodgins' investigation of the contrast between the local, with its ambiguous pleasures of repetition and domesticity, and the risks and large vistas of the surrounding world.

Toward the end of the 1980s Hodgins published two relatively unfocused novels, *The honorary patron* (1987) and *Innocent cities* (1990), which further contrasted the local and the cosmopolitan. In 1995 he returned to the up-island locale and extravagant style of his early fiction with the novel *The Macken charm*. Although lacking the narrative complexity of the two earlier up-island novels, *The Macken charm* re-asserts their emphasis on vision and imagination, and their complex and entertaining mock-epic interpretations of working-class lives. Here the son of another Barclay sister narrates his teenage struggle to believe in his dream of being an internationally successful film-maker when the only world he has experienced is that of the narrow but energetically procreative Mackens and Barclays, whose triumphs and failures have been legendary in the Comox Valley but have never survived contact with a larger world.

Hodgins has also written the children's book *Left behind in Squabble Bay* (1988), the travel narrative *Over forty in Broken Hill: unusual encounters in the Australian outback* (1992), and the textbook *A passion for narrative: a guide for writing fiction* (1994). He has edited three school anthologies: *Voice and vision* (1972) with W.H. New, *The frontier experience* (1975), and *The west coast experience* (1976).

See David Jeffrey, *Jack Hodgins and his works* (1989) and J.R. (Tim) Struthers, ed., *On coasts of eternity: Jack Hodgins' fictional universe* (1996).

See also NOVELS IN ENGLISH 1960 TO 1982: 2. FRANK DAVEY

Hollingshead, Greg (b. 1947). Born in Toronto, he was raised in Woodbridge, Ontario. When Hollingshead studied English in the late 1960s at Victoria College, University of Toronto, editor Dennis LEE featured his poems in an anthology of new poets, *T.O. now* (1968). After completing a Ph.D. thesis (1947) at the University of London, England, on philosopher Bishop Berkeley, Hollingshead began teaching English in 1975 at the University of Alberta, Edmonton, where he has since remained.

As a result of the encouragement of Matt COHEN, Hollingshead began a cycle of stories including, 'The revenge of Eddie Reeser', collected in his first book, *Famous players* (1982). His early fiction, like his poetry, owes much to the surrealism of the early lyrics of Bob Dylan and the fiction of Samuel Beckett and William Burroughs. While characters can be outwardly conventional, their lives are tumultuous with irrational events, unexplained violence, and reverses of fortune. Few characters are able to control their lives. The narratives are often so compressed they sometimes require repeated readings to sort out details. In the stories collected in his second collection, *White Buick* (1992), Hollingshead loosens his style but not the message, which, as in 'When she was gone', explores the deepest reaches of the macabre. A finalist for a regional Commonwealth Writers' Prize, *White Buick* emphasized Hollingshead's place as primarily a writers' writer. His 1992 novel *Spin dry* focused on the lives of suburbanites holding their lives together with dream therapy and eccentric encounter groups. Despite its jaunty comic tone, it failed to capture much of an audience.

Hollingshead's strong third collection of stories, *The roaring girl* (1995), was a surprise winner of a Governor General's Award and became a best-seller for twenty weeks in Canada, with editions in the USA and Britain. Reflecting a more subtle image of middle-class life than his previous work, most of the stories show an affinity with Hollinghead's earliest writing, embedding illogical and unsettling events in what appears to be perfectly ordinary life. JOHN AYRE

Hollingsworth, Margaret (b.1940). Born in Sheffield, England, and trained as a librarian at Loughborough College, she completed her education in Canada, with a B.A. (1971) in psychology from Lakehead University and an MFA (1974) in theatre and creative writing from the University of British Columbia. She has been a librarian, editor, freelance journalist, and teacher of English in Italy and Japan. She has been writer-in-residence at Concordia University, Montreal, the University of Western Ontario, and the Stratford Festival; since 1992 she has been a professor of creative writing at the University of Victoria. Her plays have been nominated for a number of awards, including the Governor General's Award; her children's play *Ring of fire* (1994) won the Jesse award.

Hollingsworth is a prolific writer of radio and television drama; her plays were performed on BBC-TV before she immigrated to Canada in 1968, and those written since have been broadcast in Canada, Britain, Australia, New Zealand, West Germany, Yugoslavia, and Denmark. Among the radio plays available in CBC archives (from 1973) are 'Prairie dive', 'As I was saying to Mr Dideron', 'Wayley's children', 'War games', 'Webster's revenge', 'The apple in the eye', 'Responsible party', 'Woman on the wire', and 'Surreal landscape'. Her television plays, 'Scene from a balcony' and 'The last demise of Julian Whittaker', were produced on CBC-TV in 1987 and 1989 respectively.

Hollingsworth's one-act stage plays excel at conveying the gist of a lifetime in a brief episode of the present. *Bushed* (1973) is set in the laundromat of a northern town; it is used as shelter and meeting-place by two retired workers whose exclusion from the world of action, except in fantasy and memory, is reflected in women's mimed sheet-folding and the relentless turning of the machines. *Alli Alli Oh* (1977) is virtually the monologue of a woman retreating to insanity from two contrasting lifestyles, neither of whose demands she is willing or able to fulfil. The companion play *Islands* (1983) focuses on a second character from the earlier play, a woman who finds freedom in her unconventional choice of life as a farmer and a lesbian.

Operators (1975; rev. 1981) is a more complex one-act play that deals with the friendship of two women, night-workers in a northern Ontario factory, who have used games and fantasies to ward off boredom, frustration, and dangerous self-knowledge. An intrusion by a third woman threatens their relationship, but this episode leads to new awareness and a positive, if ambiguous, conclusion. Hollinsgworth's most frequently produced work, *Ever loving* (1981), is a multi-scene play that uses techniques of simultaneous action, flashback, 'freezing', and the inclusion of popular songs for ironic effect in a story of three war brides of the 1940s—English, Scottish, and Italian—and their difficulties in adapting to Canada and to their husbands' lives. *Mother country* (1980) is set on an island off the British Columbia coast and captures the eccentricities of Canadians who are more English than the English. Through three adult daughters it comically portrays the attempt to break ties with both England and the mother, who embodies qualities traditionally associated with England.

War babies was published with four earlier plays in a collection entitled *Willful acts* (1985), introduced by Ann Saddlemyer. This multi-layered drama presents a play within a play, the revealed subconscious of a pregnant forty-two-year-old writer who fears entrapment in domesticity and resents her war-correspondent husband's relative freedom. At the other extreme from the sprawling complexity of this play is the spare economy of *Diving* (1985), where a woman diver, literally on the edge, suggests through her brief monologue the entire scope of woman's lot in a male-dominated society, represented by an insistent male 'voice off'.

A second collection, *Endangered species* (1988), contains four highly experimental one-act plays where the surrealism verges on nightmare. *It's only hot for two months in Kapuskasing* has a woman answering an urgent summons to the apartment of an old acquaintance where, in the middle of the night, she encounters a frightening, bizarre and inexplicable situation. In *The house that Jack built* a woman has to come to terms with a way of life based on her husband's wishes, not her own. *Prim and Duck, Mama and Frank* portrays an odd family, their eccentricities structured around four different parts of the body; *Poppycock*, which grew out of an interest in masks and clowning, explores power relationships between the sexes, one actor portraying three epitomes of male power: Ezra Pound, Hitler, and Picasso.

Two commissioned plays continue the exploration of gender conflicts. *The green line*, workshopped at the Stratford Festival Theatre in 1986, is set in a Beirut museum where a Canadian woman is unable to understand a male curator's obsession with ancient artefacts in the midst of present social devastation. *Alma Victoria*, commissioned by the Nanaimo Festival and produced in 1989, is based on the historical figures of Alma Rattenbury and her husband Francis, a Victoria architect whom her lover murdered. In 'Collaborators', an article published in *Canadian Theatre Review* (Winter 1991), Hollingsworth relates the process whereby the play as staged bore little resemblance to what she had envisioned and written.

Hollingsworth returned to a monologue form in the tragi-comic play *In confidence* (1994). Exploring the sexuality of two middle-aged women who, without speaking to one another, hold a kind of intimate mental conversation across three thousand miles, the play re-examines many of Hollingsworth's early themes: the immigrant experience, alienation and loneliness, the importance of home, the delicate balance of man/woman relations, the range of sexual tastes and the potential violence in them, the subversive strategies women adopt to counteract the narrowness of their worlds and, above all, the power of women's friendships, shared laughter, and love. This play admirably illustrates Hollingsworth's impeccable ear for the nuances of English, especially the variations brought to the language by Canadian speakers of different national origins.

Numbrains (1995) captures contemporary idiom in the short monologue of a teenage boy as he keeps vigil over a dying whale on the beach. His social alienation is counterpointed by his deep knowledge of and sympathy for other forms of life.

Hollingsworth's short stories, collected in *Swimming under water* (1989), explore similar social and psychological themes as the plays, especially relations between the sexes and the search for home.

For critical analyses see Dorothy Parker, 'Alienation and identity: the plays of Margaret Hollingsworth', *CANADIAN LITERATURE* 88 (Autumn 1988); two chapters in Yvonne Hodkinson, *Female parts: the art and politics of female playwrights* (1991); and a chapter in Cynthia Zimmerman, *Playwriting women* (1994). See also Robert Wallace and Cynthia Zimmerman, *The work: conversations with English-Canadian playwrights* (1982).

JOAN COLDWELL

Hollingsworth, Michael (b. 1950). Born in Swansea, Wales, he immigrated to Canada with his parents in 1956 and now lives in Toronto. He is a playwright and musician, primarily interested in integrating rock music, video, and live theatre. Since his first play, *Strawberry fields* (1973), premièred at Toronto's Factory Theatre Lab in 1973, his work has become exceedingly complex. With the Hummer Sisters in 1976 he formed the VideoCabaret Theatre of Science, which became VideoCabaret International—the only such group in North America and one of the pioneering theatre groups in the world experimenting with video production: pre-taped sequences interacted with live video, live actors, the audience, and theatrical aspects of rock music. Hollingsworth was a founding member of the punk-rock group The Government.

Hollingsworth's published plays include *Clear light* (1973), based on transcripts of the Watergate trials and bad LSD experiences. The Metropolitan Toronto Police Morality Squad closed the production for alleged obscenity in film sequences featuring pornographic clips. *Strawberry fields* was inspired by John Lennon's lyrics and focuses on the aftermath of a rock concert. *Transworld* (1979), like all his plays, deals with psychotics, madness, drug abuse, and political repression—representing the collective psychosis of society.

Hollingsworth's 1977 productions included *Punc rok*, *Cheap thrills*, and *White noise*, based on the life of rock singer Janis Joplin. The poor critical reception of these plays led to the founding of VideoCabaret and to *Electric eye* (prod. 1979), a multimedia study of urban depravity based on the Son of Sam murders in New York and the murder of a shoeshine boy in Toronto. Hollingsworth then moved to video adaptations of George Orwell's *Nineteen eighty-four* (prod. 1978), and Aldous Huxley's *Brave new world* (prod. 1981). A ceaseless experimenter, he frequently revises his plays. *Nineteen eighty-four*, for example, appeared in productions ranging from eighty minutes to four hours, and in taverns as well as theatrical settings.

Influenced by Peter Brook, who considers theatre a 'hot' experience, and Artaud's Theatre of Cruelty concepts—in which the audience is assaulted by the play until they receive catharsis—Hollingsworth sees the visual image as more natural than the word to an audience raised on television, and feels that the results of his experimentation will lead to a redefinition of drama.

In the 1980s and early 1990s Hollingsworth created an eight-part play, *The history of the village of small huts: parts 1-8* (1994). This work is a monumental, ironic, and unique vision of Canada's past, described by *Maclean's* as 'Pierre Berton meets Monty Python'. Starting from the idea that the word 'Canada' comes from an Iroquois word loosely translated as 'village of small huts', Hollingsworth created a satire of various colonial periods of Canadian history. Using events from the past to illuminate the difficulties of today, he re-invented Canadian history through the French and British colonial periods, from Jacques Cartier and Champlain to the end of the Second World War. The play includes nineteen separate stories, 914 scenes, over 400 characters, and a veritable encyclopaedia of theatrical styles, from burlesque and comedy of manners to puppets, masks, and computer-generated imagery.

Hollingsworth discusses his theatrical concepts with Robert Wallace and Cynthia Zimmerman in *The work: conversations with English-Canadian playwrights* (1982).

GEOFF HANCOCK

Homme et son péché, Un. See Claude-Henri GRIGNON.

Hood, Hugh (b. 1928). Born in Toronto of an English-Canadian father and a French-Canadian mother, Hugh John Blagdon Hood was educated in Catholic schools there. He earned a Ph.D. from the University of Toronto in 1955, and has spent his academic career largely at the Université de Montreal. Academic interests—his dissertation examines the psychology behind the poetry of the English Romantics—and religious convictions combined in his presenting, in many books, a fictional view of Canadian experience in this century that is realistic in detail and emblematic in intent.

Three characteristics distinguish Hood's fiction: 1. An unobtrusive but discernible Roman Catholic perspective on experience. Earthly affairs convey the symbolic weight of the spiritual. If the phrase 'natural supernaturalism' conveys the complexity of the Romantic vision, then 'supernatural naturalism' describes Hood's fictional project. 2. A close acquaintance with the material aspects of his subjects' cultures—popular culture, the technical aspects of jobs, the inner workings of the bureaucracies shaping contemporary life. 3. A concern with placing Canada's history and culture within the broader frame of Western culture. The narratives are frequently written in a flat, colloquial style that yields to lyricism during moments of intense observation and feeling.

First recognized for his often superb short fiction, Hood has produced seven collections of stories: *Flying a red kite* (1962), *Around the mountain: scenes from Montreal life* (1967), *The fruit man, the meat man and the manager* (1971), *Dark glasses* (1976), *None genuine without this signature* (1980), *August nights* (1985), and *You'll catch your death* (1992). *Selected stories* appeared in 1978; instalments in a Collected Stories series appear at intervals. Perhaps the most widely anthologized of his stories are 'Flying a red kite' and 'Recollections of the Works department', based on a summer job experience in Toronto.

Among Hood's novels, *White figure, white ground* (1964), *The camera always lies* (1967), *A game of touch* (1970), and *You can't get there from here* (1972), the first three deal with figures within what we now term the cultural industries (painting, film, cartooning), while the last presents a satirical portrait of the corporate forces (economic, philanthropic) unleashed upon a developing African country resembling Canada.

The New Age/Nouveau Siècle series (ten of its projected twelve volumes had appeared by 1996) has occupied a major share of Hood's energies, though the novella *Five new facts about Giorgione* was published in 1987. *The swing in the garden* (1975), *A new Athens* (1977), *Reservoir ravine* (1979), *Black and white keys* (1982), *The scenic art* (1984), *The Motor Boys in Ottawa* (1986), *Tony's book* (1988), *Property and value* (1990), *Be sure to close your eyes* (1993), and *Dead men's watches* (1995) form a *roman fleuve* narrated by Matthew Goderich. His ancestral memories stretch back to the 1880s, and the series will conclude with sci-fi projections of the world to come. The New Age series, then, has a Genesis-to-Revelations scope—though the narrator's response to historical shifts in the experience of central Canada during his lifetime is featured. Each volume contains a number of epiphanic, visionary scenes, counterbalanced by the doings of an extensive cast of characters, and the narrator's frequent meditations on various aspects of his culture.

In interviews Hood has compared his project to Proust's *À la recherche du temps perdu* as he has particularly sought to duplicate his formidable predecessor's 'narrative technique, the appeal to the philosophy of time, certain subtleties in the handling of the narrator'. Hood's aim in The New Age series is to represent 'historical mythology, the articulation of the past, the articulation of the meaning of our society in terms of the way we live our lives'.

No project that ambitious, and so boldly put, will elude detraction. The narrator's unengaging personality, the Laurentian viewpoint inflating itself into an all-Canadian perspective, Goderich's village-explainer disquisitions, have all attracted unfriendly notice. Hood's defenders point to the sheer bravado of the enterprise, the richness of its moments of visionary recollection, and the deftness with which the narrative relates the experience of the wide world to our national one. But Hood's abiding concern with matters of epistemology and morality, expressed within a narrative structure recalling Alice MUNRO's blending of the linear with the synchronic, continues to render his writings unique among imaginative preoccupations in current Canadian fiction.

Hood has also published three essay collections: *The Governor's Bridge is closed* (1973), *Trusting the tale* (1983), *Unsupported assertions* (1991); a sports biography (*Strength down centre: the Jean Beliveau story*, 1970); and has supplied the text for an album of paintings by Montreal's Seymour Segal (*Scoring: the art of hockey*, 1979). He was made an Officer of the Order of Canada in 1988.

Hood's 1975 interview with Robert FULFORD in the *TAMARACK REVIEW* (66) reveals his plans for The New Age. *Before the flood: Hugh Hood's work in progress*, a 1979 issue of *Essays in Canadian Writing* (13/14), edited by J.R. 'Tim' Struthers, contains criticism, a bibliography, and an important interview. See also Robert Lecker, *On the line: readings in the short fiction of Clark Blaise, John Metcalf, and Hugh Hood* (1982); Keith Garebian, *Hugh Hood and his works* (1984); Suzi Copoloff-Mechanic, *Pilgrim's progress: a study of the short stories of Hugh Hood* (1988).

See also NOVELS IN ENGLISH 1960 TO 1982; 1982 TO 1996. DENNIS DUFFY

Horwood, Harold (b. 1923). Harold Andrew Horwood was born in St John's, Newfoundland, and received his formal education at Prince of Wales College there. In 1945, with his brother Charles, he founded *Protocol*, a journal that published experimental writing. Another contributor to *Protocol* was Irving Fogwill, who, Horwood stated many years later, 'introduced me to contemporary writing.' From 1949 to 1951 Horwood was a Liberal member of the Newfoundland legislature. His important column in the St John's *Evening Telegram*—'Political notebook' (1952-8)—was at first conciliatory in its attitude towards the administration of J.R. Smallwood, but eventually became harshly critical of its policies. Horwood thus provided a voice of dissent in a decade of political domination by the Liberal party in Newfoundland. In 1958 he turned to freelance writing, a move that appears to have coincided with a growing radicalism in political outlook. In the sixties and seventies he became an apologist for the 'counter-culture' and adopted, to some extent, the hippie life-style. He was writer-in-residence at the University of Western Ontario in 1976-7 and later served in the same capacity at the University of Waterloo, Ontario. A founding member of the WRITERS' UNION OF CANADA, he was its chairman in 1980-1. He now lives in Nova Scotia.

Horwood's books show him to be a well-read man of wide-ranging intellectual interests, with a tendency to parade his knowledge before the reader and to seize upon ideas with the enthusiasm of a literary novice. He is perhaps at his best as a writer when he simply observes the natural environment and displays his sensitivity to the normally unnoticed world of flora and fauna. Yet he is rarely content to do just that. His characteristic posture is that of a harbinger of new modes of life and thought. Typically he wishes to promote what he regards as enlightened notions, while jettisoning and denouncing the old; he is less an onlooker than a kind of teacher, or even (though the word may seem odd when applied to Horwood) a preacher. Few authors of fiction so persistently editorialize about their material as Horwood. His first novel, *Tomorrow will be Sunday* (1966), is a beautifully written book spoiled for many readers by humourless sermonizing. The setting is an isolated Newfoundland outport, 'Caplin Bight', and the theme is the intellectual and physical coming-of-age of one of its inhabitants, Eli Pallisher. The outport is richly portrayed, and there are passages of lyrical and dramatic power; but the adversarial role that is adopted by the author towards religion and traditional institutions is so strident that it becomes tiresome. Moreover, the alternative views Horwood supports (for example, the idea expressed by the character Christopher Simms that sex is 'something to be enjoyed with a carefree heart, like a picnic, or a swim in the ocean') are quickly perceived as shallow. The book is, at bottom, a restatement of the stock romantic themes of the inherent goodness of the human heart and the superiority of youthful instinct and passion over conventional values and restraints.

Horwood's *The foxes of Beachy Cove* (1967) is a work of meditation and observation that invites comparison with Thoreau's *Walden*. Horwood takes us on walks through the Newfoundland countryside and on canoe trips up its rivers, impressing us with the thoroughness of his knowledge of external nature and making us see what we had not before learned to look for, with little hectoring. This is Horwood at his best, but he did not attempt this genre again. Instead, in his second novel, *White Eskimo; a novel of Labrador* (1972), we find him plunging once more into romantic excess. This time his subject is the Inuit of Labrador, who are seen as noble savages exploited by the 'white racist' Moravians and the meddling Dr GRENFELL (disguised as 'Dr. Tocsin'). It is hard to accept such extreme judgements, even from a novelist. In this book he rejected what he calls 'the sickness of Western society'. Indeed, as late as 1977 he announced in public that he remained 'deeply opposed to the way our society is organized'. Even with advancing years, Horwood has not ceased to issue his jeremiads.

White Eskimo, *Tomorrow will be Sunday*, and *Foxes of Beachy Cove* have been reprinted in PaperJacks, the first in 1972, the other two in 1975. In 1979, however, Horwood stated that the two novels were in 'a style and method that I was finished with before 1970.' His collection of short stories, *Only the gods speak* (1979), formed, in his description, 'a kind of watershed' between these books and 'the fiction I hope to go on writing the rest of my life.' In fact the seventeen stories in this volume do not strike the reader as very different from the earlier books, except in superficial matters of technique. They are all, Horwood says, 'about people seeking salvation', and they convey some of his 'deepest concerns, from the need for closer communion between people to the fear that white civilization has shot its bolt.' Horwood's hippie propagandizing reached its peak in the novel *Remembering summer* (1987), featuring the return of an unrecognizable Eli Pallisher. In *Dancing on the shore* (1987), a work of reflection on the environment at Annapolis Basin, Nova Scotia, he wrote that over the years he 'had absorbed an exaggerated view of the importance of the novel.' The flight from fiction is borne out by *The magic ground* (1996), another treatise on the natural world. In 1997 Horwood published *A walk in the dream time: growing up in old St. John's.*

Horwood has produced a number of less ambitious yet valuable books. *Newfoundland* (1969) is a traveller's guide to the province, recast from magazine articles and broadcasts. He collaborated with photographer Stephen Taylor to produce a coffee-table book on Newfoundland's Great Northern Peninsula entitled *Beyond the road: portraits & visions of Newfoundlanders* (1976). He has also written a fine biography of Captain Bob Bartlett, *Bartlett: the great Canadian explorer* (1977), and is the author of the second volume in the Canada's Illustrated History series, *The colonial dream 1497/1760* (1978). He also edited *Voices underground* (1972), a poetry anthology, and *Tales of the Labrador Indians* (1981). The phrase 'With Harold Horwood' appears on the title-page of Cassie Brown's *Death on the ice: the great Newfoundland sealing disaster of 1914* (1972). *Joey* (1989) is a stimulating biography of J.R. Smallwood.

There is a revealing interview with Horwood in *Quill & Quire* (Aug. 1972). His fiction is discussed in Joan Strong, *Acts of brief authority: a critical assessment of selected twentieth-century Newfoundland novels* (1994).

PATRICK O'FLAHERTY

Hospital, Janette Turner (b. 1942). Born in Melbourne, Australia, Janet Turner moved with her family to Brisbane at the age of seven where, in 1965, she graduated with a B.A. in English from the University of Queensland, worked as a high-school teacher, and married Clifford George Hospital. In 1967 they moved to the USA, where she worked as a librarian at Harvard University and had two children. In 1971 they moved to Kingston, Ontario, where they now reside, and where she began her studies in medieval literature at Queen's University, graduating with an M.A. in 1973. Hospital has held positions as a writer-in-residence at universities in Canada, Australia, the USA, and Britain; has been the recipient of numerous literary awards; has been twice nominated for Britain's Booker Prize; and her books have been published in several languages. Hospital's increasingly experimental approach to narrative structure and content is perhaps one reason why she has yet to be appreciated by a wider readership.

Hospital has published six novels: *The ivory swing* (1982), *The tiger in the tiger pit* (1983), *Borderline* (1985), *Charades* (1988), *The last magician* (1992), and *Oyster* (1996); three collections of short stories: *Dislocations* (1986), *Isobars* (1990), *Collected stories* (1995); a crime thriller, *A very proper death* (1990), published under the pseudonyn 'Alex Juniper'; and a novella, *L'Envolée* (1995), commissioned by Myriam Solal and published in French. Hospital's writing also includes uncollected short stories, critical essays, travel articles, and book reviews published in both mainstream magazines and academic journals.

An essential feature of Hospital's fiction has to do with characters who straddle several countries and several kinds of cultural perceptions, and do so in a way that brings to critical scrutiny the codes of knowledge and systems of order by which, and in which, people make and find themselves at home. In foregrounding codes of knowledge central to Western, Eastern, and Aboriginal thought, Hospital reveals the philosophical, psychological, and emotional implications of crossing borders. In *The ivory swing*—set in South India, where she and her family lived in 1977—Hospital documents cultural nuances while exploring their complexities, discovering that there remain certain incommensurable differences resulting from distinct world views in spite of attempts at mutual understanding. (It received the Seal First Novel Award.) She moved to the disjunction between 'reality' and one's perception of reality in *The tiger in the tiger pit*, in which the Carpenter family crosses borders of geography, memory, and emotion as they reunite for their parents' fiftieth wedding anniversary. Adopting the musical structure of a fugue, Hospital experiments with conventional narrative by shifting the narrative point of view with each chapter, revealing multiple perspectives on various past events. The reader of the metafictional narrative of *Borderline* is challenged by the difficulty of separating the imaginary from the real as apolitical characters become implicated in the lives and consequences of illegal Salvadorean immigrants who attempt to cross the American/Canadian border. Questions of personal culpability and moral responsibility abound in a work that demonstrates how even the most philanthropic acts can have political consequences.

Both medieval literature and the indeterminacies of twentieth-century quantum physics provide the narrative and metaphoric structures for *Charades* and *The last magician*. In the former the narrative parallels that of *The thousand and one nights*, but with a feminist, revisionist twist. With its metaphors of subatomic particle theory, this quest narrative shifts and turns as the protagonist, Charade Ryan, probes the mysteries of the origins of the universe, of matter, and of Charade herself. In *The last magician* the principles of quantum physics are used to reveal how two contradictory states and contestant worlds coexist simultaneously. Using familiar images and simple detail drawn from Dante's *Inferno*, Hospital exposes the subterranean world beneath the respectability of the city and reveals how the two prey on one another. Like *Borderline*, *The last magician* invites critical reflection on contemporary moral, political, and economic issues that are relevant to any metropolitan centre.

Oyster—set in Outer Maroo, a small opal-mining town in the Australian Outback—is an exploration of the complex philosophical and metaphysical issues surrounding the tremendous power and seductiveness exercised by a religious cult leader over his followers; concomitantly, the novel probes the psychology of his entourage. Powerful in its evocation of a mirage-ridden landscape that is as insubstantial and unreliable as its guru cult figure, the novel also invokes the contentious debate surrounding white Australian cattle ranchers and opal miners who are contemptuous of government accommodation to Aboriginal land-claim issues.

Hospital is also an accomplished short-story writer. *Dislocations*, as the title suggests, is a collection of stories structured thematically around characters who experience one form or other of dislocation, be it geographic, cultural, or personal. The settings are diverse (ranging across three continents), and while loneliness, fear, and death are present in many of the stories, the end result is triumph. In the interrelated narratives comprising *Isobars*, Hospital achieves a truly postmodern collection where her characters are not the detached observers of realism but appear fragmented and discontinuous as they are positioned in a larger field of events where past and present are simultaneous.

See *Literature in North Queensland* 17.1 (1990), a special issue devoted primarily to writings by and about Hospital, containing an interview with Hospital by Ron Store. Elspeth Cameron offers a biographical background on Hospital and overviews of much of her fiction in *Profiles in Canadian Literature*, no. 8 (1991). Diana Brydon interviews Hospital in *Commonwealth Novel in English* 4.1 (Spring 1991). For a comprehensive bibliography of writings by and about Hospital and their subsequent reception in North America, Australia, and Europe, see Deborah Torkko, *Borderlines and dislocations: Janette Turner Hospital, a select bibliography, 1973-1995* (1995).

DEBORAH TORKKO

Houston, James (b. 1921). Born in Toronto, he attended the Ontario College of Art. After serving with the Toronto Scottish Regiment during the Second World War he went north to Baffin Island, and for nine of his twelve years there he was the region's first civil administrator. He is generally credited with the initial development of Inuit art in Canada. Houston has travelled extensively and studied art in France, Japan, and the United States.

Best known as a writer of juvenile fiction, Houston has three times (1966, 1968, 1980) won the Book-of-the-Year Award of the Canadian Association of Children's Librarians. Beginning with *Tikta' liktak: an Eskimo legend* (1965), he has written seventeen books for children and young adults, usually with his own illustrations, all full of factual information about native customs that he has woven into the action of the stories. *The white archer: an Eskimo legend* (1967) and *Akavak: an Eskimo journey* (1968) both centre on journeys in which physical courage parallels moral development. *Wolf run: a Caribou Eskimo tale* (1971) followed. Houston's plotting is generally very loose, his emphasis being on events rather than character development; the protagonist is most often a child or young adult who, through a series of crises, grows to maturity. *Kiviok's magic journey: an Eskimo legend* (1973), which is for very young children, is the only Inuit legend that Houston did not change substantially. The writer claimed that of 100 traditional Inuit stories, perhaps only three would work for a non-Inuit writer in their present form because of differences in the literary tradition. In *Frozen fire: a tale of courage* (1977) and *River runners: a tale of hardship and bravery* (1979) Houston moved away from traditional themes and began dealing with problems in the modern Inuit world. In *Long claws: an Arctic adventure* (1981) he makes good use of the bear as a visible sign of terror. Houston considers a bear-attack a staple of Canadian children's literature about the North and says: 'The weather isn't quite enough to express the danger that is present in the Arctic, whereas a bear can symbolize that in a wonderful way. He's white and he's big; he's like a terrible storm; he's an allegorical kind of thing sometimes. And I think I've often used bears in an allegorical way.' Other books for children and juveniles include *Black diamonds: a search for Arctic treasure* (1982). Houston, who spent considerable time living in a cabin in the Queen Charlotte Islands, also wrote *Eagle mask: a West Coast Indian tale* (1966) and *Ghost paddle: a North West Coast Indian tale* (1972).

Houston's adult novels, like many of his children's books, draw on true stories of Native contact with Europeans. *The white dawn: an Eskimo saga* (1971) was based on an incident in 1896 when three New England whalers were first rescued and then killed by Inuit. Houston heard of these men from Inuit friends on Baffin Island and was later able to confirm parts of the story from the ship's log of the *Abbey Bradford*. *Ghost fox* (1977), about the abduction of a New England farm girl by the Abenaki in the 1750s, contains the historical and anthropological accuracy of his other works. *Spirit wrestler*

(1980) is a fictional examination of the spirituality and chicanery of shamanism. For *Eagle song* (1983) Houston consulted the journal of John R. Jewitt, of the American brig *Boston*, who was captured by the Nootka chief Maquinna in 1803. The story is told by Maquinna's brother-in-law. His other two novels are *Whiteout* (1988) and *Running west* (1989).

Houston's non-fiction works include *Canadian Eskimo art* (1955), *Eskimo graphic art* (1960), *Eskimo prints* (1967), the introduction to *The private journal of Captain G.F. Lyon* (1970), and *Ojibway summer* (1972). Houston frequently uses authentic Inuit and Amerindian poetry in his novels, an interest that resulted in *Songs of the dream people: chants and images from the Indians and Eskimos of North America* (1972). He has also written several screenplays, beginning with one for a film based on *The white dawn*, which was released in 1974, and another based on his novel *Whiteout*. *Confessions of an igloo dweller* (1995) is a personal account of his years in the Canadian Arctic. Houston was made an Officer of the Order of Canada in 1972 for his work as an administrator, artist, and writer.

ROBIN GEDALOF McGRATH

Howe, Joseph (1804-73). Born in Halifax, Nova Scotia, he received some formal schooling but at the age of thirteen was taken as an apprentice into the family printing and newspaper business, the same office that had earlier published the first literary journal, *The NOVA-SCOTIA MAGAZINE*. He went on to a brilliant career as an author and journalist, establishing his newspaper *The Novascotian* as the leading journal in nineteenth-century Halifax; but he is best remembered as the pre-eminent politician of nineteenth-century Nova Scotia. He was elected to the legislative assembly in 1836 and for the next twelve years fought for responsible government. He reached the peak of his provincial political career as premier from 1860 to 1863. In the Confederation debate of the mid-1860s Howe led the opposition forces in Nova Scotia and ran as an Opposition candidate in the first federal election in 1867. He won, but by 1869 became convinced that opposing Confederation was futile. He accepted an appointment to the federal cabinet as secretary of state for the provinces, and served as minister until appointed lieutenant governor of Nova Scotia in Apr. 1873, two months before his death at Government House, Halifax.

In the 1820s and 1830s Howe wrote a substantial amount of verse, most of which was published in local newspapers. It was later collected and posthumously published in *Poems and essays* (Montreal, 1874), in which there are two poems of more than passing interest: 'Melville Island', which was first published in 1825, and 'Acadia'. In the first Howe uses a description of a former military prison near Halifax as a point of departure for philosophic observations on human experience. His intention is to suggest that life in Nova Scotia should not be considered remote or isolated from the mainstream of human civilization. In 'Acadia' (probably written in the early 1830s) the frame of reference against which past and present experiences are viewed is a rather vague vision of a bright social, political, and economic future for the people of Nova Scotia. Howe's intention is not made clear; he was better equipped to pursue his vision in the world of partisan politics and through the manipulation of political power.

Howe's formal prose works, while competently written, reflect the limitations and topicality of his concerns. *The speeches and public letters of the honorable Joseph Howe* (London & Boston, 1858; Halifax, 1909) is of some historical interest, but his addresses on non-political subjects are too general and simplistic to merit much attention. Some of his early journalistic pieces, however, have a vivacity and sharpness of observation that make them a continuing delight to read. Of particular note are his 'Western rambles' and 'Eastern rambles'—which ran serially in *The Novascotian* between 1828 and 1831—where he describes two journeys in Nova Scotia employing anecdotes, commentary, and observation, in the manner of William Cobbett's 'Rural rides'. At the same time Howe contributed to 'The Club Papers', a series of satiric and witty dialogue discussions of people and events by an ostensibly fictitious group of Halifax gentlemen; the articles are not unlike the 'Noctes Ambrosianae' series in *Blackwood's Magazine*.

Howe's greatest contribution as a cultural figure, however, lay in his lifelong belief in the necessity of developing a local literature and in the encouragement he gave to those around him to write and publish. After purchasing *The Novascotian* (1824-1926) from George Renny Young in Jan. 1828, he (together with John Sparrow THOMPSON) turned the paper into a cultural and intellectual vehicle in the community, opening its weekly columns to local essayists, fiction writers, and poets. During Howe's proprietorship (and even after he sold it in 1840), *The Novascotian* actively promoted local literary activity, and counted among its contributors George Renny Young, Thomas Chandler

HALIBURTON, Angus Gidney, Andrew SHIELS, Mary Jane KATZMANN, and John MCPHERSON. Howe himself, through the 'Rambles' and 'The Club Papers' in the 1820s and 1830s, helped to set the literary tone of the times and to nurture the confidence that Nova Scotian writers developed in themselves and in the cultural potential of colonial society.

M.G. Parks edited and wrote introductions to a 1973 edition of *Poems and essays* and to *Western and eastern rambles: travel sketches of Nova Scotia* (1973). See also *The heart of Howe: selections from the letters and speeches of Joseph Howe* (1939) edited by D.C. Harvey and *Joseph Howe: conservative reformer, 1804-1848*, vol. I (1983) by J. Murray Beck.

TOM VINCENT

Howley, James Patrick (1847-1918). Born in his family's summer home, on the farm known as Mount Cashel, then near, now in, St John's, Newfoundland, he attended St Bonaventure's College in St John's, but it was after he left school that he acquired his interest in geology, from reading an article in *Chambers's Miscellany*. In 1867 he got a job as a government clerk and met Alexander Murray, the Director of the Geological Survey of Newfoundland. The next year Murray took Howley with him as his assistant on a survey party in Placentia Bay. It was the first of forty-two consecutive summers that Howley would spend in the Newfoundland bush, all of which he described in voluminous journals—later, in his old age, recast as 'Reminiscences'. A selection from this rich text, edited by William J. Kirwin, G.M. Story, and P. O'Flaherty, was published by the Champlain Society in 1997. (The 'Reminiscences' text for 1868, edited by Kirwin and Story, was published in *Newfoundland Studies*, vol. 7, no. 2, 1991.) After Murray left the Survey in 1883 to return to Scotland, Howley became the *de facto* Director, although he wasn't formally appointed as such until 1898; he left the position in 1909.

The Geological Survey of Newfoundland is perhaps the colony's principal intellectual accomplishment in the nineteenth century. Murray and Howley together, and later Howley himself, produced a large number of geological studies and maps that opened up the little-known interior of the island and prepared the way for inland enterprise. Howley also produced a *Geography of Newfoundland* (1876). But he was more than a geologist, geographer, and cartographer; he was a man of letters, as indeed were his brothers Bishop Michael F., a poet, librettist, and historian, and Richard V., a brilliant essayist and orator, whose drinking made him the black sheep in this distinguished family. J.P., too, was capable of writing charming essays, but historical controversy, booming Newfoundland, and ethnology were more his line than *belles-lettres*. His equals among contemporaries were the historians D.W. Prowse and Moses HARVEY, the first a friend, the second a rival. Howley's major non-geological work was *The Beothucks, or Red Indians, the Aboriginal inhabitants of Newfoundland* (1915), published by Cambridge University Press, a magisterial work of documentary collection and commentary. This and Prowse's *A History of Newfoundland from the English, colonial, and foreign records* (1895) are the two great pioneering works of Newfoundland historical scholarship.

PATRICK O'FLAHERTY

Huff, Tanya. See FANTASTIC LITERATURE IN ENGLISH: I.

Huggan, Isabel (b. 1943). Born in Kitchener, Ontario, she grew up in nearby Elmira, studied at the University of Western Ontario (B.A., 1965), and has lived in Kenya, France, and the Phillipines. Huggan is best known for her first collection of short fiction, *The Elizabeth stories* (1984), three of which were first anthologized by John METCALF in *First impressions* (1980). The setting is the fictional small Ontario town of Garten, and the stories chart the development of Elizabeth Kessler from pre-school to her imminent departure for university. Elizabeth is intellectually precocious but emotionally cowardly, both qualities captured in the constant references to her parents as 'Frank' and 'Mavis': the distance built into familial relations in this upper middle-class background functions as an ironic device for revealing how Elizabeth's desire to escape Garten's various claustrophobias is simultaneously underwritten by her saturation in Garten's (and her parents') ways. Subtle forms of unearned snobbery, ethnic and class prejudice, sexual repression, and an unreflective sense of self and others constitute Elizabeth's difficult inheritance. Despite her attempts to escape, she unconsciously lives by these forms and is frequently the agent, sometimes witting, of malicious practices.

The stories in *You never know* (1993) are set in such diverse places as Scotland, Canada, Kenya, and France, and are mostly told through the perspective of adult women. They immerse us in relationships that test, through carefully controlled ironies, the limits of self-awareness, especially in upper middle-class protagonists whose liberal aspirations tend to be exposed in quiet but nevertheless disturbing ways. Although these stories reflect the various adults that Elizabeth Kessler might have become, the link between the volumes is the more broadly thematic one specified by the closing lines of the second collection: 'Why we enter each other's lives and how we are meant to fit together is more than is given us to know. And yet that's what we want, isn't it? That's what we want to understand.' Huggan's stories are careful tracings of this multifaceted desire to understand how people are meant to fit together and why we often fail to do so. DONNA PALMATEER PENNEE

Hughes, Monica (b. 1925). Born Monica Ince in Liverpool, England, Hughes had lived in Egypt, England, Scotland, and Zimbabwe before coming to Canada in 1952. She married in 1957 and lives in Edmonton. Hughes speaks of the shock she felt upon entering the Canadian landscape, of the fear and loneliness created by the Laurentian Shield and the Prairies. This sense of alienation imposed by a setting recurs in her novels, especially *Earthdark* (1977), the Isis trilogy (*Guardian of Isis*, 1981; *Keeper of the Isis light*, 1982; *The Isis pedlar*, 1982), and *Beyond the dark river* (1979). One of the most important and talented writers for adolescents of the present day, Hughes has produced historical fiction (*The gold-fever trail*, 1974; *The treasure of the Long Sault*, 1982), and realistic novels (*Ghost dance caper*, 1978; *Hunter in the dark*, 1982); but she is best known for her science fiction (the Isis trilogy; *Crisis on Conshelf Ten*, 1975; *The tomorrow city*, 1978). The teenage heroes/heroines in Hughes' novels become isolated by circumstances, which force them to make choices that define their character and identity. They face the universal adolescent difficulties of parental short-sightedness, the fear and hostility aroused by being 'different', the loneliness of isolation, and the need for close friendships. Hughes insists upon a character's search for truth and humanistic values. Presented as a saving remnant against the dehumanization of modern or future mass cultures, and usually caught in a web of intolerance and power, her main characters undergo a struggle that is of importance to the survival of their civilization.

Two major themes permeate Hughes' fiction: the conflict of cultures and respect for the power and beauty of nature. These very Canadian themes are most forcefully handled in the Isis trilogy, and in *Hunter in the dark* and *Beyond the dark river*. In the conflict of cultures, those who survive do so because of their deep fidelity to the traditional humanistic values of courage, tolerance, and individual choice. Cultures that violate these values carry self-destruction within them. Culture, however, is never isolated from place and landscape—one must either adapt through knowledge to the power of Nature or succumb to it. As in most important children's literature, the value of revering nature is closely associated with development of self and respect of others.

Hughes has now written over thirty books, primarily focusing her talents on science fiction, which always contains a bedrock of realism—what she calls 'scientific facts', or perhaps simply the facts of reality. *Sandwriter* (1986) and its sequel *The promise* (1989) provide strong female heroes who experience rebirth into a new, fuller existence by being willing to accept their responsibility to a larger world than the one they have felt 'safe' and comfortable in. In *Where have you been Billy Boy?* (1995) she cleverly uses the situation of the *Wizard of Oz* to show us the hero's choice of returning to an impoverished past (the Kansas of 1908, in fact) after seeing the world of eighty-five years later and rejecting the glitter and technological glow of 1993. He chooses to return because of his attachment to the old carousel operator Johannes (the Wizard?). For Hughes, character is always determined by such choices and the power of choice is fundamental. It lies at the heart of Hughes' vision.

One of Hughes' most popular novels for young readers is *Invitation to the game* (1990), a powerful book that once again pits individual choice against a technologically closed universe (the image of enclosure, or being trapped, is one that recurs in Hughes—see *The refuge*, 1989, with its fenced-in 'garden'). *Invitation* offers us a futuristic world (twenty-second century) so dehumanized that even individual choice is almost impossible. Unemployed youths live in groups or gangs—searching for some sense to their existence. The group we follow here ironically shows us that when technology becomes so overwhelmingly anti-human, there is almost no such thing as individual choice—there can only be a shared co-operation that can act to break through the prison.

Throughout Hughes' work it is often 'setting' that readers and reviewers note as a powerful part of her creative achievements and accompanying ecological themes. Settings can be realistic, as in *Blaine's way* (1986), set in southwestern Ontario during the Depression and the Second World War; they can also be futuristic, as in *Beckoning lights* (1990), where the theme of prejudice is probed by using 'aliens' as 'others' who are feared, even hated by the antagonist, Barry Trevor, whose drive for wealth makes it impossible for him to accept the Other as just as human as he is. In *The golden Aquarians* (1994), the planet Aqua is the setting for a battle between son, Walter, and father, Colonel Elliott, who has control of Aqua and is destroying it. A poet and musician, Walter overcomes the Colonel's attempt to make him into 'a man'. Ironically, back on earth after the planet Aqua experience, Walter and his father (who has amnesia and forgets his Colonel past) are reunited and we experience one of those ambiguous endings Hughes is noted for: will the Colonel remember and return to his past?

Having become Canada's foremost science-fiction writer for young adults, with novels such as *Hunter in the dark* (1982; winner of the 1983 CANADA COUNCIL Children's Literature Award) and *My name is Paula Popowich!* (1983) Hughes became one of our finest realistic writers as well.

Known both in North America and in Europe, Hughes also received the Canada Council Children's Literature Award in 1982. See 'The writer's quest', *Canadian Children's Literature* 26 (1982) for Hughes' comments on her methods and intentions in writing; also in that magazine (no. 17, 1980), 'Monica Hughes: an overview' by Gerald Rubio; and Raymond Jones' interview (no. 44, 1986).

ROBERT LOVEJOY

Humour and satire in English. Because satire has long been a mainstay of Canadian literature, it is fair to say that an important part of the Canadian literary imagination is critical, ironic, and mockingly humorous. Among our most widely read writers are two accomplished satirists from the past, T.C. HALIBURTON and Stephen LEACOCK; while the satirical fiction of Mordecai RICHLER and Robertson DAVIES, and the satirical poetry of Earle BIRNEY and F.R. SCOTT, are much enjoyed and admired today. Non-satiric humour tends to be restrained, stressing irony, but occasionally rising to the fullness of comedy, as in other novels by Richler and those of Robert KROETSCH.

The satires of Thomas McCULLOCH and T.C. Haliburton are largely, but certainly not exclusively, topical. To modern readers the effects of humour in their work are weakened by ponderous prose, moralizing, and verbosity; but Haliburton has survived more successfully than McCulloch because Sam Slick, the central character of much of Haliburton's writing, sometimes transcends his own limitations and becomes an engaging humorist, though the humorous effects of his dialect, witty aphorisms, and figures of speech are often weighed down by repetition and archaic Tory philosophy. McCulloch's Mephibosheth Stepsure, the lame Presbyterian minister, lacks Sam Slick's verbal power, and his humour at the expense of his profligate neighbours seems condescending and self-righteous—even for a satirist. One of McCulloch's best satires points out that poetic diction and classical allusion are inappropriate to North American writing, and in a mock dream-vision Stepsure journeys to Parnassus to hear Apollo's wisdom and finds a bouquet of Parnassian flowers stuck in a pad of cow dung. Although *The letters of Mephibosheth Stepsure* (1862) is McCulloch's only publication in this genre, Haliburton wrote, besides four Sam Slick collections, several other satirical-humorous books.

Stephen Leacock's writings are often slight, their humour depending on the tedious device of nonsense created by irrelevance, puns, and ambiguity. His books, however, contain many successful sketches, and an air of near-fantasy can strengthen Leacock's best work, such as his minor masterpiece *SUNSHINE SKETCHES OF A LITTLE TOWN* (1912), in which ruinous nonsense is held in check and a subtle and carefully designed mock-heroic form dominates. The pretensions of small-town Canada (Mariposa in the satire) are contrasted with the satiric norms of New York, London, King Edward VII, Rockefeller, and Carnegie. Mariposans are seen by Leacock's unrelentingly critical eye as gullible, vain, stupid, incompetent, and self-interested. *ARCADIAN ADVENTURES WITH THE IDLE RICH* (1914) satirizes city life in sketches on social, financial, educational, religious, and political affairs. Cameo characterizations help to give unity to this work: President Boomer of the University, the Rev. Fareforth Furlong and the Rev. Uttermost Dumfarthing of the Episcopalian and Presbyterian churches, the Overend brothers, the financiers Fysshe and Rasselyer-Brown, and the Rev. McTeague, who finally reconciles Hegel and St Paul when he realizes that life is a paradox and the seemingly important things are unimportant. When he becomes concerned for ordinary people, and spends time in friendly discourse with people he meets on the streeet, he is thought to have gone mad.

Leacock's influence can be seen in the work of Paul Hiebert, author of *SARAH BINKS*

(1947), a fictional biography of the Sweet Songstress of Saskatchewan whose marvellously banal 'poetry' is analysed with suitable academic overkill. The theme of Canadian provincialism is carried on from Haliburton and Leacock, but whereas Sam Slick and Leacock's persona in *Sunshine sketches* are both worldly, Sarah's biographer is as naïve as she is. Hiebert contributes the name Willows, Saskatchewan, to Canadian fictional place-names in *Sarah Binks*; but his *Willows revisited* (1967) is less successful than its predecessor in giving humorous life to a rural area.

Salterton, Ontario, is the small city of Robertson Davies' *Tempest-tost* (1951) and *Leaven of malice* (1954). The third work in this trilogy of often forced humour, *A mixture of frailties* (1958), is less satiric than the other two; but all three attack the provincialism of Salterton, an old university town. Davies' situation humour—sometimes Leacockian in its extravagance—and characterizations of university professors, the local little-theatre group, and the town's social élite, are at times farcical. Davies also attacks Canadian cultural stagnation in *The diary of Samuel Marchbanks* (1947) and *The table talk of Samuel Marchbanks* (1949)—sketches of biting humour, most of which appeared in the Peterborough *Examiner* when Davies was editor. His satire continues in the Deptford and Cornish trilogies.

Perhaps the most successful Canadian writer of humour in prose satire is Mordecai Richler, in *The incomparable Atuk* (1963) and *Cocksure* (1968). *Atuk*, a formal satire bound only superficially by the conventions of realism, ranges from witty analogies between Jews and Eskimos to low and grotesque imagery in the activities of the gentile-hating Panofsky, in the sex lives of the various characters, and in Atuk's murder of his brother. It is one of Canada's most complete works in its use of the conventions of humorous satire. *Cocksure*, on the other hand, uses these conventions in realistic novel form and is somewhat diffuse, although its black humour is chillingly effective. There is also a Leacockian exaggeration in incidents that satirize the avant-garde in the arts, and liberalism in education and other areas: Star Maker—the ultimate narcissist Hollywood producer—possesses a surgically developed androgyneity that enables him to impregnate himself and become pregnant.

Earle Birney's *Turvey: a military picaresque* (1949) has an analogue in Jaroslav Hasek's novel *The good soldier Schweik*. Its picaresque adventures celebrate the 'naturally loving and obstinately life-preserving' forces (present in the simple and earthy Private Turvey and his friend Mac) over the 'mechanical and life-destroying' (the Army, its tests, regulations, and courts martial). Birney, however, was also a poet, and his humorous satirical poems flay the ignorant, arrogant, and bigoted prejudices of society in such poems as 'Appeal to a woman with a diaper', 'Billboards build for freedom', and 'Anglosaxon Street'. 'Twenty-third flight' and 'The way to the West' take aim at powerful business, the Kaiser Corporation and International Nickel. Birney is also sometimes satirical in his delightful experiments with language and verse forms in the collection *Rag and bone shop* (1971).

F.R. Scott was another poet who wrote effective satire, attacking with sharp and unsparing wit the CANADIAN AUTHORS' ASSOCIATION ('The Canadian authors meet'), capitalism ('Efficiency'), dehumanization in a technological society ('Mural'), prime ministers R.B. Bennett and Mackenzie King, and other subjects. Irving LAYTON's satiric humour, on the other hand, which is frequently aphoristic, is all too often pursued with the self-indulgence of a carping iconoclast. Scott and A.J.M. SMITH edited *The blasted pine: an anthology of satire, invective and disrespectful verse* (1957; rev. 1967), which contains poems by colonial writers (for example, Alex Glendinning, Alexander McLACHLAN, and Standish O'GRADY, who damn the British, the Americans, and even the climate of Lower Canada); by Archibald LAMPMAN of the CONFEDERATION POETS, a most unhumorous group; by L.A. MacKay; the McGill group (especially Smith and Scott); and, in the second edition, by contemporary poets Margaret ATWOOD, Birney, Layton, Al PURDY, and Raymond SOUSTER. Another humorous anthology is *The maple laugh forever: an anthology of Canadian comic poetry* (1981) edited by Douglas BARBOUR and Stephen SCOBIE.

In 1958 James REANEY made an ambitious attempt to use humour in his long satire *A suit of nettles* (1958; 2nd edn 1975), based on Edmund Spenser's *Shepheardes calender*. Essentially a beast fable in twelve eclogues, Reaney's work is often pedantically obscure, and the humour of geese discoursing on human affairs often suffers accordingly.

Contributions to non-satiric humour in poetry have been made by W.H. DRUMMOND and Robert SERVICE. Drummond, writing at the turn of the century, employed for comic purposes his own version of the broken English used by Quebec *habitants* in narrative poems about their courting, marriage, family occasions, and about individuals who have stirred local interest: Jean Bateese, who goes to the United States, becomes rich, but returns gratefully to Quebec after he loses his money; Madame Albani, world-famous singer, who is still just 'de Chambly girl'; and Louis Desjardin, who outwits the Devil, driving him off by enveloping himself in a cloud of smoke from the pungent local tobacco. Robert Service also sets much of his poetry in a specific locale—the Yukon, at the time of the Gold Rush and after. His few humorous poems—with their simple characters, engaging rhythms, and imagery from the difficult northern life—include two classics, 'The cremation of Sam McGee' and 'The shooting of Dan McGrew', among others that are less well known.

Nearly all our good poets include some humour in their work; but excepting that of Service and Drummond, it usually tends to be ironic—Atwood's 'They eat out', Purdy's 'Linear B', and Souster's 'The girl at the corner of Elizabeth and Dundas'. Leonard COHEN's personae frequently have a touch of ironic humour in their attitudes, and in *Death of a lady's man* (1978) the informality of the critical commentator's audacity sometimes contrasts wittily with the seriousness of the poem under discussion. Many of George JOHNSTON's poems in *The cruising auk* (1959) have an innocent humour that is ironically reminiscent of children's verse. The contemporary poet whose non-satirical poems are most pervasively humorous is Irving Layton. His witty phrases, colloquialisms, bawdy diction, and violent images often give his love poems an ironic, earthy perspective.

In non-satirical humorous prose works the image of the small town or rural community is frequent. These can be idyllic, such as in Robert Fontaine's delightful, nostalgic *The happy time* (1945); L.M. MONTGOMERY's *Anne* books, which centre on that high-spirited, intelligent, sensitive girl and young woman; and W.O. MITCHELL's *Who has seen the wind* (1947), whose Brian O'Connal, his friends, and family give imaginative definition to a small prairie town, just as Anne does to Prince Edward Island. Mitchell's *The kite* (1962), also set in a small town, uses the convention of friendship between an independent old man and a young boy. The old man's speech and confusions are often humorous, but episodes sometimes approach the tall tale, which in a realistic novel strains credibility.

Max Braithwaite's humorous novels are set in rural and small-town Saskatchewan. Although in general they lack serious thematic interest, *The Commodore's barge is alongside* (1979) and *The night we stole the Mountie's car* (1975) are two simple, unpretentious, and thoroughly funny novels.

Also giving a strong sense of place to the Prairies are some of the novels of Robert Kroetsch, particularly *The words of my roaring* (1966), *The studhorse man* (1969), *Gone Indian* (1973), and *What the crow said* (1978). Bawdy and full of ingenious, humorous incidents, they are permeated with a sense of the ridiculous. His central characters, who occupy heroically imaginative worlds surrounded by banality, are classical gods and goddesses or Odyssean wanderers embodying a vision of life that is serious, but vigorous and earthy, hilarious, but ironic and sad.

Along with Kroetsch, Mordecai Richler raises humour to its highest development in Canadian prose in *The APPRENTICESHIP OF DUDDY KRAVITZ* (1959), *St. Urbain's horseman* (1971), and *Joshua then and now* (1980). Duddy Kravitz is often humorous in his frankness, in his witticisms, and in his naïveté as he struggles to develop some sophistication. He seeks identity through owning land, while guilt-ridden Jake Hersh, in *St. Urbain's horseman*, searches vainly for a hero to worship. This novel—a superb compendium of life in the 1950s and 1960s—makes effective use of verbal irony, comedy, colourful characterizations, low language, Jewish-gentile cultural confusions, and unconventional material such as newspaper clippings and a Mensa test.

Other novels touched with the comic spirit are Sara Jeannette DUNCAN's *The imperialist* (1904), Brian MOORE's *The luck of Ginger Coffey* (1960), Cohen's *Beautiful losers* (1966), Marian ENGEL's *Lunatic villas* (1981), Morley TORGOV's *The outside chance of Maximilian Glick* (1982; Leacock Medal for Humour), and Atwood's *Lady oracle* (1976), in which the overweight heroine describes others caustically ('the indistinct wives' of businessmen) and herself ironically ('I stood in front of the mirror . . . and examined myself much as a real-estate agent might examine a swamp, with an eye to future development'). There is no humour in Atwood's *The HANDMAID'S TALE* (1985), a powerful dystopian satire on right-wing religious fundamentalism. Leo SIMPSON's *Arkwright* (1971) develops a kind of surrealism, whose effect is weakened by wordiness and extravagant conceits. Characters tend to be stereotypes, as they are in his comedy of manners, *Kowalski's last chance* (1980), which uses the 'dumb cop' convention. Though its farce is sometimes effective, this novel is too often silly rather than funny. Simpson's *The Peacock papers* (1973) mixes satirical and non-satirical humour in a work that is, at times, close to fantasy. John METCALF's *Going down slow* (1972), a more successful blend of satire and comedy, portrays the vicissitudes of a sardonic young English immigrant teaching in Montreal; but his *General Ludd* (1980), more ironic than satiric, has only a few touches of humour. Jack MacLeod's hilarious *Zinger and me* (1979) is an epistolary novel that deals with some of the vagaries of academic life, and covers a broad spectrum of deftly handled techniques, from intellectual wit to the low humour of body functions. His *Going grand* (1982) is less humorous and fails to resolve problems created by mixing comedy and pathos.

Short stories are an important part of Canadian writing, and humour has a significant place in them. W.O. Mitchell's stories in *Jake and the kid* (1961), though sometimes sentimental, have humorous moments in their depiction of the affairs of the hired man and the little boy. Ethel WILSON's *Mrs. Golightly and other stories* (1961) reveals her deft style and gentle humour, particularly in the estimable 'A drink with Adolphus'. Frederick Philip GROVE skilfully uses understated humour in 'The midwife'. Some of Margaret Atwood's stories can be said to be humorous, but her *forte* is the pointed, mocking phrase. Mavis GALLANT's exquisite stories are often touched with light irony; Shirley Faessler and Jack LUDWIG contribute to the body of Canadian humorous Jewish literature with, for example, 'A basket of apples' and 'A woman of her age' respectively. John Metcalf's 'Private parts: a memoir' is an excellent, funny fictional reminiscence.

W.P. KINSELLA has published a number of humorous books on Native people—*Dance me outside* (1977), *Born Indian* (1981), *The fencepost chronicles* (1986), and *The Miss Hobbema pageant* (1989)—which, while they have been criticized by some critics as examples of appropriation of the Native voice, are rich in humour and farce and show a sympathetic understanding of their subject-matter. H.T. Schwartz also turned to Native people for his collection of interesting, funny, and erotic Native stories, *Tales from the smokehouse* (1974), as did Basil JOHNSTON in *Moose meat and wild rice* (1978). Thomas KING, an Amerindian like Johnston, links authenticity and genial humour in *Medicine River* (1990), *Green grass, running water* (1993), and *One good story, that one* (1993).

Humorous reminiscences, sketches, and journalism, some of it fictional, abound in Canadian writing. Of these rather ephemeral forms, perhaps Don Harron and Farley MOWAT are two of the most important practitioners, with Eric NICOL, Peter McARTHUR, Gregory Clark, and R.T. Allen also making significant contributions. In Harron's series by 'Charlie Farquarson', the Parry Sound (Ontario) farmer gives us his *Jogfree of Canada, the whirld and other places* (1976), *The histry of Canada* (1972), plus his own version of the Old Testament, and his *K-O-R-N filled allmynack*. The humour in these works depends on distortion of fact, misspellings, dialect, prurience, puns, and malapropisms.

For *The boat who wouldn't float* (1969), Farley Mowat won the 1970 Leacock Medal, which is offered annually for the best work of humour by a Canadian. His entertaining reminiscences of sailing a run-down schooner from Newfoundland to (eventually) Montreal have aspects of a comic epic, including the apparent intervention by spiritual forces in the running of the ship's engine. The stark realism of every situation always gives way to humour.

Though occasionally serious and entertaining, books of newspaper humour are often sexist, condescending, moralistic, and sentimental. Eric Nicol writes 'A drag down mammary lane'; to Greg Clark, the rich are nearly always bores. R.T. Allen's wife is apparently without a sense of humour; he feels that today's children are likely to think the world of his youth stupid and funless, and he writes *We gave you the electric toothbrush* (1971) to argue his point. One exception to these writers is Peter McArthur, whose ironic, light-hearted view of life is expressed by an easy-going, very human persona. The intellectual level of his sketches—which are often bucolic and may deal with art, poetry, and nature—is higher than that of other examples in this genre. Gary Lautens, who wrote a column in the *Toronto Star* until his untimely death, brought a warm, domesticated quality to his humorous sketches in *Take my family—please* (1980, *No sex please . . . we're married* (1983), and *The best of Gary Lautens* (1995).

There is humour of a relatively sophisticated kind in John GLASSCO's fictionalized autobiography *Memoirs of Montparnasse* (1970), about a delightfully honest and indolent young man's experiences in Paris in the late 1920s, including a soirée at Gertrude Stein's where 'the atmosphere was almost ecclesiastical'. Emily CARR's frequently amusing autobiographical writings in *The book of Small* (1942) and *The house of all sorts* (1944) tell of her life in Victoria, B.C., the former of her childhood and the latter of her years as the landlady of her apartment house. *Running to paradise* (1962), a book of Kildare DOBBS' essays, begins with his childhood in Ireland, moves through his experiences as a sailor in the British navy and as an administrator in Africa, and ends with his immigration to Canada. However, these slight but often elegant and entertaining pieces are on occasion marred by racially patronizing attitudes of the time. Dobbs also wrote one of the finest modern humorous books: *The great fur opera* (1970), a comic history of the Hudson's Bay Company with illustrations by Ronald Searle. *Smiles and chukkas* (1995) is a collection of articles written for the *Financial Post*.

Humour fares less well in Canadian drama than in other forms. Of *Three plays by Eric Nicol* (1975) two are comedies: *Like father, like fun* and *The fourth monkey*. The first features clichés about preparing a young man for his initiation into sex; the second has a fairly witty use of language, but is trite in its references to the USSR. Merrill DENISON's *The weather breeder* (1923), *Brothers in arms* (1923), and *Balm* (1926) have humorous episodes.

Critics have noted James Reaney's penchant for playfulness in his dramas, but too often the deliberate obfuscation of meaning in dialogue, and the use of word games, detract from the humour. *The killdeer* (1962, rev. 1972), however, shows some effective contrast between the humorous and the dark or grotesque; *The easter egg* (1972), a comedy of manners, has Shavian repartee at times; and *One-man masque* (1962) has some good verbal humour and effective stage business.

Robertson Davies' best plays are sometimes satirical (*Overlaid*, *Hope deferred*, and *A masque for Mr. Punch*), and there are others, such as those in *Eros at breakfast and other plays* (1949) and in *Four favourite plays* (1968), that are humorous if rather slight.

A collection of Canadian plays (3 vols, 1972-8), edited by Rolf Kalman, contains some impressive comedies: Sheldon ROSEN's *Meyer's room* (1972), a fast-moving absurdist play in which humour is created by misunderstandings and confusions of meanings; Donald Jack's *Exit muttering* (1972), a sex-oriented farce of bawdy and situation humour; and Mavor MOORE's witty *The pile* (1973), based on amusing semantic and logical arguments, and *The store* (1973), a very funny play in which a woman badgers the store manager with her complaints until he goes mad and stabs her.

Three other examples of successful comedies are David FRENCH's *Jitters* (1980), which deals with the anxieties of the professional production of a play—the practical difficulties as well as those of interpersonal relationships; David FENNARIO's bilingual *BALCONVILLE* (1980), which is set in a working-class part of Montreal where, in the summer heat, problems of life are dealt with on the balconies, and in the street below, by earthy English- and French-Canadian characters; and Erika RITTER's *Automatic pilot* (1980), which deals, through themes of alcoholism, love, and homosexuality, with a comedienne's fear of success. The humour of the play, very successful at times, comes both from repartee among characters and from the frantic nightclub routines that reveal, while trying to hide, the comedienne's private agonies. Tomson HIGHWAY's *The rez sisters* (1988) is a play by a Native dramatist in which the comedy arises from both characterization and the mores of community life on a reserve.

The list of significant writers who have won the Stephen Leacock Medal for Humour, awarded annually, shows the continuing importance of humour and laughter for the Canadian imagination: Ted ALLAN (*Love is a long shot*, (1985); Paul QUARRINGTON (*King Leary*, 1988); W.O. Mitchell (*According to Jake and the kid*, 1990); and Roch CARRIER (*Prayers of a very wise child*, 1992). See R.E. Watters, 'A special tang: Stephen Leacock's Canadian humour', *CANADIAN LITERATURE* (Summer 1960); Margaret Atwood, 'What's so funny? Notes on Canadian humour', *Second words* (1982); and Beverly Rasporich, 'Canadian humour and culture: regional and national expressions', *Culture, development and regional policy* (1988), Canadian Issues Series, vol. 9. Watters proposes that the Canadian hero, as best exemplified by characters in Leacock's works, can combine self-awareness, diffidence, and self-confidence. Atwood, on the other hand, finds that our humour is often structured on the contrast of our cosmopolitan values being undercut by a certain 'irrevocable' provincialism.

In the body of Canadian writing many works of humour are interesting documents in the development of a culture, rather than significant pieces of literature. With only a few exceptions, however, the highlights are modern. But when one considers the frequency of humour in the literature of the last ten decades, and the stature of those writers who handle it well (Richler, Kroetsch, Birney, *et al.*), one can conclude that humour is a major element in Canadian literature.

VINCENT SHARMAN

Humour and satire in French. Humour and satire have been essential elements of the oral tradition in French Canada, being found in varying degrees in the traditional folksongs and numerous stories passed on from generation to generation. In the novels, poetry, and plays of the nineteenth century, however, these elements are almost entirely absent—though some early novels, dealing frequently with historical topics or preaching moral or 'patriotic' messages, sometimes incorporate rudimentary attempts to provide the reader with reason to laugh. In historical fiction set at the time of the Conquest, for example, anglophone characters, such as the haughty British officer, are invariably treated mockingly. Joseph MARMETTE adds a new twist in his *François de Bienville* (Québec, 1870) by consistently using a 'vendu'—a French Canadian sympathetic to the British troops—as his comic relief.

Negative and satirical reactions to the Anglo-Saxon 'conqueror' are found as early as 1767 when, in a poem published for New Year's Day in *La Gazette de Québec*, rhyming couplets praise the new governor with discreet, tongue-in-cheek irony. Joseph QUESNEL's one-act play *L'Anglomanie; ou Le dîner à l'angloise*, composed around 1803, pokes fun at the French-Canadian élite who only too eagerly ape British ways and customs. *Épîtres, satires, chansons, épigrammes et autres pièces de vers* (Montréal, 1830) by Michel BIBAUD reflects the influence of the seventeenth-century French writer of epistles and satires, Boileau. Louis FRÉCHETTE's bitterness at the proposed Confederation of 1867 is apparent in his poem 'La voix d'un exilé' (1866), published during his voluntary political exile in Chicago. Praising the rebellious Patriotes of 1837, Fréchette satirizes the 'sordid band' of Cartier and Macdonald as they cynically get drunk on truffles and champagne now that they have succeeded in imposing Confederation on his French-speaking compatriots. A light-hearted tone characterizes Marmette's unpublished 'comédie de salon', *Il ne faut désespérer de rien* (Québec, 1880).

In the twentieth century, humour and satire are markedly absent from the writing of Quebec poets. One notable exception is Émile CODERRE, whose poetry of social criticism derives from his sympathy for the exploited poor during the Depression. Using the pseudonym 'Jean Narrache' and the colourful language of the working class, he prefigures the 'joualisants' of the 1960s (those intellectuals preferring to write in *JOUAL* rather than in a European French). In *Quand j'parl' tout seul* (1932)—a sequence of poems in the form of tragi-comic monologues by the unemployed Jean Narrache—puns and word-play abound, though the essentially tragic tenor of the social criticism, ranging from the bittersweet to the vitriolic, is underscored by abrasive humour, irony, and sarcasm. One incident illustrates Coderre's sense of humour and recalls at the same time Roch CARRIER's short story 'The hockey sweater'. Praising the politics of a member of the Saint Jean-Baptiste Society, Jean Narrache becomes violently angry that these 'patriotic' flag-wavers on behalf of Quebec's independence buy their flags from Eaton's in Toronto. A parallel to Coderre in the evolution of Quebec song was provided by La Bolduc (Mary Travers), a popular singer during the 1930s who described scenes similar to those of Jean Narrache, singing in the language of the poor and using humour and satire to make her critical point. Jacques GODBOUT's ironic humour is tentatively present in an early volume of poetry, *Les pavés secs* (1958), and would come to fruition in his novels.

Edmond Grignon published a light-hearted collection of short stories dealing with human foibles, *Quarante ans sur le bout du banc* (1932), in which wit, maliciousness, and burlesque parody issue forth from the mouth of a narrator-judge sitting on his bench in the remote Laurentians. Abbé Lionel GROULX reveals a warm sense of gentle humour in 'Comment j'ai quitté la politique', a chapter of *Les rapaillages* (in the expanded 1935 edition), which describes his childhood and the village milieu. Groulx humorously recalls his first foray into politics at the age of twelve when, in a school election between the 'Rouges' and 'Bleus', he, the chief speaker for the 'Bleu' party, suffered ignominious defeat through the 'shameless, corrupt means' of the Liberal opposition.

When discussing the history of theatre in Quebec, one thinks automatically of historical dramas or biblically inspired pageants, but alongside the formal 'play' existed the popular monologue of 'improvisateurs'—storytellers presenting dramatic monologues in the local accent to an eager and often unsophisticated audience. From the oral literature of New France springs the long and popular tradition of the 'revue' or the 'sketch', which in the 1960s and 1970s was used by dramatist, poet, and *chansonnier* alike and later found its full expression in the 'monologuiste' movement. (See *Monologues québécois 1890-1980*, 1980, by Laurent Mailhot and Doris-Michel Montpetit.) Régis Roy's satirical description of federal politics as described by the candidate for election, Baptiste Tranchemontagne (cf. *On demande un acteur*, 1896), is typical of these presentations, which were usually topical in nature. Jean Narrache, smoking his pipe in front of the fire, became the modern prototype of these monologists. The most important writer of monologues, however, was Paul Coutlee, who provided the link between his amateurish predecessors and the more polished performances of Yvon Deschamps and Viola Léger. Coutlee's comic rendering in 1920 of 'Le recensement' ('The census'), in which the father of a large family cannot remember whether he has nine or twelve children, would be radically adapted by Antonine MAILLET in *La SAGOUINE*. Both Maillet, the author of La Sagouine's monologues, and Deschamps, creator of his own, represent the flowering of a long tradition of humour that uses popular speech, puns, invented words, and curious syntax blended with pessimistic irony and biting satire bordering on 'black humour'. Contemporary realities are perceived and interpreted by alienated and marginal characters. Clémence Desrochers and Marc Favreau (the actor Sol) follow in the same tradition. In the realm of formal theatre, Gratien GÉLINAS's annual series of amusing sketches in the 1940s, *Les Fridolinades*, and to a lesser extent his *TIT-COQ* (1950)—as well as the plays of Michel TREMBLAY, with their black humour and choral monologues—come from this same tradition. So does Jean-Claude GERMAIN's witty use of 'popular' French, though much of his humour derives from buffoonery, mockery, sarcasm, irony, and vulgarity as he unflinchingly parodies sacred cows of Quebec ideological mythology in such plays as *Un pays dont la devise est je m'oublie* (1976) and *Mamours et conjugat* (1979).

Humour and satire in Quebec fiction, until after the Second World War, appeared only occasionally. Rodolphe GIRARD injected some earthy humour and light anti-clerical comment into *MARIE CALUMET* (1904), through references by the parish priest's housekeeper to the visiting bishop's 'holy piss' and the accidental baring of her buttocks to the *curé* as his parishioners looked on. Girard's experiment in humour, however, brought swift public condemnation by Monseigneur Bruchési, the bishop of Montreal, and Girard's firing as director of *La Presse*. Abbé Groulx's controversial and best-selling novel *L'appel de la race* (1922) illustrated the dangers of cultural assimilation through marriage between English and French Canadians. Debate about Regulation 17, depriving Franco-Ontarians of an education in French, provided Groulx with grist for satiric comment: the Union Jack in his novel becomes the 'flag of the conqueror' flying haughtily over the country's capital, and Parliament itself a 'battlefield where since Sainte-Foy two races and two civilizations confront and oppose each other.' Outspoken anti-clericalism, and a scathingly satiric portrayal of the Quebec City's establishment by Jean-Charles HARVEY in *Les demi-civilisés* (1934), earned him the same fate as Girard: public clerical condemnation and loss of his job as editor of *Le Soleil*.

The widespread acceptance of Roger LEMELIN's realistic depiction of Quebec City's Lower Town in *Les PLOUFFE* (1948) not only confirmed the changing nature of Quebec society—Lemelin's satiric verve and his comic personalities enabled Québécois to laugh at themselves—but it is the first Quebec novel to be suffused with humour from beginning to end (while also retaining a critical purpose). This successful venture into social realism with a comic vein was later taken up by three major writers: Jacques FERRON, Jacques Godbout, and Roch Carrier. Ferron, in debunking traditional myths within Quebec, invented new ones based on his reinterpretation of historical fact. Good-natured humour is used in *La nuit* (1965) and *Le ciel de Québec* (1969) to poke fun at Scots and at Anglican archbishops whose ancestors have lived in Quebec since the Conquest. Anti-clerical humour, traditionally negative and biting, takes an amusing turn in *Le Saint-Elias* (1972) as the newly ordained priest, arriving in a country parish, is soon seduced by an admiring parishioner he was trying to convert and must be rapidly transferred to avoid scandal. In *L'amélanchier* (1970), however, the good-natured Dr Ferron heaps vitriolic scorn on the medical profession for its callous treatment of the mentally ill. Roch Carrier, like Ferron, has his intellectual roots in the oral tradition. In his short stories and novels he excels in the use of situation comedy; he is known particularly for his disquieting 'black humour', with its subversive undertones (*La guerre, yes sir!*, 1968) and humorously bawdy dialogue (*Le jardin des délices*, 1975).

Gérard BESSETTE and Jacques Godbout have honed the art of satire to a fine degree in their numerous novels. Malicious irony seems to be Bessette's *forte*, whether he is dissecting religious hypocrisy in *Le libraire* (1960) or mocking Orange-Loyalist families in *L'incubation* (1965) and academic colleagues in *Le semestre* (1979). In *Le couteau sur la table* (1965) Godbout prefers heavy-handed satire in sketching 'racial' (i.e. anglophone and francophone) stereotypes and expressing anti-clerical sentiments. Irony and laughter are skilfully intertwined in *SALUT*

GALARNEAU! (1967) and *D'amour P.Q.* (1972). The whimsical nature of *L'isle au dragon* (1976), with its light-hearted punishment of the American industrialist, Shaheen, for dumping atomic wastes into the St Lawrence River, represents a masterful use of humour that does not lessen the seriousness of the problems posed by multinational companies.

In recent years women writers have made significant use of humour and satire. In Antonine Maillet's novels and plays, which contain amusing dialogue and situations, the humorous weaknesses of her colourful rural characters arouse sympathetic laughter; there is none of the bitterness found in Lemelin and Carrier. Three overtly feminist writers exhibit judicious and effective use of humour as a vehicle for social criticism. In *L'EUGUÉLIONNE* (1976) Louky BERSIANIK invents an extra-terrestrial feminine version of Candide who comes from outer space to comment on the curious hierarchical relationship existing between the two sexes on the planet Earth. Iconoclastic at the ideological level, Bersianik excels in illustrating with wit and irony the absurd sexism of the French language. (As she points out, in the sentence 'Three hundred women and one cat walked down the street', the masculine cat takes grammatical precedence over the three hundred females.) Tragicomic relationships between couples illustrate feminist themes in Elisabeth Bourget's *Bernadette et Juliette* (1980); while in *La SAGA DES POULES MOUILLÉES* (1981) Jovette MARCHESSAULT amuses her theatre audiences by putting swear words in the mouth of Laure Conan (Félicité ANGERS) and four-letter ones into Gabrielle ROY's. Incidentally, while humour is not primarily associated with the fiction of Roy, her vision of life and character is often mellowed by gentle irony.

Claude JASMIN's novel *Maman-Paris, Maman-la-France* (1982) treats humorously a topic touched on by both novelists and playwrights: the amusing differences between the people and language of France and Quebec. Most refreshing and innovative is the underlying mischievous current of humour in Yves BEAUCHEMIN's *Le matou* (1981), with its voraciously hungry little boy, Monsieur Émile, who gets drunk regularly by siphoning the cook's cognac and feeds his equally hungry tomcat, Déjeuner, black pudding and sardines indiscriminately. Dany LAFERRIÈRE adds a refreshing and humorous perspective to the many fictional representations of Montreal in *Comment faitre l'amour à un nègre sans se fatiguer* (1985)—translated by David Homel as *How to make love to a Negro* (1987). Against the backdrop of the Christian cross on Mount Royal and a shining Islamic crescent moon, two young blacks in a nearby studio express their cultural alienation, torn between the spiritual lessons of Allah and the enticing theories of Freud. With tongue-in-cheek irony and humour, ranging from black to light, the Haitian-born journalist allows his protagonists to redress the evils of white colonization by seducing an interminable number of white women picked up in the bars and discos of Saint-Denis. In his politically incorrect scenario, he deftly avoids giving offence to potential francophone readers by creating a host of anglophone females from McGill, including feminists and cat-lovers, who couple enthusiastically with the narrator, confirming the myth of the sexual attraction of the female colonizer to the black male. A film version of this novel was well received in both Quebec and France. RAMON HATHORN

Hunter-Duvar, John (1821-99). John Hunter was born in Newburgh, Scotland, and after 1850 was based in Halifax as press agent for the Associated Press of New York. In 1857 he and his wife Anne Carter—who, according to a note scribbled on her husband's will, was an illegitimate first cousin of Queen Victoria—immigrated to Prince Edward Island. In 1861 he legally changed his surname to Hunter-Duvar. He served as a militia officer and a justice of the peace, edited the Summerside *Progress* (1875-9), and was Dominion inspector of fisheries (1879-89), in which post he supported conservation of the fish stocks. At his Hernewood estate he led the life of a gentleman and scholar, joined several literary societies, and corresponded with many public figures. He died at Alberton, PEI.

As a poet, Hunter-Duvar was equally at ease with short and long poems and developed two distinct voices: one of them a realistic and colloquial contemporary style, often satiric, and the other a rich, bilingual, allusive, medieval style. Both frequently avoided the cloying sentimentality of much Victorian verse. Usually ignoring Canadian subjects, he set his poems in Renaissance France and Spain, or in a fanciful 'fairyland', reflecting the Victorian fondness for medieval subjects. Yet his poems have parallels to his own life, for his protagonists are lonely travellers into new and alien lands; when they fail, they are sustained by the faith of their ladies and by their own poetic vision. *The enamorado; a drama* (Summerside, 1879), dedicated to Swinburne and based on an event in the life of the historical fifteenth-century Mazias of Gallicia, tells of the *Othello*-like betrayal of its soldier-poet hero and is written in the style of Jacobean and Restoration heroic tragedies. The title piece of *De Roberval, a drama; also The emigration of the fairies, and The triumph of constancy, a romaunt* (Saint John, 1888), with its echoes of Shakespearean tragedy, describes how the austere, aloof French nobleman's vision of a harmonious New World society is destroyed by Old World corruption. This publication includes two poems of contrasting style and subject. *The triumph of constancy* successfully recreates the language and flavour of a Chaucerian-style folktale in which a questing knight finds salvation in constancy after savouring the pleasures of promiscuity. The other is Hunter-Duvar's most anthologized poem, the humorous *The emigration of the fairies*, which may have been written as a private joke about the discovery by him and Anne (the fairies) of Hernewood. In it the world of imagination—with its ancient affinities for the woods and the sea—is transported from old England to Prince Edward Island, the Edenic New World. In all these stories of knights, explorers, and fairy folk, the saving grace is their imaginative vision.

Hunter-Duvar also published *John a' Var; gentilhomme et troubadour. His lays* (privately printed, 1874?) and *Fin de siècle; a comedy* (n.d.), which are very rare; a satiric prose work, *Annals of the court of Oberon; extracted from the records* (London, 1895); and an archaeological study of science, folklore, and legend, *The Stone, Bronze and Iron Ages* (London, 1892).

See *Hernewood. The personal diary of Col. John Hunter Duvar June 6 to September 17 1857. The story of Anne of Hernewood a fascinating lady and The emigration of the fairies* (1979) edited by L. George Dewar; Stephen Campbell, 'John Hunter-Duvar; a biographical introduction, check-list of his works and selected bibliography', an M.A. thesis submitted in 1966 to the University of New Brunswick and available on microfilm from the National Library; M.D. Edwards, *A stage in our past, English-language theatre in eastern Canada from the 1790s to 1914* (1968); Frances Frazer, 'Island writers', CANADIAN LITERATURE 68-69 (1976); [P.J.] M. Blagrave, 'Playwriting in the Maritime provinces: 1845-1903' (1983), Ph.D. dissertation, University of Toronto; and S.C. Campbell, 'John Hunter-Duvar (John Hunter)', DICTIONARY OF CANADIAN BIOGRAPHY, vol. 12 (1990). GEORGE L. PARKER

Huston, James. See ANTHOLOGIES IN FRENCH: 1, ESSAYS IN FRENCH: 1, and POETRY IN FRENCH: 2.

Huston, Nancy (b. 1953). Born in Calgary, Alberta, she grew up there and in Edmonton. Her mother suddenly left the family when Huston was six, and her relationship to her mother-tongue is related, in her accounts, to that early abandonment. Her family moved to New England when she was in her teens and she attended Sarah Lawrence College in Bronxville, New York. She moved to Paris in 1973 and still lives there. Huston studied in Paris at the École des hautes études en sciences sociales with the leaders of post-structuralism, including Roland Barthes (her M.A. thesis, published as *Dire et interdire*, 1980, dealt with profanity). A sometime teacher—she has been visiting professor and guest lecturer at numerous universities and institutions in North America and Europe—she is married to the Bulgarian-born writer Tzvetan Todorov and has two children.

Huston has published six novels. *Les variations Goldberg* (1981, self-translated as *The Goldberg Variations*, 1996) was a *tour de force*; published after Barthes' death, it was dedicated to him. The novel's action lasts exactly an hour and a half, the time it takes Liliane Kulainn to play Bach's *Goldberg Variations* on the harpsichord before thirty friends and acquaintances at her Paris apartment; thirty-two inner monologues give voice to Liliane and her guests. Most of Huston's key themes—music, words, writing, passion, sex, the body, food, the passage of time, and the relationship between time and space—are launched here. A second novel, published in 1985, *Histoire d'Omaya* (with its ironic reference to *Histoire d'O*, the classic pornographic novel of a woman in love with her own abasement), presents, through fragment and collage, the psychic collapse of an already fragile young actress who was abducted and abused by a group of men and, having pressed charges against them, found herself on trial. Against the backdrop of the Vietnam War, *Trois fois septembre* (1989) relates the descent into madness and the suicide of a young woman as seen through the eyes of a mother-daughter couple reading her journal and letters after the fact.

For *Plainsong* (1993) Huston drew for the first time on her childhood experiences of life in western Canada and found herself writing, also for the first time, fiction in English. This lyrical and desperate novel relates the narrator's attempts to reconstruct imaginatively her grandfather's life (resembling that of her father as related in *Jouer au papa et à l'amant*, 1979): an aspiring writer-philosopher, he soon found himself trapped in the role of husband, breadwinner, and father and lost the ability, but not the longing, to make an intellectual contribution. Huston rewrote the novel in French, and *Cantique des plaines* (1993) won a Governor General's Award. The prize sparked a controversy in Quebec literary circles—because it was a translation, because the author was not a Québécoise. Ironically, the angry protests from five Québécois publishers gave the novel heightened visibility, and won Huston many new readers. The lapidary and intense *La virevolte* (1994)—initially written in English, this version was not published until 1996 as *Slow emergencies*—is the story of mother-daughter love and abandonment across three generations and a meditation on the relationship between art (dance) and life. The same metamorphosis of the everyday into literature, pain into transcendence, is at the heart of *Instruments des ténèbres* (1996). The narrator, Nadia (Nada), alternately reflects on her own troubled past and present and writes a novel, inserted in the text, about a young servant girl who killed her newborn child in eighteenth-century France. It was nominated for the Prix Goncourt, won the Goncourt des lycées, and was chosen as one of the twelve best books of 1996 by the Paris magazine *Lire*. A translation, *Instruments of darkness*, was published in 1997.

Huston's greatest strength as an author of non-fiction is her ability to write both as an intellectual and as a woman who refuses the structuralist premise that the text is a purely imaginative construction with no connection to, and no impact on, real life. Much of her early non-fiction deals with the complex links between sex, language, and power, documenting male domination of women through pornography (*Mosaïque de la pornographie*, 1982) and unequal and eroticized power relations (*Jouer au papa et à l'amant*). She has returned often to the mind-body, man-woman split that permeates all Western thought and has damaged both men and women. *À l'amour comme à la guerre* (1984), letters between Huston and the American historian Samuel Kinser, looks at the symbolic relationships between Mars and Venus, and at war, motherhood, and prostitution. *Journal de la création* (1990) combines case studies of famous writing couples and the symbolic roles each member played, musings on Huston's past physical and mental ailments and their symbolic meaning and function, and the diary of her second pregnancy and its impact on her body, life, thoughts, and writing. Exile has become another important theme of Huston's work, particularly in *Lettres parisiennes: autopsie de l'exil* (1986), written with the Algerian-French writer Leïla Sebbar. In a similar vein, *Tombeau de Romain Gary* (1995) is a highly personal portrait of a writer obsessed with reinventing himself between and among languages, countries, identities, and writing styles.

Although she is spectacularly fluent in, and writes in, two languages, Huston says she is not at home in either of them. She has written movingly of her self-translation, a kind of bilingual writing and rewriting with no true source or target language, and of her hesitations, possibilities, and impossibilities in using French as a literary language. It is precisely this in-between, uncomfortable, and yet vital position that is the source of her considerable creative energy. LORI SAINT-MARTIN

Hutcheon, Linda (b. 1947). Born Linda Bortolotti in Toronto, Ontario, and educated at the University of Toronto (B.A., 1969; Ph.D., 1975), and Cornell University (M.A., 1971), she taught at McMaster University, Hamilton, from 1976 to 1988, the year she became professor of English and comparative literatures at the University of Toronto. Hutcheon is one of Canada's best-known and most frequently cited literary critics as well as an influential teacher and editor. She has popularized poststructuralist theories among the academic community and its students, and shown their relevance to contemporary Canadian concerns with identity, history, and community in her many books, including *Narcissistic narratives* (1980), *A theory of parody: the teachings of twentieth-century art forms* (1985), *A poetics of postmodernism: history, theory, fiction* (1988), *The Canadian postmodern: a study of contemporary English-Canadian fiction* (1988), *The politics of postmodernism* (1989), *Splitting images: Canadian ironies* (1991), and *Irony's edge: the theory and politics of irony* (1995). They have influenced the field of postmodern theory, cultural studies, and Canadian literary and cultural studies as they are practised in Canada and elsewhere. Hutcheon's clear stye and breadth of reference across various fields of cultural representation (notably architecture, literature, painting, and opera) provide a synthesizing overview of culture as a system governed by representation conventions that rivals Northrop FRYE's. Unlike Frye, however, Hutcheon increasingly brought formalist readings into contact with political questions, particularly those involved in the representation of history, gender, and race. Each of her books contributes a new angle to what is now emerging as the governing goal of her work:

the anatomization and investigation of complicitous critique. From her earliest work on what she calls 'narcissistic narrative' to later considerations of postmodern aesthetics, parody, and irony, Hutcheon has wrestled with her desire to celebrate self-reflexivity in contemporary art as a liberating strategy even as she recognized the limitations of such stance.

With her husband Michael Hutcheon, Linda Hutcheon has also written *Opera: desire, disease, death* (1996), an entertaining discussion of some famous operas in the contexts of the subtitle. She edited *Double-talking: essays on verbal and visual ironies in Canadian contemporary art and literature* (1992) and co-edited (with Marion Richmond) the anthology *Other solitudes: Canadian multicultural fictions* (1990), stories and interviews; (with Mark A. Cheetham) *Remembering postmodernism: trends in recent Canadian art* (1991); and (with George BOWERING) *Likely stories: a postmodern sampler* (1992). DIANA BRYDON

Hutchison, Bruce (1901-92). Born in Prescott, Ontario, he was taken to British Columbia as an infant and grew up in Victoria. He became a high-school journalist for the Victoria *Times* in 1918 and a political reporter in Ottawa in 1925; he returned to the *Times*, also reporting on the provincial legislature for the Vancouver *Province*. He was an editorial writer and columnist for the *Vancouver Sun* (1938), assistant editor on the Winnipeg *Free Press* (1944-50), and then returned to the Victoria *Times*, where he served as editor from 1950 to 1963, establishing his reputation as a leading political journalist and commentator. In 1963 he became editorial director of the *Vancouver Sun* and in 1979 editor emeritus; he wrote a weekly column for the *Sun* until his death. In addition to his newspaper work, Hutchison wrote dozens of pulp stories in the 1920s, a novel, and even a film script, 'Park Avenue Logger', which was produced in Hollywood. By the end of his career he had won three National Newspaper Awards, three Governor General's Awards, the Royal Society of Arts Award for Journalism, and the Bowater Prize. He received the inaugural Royal Society of Arts Award for Distinguished Journalism in the Commonwealth (1961), was placed on the *Maclean's* Honour Roll (1989), and received the City of Victoria Prize (1990), and the Jack Webster Foundation First Lifetime Achievement Award (1991).

In nearly seventy-five years of political reporting, spanning the careers of ten prime ministers, Hutchison developed friendships with political personalities that ranged from Louis St Laurent and Lester Pearson to Pierre Elliott Trudeau and Jean Chrétien. His writings on Canada and its political figures were characterized by the confidential vignette, but he was criticized for partisan loyalty to the Liberal party—a charge he always denied. His best-known book, *The unknown country: Canada and her people* (1943)—which won a Governor General's Award, and is still in print after several revised editions—is a delightful panorama of Canada, containing vivid descriptions of place and personality, with short lyrical vignettes between chapters. Hutchison also dealt successfully with the larger movements of politics and economics. His novel *The hollow men* (1944), the story of a newspaper correspondent disillusioned by world war, combines subtle political satire with sympathy for wilderness life.

Hutchison's other titles include *The Fraser* (1950) in the Rivers of America series; *The incredible Canadian: a candid portrait of Mackenzie King, his works, his times, and his nation* (1952; Govenor General's Award); *Canada's lonely neighbour* (1954); *The struggle for the border* (1955); *Canada: tomorrow's giant* (1957; Governor General's Award), and *Mr. Prime Minister 1867-1964* (1964), which was condensed as *Macdonald to Pearson: the prime ministers of Canada* (1967). Hutchison also wrote *Western window* (1967), a collection of essays, as well as the text for *Canada: a year of the land* (1967), a lavish picturebook on Canada produced by the National Film Board. At the age of eighty Hutchison published *Uncle Percy's wonderful town* (1981), a dozen fictional and nostalgic accounts of life in Emerald Vale, B.C., a town with the features of Merrit, Cranbrook, and Nelson in British Columbia. While short on emotional range, these stories—narrated by a fourteen-year-old boy—evoke a vanished time and place. *A life in the country* (1988) is both a memoir and a meditation on country life. Hutchison's autobiography, *The far side of the street* (1976), expressed a highly personal view of the growth of his generation, and reaffirmed his vision of a modern and responsible Canada.

See *Maclean's* (9 Dec. 1985) for an interview, and *Maclean's* (25 Dec. 1989) for the honour-roll citation. See also *Maclean's* (28 Sept. and 5 Oct. 1992) for appreciations by Allan Fotheringham and Peter C. NEWMAN.

GEOFF HANCOCK

Huyghue, Douglas Smith (1816-91). He was born in Charlottetown, Prince Edward Island, while his father was stationed there with the military, and was educated in Saint

John, New Brunswick. In 1840-1 he was living in Halifax and contributing poetry to *The Halifax Morning Post* under his pseudonym 'Eugene'. A year later he was again resident in Saint John and had become a regular contributor of poetry, fiction, and prose to the literary periodical *The Amaranth*. His activities between 1841 and 1844 included co-hosting an exhibition of Native artifacts in Saint John with New Brunswick's Indian commissioner, Moses Perley, and working with the Boundary Commission settling the border between Maine and New Brunswick after the Aroostook War. His novel *Argimou: a legend of the Micmac* (Halifax, 1847) first appeared as a serial in *The Amaranth* in 1842. Two years later he left the Maritimes and moved to London, England, where he contributed descriptive sketches to *Bentley's Miscellany* and published a second novel, *The nomads of the West; or Ellen Clayton* (London, 1850). In 1852 Huyghue immigrated to Australia and in 1854 witnessed the Eureka uprising while working as a government clerk in the goldfields at Ballarat. His impressions of the experience were recorded in a watercolour now housed in the Ballarat Fine Art Gallery and in an unpublished memoir, 'The Ballarat riots'. Huyghue held various government posts in Australia until his retirement in 1878. He died in Melbourne in 1891.

Huyghue's poems and stories reflected his lifelong interest in the culture and society of Native people. Although *Argimou* purports to be a romance set in Acadia in 1755, it is in reality an impassioned novel of conscience exploring the disintegration of Micmac culture under the influence of European settlement. One of the first Canadian novels to describe the Expulsion of the Acadians, *Argimou* was popular enough to be re-serialized in Saint John as late as 1860. Its successor, *Nomads of the West*, never achieved the same reputation, although it too reflected the author's intimate understanding of Native people 'before their ranks were thinned, or their spirit broken by aggression.' Perhaps discouraged by the novel's failure in Britain, Huyghue wrote only periodical and private pieces after 1850, and in Australia seemed to favour his art work rather than his writing.

GWENDOLYN DAVIES

Hyde, Anthony. See NOVELS IN ENGLISH 1983 TO 1996: OTHER NOVELS 4.

Hyde, Christopher. See NOVELS IN ENGLISH 1983 TO 1996: OTHER NOVELS: 4.

I

Iglauer, Edith (b. 1917). Born in Cleveland, Ohio, USA, she received her B.A. from Wellesley College and obtained a graduate degree in journalism from Columbia University, New York. During the Second World War she worked for the Office of War Information in Washington, was a war correspondent for *The Cleveland News*, and married Philip Hamburger (divorced 1966). After writing as a freelance journalist, she began contributing in 1958 to *The New Yorker*, a venue that paradoxically led her into the Canadian North. Her first two books, *The new people: the Eskimo's journey into our time* (1966)—revised in 1979 and retitled *Inuit journey*—and *Denison's Ice Road* (1975), were developed out of articles she wrote for *The New Yorker* and *Maclean's*. The first describes the meetings that led to the founding of the Inuit co-operatives for marketing goods to the south, particularly crafts; and the second describes her experience of accompanying John Denison and his crew while they built the ice-road from Yellowknife across northern lakes to a silver mine. These glimpses of Canadian life led Iglauer to move in the early 1970s to Vancouver, where she met John Daly, a commercial fisherman, whom she married in 1972.

Iglauer brought to her new life the same intense curiosity that characterizes her writing on other subjects. After Daly's death in 1978, she wrote a memoir about accompanying her husband during the fishing season that was published as *Fishing with John* (1988), which documents the fishing season off the British Columbia coast and bears many of the marks that make Iglauer's writing memorable. She is drawn to stories of energy, enterprise, and vision: both the Inuit co-operative initiative and the ice-road construction reflect these qualities, as do the subjects of other pieces, such as *Seven stones: a portrait of Arthur Erickson* (1981), her famous *New Yorker* profile of Pierre Elliott Trudeau (July 1969), and her 1972 article describing the construction of the World Trade Centre's massive foundation, which took seven years to write (since the foundation took seven years to complete): that investment of time, and degree of perseverance, characterize Iglauer's approach to her subjects. *The strangers next door* (1991), selected articles and excerpts from Iglauer's writings, illustrates her documentary impulse, her ability to catch emotional and sensory nuance, and her willingness to embrace exhausting, demanding circumstances to satisfy her desire to know. ANNE RAYNER

Ignatieff, Michael (b. 1947). Born in Toronto—the son of the distinguished Canadian diplomat George Ignatieff and the former Alison Grant, a painter—he lived in many different locations as a child, including Yugoslavia, Geneva, and Paris. He was educated at Trinity College, University of Toronto, Harvard University (Ph.D., 1975), and Cambridge University (M.A., 1978). He taught history at Harvard (1971-4) and the University of British Columbia (1976-8), and was Senior Research Fellow at King's College, Cambridge (1978-84). In 1985 he was visiting professor at the École des Hautes Études, Paris. He then, in his own words, 'climbed the monastery wall', becoming a television host for the BBC and writing the script for *Nineteen nineteen* (1985), a film whose subject was the last two surviving patients of Sigmund Freud. He was editorial columnist for *The Observer* (London) from 1990 to 1993. Ignatieff is a man for all media, bringing intelligence, warmth, urbanity, and verbal facility to everything he undertakes. He lives in London, England.

His writing career began with a history, *A just measure of pain: the penitentiary in the Industrial Revolution* (1978). He was co-author of *Wealth and virtue: the shaping of classical political economy in the Scottish Enlightenment* (1983). Ignatieff began to write for a broader audience with *The needs of strangers* (1984), a meditation on individualism in Western states, and on the attempts to institutionalize mechanisms that respond to human needs. With *The Russian album* (1987), which won a Governor General's Award, he shot into prominence as a writer. It is an intensely personal look at Russian history of the last century through four generations of his own aristocratic family. Family members included Count Paul, an education minister to Czar Nicholas, who was saved from a Bolshevik execution by admiring students. The family escaped abroad, with some difficulty, to the home of an English nanny, and from there the Ignatieffs moved to Canada, where George eventually became an important diplomat associated particularly with Lester Pearson. It is a compelling and moving story that has considerable glamour as it traces a family's fall in one country and rise in another. The appeal of the book lies in the combination of facts and personalized history that is characteristic of Ignatieff's writing since then.

Ignatieff's forays into fiction have met with a mixed response. *Asya* (1991) describes the life of a Russian *émigrée*, Princess Anastasia Vladimirova Galitzine, an aristocrat who flees the revolution to Paris, where she is finally joined by her husband, a Red spy. A failed romance, it was vilified in Britain, though less harshly treated in Canada. *Scar tissue* (1993), the story of a man who watches his mother die of Alzheimer's disease, poses questions about sentience and the self. Now came accolades in Britain—it was nominated for the Booker Prize—but Canadian reviewers were uncomfortable with it, being unpersuaded that the novel could properly be called fiction, since Ignatieff's mother had died from the same disease. Ignatieff himself said that he wanted to write 'on the edge [of non-fiction]'.

Blood and belonging: journeys into the new nationalism (1993) accompanied a series of BBC documentaries examining various 'new' nationalisms in Yugoslavia, Quebec, Germany, and elsewhere. Here Ignatieff examines the tension between 'civic' nationalism, based on consensus, and 'ethnic nationalism', based on blood. The great strength in this collection of essays is the sense of Ignatieff's own anguish and outrage as a self-avowed liberal and cosmopolitan facing the violent and irrational 'call of the blood' of drunken young soldiers on the rampage. For this work Ignatieff won the Lionel Gelber Prize for writing on international relations, and the Gordon Montador Award for writing on contemporary social issues, both in 1994. ANTANAS SILEIKA

Incubation*, *L' (1965). This novel by Gérard BESSETTE is important in modern Quebec fiction for its exploration of the depths of the human psyche—symbolized by the labyrinthine basements of the library where the narrator, Legarde, works—and for its innovative, frequently imitated, style: the text is an implosive and introspective first-person narration in one long paragraph. Legarde strives to stay afloat in a world that continually threatens to drown him, and expresses despair at the degeneration of the relationships that surround him. Long, unpunctuated sentences record the stream of his ideas and emotions (in the spirit of Claude Simon's 'nouveau roman'). He accompanies his dissolute friend Gordon to Montreal where Gordon meets his former lover, Néa, after twenty years. They are both guilt-ridden for having wished the death of Néa's husband—a wish that was fulfilled. Néa longs for some 'overwhelming confrontation', a 'catastrophic event to restore her equilibrium and moral tranquility'. Because of Néa, Gordon's wife leaves him, but Néa, realizing that Gordon no longer cares for her, commits suicide. Néa is the novel's only passionate character: the men (including the repressed narrator) are rendered helpless by acute neurosis.

In *Mes romans et moi* (1970) Bessette suggested that serious emotional crises preceded the writing of this novel: 'With a great many distortions and changes, *L'incubation* recounts a drama that I have experienced, both in reality and in fantasy.' It won a Governor General's Award and was translated by Glen Shortliffe into English as *Incubation* (1967).

LOUIS LASNIER

'In Flanders fields'. See John MCCRAE.

Influence d'un livre, L' (Québec, 1837), the first French-Canadian novel, was written by Philippe-Ignace-François Aubert de Gaspé, son of Philippe-Joseph AUBERT DE GASPÉ. Born in Quebec City on 8 Apr. 1814, Aubert de Gaspé Jr took part of his classical secondary course at the Séminaire de Nicolet before becoming a stenographer and journalist. Imprisoned for a month in 1835 following an altercation with a member of Parliament, he avenged himself by planting a stinkpot in the vestibule of the legislative assembly. He was then obliged to take refuge in the family manor-house at Saint-Jean-Port-Joli, where he amused himself by reading fiction and composing a novel of his own, which was published by subscription in Sept. 1837. The young Aubert de Gaspé subsequently worked as a journalist in Halifax, where he died at 26 on 7 Mar. 1841.

L'influence d'un livre: roman historique is a pre-Romantic novel of mystery, adventure, and love. The title refers to a popular manual of superstitious recipes that encouraged Charles Amand, an eccentric amateur alchemist living on the shores of the St Lawrence River, to seek the philosopher's stone. One of his macabre experiments requires the use of a black hen stolen at the full moon; another involves a *main de gloire*, the dried arm of a hanged man, which Amand removes from the dissection room after the execution of a murderer. Duped by practical jokers and shipwrecked off Anticosti Island, Amand suffers one disappointment after another until, after five years' absence, he finds a modest treasure of five hundred dollars. The lover in the tale is an elegant young student, Saint-Céran, who becomes a doctor and wins the hand of Amand's daughter Amélie. At least one chapter of the novel (the legend of Rose Latulippe in Chapter V) appears to have been written by Aubert de Gaspé's father, who later composed *Les ANCIENS CANADIENS*.

Published just as the Rebellion of 1837 was beginning, *L'influence d'un livre* received little attention, although one 'letter to the editor' criticized its lack of realism. Aubert de Gaspé retorted that Amand was modelled on a person he had known, and historians have since shown that certain of the events and characters are based on reality: the murder actually took place at Saint-Jean-Port-Joli in Aug. 1829, and some of the secondary characters (the giant Capistrau, la mère Nolet) are drawn from persons known in the district.

Long after its author's death, the novel was reprinted in 1864 in one of the bonus volumes offered with *Le FOYER CANADIEN*, and was later distributed as a prize in schools. But Abbé Henri-Raymond CASGRAIN, considering it too daring for the conservative tastes of that period, had expurgated the text with the approval of Aubert de Gaspé's aged father: he changed the title to *Le chercheur de trésors*, removed references to 'dangerous' European authors, and bowdlerized the love passages. Reprinted in 1968 in a facsimile of this edition, Quebec's first novel is thus chiefly known in a version very different from that composed by its young author. The original unexpurgated text of the novel has, however, been published in an annotated facsimile edition by André Senécal (1984).

The best recent studies of Aubert de Gaspé Jr and his novel are by Luc LACOURCIÈRE, 'Aubert de Gaspé, fils, 1814-1841', *Les Cahiers des Dix* (no. 40, 1975), and Maurice Lemire, '*L'influence d'un livre*' in *Dictionnaire des oeuvres littéraires du Québec, I: des origines à 1900* (1978).

DAVID M. HAYNE

Innis, Harold Adams (1894-1952). Born on a farm near Otterville, Ontario, he was educated in Otterville and Woodstock and was a scholarship student in political science at McMaster University (then in Toronto). Upon graduating in 1916 he enlisted in the army, took part in the attack on Vimy Ridge in Apr. 1917, and was wounded in the leg a few months later. He received an M.A. from McMaster and a Ph.D. from the University of Chicago with a thesis that was published as *A history of the Canadian Pacific Railway* (1923). In Chicago he met and married Mary Quayle, who later became a writer and economic historian; they had four children. In 1920 he was appointed to the department of political economy in the University of Toronto, where he remained for the rest of his life.

Simultaneously involved in research, teaching, compilation, travel, and publication, Innis became the driving force behind the intellectual development of political economy specifically, and of social science generally, in the university and throughout Canada. He devised 'a philosophy of economic history applicable to new countries' that for Canada has come to be known as the 'staple approach': an analytical method that stresses the dominance of a succession of export commodities—or staples—in Canadian development; the subordination of other activities to the production of staples; the vulnerability of an economy that grows around staples in a dependent relation with centres of Western civilization; and the political repercussions that were a consequence of that vulnerability. *The fur trade in Canada: an introduction to Canadian economic history* (1930) is his best-known publication using this methodology, but he pursued the approach in numerous papers, essays, and editing tasks, and with a major study of Canada's earliest staple, *The cod fisheries: the history of an international economy* (1940).

Innis's disillusionment with the rising irrationality expressed in world events of the 1930s and 1940s, and with the inadequate scholarly approach to such complexities, led him to consider the study of empires. Aware that the severest difficulty with this undertaking was the scholar's problem with bias, he proceeded to address 'bias' by focusing on various empirical communications systems and analysing their impact on the nature and structure of society. Two important books emerged from this field of study: *Empire and communications* (1950) and *The bias of communication* (1951).

Though Innis was not a talented writer—he often overwhelms or confuses his readers with a sometimes cryptic prose that tends to be swamped with unnecessary detail—he was one of Canada's most prolific and influential authors. He transformed Canadians' awareness of the source and basis of their nationhood, and contributed—as no other Canadian scholar has—to the discussion of important philosophical questions dealing with the human condition and survival. His creative ideas have influenced a succession of Canadian scholars (including Donald CREIGHTON and Marshall McLUHAN) and a variety of disciplines in the social sciences.

After Innis's death Mary Quayle Innis edited his *Essays in Canadian economic history* (1956). See also Jane Ward, 'The published works of H.A. Innis', *Canadian Journal of Economics and Political Science* (May 1953) for a list of Innis's extensive publications; D.G. Creighton, *Harold Adams Innis: portrait of a scholar* (1957, 2nd edn 1978); the chapter on Innis in Carl BERGER, *The writing of Canadian history: aspects of Canadian historical writing: 1900-1970* (1976); Graeme Patterson, 'Harold Innis and the writing of history', *CANADIAN LITERATURE* 83 (Winter 1979); Sally F. Zerker, 'Transportation and communication in Innis' thought', in *Change and impact: Essays in Canadian social sciences* (Jerusalem, Magnes Press, 1994) edited by Sally F. Zerker; and *Staples, markets and cultural change* (1995) edited by Daniel Drache.

SALLY F. ZERKER

Inuit literature. See ABORIGINAL LITERATURE.

Ipellie, Alootook. See ABORIGINAL LITERATURE: INUIT LITERATURE 1982 TO 1996.

Irchan, Myroslaw. Pseudonym of Andrii Babiuk. See UKRAINIAN-CANADIAN LITERATURE.

Ireland, Ann. See NOVELS IN ENGLISH 1983 TO 1996: OTHER NOVELS: 2(a).

Irving, John. See FOREIGN WRITERS ON CANADA IN ENGLISH: 2.

Isham, James. See EXPLORATION LITERATURE IN ENGLISH: 2.

Italian-Canadian literature. The writing of Italians in Canada exists in English, French, and Italian, and constitutes an identifiable body of literature that reflects both the immigrant experience and a common Italian culture. In 1653 the Italian Jesuit missionary Francesco Bressani (1612-72) published *Breve Relatione*, the first Italian-language account of life in Canada and the only part of the voluminous *JESUIT RELATIONS* that is not in French or Latin. In the 1800s there were a number of books by Italians who lived briefly in Canada. The most notable writer of this early period was Liborio Lattoni (1874-1958), who lived in Montreal and published dozens of his Italian poems and essays in Italian papers in New York, Montreal, and Toronto. Though widely read, his work was never collected into a book; but Watson KIRKCONNELL included English versions of three of Lattoni's poems in the anthology *Canadian overtones* (1935). In Toronto, First World War veteran Francesco M. Gualtieri (1898-?), who published several books of poetry in English, wrote *We Italians: a study in Italian immigration in Canada* (1928), which was one of the first examinations of the integration of newcomers in Canada. The most productive writer of the inter-war period was Mario Duliani (1885-1964), a journalist with *La Presse*, Montreal, who published plays and books of humour in French, ten in all, and translated Pirandello for Quebec theatre. He combined history, fiction, and journalism in his most important work, *La ville sans femmes* (1945), the only account of an internment-camp experience in Petawawa, Ontario, which he shared with 500 other Italians during the Second World War. (They were all arrested when Italy declared war on Great Britain in 1940.) In 1946 he produced an Italian version, *Città senza donne*. There was a controversy over whether Duliani was a fascist or an anti-fascist, and this arose once more when the first English version was published, *The city without women* (1994), translated by Antonino Mazza. Poet and journalist Filippo Salvatore (b. 1948) has produced a book of interviews with thirteen witnesses of the Italian internment in Quebec, *Le fascisme et les Italiens à Montreal* (1995). One of these witnesses was journalist Antonio Spada (1901-90), a leading anti-fascist who wrote the first English social history of Italian-Canadians, *The Italians in Canada* (1969).

After the Second World War, immigration from Italy was high, and resulted in an increase in Italian-language newspapers. In 1953, poet Gianni Grohovaz (1926-88) helped to found Toronto's *Corriere Canadese*, which became the major Italian-language paper in Canada. Grohovaz was born in Fiume when it was part of Italy (it is now part of Slovenia). This physical and psychological displacement is reflected in his novel *Strada bianca* (1989). In keeping with his own hybridity, Grohovaz published several histories of Italian regional groups such as the Friulani, but two slim volumes of poetry were his major literary achievement: *Per ricordar le cose che ricordo* (1974) and *Parole, parole e granelli di sabbia* (1980).

While Grohovaz published all his books in Toronto, Italian writers in Montreal often had their work published in Italy. *Gli Italiani in Canada* (1956) by Guglielmo Vangelisti (1883-1959), the first history of its kind, was printed in Florence but distributed by a Montreal publisher for Italian readers in North America. The first Italian-Canadian woman novelist, Elena Randaccio (1921-88), published under pen-names and lived quietly in Montreal. Under the name Elena Albani her *Canada, mia seconda patria* (1958) was published in Bologna in a romance series by Edizioni Sirio. As E. MacRan she published *Diario di una emigrante* (Bologna, 1979), which is less melodramatic than her first novel and a more realistic narrative of the immigrant experience. Some Italian-language authors continue to publish their books in Canada, but more often they choose publishers in Italy for a wider readership. In Toronto Maria Ardizzi (b. 1931) has produced five Italian books, all printed in Canada and later distributed in Italy. Her first Italian novel, *Made in Italy* (1982), won an Ontario Arts Council prize and was translated into English by Anna Maria Castrilli. The English edition, with the same title (1982), had a wide readership and became a text in many Canadian-literature courses. The story of an old immigrant mother who recalls the many events in her life with little regret reminds one of Margaret LAURENCE's Hagar Shipley. Ardizzi's second novel, *Il sapore agro della mia terra* (1984), written in a more poetic style, is the story of a young immigrant woman torn between a man in Italy and one in Canada. Like Ardizzi's later novels, it has not been translated into English, though it has great appeal.

Italian-Canadian writers began to have an impact on mainstream literature after 1978 with the publication of four titles: *Roman candles: an anthology of poems by 17 Italo-Canadian poets* (1978) edited by Pier Giorgio DI CICCO, F.G. PACI's novel *The Italians* (1978), and the stage production in 1980 of Marco MICONE's play *Gens du silence* (1982), followed by Ardizzi's novel *Made in Italy*, both Italian and English versions. Contributing to this impact was a large group of younger, university-educated authors who participated for the first time in both the growth of Canadian literature in English and French and the consciousness of a new multiculturalism. At first poets outnumbered fiction writers and were recognized through awards and inclusion in major anthologies. Di Cicco's *The tough romance* (1979), Mary DI MICHELE's *Mimosa and other poems* (1981), Alexandre Amprimoz's (b. 1948) *Sur le damier des tombes* (1983), and Filippo Salvatore's *Tufo e gramigna* (1977) and his English version, *Suns of darkness* (1980), continued the multilingual tradition. A great diversity in themes and styles is evident in Romano Perticarini's (b. 1934) *Quelli della fionda* (1981), Len Gasparini's (b. 1941) *Breaking and entering* (1980), George Amabile's (b. 1936) *Presence of fire* (1982), Fulvio Caccia's (b. 1956) French poems, *Irpinia* (1983), Mary MELFI's (b. 1951) *A queen is holding a mummified cat* (1982), Pasquale Verdicchio's (b. 1954) *Moving landscape* (1985), and Dorina Michelutti's (b. 1952) *Loyalty to the hunt* (1986). This flowering of Italian-Canadian poetry coincided with the founding in Montreal in 1980 of GUERNICA EDITIONS by Antonio D'ALFONSO. It first published the last four authors above and English translations of Micone's French plays and Salvatore's poems among many other works. D'Alfonso and Fulvio Caccia edited *Quêtes: textes d'auteurs italo-québécois* (1983), a mixed-genre anthology in French that was a response to the Italian anthology edited by Tonino Caticchio (1930-84), *La poesia italiana nel Quebec* (1983). In Toronto, Caroline Di Giovanni edited the first English anthology, *Italian-Canadian voices* (1984), which was popular for a decade. In Vancouver C. Dino Minni (1942-89) edited an anthology of short stories in English, *Ricordi: things remembered* (1989), and helped to found, in 1986, the Association of Italian-Canadian Writers to unite these disparate authors across the country and publish a newsletter. *Ricordi* included the first stories by Nino RICCI and Fiorella De Luca Calce.

While lyric and narrative poetry captured particular moments in dislocation and problems of dual identity, it was fiction that gave a new reality to the Italian presence in Canada and told the stories for the first time. F.G. Paci followed *The Italians* with *Black Madonna* (1982), his most important work, and five more novels. C. Dino Minni's stories in *Other selves* (1985) continued the realist tradition of telling the stories of immigrants trying to live in two different worlds at once. Born in Trieste, Genni Donati Gunn writes stories and poems that use humour and irony to capture the difficult position of women trying to be artists. Her poems in *Mating in captivity* (1993) recall her Italian upbringing in Vancouver. Fiction by the once-voiceless Italian-Canadian woman is making a significant impact. In Edmonton Caterina EDWARDS wrote *The lion's mouth* (1982), the first novel of an Italian immigrant girl growing up on the Prairies. Reflecting her own life experiences, much of Edwards' fiction has split perspectives and settings between Canada and Italy. In Toronto the stories of Darlene Madott (b. 1952) in *Bottled roses* (1985) recall the Italian peasant tradition of story-telling. In a similar vein Marisa De Franceschi (b. 1946), of Windsor, Ontario, recreates the life changes of women in *Surface tension* (1994). A number of Italian women in Montreal have tried different narrative forms in order to capture various states of immigrant disorientation. Mary Melfi's *Infertility rites* (1991) is a protest novel with elements of the surreal; Fiorella De Luca Calce writes about street rebellion in *Toni* (1990); Mary di Michele uses romance and horror in *Under my skin* (1994); and *Une femme à la fenêtre* (Paris, 1988) by Bianca Zagolin (b. 1952) is built on poetic meditation.

While several books by men—Duliani, Grohovaz, D'Alfonso, Micone—are in part explanations of their lives, there are few examples of life-writing by women. The most remarkable is *Breaking the mould* (1995) by Penny Petrone (b. 1930), an informal portrait of growing up as the daughter of Italian immigrants in what was then Port Arthur (now Thunder Bay) in northern Ontario. Only F.G. Paci in *The Italians* is able to capture in fiction a similarly warm family life, in Sault Ste Marie. These narratives make clear the connection between life-writing and the history of immigration, family stories, and the half-forgotten history of communities. Authors have spoken for their communities through theatre: Micone's play *Addolorata* (1984), Edwards' *Homeground* (1990), and Vittorio Rossi's (b. 1961) *Scarpone* (1990).

The most remarkable quality of Italian-Canadian writing is the unbroken tradition of linguistic diversity among the different writers, and within the work of some authors. While he first wrote in Italian, Alexandre Amprimoz now publishes his poetry in French and English, *Changement de ton* (1981) and *Fragments of dreams* (1982), and his short stories in English, *Hard confessions* (1987). In Montreal Filippo Salvatore (b. 1948) moved from Italian to English and now works in French. His play *La fresque de Mussolini* (1985) challenges Québécois nationalist assumptions by drawing parallels with fascism. Marco Micone's French plays—*Gens du silence*, *Addolorata*, and *Déja l'agonie* (1988)—have been translated into English. Antonio D'Alfonso has expressed concern that his own use of different languages makes him master of none. His novel *Avril: ou l'anti-passion* (1990) was better received than the English version, *Fabrizio's passion* (1995). Lingual versatility extends into Italian regional languages, with Dore Michelut (formerly Michelutti) including poems and stories in the Friulan language in the anthology *A Furlan harvest* (1993), which she edited from Alberta. Toni Nardi's play *A modo suo* (1990) is in Calabrian, as is the verse of Antonio Corea. Bruno Ramirez (b. 1942) and Paul Tana (b. 1947) wrote the script for their award-winning Quebec film *La Sarrasine* (1992) in French, Italian, and Sicilian. The English translation, *Sarrasine*, by Robert Gray was published in 1996.

The Italian language itself has entered English writing in Canada both consciously and unconsciously. The poems of Di Cicco, Mazza, di Michele, and Michelut are seeded with many Italian words and expressions that make readers aware of another culture in an anglophone environment. By combining the two modes of expression these poets have developed individual voices. The unique power of this approach can be felt in the emotionally charged poetry of Gianna Patriarca (b. 1955), *Italian women and other tragedies* (1994), and in di Michele's *Stranger in you: selected poems and new* (1995). This linguistic interference is also evident in the fiction of Paci, Edwards, Minni, Melfi, Amprimoz, and Nino Ricci.

Rather than language, it is Italian folklore that emerges from the short stories of Darlene Madott and from *Drowning in darkness* (1993) by Peter Oliva (b. 1964), a novel about Italian coal miners in Alberta's Crow's Nest Pass. While much of the fiction by Italian-Canadian writers respects the conventions of realism, Oliva and Genni Donati Gunn experiment with magic realism, and Antonio D'Alfonso writes prose that verges on prose-poetry, a form more successful in French than in English. Marco Fraticelli (b. 1945) has devoted his writing to haiku poems, while Pasquale Verdicchio's poems seem studies in the Latinate qualities of the English language.

This body of work, as a whole, has been described as ethnic minority writing, marginalized from mainstream literatures. But with Nino Ricci's winning the 1990 Governor General Award for fiction with *Lives of the saints* and Fulvio Caccia's receiving the same prize in 1994 for his French-poetry collection *Aknos*, and with the rise to prominence of Linda HUTCHEON as a literary scholar, Italian-Canadian writers began to receive recognition and admiration. As a group, and as talented individuals, these authors have encouraged other ethnic minority writers, and have contributed to the perception of Canadian writing as a literature of cultural pluralism and linguistic diversity. This is demonstrated by two major anthologies: Linda Hutcheon and Marion Richmond, eds, *Other solitudes* (1990), and Smaro Kamboureli, ed., *Making a difference* (1996).

See Joseph Pivato, *Echo: essays on other literatures* (1994), and a special issue, 'Italian-Canadian connections', of *CANADIAN LITERATURE* (106, Fall 1985); Pivato, ed., *Contrasts: comparative essays on Italian-Canadian writing* (1985); C. Dino Minni and Anna Foschi Ciampolini, eds., *Writers in transition* (1990); and Francesco Loriggio, ed., *Social pluralism and literary history* (1996). JOSEPH PIVATO

Itwaru, Arnold. See CARIBBEAN-CANADIAN LITERATURE.

Iwaniuk, Waclaw (b. 1915). Born in Chelm in eastern Poland, he studied at the Free University of Warsaw and contributed prose and poetry to avant-garde literary periodicals. During the Second World War he enlisted with the Polish Mountain Brigade, was captured and imprisoned in Spain, escaped, and made his way to England, where he joined the British First Armoured Division and fought in Europe. After the war he studied at Cambridge University and in 1948 immigrated to Canada, becoming a citizen in 1953. He worked as a court-room translator in Toronto until retirement in 1978. His poems, essays, reviews, and short fiction have appeared in leading Polish-language *émigré* periodicals. With the collapse of Communism, his books were acceptable again and were published or republished to acclaim in Cracow, Lublin, and Warsaw. *Wiersze wybrane* (Selected poems) appeared in 1995, with gouaches by Kazimir Glaz.

Iwaniuk wrote close to two dozen Polish-language books between 1936 and 1997, most of them volumes of poetry. The earliest and latest books appeared in Poland; the ones in between were issued by *émigré* houses in London, Paris, Brussels, and Toronto. Two books were issued in English in the latter city. *Dark times: selected poems of Waclaw Iwaniuk* (1979), edited by John Robert COLOMBO with a foreword by Zbigniew Folejewski, offers poems translated by Vancouver translator Jagna Boraks and others. The stark poem 'Carthage' talks of Poland ('A strange land / a sad land / this dark foyer / to Asia'); Canada is the subject of the magnificent 'Elegy in a Toronto cemetery' ('I was not born here, / I was not bequeathed this parcel of land, / yet my voice quivers as I speak of it'). *Evenings on Lake Ontario: from my Canadian diary* (1981) consists of meditations written in English on the cycles of impersonal history and the continuity of private life in Toronto. One poem expresses the sense of ambivalence found in a city of defiant exile and personal renewal: 'Toronto became my many graveyards / and my painful redemption. / I have never danced to music I did not like.' Iwaniuk remains the leading poet of Polish exile, despite the fact that the exilic period has now passed into history. Poland is no longer the land that was pledged, and Canada is no longer the place of exile. In common with other writers of his generation from Central and Eastern Europe, Iwaniuk feels the need to contrast pre-war and post-war life.

The critic Maja E. Cybulska has noted that Iwaniuk 'brings a sense of constancy into the uncertainty of the human predicament' and that his poetry 'exemplifies a search for lasting values in the midst of raving confusion.' The poems are characterized by intellectual imagery, measured emotion, and ironic comment in free-verse forms.

JOHN ROBERT COLOMBO

J

Jacob, Fred. See NOVELS IN ENGLISH 1920 to 1940: 3.

Jacobs, Peter (Pahtahsega or He who comes shining, Ojibwa, 1805-90). Born near Rice Lake in Upper Canada, Jacobs was trained as a Methodist missionary by William Case, who was superintendent of Native missions and schools in Upper Canada. Jacobs worked among the tribes on Lake Superior, Rainy Lake, Norway House, and Fort Alexander (Manitoba) until he left for England in 1842 for his ordination. He returned to the Rainy River region in 1844-9, and in 1852 made a tour from Rice Lake to York Factory, recorded in *Journal of the Reverend Peter Jacobs, Indian Wesleyan missionary, from Rice Lake to the Hudson's Bay territory, and returning: commencing May, 1852: with a brief account of his life; and a short history of the Wesleyan mission to that country* (Toronto 1853; 2nd edn, Boston, 1853; 3rd edn, New York, 1858), which provides a valuable account of the mission field. A dynamic orator who drew large crowds wherever he spoke, Jacobs lectured in Canada, the United States, and England. A number of his letters written during his ministry appeared in the *Christian Guardian*, founded by Egerton Ryerson in 1829 as a weekly journal for the Weslyan Methodists. Jacobs died at the Rama Indian Reserve, near Orillia, Ontario. PENNY PETRONE

Jalna (1927). Mazo DE LA ROCHE's novel, though first submitted to the American branch of Macmillan, was also entered by the author in the $10,000 *Atlantic Monthly* prize competition for a first novel. *Jalna*'s victory in the highly publicized event (through the efforts, it has been suggested, of an editor who knew of her genteel poverty) led its publisher, Little Brown, to order an initial printing of 45,000 copies in October. By Christmas sales had approached 100,000. It initiated the series, which the author had not initially planned, that ended fifteen sequels later, a year before her death. During that time the novels had become international best-sellers (11 million copies by 1966). A stage dramatization, a film, and a radio series were created in de la Roche's lifetime. Since then, two television series have appeared, one of them originating in France.

Jalna is the name of a house and property located within the Toronto region in Clarkson, Ontario (a number of residences can claim to be its original). It is named after the Indian hill-station where the soldier Philip Whiteoak and his bride Adeline passed the early years of their marriage. As the novel opens, Adeline has been transformed into the peppery matriarch Gran, who rules a household consisting of her sons and their attachments, and a parrot who swears in Hindi. Among her offspring are Renny, her headstrong likeness who will reign after her death at the age of 100, and Finch, a troubled artist who most resembles his creator.

A series of sexual intrigues preoccupies this novel, and many others in the series. Here,

Renny falls in love with the American bride of his brother Eden, who, in turn, enjoys a fling with a neighbour's daughter, who later elopes with Piers, another Whiteoak brother. Such soap-opera formulas underlie the rest of the series. It is the house that remains central. Enduring, expandable, accommodating, it survives even when American materialism (embodied in the arrival of TV) undermines the foundations of the Whiteoaks' colonial culture. Old World graciousness, New World informality and drive, the unending tensions of family life—all these forces are reconciled within Jalna's magic walls. DENNIS DUFFY

Jameson, Anna. See Writing in ONTARIO: 1, and TRAVEL LITERATURE IN ENGLISH.

Janes, Percy (b. 1922). Born in St John's, Newfoundland, Percy Maxwell Janes moved in 1929 with his family to Corner Brook—where his father, Eli Janes, a blacksmith, had found work in the new pulp-and-paper mill—and passed his formative years in this frontier boom town. From 1938 to 1940 he attended Memorial University College, St John's, but at eighteen he left for Montreal and enlisted in the Canadian Navy, serving for nearly four years in the medical corps. He then enrolled in Victoria College, University of Toronto, and became acquainted with modern literature. Graduating in 1949, he worked as a tutor, principally at Grove School in Lakefield, Ontario, and as a carpenter. In the early 1960s he dedicated his life to writing. He has travelled widely, living for many years in England, and now lives and writes in Newfoundland.

Janes' first book was the self-published *So young and beautiful* (1958), a novel set in small-town Ontario. Though largely undistinguished, it suggests the stirrings of a real talent and the germs of ideas and characters that would emerge fully in *House of hate* (1970); one character, Newfie, is of particular interest as a prefiguring of Saul Stone in the later novel. In the mid-1960s, following the death of his father, Janes decided to write about the life of his family in Corner Brook, and the result was *House of hate*, a brilliant, obsessive, bleak novel about the corrosive effects of a cantankerous father, Saul Stone, upon his wife and children. Janes take us into the lives of Saul's children to show how each in turn was twisted and coarsened by the atmosphere of recrimination, suspicion, and violence that Saul created in his home. There is artfulness in the way Janes mostly avoids the monotonous repetition that seems inherent in such a structure. He rivets our attention upon domestic scenes of frightening rawness; analyses with brutal frankness, yet with some compassion, the motives of the central character; and accurately conveys Newfoundland habits of speech. We feel that we are on the delicate boundary between autobiography and fiction and are witnessing the rare phenomenon of a man telling the whole truth about himself, his family, and his society. The novel was reprinted in the NEW CANADIAN LIBRARY in 1976, with an introduction by Margaret LAURENCE.

Janes continued to write both fiction and poetry. *Light and dark: poems* (1980) contains poems on Newfoundland themes that reveal an alert, ironic sensibility affectionately bemused by what was happening in his native province, and more personal poems in which he broods over his craft and middle age. The poetry in *Roots of evil* (1985) is less successful. His subsequent works of fiction show a growing attachment to Newfoundland. *Newfoundlanders: short stories* (1981)—three more stories are added in *A collection of short stories* (1987)—is often lighthearted and whimsical, while the novel *Eastmall* (1982), a far less impressive work than *House of hate*, focuses on local concern over large-scale municipal development in St John's. *Requiem for a faith* (1984), and *Requiem for a faith II: the rebels and the renegades* (1984), and *No cage for conquerors* (1984) show a further falling off from *House of hate*; but *The picture on the wall* (1985)—which ends with a scene of unpunished, stomach-turning violence, the like of which is rarely found in literature—has in it something of the anger and grit of his best novel. Janes edited, with Harry Cuff, *Twelve Newfoundland short stories* (1982).

Janes' work is discussed in Joan Strong, *Acts of brief authority: a critical assessment of selected twentieth-century Newfoundland novels* (1994).

PATRICK O'FLAHERTY

Jarvis, William Henry Pope (1876-1944). Born in Summerside, Prince Edward Island, he was a journalist in western and central Canada and died in Canton, Ontario. His three volumes of fiction are of interest mainly for their re-creations of local colour. *The letters of a remittance man to his mother* (1908), set in Winnipeg and on Manitoba farms, sketches with comic hyperbole the practical education of a supercilious young Englishman. *Trails and tales in Cobalt* (1908) is a collection of anecdotes from western and northern mining camps drawn loosely together within the framework of a prospecting adventure in northern Ontario. *The great Gold Rush* (1913) follows a group of Klondike stampeders through the hardships of the wilderness and of dealing with corrupt officials and noble but inflexible Mounted Policemen. In the preface to *Trails and tales in Cobalt* Jarvis claims to have known the mining regions of British Columbia and to have spent five years prospecting and mining in Alaska and the Yukon. His tales are heavy with particulars of the principles and processes of prospecting, mining, and wilderness living that continually overcome his uncertain grasp of fictional form and technique.

DICK HARRISON

Jasmin, Claude (b. 1930). Born in Montreal, he studied at the Collège Grasset and the École des arts appliqués. He has been a ceramist, actor, art teacher and critic, a television designer at Radio-Canada, and director of the literary and art pages of the *Journal de Montréal.*

Jasmin has published numerous novels, plays, collections of short stories for adults and children, and autobiographical sketches and journals. The novels—most of which are first-person narrations—reflect social hatred for the well-to-do and shame for the heroes' low social rank, as well as a strong degree of disgust for shallow intellectualism and pretension. Revolt and violence, some of it politically motivated, and revulsion against the absence or weakness of the father-figure, are other recurring features.

His first novel, *Et puis tout est silence . . .* in 1959, is based on his experiences as an *animateur de théâtre* for the Montreal Parks Department and contains reminiscences of the neighbourhood where he grew up—the multi-ethnic working-class area of north-east Montreal that reappears in many of his novels. *La corde au cou* (1960), which won the Prix du Cercle du Livre de France, is a violent novel about a schizophrenic who kills in order to achieve temporary liberation from a life of cultural and economic alienation. *Délivrez-nous du mal* (1961) deals with a homosexual relationship between the wealthy André Dastous and Georges Langis, a translator of modest origins. Jasmin's best-known, and perhaps most successful, novel is *Ethel et le terroriste* (1964)—translated by David Walker as *Ethel and the terrorist* (1965)—based on the first fatal FLQ incident in Apr. 1963. *Pleure pas, Germaine!* (1965), also partly concerned with terrorist activity, is a *JOUAL* novel in which the narrator and his family try to retrace their origins on a long auto trip through Quebec to the mother's native Gaspé.

After nine years in which Jasmin wrote no fiction, he published *Revoir Ethel* (1976), *Le loup de Brunswick City* (1976), and *La sablière* (1979), the latter winning the Prix France-Canada. The first novel—a kind of sequel to *Ethel et le terroriste*—concerns Germain (formerly Paul), who now rejects urban guerilla warfare and is drawn, against his will, into a plot to explode a bomb over Montreal's Olympic Stadium. A largely unbelievable story, it is awkwardly narrated by an impersonal, omniscient 'on'—in contrast to the palpable first-person narration of *Ethel et le terroriste.* Similarly handicapped and even less credible is the protagonist of the short novel *Le loup de Brunswick City*, which is allegedly based on the true experience of Louis Laberge, who wanders off in the Maine forest at the age of two and becomes a wolf-boy. Ten years later he and his pack frighten villagers before he is united with his parents. *La sablière* is a fine, often very moving novel. The narrator, Clovis Jhie (assonant with 'Claude J.' in French), is an imaginative sixteen-year-old whose fabulous play-acting with his younger autistic brother, Mario, cures the boy's stammer. The stammer returns, however, when the father decides to send Mario to an orphanage. Clovis manages his brother's escape from the institution—to which the child has set fire—and a kindly Cistercian monk invites Mario to live and work on the Order's communal farm.

In 1982 Jasmin published two interesting novels, though not among his best. *L'armoire de Pantagruel* is reminiscent of *La corde au cou* and *Ethel et le terroriste* in its treatment of violent crime resulting from sordid social conditions, and in its anti-intellectual tone. There is some successful play of rhythm and poetic prose and a multi-faceted use of the symbol of the title's *armoire*. But this melodramatic tale of multiple murders stretches credibility. *Maman-Paris, Maman-la-France* (1982) is about Clément Jobin (cf. Clovis Jhie), a ceramics designer, and his wife, Rachel, a publicist and amateur photographer, who take their first trip to France, where she participates in the finals of a picture contest. In diary entries Jobin waxes lyrical—but not without a certain amount of irony and satire—on the richness of continental French speech and clarity and on the ancient civilization of the 'mother' country.

Most of the ten stories in the collection *Les coeurs empaillés* (1967) are about women who hope for affection, happiness, gratitude, or social involvement and are cruelly and sadly disappointed. The stories, of uneven quality, feature surprise endings (often of gratuitous violence or suicide), the tactile presence of Montreal and its popular speech, and satire of the media, intellectual artificiality, and bourgeois 'charity'.

Three of Jasmin's plays for radio, television, and the stage have been published. *Blues pour un homme averti* (1964) portrays a sordid alcoholic, raised in an orphanage, who has never ceased to search for his father. Caught in a web of crime, he mistakes a police-inspector, pursuing him for murder, for his father. *Tuez le veau gras* (1970), whose theme is moral surrender in a labour setting, is set in a small lumbering town in the Duplessis era. The father-son conflict is again central, but the play is melodramatic, with weak characterization and artificial dialogue. Similar problems beset *C'est toujours la même histoire* (1972), which deals with a drug-free youth centre in the Laurentians organized by an American draft resister.

One of Jasmin's most convincing pieces of writing is *Rimbaud, mon beau salaud!* (1969), an imaginary dialogue between Jasmin and the French poet, which offers striking childhood reminiscences and evocations of the past, present, and future of Quebec and its people that are marked by an optimistic view of self-determination. *L'Outaragasipi* (1971), a saga of the settlers of the Portage-Assomption area of Quebec, is a thin work that fails to achieve its aim of linking history with actuality.

The title of the first of a three-part series of autobiographical sketches, *La petite patrie* (1972)—referring to Jasmin's early childhood in the Villeray district of Montreal—became a catch-phrase in Quebec, as well as the title of a 75-part TV series begun in 1974; this book had seven reprintings in seven years. The second volume, *Pointe-Calumet boogie-woogie* (1973), concerns the years 1940-6; the third, *Sainte-Adèle-la-vaisselle* (1974), leaps into 1951 and relates the events of a ten-month period. The three works develop the stages of the youth's adolescence. More recently Jasmin has published two collections of non-fiction commentaries. *Feu à volonté* (1976) reveals aspects of the author's involvement in reform politics in Montreal. The best pieces are useful documents of Quebec's socio-cultural history, though Jasmin is sometimes a simplistic and irrational polemicist. *Feu sur la télévision* (1977) advocates more public recognition for Quebec's creative writers, and increased telecasting of Quebec drama.

In 1981 Jasmin received the Prix Duvernay for the corpus of his work. During the 1980s Jasmin published four detective novels centred on Inspector Charles Asselin: *Le crucifié du sommet blue* (1984), *Des cons qui s'adorent* (1985), *Une duchesse à Ogunquit* (1985), and *Safari au centre-ville* (1987), thus achieving a shift in point of view from his earlier works dealing with crime. Another novel, *Le gamin* (1990), is the story of a mistaken child kidnapping that echoes *Ethel et le terroriste*, and especially *Revoir Ethel*.

Jasmin has also produced non-fiction books dealing with aspects of his personal history. *Deux mâts, une galère* (1983) is a dialogue with his father that reveals autobiographical elements of some of his fiction. *Pour tout vous dire* (1988) and *Pour ne rien vous cacher* (1989) constitute a two-volume journal, while *Un été trop court* (1995) is a more concentrated memoir.

For a critical evaluation of Jasmin's novels, see Gilles MARCOTTE's 'L'aventure romanesque de Claude Jasmin' in *Littérature canadienne-française, conférences J.-A. de Sève* (1969). A socio-critical evaluation is given in B.-Z. Shek's *Social realism in the French-Canadian novel* (1977), and a psychoanalytical interpretation by Jacques Cotnam in *Violence in the Canadian novel since 1960* (1981), edited by V. Harger-Grinling and Terry Goldie. See also Mireille Trudeau, *Dossiers de documentation sur la littérature canadienne-française, 9: Claude Jasmin* (1973).

See also DRAMA IN FRENCH 1948 TO 1981: 3 and NOVELS IN FRENCH 1960 TO 1982: 1, 3.

BEN-Z. SHEK

Javor, Pavel. See George SKVOR.

Jeanneret, Marsh (1917-90). Born in Toronto, he graduated from the University of Toronto in 1938 and entered publishing as a traveller in textbooks for Copp Clark Co. Ltd, rising to a senior position before joining the UNIVERSITY OF TORONTO PRESS in 1953 as its director. During the next twenty-four years, until his retirement from that position, he built the Press from modest stature to its present status as one of the largest and most respected university presses in North America. Jeanneret was the first Canadian elected president of the Association of American University Presses (1970) and was founding president of both the bilingual Association of Canadian University Presses (1972) and the International Association of Scholarly Publishers (1976). His impact on Canadian publishing extended well beyond the academic field. He served as president of the Canadian Copyright Institute (1965-7), and of the Canadian Book Publishers' Council (1968), bringing to these offices characteristic concentration, energy, and imagination. In 1970 he was appointed one of three members (and the only publisher) of the Ontario Royal Commission on Book Publishing, and was the principal author of its final report, *Canadian publishers and Canadian publishing* (1973), which offered broad recommendations to encourage Canadian publishing in its English-language centre. Jeanneret was the author of three high-school history texts—*Story of Canada* (1947), *Notre histoire* (1949), and *Canada in North America* (1961)—as well as of numerous articles on publishing and education. In 1989 he published his memoirs, *God and Mammon*.

As head of the University of Toronto Press, Jeanneret stressed the importance of international distribution and international standards in this country's scholarly publishing, and under his leadership the Press pioneered Canadian participation at the Frankfurt International Book Fair and opened its own offices in Buffalo, New York, and London, England. He also frequently stressed the importance of university publishing to Canadian self-understanding. To this end he encouraged the development of university presses, publishing in both official languages, on campuses other than his own. IAN MONTAGNES

Jean Rivard. Antoine GÉRIN-LAJOIE's *Jean Rivard: le défricheur* (Montréal, 1874), with its sequel *Jean Rivard: économiste* (Montréal, 1876), together comprise one of the foremost novels of nineteenth-century French Canada. The critical consensus on that point is due not to the work's innate literary merits but rather to the thematic influence it almost immediately exerted on socio-economic policy, and on the prose fiction that espoused that policy for two generations after its author's death. *Jean Rivard* was Gérin-Lajoie's first and only excursion into the novel, for he was primarily a social historian by background and inclination. It was conceived as a means of arresting and redirecting the immigration of rural Québécois to the U.S. Excluded from their traditional life, as land in the established parishes was all allotted, they were drawn there increasingly by the possibility of jobs in American industry. The two novels advocate, in exemplary fashion, a rural rebirth of the nation based on the land-based economics of the previous century in France.

In *Jean Rivard: le défricheur* the twenty-year-old hero, still in college, is faced with a crucial decision on his father's sudden death: should he continue his studies, entering one of the three careers to which they then led—medicine, the Church, or the law—or should he attempt to work one of the small over-crowded farms in the old parishes, shrunken now by years of subdivision? He decides against both, opting instead for the rude life of the pioneering farmer in an unsettled area of the province. Despite discouragements, taunts, and fearful challenges, he creates fertile land and bounteous harvests from the wilderness, building his own home in which his childhood sweetheart will join him. Two years later, in *Jean Rivard: économiste*, the untamed forest has become a prosperous village known as 'Rivardville', of which he is elected mayor. Rivard's pioneering zeal is now turned towards its welfare, and he constructs for it a social policy based upon the simpler views of the preceding century, according to which only the farmer is considered truly productive, a creator of wealth: all others are, in effect, parasites and must therefore be subordinate to the agricultural class. Jean Rivard's signal success in putting this theory into operation attracts much attention and he is elected to the legislature. But Rivard soon resigns—to return, as the principles of the novel demand, to the simple farming life that alone is healthy, productive, and godlike. One's garden must be cultivated with reverence, for that is the most natural and liberating task a person can perform.

The text of both novels is homespun, unembellished, and at times arid, exhibiting some of the worst qualities of the *roman à thèse* in its didacticism, its moralizing tone, the simplification of character and plot, and in the utter predictability of its hero's success in all his undertakings. But Gérin-Lajoie had no illusions about its literary worth, insisting from the beginning that he was not setting out to create a novel in any traditional sense but to portray in realistic terms what could be done to improve social conditions for his countrymen. These novels, however, had a far-reaching effect on French-Canadian literature, as the rural novel that would dominate it for so long owed much of its proselytizing zeal to *Jean Rivard*.

See M. Lemire's unpublished thesis, '*Jean Rivard* d'Antoine Gérin-Lajoie: Un plan de conquête économique' (Laval, 1962), the principal points of which are reproduced in *Dictionnaire des oeuvres littéraires du Québec* vol. I (1978). *Jean Rivard* is also discussed in every standard critical work on the literature of French Canada, especially in *Le roman de la terre au Québec* (1974) by M.M. Servais-Maquoi. See also Robert Major, *Jean Rivard ou l'art de réussir* (1991). L.E. DOUCETTE

Jenness, Diamond. See ABORIGINAL LEGENDS AND TALES: BIBLIOGRAPHY.

Jesuit Relations. This is the collective name given to a series of reports sent from Quebec to the Provincial Father of the Society of Jesus in Paris and signed by the Quebec Superior. The first collective edition (Québec, 1858) was superseded by the scholarly work of Reuben Gold Thwaites, who added to these *Relations* a mass of personal letters, memoirs, journals, and other documents. His monumental edition, the 73 volumes of *The Jesuit Relations and allied documents; travels and exploration of the Jesuit missionaries, in New France 1610-1791*, heavily annotated and with page-for-page translation, was published in Cleveland from 1896 to 1901 in an edition of 750 sets. Combining a wealth of minutiae about life in New France, and the customs of the native population, with dramatic narratives of travel, exploration, and adventure, and written by educated Europeans, these materials have provided rich source material for historians, geographers, philologists, and ethnologists—as well as for writers of creative literature. The Thwaites edition can be broken down into four fairly distinct categories:

I. The main series of *Relations* begun in 1632 by Paul Le Jeune and uniformly published in Paris by Sébastien Cramoisy and family until 1673. Notable topics here are the development of the Huron missions, and Iroquois warfare on the St Lawrence and in Huronia.

II. Earlier letters and reports by Pierre Biard from Port-Royal, and by Charles Lalemant from Kebec, dated between 1611 and 1629; some of these were published by *Mercure françois*.

III. Journals, letters, draft reports (not only in French but also in Latin and Italian), and personal and business correspondence extending as far as 1791. This category includes the *Journal des Jésuites* (the Quebec Superior's daily record of noteworthy events, management of Jesuit affairs, and observations on the colony and its public figures, 1645 to 1668). The *Journal* and the reports sent to Quebec were used in preparation of the annual *Relations*, so there is considerable duplication of material.

IV. Letters from more widespread posts in North America, giving accounts of priests, travels, mission activities, and Native populations to 1763, when the Society of Jesus was suppressed.

Assignment of authorship can seldom be definitive. The Quebec Superiors who signed the *Relations* usually had only the last hand on the copy before it went to Paris. Even when signatures appear on sections sent in to these author-editors, the exact degree of authorship is not self-evident: any of the 320 Jesuit missionaries who went to New France and Louisiana (listed in Thwaites, vol. 71) could have contributed at some time.

The best sustained passages of the *Relations* are in the central early reports (Thwaites, vols 5 to 35), from Paul Le Jeune's in 1632 to Paul Ragueneau's in 1650. Le Jeune lands at Quebec on 5 July, and after two months of domestic administration records a curious decision: the major victories for God are to take place elsewhere. While all *sauvages* are eager to be rescued from their misery, the stable Huron population, in a fertile area east of Georgian Bay (southern Ontario), offers the best chance of conversion. Hereafter the Huron missions occupy an increasing portion of the annual *Relations* until, in 1650, Ragueneau writes of the destruction in 1649 of Saint-Marie (near Midland, Ontario), where he had been superior for four years, struggling against odds and witnessing the martyrdom of his brethren. From Le Jeune to Ragueneau—via Fathers Brébeuf, Jérôme Lalemant, Garnier, Vimont, Chaumont, Lemercier, and Dablon, among others—the heroic rhetoric of conversion is mixed with the determined application of spiritual exercises. One modern critic has described this series of the *Relations*—with its exotic characters, grotesque details, and miraculous events—as a baroque drama with, at its centre, paradox and inversion of values.

The *Relations* can also be read as a record of day-to-day happenings, ranging from minute episodes to personal accounts of major events in the colony, all narrated with elegance and charm. One remembers Le Jeune's visit to a Montaignais cabin; his description of *sagamité*, the staple food; the ceremonial arrivals at Quebec of the colony's chief officers; the gatherings of Native councils for peace negotiations; the numerous descriptions of religious institutions at Quebec, such as the hospital and the Ursuline seminary; the daily routines and spiritual discipline of the Jesuits themselves; and the many accounts of Amerindian life, with emphasis on an edifying and exaggerated portrayal of the Native response to the Christian message.

Among many other memorable episodes in the *Relations* are Father Biard's account of Acadia (vol. 3), which is logically organized in chapters dealing with different aspects of the land, Native life, disputes in the embryonic colony, travel, and policy recommendations; although a personal touch is maintained and some striking characters, such as Membertou, are introduced, the aim is more scientific than conversational. Other authors of special interest are Fathers Lamberville and Cauchetière, who wrote about Kateri Tekakwitha (vol. 42); Father Jacques Marquette, who descended the Mississippi with Louis Jolliet in 1673 (vol. 59); and Father Joseph-François Lafitau, whose contribution to the myth of the *bon sauvage* is one of the major works of New France (vol. 47).

'Relation de voyage' is a standard phrase in French and is found in other writings on New France. What makes the *Jesuit Relations* original is their sustained and relatively standardized serial character. Each annual *Relation de ce qui s'est passé en la Nouvelle France* in the main series addresses the reader in a personal manner and gives an agreeable, often humorous, account of matters great and small in a curious, distant land. An official optimism sustains even the most discouraging accounts, as if to encourage the admiration and support of sponsors in France and maintain the good social tone of letters that might be read aloud in company.

The Thwaites edition is available in a 1959 reprint (New York: Pageant Book Co.); it should be supplemented by *Thwaites' Jesuit Relations: errata and addenda*, edited by Joseph P. Donnelly (Chicago, Loyola University Press, 1967). *The Jesuit Relations and allied documents* is also the title of abridged and selected editions by Edna Kenton (1954) and S.R. Mealing (CARLETON LIBRARY, 1963). Edna Kenton also published selections under the titles *Indians of North America* (1927) and *Black gown and Redskin* (1954). The *DICTIONARY OF CANADIAN BIOGRAPHY* contains authoritative articles on many of the writers in the series.

See also ABORIGINAL LITERATURE: 1.

JACK WARWICK

Jiles, Paulette (b. 1943). Born in Salem, Missouri, she grew up in the Ozarks and obtained a B.A. in Spanish literature from the University of Missouri. Jiles lived in the Canary Islands and North Africa before arriving in Canada in 1969. *Waterloo Express* (1973), her first collection of poetry, was succeeded by *Celestial navigation* (1984), winner of a Governor General's Award, and the vigorous *The Jesse James poems* (1988).

During the early 1970s, Jiles worked as a Toronto-based radio reporter and documentary-maker, then spent seven years as a media correspondent and consultant among the Cree and Ojibwa of northern Ontario, the latter experience vividly recounted in *North Spirit: travels among the Cree and Ojibway nations and their star maps* (1995). Her drama scripts for radio are adapted for print in *Song to the rising sun: a collection* (1989). Jiles has also written fiction, including a science-fiction novel, *The late great human road show* (1986), and the racy, more successful *Sitting in the club car drinking rum and Karma-Cola* (1986), published in the United States under its subtitle, *A manual of etiquette for ladies crossing Canada by train*. The non-fiction *Cousins* (1991)—part love story, part family saga—returns Jiles both to her Missouri roots and to her far-flung relatives. *Blackwater* (1988) represents a cross-section of prose and poetry. *Flying lessons: selected poems* (1995) draws from *Celestial navigation*, *The Jesse James poems*, and *Song to the rising sun*, and adds 'Ragtime', a suite of poems about Scott Joplin.

Especially in her poetry, Jiles' persona is partly that of a sardonic, streetwise pulp-fiction detective, partly a romantic drawn to violent events and oversized myths. Always, her darting imagination is yoked to shrewd observation. Jiles has lived for extended periods in southern Ontario and the Kootenays of British Columbia, and now resides in Texas.

FRASER SUTHERLAND

Joe, Rita (b. 1932). The youngest of seven children of Joseph and Annie (Googoo) Bernard, this Micmac poet and educator was born in Whycocomagh, Cape Breton Island. From the age of five, when her mother died, until she was twelve she lived with a series of foster parents. From 1944-8 she attended the Indian Residential School in Shubenacadie, Nova Scotia. In 1954 she married Frank Joe. She began writing in 1969 with a column, 'Here and There in Eskasoni', in the *Micmac News*. In 1974 she won the Nova Scotia Writer's Federation poetry competition with her collection 'The Valiant Race'. Four years later, *Poems of Rita Joe* (1978), a collection of twenty-six untitled poems, a few with Micmac translations, was published. Joe then went back to school, graduating with her Grade 12 certificate and a diploma in business education. She has made numerous personal appearances across Canada and parts of the United States, giving workshops, seminars, lectures, poetry readings, and radio/television interviews about her Micmac culture and heritage. Two more collections are *Song of Eskasoni: more poems of Rita Joe* (1988) and *Lnu and Indians we're called* (1991). Joe's poems range gracefully across many subjects from Native residential schools, battered women, the Ksan Dancers of British Columbia, to Donald

Marshall Jr, the Micmac who spent eleven years in prison for a crime he did not commit. Joe writes with spareness and dignity, gentle candour, and quiet humour as she protests past injustices and pleads for understanding and compassion for her people. Her poem 'When I was small' hangs in the Museum of Civilization, Hull, Quebec. In 1989 Joe was made a member of the Order of Canada and in 1993 she received an Honorary Doctor of Laws degree from Dalhousie University.

PENNY PETRONE

Johnson, Pauline (1861-1913). Born on the Six Nations Reserve near Brantford, Canada West (Ontario), she was the daughter of a Mohawk father and an English mother, Emily Susanna Howells (a relative of William Dean Howells). Her education was for the most part informal, but she very early became familiar with the poetry of Byron, Scott, Longfellow, Tennyson, and Keats. Her Native background was less influential than popular tradition would have it, although she knew the history of her father's family and listened as a child to tales and legends told by her grandfather.

Johnson's poems first appeared in the New York magazine *Gems of Poetry* in 1884, and thereafter in several British and North American magazines, including *The WEEK*. Two of her poems were included by W.D. LIGHTHALL in his anthology *Songs of the Great Dominion* (London, 1889), and they were praised by Theodore Watts-Dunton in his review of the book, creating Johnson's reputation as an authentic 'Indian' voice in poetry. This reputation was firmly established by her public readings, particularly after she adopted Native dress (which she wore when she recited Native poems; otherwise she wore evening dress). From 1892, until her retirement to Vancouver in 1909, Johnson was an extremely popular and compelling performer, touring not only Canada but parts of the United States; she also visited London, attracting favourable public attention there in 1894, and again in 1906. Johnson's abilities as a performer gave her poetry much of the high reputation it enjoyed during her lifetime.

Johnson's first volume of poems, *The white wampum* (London, 1895), was published by Bodley Head. Other volumes were *Canadian born* (1903) and *Flint and feather* (1912), misleadingly described as 'the complete poems'. After her retirement she produced *Legends of Vancouver* (1911), a collection of short pieces inspired by the tales and legends she heard from her friend Joe Capilano, a Squamish chief. *The Shagganappi* (1912) and *The moccasin maker* (1913) appeared posthumously: both are primarily collections of short sentimental and didactic fiction, including some previously published boys' adventure stories. *The moccasin maker* contains 'My mother', Johnson's fictionalized and romantic account of her parents' courtship and her own early years.

Today the bulk of Johnson's poetry appears derivative and shallow, echoing the styles and themes of Romantic and Victorian writers, and of such Canadian poets as Charles G.D. ROBERTS and Bliss CARMAN. The Native qualities of the verse were exaggerated, because Johnson used Native materials that for the most part lent themselves to conventional poetic expression. At times, however, she did speak for the Native in 'A cry from an Indian wife', 'The corn husker', and 'Silhouette', and she was influential in her use of Native legends. Johnson's attitude to her heritage was ambiguous. She insisted with pride and conviction on its importance—in 1886 she adopted the name 'Tekahionwake' (although not legally entitled to it), and she knew and resented the bigoted treatment that Native people often endured—yet she also wrote poems and stories that celebrated European culture, and often presented the Native in picturesque and conventional terms. Feeling the claims of both cultures, she never resolved them—a tension that occasionally found poetic expression, as in 'The idlers' and 'Re-voyage'.

Most books about Pauline Johnson deal with the legend rather than the woman. Walter McRaye's *Pauline Johnson and her friends* (1947) is in this category, but it offers insight into Johnson's career as an entertainer from a man who was for many years her performing partner. Of major importance are Norman Shrive's 'What happened to Pauline?' *CANADIAN LITERATURE* 13 (Summer 1962) and Pauline Loosely's 'Pauline Johnson' in *The clear spirit* (1966), edited by Mary Quayle Innis. Betty Keller's *Pauline* (1981) follows similar lines of interpretation in greater detail and with more documentation; her biography is also valuable for its inclusion of some of the uncollected and unpublished poems.

DAVID JACKEL

Johnston, Basil H. (b. 1929). An Ojibwa (Anishinaubae) born on the Parry Island Indian Reserve, Ontario, he received his early education at the Cape Croker Indian Reserve Public School. At the age of ten he entered the Spanish Indian Residential School in northern Ontario, graduating with his high-school diploma in 1950. In 1954 he received a

B.A. from Loyola College, Montreal, and in 1962 his secondary-school teaching certificate from the Ontario College of Education, going on to teach history at Earl Haig Collegiate, Toronto, from 1962 to 1969. He then joined the Department of Ethnology at the Royal Ontario Museum, Toronto, where he worked for twenty-five years. To reclaim and regenerate Anishinaubaek culture—its values, beliefs, customs, wisdom, and language—is Johnston's chief occupation. He has produced the most extensive Anishinaubaek language courses on tape and in print. Although Johnston writes in both English and Ojibwa, only his works in English have been published. Numerous short stories, essays, and articles have appeared in Native and mainstream newspapers, anthologies, and journals. The majority of his books—*Ojibway heritage* (1976), *How the birds got their colours* (1978), *Tales the elders told: Ojibway legends* (1981), *Ojibway ceremonies* (1982), *By canoe & moccasin* (1986), *Tales of the Anishinaubaek* (1993), *The Manitous: the spiritual world of the Ojibway* (1995)—record and enlarge the literary canon of the Anishinaubaek. His most popular book, *Moose meat and wild rice* (1978), a collection of twenty-two stories about reserve life, focuses on the humorous situations in Native-white relations. His ear for Native/English oral speech patterns and vocabulary is marvellously accurate, though enthusiasm can lead to excess—we are at times overpowered by the sheer surfeit of words. In his memoir *Indian school days* (1988) Johnston recalls his experiences as a young student during the 1940s at the Spanish Indian Residential School. Rather than attacking the government policy that regulated the Native residential school system, which was rooted in racism and ethnocentrism, Johnston writes with vigour and humour about the mischievous antics and amusing adventures of the students.

Johnston is a much sought-after speaker who has appeared publicly in both Canada and the United States. In 1967 he received the Centennial Medal in recognition of his work on behalf of his people. He was awarded the Order of Ontario in 1989; and in 1994 he received an Honorary Doctor of Laws degree from the University of Toronto. PENNY PETRONE

Johnston, George (b. 1913). George Benson Johnston was born in Hamilton, Ontario, and educated at the University of Toronto. After several years as a freelance writer in England, he joined the RCAF at the outbreak of the Second World War and served as a reconnaissance pilot in Africa. He returned to the University of Toronto for graduate studies and taught at Mount Allison University, Sackville, New Brunswick, from 1947 to 1949. He then joined the staff of Carleton College (later University) in Ottawa, where he became a popular teacher of Anglo-Saxon and Old Norse and an internationally known scholar of the Icelandic sagas. His work has been recognized by honorary degrees from several universities.

All of Johnston's poetry is informed by his intelligence, warm personality, sense of absurdity, and compassion, from the serious light verse of his early poems to the plain speech, austere forms, and sometimes complex rhythms of his later work. Although many of the poems in his first collection, *The cruising auk* (1959), were first published in journals, they seem to belong to a complete and self-sufficient world that unifies the book: a small city like Ottawa that has not yet acquired the anonymity of a huge metropolis is viewed as if through reflecting mirrors that distort and change perspectives. The central portion of the book depicts a dream world, a surrealistic landscape, with its own set of characters who are observed with affection and ironic amusement. The poems combine fantasy with direct simplicity, in the manner of James REANEY's rural fables, and comment on the desires and illusions of ordinary humanity. Their wit and satiric edge are sharpened by the apparently simple stanzaic forms, playful metres, and rhyme.

Home free (1966) includes several poems involving the same characters and displaying similar qualities of lively wit and fluent movement; but other poems—more directly colloquial in speech—experiment with varied rhythms and touch on personal experience or turn to social and political satire. Two long poems have public themes. 'Under the tree' is a passionate poem about the effects of capital punishment upon the hangman, the hanging judge, and the whole community involved in an execution. 'Love in high places', a narrative and reflective poem, concerns the transformation over two generations of love into an obsession with worldly success. Sharp in observation, often witty in expression, it has seemed to some readers to lack a central focus and a unifying emotional force.

Happy enough: poems 1935-1972 (1972) contains the two earlier collections and a number of new poems that show Johnston's delight in what language can do, even in its barest and simplest forms. Johnston adapts the rhythms and stress patterns of colloquial speech to verse in ways that show the influence of Anglo-Saxon and Norse modes. The new poems—lyrics or brief narratives about farm, sea, or rock-bound coast—move away from the urban atmosphere of his earlier work towards the elemental and primitive. However, many poems celebrate personal affection or reflect wryly and humorously on domestic occasions. *Taking a grip* (1979) shows many of the same characteristics of style and subject. Johnston has a gift for universalizing a small incident from everyday life. 'Taking a grip' suggests the need for maintaining some kind of order—in things as basic as drains and cesspit or in the whole threatened world—in the face of possible chaos. In several poems there is an elegiac quality, but Johnston's wit and humour are still evident, and there are festive celebrations of the coming together of family and friends. Most of the poems in *Ask again* (1984) were written for specific occasions, some public ('Convocation address', 'A celebration of Northrop FRYE'), others private ('Fred's sixty-fifth birthday', 'Remembering Betty'), most of them notable for employing unusual and intricate metres and verse-forms often derived from Johnston's study of early languages.

Auk redivivus: selected poems appeared in 1981, and *Endeared by dark: the collected poems* in 1990. The latter contains a group of new poems, as does *What is to come: selected and new poems* (1996)—all marked by Johnston's characteristic mixture of technical deftness with a relaxed, seemingly casual tone.

Johnston's translations from Old Norse include *The saga of Gisli* (1963), with its interpolated poems in complex patterns, *The Faroe Islanders' saga* (1975), and *The Greenlanders' saga* (1976). The last two have been revised and reprinted, with a new introduction and notes, as *Thrand of Gotu* (1994).

In recent years Johnston has also worked as a translator of modern poetry and fiction from a variety of Nordic languages. These include *Rocky shores: an anthology of Faroese poetry* (1981); *Wind over Romsdal* (1982) and *Bee-buzz, Salmon leap* (1988), both selections of poems in Nynorsk by Knut Odegard; *Pastor Bodvar's letter* (modern Icelandic, 1985), a short novel by Olafur Johann Sigurdsson; *Seeing and remembering* (Faroese, 1988), a bilingual selection of poems by Christian Matras; and *Barbara* (Danish, 1993), a novel by Jorgen-Frantz Jacobsen.

Johnston has written an engaging prose memoir of a friend, *Carl: portrait of a painter* (1986), devoted to the distinguished Canadian painter Carl Schaefer.

Articles about Johnston's poetry have appeared in *CANADIAN LITERATURE* by George Whalley (35, Winter 1968) and D.G. JONES (59, Winter 1974), and in *Canadian poetry* by W.J. Keith (31, Fall/Winter 1992). See also a special George Johnston issue of *The MALAHAT REVIEW* (78, March 1987). An illuminating discussion of his saga translations is contained in a review by George Clark of *Thrand of Gotu* in *University of Toronto Quarterly* 65 (Winter 1995/6).

JOHN MARGESON/W.J. KEITH

Johnston, Julie (b. 1941). Born in Smith's Falls, Ontario, she studied physiotherapy and occupational therapy at the University of Toronto, graduating in 1963, and worked as a physiotherapist until 1967, when the first of her four daughters was born. After moving to Peterborough, Ontario, in 1970, Johnston obtained an honours degree in English (1984) from Trent University. Using her knowledge of physiotherapy, she began writing a novel set in the Ottawa Valley in the 1946-7 period when polio was epidemic, and could kill or cripple healthy children in a matter of hours or days. This novel, *Hero of lesser causes* (1992), was published to acclaim, winning both the National IODE Book Award and a Governor General's Award. She made history by winning a second Governor General's Award with her second novel, *Adam and Eve and Pinch-me* (1994), a story about a Children's Aid ward who, angry and estranged, confides her thoughts to her computer. This book also won the CLA Young Adult Canadian Book Award and the Ruth Schwartz Award.

MARY HENLEY RUBIO

Johnston, Wayne. See NOVELS IN ENGLISH 1983 TO 1996: OTHER NOVELS: 2(b), 3.

Jonas, George (b. 1935). Born in Budapest, Hungary, he came to Canada in 1956. Since that time he has written poetry, fiction, and non-fiction; and produced and directed for radio and television in Toronto, where he is a producer with the Canadian Broadcasting Corporation.

Jonas's three volumes of poetry—*The absolute smile* (1967), *The happy hungry man* (1970), and *Cities* (1973)—revealed him as a student of modern man's bleak and lonely existence. An ironic wit offers the only relief from the monotonous vacuum depicted in his sparse and spare verse. In the first volume the protagonist leads an empty life in poems of unhappiness and alienation. Little levity or optimism appears in *The happy hungry man*, where the narrator's cynicism distances himself and his reader from the human scene.

Cities is a suite of poems that journeys from contemporary Toronto, the poet's adopted city, back through his urban haunts of New York, London, and Vienna to his Hungarian birthplace, Budapest. The autobiographical dimension underlines the prevailing self-absorption, which evokes not the world's great cities but the poet himself and his interests.

The undecorated style of Jonas's verse often borders on the prosaic, and it is no coincidence that he later turned almost completely to prose. He contributes articles and reviews to many Canadian and American magazines and writes regular columns for *Toronto Life* and *Canadian Lawyer*. With Barbara Amiel he wrote *By persons unknown: the strange death of Christine Demeter* (1977), an exhaustive prose account of the murder of a Toronto woman and the conviction of her wealthy Hungarian-born developer husband. Behind the facts is the authors' analysis of the social and ethnic backgrounds of the main characters and a scathing dissection of the complex legal processes involved in the trial. This work won the Edgar Allan Poe Award for Best Fact Crime Book. In *Final decree* (1982), Jonas's first novel, a Hungarian-born carpenter who lives in Toronto arrives home one day to find his wife and two children gone as his wife begins her search for personal fulfilment. Costly and inhumane legal machinations unfold once she files for divorce. The novel's compelling structure, weaving back and forth in time through the carpenter's mind, propels the plot relentlessly and naturally to a violent climax in which the hero, now the victim of a seemingly inexorable legal network, takes the law into his own hands.

Jonas has also written the librettos to two operas by Tibor Polgar: *The European lover* (1966) and *The glove* (1973). His play *Pushkin*, a dramatization in three acts of Pushkin's life and the conflict between Romanticism and idealism, was commissioned by Theatre Plus, Toronto, and produced in May, 1978.

Continuing to explore the world through his prose and poetry, Jonas released a collection of new and selected poems, *The east wind blows west* (1993), as well as two collections of selected essays and short journalistic pieces: *Crocodiles in the bathtub* (1987) and *Politically incorrect* (1991). He has also edited two volumes of *The scales of justice* (1983, 1986), collections of scripts recreating some of Canada's most famous criminal trials that were originally part of a CBC radio drama series with which Jonas was associated.

DAVID STAINES

Jones, Alice (1853-1933). The daughter of Lieutenant-Governor Alfred Gilpin Jones of Nova Scotia, she was born and educated in Halifax. In the 1880s and 1890s she travelled extensively to Europe, Egypt, Bermuda, and Jamaica, and contributed short fiction to the Halifax *Critic*, *Frank Leslie's Monthly*, and *The WEEK*. Her visits to Algeria, Brittany, Venice, London, and various European centres led to a series of travel essays in *The Week* in the 1890s, and later informed her short stories and novels with an intimate understanding of continental settings, customs, and social expectations.

While acting as her father's chatelaine in Government House at the turn of the century, Alice Jones turned to novel writing while continuing to contribute short fiction to journals like *The Canadian Magazine*. *The Night-Hawk: a romance of the 60's* (1901) appeared in New York under her sometime pseudonym 'Alix John' and is set in Paris, Halifax, and the Confederacy during the American Civil War. Incorporating a thinly disguised version of the famed 'Tallahassee' episode into its tale of blockade-running, it introduced the strong female figure common to all Jones' fiction. *Bubbles we buy* (1903)—reprinted in England as *Isobel Broderick* (1904)—developed a plot of international intrigue against a backdrop of Europe's fashionable society and Nova Scotia's age of sail. Successful in Britain as well as in North America, it resembled three subsequent novels—*Gabriel Praed's castle* (1904), *Marcus Holbeach's daughter* (1912), and *Flame of frost* (1914)—in counterpointing the shallowness of the international set against the vitality of Canada's less tradition-bound society. Like *Gabriel Praed's castle*, *Bubbles we buy* is also a story of young North American artists struggling to achieve recognition at the Salon in Paris. While both novels introduced strong 'new woman' figures into this environment, *Gabriel Praed's castle* expanded the international theme by exploring the vulnerability of a forthright Canadian businessman when confronted with European decadence and corruption.

In 1905 Jones moved to Menton, France, remaining there until her death. She continued to write on Canadian themes, developing, in the rugged Gaspé and wilderness settings of *Marcus Holbeach's daughter* and *Flame of frost* respectively, the strong relationship between environment and character that had entered her earlier work. Considered by *The Canadian Magazine* in 1903 to be potentially 'the leading woman novelist in Canada', she invites comparison with Sara

Jeannette DUNCAN in her emphasis on strong woman characters and in her treatment of international themes.

GWENDOLYN DAVIES

Jones, D.G. (b. 1929). Douglas Gordon Jones was born in Bancroft, Ontario, and educated at McGill University (B.A., 1952), and Queen's University (M.A., 1954). After teaching English literature at the Royal Military College (1954-5), Kingston, and the Ontario Agricultural College (1955-61), Guelph, he moved to Quebec and taught at Bishop's University (1961-3) before moving to the Université de Sherbrooke (1963-94). In 1969 he founded *Ellipse*, the only Canadian magazine in which poetry in English and French were reciprocally translated. As an anglophone teaching in a French-language university, and as an editor of a bilingual journal, he and his writings have reflected an openness to both English-Canadian and French-Canadian cultures. His translations of poems by Paul-Marie LAPOINTE, *The terror of the snows*, appeared in 1976; he edited *The march to love: selected poems by Gaston Miron* (1986), of which he translated the title suite and other poems; and was the translator of Normand de Bellefeuille's *Categorics, one, two, & three* (1992), which won a Governor General's Award for translation, and Émile Martel's *For orchestra and solo poet* (1996).

Jones first became known as a poet of unusual, if rather unfashionable, lyrical clarity and philosophic intensity. His first volume, *Frost on the sun* (1957), was followed by *The sun is axeman* (1961), *Phrases from Orpheus* (1967), *Under the thunder the flowers light up the earth* (1977), which won a Governor General's Award, and *A throw of particles: the new and selected poetry of D.G. Jones* (1983). As the title *Phrases from Orpheus* suggests, Jones has tended to see his larger, more embracing forms in mythological terms, though he has been saved from the amorphous vagueness of much mythopoeic poetry (for example, that of Charles G.D. ROBERTS) by an aesthetic precision, an economy of language, and a neo-imagistic sharpness of outline. The neo-imagism is perhaps most apparent in *Under the thunder the flowers light up the earth*, but the empathies of this book range more widely than those of the earlier volumes. The myths have not departed from the poet's vision, but they have changed their forms. The gods come this time in other guises, and often as painters, for two of the five sections of the book are devoted to poems inspired by David Milne and Alex Colville. Jones matches an appreciation of the lyrical qualities of these painters with a strong visual and 'painterly' element in his own verse. *Under the thunder* reflects the biculturalism of other aspects of the poet's life by including, along with the expected poems in English, others that are partly or wholly in French and one poem at least that is in a Caribbean patois. His later collections are *Balthazar and other poems* (1988), and *The floating garden* (1995), which includes five interesting suites of poems and a group of shorter poems that show Jones at his best, and most enjoyable.

A concern for the guiding myths of literature found a place not only in Jones' poems but in his single work of criticism, *Butterfly on rock: a study of themes and images in Canadian literature* (1970), in which he sees the dominant themes and images in the literature of Canada as emanations of the mythical and moral structure of our society when, at a critical changing point, it ceases to be the garrison society described by Northrop FRYE and enters into a dialogue with the natural world it had formerly rejected in fear.

See two essays on Jones in *CANADIAN LITERATURE*: E.D. Blodgett, 'The masks of D.G. Jones' (Issue 60, Spring 1974), and George BOWERING, 'Coming home to the world' (Issue 65, Summer 1975).

See also CRITICISM IN ENGLISH: 5(d).

GEORGE WOODCOCK

Jones, Peter (Kahkewaquonaby or Sacred Feathers, 1802-56). The son of Augustus Jones, a Welsh land surveyor, and Tuhbenahneequay, daughter of Mississauga Chief Waubanasay, he grew up among his mother's people on the northwestern shore of Lake Ontario where Hamilton now stands. When he was fourteen his father took him to his farm on the Grand River and he was sent to school. He was converted to Christianity at the age of twenty-one and nearly two years later began his missionary career as an itinerant Methodist preacher, converting his own Ojibwa band and other Ojibwa-speaking bands around Lakes Huron and Superior. So successful was his mission work that in 1833 Jones was ordained and became the first Native Methodist missionary in Canada. He preached at numerous missionary meetings in Ontario, Quebec, and the United States, where his Native and non-Native listeners were awed by his eloquence. He soon became the influential leader of a group of remarkable young Ojibwa—George COPWAY, George HENRY, Peter JACOBS, John Sunday, Allen Salt, and Henry Steinhauer—who were trained by the Wesleyan Methodist Missionary Society to become teachers, interpreters, and missionaries. Three times he visited Great Britain, where he spoke on behalf of the rapidly growing Canadian missions, delighting large audiences and fêted by royalty and distinguished men and women of the realm. In 1833, in New York, despite much opposition, he married Eliza Field, the accomplished daughter of a prominent London merchant. Jones was a prolific writer. Many of his sermons, speeches, and articles appeared in missionary publications, local newspapers, journals, and pamphlets in Great Britain and the United States. He is remembered principally for two remarkable books that were published after his death: *Life and journals of Kah-ke-wa-quo-na-by (Rev. Peter Jones) Wesleyan minister* (1860) and *History of the Ojebway Indians: with especial reference to their conversion to Christianity* (1861; rpr. 1970). Besides his writing in English, Jones' translations appear in *A collection of hymns for the use of Native Christians of the Iroquois. To which are added a few hymns in the Chippeway tongue* (1827), *Part of the Discipline of the Wesleyan Methodist Church in Canada* (1835), and *The first book of Moses called Genesis* (1835) translated into Ojibway. With his brother John, he translated into Ojibwa the *Gospels of St. Matthew* (1828) and *St. John* (1831). He also translated the *Gospel of Luke* into Mohawk and prepared a *Spelling book* (1828) and a small dictionary. *Additional hymns translated by the Rev. Peter Jones, Kah-ke-wa-quon-a-by, a short time before his death, for the spiritual benefit of his Indian brethren* (1861) was published posthumously.

Numerous letters, briefs, reports, and petitions to government officials survive that attest to Jones' unrelenting labours as spokesman on behalf of his people, as he tried to help them gain legal title to their land and to have their injustices redressed. He established a model agricultural settlement along the Credit River, where the Mississauga hunters became self-supporting Christian farmers. In his *History* he wrote: 'Oh, what an awful account at the day of judgment must the unprincipled white man give, who has been an agent of Satan in the extermination of the original proprietors of the American soil!' PENNY PETRONE

Joual. Literary *joual* came into prominence in Quebec in 1964 and was of major interest for about ten years. Before 1964 the word *joual* had been used pejoratively: its existence as a dialect pronunciation of *cheval* is well attested in rural Quebec, Normandy, and other parts of France. Claude-Henri GRIGNON and André Laurendeau had referred to it to denote not only a corrupt speech but the deprived culture that went with it. Émile CODERRE ('Jean Narrache') had developed in his poetry an orthographic and lexical style to record the resentment and frustration of the down-and-out Montrealer of the Depression years, admitting a certain sympathy and even sentimentality. Popular idioms peculiar to Canadian French had been used in other literary works but kept remote from the authorial voice. Jean-Paul Desbiens drew widespread attention to the use of *joual*, particularly in the lower-class districts of Montreal, in his *Les insolences du Frère Untel* (1960; translated by Miriam Chapin as *The impertinences of Brother Anonymous*, 1962), in which he regarded it as a disease like malnutrition. Gérald GODIN first applauded Desbiens's call for educational reform, but later criticized himself, and 'Frère Untel', for this haughty attitude (*PARTIS PRIS* II, 5 Jan. 1963). Desbiens also changed his position in later writing.

The year 1964 saw the publication of *Le cassé*, a novella by Jacques RENAUD, and in the following year a short novel, *Pleure pas, Germaine!*, by Claude JASMIN; in 1968 Michel TREMBLAY's *Les BELLES-SOEURS* (1968) was performed. For all three works the authors chose a literary form that could fully exploit the novelty of making uneducated speech the main medium of expression and standard French a marginal, usually comic, intrusion. The popularity of these works in *joual* had a major impact on Quebec letters. Marie-Claire BLAIS's *Un joualonais, sa joualonie* (1973) mocked the literary affectation of proletarian language, which by that time had become repetitious. Her bitter parody marked the beginning of the end of the literary use of *joual*, but its influence remains in a less-intensive cult of oral style.

We can distinguish certain common features of *joual* in literature, though their proportions differ considerably from one author to another: anglicisms and barely assimilated English words (frequent in Jasmin's novels, rare in the works of Tremblay); obscenities and picturesque blasphemies (intense in Renaud's novella); and non-standard syntax and orthography that often imply an erosion of basic grammar. The thematic correlatives are violence and alienation; murder, rape, abortion, perversion, and prostitution; the boredom of factory work and the hopelessness of the unemployed; unsupportive relations with family, friends, and sexual partners; lack of direction or positive awareness of social goals; and resentment, vituperation, and an inability to communicate—all are found, in different mixes, in *joual* works.

JACK WARWICK

Joudry, Patricia. See DRAMA IN ENGLISH 1953 TO 1981.

Journals of Susanna Moodie, The (1970). This sequence of poems by Margaret ATWOOD is one of the most important efforts to create a Canadian myth of the wilderness. Written at the end of the 1960s, when Canadian writers were preoccupied with the issues of cultural identity, it is based on the life of Susanna MOODIE, an English gentlewoman who immigrated in 1832 to Upper Canada (Ontario). The sequence is divided into three sections. Journal I describes Moodie's arrival in Canada, her voyage up the St Lawrence, past cities 'rotting with cholera', and her experiences during seven years of settlement in the Ontario bush. Her efforts as a pioneer failed, and Journal II records her escape to Belleville, Ont., where her husband had been made sheriff. Journal III describes Moodie as an old woman living in estrangement from the artificial civility of a Canadian Victorian town. In the last poems of the cycle she is resurrected as a spirit haunting the twentieth-century Canadian mind with accusations of its betrayal of its historical traditions. From the first poem ('Disembarking at Québec'), through 'The wereman', a poem about Moodie's husband, 'Departure from the bush', 'Death of a young son by drowning', the 'Dream' poems (which include 'The bush garden' and 'Brian the still-hunter'), and 'Thoughts from underground', this collection is one of the most memorable literary evocations of immigrant experience in modern Canadian literature.

Susanna Moodie provided Atwood with a Canadian archetype that enabled her to explore what was, in 1970, a cultural obsession with the moral and psychological problems of colonialism. As Atwood explained in her 'Afterword': 'We are all immigrants to this place even if we were born here: the country is too big for anyone to inhabit completely, and in the parts unknown to us we move in fear, exiles and invaders.' The Canadian psyche, Atwood felt, was schizophrenic, split by a deep ambivalence: while we preached ardent affection for Canada, we remained detached and critical observers. Through Moodie, Atwood revealed how this mentality was established in the process of colonization. With a fine perceptive irony she records the pathetically incongruous conjunction of a Victorian sensibility, and its world of porcelain civility, with a mysterious and hostile wilderness that made no accommodation to the human. In these poems Moodie becomes a heroic figure struggling to 'unlearn' old European codes of behaviour in order to speak a new language. At the end of the cycle she is the spirit of the land, accusing Canadians of erecting a garrison mentality: alienated in a world of concrete and glass, they remain ignorant of the wilderness that surrounds them.

See also *SURVIVAL: A THEMATIC GUIDE TO CANADIAN LITERATURE*.

ROSEMARY SULLIVAN

Juchereau de La Ferté, Jeanne-Françoise. See Writing in NEW FRANCE: 2.

K

Kalm, Peter. See TRAVEL LITERATURE IN ENGLISH.

Kamouraska (1970). Anne HÉBERT's most successful novel, *Kamouraska* skilfully combines two plots. The first—based on an actual murder-case in nineteenth-century Quebec—takes place during the Rebellion of the Patriotes in Lower Canada: in 1839 a young woman, Elisabeth, induces her American lover, Doctor Nelson, to kill her husband, a violent man who is seigneur of Kamouraska. Nelson accomplishes the dreadful deed, then flees to the USA. Elisabeth is arrested, imprisoned, and finally released. She assumes the obligatory mask of bourgeois respectability, marrying a Quebec City notary named Roland. The second plot, which reinterprets the first, is set some twenty years later. Elisabeth's second husband, gravely ill, is about to die. She will soon be free again, but what will she do with that freedom? Remain faithful to her honourable role of widow and mother, or try to rejoin her American lover? As she contemplates these choices she sees again, in the course of a single night of terrifying lucidity, all her violent past. Arriving at a dreadful realization of her sealed fate, she decides to cling to her false respectability. This devastating portrait of a woman in anguish, consumed by passion, is written in broken, telegraphic sentences that give the novel a breathlessly romantic style. It is also studded with details about the manners, dress, and customs of nineteenth-century Quebec.

A visually beautiful film directed by Claude Jutra, *Kamouraska* (1973), captures the dramatic subtleties of the novel, which was translated by Norman Shapiro (1973).

For historical background to the novel, see Sylvio Leblond, 'Le drame de Kamouraska d'après les documents de l'époque', *Cahiers des dix* 37 (1972). See also Delbert W. Russell, 'Uncovering the past: *Kamouraska*', *Anne Hébert* (1983). PIERRE H. LEMIEUX

Kane, Paul (1810-71). Born in Ireland, he came to York (Toronto) about 1819 (subsequently he claimed to have been born in York). He studied portrait painting as a young man, and lived and worked in Toronto, Cobourg, Detroit, and Mobile, Alabama. He toured Europe in 1841-2 and spent time in London in 1842-3, where he became a friend of George Catlin, who had lived and painted among forty-eight Amerindian tribes in the United States. Kane left London in 1843 determined to paint the Natives of Canada. His three-year western journey began from Toronto on 17 June 1845, and took him to Georgian Bay and thence, by way of a number of Hudson's Bay Company posts, to Fort Vancouver. From there he made sketching trips to Oregon, to the north-west region then known as New Caledonia, and to the southern part of Vancouver Island. Kane's best-known works are the 100 canvases he painted largely from sketches made during his travels; several hundred surviving sketches are important not only for their documentary value but also for their freshness and immediacy. Both sketches and canvases are an impressive artistic record of a way of life that was soon to disappear. Kane is also known as the author of *Wanderings of an artist among the Indians of North America . . .* (London, 1859), a classic of Canadian travel literature. Based on his diary—expanded with extracts from field logs, stories, and legends about the Natives he encountered—it provides extensive and careful information and description in a narrative that is free of the heavy embellishment that was characteristic of other Victorian writing. It was illustrated with reproductions of a number of Kane's sketches and paintings. The English-language edition sold out; French, Danish, and German editions appeared between 1860 and 1863; and a second English edition appeared in 1925.

See *Paul Kane's frontier: including 'Wanderings of an artist among the Indians of North America' by Paul Kane* (1971), edited with a catalogue raisonné by J. Russell Harper—a large, lavishly illustrated volume that contains a definitive biographical study by the late Dr Harper. KATHRYN HAMER

Kattan, Naim (b. 1928). Born in Bagdad, Iraq, of Jewish parents, he attended a Hebrew school, where he learned Arabic, French, and English in preparation for his studies in the law faculty of the University of Bagdad. Because of the unfavourable political climate he left Iraq at the end of the Second World War for Paris, where he studied literature at the Sorbonne before moving to Montreal in 1954. In Canada he has edited and written essays for a variety of political and literary journals, was the head of the literary section of the CANADA COUNCIL (1967-90), and in 1994 was appointed associate professor at the Université du Québec. He is an Officer of the Order of Canada.

The three worlds Kattan has lived in (the Middle East, Europe, and North America), and the cultures he has immersed himself in (Jewish, Arabic, French, and North American), inform his essays, novels, and short stories with an unusually wide range of perceptions, which he conveys with remarkable clarity. His first book of essays, *Le réel et le théâtral* (1970)—which won the Prix France-Canada in 1971 and was translated by Alan Brown in *Reality and theatre* (1972)—combines informal autobiography with formal speculation on the cultural, religious, and linguistic differences between the occidental and oriental ways of perceiving reality: the latter confronts reality directly, while the former resorts to theatrical mediation. In the tradition of the French structuralists, Kattan operates through a series of binary oppositions: the image and the unseen, object and shadow, groups and communities, actors and dictators, word and place. He repeated this method in subsequent volumes of essays—*La mémoire et la promesse* (1978), *Le repos et l'oubli* (1987), *Le père* (1990), *La réconciliation* (1993), and *Portraits d'un pays*

(1994)—as he continued to explore such dichotomies as occident and orient, Arabic and French, Jew and Arab, male and female, particular and universal, and memory and promise.

Some of these preoccupations even found their way into Kattan's autobiographical first novel *Adieu, Babylone* (1975), which appeared in an English translation by Sheila Fischman as *Farewell, Babylon* (1976). The nameless narrator recounts his childhood experiences in Bagdad during the Second World War, describing his family's fear of the Germans and the *Farhoud*, a pogrom-like attack by the Bedouins against the Jewish population. The narrator's sexual and literary apprenticeship is described with very little dialogue to interfere with the discursive narration. In *Les fruits arrachés* (1977)—*Paris interlude* (1979) in its English translation by Sheila Fischman—the protagonist Méir has a much smaller narrative role, as Kattan shifts to a more dramatic form where dialogue predominates. Having left Iraq, Méir studies literature at the Sorbonne at a time when France is recovering from the trauma of the Second World War. His alternating love affairs with a French, a Polish, and a Dutch lover symbolize the instability of post-war Europe. As in the first novel, the second ends with a departure—this time for North America, where Kattan's third novel, *La fiancée promise* (1983), is set. *La fortune du passager* (1989) and *Farida* (1991) traverse many urban centres, including Geneva, Paris, and Tel Aviv.

Kattan the short-story writer emerges with the proper balance of dialogue and narration in his collections of stories: *Dans le désert* (1974), *La traversée* (1976), *Le rivage* (1979), *Le sable de l'île* (1981), *La reprise* (1985), and *La distraction* (1994). Many of these stories focus on incomplete love affairs in which one of the lovers discovers the weakness of the other and must choose, by the end of the story, whether to depart or to renew the relationship. Settings are often bars, hotels, or airports, reflecting the transience of these liaisons, the fragility leading to departure. Some of Kattan's stories were translated into English by Judith Madley and Patricia Claxton and collected in *The neighbour and other stories* (NCL, 1982).

Kattan's short plays have been collected in *La discrétion, la neige, le trajet, les protagonistes* (1974). He has edited three volumes of literary criticism, *Écrivains des Amériques* (1976), covering contemporary fiction of the United States, English Canada, and South America; and he has also supervised the publications of Le Cercle juif de langue français, Montreal, editing and contributing to the two volumes of its Cahiers: *I. Les juifs et la communauté française* (1965), and *II. Juifs et Canadiens* (1976).

See Michael Greenstein, 'Invisible borders: Naim Kattan's internationalism', *Third solitudes* (1989). MICHAEL GREENSTEIN

Katz, Welwyn Wilton (b. 1948). Born in London, Ontario, she received a B.Sc. in mathematics (1969) from the University of Western Ontario and a Diploma in Education (1970) from Althouse Teachers College. She taught mathematics at South Secondary School, London, for seven years, turning to full-time writing in 1977.

Katz's first published novel for children, *The prophecy of Tau Ridoo* (1982), was her entrance into fantasy, a genre she would continue to develop in original ways, combining with the supernatural elements real-life issues such as moral choices, the effects of divorce on children, and male-female relationships. *Both Witchery Hill* (1984) and *Sun god, moon witch* (1986) are set in England and blend the fantasy of pagan magic with realistic adolescent dilemmas. *False face* (1987), set in Katz's hometown, is a story of a daughter of divorced parents who finds a dangerous set of Native False Face masks. It won the International Children's Fiction Award (1987) and the Max and Greta Ebel Memorial Award for Children's Writing (1988). *The third magic* (1988), a time fantasy using Arthurian material, won a Governor General's Award in 1988.

Whalesinger (1990), set on the California coast, explores adolescent emotions surrounding death and sexuality, as well as the thoughts of a mother whale with a sick calf. *Come like shadows* (1993), set in Stratford, Ontario, and in Scotland, aligns past with present, Scotland with Canada, as real witches from the past enter a production of Shakespeare's *Macbeth* that emphasizes Quebec, as well as Scottish, nationalism. *Time ghost* (1994), another time-shift story, is set in the future (and our present) through the agency of the 'timeless' location of the North Pole. In *Out of the dark* (1995), winner of a Ruth Schwartz Children's Book Award in 1996, a boy's fascination with Vikings helps him adjust to the death of his mother. With each book, Katz has enriched her style, further complicated her structure, and delved more deeply into character.

Some controversy has attached to Katz's works—over her appropriation of voice and revelation of Native ceremonies in *False face*, her evil and unpleasant mother figures, and her sometimes violent expressions of the darkness in the human psyche. She is, however, a talented writer whose books have value for young adults in not avoiding reality even while entering fantasy worlds. She won the Vicky Metcalf Award in 1994 for her body of work for young adults.

See Marianne Micros, 'When is a book not a book?: the novels of Welwyn Wilton Katz', *Canadian Children's Literature* 47 (1987); Jamie Vandermoer, 'Welwyn Wilton Katz', *The Writer, Canadian Author and Bookman* 65, no. 4 (Summer 1990); Adrienne Kertzer, 'Mad voices: the mothers of Welwyn Wilton Katz', *Canadian Children's Literature* 77, vol. 21:1 (Spring 1995). MARIANNE MICROS

Katzmann, Mary Jane (1828-90). Born in Preston, Nova Scotia, she showed exceptional intelligence at an early age, but because she was female she was not given the benefit of a formal education. In 1845 her poetry came to the attention of Joseph HOWE, who praised it in 'Nights with the muses', a series of articles on Nova Scotia writers in *The Novascotian*. In 1852, at the age of twenty-four, she became editor of a new literary magazine, the *PROVINCIAL* (Jan. 1852-Dec. 1853). As the foremost female editor of her time, she encouraged other women writers to project a humanistic vision of society through writing. She married William Lawson in 1869 and died of cancer in Halifax.

From 1848 to 1851 Katzmann published a large amount of verse in *The Guardian* (Halifax), and in the late fifties and sixties her verse appeared frequently in local newspapers. A collection, *Frankincense and myrrh* (Halifax, 1893), was published posthumously, as was her *History of the townships of Dartmouth, Preston, and Lawrencetown* (Halifax, 1893). As a poet Katzmann was prone to generalities, melodramatic effects, and dull religious and moral didacticism—characteristics that mark the verse of contemporary 'female poets' in Britain and the United States upon whom she patterned herself—but she was always technically competent, at her best when writing descriptive verse or charming song-like lyrics. TOM VINCENT

Kavanagh, Patrick. See NOVELS IN ENGLISH 1983 TO 1996: OTHER NOVELS: 1(a).

Kay, Guy Gavriel (b. 1954). Born in Weyburn, Saskatchewan, he grew up in Winnipeg, where he gained a B.A. (1975) in philosophy from the University of Manitoba. He also has an LL.B. degree (1978) from the University of Toronto. Best-known for his fantasy novels, which have achieved international acclaim, he has also worked as a producer and writer for the Canadian Broadcasting Corporation, writing for both radio and TV versions of the highly praised series 'The Scales of Justice'.

Kay first entered the world of high fantasy when he assisted Christopher Tolkien with the editorial construction of his father J.R.R. Tolkien's *The Silmarillion* (1977). Disagreeing with the son's decision to publish all of the elder Tolkien's writings, Kay turned his hand to writing his own trilogy, *The Fionavar tapestry*: the first volume, *The summer tree* (1984), was followed by *The wandering fire* (1986) and *The darkest road* (1986). This is a truly post-Tolkien fantasy that builds on, rather than simply copying, its great original; with its creation of a 'first' universe of Fionavar, from which all others depend, and with its adult approach to sexuality, it lifts fantasy to a new level of psychological complexity. As Neil Randall has pointed out, Kay developed a complex form of shifting focalization in *The Fionavar tapestry*, which has a more complicated narrative strategy than most fantasies.

Kay has said that one of his influences was the great historical novelist Dorothy Dunnett, and his three later novels reveal how much he learned from her. They are set on another world, in another universe, yet they carefully play off European history in fascinating ways, exploring human problems in a world lacking our exact religious and tribal affiliations. They also gradually rejected the usual 'magic' associated with fantasy. Kay improved on his method of deepening characterization throughout *Tigana* (1990), winner of the 1991 Aurora award for best Canadian fantasy; *A song for Arbonne* (1992); and *The lions of Al-Rassan* (1995). The first alludes to Renaissance Italy, the second to Troubadour-era France, and the third to the end of the multicultural experiment in Spain in the fourteenth century. By placing his stories in another world, Kay can interrogate questions of faith, philosophy, race, and culture—without necessarily offending readers' biases, As a result, he has enlarged the range of epic fantasy. His novels have been translated into twelve languages.

Neil Randall's 'Shifting focalization and the strategy of delay: the narrative weaving of *The Fionavar tapestry*', *CANADIAN LITERATURE* (Summer 1991), and Janeen Webb's 'Post-Romantic romance: Guy Gavriel Kay's *Tigana* and *A song for Arbonne*', *New York Review of Science Fiction* (January 1995) provide useful critical insights into Kay's work.

DOUGLAS BARBOUR

Kearns, Lionel (b. 1937). Lionel John Kearns was born and raised in the Kootenay region of British Columbia, where he was an enthusiastic student, musician, and athlete. Influenced by his father, C.F. Kearns, a former Great War flyer, outdoorsman, and short-story author, Kearns initiated his literary career in the mid-1950s by setting out on a life of travel and adventure that included playing hockey in Mexico. In the early 1960s, while studying at the University of British Columbia, Kearns became a close friend of George BOWERING, Frank DAVEY, and Fred WAH and contributed significantly to the development of their magazine *TISH*. Exposed to the ideas of both Marshall McLUHAN and the Russian Formalists, Kearns began an investigation of modern prosody that led to his proposal for 'stacked verse'—a page notation system for oral poetry that featured a 'stress axis' running vertically down the page through the most heavily accented syllable of each phrase of the poem. Kearns set out the theory of stacked verse in his M.A. thesis, and illustrated the notation in *Songs of circumstance*, published by TISHbooks in 1962 (republished in conventional notation by the RYERSON PRESS in 1967 as *Pointing*). These well-crafted poems, marked by irony and understated humour, were followed by *Listen, George* (1964), a free-flowing, long-line verse-letter recalling his youth, which Kearns wrote while studying structural and generative linguistics at the School of Oriental and African Studies, University of London. Active on the British poetry scene, Kearns came under the influence of the European concrete- and sound-poetry movements, creating the first version of his much-published mathematical mandela 'The birth of God'. Before leaving England for Trinidad, where he spent a year analysing West Indian English dialect, Kearns worked as a production assistant and bit actor in *The War Game*, Peter Watkins' controversial film about nuclear disaster.

In 1966 Kearns returned to Canada to take up a position in the English department at Simon Fraser University. *By the light of the silvery McLune: media parables, poems, signs, gestures, and other assaults on the interface* (1968) is a book of celebration and social protest rooted in the preoccupations of the 1960s. *Practicing up to be human* (1978) marked a return to the rhythmically crafted, intellectually intense poems of his early work. *Ignoring the bomb* (1982) is a collection of new and selected poems. In 1982-3 Kearns spent a year in Montreal as writer-in-residence at Concordia University. His finest work, *Convergences* (1984), is a book-length poem for voices that explores the impact of the arrival of Captain Cook's two ships on the Native people of Nootka Sound, British Columbia. It exemplifies Kearns' continuing fascination with the idea of *text* (context, subtext, hypertext) and his interest in West Coast history.

Since retiring from Simon Fraser in 1986 Kearns has become increasingly interested in the literary potential of digital media. He pioneered on-line education by teaching, from his home in Vancouver, a continent-wide graduate course, 'The Cybernetics of Poetry', for ConnecEd, the distance educational facility of the New School for Social Research, New York. In 1988 he became the first writer-in-electronic-residence, helping Trevor Owen establish an on-line creative writing program that has since flourished across Canada as the 'WIER' project.

See Lianne Moyes, 'Dialogizing the monologue of history and lyric: Lionel Kearns' *Convergences*', *OPEN LETTER* 7, 5 (Summer 1989), 15-27; and Manina Jones, 'Log entries: exploring discursive space in Lionel Kearns' *Convergences*', in Douglas BARBOUR, ed., *Beyond TISH* (1991). FRANK DAVEY

Keeshig-Tobias, Lenore (b. 1950). Born in Wiarton, Ontario, to Keitha (Johnston) and Donald Keeshig, the eldest of ten children, she is a member of the Chippewa of Nawash First Nation on the Bruce Peninsula. She attended elementary school on the Cape Croker Reserve and received her high-school education at Loretto Academy, Niagara Falls, and the Wiarton District High School. In 1983 she received a Bachelor of Fine Arts degree from York University. She has been a staff writer for *The Ontario Indian*, editor of *Sweetgrass*, and co-founder of *The Magazine to Re-establish the Trickster: New Native Writing*, as well as a founding member of the Committee to re-establish the trickster, and the founding chair for the Racial Minority Writers' Committee in the WRITERS' UNION OF CANADA.

In her poetry—which has appeared in journals and anthologies—Keeshig-Tobias tends to express herself with delicate simplicity, a gentle humour, and unpretentiousness. Much of it draws upon the realities of Native life and the mythological icons and symbols of her people. One of her favourite symbols is the trickster, considered by Canadian Aboriginal writers to be a symbol of cultural rebirth. In a long poem that is characterized by an untypical coarse virility of phrase and is divided into sixteen sections, entitled 'Trickster beyond 1992: our relationship' in *Indigena: contemporary Native perspectives* (1992), written to be performed, Tobias's narrative has a surprising twist, for it is the white man who is the trickster, from whom it is learned what *not* to do.

Keeshig-Tobias has written two bilingual (English/Ojibway) children's books illustrated by her daughter Polly: *Emma and the trees* (1996) and *Bird talk* (1991), which won the Living the Dream Book Award in 1993 for a children's book that best provides positive and authentic cultural images and dispels prejudice. (The award was sponsored by the Manhattan Country School and Public School 151 in New York, in commemoration of Martin Luther King Jr.) Keeshig-Tobias has also been instrumental in bringing the issue of cultural appropriation to public attention (causing much controversy in academic circles and the media). Strongly committed to the oral storytelling tradition, she has been untiring in encouraging First Nations writers to reclaim their own stories and myths. In her essay 'Not just entertainment' in *Through Indian eyes: the Native experience in books for children* (1992) edited by Beverly Slapin and Doris Seale, Keeshig-Tobias states that 'The issue is about culture theft, the theft of voice. It's about power.' PENNY PETRONE

Keith, Marian. Pseudonym of Mary Esther MACGREGOR.

Keith, W.J. See CRITICISM IN ENGLISH: 6(e), (g), (h), (l), (n).

Kelley, Thomas P. (1905-82). Born at Campbellford, Ontario, he travelled as a youngster with his father's medicine show, then boxed professionally in the United States. His career as a pulp writer began in 1937, when he sold the first of three fantasy adventure serials to *Weird Tales*. Using various pseudonyms, he filled many an issue of *Uncanny Tales*, the leading Canadian pulp magazine published during the Second World War. Thereafter he churned out some two-dozen paperback books, largely of the true-crime variety. *The Black Donnellys* (1954) and *Vengeance of the Black Donnellys* (1969)—his lurid accounts of the Irish blood feud and its aftermath, which took place in the 1880s in Lucan, Ontario—have sold hundreds of thousands of copies. *The fabulous Kelley* (1968; rev. 1974) is a surprisingly sensitive evocation of the life and times of his father, known as 'Doc Kelley, Canada's King of the Medicine Men'. A lively character, Thomas Kelley claimed to be 'king of the Canadian pulp writers' and 'the fastest author in the East'. He died in Toronto, leaving unpublished a fantasy-adventure novel set in A.D. 7109.

JOHN ROBERT COLOMBO

Kelly, M.T. (b. 1946). Born in Toronto, Milton Terrence Kelly was educated at Glendon College and the University of Toronto. He has lived in Edinburgh, Scotland; has been a high-school teacher in Levack, Ontario; a city-hall reporter in Moose Jaw, Saskatchewan; and a freelance writer and newspaper columnist in Toronto. Such experiences inform his fiction, three significant loci being the poor-white culture of Toronto's welfare-class neighbourhoods, Native peoples, and the North.

Constant in Kelly's fiction have been a Celtic lyricism (though in a progressively simpler style), a porousness to landscape and weather, and characters who are profoundly uncomfortable with each other. Women are ambivalent goddesses, deeply troubling to men, but also rendered with great empathy. In the title novella of *The more loving one* (1980), a collection of stories, the protagonist dabbles in psychodrama, shucks off his wife for a new woman, but finds that the latter can live only in his mind's eye. In such stories, sensations tell painful truths.

In Kelly's first novel, the often hilarious *I do remember the fall* (1977), the self-mocking Randy Gogarty moves towards a better understanding of himself amid vocational intrigues, poignant domestic politics, and low comedy in a small city called Elk Brain, Saskatchewan. His play *The green dolphin* (1982), and the stories in *The more loving one* and *Breath dances between them* (1991), return Kelly to Toronto.

The viewpoint Kelly adopts for settings outside Toronto is typically that of someone lost in alien physical and psychological terrain. For Michael Leary, the protagonist of *The ruined season* (1982), northern Ontario is 'the empty country of his imagination', an ominously enigmatic landscape. This unresolvable love and hate is reiterated in Kelly's poetry collection *Country you can't walk in* (1979).

Kelly's most popularly and critically acclaimed novel, *A dream like mine* (1987), which won a Governor General's Award and was filmed in 1989 as *Clearcut*, puts the outsider on a Native reserve in northwestern Ontario, bewildered by the violent retribution that followed a pulp mill's pollution, and by the even more confounding world of Native spirituality.

Readers who take the sparse plotting and rudimentary character development of *Out of the whirlwind* (1995) as flaws miss the point of this novel. Kelly uses the parable form to tell of an ill-fated canoe expedition of three Torontonians and a northern-Alberta teenager to depict claustrophic human conflict, and the otherness of nature, powerfully and poetically.

Kelly has also written a CBC screenplay, *Wildfire: the legend of Tom Longboat* (1983), and edited Walter Kenyon's *Arctic Argonauts* (1991).

FRASER SUTHERLAND

Kelsey, Henry. See EXPLORATION LITERATURE IN ENGLISH: 2.

Kennedy, Leo (b. 1907). Born in Liverpool, England, he moved with his family to Montreal in 1912. Though he had left school after repeating grade six, he was admitted to the Montreal campus of Laval (now the Université de Montréal), where he studied English for two years and became closely associated with F.R. SCOTT and A.J.M. SMITH of the *McGILL FORTNIGHTLY REVIEW* after they discovered Kennedy as the pseudonymous 'Helen Lawrence' in the lonely-hearts column of the Montreal *Star*. In 1928, with Scott, he founded and edited the short-lived *CANADIAN MERCURY*. In 1933 his only collection of poetry. *The shrouding*, was published by Macmillan at the urging of E.J. PRATT.

Kennedy was a modernist who sought to replace the sentimental romanticism of the 'Maple Leaf school' with objective craftsmanship. Under the influence of the metaphysical and mythic sensibilities of T.S. Eliot and Sir James Frazer, he wrote poems that sought salvation from the winter wasteland of death and oblivion by fusing Christian faith in the resurrection with the myth of renewal found in the order of nature: buried bones are like crocus bulbs awaiting the spring to sprout heavenward. By 1936, when his poems were included in the modernist anthology *NEW PROVINCES*, he was already turning his back on much of what he began, writing committed criticism of social realities for radical periodicals like *New Frontier*. Some of his socialist writings were published pseudonymously, for he was working throughout the 1930s for advertising agencies in Montreal, Toronto, and Detroit. In 1942 he moved to a Chicago agency and freelanced as a book reviewer for the Chicago *Sun*. He eventually settled in Norwalk, Connecticut, as a staff writer for *Reader's Digest*. In 1976 he returned to his literary friends in Montreal, living for ten years with his daughter-in-law, before retiring to a hotel in Pasadena, California.

The shrouding was reprinted in 1975 with an introduction by Leon EDEL, who described Kennedy as the sprightly leader of Canada's 'graveyard school' of metaphysical poetry. His short story 'A priest in the family', first published in *The CANADIAN FORUM* (April 1933), was reprinted in *Great stories of the world* (1972). For a selection of criticism by and about Kennedy, see *The McGill movement: A.J. M. Smith, F. R. Scott and Leo Kennedy* (1969) edited by Peter Stevens. Francis Zichy has written a critical survey, 'Leo Kennedy', for *Canadian writers and their works: poetry series*, vol. 4 (1990) and Patricia Morley has written a full biography, *As though life mattered: Leo Kennedy's story* (1994). DAVID LATHAM

Kidd, Adam (1802-31). Of the many early Canadian writers who produced a single volume of poetry, Adam Kidd has received more attention from modern critics than the quality of his work merits. Many others wrote equally well, on similar themes, but Kidd's flamboyant personality, and the tragedy of his early death, combine to make him a sympathetic subject for study.

Born in Ireland, he settled in Quebec with his family while in his teens. Sometime in the mid-1820s he was considered as a candidate for the Church of England priesthood, but having displeased Bishop Mountain for an undocumented reason he was rejected as unsuitable. He travelled in Upper Canada in 1828, but late in that year was living in Montreal and publishing poetry in the local radical newspaper, *The Irish Vindicator*, as well as in *The Irish Shield* (Philadelphia), both under his own name and under the pseudonym 'Slievegallin'. After his collection *The Huron chief, and other poems* (1830) appeared, he set off on a journey through Upper Canada, publicizing his book and gathering material and subscriptions for a new one, also on an Indian theme. He seems to have spent the winter of 1830-1 with friends in Kingston. Aware that he was dying—he published a farewell poem, 'Impromptu', in the *Kingston Chronicle* (12 Mar. 1831)—he returned to Quebec. He died there in July.

Another Montreal poet, W.F. HAWLEY, had also published many poems in the *Vindicator*. When Hawley's book *Quebec, the harp, and other poems* appeared in 1829, several courteous mentions in that newspaper were followed by a savage review, which one suspects was written by Kidd. *The Huron chief*'s publication in Montreal a little later provided occasion for critical revenge. The book was mockingly dissected in the *Gazette* and spiritedly defended by the author in the *Vindicator*. The *Gazette* correspondent also told of Kidd's selling subscriptions for his book from door to door. If Kidd did indeed sell 1,500 copies of *The Huron chief*, as he claimed, that number is more than double the recorded sales of any other pre-Confederation literary work.

Criticism of *The Huron chief* was not confined to the pages of local newspapers. Taking exception to a footnote that attacked Mr Buchanan, the British Consul in New York, for policies he advocated with regard to the navigation of the St Lawrence, Buchanan's sons and a 'friend' attacked Kidd on a Montreal street and subjected him to a public thrashing. There are two versions of the story: one by Kidd, in which he emerges triumphant; the other by the 'friend', who portrays the poet as beneath the notice of a gentleman. It appears that only Kidd's dignity was hurt, but the incident is a striking indication of the status of poets in early Canadian society.

The Huron chief demonstrates the nobility of the Indian in his natural state and the perfidy of the whites who attempt to convert him while seizing his land. The central figure is the chief Skenandow, a wise and peaceful man, ultimately murdered by whites whose release from captivity he has effected. Kidd, as narrator, spends much time recording details of the Native way of life and describing the scenery of the Great Lakes area. A number of shorter poems complete the volume, many of them addressed to young ladies.

An article on Kidd and his work by C.F. KLINCK appeared in *Queen's Quarterly* (Autumn 1958). A modern annotated edition of *The Huron chief*, edited by D.M.R. Bentley, was published by Canadian Poetry Press at the University of Western Ontario in 1987.

MARY LU MacDONALD

Kilbourn, William (1926-95). Born in Toronto, Ontario, he was educated there at Upper Canada College; at Trinity College, University of Toronto (B.A., 1948); at Harvard University (A.M., 1949; Ph.D., 1957); and at Oxford University (B.A., 1952; M.A., 1956). He taught at McMaster University, Ontario (1951-3, 1955-62), and from 1962 was professor of humanities and history at York University, Toronto. He was a Member of the Order of Canada and a Fellow of the Royal Society of Canada.

A passionate lover of his country and his city, and a political activist (he served on the committee that led to Pierre Elliott Trudeau's being chosen as leader of the Liberal party, and in Toronto he was both a reform alderman, 1970-6, and a Metro councillor, 1973-6), Kilbourn wrote and edited books that grew out of both these interests—all of whose texts were informed by a historian's knowledge and made readable by literary grace, wit, irony, and the infusion of drama and significance. His first book was *The firebrand: William Lyon Mackenzie and the rebellion in Upper Canada* (1956; 2nd edn, 1960), a memorable characterization of MACKENZIE that is still in print; it won the University of British Columbia's President's Medal for Biography. Other books relating to Toronto were *Toronto in pictures and words* (with photographs by Rudi Christl, 1977; rpr. 1983); *Toronto observed: its architecture, patrons, and history* (with William Dendy, 1986), which won the City of Toronto Book Award; *Intimate grandeur: one hundred years at Massey Hall* (1993); and two anthologies: *The Toronto book* (1976) and *Toronto remembered: a celebration of the city* (1994), containing pieces by himself and others. Kilbourn's books of more national interest were *The making of the nation: a century of challenge* (1966; rev. 1973), a picture-history in the Canadian Centennial Library; *Pipeline: TransCanada and the great debate: a history of business and politics* (1970); *C.D. Howe: a biography* (with Robert Bothwell, 1979); and the anthology *Canada: a guide to the peaceable kingdom* (1970), sixty-two pieces portraying Canada at the end of the 1960s. An Anglican, Kilbourn was co-author (with A.C. Forrest and Patrick Watson) of *Religion in Canada: the spiritual development of a nation* (1968) in the Canadian Illustrated Library, and edited *The restless church: a response to* [Pierre BERTON's] *The comfortable pew* (1966).

WILLIAM TOYE

King, Basil (1859-1928). Born in Charlottetown, Prince Edward Island, William Benjamin Basil King was educated locally and at King's College, Windsor, Nova Scotia. He was ordained an Anglican priest and served St Luke's Pro-cathedral, Halifax, as rector from 1884. In 1892 he became rector of Christ Church, Cambridge, Massachusetts. Failing eyesight forced him to resign his charge in 1900 and he devoted the rest of his life to travel and writing.

From his first novel, *Griselda* (1900), King worked within the conventions of popular moral fiction. Disparagement of divorce is evident in his second title, *Let not man put asunder* (1901). *In the garden of Charity* (1903), his only digression from Boston-New York settings and from the portrayal of the international world of wealthy Americans, is set among Nova Scotia fisherfolk. Its themes of love, betrayal, and marital fidelity are worked out with compelling vigour. In *The steps of honour* (1904) a Harvard professor plagiarizes scholarship in a vain attempt to win a Cambridge bluestocking. *The giant's strength* (1907) shows the richest man in America learning moral sensitivity through his daughter's suffering. King's early novels did not, however, reach a wide audience until they were reprinted after two successive best-sellers made him famous. These were *The inner shrine* (1909), a trite exercise in the Howells-James international mould, and *The wild olive* (1910), a more interesting drama of moral crisis.

King used his fiction to promote understanding across class, sex, and international barriers. But in his later work he over-exploited popular themes about the crossing of class boundaries, especially through marriage, though he was adept at portraying capable women, and was eager to explain the social background of the many Canadian characters who appear in about half of his twenty-two novels. British and American social viewpoints are contrasted convincingly in *The street called Straight* (1912). *The way home* (1913), set partly in the Canadian Northwest, but mainly filtering its social Christian issues through a New York Episcopal rectory, received high praise from W.D. Howells. Two diffuse, didactic marriage novels, *The letter of the contract* (1914) and *The side of the angels* (1916), illustrate how King's clever plots were declining into mere formulae until his response to First World War conditions gave him a renewed social conviction and a counterweight to his tedious pandering to popular morality.

The Canadian heroine-narrator of *The high heart* (1917) marries a rich American, but differs strongly in her opinions of the war from those of the British and American characters. *The lifted veil* (1917) and *The city of comrades* (1919) also portray Canadians in the USA against a wartime background. Class, and to some extent race, are the main postwar concerns in *The thread of flame* (1920). These themes recur in *The empty sack* (1921) and *The dust flower* (1922), where upwardly mobile Canadians are contrasted with new immigrants, and with wealthy establishment New Yorkers. *The happy isles* (1923), *The high forfeit* (1925), *Pluck* (1928), *Satan as lightning* (1929), and *The break of day* (1930) are, like King's other novels, parables of waywardness and redemption, but add nothing to his reputation. *The spreading dawn* (1927) is a collection of stories that gathers some of his short fiction from magazines. In the 1920s King became a kind of popular sage, issuing *The abolishing of death* (1919), an account of spiritualism; *The conquest of fear* (1921), popular philosophy; *The discovery of God* (1923) and *The Bible and common sense*, biblical commentaries; *Faith and success* (1925) and *Adventures in religion* (1929), popular theology; and *The seven torches of character* (1929). Thirty thousand copies of his best-known religious-philosophical work, *The conquest of fear*, were sold in 1930 alone.

KEN MacKINNON

King, James. See BIOGRAPHY AND MEMOIRS 1983 TO 1996: 1.

King, Thomas (b. 1943). Of Cherokee and Greek ancestry, King was raised in the central valley of California. He has held positions in Native Studies programs in the universities of Utah (where he obtained his Ph.D.), California, and Minnesota, and for ten years at the University of Lethbridge. He now teaches at the University of Guelph.

King's short stories, some of which are collected in *One good story, that one* (1993), distil the concerns, characters, and wit of all his work: they show Native people and tricksters making life out of old and new stories and undermining outsiders' expectations of them. In the title story, anthropologists listen to an old grandmother (or maybe a grandfather, or maybe a coyote) tell a 'traditional' Creation story that turns out to be a hilariously cockeyed version of the account in Genesis. In 'Joe the Painter and the Deer Island Massacre' a town pageant goes awry when the Native narrator and his oddball white friend present a different perspective on history than that anticipated.

King's first novel, *Medicine River* (1990), concerns a Toronto photographer who goes home to Alberta for his mother's funeral, whereupon his old friend Harlen Big Bear conspires to keep him there. Will, the protagonist, plays the alienated intellectual to Harlen's amusing bungling and scheming. A second novel, *Green grass, running water* (1993), is wider in scope, couching stories of domestic life, political resistance, and Native community within a coyote story of the Creation of the world. Both *Green grass, running water* and King's children's book, *A coyote Columbus story* (1992), were shortlisted for Governor General's Awards.

In his article 'Godzilla vs. Post-Colonial' (*World Literature Written in English*, 1990) King discusses what he calls interfusional literature and associational literature, applying the former term to Native literature that crosses the line between oral and written genres, and the latter to literature that emphasizes the vitality of contemporary Native communities. His own writing is both interfusional and associational. He draws on the oral traditions of many different Native peoples, bringing various trickster traditions together to challenge entrenched stereotypes, and one of his greatest talents is for creating a sense of laconic but effective spoken language. As well, his writing shows Native people living their lives with a matter-of-fact quirkiness, wrapped up in each other rather than in their relations with non-Native people.

King edited *An anthology of short fiction by Native writers in Canada* (1988), *All my relations: an anthology of contemporary Canadian Native writing* (1990), and co-edited a collection of critical articles, *The Native in literature* (1987). His poetry has appeared in *CANADIAN LITERATURE, Soundings, Whetstone*, and other periodicals. LAURA J. MURRAY

Kingsford, William. See HISTORICAL WRITING IN ENGLISH: 2.

Kinsella, W.P. (b. 1935). William Patrick Kinsella was born in Edmonton, Alberta, and spent nearly two decades in business before earning a B.A. in creative writing (1974) at the University of Victoria and an M.F.A. (1978) at the University of Iowa, where he was enrolled in the Writer's Workshop.

Kinsella's fiction—which for the most part celebrates two worlds, the Ermineskin reserve near a place he calls Hobbema in southern Alberta, and the American mid-West, where his baseball-inspired semi-fantasies are set—is marked by humour, sentiment, and compassion, with touches of mythic resonance and euphoric anti-authoritarianism. In both the Native stories and the baseball fantasies Kinsella attacks vice, prejudice, dullness, and rampant absurdity, his constant touchstone being a good heart endowed with the ability to dream.

Kinsella's Native stories, many of which feature young Silas Ermineskin and his friend Frank Fencepost, are knitted together by recurring motifs and familiar characters into a unified fictional tapestry. Ermineskin's spare but vivid idiom deftly expresses his mingled naïvety and shrewdness. Seen through his eyes, the white world is repressive, humourless, moralistic, theoretical, and legalistic; its excessive rationalism and materialism have left it loveless and sterile. By contrast the Native world is frankly sexual, pragmatic, and spontaneous, drawing its strength from joyous and resilient anarchy. Kinsella's style is primarily humorous, but he is equally adept at portraying the darker side of human nature and life on a reserve. These stories are in the collections *Dance me outside* (1977), *Scars* (1978), *Born Indian* (1981), *The moccasin telegraph* (1983), *The Fencepost chronicles* (1986), *The Miss Hobbema pageant* (1989), and *Brother Frank's Gospel Hour* (1994). While his Amerindian stories—which are very much like Native 'tall tales'—have won Kinsella high praise, they have also led to accusations by some Native critics of appropriation of voice. But this has not stopped him from writing about these characters, who are so close to his heart, nor has it stopped readers from enjoying them.

Kinsella's baseball fiction includes the story collections *Shoeless Joe Jackson comes to Iowa* (1980); *The thrill of the grass* (1984); *The further adventures of Slugger McBatt* (1988), reissued as *Go the distance* (1995); and *The Dixon Cornbelt League* (1993)—all of which display imaginative and manic verve. In the title story of *Shoeless Joe Jackson comes to Iowa*, a high-spirited blend of 'fact and fantasy, magic and reality', a Kinsella-like narrator obeys a mysterious voice that bids him construct a backyard left field as a shrine to his father's hero, Shoeless Joe Jackson, unjustly disgraced in the 1919 White Sox scandal. This touching and liberating fantasy about love, innocence, the land, and the mystique of baseball later became the novel *Shoeless Joe* (1982), in which Joe redeems himself. Other novels that are baseball connected are *The Iowa baseball confederacy* (1986), *Box socials* (1991), and *If wishes were horses* (1996). All these books, as well as the film adaptation of *Shoeless Joe* (*Field of Dreams*, 1989) made Kinsella a leading writer of baseball lore.

Three works of fiction that do not belong in the above subject categories are the story collections *The Alligator Report* (1985) and *Red wolf, red wolf* (1987), containing the story 'Lieberman in love', which was made into a live-action short film that won an Academy Award in 1996; and the novel *The winter Helen dropped by* (1995). Kinsella has also published poetry—*The rainbow warehouse* (1989)—and a biography of the Cree artist Allen Sapp, *Two spirits soar* (1990). *Shoeless Joe* won the Houghton Mifflin Literary Fellowship in 1982 and the W.H. Smith-*Books in Canada* First Novel Award in 1983. In 1987 Kinsella won the Stephen LEACOCK Memorial Medal for Humour (for *The Fencepost chronicles*), the Vancouver Award for Fiction Writing, and the Author of the Year Award from the Canadian Booksellers' Association. He was made an Officer of the Order of Canada in 1994.

JEFFREY HEATH/TARA L. CURTIS

Kirby, William (1817-1906). Grandson of United Empire Loyalists and the voice of Loyalism in his day, Kirby was born a tanner's son in Kingston-upon-Hull, England. His family immigrated to the United States in 1832, and Kirby to Upper Canada in 1839. After visiting Toronto, Montreal, and Quebec City, he settled in Niagara-on-the-Lake, Ontario (where his house still stands). Kirby practised as a tanner until he married Eliza Madeline Whitmore, one of the extensive Servos clan of Niagara Loyalists. He was editor of the *Niagara Mail*, collector of customs from 1871 to 1895, a charter member of the Royal Society of Canada in 1882, and delivered the principal address at the 1884 United Empire Loyalist Centennial celebrations.

Kirby's literary importance rests largely on his authorship of *The* GOLDEN DOG (Rouses Point, New York, 1877). It is set in New France in 1748, its characters based on historical figures and its usage of Gothic conventions highly romantic. Weighted (as its Epilogue reveals) with the ideology of a One Canada that fuses both English and French portions, attributing loyalty to British institutions as the chief characteristic of both segments, the novel's conception is ambitious. An abridgement exists (NCL, 1969), and a scholarly edition is being prepared by the CENTRE FOR EDITING EARLY CANADIAN TEXTS.

Kirby's lesser works display the contours of an Upper Canadian Tory mentality. As 'Britannicus', Kirby wrote a *Counter manifesto to the annexationists of Montreal* (Niagara, 1849). Various poems and pieces flowed from his newspaper press before and after *The Golden Dog*. *The U.E.: a tale of Upper Canada* (Niagara, 1859) is an epic in twelve cantos written in heroic couplets. Of minor formal interest, it displays the primary assumptions of the Loyalist mythology that was influential in the culture of Victorian Ontario: melding the 1837 Rebellion to the cycle of Loyalist challenges in 1776 and 1812; warning that Upper Canada is an Eden constantly threatened by marauders and traitors both inside and out; stretching the historical limits of United Empire Loyalism to include anyone defending British-Canadian institutions and territory. The poem's martyred hero, Ethelwald, is described as a Loyalist, though his father did not reach Canada until after 1812. The real Loyalist, Ranger John, who had been killing Americans since 1776, warns newcomers to Upper Canada of their American and Canadian enemies. Hugh, his son, fights in 1837 for the 'Americans' (in fact, MACKENZIE's Canadian rebels). Much of the poem pastoralizes Upper Canada. The forest, so grim in the writings of John RICHARDSON, is here a plantation for producing the Royal Navy's masts. Ethelwald and a loyal son of Ranger John die in a skirmish; the fathers close the poem with a patriotic lament.

Kirby's newspaper poems, collected in *Canadian idylls* (Welland, Ont., 1881), deal with patriotic and historical themes, including local legends. 'Spina Christi' offers a jocular account of desecrating the graves of rebels and fellow-travellers. *Annals of Niagara* (Welland, 1896) is a shapeless historical narrative of the barbarities accompanying the desultory border warfare after the battle of Queenston Heights in the War of 1812. The writings and career of Kirby reveal the extent to which the concept of Loyalty in his time changed into a rhetorical epithet expressing Tory approbation. Lorne PIERCE's biography notes how Kirby relished a souvenir that his son sent him from Regina: a piece of the rope that had hanged Riel.

See W.R. Riddell, *William Kirby* (1923); Lorne Pierce, *William Kirby: the portrait of a Tory loyalist* (1929); L.R. Early, 'Myth and prejudice in Kirby, Richardson, and Parker', *CANADIAN LITERATURE* 81 (Summer 1979); Dennis Duffy, *Gardens, covenants, exiles: Loyalism in the literature of Upper Canada/Ontario* (1982).

DENNIS DUFFY

Kiriak, Illia. See UKRAINIAN-CANADIAN WRITING.

Kirkconnell, Watson (1895-1977). Born in Port Hope, Ontario, he was educated at Queen's University, the Toronto Conservatory of Music, and Oxford University. From 1922 to 1940 he taught English, and later classics, at Wesley College, Winnipeg. From 1940 to 1948 he was head of the English department at McMaster University, and from 1948, until his retirement in 1964, he was president of Acadia University. In 1966 he came out of retirement for two years as head of Acadia's English department. A founding member of the CANADIAN AUTHORS' ASSOCIATION, he served two terms as national president (1942-4, 1956-8), and was appointed honorary president in 1968. During the Second World War he chaired the Writers' War Committee and was active in the creation of the Humanities Research Council, which led to the writing, with A.S.P. Woodhouse, of *The humanities in Canada* (1947). He was elected to the Royal Society of Canada in 1936. In addition to numerous European literary awards, he received the Lorne PIERCE Medal in 1942.

Kirkconnell was doubtless Canada's most prolific and industrious scholar, with more than 150 books and booklets and over 1,000 published articles. A tireless linguist, he translated poetry from over 50 languages. His chief works of translation are: *European elegies: one hundred poems chosen and translated from European literature in fifty languages* (1928); *The North American book of Icelandic verse* (1930); *The Magyar muse: an anthology of Hungarian poetry, 1400-1932* (1933); *Canadian overtones: an anthology of Canadian poetry written originally in Icelandic, Swedish, Hungarian, Italian, Greek, and Ukrainian* (1935); *Arany's 'The death of King Buda'* (1936); *A little treasury of Hungarian verse* (1947); *Prince Ihor's raid against the Polovisti* (1947); Mickiewicz's *Pan Tadeusz; or the last foray in Lithuania* (1962); in collaboration with Séraphin Marion, *Tradition du Québec/The Québec tradition* (1946); and in collaboration with C.H. Andrusyshen, *The Ukrainian poets, 1189-1962* (1963) and *The poetical works of Taras Shevchenko* (1964). The Széchenyi Society published his *Hungarian Helicon* in 1985.

Providing a trilogy of valuable critical aids to Milton's poetry, Kirkconnell wrote *The celestial cycle: the theme of Paradise Lost in world literature, with translations of the major analogues* (1952); *That invincible Samson: the theme of Samson Agonistes in world literature with translations of the major analogues* (1964); and *Awake the courteous echo: the themes of Comus, Lycidas, and Paradise Regained in world literature with translations of the major analogues* (1973).

Kirkconnell's major contribution to Canadian scholarship was his annual comprehensive review of Canadian writing in languages other than English and French for the 'Letters in Canada' survey in the *University of Toronto Quarterly*. Between 1938 and 1965 he supplied 28 such annual reviews, which evaluated specific works and commented upon trends and themes peculiar to the ethnic press. Characterized by a strong religious and anti-Communist bias, these reviews as a whole provide a record of Canadian literary accomplishment accessible to few. Kirkconnell's promotion of the literature of immigrant groups within their Old World traditions, as well as his translations of European poetry, and his constant championing of immigrants in the face of prejudice, were warmly appreciated by many groups. Examples of his role as an intermediary presenting European culture to Canadians include *An outline of European literature* (1927) and *The European heritage: a synopsis of European cultural achievement* (1930). To reassure Canadians of the loyalty of these immigrants in wartime, he also produced *Canadians all: a primer of national unity* (1940).

Kirkconnell's own poetry incongruously mixed classical forms with modern themes, as in *The tide of life* (1930) and *The eternal quest* (1934). *The flying bull and other tales* (1940) forces a series of western 'tall tales' into the form of the *Canterbury tales*. More poems were collected in *Manitoba symphony* (1937); *Lycra sacra: four occasional hymns* (1939); *Western idyll* (1940); *The flavour of Nova Scotia* (1976); and lastly *The coronary muse* (1977), written in hospital. *Centennial tales and selected poems* (1965) contains narrative poems on historical themes. *Titus the toad* (1939) is a children's book. A short light opera, *The mod at Grand Pré*, was published in 1955.

Kirkconnell's publications cover an astonishingly wide field, ranging from economics to natural history, pedagogy, political theory, and multiculturalism. His autobiography, *A slice of Canada* (1967), links many of his varied concerns to reveal the intellectual integrity, Christian faith, and wide knowledge of world literature that informed them. It contains a selective bibliography in its appendix. Another selective bibliography is in *The Acadia bulletin* (Jan. 1961), while J.B. Snelson prepared one for *Morning in his heart* (1985), a short biography by J.R.C. Perkin. Perkin also edited a collection of essays on Kirkconnell's life and work, *The undoing of Babel* (1975), which includes a selective bibliography compiled by H.W. Ganong. TERRENCE CRAIG

Kirouac, Conrad. See MARIE-VICTORIN.

Kiyooka, Roy (1926-94). Born in Moose Jaw, Saskatchewan, he studied art with J.E.H. MacDonald of the Group of Seven. He then studied abstract expressionism with Will Barnet, Barnett Newman, and Clement Greenburg, feeling equally at home as a painter in New York City, Moose Jaw, Vancouver, and Japan. In 1960 he began teaching at the Vancouver School of Art, and his teachings inspired many local artists. In 1966 he was awarded a silver medal at the Sao Paulo Biennial. His cool, elegant, abstracts hang in many major galleries and private collections. As a creative artist who was at home in a variety of disciplines—painter, poet, sculptor, photographer, film-maker—Kiyooka was a primal force in the artistic renaissance of Vancouver in the 1960s; he also organized many poetry readings, and was a key link between the avant-garde poets of Vancouver and the COACH HOUSE PRESS group of Toronto; for many years his partner was poet Daphne MARLATT. As a second-generation Canadian-born Japanese Canadian, Kiyooka was a singular and perhaps the most important figure in the history of Japanese-Canadian art, writing, and culture. Although better known as an artist, Kiyooka transformed language with precision; words, syntax, and space were used as instruments of artistic expression.

His poetry collections include *Kyoto airs* (1964), *The unquiet bed* (1967), *Nevertheless these eyes* (1967), *Stoned gloves* (1970), *The Fontainbleau dream machine: 18 frames from a book* (1977), and *Of seasonal pleasures and small hindrances* (1978). His *Transcanada letters* (1975) contains verbal snippets of everyday life, notes to his children, and reflections on art. These uncensored, unedited, free-flowing disclosures are playful and undisciplined, and celebrate the joy of making something—a picture, a poem, or a living. Kiyooka's free-form style fell out of favour with the more controlled poets of the 1980s and 1990s. A decade later his *Pear tree poems* (1988) were complex poems of mortality, imagination, lost love, and failed marriage; the central image of the book is a pear tree that embodies the stability of which Kiyooka was deprived. But the tree is also a muse that embraces the earth and gives him peace with 'a small garden'. A complete collection of Kiyooka's writings—including biography, bibliography, and explication of the poems—is *Pacific windows: collected poems of Roy Kiyooka* (1974) edited by Roy Miki.

See *BRICK*, Spring 1994, for a tribute and photographs. GEOFF HANCOCK

Klein, A. M. (1909-72). Abraham Moses Klein was born in Ratno in Ukraine, and in 1910 his family moved to Montreal, where he spent the rest of his life. His background was Orthodox and he received a solid Jewish education in Hebrew, the Bible, and the Talmud (his poem 'Sophist' offers an affectionately ironic portrait of his Talmud teacher, Rabbi Simcha Garber). Although Klein's Jewish teachers encouraged him to enter the rabbinate, by his high-school years he had abandoned strict religious orthodoxy, acquiring in its stead his lifelong commitment to Zionism and to his vocation as a poet. In 1926 he entered McGill University, where he met the *McGILL FORTNIGHTLY REVIEW* group: Leon EDEL, Leo KENNEDY, F.R. SCOTT, and A.J.M. SMITH. Klein never published in the *Review*; his one submission was rejected because he refused to change the word 'soul', which the editors considered insufficiently modern. However, about this time he began to publish in Canadian and American periodicals, both Jewish and non-Jewish: *Menorah Journal* in 1927; *Poetry* in 1928; *The CANADIAN FORUM* and *CANADIAN MERCURY* in 1929. (Klein continued this practice throughout his career, publishing as well in *The Canadian Jewish Chronicle*, *The Canadian Zionist*, *The Jewish Standard*, *Opinion*, *CONTEMPORARY VERSE*, *FIRST STATEMENT*, *PREVIEW*, *NORTHERN REVIEW*, and *New Directions*.) About this time he first read James Joyce's *Ulysses*, which was to influence his poetry and prose throughout his career. In 1930 he graduated from McGill and enrolled as a law student in the Université de Montréal, graduating in 1933 to practise law, a profession he never found very satisfying or remunerative. In 1935 he married his childhood sweetheart, Bessie Kozlov, and they eventually had three children. In 1936 a highly laudatory account of his work appeared in W.E. Collin's pioneering study of Canadian literature, *The WHITE SAVANNAHS*, and in the same year two of his poems, 'Out of the pulver and the polished lens' and 'Soirée of Velvel Kleinburger', were included in the anthology *NEW PROVINCES*.

In 1938, to supplement his income as a lawyer, Klein took on the editorship of a Montreal weekly, *The Canadian Jewish chronicle*, which he held until the end of his career in 1955. From this period on, the bulk of his writing consisted of his mostly ephemeral editorials for the *Chronicle*. In 1939 Klein became speech writer and public relations adviser to Samuel Bronfman, president of Seagram's and, as head of the Canadian Jewish Congress, the most powerful leader of the Jewish-Canadian community for over thirty years. Mordecai RICHLER, who owes much to Klein's groundbreaking achievement (compare, for example, Klein's *The second scroll* and Richler's *St. Urbain's horseman*) presents a cruelly satirical portrait of the relationship between Bronfman and Klein in *Solomon Gursky was here* (1989). Klein published his first volume of poetry, *Hath not a Jew. . .*, in 1940. In the early forties he came in contact with a number of younger writers involved in *Preview* and *First Statement* who encouraged his interest in modern poetry: Patrick ANDERSON, P.K. PAGE, Louis DUDEK, John SUTHERLAND, and Irving LAYTON (whom he had known for some years). In 1944 he published *Poems* and *The Hitleriad*, and in 1948 *The rocking chair and other poems*, which won a Governor General's Award. From 1945 to 1948 he was a lecturer in the English Department of McGill, an appointment made possible by Bronfman, a prominent financial supporter of McGill, who was concerned that Klein might leave Montreal to take up an offer of employment in New York. The following year he ran for the CCF in the federal riding of Cartier, where he suffered a personally devastating defeat. Soon after this he was sent by the Canadian Jewish Congress, again with the support of Bronfman, on a fact-finding trip to Israel and to Jewish refugee camps in Europe and North Africa. *The second scroll* (1951; NCL, with an Afterword by Seymour MAYNE) is a novel inspired by that trip. Not long after its publication Klein began to show signs of psychological distress, leading to several suicide attempts in 1954. After a partial recovery he became increasingly reclusive, giving up his law practice and his editorship of the *Chronicle*, avoiding contact with anyone but his immediate family, and ceasing to write altogether. The short story 'The almost meeting', by Henry KREISEL, testifies to the devastating effect of Klein's premature silence on a generation of younger Jewish-Canadian writers.

In an article reprinted as the preface to *Hath not a Jew. . .*, the prominent Jewish-American writer Ludwig Lewisohn described Klein as 'the first contributor of authentic Jewish poetry to the English language'. Although in his later poetry, especially the poems collected in *The rocking chair*, Klein leaves explicitly Jewish themes behind, this aspect of his achievement is crucial. Klein formed an important link to the vital Yiddish culture of Montreal. He was particularly close to the Montreal Yiddish poet Y.Y. SEGAL, and his translations of the poetry of Segal and of a number of other Yiddish and Hebrew writers make up a substantial and often impressive body of work. Even more important, Klein's distinctly Jewish perspective provided a stimulus to many younger Jewish writers in Montreal and elsewhere in Canada, such as Layton, Leonard COHEN, Richler, Miriam WADDINGTON, Eli MANDEL, Henry Kreisel, and Seymour MAYNE.

Hath not a Jew. . ., consisting almost entirely of poems from the late twenties and early thirties, most fully explores Klein's relationship to his Jewish heritage, whose rich diversity is the keynote of the volume (see the manifesto poem, 'Ave atque vale'). Klein's celebration of the unity underlying this diversity, of the One in the many, is the theme of the volume's finest poem, 'Out of the pulver and the polished lens', and has many parallels in Klein's later works. *Hath not a Jew. . .* contains some of Klein's most beloved poems, but there is often a quaint folkloric quality about them, reflecting the fact that most of them celebrate a way of life based in the *shtetl* of Eastern Europe, which had almost disappeared by the time most of the poems were written and which Klein never knew at first hand.

The essentially celebratory and optimistic vision of *Hath not a Jew. . .* did not survive the thirties. The Depression, the rise of Nazism, and Klein's own difficult personal circumstances seemed to overwhelm him, and he wrote relatively little (apart from his journalism) in this period: a few satirical poems and short stories in which he appears to be groping, unsuccessfully, for a tenable point of view, and a number of translations, most notably of the modern Hebrew poet Chaim Nachman Bialik, through which Klein was able vicariously to give voice to his feelings of confusion and despair. It was only with the outbreak of the Second World War that he returned to serious, sustained creative writing. *The Hitleriad*, an attack on Hitler that reflects Klein's interest in eighteenth-century satire, especially Pope's *Dunciad*, falls flat as a whole despite some witty passages. Klein the satirist is at his best when he can recognize in the object of his satire genuine human qualities, however distorted. Understandably, he cannot achieve this perspective on Hitler, and as a result is often reduced to bombast and trivial abuse. Much more impressive are the anguished, prophetic psalms that were gathered together, along with some earlier works, to form 'The psalter of Avram Haktani', the most important section of *Poems*. A note of forced rhetoric mars several of them, but in the best the immediacy of Klein's confrontation with evil gives rise to a sense of pathos and intensity that is missing in most of his earlier work.

In the early forties Klein also produced a substantial body of prose works which remained unpublished during his lifetime. They attest to a growing sense of despair, and are characterized by a disturbing, almost obsessive emphasis on isolation, futility, and self-disgust (often of a sexual nature). Klein was not able to bring any of the works of this period to completion. However by the mid-forties, beginning with 'Sestina on the dialectic' and 'Portrait of the poet as landscape', Klein's work takes on a more positive note as he begins to explore dialectical modes of thought, owing more to the Kabbalah, to which he had been introduced by Gershom Scholem's *Major trends in Jewish mysticism* (1954), than to Marx or Hegel. The negative aspects of experience, which he had been forced to acknowledge in the thirties and early forties, and which had nearly silenced him as a creative writer, now gave rise to a dialectical vision in which negation, in the form of social and spiritual fragmentation, is seen to lead inevitably to the eventual achievement of a higher unity. The most moving statement of this vision occurs in the final poem of *The rocking chair*, 'Portrait of the poet as landscape' (which, in fact, precedes the other poems in the volume chronologically), in which the poet's isolation from his community comes to be seen as a temporary stage in a process of self-transformation ('he makes of his status as zero a rich garland'). The Quebec poems in *The rocking chair* are a profoundly dialectical study of the power of community for both good and evil (see especially 'The rocking chair' and 'Political meeting)'). This is Klein's finest collection. Stimulated by modern poets such as T.S. Eliot, W.H. Auden, Dylan Thomas, and Karl Shapiro—as well as by the Metaphysicals, G.M. Hopkins, and Joyce—Klein developed a striking idiom of his own, by turns highly allusive and startlingly direct, coolly ironical and warmly sympathetic, and marked by great flexibility and subtlety of rhythm. Although there are striking differences between early and late Klein, certain features are constant: a kaleidoscopic profusion of metaphors; puns, often multilingual; a richly varied vocabulary making substantial use of foreign loanwords, archaisms, and, especially in the later Klein, Joycean neologisms; and non-linear, 'spatial' structures that work through a mosaic-like accumulation of varied perspectives. These aspects of Klein's poetic technique seem most closely related to his central vision of a unity achieved through the greatest possible diversity.

The second scroll is Klein's most complex and ambitious work, both formally and conceptually, and the most important expression of his Zionism. While writing it Klein was deeply involved in a massive, never-to-be-completed commentary on Joyce's *Ulysses*, and Joyce's influence is everywhere apparent in the novel: the structural principle of parallels between its five chapters (and glosses) and the five books of the Pentateuch recalls Joyce's extensive use of Homeric parallels; and Klein's highly wrought polyphonic prose (see especially 'Gloss Gimel') owes much to Joyce's example. Like *Ulysses*, *The second scroll* is an essentially optimistic work: it celebrates the human capacity for self-renewal, especially through language, even in the face of the apparently overwhelming evil of the Holocaust. The influence of Scholem's *Major trends in Jewish mysticism* is also evident in the novel, which draws heavily on Kabbalistic myths of Creation stressing the interdependence of evil and good, exile and redemption. Uncle Melech, the object of the narrator's search throughout the novel, embodies the Messianic yearning of the exiled many for the ideal One; but, as Melech's story and the history of his people illustrate, it is only through the dialectical process of affirmation through negation, summed up by the Kabbalistic phrase 'Aught from Naught', that this ideal is achieved.

However, Klein's celebration of 'Aught from Naught' in *The second scroll* is marked by a certain skepticism. This is present from the very beginning of his attempts to interpret experience dialectically, and intensifies until it becomes the dominant note of Klein's writings, both published and unpublished, in his final years. The short stories 'Letter from afar' and 'The bells of Sobor Spasitula', for example, present the Marxist version of the dialectic as a destructive self-delusion; and 'The Bible's archetypical poet' recasts 'Portrait of the poet as landscape' as a grim allegory of the poet's fate. Even more radical in its questioning of the attempt to impose a dialectical model—or any model, for that matter—on experience are the two completed chapters of a projected novel on the theme of the Jewish legend of the golem; their ironic exploration of the nature of creativity and the limits of art, which grew out of Klein's personal agony and self-doubt, foreshadows central concerns of much of the postmodernism of recent years. Klein wrote very few new poems during this period and no major ones, but some of the revisions of his earlier poems that he undertook in the fifties, and some of his translations of Bialik, also of this period, are among his finest creations.

The following volumes have so far appeared in the *Collected works* being published by the University of Toronto Press: *Beyond Sambation: selected essays and editorials 1928-1953* (1982) edited by M.W. Steinberg and Usher Caplan, with an introduction by M.W. Steinberg; *The short stories of A.M. Klein* (1983) edited with an introduction by M.W. Steinberg; *Literary essays and reviews* (1987) edited by Usher Caplan and M.W. Steinberg, with an introduction by Usher Caplan; *The complete poems* (1990) edited with an introduction by Zailig Pollock; *Notebooks: selections from the A.M. Klein Papers* (1994) edited by Zailig Pollock and Usher Caplan, with an introduction by Zailig Pollock. Two further volumes in the *Collected Works* are currently being edited: *The second scroll*, by Elizabeth Popham and Zailig Pollock, and the *Letters*, by

Elizabeth Popham and Harold Heft. *The second scroll* is available in the NEW CANADIAN LIBRARY with an Afterword by Seymour Mayne. *Like one that dreamed: a portrait of A.M. Klein* (1982) by Usher Caplan is an excellent biography with many photographs of Klein and his milieu and excerpts from his work, many previously unpublished. *A.M. Klein: an annotated bibliography* (1993) by Zailig Pollock, Usher Caplan, and Linda Rozmovits, with an introduction by Zailig Pollock, is the most complete and up-to-date bibliography of works by and about Klein. Miriam Waddington's *A.M. Klein* (1970) is a pioneering short study that emphasizes Klein's secular humanist side. Zailig Pollock's *A.M. Klein: the story of the poet* (1994) surveys the entire body of Klein's writing in relation to his developing vision of the poet's role. Three useful collections of studies are *A.M. Klein* (1970) edited by Tom MARSHALL; The *A.M. Klein symposium* (1975) edited by Seymour Mayne; and 'A.M. Klein's Montreal', *Journal of Canadian Studies* (Summer 1984) edited by Zailig Pollock.

ZAILIG POLLOCK

Klinck, Carl F. (1908-90). Born in Elmira, Ontario, he held a B.A. from Waterloo College (1927), Waterloo, Ontario, and an M.A. (1929) and Ph.D. (1943) from Columbia University. From 1928 to 1947 he taught at Waterloo, where he became Dean of Arts. In 1947 he began a distinguished career at the University of Western Ontario, London, where he became head of the English department (1948), professor of Canadian literature (1955), and on his retirement in 1973 Professor Emeritus. His honours included the Order of Canada (Officer, 1973) and a D. Litt. from the University of Western Ontario (1974).

Klinck became a scholar-adventurer in the field of Canadian literature—as an editor, biographer, critic, and bibliographer—long before this discipline had any academic stature. His personal bibliography is substantial. He edited books on or by Samuel Strickland, Abraham Holmes, Tecumseh, John Norton, Adam Hood BURWELL, 'Tiger' Dunlop, and John RICHARDSON. Subjects of his many articles include John GALT, Archibald LAMPMAN, Adam KIDD, Levi ADAMS, and the relationship between early-Canadian and American literatures. He edited and introduced the NEW CANADIAN LIBRARY editions of Frances BROOKE's *The history of Emily Montague* (1961), Susanna MOODIE's *ROUGHING IT IN THE BUSH* (1962), Richardson's *WACOUSTA* (1967), and Rosanna LEPROHON's *Antoinette de Mirecourt* (1973). He co-edited the college text *Canadian anthology* (with R.E. Watters, 1955), and the biographical reference work *Canadian writers/Écrivains canadiens* (with Guy Sylvestre and Brandon Conron, 1964), and published biographical and critical studies of E.J. PRATT (with Henry W. Wells, 1947), Wilfred CAMPBELL (his dissertation, 1943), and Robert SERVICE (1976). From 1959 to 1972 Klinck compiled 'Theses in preparation' for *CANADIAN LITERATURE*'s annual bibliography. He was best known, however, as general editor of the *Literary history of Canada* (1956; 2nd edn 1976), to which he contributed two chapters on literary activity in the Canadas from 1812 to 1880. His longtime importance as a senior statesman of Canadian letters cannot be overestimated: it rested on his making accessible much early writing long before it was regarded as important to the national literary consciousness. Approaching this literature and its authors from the beginning in a spirit of modest proselytizing and thorough scholarship, Klinck made contributions to the advancement, breadth, and maturity of Canadian studies that were an enduring and major academic achievement. A posthumous memoir edited by Sandra Djwa, *Giving Canada a literary history* (1991), is a characteristically modest testimony to his pivotal role in the consolidation of Canadian literary history.

See also CRITICISM IN ENGLISH: 4.

LOUIS K. MacKENDRICK

Knister, Raymond (1899-1932). John Raymond Knister was born in Ruscomb, near Stoney Point, Essex County, Ontario, and attended Victoria College, University of Toronto, and Iowa State University. He worked on his father's farm near Blenheim, Ont., from 1920 to 1923, when he moved to Iowa City to become associate editor of an avant-garde literary magazine, *The Midland*. In 1924 he lived in Chicago briefly before returning to Canada in the autumn. In 1925 his poem 'A row of horse stalls', and his stories 'Elaine' and 'The fate of Mrs. Lucier', appeared in *This Quarter*. In 1926 he moved to Toronto, where he freelanced; his work appeared in the *Toronto Star Weekly* and *Saturday Night*. The next year Knister married Myrtle Gamble and for the summer they moved to Hanlan's Point, Toronto Island, where Knister completed his first published novel, *White narcissus* (1929; NCL, with an Afterword by Morley CALLAGHAN). He edited the anthology *Canadian short stories* (1928), considered to be the first anthology of its kind; his introduction to it is still of critical interest. In 1929 the Knisters moved to a farmhouse near Port Dover, Ont., where Knister wrote *My star predominant* (1934); a daughter, Imogen, was born in 1930. Frederick Philip GROVE encouraged Knister to submit *My star predominant* to Graphic Publishers' Canadian Novel Contest, and in 1931 it won the $2,500 first prize. In 1931-2 he lived in and near Montreal, returning to Ontario after Lorne PIERCE had offered him a job on the editorial staff of the RYERSON PRESS that would allow him time to write. While swimming off Stoney Point, Lake St Clair, in Aug. 1932, Knister drowned. At the time of his death a number of his stories and poems, and two novels, were unpublished; a good deal of this material has since been published.

White narcissus was published in Toronto, London, and New York. Set in rural southwestern Ontario, it concerns a writer, Richard Milne, who returns home in order to make a final attempt to convince his childhood sweetheart, Ada Lethen, to marry him. Ada feels it is her duty to stay at home because for years, as a consequence of a quarrel, her parents have communicated only through her. The white narcissus of the title becomes a symbol of obsession, a subject given serial exploration in the course of the novel. While the novel is usually and justly considered a work of realism, it has also been suggested that it contains elements of romanticism, and that the lyricism of some passages approaches prose-poetry. It is in the NEW CANADIAN LIBRARY, with an Afterword by Morley CALLAGHAN. *My star predominant* is a well-researched novel based on the last years of the life of John Keats, in which the poet's social milieu is vividly conveyed. The unpublished novels *Soil in smoke* and *Turning loam*—both set in rural southwestern Ontario—have more of the atmosphere of the 1920s than *White narcissus*.

Of Knister's many short stories, probably the best known is 'Mist-green oats', about a young man's break with his life on the family farm. His stories recurrently focus on some form of psychological initiation. Knister also wrote novellas. In 'Innocent man' the story of a man's wedding frames the tale of his false arrest and wedding-night spent in a Chicago jail. During the night each prisoner tells the story not of his guilt but of his innocence; the tension between black and white prisoners, and between inmates and guards, threatens to explode in violence. 'Peaches, peaches' is set on a fruit farm; as an overabundant crop of peaches ripens, a young man first encounters sexual politics. A strength of these two novellas—both of which are included in *The first day of spring: stories and other prose* (1976) edited by Peter STEVENS—is the power with which atmosphere is evoked. Other stories, as well as essays, appear in *Raymond Knister: poems, stories, and essays* (1975) edited by David Arnason *et al.*, and six stories are included in *Selected stories of Raymond Knister* (1972) edited by Michael Gnarowski.

Knister is now considered one of the first modern poets in Canada. His poetry, which contains powerful descriptions of nature, is usually associated with the imagist school, although Knister also employed the forms of the prose-poem ('Poisons'), the serial poem ('A row of horse stalls'), and the longer poem ('Corn husking'). Dorothy LIVESAY edited the *Collected poems* (1949), which is actually a selection: more poems are found in *Raymond Knister: poems, stories and essays*.

See Dorothy Livesay's memoir in the *Collected poems* and 'Raymond Knister—man or myth?', *Essays on Canadian writing* 16 (1979-80), edited by Imogen Givens, Knister's daughter, which includes a diary account by her mother about the day of Knister's drowning. See also Marcus Waddington's essay 'Biographical note' in *Raymond Knister: poems, stories, and essays*. For a critique of Knister's stories, see Michelle Gadpaille, *The Canadian short story* (1988), pp. 19-21. For Knister's poetry, see David Arnason's 'Canadian poetry: the interregnum', *CVII*, vol. 1, no. 1 (Spring 1975). See also Anne Burke, *Raymond Knister: an annotated bibliography* (1981).

JOY KUROPATWA

Knowles, R.E. (1868-1946). Robert Edward Knowles was born in Maxwell, Ontario, the son of an Irish Presbyterian minister. Educated at Peterborough Collegiate under William Tassie, Queen's University, and Manitoba College, he was ordained in 1891 and served as pastor of Stewarton Presbyterian Church, Ottawa. In 1896 he married Emma Jones of North Carolina, and they had a son and daughter. In 1898 he became minister of one of Ontario's largest Presbyterian churches, Knox's in Galt.

Between 1905 and 1911 Knowles wrote seven novels, published by the evangelical publisher Fleming H. Revell in New York and reissued in Toronto, Edinburgh, and London. They gained considerable popularity—Ontario sales of *The attic quest* (1909) rivalled those of works by Ralph Connor (C.W. GORDON) and L.M. MONTGOMERY. These novels Knowles regarded frankly as an extension of his ministry. Their style owes much to biblical rhythms and phraseology and to the rhetoric of Knowles' impassioned, crowd-pleasing sermons. Interest centres on the moral crises and religious experience of the characters. The didactic plots, relying heavily on coincidence, echo biblical parables of admonitions such as 'your sin will find you out', while deathbed scenes and symbolic patterns point frequently to an extra-temporal world. Less dated is Knowles' humour, and sometimes shrewd insight into character. The novels also provide a realistic glimpse of life in the villages and towns of Ontario.

In *St. Cuthbert's* (1905), the minister-narrator frequently diverges from his plot to give humorous vignettes of the rugged Scots Presbyterians who settled what is obviously the Galt area. *The undertow* (1906), psychologically more complex, portrays a young minister torn between his ambitions in a wealthy Hamilton parish and the simpler rural values of his father. It introduces a favourite character-type, the devoted woman—here a Salvation Army girl, at other times a mother or wife. *The dawn at Shanty Bay* (1907) is more an extended parable than a novel, using the seasonal symbolism of Christmas to portray the conversion of a proud, unforgiving Scotsman. *The web of time* (1908) centres on Harvey Simmons' struggle against alcoholism when he leaves home to attend college and to work in the big city. *The attic guest* effectively uses a new narrator—a Southern girl who marries Gordon, a visiting minister—and includes a dramatic scene in which Gordon tries to stop a lynching. The chief theme, however, is Gordon's struggle with the higher criticism and religious doubt. In *The handicap* (1910) the growth of a pioneer settlement over two generations is the background to the romance of two 'handicapped' lovers, a pub-keeper's daughter and an illegitimate youth. The least church-centred of Knowles' novels, it culminates in the arrival of a sagacious John A. Macdonald, who brings the lovers together. *The singer of the Kootenay* (1911) is less remarkable for its hero, a young singer, than for its portrait of Armitage, a dry, formalistic, ageing minister. In far-off British Columbia, Armitage leads pitifully unsuccessful revival meetings, but eventually finds his own regeneration.

Difficulties probably related to alcoholism put an end to Knowles' career as a novelist and resulted in his formal retirement from his ministry in January 1915. After a period of recuperation, he began to work as a journalist: starting with mainly religious reporting for the Toronto *Star* in the early twenties, he soon became its special writer sent to interview celebrities such as Albert Einstein and Ramsay MacDonald, besides providing many short opinion pieces in his familiar rhetorical and humorous style. He was in great demand as a lecturer and after-dinner speaker. Divorced in 1923, Knowles married Georgia Hogg, and joined the United Church after its formation in 1925. He died in Galt. JEAN O'GRADY

Kobayashi, Tamai. See LESBIAN LITERATURE.

Koch, Eric (b. 1919). Born in Frankfurt, Germany, to a well-to-do Jewish bourgeois family, he was lucky enough to get out of the country in 1935 to continue his schooling in England. He attended Cambridge University, but was arrested in 1940 as an enemy alien and deported to Canada. He was released from detention camp in 1942 and continued his education at the University of Toronto. In 1944 he joined the Canadian Broadcasting Corporation, where he was a producer from 1953 to 1971 and then regional director (Montreal) until 1977.

Koch's first novel was *The French kiss* (1969), a brilliant comic version of the cause and consequences of General de Gaulle's famous 1967 'Québec Libre!' speech in Montreal. The first-person narrator of the novel, the fat, vain Jo-Jo, is a history professor at the Université de Montréal and also a secret agent for De Gaulle. Jo-Jo parallels the story about De Gaulle's attempt to aid the Quebec independence movement with a narrative about Napoleon III's endeavour to help Italy throw off the yoke of Austrian domination during the 1860s. Both men fail in their ambitions to extend French influence through intervention in other nations' affairs. The disillusioned Jo-Jo, writing in 1977 (eight years after the publication of the novel and a year after the triumph of the Parti Québécois at the polls), concludes that the Quebec separatist movement is dying. Koch may have been wrong about the future of Quebec separatism—at least in the short term—but *The French kiss* remains a *tour de force* both about history and the future: charming, funny, and pathetic by turns.

Koch's next two novels are set in the future. *Leisure riots* (1973) is narrated by a director of a think-tank, Diedrich Bierbaum, who is asked by the President to investigate and find remedies for a series of apparently random acts of violence that break out across the USA in 1979. In *The last thing you'd want to know* (1976), Bierbaum reappears as the narrator.

This time—it's 1984—he is asked by the President to find out why a number of people in the criminal class have reformed their lives on being told by a mysterious woman the date of their death. In both novels Koch pits rational problem-solving methods against the powers of the irrational. The struggles and the intrigues provide admirable arenas for Koch to demonstrate his talent for urbane satire.

In *Goodnight little spy* (1979) Koch invents a small African country, Lalonga, and sends there Monty Haynes, who is supposed to give a western spin to a PR firm that is counselling the corrupt President. This is a neat, satiric, and funny look at a developing nation.

Koch has also written three non-fiction works. *Inside Seven Days: the show that shook the nation* (1986) is a detailed examination of the rise, decline, and fall of the CBC-TV program 'This Hour Has Seven Days'. *Deemed suspect* (1980) is an autobiographical account of Koch's early years as an 'enemy alien' when he was deported to Canada, along with a number of Jewish compatriots, many of whom later played an influential role in the artistic and intellectual life of Canada. *Hilmar and Odette* (1995) tells the story of two of Koch's German relations who stayed behind in Germany during the Nazi régime. Both were illegitimate children who were unknown to Koch until the 1980s. When informed of their lives, he set out to discover what happened to them. Hilmar died in Auschwitz; Odette, unaware of her Jewishness, spent the war in affluence, hobnobbing with the Nazi élite.

Probably because of the pattern of his own life, Koch has been preoccupied with the absurdities and ironies of life, and with the intrigues necessary to cope. His imaginative agility, inventiveness, and stylish wit have enabled him to create original and highly entertaining work. His fiction fits into no acknowledged category of Canadian literature, however, which is probably why he is not as well known as he should be.

PETER BUITENHUIS

Kogawa, Joy (b. 1935). Born in Vancouver, British Columbia, she was moved with her family to the interior of the province during the evacuation of Japanese-Canadians from the West Coast during the Second World War. She has also lived in Saskatoon and Ottawa, where she worked as a writer in the Prime Minister's office (1974-6). She now lives in Vancouver.

Kogawa's first volume of poetry, *The splintered moon* (1967), established her direct, often understated voice in short-lined pieces relying on epigrammatic tightness, a transliteration of her Japanese heritage in the way these short poems express a moment's experience without comment; yet they do not, like *haiku*, summarize the transitory quality of the experience through a tight focus on one image, but rather state the experience directly in pared-down phrasing. The first half of *A choice of dreams* (1974) details a visit to Japan, but the poems often shift away from oriental feeling to a clear-eyed, undramatic sensibility. A more personal poetry appears at the end of the book. The tones and moods in this collection continue in *Jericho Road* (1977), though the language is more thoroughly metaphorical, a development that continued in her later poetry, as in *Woman in the woods* (1985).

Kogawa moved from poetry to fiction in 1981 when she published *Obasan*, which was awarded the *Books in Canada* First Novel Award and the CANADIAN AUTHORS' ASSOCIATION 1982 Book of the Year Award; it was also a featured book for the Literary Guild Book Club and the Book of the Month Club of Canada. *Obasan* has its source in her experience of the wartime evacuation of the Japanese, and derives its power from the same direct and sober language that is evident in her poetry, avoiding any excesses of bitterness or resentment. The same is true of *Itsuka* (1992), a kind of sequel in that it follows the life of one of the younger characters in *Obasan*, examining her life growing up on the Prairies and then in Toronto. There Naomi, the protagonist, involves herself in the struggle for recognition and redress for those Japanese-Canadians who were evacuated. Life on the Prairies is also featured in *The rain ascends* (1995), which recounts the struggle of a young woman whose father, a minister—a man she has been overly devoted to—is discovered to have been a child molester.

Kogawa has also written a children's book, *Naomi's road* (1986), which was based on *Obasan*.

PETER STEVENS

Kokis, Serge (b. 1944). Born in Rio de Janeiro, Brazil, he developed a strong interest in fine arts and philosophy as a young student. Involved in clandestine political activities protesting Brazil's dictatorship (sketching caricatures and political posters), he was charged with 'crimes against national security'. A scholarship to study in France enabled him to leave Brazil discreetly and complete a master's degree in psychology at the Université de Strasbourg in 1969. The same year he was offered a post as psychologist in Quebec, Canada, at the Gaspé psychiatric hospital before moving to Montreal where he completed a doctorate in clinical psychology at the Université de Montréal in 1973. Teaching psychology briefly at the Université du Québec à Montréal, he accepted another position as psychologist at Sainte-Justine childrens' hospital, where he spent twenty years before devoting himself in 1995 entirely to painting and writing.

Kokis's first novel, *Le pavillon des miroirs* (1994), published when he was fifty years old, received an enthusiastic reception from critics and public alike, winning him four of Quebec's five major literary prizes: the Grand Prix du livre de Montréal, the Prix de l'Académie des lettres du Québec, the Prix France-Québec, and the Prix du Salon du livre du Québec. Alternately describing vivid memories of childhood and the reflective judgements of the adult, the novel describes the first twenty or so years of the narrator, who lived in Brazil to the 1950s. Though many events parallel those in Kokis's own life, he insists this is not an autobiographical novel, but rather an exploration of art and creativity seen through the memories of a painter who has moved to the northern hemisphere but recalls the colours and forms of his childhood and tries to integrate them into his present work and thinking.

Against the 1972 backdrop of the red-light districts of Rio and its death squads, *Negão et Doralice* (1995) explores the sordid life of the city's underbelly. The thirty-year-old mulatto Negão, a dock-worker thief specializing in the stealing of luxury cars, kills three policemen to prevent them raping a young whore. He is pursued throughout the novel by Dr Vigario, a political officer of the current dictatorship, in a manhunt that ends brutally on the eve of Carnival, recalling at times the mood and setting of Cocteau's *Black Orpheus*. Partly a detective story, partly a critique of the violence oppressing the destitute, expressed frequently in the coarse and colourful language of its milieu, it introduces the reader to a harsh but exotic world where magic and myth are as important as reality, and love may be found even in the depths of brutality and torture.

The setting for *Errances* (1996) is East Berlin in 1986, where Boris Nikto, a Brazilian poet who has lived in exile for twenty-two years after escaping a military coup, has been granted an amnesty and an invitation to return to the land of his birth. In a successful juxtaposition of a past filled with images of the violent oppression seen in his first two novels and a present filled with self-doubts and unease, Kokis sketches vividly and convincingly the surprise and confusion overwhelming his narrator as he leaves Iron Curtain territory to return to the democratic milieu of Bremen, West Germany. Cerebral and, at times, sensual, *Errances* is both a fascinating study of exile and a disturbing questioning of the nature of reality, which the writer attempts to shape and form through the written word; it also confirms Kokis's ease with the structures of fiction and the elegance of his prose, written in a language other than his mother tongue. RAMON HATHORN

Korn, Rokhl (Rachel) H. (1898-1982). A major poet of the modern Yiddish literature that flourished in eastern Europe before the Holocaust, she was brought up on a farm and educated in Galicia, part of the Austrian Empire annexed by Poland in 1919, the year she began writing in Yiddish instead of Polish. When the Germans invaded Poland in 1939, Korn fled to the Soviet Union, where she spent the war years making her way from the refugee camps in Tashkent and Uzbekistan to Moscow. There she was welcomed and assisted by the Yiddish writers' community that included Shlomo Mihoels, Peretz Markish, and David Bergelson. After the war she returned to Poland and resumed her literary activities in Lodz, where she was elected to the executive of the Yiddish writers union. Subsequently she represented the union at a PEN Congress in Stockholm; from there, without returning to Poland, she immigrated to Canada. She settled in Montreal in 1948 and lived there until her death.

Korn was the author of nine books of poetry and two collections of short stories, as well as numerous critical essays. Two of her manuscripts, which were to be published in Kiev, were destroyed when the Nazis laid waste the city and liquidated the Yiddish publishing house and all its staff. Her first book of poems, *Dorf* ('Country', 1928), received universal critical acclaim when it appeared in Vilnius, the literary and cultural centre of Yiddish life before the advent of Hitler. Her subsequent books were published in Tel Aviv and Montreal and she remained, throughout her life, a frequent and influential contributor of essays, poems, and stories to every prestigious Yiddish journal in America, Israel, and Europe. As well, she was awarded nearly all the existing literary prizes for Yiddish literature: the Leivick prize, the Lamed prize, the Manger prize, and the SEGAL prize, among others.

Korn's poems are beloved and celebrated for their lyrical vision and realistic depiction of country life and landscape, and her stories are famous for their profound psychological penetration and dense, complex, and unsentimental style. Her themes of art and language, exile, human suffering, and endurance are reflected in the titles of her poetry collections: *Roiter Mon* ('Red poppies', 1937), *Shnitt* ('Harvest', 1941—destroyed by the Nazis), *Haym un Haymolozikeit* ('Home and homelessness', 1948), *Bashertkeit* ('Fatedness', 1949), *Fun yener Zeit Lied* ('From beyond poetry', 1962), *Shirim V'odomeh* ('Songs of the homeland', with facing Hebrew translation by Shimshon Melzer, 1966), *Die Gnod fun Vort* ('The grace of words', 1968), *Oif der Sharf vun a Rega* ('In the flash of an instant', 1972), *Farbittene Vor* ('Transformed reality', 1977); and in her short stories: *Erd* ('Earth', 1935) and *Nayn Dersteylungen* ('Nine stories', 1958). Her work has been translated into Hebrew, Polish, Russian, French, and German, and a volume of her selected poems has appeared in English translation: *Generations* (1982), edited by Seymour MAYNE. *Paper roses* (1986) is a bilingual edition of Korn's poems, selected and translated by Seymour Levitan.

See Korn's story 'Earth', translated by Miriam WADDINGTON and included in the anthology she edited, *Canadian Jewish short stories* (1990), and Waddington's memoir 'Rachel Korn: remembering a poet' in her *Apartment Seven* (1989). Korn's story 'The road of no return', translated by Waddington, is in the anthology *Found treasures* (1994).

MIRIAM WADDINGTON

Kostash, Myrna (b. 1944). Born in Edmonton of Ukrainian parents, and educated at the University of Alberta (B.A.), the universities of Washington, Seattle (graduate studies), and Toronto (M.A.), Kostash has been a freelance writer, an instructor in Women's Studies, and an associate film producer at the National Film Board. She is the author of four books of non-fiction in which she examines her subjects with the same relentlessly honest gaze that she trains on her own beliefs.

In *All of Baba's children* (1977), about the lives of Ukrainian immigrants in Two Hills, Alberta, Kostash explodes the myth of immigrant Ukrainians as docile, religious peasants and reveals the complexity of the world the immigrants left behind and the one they came to. *Long way from home* (1980) treats politics of the 1960s and the student movement in Canada. In *No kidding* (1987), an examination of the lives of teenage girls, Kostash as a feminist looks back at a younger generation to see what gains had been made for women, and finds the experience brutally sobering. The girls were often harsh with one another, locked in cruel relationships, and ignorant of basic information on sex. *Bloodlines* (1993) is a study of Slavic nations based on several years of travels in those countries shortly before the collapse of the Soviet Union and the dramatic changes that swept through the area. It is therefore a series of impressionistic snapshots of the region in the final days of Communism that includes the narrator, her relatives, hotel clerks, and various conformists and non-conformists. As in her previous books, Kostash reveals complexity without ever slipping into easy generalities.

She contributed to *Her own woman* (1975), a collection of feminist essays by Erna Paris, Valerie Miner, Heather Robertson, Melinda McCracken, and Kostash herself.

ANTANAS SILEIKA

Kreisel, Henry (1922-91). Born in Vienna, he left Austria for England in 1938 after the Nazi take-over. Sent to Canada by the British authorities in 1940, he was interned for eighteen months. He then attended Jarvis Collegiate, Toronto, and the University of Toronto. There he was introduced to the work of A.M. KLEIN, which showed him that 'it was possible and in fact quite all right for me to use my own background and traditions and yet still integrate myself with the country where I had decided I wanted to settle.' Kreisel received his B.A. (1946) and M.A. (1947) from the University of Toronto, and his Ph.D. from the University of London (1954). He began teaching at the University of Alberta in 1947, and had a distinguished career there.

Kreisel described himself as being 'one of the first people probably to bring to modern Canadian literature the experience of the immigrant.' Both of his novels have as protagonists men who find it difficult to come to terms with the contrast between the 'hell' of Austria in the 1930s and the bland, but more secure, character of Canadian life. In *The rich man* (1948) Jacob Grossman, a presser in a Toronto clothing factory, returns to Europe after more than three decades in North America. His seemingly innocent decision to 'throw money around like a rich man' becomes a trap when his Viennese relatives, in the anti-Semitic and repressive climate of 1935, turn to him for financial help he cannot provide. Grossman's growing awareness of the moral blunder into which vanity and lack of self-knowledge have led him is effectively presented, as is the tension created within a family of strong-minded individuals who are sometimes bound together and sometimes thrown apart by adverse circumstances. The novel was reissued in the NEW CANADIAN LIBRARY (1961).

The betrayal (1964), described by Kreisel as a 'morality tale', deals with moral irresponsibility in a more dramatic, less atmospheric, way. Theodore Stappler, a young Austrian seeking with his mother to escape the Nazis, is paralysed by fear when he realizes that both of them have been betrayed by a fellow Jew. Stappler survives, ultimately to confront his enemy in Edmonton. The troubled consciences of both Stappler and his betrayer, who has plausible self-justifications to offer, are powerfully rendered. The characterization of Mark Lerner, the Jewish-Canadian professor who narrates the story, is a convincing study of North American naïvety attempting to comprehend the dark European heritage.

The almost meeting and other stories (1981) brings together stories with both European and western-Canadian settings that Kreisel had written over a period of more than two decades. In the latter category is the much-admired and widely reprinted 'The broken globe', and the charmingly wry 'The travelling nude'. Kreisel's essay, 'The prairie: a state of mind' (1968), a seminal study of the literary implications of the prairie sensibility, has been reprinted several times (see Donna Bennett and Russell Brown, eds, *An anthology of Canadian literature in English: volume II*, 1983). Kreisel also edited *Aphrodite and other poems* (1959) by John Heath.

Another country: writings by and about Henry Kreisel (1985), edited by Shirley Neuman, is an excellent compilation that includes interviews given by Kreisel, his letters, creative work, and a diary of his 1941 internment, along with ten critical essays about him and a bibliography of his writings. THOMAS E. TAUSKY

Krizanc, John. See DRAMA IN ENGLISH 1953 TO 1981.

Kroetsch, Robert (b. 1927). Born and raised in Heisler, Alberta, he attended the University of Alberta (B.A., 1948), then spent the next six years working in various parts of the Canadian North as a labourer, and as a civilian information officer for the US Air Force in Labrador. In 1954 he attended McGill University for a year to study under Hugh MacLENNAN, and in 1956 completed an M.A. at Middlebury College, Vermont. He later attended the Writers' Workshop at the University of Iowa, earning a Ph.D. in creative writing in 1961. He remained in the USA, teaching English at the State University of New York at Binghamton, until the late 1970s, when he accepted a teaching position at the University of Manitoba. He is now retired from teaching and makes his home in Victoria, British Columbia.

Kroetsch's *But we are exiles* (1965) is based on his experiences working on Mackenzie River riverboats. While this novel is written in a realist manner, the epigraph from Ovid that originally appeared on its title page calls attention to parallels between the protagonist's story and the Greek myth of Narcissus; as well, some elements of the book recall Conrad's *Heart of darkness*, the most important of Kroetsch's early influences. This 'layering' of extended mythic and literary allusions to give saliency to narrative events, although rooted in well-established conventions of International Modernism, made the novel a departure in Canadian fiction. In the novels that followed, Kroetsch's interest in myth became progressively more evident in the surface of his texts, moving his writing beyond modernism's use of myth and towards the 'fabulations' that have been an important strand in English-language fiction since the 1960s. Structured by comic and surreal episodes, his Out West triptych—*The words of my roaring* (1966), *The studhorse man* (1969), and *Gone Indian* (1973)—is an extended investigation of the fabulous and mythic implications of rural life on the Prairies.

Beneath the surface of *The words of my roaring*—a historically based account of Alberta in the 1930s—Kroetsch creates an elaborate structure of myth, blending the tale of Hades' abduction of Persephone with Christian allusions, and introducing extensive patterning derived from Frazer's *The golden bough*, the Babylonian-Assyrian mythologies of Marduk and *The epic of Gilgamesh*, and other narratives to provide a complex (if to some extent invisible) grounding for this Depression-era story of John Judas Backstrom, a small-town undertaker running for office in the Alberta general election of 1935. Though a follower of a political leader named Applecart, a man who uses the Book of Revelation to turn Westerners against the East (an allusion to William 'Bible Bill' Aberhart, the evangelical founder of the Social Credit Party in Canada), Backstrom bases *his* campaign on a whimsical promise to bring rain in a way that recalls Frazer's belief that all ancient rulers were first of all rainmakers.

While this use of mythic parallels serves, as in modernism, to enrich the text, in *The words of my roaring* and in the novels that followed, Kroetsch's use of myth is also postmodern, in that there is such a superfluity of allusions and echoes that they resist a single, coherent reading. In *The studhorse man*, which won a Governor General's Award, Kroetsch uses not only Old World myths—in particular, parallels to, and parodies of, Homer's *Odyssey* and the myths of Poseidon and Demeter—but also introduces North American mythology, setting up extensive resonances with Native Trickster tales. Kroetsch became attracted to the Trickster figure after encountering Sheila WATSON's use of Coyote in *The double hook*, and it has continued to fascinate him throughout his career. He has exploited the myth for its sexual dimensions, its embodiment of comic and transformative unpredictability, and its larger vision of an inherently disorderly universe. In *The studhorse man* the Trickster is especially associated with Hazard Lepage, a breeder of horses who fails to recognize that, with the growth of technology and the end of gas rationing after the Second World War, the day of the horse is over, even in the Canadian West.

Gone Indian concludes Kroetsch's Out West triptych with the tale of an American graduate student, Jeremy Sadness, who is fascinated by Archibald Stansfeld BELANEY (the British immigrant who deceived the public in his guise as Grey Owl, a wise Indian trapper). Jeremy comes to the Canadian West seeking a vanished American frontier but finds instead a winter-carnival celebration in which he has a series of dream-like adventures. Containing allusions to several Native myths, to the Funeral Games section of Virgil's *Aeneid*, to Dante's *La vita nuova*, and to the Norse myth of Ragnarok, *Gone Indian* ends with its hero, mounted on a snowmobile and accompanied by a beautiful woman, ambiguously disappearing into the North.

In 1972 Kroetsch co-founded, with his colleague William Spanos, the influential critical journal *Boundary 2: A Journal of Postmodern Literature*. His developing consciousness of and interest in postmodernism around this time is evident in his fiction not only in the surplus of intertexts in the Out West triptych, but also in his use, in the second and third novels, of metafictional and self-reflexive techniques that introduce a high degree of indeterminacy. A mad biographer, Demeter Proudfoot, tells—or invents—the story of Hazard Lepage, while *Gone Indian* is constructed from questionable transcriptions of tapes sent by Jeremy to his Canadian-born professor teaching in Binghamton, N.Y. (a man who shares what was then Kroetsch's home address). At the same time, the Alberta settings in these and Kroetsch's later novels show him balancing against the anti-representational tendencies of postmodernism a commitment to writing into existence the unrecorded narratives of his place of origin. As a result, his writing is also been associated with postcolonial goals—a commitment visible in many of his essays and epitomized in his often-quoted remark (recorded in conversation with Margaret LAURENCE): 'We haven't got an identity until somebody tells our story. The fiction makes us real' (*Creation*, 1970). Because of its suggestion that English-Canadian writers must engage in a struggle to reclaim the language and its structures of meaning from the British and American inheritance it conceals within it, 'Unhiding the hidden' (first published in 1974), the most discussed of Kroetsch's essays, has come to be regarded as an early and influential articulation of postcolonial theory.

Like *The studhorse man* and *Gone Indian*, Kroetsch's fifth novel, *Badlands* (1975), generally parodies the male adventure quest: its river-raft journey into the Alberta Badlands variously recalls and inverts a number of tales, including the underworld descents made by both Orpheus and Coyote, the gathering of troops for the final seige of Troy, and Mark Twain's *Huckleberry Finn*. Its story of William Dawe, a paleontologist who leads an expedition in search of dinosaur bones, is reconstructed by Anna Dawe, who uses her father's field notes to recreate, a generation later, his journey of exploration. Her discovery that 'There are no truths, only correspondences' suggests much about the way Kroetsch's fiction makes it impossible to feel that any interpretation is ever final.

With its play with ideas about language and its tale of prairie people who begin a War Against the Sky, *What the crow said* (1978) continues Kroetsch's investigations of myth and his ironic reconsiderations of his literary and intellectual tradition. (He has described it as his attempt to write a 'deconstructed' work of fiction.) Located more clearly in the realm of the fantastic than any previous work, this novel shows the impact on Kroetsch of Latin American writers such as Gabriel García Márquez. In 1980 Kroetsch published *The 'Crow' journals*, selections from the journal he kept while working on the novel.

Alibi (1983) and *The puppeteer* (1992) represent two-thirds of a trilogy he has decided not to finish. In *Alibi*—a novel about gender, desire, and guilt that plays with patterns of death and rebirth, fall and regeneration—William William Dorfendorf is on a quest that carries him from the New World to the Old. In the employ of a wealthy collector, the mysterious and god-like Jack Deemer, he must find the perfect spa. (Water—and wasteland imagery—recur throughout Kroetsch's fiction.) In *The puppeteer* Deemer becomes the framing narrator of a complex story that plays with the borderlines between life and art and between metaphysics and fiction. The movement of the previous novel is reversed, so that the detective-like 'Dorf' is now accused of a crime and finds himself in flight rather than in quest, his freedom growing ever more limited.

In the seventies and eighties, Kroetsch also emerged as an important poet, working chiefly with the long poem. (*The stone hammer poems*, 1975, collects his earlier, shorter, poems.) *The ledger* (1975) and *Seed catalogue* (1977) attracted special interest for his creation of a palimpsest, in which his poem is superimposed onto found documents of an earlier era. These two poems, along with *The sad Phoenician* (1979), *The criminal intensities of love as paradise* (1981), *Letters to Salonika* (1983), *Advice to my friends* (1985), *Excerpts from the real world* (1986), and others are collected in *Completed field notes* (1989), a long poem made out of long poems, unified not by content but through juxtaposition, repetition, permutation, and voice.

Kroetsch has also been an influential critic and theorist, one who helped provoke Canadian interest in postmodernism as a literary and intellectual movement. In *Labyrinths of voice* (1981), a book-length interview with Shirley Neuman and Robert Wilson, he drew heavily on post-structuralist and other contemporary criticism to contextualize his ideas about writing. Many of the critical essays he published between 1971 to 1989 may be found, often extensively revised, in *The lovely treachery of words* (1989). Theoretically informed, they are couched in a characteristic personal voice that ranges from playful to oracular as Kroetsch traces out a Canadian tradition that is characterized by ironic indirection and gaps, and that has been shaped by fragmentation and marginality. His early travel book, *Alberta* (1968), was reissued in 1993 with a new Afterword by Rudy WIEBE. In 1995 he published *A likely story: the writing life*, a series of sketches that blend autobiographical reminisences with reflections on writing and on his reading of Laurence, Wiebe, and Wallace Stegner. He is currently in the final stages of work on his ninth novel.

Kroetsch's writing has received considerable critical attention: books, essays, special issues of journals, and academic conferences have been devoted to it. Good starting points are Robert Lecker, *Robert Kroetsch* (1986); and the two special issues of *OPEN LETTER*: 'Robert Kroetsch: Reflections' (*Open Letter* Fifth series, nos. 8-9, Summer-Fall 1984) and 'Kroetsch at Niederbronn' (*Open Letter* Ninth series, nos. 5-6, Spring-Summer 1996). An excellent and up-to-date electronic bibliography is currently maintained on-line by Dennis Cooley at http://130.179.92.25/canlitx/Robert_KroetschB.html. *The Robert Kroetsch papers: first accession* is a partial guide to his papers, held in the archives of the University of Calgary. RUSSELL BROWN

Kulyk Keefer, Janice (b. 1953). Born Janice Kulyk and raised in Toronto, Ontario, the child of a Ukrainian father and a Polish immigrant mother, she draws upon the experience of inhabiting more than one cultural world in her poetry, fiction, and critical writing. A graduate of the University of Toronto, she completed an M.A. and a Ph.D. in modern English literature as a Commonwealth Scholar at the University of Sussex, England. After a year in France, she and her husband moved to Nova Scotia, where both taught at the Université Sainte-Anne between 1982 and 1989. During this period her creativity was fuelled by isolation, and the desire to see herself in print. After winning the CBC short-story competition for two consecutive years, Kulyk Keefer published three books of short stories, *The Paris-Napoli Express* (1986), *Transfigurations* (1987), and *Travelling ladies* (1990); a book of poems, *White of the lesser angels* (1986); her first novel, *Constellations* (1988); and *Under eastern eyes: a critical reading of Maritime fiction* (1987), nominated for a Governor General's Award. She teaches creative writing and English literature at the University of Guelph, Ontario.

Kulyk Keefer's poetry is spare and elegant, and her fiction is written with a clean, precise control. Many of her short stories from this period, as well as her novel, are set on the French shore of Nova Scotia and explore the tensions and limitations within a society defined by language, history, and geography and that regards outsiders with suspicion. In *Under eastern eyes*, Kulyk Keefer analyses a body of writing often overlooked both by nationalist critics following Northrop FRYE, who read Canadian literature in terms of thematic paradigms, and by critics who favour more experimental writing than the predominantly realist traditions of the Maritimes. Her thesis is that the fiction of this region has its own themes and traditions, generated by its distinct cultural history, and she supports her claims with engaging discussions of writers from Thomas Chandler HALIBURTON to David Adams RICHARDS.

Along with reviews and articles on literature, ethnicity, and multiculturalism, Kulyk Keefer has written a second critical book, *Reading Mavis Gallant* (1989), in which she examines GALLANT's many uncollected stories, along with her more familiar collections. Gallant, the expatriate Canadian short-story writer, has influenced Kulyk Keefer's own literary development, and her third book of short stories, *Travelling ladies* (1990), uses the motif of journeying to explore her female protagonists' lives, families, and relations to culture at crucial points of transition. Her novel *Rest Harrow* (1992) continues to employ tension between movement and stasis, physical and emotional journeys. The Canadian protagonist, Anna, escapes her lover for a year's research in England, only to find new demands upon her fragile self-containment. Similarly, in *The green library* (1996)—runner-up for a Governor General's Award—the stability of the heroine, Eva, is irrevocably altered when her Ukrainian heritage is revealed to her, causing her to visit Kiev and revisit a past now equally foreign. While Kulyk Keefer has often created immigrant characters, this is the first novel to use her own ethnic heritage, and the result is a powerful look at the divided experience of one world that demands conformity as the price of acceptance and of another that equally demands loyalty and silence about the darker elements of its culture and history.

See Colin Nicholson, 'Grain of the actual: Janice Kulyk Keefer and her writing', and Coral Ann Howells, 'Janice Kulyk Keefer's *Travelling Ladies*', both published in the *British Journal of Canadian Studies* 7.2 (1992).

HEATHER SANDERSON

Kurapel, Alberto. See DRAMA IN FRENCH 1981 TO 1996: 6.

Kusugak, Michael Arvaarlok. See ABORIGINAL LITERATURE: INUIT LITERATURE 1982 TO 1996.

Kwa, Lydia. See LESBIAN LITERATURE.

L

Laberge, Albert (1877-1960). Laberge is best known for his novel *La Scouine*, but he was also the author of thirteen published volumes of stories and sketches and an unpublished novel, as well as of poems and literary articles published in periodicals. Some of his journalism appears under the pseudonym 'Adrien Clamer'. He was born in Beauharnois, Quebec, where his family had occupied the same land since 1659. While attending the Collège Sainte-Marie in Montreal, apparently expecting to prepare for the priesthood after his *cours classique*, he occasionally visited the library of an uncle who was a doctor and avidly read the French Naturalists. A confession of this 'sin' led to his expulsion from the Collège and, so far as we can judge from his story 'La vocation manquée', to his lifelong anti-clericalism. For four difficult years Laberge held odd jobs and studied law—feeling an aversion, one presumes, to returning to the family farm. In 1896 he began to work for *La Presse*, where he continued for thirty-six years, mainly as sports writer but also as art critic. In 1932 he retired to Châteauguay, where he was able to give more time to writing.

His literary talent showed early. In 1895 Laberge won a prize offered by the newspaper *Le Samedi* for a realistic story; shortly afterwards he became a frequent visitor to the ÉCOLE LITTÉRAIRE DE MONTRÉAL. A dedication to realism and a high regard for writing as an art became permanent obsessions. *La* SCOUINE (*Bitter bread*, 1977, translated by Conrad Dion)—considered to be the first realistic novel in Canada—was published in 1918 in an edition of sixty copies because it was too offensive for its time in Quebec. (Rodolphe GIRARD, after a much milder show of disrespect for the clergy, was being persecuted by loss of employment and ostracism.) All Laberge's other works were published after his retirement. But it has been argued that he could not develop fully in spare-time writing. All his books, including his novel, consist of short pieces that were much worked over and show the constraints of the author's negativism. His stories were collected in *Visages de la vie et de la mort* (1936), *La fin du voyage* (1942), *Scènes de chaque jour* (1942), *Le destin des hommes* (1950), *Fin de roman* (1951), *Images de la vie* (1952), and *Le dernier souper* (1953). He also published two volumes of sketches and prose poems: *Quand chantait la cigale* (1936) and *Hymnes à la terre* (1955); and three volumes of memoirs and criticism: *Peintures et écrivains d'hier et d'aujourd'hui* (1938), *Journalistes, écrivains et artistes* (1945), and *Propos sur nos écrivains* (1954). Thirteen of his stories and extracts from his other works are included in *Anthologie d'Albert Laberge* (1963), which has a valuable introduction by Gérard BESSETTE.

Most of Laberge's works treat village or farm life. He also wrote many urban sketches; but, unusually for his time, he made no moral opposition between city life and country life. His sketches of the country are characterized by grim realism, though he avoids all but the slightest rare hint of didacticism. His characters are determined by their narrow milieu and seem incapable of learning; often they live in a complete moral void. Laberge excels in the sharp detail—such as a set of false teeth left among wedding keepsakes in 'Le notaire'—to epitomize the grotesque incongruity between reality and our conventional images of life.

A thorough bibliography is contained in Jacques Brunet, *Albert Laberge, sa vie et son oeuvre* (1969). JACK WARWICK

Laberge, Marie (b.1950). Born in Quebec, she received her early education there and entered the École de journalisme et d'information of Université Laval in 1970, studying in several faculties; she took part as well in collective productions of the local Troupe des Treize. From 1972 to 1975 she studied acting at the Conservatoire d'art dramatique de Québec, then taught theatre at the Université du Québec à Chicoutimi and developed theatre courses for Danse-Partout. She earned an enviable reputation as actress, producer, and educationalist before launching her career as dramatist. A versatile and prolific author, Laberge has written for radio, film, and television; her professional career includes administrative positions at the Théâtre du Trident and the Centre d'essai des auteurs dramatiques (of which she was president, 1987-9). She was vice-president of the Conseil québécois du théâtre, 1983-6, and has been editor of theatre publications at Boréal since 1991.

The plays of Laberge are characterized by their intensity, emotion, and often violence: some become melodramatic; others depict human distress with convincing realism. She develops plot and structure—generally linear—with great skill, and excels in the psychological delineation of character, especially that of women, who occupy the foreground of her work. Her first published play, *C'était avant la guerre à l'Anse à Gilles* (1981; translated by Alan Brown as *Before the war, down at l'Anse à Gilles*, 1986) won a Governor General's Award. It is the sympathetic tale of a young widow who decides to free herself and an abused friend from the oppressiveness of their Quebec village life in 1936. *Ils étaient venus pour. . .* (1981) was first written for drama students in Chicoutimi. Based loosely on fact, it traces the life and death of the village of Val-Jalbert in the Lac Saint-Jean region from 1902 to 1927. *Avec l'hiver qui s'en vient* (1981) examines the breakdown in the relationship of a retired working-class couple whose life has been governed by the social norms of their generation. Even darker in mood is *Jocelyne Trudelle trouvée morte dans ses larmes* (1983) where the heroine, who has attempted suicide, hovers between life and death.

While the family was still present as a theme, through differing scenarios Laberge went on to create a portrait gallery of women—passionate, suffering, scheming, or admirable. In *Deux tangos pour toute une vie* (1985) the wife seeks fulfilment; she finds it briefly in a passionate affair, but resigns herself to ordinary life. *Le Night Cap Bar* (1987) is a suspense drama about three women who meet in a sleazy bar whose owner is found dead. In *Oublier* (1987; translated by Rina Fraticelli as *Forgetting*, 1988), the four daughters of a woman dying of Alzheimer's disease are briefly reunited on a stormy winter night; each has suppressed memories that have warped their lives. *Aurélie, ma soeur* (1988; translated by Rina Fraticelli as *Aurélie, my sister*, 1989) is set against a sombre background of complex family relations, but the figure of Aurélie stands out as a model of understanding and generosity. Laberge transforms historical figures in *Pierre; ou La consolation* (1992). Set in the twelfth century, the play centres on Héloise as she watches over the body of Pierre Abélard, which she imagines has been brought to her abbey by the Prior of the Abbaye de Cluny. Throughout the night they discuss love and desire in the divine order.

Virtually all Laberge's plays have proved popular with the Quebec public. Her first play to attract international attention was *L'homme gris* (1986; translated by Rina Fraticelli as *Night*, 1988), in which a middle-aged man harangues his victimized daughter until she rebels in a gesture of ultimate violence. The play was largely responsible for Laberge's receiving the award of the Croix de Chevalier de l'Ordre des Arts et des Lettres in France in 1989. At least four other plays have been staged successfully in Europe.

A notable feature of Laberge's theatre is the variety in language. The 'popular' dialogue, reproduced in an almost phonetic transcript of regional dialects, has been 'adapted' for French and other European productions. For *Pierre; ou La consolation* the author developed a form of speech to recreate the atmosphere of the Middle Ages.

Since 1989 Laberge has published four successful novels about self-knowledge and sexual passion: *Juillet* (1989) depicts violence in a family where the father has a passionate relationship with his daughter-in-law; *Quelques adieux* (1992, winner of the Prix des lectrices de *Elle-Québec*) traces the recovery of a woman whose late husband has been involved in an affair with one of his students; *Le poids des ombres* (1994) is about a young woman who finds herself as she learns to understand the complex life of her mother, who has committed suicide; *Annabelle* (1996) is the story of an adolescent who renounced music before her parents' divorce and now seeks her own way of living.

See Gilbert David and Pierre Lavoie, 'Marie Laberge', *Jeu*, 21 (1981); André Dionne, 'Marie Laberge, dramaturge', *Lettres québécoises*, 25 (printemps 1982); André Smith, ed., *Marie Laberge, dramaturge: actes du colloque international* (1989); Laurent Lapierre, 'La lucidité et l'intensité' and Mary Jean Green, 'Marie Laberge, une romancière passionnée', both in *Lettres québécoises*, 81 (printemps 1996).

BARBARA McEWEN

Lacerte, Alcide. See NOVELS IN FRENCH 1900 TO 1920.

Lacey, E.A. See GAY LITERATURE: 3.

Lachance, Louis (1899-1963). Born in Saint-Joachim de Montmorency, Québec, he studied at the Petit Séminaire de Québec and, after graduating in 1920, joined the Dominican Order at St-Hyacinthe, the traditional stronghold of Quebec Thomism, which sent him to study at its philosophical college in Ottawa. He remained there as a teacher until 1936, apart from the years 1929-31, when he studied in Rome. His *Nationalisme et religion* (1936)—which set out to show how nationalist convictions could be reconciled with a religion that was international in scope—provided the foundation for a nationalism based on reason, as distinct from the nationalism of Abbé Lionel GROULX, which was founded chiefly on tradition and feeling. Lachance's basic notion—which was to become influential among French-speaking intellectuals in Canada, and would help turn Roman Catholic scholars towards a friendly posture on nationalism—was that the modern nation is the most effective way of achieving the necessary collective response to modern problems, and that the nation provides a vehicle for moral action. Lachance generally expressed himself as a cautious federalist, but in Quebec his concerns about culture and language endeared him to both separatists and federalists. His thoughts on moral practice were published in *Où vont nos vies* (1934).

In 1936 Lachance was called to teach philosophy in Rome at the Angelicum University. On the outbreak of war he returned to Canada, where he served as a priest in the diocese of Sherbrooke and took part in the founding of the Séminaire Saint-Apôtres. In 1943 he moved to the Université de Montréal, first as professor, and later as dean, in the faculty of philosophy. His pioneering *Philosophie du langage* (1943) substantially predates the popularity of 'linguistic philosophy' and raises many basic questions. While in Montreal he published *Le droit et les droits de l'homme* (1959), which develops the theory that human rights are meaningless if seen merely in the context of subjects and their desires: they depend upon the community, and so must be related to the common good and to basic social responsibilities. In its emphasis on community and responsibility, Lachance's theory has affinities with the work of Simone Weil, and resembles in important respects the theory of rights put forward in English Canada by John WATSON. Lachance also wrote a historical legal study, *Le concept de droit selon Aristote et St. Thomas* (1948); a metaphysical study, *L'être et ses propriétés* (1950); and a religious study, *La lumière de l'âme* (1955).

Though Lachance read widely, was an original thinker, and built upon various philosophical traditions, St Thomas always held a central place in his writings. At the end of his life he returned to a revision of his *L'humanisme politique de St. Thomas d'Aquin* (2 vols, 1939), but did not live to finish this work; a partly revised second edition was published in 1964.

LESLIE ARMOUR

Lachance, Micheline. See NOVELS IN FRENCH 1983 TO 1996: 1, 6.

Lacombe, Patrice (1807-63). Born at Lac-des-Deux-Montagnes, Quebec, he studied first at Oka, then at the Collège de Montréal, becoming a notary in 1930 and working as an accountant for the Séminaire de Montréal until his death. His short novel, *La terre paternelle* (Montréal, 1846), the prototype of the 'roman paysan' in Quebec, began a literary tradition that was to last over 100 years and spawn some sixty variations. (First appearing, unsigned, in the *Album littéraire et musical de la Revue canadienne*, it had ten printings from 1871 to 1924; the most recent edition appeared in 1981.) Having deeded the Chauvin family's land to his eldest son, the father is compelled by the son's mismanagement to repossess it; attracted, however, by the prestige of the merchant class, he then rents out the farm and settles in the village; eventually his business there fails, he loses the farm to an 'Anglais', and the family is forced to move to a slum in the Montreal suburbs, where father and son eke out a living as carters of water. The farm is restored to the family name only when a wayward son, who has spent years with the North West Company, returns and buys it back. Basically a defence of the traditional ideological preference for the agricultural rather than the urban life, the novel also portrays peasant avarice; this element, and the tension that develops between father and son after the deeding of the land, are at odds with the attempt to idealize farm life. Lacombe sprinkles his work with many realistic touches and with popular speech—though, like other nineteenth-century authors, he sets it off in italics and adds standard equivalents.

The 1973 and 1980 editions of *La terre paternelle* contain a critique by André Vanasse, while the 1981 edition has a preface by Maurice Lemire. BEN-Z. SHEK

La Corne, Luc de (known as La Corne Saint-Luc). See Writing in NEW FRANCE: 1.

Lacourcière, Luc (1910-89). Born in Saint-Victor-de-Beauce, Quebec, the son of country doctor Henri Lacourcière and Emma Gosselin, he had an eclectic education before graduating from the École Normale Supérieure at Université Laval with his Licence ès lettres in 1934. He taught for a year in Switzerland, returning home without employment; but was offered the task of compiling the report on the second Congress on the French Language by Mgr Camille ROY, which he eagerly accepted. In this period Lacourcière had two decisive encounters: with Marius BARBEAU, author of the then recently published *Romancero du Canada*, and Félix-Antoine SAVARD, who had just published his *MENAUD, MAÎTRE DRAVEUR*.

After helping establish Laval's French-language summer school in 1938, Lacourcière began working with Barbeau on medieval ballads, while accepting in 1940 a position as a professor of French at Laval. The twin strands of folklore and literature, with the former dominant, were to govern the rest of his career. He founded the Archives de Folklore in 1944, and for the next thirty years collected vast quantities of oral data from the francophone traditions of eastern Canada, chiefly in Quebec and the Maritime Provinces. In 1946 he founded the series 'Les Archives de Folklore', which was to become the major publication in FOLKLORE IN FRENCH for the next forty years, and began work on fundamental research tools of francophone folklore scholarship: a *Bibliographie raisonnée des traditions populaires françaises d'Amérique*, a *Catalogue de la chanson folklorique française,* and the *Catalogue raisonné du conte populaire de l'Amérique française*. In 1944 he had founded the 'Nénuphar' collection, intended to publish, or republish, classics of Quebec literature; his critical edition of Émile NELLIGAN's *Poésies complètes* (1952) was highly acclaimed.

Lacourcière's career as folklore collector, teacher, administrator, editor, and defender of folklore studies did not allow him to produce a large written corpus. But his reputation brought him many deserved honours: membership in the Royal Society of Canada (1962), the Société des Dix (1966), the Order of Canada (Companion, 1970), the Lorne PIERCE medal (1972), the Order of Merit and medal of the Société Saint-Jean-Baptiste de Québec (1976), the Prix de l'Académie canadienne-française (1985), and honorary degrees from McGill (1966), Memorial (1975), and Laurentian (1977) universities, among others. In taking up Marius Barbeau's mantle, Lacourcière was the dominant figure in North American francophone folklore studies for the best part of his career, teaching or influencing almost every francophone folklorist of any note from the 1940s to the late 1970s. GERALD THOMAS

Ladoo, Harold Sonny (1945-73). Born in Couva, Trinidad, he came to Toronto in 1968 and received a B.A. in English from Erindale College, University of Toronto. He died in Trinidad under mysterious circumstances—he was presumably murdered. Ladoo's talent as a novelist was recognized and encouraged by Peter SUCH and Dennis LEE, but Ladoo found no popular acceptance as a writer while he lived. Before he left Toronto for the last time he was working as a dishwasher at a restaurant. Lee's long poem 'On the death of Harold Ladoo' is a meditation on a talent destroyed prematurely.

Although Ladoo's estate includes fragments from nine uncompleted novels, only two have been published: *No pain like this body* (1972) and *Yesterdays* (1974), published posthumously. Ladoo intended these works to form part of a Faulknerian cycle encompassing the history of the West Indies, his own biography, a history of Canada in the Caribbean, and slavery. *No pain like this body* is a plotless novel about a family of East Indian rice-growers in 1905, on an imaginary Carib island. Written in dialect, and incorporating the point of view of a child terrified by a rainstorm, the novel treats, with an engaging lyricism, brutality, death, insanity, and sickness. *Yesterdays* is about a Hindu in Trinidad in 1955 who wants to go to Canada and convert Canadians to Hinduism, in the same way Canadian missionaries went to Trinidad to convert the people there. Under a simple plot lies a fine comic sense, often bawdy or scatological, and beneath that is a bitter indictment of colonialism, poverty, and enforced religion.

See L.R. Early, 'The two novels of Harold Ladoo', *World Literature Written in English* 15 (1976); Clement C. Wyke, 'Harold Ladoo's alternative worlds: Canada and Carib island', *CANADIAN LITERATURE* 95 (1982).

GEOFF HANCOCK

Laferrière, Dany (b. 1953). Born in Port-au-Prince, Haiti, where he practised journalism, he was the co-founder of the weekly journal *Le Petit Samedi Soir*. When his colleague Gasner Raymond was found murdered during Duvalier's regime, Laferrière moved to Montreal in 1978. He then embarked, not without difficulty, on a career as a writer. In less than ten years he published the first of seven books, all of them grounded in his own life and including fictionalized memoirs of his childhood and wise and amusing takes on life as a Black in a mainly white environment. They feature a well-tuned ear for language and dialogue and an easy narrative style.

Laferrière achieved celebrity with the publication of his first book, *Comment faire l'amour avec un Nègre sans se fatiguer* (1985)—translated by David Homel as *How to make love to a Negro* (1987). Called a novel, it is made up of fictionalized autobiographical episodes, each with a colourful title, narrated by a young black immigrant who lives near Montreal's Carré St-Louis and takes pleasure from being desired by white women. While humorous, the novel also attacks racism, stereotypes, and other negative portrayals of human beings. The novel was the basis of a film (1988) directed by Jacques W. Benoît.

Éroshima (1987)—translated by David Homel as *Eroshima* (1991)—is a novel with international settings, made up of brief *pensées*, episodes, dialogues, in which the names of John Lennon and Rita Hayworth are mentioned, and Norman Mailer, Alberto Moravia, V.S. Naipaul, and the black painter Jean-Michel Basquiat make appearances. Love affairs with the Japanese-Canadian Hoki, and her friend Keiko and others, are central. The idea for this book was the image of a young couple making love in Hiroshima on the morning of the dropping of the atom bomb, which is a recurring image that fascinates the narrator, suggesting both sexual energy and 'a kind of ecstasy brought on by evil'.

In *L'odeur du café* (1991)—translated by David Homel as *An aroma of coffee* (1993)—the narrator is a ten-year-old boy who describes his childhood and his relationship with his grandmother, Da, who is the centre of life in a Haitian village. For its sensitivity and lyricism, this novel is Laferrière's masterpiece. The sequel, *Le goût des jeunes filles* (1992)—translated by David Homel as *Dining with the dictator* (1994)—is also a lyrical novel. After a dispute with one of the dictator Duvalier's *tontons macoutes* in Port-au-Prince, an adolescent boy takes refuge in Miki's house across the street, where he discovers the power of words (represented by the poetry of the Haitian Magloire Saint-Aude) and contemplates the beauty of the girls living in the house (the power of sex). This initiation into the world of women makes him feel that he has discovered the secret of life.

Cette grenade dans la main du jeune Nègre est-elle une arme ou un fruit? (1993)—translated by David Homel as *Why must a black writer write about sex?* (1994)—is called a novel on the cover of the English edition, but the first sentence says 'This is not a novel.' It is a series of chapters—conversations, anecdotes, mini-essays, portraits of black celebrities—drawn from a well-informed black writer's experiences of the 1990s. *Chronique de la dérive douce* (1994) is a collection of 365 autobiographical short poems and prose paragraphs that describe the narrator's daily life during his first days in Montreal as a Haitian immigrant, and the contradictions experienced by a young writer who has to work in a factory. He becomes a dreamer who persists in believing in the harmony and power of words. The texts also trace the complexities of co-existence between the so-called 'visible minorities' and the historical and cultural majority.

BERNARD DELPÊCHE

Lafitau, Joseph-François. See Writing in NEW FRANCE: 1.

Lahaise, Guillaume. See POETRY IN FRENCH: 4.

Lahontan, Louis-Armand de Lom d'Arce de. See Writing in NEW FRANCE: 1.

Lai, Larissa. See LESBIAN LITERATURE.

Lalonde, Michèle (b. 1937). Poet, essayist, dramatist, and writer for radio, she began writing and publishing while still a student at the Université de Montréal. After receiving a degree in philosophy in 1959 she did research at Harvard in 1960, in Baltimore (1962-3), and in London (1963-4). She wrote a series of programs on philosophers and intellectuals for Radio-Canada in 1964 and in 1965 began work at the Université de Montréal on a doctorate she never completed.

Lalonde's first book of poetry, *Songe de la fiancée détruite* (1958), a poem written for radio (produced by Jean-Guy PILON, Radio-Canada, 1958), is based on the themes of solitude and the inability of people to communicate. *Geôles* (1959) presents a 'climat cauchemardesque' (nightmare)—voids and abysses, hatred, cries, anger, violence, and destruction—and shows the influence of SAINT-DENYS-GARNEAU and Anne HÉBERT in particular. At about this time Lalonde became involved in editing, and writing essays for, intellectual reviews, first as a member of the editorial staff of *Situations* (1959) and then by contributing regularly to *LIBERTÉ*. She became a member of the editorial board (1963-4) of *Liberté* with Pilon, Jacques GODBOUT, and Fernand OUELLETTE, writing news stories and articles. Ten years later, as one of the editorial team of *Maintenant* (1973-4), she wrote a series of essays on Quebec nationalism and the linguistic debate.

A profound change occurred in Lalonde's poetic concepts in the mid-1960s. Formerly esoteric, her poems became 'committed': no longer addressed to a limited readership, they sought a wider audience and adherence to the socio-political concerns of the people. In addition, the borders between poetry and the essay began to disappear for her, 'commitment' becoming the major concern in her work. This was evident in the poem she wrote for the symphonic fresco *Terre des hommes* (music by André Prévost) that inaugurated Expo 67 in Montreal; in the celebrated poem 'Speak white' (1968) recited at the 'Nuit de la poésie' in Mar. 1970; and in her lectures, essays, manifestos, and statements on politics, the role of writers and intellectuals, and the status of women in Quebec.

The impact of Lalonde's work continued to spread in Quebec and abroad. She collaborated with writers, intellectuals, painters, and musicians to develop new means of expression, giving her a closer contact with the public. In 1977 she experimented with a historical play entitled *Dernier recours de Baptiste à Catherine* (having had her first play, *Ankrania ou Celui qui crie*, produced in 1957). She edited an important selection of texts, *Défense et illustration de la langue québécoise suivie de proses et poèmes* (1979), and was awarded the Prix Duvernay in 1980 for the body of her work.

See Jean-Pierre Faye, 'La défense de Michèle Lalonde ou le goût de POT-LAID-MICKEY' in *Liberté*, no. 129 (mai-juin 1980); François Hébert, 'Des dazibaos à Outremont' in *Liberté*, no. 127 (jan.-fév. 1980); and D.G. JONES, 'An interview with Michèle Lalonde' in *Ellipse*, no. 3 (Spring 1970).

RICHARD GIGUÈRE

Lalonde, Robert. See NOVELS IN FRENCH 1983 TO 1996: 7.

Lampman, Archibald (1861-99). He was born in Morpeth, Canada West (Ontario), where his father was an Anglican clergyman. His family moved to Parrytown in 1866 and the next year to Gore's Landing in the Rice Lake district, where Lampman came to know the Strickland sisters, Susanna MOODIE and Catharine Parr TRAILL. In 1868 he contracted rheumatic fever, which contributed to his early death. In 1874 his family moved to Cobourg and from 1876 to 1879 he attended Trinity College School, Port Hope, and then Trinity College, Toronto, where he contributed literary essays and poems to *Rouge et noir*, the college magazine. In the spring of 1880 he read, 'in a state of wildest excitement', a new book of poems, *Orion* (1880), by Charles G.D. ROBERTS, whom he would later know. In 1883, after a brief and unsuccessful attempt at teaching in Orangeville High School, he became a clerk in the Post Office Department, Ottawa, a position he held for the rest of his life. From Ottawa he made walking tours of the surrounding countryside—which he loved, and loved to describe in verse—and with his friend Duncan Campbell SCOTT (also a government employee) canoeing expeditions into the wilderness. From 1883 until the last year of his life Lampman's poems appeared frequently in Canadian, American, and British periodicals, notably *The WEEK* and the Toronto *Globe* and, in the United States, *Harper's*, *Scribner's*, and *Youth's Companion*, a Boston magazine edited by his friend E.W. THOMSON. In 1887 Lampman married Maud Playter, and with the help of a small legacy she provided he published privately *Among the millet and other poems* (Ottawa, 1888). A daughter, Natalie, was born in 1892. From 6 Feb. 1892 to 1 July 1893 he joined Scott and Wilfred CAMPBELL in writing 'AT THE MERMAID INN', a weekly column of literary and social comment that appeared in the *Globe*. In 1894 his wife bore him a son, Arnold, who died at four months. Lampman was elected to the Royal Society of Canada in 1895 and that same year *Lyrics of earth* was published by Copeland and Day, Boston. A second son, Archibald Otto, was born in 1898.

In 1889 Lampman fell in love with Katherine Waddell, a fellow clerk. The exact nature of their relationship is still unclear, but they may have lived together for a time. This attachment was a source of great distress for Lampman in his last years. He was at work on the proofs of *Alcyone*, which he intended to have published in Edinburgh, when he died. Scott, as Lampman's literary executor, ordered a printing of twelve copies (Ottawa, 1899). This was the first of several editions of Lampman's poems edited by Scott, who endeavoured, all his life, to keep his friend's reputation alive. Scott also edited *The poems of Archibald Lampman* (1900), for which he provided a memoir; *Lyrics of earth: songs and ballads* (1925); *At the Long Sault and other new poems* (1943, with E.K. BROWN); and *Selected poems of Archibald Lampman* (1947).

At present no definitive account of Lampman's work is possible because of the lack of a comprehensive study of his papers held in archives, an adequate biography, or an edition of complete poems. A substantial number of Lampman's poems in manuscript remain unpublished, although a number of these poems have been appearing piecemeal in recent years. And, although Lampman's most important poetry has been collected in *The poems* of 1900 and *At the Long Sault*, these editions are not reliable. On the basis of material available in print and in manuscript, however, the essential nature of Lampman's achievement seems fairly clear. His reputation as the finest of the CONFEDERATION POETS is largely based on a small body of nature poetry written, for the most part, relatively early in his brief career. In recent years, however, critical emphasis has shifted from Lampman as gently melancholic heir of the Romantics and Victorians to Lampman as alienated precursor of modernism, leading to a new interest in Lampman's more obviously troubled later works and to new ways of looking at many of the justly admired nature poems.

Like Keats and Tennyson, the two greatest influences on his diction, Lampman was a master of sonority with few, if any, rivals in Canadian literature. Rhythmically he is sometimes fluent to the point of monotony, but he is capable of creating, through slight rhythmic variation, the impression of an immediate notation of moment-to-moment sensation. Lampman's later poetry was often experimental in its rhythms. The classical Greek metric scheme of 'Sapphics', the seven-foot anapestic line of 'The woodcutter's hut', the complex stanzaic form of 'An ode to the hills', all suggest a deliberate effort by Lampman to submit to the discipline of unusual and challenging metres. Other poems, such as 'Alcyone' or 'Personality', display a new rhythmic freedom. 'At the Long Sault' reflects both tendencies: the striking contrast between the very free iambs of the main narrative and the much more regular anapests of the lyrical ending is one of the finest rhythmic effects in Canadian poetry.

At least as important as the music of Lampman's verse is its pictorial quality. Lampman's nature poems abound in vivid pictures of the Canadian landscape that are both objective in their precise descriptiveness and subjective in their evocation of the intensely felt essence of the scene. Lampman's ability to express his vision with great immediacy through the accumulation and arrangement of musical and pictorial effects is at its best in his sonnets (e.g. 'In November', 'Solitude', 'Among the orchards', 'Sunset at Les Eboulements', 'Winter uplands'). The restraint and discipline of the sonnet form discouraged the shapelessness and discursiveness that mar much of his verse.

Lampman's vision owes much to Wordsworth in particular and to the Romantics in general. Humanity, spiritually exhausted by an unhealthy existence in the city, must renew itself through a solitary communion with nature that in its exalted state is usually described by Lampman as a 'dream', the most charged word in his vocabulary. In this dream-state humanity's energies are no longer at odds with one another, and the self-destructive 'strife' and 'change' of the city are replaced by an exquisite balance in which opposites are taken up, into a larger whole. (Lampman's account of the 'dream' is clearly influenced by Keats; another probable influence is the German lyric poet Eduard Mörike [1804-75]. In this and other respects Mörike's poetry bears striking resemblances to that of Lampman, who was of partly German extraction and studied and wrote about German literature.) However, the Romantic influence on Lampman, important though it is, is undercut by other elements, to the ultimate enrichment of the poetry. Wordsworth's 'wise passiveness' ('Expostulation and reply') was difficult to maintain in the face of either the apparently intractable problems of late nineteenth-century society or the harsh Canadian environment. In many of Lampman's finest poems (e.g., 'April', 'Heat', 'In November', 'Winter uplands') the celebration of nature is touched by unease, even fear. In particular the passivity involved in communion with nature comes to be seen as threatening, with its final end not a higher vision but death ('Death', 'A summer evening', 'The frost elves').

If Lampman's nature poetry at its best transforms the conventions he inherited into something personal and vivid, the same cannot be said about most of the rest of his verse. In his philosophical poems, very much influenced by Matthew Arnold, Lampman turns for consolation to idealized abstractions ('Beauty', 'Virtue'), to poetry ('What do poets want with gold?'), or to hope in the future ('The clearer self', 'The largest life'). These poems tend to be conventional and characterless in thought and diction. The narrative poems (apart from 'At the Long Sault', which is in a mixed lyric-narrative mode) are even less successful. Lampman, with his meditative cast of mind, shows little skill in the creation of plot or character, and his gift for capturing immediate sensations finds no scope in these poems, with their heightened rhetoric and bookishly exotic settings. One partial exception is 'A story of an affinity', his only narrative set in nineteenth-century Canada, which seems to reflect Lampman's painful relationship with Katherine Waddell. His earlier love poems, little more than sentimental literary exercises, are less interesting than the poems inspired by Waddell, published posthumously in *At the Long Sault and other new poems* ('A portrait in six sonnets'), and, more recently, in *Lampman's Kate: late love poems of Archibald Lampman* (1975) edited by Margaret Coulby Whitridge. Lampman's strong-minded 'friend', as he calls her, is a more convincing and challenging presence than the shadowy beloved of the earlier lyrics. Even these poems, however, lack passion or sensuality, for Lampman shared the prudery of his age with regard to 'uninnocent emotion' (see his essay 'The modern school of poetry in England'). The most intense note in the late love lyrics is of frustration and despair, as in 'Man', one of his finest and most painful poems.

The darkness of Lampman's late love lyrics typifies much of the poetry of his last years, where passive acceptance of nature's healing power is rejected as Lampman becomes increasingly concerned with the value of decisive action. This development is probably a response to his growing sense of helplessness in the face of unrewarding work at the post office, his agonizing relationship with Katherine Waddell, the deaths of his son and father, and his own failing health. His espousal of socialism in these years (see 'The Land of Pallas', or the untitled essay on socialism) seems diametrically opposed to his earlier praise of the solitary dream of nature far from the world of men: there is nothing dreamy about the powerful and sometimes strident invective in much of the later verse ('To a millionaire', 'The modern politician', 'Liberty'). In most of this poetry, with the exception of some excellent sonnets, the freshness of the earlier work tends to be sacrificed for larger, more abstract effects. But Lampman's new directions led to successes that could never have been predicted on the basis of his earlier work. One of the most impressive of these is 'The city of the end of things', a visionary poem in which industrial society is presented in nightmarish terms: the 'grim idiot at the gate', with which the poem ends, is Lampman's most powerful evocation of the death-like passivity to which his society threatened to reduce man's creative powers. The finest of the late poems is the unfinished 'At the Long Sault: May 1660', which, in the version edited by Scott, has become a Canadian classic. The poem describes the successful but suicidal attempt of Adam Dollard (called Daulac) and his company to save Ville-Marie from an Iroquois attack. Even in its imperfect state the poem is outstanding, not only for its formal boldness but also for its breadth of vision. Nature here is a source of both good and evil; humanity must choose to make of the world what it can. 'Dream' is once more a key word, but there is nothing passive about the dreaming of Daulac and his men. The lyric at the close, in which a harmony between humanity and nature has been achieved through active struggle and sacrifice, is a touching statement of the vision towards which Lampman had been moving in his later years.

Much of Lampman's previously inaccessible prose has been published in recent decades. The *Selected prose* (1975), edited by Barrie Davies, contains a number of pieces that throw important light on the poetry. 'Hans Fingerhut's frog lesson', an allegorical fairy tale, explores the poet's relationship to nature and society; the essay 'On happiness' expresses faith in 'creative activity' as a means of overcoming the frustrations of existence; an untitled essay on socialism provides useful insights into Lampman's later poems of social criticism. His most intrinsically valuable prose is to be found in his letters to Edward Thomson edited by Arthur Bourinot (1956) and, in more complete form, by Helen Lynn (1980), and in his contributions to 'At the Mermaid Inn' (see *At the Mermaid Inn . . .*, 1979, with an introduction by Barrie Davies). The Lampman of these writings is more varied and attractive than we might suspect from his poetry. His range of interests is surprisingly great and he shows himself capable of an irony—sometimes gently humorous, sometimes bitter—that the poems altogether lack.

As Lampman's prose suggests, much of what was most vital in him never found expression in his poetry. This anomaly was no doubt partly owing to his difficult personal circumstances and early death, but it also reflects the state of contemporary Canadian culture. In a more critically mature milieu Lampman might not have devoted so much of his time and energy to stillborn imitations of dated Romantic and Victorian models; even his best nature poetry often falls into clichés of sentiment and morality that suggest a certain immaturity of culture. And the Canadian culture of his day could provide little support or guidance for the poetry of radical social criticism he was beginning to write in his later works. Whether he would have succeeded along these bold new lines must remain a matter of conjecture; had he done so, the development of Canadian poetry would almost certainly have been very different.

Lyrics of earth and the Scott edition of *The poems* are available in recent reprints: the first (1978) edited by D.M.R. Bentley, and the second (1974), including 'At the Long Sault', with an introduction by Margaret Coulby Whitridge, who also edited *Lampman's sonnets, 1884-1899* (1976). See also *Comfort of the fields: the best-known poems of Archibald Lampman* (1979), a selection by Raymond SOUSTER, and *Selected poetry of Archibald Lampman* (1980) edited by Michael Gnarowski.

Carl Y. Connor, *Archibald Lampman. Canadian poet of nature* (1929), is a good biography but is out of date. Two useful collections of essays are Michael Gnarowski, *Archibald Lampman* (1970), and Lorraine McMullen, *The Lampman symposium* (1976). For an excellent account of the crucial theme of the dream in Lampman's work, see Sandra Djwa, 'Lampman's fleeting vision', *CANADIAN LITERATURE* 55 (1973). The best critical overview of the life and work is *Archibald Lampman* (1986) by L.R. Early. The manuscript material relating to Lampman is summarized in George Wicken, *Archibald Lampman: an annotated bibliography* (1980), which also includes Lampman's contributions to periodicals, works on the poet, and selected reviews.

ZAILIG POLLOCK

Lane, M. Travis (b. 1934). She was born Millicent Travis in San Antonio, Texas, and her early life was characterized by many changes of residence and by education in many places. At university she specialized in English literature, receiving a B.A. from Vassar, and an M.A. (1957) and a Ph.D. (1967) from Cornell University. She moved with her husband, Lauriat Lane, Jr, to New Brunswick in 1960 and they became Canadian citizens in 1973. From 1970 until the 1990s she was the principal poetry reviewer for *The FIDDLEHEAD*, where she contributed numerous reviews of Canadian and Caribbean poets.

Lane's first anthologized poems appeared in *Five poets: Cornell, 1960* (1960); her first book, *An inch or so of garden* (1969), was published by New Brunswick Chapbooks. This chapbook was followed by several larger volumes: *Poems 1968-1972* (1973), *Homecomings* (1977), and *Divinations and shorter poems* (1980), all published by FIDDLEHEAD POETRY BOOKS, Fredericton. A leaflet, *Walking under the nebulae* (1981), was published by the LEAGUE OF CANADIAN POETS. Other volumes include *Reckonings: poems 1979-1983* (1988), *Solid things: poems new and selected* (1993), *Temporary shelter* (1993), and *Night physics* (1994).

Despite appearances in many anthologies and unstinting praise by such reviewers as W.H. New, Guy Hamel, and Patricia Monk, Lane has not been sufficiently recognized as being one of a handful of poets of the first rank writing in Canada for at least a generation. Her work can be summed up in one phrase: 'Her poetry is her life.' That life is not merely the kind of amphibian existence most poets achieve. She is a true triphibian, comprising and harmonizing a rich spirituality; an erudition that has sought out, known, and responded to the best; and an ability to bring to a poem an imaginative gusto that arises from her senses and feeling.

See W.H. New, 'M. Travis Lane', *Dictionary of literary biography*, vol. 60 (1987).

FRED COGSWELL

Lane, Patrick (b. 1939). Born in Nelson, British Columbia, and educated at the University of British Columbia, Lane has lived mostly in the West and on the West Coast, supporting himself by working in the logging, mining, and construction industries and, later, by teaching. He has been writer-in-residence at the universities of Ottawa, Manitoba, and Alberta. With bill BISSETT and Seymour MAYNE, he established the small press Very Stone House in the early 1960s. His poetry collections include *Letters from the savage mind* (1966); *Separations* (1969); *Mountain oysters* (1971); *The sun has begun to eat the mountain* (1972); *Passing into storm* (1973); *Beware the months of fire* (1974); *Unborn things: South American poems* (1975); *Albino pheasants* (1977); *Poems new and selected* (1979), which won a Governor General's Award; *The measure* (1980); *Old mother* (1982); *Woman in the dust* (1983), extensively illustrated with Lane's own drawings; *Linen crow, a caftan magpie* (1984); *Selected poems* (1987); *Winter* (1990); *Mortal remains* (1991); and *Too spare, too fierce* (1995). In 1979 he published a collection with Lorna Uher, called *No longer two people*. He has also edited the work of his brother (q.v.), who died in 1964: *Collected poems of Red Lane* (1968).

The locus of much of Lane's early poetry—particularly in *Mountain oysters* and *The sun has begun to eat the mountains*—is the West Coast and the Prairies, as he writes of logging camps and forests, Native people, hunting, and bush farming. The poems are tough-minded and anecdotal, full of narratives about working-class people; they show a remarkable and moving empathy for lives that are hard, painful, and vulnerable. Lane has a fine gift for image, and writes of the tragic not histrionically but in understatement, often deflecting attention in a poem to some small detail that is made to carry the full horror of a situation. His genuine understanding of violence—the woman who aborts herself in a dingy hotel ('There was a woman bending'); the pregnant cat dipped in gasoline and set alight ('Last night in darkness')—challenges the reader's complacency. In later books—like *Unborn things* and *Albino pheasants*—Lane's language and imagery developed in subtlety, and there is a more reflective voice, with a broader historical and literary reference. The locus of the poems also broadened to include Europe and Latin America. *Poems new and selected* demonstrates the evolution of his work from a poetry that relied on narrative impact for its effects to one that expresses a painfully achieved personal vision, in passages of lyrical beauty. In *Old mother* he grieves in sombre, elegiac poems for the violations of history and human disorder. Life is a brutal pantomime of sexual conquest and deadly combat. In allegories of slaughter and bestial rapacity, such as 'The young man' and 'All my pretty ones', Lane explores the grotesque monsters that live 'below the mind', and concludes that the atavistic root of the psyche is the lust for death. Birds, especially predators and wild fowl, are a recurring motif. Many poems, like 'Old mother' and 'The mother', undertake a generic quest for shelter, but Lane finds the archetypal mother a predator: 'your talon deep in my heart'. Yet in the most moving poem in the book, 'A red bird bearing on his back an empty cup', the bird provides a talisman that seems a source of patience. In the image of the bird, Lane finds love of a kind, a source of consolation for pain and emptiness.

Lane's talent is multifaceted. He has often illustrated his poetry with his own drawings—stark, haunting images that seem to proceed from a nightmare vision. He has also published a collection of stories, *How do you spell beautiful? And other stories* (1992), most of which are located in the working-class communities of small company towns. He captures these dying towns and their impoverished inhabitants with a precise realism; but it is his lyric images that stay in the mind, like that of the young woman wringing diapers at the sink, the 'seven-month foetus high up against her heart', who could be the presiding muse of the stories.

In 1990 Lane published *Winter*, perhaps his most powerful sequence, forty-five poems on the theme of winter. It begins: 'The generosity of snow, the way it forgives/ transgression, filling in the many betrayals.' The poems show the mature Lane, still haunted by loss and violence, but with an uncanny gentleness and grace located in the desolate landscapes. In 1992, ready to exorcise some of his ghosts, he published *Mortal remains*, poems about the death of his brother and his father's murder, twenty-five years later. 'Poetry cannot save us,' he explains, 'but it can provide us with some small redemption.'

Over three decades Patrick Lane's work has made him central to the Canadian writing community. On the occasion of his fifty-fifth birthday Susan MUSGRAVE compiled and edited *Because you loved being a stranger: 55 poets celebrate Patrick Lane* (1994). A collection of poems written about or dedicated to Lane, it is a moving tribute to one of Canada's most gifted poets.

An interesting essay by Lane, in which he describes his poetics, is 'To the outlaw', in *New: American and Canadian poetry* 15 (1971). See also *Patrick Lane and his works* by George WOODCOCK (1984).

ROSEMARY SULLIVAN

Lane, Red (1936-64). Richard Stanley 'Red' Lane, the elder brother of Patrick LANE, was born in Nelson, British Columbia, and died in Vancouver of a cerebral haemorrhage. During his short life he lived in various parts of western Canada and worked at jobs that accommodated the 'maverick' wanderings recorded in his poems. Although most of his work appeared posthumously, Lane's poems were published in little magazines in the early 1960s. The Toronto journal *Ganglia* devoted its second issue to his book *1962: poems of Red Lane*, which brought him to the attention of poets such as Milton ACORN, who later lamented Lane's untimely death in the elegiac poem 'Words said sitting on a rock sitting on a saint'. In 1968 Seymour MAYNE and Patrick Lane (who cites his brother as an important influence on his decision to write) published *Collected poems of Red Lane* under their imprint, Very Stone House. (It was reprinted in 1978 by Black Moss Press.) The poems in the first section, 'The surprise sandwich', were written for children and are statements of feelings, experiences, and observations that conclude with questions involving the reader in a game of self-reflection and response. The core of the book, however, lies in the later sections, which chronicle Lane's experiences in a manner that, although not yet fully developed, is crisp and visually powerful and sometimes experimental. The book concludes with a haunting poem, 'Death of a poet (for Milton Acorn, ultimately)', that eerily foreshadows Lane's sudden death at twenty-eight. Like Acorn, Lane viewed the world from a populist standpoint: his poems portray incidents—on street-corners, in beer parlours and cheap hotels—in detailed observations that grow out of the poet's participation in these events. *War-cry* (1973) is a long anti-war poem dedicated to Lane's father and edited from manuscripts by his brother Patrick. Much of Red Lane's poetry bears marks of the uneasiness and lack of polish of the developing poet; but his work is significant for its controlled use of colloquial speech, and its strong and direct treatment of unadorned reality.

BRUCE MEYER

Langevin, André (b. 1927). Born in Montreal, he lost both his father and mother by the age of seven. His next five years were spent in an institution that he later described as 'asylum-like', a 'locked-in world', worse than the Saint-Vincent-de-Paul penitentiary. He later enrolled in the Collège de Montréal, pursuing his studies to the level of Belles-Lettres. After a series of odd jobs, his first regular employment was in 1945 as a messenger for *Le Devoir* where, six months later, he was made responsible for the paper's literary section. He remained in that position for three years, reading voraciously and 're-educating' himself: he was influenced by the writings of Camus and Sartre, and particularly by Gabrielle ROY's *BONHEUR D'OCCASION*. He published a great many articles, mostly on literary or artistic subjects, in *Le Devoir* and *Notre Temps*, as well as literary criticism for the Canadian Broadcasting Corporation. In 1948 he joined the information staff of Radio-Canada, becoming a producer there. Langevin was awarded a Guggenheim fellowship in 1955. A frequent contributor of articles on subjects of political or social interest to periodicals, he was awarded the 1967 Prix Liberté for his articles in *Le Magazine Maclean*. In 1978 he was voted 'Grand Montréalais' of the preceding two decades in the field of literature.

Langevin has written five novels that have established him as an important contemporary Quebec writer. *Évadé de la nuit* (1951), which won him his first Prix du Cercle du Livre de France, revealed a powerful imagination that at the time outstripped his craftsmanship. Though it lacks unity, is forced in tone, and is flawed by such excesses as ten deaths—including two suicides—it is nonetheless a compelling drama of human incommunicability. Twenty-year-old Jean Cherteffe —who never knew his mother, was abandoned by his alcoholic father, and raised amid the terrors and sordidness of an orphanage—unsuccessfully attempts to rehabilitate Roger Benoît, a drunken poet he once admired and whom he gradually identifies with his father. The last two chapters relate the growing love between Jean and Micheline, the death of Micheline in childbirth, and Jean's suicide in the snow.

In *POUSSIÈRE SUR LA VILLE* (1953) Langevin relates the tragedy of Alain Dubois, a young doctor in the mining town of Macklin, and his unfaithful wife Madeleine. This short novel, which has all the elements of classical tragedy and is written in a beautifully simple style, was translated by John Latrobe and Robert Gottlieb as *Dust over the city* (1955).

Pity for his fellow men is the chief characteristic of Pierre Dupas in Langevin's third novel, *Le temps des hommes* (1956), whose title refers directly to Job, 10:5. Set in the forests of northern Quebec five years after the end of the Second World War, it portrays the fate of Dupas, a defrocked priest, who lost his faith ten years earlier when, unable to perform an expected miracle, he was obliged to watch a twelve-year-old boy die of meningitis. Framing the revelations of Dupas's personal tragedy is the conflict between Laurier and Gros Louis, foreman of the logging crew and lover of Laurier's frustrated twenty-eight-year-old wife of five years, Yolande. This novel, in which all the characters seem to be the hapless playthings of a cruel and unfathomable fate, fails to integrate the themes associated with Dupas into the plot of violence, jealousy, and revenge.

L'élan d'Amérique (1972)—which was awarded the Grand Prix Littéraire of Montreal—is infinitely complex, full of symbolic imagery, and constantly shifts back and forth between dream and reality. Here Langevin presents Claire Smith, an American with roots in Quebec on her mother's side, who is married to Stephen Peabody, the wealthy vice-president of the United States Pulp and Paper Company. Amoral, liberated, but spiritually lost and empty, she searches in vain for the male who will dominate her. Through Antoine, a guide working for an American logging company who has left his wife and children to live in the forest, she acquires dignity and strength. A tremendous moose appears in the forest—'l'élan d'Amérique'—symbolizing the perfection of creation and of man, the male, the master of the universe. The first instinctive reaction of Claire is to slaughter him; Antoine's is to protect him. But in the end the moose is killed and Antoine brings back to Claire its head and antlers. He then flees from a world full of ugliness and disorder, seeking refuge in the woods, and Claire, after shoving the moosehead out of the Cessna that was flying her back to civilization, commits suicide by jumping after it. Langevin here denounces some of the conditions that enslave the people of Quebec: existential alienation, exploitation, dispossession, and assimilation by the North American whole.

In Langevin's fifth novel, *Une chaîne dans le parc* (1974), many of the themes of *Évadé de la nuit* are dealt with in such a way as to give the impression that it was preceded by *Une chaîne*, which portrays with extraordinary vividness the violence or indifference of adults in their dealings with young children, as experienced by eight-year-old Pierrot, whose father abandoned him after his mother died of tuberculosis. Arranged in twenty-seven unnumbered chapters, the novel recounts Pierrot's experiences with his legal guardian, Uncle Napoléon, and his three old-maid aunts in the working-class district of east-end Montreal during the eight-day period between 6 June 1944 and the following Tuesday, when he is shipped off to learn a trade in another institution. In the first orphanage Pierrot, intelligent and precocious, compensated for his unhappiness by inventing a fantasy world. This imaginary universe collides with his experience of the outside world, where he must come to terms with an astounding array of human misery, venery, and brutality, as well as with some humanity, generosity, and tenderness.

The thematic continuity in four of Langevin's five novels is striking: orphaned, deserted, and dead or dying children are recurring figures. In the world they portray there are no winners: his orphans and outsiders despair at their inability to communicate or to escape from the resulting solitude. A compassionate yet bitter tribute to these losers, the novels are inspired by profound pity for their helplessness and unhappiness.

Langevin has written two stage plays. *Une nuit d'amour* (produced in 1954) was the first play by a Québécois author to be produced by the Théâtre du Nouveau Monde. The action takes place in Acadia after the Conquest. *L'oeil du peuple* (1958), a satire on municipal political corruption and leagues for moral decency, won first prize in the Théâtre du Nouveau Monde drama competition.

Langevin has also written several television dramas, which have been produced by Radio-Canada, and short stories: 'L'homme qui ne savait plus jouer' (*Écrits du Canada français*, vol. 1, 1954); 'Noce' (*Chatelaine*, vol. 2, no. 3, Mar. 1961); and 'Un parfum de rose bleue' (*LIBERTÉ*, no. 62, mars-avril 1969).

See Gabrielle Pascal, *La quête de l'identité chez André Langevin* (1976), David J. Bond, *The temptation of despair: a study of the Quebec novelist André Langevin* (1982); André Brochu, *L'évasion tragique: essai sur les romans d'André Langevin* (1985); and Karin Egloff, *L'aveugle au miroir déformant: réflexion sur le(s) regard(s) dans l'oeuvre d'André Langevin* (1990).

See also NOVELS IN FRENCH 1940 TO 1959: 2; 1960 TO 1982: 3(e).

L.W. KEFFER

Langevin, Gilbert (1938-95). Born in La Dorée, Quebec, in the Haut-Saguenay, where he received his early schooling, he went to Montreal in 1958 for further studies but did not complete them. In 1959 he founded Éditions Atys, which he directed until 1965. From this period date his encounters with other poets (Gaston MIRON, Gilles Leclerc) as well as his involvement—after a brief flirtation with the Parti communiste—in the Mouvement fraternaliste. Around 1960 Langevin began organizing poetry recitals throughout Quebec, but particularly in Montreal at the Bar des Arts and the Perchoir d'Haïti. Later he became active in the Atelier d'expression multidisciplinaire. He worked at the Bibliothèque Sulpice, the press of the Université de Montréal, and Radio-Canada. In the 1980s he mounted and starred in several shows, for example, in *Comme il parle, comme il chante*, in 1982 and 1984. For many years Langevin's name was associated with Montreal's alcoholic counter-culture.

Langevin was awarded the Du Maurier Prize for *Un peu plus d'ombre au dos de la falaise* (1965); and a Governor General's Award for *Mon refuge est un volcan* (1978, with nine illustrations by Carl Daoust)—Langevin expressed his intention to donate part of the award towards the 'defence of political prisoners in Quebec'; and the Alain GRANDBOIS Prize of the Académie des lettres du Québec for his 1993 collection *Cercle ouvert* (published with *Hors les murs*, *Chemin fragile*, and *L'eau souterraine*). His corpus includes some thirty or more collections of poetry—including three 'hors commerce': *Le vertige de sourire* (1960), *Poèmes-effigies* (1960), and *Au milieu de la nuit* (1977, with twelve original engravings)—along with four works combining prose and poetry, all sharing the same themes, characters, and style, and all attributed to 'Zéro Legel', one of the poet's eight 'hétéronymes': *Les écrits de Zéro Legel* (1972), *La douche et la seringue* (1973), *L'avion rose* (1976), and *Confidences aux gens de l'archipel* (1993). He also wrote numerous songs that he described as 'much rougher and more compact' than his poems; some of these were recorded by Pauline Julien (*Comme je crie/comme je chante*, 1969; *Le temps des vivants*, 1971; and *Dans l'temps comme dans l'temps, À la dérive*, 1974) as well as by the rock group Offenbach (*La voix que j'ai*, music by Gerry Boulet, 1977). The early songs were published in two collections: *Chansons et poèmes* (1973) and *Chansons et poèmes 2* (1974). Pauline Julien also recorded *L'étoile du nord* (1984), Marjo recorded *Celle qui va* (1986), Dan Bigras, *Naufrage* (1988), *Ange-Animal* (1990), and *Le vent bleu* (1992), and Yves Raymond, *Hôtel-vert-de-gris* (1992). Other recordings include: *Le blé des autres, Entre un scotch et du jazz, Ruelle des nos amours* (1992) and *Le train maudit* (1992). The poet himself was featured on *Le fou solidaire* (1980) and *Où mes racines parlent d'elles-mêmes* (1981), recordings produced by Radio-Canada International and Radio-Canada respectively. Langevin also appeared in a number of films and videos, either as one of a group (*Paroles du Québec, sept poètes québécois en scène à La Rochelle*, 1980; *Nuit de la poésie 80*, 1981; *Y a tant tellement d'espoir*, 1981; and *Poésie en fusion*, 1985), or as the principal interpreter (*Histoire d'aimer*, 1983; *Langevin au café du Port*, 1985).

Langevin's poetry collections include: *À la gueule du jour* (1959); *Symptômes* (1963); *Noctuaire* (1967); *Un peu plus d'ombre* (1966) and *Pour une aube* (1967)—collected in *Origines 1959-1967* (1971); *Stress* (1971); *Ouvrir le feu* (1971); *Novembre* (1973); *La vue du sang* (1973); *Griefs* (1975); *Le fou solidaire* (1980, with illustrations by Jocelyne Messier); *Issue de secours* (1981, with illustrations by the poet himself); *Fables du temps rauque* (1981, with seven original engravings by Monique Dussault); *Les main libres* (1983); *Entre l'inerte et les clameurs* (1985); *Comme un lexique des abîmes* (1986); *Au plaisir* (1987, with illustrations by Monique Bégin); *La saison hantée* (1988); *Ultimacolor/Espace appelle écho* (1988); *Né en avril* (1989); *Haut risque* (1990, with two illustrations from paintings by Laryssa Luhovy); *Les vulnérables* (1990, in collaboration with Jean Hallal); and *Le dernier nom de la terre* (1992). Selected poems translated into English by Marc Plourde appeared in 1987 under the title *Body of night*, volume 20 of the Essential Poet series. Many other poems remain unpublished. The poet's corpus constitutes a sort of inner autobiography; infused with a vibrant indignation, his poetry is distinguished by its extreme conciseness and sobriety of form, simplicity of phrase, verbal inventiveness, and tragic tone. Langevin's usual themes are those of love, anguish, dream, the opposition between light and dark, sweetness and bitterness, with the poems of his last years often haunted by the idea of illness. While critics find that his work sometimes suffers from too much virtuosity and a certain facility, critic Norman Baillargeon has called Langevin an authentic poet, one who placed his wordsmanship on an extremely high level, confronting the demands of his craft without any concessions. However, despite an abundant creative output and the praise of a few, Langevin's poetry has not aroused much interest in critical circles.

See Raoul DUGUAY, 'Littérature québécoise', *PARTI PRIS* 4, no. 1 (sept.-oct. 1966), Pierre Nepveu, 'La poétique de Gilbert Langevin', *Livres et auteurs québécois* (1973), and Claude Beausoleil, 'L'amoureuse émeute de Gilbert Langevin', *Le Devoir* (7 fév. 1981), p. 20.

ALEXANDER SOKALSKI

Language (English). For much of its history, Canadian English has been described as if either British English or American English were the norm from which it was the deviation. However, the idea that English in some sense belongs to the English and all other Englishes are derivative 'branches' has withered with the British Empire. Now the majority of first-language English-speakers live outside the British Isles, and each major national variety of English is regarded as having its own norms. In the past few decades new interest in world varieties of English, an increasingly multilingual population, and computer technology have all facilitated research into Canadian English, demonstrated by the appearance of such Canadian reference books as *A dictionary of Canadianisms on historical principles* (1967), the *Dictionary of Prince Edward Island English* (1988), the *Dictionary of Newfoundland English* (1982; 2nd ed. 1990), the *Gage Canadian dictionary* (rev. and exp. ed. 1997), the *ITP Nelson Canadian dictionary of the English language* (1997), the *Guide to Canadian English usage* (1997), and the *Canadian Oxford dictionary* (1998).

In the past, most studies focused only on the few features that distinguished Canadian English from both American and British English. Battles over the origins of Canadian English and over what is the 'correct' Canadian form often come down to arguments between those who think Canadian English is (or should be) British and those who see it as a branch of American English. These approaches have led to the overlooking of one major distinctive feature: Canadian English speakers and writers use a mix of 'British' and 'American' forms along with Canadian ones, something that is found in neither British nor American English. Because the generation that came of age in the nationalistic 1960s tended to anti-Americanism, often its educated speakers emphasize the British elements in Canadian English. The frequent choice of British pronunciations by the Canadian Broadcasting Corporation and the reversion to *-our* spellings by the Toronto *Globe and Mail* in 1990 can be seen as part of this phenomenon. However, the younger generation, unencumbered by memories of the Second World War or the Vietnam War, and exposed to a wide range of American media, has more positive attitudes to the United States and appears to be assimilating its speech to American norms. Wherever one sits in this debate, it would be foolish to attempt to describe Canadian English without reference to American and British English: Canadian English-speakers have never been isolated from either variety, although the prestige of each has varied during Canada's history.

Settlement history accounts for the homogeneity of the standard Canadian accent—the accent of educated urban Canadians—which is similar from the Ontario-Quebec border to Vancouver Island. This accent is not very different from that of speakers from the middle northern United States (Pennsylvania, New York, New Jersey, and western Vermont) because Ontario was settled by Loyalists from these states at the end of the American Revolution (1783 and after). This Canadian accent spread when the West was settled from Ontario after the Riel Rebellions (1870 and after). Most scholars accept this explanation of the origins of Canadian English. M.H. Scargill, however, locates its origins not in Loyalist speech, but in the primarily northern British accents of the half-million British immigrants who arrived between 1825 and 1851. These accents, he notes, were far from the southern accent that was later to become the British standard.

The case for Loyalist origins is based on the finding that when even large groups of people with varying accents move into a social structure where there is already a prestige accent—that is, a uniform accent spoken by the middle and upper classes, especially teachers, politician, ministers of religion, and other professionals—the children of first-generation immigrants quickly assimilate their speech to it. Walter S. Avis states that by the time the first wave of British immigrants arrived, 'the course of Ontario speech had been set, American speech habits of the Northern variety having been entrenched from the beginning' ('The English language in Canada: a report', in *Current trends in linguistics*, 1973, 10, Pt. 1, edited by Thomas A. Sebeok). Perhaps the heat generated by this debate might be lessened if Loyalist speech were not equated with 'American' speech; after all, the Loyalists left the United States in the early decades of the formation of American English out of a mix of British dialects. Canadian English was consolidated after their arrival in Canada over several generations.

Newfoundland English is the most distinctive dialect of Canadian English because

Newfoundland was settled primarily from the western counties of England and southeastern Ireland and remained rather isolated from mainland Canadian and British influences, although Irish priests and teachers often provided a prestige norm. Since the province joined Confederation in 1949, however, as the work of Sandra Clarke has made clear, speakers have been moving to the norms of mainland Canadian English. Differences in Maritimes English (rhyming *aunt* with *flaunt*, for example) are accounted for in part because early Loyalist settlers there came mainly from the New England states. English-speakers in Quebec, concentrated in Montreal, have always differed somewhat from other English-Canadians in the pronunciation of their English. Since the 1970s, with increasing emphasis on the use of French in all aspects of Quebec public life, English-speakers there have also begun to bring French words into their English, such as *caisse* (credit union) and *dépanneur* (corner store), which are not generally understood outside the province.

Although insufficient work has been done on the dialects of rural Canada, enough information exists to indicate which areas deserve further study. For example, Shana Poplack and Sali Tagliamonte have studied the African Nova Scotian English of isolated communities of people descended from Black Loyalists who arrived in the 1780s and refugee slaves who arrived after the War of 1812. Their work will cast light on the origins of African American Vernacular English. Other important dialect areas are the Ottawa Valley, Prince Edward Island, Lunenburg, and Cape Breton.

Canadian English differs from other Englishes most significantly in its sound system and its vocabulary. Very little important grammatical variation occurs among standard varieties, although apparently Canadians make more use of questions using 'have', preferring 'Have you eaten yet?' to the American 'Did you eat yet?' Canadian English also has a distinctive vocabulary; for example, *acclamation* and *riding* (both in the electoral sense), *loonie*, *wind chill factor*, and *baby bonus* are all Canadianisms. Borrowings from indigenous languages and Canadian French were common in the early period of exploration and settlement, the former giving us *chipmunk*, *moose*, *muskeg*, and *kayak*; and the latter *sault* (rapid, as in Sault Ste Marie), *gopher*, *sashay*, *voyageur*, and *toque*, for example.

Generally, the most common Canadian and Northern American accents are close enough to be indistiguishable to English-speakers from outside North America. For example, Canadians, like many Americans, have the tendency in informal speech to pronounce *t* as *d*, or omit it altogether,: thus, the familiar pronunciation of Ottawa as *Oddawa* and Toronto as *Trawna*. Sometimes there is a difference between Canadian and American speech in terms of the relative frequency of various sounds. Thus, Canadians tend to retain a *y* sound in the pronunciation of words like *tune* (tyoon), *stupid* (styoopid), *avenue* (avenyoo) more than many Americans, although this tendency is declining. Most Canadians make no distinction between the sounds in *dawn* and *Don*, *awful* and *offal*, *caller* and *collar*, etc., although Americans living along the border do. (These sounds are merged, however, in other parts of the USA, in central Ohio, Indiana, and Illinois.) Canadians tend more than Americans to make words beginning with *wh* sound as if they began with *w*, making homophones out of *Wales* and *whales*. Howard B. Woods has also shown that the commonplace assumption that Canadians, when speaking informally, pronounce the *-ing* suffix as *in* (as Americans do) is faulty; in fact, the most common variant for the Ottawa speakers he studied was *een*. Finally, most Canadians distinguish the vowels in pairs such as *knife* and *knives* and *house* and *houses*. This last feature has been called Canadian raising, and, since it affects such common words as *out* and *about*, has been one of the obvious ways of distinguishing a Canadian from an American. However, this sound feature is not stable, with differences between older and younger generations pointing to a gradual shift towards American English.

The European romantic nationalist assumption that nations required a distinctive national language (as well as a great literature) has had a great influence on the study of national languages and dialects. The presence of French as an official national language, coupled with the obvious similarity of Canadian English to American English, has clearly put a damper on this study in Canada (even when compared to Australia, with a similar number of English-speakers). Canadian English is a variety that should be studied as a whole not because it proves the distinctiveness and validity of Canadian culture; it is of considerable interest precisely because it does not do this, but rather reveals the varying influence of two other world varieties.

See J.K. Chambers, 'Canada', in *English around the world: sociolinguistic perspectives* (1991) edited by Jenny Cheshire, and Sandra Clarke, ed., *Focus on Canada*, Varieties of English around the world, G11 (1993).

MARGERY FEE

Language (Quebec). French is the second most widely spoken language in Canada (6.5 million speakers in 1991) and is represented by two distinct varieties: Acadian French and Quebec French. 'Quebec French' is a general term used for varieties spoken in Quebec, parts of New Brunswick, and the provinces west of Quebec, mainly Ontario and Manitoba. The large majority of French-speakers in Canada (5.5 million) live in Quebec and the language has long been at the centre of the socio-political debate surrounding the future of Quebec in the Canadian confederation.

French in Quebec has only recently acquired the status of an economically viable alternative to English. Since then, the main language issue in Quebec has been based on a tension between regionalization and internationalization, reflected in regularly surfacing controversies as to whether or not French-speaking Quebec should tend towards accentuating or attenuating regional characteristics. The affirmation movement culminating in the Quiet Revolution led certain writers and intellectuals in the 1960s to promote an extreme variety of Quebec French known as *JOUAL*. Today it seems that most people accept the fact that internationalization is preferable for the survival of French in the North American context, but other issues arise regularly with respect to the sanctioning of regional differences; this is illustrated by the public debate that surrounded the publication of French dictionaries such as the *Dictionnaire du français plus* and the *Dictionnaire québécois d'aujourd'hui* (*Le Robert*), which include a relatively high proportion of regionalisms and which were perceived as sanctioning through standardization the Quebec French variety to the detriment of a more standard international variety.

Language policies have played an important role in Quebec and Canada and have contributed to the maintenance of French in North America. In 1969 the Canadian government passed the Official Languages Act, which gives French and English equal status at the federal level. New Brunswick is the only province that followed suit and became officially bilingual; all other provinces, including Quebec through the 1977 charter, have adopted only one official language. The decline of French outside Quebec is probably partly due to this territorial approach to bilingualism.

It is generally assumed that Quebec French represents a regional variety of French with its own, mostly lexical and phonological, characteristics that developed in parallel with other regional varieties in France, Belgium, Switzerland, and other francophone countries. The fact that few grammatical differences exist among those varieties is often used to justify describing them as varieties of the same language as opposed to different languages.

HISTORICAL ASPECTS. Nouvelle-France, the French colony that in part became the Province of Quebec, was settled by French immigrants starting in the seventeenth century. The linguistic landscape in France in this era was extremely fragmented, with the Île-de-France dialect, which evolved to become today's French, spoken by only a fifth of the population at the end of the eighteenth century. The number of colonists speaking French (i.e., the Île-de-France dialect) in Nouvelle-France in the seventeenth century has been estimated to represent one third of the total population. Consequently, one of the most debated issues with respect to Quebec French is the question of determining how the Île-de-France dialect succeeded very rapidly in supplanting the other quite distinct dialects spoken by the rest of the settlers in Nouvelle-France. Various hypotheses have been put forward, including the high social value associated with the Île-de-France dialect, the fact that a majority of the women colonists probably spoke French, and the political will to unify the colony through the use of a single dialect. Some scholars propose that the issue is not real in that most settlers would have been exposed to the Île-de-France dialect long enough before actually leaving France to have learned the dialect and therefore be bilingual. It is likely that many of these factors contributed to the rapid spread of French in Nouvelle-France. Many characteristics of Quebec French are remnants of the most represented dialects brought by the colonists in the beginnings of the colony.

VOCABULARY. It must first be noted that the fundamental lexicon of Quebec French, i.e., the most frequently used vocabulary, is essentially the same as that of France. The differences are found in low-frequency items. The distinctiveness of Quebec French vocabulary is built upon three types of innovation. First, the particular geographic and socio-cultural context in which the variety is spoken has led to the borrowing of words denoting concrete or abstract entities that are either non-existent or different in the European context. English is the main source of borrowing; some words are borrowed directly and only adapted to the grammatical features of French: *du fun*, *un brake*, *une switch*, *watcher* (as a verb), etc.; others are more completely assimilated as French-sounding words: *poutine* (from *pudding*), *robine* (from *rubbing alcohol*), *engin* (for *locomotive*), *porche* (for *veranda*), etc. Native languages have also contributed many new words to the Quebec French lexicon: *atoca* (for *cranberry*), *achigan* (*bass*), *caribou* (*American reindeer*). Second, French evolved in Canada without sustained contact with France for many generations. This may account for the various words that have survived in Quebec but not in France: *accoter* (*to support*), *achaler* (*to bother*), *boucane* (*smoke*), *maganer* (*to mistreat*), *catin* (*doll*). Third, words have been created or existing words have developed their own meanings: *débarbouillette* (*facecloth*), *poudrerie* (*drifting snow*), *traversier* (*ferry*), *stationnement* (*parking lot*), *magasiner* (*to shop*), *briser* (*to damage*), *breuvage* (*drink*).

PRONUNCIATION. Aside from obvious but difficult-to-describe general regional accent differences between Quebec and other varieties of French, Quebec French possesses various features of pronunciation that reflect sociological differences based on geography, social class, and age. But it also has some fairly stable features that are not necessarily socially marked. The *t* and *d* consonants are pronounced as affricates (*ts* and *dz*) when they precede the vowels *i* and *u* (and corresponding semi-vowels), as in *tu* (*you*), *dire* (*to say*), *tuile* (*tile*), *diable* (*devil*). As in general spoken French, final *r* and *l* tend to drop at the end of words when preceded by stops in words such as *autre* (*other*) and *table* (*table*). The consonant *r* has two main realizations in Quebec: a fronted trill (used in the Montreal area) similar to the Spanish *r* and a trill produced with the back of the tongue as in Standard French. The vowels written as *i*, *u* and *ou* have lowered variants (similar to the vowels in the English words *pit*, *duck* and *pull*), used especially when the vowel is in the final syllable and followed by one or more consonants, as in *pipe* (*pipe*), *lutte* (*wrestling*), *toute* (*all*). When it is the final sound of a word, a back rounded variant of the vowel *a* is used (similar to the one in English *pop*); otherwise, the more standard front version (as in English *pat*) is heard. Thus, in a word such as *Canada*, the first two are front *a* but the last one is back *a*. Slightly more socially marked is a tendency to use diphthongs for some middle vowels when they are long historically or lengthened by a following consonant at the end of a word, in examples such as *mère* (*mother*), *saute* (*jump*), *beurre* (*butter*), *fête* (*party*) realized as *maère*, *sauôte*, *baeurre*, and *faête*. Many more phonological characteristics exist that affect principally the vowel system; but a large proportion of these features can be found in various other regional varieties of French across the world.

GRAMMAR. Although most differences between Standard French and Quebec French stand at the lexical and phonological level, some variation can be found in aspects of word and sentence formation; a few cases are provided here that can also be found in general spoken French but tend to appear with a higher frequency in Quebec French. Some derivational suffixes such as *-able* and *-age* are more productively used. Nouns used with a demonstrative pronoun are usually followed by *là: ces affaires-là* (*these things*). Subject noun phrases are often doubled by a corresponding personal pronoun in sentences such as *Mes enfants ils sont partis* (*My children are gone*). In questions, the interrogative particle *-tu* follows the conjugated verb as in *Il va-tu venir?* (*Will he be coming?*) and a complex form of the interrogative pronoun can commonly be found replacing the simple form: *Qui est-ce qui est venu?* (*Who came?*) as opposed to the *Qui est venu?* alternative.

The French language has long been associated with an intense and tenacious tradition of prescriptivism. Transposed to the Quebec situation, this tradition feeds the paradoxical desire to preserve regional characteristics while promoting a fairly standard variety of French.

See Philippe Barbaud, *Le choc des patois en Nouvelle-France* (1984), and Denis Dumas, *Nos façons de parler* (1987). YVES ROBERGE

Languirand, Jacques (b. 1931). Born and raised in Montreal, Quebec, he obtained a classical education at the collèges Saint-Laurent and Sainte-Croix before spending a few years (1949-53) studying theatre in Paris with Charles Dullin and Michael Vitold. Shortly after his return to Montreal he hosted a popular talk show on Radio-Canada, 'Le Dictionnaire insolite', and began writing radio dramas. In 1956 he entered the Dominion Drama Festival with his bizarre piece *Les insolites* (1962), which won first prize for the best Canadian play; its month-long run in Montreal established Languirand as the leader of avante-garde theatre in Quebec. He held this position throughout the late fifties and early sixties, for his first absurdist play was followed in quick succession by other stage and TV productions. *Le roi ivre* (1970), produced in 1956 at Languirand's own experimental but short-lived Théâtre de Dix Heures; *Les grands départs* (1958), televised in 1957; *Diogène* (1965) and *Le gibet* (1962), produced in 1958; and *Les violons de l'automne* (1962), produced in 1961.

Since 1962, when Languirand received the Governor General's Award for *Les insolites* and *Les violons de l'automne*, he has become increasingly involved with radio and television. His musical comedy *Klondyke* (1970) was well received in Montreal and at the Commonwealth Arts Festival in 1965; but his last piece for theatre—an elaborate, multimedia work, *L'age de Pierre*—has never been performed in French and failed to capture any critical or popular acclaim when it was produced in English in 1970 as *Man Inc.* at Toronto's St Lawrence Centre.

Languirand's biggest concern, in all his plays, is the lack of communication between individuals and the social and psychological forces that keep them apart. Influenced by Artaud, Beckett, Ionesco, Brecht, and the existentialists, Languirand continually experimented with new ideas and forms of expression. In *Les insolites*, the result of an experiment with automatic writing, his disorienting style creates an atmosphere of riotous folly. The action takes place in a bar where, among the people brought together by chance,an old woman is shot dead in the dark, and an innocent but agitated bartender is arrested for murder. The absurd ending is consistent with Languirand's strange world where injustice reigns, death is senseless, and communication impossible. In *Le roi ivre* a cruel tyrant irrationally abuses and exploits his subjects, his servants, and his queen, who are all too weak or too cowardly to resist. The question of individuals who do little to change their lives is taken up again in *Les grands départs*, in which an unsuccessful writer and the disgruntled members of his family day-dream about building a new life for themselves while waiting for the movers to take them to more squalid living-quarters. (It was translated by Albert Bermel as *The departures* and published in *Gambit* 5, 1966.) In *Le gibet* Languirand focuses on the vulnerability of a hopelessly idealistic character who is trying to break the world flagpole-sitting record. Alone and aloft, he observes but fails to understand the malevolence and infidelity of his friends and family. The suffering and humiliation of the old are at the centre of *Les violons de l'automne*, a cynical love story that depicts the futile efforts of an aged couple to consummate their marriage. In this absurdist poetic drama the characters are called simply 'He', 'She' and 'The Other Man'.

Though these plays make no direct reference to Quebec, they convey harsh criticism of individuals who refuse to fight the dishonesty, exploitation, and injustice of regimes similar to that of Duplessis. Languirand also deplores the moral and intellectual paralysis of those who reject innovation in the name of reason and tradition, and effectively shows that attitudes must change and communication channels must be opened if one is to thrive in the modern world. In *Klondyke* Languirand's message is more overtly topical. Set in the Yukon of the Gold Rush, the plot is loosely centred on the adventures of two prospectors who eventually leave the Klondike penniless. Although obviously interested in the American dream, Languirand was clearly warning his audience of the dangers of crass materialism at a time when Quebec was in the middle of a modernization program.

Languirand has also published a travel book, *J'ai découvert le Tahiti* (1961); a humorous dictionary, *Le dictionnaire insolite* (1961); a psychological novel, *Tout compte fait* (1963, 1985); and a futurist essay, *De McLuhan à Pythagore* (1972).

See Jean-Cléo Godin, 'Révolution dans le langage: Languirand insolite', in Jean-Cléo Godin and Laurent Mailhot, *Théâtre québécois* (1970). ELAINE NARDOCCHIO

Lanigan, George T. See 'The AHKOOND OF SWAT'.

Lapointe, Gatien (1931-83). Born in Sainte-Justine-de-Dorchester, Quebec, he was educated at the Petit Séminaire in Quebec City and continued his studies for a year at the École des Arts Graphiques, then in the Faculté des Lettres of the Université de Montréal. Between 1956 and 1962 he travelled extensively in Europe and completed a doctoral thesis on Paul Éluard at the Sorbonne, Paris. After returning to Quebec he taught at the Collège Militaire Royal, St Jean, before accepting a position at the Université du Québec, Trois-Rivières, where he remained. While devoting a great deal of his energies to writing and teaching, Lapointe also founded in 1971 a small publishing house, Les Écrits des Forges, which publishes young and unknown poets—he remained a director of the press until the end of his life.

Lapointe's first collection of poems, *Jour malaisé* (1953), reflects his early artistic training and his interest in lay-out and typography, while its title testifies to his *mal de vivre*. It also reveals the emotional climate of Quebec in the 1950s: Lapointe once referred to *Jour malaisé* as the muffled but liberating shout of a poet inhabiting the oppressive desert of the Duplessis era. Ironically, it was with *Le temps premier, suivi de Lumière du monde* (1962), which he wrote in France—an alien space—that he found his 'terra nova', his own universe and origins. It is a powerful book, one that is looked upon retrospectively as a 'founding text'—part of a ground-swelling surge of poetry that proceeded to name Quebec's trees, land, rivers, and faces because only by doing this could its inhabitants find and claim their territory: Lapointe's poems were very much part of this collective and spontaneous impulse. *L'ode au Saint-Laurent, précédée de J'appartiens à la terre* (1963)—which won a Governor General's Award—proceeds from the same instinctual needs: 'Je suis la première enfance du monde/je crée mot à mot le bonheur de l'homme/et pas à pas j'efface la souffrance.' It deciphers a primordial morning and celebrates the many joys of its coming. *Le premier mot, précédé de Le pari de ne pas mourir* (1967) shows a much more sombre and anguished mood: the certitude that writing does not allay suffering, does not relieve human loneliness or political injustices, does not even ultimately bring any satisfactory answers. But it stands as a wager against death, an attempt at holding it at bay to survive a few moments longer. With *Arbre-radar* (1980), and especially *Corps et graphies* (1981), Lapointe moved into a different territory. Barthes, Blanchot, Deleuze, and the searchings of a younger generation of poets who gravitated around the magazine *La Nouvelle* BARRE DU JOUR and the avant-garde publisher Les Herbes Rouges gave his concerns a different textual fabric. *Corps et graphies* takes us into a much more fragmented and broken-up syntax: Lapointe viewed these poems as an attempt to let the human body dance upon the white stage of pure pleasure, with no rhyme or reason and no rational finality. *Barbare inouï* (1981) and *Corps-transistor* (1981) appear to have evolved out of the same need.

In 1983 Lapointe recorded (on vinyl) *Corps de l'instant*, an anthology of his writings spanning the years 1956 to 1982. He remains a popular writer in the 1990s—such major works as *Ode au Saint-Laurent, trois poèmes* and *Arbre-radar* have been reprinted.

See the interview with Gatien Lapointe by Donald Smith, 'Le corps est aussi un absolu', in *Lettres québécoises* 24 (hiver 1981-2). See also Jean Cléo Godin, '"Le premier mot" et "Le pari de ne pas mourir"', *Études françaises*, vol. III, no. 4 (nov. 1967), Maximilien Laroche, 'L'Américanité ou l'ambiguité du "je"', *Études littéraires*, vol. 8, no. 1 (avr. 1975), and Clément Marchand, *Gatien Lapointe ou la juste mort* (1984).

CAROLINE BAYARD/FRANCESCA BENEDICT

Lapointe, Paul-Marie (b. 1929). Born in Saint-Félicien, Quebec, he studied at Collège St Laurent and the École des Beaux-Arts in Montreal before becoming a journalist with *L'Événement-Journal* (1950-4) and *La Presse* (1954-60) and co-founding, with Jean-Louis Gagnon, *Le Nouveau Journal* (1961). A freelance writer and journalist for Radio-Canada in 1962-3, and editor-in-chief of *Le Magazine Maclean* (1964-8), he joined Radio-Canada in 1968 as radio-program director in the French Services division.

Although as yet unaware of Les Automatistes, Lapointe had read the French poet Paul Éluard, and his first collection of poems, written over a three-month period in 1947, was produced in the true spirit of automatic writing. Claude GAUVREAU, to whom the manuscript was submitted, helped to publish it under the title *Le vierge incendié* in 1948. That same year Lapointe wrote a series of poems entitled 'Nuit du 15 au 26 novembre 1948', which did not appear until 1969, when it was published in a special issue of *La* BARRE DU JOUR devoted to Les Automatistes. Whereas the first collection displayed an absolute faith in poetry and the regenerating power of revolt, 'Nuit' marked a recognition of the limits of language evident in the proliferation of meaningless neologisms and the gradual disintegration of syntax which led to static repetition. The threat of silence that was present in these poems was real: Lapointe did not publish again until 1960. That year *Choix de poèmes—arbres* appeared; it was followed in 1964 by *Pour les âmes*. Both these collections—which showed a movement away from pure revolt towards reintegration—are characterized by an improvisation modelled on jazz. The poem 'Arbres', a magnificent litany, expressed a 're-appropriation', the will to retrieve one's heritage that coincided with the new socio-political climate of Quebec in the sixties: this, along with its literary merit, made it Lapointe's best-known work. All the works cited were gathered in *Le réel absolu: poèmes, 1948-1965* (1971), which had a tremendous influence on the new generation of poets of the seventies. In particular the reappearance of *Le vierge incendié*, which had until then been little read, was enthusiastically received: the exemplary freedom of the images, the glorification of revolt, the theme of the purification of dead flesh on the altar of love, the provocative mixture of the sacred and profane, all combined to make Lapointe a pioneering figure in the eyes of the new generation. *Le réel absolu* won the Prix David and a Governor General's Award.

Lapointe's writing took another new turn with *Tableaux de l'amoureuse suivi de Une unique; Art égyptien; Voyage; Huit autres poèmes* (1974) and *Bouche rouge* (1976), both illustrated by Gisèle Verreault. In the first volume the poet took his inspiration from the work of the artist; the second was a joint creation, the result of a continuing exchange between poet and artist, and is a celebration of woman through the ages. Lapointe's monumental *Écritures* (1979)—more than a thousand pages—stems from yet another creative mode: writing as a purposefully gratuitous act, devoid of meaning or coherence and designed to resist all interpretations. It is a demanding work that requires the reader to experience the presence, the materiality, of words themselves as they are actually set on paper, empty of intended reference or even expression. *Tombeau de René Crevel* (1979), with illustrations by Betty Goodwin, was written as a homage to the French surrealist who had a seminal influence on Lapointe. The text consists entirely of material extracted from Crevel's works—the process of selection being based on an arbitrarily pre-defined set of rules devised by Lapointe—and recombined into new patterns.

Lapointe's writing, consistent yet constantly renewing itself, has been a leading example for the new poetry of Quebec. In 1976 Lapointe received the prize of the International Poetry Forum in the United States and in 1980 the *La Presse* prize.

English translations of his work appear in *The poetry of French Canada in translation* (1970), edited by John GLASSCO, and in *Ellipse*, II (1972). A selection of his poems translated by D.G. JONES was published in *The terror of the snows* (1976); *The 5th season* (1985) is a revised and enlarged edition of the latter. *Le vierge incendié* is explored in an original study by Jean Fisette, *Le texte automatique* (1977), as well as in *La nuit incendiée* (1978) by Jean-Louis Major. *Études françaises* 16/2 (1980) is a special issue devoted to his work, as is *VOIX ET IMAGES* 17/3 (1992). An essay by Robert Mélançon, accompanied by a selection of Lapointe's poems, was published in Paris in the collection 'Poètes d'aujourd'hui' (1987).

MICHEL PARMENTIER

La Rocque, Gilbert (1943-84). Born in Rosemount, Quebec, the son of a blacksmith, he completed five years of an eight-year *collège classique* program and dropped out to become a clerk for the city of Montreal-Nord for eight years, spending his leisure time writing his first two novels. With the publication of *Le nombril* (1970), his life changed and he became involved in Montreal's most important publishing ventures, working for Éditions du Jour under Jacques Hébert; for Éditions de l'Homme as editor-in-chief; and for L'Aurore as literary director under Victor-Lévy BEAULIEU. After L'Aurore failed, La Rocque helped to establish the VLB publishing company, before going on to create Éditions Québec/Amérique, which became one of the most important Quebec publishing houses. Writing all the time, he waited for recognition, which came with the Prix France-Canada for his fifth novel *Les masques* (1980).

La Rocque's novels make difficult reading. He plunges his readers into a universe of pettiness generated by characters trapped in futile family or marriage problems. La Rocque was well known for his penchant for shocking descriptions (oozing garbage, rot, excrement, odours, the world of sickness, etc.), and for such scenes as the one in which Gaby, the heroine of *Après la boue* (1972), provokes her abortion (with a knitting needle) in a bathtub in which she literally swims in blood. The fact that the *dégoûtant* in La Rocque's novels demonstrates his mastery of eloquent prose does not make these passages any easier to accept.

With the first cycle of novels—*Le nombril, Corridors* (1971), and *Après la boue*—readers feared that La Rocque's talent was dwindling into mere repetition. But with the publication of *Serge d'entre les morts* (1976) there was a definite break with the past in a new quality of tenderness that raised his prose to the sublime. In this novel—about an incestuous relationship between Serge (an orphan) and his cousin Colette, which ends suddenly with Colette's marriage to another man—the world becomes wondrous, fantastic. This quality was further expressed in *Les masques,* which relates in hallucinatory prose the anguish of a narrator-hero whose son drowns while on a weekend visit with him. *Le refuge* (1979), La Rocque's only dramatic work, which was televised by Radio-Canada, sets this drowning tragedy against the background of *Le nombril*, which is about the rebellion of an office clerk. *Le passager* (1984) is a *roman à clef*, about a literary quarrel with the critic Reginald Martel.

Gérard BESSETTE, who was among the first to notice this shift in La Rocque's writing, based his novel *Le semestre* on *Les masques*, using La Rocque's novel as the object of a literary analysis, which is cleverly worked out by Bessette's hero, Omer Marin.

See Donald Smith, et al., *Gilbert La Rocque: l'écriture du rêve* (1985).

See also NOVELS IN FRENCH 1960 TO 1982: 3(a).

ANDRÉ VANASSE

La Roque de Roquebrune, Robert. See Robert Laroque de ROQUEBRUNE.

LaRue, François-Alexis-Hubert (1833-81). Born in Saint-Jean (Île d'Orléans), he was a brilliant student at the Séminaire de Québec and attracted the attention of that institution's superiors, who in 1855 persuaded him to undertake studies at Louvain and Paris with a view to teaching medicine at the newly founded Université Laval on his return. This he did, remaining professor of medicine there from 1859 until his death. He was very active in literary, cultural, and scientific circles, helping to found the influential reviews *Les SOIRÉES CANADIENNES* (1861-5) and *Le FOYER CANADIEN* (1863-6).

LaRue's many publications fall into three main categories, the first and largest comprising those of scientific, pedagogic, and social interest, such as *Éléments de chimie et de physique agricole* (Québec, 1868). Next are two historical works: *Histoire populaire du Canada; ou Entretiens de madame Genest à ses petits-enfants* (Québec, 1875 and 1913) and *Petite histoire des États-Unis très élémentaire; ou Entretiens de Madame Genest avec ses petits-enfants* (Québec, 1880). The third category is more literary and includes contributions to periodicals, notably a 'Voyage autour de l'Île d' Orléans' in *Les soirées canadiennes*, vol. I (1861), and a useful study, 'Les chansons populaires et historiques du Canada', in *Le foyer canadien*, vols I (1863) and IV (1865); two characteristically mixed volumes, *Mélanges historiques, littéraires et d'économie politique* (Québec, 1870 and 1881); a play, *Le défricheur de langue* (Québec, 1859); and a collection of essays, *Voyage sentimental sur la rue Saint-Jean: départ en 1860, retour en 1880* (Québec, 1879).

Le défricheur de langue, written in collaboration with J.-C. TACHÉ and published under the pseudonym 'Isidore Méplats', is a three-act satire (LaRue called it a 'tragédie-bouffe') directed against the immigrant French editor of the review *La Ruche littéraire*, H.-É. CHEVALIER, whose turgid style and simplistic pseudo-scientific views on the evolution of French in North America are brilliantly parodied in this fanciful closet-drama. Ever a conservative, LaRue despised the liberal, anti-clerical views espoused by Chevalier and his friends. *Voyage sentimental* is a whimsical trip in time and space along Quebec's main street, mingling the author's personal recollections, history, and popular legend in twenty short essays.

See Charles Angers ('Jean du Sol'), *Le docteur Hubert LaRue et l'idée canadienne-française* (1912) and Léon Lortie's article in the *DICTIONARY OF CANADIAN BIOGRAPHY*, vol. xi (1982).

L.E. DOUCETTE

LaRue, Monique (b. 1948). Born in Montreal, she is part of a new generation of Montreal writers who were partly educated in France. After receiving her B.Ph. from the Université de Montréal (1970), she earned her Master's degree in philosophy from the Sorbonne in the Université de Paris (1971), and in 1976 her doctorat de 3ème cycle en lettres. Since 1974 she has been a member of the French department of the Collège Edouard Montpetit, Montreal. Her first novel, *La cohorte fictive* (1979), concerns the relationship between body and language as objects of procreation. Through the eyes of Claire, a writer and future mother, the novel explores the lives of five sisters, their desires, their fears, and makes explicit a comparison between the birth of a child and the creation of a literary text. Warmly acclaimed by critics, it was nominated for the Grand Prix du livre de Montréal in 1979. With *Les faux fuyants* (1982) LaRue turns both a touching and a pitiless eye on the plight of the young and the destruction of a family. It is a text haunted by bisexuality and the figure of the double: Klaus, a disenchanted youth, and his sister Elodie flee their disinterested entourage of teachers and parents in search of a small core of reality, only to lose themselves in the vast 'nowhere' of modern society.

LaRue's third novel, *Copies conformes* (1989), earned her the Grand Prix du livre de Montréal in 1990 and remains the best known and most studied of her books. The line between fiction and reality, truth and lies, the illusions created by fictive space, the tyranny of the image, Plato's hierarchy between the original and its copy in art, and 'la paternité' of ideas—all converge in this postmodern detective story. The plot, derived from Dashiell Hammett's *The Maltese falcon*, was rewritten by LaRue with a female protagonist, a young Montreal mother in search of her husband's lost research diskette in San Francisco. It was translated by Lucie Ranger as *True copies* (1996).

LaRue's prose has been admired for its tightness of form and its control of language; she also has an acute sense of nuance, and takes care to leave to the reader the ultimate interpretation of her novels' often complex psychological framework. In the subtle and intricate *La démarche du crabe* (1995), LaRue draws a convincing portrait of a successful middle-aged dentist, Dr Santerre, for whom the visit of one young patient provokes a personal and philosophical investigation into the values of his baby-boomer generation. LaRue has also published *Promenades littéraires dans Montréal* (1989) in collaboration with Jean-François Chassay. KATHERINE ROBERTS

Lasnier, Rina (b. 1915). Born in Saint Grégoire d'Iberville, Quebec, she studied in Montreal and in England. She has worked as a journalist and has long lived in Joliette, Quebec.

Lasnier is widely recognized as one of the most accomplished poets in Quebec. Though her religious themes mark her work as marginal to contemporary Québécois poetry, her skills as a poet make her nevertheless a highly respected literary figure. She has pursued a vigorously independent course, evolving within the parameters of her personal universe rather than within the often destructive values of modernism. Her poems combine classical control with a great semantic and rhythmical density; and much of their power is drawn from the tension between their theme (the conflicting pull of this world and the other) and the great sensuality of their language. The complexity of her poetry has often been compared to that of Margaret AVISON. For instance, see D.G. JONES' essay 'Identity and difference: comparative notes on the poetry of Margaret Avison and Rina Lasnier', *Ellipse* 56 (1985).

The list of Lasnier's publications is long. *Images et proses* (1941) is largely religious in inspiration; *Madones canadiennes* (1944) is a series of lyrics written to illuminate pictures chosen by Marius BARBEAU to illustrate the art of Quebec as exemplified in statues of the madonna; *Le chant de la montée* (1947) is a series of chants inspired by the story of Jacob and Rachel. The major works of her maturity are *Présence de l'absence* (1956, rpr. 1992), *Mémoire sans jours* (1960), *Miroirs: proses* (1960), *Les gisantes* (1963), and *L'arbre blanc* (1966).

La salle des rêves (1971) won the first A.J.M. SMITH Prize for Canadian poetry. It was followed by *L'invisible* (1971), *Le rêve du quart jour* (story, 1973), *Amour* (1975), *L'échelle des anges* (prose, 1975), *Les signes* (1976), *Matins d'oiseaux* (vol. I, 1978); *Paliers de paroles* (vol. II, 1978); *Entendre l'ombre* (vol. I, 1981), and *Voir la nuit* (vol. II, 1981). Some of Lasnier's collections have been republished in *Poèmes I* (1972) and *Poèmes II* (1972). In 1987 and 1988 the publishing house Écrits des Forges, in collaboration with the Université du Québec à Trois-Rivières, re-issued *La salle des rêves*, *Les signes*, *Matin d'oiseaux,* and *Paliers de paroles* as *L'ombre jetée* (vol. I), and *Entendre l'ombre, Voir la nuit*, and *Chant perdu* (a collection from 1983) as *L'ombre jetée* (vol. II).

Lasnier has also written several plays inspired by the religious history of Quebec. *Féerie indienne: Kateri Tekakwitha* (1939) is based on the life of the celebrated Mohawk girl (1656-80?), a Native convert recently beatified; *Le jour de la voyagère* (1941) on the career of Marguerite Bourgeoys; and *Les fiançailles d'Anne de Noüe* (1943) on the work of a Jesuit missionary. *Notre-Dame du pain* (1947) was written for the Eucharistic Congress held in Ottawa. *La mère de nos mères* (1943) is a biographical essay on Marguerite Bourgeoys.

Lasnier has received many awards for her work, including the Prix David (in 1943 and 1974), the Prix Duvernay (1957), the Molson Prize (1971), the Prix France-Canada (1973-4), and an honorary doctorate from the Université de Montréal (1977).

One issue of *LIBERTÉ* (no. 108, vol. 18) is devoted entirely to Lasnier and contains an important bibliography, including her poems, journalism, and translations of poems by A.J.M. Smith (see also *CANADIAN LITERATURE* 39, Winter 1969). A special issue of the French magazine *Les Pharaons* 20 (automne 1974) is also devoted to Lasnier, as is *Ellipse* 22 (1978), containing poems by Lasnier in translation and a long interview.

See Eva Kushner, *Rina Lasnier* (1964)—more apology than criticism—and Sylvie Sicotte, *L'arbre dans la poésie de Rina Lasnier* (1977). Selections of her work are found in *Rina Lasnier: textes choisis* (1961), edited by Jean Marcel, and in *La part du feu* (1970), an anthology of her poetry that has a critical introduction by Guy ROBERT. Anne-Marie ALONZO contributed an introduction to a very fine collection of essays on Lasnier by fellow poet/critics including Monique BOSCO and André BROCHU, *Le langage des sources* (1988). This text also includes extensive primary and secondary bibliographies.

SHERRY SIMON/DAVID LEAHY

Last of the Eries, The (1849). By 'H.H.B.'. As interesting and as competently written as better-known Canadian novels of the period, it was printed at the newspaper office in Simcoe, Canada West (Ontario), and advertised for sale throughout the province. Despite the attempt to tell a story about Canada to Canadians, it does not seem to have been widely noticed at the time, and only two copies—in the libraries of the University of Western Ontario and Acadia University—are reported as surviving today.

Set in the 1750s, the novel is one of the very early English-Canadian attempts to use New France as a romantic background for fiction. The plot owes much to French-Canadian legends, beginning with 'L'Iroquoise', that revolve around the love of a young, nobly born French soldier for a beautiful Native maiden. The Erie tribe of the title has been virtually exterminated by the Six Nations. The survivors are still pursued by the villainous Iroquois Coswenago, who abducts Pale Lily, the half-white daughter of their chief. The French soldier Pierre, a friend of the Eries and sympathetic to their way of life, rescues her. Most of the action takes place in an unnamed area of the Canadian interior in 1756, some of it at Fort Frontenac, and the remainder in 1760, at Quebec, where all but seven of the remaining Eries die fighting on the French side. Pale Lily, the only convert to Christianity, marries Pierre and they settle in Lower Canada. There is little, except her forest background, to distinguish Pale Lily from a standard white heroine; and among the male characters neither villainy nor heroism is exclusive to Natives or Europeans.

The narrative device is that of a tale within a tale. One of a group of friends in present time reads on successive nights the story of the extermination of the Erie tribe a century earlier. The ensuing discussions, augmented by authorial asides, tell much about Aboriginal customs, and comment on such diverse subjects as the relations of the French to the Natives; the role of the French at Culloden; theology; and the vast improvement made by England in the civilization of North America. The narrative focuses on action rather than description, and suspense about the outcome of various crises and the fate of various individuals carries the reader rapidly forward.

MARY LU MacDONALD

Laterrière, Pierre de Sales. See BIOGRAPHY AND MEMOIRS IN FRENCH: 3.

Laurence, Margaret (1926-87). Jean Margaret Wemys was born in the prairie town of Neepawa, Manitoba, which inspired her fictional 'Manawaka'. Her parents, of Scots and Irish descent, died when she was young and she was brought up by an aunt who had become her stepmother. Having decided as a child on a career as a writer, she contributed to school and college magazines and as early as 1939 used the invented name 'Manawaka' in a story for a *Winnipeg Free Press* contest. After graduating (1947) in Honours English from United College, Winnipeg, she worked as a reporter for the *Winnipeg Citizen*. In 1947 she married Jack Laurence, a civil engineer, and in 1949 moved with him to England. From 1950 to 1957 they lived in Africa, for the first two years in the British Protectorate of Somaliland (now Somalia), then in Ghana just before its independence. Laurence's experience of these countries led to a variety of writings on African subjects over a period of some sixteen years: the first of these was *A tree for poverty* (1954), an essay on and collection of Somali poetry and prose, which she completed while in Somaliland. Two children, Jocelyn and David, were born to the Laurences before their return to Canada in 1957. While living in Vancouver from 1957 to 1962 Laurence saw the appearance in Canadian journals of her African short stories, later collected in *The tomorrow-tamer* (1963), and the publication of her African novel, *This side Jordan* (1960). At the same time she was writing a first draft of a novel set in Canada, which would eventually be rewritten and published as *The STONE ANGEL* (1964). After separating from her husband in 1962 (the Laurences were divorced in 1969), she moved with her children to England, where she lived for ten years. In this prolific decade she published a memoir of her life in Somaliland, *The prophet's camel bell* (1963); three of the four Manawaka novels, *The stone angel*, *A jest of God* (1966), *The fire-dwellers* (1969); *A bird in the house* (1970), a collection of linked stories, also set in Manawaka; a children's book, *Jason's quest* (1970); and *Long drums and cannons* (1968), a critical study of Nigerian writing in English during a fifteen-year period of cultural renaissance that was to be ended by the tribal warfare of the mid-1960s. The period also saw the publication of several magazine articles, which were later collected to form *Heart of a stranger* (1976). Between 1969 and 1974 Laurence was writer-in-residence at three Ontario universities and served as Chancellor of Trent University from 1980 to 1983. From 1974 she made her home in Lakefield, Ontario, spending summers at her cottage on the Otanabee River, near Peterborough, where most of the fourth Manawaka novel, *The DIVINERS* (1974), was written. She wrote three more children's books: *Six darn cows* (1979); *The olden days coat* (1979), which was made into an award-winning television drama in 1981; and *The Christmas birthday story* (1980). Her memoir, *Dance on the earth* (1989), was completed by her daughter after Laurence's death; it celebrates motherhood and friendship, and includes letters to her lifelong friend Adele WISEMAN.

Since 1961, when her story 'A gourdful of glory' was awarded the President's Medal, University of Western Ontario, and her novel *This side Jordan* earned the Beta Sigma Phi First Novel Award, Laurence earned numerous prizes, honorary degrees, and awards. She received a Governor General's Award for *A jest of God* and again for *The diviners*. She was made a Companion of the Order of Canada in 1971 and received the Molson Prize in 1975.

Laurence's work has been published in several languages and in a variety of paperback editions. In their English and American editions some of the books are differently titled: *The prophet's camel bell* appeared in New York as *New wind in a dry land* (1964); the English paperback of *A jest of God* was entitled *Now I lay me down* (1968), and the Warner Brothers film of this novel was called *Rachel, Rachel* (1968). In addition to radio, television, and stage adaptations of her writings, there is a National Film Board documentary on her life and work, *Margaret Laurence, first lady of Manawaka* (1979).

Laurence's African writings introduce the themes of survival, freedom, and individual dignity that dominate her major novels. In the deserts of Somaliland she translated and paraphrased the oral poems and stories of the Somali nomads, to form the first collection in English of this material. Her introduction to *A tree for poverty* tells of the harsh, drought-ridden lives and compensatory culture of the nomads; she later wrote essays on two poets who particularly fascinated her, the warrior 'Mad Mullah' and the love-poet Elmi Bonderii, and these are included in *Heart of a stranger*. The best of Laurence's African books, *The prophet's camel bell*, was written a decade after she left Somaliland and is a recollection of her experience there. A travelogue based on her diaries, it creates a vivid picture of landscape and people, including some of the most sympathetic portraits of European colonizers to be found in her work. As a personal document, it records the author's spiritual journey from naive enthusiasm and hasty judgement to a respect for the privacy and dignity of others. The two books dealing with Ghana, the novel *This side Jordan* and *The tomorrow-tamer*, are more overtly political; set in the period when the country faced its independence, they give full rein to Laurence's anti-imperialist, anti-colonial views. *This side Jordan* suffers from a rigid structure and contrived ending because it endeavours to give equal weight to two points of view: those of the white imperialists facing expulsion and of black Africans caught between the old world of their ancestors and the new world of Christianity and urban technology. Laurence sometimes attempts to see through African eyes, but is less successful in this novel than in the semi-allegorical story 'Godman's master', which appears in *The tomorrow-tamer*. Stories in this collection examine closely, and often ironically, the nature of freedom, and show special sympathy for those, both African and European, who no longer fully belong anywhere. The title story illustrates the book's main concern, the conflict between old and new ways.

Laurence's greatest achievement lies in the four Canadian novels dominated by the town of Manawaka, which is not simply a fictional version of Neepawa, though similar in many details, but an amalgam of all prairie small towns infused with the spirit of their Scots-Presbyterian founders. In this respect it is like the small-town settings of Sinclair ROSS and W.O. MITCHELL that were an early influence on Laurence. Although only *A jest of God* is set entirely in Manawaka, the town—with its paralysing, often hypocritical, respectability and harsh social divisions—represents in each novel a constricting force to be overcome by the main characters. Insofar as it shapes each protagonist, Manawaka is an aspect of her own being that must be confronted from within; at another level the town is an emblem of life itself. Laurence's chief concern as novelist is the depiction of character, and at the centre of each novel is a powerfully realized woman. Ninety-year old Hagar in *The stone angel* tries to stave off physical disintegration and death with all the dignity she can. She acquires a measure of grace in acknowledging the pride that, though it has been her strength, has shackled her emotions and stopped her from loving freely. Unlike Hagar, who has a rich and humorous zest for life, Rachel, the unmarried schooolteacher in *A jest of God*, endures a sterile, introverted living death. She is finally able to break away from Manawaka after a sexual affair and its traumatic consequences bring her a liberating self-knowledge. Rachel's sister Stacey, the protagonist of *The fire-dwellers*, is a spiritually isolated housewife and mother threatened by domestic and social chaos, which she fears as both personal hell-fire and nuclear holocaust. Experience of real tragedies and near-disasters, together with the help of a stranger (as in Hagar's case), results in a hopeful conclusion that offers the possibility of communication with others. Morag in *The diviners* faces the dilemma of trying to live her own life as a writer, while coping with the emotional and physical demands of being wife and mother. Unlike the three previous heroines, she was not brought up in a middle-class family but in the haphazard environment of the garbage-collector's unconventional home. She thus understands social ostracism, so familiar to the Métis, who are powerfully represented here, as elsewhere in the cycle, by the Tonnerre family. Morag's liaison with Jules Tonnerre produces a daughter whose consciousness of her mixed heritage, painful though it is, holds promise of a better future. Of the four novels, *The diviners* deals most richly with their shared themes of ancestral heritage and the relation of past to present. Time sequence is differently handled in each novel: *The stone angel* alternates present and past episodes; *A jest of God* is a monologue in the present tense; *The fire-dwellers* tries to capture the multiple, simultaneous workings of consciousness by rendering Stacey's inner voice, outer dialogues, dreams, and fantasies through changes of type-face and manipulation of space on the page. Time, memory, and understanding are most thoroughly explored in *The diviners*, where the narrative method is varied by such devices as 'Memory bank movies' and the use of present tense for past events, of past tense for present.

Laurence had a rich ear for nuances of speech, ranging from everyday slang to the colourful, oracular poetry of chanted myth. There is much humour in her work and a strong sense of irony. Depth is given to the prose by a wide range of metaphorical and symbolic allusion, notably to the Bible and to the natural world; names are used in full consciousness of their derivations or associations. Each of the Manawaka novels is dominated by imagery associated with one of the four elements; and this, together with numerous cross-references and the unifying presence of the town itself, justifies the reading of the four works as a unit, a tetralogy expressing Laurence's view of the human condition where grace, symbolized by water, may ultimately be offered to those who endure.

A bird in the house stands slightly apart from the four novels in that it is, as Laurence said, 'semi-autobiographical'. The short stories about the girlhood of Vanessa MacLeod recreate some of the experiences of the young Margaret Laurence, especially in facing the death of a parent and coming to terms with the autocratic spirit of a stern grandfather. The narrator is the adult Vanessa, but her voice belongs simultaneously to the young Vanessa who, as an apprentice writer, makes a point of listening and observing and so has much to report. Through her we encounter the tensions and consolations of family life and, in the later stories, social issues with the particular flavour of small-town and rural life during the Depression.

A bird in the house, *The diviners*, *The fire-dwellers*, *A jest of God*, *The prophet's camel bell*, *The stone angel*, *This side Jordan*, and *The tomorrow-tamer* are all in the NEW CANADIAN LIBRARY, with Afterwords by Isabel HUGGAN, Timothy FINDLEY, Sylvia FRASER, Margaret ATWOOD, Clara THOMAS, Adele WISEMAN, George WOODCOCK, and Guy VANDERHAEGHE respectively.

See *A very large soul: selected letters from Margaret Laurence to Canadian writers* (1995) edited by J.A. Wainwright. Laurence was generous in granting interviews, which are listed, together with critical articles on her work, in *Margaret Laurence, an annotated bibliography* (1979) by Susan J. Warwick. An interview and the title essay by Laurence are included in *A place to stand on* (1983), a collection of articles edited by George WOODCOCK. Other collections of critical articles include Kristjana GUNNARS' *Crossing the river* (1988), Colin Nicholson's *Critical approaches to the fiction of Margaret Laurence* (1990), and Christl Verduyn's *Margaret Laurence: an appreciation* (1988). Joan Hind-Smith's *Three voices* (1975) is an early biography that sometimes points to the facts behind the fiction. There is a detailed chronology, compiled by Susan J. Warwick, in *Journal of Canadian Studies* 13, no.3 (Fall, 1978), which is a special issue devoted to Margaret Laurence. Of other periodical numbers devoted to Laurence, the most notable are *Journal of Canadian Fiction* 27 (Summer, 1980), which includes four early Laurence stories not previously printed, and *Canadian Woman Studies* 8, no.3 (1987). There is a collection of reviews and articles reprinted from a variety of sources in William New's *Margaret Laurence, the writer and her critics* (1977). For book-length critical studies, see Clara THOMAS's *The Manawaka world of Margaret Laurence* (1975) and Patricia Morley's *Margaret Laurence: the long journey home* (1991). *The life of Margaret Laurence* (1997) by James King, reveals Laurence, sick with cancer, preparing to take her own life, which she did.

See also NOVELS IN ENGLISH 1960 TO 1982: 2. JOAN COLDWELL

Laurendeau, André. See ESSAYS IN FRENCH: 6.

Laut, Agnes Christina (1871-1936). Born in Stanley Township, Huron County, Ontario, she was two when the family moved to

Winnipeg, Manitoba, then a frontier town. Upon graduating from the University of Manitoba, she wrote for the *Manitoba Free Press*. When ill health caused her to spend a summer in the mountains of British Columbia, she conceived a lifelong love for the wilderness, feeling a special affinity for those who opened up the Canadian North and the Canadian and American West. She moved to the United States, where she pursued these interests in many publications. Her novel *Lords of the North* (1900), a historically accurate and action-filled story of the rivalry of the North West and Hudson's Bay companies, inaugurated her successful career as a writer, and was the first of her five novels on Canadian subjects. Among her many works of historical non-fiction, the earliest and perhaps best known is *Pathfinders of the West: being the thrilling story of the adventures of the men who discovered the great Northwest* (1904). Laut also wrote three volumes in the Chronicles of Canada series—on the northern fur trade, the pioneers on the Pacific coast, and the goldfields of British Columbia respectively—published between 1914 and 1916. Laut was the first writer permitted by the Hudson's Bay Company to use diaries and photographs from their archives in her works. She died at her estate in Wassaic, New York.

See Carole Gerson, 'Agnes Christina Laut', *Dictionary of literary biography* 92: 181-3.

LORRAINE McMULLEN

Lavallée, Ronald. See NOVELS IN FRENCH 1983 TO 1996: 7.

Lavigne, Louis-Dominique. See DRAMA IN FRENCH 1948 TO 1981: 3.

Lawrence, R.D. See NATURE WRITING IN ENGLISH: 6.

Layton, Irving (b. 1912). Born in Romania, he came to Montreal with his parents (Lazarovitch) at the age of one, and was educated at Baron Byng High School and Macdonald College, where he earned a B.Sc. in agriculture. After brief service in the Canadian Army (1942-3), he did postgraduate work in economics and political science at McGill University, obtaining an M.A. in 1946. He taught English at a parochial school in Montreal, while also teaching part-time at Sir George Williams College (now Concordia University). He was appointed writer-in-residence at Sir George in 1965, and to a similar post at the University of Guelph in the winter of 1969. That year he was appointed professor of English at York University, Toronto, from which post he retired in 1978. He was awarded a Doctor of Civil Laws by Bishop's University in 1970 and was made an Officer of the Order of Canada in 1976.

Layton was a member of the active group of young poets in Montreal who contributed to *FIRST STATEMENT*, founded by John SUTHERLAND in 1942. With Louis DUDEK in 1943 he joined Sutherland in editing the magazine and remained an editor until it merged with *PREVIEW* in 1945 to become *NORTHERN REVIEW*. He resigned in the 1950s when new editorial policies were adopted by Sutherland. In 1952 he was associated with Dudek and Raymond SOUSTER in founding CONTACT PRESS, a co-operative venture to publish the work of Canadian poets. Together with Dudek, he was instrumental in shaping the editorial policy of Aileen Collins' magazine *CIV/n* (1953-5). In 1955 he declined an invitation by Charles Olson to join the faculty of Black Mountain College, North Carolina, and the editorial board of the *Black Mountain Review*. However, he was in close contact with the American poets Robert Creeley, Cid Corman, and Jonathan Williams throughout the 1950s, and in 1956 edited a Canadian issue of Corman's magazine *Origin*. His extensive correspondence with Creeley was published in 1990 as *Irving Layton and Robert Creeley: the complete correspondence, 1953-1978*.

Layton's poetry has dazzled, puzzled, angered, and astonished its readers since its first publication. He has vigorously opposed the aestheticist concept of the poem as a paradigm of the beautiful. To Layton the poem must convey truth, which can reside in the most ignoble and 'unpoetic' subjects and be expressed in blatantly non-poetic forms. The craft of poetry lies in finding the words, however unconventional, to manifest the poet's vision.

Many of Layton's early collections of poetry were prefaced by attacks on alleged restricters of the freedom of the poet's imagination—professors, critics, clergymen, rationalist poets, puritan editors—who were, in Layton's view, abetted by women in attempting to confine the poet's Apollonian spirit to a world of comfort, convention, and predictability. In these collections Layton presented himself as defiantly breaking a puritan embargo on image, magic, and sexuality, and as making the irrational an accepted part of Canadian poetry for the first time since LAMPMAN and CARMAN. In his rehabilitation of the irrational, however, he invariably included himself among the liars, hypocrites,

Yahoos, and philistines of whom he wrote. His voice thus appeared to come from inside the primal energy and vileness of our world, as a presumably 'honest' testimony to its dangers and powers. The most impressive of Layton's poems have captured the poet's own extravagance, as in 'The day Aviva came to Paris', 'Shakespeare', and 'Keine Lazarovitch', and revealed a wit that can astonish with both its appropriateness and its reach. Layton's voice in such poems has been confident, bawdy, and at times hyperbolic, yet capable of discerning self-perception.

Layton began publishing in *First Statement* in 1943; between 1943 and 1952 he wrote relatively little, publishing three books, two of which reprinted significant portions of the first, and contributing a small number of poems to *Cerberus* (1952), a collection he shared with Dudek and Souster. From 1953 until the early 1980s he was extraordinarily productive, publishing an average of one book a year. Layton's publications in the first two decades of his career are: *Here and now* (1945), *Now is the place* (1948), *The black huntsman* (1951), *Love the conqueror worm* (1953), *In the midst of my fever* (published in Mallorca by Robert Creeley, 1954), *The long pea-shooter* (1954), *The cold green element* (1955), *The blue propeller* (1955), *The bull calf and other poems* (1956), *The improved binoculars* (published in North Carolina by Jonathan Williams, with an introduction by William Carlos Williams, 1956), *Music on a kazoo* (1956), *A laughter in the mind* (also published by Jonathan Williams, 1958), and *A red carpet for the sun* (1959, Governor General's Award). They establish the underlying dichotomies of his vision: poet v. society, poetry v. literature, the individual v. the state, passion v. reason, creativity v. order, sacrifice v. rationalization, rudeness v. decorum, imperfection v. perfection, life v. art. The later poems continually expand the amount of the ostensibly horrific, trivial, or crude that this life-affirming vision must necessarily and paradoxically include. The collections of his middle years —*The swinging flesh* (1961), *Balls for a one-armed juggler* (1963), *The laughing rooster* (1964), *Collected poems* (1965), *Periods of the moon* (1967), *The shattered plinths* (1968), *The whole bloody bird: obs, alphs, and poems* (1969), *Nail polish* (1971), and *Lovers and lesser men* (1973)—are increasingly angry and strident in tone. In later collections—*The pole vaulter* (1974), *For my brother Jesus* (1976), *The covenant* (1977), *The tightrope dancer* (1978), *Droppings from heaven* (1979), *For my neighbours in hell* (1980), *Europe and other bad news* (1981), *The Gucci bag* (1983), and *Fortunate exile* (1987)—Layton gave renewed emphasis to anti-Christian themes and to his Jewishness, using the latter as a symbol of passion, dignity, and truth. His poetry can be examined in depth in *The collected poems of Irving Layton* (1971), in several volumes of selected poems, including *The darkening fire: selected poems, 1945-68* (1975), *The unwavering eye: selected poems, 1969-75* (1975), *A wild peculiar joy: selected poems 1945-1982* (1982), *Final reckoning: poems 1982-1986* (1987), and *Fornaluxt: selected poems 1928-1990* (1992).

Layton edited *Pa-nic: a selection of contemporary Canadian poems* (1958) and *Love where the nights are long: Canadian love poems* (1962). He collaborated with Louis Dudek in editing *Canadian poems: 1850-1952* (1952). His other publications have included *Engagements: the prose of Irving Layton* (1972), a collection of ten short stories, articles, prefaces, and reviews, *Taking sides: the collected social and political writings* (1977), *Waiting for the Messiah: a memoir* (1985), and *Wild gooseberries: the selected letters of Irving Layton* (1989). International publication of Layton's work has included *Selected poems* (London, 1974), *The poems of Irving Layton* (New York, 1977), *Seventy-five Greek poems* (Athens, 1974), *Il freddo verde elemento* (Torino, 1974), *Il puma ammansito* (Milan, 1979), *Le poesie d'amore di Irving Layton* (Albano Terme, 1983), and *Il cacciatore sconcertato* (Ravenna, 1993). Other books are *Uncollected poems 1935-59* (1976); *Dance with desire: love poems* (1986, rev. 1992); a collection of letters, *An unlikely affair* (1980, with Dorothy Rath); and other anthologies he edited: *Poems for 27 Cents* (1961), *Anvil* (1966), *Anvil Blood* (1973), *Shark tank* (1977), and *Rawprint* (1989)—the latter four collecting work by his students.

See Eli MANDEL, *The poetry of Irving Layton* (1969; rev. 1981); Seymour MAYNE, ed., *Irving Layton: the poet and his critics* (1978); Elspeth Cameron, *Irving Layton: a portrait* (1985); and Henry BEISSEL and Joy Bennett, eds, *Raging like a fire: a celebration of Irving Layton* (1993).

See also POETRY IN ENGLISH 1950 TO 1982: 1.

FRANK DAVEY

Leacock, Stephen (1869-1944). Stephen Butler Leacock was born in Swanmore, England. His father, after failing at farming in South Africa and Kansas, took his family in 1876 to Canada, where they settled on a farm in the Lake Simcoe district of Ontario. It was never a success, and Leacock's father eventually abandoned his wife, leaving her to raise the family of eleven children (of whom Stephen was the third). Leacock was educated locally and then at Upper Canada College,

Toronto. After a year at the University of Toronto he became an unenthusiastic schoolteacher in 1888; from 1889 to 1899 he taught at Upper Canada College, finding time to complete a degree in modern languages at the University of Toronto in 1891. In 1899, inspired by Thorstein Veblen's *Theory of the leisure class*, he enrolled at the University of Chicago, where he did graduate work in political economy under Veblen. He married Beatrix Hamilton in 1900, and upon receiving his Ph.D. in 1903 was appointed lecturer in the Department of Economics and Political Science at McGill University. In 1906 he published his first and most profitable book: *Elements of political science* (rev. 1921), a college textbook. In 1907-8 he went on a lecture tour of the British Empire to promote Imperial Federation, and when he returned to McGill he became head of his department, helped found the University Club, and built a summer home on Lake Couchiching near Orillia, Ontario. McGill, the University Club, and the home in Orillia became the focal points of his existence. In 1910 the first of Leacock's many books of humour was published, *Literary lapses* (NEW CANADIAN LIBRARY, with an Afterword by Robertson DAVIES). Elected to the Royal Society of Canada in 1919, Leacock became a charter member of the CANADIAN AUTHORS' ASSOCIATION in 1921, and that year went on a lecture tour of England. He remained head of his department until his enforced retirement in 1936, after which he made a triumphant lecture tour of western Canada that resulted in *My discovery of the West: a discussion of East and West in Canada* (1937)—winner of a Governor General's Award. In 1937 he received the Lorne PIERCE Medal of the Royal Society of Canada. He continued to write prolifically until his final illness.

Leacock's humorous books usually gathered together, in time for the Christmas trade, miscellaneous pieces that had appeared previously in various magazines. As a result, most of them have little or no overall unifying structure. The mix in *Literary lapses* is typical: funny stories, some little more than anecdotes, others more extended; monologues and dialogues; parodies ranging from fashionable romantic novels to Euclid; humorous reflections and essays on a wide variety of topics. Much of Leacock's humour, in this book and in others, is exuberant nonsense that, like Lewis Carroll's, sometimes breaks out into a violence that would be disturbing if it were not so obviously in fun. More modern parallels might be the Marx Brothers or *Monty Python's Flying Circus*. Leacock's parodies (see especially *Nonsense novels*, 1911; *Frenzied fiction*, 1918; and *Winsome Winnie, and other new nonsense novels*, 1920), which are undervalued today, offered him an excellent opportunity to give vent to this strain of irresponsible anarchy. Lord Ronald in 'Gertrude the governess; or simple seventeen', who 'flung himself upon his horse and rode madly off in all directions', is the most famous example of this strain of Leacock's humour. Other parodies—such as 'Guido the gimlet of Ghent: a romance of chivalry' and 'Sorrows of a super soul; or, The memoirs of Marie Mushenough'—provide examples of almost equally inspired absurdity. Often, however, a more serious note mingles with the humour, and some of Leacock's funniest pieces—such as 'My financial career', 'Hoodoo McFiggin's Christmas', or any of the sketches from *ARCADIAN ADVENTURES WITH THE IDLE RICH* (1914; NCL)—show genuine sympathy for decent but ineffectual victims of a coldly indifferent or actively hostile world. It is clear from pieces such as these why Leacock considered Mr Pickwick and Huckleberry Finn to be the two greatest creations of comic literature, and why he was approached to write a screenplay for Charlie Chaplin.

The most striking aspect of Leacock's style is the illusion of a speaking voice, which is so strong in all his works. Like his masters, Dickens and Mark Twain, Leacock was a great lecturer and raconteur, and many of his pieces must be read aloud or recited for their full effect. North American humour has always been rooted in the oral tradition, from Thomas Chandler HALIBURTON (whom Leacock did not admire but with whom he had much in common) through Artemus Ward, Mark Twain, and many others, including Robert Benchley and James Thurber, who were both influenced by Leacock. But Leacock's idiom has none of the frontier raciness we associate with Sam Slick and his numerous progeny. Much of the humour of his best pieces comes from their modesty of tone. They seem to be recounted, as simply and straightforwardly as possible, by someone who is not intending to amuse us and would probably find our amusement puzzling. Leacock's finest achievement in this respect is the naively self-revealing narrator of *SUNSHINE SKETCHES OF A LITTLE TOWN* (1912; NCL, with an Afterword by Jack HODGINS). Another aspect of Leacock's humour that may also owe something to the oral tradition is the way in which he elaborates a single idea, capping one ingenuity with another until he reaches an inevitable but absurd climax (the final irrational act of the narrator that follows a crescendo of humiliations in 'My financial career') or collapses into an equally inevitable but absurd anticlimax (as in the apparent tragedy turned farce of 'The marine excursion of the Knights of Pythias' or 'The Mariposa bank mystery' in *Sunshine sketches*).

Leacock's two most important books are *Sunshine sketches* and *Arcadian adventures*. The first is a regional idyll portraying the essentially good-natured follies of Mariposa, a small Ontario town based on Orillia. The second, set in an American city, is much harsher in its criticism of a hypocritical and destructive plutocracy. These two books stand apart from the rest of Leacock's humorous writings in their artistic unity and seriousness of purpose. Apart from the works already mentioned, Leacock's thirty-odd books of humour include *Behind the beyond, and other contributions to human knowledge* (1913), *Moonbeams from the larger lunacy* (1915), *Further foolishness: sketches and satires on the follies of the day* (1916), *The Hohenzollerns in America: with the Bolsheviks in Berlin and other impossibilities* (1919), *Over the footlights* (1923), *Winnowed wisdom: a new book of humour* (1926), *Short circuits* (1928), *The iron man & the tin woman, with other such futurities: a book of little sketches of today and to-morrow* (1929), *The dry Pickwick and other incongruities* (1932), *Funny pieces: a book of random sketches* (1936), *Model memoirs and other sketches from simple to serious* (1938), *My remarkable uncle, and other sketches* (1942, NCL), and *Last leaves* (1945). An original NCL collection is *My financial career and other follies* (1993), selected and with an Afterword by David Staines.

After the appearance of *Literary lapses*, (1910; NCL, with an Afterword by Robertson Davies) Leacock published, on the average, one book of humour a year; but he found time to produce many non-humorous works as well—numerous articles, and some twenty-seven books, most of which are of little lasting interest. Two exceptions are *My discovery of England* (1922) and *The boy I left behind me* (1946). The first is based on Leacock's 1921 lecture tour of England and contains two of his best pieces: 'We have with us to-night', a hilarious account of the tribulations of a public lecturer, and 'Oxford as I see it', a powerful defence of the ideal of education as a humane experience. *The boy I left behind me* consists of the opening chapters of an autobiography that was interrupted by Leacock's death. It is shrewd and unsentimental but evocative, and even in its truncated form is one of Leacock's finest sustained pieces of writing. Leacock's other non-humorous books, while skilful and sometimes genuinely eloquent, are lacking in originality, seldom rising much above the level of competent popularizations. However, many of these works provide important insights into the issues that concerned Leacock all his life and that underlie much of his best humour.

Leacock's most dearly held belief, which links him to the Victorian age in which he spent his formative years, was in progress, which he saw as culminating in the achievements of Anglo-Saxon civilization. This belief underlies his many works of history, political science, and economics, such as *Baldwin, Lafontaine, Hincks: responsible government* (1907), *Economic prosperity in the British Empire* (1930), *Canada: the foundations of its future* (1941), and *Montreal: seaport and city* (1942), among many others. For Leacock the essence of progress was an ever-increasing capacity for human kindness, which found its highest artistic expression in Anglo-Saxon humour, especially as it is reflected in the works of Mark Twain and Dickens. He argued this thesis most notably in *Mark Twain* (1932), *Charles Dickens, his life and work* (1933), *Humour: its theory and technique* (1935), and *Humour and humanity* (1937). Leacock's belief in progress may appear complacent, but it was not lightly held. Throughout his life there was a tension between his proclaimed optimism about the continuing progress of humanity and his feeling of unease (expressed most forcefully in *The unsolved riddle of social justice*, 1920) about the triumph of materialism, with its exaltation of *laissez-faire* individualism and its undermining of traditional social ties. Leacock's particular stance in this matter has been characterized by Gerald Lynch as Tory humanism, a particularly Canadian stance that Leacock shares to some extent with other Canadian social satirists such as Thomas Chandler Haliburton, Sara Jeannette DUNCAN, and Robertson Davies, and with philosophers such as Charles TAYLOR and George GRANT.

Leacock's hostility to the chaotic forces that he saw threatening human progress was reflected in his views on imperialism. Like many of the Canadian imperialists of his day (again Haliburton and Duncan come particularly to mind), Leacock saw the British Empire, for all its failings, as a humane alternative, rooted in tradition and community, to the unfettered materialism of the American capitalist juggernaut—a kind of Mariposa writ large. To be sure, Leacock's imperialism often came out in unpleasant ways, as in his unyielding opposition to non-Anglo-Saxon immigration to Canada; but whatever the forms his world view sometimes took, it was deeply rooted in a genuine desire that the gradual progress of humanity not be brought to a halt.

Most readers of Leacock agree that his writing career shows little sign of development, either intellectual or artistic. He did, however, continue to produce excellent pieces intermittently throughout his career, such as 'Eddie the bartender' (1929), 'My Victorian girlhood by Lady Nearleigh Slopover' (1939), and 'My remarkable uncle' (1942); and in his last years he wrote some very fine essays, essentially serious but leavened with humour, among the best of which are the final chapter of *Humour: its theory and technique*, with its vision of the universe as a great cosmic joke, and two meditations on old age: 'When men retire' (1939), and 'Three score and ten—the business of growing old' (1942). Nonetheless there remains a sense of disappointment, of unfulfilled potential, in his career. It has been argued, notably by Robertson Davies, that, perhaps because of his impoverished and unstable childhood, Leacock craved the reassurance that fame and money brought, and that this led him to fall back uncritically on successful formulas. This is undoubtedly true; but another reason may be that the kindly view of an ever-progressing world that Leacock wished to maintain was at odds with his gift. Leacock's insistence that humour should be kindly is clearly wrongheaded when tested against the world's great humour, including his own, especially *Sunshine sketches* and *Arcadian adventures*, with their critique—implicit in the former and bitterly explicit in the latter—of 'money-getting in the city.' It is hard to see how Leacock could have continued in the far-from kindly direction that seemed to lie ahead of him after *Arcadian adventures* if he were to maintain his faith in progress. His emphasis on the need for kindliness in humour seems, then, a rationalization for his pulling back from the fullest implications of his essentially pessimistic vision of man in the modern industrial age. Ironically, it may have been Leacock's need to maintain his faith in the progress of humanity that thwarted his own progress as an artist and the fullest development of the gifts with which he was so generously endowed.

See D.A. Cameron, *Faces of Leacock, an appreciation* (1967); Robertson Davies, *Stephen Leacock* (1970); Carl Berger, 'The other Mr. Leacock', *CANADIAN LITERATURE* 55 (Winter 1973); David Staines, ed., *Stephen Leacock: a reappraisal* (1986); and Gerald Lynch, *Stephen Leacock: humour and humanity* (1988).

ZAILIG POLLOCK

League of Canadian Poets, The. It was founded on 20 August 1966, when Ron EVERSON, Raymond SOUSTER, Louis DUDEK, and Michael Gnarowski met at Ralph GUSTAFSON's home in North Hatley, Quebec, to discuss an organization that would serve the interests of English-speaking poets in Canada. John Robert COLOMBO became the group's first organizer, and the name was soon adopted. The League now has over 400 members. Its Founding Members and Life Members include many of the leading English-Canadian poets. Reading programs are administered by the League in the form of national poetry tours funded by the CANADA COUNCIL, school workshops in Ontario, and two reading programs in Toronto. The bimonthly *Poetry-Spoken-Here* calendar lists all readings by members and is mailed to 800 bookstores, media, and libraries, etc. Among the League's publications is the biannual *Who's who in The League of Canadian Poets*. It also sponsors the Pat Lowther Memorial Award for the best book of poetry by a Canadian woman, and the Gerald Lampert Memorial Award for the best book of poetry written by a Canadian. The League's secretariat is located in Toronto.

WILLIAM TOYE

Leblanc, Gerald. See ACADIAN LITERATURE: 3(a).

Leblanc, Raymond. See ACADIAN LITERATURE: 2(a).

Leblanc de Marconnay, Hyacinthe-Poirier (1794-1868). Born in Paris into an old aristocratic family, he immigrated to Montreal in 1834, apparently because of his involvement in suspect political activity in France. He remained in Canada until 1841 and was active in Montreal from the moment of his arrival, in journalism, politics, freemasonry, and the theatre. Initially sympathetic to the Patriote cause, he gradually turned against it as armed violence neared. His last political work published in Canada, *Réfutation de l'écrit de Louis-Joseph Papineau, ex-orateur de la Chambre d'assemblée du Bas-Canada, intitulé 'Histoire de l'insurrection du Canada'* (Montréal, 1839), shows how far the author's loyalties had evolved by then, for it is patently hostile to the rebels and their leaders.

Before leaving France, Leblanc de Marconnay had collaborated on a one-act comic opera, *L'hôtel des princes*, which was staged with some success in Paris in 1831 and published there the same year. In Canada his interest in theatre remained, as he signed his name to two plays that were published and performed in Montreal in 1836, the year he was elected president of the short-lived Société dramatique des auteurs français. The first of these, *Le soldat* (which may have been written in collaboration with Napoléon AUBIN), described as an 'Intermède en 2 parties, mêlé de chants', comprises only eight pages and one bathetic role: that of a chauvinistic French soldier. The second play, *Valentine; ou La Nina canadienne*, is much better developed and represents an important step in the evolution of theatre in French Canada. Its author has been falsely accused of plagiarizing his subject from the eighteenth-century French author Marsollier des Vivetières, whose operetta, *Nina; ou La folle par amour* (Paris, 1786), had enjoyed considerable success. In fact the indebtedness is minimal and sufficiently acknowledged in Leblanc de Marconnay's title. Acquainted with stage techniques in France, he constructed an entirely new and different play: solidly Canadian in setting, it reflects local speech patterns and includes references to Canadian history and politics, along with French-Canadian folksongs. *Valentine*, like *Le soldat*, was performed at least twice at the Theatre Royal in Montreal.

After his return to France in 1841, Leblanc de Marconnay resumed the intense masonic activity that characterized his early years there (he had already reached the 32nd degree by 1828). Although he had indicated, in his correspondence with Governor Sir Charles Bagot, his willingness to return to Canada, he never did. Ineffectual in politics and journalism, he made his major contribution to Canadian culture with his play *Valentine*.

See Claude Galarneau's article in the *DICTIONARY OF CANADIAN BIOGRAPHY*, vol. IX; and J.-N. Fauteux, 'Débuts du journalisme au Canada français', in *Le journaliste canadien-français* I (1955). L.E. DOUCETTE

LeBouthillier, Claude. See ACADIAN LITERATURE: 2(c).

Lecker, Robert. See CRITICISM IN ENGLISH: 5(f), 6(l), 6(n).

Leclerc, Félix (1914-88). Born at La Tuque, Quebec, he was educated there, at a secondary school in Ottawa, and at the Université d'Ottawa, which he attended for two years. From 1934 to 1942 he was employed as a radio announcer in Quebec City and Trois-Rivières and by Radio-Canada. He became a popular performer, reading his stories and poems and singing his own songs on the radio, and from 1942 to 1945 acting with the Compagnons de Saint-Laurent. A precursor of the French-Canadian *chansonniers* who have become internationally popular, from 1951 to 1953 he lived in Paris; he toured Europe and the Near East and was known as 'Le Canadien'. He received the Grand Prix du Disque in 1951 for his recording of *Moi, mes souliers*, and twice again. In 1966 he went to Europe, where he remained popular. A militant nationalist, he lived on the Île d'Orléans.

Leclerc was a troubador whose 'songs are on all lips', a writer who was simple without being naïve. His books of stories, fables, songs, poems, plays, and reminiscences reflected his love of nature and folklore, his lighthearted attitude to life, his humour, and a fresh and spontaneous style of writing. His popularity in Quebec was revealed by the fact that all his books were reissued several times, and by the cover blurb of one of his novels—*Carcajou; ou Le diable des bois* (1973)—which says merely: 'Félix Leclerc n'a pas besoin d'être présenté. Il est lui. Beaucoup plus qu'un célèbre, un grand Québécois.' His first publications were *Adagio* (1943; rpr. 1986), stories; *Allegro* (1944; rpr. 1974), fables; and *Andante* (1944; rpr. 1975), poems. (*Le hamac dans les voiles*, 1951, is a selection from these three books.) He wrote two memoirs: *Pieds nus dans l'aube* (1946), about his happy childhood in La Tuque, and *Moi, mes souliers: journal d'un lièvre à deux pattes* (Paris, 1955), about his careers as writer, actor, playwright, singer, etc. Other books are *Dialogues d'hommes et de bêtes* (1949), thirteen tales; *Le fou de l'île* (Paris, 1958)—translated by Philip Stratford as *The madman, the kite and the island* (1976; 1983); and *Le calepin d'un flâneur* (1961), reflections. His plays are *Théâtre de village* (1951), *L'auberge des morts subites* (1964), *Sonnez les matines* (1959), and *Le p'tit bonheur* (1959; rpr. 1966), twelve short plays that were widely performed as a group. See *Le choix de Félix Leclerc dans l'oeuvre de Félix Leclerc* (1983).

See also Jean-Claude Le Pennec, *L'univers poétique de Félix Leclerc* (1967); Jean-Noel Samson, *Félix Leclerc* (1967), in the series Dossiers de documentation sur la littérature canadienne-française; and Marcel Brouillard, *Félix Leclerc: l'homme derrière la légende* (1994).

WILLIAM TOYE

Leclerc, Gilles. See ESSAYS IN FRENCH: 5.

Lee, Dennis (b. 1939). Born in Toronto, Ontario, Lee attended the University of Toronto Schools and Victoria College, University of Toronto (B.A., 1962; M.A., 1965), where he taught for several years. He was a founder of the experimental Rochdale College, Toronto, and co-founder (with Dave GODFREY) of the House of ANANSI Press. After his association with Anansi ended, Lee embarked on a varied career, writing poems for children and song-lyrics for the televison program *Fraggle Rock*, and serving as a literary consultant for both MacMILLAN and McCLELLAND & STEWART. He was Scottish-Canadian Exchange Fellow at the University of Edinburgh (1980-1), and received an honorary degree from Trent University. An Officer of the Order of Canada, he divides his time between Toronto and Costa Rica.

A central concern in Lee's critical work *Savage fields: an essay on literature and cosmology* (1977), and in his essay 'Cadence, country, silence' (*OPEN LETTER* 2, no. 6, Fall 1973), has been to define both the creative and critical acts as fundamentally religious in nature. In his first book of poems, *Kingdom of absence* (1967), he explores 'a cosmos gone askew' in a sequence of sonnets that abound in images of alienation, absence, loss, and disinheritance. He comes armed in his next book, *Civil elegies* (1968)—and in the revised and enlarged *Civil elegies and other poems* (1972), which won a Governor General's Award—with the pessimism of George GRANT's *Lament for a nation*, and with his own sense of disappointment and complicity in charting his country's 'failures of nerve and its sellouts'. The elegies expand beyond Canada to encompass the history of material interests, imperialism, and war.

Lee's dialogue of self and soul continues through his next two works: *The death of Harold Ladoo* (1976), an elegy in which the poet examines the cultural and spiritual currents surrounding the death of his friend and fellow writer (q.v.) and declares that the notion of art as an absolute brings only 'redemptive lunacy' or 'bush league paranoia'; and *The gods* (1978), a meditation on life in the uncivil, technological space we inhabit, where, despite the absence of values and signposts, we should 'honour the gods in their former selves,/albeit obscurely, at a distance, unable/to speak the older tongue; and to wait/till their fury is spent and they call on us again/for passionate awe in our lives, and a clean high style.' These two long poems, and the earlier *Not abstract harmonies but* (1974), were revised and published together in *The gods* (1979).

Perhaps in response to the absence of a listening God, Lee is obsessed with the idea of voice. He has achieved considerable success in presenting poetically 'the texture of our being here', the 'grunts of prose', and the 'grainy sense of life'; and he has provided a moving testament of his search for authentic speech in the age of information explosion and spiritual deafness—and in a country that continues to merit the designation *colonial*. As a poet and nationalist, a man 'mortgaged to words', Lee has made a remarkable investment in the cultural life of Canada.

His later works include *Riffs* (1993), a Dantean-jazz mini-novel in verse, cast as an excursion from spiritual and erotic ecstacy to rejection and solitude, and *Nightwatch: new and selected poems 1968-1996* (1996). In addition to his varied work as an editor, which includes several high school anthologies and *The new Canadian poets 1970-1985* (1985), Lee is famous for his books of poetry for children: *Wiggle to the laundromat* (1970), *Alligator pie* (1974), *Nicholas Knock and other people* (1974), *Garbage delight* (1977), *The ordinary bath* (1979), *Jelly belly* (1983), and *Lizzy's lion* (1984). Tributes to Lee's talents as an editor and essays on his writing appear in *Task of passion: Dennis Lee at mid-career* (1982). See also Tom Middlebro', *Dennis Lee and his works* (1984).

GARY GEDDES

Lee, Sky (b. 1950). Born in Port Alberni, British Columbia, she received a Fine Arts degree from the University of British Columbia and worked as an artist on the feminist magazine *Makaral*. She also illustrated children's books. Active in the women's movement, she co-edited (with Lee MARACLE, Daphne MARLATT, and Betsy WARLAND) *Telling it: women and language across cultures* (1990), a series of papers that emerged from a 1988 conference on issues confronting minorities—Asian-Canadians, Natives, and lesbians. Her first novel, *Disappearing Moon Café* (1990), is a multi-generational saga that illuminates the dilemma of being Chinese in the twentieth century. Fifteen years in the writing, the novel describes a young Chinese woman investigating her past across five generations as it illuminates the history of the Chinese in Canada and the growth of Vancouver's Chinatown with both historical fact and elements of magic realism, and addresses, sometimes in a lecturing tone, issues of racism and cultural isolation. Her collection of four stories, *Bellydancer* (1994), is at once despairing and humorous. The stories describe a young woman who learns the art of belly-dancing from an older woman; themes include how women are abused by men, but find love and healing in the company of women.

See G. Huggan, 'The latitude of romance', *CANADIAN LITERATURE* 140 (Spring 1994).
GEOFF HANCOCK

Le Franc, Marie (1879-1964). Born in Banastère-en-Sarzeau, a hamlet in Brittany, France, she spent most of her childhood by the sea—one of the main themes in her books. After completing the École Normale in Vannes she became a teacher, but dreamed of travels in exotic lands. In 1906 she came to Montreal to marry Arsène Bessette, a journalist with whom she had corresponded. The wedding did not take place, but she remained in Montreal, where she taught privately and in a girl's school in Westmount. The first few years were hard, but she later acknowledged that they moulded her character. After twenty years in Montreal she returned to Brittany and for the rest of her life divided her time and allegiance between France and Canada. She died in Saint-Germain-en-Laye.

Marie Le Franc's first works were two volumes of conventional poetry, *Les voix du coeur et de l'âme* (1920) and *Les voix de misère et d'allégresse* (1923)—both published in Paris—whose main themes are her love for Canada, her nostalgia for Brittany, and the memory of her two brothers killed in the First World War. *Grand-Louis l'innocent* (1925)—translated by George and Hilda Shiveley as *The whisper of a name* (1928)—was unnoticed when published in Canada, but when it came out in Paris (1927) it won the Prix Fémina. The success of this novel was due mainly to the poetic and sensuous descriptions of the Breton and Canadian landscapes, which vie with each other in the heroine's mind, just as her two loves—for an English-Canadian businessman and for Grand-Louis, an amnesiac fisherman she has met in Brittany—vie in her heart. In several of Le Franc's books human beings become mere personifications of landscape, among them Grand-Louis, Hélier in *Hélier fils des bois* (Paris, 1930), and Antonin in *Le fils de la forêt* (Paris, 1952), which is a kind of remake of *Hélier*. In *La randonnée passionnée* (Paris, 1930) the thin plot is an excuse for describing the landscape of Saint-Maurice. Le Franc is at her best when depicting scenery, and no other francophone writer has captured the spirit of the Laurentian forest as she has. Some of her novels were written with a social message. in *La rivière solitaire* (Paris, 1934) she describes with deep human warmth the hardships endured by a group of unemployed workers from Hull and Montreal sent to clear land in Temiskaming, and *Pêcheurs de Gaspésie* (Paris, 1938) draws attention to the plight of the Gaspé fishermen. *Au pays canadien-français* (Paris, 1932), a book of essays, contains a powerful prose-poem, 'Chant canadien', in which she affirms her love for Canada. *Visages de Montréal* (1934) is a series of sketches of Montrealers she has known. Not all Le Franc's books have a Canadian setting: *Le poste sur la dune* (Paris, 1928), *Dans l'île, roman d'Ouessant* (Paris, 1932), and *Pêcheurs du Morbihan* (Paris, 1946) all take place in Brittany. Several works have both France and Canada as background: *Grand-Louis le revenant* (Paris, 1930), a poor sequel to *Grand-Louis l'innocent*; two books of short stories: *Dans la tourmente* (Issy-les-Moulineaux, 1944) and *O Canada! terre de nos aïeux* (Issy-les-Moulineaux, 1947); and *Inventaire* (Paris, 1930), a strange, introspective work so teeming with images that it sometimes becomes obscure. Le Franc also wrote a large number of essays and short stories that appeared in French and Canadian periodicals.

Her last publication, the charming *Enfance marine* (1959), about her childhood in Brittany, came out in Montreal, and several of her books were reissued there. Though she never became naturalized, Canadian critics have claimed Le Franc as a Canadian. W.E. Collin included a study of Le Franc's fiction in *The WHITE SAVANNAHS*. France gave her the Légion d'honneur, and Canada named a lake in the Mont Tremblant district after her.

See Paulette Collet, *Marie Le Franc: deux patries, deux exils* (1976), and Madeleine Ducrocq-Poirier, *Marie Le Franc. Au-delà du personnage* (1981).
PAULETTE COLLET

Lefrançois, Alexis (b. 1943). This is the pseudonym of Ivan Steenhout. The mystery that surrounds his birthplace is in itself emblematic of his personality and of his place among the contemporary poets of Quebec. Lefrançois is a 'nowhere man', a perpetual traveller of the real and the imaginary world. Probably born in Belgium, he lived and studied in Germany between 1955 and 1961. He then lived in Greece, which has been a kind of spiritual homeland to which he returns from time to time and whose presence can be felt in some of his poetry. Since the end of the 1960s Lefrançois has divided his time between Quebec and various parts of the world—in particular Senegal, where he was a teacher from 1971 to 1973. A translator (under his birth name), he was co-winner of the Governor General's Award for translation in 1987. He also raises mohair goats in the Eastern Townships of Quebec.

In spite of a presence in Quebec that is both infrequent and discreet, Lefrançois has established himself as an important Canadian poet of his generation, ranking with such poets as Michel BEAULIEU, Marcel Bélanger, and Pierre MORENCY. As a poet he has defied any easy definition and has shown a total indifference to the mainstream and the trends of modern Quebec poetry. His first two books, *Calcaires* (1971) and *36 petites choses sur la 51* (1971), seem to have been written by two different men. The former contains sharp images and a tense syntax to express anguish, passion, and irrationality; it is remote from any realistic or descriptive concern, almost classic in its economy. The latter is much lighter in tone, close to the tradition of such French poets as Queneau, Prévert, and Vian. Anxiety and sorrow, though very much present, are overwhelmed by a wry humour and by an irony that makes use of the elements of daily life, in particular streets and scenes of cosmopolitan Montreal. Language is made fun of by means of phonetic spellings.

Since 1971 Lefrançois's poems have kept alive these two orientations. After producing *Mais en d'autres frontières déjâ . . .* (1976) in a limited edition, he returned the next year with two books that are complementary to his first two: *Rémanences* (1977), a lyric suite that is a search for light and transparency, and *La belle été suivi de La tête* (1977), a playful collection with nursery-rhyme overtones. Lefrançois published in Paris a book of poems, *Quand je serai grand* (1978), and a tale for children, *Eglantine et Mélancolie* (1979), while continuing to contribute poetry and prose of a more classical tone to Quebec literary magazines. It is apparent that childhood is one of the keys to the unity of Lefrançois's work, to its central affirmation that life is deeply irrational but promises light, clarity, a form of rebirth. For him childhood is not merely another form of nostalgia: it is a reality that reaches through language and song and is an answer to the tragedy of life and death. A retrospective of his poetry was published in 1984 in the two-volume *Comme tournant la page*: I. *Poèmes 1968-1978*; II. *Petites choses 1968-1978*.

See Pierre Nepveu, 'Alexis Lefrançois, les mots éblouis de silence', *Lettres québécoises* 4 (oct. 1977), and *Ellipse* 46 (1991), which is devoted to Lefrançois and Michael ONDAATJE.

PIERRE NEPVEU

Leith, Linda. See NOVELS IN ENGLISH 1983 TO 1996: OTHER NOVELS 2(a).

Le May, Pamphile (1837-1918). Léon-Pamphile Le May, son of a merchant-farmer, was born in St-Louis-de-Lotbinière, Lower Canada (Quebec). After attending the Séminaire de Québec, where he studied law, he travelled to the USA and tried many jobs, eventually deciding to enter the priesthood. He enrolled at the seminary of the Université d'Ottawa, but illness obliged him to leave the priesthood and resume the study of law in 1860. Although called to the bar in 1865, Le May worked as a civil servant, first as a parliamentary translator in Ottawa, then as parliamentary librarian at Quebec, where he compiled the *Catalogue de la bibliothèque de la Législature de Québec* (Lévis, 1873, 7 supplements 1874-83). During the evenings he read his poems at Octave CRÉMAZIE's bookstore, where he met with other members of the ÉCOLE LITTÉRAIRE DE MONTRÉAL. A founding member of the Royal Society of Canada, Le May was a much-honoured poet, winning prizes and an honorary doctorate from Université Laval, and the rosette of an Officier de l'Instruction publique of France.

Le May's first collection of poems, *Essais poétiques* (Québec, 1865), lacked both originality and technical skill. Admitting his ignorance of the rules of French versification, Le May set about correcting this, revising most of his poems through subsequent editions. His translation of Longfellow's *EVANGELINE*, first published in this collection, was reissued with revisions as *Évangeline* (1870), and again in *Évangeline et autres poèmes de Longfellow* (1912). He had considerable success with the popular epic mode in his *La découverte du Canada* (1869), a 21-stanza narrative of the war against the Amerindians, and the patriotic *Hymne pour la fête nationale des Canadiens français* (1869), both of which won a Laval poetry contest and were published in *Deux poèmes couronnés par Laval Université* (Québec, 1870). In *Les vengeances: poème canadien* (Québec, 1875), a heroic poem ranging from the tragic episodes of 1837 to the pictureseque manners of Quebec life, Amerindian vengeance (the kidnapping of a child) is contrasted with the Christian miracle that brings the evil Tonkourou to repentence. Le May adapted it for the stage (Québec, 1876) and prepared two revisions: *Tonkourou* (Québec, 1888) and *Les vengeances* (Montréal, 1930). *La chaine d'or* (Québec, 1879), sold in aid of the St Vincent de Paul Society, is the true story in rhyme of a man fallen on hard times who is helped by a friend's charity. Equally didactic is *Fables canadiennes* (Québec, 1882), an immensely popular imitation of La Fontaine. After twenty years of working in other genres, Le May produced his masterpiece, *Les gouttelettes* (Montréal, 1904), a collection of sonnets, characterized by restraint and simplicity, following the Parnassian trend of the decade and featuring religious or rustic scenes transfused with emotion; these finely drawn miniatures are not unlike the work of the CONFEDERATION POETS. Le May continued polishing and condensing in his last years, bringing out two more revisions and rearrangements of earlier poems: *Les épis* (1914) and *Reflets d'antan* (1916).

Today there is more interest in Le May's fiction than in his poetry. Generally condemned in the nineteenth century for heaviness of style, his novels show subtle humour, though they have melodramatic plots, filled with endless peripeteia, complicated subplots, and improbable coincidences that rework the basic themes of the narrative poems. *L'épreuve* was serialized in *Le journal du Québec* (1863). Although written as a pair, *Le pèlerin de Sainte-Anne* (Québec, 1877) and *Picounoc le maudit* (Montréal, 1878; rpr. 1972) are connected by plot, though not style. The first tells the story of Jos, an orphan involved with the gang of the villain Picounoc the elder, and his difficulties in marrying his beloved. The sequel develops an *Othello* plot in which the son, Picounoc the damned, plays Iago to his friend Jos. In both books hypocrisy is unmasked, vice punished, and good rewarded. Undaunted by their poor critical reception, Le May went on to write *L'affaire Sougraine* (Québec, 1884)—a pioneer detective fiction in Quebec based on an actual murder committed in the forests of Lotbinière by an Amerindian, Sougraine—which retains a certain historical interest for its satirical depiction of life in Quebec City. In the same year Le May's translation of William KIRBY's *The GOLDEN DOG*—*Le chien d'or* (Québec, 1884)—did much to popularize the historical novel in Quebec.

After a lengthy silence, Le May published his major work of prose, *Contes vrais* (Québec, 1899; rev. 1907; critical edition, 1993). His tendency to digress is here accommodated: tale is embedded in tale as narrators exchange stories. Though these legends contain marvellous and supernatural elements, Le May demystifies the fantastic by placing them in real places and within actual historical events. Their variety, and the vivacity of Le May's style, have made this book a favourite nineteenth-century work.

Fêtes et corvées (Lévis, 1898) is a collection of essays that describe the calendar of rural labours and celebrations in Quebec, and includes songs, dances, and stories. Le May also wrote three comedies that were collected in *Rouge et bleu, comédies* (Québec, 1891), and a one-act vaudeville, *Entendons-nous* (1911), produced for the Royal Society.

See Anne Gagnon's introduction to the reprint of *Picounoc le maudit* (1972); Romain Legaré's introduction to that of *Contes vrais* (1973); and the entries on Le May's works in the *Dictionnaire des oeuvres littéraires du Québec* (1978). For an interesting comparative study linking Le May with his contemporaries the Confederation Poets, see Lucille Begley, 'Harmonies canadiennes: Pamphile Le May, Archibald Lampman', *Lectures*, 6 (juin 1960). The catalogue of the exhibition *Pamphile Le May, écrivain et bibliothécaire*, held at the Bibliothèque nationale du Québec in 1987 to mark the 150th anniversary of his birth, contains a biography of Le May by Maurice Péllerin and Gilles Gallichan and a complete bibliography of Le May's works. BARBARA GODARD

Lemelin, Roger (1919-92). Born in a working-class district of Quebec City, he was the eldest of ten children. He left school in eighth grade during the Depression—starting to work at fourteen, and reading and studying independently. Beginning in 1961 he was a full-time businessman, first in Quebec City, where he managed advertising, food-processing, and lumber firms, then in Montreal, where he was publisher and president of *La Presse*. His first novel, *Au pied de la pente douce* (1944), translated by Samuel Putnam as *The town below* (1948; NCL 1961), was a pioneer novel of the urban working-class in Quebec; its widely read translation provided English-speaking readers with their first insight into that milieu. It won the Prix David and a prize from the Académie française. Lemelin's second novel, *Les PLOUFFE* (1948), translated by Mary Finch as *The Plouffe family* (1950; NCL 1975) became the basis for a popular TV series on the French and English networks of the Canadian Broadcasting Corporation, beginning in 1952, the year in which Lemelin published *Pierre le magnifique*, translated by Harry Binsse as *In quest of splendour* (1955). In 1946 Lemelin was awarded a Guggenheim fellowship; in 1953 a Rockefeller Foundation grant; and in 1954 the Prix de l'Académie des Arts et des Lettres of Paris. He was made a corresponding member of the Académie Goncourt in 1974.

Lemelin's three novels, all set in Quebec City, are linked thematically and chronologically. The dominant theme is the stifling of ambition in the most gifted young people from the poor sections of the city who are frustrated in their desire to rise above their milieu (the passage upward is represented symbolically in the first two novels by the staircases and roads leading from Lower to Upper Town) and to secure a place in the prosperous secular world. The first novel treats the last years of the Depression; the second starts from that point and continues until the spring of 1945; and the third takes place between the summer of 1949 and the spring of 1950. From the crowded working-class parish in the first novel (centred on two families), the focus shifts in *Les Plouffe* to a single family in a more secular setting that includes various parts of Quebec City (though the United States and the battlefields of Europe are evoked by secondary characters), where family and parish are in a state of disintegration. In the third novel, *Pierre le magnifique*, the parish becomes ill-defined, the action taking place mostly in Upper Town, with some important events occurring at the provincial Parliament Buildings, the Petit and the Grand Séminaire, and Université Laval.

Denis Boucher (who appears in lesser roles in the other two novels) and Jean Colin in *Au pied de la pente douce* are Lemelin's most successful characters, among a group of largely one-dimensional caricatures. In Lemelin's novels the working-class family is dominated by the mother. The father—when he exists—is in the background, timid, crushed, passive, but often breaking out into fits of anger to compensate for his lack of authority. The 'couple'—as a sharing, consultative unit—is often the mother and the priest. A keen observer of French-Canadian life, Lemelin portrayed strains and conflicts between the poor and those who are somewhat better off, and sometimes between the poor and the wealthy. The suffering of the poor—who must work for well-to-do 'étrangers'—is sometimes increased by their sense of cultural alienation, symbolized in *Au pied de la pente douce* and *Les Plouffe* by allusions to a people without a flag.

A critic of the *ancien régime* and of the right-wing nationalism that held sway for so long in Quebec, Lemelin castigated—particularly through Denis Boucher—the narrowness and backwardness of the traditional rural parish transplanted into the city, and its spiritual leaders, the clergy. His social satire not only reflects the growing Americanization of Quebec and the abrupt end of its isolationism with the advent of the Second World War, but announces the modern, secular, liberal era that was to come to fruition with the Quiet Revolution in the sixties. These three novels display verve, spontaneity, humour, and satire (sometimes diminished by Lemelin's penchant for melodrama). With them Lemelin became, along with Ringuet (Philippe PANNETON) and Gabrielle ROY, an initiator of social realism in French-Canadian fiction.

Lemelin wrote the scripts for the TV version of *Les Plouffe* and for the film (1981) directed by Gilles Carle. He also published *Fantaisies sur les péchés capitaux* (1940), seven rather superficial short stories. The best, a satire on the clergy of Quebec City, is the much-anthologized 'Le chemin de la croix'. (An English translation by Mary Finch, 'The stations of the Cross', is included in *Canadian short stories* [1960; rpr. 1966] edited by Robert WEAVER.) It appeared in Lemelin's *La culotte en or* (1980), together with various reminiscences, particularly of his formative years in Lower Town. Lemelin also tells, in five episodes, of his acquaintance with the jeweller Albert Guay, who had his wife and twenty-two other passengers blown up in a DC-3 in northeastern Quebec in Sept. 1949. A somewhat transposed version of this tragedy appears in *Le crime d'Ovide Plouffe* (1982), a sequel to *Les Plouffe*. The fumbling Ovide is given some of the attributes of Guay (minus the criminality) in a very long melodrama that mixes fictional and historical characters (e.g., Pierre Elliott Trudeau, Jean Marchand), and literary genres (satire, social realism, farce). Weaknesses include frequent authorial intervention, lengthy explanations (even notes), and stiff dialogue.

Le crime d'Ovide Plouffe was adapted for a TV series by Gilles Carles in 1984. The last episode of the series became a film with the same title, directed by Denys Arcand that same year.

See also NOVELS IN FRENCH 1940 TO 1959: 1. BEN-Z. SHEK

Lemm, Richard. See Writing in the MARITIMES: 5.

LeMoine, Sir James Macpherson. See Writing in English in QUEBEC: 1.

Le Moyne, Jean (1913-96). Born in Montreal, Quebec, he almost completed a classical education under the Jesuits at Collège Sainte-Marie, but the onset of deafness obliged him to interrupt his studies. With the encouragement of his father, a physician, who fostered in him an interest in Greek culture and the Bible, Le Moyne undertook to educate himself. In his endeavour he was influenced by such diverse figures as Spinoza and Jacques Maritain; by French, English, Spanish,

Russian, and American literatures; the music of Bach, Beethoven, and Mozart; the great religious mystics; and Teilhard de Chardin. With the international perspective thus acquired, he was not affected by the nationalism of his era. He learned from Henry James, however, to identify himself as a North American without forgetting his European heritage. In *Convergences* (1961) he wrote: 'I want to keep my French heritage, but it is just as important for me to keep my English chattels and to go to the limit of my American gift of invention.'

In 1929 Le Moyne became associated with a group of dynamic young intellectuals who were to influence the literary and intellectual life of Quebec: Robert CHARBONNEAU, Claude Hurtubise, Paul Beaulieu, and the man responsible for directing the evolution of French-Canadian poetry towards modernism, Hector de SAINT-DENYS-GARNEAU. With them, and with Robert ÉLIE, he was active in founding, in 1934, the periodical *La RELÈVE*. The articles by this group—and contributions by the French writers Maritain, Daniel-Rops, and Emmanuel Mounier—helped to free Quebec from its clerical restraints and to open it up to the outside world. Le Moyne published many pieces *La Relève*; however, while his associates became increasingly interested in literature and social and political problems, he became more preoccupied with religious questions, though not to the exclusion of poetry and music.

Le Moyne began a journalistic career in 1941, working for *La Presse* and transferring in 1943 to *Le Canada*. He joined the Canadian Broadcasting Corporation in 1951 and was managing editor of *La Revue moderne* from 1953 until 1959, when he became a writer and researcher for the National Film Board. In 1969 he joined the prime minister's office in Ottawa, where he remained until his retirement in 1978.

Le Moyne's *Convergences*, a collection of essays that first appeared between 1941 and 1961, was one of the notable French-Canadian publications of its time. It is remarkable not only for being a masterpiece of essay writing, but also for its brilliant insights into French-Canadian life and literature, which are coloured by an unflinching heterodoxy. These writings were the contribution to the Quiet Revolution of a unique French Canadian: a penetrating thinker and polished literary stylist whose intellectual roots were international rather than provincial. The topics discussed include the author's early intellectual development, theology (a subject that permeates his writing), Saint-Denys-Garneau, Teilhard de Chardin, Rabelais, Pickwick, Henry James, and some great composers. But it is his aphoristic essays on aspects of French Canada—focusing on the role of religion and of women—that make the strongest impression. 'Our education', he wrote, 'was a long soak in the high water of clericalism.' Ecclestiastical authority, 'having once saved us from the peril of extinction ... kept up the habit but therafter tended to save us from life.' A major preoccupation of Le Moyne was the problem of dualism—the relation between the spirit and the flesh—which implies 'a defective attitude toward matter and toward the flesh', engendering guilt, fear, alienation, and accounting for a morbid, neurotic strain in French Canada. 'Two signs suffice to identify this dualism: it ignores Easter and it hates women.' In the French-Canadian society of which he wrote, women were relegated to fulfilling the myth of the French-Canadian mother. 'We multiplied greatly through rejecting the flesh ... we deceived ourselves by entering into a union in which the wife was the mother.' These neuroses had two main effects on French-Canadian fiction over a long period, from Laure Conan (Félicité ANGERS) to Marie-Claire BLAIS, sister-novelists who 'share the same psychological heredity': true women were absent from it, and it had a common subtext: 'It is forbidden to love and be happy because—guess why—because it is a sin.'

Such ideas, which ran counter to the current ideology, were those of a deeply religious man who criticized the Church from within; of a committed French Canadian who, dismissing nationalism as 'a kind of folklore', aspired to be a total man, while seeing for French Canada a destiny and culture of its own. With some essays deleted and replaced by others, an English translation by Philip Stratford, *Convergence: essays from Québec*, was published in 1966. All the above extracts are quoted from that edition.

Le Moyne's gifts as a writer and thinker were recognized by several awards: *Convergences* won a Governor General's Award, the Prix France-Canada, and the first prize of the Concours littéraire de la Province de Québec; and in 1968 Le Moyne received the Molson Prize for his unique contribution to Canadian arts and letters. He was made an Officer of the Order of Canada in 1982, when he was appointed to the Senate of Canada, retiring in 1988.

With Robert Élie he edited Saint-Denys-Garneau's *Poésies complètes* (1949), *Journal* (1954), and *Lettres à ses amis* (1967).

ANTOINE SIROIS

LePage, John (1812-86). Born at Pownal, Prince Edward Island, he spent most of his life as a school teacher at Malpeque and Charlottetown, where he died. He was best known to the public as an 'occasional' poet, frequently publishing verse in local newspapers under the initials P.L.I. or P.L.J. He also published several pamphlets of verse and a number of broadsheets, but his most ambitious works were *The Island minstrel: a collection of the poetical writings of John LePage* (Charlottetown, 1860) and *The Island minstrel . . . volume II* (Charlottetown, 1867). He wrote public verse for events and occasions: odes, eulogies, elegies, songs, satires. Of these, the most interesting are his satires on social and political events in the life of the Island. Here he could employ doggerel rhythms and verse forms with devastating effect, puncturing pomposity, stupidity, and greed whenever he saw it. A good example is *An authentic history of the land commission and stirring events in Prince Edward Island* (Charlottetown, 1862)—a satire on the ineffectual efforts of a Royal Commission set up to solve the province's land-tenure problem—in which he balances indignation and a wry sense of irony. TOM VINCENT

Lepage, Robert. See DRAMA IN FRENCH 1981 TO 1996: 4.

Lepage, Roland. See DRAMA IN FRENCH 1948 TO 1981: 3.

LePan, Douglas (b. 1914). Douglas Valentine LePan was born in Toronto. After obtaining degrees from the universities of Toronto and Oxford, he served as instructor and tutor in English literature at Harvard University (1938-41), leaving to become personal adviser on army education to General McNaughton. From 1943 to 1945 he served as a gunner with the First Canadian Field Regiment in Italy. At the end of the war he entered the diplomatic service as first secretary on the staff of the High Commissioner's Office in London. It was during these years that he completed and published his first volume of poems, *The wounded prince* (1948). LePan remained with the Department of External Affairs until 1959, holding various appointments, including that of special assistant to the secretary of state, counsellor and later minister counsellor at the Canadian Embassy in Washington (1951-5), secretary and director of research of the Royal Commission on Canada's Economic Prospects (1955-8), and assistant under-secretary of state for external affairs (1958-9). After five years as professor of English at Queen's University (1959-64), LePan served as principal of University College, University of Toronto (1964-70), and as University Professor (1970-9). He was appointed senior fellow of Massey College in 1970. In 1976 he was awarded the Lorne PIERCE Medal of the Royal Society of Canada for distinguished contributions to Canadian literature.

LePan's poetry, from *The wounded prince* to his recent work, is notable for its formal purity and its immaculate ordering of sight, sound, and sense. A learned poet who can see his own time and his own place from afar as well as from deep within, LePan negotiates his northern rivers with the expectant eye of the coureur-de-bois and the visionary second-sight of the myth-maker. In poems like 'A country without a mythology' and 'Canoe-trip' (*The wounded prince*), he makes us see Canada as an outsider might see it, and for the first time. But the insider with second-sight hints at the riddle of a hidden landscape of the mind, and we come to know our land as no outsider ever could. In much later poems, like 'The green man' and 'Rough sweet land', the myth-making faculty goes beyond hints into realized and original symbol.

LePan's second volume of poetry, *The net and the sword* (1953), which won a Governor General's Award, expresses the experience of transplanted Canadian men in the Old World—a world of war and desolation in which young Canadian soldiers, homesick for their own distant landscape, aliens in a world they cannot fully comprehend, live and die, brave in their fears and with compassion in their bones. There are reflective and elegiac poems here, like 'Tuscan villa' and 'Elegy in the Romagna', in which LePan contemplates the fury of the moment in the long perspective of history. As no other Canadian has done, LePan in this book has given us in a mighty paradox the utter meaninglessness of war and the indestructible meaning of the intrinsically human.

His novel *The deserter* (1964), which also won a Governor General's Award, is a quest for a sustaining faith among the broken shards of values at war's end. Pursued by the military police and by gangs of criminals, haunted by the memory of a perfect moment of love (a paradise not to be regained), the protagonist Rusty is 'away without leave' and seemingly without hope. In this nightmare underworld of pursuit and flight, evidences of simple human courage and sacrifice bring Rusty at last to the realization, in a kind of epiphany, that the rock upon which he must build his faith and rest his hope is not made from a dream of the perfect but instead, as D.G. JONES puts it (in *Butterfly on rock*), from 'the love of persons' and 'of a perishing imperfect world'.

In *Something still to find* (1982) LePan continues his quest for meaning and order. There are poems of savage irony—like 'Hideout' and 'Crackup'—in which a world 'at peace' seems more terrible than the world at war in *The net and the sword*. There are sensitive, personal poems of loss and dissolution, like 'Hysterica passio' ('O my lost kingdom'). There are poems of the land like 'The green man', which gives to this country its mythology and its meaning. And there are prayer-like poems, like 'Say in October'.

Midway in this volume and in a key quite its own is a cluster of love poems that might have been the poems of a man in the summer of his life. These poems would reappear as prelude to LePan's 1990 collection *Far voyages*, poems addressed to a young man who in 1985 died agonizingly of cancer. *Weathering it: complete poems, 1948-1987* (1987) is prefaced by a set of fifty new poems (*Weathering it*) that serve as a kind of summing up, a valediction in which old, far-off things were not forgotten, and old triumphs and sorrows are recollected sometimes in tranquillity, sometimes in pain and dark foreboding ('Now with his lover dead and death trickling through all his veins and arteries'). He concludes the set wondering 'if he could pray; what he should pray for . . . But weathering it.'

In *Far voyages* we are given the love story that had ended before the 'weathering' poems were written, and was announced in the puzzling cluster of poems in *Something still to find*. In what seems a second spring the poet exults in a burst of new energy, an exuberant lyricism shadowed at times by self-doubt and the awareness of his own mortality. When his lover is at last stricken, the poet 'goes down into dread' with him and comes to know the very taste of death. Has he 'weathered it' after all?

Perhaps the answer is to be found in LePan's most ambitious poem to date, *Macalister, or dying in the dark* (1995). A verse drama based on what is known of the life and fate of John Kenneth Macalister, it brings into play the author as poet, novelist, and dramatist. In an imaginative and experimental meta-realism LePan tells us of a young Canadian soldier who was parachuted behind enemy lines in France as a secret agent. With his comrade, Frank Pickersgill, Macalister is captured by the Nazis, tortured, and executed. The author who appears in the poem as questioner, double, and poet puts on the stage of our mind Macalister, his mother, his wife, and a military historian who gives a documentary dimension to the action. As he awaits certain death, Macalister wonders if his fate can be reconciled with any notion of faith, meaning, or purpose. Might he at least die in the light of the answers? Just before his obscene and lingering death on a meat-hook, he has a brief vision of the greenery of his home town and the church of his boyhood. But he dies in the dark, no answers given. 'What is left?' the poet asks of 'high heaven with its ragged indifferent clouds'.

Bright glass of memory (1979) is LePan's recollection of some of the central moments in his career as a public servant. The novelist is at work here in vivid sketches of General McNaughton, Lord Keynes, and Vincent Massey; and we are aware of the poet in the insets and miniatures, and in the reflective moments of self-scrutiny set down in quiet between the fusillades of the politicians. In this book, which gives us a fresh insight into some of the most significant moments in recent Canadian history, we see the man of letters and the man of affairs as one man, single and indivisible.

See S.C. Hamilton, 'European emblem and Canadian image: a study of Douglas LePan's poetry', *MOSAIC*, vol. 3, no. 2 (Winter 1970); Donald F. Priestman, 'Man in the maze', *CANADIAN LITERATURE* 64 (Spring 1975); Lord Trend, review of *Bright glass of memory*, *International Journal*, vol. XXXV, no. 3 (Summer 1980); J. M. Kertzer, 'The wounded eye: the poetry of Douglas LePan', *Studies in Canadian literature*, vol. 6, no. 1 (1981); D.I.B. Smith, 'Wild Hamlet with the features of Horatio: Canadian content in the work of Douglas LePan', *Regionalism and national identity* (1985), R. Berry and J. Acheson, eds; Ronald B. Hatch, 'Letters in Canada' (*Weathering it*), *University of Toronto Quarterly*, vol. 58 (Fall 1988); George Thaniel, 'The moon, the heron, and the thrush', *Classical and modern literature* (1989); and Robert K. Martin, review of *Far voyages*, *Arc* (Spring 1994). There are discussion of LePan's work in D.G. JONES, *Butterfly on rock* (1970), and Tom MARSHALL, *Harsh and lovely land* (1979). MALCOLM ROSS

Leprohon, Rosanna (1829-79). Rosanna Eleanora Mullins was born in Montreal, where her Irish-born father was a prosperous merchant. She attended the Convent of the Congregation of Notre Dame and, encouraged to write by the nuns who educated her, she began publishing in *The LITERARY*

GARLAND: under the initials R.E.M. two poems appeared in Nov. 1846, and a story, 'The Stepmother', was serialized in the spring of 1847. Her contributions to this periodical were soon noticed by such people as Susanna MOODIE. (In *The Victoria Magazine*, June 1848, Moodie praised R.E.M.'s 'Ida Beresford' as a 'story written with great power and vigor'.) As Rosanna Mullins she continued to contribute to the *Garland* until it ceased publication in 1851. In that year she married Jean-Baptiste-Lucain Leprohon, a medical doctor whose ancestors had come to New France in the eighteenth century. They lived in Montreal, except for a few years after their marriage, when they resided in Saint-Charles, Quebec; they had thirteen children.

Three of Rosanna Leprohon's most significant novels appeared in the 1860s: 'The manor house of De Villerai: a tale of Canada under the French dominion', which was serialized in *The Family Herald* from 16 Nov. 1859 to 8 Feb. 1860; *Antoinette de Mirecourt; or Secret marrying and secret sorrowing: a Canadian tale* (Montreal, 1864); and *Armand Durand; or, A promise fulfilled* (Montreal, 1868). Using conventional patterns of nineteenth-century fiction, each story focuses on aspects of French-Canadian society, with French Canadians as the chief characters. 'The manor house of De Villerai' is set in Canada in the years immediately preceding the Conquest, and *Antoinette de Mirecourt* in Canada shortly 'after the royal standard of England had replaced the fleurs-de-lys of France'. Both novels explore such themes as the psychological problems facing the 'old French' who stayed in 'their country' after 'it had passed under a foreign rule', and love between people of different national, religious, and social backgrounds. Using as her main plot the French Roman Catholic Antoinette's 'secret marriage' to a Protestant English army officer, Leprohon developed these themes with some complexity in what she called this 'essentially Canadian' tale. *Armand Durand*, set in the nineteenth century, traces what in many ways is a typical French-Canadian career: that of a bright young farmer's son who becomes a lawyer and then a politician. These works were well reviewed at the time of their first publication in both the English- and French-Canadian press, and a French translation of each was published. *Le manoir de Villerai* (Montréal, 1884) and the French translation of *Armand Durand* were still being published in the mid-1920s.

Leprohon continued to write for Canadian periodicals until shortly before her death. 'Clive Weston's wedding anniversary', a story dealing with the early years of a Montreal businessman's marriage, was serialized in *The Canadian Monthly and National Review* in 1872. *The Canadian Illustrated News* serialized several stories, including 'Ada Dunmore: an autobiography' (1869-70) and her last published work, 'A school-girl friendship' (1877). Edward Hartley DEWART included in his *Selections from Canadian poets* (1864) five of her poems—one, 'Given and taken', is an elegy on the death of her 'first-born'; another, 'Winter in Canada', celebrates the beauties of winter 'spite of ice and snow'. But it was only after her death that John Lovell published *The poetical works of Mrs. Leprohon (Miss R.E. Mullins)* (Montreal, 1881), compiled and introduced by John Reade.

Leprohon has never been entirely forgotten, but since the 1970s there has been renewed interest in her works in both English and French Canada. The English and French versions of each of her three Canadian novels have been reproduced on microfiche by the Canadian Institute for Historical Microreproduction. A scholarly edition of *Antoinette de Mirecourt*, prepared by John C. Stockdale, was published by the CENTRE FOR EDITING EARLY CANADIAN TEXTS in 1989. An edition of *Armand Durand* introduced by Lorraine McMullen and Elizabeth Waterston appeared in 1994. Her poems and short stories have been included in several recent anthologies of Canadian literature; 'Clive Weston's wedding anniversary', for example, was reprinted in *The evolution of Canadian literature in English*, vol. 1 (1973), edited by Mary Jane Edwards. There have been several articles and dictionary entries on Leprohon and her work in which critics have pointed to her gifts as a storyteller, her realistic portrayal of French-Canadian life and French-English relations, and her conservative but nevertheless feminist views on the education of women and on marriage as a partnership. She has also been recognized as one of the first English-Canadian writers to depict French Canada in a way that earned the praise of, and resulted in her novels being read by, both anglophone and francophone Canadians. The entries on Leprohon and her fiction in the *Dictionnaire des oeuvres littéraires du Québec*, vol. 1 (1978); the essay on her by Carole Gerson in *Canadian writers and their work: fiction series: volume one* (1983) edited by Robert Lecker, Jack David, and Ellen Quigley; and 'Rosanna Mullins Leprohon: at home in many worlds' by Lorraine McMullen and Elizabeth Waterston in *Silenced sextet: six nineteenth-century Canadian women novelists* (1992) by Carrie MacMillan,

Lorraine McMullen, and Elizabeth Waterston—are representative of these assessments of Leprohon's achievements.

MARY JANE EDWARDS

Leroux, Patrick. See DRAMA IN FRENCH 1981 TO 1996: 7, 8.

Lesbian literature. Happily the field of lesbian writing in Canada and francophone Quebec extends beyond the boundaries drawn loosely in this entry, which concentrates on writers identified as lesbian or queer and whose interventions in writing and culture are traversed by lesbian or queer desire. In the early- to mid-twentieth century the very possibility of such identifications and interventions often meant that writers displaced themselves, sometimes to centres of gay and lesbian culture, sometimes to seemingly unlikely outposts. Elsa Gidlow, once an important figure in underground artistic circles in Montreal in the 1910s, moved to the USA to explore her sense of gender as a series of 'gradations'. In Greenwich Village, New York, and then in San Francisco, Gidlow published close to a dozen volumes of poetry, available in the selection *Sapphic songs: eighteen to eighty* (1982), and an autobiography *Elsa: I come with my songs* (1986). For Jane RULE, writing entailed leaving the USA, first for England and then for Vancouver, where she wrote *Desert of the heart* (1964), her first published novel. With its positive images of desire between women—which Rule explored further in her essay collection *Lesbian images* (1975)—this coming-out novel is considered a landmark in pre-Stonewall fiction. Rule's novels and short stories, social realist in texture and democratic in vision, insist upon the need to live lesbian desire freely.

Phyllis WEBB is cited by Rule as a woman who, along with Adrienne Rich, has written poems 'of permanent importance' to her. *Naked poems* (1965) in particular refers obliquely to a lesbian lover. More able to speak about these poems and their 'erotics of restraint' in the 1990s with Janice Williamson than she was in the 1960s, Webb continues to resist any category, lesbian or other, that 'nails down' her identity (*Sounding differences*, 1993). The poetry of Dorothy LIVESAY, too, disturbs fixed definitions of lesbian writing. Written late in her life when Livesay was widowed and had had an affair with a woman, lines such as 'you must let your mouth go/you must drown in me' in *The phases of love* (1983) prefigure the intersubjective flux and sliding corporeal referents of Daphne MARLATT's lesbian love poems: 'the Fraser rushes out to sea and you, where you are I am.'

Whereas the lovers in the poems of Webb and Livesay remain unnamed, Marlatt and Betsy WARLAND publicly affirm the desire that structures the I-you relations of *Touch to my tongue* (1984) and *open is broken* (1984) through mutual dedications. Their collaborative writing in *Double negative* (1988) and *Two women in a birth* (1994) explores the specificity of each woman subject at the same time that it challenges individual authorship. Significantly, Marlatt's feminist novel *Ana historic* (1988) ends with the beginnings of a lesbian relationship. Warland's poetry (*serpent (w)rite*, 1987) and essays (*Proper deafinitions*, 1990) destructure language in an effort to break patriarchal and homophobic codes, and to make language speak a lesbian-lived body. Warland played a key role in organizing the 1983 'Women and Words' conference and in editing the proceedings, *in the feminine* (1985), and the anthology *InVersions: writing by dykes, queers & lesbians* (1991).

The 1980s and early 1990s were a period of ground-breaking anthologies and new presses and magazines. *Tessera*, a feminist magazine founded in 1984 by Barbara Godard, Marlatt, Kathy Mezei, and Gail SCOTT to foster exchanges between French- and English-speaking women, has from the outset explored the term 'lesbian' as a position of desire, a way of reading, and a relation to language. Among those published in its pages are poets Suniti Namjoshi, whose women-centred fables in *From the bedside book of nightmares* (1984) subvert conventional addressor-addressee relations, quest-narratives, and moral lessons; Janice Williamson, whose *Tell tale signs* (1991) reads culture as a weave of signs susceptible to resignification; and Erin MOURÉ, whose most recent work, *Search procedures* (1996), uses repetition, broken syntax, and non sequiturs to open a conceptual space for sexual and other differences. In 1981 the feminist quarterly *Fireweed* published an issue entitled 'Lesbiantics', featuring critical essays, poetry, soap opera, and stories, including 'A short story' by Vancouver Island writer Anne Cameron. Best known for the Aboriginal myths and stories she sets down in *Daughters of Copper Woman* (1981), Cameron has written a number of short stories that foreground the pleasure of women living together and the humour, for example, of a lesbian couple nailing the sign 'Women' over their outhouse door. A second 'Lesbiantics' issue (1988) included an essay by Makeda Silvera, a Toronto writer who helped bring about a sea-change at *Fireweed* with her analysis of the intersecting questions of race and sexuality. By the late 1980s the texts of lesbians had become integral to *Fireweed* and lesbians were articulating their differences from straight feminism.

In 1985 Silvera, author of the collection of stories *Her head a village* (1994), founded Sister Vision, a 'black women and women of colour press' for which lesbian writing is a focus. At Sister Vision in Toronto she edited the first lesbians-of-colour anthology in North America, *Piece of my heart* (1991), a momentous project given contributors' fears of loss of family and community in coming out. In a further effort to create spaces of dialogue among lesbians of colour, Silvera suggested the joint collection of poetry and prose by Toronto-born Mona Oikawa and Japanese-born Tamai Kobayashi, *All names are spoken* (1992); and, with writer C. Allyson Lee, she edited *Pearls of passion: a treasury of lesbian erotica* (1994). Also published at Sister Vision were *Beneath the naked sun* (1992), a book of poems, by Cree lesbian Connie Fife, addressed sometimes to a collective white 'you' with 'bloody hands' and sometimes to a lesbian 'beloved'; and *The very inside: an anthology of writing by Asian and Pacific Islander lesbian and bisexual women* (1994), edited by Sharon Lim-Hing, which nuances the ways in which racism and lesbian sexuality are lived by different women. The boundaries of the field of lesbian writing are questioned by the work of Sister Vision's Bisexual Anthology Collective in their anthology *Plural desires: writing bisexual women's realities* (1995).

Vancouver's Press Gang, a women's press since the mid-1970s, has a major commitment to lesbian writing. They published *Drawing the line: lesbian sexual politics on the wall* (1991) and *Her tongue on my theory* (1994) by Kiss & Tell, a collective of three Vancouver-based lesbian artists—Persimmon Blackbridge, Lizard Jones, and Susan Stewart—who are well known for their sexually explicit multi-media work and the difficult questions they raise about desire, censorship, collaborative projects, and homophobia. Press Gang is also a key site of lesbian fiction publishing in the 1990s. Marusya Bociurkiw's *The woman who loved airports* (1994) is a collection of stories—some highly cinematic, others verging on prose poetry—that track the movements and conjunctures of women lovers who refuse to settle. The conflicted process of moving on after a lover's death is the central concern of Marion Douglas's *Bending at the bow* (1995). *When fox is a thousand* (1995), a novel in three voices by Vancouver writer Larissa Lai, explores the imaginative possibilities of the Chinese myth that foxes have the power to change into women. Toronto writer Ann Decter, a co-editor with Mona Oikawa and Dionne Falconer of *Resist! essays against a homophobic culture* (1994), has published two novels with Press Gang: *Paper, scissors, rock* (1992) and a sequel, *Honour* (1996). In the stories collected in *Out on main street* (1993) and in the novel *Cereus blooms at night* (1997), Shani Mootoo writes across cultural borders and across generations to expose the ironies and the violence of racism and (hetero)-sexism.

In Toronto the Women's Press has also been active in publishing the writing of lesbians. In 1984 it created the Lesbian Writing and Publishing Collective, which compiled two anthologies of short fiction: *Dykeversions* (1986) and *Dykewords* (1990). 'Notes about racism in the process' in the introduction to the first anthology is an important document of 1980s feminism coming to terms with its exclusionary analysis and white privilege. The second anthology casts its net wider than the first to include writing by Beth Brant and Dionne BRAND. Brant, a Bay of Quinte Mohawk, has published several books with Women's Press. In her fiction *Mohawk trail* (1985) and in her non-fiction *Writing as witness: essays and talk* (1994) she writes of First Nations Two-Spirits (queers) and cross-dressing Tricksters. Brant's *A gathering of spirit: a collection by North American Indian women* (1994) is an anthology of poems and narratives that offered several women a forum to come out as Indian lesbian writers. A Toronto writer, essayist, and film-maker, Brand was guest-editor with Silvera of *Fireweed*'s 'Women of Colour' issue and director of the film *Listening for something* (1996) in which she speaks with Adrienne Rich. She has published eight books of poetry; a collection of stories, *Sans Souci* (1988); and a novel, *In another place, not here* (1996). The novel picks up the lyrical thread of her poetry and weaves it with the voices of her Island birthplace, the voices of two women lovers with very different life experiences and class backgrounds.

Since 1990 Women's Press has published a number of important first books. Finding poems in fortune cookies and insisting that English is not her language, the speaker of Lydia Kwa's *The colour of heroines* (1994) conveys the pain as well as the pleasure of self-translation. Ingrid MacDonald's *Catherine, Catherine* (1991) imaginatively constructs a lesbian of premodern history, a woman who passed as a Prussian soldier and took a wife.

Written from a butch lesbian perspective often marginalized by lesbian-feminist discourses, Karen Tulchinsky's stories collected in *In her nature* (1995) concern issues of gender and Jewish identity. Tulchinsky has also co-edited several collections of stories, including *Tangled sheets: stories & poems of lesbian lust* (1995).

For reasons related to region, genre, projected audience, cultural politics, and publishing history, some lesbian writers publish with more mainstream presses, regional small presses, or other women's presses. Beginning with *A reason to kill* (1972), Toronto writer Eve Zaremba has published her dyke detective mysteries with various presses including Paperjacks, Amanita Publications, and Second Story Press in Toronto. Sky LEE's novel *Disappearing Moon Café* (1990), published with Douglas and McIntyre, dramatizes the heroine's efforts to write an anti-racist genealogy, to document attitudes toward the Chinese in Canada, and to rethink her relationship with a woman friend and potential lover. Carolyn Gammon's *Lesbians ignited* (1992), a witty collection of poems attuned to the contradictions of lesbian desire and sexual practice, was published with gynergy books, a Charlottetown press with a strong commitment to feminist publishing. A similar sense of humour, this time directed at prevailing culture, permeates *Moon honey* (1995), by Alberta writer Suzette Mayr, in which metamorphoses—in skin colour, in species, in sexual orientation, and in narrative form—become ordinary events. Not unlike Lee's *Disappearing Moon Café*, Ann-Marie MacDONALD's *Fall on your knees* (1996) gradually exposes the 'unthinkable' (illegitimacy, same-sex desire, cross-racial affairs) within the history of a family and points to the limitations as well as the lure of the narratives through which characters understand their lives.

In her play *Goodnight Desdemona (Good morning Juliet)* (1990), first produced by Toronto's feminist theatre Nightwood, MacDonald transforms three victims—Desdemona, Juliet, and Constance, a modern-day graduate student and slave to her male professor—into women with the qualities of all three characters: courage, sensuality, and intelligence. As a reader of early versions of *Othello* and *Romeo and Juliet*, Constance is an effective agent of this transformation, inverting lines, mistaking identities, imagining alternative trajectories of desire, and overturning generic conventions. MacDonald's second play, *The Arab's mouth* (1995), finds a similar agent of discovery and change in scientist Pearl MacIsaac at work in her family's ancestral home Belle Moral on the coast of Scotland. Audrey Butler, a Cape Breton-born playright who founded Temperamental Journey Theatre and has worked with Buddies in Bad Times Theatre in Toronto, layers several coming-out stories in her play *Black Friday* (in *Radical perversions: 2 dyke plays*, 1990). In telling her mother about the texture of her life as a dyke, Terry, the play's heroine, creates a conversational space in which family secrets can be spoken. In her words, 'for some of us being private is a luxury we can't afford. We have to be public first.'

Quebec writer Nicole BROSSARD affiliates herself with an international community of lesbian writers. In *Picture theory* (1982), for example, she registers her intertextual relation to American avant-garde writers Djuna Barnes and Gertrude Stein, and in *Mauve* (1985) and *Jeu de lettres/Character* (1985) she explores an erotics of collaborative translation with Daphne Marlatt. Brossard's writing, known in the early 1970s for its departures from linguistic and novelistic codes, takes a lesbian-feminist turn in the fiction-theory of *L'amèr ou le chapitre effrité* (1977) and in the poetry of *Amantes* (1980) and *Le sens apparent* (1980). Using words to construct a passage between the virtual and the real, Brossard's texts project women beyond the patriarchal screen into scenes of erotic encounter, often valuing negatively marked spaces such as the desert (*Le désert mauve*, 1987) and the cemetery (*Baroque d'aube*, 1995). The poetry of Germaine Beaulieu (*Envoie ta foudre jusqu'à la mort, abracadabra*, 1977; *Archives distraites*, 1984; *Voie lactée*, 1991; and *De l'absence à volonté*, 1996) typically gives preference to the third person and alternates between 'elle' and 'elles'. In this way the language of the poems renders women and their desire for one another visible; as in the work of Brossard, a lesbian subject takes form with each successive line.

Jovette MARCHESSAULT, who came to the fore in the mid-1970s, has published several autobiographical fictions including *Comme une enfant de la terre* (1975), *La mère des herbes* (1980), *Tryptique lesbien* (1980), and *Les cailloux blancs pour les forêts obscures* (1987), and several plays, among them *La SAGA DES POULES MOUILLÉES* (1981), *Alice & Gertrude, Natalie & Renée et ce cher Ernest* (1984), and *Le voyage magnifique d'Emily Carr* (1990). Marchessault's fiction offers visionary alternatives to received myths of origins (birth, genesis, founding fathers). Her plays frequently bring together lesbian writers across time and place to discuss aspects of history, writing, and sexuality that would be unspeakable at other historical moments and in other contexts. Tracing her roots back through her Native grandmother to women mystics such as Mère MARIE DE L'INCARNATION, Marchessault locates her work within a hybrid tradition of writing, storytelling, and prophecy by women. Pol Pelletier, well-known for her participation in the collective play *La nef des sorcières* (1976) and for her one-woman performance of Marchessault's *Les vaches de nuit* (from *Tryptique lesbien*), founded the Théâtre Expérimental des Femmes 1979. In 1981, at TEF, she acted in her own play, *La lumière blanche* (1989), which portrays a struggle to the death between a mother, a 'femme-objet', and a woman bent on exploring the ways in which women move and inhabit their bodies when they are not playing the roles society scripts for them.

Like Brossard, Montreal poet and fiction writer Anne-Marie ALONZO has worked to create an international forum for the publication and reception of writing by lesbians. *Trois*, the French-language review (and publishing house) she co-founded in 1985 with Richard Boutin and Alain Laframboise, published a special issue entitled 'Femmes internationales: auteures de plus de vingt pays' (1989), which includes the work of many lesbians. Alonzo's own experimental fictions include the trilogy *Droit et de profil* (in *Les lèvres urbaines*, 1984), *Bleus de mine* (1985), and *Écoute, Sultane* (1987), and the collaborative texts *Nous en reparlerons sans doute* (1986), *Seul le désir* (1987), *Lettres à Cassandre* (1990), *Liens* (1990), and *Margie Gillis/la danse des marches* (1993). By way of unexpected combinations of words, genres, artists, and media, her texts stage a dance of desire among women.

The links between elements in a field of relations are equally important to the writing of anglo-Montrealer Gail Scott. In her novels *Heroine* (1988) and *Main brides* (1993), the privileged centre of consciousness is abandoned in order to explore the intersubjective connections among women characters and to make visible those subjects at the limits of the narrative consciousness. In a similarly decentralizing gesture, *À propos de Maude* (1986), one of six narratives by Montreal writer Lise Harou, presents a relationship between two women from four different angles: Elisa thinking about the absent Maude, Maude's husband recounting a brief stay with Elisa in New York, Maude's letters to Elisa, and Elisa's reflections on Maude's suicide. Everywhere present yet nowhere to be seen, Maude is the absence that drives Elisa's desire and Harou's narrative. 'Maude' returns in the work of Montreal writer Gloria Escomel, who has published two novels, *Fruits de la passion* (1988) and *Pièges* (1992); a play, *Tu en reparleras . . . et après* (1989); and a collection of short stories, *Les eaux de la mémoire* (1994). In *Fruits de la passion*, 'Maud' is both a character created by the narrator, Patricia, and an object of desire for Patricia's twin brother, Patrice; little more than a mediating figure for Patricia's desire for Maud, Patrice eventually drops out of the picture, allowing Patricia to assume her sexual/textual relationship to Maud.

Particularly in their use of a third character who disrupts the logic of the heterosexual couple, the novels of Harou and Escomel recall those of Louise MAHEUX-FORCIER's trilogy *Amadou* (1963), *L'île joyeuse* (1964), and *Une forêt pour Zoé* (1969). Like Rule in English Canada, Maheux-Forcier is the first francophone writer in Quebec to deal explicitly with lesbian relationships in terms of liberation. The major difference between the two writers lies in the poetic prose of Maheux-Forcier's symbolist novels, which foreground the work of language in constituting gender and desire. Marie-Claire BLAIS in *Les nuits de l'underground* (1978), set in a lesbian bar in Montreal, uses long, convoluted sentences that slide between interior states of emotion and exterior scenes of action to convey the story of Geneviève's passion for two women. In Blais's *L'ange de la solitude* (1989), a figure borrowed from Jean Genet follows the circulation of desire within and beyond a commune of women, each isolated in her own world, each finding identity in a lover who is in some cases a woman, in other cases a man. Longtime lover and friend of Marie-Claire Blais, Mary Meigs has written of her relationship with Blais in *Lily Briscoe: a self-portrait* (1981) and of their relationship with a third woman in *The Medusa head* (1983). In an essay in *In Versions*, Meigs offers an engaging analysis of the continuities and discontinuities between fiction and autobiography, and of the pitfalls of sealing a writer within her lesbian identity once she has publicly declared herself.

Although there are feminist presses in Quebec (Les Éditions du Remue-ménage and Éditions de la Pleine Lune), there are, to date, no francophone anthologies and very few issues of magazines devoted to the writing of lesbians. Notable exceptions are 'The Lesbian Issue' of *Resources for Feminist Research/Documentation sur la recherche féministe* (1983), and a special issue of the lesbian magazine *Treize* (1996) on literature. In Quebec the writing of lesbians has appeared in lesbian newsletters such as *Long time coming*, *Amazones d'hier et lesbiennes d'aujourd'hui*, *La vie en rose* (all no longer publishing), as well as in special issues on feminist or women's writing of *Trois*, *VOIX ET IMAGES*, *Dérives*, *SPIRALES*, and *La nouvelle BARRE DU JOUR*. In this sense, although the writers themselves are reasonably well known, lesbian writing is not as visible or as institutionalized a field in Quebec as it is in English Canada, and the focus tends to be more on issues of language, subjectivity, and representation than on issues of identity.

LIANNE MOYES,
with JENNIFER HENDERSON
and SUSAN HOLBROOK

Lescarbot, Marc. See DRAMA IN FRENCH TO 1900 and Writing in NEW FRANCE: 1.

Leslie, Kenneth (1892-1974). Born in Pictou, Nova Scotia, he was educated at Dalhousie (B.A. 1912), Nebraska (M.A. 1914), and Harvard, where he continued graduate studies in philosophy and mysticism. His marriage to Elizabeth Moir, daughter of the wealthy Halifax candy merchant, enabled him to pursue such literary interests as the Song Fishermen—a Nova Scotia literary group he formed with Charles G.D. ROBERTS, Bliss CARMAN, Charles BRUCE, and Robert NORWOOD. This period of his life culminated in his best collection of poetry, *By stubborn stars and other poems* (1938), for which he won a Governor General's Award.

As a crusading journalist, Leslie moved to New York, where he edited the radical *Protestant Digest* (later called *Protestant*) from 1938 to 1949. After Senator Joseph McCarthy and Bishop Fulton Sheen implicated him as a Communist (*Life* magazine included him with Charlie Chaplin, Albert Einstein, and Thomas Mann in a group of fifty suspected 'fellow travellers'), he returned to Halifax, where he continued to edit *Protestant* until 1953. As the editor of *Man* and *New man* from 1957 to 1972, he was subjected to RCMP surveillance. Leslie once cited Christ and the First Baptist Church as the sources for his commitment to social reform; such poems as 'O'Malley to the Reds' (inspired by Father Moses Coady of the co-operative self-help Antigonish Movement) suggests his preference for Christian socialism motivated by love, over Marxist violence motivated by rhetoric.

After *Windward rock* (1934), *Lowlands low* (1935), *Such a din!* (1936), and *By stubborn stars*, Leslie turned to political verse that was occasionally relieved by Vachel Lindsay-like African rhythms, as in 'Remember Lamumba'. His best poems, however, are steeped in the imagery of the sea. In 'Cape Breton lullaby', for which he wrote a haunting melody, the lost lambs in a shepherd's pasture remind a mother of her husband spending the night at sea. 'Halibut cove harvest' is a lament for the heroic toil of fishermen who have been replaced by sea-raping trawlers. In 'By stubborn stars', a sonnet-sequence like George Meredith's 'Modern love', Leslie charts the course of a tempest-tost love affair. After a defiant vow to go his own way—'I sail by stubborn stars, let rocks take heed,/and should I sink . . . then sinking be my creed'—he grows to realize that he will find consolation only through song, by which he recognizes his personal experience as archetypal. Sean Haldane's curiously edited selection *The poems of Kenneth Leslie* (1971) led Leslie to make his own selection: *O'Malley to the Reds and other poems* (1972).

Burris Devanney has published an introductory biography and preliminary bibliography in *Canadian Poetry* 5 (1979). See also Susan Perly's memoir, 'We bury our poets; Kenneth Leslie: a homesick Bluenoser', in *The CANADIAN FORUM* (June 1975) and Milton ACORN's tribute in his *Jackpine sonnets* (1977).

DAVID LATHAM

Lesperance, John (1835-91). An American whose family was probably French in origin, he was born in St Louis, Missouri. According to Jesuit records, after studying at St Louis University (1845-51), Lesperance entered the novitiate of St Stanislaus at Florissant, Missouri. Although he never completed his training, he studied and taught at Jesuit institutions in Missouri, Kentucky, and New York, and in Namur, Belgium, until 1865—when, owing to illness, he was 'dispensed from his vows by lawful ecclesiastical authority'. Shortly thereafter he immigrated to Canada. He settled for some time in St Johns (Saint-Jean), Quebec, where he worked on *The News and Frontier Advocate*. Later he continued his career as a journalist in Montreal. In the 1870s he helped edit *The Canadian Illustrated News* and for several years in the 1880s, using the pseudonym 'Laclède', he contributed a weekly Saturday column to *The Gazette*. In 1888, after a stint as a provincial immigration officer, he joined the staff of *The Dominion Illustrated News* as director of its 'literary portion', but ill health virtually ended his career early in 1889.

Lesperance made a not-unimportant contribution to late nineteenth-century Canadian culture as an editor and critic. He had an eye for literary talent and regularly published works of poetry and fiction by such writers as

Rosanna LEPROHON and Charles MAIR. In a letter to George Taylor Denison in 1889 he reminisced about his 'friend Mair, for whom [he] published, for the first time, his "Last Bison", and "Kanata" in the [*Dominion*] *Illustrated*'. Elected a founding member of the Royal Society of Canada in 1882, Lesperance read at its annual meetings papers on such subjects as 'The literature of French Canada' (1883) and 'The poets of Canada' (1884); in the latter he asked the Society to 'send a word of greeting' to Charles G.D. ROBERTS—whose *Orion* had been published four years before—and to 'encourage him to go on cultivating a talent which must inevitably lead him to fame.'

Lesperance achieved some fame himself for the drama, fiction, and poetry that he wrote after he came to Canada. Although he never forgot his Missouri background—his story 'My Creoles', a fictionalized autobiographical memoir of the Mississippi Valley, was serialized in the St Louis *Republican* in 1878, over a year before it appeared in *The Canadian Illustrated News*—most of his creative writing had a strong Canadian content. 'Rosalba; or Faithful to two loves. An episode of the Rebellion of 1837-38' (*Canadian Illustrated News*, 1870), published under the pseudonym 'Arthur Faverel', explores English-French relations by dealing with the marriage of a French-Canadian girl first to a Patriote and then to an English-Canadian loyalist. His most popular work, *The Bastonnais: a tale of the American invasion of Canada in 1775-76* (Toronto, 1877), focuses mainly on events in Quebec and on a complicated series of romantic entanglements featuring English and American—or, as the French Canadians called them, *Bastonnais*—officers and French-Canadian women. Gothic motifs and legends are used to build suspense and mystery in this novel, which appeared originally as a serial in *The Canadian Illustrated News* (1876-7). *One hundred years ago* (Montreal, 1876), a drama set during the American Revolution and dealing with themes similar to those of *The Bastonnais*, was composed by Lesperance to help celebrate the centennial of the Revolution. French translations of 'Rosalba', *The Bastonnais*, and the drama were also published. Among his other works was *Tuque bleue; a Christmas snowshoe sketch* (Montreal, 1882), which uses the courtship of two young couples to describe the activities of the 'Old Montreal' and other snowshoe clubs during the winter of 1872-3. William Douw LIGHTHALL included three poems by Lesperance in *Songs of the great Dominion* (London, 1889).

Although he is not a well-known figure in Canadian literature, Lesperance is regularly included in such reference works as the *Dictionnaire des oeuvres littéraires du Québec*, vol. I (1978). The most accurate account of his life is the biography by Mary Jane Edwards in the *DICTIONARY OF CANADIAN BIOGRAPHY*, vol. 12 (1990), which also assesses his literary achievements. Several of his works have been reproduced on microfiche by the Canadian Institute for Historical Microreproductions.

MARY JANE EDWARDS

LeSueur, William Dawson. See BIOGRAPHY AND MEMOIRS IN ENGLISH: 2 and HISTORICAL WRITING IN ENGLISH: 4.

Levenson, Christopher (b. 1934). Born in London, England, he studied at Cambridge University and the University of Bristol, England, and at the University of Iowa, USA. His first two books of poems, *Cairns* (1969), and *Stills* (1972), were published in England. He came to Canada in 1968 and since then most of his books—including *Into the open* (1977), *The journey back* (1978), *Arriving at night* (1986), *Half truths* (1990), and *Duplicities: new and selected poems* (1993)—have been published in Canada. He teaches at Carleton University, Ottawa.

Levenson has published widely in journals, both poetry and criticism, and he co-founded and served as editor of *Arc*, an Ottawa-based poetry magazine. He is currently general editor of the Harbinger Poetry Series, devoted to publishing first books of poetry; poetry editor of Bayeux Arts Press, Calgary; and co-editor of poetry for the *Literary Review of Canada*.

Much of his poetry focuses on his English background and his response to his Canadianness, with both a serious intent and a playful wit. He searches for value in his past as well as in the world around him, and it is that constant, often mysterious search that his poems return to: worrying about what constitutes external reality without, and his own darker elements within, in an effort to understand, as he states in one poem, 'leaving/the lairs of secrecy, taking/all that we have and are/ into open night.'

Levenson has travelled widely, and his response to places and their people looms large in his poetry. He has also published two volumes of translations from seventeenth-century Dutch poetry, *Seeking heart's solace* (1981) and *Light of the world* (1982).

PETER STEVENS

Levesque, Anne. See ACADIAN LITERATURE: 2(c).

Levi, Helen. See NOVELS IN ENGLISH 1960 TO 1982: OTHER TALENTS, OTHER WORKS: 5.

Levine, Norman (b. 1923). Born and brought up in Ottawa, Ontario, he served in the RCAF during the Second World War and afterwards studied at McGill University. He went to England in the late 1940s and lived there—for most of the time in St Ives, Cornwall—until his return to Toronto, Canada, in 1980. Later he moved to France, and is now living in the north of England.

Levine's first two books were poetry collections: *Myssium* (1948) and *The tight-rope walker* (1950), in which many of the poems are about the physical presence of St Ives. *I walk by the harbour* (1976) was mostly written in St Ives in 1949. He and the Canadian painter Ron Bolt collaborated on *The beat and the still* (1990), a book about St Ives in which the text is drawn from all of Levine's books. His war novel, *The angled road* (1952), was quite unlike the naturalistic and panoramic war novels of such American writers as Norman Mailer and James Jones. Small in size and scope, sensitive and personal, it is the story of the coming-of-age of David Wrixon, who is commissioned in the RCAF and has two youthful love affairs in England; the dramatic events of life in wartime usually take place offstage.

In the tradition of Henry Miller (mentioned in the Author's Note) and Graham Greene, the autobiographical *Canada made me* (1958) sets out to examine Canadian society from the underside as Levine observed life in Canada in the 1950s from a consistent if unfashionable point of view. 'I like the lower towns,' he wrote, 'the place across the tracks, the poorer streets not far from the river. They represent failure, and for me failure here has a strong appeal.' Setting out on his journey of rediscovery with very little money, he lived in cheap hotels and rooming houses, waiting anxiously for small cheques to reach him, eating in greasy spoons and drinking beer in barren beverage rooms. By the time his journey ends in Quebec City, both the book and its author seem to have been nearly overcome by exhaustion. Levine's portrait of the optimistic and often complacent society of Canada in the 1950s offended some Canadians. Though both English and American editions of *Canada made me* were published in 1958, only a few copies of the English edition were distributed in Canada. While it began to have an underground reputation here, the first Canadian edition of *Canada made me* didn't appear until 1979, when his own country, in which profound changes had taken place, finally caught up with Levine.

In his fiction Levine has been preoccupied with what he describes as 'the precarious existence' of the writer, with the abrasions and the loving closeness of marriage and family life, and the need to come to terms with the past. He writes autobiographical fiction in the modern manner—examining the details and the repetitions of daily life in an often deliberately fragmentary prose. His novel *From a seaside town* (1970) is about Joseph Grand, who was born in Canada, served in the RCAF during the Second World War, and lives in England with a wife and children while he pursues a precarious career as a travel writer. But as a writer of fiction, Levine is best known for his short stories published over thirty years in a half-dozen collections: *One way ticket* (1961), *I don't want to know anyone too well* (1972), *Selected stories* (1975), *Thin ice* (1979), *Champagne barn* (1984), and *Something happened here* (1991). His stories have appeared in both popular and small-circulation magazines in England and Canada; many of them have been broadcast by the CBC and BBC; and his collections have been widely translated in Holland, Switzerland, and Germany. A book of his stories in French translation, *Pourquoi habitez-vous si loin?*, was published in Paris in the spring of 1997 and is being distributed in Quebec. He edited the anthology *Canadian winter's tales* (1968).

See Frederick Sweet, *Norman Levine* (1983), in Profiles in Canadian Literature, vol. 4; Lawrence Mathews, *Norman Levine and his works* (1990); and Simone Vauthier, 'Portrait of the artist as a (no longer) young man: Norman Levine's "We all begin in a little magazine"', *New directions from old* (1991).

ROBERT WEAVER

Lewis, Wyndham. See FOREIGN WRITERS ON CANADA IN ENGLISH: 1.

Liberté (1959-). Founded by Jean-Guy PILON, it originally set out to become a 'national magazine', featuring contributions by writers—both French- and English-speaking—from across Canada that would establish a 'forum for the discussion of cultural matters, hoping to attract worthwhile ideas and to promote dialogue'. Very soon, however, with the advent of the Quiet Revolution in the sixties, the magazine ceased to be apolitical and, counting among its contributors some of the founders of the Rassemblement pour l'Indépendance National (RIN), became neo-nationalist and secular; along the lines of the magazine *Cité libre*, it began to advocate the democratization of Quebec's political institutions, reform of the educational system, and greater state intervention in the economy. When the Parti

Québécois came to power in the 1970s, *Liberté* became less reformist and nationalist and gradually reverted to its origins as a cultural and literary magazine, featuring the work of leading French-Canadian writers in an elegant small format, along with special issues such as one on 'The Quebec Literary Movement' in 1981.

In the 1990s, under an editorial committee that included François Hébert, Yvon RIVARD (until the end of 1995), and Pierre Turgeon, and publishing six times a year, *Liberté* remained a distinguished literary magazine, maintaining high quality in content and appearance. Without neglecting French-Canadian writing it published special issues on such subjects as 'European Writers', 'Literature of Brazil', 'Literature and Theory', 'Italian Poets', and 'New Writing in French' (featuring twenty-one French authors). As an example of the magazine's long-standing interest in the visual arts, in the June 1997 issue (vol. 39) it published a feature on the Quebec painter Rodolphe Duguay (1891-1972).

See also LITERARY MAGAZINES IN QUEBEC: 3.

JACQUES PELLETIER/WILLIAM TOYE

Lighthall, William Douw (1857-1954). Although he was born in Hamilton, Ontario, Lighthall's career was closely associated with Montreal and the province of Quebec. Educated at the Montreal High School and McGill University (B.A., 1879; B.C.L., 1881; M.A., 1885), he practised law in that city until 1944 and held offices in local historical and literary societies and on municipal commissions and military bodies. Mayor of Westmount from 1900 to 1903, he helped to found the Union of Canadian Municipalities. He wrote three historical sketches of Montreal: *A new Hochelagan burying-ground discovered at Westmount on the western spur of Mount Royal, Montreal, July-September 1898* (Montreal, 1898); *Montreal after 250 years* (Montreal, 1892); and *Sights and shrines of Montreal: a guide book for strangers and a handbook for all lovers of historic spots and incidents* (1907). Lighthall was elected to the Royal Society of Canada in 1905 and became its president in 1918.

The underpinning for Lighthall's literary career was a rather abstract philosophy of idealism, which he described in *Superpersonalism. The outer consciousness, a biological entity: reflections on the independence of instinct and its characteristics in evolution* (1926). In the earliest phase of his writing career he mixed this idealism with a strong dose of Canadian nationalism to produce a novel, *The young seigneur; or, Nation making* (Montreal, 1888)—written under the thin pseudonym 'Wilfrid Châteauclair'—in which a young French-Canadian politician describes to his colleague from Ontario his spiritual growth towards an ideal of national service. The ideal is frustrated, for the young man falls victim to corrupt political practices; but his accidental death rescues the situation by removing him to a plane beyond this world so that he may become an inspiration to all. Death also saves the situation in Lighthall's second novel, *The false chevalier; or, The lifeguard of Marie Antoinette* (Montreal, 1898). A young French Canadian with a prosperous merchant father finds himself in France just prior to the Revolution and succeeds in introducing himself into society as a noble. Brought to trial by the revolutionaries, he chooses to maintain his personal integrity by withholding the truth about himself and accepting execution. Lighthall's idealism found a more remote expression in *The master of life: a romance of the Five Nations and prehistoric Montreal* (1908). Here Lighthall turned the story of Hiawatha, and the founding of the Iroquois confederacy in the sixteenth century, into an object lesson in the power of pure ideals to influence history. The hero's true significance, as in the other novels, comes as much from his death as his deeds.

Lighthall's occasional verse, collected in *Old measures: collected verse* (1922), ranges over similar ground—from inspirational pieces on Canada, the Empire, and the war to expressions of man's unity in a greater Spirit and a struggle to rise above the commonality of everyday life.

Lighthall is usually remembered today as editor of the second major anthology of Canadian poetry (the first being that by Edward Hartley DEWART)—*Songs of the great Dominion: voices from the forests and waters, the settlements and cities of Canada* (London, 1889; rpr. 1971). In his introductory essay Lighthall highlighted the new tone of national confidence, while he lamented the editorial limitations that prevented him from including subjective pieces in addition to those descriptive of Canadian life. Nevertheless, the anthology—which includes the poets of the time who are still respected, and many others now forgotten—enjoyed some success and was reissued in a reduced form in The Canterbury Poets as *Canadian poems and lays: selections of native verse, reflecting the seasons, legends, and life of the Dominion* (London and New York, 1893).

Lighthall affirmed many of the national and humanistic ideals of late-nineteenth-century

Canada and saw literature as the active promoter of such values. CAL SMILEY

Lill, Wendy (b.1950). Born in Vancouver, she grew up in London, Ontario, and in 1971 graduated from York University, Toronto, with a degree in political science. In 1977 Lill moved to northern Ontario to serve as a consultant for the Canadian Mental Health Association. Leaving after six months, she remained in Kenora working as a reporter for a Native newspaper and writing radio documentaries for the Canadian Broadcasting Corporation ('Our native land'). Moved by what she learned and experienced, she committed herself to telling the stories 'that are already out there', to fictionalizing real incidents and events. In 1979 she moved to Winnipeg, where for four years she worked as a freelance broadcaster and journalist. Her radio documentary *Who is Georges Forest?* (1981), about an insurance salesman who challenged the legality of his unilingual traffic ticket, won an ACTRA award, as did her CBC radio drama *Shorthanded* (1981). Her 1980 series of reports for Information Radio, 'The native urban migration', led to her collaboration with filmmaker Norma Bailey on *Daughters of the country*, a four-part National Film Board series about Métis women. Her script for *Ikwe*, which she wrote after moving to Nova Scotia in 1984, won the 1986 Golden Sheaf Award. She became a member of Parliament (NDP) for Dartmouth, N.S., in the 1997 federal election.

Lill's first stage play, *On the line* (produced in 1982), is agitprop, a theatre piece dramatizing the exploitation of immigrant women in the Winnipeg garment industry. *The fighting days* (1985) features figures from Manitoba history. Spanning the years 1910 to 1917, it tells the story of the idealistic journalist Frances Beynon, who held some prominence in the suffragist movement until she broke with her famous colleague Nellie McCLUNG over the issues of pacifism and immigrants' rights.

The occupation of Heather Rose (1987), which began as a short-story idea, was nominated for a Governor General's Award. Now widely produced, this monodrama relates the psychic journey of a cheerfully naive and altruistic white nurse while on the Snake Lake Reservation, and how the isolation, her alien sensibility, and her own irrelevance overwhelm her. Toronto's Tarragon Theatre produced a revised version in 1988.

Memories of you (1989), nominated for a 1989 Chalmers Canadian Play Award, focuses on the controversial life of Elizabeth SMART, the author of *BY GRAND CENTRAL STATION I SAT DOWN AND WEPT*. In Lill's play, Smart is confronted by her enraged daughter, Rosie, who accuses her of having lived a vacuous and selfish life. Smart's own version of her romantic obsession with poet George Barker alternates with scenes in the present. The play concludes with its central moral issues unresolved.

A play based on the 1972 burning of a Shubenacadie residential school for Native children, *Sisters* (1991), presents the story through the memories of Sister Mary, a nun who admitted to arson. 'I wanted to tell the story from the other side,' says Lill. 'What was going on in the hearts of those who were guardians?' In this play, as in the earlier ones, Lill uses history and memory to allow the necessary distance that permits reflection, doubt, and revisionist thinking. The CBC television adaptation of *Sisters* won a 1992 Gemini Award.

All fall down (1994) dramatizes the escalation of hysteria that occurs when a daycare-worker is charged with sexual abuse. Connors, whose comments provide the frame of the play, expresses in the present the doubts he had set aside in the past. The accused never appears on stage, but Lill's point is the damage such occurrences do to the entire community. As in *Sisters*, her focus is not on the victims but on those whose past convictions are revisited. Lill has won praise for her courageous exploration of the emotional truths that drive ideological positions and for the political commitment at the heart of her work.

Lill has adapted her own plays for CBC Radio as well as Sheldon Currie's *The Glace Bay miner's museum* (broadcast 1991) and Robert MacNeil's *Burden of desire* (broadcast 1992). CYNTHIA ZIMMERMAN

Lillard, Charles (1944-97). Born in Long Beach, California, he was educated at the University of Alaska and the University of British Columbia (B.A., 1969; M.F.A., 1973). He lived in dozens of locations in Alaska and B.C., working in the bush and on the water. His poems, essays, and books were attempts to understand what he called the last frontier of the Pacific Northwest; he found his calling not only as a poet and student of Native lore, but as a popular regional historian. Lillard wrote out of a strong sense of place, but his combination of regionalism and Native mythology had a link with European classicism. He was therefore not a typical bush poet who celebrated the lonely life of a man in the wilderness: his poems are neither romantic nor understated. In the last frontier of the Canadian wilderness, he found a frontier of the human spirit.

Lillard's first collection, *Cultus coulee* (1971), incorporated West Coast Native mythology. His more disciplined and mature collections—*Drunk on wood* (1973), *Voice, my shaman* (1976), *Coastal sanctus* (1983), *A coastal range* (1984), and *An early morning fragment* (1993)—found a balance between Native mythology and the poetic lessons learned from classical European literature. His major long poem, *Jabble* (1976)—privately printed—was followed by other privately printed collections: *Poems (Mythistoria-I)* (1979) and *Green weather country: dramatis personae* (1991). The imagery of his poems—which are often evocations of rugged landscape—includes rivers, logging trucks, ravens, and totems. Myths intersect with reality as he writes about the wildness of landscape, the wildness within men and women, and the wildness of mythology. As the poet, who was 'born with a landscape', meditates on the power of nature without, he finds spiritual strength within. Lillard's seventh collection, *Circling Worth* (1988), won the fifth annual Dorothy LIVESAY Poetry Prize. *Shadow weather: poems selected and new* (1996) contains powerful evocations of the wilderness (especially in poems such as 'Petroglyph at tidemark', 'Encounter, Waldron Island', and 'Closing down Kah Shakes Creek') and expressions of helplessness at being cold and alone in remote areas.

Lillard was a serious West Coast historian, who became well acquainted with eighteenth- and nineteenth-century unpublished missionary accounts, and he produced many historical books as editor, collaborator, or sole author.

He elaborated on his attitude towards the West Coast of Canada as guest editor of 'The West Coast Renaissance' in issues 45, 50, and 60 of *The MALAHAT REVIEW*. He also co-edited, with J. Michael YATES, *Volvox* (1971), the first collection of poetry in translation from the unofficial languages of Canada; and, with Geoff Hancock, the first collection of fiction in translation from the unofficial languages of Canada in *CANADIAN FICTION MAGAZINE* (1976). GEOFF HANCOCK

Linteau, Paul-André. See HISTORICAL WRITING IN FRENCH 1980 TO 1996.

Literary Garland, The (1838-51). This monthly magazine was begun in Dec. 1838 by Montreal publisher John Lovell—an Irishman who came to Canada in 1820 and later made a reputation as a publisher of directories, school texts, and gazetteers—and his brother-in-law, John Gibson, who served initially as editor and after 1842 as co-publisher. For its time the *Garland* was the leading literary journal in British North America, and had the longest lifespan. Taking seriously James Holmes' assertion that 'the literature of a country is the *measure* of its progress towards refinement' (Aug. 1840), it set about providing, in the early numbers, a mix of poetry, book reviews, essays, prose, fiction, news of the arts, jokes, anecdotes, helpful household hints ('make your own catsup'), and music scores designed to appeal to a wide range of readers. Eventually the *Garland*'s pages were filled with essays on linguistics, dramatic sketches (often with a biblical setting), poems of Victorian gift-book calibre, and a plethora of formulaic romantic-historic fiction—material that appealed only to a small coterie of readers and contributors who saw themselves as upholders and promoters of a genteel tradition. Parts of John RICHARDSON's *The Canadian brothers* appeared in the *Garland* (1839); Rosanna Mullins LEPROHON contributed poetry and prose from an early age; and Charles SANGSTER contributed poems. But apparently few Canadian writers could produce what the *Garland* thought to be worthy of publication: too rarely did such material as Susanna MOODIE's six sketches—published in 1847 (Jan., Mar., June, Aug., Oct.), and later to reappear in *ROUGHING IT IN THE BUSH*—find its way there. Many of its writers, not surprisingly, had cultural allegiances and values that were located elsewhere, and they were not interested in making the *Garland* a vehicle of Canadian literary expression, which was one of its declared aims. There was, finally, little to distinguish the *Garland* from its American competitors. With John Gibson's death in the fall of 1850, it lost its chief moving force. There were simply not enough subscribers who shared, and were willing to pay for, the cultural values evidenced by the *Garland*'s principal contributors, and the financial problems became too daunting. With no. 12 of vol.IX (Dec. 1851) it succumbed to the indifference of those for whom it was to have been a voice, and to foreign competition—a pattern that was to be repeated again and again in Canadian periodical publishing.

See Mary Markham Brown, *An Index to The Literary Garland, Montreal, 1838-1851*. Toronto: Bibliographic Society of Canada (1962); Carl F. KLINCK, ed., *Literary history of Canada* (2nd edn, 1976), vol. I, pp. 159-61, 195-6; and the article on John Lovell by George F.

Parker in the *DICTIONARY OF CANADIAN BIOGRAPHY*, vol. XII (1990), p. 570.

S.R. MacGILLIVRAY

Literary magazines in English: 1. THE EIGHTEENTH AND NINETEENTH CENTURIES. The first British North American periodical in English was *The NOVA SCOTIA MAGAZINE* (1789-92). Claiming to be 'a comprehensive review of literature, politics and news', this monthly consisted chiefly of reprinted articles and extracts, both domestic and foreign. *The Quebec Magazine* (1792-4), also a monthly, was our first bilingual magazine. Also depending mostly on reprints, it was described as a 'useful and entertaining repository of science, morals, history, politics, etc., adapted for use in British America'.

After a dry period of two decades the literary community was enlivened by *The Scribbler* (1821-7), 'a series of weekly essays on literary, critical, satirical, moral, and local subjects, interspersed with pieces of poetry', emanating from Montreal. Its editor, Samuel Hull Wilcocke, under the pseudonym 'Lewis Luke McCulloch, Esquire', enjoyed gossiping in print about Montreal businessmen and was also notorious for his political lampoons. On the other hand he kept a close watch on the literary scene and reviewed every Canadian book he could find. He claimed, with some justification, to be 'the first that regularly assumed the critic's chair in Canada'. *The Canadian Literary Miscellany* (1822-3) also appeared in Montreal but survived for only six issues. Wilcocke was scornful of the *Miscellany*, claiming it was 'too much occupied with newspaper controversy, and newspaper criticism, both objects that are, in most cases, beneath the dignity of an essayist.'

Other magazines of the 1820s with some literary dimension include *The Christian Examiner* (1819-20) from Kingston; *The Enquirer* (1821-2) from Quebec; and *The ACADIAN MAGAZINE; or Literary Mirror* (1826-8) from Halifax. *The Christian Guardian*, a religious and cultural magazine, appeared in York (Toronto) in 1829. It was launched by Methodist minister, writer, and educator Egerton Ryerson; and it was the first publication of the Methodist Book and Publishing House, of which Ryerson was the founder and editor. After almost a century of activity, this press, called by Lorne PIERCE the 'Mother Publishing House of Canada', was renamed The RYERSON PRESS in 1919, in honour of its prestigious founding editor. The two most ambitious magazines of the 1820s were *The Canadian Magazine and Literary Repository* (1823-5), a monthly, and its rival *The Canadian Review and Literary and Historical Journal* (1824-6), a quarterly that was renamed *The Canadian Review and Magazine*. Both of these Montreal periodicals aimed to 'equal' the great British reviews such as *Blackwood's, The Edinburgh Review*, and *The Quarterly*. The first was devoted 'to all that tends to improve the mind, and develope [*sic*] the moral and physical history of this colony...', and 'the diffusion of useful knowledge throughout this country.' The second made a more determined effort to attract Canadian writers. Its literary policy was quite clear: '... we prefer the substantial realities of a virtuous education ... and useful learning, to the evanescent and fanciful colouration of *modern* polite literature.'

The conservatism of these early Canadian magazines may be explained by the fact that the editors themselves were most often immigrants whose tastes had been formed abroad. Their antipathy to Romantic literature, for example, was a reflection of that expressed in the prestigious (and conservative) British quarterlies they sought to emulate. The conditions of the colony simply strengthened such prejudices and confirmed the need for practical counsel, moral firmness, and sobriety of tone. Fiction, for example, especially of the Gothic kind, was firmly discouraged as tending to distract the mind from 'more useful pursuits'. Poetry was welcomed, providing it was 'decorous', or 'graceful', and morally refined. (Poets were urged to avoid high flights of fancy, to ground their verse in their colonial experience, and to lend their talents to the description and celebration of the true beauties and resources of this fair land.) Most of the material of these early magazines, however, was expository, and aside from those pieces written by the editors themselves, much of it was not native, or 'original'. It would be another decade before any editor attempted to rely solely on 'domestic' talent.

In the 1830s several new magazines appeared. These included *The Halifax Monthly Magazine* (1830-3); *The MONTREAL MUSEUM* (1832-4), a monthly devoted to fiction, poetry, and non-fiction directed to female readers; *The Bee* (1835-8), 'a Weekly Journal devoted to News, Politics, Literature, Agriculture, Etc.'; and *The Colonial (or Halifax) Pearl* (1837-40). Two monthlies emanating from York in 1833 expired within the year: *The Canadian Magazine* and *The CANADIAN LITERARY MAGAZINE*. The latter is of interest for its intention to publish only 'fine Canadian writing'.

Literary magazines in English 1

The only successful magazine of the pre-Confederation period was *The* LITERARY GARLAND (1838-51), a monthly from Montreal. Patterned after British popular journals like *Godey's Lady's Book*, the *Garland* provided original tales, sketches, and sentimental romances in fiction and verse. Its chief value lay in the encouragement it offered to Canadian writers such as Susanna MOODIE and Catharine Parr TRAILL.

Except for the short-lived *Amaranth* (1841-2), from New Brunswick, the *Garland* was the only literary magazine extant between 1840 and 1845. In 1846 *BARKER'S CANADIAN MONTHLY MAGAZINE* was founded in Kingston. This, claimed Mrs Moodie, was 'decidedly the best magazine that had appeared in the Upper Province'. However, *Barker's* ceased publication in 1847. In that year Mrs Moodie and her husband launched *The Victoria Magazine* from Belleville, with the hope of 'inducing a taste for polite literature among the working classes'. It too lasted but one year. (When this magazine was reprinted in 1968 George WOODCOCK described it as representing 'the dregs of early Victorian genteel writing'.) *The Magic Lantern* (1848), though it lasted only six months, is perhaps worth noting for its opposition to the romanticism and sentimentality of the young ladies publishing in such magazines. One other magazine to appear in the 1840s was *The Canadian Gem and Family Visitor* (1848-50), notable chiefly as an indication of a trend towards the popular magazine.

When, mainly because of financial difficulties, the *Garland* folded in 1851, its editor expressed 'the hope that the day will yet come, when Canada will be able to support, not one, but several periodicals, although at present the abundance and cheapness of foreign publications, render it difficult.'

The number of literary magazines did increase in the next quarter of the century. As one might expect, during the decades before and after Confederation their thrust was strongly political. Several were launched and edited by newspapermen; brilliant political journalists like D'Arcy McGEE and Goldwin SMITH were frequent contributors. Their main concern was to foster an independent Canadian literature, which they considered to be essential to the growth of a national consciousness, the necessary correlative of political independence. Hence many pages of their magazines were devoted to problems of the publishing trade, the state of libraries, the encouragement of literary societies, and the need for copyright laws and for legislation to protect Canadians against the flood of British and American books and periodicals. These magazines also published reviews of Canadian books and as much creative material by Canadians as space allowed. Clearly their importance is that they attracted talented writers and intellectuals and helped to prepare a climate for the 'first flowering' of Canadian literature in the 1880s and 1890s.

A selection follows of the more important magazines launched between 1850 and 1875. Their very titles are often an indication of the various concepts of nationalism current at the time: *The* PROVINCIAL: *or Halifax Monthly Magazine* (1852-3); *The Canadian Journal* (1852-78); *The British Colonial Magazine* (1852-3), a weekly from Toronto; *The Anglo-American Magazine* (1852-5), a Toronto monthly; *The British Canadian Review* (1862-3), a Quebec monthly devoted exclusively to Canadian literature; *The British American Magazine* (1863-4), a Toronto monthly; *The British American Review* (1865-7), Toronto; *The Canadian Quarterly Review and Family Magazine* (1864-6), Hamilton; *STEWART'S LITERARY QUARTERLY* (1867-72), Saint John, New Brunswick; *The New Dominion Monthly* (1867-79), Montreal; *The Family Herald and Weekly Star* (1869-1968), Montreal; *The Canadian Illustrated News* (1869-83), 'Canada's First National Magazine', a Montreal weekly; *The Canadian Literary Journal* (1870-1), 'devoted to select original literature and the interest of Canadian Literary Societies', Toronto; *The Canadian Literary Magazine* (1871-2), and *The Maritime Monthly* (1873-5), a journal of 'light' literature, science, and art.

Certain trends may be observed among the publications of this period. One is the growth of the popular family magazine and the mass-circulation illustrated periodical. Both favoured news, human-interest stories, and the literature of entertainment over the more serious intellectual fare provided by the reviews. A second trend is towards diversification. Special areas of interest—such as history, religion, and science—were beginning to generate their own journals. Politics also had its own magazines, such as *The Nation* (1874-6) and *The Bystander* (intermittently between 1880 and 1890). The prototype of the academic journal also emerged at this time. *The Canadian Journal* (1852-78) is an example. Subtitled 'A Repertory of Industry, Science and Art', this periodical was dominated by academics, notably from the University of Toronto. It did not include creative work. Its broad range of topics was balanced by scholarly depth; and it was directed to the intelligent reader who had not succumbed to the 'invidious habit' of reading for pleasure.

Such diversification clarified (and narrowed) the role of the literary periodical, leaving it to concentrate on the cultivation of polite letters and the dissemination of informed opinion on social, political, and cultural issues. *The Canadian Monthly and National Review* (1872-8), which was continued as *ROSE-BELFORD'S CANADIAN MONTHLY* (1878-82), was founded 'to deal with Canadian questions and to call forth Canadian talent'. This review provided a forum for the best minds of the decade, including a core of artists and writers involved with the 'Canada First' movement.

In the last quarter of the century only two magazines of comparable stature emerged. *The WEEK* (1883-96), which inherited contributors and subscribers from *The Canadian Monthly*, saw itself as a bastion against the erosion of literary standards, refined taste, and informed opinion. For thirteen years it was the main vehicle for the work of the major poets and essayists of the Confederation period. During the 1890s this central function of the literary periodical was maintained by *The Canadian Magazine* (1893-1939), though it gradually assumed the character of a popular magazine. (During the 1930s it reached a circulation of 90,000.)

Other magazines that flourished in the 1890s followed a similar course. *The Dominion Illustrated Monthly* (1888-95) deliberately broke with the genteel tradition, emphasized a 'masculine' journalism, and unabashedly encouraged fiction as entertainment. *Saturday Night* (1887-) was from the beginning a 'Busy Man's Magazine'; during various periods in its subsequent history, however, it has played a significant literary role. *Maclean's* (1896-) and *Westminster* (1897-1916) had few literary pretensions but they did provide outlets for popular fiction during the early years of the new century. No new review comparable to *The Week* appeared in the next two decades. A very small intellectual minority was served, however, by the new academic quarterlies, which preserved the broad concept of literature as 'letters', providing erudite articles on topics drawn mostly from the humanities. *Queen's Quarterly*, founded in 1893 as an alumni journal, did not become a significant literary periodical until 1920. Since then it has functioned both as an academic review and as an outlet for new Canadian poetry and fiction. *The University of Toronto Quarterly* (1895-) has retained its scholarly character and still does not accept creative material; however, since the 1930s it has performed a valuable service by devoting most of one issue annually to a survey of letters in Canada. *The McGill University Magazine* (1901-6), a semi-annual that lasted for ten issues, was succeeded by *The UNIVERSITY MAGAZINE* (1907-20), a quarterly edited by Andrew MACPHAIL that set out to provide 'lengthy treatments of subjects of general interest in literature and science'. It took over the *McGill University Magazine*'s subscription list and numbered its issues consecutively, beginning with vol. VI. *The Dalhousie Review* (1920-) has been faithful to its chosen role as 'A Canadian Journal of Literature and Opinion'. For several years it carried, in addition to academic essays, a column devoted to 'Topics of the Day', and another devoted to 'Current Magazines'. It reserved several pages too for reviews of current Canadian books.

2. THE TWENTIES AND THIRTIES. No new literary magazines of note appeared in the first two decades of the twentieth century. Canada was still culturally insecure, its literary development still dependent on the growth of a national consciousness. Moreover, a lingering taste for late-Victorian Romanticism, a persistent pragmatic bent, and a puritanical distrust of the arts combined to favour conservative writing and to delay the acceptance of modernism in this country. Two magazines emerged in response to these conditions. *The Canadian Bookman*, 'a quarterly devoted to Literature, The Library and The Printed Book', was established in 1919. Its aim was to encourage and protect Canadian writers by attending to such practical matters as marketing, distribution, and copyright; it also promised to provide much-needed criticism, but this aim was not realized. In 1921 it became the organ of the CANADIAN AUTHORS' ASSOCIATION, which it had helped to found. Thereafter the policy of the magazine was adapted to the needs of that essentially conservative and professionally oriented organization, resorting in the twenties to a noisy boosterism that favoured quantity over quality and patriotism over literary worth. Deservedly or not, the reputations of both the Association and its house-organs have suffered from this stigma ever since. The *Bookman* became *The Canadian Author and Bookman* in 1943. Another CAA publication, *The Canadian Poetry Magazine*, founded in 1936 (the first all-poetry magazine in Canada), was absorbed by the *CA&B* in 1969.

The CANADIAN FORUM (1920-) was founded as an élitist magazine resembling *The Week* in format and was equally proud of its minority position. Though openly nationalistic, it maintained a critical stance politically and was strongly opposed to literary boosterism and the mediocrity that policy had encouraged. Its most notable service to Canadian literature in the twenties was its encouragement of rigorous criticism and its openness to the work of the first generation of Canadian modernists. The *Forum* has remained consistent in policy and format, resisting the trend towards specialization and especially deploring the divorce of literature from the broader (social and political) cultural context.

In the late twenties two other élitist magazines emerged, both from Montreal. During their brief lives neither the *McGILL FORTNIGHTLY REVIEW* (1925-7), founded by A.J.M. SMITH and F.R. SCOTT, nor *The CANADIAN MERCURY* (1928-9), created and subsidized by Louis Schwartz, had the breadth of influence of the *Forum*; but in retrospect they are significant as having been the prime vehicles for the early work of the Montreal modernists headed by Smith and Scott. Because of their aggressive defence of modernism, these two magazines are sometimes regarded as precursors of the 'littles' of the forties. However, both in appearance and in breadth of content they were much closer to the *Forum* and to such foreign models as *The Nation* and *The New Republic*.

During the thirties, aside from *The Canadian Poetry Magazine*, only two new literary journals were launched. *The Masses* (1932-4) was primarily political. *The New Frontier* (1936-7), which mixed politics with socially oriented poetry and criticism of a more radical cast than to be found in the *Forum*, is notable for having published such writers as A.M. KLEIN, Dorothy LIVESAY, and Leo KENNEDY. *Quill & Quire*, a journal geared to the needs of booksellers and librarians, was founded in 1935; in 1969 it expanded its format to interest publishers and writers and in 1972 introduced formal book reviews.

3. THE FORTIES TO THE SIXTIES. In the forties a new trend became evident. Within the decade about a dozen mimeographed poetry-centred 'little' magazines were founded to challenge the conservatism of the literary establishment. They were distinguished from the traditional minority review by their modest format, their narrower literary focus, and their emphasis on modern poetry. Not all of these 'littles' were militantly avant-garde, but all were of service in providing much-needed outlets for Canada's second wave of Modernists such as Raymond SOUSTER, Louis DUDEK, Irving LAYTON, Patrick ANDERSON, P.K. PAGE, and Miriam WADDINGTON. *CONTEMPORARY VERSE* (1941-52), and *The FIDDLEHEAD* (1945-), both eclectic from the start, proved to be the more durable, the latter eventually becoming a full-fledged review that is still very much alive. *PREVIEW* (1942-5) and *FIRST STATEMENT* (1942-5), both more aggressively modern, were short-lived. By the time these two merged to become *NORTHERN REVIEW* (1945-56), the forties' movement had begun to flag. *Northern Review* became increasingly conservative, thus losing its character as a 'little' and evolving, in the fifties, into something more closely resembling the traditional minority review. *Here and Now* (1947-9), designed and edited by Paul Arthur in Toronto, was distinguished for its large, handsome format, typographic flair, and interesting contents, which included stories, poems, and articles. It lasted for only three issues.

During the fifties over a dozen new magazines appeared. Among the more durable, *Quarry*, founded as a student periodical at Queen's University in 1952, later acquired status as an eclectic review. *The TAMARACK REVIEW* (1956-82), an independent quarterly, was one of the prime outlets for 'cosmopolitan' Canadian writing. *Prism* (1959-) began as an independent magazine of contemporary writing and later became associated with the creative-writing program at the University of British Columbia. *CANADIAN LITERATURE* (1959-) emerged from the same university.

Among several new 'littles', *CONTACT* (1952-4) and *COMBUSTION* (1957-60) from Toronto, favoured international (mainly American) new writing. *CIV/n* (1953-5) and *Yes* (1954-70) focused on Montreal poets and the eastern-Canadian tradition of social realism. *DELTA* (1957-66) was unique. Its editor, Louis Dudek, encouraged the search for new techniques that would serve to extend the tradition of modernism in Canada without sacrificing ideational content and social relevance. Unlike most other 'littles', *Delta* sought to maintain a broad cultural context for the new poetry.

In the sixties Canadians experienced a new surge of nationalism—encouraged, no doubt, by preparations for the celebration of the Centennial in 1967. The new nationalism coincided with a period of affluence and with an increase in the numbers of college-age young people. In various combinations these factors account for the sudden growth in quantity, size, and quality of literary magazines. For example, the unprecedented increase in the student population required the expansion of colleges and universities throughout the country; and the new nationalism favoured the introduction of Canadian studies and Canadian literature into the curriculum. In response to the market thus engendered, commercial publishers engaged in a spate of activity to make new and out-of-print Canadian texts available. Scholars now turned their attention more zealously to the provision of histories, bibliographies, and criticism of Canadian writing. And, most importantly, a new generation of talented writers joined their seniors in an enthusiastic exploration of Canadian themes.

The sixties thus witnessed both a burgeoning of scholarship and creativity and the enlargement of a reading public eager to discover its 'Canadian identity' and predisposed towards any writing that explored the 'Canadian imagination' or fostered 'Canadian unity'. Magazines were divided (as they had been from the beginning of Canadian literary history) on the question of how the development of literature in Canada might best be served—whether by deliberate fostering of 'native' talent or by exposure to international 'cosmopolitan' standards.

During this decade *Canadian Literature* had a singular importance. It was the first critical journal exclusively devoted to Canadian literature. With a policy that avoided both chauvinism and academicism, *CL* helped to shape as well as to reflect the new literary nationalism. *Edge* (1963-9) was an independent journal of opinion and the arts. Its policy (and mission) was to confront those elements of the Canadian psyche that had so far inhibited the creative imagination: namely, conservatism, conformity, and puritanism. *The University of Windsor Review* (1965-) combined the function of an academic journal with that of a magazine of new Canadian writing. *The Journal of Canadian Studies* (1966-) from Trent University reserved some pages for topics related to Canadian literature. *Wascana Review* (1966-) addressed itself 'not to residents of Saskatchewan only, or of Canada, or of North America, but to whatever general audience our particular human voice will reach'. *West Coast Review* (1966-), from Simon Fraser University, was devoted to 'contemporary North American' writers. *MOSAIC* (1967-) was founded at the University of Manitoba as a scholarly quarterly for the comparative study of literature. *Contemporary Literature in Translation* (1968) from the University of British Columbia provided a wide sampling of foreign writers. (*Prism*, too, which became *Prism International* in 1969, offered many translations along with indigenous writing.) *Ellipse* (1969-), from the University of Sherbrooke, was the first journal to be devoted to the translation of French- and English-Canadian work. *The MALAHAT REVIEW*, from the University of Victoria—founded in 1967 to celebrate 'the coming of age' of our country—was subtitled 'An international Quarterly of Art and Life' and soon gained an international reputation for cosmopolitan excellence.

Three other magazines of this decade deserve special mention. *Evidence* (1960-7), a lively independent review from Toronto, was designed to offer 'evidence' of vigorous new writing in Canada and at the same time give serious attention to the state of cultural institutions in this country. It was eclectic, hoping to provide a bridge between older and younger writers, between the east- and west-coast orientations, and between tradition and contemporary developments. It took a strong stand, however, against experimental writing as an end in itself and expressly declined the role of an avant-garde magazine.

ALPHABET (1960-71), from the University of Western Ontario, was dedicated to the 'iconography of the imagination'. Each issue juxtaposed a particular myth with illustrative documents chosen from local history. Each theme was then reflected in a selection of contemporary verse and prose by Canadian authors. Far from being an academic journal, *Alphabet* played an important role in the ferment of creativity in all the arts in London, Ontario, and the surrounding region—an early example of what editor James REANEY has called 'the regional liberation front'. Reaney's fascination with the magical and incantatory powers of language made him more receptive to forms of experimental writing than were the more conservative reviews. Frank DAVEY's *OPEN LETTER* (1965-9, 1971-) is staid in appearance; but its contents are intellectually most challenging. Subtitled 'A journal of writing and sources', it explores the philosophical assumptions and the theoretical and critical implications of postmodernism, as well as the more esoteric reaches of the language revolution, and is one of the most advanced journals of its kind anywhere in the world.

Though these magazines existed on the fringe of the new establishment, they were known, or at least accessible, to the literary community. By contrast, an extraordinary number of other magazines of the decade remained virtually unknown and inaccessible to the general reading public. These were the new littles—ephemeral, mostly mimeographed, poetry-centred, often 'unperiodical' publications that, taken singly, seem to have small importance but collectively proved very significant. Numbering at least sixty (closer to ninety if we include those that published fewer than four issues), and appearing sporadically throughout the country, they constituted an informal network of little magazines and presses that before the decade was over would redirect the course of poetry in Canada. Generally speaking these new 'littles' were indifferent, if not antipathetic, to both nationalism and tradition, whether cosmopolitan, native, or any other. Rather, they were linked in spirit with literally thousand of similar underground publications in various languages, and in other countries throughout the world—publications that were not only anti-establishment and anti-academic but also anti-literary. Refusing to be bound by traditional literary forms, categories, conventions, proprieties, and standards, and disdaining the usual criteria of 'successful' publishing, such as regularity of appearance and format, consistent editorial policy, professional production, and financial stability, the 'little mags', here and abroad, were an affront to the literary establishment. They did not, in fact, address themselves to the literary community but to each other. Their young writers, editors, and publishers were intent upon developing not simply new writing but writing that would reflect a whole new vision of reality, cosmic in its reach, and profoundly challenging to existing values. It would be too much to assume that every little-mag editor entertained such an awesome vision, but it is certainly true that most of them were deliberately (and sometimes gleefully) playing a subversive role. They were an integral part of that international revolutionary subculture that served so effectively during the sixties to disseminate the values of the so-called new consciousness. The new titles reflected a radical and irreverent attitude (*Bust*, *Weed*, *Luv*, *Gronk*, *Laid Bare*, *Mainline*, *Up the Tube with One I Open*), and were often cryptic (BLEW OINTMENT, *Elfin Plot*, TISH, *Is*, *Imago*). The writers who published in such magazines represented the first wave of postmodernism; and their most influential poet-editors—Frank Davey, George BOWERING, Victor COLEMAN, bill BISSETT, and bp NICHOL—were to continue to be in the vanguard of that movement throughout the seventies.

The established literary community of the sixties—absorbed in the definition, defence, and cultivation of 'Canadian Literature'—took little notice of the underground movement. Only one 'little mag' drew serious attention. *Tish*, founded in 1961, was seen to be most flagrantly under the influence of the 'new poetry' from the United States, loosely identified as 'Black Mountain'. Fear of American imperialism made *Tish* the centre of a controversy that was to be echoed in numerous magazines (and books) well into the seventies. But the issue was spurious, and the notoriety it engendered served mainly to obscure the broader implications of the little-magazine/small-press movement of the sixties.

The aesthetic to which both the *Tish* poets and their American mentors subscribed simply reflected a multi-faceted movement operating in all the arts and in most countries of the Western world. Its values called for a total transformation of Western consciousness—an ideal that transcends all nationalism and all languages. Proof of this lay very close to home: nationalists from English Canada who attacked the Vancouver poets overlooked the fact that the young avant-garde Québécois writers and editors of the early sixties—spokesmen for the Quiet Revolution—were deeply imbued with the 'new zeitgeist' (as one of them called it), yet their writing owed nothing to *Tish*, nor to any North American influence. Even more significant was the commitment of several of the most conspicuously avant-garde writers in both English Canada and Quebec to the 'language revolution', a radically experimental movement that was more advanced in South America and Europe than in the United States. In fact, of the many new poetries to emerge during the decade—sound, found, visual, kinetic, typographic, video, etc.—the *Tish*/Black Mountain variety was the most conservative and, perhaps because of its sense of place, proved to be the most adaptable to a 'Canadian' regionalist orientation.

By the end of the 1960s the subculture had surfaced. The underground, as such, no longer had a function, and the guerilla fighters (the 'little mags' typical of the decade) died with it.

WYNNE FRANCIS

4. THE SEVENTIES will be remembered as a period of intense literary activity in Canada: there were more active writers than at any other time in Canadian history, and there were more magazines available to publish their work than ever before. In this decade the experimental and fledgling voices of the sixties joined a relatively strong literary community that spoke not only to the Canadian audience but to an international readership. Literary magazines during the seventies—surmounting the challenge of limited financial

resources with craft, elegance, and determination—fell into three distinct groups: university-sponsored journals, student magazines, and independent reviews. Physically the magazines took many shapes, ranging from 'perfect-bound' book formats of up to 400 pages to small saddle-stitched (stapled) pamphlets of under twenty pages. As the forum where new authors tested their skills and ideas, and where established authors broke in new work for public viewing, they had a significant influence on Canadian literature.

Long the mainstay of the Canadian literary-magazine community, university magazines continued to maintain their presence, offering not only scholarly criticism but poetry, fiction, and reviews. Journals such as *The Fiddlehead* and *The Dalhousie Review* in the Maritimes were joined by *The Antigonish Review* (1971-) from St Francis Xavier University, which extended its Canadian content by introducing many overseas authors to Canadian readers.

Along with the bilingual journal *Ellipse*, *Le Chien d'Or/Golden Dog* (1972-5) and *Outset* (1973-4) from Sir George Williams University, and *Matrix* (1975-) from Champlain College, also helped to maintain the presence in Quebec of creative writing in English.

In Ontario established literary/scholarly journals such as *The University of Toronto Quarterly* and *Queen's Quarterly* continued their leadership in a field that expanded to include *Arc* (1979-) at Carleton University; *Waves* (1972-), which began at York University and later became a front-running independent quarterly; *The University of Windsor Review* (1965-), which publishes both criticism and creative writing; *Lakehead University Review* (1968-77); and *The New Quarterly* (1980-) from Waterloo University.

In the West, *Ariel: A Review of International English Literature* (1970-), from the University of Calgary, took a commanding position on the merit of its literary contributions and the quality of its criticism. The University of Manitoba was the centre for three significant periodicals: *The Far Point* (1968-73), *Northern Light* (1975-7; 1981-), and *CV/II* (1975-)—a revival of its influential namesake, *Contemporary Verse*.

Magazines published from such institutions as the University of British Columbia and the University of Victoria present a stunning portrait of the wide variety of writing produced on the west coast during the decade. While *Prism* and *Canadian Literature* at UBC maintained their importance, new magazines such as *event* (1971-) at Douglas College, the *West Coast Review* at Simon Fraser University, *The Malahat Review* at the University of Victoria, *Capilano Review* (1972-) at Capilano College, and *Writing* (1979-) at David Thompson University published not only west-coast writing but serious work from the other provinces and abroad.

Scholarship in Canadian literature, particularly in poetry, was noteworthy during the seventies because of the efforts of such journals as *Canadian Poetry: Studies, Documents and Reviews* (1977-) from the University of Western Ontario and *Studies in Canadian Literature* (1976-) and the *Journal of Canadian Poetry* (1978-) from the University of New Brunswick. An important journal of Canadian literary criticism, *Essays on Canadian Writing* (1974-), is published at York University, and ECW PRESS has evolved from it. Also published at York is *CTR: Canadian Theatre Review* (1974-). Two other important magazines in the same field are *Canadian Drama/L'Art dramatique canadien* (1975-90) and *Theatre History in Canada/Histoire du Théâtre au Canada* (1980-).

The student population of Canadian universities also became more active in the publication of literary journals during the seventies. Magazines such as Canada's oldest literary publication, *Acta Victoriana* (1878-), at Victoria College, University of Toronto, provided a model for other student periodicals by offering opportunities for young writers and editors to test and polish their skills. Many were well produced and proved that new ideas and energies could be infused into the Canadian literary scene from this quarter. Ontario universities were probably the most lively centres for student publications during the decade, with a large number issuing from the University of Toronto. From 1975 to 1980 no less than seven reputable journals were produced by students at U of T colleges. *The University of Toronto Review* (1975-), founded as a focus for creative writing on the campus, joined *The Grammateion* (1974-) and *Rune* (1974-) from St Michael's College; *The University College Review* (1971-); *Laomedon Review* (1972-9) and later the *Erindale Review* (1981-); *Writ* (1970-) from Innis College; and *Scarborough Fair* (1974-). Ryerson Polytechnical Institute's undergraduates published the finely crafted *White Wall Review* (1973-) and students at the University of Western Ontario produced *The Pom Shed* (1974-). Other Ontario journals included *Portico* (1975-82) at Sheridan College, *Poetry WLU* (1981-) at Wilfrid Laurier University, and *Direction* and *Skatwin*, both published at York University. Noteworthy

Maritimes publications included *Sift* (1974-80) at St Mary's University; *Alpha* (1976-9), which succeeded *Either/Or* at Acadia University; *Skylight* (1976-8) at Dalhousie; and *First Encounter* (1969-) at Mount Allison. In Quebec, *Los* (1975-82) from Loyola College was contemporary with the McGill publications *Cyan Line* (1975-6), *Scrivener* (1981-), and *Atropos*. *Ion* (1976-8) and *From an Island* (1980-) were produced at the University of Victoria.

Assistance from arts councils, both national and regional, coupled with a new public awakening to the virtues and importance of Canadian writing, plus the demand for opportunities to present new authors, sparked numerous enterprises by individuals who believed that they could create journals that had something unique and important to say. In the Maritimes *Germination* (1974-) from River Hebert, N.S., *Pottersfield Portfolio* (1980-), also from Nova Scotia, and *Iconomatrix* (1975-) from Fredericton, New Brunswick, became significant forums for poetry, fiction, and reviews on the east coast. In Quebec, journals such as *Cross Country* (1975-), *Athanor* (1978-82), and *The Alchemist* (1974-) brought renewed energy to the Montreal scene, while *The Moosehead Review* (1977-), a lively journal of poetry and fiction, appeared from Waterville, Quebec.

Ontario cities—Toronto, Hamilton, and London, in particular—became centres for a large number of independent magazines, partly because of the number of editors there who were able to devote their time to such publications and the abundance of writers who could contribute to them, and partly because of the readership that was at hand. Of the Toronto periodicals. *DESCANT* (1970-) emerged from its origins as a graduate-student magazine at the University of Toronto to become one of Canada's leading magazines for poetry and fiction. *CANADIAN FICTION MAGAZINE* (1971-), also based in Toronto, took the lead in the publication of short stories and fiction-related articles. *Poetry Canada Review* (1979-) appeared quarterly in tabloid format and featured new writing by both established and younger poets, as well as articles on poetry activities from across the country. *Cross Canada Writers Quarterly* (1979-) published a newsstand magazine that offered articles, creative writing, and reviews, as well as the first cross-country workshop by mail. *Poetry Toronto* (1975-) served as a vital instrument for poets and writers by providing monthly market information and listings of literary activities. *EXILE* (1972-), although Toronto based, expanded its horizons to the international sphere and published outstanding works of major authors, as did *Intrinsic* (1975-9). The Haiku interests on the Toronto scene were served by *Cicada* (1976-81) and later *Inkstone* (1982-). Doubleday Company Limited, based in Toronto, published the annual anthology *Aurora* (1977-80), which was considered by many to be the finest bridge between book-style literary magazines and actual books. *The Canadian Literary Review* (1982-), published in Toronto, was designed as a national literary review with editorial input from across the country. Other Toronto magazines included the feminist journal *Fireweed* (1975-), *Harvest* (1977-82), *Nimbus* (1979-82), *Another Poetry Magazine* (1970-71), and *Acanthus* (1978-80), all of which featured poetry and short fiction in saddle-stitched formats. Having been founded in Victoria (1965), *Open Letter* began to be published in Toronto in 1971. *Ethos* (1983-7) was devoted to literature and the arts, with an international perspective. Hamilton and London boasted several small but lively journals during the seventies and early eighties. In Hamilton *Wee Giant* (1977-82) and *Origins* (1967-83) published poetry in quarterly formats, while the London literary scene featured several journals: *Stuffed Crocodile* (1972-8); *Jubilee* (1973-5); *SWOP* (1977-80), which also featured information on markets and short reviews; *Applegarth's Folly* (1973-9); *Brick* (1978-), a fine journal of reviews and literary articles; *Other Voices* (1965-75); *Twelfth Key* (1975-8); and *Watchwords* (1982-). Northern Ontario was represented by the visually beautiful *Northward Journal* (1975-) from Moonbeam; *Copperfield* (1969-76), which, like *Northward Journal*, focused on northern themes and issues; and the North Bay magazine *Nebula* (1974-). Ottawa was the centre for several magazines that included *Manna* (1972-4), *Northern Journey* (1971-7), *Review Ottawa* (1977-8), and its successor *Anthos* (1978-). *Canadian Children's Literature* (1975-), published at the University of Guelph, is a journal of criticism and review.

Manitoba, Saskatchewan, and Alberta were also part of the literary explosion of the seventies. Of the magazines that appeared from the West during the decade, *Grain* (1973-), published in Saskatoon, evolved as the leader in western writing and featured some of the most important prairie authors. Also significant were *Imago* (1965-73), which began in Calgary and later moved between Montreal and Vancouver; *Dandelion* (1975-), published in Calgary; *Poetic License* (1977-80) from Edmonton; *White Pelican* (1971-8), also from Edmonton; *Salt* (1972-80) from Moose Jaw;

The Camrose Review (1981-) from Camrose, Alberta; *Worldloom* (1981-) from Winnipeg; and *The Alberta Poetry Yearbook* (1927-), an annual publication of the CANADIAN AUTHORS' ASSOCIATION.

On the west coast the feminist magazine *Room of One's Own* (1974-), published in Vancouver, consistently offers fine writing and editing. Other notable independent west-coast literary magazines from the seventies and early eighties include *WOT* (1979-81), *Karaki* (1976-9), *Periodics* (1977-80), *Tuatara* (1969-72)—all from Victoria—and *Blackfish* (1971-5) from Burnaby and *Air* (1971-5) from Vancouver.

By 1980 Canada had as many literary magazines per capita as the United States—a fact that was a testament to the energies of those involved in their publication and to the productivity of Canadian writers. The most startling characteristic of these magazines was their range of content. The sudden rise in the number of journals stimulated the pursuit of excellence.

5. THE EIGHTIES AND NINETIES. While the period signalled a decline in arts funding for literary periodicals, and shrinking market interest, the number of Canadian literary periodicals actually grew—a reflection, perhaps, of the constant flow of energy these publications brought to the national literature, and of the indomitable need for the written culture to find forums for expression. James Deahl's editions of *Poetry markets for Canadians* (1989, 1992, 1996), which have been very profitable, are not only useful guides—particularly for new writers, many of whom await publication in book form—but an indicator of the sheer number of literary periodicals. Aside from the fact that the energy of the literary magazines failed to translate into the growth of literary publishing at a grass-roots level (as demonstrated in the past by the growth of *Quarry*, EXILE, and *Black Moss* into key publishing houses), the impact of this 'bottlenecked' literary development in Canadian culture will likely be felt well into the twenty-first century; or the situation may be read as indicative of the maturing of Canadian literature, where the climate has imposed a structure of selectivity on the literary scene as a whole. The difficulties in translating work from magazine publication to finished book are also symptomatic of an undervalued and underfunded literary culture.

For those magazines that pursued excellence, married strong content to striking design, and balanced funding, the 1980s and 1990s were periods of some achievement. Among the most notable and consistently good magazines are three that were edited by prominent writers: Barry CALLAGHAN's *Exile* (1972-), which has featured not only Canadian work but also a superb selection of international authors and translations; Karen Mulhallen's *Descant* (1971-), which presented special theme issues on Japanese Literature, Travel Writing, and Male Desire; and M.G. VASSANJI's *The Toronto Review of South Asian Literature* (later *The Toronto Review of Contemporary Literature Abroad*). Like *The Tamarack Review* of the 1960s and 1970s, both *Exile* and *Descant* published anthologies to celebrate their success: the two-volume *Fifteen years in Exile* (1992) and *Paper guitar: 27 writers celebrate 25 years of Descant magazine* (1995).

On the university scene there were a number of notable journals in spite of budget cutbacks. The mainstay quarterlies that offered both scholarly and literary work remained a vital part of the total picture. In Nova Scotia, at St Francis Xavier University, *The Antigonish Review* (1971-), edited by R.J. MacSween and later George Sanderson, flourished and featured the work of Canadian authors as well as many British writers. At the University of New Brunswick the tradition of *The Fiddlehead* (1945-), once the work of Alfred BAILEY and Fred COGSWELL, was continued by Robert GIBBS and Don McKAY, among others, and provided a forum for many new voices, reaching a crescendo in 1995 with the celebratory fiftieth-anniversary issue. The stalwarts of Canadian literary/academic publishing—*The Dalhousie Review*, *Queen's Quarterly*, and *MATRIX* (1975-), at Concordia University—continued, as did the *Windsor Review* (formerly *The University of Windsor Review*, 1965-) and Waterloo's *The New Quarterly* (1981-). The University of Lethbridge contributed *Whetstone* (1971-), and the *Wascana Review* (1966-) continued at the University of Regina. *Ariel: A Review of International Engish Literature* (1970-) at the University of Calgary continues to be an important source for Commonwealth and prairie literature. *Canadian Literature* (1957-), edited by W.A. New from 1977 to 1995, and then by Eva Marie Kröller, remained a key source for criticism of Canadian literature and new poetry. *The Malahat Review* (1967-) at the University of Victoria, founded by Robin Skelton and edited for a time by Constance Rooke and since 1992 by Derk WYNAND, continued to be prominent on the literary-magazine front and featured items such as an intriguing interview with P.K. PAGE by Eleanor Wachtel. Other strong West Coast journals are *Prism international* (1959-) from the University of British Columbia's Department of Creative Writing, *West Coast Line* (1966-), edited by Roy Miki, published at Simon Fraser University, and *The Capilano Review* (1983-) at Capilano College in Vancouver: all continued to maintain high standards in content and quality of production.

Among the independent magazines, the most significant players were Geoff Hancock's *Canadian Fiction Magazine*, which continued to publish the very best in short stories and interviews with fiction writers. With funding cuts in the late 1990s, the future of the magazine is tenuous. Bob Hilderley, publisher of QUARRY PRESS in Kingston, Ontario, entered the Canadian literary magazine scene during the 1980s and 1990s when he became publisher, then owner, of *Canadian Fiction Magazine*. He also acquired *Poetry Canada Review* (founded by Clifton Whiten, Ted Plantos, and Peter SUCH in 1979 and edited successively by Beverley Daurio, Maggie Helwig, and Barry Dempster). Quarry Press also continued the tradition of *Quarry* (1952-), most notably under the editorship during the early nineties of Steven HEIGHTON, who took the magazine to new heights of excellence, including a British/Irish poetry issue edited by Bruce Meyer and Carolyn Meyer and a Scottish poetry issue. Poet and critic Di BRANDT was poetry editor of Winnipeg's *PRAIRIE FIRE* (1978-). Other notable magazines were: Ottawa's *Arc* (1978-), originally founded at Carleton University by Christopher Levenson and edited during the 1990s by poet John Barton; *CONTEMPORARY VERSE II* (1975-) from Winnipeg; *Dandelion* (1974-) from Calgary and originally edited by poet Robert HILLIES; the feminist magazines *Fireweed* (1975-) from Toronto and *Room of One's Own* from Vancouver; *GRAIN* (1973-) from Regina, which featured Governor General's Award winner Tim Lilburn as poetry editor; the surprisingly energetic yet low-key *Jones Ave.* (1994-) from Toronto; the impressive and well-edited *Pottersfield Portfolio* (1979-) from Halifax; and *sub-TERRAIN* (1988-) from Vancouver. From Sault Ste Marie, Ontario, Karl Jirgen's *Rampike* (1979-) presents a fine array of work by leading Canadian and international writers. Of special note is Toronto's *Blood and Aphorisms* (1994-), which presents emerging authors. Beverley Daurio's fiction magazine, *Paragraph* (1990-), from Stratford, Ontario, rose out of the ashes of Ted Plantos' *Cross-Canada Writers' Quarterly* (1982-9).

Unfortunately and inevitably, a large number of magazines flourished and faded, or simply faded, during this period—an indicator of the brief life-expectancy for such publications (which now average about two issues). Most notably mourned among the lost publications were Marco Fraticelli's *The Alchemist* (1974-*c*.90), which was an important source for poems and translations by the Italian writers of Canada; Nova Scotia's *Germination* (1974-*c*.90), which published many new and emerging poets; Bernice Lever's *Waves* (1972-86); Sonja Skarstedt's *Zymergy* (1987-90) from Montreal; and *The Moosehead Review* (1977-*c*.86). There were, in fact, more magazines; but their importance remains largely unmeasured and unqualified because of the briefness of their existence and a general lack of scholarly interest in Canada in contemporary literary-magazine publishing—a problem of weak critical energy rather than a failure of the creative and artistic energy that lies at the root of the literaries. BRUCE MEYER

Literary magazines in Quebec. Periodicals have always been instrumental in the dissemination, and even in the creation, of Quebec literature. In the nineteenth century book publishers were reluctant to produce works of fiction. To compensate, several newspapers brought out serially either complete novels or shorter pieces, such as stories and poems. When specifically literary magazines began to appear, they functioned as organs for various groups that pointed to important movements in Quebec literature.

1. THE NINETEENTH CENTURY. The first goal of one of the earliest periodicals, *La Ruche littéraire illustrée* (1853-9), was to bring together Canadian literary works, but it soon began to include works translated from other languages as well; and in fact it specialized in stories with a romantic tinge by writers newly arrived from France, of whom the best known was Henri-Émile CHEVALIER. Three publications that first appeared in the mid-nineteenth century, at the time of the MOUVEMENT LITTÉRAIRE DE QUÉBEC, made the first real attempts to become established. *Les SOIRÉES CANADIENNES* (1861-5), subtitled 'a compendium of national literature', had as an epigraph Charles Nodier's celebrated remark: 'Let us make haste to recount the charming stories of the people before they are forgotten.' Its goal was 'to rescue our fine Canadian legends from the oblivion which now threatens them more than ever, thereby maintaining those memories that have been preserved by our old storytellers and making popular certain little-known episodes in the history of our country.' The first issue contained 'Trois

légendes de mon pays' by Joseph-Charles TACHÉ and 'La jongleuse' by Abbé CASGRAIN; among the other contributors and editors were Hubert LaRUE and Antoine GÉRIN-LAJOIE. *Les Soirées canadiennes* sought to promote a literature based on folklore and banished from its pages any political discussion. Founded as a result of dissent within the group at *Les Soirées*, *Le FOYER CANADIEN* (1863-6) was a literary and historical compendium with the same objectives, while it also aimed to publish 'any Canadian work distinguished by originality in point of view, thought, or style'—one of which was Antoine Gérin-Lajoie's *JEAN RIVARD, économiste*. These two periodicals were succeeded by *Les Nouvelles Soirées canadiennes* (1882-8), which sought to encourage original literary works with the aim of 'strengthening our institutions and our language', even stating that it would 'be first and always Canadian and Catholic, or, in other words, essentially national.' Expressing a concept of literature that was basically moral and nationalist, it promoted a sense of rootedness and articulated a Canadian specificity that was most often evoked through folkloric themes. In a general way these leanings were shared by *L'Opinion publique* (1870-83), a political and literary magazine, *L'Album universal* (1884-1902), and *La Revue canadienne* (1864-1922), which was more open to the overall intellectual life of French Canada.

2. THE EARLY TWENTIETH CENTURY. The question of a national literature was being examined in terms of the regional, as opposed to the universal, option when in 1909 a group of writers founded *Le Terroir*, which set out to give prominence to 'the French-Canadian soul', as well as to make possible 'the exaltation of our native soil' and the 'bringing together of Canadian literary youth'. Under the direction of members of the ÉCOLE LITTÉRAIRE DE MONTRÉAL, including Charles GILL and Albert Ferland, the contents of the magazine were very eclectic and it lasted only one year. Some ten years later an equally short-lived publication, *Le NIGOG* (1918), echoed *Le Terroir* by opting for a certain universalism and declaring the need to relate to modern times and contemporary literature. The debates stirred up by these magazines were to be continued in the work of such essayists and pamphleteers as Victor Barbeau and Claude-Henri GRIGNON in the 1930s and centred on the question of the kind of French to be used for writing.

At this time other periodicals were integrating literature into a broader perspective. *Les Idées* (1935-9), edited by Albert Pelletier, attacked the 'lack of a life of the mind' and spoke of an intellectual life that was getting soft as it moved 'gradually into the limbo of instinct'. *La RELÈVE* (1934-41), the most important cultural magazine of the first part of the twentieth century, was put out by Robert CHARBONNEAU, Paul Beaulieu, Hector de SAINT-DENYS-GARNEAU, and Robert ÉLIE. It aimed at a spiritual and humanistic renewal to which art would be a privileged witness: 'In the great revolution that is taking shape and that should signify humanity's return to spiritual concerns', wrote Saint-Denys-Garneau, 'it is essential that art—that crown of man, the supreme expression of his soul and of his will—rediscover its lost meaning and become the splendid expression of that upward striving.' The literary works of this group were far removed from folklore: they focused on the expression of the ego, the inner life, and those spiritual problems that affected modern civilization. *Amérique française* (1941-64) would pursue these themes, while posing the problem of twin loyalties, both French and American. *Les ÉCRITS DU CANADA FRANÇAIS* (1954-), after a break of several years, continues to publish fiction, poetry, and essays.

3. THE MID-TWENTIETH CENTURY. As they were moving progressively away from a narrow notion of a 'national literature', later twentieth-century periodicals continued to bear the mark of a certain sort of Catholicism. Even *Cité libre* (1950-66) did not escape. This magazine—founded in the midst of the Duplessis period by Pierre Elliott Trudeau, Jean Marchand, and Gérard Pelletier, who later were better known for their subsequent political careers—opposed the conservative ideology that had dominated Quebec for more than a century, advocating a form of internationalism at the expense of the concept of 'nation'. More political than literary, *Cité libre* nonetheless left a mark on Quebec's cultural history by declaring—two years after the publication of *REFUS GLOBAL* (1948)—the right to speak and to dissent. The group would soon become the favourite target of the editors of *PARTI PRIS* (1963-8), a political and cultural periodical with a threefold objective: an independent, socialist, and secular Quebec. Most of its editorial committee was composed of writers: Paul CHAMBERLAND, Jacques RENAUD, André MAJOR, *et al.* The *parti pris* group differed from earlier movements because they moved the national question to the left, considering the case for Quebec without confining it to a hidebound nationalism. Important as well for articulating

the relations between literature and politics—and for challenging both—*parti pris* was concerned with both the literary *fact* (that is, literature as an institution) and the *making* of literature, bringing together the practice of fiction and a theory to explain this practice. Among the questions frequently taken up in its pages were the status of the writer, the situation of culture and literature in a colonial context, and the sort of French to be used. *parti pris* is particularly well known for having briefly, and for political reasons, espoused *JOUAL*; its writers sought as well to take up Sartre's great themes—namely, 'For whom and for what do we write?'—in the practice of a literature that would be known henceforth as Québécois.

Between the founding of *Cité libre* and *parti pris* another periodical appeared, which is still one of the most prestigious literary magazines in Quebec. *LIBERTÉ*, founded in 1959, described itself first as 'a centre for the discussion of cultural problems, which intends to welcome all valid ways of thinking as well as to encourage dialogue'. Far from being 'the organ of a closed group', it intended to be 'open to everyone with something to say'. *Liberté*—whose editors specified at the outset that it would not be associated with any political position—was a meeting-place and crossroads for various literary and cultural currents. An issue from 1961 does, however, contain a sort of manifesto: 'We are for: total, universal, immediate disarmament; love, liberty, friendship; jazz; those who have the youth of Varèse, Russell, Henry Miller, Abel Gance; a Department of Public Education; respect for consciences; cultural democracy; secular universities; the refined use of sex.' In its early years *Liberté* strove to denounce the problems of 'cultural fatigue'. In 1963 it published the first writings of the *parti pris* group, and titled one of its issues 'Québec and the language struggle'. Among more recent special issues, the Acts of the various meetings organized by the editorial board each year are important documents. Although *Liberté* publishes works from such countries as Israel, the United States, France, and Romania, it still reserves a select spot for young local writers. After several years in transition, the editorship of the magazine passed from Jean-Guy PILON to François Ricard; the editorial committee was reorganized and the magazine got its second wind. In 1981 a highly valued issue appeared on 'The Québec literary institution'. Under the direction of François Ricard, *Liberté* became more polemical, more concerned with socio-political debates. François Hebert and Marie-Andrée Lamontagne, who actually edited the review, have succeeded him.

4. THE MODERNIST PERIOD. The average life-span of a literary generation, particularly in Quebec, is about ten years. Thus, while *parti pris* rebelled against *Cité libre* and took a position to the left of *Liberté*, *La BARRE DU JOUR* (1965-76), founded by Nicole BROSSARD and Roger Soublières, broke with a certain social concept of literature, claiming that the writer was no longer a seismograph to measure society's pain but was concerned with his or her own urges. After a few years and a change in editorial committee, *La Barre du jour* became *La Nouvelle Barre du jour* (1977-90), and the writing expresses a modernism midway between theory and fiction; theory, considered a form of fiction, even becomes fiction—hence its inevitable step into formalism that led to charges of mandarinism and class-specific writing. To such criticisms the new writers reply that reading habits inculcated by bourgeois culture must be changed. For more easily located and recognizable codes they substitute the notion of the text; over linear, absolutist writing, they prefer the fragment. Successive editorial teams have become involved in a series of renewals, violations, and reversals of language. Nothing is self-evident: in the beginning is the 'game', which leads to the 'fabrication' of fables and tales written 'literally', to the 'page/image' and to 'diasynchronic chronicles'. The challenge is considerable. Each text must reinvent itself, under penalty of falling into the comfortable purr of the familiar. Inevitably the challenge is not always successful.

Alongside *La Barre du jour*, *Les Herbes rouges* (1968-), under Marcel and François Hébert, devotes each issue, in the form of a small volume, to work by a single writer. Addressing the central questions of modernism, it offers no programmatic utterances: practice is enough. Concerning this practice, Roger DesRoches, like the editors of *La Barre du jour*, talks of the materiality of the text as a place for questioning and for play, of the intention to 'illustrate the particularities of pleasure and desire, of the body as the seat of thought, thinking of its fine deaths', and also of 'differences in all manner of madness'. The contents of *Les Herbes rouges* are usually more provocative than those of *La Barre du jour*; more subversive and more playful too; more counter-cultural and mythic. Everything is raw material for texts, for poetry—from advertising to comic strips, from social discourse to political awareness.

Estuaire (1976-), the product of a group that calls itself 'poètes sur parole', is essentially a poetry magazine, publishing work based on the oral tradition, on proclamation and sharing. Pierre MORENCY, one of its guiding lights, once rented a billboard in the heart of Quebec City and had his poems printed on it. Other members of the group have constructed picture-poems and poster-poems. *Estuaire* reserves a special place for poetry for the eye and the voice, and for a mode of speech that has deep roots in the heart of the land and the landscape. It is no coincidence that the magazine has published interviews with Gaston MIRON, Hélias and Pierre PERRAULT—all craftsmen of the word who were moulded initially by the heritage of folklore. This initial orientation, however, seems to be gradually giving way as *Estuaire* turns to a more modern poetry that nonetheless remains to some extent accessible to the reader.

5. CROSS-CULTURAL VENTURES. Between 1960 and the 1980s other magazines were born, only to live somewhat ephemeral lives. *Maintenant* (1962-75) attempted to reconcile the national question and left-wing Catholicism. *Mainmise* (1970-8) made itself the organ for an American-style counter-culture attempting to take root in Quebec, while *Presqu'Amérique* (1970-3) sought to define new kinds of local identification. *Brèches* (1973-7) examined literature and culture in the wake of Parisian critical currents. Both *Chroniques* (1975-8) and *Stratégie* (1972-7) analysed the literary object and its surrounding critical discourses from a Marxist perspective. *Les Têtes de pioche* (1976-9) brought together the most radical elements of the women's movement, then in full bloom. *La Vie en rose* (1980-7), a feminist magazine aimed at a much larger public, published pieces that were in turn humorous, journalistic, or subversive. *Arcade* (1982-) describes itself as the only francophone journal in North America entirely devoted to women's writing. *La Parole métèque* (1986-) is dedicated to 'un nouveau rêve féministe'.

Informational literary periodicals are *Livres et auteurs québécois* (1961-), an annual collection of critical writing on Quebec literary production; *Lettres québécoises* (1976-), a systematic review of current publications; and *SPIRALE* (1979-), in which literary criticism runs counter to clichés and conventional wisdom. In the field of theatre the excellent *Jeu* (1976-) makes the link between theory and practice, keeps a close watch on theatrical productions, interviews troupes, and provides an account of what is at stake in theatrical activity in Quebec.

Various scholarly periodicals put out by the universities are generally devoted to the study of one theme, one writer, or one question. This is the case for *Études littéraires* (Laval) and *Études françaises* (Université de Montréal), which celebrated its thirtieth anniversary in 1995. *VOIX ET IMAGES* (1968-), published by Les Presses de l'Université du Québec and born out of *Voix et images du pays*, the only publication devoted entirely to Quebec, allots part of each issue to one writer. *Ellipse* (Université de Sherbrooke) is of singular importance in presenting literary works, generally poetry, in both French and English, with the original versions on facing pages. *Présence francophone* provides an account of literary activity in French-language countries. In Ottawa *Incidences* and *La Revue de l'Université d'Ottawa* open their pages to literary questions and at the Université du Québec à Rimouski, *Tangence* (1992-) has replaced *Urgence* (1981-92).

A number of new publications have appeared since 1975: *Dérives* (1975-87), *Possibles* (1976-), *Intervention* (1978-), *Le Temps fou* (1978-83), *Focus* (1978-). Reflecting a spirit of anti-dogmatism, they share a desire to tear down the walls dividing various fields of cultural activity. Although *Intervention* is primarily concerned with various artistic activities, it also deals with such related matters as distribution, galleries, publishing, etc., as well as with current sociological issues and government policies. *Dérives* was an interdisciplinary publication that attempted to establish a dialogue between Quebec and the Third World and published articles by very diverse contributors. Two transcultural journals, *Vice Versa* (1989-) and *Ruptures* (1992-), do the same today. *Possibles*, which brings together sociologists and literary writers, has since its inception been musing over Quebec, its political future, and the self-management practices that are becoming established there; literary and artistic creation is viewed as an essential component of the societal imagination, a kind of preferred meeting-ground for both individual and joint 'possibilities'. *Le Temps fou*, the only one of these periodicals to appear monthly, systematically detected what was innovative in different areas of culture and society, while *Focus* provides an account of activities in the Saguenay-Lac Saint-Jean area. In these interdisciplinary times new periodicals are integrating literary creation in a global social project—*Trois* (1985-) and *Zéro de conduite* (1995-), for example. In a different context, readers who want news can turn to

XYZ (1985-) and *Stop* (1986-). In keeping with the widespread interest in the extraterrestrial, two publications are devoted to science fiction: *Solaris* (formerly *Requiem*, 1975) and *Imagine* (1979). The Acadian journal *Héloises* (1981-) has devoted an entire issue to new francophone writing from Louisiana.

An analysis of cultural periodicals shows that several trends coexist, survive, and struggle for symbolic recognition, whereas the literary history of Quebec had accustomed us to seeing a single dominant group arise in any one period. These many facets make generalization difficult, but several conclusions may be drawn. Between 1960 and the 1980s the writer generally shed his bad conscience and moved away from the national 'wailing wall'; writing became a matter of craft, with roots in a social and political context, in which it is easier to say *I* than *we*; and where groups are concerned, ruptures are less violent than at the time of *Refus global* and *parti pris*. Opposition has now given way to transposition and transgression. LISE GAUVIN

Little, Jean (b. 1932). One of four children born in Taiwan to parents who were both Canadian medical doctors serving as missionaries for the United Church, she moved to Canada shortly before the Second World War erupted. Almost blind since birth, Little was educated in Guelph, Ontario, and at Victoria College, University of Toronto, studying under Northrop FRYE and receiving an Honours B.A. in English (1955). After training as a 'Special Education' teacher in the USA, she combined teaching and writing until royalties made full-time writing possible. Her extensive international travel includes two years in Japan, and she has lectured widely in the USA, the UK, and across Canada, usually accompanied by a Labrador guide dog—first 'Zephyr' and then 'Ritz', both essential elements of her public persona. She has honorary degrees from the universities of Guelph, Nippissing, and Mount Saint Vincent, and was made a Member of the Order of Canada in 1993. After her mother's death in 1991 she began, with her sister Pat, a new life on a century-farm outside Guelph: they joined households, then began raising two of Pat's young grandchildren.

By early 1997 Little had published eleven novels, two books of autobiography, two books of historical fiction, two books of poetry, and six picture books, plus several 'I Can Read' titles. Her novels are *Mine for keeps* (1962), *Home from far* (1965), *Spring begins in March* (1966), *Take wing* (1968), *One to grow on* (1969), *Look through my window* (1970), *Kate* (1971), *From Anna* (1972), *Stand in the wind* (1975), *Listen for the singing* (1977), and *Mama's going to buy you a mockingbird* (1984). Her autobiographies are *Little by Little* (1987) and *Stars come out within* (1990); her two historical-fiction novels are *His banner over me* (1995), based on her mother's life as a daughter of foreign missionaries, and *The belonging place* (1997), based partly on her own Scottish ancestors. Several short novels and picture-books include *Lost and found* (1985); *Different dragons* (1986); *Once upon a golden apple* (1991), with Maggie DeVries; *Jess was the brave one* (1991); *Revenge of the small Small* (1992); *Bats about baseball* (1995), with Claire Mackay; *Jenny and the Hanukkah Queen* (1995); and *Gruntle Piggle takes off* (1996). She has won the Little, Brown Canadian Children's Book Award (1961), the Vicky Metcalfe Award (1974), the CANADA COUNCIL Children's Literature Prize (1977), the German 'Youth Literature Prize' (1981), the Canadian Library Association Children's Book-of-the-Year Award (1984), the Ruth Schwartz Award (1984), the Boston *Globe* 'Horn Book' Award (1988), and two ALA Notable Book Awards. Her books have been translated into French, German, Danish, Dutch, Japanese, Greek, Welsh, and Norwegian, and are available in Braille. Two have been made into movies. Little's books, grounded in the emotional and psychological lives of children, explore both self-defeating and successful ways of coping with threatening events.

MARY HENLEY RUBIO

Livesay, Dorothy (1909-96). Born in Winnipeg, she came to Toronto in 1920 when her father, J.F.B. Livesay, became manager of the Canadian Press. She attended Glen Mawr private school for girls, where she met women teachers who—together with her father—encouraged her to consider questions of atheism and socialism. Influenced by Shaw, Ibsen, and Emma Goldman, whose lecture series in Toronto she attended early in 1926, she enrolled in the fall of that year in French and Italian at Trinity College, University of Toronto, where her evolving ideas about socialism and women's rights led her to study privately Emily Dickinson, H.D., Katharine Mansfield, and the sociological writings of Friedrich Engels. When only eighteen she published her first poetry collection, *Green pitcher* (1928) which later disappointed Livesay by its failure to deal openly with social issues. Nevertheless these were well-crafted poems that not only showed skilled use of the imagist technique but prefigured Margaret ATWOOD's condemnations of exploitative and fearful attitudes to the Canadian landscape. Livesay spent 1929-30, her junior year of university study, in the south of France, and on graduation (B.A., 1931) went to Paris to study at the Sorbonne (Diplôme d'études supérieures, 1932). Deeply moved by the poverty and violence created by the Depression, she returned in 1932 to the University of Toronto, where she entered the School of Social Work and shortly after joined the Communist Party. But her second book, *Signpost* (1932), reflected few of these interests; rather it showed the increasing sophistication of her imagist skills, as in 'Green rain', and an original sense of feminine sexuality.

As is now well documented in her retrospective collection of essays, poems, letters, and reminiscences, *Right hand left hand: a true life of the thirties* (1977), Livesay spent the thirties organizing for the Party; employed as a social worker in Montreal, in Englewood, New Jersey, and in Vancouver; writing for the Marxist news magazine *New Frontier*; and learning from Auden, Spender, and C. Day Lewis how to marry political ideas to poetic craftsmanship. Although Livesay's powerful poems from this period, focusing on Depression conditions and the Spanish Civil War, did not see book publication until *Selected poems* (1957) and *Collected poems: the two seasons* (1972), they appeared throughout the thirties in periodicals such as *New Frontier*, *The CANADIAN FORUM*, and *Canadian Poetry Magazine*.

In the 1940s Livesay continued to publish overtly political poetry: *Day and night* (1944, Governor General's Award), concerning workers' contributions to wartime industry; *Poems for people* (1947, Governor General's Award), *Call my people home and other poems* (1950), which includes the title verse-play for radio, dramatizing the persecution of Japanese-Canadians during the Second World War. Most of this work was marred by unconvincing dramatic voices and simplistic political diction.

After an extended residence in Vancouver, where she married Duncan Macnair and raised two children, Livesay travelled to Zambia, where she taught English for UNESCO from 1960 to 1963. In the mid-1960s, stimulated by the rapidly evolving Vancouver poetry scene and by her study of linguistics while earning an M.Ed. (1966) from the University of British Columbia, Livesay began writing a new kind of poetry, concrete and phenomenological in style, and in content centring on womanhood and physical love. These changes resulted in her two finest books: *The unquiet bed* (1967) and *Plainsongs* (1969). A new concern to give voice to vigorous old age appeared in *Ice age* (1975) and *The woman I am* (1977). Overall, Livesay's career had a remarkable range, spanning—as she noted herself in *Right hand left hand*—the imagist lyric of *Green pitcher*, political polemic in the poems of the 1930s, documentary realism in *Day and night* and *Call my people home*, and the lyric confessional in her later work. Livesay's other poetry collections include the long-poem collection *The documentaries* (1968), *Plainsongs extended* (1971), *Nine poems of farewell* (1973), *The raw edges: voices from our time* (1981), *Phases of love* (1983), *Feeling the worlds* (1984), and *The self-completing tree* (1986). Prose writings include *A Winnipeg childhood* (1973), fictionalized reminiscenses expanded in *Beginnings* (1988), and *The husband: a novella* (1990). She also edited the anthology *Forty women poets of Canada* (1972) and in 1975 founded the important magazine of poetry and poetry criticism *CV/II*, the title of which is a tribute to Alan Crawley's *CONTEMPORARY VERSE*.

Livesay was writer-in-residence and professor of English at several Canadian universities and was the recipient of a number of honorary degrees. She was appointed an Officer of the Order of Canada in 1987.

A special issue of *A Room of One's Own*, vol. 5, no. 1/2 (1979) is devoted to Livesay. See also Susan Zimmerman, 'Livesay's houses', *CANADIAN LITERATURE* 61 (Summer 1974), and Lee Briscoe Thomspon, *Dorothy Livesay* (1987). FRANK DAVEY

Llewellyn, Edward. Pseudonym of Edward Llewellyn-Thomas. See FANTASTIC LITERATURE IN ENGLISH: 1.

Lochhead, Douglas (b. 1922). Douglas Grant Lochhead was born in Guelph, Ontario, and was raised for the most part in Ottawa, where his father was Dominion Agricultural Bacteriologist. Through his New Brunswick-born mother, Helen Louise Van Wart, Lochhead's childhood was also shaped by the experience of Canadian Maritime rural life. He received a B.A. (1943) and a B.L.S. (1951) from McGill University and an M.A. (1947) from the University of Toronto. Between 1943 and 1945 he served in the Canadian army, eventually obtaining the rank of lieutenant. His marriage in 1949 to the late Jean St Clair of Sydney, Nova Scotia, further deepened and extended Lochhead's personal and imaginative associations with the Maritimes.

Following a stint working in advertising and publicity, Lochhead became Librarian at Victoria College in British Columbia in 1951. Subsequently he held library appointments at Cornell University (1952-3); Dalhousie University, Halifax, Nova Scotia (1953-60); and York University, Toronto (1960-63). Between 1963 and 1975 he worked closely with Robertson DAVIES as the Librarian and a Fellow of Massey College, simultaneously serving as a Professor of English in University College, University of Toronto. From 1975 until 1987, when he retired and became Professor Emeritus, Lochhead was Davidson Professor of Canadian Studies and Director of the Centre for Canadian Studies at Mount Allison University, Sackville, New Brunswick.

The full furnace: collected poems (1975) and *Tiger in the skull: new and selected poems: 1959-1985* (1986) offer similar and representative selections of Lochhead's first poems followed by differing selections of his later, steadily maturing work. Both collections contain generous samplings from *The heart is fire* (1959) and *It is all around* (1960). The poems of these earliest books are heavily and distractingly influenced by Dylan Thomas, Auden, Yeats, Roethke, and E.J. Pratt. The best of them either are set in the Maritimes or concern Lochhead's experiences in the army. In *Millwood Road poems* (1970), whose contents are fully reprinted in the collected volume of 1975, Lochhead found the voice of his early maturity. Set in his Toronto home of the 1960s and 1970s, located on Millwood Road, his poems in this collection are understated, gentle, frequently comic vignettes of domestic life, animated by the unpredictable presences of Lochhead's two very young daughters and assorted suburban flora and fauna. They are written in accurately stressed and convincingly lineated free verse, and indicate what subsequent work has confirmed: Lochhead has a remarkable gift for appropriate rhythm and pace.

Lochhead's move to Sackville in 1975 and the self-renewal he experienced in its surroundings helped impel the prolific poetic activity that immediately followed. Close friendship with the poet John THOMPSON also had an immediate effect on his work. Thompson's attritional dedication to poetry, the circumstances of his death, and the stylistic example of his posthumously published poetry collection *Stilt Jack* (1978), a typescript copy of which Thompson entrusted to Lochhead to ensure its survival, all left their mark on Lochhead's *High Marsh Road* (1980, 1996). This book consists of a series of dated prose-poem journal entries (actually written in 1976) whose setting is the Tantramar Marsh. It marks the emergence of a new poetic persona. Lochhead is as colloquial and frequently as engaging as the writer of *Millwood Road poems*, but he is also far more deeply conscious of personal loss, missed opportunities for love, self-betrayal, and guilt.

In 1980 Lochhead published *A & E* and the chapbook *Battle sequence*. Written in free-verse tercets, *A & E* is a six-part monologue delivered by 'A', or Adam or Albert or Robert Hooke, to his wife 'E', or Eve or Ellen or Mrs Hooke. The subject is love and its evanescent revelation in the natural order of the cosmos. *A & E* was originally written in 1966 and is charged with the same kind of light-hearted virtuosity as many of Lochhead's other Toronto poems. *Battle sequence*, by contrast, a collection of eight semi-prose-poems, is voiced by a poetic persona more bitter and despairing than the one in *High Marsh Road*. His voice speaks also in many prose-poems in *The panic field* (1984), particularly in the book's title sequence, which is a meditation on Lochhead's wartime experiences, and in 'In a winter apartment', where the protagonist tries and fails to recover the kind of balance *A & E* enacts.

Upper Cape poems (1989) is a reflective and miscellaneous collection that is notable for the elegy 'John Thompson' and for a lyrical sequence, 'Words in winter—six poems'. *Dykelands* (1989) is one of the most elaborate books of poetry published in Canada, containing a sequence of twenty-six poems written to accompany photographs by Lochhead's friend, the landscape photographer Thaddeus Holownia. The poems, written in free-verse couplets resembling John Thompson's ghazals, succinctly celebrate the immense openness and layered natural and human history of the Tantramar Marsh.

Black festival: a long poem (1991), privately issued in a limited number of copies by Lochhead using his Harrier Editions imprint, is a fifty-three part elegy for his wife. Together with *High Marsh Road*, it is among the works that are Lochhead's primary accomplishment. Few of the lines in *Black festival* are more than three words; few of the stanzas in it are longer than six lines—its diction is of the utmost simplicity.

During the latter part of the 1980s Lochhead worked on a sequence of prose-poems devoted to the Nova Scotia Baptist preacher and visionary Henry ALLINE. *Homage to Henry Alline & other poems* (1992) contains not only the thirty-part main title sequence but also a related work of equal complexity, 'Vigils & Mercies 1-30', together with several other shorter sequences and miscellaneous poems. Although it is scarcely visible in the early books, a persistent vein of religious feeling becomes obvious in later books in the form, often, of a punitive introspection that may well have been inherited in part from a Presbyterian family background. The sequence 'Homage to Henry Alline', while taking into account the ambiguities and limitations of its protagonist, including the unintentional comedy of some situations Alline himself contrived, presents Alline as a Blakean force of positive energy and imagination. In the sequence 'Vigils & mercies' Lochhead drops the mask of Alline, depicting himself overtly as a pilgrim undergoing an explicitly Dantean journey during which he is his 'own Virgil', finding and feeling his way into the balanced cosmos improvisationally. Although *Breakfast at Mel's and other poems of love and places* (1997) contains several sequences that are as concerned with relationships as baffling as the ones depicted in 'In a winter apartment' and in parts of *High Marsh Road*, its dominant tone is celebratory.

See *The red jeep and other landscapes: a collection in honour of Douglas Lochhead* (1987), edited by Peter Thomas, which contains a full bibliography of Lochhead's articles, poems, and books. See also Ann Munton's 'Return, Toronto to the Tantramar: regional poetics, the long poem and Douglas Lochhead', *Essays on Canadian Writing* 31 (1985); Peter Sanger, 'The real round of the saying: an introduction to the poetry of Douglas Lochhead', *The Antigonish Review* 76 (Winter 1989), and *As the eyes of Lyncaeus: a celebration for Douglas Lochhead* (1990). PETER SANGER

Lodge, Rupert C. (1886-1961). Born in Manchester, England (a nephew of Sir Oliver Lodge, the physicist and spiritualist), Rupert Clendon Lodge came to North America in 1914 and taught at the University of Minnesota and the University of Alberta, before moving in 1920 to the University of Manitoba, where he remained (apart from a year as visiting professor at Harvard, and other occasional absences) until he retired in 1947. Later he taught at Queen's University, Kingston, Ontario, and at Long Island University, New York. He died in St Petersburg, Florida.

Probably the most widely read philosopher to work in Canada, Lodge played an important role in the development of pluralist ideas, in bringing philosophy to the Canadian West, and in the development of the 'philosophical federalism' that characterized Canadian thought in the inter-war years. His *Introduction to modern logic* (1920) shows the influence of the British idealists. Thereafter he pursued his own ideas, maintaining that philosophy was irreducibly pluralistic, and that every philosophical question could be answered from the viewpoint of a realist, an idealist, and a pragmatist: one may view the world either as a collection of objects that are simply 'there', as a system of experiences, or as something whose nature cannot be objectively defined but can be used in the furtherance of one's goals. His books—beginning with *The questioning mind* (1937) and *The philosophy of education* (1937)—develop this theme across a wide range of philosophical issues. *The philosophy of business* (1945) applies this trichotomy to practical life and to the theory of business, and *Applying philosophy* (1951) extends the thesis to other workaday domains. Lodge wrote with great clarity and simplicity and conveyed ideas to a wide audience; his books achieved a popularity that is rare in modern books in philosophy. *The philosophy of education* was widely consulted in colleges and faculties of education, especially in the United States. *The great thinkers* (1949), in which he discussed the major philosophers from the past in an easygoing style almost wholly without technical jargon (though with a good deal of scholarly acumen), continues to be widely read. It illustrates Lodge's thesis that philosophy is a continuing enterprise whose past actively influences its present. This belief was widely criticized (especially by G.S. BRETT), but Lodge defended it with skill and persistence.

Lodge is also remembered for his *Plato's theory of education* (1947), *Plato's theory of art* (1953), and *The philosophy of Plato* (1956).

LESLIE ARMOUR, ELIZABETH TROTT

Logan, John. See CRITICISM IN ENGLISH: 2.

London, Jack. See FOREIGN WRITERS ON CANADA IN ENGLISH: 2.

Lonergan, Bernard, J.F. (1904-84). Born in Buckingham, Quebec, he taught at Jesuit seminaries in Montreal and Toronto, and at the Gregorian University, Rome (1953-65), Harvard University (1971-2), and Boston College (1975-83). He is thought by some enthusiasts to be among the greatest philosophers of the twentieth century: the Lonergan Research Institute at Regis College, Toronto, is one of many such institutions throughout the world that study his work. Lonergan had a lifelong ambition to provide an up-to-date and comprehensively critical method for

Catholic theology that culminated in *Method in theology* (1971). In *Insight: a study of human understanding* (1957; 2nd edn 1992), he prepared the way with a study of the mind when it attains moments of understanding in mathematics, natural science, the realm of common sense, psychotherapy, political theory, epistemology, metaphysics, hermeneutics, ethics, and natural theology. This study had been preceded by two sets of articles on the work of Thomas Aquinas, one concerned with his theory of grace, the other with his notion of the 'inner word' as applicable both to human psychology and to Trinitarian theory. (Both were later published in book form, the former as *Grace and freedom*, 1971, the latter as *Verbum, word and idea in Aquinas*, 1967.) According to Lonergan, the experience of seeing into the nature of things is the ultimate experience of God, understood as an intelligent will underlying world process. Four basic types of activity are involved in human knowing and doing, described in his later writings as 'four transcendental precepts': 'Be attentive, be intelligent, be reasonable, be responsible.' The foundation of his thought is thought itself: we get at the truth about things by applying our minds correctly. 'This man does not think, therefore this man is not to be listened to.' The intellect is superior to the will (Thomas Aquinas) and God is the source of understanding: it is reasonable to believe that God exists in order fully to explain our universe, divine intelligence accounting for its intelligibility, divine will for its having the particular kind of intelligibility that science progressively finds it to have. It is to be admitted, too, that God is revealed more or less directly in other religions, and is active in the hearts of all those who love truth and justice, whether acknowledged explicitly or not.

See Frederick E. Crowe and Robert H. Doran, eds, *The collected works of Bernard Lonergan* (1988); F.E. Crowe, *Lonergan* (1992); and H.A. Meynell, *An introduction to the philosophy of Bernard Lonergan* (2nd ed. 1992).

HUGO A. MEYNELL

Longfellow, Henry Wadsworth. See *EVANGELINE: a tale of Acadie* and FOREIGN WRITERS ON CANADA IN ENGLISH: 2.

Longmore, George (1793-1867). Born in Quebec City, the son of a British army doctor stationed there, he spent part of his youth in Quebec before he was commissioned ensign in the Royal Staff Corps, a military engineering unit, at Hythe, England, in 1809. He served in the Peninsular War and in 1820 was posted to Montreal, where he was engaged in supervising construction of the Lachine Canal, and the Grenville Canal on the Ottawa River. He returned to England in 1824. Longmore never again resided in his native land, although he did seek an appointment there in the late 1840s, and a younger brother settled, and both his parents died, in Canada. Before going on half-pay with the rank of major in 1832, he had been acting surveyor-general of Mauritius for three years. In 1834 he received an appointment in Cape Colony, where he served successively as stipendiary magistrate, as aide-de-camp to two governors, and finally as librarian and sergeant-at-arms to the legislative assembly of the colony. He was also active in the cultural life of the Cape, publishing many uncollected poems and stories in periodicals, in addition to seven volumes of poetry.

In the early 1820s, while he was in Montreal, Longmore published anonymously *The charivari; or Canadian poetics: a tale after the manner of Beppo* (Montreal, 1824), by 'Launcelot Longstaff'. A humorous poem in 179 *ottava rima* stanzas, it is modelled on Byron's *Beppo* (1818) and tells of the courtship and marriage-day of an old bachelor, Baptisto, and the young widow of his choice, Annette. The protagonists were said, at the time, to be well-known Montreal residents, and the work itself comments satirically on many aspects of Montreal life. A charivari—in its earliest form the noisy serenading of a newly married couple on their wedding night—had become in Montreal the means by which mobs, not always good-humoured, extorted funds for drink or charity from well-to-do bridegrooms. During a riotous charivari in 1823 a passerby had been shot, a house destroyed, and participants on both sides were forced to flee the country. There were public demands that charivaris be outlawed. Longmore's portrayal of a charivari with a happy ending was intended to suggest that the custom was an innocent one that did not necessarily lead to riot and destruction. Before Longmore's identity as the author of *The charivari* was established, an attribution of the work to Levi ADAMS had long been accepted.

Another work of Canadian interest by Longmore is 'Tecumthé', a poem as long as *The charivari*, which appeared in *The Canadian Review and Literary and Historical Journal* (Dec. 1824). An account of the great chief's life and death, and of the early years of the War of 1812, 'Tecumthé' focuses principally on its hero and his life—unlike John RICHARDSON's *Tecumseh*, published four years later, in which the events of the war have as much prominence as the life of Tecumseh. It was included in the anonymous *Tales of chivalry and romance* (Edinburgh and London, 1826), along with other long and short poems, many of which had been published in Montreal periodicals.

Longmore also published, under his own name, a 250-page verse account of the Peninsular War, *The war of the isles* (Edinburgh and London, 1826), and a play, *Mathilde; or the Crusaders* (Edinburgh and London, 1827).

In verse form, and in their Romantic subject matter, all Longmore's works owe much to the influence of Byron and Scott. At his best when writing about people, places, and events of which he had first-hand knowledge—and showing flashes of wit in his early works that seem to have disappeared in his later publications—Longmore was an amateur versifier, but an unusually competent one: rough metre or awkward rhymes are rare in his poetry.

See M.L. MacDonald, 'George Longmore: a new literary ancestor', *Dalhousie Review* (Summer 1979), and 'Further light on the life: George Longmore in Cape Colony', *Canadian Poetry*, no. 24 (Spring/Summer 1989). The Canadian Poetry Press at the University of Western Ontario has published modern annotated editions of *The charivari* and *Tecumthé* edited by D.M.R. Bentley.

MARY LU MacDONALD

Loranger, Françoise (1913-95). Born in Saint-Hilaire, Quebec, she studied literature and science in Montreal and then began working in 1939 as a writer for the CBC in Montreal. Her early radio dramas (*L'école des parents, Ceux qu'on aime, La vie commence demain*) showed her gifts for authentic dialogue and psychological penetration. Her first published work, *Mathieu* (1949), is a well-written novel that describes the anguish of a young man in revolt against the repressive atmosphere of Duplessis's Quebec. Critics praised its free-flowing style and the refined psychological observation of Mathieu. Loranger's career moved quite naturally towards the spoken word and she became a key figure in French-Canadian television drama. In the 1950s, 1960s, and early 1970s her television plays (*Madame la présidente*; *Georges... oh! Georges*, 1965; *Un cri qui vient de loin*, 1966; *Un si bel automne*, 1971; *Jour après jour*, 1971); and serials (*À moitié sage and Sous le signe du lion*) helped her to perfect her skills as a playwright. In a province where the family was seen to be eternal and untouchable, she was regarded as having been prophetic in her descriptions of family break-ups and strife.

Loranger became known internationally in 1965 when the Théâtre du Rideau Vert performed *Une maison ... un jour* (1965) in Montreal, France, and Russia. In this very successful play, centred on the theme of departure—departure from one's parents and ultimately from life itself—the dialogue is poetic and lyrical and the various episodes comment on the decaying morals and values of bourgeois Québécois. *Encore cinq minutes* (1967), which won a Governor General's Award, is another psychological play (with feminist overtones) that describes a family break-up symbolized by the cracking walls of the house. A critical and box-office success, it is perhaps Loranger's best traditional play.

Le chemin du roi (1969), which Loranger wrote with Claude Levac, represented a turning-point in her career as a playwright: it shows a change of themes (anti-bourgeois theatre giving way to political theatre) and of technique (towards participatory theatre). Lester B. Pearson, John Diefenbaker, Jean Marchand, and Judy LaMarsh (prominent Ottawa politicians) play a hockey game against Daniel Johnson, Jean Lesage, and René Lévesque (Quebec politicians), while General de Gaulle acts as a kind of referee. Fast-paced and elaborately staged, and requiring the actors to change roles continually, *Le chemin du roi* (the King's Highway, on which de Gaulle travelled from Quebec to Montreal in 1967) shows the influence of Brecht, Artaud, Pirandello, Grotowski, the Living Theatre, and the Open Theatre, though it develops an original approach to the relationship between actors and audience, exploiting identification and physical participation to the utmost. It was first produced at the Theâtre de Gésu, Montreal, in 1968 and was a commercial success.

In *Double jeu* (1969), performed by La Comédie canadienne, Loranger attempted to create a 'happening' (audience participation) and a psychodrama (therapeutic acting-out of a situation to allow the spectators to learn more about themselves). Unfortunately the story of impossible romantic love that the audience is supposed to enact is too mystical and abstract to permit effective and spontaneous participation. *Médium saignant* (1970), 'a patriotic play' about the 'good guys' who favour French unilingualism and the 'bad guys' who believe in freedom of choice for the language of education, is too simplistic and stereotyped to endure. It had a brief success, but it lacks the nuanced ideology and effective caricature used in *Le chemin du roi*.

Loranger left behind a body of work that, in the minds of most Quebeckers, remains resolutely inscribed within the social events of the Quiet Revolution and the political debates of the early 1970s. While few of the political and linguistic issues raised in plays such as *Double jeu* or *Médium saignant* have been resolved, her theatre continues to resonate within Quebec, as a highly successful collage of her texts, *Signé Loranger*, mounted in 1994 and in 1995, revealed. Some saw Loranger's silence in her later years as a reaction to the general incomprehension of her support of an incident surrounding a 1970 performance of *Double jeu* in which a group from the audience mounted the stage, undressed, and then wrung the neck of a dove. Loranger, present at the performance, understood the gesture as a subversive act of theatrical sublimation and defended the group in a text published in LIBERTÉ (1970).

See J.-C. Godin and L. Mailhot, 'Françoise Loranger ou la maison éclatée', *Théâtre québécois* (1970); Jean-Pierre Crête, *Françoise Loranger, à la recherche d'une identité* (1974); J-M. Duciaume, 'Françoise Loranger: du théâtre libre au problème de la liberté', *Le théâtre canadien-français: archives des lettres canadiennes* (1976); *Québec français* 28 (1977), a special issue on Loranger; C.F. Coates, 'From feminism to nationalism: the theatre of Françoise Loranger', in Paula Gilbert Lewis, ed., *Traditionalism, nationalism and feminism: women writers of Quebec* (1985); and T. Marois, 'Recherche et affirmation d'une identité québécoise dans l'oeuvre de Françoise Loranger', *The French Review* 59, 6 (1986).

DONALD SMITH/SHAUN HUFFMAN

Loranger, Jean-Aubert (1896-1942). Born in Montreal, Quebec, into a well-known family of writers and jurists, he received a private education. After a few brief jobs he began a career as a journalist that led him successively from *La Patrie* (1923-7) to *La Presse* (1927-30) and—after a two-year interruption as private secretary to the minister of marine in Ottawa—to Jean-Charles HARVEY's weekly, *Le Jour* (1938-9), then back to *La Patrie* (1939-42). He became news editor of *Montréal-Matin* just before his sudden death.

At the end of the First World War Loranger's cousin Robert Laroque de ROQUEBRUNE introduced him to the Montreal literary milieu through a group of intellectuals that met in Fernand Préfontaine's Westmount literary salon. In 1918 this group founded *Le* NIGOG, an avant-garde review that extolled freedom of inspiration and expression in the arts. An avid reader of *La Nouvelle Revue Française* and of contemporary French writers (Apollinaire, Proust, Saint-John Perse), Loranger was influenced for a time by the *unanimiste* doctrine of such writers as Charles Vildrac and Jules Romains, and published in quick succession *Les atmosphères. Le passeur. Poëmes et autres proses* (1920) and *Poëmes* (1922). The critics were nonplussed by these collections. Their themes, however, were not so astonishing: obsession with departures for foreign shores; disillusionment and despair in the face of unfulfilled longing; loneliness; marking time; old age and the pangs of death. Loranger's modernity was rather a matter of form: a foreshortened elliptical quality; succinct, incisive imagery; bold metaphors; and simple, anti-declamatory syntax.

Besides poetry, Loranger published between 1918 and 1942 many stories. They were first collected in *À la recherche du régionalisme. Le village. Contes et nouvelles du terroir* (1925), and then many more appeared in the review *Les Idées*, in the weekly *Le Jour*, and in the daily *La Patrie*. In these stories the experimental poet, surprisingly, is a traditional storyteller 'in search of a certain regionalism'. Loranger's tales of local customs and anecdotes make use of traditional themes and characters, local colour, and the rich lexicon of colloquial language.

In the seventies critics granted Loranger a place between NELLIGAN and SAINT-DENYS-GARNEAU in modern Quebec poetry, noting the reconciliation he had attempted between the regional and the exotic in literature between the wars. Gilles MARCOTTE wrote a preface to a new edition of Loranger's poems, *Les atmosphères, suivi de Poëmes* (1970)—though this does not include the remaining fragments of a lost manuscript, 'Terra nova'—and Bernadette Guilmette edited and introduced a complete edition of the *Contes* (1978). *Ellipse*, no. 20 (1977) contains poems and prose by Loranger (with translations) followed by a study of his work.

See Marcel DUGAS, *Littérature canadienne, aperçus* (1929); Robert Giroux, 'Patterns in Jean-Aubert Loranger' in *Ellipse*, no. 20 (1977); Gilles MARCOTTE, 'Jean-Aubert Loranger' in *Écrits du Canada français*, no. 35 (1972); and Bernadette Guilmette, 'Jean-Aubert Loranger, du *Nigog* à l'École littéraire de Montréal', in *L'École littéraire de Montréal* (1972).

RICHARD GIGUÈRE

Loved and the lost, The (1951). One of Morley CALLAGHAN's most successful novels, *The loved and the lost* is set in downtown Montreal:

the Ritz Carlton Hotel, the Montreal Forum where the Canadiens play, the night clubs and restaurants of the inner city, and the grand residences of upper Westmount. Jim McAlpine, an ambitious former university professor who is hoping to become a political columnist on the Montreal *Sun*, has come to the city at the invitation of the newspaper's publisher Joseph Carver. He is attracted to Carver's wealth and power and by his daughter Catherine. But he also becomes involved with another woman, Peggy Sanderson, who has dropped out of middle-class society (long before that became a life-style) and spends much of her time in the city's small black community. Trying at one point to explain herself to McAlpine, Peggy says that 'all kinds of people walk in on me.' Finally the wrong person walks in and she is brutally murdered. McAlpine's involvement with her destroys his prospects at the *Sun*, but he has already been destroyed by her death, and by his conviction that he has betrayed her by not being constant. Admired and enjoyed for its elements of an urban thriller, for its affecting love story and the subtle exploration of Peggy Sanderson, *The loved and the lost* won a Governor General's Award, and a paperback edition sold half a million copies in Canada and the United States. It was in large part because of reading this book that the American critic Edmund Wilson described Callaghan in *The New Yorker* as 'perhaps the most unjustly neglected novelist in the English-speaking world . . . a writer whose work may be mentioned without absurdity in association with Chekhov's and Turgenev's.'

ROBERT WEAVER

Lowell, Robert Traill Spence. See FOREIGN WRITERS ON CANADA IN ENGLISH: 2 and Writing in NEWFOUNDLAND.

Lowry, Malcolm (1909-57). Clarence Malcolm Lowry—who also went by the name of Malcolm Boden Lowry—was born in Birkenhead, England, a Cheshire dormitory-town to Liverpool, where his father was a wealthy cotton-broker with Methodist affiliations. Educated in upper-middle-class schools, Lowry early displayed—especially in an enthusiasm for jazz, which led him in his teens to attempt a career as a song-writer—an inclination to break away from the business life his family assumed he would follow and that his brothers accepted. This inclination to escape was first expressed actively when, in 1928, he signed on as a cabin-boy on a freighter bound for the China coast, an experience whose more harrowing aspects found a place in his first novel, *Ultramarine* (1933); however, it did not prevent him from sailing two years later as deckhand on a ship bound for Oslo, where he sought the Norwegian novelist Nordahl Grieg, whose novel *The ship sails on* (1927) greatly influenced Lowry's early work. Already Lowry's growing enthusiasm for literature had led him into a correspondence with the American poet and novelist Conrad Aiken, who took him as a paying guest in the summer of 1929 and whose *Blue voyage* (1927) impressed Lowry and finds an echo in *Ultramarine*. In the autumn of 1929 Lowry entered St Catherine's College, Cambridge, graduating in 1932; but his encounters with Aiken, Grieg, and younger writers he met at Cambridge contributed far more to his literary persona than did his academic studies.

At Cambridge, Lowry began seriously to write. *Ultramarine* was completed in 1932; rewritten after the manuscript had been stolen from the car of a publisher's reader, it finally appeared in 1933. This was the unusual beginning of a strange literary career that was marked by intense industry and little apparent production. Lowry published only two books during his lifetime: *Ultramarine* (which he later rejected as immature) and *Under the volcano* (1947). Another of his novels, *In ballast to the white sea*, was lost, this time irretrievably—burnt in 1945 when a fire destroyed the shack Lowry inhabited at Dollarton, British Columbia. But his scanty publication was due mainly to an obsessional inability to complete to his own satisfaction any work longer than a short story. During the years following the completion of *Under the volcano* in 1945, he worked on a whole cycle of novels, of which it would form part: this was to be entitled *The voyage that never ends*.

Two of the novels intended for inclusion in this cycle—*Dark as the grave wherein my friend is laid* and *October ferry to Gabriola*—were published posthumously, in 1968 and 1970 respectively; but in neither case was the final form Lowry's own, for the editors (Margerie Lowry, his wife, and Douglas Day in the first case and Margerie Lowry in the second) had to deal with chaotic manuscripts offering alternative versions of many passages. Other works by Lowry published after his death are *Lunar caustic* (1963), a novella; *Hear us O Lord from heaven Thy dwelling place* (1961), a collection of short stories; *Selected poems* (1962), edited by Lowry's friend Earle BIRNEY; *Selected letters* (1965), edited by Harvey Breit and Margerie Lowry; and *Psalms and songs* (1975), edited by Margerie Lowry, a miscellany bringing together some early and late stories, most of them previously uncollected, with a few recollections by friends and acquaintances. *La mordida* (1996), a scholarly edition prepared by Patrick A.McCarthy, was meant to be part of *The voyage that never ends* cycle.

In these works one can trace Lowry's physical journey through life, shadowed by alcoholism and paranoia, and an inner journey marked by spiritual hopes and terrors. His life, between leaving Cambridge and his death twenty-five years later, falls into three periods. First was the time of wandering, in Spain and France, Mexico, and the United States. During this period he married his first wife, Jan Gabrial, in 1933; went to Hollywood in 1935; and in 1936 travelled to Mexico, which made a profound and morbid impression on him and inspired *Under the volcano*, the first draft of which he completed in 1937. In 1938—his first marriage having foundered—he left Mexico for the United States and in 1939 reached Canada, where he married Margerie Bonner in 1940 and lived until 1954, mainly in a beach shack at Dollarton. The profound impression his Canadian years made on him is shown not only in the stories contained in *Hear us O Lord* but also in *October ferry to Gabriola*. There were interludes spent in Oakville and Niagara-on-the-Lake, Ontario, and again in Mexico (a disastrous second journey which was the basis of *La mordida*) and in Haiti, before he left Canada in 1954. He died—apparently of a combined overdose of alcohol and barbiturates—at Ripe, Sussex, in the summer of 1957. The coroner's verdict was 'Death by misadventure'.

Under the volcano has often been treated as Lowry's only successful work; it is without doubt his best. In this story of the murder of an alcoholic British consul, the human drama is integrated in a closely knit formal and metaphorical structure, and the sinister aspects of Mexico are used admirably to symbolize the metaphysical overtones; the strong autobiographical element is admirably subsumed in the fiction. In none of the other novels is the structural integration so complete. The facts and preoccupations of Lowry's life are insistently obvious in all, though *October ferry to Gabriola* presents a deeply moving, if imperfect, counterpart to *Under the volcano* and represents Lowry's Paradiso as compared with his Inferno.

Critical studies include Sherrill E. Grace, *The voyage that never ends: Malcolm Lowry's fiction* (1982), C.J. Ackerley and Lawrence J. Clipper, *A companion to Under the Volcano* (1984), Sherrill E. Grace, ed., *New perspectives on Malcolm Lowry* (1992), and Patrick A. McCarthy, *Forest of symbols: world, text, and self in Malcolm Lowry's fiction* (1994). Biographies are Douglas Day, *A biography of Malcolm Lowry* (1973) and Gordon Bowker, *Pursued by furies: a life of Malcolm Lowry* (1993). For Lowry's correspondence see Cynthia Sugars, ed., *The letters of Conrad Aiken and Malcolm Lowry* (1992), and Sherrill E. Grace, ed., *Sursum corda! The collected letters of Malcolm Lowry* (two volumes, 1991, 1994). See also *The collected poetry of Malcolm Lowry* (1992), edited by K.D. Scherf and C.J. Ackerley.

GEORGE WOODCOCK

Lowther, Pat (1935-75). Born in Vancouver, Patricia Tinmuth came from a working-class background. Her mother was a dancer and her father was a sheet-metal worker who suffered spinal meningitis shortly before her birth. She left school at sixteen and took office jobs to support her writing. At eighteen she married Bill Domphousse, a fellow worker at the North Vancouver Shipbuilding Company, with whom she had two children. They were divorced, and in 1963 she married Roy Lowther, a public-school teacher and activist who was eventually dismissed for his radical politics. Before her untimely death, Pat Lowther had been elected president of the LEAGUE OF CANADIAN POETS and was teaching creative writing at the University of British Columbia. In 1977 her husband was convicted of her murder.

Pat Lowther published three books of poetry in her lifetime: *This difficult flowring* (1968), *The age of the bird* (1972), and *Milk stone* (1974). *A stone diary* (1977) was accepted for publication by Oxford University Press Canada before she died and was published posthumously. A last collection, *Pat Lowther: final instructions: early uncollected poems*, edited by Dona Sturmanis and Fred Candelaria, was published as an issue of *West Coast Review* in 1980.

This difficult flowring, illustrated by S. Slutsky and published by Very Stone House, is a vindication of the small publishing house: drawings and poems work in a fine balance. Lowther began tentatively as a poet with a variety of technical experiments in image and form (chants, poems for voices, compositions by field in the style of the American Black Mountain school of poetry). The poems explore varieties of female experience, and include some of the more convincing poems about motherhood—the body occupied by new life as the mind is by the poem. They try to make sense out of the pain, and normalcy, of private domestic life. Deeply influenced by the Chilean poet Pablo Neruda, Lowther had a political motive: the poems search for a new celebratory attitude to the body, to oppose the chameleon-like conformity that defines modern social life. Their directive cry is 'Be human'.

In her later books Lowther discovered the enduring obsessions that was to become a focus in her poetry: life juxtaposed with the natural cycle; atavistic relations between man and woman as primitive giants trapped in the 'Janus-pain' of love. West Coast Native mythology provided metaphors for her themes. Animals become spirit symbols of an elemental liberty that is destroyed by domestic rituals. *A stone diary* contains Lowther's best work. Here the poems have the directness and authority of an assured and sophisticated voice; they are simpler in style, and more anecdotal and personal. Their controlling metaphor is the quest for a symbiotic relationship with the landscape, where psyche and landscape engage in a fluid interchange as the poet aligns herself with nature's resistance to the encroachments of technology and mechanism. A sequence dedicated to the memory of Pablo Neruda identifies Lowther's need to assert the poet's political voice. The poems are also preoccupied with pain and violence, and inevitably have a prophetic, elegiac tone: 'Love is an intersection/where I have chosen/unwittingly to die.' Although silenced prematurely, Lowther achieved in this book a range and depth that will give her work a permanent place in Canadian poetry.

See Paul Grescoe, 'Eulogy for a poet', *Canadian*, 5 June 1976, pp. 13-19; and Margaret ATWOOD, 'Last testaments: Pat Lowther and John THOMPSON', *Second words: selected critical prose* (1982). ROSEMARY SULLIVAN

Lozeau, Charles-Joseph-Albert (1878-1924). Born in Montreal, Quebec, he contracted Pott's disease (spinal tuberculosis) at age thirteen and was paralysed and bedridden from 1896. He thus attended only primary school with any regularity, and was largely self-taught. His writing was published in various periodicals in the 1890s, and his friend Charles GILL, who guided his continuing literary education, arranged to have his work included in the ÉCOLE LITTÉRAIRE DE MONTRÉAL's *Soirées du Château de Ramezay* (1900). Lozeau was a corresponding member of the École from 1904 to 1907. In 1911 he was made a member of the Royal Society of Canada, and in 1912 he was honoured by the French government. At the time of his death he was editing his *Poésies complètes* (3 vols: *L'âme solitaire*, 1907; *Le miroir des jours*, 1912; and *Lauriers et feuilles d'érable*, 1916), published in 1925-6.

Lozeau's views of the world and society were circumscribed by the view from his window and the visits of a few friends. In his subtle, understandably intimate poetry, he reflects on time and the melancholy of the seasons, evoking the 'dangerous charm' of autumn, with its skeletal trees and bare roofs, its muffled grey shades of dust and ashes, smoke and fog: 'Et du gris sur du gris comme une cendre pleut.' Lozeau's 'I' is exceptionally subjective for its time and gives expression to the genuine feelings and private vision of a definite personality: 'Tout l'espace est en moi, qui vibre clairement;/Je l'ai bu du regard de moment en moment.' Lozeau avoided any patriotic or regionalist tendencies in his treatment of nature and the land.

An anthology of his work, *Albert Lozeau* (1958), is available in the 'Classiques canadiens' series. The editor, Yves de Margerie, also published an article about Lozeau in volume 2 of the *Archives des lettres canadiennes* (1972).

MARTA HORBAN-CARYNNYK

Ludwig, Jack (b. 1922). A native of Winnipeg, he graduated from the University of Manitoba in 1944 and moved to California to pursue a career as a writer. He later took a Ph.D. in English at UCLA (1953) and taught at Williams College (Mass.), Bard College (N.Y.), the University of Minnesota, and the State University of New York at Stony Brook. (While at Bard he co-founded, with colleagues Saul Bellow and Keith Botsford, the little magazine *The Noble Savage*.)

Ludwig achieved prominence at the end of the 1960s with two novels that brought a ribald tall-tale quality to the mordant, self-ironizing tradition of social satire also visible in work of such Jewish contemporaries as Bellow, Philip Roth, and Mordecai RICHLER. The first of these, *Confusions* (1963), is a comedy of manners and academic satire that details the confusion and cultural dislocation of an American Jew who tries to master the 'Ivy League mythology' of Harvard, only to wind up on the faculty of a California university for which neither his working-class Jewish background nor his Harvard-acquired credentials and style have prepared him. *Above ground* (1968) is another story of confusion and constant change, the semi-autobiographic account of a boy who, despite a childhood injury that hospitalizes him for an extended period and leaves him permanently lame, pursues the 'bait of life' and grows into a man who falls in love with one woman after another. Like *Confusions*, *Above ground* is a comic monologue delivered by a man trying to sort out the dark and consuming reality that he believes lurks behind life's everyday appearances. Although this novel is partly, in the modernist tradition, a descent beneath the surfaces of life, it also anticipates the pattern of Margaret ATWOOD's *Surfacing* by showing its protagonist's struggle to emerge back into a daylight world 'above ground'. (Ludwig's title responds to Dostoyevsky's 'Notes from underground'.) In an early critical monograph, *Recent American novelists* (1962), Ludwig wrote that the novelists of his generation were 'turning from the Kafkaesque "Underground Man" towards an "Aboveground Man"', the hero who breaks out of his real, or symbolic, sealed-off room to re-enter the world of action and history.'

In Ludwig's novella *A woman of her age* (1973) the central character makes just such a re-entry—in her 85th year. This expansion of a short story, first published in *The TAMARACK REVIEW* 12 (1959), offers an affecting portrait of Doba Goffman, an old woman in the Montreal Jewish community. The 'confusions' of Ludwig's earlier novel recur as Doba tries to understand her perplexing metamorphosis from youthful radical to wealthy matron.

Around this time Ludwig turned from fiction to a literate sports journalism with *Hockey night in Moscow* (1972; expanded and published in the USA as *The great hockey thaw, or the Russians are here*, 1974). His essays, published in *Maclean's* and *The Canadian*, were collected in *Games of fear and winning* and published in 1976, the year Ludwig also published *Five-ring circus*, about the Montreal Olympics, and *The great American spectaculars*, a chronicle of a year's 'big events' in America—such as the Kentucky Derby, the Indianopolis 500, the political conventions, and the Rose Bowl.

Critical pieces on Ludwig include 'Anatomy of confusion: Jack Ludwig's evolution' by Lila Stonehewer (some have suspected this name of being a pseudonym for Ludwig himself), *CANADIAN LITERATURE* 29 (Summer 1996); E. James, 'Ludwig's confusions', *Canadian Literature* 40 (Spring 1969); Russell Brown, 'The Canadian eve', *Journal of Canadian Fiction* 3, no. 1 (1974); and Margaret LAURENCE's introduction to the 1974 NEW CANADIAN LIBRARY edition of *Above ground*.

RUSSELL BROWN

Lunn, Janet (b. 1928). Born Janet Louise Swoboda in Dallas, Texas, she attended high school in Ottawa, and Queen's University, Kingston, Ontario. She married the late Richard Lunn in 1950 and lives in Ontario's Prince Edward County, a location that provides the background for much of her writing. Her first novel for children, *Double spell* (1968), is the story of twin girls who find an antique doll that leads them into the past, to 1840s Toronto. A highly readable, neatly constructed tale, it combines elements of traditional domestic fiction—big happy family, rambling ramshackle house, rambunctious dog—with conventions of the ghost story: unseen forces and psychic disturbances. More ambitious in narrative and emotional scope are the two novels set in Lunn's home territory. *The root cellar* (1981) is a time-travel narrative in which young Rose travels geographically from southern Ontario to Washington, D.C., and historically from the present to the period just after the American Civil War. Rose, a neglected orphan, finds in her journey a sense of companionship, a realization of her own strengths and the means to integrate facets of her fragile personality. Lunn's able manipulation of the mechanics of time travel and her confident use of historical detail add up to a suspenseful narrative exploring time, continuity, and change. In *Shadow in Hawthorn Bay* (1986) Lunn creates a passionate, almost Gothic tale of a young woman, a Scottish immigrant, who travels to Canada in pursuit of her one true love. Lunn's re-creation of life in the period around 1815 and her powerful evocation of a malevolent landscape provide a vivid background for this story of longing and redemption. Her gift for presenting the past to children is also shown in her pioneer story *One hundred shining candles* (1990), in a collection of historical vignettes, *Larger than life* (1979), and in *The story of Canada* (1992), a lively and substantial illustrated history, written with Christopher Moore. Her picture-book stories—*The twelve dancing princesses* (1979), *Amos's sweater* (1988), and *Duck cakes for sale* (1989)—reveal a pawky wit and expertise in the highly patterned rhythmical prose of children's tales. Lunn, whose books have received many awards, has contributed greatly to the development of children's literature in Canada not only in her writing, but in her longstanding support of the literary community. She was Chair of the WRITERS' UNION OF CANADA for 1984-5.

SARAH ELLIS

Lyall, William (1811-90). Born in Paisley, Scotland, and educated at the universities of Glasgow and Edinburgh, he was ordained into the Church of Scotland and took the part of the Free Church in the Great Disruption of

1843. He came to Toronto as a tutor at Knox College in 1848. In 1850 he moved to Halifax, Nova Scotia, and remained there for the rest of his life, apart from three years in Truro. After a decade at the Free Church College, he taught philosophy at Dalhousie University until his death.

Lyall's major work, *Intellect, the emotions and the moral life* (Edinburgh, 1855)—which was widely read and used in colleges of the Maritime Provinces for half a century—set out to bridge the gap between the intellect and the emotions that had played a central role in philosophy since Plato. Weaving a complex synthesis of common-sense realism and Augustinian neo-Platonism, Lyall argued that the emotions in general, and love in particular, were crucial sources of knowledge and formed an essential basis for action. In Lyall's theory the direct object of an emotion (the source of joy or anger, or the object or person loved or hated) affects the indirect object—the state of mind and character of the person who has that emotion. With the education of the emotions and the imagination, the individual may become aware of more appropriate direct objects; sexual love, for instance, may develop into love of God. (The wide diffusion of Lyall's ideas helps to explain the 'moralistic' trend in Maritimes fiction described by Fred COGSWELL in the *Literary history of Canada*, vol. 1, 2nd edn, 1976.) Lyall's Augustinian political thesis—that the state, though necessary to human beings in their fallen condition, is to be regarded with a measure of suspicion—contrasts sharply with that of his predecessor at Dalhousie, Thomas McCULLOCH, who sought a political order based on a natural relation between human beings and their physical environment. Lyall saw fallen humanity as needing an elaborate political organization, and saw the isolated communities of the Maritimes in the context of a larger world. His ideas thus mark a passage in political thought in the Maritime Provinces towards the era of compromise and negotiation that led to Confederation.

One copy of Lyall's *Sermons* (Edinburgh, 1848) is in the British Museum.

LESLIE ARMOUR, ELIZABETH TROTT

Lysenko, Vera. See UKRAINIAN-CANADIAN LITERATURE.

M

McArthur, Peter (1866-1924). Peter Gilchrist McArthur was born in Ekfrid Township, Middlesex County, Canada West, in a log house now standing at Doon, Ontario, and attended local schools; in 1887 he received a teacher's certificate at the Strathroy Model School. In 1888, after teaching for six months, he entered the University of Toronto—to make ends meet he contributed jokes to *GRIP*—but in 1890 he became a reporter for the *Toronto Mail*. From 1890 to 1895 he freelanced in New York, largely as a jokesmith for *Judge*, *Life*, and *Town Topics*, and then became editor of *Truth* (1895-7). After another period of freelancing in New York, he went to England (1902), where he wrote for Punch and worked on W.T. Stead's *Review of Reviews* and *Daily Paper*. He returned to New York (1904) and opened an advertising agency. It failed, and in 1909, without work or funds, he had to take refuge on the Ekfrid homestead.

While in New York, McArthur had written short stories for *Truth*; a book, *The prodigal and other poems* (1907); and articles for *Ainslie's Magazine* and the *Atlantic Monthly*; in England he had published a satire on Canadian-British relationships, *To be taken with salt; being an essay on teaching one's grandmother to suck eggs* (1903). McArthur made his name at Ekfrid, however, with his articles for the Toronto *Globe* (1909-24) and the *Farmer's Advocate* (1910-22). From these were drawn *In pastures green* (1915), *The red cow and her friends* (1919), *Around home* (1925), and *Friendly acres* (1927). Centring on pioneers and the simple life, farm activities, and farm animals (which he treats mainly as comic characters), the delights of nature and an almost Messianic 'back- to-the-land' message, these essays made him the leading Canadian writer in the rural tradition. They also disclosed his gift for humour, which gave him special insight for his critical study *Stephen Leacock* (1923).

McArthur also wrote many essays about politics and economics—subjects that were central to *Ourselves* (1910-12), his farm magazine for 'Cheerful Canadians'; his eulogistic *Sir Wilfrid Laurier* (1919); and his commentary on American society and the threatened decay of its cities, *The affable stranger* (1920). McArthur's attacks on big business notwithstanding, he was always devising schemes (even one for Henry Ford to make money), and in 1922 became a trust-company executive. Inconsistent as this may seem, McArthur considered insurance to be peoples' capitalism, protecting farmers and thereby rural independence—his favourite form of financial organization. McArthur's discussions of farm politics and economics, despite questionable arguments (and heavy-handed satire), add much to the vital and imaginative treatment of old-time rural life. ALEC LUCAS

Macbeth, Madge (1881-1965). Born in Philadelphia, USA, Madge Hamilton Lyons was educated at Hellmuth Ladies' College, London, Ontario. She then married Charles Macbeth and moved in 1904 to Ottawa, where she supported her two young sons as a writer when she became a widow, and where she remained until her death. The granddaughter of Louisa Hart Maffitt, one of the first professional American press women, Macbeth began working as an Ottawa journalist in 1908. She wrote several regular columns in magazines and newspapers, including 'Over my shoulder', which was featured in the *Ottawa Citizen* throughout the 1950s.

'Frieda's engagement' (1908)—included in *New women: short stories by Canadian women, 1900-1920* (1991), edited by Sandra Campbell and Lorraine McMullen—was Macbeth's first short story published in Canada. Hundreds of magazine articles, and stories and twenty novels, appeared between 1910 and 1965. Among her early works are the novels *The changeling* (1909), *The winning game* (1910), and *The Patterson limit* (1923). Macbeth used various pseudonyms throughout her career, notably 'Gilbert Knox' for her satires *The land of afternoon* (1924), a scathing and controversial commentary on political and social intrigue at Government House, Ottawa, and *The kinder bees* (1935), also about life in Ottawa. She created controversy through her frank discussions of sexuality, particularly in *Shackles* (1926), *Lost: a cavalier* (1947), and *Shreds of circumstance* (1947).

A fervent nationalist and outspoken advocate of a national radio system, Macbeth was a key figure behind the establishment of what would become the Canadian Broadcasting Corporation as well as being instrumental in the creation of the CANADIAN AUTHORS' ASSOCIATION (and its first female, and only three-time national president).

Macbeth's 'The superwoman' (1926) is reputed to be the first Canadian play written for radio, and her novel *Kleath* (1917) was adapted for film in the 1920s. She published two travel books and two autobiographies—*Over my shoulder* (1953) and *Boulevard career* (1957)—which provide accounts of changes occurring in Canada and elsewhere between 1920 and 1950. TARA L. CURTIS

McCaffery, Steve (b. 1947). Born in Sheffield, England, he became interested in alternative poetry while studying at the University of Hull. Immigrating to Canada in 1968, and specializing in linguistics, epistemology, and literary criticism, he conducted graduate studies at York University. McCaffery has since taught at the University of California, and Queen's University, Kingston, Ontario. Early in his career he moved from text to performance as a condition of writing beyond the book. His collaboration with the sound-poetry group the FOUR HORSEMEN began in 1970. He has published nearly twenty books, however, including *Theory of sediment* (1991), nominated for a Governor General's Award, and *The black debt* (1990), nominated for the Before Columbus Award (USA).

Influenced by Dadaism, Surrealism, and 'pataphysics' (a late nineteenth-century absurdist movement initiated by the French dramatist Alfred Jarry), and applying theories of Wittgenstein, Barthes, Derrida, Bataille, Deleuze, and Guattari, McCaffery abandoned mainstream conventions of genre and logic. In his often satiric performances at international festivals of poetry, he dislocates narrative through multiple perspectives and shifting voices, thereby redefining boundaries between artist and audience through sound-poetry, video, film, audio-recording, choreography, and performance art. He is documented in Michael ONDAATJE's film *Sons of Captain Poetry* (1971). In the mid-1970s and early 1980s, with Charles Bernstein and others, McCaffery developed the L=A=N=G=U=A=G=E school of writing, which investigates connections between cognition and linguistics. McCaffery's *Rational geomancy* (1992), a collection of reports, essays, and manifestos co-written with bp NICHOL under the name TRG (Toronto Research

Group), is both a logical and an intuitive inquiry into the multiple forms of postmodern writing. Partly in response to MCLUHAN's notion that the 'medium is the message', McCaffery engages the reader in a satiric, self-reflexive, and often parodic loop through his analyses of performance, pataphysics, the book as machine, visual and sound poetry, anti-narrative, and a host of contemporary writers and theoreticians. A frequent writer/artist-in-residence, McCaffery has lectured widely on postmodern literature at Oxford University (1992), the Modern Languages Association (1994), and Yale University (1995). He helps edit the magazine *OPEN LETTER*, and has edited several anthologies of sound poetry and language poetry, including *Imagining language* (1996). McCaffery's recent collection of poetry *The cheat of words* (1996) exemplifies Umberto Eco's innovative notion of the open text by illustrating how layers of surprisingly ironic meanings are generated when the conventional meaning of language is unsettled.

See Clint Burnham, *Canadian writers and their works* (vol. 12, 1996); Frederick Garber, *Repositionings* (1995); and Marjorie Perloff, *Radical artifice* (1991). See also POETRY IN ENGLISH 1950 TO 1982: 3.

KARL JIRGENS

McCall, Christina (b. 1935). Born in Toronto, Ontario, she attended Jarvis Collegiate and in 1956 graduated in English Language and Literature from Victoria College, University of Toronto, where her professors included Northrop FRYE, E.J. PRATT, and Kathleen Coburn (English); Donald CREIGHTON and Bertie Wilkinson (history); and C.B. Macpherson (political science). During her marriage (1959-77) to Peter NEWMAN, she pursued a career as an increasingly influential political journalist known for the grace and clarity of her writing and for her skill as a researcher and analyst. She was associate editor, then Ottawa editor, of *Chatelaine* (1958-62); Ottawa columnist for *Saturday Night* (1967-9) and executive editor (1976-80); associate editor of *Maclean's* (1971-3); and National Reporter for Toronto's *Globe and Mail* (1975-6). From 1962 to 1975 she was a researcher and creative editor for her husband, contributing substantially to his articles and books, and was under contract to co-author with him a work to be called *The anatomy of Canada*, which was later published in two volumes by Newman as *The Canadian establishment* (1975, 1981). She spent two years writing *Grits: an intimate portrait of the Liberal Party* (1983), the 'intimate portrait' of the subtitle having been made possible by the author's first-hand acquaintance with Ottawa in the Lester Pearson/early Trudeau years, her skilled use of 174 interviews, and her gift for weaving subtle political analyses, probing character sketches, and memorable anecdotes into a compelling narrative. It won a CANADIAN AUTHORS' ASSOCIATION Award and was short-listed for a Governor General's Award.

In 1978 McCall married Stephen Clarkson (b. 1937), professor of political science at the University of Toronto, and from 1984 to 1994 she collaborated with him on *Trudeau and our times*, a masterly two-volume study of the Trudeau era that is partly a political/intellectual biography of Pierre Elliott Trudeau. Volume 1, *The magnificent obsession* (1990), which won a Governor General's Award, covers the Trudeau ministry from 1968 to 1979 and describes his prolonged effort to fulfil his obsession for patriating the Canadian constitution and entrenching within it a charter of rights and freedoms. Volume 2, *The heroic delusion* (1994), in which this goal was achieved, deals mainly with his ministry from 1980 to 1984, which reflected his mistaken belief that Canada could remain both liberal and autonomous in an increasingly integrated North America. Illuminating their eminent subject and those who served him, and clarifying political intricacies—and the impact on Canadians of the Trudeau era—the authors elevated the writing of Canadian political history by combining literary distinction, original perceptions, and unimpeachable scholarship. A French translation was published in Montreal under the titles *Trudeau: l'homme, l'utopie, l'histoire* (1990) and *Trudeau: l'illusion héroique* (1995).

WILLIAM TOYE

McCarroll, James (1814?-92). Born in County Longford, Ireland, and educated in the classics and music, he immigrated to Canada in 1831. He settled in Peterborough, Upper Canada (Ontario), and taught music in a grammar school. In the early 1840s he began to publish poetry and developed local political notoriety as the outspoken owner-editor of the pro-Reform Peterboro *Chronicle* (1844-6). When a fire left him bankrupt, McCarroll moved to Cobourg, again teaching music and editing the Newcastle *Courier* (1847-8). Appointed to the Customs Service in Cobourg in 1849, he at last found steady employment to support his growing family. Subsequent postings took him to Port Stamford (Niagara Falls), Port Credit, and Toronto. In each he was active in music and writing.

By 1860 his fame as a flautist and as a poet and story writer was widespread. Settling in Toronto in 1856, he was a music critic for several papers, contributed poems to the *Leader*, and wrote for the *Anglo-American Magazine*, *Home Journal*, and *British-American Magazine*.

McCarroll's literary fame reached its zenith in the early 1860s with the weekly publication of letters to Thomas D'Arcy MCGEE from 'Terry Finnegan'; these appeared in several Toronto satiric magazines, notably the *Grumbler*. Writing in a spirited Irish vernacular, Finnegan identified himself as McGee's 'lovin cousin': his letters paid particular attention to Canadian socio-political conditions and the vulnerable situation of the Irish in the Canadas. McCarroll's Finneganesque attacks on the activities of then-premier John Sandfield Macdonald in the summer of 1863 cost him his Customs position. The 'first series' of the Finnegan letters were published as a book in Toronto in 1864.

A passionate Irish nationalist, McCarroll continued to write for the *Leader* and the *Irish Canadian* (1863) and his own *Latch-Key*, even as his financial situation deteriorated. Finnegan continued to serve as his mouthpiece. Hoping for patronage help from John A. Macdonald and the Conservatives he supported, McCarroll stewed impatiently as his savings vanished and his wife's health deteriorated. To get by, he travelled the province performing a musical-literary show that included Finnegan readings and virtuoso flute solos. With no help forthcoming and virtually penniless, he went to Buffalo to perform in February 1866; he stayed there, becoming editor of the *Fenian Volunteer*. Viewed as a traitor by Canada, he had no choice but to make the United States his home. He took out his frustration and anger on John A. Macdonald in *Ridgeway: an historical romance* (1867), the introduction to which celebrates the many achievements of the Irish and condemns Canada's leaders for so mistreating them.

McCarroll had to recreate himself in New York by means of his pen. After years of journalistic gypsying, he moved to New York City, where he held an editorial position with Frank Leslie's *The Chimney Corner*. He was active in the music and theatrical scene, publishing one play, *Nearly a tragedy: a comedy* (1874), nurturing many friendships among the leading musicians of the day, and working on several inventions. His collected poems, *Madeline, and other poems*, appeared in 1889 when he was working for *Belford's Magazine*.

See Nora Storey, *Oxford Companion to Canadian History and Literature* (1967); Michael Peterman, *James McCarroll, alias Terry Finnegan: newspapers, controversy and literature in Victorian Canada* (1996). MICHAEL PETERMAN

McClelland, Jack (b. 1922). John Gordon McClelland was born in Toronto, the only son of John McClelland, who owned and ran the publishing firm MCCLELLAND & STEWART LIMITED. After attending the University of Toronto Schools and St Andrew's College, he enrolled in maths and physics at the University of Toronto in 1940 and the next year enlisted as a commissioned officer in the Royal Canadian Navy. A skipper on torpedo boats in the English Channel, he was mentioned in dispatches. In 1946 he completed a B.A. at Trinity College, University of Toronto, and married Elizabeth Matchett; they have four daughters and one son.

Jack McClelland joined his father's firm in 1946. Early on he pressed his father to rely less on the distribution of British and American books and to work towards establishing a solid list of Canadian authors. In 1952, when he had become familiar with all aspects of the business, he became president. His intuitive sense of what makes a good manuscript, his formidable energy, and his genius for friendship enabled him to enlist many of the best Canadian authors of his time: Irving LAYTON, Earle BIRNEY, Gabrielle ROY, Leonard COHEN, Sheila WATSON, Roger LEMELIN, Mordecai RICHLER, Margaret LAURENCE, Margaret ATWOOD, and Michael ONDAATJE, to name but a few. With some authors, such as Pierre BERTON and Farley MOWAT, he formed enduring friendships. His motto was 'McClelland and Stewart publish authors, not books.'

A colourful maverick, McClelland was known in publishing circles for the flamboyant gimmicks he used in promotion. His 1982 Molson Prize, however, attested to the enormous contribution he made not only to Canadian publishing, but to Canadian culture in producing a large and diverse list of books that collectively represent the cornerstone of Canadian literature.

In 1982 he appointed his former vice-president of publishing, Linda McKnight, president of the firm, and became chairman of the board and president of Seal Books, a collaborative paperback venture between McClelland & Stewart and Bantam Books.

ELSPETH CAMERON

Even for a man once described as 'the mercurial helmsman' of Canada's most influential publisher, the year 1985 can be best described as volatile. Beginning with the sudden resignation of Linda McKnight, the year ended with the sale of the company, which had been in the McClelland family for almost 80 years. Plagued by financial difficulties that had led a 21-member consortium of investors to step forward the previous year with $1 million in rescue capital, McClelland & Stewart was purchased by Toronto real-estate developer Avram (Avie) Bennett. Although he extended to McClelland a five-year consultancy contract, the full term of this agreement was never realized; McClelland severed all ties with the company after only two years, following a much-publicized and at times publicly antagonistic relationship with Bennett.

In 1987 McClelland sold his controlling interest in Seal Books to Anna Porter, a former M&S executive. Following an ill-fated attempt to establish a Canadian fiction series with HarperCollins publishers in 1989 (M&S threatened a lawsuit under the terms of a non-competition clause signed by the former president), McClelland continued to function as a literary agent until his retirement in 1991.

Criticized at times for his almost fearless disregard for public decorum, McClelland is remembered by many for a lifelong dedication to Canadian writing that the writers Farley and Claire Mowat once described as fueled by equal parts 'faith and conviction and pizzazz'. This lifetime of achievement has been recognized with a host of local and national awards, including McClelland's being named an Officer of the Order of Canada (1976). KLAY DYER

McClelland & Stewart Limited. Founded in 1906 by John McClelland, formerly manager of the library department of the Methodist Book Room (later the RYERSON PRESS), in partnership with Frederick Goodchild from the same company, it began as a library supply house selling books secured from foreign publishers. The imprint 'McClelland and Goodchild' was initiated three years later. In 1910 the new company's first Canadian book, L.M. MONTGOMERY's *Kilmeny of the orchard*, appeared. Three years after it was incorporated in 1911, George Stewart, a Bible salesman from the Methodist Book Room, joined the firm. In 1918 Goodchild formed his own company (Frederick D. Goodchild) and the firm became McClelland & Stewart Limited.

Before the First World War, M&S expanded its activities as agents for British and American firms by starting to build a list of Canadian publications. In 1917 it became the publisher of Ralph Connor (Charles William GORDON); its other Canadian authors at that time included Bliss CARMAN, Marjorie PICKTHALL, Marshall SAUNDERS, Duncan Campbell SCOTT, Isabel Ecclestone MacKay, and Marian Keith (Mary Esther MacGREGOR). Between the wars, books by Stephen LEACOCK, Arthur STRINGER, Frederick Philip GROVE, Laura Goodman SALVERSON, and Thomas H. RADDALL were added to its list.

After the Second World War—under the direction of John (Jack) McCLELLAND, who joined his father's firm in 1946 and became president in 1952—M&S began its steady shift away from handling agencies to concentrate on its Canadian publishing. Three celebrated Quebec novels were published in translation: Gabrielle ROY's *The tin flute* (*BONHEUR D'OCCASION*), which appeared in 1947, and Roger LEMELIN's *The town below* (*Au pied de la pente douce*) and *The Plouffe family* (*Les* PLOUFFE), which appeared in 1948 and 1951 respectively. In the late forties, also, the beautifully designed Indian File Series of poetry books—including collections by James REANEY, Robert FINCH, and Phyllis WEBB—began the strong commitment of M&S to poetry publishing that continues to this day. By 1954 forty per cent of the firm's revenues came from Canadian publications. In 1958 the famous NEW CANADIAN LIBRARY reprint series of major Canadian works was started, and the following year M&S published Irving LAYTON's *A red carpet for the sun*, Mordecai RICHLER's *The APPRENTICESHIP OF DUDDY KRAVITZ*, and Sheila WATSON's *The double hook*. By 1962 it had dropped most of its foreign agencies, a decision that seemed well justified by the commercial success of books by Pierre BERTON, Farley MOWAT, of Peter NEWMAN's *Renegade in power* (1963), Margaret LAURENCE's *The STONE ANGEL* (1964); and, in the years that followed, of subsequent works by these authors and books by Margaret ATWOOD, Earle BIRNEY, Marie-Claire BLAIS, and Leonard COHEN, among other well-known writers. In the area of scholarship, M&S published in 1963 the first two volumes in its 18-volume history of Canada, The Canadian Centenary Series, under the editorship of W.L. MORTON and Donald CREIGHTON. Despite severe financial difficulties (government grants had been successfully sought in 1970 and 1978 to keep the company from folding), there was hardly an area of literature, and of Canadian life, that was not represented by M&S books—which included not only fiction and poetry and a wide range of non-fiction, but children's literature, and school and college textbooks.

In 1982 McClelland appointed his vice-president of publishing, Linda McKnight, president of the firm, and became chairman of the board. He also became president of Seal Books, a collaborative paperback venture between M&S and Bantam Books.

AFTER 1982. In 1985 president and publisher Linda McKnight resigned over a dispute with company chairman Jack MCCLELLAND. This parting marked a kind of sea-change for the publisher, for in December of the same year the company was purchased by Avram (Avie) Bennett, a Toronto real-estate developer whose company had been part of a consortium of twenty-one investors that had raised more than $1 million to save M&S from financial collapse a year earlier. The transition was not without turmoil. Although Bennett signed McClelland to a five-year consultancy contract, they parted after only two years in a much-publicized, and at times publicly acrimonious, falling-out.

Early in 1987 Bennett named former television journalist Adrienne Clarkson as the company's president and publisher. It was during her tenure that M&S's flagship NEW CANADIAN LIBRARY series was redesigned and reset after thirty years; most significantly, a new general editor, David Staines, and an advisory board were brought in, almost all the old titles were allowed to go out of print, and a new format was introduced for the new series, launched in October 1988, that included Afterwords by distinguished writers, critics, and scholars. It was at this time that the company announced its purchase of the prized Canadian rights to James Michener's novel *Journey*. The much-publicized signing included Michener's promise to donate royalties from the Canadian edition to a fund for promising new writers; in 1989 these proceeds were used to establish *The Journey Prize Anthology*, an annual M&S collection of short fiction by young Canadian writers.

September 1988 saw another major redistribution of power within M&S, with Clarkson relinquishing her dual role after only eighteen months. Bennett subsequently resumed the presidency and named Douglas Gibson as his new publisher. Gibson has maintained his own imprint under the M&S banner since 1986, following success in various editorial and publishing capacities at Doubleday (1968-74) and MACMILLAN (1974-86).

While these years of change saw M&S continue to publish such high-profile nonfiction writers as Pierre Berton, Farley Mowat, and Peter Newman, the company was quickly establishing itself as the pre-eminent publisher of Canadian fiction; indeed, many of Canada's best-known writers have attained international distinction under the M&S banner, including Margaret Atwood and Michael Ondaatje. Freelance editor Ellen Seligman, who joined the firm full-time in 1977, rising to the position of editorial director, has provided editorial guidance to a new generation of exceptional fiction writers, including David Adams RICHARDS (*Nights below Station Street*, 1988), Jane URQUHART (*Away*, 1993), and Rohinton MISTRY (*A fine balance*, 1995)—all of whom have garnered prestigious national and international awards for their writing.

The 1990s began at M&S with a high-profile $1.5 million libel suit launched against the company and author Ron GRAHAM by Canadian media mogul Conrad Black for a passage in Graham's book, *God's dominion*, that Black claimed was libelous; in a much-publicized stand, Bennett refused to withdraw copies of the book or delete the passage in question. The suit was finally settled out of court in February 1992. It was also during this time that Bennett established M&S as a key and sometimes controversial player in a number of long-standing battles facing Canadian publishers, notably the struggle to safeguard Canadian copyrights and rights of distribution, and against an increasing governmental inclination to relax limits on foreign investment in the Canadian book business.

Despite these protracted legal scuffles, the company continued to expand. In May 1991, for instance, Bennett ended months of speculation by announcing the purchase of the financially troubled Hurtig Publishers of Edmonton—home to such publishing megaprojects as *The Canadian encyclopedia*, which M&S continued to develop, using CD-ROM technology. More recent moves include the 1995 purchase of Montreal-based Tundra Books, a small but prestigious Montreal publisher specializing in beautifully illustrated children's books, and the acquisition of Reed Books Canada in 1996. The latter move brought to M&S a strong international agency list that includes such luminaries as Margaret Drabble and Roddy Doyle.

No success comes without stumbles. Some once-durable relationships proved difficult to maintain: Pierre Berton, for example, broke his almost four decade-long association with the company in 1995. But as Margaret Atwood said in a speech given to mark the company's ninetieth year: 'That any business has lasted this long is astounding; that the business is a Canadian publishing house is more astounding still.'

ELSPETH CAMERON/KLAY DYER

McClung, Nellie L. (1873-1951). Nellie Letitia Mooney was born on a farm near Chatsworth, Grey County, Ontario, the youngest of six children of Methodist Scotch-Irish parentage. The family moved to Manitoba in 1880 and took up homestead land on the Souris River. Attending school for the first time at age ten, Nellie was enrolled in Winnipeg's Normal School within six years. She taught at rural schools in Manitoba, returning to Winnipeg in 1893-5 to complete high school at the Collegiate Institute. In 1896, having picked out her mother-in-law several years before, she married pharmacist Wesley McClung.

An avid reader of fiction, with a lively imagination and easily stirred sympathies for the voiceless, downtrodden, and unfortunate, Nellie was caught up by the novels of Charles Dickens and the serials in the weekly *Family Herald*. Early ambitions to write stories about the Manitoba country-people she lived among were sidetracked by the responsibilities of her growing family and by her widening activism in temperance and suffrage organizations. She achieved commercial success as a writer with her first book: *Sowing seeds in Danny* (1908; rpr. 1965), which sold over 100,000 copies and helped pave the way for her rise soon afterwards to political prominence. Her political achievements were numerous: she was a prominent member of Winnipeg's Political Equality League, Women's Press Club, Women's Christian Temperance Union, and the CANADIAN AUTHORS' ASSOCIATION, and was a front-line campaigner in the Manitoba elections of 1914 and 1915 that led to the enfranchisement of the province's women in 1916. She gave equally effective leadership in the Alberta suffrage cause after the McClung family's removal to Edmonton (1914), and unrelenting platform service in the campaign for prohibition; was elected to the Alberta legislature as a Liberal in 1921 (she was defeated in 1925); and was one of the 'famous five' who pursued the Persons Case to its successful conclusion in 1930. On her husband's retirement in 1935 the McClungs moved from Calgary, where they had lived since 1923, to Gordon Head, near Victoria, B.C. Here Nellie combined gardening, writing, and continued public service. In 1936 she began a six-year term on the newly formed CBC's Board of Governors, and in 1938 was named a Canadian delegate to the League of Nations conference in Geneva.

McClung published sixteen books and numerous uncollected stories and articles for newspapers and magazines. Her dramatic flair, charisma, and wit reached large audiences across Canada and the USA through her public readings from *Sowing seeds in Danny*, a loosely knit novel about Danny's sister, the dauntless twelve-year-old Pearlie Watson, and her irrepressible Irish family. Two later novels, *The second chance* (1910) and *Purple Springs* (1921), take Pearlie—whose temperament, philosophy, and adventures closely matched those of McClung's—through an independent young womanhood as a teacher and a campaigner for temperance and suffrage, ending with her marriage to an idealistic, progressive doctor. *Painted fires* (1925), McClung's last full-scale novel, showed her lifelong concern for immigrant groups in Canada through the trials of Helmi, a young Finnish girl. McClung's other fiction includes two novellas, *The Black Creek stopping-house and other stories* (1912) and *When Christmas crossed 'The Peace'* (1923), as well as short sketches mixed with personal essays in volumes like *The next of kin* (1917) and *All we like sheep* (1926). *Three times and out* (1918) was her rendition of an escaped prisoner-of-war's experiences in the First World War.

Although McClung's penchant for pathos and moral uplift dates her fiction, the humour and sprightliness of her stories and characters can still offer amusement. McClung could effectively puncture stuffiness and pretension, and she had an ear for the colloquial rhythms and usages of turn-of-the-century westerners. Epigrammatic wit enlivens her novels, stories, sketches, and polemical writing alike, and it is clear that neither McClung nor her early readers cared much for the distinctions of prose forms. She was also adept at sentimental and satiric verse.

Present-day readers will find abundant evidence of McClung's common sense and vivacity in her four collections of newspaper sketches and stories: *Be good to yourself* (1930), *Flowers for the living* (1931), *Leaves from Lantern Lane* (1936), and *More leaves from Lantern Lane* (1937). Of more enduring value, however, are her two fine volumes of autobiography, *Clearing in the West* (1935; rpr. 1976) and *The stream runs fast* (1945; rpr. 1965). *In times like these* (1915), a classic statement of Canadian feminism, was reprinted in 1972 by the University of Toronto Press, with an introduction by V. Strong-Boag.

In *Our Nell: a scrapbook biography of Nellie L. McClung* (1979) Candace Savage has brought together excerpts from McClung's writings, excellent illustrations, and a good bibliography. Mary Lile Bentham's *Nellie McClung* (1975) is a reliable booklet for schools. See also Mary E. Hallett, *Firing the heather: the life and times of Nellie McClung* (1993) and R.R. Warne, *Literature as pulpit: the Christian social activism of Nellie L. McClung* (1993).

SUSAN JACKEL

McCormack, Derek. See NOVELS IN ENGLISH 1983 TO 1996: OTHER NOVELS 2(b).

McCormack, Eric. See NOVELS IN ENGLISH 1983 TO 1996: OTHER NOVELS 4.

McCourt, Edward (1907-72). Edward Alexander McCourt was born in Mullinger, Ireland, and brought to Canada in 1909; he grew up on a farm outside Kitscoty, Alberta. After taking his high-school education by correspondence, he studied English literature at the University of Alberta and, as a Rhodes Scholar, at Oxford University, from which he received an M.A. in 1937. On returning to Canada he taught English at Ridley College and Upper Canada College in Ontario, at the University of New Brunswick, and Queen's University, Ontario, before accepting a position at the University of Saskatoon, where he taught from 1944 until his death.

McCourt's writing is rooted in the Prairies. His novels are character studies that test the truth of Dr Fotheringham's declaration in *The wooden sword* (1956) that 'The life of everyman is no more than a succession of disillusionments. Each disillusionment constitutes a crisis. And a man's happiness—a relative term only—depends on the success or otherwise with which he meets each crisis.' McCourt's first and best-known novel, *Music at the close* (1947), traces the progressive disillusionment of Neil Fraser, an orphan given to romantic dreams, from his arrival on his great-uncle's prairie farm at the age of twelve until his death in the Second World War. A winner of the Ryerson All-Canada Fiction award, it was reprinted in the NEW CANADIAN LIBRARY (1966) and in the Alberta Heritage Series (1979). *Home is the stranger* (1950) focuses on Norah Armstrong, an Irish war bride struggling to make a new life for herself in a small prairie farming community; disillusioned by her failure as a wife and a mother, she attempts suicide. A prairie university is the setting of *The wooden sword*, a psychological case-study of Stephen Veneer, a professor of English whose adolescent dreams of heroism have been shattered by his war experiences, and whose unwillingness to come to terms with those experiences has driven him to the verge of a mental breakdown. It was reprinted in the New Canadian Library (1975). *Walk through the valley* (1958) focuses on fourteen-year-old Michael Troy, whose faith in his father, Dermot, and in the romantic tales of adventure with which his father regales him, are all but destroyed when the police close in on Dermot's whiskey-running operation. In *Fasting friar* (1963), published in England as *The Ettinger affair*, the process of disillusionment is reversed: Walter Ackroyd, an aging, fastidious, and ascetic professor of English at a prairie university, finds new hope and courage when he falls in love with Marion Ettinger, wife of a colleague dismissed for writing a racy novel. In addition to these five novels, McCourt published forty-three stories, most of which are set in western Canada. None of his novels are currently in print.

As a literary critic McCourt is best known for *The Canadian West in fiction* (1949), a pioneering study of prairie writers that focuses on Ralph Connor (Charles W. GORDON), Frederick NIVEN, and Frederick Philip GROVE, but also includes discussions of such writers as Nellie McCLUNG, Sinclair ROSS, and W.O. MITCHELL. A revised edition appeared in 1970. McCourt also wrote *Remember Butler: The story of Sir William Butler* (1967), a biography of the author of *The great lone land*. (See FOREIGN WRITERS ON CANADA IN ENGLISH: 1.)

The North West Rebellion of 1885 is the subject of three books McCourt wrote for young people. *The flaming hour* (1947) is a tale of cattle-rustling, gun-running, and romance set in the Cypress Hills at the outbreak of fighting. The other two are volumes in the Great Stories of Canada series: *Revolt in the West: the story of the Riel Rebellion* (1958) recounts the events of that defining moment in Canadian history, and *Buckskin brigadier: the story of the Alberta Field Force* (1955) concerns the role played by General Tom Strange's expeditionary force in the suppression of the rebellion.

McCourt is also the author of three travel books. *The road across Canada* (1965) is an account of his trip across the country on the newly opened Trans-Canada Highway. Both *Saskatchewan* (1968) and *The Yukon and the Northwest* (1969) are volumes in the Traveller's Canada series, and combine local history and travelogue in a celebration of place.

McCourt's fiction has received scant critical attention. His work is examined in Laurie Ricou's *Vertical man/horizontal world* (1973) and in Richard Harrison's *Unnamed country: the struggle for a Canadian prairie fiction* (1977).

See also CRITICISM IN ENGLISH: 4, 5(g).

PAUL HJARTARSON

McCrae, John (1872-1918). Born in Guelph, Ontario, he grew up under the influence of his military-minded father, and as an adolescent belonged to the Guelph Highland Cadets. His poems began to appear in periodicals as early as 1894. Graduating in medicine from the University of Toronto in 1898, he worked during that year at the Toronto General Hospital, and spent part of 1899 at John Hopkins University, Baltimore, USA. After serving in South Africa (1899-1900), McCrae became a pathologist at McGill University; he was later associated in Montreal with the General Hospital, the Alexandra Hospital, and the Royal Victoria Hospital. (He also published several medical works.) In Sept. 1914 he embarked as a medical officer for the European theatre of war. His best-known poem, 'In Flanders fields', was written during the second battle of Ypres in the spring of 1915 and first appeared in *Punch*, in Dec. 1915. In June 1915 McCrae left the Front for the military General Hospital in Boulogne, where he died of pneumonia in Jan. 1918. Sir Andrew MACPHAIL published twenty-nine of McCrae's poems, which had appeared in periodicals during 1894-1917, as *In Flanders fields and other poems* (1919). They demonstrate McCrae's careful attention to poetic craft, his commitment to fruitful labour, and his profound concern for the fellowship of the dead, whom he portrays as wakeful and anxious lest their labours have been in vain. In his later poems these labours specifically include British Imperial military service. Only rarely, as in 'Flanders fields', does McCrae fuse his craft and concern for worthwhile service into an evocative statement on sacrifice for a higher principle. *In Flanders fields and other poems* concludes with a memorial tract by Macphail, 'An essay in character', which includes biographical information as well as extracts from McCrae's journal and letters. See John F. Prescott, *In Flanders fields: the story of John McCrae* (1985) and Peter E. Greig, *John McCrae (1872-1918): selected sources* (1990).

KEITH RICHARDSON

McCulloch, Thomas (1776-1843). Born in Ferenze, Renfrewshire, Scotland, he was educated at the University of Glasgow and at Divinity Hall, Whitburn. A member of the secession branch of the Presbyterian Church, he was ordained in 1799 and in 1803 was sent to Prince Edward Island. He was unable to reach his destination and stopped in Pictou, Nova Scotia. After a year, despite entreaties to move to P.E.I., McCulloch accepted a call to remain there. A frail man, but with incredible energy, McCulloch soon became involved in many activities outside his ministry. He founded Pictou Academy (incorporated 1816) and became caught up in the Anglican Church's endeavours to dominate education in the province: he was unable to obtain funds for the academy or the power to grant degrees. McCulloch was a natural reformer, and under his leadership Pictou became a centre of protest against the Establishment. *The Colonial Patriot*, founded there in 1827, was edited anonymously by one of McCulloch's former pupils and financial supporters, Jotham Blanchard. McCulloch's skill as a teacher and public speaker was widely recognized. In 1838 he became the first president of Dalhousie University, a non-sectarian institution of higher learning in Halifax, and remained in this post until his death. He founded a theological seminary at West River, Pictou County, which was moved after his death to Truro in 1858 and two years later joined with the Free Church Seminary to form the Halifax Presbyterian College. In 1925 this institution amalgamated with the Mount Allison Faculty of Theology to form Pine Hill Divinity Hall of the United Church of Canada. McCulloch's influence is even felt in the Atlantic School of Theology, founded in 1970. McCulloch was also a naturalist in the nineteenth-century tradition. His collection of bird specimens attracted the attention of John James Audubon, who visited him in 1833.

McCulloch was a prodigious letter-writer and pamphleteer on a wide range of subjects who managed also to write books of general as well as educational and theological interest, often driving himself to the point of exhaustion. As a writer he is best known for his *Letters of Mephibosheth Stepsure*, which first appeared in serial form in the *Acadian Recorder* between 22 Dec. 1821 and 11 May 1822 and in Jan. and Mar. 1823. The letters were reprinted in 1862 and, as *The Stepsure letters*, in the NEW CANADIAN LIBRARY in 1960. A superb edition of this work, entitled *The Mephibosheth Stepsure letters* (1990, CEECT 7), edited by Gwendolyn Davies, contains considerable material about McCulloch's life as a clergyman and writer in nineteenth-century Nova Scotia and is the most detailed and scholarly study of McCulloch to date. McCulloch's satiric and humorous account of the rural life of Pictou County in the 1820s created a furore in the newspaper columns of the time. Northrop FRYE, in his Introduction to the 1960 NCL edition, describes McCulloch as 'the founder of genuine Canadian humour; that is, of the humour which is based on a vision of society and is not merely a series of wisecracks on a single theme.' *The Stepsure letters* had a strong influence on HALIBURTON's Sam Slick sketches, and it can be stated that McCulloch wrote in the tradition that had its flowering in LEACOCK. In 1824 he published in *The Novascotian* the moral tale 'William', depicting the fortunes of an emigrant and the difficulties awaiting those who were not prepared to work hard in the New World. 'William' was joined with a similar work and reprint as *Colonial gleanings: William and Melville* (Edinburgh, 1826).

McCulloch also wrote in the fields of education and religion. He was a strong proponent of liberal education and published his ideas in *The nature and uses of a liberal education* (Halifax, 1819). While advancing the cause of Presbyterianism and public education, he ran afoul of the Roman Catholic bishop Edmund Burke. In two major works, amounting to over 800 pages—*Popery condemned by scripture and the fathers* (Edinburgh, 1808) and *Popery again condemned* (Edinburgh, 1810)—McCulloch out-thought and out-wrote his Catholic opponents in an astonishing display of theological argument. Posthumously published was *Calvinism: the doctrine of the scriptures* (Glasgow, 1849). In this 270-page work he outlined his own faith in his typically vigorous and authoritative style. McCulloch's correspondence was wide and varied. He maintained his connections in Scotland and contributed letters on political, economic, and social subjects to *The Pictou Herald* and *The Acadian Recorder*. Lucid and well conceived, his correspondence (now being collected) provides a wide and penetrating view of nineteenth-century life in the Maritimes, and of McCulloch's central role.

The only book-length biographical study is *Life of Thomas McCulloch, D.D. Pictou* (1920) by his son William McCulloch D.D.; it was unfortunately heavily edited by his granddaughters. DOUGLAS LOCHHEAD

MacDonald, Ann-Marie (b. 1959). An actor, playwright, television-writer, and novelist, she was born on a Canadian Air Force base in West Germany; the family moved frequently during her childhood, but their roots are in Cape Breton Island. MacDonald attended high school in Ottawa, studied a year at Carleton University, and then enrolled at the National Theatre School, graduating in 1980. After graduation she moved to Toronto to begin her acting career. She has performed in films such as *Island love song* (CBC-TV, produced in 1987), *I've heard the mermaids singing* (1987, Genie nomination), and *Where the spirit lives* (CBC-TV, produced in 1990, Gemini Award) and in theatre pieces such as Banuta Rubess' *Boom, baby, boom!* (1993) and the 1989 Toronto production of Maria Irene Fornes' *Abingdon Square* (1989).

The transition to writing for the stage happened naturally through her involvement with Toronto's feminist fringe theatre. Starting as an actor and collaborative creator with Nightwood Theatre's *Smoke damage* (1985), she was also an actor/writer of *This is for you, Anna* (1985), a collective creation that began as a short for the 1983 Women's Perspective Festival. An imagistic political performance piece revolving around a mother's actual revenge on her daughter's murderer, it toured provincially in 1984, in Britain in 1986, and nationally in 1990. It won a Dora nomination for theatrical innovation. *Clue in the fast lane* (produced in 1984) was co-written and co-performed with Beverley Cooper. A spoof on the Nancy Drew detective genre, it began as a series of late-night performances before its production at the 1984 Rhubarb Festival and then at Theatre Passe Muraille, Toronto, in 1985. *The road shows* (produced in 1986), a satirical spin on regular 'road movies' featuring a pair of wily and witty sisters, was also co-written and co-performed with Cooper.

Goodnight Desdemona (Good morning Juliet) (1990) is an ingenious piece, written entirely in blank verse, in which a beleaguered academic literally falls into the worlds of Othello and Romeo and Juliet, altering their stories and her sense of herself. Revised and remounted for a national tour in 1990, it has had over fifty productions worldwide. The play won the Chalmers Canadian Play Award, a Governor General's Award, and the CANADIAN AUTHORS' ASSOCIATION Award.

The Arab's mouth (1995)—an amalgam of Gothic mystery, Freudianism, feminism, myth, magic, and nineteenth-century rationalism—won a Dora nomination for best new play. In 1992 MacDonald was the librettist for *Nigredo Hotel* (produced in 1992), a chamber opera created with musician Nic Gotham, which also was nominated for a Dora. Inspired by the Biblical story of Job, it is a Jungian-influenced tale about the journey to self-knowledge. In 1995 she was a co-writer and performer of *The attic, the pearls, and three fine girls* (produced in 1995). In 1996, the same year she performed in Alissa Palmer's *The bitch* (unpublished) during the Toronto Fringe Festival, her first novel, *Fall on your knees*, was published to great praise (it was nominated for the Giller Prize). Macdonald's experience as a playwright and an actor may have given her the compelling, intimate narrative voice that recounts an epic family history, set mostly in New Waterford, Cape Breton Island. The family is Scottish-Lebanese: in 1898 thirteen-year-old Materia Mahmoud elopes with eighteen-year-old James Piper, a piano tuner, and they have four daughters. *Fall on your knees* is an emotionally rich, often surprising and disturbing saga of four generations. It won the Commonwealth Writers best-first-book prize in 1997.

CYNTHIA ZIMMERMAN

MacDonald, Ingrid. See LESBIAN LITERATURE.

Macdonald, John. See PHILOSOPHY IN CANADA: 6.

MacDonald, Laura. See NOVELS IN ENGLISH 1983 TO 1996: OTHER NOVELS 3.

Macdonald, Malcolm. See FOREIGN WRITERS ON CANADA IN ENGLISH: 1.

MacDonald, Wilson (1880-1967). Wilson Pugsley MacDonald was born in Cheapside, Ontario, and educated at Woodstock College and McMaster University, Hamilton. In *The song of the undertow* (1935), he wrote: 'I have been, in my varied career, a view agent, seaman, cabin-boy, bartender (one night), schoolteacher, actor, inventor, producer, playwright, composer, advertisement writer, newspaper reporter, editorial writer, columnist, banker, and poet. When my poetry would not sell, circumstances forced these other tasks upon me.'

A minor poet who satisfied the public taste with his 'romantic sensibility' and came into prominence just after the First World War, MacDonald had a strongly religious and Anglo-oriented background that influenced much of his early work. Today he appears as the last Canadian writer of a brand of romantic verse that was rooted in the nineteenth century, its most obvious characteristics being its abundance of colour and its musical quality. The poems are invariably well balanced because of his musical interest; parts of stanzas are repeated for emphasis and direction—as major melodies in music would be—with other lines juxtaposed to heighten the emotional effect. For MacDonald, civilization eventually was an evil; man had made a mockery of life in art, religion, and education and must return to the soil if he was not to be destroyed by his own vanity. *Comber cove* (1937) reflects his disappointment in society and the people who corrupt it. While his contemporaries were invoking universal love and compassion, MacDonald drew upon his Christian beliefs to expose hypocrisy and smugness—the marks, in his view, of twentieth-century man. Towards the end of his life he became known as a satirist, but much of what he wrote was petulant and bitter; he held strong, frequently unpopular, opinions, and did not care what others thought of him. His collections of verse are: *The song of the prairie land, and other poems* (1918); *The miracle songs of Jesus* (1921); *Out of the wilderness* (1926); *A flagon of beauty* (1931); *Quintrains of 'Callender' and other poems* (1935); *The song of the undertow, and other poems* (1935); *Comber cove* (1937); *Greater poems of the Bible: metrical versions, biblical forms, and original poems* (1943); and *The lyric year. Poems and pen-work* (1952).

MacDonald attained a popular following in Canada and abroad, but received little critical acclaim from those, in the 1930s, who preferred F.R. SCOTT, A.J.M. SMITH, and Dorothy LIVESAY. Beginning in the early twenties, he went across the country reading his poetry to audiences in large cities and small towns. His personal shyness disappeared on stage, where he became dynamic; humming, chanting, and singing, he synchronized his whole performance to make poems come alive for his audience. On one of his tours he kept a notebook record of his journey, embellished with illuminations and drawings that showed his versatility in the arts. It is described by Stan Dragland in *Wilson MacDonald's western tour, 1923-24* (1976).

DONALD STEPHENS

McDougall, Colin. See NOVELS IN ENGLISH 1940 TO 1960.

McDougall, E. Jean. (pseudonym of Jane Rolyat). See NOVELS IN ENGLISH 1920 TO 1940: 2.

McDougall, John (1842-1917). Born in Owen Sound, Canada West (Ontario), John Chantler McDougall grew up on the Methodist mission stations conducted by his father, the Rev. George Millward McDougall, among the Ojibwa of the Great Lakes. His formal education was limited to backwoods schools and two terms at Victoria College, Cobourg. The eldest of eight children, he left college at sixteen to accompany the mission family to Norway House on Lake Winnipeg. There he served as schoolteacher to the Native children, becoming fluent in Swampy Cree.

Beginning in 1862 McDougall worked for ten years as translator, provisioner, and apprentice missionary in the McDougall mission network, now moved inland to stations on the North Saskatchewan River. Whitefish, Victoria (Pakan), Edmonton, and Pigeon Lake were his homes, but he led a life of constant travel, following the Native camps as they in turn followed the buffalo. In 1865 he married Abigail Steinhauer, daughter of the Ojibwa missionary Henry Bird Steinhauer and his Cree wife, and they had three daughters. Abigail died in Apr. 1871 and McDougall remarried in 1872, shortly after his ordination as a Methodist minister.

McDougall's familiarity with northwest travel routes and methods, as well as his position of trust among the Cree and Stoney tribes, involved him in government commissions, treaty negotiations, and a complex array of educational, social, and religious measures affecting the region's Native and mixed-blood inhabitants. An accomplished linguist, especially in the several dialects of Cree, he and a colleague, the Rev. E.B. Glass, published a *Primer and language lessons* and a revised Cree *Hymn book*, both in 1908. However, John McDougall is primarily known for six other books that made him a favourite with the turn-of-the-century Canadian reading public. A biography of his father, *George Millward McDougall: pioneer, patriot and missionary* (Toronto, 1888), was followed by five books of memoirs detailing his own adventurous life on the frontier among the Indians. The entire series is marked by surprising consistency of tone and freshness of recall. *Forest, lake and prairie: twenty years of frontier life in western Canada, 1842-62* (Toronto, 1895) describes his boyhood and youth; *Saddle, sled and snowshoe: pioneering on the Saskatchewan in the sixties* (Toronto, 1896) covers the years from 1862 to McDougall's first marriage in 1865. *Pathfinding on plain and prairie: stirring scenes of life in the Canadian North-west* (Toronto, 1898; rpr. 1971), which recounts events from 1865 to 1868, went into several printings and was given a facsimile reprint. The most consciously structured and most satisfying of the series, *In the days of the Red River rebellion: life and adventure in the far west of Canada (1862-1872)* (1903), tells of the mounting strains on the interior region's residents during the period of unrest and uprising at Fort Garry. *On western trails in the early seventies: frontier life in the Canadian North-west* (1911) carries the story to 1875. J.E. Nix edited a sixth volume of memoirs, *Opening the great West* (1970), which had been left in manuscript at McDougall's death. It describes the events of 1876, chief among which was George McDougall's death on the plains near Calgary.

The little-known *Wa-pee Moos-tooch; or, White Buffalo, the hero of a hundred battles: a tale of Canada's great west during the early days of the last century* (1908)—privately printed by the author in Calgary—is an episodic narrative of a young chief's education and testing, remarkable for being both ethnologically sound and competent as a work of historical fiction. The occasional idiomatic aberration in the prose style can be explained by McDougall's imaginative engagement with his young Cree hero, whose thoughts and speech reflect the customs and phrasing of the woods-and-plain Cree.

The only full-scale biography, *McDougall of Alberta: a life of Rev. John McDougall, D.D., pathfinder of empire and prophet of the plains* (1927), by his co-religionist John Maclean, needs updating. A useful brief book on the historical place of the two McDougalls, George and John, is J.E. Nix's *Mission among the buffalo* (1960). SUSAN JACKEL

McDowell, Franklin Davy. See NOVELS IN ENGLISH 1920 TO 1940: 2.

MacEwen, Gwendolyn (1941-87). Born in Toronto, Ontario, she attended schools there and in Winnipeg, Manitoba. She published her first poem in *The CANADIAN FORUM* when she was seventeen and left school at eighteen to pursue a literary career. She taught herself Hebrew, Arabic, Greek, and French, translating writers from each of these languages. She published over twenty books, in a variety of genres, and also wrote numerous radio docudramas for the Canadian Broadcasting Corporation. She was married for six years to the Greek singer Nikos Tsingos, and in 1972 they operated The Trojan Horse, a Toronto coffee house. Her links with Greece led her to write a volume of travel recollections, *Mermaids and ikons: a Greek summer* (1978), and to translate with Tsingos two long poems by the contemporary Greek writer Yannis Ritsos. These were published in *Trojan women* (1981), which included MacEwen's new version of Euripides' *The Trojan women*. She also published a modern adaptation of Aristophanes' *The birds* in 1983.

MacEwen published two novels, *Julian the magician* (1963) and *King of Egypt, king of dreams* (1971), as well as two collections of short stories, *Noman* (1972), and *Noman's land* (1985), and three children's books: *The chocolate moose* (1979), *The honey drum: seven tales from Arab lands* (1983), and *Dragon sandwiches* (1987). Her verse includes two early privately published pamphlets, *Selah* (1961) and *The drunken clock* (1961), and nine larger volumes: *The rising fire* (1963), *A breakfast for barbarians* (1966), *The shadow-maker* (1969)—winner of a Governor General's Award—*The armies of the moon* (1972), *Magic animals: selected poems old and new* (1974), *The fire-eaters* (1976), *The T.E. Lawrence poems* (1982), *Earthlight: selected poetry 1963-1982* (1982), and *Afterworlds* (1987), which also won a Governor General's Award. Two volumes of her poetry, edited by both Margaret ATWOOD and Barry CALLAGHAN, appeared posthumously: *The poetry of Gwendolyn MacEwen: the early years* (1993) and *The poetry of Gwendolyn MacEwen: the later years* (1994).

In approaching MacEwen's verse and prose alike, the reader is tempted, as Margaret Atwood has said, 'to become preoccupied with the brilliant and original verbal surfaces she creates'. But this bright enamel of words and images, which woos the reader's initial pleasure, overlies profundities of thought and feeling. The extraordinary feat of empathy represented by *The T.E. Lawrence poems*—the voice seems to be Lawrence's own—suggests the oracular seriousness in her verse, and a growing inclination to move away from the elusive introspection of the first poems. This development can be seen by comparing the selections included in *Magic animals* with those in *Earthlight*, published seven years later. The poems in the latter volume have a greater solidity of texture and concreteness of imagery, a sharper visualness; they reveal a preoccupation with time and its multiple meanings, with the ambivalences of existence, with the archetypal patterns that emerge and re-emerge from ancient times to now, but also with the actual human lives that carry on in their mundane way within such patterns. There are few Canadian poets with a grasp as broad as MacEwen's of the poetic dimensions of history—the realm of the muse Clio—and of its necessarily Zoroastrian duality, expressed in the last line of *The T.E. Lawrence poems*: as T.E. Lawrence dies, his mind exclaims, 'Night comes and the stars are out. Salaam.' Light lives in darkness; darkness nurtures light.

Such concerns, recurring throughout her poetry, take personified form in MacEwen's novels, which blend fantasy with history: *Julian the magician*, with its early-Renaissance preoccupation with hermetic quasi-philosophies and their ambiguous relationship to Christianity; *King of Egypt, king of dreams*, with its imaginative reconstruction of the gallant and eventually futile life of the heterodox pharaoh Akhnaton. The stories in *Noman* are united by the central enigmatic character who names the book, and here the protean quality of MacEwen's talent takes full flight as her vision of 'Kanada' whirls in a mythological carousel whose turning unites us with every temporal past and every spatial present.

MacEwen's last book, *Afterworlds*—published in the year of her death—seems, uncannily, to be a summing up of her work. It includes her much-admired radio drama, *Terror and Erebus*, written in 1965; poems to lost lovers; and political poems lamenting the nuclear terror into which the world is plunging. And yet she seemed to have found a new affirmative direction for her work through her reading of modern physics, which confirmed her sense of the mystery inherent in the material world. This is evident in her last poem, 'The Tao of physics', which concludes with the remarkable challenge: 'Here where events have a tendency to occur/ My chair and all its myriad inner worlds/ Whirl around in the carousel of space; I hurl/ Breathless poems against my lord Death, send these/ words, these words/ Careening into the beautiful darkness.'

See Margaret Atwood, 'MacEwen's muse', *CANADIAN LITERATURE* 45 (Summer 1970), reprinted in Atwood, *Second words* (1982), which contains a further discussion of MacEwen's work in 'Canadian monsters'; Frank DAVEY, 'Gwendolyn MacEwen: the secret of alchemy', *OPEN LETTER* (Spring 1973); Jan Bartley, *Invocations: the poetry and prose of Gwendolyn MacEwen* (1983); and Rosemary SULLIVAN, *Shadow maker: the life of Gwendolyn MacEwen* (1995).

See also POETRY IN ENGLISH 1950 TO 1982: 2 and FANTASTIC LITERATURE IN ENGLISH.

GEORGE WOODCOCK/ROSEMARY SULLIVAN

McFadden, David (b. 1940). Noted for his poetry of pop-art image and ironic ingenuousness, he lived his first thirty-nine years in Hamilton, Ontario. He joined the staff of the *Hamilton Spectator* as a proofreader in 1962, became a reporter for the paper in 1970, and resigned in 1976 to take up freelance writing and editing. McFadden's poetry appeared first in *TISH*, *Is*, *Evidence*, *Weed*, *Talon*, and in his own mimeographed magazine, *Mountain* (1962).

The poems of McFadden's first major collections—*Letters from the earth to the earth* (1968), *Poems worth knowing* (1971), and *Intense pleasure* (1972)—use his family life with his wife and two daughters as their central symbol. Details about cooking meals or repairing toys are affirmed as important, despite the larger twentieth-century context of brutality and commercial exploitation. McFadden personified this conflict between family life and North American media advertising in his characterization of Ricky Wayne, the protagonist of his first novel, *The great Canadian sonnet* (1970).

In the seventies his writing shifted its focus from the family home to the family's exploration of the outside world. The major poems of *A knight in dried plums* (1975) are the marvellously comic tourist poems 'Somewhere south of Springhill' and 'A typical Canadian family visits Disneyworld', in which an ostensibly naïve narrator satirizes both the conventional expectations of the tourist and the outside world's eager fulfilment of these expectations. *On the road again* (1978) continued this exploration, although without the family as a central image.

McFadden followed these books with three comic 'novels': *A trip around Lake Erie* (1980), *A trip around Lake Huron* (1980), and *A trip around Lake Ontario* (1988). In exceedingly brief, discontinuous chapters, these picaresque works illustrate the struggle of the small man to make sense of an increasingly surreal and commercialized century. The subtitle 'Curious rambles and singular encounters' is an apt description of his delightfully whimsical *An innocent in Ireland* (1995). *Animal spirits: stories to live by* (1983), published with drawings by Greg Curnoe, is a retrospective collection of McFadden's short stories.

Other books by McFadden are *The poem poem* (1967); *The Saladmaker* (1968); *The ova yogas* (1972); *The poet's progress* (1977); *I don't know* (1978); *A new romance* (1979); *My body was eaten by dogs* (1981), a selected poems edited and introduced by George BOWERING; *Country of the open heart* (1982), a book-length poem; *Three stories and ten poems* (1982); *A pair of baby lambs* (1983)—which contains two long, charming, funny poems, 'The cow that swam Lake Ontario' and 'Stormy January'; *The art of darkness* (1984); *Gypsy guitar: one hundred poems of romance and betrayal* (1987); *Anonymity suite* (1992); and *There'll be another* (1995), which begins with a moving remembrance of his close friend Greg Curnoe.

FRANK DAVEY

McFarlane, Leslie (1903-1977). Born in Carleton Place, Ontario, and raised in Haileybury, he worked as a reporter on the Cobalt *Nugget* and other newspapers before contributing to American pulp magazines under such pseudonyms as 'Roy Rockwood' (for juveniles), 'James Cody Ferris' (westerns), and 'Bert Standish' (general articles). In 1926, answering an advertisement ('Experienced Fiction Writer Wanted to Work from Publisher's Outlines'), placed in an American trade paper by the Stratemeyer Syndicate, he commenced two decades of ghost-writing. In his lively autobiography, *Ghost of the Hardy Boys* (1976), he explained how he wrote the first Hardy Boy book under the house name 'Franklin W. Dixon' in his room above a bank in Haileybury. He began with *The tower treasure* (1926) and completed twenty volumes in the popular boys' adventure series. As well, he was the first writer to use the name 'Carolyn Keene', the byline later identified with the Nancy Drew detective books for young girls. Under his own name he wrote *Streets of shadow* (1930), a romantic novel, and *McGonigle scores!* (1966), a hockey juvenile that continues to find readers. He scripted documentary films for the National Film Board and contributed dramatic scripts to CBC-TV, serving as the Corporation's chief drama editor in 1958-60. McFarlane retained a secure place in the affections of three generations of North American youngsters from the moment they opened the first of the Hardy Boy books and began to read with breathless excitement: 'Two bright-eyed boys on motorcycles were speeding along a shore road.' McFarlane was the father of Brian McFarlane, the sports personality who created the 'Peter Puck' hockey books for youngsters.

JOHN ROBERT COLOMBO

McGee, Thomas D'Arcy (1825-68). Born in Carlingford, Ireland, he immigrated in 1842 to the USA, where he worked for the Boston *Pilot*, and began his professional life as a spokesman for, and interpreter of, Ireland in New England. After three years he returned to Ireland as a political journalist, became involved in the Young Ireland movement, and when sought by the British as one of the leaders in the abortive 1848 revolution, escaped to the USA. He continued his activities as a political journalist in New York and Buffalo until 1857, when he left for Canada, after having earlier offended the Roman Catholic bishop of New York by attacking the Irish clergy for discouraging rebellion, and then progressively alienating Americans by criticizing their anti-Roman Catholicism, their anti-foreign bias, and the corruption and bullying of American ward politics.

Though McGee has sometimes been accused of subordinating political and cultural ideals to considerations of personal advantage, he had been consistent in his efforts on behalf of the disadvantaged Irish, as he saw them, and continued to further their cause upon his arrival in Montreal in 1857, when he founded *The New Era*. Elected to the House of Assembly in 1858 as an independent representing the Irish and Roman Catholics of his Montreal constituency, he first favoured the reformers and achieved initial success through their patronage, serving as president of council in 1862. He subsequently aligned himself with the conservatives and enjoyed even greater success, serving as minister of agriculture in 1864. He was an influential participant in the Charlottetown and Quebec conferences that laid the groundwork for Confederation, achieving fame as an oratorical proponent of Confederation in the years immediately preceding its establishment in 1867. He was elected to the first Canadian Parliament in 1867. In the cause of advocating full Irish support for Confederation, McGee had joined battle against the North American Fenian movement and was assassinated by one of its adherents, Patrick James Whelan, on 7 Apr. 1868.

Many of his publications were directly related to his political activities, and to his attempts to further Irish knowledge of, and pride in, Irish culture, in whatever nation Irish people lived. Such works include *Eva MacDonald; a tale of the united Irishman* (Boston, 1844), *The Irish writers of the seventeenth century* (Dublin, 1846), *A history of the Irish settlers in North America . . .* (Boston, 1851; 2nd edn 1852), and *A popular history of Ireland . . .* (2 vols, New York, 1863). The second most frequent subject of McGee's publications in prose was Canada: *Two speeches on the union of the provinces* (pamphlet, Quebec, 1865); *Speeches and addresses, chiefly on the subject of British American union* (London and Montreal, 1865), translated by L.G. Gladu (St Hyacinthe, 1865); and *The mental outfit of the new Dominion* (pamphlet, Montreal, 1867).

McGee also enjoyed, and still bears, a reputation as a poet, but during his life he published only one collection of verse, *Canadian ballads and occasional verses* (Montreal, 1858). Few of these poems are actually on Canadian subjects; many express his love for Ireland and for things Irish; some articulate a rather conventional religious faith. The strongest are his most personal—evocations of his love for his wife. After his death his poems were assembled by Mary Anne Sadlier in *The poems of D'Arcy McGee* (New York, 1869).

McGee's life and significance have received occasional scholarly comment over the years, most extensively in the centenary works of Alexander Brady, *Thomas D'Arcy McGee* (1925), Isabel Skelton and *The life of Thomas D'Arcy McGee* (1925), and in Josephine Phelan, *The ardent exile: the life and times of Thomas D'Arcy McGee* (1951).

CHARLES R. STEELE

McGill Fortnightly Review (1925-7). Founded by A.J.M. SMITH and F.R. SCOTT, then graduate students at McGill University, Montreal, it was described by Leon EDEL, a contributing editor, as representing 'the innovative spirit of the 1920s in Canada'. Other writers associated with the journal were A.M. KLEIN and Leo KENNEDY. It developed out of the modernist movement of the early twentieth century associated primarily with James Joyce and T.S. Eliot—Smith's second article in the *Review* was an analysis of Eliot's *The wasteland* (1922). In various editorials, Smith argued that Canadian poets must go beyond the 'maple-leaf school' of Bliss CARMAN, Archibald LAMPMAN, Duncan Campbell SCOTT, and Charles G.D. ROBERTS in favour of free verse, imagistic treatment, displacement, complexity, and a leaner diction free of Victorian mannerisms. One target of the *McGill Fortnightly Review* was the CANADIAN AUTHORS' ASSOCIATION, founded in 1921. The last issue of the journal included F.R. Scott's much-anthologized satirical poem 'The Canadian authors meet', which pilloried the Association as representing amateurism in art. While short-lived, the journal was important in first articulating the new ideas of modernism that were to influence Canadian literature beginning in the 1940s.

See Ken Norris, *The little magazine in Canada, 1925-80* (1984). GEOFF HANCOCK

McGill Poetry Series. See Louis DUDEK.

McGill-Queen's University Press. The venture of two Canadian universities, McGill-Queen's University Press (MQUP) was established in 1969. MQUP's first director, Robin Strachan, was the former director of McGill University Press (est. 1960) and proposed the joint operation. Endeavouring to attract a broad cross-section of Canadian academics, Strachan sought to establish a press with international distribution potential. In its early years an office in London, England, was maintained to facilitate that objective and to provide the press with dual English and Canadian imprints. During the mid-1970s, even as it enjoyed the prestige of at least five design awards, MQUP became beleaguered by financial difficulties brought on by increases in production and staffing costs. Reorganizational efforts in 1977 reduced the staff by approximately 60 per cent, encouraged the publisher to seek co-publication arrangements with overseas presses, and forced it to contract out its fulfilment operation to the UNIVERSITY OF TORONTO PRESS (UTP). Financial problems persisted, however, and MQUP temporarily suspended operations in 1980. After committing to an extensive contract with UTP for production, promotion, marketing, and fulfilment services while MQUP maintained control over acquisition and selection of manuscripts, it began publishing again in 1981. In 1987 it repatriated the non-fulfilment aspects of its operation from UTP. During its history MQUP has published broadly in the humanities and social sciences. Notable is the number of series it has produced, among them Studies in the History of Ideas, Studies in the History of Religion, and Native and Northern Series. Its titles of Canadian literary criticism include Michael Greenstein's *Third solitudes* (1989), Helen Buss's *Mapping our selves* (1993), and Christl Verduyn's *Lifelines* (1995). MQUP also published the first work of fiction in English by an Inuit of Canada, Markoosie's *Harpoon of the hunter* (1970). JANET FRISKNEY

McGrath, Robin Gedalof. See ABORIGINAL LITERATURE: INUIT LITERATURE 1982 TO 1996.

MacGregor, Mary Esther (1876-1961). Born Mary Esther Miller in Rugby, Ontario, she was educated in Orillia and at the Toronto Normal School. She married a Presbyterian minister, the Rev. Donald MacGregor, in 1909, residing in first in London, Ont., then in Brantford and Owen Sound, where they retired. In 1911 she met L.M. MONTGOMERY at a Toronto Women's Press Club reception and the two, having much in common, became lifelong friends. Under the pseudonym 'Marian Keith', MacGregor was a prolific writer of popular fiction. Most of her stories depict rural life, particularly in predominantly Scottish settlements in Ontario in the 1880s, where conflicts among English, Irish, and Scottish settlers, and between Methodists and Presbyterians, served as her focus. *Duncan Polite, the watchman of Glenoro* (1905) is about a minister whose desire to install an organ in the church causes a furore. It was followed by *Treasure valley* (1908), *'Lizbeth of the dale* (1910), *The end of the rainbow* (1913), *In orchard glen* (1918), *Little Miss Melody* (1921), *The bells of St. Stephen's* (1922), and *The forest barrier* (1930). Her trilogy—consisting of *As a watered garden* (1947), *Yonder shining light* (1948), and *Lilacs in the dooryard* (1952)—set in a community near Georgian Bay, continued to stress her central themes of goodwill and community co-operation. Other novels, such as *The silver maple* (1906), depicting a Canadian expedition to rescue General Charles Gordon at Khartoum, and *A gentleman adventurer: a story of the Hudson's Bay Company* (1924), have a somewhat broader focus.

In all, MacGregor wrote fourteen novels—the last, *A grand lady* (1960), was published a year before her death. Although overly didactic, sentimental by modern standards, and slim and formulaic in plot, her books retain some value as regional idylls rich in quotidian detail regarding life in small Ontario communities before the turn of the century.

MacGregor also wrote short stories, religious biography such as *Glad days in Galilee* (1935), and a travel book, *Under the grey olives* (1927), about a visit to the Holy Land. With L.M. Montgomery and Mabel Burns McKinley, she co-authored *Courageous women* (1934), a collection of biographical sketches designed for use in schools. MARILYN ROSE

Machar, Agnes Maule (1837-1927), who sometimes used the pen-name 'Fidelis', was born in Kingston, Upper Canada (Ontario), and spent her life there. Her father, the Rev. Dr John Machar, was minister of St Andrew's Presbyterian Church for over thirty-five years (1827-63) and principal of Queen's University (1846-53). Learning, Christian piety, and social service were the cornerstones of her upbringing. As a writer of poetry, fiction (both juvenile and adult), verse-drama, biography, history, and essays for American, British, and Canadian journals on such issues as public education, the co-education of women, social justice for the poor, and Christian belief, she revealed a lively intellect, wide reading, and a commitment to non-sectarian Christian humanism.

Machar wrote eight novels, of which five—*Katie Johnson's cross, a Canadian tale* (Toronto, 1870), *Lucy Raymond; or The children's watchword* (Toronto, 1871), *For king and country; a story of 1812* (Toronto, 1874), *Lost and won; a story of Canadian life* (issued serially in *The Canadian Monthly*, Jan. to Dec. 1875), and *Marjorie's Canadian winter; a story of the northern lights* (Boston, 1892)—were for children. Of the other three—*Roland Graeme, knight: a novel of our time* (Montreal, 1892), *Down the river to the sea* (New York, 1894), and *The heir of Fairmount Grange* (Toronto, 1895)—only the first is of interest today. *Roland Graeme* is a serious attempt to deal with socio-economic issues, especially as revealed in the activities of the Knights of Labour Movement. A travelogue posing as a novel, *Down the river to the sea* celebrates, in a manner reminiscent of Charles SANGSTER's 'The St. Lawrence and the Saguenay', the beauties of the Canadian landscape from Niagara to the Gaspé. *The heir of Fairmount Grange* is a forgettable society novel of the sort so popular in the late nineteenth century. Machar's fiction uses stereotyped characterization, faint plot lines, and the familiar Victorian mixture of Protestant piety and commitment to social justice.

A representative selection of her poems, *Lays of the 'true north' and other Canadian poems* (1892)—which appeared in an enlarged edition that includes her verse-drama *The winged victory* (London, 1902)—reveals a competent, if typically minor, Victorian poetry that celebrates British-Canadian nationalism and the joy, peace, and wonder to be found in nature.

Machar also wrote, or co-authored, two biographies: *Faithful unto death; a memorial of John Anderson* (Kingston, 1859); and, with her mother, *The memorials of the life and ministry of the Reverend John Machar, D.D.* (Kingston, 1873); histories for young readers, *Stories of New France* (Boston, 1890), and *Stories of the British Empire for young folks and busy folks* (1913); and a still valuable account of the early history of her home city, *The story of old Kingston* (1908). At the age of 82 she published *Young soldier hearts of France* (1919), a series of letters from two young French soldiers to their families during the First World War.

Always ready (with her pen or through good works) to advance causes in which she believed, Machar was the first Canadian to be named a life member of the International Council of Women. After her death funds from her estate were used to establish a home for indigent elderly widows.

See Henry Morgan, *Canadian men and women of the time (1912)*; F.L. MacCallum, 'Agnes Maule Machar', *Canadian Magazine* 62 (Mar. 1942); Rosa L. Shaw, *Proud heritage* (1957); and Carole Gerson, 'Three writers of Victorian Canada: Rosanna Leprohon/James DeMille/Agnes Maule Machar', *Canadian writers and their works*, Fiction series, vol. 1 (1983), edited by Robert Lecker, Jack David, and Ellen Quigley. S.R. MacGILLIVRAY

McIlwraith, Jean Newton (1859-1938). Born in Hamilton, Canada West (Ontario), she was educated at the Ladies' College, Hamilton, and through the correspondence program in modern literature offered by Queen Margaret College, Glasgow University, Scotland. From 1902 to 1919 she worked as a publisher's reader in New York while establishing herself as a writer of literary criticism, biography, and fiction. She returned to Canada in 1922 and died in Burlington, Ont.

McIlwraith is best known for her historical romances. Her earliest works included *The making of Mary* (1895), written under the pseudonym 'Jean Forsyth', and a libretto for the comic opera *Ptarmigan* (1895). *The curious career of Roderick Campbell* (1901), her most substantial work, is about three Scottish families who immigrate to North America and find themselves on differing sides in the Seven Years' War. *A Diana of Quebec* (1912) is a romance set in Quebec during the American Revolution, while *Kinsmen at war* (1927) is a sentimental tale of conflicting localities during the War of 1812. McIlwraith also collaborated with William McLENNAN on *The span o'life: a tale of Louisbourg and Quebec* (1899). Her novels are well documented in terms of historical detail, though plot and characterization tend to be formulaic and overwhelmed by historical minutiae.

In keeping with her interest in and knowledge about the colonial period in Canadian history, McIlwraith wrote a well-regarded biography, *Sir Frederick Haldimand* (1904), for the Makers of Canada series. She was also the author of several books for young people, including *Canada* (1899), *A book about Shakespeare* (1898), *A book about Longfellow* (1900), and *The little admiral* (1924), which is set in the period of the fall of Quebec and won the Hodder and Stoughton prize novel award in 1923.

See Wendy Ratkowski Huyck, 'Jean McIlwraith and *The little Admiral*', *Canadian Children's Literature* 59 (1990). MARILYN ROSE

MacInnes, Tom (1867-1951). Born in Dresden, Ontario, Thomas Robert Edward MacInnes was a son of Thomas McInnes, a lieutenant-governor of British Columbia (1897-1902) (he changed the spelling of his family name). He went with his family to New Westminster, British Columbia, in 1881, was educated at the University of Toronto, and was called to the bar in 1893. He was secretary to the Bering Sea Commission (1896-7) and helped supervise the importation of goods to Skagway (1897) for members of the Klondike Gold Rush. He practised law in Vancouver and was involved with the drafting of immigration laws in 1910, and with import regulations and the control of narcotics. From 1916 to 1927 MacInnes spent long periods in China, where he had business interests. As a result he developed a sympathy for Orientals living in British Columbia; his views of British Columbia prejudice appeared in the pamphlet *Oriental occupation of British Columbia* (1927). MacInnes's autobiographical *Chinook days* (1926) contains his impressions of people, places, and events in British Columbia history. He died in Vancouver.

MacInnes's narrative poems—concerned with adventure or dramatic situations in strange environments (his attitude is bohemian), and expressing his enjoyment of life—were highly popular in his lifetime. He wrote light, easy verse that dismissed smugness and respectability with unconcerned humour, as Stephen LEACOCK did in his short anecdotes. Even when MacInnes is sometimes serious, an amused detachment underlies his work, as though poetry were merely one form of expression, as good as any other. He felt that any subject was appropriate for poetry and was especially interested in examining man within a natural landscape, on the fringes of society. Though uninterested in poetic subtleties—his rhythms are often forced and pedantic, his rhyme-schemes careless and rough—he was intrigued with elaborate poetic forms, such as the villanelle, and with a five-line stanza of his own he called the 'mirelle'. His belief that joy and delight, rather than the prevalent melancholic outpourings of the soul, were essential to poetry was expressed in one of his later and best-known poems, 'The tiger of desire', which fits an allusion to the past (Blake) and to contemporary concerns (a type of Darwin-mysticism) into his usual structure, the villanelle. His collections are *A romance of the lost* (1908), reprinted with other poems in *Lonesome bar, A romance of the lost, and other poems* (1909); *In amber lands* (1910); *Rhymes of a rounder* (1913); *The fool of joy* (1918); *Roundabout rhymes* (with a Foreword by Charles G.D. ROBERTS, 1923); *Complete poems of Tom MacInnis* (1923); *High low along: a didactic poem* (1934); and *In the old of my age* (1947). DONALD STEPHENS

McKay, Don (b. 1942). Donald Fleming McKay was born in Owen Sound, Ontario, and raised in Cornwall, Ontario. He attended Bishop's University and the University of Western Ontario (M.A., 1966), and completed a Ph.D. at Swansea University College, Wales. He has taught Canadian literature and creative writing at the University of Western Ontario and, from 1990 to 1996, at the University of New Brunswick, where he edited *The FIDDLEHEAD*; he has also been an editor and publisher of BRICK Books, a small literary press. He now lives in British Columbia.

McKay has written seven books of poetry: *Air occupies space* (1973); *Long Sault* (1975), a long poem; *Lependu* (1978); *Lightning ball bait* (1980); *Birding, or desire* (1983), which won the CANADIAN AUTHORS' ASSOCIATION prize; *Sanding down this rocking chair on a windy night* (1987); and *Night field* (1991), which won a Governor General's Award. McKay's gift for metaphor—which he calls 'anthropomorphic play'—produces in his work delightful and startling portraits of familiar objects, rivers, trees, and small creatures, birds especially. His poetry is informed by his concern for the natural environment—for the ways in which wilderness coexists with us, teasing and frustrating our need for firm understanding, or for knowledge as a kind of ownership. McKay conceives of 'wilderness' not solely as the threatened ecosphere but as the elusive quality of otherness in all things, even tools: the things we have our hands on, but cannot grasp in the full sense. His ironic sense of humour, deadpan delivery, and knack for overturning clichés give some of his work a deceptively light tone.

See *Studies in Canadian literature/Études en littérature canadienne* for informative discussion of his poetics: Don McKay, 'Baler Twine: thoughts on ravens, home, and nature poetry', vol. 18, no. 1 (1993); Alana F. Bondar, '"That every feather is a pen, but living,/flying"—Desire: the metapoetics of Don McKay's *Briding, or desire*', vol. 19, no. 2 (1994); and Kevin Bushell, 'Don McKay and metaphor: stretching language toward wilderness', vol. 20. no. 2 (1996). SUSAN ELMSLIE

MacKay, L.A. See POETRY IN ENGLISH 1900 TO 1950: 3.

Mackenzie, Sir Alexander. See EXPLORATION LITERATURE IN ENGLISH: 2.

Mackenzie, William Lyon (1795-1861). Born in Scotland, where both his grandfathers had fought for the rebel cause at Culloden, Mackenzie immigrated to Upper Canada in 1820. He founded *The Colonial Advocate* (Queenston, 1824; York, 1824-34) and a succession of other newspapers, which he edited, published, and wrote much of the copy for: *The Correspondent and Advocate* (Toronto, 1834-6); *The Welland Canal* (Toronto, Dec. 1835); *The Constitution* (Toronto, 1836-Nov. 1837);

Mackenzie's Gazette (New York 1838-39; Rochester, 1839-40); *The Volunteer* (Rochester, 1841-42); *The New York Examiner* (New York, 1843); *Mackenzie's Weekly Message* (Toronto, 1852-6); and *The Toronto Weekly Message* (1856-60). In his career as a radical politician and agitator, Mackenzie was elected to—and expelled from—the Upper Canada house of assembly several times, and was the first mayor of Toronto (formerly York) for nine months in 1834-5. A leader in the 1837 Rebellion, which collapsed following skirmishes with government forces near and in Toronto on 7 Dec., Mackenzie escaped to the United States, where he felt the influence of the editor and journalist Horace Greeley. He returned to Canada under the Amnesty Act of 1849, was re-elected to the assembly in 1851, and resigned in 1858.

Mackenzie's interests were wide-ranging, as the titles of some essay collections and almanacs suggest: *Essay on canals and inland navigation* (Queenston, 1824); *Catechism of education* (York, 1830); *Sketches of Canada and the United States* (London, 1833); *Poor Richard; or the Yorkshire Almanac . . . by Patrick Swift* (New York, 1831?). All of his work was in large part polemical, and the following titles indicate the prevailing tone: *The legislative black list of Upper Canada; or, Official corruption and hypocrisy unmasked* (York, 1828); *Celebrated letter of Joseph Hume, esq., M.P., to William Lyon Mackenzie* (Toronto, 1834); *The Seventh Report from the select committee of the House of Assembly of Upper Canada on grievances* (Toronto, 1835). Mackenzie was at heart an agrarian Utopian, in the vein of Cobbett, Burns, and the Walter Scott of the *Waverley* novels, and this yearning places him in the Canadian pastoral tradition expressed in such contemporary works as Thomas McCULLOCH's *Stepsure letters*, and parts of Oliver GOLDSMITH's *The rising village*. During a lifelong messianic quest to make of his nation a genuinely charitable community, reckless, impulsive, opinionated personality became itself a main cause of the controversies that surrounded him.

Mackenzie was also a raconteur: of tales of war and intrigue (*Head's flag of truce*, Toronto, 1853?); of frontier rowdiness (*The history of the destruction of the 'Colonial Advocate' press*, York, 1826); of escape and adventure (*Mackenzie's own narrative of the late rebellion*, Toronto, 1838). He wrote memorable character sketches of some of his Canadian and European contemporaries; of Andrew Jackson (*Life and opinions of Andrew Jackson*, York, 1829); and *The sons of the Emerald Isle; or Lives of one thousand remarkable Irishmen* (New York, 1845). He also wrote vivid, concrete, observant accounts of Upper and Lower Canada, its scenes and people, that earn him a place among significant travel writers of Canada. He was a puritan moralizer; and a furious, chronic, Juvenalian satirist—of the Family Compact of Upper Canada, and of several Americans (*The life and times of Martin van Buren*, Boston, 1846; *The lives and opinions of Benjamin Franklin Butler, United States district attorney, and Jesse Hoyt, counsellor at law, formerly collector of customs for the port of New York*, Boston, 1845).

Mackenzie's work mixes shrill invective with a prophet's exalted visions and a Calvinist sense of good v. evil—which, for Mackenzie, meant poor v. established rich. He often presents his enemies in diabolic images drawn recognizably from eighteenth-century Gothic works like Mrs Ann Radcliffe's *The mysteries of Udolpho* (1794). In one aspect an anti-rational, anti-institutional Romantic, with a Byronic zeal for unattainable political and personal liberty, Mackenzie also shows affinities with the Scottish-enlightenment thinkers Adam Smith and Joseph Hume, and with Jeremy Bentham.

Mackenzie's writing is quite as eclectic in style as in subject. Wide reading enabled him to mix homely similes from Scottish folklore, poetic quotations, rustic-frontier anecdotes, and biblical analogies with elevated declarations of abstract political principle. His expository and polemical pieces, at their best, proceed via methodical arguments buttressed with fact, example, and illustration. Long periodic sentences with sustained parallelisms and subordinations build in rhythm and sound toward conclusions as climactic in cadence as in meaning. Elsewhere he uses such techniques as sarcasm, rhetorical questions, catalogues, and brief emphatic sentences. Often his rhetoric is oral and spontaneous in effect, invoking for the reader images of Mackenzie the vivid orator. Some of his work has the quality of poetry: see John Robert COLOMBO's selection of 'redeemed prose', *The Mackenzie poems* (1960), and the 'found poem' from Mackenzie's 1837 Navy Island proclamation in Raymond SOUSTER's *Hanging in* (1979).

The colourfully heroic Mackenzie often appears as a character in Canadian literature. See, for example, Rick SALUTIN's drama *1837*, subtitled *The farmers' revolt* (1975); James REANEY's children's novel *The boy with an R in his hand* (1965); and William KILBOURN's *The firebrand* (1956), a biography that, like the writings of its subject, often achieves literary stature. In Dale Hamilton's 1990 agit-prop community play *The spirit of Shivaree*, Mackenzie inspires a 1980s farmers' revolt against a modern oligarchy turning farmland into suburban real-estate. However controversial, Mackenzie will always be needed (as Dennis LEE writes in *Nicholas Knock and other people*, 1974), in the way that every nation needs its millennialists.

See *The selected writings of William Lyon Mackenzie: 1824-1837* (1960) edited by Margaret Fairley, and the passages by Mackenzie in A.J.M. SMITH's *The book of Canadian prose, vol. I: early beginnings to Confederation* (1965).

WILLIAM BUTT

M'Kinnon, William Charles (1828-62). Born near North Sydney, Cape Breton, Nova Scotia, into a military family of Loyalist and Scottish background, he was educated in a rural Cape Breton schoolhouse. Between 1846 and 1850 he founded and edited three partisan Liberal newspapers: *The Cape-Breton Spectator* (North Sydney), *The Times* (North Sydney), and *The Commercial Herald* (Sydney). Following the demise of the *Herald* he tried unsuccessfully to establish a literary career in Boston, Halifax, and Sydney, at one point editing the Halifax *New Era* while continuing to write fiction and poetry. After entering the Methodist ministry in 1853, he abandoned creative writing and channelled his literary energies into works of a theological and geological nature. He died of tuberculosis at the age of thirty-four while serving the Methodist circuit of Shelburne, N.S.

M'Kinnon's first literary publication was a collection of poems, *The battle of the Nile* (Sydney, 1844), which revealed a precocious and sophisticated understanding of poetic convention for a youth of sixteen. He next published two historical novellas—*Castine: a legend of Cape Breton* and *The midnight murder: a legend of Cape-Breton*—in *The Commercial Herald*, and then in *The Waverley Magazine* of Boston (1850). *Castine* was also serialized in *The Eastern Chronicle* of Pictou in 1850 and published in book form as *St. Castine* (Sydney, 1850). Set in Louisbourg at the time of the 1758 siege, *St. Castine* is typical of M'Kinnon's narratives in weaving melodrama, disguise, intrigue, and romance into a fabric of actual events and characters. *The midnight murder*, based on Sydney's 1833 Flahaven murder, illustrates the author's penchant for lecherous villains and exotic background characters and introduces a Yankee sailor, a Gaelic backlander, and thinly disguised local figures into a busy plot of blood, betrayal, and vindication. Probably the first fictional interpretation of contemporary Cape Breton, it enjoyed a readership of 13,000 in Boston alone. On returning to Nova Scotia from Boston in 1851, M'Kinnon wrote *Francis; or Pirate Cove, a legend of Cape-Breton* (Halifax, 1851), a somewhat melodramatic historical romance about the activities of Jordan the Pirate off Cape Breton and New England in the eighteenth century. His most ambitious effort, however, was *St. George; or The Canadian league: a tale of the outbreak* (Halifax, 1852), a two-volume work about a secret society in Lower Canada during the Rebellion of 1837. Although M'Kinnon introduced historical figures like Papineau and MACKENZIE into the novel, and defended the historical accuracy of his tale in a lengthy introduction, he could not make the hypnotic powers and villainy of his central character seem credible. His entry into the ministry, and disappointment over the book's reception, resulted in his eschewing romances and destroying his published novels. These works had emerged from his avowed interest in Sir Walter Scott and Bulwer-Lytton and provide yet another illustration of the influence of the Scott tradition on the popular literature of nineteenth-century Canada.

GWENDOLYN DAVIES

McLachlan, Alexander (1818-96). Born in Johnstone, Scotland, he worked in a cotton factory until he was apprenticed to a tailor in Glasgow. In 1840 he immigrated to Caledon, Upper Canada (Ontario), to take possession of the farm of his father, who had died. He sold it the next year and cleared land for three other farms before moving in 1850 to Erin Township, where he worked as a tailor to support his family of eleven children; achieving a reputation as a speaker, he also gave lectures for the Mechanics' Institute. Through his friendship with D'Arcy McGEE, he was made immigration agent for Canada in Scotland in 1862. In 1877 he moved to a farm in Amaranth Township, Ontario, where he remained until he retired to a house nearby Orangeville in 1895.

For his idylls about log houses, 'hosses', and oxen in the bush, McLachlan is the poet of the backwoods pioneers; in his time he was known as 'the Burns of Canada' for his celebration of the democratic spirit of brotherhood and the toil of the common man. 'A backwoods hero' celebrates the steadfast work of the pioneer—'he chopped, he logg'd, he cleared his lot'—who turns the backwoods into a prosperous and charitable farming community. McLachlan was at his best in light lyrics that document the customs of country life, as in 'Sparking' (the pioneers' slang for courtship). Like Burns, he complements his reverence for the common man with kindly humour, satirizing skinflints and mistreaters of oxen. Occasionally, as in 'We live in a rickety house', he rises to the ironic pitch of a Blakean nursery song in condemning the naïvety of pious charity workers who fail to recognize the church's responsibility for the ignorance and crime that exist among the poor. Of his five volumes of verse—*The spirit of love and other poems* (Toronto 1846), *Poems* (Toronto 1856), *Lyrics* (Toronto 1858), *The emigrant and other poems* (Toronto, 1861), and *Poems and songs* (Toronto 1874)—the 1874 volume is his best collection, while 'The emigrant' is his most ambitious single poem, an unfinished epic in narrative couplets and songs telling of the Scottish immigrants who sailed across the ocean to clear land for a home in the backwoods of Upper Canada. McLachlan wrote many poems about Scotland: the elegaic song 'The halls of Holyrood' won *The British Workman*'s prize for the best poem about Queen Mary's palace; other Scottish poems, like the rousing 'Curling song', are in dialect.

McLachlan, like Burns, was interested in the delineation of character, but his gift for characterization was that of the mimic. The probing of character achieved no more depth than the glimpse at the faith that sustains a long-suffering widow in 'Old Hannah'. As E.H. DEWART noted in his introduction to the posthumous collection *The poetical works of Alexander McLachlan* (Toronto, 1900), McLachlan 'was too often satisfied with putting the passing thoughts that occupied his mind into easy, homely rimes.'

A 1974 reprint of *The poetical works of Alexander McLachlan* includes an introduction by E. Margaret Fulton and Dewart's 'Introductory Essay and Biographical Sketch' from the original edition. Her appendix of eight poems regrettably omits 'We live in a rickety house'. For his scholarly edition of *The emigrant* (1991), D.M.R. Bentley has written a detailed introduction. DAVID LATHAM

McLaren, Floris Clarke. See POETRY IN ENGLISH 1900 TO 1950: 2(a).

MacLennan, Hugh (1907-90). Born in Glace Bay, Nova Scotia, the son of a medical doctor, he grew up in Halifax, was educated at Dalhousie University and, as a Rhodes Scholar, at Oxford, and travelled in Europe before taking his doctoral degree in classical studies at Princeton. His dissertation, published as *Oxyrhynchus: an economic and social study* (1935; rpr. 1968), showed a leftist bias that was later cured by MacLennan's visit to Russia in 1937; but some critics point to the relevance for his fiction of its analysis of the decay of a Roman colony cut off from its roots in the parent civilization. While at Princeton, MacLennan also began writing fiction but, out of economic necessity, turned to the teaching of Latin and history at Lower Canada College, Montreal, in 1935. Originally encouraged to write by the American writer Dorothy Duncan, whom he married in 1936, he made two abortive attempts at novels with international settings. According to MacLennan, Dorothy directed him to the national theme and setting that he knew, and the result was *BAROMETER RISING* (1941), which drew on his boyhood experience of the Halifax explosion of 1917. On the strength of its *succès d'estime* he spent a year in New York on a Guggenheim Fellowship. He returned reluctantly to Lower Canada College, but then *TWO SOLITUDES* (1945) became a commercial success and won a Governor General's Award, as did *The precipice* (1947) and his first volume of essays, *Cross-country* (1949). MacLennan was now a celebrity, writing regularly for *Maclean's* and other national magazines; in 1952 he received the Lorne Pierce Medal and in 1953 he was elected to the Royal Society of Canada. His second volume of essays, *Thirty and three* (1954), brought him a fourth Governor General's Award; but by this time financial pressure and Dorothy's chronic illness obliged him to seek academic security and he began lecturing part-time in the English department of McGill University. The impact on MacLennan of Dorothy's death is apparent in the emotional intensity of *The watch that ends the night* (1959), the novel—for many readers his best—that brought him a record fifth Governor General's Award. He followed it the next year with a third volume of essays: *Scotchman's return and other essays* (1960). In 1967 he became a Companion of the Order of Canada; in 1968 he was made a full professor at McGill and received his seventh honorary degree. He retired as professor emeritus in 1979 and lived until his death with his second wife, Frances Walker, in North Hatley, Quebec.

Though MacLennan's public honours were closely associated with his reputation as a nationalist, his larger subject was Graeco-Roman civilization and its long decline to the present. This Spenglerian view—in which the key to survival and to more fulfilling lives may be found in learning the lessons of history and the wisdom taught by both classical and

Judaeo-Christian writers—accounted for MacLennan's vision, in the early novels, of Canada, heir of European culture, as a mediator between the crude, vital New World and an Old World informed by classical ideals; and it justified his use of classical models, particularly the Homeric epic. George WOODCOCK and others have pointed to the prominence in MacLennan's fiction of the Odyssean archetype—a figure that is often not simply a homeseeker but an emissary of civilization to an increasingly indifferent world.

Though a self-conscious nationalism has always been an element in our literature, MacLennan's deliberate choice of Canadian concerns for his subjects, and his early view of Canada as mediating between an inherited culture and North American obsessive materialism, earned him a too-facile reputation as a crusading nationalist. Of course he was a nationalist. Neil Macrae of *Barometer rising* could have no identity until the colonial past, engendered in violence, had been violently destroyed. As Neil's identity is acknowledged, so is that of the nation: it has earned the right to be itself. In *Two solitudes* Paul Tallard and Heather Methuen combine artistic creativity with a symbolic marriage of the two founding peoples, and Paul determines to write a novel about Canada. In *Each man's son* (1951), which features the Cape Breton of MacLennan's childhood, Alan MacNeil is saved from the crippling life of the mines and taught the privilege of belonging to civilization, especially in Canada, respected honest broker of the post-war world, where the past can meet the energy of the future. However, the optimism inherent in MacLennan's early nationalism soon soured. In *The precipice* there is already a sense of dismay at the destructive power of American industry and less confidence in Canada's ability to meliorate it. The small Ontario town in which the action begins has only potential; not even the Second World War can arouse it until American energy, in the person of Stephen Lassiter, invades it. In *The watch that ends the night* it is openly acknowledged that scientific, military, economic, and even political power ultimately reside outside Canada; salvation is not national but an individual and a personal dream. Jerome Martel—doctor, saviour, man of violence—returns, almost from the grave, to threaten the happiness of timid, bourgeois George Stewart and his sick wife Catherine, who was once married to Jerome. But through him, George and Catherine—who represents what is gracious and civilized in a declining world—learn to accept her death.

The tone of MacLennan's last two novels is much darker. *Return of the Sphinx* (1967) deals with the nation's failure to heal the rift between French- and English-speaking Canadians, and with the perpetuation in the New World not of the values but of the hatreds of the Old. With this novel MacLennan conceded that Canada's future, like its politics and economics, was beyond our control: everything the protagonist, Alan, had stood for seemed lost, the only hope being represented by a rural French-Canadian wedding and Alan's awareness of love for his children. *Voices in time* (1980), set in Montreal fifty years after it was destroyed by a nuclear holocaust, portrays a world like that of Orwell's *Nineteen eighty four* as John Wellfleet, like Orwell's Winston, finds and puzzles over the evidence of his family past and a former civilization: decline and fall are here complete. MacLennan moved back and forth in time and space to repeat his major theme: that the failures to learn the lessons of the past and to guarantee civilized values made the destruction of the West—like the destruction of the classical world—inevitable.

MacLennan endowed his writing with a strong element of regionalism, in the conviction that place too has its personality; this finds its most sustained expression in *The rivers of Canada* (1974) but pervades the fiction as well. Included in the regional 'personalities' of his novels is the local manifestation of general attitudes, particularly the puritanism that MacLennan, perhaps naïvely at first, thought of as Canadian and tended to associate with the Scots and the Presbyterian church. All his protagonists are prone to puritanical self-examination, and *The precipice* and *Each man's son* are explicit analyses of inherent guilt in the individual and the community. The early MacLennan seemed to see the joylessness of Calvinism as inimical both to the arts and to individual expression. Usually his puritans are men; his female protagonists embody life-giving joy, creativity, sensuousness, and love.

MacLennan's novels have been criticized for their didacticism, the tendency to tell us rather than show us. Too often the author stops to reflect on national and historical issues or to explain in laboured dialogue or monologue what his characters are supposed to mean. Though he can be sensitive, he sometimes becomes embarrassed and rhetorical in intimate scenes, especially sexual ones. Generally well within the realistic mode, his protagonists (notably Jerome Martell) sometimes seem more romantic than real. Some of them, however—George Stewart, Athanase

Tallard—are memorable as well as representative, and each of the novels does address a technical as well as a thematic problem. The Halifax explosion in *Barometer rising*, Jerome's recollection of his escape from the lumber camp in *The watch*, and Archie MacNeil's decline in *Each man's son* show MacLennan's gift for fast-paced, exciting narrative. With *The precipice* the characterization becomes more overtly psychological, and in all the novels a sustained structure of imagery reinforces character and theme.

MacLennan's essays, most of which are journalistic and occasional pieces dealing with politics, contemporary personalities, and comparative Canadian-American attitudes, tended to date rather quickly. Those concerned with his own writing and with literature (e.g., 'My first novel'), those narratives that suggest MacLennan's potential in the short story (e.g., 'An orange from Portugal' and 'The lost love of Tommy Waterfield'), and the later social vignettes and commentary, such as 'Have you had many Wimbledons?' and 'The curtain falls on the grand style', are often whimsical, humorous, and urbane. One understands some critics' preference for MacLennan as essayist, where he is often more professional than he is in the novels, but the unity of purpose the essays share with the novels should not be overlooked; they too champion civilized values in a philistine world, and though less intense than the novels, they also express a lament for civilization. Related to the three volumes of essays are the texts for *The colour of Canada* (1967); *McGill: the story of a university* (1961); and *The rivers of Canada*, which is a much-revised version of *Seven rivers of Canada* (1961). Its introductory essay, 'Thinking like a river', acknowledges the 'watershed of the '60s' that changed the writer's, and our, world: MacLennan's realization that for Canada and the Western world a cycle of civilization, or order and human values, was ending, to be replaced by the violent era of the 'rough beast'. This realization informed the fiction and the non-fiction alike and gave unity to MacLennan's work. His essays on the rivers, like those on Canadian cities, effectively personify characteristics of the landscape he loves. *The other side of Hugh MacLennan* (1978), essays edited by Elspeth Cameron, selects the best of the non-fiction and testifies to MacLennan's skill in the shorter form. *Dear Marian, Dear Hugh: the MacLennan-Engel correspondence* (1995), edited by Christl Verduyn, contains mostly letters from MacLennan to Marian ENGEL.

For some years MacLennan enjoyed more critical attention than most of his Canadian contemporaries. Significantly the first full-length study, by Paul Goetsch, appeared in Germany (1961); Goetsch subsequently edited the MacLennan volume (1973) in the McGraw-Hill Ryerson Critical Views series. George Woodcock's *Hugh MacLennan* (1969) first demonstrated the Odyssean parallel; Alec Lucas's *Hugh MacLennan* (1970) draws on the relevance of *Oxyrhynchus*; Peter Buitenhuis's *Hugh MacLennan* (1971) relates the essays to the fiction; Robert Cockburn's *The novels of Hugh MacLennan* (1971) has useful critical analyses; Patricia Morley's *The immoral moralists* (1972) is a helpful summary of characteristics of puritanism but links MacLennan and Leonard COHEN unconvincingly. Elspeth Cameron's *Hugh MacLennan: a writer's life* (1981) provides a wealth of personal data and anecdotes with careful documentation. *Hugh MacLennan: 1982*, edited by Elspeth Cameron, makes available the papers and personal reminiscences from the MacLennan Conference at the University of Toronto. See also T.D. MacLulich, *Hugh MacLennan* (1981) and Marie Peepre-Bordessa, *Hugh MacLennan's national trilogy* (1990).

See also ESSAYS IN ENGLISH: 3 and NOVELS IN ENGLISH 1960 TO 1982: 1.

D.O. SPETTIGUE

McLennan, William (1856-1904). Born in Montreal, McLennan was educated at the Montreal High School and at McGill University (LL.B., 1880). He was a senior partner in a firm of notaries until 1900, when ill health forced him to move to Italy. He died there, and is buried in the English cemetery at Florence.

Elected a fellow of the Royal Society of Canada in 1899, McLennan was considered one of Canada's finest writers of historical fiction. He saw himself as preserving the folktales, songs, and myths of French Canada in his translations, short stories, and longer fiction. His translations of French-Canadian songs were collected in *Songs of Old Canada* (Montreal, 1886), but he made his greatest impact on the public with a series of short stories about French-Canadian life that appeared in *Harper's Magazine* in 1891-2. Based on personal research into the traditions of his native province, they were combined with other stories set in revolutionary France and collected in *In Old France and New* (Toronto, 1900).

Two of McLennan's finest stories are 'The indiscretion of Grosse Boule', a comic tale in the *fabliaux* tradition, and 'Le coureur-des-neiges', an interesting blend of history and the supernatural. In his stories historical research supported but did not dominate the romantic legends. This was not true of *Spanish John* (New York, 1898), a crude reworking of the memoirs of Captain John McDonnell (1728-1810), which were originally published in *The Canadian Magazine* (1825). The novel lacks any effective literary design, and the critics were quick to point out the absence of a love plot, considered mandatory in a historical novel. In apparent response to this criticism, McLennan collaborated with Jean MCILWRAITH on his next novel, *The span o' life: a tale of Louisbourg and Quebec* (New York, 1899). He found his character and setting in the autobiography of Chevalier Johnstone, a Scotsman who fought in the Old World and the New in support of the Jacobite cause. McLennan provided the historical setting and McIlwraith the love story, but their united efforts produced a sprawling work that adhered to the formula for historical fiction without achieving a satisfactory resolution of its elements.

Although today McLennan is forgotten, the praise and recognition he received in his lifetime—justifiably so for his short stories—are captured in Duncan Campbell SCOTT's poem 'At William Maclennan's grave' (*The poems of Duncan Campbell Scott*, 1926).

CAL SMILEY

MacLeod, Alistair (b. 1936). Born in North Battleford, Saskatchewan, he grew up in Alberta until he was ten. In 1946 his parents took their family back to their Cape Breton ancestral farm. MacLeod studied at the Nova Scotia Teacher's College, St Francis Xavier University, the University of New Brunswick (M.A., 1961), and the University of Notre Dame (Ph.D., 1968). He taught English at the University of Indiana for three years and then moved to the University of Windsor in 1969 where he now teaches English and creative writing. He was selected as the Canadian participant in the Canada/Scotland Writers in Residence Exchange Program for the year 1984-5. He has received honorary degrees from St Francis Xavier University (1987) and University College of Cape Breton (1991), and was appointed University Professor by the University of Windsor in 1993. He has been the fiction editor of *The University of Windsor Review* for the past twenty-five years.

MacLeod began publishing short stories in Canadian and American journals in the 1960s and 1970s. International recognition for his talent as a storyteller came early with his second published short story, 'The boat' (*Massachusetts Review*, 1968), which was selected for Houghton-Mifflin's annual collection *Best American short stories* (1969). MacLeod again received this high distinction when 'The lost salt gift of blood' was selected for *Best American short stories* (1975). Many of MacLeod's stories have been frequently anthologized (to date 'The boat' has appeared in sixteen anthologies) and read on CBC and BBC. 'In the fall' was adapted into a moving short film (1983) by Allan Kroecker.

MacLeod's *The lost salt gift of blood* (1976; NEW CANADIAN LIBRARY, with an Afterword by Joyce Carol Oates) brought together seven of his stories. It received high praise from both critics and the writing community. *As birds bring forth the sun and other stories* (1986; NCL with an Afterword by Jane URQUHART) brought together another seven stories and again received critical acclaim. Joyce Carol Oates introduced MacLeod's work to a larger American audience with her selection of his stories, *The lost salt gift of blood: new and selected stories* (1988). This collection (which includes four of the *Blood* stories, six of the *Sun* stories, and a new long story, 'Island') was chosen by *Publisher's Weekly* as one of the best books of 1988. Following the 1991 British publication of *The lost salt gift of blood*, MacLeod's stories found a large and admiring audience in Scotland—six were translated into Gaelic. Two of his stories have also been translated into Russian, and the collection has been translated into French (Quebec, 1994; Paris, 1995), as has *As birds bring forth the sun* (Quebec, 1995).

MacLeod's stories grow slowly. In the last thirty years he has published only sixteen stories, which on the surface appears to be a rather thin output. But as Oates points out, one senses that MacLeod's intensely compacted stories 'might have been expanded into novels.' He works slowly, but with lapidary sureness, cutting and polishing each word, phrase, sentence, and paragraph to achieve rhythms and density characteristic of poetry (he has, in fact, published about fifteen poems).

MacLeod's deep identification with the geography and culture of Cape Breton—its Gaelic heritage, the working life of the farm, mine, bush, and sea—lies at the centre of his stories, which draw on the oral tradition of storytelling. MacLeod's narrators are also haunted by their pasts, immediate and ancestral, and they elegiacally reflect on their pasts in what appears to be the immediate present, in a kind of eternal 'nowness' in which their pasts bleed persistently into their present.

Many of his narrators attempt to free themselves from their families, from the traditional island professions of mining, farming, and fishing, and from the close-knit Cape Breton culture, by leaving for the eastern or mid-western cities. In these stories ('The vastness of the dark', 'The lost salt gift of blood', 'The boat', 'The return', 'The road to Rankin's Point') MacLeod explores a kind of triple paradox: you have to leave home, but you can never leave home, and when you leave home you cannot come back home.

See Colin Nicolson, 'Signatures of time: Alistair MacLeod & his short stories', *CANADIAN LITERATURE* 107 (Winter 1985), and 'Alistair MacLeod' in Andrew Garrod, *Speaking for myself: Canadian writers in interview* (1986). ORM MITCHELL

MacLeod, Jack. See HUMOUR AND SATIRE IN ENGLISH and NOVELS IN ENGLISH 1960 TO 1982: OTHER TALENTS, OTHER WORKS: 3.

MacLeod, Joan (b.1954). Born in Vancouver, British Columbia, she has creative writing degrees from the University of Victoria (B.A., 1978) and the University of British Columbia (M.F.A., 1981). A published poet, MacLeod entered the world of theatre as librettist for *The secret garden* (prod.1985, Comus Music Theatre), an opera adaptation of the classic Victorian novel. Written with composer Stephen MacNeff, it won a 1986 Dora Mavor Moore Award for Best New Musical. She moved to Toronto in 1985 to join Tarragon Theatre's Six Playwrights Unit and then became playwright-in-residence until 1992, when she returned to British Columbia.

Tarragon premièred both *Jewel* (1989) and *Toronto, Mississippi* (1989) in 1987—both of which have had many productions. The former is the poignant 'conversation' that a young widow has with her husband, a casualty of Newfoundland's 1984 Ocean Ranger oil-rig disaster. The Canadian Broadcasting Corporation radio adaptation, *Hand of God*, was aired in 1988. This lyrical solo for a single voice provided a natural transition to MacLeod's first 'real' play, *Toronto, Mississippi*. Mining her own experiences as a life-skills teacher, it tells the story of a single mother trying to raise her difficult, mentally handicapped daughter. The crisis occurs when Jhana's flamboyant father, an Elvis Presley impersonator, shows up and decides not to leave.

MacLeod's *Amigo's blue guitar* (1992), which won a Governor General's Award, juxtaposes cultures and complicated personal motives while dealing with the consequences for a Gulf Island (British Columbia) family when they sponsor a Salvadorean refugee. *The hope slide* (1994), which began as a 1992 CBC radio drama called 'Teenage Doukhobor', won the 1993 Chalmers Canadian Play Award. It returns to the monologue form, but this time the speaker plays not only herself but other characters: embarked on a tour of her one-person show about the Doukhobors, an actress experiences a dark night of the soul. The controlling metaphor is loss, but her reverie weaves together memories of coming of age in the 1960s, the famous landslide outside Hope, British Columbia, untimely deaths from AIDS, and persecution of the Doukhobors community.

Little sister (1994) also began as a monologue, and won the 1995 Chalmers Award in the Theatre for Young Audiences category. Inspired by Katherine Gilday's documentary *The Famine Within* and intended for teenage audiences, its subject is self-image, body image, and eating disorders. MacLeod's *2000* (produced in 1996) is less about particular issues than about a general anxiety for the future. Living on the edge of a century, on the edge of a ravine, a middle-aged couple are totally immersed in their own hectic present as urban planners. But, as a result of various intruders, they become painfully aware of their own estrangement.

CYNTHIA ZIMMERMAN

McLuhan, Marshall (1911-80). Herbert Marshall McLuhan was born in Edmonton, Alberta, and spent his youth in Winnipeg. He graduated from the University of Manitoba (B.A., 1933, M.A., 1934) and received a doctorate in English literature from Cambridge University in 1943. In 1944, after teaching English at Saint Louis University, a Jesuit institution in St Louis, Missouri, he returned to Canada to teach at Assumption College (now the University of Windsor). From 1946 until shortly before his death he taught English at St Michael's College, University of Toronto, where he became interested in media of communication, culture, and technology, organizing an interdisciplinary seminar in 1953-4 under the sponsorship of the Ford Foundation. Outgrowths of this project included the innovative periodical *Explorations*, which he co-edited with Edmund (Ted) Carpenter from 1953 to 1959, and the Centre of Culture and Technology (1963-81), at the University of Toronto, of which he was founding director. One of the first scholars to occupy the Albert Schweitzer Chair at

Fordham University, New York, in 1967, he was elected FRSC in 1964, and named a Companion of the Order of Canada in 1970.

Although usually described as a communications scholar, McLuhan made major contributions to literary and cultural studies, and to the understanding of the role of media and the effects of technology in society. His first work, *The mechanical bride: folklore of industrial man* (1951), applied the strategies of a satirically focused critical interpretation to products of popular culture and the media industries. As early as 1959 (writing presciently about the 1990s), he said in a letter that in the electronic age 'we are returning to the old tribal patterns, abandoning the highly individualistic ways of the Western World. . . . The tribe is a unit, which, extending the boundaries of the family to include the whole society, becomes the only way of organizing society when it exists in a kind of Global Village pattern . . . caused by the instantaneous movement of information from every quarter to every point at the same time. Tribal man, or family man, is characterized by certain basic outlooks and strategies, of which perhaps the most obvious is a deep sense of togetherness, a strong resistance to change.'

McLuhan's international reputation was established by two works bridging historical and theoretical problems. *The Gutenberg galaxy: the making of typographic man* (1962) analyses the pre-print, oral/aural culture and the cultural changes brought about by Gutenberg's invention of movable type and the mass production of books; it introduced publicly one of McLuhan's most famous phrases in stating that the world had become a 'global village' in its electronic interdependence. *Understanding media: the extensions of man* (1964) examines the radical changes in human responses caused by electronic communications and contains one of his most celebrated aphorisms, 'the medium is the message'. After the publication of these books McLuhan's name became a word in itself (e.g., *mcluhanisme* in France). His work paralleled the interests of other Canadian scholars, particularly H.A. INNIS—who has often been described, erroneously, as his mentor. (McLuhan did share with Innis a realization of the importance of technology in shaping human cultural development.) While McLuhan, like Northrop FRYE, was interested in problems of interpretation and symbolism, he had a broader scope, seeking a total cultural criticism. McLuhan emphasized the way polysemy in language (e.g., puns, ambiguity, metaphor) reveals the continuum between all orders of cultural expression.

Influenced by the work of avant-garde writers such as Wyndham Lewis and James Joyce, McLuhan created a series of *essais concrètes* combining photography, layout, advertising techniques, headlines, typography, and visual arrangement: e.g., *The medium is the massage* (1967) and *War and peace in the global village* (1968). Other books by McLuhan include: *The literary criticism of Marshall McLuhan 1943-62* (1969); *Counterblast* (1969); *Culture is our business* (1970); and *The city as classroom* (1977). *Verbi-voco-visual* (1967) was originally Issue 8 of *Explorations*. He co-authored (with Wilfred WATSON) *From cliché to archetype* (1970), (with Barrington Nevitt) *Take today: the executive as dropout* (1972), and (with Harley Parker) *Through the vanishing point* (1968), a study of the contemporary revolution by media and the avant-garde against the assumptions of Renaissance perspective and print culture. In addition to *Explorations*, McLuhan co-edited with his son, Eric, *The Dew Line*, an important information letter for those involved in government, business, and academia. Eugene McNAMARA edited *The interior landscape: the literary criticism of Marshall McLuhan 1943-62* (1969). Two posthumous publications have appeared: *Laws of media: the new science* (1988), co-authored with Eric McLuhan, and *The global village: transformation in world life and media in the 21st century* (1989), co-authored with Bruce Powers. The letters of McLuhan were also published posthumously (see below).

McLuhan conceived of himself as a 'poet *manqué*' who produced do-it-yourself creativity kits. Despite obvious weaknesses in his writing (such as a tendency towards technological determinism), their perceptions, theoretical suggestivity, and paradoxes are distinctive, inventive, and very much a product of his having pursued his career in Canada. Possessing a typical Canadian sensitivity to the way in which technology, cultural products, and media affect the quality of life, McLuhan was one of the first scholars to recognize that technology had become a major factor in human evolution and in the changing shape of modern culture. As his literary criticism and concern with history suggest, his thought was rooted in humanism, modernist art, and literature, and in an avant-garde version of Thomism that grew out of his conversion to Catholicism.

While in the late 1970s and in the 1980s there was a decline of interest in McLuhan (though his name never ceased to be mentioned in print media), his influence among artists, film-makers, and multi-media artists persisted. In *The media lab* (1987) Stuart Brand first called attention to McLuhan's important influence among researchers at the MIT Media Lab—such as its former director, Nicholas Negroponte. In the 1990s McLuhan has re-emerged as a major influence with the appearance of the new cyberworld of the Internet and Virtual Reality: *Wired* magazine's premier issue opened with five pages of elaborate visual display incorporating quotations from McLuhan, and on the masthead he is named the magazine's 'patron saint'. Since early 1994 a miniature photo with a short aphorism has been added. *Mondo 2000* has declared him to be 'a man for all media', and an article in the second issue of *Post-modern culture* linked McLuhan to James Joyce and modernist art as an important figure in the pre-history of cyberspace. McLuhan, whose works continue to assist us in understanding our global technoculture of computers and telecommunications, has assumed a new importance.

McLuhan's theoretical contributions to the interface between rapidly evolving technology and human culture have been recognized by the McLuhan Teleglobe Canada Award sponsored by UNESCO.

The primary writings on McLuhan's work are: Jonathan Miller, *McLuhan* (1971); Donald Theall, *The medium is the rear view message: understanding McLuhan* (1971); Jacques LANGUIRAND, *De McLuhan à Pythagore* (1972); Arthur Kroker, *Technology and the Canadian mind: Innis, McLuhan, Grant* (1984); and Graeme Patterson, *History and communications: Harold Innis, Marshall McLuhan, the interpretation of history* (1990). Three excellent collections of essays and reviews are *McLuhan hot and cool* (1967), edited by Gerald E. Stearn; *McLuhan: pro and con* (1968), edited by Raymond Rosenthal; and a special issue of the *Canadian Journal of Communications* (December 1989), edited by Donald Theall. For McLuhan as a cultural critic and literary theorist, see John Fekete, *The critical twilight* (1977), and Donald Theall, *Beyond the word: reconstructing sense in the Joyce era of technology, culture, and communication* (1995). Biographical information may be found in Philip Marchand's *McLuhan* (1989). Remarks and reminiscences by many of those who knew McLuhan appear in *Who was Marshall McLuhan?* (1994), edited by Barrington Nevitt and Maurice McLuhan. Important biographical and critical commentary and annotations by William Toye are to be found in *Letters of Marshall McLuhan* (1987), selected and edited by Matie Molinari, Corinne McLuhan, and Toye.

DONALD F. THEALL

MacMechan, Archibald (1862-1933). Born in Berlin (Kitchener), Ontario, Archibald McKellar MacMechan was educated at the University of Toronto and Johns Hopkins University, and was professor of English at Dalhousie University, Halifax, from 1889 until two years before his death. He was made a Fellow of the Royal Society of Canada in 1926 and was awarded the Lorne PIERCE medal for distinguished service to Canadian literature in 1931.

MacMechan is principally known for his engaging familiar essays. Three early collections are *The porter of Bagdad and other fantasies* (1901), a small volume of typically late-Victorian whimsical essays; *The life of a little college* (1914), the title essay of which deals with MacMechan's affectionate ties with Dalhousie University; and *The book of Ultima Thule* (1928), essays concerned mostly with the author's personal response to Nova Scotia geography and history. His familiarity with the sea, and the local history relating to it, is central to three historically based collections that represent the writing he considered to be of most lasting value: *Sagas of the sea* (1923), *Old Province tales* (1924), and *There go the ships* (1928). *Tales of the sea* (1947), edited by Thomas RADDALL, is a posthumous collection of essays drawn from these books. MacMechan's critical survey of the principal works of English- and French-Canadian authors, *Headwaters of Canadian literature* (1924; NCL 1974), sets forth his strongly held views concerning the need for a native literature worthy of international recognition. His adherence to idiosyncratic standards, and his recognition of the dual national culture, make this book an important contribution to early Canadian literary criticism. On local history MacMechan also wrote *Red snow on Grand Pré* (1921) and *The Halifax explosion* (unpublished); and on political history, *The winning of popular government* (1916) in the Chronicles of Canada series. His published verse includes *Three sea songs* (1919) and the posthumous *Late harvest* (1934). As a scholar of non-Canadian literature he published his doctoral dissertation, *The relation of Hans Sachs to the Decameron as shown in an examination of the thirteenth Shrovetide plays from that source* (1889); and he edited editions of two works by Thomas Carlyle, *Sartor resartus* (1896) and *Heroes and hero worship* (1901), the *Select poems of Lord Tennyson* (1907), and the Thoreau chapter in the *Cambridge history of American literature* (1916). From 1907 until his death, MacMechan was a weekly book reviewer for *The Montreal Standard*, writing under the nom-de-plume 'The Dean'.

See also CRITICISM IN ENGLISH: 2 and ESSAYS IN ENGLISH: 2. JANET BAKER

Macmillan Company of Canada, The. Like a number of other Canadian branches of English publishing companies, the Macmillan Company of Canada owes its existence to the absence of copyright protection in the United States for foreigners in the nineteenth century. Alexander Macmillan visited the USA at the end of the Civil War to look into the prospects for setting up a North American establishment to stock and sell his books, and so discourage 'pirates' from producing unlicensed editions. He found the right man to head such a business in George Edward Brett, who was succeeded by his son, and then by his grandson. The New York firm worked Canadian territory; but when it rose to the front rank of American publishers, it became necessary to have a house in Canada that would incidentally enable Macmillan's to obtain imperial copyright, an ironic reversal of the purpose that had brought it into existence. The Canadian Macmillan Company was incorporated in 1905, as one of a chain of branches and depots then being established around the Empire. The New York company, because of its size, was permitted to hold an interest in it.

Macmillan of Canada took off well, and within two years had put up a building at 70 Bond Street, Toronto, where the company was to remain until 1980. During the First World War the management under Frank Wise had become slack. In 1917 a young Yorkshireman, Hugh Eayrs (1894-1940), who had been in Canada for five years with Maclean-Hunter, joined Macmillan, and in 1921 he succeeded Wise as president. The elderly London partners were deriving a good profit from the great American business they had founded, which was now entirely self-managing but still subject to London's control. Eayrs impressed them with his youthful vigour, his brilliant, though sometimes impractical, plans, and his evangelistic belief in the future of Canada. Within two years he had published W.H. BLAKE's translation of Louis HÉMON's *MARIA CHAPDELAINE*, which became a great success in Britain and the USA, as well as in Canada. Encouragement of their aggressive young Canadian manager must have seemed to the London partners a way of keeping the American Bretts—who appeared to be growing too big for their boots—in order. Eayrs was allowed his head, acquiring the agency for Cambridge Bibles and prayer-books as well as for a whole group of British medical publishers, and even for one or two of Brett's American rivals.

When, in 1950, the London partners decided to sell the Macmillan Company, New York—now a giant bigger than themselves and impossible to control—they bought back, as part of the deal, the interest the American company had been allowed to have in the Canadian company. Eayrs had died during the war and was succeeded in 1946 by John GRAY. From that point on, until Gray's retirement in 1973, Macmillan Canada, riding the crest of the wave of Canada's postwar publishing expansion under Gray's expert leadership, became one of the largest and most successful publishing companies in Canada. Its list of Canadian authors included Mazo DE LA ROCHE, Morley CALLAGHAN, Hugh MacLENNAN, Robertson DAVIES, and Donald CREIGHTON.

Difficulty in finding a suitable successor to John Gray caused the London partners to sell Macmillan Canada to Maclean-Hunter in 1973. In 1980 Macmillan of Canada was taken over by Gage Publishing Limited, who retained the imprint but made the trade publishing a division of its educational business. Macmillan Canada is now a division of Canada Publishing Corporation. LOVAT DICKSON

McNamara, Eugene (b. 1930). Born in Oak Park, Illinois, and educated in the Chicago area, he came to Canada in 1959 to teach English at the University of Windsor (then Assumption University), where he was instrumental in 1967 in starting the Creative Writing Program, of which he was director until his retirement in 1995. He is now Professor Emeritus. He has long been associated with the academic and cultural life of Windsor, editing the *University of Windsor Review* for many years from its inception in 1965, and co-founding Sesame Press in 1973 with Peter STEVENS and Dorothy Farmiloe; he has also been connected with various Windsor little magazines, including *Mainline* and *Connexion*.

The dominant mood of McNamara's poetry in *For the mean time* (1965), *Passages* (1972), *Hard words* (1972), and *In transit* (1975) is one of gently brooding melancholy about the passage of time, though this overall tone does not preclude another of tough irony and satire as well. Other poems concentrate on external reality, both on and below the surface, often centring on the joys and pains of family and human love as the titles of some volumes suggest: *Love scenes* (1970), *Diving for the body* (1974), and *Forcing the field* (1981). His poetry of the last fifteen years is more pervasively personal, while continuing with these same themes—as in *The moving light* (1986);

though *Call it a day* (1984) concentrates more on the depiction of physical labour and work in factories.

For many years McNamara was a film critic, writing a weekly column for the *Windsor Star* and reviewing movies for CBC radio. He sees movies as mythic reflections of our world: *Dillinger poems* (1971) and *Screens* (1977) show both a fondness for the movie vision and a perception of film's romantic expression and falsifications: movies are a way into life, while at the same time they are a barrier to reality. The poems in these books are full of clear, direct imagery with a filmic sharpness, even as they are grounded in a documentary realism that also takes on some of the glamour associated with movies.

McNamara's early fiction was collected in two volumes—*Salt: short stories* (1975) and *The search for Sarah Grace and other stories* (1977). His stories have the same clarity as his poetry, though often they veer off into mysteries and ambiguities of character and event. *Spectral evidence* (1985) and *Fox trot* (1994) contain stories that are fictional extrapolations from various factual events and characters (he calls them 'factions'). The disparities between facts and fiction allow the stories to expand those ironic shifts and ambiguities that are present in the earlier work, as well as to undermine the nature of both fact and fiction with parodic patterns. McNamara's stories appeared in *Best Canadian Stories* in 1979, 1987, 1991, and 1994.

McNamara has published critical articles in numerous academic journals on modern literature, particularly American. He edited *The interior landscape: the literary criticism of Marshall McLuhan, 1943-1962* (1969).

PETER STEVENS

McNeil, Florence (b. 1940). Born in Vancouver and educated at the University of British Columbia, where she studied under Earle BIRNEY, McNeil is the daughter of Scottish Hebridean emigrants. To her ancestry may be attributed her interest in narrative and in how the past impinges on the present. The poems in McNeil's collections—such as *Walhachin* (1972), *Ghost towns* (1975), *Emily* (1975), and *Barkerville* (1984)—often take the form of linked sequences, typically grounded in a historical person, tribe, place, or event. *Walhachin* and *Barkerville* (later adapted as a stage production and radio play) deal with specific extinct communities in the British Columbia interior; the title of *Ghost towns* is self-explanatory; and *Emily* is based on the life of Emily CARR. *The overlanders* (1982) is based on the trek of settlers from Canada West (Ontario) to the B.C. interior in 1862. The documentary impulse even extends to *The rim of the park* (1972), drawn from her own life. Besides the sense of historical wonder, her work is marked by imagistic incisiveness and, in later collections, by fluid diction and increased openness of form. *Swimming out of history* (1991) gathers selections from six previous collections and adds new poems.

McNeil, who lives in Delta, British Columbia, has taught at Western Washington State College (now University), the University of Calgary, and the University of British Columbia, but has been a full-time writer since 1976. She is also active as a writer for children, having published *Miss P. and me* (1982), *All kinds of magic* (1984), *Catriona's island* (1988), and *When is a poem: creative ideas for teaching poetry collected from Canadian poets* (1980), besides editing the anthologies *Here is a poem* (1983), and *Do whales jump at night? Poems for kids* (1990). She won the Sheila A. Egoff Prize for children's literature in 1989.

FRASER SUTHERLAND

Macphail, Sir Andrew (1864-1938). He was born John Andrew McPhail at Orwell, Prince Edward Island. Following grammar school he won an entrance scholarship to Prince of Wales College, Charlottetown. The excellent teaching and classical ideals he encountered in his two years there influenced him permanently. After three years as a teacher in rural Prince Edward Island, he proceeded to McGill University, where he received a B.A. (1888) and an M.D. (1891). He married Georgina Burland of Montreal in 1893, and practised medicine for about ten years, while also teaching in the medical faculty of the University of Bishop's College, Montreal, from 1893 to 1905. In 1907 he was appointed McGill's first professor of the history of medicine, a chair he held for thirty years. He had become editor of the monthly *Montreal Medical Journal* in 1903; when it merged with another medical periodical eight years later to establish the *Canadian Medical Association Journal*, Macphail was made editor of the new monthly. Serving overseas in the Canadian army medical services (1915-19), he attained the rank of major. He was knighted in 1918.

After the death of his wife in 1902, Macphail published more than ten books and scores of shorter pieces. *The vine of Sibmah; a relation of the Puritans* (1906) is a romantic novel set in the Restoration period. In 1921 he published the first translation of Louis HÉMON's classic *MARIA CHAPDELAINE*, which he described as 'the book that has interested me most in all my lifetime'—a fondness that reflected his deep commitment to a rural and traditional way of life, and his sentimental admiration for French Canada. (Macphail had attempted to collaborate with W.H. BLAKE on a translation, but they were unable to agree on stylistic matters. Macphail's translation preceded Blake's by a matter of months, but Blake's has become the standard one.) Macphail published four one-act plays—'The land' (1914), 'The last rising' (1930), 'Company' (1936), and 'The new house' (1937)—none of which were performed.

A prolific and forceful writer and an accomplished stylist, Macphail was the best Canadian personification of the nineteenth-century ideal of the non-specialist man-of-letters who wrote in a confident tone on a wide range of subjects. His favourite and most successful medium was the essay. *Essays in puritanism* (1905) is a series of biographical studies of literary and religious figures; *Essays in politics* (1909) is about contemporary political issues, particularly the nature, real and ideal, of the imperial connection between Canada and Great Britain; *Essays in fallacy* (1910) offers lengthy polemical critiques of feminism, modern education, and modern theological trends; and *Three persons* (1929) is made up of extended reviews of memoirs by three figures of the First World War, including T.E. Lawrence. Most of the essays in the second and third collections had already appeared, in whole or in part, in *The UNIVERSITY MAGAZINE*, a quarterly Macphail edited from 1907 to 1920, with the exception of the time he spent overseas. In many respects this magazine was his most remarkable achievement.

The book to which Macphail devoted most care, and which he considered his best, was published posthumously: *The master's wife* (1939; NCL 1977; Institute of Island Studies, 1994). An autobiographical reminiscence of Prince Edward Island, it focuses particularly on his father, who was a school inspector ('the master' of the title), on his mother, and on Orwell. The characters in the book are real: as well as his parents and local people, they include literary and academic figures like Edward William THOMSON (disguised as 'the Old Gentleman'), and James Mavor, professor of political economy at the University of Toronto. For Macphail, his native province represented a way of life—emphasizing stability and traditional ties, and a relative lack of materialism—that provided the basis for the romantic anti-industrial sensibility that formed the core of his social criticism.

For many years *The master's wife* was a hidden treasure of Canadian writing. There were several reasons for this obscurity. His two children published the novel through a private arrangement with a printer, and this method, with its lack of linkage to a system of distribution, combined with the outbreak of war in 1939 to bury it in terms of public consciousness. In the first edition of this *Companion*, historian J.M. Bumsted drew attention to another cause for its neglect: its defiance of neat categorization as either history or literature or biography or memoir. The 1977 NCL reprint provided national distribution for the book, which at last began to receive the circulation and recognition it merited. Because of *The master's wife* Janice KULYK KEEFER, in her *Under eastern eyes* (1987), ranks Macphail with such major Maritime writers as Thomas McCULLOCH, T.C. HALIBURTON, and Joseph HOWE. With its power, its rich texture, and its complexity, the book in her view is 'one of the finest and oddest pieces of prose to be found in Maritime, or Canadian literature as a whole'.

The book of sorrow (1916), an anthology of poetry that Macphail had initially compiled after the death of his wife, includes two Petrarchan sonnets by himself. He also edited *In Flanders fields and other poems* (1919), a collection of John McCRAE's verse, with a 95-page essay on the poet; the *Official history of the Canadian forces in the Great War, 1914-1919: the medical services* (1925); and *The Bible in Scotland* (1931).

Since the middle of the 1970s Macphail has reached a new level of public recognition in modern Prince Edward Island, in part because of *The master's wife*, but also because of his significance in defining a distinctive Prince Edward Island identity, which values the non-material aspects of life, and his importance as an eloquent spokesman for rural Canada in general. This intense interest, and a growing perception that he stands with Milton ACORN and Lucy Maud MONTGOMERY at the summit among writers rooted in Prince Edward Island, led to deep concern over the fate of his family property, which had been given to the provincial government in 1961, in the expectation that it would be used as a park for the benefit of the public. An informal group known as 'Friends of Macphail' pressured the government into making a commitment in 1989 to save the house and to keep the property intact. Since then, the Friends have established the 'Sir Andrew Macphail (of Orwell, P.E.I.) Foundation Inc.' and have restored the house beautifully. In 1994 the Institute of

Island Studies at the University of Prince Edward Island published a facsimile reprint of the original edition of *The master's wife*, including the same photographs of the main characters, and an expanded introduction.

See Ian Ross Robertson, 'Sir Andrew Macphail as a social critic' (unpublished Ph.D. thesis, University of Toronto, 1974), which contains a complete bibliography of Macphail's published and unpublished works.

IAN ROSS ROBERTSON

Macpherson, Jay (b. 1931). Born in England, she came to Newfoundland with her mother and brother at the age of nine, and in 1944 the family settled in Ottawa. She studied at Carleton College (1951-2), McGill University (1953), and the University of Toronto (M.A. 1955; Ph.D. 1964), where, until her retirement in 1996, she was professor of English at Victoria College. Her first poems were published by Alan Crawley in *CONTEMPORARY VERSE* when she was eighteen. Her first poetry collection, *Nineteen poems* (1952), was published by Robert Graves' Seizin Press. *O earth return* (later to become section two of *The boatman*) came out in 1954 under the imprint of her own small press, EMBLEM BOOKS. Macpherson has not published a great deal of poetry, yet her reputation as an important Canadian poet was firmly established with her first commercially published book, *The BOATMAN* (1957), which won a Governor General's Award. In this collection she was revealed as a poet of wit and erudition who—influenced by Northrop FRYE's theory of mythic displacement—rewrote mythological themes in colloquial style. *The boatman* was reissued in 1968 with sixteen new poems. Her next book, *Welcoming disaster* (1974) was privately published. Both volumes—including the 'new poems' in the second edition of *The boatman*—were reissued in 1981 under the title *Poems twice told*, with decorations by the author. *Four ages of man: the classical myths* (1962) is Macpherson's retelling of Greek myths for young people. In 1982 she published a scholarly study, *The spirit of solitude: conventions and continuities in late romance*, in which she examines traditional pastoral romance conventions in nineteenth- and twentieth-century narratives, including Mary Shelley's *Frankenstein*, and explores their evolution in Canadian literature from Oliver GOLDSMITH to James REANEY.

The poems in *The boatman*, and some of Macpherson's later poems, have the resonance of archetypal experience in the manner of William Blake's more epigrammatic pieces. In *Welcoming disaster*, a complex and difficult work, the poems record a psychological struggle against poetic silence in a personal wasteland. Composed of five parts plus an epilogue, the book follows a traditional mystical pattern: the way up and the way down are the same. The sequence begins in a dark night of the soul, with the poet metaphorically orphaned. The controlling symbol, a child's teddy-bear called Tedward, functions as a substitute for 'Him not there' (father, lover, God), an embodiment of a childish need in the adult psyche and of a metaphysical longing. The struggle towards 'Recognitions' (Section IV) is realized when the child's bear is transformed into the constellation Ursa Major. The poet recognizes that direction can be found only when the dark impulses in the self are acknowledged and explored. As the critic Sherrill Grace has made clear, the poems achieve a profound cultural and archetypal resonance by their allusions to Sumerian and Babylonian myth. The female persona is identified with the goddess Inanna who, in the tradition of fertility cults, must annually search the underworld for the lost god, Dumuzi or Tammuz. But the peculiar originality and poignancy of the poems comes from a second level of allusion: to the world of fairy tale and nursery rhyme. Grace suggests convincingly that Tedward can be associated with the Teddy Bear of A.A. Milne's *When we were young*. Macpherson's extraordinary gnomic gifts are demonstrated by the way that even her notes and acknowledgements at the end of *Poems twice told* are rendered humorously in rhyme.

For discussions of Macpherson's poetry, see James Reaney's 'The third eye', *CANADIAN LITERATURE* 3 (Winter 1960); Northrop Frye's review of *The boatman* reprinted in *The bush garden: essays on the Canadian imagination* (1971); Sherrill Grace, 'Jay Macpherson', *Dictionary of literary biography*, vol. 53; and Lorraine Weir, *Jay Macpherson and her works* (1989).

See also POETRY IN ENGLISH 1950 TO 1982: 1.

ROSEMARY SULLIVAN

McPherson, John (1817-45). Born in Liverpool, Nova Scotia, he received his early schooling there. At about the age of seven, following the death of his parents, he went to live with his uncle at North Brookfield, a farming area inland from Liverpool, and there he met Angus M. Gidney, a young school teacher and poet, who recognized his gift for verse. In the late 1830s Gidney went on to become an editor of several newspapers in Halifax and was instrumental in introducing McPherson to other literary-minded people whenever he visited the city. Encouraged by this attention, McPherson decided to dedicate himself to writing poetry. Neither through poetry nor through a variety of jobs could he support himself, however, and in 1841 he returned to North Brookfield, settled on schoolteaching, married, and fathered a daughter. He soon found his work onerous, his income insufficient, and his health (always delicate) failing, though he managed to sustain a high level of poetic activity, publishing verse in Halifax newspapers and a prize poem, *In praise of water* (Halifax, 1843). In 1843, when poverty and sickness made his situation desperate, friends in Halifax raised a small sum to help him build a cottage near North Brookfield, but by the time he and his family moved in (Dec. 1844), his health was broken and the place was found to be unfit for winter habitation. In May 1845 McPherson was carried to his uncle's home and died there on 26 July. His poems were collected and edited by John Sparrow THOMPSON and ultimately published under the title *Poems, descriptive and moral by John McPherson* (Halifax, 1862).

As with Grizelda TONGE, much of McPherson's local fame rested on the tragic circumstances of his life. But there is more to McPherson than myth: he left a substantial body of verse. Apart from a large number of conventional poems on moral and religious subjects (especially temperance), there is a group that can be loosely classified as nature poems in which an intense awareness of mortality introduces elements of nostalgia and melancholy into the tone and mood. The poems are sentimental in character, but in the best of them the sentiment is counterbalanced by an intellectual appreciation of ideal harmony between humanity and nature.

TOM VINCENT

MacSkimming, Roy. See NOVELS IN ENGLISH 1983 TO 1996: OTHER NOVELS: 2(b).

McWhirter, George (b. 1939). Born in Belfast, Northern Ireland, he was educated at Queen's University, Belfast, where he taught high school. After teaching at the Berlitz School in Barcelona, Spain, he immigrated to Canada in 1966, taught in Port Alberni, British Columbia, and since 1968 has lived in Vancouver. He has taught at the University of British Columbia since 1970, and became head of the department of creative writing in 1982. He is one of Canada's most original poets and fiction writers, as well as a frequent contributor to radio broadcasting as playwright, poet, and interviewer. His poems and stories, which have been included in several anthologies, are characterized by strongly textured detail, alien or grotesque characters, and the surreal influences of Spain and Latin America. His viewpoint is always unexpected.

McWhirter's first book, *Catalan poems* (1971, co-winner of the Commonwealth Poetry Prize), was deeply immersed in his Spanish experiences; the poems work backward from the deathbed of Eduardo Valls to his marriage bed, in sometimes oblique language. McWhirter has also published a small chapbook, *Bloodlight for Malachi McNair* (1974).

The sharp imagery, strong physical detail, and the precise style of these poems continued in McWhirter's partly autobiographical book-length cycle of fifty-two poems, *Queen of the sea* (1976), in which the technology of the shipbuilding trades in his native Belfast, where the ill-fated *Titanic* and the *Reina del Mar* were built, provided extended metaphors. *Twenty-five* (1978) is a small collection of twenty-nine free-verse poems on the central themes of village life and Catholicism in Mexico. *The island man* (1981) is a poem-cycle set on Vancouver Island in the 1930s and based on motifs derived from *The Odyssey* and the Spanish explorers of early British Columbia. *Fire before dark* (1983) examines an Irish childhood and the Canadian landscape, character, and identity. The longest section describes the experience of Greek, Vietnamese, Japanese, and Irish immigrants both learning a new language and adapting to the new world of Canada. Recent collections include *A staircase for all souls* (1991), *The British Columbia suite: a wooded masque for readers and listeners* (1993), and *Incubus: the dark side of the light* (1994).

McWhirter's short stories are among the most innovative and experimental in Canada. The nineteen poetic, sometimes obscure, stories in *Bodyworks* (1974)—about a character named Hermione who lives in a mythological country, Sarne—are enriched by water imagery, an Irish comic vision, and heroic gods, as well as scatological and sexual humour. *God's eye* (1981) contains eleven stories set in Mexico. *Coming to grips with Lucy* (1982) is a series of reminiscences about the perils of growing up in Ireland and growing old in B.C. The Irish stories are poetic, textured, and use intercut storylines, while the B.C. stories are often hard-edged and brutal, with an emotional undercurrent suggested by animal imagery. *A bad day to be winning* (1991) is a self-conscious poetic collection of character sketches set in Northern Ireland.

Paula Lake (1984) is a stylish novella set in B.C. with an unsympathetic main character—a disturbed lifeguard who kidnaps a Japanese boy; the story is told with complex time-shifts, striking imagery and metaphor, and surreal incident. McWhirter's masterpiece, *Cage* (1987)—which received the Ethel WILSON British Columbia Book Prize—refers to the moral dilemma of the Reverend Benjamin Carragher, assigned to a parish in a superstitious Mexican town. To overcome the poverty he works with his parishioners to build bird cages for tourists. But he has also built a cage for himself. In this difficult novel, dreamscape and reality intermingle, as do past and present. McWhirter's third novel, *The listeners* (1991), tells the story of two musicians—a lute-playing father and a tuba-playing son, the Kerrs—in a series of flashbacks as they watch the parade that marks the Belfast celebration of the twelfth of July.

A renowned translator from the Spanish who maintains close contact with many writers in Mexico, McWhirter edited and translated many of the poems in *The selected poems of José Emilio Pacheco* (1987). In 1988 he won the F.R. SCOTT Translation Prize. With J. Michael YATES he co-edited *Contemporary poetry of British Columbia* (1970), and he also edited *Words from Inside* (1974, 1975), a magazine of prison writings. He is an advisory editor of *Prism International*, and a member of the board of directors of *CANADIAN FICTION MAGAZINE*. GEOFF HANCOCK

Maharaj, Rabindranath. See CARIBBEAN-CANADIAN LITERATURE.

Maheu, Gilles. See DRAMA IN FRENCH 1981 TO 1996: 4.

Maheux-Forcier, Louise (b. 1929). Born in Montreal, she studied at the École supérieure Sainte-Croix and at the Conservatoire de musique et d'art dramatique de Québec, and spent two years studying music in Paris on a Quebec government scholarship (1952-4). After courses in art history at the Université de Montréal, and another brief period in Europe in 1959, she abandoned music for writing.

Maheux-Forcier's three novels of the 1960s—*Amadou* (1963), *L'île joyeuse* (1964), and *Une forêt pour Zoé* (1969), which won a Governor General's Award—form a triptych evoking a gradual move from paralysis and violence to the discovery of a sacred woman-centred world. The opening line of *Amadou*—in which the narrator, symbolically isolated in a house in the Quebec countryside, announces she has killed her husband—signifies a violent rejection of the traditional patriarchal value system and inaugurates a process of birth that will continue throughout the triptych. Although the nostalgia for a childhood paradise, symbolized by the sandy island of *L'île joyeuse*, remains a constant in Maheux-Forcier's work, the succession of goddess figures in *Une forêt pour Zoé* marks a reconciliation with time and process and an ever-more-joyous rejection of traditional societal structures. In the 1970s Maheux-Forcier became more explicitly concerned with her own art and its relation to life. In *Paroles et musiques* (1973) a woman writer facing death attempts to evaluate her life and finds its meaning in her loves, her refusal to compromise, and above all in her writing. In *Appassionata* (1978) the author plays ironically on the relation between autobiography and fiction. The novel opens with a letter from Maheux-Forcier to her publisher in which she reflects on her literary career and presents the novel as the manuscript of a friend who has committed suicide and who had lived in the shadow of Maheux-Forcier's own success. Again the theme of the feminine couple captures the nostalgia for a unity that transcends time, and the rich sensuality of Maheux-Forcier's evocations contradicts the tragic destinies of her characters. *Appassionata* introduces humour in Maheux-Forcier's work. This quality is further developed in *En toutes lettres* (1980), a collection of wry, anecdotal, elegant short stories—whose titles follow the letters of the alphabet—that treat different facets, and different relationships, in the lives of women; it has been translated by David Lobdell as *Letter by letter* (1982). Maheux-Forcier is also the author of several television and radio plays, and of two stage plays: *Un parc en automne* (1982) and *Un jardin défendu* (1988).

See Jean-Guy Blondin, 'Aux sources de la rêverie poétique chez Louise Maheux-Forcier' in *Livres et auteurs québécois* (1971); Paulette Collet, 'La notion du bien et du mal chez Louise Maheux-Forcier', *Presénce francophone* (printemps 1976); and André Renaud, 'Les confidences de Louise Maheux-Forcier', *Lettres Québécoises* 37 (printemps 1985).

See also DRAMA IN FRENCH 1948 TO 1981: 4. PATRICIA SMART

Mailhot, Michèle. See NOVELS IN FRENCH 1960 TO 1982: 3(g).

Maillard, Keith (b. 1942). Born in Wheeling, West Virginia, he studied at West Virginia University and Vancouver Community

College, graduating with a degree in music (1977). After travelling extensively in North America and working in the anti-Vietnam War movement, he immigrated to Canada in 1970. A musician by profession, he taught lyric songwriting in the Creative Writing department of the University of British Columbia and in 1989 was made associate professor of creative writing.

Heavily influenced by Henry Miller and Jack Kerouac, Maillard is an obsessive overwriter: his novels are plotted with colour-coded note cards on storyboards, then edited down by hundreds of pages and rewritten dozens of times. A sensual writer, with great storytelling skills, and a moving sense of lucidly expressed emotions, he has been compared to the magic realists. Maillard is especially interested in the coming-of-age novel, with emotionally crippled parents and distorted memories; his books challenge the meaning of 'autobiography', since they are fictionalized accounts of his own experiences.

His first novel, *Two Strand River* (1976), is an adult fairy tale with the theme of androgyny on British Columbia's west coast. *Alex driving south* (1980) tells the story of a man coming to Canada to escape the draft. A long manuscript tentatively entitled 'Difficult beginnings' became two novels: *The knife in my hands* (1981) describes five years in the life of John Dupré up to 1963 as he deals with his androgyny, American violence, and arcane spirituality; and *Cutting through* (1982) is the sequel, as Dupré searches for his ancestral roots, comes to terms with his sexuality and American politics, and moves to Toronto to work on an underground paper. *Motet* (1980; rpr. 1997) was the first of a planned series of five novels (a motet is a sacred choral improvisation with several voices). Its complex plot tells the story of Paul Crane, a classical-music teacher, his family, his mid-life crisis, and has the psychedelic 1960s in Vancouver as background. Set in the fictional steel milltown of Raysburg, West Virginia, *Light in the company of women* (1993) is a superbly researched, meticulously plotted *tour de force*, written in the style of a nineteenth-century historical novel, that tells the story of an aristocratic family and their submerged traumas. The sequel, *Hazard zones* (1995), describes a contemporary researcher in areas subject to floods, which become a metaphor for a destructive past filled with alcoholism, self-defeat, and suppressed sexuality. There is an emotional resolution helped by therapy, and what could have been clichéd becomes a vital and absorbing narrative of redemption and inspiration.

See Peter Hinchcliffe and Ed Jewinski, eds, *Magic realism and Canadian literature* (1986).

GEOFF HANCOCK

Maillet, Andrée (1921-96). Born in Montreal, she was a journalist and lecturer as well as the writer of poetry, novels, short stories, and plays for theatre, television, and radio. Her writing appeared in numerous journals. After several years' residence in France, she became a member of L'Association de presse anglo-américaine in Paris following publication of her series of articles written on the Russian army of occupation in Germany. From 1952 to 1960 Maillet was editor of *Amérique française*, and in 1960 she was awarded the Prix Athanase-David for her *oeuvre*. In 1972 she was elected to the Académie canadienne-française. She also became a member of PEN and, amongst other honours, was made an Officer of the Order of Canada (1978), a Grand Officier de l'ordre du Québec (1991), and was awarded the Prix David (1990).

Maillet's first two novels, *Profil de l'orignal* (1953) and *Les remparts de Québec* (1965), were both reissued by Éditions de l'Hexagone, the first (1974) with a preface by Gilles MARCOTTE, the second (1977) with a preface by François Ricard. *Profil de l'orignal* is Maillet's most original work, a complex symbolic novel of quest in which, in a series of independent sketches, the hero, Paul Bar, moves from one identity to another—from hunter to professor to urbane literary critic. It is at once mystical, fantastic, and satirical. *Les remparts de Québec* is a penetrating portrait of a young girl, rendered in prose of great pathos and beauty. Indeed, it is Maillet's language—speaking forcefully in her poetry and in some of her novels and stories—that creates the interest of her best work. Subsequent novels are *Le bois-pourri* (1971), *Le doux mal* (1972; rpr. 1991), *À la mémoire d'un héros* (1975), *Lettres au surhomme* (vol. I, 1976; rpr. 1991), and *Miroir de Salomé* (*Lettres au surhomme*, vol. II, 1977; rpr. 1991).

Maillet's collections of poetry are *Elémentaires* (1964), *Le paradigme de l'idole* (1964), *Le chant de l'Iroquoise* (1967), and *Ski nocturne dans les Laurentides* (1976). Her short-story collections are *Ristontac* (1945), *Les Montréalaises* (1963), *Le lendemain n'est pas sans amour* (1963), *Le chêne des tempêtes suivi d'autres contes* (1965), *Nouvelles Montréalaises* (1966), and *Les bois de renards* (1967). *Les Montréalaises* and *Nouvelles Montréalaises* were twinned in a popular 1987 edition called *Les Montréalaises*; critic Gilles Marcotte perceptively characterized the stories as discovering and prophesying in the

Montreal of the 1960s the city of the 1980s, 'le Montréal pluri-ethnique, pluri-culturel dans lequel nous nous habituons peu à peu à vivre.' Maillet's plays are *Le meurtre d'Igouille* (1965), *La Montréalaise* (1968), *Souvenirs en accords brisés* (1969), and *La dépendance* (1973). Her children's books are *Le marquiset têtu et le mulot réprobateur* (1944, rpr. 1965) and *Le chêne des tempêtes* (1944; tr. by F.C.L. Muller as *Storm oak*, 1972). Excerpts from Maillet's 'Journal intime' were read in a series on Radio-Canada, and several of her works, such as *Le doux mal*, were adapted for television and radio. SHERRY SIMON/DAVID LEAHY

Maillet, Antonine (b. 1929). Born in Bouctouche, New Brunswick, she was educated at the universités de Moncton, N.B., and Montréal and Université Laval, where she received a Doctorat ès Lettres in 1970. She taught literature and folklore at Laval and Montréal and is now Chancellor of the Université de Moncton. The recipient of many honorary degrees and awards, she is a Companion of the Order of Canada and a member of the Queen's Privy Council for Canada.

Antonine Maillet is the leading writer of Acadia. She has revealed to a large public—through her books, and particularly through many performances (in both French and English) by Viola Léger of *La SAGOUINE*—the striking character of Acadian oral culture and language, which is a version of the sixteenth-century French of her ancestors, somewhat 'distorted by the climate and sharpened by the sea; by the salty air in the larynx and the obsessive beating of the waves in the ears'. The success of *La Sagouine* (1971) aroused interest in all her novels. *Pointe-aux-Coques* (1958), a village chronicle, was unnoticed when it first appeared, but was reissued by the publisher Leméac in 1972. *On a mangé la dune* (1962), tales about children, and *Par derrière chez mon père* (1972), a collection of picturesque, boisterous sketches and lively portraits (e.g. 'Soldat Bidoche'), are in the same humorous, touching, folkloric vein. Maillet's *L'Acadie pour quasiment rien* (1973) is a very personal travel guide. Her thesis *Rabelais et les traditions populaires en Acadie* (1971) collects for the first time more than 500 archaisms (from Touraine and Berry) still used in the francophone ghettoes of the Atlantic provinces.

Maillet, who was an observant storytelling child, learned her craft as an adult storyteller from her pioneer relatives, from rural folklore, village entertainers, and at election meetings and social gatherings. At once direct, spicy, and learned, Maillet's writings are meant to be narrated, performed. Her language is not *chiac* (from Shediac, the small fishing port near Moncton)—the equivalent of the most anglicized urban *joual*—but an old domestic French, coloured (and somewhat gratingly roughened, coarsened) by her personal touch and a special local intonation and accent. *La Sagouine* (freely translated as The Slattern) is a series of sixteen monologues that offer the reminiscences, grievances, anecdotes, and homilies of a seventy-two-year-old charwoman, a former prostitute, the wife of an Acadian fisherman. (An English edition, translated by Luis de Céspedes, was published in 1979.) *Les crasseux* (1968), a dialectal drama, and the fantasy *Don l'Orignal* (1972, translated as *The tale of Don l'Orignal* by Barbara Godard, 1978)—which won a Governor General's Award—treat similar themes and have recurring types. The 'gens d'En-bas' (those who live on the other side of the tracks) fight with the big-shots, the powerful, who are named for their occupations—the Mayoress, the Barber, the Milliner, the Playboy—while Noume, Citrouille, General Michel-Archange, La Sainte, La Cruche, and other 'Sagouins' are given nicknames. These actor-storytellers appear in one work after another—indestructible, welcomed, having echoes of Homer, Rabelais, Balzac, and of characters in a picaresque novel, while remaining Acadians, a minority within a minority. The play *Gapi et Sullivan* (1973), retitled *Gapi* (1976)—translated as *Gapi and Sullivan* by Luis de Céspedes, 1986—portrays two contrasting characters: the settled Acadian, a former fisherman who is now a lighthouse keeper, and the wandering Irishman, a sailor with exotic memories and imagination. In the novel *Mariaagélas* (1973; translated by Ben-Z. Shek, 1986), and in the play *Evangéline Deusse* (1975; translated by Luis de Céspedes, 1986) Maillet again creates indomitable, marginal women, who remain upright and haughty despite their illegal traffic in alcohol and flesh. They sell, but they never truly sell themselves. Their plain language, their faces, and their demeanour evoke scenes from the Flemish school of painting.

After completing several quick and easy projects, one of which was *Le bourgeois gentleman* (1978), a most un-Molière-like play, Maillet undertook the ambitious task of chronicling the return of the Acadians—French settlers of what is now Nova Scotia who were expelled by British troops in the 1750s and scattered throughout British colonies in America and the West Indies. *Pélagie-la-Charrette* (1979) recounts the odyssey and tribulations of one woman and a small group of outcasts who, picking up scores of other displaced Acadians, make their way over a period of ten years from the southern United States towards their ancestral homeland. It won the 1979 Prix Goncourt (the first time this prize had been awarded to an author who was not a native of France), became a best-seller, and was translated by Philip Stratford as *Pélagie: the return to a homeland* (1982). *Cent ans dans les bois* (1981), a title reminiscent of Gabriel García Marquéz, is another epic and picaresque novel, whose action occurs in 1880, near the New Brunswick border. Its use of folklore sometimes enhances and sometimes obscures the narrative.

Always lively and engaging, Maillet has become a personality, an institution. A street (where she lives) has been named after her in the Outremont district of Montreal. Her work continues to develop. In the theatre she has presented adaptations of Rabelais and Shakespeare (*William S.*, 1991) as well as her own plays—*La contrebandière* (1981), *Garrochés en paradis* (1986), and *Margot la Folle* (produced in 1987). Her picaresque and picturesque novels include *Crache-à-pic* (1984), translated as *The devil is loose* (1986) by Philip Stratford, and *Le huitième jour* (1986), translated as *On the eighth day* (1989) by Wayne Grady. *Les confessions de Jeanne de Valois* (1992)—a regal title for an original work—is both memoir and history, biography and autobiography. The writer, the former pupil, mingles her voice with that of a ninety-year-old woman, a pioneer, still lucid about matters of religion, pedagogy, culture, and the feminine and feminist in Acadia.

See also ACADIAN LITERATURE: 2, DRAMA IN FRENCH 1948 TO 1981: 3, and NOVELS IN FRENCH 1960 TO 1982: 3(c).

LAURENT MAILHOT

Mair, Charles (1838-1927). Born in Lanark, Upper Canada (Ontario), a timber town in the Ottawa Valley, Mair began medical studies in 1856 at Queen's University, Kingston, but left in 1857 to work for ten years in his family's timber business. In 1868, after another year at Queen's, he went to Ottawa, where he became one of the founders of the Canada First movement. He then accepted a job as paymaster to a government road party at the Red River Settlement (present-day Winnipeg). His vividly descriptive letters to his brother, who forwarded them to the Toronto *Globe*, praised the Northwest but insulted the Métis, particularly the women, and caused a furore in the Settlement. In Dec. 1869, during the Red River Rebellion, Mair was imprisoned and sentenced to death by Louis Riel. Escaping from Fort Garry, he later made his way east, to Toronto, where he roused Ontario's Orangemen over Riel's execution of Thomas Scott. Angry over Riel's confiscation of his poems, Mair returned to the West to join the suppression of Riel's North West Rebellion of 1885. Back in Toronto, he received a medal of honour and was proclaimed the 'warrior bard'.

Dreamland and other poems (Montreal, 1868), written before Mair joined Canada First, reveals a conventional imitator of Keats. Its preface, asking for guidance through candid criticism, is the first indication of Mair's method of composing poetry—creativity through consensus. R.G. Haliburton urged Mair to Canadianize his subject matter, to look to the Prairie buffalo rather than to Milton's 'Comus' for inspiration. Leaving the Northwest, where he had been a storekeeper in Portage la Prairie and Prince Albert, Mair moved to Windsor in 1822 to do research for *Tecumseh: a drama* (Toronto, 1886), a verse-play based on a central event for nineteenth-century writers, the War of 1812. This work (which benefited from the advice of George Denison, Goldwin SMITH, Daniel Wilson, Charles G.D. ROBERTS, and even Matthew Arnold) contrasts what Mair saw as the Canadian tradition of co-operative self-sacrifice with the American tradition of divisive self-interest. He identifies both Tecumseh and Isaac Brock as exemplars of self-sacrifice—'the spirit and springs of actions which have made Canada what she is.' A Shakespearean model is effective in Mair's description of the Northwest as being vast as an ocean, with its shoreless prairies and roaring waves of earth-rumbling bison, and as he depicts low Yankee ruffians using slang mimicked from T.C. HALIBURTON's Yankee pedlar. The play's central metaphors are the axe as both tool and weapon, and water as both redemptive stream and drowning flood. Its occasional flaws now look quaint and comical: one Byronic character enters 'carrying his rifle, and examining a knot of wild flowers'.

All of Mair's other poems repeat the flaws rather than the epic strengths of *Tecumseh*. The revisions recorded in *Tecumseh: a drama, and Canadian poems* (Toronto, 1901) reveal Mair's effort to Canadianize his earliest poems by replacing medieval knights with the warriors and heroines of 1812. 'The last bison' presents a hermaphrodite bison singing a conservationist song before it dies. Mair supported the concern of this poem with an essay, 'The American bison', that led to the federal government's establishment of a sanctuary for the world's last bison herd. Another prose work was *Through the Mackenzie Basin; a narrative of the Athabaska and Peace River Treaty Expedition of 1899* (1908)—Mair was secretary of the commission that was sent to negotiate land transfers with the Natives there. Appointed in 1898 to the federal immigration service in the West, he retired in 1921 to Victoria, British Columbia.

For a well-balanced view of the warrior bard, see Norman Shrive's biography, *Charles Mair: literary nationalist* (1965), and its revised edition, *The voice of the burdash: Charles Mair and the divided mind in Canadian literature* (1995). See also Shrive's introduction to *Dreamland and other poems/Tecumseh: a drama* (1974), and Leslie Monkman's succinct critical overview *Charles Mair*, vol. 5 (1986) in the series *Profiles in Canadian Literature*, edited by Jeffrey M. Heath. DAVID LATHAM

Major, André (b. 1942). Born in Montreal, he early became interested in separatist politics and was expelled from the Collège des Eudistes for his writings in leftist student publications. He was a contributor to *PARTI PRIS*, but broke with the group in 1965, after an ideological quarrel, to become editor of the literary section of *L'Action nationale*, the organ of the older Catholic nationalists of the right. He has been an arts editor of the weekly tabloid *Le Petit Journal*, a publisher's reader, a theatre and book critic for *Le Devoir*, and a radio producer.

A precocious poet, Major had his first collection, *Le froid se meurt*, published in 1961. This was followed by *Holocauste à 2 voix* (1961) and *Poèmes pour durer* (1969), his own selection from his earlier work, with new poetry. He writes of winter and coldness, usually as metaphors for Quebec and its people, of the everyday life of city streets, and of love and the flight of time. Some of his poems are personal, others political. All are marked by great energy and simplicity, hard, clear images, and an assured use of language.

Major's early short stories, most of which deal with Montreal slum life, were published—along with those of Jacques BRAULT and André BROCHU—in *Nouvelles* (1963), and in his own first collection *La chair de poule* (1965). A story from the latter group, 'La semaine dernière pas loin du pont', was made into a short film; another, 'Mental test pour tout le gang', is a thinly disguised account of the arrest of Hubert AQUIN. *La folle d'Elvis* (1981) is a less political collection, with wry, often slight stories about possible encounters that fail to take place, or when they do take place are merely tentative or disillusioning. It was translated by David Lobdell as *Hooked on Elvis* (1983). Major's novel *Le cabochon* (1964), written while he was still a member of the *parti pris* group, is the ideological and personal history of a young Montreal slum-dweller's progress towards revolutionary politics. *Le vent du diable* (1968), a love-triangle with a rural setting, may be read symbolically, the two young women involved representing two aspects of the hero's love for his 'native land' of Quebec. In his most mature and ambitious work, the trilogy *Histoires des déserteurs*, Major makes nominal and somewhat eccentric use of the classic police-chase form to make a sociological and psychological statement about rural Quebec life. In these three novels—*L'épouvantail* (1974), *L'épidémie* (1975), and *Les rescapés* (1976), which received a Governor General's Award—he weaves a tale of lust, murder, suicide, and violence of every sort to depict a society severed from its roots and yet still obsessed by a past that is at once too distant and too close. *L'épouvantail* has been translated by Sheila Fischman as *The scarecrows of Saint-Emmanuel* (1977) and *L'épidémie* by Mark Czarnecki as *Inspector Therrien* (1980). *L'hiver au coeur* (1987), translated by David Lobdell as *Winter of the heart* (1989), tells a rather simple story, which manages to escape sentimentality, about a man who leaves his wife and his job in publishing, settles into a furnished room, encounters his childhood sweetheart and finds happiness with her. *La vie provisoire* (1995) is a more complex account of disillusionment and attempted escape. Flee as he may, the protagonist is never able to achieve more than provisional freedom from an unhappy marriage and a sense of emptiness. Major has also published a stage play, *Une soirée en Octobre* (1975), and two radio plays, *Le désir suivi de Le perdant* (1973), the latter with a preface by François Ricard.

Major's *Félix-Antoine Savard* (1968), in the collection 'Écrivains canadiens d'aujourd'hui', is a critical biography of the late nationalist writer (q.v.), to whom Major felt deeply indebted.

Major was one of the six young French-Canadian poets included by Jacques GODBOUT and John Robert COLOMBO in the bilingual anthology *Poésie/Poetry 64* (1964). Translations of some of his poems have also been published in *The poetry of French Canada in translation* (1970) edited by John GLASSCO. An account of his ideological shift, with translations of extracts from his poetry and prose, can be found in *The shouting signpainters* (1972), Malcolm Reid's study of the *parti pris* writers.

See also NOVELS IN FRENCH 1960 TO 1982: 3(a). JOYCE MARSHALL

Major, Kevin (b. 1949). Born in Stephenville, Newfoundland, a small coastal outport with its local dialect and way of life, he graduated with a B.Sc. (1972) from Memorial University, St John's. An awareness of the dearth of literature for young people set in Newfoundland resulted in his becoming one of Canada's foremost authors of books for adolescents. As a high-school teacher he learned the idiom and perspectives of teenagers, qualities that characterize his novels, beginning with *Hold fast* (1978)—winner of a Governor General's Award—*Far from shore* (1980), and *Thirty-six exposures* (1984). To reveal the intense feelings of a lonely teenage boy, he used fictitious letters to 'The Boss' in *Dear Bruce Springsteen* (1987). They all reflect Major's own memories of his confusing, perplexing teenage years, and those of his friends. These and subsequent novels were also creatively shaped by such troubling circumstances as intolerance, economic and political changes threatening the traditional life of Newfoundlanders, province-wide unemployment, and the uncertain future facing young people today.

Disturbing historical events have also been an inspiration. In *Blood red ochre* (1989) Major used a literary time-slip device to take the reader back to Newfoundland's Beothuk, who were annihilated by settlers through starvation, disease, and murder. Another tragic historical event is the focus of his powerful novel *No man's land* (1995), about the Battle of the Somme during the First World War. Describing it as a battle that should never have happened, he reconstructs the events and human emotions that culminated in the slaughter of the Newfoundland regiment.

Incidents of censorship in Newfoundland involving his first three novels led to Major's comic fantasy *Eating between the lines* (1991), in which the young protagonist finds himself physically projected into the book he is currently reading. Humour also characterizes his novel *Diana: my autobiography* (1993), a parody of people's obsession with royalty that introduces his first female protagonist and fictional daughter, Diana (named after 'Princess Di'), who contrives to realize her imagined royal connections. *Gaffer: a novel of Newfoundland* (1997) is an imaginative, surreal story for adults about a boy and the sea.

Books by Major have been translated into French, Spanish, German, and Danish.

WENDY K. SUTTON

Makeda, Silvera. See LESBIAN LITERATURE.

Makers of Canada. See BIOGRAPHY AND MEMOIRS IN ENGLISH: 1.

Malahat Review, The (1967-). Conceived in 1965 by Robin SKELTON and John Peter (1921-83) as an international quarterly of life and letters, the first issue—published under the auspices of the University of Victoria—appeared in 1967. The title suggests the regional basis that complements the *Malahat*'s cosmopolitan ambitions (the Malahat is a mountain near Victoria, British Columbia, over whose slopes the main road runs northward up Vancouver Island). Skelton and Peter shared the editorship until the nineteenth issue (1971), when Skelton became editor (assisted at times by Derk WYNAND, Charles LILLARD, and William David Thomas). When the university nearly withdrew its support—a Committee to Disband *The Malahat Review* was actually struck—Skelton resigned and was succeeded in 1982 by Constance Rooke, who brought the magazine to the University of Guelph for part of her tenure. With the 100th issue the magazine returned to the University of Victoria, and Derk Wynand became editor in 1992.

What has made *The Malahat Review* exceptional, and important among Canadian magazines, has been its policy of printing the best of Canadian writing alongside the best that could be obtained internationally. Equally important has been the publication of English versions of foreign works never before translated, and of special book-length issues relating to specific authors or areas of literature. These include the 'Herbert Read memorial symposium' (no. 9, 1969; reprinted as a book, 1970); the 'Friedrich Nietzsche symposium' (no. 24, 1972); the 'Gathering in celebration of the 80th birthday of Robert Graves' (no. 35, 1975); 'Austrian writing today' (no. 37, 1976); the 'Margaret Atwood symposium' (no. 41, 1977); and an issue on the famous Spanish poet 'Rafael Alberti' (no. 47, 1979), with a specially designed cover by Miró.

In the early years of the magazine, Skelton was often criticized for featuring English writers like Lawrence Durrell, Anthony Burgess, D.H. Lawrence, Robert Graves, and Herbert Read, whose papers were in the University of Victoria's Special Collections (the idea for which was Skelton's). But Skelton also published complete issues devoted to Canadian writing (no. 26, April 1970; no. 31, July 1974). The tenth-anniversary ATWOOD issue marked a turning point, when the magazine began to focus on Canadian writing. A brief history and Index to issues 1-42 were published, and then came new changes in management and funding. Up to that point the publication of the magazine three times a year was funded totally by the University. From then on it sought out grants, increased subscriptions, and acquired funding for special issues.

The most ambitious special project was a group of three issues (nearly 900 pages) devoted to 'The West Coast renaissance' (no. 45, 1978, no. 50, 1979, and no. 60, 1981). Under Rooke's editorship the magazine continued to be stylish, with arresting covers, often featuring photographs by Michael ONDAATJE, and publishing a distinguished cross-section of new and established Canadian poets and fiction writers. Special issues have featured the work of John METCALF (no. 70), Sharon THESEN, Paulette JILES, Diana Hartog (no. 85), and P.K. PAGE (no. 117). By 1985 the magazine was a quarterly publication. In the 1990s it became a regular finalist or winner for poetry, fiction, or magazine-of-the-year in the annual Western Magazine Awards and the National Magazine Awards; its fiction frequently appeared in *The Journey Prize anthology*.

GEORGE WOODCOCK/GEOFF HANCOCK

Mandel, Eli (1922-92). Elias Wolf Mandel was born in Estevan, Saskatchewan. He left the University of Saskatchewan to serve in the Army Medical Corps during the Second World War. He then studied at the universities of Saskatchewan (B.A., 1949; M.A., 1950) and Toronto (Ph.D., 1957), and taught English at the Collège militaire royal de St-Jean, the University of Alberta, and York University, Toronto.

Mandel began publishing poetry in the early 1950s in magazines such as *CIV/n* and *CONTACT*; his first significant collection, 'Minotaur poems', appeared (together with poems by Phyllis WEBB and Gael Turnbull) in the CONTACT PRESS anthology *Trio* (1954). His first book was *Fuseli poems* (1960); this was followed by *Black and secret man* (1964); *An idiot joy* (1967), which won a Governor General's Award; *Stony plain* (1973); *Crusoe* (1973), a selected poems; *Out of place* (1977); *Mary Midnight* (1979) *Life sentence* (1981); and *Dreaming backwards: selected poems* (1981). Mandel was also extremely active as an editor and critic. *Criticism: the silent-speaking words* (1966), a collection of eight essays—previously presented as radio talks on the Canadian Broadcasting Corporation—called for an emotionally engaged criticism that recognizes that poetry is 'beyond system'. In 1969 he published a monograph on his fellow-poet and colleague at York, Irving LAYTON (rev. 1981). *Another time* (1977) and *The family romance* (1986) are collections of essays that assert the fictive nature of literary reality and explore the nature and origin of writing. Mandel's editing has been instrumental in shaping the canon of Canadian poetry. His first anthology, *Poetry 62/Poésie 62* (1961), which he co-edited with Jean-Guy PILON, brought to public attention a number of neglected newcomers of the 1950s—Al PURDY, Milton ACORN, D.G. JONES, Alden NOWLAN, Leonard COHEN, and John Robert COLOMBO. A later anthology, *Poets of contemporary Canada: 1960-1970* (1972), in the NEW CANADIAN LIBRARY, gave Joe ROSENBLATT and bill BISSETT their first significant publication. Mandel's other anthologies include *Five modern Canadian poets* (1970); *English poems of the twentieth century* (1971), which he co-edited with D.E.S. Maxwell; and *Eight more Canadian poets* (1972), with Ann Mandel. He also edited *Contexts of Canadian criticism* (1971) in the University of Chicago Press series, Patterns of Literary Criticism.

The Second World War, and the horrors of the Jewish concentration camps in particular, appear to have profoundly affected Mandel's poetry. Although specific references to the war do not occur until 1973 and *Stony plain*, all of his work is characterized by macabre images of suffering and destruction, and by a pervasive pessimism. The 'Minotaur poems' of *Trio* are concerned with the brutality of the western Canadian landscape, a land of 'sharp rocks . . . /cold air where birds fell like rocks/and screams, hawks, kites and cranes.' *Fuseli poems* is titled in honour of the eighteenth-century Swiss-born English painter Henry Fuseli, whose work frequently depicted tragic subjects fantastically contorted by desperation, isolated in wildly Gothic backgrounds. The poems here speak of horrifying violence, despair, self-accusation, 'fables of indifferent rape/and children slain indifferently/and daily blood'. The succeeding volumes—*Black and secret man*, *An idiot joy*, *Stony plain*—suggest little change in this bleak outlook. *Out of place*, a long meditative poem that focuses on failed Jewish settlements in Saskatchewan, and *Life sentence*, a collection of travel poems and journal entries largely set in India, Peru, and Ecuador—while less dramatic in their presentation of human misfortune—sustain a quietly pessimistic vision. In the lengthy poem/essay 'The long poem: journal and origin', included in *The family romance*, Mandel focused painfully on both the Canadian long poem and Stalin and Dachau. For Mandel the world was static, an arena of eternal and meaningless persecution. In Poland there was Auschwitz; in Estevan, Saskatchewan, a sun that kills 'cattle and rabbis . . . in the poisoned slow air'.

In style, Mandel was intellectual and contemplative—an ironic poet rather than an angry one. A central feature of his work is a deliberate lack of emotion, which amplifies the stark hopelessness of his outlook. His early work, exceedingly complex in syntax, formal in prosody, and literary in references, appears written for a scholarly rather than a public audience. Here, as in most of his poetry, Mandel saw ancient myths and literary stories as being alive in contemporary actuality, but obscuring the actual and personal. Because the poems lack a strong sense of the actual events that brought the particular myths to the poet's attention, many of the myths seem arbitrarily applied. However, beginning with the poetry of *Black and secret man*, Mandel enriched his work by introducing open verse-forms, spare but colloquial language, simplified syntax, and reportorial detail. While the meditative style remained, a resourceful, witty tone replaced the earlier sombreness. Mandel's later poetry became increasingly experimental: prose poems, concrete poems, and found poems can be seen in both *An idiot joy* and *Stony plain*; lists and found materials punctuate the intentionally flat tones of *Out of place*. Mandel maintained his black and mythological vision of the present, but the mythology was now rooted in anecdotal actuality.

See Peter STEVENS, 'Poet as critic as prairie poet', *Essays on Canadian Writing* 18/19 (Summer/Fall 1980) and an interview in the same issue; Julie Beddoes, ed., Essays on Canadian Writing 45-6 (1991-2), special issue on Eli Mandel; and Andrew Stubbs, *Myth, origins, magic: a study of form in Eli Mandel's Writing* (1993).

See also CRITICISM IN ENGLISH 5(d), 5(f), 5(g), and POETRY IN ENGLISH 1950 TO 1982: 2.

FRANK DAVEY

Manguel, Alberto (b. 1948). Born in Buenos Aires, Argentina, he fell as a student under the sway of the blind Jorge Luis Borges, to whom he read, and was influenced by the Argentine poet's personal charm, multilingualism, love of reading, sense of style, and fantastic imagination. Manguel worked as a writer and editor in Milan and Tahiti before moving in 1982 to Toronto, where he was active as a reviewer, writer, and editor. He moved to Switzerland in 1992 and since 1996 has resided in London, England. With Gianni Guadalupi he composed *The dictionary of imaginary places* (1980; expanded ed., 1987), a reader's guide to realms of the fantastic imagination. His internationally acclaimed anthologies *Black water: the anthology of fantastic literature* (1983) and *Black water II: more tales of the fantastic* (1990) include stories written by some Canadian writers and a good many writers from Latin America. His theme anthologies include *The Oxford book of Canadian ghost stories* (1990) and *Canadian mystery stories* (1991) as well as collections of erotic and homosexual fiction. His novel *News from a foreign country came* (1991), set largely on the Gaspé Peninsula of Quebec, reveals how a man's actions in Algeria and Argentina in earlier years affected him and his wife and daughter in later years. Manguel devoted seven years to the research and writing of *A history of reading* (1996), a work of considerable elegance and erudition.

JOHN ROBERT COLOMBO

Maracle, Brian. See ABORIGINAL LITERATURE: 4.

Maracle, Lee (b. 1950). She grew up in a poor working-class district adjacent to the Burrard Reserve in North Vancouver and attended local elementary schools and Argyle Secondary School. But her education was obtained, she says, 'from lots of books, dictionaries and talking to my elders'. She spent a difficult adolescence and youth filled with frustration, anger, and hatred towards whites, drifting from California's world of itinerant farm workers to Toronto's hippy/drug scene. She chronicled the frightful injuries of these times in *Bobbie Lee: Indian rebel* (1975; rev. 1990). Shrill and shocking, this searing memoir has become a popular social document of the period for students of contemporary Native issues. In *I am woman* (1988), a collection of autobiographical essays, her suffering and pain do not mean hopeless doom, for her resilience and tenacity enable her to emerge free and triumphant. Unapologetic in her wrath, Maracle subjects her readers to a remorseless exposé of the contemporary state of Native women. From 1989 to 1990 Maracle worked at the En'owkin Centre in Penticton, British Columbia, as a teacher of creative writing. She herself has been one of the most productive Native writers in Canada in the nineties. In *Sojourner's truth and other stories* (1990), she tries to integrate two mediums, 'oratory and European story', in narratives and essays that depict the plight of Native children in school, and Native women (doubly victimized as Natives and women); but she also portrays cross-cultural relationships. Her novel *Sundogs* (1991) focuses on the effects on Canada's Aboriginal people of two events that happened in 1990: Elijah Harper's filibuster in the Manitoba legislature and the Oka crisis in Quebec. The novel is told from the point of view of a naive Native college student, living with her mother in Vancouver, who joins the Run for Peace that crosses Canada in support of the Oka freedom-fighters: within the space of a year she experiences a virtual rebirth as a Native person. In *Ravensong* (1993) Maracle portrays the lives of Natives in a West Coast village during the 1950s when a flu epidemic devastates their community—while doctors in a nearby white village do nothing because the Native village is outside their jurisdiction. The novel explores the emotions of guilt and shame suffered by both white and Native characters.

Maracle has co-edited two books: *We get our living like milk from the land* (1993), a historical overview of the Okanagan nation from the Creation story and first contact, to colonization and the present, and *Telling it: women and language across cultures* (1990), chronicling the 'Telling It' conference held in Vancouver in November 1988, which brought together prominent Native, Asian-Canadian, and lesbian writers debating the women's movement. Maracle believes implicitly that words are a form of empowerment, and in her idiosyncratic style and language, as she writes outside the literary mainstream, she condemns inequities that go deeper than immediate quarrels and grievances, providing insights into Canada's dilemmas of race and culture.

PENNY PETRONE

Marchand, Clément (b. 1912). Born in Sainte-Geneviève de Batiscan, Quebec, he has been a poet, journalist, publisher, and an editor of two magazines and one newspaper. In 1933, after completing his studies at the Séminaire de Trois-Rivières, he joined the editorial staff of the regional weekly newspaper *Le Bien Public*. He became its co-owner with Raymond Douville, and at the same time managed the printing plant as well as Les Éditions du Bien Public. He wrote poems, news items, articles, and short stories that were published either in his weekly, in the review *Le Mauricien* (founded in 1937, it became *Horizons* in 1940), or in book form. In forty years Les Éditions du Bien Public published nearly 200 titles, from history to the work of young poets, making Marchand one of the chief promoters of literature and culture. His reputation extended beyond his region after he became a member of the Royal Society of Canada in 1947, and later president of the Comité consultatif du livre. In 1959 Marchand became the sole owner of *Le Bien Public*; he sold the newspaper and printing plant in 1978, remaining head of Les Éditions du Bien Public.

Bas-reliefs (1932), a collection of poetry and prose written by three authors for the tricentenary of Trois-Rivières, contains a series of twelve sonnets by Marchand entitled 'Le geste de la croix'. Recounting the story of the erection of a cross by the captain of the *Émerillon* on Cartier's expedition of 1534-5, the series is an epic with strong religious and patriotic overtones whose alexandrines attest to the young poet's technical mastery. In 1939 Marchand was awarded the Prix David for the manuscript of *Les soirs rouges*, which, though written in the 1930s, was not published until 1947. Describing the 'factory nights', the 'nights reddened by the high flames of the iron works' during the Depression, the poet cries out in revolt, in the name of the displaced peasant become labourer in a city that exploits him. The collection was a first for Quebec literature in expressing interest in urban labourers and in openly taking the side of the proletariat. *Courriers des villages* (1940) is a collection of news items, articles, and short stories by Marchand that had first appeared in *Le Bien Public*, describing the habits and psychological make-up of rural characters. It was awarded the Prix David and was reprinted several times during the forties.

Marchand demonstrated his admiration for the regionalist poetry of Nérée BEAUCHEMIN by editing a collection of his works: *Nérée Beauchemin: textes choisis* (1957).

See Jacques Blais, *De l'ordre et de l'aventure. La poésie au Québec de 1934 à 1944* (1975), and Claude-Henri GRIGNON, 'Clément Marchand, peintre de la campagne' in *Les pamphlets de Valdombre*, series 4, no. 6-7 (nov.-déc. 1940).

RICHARD GIGUÈRE

Marchand, Félix-Gabriel (1832-1900). Born in Saint-Jean d'Iberville, Quebec, he was educated at local schools and at the Séminaire de Saint-Hyacinthe. He became a qualified notary, but found that profession less attractive than politics, journalism and the theatre. His political career spanned thirty-three years, from 1867 to his death, during which time he occupied various cabinet posts before becoming, in 1892, leader of the provincial Liberal party and, in 1897, premier of Quebec, the post he held at the time of his death.

Marchand helped found the newspaper *Le Franco-Canadien* in 1860, and became editor of Montreal's *Le Temps* in 1883. In literature he is best remembered for his five plays: the one-act comedy *Fatenville* (Montréal, 1869); the vaudeville *Erreur n'est pas compte; ou Les inconvénients d'une ressemblance* (Montréal 1872); two verse comedies, *Un bonheur en attire un autre* (Montréal, 1883) and *Les faux brillants* (Montréal, 1885); and a comic operetta, also in verse, *Le lauréat* (Montréal, 1899). All of these were republished in his *Mélanges poétiques et littéraires* (Montréal, 1899), along with various occasional poems—some satirical ('Les travers du siècle', 'Nos ridicules'), some patriotic ('Hymne aux martyrs de 1837', etc.)—and essays on political and social topics. His theatre shows the influence of the popular Parisian stage and is characterized by its lightness of touch and the distance it establishes, especially in his verse-plays, between itself and its public's everyday preoccupations. His best-known work is the three-act *Les faux brillants*, reminiscent of Molière's *Tartuffe* with its theme of an intriguing schemer who insinuates himself into a wealthy bourgeois family and attempts to subvert its resources to his own ends. The play was revived in an adapted version by Jean-Claude GERMAIN in Montreal in 1977.

See L. Fortin, *Félix-Gabriel Marchand* (1979), and the entry on Marchand in *The Oxford Companion to Canadian Theatre* (1989).

L.E. DOUCETTE

Marchbanks, Samuel. See Robertson DAVIES.

Marchessault, Jovette (b. 1938). Born in Montreal, Quebec, she was obliged to leave school at thirteen and go to work in a textile factory. Self-taught, she is a visual artist, novelist, and playwright. Her paintings, sculptures, and masks of telluric women have been widely shown in Toronto, Montreal, New York, Paris, and Brussels. A radical lesbian feminist, proud of her Aboriginal heritage and the spiritual traditions upon which it is based, she produced during her first long creative period a multi-faceted and highly original body of novels and plays evoking a world in which divine and human power is predominantly female and bonds among women exist across time and space, whether these be personal, social, or cosmic. During this first period, her focus was on matrilinear bonds and women's culture, which includes women's knowledge, vision, energy, memory, and all women's production: in kitchens, salons, schools, hospitals, factories, offices, or in birthing and painting. Her most recent work continues to show her preoccupation with culture and spiritual vision, but moves away from gender analysis in favour of a global view of human relations. A visionary, utopian project, as well as trenchant social commentary, is evident in all of her work.

Marchessault's autobiographical novel *Comme une enfant de la terre/1. Le crachat solaire* (1975, Prix France-Québec; *Like a child of the earth*, 1988) is the first volume of a trilogy. (All Marchessault's fiction has been translated into English by Yvonne M. Klein.) Based on the theme and structure of a quest or initiatory journey, the trilogy is an exploration of human relations and of the bonds linking humans to spiritual, animal, vegetable, and mineral worlds. The autobiographical exploration undertaken occurs not only in the past and the present, but also in the future of a world that does not yet exist, but that can be made to exist through human creativity in mystical union with cosmic forces. Marchessault has her narrators relate the odyssey through evocations of events in the life of her, her family, and Amerindian societies and their cultures. *Comme une enfant* recounts metaphorically and allegorically the birth and the memories of the narrator, whose origins are in 'solar spittle' and in the stars. *La mère des herbes* (1980; *Mother of the grass*, 1989) combines the poetic qualities of the mystic quest with explicit and angry social commentary. In the third volume of the trilogy, *Les cailloux blancs pour les forêts obscures* (1987; *White pebbles in the dark forests*, 1990), the narrator, a writer, and her visionary companion, an aviatrix, continue in dialogue the cosmic quest for mystic union and for understanding human existence, death, and evil. The trilogy is a rich exploration of women's experience, community, tradition, vision, spirituality, suffering, and solitude. It opens in this third novel to a new dimension through a question, 'What about the Fathers?' By the end of the novel, the terrible gulfs between men and women have been addressed, although not resolved. These gulfs are seen to render impossible personal and spiritual fulfilment for either sex.

'Chronique lesbienne du moyen-âge québécois' in another work of fiction, *Tryptique lesbien* (1980; *Lesbian triptych*, 1985), is structured around a genealogy of generations of women; it celebrates women's power and vehemently denounces destructive forces in male-dominated society. 'Les vaches de nuit' in *Tryptique lesbien* has become best known as a dramatic monologue. It is an extended metaphor in which the narrator identifies herself as a calf and her mother as a milk cow. The text has been performed to powerful effect in French and English ('Night cows') by Pol Pelletier in Montreal, New York, Paris, Italy, Toronto, and Vancouver. The theme of the third text in *Tryptique lesbien*, 'Les faiseuses d'anges', which has also been performed in Montreal as a dramatic monologue, is abortion: the narrator's mother is an abortionist, or 'angel-maker', who expresses her creative energy in knitting as well as in using her needles to produce abortions. Through an original use of extended paradox, Marchessault argues poetically in favour of women's rights to control their own bodies.

Marchessault's plays frequently offer fictional re-creations of real, historical women, particularly of authors, whose texts she cites extensively while situating them in the context of her dramatic universe. As a result of this original strategy, works from the past that were poorly read by critics are received in surprisingly fresh and new perspectives. The four protagonists of *La SAGA DES POULES MOUILLÉES* (1981, 1989), which had a successful 1981 run at Montreal's Théâtre du Nouveau Monde and, as *Saga of the wet hens* (1983) in a translation by Linda Gaboriau, at Toronto's Tarragon Theatre in 1982, are dramatizations of four of Quebec's best-known writers: Laure Conan (Félicité ANGERS), Germaine GUÈVREMONT, Gabrielle ROY, and Anne HÉBERT. They meet in a mythic space where each assumes a poetically established totemic identity. The play offers an imaginative reading of their works and a reinterpretation in a feminist frame of their creative experience. *La terre est trop courte, Violette Leduc* (1982), which also offers a re-vision of women's history and their place in literature and culture, dramatizes turbulent events and commitment to writing in the life of French author Violette Leduc. It was performed at Montreal's Théâtre Expérimental des Femmes (1981) and in an English translation by Suzanne de Lotbinière-Harwood in Montreal and Toronto. *Alice & Gertrude, Natalie & Renée et ce cher Ernest* (1984) is a dramatization of a fictitious meeting in 1939 of Alice B. Toklas, Gertrude Stein, Renée Vivien, and Ernest Hemingway in the Paris salon of Natalie Barney. The characters' actions and dialogue form a celebration of women's culture and history, particularly as created by lesbian writers. *Anaïs, dans la queue de la comète* (1985, Prix du *Journal de Montréal*) dramatizes fictitious meetings of writers Anaïs Nin, June Miller, Henry Miller, Antonin Artaud, and Otto Rank. The play is an imaginative exploration through many times, many places, and many characterizations of the complex socio-cultural values, practices, and evils that allegedly prevented Anaïs Nin from realizing her full potential as a writer and artist.

Demande de travail sur les nébuleuses (1988, Grand Prix Littéraire de la Ville de Sherbrooke) is a new-age, visionary play that takes place at the eleventh hour in a North American house floating in space, no longer of this world. A family—father, mother, daughter, son—dominated by patriarchal traditions and memories, is seeking the vision and strength to move into the future, despite severe handicaps created by the values and roles that have structured their lives and relationships to date. *Le voyage magnifique d'Emily Carr* (1990, Governor General's Award; translated by Linda Gaboriau as *The magnificent voyage of Emily Carr*, 1992), is a homage to the telluric and cosmic vision of the painter and a dramatic reflection on life, creativity, solitude, and death. While Emily's sister seeks to restrain Emily within the norms of Victorian family and society, the voices of her Aboriginal friend, of the Aboriginal goddess La D'Sonoqua, of a young Lawren Harris, and of the Soul Tuner support her in her cosmic struggle to share nature's secrets and to make her art. *Le lion de Bangor* (1993) gives dramatic form and continuation to the characters first created in *Des cailloux blancs pour les forêts obscures*. Together they struggle with the forces of the abyss in themselves, in society, and in the universe, while never losing their grip on their vision of transcendence.

Lettre de Californie (1982) is a short work that pays homage to radical American feminist Meridel Le Sueur. It contains a long poem inspired by Le Sueur and ten portraits of heroic and creative women of the past.

Several of Marchessault's books include texts and critical commentary by people with whom she has worked. Of particular interest are those by Gloria Feman Orenstein in *La mère des herbes*, *Tryptique lesbien*, and *La saga*; by Michelle Rossignol in *La saga*; by Francine Pelletier in *La terre est trop courte*; by Barbara Godard in *Lesbian triptych* (includes bibliography); and by Pierre Filion in *Le lion de Bangor*. See also the NFB/ONF film *Firewords/Les terribles vivantes* (1986) by Dorothy Todd Hénaut; *Dramaturges québécoises. Dossier de presse* (1986); the special issue on Marchessault prepared by

Claudine Potvin in VOIX ET IMAGES, *Littérature québécoise*, 47 (1991, includes extensive bibliography); and Barbara Godard, 'En mémoire de l'avenir: les stratégies de transformation dans la narration de Jovette Marchessault', *Voix et images*, 49: 100-115.

LOUISE FORSYTH

Marcotte, Gilles (b. 1925). Born in Sherbrooke, Quebec, he was educated there and at the Université de Montréal. Literary critic for *Le Devoir* for seven years, then literary editor of *La Presse*, he taught in the French department of the Université de Montréal from 1966 until his retirement. One of the most prominent literary critics in Quebec today, Marcotte is probably the most prolific, having published some 1500 texts, most of them articles, as of 1996.

Marcotte's first work of criticism, *Une littérature qui se fait* (1962; rev. 1968 and 1995), which won a Governor General's Award, was an important beginning in the development of Québécois criticism. Along with his *Le roman à l'imparfait* (1976; rev. 1989), essays on the contemporary Quebec novel, it is considered the most important of his books. Other critical works are *Présence de la critique* (1966), an anthology of critical texts that he edited; *Le temps des poètes* (1970), a survey of modern Quebec poetry that won the City of Montreal Prize for Literature; and *Les bonnes rencontres* (1971), a collection of Marcotte's literary journalism. Marcotte was the senior editor for the massive four-volume *Anthologie de la littérature québécoise* (1978).

Marcotte is highly respected for the acuity of his judgement and the wide range of his knowledge. He has maintained a basically socio-critical approach, although he was tempted—but only briefly—by a more modish formalist approach in *Le roman à l'imparfait*, an approach he has increasingly opposed, as he does 'ideological' readings. In general Marcotte is not anguished by the exigencies of theory, opting for the 'universal' values of international humanism and remaining committed to thematic concerns. *La littérature et le reste* (1981), an epistolary exchange with critic André BROCHU, is an occasionally prolix but generally interesting and serious examination of the activity and role of the Québécois critic. Marcotte shows himself to be master of his own territory but never afraid to admit the limits of this ground. As he has often said of socio-criticism (and other such approaches), it risks making literature lose its sovereignty. He is a receptive, generous, and incisive critic—at home both in scholarly criticism and in journalism. This ongoing range has continued to be evident in his *La prose de Rimbaud* (1983), his many popular book reviews in *L'Actualité*, the publication of fifteen years of selected essays in *Littérature et circonstances* (1989), his involvement with the research group 'Montreal Imaginaire' and its publication *Montréal imaginaire: ville et littérature* (1992, co-edited with Pierre Nepveu), as well as in Pierre Popovic's absorbing, entertaining interviews with Marcotte in *Entretiens avec Gilles Marcotte. De la littérature avant toute chose* (1996).

Marcotte has also written three novels. *Le poids de Dieu* (1962) describes the crisis of Claude Savoie, a young priest from a middle-class family who is confronted with the problems of a working-class parish. It was translated into Spanish by Jesus Lopez Pacheco as *El peso du Dios* (Barcelona, 1963) and into English by Elizabeth Abbott as *The burden of God* (New York, 1964). In *Retour à Coolbrook* (1965) the protagonist, Marcel Parenteau, is destroyed by his attempt to cut himself off emotionally. *Un voyage* (1973) tells of the possibility of transcendence in the mediocre life of a Quebec civil servant. The collection of stories *La vie réelle: histoires* (1989) frequently centres upon a self-reflexive older man, sometimes a professor, sometimes a bureaucrat, who luxuriates in the grace of contemplation and the wonder at how 'real life' can suddenly take us by the throat with love and desire. These apparent glosses on Marcotte as a private, contemplative man are sometimes reflected in the much-deserved collective academic homage to him on his retirement from teaching: *Miscellanies en l'honneur de Gilles Marcotte* (1995) edited by Benoît Melançon and Pierre Popovic.

See 'Dossier: Gilles Marcotte', VOIX ET IMAGES 6, no. 1 (automne 1980).

SHERRY SIMON/DAVID LEAHY

Maria Chapdelaine (1916). A widely read classic of world literature, this novel by Louis HÉMON was published first in France in serial form in 1914, then in Montreal as a book in 1916. It is set in the Lac Saint-Jean region of Quebec and portrays the farmers' attempts to tame the harsh land. On the death of the man she loves, and to whom she was betrothed, Maria is faced with the choice of marrying Lorenzo Surprenant, who would take her to a much easier life in the United States, or Eutrope Gagnon, who can offer her nothing better than the same difficult life she and her family have always known. In rejecting the opportunity to flee, she sacrifices herself in order that the values of her family and her community may be safeguarded. This devotion symbolizes Quebec's determined struggle to secure a foothold for rural, Catholic, French society away from the onslaught of modern, urban, English-dominated life. Although Hémon had been living in Canada for less than three years when he began to write the novel, he succeeded in capturing the essence of Quebec's cultural ideal as it was promoted at the beginning of the twentieth century.

Maria Chapdelaine: récit du Canada français is a masterpiece that belongs solidly within the tradition of the *roman de la terre* or 'agricultural novel', and may even be said to represent its perfected form. Among its many literary qualities are its range of styles, from the lyrical prose describing springtime and Maria's exchange of vows, to the muscular, spare accounts of the harsh winter and the death it brings; its sharply drawn characters; and its convincingly rendered scenes. The novel has been transformed into a political football, its literary merits virtually ignored, first by ideologues anxious to celebrate the characters' fidelity and to propose this as an ideal worthy of emulation, and more recently by critics intent on proving that the characters' submissiveness only enslaved them. The novel may indeed crystallize, as Nicole Deschamps has suggested, 'a moment in the collective history of French Canada and thereby have become inseparable from the debate on that history.' What has been sacrificed during the heated 'political' debate about *Maria Chapdelaine* is an appreciation of it as a work of art, an aspect that one presumes has not eluded its readers in more than twenty languages.

An English translation (1921) by William Hume BLAKE, with the subtitle *A tale of the Lake St. John country*, remains the standard one; it is available in the Laurentian Library. *Marie Chapdelaine* has been filmed three times: in 1939 (with Madeleine Renaud and Jean Gabin; Julien Duvivier dir.); in 1949 (with Michèle Morgan and Phillipe Lemair; Marc Allegret dir.); and in 1983 (with Carole Laure and Nick Mancuso; Gilles Carle dir.).

See Guy Laflèche, 'L'édition critique de *Maria Chapdelaine* par Ghislaine Legendre', *VOIX ET IMAGES*, VIII/1 (automne 1982); Réal Ouellet, 'Débat: Brève réponse à une longue diatribe de Guy Laflèche sur une réédition récente de *Maria Chapdelaine*', *Voix et Images*, VIII/3 (printemps 1983); Ben-Z. Shek, '*Maria Chapdelaine* in Iberoamerica', *CANADIAN LITERATURE* 142-3 (Fall-Winter 1994).

See also NOVELS IN FRENCH 1900 TO 1920. PAUL SOCKEN

Marie Calumet (1904). This satirical novel by Rodolphe GIRARD is set in the Quebec countryside of 1860. Father Lefranc, the parish priest of St-Apollinaire, visits his neighbour, Father Flavel, the pastor of St-Ildefonse, whose rectory is in chaos. Lefranc sends him Marie Calumet, a still-comely forty-year-old woman who is a remarkable housekeeper. She soon has the presbytery running like clockwork, while unwittingly attracting the romantic interest of Narcisse, the hired man, and Zéphirin, the verger. Narcisse wins her hand and Zéphirin avenges himself by pouring a laxative into one of the dishes at the wedding feast. Most of the characters are naïve, but sensitive and warmhearted. Marie has an exaggerated admiration for all things connected with the Church and its priests. During the bishop's pastoral visit she asks where to put Monsignor's 'holy piss', after pondering whether to save it; and wearing a crinoline and no underwear at the harvest feast, she trips on a walnut-tree root and scandalizes the pastor, who threatens excommunication. Another scandalous episode occurs when the pastor's teenage niece reads the most sensual verses (taking up thirteen pages in the novel) from J.F. Ostervald's version of the 'Song of Songs', which had been forbidden to the masses. These and other scenes are described by Girard both satirically and humorously.

When *Marie Calumet* was published in 1904, 1000 copies were sold almost immediately; but it was condemned by the Church as 'gross, immoral and impious'. For the 1946 edition Girard, in addition to making many stylistic improvements, modified many irreverent religious references and omitted the final chapter, with its scatological description of the consequences produced by the laxative. Even in the revised version, however, the novel conveys a realistic depiction of the customs, language, and morality of Quebec around 1860. *Marie Calumet* is the first major French-Canadian novel to treat the Church and clergy in a humorous way. A translation of the expurgated edition, by Irène Currie, appeared in 1976.

See André Vanasse, '*Marie Calumet*', *Dictionnaire des oeuvres littéraires du Québec*, II (1980).

See also NOVELS IN FRENCH 1900 TO 1920. MADELEINE DIRSCHAUER

Marie de l'Incarnation (1599-1672). Born Marie Guyart in Tours, France, she was married at eighteen and widowed two years later. In 1633 she entered the Ursuline monastery of Tours and in 1639 sailed for Quebec, with three other Ursulines and Madame de la Peltrie, to found a 'seminary' for Native children and a boarding school for French girls. For more than thirty years, while she alternated as head of the monastery, she wrote thousands of letters to her son, Claude Martin, a Benedictine priest, and to various benefactors in France. Though a cloistered nun, Marie de l'Incarnation was in touch with everyone in the colony—the Jesuits, the governors and other notables, the Native converts, and common people. Her letters rank with the *JESUIT RELATIONS* as source material for the period. Because not intended for publication, they are more personal and informal and cover not only the triumphs and tragedies of the Jesuit mission but such mundane matters as the earthquake of 1663, the weather, the crops, the coming of the 'filles du roi', and the fire that destroyed the Ursuline monastery in 1650. The style is lively, at times hasty and even breathless, shrewd and often tart in its observations, by turns practical and high-minded. Marie de l'Incarnation was the first social historian of Canada, and the breadth and vividness of the picture provided is remarkable in view of the fact that she frequently wrote of events she had not personally witnessed.

After Marie de l'Incarnation's death Claude Martin published 228 of her letters in *Lettres de la vénérable mère Marie de l'Incarnation . . .* (Tournai, 1876). Albert Jamet's more scholarly four-volume edition—*Marie de l'Incarnation, fondatrice des Ursulines de la Nouvelle France* (1923-39)—adds four more letters and some devotional writing but covers only the period 1639-52. *Word from New France: the selected letters of Marie de l'Incarnation* (1967), Joyce MARSHALL's translation of 66 letters, includes a complete biography and historical introduction.

Other source material includes Claude Martin's life of his mother, *La vie de la vénérable Mère Marie de l'Incarnation* (Paris, 1677), and *The autobiography of the Venerable Marie of the Incarnation* (1964), John J. Sullivan's translation of her 'spiritual autobiography'.

JOYCE MARSHALL

Marie-Victorin (1885-1944). Born Conrad Kirouac at Kingsey Falls in the Eastern Townships, Quebec, he moved with his family to Quebec City as a child and was educated first at the parish school of Saint-Sauveur and later at the Académie commerciale. In 1901 he entered the Order of the Brothers of the Christian Schools and took the name (in religion) of Marie-Victorin. In the following years he taught at Saint-Jérôme, Westmount, and Longueuil. After becoming interested in botany, he was appointed professor of botany at the Université de Montréal in 1920 and in 1922 received his Ph.D. in sciences from that university, where he would teach for the rest of his life. In 1923 he founded the ACFAS (Association canadienne-française pour l'avancement des sciences) and he was elected to the Royal Society of Canada the following year. In 1939 he founded the Botanical Gardens of Montreal. He received the Prix David twice (1923, 1931) and several provincial, national, and international distinctions for his scientific contributions.

Récits laurentiens (1919), translated by James Ferres as *The chopping bee and other Laurentian stories* (1925), is a collection of nine short stories in which Marie-Victorin often recalls the years of his childhood in developing themes of the then-popular *terroir* school. *Croquis laurentiens* (1920) is a collections of picturesque sketches that describes, with a remarkable mixture of poetic images and precise terminology, the Laurentian landscape and the land that had been settled by French Canadians for centuries. *Peuple sans histoire* (1925), an adaptation for the stage of a short story included in *Récits laurentiens*, and first performed on 31 Jan. 1918, portrays Lord Durham as a man who was not an enemy of the French-Canadian people but rather was ignorant of their history. *Charles Le Moyne* (1925) is a patriotic historical drama that was performed at the Collège de Longueuil, 13 and 14 May 1910. Marie-Victorin's most important book is *Flore laurentienne, illustrée 22 cartes et de 1800 dessins* (1935; rpr. 1947; rev. 1964), an inventory of 1,917 plants found in Quebec that describes these plants with a rare mixture of scientific precision and poetry and reveals the richness of the French-Canadian vocabulary for naming plants. Other works include *Itinéraires botaniques dans l'île de Cuba* (1942), *Les filicinées du Québec* (1923), *Études floristiques sur la région du Lac Saint-Jean* (1925), *Les équisétinées du Québec* (1927), *Le dynamisme dans la flore du Québec* (1929), and *Histoire de l'Institut botanique de l'Université de Montréal* (1941). *Confidences et combat* (1969) is a selection of Marie-Victorin's letters, written between 1924 and 1944; they were annotated by Gilles Beauder.

See M. Gauvreau, *Le Président de l'ACFAS* (1938); L.-P. Audet, *Le Frère Marie-Victorin* (1942); and Robert Rumilly, *Le Frère Marie-Victorin et son temps* (1949).

JACQUES COTNAM

Maritimes, Writing in the. 1. 1749 TO 1830. In February 1750 *The Gentleman's Magazine* of London published 'Nova Scotia. A New Ballad', which offered the settlers of Halifax (founded in 1749) the promise of dignity, plenty, and prosperity. After the first printing press was brought to Halifax by Bartholomew Green in 1751, this 'literature of empire' was soon replaced by locally written prose and poetry. From the 1752 founding of John Bushell's *The Halifax Gazette* onward, Maritime newspapers and periodicals stimulated literary life by providing publishing outlets for regional authors and by excerpting the latest writing from Britain and America. *The Nova-Scotia Magazine and Comprehensive Review of Literature* (1789-92), established by scholar William Cochran, and later edited by Joseph HOWE's father, John, set a standard of professionalism among literary journals to which successive Maritime periodicals turned. By January 1827 a publication such as Halifax's *The ACADIAN MAGAZINE; or Literary Mirror* (1826-8) could produce an 'entirely original' issue written by local contributors. Edited successively by lawyers Beamish Murdoch and J. Scott Tremain, *The Acadian Magazine* reviewed and excerpted the poetry of Oliver GOLDSMITH, Jr, published the Truro-based essays of former *Blackwood's* contributor James Irving, and included the illustrations of Halifax engraver Charles W. Torbett. Although almanacks, monographs, and a few newspapers had included illustration prior to 1826, *The Acadian Magazine* was the first Maritime literary periodical to be embellished by visual art.

Most broadsheets, pamphlets, and books published in the eighteenth and early nineteenth centuries fell into the category of government documents, almanacks, electioneering material, or sermon literature. Typical were Henry ALLINE's sermons *Two mites on some of the most important and much disputed points of divinity* (Halifax, 1781) and *The anti-traditionalist* (Halifax, 1783), and his poetical book *Hymns and spiritual songs*, published in Halifax in 1782 before being reprinted in Vermont in 1796 (a different Alline work with the same title appeared in Boston in 1786). One of nearly 8000 Connecticut and Rhode Island 'Planters' who in 1760 took up the lands of the deported Acadians in Nova Scotia and New Brunswick, Alline remains the most significant literary figure on the eighteenth-century Maritime landscape before the American Revolution. However, with the arrival of approximately 30,000 Loyalist refugees in the region between 1779 and 1783, the literary and cultural character of the Maritimes changed dramatically. Arriving in the region with established standards of cultural expectation, the Loyalists organized schools, universities, journals, reading societies, and theatrical opportunities that encouraged the growth of a regional literature. While Loyalist authors were always to be too geographically dispersed to coalesce as a literary school, individual writers reconfirmed for subsequent generations the cultural validity for which they wrote. It is interesting to note, for example, that Oliver Goldsmith, Jr, Joseph Howe, Grizelda TONGE, and Thomas Chandler HALIBURTON were all of Loyalist descent, and that in the 1890s writers such as Bliss CARMAN, Charles G.D. ROBERTS, Sophia Almon HENSLEY, and Alice JONES looked with pride to their Loyalist literary antecedents.

Amongst the Loyalist poets who removed to the Maritimes after the American Revolution were Deborah (How) Cottnam, Roger VIETS, Jonathan ODELL, Mather Byles II, Jacob BAILEY, and Joseph STANSBURY. Of these, Cottnam and Viets were to preach an eighteenth-century social vision of order and renewal through their poetry, she in her schools for girls in Halifax and Saint John and he through his *Annapolis Royal: a poem* (Halifax, 1788), the first poetry pamphlet published in Canada. Already established as trenchant Tory satirists during the Revolution, Bailey and Odell continued their satirical thrusts against republicanism and levelling principles by directing their waspish pens to such subjects as non-conformist religions and the War of 1812 respectively (for example, see Bailey's 'The Adventures of Jack Ramble, the Methodist Preacher,' *c.* 1787-95). Stansbury—whose poem 'To Cordelia' (*c.* 1783) is often read as an archetype of Loyalist experience—was the only one of the Tory writers to return to America.

Satire continued to be a dominant mode in the first two decades of the nineteenth century. Alexander Croke's mock-heroic poem 'The Inquisition' (1805) wickedly exposed the vanities and peccadillos of Halifax society (an implied target was the Governor's wife, Lady Frances Wentworth, the subject of Thomas H. RADDALL's 1959 novel *The Governor's lady*). The survival of five handwritten copies of the poem suggests its mode of circulation prior to being published with alterations in Britain in 1841. Pseudonymous sketches in newspapers such as the *Acadian Recorder* of Halifax or the *P. E. I. Register* of Charlottetown poked fun at the follies and foibles of society in the post-Napoleonic period, making manners and mores far more a preoccupation of writers and readers of this period than were the wilderness themes identified by Northrop FRYE as a characteristic of central-Canadian writing. The untitled 'Mephibosheth Stepsure letters', published in Halifax's *Acadian Recorder* (1821-23) and written by the Reverend Dr Thomas McCULLOCH of Pictou, were a combination of moral tale, double-edged satire, and social commentary. Described by Frye as typical of all subsequent Canadian humour with their dry asides and social vision, the Stepsure letters proved the efficacy of using the newspaper sketch form, an eccentric protagonist, and distinctive speech patterns in achieving satirical effect. This example was not lost on the writers of the comic 'Club Papers', published in Joseph Howe's *Novascotian* from 1828 to 1831, or on Thomas Chandler Haliburton in the creation of his 1835 'Recollections of Nova Scotia', also published in Howe's newspaper. Already the author of two histories of Nova Scotia (1823, 1829), Haliburton caught in the vitality of language and double-edged satire of his Yankee pedlar Sam Slick the energy that would propel Slick and his 'go-ahead' philosophy to international fame. Published in Halifax in book form in 1836 and in London and Philadelphia in 1837 as *The clockmaker*, the Sam Slick stories gave birth to a series of books that helped to cement Haliburton's place on the international literary map. Haliburton also wrote an insightful, humorous cultural exploration of Nova Scotia, *The old judge; or Life in a colony* (London, 1849).

By the end of the 1820s, notes D.C. Harvey, Nova Scotia had experienced an 'intellectual awakening' marked not only by political debate and satire but also by its social and economic expansion. John Young's 'The Letters of Agricola on the principles of vegetation and tillage', published in *The Acadian Recorder* from 1818 to 1821 (Halifax, 1822), stimulated agricultural movements in essays that were classics of their genre, and Joseph Howe's *Novascotian* sketches 'Western Rambles' (1823) and 'Eastern Rambles' (1829-31) were typical of a zest for travel-writing that ranged from newspaper columns to published works (for example, William Scarth Moorsom's *Letters from Nova Scotia*, London, 1830). In the field of fiction, Julia (Beckwith) HART, originally from Fredericton, published by subscription in 1824 *ST. URSULA'S CONVENT; or The nun of Canada*, the first Canadian novel written by a Canadian. A romance, it nonetheless contained the moral elements that also dominated tales such as Joseph Howe's 'The Locksmith of Philadelphia' and Thomas McCulloch's immigrant fiction, *Colonial gleanings: William and Melville* (Edinburgh, 1826). Poetry was considered the genteel art, however, whether it was Lieutenant Adam Allan's translation of Allan Ramsay's *The gentle shepherd* from Lowland Scots (*The new gentle shepherd*, London, 1798), the Spenserian stanzas of Grizelda Tonge's 'To my dear Grandmother, on her 80th birth day' (*Acadian Recorder*, 1825), or the settlement poems of Joseph Howe ('Acadia') and Oliver Goldsmith, Jr (*The rising village*). Goldsmith's poem, published in London in 1825, enjoyed the fame of being the New World revision of his great-uncle's well-known *The deserted village*, although it introduced an element of romance not found in the older, more ironic poem. James Irving's twenty-five 'Letters on the present state of English poetry, as exemplified in the works of the living poets', published in *The Acadian Recorder* from 1820 to 1822, introduced critical analysis to newspaper readers and generated considerable discussion about the Romantic poets. With other Scottish and Irish writers of non-conformist or non-Loyalist background, such as Thomas McCulloch of Pictou, James Hogg of Fredericton, and Andrew Shiels of Halifax, Irving added to the complexity of influences helping to shape Maritime writing by the 1830s.

2. 1830 TO 1880. Although Nova Scotia continued to enjoy an active literary life in the 1830s and 1840s, New Brunswick had increasingly taken centre stage by the 1840s when Saint John periodicals and newspapers, such as *The Amaranth* and the *Morning News*, encouraged regional writing and fed an emerging rivalry between Halifax and Saint John as progressive leaders of Maritime society. Emily Beavan, appearing first in the pages of *The Amaranth* as a writer of romantic poetry and fiction, wrote a culturally revealing account of *Life in the backwoods of New Brunswick* (London, 1845), in which she detailed the growth of a settlement around Lake Washademoak. Also establishing a reputation in *The Amaranth* as a poet and fiction-writer was Douglas S. HUYGHUE ('Eugene'), whose *Argimou. A legend of the Micmac* (Halifax, 1847) was serialized in the magazine between May and September 1842. Both a romance and a novel of social concern about the loss of Micmac and Maliseet cultures after European settlement, *Argimou* was followed by the novel *Nomads of the West; or, Ellen Clayton* (London, 1850), and a series of essays about the Upper Saint John River published in *Bentley's Miscellany* (London) in 1849-50.

Huyghue's sympathy for First Nations culture was echoed by his friend Saint John lawyer Moses H. Perley, who published a series of 'Sporting sketches from New Brunswick' in local periodicals and in *The London Sporting Review* in the 1830s-1840s. Cited as one of the leading international practitioners of the sporting sketch in his day, Perley was one of a number of sportsmen who gave the genre a particularly New Brunswick character in mid-century. In later years Albert Bigelow Paine's *The tent dwellers* (1908) and Frank Parker DAY's *The autobiography of a fisherman* (1927) were to be popular Nova Scotian representatives of the genre.

Common to all three provinces in mid-century was a taste for religious and moral writing that spoke of the pious earnestness of Victorian Maritimers. Mary Coy Bradley's *A narrative of the life and Christian experience of Mrs. Mary Bradley* (Boston, 1849) was typical in recounting her conversion and everyday spiritual experiences in Gagetown and Saint John in the late eighteenth century; but it also provides glimpses into feminist history by revealing her frustration at being denied preaching rights in the Methodist chapel. Methodist author William Charles M'KINNON, abandoned his writing of historical poems (*The battle of the Nile*, 1844) and novels as frivolous once he entered the ministry. In Halifax, sisters Sarah and Mary Eliza HERBERT contributed to religious periodicals such as *The Wesleyan Magazine* and encouraged struggling fellow poets such as John McPHERSON (*In praise of water: a prize poem*, 1843). Editor and sometime proprietor of the temperance newspaper *The Olive Branch*, Sarah Herbert is often remembered for her poems in *The Aeolian harp; or miscellaneous poems* (Halifax, 1857) containing the work of both sisters and published after Sarah's death. Mary Eliza Herbert's romances, such as *Belinda Dalton; or Scenes in the life of a Halifax belle* (Halifax, 1859), frequently identify the difficulties facing unmarried genteel women but never rise above their pietistic purposes. Neither her periodical for women, *The Mayflower* (Halifax, 1851-2), nor Mary Jane KATZMANN's more intellectual *The Provincial; or Halifax Monthly Magazine* (1852-53), could compete with inexpensive American magazines flooding the Maritime market; but they represented the increasing attempts by Maritime women to carve professional careers for themselves as writers and editors. While many writers, such as Fredericton's Agatha Armour (author of *Lady Rosamund's secret*, 1880) still struggled with writing as an avocation, the success of Saint John's May Agnes FLEMING in selling her escapist domestic fictions in New York (for example, *A mad marriage*, N.Y., 1875; *The heir of Charlton*, N.Y., 1878) signified the process of professionalization taking place among a number of writers of Maritime origin. Fellow Saint John native James DE MILLE also enjoyed financial success in the American market with satirical novels such as *The Dodge Club; or, Italy in MDCCCLIX* (serialized in *Harper's* in 1867; N.Y. 1869) and with the posthumous dystopia *A strange manuscript found in a copper cylinder* (N.Y., 1888). His B.O.W.C. (Brethen of the White Cross) books for children was 'The Hardy Boys' series of its era. Set in the Bay of Fundy area, these books provided more exciting reading than did other children's works of the period, such as Hannah Pickard's *The widow's jewels* (Boston, 1844) or Miss Grove's *Little Grace; or, Scenes in Nova Scotia* (Halifax, 1846), a tutorial organized around Haliburton's 1829 *An historical and statistical account of Nova Scotia*.

An enduring literary influence to emerge from the 1830-80 period was Henry Wadsworth Longfellow's *EVANGELINE* (Boston, 1847). Written by an American who had never set foot in Nova Scotia, the poem nonetheless created a mythology about the 1755 Acadian Expulsion that informed countless poems in the Victorian period, stimulated Clotilda Jenning's prize-winning tale *The white rose in Acadia* (Halifax, 1855), and inspired a reworking of the Acadian story by a series of historical novelists at the end of the century: for example, Carrie Jenkins Harris's *A modern Evangeline* (Windsor, N.S., 1896), Marshall SAUNDERS' *Rose à Charlitte* (Boston, 1898), Charles G. D. Roberts' *A sister to Evangeline* (Boston, 1898), and John Frederic Herbin's *Jen of the marshes* (Boston, 1921).

3. 1880 TO 1940. Many of the writers who came to prominence in the late nineteenth century had been born in the decade surrounding Confederation (1867), and reflected the changes taking place in Maritime literary life as the focus shifted from regional identity to a national one. George STEWART had tried to reinforce local writing with *STEWART'S LITERARY QUARTERLY* (1867-72) in Saint John, but he was typical of Maritime writers and editors, who by the 1880s and 1890s had often relocated to Quebec, Ontario, Boston, or New York. Two of the best-known post-Confederation writers who were eventually to follow this pattern were Charles G.D. Roberts and his cousin Bliss Carman, who, with Barry Straton and Francis SHERMAN, emerged from what has been called the post-Confederation

literary 'flowering of Fredericton'. However, it was particularly in the 1885-95 period of Roberts' professorship at King's College, Windsor, Nova Scotia, that he was consistently to attract around him the 'King's Circle' of friends (Carman, Richard Hovey), protegées (Sophia Almon Hensley), students (Robert NORWOOD, H.A. CODY), and visiting British admirers (Douglas Sladen, William Sharp). Roberts' *Orion and other poems* (Philadelphia, 1880), *In divers tones* (Boston, 1886), *Songs of the common day* (Toronto, 1893), and *New York nocturnes and other poems* (Boston, 1898) reflected variously his classical, Romantic, and transcendental interests, including a symbiotic relationship with nature. However, in his influential wilderness stories, collected first in *Earth's enigmas* (Boston, 1896), he expanded the boundaries of the genre by developing Darwinian portrayals of creatures caught in the chain of survival, and by exploring animal psychology. His historical romances, little more than costume dramas, successfully appealed to the post-Confederation appreciation of this genre in Canada. Roberts' potential for addressing more serious themes in fiction emerged in the story of an unwed mother in *The heart that knows* (1906); but here, as in his other novels, romance won out over realism.

Of Roberts' circle, Bliss Carman remains by far the best known. His mystical, pantheistic and transcendentalist sense of nature informed the lyricism of, among other works, *Low tide on Grand Pré* (New York, 1893), *Ballads of lost haven: a book of the sea* (Boston, 1897), and *Sanctuary: Sunshine House sonnets* (1929). His collaboration with Richard Hovey on *Songs from Vagabondia* (Boston, 1894) was the first of three collections in which the vigorous joys of the open road produced an optimistic, physical poetry that was quite different in tone from Carman's more classically inspired *Sappho: one hundred lyrics* (1904). Carman spent most of his career in America, often as an editor of periodicals and books, but returned to the Maritimes for readings as late as 1928 (a year before his death).

The Song Fishermen were a loose assembly of regional poets that included Charles G.D. Roberts, Charles BRUCE, Kenneth LESLIE, and Robert NORWOOD (and Carman) who celebrated romantic lyricism, Gaelic traditions, and Maritime camaraderie in poems completely antithetical to the modernist emphasis of the contemporaneous MONTREAL GROUP. Norwood—rector of St Bartholomew's Church, New York, and Roberts' former student—published dramatic monologues, blank-verse drama, sonnet sequences, and religious poetry, including a narrative poem (*Bill Boram*, 1921) and a spiritual long poem (*Issa*, 1931) that drew on his Nova Scotian background. Kenneth Leslie, who celebrated Norwood in his poem 'The Shaunachie man', showed early in his 'Song sheets' the influence of Gaelic rhythms and the socialist conscience that were to inform his later collections, including *By stubborn stars* (1938, Governor General's Award). Charles Bruce's first collection of poems, *Wild apples* (1927), was sponsored by Norwood.

Roberts' continuing influence as international editor and poet (*The iceberg and other poems*, 1934), cultural nationalist, and man of letters earned him a knighthood in 1935, but many of his late-nineteenth-century contemporaries had followed different literary paths. Sophia Almon Hensley's volumes of poems and essays, including *A woman's love letters* (New York, 1895) and *Love and the woman of tomorrow* (1913), reinforced the work of other feminist writers of the 1890-1920 period with their frank celebration of female sensuality and their criticism of social hypocrisy in the treatment of women. Amelia Fytche's *Kerchiefs to hunt souls* (Boston, 1895) provided a conventional conclusion for its Nova Scotian 'New Woman' heroine in Paris, but Marshall Saunders' novels for young women (including *The story of the Gravelys*, 1903, and *The girl from Vermont: the story of a vacation school teacher*, 1910) showed women spiritedly fighting for the playground movement, better working conditions, and political recognition. Saunders' use of an orphan figure in *Tilda Jane* (Boston, 1901) never captured international imaginations as successfully as did L.M. MONTGOMERY's *ANNE OF GREEN GABLES* (Boston, 1908), which became a symbol to generations of girls of the threat to individuality posed by convention. Of the five 'Anne' books that followed, none achieved the sense of irony of the first, but scholarship has redirected attention to Montgomery's novels set during the Great War (*Rainbow Valley*, 1919; *Rilla of Ingleside*, 1920); to the domestic realism of the 'Emily' books (*Emily of New Moon*, 1923; *Emily climbs*, 1925; *Emily's quest*, 1927); and to the importance of Montgomery's journals.

Published in London, America, and Toronto were the novels of Halifax cousins Alice Jones and Susan Morrow Jones ('Helen Milecete', 'S. Carleton'). Alice Jones often portrayed Canadians as energetic forces when juxtaposed against the amorality of Europe (*Bubbles we buy*, 1903; *Gabriel Praed's castle*, 1904). Susan Jones integrated First Nations themes into her short stories, and brought international settings to novels such as *A detached pirate* (London, 1900). On a more moralistic note were the romances of Anglican clerics Hiram A. CODY and Basil KING. Cody published twenty-three romantic novels of 'muscular Christianity', with titles such as *The long patrol; a tale of the Mounted Police* (1912). King's many novels, appearing after he had moved to Boston, included the specifically Canadian work *In the garden of charity* (1903), set on the South Shore of Nova Scotia; class issues, cross-border characters, and Christian social themes informed fiction as varied as *The way home* (1913) and *The thread of flame* (1920), and in a few cases attracted the attention of Hollywood.

Sea tales often characterized the prose published from the 1890s to 1940. Although Joshua Slocum gave up his Canadian citizenship to sail American tall ships, *Sailing alone around the world* (1900), based on his personal exploits in the sloop *Spray*, acknowledged in its opening line his Bluenose background. William Albert Hickman's fictional *The sacrifice of the Shannon* (1903), set on an ice-breaker in the Northumberland Strait, resembles some of his magazine stories in relying on sea knowledge gleaned from his family shipbuilding background. Frederick William WALLACE published classics of a disappearing way of life in *Blue water: a tale of the deep sea fishermen* (1907), *The shack-locker: yarns of the deep sea fishing fleets* (1916), and *Wooden ships and iron men* (1923). Of the Maritime fiction written after the First World War, Frank Parker DAY's controversial *Rockbound* (1928) best caught the tension between realism and romance as it detailed the backbreaking toil of inshore fishing families on an island off the Aspotagon Peninsula of Nova Scotia, while at the same time developing in its protagonist, David Jung, a hero of epic proportions. Theodore Goodridge ROBERTS, younger brother of Charles G. D. Roberts, caught a sense of Newfoundland idiom and outport life in *The harbour master* (1913), and utilized his experience sailing on a barkentine in the West Indies and South America as the background for his sea adventures *The wasp* (1914) and *The islands of adventure* (1918).

Theodore Goodridge Roberts was typical of the versatility of the Roberts family. (A sister, Elizabeth Roberts Macdonald, and a brother, William, published with Charles, T.G., and Bliss Carman in *Northland lyrics*, Boston, 1899; T.G.'s daughter, Dorothy Roberts Leisner and grandson, Goodridge MacDonald, published poetry in the next two generations.) Like other writers of the 1880-1940 period, T.G. Roberts often combined journal editing in Canada or the United States with publication in book and periodical form to sustain a writing career. He prolifically published poetry, Great War material, historical romances, local-colour fiction, and First Nations myths and tales (*The red feathers*, 1907) among other genres, including nature stories such as *The master of the moose horn, and other backcountry stories* (1919). Some of Roberts' work appealed to juveniles, as did the fiction of James MacDonald OXLEY (*The wreckers of Sable Island*, London, 1891; *Fife and drum at Louisbourg*, London, 1899), and William Alexander FRASER (*Mooswa and others of the boundaries*, 1900). In *Mooswa*, Fraser gave anthropomorphic qualities to animals, as did Marshall Saunders in her prize-winning story of an abused dog, *BEAUTIFUL JOE* (Philadelphia, 1894). Selling over a million copies and translated into over fifteen languages, *Beautiful Joe* superseded in popularity Saunders' later juvenile animal stories such as *Golden Dicky; The story of a canary and his friends* (1919) or *Jimmy Goldcoast; or, The story of a monkey* (1924). After the First World War, shifting standards of reading taste often made the high idealism of the late-Victorian period seem dated, and Saunders was among those who declined in popularity in the period between the wars. However, New York- and Boston-based Arthur Wentworth Hamilton EATON enjoyed a long career, extending from his historical *Acadian legends and lyrics* (London, 1889) to a collection of his most representative poems, *Acadian ballads and lyrics in many moods* (1930). Eaton also wrote the *History of King's County, Nova Scotia* (1910) and a respected biography, *The famous Mather Byles, the noted Boston Tory preacher, poet and wit, 1707-1788* (1914). Francis Sherman, Roberts' boyhood Fredericton friend, was particularly noted for his fine sonnet sequence, *In memorabilia mortis* (Cambridge, Mass., 1896), in honour of William Morris, and for his disciplined sonnets on love and faith in *The deserted city* (Boston, 1899). Eleven years after his death he was memorialized by Lorne PIERCE's edition of *The complete poems of Francis Sherman* (1935).

Economic decline in the Maritime Provinces in the 1920s and 1930s, accompanied by massive outmigration, did not enhance the climate for writing or for literary experimentation. The Great War gave rise to a range of war literature stretching from Edgar Wardell McInnis's *Poems written at 'The Front'* (1918) and *Road to Arras* (1920) to Dawn Fraser's vernacular verse, *Songs of Siberia* (1919). Fraser graphically caught the plight of disaffected soldiers, and in *Echoes from labour's war* (1926) played a bardic role as a voice for hungry strikers on the streets of Cape Breton ('He starved, he starved, I tell you'). Sensitivity to modernist trends emerged in Florence Ayscough's translations from the Chinese (with Amy Lowell) in *Fir-flower tablets. Poems* (1921), and Frank Davison ('Pierre Coalfleet') came close to a novel of psychological realism in *Solo* (1924), an account of a sensitive, gifted boy growing up in Davison's home-town of Hantsport, Nova Scotia. Davison, whose friendship with Marsden Hartley in Paris inspired the American artist's paintings and poetry on Nova Scotia, was also the author of three other prose works, including *Sidonie* (1921) and *Hare and tortoise* (1925). *The Dalhousie Review*, founded in Halifax in 1921, provided a rare forum for Maritime essayists and poets in the years between the wars. It included feminist essayist Professor Eliza Ritchie on its editorial board from 1921 to 1933. Ritchie's edited anthology of poems, *Songs of the Maritimes* (1931), gave voice to numerous younger poets. By and large, however, traditional lyric poetry and romantic historical fiction dominated the between-the-wars period, including *The token* (1930) by Edith Archibald (on nineteenth-century Cape Breton) and *Fog over Fundy* (1936) by Louis Arthur Cunningham, one of many popular fictions produced by the Saint John writer.

4. 1940 TO 1982. In the aftermath of the Second World War a sense of Maritime regional identity began to be constructed, both in historical writing and in poetic evocations of a disappearing way of rural life. In 1941 Cape Breton-born Hugh MacLENNAN struck a note of renewal in his First World War novel *BAROMETER RISING*, in which he employed the 1917 Halifax explosion as a catalyst for exploring themes of class, the integrity of Gaelic culture in Nova Scotia, and cultural nationalism. His other major Maritime novel was *Each man's son* (1951). Set in a mining community in Cape Breton, it successfully revealed class tensions but overdramatized the soul-crippling effects of Calvinist guilt on the Highland descendants in the novel. Along with Andrew MacPHAIL's Prince Edward Island novel *The master's wife* (1939), MacLennan's work invites comparison with Alistair MacLEOD's *As birds bring forth the sun* (1986) and Sheldon Currie's novella *The Glace Bay miners' museum* (1995) in providing imaginative insight into the loss of a distinctive Maritime Gaelic culture in an industrialized world.

Historical novelists Will R. BIRD, Evelyn Eaton, and Thomas H. Raddall spoke to historical parallels during the war years and provided readers with an escape to a more understandable past. Bird drew on his own ancestral rootedness in the Chignecto area to write popular Yorkshire settler novels such as *Here stays good Yorkshire* (1945), *Judgement Glen* (1947), and *The shy Yorkshireman* (1955), although he also published travel works, local histories, and memoirs of the First World War. Evelyn Eaton's highly readable historical romances of colonial Nova Scotia included *Quietly my captain waits* (1940), which was chosen by the Literary Guild of New York; *Restless are the sails* (1941); and *The sea is wide* (1943). Some of Eaton's later works, including her autobiography, explored her return to her First Nations roots and spirituality. Thomas H. Raddall's meticulously researched historical romances, written in the Sir Walter Scott tradition, included *His Majesty's Yankees* (1942), *Roger Sudden* (1944), and *Hangman's Beach* (1966). They resembled Raddall's *The nymph and the lamp* (1950) in projecting a regenerative social vision, although in the latter more contemporary novel that can be achieved only by the characters' retreating to an anti-modernist Sable Island-like environment. Twice winner of a Governor General's Award, Raddall also published histories and a memoir, *In my time* (1976).

Contributing to the anti-modernist image of the region after 1940 were Evelyn Richardson's account of isolation in *We keep a light* (1945, Governor General's Award) and Helen Creighton's folk collections, including *Songs and ballads from Nova Scotia* (1932), *Folklore of Lunenburg County, Nova Scotia* (1950), and *Bluenose ghosts* (1957). Like Cyrus MacMillan in *Canadian wonder tales* (1918) and *Canadian fairy tales* (1922)—and in the selection from these books, *Glooskap's Country and other Indian tales* (1955)—and Louise Manny in her work on the Miramichi River, Creighton helped to identify the importance of an oral tradition in the region. A challenge to Creighton's construct of Nova Scotian folk life emerges in Ian McKay's *The quest of the folk* (1994).

The impact of change on regional life was measured in the poetry and prose of lyricist Charles Bruce and in the lushly written but inherently ironic fiction of Ernest BUCKLER. In poetry collections such as *The flowing summer* (1947) and *The Mulgrave Road* (1951), which won a Governor General's Award, Bruce explored the fusion of sea, land, and family tradition to produce the 'salt in the blood' that binds Nova Scotians to their province ('Words are never enough'). His novels *The Channel Shore* (1954) and *The township of time* (1959) further delineated the importance of place, communal memory, and family connections, all revealed through Bruce's sure handling of time. In Buckler's novels *The MOUNTAIN AND THE VALLEY* (1952) and *The cruelest month* (1963), and in *Oxbells and fireflies: a memoir* (1968), rural pastoralism is eroded by contemporary urban values. *The mountain and the valley*, however, transcends regional concerns by exploring the interiority and self-delusion of a writer sustained by his love of the land but isolated in his pursuit of the imaginative. *Oxbells*, partly a nostalgic elegy for the past, is also a record of regional idioms, customs, and institutions written in an incremental, lyrical prose style.

In New Brunswick in the post-war years the focus for many writers was on Fredericton, where *The FIDDLEHEAD* had been founded as a journal in 1945. Associated with its early years were poets Alfred BAILEY, Elizabeth BREWSTER, and Fred COGSWELL, among others. Bailey, who published the influential *The conflict of European and eastern Algonkian cultures, 1504-1700* (1937; 1969) and *Culture and nationality* (1972), wrote polished, intellectual poetry found in *Thanks for a drowned island* (1973) and *Miramichi lightning* (1981). Brewster's understated, ironic voice shaped lyrics of ordinary (and therefore universal) experience in collections such as *Passage of summer* (1969), *Sunrise north* (1972), and *The way home* (1982). Her novel *The sisters* (1974) and her short stories, collected in *It's easy to fall on the ice* (1977), explored 'every woman's' experiences in growing up, working, and coping with life. Cogswell, who edited *The Fiddlehead* from 1952 to 1967, and until 1981 published countless young Canadian writers in Fiddlehead Books, brought both irony and a passionate sense of place to his finely crafted first collection, *The stunted strong* (1954). Many volumes of traditional and experimental poetry followed, including *A long apprenticeship: collected poems* (1980) and the deeply moving *Pearls* (1983). A fine translator of francophone verse (for example, *One hundred poems of modern Québec*, 1970), Cogswell also played an influential role as critic in his Maritime Provinces contributions to the *Literary history of Canada* (1965; 1976).

In the period leading up to the 1980s a number of other writers associated with New Brunswick locations emerged. In Fredericton they included Robert Hawkes, Peter Thomas, Tony Brennan, Dale Estey, William Bauer, Nancy Bauer, M. Travis LANE, Kent THOMPSON, and Robert GIBBS. Kent Thompson, than a teacher of creative writing at the University of New Brunswick, published novels such as *The tenants were Corrie and Tennie* (1973) and *Shacking up* (1980). M. Travis Lane's *Poems: 1968-1972* (1973), *Homecoming* (1977), and *Divinations and shorter poems* (1980) established her as a cerebral poet of technical craftsmanship, while Robert Gibbs' books of subtle poetry ranged from *The road from here* (1968) to *A space to play* (1981). Gibbs' short stories, narrated by a perceptive, wry child, evoked a sense of an irretrievable 1930s-1940s New Brunswick past in *I've always felt sorry for decimals* (1978) and invite comparison with Brewster, Buckler, and Bruce.

Two of the most significant writers to emerge from the Fredericton environment of the post-war period were Alden NOWLAN and David Adams RICHARDS. Nowlan, writer-in-residence at the University of New Brunswick from 1969 until his death in 1983, drew upon his rural Nova Scotian childhood and his knowledge of Upper Saint John River society to inform novels such as *Miracle at Indian River* (1968), *Various persons named Kevin O'Brien* (1973), and the posthumously published *The wanton troopers* (1988). The destructive effects of poverty, puritanism, alcohol-abuse, and parochialism on human dignity and on the development of the imagination form a central motif in his fiction and explain why ironic masks and self-parody often characterize the personae of both the poetry and the fiction. Nowlan's ironic, conversational lyrics appeared in collections such as *The mysterious naked man* (1969), *Between tears and laughter* (1971), and *I'm a stranger here myself* (1974), and were collected by Lorna CROZIER and Patrick LANE in *Alden Nowlan: selected poems* (1996). Both Nowlan and Buckler encouraged young novelist David Adams Richards, who studied at St Thomas University, Fredericton, before publishing the *Coming of winter* (1974), *Blood ties* (1976), and *Lives of short duration* (1981). Exploring lives of frustration, inarticulacy, and pathos similar to those that had preoccupied Nowlan, Richards created in his stylized Miramichi setting an almost mythic world where elemental emotions are played out in a powerful incremental narrative style.

In Sackville, New Brunswick, a number of writers emerged in the 1970s, although their responses to the Tantramar Marsh rather than their affiliation with Mount Allison University often seemed to be the common denominator. John THOMPSON's sophisticated use of concentrated imagery informed *At the edge of the chopping there are no secrets* (1973) and the posthumous *Stilt Jack* (1978). Liliane Welch and Michael Thorpe, both polished, intellectual writers, integrated international and regional experience into their respective collections. Alan Cooper, a graduate of the university, assumed the editorship of the poetry journal *Germination* from poet Harry Thurston in 1982, and published *Bloodlines* (1978) and *Hidden River poems* (1982). Most prolifically responding to the Tantramar Marsh environment, however, was poet Douglas LOCHHEAD (*The full furnace*, 1975), whose *High Marsh Road* (1980) was nominated for a Governor General's Award. In a series of verse diary entries that revealed a sensual, often elliptical response to the land and all that its continuity signified, Lochhead stressed the relationship between visual image and the word not only in the design of *High Marsh Road* but also in his collaboration with photographer Thaddeus Holownia in the collection *Dykelands* (1989).

Part of a group of young artists and writers in Saint John in the late 1930s (including P.K. PAGE, *The sun and the moon*, 1944), Kay Smith published modernist, spiritually affirming poems in *Footnote to the Lord's Prayer* (1951), *At the bottom of the dark* (1971), *When a girl looks down* (1978), and *White paper face at the window* (1987). In Prince Edward Island the 1970s and early 1980s saw publishing activity focus on such catalytic figures as Reshard Gool (Square Deal Press) and Libby Oughton (Ragweed Press). Poets such as Wayne Wright (*The girl in the brook*, 1980), Richard Lemm (*Dancing in Asylum*, 1982), and Joseph Sherman (*Birthday*, 1969; *Chaim the slaughterer*, 1974) were then, or have since been, associated with 'the Island'. The best-known P.E.I. writer of the 1960s-1980s period was Milton ACORN, whose poetry, built around dialectical opposites, included *I've tasted my blood: poems 1956 to 1968* (1969), *The island means Minago* (1975, Governor General's Award), *Jackpine sonnets* (1977), and *Dig up my heart: selected poems of Milton Acorn: 1952-1983* (1983).

The period of the 1970s and early 1980s saw the first publications of a group of writers who by the 1990s would be firmly established on the Canadian literary landscape: Brian Bartlett, Don Domanski, J. A. Wainwright (*After the war*, 1981), Elizabeth Jones (*Nude on the Dartmouth ferry*, 1980), 'Silver' Donald Cameron (*Seasons in the rain*, 1978), George Elliott CLARKE (*Saltwater spirituals and deeper blues*, 1983), Lesley CHOYCE, Greg Cook, Fraser SUTHERLAND, and Harry Thurston (*Barefaced stone*, 1980; *Clouds flying before the eye*, 1985). Strong female voices in prose also emerged in this period, including that of Donna Smyth in her feminist novel *Quilt* (1982). Often treating the world of the religious cloister, Ann COPELAND published *At peace* (1978) and *The back room* (1979). Beth HARVOR and Joan CLARK revealed the understated ironies of ordinary female lives in *Women and children* (1973) and *From a high thin wire* (1982) respectively. (Clark's *Swimming toward the light*, 1990, developed further the paradoxes of a young girl's growth to discovery in the Maritimes.) Susan Kerslake's *Middlewatch* (1976) and *Penumbra* (1984) intricately explored aspects of female voicelessness, darkness, and language recovery in intense prose. Also complexly crafted were Ray SMITH's postmodernist experimental stories in *Cape Breton is the thought control centre of Canada* (1969), and his ironic, playful linked fictions in *Lord Nelson Tavern* (1974). Completely different in tone were Alistair MacLEOD's two collections of short stories, *The lost salt gift of blood* (1976) and *As birds bring forth the sun* (1986). These books hauntingly exposed the personal and cultural loss generated by Cape Breton's economics of outmigration, with the second book particularly emphasizing Gaelic language, folklore, superstition, and music as part of the island's threatened Highland heritage.

The 1940-82 period in the Maritimes saw a growth in literary activity nourished by the support of the CANADA COUNCIL and the Canadian Broadcasting Corporation, by the presence of regional literary journals (for example, *The Fiddlehead*, the *Antigonish Review*, *Pottersfield Portfolio*, *Germination*, *The Dalhousie Review*), and by the encouragement of regional publishers (for example, Fiddlehead, Formac, Ragweed, Petheric, Nimbus, Lancelot, Harrier Editions, Wombat). During the two hundred and thirty years that had passed since the first newspaper offered Maritime writers an opportunity to publish, a distinctive body of writing had developed marked by a sense of place and a focused, self-conscious sense of literary culture.

GWENDOLYN DAVIES

5. 1982 TO 1996. The appearance of criticism in book form is an indication of a focused and self-conscious literary culture. This period saw the publication of the first volume of Maritime literary criticism by a single author, *Under eastern eyes: a critical reading of Maritime fiction* by Janice KULYK KEEFER. In this ground-breaking study Kulyk Keefer perceives, as have other critics, that

all-purpose descriptions of Canadian literature apply inadequately to the long and sturdy literary traditions of the Maritimes. She suggests that this failure occurs because the Maritime ethos grew out of, and is still to some extent based on, Enlightenment principles, whereas that of southern Ontario, the source of these blanket descriptions, is based on nineteenth-century ideals. Kulyk Keefer identifies characteristic themes of Maritime authors: the question of whether to stay at home or leave; the sense of economic and spiritual connection with (rather than fear of) nature; and the continuum of history. These themes, she shows, remain pervasive even though different writers in their times treat them differently. Supplementing *Under eastern eyes* are *Myth and milieu: Atlantic literature and culture, 1918-1939* (1994) by Gwendolyn Davies, who edited *Studies in Maritime literary history, 1760-1930* (1991), and *Down east: critical essays on contemporary Maritime Canadian literature* (Trier, Germany, 1996) edited by Wolfgang Hochbruck and James O. Taylor.

The establishment of two significant annual awards for published books strengthened Maritime literary culture: the Dartmouth Book Awards of $1000 each, initiated in 1989 and offered by the Halifax Regional Municipality and the Halifax Regional Library; and the Thomas Raddall Atlantic Fiction Award of $4000, presented since 1990 by the Writers' Federation of Nova Scotia. The Maritime Writers' Workshop, founded by Nancy Bauer in Fredericton in 1975, has continuously offered one of Canada's finest residential writers' programs, developing in particular the craft of Maritime poets and fiction writers.

The pre-eminent Maritime fiction writer is David Adams Richards, whose novels are grounded in the Chatham-Newcastle area of New Brunswick, on the Miramichi River. His characters range from workers to welfare recipients to returnees from the city, the university, or even prison with enough money and power to bully or corrupt their former neighbours. Protagonists tend to stay put rather than leave, passionately connected to their own homes and societies. The most powerful qualities of Richards' writing are subtle dialogue, deceptively rough, through which character gradually emerges, and a dark, cumulative humour. In the 1990s the reissue of his three earliest novels and the strength of his trilogy—*Nights below Station Street* (1988), *Evening snow will bring such peace* (1990), and *For those who hunt the wounded down* (1993)—reinforced his stature as a writer who, while commanding national and international attention, has remained true to his Miramichi roots and his literary and social vision. In recognition of this he was awarded the Alden Nowlan Award for Excellence in English Literary Arts by the New Brunswick government in 1993. His most recent novel is *Hope in the desperate hour* (1996).

Herb Curtis, also from the Miramichi area, has written four poignantly humorous novels: the Brennen Siding trilogy—*The Americans are coming* (1989), *The last Tasmanian* (1991), and *The lone angler* (1993)—and *The silent partner* (1996). *The last Tasmanian* won the 1992 Thomas Raddall Atlantic Fiction Award and was shortlisted for a Commonwealth Book Award. Curtis deals with his characters' love of the river, their seasonal jobs as fishing guides and woods workers, and the simultaneous lures of leaving and staying home. Wayne Curtis (Herb Curtis's brother), best known for insightful and beautiful essays about the Miramichi and its people, has published a novel, *One Indian summer* (1994), about a young man who leaves the family farm just as mechanization becomes inevitable.

Lesley Choyce's adult fiction is characterized by male protagonists in retreat from urban pressures to the shore or countryside, a flexible sense of reality, and a taste for the absurd. His two adult literary novels, *The second season of Jonas MacPherson* (1989) and *The republic of nothing* (1994), each won a Dartmouth Book Award. *Dance the rocks ashore: stories new and selected* (1997) shows a continuous growth in technique and complexity of vision. The poems in Choyce's sixth collection, *The coastline of forgetting* (1995), meditate on humanity's connection with the elemental force of the sea.

Ann Copeland's story cycle *The golden thread* (1989), shortlisted for a Governor General's Award, follows Sister Claire Delaney through her youth and her life as a nun until she leaves the convent. A second cycle, *Strange bodies on a stranger shore* (1994), follows Claire into middle age. The stories in *Season of apples* (1996) leave the convent behind, but they continue Copeland's exploration of the complex connections between body, intellect, and spirit.

Nancy Bauer followed *Flora, write this down* (1983) with *Wise ears* (1985), *The opening eye* (1988), *Samara the wholehearted* (1991), and *The irrational doorways of Mr. Gerard* (1994). Mingling an updated New England transcendentalism with New Brunswick pragmatism, they deal with the adventures and the peace achieved by women who choose to let faith and instinct control their lives. M.T. Dohaney, a Fredericton writer who often sets her fiction in her native Newfoundland, has published three novels about women struggling with their decisions to stay at home or leave: *The Corrigan women* (1988); its sequel, *To scatter stones* (1992); and *A marriage of masks* (1995), winner of the 1996 Thomas Raddall Atlantic Fiction Award.

Important story collections include Alistair MacLeod's *As birds bring forth the sun* (1986); Leo MacKay, Jr's *Like this: stories* (1995), which won the 1996 Dartmouth Book Award for Fiction; and Carol Bruneau's *After the Angel Mill* (1995), stories about four generations of women arriving at, staying in, or leaving industrial Cape Breton. Sheldon Currie's novella *The Glace Bay miners' museum* (1995) was the basis for the hit movie *Margaret's museum*. Collections of J.J. Steinfeld's mordant, carefully crafted stories, many of which feature young Jewish men, include *Our hero in the cradle of Confederation* (1987), *Forms of captivity and escape* (1988), and *Dancing at the Club Holocaust* (1993).

Brian Bartlett has three books of strong, sensitive poetry to his credit: *Planet Harbor* (1989), *Underwater carpentry* (1993), and *Granite erratics* (1997). Lesley-Anne Bourne, a professor at the University of Prince Edward Island, has also published three collections, *The story of pears* (1990), *Skinny girls* (1993), and *Field day* (1996). Although Elizabeth Brewster has lived in Saskatoon for many years, she remains very much a Maritimer. Her poetry books since the mid-1980s include the two-volume *Selected poems of Elizabeth Brewster, 1944-1984* (1985); *Spring again* (1990), shortlisted for the 1991 Pat LOWTHER Award; and the Governor General's Award finalist *Footnotes to the Book of Job* (1995). George Elliott Clarke, a popular spokesman for the black Nova Scotian experience, has published three books of vibrant poetry, *Saltwater spirituals and deeper blues* (1983), *Whylah Falls* (1990), and *Lush dreams, blue exile* (1994), and he has edited the two-volume *Fire on the water: an anthology of Black Nova Scotia writing* (1991, 1992) and *Eyeing the North Star: directions in African-Canadian literature* (1997). David Woods, a poet and playwright who is active in the Black cultural community of Halifax, published *Native song* (1990).

Fred Cogswell published six books of poems between 1990 and 1996, including *In praise of old music* (1992), *When the right light shines* (1992), and *The trouble with light* (1996). His translations of Acadian poetry embody New Brunswick's bilingual culture; with Jo-Anne Elder he selected and translated *Unfinished dreams: contemporary poetry of Acadie* (1990), which was published simultaneously in French as *Rêves inachevés* (1990). Allan Cooper has continued to encourage the work of other poets while publishing new books, including *Poems released on a nuclear wind* (1988) and *The pearl inside the body: poems selected and new* (1990). An intense physicality characterizes the poetry of Don Domanski, whose sixth book, *Stations of the left hand* (1994), was shortlisted for a Governor General's Award.

Two Mi'kmaq poets strive to express and validate the experience of their people: Chief Lindsay Marshall in *Clay pots and bones* (1997) and Rita JOE in *Song of Eskasoni* (1988) and *Lnu and Indian we're called* (1991). M. Travis Lane's recent books include *Reckonings: poems 1979-1985* (1986), *Temporary shelter* (1993), and *Night physics* (1994); she is an astute critic as well as one of Canada's most skilled poets. Richard Lemm has served as president of the League of Canadian Poets and head of poetry at the Banff Centre of the Arts; his recent books are *A difficult faith* (1985) and *Prelude to the bacchanal* (1990). Douglas LOCHHEAD, one of Canada's most respected poets and a supreme craftsman, often explores the human spirit in the context of the Tantramar Marsh. Recent books include the sumptuous *Dykelands* (1989), with photographs by Thaddeus Holownia; the cerebral yet passionate *Homage to Henry Alline* (1992); and *Breakfast at Mel's* (1997). Heather Browne Prince's spare, carefully honed *Knowledge in the hands* (1994) was shortlisted for the Gerald Lampert Award.

Peter Sanger has published one book of his own poetry, *Earth moth* (1991); founded the Elizabeth Bishop Society of Nova Scotia for the repatriation of that poet's works (1994); and edited *John Thompson: collected poems and translations* (1995). His strange and beautiful experimental works include *The third hand* (1994) and *Ironworks* (1995), with photographer Thaddeus Holownia, and *Stone notes*, twenty one-to-three-line poems engraved on sandstone by Heather Lawson. Maxine Tynes, an Africadian feminist poet, writes dramatically about social as well as personal issues. Her first book, *Borrowed beauty* (1987), won the Milton Acorn People's Poet of Canada Award; her two subsequent volumes, *Woman talking women* (1990) and *The door of my heart* (1993), include both poems and stories. *The incorrupt tables* (1995) and *A selection of dazzling scarves* (1996) launched the career of iconoclastic gay poet R.M. Vaughan. Lilianne Welch's uncompromising voice is as well known in Europe as in Canada. *Life in another language* (1992) won the F.G. Bressani Prize, and other recent books are *Fire to the looms below* (1990) and *Dream museum* (1995).

Three substantial anthologies of contemporary Maritime literature have been published since the mid-1980s: *Best Maritime short stories* (1988) edited by George Peabody; *Poetic voices of the Maritimes* (1996) edited by Allison Mitcham and Theresia Quigley; and *Fiddlehead gold* (1996) edited by Sabine Campbell, Don MacKAY, Roger Ploude, and Demetres Tryohonopoulis, a selection of poetry and fiction from fifty years of *The Fiddlehead*.

Most Maritime literary presses maintain strong regional lists while also publishing books by writers from elsewhere. In 1982 publisher Peter Thomas added the GOOSE LANE EDITIONS imprint to Fiddlehead Poetry Books for prose titles; in 1996 a WRITERS' UNION OF CANADA survey named Goose Lane Editions Canada's best publisher. Since 1985, using several imprints including Wild East and Broken Jaw, Joe Blades has published about forty poetry chapbooks by new writers and established poets such as Robert Gibbs and Robert Hawkes, along with several essay and fiction titles. 1996 saw the closing of Lancelot Press, which had published a few literary titles each year since 1966. Lesley Choyce's Pottersfield Press, established in 1978, has published about twenty-five books of poetry, fiction, and literary biography. Two Cape Breton presses publish fiction, poetry, and drama about Cape Breton by Cape Breton authors along with their non-literary lists: Breton Books, founded in 1988 by Ronald Caplan as an outgrowth of *Cape Breton's Magazine*, and University College of Cape Breton Press, founded in 1974. Prince Edward Island's Ragweed Press publishes mainstream poetry and fiction and, under the Gynergy imprint, feminist and lesbian fiction, poetry, and other books. Perhaps the strength of book publishing in the Maritimes is due in part to the region's long intellectual history and its continuous literary tradition. LAUREL BOONE

Marlatt, Daphne (b. 1942). Born Daphne Buckle in Melbourne, Australia, to English parents who had been evacuated from Penang, Malaya, in advance of the Japanese occupation, Daphne Marlatt spent six postwar years in Penang before her family moved to North Vancouver, British Columbia, in 1951. She enrolled in English at the University of British Columbia in 1960, became an editor of *TISH* in 1963, and on graduation in 1964 went to the University of Indiana, where she completed an M.A. (1968) in comparative literature. Following the breakup of her marriage she returned to British Columbia, where she lives in Victoria. From 1973 to 1976 she was an editor of *The Capilano Review*; from 1977 to 1981 she co-edited with Paul de Barros the prose magazine *Periodics*. She was a founding co-editor of *Tessera*, a feminist journal.

Marlatt's first widely published works were the novella 'Sea Haven', in Giose Rimanelli's and Roberto Ruberto's *Modern Canadian stories* (1966), and fifteen poems in Raymond SOUSTER's *New wave Canada* (1966). These were followed by the long poems *Frames of a story* (1968) and *leaf/leaf/s* (1969), which are highly contrasting experiments in language and form. *Frames*, written in a long prose line, retells Hans Christian Andersen's 'The Snow Queen', using the tale to reinterpret events in the author's life. *leaf/leaf/s*, written in lines of single words and syllables, accentuates minute fragmentary features of syntax and morphology so that at times they become the writing's primary content. While one work engages language at the level of sentence rhythm and narrative voice, and the other at that of phoneme and syntactic connection, each uses language to divine meaning through recurrence and resemblance. Each also follows American poet Charles Olson in seeing language as a potential twin to the processes of consciousness.

These tentative and visibly technical works were succeeded in the next decade by a number of long poems and related texts that explored phenomenology, autobiography, and the politics of the local—*Rings* (1971), *Vancouver poems* (1972), *Steveston* (1974), *Our lives* (1975), *Zócalo* (1977), and *What matters* (1980)—and culminated in *Selected writing: net work* (1980). While all of these—except the journal *Zócalo*—were presented as 'poems', their dominant feature was the long verse line, minutely punctuated, which suggests both the linguistic precision of poetry and the sequential motion of prose. All were written from inside a single consciousness and used linguistic structure to map perceptual processes in detail. *Rings* presents the images and fragmentary reflections in the mind of a woman whose marriage is crumbling and whose first child is about to be born. Puns, shards of words, metaphors, enigmatic images, and broken sentences combine to give a dense physical rendering of her simultaneous experience of pregnancy, memory, her husband's hostility, and her physical surroundings. *Vancouver poems* encounters that city through the subjective vision of someone freshly experiencing its geography, climate, and historical and political documents as interwoven, nearly co-present, phenomena. Marlatt's major work of this period, *Steveston*, presents the history and present of this Japanese-Canadian fish-cannery town as alive in the 'net' of consciousness cast by the writer. *Zócalo*'s very different images and denser, more extended prose line give form to the intense experiences of a woman travelling in the Yucatán (Mexico), who is separated by language, race, gender, and class, yet not by eye or ear, from the scenes she witnesses.

In the 1980s Marlatt's public affiliation with lesbian communities marked a sharp change in the political perspectives and implied readership of her writing. This period saw Marlatt undertake reconsiderations of some of her earlier writing and extend and re-focus her autobiographical inquiries. The long-poem/journal *How hug a stone* (1983), with its critical examination of early moments in her mother's marriage and its invocation of a hypothetical feminine presence at Avebury, announced Marlatt's new interest in various feminisms. This book was quickly followed by the lyrical lesbian love texts of *Touch to my tongue* (1984), and its accompanying essay/meditation on feminist theorists Julia Kristeva and Mary Daly, 'Musing with Mother Tongue'. In 1988 Marlatt published, with Betsy WARLAND, *Double negative*, a collaborative long-poem/journal about two lesbians crossing Australia's Nullarbor Desert that draws comparisons between the theft of Aboriginal lands and the denial of space to women who are lesbians. Later that year she published her best-received work to date, the novel *Ana Historic*, which continued Marlatt's autobiographical investigations and linked semi-fictionalized accounts of her early family life to the erasure of women from the official early history of Vancouver. In 1991 she published *Salvage*, a collection of texts 'salvaged' and expanded from those she had deleted more than a decade earlier from *Steveston*—which would have given it a more feminist emphasis. In 1993 she released *Ghost works*—a collection that recasts *Zócalo*, *How hug a stone*, and her 1976 Penang journal, 'Month of hungry ghosts'—which, as Marlatt's introduction argues, illuminates the extreme difficulty of women's autobiography in cultures where the systemic erasing of women's activities leaves them only the ghosts of lives to reclaim or imagine. This theme—that women, lacking documentary accounts of their own or their mothers' lives, must re-imagine or fictionalize their pasts—is central to Marlatt's second novel, *Taken* (1996), which focuses on characters who strongly resemble Marlatt's parents during their Penang and Australian years.

Marlatt's work during the 1970s with the British Columbia Archives' oral history project resulted in two important documentary publications: *Steveston recollected: a Japanese-Canadian history* (1975, with M. Koizumi) and *Opening doors: Vancouver's East End* (1979, with Carole Itter).

See Smaro Kamboureli and Shirley Neuman, eds, *Line* 13 (1988), a special issue on Marlatt.

See also POETRY IN ENGLISH 1950 TO 1982: 3.

FRANK DAVEY

Marleau, Denis. See DRAMA IN FRENCH 1981 TO 1996: 3.

Marlyn, John (b. 1912). Born in Hungary (family name: Mihaelovitcz), he came to Canada as an infant and grew up in Winnipeg's north end. He attended secondary school in Winnipeg, leaving at the age of fourteen, and beginning in 1930 studied literature at the University of Manitoba for a short period. Unable to find employment in Canada during the Depression, he moved to England where he became a script reader for a film company, Gainsborough Studios. He returned to Canada just before the Second World War and worked as a writer for various government departments in Ottawa, where he also taught creative-writing courses. He now lives on Gran Canaria, Canary Islands.

Marlyn's *Under the ribs of death* (1957; NCL, with an Afterword by Neil BISSOONDATH) is one of the earliest Canadian novels to deal with what has been called the 'third solitude'—life within ethnic cultures outside the Canadian mainstream. It is the story of Sandor Hunyadi, the son of an idealistic Hungarian immigrant, who is determined to escape the poverty and humiliation he associates with his immigrant background. Changing his name to Alex Hunter, he becomes a successful and ruthless businessman, only to be ruined in the Depression, a reversal that forces him to return to his family and the humanistic values he had earlier rejected. In spite of a somewhat facile ending, the novel is a powerful portrait of the hardships endured by immigrants, and of the driving ambition and susceptibility to materialistic values that can be triggered by such an experience.

Marlyn's second novel, *Putzi, I love you, you little square* (1981), is a surrealistic satire set in the 1970s dealing, once again, with Hungarian immigrants in a city resembling Winnipeg. It is about a precocious fetus who speaks from his virgin mother's womb, advising her on the unworthiness of her suitors, quoting Shakespeare, Donne, Wordsworth, and other classical writers at length, and commenting tartly on life in the world beyond the womb, with special attention to the threat of technological incursions upon human privacy. While slight, the novel is nonetheless a witty fable that argues for the same humanistic values (here personified in the character of Julian, a doctor) as did Marlyn's earlier novel.

See John Roberts, 'Irony in an immigrant novel: John Marlyn's *Under the ribs of death*', *Canadian Ethnic Studies* 14, no. 1 (1982), and Marlene Kadar, 'Reading ethnicity into life writing: Bela Szabados's narrator rewrites Sandor Hunyadi', *Essays on Canadian Writing* 57 (Winter 1995). MARILYN ROSE

Marmette, Joseph-Étienne-Eugène (1844-95). The son of a physician, he was born at Montmagny, Canada East (Quebec). He studied at the Séminaire de Québec, spent one year at the Royal Military College in Kingston (Ontario), and one year in the law school of Université Laval. In 1866 he took a job as a clerk-bookkeeper in the Provincial Treasury department and retained this position until 1882. Such was his first career, during which he managed to fill his leisure hours by reading novels and histories, writing serial romances, and collaborating with Henri-Raymond CASGRAIN (who used his pseudonym 'Placide Lépine') on the literary profiles *Silhouettes canadiennes* (Québec, 1872). He married Joséphine, daughter of the historian François-Xavier GARNEAU, in 1868 and they had one daughter. In May 1882 he was appointed by Ottawa as a special immigration agent in Europe for France and Switzerland and left for Paris, where he worked for the Public Archives of Canada, transcribing documents relating to Canadian history. In the same year he became a charter member of the Royal Society of Canada. Between 1884 and 1887 he made three trips to Paris and also spent some time in London, where he was in charge of the library for the Canadian pavilion of the Colonial Exhibition of 1886. After 1887 he never again left Ottawa.

Between 1866 and 1895 Marmette published, besides *Silhouettes canadiennes*, a light comedy, *Il ne faut désespérer de rien* (Québec, 1880), and *Récits et souvenirs* (Québec, 1891), travel articles chiefly about London and Paris, most of which had already appeared between 1884 and 1888 in *Mémoires de La Société Royale du Canada*. But Marmette was most prominent for his historical novels; indeed, he was one of those who introduced the genre to his era. Unfortunately, his wide reading of such historians as Charlevoix, Garneau, Ferland, La Pothérie, Jean-Claude Panet, Casgrain, Francis Parkman, and the *JESUIT RELATIONS*, his use of historical figures, and his attempts to reconstruct the Canadian cultural scene, were all in vain: his plots were ill-contrived and his characters neither well drawn nor sufficiently brought into the foreground. Inept at originating his own stories or at bringing history to life, he merely repeated himself endlessly. *Charles et Eva*, a story about a raid on Schenectady in 1890, which appeared in *La Revue canadienne* (Dec. 1866-May 1867; rpr. 1945), *François de Bienville: scènes de la vie canadienne au XVII*[e] *siècle* (Québec, 1870), *L'intendant Bigot* (Montréal, 1872), *Le chevalier de Mornac: chroniques de la Nouvelle-France* (Montréal, 1873), *Le tomahahk et l'épée* (Québec, 1877), *Les Machabées de la Nouvelle-France: histoire d'une famille canadienne 1641-1768* (Québec, 1878), and *Héroisme et trahison* (Québec, 1878) are all cloak-and-dagger adventure fiction and anything but models of composition and style. But they were extremely popular in the nineteenth century: despite his fatuous and pompous style and his primitive psychology, Marmette had a large audience. Apparently modelling himself on the French dramatist Pixerécourt (1773-1844), he was skilful in exploiting the nostalgia felt by so many of his compatriots for the seventeenth and eighteenth centuries, but he is hardly read today. His two best works are *La fiancée du rebelle: épisode de la guerre des Bostonnais*, which appeared in instalments of *La Revue canadienne* (vol. XII, jan.-oct. 1875), and *À travers la vie: roman autobiographique*, which was first published in fragments in 1881, 1886, and 1892, and then in its entirety in *La Revue nationale* (vols I-II, 1895-6).

MAURICE LEBEL

Marquis, Thomas Guthrie (1864-1936). Born in Chatham, New Brunswick, he graduated from Queen's University, Kingston, and taught English in Ontario schools until 1901. He then became a freelance writer, an editor, and a well-known figure in the Toronto book trade. He first came to public attention as a writer of popular historical tales. His *Stories of New France: being tales of adventure and heroism from the early history of Canada* (Boston, 1890), the second in a series (Agnes MACHAR wrote the first volume), was followed by *Stories from*

Canadian history (Toronto, 1893; rpr. 1936). His one full-length historical romance, *Marguerite de Roberval; a romance of the days of Jacques Cartier* (Toronto, 1899), told in an old-fashioned intrusive manner, explains the failure of the Cartier-Roberval expedition to New France. A second work of prose fiction, *The king's wish* (1924), is a charming pastoral allegory for children.

Marquis began his historical work with a book on Canadian activity in the Boer war, *Canada's sons on kopje and veldt: an historical account of the Canadian contingents* (1900), and *Presidents of the United States from Pierce to McKinley* (1903), vol. XXI in the prestigious 26-volume Nineteenth-Century Series edited by Justin McCarthy (Charles G.D. ROBERTS and Marquis were among the four international associate editors of the series). A number of Canadian biographies and histories for the popular and school markets followed: *Brock, the hero of Upper Canada* (1912); *The war chief of the Ottawas: a chronicle of the Pontiac war* (1915); *The Jesuit missions: a chronicle of the cross in the wilderness* (1916); and four brief textbooks in the Canadian History Reader Series: *Sir Isaac Brock* (1926), *Naval warfare on the Great Lakes, 1812-14* (1926), *Battlefields of 1813* (1926), *George Monro Grant* (1926), and *The voyages of Jacques Cartier in prose and verse* (1934), with sonnets by S.C. Swift and prose sketches by Marquis.

Marquis's *English-Canadian literature* (1913), a valuable overview of its subject, was prepared first as a lengthy chapter in *Canada and its provinces*, vol. XII (1914). His long poem, *The cathedral* (1924), an effective blank-verse dramatic monologue, was republished posthumously in *The cathedral and other poems* (1936), a collection edited by his wife, and introduced by Sir Charles G.D. Roberts. Marquis also edited *Builders of Canada from Cartier to Laurier* (1903), consisting of 33 lives of historical personages and published in the USA as *Giants of the Dominion from Cartier to Laurier* (1905); and in 1929 he edited and introduced the re-publication of Georgiana M. Pennée's 1864 translation of Philippe AUBERT DE GASPÉ's *Les ANCIENS CANADIENS: Seigneur d'Haberville (The Canadians of Old)*.

KEN MacKINNON

Marriot, Anne (b. 1913). Born in Victoria, British Columbia, she was educated at The Poplars and at the Norfolk House School for Girls in Victoria, and took summer courses in creative writing at the University of British Columbia. The first person to interest her in modern poetry was Ira Dilworth. She was further encouraged by Alan Crawley, and was on the founding committee of Crawley's *CONTEMPORARY VERSE* in 1941. She wrote dozens of school broadcasts for CBC radio and the B.C. Department of Education, largely on creative writing or historical subjects. In 1943-4 she edited a poetry column for the *Victoria Daily Times*. From 1945 to 1949 she was a script editor for the National Film Board in Ottawa. From 1950 to 1953 she was women's editor of the Prince George *Citizen*. In the 1970s she conducted poetry-writing workshops with elementary-school students in libraries around Vancouver, producing in 1977 a poetry-writing handbook.

Marriot's best-known work is the long narrative poem 'The wind our enemy', which describes drought on the Prairies during the 1930s and was the title poem in a Ryerson Poetry Chapbook (1939). Subsequent collections include *Calling adventurers!* (1941), for which she won a Governor General's Award; *Salt marsh* (1942); and *Sandstone and other poems* (1945).

After a long silence, Marriot published *Countries* (1971), a series of moving poems in which the narrator, confined by a serious illness, investigates the memories of countries she has known. Then, working with the materials of everyday life as Marriot travels about in her mental landscape, she discovers the heart of love. *The circular coast: poems new and selected* (1981; GGA nominee) includes the best poems from the earlier collections and some new works that reveal a unified whole in which Marriot seeks, with complex imagery and perfectly observed detail, the core of stability within a changing world. Her subjects are time, youth, and fulfilling dreams; aging and death are also prominent. With a chant she speaks a mantra to death: 'That is the timeless clock/that tells no hours/set to its/certain time.'

In 1992 Marriot published a new collection, *Aqua*, a mature work that continued the tone of farewell. Meditations on death and a celebration of water as a spiritual force, the poems at the same time sparkle with vitality, courage, and strength. The book includes a funny play and a sad love story. Marriot's short stories were collected in *A long way to Oregon and other stories* (1984).

See Andrew Stubbs and Jeanette Seim, 'Anne Marriot, frontier poet', *Canadian Poetry* 15 (Fall/Winter, 1984). GEOFF HANCOCK

Marshall, Joyce (b. 1913). Born in Montreal and educated at McGill University, she has lived in Toronto for many years. She is the author of two novels and three collections of short stories and has been a freelance editor for book publishers and the Canadian Broadcasting Corporation; she has also translated fiction by Gabrielle ROY and other French-Canadian writers. Her first novel, *Presently tomorrow* (1946), is set in the Eastern Townships of Quebec, in an English-speaking enclave in the southwest corner of the province. The story takes place in the early 1930s, when the Depression has caused political and social turmoil throughout Canada. Craig Everett, an idealistic but naïve Anglican priest, whose social conscience has become an irritant to his superiors, has been sent from Montreal to conduct a retreat at St Ursula's, a boarding-school for girls. Before the retreat has ended he is seduced by one of the students, a schoolgirl who is already more knowing than Craig will ever be.The fine prose and the subtle exploration of character and motivations that distinguish *Presently tomorrow*—which achieved some notoriety on publication because of its subject matter—are noticeable once again in *Lovers and strangers* (1957), which takes place in the latter half of the 1940s in Toronto. Katherine, a diffident young woman who bear the faint after-effects of polio, impulsively marries Roger Haines, an architect who seems to be already launched on a successful career. But Roger, although he appears to be outgoing, busy, and affluent, suffers from his own insecurities, and the novel becomes a study of marriage and a career that are both going badly.

Marshall's short-story collection *A private place* (1975) brings together seven stories that appeared in magazines or were broadcast by the CBC at various times from the early 1950s to the 1970s. One story is set in Norway, another in Mexico; a third story, about childhood, takes place in the Eastern Townships; and 'The old woman', a study of an obsession that ends in madness, has as its background a remote village in northern Quebec. But the tone of *A private place* is really established by the three remaining stories—'The enemy', 'Salvage', and 'So many have died'—about urban life in North America in the second half of the twentieth century; even more specifically, they are stories about the lives that women lead who must live alone in big cities, solitary, vulnerable, sometimes physically endangered.

Joyce Marshall's second collection, *Any time at all and other stories* (1993; NCL, with an Afterword by Timothy FINDLEY), was selected by Findley. Among the twelve stories included are the well-known 'The old woman', 'So many have died', and five 'Martha' stories, perceptive and tough-minded short fictions about childhood and growing up, written between the 1970s and the 1990s, with two of them published here for the first time. The Martha stories are linked to three summers spent 'on one of the English streets at the edge of that French-Canadian village on the Ottawa River'—not a welcoming place to be.

Marshall's third collection of short fiction, *Blood and bone/En chair et en os* (1995), contains seven stories in English and their French versions, each by a different translator. In recent years Marshall has also published in literary journals essays about a number of her fellow writers, including Ethel WILSON, Gwendolyn MacEWEN, Gabrielle Roy, Gérald GODIN, and Morley CALLAGHAN.

Marshall edited and translated *Word from New France: the selected letters of Marie de l'Incarnation* (1967), for which she wrote a lengthy and important historical introduction, and *No passport: a discovery of Canada* (1968) by the prolific Quebec travel-writer Eugène Cloutier. Her translations of three books by Gabrielle Roy—*The road past Altamont* (1966), *Wildflower* (1970), and *Enchanted summer* (1976)—involved her in a close and sympathetic collaboration with the author. Marshall was awarded the CANADA COUNCIL Translation Prize (1976) for her translation of Roy's *Cet été qui chantait.*

ROBERT WEAVER

Marshall, Tom (1938-93). Born in Niagara Falls, Ontario, he lived in Missouri and Tennessee, USA, where his father was a chemical engineer. He was educated at Queen's University, Kingston, where he he obtained a B.A. in history, and wrote an M.A. thesis on A.M. KLEIN. In 1964 he became a member of the English department at Queen's. He edited the literary magazine *Quarry* and was poetry editor for *The CANADIAN FORUM.*

Marshall's first four mature poetry collections—which form an interlocking cycle of earth, air, fire, and water imagery—are *The silences of fire* (1969), *Magic water* (1971), *The earthbook* (1974), and *The white city* (1976); selections from these make up *The elements: poems 1960-75* (1980). Marshall explored history, pain, and the human condition against a backdrop of the history, artists, and historical figures of Canada, a country that he regarded as 'a second chance' for humanity to redeem itself, since that opportunity was lost by Europeans: 'the garden of the gods is here'. Marshall moved easily 'between two worlds, the ordinary and the cosmic'. *Playing with fire*

(1984), and *Dance of the particles* (1984) are lyrical longer poems that elaborate his established themes.

Much of Marshall's fiction, and many of his essays, celebrate collective heroes and a sense of community. In his early fiction he often gently satirized inadequate academics and Toronto artsy types. He moved on to provocative character studies and complex narrative structures in his final works. His style was gentle, in the comic burlesque tradition. He explored sadness and loss in his quiet lyrical tone. Later fictions show a concern with spiritual and ecological issues.

Marshall's first novel, *Rosemary Gaol* (1978), is a flawed though interesting comedy of manners about men and women in their early thirties making a bid for career and personal fulfilment before the onslaught of middle age. His protagonist is a teacher and amateur novelist who is writing a dull novel within the novel. Marshall wittily juxtaposes narrative styles to portray the pretensions of the university milieu. The five stories in *Glass houses* (1985) represent a serio-comic examination of characters going through upheavals in relationships. Two of the stories feature characters from *Rosemary Gaol*, and were intended to be part of an uncompleted sequel novel. The most memorable stories are about a mildly disturbed child and a man with an obsession for the movie star Elizabeth Taylor. *Adele at the end of the day* (1987), a psychological novel, is a bittersweet masterpiece about an older woman, Adele Driscoll, who fades in and out of reverie. The past events of her life are seen from the point of view of Barney, her estranged son, a middle-aged man disappointed by his life and career. Marshall effortlessly handles shifting points of view from first to third person, inner monologue, and Joycean stream of consciousness. *Voices on the brink: a border tale* (1989) is a coming-of-age novel, with rich metaphoric associations, set in Niagara Falls. A combination of fiction, essay, poetry, and drama, it has a narrator who muses on the death of his father, the murder of a friend, and the ills of the USA and American pop culture represented by Marilyn Monroe, in Canada to make a film. Its complex structure includes alternating chapters told in the first person by the middle-aged narrator and from the third-person point of view of his younger self, as the narrative moves from disillusionment to tragedy. *Changelings: a double fugue* (1991) is a provocative psychological study of multiple personalities in a brother and sister. The novel unfolds like a fugue as the various characters overlap and move towards a brilliant resolution. Unlike horror writers such as Edgar Allan Poe or Stephen King, Marshall sees possession as a spiritual problem linked to a mystical world view. In *Goddess disclosing* (1992) Marshall continued to explore the female voice. A loosely structured novel, with flashes of brilliance and an unsuccessful plot, the book blends ecological and feminist themes in his study of a small-time movie actress who could be Gaia, the female spirit of earth. The opening chapter, 'The other Mexico', is a splendid, haunting, and melancholy plea for the earth.

Marshall's posthumously published postmodern novel *The adventures of John Montgomery* (1995) tells an amusing story of Canada from the War of 1812 and the Rebellion of 1837 to the FLQ crisis of 1970 and the Oka crisis of 1990, through the central character and his descendants (including Lucy Maud MONTGOMERY and the author of the novel in hand), all of whom happen to become distinguished Canadian writers.

With Stuart McKinnon, Gail Fox, and David HELWIG, Marshall recorded an album of poetry, *Four Kingston poets* (1972). His prolific critical writings include *Psychic mariner: a reading of the poems of D.H. Lawrence* (1970) and *Harsh and lovely land: the major Canadian poets and the making of a Canadian tradition* (1979). Marshall also edited, and wrote the postscript to, *A.M. Klein* (1970), a compendium of Klein criticism. His collection of essays *Ghost safari* (1990) reflects on his literary friendships with Margaret ATWOOD, David Helwig, Gwendolyn MacEWEN, and Bronwen WALLACE. *Multiple exposures, promised lands* (1992) is a series of reflections on the lives and work of Atwood, Michael ONDAATJE, Al PURDY, Margaret LAURENCE, Leonard COHEN, Mordechai RICHLER, and other poets and fiction writers.

Marshall was the co-editor, with Helwig, of the anthology *Fourteen stories high* (1971), which evolved into the Oberon annual anthology, *Best Canadian stories*. See Stan Dragland, 'Tom Marshall's *The white city*', *Essays on Canadian Writing* 12 (1978) and Bronwen Wallace, 'Community', *Cross-Canada Writer's Quarterly*, vol. 8, 3/4 (1986). See also Jon Pearce, ed., *Twelve voices: interviews with Canadian poets* (1980). GEOFF HANCOCK

Marsh Hay (1923). A four-act play by Merrill DENISON, first published in his *The unheroic north: four Canadian plays* (1923), it was not produced until 1974 (Hart House Theatre, Toronto), directed by Richard Plant. Denison examines not only the inhumane conditions of farm life in the Ontario backwoods, but also the sociological and economic factors causing them. Set in the dirty kitchen of a backwoods farmhouse, *Marsh hay* depicts the aimless existence of the Serang family. The parents, Lena and John, in their early forties, are worn-out, crushed by their hopeless twenty-year struggle with poor land. Lena blames John for not going west; John blames Lena for not wanting to leave relatives and friends. Of their twelve children, five are dead and three have run away. Those remaining are intent only on avoiding work. The neighbours are narrow and uneducated—with the exception of Andrew Barnood, a placid, kindly man. He and William Thompson—an elderly lawyer who comes for the hunting season—are foils against which the family's deterioration is emphasized.

Naturalism, in which heredity and environment so determine life that nothing one can do can alleviate or change the pattern, is clearly the philosophy behind *Marsh hay*. There is no hope for the future. The misery of the Serang family is climaxed by the unwanted pregnancy of fifteen-year-old Sarilin, a subsequent abortion, and her return to sexual promiscuity. The title of the play is symbolic of destitution. The wild marsh hay growing in the cedar swamps, so vital for the cattle's winter fodder, is often destroyed by beavers building their dams.

A powerful statement of the ills of Ontario farmers in the early 1920s, *Marsh hay* is a tightly constructed play with sharp dialogue and powerful characterization in the portrait of John Serang. That the play had to wait fifty years for its première is probably explained by the reluctance of the country's amateur theatres to promote such a bitter and bleak view of Canadian rural society. But it did receive a much-praised production in the summer of 1996 at the Shaw Festival, Niagara-on-the-Lake, Ontario. GERALDINE ANTHONY

Martel, Suzanne. See CHILDREN'S LITERATURE IN FRENCH: 3.

Martel, Yann. See NOVELS IN ENGLISH 1983 TO 1996: OTHER NOVELS 2(b).

Martin, Claire (b. 1914). Born in Quebec City, she was educated by the Ursuline nuns and the Sisters of the Congrégation de Notre-Dame. After a career as a radio announcer, first in Quebec City and then with Radio-Canada in Montreal, she married Roland Faucher, a chemist with the ministry of health in Ottawa and, while living there, began to write. Her first work was a collection of stories, *Avec ou sans amour* (1958), for which she won the Cercle du Livre de France award. Martin and her husband lived in the south of France from 1972 until 1982. She lives in Quebec City.

From the outset Martin's writing has focused on brief depictions of love, always shown to be fragile, threatened, ephemeral: her gift is for the bold stroke, for precise observation, and for fusing irony with tenderness. Her best work was published during the sixties: two novels, *Doux-amer* (1960) and *Quand j'aurai payé ton visage* (1962), and two famous books of memoirs, *DANS UN GANT DE FER* (1965) and *La joue droite* (1966), for which she received the Prix de la Province de Québec and a Governor General's award (for fiction!). A novel with overtones of tragedy, *Les morts* (1970) was adapted for the stage under the title *Moi je n'étais qu'espoir*, which was produced by Montreal's Théâtre du Rideau Vert in 1972. While writer-in-residence at the Université d'Ottawa in 1972, Martin wrote a short essay, *La petite fille lit* (1973), which offers an exquisite description of the way she was captivated and fascinated by the magic of books when she was a little girl. Beginning in 1972 she devoted herself to translating: among the works she translated are Margaret LAURENCE's *The STONE ANGEL* (*L'ange de pierre*, 1976), Robertson DAVIES' *The manticore* (*Le lion avait un visage d'homme*, 1978), *World of wonders* (*Le monde des merveilles*, 1979), and Clark BLAISE's *Tribal justice* (*Le justice tribale*, 1985).

In both her fiction and her autobiographies Martin relentlessly pursued topics that have traditionally been proscribed for Quebec literature: extramarital love and the demythologizing of the sacrosanct image of the father as noble and good, the rightful holder of authority and knowledge. She showed a preference for the first-person narrative and for presenting multiple viewpoints, techniques that enabled her to probe the inner depths of human nature, bringing to light its complexity and giving the individual primacy over the group.

Doux-amer—translated by David Lobdell as *Best man* (1983)—portrays a writer who lays claim to her rights to freedom by putting her career before love, by allowing herself to be unfaithful, and by marrying a man younger than herself—all time-honoured actions and privileges reserved for men. As traditional roles are reversed, abilities and temperaments—rather than gender—govern behaviour: the male protagonist, the writer's lover and editor, plays the role usually played by women, that of the Other—submissive, faithful, devoted. He is the narrator, the one who confides his suffering, openly pouring out his feelings about being a too-frequently obliging victim. The emphasis on individual confrontation and on subjectivism is even more apparent in *Quand j'aurai payé ton visage.* About a love triangle involving two brothers and the wife of one of them, it reveals a tangle of family relations that touches on incest and other taboos, giving the author an opportunity to criticize the family and society. The narrative unfolds in the words of Catherine, Robert, and Jeanne Ferny respectively, providing a compressed and varied perspective, and throwing into relief the profound isolation of each person locked into his or her own world. In *Les morts* reminiscences and confessions abound as the young narrator tries desperately to relive her youthful passion for a man killed in the war: once again, love is inseparable from separation. But Martin's major works are indisputably her books of memoirs, *Dans un gant de fer* and *La joue droite,* two powerful and frank recreations of a painful and oppressive childhood and adolescence in which Martin was exposed to violence and every kind of humiliation. The maleficent and terrifying figure of a despotic father can be seen as embodying the paralysing monolithic structure that for so long tyrannized Quebec society and prevented its flowering. The books also expose, with merciless clarity, the situation of women—treated as inferior, incompetent, enslaved. This autobiography, which reveals the hell that can exist in the realm of intimacy, provides the key to the relentless quest for love that governs all Martin's work.

Dans un gant de fer and *La joue droite*, translated by Philip Stratford, were first published in one volume, *In an iron glove* (1968), and later separately as *In an iron glove* (1973) and *The right cheek* (1975).

See *VOIX ET IMAGES du Pays*, VIII, 1974; Robert Vigneault, *Claire Martin: son oeuvre, les réactions de la critique* (1975); and Françoise Kaye, 'Claire Martin ou le "je" aboli', *Incidences*, vol. IV (mai-déc.) 1980.

NICOLE BOURBONNAIS

Marty, Sid (b. 1944). Born in South Shields, England, he was raised in Medicine Hat, Alberta, and educated in Calgary at Mount Royal Junior College. His grandparents were homesteaders of Swiss stock from Minnesota who were lured to Canada by the Canadian Pacific Railway and by useless promises of good farmland in the arid Palliser Triangle of southern Alberta—a background that inspires his best work. Marty received an honours degree in English from Sir George Williams University, Montreal, before deciding to work full-time as a park warden and writer. He was a season ranger in Yoho and Jasper National Parks from 1966 to 1973. Since then he has worked as a park warden in Banff National Park. As writer, poet, conservationist, and critic of development in the national parks, Marty is a tireless supporter of an unspoiled natural world.

His first chapbooks, undated—*Carbon copies* and *The dream horseman*—were followed by a modest ten-page collection of poems, *The tumbleweed harvest* (1973). The poems in *Headwaters* (1973) draw upon Marty's Rocky Mountain experiences to remind readers that loneliness, death, and madness are part of the accepted life cycle. A deceptively simple stylist, Marty sees love, death, forest, fires, children—whether in urban or wilderness settings—as occurrences in a natural cycle. He developed these themes in *Nobody danced with Miss Rodeo* (1981), a three-part collection that again captures the sounds and elements of the Rocky Mountains. In the first sequence he contemplates the technological invasion of the wilderness by search and rescue aircraft, chainsaws, power boats, ski-lift operators, and helicopters. The title sequence includes bittersweet or humorous accounts of urban dwellers misplaced in a mountain setting. *Men for the mountains* (1978) is a prose documentary about the wardens in Canada's national parks, drawing on Marty's work in Banff. He eloquently describes his aesthetic of the intimate, ancient, and still essential interdependence between humanity and the natural world, while discussing isolation, grizzly bears, forest fires, tourists, the negative effects of the Trans-Canada highway, the hunting season, and certain park-administration policies.

Leaning on the wind, under the spell of the Great Chinook (1995), describing Marty's passion for southern Alberta, is a chronicle of its history and a plea for its future. It was nominated for a Governor General's Award.

GEOFF HANCOCK

Mathews, Robin. See CRITICISM IN ENGLISH: 5(e).

Mathieu, Claude. See FANTASTIC LITERATURE AND SCIENCE FICTION IN FRENCH.

Matrix (1975-). This magazine of critical and creative writing was first published by the Champlain College Department of English in

Lennoxville, Quebec. Under editor Philip Lanthier, it was a biannual publication of poetry, short fiction, essays, and reviews. In 1988 co-editors Linda Leith and Kenneth Radu moved the magazine from Lennoxville to John Abbot College, Sainte-Anne-de-Bellevue. *Matrix* was enlarged, broadened, and modernized as a three-times-a-year glossy publication focusing on a revival of writing in English and non-francophone writers in Quebec, for a community who felt cut off as a result of the 1980 referendum and the language laws. In 1995 the magazine relocated to Concordia University, Montreal, under editor-in-chief Robert Allen. GEOFF HANCOCK

Mayne, Seymour (b. 1944). Born in Montreal, Quebec, he did undergraduate studies at McGill University and doctoral studies at the University of British Columbia. He taught briefly at UBC before joining the faculty of the University of Ottawa (1973), where he is presently associate professor of English. He has been visiting professor at the Hebrew University of Jerusalem (1979-80) and at Concordia University, Montreal (1982-3).

In his earliest collections of poetry—*That monocycle the moon* (1964), *Tiptoeing on the mount* (1965), *From the portals of mouseholes* (1966), and *I am still the boy* (1967)—Mayne is a frequently lighthearted explorer of human passion and sensuality. Discipline and intelligence stand behind his carefully controlled poems. *Manimals* (1969) is a comic diversion in poetry and prose. In later volumes—*Mouth* (1970), *For stems of light* (1971), *Face* (1971), and especially *Name* (1975)—the celebratory exploration in the earlier collections gives way to a more personal and painful probing. Mayne's vision, founded in a Jewish mysticism of the body, studies man's relations with himself and the world around him. His poetry reveals a new consciousness of his Jewishness and a concern with social issues that always focuses on the human dimension. The sexuality of the early romantic poetry is replaced by pain and melancholy about the transience and mortality of the human condition. *Name* received the J.I. SEGAL Prize in English-French literature and the York University Poetry Workshop Award.

Diasporas (1977) and *The impossible promised land: poems new and selected* (1981) herald the secure voice of a mature poet conscious of his heritage and his calling. Here Mayne is the literary descendent of A.M. KLEIN, the friend of Irving LAYTON and Leonard COHEN—the youngest poet of this quartet from the Montreal Jewish community. Though a bleak and pessimistic vision of life now permeates his poetry, Mayne finds hope in his commitment to Jewish traditions and in man's awareness and acceptance of the cycle of time. As impassioned and indignant about the Holocaust as Layton, he never indulges in the 'gorgeous rant and offensive irony' that characterize much of Layton's later verse. The disciplined control of Mayne's poetry is reminiscent of Klein's later verse, though the increase in Jewish allusions and terminology in Mayne's recent volumes recalls Klein's early work.

In Montreal in the early sixties Mayne was one of the editors of *Cataract* and later of *Catapult*. He was one of the founders of Very Stone House Press (Vancouver) and later of Ingluvin Publications (Montreal). For the former he edited, with Patrick LANE, *The collected poems of Red Lane* (q.v., 1968). He was also one of the founders of Mosaic Press/Valley Editions (Oakville and Ottawa, Ontario). For these three presses he edited many volumes of poetry and prose. Organizer of the University of Ottawa's A.M. Klein Symposium (1974), the first reassessment of Klein's literary stature, Mayne edited, and wrote the introduction to, *The A.M. Klein symposium* (1975). He has also edited *Engagements: the prose of Irving Layton* (1972) and *Irving Layton: the poet and his critics* (1978).

While Mayne's poetry has been translated into Hebrew and Spanish, he himself has co-translated poetry from Yiddish, Polish, and Russian. With Catherine Leach he translated the Polish verse of Jerzy Harasymowicz, *Genealogy of instruments* (1974). From the Yiddish he translated *Burnt pearls: ghetto poems of Abraham Sutzkever* (1981), and he was the editor of *Generations: selected poems of Rachel Korn* (q.v., 1982).

Given Mayne's close personal and poetic affiliations with early Canadian modernists, it is not surprising to find that the bleak and pessimistic vision of life that characterized his early poems persists in more recent works. Visiting and revisiting biblical sources and stories in such collections as *Children of Abel* (1986) and *Killing time* (1992), his poems increasingly deal with the paradoxes that have long troubled people of deep faith: the coexistence of a benevolent god and the legacy of violence informing almost all world religions; ideas of innocence and evil; and, of course, the tensions between common language and the Word. Mayne's most recent book of poems is *The song of Moses and other poems* (1995).

Mayne also continues to contribute valuable work as an editor, anthologist, and translator. He has edited or co-edited two anthologies of Jewish-Canadian poetry (*Essential words*, 1985, and *Jerusalem*, 1996) as well as a volume of selected poems by the poet Moshe Dor (*Crossing the river*, 1989). His recent co-translations include *Jerusalem as she is: new and selected poems of Shlomo Vinner* (1990), Melekh RAVITCH's *Night prayer and other poems* (1993), both from the original Yiddish, and Jerzy Harasymowicz's *I live on a raft* (1994) from the Polish. DAVID STAINES

Mayr, Suzette. See LESBIAN LITERATURE.

Meigs, Mary. See BIOGRAPHY AND MEMOIRS IN ENGLISH 1983 TO 1996: 2 and LESBIAN LITERATURE.

Melanson, Laurier. See ACADIAN LITERATURE: 3(c).

Melfi, Mary (b. 1951). Born near Rome, Italy, she immigrated to Montreal, Quebec, with her family at the age of six. She obtained a B.A. in English from Concordia University and a Master of Library Sciences from McGill University. Her writings are characterized by an avant-garde sensibility that transgresses the conventions of a given literary form (whether it is poetry, drama, or fiction). In each of her works poetry verges on prose, fiction is penetrated by poetic and dramatic devices, and a play has poetic and narrative elements—though the distinctiveness of the given form is not erased. Ideas about identity and culture that flow out of English-Canadian and Italian-Canadian/Québécois experiences interpenetrate each other. Melfi is interested in the metaphysical side of human existence, the difficulties of establishing a coherent feminine identity, cultural dislocation, and the artist's attempt to create a new reality.

A bride in three acts (1983), a sardonically humorous long poem, looks at the private realm of heterosexual relations and relies on parody, the use of prose, and the intermixing of voices, and employs surreal imagery that veers towards the grotesque and the violent. Not only a tirade against the oppressiveness of patriarchy, it is a metaphysical view of the impossibility of fulfilling one's desire and the delusions that arise as a result. *Infertility rites* (1991), a novel about a woman's obsession with having a child, replays in different ways the formal and thematic preoccupations of *A bride*. Driven to motherhood by her need to construct a world where she feels at home, the central character accepts ideas of traditional womanhood that come out of her ethnic background and are reinforced by patriarchal mainstream society. The juxtaposition of styles and the self-consciousness of the writing mirror the unreality of the protagonist's life and her obsessive self-awareness. This sensibility recurs in *Sex therapy* (1996), a play that verges on absurdist drama in which the roles of therapist and patient are continually subverted and inverted. MARINO TUZI

Memoirs of Montparnasse. See John GLASSCO.

Menaud, maître-draveur (1937). Félix-Antoine SAVARD's first novel, this classic of French-Canadian literature, set in the lumbering region of Charlevoix County in north-eastern Quebec, is about a veteran of the log-drive who—incensed by the foreign (Anglo-Canadian) businessmen exploiting Quebec's resources—is fired by words he reads in Louis HÉMON's *MARIA CHAPDELAINE*: 'Around us have come strangers we scorn as foreigners. They have taken all the money. Yet in the land of Québec nothing will change . . .' Misfortune comes to Menaud in the harshest fashion when his son Joson drowns while trying to free a log jam—a powerfully depicted episode. Menaud's efforts to rally people to oppose the foreigners meet with no success. When, distraught, he goes into the forest during a snowstorm in search of the 'stranger' who has threatened to cut off the local people from access to the territory, he is barely saved from freezing to death. After this he sinks into madness, repeating incessantly: 'Strangers came! Strangers came!' The novel ends with the words of a farmer: 'This is no ordinary madness! It is a warning!'

The last in a long line of traditional novels on French-Canadian nationalism—though in its conflicts and its portrayal of madness it is far removed from the rural idylls of the past—*Menaud* was applauded by critics for its nationalistic spirit, but above all for its profuse and vivid imagery, and for Savard's skill in incorporating French-Canadian regional expressions into a text of essentially classical texture. In 1938 Savard published a second version, correcting misprints that marred the original edition; making stylistic revisions; changing to roman type the regional expressions that had appeared in italics; and adding a short glossary. Some critics had expressed reservations about an excessive richness of style, an exaggeration of ornamentation, and in 1944 Savard produced a 'more concise and simple text', which he called the 'definitive edition'. In 1960 he produced a fourth version in the 'Alouette bleue' collection published by Fides. Under the title appeared the words, 'In conformity with the first edition'—though this version is by no means identical with the original. Finally in 1964 Savard reshaped his novel for the fifth time.

The 1937 version was translated into English by Alan SULLIVAN under the title *Boss of the river* (1947). The most recent translation, by Richard Howard—*Master of the river* (1976)—is based on the 1964 version.

See François Ricard, *L'art de Félix-Antoine Savard dans 'Menaud, maître-draveur'* (1972), and a theme issue of the *Revue d'histoire littéraire du Québec et du Canada français*, no. 13 (hivers/printemps 1987), entitled 'Histoire de *Menaud*'. JULES TESSIER

Mercer plays. There are few rivals in Canadian theatre for the importance and influence of David FRENCH's Mercer plays as a body of connected works. The first play, *Leaving home* (1972), is credited with consolidating the reputation of the Tarragon Theatre, Toronto—where it opened on 16 May 1972—in raising the credibility of Canadian drama, and encouraging the development of a Canadian neo-realistic 'school'. As a whole, the Mercer plays document a Canadian social phenomenon, the culture shock experienced by people moving within Canada from one region (Newfoundland) to another.

Set in a Toronto working-class household in the late 1950s, *Leaving home* pits Jacob Mercer, the patriarch carpenter, against his eldest son, Ben, while the long-suffering mother, Mary, tries to keep the peace. The Mercers had moved to Ontario from Newfoundland when their sons were small, and the father/son conflict is both extended and localized by the clash between the values of outport Newfoundland and those of Toronto. The boys have grown up as urban North Americans and resent Jacob's old outport standards, especially those that define a 'man'. Most of the characters 'leave home' in the course of the play. Billy and Ben leave physically, Billy to marry a girl pregnant by him, Ben to escape his father's tyranny; Jacob leaves home spiritually in abandoning the values of the fishing village he had left many years before—with his sons gone, there was no one to whom he could pass them on. Father/son conflict is paralleled and reinforced by mother/daughter tension between Kathy, Billy's fiancée, and her mother Minnie, a flamboyant former flame of Jacob's. Much of the play's comedy is provided by Minnie and her silent undertaker boyfriend, Harold, while contrast between the old and the new is given vivid aural presence through the sharp contrast between the Newfoundland accents of the older generation and the Torontonian speech of the younger. *Leaving Home* received over thirty productions across the country in the season following its première.

Of the fields, lately (1973) opened at Tarragon on 29 Sept. 1973. Two years after the events depicted in *Leaving home*, Ben returns from Regina, Saskatchewan, to attend an aunt's funeral. Father and son are as far apart as ever, but in the course of the play Ben discovers that Jacob has suffered a heart attack. He decides he will find work in Toronto so his father will not have to return to his potentially dangerous job. However, Ben does come to some understanding of his father's values; and knowing that his father's work is necessary to Jacob's sense of self, changes his mind and once again leaves home. The play is a 'memory play', framed by direct address to the audience, placing some events in the past. The core of the play is to be found in three scenes between father and son, marvellously detailed but oblique—among the most effective uses of sub-text to be found in Canadian dramatic literature. *Of the fields, lately* won the Chalmers Award for 1973.

Salt-water moon (1985) opened at Tarragon on 2 Oct. 1984. This long one-act two-hander is a 'prequel' set in Coley's Point, Newfoundland, in 1926. Jacob has returned from a year in Toronto to discover that his former sweetheart, Mary, is engaged to Jerome McKenzie, a school-teacher Jacob despises. Jacob finds Mary in the yard of the house where she works as a domestic, looking at the stars through a telescope; in the course of the evening he woos her back. While the essence of the play is this lyrical courtship, we get an insight into social conditions of place and time. In this play we see the reality behind Jacob's 'mythic' Newfoundland.

A fourth Mercer play, *1949* (1989), premièred at Toronto's St Lawrence Centre on 20 Oct. 1988. With a cast of twelve, it is set on the eve of Newfoundland's entering Confederation, and incorporates a number of the characters seen or mentioned in the previous Mercer plays.

Selected criticism of *Leaving home* and *Of the fields, lately* is included in *Canadian drama and the critics* (rev. ed. 1995), edited by L.W. Conolly. CHRIS JOHNSON

Mercier, Serge. See DRAMA IN FRENCH 1948 TO 1981: 3.

Mercure, Marthe. See DRAMA IN FRENCH 1981 TO 1996: 7.

Merril, Judith (1923-97). Born in New York City, she acquired an international following among science-fiction enthusiasts for her stories, novels, reviews, and anthologies before she settled in Toronto in 1968, becoming a Canadian citizen in 1976. Her personal library of over five thousand SF books and periodicals formed the basis of the Spaced Out Library, established at Rochdale College in 1969. The following year it became part of the Toronto Public Library system. Now the world's largest public collection of such literature, it is known as the Merril Collection of Science Fiction, Speculation and Fantasy. From the first, Merril's fiction combined 'a sense of wonder' with 'a sense of gender'. Her influential anthologies cut across literary genres and championed the works of new and experimental writers. After coming to Canada she published *Survival ship and other stories* (1973), *The best of Judith Merril* (1976), and *Daughters of earth and other stories* (1985), and compiled the first of the *Tesseracts* anthologies devoted to new Canadian SF. A social activist, Merril drew public attention to the SF field, to the work of new writers, to the need for professional standards, and to a proper appreciation of the genre.

JOHN ROBERT COLOMBO

Metcalf, John (b. 1938). Born in Carlisle, England, he came to Canada in 1962, having received an Honours B.A. (1960) and a certificate in education (1961) from the University of Bristol. He taught at high schools in Montreal and Cold Lake, Alberta, before accepting in 1969 a position at Loyola College, Montreal. Since 1971 he has devoted his time to writing, supplementing his income with part-time teaching, editing, and as writer-in-residence at a number of Canadian universities.

Metcalf's five stories in *New Canadian writing, 1969* reveal a disciplined prose style and, in 'The children green and golden', an early attention to sound, smells, and texture—elements designed to elicit an emotional as well as an intellectual response. 'The estuary', which focuses on a potential suicidal but vitally alive young man, won the President's Medal of the University of Western Ontario for the best story of 1969. Metcalf's first short-story collection, *The lady who sold furniture* (1970), contains—besides the title story, a novella—five stories set in England. Employing a fairly traditional technique and vivid observations, Metcalf injects a note of uneasiness into these stories that sometimes explodes in a macabre or gruesome scene. *The teeth of my father* (1975) is a more uneven collection, though the control of tone and mood remains and there are touches of humour. In the moving 'Beryl' two characters come together but ultimately are unable to relieve each other's loneliness—a popular Metcalf theme.

In Metcalf's first novel, *Going down slow* (1972), set in Montreal, he ridicules both the self-important staff of a high school and a society that would reward efficiency at the expense of intelligence and humanity. David Appleby is a recent English immigrant who battles the system in a series of fast-moving skirmishes, in contrast to his mistress Susan, who stays outside it, and his roommate Jim, who rises through the educational establishment. *Girl in gingham* (1978)—reprinted as *Private parts: a memoir* (1980)—contains two novellas with these titles. 'Girl in gingham'—first published in *Dreams surround us* (1977), which also contains poems by John NEWLOVE—features a nearly flawless setting and dialogue, in addition to excellent satire. Peter Thornton, an appraiser of antiques who is slowly rebuilding his life after a traumatic divorce, is paired (after several computer-date mismatches) with his ideal woman, Anna, a rare-books librarian with a similar regard for the past. The title of 'Private parts' alludes both to sex, which is treated lightly and entertainingly, and to the narrator's preservation of his inner self in a life-denying, puritanical milieu. About the coming-of-age of a precocious youth, it concludes with a sad irony: adulthood has brought not liberation but disillusionment and boredom. The novel *General Ludd* (1980) combines vehement wit, understated humour, a black comedic vision, and occasional absurdity. Its hero, James Wells, poet-in-residence at St Xavier University—which, like society at large, has little appreciation for true poetry—becomes a modern-day Luddite and attempts to forestall the future by destroying the highly sophisticated Communication Arts Centre, the false idol of campus technocrats. Although the novel occasionally rambles and has an ending reminiscent of Ken Kesey's *One flew over the cuckoo's nest*, it has passion and emotional range and offers a brilliant satire of a fast-food society oblivious of traditional values, art, and culture. In 1982 Metcalf published his first book of essays, *Kicking against the pricks*, and *Selected stories*, and edited *Making it new: contemporary Canadian stories*. He co-edited *Best Canadian stories* from 1977 to 1982.

Since 1983 Metcalf has laboured mightily as editor, anthologist, and cultural critic, publishing and promoting the work of other Canadians, particularly in the short-story form. He has produced nearly thirty anthologies over the course of his career and 'readied' several score of books for press, most recently for The PORCUPINE'S QUILL. His anthologies often include critical or authorial comment on the formal aspects of the writing, a practice extended in *How stories mean* (1993), a gathering of reflections by writers on questions of technique.

Metcalf's effort to create a receptive climate for this work has led him into what he calls a guerilla campaign against academic critics who evaluate books from an extra-literary perspective. In *Freedom from culture* (1987), *What is a Canadian literature?* (1988), and *Volleys* (1990)—an exchange with academicians Sam Solecki and W.J. Keith—he attacked the twin shibboleths of literary nationalism and government patronage of the arts. To further encourage spirited and accessible literary debate, Metcalf compiled two books of 'contentious essays and squibs': *The bumper book* (1986) and *Carry on bumping* (1988).

He has published only one collection of stories in the past decade, *Adult entertainment* (1986), though to put it thus is to diminish the fact that it shows a master stylist confidently at work in his favoured form. Its three short stories and two novellas are characterized by an episodic structure that achieves its effect through juxtaposition of images and scenes rather than narrative exposition; by dialogue that is nuanced and suggestive of unarticulated thought and feeling; by a cherishing of the particular and a concomitant fondness for lists; by a careful control of mood and pacing; by a comedic sense that is here more poignantly ironic than sharply satiric; and by a sensitivity to the artifice involved in any attempt at the real. Sometimes this artifice is brought to the fore, as in 'The Eastmill reception centre', where the narrator interrupts his story in order to comment on the inadequacy of its ending, proposes several alternative effects, dismisses the last and best of these on the grounds that he 'can't be bothered', then brings off a version of the ending he has just dismissed. Such metafictive effects are not unique in Metcalf's writings and demonstrate that he is by no means bound by the modernist tradition he extols.

'Forde abroad', a sequel to 'Travelling northward' (the novella that closes *Adult entertainment*), won the 1996 gold medal for fiction at the National Magazine Awards. The Porcupine's Quill republished three earlier novellas under the title *Shooting the stars* (1993), with an introduction by Michael Darling, a guide to the 'deflationary structures' that characterize Metcalf's work.

For extended treatment of his fiction see Douglas Rollins' and Barry Cameron's entries on Metcalf in *Canadian writers and their work* (1985) and the Twayne World Author Series (1986). A number of literary magazines have devoted special issues to Metcalf (*The MALAHAT REVIEW* 70, *CANADIAN FICTION MAGAZINE* 65, and *The New Quarterly* 16.3, Fall 1966, which focuses on his influence as an editor). For biographical details see *The Montreal story tellers: memoirs, photographs, critical essays* (1985), edited by J.R. (Tim) Struthers.

See also NOVELS IN ENGLISH 1960 TO 1982: 4.

DAVID O'ROURKE/KIM JERNIGAN

Meunier, Claude. See DRAMA IN FRENCH 1948 TO 1981: 4.

Michaels, Anne (b. 1958). Born in Toronto of Jewish parents, her father a Russian immigrant, she was educated in the city's schools and at the University of Toronto (B.A., 1980). For several years she has taught a course in creative writing there.

Michaels has published two important collections of poems, *The weight of oranges* (1985) and *Miner's pond* (1991), which was short-listed for a Governor General's Award. Most of her lyrics—several of them complex, multi-layered sequences—can be categorized as love poems, elegies, or dramatic monologues, often about artists and historical figures. The love poems tend to be shorter, more purely lyrical, and to focus on what Michaels calls 'the passionate world' in which a relationship moves 'past the last familiar outpost', almost beyond space and time into a privacy available only to the lovers. In the longer poems, love and ecstasy are often celebrated as something lost, and her characteristic tone—despite the powerful verbal music and sensuous, natural, often visceral imagery—is a plangent one. Several of the most memorable poems—'Lake of two rivers', 'Words for the body', 'Miner's pond', 'Modersohn-Becker', and 'What the light teaches'—are retrospective meditations on something that has already happened and that is irretrievably lost, even though the words attempt to restore it. The longer poems show a tense interplay between a lyric intensity and an understated narrative drive. Their form, as well as some of the imagery—especially the concern with light—reflects Michaels' interest in music and painting. Both books were reissued in one volume, *The weight of oranges* (1997).

Though most of Michaels' poems are written in the first person, they are almost never directly autobiographical or confessional. In the more personal poems the 'I' maintains a taut balance between the subjective self and a more objective persona. In the historical dramatic monologues the speakers are individuals like Isak Dinesen, the artist Paula Modersohn-Becker, the Russian poet Marina Tsvetaeva, and Marie Curie. The language of these poems—though characterized by a deceptively simple diction and syntax, and verse forms built on enjambment—communicates alternately with disarmingly simple sentences: 'No matter where you are/or who you're near,/we come up for air together'; and stanzas taut and highly metaphoric: 'There are nights in the forest of words/when I panic, every step into thicker darkness,/the only way out to write myself into a clearing,/which is silence.' Without being overtly about history, Michaels' poems are often suffused by a historical sense, an awareness of the ineluctable presence of the past in our lives. This is accompanied, however, by a concomitant awareness of how difficult it is to give adequate expression to the past, whether private or public, in words.

The concern with time, memory, and history is also evident in *Fugitive pieces* (1996), Michaels' remarkably strong first novel. It is made up of two closely related first-person narratives, the first by Jakob Beer, who is rescued by an archaeologist from the Nazi genocide of the Polish Jews, the second by Ben, a young Canadian professor, whose parents survived the death camps. Each narrative reveals an individual trying to understand a tragic, almost incomprehensible past in order to free himself to live in the present. Though the novel focuses on a handful of characters, it leaves one with the impression of a work that is much more inclusive and larger in scope—partly due to the shifts in setting from wartime Poland and post-war Greece to Toronto and back again to Greece; to Michaels' ability to sketch suggestively the lives of related minor characters; and to the fact that she situates the events not only against the background of the war—often registered in telling casual details—but also within the context of discussions of theology, geology, and art. *Fugitive pieces* has been translated into all the major European languages. In 1997 it won both the Chapters/*Books in Canada* First Novel Award and the British Orange Prize for Fiction, given to women writers.

See also Michaels' essays on poetry in *Sudden miracles: eight women poets* (1991), edited by Rhea TREGEBOV, and *Poetry and knowing* (1994), edited by Tim Lilburn.

SAM SOLECKI

Michener, James. See FOREIGN WRITERS ON CANADA IN ENGLISH: 2.

Micone, Marco (b. 1945). Born in Montelongo, Italy, he immigrated to Montreal with his family in 1958. His education includes an M.A. (1969) from McGill University with a thesis on the theatre of Marcel DUBÉ. While he was teaching Italian at Montreal's Vanier College, his first play, *Gens du silence*, was staged there in 1980 by Le Théâtre de l'Ouverture and published in 1982. The English translation by Maurizia Binda, *Voiceless people* (1984), was premièred in Vancouver during Expo '86. The first French-language playwright to examine the immigrant experience in Quebec, Micone achieved critical and popular success with repeated productions of *Gens du silence*, the more feminist *Addolorata* (1984), and *Déjà l'agonie* (1988), translated by Jill MacDougall as *Beyond the ruins* (1995). The English translation of *Addolorata* (1994) by Maurizia Binda has the same title. All Micone's plays engage the polemics of Quebec politics and the problematic place of immigrants in a nationalist country; they also recall the realism of Marcel Dubé's early works. *Addolorata*, which premièred in 1983 with the troupe LaManufacture at La Licorne theatre, Montreal, deals with a young woman who feels three-times marginalized: as an immigrant in Quebec, as an Italian in Canada, and as a woman in a male-dominated society. These issues are explored in Micone's book of essays and narratives, *Le figuier enchanté* (1992). The great appeal of his drama is in part due to his effective use of an almost literary everyday French, with the occasional word of English or Italian. The success of his plays has been matched by his award-winning French translations of Goldoni, Pirandello, and Shakespeare.

See Sherry Simon, 'Speaking with authority: the theatre of Marco Micone', *CANADIAN LITERATURE* 106 (Fall 1985); 'Le théâtre des Italiens', *Lettres québécoises* 36 (1984-5); Minni and Foschi Ciampolini, eds, *Writers in transition* (1990); and Joseph Pivato, 'Famiglia', *Echo: essays on other literatures* (1994).

JOSEPH PIVATO

Millar, Margaret (1915-94). Born Margaret Sturm in Kitchener, Ontario, she studied at the Kitchener Collegiate Institute, and then at the University of Western Ontario. While still a student in Kitchener, she met Kenneth Millar (1915-83), an American-born fellow-student. They were married in 1938 and the following year the couple taught English and history at KCI and then moved permanently to Santa Barbara, California, where they pursued parallel careers as writers of mystery fiction. (Kenneth Millar, who wrote as 'Ross Macdonald', created the private detective Lew Archer, who was renamed Harper for screen performances by actor Paul Newman.) Margaret Millar claimed she was a mystery fan years before she met her husband, avidly reading the detective magazines purchased by her two older brothers. She worked briefly as a screenwriter for Warner Brothers, but preferred to concentrate on her own mystery novels, which are prized for their psychological penetration of the hearts and minds of murderers. Her first novel was *The invisible worm* (1941), but she came to prominence with *Beast in view* (1955). Among her later novels are *Banshee* (1983) and *Spider webs* (1986). Margaret and Kenneth Millar were honoured independently by the Mystery Writers of America as Grand Masters.

JOHN ROBERT COLOMBO

Mills, John (b. 1930). Born in London, England, he came to Canada in 1953. While travelling widely in Canada and Europe, he held a striking variety of manual and technical positions. After he earned a B.A. from the University of British Columbia (1964) and an M.A. from Stanford University (1965), he began his present career as a teacher of English at Simon Fraser University, Burnaby, British Columbia. Mills is a sophisticated satirist of considerable forcefulness, and his novels are also assured parodies of literary conventions. *The land of is* (1972) is a blackly comic subversion of *The tempest*, transposed to contemporary Vancouver; *The October men* (1973), set during the 1970 FLQ crisis, features a small-time confidence man whose associates, schemes, and fantasies imitate the stereotypes of pulp fiction. *Skevington's daughter* (1978), an inventive epistolary novel, is a caustic academic caricature, riddled with violence in action and rhetoric, which incidentally echoes late-Romantic travel writing. *Runner in the dark* (1992), with its subtext of literary allusion, is a somewhat archetypal thriller with a psychologically confounded hero, involuntary derring-do, and a spiritual climax set in a bleak New Mexican landscape. *Lizard in the grass* (1980) is a collection of Mills' amusing and unsentimental autobiographical pieces and some characteristically mordant and informed literary reviews. His later interesting and poised autobiographical essays, several prompted by his Christian conversion, appeared in *Thank your mother for the rabbits* (1993). Both Mills' fiction and criticism often display a tone of articulate mockery that suggests uncompromising standards and complete individuality.

LOUIS K. MacKENDRICK

Miron, Gaston (1928-96). Born in Sainte-Agathe-des-Monts, Quebec, he attended the Collège des Frères du Sacré-Coeur until 1946; the following year he went to Montreal, where he worked at various jobs and befriended Louis Portuguais, Gilles Carle, Mathilde Ganzini, and Olivier Marchand. In 1953 he was one of the founders of Les Éditions de l'Hexagone, a publishing house devoted to the printing and distribution of poetry that influenced Quebec's literary life for the next three decades. L'Hexagone was to become a convenient term not only for this business venture but also for the generation of poets it published (Jean-Guy PILON, Fernand OUELLETTE, and Paul-Marie LAPOINTE, to name only a few). Miron invested a considerable amount of energy in the everyday running of L'Hexagone, of which he was still the editor in the early 1980s; as a result, his own poetic output suffered. Apart from *Deux sangs* (1953)—jointly produced with Marchand—most of his poetry appeared in reviews, periodicals, magazines, and anthologies during the sixties. It was only in 1970, thanks to the initiative of the Presses de l'Université de Montréal, that *L'homme rapaillé* appeared to great critical and public acclaim. In 1980 a long-awaited translation by Marc Plourde of one of the sections of *L'homme rapaillé*—with other poems not included in that volume—was published under the title *The agonized life*. In 1975 the Université d'Ottawa published *Contrepointes*, a collection of poems written between 1954 and 1968 that had appeared in various magazines around the world, but never in book form.

Miron's selflessness, and maybe his ambivalence about his own writing, were illustrated by his concentration on political action. In the late 1950s he ran twice as an NDP candidate, but from 1962 he devoted his energy to separatist movements. In Oct. 1970 he was jailed for ten days on account of his political opinions. But that same year he received two literary awards—the Prix de la Revue *Études françaises* and the Prix France-Canada—for *L'homme rapaillé*. Other international awards followed: the Prix Belgique-Canada (1972) and the Prix Guillaume Apollinaire (1981), which traditionally goes to one of the great poets in the French language. In 1983 he was awarded Quebec's Prix David, in 1990 the Medal of the Académie des lettres du Québec, and in 1993 he was named Commandeur des Arts et des Lettres de la République française.

Miron's relationship with writing bore the mark of a mind distressed by 'the semantic perversion of Quebec's language'—his description of the linguistic syndrome of the 1950s and 1960s. Indeed, he felt devastated at that time by the disruption of the French language under the inevitable pressures of English, which was then the functional idiom of work, media, advertising, and trade. Three of his political essays in *L'homme rapaillé*—'L'alienation délirante', 'Un long chemin', and 'Notes sur le non-poème et le poème'—explicitly detail his position on this issue. (See Marc Plourde's translation of the second, 'A long road', in *The agonized life*.) Consequently he determined to avoid what he saw as two equally disastrous pitfalls: regionalism and universalism. Miron never adopted the abstract humanism of the previous generation of poets, nor did he embrace *JOUAL* as a mode of communication. His language articulated a specific territory as well as a unique moment in time, yet it also transcended these and reached for all alienated, dispossessed human beings. Two images recur in Miron's work: one is of a woman—usually estranged, distant, and lost to the narrator; the other is of the land of Quebec and its collective destiny. Both evoke unhappy ties, alienating and schizophrenic emotions; but they are also linked to a reconstruction process, a reconciliation of all forces. Man is 'rapaillé': his life-giving faculties are gathered once more, just as old bits of straw are picked up from the autumn fields of rural Quebec. Though Miron's texts contend against the injustices of history and the plight of the Quebec people, they include a message of invincible hope. The fact that his own writing destiny was inextricably linked to a specific historical situation made him one of the most visible and listened-to spokesmen for Quebec's independence. But he also attracted more international attention perhaps than any Québécois poet. His poetry has been linked to that of Pablo Neruda and Aimé Césaire, who also expressed ideals of nationalism and social justice.

Miron's perception of language was such that his later publications were, in fact, rewritings. The three version of *L'homme repaillé* (1970, 1981, and 1994)—the 1994 version includes material from *Deux sangs* and *Contrepointes*—attest to this, as do his numerous versions of 'La marche de l'amour', first published in 1962 in *Le Nouveau Journal*, later made available on videotape (1990) and on CD (1992).

A leader in Quebec's cultural and political scene, Miron emphasized the role of the poet in expressing the reality of the 'nation' of Quebec. This may be seen in the two anthologies he co-edited. *Écrivains contemporains du Québec depuis 1950* (1989), with Lise Gauvin, was intended to showcase Quebec's 'modern' literature. *Les grands textes indépendantistes: écrits, discours et manifestes québécois, 1774-1992* (1992), co-editor Andrée Ferretti, is a compilation of major texts, speeches, and manifestos addressing the issues of Quebec autonomy, independence, and separation. The texts begin with a letter from the American Congress dated 1774 and presents a wide range of authors.

Jacques BRAULT's *Miron le magnifique* (1969) and Eugène Roberto's *Structure de l'imaginaire dans 'Contrepointes' de Miron* (1979) testify to the impact Miron had on the Quebec literary scene for fifteen years. One issue of *La BARRE DU JOUR* (no. 26, Oct. 1970) was devoted to a critical examination of his writings and of his role as editor, publisher, and ideologue. Abroad, one essay by John Beaver, 'Gaston Miron', *The language of poetry: crisis and solution* (Amsterdam: Rodopi, 1980), is an interesting tribute to Miron's role as a contemporary writer in French. Apart from Marc Plourde's *The agonized life*, numerous other translations of his works have been published. See Gertrude Sanderson's translation in *The Antigonish Review* 18 (Summer 1974); Fred COGSWELL's in *The poetry of French-Canada in translation* (1970); John GLASSCO's in *Ellipse* 1 (Fall 1969); and the bilingual edition, *L'homme repaillé/Embers and earth: selected poems* (1984), translations by D.G. JONES and Marc Plourde. See also Jean-Louis Major, 'L'Hexagone: une aventure en poésie québécoise' in *La poésie canadienne-française*, vol. 4 (1969).

CAROLINE BAYARD/FRANCESCA BENEDICT

Mistral, Christian. See NOVELS IN FRENCH 1983 TO 1996: 5.

Mistry, Rohinton (b. 1952). Born in Bombay, India, he completed his bachelor's degree at St Xavier's College, University of Bombay. He immigrated to Canada in 1975, worked for a time as a bank clerk, and also earned a B.A. (1982) at the University of Toronto. He lives in Brampton, Ontario, and is a full-time writer.

Mistry's gift for writing fiction became evident when, as an undergraduate, he won the prestigious short-story contest conducted by Hart House at the University of Toronto in both 1983 and 1984. Since then he has published a collection of short stories entitled *Tales from Firozsha Baag* (1987) and two novels, *Such a long journey* (1991), which won a Governor General's Award, and *A fine balance* (1995), which won the Giller Prize.

Very few writers—Bapsi Sidhwa (b. 1938) is a notable exception—have so consistently and so rigorously dealt with the Parsi community as Mistry has. A Parsi himself, Mistry for the most part has set his fiction in India, and has focused on the aspirations, heroism, weaknesses, and marginality of the Parsi community with sympathy, humour, and love. Very much a realist, his strength lies in his capacity to create a strikingly referential surface and to draw his readers into the complex world he creates. In both his novels the political—particularly the period dominated by Indira Gandhi—and the personal intersect, and if at times the connection seems forced, it certainly leads to a completeness without which his characters would seem less engrossing. *A fine balance* also marks a growing point in that it reveals a desire to move beyond the Parsi community to extend the scope of his fiction.

Mistry's work lacks the metafictional quality of Salman Rushdie or the artifice of Amitav Ghosh, yet his work is no less important in the way it chooses to reflect, in the lives of a small community in India, the concerns that confront diasporic communities. Issues of marginality, essentialism, hegemony, and assimilation are not foregrounded in his writing, but reading about the lives of the characters he so painstakingly creates is to recognize what it means to live on the cusp and to assert one's identity in the face of opposition that threatens to engulf it.

See Ajay Heble, '"A foreign presence in the stall": towards a poetics of cultural hybridity in Rohinton Mistry's migration stories', CANADIAN LITERATURE (Summer 1993); Arun Mukherjee, 'Narrating India: Rohinton Mistry's *Such a long journey*' in *Oppositional aesthetics: readings from a hyphenated space* (1994); Gordon Ekelund, 'Left the station: the portrayal of women in Mistry's *Such a long journey*', *The Toronto Review of Contemporary Writing Abroad* (Summer 1995); Nilufer Bharucha, '"When old tracks are lost": Rohinton Mistry's fiction as diasporic discourse', *The Journal of Commonwealth Literature*, 30/2 (1995).

CHELVA KANAGANAYAKAM

Mitchell, John (1880-1951). Born on the farm purchased by his grandfather in the Caledon Hills near Mono, Ontario, he moved in 1894 with his mother to Toronto, where he attended Harbord Collegiate; Victoria College, University of Toronto; and Osgoode Hall Law School. He practised law in Toronto for twenty-eight years, for the most part independently. Reticent, reclusive, and careless about the management of his personal affairs, Mitchell destroyed his professional standing in 1935 by confessing publicly to the misappropriation of trust funds. He was convicted, imprisoned for six months, and disbarred. Upon his release, he lived the rest of his life in obscurity.

Mitchell had begun writing after the death of his beloved mother in 1928. His first work was *The kingdom of America* (1930), a privately printed nationalistic manifesto in which Mitchell proclaimed his allegiance to a Canada that was not a dominion but an autonomous and monarchical kingdom. Under the pseudonym 'Patrick Slater' he next wrote *The yellow briar: a story of the Irish in the Canadian countryside* (1933; rpr. 1971), a fictional autobiography narrated by the Irish orphan 'Paddy Slater'. The book was initially accepted as genuine autobiography because it contained much authentic detail drawn from the experiences of Mitchell's grandparents. An engaging story of pioneering and early settlement in the Caledon region of southern Ontario and of life in Toronto, mainly in the 1840s, it captures and celebrates the seasonal and generational cycles with originality, tolerance, and garrulous good nature. It was an immediate success. Mitchell also wrote *Robert Harding* (1938), an unsuccessful novel about a man wrongly imprisoned for murder; *The water-drinker* (1938), a collection of sentimental verse; and a work of local history, *The settlement of York County* (posthumously published in 1952).

'The story of John Mitchell', an account of his life by Dorothy Bishop, appeared in the 1971 edition of *The yellow briar.*

JOHN LENNOX

Mitchell, Ken (b. 1940). Born in Moose Jaw, Saskatchewan, he attended the University of Saskatchewan (B.A., 1965; M.A., 1967) and while still a student began publishing short fiction and writing radio plays for the regional and international networks of the Canadian Broadcasting Corporation. In 1967 he joined the English department of the University of Regina, where he still teaches creative writing and Canadian literature (and served as Chair of the department in the early 1990s). In 1970 he wrote his first stage play, *Heroes* (1973), which won first prize in the Ottawa Little Theatre Play competition of 1971. In 1979-80 he was the Scottish-Canadian Exchange Fellow at Edinburgh University and the following year he was visiting professor of English, University of Nanking. He has returned to China many times since. He has also taught writing at the Saskatchewan Summer School of the Arts and the Banff Centre of the Arts, and in the early 1970s he helped found the Saskatchewan Writers' Guild.

Mitchell has described himself as 'a popularist by nature', and his work makes clear that he is a populist writer as well. He is also an almost paradigmatic example of the regionalist artist; although his works are universal in appeal, it is difficult to conceive of them outside their prairie context, which is sometimes palpably physical and at other times little more than a mood or an attitude (as in his more recent works set outside the region, and even outside the country). In terms of characterization, this attitude appears in Mitchell's choice of protagonists—people who are, as he says, 'eccentric in the sense that they automatically resist being part of a consensus or any kind of conforming society.' Mitchell's love for, and enjoyment of, such people can be felt in his first novel, *Wandering Rafferty* (1972), in which the eponymous protagonist and his young sidekick endure a series of comic misadventures as they travel across the western provinces. Even the foolish young RCMP constable of the slapstick *The Meadowlark connection* (1975) is a bit of a nonconformist, albeit one who wants to belong. The stories collected in *Everybody gets something here* (1977) are essentially comic, though many have rather bleak subtexts. The protagonists, however, are always willing to flout authoritiy. In *The con man* (1979) the rebel figure is a half-breed who spends much of his time in jail because the people he meets keep insisting that he offer them something for nothing: he becomes the comic victim of a society that pretends to despise him but cannot do without him.

Although Mitchell is an accomplished fiction writer, he feels that 'theatre is ... the most powerful form of communication that there is.' He has therefore especially enjoyed working on projects that involve various degrees of collaboration with other artists. One of his first major efforts was *Cruel tears* (1976), a Country and Western 'opera' that transformed *Othello* into a tragi-comic tale about truckers and their politics and jealousy over women. It had songs by Humphrey and the Dumptrucks, who provided a kind of musical commentary on stage in an almost Brechtian manner. *Davin: the politician* (1979) recovers from Victorian silence the story of an early prairie politician and writer, Nicholas Flood DAVIN, and his feminist lover Kate Simpson-Hayes—both fitting Mitchell nonconformists. *The shipbuilder* (1979), written for actors and a percussion ensemble, is about a Finnish farmer who decides to build a ship by hand on his Saskatchewan farm in order to sail back to his homeland; unlike Mitchell's earlier plays, it is a stark tragedy of pride. In *The medicine line* (1976) Mitchell created an epic outdoor drama about Major James Walsh of the North-West Mounted Police and Chief Sitting Bull. *The great cultural revolution* (1980) sets a version of a *kunchu*-style Chinese opera inside a play about its staging in China in 1966; here he collaborated with the Chinese-Canadian composer David Liang. Mitchell has continued to explore the medium of drama, with musicals and revues, and especially in the startling and very popular one-man show based on the life of Norman Bethune, *Gone the burning sun* (1985), which he even toured in China, during his second visit there in 1986-7. *Chatauqua girl* (1982) is his one (musical) drama with a woman as the rebel hero. As Mitchell says in his Preface to *Rebels in time: three plays by Ken Mitchell* (1991), 'I have always been fascinated by rebels,' and the three revised plays in this anthology—*Davin: the politician*, *Gone the burning sun*, and *The great cultural revolution*—present heroic, rebellious, and tragic figures who insist on holding centre stage.

Mitchell has also published poetry. *Through the Nan Da gate* (1986) is a collection of mainly descriptive poems, with his own photographs, based on his first trip to China. *Witches & idiots* (1990) is in two sections, 'Coming of age in Saskatchewan', poems about his childhood on the Prairies, and 'Pilgrimage', more poems about his travels in China and elsewhere.

Ken Mitchell country (1984) is his own anthology of his work. Mitchell has edited an anthology, *Horizon: writings of the Canadian Prairies* (1977); published a critical study, *Sinclair Ross: a reader's guide* (1981); and written several screenplays, including *The train* (CBC, 1977), *Striker* (NFB), and *The hounds of Notre Dame* (Fraser Films, 1980). He is the subject of critical interviews in Alan Twigg, *For openers* (1981), and Robert Wallace and Cynthia Zimmerman, eds, *The work: conversations with English-Canadian playwrights* (1982).

See also NOVELS IN ENGLISH 1960 TO 1996: OTHER TALENTS, OTHER WORKS: 6(b).

DOUGLAS BARBOUR

Mitchell, W.O. (b. 1914). Born and raised in Weyburn, Saskatchewan, William Ormond Mitchell, the second of four sons of Ormond and Maggie Mitchell, lost his father in 1921. He was raised thereafter in a largely female environment, though his boyhood was disrupted when he was diagnosed in 1926 as having bovine tuberculosis in his wrist. On medical advice his mother took him to the warmer climate of St Petersburg, Florida (and later California), where he attended high school. Throughout the 1930s he mixed formal education with travel and odd jobs. His pursuit of a medical degree at the University of Manitoba was interrupted by a further flare-up of the disease, whereupon he travelled through North America and Europe and worked at various jobs in Seattle and Calgary. In the early forties he completed his undergraduate studies and education degree at the University of Alberta, married Merna Hirtle, and began teaching in 'composite schools' in rural Alberta. At the same time he was experimenting in fiction, playwrighting, and journalism, stimulated by his creative-writing training under Professor F.M. Salter of the University of Alberta and his Seattle theatre experience with the Penthouse Players. In the mid-forties, having been published in magazines like *Maclean's* and *The Atlantic Monthly* (his first three stories appeared in 1942), he determined to risk it as a full-time writer; hence, he gave up teaching and moved his family to High River, Alta. A year after the publication of his first novel, *WHO HAS SEEN THE WIND* (1947), the Mitchells moved to Toronto, where he became fiction editor of *Maclean's* (1948-51). From 1950 to 1956 he wrote over 300 weekly scripts for the popular Canadian Broadcasting Corporation radio series 'Jake and the Kid'—thirteen of which, originally written as short stories, were collected in *Jake and the kid* (1961), which won the Stephen LEACOCK Medal for Humour. Since 1951 he has lived mainly in Alberta, though he has enjoyed an immense popularity across the country over the past five decades. He has often served as a writer-in-residence at Canadian universities (among them Alberta, Calgary, Trent, Massey College at the University of Toronto, and Windsor, where he spent eight years); he was a leading force from 1975 to 1985 in the creative-writing division of the Banff School of Fine Arts; and, in his efforts to promote his books and Canadian writing in general, he became a radio and television personality, a popular lecturer, and a much sought-after speaker and performer. He is an Officer of the Order of Canada (1973), a Member of the Privy Council of Canada (1992), and the subject of an NFB film, Robert Duncan's 'W.O. Mitchell: A Novelist in Hiding' (1980).

Though concerned with death, destructiveness, and negative values, Mitchell's work bubbles with energy and a persistent sense of joy: he is at heart a comic writer. His novels are remarkable for their exuberant talk, reflecting his fascination with oral tradition, inherited in part from Mark Twain and western American humour. Much influenced as well by the Romantic poets, particularly Wordsworth and Blake, Mitchell cherishes innocence, spontaneity, and natural freedom, championing these virtues in the face of darkness, artificiality, and various forms of social restraint.

Who has seen the wind was followed by *The kite* (1962), which is made memorable by the vibrant presence of Daddy Sherry, an irrepressible old maverick whose lifetime spans the 'white' history of the West and whose birthday provides the novel's focus. This novel, however, is somewhat weakened by Mitchell's emphasis on David Lang, a repressed middle-class journalist sent out west to cover Daddy's celebration. A similar theme and problem appear in *The vanishing point* (1973), Mitchell's most ambitious and intriguing novel. A reworking of material in *The alien* (serialized, but not completed, in *Maclean's* in 1953-4), it is the story of Carlyle Sinclair's attempts as teacher and administrator on a Stony Native reserve to bridge the cultural gap between himself and the Stonys, to break through his own puritanical inhibitions and recognize his love for a Native girl in a way that is neither paternalistic nor condescending. But the book's energy and power lie less with the agonies and earnestness of the middle-class protagonist than with the enterprising and clever Archie Nicotine and the self-serving evangelist Heally Richards—characterizations that again reveal Mitchell's creative exuberance and his gift for dialect and comic situations. *How I spent my summer holidays* (1981) returns to the rich, sensory world of prairie boyhood, taking up where *Who has seen the wind* leaves off in dramatizing not the recognition of life, death, and the natural cycle but the struggle a youth faces in discovering the presence of evil in a man he has romantically idolized.

In the 1980s and 1990s Mitchell was most prolific, writing novels that have near their centres the problems of ageing, especially as they relate to the creative spirit and the need to build bridges of communication. *Since Daisy Creek* (1984) has a university setting, as do *Ladybug, ladybug*. . . (1988), which is in part about a retired Canadian professor's attempt to complete a biography of Mark Twain, and *For art's sake* (1992). *Roses are difficult here* (1990), which was first drafted in 1959, involves a return to the Alberta town of Shelby and to popular characters and character types from his earlier writing. Recent years have also seen the publication of a new edition (one that restores Mitchell's original text) of *Who has seen the wind* (1991), which includes paintings by William Kurelek, and a second collection of adapted 'Jake and the Kid' radio scripts, *According to Jake and the Kid* (1989), which earned Mitchell another Stephen Leacock Award for Humour.

At present there is no complete account of the numerous radio scripts Mitchell contributed to the CBC. His only collection of plays, *Dramatic W.O. Mitchell* (1982), includes five: two had been previously published in small editions—*The devil's instrument* (1973) and *The black bonspiel of Wullie MacCrimmon* (1965); the latter was rewritten as a novella in 1993—while three were new: *The kite, For those in peril on the sea*, and what is perhaps Mitchell's most serious and affecting drama, *Back to Beulah*, which was effectively dramatized for CBC television by Eric Till.

See Donald Cameron, 'W.O. Mitchell: sea caves and creative partners', *Conversations with Canadian novelists* (vol. 2, 1973); Dick Harrison, '*W.O. Mitchell*' in *Canadian authors and their works, fiction series*, vol. 4 (1991), eds, Robert Lecker and Jack David; Sheila Latham, 'W.O. Mitchell: an annotated bibliography' in *The annotated bibliography of Canada's major authors*, vol. 3 (1981); Marlys Chevrefils *et al.*, *The W.O. Mitchell papers: An inventory of the archive at the university of Calgary*; and Sheila and David Latham, eds, *Magic lies: the art of W.O. Mitchell* (1997). Mitchell's son Orm and daughter-in-law Barbara are currently preparing an authorized two-volume biography.

See also NOVELS IN ENGLISH 1960 TO 1982.

MICHAEL PETERMAN

Mojica, Monique. See ABORIGINAL LITERATURE: 4.

Monette, Hélène. See NOVELS IN FRENCH 1983 TO 1996: 2.

Monk, Maria. See *AWFUL DISCLOSURES OF MARIA MONK*.

Montgomery, L.M. (1874-1942). Born at Clifton (now New London), Prince Edward Island, Lucy Maud Montgomery was raised by her maternal grandparents after her widowed father moved to Prince Albert, Saskatchewan. Educated at Prince of Wales College, Charlottetown, and at Dalhousie University, Halifax, Nova Scotia, she taught for some years; then, apart from working briefly for the Halifax *Daily Echo* (1901-2), she looked after her grandmother at Cavendish, P.E.I., from 1898 to 1911. Meanwhile, determined to become a writer, she wrote for American and Canadian children's magazines and gained international recognition with her first novel, *ANNE OF GREEN GABLES* (1908). In 1911 she married the Rev. Ewan Macdonald, and while she pursued her writing career in her husband's charges at Leaskdale and Norval, Ontario, she performed her other roles as the minister's wife and as mother of a young family. In 1935 she was awarded the OBE, elected a Fellow of the Royal Society of Arts and Letters, and made a member of the Institut des Lettres et des Arts (France), which later awarded her a silver medal. The Macdonalds retired to Toronto in 1935. Their last years were plagued by her husband's deteriorating mental health and by Montgomery's severe depression over the outbreak of the Second World War. Both Montgomery and her husband died in Toronto and were buried in Cavendish. Several places associated with her are now museums: her birthplace at New London; her grandmother Macneill's homestead at Cavendish, where she wrote *Anne*; a house in Bala, Ontario, which is associated with her inspiration for *The blue castle*, her only Ontario novel; and two national historic sites, the 'Green Gables' farmhouse at Cavendish and the Presbyterian manse at Leaskdale.

Anne of Green Gables introduces the central situation in Montgomery's fiction: the imaginative adolescent girl's search for self-knowledge that results in liberation from adult authority and success in the male-female clash. An adoring public devoured not only this novel but seven sequels about Anne's teaching career, her marriage to Gilbert Blythe, their family, and her responses to the changes wrought by the First World War and its aftermath in *Anne of Avonlea* (1909), *Anne of the Island* (1915), *Anne's house of dreams* (1917), *Rainbow valley* (1919), *Rilla of Ingleside* (1921), *Anne of Windy Poplars* (1936), and *Anne of Ingleside* (1939). Anne, the spirited child, necessarily grows into a married matron who is highly conventional—to compensate, the later books develop sharp portraits of eccentric characters and rhapsodic descriptions of nature. The enduring quality of the Anne books is in their intense evocation of landscape and in their representation of female aspiration and power.

Following the success of *Anne of Green Gables*, Montgomery wrote several collections of stories, including her own favourite, *The story girl* (1911). In 1917, after a bitter lawsuit, she broke with her first American publisher, L.C. Page, and moved to a Canadian publisher. Page's unauthorized publication of her stories, *Further chronicles of Avonlea* (1920), embroiled her in a further nine-year court battle that she finally won.

The Emily series is somewhat more autobiographical than the Anne books, and its themes are more deliberately feminist. Montgomery utilizes her own reading of Charlotte Brontë's *Jane Eyre*, Elizabeth Barrett Browning's *Aurora Leigh*, and Olive Schreiner's *The story of an African farm* to write about Emily Byrd Starr's own reading and her discovery of her vocation. *Emily of New Moon* (1923) balances the child Emily's first-person journals against the author's third-person narrative. Misled by her male 'suitors', but sustained by her own Wordsworthian 'flashes' of creative insights, Emily's struggles as an adolescent and woman to understand her visions and find her voice as a writer are continued in *Emily climbs* (1925) and *Emily's quest* (1927). In deference to her publisher and demanding readership, Montgomery eventually marries Emily to a suitor to end the trilogy, rather than focusing on her achievement and potential.

Never comfortable with the frank realism of fiction after the First World War, Montgomery recognized that her talent lay in employing humour for the purpose of satirizing society. Montgomery wrote two fictions aimed at a mature audience. They were well reviewed and sold well. The heroine Valancy of *The blue castle* (1926), the only novel without a P.E.I. setting, leaves her unhappy home in the Muskoka district of Ontario to care for a dying 'fallen woman' and child, and then to marry a local man who is suspected of being a shady character. He is revealed to be Valancy's favourite nature writer in disguise, as well as a millionaire's son. *A tangled web* (1931) depicts a manipulative, powerful old woman making sport of prospective heirs to a family heirloom. Montgomery then returned to two more adolescent heroines in *Pat of Silver Bush* (1933), *Mistress Pat* (1935), and *Jane of Lantern Hill* (1937). The latter work establishes a fascinating contrast between the city (Toronto) as a sterile wasteland of domineering adults and the P.E.I. countryside as an Edenic, organic community where self-realization is achieved. Montgomery also wrote *The watchman and other poems* (1916) and co-authored *Courageous women* (1934) with Marian Keith (Mary Esther MACGREGOR) and Mabel Burns McKinley. Posthumous collections include *The road to yesterday* (1974), Catherine McLay's compilation *The doctor's sweetheart: and other stories* (1979), and Rea Wilmhurst's editions of stories (seven to date), published by MCCLELLAND & STEWART. *The Alpine path; the story of my career* (1974) is a collection of magazine articles from 1917.

Early in the century Montgomery began a life-long correspondence that—along with her journals, of which she left some ten volumes covering the years 1889 to 1942—provided her with much-needed intellectual and emotional outlets. Her letters were edited by Wilfrid Eggleston in *The Green Gables letters from L.M. Montgomery to Ephraim Weber 1905-1909* (1960) and by Francis W.P. Bolger and Elizabeth R. Epperly in *My dear Mr. M.: letters to G.B. MacMillan* (1980). *The selected journals of L.M. Montgomery. volume I: 1889-1910* (1985), *Volume II: 1910-1921* (1987), and *Volume III: 1921-1929* (1992), edited by Mary Rubio and Elizabeth Waterston, provide far more than insights into Montgomery's writing. They are a powerful account of the tensions between her public image as minister's wife and successful author and her private life as wife, mother, and artist. Volumes II and III are a detailed record of the changes in Canadian society as Montgomery experienced them day by day; through these volumes Montgomery achieved a new reputation as a journal writer. Volumes IV and V are in preparation.

As Elizabeth Epperly has demonstrated, Montgomery's fictions are psychic biographies in which the self is idealized. She took over the Victorian fiction formulas of her youth and transformed them into romances of enduring appeal, which narrate the heroine's quest for empowerment; her tangles with parental authority figures; her rivalries with, and sexual attraction towards, males; and her triumph through marriage and the artist's vocation. At the same time, Montgomery's narrative strategies, as Mary Rubio has explained, rework the conventions of romance patterns in order to make 'serious social criticism' and permit women readers an ironic recognition of how their culture oppresses them. Thus the continuing appeal of Montgomery's works lies in her ability to dramatize the psychology of adolescent girls and to be both empathetic and objective about them, in her depiction of home and community that is an integral part of almost every story, in her humour and irony, and in the *Journals*' portrait of a remarkably passionate and intelligent person.

All twenty volumes of fiction and stories published in Montgomery's lifetime are in print, including many titles in translation, a testimony to their popularity around the world and to Anne's almost legendary status in Japan and Poland. The Signet editions of *Anne of Avonlea* (1987), *Anne of Green Gables* (1987), *Anne's house of dreams* (1988), *Chronicles of Avonlea* (1988), *Anne of the Island* (1991), and *The story girl* (1991) contain 'Afterwords' by Mary Rubio and Elizabeth Waterston; the NEW CANADIAN LIBRARY editions of *Anne of Green Gables*, *Emily of New Moon*, *Emily climbs*, and *Emily's quest* contain Afterwords by, respectively, Margaret ATWOOD, Alice MUNRO, Jane URQUHART, and P.K. PAGE. There seems no end to the spinoffs. *Anne of Green Gables* was filmed in 1919 and 1934, and *Anne of Windy Poplars* in 1940. The musical version of *Anne* by Mavor MOORE, Donald Harron, and Norman Campbell has been performed annually at the Charlottetown Confederation Centre since 1965; stage versions of both *Anne of Green Gables* and *The blue castle* have been widely produced in Poland for several decades. The television movies *Anne of Green Gables* (1985), the sequel *Anne of Avonlea* (1987), and the ninety-one episodes of *The road to Avonlea* (1989-96) have been seen around the world and produced a generation of performers who enhanced live theatre in Canada. Other television versions include *The blue castle* (1993) and the *Emily* series (1997-8). Craft shops on Prince Edward Island sell Anne dolls, soap, and other merchandise associated with the red-haired heroine. There is a charming realization of cooking and recipes by Kate Macdonald, Montgomery's granddaughter, in *The Anne of Green Gables cookbook* (1985), illustrated in colour and black and white by Barbara Di Lella. Elaine and Kelly Crawford published *Aunt Maud's recipe book* in 1996. George and Maureen Campbell of Park Corner, P.E.I., issue the newsletter *Kindred spirits of P.E.I.* (1990-). The L.M. Montgomery Institute, established at the University of Prince Edward Island in 1993, has sponsored symposiums on Montgomery and her contemporaries. One can browse the World Wide Web for information on Montgomery's books and her literary clubs. Large collections of archival materials about Montgomery are held by the National Archives, Ottawa, by the Confederation Centre, Charlottetown, and by the University of Guelph, Ontario.

Biographies include F.W.P. Bolger, *The years before 'Anne'* (1974); Mollie Gillen, *The wheels of things: a biography of L.M. Montgomery* (1975); and Mary Rubio and Elizabeth Waterson, *Writing a life: L.M. Montgomery* (1995).

Serious critical interest in Montgomery began with Elizabeth Waterston's essay in *The clear spirit: twenty Canadian women and their times* (1966), edited by Mary Quayle Innis. Other studies include John Robert Sorfleet, ed., *L.M. Montgomery: an assessment* (1976); Gabriella Ahmansson, *A life and its mirrors: a feminist reading of L.M. Montgomery's fiction* (1991); Elizabeth R. Epperly, *The fragrance of sweet-grass; L.M. Montgomery's heroines and the pursuit of romance* (1992); Mavis Reimer, ed., *'Such a simple little thing': critical responses to L.M. Montgomery's Anne of Green Gables* (1992); Elizabeth Waterston, *Kindling spirit: L.M. Montgomery's Anne of Green Gables* (1993); and Mary Henley Rubio, ed., *Harvesting thistles: the textual garden of L.M. Montgomery, essays on her novels and journals* (1994). The major source of articles is the journal *CCL: Canadian Children's Literature*, published at the University of Guelph, Ontario. See Yuko Katsura, 'Red-haired Anne in Japan', *CCL* 34 (1984); Barbara Wachowicz, 'L.M. Montgomery: at home in Poland', *CCL* 46 (1987); Gabriella Ahmansson, 'The survival of the artist: L.M. Montgomery and the attempted murder of Emily Byrd Starr', *Literary responses to Arctic Canada* (1990); Mary Rubio, 'Subverting the trite: L.M. Montgomery's "Room of her own"', *CCL* 65 (1992); Douglas Baldwin, 'L.M. Montgomery's *Anne of Green Gables*: the Japanese connection', *Journal of Canadian Studies* 28, no.3 (Fall 1993); Alan R. Young, 'L.M. Montgomery's *Rilla of Ingleside* (1920): romance and the experience of war', and Diana Tye, 'Women's oral narrative traditions as depicted in Lucy Maud Montgomery's fiction, 1918-1939', both in *Myth and milieu: Atlantic literature and culture 1918-1939* (1993), edited by Gwendolyn Davies; Lorna Drew, 'The Emily connection: Ann Radcliffe, L.M. Montgomery and "The female Gothic"', *CCL* 77 (1995); and Martin Knelman, 'Mickey on the road to Avonlea', *The Financial Post Magazine* (March 1996). A useful bibliography is Ruth Weber Russell, D.W. Russell, and Rea Wilmshurst, *Lucy Maud Montgomery: a preliminary bibliography* (1986, University of Waterloo Library).

See also CHILDREN'S LITERATURE IN ENGLISH: 1. GEORGE L. PARKER

Montpetit, Edouard. See BIOGRAPHY AND MEMOIRS IN FRENCH: 8 and ESSAYS IN FRENCH: 3.

Montreal Group, The. This influential group of students, with shared literary interests, at McGill University in the 1920s existed in four phases. The first was the founding by A.J.M. SMITH of the *Literary Supplement* (eighteen issues, 1924-5) to the *McGill Daily*, where he began his prolonged effort to introduce a modernist sensibility into Canadian writing. When the *Supplement* was abolished, probably because it was considered too 'highbrow', Smith and F.R. SCOTT—both graduate students—founded *The McGILL FORTNIGHTLY REVIEW* (1925-7) as an independent journal, though it was supported by the student body. It attracted other young writers—among them A.M. KLEIN, Leo KENNEDY, John GLASSCO, Eugene FORSEY, and Leon EDEL, who was made managing editor. Here, too, Smith was the moving literary spirit, demanding high standards of taste and style, and precision of word and thought. A third phase, after the *Fortnightly* had run its course, was the *CANADIAN MERCURY*, subsidized and created by Louis Schwartz, who had been on the *Fortnightly* staff. Smith, Scott, Klein, Kennedy, Edel and others participated—Smith writing from Edinburgh, where he was working towards his Ph.D., and Edel from Paris. The final phase was the publication in 1936 of the seminal anthology of early Canadian modernism: *NEW PROVINCES: poems of several authors* 1936; rpr. 1976).

See Leon Edel, *Memories of the Montreal Group* (Memorial University of Newfoundland, 1986). LEON EDEL

***Montreal Museum*, *The*.** This was the first periodical in British North America directed to female readers by a female editor and proprietor. It was typical of its genre in its short publication span (Dec. 1822-March 1834) and its broad content—poetry, moralistic fiction, didactic and improving non-fiction, and supposedly true stories about historical figures—and was unique for its time and place in providing its readers with a monthly account of London fashions, and with material translated from French sources. The editor, Mary Graddon Gosselin, was the daughter of a Quebec merchant who, in 1830, married Léon Gosselin, a Montreal lawyer, prominent reformer, and editor. She was initially assisted by Elizabeth Tracey (sister of the reform politician Daniel Tracey), who withdrew after two numbers. *The Montreal Museum* was printed on the press of the newspaper *La Minerve*, of which Mme Gosselin's husband was editor, and its termination may have been related to his departure from that position. The principal identified contributor was Mrs H. (Diana) Bayley, who had published several books in England before accompanying her husband, an officer in the Commissariat, to Canada. The content was produced by writers of both sexes, most of them residents of the colony, although the poetry and fiction rarely had to do with anything distinctively Canadian. Women were more often the principal protagonists of stories than men, and were always depicted in a family context, as wives, mothers, daughters, or aunts, capable of independent action only within a limited sphere, where they are generally portrayed as strong, nurturing, sensible, and sensitive. A number of articles instruct women in their proper role as submissive wives. Articles on the education of daughters emphasized the moral and practical, rather than frivolous accomplishments.

Initially, and throughout its duration, *The Montreal Museum* was well received by the press of both languages and all political interests. In winding up the periodical, Mme Gosselin attributed its demise to a lack of subscribers. Its termination was publicly regretted.

MARY LU MacDONALD

Montreuil, Gaëtane de. See NOVELS IN FRENCH 1900 TO 1920.

Moodie, Susanna (1803-85). Born near Bungay, Suffolk, England, Susanna Strickland lived mostly at Reydon Hall, near Southwold, until her immigration to Canada in 1832. The last-born of the six Strickland daughters, five of whom became writers, she was educated by her parents and, as her father's health began to fail, by her elder sisters, notably Elizabeth, who, with Agnes, later gained fame and social status in England as authors of *Lives of the Queens of England* and other popular multi-volumed biographies of royalty and Anglican leaders. Like her sisters at isolated Reydon, Susanna began writing at an early age. She was especially attracted to heroic figures of history she judged to have been misunderstood. Her first narrative for young people, *Spartacus: a Roman story* (London, 1822), was published through the efforts of a family friend. It was followed by a number of didactic stories for children and adolescents, among them *The little Quaker; or, The triumph of virtue* (London, n.d.), *The little prisoner; or, Passion and patience* (London, n.d.), *Hugh Latimer; or, The school-boy's friendship* (London, 1828), *Roland*

Massingham; or I will be my own master (London, n.d.), and *Profession and principle; or, The vicar's tales* (London, n.d.). Markets of a more diverse kind opened up for her when a family friend, Thomas Harral, moved from Suffolk to London to edit *La Belle Assemblée*, a fashionable court and literary magazine. From 1827 to 1830 Susanna contributed poems, sketches, and stories to Harral while also submitting her work to several of the then-popular annuals in London. By 1830 she was also writing occasionally for *The Athenaeum* and *The Ecclesiastic*, with which her friend the Scottish poet Thomas Pringle was involved, and *The Lady's Magazine*. Under Pringle's paternal direction and while a visitor in his London home, she was introduced to the injustices of slavery—Pringle had been in South Africa in the 1820s and was the secretary of the Anti-Slavery Society in England—and wrote separate pamphlets describing the lives and sufferings of two Caribbean slaves, Mary Prince and Ashton Warner. In 1830 she also collaborated with her sister Agnes to write a slim volume called *Patriotic songs* and a year later, again with Pringle's help, she brought out by subscription her own collection of poetry, *Enthusiasm, and other poems* (London, 1831).

Susanna Strickland's life changed radically when, in 1830, she met Lt John Wedderburn Dunbar Moodie at the Pringles'. An Orkney gentleman and half-pay military officer, he had come to London from his Groote Valley farm to write an account of his ten years in South Africa. They married in London in April 1831, and later moved to Southwold, where their first child was born. After weighing alternatives and carefully considering their options, they decided to immigrate to Canada in the spring of 1832. Arriving in Cobourg, Upper Canada (Ontario), in September, John Moodie chose not to take up their backwoods land-grant near Susanna's brother, Samuel Strickland; rather, he bought a partially cleared farm near Lake Ontario and 'the Front'. 'Melsetter' (eight miles northwest of present-day Cobourg) is described in the first half (volume) of *ROUGHING IT IN THE BUSH*. The problems of adjustment the Moodies faced there, compounded by a failed steamboat investment and the more encouraging prospects for a northern waterway (now the Trent-Severn system), prompted them to sell the farm and move in Feb. 1834 to their land-grant, north of what is now Lakefield in 1834. Here they would be close to both Sam and Susanna's sister Catharine Parr TRAILL. They remained on their 300-acre bush farm for nearly six years, including the fearful days of the Rebellion of 1837, struggling to make ends meet on a farm distinguished more by cedar forest and rock deposits than by arable land. Only with Moodie's appointment as sheriff of the newly established county of Hastings were Susanna and her five children finally able to leave the backwoods. They moved to the growing town of Belleville, where they lived until John Moodie's death in 1869.

Though she endured a great deal in her 'bush' experiences, Moodie never weakened in her literary aspirations. Initially few markets were available in Upper Canada. Only with the invitation of John Lovell to write for *The LITERARY GARLAND* (Montreal) did she at last find a sustained, paying outlet. During the life of that magazine (1838-51) she was its most prolific contributor, specializing in serialized fiction. As well, in 1847-8 Susanna and John Moodie jointly edited *The Victoria Magazine* in Belleville. The original sketches for *Roughing it in the bush* appeared in both *The Literary Garland* and *The Victoria Magazine* in 1847.

The high point of Moodie's literary career occurred during the 1850s when, through her husband's publisher Richard Bentley, her writing again found English publication. Her most enduring work is autobiographical in nature and includes her best-known book, *Roughing it in the bush: or, Life in Canada* (2 vols, London, 1852; NCL); its hastily put-together sequel, *Life in the clearings versus the bush* (London, 1853; NCL, with an Afterword by Carol SHIELDS); and a fictionalized narrative, *Flora Lyndsay; or, Passages in an eventful life* (London, 1853). Together the three form a loose trilogy, *Flora Lyndsay* in fact recounting the events leading up to the Moodies' move to Canada and concluding with their journey up the St Lawrence River. Marked by humour and an unusual frankness concerning pioneering experience, Susanna Moodie's extended account of her difficult adaptation from England to Canada has a dramatic force as narrative and a perspicacity of observation rare in the literature of emigration and settlement.

In the 1850s Moodie wrote several long-winded novels for Bentley that drew heavily on Gothic and sentimental conventions. The first was *Mark Hurdlestone; or, The gold worshipper* (London, 1853). It had begun as a short tale in *The Lady's Magazine* (Nov. 1833) and grew first into a serialized novel in *The Literary Garland*, then into a two-volume Bentley novel. The three stories that make up *Matrimonial speculations* (London, 1854) and the narrative of *Geoffrey Moncton; or, The faithless guardian* (New York, 1855) also had previously appeared in the *Garland*. These elaborate and moralistic novels, marked by murder, intrigue, family tyranny, and mistaken identity, had less appeal for the English literary audience of the 1850s than Moodie and Bentley hoped. The fact that they were more successful when reprinted in the United States is evinced by the decision of the New York firm of Dewitt and Davenport to publish *Geoffrey Moncton* prior to its release by Bentley; the English edition thus appeared a year later as *The Monctons* (2 vols, 1856). Bentley also published Moodie's novel *The world before them* (3 vols, 1868), mostly as a gesture of friendship to his long-standing and now needy correspondent.

While the Belleville years appear to have been a generally stable and comfortable period for the Moodies, their finances were seldom secure and they were often the target of Tory lawyers who resented their reform (Baldwinite) politics and the advantages conferred upon them through John's appointment as Sheriff by Sir George Arthur. Moreover, they suffered great personal losses in Belleville, first in a house fire in 1840 and then as a result of the drowning death of their five-year-old son John in 1844. Late in the 1850s, those old political and personal grievances resurfaced in the form of a dubious charge against the ageing sheriff for the 'farming' of his office. After having exhausted much money and his legal recourses to appeal, John Moodie was at last forced to resign in 1863. After his death in 1869, Susanna outlived him by seventeen years, staying mostly with the families of her married children, though she often visited her sister Catharine Parr Traill in Lakefield.

She wrote little during these later years, turning increasingly to flower painting, a skill she had learned as a girl and had passed on to her daughter, Agnes (Moodie) Fitzgibbon (later Chamberlain), who illustrated *Canadian wildflowers* (1868), the text of which was written by Catharine Parr Traill. Moodie, however, made minor revisions to *Roughing it in the bush* for the first Canadian edition, brought out by Toronto publisher George Rose in 1871. During her last year she was bedridden, suffering in her final days from what her sister Catharine called brain-fever. She died in Toronto at the home of her eldest daughter, Katie Vickers.

See Audrey Morris, *The gentle pioneers: five nineteenth-century Canadians* (1968); Clara THOMAS, 'The Strickland sisters' in *The clear spirit* (1966), edited by Mary Quayle Innis; Michael Peterman, 'Susanna Moodie' in *Canadian writers and their works: fiction series: vol. 1* (1983), edited by Robert Lecker, Jack David, and Ellen Quigley; Marian Fowler, *The embroidered tent: five gentlewomen in early Canada* (1982); and John Thurston, *The work of words* (1996). Much valuable information about Moodie's life and writing can be found in two collections of letters edited by Carl Ballstadt, Elizabeth Hopkins, and Michael Peterman: *Susanna Moodie: letters of a lifetime* (1985) and *Letters of love and duty: the correspondence of Susanna and John Moodie* (1993). See also the Moodie collections in both the National Library and the National Archives of Canada. MICHAEL PETERMAN

Moore, Brian (b. 1921). Born and educated in Belfast, Northern Ireland, he served as a civilian employee of the British Ministry of War Transport during the Second World War in Algiers, Naples, and Marseilles, then for the United Nations commission for the resettlement of refugees (UNRRA) after the war, primarily in Warsaw. He immigrated to Canada in 1948, where he worked for the *Montreal Gazette* from 1948 to 1952 while writing his brilliant first novel, *Judith Hearne* (1955; US title *The lonely passion of Judith Hearne*), about a Belfast spinster whose feelings of loneliness and isolation are briefly and pathetically assuaged by an imaginary romance. A great critical success (and made into a 1987 film starring Maggie Smith), that novel was followed by *The feast of Lupercal* (1957) and *The luck of Ginger Coffey* (1960), which won a Governor General's Award. Moore moved to the USA in 1959 but retains Canadian citizenship. References to Canada and Canadian experience continue to appear in his fiction, as in *The great Victorian collection* (1975), which also won a Governor General's Award and deals with a McGill University history professor, who, while visiting California, dreams about a 'Victorian collection' and awakens to find that his dream, to somewhat perverse effect, has come true. *The lonely passion of Judith Hearne* and *The luck of Ginger Coffey* are both in the NEW CANADIAN LIBRARY, with Afterwords by Janette Turner HOSPITAL and Keath FRASER respectively.

Moore's other novels include *An answer from Limbo* (1962), *The emperor of ice-cream* (1965), *I am Mary Dunne* (1968), *Fergus* (1970), *Catholics* (1972), *The doctor's wife* (1976), *The Mangan inheritance* (1979), *The temptation of Eileen Hughes* (1981), *Cold heaven* (1983), *The colour of blood* (1987), *Lies of silence* (1990), *No other life* (1993), and *The statement* (1995). Of

Moore's eighteen novels, *Black Robe* (1985) seems his greatest departure. His only historical fiction, it portrays the mission of seventeenth-century French Jesuits to convert Native tribes in Canada and was made into a film (directed by Bruce Beresford, 1991).

In fact, all Moore's novels deal in some way with dilemmas of faith triggered by what he has called 'moments of crisis' that bring the accustomed into question. While his early Belfast-set novels assail a tyrannical version of Irish Catholicism that seems rooted in his own harshly clerical education there in the 1930s, his later books (beginning with *An answer from Limbo*) reveal the limitations of an opposite orientation, the attempt to find happiness through secular self-absorption. The books of this middle period betray a deep yearning for mystical and spiritual affirmation on the part of even his most rootless and worldly characters. Beginning with *The colour of blood*, Moore turned to the thriller genre as a way of exploring issues of conscience within the context of contemporary politics, from an uneasy complicity between Church and state in the case of a French war criminal (*The statement*) to hostage-taking in Northern Ireland (*Lies of silence*).

While not equally successful as literary productions, Moore's novels are on the whole remarkable for their transparency of style, and a leanness and dramatic economy of expression (perhaps honed by his occasional forays into script-writing) that manage to convey exceptional levels of nuance and psychological complexity. Moore is also notable for his success in depicting female characters and female sexuality, relating sexual autonomy for women to issues of identity and self-expression—and ultimately to their capacity for independent moral choice and moral responsibility.

Moore has also written *Canada* (1963; rev. 1968) with the editors of *Life*, and *The revolution script* (1971), a fictionalized account of the kidnapping of James Cross in Montreal by the FLQ in Oct. 1970.

See Jo O'Donoghue, *Brian Moore: a critical study* (1991). MARILYN ROSE

Moore, Mavor (b. 1919). Born in Toronto to the Anglican clergyman Francis John Moore and the actress Dora (née Mavor) Moore, he grew up in Toronto where he attended university, graduating with a B.A. (1941). Following service in Canadian army intelligence during the war, he and his mother founded the New Play Society in Toronto in 1946. He also worked for the Canadian Broadcasting Corporation during the 1940s and 1950s, becoming chief producer for CBC-TV (1950-4). He was Professor of Theatre at York University, Toronto, between 1970 and 1984. Throughout his career he was actively involved in the theatre, acting as producer and director of the annual revue 'Spring Thaw' between 1948-57 and 1961-5. He was the founding artistic director of the Charlottetown Festival (1964-8), general director of the St Lawrence Centre (1965-9), founding chair of the Guild of Canadian Playwrights (1977), and chair of the CANADA COUNCIL (1979-83). In 1996 he became co-chair of the B.C. Arts Council.

Moore was the librettist for a number of musicals and operas including *Sunshine town* (produced in 1954), *The Ottawa man* (produced in 1958), *Johnny Belinda* (produced in 1968), and *Fauntleroy* (produced in 1980). Perhaps his most important work in this genre was his libretto for Harry Somers' opera *Louis Riel* (1967), commissioned by the Canadian Opera Company for the centenary celebrations. A number of Moore's stage plays have been published in *Three one-act plays by Mavor Moore* (1973) and *Six plays* (1989).

Moore is the recipient of a number of honorary degrees. He was made an Officer of the Order of Canada in 1973 and in 1986 was awarded the Molson Prize for his outstanding achievement in the arts. He has published his memoirs under the title *Reinventing myself* (1994). His papers are in the archives of York University. STEFAN HAAG

Moore, Thomas. See FOREIGN WRITERS ON CANADA IN ENGLISH: 1.

Mootoo, Shani. See CARIBBEAN-CANADIAN LITERATURE and LESBIAN LITERATURE.

More joy in heaven. From the publication of his first novel, *Strange fugitive* (1928), until that of *A time for Judas* (1983), one of the preoccupations of Morley CALLAGHAN's fiction has been the world of the criminal. Most concerned with this subject is *More joy in heaven* (1937; NCL, with an Afterword by Milton Wilson), the last and possibly the best novel by Callaghan from his most prolific period as a writer. It was clearly inspired by the life of the notorious bank robber Red Ryan, who was released from Kingston (Ont.) Penitentiary in the summer of 1935 after serving almost a dozen years of a life sentence. Ryan claimed that he had reformed, and his supporters included a priest, a senator, other citizens interested in prison reform, and even Prime

Minister R.B. Bennett. The welcome that Ryan was given on his return to Toronto was equalled only by the bitterness that greeted the news, in May 1936, that he had been shot to death by police as he attempted to rob a liquor store in Sarnia, Ont.

In *More joy in heaven* Red Ryan becomes the fictional Kip Caley, whose release from prison is also aided by a senator and a priest. Caley, however—unlike Ryan—has truly reformed. Having been turned into a celebrity by the press and the public, he begins to believe he has a mission to reform society, but is eventually overcome by its cynicism and violence. On one level *More joy in heaven* may be read as a novel of social comment; on another it is a religious parable, with the redeemed sinner being destroyed both by his illusions and by his fellow men. It has been dramatized for both radio and television.

See George WOODCOCK, *Moral predicament: Morley Callaghan's 'More joy in heaven'* (1993). ROBERT WEAVER

Morency, Pierre (b. 1942). Born in Lauzon, Quebec, he studied at the Collège de Lévis and Université Laval. His early poetry was collected in *Au nord constamment de l'amour* (2nd edn, 1973). He then published *Lieu de naissance* (1973), *Le temps des oiseaux* (1975), and *Torrentiel* (1978), as well as a number of children's plays and, with Paul Hébert, a highly acclaimed French adaptation (1974) of J.T. McDonough's *Charbonneau and Le Chef* (1968), a play about Maurice Duplessis's clash with the Archbishop of Montreal. In 1976 he co-founded *Estuaire*, which remains the only magazine devoted exclusively to poetry, and in 1978 he wrote a play, *Les passeuses*, which was eventually produced. Morency then concentrated on his career as a broadcaster, producing programs and records on the birds of the St Lawrence and using to good effect his poetic gifts and his splendid speaking voice.

Morency belongs to the generation of poets determined to end Quebec's atavistic enslavement to the dualism of flesh and spirit. He rejects cerebral and disincarnated art. The head, he complains, has snapped its moorings with the heart. The consequence is that the imagination is adrift and the senses vacillate without engaging the real world. He revels in a sensual delight in words, 'le simple plaisir de prononcer'. His poetry celebrates the world of things and people—the city, but above all the country, the Île d'Orléans, the North Shore, and the wildlife of the region. He blatantly adopts a technical wildlife vocabulary in his poems to express his holistic vision of the human struggle against alienation and a reconciliation with the environment. He has also challenged the commercialization of language and communication in North America by producing poems in the form of huge street hoardings, or of picture postcards to send to his friends, aiming to beat the commercial world at its own game. Nevertheless Morency's poetry is suffused with an undercurrent of dedication and high seriousness. In his early period Morency also wrote a poetic, or 'free', novel, *L'ossature* (1972).

Starting with the poems in *Torrentiel*, the scansion of which was somewhat derivative of the Hexagone poets, the collections that followed, *Effets personnels* (1987) and *Les paroles qui marchent dans la nuit* (1994), show a clear propensity for poetic prose, with an attraction to the narrative form. For Morency, prose seemed the right vehicle for the life lesson he wanted to transmit through his rich evocations of rivers, light, and desire represented by, among other things, the image of the arrow. His poetry in verse tends in the direction of the maxim. Clearly for Morency poetry is closely bound up with the meaning of existence, and the poet's quest is to inhabit language as he would inhabit a house filled with light. His love of nature, and birds in particular, has inspired stories in which he invites readers to look more closely at the world around them: *L'oeil américain: histoires naturelles du Nouveau Monde* (1989) and *Lumière des oiseaux: histoires naturelles du Nouveau Monde* (1992). Pierre Morency is one of the few renowned Québécois writers who live and write in Quebec City, and have the courage and skill to take poetry from the private realm to public space—in Europe as well as Quebec.

C.R.P. MAY/JACQUES PAQUIN

Morgan, Bernice (b. 1935). Born in St John's, Newfoundland, where she still lives, she occupied several jobs until 1986, when she resigned as communications director of the Newfoundland Teacher's Association to devote herself full-time to writing (while being married with three children). Her short stories won awards in literary competitions and were published in anthologies such as *From this place: a selection of writing by women of Newfoundland and Labrador* (1977), which she edited with Helen Porter and Geraldine Rubia. She has also written several radio plays for the CBC.

Morgan's two novels tell a linked story about the families of Cape Random, an isolated, exposed point in the northeastern part of Newfoundland. She draws upon the history of her mother's family in Cape Island, a now deserted outport, combining elements of Gothic romance with historically accurate and realistic details to form a sweeping narrative. *Random passage* (1992) begins with the arrival of the Andrews family in 1824, and takes the form of a journal written chiefly by Lavinia Andrews in a shipping-records book. *Waiting for time* (1994), which won the 1995 CANADIAN AUTHORS' ASSOCIATION Award and the 1995 Thomas RADDALL Atlantic Fiction Prize, brings the narrative into the present with Lav Andrews, who is transferred from Ottawa to St John's to co-ordinate a report on the troubled cod fishery, and also recounts the story of Mary Bundle, one of the early settlers in Cape Random, that is inscribed in the margins of, and contests, the original journal that Lav finds. The interwoven stories layer fiction and history, evoking the tenuousness of life in the outports and the strength for survival that comes largely from the women. Morgan blends fast-paced narrative with haunting images of the people, land, and sea.

See Helen Fogwill Porter, 'To rearrange the past', *Books in Canada* 23.1 (February 1994).

HEATHER SANDERSON

Morin, Marie. See Writing in NEW FRANCE: 2.

Morin, Paul (1889-1963). Born in Montreal, Paul Morin attended the Académie Marchand, a girl's school founded by his maternal grandmother, before beginning his secondary education at the Collège Sainte-Marie; he published his first poems in *Le Journal de Françoise* when he was fourteen. In 1907, after receiving his bachelor's degree, he entered the law faculty of Université Laval in Montreal and was admitted to the bar in 1910 at the age of twenty. He immediately left Quebec for Paris to enrol at the Sorbonne. That winter he put the finishing touches on his first collection of poetry, *Le paon d'émail* (1911), in which outlandish, imaginary oriental settings evoke a luxuriant sensuality. Morin's flight to foreign parts was also a flight from the moral establishment of his homeland, and in this book he gave free rein to his youthful ardour. Despite his use of themes that could hardly be considered suitable in ultra-Catholic Quebec, his deft handling of the alexandrine and his cleverness with words and rhymes in conveying extraordinary sensations delighted the champions of 'art for art's sake' and won the approval of even the most stubborn nationalists—who were, after all, not immune to Parnassian aesthetics.

In July 1912 Morin received a doctorate from the Sorbonne with his thesis *Les sources de l'oeuvre de Henry Wadsworth Longfellow* (1913), a 600-page work that is still considered to be one of the major studies of the poet, in whom Morin found a kindred spirit. At the onset of the First World War he returned to Canada and devoted himself chiefly to teaching literature at McGill University (1914-15), Smith College, Massachussetts (1915-16), and the University of Minnesota (1916-17), where he met and married in 1917 a young American girl, Geneviève van Rennslaer-Bernhardt. He left teaching in 1918 and began to work as a translator. He was a co-founder of *Le NIGOG* and published a second collection, *Poèmes de cendre et d'or* (1922), which won the Prix David in 1923. It contained more of his finely crafted, opaline verse, along with some melancholy, disillusioned confessional poetry in which he recalled his difficults years as a teacher and translator—though he also celebrated his happiness with Geneviève. The sensual youth had become a faithful lover, the peacock a clumsy bird ('La revanche du paon').

In 1922 Morin became librarian and secretary of the École des Beaux-Arts, Montreal, where he remained until 1928. In this period he published an English translation of Louis Bertrand's *The private life of Louis XIV* (1920) and a French translation of Longfellow's *EVANGELINE* (1924). He also worked with the painter Suzor-Côté on a tourist brochure, *Héroisme d'antan, victoires d'aujourd'hui* (1923), that was commissioned by the Canadian National Railways. To make ends meet during the Depression, Morin became a court interpreter and almost ceased writing : from 1930 to 1940 he published only a few poems. By the end of the thirties he was almost destitute. He continued, however, to work as an interpreter and translator; but, after suffering from angina in 1944, both his health problems and his financial situation grew steadily worse. In 1952 Morin lost his wife, and the accumulation of calamities plunged him into a depression from which he never recovered. In 1957 a fire destroyed his possessions, including several valuable manuscripts.

Jean-Paul Plante edited a small anthology, *Paul Morin: textes choisis* (1958), and later Morin published a final collection, *Géronte et son miroir* (1960), which brought together work published in reviews and newspapers since 1920: some autobiographical free verse, sonnets, epigraphs, and an exotic bestiary, showing that Morin never entirely broke with the classical aesthetic and his early aristocratic period, though the ironic, mocking tone of these poems indicates his awareness of being anachronistic and in decline. Plante re-edited Morin's first two collections and had them published under the title *Oeuvres poétiques* (1961). Although these late publications placed Morin at the forefront of the Quebec literary scene in the sixties, they did not attract much interest. Consequently he died in almost total oblivion. A critical edition of Morin's poetry is being prepared for the Bibliothèque du Nouveau Monde.

See Victor Barbeau, 'Paul Morin', *Cahiers de l'Académie canadienne-française* 12 (1970); and Jean-Paul Morel de la Durantaye, 'Paul Morin, l'homme et l'oeuvre' (1975), a doctoral thesis for the Université d'Ottawa.

JACQUES MICHON

Moritz, Albert F. (b. 1947). Born in Warren, Ohio, he was educated at Marquette University, Milwaukee, Wisconsin (B.A., 1969; M.A., 1971), and has been a resident of Canada since he received his Ph.D. in 1975. In his early career he was a prolific journalist, film columnist, and copy writer. Since 1986 he has taught a variety of literature and creative-writing courses at the University of Toronto.

As a poet Moritz is in the tradition of the Romantics. His poems are often philosophically dense meditations on visionary states in a nature increasingly threatened by the mechanical world. His nine books of poetry include *Here* (1975); *Signs and certainties* (1979), *Between the root and the flower* (1982), *The visitation* (1983), *The ruined cottage* (1993), and *Mahoning* (1994). In the latter, named after the river of his birthplace in Ohio, the poet seeks out the spirit of nature in a landscape blighted by the steel industry; this long poem was inspired by William Carlos Williams' *Paterson*. Michael Cameron, in his Introduction to *Black orchid* (1981), wrote that 'Moritz's mental world has a haunted and haunting quality: the images are billiant and correct as if seen in too harsh sunlight.' This collection and *The tradition* (1986), *Song of fear* (1992), and *Phantoms in the ark* (1994) form an extended work, *Lucretius in the New World*. The poems continue the theme of seeking a pure natural spirit in a mechanical and industrialized world. A selected poems has appeared in Spanish translation, *Ciudad interior* (1993). Moritz has also translated several volumes from modern French and Spanish-American poetry, and especially the work of Ludwig ZELLER, with whom he has collaborated on several occasions. *Phantoms in the ark* includes Zeller's Dada-inspired collages, and an interview on the genesis of poems and art. Moritz has received several distinctions for his poetry, including selection in 1986 for the Princeton Series of Contemporary Poets, and a 1990-1 Guggenheim Fellowship and a 1993 Fellowship from the Ingram Merrill Foundation. In 1993-4 he was the Northrop FRYE Visting Lecturer in Poetry at the University of Toronto.

Moritz co-authored with his wife, Theresa Moritz, *Leacock: a biography* (1985), *The Pocket Canada: a guidebook* (1982), and *The Oxford illustrated literary guide to Canada* (1987).

GEOFF HANCOCK

Morton, W.L. (1908-80). Born in Gladstone, Manitoba, William Lewis Morton was educated at the University of Manitoba and Oxford University, where he was a Rhodes Scholar. He held various university teaching appointments in Manitoba until settling in the history department at the University of Manitoba in 1942, serving there until 1966 (from 1950 to 1964 as head). He then moved to Trent University, Peterborough, Ontario, as Master of Champlain College and Vanier Professor of History. After formally retiring from Trent in 1975, he returned to the University of Manitoba and continued to teach there until his death. Morton received many honours, including a Governor General's Award for *The Progressive Party in Canada* and the Tyrell Medal of the Royal Society in 1958. He was made an Officer of the Order of Canada in 1969.

Although his earliest historical research was on imperial themes (including an Oxford thesis on the Newfoundland fishery), Morton first found his métier in the study of his native district. Collaborating with his sister Margaret Morton Fahrni, he published *Third crossing: a history of the town and district of Gladstone in the Province of Manitoba* (1946), which celebrated the 'privileged settlers'—as L.H. Thomas called them—of British Protestant background who had established rural communities in the province. Gladstone's founders were devoted to family, to nation, and to Empire, loyalties Morton never questioned. In the late 1940s he published a number of articles that pointed to *The Progressive Party in Canada* (1950; rev. 1967), a book that was part of the working-out of the Morton family past: the author's father had been elected to the Manitoba legislature as a Progressive and the study is deeply sympathetic to both regional grievances and the positive reforms of the movement. By this time, however, Morton had broken with his family's traditional political allegiances and become an active supporter of the Conservative party; many of his later writings attempted to delineate a philosophy for Canadian Conservatism.

Beginning in the mid-1950s Morton entered upon a decade of prodigious output, which saw him publish most of his major works and gradually change from a regional to a national historian. In 1956 he published two vital studies on early Manitoba in the form of lengthy introductions to collections of documents. The introduction to *The London correspondence inward from Eden Colvile 1849-1852* for the Hudson's Bay Record Society revealed Morton's prose style—graceful yet analytical—at its best; the work is a masterpiece of delineation of the problems facing Red River in the transitional period from fur trade to agriculture and commerce. His introduction to *Alexander Begg's Red River journal and other papers relative to the Red River resistance of 1869-70* for the Champlain Society brilliantly synthesized the developments that led to the Riel uprising. Both these works have been unjustly neglected. Building upon his own research and that of others, Morton then produced what many regard as his finest book, *Manitoba: a history* (1957; rev. 1967), which has remained the model provincial history. Stronger on the Red River period than the post-1870 one, it illustrated again Morton's strong identification with the agrarian origins of the province, as well as his growing sense of Manitoba's cultural distinctiveness. (Morton later wrote another brilliant introduction to a related collection of documents: *Manitoba: the birth of a province*, 1965, for the Manitoba Record Society.) In 1957 he also published *One university: a history of the University of Manitoba, 1877-1952*, which—while inevitably institutional in approach—captured the flavour of the disparate educational and cultural traditions in Manitoba that Morton always celebrated.

After this outpouring of major writings on Manitoba, Morton turned to larger themes. An invitation to deliver a series of lectures in 1960 at the University of Wisconsin produced the bulk of *The Canadian identity* (1961; rev. 1972). In these lectures, and in his 1960 Canadian Historical Association presidential address, Morton sought to provide Canada with 'a self-definition of greater clarity and more ringing tone', emphasizing the nation's northern character, historical dependence, monarchical commitment, and special relationships with other states. These themes became the basis of his large-scale history *The kingdom of Canada* (1963), although they often tended to become lost in a morass of encyclopaedic and ill-digested detail. This work did not display Morton's abilities to best advantage, nor did *The critical years: the union of British North America, 1857-1873* (1964), a volume in the Canadian Centenary Series, of which he was co-editor with Donald CREIGHTON. More than other studies of the Confederation period, *The critical years* focused on the aspirations of the outlying regions, stressing the cultural (rather than political) duality of Canada, a major preoccupation of Morton's later works. When he came to deal with regions outside Manitoba, however, Morton self-confessedly had difficulty in achieving the same understanding he displayed about this native province. His study with Margaret MacLeod, *Cuthbert Grant of Grantown: Warden of the Plains of Red River* (1963; rev. 1973), marked a return to earlier interests, its great virtue being its sympathetic understanding of Métis aspirations. His most insightful analysis and most stylish—often lyrical—prose is to be found in his writings on the early history of Manitoba. Although Morton was far more than merely a regional historian, it was as a regional historian that he produced his most enduring and endearing work.

Morton was an essayist of considerable charm and ability. His shorter writings are accessible in A.B. McKillop, ed., *Contexts of Canada's past: selected essays of W.L. Morton* (1980).

See Carl BERGER, 'William Morton: the delicate balance of region and nation' in *The West and the nation: essays in honour of W.L. Morton* (1976), edited by Carl Berger and Ramsay COOK. J.M. BUMSTED

Mosaic (1967-). Founded by the University of Manitoba in Canada's centennial year, it was originally intended to be a quarterly for the study of literature and ideas; its name suggests the cultural concept associated with Canada as a 'mosaic' of different ethnic groups rather than the American 'melting pot'. In 1980, however, the magazine changed direction to become 'A journal for the interdisciplinary study of literature', edited by Dr Evelyn Hinz. One issue each year focuses on a topic of concern, such as multiculturalism, literature and the law, or relationships between literature and the other arts within a Canadian context.
GEOFF HANCOCK

Moses, Daniel David (b. 1952). A registered Delaware, the elder of two children of David Nelson Moses and Blanche Ruth Jamieson, he was born in Ohsweken, Ontario, on the Six Nations Reserve. He grew up on a farm there, attended elementary school on the reserve, and received his secondary education at Caledonia High School. He graduated with an Honours B.A. in general fine arts from York University, Toronto, and received a Master of Fine Arts degree in creative writing from the University of British Columbia, winning the department's prize for playwriting in 1977. His first collection of poetry, *Delicate bodies* (1980), was followed by *The white line* (1991). He has also published four plays: *The Dreaming Beauty*, a one-act play in twelve scenes, published in *Impulse*, vol. 15, 3 (1989), which was produced in a French version, 'Belle fille de l'Aurore', by the Théâtre du Jour of Saskatoon and toured Canada in 1991; *Coyote City* (1990), produced by Native Earth Performing Arts, Toronto, in 1988; *Almighty Voice and his wife* (1992), produced in 1991 by the Great Canadian Theatre Company, Ottawa, and in 1992 by the Native Earth Performing Arts, Toronto; and *The Indian medicine shows* (1995)—two linked one-act plays, *The moon and dead Indians* and *Angel of the medicine show*—produced by Theatre Passe Muraille, Toronto, in 1996. His *Big Buck City*, produced by the Cahoots Theatre Project at the Tarragon Theatre, Toronto, in 1991, has not yet been published. The following unproduced plays are available in script format: *Kyotopolis*, workshopped by the University of Toronto's Centre for Drama (1993); *City of shadows*, workshopped at the School of Dramatic Art, University of Windsor, in 1995; and *Brébeuf's ghost*, workshopped at the University of Windsor's School of Drama in 1996.

Although Moses has one foot planted in a world of tribal tradition and the other washed by the eddies and currents of mainstream Canada, he does not seem to be caught between the two worlds in a cultural divide. In his poetry he probes his world, trying to find meaning from it, but there is no outrage; the message is submerged in surreal images characterized by unembittered wit and trickster wisdom. His lyrical use of English seems to be inspired by the King James version of the Bible, Gerard Manley Hopkins, and e.e. cummings.

Moses' plays are boldly didactic, but the creative way he uses his Native background as material for his settings, characters, images, and humour is remarkable. For example, his theme in *The Indian medicine shows*, set in New Mexico in the late nineteenth century, draws upon contemporary Native thought about homosexuality, which implies that gay people have a dual nature, the male and the female inhabiting one body. According to Moses, the first of the two plays represents the destruction of the feminine; the second represents its resurrection. Add to these themes the fast-paced action, special lighting and sound effects typical of theatre in the television age, and the result is spectacular. Moses' plays are profoundly imagined, the work of a circumspect and strong intelligence.

Moses co-edited *An anthology of Canadian Native literature in English* (1992) and is currently playwright-in-residence at the University of Windsor, Ontario.

PENNY PETRONE

Moss, John. See CRITICISM IN ENGLISH: 5(d).

Mouawad, Wajdi. See DRAMA IN FRENCH 1981 TO 1996: 6.

Mountain and the valley*, *The (1952). Though drawing on themes, characters, and plot situations explored in his earlier stories, Ernest BUCKLER's first novel developed out of his desire to write about the Second World War as perceived through the psyche of a character who remains at home and suffers the frustration that 'everything was somewhere else'. This underlying idea, however, was ultimately subsumed within Buckler's powerful combination of certain literary paradigms that give the book its structure, and in part account for its strong and universal appeal. Most noticeably, it portrays the complex psychological development of its semi-autobiographical protagonist, David Canaan, from childhood to adulthood, and delineates the slow emergence of David's aspirations to be a writer within a hostile rural culture—a situation that Margaret ATWOOD (*SURVIVAL*, 1972) and others have suggested is a paradigm of the condition of the artist within early Canadian culture.

Using a frame formed by a Prologue and Epilogue that show the alienated and unfulfilled David on the day of his death, Buckler presents six intervening sections that portray David's childhood, his sexual awakening, and growing awareness of the world outside the rural valley in which he lives; the end of his childhood and his guilt for his girlfriend's death; the conflict with his father (never to be fully resolved); his realization that leaving the valley for another way of life cannot be, since 'he was neither one thing nor the other'; his discovery of the power of the written word; and the wartime crisis brought on by the visit of his friend and brother-in-law Toby, who comes from outside the valley and is serving in the navy. In addition, Buckler shows not only David's pain as his family disintegrates, but his growing psychological and cultural alienation. We are also made witness to the momentous changes affecting rural life in the period between the two world wars, the novel in part being a moving elegy on aspects of Canadian rural life now gone forever. Where the Prologue depicts David as about to climb the mountain to the south of his home, and so fulfil a life-long dream, the Epilogue describes the climb itself. David's visionary experience, preceding his death at the summit, reveals to him his destiny as a writer. That he dies before writing his promised book is a paradox, and that he is not the artist he believes himself to be is a profound irony, though not one that affects the uplifting mood of the climax—where we realize that this has been David's book. The novel is in the NEW CANADIAN LIBRARY, with an Afterword by Robert GIBBS.

See Alan R. Young, *Ernest Buckler* (1976), Robert Chambers, *Sinclair Ross and Ernest Buckler* (1978), and Claude Bissell, *Ernest Buckler remembered* (1989). ALAN R. YOUNG

Mouré, Erin (b. 1955). Born in Calgary, Alberta, she was educated at the universities of Calgary and British Columbia. She has been living and working in Montreal since 1984. Although often conscious of her western roots, the cultural, political, and social vibrancy of Montreal seems to have fired much of Mouré's work. She shares with other well-known women writers in that community, notably Nicole BROSSARD and Gail SCOTT, an intensely urban-edged appreciation of life's confusions, as well as a fascination with the ways identity is shaped by the double-play of memory and experience. Broadly speaking, one could say that the span of Mouré's poetry tracks the progress of a woman's move from west to east, from prairie grass to urban concrete, from heterosexual divorce to lesbian love. But such a sweeping biographical formulation ignores the intensely experiential quality of Mouré's work, which has almost always conveyed a high charge of immediacy, demanding from the reader an uncompromising commitment to the page. Her first book of poems, *Empire, York Street* (1979), was nominated for a Governor General's Award. A chapbook, *The whisky vigil* (1981), conveyed the pain of divorce, but not without a characteristic comingling of rage and laughter. *Wanted alive* (1983) marks a strengthening of voice, an affirmation of the power of language, and an acknowledgement of the daily grind of work informed by Mouré's own experience as a CN/VIA Rail employee. *Domestic fuel* (1985) activates a passionate awareness of the life of women, and a struggle with the paradox of creating a world of collective challenge through private voice. *Furious* (1988), a witty, fervent, and intellectually intense appreciation of material integration, and of memory, language, and desire ('Your blue sweater bunched up in the garden/& you in it, squatting over lettuce'), won a Governor General's Award. *WSW (West South West)* (1989) extends these preoccupations through a clever series of linked poems. A further poetic cycle, *Sheepish beauty, civilian love* (1992), continues to map the spaces where the personal and the political intersect. *Search procedures* (1996), Mouré's most complex set of lyrics, contends that 'the creation of experience is what the brain *does*', a succinct manifesto of Mouré's own writing principle. See also *The green world: selected poems* (1994).

NOREEN GOLFMAN

Mouvement littéraire de Québec, Le. When the itinerant parliament of United Canada (1840-67) moved to Quebec City in 1859, it brought with it an influx of educated persons with varied cultural interests who would be making their home in the old French capital until the new federal government moved to Ottawa in 1867. In May 1860 there arrived Abbé Henri-Raymond CASGRAIN, an energetic twenty-eight-year-old priest, newly returned from Europe, who, eager to make his mark in literature, set about stimulating literary activity among his new acquaintances.

About a dozen aspiring writers, most of them born in the 1820s, gathered from time to time in the back room of Octave CRÉMAZIE's bookstore on the Rue de la Fabrique, and elsewhere, to discuss literary matters and to encourage one another's efforts at writing. According to Casgrain's romanticized account in his memoirs, the group included two professors at the newly founded (1852) Université Laval, the historian Abbé Jean-Baptiste-Antoine Ferland and a medical doctor, François-Alexandre-Hubert LaRUE; the superintendent of public education for Lower Canada, Pierre-Joseph-Olivier CHAUVEAU; the founding editor of the Conservative newspaper *Le Courrier du Canada*, Dr Joseph-Charles TACHÉ; the government librarian and journalist Antoine GÉRIN-LAJOIE; the new French consul at Quebec City, Charles-Henri-Philippe Gauldrée-Boilleau; and Étienne

Parent, under-secretary for Lower Canada and a celebrated public lecturer on economic questions. Younger members of the group were Louis FRÉCHETTE, Léon-Pamphile LEMAY, and Alfred Garneau, son of the 'national historian', François-Xavier GARNEAU.

At its high point in the early 1860s the Mouvement littéraire de Québec was an impressive and largely successful effort by a handful of Quebec intellectuals to found a national literature in French which, although inspired by the French Romantic movement of thirty years before, was genuinely French-Canadian, both in its collective concerns and in its rejection of the 'dilettantism' and 'unhealthy realism' of contemporary French literature.

The first joint project was the founding of a monthly literary magazine, *Les SOIRÉES CANADIENNES* (1861-5); after a squabble over ownership and policy, three members of the editorial committee (Casgrain, La Rue, and Gérin-Lajoie) broke away and founded *Le FOYER CANADIEN* (1863-6). At the same time, book-length works by members of the group appeared. Gérin-Lajoie's colonization novel in two volumes, *JEAN RIVARD* (1862-4), and Philippe AUBERT DE GASPÉ's historical romance *Les ANCIENS CANADIENS* (1863) were the most durable of these. Others included Taché's *Forestiers et voyageurs* (1863); Ferland's two-volume *Cours d'histoire du Canada* (1861-5); and Casgrain's *Histoire de la Mère Marie de l'Incarnation* (1864), which was widely circulated in Europe. Quebec's first two collections of lyric poetry, Fréchette's *Mes loisirs* (1863) and Lemay's *Essais poétiques* (1865), also issued from the Mouvement, although their success was more limited.

After this shower of publications the Quebec City group gradually broke up. Crémazie had already gone into exile (1862) and Ferland died of a stroke in 1865. Taché and Gérin-Lajoie, appointed to federal government posts, moved to Ottawa; Chauveau became the new Province of Quebec's first prime minister; and Fréchette, disgusted by the Conservatives' confederation schemes, immigrated to the United States (1866-71). By the time Casgrain published an important essay on 'Le mouvement littéraire au Canada' in *Le foyer canadien* in Jan. 1866, the Quebec movement had already spent itself; the relocating of the national capital in Ottawa, and the increasing commercial importance of Montreal, condemned Quebec City to a declining role as a literary centre. The main features of this movement, however—its Romantic inspiration, its historical and patriotic orientation, and its profoundly Roman Catholic spirit—continued to dominate French-Canadian writing for more than a quarter of a century.

There is no history of the Mouvement, although several useful studies appear in the first volume of the collection 'Archives des lettres canadiennes' published by Fides.

DAVID M. HAYNE

Mowat, Farley (b. 1921). Born in Belleville, Ontario, he grew up in Saskatoon and was educated at the University of Toronto. After serving in the Hastings and Prince Edward Regiment during the Second World War, he spent two years in the Arctic before completing his degree and becoming a freelance writer. Mowat's first book, *People of the deer* (1952; rpr. 1975), caused much controversy by blaming government officials and missionaries for the plight of the caribou-hunting Ihalmiut Inuit, and was severely criticized for its obvious bias. Its sequel, *The desperate people* (1959), is more moderate and much better researched, but lacks the impact of the first book, which sincerely and eloquently conveys the writer's sympathy for, and understanding of, a people whose culture and very lives were threatened by contact with European civilization.

Mowat's involvement with the North is a recurring theme in his books. *Coppermine journey* (1958) is an edited version of the narrative of Samuel Hearne; and the works known as the Top of the World Trilogy—*Ordeal by ice* (1960), *The polar passion* (1967), and *Tundra* (1973)—are edited journals of both famous and unknown explorers, with a linking commentary by Mowat. *Siber: my discovery of Siberia* (1970) is an account of the author's trips to the Soviet Union in the late 1960s, and *Snow walker* (1975) is a collection of stories about Canadian Inuit. *Canada North* (1967), a pictorial book with text by Mowat, was followed by *Canada North now: the great betrayal* (1976), an examination of living conditions in the Arctic during the 1970s. Mowat felt in retrospect that he did the Inuit a great disservice, after his first book about them encouraged assimilation: 'the government saw to it that no Eskimo died of malnutrition and the medical services were improved and nobody froze to death. But they turned the whole of the Canadian Arctic into a charity ward.'

Mowat's sympathy for the dispossessed is evident in the texts he wrote for two pictorial books about Newfoundland. In *This rock within the sea: a heritage lost* (1968), John de

Visser's photographs are accompanied by Mowat's lament for a vanishing outport culture and a characteristic attack on Joseph Smallwood and the relocation program that wiped thousands of small communities off the map. In *The wake of the great sealers* (1973), David Blackwood's prints and drawings of nineteenth- and early twentieth-century seal fishing are complemented by a narrative in which Mowat draws on literature, folklore, and his own imagination to convey the heroism and tragedy of the sealing industry. Mowat's love affair with the people of Newfoundland, whom he described as 'the last primordial human beings left in our part of the world', was shattered after the events he describes in *A whale for the killing* (1972). His failed attempts to save the stranded whale and his account of the affair alienated him from the people he had been living among.

Mowat has been greatly criticized for his belief that one should never spoil a good story for lack of exaggeration. He has responded to a description of his work as 'subjective non-fiction' by saying that 'I try to tell the truth about the human condition without, on the one hand, letting the facts get in my way and, on the other hand, inventing situations which might suit my purpose.' Mowat's concern for endangered species has run the full gamut from Inuit to outporter, to whales and wolves. In 1983, Disney made *Never cry wolf* (1963) into a heartfelt and convincing film conveying the book's message that wolves are not vicious but a necessary and useful element in the natural cycle.

Sailing has always been important to Mowat and he has written vividly about it in several books. *The grey seas under* (1959) is a history of the Foundation Company's salvage tug, and *The serpent's coil* (1961) is another sea narrative about a daring rescue accomplished during a hurricane. *Westviking: the ancient Norse in Greenland and North America* (1965) is a popular account of Viking exploration and settlement; the liberties Mowat took in this work did not endear him to historians or archaeologists.

Mowat's broad definition of poetic licence has been more enthusiastically received in his novels for young people: *Lost in the barrens* (1956), earned Mowat a Governor General's Award and was later made into a television film. Its sequel, *Curse of the Viking grave* (1974), and *The black joke* (1962), about rum-running off the coast of Newfoundland, reflect the interests apparent in his books for adults. But his reflections on his own childhood in Saskatoon best display his abilities as a storyteller. Mutt, a canine of remarkable personality, is featured in *The dog who wouldn't be* (1957), along with Weep and Wol, who appear again in *Owls in the family* (1961). The same wonderful light humour is evident in *The boat who wouldn't float* (1969), for which he was given the LEACOCK Medal for Humour.

In the early 1980s, Mowat turned again to his own youth for inspiration with *And no birds sang* (1979), about his experience of the Second World War, which covers essentially the same subject-matter as *The regiment* (1955). The former work won in 1981 the Periodical Distributors of Canada award for best non-fiction book. It was followed by *The world of Farley Mowat* (1980). *The sea of slaughter* (1984), again winner of the Periodical Distributors of Canada award, marked a return to discussions about the environment.

Mowat has continued to produce critically acclaimed and financially successful books throughout the 1980s and 1990s, including *My discovery of America* (1985); *Virunga: the passion of Dian Fossey* (1987); *Woman in the mists: the story of Dian Fossey and the mountain gorillas of Africa* (1987); *The new founde land* (1989); *Rescue the earth* (1990); *My father's son* (1992); *Born naked* (1993); and *Aftermath* (1995).

He has received numerous awards, including the Canadian Library Association's Book of the Year Medal (1958); the Hans Christian Andersen International Award (1958); the Canadian Centennial Medal (1967); The Vicky Metcalfe Award (1970); the Mark Twain Award (USA, 1971); and the Queen Elizabeth II Jubilee Medal (1978). He has also been named Knight of Mark Twain (1980), Officer of the Order of Canada (1981), and Author of the Year (1988). In 1997 Mowat was featured on the CBC television program 'Life and Times'.

ROBIN GEDALOF McGRATH/TARA L. CURTIS

Multicultural writing in English. See CARIBBEAN-CANADIAN LITERATURE, ITALIAN-CANADIAN LITERATURE, SOUTH ASIAN-CANADIAN LITERATURE, UKRAINIAN-CANADIAN LITERATURE.

Multicultural writing in French. In recent decades some two hundred fresh voices have been making themselves heard in Quebec, expressing a new reality in which a variety of cultures, languages, and beliefs all contribute to the shaping of a different future. Some are of European stock: Régine ROBIN (France); Monique BOSCO (Austria); Alice PARIZEAU (Poland); Marco MICONE (Italy). An impressive contingent from Haiti includes Émile

OLLIVIER, Dany LAFERRIÈRE, Gérard ÉTIENNE, Marie-Célie Agnant, Stanley Péan, and Anthony PHELPS. Others are from Latin America, the Middle East, North and sub-Saharan Africa, and Asia: Sergio Kokis (Brazil), Nadine Ltaif (Egypt and Lebanon), Nadia Ghalem (Algeria), Maguy Kabamba (Zaire), Ying Chen (China). The list is long, and only a few writers can be mentioned here.

The actual process of becoming an immigrant, and the period of adapting to, and learning, a new culture, are frequently, though not always, at the heart of their writing. Régine Robin is very much preoccupied by a sense of foreignness, as in her novel *La Québécoite* (1983). The ambiguous title, with its possible play on the word *coi/coite* (silent or nonplussed), refers to the main character who, because she is an immigrant and unable to comprehend or participate fully in her new society, is not quite Québécoise; it may also be read, of course, as the name of the condition itself. Each in her own way, Monique Bosco (*Un amour maladroit*, 1961; *Babel-Opéra*, 1989) and Alice Parizeau (*Fuir*, 1963; *Blizzard sur Québec*, 1987) speaks to her experience of exile, war, culture, and religion. In *Babel-Opéra*, Bosco emphasizes the narrator's choice of freedom, the refusal to be confined by any god, in any language, in any country. Marco Micone (*Gens du silence*, 1982; *Addolorata*, 1984) frequently studies the fate of the immigrant in relation to class. The mix of languages used by the characters in the drama *Addolorata*—French, English, Italian, and Spanish—reveals their inability to master any tongue, their failure to work with words. Dany Laferrière, a master of good-humoured derision, often plays with clichés in relation to questions of race and sex in *Comment faire l'amour avec un nègre sans se fatiguer* (1985) and *Cette grenade dans la main du jeune nègre est-elle une arme ou un fruit?* (1993). Sergio Kokis (*Le pavillon des miroirs*, 1994; *Negão et Doralice*, 1995) holds up his adult life in Montreal as a mirror to the sounds, colours, and experiences that accompanied his coming of age in Brazil. Nadia Ghalem (*Les jardins de cristal*, 1981; *La villa Désir*, 1988) and Nadine Ltaif (*Entre les fleuves*, 1991; *Élégies du Levant*, 1995) are concerned with the meeting and merging of cultures, as the first of these last two titles in particular reveals. Maguy Kabamba (*La dette coloniale*, 1995) and Ying Chen (*La mémoire de l'eau*, 1992), from their divergent perspectives, stress the importance and perhaps the mythification of images of the West in the minds and hearts of those who are preparing to immigrate. All these writers, however, address other themes not linked to their status as immigrants, including love, death, writing, childhood, history, maternal love, and patriarchy. Most of them wish to be defined as writers without any prefix; their first and only country is writing itself.

The literary and cultural establishment of Quebec has begun to recognize and reward the contributions of those writers whose roots lie outside the province. Both Émile Ollivier (1992) and Sergio Kokis (1994) have won the Grand Prix du Livre de Montréal. Ying Chen was awarded the Prix Québec-Paris for the her third novel, *L'ingratitude* (1995). The highly respected journal *VOIX ET IMAGES* has published special issues on the writings of Monique Bosco (IX, 3), Naim KATTAN (XI, 1), and Anne-Marie ALONZO (XIX, 2). Born in Egypt, Alonzo is the author of many books, including narrative prose-poems (*Geste*, 1979; *Écoute, Sultane*, 1987), poetry (*Bleus de mine*, 1985), and letters (*L'immobile*, 1990). She is also the editor of the literary journal *Trois*, founder of the publishing firm Les Éditions Trois, and the organizer of an annual poetry festival in Laval, Quebec. Immobilized as the result of an accident, Alonzo, a modern-day Scheherazade, meditates not only on the various forms of female love but also on the mingling of history and memory, of personal and universal myth.

The influence of these writers in the Quebec context is undeniable. Readers are now confronted by unfamiliar sights and sounds: the evocation of orange groves (Mona Latif Ghattas, born in Egypt, in *Le double conte de l'exil*, 1990 and *Les lunes de miel*, 1996); the perfume of bougainvilleas (Ghalem); the aroma of freshly roasted coffee (Laferrière); the harmonies of Eastern music (Alonzo); the rhythms of the Americas (Kokis). But such writers also offer new visions, both of Quebec itself and of the rest of Canada, and reveal a different understanding of these societies and how they function: *Le double conte de l'exil* by Mona Latif Ghattas, for example, brings together the internal exile of a Canadian First Nations woman and the physical exile of an illegal immigrant. Because of these changes, even the vocabulary has undergone important modification as other words, other concepts, infiltrate the language.

In exchange, writers with Quebec roots find themselves responding to such challenges, bringing a new distance to their own self-concepts and widening their own horizons. The outside world—long the prerogative of neo-Québécois like Naim KATTAN

(Iraq), or such Haitian writers as Anthony Phelps, who immigrated in 1964 and is the author of a political novel, *Mémoire en colin-maillard* (1976), set in Haiti; Gérard Étienne (*Un ambassadeur macoute à Montreal*, 1979); Émile Ollivier; and Marie-Célie Agnant, author of *La dot de Sara* (1995), which moves with its characters, both willing and unwilling immigrants, between Haiti and Quebec—now informs and shapes the writing of a whole generation of all origins. The French-Canadian writers Jacques POULIN (*Volkswagen blues*, 1984) and Monique LaRUE (*Copies conformes*, 1989) set their novels partly, or totally, in the United States; their characters are no longer only French Canadians, and the question of uncertain identity is both feared and desired because the undefined may now be a dynamic component of one's own identity. Both, in different ways, show the importance of experiencing the feeling of being different, of being foreign, while simultaneously feeling at home. Hugues Corriveau's *La maison rouge au bord de la mer* (1992), which describes the sexual awakening of two adolescents, is set in North Africa and the characters are mainly Arabs. Corriveau, like other writers, no longer feels impelled to respond to a specific social, territorial, or nationalist demand. And writers feel freer to take liberties with their language. In *Le désert mauve* (1987), partly set in the United States, Nicole BROSSARD plays with the relationship between English and French. As borders/barriers fade into relative insignificance, as the writers incorporate into their consciousness a new and shifting population, the world at last becomes their oyster.

Thanks to the neo-Québécois writers, the way Quebec is perceived has also undergone transformation. As can be seen from the new plurilingual magazines mentioned below, cultures now meet and marry in Québécois literature, and there is emerging a new hybrid mix that, like many hybrids, is stronger than its component parts. For example, Stanley Péan (*L'emprise de la nuit*, 1993; *Zombi Blues*, 1993), whose family entered Canada from Haiti when he was one year old, paints a portrait of the Haitian community in Quebec in which the younger generation freely assumes its double identity as Haitian and Québécois, while simultaneously creating links with others from the mainstream or from other cultural communities. *L'emprise de la nuit* deals with gang wars, but at the centre is a black teen, searching for his roots, who is able to develop a close friendship with a white teenager. A different, chameleon culture is coming into existence.

Some Québécois writers, women in particular, have always been anxious to show that Quebec was never entirely homogeneous. In the early 1950s Charlotte Savary, to name but one, was already describing a world in which immigrants and their specific problems figure prominently. In *Isabelle de Fréneuse* (1950) she wrote of the gulf separating the official discourse that welcomed newcomers and the harsh reality that governed their lives, immigrants tending to be either token and exotic guests at dinner parties or, more often, servants. In neither case were they recognized as equals. She also showed that women immigrants had more difficulty than men in finding their own place in the new country.

In today's writing, however, the emphasis is different. Immigrants or neo-Québécois are no longer depicted as marginal or outside the mainstream: as in new physics, the centre itself has shifted. Gone are the traditional definitions based on name or place of birth. Quebec is no longer a space to be monopolized by a fixed group; it has become, on the contrary, not only the soil that produces the hybrid mix, but also an *agora* for all peoples, a space from which to write, to redefine oneself and the world.

Diverse origins may contribute to the emerging culture, but they are not necessarily significant in and of themselves. Désirée Szucsany, born of a Hungarian father, in *Beau soir pour mourir* (1993) portrays a world composed of young intellectuals and artists, unemployed and deprived of hope for their future. Only their names give any indication that not all have their family root in Quebec; any possible differences are subsumed under the common problems confronting the young.

While French is naturally the common language of the neo-Québécois writers, many have chosen to play on the interaction between French and the language(s) of their ancestors. Marco Micone includes Italian expressions and vocabulary in his writings. Anne-Marie Alonzo transcribes words of Arabic origin. Others publish in more than one language. The 'transcultural' magazine *Vice-Versa* (1989-) includes texts in English, French, and Italian; *Ruptures* (1992-), published in conjunction with various Latin-American countries, includes texts in Spanish, Portuguese, French, and English. Quebec space has become multilingual as well as multicultural.

These transformations have not always taken place smoothly. There are still those in Quebec who are unwilling to recognize writers of foreign descent and wish Quebec literature to reflect only past reality. This reaction is symptomatic of the growing pains that accompany any major change, but the change is under way, and cannot be reversed.

Immigrant writing in French is not, of course, confined to Quebec. A number of writers from the French-speaking world have settled in English-speaking Canada. They include Hédi Bouraoui (Tunisia) of Toronto, whose work, mainly poetry—such as *Éclate-Module* (1972), *Echosmos* (1986)—has met with wide recognition at home and abroad; Thuong Vuong-Riddick (Vietnam), now living in Vancouver, author of *Two shores/Deux rives* (1995), a book of bilingual verse recounting her experiences in Vietnam, France, and Canada; Annick Perrot-Bishop (Vietnam), living in Newfoundland, author of a number of short stories and poems as well as a collection of short texts belonging to the category of speculative fiction, *Les maisons de cristal. Récits* (1990); Pierre Léon (France), settled in Ontario, whose novel *Sur la piste des Jolicoeur* (1994) won the Prix Rabelais in France; Monique Genuist (France), now a resident of British Columbia (formerly of Saskatchewan), author of *Le cri du loon* (1993), in which a young Frenchwoman is confronted by the choice between her native France and Canada, and *C'était hier en Lorraine* (1993), which recalls the Second World War; Evelyne Voldeng (France), now living in Ottawa, author of a number of volumes of verse, including *Keranna* and *Mes Amérindes* (1995). One might also note the presence in Ontario of a writer from Germany, Marguerite Andersen, who has chosen to write in French and whose first novel, *De mémoire de femme* (1982), won the Prix des Jeunes Écrivains du *Journal de Montréal* in 1983.

For writers publishing in Quebec, see *Romanciers immigrés: biographies et oeuvres publiées au Québec entre 1970 et 1990* (1993) edited by Denise Helley and Anne Vassal.

MAÏR VERTHUY/LUCIE LEQUIN

Munro, Alice (b.1931). Born Alice Laidlaw in Wingham, southwestern Ontario, Alice Munro started writing in her early teens. After studying English for two years at the University of Western Ontario, she left to marry James Munro in 1951 and moved to Vancouver and then to Victoria, British Columbia, where her husband opened a bookstore. While helping with the business and raising three daughters, Munro began her writing career with short stories published in magazines—a well-known early story, 'The peace of Utrecht', appeared in Issue 15 (1960) of *The TAMARACK REVIEW*—and broadcast on the Canadian Broadcasting Corporation (CBC). Divorced in 1976, she returned to live in southwestern Ontario with her second husband, Gerald Fremlin; they divide their time between Clinton, Ont., and Comox, B.C.

In 1968 Munro published her first collection, *Dance of the happy shades* (translated as *Danse des ombres*, 1980), which won a Governor General's Award. *Lives of girls and women* (1971), which received the Canadian Booksellers Award, is Munro's only novel; but even here there is a story-like shape to the chapters. (The CBC filmed a dramatization of this work in 1973, with Munro's daughter Jenny in the main role.) A second collection of stories, *Something I've been meaning to tell you* (1974), was followed by *Who do you think you are?* (1978), a group of stories held together, like *Lives of girls and women*, by a single protagonist whose experiences are presented more or less chronologically. This book—which in the American and English editions is entitled *The beggar maid*, and in the German translation *Bettelmädchen* (1980)—also received a Governor General's Award. Some of the stories in *The moons of Jupiter* (1982) previously appeared in *The New Yorker*, where Munro has continued to publish much of her work. The book presents a variety of minutely observed characters dealing with familiar situations of everyday life. *The Progress of love* (1986), winner of a Governor General's Award, explores relationships between the sexes and among families, with an increasing focus on the nature of story-telling. The French translation of this book uses the title of one of its stories, *Miles City, Montana*. The stories in *Friend of my youth* (1990) focus almost exclusively on adult situations, in increasingly complex, multi-layered narratives. In *Open secrets* (1994) Munro pushes her fiction beyond realism, allowing for a variety of possible interpretations of 'truth'; the title is ironic, in that many of the stories do not fully reveal their secrets. Munro chose twenty-eight stories from the earlier books and arranged them in chronological order for her *Selected stories* (1996). She has written a number of television scripts, including one on Irish immigrants for the CBC series *The newcomers*; a story version, 'A better place than home', is included in the book based on the series, *The newcomers* (1979). Her television play 'How I met my husband' is published in the collection *The play's the thing* (1976), edited by Tony Gifford.

By a careful focus on the telling action or statement, Munro excels at revealing the surprising depth and complexity in the emotional lives of ordinary people. In the earlier books such revelations are often filtered through the consciousness of a girl who feels herself to be 'different' from those around her, usually because she is a secretly developing artist in an environment hostile to art. An imaginative girl's response to social pressures and the expectations of others, especially her mother, is the central subject of *Lives of girls and women*, as it is of many of the stories. The girl's steady desire to be like everyone else, to avoid mockery and humiliation, persists in many of Munro's adult women. Munro is *par excellence* the artist of social embarrassment and unease, capturing the obscure moments of shame that plague both child and adult. In the later stories her adult writer figures suffer from a sense of shame at being professional *voyeuses* who open secrets and lay things bare. Munro also depicts, with wry humour, the nuances of female response to what she sees as the pleasurable tyranny of sex. Del's mother in *Lives of girls and women* foresees a time when women will not assess their own worth only through their relationship with men; but in the life story of Rose in *Who do you think you are?* Munro shows how difficult it is for even the most competent women to break that 'connection'. Without a man Rose feels undefined; an uncertain affair with a distant married man can validate her identity. Munro continues to explore this theme in several of the stories in *The moons of Jupiter*. The title story celebrates the father when a daughter must come to terms with his approaching death. (Munro's own father, shortly before his death, wrote a novel entitled *The MacGregors: a novel of an Ontario pioneer family*, 1979.) Although she creates accurate portraits of men, particularly in this volume, Munro only occasionally writes from a male point of view; her chief interest is in the lives of girls and women and in their influence on one another. The mother-daughter relationship is the central female connection; in the title story of *Friend of my youth*, the narrator accepts the fact that she will never fully understand or accurately describe her mother, never exorcize her guilt about their mutual past. In several of the later stories the narrator is herself a mother, painfully aware of the difficulty of communication across the generations. From her earliest stories, Munro has portrayed characters who have an interest in story-telling, whether as an art form or as an instinctive shaping of reality to make it understandable, bearable, or simply more dramatic. In the later work, especially in *Open secrets*, she experiments with an apparent realism that nevertheless moves to an area where seemingly contradictory interpretations are possible. Her narrators often seem puzzled by what they are telling; their non-linear accounts give the illusion of several stories being told at once, story lying behind or beside story. Letters, diaries, dreams, poems are devices to explore the mystery of communication, underscoring the notion that we can never know what 'really' happened, never fully understand other people or even ourselves. The title story in *Open secrets* highlights the difficulty of 'getting it all', in that some of the characters simply cannot tell their stories in words; gestures are scrutinized for meaning, in a reprise of the epiphanic moment at the end of *Lives of girls and women*.

Munro has set some of her stories in British Columbia, Toronto, and elsewhere—one even as far afield as Albania—but it is with rural southwestern Ontario that she is most closely identified. She captures the look and atmosphere of small towns that resemble her birthplace, of the ramshackle dwellings at their outskirts and the rundown farms nearby. Reality is heightened with such clarity of remembered detail that it is, in Munro's words, 'not real but true'. (Her techniques of photographic realism are in some respects like those of two writers of the American South whose work she admires, James Agee and Eudora Welty.) She achieves her vivid re-creations of place and people by complete detailing of all that the senses might register in a room, a street or on a person; she often lists objects, or qualifies a noun with a catalogue of adjectives that usually contains at least one surprising and satisfying oddity or paradox. It is characteristic of Munro's wit that a single word will strike home forcefully because it is both unexpected and yet completely right. Quasi-conversational repetition gives the appearance of artlessness to the prose, making the narrative seem spontaneous and immediate.

Some of the many critical articles on Munro's work are collected in L.K. MacEndrick, ed., *Probable fictions: Alice Munro's narrative acts* (1983) and J. Miller, ed., *The art of Alice Munro: saying the unsayable* (1984), both of which contain interviews with the author. Eleanor Wachtel's interview with Munro is included in *The BRICK reader* (1991), edited by Linda SPALDING and Michael ONDAATJE. Recent books on Munro include I. de Papp Carrington's *Controlling the uncontrollable* (1989), B.J. Rasporich's *Dance of the sexes* (1990), M. Redekop's *Mothers and other clowns* (1992), James Carscallen's *The other country* (1993), and Ajay Heble's *The tumble of reason: Alice Munro's discourse of absence* (1994).

JOAN COLDWELL

Munsch, Robert (b. 1945). He was born in Pittsburg, Pennsylvania, USA, as a middle child in a family of nine children. He devoted seven years of study towards becoming a Jesuit priest, and taking a B.A. in history, an M.A. in anthropology, and an M.Ed. in early childhood education. Later, employed at the University of Guelph, Ontario, in the Laboratory Preschool, at the urging of his department Chair he submitted for publication some of the stories he had made up and told to children. Now a full-time writer and oral performer based in Guelph, Munsch has sold over twenty million books in North America. His storytelling performances are unique in that he often selects a child and makes up a story from details he elicits on the spot. Children like the respect he shows them in stories: they always cope successfully when events spin out of control. His stories usually contain repeated motifs, extraordinary vocal sound effects, surprise turns of event, humour that appeals to children, and something he calls an 'adult twist'. His first two books—*Mud puddle* (1979) and *The dark* (1979)—were followed by the immensely popular *The paper bag princess* (1980), a feminist fairy-tale retelling. His best-selling book, *Love you forever* (1986), which has sold over ten million copies and was on the *New York Times*' bestseller list of children's books, has also been controversial. Other books include *Show and tell* (1991) and *Get me another one* (1992). By early 1997 his twenty-eight titles had appeared as tapes, filmstrips, movies, and plays, and been translated into French, Spanish, Chinese, Hebrew, German, Armenian, Danish, Dutch, Swedish, and Inuktituut.

MARY HENLEY RUBIO

Murray, John Clark (1836-1917). Born at Thread and Tannahill, near Paisley, Scotland, he was educated in religion and philosophy at Edinburgh, Scotland, and Heidelberg and Göttingen, Germany. In 1862 he came to Canada to teach at Queen's University, Kingston. Ten years later he moved to McGill University, Montreal, where he remained until his retirement. His *Outline of Sir William Hamilton's philosophy* (Boston, 1870) is a faithful presentation of the beliefs of his teacher at Edinburgh, but Murray had already begun to react against the 'common sense realism' of Hamilton. He emphasized the rational order and ultimate unity of reality in a manner closer to Hegel and the British idealists, and akin to that of his successor at Queen's, John WATSON. His theory is outlined in his two works on philosophical psychology: *Handbook of psychology* (London, 1885) and *Introduction to psychology* (1904), in which Murray denied the possibility of a mechanical explanation of the human mind, argued that the concept of personality was central to psychology, and laid some of the foundations of his theory of value. His books were widely translated.

Murray's *Industrial kingdom of God*—probably written in 1887, but not published until 1982—advances proposals for economic reform that envisage chiefly a co-operative society and a system for the public determination of certain wages and prices. Murray read and commented on Marx and Henry George, but the main inspiration for this book was evidently the co-operative movement and his belief that Christianity provided the only basis for a just society of free human beings. Though he frequently quoted scripture in his social commentaries, he tried to develop his ethical theory from an analysis of the concept of person; he praised Christianity chiefly for having made the concept of person central to Western thought. Murray fought early, long, and hard for the education of women. His writings on this subject, and his defence of Canadian nationhood, are contained in letters, occasional newspaper and magazine articles, and handwritten notes.

The basis of Murray's moral theory can be found in his *Introduction to ethics* (London, 1891) and *Handbook of Christian ethics* (Edinburgh, 1908), as well as in his social-gospel novel *He that had received the five talents* (1904), which undoubtedly helped to make popular the reformist views of Christianity that figured in other social-gospel novels. Murray also published a volume of verse, *The ballads and songs of Scotland* (London, 1874).

LESLIE ARMOUR, ELIZABETH TROTT

Murrell, John (b. 1945). Born in Lubbock, Texas, he received a B.F.A. from Southwestern University, Texas (1966), after which he came to Canada and studied at the University of Calgary (B.Ed., 1969). Murrell has been associated with a number of major Canadian theatres, including Alberta Theatre Projects, Calgary, as playwright in residence (1975-6); the Stratford Festival as an associate director (1977-8); Theatre Calgary as a dramaturge (1981-2), and the Banff Centre School of Fine Arts Playwrights Colony as Head (1986). From 1988 to 1992 he was the Head of the CANADA COUNCIL's Theatre Section.

Murrell is one of Canada's most acclaimed and widely produced playwrights. In 1975 he won the Clifford E. Lee Playwriting Award for *Power in the blood*, about a woman evangelist. The following year, Alberta Theatre Projects produced *A great noise, a great light*, which is set in 1937 and deals with the politician William Aberhart. This play marks the beginning of Murrell's recurring theatrical explorations of historical figures. Other early plays, which were produced, include *Haydn's head* (1973), *Teaser* (1975, with Kenneth Dyba), and *Arena* (1975).

Murrell received international acclaim for *Memoir* (1978), which was produced at the Guelph Spring Festival (1977) in a production that starred the late Irish actor Siobhan McKenna as Sarah Bernhardt. The play is starkly simple, a depiction of the reminiscences of the aging Bernhardt, who is attended by the play's only other character, her faithful secretary and servant Pitou, played in the original production by Gerard Parkes. The two actors reprised their roles in Dublin (1977) and London (1978). *Memoir* has been produced throughout Canada and was adapted for a CBC radio production (1980). It has also been translated into a number of languages, and published in German (1979) and French (1979). An abridged French version, *Sarah et le cri de la langouste*, enjoyed a run of three years in Paris before being featured in the 1984 Edinburgh Festival.

The success of *Memoir* is evidence of Murrell's gift for precise, elegant dialogue that reveals nuances of character with an often understated, poignant humour. These qualities are apparent in *Waiting for the parade* (1980), a study of five women living in Calgary during the Second World War. In *Farther west* (1986), May, a prostitute, moves 'farther west' in an attempt to escape the social and sexual constraints imposed by men who fall in love with her and demand that she settle into domesticity with them. Like many of Murrell's plays, *Farther west* deals with the character's fear of being constrained, which the playwright explores through spatial metaphors. When May finally reaches the Pacific Ocean she meets her death. In *Memoir* the mobility of the aging Bernhardt is impaired by her amputated leg, but she will not be confined to a wheelchair, as if her spirit refuses to be contained. In *New world* (1986) the three Rennie siblings gather at the edge of Canada, on the southwest coast of Vancouver Island, which serves as a metaphor for the edge of the world. On a single day—in contrast to the years during which the action of *Farther west* unfolds—the three speak of their yearnings, which amount finally to a longing for stability.

Democracy (1992) depicts an exchange between Ralph Waldo Emerson and Walt Whitman, who is attending two young men, Pete and Jimmy. Set during a day spent by the characters at the side of a pond—evocative of Waldon Pond—Whitman's idealism seems to flourish only in this natural idyll, removed from the violence and inhumanity of daily life.

Murrell admits to an admiration for artists whose work has nourished him. Not surprisingly, two of his other plays, *October* and *Faraway nearby* (both produced by Tarragon Theatre, the former in 1988, the latter in 1995), depict artists. *October* offers an encounter between Eleonora Duse and Isadora Duncan, and *Faraway nearby* portrays the last year of the reclusive Georgia O'Keeffe and her friendship with the much younger artist, Juan Hamilton. Murrell's admiration of artists—and his linguistic facility, with fluency in French and Italian—has resulted in his translation of many works, including Machiavelli's *Mandragola*, Racine's *Bajazet*, and Sardou's *Divorçons*. He has also translated Chekhov's *Uncle Vanya* and *The seagull*, Ibsen's *The master builder*, and Sophocles' *Oedipus Rex*.

ANN WILSON

Musgrave, Susan (b.1951). Born in California of Canadian parents, she is the fourth great granddaughter of Sir Anthony Musgrave, governor of the Crown colony of British Columbia, 1869-71. Musgrave is one of the foremost and most popular poets of her generation.

Musgrave left school at fourteen, and was briefly treated in a psychiatric ward for drugs and depression. Mentored by Robin SKELTON, whom she met as babysitter of his children, she had poems published in *The MALAHAT REVIEW* at sixteen. She travelled widely, living in California (1967-9); Ireland (1970-2); and her 'spiritual home', the Queen Charlotte Islands of B.C. (1972-4). She now lives in Sidney, B.C.

Musgrave had a flamboyant and notorious public personal life. Her three husbands include a lawyer; one of his clients, a drug dealer; and the third a convicted bank robber, Stephen Reid, author of *Jackrabbit parole* (1988), whom she met through a correspondence writing course; their marriage was nationally televised from a maximum-security prison. Discreet nude photos of her have appeared in a *Saturday Night* profile. Up to mid-career, then, Musgrave's career can best be seen in three phases: the gifted and troubled 'sea-witch' of adolescence; the *femme fatale*; and earthbound mother and wife.

Musgrave's first poetry collection, *Songs of the sea-witch* (1970), published when she was eighteen, introduced many of her subsequent themes: roots, witches, fire, water, eroticism, and death. The landscape of the West Coast permeates her writing. Her poetic persona often searches for an identity against a mythological landscape of animated rocks and water. Her sensibilities incline towards both the contemporary and the Aboriginal; her response to the modern urban world is either outrage or witty denunciation, though her often beautiful lyrics can slip into vagueness. *Entrance of the celebrant* (1972) celebrates the will of the imagination in brooding, mystical, ritualistic poems. *Grave-dirt and selected strawberries* (1973) includes a poetic sequence entitled 'Kiskatinaw songs', written in collaboration with Seán VIRGO during a period of homesickness in Cambridge, England. Originally published as a pamphlet, the poems were unsuccessful until they were republished under the Amerindian pseudonym 'Moses Bruce'. The 'strawberry poems' were inspired by a road sign. While most poets prefer a selected poems, Musgrave jokingly published *Selected strawberries* (1973), a book-length satire with gleanings from *The golden bough*, *Everything you always wanted to know about sex*, the journals of Anaïs Nin, *The Guinness book of records*, cookbooks, and self-help manuals. Beneath this satirical mythology, the strawberry emerges as a likeable main character. The collection, with minor revisions, was republished as *Selected strawberries and other poems* (1977), which includes *Entrance of the celebrant.*

The impstone (1976) is a transitional book. More intimate, more approachable, more restrained and mature, Musgrave drew inspiration from the imp, the animal that helps a witch cast spells. These fifty-three Gothic poems employ strong, sometimes violent images. Her evocative and suggestive vocabulary of earth, stone, water, evil, witches, ghosts, moon, shadows, graves, dreams, night, and animals is utilized in a ritualistic manner to evoke an animistic landscape. Several of the poems deal with the problems of relationships. With mature poems like 'Fishing on a snowy evening', Musgrave moved from the sea-witch of youth to a more confident voice. In *Becky Swann's book* (1977), reprinted in *A man to marry, a man to bury* (1979), familiar images and simple detail move quickly to a Dantesque moral vision in a Canadian setting, with scathing commentary on contemporary moral issues. The first poems are some of the most haunting love poems in Canadian letters, but they quickly move into a depressing world of loveless marriage, breakup, bizarre murder, degenerate ways among Native people, deformity, abortion, and death. Musgrave counterbalances these with poems of genuine friendship (especially with the poet Marilyn BOWERING), caring, love, and acceptance in a carefully constructed sequence, 'Salmonberry Road', which explores friendship from delight to murderous fantasy to profound loss. *Tarts and muggers* (1982)—mostly a selection from previous books—relies on shock (rats on a face or dead-animal imagery) that produce a vision of an empty, hostile, loveless world. The best poem, 'Woodcutter, river God, and I', is a classic of mythological understatement. Musgrave's tenth collection, *Cocktails at the mausoleum* (1985), deals with the psyche, relationships, and her response to places where she has lived. A powerful awareness of being alone is countered with a tinge of hope in a deep need to love another person. She also includes a deeply felt Queen Charlotte Island poem, 'Requiem for Talunkwun Island', a lament for the loss of the forest to loggers and of a simple primordial life. *The embalmer's art* (1991) is a well-chosen selection from collections published between 1970 and 1991, with half a dozen new poems.

Musgrave has published several collections in limited editions, including *Skuld* (1971), *Birthstone* (1972), *Equinox* (1973), *King* (1973), *Two poems* (1975), and the award-winning *In the small hours of the rain* (1991). She has also published three children's books: *Gullband* (1974), which includes thirty-two poems about a cat, a frog, and a lizard; *Hag head* (1980), a Hallowe'en story about children who are followed by demons; and *Kestrel and Leonardo* (1990).

Musgrave's interest in West Coast mythologies, Frazerian symbolism, militant feminism, and the mysterious is also evident in her first novel (which she calls an apprentice work), *The charcoal burners* (1980), a modern horror story and a study in depravity, in which Musgrave's black humour carries Margaret ATWOOD's edible-woman thesis to the extremes of violent and bloody death, bestiality, and cannibalism. Matty, a sociologist married to an Amerindian living in East Oyster, B.C., is led by her lover, Christian Hawker, into the wilderness, where she meets a band of feminist crazies from California who live off the land and practise a ritualistic religion based on ancient fertility rites and radical feminist ideology. Nearby live the charcoal burners, twentieth-century dropouts led by a Mansonesque madman known as the Chela. A powerful and original first novel, it has a serious structural flaw, with a naturalistic first half clumsily connected to a bizarre, almost surreal conclusion. Musgrave's second novel, *The dancing chicken* (1987), which describes the degenerate life of a lawyer and his emotionally crippled family, was savagely reviewed and dismissed as clichéd and stilted, though it is a funny comedy of manners.

Behind Musgrave's intelligence and often dark tone, there is charm and humour that surface in her journalism. Two collections of her insightful, practical, entertaining newspaper and magazine articles, *Great Musgrave* (1989) and *Musgrave Landing: musings on the writing life* (1994), present her always enjoyable, sometimes sarcastic thoughts on the often difficult life of a writer. Described in the first book are several love affairs and her wedding in prison. Musgrave edited a celebration anthology, *Because you loved being a stranger* (1995), in honour of Patrick LANE's fifty-fifth birthday.

Musgrave has discussed her work in *CANADIAN FICTION MAGAZINE* 30/31 (1979). Her interest in myth, magic, and shamanism are explored by Sharon McMillan in *The MALAHAT REVIEW* 45 (1978); she is the subject of an article by Dennis Brown in *CANADIAN LITERATURE* 79 (Winter 1978). Alan Twigg interviewed her in *For openers* (1981) and *Strong voices* (1988). GEOFF HANCOCK

Myers, Martin. See NOVELS IN ENGLISH 1960 TO 1982: OTHER TALENTS, OTHER WORKS: 1.

Mysterious stranger, The. See Walter BATES.

Mystery and crime. Canada has no real tradition in the genre of mystery and crime fiction. Derrick Murdoch, longtime reviewer of spy novels and crime fiction for the Toronto *Globe and Mail*, wrote in 1981 that 'for nearly half a century—roughly, say, from the dawn of Sherlock Holmes until the twilight of Sam Spade—the only notable contribution from Canadians came from expatriates.' In the preface to his anthology *Maddened by mystery: a casebook of Canadian detective fiction* (1982)—the title was suggested by Stephen LEACOCK's spoof of Sherlock Holmes, 'Maddened by mystery, or the defective detective', in *Nonsense novels*—Michael Richardson remarked that only two of its thirteen stories were set in Canada and one of those was by a non-Canadian. He had discovered that expatriate Canadian mystery writers, who were contributing to popular magazines in Britain and the United States, felt little compulsion to draw upon their Canadian background.

One of the authors represented in *Maddened by mystery* was Grant ALLEN, who was born in Kingston, Ontario, but lived in England for most of his adult life. His *An African millionaire* (London and New York, 1897)—republished in the United States, England, and Canada in 1980—is an amusing and cynical study of hypocrisy and fraud in late-Victorian England and America, with an attractive English villain, Colonel Cuthbert Clay. It managed the sea change to the 1980s remarkably well—though perhaps only for readers who have some historical interest in mystery fiction. Another Canadian expatriate, Frank L. PACKARD, who was born in Montreal and moved to the United States, created another attractive rogue for a series of books beginning with *The adventures of Jimmy Dale, detective* (1917). Toronto-born Vincent Starrett was the creator of an American detective, Jimmie Lavender (*The casebook of Jimmie Lavender*, 1944), and the prolific Arthur STRINGER worked both sides of the border with detective stories set in the United States, beginning with *The wire tappers* (1906), and crime fiction about the Canadian North, beginning with *Empty hands* (1924). Robert BARR, born in Glasgow but living in Canada until 1881, when he moved to England, began a prolific writing career there. He was known particularly as a writer of detective stories, some of which were collected in *The triumphs of Eugène Valmont* (1906), featuring a humorous French detective who worked in a cold and foggy England (several decades before Agatha Christie introduced her Hercule Poirot).

In the 1940s Margaret MILLAR began writing remarkable psychological mystery novels set in Toronto and Georgian Bay, Ontario. More than twenty were published, beginning with *The devil loves me* (1941) and concluding with *Banshee* (1983). At the University of Toronto she met her future husband, Kenneth Millar (1915-83), who was born near San Francisco and educated in Canada. They moved to California, where he began a very successful career as a writer of crime fiction under the pen-name Ross Macdonald, creating the California private eye Lew Archer and becoming the much-admired successor to Dashiell Hammett and Raymond Chandler.

In Montreal John BUELL began his writing career with *The pyx* (1959), which was made into a film that enjoyed some critical but no great popular success. His second novel, *Four days* (1962), was followed by two more titles in the 1970s. Buell appeared to be striving for 'entertainments' of Graham Greene quality, and his first two books attracted the attention of the American critic Edmund Wilson (who was not usually interested in thrillers); but

Buell's career never really developed as might have been expected. Another promising mystery writer, Toronto-born John Norman Harris, died unexpectedly soon after publishing *The weird world of Wes Beattie* (1963), about the ne'er-do-well member of an old Toronto family accused of murdering his uncle. Written in the civilized manner of English mystery fiction from between the wars, it captures well the atmosphere of Toronto in the 1950s, but the plot is too elaborate and the book, while amusing, is too wordy.

In the 1970s Hugh GARNER undertook a new and somewhat surprising departure in his writing when he published the first of three police procedural novels. *The sin sniper* (1970), whose central character is Inspector Walter McDumont of the Toronto Police Force, is the most successful of these books. It is set in an area of downtown Toronto inhabited by petty criminals, prostitutes, homosexuals, and greasy-spoon restaurants. (A film based on it, *Stone cold dead*, released in 1980, preserved the locale but altered the story radically.) In *Death in Don Mills* (1975) and *Murder has your number* (1978) Garner seemed to have lost interest in the genre, allowing McDumont to become increasingly garrulous. However, he was at work on a fourth police novel when he died in 1979: *Don't deal five deuces* (1992) was completed by Paul Stuewe—who wrote *The dark embrace* (1996) to end the series.

So many thrillers and mystery novels were published in Canada after the early 1970s that the problem of selection is difficult. There are still one or two expatriates, the most interesting and mysterious of them being Donald MacKenzie, who published nearly thirty crime novels in England. Canadians turn up as secondary characters in some of them, though they are mainly about the criminal world of London. His skimpy biography identifies him as Canadian, and notes that he spent time in prison.

Particularly among writers of thrillers, the setting is quite often foreign; or Canada becomes a part of international espionage operations. James Henderson's highly professional *Copperhead* (1971) takes place in Canada and the Caribbean. The violent, Bond-like *Dreadlock* (1981), by 'Lew Anthony' (the pen-name of Robert Miller and William Marshall), which was supposed to be the first in a series of spy thrillers, also uses Canada and the Caribbean as backgrounds. The team of Gordon Pape and Tony Aspler uses the Tchaikovsky International Music Competition in Moscow as the scene in their third and most successful thriller, *The music wars* (1982).

Some of our best writers of spy novels have come from abroad to live in Canada. Chris SCOTT was born in Hull, England, and his complex thriller, *To catch a spy* (1978), traces the life story of an Englishman who turns up in Moscow as an apparent traitor and then mysteriously dies there. Ian McLachlan, the author of *The seventh hexagram* (1976), a richly textured political thriller set in Hong Kong, was born in London, England, and now teaches at Trent University in Peterborough, Ontario. More prolific than these writers is Shaun Herron, who was born in Northern Ireland, served in the Republican Army during the Spanish Civil War, and has been a broadcaster and controversial United Church minister and an editorial writer and columnist for the Winnipeg *Free Press*. It was in Winnipeg that Herron wrote *Miro* (1969), the first of half-a-dozen sophisticated thrillers. The character Miro was described in the *Toronto Star* as 'the personification of that burnt-out case, the cold war spy for whom betrayal has become a way of life, existing on an ambiguous plane where neither side has a moral exclusive'. A long section of *Miro* takes place in Quebec; Herron's later books moved on to England, Ireland, and Spain. William DEVERELL's exuberant thriller *High crimes* (1981), about the international drug trade, encompasses a variety of surroundings: Toronto and Ottawa, Colombia, Miami, and Newfoundland.

Canadian-born writers of mystery novels seem quite homey after consideration of the international scope of the thrillers. Ellen GODFREY's two novels, *The case of the cold murderer* (1976) and *Murder among the well-to-do* (1977), have an exotic amateur sleuth—Rebecca Rosenthal, in her seventies, anthropologist, survivor of the Holocaust—but in all other respects both are solidly grounded in Toronto. *The case of the cold murderer* has some interest as a *roman à clef* for those who know something about small-press publishing in Canada. In both books not only is Rebecca Rosenthal not very interesting, despite her background; she is an irritating meddler. But the two novels led to a third and much better book by Godfrey: *By reason of doubt* (1981), a true-crime investigation of the murder trial in Switzerland of Professor Cyril Belshaw of the University of British Columbia.

Marion Rippon, who lives in Victoria, British Columbia, published several books, including *The hand of Solange* (1969) and *Lucien's tomb* (1979), about a retired French gendarme, Maurice Ygrec. For some reason her novels, which have a certain Simenon quality and are published in New York, have attracted little attention in Canada.

While the early 1970s produced no significant centre of Canadian crimewriting, there were isolated pockets of activity. Niagara-on-the-Lake had two resident writers. Sara Bowen-Judd (1922-85) was born in England but launched her writing career when she immigrated to Canada in 1958. Writing as Sara Woods she published *Bloody instructions* (1962) and became well known in the USA and the UK for a series of more than forty family-based legal mysteries starring British barrister Antony Maitland. J. Robert Janes, who published young people's books and suspense fiction during this period, maintained a steady, if generally unacclaimed, output. He finally achieved international recognition in 1992 with his Second World War detective series set in Occupied France, featuring French policeman Jean-Louis St-Cyr and Gestapo investigator Hermann Kohler.

Two Toronto writers were working in this period, but both seemingly have abandoned mysteries. John Reeves, who created the Toronto police detective duo of Coggin and Sump in the quirky *Murder by microphone* (1978), wrote three further episodes of their adventures in the next decade that never seemed to catch on outside Canada. Similarly, L.A. Morse, the writer of tough, private-eye detective fiction, won an Edgar from the Mystery Writers of America for his first book, *The old dick* (1980). *An old-fashioned mystery* (1983), his hilarious send-up of the classic crime novel, written under the pseudonym 'Runa Fairleigh', is a classic of the genre, but he has written nothing in the crime genre since *Sleaze* (1985)

In the United States expatriate Canadian Charlotte McLeod began to establish a reputation with three humorous, cosy mystery series set in New England. They variously featured Peter Shandy and the campus of Balaclava Agricultural College starting with *Rest you merry* (1978); Boston art-scene detectives Sarah Kelling and Max Bittersohn beginning with *The family vault* (1979); and (under the pseudonym 'Alisa Craig') the Grub and Stakers Garden Club beginning with *The grub and stakers move a mountain* (1981). McLeod's sole Canadian-based series (also written as Alisa Craig) started in 1981 with *A pint of murder* and was set in New Brunswick; it featured Mountie sleuth Madoc Rhys.

ROBERT WEAVER/JOHN NORTH

1980 to 1996. The late 1970s and early 1980s saw Canada join in a worldwide surge of unparalleled popularity for crime fiction. The genre, always popular with book buyers and library users, had at last become a respectable part of the Canadian literary landscape. During this boom publishers eagerly sought mystery and crime titles, new crime-writers appeared, and the first specialist bookstore, Sleuth of Baker Street, opened in Toronto in 1979.

The first significant and enduring modern Canadian sleuth created by a resident Canadian author was Howard ENGEL's Benny Cooperman (*The suicide murders*, 1980), an eminently Canadian Jewish private eye operating from the fictional town of Grantham (St Catharine's, Ontario). The Cooperman novels take massive liberties with the private-eye genre (and Jewish family myth), but each is a complete, competent, and usually witty mystery. In 1983, hot on the heels of Cooperman, came two police detectives also destined for long-lasting series. Eric WRIGHT created Charlie Salter, a Toronto police inspector who first appeared in *The night the gods smiled* (1983), while for *Dead in the water* (1983)—and nine later novels—Ted WOOD dreamed up Reid Bennett and his police dog Sam, who made up the entire police presence of Murphy's Harbour, a fictional town set in the Kawartha area of Ontario.

By 1982 there were enough crime and mystery writers resident and working in Canada (mostly in the Toronto area) to found the Crime Writers of Canada—of which, by late 1996, there were 180 members (mostly working writers) spread across the country from Vancouver Island to the Maritimes. The CWC had the twin benefits of providing prospective crime-writers with a peer group and introducing the Arthur Ellis Awards (named for the *nom-de-travail* of Canada's official hangman) to recognize excellence for each year's best novel, best first novel, short story, and non-fiction. While two locations (Vancouver/Victoria and Toronto) now have enough members to support local chapters, isolated members between and beyond these points participate through electronic mail.

The national and international success of the trail-blazing 'big three' of Engel, Wright, and Wood spurred a second wave of Canadian crime-writers producing first novels. Some, such as Nora Kelly (*In the shadow of kings*, 1986), Anna Porter (*Hidden agenda*, 1986), and Ellen GODFREY (*Murder behind locked doors*, 1988), had a relatively limited published output despite general critical acclaim; while others—such as L.R. WRIGHT, Medora SALE, Peter ROBINSON, Laurence GOUGH, John

BRADY, John Lawrence Reynolds, Alison GORDON, Eve Zaremba, and Edward PHILLIPS—continued to publish and gained an international readership.

The female protagonists of four of the new writers (all women) encroached on the male-dominated fictional turf of southern Ontario so firmly staked out by Cooperman, Salter, and Bennett. Eve Zaremba was one of the first to develop the tough female private-eye sub-genre and in *A reason to kill* (1989) used Toronto as the main centre of activity for her hard-boiled lesbian investigator Helen Keremos. *The butterfly effect* (1994) is the fifth of the novels that followed. Medora Sale's peripatetic photographer/sleuth Harriet Jeffries, introduced in *Murder on the run* (1986), is also located in Toronto, close to her policeman partner, John Sanders. Alison Gordon's baseball writer/sleuth Kate Henry is another Toronto resident, and since her first appearance in *The dead pull hitter* (1988) her adventures have been closely linked to the fortunes of a Toronto baseball team called the Titans. Gail BOWEN's five novels—from *Deadly appearances* (1990) to *A colder kind of death* (1994), which won an Arthur Ellis Award—feature the detective work of Joanna Kilbourn and are centred in Regina, Saskatchewan.

Most of the new writers staked claims further afield. The first female Canadian crime-writer to achieve major status was L.R. Wright, who became only the second Canadian winner of the prestigious Edgar from the Mystery Writers of America with her prize-winning first mystery novel *The suspect* (1985), a classic whydunit featuring a geriatric killer. Along with its successors, all featuring RCMP Sergeant Karl Alberg and librarian Cassandra Mitchell, it is set on the coast of British Columbia. Her western territory was later shared by Laurence Gough, who located his police detectives Claire Parker and Jack Willows in nearby Vancouver in his first novel, *The goldfish bowl* (1987).

While Edward Phillips set the activities of his lawyer/sleuth Geoffry Chadwick in Montreal's gay community and Anglo enclave of Westmount (*Buried on Sunday*, 1986), three notable police detective series used foreign locations. Peter Robinson set his Inspector Banks series (beginning with *Gallow's view*, 1987) in the dales of his native Yorkshire; John Brady used his hometown of Dublin as the background for his Inspector Matt Minogue series, which began with *Stone of the heart* (1988) and led to *The good life* (1994); and John Lawrence Reynolds used detective Joe McGuire, with Boston as the locus, for *The man who murdered God* (1989), a dark series that continued with *And leave her lay dying* (1990).

In the 1990s the general economic recession had an impact on Canadian mystery fiction. New authors found it difficult to find publishers or agents, and as publishers cut back fiction lists, and in some cases abandoned them altogether, several established writers found themselves without publishers.

Nevertheless, the current ranks of new Canadian mystery writers are replete with potential and accomplishment. Depending on staying power and the quality and quantity of their extended output, the following might be among contenders for the still-to-be founded Canadian Crimewriters Hall of Fame.

Retired sportswriter Scott Young introduced Inuk RCMP Inspector Matteesie Kitologitak in *Murder in a cold climate* (1990), followed by *The shaman's knife* (1993). This unusual detective may become an unfortunate victim of his creator's advancing years, although the many fans of this uniquely Canadian sleuth hope Young lives long enough to write more titles. Carsten Stroud, a converted non-fiction writer, has written two crime novels set in the USA: *Sniper's moon* (1990) and *Lizardskin* (1992), which both won Arthur Ellis Awards.

Hamilton psychiatrist David Laing Dawson's first novel, *Last rights* (1990), dealt with a geriatric sleuth puzzled by a series of murders in a home for the aged, but Dawson's later novels are darker stories dealing with various aspects of hospital work. Arthur Eddenden's *A good year for murder* (1988), *Murder on the thirteenth* (1992), and *Murder at the movies* (1996) are humorous mysteries set in Fort York (a thinly disguised Hamilton, Ontario) just prior to the Second World War, where Inspector Albert Tretheway practises a kinder, gentler brand of policing than that seen today.

Two other noteworthy writers with great crime-writing potential are Robert J. SAWYER and Gregory Ward. Sawyer's books, due mainly to their settings and characters, are generally labelled as science fiction, although a strong mystery/suspense theme is evident in all of them to date. His futuristic first novel, *Golden fleece* (1990), features a computer that kills the passengers on a long star-ship voyage. *Fossil hunter* (1993) is centred on scientist Afsan the Far-Seer, an intelligent saurian and the first dinosaur/detective. Already in his six-year writing career Sawyer has won multiple awards, including a Nebula for *The terminal experiment* (1995), featuring Detective Inspector Sandro Philo in pursuit of a murderous artificial intelligence in a future Toronto. Gregory Ward's *The carpet king* (1991) and *Water damage* (1993) are two literate and creepy Toronto-set suspense stories that may make Ward a force to be reckoned with if his future output continues at this level.

Three other prolific Canadians deserve mention in any overview of the mystery and crime genres. Two, who are currently living and writing abroad, are Lia Matera and David M. Pierce. Matera, now a California resident, has two series starring American lawyer/sleuths Laura Di Palma and Willa Jansson; while Pierce a resident of Paris, France, has written a series featuring Los Angeles private-eye Vic Daniel. The third, Eric Wilson, one of Canada's most successful crime-writers, is relatively unknown (except to his avid readers), because he writes exclusively for the children's market. Since he started publishing in 1976, Wilson has written a long series of internationally acclaimed juvenile mysteries starring child sleuths Tom and Liz Austen, as well as several non-series titles.

For additional titles and authors, see *In cold blood: a directory of Canadian crime writing and crime writers*, published occasionally by Crime Writers of Canada and the Metropolitan Toronto Reference Library. See also Michael Richardson, *A casebook of Canadian detective fiction* (1982), and David Skene-Melvin, ed., *Canadian crime fiction: an annotated comprehensive bibliography of Canadian crime fiction from 1817 to 1996 and biographical dictionary of Canadian crime writers, with an introductory essay on crime writing* (1996). JOHN NORTH

N

Namjoshi, Suniti. See LESBIAN LITERATURE.

Narrache, Jean. Pseudonym of Émile CODERRE.

Nature writing in English. Canadian nature writing had a rudimentary beginning as comments and observations in books by explorers and settlers. Not until the mid-nineteenth century did it develop into nature writing proper: prose that fuses facts about nature with an emotional and imaginative response to them. It reached a peak of popularity in the first decades of the twentieth century; then interest in it waned until the 1950s, when it regained much of its former favour and status. The following discussion of the main trends in this writing refers to only a few of the many titles that have been published.

1. SPORTSMAN'S BOOKS. These were the first books to focus on individual species of animals and birds, shifting emphasis from wildlife as food to wildlife as game and sport, and at least hinting at a different appreciation of nature.

Not Fredrick Tolfrey's *The sportsman in Canada* (London, 1845)—despite the title—but William 'Tiger' Dunlop's *Statistical sketches of Upper Canada, for the use of emigrants* (London, 1832), with a short chapter called 'Field sports', marked the beginning of the sportsman's book in Canada, and, more significantly, suggested a different perspective for writing about wildlife. While Tolfrey restricted his interest in nature to game, the kill, and the number killed, Dunlop wrote in the genteel tradition of describing favourite dogs, favourite guns, and favourite game. The restraint and sensitivity of his treatment of hunting distinguished it from that of Tolfrey, and from earlier books that stressed the barbarous pleasure the authors got from the slaughter of birds and animals. Dunlop, however, had no immediate effect on writing about nature, but something of his attitude eventually became integral to Canadian sportsman's books. In Dunlop's own time the Romantic movement—ushered into Canadian literature so passionately by Susanna MOODIE in *ROUGHING IT IN THE BUSH* (London, 1852), with its exaltation of the sublimity of the river cliffs at Quebec—began to affect descriptive writing about nature. Now appreciation of the environment, even the wilderness, became an acceptable human response to the non-human world.

By the late nineteenth century, Romanticism was widespread in writing about Canadian nature. Sidney C. Kendall in *Among the Laurentians* (Toronto, 1885) made much of wilderness scenery, but mainly as a backdrop or a stage where a sportsman could follow his fancy, recognizing that Canada was a sportsman's paradise even if a wilderness and a country of no international significance. The same general characteristics mark George Moore Fairchild's *Rod and canoe, rifle and snowshoe in Quebec's Adirondacks* (Quebec, 1896). But it made less of sport than of an environment where an (American) sportsman-tourist, lured by the title of the book, might yet indulge his feelings for the romantic in an untouched and unknown wilderness—his own, in the eastern United States, now fast disappearing, though once readily accessible.

Despite the tenor of such books, the hardy and the red-blooded continued to boast of their robust outdoorsman's prowess with rod and gun, as in Campbell Hardy's *Sporting adventures in the New World; or, Days and nights of moose-hunting in the pine forests of Acadia* (2 vols, London, 1855); even in the Rev. Joshua Fraser's *Three months among the moose* (Montreal, 1881), and in T. R. Pattillo's catch-all, *Moose hunting, salmon fishing and other sketches of sport* (1902)—all of which endorse, if not advocate, a brutal exploitation of wildlife.

The sportsman's book has maintained its popularity, despite (or because of) the development of a more sympathetic attitude towards nature. Edwyn Sandys' *Upland game birds* (1902), autobiographical and anecdotal, as is typical of the genre, reveals traces of this new approach to hunting. In keeping with its subject, it is less grisly than B. Williams' serious *Game trails of British Columbia* (1926) and Neville A.D. Armstrong's *After big game in the upper Yukon* (1937). Each tries to emphasize the dignity of sport-hunting. Though without the lion or tiger, big-game hunting in the Rockies, they imply, is still regal and prestigious.

Mike Crammond, a prolific western sportsman-author who really knows game and the 'science' of sport, with books on hunting birds and animals of many sorts and sizes, writes fluently of the benefits of 'harvesting' them in such books as *Game bird hunting in the West* (1976) and *Fishin' holes of the West* (1973). As if to attest to the sagacity of wildlife, he stresses the skill needed in hunting and includes fine descriptions and pictures (not photographs) of game, not in appreciation of the animals' beauty but largely as a guide to the hunter in identifying a legal bag. Jack Hambleton's *Hunter's holidays* (1947) takes a flippant approach to hunting: his book is boisterous and tends to trivialize the sportsman and his quest.

Almost all sportsman's books are pots-pourris of anecdotes, expert advice on methods, comments on natural history, and character sketches threaded on a string of memorable outdoor experiences climaxing in a proud accumulation of trophies of the hunt, or a prize mounted to stare glassy-eyed from a mantel in a games-room. Undoubtedly hunting has changed and the sportsman's book is far removed from Dunlop's 'Field-sports'. Yet it has not reverted to Tolfrey's kind of book; hunting has become methodized and commercialized, a business.

2. FISHERMEN-WRITERS. Since it is harder to think of a fish than of a bird or animal as a kindred of the wild, fishing has always seemed beyond the scope of nature writing. As if to compensate for any want of emotional involvement with nature, however, fishermen-writers try to substitute for it the thrill of the strike, the fight to avoid the landing net, and the nervous and exciting uncertainty that precedes bringing in an impressive creature of sleek symmetry and vitality.

The first noteworthy book specifically on fishing in Canadian literature is the Rev. William A. Adamson's *Salmon fishing in Canada* (London, 1860), an unpretentious treatise on fishing interwoven, like Isaac Walton's *The compleat angler* (1653), with discussions of literature and religion. It established the fast-flowing rivers of Canada, rather than Walton's streams and ponds, as appropriate locations for fishing narratives. It gave rise eventually to several remarkable books: W.H. BLAKE's *Brown waters and other sketches* (1915) and *In a fishing country* (1922); and Roderick HAIG-BROWN's *A river never sleeps* (1946) and his seasonal tetralogy commencing with *Fisherman's spring* (1951). Both men wrote sensitive and lucid prose, though Haig-Brown's tends to have a harder surface. Like Adamson, both men display remarkable rapport with the natural world, and never consider fishing simply a matter of the catch. For Adamson, fishing meant friendly chats; for Blake, *habitant* guides, somewhat romanticized, pleasant sojourns in their countryside, and such reflections as he mulls over in *A fisherman's creed* (1923), where he considers the significance of the spiritual in his life and the wonders of unceasing creation in nature.

For Haig-Brown, a recognized ichthyologist and a more serious (or at least less gregarious) angler than Blake, fishing ritualizes techniques of the art of fishing for a solitary fisherman (not the chatty group) in the mountain fastness, where a thoughtful man can learn about himself and take time to meditate in a world free of human pretences.

Books on fishing have become increasingly popular as sportsmen find vicarious pleasures in reading and day-dreaming about exploits that could never be theirs, and about the freedom the outdoors gives. As an antidote to the high seriousness of many fishermen's books, with their instructions bristling with technicalities, *The incomplete angler* (1943), by the university professor and humorist John D. Robins, humanizes the sport, for it evokes the non-solemn attitude that should inform a pleasurable avocation and nature writing itself.

3. LITERARY-SCIENTIFIC ESSAYS. As the population of pioneer Upper Canada increased in the early nineteenth century, so too did its response to nature change from a pioneer sensibility to a British one. As the settlements attracted more refined and educated people, many began to wonder whether quill and brush, not rod and gun, could give a better sense of control over the myriad forms and abundances of the wilderness. Among these newcomers was the Otonabee school of writers, the Stricklands, Thomas Need, the Stewarts, the Moodies, and the Traills—one of whom, Catharine Parr TRAILL, wrote the text of *Canadian wild flowers* (Montreal, 1869), with illustrations by her niece Agnes (Moodie) Fitzgibbon. This book was to establish her significance as a field naturalist and give nature writing a form—the literary-scientific essay—and a new attitude. It celebrated not conquest of, but communion with, nature. Although Traill made botany her special interest, as she again demonstrated with *Studies of plant life in Canada* (Ottawa, 1885), she was a sensitive, articulate, and sympathetic observer of nature, as she disclosed in *Pearls and pebbles: or, Notes of an old naturalist* (London, Toronto, 1894), even if it could be argued that gathering wild flowers was but a more gentle way (than shooting birds and animals) of expressing control over the natural world. Like Gilbert White in *The natural history and antiquities of Selborne* (1789), Traill combined the personal and impersonal in describing nature; perhaps influenced by current Romanticism, she tended to personify wild creatures, a trait she first developed in *Cot and cradle stories* (Toronto, 1895), a book of nature studies for children, similar in attitude to Philip H. Gosse's little-known but more scientific study *The Canadian naturalist: a series of conversations on the natural history of Lower Canada* (London, 1840). Her bird was a 'feathered friend'; her spider 'a surly fellow'; her pole cat 'a horrid creature'. All, however, were God's creatures in a providential world. Her kind of essay became the standard and most popular form of writing about nature.

During Traill's time nature writing became more popular and more wide-ranging. William Lett wrote, but not as hunter, of Ottawa Valley deer in *The antlered kings* (Ottawa, 1884). Grant ALLEN changed direction and devoted his nature writing to Darwinism in several books from *Vignettes of nature* (New York, 1888) to *In nature's workshop* (1901). Ernest Thompson SETON, uncertain about the role of science in nature study, moved from fiction in *WILD ANIMALS I HAVE KNOWN* (New York, 1898) to natural history in *The life histories of northern animals: an account of the mammals of Manitoba* (1908). His work is marked by a romantic primivitism that resulted from his efforts to link Native life with natural history, though in the short story 'Redruff', Seton, an avowed Darwinian, describes a predacious squirrel as a 'bloodthirsty villain'. During the same period Samuel Wood, in the manner of natural philosopher John Burroughs, made many woodland trips the centre of his *Rambles of a Canadian naturalist* (1916). Others of the time took up particular places and themes. D. McCowan and H.J. Parham write of the Rockies and the forests of British Columbia in *Animals of the Canadian Rockies* (1936) and *A nature lover in British Columbia* (1937) respectively. Lorus and Margery Milne discuss nature at night in *The world of night* (1948) and Franklin Russell aquatic life in *Watchers at the pond* (1961), a kind of dramatized biology textbook designed to demonstrate Darwinian theory.

By far the most renowned Canadian nature writer of the twentieth century is Grey Owl (Archibald Stansfeld BELANEY). He was once called the Canadian Thoreau, a name often given in Canada to anyone who writes sympathetically of nature. But Grey Owl was no transcendentalist like Thoreau. He never looked for the bird behind the bird, but directly at it; it was never for him the embodiment of an ideal. Thoreau kept journals in hopes that someday facts would blossom into meaning; Grey Owl 'kept' beavers—McGinnis, Jelly Roll, and Rawhide—because each was a meaning in itself, a celebration of the vitality of the natural world. He kept his journals and wrote his autobiographical *Pilgrims of the wild* (1934) and *Tales of an empty cabin* (1936) as atonement for, or in reaction to, his life as trapper.

Despite masquerading as an Amerindian in order to identify with the spirit of the wilderness, Grey Owl seems to convey a factitious not a Native's view of nature, if John Tetso's *Trapping is my life* (1970) is to be believed. This is an account of the harshness of life in the woods; Tetso, a Native, finds a sunset interesting, but as a 'weather picture', not as a magnificent view of the natural world. Arthur Heming's *The living forest* (1925) and *The drama of the forests* (1928) also present winter life in northern Canada realistically.

Since Grey Owl's time studies of other 'wild pets', such as wolves and foxes, have appeared; but it is a new-style life history of animals in the wild that has proven most popular, as demonstrated by Farley MOWAT's *Never cry wolf* (1963). Despite a fine discussion of wolf family life, the author's account of crawling into the dens of wintering wolves made the book sensational and has caused some critics to question the accuracy and depth of his research; by careful study of pack behaviour, however, Mowat does disclose the falsity of the myth that the wolf is the embodiment of savagery. The nature writer R.D. Lawrence is best known for his account of wolves in *Cry wild: the story of a Canadian timber wolf* (1970) and *In praise of wolves* (1986).

George W. Calef's *Caribou and the Barrenlands* (1981), a coffee-table book, approaches nature quite differently from Mowat's study of wolves. It uses photographs as effective comments on exposition and narrative in a magnificent pageant of the natural history of the last of the great herds of big-game animals in Canada.

A westerner and 'mountain man', Andy Russell has made grizzly country his home. It also gave him the title of one of his eleven books on the area, the thrilling *Grizzly country* (1967), a wide-ranging study of one of the world's biggest carnivores. In addition to his talent as a naturalist, Russell's marked ability as a photographer gives his nature writing a convincing double focus. Following many years of study of orca populations off the B.C. coast, Alexandra Morton published *In the company of whales* (1993).

Wayne Grady has also demonstrated the continued and, indeed, intensified concern for nature. Widely recognized for science writing, he has combined that ability with an appreciation of a much-abused and persecuted animal in *The nature of coyotes* (1994). After careful field work, he presents a remarkable creature worthy of respect for its intelligence and pertinacity in defiance of poison, traps, and guns.

4. REALISTIC ANIMAL STORIES. The animal story was one of the most important developments of nature writing in the late nineteenth century. Charles G.D. ROBERTS and Ernest Thompson Seton, both of whom had published in sportsmen's magazines, felt the influence of both Romanticism and the nature essay. Roberts' sketch 'Do seek their meat from God' (1892), later published in *Earth's enigmas: a book of animal and nature life* (Boston, 1896), and Seton's *Wild animals I have known* mark the beginning of a new literary genre, the realistic animal story. Each writer refused to follow Kipling and his *Jungle book*, after the fashion of W.A. FRASER and his intelligent talking animals in *Mooswa and others of the boundaries* (1900). Roberts continued with animal stories until 1936, when he published the last of nineteen volumes of them, *Further animal stories*. He had learned how the short story works and quickly recognized how very popular it was at the time. Unfortunately, this knowledge, along with an unrelenting Darwinism, tended to bring about formula-writing of courageous animals fighting to the death as if to demonstrate Darwin's theory of natural selection. At the same time, Roberts examines the motives and reactions of his protagonists as personalities and becomes unduly anthropomorphic. Though he preferred the short story, he may well have done his best work in *Red Fox* (1905), a convincing animal biography of both interest and insight. His awareness of the irony and amorality of life in the natural world prevented him from resorting to sentimentality.

If Roberts, a man of letters, wrote formally structured stories that illustrate the principles of biological theory, Seton, a naturalist from boyhood—as his fascinating fusion of woodlore and adventure in the autobiographical *TWO LITTLE SAVAGES* (1906) makes clear — recorded the lives of creatures known to him. Roberts saw humans as superior moral beings and animals as living according to nature's law, yet motivated by hate, love, loyalty, and bravery. Like many late-Victorians, Seton attempted a compromise between Christian belief and the new biological theory. In *The natural history of the Ten Commandments* (1907), he argued for evolutionary morality and, caught up in the conservation movement, treated his animal-hero victims sympathetically and their deaths as hunter-perpetrated tragedies that broke the moral link between man and nature. Testaments to this conviction are his most impressive books, *Wild animals I have known* and especially *Lives of the hunted* (1901), which contains his superlative story of a mountain ram ('Krag'). Seton's favourite mode was the full-length animal biography—*The biography of a silver-fox* (1909) and *Bannertail* (1922)—but he also turned to woodland tales and books of woodcraft in his later years, and to many-volumed scientific studies of lives of game animals.

With Roderick Haig-Brown's *Panther* (1934), about a cougar, the fictional animal biography broke new ground. Lacking the romanticism of Roberts and Seton, Haig-Brown reverted to realism and autobiography in a cruel and authentic account of hunter-animal relationships. In *Return to the river* (1941) he again gave animal biography new direction in a most difficult form, the fictional biography of a fish. Here the fish is an individual, in a narrative vividly dramatizing the piscine life-cycle and the fight of the 'fittest' to survive; but for the first time in the genre, game-management people had roles, and conservation is a theme, not implicitly through the plight of the individual (as in Seton), but explicitly through a species.

In the 1940s and 1950s the fictional animal story regained popularity and assumed, as in Fred BODSWORTH's *The last of the curlews* (1954), a Seton-like sentiment towards the wild. In the past, the genre came under attack for anthropomorphism, and even President Theodore Roosevelt dismissed Roberts and Seton as 'nature fakirs' in an article in *Everybody's Magazine* (1907). Today, however, some critics accept the anthropomorphic view and see the animal (the victim) as a symbol of people struggling for survival against inimical forces of history and nature. In such an interpretation the animal story has come full circle. It has become a modern version of the beast fable.

5. THE RURAL AND THE PASTORAL TRADITIONS. Books in the rural tradition (agrarianism) arose only after the farming community became aware of the alienating influence of the urban, an awareness that is central to almost all Peter McARTHUR's books, which established him as the first, and certainly one of the best, rural nature writers. Dedicated to farm life, he tried, like William Cobbett in his *Rural rides* (1830), to prove the truth behind the agrarian myth that the simple life close to nature is a social ideal, since man is happiest when farming. However, despite his love of the bucolic, McArthur never wrote of the farm as an Eden because he knew farm life too well to present it as such. His 'friends' the trees and his 'neighbours', his farm animals, were soon to become subjects of lively, witty, and popular books, from *In pastures green* (1915) to *Friendly acres* (1927). To support his agrarianism, McArthur campaigned in these books for a back-to-the-land movement, enlivening his campaign with humorous vignettes of a red cow, Socrates, a ram, and a 'lordly' turkey-gobbler, to counter the opinion of many who considered farm life unceasing drudgery. However, he never created a Black Beauty or any other noble creature as propaganda for the pleasures of farm life. McArthur's last book, *The affable stranger* (1921), sums up a life-long dedication to the country by juxtaposing his concern for it with a most penetrating discussion of the impending decay of city life in the United States.

Like McArthur's books, Frederick Philip GROVE's *Over prairie trails* (1922) belongs in the rural tradition, though it says little of farming except for the problems of travelling by horse and cutter through the farming country of southern Manitoba. Grove, however, as rural teacher and amateur meteorologist, writes realistically about weather as central to the winter prairie environment. Despite its harsh setting, the book affirms farm life, for its core is the farm home, a haven where love and comfort hold the winter at bay. *The turn of the year* (1923), Grove's second treatment of the mid-western farm world, is a book for all seasons, as if to counterbalance *Over prairie trails*, though Grove writes as observer, not as farmer. Despite his intention to relate nature to man, his characters (a sower, a reaper, young lovers) are interesting largely as cosmic figures, subject to natural forces that are always authentically described.

Between the 1950s and the 1980s the rural book took two different directions. One was represented by Kenneth McNeill WELLS' once-popular *The owl pen* (1947; rpr. 1995), *By Moonstone Creek* (1949), *Up Medonte way* (1951), and *By Jumping Cat Bridge* (1956), which deal with his misadventures as an apiarist and portray rustic life facetiously, presenting self-ridicule as humour, and ineptitude in farm work as funny and without social stigma, hence implying the superiority of the urban. Opposed to this frothy approach are books of another purpose, such as Philip W. Keller's *Splendour from the land* (1963), in which the farmer becomes an economic figure and farming a machine-based occupation. It extols not the pleasant life of agrarianism, but the financial profits of agri-business.

With the decline of non-urban population, rural writing seemed to have lost its popularity until the appearance of Marsha Boulton's *Letters from the country* (1995), a collection of witty and interesting commentaries that treat her particular rural life as a private/public entertainment. Despite its title, it differs greatly from Wayne Grady's *From the country* (1991). Boulton focuses on her farm animals and her neighbours; Grady's book, a collection of short stories about villagers and rural residents, depicts them as protagonists. In Marsha Boulton's book the rural tradition is modernized, if not urbanized, in the manner of many Harrowsmith publications.

Closely related to the rural essay, which celebrates farm-life, is the pastoral, which celebrates country living: it leads to the romantic escapism of the memoir—or to residence in cottage country. Memories of farm life or the beauty of the countryside influenced nature writing for a century. A.D. Wood's *Old days on the farm* (1918), for example, comprises recollections of a farm boyhood that says little about nature except that as environment it made growing up in the country an enduring memory. The reading of such books has declined with erosion of the rural world, but Wood discloses the vitality it once had. *T'aint running no more: the story of Grand Bend, the Pinery, and the old river bed* (1946), by William Sherwood Fox, then president of the University of Western Ontario, portrays the delights of fishing the Aux Sables River and recreates the history of that country world. Fox's best-known nature book, however, is *The Bruce beckons: the story of Huron's great peninsula* (1952). Grant Madison, in *River for a sidewalk* (1953), like Thoreau, tried to live a life of self-reliance in a log house, not near a pond but in the great forests and mountains of British Columbia, far from the gadgetry of civilization. Freedom from restraints motivates Gilean Douglas in *Silence is my homeland* (1978), also set in British Columbia, where she finds spiritual sustenance in the wilderness. In *The protected place* (1979) Douglas uses the pastoral motif of the annual cycle of seasons to structure her observations on nature as seen from her house on Cortes Island, B.C. Chris Czajkowski wrote two books about building a house in the B.C. wilderness: *Cabin at Singer River* (1991) and *Diary of a wildreness dweller* (1996).

Among later pastorals, three stand out for their perceptiveness and originality: William Arthur Breyfogle's *Speak to the earth* (1961), Harold HORWOOD's *The foxes of Beachy Cove* (1967), and Ernest BUCKLER's *Ox bells and fireflies* (1968). Breyfogle, a well-read field naturalist and amateur anthropologist, wrote discerningly of people-nature relationships that illuminate both human and natural history, as the brilliant chapters 'Running water' and 'April sun and adding machines' so clearly illustrate; *Speak to the earth* makes a most persuasive case for the need to recognize one's symbiotic kinship with the whole natural process, which humans neglect to their own great loss. Horwood, like Breyfogle, is never negative; Beachy Cove in Newfoundland is no Shangri-La, but a calm centre amid ceaseless activities of the organic world. He keeps nature clearly in focus, and his birds and animals never lose their identities in the specifics of science or in the vagueness of romantic idealism. A vitalist, Horwood needs no external system as explanation: life itself is the supreme revelation of the creative force of nature.

Buckler called *Ox bells and fireflies* a 'fictional memoir', but it might also be defined as a book in the rural-pastoral tradition, for it combines the realism of the one with the romanticism of the other in relating the author's memories of a lifetime spent as a farmer in rural Nova Scotia. Although a record of the past, and sparing in descriptions of nature, it is a richly rewarding depiction of a man living in harmony with the forces of the natural world. It gains its power as nature writing not by describing species and their behaviour, but by presenting the past as a living present in metaphysical language of apt images and metaphors. Buckler gives the natural world life so that it exists not as nostalgia, but as evidence of the permanence of its beauty and vitality. In *The perfection of the morning: an apprenticeship in nature* (1994), Sharon BUTALA writes of her years of struggle to feel at home on her husband's Saskatchewan farm, and of the mystical and spiritual aspects arising from human contact with nature. Other important books dealing with the Prairies are Sid MARTY's *Leaning on the wind: under the spell of the great chinook* (1959) and Don Gayton's *The wheatgrass mechanism: science and imagination in the western Canadian landscape* (1990) and *Landscapes of the interior: re-explorations of nature and the human spirit* (1995).

6. CONSERVATION. Sportsmen as members of the prosperous middle class have long promoted hunting as a gentlemanly sport and, to help establish it as such, have talked of their interest in the conservation of game. But in defending their practice and accounting for scarcity of game they have shifted the blame to predatory animals and birds—vermin, as they designate such creatures. However, in *Sportsman Joe* (1924) Edwyn Sandys made a case for both hunters and predators. Since the latter had become scarce, hunters, he argued, should assume the role of predator, because hunting 'makes for the preservation and increase of species'. Whatever the grounds for such logic, it centred on a topic of great interest to sportsmen and a concern that C. Gordon Hewitt made the subject of a challenging

study, *The conservation of the wildlife of Canada* (1921). Arguing on economic grounds, he strongly advocated the destruction of all 'vermin'. The book must have stirred Jack Miner, the famous 'goose man' and ardent conservationist, for in newspaper articles and public speeches he set about inciting farmers and hunters to wage war on all predators, especially hawks; they fed on grouse and other of his favourite game birds.

Hewitt's book has been followed by many others in the area of conservation. Daryll Stewart's *Canadian endangered species* (1974) sounded a loud alarm that was echoed by David Grainger's *Animals in peril* (1978), as if the author feared Stewart had gone unheard. The renowned naturalist R.D. Lawrence has published a number of books cataloguing the varieties of wildlife—*Wildlife in North America: birds* (1974) and *Wildlife in North America: mamals* (1974), for example—but his primary interest has always been conservation. This is evidenced in *The poison makers* (1969), about the environmental degradation caused by pesticides, *The zoo that never was* (1981), about rescuing wildlife in Ontario, and *A shriek in the night: wilderness encounters* (1996), which, in twenty-four profiles, relates various animals to their specific environment with the purpose of broadening the boundaries of biology so that we can learn to see animals and insects as 'an integral and essential part of a whole environment'. Even a hunter-author like Mike Crammond, who in addition to the books previously mentioned wrote *Of bears and men* (1986), can now focus on the welfare of wildlife and call for harvesting game for its own good. In this way hunters have become ecologists in wildlife management programs in which game is a 'gun crop'—a strange but revealing way of linking the sportsman's love of hunting and the outdoors with conservation. Valuing wildlife for itself, which is central to conservation (and nature writing), has given way to a rationalized solution of the problem. Farley Mowat gets at the root of the matter in his moving and perspicacious *A whale for the killing* (1972). A study of the life and agonizing death of a bay-locked whale, it is also a symbolic treatment of the plight of all wild creatures in the modern world. It combines angry protest and shock therapy to oppose the view that animals are insensitive and thus inferior, and are justifiably subject to heartless treatment. The term 'conservation' has thus come under attack in the 1980s on the grounds that it suggests conserving nature in order to make use of it later, to exploit it more fully. The environmental crisis is now understood to be ecological in nature; that is, to concern the entire interconnected web of relationships among species, climate, topography, and human intervention. A crucial work in this regard is Alexander Wilson's *The culture of nature: North American landscape from Disney to Exxon Valdez* (1991).

The natural world has dominated the Canadian imagination from the beginning of our history, explicitly or implicitly influencing almost all our writing. Nature writing itself tries to give us a knowledgeable and imaginative hold on our natural environment. The strength of our wish to retain this hold is demonstrated by the great number of nature books (exclusive of outdoors books) published in Canada between the 1970s and the 1990s, of which many have centred on the need to protect our natural heritage and many others on the satisfactions of rural or wilderness living. Nature writing may be a small current, but it is in the mainstream of both our literature and our national consciousness.

See John A. Murray, ed., *A republic of rivers: three centuries of nature writing from Alaska and the Yukon* (1990); Wayne Grady, ed., *Treasures of the place: three centuries of nature writing in Canada* (1992); and Andrea Lebowitz, *Living in harmony: nature writing by women in Canada* (1996). ALEC LUCAS

NCL. See NEW CANADIAN LIBRARY.

Neatby, Hilda (1904-75). Born in Sutton, Surrey, England, and brought to a small Saskatchewan town two years later, she was educated at the University of Saskatchewan (B.A., 1924; M.A., 1927), at the Sorbonne, Paris, and at the University of Minnesota (Ph.D., 1934), supported by scholarships. Her doctoral thesis was published as *The administration of justice under the Quebec Act* (1937). Neatby was determined to invade the male preserve of historical scholarship, but it was not until 1945 that she secured a position as associate professor in the history department of the University of Saskatchewan, where she spent most of her academic career as a specialist in the history of Quebec.

Iconoclastic writings on education brought Neatby to the attention of Vincent Massey and appointment in 1949 to the Royal Commission on National Development in the Arts, Letters and Sciences. Her contributions were central to the Commission's report and Neatby became a speech-writer for Massey while he was governor general. In *So little for the mind* (1953) and *A temperate dispute* (1954), which aroused enormous debate, Neatby decried the emphasis placed in public education on physical facilities and administration at the expense of curriculum. She wrote for The Canada Centenary Series *Quebec: the revolutionary age, 1760-1791*, which was published in 1966. The following year she was made a Companion of the Order of Canada.

Frequently encountering male prejudice, and interested in promoting the place of women in intellectual life, Neatby was nevertheless typical of her generation in toeing the line of male consensus in her historical work. Her last book, *Queen's University*, published posthumously in 1978, was subtitled *to strive, to seek, to find, and not to yield*, words from Tennyson's 'Ulysses' that conveyed her own tenacity. *So much to do, so little time* (1983) is a selection of her writings edited by Michael Hayden. TERRY CROWLEY

Nelligan, Émile (1879-1941). Born in Montreal, he was the son of David Nelligan, a postal inspector of Irish extraction, and Émilie-Amanda Hudon. He acquired his early education at Montreal's École Olier (1886-90) and Mont Saint-Louis (1890-3). His numerous absences set him back in his studies and forced him to repeat his third year. His secondary education was equally undistinguished: at the Collège de Montréal (1893-5) he twice repeated his course in elementary Latin and, after a six-month delay, registered at the Collège Sainte-Marie for two semesters (Mar. 1896-Feb. 1897). At 17 he was two years behind his schoolmates and, against his parents' wishes, decided to abandon his studies. He wished only to be a poet; he was already writing verses and could envision for himself no other profession than that of an artist.

In 1896 he answered a call for poems from *Le Samedi* and published his first poems, under the pseudonym 'Émile Kovar' (June 13-Sept. 19), which plainly show the influence of Verlaine and Baudelaire. Nelligan introduced a 'frisson nouveau' into a literary milieu dominated by the Romantic and patriotic epic. If he is sometimes Parnassian in his descriptions, he is so in the Symbolist manner, stressing the subjective impression ('Rythmes du soir', 'Rêve de Watteau'). Unlike such contemporairies as Jean CHARBONNEAU and Lucien Rainier, who produced philosophical and moralistic poetry, Nelligan showed a remarkable sensitivity to the power of words and the music of language. He adhered to Verlaine's precept, 'Music above all', and his revisions show a preoccupation with the evocative power inherent in sonority. Like his French masters he expressed, in poems of melancholy ('Soir d'hiver') and nostalgia ('Le jardin de l'enfance'), an essential unfitness for life that was bound up in the demands of poetry itself.

In 1897, through the intervention of his friend Arthur de Bussières, Nelligan attended the recently founded ÉCOLE LITTÉRAIRE DE MONTRÉAL, but withdrew almost immediately. Poems published in *Le Monde illustré* (1897-8) appeared for the first time under his real name, which was sometimes modified to 'Émile Nellighan'. In 1898 Nelligan's poetic output fell off, possibly because of a journey he planned to make to England. His father, not content with his son's total preoccupation with poetry, would have found him a place in the Merchant Marine—a venture that never took place, however, since in October Nelligan was publishing poems in *La Patrie*. At this time he contemplated gathering a collection of his verse under the title *Récital des anges*. He worked on it in 1899, but it never progressed beyond the stage of a rough draft and has not been published.

At the end of 1898 Nelligan was readmitted to the École littéraire de Montréal, which was increasingly becoming an important intellectual movement. By bringing together poets of diverse leanings, and refusing to address political and religious matters, the group declared its intention of giving special rules and autonomy to literature. During its heyday in 1899, when Nelligan was participating in the group's public readings, he achieved a great triumph after having recited his 'La romance du vin', an impassioned reply to detractors of poetry. But this, his most glorious moment as a poet, was his last public appearance. He was confined to the Saint-Benoît asylum, apparently for exhibiting signs of derangement.

Nelligan had published only twenty-three poems, but in 1903, thanks to the devotion of his friend Louis Dantin (Eugène SEERS), and with his mother's help, 107 poems were collected in *Émile Nelligan et son oeuvre*. This book revealed his lyricism, his melancholy, and his nostalgia for childhood; it also contained 'Le vaisseau d'or', which has been perceived as a premonition of his madness.

During more than forty years of confinement, Nelligan continued to write; but, having lost the capability to create a body of work, he contented himself with rewriting poems and fragments. Dr Ernest CHOQUETTE, who visited him in 1909, remarked that 'he showed an undeviating obsession with literature'. After his father's death in Oct. 1925, Nelligan was transferred to the public ward of the Saint-Jean-de-Dieu hospital. But all that emerged from this period were notebooks containing the poet's revised versions —some with faulty titles—of earlier poems and versions of Baudelaire, Gregh, Rodenbach, Crémazie, *et al.* It is likely that he also wrote many delirious texts that have been destroyed. His sister Eva visited him regularly and provided him with writing materials. The increased number of visitors Nelligan received during the thirties attests to the growing public interest in *Émile Nelligan et son oeuvre*, which came out in its third edition in 1932. The last thing he worked on was a version of 'La Bénédictine', dated 5 Apr. 1941, seven months before his death in November.

The most comprehensive editions of Nelligan's poems were compiled by Luc LACOURCIÈRE in 1952, *Poésies complètes 1896-1899*; and by Réjean Robidoux and Paul Wyczynski in 1991, *Poésies complètes*, in *Oeuvres complètes I*. The hospital notebooks were compiled by Jacques Michon in *Oeuvres complètes II: poèmes et textes d'asile, 1900-1941* (1991). P.F. Widdows translated a few of Nelligan's poems into English under the title *Selected poems* (1960), and in 1983 Fred COGSWELL published *The complete poems of Émile Nelligan*.

See Paul Wyczynski, *Bibliographie descriptive et critique d'Émile Nelligan* (1973) and *Émile Nelligan, 1879-1941, biographie* (1987).

JACQUES MICHON

New, W.H. See CRITICISM IN ENGLISH: 5(c), 5(f); 6(c), 6(f), 6(l).

New Canadian Library. Officially launched on 17 January 1958, McCLELLAND & STEWART's New Canadian Library is a quality paperback reprint series of outstanding or significant Canadian literary works. Malcolm Ross, its general editor until 1978, conceived the idea in the early 1950s when he became frustrated by the lack of available texts to facilitate the teaching of Canadian literature in universities. While publisher and editor perceived post-secondary classes as the series' major market, they also hoped that some titles would appeal to secondary-school teachers and the public. An introduction, usually written by an academic, accompanied each of the more than 150 books issued under Ross's editorship. Mainly prose fiction, titles ranged from eighteenth-century works (Frances BROOKE's *The history of Emily Montague*) to such contemporary titles as Margaret LAURENCE's *The DIVINERS*. Financial concerns, related to book length, led to the abridgement of some works. This period also saw the emergence of two sub-series: NCL Originals, collections of poems or criticism, such as *Poets of the Confederation* and *Masks of fiction*; and the Canadian Writers Series, under the editorship of Dave GODFREY until the twelfth volume, consisting of brief monographs on Canadian writers. The NCL's success and the expansion of the study of Canadian literature encouraged other publishers to undertake similar reprint series, creating competition both in terms of sales and in the acquirement of titles. By the time of Ross's retirement in 1978, these circumstances had become troubling and provoked within M&S a lengthy period of reassessment. Titles added in the early 1980s were included at the publisher's sole discretion. After M&S's 1985 sale to Avie Bennett, plans for a revised NCL were initiated. David Staines was retained as general editor, an advisory board—Alice MUNRO, W.H. New, and Guy VANDERHAEGHE—was established, cover designs were in colour, most titles in the original series were allowed to go out of print, introductions were abandoned in favour of Afterwords, and full texts replaced abridgements. The series was relaunched in 1988.

JANET FRISKNEY

Newfoundland, Writing in. Newfoundland, Canada's most easterly province, was visited and settled by the Norse around A.D. 1000; remains of their settlement, near L'Anse aux Meadows on the island's Northern Peninsula, have been uncovered by archaeologists, and the sod huts reconstructed. It is possible that this site is itself 'Vinland', the colony described in such detail in the Norse sagas. It would, however, be another five centuries before Europeans established permanent contact with North America. The writing about Newfoundland that survives from this second period of discovery consists of a few letters, extracts from ships' logs, and other such bald documents. John Rut's voyage of 1527 gives us what appears to be the earliest first-hand English description of the coast of Newfoundland, which Rut gloomily pictured as 'all wildernesse and mountaines and woods, and no naturall ground but all mosse, and no inhabitation nor no people.' The most important descriptions of Newfoundland from the sixteenth century are those of Jacques Cartier (1534), Anthony Parkhurst (1578), Edward Hayes (1583), and Stephen Parmenius (1583), all printed in the 1599-1600 edition of Richard Hakluyt's *Principal navigations*. These convey the initial shocked, amused, and occasionally hopeful European responses to Newfoundland's grim offerings. They sometimes present more accurate ideas about the country's resources than the books of early-seventeenth-century propagandists for settlement, such as Richard Whitbourne's *A discourse and discovery of Newfoundland . . .* (London, 1620), John Mason's *A briefe discourse of the New-found-land* (Edinburgh, 1620), Richard Eburne's *A plain pathway to plantations* (London, 1624), William Vaughan's *The golden fleece . . .* (London, 1626), and Robert HAYMAN's book of poems *Quodlibets* (London, 1628). These were flowery accompaniments to the attempts to plant colonies in Newfoundland. Of the prose works, Whitbourne's is the most elaborate and intriguing. Among the adjectives he applies to Newfoundland are 'excellent', 'wholesome', 'enticing', 'delightful', and even 'beautiful', words later writers would not readily use of the island's stern coastline. By 1660 it was apparent that the early efforts to establish formal colonies had failed. Nevertheless, a small resident European population was left behind on the island. (Whitbourne's *Discourse* and other documents relating to the seventeenth-century efforts to found colonies in Newfoundland are included in *Newfoundland discovered*, 1982, edited by Gillian T. Cell.)

For the remainder of the seventeenth century and the whole of the eighteenth, Newfoundland's history was one of neglect and obscurity. British policy after 1699 was to permit settlement but to withhold year-round residential government in order to keep settlers to a minimum. As a consequence, almost no amenities of civilization existed on the island. There was no context in which an indigenous literature could develop, and few visitors thought enough of the place to write about it at length. However, James Yonge's *Journal*, which was not published until 1963, describes his experiences as a physician with English West Country migratory fishermen in Newfoundland from 1660 to 1670. B. Lacy's *Miscellaneous poems compos'd at Newfoundland* (London, 1729) provides a grimly realistic picture of St John's in clumsy heroic couplets. Another poet, the Irishman Donnach Ruah MacConmara, wrote macaronic verses in English and Irish about Newfoundland in the 1740s. The Methodist Laurence Coughlan's *An account of the work of God in Newfoundland* (London, 1776) contains an early recognition of the distinctiveness of the Newfoundlander, while George Cartwright's huge *A journal of transactions and events, during a residence of nearly sixteen years on the coast of Labrador* (3 vols, London, 1792) conveys with great immediacy and detail what life was like for an English trapper and fisherman in Labrador from 1770 to 1786. Cartwright's *Journal* is a classic in the pioneer literature of Canada. An important early book that had a formative influence on the writing of Newfoundland history was John Reeves' *History of the government of the island of Newfoundland* (London, 1793). Reeves saw the history as a struggle between the inhabitants and the West Country merchants—a theme that, though it contains much truth, would be endlessly reiterated and exaggerated by nineteenth-century nationalist historians.

The period 1775-1815 saw the continuing evolution of St John's as the principal port of Newfoundland, an increase in settlers, and the appearance of a resident, somewhat prosperous middle class. Britain was at war for much of the period, and this was mostly good for Newfoundland. John Ryan, a Loyalist from Rhode Island who had first settled in New Brunswick, established in 1807 Newfoundland's first printing press and newspaper, the *Royal Gazette*. Other St John's papers followed: the *Newfoundland Mercantile Journal* (1815), *Newfoundland Sentinel* (1818), *Public Ledger* (1820), *Newfoundlander* (1827), and the *Times* (1832). The first Conception Bay newspaper, the *Harbour Grace and Carbonear Weekly Journal*, appeared in 1828. The Scottish doctor William Carson's first two pamphlets, *A letter to the Members of Parliament of the United Kingdom* (Greenock, Scot., 1812) and *Reasons for colonizing the island of Newfoundland, in a letter addressed to the inhabitants* (Greenock, 1813)—the earliest literary expression of the need for political reform in the island—were printed abroad for local distribution; but by the 1820s such tracts were being printed in the colony, and Henry Winton, a 'Printer and Publisher' in St John's, was capable of producing large books. Another pamphleteer of the 1820s was the garrulous Irishman Patrick Morris, Carson's supporter in the agitation for representative institutions. A 'St John's Library' existed as early as 1810, and a visitor in 1813 noted that the city had a 'public reading room' displaying English newspapers and British monthlies. The youthful naturalist Philip Henry Gosse found in 1827 that it was possible to glean 'a sound knowledge of contemporary literature' from works available through the 'Carbonear book club'. In fact, when the colony was granted representative government in 1832 it possessed some of the rudiments of literary culture: a lively press, a growing interest in education, and an awareness of cosmopolitan ideas. Amateur theatre was now a feature of life in St John's, and Harbour Grace had a

'Play House' in 1824. There was even a monthly *Farmer's Journal* published in St John's in 1842. The first Newfoundland-born authors were: William Cormack, whose account of a coast-to-coast walk in 1822, *Narrative of a journey across the island of Newfoundland*, first appeared in abbreviated form in the *Edinburgh Philosophical Journal* of 1824 and was later published as a book in St John's (1856; D.W. Prowse, however, lists an Edinburgh edition of 1836); R.J. Parsons, editor of the *Newfoundland Patriot*, an important reform newspaper founded by Carson in 1833; William Charles St John, who wrote a *Catechism of the history of Newfoundland* ([St John's], 1835); and Philip TOCQUE, whose first book, *Wandering thoughts, or solitary hours*, was published in London in 1846. Tocque, a belletrist of considerable charm and ability, has been called the first Newfoundland-born man of letters, though most of his writing was done in the United States and Canada. Notable in Tocque is his romantic response to Newfoundland scenery, a tendency in which, however, he was anticipated by Cormack and Henrietta Prescott, author of *Poems, written in Newfoundland* (London, 1839). Mrs M.S. Peace, too, in *The convict ship and other poems* (Greenock, 1850), noted that 'Nature's pencil' had thrown 'a glory bold, sublime/And majestic o'er this land.' But, she added mournfully, ''Tis not, 'tis not my home.' She longed for Scotland, saying of her adopted country: 'this land is cold to me.' It took some doing for even Scots and Irish to grow attached to Newfoundland. One early Irish bishop, James O'Donel, though presumably well used to rock, bog, and fog at home, complained of having to live 'in this dismal & dreary country'.

From 1832 to 1855, when responsible government was inaugurated, there was such fierce sectarian and partisan rivalry in the colony that the intellectual energies of many of the most talented writers seem to have been consumed by politics. Some of the liveliest writing of the day is to be found in the newspapers—in, for example, John Valentine Nugent's *Newfoundland Vindicator* (1841-2) and Henry Winton's *Public Ledger*. Such literature, remaining at the level of commentary upon events, is not to be dismissed as trivial. (A study of nineteenth-century Newfoundland journalism is a great desideratum.) The first novel with a Newfoundland setting appears to be Charles A. Murray's *Ottawah, the last chief of the Red Indians of Newfoundland* (London, 1847); but the earliest novel to be based upon prolonged, first-hand experience of life in the colony was by a New Englander, Robert Traill Spence Lowell, whose *The new priest in Conception Bay* (Boston, 1858; rev. 1889) sprang from his missionary work in Bay Roberts in the 1840s. Though marred by bigotry against Roman Catholics, the book brilliantly duplicates dialects in the Conception Bay region and evokes the distinctive way of life of the fishermen. Two striking poems by Lowell about Newfoundland are printed in *Fresh hearts that failed three thousand years ago* (Boston, 1860) and *Poems* (Boston, 1864). The ode called 'Newfoundland' in the latter volume, though soddenly pious towards the end, is one of the finest poems ever written about the island. A long story by Lowell, 'A raft that no man made', recounting a sealing adventure, appeared in the *Atlantic Monthly* (1862). Lowell's literary interest in the colony foreshadows that of authors of fiction such as R.M. Ballantyne (*The crew of the Water Wagtail*, 1889); Rudyard Kipling, in whose *Captains courageous* (1897) a child of privilege falls overboard from a liner passing over the Grand Banks and is taught lessons about life by Newfoundland fishermen; J.B. Connolly, a Boston storyteller (*The crested seas*, 1907), who had been stirred by the romance of the Gloucester herring fishery off Newfoundland; Theodore Goodridge ROBERTS; and especially Norman DUNCAN, whose evocation of outport life in *The way of the sea* (1903) remains, in many respects, unsurpassed. As the nineteenth century ended, Newfoundland had become a well-used setting for tales of adventure. There was also much scientific interest in exploring both the island and Labrador. A book of permanent value sprang from such interest: Dillon Wallace's account of the ill-fated expedition of 1903, *The lure of the Labrador wild* (1905).

In the meantime the closing decades of the century were noteworthy for an outburst of scholarly and patriotic writing by resident authors anxious to establish Newfoundland's nationhood, or at least to prop it up. The period 1875-1915 was possibly the most fertile in the colony's literary history—although, as in earlier decades, the bulk of the writing was descriptive and topical rather than imaginative. Among native-born writers the most outstanding were the three Howley brothers Richard V., Michael F., and James P.; the historian D.W. Prowse, a scholar and prose stylist of superb gifts; and the journalists P.T. McGrath and P.K. Devine. They produced a rich and varied body of writing. Such works as M.F. Howley's *Ecclesiastical history of Newfoundland* (Boston, 1888), Prowse's *A history of Newfoundland from the English, colonial, and foreign records* (London, 1895), McGrath's *Newfoundland in 1911* (1911), and J.P. HOWLEY's *The Beothucks or Red Indians of Newfoundland* (1915) are irreplaceable contributions to local letters. J.P. Howley was also a diarist of exceptional talent whose numerous journals have only recently been released by the Howley family; that for 1868 was printed in *Newfoundland Studies*, vol. 7, no. 2 (1991). For his part, Richard V. Howley wrote, among many other pieces of journalism, an essay in the magazine *Month* (1887) containing a provocative definition of the Newfoundland character; he was a brilliant phrase-maker and fearless patriot. P.K. Devine, a member of a celebrated literary family from King's Cove, Bonavista Bay, was an author in a number of genres; his evocative pieces on the old fishery, contributed to the St John's *Trade Review* in 1915, were printed in *In the good old days!* (1990). Moses Harvey, an Irishman of Scottish descent, and Wilfred GRENFELL, the author of over thirty books, were also prominent prose writers of the day. The Bermudian W.G. Gosling, who wrote the imposing *Labrador: its discovery, exploration, and development* (1910) and *The life of Sir Humphrey Gilbert* (1911), was another scholar of significance. This heady time in Newfoundland letters was marked by the founding of three periodicals: the *Centenary Magazine* (1896), *Newfoundland Magazine* (1900), and *Newfoundland Quarterly* (1901). The first two were ephemeral; the third, established by printer John Evans, is still in existence. Nor were poetry and fiction absent from this small renaissance. Isabella Rogerson, M.F. Howley, F.B. Wood, and R.G. MacDonald produced volumes of verse between 1898 and 1908, while W.B. Stabb, Anastasia M. English, and J.A. O'Reilly wrote romances loosely based on Newfoundland life and history. Stabb's *Florimel Jones* (London, 1876), appears to be the first novel written by a Newfoundlander; he also wrote *Hard hit* ([London], 1880) and *Wreaths of smoke* (London, 1880). He was, however, a writer without distinction. George J. Bond's *Skipper George Netman: a story of out-port Methodism in Newfoundland* (London, 1887) was another early, if rudimentary, novel by a native son. This formal literary activity was matched, at a different and not necessarily lower level, by a flurry of ballad writing. G.M. Story has stated that the decades between 1850 and 1914 were the 'golden age of the St John's ballads and composed songs', and it is to that fertile period that we owe, for example, three of Newfoundland's most cherished poems: John Grace's 'Petty Harbour bait skiff' (*c.* 1852), Johnny Burke's 'The Kelligrews' Soiree' (*c.* 1904), and John V. Devine's 'The Badger drive' (c. 1915). All three are in *Old-time songs and poetry of Newfoundland* (4th edn, 1966), edited by Gerald S. Doyle, a famous songbook. A collection of Burke's songs, edited by W.J. Kirwin, appeared in 1982; there is an article on Burke by Michael Taft in *Newfoundland Studies*, vol. 6, no. 1 (1990).

All this held promise for the future; but the promise was not to be quickly fulfilled. The departure of E.J. PRATT for Canada in 1907, at the age of twenty-five, could be seen as symbolic of Newfoundland's failure to nurture literary genius (though he was far from being the first literary man to leave for Canada; to name just one other besides Tocque, Placentia-born Joseph Edmund Collins, biographer of Sir John A. Macdonald, left Newfoundland in the mid-1870s). The Newfoundland that would later be pictured in Pratt's *Rachel* (1917), *Newfoundland verse* (1923), and other volumes was often the bare, pitiless rock that he saw struggling against economic setbacks in the early to mid-1890s. Ahead lay the Great War—memorably evoked in Jack Turner's *Buddy's blighty and other verses from the trenches* (1918)—and a decade-and-a-half of further economic uncertainty that would call into question the dominion's ability to survive as a separate national identity. (Newfoundland started calling itself a dominion after the war.) Elizabeth Miller has collected *Arms and the Newfoundlander: poetry of the Great War* (1994).

The twenties and thirties were not rich in literature, though the appearance of Irving Fogwill's *Prelude to doom and other poems* (1931), perhaps the first sign of a modernist tendency in Newfoundland letters, should be noted. (A selection of Fogwill's prose and poetry, edited by Daphne Benson, appeared in 1981.) A fine lyric poet who emerged in the 1930s was Gregory Power (collected in *The Power of the pen*, edited by Harold Horwood, 1989). J.R. Smallwood was now also active as a writer, his earliest books being a biography of the founder of the Fishermen's Protective Union, *Coaker of Newfoundland* (1927), and *The new Newfoundland* (1931), a work predicting that the dominion would become 'one of the great small nations of the world'. Instead the country relinquished its independence in 1934. In the late thirties, during Newfoundland's period of rule by a British-appointed Commission, the novels of Margaret DULEY appeared in what seemed to be a literary vacuum. Her *Cold pastoral* (1939) and *Highway to valour* (1941), presenting an ambivalent attitude towards her Newfoundland heritage, provide an image of a country—or, rather, colony, for such it now was again—uncertain of itself, plagued by doubt, yet somehow stiffly proud and enduring.

The wartime boom in Newfoundland, from 1941 to 1945, expanded mental horizons and provoked renewed literary activity. New magazines such as the *Courier* (1941-6), *Atlantic Guardian* (1945-57), and the avant-garde *Protocol* (1945-9) signalled the appearance of new talent in verse and prose. The *Guardian* was especially important insofar as it gave expression to a mood of nostalgia for what was thought to be the simple and decent life of the old outport village. Montreal teacher Arthur Scammell, some of whose writings are assembled in *My Newfoundland* (1966), and New Yorker Ron Pollett, who wrote *The ocean at my door* (1956), were the two principal authors in this still as yet unfamiliar genre of sentimental *emigré* reminiscence. The stories of Edward RUSSELL, which he began to write in the 1950s, were similar in spirit and theme, though they were rooted in the practical affairs of contemporary life rather than in the past. All three writers celebrated the outport, giving authentic literary expression—in formal as opposed to folk literature—to the peculiar outharbour way of viewing the world: a way that combines shrewd understatement, funmaking, homely wisdom, acceptance, and stubborn pride. In fact, after Newfoundland's confederation with Canada in 1948-9—a climactic event depicted in Tom Cahill's play *As loved our fathers* (1974), and more soberly considered in Albert B. Perlin's *A clear head in tempestuous times* (1986), edited by Francis Hollohan and Melvin Baker—the outport became one of the chief subjects of Newfoundland writing. A fast-changing lifestyle, which seemed to make the place and people more and more North American, forced a re-examination of discarded, yet longed-for, ancient verities. The happy outport of long ago became one of the myths of the literary scene.

The post-Confederation period in Newfoundland has been marked by novelty and dislocation, as an old British colony somewhat reluctantly entered the mainstream of Canadian life. Witnessing this collision between new habits and ancient ways, writers have made it one of their central concerns. This theme is prominent, for instance, in four of the chief literary interpreters of modern Newfoundland: the outsiders Farley MOWAT and Franklin RUSSELL, and native-born novelists Harold HORWOOD and Percy JANES. Mowat, in books such as *This rock within the sea* (1968) and *A whale for the killing* (1972), pictures outharbour Newfoundlanders as a people who once 'partook of the primal strength of rock and ocean', but now are becoming dangerously infected by American diseases like 'compulsive consumerism'. A corrective to this view may be found in Russell's masterful *The secret islands* (1965), a journal of a mid-life trip to Newfoundland and other islands. In *Tomorrow will be Sunday* (1966), Horwood's first novel, the new ideas in the great world outside Newfoundland are uncritically embraced, and the outport in which the story is set is seen as one of 'the backwaters of civilization', inhabited by 'almost a lower species'. Janes, in *House of hate* (1970), expresses a similarly benighted view of his heritage, ending the novel with a devastating critique of the character of oldtime Newfoundlanders. (His opinion of contemporary Newfoundlanders, as delivered in *The picture on the wall*, 1987, isn't flattering either.) But most new writers saw the old outport as a symbol of strength and cohesiveness. In the plays of both Michael COOK and David FRENCH, the old attitudes and dialects have great attraction, while in Thomas Dawe's *Island spell* (1981), one of a number of books by this gifted poet, abandoned outports are described with poignancy. Dawe's best work has been collected in *In Hardy country* (1993). The fine times in Newfoundland's imagined past are evoked as well by the poets Enos Watts, in *After the locusts* (1974), and Al Pittman, whose best work is in *Once when I was drowning* (1978). Depicting the old outport as joyful pastoral has been a favourite activity of columnist Ray GUY, who has been writing in newspapers and magazines since the 1960s. The pieces he calls 'juvenile outharbour delights' recreate in exquisite detail his boyhood experiences in Placentia Bay in the 1940s and 1950s.

The most recent Newfoundland literature has exhibited more complexity and ambiguity. Fiction has been especially strong, with Kevin MAJOR, Bill Rowe, Wayne Johnston, Helen Porter, Bernice Morgan, Joan CLARK, and Kenneth J. Harvey leading the field. Scholarly writing has also shown great vigour in the past two decades. The magisterial *Dictionary of Newfoundland English* (1982; 2nd edn 1990), edited by G.M. Story, W.J. Kirwin, and J.D.A. Widdowson, has affirmed, once and for all, the validity of Newfoundland language, literature, and culture as worthy objects of study.

See Margaret Duley, 'Glimpses into local literature', *Atlantic Guardian*, vol. 13, no. 7

(1956); *Bibliography of Newfoundland* (2 vols, 1986), compiled by Agnes C. O'Dea, edited by Anne Alexander; G.M. Story's provocative 'Notes from a berry patch', *Proceedings of the Royal Society of Canada*, Series 4, vol. 10 (1972), responded to by Patrick O'Flaherty in 'Looking backwards: the milieu of the old Newfoundland outports', *Journal of Canadian Studies* (1976); for a survey of history and culture, see G.M. Story, 'Newfoundland: fishermen, hunters, planters, and merchants', in *Christmas mumming in Newfoundland* (1969), edited by Herbert Halpert and G.M. Story; and Patrick O'Flaherty, *The rock observed: studies in the literature of Newfoundland* (1979). For an anthology, see Peter Neary and O'Flaherty, *By great waters* (1974). PATRICK O'FLAHERTY

New France, Writing in. 1. EXPLORATION LITERATURE forms the major part of writings related to New France. It was produced by leaders of expeditions, missionaries, or ghost-writers (partisans, compilers, printers)—exact attribution is frequently unclear. Most writers aimed to uphold the authority or defend the interests of an individual or group with business in New France, while also appealing to a public interested in new scientific information and exotic descriptions. Adopting one or more of numerous genres—chronicle, history, treatise, Utopia, satire, autobiography, official reports—this literature frequently projects a narrator's personality; it can also relate, as if it were the narrator's own experience, information acquired from various sources. Questions of veracity, plagiarism, or embellishment assail most of these books, which can rarely be understood simply as records of fact.

In the discussion that follows, long titles indicating the countries visited, the type of thing observed, and the authority of the observer will usually not be quoted fully. The *JESUIT RELATIONS* are treated in a separate article. Compilers whose contact with Canada was second-hand, like Father Du Creux, will not be included.

Jacques Cartier (1491-1557) did not publish the accounts of his three journeys; in *Relations* (1986) Michel Bideaux defends their authenticity against the long-standing doubts of authorship reasonably raised by H.P. Biggar in his bilingual *The voyages of Jacques Cartier* (1924). The same title is given to an edition of the English translations in Biggar's book, with an introduction by Ramsay COOK, published in 1993; it includes documents relating to Cartier and the Sieur de Roberval. The first published work bearing Cartier's name, the *Bref récit...* (Paris, 1515), is a third-person account of the second voyage (1535-6). It was followed by posthumous accounts of the first (1534) and third (1541-2) voyages. The latter is known only through fragments published in 1600 by Richard Hakluyt, while the account of the first voyage has an extremely complex publication history. The terse style of these works has led to the suggestion that they were derived from a ship's log, but the range of interest is fully that of a travel book, containing many memorable incidents and descriptions. Among these are the first meeting with an Iroquoian fishing party in the Baie des Chaleurs, the first sight of Stadaconé (Quebec), the naming of Mont Royal, and the discovery of the much-needed cure for scurvy. Certain aphorisms, such as 'the land God gave to Cain', have become legendary, while data concerning vegetation, the Iroquoian language, and European adaptation are still prime information.

Marc Lescarbot (*c.* 1570-1642) was a Parisian lawyer and a writer before he was a traveller. His declared reason for going to Canada (at the invitation of Jean de Biencourt de Poutrincourt, who was one of his clients) was disgust with corrupt European society, particularly its courts (he had just lost a case). This was a conventional sentiment, but Lescarbot's originality lies in being the first writer in French to envision the New World as a desirable escape from the Old. Sailing for Acadia in 1606, he at once composed a poem, 'Adieu à la France', announcing a personal search for a lost Edenic paradise. In Port Royal he wrote commemorations of notable men and occasions. 'La défaite des sauvages armouchiquois' describes Native warfare in epic style. In his 'Le théâtre de Neptune', which was given the first theatrical performance in North America (1606), volleys of cannon and musket shot, trumpet fanfares, and the tomfoolery of sailors were ingeniously combined with verse speeches to mark the lieutenant-governor's return from an expedition. The written text, a mere 243 lines, has Neptune, 6 Tritons, 4 'sauvages', and one cheery companion offering fulsome tribute to Poutrincourt. Native words and local objects are combined with classical poetic conventions; for example, a Native expresses affection by presenting 'matachias' to the 'Sagamos' and explaining that these signify Cupid's flames. A Triton speaking Gascon dialect makes innuendoes about old Neptune's love life. It was obviously meant for fun, but the mock-pompous style contains a serious declaration of colonial ambitions for France. On his way to and from Acadia,

Lescarbot also wrote twelve poems—later collected in *Les muses de la Nouvelle France* (Paris, 1609), which included 'Le théâtre de Neptune'—expressing enthusiasm for exploration. His clear, declamatory verse has no obvious continuity in Canada.

After returning to France in 1607 Lescarbot continued to write on a variety of topics, including travel in the Americas, Germany, and Switzerland. His general ideas show the world progressing from childhood into an era of expanding civilization, which he linked with the urge to colonize. In his *Histoire de la Nouvelle-France* (three Paris editions: 1609, 1611-12, and 1617-18) he brought together in a repetitious monument all discovery materials available to date, and included his 'Muses de la Nouvelle France'. Books I to III reproduce accounts by French explorers in the Americas, with some editing and collation: Laudonnière, Ribaut, Gourgues, Villegagnon, Cartier, and Roberval. Book IV recounts the abortive expedition of 1604 and the 1606-7 expedition in which Lescarbot took part; this book is marked by his indignation at failures. Book V recounts Champlain's voyages from 1608 to 1613, and those of the two Biencourts (father and son, 1610-15). Book VI contains 'the Manner, Customs, and fashions of Life of the Western Indians of New France, and a comparison of them with those of the people of the old world. . .'. (While preparing this work, Lescarbot also wrote two pamphlets: *La conversion des sauvages*, 1610, and *Relation dernière*, 1612.) The three editions of the *Histoire* testify to its popularity. Writing in a cultivated style, Lescarbot combined elements of ethnography and documentation with classical allusions and moral comment tending towards the myth of the 'bon sauvage' and the regenerative power of the new land (Frenchmen become visibly more virtuous away from home). *The history of New France* (Toronto, 3 vols, 1907, 1911, 1914), translated for the Champlain Society and edited by W.L. Grant, follows Lescarbot's third edition; it contains 'Les muses de la Nouvelle France' without translation. An English translation by Pierre Erondelle of Books IV and VI of the first edition of the *Histoire* was published under the title *Nova Francia* (1609) and is available both in a modern edition (London, 1925) and in reprint (Amsterdam, 1977). *The theatre of Neptune* (1927) is a translation by Harriette Tabor Richardson; a contemporary translation by Eugene Benson and Renate Benson can be found in *Canada's lost plays*, vol. 4 (1982), edited by Anton Wagner.

Samuel de Champlain (*c.* 1570-1635) is celebrated as the explorer and navigator whose tireless efforts shaped the earliest successful colony in Canada. His prose is that of a man of action: terse, organized, sometimes peremptory. His life and works present some major mysteries. Was he a Protestant apostate? How did he appropriate the particle 'de' to his name? What was his status before 1608? What part did he have in writing 'his' first and last works? Did he make all the journeys described in them? His many biographers (listed in the *DICTIONARY OF CANADIAN BIOGRAPHY*, vol. 1) reach no precise consensus. The available facts about Champlain's activities and writing may be summed up as follows. His earliest voyages were probably made on Spanish ships to the West Indies, and he had some hand in compiling travel literature about these. His first voyages to the St Lawrence (1603) and Acadia (1604 and 1606) gave him an opportunity, perhaps a motive, to display his knowledge. As the lieutenant of de Monts, Champlain returned to the St Lawrence in 1608 and established a trading-post at Quebec called the *Habitation*. In the years that followed he laid the foundations of New France, leading expeditions up the main inland water routes, crossing the Atlantic frequently, and writing and publishing his three volumes of *Voyages*.

The first work undisputably by Champlain is *Des sauvages* (Paris, 1603), which offers a wealth of information on topography and commercial potential and succinct descriptions of rival Amerindian nations in the St Lawrence area. The first *Voyages*. . . (Paris, 1613) is regarded by some as Champlain's best work, mainly because of its highly factual character, covering the voyages from 1604 to 1612 (and using partly corrected material from *Des sauvages*). For the general reader what stands out most is the narration of striking episodes (such as the starving Natives crossing the ice floes in Feb. 1609) where the setting in the new country comes alive in action. Champlain's comments are usually curt: 'There are six months of winter in this country' (Ste-Croix, 1605) is typical of how he sums up a season of disasters.

In the second volume of *Voyages*. . . (Paris, 1619) the canvas is richer, and the reader is better able to imagine the life of the little society at Quebec. Here too are fuller descriptions of the Hurons, whom Champlain had at last seen in their own country (around Georgian Bay). They are no longer lost in vague generalities about 'sauvages' (though some of these persist), nor reduced to physical measurements (though these are plentiful), and we get a lively impression of life in a longhouse with its fleas, spoilt children, and thick smoke. Champlain's account of his disputes with the fur-trading company, on the other hand, is a careful statement of legal positions without the drama and the personal clashes that must have accompanied them.

The last volume of *Voyages*... (Paris, 1632), purporting to cover the period 1603 to 1631, presents the greatest complications. It contains a rewritten version of the voyages from 1603 (the rewriting is almost certainly not by Champlain, or not completed by him; the Jesuit Fathers in France and Champlain's young wife have both been suggested as possible ghost-writers); the new voyages to 1629; business surrounding the Treaty of St-Germain-en-Laye; and a retrospective account of French exploration since 1504. It looks like a hasty job of rewriting Champlain's own accounts and runs into inconsistencies, particularly in trying to suppress all references to Recollect missionaries. Above all, a mellifluous moralizing tone seems quite unlike the brusque style of the two earlier *Voyages*. Whenever the 1632 *Voyages* sound patronizing or didactic we suspect a foreign hand, but Champlain himself can be recognized in places: the perfect navigator, he says, must be a decent God-fearing man and emulate Flemish cleanliness. This book also contains an appendix that might have been a separate work, the *Traitté (sic) de la marine et du devoir d'un bon marinier*, a catechism translated into Huron by Father Brébeuf, and similar material translated into Montagnais by Father Massé.

H.P. Biggar's bilingual edition in the Champlain Society series, *The works of Samuel de Champlain* (6 vols, 1922-36), is authoritative. Among the selections published in English, the most recent is the translation by Michael Macklem—*Voyages to New France* (1970), with an introduction by Marcel Trudel—which lends Champlain's accounts of the years 1615 to 1618 a liveliness that is not always present in the original.

Gabriel Sagard (*fl.* 1614-38) was a simple though highly literate *Frère convers* in the Recollect branch of the Franciscan Order. He seems to have joined the Recollects about 1610, at the dawn of their existence as a strictly reformed branch, and he defected before 1638, when they were fully established. *Le grand voyage au pays des Hurons*... (Paris, 1632) is virtually a straightforward account of Sagard's own voyage to New France. He embarked at Dieppe in 1623 (his printer gives the wrong year) and describes all the stages of the journey to Ossossane in Huronia. His narrative gradually gives way to the need to describe things by categories, such as flora and fauna, burial customs, sexual behaviour, and family life. The book was written in a hurry; the Recollects needed publicity to make their presence and achievements in Canada known, since they had just been excluded from their mission. This may account for the frank spontaneity that most readers find in Sagard's narrative. Sagard's accounts of life in the longhouse are often unflattering, but nonetheless sympathetic, to the Hurons, of whom he gives the most integrated picture. In his next book (below) Sagard had to defend his favourable impressions of the unregenerate 'sauvages'. His emphasis on their internal harmony is important in literary history because it gives observer support to the myth of the 'noble savage': Sagard was read and imitated down to the time of Voltaire. *Le grand voyage* was translated for the Champlain Society by H.H. Langton as *The long journey to the country of Hurons* (1939).

Sagard's *Histoire du Canada*... (Paris, 1636), in four parts, does not recapture the fresh feeling of a personal journey. Book I gives a panorama of Franciscan missions and includes relations attributable to Father Joseph Le Caron and derived from a letter by Father Denis Jamet. These present a striking contrast: Le Caron gives a gloomy but perspicacious view of the conditions and the Native peoples, while Jamet waxes optimistic about Notre-Dame-des-Anges, Quebec, the prosperous religious residence in the wilderness. Book II expands on Sagard's 1632 relation, often tediously, but correcting many details. Books III and IV continue the Recollects' version of history down to their exclusion from Canada in 1629, and include complete relations not published elsewhere (notably Joseph de la Roche Daillon's account of his journey to present-day southern Ontario in 1627). Some portions may have been written with direct help from other Recollects in Paris, giving them the character of eyewitness narrations.

The *Histoire* is valued for its ethnographic information about the early discovery period, while also showing how Sagard's criticism of the authorities had boldened, as his appreciation of the 'sauvages' increased. Most subsequent Recollect writings were more embittered about loss of property and honour in New France, notably an anonymous *Mémoire* of 1637 (Paris, 1879). Sixte Le Tac's *Histoire chronologique de la Nouvelle France* (MS, 1689), published by Pierre Margry (Paris, 1888), is a forthright defence of the Recollects and an attack on the Jesuits. A more balanced but less reliable account covering the period 1615-90, *Établissement de la foy dans la Nouvelle France*... (Paris, 1691; translated by John G. Shea, New York, 1881) appears over the name of Chrestien Le Clercq. The unknown compiler mixes genuine and spurious relations of several Recollects' travels, including two falsely attributed to Joseph Le Caron, with dubious accounts of the discovery of the Mississippi. The real Le Clercq wrote about his own travels in *Nouvelle relation de la Gaspésie* (Paris, 1691).

The last of these Recollect explorers is Louis Hennepin (1627-*c.*1705), whose *Description de la Louisiane*... (Paris, 1683) describes a journey from Quebec to Louisiana, with observations of Niagara Falls and on various Native peoples. Hennepin is very insistent on his own part in the journey he undertook under the leadership of René-Robert Cavalier de La Salle. After La Salle was murdered in 1687, Hennepin claimed to have reached the mouth of the Mississippi in his augmented version, *Nouvelle découverte d'un très grand pays*... (Utrecht, 1697). This constitutes one of the most disputed travellers' tales, mingling falsehood and fact in a very egocentric story. It appears that the Mississippi section was lifted from the notes of Hennepin's fellow Recollect, Zénobé Membré, who was killed on the expedition.

The most flagrant mixture of fact and fiction is in three volumes of voyages by Louis-Armand de Lom d'Arce, baron de Lahontan (1666-1716). Lahontan's military career in Canada gave him first-hand knowledge, while his quarrel with J.F. de Mombicon de Brouillan, his senior officer in Newfoundland, drove him into exile and motivated his witty criticisms of the colonial administration. These constitute the main literary interest of *Nouveaux voyages*... (The Hague, 1703), *Mémoires de l'Amérique septentrionale* (The Hague, 1703), and *Supplément ... où l'on trouve des dialogues curieux*... (The Hague, 1703). (The *Dialogues* also appear in separate editions, and there are variant titles.) The use of dialogue instead of narrative represents an important change in the history of the genre. Adario, a full-fledged 'bon sauvage', confounds his European interlocutor's inept attempts to defend French civilization. Much of what he says could be accurate description, but his own loquacious personality seems improbable for a Huron. It was a provocative satirical device and much imitated in the Enlightenment. There are several English translations of the *Nouveau voyages*: *New voyages*... (London, 1703; London, 1735; Chicago, 1905) and *Voyages* (1932), translated by Stephen LEACOCK.

Joseph-François Lafitau (1681-1746), a Jesuit who spent some six years in Canada (1711-17), also has a prominent place in developing the literary figure of the 'sauvage'. His *Moeurs des sauvages amériquains comparées aux moeurs des premiers temps* (Paris, 1724) continues the work begun by Lescarbot and Sagard but carries it, as his title indicates, to outright primitivism (the belief that man's original state, true human nature, is visible in 'uncivilized' peoples). Like his predecessors, Lafitau selects those features of Amerindian culture that look most admirable in a European context, and confirms their basic naturalness by reference to classical writers, suggesting that naturalness is a source of authentic virtue.

Pierre-François-Xavier de Charlevoix (1682-1761) was one of the great Jesuit historians, known for his works on Japan and Paraguay. His two visits to Canada in 1705-9 and 1720-3 were backed up by his thorough use of Jesuit library resources, and he was actively concerned with the search for the Western sea. His *Histoire et description générale de la Nouvelle France ... avec le Journal ... d'un voyage*... (Paris, 1744) was a long-standing authority and a model of literary style. Some passing remarks about the *Canadiens*, and the transfer to them of a name that had previously designated an Indian nation, suggest the emergence of a new people. Charlevoix is also the author of *La vie de Marie de l'Incarnation*... (Paris, 1724), of a geographical report (published by Pierre Margry in his *Découvertes et établissements*... (Paris, 1879-88), and of contributions to the *Journal de Trévoux*, a Jesuit periodical. There are separate English translations of the *Journal ... d'un voyage* (London, 1761; Chicago, 1923; and others), and of the *Histoire* as the *History and description*... (New York, 1866-72; rev. 1900).

Other writers dealing directly with the discovery of the new or not so new continent have attracted less attention in literary discussion. Pierre-Esprit Radisson (*c.* 1640-1710) mingles fiction with vivid fact, visibly in the hope of attracting financial support for his expeditions. His work is known only through an English version of 1669: *Voyages of Peter Esprit Radisson* (Boston, 1885, and New York, 1943), and *The explorations of Pierre Esprit Radisson* (1961) edited by Arthur T. Adams. Louis-Henri de Beaugy (d. 1720) wrote *Journal d'une expédition contre les Iroquois en 1687* (Paris, 1883; trans., Rochester, N.Y., 1922).

Henri de Tonty (*c.* 1650-1704) is the presumed author of *Dernières découvertes . . . de M. de la Sale* (*sic*; Paris, 1697), a work whose value has been found dubious, as both history and literature. Claude-Charles Le Roy (*dit* Bacqueville) de la Potherie (1663-1717), who was in New France from 1697 to 1701, wrote a four-volume *Histoire de l'Amérique septentrionale* (Paris & Rouen, 1722; Paris 1753). Dière de Dièreville (*fl.* 1699-1711) travelled to Port Royal in October 1699, and returned to France one year later. His *Relation* of that journey (Rouen, 1708; 2nd edn, Québec, 1885) is expurgated, but the English translation (Toronto, 1933) includes the complete French text.

Of many other accounts of New France—having perhaps less literary than documentary and historical interest—five will be mentioned here. Nicolas Jérémie (1669-1732), who served in Hudson Bay from 1694 to 1714, wrote 'Relation du Détroit et de la Baie d'Hudson', which was published in *Recueil d'arrests et autres pièces pour l'établissement de la Compagnie de l'Occident* (Amsterdam, 1720), the fourth edition of which was published in English: *Twenty years of York Factory, 1694-1714: Jérémie's account of Hudson Strait and Bay* (1926), translated by Robert Douglas and J.N. Wallace. Letters attributed to the Jesuit missionary Antoine Silvy (1689-1711) were published in *Relation par lettres de l'Amérique septentrionale, années 1709 et 1710* (1904) and were included in translation in *Documents relating to the early history of Hudson Bay* (1916), edited by J.B. Tyrrell. Nicolas Perrot (*c.* 1643-1717), who had a chequered career that included being governor of Montreal (appointed 1670) and of Acadia (appointed 1684), and being arrested and imprisoned for illegal trade with the Native peoples, wrote *Mémoire sur les moeurs, coustumes et religion des sauvages de l'Amérique septentrionale* (Leipzig & Paris, 1864; rpr. 1968). Louis Franquet (1697-1768), a military engineer who is associated with improving the defences of Louisbourg, wrote journals of his tour of Québec, Trois-Rivières, and other towns and forts in 1752-3 that were published as *Voyages et mémoires sur le Canada* (Québec, 1889). In the realm of early western exploration the writings of Pierre Gaultier de Varennes et de La Vérendrye (1685-1749), and his sons, are important. These were translated and edited by L.J. Burpee for the Champlain Society in *Journals and letters of Pierre Gaultier de Varennes de La Vérendrye and his sons with correspondence between the governors of Canada and the French court, touching the search for the western sea* (1927).

The *Journal du voyage de M. Saint-Luc de la Corne . . . 1761* (Montréal, 1778; Québec, 1863) relates the ill-fated journey of the *Auguste*, carrying émigrés to France after the Conquest. La Corne Saint-Luc (1711-84), born in Canada and one of the few survivors of the shipwreck, wrote of his hardships in a fine measured style. The shipwreck is exploration literature in reverse, best known through the fictionalized version in a chapter of Philippe AUBERT DE GASPÉ's *Les ANCIENS CANADIENS*.

2. ANNALS. Pierre Boucher (1622-1717) arrived in Canada with his parents in 1635, worked for a time for the Jesuits, and became Indian interpreter, captain, and later governor of the trading post at Trois-Rivières while farming his own land. He was sent to Paris in 1661 to explain the settlers' situation with a view to reforming the fur trade. After his return the following year he wrote his *Histoire véritable et naturelle . . . de la Nouvelle France . . .* (Paris, 1664), a naïve mixture of memoirs, natural history, and description. Boucher's point of view is not that of an explorer but of a resident adapted to the land, which has a distinct presence and varied character in his work. His admiration for the English colonies, and his vehement hatred of the Iroquois, give a clear impression of the colonist's ideal of development. *Histoire véritable et naturelle* was translated by Edward Louis Montizambert under the title *Canada in the seventeenth century . . .* (Montreal, 1883).

Annals survive for the hospitals of Quebec and Montreal that are much more than annual accounts of main events in specific institutions. *Histoire de l'Hôtel-Dieu de Québec* (Montauban, 1751) was the collaborative work of Jeanne-Françoise Juchereau de la Ferté (1650-1723) and Marie-Andrée Regnard Duplessis (1687-1760). One surmises that the older woman dictated her memoirs and elaborated on other sources, such as the *Jesuit Relations* and older manuscript annals, and that the younger woman completed the work. Sister Juchereau was born in Quebec, took her vows at fourteen, and was superior from 1683 until her death; she was succeeded by Sister Regnard, who had arrived at Quebec from Paris at the age of fifteen. The *Histoire* is edifying and abounds in panegyrics of illustrious visitors and patients (including Kateri Tekakwitha), as well as of the founders of the hospital, while also commenting on great events in the life of the colony, such as the arrival of ships, epidemics, English attacks, and the earthquake of 1663.

Marie Morin (1649-1730) was also born in Quebec, like her mother (*c.* 1620), but went to the new settlement at Montreal. At twenty-two she became the first cloistered nun in Montreal and was playing an active part in directing the Hôtel-Dieu, where she elected the first Canadian superior in 1693; she was elected again in 1708. In 1697, at the request of her Order in France, she began to write annals, which she addressed to 'mes tres cheres soeurs qui lise cesy ou qui l'ecouteré lire' (*sic*). They were meant to be read aloud in other convents, like the lives of saints. Basically the work presents the lives and devotion of outstanding persons; but it includes substantial background on the foundation of Montreal and events of public interest, such as English attacks, major fires, and even a personal visit by the devil. Morin's narrative of the fire of 1695 is outstanding; she gives a vivid picture of all levels of disaster, explaining the measures that should have been taken to prevent spread of the fire and commenting wryly on the looters who sampled strong purgatives rescued from the pharmacy. Her portraits constitute a gallery of Christian Amazons (her expression). These annals were continued by Véronique Cuillerier and Catherine Porlier, but most of what survives is Marie Morin's. First published as *Annales de l'Hôtel-Dieu de Montréal* (Montréal, 1921), then as 'Pages inédites du premier écrivain canadien' (in the *Journal de l'Hôtel-Dieu de Montréal*, 1937), the critical edition is entitled *Histoire simple et véritable* (1979).

3. OCCASIONAL VERSE AND PROSE survive sporadically from the period of New France. Lescarbot's poems and masque have been mentioned above (1). Another dramatic composition, staged in 1658, was later published under the title *Réception de Mgr d'Argenson* (Québec, 1890). The anonymous author displays great ingenuity in combining allegorical figures and characters representing different sectors of the population; some of the speeches were composed entirely in Amerindian languages adapted to French verse. Elements of historical realism are combined with ceremonious statements of official optimism for the benefit of the new Governor.

Jean-Bernard Bossu (1720-92) travelled in Louisiana and the Miami country. His fables seek originality by using American content in the form created by La Fontaine, and are included in his *Nouveaux voyages aux Indes occidentales* (Paris, 1768) and *Nouveaux voyages dans l'Amérique septentrionale* (Amsterdam, 1777; trans. London 1771; New Orleans, 1940).

More strictly occasional verse is to be found about the Seven Years' War. A witty play on the word *carillon* and the French victory of that name is ironically addressed by an anonymous officer to the English soldiers: 'Le carillon de la Nouvelle-France'. Sister Marie-Hélène, less witty but more belligerent, adapted a well-known French lampoon for the victory of Chouaguen. Materials of this kind were collected by F.-A.-H. LARUE in *Le FOYER CANADIEN* (1865) and by Antoine Roy in *Les lettres . . . au Canada* (Paris, 1930).

Sermons composed for special occasions have been retrieved and published by later historians. Joseph de la Colombière (1651-1723) is the subject of a biography by Ernest Myrand (Montréal, 1898), who includes the text of a victory sermon delivered in 1690. A funeral sermon for Frontenac (1698), accompanied by a contemporary ironic comment, was first printed in *Bulletin de recherches historiques* (1895). The sermon is by Olivier Boyer (1663-1721); the wit is anonymous. The full range of this important element in the cultural life of the country is not known.

4. LETTERS from the French régime have a highly varied literary interest. Those of MARIE DE L'INCARNATION are described in the entry on her. Marguerite Bourgeoys (1620-1700) is known for her administrative vigour. Some of her letters have been collected and published in *Histoire de la Congrégation de Notre-Dame de Montréal* (Montreal, 1913) by Sister Sainte-Henriette. Jean Talon (1625-94) was the main administrative officer in Canada for most of the years between 1665 and 1672 and took a keen interest in all aspects of the colony. His letters and reports vary from perfunctory to highly discursive.

The letters of Élisabeth Bégon (1696-1755) were strictly private. Born in Canada, she had been married to the governor of Trois-Rivières. After his death in 1748 and the departure of their protector, she was sensitive to her loss of status and critical of the increasingly active social life of the colony. When her daughter—married to an army officer, Michel de La Rouvillière—died, she left a young girl and boy, who were brought up by Madame Bégon in endless consultation with the widower—a man near her own age who was posted to Louisiana in 1747—with whom Madame was in love. Her letters to him display many facets of her rich personality and of the life around her, as well as gradually disclosing a narrative in the manner of the epistolary novels of the time. Her 'cher fils' did not join her when she moved in 1749 to Rocheport, France, where she experienced an evident culture shock: 'I must seem like an Iroquois,' she comments. Mme Bégon's style, often vivid and biting, gives the reader a feeling of real presence. Her letters were first published in the *Rapport de l'archiviste de la Province de Québec* (1934-5); a modern edition appeared under the title *Lettres au cher fils* (1972).

The most elegant, polished letters of New France come from the two generals: Louis-Joseph, marquis de Montcalm (1712-59), and François-Gaston, duc de Lévis (1720-87). Each left a *Journal* of his campaigns, mainly of interest to military historians, and a volume of *Lettres...* that show an admirable range of style. Lévis in particular suits the tone to the correspondent: a dignified delicacy for the circumstances in which he had to write to General Murray, a friendly open manner to Montcalm, elegant showing off to Bigot, and so on. The journals and letters of both generals were selected for publication under the titles *Journal... de Lévis en Canada* (Montréal, 1889), *Lettres... de Lévis concernant la guerre au Canada* (Montréal, 1889), *Journal... de Montcalm (1756-59)* (Québec, 1895), and *Lettres... au Chevalier de Lévis* (Québec, 1894).

Detailed analyses of most of the works and authors mentioned in this article will be found in the *Dictionnaire des oeuvres littéraires du Québec*; information about most of their authors, with bibliographical notes, appears in the *DICTIONARY OF CANADIAN BIOGRAPHY*.

JACK WARWICK

Newlove, John (b. 1938). Born in Regina, Saskatchewan, and raised in communities in that province, where his mother was a schoolteacher, Newlove travelled extensively in Canada, living for three years in Vancouver. He was an editor for McCLELLAND & STEWART in Toronto, a teacher, and a writer-in-residence at various institutions. He now lives in Ottawa, where he works as an English editor for the Official Languages sector of the federal government. He edited the anthology *Canadian poetry: the modern era* (1977).

Newlove's books of poetry include *Grave sirs* (1962), *Elephants, mothers & others* (1963), *Moving in alone* (1965), *Black night window* (1968), *The cave* (1970), *Lies* (1972), *The fat man: selected poems, 1962-1972* (1977), *The green plain* (1981), *The night the dog smiled* (1986), and *Apology for absence: selected poems 1962-1992* (1993). Newlove won a Governor General's Award for *Lies*.

Two impulses dominate Newlove's poetry, the lyrical and the historical. As a lyric poet, Newlove is anything but precious and self-absorbed. While his work includes delicate musings on such traditional themes as love, beauty, and loss, moving away from cliché and towards ever-finer discriminations of thought and feeling, Newlove the singer also has a playful side, where he assumes the stance of stand-up comic, employing self-deflation, hyperbole, fantasy, and—especially in the treatment of domestic or mundane subjects—a deliberate rhetorical excess and archaic diction. Newlove is Canada's most gifted and meticulous prosodist. Not only do words such as *song*, *music*, *melody*, and *measure* recur frequently in his poems, but his best lyrics are characterized by a subtle modulation of image, idea, and sound, 'the single, faltering, tenuous line of melody' that holds the listener in its spell; or, to use his own phrase, by a form of 'running verse' whose headlong movement recalls Charles Olson's description of the good poem: 'A high-energy construct' where 'one perception must lead immediately and directly to a further perception.'

In 'No song', Newlove proposes to seek out a newer, more jagged music, appropriate for an age that has become increasingly violent and discordant. Like the crow perched on a branch, he must decline 'the privilege of music/or melody', instead 'fingering the absolute/wood/beneath.' That wood represents the spiritual or psychological truth embodied in private and collective experience, which the poet must record. Thus Newlove assumes his second role, that of archivist of human consciousness, concerned to preserve history, to discover both the pride and the shame of his people, the nature of their origins and inheritance. In a number of fine poems—such as 'Ride off any horizon', 'Crazy Riel', and 'The pride'—he attempts to understand the contemporary relevance of Canada's Aboriginal heritage and its terrible burden of racial violence and social and economic oppression. The stories, 'whatever is strong enough/to be remembered', are everywhere, the poet says. In such historical meditations, the concrete rendering of fact and the temperamental scoring of emotion bring an almost perfect fusion of the lyrical and the documentary modes.

See 'How do I get out of here: the poetry of John Newlove' in Margaret ATWOOD, *Second words: selected critical prose* (1982) and Brian Henderson, 'Newlove: poet of appearance', *Essays on Canadian writing* 2 (Spring 1975).

GARY GEDDES

Newman, Peter C. (b. 1929). Born in Vienna, Austria, Newman came to Toronto in 1940 and was educated at Upper Canada College, and the University of Toronto (B.A., 1950; M. Com., 1954) before becoming an assistant editor at the *Financial Post* in 1951. His career has included executive positions in mass journalism, particularly as editor-in-chief of the *Toronto Star* (1969-71) and as editor of *Maclean's* (1971-82). His main interests, however, have always lain in distinct areas of political and financial journalism. His first book, *Flame of power: intimate profiles of Canada's greatest businessmen* (1959), is the embryo of the type of minutely detailed, anecdotal personality study he later combined with analyses of events. *Renegade in power: the Diefenbaker years* (1963) and *The distemper of our times* (1968), about the Pearson government, are stately testaments to Newman's belief that the fate of nations is often the inevitable consequence of individual traits of personality acting in collusion; both books are wonderfully readable works of popular criminology. *Home country: people, places and power politics* (1973), a collection of magazine pieces, seemed to signal the end of Newman's life as a political analyst and the beginning of his career as the primary folklorist and explainer of Canada's proprietary class. *The Canadian establishment, vol. 1* (1975) and *The acquisitors: the Canadian establishment, vol. 2* (1981) tell of the transition in Canadian entrepreneurship from owners to professional managers, and the not-completely-unrelated partial shift in economic power from central Canada to the western provinces. Publication of the two volumes was separated by *Bronfman dynasty: the Rothschilds of the new world* (1978), the story of the rise to wealth and influence of the Montreal distilling family, so characteristic—in everything, perhaps, but scope—of Ontario and Quebec financial life as it had been traditionally carried out. *The establishment man: a study of personal power* (1982) is a biography of Conrad Black, the prominent Canadian capitalist and the subject of some attention in *The acquisitors*.

Other books include two volumes on the Hudson's Bay Company—*Company of adventures* (1985) and *Caesars of the wilderness* (1987). *True North, not strong and free* (1983), *Sometimes a great nation: will Canada belong to the 21st century?* (1988), and *Canada 1892: portraits of a promised land* (1992) signal Newman's return to political analysis and history.

The recipient of a number of honorary doctorates, Newman was promoted to Companion of the Order of Canada in 1980.

DOUGLAS FETHERLING

New provinces: poems of several authors (1936). This landmark anthology, illustrating the advances of the early Canadian modernists in terms of technique, subject, and poetic perspective, contains eleven poems by Robert FINCH, ten by Leo KENNEDY, two by A.M. KLEIN, eight by E.J. PRATT, ten by R.R. SCOTT, and twelve by A.J.M. SMITH. In 1931 the Montreal poets began to collect their own work and in 1934 invited the Toronto poets, Pratt and Finch, to join them in a proposed anthology. Although collaboration began optimistically under Smith's instruction to 'avoid being merely Georgian', there was some debate between Smith and Scott over the selection. Smith wanted the volume to offer an up-to-the minute statement on the contributors' work, while Scott wanted it to offer a more historical statement on the development of the contributors' poetry, in hopes of calling forth other, unknown modernist poets-in-the-making. There was also intense disagreement over Smith's proposed preface, which attacked the poetic achievements of the older Canadian poets. Without the placating, cajoling, and sometimes arbitrary insistence of Scott, *New provinces* would have foundered over this. When the anthology was finally published by MACMILLAN, Smith's lengthy Preface had been replaced by Scott's short one. A 1976 reprint contains an introduction by Michael Gnarowski that provides a history of the anthology's evolution, with particular reference to the incident of Smith's 'Rejected Preface' (which is included), laying the blame for its rejection at the feet of Pratt and Finch, who objected to his stringent attack on earlier Canadian poetry. The correspondence concerning *New provinces* reveals Scott's own reservations about it, which invited and strengthened the attack by Pratt and Finch. Smith's 'Rejected Preface', should be seen as an extension of his earlier article 'Wanted: Canadian criticism', *The CANADIAN FORUM* (Apr. 1928), to which Scott had taken exception in the next month's *Forum* (June 1938).

See Ken Norris, *The little magazine in Canada: 1925-80* (1984).

KEITH RICHARDSON

Nichol, bp (1944-88). Barrie Phillip Nichol was born in Vancouver, British Columbia. He grew up there, in Winnipeg, Manitoba, and Port Arthur (now part of Thunder Bay), Ontario, returning to Vancouver in 1960. He entered the education faculty of the University of British Columbia in 1962 and received an elementary basic certificate in 1963. While there he audited creative-writing classes attended by younger members of the *TISH* group. After a difficult year in Port Coquitlam, B.C., where he taught a Grade 4 class, he moved to Toronto and began work as a book searcher at the University of Toronto and entered therapy with the lay analyst Lea Hindley-Smith. His inclusion in 1965 in a therapy-learning group taught by Hindley-Smith led Nichol to join in 1967 in the establishing of the lay-therapy foundation Therafields, and to work as a therapist and an administrator of this therapeutic community until 1983.

Although Nichol had been writing since 1961, he first attracted public notice in the mid-1960s with his hand-drawn or 'concrete' poems. He valued particularly the personal aesthetic ground that concrete poetry gave him amid that period's various controversies about poetic theory. With its informal postal network that reached from Switzerland to Brazil, concrete poetry also gave him almost immediately an international audience and reputation.

The large range of Nichol's writing began to become apparent only with the publication of the relatively conventional free verse of *Journeying and the returns* (1967) and *Monotones* (1971)—which developed into Nichol's best-known work, *The martyrology*, published as *The martyrology: Books 1 and 2* (1972); *Books 3 and 4* (1976); *Book 5* (1982); *Book 6* (1987), and the posthumously published *Gifts: the martyrology book[s] 7 & 8* (1990). Between 1967 and his death in 1988, Nichol produced a prodigious number of books and pamphlets in a variety of genres. These included the prose text *Two novels* (1969); the essay collection *Craft dinner* (1978); the novels *Journal* (1977) and *Still* (1983); the poetry collections *Love: a book of remembrances* (1974), *Extreme positions* (1981), *Continental trance* (1982); the visual books *Still water* (1970), *ABC: the Aleph Beth book* (1971), and *Unit of four* (1974); the prose poems *Selected organs* (1988), the 'pataphysical' collections *Zygal* (1980), *Art facts* (1990), and *Truth: a book of fictions* (1993); a memoir, *Selected organs: parts of an autobiography* (1988); and the children's books *Moosequakes and other disasters* (1981), *ONCE: a lullaby* (1983), *The man who loved his knees* (1983), and *To the end of the block* (1984). *Still water*—together with the booklets *The true eventual story of Billy the Kid* (1970), *Beach head* (1970), and his collection of concrete poetry, *The cosmic chef* (1970)—won a Governor General's Award for poetry. Nichol also wrote a number of scripts for the television programs Fraggle Rock and The Racoons, and librettos for the musical-comedies *Group* (staged by Therafields in 1980) and *Tracks* (staged in Cobourg in 1986).

All of Nichol's work was stamped by his desire to create texts that were engaging in themselves as well as in their content, and to use indirect structural and textual devices to carry meaning. In *The martyrology* different ways of speaking testify to a journey through different ways of being. Language is both the poet's instructor and, through its various permutations, the dominant 'image' of the poem. The books of *The martyrology* document a poet's quest for insight into himself and his writing through scrupulous attention to the messages hidden in the morphology of his own speech.

This attention to syntax and morphology characterizes both Nichol's concrete poetry and his prose fiction. His concrete poems were typically written as sequences, and involve the sequential development of syllabic relationships (*Still water*) or of alphabetic shapes (*Unit of four* and *Aleph unit*, 1973). His prose fiction employs Gertrude Stein's technique of using evolving yet repetitive syntax to develop language both as a correlative for intense emotional states, as in *Journal*, and as a medium to divine meaning, as in *The true eventual story of Billy the Kid*.

Nichol first began performing as a sound poet in the mid-1960s. His early work in this medium was documented, together with early reflective poems, in Michael ONDAATJE's film *Sons of Captain Poetry* (1970); in 'Borders', a small phonodisc included with *Journeying and the returns* in 1967; and in the long-playing record 'Motherlove' (1968). In 1970 Nichol began what proved to be an extended collaboration with fellow poets Rafael Barreto-Rivera, Paul Dutton, and Steve MCCAFFERY, forming the sound-poetry group The FOUR HORSEMEN. Together with McCaffery in 1973 he began the intermittent 'TRG' (Toronto Research Group) project of theoretical and 'pataphysical' writing—a project that McCaffery brought to a close in 1992 with the publication of *Rational geomancy: the kids of the book machine. The collected research reports of the Toronto Research Group 1973-1982*.

In addition, Nichol was also one of the most energetic and effective editors of the 1970s and 1980s. He founded Ganglia Press in 1965 and the grOnk series of pamphlets in 1969. He joined COACH HOUSE PRESS in 1974 as an unpaid volunteer editor, and personally acquired and edited approximately one-quarter of the titles the press published between then and his death. In the early 1980s he helped found and fund the small writers' co-operative Underwhich Editions.

See Stephen SCOBIE, *bp Nichol: what history teaches* (1984); Roy Miki, ed., *Tracing the paths: reading & writing the martyrology* (1988). See also POETRY IN ENGLISH 1950 TO 1982: 2.

FRANK DAVEY

Nichols, Ruth (b. 1948). Born in Toronto and influenced by her mother's interest in literature, she began writing as a teenager and published her first novel at the age of twenty-one. Now married and living in Ottawa, she has written five novels: *A walk out of the world* (1960), *Ceremony of innocence* (1969), *The marrow of the world* (1972), *Song of the pearl* (1976), and *The left-handed spirit* (1978). She gained recognition as a remarkable writer of fantasies for children with her first, third, and fourth books. The central figures in these novels are young girls searching for a place or true home where they can be redeemed from the constrictions of a divided self. Like many fantasy writers, Nichols is steeped in the tradition of Tolkien, Lewis, Spenser, and the King James Bible; her interest in the Renaissance and the history of religion are reflected throughout her work. The search for a spiritual home leads Judith, in *A walk*, and Linda, in *The marrow*, into fantasy landscapes. Restless, troubled, near despair over the condition of their 'real' lives, they find self-awareness and redemption in the world of fantasy.

In *Song of the pearl* Nichols' use of metaphoric landscapes reaches a new level of power. Filled with hatred and melancholy, Margaret drifts calmly into death—which is her entrance into the realm of fantasy and a kind of heaven that is, ironically, both earth and the world of memory. Painfully she discovers that she has lived before—as Zawumatec, an Iroquois slave, and as Elizabeth, in Renaissance England—and learns that the uncle who raped her when she was Margaret, aged fifteen, was led to his fall by her own lust. After grappling with feelings she has denied or repressed, she gains another chance at life on earth. In this novel Nichols, putting the Tolkien-Lewis matrix behind her, succeeds in creating a powerful vision of the pilgrimage of the soul.

Nichols' writing for children was always full of mystery, intrigue, and skilful plotting. She has also extended her interests and skills into historical fiction for adults. *The burning of the rose* (1990) and *What dangers deep* (1992) take us into Tudor and Elizabethan England. The latter novel is a fascinating study of Sir Philip Sidney's role as spy in the Polish capital Krakow in 1574 while he was attending the wedding of his godfather, the English ambassador. Told as Sidney's first-person account, the novel is clever and revealing, both as a character study of Sidney and as a portrait of some aspects of Elizabethan England that always fascinate: court drama, spying, power, and the search for truth.

See Ruth Nichols, 'Fantasy and escapism', *Canadian Children's Literature* 4 (1976), and an interview with Jon Stott in that magazine (no. 12, 1978); and Ruth Nichols, 'Something of myself', in Sheila Egoff, ed., *One ocean touching: papers from the first Pacific Rim Conference on Children's Literature* (1979).

ROBERT LOVEJOY

Nickson, Elizabeth. See NOVELS IN ENGLISH 1983 TO 1996.

Nicol, Eric (b. 1919). One of Canada's most prolific and versatile humorists, he was born in Kingston, Ontario, but his family moved to Vancouver when he was six. He served in the RCAF for three years during the Second World War and spent some time as a comedy writer for the BBC and as a student at the University of British Columbia (where he wrote a column for the student newspaper) and at the Sorbonne. He has written for radio, television, and the stage; but his syndicated column in the *Vancouver Province* and his many books of humour have brought him the most widespread attention, three of them winning the LEACOCK Medal for Humour. These include: *Sense and nonsense by E.P. Nicol (Jabez)* (1947); *The roving I* (1950); *Twice over lightly* (1953); *Shall we join the ladies?* (1955); *Girdle me a globe* (1957); *In darkest domestica* (1959); *An uninhibited history of Canada* (1959); *Space age, go home!* (1964); *Don't move! Renovate your house and make social contacts* (1971); *Letters to my son* (1974); *There's a lot of it going around* (1975); *Canadadide: a patriotic satire* (1983); and *Back talk* (1992). He has published a number of works in collaboration, beginning with *Sez we* (1943), a collection of columns from the *Vancouver News-Herald* by 'Jabez' (Nicol) and Jack Scott. He has collaborated with the cartoonist Peter Whalley on *Say, uncle* (1961), *Russia, anyone?* (1963), *100 years of what?* (1966), and *Canada cancelled because of lack of interest* (1977); and with Dave More on *The joy of hockey* (1978) and *The joy of football* (1980). His work has been anthologized in *A herd of yaks: the best of Eric Nicol* (1962) and *Still a Nicol* (1972). He has written a history of his city, *Vancouver* (1970; rev.1978) and a book on his own profession, *One man's media, and how to write for them* (1973).

Without having the highly individual view of the world that makes for a great humorist on the order of Leacock, Thurber or Twain, Nicol has a distinctive voice—fast-talking, wisecracking—and the consistency and durability of his work, rare in the field, proclaim his professional skill. Even the conventional pieces in which he pictures himself struggling with social embarrassments and domestic misfortunes stand up to rereading. His main strength is verbal inventiveness, shown in outrageous puns and verbal zig-zags that take the reader by surprise: for example, the title essay of *Shall we join the ladies?* refers not to after-dinner rituals but to sex-change operations.

As a playwright Nicol has had mixed success. *Like father, like fun* (1975, prod. 1966), about the attempt of a crass businessman to contrive his son's sexual initiation, was a hit in Vancouver, but (rewritten as *A minor adjustment*) flopped on Broadway, becoming a classic instance of the dangers of transplanting a play from one community to another. Nicol characteristically got a ruefully funny book out of the experience, *A scar is born* (1968). The scars also show on the central character of *The fourth monkey* (1975, prod. 1968), a frustrated playwright. Both plays combine frequently witty dialogue with structural weakness and arbitrary characterization.

Nicol has also used drama as a vehicle for ideas, as in his contribution to *The centennial play* (prod. 1967) and *The citizens of Calais* (1975, prod. 1974) where, through the comic squabbling of characters putting on a play, Nicol reflects on the cynicism and petty-mindedness that threaten Canada, and enters a plea for tolerance and common sense. *Pillar of sand* (1975, prod. 1972) pits the unreason of early Christian mysticism—for which we may read the unreason of Nicol's own time—against the rationality of a Roman soldier. Comedy and serious comment blend uneasily here; the mix works better in Nicol's childrens' plays, *The clam made a face* (1972, prod. 1967) and *Beware the quickly who* (1973, prod. 1967), which celebrate the creative, playful side of life against the spoilsports who threaten it; and in the television play *The man from inner space* (1976, prod. 1973), whose hero tries unsuccessfully to escape to a mechanically created private world.

Nicol's most substantial achievement to date is *Dickens of the Mounted: the astonishing long-lost letters of Inspector F. Dickens NWMP 1874-86* (1989), in which he presents himself as editor of the recently discovered letters of Frank Dickens, son of the great novelist, from his time as an officer of the North-West Mounted Police. 'Dickens' writes in a modified version of Nicol's own wisecracking, pun-laden style, and shows a thoroughly modern anger at the government's treatment of Native people, combined with a wry affection for the parts of Canada that lie outside Ottawa. While he has a curious knack for bumping into famous people—like Gabriel Dumont, Louis Riel and Harry Flashman—he is also ruefully aware of his own role as the unsatisfactory son of a great man. The result is an engaging blend of history, political commentary, fiction, and mischief.

ALEXANDER LEGGATT

Nigog, Le (1918). The first arts magazine in Quebec, it grew out of Thursday-evening meetings held by the architect Fernand Préfontaine in his Westmount (Montreal) home. Among those present were Robert Laroque de ROQUEBRUNE, historian and man of letters; Adrien Hébert, painter; his brother Henri Hébert, sculptor; Louis Bourgoin, chemist; and Léo-Paul Morin, composer and pianist. The name 'Nigog' is an Aboriginal word meaning fishing-spear. The editorial committee was made up of Préfontaine, Laroque de Roquebrune, and Morin. The twelve numbers that were published (financed by Préfontaine) contained 108 articles on music, literature, the plastic arts and art in general, and some dozen poems, accompanied by art work of various kinds. Though it never claimed to be bilingual, it published some articles in English. The magazine was a polished showcase that highlighted the group's conception of art: namely that manner of presentation was more important than subject matter. Wishing to disseminate modern ideas about art, its founders were led to denounce the regionalists and their taboos, thereby producing a major disturbance in the artistic and intellectual climate because they were, in effect, urging the regionalists to forsake the sources of their inspiration—the official utilitarian themes.

Though its circulation was less than 500, *Le Nigog* exerted a far-reaching influence. It helped to change the intellectual and artistic atmosphere in Quebec, purging it of its habitual optimism and *joie de vivre*, its impressionism, and its addiction to copying nature. It set in motion the irreversible process of literary liberation from the ultra-conservative reign of the worship of the small patch of land and 'l'heure des vaches'.

ARMAND GUILMETTE

Niven, Frederick (1878-1944). Born to Scottish parents in Valparaiso, Chile, Frederick John Niven was taken to Glasgow at age five and educated in Hutcheson's Grammar School and the Glasgow School of Art. In his late teens he was sent to visit friends in the Okanagan Valley, British Columbia, as a treatment for a lung ailment. He spent what he described as 'a year or two' travelling in Canada and taking odd jobs, an experience that drew him into journalism on his return to Scotland. In 1908 he began his career as a novelist with the publication of *The lost cabin mine*, one of many adventure stories he set in the Canadian West. Married in 1911, he spent several months in 1912 and 1913 travelling as a freelance writer in Canada. In 1920 he and his wife immigrated to Canada, living near Nelson, B.C., and in Vancouver until Niven's death.

Before emigrating, Niven had established himself as a minor but promising novelist in Britain. His writing was stimulated by his Canadian travel, and more than half of his early publications include New World settings, some Canadian, some in an indeterminate 'West': two volumes of short stories, *Above your heads* (1911) and *Sage-brush stories* (1917); a book of poems, *Maple-leaf songs* (1917); a fictionalized personal experience, *The S.S. Glory* (1915); and four novels: *The lost cabin mine* (1908), *Hands up!* (1913), *Cinderella of Skookum Creek* (1916), and *Penny Scot's treasure* (1919). Some of these books were adventure romances written 'to keep the wolf from the wife', to use Niven's phrase. His more realistic novels had Old World settings and, like *A wilderness of monkeys* (1911), treated themes of isolation, especially that of the artist championing spiritual values in a materialistic society.

After settling in Canada, Niven used Old World settings for eleven of seventeen remaining novels. He used the New World for one volume of poetry, *A lover of the land and other poems* (1925); one fictionalized personal experience, *Wild honey* (1927); and six novels: *The wolfer* (1923), *Treasure trail* (1923), *The flying years* (1935), *Mine inheritance* (1940), *Brothers-in-arms* (1942), and *The transplanted* (1944). These later novels include Niven's chief contribution to Canadian literature: a trilogy spanning the settlement of the West and incorporating his most serious themes. *Mine inheritance* is a historical romance of the struggle to establish the Selkirk Settlement amid the fur-trade wars on the Red River. Wholly sympathetic to the colonizers, it dramatizes their need to adapt mentally and spiritually, as well as physically, in order to overcome the isolation of the new land. *The flying years* is a panoramic narrative extending from the 1850s to the 1920s. Its protagonist, though not strongly characterized, becomes a representative immigrant, subject to the trials of adaptation through all stages of settlement, and of his life. He makes the Prairies his home without altogether relinquishing Scotland as that 'country of the mind' from which the Highland Clearances had driven him. *The transplanted*, which depicts the development of a settlement in the lumbering, mining, and ranching area of central British Columbia, completes the pattern by concentrating its thematic emphasis on the need for community to combat the destructive isolation that comes from seeking the freedom of the natural environment.

Niven also published a good deal of nonfiction, including *Canada West* (1930); *Colour in the Canadian Rockies* (1937), with illustrations by Walter J. Phillips; *Coloured spectacles* (1938), autobiographical reflections; *Go North, where the world is young* (n.p., n.d.); and *A lady in the wilderness* (n.p., n.d.). Niven remains important to Canadian literature because he brought to bear on Western experience a developed writing talent influenced by British literary and cultural traditions. He became an immigrant, as distinct from a colonial writer—recreating the West in a Canadian perspective.

See Jan de Bruyn's introduction to the 1974 reprint of *The flying years* in the NEW CANADIAN LIBRARY. DICK HARRISON

Noël, Francine. See NOVELS IN FRENCH 1983 TO 1996: 7.

Northern Review (1945-56). The result of a merger between two Montreal literary magazines, *PREVIEW* and *FIRST STATEMENT*, it was edited by John SUTHERLAND (managing editor), F.R. SCOTT, A.M. KLEIN, Irving LAYTON, Patrick ANDERSON, A.J.M. SMITH, Audrey Aikman, R.G. Simpson, and Neufville Shaw; regional editors were P.K. PAGE, Dorothy LIVESAY, James Wreford, and Ralph GUSTAFSON. The first issue appeared in Dec. 1945-Jan. 1946. The amalgamation was made uneasy by differences in literary philosophy among its editors. More significant, however, was the fact that the more nationalistic *First Statement* poets viewed Sutherland as editor-in-chief, whereas the *Preview* poets, used to Anderson's democratic editorial policies, saw Sutherland simply as a fellow editor in charge of production. The tension came to a head with Sutherland's aggressively critical review of Robert FINCH's Governor General's Award-winning book, *Poems*, in the issue of Aug.-Sept. 1947. Scott, Klein, Anderson, Smith, Shaw, Page, Livesay, and Gustafson all resigned in protest at not having approved the review. A year later, in the issue of Sept.-Oct. 1948, Layton's name disappeared from the masthead; the magazine subsequently became more conservative. Sutherland continued to publish *Northern Review* with the help of Aikman and Simpson and, in the issue of April-May 1951, announced the incorporation of *The Canadian Review of Music and Art*, through the generosity of Lorne PIERCE. Simpson retired from the editorial board with the Oct.-Nov. 1951 issue and his eventual replacement, A.E. Farebrother, withdrew when the magazine moved to Toronto in the spring of 1955 and changed from a bi-monthly to a quarterly. *Northern Review* ceased publication with Sutherland's death in Sept. 1946, after forty issues.

Northern Review had the largest circulation of any literary journal in the country and maintained a high quality of poetry, short stories, essays, and book reviews. Mavis GALLANT, Norman LEVINE, Brian MOORE, George WOODCOCK, Robert WEAVER, and Marshall McLUHAN are only a few of the contributors who appeared in its pages.

See Robert WEAVER, 'John Sutherland and *Northern Review*', *The TAMARACK REVIEW* 2 (Winter 1957), and Ken Norris, *The little magazine in Canada, 1925-80* (1984).

DAVID O'ROURKE

Norwood, Robert (1874-1932). Born at New Ross, Nova Scotia, Robert Winkworth Norwood was educated at Coaticook Academy and Bishop's College in Quebec, at King's College, Windsor, N.S., and at Columbia University, New York. Ordained in the Anglican Church in 1898, he served in Canadian parishes in Nova Scotia, Quebec, and Ontario before moving to the USA in 1917. In Philadelphia and, after 1925, at St Bartholomew's Church in New York City, Norwood became famous as one of the most eloquent metropolitan pulpit orators of his day. He died suddenly in New York upon his return from his summer residence in Nova Scotia.

Encouraged in his verse-writing as a student at King's by his professor, Charles G.D. ROBERTS, Norwood collaborated with his college roommate Charles W. Vernon in issuing *Driftwood*, a slim volume of poems privately printed in 1898. Essentially a lyric poet, he nevertheless preferred to objectify his sensibility in dramatic monologues, sonnet sequences, poetic dramas, and narrative verse. *His lady of the sonnets* (1915) contains, besides the title sonnet sequence, three other sequences of lyric poems that are both unified and diversified by the poet's varied concepts of love; a final section of religious songs and sonnets completes the volume. *The witch of Endor* (1916) is a five-act closet drama in rhetorical blank verse celebrating the transcendent power of love. Another book of poems, *The piper and the reed* (1917), continues an almost too-forceful lyric expression of Norwood's muscular Christianity. This was followed by *The modernists* (1918), a collection of dramatic monologues in which speakers express human ideals in a progression from the cave-man through historic figures to the voice of the twentieth century. The five-act poetic drama *The man of Kerioth* (1919) explores the motives of Judas in betraying Jesus.

Bill Boram (1921), a narrative poem about the humanity hidden in the heart of a brutish sea-captain, draws on Norwood's experience of the Nova Scotia coast, and his descriptions are therefore more vivid than those in his earlier works, which abound in classical settings. The poems in *Mother and son* (1925) reflect the sorrow Norwood felt over the death of his son in a hunting accident. 'The spinner', a poem in this collection, shows the power of his mature lyricism, with its direct imagery and swiftly varying moods. *Issa* (1931), an 1800-line meditative poem employing a six-line rhymed stanza, is a highly personal exploration of Issa (or Jesus) as a presence guiding both the poet's flights into contemplation of the Godhead and his descent into communion with the earth, with human things and human beings. It is the work that best justifies Charles G.D. Roberts' high praise of Norwood 'as a great religious poet'.

Several books of prose, written in the last years of his life, express his liberal view of Christianity. These include *The heresy of Antioch* (1928), *The steep ascent* (1928), *The man who dared to be God* (1929), *His glorious body* (1930), *Increasing Christhood* (1932), and *The hiding God* (1933). A.D. Watson's *Robert Norwood* (1923) is an appreciation of the poet in the Makers of Canadian Literature series.

KEN MacKINNON

***Nouvelle Barre du Jour*, *La*.** See *La BARRE DU JOUR* and LITERARY MAGAZINES IN QUEBEC: 4.

***Nova-Scotia Magazine and Comprehensive Review of Literature, Politics, and News, The*.** Published in Halifax between July 1789 and Mar. 1792, it was the first literary journal in Canada. It was issued monthly, printed by John Howe (father of Joseph HOWE), and edited by the Rev. William Cochran, first president of King's College, Windsor, Nova

Scotia. Thirty-three numbers appeared; the first eighteen averaged over eighty pages in length, the last fifteen over sixty pages. The bulk of each issue was made up of material Cochran found in British and American books and magazines: passages by such well-known authors as Edward Gibbon, Richard Cumberland, Hester Piozzi, William Cowper, Dr Benjamin Rush, Joseph Priestley, and Benjamin Franklin, as well as little-known journalists. Prose fiction and poetry were prominently featured, and there were brief notices of new books; in addition there were detailed reports on the political scene in both Nova Scotia and Great Britain and a 'Chronicle' of current events, domestic and foreign. Of the few local contributions, all of which appeared anonymously, the best-known pieces are 'A plan of a liberal education' by 'W.' (possibly Cochran himself) and the poems of 'Pollio'. *The Nova-Scotia Magazine* was valuable for opening windows on the great world of science and literature that lay beyond Nova Scotia, and for attempting to draw Nova Scotian minds into that world.

TOM VINCENT

***Novascotian*, The.** See Joseph HOWE.

Novels in English. Beginnings to 1900. When, during her stay in Quebec in the mid-1760s, Frances BROOKE began writing the work that has come to be called the first Canadian novel, there was little in this British North American society to encourage the creation of Canadian fiction in English. The newly acquired colony of Canada had a large French-speaking population. Its few anglophone inhabitants were mostly British military personnel who, birds of passage themselves, had little use for such cultural institutions as libraries and schools, or for such locally produced reading material as newspapers, magazines, and books. It therefore took several decades of exploration, immigration, and settlement—throughout what remained of British North America after the American Revolution—to produce a recognizably indigenous English-Canadian fiction. Even then, many of the short stories and novels that emerged often seemed little more than new cloth cut to old styles.

One step towards the development of early English-Canadian fiction was the use of Canadian content in works published in the United Kingdom and the United States and written by British and American authors after they had temporarily lived in, or briefly visited, British North America. The earliest of these works was Frances Brooke's *The history of Emily Montague* (London, 1769)—one of the few novels about North America published in the eighteenth century. In the nineteenth century many such works followed, including John GALT's *Bogle Corbet; or, The emigrants* (London, 1831), Frederick Marryat's *The settlers in Canada* (London, 1844), R.M. BALLANTYNE's *Snowflakes and sunbeams; or, The young fur traders. A tale of the far North* (London, 1856), and William Dean Howells' *Their wedding journey* (Boston, 1871), with its lengthy chapter on 'The sentiment of Montreal'. All popular works by well-known writers, they not only helped to introduce various images of Canada to such groups as potential British immigrants and American tourists, but they also prepared an international market for fiction written by Canadians, and provided models of forms and suggestions of themes for these writers. There is no doubt, for example, that Frances Brooke's portrait of the 'divine' Emily's experiences of French-Canadians in Quebec in the 1760s promoted English-French relations in Canada as both a saleable and significant theme in early Canadian fiction.

The thousands of United Empire Loyalists who came north during the 1770s and 1780s benefited both Canada and the older colony of Nova Scotia. This migration, and the migrations from Europe during the nineteenth century, meant that communities throughout the colonies acquired people with the education, enthusiasm, and expertise to embark on, and to endeavour to sustain, the newspapers and magazines that published most of the indigenous early Canadian fiction. Because many of these early periodicals have not survived, much of this fiction is lost, but enough of it remains to indicate the crucial role that this mode of publication played in the development of Canadian literature in English. For example, the only version of Thomas McCULLOCH's comic masterpiece 'The Mephibosheth Stepsure letters' to appear during his lifetime was published in *The Acadian Recorder* (Halifax) in 1821-3; and part of Thomas Chandler HALIBURTON's *The clockmaker, series one* was serialized initially in *The Novascotian* (Halifax) in 1835-6. *The LITERARY GARLAND* (Montreal) was the most successful of the early monthly magazines in actively seeking the work of new Canadian writers—among others, Rosanna Eleanora Mullins LEPROHON had her first stories published there—but there were similar endeavours in many of the country's towns and cities. The man who produced the local newspaper and magazine, moreover, often printed the local books as well. Thus Hugh C. Thomson, publisher of *The Upper Canada Herald* (Kingston), printed by subscription the first novel published in Canada and written by a native-born Canadian, Julia Catherine Beckwith HART's *ST. URSULA'S CONVENT; or, The nun of Canada* (1824); and Joseph HOWE, the publisher of *The Novascotian*, printed the first book edition of *The clockmaker, series one* (1836), thereby starting Sam Slick and his author on their way to international fame.

For commercial and psychological reasons most early Canadian writers eventually sought publication abroad. Publication in either London or New York guaranteed large markets, good distribution, and sometimes favourable copyright arrangements. Publication in Great Britain had the further advantage of allowing authors to feel that they were writing for people who, because of their position at the artistic and intellectual centre of the British Empire, set the fashions for the fiction that they tried to create. Some writers in the colonies gained access fairly easily to these markets because they had published works in London before immigrating to Canada. Catharine Parr Strickland TRAILL, for instance, who had had several works issued in Great Britain before she moved to Upper Canada in 1832, had *Canadian Crusoes: a tale of the Rice Lake plains* (1852) first published in London. Native-born Canadians had works first published abroad as well. John RICHARDSON, who was living in England at the time as a half-pay army officer, had *WACOUSTA; OR, THE PROPHECY. A tale of the Canadas* (1832) published jointly by Cadell (London) and Blackwood (Edinburgh) and was, thus, assured of a number of reviews in good magazines—and (alas for his personal fortunes) the immediate piracy of the novel by American publishers. In the mid-nineteenth century James DE MILLE and May Agnes Early FLEMING, two natives of New Brunswick, were both extraordinarily successful writing directly for the American market. Fleming eventually moved to Brooklyn, New York, where she died a wealthy woman at the age of thirty-nine. De Mille remained in Nova Scotia, but in the 1870s he became one of Harper's most productive writers, and it was they who published his most fascinating novel, *A strange manuscript found in a copper cylinder* (New York, 1888), eight years after he died. At the end of the century Gilbert PARKER, who was then living in London, gained direct international acclaim when he published *Pierre and his people: tales of the Far North* (1892) with Methuen. Most authors, however, wrote first for the Canadian periodical press and only later tried for publication outside the country. Sometimes they were published in New York or London, but as the nineteenth century progressed, their works were more frequently published in Canada. After *The Literary Garland* ceased publication in 1851, Leprohon's fiction appeared in both American and Canadian periodicals; but her most important novels, including *Antoinette de Mirecourt; or, Secret marrying and secret sorrowing. A Canadian tale* (1864), were published by John Lovell in Montreal. Still, the kind of fiction that was selling elsewhere certainly influenced various aspects of Leprohon's works. The lure of the international market was probably the most important influence on the evolution of early Canadian fiction.

This international influence shaped early English-Canadian fiction in several ways. It provided specific authors—British, American, and occasionally French—as models for the local writers. The most important was Sir Walter Scott (whose story, 'Mortal exit' of 1832 was compared by 'A Scotchman' writing in *The Canadian Magazine* [York, 1833] to a 'shock!—that will only be surpassed when the last trumpet shall sound'), whose historical romances were obviously studied in great detail by such writers as John Richardson and William KIRBY. James Fenimore Cooper, Honoré de Balzac, Charles Dickens, and Mark Twain were also among the many authors cited directly by Canadian writers. Leprohon, for example, describes a character in *Antoinette de Mirecourt* as 'an elegant looking woman, on the shady side of Balzac's admired feminine age of thirty'. Stephen LEACOCK, whose early humorous sketches first appeared in Canadian and American magazines in the 1890s, later wrote critical studies of both Dickens and Twain, the two authors who most influenced his own career as a humorist.

From these models Canadian authors also learned about the kinds of fiction one could—and should—write. Historical romances were perhaps the most popular until late in the nineteenth century. But humorous sketches and novels, domestic romances of high society, animal and other tales for children, and adventure stories could all find markets. Many stories written by Canadians in these genres were very popular, and sometimes became international bestsellers. One thinks most readily of such historical romances as Richardson's *Wacousta*, William Kirby's *The GOLDEN DOG* (*Le chien d'or*). *A legend of Québec* (Montreal, 1877), and Gilbert

Parker's *The seats of the mighty* (London, 1896). But Haliburton's *Clockmaker*, created initially to satirize Nova Scotians, quickly reached an international audience after 1836, as did his subsequent 'Sam Slick' books. May Agnes Fleming's domestic romances were published simultaneously as serials and as books in the United States and Great Britain. Traill's *Canadian Crusoes* remained a popular adventure story for children, even after its title was changed to *Lost in the backwoods. A tale of the Canadian forest* (London, 1882), and Marshall SAUNDERS' *BEAUTIFUL JOE. An autobiography* (Philadelphia, 1894) about a dog, was a best-seller when it was first published. Two years before, Charles G.D. ROBERTS' 'Do seek their meat from God', an animal story for adults that owed its origin at least partly to the hunting stories popular in the late nineteenth century, had been published by *Harper's Magazine* (Dec. 1892).

In addition, the international influence encouraged the treatment of certain themes. Stories about North Americans going abroad became popular. James De Mille's *The Dodge club; or, Italy in 1859* (New York, 1869) is a comic rendering of this theme, but the Canadian writer most identified with the international theme is probably Sara Jeannette DUNCAN. *An American girl in London* (London, 1891) and *A daughter of to-day* (London, 1894) treat this theme conventionally by taking Americans to Europe. Duncan moved to India in the early 1890s, however, and her experiences of British India produced a series of novels beginning with *His honour and a lady* (London, 1896) that dealt with the triumphs and tensions of that international society. In *A daughter of to-day* she also explored another important late nineteenth-century theme, that of the independent career woman.

Throughout the century stories about the past and present of French Canada, the American Revolution, the War of 1812-14, and the opening of the Canadian West and North were almost guaranteed success. John LESPERANCE's *The Bastonnais: a tale of the American invasion of Canada in 1775-1776* (Toronto, 1877) focuses on Montgomery's siege of Quebec during the American War of Independence. Francis William GREY's *The curé of St Philippe: a story of French-Canadian politics* (London, Ont., 1899) depicts an election in contemporary Quebec. John Richardson's sequel to *Wacousta, The Canadian brothers; or, The prophecy fulfilled: a tale of the late American war* (Montreal, 1840) is set during the War of 1812-14 in areas where Richardson himself served or was later imprisoned. Charles E. Beardsley's *The VICTIMS OF TYRANNY* (Buffalo, 1847), Agnes Maule MACHAR's *For King and country: a story of 1812* (Toronto, 1874), and William Henry WITHROW's *Neville Trueman, the pioneer preacher. A tale of the War of 1812* (Toronto, 1880) also cover this war. In choosing as his chief character an itinerant Methodist preacher, Withrow combined two popular themes: the War of 1812-14 and religion. *Black rock: a tale of the Selkirks* (Toronto, 1898)—the book version of the sketches that Ralph Connor (Charles William GORDON), a Presbyterian minister, originally wrote for his church paper in 1897—describes in detail the mining and ranching country around Banff in the North-west. All these and many more novels and short stories on similar themes were generally well received by Canadian and non-Canadian readers alike.

Finally, the fact that Canadian authors wrote for popular publications and, thus, a wide range of readers at least partly explains the high moral tone of much of this fiction, which was usually intended to teach and inspire as well as to entertain; a large dollop of justice offset a sprinkling of scandal and adventure. Saunders expresses one version of this typically Victorian recipe in *Beautiful Joe* when she creates a heaven for good animals and dispenses cruel punishment to evil people. Ralph Connor, who became a millionaire from his writings, mixed the recipe even more skilfully with courageous missionaries and corrupt alcoholics, sentimental sermons and lively brawls, in a manner characteristic of 'muscular Christianity' that still titillates and entertains readers.

In some ways the circumstances that allowed these early Canadian writers to publish internationally militated against their being able to develop a Canadian fiction in English that dealt subtly with serious themes of national cultural significance. It was often easier to follow well-established formulas than to adapt the old patterns to suit new shapes. Still, from its beginnings to 1900 there were works of Canadian fiction that did at least isolate important Canadian themes and play with their significance. The following is one critic's choice of some of these works.

Frances Brooke's epistolary novel *Emily Montague*, even though written by an Englishwoman and published in England, is, for several reasons, the foundation work of Canadian fiction in English. It introduces themes that inspired some of the most subtle responses from later writers of this fiction, including the Aboriginal people and their life in a Canada being Europeanized; the relations of Canada to the other British North American colonies that became the United States, and to Great Britain; the shape of the Canadian economy; and the nature of the rapport between (French) Canadians and the English. Although Brooke's letter-writers act more as reporters than as interpreters, it is her identification of these Canadian themes, not their resolution in her novel, that is significant.

Aboriginals also turn up in Traill's *Canadian Crusoes*, Kirby's *The Golden Dog*, and Parker's *Pierre and his people*. Perhaps the most complex treatment of this theme occurs in *Wacousta* and *The Canadian brothers*, in which Richardson places at the dramatic centre of these stories a Welshman who has disguised himself as a Native warrior to seek revenge on his fellow Europeans. The ironies and ambiguities that develop suggest a good deal about the nature of racial tensions in Canada and the psychological destruction that often resulted.

Since Richardson placed his novels on the Canadian-American frontier, he also explored Canadian-American relations, especially in *The Canadian brothers*, the final lines of which describe 'the picked and whitened bones' of the Americans killed during the Battle of Queenston Heights. One of the most interesting—and comic—treatments of this theme is that of Haliburton in *The clockmaker*. Through Sam Slick, the Connecticut Yankee who travels around Nova Scotia employing *soft sawder* and a knowledge of *human nature* to sell unnecessary clocks at inflated prices to improvident 'Bluenoses', Haliburton, himself of American ancestry, suggests the ambivalent feelings of British North Americans about their Connecticut Yankee brethren. He also contemplates the economic future of the unenterprising Nova Scotians, living on top of a nation of Slick (Uncle) Sams whose belief in progress would lead them to develop the province's natural resources, build railways, and begin industries. The polite country squire who acts as the narrator of the sketches provides an English, conservative dimension to the theme of the political future of Nova Scotia.

The 1860s not only produced a new country in North America but gave produced a fresh impetus to the old theme of English-French relations in Canadian fiction. One major work that appeared on this theme in the 1860s was Leprohon's *Antoinette de Mirecourt*. Set in Montreal shortly after the Conquest, it presents a complex view of some of the consequences for the British, the French, and the Canadians of Great Britain's acquisition of New France. Like so many historical romances, furthermore, it uses a past event to contemplate a present reality, in this case the political future of the Canadas, which, since their creation in 1784, had been working out ever-more-unworkable relationships. Perhaps because she herself was an English Canadian married to a French Canadian, Leprohon seems optimistic about an eventual reconciliation between the two groups.

An even more sacramental vision of the future of the two peoples in one Canada comes towards the end of what is probably the most appealing work of early Canadian fiction, William Kirby's The Golden Dog, set in New France just before its fall. In true epic fashion Kirby reshapes historical facts to suggest that the British Conquest was ordained by God to save the Canadians—conservative, hierarchical, and monarchical—from the corrupt monarchy of France, and the evil republicanism that followed with the French Revolution, by placing them in the benevolent hands of the good monarchy of Great Britain. Designed as much to give English Canadians a national mythology as to reconcile the two 'nations', this novel thus transforms the conventions of the historical romance into a marvellously imagined heroic vision that embodies the best that was thought and said about the new nation in the years following Confederation. Subsequent events, of course, cast doubts on the validity of the vision, and new fashions in fiction devalued its expression in Kirby's novel, but The Golden Dog remains the work of early Canadian fiction in English that most successfully fits old international patterns to new national myths.

MARY JANE EDWARDS

1900 to 1920. In the first two decades of this century economic, political, and philosophical forces transformed Canadian society. It was a time of economic prosperity, marked by the emergence of powerful new financial classes, development in the West, and rapid urbanization in the East. While the world was coming to Canada with the arrival of large groups of non-English-speaking immigrants, Canada was going out to see the world as its people, especially artists and authors, went abroad to study and to live. The Great War sealed Canada's relationship with the larger world. In these and the preceding years the most favoured image for Canada—and its literature—was that of youth struggling to grow into manhood.

Writers of fiction, caught up in this social transformation, were equally involved in the theoretical and practical issues of the international literary world. Traditional concepts of fiction were being challenged by writers like James, Conrad, Joyce, and Woolf. The merits of 'realism' and 'naturalism' were under debate, and both were challenged by the advocates of 'idealism' and 'romance'. The preponderant weight of Canadian literary opinion was in favour of 'idealism'. Literature was not a personal expression of a peculiarly sensitive individual who could unmask his own and society's soul, but a social force that would entertain while instructing, leading, and inspiring. At a time when fiction was considered to be a low literary form by the classically educated, and a vehicle for frivolity and vice by religious people, the instructional aspect became important as a defence of fiction. Nevertheless some of the literary techniques developed by the maligned 'realists' became important to those authors who chose to write inspirational fiction from the basis of their own experience.

A large market for fiction was developing in the newspapers and magazines of Britain and the United States, enabling authors to make writing a profession that brought a full or partial income. Sensation, sentiment, and melodrama were the prevailing qualities of this fiction, which sought to heighten readers' emotional experience with fast-paced action, idealized characters, exotic settings, and reinforced morality. Canadian writers found that they could use scenes and characters from their own country to speak to their international audience—and they may have been more widely read by their contemporaries than any fiction writers before or since.

Both the historical and contemporary Canadian scene provided ample material for these authors, whose works helped to shape the world's image of Canada. Interest in historical fiction dropped off sharply after 1900, although Jean MCILWRAITH's *A Diana of Quebec* (1912), and some of the works of Charles G.D. ROBERTS and Theodore Goodridge ROBERTS, indicate that the nation's past—most specifically that of New France—was still a source for material. However, the more popular genre in exploiting Canada as a literary resource was that of the local-colour sketch. Canadian writers turned to all parts of the country for their material. Contemporary Quebec, both rural and urban, found its way into two of the later novels of Sir Gilbert PARKER, *The right of way* (1901) and *The money master* (1915), and into the stories and sketches of other authors. Nova Scotia provided the setting for Basil KING's *In the garden of Charity* (1903) and *The high heart* (1917) and for Alice JONES's *The bubbles we buy* (1903). The Gaspé and New Brunswick provided the background for many novels by T.G. Roberts and Hiram CODY, as well as for the animal stories of Charles G.D. Roberts. Starting with *ANNE OF GREEN GABLES* (1908), Lucy Maud MONTGOMERY made Prince Edward Island famous to the world. The lives of the people of Newfoundland and Labrador were captured by Norman DUNCAN in *The way of the sea* (1903), and by Wilfred GRENFELL and T.G. Roberts.

Ontario supplied some of the richest territory to the local-colour writers. Ralph Connor (Charles W. GORDON) used memories of his boyhood in Glengarry County, Ontario, for portions of *The man from Glengarry* (1901) and *GLENGARRY SCHOOL DAYS* (1902). In *Duncan Polite* (1905) and her later novels Marian Keith (Mary Esther MacGREGOR) portrayed life in the Scots villages of southwestern Ontario. Robert E. KNOWLES' *St. Cuthbert's* (1905), W.A. FRASER's *The lone furrow* (1907), Sara Jeannette DUNCAN's *The imperialist* (1904), Kathleen and Robina Lizars' *Committed to his charge* (1900), Stephen LEACOCK's *SUNSHINE SKETCHES OF A LITTLE TOWN* (1912), and numerous other works examined the pleasures and frustrations of life in the small towns of Ontario. The large cities play only a passing role, usually as the site of the protagonist's college years, as in Ralph Connor's novels or Robert BARR's *The measure of the rule* (1907), which uses life at the Toronto Normal School as its background.

The most exciting territory for the local colourist was the new land opening up in the West and the North. Sir Gilbert Parker had worked this foreign territory well prior to 1900, and he continued to use it as a backdrop in books like *Northern lights* (1909), *You never know your luck* (1914), *The world for sale* (1916), and *Wild youth and another* (1919). Samuel Alexander White's *The stampeder* (1910) and Agnes LAUT's over-written epic *Lords of the North* (1900) contain a similar sense of distance from the reality of western life, but the western novels of Ralph Connor—including *The sky pilot: a tale of the foothills* (Toronto, 1899) and *The foreigner* (1909)—Nellie MCCLUNG's *Sowing seeds in Danny* (1908), Robert STEAD's early novels, and the ranching novels of Arthur STRINGER reveal a more intimate knowledge of the region. British Columbia, especially its mining and logging areas, provided inspiration for Frederick NIVEN, Bertrand Sinclair, and others. Sinclair's *Burned bridges* (1919) is an especially interesting study of the power of the environment as a redemptive force in the life of a disillusioned minister who has retreated from eastern cities. Martin Allerdale GRAINGER's single work, *Woodsmen of the West* (1908), provides perhaps the best picture of life in the forests of British Columbia. The Yukon and the rest of the North influenced several writers, both Canadian and American, but Robert SERVICE's *The trail of '98* (1911) is the most memorable novel about this region.

For many authors who wrote about these various parts of Canada, the country provided a useful backdrop for action and adventure stories. Susan Jones used Halifax and the North in *A detached pirate* (1903) and *A god of the North* (1900) respectively; William Amy ('Luke Allan') exploited the West and Roger Pocock the Far West, the Rockies, in *Jesse of Cariboo* (1911). (On the other hand, Frank PACKARD, in his series of Jimmie Dale crime novels, exploited the New York underworld.) For some writers, however, setting became a starting-point for the exploration of thematic material as they looked outside themselves for themes that reflected their society, and saw almost everything in an optimistic light. Friction between French and English in Canada was destined to disappear, according to the works of Sir Gilbert Parker, as the best qualities of both races blended in new generations of Canadians. Likewise the conflict between religious and social groups in the small-town novels of W.A. Fraser, Marian Keith, and others diminished as individuals overcame inherited prejudices. The new communities growing in the West would be integrated into the older civilization of the East, to their mutual benefit. Connor's missionary preachers were especially adept at interpreting the two regions to each other. The social discontent that grew with urbanization, industrialization, and the appearance of new classes was expressed in the wit and satire of Leacock's *ARCADIAN ADVENTURES WITH THE IDLE RICH* (1914); but the fundamental goodness of individuals on both sides of the conflict determined the conclusion of most novels that examined the issue. Even the animal stories of Charles G.D. Roberts show man as the unchallenged master of this earth, able to overcome all dangers and difficulties with his intelligence and wit.

Any literary theory that appeared to focus on man's frailty or the hollowness of his ideals found little support in Canada. The realism of Émile Zola was anathema to the Canadian literary community at this time, and the late-nineteenth-century American realism of William Dean Howells was imported only rarely, as in Duncan's *The imperialist*. The idealism of Canadian authors was inextricably linked to the conventions of the literary romance. Larger-than-life characters, exaggerated emotions, episodic plots, a central love story, and the neat resolution of all story elements were the basic ingredients of most novels. Still, the inspiration for many works changed as writers shifted towards characters and incidents based on their own observations. Connor drew on his recollections of life in Glengarry, his experiences as a missionary, and his work as a pastor in Winnipeg, and Charles G.D. Roberts stressed constantly that his stories of animal life were based on his close observations in the New Brunswick woods of his youth. Writers increasingly insisted on the 'reality' of their stories. They did so, however, while staying within the limitations of the romantic conventions that supported their idealism and generated sales. The best writers of this period were able to adapt inherited literary conventions to the expression of their observations of contemporary experience. CAL SMILEY

1920 to 1940. As more than 750 novels were published in this period, the discussion that follows is necessarily selective. Nevertheless, it reflects a period in Canadian fiction when the realistic novel emerges, the regional novel reaches its high point, and the psychological influences of the twentieth century begin to be felt. Nature moves to the background as man moves to the centre; yet the acute sense of place on which Canadian fiction is based continues to dominate. The period contains many literary curiosities because of the strangely fragmented fiction of the time.

1. WESTERN NOVELS. The Prairies are the dominant setting of these twenty years. In 1920 Arthur STRINGER published *The prairie mother*, the second book—coming between *The prairie wife* (1915) and *The prairie child* (1922)—in his sprawling trilogy dealing with the harshness of the environment and asking questions about the reasons for marriage, and why opposites attract, only to create impossible situations. Robert J.C. STEAD's *Neighbours* (1922), one of his romances about prairie life, was followed by *The smoking flax* (1924), a novel that offers a credible social portrait of the time, though the plot is too romantic for today's taste. In Stead's most significant book, *Grain* (1926)—an examination of why young men leave the farm—his writing is more mature and precise. Nina Jamieson's *The hickory stick* (1921) focused more on a moral—that life's greatest moments are those spent in

service to others—than on a setting. In the same year William Lacy Amy ('Luke Allen') romanticized the prairie setting with his *Blue Pete, half breed* (1921), the first of a series, whose hero is a reformed cattle rustler from the USA who becomes an agent for the North West Mounted Police—an attempt to give to western Canada some of the frontier quality of the American 'wild west'. William DURKIN, conversely, focused on an urban centre, Winnipeg, in *The magpie* (1923), the story of a veteran of the Great War who witnesses social unrest in the city and decides to return to his home farm, where he can maintain his integrity.

In terms of form and content the most successful and popular prairie fiction in this period was by Laura Goodman SALVERSON, Martha OSTENSO, and Frederick Philip GROVE. In *The Viking heart* (1923) Salverson discusses the first Icelandic colony's problems in the lake area of Manitoba; its psychological subtleties have stood the test of time. Martha Ostenso's *Wild geese* (1925), which won an important American first-novel prize that brought attention to Canadian writing in the rest of the world, is a story of harsh pioneer life, with a complex plot and psychologically interesting characters. Grove, of course, is the dominant voice of prairie fiction in this period. His *Settlers of the marsh* (1925) is an attempt to portray pioneer life realistically, though the characterizations are too grotesque to be true; it was followed by *Our daily bread* (1928), *The yoke of life* (1930), and *Fruits of the earth* (1933). Other writers who used the prairie landscape as setting were Beaumont Cornell in *Lantern marsh* (1923), which presents some amateur psychology in the life of a minister and teacher; Ethel Grayson in *Willow smoke* (1928), an excellent study of prairie immigrant life; and John Beames, whose trilogy about 'Gateway', Saskatchewan—*An army without borders* (1930), *Gateway* (1932), and *Duke* (1933)—are about farming in the West, grain, and hardships. Winifred Reeve ('Onoto Watanna') wrote a less realistic account of immigrant life in *Cattle* (1932), which focused on American-type violence in the West. Harold Baldwin's *Pelicans in the sky* (1934) attempted to counterbalance those books that talked of life on the Prairies as idyllic by exposing the harrowing homestead conditions of the immigrant. Alberta was the special focus for John Herries McCullock when he told of English immigrant life there in *Dark acres* (1935). Jessie L. Beattie took a melodramatic approach to the conflicts of religion and art in prairie life in *Hill-top* (1935), to be followed by *Three measures* (1938) on a similar theme. By far the most interesting of all the prairie novels of this period is *Forgotten men* (1935) by Claudius Jabez Gregory, who used his novel for social criticism in a story of a man who creates a society of twelve for performing good works among the poor, is betrayed to the capitalist system by 'Jude', and eventually dies in prison: an interest in myth was making an appearance in Canadian fiction. A literary curiosity of the Prairies is Bertram BROOKER's *Think of the earth* (1936), a story of hallucination and mystery on a small Manitoba farm that won the first Governor General's Award for fiction. A writer who devoted her time to extolling the importance of community service within new pioneer settlements, and its strengthening effect on the family unit, was Ethel Chapman in *God's green country* (1922), *The homesteaders* (1936), and *With flames of freedom* (1938). Wilfrid Eggleston in *The high plains* (1938) attempted to portray the hard life of new settlers of the dry prairie; its imagery is reminiscent at times of T.S. Eliot.

Few novelists in this period used British Columbia as a setting. Among those who did was Bruce McKelvie in *Hulgowet: a story of the North Pacific Coast* (1926), an intriguing account of the Natives and the magic and mystery of their culture; this was followed by *The black canyon* (1927), a story of western settlement, and *Pelts and powder* (1929), about the western pioneer. Alexander Maitland Stephen wrote *The kingdom of the sun* (1927), a romance of early British Columbia with good characterizations, and *A gleaming archway* (1929), a carefully plotted novel that focuses on the labour movement in Vancouver. An important book to come out of British Columbia in this period was Irene BAIRD's *Waste heritage* (1939), a most impressive examination of Depression tensions in Vancouver; this well-written, solid work is frequently cited as the best social-history novel of its time.

2. HISTORICAL FICTION. Historical romances were highly popular in this period. While most treated Canadian subjects, several authors offered fictional treatments of a wide variety of foreign places in historical times. Lily Adams BECK ('E. Barrington') wrote a long list of popular historical romances with an emphasis on love interest. Virna Sheard wrote a peculiar Elizabethan romance, *Fortune turns her wheel* (1929); and W.G. Hardy, a professor of classics at the University of Alberta, began his career of writing lusty novels on biblical and classical themes with *Father*

Abraham (1935), about the Old Testament patriarch, and *Turn back the river* (1938), a novel of ancient Rome.

Among Canadian subjects, New France was by far the most popular, inviting easy exploration of a picturesque setting, quaint customs, adventurous deeds, and high drama. Most such books were sentimental romances of no real literary merit: Joseph P. Choquet, *Under Canadian skies: a French-Canadian historical romance* (1922); Edward Montague Ashworth ('John Abbot'), *La Roux* (1924) and *The seigneurs of La Saulage: gentlemen adventurers of New France* (1928); Anna Ermatinger Fraser, *The drum of Lanoraye: a narrative of the days of Talon, the Great Intendant* (1932); John C.L. Hudgson, *Lion and Lily: a story of New France* (1935); and Leslie Gordon Barnard, *Jancis* (1936). Two novels of New France, however, had a more serious purpose than popularizing a colourful period in Canadian history. Franklin Davey McDowell's *The Champlain road* (1939), winner of a Governor General's Award, is the story of the variety of religious aspirations and personality conflicts of the major characters at the time of the martyrdom of Brébeuf and the destruction of the Huron missions. Philip CHILD's *The village of souls* (1933), which also takes place in the seventeenth century, is coloured by the twentieth-century values of a Christian humanist. The West was a favourite region for treatment by historical novelists (some of whose works have already been mentioned). For a moment in 1930—to judge by reviewers' praise—it seemed that the great Canadian novel had been written and the great Canadian novelist discovered when E. Jean McDougall ('Jane Rolyat') published *The lily of Fort Garry* (1930), a novel whose convincing background of life in the Red River Settlement is vitiated by romantic sub-plots related in sonorous prose—of which this novelist's fickle public seemed to have tired when she presented them with *Wilderness walls* (1933), a romantic novel about a Hudson's Bay Company post on Lake Huron in the 1860s.

The history of Ontario and the Atlantic provinces provided fewer examples of straight historical fiction than of the regional idyll set in the past. The leading exponent of this genre was Mazo DE LA ROCHE, who focused on southwestern Ontario in *Possession* (1923), *Delight* (1926), and *JALNA* (1927), the award-winning novel that began the Whiteoak family saga. Augustus Bridle (1869-1952), in *Hansen: a novel of Canadianization* (1924), treated the problems of a farm labourer of Swedish origin in southwestern Ontario whose progress paralleled that of his adopted country. John Elson's *The scarlet sash: a romance of the Niagara frontier* (1925), about the War of 1812, and Mabel Dunham's *The trail of the Conestoga* (1924), about the trek of Mennonites to Ontario's Grand River district, are straight historical novels. The classic account of pioneer life in Ontario, however, is *The yellow briar* (1933; rpr. 1971) by John MITCHELL ('Patrick Slater'), a book that is still read with enjoyment. Moving to the east, Jessie Archibald's *The token: a tale of Cape Breton Island in the days before Confederation* (1930) is a melodramatic tale of survival that appealed to Canadian readers at the beginning of the Depression. Frank Parker DAY in *John Paul's rock* (1932) told the story of the plight of a Native banished to a rock on the Atlantic coast; and in *The eyes of the gull* (1936) and *Cold pastoral* (1939) Margaret DULEY wrote very convincingly of isolation, survival, and alienation in Newfoundland outposts.

3. OTHER FICTION. Spurning the historical and idyllic themes of popular novelists, one of the leading writers of this period, Morley CALLAGHAN, turned to the urban environment and the psychological problems of his characters to produce modern fiction reflecting the concerns of the time in which it was written. His *Strange fugitive* (1928), which examines the question of how one fits into city life, was followed by *A native argosy* (1929), a collection of short stories; *It's never over* (1930), about the reaction to a criminal's execution for murder; *A broken journey* (1932), about the relationship of a mother and daughter with the daughter's suitor; *Such is my beloved* (1934), one of his best novels, about two prostitutes and a priest driven mad by society's hypocrisy; *They shall inherit the earth* (1935), about a guilt-ridden hero's destruction by society; and *MORE JOY IN HEAVEN* (1937), which portrays the hero/saint/sinner conflict. Psychological tension was also portrayed in Raymond KNISTER's *White narcissus* (1929), which centres on the difficult relationship between parents and daughter in rural Ontario. Other novels of the period that have psychological overtones are Ethel Grayson's *Apples of the moon* (1933), a university novel in which a professor's bitter wife kills herself; and *The new front line* (1927) by Hubert EVANS, a study of a man who hates to make decisions and whose mental paralysis is solved by chance.

As the focus shifted from the country to the city, some writers, grasping a satirical pen, examined the ridiculous in contemporary society. Madge Macbeth in *The land of afternoon* (1924) ironically examined the political/

social life in Ottawa, but her wit was buried by heavy characterization; her novel *The kinder bees* (1935) used a similar theme. There were also Victor Lauriston's *Inglorious Milton* (1934), a mock epic of small-town *literati*, and the first two novels by Fred Jacob (1882-1926) of a planned (but never completed) four-part satire of Canadian life in the first quarter of the twentieth century: *Day before yesterday* (1925), about the decline of upper-class domination in a small Ontario town, and *Peevee* (1928), about the posturings and affectations of a rising middle class. Francis Pollock's *Jupiter eight* (1936) also exposes the ridiculous in a society undergoing rapid social change.

Though Canadian fiction in this period lacked originality, there was no question of its survival. Popular fiction was rife in these two decades, meeting the demands of a public who loved to read and to be entertained by simple action and everyday characters. But it should not be forgotten that even though most writers of 1920 to 1940 did not turn their novels into achievements of enduring significance, the fiction of this time was grasping at new forms and insights that would provide the basis of the 'new' fiction of the forties and onwards. DONALD STEPHENS

1940 to 1960. English-Canadian fiction in this period shows few signs of forming a coherent literary pattern. There is no sense of a national movement, of predominant themes and approaches, of an accepted novelistic technique, or even of a concerted attempt to express Canadian or mid-twentieth-century consciousness. Instead, individual writers go their own ways, searching for the fictional modes that suit them best, and sometimes finding them. The two decades produced some major works—*AS FOR AND MY HOUSE* (1941), *WHO HAS SEEN THE WIND* (1947), *The MOUNTAIN AND THE VALLEY* (1952), *The double hook* (1959), *The watch that ends the night* (1959), and (if Malcolm Lowry counts as Canadian) *Under the volcano* (1947). They also saw the emergence of several important novelists: Hugh MacLennan, Ethel Wilson, Robertson Davies, and Mordecai Richler. But these titles and names provide evidence of an abundant but bewildering variety of response about which generalizations are well-nigh impossible.

The period opens, of course, at the end of one traumatic national experience, the Depression, and the beginning of another, the Second World War. Such crises offer rich subject-matter for novelists. The Prairies were especially vulnerable to the hard times of the 1930s, and Sinclair ROSS provides an unforgettable image of the effects of the Depression, psychological as well as social, in *As for me and my house*. Unemployment in urban areas is another prominent topic, and Hugh MacLENNAN's vivid descriptions of Montreal at this time create a memorable background to the main action in *The watch that ends the night*. But, with the notable exception of Hugh GARNER's *Cabbagetown* (which appeared in a shortened version in 1950, the complete text not being published until 1968), the emphasis falls rarely on social issues as such. The writers of this period use the Depression years as a time in which public issues inevitably impinge upon the private lives of their characters. As for war, MacLennan subtly and effectively wrote of the First World War in *BAROMETER RISING* (1941) and also in *TWO SOLITUDES* (1945), which begins in 1917 and ends in 1939, but invited his contemporary readers to compare the effects of the earlier conflict with those of their own time. The most impressive fictional record of Canadian participation in the Second World War is to be found in Colin McDougall's *Execution* (1958), which chronicled the Italian campaign with documentary detail and imaginative force.

There is one general trend, moreover, that needs to be noticed. The two novelists who had established themselves as pre-eminent in the previous twenty years were Frederick Philip GROVE and Morley CALLAGHAN. Callaghan had always been an urban novelist and continued to write, primarily about Montreal, in our period. Grove was known as a novelist of farm and prairie, but in his last conventional novel, *The master of the mill* (1944), he turned his attention to the industrial processes that transform farm produce into marketable commodities. It is a saga of the Industrial Revolution, and although many writers continue to find congenial and absorbing material in rural areas, the fiction of 1940-60 begins to show an increasing awareness of the fact that Canada was rapidly being transformed into a modern industrial nation.

It has often been remarked that, because Canada is a vast country composed of scattered pockets of population, its literature is inevitably regional in inspiration and character. Certainly geographical areas (even excluding the special circumstances of language and culture in Quebec) vary in ways that, in other parts of the world, are reflected in different countries rather than different provinces, and in Canada this characteristic is not so obviously offset, as it is in the United States, with a drive towards cultural uniformity. The diversity of regions attracted a comparable diversity of immigrants whose literature was naturally influenced by their different origins and traditions and, although the individual writer does not necessarily portray or reflect his/her own region, a regional breakdown of the novelists of this period is as convenient a division as any.

Since the Maritimes have a long history of fortified settlements and national rivalries for command of the Atlantic seaboard, it is not surprising that the region should produce a number of historical novelists. The most important of these is undoubtedly Thomas H. RADDALL. His stories are more properly classified as romances, since they involve strong plots, heroes and villains, action and excitement; but his historical research is impeccable, and in novels like *His Majesty's Yankees* (1942), *Roger Sudden* (1944) and *Pride's fancy* (1946) he tapped a rich vein of novelistic ore that he skilfully blended with authentic local history. His short stories are equally impressive, and although his more modern novels have been less successful, *The nymph and the lamp* (1950) is a deeply moving study in loneliness and personal relationships. In *The MOUNTAIN AND THE VALLEY* (1952), Ernest BUCKLER succeeded in catching the essence of a sensitive childhood in the Annapolis Valley through verbal pyrotechnics that dazzle some and weary others. David Canaan, like his creator, is fascinated by words and their capacity to reflect and encompass his community. In this Maritime *Bildungsroman* technical sophistication raises local subject-matter to universal relevance. Charles BRUCE's *The channel shore* (1954) just fails to transcend its regional matrix. Because it is written in an unostentatious, rather flat prose, the book has been unjustly neglected; but it succeeds admirably in conveying a sense of place and period that is at the same time representative of a broader human experience. In *Barometer rising* Hugh MacLennan demonstrated that a local setting, Halifax at the time of the great explosion in 1917, could be the subject for a significant fiction, and both here and in *Each man's son* (1951), set in his native Cape Breton, he explored the Puritan heritage that other writers—Robertson Davies, for instance—have seen as a central experience for Canada as a whole.

Though a Maritimer by birth, MacLennan lived most of his life in Quebec. *Two solitudes* embodies the tensions between Anglo-Canadian and French-Canadian in a work that, while still impressive, seems too obviously didactic and too artificially resolved to fit the complexities of the contemporary situation. His best novel, *The watch that ends the night*, is more personal in its origins, and effectively catches the dilemma of an ordinary decent man trying to make sense of a bewildering, hostile world. Above all, it combines social and political concerns with a personal religious urgency. None the less, MacLennan has always been a somewhat stiff novelist whose matter is invariably more important than his manner. Mordecai RICHLER, on the other hand, began with an awesome mastery of the craft of fiction, which predominates over his material in his first novel, *The acrobats* (1954), about expatriates in Spain. Unparalleled for his energy and his ability to catch the essence of ordinary life and speech, Richler focused his attention on Jewish life and morality in *Son of a smaller hero* (1955) and *The APPRENTICESHIP OF DUDDY KRAVITZ* (1959). In so doing he portrayed a very different Montreal from that of MacLennan and Callaghan, who in *The LOVED AND THE LOST* (1951) and *The many colored coat* (1960) built strong if somewhat diffuse stories against backgrounds of racial and class tensions respectively.

The fictional production of Ontario during this period is decidedly disappointing. The only event of permanent literary interest was the emergence of Robertson DAVIES, who became known as a playwright during the 1940s and went on to publish his first three novels—the 'Salterton trilogy'—in the 1950s. In *Tempest-tost* (1951) his dramatic interests provide the subject-matter for the fiction, since the plot revolves around an amateur production of *The tempest* in Davies' imaginary small city modelled on Kingston. It is a polished, witty, satiric, but for the most part good-natured, comedy of manners that deftly pokes fun at characteristic Anglo-Canadian attitudes. Davies takes over the mantle of Stephen LEACOCK, but shows a capacity for sustained narrative that Leacock never possessed. The two later books, *Leaven of malice* (1954) and *A mixture of frailties* (1958), maintain the standard of wit and comedy but simultaneously sound deeper notes. The former touches upon the nature of evil, which was to absorb Davies in his subsequent fiction; and the latter, the story of a young Canadian singer who gains a scholarship to study in London, may be seen as a Canadian version of Henry James's exploration of innocence and experience in his stories about Americans in Europe. There is nothing like Davies' work elsewhere in Canada. The combination in these early novels of high-spirited amusement, elegant prose, and especially a confidence in the ability of Canadians to laugh at themselves, was an essential ingredient in the maturation of Canadian fiction in English.

By contrast with Ontario, the Prairie Provinces enjoyed a fictional renaissance during these decades. The isolated prairie town or settlement offers a promising microcosm for the novelist, and the best-known of these is Sinclair ROSS's Horizon in *As for me and my house* (1941), with its grain-elevators, railway-tracks, chapel, and symbolic false-fronts. Ross achieves a claustrophobic intensity here, and the story of a minister's wife encountering hypocrisy in the community and in her own home finds a suitable, even inevitable setting for pent-up emotions and a sense of hopeless entrapment. But prairie towns need not resemble Horizon. W.O. MITCHELL's *Who has seen the wind* presents a more positive picture. The egregious Mrs Abercrombie would have been at home in Ross's novel, but Mitchell's book encompasses the decent as well as the tyrannical, the touching as well as the depressing, the hilarious as well as the gloomy. Like Buckler's *The mountain and the valley*, it is a story of childhood, and Mitchell offers a sense of wonder, even a quest for godhead, alongside more traditional childhood subjects like gopher hunting and troubles at school. Mitchell writes with grace and eloquence, and communicates—as Ross does not—the ethnic variety of his prairie town, which includes Irish, Ukrainians, and Chinese.

Novels about immigrant settlers have always been frequent on the Prairies from the period of Frederick Philip Grove, Martha OSTENSO, and Laura SALVERSON onwards. During our period the tradition is maintained by Adele WISEMAN in *The sacrifice* (1956), a powerful if dour story of Jewish Ukrainian immigrants, and also by John MARLYN in *Under the ribs of death* (1957), which portrays the difficulties of a young Hungarian in rising from his humble ethnic origins. It is symptomatic of the times that, whereas earlier fictional treatments of immigrants generally focused on farming communities, both these novels are set in Winnipeg. Finally, no survey of prairie fiction would be complete without mention of the posthumously published *A candle to light the sun* (1960) by Patricia Blondal (1927-59), a hauntingly memorable, darkly effective story of a small town (Mouse Bluffs-Souris, Manitoba) that deserves to stand alongside the established fictional small towns of Ross, Mitchell, and (later) Margaret LAURENCE.

British Columbia in the 1940s and 1950s is dominated, so far as fiction is concerned, by three writers totally unlike each other. Malcolm LOWRY moved to Vancouver in 1939, and it was in a squatter's shack at Dollarton that the bulk of his masterpiece, *Under the volcano* (1947), was written. This richly textured, technically innovative story of the last day in the life of Geoffrey Firmin, an English ex-consul in Mexico, contains little that is Canadian save the sense of peace that made the writing possible. British Columbia always represented an idyllic haven for Lowry, and it became the setting for the completed but not finally polished novel, *October ferry to Gabriola*, which did not appear until 1970, thirteen years after Lowry's death. Lowry was a harried, tormented genius. By contrast, Ethel WILSON lived a quiet, uneventful life in Vancouver writing her serene, compassionate, beautifully cadenced novels, all of which fall within this period. In her full-length fiction she writes almost exclusively of women with a dextrous combination of sensitivity and acute intelligence. Since she strove for quality rather than quantity, her output (five novels and a volume of short stories) is small but consistently excellent. Her abilities are shown at their best in *The innocent traveller* (1949), a gentle and amusing story of a centenarian, and *Swamp angel* (1954), about two women who must find their satisfaction in lives of contrasting solitude. Sheila WATSON, even less productive than Wilson, established a well-deserved reputation with *The double hook* (1959), a spare, unsophisticated work set in the Cariboo district that uses the techniques of poetry to achieve fictional complexity and economy. Details and words are reduced to a minimum, and the basic human emotions become all the more powerful when filtered through the highly metaphorical but firmly controlled prose.

Naturally there are a number of significant novels that bear no relation to their area of origin. Philip CHILD's *Day of wrath* (1945), set in Nazi Germany; A.M. KLEIN's *The second scroll* (1951), concerned with the founding of modern Israel; Earle BIRNEY's *Turvey* (1949), a comic novel about the Second World War; Fred BODSWORTH's *The last of the curlews* (1954), continuing the worthy tradition of the Canadian animal story—all transcend or elude any regional category. Brian MOORE, a 'bird of passage' like Lowry, first attracted attention with *Judith Hearne* (1955) but wrote of Canada only at the close of this period in *The luck of Ginger Coffey* (1960). Even Henry KREISEL's *The rich man* (1948), though portraying a Canadian immigrant, takes place for the most part in Austria on the brink of Nazi occupation. And Frederick Philip Grove's *Consider her ways* (1947) is the account of an expedition of Venezuelan ants to New York City.

The literary historian can point to general trends and trace certain significant developments, but the course of literary history is never smooth. The period 1940-60 is especially muddied. It produced a number of novelists who were aware of exciting possibilities and by no means prepared to subordinate their individual preferences to a communal literary theory. All that can be said in conclusion is that a literature that encompasses the work of Buckler, MacLennan, Callaghan, Richler, Davies, Ross, Mitchell, Lowry, Wilson, and Watson may seem chaotic and directionless to a systematizer but is none the less in a healthy creative state. Many of these writers—notably MacLennan, Richler, and Davies—have extended their reputations in the years since 1960. Others can now be regarded as significant influences on younger writers; examples include Grove's impact upon Rudy WIEBE, and the encouragement Margaret Laurence derived from the praise of Wilson and the achievement of Ross. The flowering of the Canadian novel in English since 1960 was made possible by the all-important solid foundation laid by the talented, persistent, often lonely writers of the previous two decades. W.J. KEITH

1960 to 1982. With a handful of exceptions Canada's best novels and stories so far were written in these decades. One very clear indication of this is that Canadian fiction writers became better known abroad than at any time since the heydays of Mazo DE LA ROCHE and Stephen LEACOCK: Margaret LAURENCE, Robertson DAVIES, Mordecai RICHLER, Mavis GALLANT, Margaret ATWOOD, Alice MUNRO, Norman LEVINE, and Michael ONDAATJE all gained international reputations. Another is the large number of interesting second-order writers who appeared during the period whose work showed more than just competence or mere craftsmanship.

There is now enough modern Canadian fiction of high quality to render inapplicable Northrop FRYE's observation of 1965 that 'if evaluation is one's guiding principle, criticism of Canadian literature would become only a debunking project, leaving it a poor naked *alouette* plucked of every feather of decency and dignity' ('Conclusion', *Literary history of Canada*). The evaluative principles underlying the following assessment of the Canadian fiction of this period are intended to suggest, among other things, how far we have come since then. (This discussion is supplemented by another following: OTHER TALENTS, OTHER WORKS.)

1. What may seem like an arbitrary date, 1960, chosen for convenience, marks the vague boundary between the old and the new in Canadian fiction. Between 1960 and 1980 almost none of the writers whose reputations were established between 1930 and 1960 produced work that reached the standard set by their earlier major fiction, or that would cause us to revise significantly our critical opinions about them. After 1960 Morley CALLAGHAN, for example, wrote novels as different as *A passion in Rome* (1961) and *Close to the sun again* (1977), but his now-precarious reputation mainly rests on the moral fables of the 1930s. Similarly, Ernest BUCKLER's ambitious novels *The cruelest month* (1963) and *The rebellion of young David and other stories* (1975) simply restate, with interesting variations, the rural situations, and moral and aesthetic concerns, of *The MOUNTAIN AND THE VALLEY* (1952). In Callaghan there is an almost embarrassing decline, most obvious in an element of near self-parody; in Buckler, as in Sinclair ROSS (*Sawbones memorial*, 1974), there is modulated repetition.

The cases of Adele WISEMAN, W.O. MITCHELL, and Hugh MacLENNAN are more complicated. Wiseman's *The sacrifice* (1956) is still her most completely successful and challenging novel; but, though its scope is less ambitious, *Crackpot* (1974), also set in Winnipeg, has Wiseman's most vividly realized character: Hoda, the fat daughter of physically disabled Jewish immigrant parents, who drifts into adolescent sexuality and prostitution. Though the strength and success of this realistic and formally conventional novel depend on its creation of the central figure—a fully human individual whose life, though characterized by deprivation and pain (in one scene she delivers her own child), is paradoxically affirmative—the author also deals with large social issues: immigration, lower-class life, the Winnipeg General Strike, and the Depression.

W.O. Mitchell's most ambitious novel of the period, *The vanishing point* (1973), set largely on a Stony Indian reservation, deals with a white administrator-teacher's attempts to bridge the gap between the white and Native ways of life, one of which is through his love for a young Native girl, symbolically named Victoria, whose disappearance into the city instigates a desperate search. The search lends an air of compelling mystery to a novel imbued with crucial social issues. Though *The vanishing point* is weakened by Mitchell's failure to portray the well-meaning Sinclair as successfully as some secondary characters (the canny Native, Archie Nicotine, and the evangelical con-man Heally Richards), parts of the novel are characteristically lively, and its perceptions and dramatizations of contemporary Native life are always convincing. The ironic grade-school title of Mitchell's *How I spent my summer holidays* (1981) suggests a reprise of his classic *WHO HAS SEEN THE WIND* (1947). But despite the similarities in setting, character, and theme—both these prairie novels present a boy's growth into adult awareness—*How I spent my summer holidays* is a sombre mystery novel involving murder, insanity, and suicide as seen from the points of view of a boy and of the man he becomes. The 'adult' narrative frame, which emphasizes the difficulty of recalling and interpreting the past, is solemn and deliberately Proustian; the middle is lighter in tone, occasionally farcical, with much of the social comedy one expects from Mitchell. Mitchell's later novels, however, are overshadowed by *Who has seen the wind*.

Hugh MacLennan's futurist novel *Voices in time* (1980) envisions the end of Western civilization, and even of man. The setting is Quebec, the year is 2030, and the world has survived the great devastation of the cities around the year 1990. The novel's past is our present, and the attempt by the hero, John Wellfleet, to reconstruct the past from tapes, diaries, letters, and documents—the 'voices in time'—constitutes MacLennan's analysis of a self-destruction that derives from the crumbling of traditional values and beliefs, and the waning of the Graeco-Christian world view. The novel's real hero is Western man, and its tragedy is man's persistence in repeating history. As one would expect of MacLennan, this is a didactic and unrelievedly solemn book. Less a novel than a fictionalized treatise, *Voices in time* should be read as a *summa* of MacLennan's values—articulated more explicitly and more dogmatically here than in any of his other novels.

2. Robertson Davies published his first three novels in the 1950s, but unlike the writers discussed above, he earned his reputation as a major novelist, as well as his almost unchallenged status as a serious popular thinker or pundit, for his work of the 1970s and 1980s, including *The REBEL ANGELS* (1981). Discussion of his first three novels—*Tempest-tost* (1951), *Leaven of malice* (1954), and *A mixture of frailties* (1958), with which Davies began to introduce ideas and concepts into his fiction—tended to focus on his comic vision. By contrast, criticism of the Deptford trilogy—*FIFTH BUSINESS* (1970), *The manticore* (1972), and *World of wonders* (1975)—emphasized their psychological and religious dimensions and Davies' substantial debt to C.G. Jung: although still often comic and satiric, they are as explicitly ideological as any novels in Canadian literature. Davies' concern in these works was with man's need to acknowledge the emotional, irrational, and unconscious side of the self: as Liesl tells Dunstan Ramsay in *Fifth business*, it is necessary to shake hands with one's own devil—advice that could stand as an epigraph for the novels that follow, whose heroes or heroines try to come to terms with the darkness within. All the Deptford novels take the form of a confession, have essentially the same theme, and are written in the same easy, witty, and aphoristic style, borrowing their images and symbols from a common store of relatively arcane lore. There is little doubt that *Fifth business* is Davies' masterpiece. After this the scholar-didact overruled the novelist and the reader sits through painless, often witty, lectures on psychology, religion, and art. Davies' novels are elegant, informed, and entertaining; but they share a certain disconnection between the potentially disruptive subject matter and the restrained if magisterial manner of telling.

Like Davies, Mordecai Richler established his reputation in the 1950s with four novels, the last of which, *The APPRENTICESHIP OF DUDDY KRAVITZ* (1959), is perhaps the most successful. *St. Urbain's horseman* (1971) and *Joshua then and now* (1980) mine deeper in the same vein. Richler has called them 'naturalistic novels', or novels of 'character', to distinguish them from his 'straight satires'—*The incomparable Atuk* (1963) and *Cocksure* (1968)—which tend towards the fantastic, grotesque, and farcical. Yet the strain of black humour is already present in the Virgil Duff episodes in *Duddy Kravitz*, and much of Richler's moral concern in *Horseman* and *Joshua* is expressed through satire. His disgust with the attitudes and values of civilization—virulent and direct in the satires and in his essays—finds a more controlled and sublimated expression in the novels proper. *St. Urbain's horseman*, Richler's best novel since *Duddy Kravitz*, is his most ambitious in theme and most complex in form. The central concern, common in Richler's work, is the individual's preoccupation with his personal, socio-historical, and generic or racial pasts. (His heroes' struggles for freedom are a function of their attempts to understand the past.) In *Horseman*, as in the disappointingly predictable *Joshua*, Richler made modern society and modern history his subject, and within that larger canvas completed his most significant work of this period.

Irish-born novelist Brian MOORE lived in Canada between 1948 and 1959, and his writing career began here with the publication in 1955 of *Judith Hearne*. Moore is one of the most natural and readable novelists on the contemporary North American literary scene in the sense that he's so obviously comfortable with the telling of a story. His early novels, like *Judith Hearne* (still considered by many to be his finest), dealt with shabby, frustrated lives in which the individual struggles unsuccessfully for self-definition and fulfilment; the best that can be hoped for is a clearing away of illusions and a recognition of the personal and public constraints upon the self. This holds as well for novels like *The doctor's wife* (1976), *The Mangan inheritance* (1979), and *The temptation of Eileen Hughes* (1981), the first and third of which move from the mundane to the spiritual in a way that recalls the fiction of Graham Greene. But Moore is much more committed to exploring the play between eros and society, and the resultant frustrations and renunciations. His major characters, who are usually women, often discover themselves—or the possibilities of a fuller life—by discovering their own sexuality. His later characters, like Sheila Redden in *The doctor's wife*, also discover the proximity between profane and sacred love, and the complications arising out of the quest for freedom and/or fulfilment.

Mavis Gallant is best known for her short stories, most of which first appeared in *The New Yorker*. Living in Paris, she was not an influential presence in Canada during the 1960s and 1970s, yet one could not ignore her unique importance, both for her ironic world view and as a stylist among Canadian writers of fiction. The epigraph, from Edith Wharton, to her novel *A fairly good time* (1970)—'If you make up your mind not to be happy, there's no reason why you shouldn't have a fairly good time'—might apply to all her fiction. Happiness is beyond reach of most of her characters, who are for the most part discontented expatriates (physically or psychologically or both), unable to overcome the restraining habits, attitudes, and beliefs imposed by relationships, families, class, or history. Gallant's style—exemplary in its control of tone, telling detail, balance, and economy—depends, like her vision, on nuance, on slightly disconcerting qualifications and shifts of syntax and meaning that sometimes evoke an ambivalent response in the reader. Gallant is usually content to dramatize and describe a complex situation without bringing it to any resolution. The full meaning and significance of her stories, which often have endings without closure, resist easy summation.

Unlike Gallant, Margaret Laurence had a central influence during the literary renaissance of the 1960s and 1970s. Showing the way by example, she became a creative godmother to an entire generation. Her four Canadian novels and one collection of stories that are set in the fictional town of Manawaka, Manitoba, represent an ambitious and impressive attempt to write a comprehensive regional fiction that ultimately has universal concerns. Manawaka embodies both an era and a way of life. Laurence was also a feminist writer of authority who, implicitly and explicitly, anticipated the work of later writers as different as Marian ENGEL, Margaret Atwood, Jane RULE, Audrey THOMAS, and Margaret GIBSON. If, however, her recurring central theme is a woman's search for self-understanding and personal fulfilment, this always hinged on a simultaneous concern with the self's problematic relationship to her community: self and community, or society, are ultimately inseparable. This emphasis stands out in Laurence's most ambitious novel, *The diviners* (1974). Not as formally unified or as successful as her masterpiece *The* STONE ANGEL (1964), *The diviners* brings together all of Laurence's concerns; in effect it is a summary of her Manawaka world and is one of those works—*TWO SOLITUDES* is another—that marks, by its emphases and comprehensiveness, a moment in the evolution of a society's self-consciousness. Particularly significant is Laurence's attempt to articulate, through her semi-autobiographical heroine, Morag Gunn, the Canadian writer's struggle to deal with his or her past as both fiction and history. Laurence's act of divining involves remembering and interpreting 'private and fictional worlds', and worlds within which the private, communal, and historical combine. Where Hagar Currie in *The stone angel* and Rachel Cameron in *A jest of God* (1966) can be discussed and understood within an immediately personal context, Morag, through her relationships and her internal dialogues with the nineteenth-century pioneer Catharine Parr TRAILL, involves us in two centuries of Canadian life.

Rudy WIEBE, like Laurence, is a western novelist whose work also centres on interpreting the personal and historical past. Wiebe is a Mennonite for whom the central fact of his experience is his belief in what he calls 'the Jesus vision'. This translates into a sometimes didactic, often innovative, fiction (his major novels and best stories are among our most successfully experimental) that is committed to a radical Christian vision. Seeing himself as doubly an outsider—a Christian and a westerner—he writes in opposition to the literary, social, political, and religious ideologies that he finds dominant in Canada. Wiebe's first important novel, *The blue mountains of China* (1970), takes place over almost a century of Mennonite history, including the heroic 1920s emigration from the Soviet Union to Canada and, later, to Paraguay. His fascination with communities anchored in a spiritual vision of the world underlies his interest in Canadian Native people who resemble the Mennonites in this, and in the fact that they, too, exist on the periphery of official history. *The temptations of Big Bear* (1973) —a difficult, often brilliant, novel that uses a complex polyphonic structure, incorporating much documentary material—covers the twelve years from Big Bear's refusal to sign a treaty in 1876, through his inadvertent involvement in the killings at Frog Lake in 1885, to his imprisonment and death. *The scorched-wood people* (1977), Wiebe's masterpiece and thought by some to be the finest Canadian novel of its generation, returns to the same period of history to focus on Louis Riel and the Métis. His portrait of Riel—historical revisionism with a vengeance—refuses to accept traditional interpretations: instead of presenting him as a madman, Wiebe depicts him—often in Christological images—as a visionary, the prophet of a vision of community. The posthumous narrator, Pierre FALCON, exists both in the novel's present time and in our own.

Several other novels have also dealt with minorities, or groups on the periphery of the Canadian mosaic, including Peter SUCH's *Riverrun* (1973), about the Beothuk of Newfoundland, and Austin CLARKE's *Storm of fortune* (1971), about Barbadians living in Toronto. Particularly impressive—and as a first novel very promising—was Joy KOGAWA's docu-fiction *Obasan* (1981). Narrated by the teacher Nomi Nakane, it immerses the reader in the lives of Japanese Canadians interned during the Second World War.

Although one almost instinctively assigns Margaret Laurence (b. 1926) and Margaret Atwood (b. 1939) to separate generations of writers, their careers for the most part overlap: Laurence's *The stone angel* (1964) and Atwood's first book of poems, *The circle game* (1966), appeared within two years of each other. Since then, Atwood went on to achieve substantial critical reputation and wide popularity with her prolific output of both poetry and fiction: 17 books in 16 years. One of the recurring themes or concerns in her fiction is the survival of the self, usually female, in a society whose personal and public relationships are characterized by alienation, domination, and exploitation. Her heroines often flee from a male-dominated society (frequently described in imagery of machines, guns, and cameras) that is inimical both to nature and to all that is natural within the self; and/or they withdraw into the self, as in *Surfacing* (1972), *Lady oracle* (1976), and *Bodily harm* (1981). The flight from society (a job) or a man (an affair or marriage) is often a rejection of an inauthentic self that the woman recognizes as having been formed in response to ultimately dehumanizing demands. A capitalist and patriarchal society dominated by rationality, industrialism, and conspicuous consumption has no place for the attitudes and desires expressed by Atwood's central figures. Her heroines are articulate, sensitive, and self-reflective. Where there is first-person narrative, the voice is usually laconic, ironic, and restrained, even flat, though capable of an occasional dark lyricism—the voice of someone who, if not actually frightened, is guarded or anxious, sensing the hostility latent in the society around her. In *The edible woman* (1969) and *Surfacing* anxiety becomes a neurosis as the sensitive and sympathetic heroine fails to cope with the demands of a dehumanizing reality. Atwood's fiction concentrates on the existential situation, on the individual's essential isolation: all relationships are at best tenuous and tentative; the self is radically isolated both when it withdraws from, and when it returns to, society. The emphasis is predominantly subjective and psychological; we tend to remember the voices and emotional landscapes rather than the events of her novels in this period, which nevertheless offer a wide-ranging criticism of contemporary Western society.

In most contemporary novels by women the point of view or 'voice' of the heroine usually assumes what Sartre called a 'contestational' attitude towards society. One result of this has been the inability of most women novelists to create fully realized and memorable male characters. The major Canadian exception to this generalization is Alice Munro. Although her primary concern has always been with the 'lives of girls and women', some of the more memorable moments in her fiction have depended on exchanges between her heroines and sympathetically rendered males. The title story of *Who do you think you are?* (1978) recalls a casual middle-aged encounter between Rose, a successful actress visiting home, and Ralph Gillespie, a school friend now living on a navy pension. For Rose, as for the reader, the rather ordinary Gillespie is a mystery and remains elusive to the end; yet he is fully *there*. Sympathy for her subjects characterizes Munro's fiction. Her best work, *Lives of girls and women* (1971), is narrated by Del Jordan, a sensitive and articulate young woman who describes in eight interconnected stories her growth from childhood to early womanhood in the southwestern-Ontario town of Jubilee. Del becomes aware that 'People's lives, in Jubilee as elsewhere, were dull, simple, amazing and unfathomable—deep caves paved with kitchen linoleum.' Despite her simple and realistic style, Munro is capable of surprising the reader with a supple and sensuous lyricism. Fidelity to the texture of female experience is balanced in Munro's work by an equal concern with evoking (not simply transcribing realistically) the feel of life in southwestern Ontario, an area with its own specific traditions and history where 'everything is touchable and mysterious'.

The emphasis on a place, area, or locale, rather than on the more inclusive 'region', gives Munro's fiction an understated unity. That kind of unity is more apparent in the comic stories and novels of Jack HODGINS, for whom Vancouver Island has functioned both as a setting and as a subject with its own inherent interest. Hodgins repeatedly deals with a character, often an artist, who attempts to describe the island and its way of life. Maggie Kyle, the vital and erotic heroine of Hodgins' complex and entertaining *The invention of the world* (1977), alerts the reader to the fact that while the Island can be described in many modes of discourse and representation—maps among them—its ultimate reality eludes everyone. Yet, as W.J. Keith has suggested, Hodgins' Vancouver Island must be approached primarily, or at least initially, as a fictive creation, a geography of the mind, much like Marquéz's Macondo. Each of Hodgin's novels is organized, as Keith has pointed out, around a single unifying idea or image (separation, invention, resurrection, and invasion) embodied in situations usually dealing with the problematic and comic relationship between self and community. Roughly analogous to what his exuberant characters represent is the 'green island' itself, which, despite humanity's inroads and invasions, is an always pristine reminder of the promise or possibility of Eden within and outside the self. Though fundamentally comic, Hodgins' vision is capable of embracing and dealing with a wide range of human emotions and experiences, while reminding us of aspects of life, from the poignant to the tragic, that normally resist the comic vision.

3. The writers discussed above in this survey were those considered to be the major fiction writers of the period. There are writers discussed below who might be included in this category by some commentators, but none have written a work of such scope, power, and human significance as to place it in the company of *The stone angel*, *Fifth business*, *The invention of the world*, or *The scorched-wood people*. Such discrimination between major and minor works recalls Northrop Frye's remark in his *Anatomy of criticism* about evaluative criticism's smacking of the stock market; yet criticism, after performing all of its other functions, inevitably judges and places the individual work of art within the tradition.

The most problematic moment in a critic's reading of contemporary literature occurs in the confrontation with an innovative text that challenges and rejects the presuppositions of the past. Robert KROETSCH, for example, is as determined as John Barth and Gabriel Garciá Marquéz to resist and even reverse the conventions of traditional fiction. He writes in *The crow journals* (1980) that 'Symbolism may have spent its force, in its present form. But realism is not the answer. Rather a new version of the fabulist.' Rejecting realistic characters, linear narrative, and conventional plots, the fabulist creates a fiction of pure contingency, an imagined world in which everything is possible. After two relatively traditional works, Kroetsch produced four novels —*The studhorse man* (1969), *Gone Indian* (1973), *Badlands* (1975), and *What the crow said* (1978) —that are self-consciously postmodernist (and therefore usually parodic) in their approach. Despite the presence of macabre, grotesque, and surreal elements in his fiction, Kroetsch's vision, like Jack Hodgins', is essentially comic. Although set in Alberta and Saskatchewan, Kroetsch's novels are about a fictional West that owes more to the personal inflections of memory and imagination than to geography and history. They are usually organized around a quest that has mythic overtones; mythic allusions, motifs, and narrative patterns abound, along with such antithetical yet dialectically related concepts as coyote man and educated man, woman and man, community and exploration or flight, dream and reality, the natural and the cultural, eros and thanatos. They are concerned with Kroetsch's version of 'the one story and one story only': desire's attempt to achieve fulfilment by evading the entangling and repressive meshes of social reality. For Kroetsch, as for other postmoderns, the novel becomes the locus for the play and playfulness of language. The style is energetic, witty, punning, and occasionally seems to be out of control, especially in the too-obviously punning name (Roger Dorck, Miss Petcock). Missing from Kroetsch's fiction, however, is the sense—always present in Marquéz, one of his masters—that there is a significance in the characters' actions and thoughts beyond the purely literary and formal one.

One senses a roughly analogous attitude to character as a function of narrative in the fiction of Hugh HOOD, who has done his best work in several short stories and in the first four instalments of the flawed but consistently interesting Proustian *roman fleuve* about Canada in the twentieth century: The New Age/Le Nouveau Siècle (projected for 12 volumes). A Roman Catholic for whom, as he put it in an early essay ('The absolute infant'), 'everything is full of God', Hood sees art as the revelation of the sacred within the profane; or as Matt Goderich describes his mother-in-law's visionary painting in *A new Athens* (1977), art is the founding of 'heavenly inventions on ordinary life in an ordinary world'. This attitude has produced fiction that is uncomfortable with realistic plots and characters and strains towards symbolism and allegory. The early novels—*White figure, white ground* (1964), *The camera always lies* (1967), *A game of touch* (1970)—reveal Hood's sacramental and therefore optimistic view of life, and view art as performing an ultimately spiritual function; but the plots often seem imposed upon events and characters (as in the novels of Robertson Davies). This tension between vision and form, only occasionally evident in the short stories, disappears in the plotless, though not formless, novels of *The new age*. The unity of this ambitious project, as well as of its individual instalments, depends on repeated motifs, images, symbols, and emblems, and on the first-person narrative voice of Matthew Goderich, the novel's flawed, symbolically named, central figure. As an art historian with a wide range of intellectual interests—including the writing of a history of house design in eastern Ontario—he enables Hood to introduce digressive musings on Canadian architecture, art, landscape, the names of flowers, the writing of history, which (though occasionally tiresome) for the most part are formally integrated and thematically justified. However, while Hood's commitment to an affirmative and religious vision is admirable (it's refreshing to read a contemporary writer who actually believes in something), his central characters, especially the pivotal Goderich, lack a shadow side and are usually almost too good to be true. Hood has not taken into account 'the evil facts which are a genuine portion of reality' (William James). As well, since *The new age* is committed to an examination of history, the reader has the right to expect a more profound sense of social relations and historical conflict than has so far been offered.

A turn towards history also marks Timothy FINDLEY's novels *The WARS* (1977) and *Famous last words* (1981). Findley established his reputation with *The last of the crazy people* (1967), a fine psychological novel about the gradual disintegration, psychological and social, of the almost Gothic Winslow family. Particularly memorable is the portrait of the young Hooker Winslow, who observes the decline, and—in an act of violent and loving expiation—completes the fall, of his family. The novel has a quiet, understated perfection absent from Findley's later and more ambitious novels that share its motif of a family flawed or doomed for unknown reasons. For all their historical detail, *The wars* and *Famous last words* are essentially psychological novels whose history often seems decorative. Both deal with emotionally and intellectually troubled individuals. Both are narrated in such a technically complex manner that the telling becomes interesting for its own sake and, as in so much contemporary fiction, is part of the theme itself. *The wars* is narrated, in a clear though often magniloquent style, by an anonymous present-day archivist assembling the available facts about Lieut. Robert Ross, who suffered a nervous breakdown during the First World War. Ross, however, remains distant and enigmatic, though he is portrayed in both private and public life: we see him in the midst of the novel's absolutely convincing battle scenes—yet he remains a strangely static figure. Findley's novels rarely move us: with the possible exception of Kroetsch, Findley may be the Canadian novelist who is most detached from his characters, preventing the reader from making the leap of sympathy and recognition to the characters and the novel's world. His *Famous last words*—which examines, within the frame of a spy novel, the relations between Fascism and art—is ingeniously constructed but strangely lifeless.

Whereas Findley's detachment conveys little or no connection between the writer's life and his work, Clark BLAISE returns almost compulsively to focal childhood situations, suggesting a fiction insistently shadowed by autobiography. He creates scenes, often having a young boy as their focus, in which an almost unbearable knowledge—a violent and terrifying event—intrudes without warning into an otherwise peaceful existence. The opening scene of *Lunar attractions* (1979) is illustrative: David Greenwood (Boisvert) is fishing quietly with his salesman father in a Florida swamp when their boat suddenly lurches as an alligator's tail arches menacingly above them. In the story 'How I became a Jew' (*Tribal Justice*, 1974) Gerald Gordon, a Southerner now living in Cincinnati, enters grade seven and encounters brutal students and a sadistic teacher. The hero of 'A North American education' stands for all of Blaise's protagonists when he gradually realizes that 'whatever the comforting vision before him . . . something dreadful could suddenly cut him down without warning.' Knowledge of the dark side of reality produces neither enlightenment nor philosophical resignation; more often, as in 'Words for the winter' (*A North American education*, 1973), it leaves only the searing realization that 'reality hurts like nothing in this world', and that nothing can be done about it.

Matt COHEN's best works in this period are the novels *The disinherited* (1974), *The sweet second summer of Kitty Malone* (1979), and the Gothic *Flowers of darkness* (1981), all set in the fictional town of Salem, north of Kingston, Ontario—'a small town that closed its eyes to the present, let alone the future'—and dealing with the lives of several generations of local inhabitants. The emphasis is usually on ordinary lives—another novel, *The colours of war* (1977), is an exception—caught during a period of personal and/or social transition when rural and urban values conflict. This is most memorable in *The disinherited*, in the irreconcilable clash between the critically ill farmer Richard Thomas and his son Erik, who left the family farm to attend university in Toronto. Cohen's themes are often large ones, but his language seldom succeeds in embodying his concerns in a felt human drama; usually the novels leave an impression of a vaguely diffused portentousness, a sentimental fatalism without substance.

Marian Engel produced a substantial body of work, commencing with her first novel, *No clouds of glory!* (1968). Though her pellucid and deceptively simple prose style is impressive, she was essentially a one-note writer, treating emphathetically and almost obsessively a woman's search for self-fulfilment, and strongly portraying a female sensibility. Engel's heroines—like those of Margaret Atwood and Audrey Thomas—are usually caught at a moment of crisis. From Sarah Porlock in *No clouds of glory!* to Rita Heber in *The glassy sea* (1978), the central characters have just survived a divorce, a separation, or a catastrophic love affair; they are shown withdrawing from men and a male-dominated and male-defined society in order 'to go looking for themselves' (*No clouds of glory!*). In the slightly silly but persuasively narrated fable *Bear* (1976) Lou 'finds' herself in an affair of heart and body with a tame, rather mangy bear in northern Ontario. The other novels—usually short, almost novellas—lack this fabular dimension, but they assume a moralistic, even didactic tone. Too often in Engel's fiction the intention to make a general comment about women, the relations between women and stereotyped men and between women and society, overdetermines and simplifies the nature of the characterization (particularly of men), the symbolism, and plotting.

Audrey Thomas was seen to be a very talented and innovative writer whose stories—collected in *Ten green bottles* (1967), *Ladies and escorts* (1977), and *Real mothers* (1981)—tend to be more conventional, in their approach to character and narrative, than her longer fiction. They explore and often 'rewrite' the same situations dealt with in the novels *Mrs. Blood* (1970) and *Blown figures* (1974), both of which are set in West Africa, where Thomas lived in the 1960s. Most of her fiction is written from a woman's point of view (the hauntingly suggestive story 'Aquarius' is one of the few important exceptions) and attempts to render, in a supple and sardonically witty style, a woman's sense of reality. Her women are shown at a critical, and therefore revealing, moment in their lives: *Mrs. Blood* follows a woman through a painful and complicated miscarriage, and focuses on her increasing disgust with her body, which results in a crisis of identity—she alternately refers to herself as Mrs Blood and Mrs Thing; *Blown figures* deals with Isobel's attempt to understand a past love affair and the birth of her stillborn child in Africa; and *Latakia* (1979) presents Rachel's first-person account ('a letter') of her affair with Michael. Drastic shifts in style, time, and narrative viewpoint are aspects of Thomas's attempts to evoke a particular emotional and psychological condition; the emphasis often falls on a *post mortem* analysis of, or response to, an event rather than on a situation unfolding in present time. The novels tend toward solipsism as the world disappears into the subjective vortex of the woman's point of view. Stories like 'Aquarius', 'Kill day at the government wharf', and 'Crossing the Rubicon' have charged dramatic situations involving realistic characters. Though complex in emotion and tone, they hold the reader's attention—something the novels often fail to do.

Helen WEINZWEIG wrote two slim, original novels: *Passing ceremony* (1973) and *Basic black with pearls* (1980). Less indebted to any indigenous Canadian or North American tradition than to modern painting, music, and the French *nouveau roman*, they are almost plotless, although *Passing ceremony*'s brief, often elliptical, chapters are organized around a bizarre wedding; and *Basic black with pearls* follows the schizophrenic heroine's fantasies about her love affair with an international spy named Coenraad. Both novels are narrated in a cool, even austere style, with intermittent flashes of mordant wit. These are exemplary 'modernist' novels, requiring the active, creative engagement of the reader who 'assembles' and interprets the information presented in the often untagged first-person narratives of the first novel and the often puzzling events of the second. In these spare texts, populated by reticent, anxious characters dissatisfied with their lives and feeling homeless in the world, 'nuance is everything'. If there is a dominant theme, it is the tyranny of memory, the inescapable burden the past imposes on the present.

With the possible exception of Audrey Thomas's *Blown figures* and Leonard COHEN's *Beautiful losers* (1966), no Canadian novel of this period was as challengingly innovative in style and structure as Dave GODFREY's *The new ancestors* (1970). Set on the 'Lost Coast' of Africa, Godfrey's political novel is closer to Hugh Hood's African novel *You can't get there from here* (1972) than to the African novels of Margaret Laurence (*This side Jordan*, 1960) and David Knight (*Farquharson's physique*, 1971), in that its implicit subject is as much Canada's cultural and political situation as that of the Lost Coast. At its centre are the related motifs of colonialism, revolution, and identity. The stylistic and structural virtuosity is meant to be unsettling to prevent expectations of a traditional African novel, such as those of Joyce Cary and Graham Greene, that will simply confirm the reader's preconceptions. Shifts in time and viewpoint (a different character dominates each of the four sections), surreal scenes, parodies of other works (in particular Malcolm LOWRY's *Under the volcano*), and obscurities in the story all compel one to enter and even become lost in the chaotic reality of a society caught between conflicting identities. Like Michael Burdener, the novel's European hero, we have to *place* ourselves in a colony in which all languages, identities, and ideologies, both indigenous and imported, are caught in the process of change.

4. John METCALF is a comic, often satiric, writer who, in addition to two collections of short stories, published two novels, *Going down slow* (1972) and *General Ludd* (1980), that use the Canadian educational system as a basis for satirizing everything Canadian from bilingualism to computerized society to the CANADA COUNCIL. (Leo SIMPSON's *The Peacock papers* (1973) and his short story 'The savages' show another comic writer engaged in a similar project.) Metcalf's novels tend to generate their own kind of frenetic energy; but because they break down into episodes they remind us that his shorter fiction, especially two novellas—'Private parts: a memoir' and 'Girl in gingham', which appeared in *Girl in gingham* (1978), reprinted as *Private parts: a memoir* (1980)—represents his best work. The exquisitely controlled and elegant 'Girl in gingham' follows the life of Peter Thornton, an appraiser of antiques, trying to rebuild his life after an emotionally shattering divorce. Within a very brief compass Metcalf creates a fully rounded central character, a personal and social milieu, and a story encompassing both light comedy and tragedy.

Leon ROOKE is another writer who is at his best in the short-story form, although his novel *Shakespeare's dog* (1983) won a Governor General's Award. Perhaps the most unpredictable and innovative writer on the Canadian scene, Rooke is a playful raconteur who teases the reader with the 'and then, and then' factor, while showing off his arsenal of technical devices. His characters are less social personae than voices and tones; his fictional universe is one of pure contingency whose dominant moods are anxiety, fear, and paranoia.

Ray SMITH, like Dave Godfrey and Leon Rooke, absorbed the lessons of postmodernism and is committed to what he calls 'speculative fiction. Generally ironic in tone. Aesthetic in approach.' Smith has produced two very different books: a collection of experimental stories, *Cape Breton is the thought control centre of Canada* (1969), and *Lord Nelson Tavern* (1974), a novel composed of interlocking unconventional love stories about a group of characters who went to university together. Despite the brilliance of the title story in the first volume, the novel is Smith's most successful work. Writing in different voices and modes, Smith offers various perspectives on individual relationships, and managed to create an original work that is almost simultaneously ironic and sentimental (he refuses to show a preference) about love and creativity.

Lord Nelson Tavern, George ELLIOTT's dreamlike *The kissing man* (1962), and Wayland Drew's apocalyptic *The Wabeno feast* (1973) are among Canada's few truly neglected works of literature. Elliott's collection of haunting, interconnected stories has affinities with Stephen Leacock's *Sunshine sketches*, but its dark yet affirmative vision is distinctive and—while taking liberties with time and space in dealing with the lives and deaths of the inhabitants of a town in southwestern Ontario during the early part of this century—essentially innocent.

Wayland Drew is the author of a single book of fiction, *The Wabeno feast*, a complex and challenging novel that tells three related stories: a historical adventure tale involving white explorers, whose journey into the interior is also a journey into the self; a post-war narrative set in a northern-Ontario industrial town called Sable Creek; and a futuristic story in which Paul and Liv Henry are shown escaping from cities menaced by an unspecified but palpable industrial disaster. As in Peter Such's ecological novel *Fallout* (1969), the concern is with man's ability to destroy both himself and the life of nature around him. Despite the slightly forced, didactic quality of some of Drew's symbolism, *The Wabeno feast* is an intricately organized and powerful novel that addresses important psychological and social issues.

Leonard Cohen's *Beautiful losers* (1966)—about the saintly Catherine Tekakwitha, an Iroquois who died in 1680—is easily the most controversial Canadian novel of the period. Cohen was concerned here with a vision of unity and wholeness. His characters belong to his private, idiosyncratic martyrology, in which sainthood is bestowed on those lovers and losers who have 'achieved a remote human possibility . . . that . . . has something to do with love.' Cohen's saint has seen beyond the conventional possibilities for fulfilment. In *Beautiful losers*, as in Sartre's *Saint Genet*, canonization is contingent upon transgression of the acceptable, the normal, the bourgeois; the liberated self can only achieve fulfilment outside of reason, historical time, and the values of contemporary society. Much of the romantic and surreal writing is as self-indulgent as Cohen's later poetry, and the novel, which is neither as shocking nor as disturbing now as it was when it first appeared, seems to express the spirit of a very particular time.

The dark or 'black' romanticism of *Beautiful losers* is also present in Michael Ondaatje's *Coming through slaughter* (1976), a powerful exploration of the ambiguous sources of creativity. Written in the form of a discontinuous yet closely organized narrative ostensibly about the career of the legendary New Orleans jazz cornetist Buddy Bolden, 'facts have been expanded or polished to suit the truth of fiction'. The historical Bolden, about whom little is known, became a fictional exemplar through whom Ondaatje explored the dilemma of the modern poet/musician *maudit* who is not only ontologically alienated from his society but for whom 'making and destroying come from the same source, same lust. . . .' Portraying a debilitating creativity dependent on a suffering self, Ondaatje relied on a taut, austere, often jagged style; his chapters are brief, often fragmentary, units of prose related to each other by clusters of reiterated images (stars, webs, photographs, ice) and the impersonal yet paradoxically sympathetic narrative voice. Both form and style are aesthetically successful.

Despite suggestions that Canada's major fiction (or literature) could be characterized thematically in this period on the basis of the garrison mentality, or survival, or patterns of isolation, or the new hero, there was no single overview that commanded sufficient authority to gain general consensus. This was perhaps inevitable in a country that—lacking a rich cultural heritage formed over several hundred years, and a language clearly distinguishing it from other nations—has been traditionally unsure of its own identity, or defining self-image or myth. Some of our most impressive novels of the 1960s and 1970s implicitly raised the possibility that an identity or sense of place could be established only locally or regionally, never nationally. Thus the national definition could be no more than a 'collective consciousness' (George WOODCOCK's term) based on various regionalisms. Images of displacement, immigration, and exile in English-Canadian fiction were reminders of lost or abandoned 'foreign' identities, while alerting us to the fact that these hadn't been replaced by something indigenous. The adjective 'Canadian', as used in 'the Canadian novel' and 'the Canadian identity', seemed to have little meaning in this period, apart from the problematic local definitions offered by individual texts—leaving us to agree with Northrop Frye's claim that 'there does seem to be such a thing as an imaginative continuum' in Canadian literature, without being certain what the individual elements of that continuum have in common.

SAM SOLECKI

Other talents, other works: 1960 to 1982. In this period the Canadian novel became too plentiful and too diverse in its forms to be considered under one heading. After the major writers and their works have been singled out, there remains a considerable body of lesser-known fiction, often the product of Canada's flourishing small presses. In this category are included the one-novel writers, the regionalists, the experimenters, the minority writers—all those who, for one reason or another, reached a limited audience. Some of these novels, however, attained great popular success, while others were highly praised by the critics but were little known to the public.

This lesser-known fiction often followed patterns of exploration laid down by the major novelists: Rudy WIEBE, for example, fathered a dynasty of novels about Canada's Native people, many of which owe form as well as content to the influence of his *The temptations of Big Bear* (1973); Robertson DAVIES put his stamp on a certain tradition of university satire; Margaret ATWOOD and Marian ENGEL wrote the archetypal novels of female experience in the modern world; of the novels of childhood listed here, many owed their lifeblood to W.O. MITCHELL. Beyond the serious minor writers in the great traditions, however, lies that much-maligned body of fiction called 'popular'. Here too there was good writing, in an array of styles that often reflected the preoccupations of Canadian society in the years of their publication.

Because of its diversity, lesser-known fiction since 1960 will be discussed under a series of convenient though not definitive headings: 1. Experimental Fiction; 2. Minority Fiction; 3. Satire; 4. The Novel of Childhood; 5. Women and Fiction; 6. Regional Fiction; and 7. Popular Fiction.

1. EXPERIMENTAL FICTION. Although the 1960s were exciting years for the Canadian novel, truly experimental fiction arrived only with Graeme GIBSON's *Five legs* (1969). Before that there had been the tepid innovations of Peter Taylor in his *Watcha gonna do boy . . . watcha gonna be?* (1967), a picaresque pastiche of a young man's discovery that digression—in life as in railroads—is, though anathema to parents, a sweet and necessary thing. Appearing in the shadow of Kerouac and the Beat generation, Taylor's novel proclaimed its avant-garde nature as much by its youthful subject matter as by its formal innovations. A more daring explosion of form characterizes J. Michael YATES's *Man in the glass octopus* (1968), which heralded a West Coast attempt to offer Canada 'a fiction of a different order'. Yates's 'Man' appears in each of a sequence of dream-like allegories of futility, drawing the reader insistently into new considerations of ontology and of the place of fiction-making in human existence. In 1969, a year marking a burst of activity in Canada's small presses, Russell Marois used fragmented communication as the basis for the form and content of his novel *The telephone pole*. Graeme Gibson's *Five legs*, however, was heralded as the decade's crowning achievement in the experimental mode: style and content were welded to create an impression of the fragmentation of experience in the consciousness of the book's two main characters, Lucan Crackell and Felix Oswald. The interior isolation of the two men emerges on a funeral journey in the dead of winter, working against a deep underlayer of unifying mythological truth, suggested by the novel's title image.

In the 1970s Gibson continued to demonstrate that experiment in fiction need not mean gimmickry. *Communion* (1971), a 'sequel' to *Five legs*, brought back Felix Oswald with two other characters, Fripp and Ritson, intertwining their experiences in a manner as much magical as mystical. At first the reader clings to repeated motifs that seem to identify and fix the characters, but Gibson progressively withholds certainty, and the three separate experiences finally merge into one communion of violence. A similar technique—not as well or as economically handled—characterizes Robert HARLOW's *Scann* (1972), where the complex, web-like vision of reality filters through the mind and perceptions of the central character, Scann. Harlow created wonderful mythologies to people Scann's past and the past of British Columbia, breaking down all sense of linear time's relevance to perceptions of reality. A later example of experiment in Gibson's mode—perhaps a logical extension of that tradition—is Derk WYNAND's *One cook, once dreaming* (1980), which exists on the edge of any conventional definition of the novel; almost novella-length, it is a series of linked prose 'poems' that explore the impulse towards artistic creation through the metaphor of a master cook, whose skills of shaping and creating are as visible in his dreams as in his iced wedding-cakes.

A separate tradition of experiment followed the footsteps of Thomas Pynchon towards a type of fiction depicting a world where to exist is to be paranoid. In *The assignment* (1971) Martin Myers created the mysterious Spiegel, code-named Gimmel, dispatched on assignment to different lifetimes in different ages since the world began. Spiegel is either a radical schizophrenic or the only man brave enough to acknowledge that the world is arranged, under the direction of a Chief Assigning Officer, in patterns of meaning at once too seductive and too terrifying to face. In 1972 John MILLS' *The land of is* presented a similarly paranoid look at the underside of the West Coast, polarized by a split protagonist in the form of twins, one diabolically successful, the other weak and ineffectual. Mills experimented here, as elsewhere in his works, with the technique of the 'found' manuscript—letters and documents edited by a mediating narrator into an unreliable postmodernist text. Like Pynchon, Mills reached back to the Second World War for horrific images of dislocation and dismemberment to anchor his satire on modern society. The satiric bent reappeared in Jim Willer's *Paramind* (1973), along with the preoccupation with man as the game, and life as the player. By the 1980s the genre took on a new complexity, if not vitality, in the ponderous twin volumes of Robert Allen's *The Hawryliw process: part I* (1980) and *The Hawryliw process: part II* (1981), in which life, to the protagonist Minden Sills, means life inside the Hawryliw Institute, a self-proclaimed 'concatenation of whimsies'.

Yet a third experimental tradition, visible in the Canadian novel of the 1970s, exhibited a deconstructionism of the novel form that was not entirely alien to *The Hawryliw process*, with its pages of geometry and diagrams, and its chapter on 'How to read this novel'. Chris SCOTT's *Bartleby* (1971) launched the genre, with its self-conscious narrator engaged in (and sometimes disengaged from) a maniacal spoof of literary types and styles. A much more sober invasion of the novel's territory was Dave GODFREY's *I Ching Kanada* (1976), a text made not to be read sequentially from cover to cover but to be consulted in a form of mystical divination. Perhaps the most successful and exciting work in this group is George BOWERING's *A short sad book* (1977), which, though short, is never sad. Bowering's chatty, tricky narrator barges irreverently through the immensity of Canadian geography, history, and culture, as if it all existed simultaneously on one plane: all is grist for his mill as he anatomizes the literary genres, from the love story and the short story through the *roman à clef* to the Pretty Good Canadian Novel.

The early 1980s saw the rising popularity of a form that bore a close external resemblance to the conventional historical novel, but used this base of history to raise philosophic questions that still burned in the contemporary world. Gwendolyn MacEWEN's *King of Egypt, King of dreams* (1971) was perhaps a very early precursor of the genre of which George Bowering's *Burning water* (1980) was the first real example. Bowering's novel about Captain George Vancouver, and his arrival on Canada's west coast, stands the historical novel on its head, questioning its methods and assumptions at every turn and giving to eighteenth-century Amerindians the dialogue of twentieth-century psychology majors. In *The king's evil* (1981) David HELWIG used a related form—that of the historical detective novel, on the Josephine Tey model—to explore a catalogue of obsessions in the mind and life of a contemporary radio producer who discovers clues suggesting that Charles I was not beheaded but spirited off to Virginia to found a secular dynasty. Here art-forgery and human impersonation combine through the years following the interregnum to raise questions on the nature of proof and the validity of 'restoration'. Chris Scott delved even further into history, back to the Renaissance, for the matter of *Antichthon* (1982), where the heretic Giordano Bruno threatens to undermine the doctrines of the Roman Catholic Church by reconstructing the universe as a 'system ... to pick out the colours of the mind'. Graeme Gibson reappeared to crown the achievements of this hybrid genre with his novel *Perpetual motion* (1982). Like Scott's, his hero seeks the perfect system, this time against the background of nineteenth-century optimistic rationalism and the carnival and chicanery of southwestern Ontario small towns.

2. FICTION ABOUT AND BY MINORITIES. Alan Fry's *How a people die* (1970) ushered in a decade that saw the unprecedented blossoming of Native people into a major fictional subject deserving a category to itself. Fry's well-documented fictional treatment of a British Columbian resettlement village hovers at the edge of the sociological to present the economic and ethical problems surrounding the death of an eleven-month old Kwakiutl girl. Moving between the points of view of the local RCMP officer, the harried and helpless Indian agent, and the dead girl's sister,

Fry tangles questions of resettlement, responsibility, and survival to provide what is almost a problem novel.

In the previous decade the Canadian Native had continued to occupy a traditional, somewhat romantic and idealized place in the literature. Fred BODSWORTH's *The strange one* (1959) offers a mélange of animal tale and love story as he creates allegory out of a strained analogy between the courtship of barnacle geese and that of a young couple—Rory Macdonald and Kanina, a Native maiden. There is less of Hollywood in Bodsworth's later novel, *The sparrow's fall* (1967), although this story of the survival of Jacob Atook remains a fable of the primitive. In 1966 Paul St Pierre, a Vancouver author, published *Breaking Smith's quarter horse*, an excellent novel derived from an award-winning television show. Its small-farmer protagonist, the almost nameless Smith, is eclipsed by the Native characters Ol Antoine, the outlaw Gabriel Jimmyboy, and the slippery court interpreter Walter Charlie. St Pierre's evocative use of the voices and the silences of these Natives brings a vitality to the stereotypes that, married to the novel's overall metaphor of 'breaking'—not only of horses but of the human spirit—creates a fiction whose quality surpasses that of Alan Fry's later *How a people die*. But Fry's serious use of the Native point of view, and of documentary history, pointed onwards to the 1970s when, in the shadow of Rudy WIEBE's *The temptations of Big Bear*, David WILLIAMS' *The burning wood* (1975) depicted the confrontation between Saskatchewan Natives and the religious fundamentalism of the local white population. Young Joshua Cardiff, left bald by disease and rejected by his peers, turns in defiance of his family to the nearby reserve, where his baldness has a rational and even exalted explanation: he is accepted as Scalp-by-Manitou, a person singled out by the gods for special privilege. Williams' portrayal of the patriarchal, devout family, ridden by the past and riven by contact with another more 'pagan' race, recalls the work of South Africa's Alan Paton. Byrna Barclay took the Big Bear tradition a step further with her *Summer of the hungry pup* (1981), in which the nonagenarian First Woman, or Medicine Woman, relates to her Other Granddaughter the story of the Cree exile in Montana in the 1880s and 1890s. Barclay's poetic gifts enabled her to create for the generically named Old Woman a voice at once believable and inimitable to carry the monumental mythic stature of the protagonist—as Wiebe did for Big Bear. A further development is evident in James Polk's novel *The passion of Loreen Bright Weasel* (1981) which, despite its echoing title, eschews the mythic and explores the predicament of the contemporary Native in a tone of irony; the humour is often at the expense of whites, Natives, religion, local government, and contemporary society and culture. Set in the town of Hebb, Montana, the novel follows the unattractive adolescent Loreen from reservation, to convent, to pregnancy, to servitude with the well-meaning Triumph family. Loreen pursues the good with passionate ineptitude, leaving a trail of the bad behind her, and by the end of the novel all things have become their opposites: the thin become fat; the fat become thin; the madam of the local brothel joins the convent; the nuns become liberated and start wearing halter tops. Loreen's miracle is that she changes everything, but in the end all is as before.

Another kind of minority fiction emerged during the last two decades from the Caribbean immigrant community. Harold Sonny LADOO, who produced only two novels before his death in 1973, forged a new language in *No pain like this body* (1972), using a new richness of simile and onomatopoeia to depict the nightmare world of growing up in a shack in the middle of a Caribbean cane field. Ladoo's young hero is beset by thunder, rain, flood, scorpions, and insanity—ordeals presented not as exceptional or unusual, but as the inevitable concomitants of a childhood of poverty. *Yesterdays* (1974) provided a less nightmarish vision of island life, satirizing foreign planners, developers, and educators, and employing richly sexual and scatological humour.

3. SATIRE. The purest strain of satire in Canadian fiction of the last two decades surfaces in the novel of academia. In the tradition of Stephen LEACOCK and Robertson Davies, Jack MacLeod produced two hilarious novels set in 'Chiliast University' in Toronto. In *Zinger and me* (1979) he used an epistolary format to set up tension between its two heroes—the 'me' of the title, J.T., the tenure-seeking academic in the economics department, and Zinger, his alter-ego, the foul-mouthed, limerick-loving newspaperman, cast in the Gulley Jimson mould. Academic politics continued to provide fodder for MacLeod's grimmer satire *Going grand* (1982); here 'Zinger' and 'me' merge to give the novel a more conventional third-person format, and satire on the Canadian lack of cultural identity is delivered through the agency of the new foreign professor, Nalorian. An earlier, more diluted form of academic satire was

Saros Cowasjee's *Goodbye to Elsa* (1974), where the history department of a prairie university, 'Erigon College of Liberal Arts', is dissected under the one-eyed view of Tristan Elliott, the new Anglo-Indian professor. Cowasjee ranges as far afield as the Indian army, and the whole is washed in an overall tone of macabre humour that finally sobers the reader.

Despite the primacy of academia in recent Canadian satire, other targets have served. Daryl HINE wrote the most literary of Canadian satires, *The prince of darkness & co.* (1961), a *roman à clef* set in Capri. The enjoyment of its outrageous main character depends on knowledge of its dual prototypes (Norman Douglas and Aleister Crowley). In the same year William WEINTRAUB's *Why rock the boat* (1961) burlesqued the Montreal newspaper world in a gentle satire with strong romantic underpinnings. Both the romance and the gentleness disappear in Weintraub's later novel, *The underdogs* (1979), a strident and unconvincing presentation of a future in which Quebec is independent and the rest of Canada has been swallowed by the United States. A much more successful political satire is the earlier novel *My sexual and other revolutions: the memoirs of Donald Johnson* (1971), in which David Lewis STEIN captured the Messianic merger of sexual and political liberation that characterized the sixties.

4. THE NOVEL OF CHILDHOOD. In this period Canadian writers produced novels of childhood set in almost every inhabited nook and cranny of the country. The genre is best defined by a book that is less a fiction than a memoir: Fredelle Bruser Maynard's *Raisins and almonds* (1973). This meditation on the childhood of the daughter of a roving prairie shopkeeper sets out the touchstone of the genre: the recollective anecdotal concern with those little re-enactments of the Fall that mark the passing of childhood. The novel of childhood of the 1960s and 1970s might more accurately be termed a novel of growing up. Harold HORWOOD's *Tomorrow will be Sunday* (1966), for example, presents a teenage hero, Eli Palliser, fighting for his own sexual identity in the straitened moral climate of a Newfoundland outport. Though stiff in places, it is memorable for its straightforward treatment of homosexuality. In her first novel, *Pandora* (1972), Sylvia FRASER, though dealing mainly with a very young heroine, reveals her world (in 'Steeltown', or wartime Hamilton) to be a microcosm of the adult world, with its own cruelties, predicaments, systems of order, power struggles, triumphs, and defeats. Though Fraser at times weights her novel too heavily with descriptive sociology, her finely observed calculus of playground behaviour is nothing if not accurate. *Pandora* shares with Cecelia Frey's *Breakaway* (1974) a floridity of language that is particularly evident in their opening pages. Frey's novel, set in northern Alberta, is a somewhat wooden parade through the realizations that accompany and define the process of growing up: life, death, and change are experienced and assimilated in orderly turn by the protagonist, Lia. In Ontario, Dennis T. Patrick Sears' *The lark in the clear air* (1974), takes its adolescent hero, Danny, to young manhood through a series of riotous and somewhat improbable incidents, mostly sexual in nature. The sheer vitality of Sears' work contrasts with the bitter intensity of Betty Wilson's *André Tom Macgregor* (1976), which charts much the same period of time in the life of a young Métis from northern Alberta, seeking an education and finding a circumscribed life in Edmonton.

Another prairie novel combining childhood and social commentary is Mary Ann Seitz's *Shelterbelt* (1979), in which the conventional revelations that mark the growing up of Francie Polanski are eclipsed by the central and gradual realization that she is female in a male world—'just an ordinary girl' in a northern Saskatchewan family with nine brothers. In 1978 Stan Dragland crowned the achievements of the growing-up-in-the-West novel with his *Peckertracks: a chronicle* (1978). Though loosely structured—almost a series of vignettes—*Peckertracks* is held together by its extremely funny cast of high-school characters. Dragland's Depot, Alberta, in 1959 owes its economic existence to the railroad tracks; but to the hero, Percy Lewis, and the other sex-starved adolescents, 'peckertracks' are just as vital to the town's human economy. The voices—funny, anecdotal, wry, dead-pan, casually obscene—unite Dragland's prose pieces into a vigorous chronicle of growing up. A more literal example of the chronicle form appears in another novel from the same period, Hubert EVANS' *O time in your flight* (1979), in which Evans arrests time in the 1890s for a sustained look at small-town Ontario through the eyes of a child.

5. WOMEN AND FICTION. Although 'lady novelists' and the 'ladies' novel' have disappeared from the pages of serious literary criticism, one can still identify in Canadian fiction a body of serious novels written by women that concern and identify themselves with a female consciousness and its relationship to a largely male world.

In 1964 Jane RULE produced in *Desert of the heart* a memorable novel that sought a language for the unmarried woman living in a desert world where marriage is 'the idiom of life'. A decade later Constance BERESFORD-HOWE's *The book of Eve* (1973) presented the sexagenarian Eva, who runs away from a querulous invalid husband to freedom and poverty in a Montreal slum. Eva's refusal to continue to be what the male world of husband and son demands is an action that becomes the cornerstone of some later fiction. Both Joan BARFOOT's *Abra* (1978) and Aritha VAN HERK's *Judith* (1978) provide their heroines with an opportunity to escape to a healing, female world, patiently and painfully pioneered beyond the borders of the male establishment. Van Herk's Judith leaves the city for a pig farm and names her sows, one by one, after female figures from history and myth, a list—going from Marie Antoinette to Venus, via Daisy Buchanan—that charts her own transformation from siren to woman. In *Abra*, a much bleaker novel, the heroine abandons husband, children, and dog for a spare country existence—a nine-year night of the soul during which her children grow up and away from her. Van Herk's less successful second novel, *The tent peg* (1981), inspired by the Old Testament story in Judges 4, is saved from its bizarre heroine—J.L., or Ja-el, an androgynous witch-goddess with mysterious powers over men and beasts—by its multiple points of view, which move among the various members of a geological expedition to provide an interesting texture of voices, mostly male.

In 1977 the *Books in Canada* First Novel Award went to Oonah McFee's *Sandbars* (1977), a novel of memory, of the search in the past for the expectations of the past. Katherine GOVIER's heroine in *Random descent* (1979) reaches beyond her own memory to the past of her ancestors, exploring the meanings of family through the lives of women—with evocative names such as 'Constance' and 'Submitta'—who make families and hold them together.

Yet another type of fiction should be considered here—those finely observed studies of ordinary life that often constitute the novel of manners. Helen Levi's three novels—*A small informal dance* (1977), *Tangle your web and dosey-do* (1978), and *Honour your partner* (1979)—form a trilogy depicting life in a small Manitoba town as a ritual of tea and sandwiches, where partners are decorously chosen, and the young become old in the perennial dance of birth, love, and death. Another writer whose fictions seem to belong in this category is Carol SHIELDS. Her *Small ceremonies* (1976) pairs with *The box garden* (1977) to explore the manners and mores of middle-class suburbia. Urban life in Shields' two novels appears as constrained and ritualized as small-town life in Levi's trilogy.

6. REGIONAL FICTION. Most Canadian fiction is in some sense regional. Three regions have been singled out here because they have produced fictions in which the sense of place forms a unifying undercurrent to novels that sometimes vary widely in subject matter. It is perhaps surprising to find Toronto fiction described as regional, but it is an apt term for a kind of city novel that emerged during the last few decades, depicting the urban area as a landscape and producing a neighbourhood fiction strongly imbued with the regionalists' sense of place.

6(a). *Urban Toronto.* Toronto's fictional debut dates back to the early novels of Morley CALLAGHAN, where it is a nameless though not unrecognizable city, but could well be any big city in the North American midwest. By the beginning of the sixties Toronto emerged, in the fiction of Hugh HOOD and others, as a valid fictional locale, and with the Cabbagetown explosion a few years later it was anatomized to contribute to a new fiction of neighbourhoods. An early Toronto novel, Phyllis Brett Young's *The Torontonians* (1960), overhauled the upper-middle-class areas of the city, doing its best to give the ivied streets of 'Rowanwood' an aura of sin and *angst.* Hugh GARNER's *Silence on the shore* (1962) took urban fiction down the social scale to explore the volatile, decaying neighbourhood of the Toronto Annex, through the lives of the assorted inhabitants of a single rooming-house. Though Garner's characters and plot were predictable, he captured succinctly the dynamics of a neighbourhood in transition, where those on the way up mingle briefly with those on the way down. Originally published in 1950, Garner's *Cabbagetown*, which is the common ancestor of all the Toronto novels of urban grit, was substantially revised and expanded and re-issued in 1968, when it created renewed interest in the genre. Two years later Juan BUTLER reconstructed the Cabbagetown of the sixties in his *Cabbagetown diary: a documentary* (1970). With its diary-entry format, the novel used the irreverent, off-hand, 'macho' voice of the rootless Michael, a voice that seemed to speak for its time and place and was the novel's *tour de force.* Toronto novelists continued to explore the pocket neighbourhoods of the city, discovering local colour in a widening variety of urban areas and periods. Alice Boissonneau's *Eileen McCullough* (1976), for example, depicted life in the industrial Queen Street district during the Second World War. In the seventies a different kind of Toronto fiction appeared in the novels of Richard B. WRIGHT. With *The weekend man* (1970) Wright, working in the tradition of Callaghan's early novels, created the unselfconscious Toronto novel, where the shape of the city is wedded to the shape of the characters' lives. In two later novels, *In the middle of a life* (1973) and *Final things* (1980), Wright's unprepossessing heroes continue to define their failed lives in terms of the novels' spatial and temporal metaphors.

6(b). *The West.* Patricia Blondal's *A candle to light the sun* (1960) began the decade by epitomizing prairie fiction in its earlier and gentler phase. A thorough exploration of community—the small town of Mouse Bluffs, Manitoba—provided a background for a portrait of the young artist David Newman. This phase disappeared in George RYGA's two short prairie fictions. *Hungry hills* (1963) offered a grittily realistic picture of Depression-era Alberta, in which the earnest clichés of realism weigh down the slangy dialogue. Ryga's more successful and appealing *Ballad of a stonepicker* (1966), though set in the same time and place, avoided the worst pitfalls of cliché by harnessing its confessional tone to a ballad-like form—aimless and anecdotal, yet rhythmic. Echoes of this form recur in prairie fiction. Ken MITCHELL's *Wandering Rafferty* (1972)—whose title, while recalling Celtic romanticism, also betrays its form—follows middle-aged, mad, poetic Rafferty and young, rootless, revolutionary Archie Payne as they bumble their way across the West, exploring the nature of 'two kinds of romanticism'. In a later Mitchell novel, *The con man* (1979), the itinerant hero resurfaces in Gilly Savard, reluctant con-man in a world that Mitchell suggests makes con men of us all. Gilly escapes the law by placing his confidence in the eccentricities of language, particularly of names, as he meanders across Saskatchewan, lured by the sound of place names such as 'Elbow' and 'Eyebrow', in a pattern of illogic that baffles the exponents of purpose and straight highways. David Williams used a form reminiscent of all these prairie forerunners in *The river horsemen* (1981). His four wanderers—two Natives, a lapsed evangelist, and a stubble-cheeked Ukrainian youth—navigate a perilous river journey in 1930s Saskatchewan. Each member of the unlikely company speaks in his own voice, weaving a pattern of betrayal and violence on the river road to Saskatoon and apocalypse.

Farther west, British Columbia fiction of the 1960s was anchored by Robert Harlow's *Royal Murdoch* (1962) and *A gift of echoes* (1965). With their shared characters and locale (a mill town in the foothills of the Rockies), the two novels could have formed a diptych, but Harlow never successfully developed the possibilities inherent in his material, and the regional mythology he sought remained elusive until his later, and larger, novel *Scann*. A less serious, but still popular British Columbia writer is Margaret Craven, whose lightweight fiction *I heard the owl call my name* (1967) alternates intense natural lyricism with a sentimental view of a British Columbian coastal tribal village. The hero of this short novel, an Anglican priest with a mortal illness, comes to live and to die in the village, learning along the way to respect its ways and earning, in turn, the respect of the Native people.

Poet Susan MUSGRAVE, in her novel *The charcoal burners* (1980), rejected sentimentality in favour of the sensational and hacked away at any remaining romanticization of the modern Native condition. Her heroine, Matty, a former student of anthropology, furnishes ironic commentary on Aboriginal custom, but her detachment fails her when she is imprisoned in the cannibalistic commune of Ephratah in the British Columbia interior. Musgrave's horrific vision—of a woman caught between the vegetarians and the meat-eaters, and sentenced to die by one or the other—is most horrifying for the suggested universality of its application.

6(c). *The East.* In the 1960s and 70s English-language fiction set in Quebec was no longer exclusively of a high romantic nature. Robert Goulet's *The violent season* (1961) depicted the cyclical purgings by *charivari* of the pent-up frustrations of a small Quebec logging town, La Buche. Caught between seminary and logging camp, the village longs for a saint; the Curé founds a brothel in an attempt to break a vicious circle that dooms foundling girls to become mothers of more illegitimate babies. By *charivari* the brothel is destroyed, and the saint is created with much wasteful loss of life. In John Mills' *The October men* (1973) violence again characterizes the vision of Quebec. Mills uses the October Crisis (1970) as background for a novel that, on one level, is as fast, bold, and violent as any pulp thriller; but he also uses the postmodern device of the self-conscious fiction commenting upon itself to make us aware of the many fictional forms possible within the bare framework of event, thereby distancing the violence from us and making some of the violent acts seem ordered by a necessity as much fictional as political. Between these two novels of violence is the bicultural *Lark des neiges/Snow lark* (1971) of Ronald SUTHERLAND, whose Suzanne Laflamme, alias Susy MacDonald, epitomizes the duality of her society. Her narrative is a carefully crafted jumble of French and English phrases that presents a picture of Montreal life that is as schematized as anything since Hugh MacLENNAN's *TWO SOLITUDES* (1945).

Quebec appears more benign in Bernard Epps' depiction of the Eastern Townships, *Pilgarlic the death* (1967). Despite its title it is a lyrical, somewhat idealized version of small-town pastoral, recalling Dylan Thomas in the names of its characters: Dougal the School, John the Law, Long George. The town has its poachers and policemen, its sluts and saints, its sinners and sin-eaters, and offers to all its inhabitants the possibility of harmony, if not happiness, in its ordered world.

A tough, sinewy fiction emerged in Canada's Atlantic provinces in this period. Percy JANES' *House of hate* (1970) depicted the claustrophobic life of a Newfoundland mill town between the wars. The hard and bitter patriarch Saul Stone dominates this novel as he dominates the lives of his six children—a family of Stones bred in an emotional soil as barren as the rocky land around their fortress-like house. David Adams RICHARDS created a similar fiction of entrapment set in northern New Brunswick. His novels—*The coming of winter* (1974), *Blood ties* (1976), and *Lives of short duration* (1981)—explored the intricate family relationships that sustain a rural community, economically and culturally circumscribed and awaiting escape to the outside world. *Lives of short duration* is a particularly fine depiction of the tangled generations of the Terri family in a world of ignorance and casual cruelty.

7. POPULAR FICTION. Over these two decades Canadian writers of popular fiction demonstrated mastery of all the popular modes—often providing, along the way, a map of the social and cultural preoccupations of their day and time. Sheila Burnford capped the animal adventure story with her novel *The incredible journey* (1961); Donald Jack's farcical but enduring *Three cheers for me: the journals of Bartholomew Bandy, R.F.C.* (1962) was a humorous look at the Great War. Arthur Hailey's *In high places* (1962) began a tradition of political suspense novels that produced Charles Israel's *The hostages* (1966) and Charles Templeton's *The kidnapping of the President* (1974). Though Hailey went on to found another dynasty of formula novels with the publication of *Hotel* (1965), his real contribution to the popular novel is the carefully researched social and political realism of *In high places*, where the contemporary and controversial nature of the subject matter adds to the novel's suspense. After Templeton's timely and convincing recreation of the drama of a presidential kidnapping attempt, the political suspense novel ventured abroad with Ian McLachlan's *The seventh hexagram* (1976), whose setting for international intrigue was Hong Kong. David Gurr's novel *Troika* (1979) took the international thriller successfully to a Baltic setting, using front-page news as the basis of his fiction.

The familiar, ever-popular genre of the historical novel produced two works of note: Pauline GEDGE's *Child of the morning* (1977) and Sylvia Fraser's *The Emperor's virgin* (1980). Gedge, an Albertan, recreated the courts of Egypt's pharaohs Thothmes I and II, taking as her focus the story of the historically androgynous Hatshepsu, whom Gedge fashions into a female Pharaoh of great power and fascination. There is little of Gedge's nod to feminism in Fraser's tale of debauchery and decadence in Rome of the first century A.D., whose heroine, Cornelia, is a vestal virgin. A much more joyful and enjoyable exercise in eroticism was the extremely successful *In praise of older women: the amorous recollections of András Vajda* (1965), in which Stephen VIZINCZEY chronicles the amorous exploits of a Hungarian survivor of the Second World War. Though written rather in the style of a commentary on a hockey match—with a chapter for each period, and a careful charting of goals scored and assists—this hymn to older women had sufficient vitality and timeliness to be made twice into a film.

Another popular format began to flourish in the early 1980s when Howard ENGEL resurrected the Hammett-style detective novel with *The suicide murders: a Benny Cooperman mystery* (1980), and *The ransom game* (1981), whose most memorable feature is the harried, mother-ridden private eye Benny Cooperman, from Grantham, Ontario. The psychological thriller, mastered early by John BUELL in his *Four days* (1962), later produced two good examples: Tim WYNNE-JONES' *Odd's end* (1980)—winner of the 1979 Seal Book Award—and *The knot* (1982). Both works contain a skilful and unpredictable blend of the criminal, the mysterious, and the subtly horrific.

MICHELLE GADPAILLE

1983 to 1996. If the writing of Canadian literary history, from its beginnings in the nineteenth century through to some of its twentieth-century manifestations, has tended to remain rooted in a notion of national self-definition and consciousness, then this particular entry constitutes one possible attempt to inventory a slightly different history, to map some of the conditions under which our conventional understanding of terms such as 'nation', 'identity', and 'history' has recently been called into question. While the range of Canadian novels in English published between 1983 and 1996 clearly militates against routine generalizations and renders impossible any attempt to document a comprehensive history, it can be argued that many texts published during this period by both new and more established writers have invited a reassessment of received models of inquiry and facilitated a broadened set of strategies for reading representations of Canada. These texts invite us to probe the ways in which representations construct meaning, and to ask whose interests these representations serve. What sorts of cultural assumptions, for example, are encoded in representations of Canada, of Canadian history, or of other histories and identities? After the fashion of Joy KOGAWA's important earlier novel, *Obasan* (1981), these texts often attend to pasts or modes of experience that have been silenced, repressed, forgotten, or misrepresented in dominant forms of representation.

Daphne MARLATT's *Ana Historic* (1988), for example, focuses on the exclusion of women as active subjects in the writing of history. Arguing for a need to resist the confining structures of representation perpetuated by dominant histories, the novel encourages us to ask: Who has the institutional power to determine who speaks (and who doesn't speak) and to determine whose voices count as knowledge? The novel's protagonist, Annie, while working as a research assistant for her husband's 'big book' on Vancouver history, comes across a passing reference in the archives to a Mrs Richards, which leads her gradually to become more and more disengaged from her husband and his project. In rejecting the code of dominant history elaborated, for example, by Annie's husband, Marlatt, in the very writing of her own text, fashions alternative constructs of representation: reacting against the language of fact, documentation, continuity, and *telos*, Marlatt celebrates the possibility of an unconditioned language associated with women's bodies.

Margaret Sweatman's *Fox* (1991) is another experimental, fragmentary, and non-linear novel that, like Marlatt's, uses multiple points of focalization to offer a revisionary account of history. Its retelling of the events leading up to Winnipeg's 1919 General Strike also constitutes an attempt to recover voices and experiences that are conspicuously absent from traditional documentary representations of the event: here, too, for instance, Sweatman challenges the writing of history as a male-dominated discourse by using the contrasting political sensibilities of the two main women characters, Eleanor and Mary, as a way of opening up questions about the kinds of class divisions that gave rise to the strike, and, more generally, about the cultural construction of a nation in which strikers and revolutionaries were represented in both public and private discourses as 'enemy aliens' rather than Canadians.

Among the writers who established their reputations in the 1970s and early 1980s, Michael ONDAATJE has perhaps been the most consistent in seeking to incorporate marginalized (though often semi-legendary) figures and experiences from history into his fictional narratives. In *In the skin of a lion* (1987) and *The ENGLISH PATIENT* (1992), Ondaatje once again used actual persons and events from the historical past to invite us to reflect on both the powers and the limits of cultural representation. *In the skin of a lion* is about the displaced working-class immigrants who participated in the building of Toronto during the early decades of the twentieth century, but whose voices remain absent from the officially recorded history. Like *Obasan*, *Ana Historic*, and *Fox*, Ondaatje's novel invites us to ask: Who writes Canadian history? Who has the power to determine what counts as knowledge about Canada? What has been left out of the official versions of Canadian history? And whose interests have been served by those versions?

The English patient also deals with the retelling of history, and with the agential function of the imagination in reconstructions of the past. It too is a novel about displaced characters, disappearances, and uncertain identities. If, in *Lion*, Patrick Lewis is both the 'searcher' trying to find Ambrose Small, and the 'researcher' trying, as are we as readers, to reconstruct Alice Gull's history, *The English patient* documents two more disappearances: those of Katharine Clifton and, of course, the burned aviator of the title, the explorer who disappeared when he turned from Cairo and returned into the desert. As various narratives unfold, as characters gradually 'shed their skins', we begin to move towards a resolution, yet the new knowledge that the patient is, indeed, not an Englishman, but a Hungarian desert explorer who worked for the Germans during the war, seems curiously inconsequential: somehow, the revelation of his identity (and his nationality) seems not to matter anymore.

Both these novels unsettle customary notions of identity by destabilizing our desire to see nations as determinate sites of cultural belonging. Another text engaged in probing the intersections between identity and nationhood is Shyam Selvadurai's *Funny boy* (1994). Selvadurai, like Ondaatje, is a Sri Lankan Canadian, and his novel, a series of linked stories somewhat after the fashion of Alice MUNRO's *Lives of girls and women*, tells the tale of a young Tamil boy, Arjie, growing up and becoming aware of his homosexuality in the midst of Sri Lanka's political tensions in the 1970s and early 1980s. Of particular interest here is the cultural construction of nationhood *within* the borders of the nation state. National identity, this novel suggests, is not only a matter of representational acts that define nationality in opposition to other nation spaces *beyond* one's national borders; it is equally dangerously premised on cultural representations that mark out patterns of identity-formation in opposition to others situated within the context of the nation-state. Much of the force of the novel resides in the way it negotiates between, on the one hand, exposing the constructedness of the nation and, on the other, showing us just what is at stake when people insist that their most enduring attachments are inherited rather than selected. By further associating attempts to construct a homogeneous national community with the familial, institutional, and social containment of Arjie's homosexuality, Selvadurai's text denaturalizes structures of representation that are predicated on processes of exclusion and marginalization.

Funny boy, like a number of other important novels published during the period, has little to do directly with Canada. In *The doctor's house* (1996), Cary Fagan tells the story of a young boy seeking shelter in the house of a Jewish doctor in 1930s Warsaw. Mark Frutkin, in *Atmospheres Apollinaire* (1988), transports us to Paris at the beginnings of the twentieth century to document a metafictive history of Guillaume Apollinaire. And Nancy HUSTON, a Canadian-born expatriate writer, sets *The Goldberg Variations* (1996) in Paris, where she has lived for over twenty years. Along with this increasing interest, on the part of Canadian-born writers, in setting novels outside of Canada, the tendency for novelists born outside Canada—such as Selvadurai, Rohinton MISTRY, and M.G. VASSANJI—to write Canadian novels (which win Canadian literary prizes) but yet *not* write about Canada, has encouraged us to rethink our understanding of what it means to call something a Canadian text, to interrogate our assumptions about Canadian national identity and its relation to Canadian culture.

Mistry's writing is, perhaps, exemplary in this regard. In his novels *Such a long journey* (1991) and *A fine balance* (1995), Mistry shifts his focus away from the cultural in-betweenness that results from emigration (a theme developed in his collection of short stories *Tales from Firozsha Baag*, 1987), opting instead to situate his narratives in the context of specific moments in recent Indian history. Set in Bombay in 1971, when India went to war with Pakistan over what was to emerge as the new nation-state of Bangladesh, *Such a long journey* uses the political landscape of India to expose some of the forces controlling the lives of innocent people and communities. *A fine balance* is also set in India: this time the India of the mid-1970s, when Indira Gandhi's government declared a State of Emergency. The novel charts the devastating consequences of this repressive measure on the lives of its four main characters, and also documents a history and a legacy of caste, class, and communal conflicts.

As important texts in an ever-evolving literary history, these novels are hugely instructive because they provoke a questioning of the kinds of nationalist assumptions that have governed our thinking about Canadian identity; and, indeed, because they remind us that identity cannot be reduced to a single or authoritative horizon of meaning, such as nationality. However fragile, the sense of community that develops between the two tailors, the student, and the widow in *A fine balance* might serve as a kind of microcosm for the critical shift that the novel itself, when read in a Canadian context, envisions: the move in literature from seeing identity as something natural, inherited, or deep within us, to recognizing the extent to which relations between horizons of meaning (race, class, caste, gender, nation, etc.) necessitate newly articulated modes of theorizing constituency. Though set a quarter-century ago in India, these novels, like many other novels mentioned in this entry, are informed by contemporary concerns about the writing of history—concerns that are part of the Canadian cultural context today. These novels have entered the context of scholarship and critical practice in contemporary Canadian literary history, to remind Canadians that they are members not only of a particular nation, but of a broader human community.

Vassanji's two award-winning novels about Asian communities in East Africa—*The gunny sack* (1989) and *The book of secrets* (1994)—might also be read in this kind of context, for they too have implications for the way we understand the cultural construction of Canada. In *The book of secrets*, a diary belonging to Alfred Corbin, a British colonial administrator in Kikono in 1913, turns up in 1988 and is entrusted to a retired Goan history teacher who tries to unravel its mysteries. Like a number of other texts written during the period, the novel explores the clash between dominant and secondary cultures; but here that clash is further intensified by a detailed consideration of the ways in which European conflicts (between the British empire in Kenya and the German empire in Tanganyika) are fought at the expense of East African communities.

Other novels that probe similar kinds of questions about cultural belonging and cultural dislocation are Vassanji's *No new land* (1991), a text about Asian immigrants from Africa who have settled in a Toronto suburb; Sky LEE's *Disappearing Moon Café* (1990), an account of four generations of women in a Chinese-Canadian family; Wayson Choy's *The jade peony* (1995), a novel that focuses on three young children in an immigrant family growing up in Vancouver's Chinatown in the 1930s and early 1940s; and Hiromi Goto's novel about three generations of Japanese-Canadian women on the Prairies, *Chorus of mushrooms* (1994). These texts open up resonant questions about how best to negotiate between inherited ethnic identities and a different system of cultural referents in the West. In exploring the efficacy of holding on to old cultural identities in the context of a new home in Canada, in asking what it means to live on the margin with a hyphenated or hybrid identity, these novels (along with those of Mistry and Selvadurai) remind us of the impossibility of writing a single, monolithic Canadian literary history, and of the need to attend to the plurality of voices that define the Canadian literary landscape. The histories of other cultures have become part of the Canadian context. What does this do to our understanding of Canadian identity-formation?

Two other novels that explore the relations that develop when disparate cultures intersect are John STEFFLER's *The afterlife of George Cartwright* (1992) and Rudy WIEBE's *A discovery of strangers* (1994). Again, both texts are rooted in history, and both suggest that imaginative reconstructions of the past can tell us more about history than most traditional documentary accounts can. In fact, Steffler's narrative—presented as it is from the point of view of the eighteenth-century British adventurer and entrepreneur George Cartwright after his death—insists, through its very violation of a conventional point of view, on the agential power of imaginative histories, on the need to call into question our assumptions about the time-honoured distinction between history and fiction. It is a critique of expansionism and of dominant European knowledge-making systems, using as its point of departure the relations between imperial adventurers like Cartwright and the Inuit of Labrador whom he sought to use as allies and interpreters for the purposes of trade and exploration. Wiebe's novel, somewhat similarly, traces the early stages of contact between members of the first Franklin expedition and the Natives on whose knowledge and skills they so heavily depended.

Beatrice Culleton's *In search of April Raintree* (1983) also traces the implications of cultural contact by focusing, in a contemporary context, on the lives of two Métis sisters whose varied responses to their shared past point to what is at stake in the process of negotiating between opposed sets of cultural values. Demonstrating the impossibility of the two positions—essentialism and assimilation—espoused by the sisters, the novel is largely about the struggle for power of self-representation. How, it asks, can oppressed peoples, here the Métis, make history their own, how counter the dehumanizing and oppressive effects of dominant constructions of self and other?

Richard Wagamese's *Keeper 'n me* (1994) also comes to a focus on its protagonist's attempts to reconnect with a lost community. A novel of Native homecoming, it tells the story of Garnet Raven, who, as a child, was taken from his home on an Ojibway reserve and, like the sisters in Culleton's novel, placed in a series of foster homes. Growing up with no sense of his Native identity, he returns home after many years and, through his contact with one of the elders on the reserve, renews his sense of place and belonging. Like Culleton's, Wagamese's novel raises important questions about how best to challenge representations of the Native as other in dominant discourses.

Thomas KING's response to such a question, in his two novels, *Medicine River* (1989) and *Green grass, running water* (1993), involves an insistence that we take his novels on their own terms. Like Rohinton Mistry, King refuses to make concessions to his readers, refuses to bow to the kinds of expectations generated by the construction and stereotyping of the Native in dominant cultural and historical discourses. Unlike many other texts probing the intersections between cultures, King's novels are less explicitly concerned with the history of domination and resistance. In *Medicine River*, for example, that history of relations between whites and Natives is encoded in unstressed places: in the way King uses parallel and overlapping narratives to de-hierarchize relations between cultures; in the ways, also, that he plays with our readerly expectations and assumptions about Native literature. Similarly, in *Green grass, running water* resistance is subtly encoded, this time in the complex sets of negotiation between the mythic and the historical, and in King's defamiliarization of both the Genesis story and Hollywood Westerns. By using intertextuality and parody to intervene in our understanding of historical processes, *Green grass*, like several other novels mentioned in this entry, rewrites history from the point of view of those who have traditionally been silenced or misrepresented.

Throughout his career Timothy FINDLEY has also been engaged in an attempt to encourage us to revise our understanding of received texts and traditions. This is perhaps most evident in *Not wanted on the voyage* (1984), a novel that also rewrites a familiar history (in this case the biblical story of Noah and the flood), and challenges us to think rigorously about (and to question) the kinds of dominant values and oppressive social roles that it legitimizes. Findley's novel, moreover, like much of Rudy Wiebe's fiction, uses events from a distant past to comment on contemporary social and cultural issues.

Elizabeth Nickson's *The monkey-puzzle tree* (1994) is a fictionalized account of a more recent, but little remarked upon, event in Canadian history, the CIA sponsored brainwashing experiments carried out by Dr Ewen Cameron at the Allan Memorial Institute, Montreal. While the novel's reconstruction of actual events lends itself to a consideration of the uses to which history can be put in fiction, Nickson's harrowing account of the Montreal experiments should also reinvigorate our understanding of art's social function.

In *The biggest modern woman of the world* (1983), Susan SWAN also turns to the past. Like *Ana Historic*, this novel is an attempt to recover women's history, by writing *into* history the real-life nineteenth-century Nova Scotian giantess Anna Swan. But it is also a text that is deeply suspicious of authority (including the author's own) and thus recognizes the impossibility of such a thing as the 'true' history of its subject. Indeed, we encounter in this novel a paradox that, though variously manifested, is central to many of the texts considered here. How does one recover history while, at the same time, recognizing that history is suspect? How make claims about the past (which, in some way, all of these novels do) while also insisting that truth and knowledge are functions of discourse?

In a short introduction to *The growing dawn* (1983), his novel about Marconi, Mark Frutkin suggests that 'all literature is biography (or autobiography), speaking as it does of the lives of men and women, or of the life of the author.' In that same introduction he also tells us, though, that 'every biography is ultimately myth.' Particularly resonant explorations of the conventions of (auto)biography can be found in Yann Martel's *Self* (1996) and Carol SHIELDS' *The stone diaries* (1993). Martel's fictional autobiography, or portrait of the transformations in the life of a peripatetic young writer, unsettles customary notions of identity through its handling of the protagonist's startling transformations and bizarre personal boundary-crossings. Similarly Shields' novel, with its use of a shifting and self-conscious narrative, repeatedly calls attention to its gaps, discontinuities, and distortions, and shows us that we can no longer take for granted notions of stable identity or reliable point of view. For example, we are told of its first-person narrator, Daisy Goodwill, that 'she is not always reliable when it comes to the details of her life,' that she has a little trouble with the truth, that we need to take her representations of events with a grain of salt. It is also a text, *à la Tristram Shandy*, that has Daisy narrate with precision the everyday events leading up to her birth. Shields' accomplishment, then, is to show us that daily (Canadian) life is itself an invented thing, and in this sense *The stone diaries*, like the other fictions under consideration, calls attention to the constructedness of history.

The above novels consider the relationship between real and invented worlds. Many expose the ideological workings of history (of a discourse of 'the real') by showing us how dominant representations have worked to naturalize and legitimize relations of power and oppression. Many manifest what Linda

HUTCHEON, in her important study *The Canadian postmodern* (1988), identifies as 'a postmodern urge to trouble, to question, to make both problematic and provisional any . . . desire for order or truth'. But, while problematizing history, knowledge, identity, and nationhood in this way, many of these same texts also want to insist, as Aunt Emily, a character in Kogawa's *Obasan* puts it, that 'it matters to get the facts straight.' By opening up such questions as those discussed here, the above novels suggest that Aunt Emily's ethical imperative may well constitute both the most important challenge and the most compelling area of inquiry for contemporary Canadian literary history as it looks towards its future rewritings. AJAY HEBLE

Other novels: 1983 to 1996. In this period the English-Canadian novel developed in several directions. First, novelists adopted less experimental techniques than in the previous period, often to express contemporary concerns with history, identity, labour, immigration, family, mourning, photography, cinema, and mass culture. As the lessons of the modern period were absorbed into the postmodern, and as the postmodern itself became familiar —even comfortable—writers moved away from fractured narratives, collage, and wordplay to more conventional techniques. If broken narratives once represented the dislocations of twentieth-century experience, those dislocations no longer frightened average Canadian writers or readers; consequently, contemporary narratives have abandoned defamiliarization in style and have resumed, as in the works of Rohinton MISTRY and Barbara GOWDY, continuity of plot as the backbone of the novel. Moreover, many writers made excursions from poetry to prose, yet retained a lyrical, exact, poetic language in their narrative work: Diana Hartog, Mary DI MICHELE, Kenneth Radu, John STEFFLER, among others, employ intense, imagistic prose styles.

Second, comedy did not disappear from the English-Canadian novel, as the works of Matthew Hart and Mordecai RICHLER attest. However, comedy yielded to well-made, earnest narratives about pursuing love or recovering from love. Such novels take as their domain the erotic and the pathological, which often go hand-in-hand, and treat objects of love (parents, partners, children) as foundations of personal identity.

Third, the distinction between urban and regional fiction lost significance as writers assumed more mobile and worldly stances. Montreal drew fewer young writers than it once did; Toronto attracted more. Yet fine, urbane writing has come out of Saskatchewan (Guy VANDERHAEGHE, Sharon BUTALA), Alberta (Thomas Wharton), British Columbia (Audrey THOMAS, George BOWERING), Newfoundland (Patrick Kavanagh), and other provinces. Fictional characters may be fixed in specific places, but they express little anxiety about regional roots. Cosmopolitanism, not regionalism, marks the work of new and established writers.

Finally, an exuberant market for popular fiction sustained an assortment of genres, such as espionage thrillers, Gothic novels, and techno-thrillers. Falling outside the purview of 'serious' literature, these novels tended to document Canadian fantasies about technology, medicine, supernaturalism, and ideology.

1(a). THE END OF EXPERIMENTALISM. Experimentalism, in the sense of the playful and the visual, diminished in novelists' repertories between 1983 and 1996. To get a sense of the changes that have altered the complexion of Canadian fiction, one can compare Michael ONDAATJE's early cross-generic books, *The collected works of Billy the Kid* (1970) and *Running in the family* (1982), with his later novels, *In the skin of a lion* (1987) and *The ENGLISH PATIENT* (1992). The former contain mixtures of dialogue, photographs, prose, anecdotes, tall-tales, and graphics. The novels refer to photographs and have a strong anecdotal tendency, but they do not dabble in boundary-crossing and visual referents to the extent the earlier works do. The disappearance of this kind of visual experimentalism may be the result of changing conditions in Canadian publishing and a paring down of the number of small presses willing to take risks with avant-garde fiction. It may also have to do with a culture less interested in challenging narrative conventions. Ondaatje is not alone in relinquishing experimentalism at a formal level. Whereas shattering narratives or mixing genres once expressed counter-cultural rebellion, or opened up new ways of recording experience that lie beyond the range of words, writers in this period used experimentation for aesthetic rather than defiant political ends. To take another example of the shift away from such experimentalism, one could set Audrey Thomas's *Blown figures* (1974)—replete with 'ads,' cartoons, and ample white space—against her *Coming down from Wa* (1995), which makes its point through narrative, not through pictures.

Experimentation still exists in terms of fractured points of view and radical shifts in focus, but this can hardly be described as innovative in the dying decades of the twentieth century. Quirky typefaces, generated electronically, and images derived from commercial advertising replace photographs and signal an escalating awareness of the computerized world. Matthew Remski in *Dying for Veronica* (1997) plays with typefaces to express differences in characters' personalities. Douglas COUPLAND uses sidebars and headlines in *Generation X* (1991) to convey the fragmentation of identity under the competing forces of commerce and culture. In David Young's *Incognito* (1982)—a book that combines a telephone directory, photographs, recollections, and essays—the author confesses his interest in 'the border-blur between autobiography and fiction'. Indeed, the experimental fiction of the 1970s often assumes the 'I' of the writer as its point of departure. Instead of pretending a lofty, abstracted, modernist distance from its subject, *Incognito* makes Young's changing and challenging personae the topic of investigation.

Like Ondaatje's early books of poetry and Young's quasi-autobiography, two books by Ann Rosenberg, *The bee book* (1981) and *Movement in slow time* (1988), were published by COACH HOUSE PRESS in Toronto. Rosenberg's first book—in which a ten-year-old girl named Habella begins to understand her complicated sexuality through bee lore—meditates on the relations between the sexes through rituals of mating and flights of bees. *The bee book* contains photographs, diagrams, musical scores, and concrete poems. Rosenberg takes another animal, the wolf, as the central metaphor and analogue for human experience in *Movement in slow time*. In this whimsical and delightful novel, the female protagonist, in love with a gay man named Aaron, wanders through Vancouver and meditates on historical and mythic lovers. Vancouver intertwines in her imagination with Dante's *Divine Comedy* and Hieronymous Bosch's *Garden of Earthly Delights*. When an acquaintance named John flirts with her and regales her with stories about his marriage, and when Aaron stands her up for an appointment, she realizes she is better off without men, whether gay or straight.

Ondaatje's way of talking about immigrant experience in a poetic and expressive manner in *In the skin of a lion* has been adapted by Peter Oliva in *Drowning in darkness* (1993), which takes place in the coal-mining community of Crowsnest Pass, Alberta. Threatened by methane gas and collapsing rock-faces inside the mine, miners learn to hear the distant rumblings of underground catastrophes that imperil their lives. An Italian miner named Celi gets trapped when tunnels collapse. He invents—or remembers—an Italian couple named Sera and Pep. Wounded, Celi dreams of his younger self, of the love between Sera and Pep, of a horse brought out of the mountain after two weeks of being trapped, of a doctor named Sunderd who walks out with Sera, of snowstorms and landslides. Oliva's novel combines history and dream in a complex meditation on suffering and love.

Thomas Wharton acknowledges indebtedness to Ondaatje in the epigraph to *Icefields* (1995), an exquisitely crafted first novel, and arguably the best novel written during this period. Wharton's book concerns an English botanist and explorer who slips on a glacier and finds himself lodged in a crevasse in the uncharted ice-world of Alberta. Compelled by this experience to study glaciers, Edward Byrne sets up an observation shack on a rock spur that juts above the glacier's path. The characters in *Icefields* have a heroic, even Wagnerian stature, especially Freya, who blithely treks across ice-floes and scales mountains, then dies in an avalanche. The Alberta mountains are Robert KROETSCH country (Kroetsch's novel *Alibi* takes place at spas near Banff), and Wharton shares Kroetsch's sense of mythic character and place. Whereas Kroetsch creates a landscape of intrigue and romance, Wharton shows the landscape under development. In particular, the entrepreneur Frank Trask sets up tourist attractions around Jasper that make nature accessible, but also make it less rugged. Wharton's style is characterized by lyrical outbursts, and an economy of phrase and insight that centres on telling images: red paint flecked on a boulder, an orchid growing in grit next to a glacier.

Wharton's novel shares with John Steffler's *The afterlife of George Cartwright* (1992) an interest in early settlement in Canada and its impact on the environment. George Cartwright reminisces, after his death, about his feckless pillaging of Labrador resources in the late eighteenth century. Historical verisimilitude permits descriptions of smallpox, the putting up of jam, the massacre of animals, and, rather surprisingly, the preservation of condoms. Cartwright, who scarcely understands his own behaviour or motives, survives Labrador winters only with the help of his common-law wife and Native know-how. Cartwright's character resembles the Labrador landscape: it combines the caprice of clouds with the unyieldingness of granite.

Another East Coast novelist, Patrick Kavanagh, offers a different version of weather and ice in *Gaff topsails* (1996), in which an iceberg unexpectedly drifts into an Atlantic fishing port. Michael Barron, out fishing with two mates, lands on the iceberg and climbs it. The action is confined to a single day in the year that Newfoundland and Labrador joined the Dominion of Canada. As in Joyce's *Ulysses*, to which *Gaff topsails* is overtly indebted for its Catholic sensibility and narrative technique, characters' private ambitions, bodily pains, and religious longings get described in indirect discourse. Kavanagh uses salty colloquial language to present the everyday anguish of spiritual life, epitomized by the mysterious and unforgiving iceberg that invades the port. Like Oliva, Steffler and Wharton, Kavanagh creates figures subject to the forces of history. Although these four books are, in each case, 'first' novels, they also stand as the most technically and imaginatively accomplished novels produced in this period.

1(b). The historical novel also developed a vein of curiosity about the nature of work. Each of the following postmodern narratives treats labour as an essential image of the past. In *Alias Grace* (1996), for example, Margaret ATWOOD minutely catalogues the labours of maids in the houses of Upper Canada landowners. Whether work determines character, or whether character determines choice of work, is a central conceit of Guy Vanderhaeghe's *The Englishman's boy* (1996), which divides into two narrative halves, devoted to two connected characters, a screenwriter and a rodeo hand. In a less obvious way Merilyn Simonds' *The convict lover* (1996)—set, like parts of *Alias Grace*, in and around Kingston Penitentiary—deals with the nearly impossible thriving of love between a convict and a girl who lives near the prison. Simonds elaborates characters, events, and outcomes from a batch of notes she retrieved from a Kingston attic to create, in effect, a 'real' historical novel. In this remarkable book Simonds allows spelling errors and idiosyncratic grammar to stand as they do in the found letters, yet she embroiders around those letters a complex psychology of reliance and duplicity between the convict enduring hard labour and the girl who loves him.

Work and history are the subjects of Margaret Sweatman's *Fox* (1991), which covers the turbulent politics of the labour movement that culminated in the Winnipeg General Strike of 1919. Sweatman evokes the escalating anti-immigrant passions that underlay Canadian politics after the Great War. Eleanor—who develops a conscience about workers despite being the daughter of a factory owner—falls in love with a socialist leader and bookseller named MacDougal. Her friend Meg, daughter of a meat-packing magnate, blithely marries an upper-crust swell named Drinkwater. Enraptured by each other and smug about their status, the newlyweds ignore the plight of the poor. In Sweatman's second novel, *Sam and Angie* (1996), she again takes wealth and work as her subjects. Angela is a lawyer, 'a profession that suited her temperament, like a talent, like an attribute, so she'd nearly had no choice in the matter.' To the vexation of her husband, Angela buries herself in a legal case that involves a trespasser. Women who work, or women who live lives of leisure, define the limits of acceptable or transgressive behaviour. Civic duty and personal passion conflict in these socially savvy narratives. Neither novel resolves the moral issue of whether political engagement takes precedence over personal commitment. Unlike other writers, however, Sweatman makes morality a pressing concern in her fiction.

Labour is sometimes an artistic endeavour. In Ondaatje's *In the skin of a lion*, a newspaper photographer captures a bicyclist whirring across the Bloor Street Viaduct before it officially opens. Another photographer descends into the tunnel being built beneath Lake Ontario to photograph the men who are digging into the oozing earth. The photographer's job of recording history is juxtaposed with the physical labour of the tunnel-diggers. This juxtaposition suggests that photography requires as much craftsmanship and painstaking effort as manual labour. Photographers, or sorters of archival photographs, show up throughout Canadian literature—in, for example, Timothy FINDLEY's *The WARS* (1977) and *You went away* (1996), Katherine GOVIER's *The immaculate conception photography gallery* (1994) and *Angel walk* (1996), and Diana Hartog's *The photographer's sweethearts* (1996). The photographer in Hartog's novel, a Dane named Louie, settles in California at the turn of the century, bribes children with candy, and takes their pictures. He explains physiology to them and recounts fairy tales. Louie narrates the novel in broken English, full of grammatical tics and misunderstood idiomatic expressions. He converts his obsessions with children and innocence into photographs. The photographer thus represents an attempt to freeze the past into an image, and to make *eros* stand still so that it can be savoured. Photography, in Hartog's novel, is literally a labour of love, or, in the hands of Ondaatje, a love of labour.

Labour defines Trevor Ferguson's several novels published over the last two decades. *High water chants* (1977) was followed by *Onyx John* (1985), *The Kinkajou* (1988), *The true life adventures of Sparrow Drinkwater* (1993), *The timekeeper* (1995), and *The fire line* (1995). Ferguson's characters tend to be soul-searching men who tough it out in difficult circumstances: fire-fighters, inn-keepers, railway crew workers. The youthful hero of *The timekeeper*, for instance, points out the immorality of his boss's actions and faces the consequences of speaking out against authority. Ferguson's narrators also tend to be garrulous storytellers, such as Reed Kitchen, a fabulist in *The fire line* who invents larger-than-life frontier tales. Effusively written, Ferguson's novels are dark, realistic, plot-driven, and concerned mostly with male characters.

2. EROS AND ILLNESS. Families and love affairs are basic ingredients of the novel. However, love is neither exultant nor straightforward in Canadian fiction between 1983 and 1996. Some novels, such as Joy KOGAWA's *The rain ascends* (1995), Barbara Gowdy's *Mister Sandman* (1996), and Ann-Marie MacDONALD's *Fall on your knees* (1996), treat the family as a sordid, secretive system where love falters and incest lurks. Canadian fiction poses questions about why people fall in love, why people fall in love with the wrong partners, why people don't fall in love, why people fall in love and then are desperately unhappy, why people fall in love and then are left, why love is pathological. In short, the novel makes *eros* and *agape* the stuff of psychological case studies in either comic or serious modes. Love is often represented as a kind of illness, and also as an inevitable part of identity. Often the 'family novel' deals with recuperation from the devastating effects of loving the wrong person or wronging a loved person. Two trends emerge in this genre: novels by women that emphasize independence and strength; novels by men that emphasize independence and dismal self-absorption.

2(a). Women writers, affected by feminism and changing conditions of parenthood, write about the difficulties of being mothers or the desire to become mothers. Cordelia Strube combines questions of love with issues of poverty and recovery. In *Alex & Zee* (1994), lawyer Zee (a nickname derived from Theodore) separates from his wife Alex and moves in with his mother. Alex, a social worker with a muffin business, tries to get pregnant, and sleeps with three men to accomplish that goal. In Strube's *Milton's elements* (1995), a dyslexic factory worker named Milton mourns his daughter Ariel, who died in a freak accident at the age of three. Milton's wife Judith works as a grocery-store cashier and begins to see another man. When Milton strikes Judith, she moves out, leaving him alone and bereft. A sense of damage and vulnerability also marks Rita in *Teaching pigs to sing* (1996). The mother of six-year-old Max, Rita copes with single-motherhood by trying to protect Max from too much knowledge of the world. She slowly integrates Max's father Nolan, an itinerant surgeon, back into her life when he returns from abroad. In each of Strube's novels, central characters face decisions about whether they can survive alone or whether they are too reliant on children or partners. Couples separate . . . then yearn for reunion. Strube's novels provide examples of 'how we live now'. On the whole, they express the difficulties and unhappiness of contemporary urban life and are, consequently, not joyous in tone or outcome.

Happiness eludes Margaret Fisher also in Claudia Caspar's *The reconstruction* (1996). Margaret, a sculptor, is hired to create a museum model of the three-million-year-old primate known in anthropological circles as Lucy. Using only a few fossilized footprints, some bones and some teeth, Margaret has to invent a convincing model of Lucy, the hairy forerunner of *homo sapiens*. Creating Lucy parallels the reconstruction of a life and an identity for Margaret, whose husband John has moved out after ten years of an unsatisfactory marriage. John couldn't bear to touch or be touched by Margaret. Lucy becomes the tangible sign of Margaret's reconstituted life.

Three novels by two authors make eros a pedagogical matter. In Ann Ireland's *A certain Mr. Takahashi* (1985) and *The instructor* (1996), the objects of affection are, respectively, a pianist and a painter. In both novels, younger women fall in love with older male artists. In Ireland's first book, two sisters vie for Takahashi's attentions. In *The instructor*, an aspiring and naive art student seeks adventure and knowledge by moving to Mexico with her teacher, a dissolute artist named Otto Guest. Simone leaves Otto in Mexico. He seeks her out six years later to ask her for work. Whether the student can overmaster the teacher's influence—an influence both artistic and erotic—is the subject also of Sarah Sheard's *Almost Japanese* (1985). Emma, at fourteen, falls in love with Akira Tsutsuma, conductor of a local symphony. Emma studies Japanese for the sake of Tsutsuma and chronicles her lyrical despair in a diary. Years later, she pursues him to Japan, where she discovers she no longer has a crush on him. (When younger, both Sheard and Ireland were attracted to Seiji Ozawa, conductor of the Toronto Symphony Orchestra.)

Sheard's second novel, *The swing era* (1993), concerns a daughter who tries to cope with her mother's madness. Frederika turns to religion for solace when her mother's mental illness overpowers her sense of self. According to a psychiatrist, the mother's illness may be hereditary. The need to calm her own feelings of despair motivates Frederika, who flees to a Buddhist monastery in Nepal and returns when her mother dies suddenly in her bath by electrocution. The title refers to the moments of madness experienced by her mother, when she does not see Frederika, or when she locks herself in the laundry room to play records and shout abuse over loud music at her daughter.

Gail Anderson-Dargatz's *The cure for death by lightning* (1996) begins with a messy scrapbook kept by Beth Weeks's mother. Containing odds and ends of paper, with recipes written on them, the book smells of vanilla, almonds, butter, flour. This coming-of-age novel includes recipes from that scrapbook that form a diary of sorts. Beth's father forbids cosmetics and frivolity whereas her mother supports and nurtures with food. A powerfully written novel about the enigmas of adolescence, *The cure for death by lightning* sets a benchmark for other mother-daughter novels by virtue of its exact rendering of psychology among the principal characters. It was a finalist for the 1996 Giller Prize.

A mother's actions colour the lives of two sisters in Carole Corbeil's *Voice-over* (1992), a well-crafted, uncompromising novel that deftly interweaves past and present. Claudine and Janine are French-Canadian women who have different perceptions of their girlhood in Montreal. Their mother, Odette, attempted suicide in 1962, and each daughter is marked permanently by that event. The emotional Janine tries to forgive her mother, while rational Claudine talks to her rarely, believing that her mother is ashamed of her. She becomes a documentary film-maker who specializes in 'unsentimental' programs about prostitutes, drug-users, and female inmates, while wandering from lover to lover. In part, the mother's alienation from her daughters breeds in them a sense of alienation from everyone else.

Family breakdown structures two novels by Rita Donovan. *Dark jewels* (1990) chronicles the loss of Murdoch MacFarland's first wife and eldest son. Told as a sequence of monologues by all the main charactes, the novel draws unflattering portraits of the secretive MacFarland, his second wife, his sons, and his daughter. In *Daisy Circus* (1991) a rejected daughter becomes a comedian. When her beloved brother Drake is crippled and hospitalized she fulfils a need to care for him. The presiding genius of the novel is e.e. cummings, whose poetry inflects Daisy's thinking, especially cummings' poetry about love that stirs ecstasies of the senses.

Linda Leith makes Hungary in 1990 the setting for *Birds of passage* (1993), a novel about the marriage of playwright Gábor Marton, aged 43, and his out-of-work actress wife Veronika, aged 27. Gábor opposed the Communist government for years and now sits as an opposition member in the democratically elected parliament. Gábor absolves himself of responsibility when Veronika gets pregnant. Meanwhile, Veronika 'is full of wishes—she wishes Gábor were kinder to her. She wishes Gábor were different. She wishes she could just leave Gábor now, at least make him worry that she would leave him, get back at him somehow.' Political democracy permits freedom of opinion; the democracy of marriage permits divisive opinions and a dispersal of partners. In Leith's second novel, *The tragedy queen* (1995), *eros* disturbs the middle-aged women of Pointe Claire, Quebec, when Vince Carlson rides into town on his Harley motorcycle. Vince 'prides himself on knowing a lot about middle-aged women. Young women are easy enough, but they bore him.'

2(b). Novels centred on identity and family are not the exclusive prerogative of women writers. Keith Oatley, a professor of psychology, has published four books of psychology and a single novel, *The case of Emily V.* (1993), which begins with the premise that an unpublished case study by Sigmund Freud and a newly discovered manuscript about detective Sherlock Holmes are found bundled together. The novel includes the manuscript of Emily Vincent, subject of parallel investigations by Freud and Holmes, in which Vincent writes that she was seduced at the age of fourteen by her guardian.

Whereas Oatley used the case study and the detective genre to structure his novel about seduction, three gay novelists used structures of interconnected short stories that accumulate into novels. Shyam Selvadurai's *Funny boy* (1994) takes a central character through six stories set during political upheaval in Sri Lanka. Wayson Choy's *The jade peony* (1995) is about an extended family in Vancouver's Chinatown in the late 1930s and early 1940s. In Choy's novel, characters are identified by their position in the family: 'First Brother,' 'Only Sister,' 'Second Brother.' Divided according to character, the novel is a study of several identities that take their meaning from their relation—adopted, biological, loved, rejected—to other people. Each section of this extraordinary novel moves towards a moment of intensity that reveals, as if by magic, the secret longings or private distress of each character. In *Dark rides* (1996) Derek McCormack builds up the identity of a gay character named Derek through a series of short prose snippets and photographs. Set in Peterborough, Ontario, in 1952, the interlocking pieces draw a portrait of a teenager obsessed by midways, fireworks, and carnivals. This 'novel in stories' allows different perspectives on gay identity to emerge with regard to love and family; what falls between the gaps in the stories is the repressed or inexpressible part of identity.

Kenneth Radu and Alan Cumyn treat families in terms of sexual identity and longing. Cumyn's *Waiting for Li Ming* (1993) plays with the tension of thwarted reunion. A teacher returns to Canada after working for a year in China; he waits for his lover Li Ming, held up by complications of emigration, to join him. In *Between families and the sky* (1995) Cumyn documents the lives of two principal characters who are shaped by their parents. In one case, James Kinnell's father dies and his mother has a new romance; in the second, Garland Rose's mother dies and her father pursues a romantic interest in Garland's teacher. Two novels by Kenneth Radu make sexuality the key to identity. In *Distant relations* (1989) Vera keeps an escort agency in her basement. In *Home fires* (1992) Nick keeps two sex shops in Montreal, and other male characters strut through the novel selling themselves or answering personal ads.

Canadian masculinity, in some cases, is based on a renunciation of female companionship. Many fictional men have little self-awareness. Because they repudiate their spouses or families, they end up alone, as in *A year of lesser* (1996) by David Bergen. The sexual excitement of Johnny Fehr cools down whenever he recalls that he is a born-again Christian. Married to Charlene, he has an affair with Loraine, who becomes pregnant. Charlene feels rejected; Johnny sulks; Johnny gets re-baptized; Charlene dies in a fire during a blizzard; Johnny grieves; Loraine gives birth. Johnny, who leaves everyone in the lurch in this dispiriting and mildly satirical novel, does not seem the least bit equipped to deal with any emotion, great or small, and consequently creates suffering in all the people he supposedly loves. In short, he's a loser.

The pathology of masculinity takes a stranger turn in Douglas Cooper's *Amnesia* (1992). The Jewish protagonist, Izzy, lives in a house split in two by his architect father. His brother Josh and his grandfather Abba, a kindly watch-collector who tries to keep Jewish traditions alive, both die. Izzy's other brother Aaron builds a machine that registers the emotions of everyone in the partitioned house. When the father announces he's leaving for good, the house collapses. Utterly disconnected from his family, Izzy devotes most of his time to crime and self-pity. Cooper's second novel, *Delirium* (1994), was released exclusively on the Internet.

The self-indulgent male with a split personality returns in Yann Martel's *Self* (1996). Like Corbeil's *Voice-over*, Martel's novel shifts between French and English, appropriate to the bilingual child of diplomats. As a boy in kindergarten the narrator falls in love with an Israeli diplomat's son, whom he wants to marry. Later, the narrator says, 'I felt neither masculinity nor femininity, I only felt desire, I only felt humid with life.' Overnight he transforms into a woman, just as Virginia Woolf's Orlando does: 'I was a woman, that also. English-speaking and a woman. That was the core of my being.' Polymorphously adventurous, she takes both male and female lovers. Dissatisfied with womanhood after these escapades, she becomes a man again. The novel is a portrait of fluid and not altogether interesting sexual identity, and the title is adequately close to 'self-centred' and 'selfish', expressing the narrator's sense of overweening self-esteem.

In Richard Scrimger's first novel, *Crosstown* (1996), Donald Mitchell splits into two identities (without changing sex). In early adulthood he's a gynecologist who works at Civic Hospital in Toronto. In his second persona he's a down-and-out drunk who lives in missions and huddles in alleys around the city. Mitchell's narrative reveals how he lost his profession and respectability. Hapless and ambitious as a young doctor, Mitchell is coerced by Leon Opara, member of the hospital board, to perform an abortion for his daughter. Complying with Opara's wishes costs Mitchell his family and his career. He lands on the streets, alone. Technically accomplished, *Crosstown* cuts across lines of wealth and poverty, health and sickness, to show how perilously close such opposites are in the postmodern city.

Roy MacSkimming's *Out of love* (1993) begins with the separation of a family and a father already experiencing solitude and nostalgia. James Urquhart's son Nick is detained in a Greek prison in 1974. Urquhart flies to Athens to help him, and to reconnect with a passionate past that he shared with his first love, Una.

Matthew Hart lightens the dilemma of erotic vexation in his comic novel *The male of the species* (1993). Two brothers, Dave and Bill, learn about sex via rumours and dictionaries. Bill looks up dirty words in the hope that he will make sense of sexual destiny through language. Dave speaks portentously about 'coming into man's estate' and 'the currents of desire that seethe in the male.' Dave's gravity, even when he's uncertain about matters sexual, makes this novel refreshingly witty, and reminiscent of Mordecai Richler's best comic works. The novel also features a bewildered father and two ancient, dipsomaniacal sisters who concoct homemade flavoured wines. *Into the purple duchy* (1995), Hart's second novel, plays with the conceit that two Second World War battleships reappear in the St Lawrence River. The ships are boarded by two female journalists, who convert the war machines into vessels of love. In Hart's novels, men are baffled by, but do not reject, women, which may account for their engaging and humorous qualities.

3. THE NEXT GENERATION AND THE MEDIA. The frenzy that goes hand-in-glove with the pursuit of fame is a fictional concern of emerging Canadian writers. Youthful characters, thinking they are happy, lose themselves in alcohol or pounding rock music. Most often urban, this hedonistic fiction involves party-going and club-hopping. It glamorizes youth, especially teenagers and adults in their twenties who busily make a virtue of 'fun', in the sense of indulgence and amusement.

Douglas Coupland shoved Canadian fiction in a new direction with *Generation X: tales for an accelerated culture* (1991). The relentless listing of brand-name products coupled with idiomatic conversation and startling comparisons to movie stars and magazines made it a cult sensation. Coupland's *Shampoo planet* (1992), *Life after god* (1994), and *Microserfs* (1995) acknowledge through satire the perils of being born at the tail end of the Baby Boom. In all these novels, culturally hardened twenty-somethings look at chemically hardened environments on the West Coast (usually Vancouver or Seattle). They eat fast food and keep up with the latest computer games. As if they have undergone slow cultural transfusion, their personalities are replaced by references to TV shows and popular songs. Indeed, Coupland urgently poses the possibility that personality is nothing more than fragments of media blended with remembered snatches from Top Forty tunes and media memories.

Christine Slater makes the effects of media and the pursuit of fame central to three novels written in a pared-down style. Like the startled and tough heroines who populate Joan Didion's books, Slater's protagonists—Anita Asher, a famous painter in *Stalking the gilded boneyard* (1993), and Mal Sully, who experiences sudden success as a writer in *The small matter of getting there* (1994)—suffer from world-weariness in New York and London. *Certain dead soldiers* (1995), set in Ireland, grapples with the notoriety of a hard-drinking smart aleck named Eric Maguire. A witty ne'er-do-well with literary penchants, Eric spirals into a state of desperate alcoholism despite the love offered him by a solid and conventional woman named Arabel.

Slater's international settings are indicative of the next generation of writers who feel at home anywhere in the world. Cosmopolitanism also happens on native soil. Toronto in particular has produced a group of diverse novelists publishing début novels about people who are always on the move. Catherine Bush creates a technologically sophisticated family riven by the separation of parents in *Minus time* (1993). Helen and her twin brother Paul live in transit, settling now in Montreal, now in downtown Toronto, now in sublets, now nowhere. Helen's mother, an astronaut, communicates with her children via satellite hook-up from outer space.

Urban anomie overwhelms the drifters in Russell Smith's *How insensitive* (1994). 'But Toronto,' says a Vancouverite as the novel opens, 'I don't know how anyone could live there.' Ted Owen, however, does. He flops at a friend's house in Toronto and tries to begin his life. Paced by the hope that something is about to happen, perhaps a phone call from a stranger met on a train, perhaps unpredicted success, *How insensitive* lives out the anxieties of meeting parents, going to clubs, and finding a job in a city hostile to all signs of uncoolness.

Toronto receives chilly treatment in novels by two Caribbean writers who moved to the city. Cecil Foster's *Cry on, beloved* (1995) and Dionne BRAND's *In another place, not here* (1996) both arraign Canada's largest city for being unfriendly to newly arrived inhabitants, a sinkhole of expectations. In Foster's novel a Jamaican women struggles for twelve years in Toronto before she can afford to bring her daughter to Canada. Brand makes Toronto a city of desolate back alleys and cement high-rises: 'The width of the streets devastate you, the concrete-grained deserts high and wide sap your will, the marvel of them withers after nine months on the Jane Street bus. . . . Here, there were many rooms but no place to live.' The city absorbs the animosity of those who feel ill at ease, and have no sympathy for an alien culture.

Toronto the grey, Toronto the despised, is very different from Toronto the good, Toronto the beautiful, city of ravines and grand homes, which marks Timothy Findley's and Margaret Atwood's novels. Another Toronto, the city as a site of meetings and partings, immigration and execration, takes its cue from *In the skin of a lion*, which provides a map of the metropolis as a place of sweat, love, loss, rejection, work. In the postmodern city, women worry about pregnancy, gay men worry about finding lovers, spiritualists worry about university courses, and some worry about movie scripts. Alex Pugsley and Laura MacDonald, collaborative authors of *Kay darling* (1994), detail the comings and goings of Kay Pritchard who works at the CBC in Toronto, her sister Claire who is trying to finish her degree, and Kay's gay friend Will who is eager to strike it rich as an actor. *Kay darling* mocks the pretensions and ambitions of those who congregate around the entertainment business. Will shows Kay's movie script to an agent without Kay's knowledge, sparking messages and trips to Los Angeles.

Novels written between 1983 and 1996 refer increasingly to the effects of video culture. Although knowledge of television supposedly smooths away differences between strangers and links people from diverse backgrounds, idle chitchat about popular entertainment often preserves distance between fictional characters. They may have the same points of reference, but that does not confer mutual understanding. Several novels use television and film in their plots as a critique of media communication. The heroine of Mary di Michele's novel *Under my skin* (1994) works for a film agency, but longs to write novels. References to television series crisscross James Wallen's *Boy's night out* (1994), in which dissipated, priapic Abel wanders from bar to bar in search of amusement, yet finds out that 'life is no more than an accumulation of lost moments.' For Abel and his friends, the last vestiges of common memory seem to reside in humorous recollections of *The Brady Bunch* and *Star Trek*. After a solid night of drinking and disappointment, Abel falls from a fifteenth-storey balcony.

Wayne Johnston's fourth novel, *Human amusements* (1994), speculates on the importance of television to memory. As a departure from issues of property and Catholicism in his earlier novels—*The story of Bobby O'Malley* (1985), *The time of their lives* (1987), and *The divine Ryans* (1990)—*Human amusements* concerns a mother who creates a television show in which she and her son star. Television and cinema often exist as an elaborate and unbreachable code that characters use to represent their cosmopolitanism, but the code of glamour and ease that filmic entertainment conveys is not easy to crack.

4. SENSATION. Cult, crime, espionage, and other popular genres embody the fears and fantasies of a culture. Nancy Baker has carved out vampire thrillers as her domain in three novels: *The night inside* (1993), *Blood and chrysanthemums* (1994), and *A terrible beauty* (1996). The settings of these novels vary from forested wilderness in Alberta to dark dungeons in Toronto, yet the characters remain stock: scholars of antiquity, suave vampires, bumptious heroes, duplicitous women.

Eric McCormack specializes in Gothic fiction, with an emphasis on twins, dead mothers, dismemberment, and cold-blooded thrills. McCormack's Gothic imagination is exercised in a collection of short stories, *Inspecting the vaults* (1987). His first novel, *The Paradise Motel* (1989), is indebted to Robert Louis Stevenson. Ezra Stevenson, the protagonist, doubles for his dead grandfather Daniel. The novel drops heavy-handed clues about dark secrets from its opening pages: 'I never asked him why he ran away from Muirton, thirty years before.' Muirton, the narrator says, 'could be relied on for good funeral weather.' McCormack introduces a birth, death, burial, escape, or grotesquerie every few pages. In *The mysterium* (1992), a news blackout is imposed on a town suffering from a mysterious plague. In *First blast of the trumpet against the monstrous regiment of women* (1997)—a title borrowed from a pamphlet by John Knox—Andrew Halfnight is born with a large purple birthmark on his chest where his twin sister pressed against him. His sister dies on the day of her baptism; his father dies mysteriously the same day; his mother dies when Andrew is eleven. Expecting the best, orphan Andrew heads into the world where he has misadventures and meets madmen. He does not live happily ever after.

Another kind of thrill is provided by espionage fiction. Margaret Atwood, in a speculative essay on the creation of plots called 'Happy endings' (in *Murder in the dark*, 1983), intimates that bourgeois Canada cannot produce spy novels with male revolutionaries and female counterespionage agents. Despite Atwood's caveat, Canadians have produced numerous espionage novels, including Igor Gouzenko's Governor General's Award-winning *The fall of the titan* (1954) and Mordecai Richler's Berlin spy novel *A choice of enemies* (1957). That tradition has been continued with Wilma Riley's tale of a female double agent in *Cut-out* (1993) and, in a deconstructive mode, George Bowering's *Harry's fragments* (1990). Expecting cloak-and-dagger action, Bowering's Harry discovers in East Berlin that 'none of it had been anything like a movie of "international intrigue."'

Vying for commercial popularity in the espionage genre, Anthony Hyde and Christopher Hyde, Ottawa-based brothers, have perfected the plot of political secrecy and dangerous double-crosses. Anthony Hyde's novels include *The red fox* (1985), *China Lake* (1992), and *Formosa Straits* (1995). Christopher Hyde's are numerous. A partial list includes *The tenth crusade* (1983), *Maxwell's train* (1985), *Jericho Falls* (1988), *Black dragon* (1992), and *A gathering of saints* (1996). The suspense plots of all of these novels adhere to the conventions of espionage: missing people, labyrinthine conspiracies, double agents, conflicted lovers. The Cold War inspiration of John LeCarré, Len Deighton, and other international espionage novelists is visible in the Hyde brothers' construction of plots. Characters are American, Russian, and German; intrigue occurs across borders.

One noticeable strength of novels in this period is the shift away from parochialism to internationalism, a disentanglement from the long-lived but false notion that Canadian identity is something that can be defined only from within, and by region, and not in relation to other literatures and cultures from around the world. Despite prevailing wisdom that maintains that the best, most postmodern fiction is intertextual, metahistorical, and politically disruptive, Canadian novelists persist in writing compelling tales about heartbreak and breakdown, love and loss, family and foes.

See also ABORIGINAL LITERATURE, CARIBBEAN–CANADIAN LITERATURE, FANTASTIC LITERATURE IN ENGLISH, ITALIAN–CANADIAN LITERATURE, MYSTERY AND CRIME, SOUTH ASIAN–CANADIAN WRITING and, UKRAINIAN-CANADIAN LITERATURE.

ALLAN HEPBURN

Novels in French. Beginnings to 1900. The first French-Canadian novel, *L'INFLUENCE D'UN LIVRE*, was published in 1837. Its author, Philippe-Ignace-François Aubert de Gaspé, a twenty-three-year-old journalist—not to be confused with his father, who was to write *Les ANCIENS CANADIENS* (Québec, 1863)—stated that he wanted to be useful to his compatriots by contributing to the birth of a French-Canadian literature. In those troubled times the publication of a French-language novel in Canada was also a kind of encouragement to the people, who had reasons to fear for their survival. According to the author, *L'influence d'un livre* was true to life; but in fact this novel of the *fantastique*, with a most unlikely plot and improbable characters, was full of references to local superstitions and witchcraft.

Joseph Doutre, a nineteen-year-old journalist, claimed to be preoccupied with the promotion of French-Canadian literature when he wrote *Les fiancés de 1812* (Montréal, 1844), a 500-page adventure story that takes place during the War of 1812. Rather sententious and far-fetched, with incredible characters and very involved composition, it could hardly compete, as it was intended to, with the novels of Eugène Sue and Alexandre Dumas.

L'influence d'un livre, *Les fiancés de 1812*, and *La fille du brigand*—another far-fetched story written by a twenty-two-year-old student in law, under the pseudonym 'Pietro' (Eugène L'Écuyer), and published in *Le Ménestrel* from 29 Aug. to 19 Sept. 1844—inaugurated a major trend in the French-Canadian fiction of the last century: that of the adventure story. Usually melodramatic, these unbelievable stories were normally in keeping with moral standards, when they were not moralizing openly. Examples of further novels of this type are numerous, the best known probably being those written by Henri-Émile CHEVALIER: *La Huronne de Lorette* (Montréal, 1854), *L'héroïne de Châteauguay* (Montréal, 1858), *Le pirate du Saint-Laurent* (Montréal, 1859), and *L'île de sable* (Montréal, 1854); by Eugène Dick: *Le roi des étudiants* (Montréal, 1871), *L'enfant mystérieux* (Québec, 1880), and *Un drame du Labrador* (Montréal, 1897); and by Georges Boucher de Boucherville: *Une de perdue, deux de trouvées* (Montréal, 1874).

As Yves Dostaler has shown in *Les infortunes du roman dans le Québec du XIXe siècle* (1977), there was soon a lot of suspicion levelled against the novel in French Canada. In *La Gazette des Trois-Rivières*, as early as 14 Oct. 1817, Ludger Duvernay was advising future novelists to observe high moral standards and urging his readers to be careful when selecting a novel lest they be exposed to immoral ideas and descriptions. In 1846 Étienne Parent denounced the reading of European novels—there were, of course, very few Canadian novels—as a waste of time. These novels, he argued, were unable to give anything to Canadians, except perhaps immoral thoughts and false expectations, by describing a society and habits that were not their own. The novel continued to be attacked throughout the century. It is not surprising, therefore, that many French-Canadian novelists of the last century tried to justify themselves for writing a novel in a preface stressing the purity of their intentions. Guildo Rousseau collected most of these prefaces in *Préfaces des romans québécois du XIXe siècle* (1970).

A good novel was soon defined as one that was didactic, patriotic, and edifying. In such a context it is easy to understand that historical novels, and novels of the land—that is, novels promoting an agricultural ideology and fidelity to traditions—were largely favoured in Quebec. The first *roman de la terre* was *La terre paternelle* (Montréal, 1846) by Patrice LACOMBE. While depicting rural life, it tells the dramatic story of a father who made the mistake of giving his farm to his son with the intention of preventing his leaving home to seek adventure and fortune in the fur trade: the father pays a high price for having been unfaithful to his land. More interesting and more developed is the portrayal of French-Canadian manners in *Charles Guérin* (Montréal, 1853) by Pierre-Joseph-Olivier CHAUVEAU. Like this novel, *JEAN RIVARD: le défricheur* (Montréal, 1874) by Antoine GÉRIN-LAJOIE develops a thesis to prove that immigration of French Canadians to the United States could be stopped by opening settlements in the back districts of the province. *Jean Rivard, économiste* (Montréal, 1876), though fiction, is really a treatise on colonization. *Jeanne-la-fileuse* (Fall River, 1878) by Honoré BEAUGRAND, and Ernest CHOQUETTE's *Les Ribaud* (Montréal, 1898) and *Claude Paysan* (Montréal, 1899) are also didactic. *POUR LA PATRIE* (Montréal, 1895) by Jules-Paul Tardivel is in a special category: it is mainly of interest because it is the first novel to promote a separatist ideology.

After the success of *Les anciens Canadiens* by Philippe-Joseph AUBERT DE GASPÉ—who was seventy-seven when his novel was published—the historical novel began to flourish in Quebec (though no one could equal Aubert de Gaspé's skills in re-creating past times). Among the many historical novels that followed were *Jacques et Marie* (Montréal, 1866), by Napoléon Bourassa, which is a real melodrama; Joseph MARMETTE's *Charles et Eva* (Montréal, 1866-7), *François de Bienville* (Québec, 1870), *L'Intendant Bigot* (Montréal, 1872; serialized in *L'Opinion publique*, Mai-Oct. 1871), *Le Chevalier de Mornac* (Montréal, 1873), and *Le tomahahk et l'épée* (Québec, 1877). Also to be mentioned are Edmond Rousseau's *Le Château de Beaumanoir* (Lévis, 1886), *Les exploits d'Iberville* (Québec, 1888), and *La Monongahéla* (Québec, 1890), and Laure Conan's *À l'oeuvre et à l'épreuve* (Québec, 1891; *The master-motive*, 1909) and *L'oublié* (Montréal, 1900). Laure Conan (Félicité ANGERS) is best known, however, for *ANGELINE DE MONTBRUN* (Québec, 1884), the first French-Canadian psychological novel, the theme of which is self-sacrifice. Maurice Lemire has analysed *Les grands thèmes nationalistes du roman historique canadien-français* (1970).

See David M. Hayne and Marcel Tirol, *Bibliographie critique du roman canadien-français, 1837-1900* (1968); Mireille Servais-Maquoi, *Le roman de la terre au Québec* (1974); Aurélien Boivin, *Le conte littéraire québécois au XIXe siècle* (1975); Maurice Lemire, *et al.*, *Dictionnaire des oeuvres littéraires du Québec*, vol. 1 (1978). Madeleine Ducrocq-Poirier, *Le roman canadien de langue française de 1860 à 1958* (1978); Réjean Beaudoin, *Le roman québécois* (1991); Maurice Lemire, *Formation de l'imaginaire littéraire au Québec, 1764-1867* (1993); and Maurice Lemire, ed., *La vie littéraire au Québec* (1993).

JACQUES COTMAN

1900 to 1920. In his *Manuel d'histoire de la littérature canadienne-française* (1920) Abbé Camille Roy, the leading literary critic of the time, echoed the sentiments of most of his colleagues when he observed in passing that, despite several 'laudable efforts' by Adolphe-Basile Routhier, Hector Bernier, Ernest CHOQUETTE, and Ernest Chouinard, the novel had enjoyed little success in Quebec in the preceding two decades.

At the beginning of the twentieth century, novels continued in fact to encounter widespread suspicion, and authors of books that might be construed as such usually felt obliged to intervene in the narrative in order to insist on the 'reality', social usefulness, and moral qualities of their works. Abbé P.-E. Roy, in his preface to *Le vieux muet; ou Un héros de Châteauguay* (1901) by Jean-Baptiste Caouette, frankly admits that he has been asked, as a priest, to reassure prospective Catholic readers who have learned to avoid the corruptive influence of the novel form, 'un des plus exécrables dissolvants de la morale publique'. This doubtless helps to explain why, at a time when poetry, in the wake of Émile NELLIGAN, was producing works that were widely and vigorously discussed, the forty-odd novels published in Quebec between 1900 and 1920 generally received little more than a brief mention in one or two periodicals.

As for the four writers faintly praised by Camille Roy, their works mainly distinguish themselves by pushing to new extremes the sermon-like qualities previously mentioned. Most fiction writers of this period insist heavily on the Catholic virtues of their characters; A.-B. Routhier in *Le centurion: roman des temps messianiques* (1909) and *Paulina: roman des temps apostoliques* (1918) simply produces paraphrases of the Bible with Christ and Saint Paul as protagonists. The youthful Hector Bernier—who at least has the merit of clumsily incorporating his didactic messages into the dialogue—preaches nationalism, Catholicism, and fear of modern France in *Au large de l'écueil* (1912) and *Ce que disait la flamme* (1913), to a degree that caused Jules Fournier to despair at the fanatical education given young French Canadians.

Similarly *La terre* (1916) by Ernest Choquette carries the tradition of the rural novel inaugurated by Patrice LACOMBE's *La terre paternelle* in 1846 to new melodramatic heights. Although other works of the period, such as *Restons chez nous!* (1908) and *L'appel de la terre: roman de moeurs saguenayennes* (1919) by Damase Potvin, naïvely preach the dominant agriculturist ideology by glorifying life in the country while presenting the city as 'hell on earth', Choquette's *La terre* openly asks French Canadians to confine themselves to agriculture because they have no talent for industrial success.

Curiously, not one of the seven historical novels produced at this time found favour in Camille Roy's *Manuel*, though this tendency seemed to be what he had most appreciated in the preceding period. It is true, of course, that most of these works based on the heroic sacrifices of New France or the Rebellion of 1837 accorded a much greater importance to the theme of passionate (though chaste) love than was then considered desirable by the critics. Gaëtane de Montreuil's *Fleur des ondes: roman historique canadien* (1912), perhaps the best-received of the group, was criticized not so much for its lack of unity as for representing a Native maiden who commits suicide for love.

L'arriviste: étude psychologique (1919) by Ernest Chouinard belongs to the category of the surprisingly numerous novels (ten in all) situated in contemporary urban Quebec society. The protagonist is almost invariably a young lawyer and/or journalist who is in danger of falling victim to, or fighting a quixotic battle against, political corruption. Chouinard, however, paints the blackest picture of such a situation, condemning from the outset 'l'arriviste', an ambitious young lawyer and politician, while condoning his intelligent friend who retires to a monastery. Robert-Errol Bouchette's *Robert Lozé: nouvelle* (1903) adopts a more optimistic, though just slightly less didactic, approach by proposing that the true prosperity of French Canada lies in locally developed industries, modern agricultural techniques, socially conscious lawyers, and honest politicians. Perhaps the most unusual novel in this group is Ulric Barthe's *Similia similibus; ou, La guerre au Canada: essai romantique sur un sujet d'actualité* (1916), which describes the capture of Quebec by the Germans during the First World War and its subsequent liberation due to the efforts of two young journalists, one French Canadian and the other English Canadian.

The best of these 'urban' novels is without doubt *Le débutant: roman de moeurs du journalisme et de la politique dans la province de Québec* (1914) by Arsène Bessette. Completely ignored at the time of its publication—as much because of the author's radical reputation and his known affiliation with the Freemasons as because of the novel's criticism of the conservatism and intolerance of French-Canadian society and its realistic (though sober) presentation of an earnest young journalist's love affair with an older widow—this work, despite an occasional tendency to labour a point, is perhaps the only true novel (in the strict sense of the word) of quality produced by a French Canadian during this period.

The other two fictions that stand out head and shoulders above their contemporaries are *MARIE CALUMET* (1904) by Rodolphe GIRARD and *La SCOUINE* (1918) by Albert LABERGE. They too were surrounded by silence, but a silence imposed this time by the public disapproval of the Catholic Church of Quebec. It is difficult for modern readers to understand why *Marie Calumet*—an amusing and well-written story about the adventures and misadventures of the lively but profoundly religious forty-year-old housekeeper of the endearing priest of Saint-Ildefonse, Abbé Flavel—encountered such wrath on the part of the clergy. Admittedly, realism was at that time frowned upon by critics (Camille Roy recommended a technique of 'idealistic realism'!), but that hardly explains such an extreme reaction. Ironically, Girard himself gives the key to the enigma when Abbé Flavel, upon discovering his beautiful niece poring over the 'Song of Solomon' (reproduced in the novel), decides from then on to keep the Scriptures under lock and key. Since the Bible was at that time forbidden reading for Roman Catholics, it was most likely fear of the curiosity that might be kindled by this sensuous biblical text that caused the condemnation of *Marie Calumet*.

Girard's fate, which never really improved despite the numerous novels he published, can also be partly attributed to his predilection for the theme of passionate love—always poorly received! In using this theme, Girard's *L'Algonquine: roman des jours héroiques du Canada sous la domination française* (1910) is remarkably similar to Adèle Bibaud's *Avant la conquête: épisode de la guerre de 1757* (1904). This predilection was more common in women writers. Though Laure Conan (Félicité ANGERS) had learned to minimize passion by 1900, other women writers continued to cultivate it. With *Nemoville* (1917) Madame Alcide Lacerte even began a series of popular exotic love novels that might be loosely compared to today's Harlequin romances.

Although *Marie Calumet* is not quite the 'masterpiece' Albert Laberge proclaimed it to be in 1946, it is a well-written and entertaining story that successfully portrays the 'joie de vivre' of a rural French-Canadian community at the turn of the century. Ironically, Laberge himself wrote the novel that gives the most negative picture of precisely the same setting. Written in reaction to the idealistic and didactic rural novels that preceded it, *La Scouine* describes in the best naturalist technique a series of loosely connected events in the life of the Deschamps family. Almost all the characters lead a miserable, unthinking, and senseless existence, upon which, however, the narrator almost never permits himself to comment. If *Marie Calumet* can be said to illustrate facetiously the sexual repression of a small parish, *La Scouine* describes a totally castrated and isolated society resigned to its fate. At a time when rural life was the only area in which French Canada could be autonomous, the acceptance of the view presented in this work would have been equivalent to genocide. Not surprisingly, the first extract published in *La Semaine* was condemned by Mgr Bruchési, and Laberge finally published his book privately for a circle of intimate friends, whence its influence (perhaps greater than many realize) on Claude-Henri GRIGNON's *Un homme et son péché* (1933), and on *TRENTE ARPENTS* (1938) by Ringuet (Philippe PANNETON).

The fact remains that the three outstanding fiction works of this period—*Le débutant*, *Marie Calumet*, and *La Scouine*—chose to ignore the ideological dogmatism of the time, and were suppressed for that reason. The fate of other novels, however, was scarcely more enviable. Clearly the novel as a social form presenting conflicting ideologies (that of the protagonist and that of the society in which he lives) was unacceptable in a society that, in its fight for survival, had become protectionist and monolithic. It is significant that in *Le débutant*, where two conflicting value systems are effectively illustrated, the final solution adopted by the protagonist is immigration to the USA (and therefore assimilation).

More acceptable, and frequently acclaimed as masterpieces, were the collections of descriptive essays such as *Propos canadiens* (1912) by Camille Roy, *Chez nous* (1914) and *Chez nos gens* (1918) by Adjutor Rivard, *Les rapaillages* (1916) by Lionel GROULX, and *Récits laurentiens* (1919) and *Croquis laurentiens* (1920) by Frère MARIE-VICTORIN. Many even hoped that these nostalgic portraits of the 'good old days' and of rural Quebec, seasoned with a generous sprinkling of italicized local expressions, would lead to a distinctively French-Canadian genre.

This unrealistic attitude may be traced to the increasing efforts of a group known as the 'regionalists' to impose on Quebec writers an idealistic nationalist vision of French Canada as an exclusively rural, traditional, Catholic, and highly moral society. Though reminiscent of views espoused by Abbé CASGRAIN in the nineteenth century, the decided regionalist trend at the beginning of the twentieth century is usually dated back to a speech given in 1904 by Abbé Camille Roy, entitled 'La nationalisation de la littérature canadienne', which was in large part a reaction to the threat of more modern literary tendencies—dangerously well represented by some Montreal writers, Nelligan in particular.

Despite attempts by the regionalists to disregard all opponents to this highly dogmatic approach as 'exotics' or 'Francissons' (and therefore, so to speak, traitors to the national cause), there gradually evolved a conflict known as the Quarrel between the regionalists and the 'exotics' that finally exploded into the open towards 1918. As a result, literature became one of the main arenas where two distinct conceptions of the essence and future of French Canada—at the risk of oversimplification, a distinctive, traditional, rural, Catholic society versus a more modern, twentieth-century, cosmopolitan one—battled for their very existence. The monolithic tendencies of the regionalist view help explain much of the suspicion encountered by the critical function that is inevitably performed by a true novel.

A new era for fiction was to begin, however, with the critics' discovery of Louis HÉMON's *MARIA CHAPDELAINE: récit du Canada français* (1916) towards 1918. At last it seemed possible to write quality novels in French Canada that would effectively reinforce agriculturist and traditional values. Ignoring the fact that Hémon was a foreigner, the regionalists glorified *Maria Chapdelaine* as proof that their theories on the necessity of treating local subjects and rural Quebec could produce first-class literature. The 'exotics' retorted that, since Hémon came from France, the work in fact belonged to exotic literature. (This exchange is very revealing, since regionalism and exoticism are in fact both based on the accentuation of local, or foreign, peculiarities.) From then on *Maria Chapdelaine* became the measuring stick by which every French-Canadian novel published in the following twenty years would be judged. Since it was known in some circles, however, that the author had not been a practising Catholic, a few attempts were apparently made to have the book condemned, and this novel might easily have suffered the same fate as *Marie Calumet*, *Le débutant*, and *La Scouine* if Hémon had not died prematurely, if the book had not ended with the glorification of conservatism and heroic patriotism, or if it had not rapidly become a best-seller in Europe. This combination of circumstances, in any case, helped to create a success that did much to alleviate the anathema surrounding the novel form in Quebec. Not only did French-Canadian fiction increase dramatically over the next decade in quality and number of works published, but the reception accorded new fiction improved.

Obviously changes in Quebec society also played an important role in this change of attitude. As more and more French Canadians moved to the city and adapted to modern industrial society, it became increasingly difficult to impose a monolithic, tradition-oriented view of their collective future. The dogmatic excesses revealed by the Quarrel between the regionalists and the 'exotics' also contributed to the waning of a rigid view of what Quebec literature should be. More and more writers—in particular those referred to by Alfred DesROCHERS in *Paragraphes: interviews littéraires* in 1931 as the 'post-war generation'—chose to combine local subject matter with modern and varied literary techniques. It might therefore be said that the extreme opinions upheld at the beginning of the twentieth century sowed the seeds of a new literary consciousness in Quebec.

ANNETTE HAYWARD

1920 to 1940. The number of works of fiction published during this period almost tripled the number produced in the first twenty years of the century: some 400 titles, including children's stories and story collections. The novels seem to be characterized by conventionality on the one hand and by a marked deviation from it on the other. The deviation, which consisted chiefly of innovative literary techniques, was salutary because it finally broke down the norms established by the nationalistic ideology of conservatism. The traditional image of French-Canadian society's having been fragmented by disruptive change—the growth of urbanism, English-speaking economic dominance, the Depression—the élite of this society, led by the clergy, had promoted the sanctification of the past and of ancestral characteristics; the redemptive mission of a chosen people who were Catholic and French in a Protestant, Anglo-Saxon, and materialistic North America; moral idealism and rigidity; and distrust of outsiders and the modern world. In this context literature became a weapon for combat, and the fiction of the period usually presents characters that are more ideas than living people.

Their psychology is often sketchy and usually unconvincing, their emotions mere pretexts for philosophical dissertations or ideological sermonizing. The plot of the novels, illustrating a thesis rather than telling a story, often gets sidetracked into badly integrated digressions, while the author—more knowledgeable than the omniscient narrator—constantly forces the truth upon the reader in a linear delivery that is frequently marred by grammatical errors.

1. NOVELS OF THE LAND. Since a magnification of the rural world is one of the components of the ideology of conservatism, this period saw the novel of the land reach its highest point, both quantitatively (by following the ideological norm) and qualitatively (by deviating from it through realism). The prototype of the genre, on which there was

little variation, is to be found in *La terre paternelle* (1846) by Patrice LACOMBE, and in the romantic dilemma portrayed in *MARIA CHAPDELAINE* (1916; trans. 1921) by Louis HÉMON. The plot is easily summarized: an individual (or a family), living happily on the farm, leaves it out of disillusionment or lack of judgement; he also leaves behind someone he loves, who is associated with rural life; he then settles in the city or abroad, where he lives unhappily, very often with an unsuitable woman; finally, after many mishaps and adventures, he realizes his initial mistake, returns to the land, and regains his first love—or else resigns himself to a life of misfortune and disappointment. In sociological terms, leaving the farm appears to be unavoidable, inevitable, and more or less imposed upon the character; the return, however, results from a series of disordered and unconvincing events. Because the ideological norms cannot completely hide the harsh realities, the coherence of the novel suffers. This is particularly apparent in *La campagne canadienne* (1925) by Adélard Dugré and in *L'erreur de Pierre Giroir* (1925) by J.E.A. Cloutier. The standard plot is repeated in a whole series of perfunctory novels from this period: *Un coeur fidèle* (1924) and *La petite maîtresse d'école* (1929) by Blanche Lamontagne; *L'enjoleuse* (1928) and *Celle qui revient* (1930) by Mme Elphège Croft; *La terre que l'on défend* (1928) by Henri Lapointe; and *La terre vivante* (1925) by Harry BERNARD.

As a variation on the novel of the land, the pioneer novel almost totally eliminates plot; it simply glorifies the return to the land and skips over any possible difficulties. Novels such as *Le Français* (1925) or *La Rivière-à-Mars* (1934) by Damase Potvin, and *Le p'tit gars du colon* (1934) or *Un sillon dans la forêt* (1936) by Benoît Desforêt, pretend to capture the essence of French-Canadian rural life while actually revealing the absurdity of their theses.

2. NOVELS OF IDEOLOGICAL OR REALISTIC DEVIANCE. While the writers of idealized novels of the land were firmly in the foreground, the background belonged to Albert LABERGE, whose collection of short stories portraying rural and urban settings, *Visages de la vie et de la mort* (1936), ran counter to the prevailing literary fashions. Both the aesthetic orientation of his work and his profound pessimism were not to be tolerated, and Laberge himself limited the impact of his book by having only fifty copies of it printed. Jean-Charles HARVEY was not so careful: his *Les demi-civilisés* (1934; *Fear's folly*, 1982), a veritable satiric tract in the form of a novel, was consigned to the Index as forbidden reading. Using a first-person narrator who gave unfettered expression to his liberty, his sensuality, and his opinions, Harvey openly attacked the shortcomings of a society dominated by those who had used conservatism to further their hypocritical and sterile domination. An ideological bombshell, Harvey's novel, in its own way, was just as excessive and unconvincing in a literary sense as were the more orthodox pronouncements disguised as novels. Much more effective, because they were novels above all else, were *Un homme et son péché* (1933; *The woman and the miser*, 1978) by Claude-Henri GRIGNON; *MENAUD, MAÎTRE-DRAVEUR* (1937; *Master of the river*, 1976) by Félix-Antoine SAVARD; and *TRENTE ARPENTS* (1938; *Thirty acres*, 1940) by Ringuet (Philippe PANNETON). They reveal the failure of the ideology of conservatism, while appearing to pay it respect.

For a variety of reasons the world that most of these novels are concerned to defend is a world that is breaking apart. Sometimes the causes of this are internal, as with the psychological flaw in the hero of *Un homme et son péché*; sometimes they are external, as with the intrusions by outsiders in *Menaud, maître-draveur*. Sometimes, both causes are involved; the hero in *Trente arpents*, for example, is a victim both of his biological age, since he is growing old, and of his economic age, since he is suffering the effects of the Depression. Still, most of the novels of the period refuse to admit that the changes in their world stem from within the society they describe, or are directly related to the individuals making up that society. The changes are thus attributed to the pernicious influence, malicious intent, and even in some cases the inherently evil nature of outsiders.

3. TRADITIONAL VALUES AND THE OUTSIDER. The presence of the outsider leads to the repeated theme of resistance, a theme that *Menaud, maître-draveur* illustrates magnificently, at the same time as it shows its futility. The frequent references to mismatched or mixed marriages (different religious or ethnic groups) are thematically connected to the presence of outsiders and the resulting resistance. Such is the case in *La terre se venge* (1932) by Eugénie Chenel and *La campagne canadienne* (1925) by Adélard Dugré; in both novels the hero has married an outsider and his family is being assimilated. The same theme was taken up by Harry Bernard in *L'homme tombé* (1924) and *La maison vide* (1926); here the wife, who has come from a lower social class, gets caught up in the frivolities of city life and destroys both the family

home and the ancestral traditions. More than simply a lesson in the traditional bourgeois morality of French-Canadian Catholics, this theme by its very frequency expresses the anguish of a society forced to live in a modern world that is both strange and foreign. The voices of *Maria Chapdelaine* were being heard less and less, and this, from the traditional point-of-view, was a bad sign for the children of the future.

In *L'appel de la race* (1922) Lionel GROULX, under the pseudonym 'Alonié de Lestres', joined the theme of the mismatched marriage to an openly racist sanctification of national values. This novel was intended for use as a weapon; and although its plot was based on, and inspired by, the Franco-Ontarians' struggle against Regulation Seventeen, which effectively suppressed the teaching of French in Ontario, its general spirit connected it with the ideology of conservatism, which had become a veritable religion. After hesitating for a long time, the protagonist obeys the dictates of his superior bloodlines, makes part of his family French again, and becomes a spokesman for the French-Catholic cause to which he has sacrificed his marriage. Thus he fights against the influence of the Outsider—represented mainly by his converted English-speaking Protestant wife and the tainted lineage she has passed on to the hero's children. After this reconquest of the family, Groulx moved on to a reconquest of the territory. In *Au Cap Blomidon* (1932) a descendant of the Acadians expelled from their lands in the Great Expulsion manages to regain possession of the ancestral farm. However, the success of this undertaking, while ideologically desirable, is somewhat unrealistic: the plot necessitates not only an appearance by a ghost but also the intervention of a witch. With its long historical digressions, Groulx's second novel is of less interest than his first, which provided the most coherent illustration of the ideological sermonizing so often found in the writings of this period.

Harry Bernard, in *La ferme des pins* (1930), also dealt with repossession by the French, as seen through the eyes of an old English-Canadian from the Eastern Townships who watches his family being assimilated into the French-speaking community. The character has enough psychological credibility to win the reader's sympathy, even though the author's apparent intention was to proclaim the glory of the French reconquest. This Englishman, who speaks—strangely, with a French accent—of dispossession, occasionally attains the realistic grandeur of Euchariste Moisan in *Trente arpents*, and also foreshadows the tragic epic of Menaud. Perhaps the reality of the situation was so painful that it had to be expressed by being projected onto the Outsider.

The cult of traditional values and the sanctification of the French-Canadian race produced a spate of minor novels, each more insipid, awkward, and narrowly moralistic than the others. Examples of this genre include *La plus belle chose du monde* (1927) and *Le nom dans le bronze* (1923) by Michelle Le Normand, *À la hâche* (1932) by Adolphe Nantel, *L'unique solution* (1925) by Arsène Goyette, and *Le spectre menaçant* (1932) by Joseph Lallier.

4. HISTORICAL NOVELS. The historical novel, already much in vogue in Quebec literature, was able to maintain its important position in this period because the ideology of conservatism held to a vision of the world that was excessively oriented towards the past. As a vehicle for the cult of traditional values, it tended towards formula writing and sank to the level of para-literature, or popular literature, as in the novels of Jean Féron, or became a means for educating and indoctrinating young people, as in those of Eugène Achard. Where historical anecdote was used as a pretext for an exercise in style, the primary result was, fortunately, a novel rather than simply a historical illustration. Novels in the latter category deviated from the established norms and testified to the inevitable disappearance of the past.

Although *Les habits rouges* (1923) by Robert Laroque de ROQUEBRUNE deals with the troubles of 1837-8, it avoids nationalistic sermonizing and manages to tell a love story. *Les dames Le Marchand* (1927) by the same author portrays one side of the traditional world—a seigneurial family—that the heir refuses to perpetuate either materially by marrying a rich woman or spiritually by becoming a priest. In *Nord-Sud* (1931), by Léo-Paul DESROSIERS, the hero's decision to leave his native land is accepted without condemnation, and in *Les engagés du Grand Portage* (1938; *The making of Nicolas Montour*, 1978) Desrosiers presents the victory of a protagonist who would not meet with the approval of traditional morality. *D'un océan à l'autre* (1924) by Roquebrune tries to bring to life the conquest of the West and to honour the missionaries who brought Catholicism and the French tradition; in retrospect, however, the novel's final sentence seems bitterly ironic: '. . . with an instinctive gesture, the old missionary raised his hand and, in the direction of the disappearing train, made a broad sign of benediction.' This blessing is bestowed on the very weapon that would destroy the old dream of a French, Catholic America. The exceptional stylistic qualities of *Né à Quebec* (1933; *Born in Quebec*, 1964) by Alain GRANDBOIS made readers realize that simply choosing a historical subject could no longer excuse awkward writing. As with the rural novels, the successful historical novels showed that true art could not be harnessed to a cause without falling into decline; they also indicated that ideological distortions of reality lead to narrative or psychological incoherence, and to a world of cardboard-like artificiality.

5. THE PRESENCE OF THE MODERN WORLD. Moving away from history and the land, a few novels attempted to provide an accurate description of the modern world disparaged by others. For example, *Jules Faubert, le roi du papier* (1923) by Ubald PAQUIN tells of the exploits of a French-speaking industrialist; Faubert's success, however, is as unbelievable as his final failure, suggesting that control of the modern world remains in the realm of good intentions. The same theme is taken up by Jean-Charles Harvey in *Marcel Faure* (1922), a Utopian novel that inverts the dominant ideological vision of the period.

6. WOMEN'S NOVELS AND ROMANCES. In this category deviance of expression was all the more effective for being less strident. Although they were never unqualified triumphs, and although they often indulged in the worst melodrama (for example, *Peuvent-elles garder un secret?* 1937, by Adrienne Maillet), these novels provided descriptions and analyses of seduction, jealousy, and—as with *La chair décevante* (1931) by Jovette-Alice BERNIER—illicit love. Some, like *Seuls* (1937) by Lucie Clément, or *À deux* (1937) by Laetitia Filion, portrayed the powerlessness of women in society. Others, such as *Mon Jacques* (1933) by Eva Sénécal, went so far as to deal with bigamy. Still others described urban life and spoke of women's suffrage, as in *L'oncle des jumeaux Pomponelle* (1939) by Adrienne Maillet. Together these novels constituted a kind of ideological erosion through which the forms of deviance and the presence of the real world gradually made themselves felt. Although a novel by Lucie Clément was entitled *En marge de la vie* (1934), these novels were actually on the fringes of the official ideology and closer to life, opening the way for the psychological novel, which was more impervious to ideological dictates. *ANGÉLINE DE MONTBRUN* (Québec, 1884) by Laure Conan (Félicité ANGERS) had been the first of such psychological novels, a vein of writing that was quickly smothered by the pressure of established norms, as shown by Conan's last novel, *Le sève immortelle* (1925), in which the love plot took second place to a glorification of ancestors, rural life, and nationalistic loyalty.

7. TECHNICAL INNOVATIONS. At the level of style, several of these novels used a first-person narration similar to that of Harvey's *Les demi-civilisés*. Others insisted on an individualized presence that sought to establish its own norms; *Mon Jacques* (1933) by Eva Sénécal was in this regard the most successful of the women's novels. Rex DESMARCHAIS also used a first-person narrator in *L'initiatrice* (1932); with the text carrying not only the narrative line but the story of the narration itself, it is a piece of writing that is almost self-consciously a novel. Harry Bernard adopted this technique in *Juana, mon aimée* (1931) and *Dolorès* (1932), two novels that were intended to be regional portraits but rose to the level of psychological analysis. An 'ego' makes itself felt in these works—which breaks through, for example, in *La pension Leblanc* (1927) by Robert CHOQUETTE, another regionalist work that transcended its genre to become a novel of manners and psychological analysis.

This human presence, and this density of the fictional world, are characteristic of Grignon's *Un homme et son péché* (1933) and Ringuet's *Trente arpents*. As for Savard's *Menaud, maître-draveur* (1937), even though its main character cannot be considered a complete 'ego', the novel's ideological expression is so intensely poetic that Menaud becomes a symbol rather than a painfully personified idea. The swan-song of traditional nationalistic sermonizing, this novel, with its powerful ending and its poetic nature, revealed the social and literary dead-end in which the ideology of conservatism had become trapped. The literary regionalism implied by this ideology was condemned to be no more than a form of internal exoticism, badly integrated into the action of the novels. Savard imposed the presence of the Laurentians to the point that Menaud becomes part of the landscape; similarly, in the novels of Grignon and Ringuet, a natural world that is both omnipresent and indifferent to the characters' passions becomes the centre of the action, either as a witness to, or as the representative of, a relentless fate.

Beneath the appearance of uniformity, the literary scene from 1920 to 1940 actually underwent some profound changes. Writers came to learn that no matter how orthodox the subject was, there was no excuse for bad writing. They also learned that to serve a cause too closely is a disservice to literature.

Beginning with a character on whom they imposed a story, not to mention a ready-made morality, they advanced to the stage of creating a character who assumed his own history, and to the kind of writing that imposed its own universe. By obeying the logic of fiction, the most successful of their novels broke apart the stereotyped images and opened a door on reality.

8. BIBLIOGRAPHY. It is useful to consult the second volume of the excellent *Dictionnaire des oeuvres littéraires du Québec 1900 à 1939* (1980), published under the direction of Maurice Lemire, as well as the third volume of the *Archives des lettres canadiennes: le roman canadien-français* (1977). Essential aids to an understanding of this period are *Le roman de la terre au Québec* (1974) by Mireille Servais-Maquoi, *Les grands thèmes nationalistes du roman historique canadien-français* (1970) by Maurice Lemire, and 'Evolution de la technique du roman canadien-français', an unpublished doctoral thesis by Henri Tuchmaïer (Laval, 1958). A rapid survey of the subject is provided in the second volume of the *Histoire de la littérature française du Québec (1900-1945)* (1968), edited by Pierre de Grandpré, while developments in the literature of this period are sketched in *Le roman canadien-français du vingtième siècle* (1966) by Réjean Robidoux and André Renaud. Historical and ideological considerations are effectively dealt with in André Linteau, *et al.*, *Histoire du Québec contemporain. De la Confédération à la crise 1867-1929* (1979); Denis Monière, *Le développement des idéologies au Québec des origines à nos jours* (1977); André J. Belanger, *L'apolitisme des idéologies québécoises. Le grand tournant de 1934-1936* (1974); and Fernand Dumont, *et al.*, *Idéologies au Canada français 1900-1929* (1974).

GUY MONETTE

1940 to 1959. The rapid industrialization and urbanization of Quebec society during this period had significant effects on the culture of francophone Quebec, and on its literature in particular. In the intellectual sphere a capital event was the publication in 1948 of the manifesto *REFUS GLOBAL*, which had a lasting effect on cultural effervescence. *La RELÈVE*, a journal founded by Catholic intellectuals in 1934, became the monthly La *Nouvelle Relève* in 1941 and reflected the malaise over the crisis of values in Quebec society. *Cité libre*, founded in 1950 by a similar group, was more oriented to political opposition to Premier Duplessis but also gave space to literary and artistic reviews, marked for the most part by philosophical personalism and universalism. The war had brought a number of exiled French writers and artists to Quebec; books by French classical writers that were on the Index were published; and plays by Jean-Paul Sartre were performed during this period. The advent of television in 1952 also significantly shaped cultural habits and tastes. In this atmosphere literary publication grew extensively. A reading public was thus established, and several major writers were able to live from their work.

The major trends in fiction writing in this period can be grouped under five categories that sometimes interweave; urban social realism; the psychological-moral novel; works treating industrial conflict; transformed 'traditional' novels; and an important sphere of 'independent' creativity.

1. URBAN SOCIAL REALISM. As the Second World War was drawing to a close two young writers, in Quebec City and Montreal, turned the Quebec novel resolutely towards the teeming working-class areas of these two cities. Roger LEMELIN's *Au pied du la pente douce* (1944; *The town below*, 1948), an instant best-seller, was refused a literary prize because it was not centred on the countryside. Gabrielle ROY's *BONHEUR D'OCCASION* (1945; *The tin flute*, 1947) was honoured in France and the USA, and was eventually translated into nine languages. Both these novels drew sustenance from the Depression, from the tensions between sociophysical topographical entities, and from the desire of youth to break out of a claustrophobic trap.

A regionalist satirist, Lemelin continued to dwell on opposition between Quebec City's Lower and Upper Town societies in *Les PLOUFFE* (1948; *The Plouffe family*, 1950) and *Pierre le magnifique* (1952; *In quest of splendour*, 1955); while Roy, who had touched more universal chords and developed characterization to an unmatched degree in *Bonheur d'occasion*, produced a second major novel with a Montreal setting, *Alexander Chenevert* (1954; *The cashier*, 1955). Through the life and death of her bank-teller hero she developed her treatment of economic and cultural alienation, and in her religious theme she anticipated Vatican II and the *aggiornamento* of the Catholic Church. Roy's urban-realist work, like Lemelin's, also anticipated the vast changes of the Quiet Revolution. Roy returned to her Manitoba childhood and youth in creating *La petite poule d'eau* (1950; *Where nests the water hen*, 1951) and *Rue Deschambault* (1955; *Street of riches*, 1957), launching the theme of a quest for an ideal world of human solidarity that would become dominant for her in the sixties and seventies. Other writers who followed the general path of urban social realism were Ringuet (Philippe PANNETON), Roger Viau, and Jean Pellerin. Ringuet's *Le poids du jour* (1949), though less skilfully crafted than his classic *TRENTE ARPENTS*, is an interesting novel on the making of an industrialist in the period between the wars. Viau's *Au milieu la montagne* (1951) has echoes of Roy and Lemelin in its irreconcilable tensions between the east-end and Outremont districts of Montreal. Pellerin's *Le diable par la queue* (1957) presents a Quebec family that immigrates to New York during the Depression, only to be caught up in the temporary work of the sweatshop before responding to the nostalgic call of the native rural parish.

2. THE PSYCHOLOGICAL-MORAL NOVEL. An important group of Quebec writers was concerned less with external social reality than with the internal turmoil caused by what they perceived as the surrounding cultural and ethical wasteland: Robert CHARBONNEAU, André Giroux, Robert ÉLIE, all of whom were connected with *La Relève* and *La Nouvelle Relève*; André LANGEVIN; and satirists Jean SIMARD and Pierre Baillargeon. Their works —labelled 'romans du cas de conscience' by Jacques Michon—treat the anguish of characters in search of vital spiritual values in a world of hypocrisy, materialism, and expediency. Charbonneau published three novels in the 1940s: *Ils posséderont la terre* (1941), *Fontile* (1945), and *Les désirs et les jours* (1948). In the first two, set in the imaginary provincial town of Fontile in the Depression years, the author concentrates on the internal tensions, moral conflicts, and religious preoccupations of his characters. While there are temporary pulls towards political action in all three, the heroes are strangely introverted and troubled beings. Similar conflicts and tensions tear at the characters of Robert Élie's *La fin des songes* (1950), which ends with the suicide of the hero, but in his *Il suffit d'un jour* (1957) the heroine comes to terms with life, having rejected its absurd realities.

André Giroux's *Au delà des visages* (1948) and *Le gouffre a toujours soif* (1953) combine social criticism with such themes as religious hypocrisy, metaphysical anguish, and the search for authenticity. The author flays 'Christian' anti-Semitism in the first, and servility in both. In *Au delà des visages*, as in Eugène Cloutier's *Les témoins* (1953)—both of which use an innovative form of internal monologue—the heroes kill not out of hatred but in a certain ritualistic revolt against the human condition. In *Le gouffre* Giroux deals with the long agony of a cancer sufferer who, finding that his marriage partner is a stranger, is crushed by incommunicability.

André Langevin's three novels—*Évadé de la nuit* (1951), *POUSSIÈRE SUR LA VILLE* (1953; *Dust over the city*, 1955), and *Le temps des hommes* (1956)—have been seen as forming a trilogy with recurring motifs of suicide, pity, resignation, and failure to find meaningful values and human communion; the repeated appearance of the orphan figure, undoubtedly inspired in part by the author's biography, has been thought by some critics to symbolize the French Canadian in search of himself. Failure to communicate with others is summarized thus in the first novel, 'Jamais nos courbes ne se sont rencontrées . . .', and in *Poussière* by the image of the parallel lines along which the narrator, Alain Dubois, and his wife Madeleine travel, never able to meet. Langevin's work differs from that of most of the writers of the 'roman du cas de conscience' in that traditional religion is totally rejected in favour of a pessimistic existentialist outlook that recalls Camus's Sisyphus. In *Poussière* and *Le temps des hommes* the hero questions Providence by revolting against the unacceptable death of a young child, and seeks solace in the purely human. The absentee economic force lurking in the background of these two novels—the Benson Mine in Macklin, and Scott Power and Paper in Scottville—adds to the already profound ontological alienation.

A satirical tone modulates the sombre, serious subject-matter in the work of Jean Simard and Pierre Baillargeon. Simard in *Félix* (1947), *Hôtel de la reine* (1949), and *Mon fils pourtant heureux* (1956) excoriates the French-Canadian petty bourgeoisie, provincialism, official ideology, the clergy, and the educational system. In his *Les sentiers de la nuit* (1959), which centres on an Anglican family in lower Westmount, and on the anglophone banking milieu, many critics have seen a veiled transposition of pre-Quiet Revolution francophone society. Pierre Baillargeon (1916-67) attacked similar targets in *Les médisances de Claude Perrin* (1945), *Commerce* (1947), and *La neige et le feu* (1948). The spicy satire *Saint-Pépin, P.Q.* (1955) by Bertrand Vac (Aimé PELLETIER) ridicules electoral mores and the false piety of two 'dévotes'.

3. NOVELS OF INDUSTRIAL CONFLICT. While there were instances of industrial conflict in the first works of urban social realism—especially in Lemelin's *Les Plouffe* (the printer's strike at *L'Action chrétienne*) and *Pierre*

le magnifique (the loggers' walkout at the Savard camp), and in Ringuet's *Le poids du jour* (protest marches of the unemployed in the Depression)—it was not until the 1950s, when labour tensions became volatile in Quebec, that novels concentrated on such events. Most important among these are Jean-Jules RICHARD's *Le feu dans l'amiante* (1956), Pierre Gélinas's *Les vivants, les morts et les autres* (1959), and Gérard BESSETTE's first novel, *La bagarre* (1958). The distinguishing feature of these works is the collective form of social protest, as contrasted with the individual revolt in the earlier work of social realism. Richard's fictionalized treatment of the seminal Asbestos strike of 1949 contains vivid scenes of feverish labour amid mounds of dust in a town whose rhythm is marked by three daily dynamite blasts, and of the march of miners' wives and children, led by the priest, to confront the provincial police. This book, however, is too close to reportage to be an effective 'roman social'. (Richard was one of three authors to write a memorable Second World War novel in French. His *Neuf jours de haine*, 1948, Bertrand Vac's *Deux portes . . . une adresse*, 1952, and Jean Vaillancourt's *Les Canadiens errants*, 1954, are the best treatments of this theme.) Historical labour struggles—the long conflicts in 1952 at Dominion Textile and the Dupuis Frères department store—mark Pierre Gélinas's *Les vivants*. Gélinas also intersperses his *Bildungsroman*, centred on a well-to-do-hero-turned-radical, with elements of contemporary political history such as the Korean War and the Khruschev report denouncing Stalin's crimes, along with the riot that followed Maurice Richard's suspension from the National Hockey League. In Bessette's *La bagarre*, labour conflict—a strike by sweepers at the Metropolitan Transport Company—and the events that surround it are central to the evolution of the hero, Jules Leboeuf. This novel is important for its creative transcription of *JOUAL*, its use of several levels of speech, and its revival of naturalism, which had been squelched in Quebec during the First World War. Dealing with the (failed) writing of a novel, *La bagarre* announces a key aspect of Bessette's work in being reflexive, and anticipates a major preoccupation of Quebec fiction from the 1960s on.

4. TRANSFORMED 'TRADITIONAL' NOVELS. Rural and historical novels, mainstays of the traditional mode of expression, underwent important transformations in this period. Historical novels by Charlotte Savary, Pierre Benoît, and Gérard Morriset, among others, were active elements in the process of demythifying the origins of New France. After Ringuet's *Trente arpents* it had become difficult to pursue the model of the consecrated 'roman de la fidélité'. Thus Jean Filiatrault's *Terres stériles* (1953) showed the blind revolt of the younger farming generation against the dominant father figure, and continued the tendency to desanctify the rural milieu. The most important work in this mould is that classic of Quebec literature, Germaine GUÈVREMONT's *Le survenant* (1945). Although dealing with the well-worn theme of a family dynasty threatened by a break with continuity on the ancestral land, this novel, and its sequel *Marie-Didace* (1947)—published together in English as *The outlanders* (1950)—presented the rural parish as a stifling milieu dominated by pettiness and prejudice. The outlander, a transient and suspicious figure in the rural novel, moves to the centre in the person of the 'Survenant', who brings the free air of the outside world into a static community. His openness to nature and love, his skills, interest in science, musical talents, and generosity provoke the repressed dreams of those around him, particularly the women. But he finds the narrowness of the Chenal du Moine (near Sorel) too constricting and takes to the road once more.

5. 'INDEPENDENT' CREATIVITY. Some important writers who began to publish their first works of fiction in the period under review are hard to classify under the previous headings because they chose a highly independent approach to writing. Four of them—Yves THÉRIAULT, Anne HÉBERT, Antonine MAILLET, and Marie-Claire BLAIS—remain today among the major French-language writers of Canada.

While Guèvremont and Roy were among the first francophone writers to present positive, though episodic, portraits of cultural strangers to the milieu—Gypsies, Blacks, Jews, Italians, Ukrainians, etc.—and Bertrand Vac and Louis Dantin (Eugène SEERS) made major characters of a Métis and a Black respectively (*Louise Genest*, 1950; *Les enfances de Fanny*, 1951, translated by Raymond Chamberlain as *Fanny*, 1974), it was Yves Thériault who was most innovative in this context when he chose key figures for many of his works from among the ethnic and racial minorities of Canada. Thériault's first novel, *La fille laide* (1950), staked out his claim to 'primitivisme', giving ample room for psychoanalytic criticism. This violent story of a struggle between dwellers of a vague plain and mountain region was quickly followed by *Le dompteur d'ours* (1951), in which the 'survenant', Hermann, comes to an anonymous mountain village in Quebec, promising to wrestle a bear. His presence transforms village life in a way similar to that of Guèvremont's hero, but he flees before the promised match, thus proving himself a fraud. Thériault next published *Les vendeurs du temple* (1951), whose biblical title refers to the higher clergy's collusion in political corruption in a rural setting during the Duplessis years. Thériault reached the pinnacle of his career with *Aaron* (1954), set in the 'exotic' milieu of Jewish immigrants in Montreal, and *Agaguk* (1958), which allegedly takes place in the tundra of the Labrador-Ungava peninsula. In both works there is a struggle between the generations: grandfather versus grandson torn between tradition and modernism in *Aaron*, and in *Agaguk* son versus father, the tribal 'chief', in a similar struggle between corrupted tradition and desire for renewal. These two books are replete with (sometimes erroneous) ethnographic details, and some critics have seen in them a transposition and masking of aspects of the Quebec francophone reality. *Agaguk* has been hailed for presenting the first authentic lovers in Quebec fiction. Anne Hébert, who evolved from a first-rank poet to a brilliant short-story writer with *Le torrent* (1950), in 1958 produced her first novel, *Les chambres de bois*, the slightly altered title of one of her best-known poems, echoing its foreboding atmosphere. Catherine, a working-class girl from a northern mining town in France, meets her Prince Charming, the aristocrat Michel, marries him, and moves to the panelled rooms of his Paris apartment. Soon his sister Lia joins them, creating a strange triangle; profound feelings of guilt pervade the atmosphere, and Michel is obsessed with the fear that the flesh is the devil's domain. Catherine flees to the sunny south, where she finds love and the beginnings of liberation. Michel bears a strong resemblance to the author's cousin, SAINT-DENYS-GARNEAU; and other elements, too, suggest a possible allegory of pre-Quiet Revolution Quebec.

The Acadian-born writer Antonine Maillet began her splendid career with the rudimentary novel *Pointe-aux-Coques* (1958). Set in a New Brunswick fishing village, its heroine is the teacher Mlle Cormier (Maillet's mother's name). The speech of certain characters reflects Maillet's early interest in the Acadian dialect, and the novel presents various types who reappear in her later work: men of the sea, wild outlanders, the dispossessed, and the snob. Marie-Claire Blais published *La BELLE BÊTE* (1959; *Mad shadows*, 1960) when she was just twenty. A tale of ugliness, idiocy, sadism, suicide, family breakdown, and physical decomposition, it was generally received with shock by conservative and clerical critics, but was hailed by reviewers in both French and English. Fortunately it was frequently reprinted and Blais was encouraged to continue her career, which has since flourished.

See Maurice Lemire, *et al.*, *Dictionnaire des oeuvres littéraires du Québec*, vol. III (1982); Jean-Charles Falardeau, *Notre société et son roman* (1967); Ben-Z. Shek, *Social realism in the French-Canadian novel* (1977) and *French-Canadian and Québécois novels* (1991); André Belleau, *Le romancier fictif: essai sur la représentation de l'écrivain dans le roman québécois* (1980); and a special issue of *Études littéraires* (avr. 1981) entitled 'Sémiotique textuelle et histoire littéraire du Québec'. BEN-Z. SHEK

1960 to 1982. One of the most striking and important features of Quebec fiction in the sixties and seventies was its apparent desire to free itself in terms of both form and content. After 1960 the novel increasingly became an instrument of protest and of liberation. Often using a first-person narrator, and at times focusing on problems connected with the act of writing, novelists tended to reject traditional styles in favour of *JOUAL*, and popular levels of language more appropriate for describing the humble living conditions of a significant portion of the population. Traditional plot-lines and narrative techniques were dispensed with, particularly in the 1970s, when the usual psychological and social descriptions gave way to irony, caricature, satire, eroticism, violence, dreams, and self-scrutiny. Marginal characters and situations came into prominence, with descriptions of economic poverty, social dependence, and frustration, and with a variety of emotional problems connected with death, separation, suffering, madness, and depression. As in the cinema, marginal states of the imagination were also explored, producing a vein of fantasy/fantastic fiction that may have stemmed from a need to escape the confines of everyday experience.

In this period realism held more sway than symbolism, even if the realities described tended to be rather strange or unusual. Marie-Claire BLAIS, for example, moved from poetic romanticism towards hyper-realism, bleak caricature, and the grotesque; while Gérard BESSETTE's work went beyond social realism into the inner realism of analytic introspection. To a large extent Quebec fiction avoided the here-and-now; anger and revolt led it in the direction of more radical forms of escape and protest. At the same time there was a movement towards the outside—beyond the immediate borders of Quebec and into the vortex of history.

Among the most important novelists of the period, few except Michel TREMBLAY were traditional realists. Jacques FERRON, Roch CARRIER, and Jacques GODBOUT, for example, all took a playful or surrealistic approach; Victor-Lévy BEAULIEU, Yvon RIVARD, Jacques Benoît, and Roger Fournier relied on myth and fantasy; and Hubert AQUIN and Yolande VILLEMAIRE explored the dimensions of form. Introspection was frequent, as in the novels of Anne HÉBERT, Bessette, Réjean DUCHARME, and Jacques POULIN, while action often took place in a context of fantasy, history, or legend—as in novels by Antonine MAILLET, Jean-Yves Soucy, Yves BEAUCHEMIN, Bessette, and Benoît. In this way everyday life was transformed by exceptional circumstances.

This survey covers only the most prominent authors, and those novels that indicate the directions, focuses, currents, and developments in the literature and culture of the period.

1. THE EARLY SIXTIES. The Duplessis period was followed by a new and urgent desire to communicate; the despair, passivity, and existential awkwardness that had been so characteristic of previous novels were suddenly transformed with a vengeance after 1960, when the hidden corners of Quebec society began to emerge. Because 1960 marked an opening-up to the world and to history, literature began to present a new reflection of society and a critical awareness of previous limitations. *Le libraire* (1960; *Not for every eye*, 1962) by Gérard Bessette satirizes a mean, provincial society in the grip of clerical censorship. The anti-hero never directly criticizes or confronts the hypocrisy in his milieu; rather, he ironizes and avoids it, taking action by running away with the stock of books on the Index and selling them off at bargain prices. *Les pédagogues* (1961), which attacks the teaching world through caricature, is a conventional novel and less successful than the diary format of *Le libraire*. *Le poids de Dieu* (1962; *The burden of God*, 1964) by Gilles MARCOTTE shows the old world unravelling by describing a young priest's crisis of faith, which strengthens his vocation 'on the side of man'. In *L'aquarium* (1962) Jacques Godbout depicts the slow moral disintegration of a group of whites in the Third World: only the narrator will be saved. Passion explodes on the scene with *Le temps des jeux* (1961) by Diane Giguère: jealousy provokes an incestuous, suicidal girl, looking for her lost father, into having her older lover kill her mother (from whom she has stolen him); her hate is the other side of an immense, anguished love. Claire MARTIN dares to tell of the love affair between a publisher and his mistress in *Doux-amer* (1960): both characters narrate the events. Multiple narration was also used in Martin's *Quand j'aurai payé ton visage* (1962), which tells of a woman's passion for her brother-in-law.

As the old ideologies based on agriculture, free enterprise, and Messianism were replaced by industrialism, technocracy, socialism, anti-clericalism, and state control, and Catholic monolithism gave way to ideological pluralism, the term 'French-Canadian' gave way to 'Québécois'. A movement towards reappropriating the Québécois environment had already been reflected in poetry and film; it now appeared in fiction as well. Claude JASMIN's *Pleure pas, Germaine!* (1965), written in *joual*, is both a trip through the province and an account of a father's search for his daughter's murderer. *Le couteau sur la table* (1965; *Knife on the table*, 1968), by Jacques Godbout, involves a trip across Canada and then back to Quebec, as well as the transfer of the hero's affections from an English-speaking to a French-speaking woman while the first terrorist bombs explode. Jasmin's *Ethel et le terroriste* (1964; *Ethel and the terrorist*, 1965) depicts everyday life in the city but also concerns an FLQ member's flight to New York. Doubts about terrorism inspired *Mon cheval pour un royaume* (1967) by Jacques Poulin: the narrator, wounded by the bomb he is carrying, is given to much soul-searching, as is Jasmin's terrorist.

Jasmin's early works sprang from an old world that had to be destroyed. The hero in *La corde au cou* (1960) commits a crime of passion and blind revenge. His flight and subsequent death are similar to those of the hero in *Délivrez-nous du mal* (1961), in which André wants to get free of both Georges and his own past; perhaps the escape suggests a search for independence. Jasmin's early heroes are ready to commit murder; their lives are filled with degradation and introspection; sometimes they die surrounded, like the hero of *Et puis tout est silence . . .* (1965; *The rest is silence*, 1965), caught in the timbers of a fallen-down barn. There are similarities here with the position of the dying imprisoned engineer in Yves THÉRIAULT's *Cul-de-sac* (1961) who is caught in the dead-end of a nervous breakdown, looking over his past.

Besides dealing with repossession of the land, the novel became preoccupied with the language in which this activity is given expression. Prior to the sixties, fictional heroes tended to be dreamers incapable of action; but as their dreams became increasingly and consciously discredited, the descent into hell began. In *Le cabochon* (1964), by André MAJOR, the oral style of the writing matches the violence of the scenes, both in order to symbolize the fragmentation taking place and to provoke resistance and revolt. Jacques Godbout also uses popular French in his best novel, *SALUT GALARNEAU!* (1967; *Hail Galarneau!*, 1970), which tells the story of the King of French Fries on Île Perrot, a dreamer and outcast whose desire to live and whose dreams of writing lead him to wall himself up in his house.

As the official culture and the counter-culture began to merge, Quebec literature was written for the first time in a Quebec language, *joual*, its fractured nature reflecting a fractured reality. Meanwhile, as writers began to master the techniques of the realistic novel and to inject it with the hyper-realism of popular language, they also abandoned traditional forms of narration in favour of the interior monologue. The novels of Gérard Bessette exemplify this change: *L'INCUBATION* (1965; *Incubation*, 1967) consists of a long sentence with verbs and adjectives repeated and most of the punctuation eliminated. The form is both an extension of Hervé Jodoin's first-person diary in *Le libraire* and a preview of the dashes and brackets in Bessette's *Le cycle* (1971)—the dashes identifying physical sensations while the single or double brackets enclose the subconscious and unconscious levels of a continuous psychic voice (in seven interior monologues dealing with the death of the father). *Quelqu'un pour m'écouter* (1964), by Réal Benoit, tells of the childhood traumas of Rémi, who decides to run away; in the middle of the story we find a change of perspective and a first-person reflection on its writing. Dream and reality intertwine to reveal the author-narrator's unconscious, thus prefiguring future adaptations of the interior monologue. In these ways writing became increasingly self-analytic and self-conscious, culminating in the rampant formalism of the later sixties.

Gabrielle ROY, whose prairie background and fully bilingual writing skills set her apart from the regional preoccupations common among French-Canadian writers, concentrated on the human quest for joy and for a mutual understanding that is all too often ephemeral or belated. In *La montagne secrète* (1961; *The hidden mountain*, 1962) a young painter travelling in the Arctic finds, loses, and finds again a mountain that symbolizes his quest for both a subject and the means of expressing it.

By the early sixties the novel had become the predominant literary genre in Quebec. Whereas in the entire nineteenth century only 52 novels (and 22 new editions) had been published, the number of novels published annually in Quebec rose from 27 in 1961 to 100 in 1974.

2. 1965 TO 1970. In 1965 Gérard Bessette's *L'incubation*, Hubert Aquin's *PROCHAIN ÉPISODE*, and Marie-Claire Blais's *Une saison dans la vie d'Emmanuel* were published, followed in 1966 by Réjean Ducharme's *L'avalée des avalés*. Described as obsessive and outrageous, these *nouveaux romans* were both lyrical and denunciatory. Bessette's narrator, Lagarde, watches the slow degradation of the human relationships around him, including that of his friend Gordon with Néa, a prodigal mistress. Their reconciliation proves impossible and Néa commits suicide. The sumptuous, lyrical writing of *Prochain épisode* (1965; *Prochain épisode*; trans. 1967) not only deals with the act of writing but makes connections between the woman and the land, and the symbolic value of the landscape. Later, with *Trou de mémoire* (1968), Aquin continued his baroque exploration of the *Doppelgänger* theme by presenting the scrambled story of an African revolutionary; a dope-addict pharmacist and the rape of his English-Canadian girlfriend (reported by a publisher); and the completion of the story's missing sections by the girl's sister. In *L'antiphonaire* (1969; *The antiphonary*, 1973) extreme situations (such as rape and epilepsy) parallel historical periods (such as the Italian Renaissance or the American twentieth century). Aquin's final novel, *Neige noire* (1974), juxtaposed the text of a film script with a commentary upon it.

In *Une saison dans la vie d'Emmanuel* (1965; *A season in the life of Emmanuel*, 1966) Marie-Claire Blais showed how poverty engenders sordidness and squalor. A last child with a Messianic name is born into a large rural family; his father is severely limited, his mother lost in her melancholy; the priesthood is the only way out for the poetic Jean-le-Maigre, who is crushed by tuberculosis. The novel, composed like a mosaic, is by turns erotic, naturalistic, surreal, or hyper-real. The author presents a world in which existence itself has become impossible. Many of Blais's novels are descriptions and consecrations of childhood (*La BELLE BÊTE*,

1959; *Mad shadows*, 1960; *Tête blanche*, 1960; trans. 1961), or adolescence (*Le jour est noir*, 1962; *L'insoumise*, 1966, *The fugitive*, 1978). In *David Sterne* (1967; trans. 1973)—an exploration of 'all the vices'—a son rebels against his father, and in *Les manuscrits de Pauline Archange* (1968; *The manuscripts of Pauline Archange*, 1969) a problem child is badly treated by her father and her teachers. After exorcizing the experiences of youth, characteristically through suffering and revolt, Blais moved towards descriptions of romantic, sexual, and lesbian relationships in *Le loup* (1977; *The wolf*, 1974), *Une liaison parisienne* (1975; *A literary affair*, 1979), and finally *Les nuits de l'underground* (1978; *Nights in the underground*, 1979).

Réjean Ducharme also portrayed children or adolescents rebelling against adult society and suffering from an inability to express their love. In *L'avalée des avalés* (1966; *The swallower swallowed*, 1968) Bérénice Einberg's monologues are aggressive; with her insufferable parents, her lack of love, her rejection, she takes vengeance on language itself by turning it into banter. This novel, though not the first to portray Jewish characters and milieux, most dramatically illustrated the impact of internationalism on Quebec fiction. *L'océantume* (1968) deals with bitterness: Ina Ssouvie's daughter dreams of winning over her neighbour Asie Asothe and rejecting the world with her. They journey to the sea, and the ocean's surge at the end of the novel, obliterating the distinction between subject and object, is a sort of *leitmotif* that appears throughout Ducharme's work. *La fille de Christophe Colomb* (1969), Ducharme's most radically unconventional book, is a mock epic in deliberately ridiculous verse, in which the daughter of Columbus wanders the world in search of friendship.

Jacques Ferron's best novel, *L'amélanchier* (1970; *The juneberry tree*, 1975)—named for a tree that, like childhood, flowers early and briefly in springtime—reveals a nostalgia for childhood and the land. Ferron's verve, fantasy, and gift for satire made him a fine polemicist. A prolific writer, he drew on nationalistic themes and his own tragi-comic folklore. The need for a doctor to remain close to the people and to champion freedom is the theme of *Cotnoir* (1962; *Doctor Cotnoir*, 1973), about the death and funeral of an alcoholic doctor in Longueuil. Increasingly Ferron became the spokesman for a mythic country whose oral tradition and everyday history provided the verisimilitude apparent in *Le ciel du Québec* (1969), a picture of Quebec in the pre-war years. His experience as a doctor also served him in such novels as *Les roses sauvages* (1971; *Wild roses*, 1976), a political allegory about the end of a couple's relationship.

The October Crisis of 1970 marked the end of an era and of a certain kind of literature: it was the end of folklore and nationalism in literature. The next five years or so were a transitional period during which, however, important changes took place, as witnessed by the gradual disappearance of *joual* as a literary medium.

3. THE SEVENTIES. In this decade the most significant fiction seemed to come initially from writers whose reputations were already established. Claude Jasmin moved towards autobiography and resurrecting the past: in *L'Outaragasipi* (1971) he undertook a quest for the ancestors who settled in Assomption in 1717; in *La petite patrie* (1972), *Pointe-Calumet boogie-woogie* (1973), *Sainte-Adèle-la-vaisselle* (1974), and *La sablière* (1979) he resumed his search for the innocent childhood he had avoided and rejected during his revolt in the sixties. *Revoir Ethel* (1976) is a clumsy attempt to revisit characters from earlier works. In Jacques Godbout's *D'amour, P.Q.* (1972), a priggish writer is seduced by two domineering secretaries (symbols of feminism), who rewrite his unrealistic, intellectual novel—forcing a confrontation between 'high-class literature' and popular language. In *Les anthropoïdes* (1977) Gérard Bessette used interior monologues to convey the emergence, in the horde of our primitive ancestors, of historic, social, and personal consciousness; in *Le semestre* (1979) interior monologues present the emotional and intellectual state of mind of a university professor who is about to retire. Réjean Ducharme's *L'hiver de force* (1973), a satire on Montreal's culture and politics in the 1970s, portrays a young couple caught in a straitjacket of solitude: two proofreaders, André and Nicole, kill time by watching TV, smoking, reading MARIE-VICTORIN's *Flore laurentienne*, looking for affection, and doing nothing. *Les enfantômes* (1976) evokes the childhood ghosts of Vincent and Fériée, a brother and sister who are united against the world by their mother's suicide. Here again we find Ducharme's characteristic language games, satirical wordplay, puns, and linguistic virtuosity.

Among the few novels dealing with the October Crisis is Yves Beauchemin's *L'enfirouapé* (1974), which describes the historical events in a playful manner, mixing them up with a love affair and involving a poet in police interrogations, imprisonment, and a ridiculous, grotesque judicial system. *Le matou*

(1981) is the jumbled story of a boy deserted by his mother; a thief and an alcoholic, he takes refuge in a cheap restaurant and gets involved in various adventures to save it. A realistic novel, it describes external surroundings only, but in a straightforward manner and with imagery that conveys delicate touches of humour.

The major changes in fiction of the seventies had to do with form. Instead of characters with their usual passions gradually developing as the story unwinds, we see abrupt changes that often cannot be explained by traditional psychology; mythic, poetic, or lyric elements invade the text, together with magical reconstructions of worlds that are strange or violent. Clarity of style and straightforward, easily understood linear plots were no longer in fashion; sequence was based on breaks and repetitions, on interpolated links in a texture that resembles a mosaic. Content came to depend on form. This was particularly apparent after 1975 when, during the vogue for autobiographical influences and for novelists who become their own characters, the novelist self-consciously searched for a form; the process of writing became its own subject and the authors became their own narrators. In this period, fantasy and realism existed side by side, and the theme of articulating the land was reduced to the level of village realism, family life, or interpersonal relations. As the decade progressed, novelists continued to explore the links between narrative and history, but the period was marked chiefly by new directions and diversity, anarchy and individualism. Accordingly, discussion of this later period is divided into categories that reflect this diversity.

3(a). *The realists.* Victor-Lévy Beaulieu oscillated between the two major poles of Quebec literature. Concerned on the one hand to describe or to bring into being the reality of Quebec or 'the land', he also wanted to drift into dreams, fantasy, drunkenness, and nightmare. An admirer of Jack Kerouac (whose French-Canadian parentage and significance for Québécois obsessed him) and Victor Hugo, Beaulieu used torrents of language, including *joual*, to tell the saga of the Beauchemin family—especially of their young son Abel—from the Lower St Lawrence. *Race de monde* (1969) and *Jos Connaissant* (1970; Eng. trans. 1982) introduce this fictional world, and the series is completed—following a return to the countryside in *Les grand-pères* (1971; *The grandfathers*, 1975)—in *Un rêve québécois* (1972; *A Québécois dream*, 1978) and *Oh Miami, Miami, Miami* (1973). Jos, a heavy drinker who often meditates before a Buddha, has an unhappy relationship with a waitress whom he treats badly. *Un rêve québécois* culminates in orgies, masturbation, and hints of sadism; the hero ends up killing his wife in a delirious and revolting bedroom scene that reflects the concurrent events of the October Crisis. *Don Quichotte de la démanche* (1974; *Don Quixote in Nighttown*, 1978) seems to indicate a desire to create a mythology and an imaginary country. Abel Beauchemin, a megalomaniacal novelist who is obsessed with the idea of writing a colossal work of literature, becomes anxious and full of doubts about his project because his books will only bear witness to a people on the road to extinction.

Beaulieu's realism extended to his language. Along with several other writers, he established the validity—and the humour—of popular spoken French in literary writing. A new cycle of 'Voyageries' got underway with *Blanche forcée* (1976), *N'évoque plus que le désenchantement de ta ténèbre, mon si pauvre Abel* (1976), *Sagamo Job J* (1977), and the three volumes of *Monsieur Melville* (1978). In these novels we see Beaulieu's myth-making in action; the origins he tells of are collective, national, and literary, as though he were constructing cultural forefathers to replace missing personal, social, or familial antecedents.

Gilbert LA ROCQUE provided a less frenetic series of novels about a childhood that had been rediscovered and redigested. *Le nombril* (1970) opened the cycle with the disappearance of a still-born sister. *Corridors* (1971) introduced a pacifist revolutionary who imagines himself to be a foetal phallus adrift inside his aunt (a mother substitute). *Après la boue* (1972) and *Serge d'entre les morts* (1976) were more successful. In the sooty, vulgar, animalistic city, Gabrielle experiences the horror of penetration, pregnancy, and abortion. Serge advances beyond his childhood by reliving his father's death, his mother's remarriage, his cousin's rejection, and his grandmother's death. *Les masques* (1980) tells of a motherless child, deserted by his father and taken in by his grandparents; he grows up to be a writer, is divorced from his wife, and loses his only child in a drowning accident the day of his grandfather's ninety-first birthday. The emotional intensity of the narration increases as plot sequences are revised and repeated until a missing link ties them all together.

André Major gained a certain fame with his protest novel *Le cabochon* (1964), but turned towards rediscovery of the countryside in *Le vent du diable* (1968), a story of the death of a young orphan girl that verges on fantasy and myth. It also pointed towards the despairing realism (concerning the impossible dream) found in the *Histoires des déserteurs* trilogy: *L'épouvantail* (1974; *The scarecrows of Saint-Emmanuel*, 1977), *L'épidémie* (1975; *Inspector Therrien*, 1980), and *Les rescapés* (1976) are set in the little village of Saint-Emmanuel de l'Épouvante. Momo Boulanger, who has been released from prison, kills Gigi, and owing to the efforts of Inspector Therrien is given a life-sentence. After the inspector retires and marries, Momo escapes from prison and returns to prowl around the village. Particularly impressive are Major's descriptions of an entire social milieu, and of the conflict between the city and the country.

Michel Tremblay's fiction moved away from such fantasies as *La cité dans l'oeuf* (1969) towards the greater realism of *C't'à ton tour, Laura Cadieux* (1973). *La grosse femme d'à côté est enceinte* (1978; *The fat woman next door is pregnant*, 1981), *Thérèse et Pierrette à l'école des Saints-Anges* (1980; *Thérèse and Pierrette and the little hanging angel*, 1982), and *La duchesse et le roturier* (1982) continued in this vein, using a transcription of popular speech for the dialogues, and standard French for the narration. These novels, in which the female characters typified in his play *Les BELLES-SOEURS* (1968) were given greater depth, vividly portray the atmosphere of east-end Montreal in the early forties.

Pierre Turgeon increasingly turned to the action novel. In *Faire sa morte comme faire l'amour* (1969) a family is cruelly liquidated, while in *Un, deux, trois* (1970) a whole village is condemned to die. *Prochainement sur cet écran* (1973) deals with a murder-mystery and the police; *La première personne* (1980; *The first person*, 1982), more sober but equally violent, is another detective story.

3(b). *Comic or caricatured realism.* For writers describing the rural, folksy past of an urban society, realism may become essentially comic or fantastic in nature. Adrien Thério's *Le printemps qui pleure* (1962) and *La colère du père* (1974) looked back towards lost childhoods, but Thério's abundant humour was given freer rein in *Le mors aux flancs* (1965), *Un païen chez les pingouins* (1970), and *Les fous d'amour* (1973). *Soliloque en hommage à une femme* (1968) remains his most convincing novel, however, telling the story of a history professor who pays a childishly sentimental visit to the rural poverty of his childhood.

Roger Fournier's adventure novels are picaresque, erotic, and ribald, although banality and tedium diminished the effect of *Inutile et adorable* (1963), *À nous deux* (1965), *Journal d'un jeune marié* (1967), *La voix* (1968), and *La marche des grands cocus* (1972). *Moi mon corps mon âme Montréal etc.* (1974) is a first-person tale of hatred and social degradation played out against the background of the October Crisis. Fournier's talent and technique showed progress, however, in *Les cornes sacrées* (1977): leaving the backwoods of Quebec, a farmer's son, Norbert, takes his bull along on an epic journey through the mythic realms of Crete, and the pagan world, in a quest for the origins of life.

Jean-Marie Poupart seemed to enjoy making an inventory of the verbal eccentricities and particularities of popular Quebec French, as indicated by such titles as *Angoisse play* (1968), *Que le diable emporte le titre* (1969), *Ma tite vache a mal aux pattes* (1970), *Chère Touffe, c'est plein plein de fautes dans ta lettre d'amour* (1973), and *C'est pas donné à tout le monde d'avoir une belle mort* (1974). Poupart, who published an essay on the detective novel, oscillated between that genre and the unfinished novel disguised as a diary in *Ruches* (1978) and *Le champion de cinq heures moins dix* (1980), which described the author's disillusionment with the business of writing.

Roch Carrier's first three novels form a trilogy. In *La guerre, yes sir!* (1968; trans. 1970), *Floralie, où est-tu?* (1969; *Floralie, where are you?* 1971), and *Il est par là, le soleil* (1970; *Is it the sun, Philibert?* 1972), the characters are caricatures, the descriptions extravagant, and the action symbolic. *Le deux-millième étage* (1973; *They won't demolish me!*, 1974) centres on a building that is to be demolished to make way for a high-rise, and on the tragi-comic efforts of Dorval to mobilize a group of tenants against the forces of speculative capitalism. This novel, however, turns into farce and the characters become one-dimensional personifications of ideas. In *Il n'y a pas de pays sans grand-père* (1979; *No country without grandfathers*, 1981), Thomas, an old forest-ranger who has already had run-ins with Anglos, reflects on his own youth and on his grandson Jean-Thomas, who is in prison for having taken part in a demonstration against the Queen. *Le jardin des délices* (1975; *The garden of delights*, 1978) presents a tenderly ironic story of truculent characters involved in a tragi-comic burlesque; Carrier's *La dame qui avait des chaînes aux chevilles* (1981) is almost epic in scope and metaphorical in tone.

The novels of Jacques Poulin, often characterized by critics as 'roman-poèmes', emphasise simplicity, sweetness, tenderness, childhood, anguish, death, bitterness—and fantasy. *Mon cheval pour un royaume* (1967) is set on the borderline between dream and reality. Pierre Delisle, who was wounded by the bomb he was using to blow up a statue, is undergoing psychiatric treatment. Hanging out in Old Quebec, he becomes involved in a love triangle that has lasting and tragic consequences. *Jimmy* (1969) tells of an eleven-year-old boy who, during a summer spent in Cap Rouge while his parents' marriage is breaking up, identifies with a famous car racer, Jimmy Clark. In *Le coeur de la baleine bleue* (1970), a study of sexual identity, the hero, Noël, undergoes a transplant operation in which he is given the heart of a sixteen-year-old girl, Charlotte. Thereafter his relations with his wife, Élise, change as she notices him drifting passively into love with a hockey-player named Bill. When she leaves him for Bill, Noël feels all the temptations of death. The three novels were translated as *The 'Jimmy' trilogy* (1979) by Sheila Fischman. After *Faites de beaux rêves* (1974), about a group of car-racing fans who spend a frenetic weekend in Mont-Tremblant, Poulin's writing became sparer, presenting a mythic Québécois vision of America. In *Les grandes marées* (1978) the hero, Teddy Bear, is sent to an island where he can continue his work (translating comic strips); but he is forced to leave the island when a number of visitors seek him out. The charm of this story lies in its tenderness, imagination, and flights of fantasy.

3(c). *Regional realism.* The first-person narration used by Yves Thériault to create the long lyric cry of *Ashini* (1960; Eng. trans. 1972)—the Amerindian through whom he explores basic and primitive psychology—continued in *Agoak, l'héritage d'Agaguk* (1975; *Agoak*, 1979). Agaguk, the hero of Thériault's famous novel of the same name (1958; trans. 1967), had left his village and its ancient customs in order to make a home where he would not have to share his wife; in *Agoak* the Inuit, instinctively struggling against reason and domination, leave white society, which is civilized in name only. Thériault manages to convey instincts in language that evokes their deepest origins. Wishing to describe 'man, battling against what he believes to be his fate', he uses a style that oscillates between a staccato primitivism and a gentle lyricism. After her early autobiographical novels, Antonine Maillet turned to novels in the form of folktales. *Don l'Orignal* (1972; *The tale of Don l'Orignal*, 1978), which tells of a struggle for the possession of an island, won a Governor General's Award. *Pélagie-la-charrette* (1979; *Pélagie: the return to a homeland*, 1982), which won the Prix Goncourt, is peopled by legendary characters and fairy-tale heroes and tells the epic story of a mythical country that now exists only in words. Written in the style of spoken language, it describes the odyssey of the Acadians, expelled from their homeland in 1757, as they return to Acadia from Georgia, USA. A fierce enemy of acceptance and resignation, Pélagie LeBlanc leads her family and others on this ten-year journey. In *Cent ans dans les bois* (1981) Pélagie's granddaughter takes charge of the former deportees to transform them from sailors into pioneers and settlers. This work is typical of Maillet's storytelling, using old sayings, proverbs, legends, history, and folktales.

Jean-Yves Soucy's prize-winning novel *Un dieu chasseur* (1976), translated by John GLASSCO as *Creature of the chase* (1979), offers lyrical descriptions of pantheistic primitivism. A 'male supremacist' trapper who dreams of absolute liberty brings a schoolteacher into the forest, but her suicide leaves him with his freedom intact. *Les chevaliers de la nuit* (1980), set in the Abitibi region, tells how two children's voyeuristic escapades lead to their discovery of darkness and adolescence. The style is sumptuous and natural, with lyric descriptions of the landscape.

Louis CARON leaned towards fantasy and the folktale. In *L'emmitouflé* (1977; *The draft dodger*, 1980) a Franco-American draft-dodger tells the story of his Uncle Nazaire from Nicolet who, refusing to be conscripted in 1914, moved to a farm in New Hampshire in the 1950s; an enigmatic and solitary man, he is on the run throughout this excellent documentary novel. In *Le bonhomme sept-heures* (1978) Caron wrote with playful compassion of the 1955 landslide that swept part of Nicolet into the river. In the poor part of town, a gang of rowdy youths makes life miserable for a disreputable churchgoer, Augustin Lenoir; trapped in the debris caused by the landslide, Lenoir ascends into heaven. In *Le canard de bois* (1981) Bruno Bellerose returns from the lumber-camps in 1935 and is given a wooden decoy that had been carved by his ancestor, Hyacinthe, whose progressive involvement in the Rebellion of 1837-8 is recounted as a parallel narrative to that of Bruno. The style—neutral, efficient, and spare—maintains considerable evocative power.

Jean-Paul Filion used his own childhood as an inspiration for *Saint-André-Avelin* (1976) and *Les murs de Montréal* (1977). *Cap Tourmente* (1980) is a long, tension-filled love letter, while *Il est bien court le temps des cerises* (1981) shows to advantage the author's good humour and crude language in a documentary portrait of life in a Charlevoix village in the early 1950s. Noël AUDET's *Quand la voile faseille* (1980) is a superbly written account of a Gaspé childhood, a father, a resourceful uncle, and various life crises. *Ah, l'amour, l'amour* (1981) tells of love-affairs with two vastly different women, the one repressed and the other a liberating spirit.

3(d). *A new liberation of language.* Around 1973-4 the debate over *joual* ceased. After endless discussions, position-papers, and controversies, the novel reverted to traditional French, and popular forms of speech were relegated chiefly to dialogue. Nevertheless Quebec literature had won the right to speak in the language of the people.

Even Jacques RENAUD reversed his earlier position and came out against the 'sick' and 'suicidal' use of *joual. En d'autres paysages* (1970) and *Le fond pur de l'errance irradie* (1975) introduced the mysticism of the Orient—in standard French—while *La colombe et la brisure éternité* (1979) tended towards a positive, poetic lyricism. *Clandestine(s) ou la tradition du couchant* (1980) is an 'explorean' novel about the FLQ that also provides an exploration and exorcism of revolutionary violence. The language of fiction in Quebec in this period was increasingly exuberant, baroque and idiosyncratic, moving in many directions simultaneously.

3(e). *The fantastic.* Jacques Benoît, in *Jos Carbone* (1967; trans. 1974), presented a sort of post-apocalyptic vision in which his characters seem stranded in a timeless forest, or underground, or on a raft moored in a marsh. In this world, action, surrealism, violence, cruelty, and death replace psychological reflection. In *Les voleurs* (1969) the narrator Émile and his kindly uncle and aunt are caught up in a plot involving extravagant, burlesque thieves and a sadistically cruel policeman. *Patience et Firlipon* (1970) also provides a mixture of realism and fantasy: a couple of offbeat characters—a country woman and a crazed, sexually aggressive gorilla—and an atmosphere of science fiction. *Les princes* (1973; *The princes*, 1977) is set in a mysterious city reminiscent of a South-American slum neighbourhood; two opposing organizations, the one composed of men and the other of dogs, are engaged in a battle to the death. Simplicity of style heightens the impact as political and social transformations are suggested in a context of dreamlike reality. In *Gisèle et le serpent* (1981) a girl takes a serpent to her bosom in order to gain its powers, which leads inevitably to more cruelty and mutilation. Typical of Benoît's work, this novel contains fantasy infused with social criticism, although in this case there is a happy ending.

Anne Hébert moved from the purely historical novel, *KAMOURASKA* (1970; trans. 1974), to a mixture of history and the supernatural in *Les enfants du sabbat* (1975; *Children of the black sabbath*, 1978). Aurélie, the servant in *Kamouraska*, has become soeur Julie, a nun and witch, in the latter novel. The havoc she wreaks upon her convent is seen to stem from an obsessive and incestuous attachment to her brother and the strange ceremonies of initiation conducted by her primitive, poverty-stricken parents. *Héloïse* (1980; trans. 1982) is a novel of the fantastic. Bernard, who lives with his wife Christine in a Paris apartment formerly inhabited by Héloïse, is gradually seduced by a vampire woman. Here the world of dreams and fantasy is balanced against reality by means of a fast-paced style that is sober, sumptuous, metaphorical, and evocative. Hébert's *Les fous de Bassan* (1982), which won the prestigious Prix Fémina in France, is set on the North Shore of the Lower St Lawrence; it treats poetically two recurring themes of her novels: violence and the victimization of women.

A preoccupation with origins and beginnings often leaned towards the fantastic, but Charles Soucy's *Le voyage à l'imparfait* (1968) owed more to fantasy than to the fantastic, with its narrator presenting the thoughts of a foetus, and later a child trying to escape from a possessive mother. *Heureux ceux qui possèdent* (1973), set in a mythic land at the dawn of time, concerns a primitive family's response to a stranger who brings progress and science. In Soucy's best novel, *À travers la mer* (1975), a Gaspé fisherman tries to please his wife by moving into a small apartment in Montreal's Rosemont district. Losing everything, but discovering his imagination, he dies in a final embrace with the natural world.

The fantastic verges on lyric abstraction in the fiction of Jacques Brossard, with its investigations of the strange connections between reason and the unconscious, control and explosion. Written in a fluid, supple, and carefully crafted style, *Le sang du souvenir* (1976) features a narrator who seesaws between landscapes that are alternately real and imaginary, violent and nightmarish. After sixteen years of silence André LANGEVIN produced *L'élan d'Amérique* (1972), a complex novel, violent and difficult to read, that symbolically denounces the alienation, exploitation, dispossession, and assimilation of Quebec by the North American whole. *Une chaîne dans le parc* (1974) combines dream and reality in the tale of an orphan who has lived a brutal life in an orphanage since he was four years old; he escapes for one week, only to find the outside world even more terrifying, and returns to another boarding school.

3(f). *Myth-makers, the poetic, and the counter-culture.* A tendency to invent myths or to amplify existing archetypes appeared in the writings of Pierre Châtillon, who is primarily a poet. *La mort rousse* (1974) tells of an old house-painter who, during an operation, dreams of a trip to sunny Florida, of a marvellous girl with red hair, and recalls his love of life and deep-rooted memories of his childhood. In *Le fou* (1975) an old farmer sets out in the snow with his tractor to look for his wife, who has been carried away by the north wind. Helped—or hindered—by such legendary folk characters as La Corriveau, Rose Latulipe, the giant of Beaupré, the devil, and so on, his odyssey takes the form of an exploration of the collective unconscious and the traditional folklore of Quebec. *La tourbière* (1975), by Normand Rousseau, uses archetypes, poetry, and symbols such as the white virgin or the red devil. Yvon Rivard's *Mort et naissance de Christophe Ulric* (1976) is both a magical voyage and a search for national identity; everyday reality is replaced by a torrent of dreamlike elements. Rivard's *L'ombre et le double* (1979) takes the form of a quest—complete with delirious, animistic, cosmic, and metaphysical dimensions—for the spatial, temporal, and psychic borders of Quebec, involving *coureurs de bois* ancestors and a surreal voyage down the Saint Lawrence River towards the sea. Jacques Garneau's novels describe the world of voyeurism, madness, and traumatic mother-child relationships. *Mémoire de l'oeil* (1972), written in dialogue, tells of a voyeur who has supposedly murdered Véronique and destroyed Françoise, but its deeper meaning concerns a search for freedom through the annihilating effects of distance. In *Inventaire pour St-Denys* (1973) Michel, confined to a mental hospital, draws nationalistic masterpieces on the walls and dreams of escape into childhood and death. In *La mornifle* (1976) the midwife of the title must kill her own children who were born deformed. A novel of initiation, its ten chapters look at the soul through ten different windows. *Les difficiles lettres d'amour* (1979) presents the fantasies of a sequestered child, his hated father, and his distant mother. The passage into adolescence and adulthood is marked by retreat into a world devoid of language or speech; but these—and love—are restored in the latter part of the novel.

Suzanne PARADIS displayed the poetic vein of fiction in such works as *Les hauts cris* (1960), *Il ne faut pas sauver les hommes* (1961), and *François-les-oiseaux* (1967). In *Les cormorans* (1968) the characters have turned their backs on life and chosen exile on an island of sand in order to recover their memories. *Miss Charlie* (1979) juxtaposes the heroine's diary with excerpts from her neighbour's novel: the attractions and rivalries of the two writers blend into a sensuous and beautiful text. Poetic elements can also be used to break up the traditional continuity of the story, as in Jacques Lanctôt's *Rupture de ban* (1979), in which the explanation of the author's activities in the FLQ is interrupted or replaced by the lyric thrust of 'words of exile and love'. The 'free novel' (as in free verse) may be marked by a poetic style that leads to confusion between subject and object, or that heightens incoherence and tension. Novels in this vein included *L'ossature* (1972) by Pierre MORENCY, *La brunante* (1973) by Pierre Filion, and Jean-Pierre Guay's *Mise en liberté* (1974).

The counter-culture was no longer an underground phenomenon. Daniel Gagnon indulged his delirious hyperphallism and absurd narcissism—not to mention a hatred of the mother as saint, madonna, and martyr—in *Surtout à cause des viandes* (1972). As in *Loulou* (1976), 'good or evil, it doesn't make any difference.' Pierre Corbeil's *La mort d'Auline Aquin* (1975) tells of a murder in a motorcycle gang from Trois-Rivières; the main suspect, though innocent, commits suicide. In *Sivis pacem et para bellum* (1970), Louis Gauthier presents two characters whose adventures depend heavily on word-games. His more successful *Souvenir de San Chiquita* (1978) is an action novel about an ordinary man's memories of a banana republic: love, drugs, revolution, and fun. Emmanuel Cocke also had fun with fantasy and surrealism in *Emmanuscrit de la mère morte* (1972); the word-games and phonetic or semantic puns are clearly reminiscent of Réjean Ducharme. *Va voir au ciel si j'y suis* (1971) continues in the same vein, as does *Louve storée* (1973). *Sexe pour sang* (1974) is a detective novel; dealing with espionage and eroticism, it is both humorous and psychedelic.

3(g). *Feminist novels.* One of the central themes in the nationalistic writing of the 1960s was an identification of women with the land. In the seventies, however, women emerged on their own, writing about themselves in a process of discovery, exploration, and emancipation. Michèle Mailhot told the story of an unhappy woman in *Dis-moi que je vis* (1964). *Le fou de la reine* (1969) and *La mort de l'araignée* (1972) both deal with problems between couples, while in *Veuillez agréer . . .* (1975) a forty-year-old woman sets out on an entertaining road to liberation and divorce. In *Aldébaran ou La fleur* (1968) the prolific Claire de Lamirande tells of two vaguely discontented couples on holiday in Percé; there is little action, the style is choppy, and the tone artificial. Perhaps Lamirande's best novel, *Jeu de clefs* (1974)—written in short, verbless sentences that detract from the narrative—is a love story combined with a mysterious plot about a man who is haunted by the ghost of his former boss (a woman who had been murdered). *La pièce montée* (1975), which dwells on the oppression of women, contains many female characters of different generations; since they all speak in the first person, this leads to some confusion. *Signe de biais* (1976) oscillates between psychological fiction and the detective novel, while *Papineau ou L'épée à double tranchant* (1980) is a historical tale told by several narrators.

Hélène Ouvrard stuck to decorative, bourgeois romanticism in *La fleur de peau* (1965), a story of a rebellious young woman's maternal love for a sexual invert. *Le coeur sauvage* (1967) evokes the primitive, savage nature of the Gaspé in the character of Adèle, a wild creature whose fate is at the centre of the plot. *Le corps étranger* (1973) tells of a woman's struggle to regain possession of herself, while *L'herbe et le varech* (1977) is a sort of non-novel about the forty-year-old narrator's attempt to make her life over and escape male domination. In *La noyante* (1980), which describes the growing intimacy between Eléonore and a mother/goddess character named Léonor, feminism was juxtaposed with nationalism. Madeleine OUELLETTE-MICHALSKA's *La femme de sable* (1979) is a painful socio-political novel, set in Algeria during the sixties, that deals with the eternal, violated mother/earth at odds with man. *Chez les termites* (1975) is an attack on the alienation produced by the modern school system in which communication, contact, and a sense of community are all lacking. *Le plat de lentilles* (1979) is a quest for the meaning of femininity.

The message of the many female voices that made themselves heard towards the end of the decade was one not only of protest and revolt but also of self-affirmation. As well as decrying the historical alienation of women, they told of the new woman—and often of old women. Carole Dunlop, for instance, wrote of a decrepit old lady who seems to be the conscience of everything around her in *Mélanie dans le miroir* (1980). Huguette Le Blanc's *Bernadette Dupuis ou La mort apprivoisée* (1980) described an old widow's struggle against death and dispossession. Jovette MARCHESSAULT's trilogy in honour of the Great Mother, *Comme une enfant de la terre*, began with *Le crachat solaire* (1975) and *La mère des herbes* (1980). Creating a world that blends myth and autobiography, the author drew on the history of Quebec, the history of America, and the genesis of humanity. In *Un cri trop grand* (1980) Gabrielle Poulin told the story of three generations of women; as is often the case with Quebec fiction, there seems to be a superabundance of metaphor. *Lueur* (1979), by Madeleine GAGNON, is an 'archeological novel' with 'multiple' references—an allegory based on the history of a character and a family, of women and the world. *Retailles* (1977), written with Denise BOUCHER, is more a poetic and political journal than a novel in the traditional sense. In *La cohorte fictive* (1979) all the characters have gathered for a final Thanksgiving dinner at a widow's home in the Laurentians. Incest, suicide, and a whole complex of family relationships are described in long, sinuous sentences.

Yolande VILLEMAIRE's *La VIE EN PROSE* (1980) was warmly received by critics, who saw in it a blend of mysticism, memory, myth; it is also highly enjoyable reading. Having American, Amerindian, and counter-cultural antecedents, it is a playful, optimistic story of several women writers and involves multiple identities. *La pique-nique sur l'Acropole* (1979) is Louky BERSIANIK's antithetical version of Plato's *Phaedra*. An invocation to the Great Goddess, it enters a plea on behalf of all women—whether crazed, raped, mutilated, used, abused, or ignored—who have refused to be subjected to procreation. *Une voix pour Odile* (1978), by France THÉORET, is composed of twelve monologues, each of which asks agonizing questions about the fragmentation of life and female identity.

The search for modernism was influenced by both American and Parisian models, the latter being more pronounced in the writings of Nicole BROSSARD. *Un livre* (1970; *A book*, 1976) is a blend of love or eroticism and political activism that is merely a pretext for a series of musings on the art of writing a novel—a self-conscious examination of itself as process and object. *Sold-out/étreinte illustration* (1973) is another fiction that contains its own story, which may be said to take place in Montreal simultaneously in 1971 and 1941. *Étreinte illustration*, in the same volume, is an experimental piece in which language becomes its own raw material, deprived of its referential and communicative functions. *French kiss/étreinte exploration* (1974) explores both the body and Sherbrooke Street in a series of fitful and fragmented narratives that constantly scrutinize themselves. *L'amèr; ou Le chapitre effrité* (1977) presents fragments of a narrative about writing a book, various theoretical reflections, and a lesbian critique of feminism. In *Flore Cocon* (1978), by Suzanne Jacob, the heroine is a warmhearted waitress who finds in her relationship with Louanne a counterbalance to the social alienation of women.

See Gérard Bessette, *Une littérature en ébullition* (1968), *Trois romanciers québécois* (1973); Gilles Marcotte, *Le roman à l'imparfait* (1976); Jacques Allard, 'Les lettres québécoises depuis 1930', *University of Toronto Quarterly*, vol. 50, no. 1 (1980); André Belleau, *Le romancier fictif* (1980); Ben-Zion Shek, *Social realism in the French-Canadian novel* (1977) and *French-Canadian and Québécois novels* (1991).

LOUIS LASNIER

1983 to 1996. Pundits and commentators agree in seeing the 1980 referendum proposing the separation of Quebec from the rest of Canada as a major sociological event in recent Canadian history. Despite this fact, the divide between the literary culture of the 1970s and the 1980s was neither a radical nor an absolute one. While it is true that the engaged novel, so popular in the past few decades, all but disappeared, the eighties were, in many ways, the continuation and the intensification of the trends of the previous sixties and seventies. Many of the writers who became famous in that era continued writing, but without any significant change in style or interest. Roch CARRIER, Claude JASMIN, and Victor-Lévy BEAULIEU, for example, remained as prolific as before; after fourteen years of silence, Réjean DUCHARME made an unexpected return in 1990 with *Dévadé*, but not without encountering some harsh criticism; Jacques GODBOUT resumed his quest for happiness in *Une histoire américaine* (1986) and offered a sequel to his famous *Salut Galarneau!* in *Le temps des Galarneau* (1993). Nonetheless, these writers did not lead the intellectual debate that revolved around the novel in the 1980s and 1990s, nor do they receive the same kind of acclaim they once did. Exceptions are Anne HÉBERT (*Le premier jardin*, 1988; *L'enfant chargé de songes*, 1992) and Jacques POULIN (*Volkswagen blues*, 1984; *La tournée d'automne*, 1993, among others), who continued to experience success and recognition through their very intimate exploration of the human soul. Unfortunately, many well-known, established novelists died during this period: Gabrielle ROY and Yves THÉRIAULT in 1983, Gilbert LA ROCQUE in 1984, Jacques FERRON in 1985, Alice PARIZEAU in 1990, Françoise LORANGER in 1995, and Andrée MAILLET in 1996.

Language was no longer at the forefront of the intellectual debate. From being an instrument of shame for some in the sixties, a symbol of alienation for most, *JOUAL* achieved respectability among such writers as Michel TREMBLAY. From the middle of the 1970s on, *joual* became less pre-eminent in the novel and virtually ceased to be used in its narrative. Characters continued to express themselves in a familiar language made up of *québécismes*, occasional regional turns of phrases, and some elements of *joual*; but pure and constant *joual*, as encountered in *PARTI PRIS*, all but disappeared. Except for feminism, language itself was now rarely an issue. Two publications nonetheless stirred the pot of linguistic debate for a time: Noël AUDET's essay on the Quebec novel, *Écrire de la fiction au Québec* (1990), in which he suggested new linguistic norms for writers, and the 1993 publication of the *Dictionnaire du québécois d'aujourd'hui*, which gave much-criticized institutional recognition to the anglicisms and the *joual* used in the general population.

Advances in technology (micro-computers) and the reorganization of the publishing industry led to an unprecedented rise in the number of novels published, accompanied by a concomitant increase in the number of themes, types of styles and discourses, and sources of inspiration. The copyright registration service of the Bibliothèque Nationale du Québec received a total of 5,276 books in 1995, a 21.7 per cent increase over 1982. Nationalism and the quest for identity were no longer the driving forces behind the French-Canadian novel, and were slowly replaced by feminism and a new taste for realism. These last two tendencies, already perceived in the seventies, imposed their own conventions and themes: a review of history, an opening to the world outside Quebec, explicit expressions of sexuality, and an exploration of the relationships between men and women, dysfunctional families, and the rebellion of youth, all this through a renewed exploration of time and space. Nonetheless, the novel of this period was above all marked by a new 'américanité', wherein the author chose to return to plot, concentrating more on the story line than on the search for new forms that was so popular during the previous two decades.

1. THE EMERGENCE OF FEMINISM. In this period feminism took a leading role in the evolution of the Quebec novel, representing the only literary movement for which formalism (and engaged literature) remained of utmost interest. Feminist novels imposed themselves through a mental 'déconditionnement' (Derrida) from what was considered a patriarchal language and literary establishment. The result was a continuous search for a positive 'new' woman within a newly defined and constantly questioned French vocabulary and syntax. New and/or less patriarchal aesthetic forms were encouraged, such as fiction/theory, poetic prose, correspondence, diaries, etc. The lines dividing traditional literary genres consequently became somewhat blurred.

Extremely prolific and well organized, feminist writers had their own publishing houses (Remue-Ménage, Pleine Lune), their own journals (including *La Vie en rose*, 1980-7, and *Arcade*, 1981-), and were very much present in other publishing houses, such as Les Herbes Rouges and L'Hexagone, and in renowned journals such as *VOIX ET IMAGES* (UQAM) and *Quebec Studies* (USA). Among many authors and titles representing the search for meaningful new forms were France THÉORET, who illustrated the quest for a feminine identity (*Nous parlerons comme on écrit*, 1982); Régine ROBIN, who reflected on the Montreal she had come to live in (*La Québécoite*, 1983); Marie-Claire BLAIS, who created a three-hundred-page one-paragraph novel (*Soifs*, 1995); and Nicole BROSSARD, who published two complex novels, each of which is a novel within a novel within a novel (*Le désert mauve*, 1987, and *Baroque d'aube*, 1995). Also exemplary of this formal search were Suzanne Jacob's *Laura Laur* (1983), Anne Élaine Cliche's *La pisseuse* (1992), and, of course, Yolande VILLEMAIRE's celebrated *Vava* (1989).

History was one of the favourite subject areas of feminism, with several authors rewriting it from the angle of the role and position of women in society. In *Marie-Laflamme* (1991), followed by *Nouvelle-France* (1992) and *La renarde* (1994), Chrystine Brouillet took her readers from the French Inquisition and witch trials to the New World. Micheline Lachance wrote about the wife of one of the leaders of the 1837-8 rebellion, Louis-Joseph Papineau (*Le roman de Julie Papineau*, 1995). Similarly, Annick Hivert-Carthew, in her novelized biography, *Antoine de Lamothe Cadillac* (1996), placed great emphasis on the wife of Detroit's founder. One of the pioneers of women's journalism, Françoise de Guise, was also the centrepiece of Louise Simard's prize-winning novel *Le médaillon dérobé* (1996).

A new generation of young feminist/female writers emerged, often less involved in theoretical or dogmatic activities. Their novels mainly examined friendship, sexual identity, and the new relationship to be established between men and women. Pauline Harvey's philosophical novels—including *Encore une partie pour Berri* (1985), *Un homme est une valse* (1993), and *Les pèlerins* (1996)—were fine examples of novels that did so in a lyrical, dreamlike style. Scriptwriter José Fréchette's *Le père de Lisa* (1987), which discreetly examines the relationship between a little girl, her companionless father, and a woman she meets on a bus, remains one of the most beautiful novels of this period. Following her *Sans coeur et sans reproche* (1983), Monique PROULX burst on the literary scene with *Le sexe des étoiles* (1987), the strange story of a divorced male chemist who decides to become a woman, and his/her relationship with his/her daughter and his/her ex-wife.

2. EXPLICIT EXPRESSION OF SEXUALITY. Desire, pleasure, and relationships are never far removed from sexuality, and female and feminist writers soon ventured down this once taboo literary path. From radical feminism surfaced the erotic novel, or the erotic in the novel. The intent of the older generation of feminists was to create a new type of sexuality, purely 'feminine', where softness, tenderness, an absence of sexual power or struggle, and total communication would reign supreme. Though not exclusively so, a large number of these novels/short stories dealt with lesbian love (or the love of the woman within the man) as one of the solutions to patriarchy. Hélène Monette's first two novels (*Le double suspect*, 1980; *Petites violences*, 1982), and many works of Nicole Brossard, France Théoret, Anne-Marie ALONZO, and Madeleine GAGNON, among others, reflected this tendency.

However, it was *La Vie en rose*'s debate on the subject of pornography and its publication of Anne Dandurand's sadistic short story 'Histoire de Q' (July-August, 1985) that constituted the first major manifestation of eroticism/pornography on the new Quebec literary scene. Afterwards, as was the case in France and the USA, explicit sexuality and other boudoir activities became more and more present in feminist/feminine writings. In *Un homme est une valse* (1993), one of

Pauline Harvey's female characters even suggests that it is more interesting for a woman to be a woman than an intellectual. Sexuality is also omnipresent in Charlotte Boisjoli's *Jacinthe* (1990), Brigitte Caron's *La fin du siècle comme si vous y étiez* (1995), and in many of Anne Dandurand's books, including *Diables d'espoir...* (1988) and *Un coeur qui craque* (1990). Louise Anne Bouchard even examined love within an incestuous relationship in *La fureur* (1983). The most famous and popular erotic writer of the time remains Diane Boissonneault. Her humorous, carefree, fun-loving *Lilli Gulliver* series (*Paris*, 1990; *La Grèce*, 1991; *Bangkok*, 1993; *L'Australie sens dessous dessus*, 1996) succeeded in reaching a public no other Quebec writer had been able to reach.

Strangely enough, aside from Roger Fournier (*Le cercle des arènes*, 1982), Roger Des Roches (*La femme et la pornographie*, 1991; *Le rêve*, 1997), and a few other minor authors, male writers seemed much more reluctant to include, or even to address, explicit sexuality in their novels.

3. RETURN TO THE STORY. Already perceptible in such best-sellers as *La grosse femme d'à côté est enceinte* (1978) and *Thérèse et Pierrette à l'école des Saints-Anges* (1980) by Michel Tremblay, and *L'enfirouapé* (1974) by Yves BEAUCHEMIN, a return to a literature oriented towards the development of a more traditional dynamic marked this period, even if the authors were still very much aware of the formal discoveries of the previous generation. The novelist no longer wished to keep in touch with a readership perceived as a collectivity driven towards a common set of objectives. There was no more room for a 'parti pris' in the 1980s. The defeat of the *Oui* side in the 1980 Quebec referendum, which remained a major sore point for most writers of the time, and the decade's emphasis on the entrepreneur and individual success, all but provoked the disappearance of the engaged novel. It is thus understandable that French and European influences became less exclusive, and were replaced by trends and ideas from the much more capitalistic USA. To many writers French culture and language were no longer sufficient to explain the relationship between objects and their world. The 1980s became known as the 'greed generation', one in which material values and individualism were glorified. All this was called the new 'américanité'.

No work better than Jacques Poulin's *Volkswagen blues* (1984) expressed the painful split between the collectivist sixties and seventies and the individualistic eighties and nineties. In this novel, writer Jack Waterman, a man in his forties, leaves Quebec in search of a new identity. Accompanied by the Grande Sauterelle, a young Métis woman, he looks back at his life, and at the life of his people, through the traces left by his own brother Théo, who had disappeared more than fifteen years before. The search takes them through North America, where they discover that the famous heroes of history whom they thought they knew were not at all what or whom they seemed to be. The real heroes are the common people, a concept Waterman will come to fully understand in San Francisco, where his brother, an ex-member of the terrorist group FLQ, is finally found, paraplegic, and incapable of remembering a single word of that native tongue he had at one time so desperately tried to defend.

Volkswagen blues was the last major expression of the collective versus the individual self. Already Yves Beauchemin's *Le matou* (1981) had 'officially' inaugurated this new period in Quebec literature; in a stylized universe of realism and humour, he created Florent Boissonneault, an ambitious and slightly dishonest young man striving for material success and personal happiness. The same taste for action and individual fulfilment can be found in Beauchemin's two subsequent novels, *Juliette Pomerleau* (1989) and *Le second violon* (1996), and in the three main female characters of *Myriam première* (1987) by Francine Noël. Quebec readers finally had access to positive heroes and heroines whose main purpose was not to reflect, or be a reflection of, a colonized state, but rather to act, and to attempt to succeed in life.

4. THE BEST-SELLER SYNDROME. Greatly inspired by the style of famous, though very different, American authors such as John Irving and Danielle Steel, the novel's return to plot and to non-naturalist realism led the way to a more populist style of writing in Quebec. A number of very successful novels came to rule the literary scene of the period. Quite often they explored, in one way or another, the break-up of the couple and the family, a logical extension of an already popular topic from the 1960s onward. Many of the writers of these novels saw their literary careers boosted by television and cinema. These media were quick in adapting their novels to the screen, thus playing a major role in the creation of best-sellers, often before the novels' literary qualities or lack thereof had even been recognized. Yves Beauchemin's *Le matou* (1981) was turned into a film and a miniseries; scriptwriter Jacques SAVOIE was recognized as

a major author only after his novel *Les portes tournantes* (1984) was brought to the screen in 1988 by Francis Mankiewicz. Monique Proulx's *Le sexe des étoiles* (1987) also became a movie. Arlette Cousture, widely criticized for her poor writing style and her tear-jerker stories, nevertheless wrote the most commercially successful novels of the period: *Les filles de Caleb I* and *II* (1985), which sold over a million copies, and *Ces enfants venus d'ailleurs I* and *II* (1992, 1994), which reached sales of 400,000 by the end of 1996. These novels also became extremely popular television series. Chrystine Brouillet's numerous children's books, published by Éditions la Courte Échelle, became a Télé-Québec series in the mid-1990s. Other novels by more established writers were also eventually turned into television series or motion pictures—among them Victor-Lévy Beaulieu's *L'héritage (automne)* (1987) and *L'héritage (hiver)* (1991), Louis CARON's *Canard de bois* (1981), Anne Hébert's *Les fous de Bassan* (1982), and Claude Fournier's *Les tisserands du pouvoir* (1988).

Other writers, less embraced by the media, nevertheless met with success, thanks to the influence of the sentimental type of novel written by such celebrated American authors as Danielle Steele and Judith Krantz. Their works dealt with love, dreams, aspirations, ambitions, relationships, and personal or family dramas. While no movies or television series were made of her novels, Marie LABERGE produced well-received tragic psychological novels such as *Juillet* (1989), *Quelques adieux* (1993), *Le poids des ombres* (1996), and *Annabelle* (1996), while Francine Ouellette specialized in such lengthy sagas as *Au nom du père et du fils* (1984), *Le sorcier* (1985), *L'ansine* (1992), and *Les ailes du destin* (1992). Although less well known, Franco-Ontarian writer Jean-Claude Boult obtained some recognition with *Quadra I* and *II* (1989, 1995), in which he explored how a young criminal could become a loved member of a single-parent family, even after shooting one of the children during a hold-up, leaving the latter a paraplegic.

Popular, widely successful, more often than not written in a functional style in which action and suspense and/or drama dominate, most of these best-sellers were criticized because of their sentimentality, lack of psychological depth, abundance of stereotypes, and too-obvious use of *deus ex machina* solutions.

5. REBELLION AND THE NEW GENERATION. The media were also instrumental in producing their own literary celebrities, thanks to some strong personalities. Christian Mistral, the colourful anarchist writer whose works reflect the desperate feelings of Generation X, the lost generation, had some notoriety with such novels as *Vamp* (1988) and *Vautour* (1991). Dany LAFERRIÈRE, born in Haiti and first known as a member of Bleu Poudre, a group of satirists who poked fun at politicians and other public people, achieved celebrity with a 'scandalous' novel entitled *Comment faire l'amour à un nègre sans se fatiguer* (1985), which also became a movie a few years later and helped launch a successful writing career. Like Chrystine Brouillet and Marie Laberge, Mistral and Laferrière became popular fixtures on radio and television talk shows.

Other new young writers also expressed the disillusionment of their generation. In Mistral-like fashion, dominated by an overabundance of metaphors, Stéphane Bourguignon led one through the life of Julien, an unemployed 26-year-old who has just become single again, in *L'avaleur de sable* (1993). Louis Hamelin broke onto the scene with *La rage* (1989), a much-criticized exercise in style dealing with the generation of those in their twenties and thirties. This quest for a place in a brutal society continued in *Ces spectres agités* (1991). In *Love & rage* (1995), François Dupuis-Déris told the story of an ex-convict working in an bookstore specializing in erotic literature. Acadian writer Martin Pître also exemplified the boredom and disenchantment of the young generation in a small isolated village in New Brunswick in his *L'ennemi que je connais* (1996).

More established writers also followed this lead. Marie-Claire Blais, in *Visions d'Anna* (1982), expressed the confusion and helplessness of the younger generation in its struggle to find a place in society's prevalent atmosphere of decadence and violence. Réjean Ducharme's only two novels of this period also voiced this dark feeling of the soul: a nihilist attitude submerged the poverty-stricken, alienated characters of *Dévadé* (1990), a work in which the 'hero', Bottom, was shown to be a passive rebel at the domestic and sexual service of a young bourgeoise. The same irony and despair can be found in his *Va savoir* (1994); Noël Audet also scrutinized the lives of the poor and marginal of Montreal in his second novel, *La parade* (1984).

6. DYSFUNCTIONAL FAMILIES. The state of contemporary families was the novel's favourite topic in this period. If the 1960s and the 1970s saw the appearance of cracks in the framework of the traditional nuclear family, the 1980s and 1990s witnessed the break-up

of the couple and the establishment of dysfunctional families. Monique LA RUE addressed the problems of a high-school drop-out in a family where the father turns out to be gay and the mother alcoholic (*Les faux-fuyants*, 1982). Jacques Savoie's *Les portes tournantes* (1984), *Le récif du prince* (1986), *Le cirque bleu* (1995), and *Les ruelles de Caresso* (1997) are concerned with fragile and often less-than-conventional families. Claude Jasmin's *L'armoire de Pantagruel* (1982) also evolves around a family drama, as does Yves Beauchemin's *Second violon* (1996). In *Terre du roi Christian* (1989), Sylvain Trudel showed the difficulties and anxieties of a young boy trying to become an adolescent without the presence of a father. Raising a child without a husband was at the core of Élise Turcotte's well-received poetic novel *Le bruit des choses vivantes* (1991); and Louise Anne Bouchard, Pierre Gobeil, and Chrystine Brouillet studied paedophilia and incest respectively in *La fureur* (1993), *La mort de Marlon Brando* (1989), and *C'est pour mieux t'aimer mon enfant* (1996).

7. TIME AND SPACE. The newly accepted and discovered 'américanité', together with a diminished literary enthusiasm for nationalism, provided the occasion for Quebec writers to explore, or re-explore, concepts of space and time. Boundaries tended to disappear or to become meaningless. Quebec novelists opened up to the world. Jacques Poulin's *Volkswagen blues* reminded readers of the French and Native presence throughout North America. A Native influence was also omnipresent in many of Robert Lalonde's works (*Le dernier été des Indiens*, 1982; *Sept lacs plus au nord*, 1993). Michel Tremblay's *Des nouvelles d'Édouard* (1984) turned to the New York and Paris of the forties, while in *L'ours et le kangourou* (1986), Roch Carrier invited readers on a jeep trip through Australia. Sylvain Trudel opened up a world of fantasy in what turned out to be the revelation of the 1986 literary season, *Le souffle de l'Harmattan*, in which two children dig a tunnel leading to China and drive a car whose tires are filled with helium. Vietnam was the main interest of Pierre Gobeil's diary *Cent jours sur le Mékong* (1995), while Yvon RIVARD's *Le milieu du jour* (1996) took its readers through Italy, France, Greece, and other European countries.

Time also became a major concern of Quebec novelists—not in its pure form, as in the sixties and seventies, but as a way to relive a particular sociological aspect of history, or more simply as the subject of strictly fictional purposes. Francine Noël's *Maryse* (1983) is a realistic chronicle of the late sixties and early seventies. Yolande Villemaire, through the life of her fictional creation Vava Lafleur, explored the period between 1968 and 1986 in *Vava*. Michel Tremblay's 'Chroniques du Plateau Mont-Royal' series (1978-89) is situated in the forties and fifties, as are many of his subsequent novels, such as *La nuit des princes charmants* (1995) and *44 minutes, 44 secondes* (1997), where young homosexuals try to find a place of belonging in the still narrow-minded sixties. Much less based on realism were Roch Carrier's *De l'amour dans la ferraille* (1984), set in the Duplessis era. Other such novels included *Le bateau d'Hitler* (1988), in which Pierre Turgeon created a spy novel in a Nazi setting; Robert Lalonde's *Le diable en personne* (1989), a literary journey that fictionalized the life of a Métis from the end of the Second World War; and Jacques Savoie's *Les portes tournantes* (1984), which treats the era of ragtime music and the silent movies of the 1920s. Examples are endless of these returns to a partly fictional or sociological past.

Some novelists also chose to engage in writing more traditional historical novels. Aside from feminist writers, who made rewriting history a duty, Louis Caron led the way with his highly popular trilogy 'Les fils de la liberté' (1981, 1989, and 1990), whose three volumes move from the 1837 Rébellion des Patriotes to the FLQ crisis of 1970. In a finely documented novel, *Dernier blues pour octobre* (1990), Pierre Turgeon took his readers back to the 1970 October Crisis. Claude Fournier's *Les tisserands du pouvoir* (1988) relives the harsh working conditions of exiled French Canadians in the sweat shops of New England's nineteenth century; and Franco-Manitoban Ronald Lavallée's *Tchipayuk ou le chemin du loup* (1987) has as its focus the Métis struggle of the 1880s.

The history of Quebec (or French Canada) was not the only historical period that attracted novelists. The French Middle Ages also interested such new writers as Maryse Roux (*Azalaïs ou La vie courtoise*, 1995) and Rodrigue Lavoie (*Les sentiers de la volupté*, 1995). For his part, Georges-Hébert Germain rediscovered America through the eyes of a European explorer (*Christophe Colomb. Naufrage sur les côtes du paradis*, 1991). But perhaps no one exemplified this cultural opening towards the world and its history better than popular novelist Paul OHL. With remarkable erudition he took his readers to feudal Japan (*Katana*, 1987), to the time of the Vikings (*Drakkar*, 1989), to Peru and the conquistadores (*Le soleil noir*, 1991), and to China (*L'enfant dragon*, 1994). During this period, the return to a more traditional form of novel, combined with a diminished eagerness for engaged nationalist literature and a more universal artistic interest, also paved the way for new immigrant francophone writers.

See Janet Paterson, *Moments postmodernes dans le roman québécois* (1990); Jean Royer, *Romanciers québécois* (1990); Ben-Z. Shek, *French-Canadian & Québécois novels* (1991); Patricia Smart, *Writing in the father's house* (1991); Réjean Beaudoin, *Le roman québécois* (1991); Jacques Pelletier, *Le roman national. Néo-nationalisme et roman québécois contemporain* (1991); Réginald Martel, *Le premier lecteur. Chroniques du roman québécois 1968-1994* (1994); and Gérard Étienne, *La question raciale et raciste dans le roman québécois. Essai d'anthroposémiologie* (1995). JEAN LEVASSEUR

Nowlan, Alden (1933-83). Born in Windsor, Nova Scotia, he began working at fifteen in lumbermills and on farms. He completed his formal education at eighteen and left Nova Scotia for New Brunswick, where he became editor of the *Hartland Observer* and night-news editor of the *Saint John Telegraph-Journal*. Beginning to publish poetry and short stories in the mid-1950s, he was honoured with a Guggenheim Fellowship, a Governor General's Award (for *Bread, wine and salt*, 1967), and a Doctor of Letters from the University of New Brunswick. From 1969 he was writer-in-residence at the University of New Brunswick.

From the publication of Nowlan's first collection of verse, *The rose and the Puritan* (1958), his poetry was consistent in style and theme. The bulk of his poems are short anecdotal lyrics, conversational in tone and frequently directed towards some moral perception. He wrote chiefly about small-town New Brunswick, the constricted lives of its inhabitants, and the complexity of his own role as its compassionately observing poet—indicated by the title of his selected poems, *Playing the Jesus game* (1970); like Christ, Nowlan found that he must not only pity and forgive his fellow humans, but share personally their limitations and tragedies. Nowlan's emphasis on the essential innocence and helplessness of his variously benighted characters—escapist, credulous, treacherous, adulterous, murderous, insane—gives to many of his poems a suggestion of sentimentality that the poet must work to dispel through realistic imagery and colloquial dialogue. Nowlan's other collections of poetry are *A darkness in the earth* (1959), *Under the ice* (1960), *Wind in a rocky country* (1961), *The things which are* (1962), *The mysterious naked man* (1969), *Between tears and laughter* (1971), *I'm a stranger here myself* (1974), *Smoked glass* (1977), and *I might not tell everybody this* (1982).

In his later years Nowlan began writing in a number of other genres. His autobiographical novel *Various persons named Kevin O'Brien* (1973), recounts his childhood struggle against poverty in an ambitious, though not entirely successful, juxtaposition of adult and child viewpoints. The collection of short stories *Miracle at Indian River* (1968)—technically less interesting than the novel—offers close-up views of the economically oppressed characters who populate much of his poetry. In the 1970s Nowlan collaborated with Walter Learning to write three stage plays: *Frankenstein* (1976), *The incredible murder of Cardinal Tosca* (1978), and *The dollar woman* (1981). Nowlan also wrote a travel book, *Campobello, the outer island* (1975), and collected twenty-seven of his magazine articles in *Double exposure* (1978). The following titles were published posthumously: *Alden Nowlan, early poems* (1983); *Will ye let the mummers in?* (stories, 1984); *An exchange of gifts: poems new and selected* edited by Robert GIBBS (1985); *The wanton troopers* (novel, 1988); *The best of Alden Nowlan* (1993) edited by Allison Mitcham; and *Alden Nowlan: selected poems* (1995) edited by Patrick LANE and Lorna CROZIER. *Nine Micmac legends*, children's stories, was published in 1983.

See Michael Oliver, *Poet's progress: the development of Alden Nowlan's poetry* (1978), and Fred COGSWELL, 'Alden Nowlan as regional atavist', *Studies in Canadian literature* 2 (1986).

See also POETRY IN ENGLISH 1950 TO 1982: 2. FRANK DAVEY

Oatley, Keith. See NOVELS IN ENGLISH 1983 TO 1996: OTHER NOVELS 2(b).

Oberon Press. One of the leading literary publishers in Canada, Oberon is a family company run by Michael Macklem and his son Nicholas, and was founded in 1966. It has a backlist of some 525 titles—all designed and many set in hot metal in house. It specializes in fiction and poetry, though it also publishes history, biography, and criticism. Its best-selling title is *Where to eat in Canada* by Anne Hardy, which has been published annually since 1971. Among the writers of fiction on its list are Marie-Claire BLAIS, George BOWERING, Margaret GIBSON, Isabel HUGGAN, W.P. KINSELLA, John METCALF, David Adams RICHARDS, Leon ROOKE, Audrey THOMAS, and W.D. VALGARDSON. Among the poets are Elizabeth BREWSTER, R.G. EVERSON, David HELWIG, Gwendolyn MacEWEN, Tom MARSHALL, bp NICHOL, Raymond SOUSTER, and Bronwen WALLACE. WILLIAM TOYE

Ocean to ocean (London, 1873). This enduring travel classic, subtitled *Sandford Fleming's expedition through Canada in 1872*, was written by George Monro Grant (1835-1902), who was president of Queen's University, Kingston, from 1877 until his death. He acted as secretary to Sandford Fleming, chief engineer of the Canadian Pacific Railway—and one of Grant's parishioners at St Matthew's Presbyterian Church, Halifax—when Fleming made an exploratory journey to the Pacific Ocean in search of a route. Grant's book ('simply a Diary written as we journeyed') is a record of the expedition's progress by train, steamer, canoe, wagon, and horseback from Halifax to Victoria between 1 July and 11 Oct. 1872. It presents memorable descriptions of the landscape, the weather in different regions, various modes of travel, and personalities met en route; carefully records local place-names and idioms; presents and analyses the Native and Métis cultures; and constantly assesses the land's suitability for settlement. The members of the expedition themselves become vivid characters in a narrative that mingles humorous incidents with accounts of the unavoidable hardships of travel. Grant's delight in what he encounters is infectious, and his personal enthusiasms (including several rhapsodic comments about the merits of pemmican) make the book appealing.

Two volumes of the actual diary are among the Grant papers in the National Archives of Canada, and their records of the expedition often differ from the published version. It is apparent that Grant revised and expanded rough notes and structured his materials with some care for the purpose of defending both the proposed transcontinental railroad—which would firmly unite Canada, make possible the settlement of the West, and keep the Americans at bay—and the expansionist aspirations of English-speaking Canada. The Prairie West is seen as a potential garden, with the railroad as the means of bringing in settlers to make it bloom. Though treated with sympathy by Grant, the Métis and Native cultures stand in the way of necessary 'progress' and will need to be absorbed or controlled, paternalistically, by the new order. The new West, as Grant envisions it, will be in effect a colony of Ontario, a hinterland feeding the manufacturing metropolis of the East. Although *Ocean to ocean* did not save the Macdonald government from defeat in 1873, it was a defence of the prime minister's policies; perhaps not coincidentally, a second edition (Toronto, 1879) appeared soon after Macdonald's return to power.

There is a facsimile reprint (1967) of the second edition, with an introduction by L.H. Thomas. For a discussion of Grant's revisions and intentions, see David Jackel's article in *CANADIAN LITERATURE* 81 (Summer 1979). The larger context is well examined by Doug Owram in *Promise of Eden: the Canadian expansionist movement and the idea of the West, 1856-1900* (1980). DAVID JACKEL

Odell, Jonathan (1737-1818). Born in Newark, New Jersey, he was educated at the College of New Jersey (now Princeton University), graduating in 1759 with an M.A. in medicine. After serving as a surgeon in the British army in the West Indies, he went to London in 1763 to prepare himself for the Church of England ministry and was ordained in 1767; he was parish priest at St Mary's Church, Burlington, N.J., until Dec. 1776. His loyalist political sympathies led to his being forced to flee behind British lines to New York, where he was regimental chaplain, secretary to the chief British administrator, and a key intermediary in the espionage activities of Benedict Arnold and John André.

After the evacuation of New York in 1783 he lived in England for a year before being appointed secretary to the newly formed Province of New Brunswick. He arrived there in Nov. 1784 and served as provincial secretary, an influential political post, until 1812, at which time the position was passed on to his son. He died in Fredericton.

Odell was the most skilled and trenchant of the loyalist satirists. His satiric activity reached its peak in 1779-80 with the publication of four major verse satires: 'The word of Congress' (1779), 'The congratulation, a poem' (1779), 'The feu de joie, a poem' (1779), and *The American times* (1780), all written in heroic couplets. The first three were published in a New York newspaper; *The American times* was issued as a pamphlet in both London and New York. Perhaps the finest of the loyalist satires, it consists mainly of a series of biting satiric portraits of the chief participants in the rebel cause, culminating in an attack on personified Democracy. Odell's poetic activity declined after he moved to New Brunswick. There is an interesting series of poems dealing with the ethics of Thomas Carleton's absentee governing of New Brunswick (Carleton left in 1803 never to return, although he remained governor until 1817) and a small group of satiric poems inspired by the War of 1812. The most ambitious of these, 'The agonizing dilemma' (1812), is an extended travesty of the American general's report on his defeat at Queenston Heights.

In addition to poetry, Odell also produced *An essay on the elements, accents, and prosody of the English language* (London, 1805; rpr. New York, 1969).

Odell's satires were collected by Winthrop Sargent in *The loyal verses of Joseph Stansbury and Doctor Jonathan Odell* (Albany, 1860). See also M.C. Tyler, *The literary history of the American Revolution* (New York, 1897), and B.I. Granger, *Political satire in the American Revolution* (1960). TOM VINCENT

O'Flaherty, Patrick. See CRITICISM IN ENGLISH: 5(g).

Ogden, Peter Skene. See EXPLORATION LITERATURE IN ENGLISH: 2.

'O God! O Montreal!' (1874)—the refrain from 'A psalm of Montreal' by the English writer (and sometime painter) Samuel Butler (1835-1902). This poem was circulated privately in England (to Matthew Arnold, among others) and was published in *The Spectator* on 18 May 1878. Butler composed it in 1875 while he was in Canada for several months overseeing a foundering business in which he had investments. His view of Montreal as provincial was strengthened when, on a visit to the Museum of Natural History, he found a copy of the Discobolus relegated to a storeroom, among stuffed animals. The curator in the poem says, 'The Discobolus is put there because he is vulgar,/He has neither vest nor pants with which to cover his limbs.'

There is a resemblance between 'A psalm of Montreal' and Butler's painting 'Mr. Heatherley's holiday', which hangs in the Tate Gallery. It shows Mr Heatherley, whose art school Butler attended, repairing a human skeleton amid pots and vases, the Discobolus, and other statuary. VINCENT SHARMAN

O'Grady, Standish (*fl.* 1793-1841). A native of Ireland and a graduate of Trinity College, Dublin, he became a Church of Ireland minister and was forced to emigrate in 1836, when he was unable to collect his tithes. He settled on a farm on the south bank of the St Lawrence River near Sorel. His one printed work, a long narrative poem in rhymed couplets, was self-published, dated 1841, and entitled *The emigrant: a poem in four cantos* (printed in Montreal by John Lovell). Despite the title, the work has only one canto—about 2,100 lines on 117 pages—followed by 61 pages of notes that are frequently long anecdotal diversions with incidental verse incorporated; thirteen 'Miscellaneous poems' occupy an additional 12 pages—one of these, 'Old Nick in Sorel', is reprinted in A.J.M. SMITH's *The book of Canadian poetry* (3rd ed., 1957).

As a would-be man of letters O'Grady provides early evidence of how the lack of a congenial cultural climate limited pioneer literary effort. As a Protestant, clergyman, and non-francophone he was triply displaced. Inexperienced at farming, he lived at Sorel among farmers who were experienced, French-speaking, and Catholic. His literary environment was equally unpromising. He dedicated his poem to 'Nobody', as no patron had offered himself 'on this vast portion of the globe to which myself and my Muse are perfect strangers'.

O'Grady's use of heroic couplets, mostly competent, allows him to express his disillusionment in epigrams, hyperbole, and some whimsy:

With vile mosquitoes, lord deliver us,
Whose stings could BLISTER A RHINOCEROS.

The received nature of the verse-form is nonetheless an indication of the pervasive effect of his cultural displacement; his dependence upon conventional and remote rhetoric reveals his distance from the immediate Canadian context. To express his opinion of specific local and Canadian matters, O'Grady resorted to prose. For example, the couplet

Revolving years maternal care may mock
And spurn alike the monument of Brock

is expanded in this note: 'The monument of General Brock lies at present shamefully injured by the daring hands of the disloyal; a contribution has been levied to erect a new one worthy of his memory.'

This reticence in O'Grady's poetry about things Canadian, and the frequent references to things Irish, testify to his continuing and limiting sense of displacement. Though his retrospection about life in Erin was also gloomy, O'Grady warned Irish, Scots, and Britons to 'best engage your husbandry at home' rather than in a wintry country 'where nature seems one *universal blank*.' Along with winter's discomforts, he expressed dislike for French-Canadian law, education, and religious practice. Nonetheless he felt sure that eventually 'this expanded and noble continent will no doubt furnish fit matter for the Muse.'

GERALD NOONAN

O'Hagan, Howard (1902-82). He has been called 'the writer Canadian literature forgot'. Born in Lethbridge, Alberta, he received a degree in law from McGill University in 1928 and while in Montreal began a long friendship with Stephen LEACOCK and A.J.M. SMITH. After practising law without having been called to the bar, he became a tour guide in Jasper National Park. He then travelled to Australia, where he began to write short stories; he returned to Montreal, where Leacock helped him get a job with the Canadian Pacific Railway, recruiting farm labourers from England; he later worked in New York and Jasper, Alberta, as a publicist for the Canadian National Railways, and in Buenos Aires for the Argentine Central Railway. While living in San Francisco he began the series of notes about Mounties, trappers, Natives, guides, mountain men, and railway workers that were used for his first novel, *Tay John* (1939), which he completed on an island in Howe Sound, on the coast of British Columbia. During the 1950s O'Hagan was an occasional journalist for Victoria newspapers and also took odd jobs on the waterfront, in Gyproc mills, and on survey crews. Between 1963 and 1974 he and his wife lived in Sicily, until he decided to settle in Victoria, B.C., where he lived in poor health and semi-retirement while continuing to write. At the request of Margaret LAURENCE, George WOODCOCK, and Ken MITCHELL, O'Hagan was made an honorary member of the WRITER'S UNION OF CANADA in 1979; in 1982 he received an honorary degree from McGill University.

O'Hagan's writings are dominated by the Rocky Mountains. As he continued to write, even though he suffered from the lack of a supportive community, he became known as the mountain man of Canadian letters, and one of the best prose stylists of western Canada. He had a strong influence on Rudy WIEBE, Robert HARLOW, Jack HODGINS, Don GUTTERIDGE, and Michael ONDAATJE, who wrote the first critical study of O'Hagan, which appeared in *CANADIAN LITERATURE* 61 (Summer 1974).

Tay John—a remarkable novel that was possibly influenced by O'Hagan's reading of Joseph Conrad—is about a halfbreed Native, welcomed as the Messiah, who will lead his people across the Rocky Mountains to be reunited with the people of the B.C. coast. Born in his mother's grave, Tay John disappears into the earth with the body of a pregnant woman—O'Hagan touches on mythology and magic in this novel. A blend of fact, fiction, and historical re-creation, *Tay John* was reviewed favourably when it was published in England, but received little publicity because of the war. It was reprinted in the 1960s but remained relatively unknown until 1974, when it was reissued in the NEW CANADIAN LIBRARY; this edition now has an Afterword by Michael Ondaatje.

During the 1950s O'Hagan wrote wilderness articles for adventure magazines, some of which were collected in *Wilderness men* (1958). Although he referred to them as potboilers, they included incisive stories about such wilderness figures as Grey Owl (Archie BELANEY), Albert Johnson, the 'mad trapper of Rat River', and 'Almighty Voice'. O'Hagan also wrote excellent short stories that were widely published. Some were broadcast on CBC Radio, and Issue 9 of *The TAMARACK REVIEW* (1958) contained 'Trees are lonely company', which was awarded the President's Medal of the University of Western Ontario. The best of these stories were collected as *The woman who got on at Jasper station* (1963; rpr. 1978). This and *Wilderness men* appeared together as *Trees are lonely company* (1993). Another novel, *The school marm tree* (1983), was first published in *event: a journal of the arts*, vol. 5/3 (1976), along with an interview and critical commentary. *Coyote's song* (1983), edited by Gary GEDDES and published as a memorial, is a collection of essays, and includes O'Hagan's word-portrait of Leacock. *Silence made visible: Howard O'Hagan and Tay John* (1992), edited by Margery Fee, includes an essay by W.J. Keith, a memoir, and O'Hagan's spoofs of Arts Club meetings.

GEOFF HANCOCK

Ohl, Paul (b. 1940). Born in Strasbourg, France, he immigrated to Canada in 1951, completing his secondary schooling in Beloeil, Quebec. After spending two years at the Collège militaire de Saint-Jean (1957-9), and time at the Officers' Training School, Camp Borden, Ontario, he received his commission in 1960 and subsequently spent time as an officer and parachutist in the Royal 22nd Regiment. After leaving the army, he studied social sciences at the Université du Montréal (1963-4), and in 1965 joined the Quebec civil service, where he occupied various positions, studied public administration at the Université du Québec à Montréal (1972-3), and was appointed Director General of the High Commission for Youth, taking on responsibilities as well for the promotion of sports in the province.

Ohl's athletic skills (karate, speed skating, boxing) and his concerns about the rights of athletes soon led to numerous articles in the major Quebec newspapers and his first book, *Les arts martiaux: l'héritage des Samourai* (1975). *Les gladiateurs de l'Amérique* (1977), *La guerre olympique* (1977), and *Le dieu sauvage* (1980) attracted an international readership. His first novel, *Knockout Inc.* (1979), documented in fictional form the systemic slavery inflicted upon boxers; a well-documented essay, *La machine à tuer* (1981), enlarged on this theme, condemning commercial boxing as 'organized murder'. An angry biography, *Le dieu sauvage* (1980), led to the rehabilitation of the reputation of the Amerinidian athlete Jim Thorpe.

Ohl subsequently turned his attention to ancient civilizations. In the first of four historical novels, *Katana. Le roman du Japon* (1987), his authentic fictional recreation of seventeenth-century Japan reflects his personal interest in the martial arts and the science of war, as well as his appreciation of the philosophical values of the feudal Shogunate. In *Drakkar. Le roman des Vikings* (1989), he skilfully juxtaposes the Christian beliefs of medieval Europe with those of pagan Scandinavia in the year 1000; it was inspired by the film *The Vikings* (1958), starring Kirk Douglas, which he had seen as a child. In *Soleil noir. Le roman de la Conquête* (1991), Ohl focuses on sixteenth-century Bolivia and Peru as discovered through the eyes of Vadim Herzog, who in 1989 visited Bolivia to research the capture of the last Inca in 1532, only to find horrendous exploitation at the Potosi mine in the Andes and a revolutionary priest who gradually reveals to him the magnificent culture and beliefs of his ancestors, the Incas, who had been brutally annihilated by the Spanish Conquest. Ohl's *L'enfant dragon* (1994) is set in the 1920s in Canton, China, where a Scottish paleontologist and his Canadian wife, in defending Chinese culture, criticize Western influences and the British occupation. In all his novels Ohl's admiration of, and sensitivity to, other cultures, ancient and modern, is balanced by powerful descriptions, well-constructed plots, and an elegant use of language. In the latter two, his anger at the exploitation and suffering of earlier and present generations tends to intrude. But his research of his topic, always complemented by a lengthy stay in the geographical setting of his novel and his sense of the sweep of history, has renewed the historical novel in Quebec, providing a North American francophone parallel to Clavell and Michener.

RAMON HATHORN

Oikawa, Mona. See LESBIAN LITERATURE.

Oliva, Peter. See NOVELS IN ENGLISH 1983 TO 1996: OTHER NOVELS 1(a).

Ollivier, Émile (b. 1940). Born in Port-au-Prince, Haiti, he has lived in Montreal since 1965 and teaches at the Université de Montréal. He has written five novels that treat exile and alienation. *Paysages de l'aveugle* (1977) deals largely with the quest for inner social equilibrium of three characters who are faced with the cultural disparities between Haitian folklore and Canadian routine, and inaugurate a form of allegory to signify their presence in Montreal. This novel contains some psychological images of migration and exile that are a paradigm of Ollivier's literary works. *Mère-Solitude* (Paris, 1989)—translated by David Lobdell as *Mother Solitude* (1989)—portrays the search for past and future (in a fictional Caribbean city), contrasted with the social present. The success of this novel lies in the characters' retracing the history of Haiti, and the collective consciousness of Haitian people. In *La discorde à cent voix* (Paris, 1986), *Passages* (Paris, 1991), and *Les urnes scellés* (Paris, 1995), Ollivier explores the back-and-forth movement between their native island and the land to which his characters migrate, and the absence of a history of Haitian social classes.

BERNARD DELPÊCHE

Ondaatje, Michael (b. 1943). Born in Ceylon (now Sri Lanka), he joined his mother in England in 1954 and moved to Canada in 1962. After taking his B.A. at the University of Toronto and his M.A. at Queen's University, Kingston, Ontario, he taught at the University of Western Ontario (1967-70) before joining the Department of English at Glendon College, York University, Toronto, in 1971.

Ondaatje has published six books of poetry—*The dainty monsters* (1967), *The man with seven toes* (1969), *Rat jelly* (1973), *There's a trick with a knife I'm learning to do: poems 1963-1978* (1979), *Secular love* (1984), *The cinnamon peeler* (1992)—and two chapbooks, *Elimination dance* (1980) and *Tin roof* (1982); a collage of poetry and prose, *The collected works of Billy the Kid* (1970); an autobiographical work, *Running in the family* (1982; NCL, with an Afterword by Nicole BROSSARD) combining verse and prose; and three novels—*Coming through slaughter* (1976), *In the skin of a lion* (1987), and *The ENGLISH PATIENT* (1992). Three of these works—*Billy the Kid*, *The man with seven toes*, and *Coming through slaughter*—have been performed as plays, while *The English patient* has been filmed. He has received Governor General's Awards for *Billy the Kid*, *There's a trick with a knife*, and *The English patient*, which was also a co-winner of the Booker Prize. It is worth noting that *In the skin of a lion* finished in a tie with works by Nadine Gordimer and Toni Morrison for the Ritz-Hemingway prize; because the judges could not decide among the three, the prize was not awarded. Ondaatje has also received Germany's Nelly Sachs Prize. Several of his books have been translated.

With the exception of *In the skin of a lion*, Ondaatje's work is among the least obviously Canadian, as far as subject-matter, vision, and verbal texture are concerned. His books include as central characters a Victorian Englishwoman and convict (*The man with seven toes*), a nineteenth-century American outlaw (*Billy the Kid*), a New Orleans jazz musician of the turn of the century (*Coming through slaughter*), and a Hindu bomb-disposal expert and a Hungarian flier (*The English patient*). His style, owing almost nothing to an indigenous Canadian tradition, shows the influence of Wallace Stevens and of contemporary cinema artists, especially Louis Malle, Alfred Hitchcock, and Sergio Leone. His vision has been steadily directed at compelling the reader, by means of unusual settings and unexpected thematic, narrative, and stylistic shifts, to see reality as surreal, inchoate, and dynamic. His poetic universe is filled with suicidal heroes and trumpet players, mythic dogs, tortured people, gorillas, dragons, poetic spiders, and imploding stars. Ondaatje's extraordinary settings, characters, and narratives function as a metaphoric or symbolic shorthand leading the reader to perceive reality anew. The central tension in his work, between self and reality, or between two aspects of self, results in a fascination with borders—between rationality and unconsciousness ('Dragons', 'White dwarfs', 'Letters and other worlds'), peace and violence ('The time around scars', *The man with seven toes*), or reality and art ('Light', 'Spider blues', *Coming through slaughter*). The early interest in the relationship between legend and 'truth' or reality develops in *In the skin of a lion* and *The English patient* into a questioning of history and ideologies: the former novel focuses on history's lacunae and deliberate omissions, while the latter implicitly and ambiguously engages issues of nationalism and postcolonialism.

With his lyric poetry, Odaatje has written a body of work as impressive as any among the poets of his generation. *Rat jelly* collects the best of the early poems, many of which are self-reflexive meditations on creativity: 'Letters and other worlds', 'King Kong meets Wallace Stevens', 'Spider blues', '"The gate in his head"', 'Burning hills', and 'White dwarfs', all written between 1967 and 1973. These lyrics—for the most part in the first person—are his most self-reflexive poems; whatever their surface or narrative concerns, they are ultimately about poetry, and constitute Ondaatje's most explicit and complex exploration of the relationship between life and art. Ondaatje's most ambitious work in verse, and also his most personal, is *Secular love* (1984), a book-length sequence made up of four chronologically arranged sections telling the story of the break-up of a marriage, the poet's own near-breakdown, and, finally, after what one section calls 'Rock bottom', his recovery and return through the love of another woman. The book should be read as a poetic journal rather than as a collection of discrete lyrics. Some of the poems, like the lovingly nuanced and mutedly elegiac 'To a sad daughter', can be read by themselves, yet the volume is so closely organized with so much of the overall emotional and artistic effect depending on repetitions and echoes of sound, image, situation, and emotion that the poems often seem more like the chapters of a narrative than parts of a collection.

Billy the Kid uses a temporally discontinuous narrative with multiple viewpoints, and includes lyrics, photographs, prose passages, interviews, a play, and deliberately blank pages. The events are consistently ambiguous; and the central characters, Billy and Pat Garrett—drawn from history, legend, and fiction, and given a touch of autobiography—are both paradoxes. In Ondaatje's slightly romanticized narrative, Billy, certainly a killer, is described by Sallie Chisum as 'the pink of politeness/and as courteous a little gentleman/as I ever met'; while Pat Garrett, the sheriff, is a 'sane assassin' whose compulsive sanity and order bear traces of insanity.

Coming through slaughter fictionalizes the life of Charles 'Buddy' Bolden (1876-1931), a legendary jazz cornetist who, like Billy the Kid, lived 'away from recorded history'. Ondaatje admires Bolden because for him art and life became almost indistinguishable. Bolden's sensibility is so compulsively responsive to the shifts and nuances of the lived moment that his self disappears into his art and, during the novel's climactic parade through Storyville, he loses his sanity. The book's most disturbing suggestion is that in certain kinds of creativity, and in certain artists, 'making and destroying' are of necessity almost co-extensive: the tensions within them can be resolved only by being transmuted into art or madness.

A visit to Sri Lanka to recapture the family past gave rise to *Running in the family*, a work that is ostensibly autobiographical, described in an authorial note as 'not a history but a portrait or "gesture"'. The various self-contained but interrelated sketches, stories, poems, and photographs offer a compassionate fictionalized portrait of Ondaatje's family's past in Sri Lanka. By the book's end the family exists for the reader somewhere between reality and legend, and we recognize that Ondaatje has quietly erased the boundary between autobiography and fiction.

In the skin of a lion offers a similar and equally challenging blurring. Ondaatje's multi-textured and intricately structured semi-historical novel about Toronto in the 1920s, though ostensibly focused on a young man named Patrick Lewis, presents a cross-section of Toronto life, interweaving scenes dealing with immigrant workers building the Bloor Street viaduct, and digging a two-mile tunnel to bring water into a filtration plant, with the widely publicized search for a missing business tycoon named Ambrose Small. Based on Ondaatje's research in Toronto's archives, the book nevertheless subsumes the historical facts and names into a complex and challenging fictional vision of individuals in a rapidly changing society. *In the skin of a lion* marks a turn in Ondaatje's fiction towards social and political concerns: though it is by no means a novel of ideas, it does reveal a degree of social engagement only hinted at in the earlier work, Two of the characters, the thief Caravaggio and Patrick's daughter Hana, appear again in *The English patient*, which established Ondaatje's international reputation by winning the Booker Prize. The continuities between it and *In the skin of a lion* are immediately obvious: a prose style that is often memorably metaphoric and lyrical; the mixing of fact and fiction; the discontinuous narrative; the structuring of the story around a central mystery; and the reappearance of characters from the earlier novel in its successor. *The English patient* is set in a Tuscan villa during the last days of the Second World War, and involves four people brought together by chance: a young Canadian nurse, a Canadian soldier, an Indian soldier in the British Army who is a bomb-disposal expert, and the mysterious English patient of the title, injured and burned in an airplane crash. And though parts of the novel are set in England, Egypt, the Sahara and Italy, it is ultimately less about geography and history than about the complex personal relationships of the main characters.

Ondaatje has also published a book of criticism, *Leonard Cohen* (1970), and edited several anthologies, including *Personal fictions* (1977), stories by MUNRO, WIEBE, THOMAS and BLAISE; *The long poem anthology* (1979); and *From ink lake* (1990), an anthology of Canadian short fiction. He has also made four films —including one on bp NICHOL (*The sons of Captain Poetry*)—and was involved for over twenty years as an editor with COACH HOUSE PRESS. Among Ondaatje's essays, 'O'Hagan's rough-edged chronicle', in *CANADIAN LITERATURE* (Summer 1974), is, like the book on Cohen, an implicitly informative commentary on his own work. Also of interest is his essay on Gabriel Garciá Marquéz, an important influence on *Running in the family*, in *Figures in a ground* (1978), edited by David Jackel and Diane Bessai.

Essays on Ondaatje's work have been collected in *DESCANT* (Fall, 1982), *Spider blues* (1985), edited by Sam Solecki, and the *Essays on Canadian Writing* Ondaatje issue (Summer 1994). There are informative interviews with Ondaatje in *Rune* (Spring 1975), *Spider blues*, and *Other solitudes: Canadian multicultural fictions* (1990), edited by Linda HUTCHEON and Marion Richmond. Dennis LEE's *Savage fields* (1977) includes a monograph on *Billy the Kid*; Ed Jewinski's *Michael Ondaatje: express yourself beautifully* (1994) is a useful and sensitive short biography; Nell Waldman's *Michael Ondaatje*

(1982) and Douglas BARBOUR's *Michael Ondaatje* (1993) offer useful and comprehensive overviews of the work and career.

See also NOVELS IN ENGLISH 1960 TO 1982: 4 and POETRY IN ENGLISH 1950 TO 1982: 2.

SAM SOLECKI

Ontario, Writing in. To 1983. As the most heavily populated part of English Canada, and with a capital, Toronto, that is the centre of English-language publishing, Ontario has experienced a great deal of literary activity since the early nineteenth century. The survey that follows is an attempt to bring together some of the best-known authors, books, and literary periodicals. They, and other aspects of writing activity in the province—including early writings—are also discussed elsewhere in the *Companion*, not only in author-entries but in other surveys: DRAMA, EXPLORATION LITERATURE, LITERARY MAGAZINES, NOVELS, PIONEER MEMOIRS, POETRY, SHORT STORIES, and TRAVEL LITERATURE.

1. EARLY WRITINGS. Inaugurated by the Jesuits' narratives of their mission to the Hurons in the *JESUIT RELATIONS*, 1635-50, and continued through the exploration period by Alexander Henry's *Travels and adventures in Canada and the Indian territories between the years 1760 and 1776* (New York, 1809), writing in Ontario first flowered in the period of settlement. The diary for the years 1791-6 of Elizabeth Simcoe, wife of the first lieutenant-governor of Upper Canada—published complete as *Mrs. Simcoe's diary* (1965) edited by Mary Quayle Innis—describes the early days of York (Toronto). A few decades later, in *Winter studies and summer rambles in Canada* (London, 1838), a nineteenth-century writer and art critic, Anna Jameson, portrayed life in Toronto's by then close-quartered colonial society, set against the awesome vastness and variety of the new land. Among pioneer settlers, Samuel Strickland and his sisters Susanna MOODIE and Catharine Parr TRAILL—members of a prolific English writing family—recorded their experiences with an eye to English readership. Strickland's *Twenty-seven years in Canada West; or, The experiences of an early settler* (London, 1853), and Traill's *The BACKWOODS OF CANADA; being letters from the wife of an emigrant officer; illustrative of the domestic economy of British America* (London, 1836) and *The female emigrant's guide, and hints on Canadian housekeeping* (Toronto, 1854) carried sensible and optimistic advice for immigrants. Moodie's compelling combination of dismay at her surroundings, lively involvement with her new life, and real writing talent have made her *ROUGHING IT IN THE BUSH; or, Forest life in Canada* (London, 1852) an enduring nineteenth-century Canadian classic. William 'Tiger' Dunlop of Goderich—a medical doctor, an adventuring Scot, and the most entertainingly eccentric of Ontario's writing settlers—left an idiosyncratic, humorous, and quite unstatistical mark with his *Statistical sketches of Upper Canada, for the use of emigrants* (London, 1832).

2. FICTION. John RICHARDSON's Gothic and demonic *WACOUSTA; or, The prophecy fulfilled: a tale of the late American war* (Edinburgh, 1832) began a tradition of historical romances that includes William KIRBY's *The GOLDEN DOG (Le chien d'or); A romance of old Quebec* (New York, 1877) and Franklin Davey McDowell's *The Champlain road* (1939). Among John GALT's many novels is *Bogle Corbet; or, The emigrants* (London, 1831), a comic treatment of the immigrant theme arising out of Galt's experience as agent for the Canada Company. In *Canadian Crusoes: a tale of the Rice Lake plains* (London, 1852), a story of four lost children, Catharine Parr Traill wrote the first children's book with an Ontario setting.

The fiction of settlement, almost always written as romance, has been one of the most vital and enduring strands in Ontario writing. In *The man from Glengarry: a tale of the Ottawa* (1901) and *GLENGARRY SCHOOL DAYS: a story of early days in Glengarry* (1902), Charles W. GORDON ('Ralph Connor') celebrated the strength and piety of the pioneering Scots of the Ottawa Valley, as did Mary Esther MacGREGOR ('Marian Keith') in *Duncan Polite; the watchman of Glenoro* (1905) and *'Lizbeth of the dale* (1910). Four decades later Grace Campbell harked back to Glengarry's early days in her *Thornapple tree* (1942) and *The higher hill* (1944). *The yellow briar; a story of the Irish in the Canadian countryside* (1933) was written by Toronto lawyer John MITCHELL but published under the pseudonym 'Patrick Slater', the name of the narrator. Mitchell made a comic hero of 'Paddy', who tells a warm and charming story of pioneering and settlement in the Caledon region of southern Ontario. Similarly, Mabel Dunham's *The trail of the Conestoga* (1924) and Luella Creighton's *High bright buggy wheels* (1951) depicted Mennonite settlement in southern Ontario.

The small town, treated with affectionate irony, provides an important subject area of Ontario fiction, from Sara Jeannette DUNCAN's Elgin (Brantford) in *The imperialist* (1904); through Stephen LEACOCK's Mariposa (Orillia) in *SUNSHINE SKETCHES OF A LITTLE TOWN* (1912); to Robertson DAVIES' Salterton

(Kingston) in *Tempest-tost* (1951), *Leaven of malice* (1954), *A mixture of frailties* (1958), and his Deptford *in FIFTH BUSINESS* (1970), *The manticore* (1972), and *World of wonders* (1975); to Alice MUNRO's Jubilee (Wingham) in *Dance of the happy shades* (1968), a collection of short stories, and her other fiction. *White narcissus* (1929), Raymond KNISTER's probing of the repressions and distortions of Ontario rural life, anticipated works like Matt COHEN's *The disinherited* (1974) and *The sweet second summer of Kitty Malone* (1979), which take place on the confining ancestral farmland of south-eastern Ontario.

Toronto—though it is never named—is the setting of Morley CALLAGHAN's novels *Strange fugitive* (1928), *It's never over* (1930), *A broken journey* (1932), *Such is my beloved* (1934), *They shall inherit the earth* (1935), and *MORE JOY IN HEAVEN* (1937), and of many of his short stories. Hugh GARNER also set much of his fiction in Toronto. A former working-class area of the city is referred to in the titles of his well-known *Cabbagetown* (1950; 1968), a novel about Toronto in the thirties, and of Juan BUTLER's *Cabbagetown diary: a documentary* (1970). And the city is celebrated in Hugh HOOD's documentary fantasy The New Age, of which ten of the projected twelve novels had been published by 1996, beginning with *The swing in the garden* (1975). A fascination with documentary and history, so visible in Hood's fiction, is also an important feature of Timothy FINDLEY's *The WARS* (1977) and *FAMOUS LAST WORDS* (1981), which move out from Toronto and Canada into an international arena of war and violence.

From the days of Moodie and Traill, women writers have been prominent: Madge MACBETH's *Land of afternoon* (1924) was our first social satire; Mazo DE LA ROCHE's *JALNA* (1927) still draws an international readership; and Margaret ATWOOD's prolific versatility gradually gained for her a world-wide reputation with the publication of *The edible woman* (1969), *Surfacing* (1972), *Lady oracle* (1976), *Life before man* (1979), and *Bodily harm* (1981). Marian ENGEL in *The Honeyman festival* (1970), *Bear* (1976), *The glassy sea* (1978), and *Lunatic villas* (1981); Carol SHIELDS in *Small ceremonies* (1976), *The box garden* (1977), and *Happenstance* (1980); and Sylvia FRASER in *Pandora* (1972) and *The candy factory* (1975)—all these writers share contemporary concerns, though the latter's *The emperor's virgin* (1980) is an excursion into historical romance. Alice Munro's delicacy of perception and skill with language are evidenced in her linked short-story sequences *Lives of girls and women* (1971) and *Who do you think you are?* (1978).

2. SHORT STORIES. This is a flourishing form in Ontario, as it is in Canadian writing in general. Early works in this genre include Susie Frances HARRISON's *Crowded out and other sketches* (Ottawa, 1886), E.W. THOMSON's *Old man Savarin and other stories* (Toronto, 1895), Duncan Campbell SCOTT's *In the village of Viger* (Boston, 1896) and *The witching of Elspie* (1923); and Ernest Thompson SETON's *WILD ANIMALS I HAVE KNOWN* (New York, 1898). The short story flowered in the 1920s with Morley Callaghan's *A native argosy* (1929) and with the work of Raymond Knister, published in that decade in *The CANADIAN FORUM* and *This Quarter* and collected in 1972. The first collections of Norman LEVINE (*One way ticket*, 1961), George ELLIOTT(*The kissing man*, 1962), Hugh Hood (*Flying a red kite*, 1962), Alice Munro (*Dance of the happy shades*), Dave GODFREY (*Death goes better with Coca-Cola*, 1967), David HELWIG (*The streets of summer*, 1969), Austin CLARKE (*When he was free and young and he used to wear silks*, 1971), Gwendolyn MacEWEN (*Noman*, 1972), Margaret Atwood (*Dancing girls and other stories*, 1977), and Margaret GIBSON (*The butterfly ward*, 1976), offer abundant evidence of variety in theme and sophisticated skill in craftsmanship.

3. POETRY. Like prose writers, early poets focused on narrative treatment of the land and its settlement, from Adam Hood BURWELL's 'Talbot Road' (*The Scribbler*, 1822), William KIRBY's Tory epic, *The U.E.: a tale of Upper Canada* (Niagara, 1859), Alexander McLACHLAN's celebration of the Scots in *The emigrant and other poems* (Toronto, 1861), Charles SANGSTER's *The St. Lawrence and the Saguenay, and other poems* (Montreal, 1856), and Charles MAIR's *Dreamland and other poems* (Montreal, 1868), to the beautiful and startling evidence of genius in Isabella Valancy CRAWFORD's 'Malcolm's Katie', published in *Old Spookses' Pass, Malcolm's Katie, and other poems* (Toronto, 1884).

The three CONFEDERATION POETS associated with Ontario, Archibald LAMPMAN, Duncan Campbell SCOTT, and Wilfred CAMPBELL, explored lyric and subjective themes and patterns with talent and sensitivity. Lampman's *Among the millet* (Ottawa, 1888) and *Lyrics of earth* (Boston, 1895) set high standards for contemporary and later poets, while Scott moved from the lyrics of his early work, *The magic house and other poems* (Ottawa, 1893), which included the uniquely haunting 'Piper of Arll', to powerful and dramatic poetic studies of Native people (for example, 'The forsaken'), with whose tragic predicaments he became familiar in his work in the Department of Indian Affairs. Wilson MacDONALD's romantic *Whitmanesque voice* was first heard in *Song of the prairie land* (1918).

The strong narrative tradition in nineteenth-century Ontario poetry climaxed in the twentieth century in the work of E.J. PRATT. A Newfoundlander, but by adoption an Ontarian, Pratt became a public and an epic poet, his work moving from *Newfoundland verse* (1923) to the high comedy of *The witches' brew* (1925), the tragedy of *The Titanic* (1935) and *Brébeuf and his brethren* (1940), to the epic national range of *Towards the last spike* (1952). The atmosphere of southwestern Ontario provided rich material for the work of James REANEY—in *A suit of nettles* (1958), *Twelve letters to a small town* (1962), and *The dance of death at London, Ontario* (1963)—and in Reaney's poetic dramas. Frank DAVEY in *Griffon* (1972), and Don GUTTERIDGE in *Tecumseh* (1976) and *The true history of Lambton County* (1977) continued the narrative genre in Ontario settings.

The tradition of the lyric remained strong and effective in volumes like Robert FINCH's *Poems* (1946) through his *Variations and theme* (1980), and in Douglas LePAN's *The wounded prince and other poems* (1948). The colloquial and detailed sense of the city life of Toronto marked the work of Raymond SOUSTER, from the publication of the first of his many collections in 1946. Al PURDY's ability to capture a sense of place and of local history is evident in volumes like *The Cariboo horses* (1965) and *Wild grape wine* (1968). A disturbing awareness of human duality and meditative despair characterized much of the poetry of Eli MANDEL, as in *Dreaming backwards* (1981). Within the context of the poetic explosion in the ebullient, nationalistic climate of the sixties and seventies, Dennis LEE, in *Civil elegies, and other poems* (1972), was as distinguished for his depth of feeling as, in *Alligator pie* (1974) and *Nicholas Knock and other people* (1974), he was memorably inventive and lighthearted as a poet for children. Witty, idiosyncratic, and unique are the works of Joe ROSENBLATT (*Bumblebee dithyramb*, 1972). Michael ONDAATJE, the author of several brilliant poetry collections and a novel, *Coming through slaughter* (1976), was best known in this period for the evocative, violent collages that make up *The collected works of Billy the Kid* (1970).

As with fiction writers, women have been prominent among Ontario poets since the days of Isabella Valancy Crawford. Pauline JOHNSON's *The white wampum* (London, 1895) at once romanticized and individualized the life of the Canadian Indian, while Marjorie PICKTHALL's *The drift of pinions* (1913) established her mystical and lyrical voice. *Counterpoint to sleep* (1951) by Anne WILKINSON combined the sensual and the intellectual in its effects, and in *The BOATMAN* (1957) Jay MACPHERSON's wit and poetic skill played with biblical archetypes in patterns of quest and redemption. Though Margaret AVISON's spare, intellectually demanding poetry was first published in 1939, her first collection, *Winter sun*, did not appear until 1960. Margaret Atwood's versatile talent was announced in *Double Persephone* (1961), followed by many collections, including one—*The JOURNALS OF SUSANNA MOODIE* (1970)—that is a classic poetic interpretation of the immigrant experience in Ontario. Phyllis GOTLIEB's *Who knows one?* (1961) exuberantly described her Jewish childhood in Toronto, and Gwendolyn MacEwen's first volume, *The rising fire* (1963), characteristically drew dominant image patterns from the mystical and the ritualistic.

4. LITTLE MAGAZINES AND SMALL PUBLISHERS. Among the several early 'little' or literary magazines published in Ontario were the short-lived *CANADIAN LITERARY MAGAZINE* (York, 1833), *BARKER'S CANADIAN MONTHLY MAGAZINE* (Kingston, 1846-7), *The Victoria Magazine* (Belleville, 1847-8), and *The British American Review* (Toronto, 1865-67). After Confederation other periodicals appeared, including *The Canadian Monthly and National Review* (Toronto, 1872-8), which combined with Belford's *Monthly Magazine: a Magazine of Literature and Art* (Toronto, 1876-8) to become *ROSE-BELFORD'S CANADIAN MONTHLY* (Toronto, 1878-82). Other nineteenth-century periodicals of note were *The WEEK: An Independent Journal of Literature, Politics and Criticism* (Toronto, 1883-96), founded and edited by Goldwin SMITH, and *The Canadian Magazine* (Toronto, 1893-1939). In 1920 The *CANADIAN FORUM* was established as 'An Independent Journal of Opinion and the Arts'; its longstanding commitment to the publication and discussion of Canadian literature is well known. Following the Second World War more little magazines appeared: *Here and Now* (Toronto, 1947-9); Raymond Souster's *CONTACT: an international magazine of poetry* (Toronto, 1952-4) and his *COMBUSTION* (Toronto, 1957-60); *The TAMARACK REVIEW* (Toronto, 1956-82); and James Reaney's *ALPHABET: A semi-annual devoted to the iconography of the imagination* (London, 1960-71). Founded in the 1960s were *Evidence* (Toronto, 1960-7); *Quarry* (Kingston, 1965-); *Origins* (Hamilton, 1967-); *Northern Journey*

(Ottawa, 1971-6); *EXILE* (Toronto, 1972-); *Waves* (Downsview, 1972-); *OPEN LETTER* (Toronto, 1965-). Academic journals that could be mentioned here are *Queen's Quarterly* (Kingston, 1893-), which began publishing fiction and poetry in the 1920s. In 1936 the survey 'Letters in Canada' made the first of its annual appearances in *The University of Toronto Quarterly* (1931-). Other major journals include *The University of Windsor Review* (Windsor 1965-), *Journal of Canadian Studies* (Peterborough, 1966-), *DESCANT* (Toronto, 1970-), *Essays on Canadian Writing* (Downsview, 1974-), *Canadian Poetry* (London, 1977-), *Canadian Theatre Review* (Downsview, 1975-), *Journal of Canadian Poetry* (Ottawa, 1978-), and *CANADIAN FICTION MAGAZINE* (Vancouver/Toronto, 1971-). (See also LITERARY MAGAZINES IN ENGLISH.)

By 1900 a number of small publishing houses had grown and flourished, among which were the *Methodist Book and Publishing House* (later RYERSON PRESS), William Briggs, and Copp, Clark. An overview of small Ontario publishers in this century begins with GRAPHIC PUBLISHERS of Ottawa (1925-32), which in the late 1920s and early 1930s devoted itself exclusively to the publication of Canadian works in all fields. With its collapse, small publishing houses effectively disappeared until the mid-1960s, when an explosive renaissance took place. COACH HOUSE PRESS, and the more inclusive Peter Martin Associates, were established in 1965, followed a year later by OBERON PRESS and in 1967 the House of ANANSI. Their enthusiasm and success in publishing new Canadian writing inspired the founding of other houses. Among these were James Lorimer and Company (1969), New Press (1969), NC Press (1970), Borealis (1972), Women's Press (1972), PORCUPINE'S QUILL (1973), Playwrights Co-op (1973), Mosaic Press/Valley Editions (1974), and ECW PRESS (1979).

JOHN LENNOX

5. DRAMA. While stage performances occurred in Ontario as early as a 'Puppet Shew' in York on 3 October 1800, and *The school for scandal* was performed by 'New York comic gentry' on 11 February 1809, the first known drama published in Ontario was *The convention*, an anonymous political squib that appeared in the *Niagara Gleaner* (3 July 1818) 'now acting with great applause in Upper-Canada'. *Captain Plume's courtship by John Simpson* (*Canadian forget me not for 1837*, Toronto, 1837) and Hugh Scobie's *Provincial drama called the Family Compact* (*British Colonist*, 19 June-31 July 1839) are two other early topical satires in dramatic form of a type that continued to appear throughout the rest of the century in newspapers, pamphlets, and in some cases successfully on stage. Early examples of local domestic comedy appear in *The husking bee; or Courtship in the woods*, staged by amateurs in Guelph (10 Jan. 1829), and Dr Edward Barker's *The bridegroom*, which was wisely rejected by a Philadelphia theatre before he published it in his own Kingston newspaper, the *Whig* (10 Feb. 1836). By mid-century many more plays were in evidence. *Fiddle, faddle and foozle*, by Graves Simcoe Lee, is recorded to be the first drama by an 'Upper Canadian' on the Toronto stage (April 1853), and was followed by his *Saucy Kate* (June 1853). *Fiddle, faddle* was a formulaic light English comedy criticized at the time for its derivative nature. Adaptations of Dickens, such as noted Hamiltonian J.B. Harrison's *Comedy—the battle of life* (1847), were also beginning to appear, as well as more works aimed at specific local circumstances. Thus we find in *The female consistory of Brockville* (Brockville, 1856), whose lightly disguised references to personalities in the town were likely to keep this attack on hypocrisy (by 'Caroli Candidus', pseud.) both anonymous and off the stage. One playwright demonstrated sophisticated dramaturgy in a piece that has since been successfully staged. William Henry Fuller's *Unspecific scandal* (Ottawa, 1874) is a witty satire about the Pacific Scandal; his *HMS Parliament; or, The lady who loved a government clerk* (Ottawa, 1880) is an adaptation of Gilbert and Sullivan's *HMS Pinafore*, with John A. Macdonald, Alexander Mackenzie, and Canadian politics providing characters and subject matter; it was taken in 1880 on a successful national tour (Saint John to Winnipeg) by Eugene A. McDowell and his company. Fuller's attacks are decidedly mild-mannered in comparison with the vituperativeness of Nicholas Flood DAVIN, a politician himself, in *The fair Grit; or The advantages of coalition* (Toronto, 1876). Poetic drama, such as Charles SANGSTER's *Bertram and Lorenzo* (in *The St Lawrence and the Saguenay and other poems* (Kingston, 1856) was also a major form in the century. The generally negative impression held by mid-twentieth-century scholars concerning poetic dramas has given way to recent research that has reconsidered a number of these texts. Charles MAIR's *Tecumseh: a drama* (Toronto, 1886) and Sarah Anne CURZON's *Laura Secord, the heroine of 1812* (Toronto, 1887) are among those that have been found valuable and engaging, the latter particularly in the light of feminist studies. (Curzon's *The*

sweet girl graduate, 1882, is a sprightly prose play concerning Kate Bloggs, who disguises herself as a man, enters the male domain of the University of Toronto, and comes first in her class.) However, Wilfred CAMPBELL's tragedies, such as *Mordred and Hildebrand* (Ottawa, 1895), remain among those considered ponderous and sententious. The prose drama *When George the Third was King* (Toronto, 1897) by Catharine Nina Merritt was less exalted, and more effective, in celebrating a United Empire Loyalist's escape from a repressive America. It remained unstaged, but Gilbert PARKER's adaptation of his *Seats of the mighty* (Toronto, 1896) was the play that opened Herbert Beerbohm Tree's second American tour (1896) and then opened Her Majesty's Theatre in London, with theatre-owner Tree in the title role.

The opening of Hart House Theatre, University of Toronto, in 1919 provided a stage for plays such as Marjorie PICKTHALL's lyric tragedy *The woodcarver's wife* (1922) and Duncan Campbell SCOTT's *Pierre* (1926). The 1920s also saw a much-needed reaction against sentimental romance in Merrill DENISON's realistic backwoods dramas *From their own place* (1922) and *Brothers in arms* (1924). In the early 1930s Herman VOADEN founded the Play Work-shop in Toronto, a forum for experimental drama and acting. In 1932 amateur theatre was given a powerful nation-wide boost with the formation of the annual Dominion Drama Festival. The post-war period brought more opportunities with the establishment of Dora Mavor Moore's New Play Society (1946-71) and the popular annual review, Spring Thaw (1948-71), in Toronto.

In 1953 were established the Crest Theatre, also in Toronto, and the Stratford Shakespearean Festival, which has since won for itself an international reputation. John COULTER's Canadian career began in the 1930s, and in the next decade Robertson DAVIES introduced his series of ironic comedies, including *Fortune my foe* (1949); he continued writing and publishing plays through the 1970s. With the 1960s came Coulter's *Riel* (1962) and James REANEY's début as a playwright of southwestern Ontario with *The killdeer and other plays* (1962), which was followed by the innovative, poetic collage, *Colours in the dark* (1967), and *The Donnellys: a dramatic trilogy* (1975-7). John HERBERT's explicit and brutal *Fortune and men's eyes* (1967), with its prison theme, introduced a new gritty realism. The 1970s exploded with activity in drama. Toronto Workshop Productions, founded in 1958, was followed over the next two decades by many other Toronto theatres, among them Theatre Passe Muraille, Tarragon, the St Lawrence Centre for the Performing Arts, Young People's Theatre, and Factory Theatre Lab; and an array of new regional and festival theatres sprang up throughout the province.

RICHARD PLANT/JOHN LENNOX

1983 to 1996. I. NOVELS. Two canonical authors wrote their last novels in this period: Morley CALLAGHAN (*A time for Judas*, 1983) and Robertson DAVIES (*The lyre of Orpheus*, 1988; *Murther and walking spirits*, 1991; *The cunning man*, 1994). To these names must be added Tom MARSHALL (*Goddess disclosing*, 1992; *The adventures of Tom Montgomery*, 1995).

There is a large concentration of novelists and short-story writers in Ontario, and this brief survey can draw attention only to some. Perhaps the most striking thing about this period is the high productivity of some writers. Margaret ATWOOD led them all in publishing *The HANDMAID'S TALE* (1985), *The robber bride* (1993), and *Alias Grace* (1996)—three novels that produced a crescendo of international fame for the author—plus *Cat's eye* (1988), four works of short fiction, two collections of new poetry, one work of criticism, and two children's books. Janette Turner HOSPITAL followed with *The tiger in the tiger pit* (1983), *Borderline* (1985), *Charades* (1989), *The last magician* (1992), and *Oyster* (1996), plus three collections of short stories, a crime thriller, and a novella in French. Timothy FINDLEY published *Not wanted on the voyage* (1984), *The telling of lies* (1986), *Headhunter* (1993), *The piano man's daughter* (1995), *You went away: a novella* (1996), plus two collections of short stories, a memoir, and a play. Joan BARFOOT wrote four of her six novels in this period: *Duet for three* (1985), *Family news* (1989), *Plain Jane* (1992), and *Charlotte and Claudia keeping in touch* (1994); and Susan SWAN published *The biggest modern woman of the world* (1983), *The last of the golden girls* (1989), *The wives of Bath* (1993), and *Stupid boys are good to relax with* (1996). Three-novel authors included Barbara GOWDY (*Through the green valley*, 1988; *Falling angels*, 1989; and *Mister Sandman*, 1995); Katherine GOVIER (*Between men*, 1987; *Hearts of flame*, 1991; *Angel walk*, 1996—plus three collections of stories); M.G. VASSANJI (*The gunny sack*, 1989; *No new land*, 1991; *The book of secrets*, 1994—plus a collection of stories); and Richard B. Wright (*Tourists*, 1984; *Sunset Manor*, 1990; and *The age of longing*, 1995).

Writers who wrote two novels in this period included Barry CALLAGHAN, Graeme

GIBSON, Ann Ireland, Janice KULYK KEEFER, Rohinton MISTRY, Michael ONDAATJE, Rick SALUTIN, Sarah Sheard, Josef ŠKVORECKÝ and Jane URQUHART.

Another notable characteristic of the period is the number of writers who published highly successful first novels: Dionne BRAND (*In another place, not here*, 1996); Wayson Choy (*The jade peony*, 1995); Ann-Marie MacDONALD (*Fall on your knees*, 1996); Anne MICHAELS (*Fugitive pieces*, 1996); Rohinton Mistry (*Such a long journey*, 1991); Nino RICCI (*Lives of the saints*, 1990); Shyam Selvadurai (*Funny boy*, 1994); Diane SCHOEMPERLEN (*In the language of love*, 1994); Richard Scrimger (*Crosstown*, 1996); and Cordelia Strube (*Alex and Zee*, 1995). Mistry, Ricci, and Strube went on to publish other novels.

The prizes that came to some of these authors deserve mention: Commonwealth Writers Best First Novel Prize (MacDonald, Vassanji), the British Booker Prize (Ondaatje co-winner) and Orange Prize (Michaels); the Giller Prize (Vassanji, Mistry, Atwood), the Governor General's Award (Škvorecký, Atwood, Ricci, Mistry, Ondaatje), the Smith/Chapters *Books in Canada* First Novel Award (Salutin, Mistry, Selvadurai, Michaels).

The subjects and interests of Ontario novelists are of course various, but prominent is a frequent and relatively recent treatment of an old tradition, called SOUTHERN ONTARIO GOTHIC, in work by Atwood, Barfoot, Marian ENGEL, MacDonald, Findley, Marshall, Swan, Scott SYMONS, Urquhart, and others.

A sharp departure in subject matter has been provided by writers who live in Ontario but were born elsewhere. The homeland settings of their books, and their imagination, social insights, and mastery of language, have introduced a fresh, salutary, and even exotic element into the literature. The books of Brand (Jamaica), Mistry (India), Selvadurai (Sri Lanka), and Vassanji (Tanzania) quickly found a readership in Canada and in some cases internationally. Wayson Choy is Canadian-born, but *The jade peony* is about Vancouver's Chinatown.

Another striking development over the past fifteen years has been the enormous increase in the number of Canadian writers who specialize in the MYSTERY AND CRIME genre (those from Ontario including Howard ENGEL, Alison GORDON, Peter ROBINSON, and Medora SALE) and the international popularity of some Ontario authors whose books are associated with FANTASTIC LITERATURE (including Guy Gavriel KAY, Terence M. GREEN, and Robert SAWYER).

2. SHORT STORIES. Alice MUNRO, the pride of Ontario (and the rest of Canada), published in this period *The progress of love* (1986), *Friend of my youth* (1990), *Open secrets* (1994), and the triumphant *Selected stories* (1996), which garnered superb international reviews that invariably turned into tributes; in December 1996 the *New York Times Book Review* named it one of the eight best books of the year.

It has often been remarked that Canadian writers have an extraordinary gift for the short story. In this period Margaret Atwood published two collections, *Bluebeard's egg* (1983) and *Wilderness tips* (1991), and two collections of very short fiction: *Murder in the dark* (1983) and *Good bones* (1992). Among other Ontario writers who published with distinction in this genre were Bonnie BURNARD (*Women of influence*, 1988; *Casino & other stories*, 1994); Matt COHEN (*Café le dog*, 1983; *Lives of the mind slaves: selected stories*, 1994); Marian Engel (*The tattooed woman*, published posthumously in 1985); Margaret GIBSON (*Sweet poison*, 1993; *The fear room*, 1996); Katherine Govier (*Fables of Brunswick Avenue*, 1985; *Before and after*, 1989; *The Immaculate Conception Photograph Gallery*, 1994); Barbara Gowdy (*We so seldom look on love*, 1992); Elisabeth HARVOR (*If only we could drive like this forever*, 1988; *Our lady of all the distances*, 1991; *Let me be the one*, 1996; nominated for a Governor General's Award); Steven HEIGHTON (*Flight paths of the emperor*, 1992; *On earth as it is*, 1995); Janette Turner Hospital (*Dislocations*, 1986; *Isobars*, 1991); Isabel HUGGAN (*The Elizabeth stories*, 1984; *You never know*, 1993); Janice Kulyk Keefer (*The Paris-Napoli Express*, 1986; *Transfigurations*, 1987; *Travelling ladies*, 1990); Alistair MacLEOD (*As birds bring forth the sun*, 1986); Joyce MARSHALL (*Any time at all and other stories*, 1993; *Blood and bone/En chair et en os*, 1995); John METCALF (*Adult entertainment*, 1986); Rohinton Mistry (*Tales from Firozsha Baag*, 1987); James REANEY (*The box social and other stories*, 1996); Leon ROOKE (*Sing me no love songs, I'll say you no prayers*, 1984; *A bolt of white cloth*, 1984; *Why do you love?*, 1992); Diane Schoemperlen (*Double exposures*, 1984; *Frogs and other stories*, 1986); *Hockey Night in Canada*, 1987; *The man of my dreams*, 1990); Richard Teleky (*Goodnight, sweetheart and other stories*, 1993); Jane Urquhart (*Storm glass*, 1987); M.G. Vassanji (*Uhuru Street*, 1992); and Bronwen WALLACE (*People you'd trust your life to*, published posthumously in 1990).

WILLIAM TOYE

3. POETRY. Bronwen Wallace and Gwen MacEWEN were two Ontario poets whose deaths were mourned in this period.

Toronto continues to play a crucial role in fostering the growth of poetry in a province that has produced many of Canada's finest writers. Margaret Atwood and Michael Ondaatje are Toronto's, Ontario's, and Canada's best-known poets. Atwood's volumes have appeared at a fairly steady rate over the last thirteen years and include *Murder in the dark: short fictions and prose poems* (1983), *Interlunar* (1984), *Morning in the burned house* (1995), and two volumes of selected verse. Ondaatje's output has been significantly smaller but influential nevertheless. *Secular love* (1984) was followed by *The cinnamon peeler: selected poems* (1991). Both Atwood and Ondaatje have shown an increasing interest in weakening the boundaries between prose and lyric.

Other Ontario poets of reputation such as Dennis LEE, Christopher DEWDNEY, Dionne BRAND, Don COLES, Roo BORSON, Douglas LePAN, Steve McCAFFERY, Richard OUTRAM, W.J. Keith, David DONNELL, and Fraser SUTHERLAND have published well-received works in the period under consideration. Less widely known but talented writers during this period include John Reibetanz, the award-winning Roger Greenwald, Richard Lush, and the devotional poet Margo Swiss. A.F. MORITZ is a Toronto poet with numerous volumes of poetry to his credit who deserves to be better known in Canada. His extremely fine work has appeared in *The best American poetry* (1991 and 1993) as well as in other important Canadian and American publications.

Like Montreal in the 1940s and Vancouver in the 1960s, Toronto is, despite the closure of COACH HOUSE PRESS and dramatic funding cuts, currently producing some of the most innovative poetry in Canada. Interesting and varied work is coming from new writers. Of those who published first books in the 1980s and 1990s, three talented Toronto poets represent the distinct traditions out of which Canada's finest writing is emerging. Among the best new free-verse poets is Anne Michaels, whose lyric intensity and skill with the image have brought her wide acclaim. Her first volume, *The weight of oranges* (1985), was awarded the Commonwealth Poetry Prize for the Americas; *Miner's pond* (1991) won the CANADIAN AUTHORS' ASSOCIATION Award for Poetry. (Both volumes were reprinted in one edition in 1997.) Representing a completely different tradition, *Crystallography* (1994) established Christian Bök as a potential leader in the poetics of the late twentieth-century avant-garde. Finally, Jeffery Donaldson's *Once out of nature* (1991) represents a renewed interest in a formalist poetics. His carefully modulated voice and his attention to metre, stanzaic pattern, and rhythm reveal the growing influence on Canadian writing of American poets such as the late James Merrill.

Governor General's Awards for Poetry went to David Donnell (1983), Al Purdy (1986), Gwen MacEwen (1987), Margaret Avison (1990), and Don Coles (1993).

CYNTHIA MESSENGER

4. DRAMA. In the 1980s a new generation of artists joined the scene, and with them not only new issues and dramatic expression but new venues for staging their works. Despite serious cuts to public funding for the arts through and after the 1980s, Ontario remained a very active playwriting centre. Many Ontario theatres have staged Ontario-written plays and instituted programs to develop new drama. The PLAYWRIGHTS' UNION OF CANADA remains headquartered in Toronto; universities and community colleges have programs in drama with playwriting as a subject of study; and a network of support exists in the theatre community. Many playwrights originally from outside Ontario—such as Carol BOLT, Anne CHISLETT, Sally CLARK, Larry FINEBERG, Sky GILBERT, Linda Griffiths, Tom HENDRY, Margaret HOLLINGSWORTH, Tomson HIGHWAY, Lawrence Jeffery, Hillar Liitoja, Ann-Marie MacDONALD, Daniel MacIvor, Joan MacLEOD (7 seasons with Tarragon), Arthur Milner, Erika RITTER, Djanet Sears, George Seremba, and Jason SHERMAN—moved permanently or for sizeable periods of time to Ontario, especially to the Toronto area. In a generally supportive climate they have joined Ontario-born (or -raised) writers, such as Hrant ALIANAK, Jean-Marc DALPÉ, Norm Foster, David FREEMAN, Ken Gass, Michael HOLLINGSWORTH, Ted Johns, John Krizanc, John Mighton, Daniel David MOSES, Dan Needles, Banuta Rubess, and Drew Hayden TAYLOR. These playwrights joined colleagues who had been among the most prominent Ontario dramatists since the early 1970s: Judith THOMPSON, David FRENCH (who arrived in Toronto from Newfoundland when he was seven), James REANEY, and George WALKER.

RICHARD PLANT

Open Letter (1965-). This journal of experimental writing and criticism was founded in Victoria, British Columbia, by Frank DAVEY as a research project into 'open' form. The first series (each 'series' has contained nine issues) was titled 'The open letter' and offered selections from the current writing, reading, and correspondence of its contributing editors (George BOWERING, Daphne MARLATT, Fred WAH, David Dawson, and latterly Ted Whittaker). In typewritten format, this series served as a transitional publication between *TISH*, in which most of the editors participated, and the much larger and professionally printed issues that Davey later produced in eastern Canada. Numbers 5 and 6 of the first series were edited by Ted Whittaker.

The main period of *Open Letter* began when Davey moved to Toronto in 1970 and became associated with bp NICHOL, Victor COLEMAN, and the COACH HOUSE PRESS. Beginning in 1971, the second series featured Nichol, Coleman, Bowering, Wah, and Steve McCAFFERY as contributing editors and limited its contents to experimental criticism, literary theory, and reviews. Coach House Press acted as publisher from 1971 to 1977. In the fourth (1978-81) and fifth (1982-4) series the magazine ceased publishing reviews and devoted itself to special issues on such topics as performance art, 'pataphysics', poetry and painting, prosody, or on single authors. After the death of bp Nichol in 1988, the editorial board was reorganized to include Davey, Barbara Godard, Terry Goldie, Smaro Kamboureli, Steve McCaffery, Lola Lemire Tostevin, and Fred Wah. In its various editorial initiatives *Open Letter* has endorsed textual and phenomenological criticism, supported interchange between the Canadian and international avant-gardes, proposed a linguistic foundation for both writing and criticism, championed western-Canadian writing, and argued against the centralization of the Canadian literary tradition that it saw implicit in both the Canadian nationalist movement of the 1970s and the 'thematic' criticism of Northrop FRYE, D.G. JONES, and Margaret ATWOOD. After its 1988 reorganization, many of its issues examined questions of feminism and the writing of younger members of racial minority communities. Noteworthy issues include 'Sheila WATSON: a collection' (ser. 3, no. 1), 'Warren Tallman: collected essays' (ser. 3, no. 6), 'Louis DUDEK: texts and essays' (ser. 4, nos. 8-9), 'Notation' (ser. 5, no. 2), 'Robert KROETSCH: essays' (ser. 5, no. 4), 'bp Nichol Festschrift' (ser. 6, nos 5-6), 'Steve McCaffery' (ser. 6, no. 9), 'Bronwen WALLACE' (ser. 7, no 9), 'Canadian? Literary? Theory?' (ser. 8, no. 3), and 'Interventing the text' (ser. 8, nos. 5-6).

See *Ellipse* 23/24 (1979), a special issue on *Open Letter* and *La BARRE DU JOUR*.

See also LITERARY MAGAZINES IN ENGLISH: 3.

FRANK DAVEY

Ormsby, Eric. See POETRY IN ENGLISH 1983 TO 1996: 3.

Ostenso, Martha (1900-63). Born near Bergen, Norway, she came to North America with her parents at the age of two and lived in various towns in Minnesota and North Dakota. Her family moved to Brandon, Manitoba—where Ostenso attended Brandon Collegiate and became interested in writing and painting—and then to Winnipeg, where she attended Kelvin Technical High School and the University of Manitoba. She taught school briefly about 100 miles northwest of Winnipeg—an experience that was to provide the background for her novel *Wild geese* (1925; NCL)—and worked as a reporter on the *Winnipeg Free Press*. She later joined Douglas DURKIN in New York and attended his course on 'The technique of the novel' at Columbia University, possibly in 1921-2. (It is now thought that the novels published under Ostenso's name were actually co-authored by Durkin, although *Wild geese* is considered to be primarily by Ostenso.) For two-and-a-half years she was a social-worker in New York. Ostenso then went with Durkin to Gull Lake, Minnesota, in 1931; they married in 1945 and moved to Seattle in 1963. Besides *Wild geese*, Ostenso published over a dozen volumes of fiction, a collection of poetry, *A far land* (1924), and a co-authored biography of Sister Elizabeth Kenney. Her work appeared in *The Scandinavian Review* and *Poetry* (Chicago).

Wild geese, which was originally called 'The passionate flight', the title of its English edition, was well received and won the $13,500 prize for a best first novel offered by *The Pictorial Review*, the Famous Players-Lasky Corporation, and Dodd, Mead & Company. It is set in the period between the arrival of the geese in the spring and their departure in the autumn. Lind Archer comes to teach at Oeland, Manitoba, and boards with the Gares. Caleb Gare controls his family as a means to the smooth and successful operation of the family farm. Described as 'a spiritual counterpart of the land, as harsh, as demanding, as tyrannical as the very soil from which he drew his existence', he exerts his power in part by emotional blackmail of his wife, Amelia, knowing that she has had, by her lover, a son, Mark Jordan, now an adult but still unaware of who either of his real parents are. When Mark comes to Oeland to manage the homestead of an ailing neighbour of the Gares, he and Lind meet and fall in love. A major figure in the novel is the Gares' daughter, Judith, beautiful as 'some fabled animal';

she is also described as 'vivid and terrible', and her strength and sexuality are contrasted with Lind's delicacy and capacity for fine feeling. A counter-example to the isolation experienced by the Gares, individually and as a family, is provided by the neighbouring Bjarnasson family, in which four generations live in harmony. While *Wild geese* has elements of romanticism, it represents a major development in the Canadian movement towards realism.

For a detailed discussion of *Wild geese* and its role in the movement towards realism, see the unpublished Ph.D. thesis of David Arnason, 'The development of prairie realism' (University of New Brunswick, 1980); about the genesis of *Wild geese*, see Robert G. Lawrence, 'The geography of Martha Ostenso's *Wild geese*', *Journal of Canadian Fiction* 16 (1976). JOY KUROPATWA

Other Canadians: an anthology of the new poetry in Canada. See John SUTHERLAND.

Ouellet, Fernand (b. 1926). He was born in Lac-Bouchette, Quebec, and educated at Université Laval (B.A., 1948; L. ès L., 1950, D. ès L., 1965) He was professor of history at Laval (1961-5); Carleton University, Ottawa (1965-75); Université d'Ottawa (1975-85); and in 1985 he moved to York University, Toronto. He was made an Officer of the Order of Canada in 1979.

No historian achieved more after the Second World War to alter the understanding of the first century of British rule in Canada than Fernand Ouellet. Through his writing, previous preoccupations were overturned or altered by fresh approaches and new research. Foremost among his concerns was the majority—Quebec farmers and rural dwellers—but the activities of other groups such as merchants, politicians, and churchmen, whether francophone or anglophone, were not neglected. Since little had been written about ordinary people (most of it condescending), Ouellet plumbed hitherto neglected contemporary primary sources to provide a portrait of people on their own terms.

Ouellet's *Histoire économique et sociale du Québec: 1760-1850: structures et conjoncture* (1966) and his *Le Bas-Canada: 1791-1840: changements structuraux et crise* (1976)—which won a Governor General's Award—not only were comprehensive, but also countered the emphasis that the Montreal school of history placed on the negative effects of the British conquest. The 1966 work was translated as *Economic and social history of Quebec, 1760-1850* (1980, CARLETON LIBRARY), and the translation/adaptation of both books by Patricia Claxton resulted in *Lower Canada 1791-1840: social change and nationalism* (1980) in The Canadian Centenary Series. In Ouellet's view, the principal forces altering Quebec were changes in the nature of the fur trade, population increase, and the advent of the timber trade at the beginning of the nineteenth century. The rise of nationalism and the formation of political parties in the decade after 1800 allowed Ouellet to provide explanations of the intricate interplay of ethnicity and social class before the Rebellions of 1837-8. In concert with Ouellet, Marcel TRUDEL, and Jean HAMELIN, the Laval school of history forged a perspective at odds with that expounded by its Montreal counterparts.

Ouellet's biography *Julie Papineau: un cas de mélancolie et d'éducation janséniste* (1962) resulted in a lawsuit brought by the daughters of Henri Bourassa—the great-granddaughters of Julie—and the book's being withdrawn from sale. TERRY CROWLEY

Ouellette, Fernand (b. 1930). Born in Montreal, Quebec, he believed through his early years that he was destined for a sacerdotal career. However, after completing secondary studies in 1947 at the Collège séraphique des Capucins, Ottawa, he returned to Montreal to obtain a Licence en sciences sociales at the Université de Montréal (1952). He married Lisette Corbeil in 1955. They have two daughters and a son. For more than thirty years (1960-91) he directed and produced cultural programs for Radio-Canada. He has collaborated with musicians, artists, and film-makers and written extensively in a wide range of media about the process of artistic creation. He has contributed regularly throughout his career to literary journals and magazines, has been invited to teach in several universities in Quebec and elsewhere, and has received many awards.

Ouellette's work—which has been translated into a dozen languages—is characterized by its compelling integrity and its quest for mystical union, known in advance to be necessarily fleeting, combining sensual and sensuous experience with spiritual vision. Like the poets and artists he admires, who range across many historical periods and cultures, Ouellette chooses his words with reverence and respect. The radiant body of the beloved woman frequently represents in his work, which is rich in eroticism, the object of his search for a flashing glance of the infinite. The impact of modernity was evident from the start. Throughout his career he has explored dimensions of reality that include the realms of nature, culture, and the spirit.

Ouellette was one of the first poets of the Hexagone group to publish a collection of poetry: *Ces anges de sang* (1955). In 1959 he joined Jean-Guy PILON and other young poets to found the influential literary journal *LIBERTÉ*, of which he has served as editor and to which he continues to contribute. Between 1956 and 1970 Ouellette wrote texts for Radio-Canada and articles on poetry, on the socio-political situation in Quebec, on questions of language and culture, and on European writers and artists such as Varèse (*Visage d'Edgard Varèse*, 1959), Novalis, Jouve, Kierkegaard, and Dostoyevsky, whom he acknowledged as seminal influences in his own evolution. The texts Ouellette wrote revealed his unique approach to the question of *engagement*. He saw the writer as profoundly and immediately involved in his troubled society, yet he did not accept either violence or literature based on explicit social commentary as acceptable or adequate responses to social injustice. Several of these articles were published together as *Les actes retrouvés* (1970), for which Ouellette was awarded but declined a Governor General's Award—offered to him a few months after the 1970 October Crisis and the declaration by the federal government of the War Measures Act. He explained this refusal in 'Le temps des veilleurs', published in *Liberté* (jan.-fév. 1971) and reproduced in *Journal dénoué* (1974).

In 1972 Ouellette, Pilon, and André Belleau founded the annual conference that became one of the main literary events in Quebec: Rencontre québécoise internationale des écrivains. The same year L'Hexagone published a retrospective, *Poésie: poèmes 1953-1971*, containing Ouellette's first four poetry collections: *Ces anges de sang*, *Séquences de l'aile* (1958; rpr. 1995), *Le soleil sous la mort* (1965; rpr. 1995), and *Dans le sombre* (1967). This volume—in which Ouellette included several pieces that were either unpublished or did not appear in earlier collections, as well as modifications of his previous work—contains 'Le poème et le poétique', a short, frequently cited statement on his conception of the poem, which he called 'le langage de la fulgurance'. *Poésie* brought him the France-Canada award for the second time, the first being for *Edgard Varèse* (1966; rpr. 1989; translated by D. Coltman, 1968). *En la nuit, la mer: poèmes 1972-1980* (1981), a second retrospective, is made up of four collections: *Ici, ailleurs la lumière* (1977), *À découvert* (1979), *En la nuit, la mer*, and *Départs* (most of the latter two collections were previously unpublished). Another volume of the same period, *Errances* (1975), is not included in the retrospective. *Les heures* (1987), a sustained reflection on death and the spiritual significance of life's journey, earned Ouellette a Governor General's Award, as well as the first prize for poetry offered by the *Journal de Montréal*, and the Suisse-Canada prize. A volume of Ouellette's poetry in translation, *Wells of light: selected poems by Fernand Ouellette (1955-1987)* (1989), was prepared by Barry CALLAGHAN and Ray Ellenwood.

Ouellette's themes are life, death, artistic creation, love, sensuality, spiritual quest, and solitude. His images are those of light, sun and flame, night, the female body and the erotic experience, and nature perceived in material and symbolic landscapes. His poetry is highly condensed, its syntax reduced to the most basic structures with few modifiers. Ouellette makes frequent use, in both form and content, of seeming contradictions in theme, image, or structure to produce a metamorphosis and new syntheses through unresolved tensions.

Journal dénoué is a spiritual and intellectual autobiography for the period up to 1973 and contains a full bibliography to that date. It won the Études françaises prize. Throughout the 1970s Ouellette continued to reflect on the nature of poetry and its language in essays, collected in *Écrire en notre temps* (1979), that addressed the question of how one can write with lucidity, authenticity, and sincerity in a time of violence and evil, from which there is no exit. (The entire body of Ouellette's writing is a passionate exploration of this question.) He also studied the creative process in writers, musicians, and painters for whose complex work he felt sympathy: for example, *Depuis Novalis, errance et gloses* (1973). *Ouvertures: essais* (1988), the first part of which reprints *Depuis Novalis*, is a personal reflection by Ouellette on his works, his career as a writer, the writers and artists who have influenced his work, and the sacred. *Commencements: essais* (1992) is a collection of articles, originally published in *Liberté*, on the works of painters (mostly European, going back as far as the Middle Ages), that reveal once again Ouellette's passionate search for light that transcends the immediately visible, and his feeling for artists who have captured such light in their works. *En forme de trajet: essais* (1996) is a new edition of the second part of *Ouvertures*, with additions and deletions producing revisions in more than half the work. In the first article Ouellette offers his reflections on his books and his career as a writer; interviews and several occasional pieces follow.

Ouellette's work took on a new dimension with the appearance of his first novel, *Tu regardais intensément Geneviève* (1978; rpr. 1990), in which he uses the unusual narrative technique of having the main character reveal his essential fragmentation through alternation between the pronouns *je* and *tu* to express and address himself and to evoke his situation. It recounts the search for meaning and wholeness of an intellectual after his wife, upon whom he has unthinkingly depended for his practical, sensual, and spiritual needs, seeks to move into an autonomous personal space. As in Ouellette's second novel, *La mort vive* (1980, 1992), the emotional and spiritual experience of the main character is presented with depth and clarity, but there is a failure to create other credible characters. The main female characters, for the most part, are projections of the male character's desire and inability to transcend his own subjective obsessions. *La mort vive* is written in the third person, with passages in the first person taken from the diary of the protagonist (and from frequently interspersed letters to other characters), an artist who seeks to paint the perfect canvas and to achieve the glory of union with the body of his beloved—both wishes closely associated with the desire for death. His final complete isolation and presumed suicide might signify defeat, or apotheosis, as he succeeds in ridding himself of the imperfections of material form. Ouellette has said that his third novel, *Lucie ou un midi en novembre* (1985, Governor General's Award), is a reflection on form. Once again the main character, a writer and professor, is engaged in a quest for sensual and mystical union, for which the female character holds the inaccessible key. The voices of both are heard throughout, thanks to a narrative technique that combines first-person narration and extracts from journals and letters. The ultimate death of the female character, an artist, confirms the terrible spatial and spiritual separation and solitude with which both struggle throughout the novel.

Because of the quality, vision, and courageous affirmation of human freedom found consistently throughout his work, Ouellette must be seen as one of Quebec's leading writers, who has had a significant impact on the direction of poetry in Quebec since the 1960s.

See the special issue, 'Fernand Ouellette, poète', VOIX ET IMAGES. *Littérature québécoise*, 5.3 (printemps 1980), which contains interviews with Ouellette and a fairly complete bibliography after 1974. See also Paul Chanel Malenfant, *La partie et le tout. Lecture de Fernand Ouellette et Roland Giguère* (1983); Pierre Nepveu, *Les mots à l'écoute, poésie et silence chez Fernand Ouellette, Gaston Miron et Paul-Marie Lapointe* (1979), *Poètes québécois II. Dossier de presse* (1981), *La poésie de l'Hexagone* (1990); and Joseph Bonenfant, *Passions du poétique* (1992). LOUISE FORSYTH

Ouellette, Francine. See NOVELS IN FRENCH 1983 TO 1996: 4.

Ouellette-Michalska, Madeleine (b. 1930). She was born in Saint-Alexandre-de-Kamouraska, Quebec. As a child she was self-taught, receiving formal education only after enrolling at the Université de Montréal, where she received her Baccalauréat ès arts (1965) and her Licence ès lettres (1968). She earned her Master's degree (1978) from the Université du Québec à Montréal and her doctorate in French studies (1987) from the Université de Sherbrooke.

As a journalist and literary critic Ouellette-Michalska has worked for Radio-Canada and, until 1994, was a regular contributor to the magazines *L'Actualité*, *Châtelaine*, *Perspectives*, and *Lettres québécoises*, as well as to the newspaper *Le Devoir*. She has taught at the Institut de technologie de l'éducation in Algeria (1970-2) and the Université de Montréal (1980-7). She has also been a guest professor at the University of Albuquerque, New Mexico (1984), and writer-in-residence at the Université d'Ottawa (1983). In 1985 she was appointed to the Académie canadienne-française.

Ouellette-Michalska's first book, a collection of short stories entitled *Le dôme* (1968), was followed by her first novel, *Le jeu des saisons* (1970). *La femme de sable* (1979), a slim collection of short stories inspired by her stay in Algeria, was translated by Luise von Flotow under the title *The sandwoman* (1990). Upon her return to Montreal, Ouellette-Michalska published two novels: *La termitière* (1975, rpr. 1989) and *Le plat de lentilles* (1976, rpr. 1987). The preface to the second edition of the latter novel includes a useful introduction. Her first book of poetry, *Entre le souffle et l'aine* (1981), was translated by Wilson Baldridge under the title *Between breath and loins* (1990). Translations of her stories have appeared in *More stories by Canadian women* (1987); *Antologija Kratke Price Kanade* (Belgrade, Bagdala, 1986); and *A decade of Canadian fiction* (CANADIAN FICTION MAGAZINE, 1981).

Forays into other genres have yielded an 'essai-journal', *La tentation de dire* (1986), and a play, *La danse de l'amante* (1987). Her second book-length essay, *L'amour de la carte postale: impérialisme culturel et différence* (1987), was followed by her fifth novel, *La fête du désir* (1990).

In 1982 Ouellette-Michalska received a Governor General's Award for *L'échappée des discours de l'oeil* (1981, rpr. 1990). In this lyrical, unorthodox essay she explores the various strategies that, over the centuries, have placed female reproductive forces under the control of masculine discourse. A mosaic of impressive historical and cultural scope, it embraces philosophy, psychoanalysis, sociology, ancient and modern mythologies, and literature, with an emphasis on the depiction of the 'éternel féminin' from the Middle Ages to the present.

La maison Trestler ou le 8e jour d'Amérique (1984, rpr. 1995) and *L'été de l'Île de Grâce* (1993) are perhaps her best-known and best-received novels, garnering accolades on both sides of the Atlantic with the former winning the Prix Molson de l'Académie canadienne-française, and the latter the prestigious Prix France-Quebec. In both these works history, as a legitimizing, inherently objective narrative, is subverted and transformed into a tapestry of stories (*histoires*) that erode the boundaries between reality and fiction, narrator and author, subject and object. In Ouellette-Michalska's vision of history, genealogy replaces chronology, giving voice(s) and substance to the muted anguish and desires of generations past. Indeed, her writing as a whole is infused with desire, as reflected in a strongly sensual, corporeal language.

STEPHANIE NUTTING

Outposts. This British literary magazine founded by Howard Sergeant in 1944 to promote the work of younger poets (notably Muriel Spark) was the first foreign poetry journal to devote an entire issue solely to the work of Canadian poets. *Outposts 10*, Summer 1948, was edited by Earle BIRNEY (editor of *Canadian Poetry Magazine*), whom Sergeant had met during the Second World War. By 1948, *Outposts* had become a vehicle for the British Poetry Association, a London-based group dedicated to opening the horizons of national poetries to an international poetic and an international audience. *Outposts 10* contained poems by Patrick ANDERSON, Louis DUDEK, Birney, E.J. PRATT, Malcolm LOWRY, P.K. PAGE, Robert FINCH, A.M. KLEIN, Dorothy LIVESAY, James REANEY, Roy DANIELLS, Miriam WADDINGTON, R.A.D. FORD, and Ralph GUSTAFSON. Space limitations precluded the inclusion of work by Margaret AVISON, Anne WILKINSON, and Raymond SOUSTER. Of the poems included, the most important, from a historical perspective, are Klein's satirical 'Quebec Liquor Commission', which appeared as 'Quebec Liquor Commission store' in his *The rocking chair and other poems* (1948), and Pratt's uncollected 'Lake Success'. Also of interest is Livesay's sonnet 'London rain'.

Useful as a barometer of the energy and concerns of the period, the issue was introduced by Birney with a brief essay, 'Contemporary Canadian poetry', in which he charted the rise of modernism in Canadian poetry, from the MONTREAL GROUP to the late 1940s, and where he noted the intense activity of such journals as *FIRST STATEMENT*, *Here and Now*, *PREVIEW*, *CONTEMPORARY VERSE*, and the then new *FIDDLEHEAD*. What makes this issue of *Outposts* a notable document, aside from the editorial observations and the poets represented, is that it anticipates the overwhelming importance that small magazines would play in the shaping of the Canadian literary identity during this era.

BRUCE MEYER

Outram, Richard (b. 1930) Born in Oshawa, Ontario, he attended Victoria College, University of Toronto (1949-53). He worked on technical crews for CBC-TV from 1956 to 1995, when he retired. With his wife he operates Gauntlet Press, founded in 1960. Outram's first book-length volumes, including *Exultate, jubilate* (1966) and *The promise of light* (1980), contain poems that are written in a loosely metaphysical mode, teasing out paradoxes and polarities with a meticulous playing with language, conceits, and mythological references. His poetry centres on the theme of the discrepancy between human aspirations and spirituality and the gross reality of the world. The ambivalencies of life—dark and light, real and ideal, spiritual and physical—are expressed in controlled structures.

The poetry of these years is contained in *Selected poems 1960-1980* (1984), a book that indicates in some of its poems a new direction in his work. While retaining Outram's delight in metaphysical paradox, it shifted towards a more open form without losing its hold on structure. In the same way Outram's language also opened into a more conversational and informal diction without letting go of formal elements. This newer style can be seen in *Hiram and Jenny* (1988), a series of poems about the lives and times of the two title characters in a small town in the Maritimes; in 1993 Outram published *Mogul recollected*, poems focusing on a shipwreck off the coast of New Brunswick, and in particular on an elephant drowned in that disaster. These two books approach the subject matter with both seriousness and humour. Outram's own Gauntlet Press has also published his *Around and about the Toronto islands* (1993), *Tradecraft* (1994), and *Eros descending* (1995).

PETER STEVENS

Ouvrard, Hélène. See NOVELS IN FRENCH 1960 TO 1982: 3(g).

Oxley, James MacDonald (1855-1907). Born into a relatively wealthy Halifax family, Oxley was educated at Halifax Academy, Dalhousie University, and Harvard. He was admitted to the Nova Scotia Bar in 1878 and practised law in Halifax for five years before becoming a legal adviser to the federal Department of Marine and Fisheries. In 1891 he moved to Montreal to join the staff of the Sun Life Assurance Company. He spent the final years of his life in Toronto.

Oxley wrote thirty-one books for boys, published between 1889 and 1905—unabashed adventure tales exploiting the northern and seafaring settings already made popular by G.A. Henty, R.M. BALLANTYNE, and Frederick Marryat. In general, as many of their titles indicate, his stories turn on themes of initiation and the experience of a personable boy-hero whose physical courage is tested in an exotic setting. He usually set them in a remote historical period, though he occasionally used his native Nova Scotia as a backdrop. Among his titles are: *Bert Lloyd's boyhood* (London, 1889); *Up among the ice floes* (London, 1890); *The wreckers of Sable Island* (London, 1891); *Archie of Athabaska* (Boston, 1893), published in London, 1894, as *Archie Mackenzie, the young Nor'wester; The good ship Gryphon; or On the right track* (Boston, 1893); *Fife and drum at Louisbourg* (London, 1899); and *L'Hasa at last* (1900).

GILLIAN THOMAS

P

Pacey, Desmond (1917-75). Born in Dunedin, New Zealand, William Cyril Desmond Pacey lived in England from 1924 to 1931, when he came to rural Ontario, where he finished school. He took his B.A. in English and Philosophy at the University of Toronto in 1938 and his Ph.D. from Cambridge University in 1941. He was professor of English at Brandon College, University of Manitoba, from 1941 to 1944, and then moved to the University of New Brunswick, where he remained until his death, serving as head of the Department of English (1944-69); dean of graduate studies (1960-70); vice-president academic (1970-5), and University Professor (1974-5). He was made a Fellow of the Royal Society of Canada in 1944 and received its Lorne PIERCE medal in 1972. Writing criticism that, like his teaching, was lucid, moderate, and modest in its claims, he helped to establish Canadian literature as a legitimate field of study in both schools and universities.

Pacey's publications in Canadian literature began with his *Frederick Philip Grove* (1945), which reflected an interest that continued with a selection of GROVE's stories, *Tales from the margin* (1971); an anthology of critical essays on Grove in the Critical Views of Canadian Writers series (1970); and his edition of *The letters of Frederick Philip Grove* (1976). His *Creative writing in Canada: a short history of English Canadian literature* (1952; rev. and enlarged, 1961) was the only handbook of its kind for many years. His *Ten Canadian poets: a group of biographical and critical essays* (1958) allowed him to treat more fully the work of SANGSTER, ROBERTS, CARMAN, LAMPMAN, D.C. SCOTT, PRATT, SMITH, F.R. SCOTT, KLEIN, and BIRNEY. He contributed two chapters—'The writer and his public', and 'Fiction 1920-1940'—to the *Literary history of Canada* (1965), of which he was an editor. His *Essays in Canadian criticism: 1938-1968* (1969) and *Ethel Wilson* (1968), in the Twayne World Authors Series, contain some of his best critical writing. He edited *A book of Canadian stories* (1947; 4th edn 1967) and *The selected poems of Sir Charles G.D. Roberts*

(1956), as well as the school anthology *Our literary heritage* (1966).

Pacey also published two collections of stories, *The picnic and other stories* (1958) and *Waken, lords and ladies gay* (1974), and two books for children: *The cow with the musical moo and other verses for children* (1952) and *Hippity Hobo and the bee* (1952). Two scholarly editions he was preparing at the time of his death were published posthumously: *The collected poems of Charles G.D. Roberts* (1985), completed by Graham Adams, and *The collected letters of Charles G.D. Roberts* (1989), completed by Laurel Boone. The exchange of letters between him and Irving LAYTON, edited as a dissertation for the University of British Columbia by Michael Pacey, is in press. ROBERT GIBBS

Paci, F.G. (b. 1948). Born in Pesaro, Italy, he immigrated to Canada with his parents in 1952 and grew up in Sault Ste Marie, Ontario. His education includes a B.A. (1970), and B.Ed. (1975) from the University of Toronto, where he was encouraged by Margaret LAURENCE, who was writer-in-residence; and an M.A. (1980) from Carleton University. Paci is the most important Italian-Canadian novelist writing in English, both because of the number of his publications and the consistent quality of his writing. His first novel, *The Italians* (1978), is a realistic representation of a large and diverse Italian immigrant family in Sault Ste Marie, and became a best-seller; it was translated into French by Robert Paquin as *La famille Gaetano* (1990). His best novel is *Black Madonna* (1982), the story of a young Canadian woman who totally rejects her Italian background and abandons her old-fashioned Italian mother to go off to university. Feminist ideas are also examined in *The father* (1984), where a strong mother takes over the family business. Following the conventions of realism, Paci's novels explore the struggle of Italian immigrant families in northern Ontario and the children of these families in Toronto. He has argued that his work is not so much about ethnic duality as about the essential self and the ultimate search for truth. Existentialist philosophical ideas are explored in a series of related novels beginning with *Black blood* (1991), followed by *Under the bridge* (1992), *Sex and character* (1993) (which recreates a scene with Margaret Laurence), and *The rooming-house* (1996).

See Joseph Pivato, ed., *Contrasts: comparative essays on Italian-Canadian writing* (1985); Joseph Pivato, *Echo: essays on other literatures* (1994); and Martin Waxman, 'The discipline of discovery', *Books in Canada* (Nov., 1994).

JOSEPH PIVATO

Packard, Frank (1877-1942). Born of American parents in Montreal, Frank Lucius Packard was one of the first Canadian authors to reach a wide audience outside Canada. He trained as an engineer, attending Montreal High School, Woodstock College, McGill University (B.Sc., 1897), and L'Institut Montefiore, Liège. While working as a civil engineer in the USA, he used to rise at 4 a.m. to write; in 1906 his first short story was published in *Munsey's Magazine*, and in 1911 a collection of his magazine fiction was brought out by Thomas Crowell of New York. Having married in 1910, Packard settled in Lachine, Quebec, and wrote his first novel, *Greater love hath no man* (1913). His next novel, *The miracle man* (1914), which originally appeared in *Munsey's*, was a great success. Adapted for the stage by George M. Cohan, it played at the Astor Theatre, New York, and was made into a popular silent film. In 1917 Packard published another best-seller, *The adventures of Jimmy Dale*, which set a pattern for his crime fiction. Thereafter he produced about a novel a year, all originally published in New York by Doran but reprinted in both Toronto and London.

Packard used several formulas to gain mass-market appeal for his novels. He drew on his experience with railroads for *The wire devils* (1918), a crime novel with a surprise ending, and for many of the stories in his first book, *On the iron at Big Cloud* (1911), which were reprinted, with additions, in *Running special* (1925). The same characters people the stories in *The night operator* (1919), tales stressing the technical competence and toughness of the railwaymen in the foothills of the American Rockies; despite melodramatic incidents, they present a believable social spectrum and suggest a heroic struggle to conquer a continent.

For his highly successful series of Jimmy Dale crime novels (five were published between 1917 and 1935), Packard haunted the streets of New York and joined police raids; but for all their authentic atmosphere, they have conventional plots that rely heavily on impenetrable disguise, miraculous escapes, and vital information overheard. Their chief character is a millionaire clubman and champion of honour and fair play who inhabits the underworld under various disguises and foils crime through his expertise in safe-cracking and lock-picking. By 1942 the series had sold an estimated three million copies and been made into a silent serial and a CBC radio series (1942-5). Similar motifs were used with other settings, such as the north shore of the Gulf of St Lawrence in *The hidden door* (1933). *The white moll* (1920) and *The big shot* (1929) both feature rather improbable female versions of Jimmy Dale. *The red ledger* (1926), containing stories of revenge for childhood wrongs, was adapted for serial presentation on CBC radio in 1937-8, with brief moralizing introductions spoken by Packard himself.

Another group of Packard's novels, labelled 'romances' by his publisher, are also crime novels but with more claim to serious consideration: they stress psychological themes of repentance, self-sacrifice, and redemptive love. In *Greater love hath no man* (1913),Varge shields his beloved foster-mother by confessing to a murder he did not commit. Characteristically, Packard imbibed the atmosphere for this novel by visiting the St Vincent de Paul Penitentiary in Montreal, but he transferred the setting to an unnamed American location. *The miracle man* (1914) and *The sin that was his* (1917) describe the experiences of wrongdoers who are gradually converted by a religious power they set out to mock. Other such novels are *The beloved traitor* (1915), *From now on* (1919), and *Pawned* (1921).

Packard visited the South Seas in 1912, and in the 1920s he began to use them as a setting for novels with exotic titles like *Two stolen idols* (1927) and *The gold skull murders* (1931). Packard's adventure fiction also includes two collections of short stories, *Shanghai Jim* (1928) and *More knaves than one* (1938), and a novel, *The four stragglers* (1923), set in the Florida Keys. These later works, like the crime novels, are on the whole perfunctory, though skilfully plotted. Packard's enormous output shows invention and careful attention to local colour hardening into formula.

JEAN O'GRADY

Page, P.K. (b. 1916). Patricia Kathleen Page was born at Swanage in the south of England. Her family came to Canada in 1919 and settled in Red Deer, Alberta. She was educated at St Hilda's School, Calgary, and, in later years, studied art under Frank Schaeffer in Brazil and under Charles Seliger in New York. She also attended the Art Students' League and Pratt Graphics in New York. During the late 1930s she worked as a shop assistant and a radio actress in Saint John, New Brunswick; she then moved to Montreal and worked there as a filing clerk and a historical researcher. There, in the early 1940s, she associated with the writers who, for a time, made that bilingual city the most important centre of English-language poetry in Canada.

Page published her first poems in Alan Crawley's *CONTEMPORARY VERSE* before she joined the MONTREAL GROUP that had founded *PREVIEW*. There she was associated with Patrick ANDERSON, F.R. SCOTT, and Neufville Shaw, and it soon became apparent that among the younger poets of the group, she was the most accomplished. Outside periodicals, her verse was first published in *Unit of five* (1942), which Ronald Hambleton edited and in which he introduced not only Page's poetry and his own, but also that of Louis DUDEK, Raymond SOUSTER, and James Wreford.

The first book entirely made up of Page's poetry, *As ten as twenty* (1946), showed a strong awareness of English poetic trends in the 1930s; and while Page did not make the extreme political commitments of those who at this time entered the Communist Party, it was evident that she had taken sides against the Anglo-Canadian establishment that then seemed to rule in Montreal. She also shared the psychoanalytic preoccupations of contemporary English poets, and some of the best of her early verse deals with various forms of neurosis. In terms of lyrical vision, the best piece of this first volume is undoubtedly the haunting 'Stories of snow', in which legend and dream and child memories are mingled—to quote A.J.M. SMITH—in 'a crystal clairvoyance'.

In 1946 Page started to work as a scriptwriter for the National Film Board, and remained there until 1950, when she married William Arthur Irwin, at that time commissioner of the NFB. In this period she wrote the poems that appeared in *The metal and the flower* (1954), which won a Governor General's Award. In their sharply visual presentations of concrete situations, and perhaps influenced by the space created in poetry by W.H. Auden for social commentary, the poems reflect the social concerns of a post-war world. They consider not ordinary political commitments but the plights of lonely people, or those whom circumstances have condemned to appear contemptible; some are miniature imaginary biographies that come as near as any writer can to the meeting of satire and compassion.

In 1944, under the *nom-de-plume* 'Judith Cape', she published a novel—or perhaps a romance—called *The sun and the moon*. Page has never explained her pseudonym, but Margaret ATWOOD noticed 'the visions of cloak-and-dagger and Holofernes' severed head raised by the last and first names respectively', and such associations are appropriate to a novel that deals with a young girl in touch with mysterious forces that almost destroy her artist husband. It was republished under Page's name in *The sun and moon and other fictions* (1973), which includes other stories from the 1940s that are less strained in credibility and at the same time more tightly organized. The best of them, as Atwood has said, are characterized by 'the bizarre perspectives and the disconcerting insights' that distinguish Page's best poems. Some, like 'The green bird' and 'George', project a wild yet pathetic sense of comedy. Others, such as 'The glass box', resemble early poems, like 'The landlady' and 'The stenographers', in their power to convey the sadness of lonely people trying to snatch a little meaning from their lives in the unfriendly city.

From 1953 to 1964—when W.A. Irwin acted as Canadian ambassador in Australia, Brazil, and Mexico—Page lived away from Canada and wrote comparatively little poetry, concentrating on paintings and intricate drawings she made under the name of P.K. Irwin—works that show how her various arts reflect each other, for they evoke poetic as well as aesthetic images. The unity of her arts is stressed in the new poems she included in *Cry Ararat!* (1967) and *Poems selected and new* (1974), both of which consist largely of works chosen from her first books, for she had written less abundantly in the sixties and early seventies than in the forties. *Cry Ararat!* includes reproductions of Page's paintings and drawings. Although in black and white, and thereby missing the colour that is Page's distinctive signature as an artist, the reproductions do give a sense of the dynamic movement and exquisitely detailed precision of her landscapes. The connections and correspondences between writing and painting are clear in 'Bark drawing', which shows her affinity with Australian native art, and evokes with marvellous economy her double talents: 'an alphabet the eye/lifts from the air/as if by ear/two senses/threaded through/a knuckle bone.'

The newer poems demonstrate a movement towards verbal economy that one can link with Page's later philosophic inclination towards the mystical tradition of Sufism. In *Evening dance of the grey flies* (1981), which consists entirely of uncollected works, there is an ever-increasing purification of the line. In the early poems the line was long and flowing, with the kind of full eloquence that belonged to the 1940s (in Canada and England alike). In the newer poems there is still a fluidity, but it is more controlled, sparser, yet ever-moving. Similarly the pattern of thought is modified, and filled with a metaphysical intent that shifts its direction from the inward images of the earlier poems to the images of natural sublimity that pose a way of liberation from the alienated, imprisoned self. Increasingly Page's poems carry a kind of Delphic utterance, almost a possession by the vision; though the poems are perhaps more sharply and intensely visual than ever in their sensuous evocation of shape and colour and space, their imagery takes us magically beyond any ordinary seeing into a realm of imagining in which the normal world is shaken like a vast kaleidoscope, and revealed in unexpected and luminous relationships. The centre-piece of *Evening dance of the grey flies* is a remarkable futurist story, 'Unless the eye catch fire . . .', which ostensibly deals with the death of earth as a habitation of man, and the end of time as man dies; but on another level it projects a visionary perception, suggesting that one does not have to wait for the end of time to apprehend eternity.

The glass air: selected poems (1985) ranged retrospectively over Page's body of work and included drawings and two eloquent essays on the genesis of her art(s):'Questions and images' and 'Traveller, conjuror, journeyman', which develop Page's idea that 'in all essential particulars writing and painting are interchangeable. They are alternate routes to silence.' In 1991 the book was reissued as *The glass air: poems selected and new* (1991) which contained a number of new poems such as 'A little fantasy' and 'I-Sphinx' that demonstrate Page's gift for creating dramatic voices in her poetry. *Hologram: a book of glosas* (1994) is a selection of fourteen elegant and intricate poems that resuscitate the late fourteenth-century Spanish poetic form, the *glosa*—which begins with a short stanza or *cabeza* of four consecutive lines taken from another poet, followed by four ten-line stanzas, each of which ends with a line from the *cabeza*. As Page explains in her preface, the poems allowed her to pay homage to those poets whose work she 'fell in love with' in her formative years. There is an elegiac quality to the poems as the poet looks back over a lifetime of experience, yet they build to a celebratory affirmation of the mystery of being human: 'We are the sea's, and as such we are at its beck./We are the water within the wave and the water's form./And little will man—or woman, come to that—/know what he shall dream when drawn by the sea's wrack/or what he shall hope for once it is clear that he'll never go back.'

Page has written two books of fairy tales for children: *A flask of sea water* (1989) and *The goat that flew* (1993). She has also edited an anthology of short poems, *To say the least; Canadian poets from A to Z* (1979). Her poetry has been set to music by composers as various as Murray Adaskin, Bernard Naylor, Ruth Waterson Henderson, and Harry Somers. She was made an Officer of the Order of Canada in 1977 and has received honorary degrees from four universities.

See *Still waters: the poetry of P.K. Page* (1991), a National Film Board Documentary on her life and work; and *The MALAHAT REVIEW, P.K. Page/A Special Issue*, no. 117 (Winter, 1996).

See also POETRY IN ENGLISH 1950 TO 1982: 2.

GEORGE WOODCOCK/ROSEMARY SULLIVAN

Page, Rhoda Anne (1826-63). Probably the best-known Canadian poet for a brief period in the late 1840s, Page was brought to Canada from her native England at the age of six, when her family immigrated to a farm near Cobourg, Canada West (Ontario). Beginning in 1846, using the initials R.A.P., she published her poetry regularly in *The Cobourg Star*, from which other newspapers copied it; her writing was therefore widely circulated through the Canadas. Her verse also appeared in *The Victoria Magazine*, *The Church*, and *The Maple Leaf Annual*. A pamphlet collection, *Wild notes from the backwoods*, was published in Cobourg in 1850. In 1856 she married William Faulkner and moved to the Rice Lake area. Eight children were born before her death. E.H. DEWART included five of her poems, using her married name, in his anthology *Selections from Canadian poets* (1864). Although a melancholy preoccupation with death runs through much of her work, Page was essentially a poet of nature. The Canadian backwoods she described as a tranquil world that owed its beauty and life to a genteel God. Her descriptive poem 'Rice Lake by moonlight: a winter scene' was the most widely reprinted Canadian work of its day. Page was one of the multitude of female lyric poets who peopled the literary world of the early nineteenth century. Although a modern reader becomes impatient with the correctness of the sentiment expressed, and with the restraint one feels in the poet's response to her subjects, at their best her verses flow smoothly and effortlessly, with great lyric charm. The Upper Canada she described is recognizable today.

MARY LU MacDONALD

Palermo, Sharon Gibson. See CHILDREN'S LITERATURE IN ENGLISH 1970s TO 1996: 1(c).

Panneton, Philippe (1895-1960). Better known under his pseudonym 'Ringuet' (his mother's family name), he was born in Trois-Rivières, Quebec. After completing his 'cours classique', he studied medicine at Université Laval, first in Quebec City, then in Montreal, and obtained his degree in 1920. He then left for Paris, spending three years on postgraduate studies in otorhinolaryngology. He travelled widely and, free of the restrictions imposed by the Catholic Index, was able to indulge his insatiable appetite for books. It was in this period that he started to keep a diary. (The 2,390-page diary that he left at his death has never been published.) Upon his return to Canada in 1923 he practised medicine in Montreal; until 1940 he was also consultant at the Hôpital Saint-Eusèbe, Joliette. Author of several specialized articles in medical journals, he was invited, in 1935, to become professor in the faculty of medicine at the Université de Montréal. In 1956 he was appointed ambassador to Portugal, where he died. He received the Prix de l'Académie française in 1953, the Prix Duvernay in 1955, and the Lorne PIERCE Medal in 1959; and he was president of the French-Canadian Academy from 1947 to 1953.

Panneton was very proud of being a physician: 'I am first a doctor and then a writer. Literature interests me like a sport. It is a distraction in my leisure time' (*La Revue populaire*, juillet 1939, p. 6). Nevertheless he diligently pursued this 'distraction'. From among his early writings, about thirty poems were published between 1917 and 1925 in periodicals and newspapers. Panneton's first book, *Littératures . . . à la manière de . . .* (1924), written in collaboration with Louis Francoeur, presented a series of parodies of well-known French-Canadian writers and prominent politicians of the time, such as Henri Bourassa, René Chopin, 'Valdombre' (C.-H. GRIGNON), Paul MORIN, Camille Roy, and Lionel GROULX. Several critics reproved the authors for having shown little respect for Abbé Groulx by making fun of his books *Rapaillages* and *L'appel de la race* in the pages entitled 'Rabâchages' (literally 'harping on the same string'), which ended with a scene called 'Appel de la crasse'. Nevertheless, the book was generally well received and was awarded the Prix David. Panneton's only other literary work at this time was an undistinguished play, *Je t'aime . . . Je ne t'aime pas*, performed at the Monument National on 28 April and 19 May 1927.

Panneton achieved his greatest success as a writer with the publication of *TRENTE ARPENTS* (1938). A portrait of a rural and traditional society in the process of change, it was an immediate success with both French and French-Canadian critics. It was translated almost immediately into English by Felix and Dorothea Walter—*Thirty acres*, 1940; Governor General's Award—and German.

L'héritage et autres contes (1946), a collection of nine stories that stress the characters' alienation and their insatiable need to escape their milieu, was given a poor reception. The title story, which is reminiscent of *Trente arpents* and was Panneton's favourite, was made into a short movie by the National Film Board in 1960. In the same year Morna Scott Stoddart published a translation in *Canadian short stories* (1960) edited by Robert WEAVER.

Panneton's second novel, *Fausse monnaie* (1947), which depicts the empty lives of a group of well-to-do young people, concerns a Don Juan who rediscovers during a weekend in the Laurentians a childhood friend whom he had considered vain and superficial; they seem briefly to be smitten with each other but their love does not endure. This novel, which Ringuet said was written primarily to describe the Laurentians, is full of hackneyed characters and commonplace expressions and had no success. *Le poids du jour* (1949) was much more ambitious. After the death of his beloved mother, Michel Garneau learns that his real father is not Ludovic Garneau, whom he has come to detest, but rather Monsieur Lacerte, his godfather and benefactor whom he loves. Imagining that everyone has known of his illegitimacy and been laughing at him all these years, he instantly hates what he has once loved, including Monsieur Lacerte. Wanting to be admired and feared, he changes his name to Robert M. Garneau and adopts the motto: 'To be happy, you must be rich. To be rich, you must be powerful.' Though he accumulates a large fortune in Montreal, he does not find contentment until, after a series of setbacks, he moves to the country. *Le poids du jour* often seems to use the story of Garneau merely as a pretext for the description of, and commentary on, the changes in Quebec society between the two world wars.

Un monde était leur empire (1943) is an unsuccessful popular history of pre-Columbian Mexico that grew out of Ringuet's visit to that country in 1934. *L'amiral et le facteur; ou Comment l'Amérique ne fut pas découverte* (1954) discusses the relative contributions of Christopher Columbus and Amerigo Vespucci in the discovery of the American continent. *Confidences* (1965), which was originally intended for radio broadcast, is a series of recollections of Panneton's childhood and youth, narrated with much humour and charm.

Panneton was well advised not to publish in 1926 his *Carnet du cynique*; these ninety pages from his diary raise unsparing questions about sacred values of his society and would probably have ruined his medical career.

Jean Panneton's *Ringuet* (1970) gives the best summary of his life and works. See also G. Rousseau and Jean-Paul Lamy, *Ringuet en mémoire* (1989). JACQUES COTNAM

Panych, Morris (b. 1952). Born in Calgary, Alberta, he studied creative writing at the University of British Columbia (B.F.A., 1977) and acting at the E.15 Acting School in London, England. Working initially as an actor (he has performed in more than fifty plays), Panych first achieved prominence as a playwright in 1982 at Tamahnous Theatre, Vancouver, British Columbia, with *Last call: a post-nuclear cabaret* (1983). This two-man musical, which he performed with Ken MacDonald (a frequent future collaborator), features the final two survivors of a nuclear holocaust, and plays with metatheatrical devices, such as a double ending to foreground the process of performance. Later plays continue to exploit the last stages of life as a convenient context for comic exaggeration. As Artistic Director of Tamahnous Theatre from 1984 to 1986, Panych turned the group away from its collective roots to produce instead musicals he created, such as the 1985 'Cheap Sentiment' and 'Contagious' (with Ken MacDonald). *Seven stories* (1990) moves into the surreal, isolating a solitary figure (The Man) on a ledge to contemplate suicide, while bizarre characters pop out of windows to play out their seven stories behind, across, and through him. Satiric references to philosophy, literature, politics, and art make highly comic the audience's attempts to fix meaning. *The ends of the earth* (1993) continues Panych's delight in comic philosophizing, and won a Governor General's Award. In *Vigil* (1996) Panych once more finds black comedy in imminent death, as an old aunt refuses to die as scheduled, despite the ingenuity of her impatient nephew. Panych also directs—for example, the remount of Judith THOMPSON's *White biting dog* at Tarragon Theatre, Toronto, in 1994

LISBIE RAE

Pâquet, Louis-Adolphe (1859-1942). Born in St-Nicholas, Quebec, and educated at the Séminaire de Québec and in Rome, Pâquet became professor, then dean, of theology, and director of the graduate school of philosophy at Université Laval, where his scholarship and his gifts as an orator made him one of the decisive influences on the intellectual life of Quebec. His writings on social questions and his influence within the Church also made him a formative influence on the character of the social order in Quebec, especially from the turn of the century to the Second World War. His six-volume study of St Thomas, *Disputationes theologicae seu commentaria in summam theologicam d. Thomae* (Québec, 1893-1903; 2nd edn, 1920-3), one of the great monuments of Thomist scholarship, gave Pâquet his authority as a philosopher. His interest, however, quickly turned to popular public issues. Yvan Lamonde—who gathered some of his short writings in *Louis-Adolphe Pâquet, textes choisis* (1972), and wrote the chapter on Pâquet in *Les idéologies au Québec, 1900-1929* (edited by Fernand DUMONT, 1973)—wrote that he 'personifies the passage from political and religious preoccupations to social questions' in Quebec.

Pâquet had a strong feeling for the land and for rural life in Quebec, and a powerful determination to maintain a culture that was both French and Catholic. He understood the need for, and the pressures towards, industrialization; but he sought to minimize its destructive impact by supporting the traditional family with a charitable and social order led by the Church. These general concerns were set out in a four-volume study, *Droit public de l'Église (Principes généraux*; *L'organisation religieuse et le pouvoir civil*; *L'action religieuse et la loi civile*; and *L'église et l'éducation*, 1908-15). Many of his published works were collections of essays and speeches: *Discours et allocutions* (1915), *Études et appréciations* (6 vols, *Fragments apologétiques*, *Nouveau fragments apologétiques*, *Mélanges canadiens*, *Nouveaux mélanges canadiens*, *Thèmes sociaux*, and *Nouveaux thèmes sociaux*, 1917-32), and *Au soir de la vie; modestes pages philosophico-religieuses* (1938). Frequently, as in his pamphlet *Sainte Anne et le peuple canadien-français* (1925), and his celebrated essay 'La vocation de la race français en Amérique' (edited by Émile Chartier and issued in 1925 as a pamphlet for youth movements in Quebec entitled *Bréviare du patriote canadien-français*), he tried to combine religion and national feeling. Deeply conservative, he opposed socialism with vigour but was equally opposed to *laissez-faire* capitalism, and wrote essays on the mutual responsibilities of capital and labour.

Pâquet wrote three other large works: *La foi et la raison en elles-même et dans leurs rapports* (Québec, 1890), *Cours d'éloquence sacrée* (2 vols, 1925-6), and *La prière dans l'oeuvre du salut* (2 vols, 1925-6). Besides the two pamphlets mentioned, at least eight other essays were published as small pamphlets, but most of this material appears in one or other of the collections. In the archives of the Séminaire de Québec there are personal diaries for extended periods (1883-1906, 1911-27, and 1940-1), as well as an extensive correspondence.

LESLIE ARMOUR

Paquin, Ubald (1894-1962). Born in Montreal, he worked as a journalist for *Le Devoir*, *La Patrie*, *Le Canada*, and *Le Nationaliste* successively, and in 1916 founded *La Bataille*. Implicated in the bombing of the home of the owner of the *Montreal Star* in 1917, he sought refuge in Abitibi, returning to Montreal in 1920 to open a bookstore, at which time he began his friendship with Claude-Henri GRIGNON. An unsuccessful nationalist candidate in the 1921 provincial elections, he spent the remainder of his life as a civil servant, trying to reconcile this career with his literary ambitions. He died in Montreal.

Paquin's fierce nationalism informs all his novels: *Jules Faubert* (1923), *La cité dans les fers* (1926), *Le lutteur* (1927), *Les caprices du coeur* (1927), *Le massacre dans le temple* (1928), *La mort qu'on venge* (1929), *La mystérieuse inconnue* (1929), *Le mirage* (1930), *Oeil pour oeil* (1931), and *Le paria* (1933). The muddled concepts and odious fascist ideology of these works can only be understood in the historical context of the 1929 stock-market crash and the rise of fascism, which cast a spell over some Quebec intellectuals; yet in several of them passion and instinct became a source of positive energy and presented a complex psychology that merits a serious psycho-critical reading. In *La cité dans les fers*, the hero masterminds a nationalist *coup d'état*, inspired by fascist militarism. *Jules Faubert* and *Le lutteur*, whose heroes are both self-made men, probe the psychology of the superman. The hero of *Le lutteur*, Victor Duval, inherits the physical strength and stamina of peasant forebears and, through will and self-denial, becomes a Quebec shipping magnate. In a sense, Paquin radically rethought the Québécois Messianism of the nineteenth century, being one of the first to value the French-Canadian businessman—whom he saw as responsible for the cultural and social progress of the race, provided he served the higher patriotism and embraced fascism. An unconscious death-wish is important in Paquin's work, the psychology of his characters being defined largely through the relations between the dominating and the dominated. Like *Le lutteur*, *La mystérieuse inconnue* and *Le mirage* focus on such preoccupations, but they lack *Lutteur*'s psychological complexity. The hero of *Le massacre dans le temple* pushes self-denial to its extreme: following a period of asceticism that amounts to self-mutilation, he ends up with the Trappists. Yet it is not clear that Paquin espoused Christianity: his ethics of race and moral force—surprisingly for his time—took the place of religion in his novels. Equally surprising is the influence of Zola on *Le paria* (written at a time when the naturalist novel was little esteemed in Quebec). Perhaps only in *Les caprices du coeur* did Paquin question the ideal of the superman: neither confident nor self-made, the hero is a nervous, hypersensitive character who finally yields to the need—latent in the superman—to kill. Paquin had no love for the masses whose will to power in the class struggle is unstable, leading to revolutionary carnage and anarchy. Nor was he a monarchist: the king in *Oeil pour oeil* would qualify as a superman, except that he yields his political power to the will of his mistress. In this novel Paquin shows a preference for a republic organized and run by aristocrats: only the élite possess the psychological ambivalence—love and hatred, refinement and primitivism—in the service of a higher principle, the state, that characterizes the superman. CLAUDE FILTEAU

Paradis, Suzanne (b. 1936). Born in Beaumont, Quebec, she graduated from the École normale in Quebec City, and was for a time in charge of the Centre d'art at Val-Menaud, in the Lac Saint-Jean region. She married the poet Louis-Paul Hamel in 1961. Her poetry, which is rhythmic and usually set in conventional rhymed hexameters, is notable for its abundance of metaphors and for a wealth of imagery that, though sometimes barely under control, is always evocative. She writes with great verve and passion of the quest for individual freedom, of the celebration of life and nature in all their aspects, and of love and personal fulfilment.

Paradis's collections are *Les enfants continuels* (1959); *À temps, le bonheur* (1960); *La chasse aux autres* (1961); *La malebête* (1963); *Pour les enfants des morts* (1964), which was awarded the Prix France-Canada; *L'oeuvre de pierre* (1968), winner of the Prix Du Maurier; *Pour voir les plectrophanes naître* (1970); *Il y a eu une maison* (1972); *La voie sauvage* (1972); *Noir sur sang* (1976); *Les chevaux de verre* (1979); *Un goût de sel* (1983), and *Effets de l'oeil* (1986). She has also published two books of short stories, *François-les-oiseaux* (1967) and *Grain de riz* (1977); and eleven novels: *Les hauts cris* (1960), *Il ne faut pas sauver les hommes* (1961), *Les cormorans* (1968), *Emmanuelle en noir* (1971), *Quand la terre était toujours jeune* (1973), *L'été sera chaud* (1975), *Un portrait de Jeanne Joron* (1977), *Miss Charlie* (1979); *Les Ferdinand* (1984), *La ligne bleue* (1985), and *Un aigle dans le basse-cour* (1986). The novella *Quand la terre était toujours jeune* was translated by Basil Kingstone as *When the earth was still young* in *CANADIAN FICTION MAGAZINE* 26 (1976).

The fluid style of Paradis's poetry becomes too studied in her fiction. Her gifts for metaphor and image-making overpower her novels and stories and make them unduly pretentious and obscure. The subject-matter is melodramatic. *Emmanuelle en noir* is a study of incest, madness, and violence, told through interior monologue and letters. In *Les cormorans* the inhabitants of a lonely island are destroyed gradually by murder, suicide, and natural disaster, leaving only a boy and girl to set off together in a skiff in search of a new life.

Paradis is also the author of *Femme fictive, femme réelle* (1966), a study of the female characters in the novels of French-Canadian women writers, and *Adrienne Choquette lue par Suzanne Paradis* (1978).

See also NOVELS IN FRENCH 1960 TO 1982: 3(f). JOYCE MARSHALL

Parameswaran, Uma. See SOUTH ASIAN-CANADIAN LITERATURE.

Parizeau, Alice (1930-90). Born Alicja Poznanska in Luniec, Poland, she grew up in Cracow. She participated in the Polish resistance movement, and was sentenced to a German work camp. After the war, in 1945, she went to Paris, where she studied literature, political science, and obtained a master's degree in law (1953). She then immigrated to Canada and began a career as a journalist in Montreal, contributing articles to *Châtelaine*, *Cité libre*, *La Presse*, *Le Devoir*, *La Patrie*, and *Maclean's*. In 1956 she married Jacques Parizeau (premier of Quebec, 1994-5), with whom she had a son and daughter. In 1970 Alice Parizeau joined the criminology faculty of the Université de Montreal, and in 1972 she became the secretary general of the Centre international de Criminologie comparée. Apart from her literary works, she was the author of numerous books and articles on criminal justice, juvenile delinquency, and children's rights.

Parizeau's first novels—*Fuir* (1963), *Survivre* (1965), *Rue Sherbrooke Ouest* (1967), and *Les militants* (1974)—though stylistically unsophisticated, reflected her dual allegiance to

Poland and Quebec, and illustrated what would become recurrent themes in her work: human suffering and forced exile in the aftermath of the Second World War, political commitment v. individual happiness, and the affirmation of Quebec identity. Her only collection of stories, *L'envers de l'enfance* (1976), evokes, through the eyes of a journalist with little or no literary artifice, the misery of Montreal's impoverished children.

In 1981 Parizeau published *Les lilas fleurissent à Varsovie* (translated by A.D. Martin-Sperry as *The lilacs are blooming in Warsaw*, 1985), for which she received le Prix de l'Association des écrivains de la langue française. This was the first of the three novels—including *La charge des sangliers* (1982) and *Ils se sont connus à Lwow* (1985)—that make up her ambitious 'cycle polonais'. Her subject is no less than the history of the Polish people, from the German occupation during the Second World War through Sovietization to the 1980s Solidarity movement. Told through the experiences of one family, in which the characters' individual happiness often conflicts with collective aspirations to political autonomy, this saga confirmed Parizeau as a master of short scenes, and of character and detail. Although her last novels, *L'amour de Jeanne* (1986) and *Nata et le professeur* (1988), and her play *Mais comment tuer le dogme?* (1989) returned to the emigré milieu, Parizeau's *Côte-des-neiges* (1983) and *Blizzard sur Québec* (1987) focused exclusively on Quebec. The former rewrote a critical period of Quebec history, the birth of its middle class during the Depression, while the latter in part redefined Quebec nationalism in dramatizing one of that society's most important collective projects: the founding in the 1940s of Hydro-Québec.

KATHERINE ROBERTS

Parker, Sir Gilbert (1862-1932). The son of a small-town storekeeper and former NCO, Horatio Gilbert Parker was born in Camden Township East, Canada West (Ontario). After graduating from Trinity College, University of Toronto, he taught elocution there; he was later ordained a deacon in the Anglican Church. A short period as a parish assistant in Trenton, Ont., concluded with his departure in 1885 for Australia, where he rapidly rose as a journalist, becoming assistant editor of the Sydney *Morning Herald*. Before his departure for England in 1889 he travelled extensively in the South Pacific, penning romantic accounts of the spots he visited. In England his skills as a writer of popular fiction, his position as a member of Parliament (1900-18), and his 'good' marriage advanced him steadily. A knighthood (1902), a baronetcy (1915), and membership in the Privy Council (1916) testify that a bright colonial son like Parker (along with Bonar Law and Max Aitken) could aspire to the inner circles of the Imperial motherland. During the Great War, Parker directed the British government's vast propaganda effort to move American public opinion in a pro-British direction, a project that was ultimately successful. Parker's last years were spent in California with the family of his brother.

Parker's *Works* (1912-23) comprise 23 volumes, most of them historical novels of romance and adventure, and two volumes of poetry, *A lover's diary* (Chicago, 1894) and *Embers* (1908). Some of the lyrics in *Embers* were set to music by Sir Edward Elgar.

Parker's contribution to Canadian letters rests on his fictional treatment of three subject areas: the romantic Northwest, picturesque Quebec, and heroic New France. *Pierre and his people* (London, 1892), a collection of adventure tales about the colourful Métis, Amerindians, Mounties, and Imperial adventures in a Northwest he had never visited, appeared originally in the New York *Independent* (whose assistant editor at that time was Bliss CARMAN). It put Parker on the map of literary London and was reprinted many times. Parker's Quebec—the subject of *When Valmond came to Pontiac* (London, 1895), *The pomp of the Lavilettes* (Boston, 1896), *The lane that had no turning* (London, 1899), and *The money master* (1915), among other novels—is a quaint, agrarian society filled with simple rustics whose lives become momentarily ruffled by scheming villains, hot-headed lovers, and restless adventurers. It is the Quebec celebrated by William Henry DRUMMOND, Louis HÉMON, and the painter Cornelius Krieghoff. New France offered an arena for heroic action in *The trail of the sword* (New York, 1894), *The seats of the mighty* (London, 1896), and *The power and the glory* (1925). *The seats of the mighty*, which is still available in a paperback reprint (NCL, 1971), stemmed from the same source book as *The GOLDEN DOG* by William KIRBY. Set at the time of the Conquest, it concerns the adventures in love and war of a British Army spy, Robert Moray, and was based partly on the *Memoirs* of Robert Stobo (1727-70). Moray finally wins Alixe and defeats his rivals; the British take Quebec; and English daring, drive, and hardihood are wedded to French charm, beauty, and emotional richness. No other novel quite sums up with such vigour and aplomb the Imperialist view of Quebec's role in Canada.

See John C. Adams, *Seated with the mighty: a biography of Sir Gilbert Parker* (1979) and Elizabeth Waterston, *Gilbert Parker and his works* (1989). DENNIS DUFFY

Parkman, Francis. See FOREIGN WRITERS ON CANADA IN ENGLISH: 2.

Parr, Joy (b.1949). Born in Toronto, Ontario, she was educated at McGill University, Montreal (B.A., 1971), and Yale University (M.Phil., 1973; Ph.D., 1977). She taught at Queen's University, Kingston, Ontario, at Yale, and at the University of British Columbia, before joining the department of history at Queen's (1982-92), becoming professor there in 1988, and then Farley Professor of History at Simon Fraser University, Burnaby, British Columbia.

Indicative of the fresh approaches to Canadian historical scholarship in the late twentieth century are the subjects Parr has drawn attention to: the ways in which children, women, gender, and consumerism figure in the past. *Labouring children: British immigrant apprentices to Canada, 1869-1924* (1980, rev. edn 1993) was the first thoroughly documented examination of the subject of dumping the unwanted offspring of industrial Britain on its North American colony ended. Unlike popular historians of this emotional subject who had recounted the story in journalistic manner, Parr's informative and dispassionate analysis revealed the critical stages in which immigration had occurred and the means taken to govern it. With children rather than politicians as her focus, Parr concluded that while there had been injustices, sometimes so severe as to bring premature death, the movement of young people had transpired with increasing attention to their needs. The book was decentring: children, rather than economics or politics, became the criterion on which historical judgement was based. Parr also edited *Childhood and family in Canadian history* (1982).

Parr conceived a seminal study that was published as *The gender of breadwinners: women, men and industrial change in two Ontario towns, 1880-1950* (1990). Mastering industrial processes in textiles and furniture-making, social structures, and economic change in the United Kingdom and Canada, she was able to show for the first time the gendered consequences of technological transfer and immigration as they were experienced in Paris and Hanover, Ontario. New directions were also indicated in her *A diversity of women: Ontario, 1945-1980* (1995). TERRY CROWLEY

parti pris (1963-8). Founded by Pierre Maheu, André MAJOR, and Paul CHAMBERLAND, *et al.*, it was a highly influential political and cultural review published in Montreal. Its founders reacted against the generation of intellectuals that preceded them, and especially those around the review *Cité libre*, reproaching them for denouncing the political corruption of the Duplessis régime and particular cases of injustice without attacking the fundamental injustices rooted in the economic and social structure of Quebec society. This initial ideology, mainly centred on the idea of decolonization, later developed into a certain radicalization. The leaders of the review defined the situation in a Marxist perspective: the struggle for political independence appeared only as the first step towards social revolution. An internal conflict over whether René Lévesque's Mouvement souveraineté-association (1968, later the Parti Québécois) should be supported tactically or a new radical party founded, and the editors' view that the main aims of *parti pris* (independence, secularism, and socialism) had been widely disseminated, led them to cease publication.

The magazine, and the publishing house Les Éditions parti pris (founded in 1961)—which was active for some three decades—played an important role in the literary and artistic development of Quebec. The literary theories of *parti pris* were outlined by the above-mentioned collaborators and others in the Jan. 1965 issue entitled 'Pour une littérature québécoise'. There it was proposed that the vehicle for a new orientation in creative writing should be *JOUAL*; the use of international French, it was felt, would be a travesty and would not allow Québécois to recognize their colonized status. Among the creative writers whose works were published under the auspices of the review were novelists Jacques RENAUD, André Major, and Laurent Girouard, and poets Paul Chamberland and Gérald GODIN. Contributing to the review were poet Raoul DUGUAY and film-makers Denys Arcand and Pierre Maheu. Although older than the founders and editors of *parti pris*, Claude JASMIN and Jacques FERRON also had some of their prose works published by Les Éditions parti pris. The publishing house later specialized in poetry, and in essays on political, economic, and social topics, including translations of books by radical English-language authors like Stanley B. Ryerson and James Laxer.

For more information on the political and literary importance of *parti pris*, see Malcolm

Reid's *The shouting signpainters: a literary and political account of Quebec revolutionary nationalism* (1972); issue 31-2 of *La* BARRE DU JOUR (hiver 1972), devoted entirely to *parti pris*; Joseph Bonenfant's *Index de parti pris 1963-1968* (1975); Lise Gauvin's *parti pris littéraire* (1975); B.-Z. Shek's *Social realism in the French-Canadian novel* (1977, chap. 9); and especially Robert Major's *parti pris: idéologies et littérature* (1979). See also studies of *parti pris*'s political and cultural orientations, respectively, by two of its most active collaborators, Jean-Marc Piotte (*Un parti pris politique*, 1979) and Paul Chamberland (*Un parti politique anthropologique*, 1983).

CLAUDE TROTTIER/BEN-Z. SHEK

Pearson, Kit (b. 1947). Kit (Kathleen Margaret) Pearson was born in Edmonton, Alberta. She worked as a children's librarian in the public libraries of St Catharines and North York, Ontario, and Burnaby, British Columbia. After receiving her M.A. in children's literature from Simmons College, Boston, she settled in Vancouver, British Columbia.

Pearson's first novel for children, *The daring game* (1986), is an exploration of boarding-school life in 1960s Vancouver. In *A handful of time* (1987) Pearson blends fantasy and social history with the dynamics and secrets of family life. She has written a historical trilogy—*The sky is falling* (1989), *Looking at the moon* (1991), and *The lights go on again* (1993). Pearson's latest novel, *Awake and dreaming* (1996), is a ghost fantasy.

Pearson's novels are straightforward, clear, and tightly written with a gentle pace and, most often, episodic plots. A recurring theme is that of children being uprooted, leaving their homes, and forming their own societies as separate tribes apart from the intervention of parents and other adults. Another pattern is the exploration of personal integrity and courage as child characters become involved in moral choice and dilemmas. The novels have strong, memorable characters, usually eleven- or-twelve-year-old girls in the pre-pubescent stage of personal strength, confidence, and imagination. All the novels are rooted in the history and landscape of different parts of Canada.

The singing basket (1990) is a picture-storybook that retells a French-Canadian folktale of deceit and trickery as a woodcutter husband outwits his wife in a clever, lively manner. The text is a rewriting of the story that accompanied Ann Blades' fine watercolour paintings for an earlier edition of the tale.

Pearson has received the Canadian Library Association Book of the Year Award for Children, the Mr. Christie's Book Award, the Geoffrey Bilson Award for Historical Fiction for Young People, the IODE Violet Downey Book Award, and the Manitoba Young Reader's Choice Award. JUDITH SALTMAN

Pelletier, Aimé (b. 1914). A Montreal physician and surgeon who wrote under the pseudonym 'Bertrand Vac', he was born at Saint-Ambroise-de-Kildare, Quebec, a small village about sixty-five kilometres north of Montreal. Between periods of medical studies in Montreal and Paris, he joined the Canadian army (1942-6) and was attached to the general staff in northern France and Belgium. Upon returning to Canada he resumed his career in medicine, while at the same time travelling widely and devoting part of his leisure to writing.

Despite winning three times the Prix du Cercle du Livre de France (1950, 1952, 1965), Vac is relatively little known. His first novel, *Louise Genest* (1950), won the Prix the first year it was offered. Set in the village of Saint-Michel-des-Saints and the surrounding forest area north of Joliette, it relates the drama of a woman married at the age of seventeen to the owner of the general store, Armand Genest, a coarse, brutal, miserly man who makes her life unbearable. When Louise leaves her husband to seek happiness in the forest with a young half-breed hunter and trapper, Genest, to punish her, withdraws their sixteen-year-old son from the college where he is studying and the boy winds up working in a logging camp. When he fails to return from a hunting expedition, Louise—tortured by guilt, remorse, and the conviction that she has abandoned him—sets out alone to search for him. Finding only his rifle, she suffers from hallucinations, succumbs to the elements, and dies of exhaustion. The forest, and the myth of the noble savage living a life of freedom and contentment in the heart of nature, are both important in this novel; but elements of social criticism are even more significant: tragedy springs from the guilt Louise suffers as a result of her upbringing and social and psychological pressures.

In *Deux portes . . . une adresse* (1952), one of the few French-Canadian novels based on the Second World War, Captain Jacques Grenon, a twenty-seven-year-old engineer who is unhappily married and the father of two young sons, has been in the army for four years and falls in love with Françoise Clair, a charming, cultivated, wealthy young widow.

Much of the evolution of their love is revealed in a year-long exchange of letters between their infrequent meetings. The captain finally decides not to return to his wife, but she writes to his commanding general and has him repatriated against his will. Back in Montreal, he is swallowed up in the quagmire of his former existence.

In *Saint-Pépin, P.Q.* (1955) satire and caricature enliven this story of political antics in a small Quebec town. The main character, Polydor Granger, becomes an election candidate in spite of himself, attracting in his wake a colourful collection of local bigots, opportunists, malcontents, and hypocrites. The election campaign, in which Granger is successful, is preposterous and unleashes all sorts of passions—some shameful, some comic.

L'assassin dans l'hôpital (1956), Vac's detective novel about an Ungava mining fortune and triple murder, was awarded the Prix du Cercle du Roman policier and was adapted for television by Radio-Canada (1956). *La favorite et le conquérant* (1963) is a painstakingly documented historical novel whose action begins in 1397 during the reign of the famous Tartar chieftain Tamerlaine, ruler of Samarkand. The action flags at times, but the vast and exotic narrative—interspersed with passages of crude, erotic, and almost scabrous violence—is deftly handled.

In 1965 Vac was awarded his third Prix du Cercle du Livre de France for *Histoires galantes* (1965), a collection of eight short stories varying in length from six to thirty-six pages. Light and licentious, sometimes amusing, occasionally unpredictable, they constitute a series of variations on the theme of not-so-serious sex.

Mes pensées 'profondes' (1967) is a tongue-in-cheek collection of maxims, aphorisms, and witticisms arranged chronologically from 1958 to 1966. *Le carrefour des géants* (1974), a social history of Montreal between 1820 and 1885, may also be construed as a history of Canada seen through the eyes of Montrealers. Avoiding the rigorous methodology of the professional historian, Vac succeeds in painting a fascinating, albeit ironic picture of Montreal and its inhabitants.

See Guy Robert, 'Trois livres de Bertrand Vac', *La Revue dominicaine*, LXII, tome 1, (jan.-fév., 1956). L.W. KEFFER

Pelletier, Pol. See DRAMA IN FRENCH 1981 TO 1996: 5.

Péloquin, Claude (b. 1942). Born and raised in Montreal, he began to write at thirteen and gave his first poetry reading shortly after his seventeenth birthday. He co-founded in 1964 a group called 'L'horloge du nouvel-age', whose presentations combining electronic music, slides, films, dance, and poetry gave birth to the era of COLLECTIVE CREATIONS and multi-dimensional shows in Quebec. A year later he founded another group, 'Le Zirmate', whose collective multi-media creations, produced at the Musée de l'art contemporain, were greeted by critics as courageous pioneering attempts to synthesize different modes of artistic expression.

But these activities did not hinder Péloquin's commitment to writing. After the publication of his first volume of poetry, *Jericho* (1963), in which he wove surrealist images, *Les essais rouges* (1964) and *Les mondes assujetis* (1965) explored other stylistic possibilities: automatic writing, wildly opposed semantic connotations, and nonsensical sound patterns frequently joined by a single metaphor. Péloquin was then described by French poet Alain Bosquet as 'the most seductive of all avant-garde poets' and won a place in Pierre Segher's Parisian anthology of the best poets of 1966. In the late sixties and early seventies he performed in the Zirmate's productions, wrote the words of Robert Charlebois's famous song 'Lindbergh', and also wrote the text that was incorporated in a mural displayed in front of Quebec City's Grand Théâtre in 1967. He continued to publish collections of prose-poems: *Manifeste infra suivi des Émissions parallèles* (1967), dedicated to the NASA scientists; *Pyrotechnics* (1968); *Pour la grandeur de l'homme* (1969); and *Mets tes raquettes* (1972), in which he stated and developed the main themes of his poetry: his struggle against death, his passionate rejection of human finitude, and his plea for the biological continuation of our species. He has been called by some critics a 'death-obsessed poet', and by others 'an eternalist', descriptions that often tend to draw attention away from his essential concern: the conscious exploration of what he calls our 'infra-structures'. Péloquin urges us to transcend rational limits, to imitate the scientists' open-mindedness to new laws, based on new empirical evidence, and to decipher the 'incommensurable' within us. This concern is also manifested in the very form of his writings: his texts are strewn with graphs, diagrams, and mathematical equations; a number are open-ended; most urge readers to apply their own method of reading—to backtrack, skip, fill in the blanks. *Manifeste infra* is described on the dust jacket as 'an open work', an explicit reference to the Italian philosopher and semiotician Umberto Eco. Indeed, Péloquin strives to arouse his readers' creative capacities, to stimulate their cerebral powers, and to enlist their collaboration in the making of a work, thereby replacing the traditional process of communication between creator and audience with a new mode of participation. The calligraphic aspects of the poems echo those of other contemporary poets (Raoul DUGUAY and Paul CHAMBERLAND in Quebec, and bp NICHOL in English Canada, to mention only a few). But Péloquin's passion for rejecting conventional typography reveals the need to express himself beyond the confines of the written word through visual forms, artefacts, and sculptures. In 1974 he exhibited some of his montages—surgical instruments mounted under glass—at the Galerie Martal and Espace 5 in Montreal. In 1976 he exhibited his first lithographs at the Jolliet Gallery, Quebec City. His *Le premier tiers, oeuvres complètes, 1942-1975* was published in three volumes in 1976. There followed *Inoxydables* (1977) and *L'autopsie merveilleuse* (1979); at the time neither book attracted much critical attention.

Peloquin's artistic development led him much farther than Chamberland's spiritualism. By the mid-1980s, in keeping with his acute awareness of death, he came to embrace a somewhat more Christian approach, as can be seen in *Une plongée dans mon essentiel* (1985), which has been termed an autobiographical manifesto; it reproduces the 'open' character of the work published in the late 1970s and was prefaced by Roger LEMELIN, who had been critical in 1969 of Peloquin's anti-conformists texts. In *L'ouragan doux: éternitextes 1970-1990* (1990) Peloquin opens with a text on the issue of national identity, which is followed by a collocation of narrative prose texts and poetic texts. Texts written in his later years describe his travels, his ideas on the nature of writing, the Zirmate movement, and include a religious poem, 'Prière'. Some essays and poems are in English.

Clément Moisan, in his *Poésie des frontières* (1979), devotes a chapter to Péloquin, bill BISSETT, and bp Nichol. An interview with Péloquin can be found in Caroline Bayard and Jack David, *Out-Posts/Avant-postes* (1978).

CAROLINE BAYARD/FRANCESCA BENEDICT

Percy, H.R. (1920-96). Born in Burham, Kent, England, he served in the Royal Navy from 1936 to 1952 and in the Royal Canadian Navy until 1971. He edited the *Canadian Author and Bookman* from 1962 to 1965 and in this period wrote a column for the *Ottawa Journal*. He was founding chair of the Writers' Federation of Nova Scotia.

Percy's essays and short stories appeared in many British and Canadian anthologies and magazines. His collection of stories *The timeless island* (1960) largely features bittersweet romances and sentimental idylls in formally controlled language. In his novel *Flotsam* (1968) David Bronson's memories of social and nautical experiences are developed in an alternately lyric and realistic narrative. The memories of a dying painter, Emile Logan, structure Percy's second novel, *Painted ladies* (1983), which considers art and life with a characteristic poetic intensity of expression. Percy's mature, uncollected stories reflected his developing concern with the fluidity and 'emotional cargo' of language. *A model lover* (1986) collected most of his short stories. His evocative and sometimes puckish narratives are particularly distinguished by their metaphoric richness: three of his most accomplished, psychologically focused, and highly contained stories are 'An inglorious affair', 'Falling for Mavis', and 'A model lover'. The novel *Tranter's tree* (1987), a historical romance written in a whimsical, self-conscious style, with eccentric characterization, is an archly comic and sentimental Maritime tall tale about continuity and the spirits of place. Percy also wrote two short biographies, *Joseph Howe* (1976) and *Thomas Chandler Haliburton* (1980), for The Canadians series.

LOUIS K. MacKENDRICK

Perrault, Pierre (b.1927). Born in Montreal, Quebec, he was educated there in various classical colleges—where he met Hubert AQUIN and Marcel DUBÉ, with whom he published *Les cahiers d'Arlequin*—and then in law at the universities of Montreal, Paris, and Toronto. He paid his way though university as a hockey player and coach.

The brilliant reconstructions in his films of traditional life on the Île-aux-Coudres and in the Abitibi region have earned Perrault an international reputation. Also, as a poet, dramatist, and broadcaster, he has published two collections of verse—*Chouennes* (1975) and *Gélivures* (1977)—and several film scenarios: *Le règne du jour* (1968), *Les voitures d'eau* (1969), and *Un pays sans bon sens* (1972). His best-known play is *Au coeur de la rose* (1964), a three-act poetical drama set against a background of gulls, gannets, divers, flowers, and islands, in which people try to find significance in nature and the collective folk memory; it was performed in 1963 and 1974.

Perrault has made himself the memory of a people, teasing out from the past of a tiny down-river kingdom a saga of human wit, skill, and energy, enlivened with music and anecdote. Though his poetry deals with a cold, northern world of nostalgia and struggle, it is humorous, lyrical, and surprisingly unsentimental. *Gélivures*, a long poem in three cantos, is both a hymn to the wintry northlands and a reflection on the difficulty of authentic recall. A strident tone in Perrault's poetry, which he calls 'joualeresque', is tempered with the humour of his 'chouennes'—his amiable tall stories. His films on the Île-aux-Coudres succeed perfectly in overcoming self-consciousness and doubtful recall by evoking the past preserved in traditional pursuits. In innocently asking his interlocutors to recreate the beluga hunt or to hand-build a small boat, Perrault triggers off a chain of involuntary memory and restores the vocabulary of many crafts and the vital speech of the isolated communities whose chronicler he became. He did this 'pour la suite du monde', convinced that continuity, and a national memory, living and actualized in terms of real people and tangible phenomena, are an antidote to melancholy, alienation, and bitter resentment.

La bête lumineuse (1982) is a transcription of the scenarios for the film of the same title, and contains Perrault's commentary on its exploration of the relationships among a group of hunters, and of the primordial nature of murder, violence, and domination, themes that also figure in his 1993 film *L'Oumigmag*. *Caméramages* (1983) is a collection of texts that focus on his approach to, and theories on, film-making, where he revealed both a political and an aesthetic concern for the context of Québécois culture and what he considered its colonized people. Perrault wrote of his extensive travels in *Le Saint-Laurent/Mia et Klaus* (1984). His expedition across the Atlantic, as he retraced Jacques Cartier's discovery route, is featured in *La grande allure* (1989, 2 volumes), which is also a transcription of Perrault's 1985 film of the same title. This work originated in his 1983 film *Les voiles bas et en travers*, and again reveals Perrault's thoughts on the question of Quebec. His militant stance throughout the mid-1960s to the late 1970s on the issue of Quebec's independence was articulated in the essays collected in *De la parole aux actes* (1985), which also includes texts on Hubert AQUIN, Félix-Antoine SAVARD, and Gaston MIRON. In 1988 Perrault published a third version of *Au coeur de la rose: pièce en trois actes*. *Toutes îles: récits* (1990) is a reissue of 1963 and 1967 works of the same title. Another film-scenario, *Pour la suite du monde* (1992), is a poetic account of his 1963 'cinematographic fable' of the fishermen of l'Île-aux-Coudres, their everyday speech and activities. Throughout his work Perrault stresses the importance of discovery, and of the open spaces necessary not only for the survival, but for the strength and freedom, of the people and culture he represents and chronicles.

See the interview with Paul Warren in *Cinéaste de la parole* (1996). For an analysis of Perrault's work, see Gilles Thérien, 'La bête lumineuse ou le gibier imprévu', *VOIX ET IMAGES* 8.1 (1982) and 'Les Indiens du celluloïd', *Revue d'histoire littérature du Québec et du Canada-Français* 11 (hiver-printemps 1986); Yves Laberge, 'La grande allure', *Séquences* 128 (février 1987); Jean-Daniel Lafond, *Les traces du rêves* (1988); Lucie Robert, 'Constellation classique', *Voix et images* 14.2 (1989); and Claude Albert, 'Poésie et réalité, le sens caché de L'Oumigmag de Pierre Perrault', in *Cinémas* 5.3 (1995). See also *VO: Le magazine de vie ouvrière* 243 (juillet-août 1993) for comments on Perrault's work as a film-maker.

C.R.P. MAY/MARIE J. CARRIÈRE

Perrot, Nicolas. See BIOGRAPHY AND MEMOIRS IN FRENCH: 6 and Writing in NEW FRANCE: 1.

Persaud, Sasenarine. See CARIBBEAN-CANADIAN LITERATURE.

Persky, Stan. See GAY LITERATURE: 1.

Peterson, Len (b. 1917). Leonard Byron Peterson was born in Regina, Saskaschewan, of Norwegian stock. He received a B.Sc. (1938) from Northwestern University, Illinois, USA. For over four decades he has been a professional man of letters and the theatre. He established his reputation as a radio dramatist in the forties, collaborating with Andrew Allan and Esse Ljungh; he has also written documentary films, musicals, novels, stage plays for both children and adults, and has adapted French-Canadian and European authors. During his long career he has produced more than 1,200 scripts.

The 1930s left an indelible stamp on his work. A recurring theme in his plays is the destruction of the individual or the small community by impersonal states or societies. Variations on this theme are present in *Burlap bags* (1972), which presents a vertiginous vision of the world's absurdity and human insensitivity; *Almighty voice* (1974), a one-act children's play produced for Young People's Theatre, Toronto, in 1975, about the government's hunt for a Cree who stole a cow to feed his starving people; *They're all afraid* (1981), which concerns a young man's alienation in a society governed by neurotic anxieties; and *The trouble with giants* (1973), a radio play—winner of a 1973 ACTRA award—that touchingly evokes the erosion of a unique Lithuanian culture by the acquisitive ruthlessness of both Germany and Russia. Peterson's passionate identification with the underdog in his struggle against depersonalizing institutions lends energy to his plays, but sometimes his presentation of the conflict is simplistic. His best stage piece is *The great hunger* (1967), first produced by the Arts Theatre, Toronto, Nov. 1960. Set in the Arctic, and about retribution for a killing, its theme is the importance of communal myths by which men—white or Inuit—live or perish.

In attempting to explore the complexity of the self, Peterson frequently resorted to psychodrama in which fragments of the psyche assume distinct identities. *Women in the attic* (1971)—about a newspaperman who, while covering the funeral of a celebrated lady of pleasure, enters the reality of her life as it is revealed in her diary—and *Burlap bags* (1973) both use this expressionistic device in combination with moments of theatrical realism.

In addition to writing instructional scripts for young people that were produced on CBC radio, Peterson has written several one-act plays produced by Young People's Theatre, notably *Billy Bishop and the Red Baron* (1975), about the Great War flying aces Billy Bishop and Baron von Richthofen. In 1984 he won an ACTRA award for best radio drama for *Evariste Galois*, and he wrote the libretto for the chamber opera *Clear sky and thunder*, music by Ruth Watson Henderson, which was performed at Vancouver's Expo '86.

MICHAEL TAIT

Petitclair, Pierre (1813-60). Born of illiterate parents at Saint-Augustin-de-Portneuf, near Quebec, he attended local schools and the Petit Séminaire de Québec, which he left in 1829 without completing his studies. He then worked as a copyist and notary's clerk before accepting, in 1838, a position as tutor to the twelve children of a wealthy family trading in Labrador. He spent most of the rest of his life there, returning occasionally to Quebec City. Petitclair was the author of three published plays: *Griphon; ou La vengeance d'un valet* (Québec, 1837); *La donation* (Québec, 1842), and *Une partie de campagne* (Québec, 1865); of a short story in verse, *Le revenant* (*Le Canadien*, 27 July 1831), and one in prose, *Une aventure au Labrador* (*Le Fantasque*, 2 nov. 1840); and a half-dozen poems.

Petitclair is remembered primarily as a dramatist, his *Griphon* being generally acknowledged as the first play published by a native French Canadian (an identification that is appropriate only if one disqualifies the five anonymous 'Comédies du statu quo', 1834, as being more politics than theatre). This play—although published, it was never performed—is a three-act comedy with strong farcical elements, many of them inspired directly by Molière (*Tartuffe*, *Les fourberies de Scapin*) and by Shakespeare in the Falstaff plays, which had been introduced to French Canada in the Ducis translations. A valet enlists a friend's support in seeking revenge against his master, Griphon, an aged, lusting hypocrite. The disguises and the pratfalls they prepare for the old man quickly become repetitive, as the structure of the play deteriorates towards its artificial moralizing end, where all is set right. *La donation*, performed several times in the 1840s before its second publication in James Huston's *Répertoire national* (Montréal, 1848), is a two-act play strongly influenced by melodrama, with concomitant simplification of character and plot, and many monologues and asides. A wealthy merchant, Delorval, is persuaded by an intriguer, Bellire, to dispossess his niece and to forbid her marriage to the hero, Auguste, as a result of false rumours Bellire has spread about the latter. The calumny is unmasked in time, with heavy reliance upon melodramatic *coups de théâtre*. Despite its defects, the play seems to have been well received by contemporary audiences. Petitclair's last surviving dramatic work (only the titles of two other plays are known), the two-act comedy *Une partie de campagne*, was written in 1856, first performed in 1857, and published posthumously in Quebec in 1865. Its theme is similar to that of Joseph QUESNEL's *L'anglomanie* (1803), depicting the evils inherent in aping English manners and speech. Better constructed than his preceding works, this play establishes the full extent of the protagonist's infatuation with all that is English, and then in Act II ridicules and finally punishes him for it. Petitclair here demonstrates a keen ear for rural accents and diction, while breathing more life into his characters than before.

Both his short stories deal with superstitions and their effects. *Le revenant*, his first published work, tells of a prisoner who escapes by taking the place of a body that is removed from prison in a coffin, and whose 'resurrection' consternates the assembled mourners. *Une aventure au Labrador* combines a ghost story with an account of a curious hunting accident and is remarkable chiefly for its romantic description of Labrador itself. Of the six poems credited to Petitclair, one, 'Le bon parti', is a comic song; three ('La somnambule', 'À Flore', and 'Sombre est mon âme comme vous') are Lamartinian in tone, dealing with the sorrow of unfaithful love; a fifth is in praise of Governor Sir Charles Bagot ('Le règne du juste'); and the last, 'Pauvre soldat! qu'il doit souffrir', describes the heroism of a patriotic soldier. All except the first are reproduced in both editions of Huston's *Répertoire national* (1848-50, 1893).

See L.E. Doucette, *Theatre in French Canada, 1606-1867* (1984) and the entry on Petitclair in *The Oxford companion to Canadian theatre* (1989). L.E. DOUCETTE

Petrone, Penny. See ABORIGINAL LITERATURE: NATIVE AND MÉTIS LITERATURE: 4 and ABORIGINAL LITERATURE: INUIT LITERATURE 1982 TO 1996.

Phelps, Anthony (b.1928). Born in Port-au-Prince, Haiti, he completed a humanities program at the Collège Saint-Louis-de-Gonzague (1947), studied chemistry at Seton Hall University, New Jersey, USA (1950-3), and ceramics at Montreal's École des Beaux-Arts (1953). Returning to Haiti, he became director of cultural programming at Radio-Cacique, where he produced a weekly program of poetry and theatre. In the early 1960s Phelps founded the journal *Semences*, directed Prisme, a theatre troupe, and was heavily involved with the group of poets known as Haïti littéraire. During this period he published three volumes of poetry: *Été* (1960), *Présence* (1961), and *Éclats de silence* (1962). In 1964 he immigrated to Quebec, first working as a cameraman with Productions Ville-Marie and acting at Le Théâtre de l'Estoc (Quebec City), before joining Radio-Canada in Montreal, where he has worked as a news journalist since 1966.

Phelps' interest in various literary genres soon became evident. Two volumes of short stories were published in Paris and Montreal respectively: *Mon pays que voici, suivi de Les dits du feu-aux-cailloux* (1968) and *Et moi je suis une île* (1973). A first play, *Le conditionnel*, was produced at Hull's L'Escale (1970) and Toronto's Théâtre du P'tit Bonheur (1977). His first novel, *Moins l'infini. Roman haïtien* (1973)—which has been translated into Spanish, Russian, and German—is the first of several works that reflect his ongoing concern with conditions in the land of his birth. His second, *Mémoire en colin-maillard* (1976), in which the narrator-protagonist seeks to identify the person who betrayed two children to the political police of a country strongly resembling Haiti, illustrates the author's mastery of language and his penchant for poetic prose. The same year he also edited a volume of essays, *Trente ans de pouvoir noir en Haïti*, and in 1985 published another novel, *Haïti! Haïti!*

Best known for his poetry—which has been translated into English, Spanish, and Russian—Phelps has published poetic texts in many journals, such as *Conjonction* (Haiti), *Marginales* (Belgium), and *Présence africaine* (France).

The poetry collection *Motifs pour le temps saisonnier* (1976) was followed by *La bélière Caraïbe* (1980), published in Montreal and Havana, in which the poet comes to terms with the complexities of his people, emerging from the trifold mix of Indian, African, and European ancestry into what he calls the Caribbean man. Reflecting the poetic maturity of a poet in exile, *La bélière Caraïbe* was awarded the Cuban poetry prize, Casa de las Americas. Phelps's most powerful poetry is found in *Orchidée nègre* (1987), which is divided into two parts: 'Typographe céleste' contains a selection of texts written from 1981 to 1983, while 'Orchidée nègre' conjures up a litany of sensuous evocations of the erotic beauty of *Caraïbe*, his Caribbean lover and homeland—confirming Phelps' mature nationalism and his mastery of the poetic art.

RAMON HATHORN

Philip, Marlene Nourbese (b. 1947). Born Marlene Irma Philip in Tobago, and raised in Trinidad from the age of eight, she adopted the name 'Nourbese', a Benin name from Nigeria, and now signs her work M. Nourbese Philip. She earned a B.Sc. in economics at the University of the West Indies (1968), then immigrated to Canada, where she completed an M.A. in political science (1970) and an LL.B. degree (1973) at the University of Western Ontario. She practised law in Toronto from 1973 to 1982, working in the areas of immigration and family law, primarily as a partner in the firm Jemmott and Philip, the first black women's law partnership in Canada. During this period she also wrote the poetry that appears in two collections, *Thorns* (1980) and *Salmon courage* (1983).

Since she turned to writing full-time in 1982, Philip's publications include *Harriet's daughter* (1988), a novel for young people; *She tries her tongue, her silence softly breaks* (1989), a poetry cycle that won the Casa de las Américas Prize for English-language Caribbean poetry; *Looking for Livingstone: an odyssey of silence* (1991), an epic narrative in poetry and prose; and two collections of essays, *Frontiers: essays and writings on racism and culture* (1992) and *Showing grit: showboating north of the 44th parallel* (1993). She was awarded a Guggenheim Fellowship for Poetry in 1990, is a charter member of Vision 21 (a coalition of writers and artists opposing racism in the arts in Canada), and has taught creative writing and women's writing at several Canadian universities.

The poems in Philip's early collections deal powerfully with the experience of colonialism in the Caribbean, and particularly imperial attempts to smother a living, resonant culture under the spurious cover of transplanted hegemonic rituals and symbols—such as the English Queen's state visit, which is cleverly repudiated in the poem 'Oliver Twist'. In *She tries her tongue*, Philip portrays the English language itself, along with its literary conventions, as an instrument of colonization, a 'father tongue' that is inescapable yet patriarchically abusive in its systematic erasure of the native tongues of those under its sway—unlike the subversive tongue of the mother, which can blow into infant mouths an oppositional counter-speech with which to resist imperial fathers. Her most ambitious text, *Looking for Livingstone*, records a woman traveller's epic journey across time (18 billion years) and space (much of Africa) as she visits a series of mythic tribes, all of whose names are anagrams of the word SILENCE, who teach her the power of self-imposed and self-exploratory silence, the true 'dark continent' out of which full-voiced counter-discursive identity can ultimately emerge.

Philip's powerfully written essays about issues of race, gender, and class speak particularly of the marginalization of writers of colour in Canada, a 'bordering' that must be countered, in her view, by reconstructing those borders as 'frontiers'. Referring to herself as 'Afrosporic', Philip sees herself, along with all other 'New World Africans', as exiled because severed from a nurturing linguistic and historical African past. Her children's story *Harriet's daughter* dramatizes the need for active reconstruction of black histories for African-Canadian children.

Philip's work is featured, along with that of Dionne BRAND and Claire HARRIS, in *Grammar of dissent: poetry and prose by Claire Harris, M. Nourbese Philip and Dionne Brand* (1994), edited by Carol Morrell. See also Brenda Carr, 'To "heal the word wounded"', *Studies in Canadian Literature* 19 (1994).

MARILYN ROSE

Phillips, Edward (b. 1931). He was born in the Westmount district of Montreal, Quebec (where he still lives), was educated at McGill University Montreal (B.A., 1953) and graduated in law (1956) from the Université de Montréal. He also has an M.A. in teaching (1957) from Harvard, an M.A. in English literature (1962) from Boston University, and a Diploma from the Montreal Museum of Fine Arts School of Art and Design (he has had several one-man exhibitions of his paintings). He taught English in Boston and Montreal (1957-65), but is now a full-time writer.

No one was more surprised than Phillips himself when he won an Arthur Ellis Award from the Crime Writers of Canada for *Buried on Sunday* (1986) because he saw himself not as a crime writer, but as the author of comic novels of manners (he is both). *Buried on Sunday* is set in Quebec cottage country north of Montreal, and features Westmount lawyer Geoffry Chadwick, who was introduced getting away with murder in *Sunday's child* (1981). *Buried on Sunday* is replete with black humour and pokes wicked fun at Anglo pretensions, while being a cracking good mystery yarn.

Before re-introducing Geoffrey Chadwick in *Buried on Sunday*, Phillips published *Where there's a will* (1984), a hilarious *tour de force*. Subsequently, he brought out *Hope springs eternal* (1988), and brought Chadwick back in *Sunday best* (1990). Phillips then turned to a humorous novel in the witty and entertaining *The landlady's niece* (1992), in which Elinor Richardson, an engaging heroine for the 1990s, inherits a dilapidated apartment house in Montreal. *The mice will play* (1996) is another comedy of Westmount manners.

DAVID SKENE-MELVIN

Philosophy in Canada. 1. ORIGINS OF PHILOSOPHY IN FRENCH CANADA. Philosophy was first taught at the Jesuit College in Quebec in 1665; the first official teacher was appointed in 1665. The early teachers were French Jesuits, some of whom had been educated at La Flèche, France, where René Descartes had been a student. Cartesian ideas about the nature of knowledge and the distinction between mind and body arrived in Quebec in the brief period between the death of Descartes and the placing of his works on the Index in 1666. Though generally expounded by clerics doubtful of their validity, at least as they were being commonly read in France, they played a crucial part in defining the philosophical themes of the New World. Descartes's thesis was that each person is certain only of his own existence and of certain powers of reasoning: the existence of others needs to be inferred and that of God needs to be argued for. He was often read as supposing an ultimate sense in which the human person is alone, for we are never as certain of the reality of others as we are of our own existence. In Canada this struck home when people—uprooted from their natural communities, and stripped of the cultural surroundings that might reassure them about the existence of others past and present—faced a hostile environment. (English-Canadian literary theorists, including Northrop FRYE and Margaret ATWOOD, have written of the impediments to self-definition, the preoccupation with survival, and the defensive attitudes of isolated people and isolated communities.) From the beginning in Quebec there was an attempt to rebut readings of Descartes about the primacy of individual experience and establish the existence of a public experience on which an isolated society could rely. Quebec Cartesians argued that the Cartesian notion of reason was universal and that the ideas we all share form the basis of a natural community. The records of the Séminaire de Québec, founded in 1668, testify both to the importance of Descartes and to the attempts to refute some readings of his doctrines. In the English-speaking world the individualist Cartesian perspective passed into common usage (though in English Canada, despite some influence of thinkers like David Hume, it came to be strongly resisted). In Quebec it was opposed by the clergy—Cartesian or not—as long as they dominated intellectual life. Philosophical studies at the Séminaire de Québec, which eventually became Université Laval, were surprisingly eclectic and included the ideas of Locke and Hume as well as those of Descartes (critically treated) and Nicolas Malebranche. They are represented in the *Compendium philosophicae ad usum studiosae juventutis* (Québec, 1835) of Jérôme DEMERS, a widely used manual in Quebec.

From the beginning, much of the philosophical concern was political. In the uncertainties of the New World, traditional foundations for authority were weakened by distance, and by the intrusion of political structures controlled by the British. The only institution that survived the Conquest intact was the Church, which could make its authority the basis for a functioning community only by creating a climate of belief anchored in a coherent and generally intelligible philosophy. Thus the basic concern was to find a set of ideas through which the political system could be ordered and the goals of both educational and charitable institutions established. In *Savoir et pouvoir* (1972) Pierre Thiebault describes the philosophical ideas that developed in Quebec in this early period, and their use by the Church in what he calls 'a system of indirect control'.

2. THE COMING OF THOMISM IN FRENCH CANADA AND THE BEGINNINGS OF NATIONAL THOUGHT. The first major French philosophical work that seems to have had its roots in predominantly native conditions was the *Essai sur la logique judiciaire* (Montréal, 1853). In it, François-Marie-Uncas-Maximilien Bibaud (1824-87), a Montreal lawyer (and son of the historian Michel BIBAUD) who also taught law at the Collège Sainte-Marie, raised the question of whether or not one should have two logics to accommodate the legal systems of the two major cultures in Canada. Although he answered 'no', he questioned the proposition that the intellect can transcend the 'two solitudes'.

About the same time the Church was faced with the growing conflict between science and religion and turned to the doctrines of Thomas Aquinas, who had coped with the medieval clash of Arab science and Christianity by postulating two distinct spheres, one for faith and one for reason. The Thomists insisted that reason was the same for all human beings, that it could provide a foundation for moral action, the basis of a political order, and grounds for belief in the existence of God. But they denied that certain central doctrines—including that of the Trinity and the necessity of the sacraments—could be shown by reason alone. Thus faith had its own sphere. Thomism had become firmly entrenched in Quebec well before it became the recommended doctrine in 1879. Its chief spokesmen, however, developed positions of their own, often by exploring regions—chiefly nationalism and the understanding of history—that had not been central to Thomistic doctrines. An example is Mgr Louis-Adolphe PÂQUET, a deeply conservative and orthodox thinker, who explored the relation of the human race to nature and the land. He was firmly convinced that a stable social order would develop only out of continuing devotion to the land and its responsible working: urbanization held dangers that included the creation of an environment in which families need not, and perhaps could not, work together. In essays, especially in the collection *Mélanges canadiens* (1918), he urged upon French Canadians devotion to 'the land, the past and the language'. As the most highly thought-of official spokesman for the Church in Quebec, he gave respectability to this adherence to traditional values, and of course approved their celebration in literature.

Pâquet was active in the day-to-day life of the Church in Quebec, and many of his social theories were expressed only in occasional essays. A much more systematic thinker was Louis LACHANCE, also a Thomist, who developed a rational nationalism that would justify the idea of cultural independence within a universal Christian framework, presenting a doctrine quite different from the strongly emotional nationalism of Lionel GROULX. Lachance's *Nationalisme et religion* (1936) argued that nationalism was justified, because even though all peoples must share in the same ultimate goal (happiness in this life and the beatific vision in the next), the diversity in patterns of human development meant that different groups of human beings must necessarily follow different paths, though in full recognition of the responsibility of all people to each other. By contrast Groulx relied more strongly—especially in his much-discussed and influential novel *L'appel de la race* (1922)—on notions of racial homogeneity among French Canadians, and on feelings of solidarity and distinctness from English Canada.

3. ORIGINS OF PHILOSOPHY IN ENGLISH CANADA. The first professional philosophical work written in English seems to have been *Elements of natural theology* (London, 1855) by James Beaven (1801-75), who taught at University College, University of Toronto. lt exhibits the passion for systematic order that Northrop Frye has noted as a characteristic of Canadian thought (and that continued in English Canada down to Frye himself.) Before his arrival in Canada from England, Beaven had been a rather disputatious defender of Anglican orthodoxy; but his *Elements* is an attempt to examine religious belief from a philosophical standpoint, and to find a rational basis for it that is not subject to doctrinal emendation. William LYALL, of Dalhousie University, Halifax, wrote his *Intellect, the emotions and the moral nature* (Edinburgh, 1855) in the same non-doctrinal spirit, stating that the emotions were an important source of information and were fundamental to human nature. This notion was not uncharacteristic of Maritime literature: the claim that the understanding of the emotions is a crucial human need is a theme that runs through the stories of Thomas McCULLOCH, a respected theologian (and first president of Dalhousie University) who wrote the first book of Canadian humour, *The letters of Mephibosheth Stepsure* (Halifax, 1862).

4. THE IDEALIST MOVEMENT IN ENGLISH CANADA. The need for a common morality was emphasized by George Paxton Young (1818-89), of Knox College, and then University College, University of Toronto, whose few published works—among them *Freedom and necessity* (Toronto, 1870) and *The ethics of freedom* (1911), with notes edited by his pupil James Gibson Hume—are mere tokens of his stature, and of his impact as a teacher. Young paid little attention to the then-popular Scottish philosophy of 'common sense' (an important ingredient in the synthesis found in William Lyall's *Intellect*), and favoured instead a Hegelian idealism that had much in common with that of T.H. Green in England. Essentially a realist metaphysics contrived in Scotland by philosophers like Thomas Reid and Dugald Stewart to counteract the skepticism of David Hume, this philosophy supposed that common sense was strong enough to assure us the reality of the external world. In moral theory it was allied to the notion of a 'moral sense' that gave people assurance of the soundness of generally agreed-upon experiences.

However, as science and industry alike created sharp distinctions between the experiences of human beings in the industrialized world and of their predecessors, who came to be thought of as 'primitive', it became hard to believe that there was really a natural experience common to all human beings. From Hegel to Marx the belief developed that there had been a historical development in human life, and that experience was relative to one's place in time.

In Quebec the somewhat similar philosophy of the French thinker Felicité de Lamennais (1782-1854)—based on the notion of the naturally unfolding common human tradition—created some interest at the end of the first third of the nineteenth century, and this has been documented in Yvan Lamonde's *La philosophie et son enseignement au Québec, 1665-1920* (1980). But it was short-lived, not only for the reasons that doomed common-sense philosophy in English Canada, but because it ultimately led to de Lamennais's denial of the rational function of the Church—which cut against common experience, common sense, and tradition, and was condemned by Rome. Fundamentally the nineteenth century was a time of novelty and ideological innovation: 'common sense', in whatever guise, could not prevail against it.

The 'idealist movement'—which sought to understand experience as a historical development, and tended to deny that there was a 'reality' independent of that developing experience—quickly took hold in Canada. 'Idealism' in this sense was the doctrine that ideas are more real than things—indeed, that ideas shape all our knowledge of things. In moral theory it oriented itself around the notion that principles of action derive not from raw experiences, but from a rational understanding of the meaning and progressive evolution of experience. Young and John Clark MURRAY, who made the idealist movement dominant in Canada, exemplified the Scots tradition of rational religion, which was an outgrowth of the schism between the Church of Scotland and the Free Church. This schism had centred on disputes about the relation of church and state and was kept alive by the Presbyterian tradition of sermons, in which the minister attempted to establish his point by a series of logical deductions (usually starting from a biblical text and influenced by Hegel). The clergyman-teacher in *ARCADIAN ADVENTURES WITH THE IDLE RICH* (1914) by Stephen LEACOCK (a pupil of Murray's), who offered three parts Hegel and two parts St Paul on weekdays and reversed the mixture on Sundays, is probably a justly drawn and apt exemplar of generations of pupils who went forth from Murray's classes at McGill and from those of John WATSON at Queen's. In the similarly idealist philosophy of George Blewett (1873-1912), of Victoria College, University of Toronto, the attitude to nature becomes the issue of central concern. In the history of the Christian West there have been two dominant views of nature: that nature, apart from humanity, is the perfect creation of God, and the human animal, with its free will and habit of disobedience, brings nature into disarray; and that nature, into which people were thrown after the Fall, is specifically designed to be struggled against—it is for human beings to overcome nature as part of their preparation for rehabilitation and ultimate salvation. From the first attitude the philosophical strands of nineteenth-century Romanticism, and of much contemporary environmentalism, descend. From the second stems a variety of attitudes, including the view of the American pragmatists that nature is essentially there for us to use. For Blewett, who rejected both these postures, nature was a distinct entity with its own proper goal, He was perhaps the first thinker to speak of the 'earth' as having its own 'rights'. His experiences of the Canadian West convinced him that nature, in Canada, is very fragile and easily damaged. But he was also convinced that it could not simply be left alone. His *The study of nature and the vision of god* (1907) and *The Christian view of the world* (1912) were major influences on his students, and Blewett was quoted in university classrooms and churches from Toronto to Halifax and Vancouver. His focus on nature was balanced by his concern with the idea of community as the human counterpart to a complex physical world, providing the obvious mode of survival amidst nature's powers. In fact all the idealist philosophers emphasized the primacy of community over individuality, and foreshadowed a Canadian literary tendency—noticed by Frye and Atwood—to champion collective values and common causes rather than individual heroes.

The influence of evolutionary theories produced other direct responses. Jacob Gould Schurman (1854-1942) of Dalhousie (later president of Cornell University) sought to defend traditional values, and in his *Ethical import of Darwinism* (New York, 1887) did battle against the doctrine that the 'survival of the fittest' ought to hold in the social order. Nonetheless he accepted an evolutionary metaphysics to which, in *Belief in God, its origin, nature and basis* (New York, 1890), he added an evolutionary theism. Richard Maurice BUCKE, whose *Cosmic consciousness* (1901) has remained in print, sought to extend the idea of evolution into the spiritual realm. William Douw LIGHTHALL attempted, in his *Person in evolution* (1933), to extend this theme in a less mystical way that has affinities with the philosophies of Henri Bergson and Alfred North Whitehead.

5. THE RECOVERY OF HISTORY AND THE ENTRENCHMENT OF PLURALISM IN CANADA. The efforts of the Thomists in French Canada and the idealists in English Canada to reconcile science and religion led to some frustration. As science advances and explains the origins of the stars, the history of the earth, and the chemistry of life, should religion retreat from its claims about these matters? If so, at what point? If not, by what means can it resist? Can philosophers determine, by their study of history, what is sound and central in religion? Biology, archaeology, and anthropology all focused attention on time. For the philosopher this meant that the

study of human nature could no longer easily be regarded as the study of a set of permanent properties. History—once chiefly the study of names, dates, and battles—became a central concern for anyone seeking a picture of human nature. Hegel advanced the view that there is a natural (some of his followers thought inevitable) path of human history that is always progressive. But in French Canada the view developed early that Quebec was special and had a history of its own, which was not dominated by the European history that centrally concerned Hegel. In *Des influences françaises au Canada* (3 vols, 1916-20) the poet-philosopher Jean CHARBONNEAU carried the argument one step further. He believed that the firmest grasp on the historic mainstream of Western thought—which in France had been deflected into new courses that radically changed its nature—was held in Quebec. In English Canada, George BRETT, in his massive *History of psychology* (3 vols, 1912-21), sought to trace the development of views of the human mind itself. Brett's work was to dominate the philosophy department of the University of Toronto for two generations and to turn it into a major centre for the study of the history of thought. The historical turn given to thought by Charbonneau in French Canada and Brett in English Canada drew upon an existing tendency to see thought in terms of history, and attracted widespread support from other scholars. For the Canadian identity is above all historical. It must be specified not in terms of a single culture, race, or language but of a common experience and a common response to surrounding cultures. The result was that historians—François-Xavier GARNEAU, Lionel-Adolphe Bergeron, and Fernand OUELLET in French Canada; Donald CREIGHTON, A.R.M. LOWER, W.L. MORTON, Ramsay COOK, and Carl BERGER in English Canada—came to occupy an increasingly important place in Canadian intellectual life, while philosophers faded from view. Rupert LODGE, teaching primarily at the University of Manitoba, accepted the diminished role of philosophy, and claimed to be able to show that no single philosophical system could prevail and, therefore, that philosophy could not solve some of its most fundamental problems. He reacted quite differently to the difficulties involved in reconciling opposing fundamental views of the world, and ultimately saw philosophy as irreducibly pluralistic. He believed that there are always at least three equally valid responses to any basic question: the idealist, the realist, and the pragmatic. The concern with the history of philosophy implied a concern with a plurality of views or perspectives. Despite the fact that Lodge's form of it attracted few supporters, pluralism itself became deeply entrenched.

6. TRADITION AND CHANGE IN PHILOSOPHICAL THEMES. Brett and Lodge, along with more traditionally oriented idealist philosophers such as John Macdonald (1887-1972) at the University of Alberta and Herbert Stewart (1882-1953) at Dalhousie University, played leading roles in English Canada until the Second World War and beyond. Macdonald's *Mind, school and civilization* (1952), a defence of an educational system aimed at the traditional 'civilizing' virtues and dedicated to the transmission of a developed, inherited culture, was welcomed by many intellectuals who suspected that the philosophy of John Dewey, then gaining strength among professional educators, threatened the aims for which public education had been established. Irish-born Stewart, who became an influential spokesman for the idea of a revitalized British Commonwealth, was familiar to radio listeners, and many of his radio talks on a wide range of subjects were assembled into a book, *From a library window* (1940). His most widely read philosophical work was a biting study entitled *Nietzsche and the ideals of modern Germany* (1915), which, while it calls attention to the many (often contradictory) strands in Nietzsche's thought, endeavours to establish Nietzsche as a thinker who stimulated the thirst for power that led to the devastation of Europe.

Thomist theses were developed and defended by Charles DE KONINCK, whose *The hollow universe* (1960), written in English, was widely influential in both English and French Canada, and was also read in the United States. De Koninck's influence in French Canada stemmed partly from his close relations with the hierarchy of the Catholic Church and his position as dean of philosophy at Université Laval, but chiefly from the fact that he opened new possibilities for the reconciliation of philosophy, science, and religion. His thesis was that there are ways of knowing the world, and especially living things, that complement rather than confront scientific knowledge. De Koninck argued that the scientific world is a hollow shell of abstraction until it is made concrete by human feeling, understanding, and immediate experience. He illustrated this principle by the idea of 'life', which, even in its developed forms, is described in scientific biology as a matter of atoms and molecules.

After the war, most leading English-language works examined philosophy and philosophers from an essentially traditional, even conservative, standpoint. George GRANT's *Philosophy in the mass age* (1959) is a plea for a return to classical values and modes of knowing. William Dray (b. 1921), the University of Ottawa, wrote *Laws and explanation in history* (1958) as an eloquent defence of the humanities against the claims of those who believe that all knowledge must be expressed as scientific laws.

Both the Canadian interest and the concern with Hegel are reflected by Emil FACKENHEIM, who taught for many years at the University of Toronto. His *Religious dimension of Hegel's thought* (1968) and *Metaphysics and historicity* (1961) continue to be read and cited. In *Collingwood and the reform of metaphysics* (1970) Lionel Rubinoff (b. 1930), Trent University, reflects many of the interests of the Canadian idealists of an earlier period, but in a form intended to take account of recent criticisms of idealist metaphysics. Rubinoff has also had interests in Heidegger and continental philosophy; but the most original Canadian contributor to this field has been Graeme Nicholson (b. 1936) of the University of Toronto. His *Seeing and reading* (1984) has been particularly influential. Charles TAYLOR, McGill University, first made his name in philosophy with his *Hegel* (1976), which did much to make Hegel interesting to analytic philosophers. A good sample of his wide interests can be found in *Philosophical papers* (1985) and *Philosophical arguments* (1995). His *Sources of the self* (1989) and his work on culture and community in *The malaise of modernity* (1991) and *Reconciling the solitudes* (1993), reflecting his long interest in moral theory and political life, have attracted international attention. Taylor continues many traditional Canadian themes, but does so in the context of recent analytic philosophy. John Leslie (b. 1940), the University of Guelph, has returned to metaphysical themes that derive from eighteenth-century rationalism and applied his work to recent physical cosmology. His *Value and existence* (1979) reflects his metaphysical work, while *Universes* (1989) reflects his cosmological concerns.

Taylor and Leslie both suggest that there are rich possibilities remaining for philosophical theology. Two works by Bernard LONERGAN—his great *Insight: a study of human understanding* (1954) and *Method in theology* (1971)—attempt to demystify Catholicism by suggesting that the continuing pursuit of understanding the nature of things, through studying a wide range of disciplines and employing common sense, brings one closer to experiencing the meaning of God and of the divine will. Hugo Meynell (b. 1940), the University of Calgary, in his *Introduction to the philosophy of Bernard Lonergan* (1976; 2nd edition 1991) wrote the standard explication of Lonergan's thought. Meynell's *Religion and irreligion* (1986) and *The nature of aesthetic value* (1986), though mindful of analytic tradition, seek to connect human judgements to a genuinely experienced world. The main critic of philosophical theology has been the American-born militant atheist Kai Nielsen (b. 1926), author of *God and the grounding of morality* (1991).

The University of Toronto has been a major source of political philosophy with important work being produced by Frank Cunningham (b. 1940), *Democratic theory and socialism* (1989) and Wayne Sumner (b. 1941), *The moral foundation of rights*. Will Kymlicka (b. 1962) at the University of Ottawa is the author of *Justice in political philosophy* (1992), *Liberalism, community and culture* (1989), and *Multicultural citizenship: a liberal theory* (1995). All have figured in public debates on multiculturalism and liberalism in Canada.

Logic and the philosophy of science have become increasingly important. Also at Toronto, Ian Hacking (b. 1936), author of *Emergence of probability* (1975), *Scientific revolutions* (1981) and *Rewriting the soul* (1995), and Bas Van Fraassen (b. 1941), author of *Current issues in quantum logic* (1981) and *Laws and symmetry* (1989), have developed international reputations; while Douglas Walton (b. 1942) of the University of Winnipeg has developed the field of informal logic in *Argument: The logic of the fallacies* (1982) and *Begging the question* (1991), a field that responds to practical concerns about reason.

Among Francis SPARSHOTT's several books of the 1970s, his *Looking for philosophy* (1972) explores the interests of analytic philosophy by examining the works of Bertrand Russell, G.E. Moore, Ludwig Wittgenstein, Gilbert Ryle, and J.L. Austin, applying to them a skeptical eye and a critical wit. An earlier work, *The structure of aesthetics* (1963), emphasizes the essential plurality of theories of the arts. Since then Sparshott has written major works on the philosophy of dance and on Aristotle's ethics. Terence Penelhum (b. 1929), the University of Calgary, used Wittgensteinian techniques in his *Survival and disembodied existence* (1970), which analyses claims to life after death. In Quebec, Fernand DUMONT developed general critiques of the social order, using a variety of modern techniques, in *Le lieu de l'homme* (1967) and *La dialectique de l'objet économique* (1970). Various strands of existentialist as well as Thomist thought can be found in the work of Benoît Pruche (b. 1914), Université de Sherbrooke. His *Existant et acte d'être* (2 vols, 1977-80) is one of the most ambitious metaphysical studies produced in French Canada. A principal concern among writers there has been the problem of selfhood and self-identity. Important work on these themes has been done by René Écuyer (b. 1938), also Université de Sherbrooke, whose *La genèse du concept de soi* (1975) deals with questions on the border of philosophy and psychology; and Jacques Croteau (b. 1921), Université d'Ottawa, whose *L'homme: sujet ou objet* (1982) combines traditional Thomist ideas with recent notions borrowed from Husserlian phenomenology. Thomas De Koninck (b. 1934), Université Laval (the son of Charles de Koninck), has published *La dignité humaine* (1995), a work that opens new ground on questions of human rights. Problems stemming from the philosophy of Thomas Aquinas and its development in the writings of Jacques Maritain are dealt with in the work of Jean-Louis Allard (b. 1926), Université d'Ottawa. His *L'éducation à la liberté* (1978)—translated by Ralph Nelson as *Education for freedom* (1982)—defends a Maritainist conception of education and society. Traditional questions about philosophical theology are looked at anew by Laval philosopher Henri-Paul Cunningham (b. 1941) in *Les impasses de la raison: le véritable athéisme* (1989). The philosophical spirit of the Quiet Revolution is obvious in the work of André Dagenais (b. 1917), who has taught at the Université de Montréal and in Argentina. His *Vingt-quatre défauts Thomistes* (1964) is a vigorous attack on the philosophy that had prevailed in Quebec for nearly a century. His *Le Dieu nouveau* (1974), however, shows a fundamental interest in religion, combined with a desire to reconceptualize its problems. At the Université du Québec à Trois-Rivières, Alexi Klimov (b. 1937)—in *Dostoievski; ou Le connaissance périlleuse* (1971), *Éloge de l'homme inutile* (1983), and *De la philosophie compassion de la liberté* (1984)—has contributed significantly to the combined subjects of philosophy and literature; and at the Université de Montréal, Venant Cauchy (b. 1924), though he has published no books, has been an important figure as the president of the World Federation of Philosophy, and for his philosophical explorations of violence.

LESLIE ARMOUR, ELIZABETH TROTT

Piché, Alphonse (b. 1917). Born in Chicoutimi, Quebec, he studied classics in Trois-Rivières, where he made his home and worked in various occupations, including accounting.

His first collection of poems, *Ballades de la petite extrace* (1946), with a preface by Clément MARCHAND, was followed by *Remous* (1947) and, in 1950, by *Voie d'eau*. In 1966 these three collections were reissued in a single volume as *Poèmes, 1946-1950*. They form a fairly homogeneous triptych: Piché's poetry is explicitly inspired by Villon and Ronsard and draws freely on the forms of the ballad and the song. More recent poems were added for the retrospective published by Les Éditions de l'Hexagone under the title *Poèmes (1946-1968)* (1976), which won a Governor General's Award. This body of work constitutes what could be called Piché's 'first style', for his writing was to take quite a different direction in the early 1980s.

Beginning in 1982, Piché abandoned the rather light and nostalgic work of his first period for a much more sombre and sometimes harsh poetry centred on illness and approaching death. Published by Écrits des Forges, the small collections *Dernier profil* (1982) and *Sursis* (1987) are very spare and direct; in them the author confronts the process of aging with a clear eye, resisting any sense of complacency. These two collections were reissued, with some previously unpublished poems, in 1991. In 1989, Les Éditions de l'Hexagone published *Fables,* in which Piché returns to the figure of Jean de La Fontaine and the mocking tone of some of his earliest work.

Little studied, although it has often been warmly acclaimed (Prix David, 1946; Prix Duvernay, 1966; Governor General's Award, 1976), Piché's work is somewhat marginal to the main currents of poetry in Quebec, but there is no doubt that it will remain one of the most accomplished examples in Quebec literature of inspiration drawn from the tradition of French poetry.

See André Gaulin, 'Alphonse Piché, Poèmes (1946-1968)', *Livres et auteurs québécois* (1976), pp. 151-3; André BROCHU, *Tableau du poème* (1994), pp. 26-7.

FRANÇOIS DUMONT

Pickthall, Marjorie (1883-1922). Born in Gunnersby, Middlesex, England, Marjorie Lowry Christie Pickthall immigrated with her family to Toronto in 1889. Educated at St Mildred's Girls School and the Bishop Strachan School for Girls, she was encouraged by her indulgent parents in writing, reading, and music (she studied the violin until she was nearly twenty), though she always had delicate health. Her literary career began with the publication of her story 'Two ears' in the Toronto *Globe* in 1898; but her mother's death in 1910 so devastated her that it took the efforts of many prominent friends to encourage her to write again. She worked for a time in the library of Victoria College, University of Toronto, and in Dec. 1912 sailed for England to live with relatives and complete her recovery. During the war she trained as an ambulance driver, worked as a farm labourer, and assisted in the library of the South Kensington Meteorological Office. By 1920 she was, as she said, 'Canada sick', and sailed for home. After a brief visit with her father and friends in Toronto, she went to Vancouver, to indulge a long-cherished wish to see the West at first hand. Eventually she settled in a small cottage on Vancouver Island and resumed writing. Surgery to correct her continuing ill-health was carried out in Vancouver in April 1922; but the initial rapid recovery was ended by an embolus. She was buried beside her mother in St James' Cemetery, Toronto.

Pickthall's literary reputation rests ultimately on the two major collections of poetry published during her lifetime: *The drift of pinions* (1913) and *The lamp of poor souls* (1916; rpr. 1972), which includes the poems published in the earlier volume. *The complete poems of Marjorie Pickthall* (1925), compiled by her father, includes the material of the earlier volumes and other 'fugitive and hitherto unpublished poems'. A 1936 edition, now regarded as definitive, includes the posthumously published *Little songs* (1925) and *The naiad and five other poems* (1931). *The selected poems of Marjorie Pickthall*, edited and with a sympathetic introduction by Lorne PIERCE, appeared in 1957. The penchant for locations remote in place and time, the use of incantatory rhythms, a persistent sense of *ennui*, the evocation of an insular world of muted lights and a hushed atmosphere, and the recurrence of words such as 'silver', 'rose', and 'gold', suggest a perception of a world of ideal beauty and a literary practice that originate at least as far back as the Pre-Raphaelite Brotherhood. To these mannerisms Pickthall added her own Anglo-Catholicism. The result is a poetry that evokes a dream-like world that, although removed from the world of ordinary experience, only halfway approaches a more perfect existence in God. Poems such as 'Golden dawn', 'Dream river', and 'The garden of weariness' are entirely representative. The frequently anthologized 'Père Lalement', 'The bridegroom of Cana', and 'Resurgam' show Pickthall's success in using cadence, delicate colouring, and apt word choice to create sustained moods. At their best the poems achieve a vision of beauty in earthly things that suggests a higher spiritual life; at their least inspired they are little more than versifications of poetic mannerisms.

Like others of her generation, Pickthall wrote verse-drama. *The woodcarver's wife*, begun in England in 1919 and finished in Victoria in 1920, was first presented by the Community Players of Montreal at the New Empire Theatre. It appeared in published form in *The woodcarver's wife and other poems* (1922). Despite its convincing handling of incident and its contemporary issues (an artistic figure who can cope with aesthetics but not with life; a confined yet aspiring wife; and a chivalrous rescuer with fleshly appetites), this four-character one-act play, set in pre-Conquest days, is an academic exercise in which the characters mechanically mouth lines of verse to one another.

Pickthall also completed over 200 short stories, three juvenile novels, and two adult novels. The short stories—many of which were written during the war years in England and submitted to various publications there, and suggest Pickthall's debt to Joseph Conrad, whose work she greatly admired—frequently imply deliberate manipulation of often violent incidents, or convey a facile conception of character. A representative selection of twenty-four stories was published posthumously in London under the inapt and misleading title *Angel's shoes* (1923).

Three of Pickthall's contributions to *East and west*, a young people's paper sponsored by the Presbyterian Church, appeared in book form: *Dick's desertion; a boy's adventures in Canadian forests* (1905), *The straight road* (1906), and *Billy's hero; or The valley of gold* (1908), the last two illustrated by C.W. Jefferys. In each book a boy or young man, isolated by orphanhood or financial straits, is forced to undertake a journey, during which he must solve a trying problem; its solution, through a combination of luck ('Providence'), a new spiritual and moral rectitude, and a fresh sense of duty, leads to his re-integration into the family or society.

Of Pickthall's adult fiction, *Little hearts* (1915), set in the eighteenth-century Devonshire countryside, and *The bridge; a story of the Great Lakes* (1922), employ melodramatic incident. (*The bridge*, begun during the war years in England, and completed and revised on Vancouver Island, was published serially in

Everybody's, New York, and the London *Sphere* in 1921.) As in most of her short stories, Pickthall in these novels fails to integrate fully descriptive detail, character, and incident. At the time of her death she was working on another novel, 'The beaten man', of which a 30,000-word fragment and the author's working notes are extant.

Pickthall was undoubtedly the most gifted of a group of minor writers who owed their inspiration, and a good deal of their literary practice, to the vestiges of romanticism. There have been attempts to read in some of Pickthall's poetry the stirrings of late twentieth-century feminist sensibility, but it seems likely that Pickthall will continue to be regarded as part of the fading light of an earlier day and not as part of the initial light of our own.

See the entry on Pickthall by Lorne Pierce in *A standard dictionary of Canadian biography*, vol. II (1938), and Pierce's *Marjorie Pickthall; a book of remembrance* (1925); W.E. Collin, 'Dream-gardens', *The WHITE SAVANNAHS* (1936; rpt. 1975); Alex Kizuk, 'The case of the forgotten Electra: Pickthall's apostrophes and feminine poetics', *Studies in Canadian literature* 12, no. 1 (1987); and Diana M.A. Relke, 'Demeter's daughter: Marjorie Pickthall and the quest for poetic identity', *CANADIAN LITERATURE* 115 (Winter, 1987).

S.R. MacGILLIVRAY

Pierce, **Lorne** (1890-1961). Born in Delta, Ontario, he was educated at Queen's University, Victoria University (University of Toronto), the Union Theological Seminary of New York, New York University, and Wesleyan Theological College, Montreal. He became a minister of the Methodist Church and later of the United Church of Canada. In 1916 he married Edith Chown, a member of a prominent Kingston family. In 1920 he was named literary adviser to the RYERSON PRESS, and from 1922 to 1960 was its editor. In 1926 he was elected to the Royal Society of Canada.

As an editor at Ryerson who was also an ardent Canadian nationalist, Pierce consistently used his authority to encourage Canadian writers by both publication and advice. Among the poets he introduced were E.J. PRATT, Raymond KNISTER, Earle BIRNEY, A.J.M. SMITH, Dorothy LIVESAY, Louis DUDEK, and P.K. PAGE; and he was the first editor to accept a novel (*Settlers of the marsh*, 1925) by Frederick Philip GROVE. His desire to stimulate Canadian writing, however, led him to rely heavily on copy-editors to redeem manuscripts of questionable promise.

His sentiments and interests were expressed early in his editorial career when he instigated three series of short books on Canadian subjects: *Makers of Canadian literature* (from 1925), the *Ryerson Canadian history readers* (from 1926)—to celebrate past achievements—and the Ryerson poetry chapbooks (from 1925) to stimulate future efforts. In order to familiarize school-children with the native literature Pierce edited the *Ryerson* (later *Canada*) *books of prose and verse*, which began to appear in 1927. For adult readers he edited, with A.D. Watson, *Our Canadian literature: representative prose and verse* (1922). Its poetry section, edited with Bliss CARMAN, later became *Our Canadian literature: representative verse, English and French* (1922), and was revised in 1954 by V.B. Rhodenizer as *Canadian poetry in English*. Pierce was the author of *Fifty years of public service: a life of James L. Hughes* (1924); *Marjorie Pickthall: a book of remembrance* (1925); *An outline of Canadian literature (French and English)* (1927); and *William Kirby, the portrait of a Tory loyalist* (1929). He also wrote two histories of the Ryerson Press: *The chronicle of a century, 1829-1929: the record of one hundred years of progress in the publishing concerns of the Methodist, Presbyterian and Congregational churches in Canada* (1929) and *The House of Ryerson, 1829-1954* (1954). *Three Fredericton poets* (1933) reflected his close friendship with Sir Charles G.D. ROBERTS and Bliss Carman (who made him his literary executor). In numerous pamphlets Pierce urged upon Canadians the possibility of national greatness, to be achieved through awareness of spiritual foundations and the cultivation of *bonne entente* between English- and French-speaking Canadians.

His many publications aside, Pierce has a claim to remembrance as a literary entrepreneur who unstintingly devoted his time and money to the promotion of Canadian literature and art. To this end he donated to the Royal Society of Canada the Lorne Pierce medal for distinguished service to Canadian literature; took a leading part in founding several organizations, including the Canadian Writers' Foundation; and built up an important collection of Canadian books, manuscripts, and correspondence that is now deposited at Queen's University. His career is described appreciatively by C.H. Dickinson, the Book Steward of the Ryerson Press from 1937 to 1964, in *Lorne Pierce: a profile* (1965).

See also CRITICISM IN ENGLISH: 2.

JOHN WEBSTER GRANT

Pilon, **Jean-Guy** (b. 1930). Born in Saint-Polycarpe, Quebec, he graduated in law from the Université de Montréal. He has been editor of Éditions de l'Hexagone and Éditions de l'Actuelle and was co-organizer, in 1958, with Gaston MIRON and Louis Portugais, of the first Quebec poets' conference, which later became the Rencontre internationale québécoise des écrivains, a cultural forum of which he is secretary-general. In 1959 he became a founder-director of *LIBERTÉ*. He has been in charge of Radio-Canada's cultural programming since 1960. An indefatigable 'homme de lettres', Pilon was elected a member of the Royal Society of Canada in 1967 and has received many awards, including the Prix de la Province de Québec (1955), the Prix David (1956), and a Governor General's Award for *Comme eau retenue: poèmes 1954-1963* (1968). With Eli MANDEL he edited an anthology of new Canadian poetry, *Poetry 62/Poésie 62* (1962).

Employing a vocabulary of such basic words as 'bread' and 'friendship' to exorcise death and alienation, Pilon's poetry, while denouncing the past, is a brotherly urging of his fellow Québécois to name and build the country, at the risk of becoming redundant, in order to create a habitable place. The poetry has been influenced by Alain GRANDBOIS as well as by René Char, who wrote a preface for Pilon's second collection, *Les cloîtres de l'été* (1954), the first being *La fiancée du matin* (1953). These early poems celebrate the body, nature, and woman, and express the poet's desire to confront heaven with the 'naked act of persistence'. In *L'homme et le jour* (1957)—long verses that are reminiscent of Anne HÉBERT's *Mystère de la parole*—man emerges from the ashes of the past 'to resume his beneficial watch over things'. The poems in *La mouette et le large* (1960), with their simple, warm grace, lend a more inclusive tone to the quest for life by introducing a 'nous' that strives 'to name the evil, to draw it out of the flesh' and call for a new dawn in a country whose 'soul has been frozen' by its lack of life and history. *Recours au pays* (1961) and *Pour saluer une ville* (1963) consider ways of creating a new land: 'Comment réussir à dompter les espaces et les saisons, la forêt et le froid? Comment y reconnaître mon visage?' Affirmation begins to take hold in 'Poèmes pour maintenant' (included in *Pour saluer une ville*), in which the fraternal 'nous' discards the shame of the past to open 'des bras nouveaux sur une terre habitable'. In words and in woman Pilon sees salvation, sees himself 'clutching the logbook and the woman's hand despite the shipwreck.' The eroticism and earthy sensuality in *Recours au pays* and *Pour saluer une ville* find their full expression in *Saisons pour la continuelle* (1969), in which Pilon celebrates the union of the poet with the seasons of his country and with woman, and shows a desire to savour the simple things of life—a desire that pervades all of his later work, including *Silences pour une souveraine* (1972) and *Comme eau retenue, poèmes 1954-1977* (1985). Pilon also wrote a novel, *Solange* (1966).

See Axel Maugey, 'Jean-Guy Pilon', in his *Poésie et société au Québec (1937-1970)* (1972), and Jean-Louis Major, 'L'Hexagone: une aventure en poésie québécoise', *La poésie canadienne-française* 4 (1969). MAROUSSIA AHMED

Pioneer memoirs. The accurate tales by pioneers of their heroic battles against harsh climate, homesickness, isolation, and poverty are the epics of Canadian literature. The magnitude of the struggle for survival demanded to be recorded, even though many of the memoirists were not professional writers: they had only this one tale to tell. Pioneers faced two struggles. First they had to tame the land, to wrest a living from it. Many memoirs, journals, and letters don't go beyond this level, particularly those written by lower-class settlers of limited education. Already used to privation and manual labour, they accepted these conditions and went on to prosper materially; but their memoirs pall because they are often mere ledger-like accounts of mounting assets. Erudite, upper-class settlers, on the other hand, usually failed as homesteaders in the external battle of taming the land; but they engaged strenuously in the second, more exciting internal battle of mapping it in the mind. Their memoirs are full of the clash and conflict of Old World polish and refinement meeting New World primitivism and roughness—an unresolved dichotomy that is still at the heart of Canadian consciousness. Their crops may have failed, but their sensibilities flowered into fine autobiographical prose.

The flood-tide of frontier living in English Canada moved slowly from east to west across the country, and covered a span of roughly 140 years, from the 1780s to the 1920s.

1. THE MARITIME PROVINCES. The main thrust of settlement in the Maritimes came from the United Empire Loyalists, from 1783 to 1812, but few recorded the pioneer experience, perhaps because they were already old hands at it—on their second lap, as it were. Later memoirs include William T. Baird's *Seventy years of New Brunswick life; autobiograhical sketches* (Saint John, 1890). Baird claims that 'the training of a young mind in log cabin life' leads to early maturity; at the age of six he

confronted his first bear and chopped down his first tree. Aeneas McCharles's *Bemocked of destiny; the actual struggles and experiences of a Canadian pioneer, and the recollections of a lifetime* (1908) describes his childhood years on a Nova Scotia farm in the 1840s and 1850s.

2. QUEBEC AND ONTARIO. Quebec memoirs in English are equally scant. By far the liveliest record is *Lifelines; the Stacey letters: 1836-1858* (1976) edited by Jane Vansittart, who found the letters advertised for sale in a stamp catalogue. Rakish young George Stacey, perenially in debt and in love, is dispatched from London by his desperate father to farm in the Eastern Townships. There George encounters all the disasters that usually befall an inexperienced farmer, and such extra ones as imprisonment for debt in Sherbrooke jail. Mary Gillespie Henderson's *Memories of my early years* (1937) briefly records her childhood on the farm at Little River, Quebec, where her Irish parents homesteaded in the 1840s.

Ontario yields a large crop of pioneer memoirs, most of them from the 1815-50 period, when British immigrants poured into its fertile southern half. The finest 'nest of singing birds' among memoirists was to be found in the backwoods near Peterborough. Susanna MOODIE's *ROUGHING IT IN THE BUSH; or Forest life in Canada* (London, 1852; NCL) shows her to be half the delicate, sentimental English heroine and half the stalwart Canadian pioneer, holding the split self together by means of irony, her sensibility gradually expanding to meet the challenge of white water and waving pines. Her sister, Catharine Parr TRAILL, in *The BACKWOODS OF CANADA; being letters from the wife of an emigrant officer* (London, 1836; NCL), is all sense, a female Robinson Crusoe of scientific curiosity and practicality. In contrast to Susanna's imagination, Catharine's ultimately retreats from the tangled mystery of dense forest to its small, decorative delights—wildflowers, birds, insects—or to snug indoor domesticity. Their brother Samuel Strickland, one of the few gentry who succeeded in the backwoods, gives in *Twenty-seven years in Canada West* (London, 1853) a much less interesting account than those of his 'Sense and Sensibility' sisters. Other Peterborough memoirs include *Our forest home; being extracts from the correspondence of the late Frances Stewart* (Toronto, 1889), compiled and edited by Frances Stewart's daughter, E.S. Dunlop, and Thomas Need's *Six years in the bush; or Extracts from the journal of a settler in Upper Canada 1832-1838* (London, 1838). Modern critical and biographical studies of the Peterborough group include Marian Fowler's *The embroidered tent: five gentlewomen in early Canada* (1982), G.H. Needler's *Otonabee pioneers: the story of the Stewarts, the Stricklands, the Traills, and the Moodies* (1953), and Audrey Y. Morris's *Gentle pioneers* (1968).

Masculine accounts of pioneering tend to be extroverted and pragmatic. Typically down-to-earth are *Authentic letters from Upper Canada; including an account of Canadian field sports by Thomas William Magrath; the whole edited by the Rev. Thomas Radcliffe* (Dublin, 1833; rpr. 1953), John C. Geikie's *Adventures in Canada; or life in the woods* (London, 1874), Samuel Thompson's *Reminiscences of a Canadian pioneer for the last fifty years* (Toronto, 1884; rpr. 1968), and David Kennedy's *Country life in Canada fifty years ago: personal recollections and reminiscences of a sexagenarian* (Toronto, 1885; rpr. 1971). More interesting, because more introspective, are *A gentlewoman in Upper Canada; the journals of Anne Langton* (1950), edited by H.H. Langton, and *The journals of Mary O'Brien 1828-1838* (1968), edited by Audrey Saunders Miller. Both writers possess a fine Jane-Austen-like wit and irony.

By 1850 all the green belt of southern Ontario (then Canada West) was under cultivation, so that new settlers had to trek north to rockier terrain. To Madoc came the courageous Anna Loveridge, whose letters comprise *Your loving Anna; letters from the Ontario frontier* (1972), edited by Louis Tivy. To Muskoka in 1878 came Roger Vardon, fresh from an English public school, author of *English bloods* (1939). Ann Hathaway's father, a distant kin of Shakespeare's wife, had a cabin on Lake Joseph, described by Ann in her *Muskoka memories; sketches from real life* (1904).

3. MANITOBA, SASKATCHEWAN, ALBERTA. Prairie settlement followed the new railways and peaked between 1895 and 1914. More than three million people poured in from the USA, Britain, Scandinavia, Russia, Poland, and Ukraine, many of them in response to offers of free land, a quarter-section (160 acres) for each homesteader. In the battle with the land their only weapons were high hopes and strong backs, and their adversaries were formidable: intense cold, blinding blizzards and dust-storms, hailstones bigger than bullets, and long periods of drought. In the flatness of that prairie world, men and women were the only upright things, casting a long shadow, gradually making their mark. Ego counted; perhaps that is one reason why there are far more memoirs from the Prairies than the Maritimes, where sea and mist swamped and dissolved any sure sense of self.

Among the best Manitoban memoirs are Mrs Cecil Hall's *A lady's life on a farm in Manitoba* (London, 1884) and Billie Lamb Allan's warm and homey *Dew upon the grass* (1963). From Saskatchewan come the delightful *Pioneer girl* (1964), fourteen-year-old Maryanne Caswell's letters to her grandmother, edited by Grace Lane; Mary Hiemstra's vividly written *Gully farm* (1955); Georgina Binnie-Clark's *Wheat and woman* (1914; 1979), chronicling the heroic feats of a woman farmer on her own; and James M. Minifie's *Homesteader: a prairie boyhood recalled* (1972). Interesting Albertan memoirs include Sarah Ellen Roberts' *Of us and the oxen* (1968); Hilda Rose's *The stump farm; a chronicle of pioneering* (1928), a remarkable saga of a ninety-pound woman alone in the northern wilderness with a child and invalid husband; H.E. Church's *An emigrant in the Canadian Northwest* (1929); R.M. Patterson's *Far pastures* (1963); John H. Blackburn's *Land of promise* (1970), edited by John Archer; and Peggy Holmes's hilarious *It could have been worse* (1980).

4. BRITISH COLUMBIA. A fascinating West-Coast memoir is *A pioneer gentlewoman in British Columbia; the recollections of Susan Allison* (1976) edited by Margaret A. Ormsby. Mrs Allison came from England to Hope in 1860, married there, and made the treacherous 75-mile trek across the Hope mountains on horseback—the first white woman to do so—to a 'wild, free life' in the Similkameen Valley. On the Canadian frontier women found new strengths and freedoms, surprising no one quite as much as themselves. Other memoirs of note are Florence Goodfellow's slim volume, *Memories of pioneer life in British Columbia* (1945), and C.W. Holliday's *The valley of youth* (1948), a nostalgic and amusing account of farming in the Okanagan Valley in the 1890s.

To date the field of pioneer memoirs is virtually untilled by literary scholars, even though it contains rich insights into the nature of the collective Canadian psyche and its relationship to the land. It is high time we turned the first critical sod.

MARIAN FOWLER

1983 to 1996. Since 1983 scholarly enquiry in the field of pioneer memoirs has been dominated by an interest in the women of the nineteenth century that is reflected both in scholarly editions and reprints of original texts and in critical scholarship on the pioneer texts. Three women who have received the lion's share of attention are Susanna MOODIE, Catharine Parr TRAILL, and Anna Jameson. In 1988 Carleton University Press published a critical edition of *ROUGHING IT IN THE BUSH*, the fifth text produced by its CENTRE FOR EDITING EARLY CANADIAN TEXTS, which used as its basic copy-text the 1852 Richard Bentley edition, since there is no known surviving manuscript or proof; it replaces the previously widely used NEW CANADIAN LIBRARY edition (1967) abridged by Carl KLINCK. Edited by Carl Ballstadt, this volume also provides useful documentation on the book's publication history and its reception by Moodie's contemporaries, and a brief review of twentieth-century critical responses to Moodie and *Roughing it in the bush*. McCLELLAND & STEWART's New Canadian Library series (with afterwords by Canadian critics and authors) has reprinted original texts of Moodie's *Roughing it in the bush* (1989, Afterword by Susan Glickman) and Moodie's *Life in the clearings* (1989, Afterword by Carol SHIELDS). This series has also reissued Catharine Parr Traill's *The backwoods of Canada* (1989, Afterword by D.M.R. Bentley) and Anna Jameson's *Winter studies and summer rambles* (1990, Afterword by Clara THOMAS). Virago Press has also issued an abridged facsimile of *Roughing it in the bush* with an introduction by Margaret ATWOOD (1986). Two collections of Susanna Moodie's letters have been edited by Carl Ballstadt, Elizabeth Hopkins, and Michael Peterman: *Susanna Moodie: letters of a lifetime* (1985) and *Letters of love and duty: the correspondence of Susanna and John Moodie* (1993).

A small number of pioneer memoirs by other women have been published, including *Eleanora's diary: the journals of a Canadian pioneer girl* (1994) edited by Caroline Parry and *A new life in Canada: the letters of Sophia Eastwood, 1843-1870* (1989) edited by Susan Beattie. The Canadian Plains Research Center has published correspondence between William and Maggie Wallace: *My dear Maggie—letters from a Manitoba pioneer* (1991).

Marian Fowler's call, in the conclusion of her 1983 entry (above), for literary scholars to begin to till the rich but relatively untouched soil of pioneer writing has been answered in a number of studies that focus particularly on the women of the nineteenth century. The first volume of *Canadian writers and their works: fiction series* (1983), edited by Robert Lecker, Jack David, and Ellen Quigley, includes an entry on Moodie (by Michael Peterman) and one on Traill (by Carl Ballstadt) that provide biographical, contextual, and bibliographic information, as well as critical analyses of the primary texts. In *Re(dis)covering our foremothers: nineteenth-century Canadian women writers*

(1990), editor Lorraine McMullen asserts that 'rescuing nineteenth-century women writers from anonymity is one of the tasks of today's scholars'. The essays in this volume contribute significantly to the work of recuperating and reassessing—often from a feminist perspective—women's memoirs, letters, and creative writing from the nineteenth century. Helen Buss's *Mapping ourselves: Canadian women's autobiography in English* (1993) sets out to 'better understand the complex subjectivity of women writing themselves into the literature and history of [Canada]', and argues that nineteenth-century women were able to 'shift the terms of representation [within patriarchal discourse] to [their] own autobiographical needs, to undercut old identities and build new ones'. Buss writes about a number of nineteenth-century women: Elizabeth Simcoe, Mary O'Brien, Sarah Ellen Roberts, Elizabeth Lichtenstein Johnston, Susan Sibbald, Susan Allison, Susanna Moodie, and Anna Jameson. (See also Buss's *Canadian women's autobiography in English: an introductory guide for researchers and teachers*, 1991.)

Half of Buss's book, *Mapping ourselves*, addresses twentieth-century women's autobiography, and the link she makes between the centuries is another defining feature of how twentieth-century scholars—and creative writers—conceptualize nineteenth-century writers. In *The pioneer woman: a Canadian character type* (1991), Elizabeth Thompson argues that the Canadian pioneer woman, particularly as she is characterized in Catharine Parr Traill's writing, breaks with the conventions of British nineteenth-century femininity and establishes a type of Canadian woman who has been 'an accepted and essential aspect of female characterization in Canadian fiction' from the nineteenth century to the present, and she traces this figure as it appears in the works of Sara Jeannette DUNCAN, Ralph Connor (Charles W. GORDON), and Margaret LAURENCE. Certainly an interest in nineteenth-century women—and links between those women and present-day women— is evident in a number of literary texts since 1983: Daphne MARLATT's *Ana Historic* (1988), Alice MUNRO's short story 'Meneseteung' (in *Friend of my youth*, 1990), Jane URQUHART's *Away* (1993), and Margaret Atwood's *Alias Grace* (1996).

Much of the critical work on pioneer writing since 1983 has been a feminist recuperation and reassessment of nineteenth-century women's texts and lives. More of this important work needs to be done. But it is also time for a post-colonial perspective to be brought to bear on the texts of pioneer writers, both male and female, that will situate their works more clearly than has been done to date in the historical context of colonial expansion.

GILLIAN SIDDALL

Plante, Raymond. See CHILDREN'S LITERATURE IN FRENCH 1980s TO 1996.

Plouffe, Les (1948). This second novel by Roger LEMELIN—translated by Mary Finch as *The Plouffe family* (1950; NCL, 1975)—follows chronologically *Au pied de la pente douce* (*The town below*, 1948). Structured in four parts, with the action stretching from summer 1938 to summer 1940, it ends with a brief epilogue dated May 1945. Its setting—a working-class district of Quebec City's Lower Town—is less important than in the first novel (more events occur in Upper Town), and attention centres on a single family. The nominal head of the Plouffe family is the father, Théophile, a typesetter; but the real power is held by his wife, Joséphine. Three of their children—Cécile, forty; Napoléon, thirty-two; and Ovide, twenty-nine—work in shoe factories; nineteen-year-old Guillaume, a baseball star, is unemployed. As the novel unfolds, the family disintegrates: Théo dies; Ovide and Napoléon marry and have families of their own; Cécile occupies herself with her newly adopted child; and Guillaume goes to war. Joséphine is left alone, although her two married sons remain nearby. The plot is fan-shaped, with the characters each living out his or her drama over a period of seven years. Less spontaneous than the characters in the first novel, they each have a caricature-like quirk or label: Guillaume, 'le sportif'; Napoléon, 'le collectionneur', with a mania for ice-cream cones; Ovide, the 'mélomane' and frustrated opera star; Joséphine, habitual gum-chewer; Théophile, tippler and admirer of Kaiser Wilhelm II; Cécile, penny-pincher and lover of bus-rides. *Les Plouffe*, however, shows Lemelin's keen awareness of the impact on Quebec of the Second World War and the Conscription Crisis; the changing character of the Catholic syndicates; the influence of the Church and the disintegration of the parish; and the growing Americanization of Quebec. The ironic discrepancy between the Plouffes' heroic-sounding given names and their commonplace family name—which resembles in sound the deflation of their dreams—echoes the theme of failure and demoralization.

The basis for a very popular TV serial on both the French and English CBC networks,

Les Plouffe also became, in 1981, a widely acclaimed film directed by Gilles Carle—both with scripts by Lemelin. In the film the satirized priest of the novel, Father Folbèche, and the language of the characters are somewhat idealized, and the dominating Mme Plouffe is more benign.

A sequel to *Les Plouffe, Le crime d'Ovide Plouffe*, was published in 1982.

BEN-Z. SHEK

Pocock, Roger. See FOREIGN WRITERS ON CANADA IN ENGLISH: 1.

Poetry in English. To 1900. 1. THE PRE-SETTLEMENT PERIOD. Before the founding of Halifax (1749) and the garrisoning of Quebec (1760), the English presence in Canada was small and scattered, lacking the communal cohesiveness and mechanisms of communication (presses and newspapers) necessary to stimulate an indigenous literature. Poetry written in and of the area was composed by visitors who reported their observations and experiences back to a more coherent and literate society (usually in England) with the intention of satisfying their readers' inherent curiosity about distant lands and events. These visitor-poems are mainly of two types: descriptions of the land and its settlement, and narratives of military actions.

The earliest descriptive verse was written by seventeenth-century visitors to Newfoundland. William Vaughan's *The golden fleece* (London, 1626) and Robert HAYMAN's *Quodlibets, lately come over from New Britaniola, Old Newfoundland* (London, 1628) project an idyllic vision of Newfoundland's potential and a Utopian view of the possibilities of settlement. This optimistic and idealized perspective sets the tone for most of the descriptive poetry composed by subsequent visitors. B. Lacy's *Miscellaneous poems compos'd at Newfoundland* (London, 1729), which vividly describes the hardships of settlement, is an unusual exception. The anonymous *Nova Scotia: a new ballad* (London, 1750), J. Patrick's *Quebec: a pastoral essay* (London, 1760), and George Cartwright's *Labrador: a poetical epistle* (London, 1792) sustain an optimistic picture of settlement, while replacing the earlier idyllic view of the land with an eighteenth-century appreciation of the sublimity of nature. This combination of optimism and sentiment may be found as late as Cornwall Bayley's *Canada: a descriptive poem* (Quebec, 1806), Thomas D. Cowdell's *The Nova Scotia minstrel* (Dublin, 1809), and in the verses included by Methodist missionary Joshua Marsden in his *The narrative of a mission to Nova Scotia, New Brunswick, and the Somers Islands, with a tour to Lake Ontario* (Plymouth Dock, 1818). The other subject that early poets reported on was military activity in Canada. Martin Parker's *England's honour revived* (London, 1629) is a ballad on Sir David Kirke's victory at Quebec. Valentine Neville, a naval officer who participated in the capture of Louisbourg, described that event in *The reduction of Louisburg* (London, 1759). George Cockings follows a similar pattern in *War: an heroick poem* (London, 1762), in his verse-drama *The conquest of Quebec* (London, 1766), and in his later poem *The American war* (London, 1781). As late as the War of 1812 the anonymous poem *A poetical account of the American campaigns of 1812 and 1813* (Halifax, 1815) approached its subject in a reportorial manner. This type of detached perspective characterizes all the visitor-poetry of this period. In spite of occasional didacticism, both the descriptive and narrative poems are aimed more at informing a remote readership than at shaping local response to a new reality.

2. 1749 TO 1815. With the development of substantial English communities in Quebec, Nova Scotia, and New Brunswick, locally written verse intended for a local readership began to emerge. This activity increased markedly towards the end of the century with the influx of thousands of Loyalist refugees displaced by the American Revolution. Very quickly the inhabitants of these loyal colonies established themselves as cohesive economic, political, and social entities. At the same time they developed a remarkably coherent concept of the ideological basis of their society. Not surprisingly, as eighteenth-century conservatives thay had an understanding of reality characterized by well-established sets of social, political, moral, and religious assumptions in which the idea of order and propriety was central; man's relationship to his natural environment was less important than his awareness of the ordered structure of civilization. Poetry, because it could be readily created under local conditions, played a significant role in the cultural development of these colonies: it became a sophisticated means of expressing local social and cultural expectations. Consciously imitating established verse-forms and poetic sentiments, colonial poets explored and described local experience in relation to universal frames of reference; their subjects revolved around the social, political, moral, and religious ideals of their time. In its similarity to prevailing forms, local poetry thus reflected the colonial desire to be part of

a universal cultural reality—one that was perceived to be most clearly expressed in European (particularly English) literature. This poetic perspective dominated Canadian poetry until the end of the Napoleonic Wars.

The poetry of this period is inherently didactic in almost all its forms. Descriptive works and topographical poems, such as Roger VIETS' *Annapolis Royal* (Halifax, 1788), Thomas Cary's *Abram's Plains* (Quebec, 1789), J. Mackay's *Quebec Hill; or Canadian scenery* (London, 1797), and Adam Allan's *A description of the great falls of the River St. John* (London, 1798) essentially had a moral purpose: integrating the character of colonial life with prevailing moral ideals. In occasional poems, such as Stephen Dickson's allegorical eulogy *The union of taste and science* (Quebec, 1799), the moral didacticism was even more overt, as it was in the numerous elegies, lyrics, and songs published in local newspapers. Religious values were another important subject for didactic treatment. Henry ALLINE's *Hymns and spiritual songs* (Boston, 1784) is the best example: the collection is a cross between a spiritual autobiography and a guide to religious life. Finally, social and political concerns were often treated, with an implicitly didactic purpose, in satiric terms; specific social, moral, and religious values were promoted by attacking those who failed to live up to the desired ideal. The social, political, and religious satires of Jacob BAILEY, Jonathan ODELL, Samuel Denny Street, and Alexander Croke were grounded in a moral vision of society drawn from eighteenth-century English conservatism.

3. 1815 TO 1840. While the conservative mentality of the eighteenth century lingered after 1815, the imagination of a new generation of writers was excited more by the apparent uniqueness of colonial experience than by its connection with ideal universal realities. This shift in perspective was not sudden and radical but gradual, often halting; it emerged as a growing awareness of colonial social and cultural autonomy in the face of continuing emotional attachments to the culture of Great Britain. In political terms it manifested itself in the movement towards responsible government, particularly in Nova Scotia. In the poetry of the period it was most clearly demonstrated in a new-found interest in the legends, customs, and historical background of colonial life. Native poets began to write of the struggles and hardships of early settlement as part of a process of historical development: Adam Hood BURWELL's 'Talbot Road' (1820), Oliver GOLDSMITH's *The rising village* (London, 1825), and Joseph HOWE's 'Acadia' (*c.* 1832) all reflect emerging colonial interest in social, political, and cultural identity. At the same time poets also turned to North America's Native peoples as a subject for verse. In the anonymous captivity tale *The lay of the wilderness* (Saint John, 1833), hostile relations with Native people are treated as a significant part of the romantic history of early settlements; in John RICHARDSON's *Tecumseh; or, The warrior of the West in four cantos with notes* (London, 1828) and Adam KIDD's *The Huron chief and other poems* (Montreal, 1830), the Native is depicted as a noble savage whose culture is essentially compatible with the central values of European civilization. In both cases the poetry integrates Native people into a perceived pattern of historical development. This is also true of the verse dealing with local customs and legends: George LONGMORE's *The charivari; or Canadian poetics: a tale after the manner of Beppo* (Montreal, 1824), Levi ADAMS' *Jean Baptiste* (Montreal, 1825), and Andrew SHIELS' *The witch of the Westcot* (Halifax, 1831)—all attempt to identify and promote the special texture of social life unfolding in British North America.

In addition to poetry that dealt specifically with colonial life, native poets continued to produce didactic verse prescribing accepted moral and religious values, and lyrics that projected universal social and cultural values. The poetry of such writers as Joseph Hart Clinch, William Martin Leggett, J.M. Cawdell, Angus Gidney, and Adam Hood Burwell sustained the didactic character of eighteenth-century verse, but was generally more sentimental in tone. This is true of the work of such lyricists as James Hogg, W.F. Hawley, Margaret Blennerhasset, James Redfern, and John Laskey. Under the influence of Robert Burns and Thomas Moore, these poets cultivated a range of sentimental poetic responses and applied them to colonial social life and to the natural environment. The picture of cultural life that emerges is one marked by a self-conscious appreciation of all forms of emotional and moral sensitivity. These native lyricists strove to demonstrate that colonial sensibilities were not blunted by the unsophisticated conditions in which they were nurtured.

4. 1840 TO 1860. The poetic subjects of the 1820s and 1830s continued to attract attention in mid-century. G.A. Hammond's verses on New Brunswick Natives, William KIRBY's *The U.E.: a tale of Upper Canada* (Niagara, 1859), and Archibald Grey's view of village life in *Shades of the hamlet* (Woburn, Mass., 1852) reflected a continuing need to project a vision of historical and social development. Added to

this was a new dimension in the colonizing process—large-scale immigration, starting in the 1830s. Standish O'GRADY's *The emigrant* (Montreal, 1842) was the first of many poems to explore the role of the immigrant in colonial life. Also, moral and religious didacticism continued to find expression in the poetry of Andrew SHIELS, Samuel Elder, A.K. Archibald, and Sarah and Mary E. HERBERT, among others; the subject of temperance was of special interest. At the same time, Charles HEAVYSEGE's *Saul; a drama in three parts* (Montreal, 1857) demonstrated a lingering interest in biblical subjects.

But the most significant poetic development of the mid-century was a growing interest in the landscape and natural environment of Canada, probably stimulated by the importance of nature in British Romantic poetry. This trend is evident in books published from the Maritimes to Upper Canada: M.A. Wallace's *Hymns of the Church, Nativity, and other poems* (Portland, Me., 1853), which contains secular verse; Clotilda Jennings' *Linden rhymes* (Halifax, 1851); Bishop G.J. Mountain's *Songs of the wilderness* (London, 1846); W.A. Stephens' *Hamilton and other poems* (Toronto, 1840); James Liston's *Niagara Falls* (Toronto, 1843); and in the early Canadian verses of Alexander McLACHLAN. But of special interest is the nature poetry of John McPHERSON, posthumously collected in *Poems, descriptive and moral* (Halifax, 1862); of Peter John ALLAN in *Poetical remains* (London, 1853); and of Charles SANGSTER in *The St. Lawrence and the Saguenay, and other poems* (Kingston and New York, 1856) and *Hesperus, and other poems and lyrics* (Montreal, 1860). Their poetic perspectives are complex and their poetic 'voices' seem uniquely North American. Where others tend to sentimentalize their responses to nature, these poets strove to articulate man's ability to identify himself emotionally with, and to explore, the unique character of the natural world around him.

Finally, the publication of D'Arcy McGEE's *Canadian ballads, and occasional verses* (Montreal, 1858) introduced a strain of self-conscious patriotic nationalism into Canadian poetry. Although McGee drew on his Irish experience to shape this perspective, the rapid movement of colonial North America towards nationhood created conditions amenable to patriotic and nationalistic verse.

5. 1860 TO 1880. Poetically, the years on either side of Confederation appear to lack clear focus and direction, as if poets were not quite sure how to come to terms with the new social and political realities of Canada. Certainly poets such as Charles MAIR, Mrs LEPROHON, and a host of lesser names tried to articulate the new sense of Canadian nationalism that logically ought to have been a part of the attainment of nationhood; but their efforts appear formulaic, projecting an abstract patriotism at best. Indeed, in Mair's case this nationalistic focus seems to have deflected him from exploring his response to the natural environment, the subject of his early verse in *Dreamland and other poems* (Montreal, 1868). The desire to project a national voice drew him away from his poetic strength.

This period also saw the publication of the first significant anthology of Canadian verse, E.H. DEWART's *Selections from Canadian poets* (Montreal, 1864). Like contemporary poets, Dewart saw his work as part of a growing sense of Canadian nationalism, arguing that 'A national literature is an essential element in the formation of national character.' A third of the selections are nature poems, another third moral and religious verse, and the remainder 'miscellaneous pieces'. Despite Dewart's claims, it is very difficult to draw an impression of national character from the collection, and even more difficult to ascertain the direction in which Canadian poetry was moving. Much the same may be said of W.D. LIGHTHALL's later anthology, *Songs of the great dominion* (London, 1889), although Lighthall more consciously organized his selections around what he perceived to be aspects of Canadian national identity.

Aside from nationalistic verse, the period was dominated by Scottish immigrant poets and by women magazine-writers. Alexander McLachlan's *The emigrant, and other poems* (Toronto, 1861) and *Poems and songs* (Toronto, 1874), William Murdoch's *Poems and songs* (Saint John, 1860 and 1872), and Evan McColl's poetry (collected in 1883), all reflect the adaptation of Lowland Scots lyric verse to Canadian subjects. At their best these poets projected a vision of social, economic, and political progress in the new Canada. But their perceptions of human character, and of society, often seem to be grounded in Scottish rather than Canadian cultural experience; consequently they seem to be imposing patterns of perception rather than exploring the character of Canadian life. Since Canadian poetry had effectively gone beyond the stage of prescribing notions of social, moral, and cultural experience, these Scottish poets often appear somewhat removed from the direction that had been developed in the earlier part of the century. Much the same may be said of the women poets, such as Mary Jane KATZMANN, Agnes MACHAR, and M.G. Currie. Their poetic voices were those of the popular magazine poetesses of Britain and America, presenting sentimentalized images of moral and religious propriety—an abstraction of civilized life applied to a Canadian context.

6. 1880 TO 1900. The last two decades of the century were marked by the emergence of a group of poets who, though fully aware of intellectual and artistic developments in New York and London, confidently turned to their own experience, trusting their perceptions (particularly of the natural world) to provide the subjects and images of their poetry. Not surprisingly they found in the natural environment of Canada a fundamental source of poetic inspiration.

It was Charles G.D. ROBERTS' *Orion, and other poems* (Philadelphia, 1880) and *In divers tones* (Boston, 1886) that signalled the presence of this new poetic perspective in Canadian verse. His efforts were joined by those of Isabella Valency CRAWFORD in *Old Spookses' pass, Malcolm's Katie, and other poems* (Toronto, 1884); and by Archibald LAMPMAN in *Among the millet* (Ottawa, 1888), *Lyrics of earth* (Boston, 1895), and *Alcyone* (Edinburgh, 1899). Further, the early verse of Roberts' cousin Bliss CARMAN in *Low tide on Grand Pré* (New York, 1893), and of Duncan Campbell SCOTT in *The magic house, and other poems* (Ottawa, 1893) and *Labor and the angel* (Boston, 1898), formed part of a relatively cohesive body of verse that focused on Canadian landscape and its effect on Canadian consciousness. (See CONFEDERATION POETS.) In this poetry there are strains of the poetic sensibilities of P.J. Allan, John McPherson, and Charles SANGSTER; but for the later poets nature has become a much more complex and mysterious phenomenon than the earlier writers had imagined. Where earlier generations treated nature descriptively as topography, or sentimentally as an extension of their emotional sensitivity, Roberts' generation approached nature as an embodiment of the spirit of being informing all human reality and around which human consciousness was shaped. In other words Canadian poets, responding to Canadian landscapes, now confronted a universal reality that was immediate and profound, and their fundamental perceptions were not borrowed or channelled through aesthetic assumptions formulated in foreign centres of culture. Although their poetic language may have been influenced by prevailing poetic fashion, their primary perceptions—the source of their poetry—remained individualistic, immediate, and original. In the verse of all five poets, the disarming simplicity of their presentation of nature is its most attractive feature, but behind that simplicity lies a disturbing ominousness. In an increasingly utilitarian world struggling with a Darwinian vision of human reality, the need to seek and assert the essential spirituality of nature emerged as a basic intellectual, aesthetic, and humanistic responsibility that the poet could not ignore. This poetic responsibility linked Roberts, Crawford, Lampman, Carman, and Scott to an international brotherhood of poets, but it did so in specifically Canadian terms. Their awareness of the spirit of reality was shaped by the natural forms in which they perceived it. For these poets the forms were Canadian, their perceptions were Canadian, and their poetic response had a specifically Canadian character.

Less perceptive, but often touched by the same sense of transcendental truths in nature, were the verses of Wilfred CAMPBELL in *Lake lyrics and other poems* (Saint John, 1889), of Frederick George SCOTT in *The soul's quest* (London, 1885), and of Francis SHERMAN and Pauline JOHNSON. These poets, however, often appear more concerned with accommodating their poetic presentations to one contemporary literary fashion or another than with exploring and articulating the character of their personal experience of nature. Much the same may be said of G.F. CAMERON's *Lyrics on freedom, love, and death* (Kingston, 1887). Indeed, the temptation to imitate internationally recognized poetic patterns and apply them to ostensibly Canadian subjects tended to undermine the impulse to establish a viable set of indigenous poetic perspectives. In the late eighteenth and early nineteenth centuries the adoption of borrowed poetic forms and stances was central and necessary to the development of Canadian poetry; in the late decades of the nineteenth century this kind of imitation betrayed an unnecessary aesthetic insecurity that haunted Canadian verse well into the twentieth century.

TOM VINCENT

1900 to 1950. 1. THE ROMANTIC AND VICTORIAN HERITAGE. The dominant voices in Canadian poetry at the turn of the century were heavily influenced by the concerns, verse forms, and diction of English and American Romantic and Victorian poetry. Archibald LAMPMAN's *Poems* (1900), Charles G.D. ROBERTS' *Poems* (1901), Duncan Campbell SCOTT's *New world lyrics and ballads* (1905), and Bliss CARMAN's *Pipes of Pan*

(1906), while showing the results of the poets' classical training, also clearly illustrate their stylistic and philosophical debts to nineteenth-century British and American writers. Though some of the later work of these poets exhibit a slight loosening of formal constraints, Canadian life and landscape, spirituality, and patriotism remain central to their poetry. Roberts, Carman, and Scott continued to publish into the second quarter of the century, Scott himself doing much to foster Lampman's reputation by editing four posthumous collections of Lampman's verse.

Women writers of this period were building networks and a female tradition, as is evidenced in A. Ethelwyn WETHERALD's introduction to *The collected poems of Isabella Valancy Crawford* (1905), and in CRAWFORD's presence in a literary community that included among others Marjorie PICKTHALL, Agnes Maule MACHAR (*Lays of the 'True North,' and other Canadian poems*, 1899), Helena Coleman (*Songs and sonnets*, 1906), and Isabel Ecclestone MacKay (1875-1928). Her *Complete poems* (1930) includes two winners of the *Globe*'s historical poem contest and an elegy, 'Vale', for her friend Pauline JOHNSON. Wetherald's own representations of female desire and nature were collected in *Lyrics and sonnets* (1931).

Pickthall's *Complete poems* (1925) shows her to be in the forefront of the minor poets of this period (among whom were Wilson MacDONALD and Francis SHERMAN) who inclined to a mystical and lyrical aestheticism that has been linked both to the Celtic twilight and to the Pre-Raphaelite school. Mellifluous and charming, her largely woman-centred poetry often recounts biblical, classical, and Canadian historical narratives.

Popular poets in the early years of the century were conservative in their prosody, and chose subjects that would have been exotic to most white anglophones. *The poetical works* (1912) of William Henry DRUMMOND brings together dialect portraits of French-Canadian characters; and Robert SERVICE's *Songs of a sourdough* (1907) is memorable for its humorous Gothic tales of the Yukon at the time of the Gold Rush, such as 'The shooting of Dan McGrew', work that overshadowed his more serious side. His later work, of which *Bar-room ballads* (1940) is representative, depicts a world-ranging bohemian way of life. Ambivalent in her attitudes to and presentation of her dual British and Mohawk heritages, Pauline Johnson (Tekahionwake) popularized her poetry, collected in *Flint and feather* (1912), in many public readings throughout Canada and in England. Once calling herself 'sad historian of her own race', Johnson both critiques white racism and articulates a loyalty to Crown and Empire.

The work of both established and newer poets of the first quarter of the century can be sampled in Albert Watson's and Lorne PIERCE's *Our Canadian literature: representative prose and verse* (1922). This book became, in 1935, exclusively an anthology of poetry under the editorship of Pierce and Bliss Carman, and in 1955 was revised and updated by V.B. Rhodenizer as *Canadian poetry in English*. The enervation of Canadian poetry by sentimental versifiers, and its freighting with imperial ideology, are painfully evident in much of Wilfred CAMPBELL's *The Oxford book of Canadian verse* (1913) and John Garvin's *Canadian poets* (1916; rev. 1926).

2. NEO-COLONIAL MODERNISM. Although in the twenties and thirties Canadian poetry gained a new life and direction as the cramping prosody, idiom, and Romantic worldview of the last century were left behind, the majority of poets still looked to Europe or, in fewer cases, America, to provide them with poetic models for the expression of contemporary experience. Learning from the Imagists, experimenters in free verse, and British and American poets who had a social orientation, Canadian writers broadened their concept of what was suitable subject-matter for poetry, discovered a diction and imagery appropriate to contemporary concerns, and freed themselves from the strictures of rhyme and conventional metres.

2(a) *Transitional figures*. E.J. PRATT is the quintessential transitional figure. The life of his early work *Newfoundland verse* (1923) is largely attributable to its gripping images of humanity confronting an overwhelmingly powerful nature, though it is sometimes choked by diction and sentiments inherited from an outworn tradition. Pratt was not a metrical or formal innovator—as his *Many moods* (1932) and his narratives *Titans* (1926) and *The Titanic* (1935) amply testify. But the scope of his vision and his epic scale were appropriate reflections of Canadian experience, while his attempts to bridge the gap between the sciences, technology, and the humanities—reflected most clearly in his choice of subject and in his diction—show him to be vitally engaged with twentieth-century life. In his later work Pratt mythologized the male Canadian experience in meticulously researched narratives: *Brébeuf and his brethren* (1940) and *Towards the last spike* (1952). Pratt's verse (*Complete poems*, 1989) is a culmination and summation of a phase in the developing Canadian imagination that saw Canada as a land characterized by an often beautiful and always powerful and indifferent nature that both threatened to crush the human spirit and challenged it to reach sacrificial heights of nobility.

The 'poet of the Laurentians', F.G. SCOTT, also wrote *In the battle silences: poems written at the front* (1916), and Helena Coleman (1860-1953) offers a woman's view of the Great War in similarly conventional prosody in *Marching men* (1917). Frank PREWETT's responses to Great War experiences (*Poems*, 1922), by contrast, are in the manner of Georgian poet Siegfried Sassoon.

Tom MacINNES's *Rhymes of a rounder* (1913) shows this highly individual poet—best known for his villanelle 'The tiger of desire' —going to French verse-forms to structure his exuberantly irreverent view of life. *Frozen fire* (1937) by Floris Clarke McLaren (1904-?) dramatizes attitudes towards British Columbian landscapes and the north country, while the terse, sometimes prosaic, qualities of Charles BRUCE's realistic portraits of Maritime life and landscapes can be sampled in their early form in *Wild apples* (1927). The early work of Kenneth LESLIE, also a Maritimer with a strong regional awareness, echoes the themes and voices of Carman and Roberts, but his polished sonnets of passion *By stubborn stars and other poems* (1938) showed that conventional forms could still structure genuine feeling. Fellow Maritimer Alfred Goldsworthy BAILEY, who would help found the Fredericton magazine *The FIDDLEHEAD*, published the conventional *Songs of the Saguenay and other poems* (1927) before being influenced by modernist forms. Ralph GUSTAFSON similarly showed an early fascination with the manner of late Romantic poetry in *The golden chalice* (1935); but in *Flight into darkness* (1944) the elliptical quality of the syntax and the erudite vocabulary of his new poems reflected contemporary influences.

2(b) *The free-versists*. Evidence of formal innovation can be found as early as 1914 when Arthur STRINGER defended his free-verse style in a preface to *Open water*; but early Canadian reaction was often hostile, though never so well and self-subvertingly expressed as in Lucy Maud MONTGOMERY's *vers libre*, 'I feel' (1920). Not until W.W.E. ROSS blended this style with what he had learned from the American Imagist Marianne Moore was free verse significantly used in Canadian poetry. Ross wrote most of his important poetry during the twenties, attempting to capture 'something of/what quality may mark us off/from older Europe,—/something "North American"—/and something of/the sharper tang of Canada.' He quietly published *Laconics* (1930) and *Sonnets* (1932), but *Experiment 1923-1929* did not appear until 1956. The poems of a fellow free-verse Imagist of the 1920s, Raymond KNISTER, were similarly delayed in gaining broad exposure: his only volume of poems, which concentrated on farm life, *The collected poems of Raymond Knister*, edited and with a memoir by Dorothy LIVESAY, was published posthumously in 1949.

Critic Arthur Phelps, painter Lawren Harris, and poet Louise Morey Bowman (1882-1944) all used free verse in their poetry, which has more historical than aesthetic importance. The title *Acanthus and wild grape* (1920) by Frank Oliver Call (1878-1956) represents his book's mix of formally stylized and free-verse forms, and Arthur BOURINOT left behind his early plodding adherence to conventional rhythms and rhyme—evident in *Laurentian lyrics and other poems* (1915)—for a freer verse style in *Under the sun* (1939).

Free-verse techniques were blended with more conventional prosody to translate and adapt First Nations' texts in *Songs of the coast dwellers* (1930) by Constance Lindsay Skinner (1879-1939) and in Hermia Harris Fraser's *Songs of the western islands* (1945). These books continued a tradition of making available to English-speaking readers the poems of Canada's non-English poets. This tradition extends at least as far back as 1916, when *Songs of Ukraina, with Ruthenian poems* by Florence Randal Livesay (1874-1953) appeared, and includes Watson KIRKCONNELL's *Canadian overtones: an anthology of Canadian poetry written originally in Icelandic, Swedish, Hungarian, Italian, Greek, and Urkrainian, and now translated* (1935).

2(c) *Lorne Pierce and the Ryerson Press*. Hermia Fraser's book is one of the Ryerson poetry chapbooks, a series under the general editorship of Lorne PIERCE. As editor for RYERSON PRESS from 1920 to 1960, Pierce did much to aid the growth of Canadian poetry, initiating the chapbook series in 1925 with Sir Charles G.D. ROBERTS' *The sweet o' the year and other poems*. Roberts was also the first recipient of the Lorne Pierce medal, donated by the editor to recognize a significant and sustained contribution to Canadian letters. Important later volumes in the chapbook series include Bliss Carman's *The music of earth* (1931), Ann MARRIOTT's ten-poem sequence describing the hardships of farming in Saskatchewan during the dirty thirties, *The wind our enemy* (1939), and Dorothy Livesay's documentary radio poem about the internment of Japanese Canadians during the Second World War, *Call my people home* (1950). Pierce was also general editor for the nationalistic Makers of Canadian Literature series, which published appreciative biographies of several Canadian poets.

3. THE MONTREAL MOVEMENT AND OTHER THIRTIES' ACTIVITY. Founded by F.R. SCOTT and A.J.M. SMITH, The *McGILL FORTNIGHTLY REVIEW* (1925-7) was a Montreal-based periodical that published poems, poetic manifestors, and critical articles sympathetic to the aims and techniques of modernist poetry. In articles like 'Wanted: Canadian criticism' (*Canadian Forum*, Apr. 1928), Smith was also instrumental in articulating what was wrong with Canadian poetry: too self-conscious of its position in space, it was hardly conscious of all of its position in time. 'Sensibility is no longer enough, intelligence is also required. Even in Canada,' Smith proclaimed.

The short-lived successor to the McGill paper, *The CANADIAN MERCURY: a monthly journal of literature and opinion* (1928-9), edited by Scott and Leo KENNEDY, kept up the attack on the mediocrity of much Canadian verse and gave space to many of the important poets whose work later appeared in the commercially unsuccessful but critically important anthology *NEW PROVINCES: poems of several authors* (1936). The voices of Yeats, Eliot, Pound, and Auden could clearly be heard in the cadences of many of the anthology's poems, while the spare style and irregular rhythms and forms of the free-versists proved effective in rendering the quality of the Canadian landscape in such poems as 'Trees in ice' by Scott and 'The lonely land' by Smith, visions of Canadian nature shaped by painters in the Group of Seven. Scott contributed several satirical pieces and poems examining people as social beings, modes that were continued in his *Overture* (1945). Kennedy and Smith both employed metaphysical images in their poems, the former having already published *The shrouding* (1933), with its poems centring on fertility cycles, and the latter continuing to work the metaphysical and psychological veins in *News of the phoenix and other poems* (1943). Robert FINCH was the most stylistically traditional of the contributors, and a neo-classical spirit informed his first two individual collections, *Poems* (1946) and *The strength of the hills* (1948). Both in *New provinces*, and in the poems of *Hath not a Jew* (1940), A.M. KLEIN wrote about his Jewish heritage, creating portraits of imagined or real individuals such as Baruch Spinoza in the justly celebrated 'Out of the pulver and the polished lens'. Klein's relatively brief but intense publishing career as poet culminated in *The rocking chair and other poems* (1948), in which his concern for members of minority groups extended to both French Canadians and the ultimate 'minority of one' figure, the artist, in 'Portrait of the poet as landscape'. (See also the MONTREAL GROUP.)

The interdisciplinary magazine *CANADIAN FORUM* published in the thirties not only many important poems (especially under the literary editorship of Earle BIRNEY from 1936 to 1940), but also two series of critical essays of note: 'The new writers of Canada' (1932) and 'Canadian writers of the past' (1932-3). Both poems and articles made clear the prevalent anti-Romantic stance of the poets and critics of the era. One poet whose work was discussed in the former series and who later proved to be a major talent was Dorothy Livesay. Her irregularly rhymed and Imagist-influenced free-verse collection *Green pitcher* (1928) was followed by the socially conscious poems of *Signpost* (1932) and *Day and night* (1944), in which subject matter clearly determines form, though angry leftist rhetoric sometimes detracts from the impression created by the effective use of mimetic rhythms. L.A. MacKay (1901-?) was a contributor to both series of essays, assessing past writers Bliss Carman and Wilfred Campbell and the more recent poet Audrey Alexandra BROWN, whose *A dryad in Nanaimo* (1931, rpr. and enlarged 1934) included the noteworthy romance narrative 'Laodamia', and showed her in both strengths and limitations to be a successor in mode to Marjorie Pickthall. A professor of classics and a poet in his own right, MacKay had published his love poems, sonnets, and neo-classical satires under the pseudonym 'John Smalacombe' in *Viper's Bugloss* (1938) and, using his own name, in *The ill-tempered lover and other poems* (1948).

The thirties saw the birth of many supports to the renaissance in Canadian poetry, 1936 being a particularly fruitful year as W.E. Collin's landmark book of essays on Canadian poetry, *The WHITE SAVANNAHS*, appeared; *The Canadian Poetry Magazine* was founded by the CANADIAN AUTHORS' ASSOCIATION under the editorship of E.J. Pratt, and in its first number published Livesay's 'Day and night', as well as poems by F.R. Scott, Finch, and Kennedy; *The University of Toronto Quarterly* began its annual review of Canadian poetry in its 'Letters in Canada'; the GOVERNOR GENERAL'S LITERARY AWARDS were instituted;

and the Canadian Broadcasting Corporation was becoming an important disseminator of poems and critical commentary. Few poetry anthologies of any real merit were published in this decade, though Ethel Hume Bennett's anthology, *New harvesting: contemporary Canadian poetry 1918-1938* (1938), gives a representative sampling of the then-recent work of Canadian poets who were still living.

4. THE FORTIES. Montreal continued to be a centre of poetic activity in this decade as two literary magazines provided an outlet for two groups of poets, both concerned with raising public consciousness about social issues. *FIRST STATEMENT: A magazine for young Canadian writers* (1942-5), founded by the poet-critic John SUTHERLAND—later joined by Irving LAYTON and Louis DUDEK—was avowedly proletarian, and its poets used a colloquial idiom and a detailed realism to evoke their Canadian environment. *PREVIEW* (1942-5) was a work-in-progress mimeo-magazine established by the English expatriate Patrick ANDERSON and put together by a group that included F.R. Scott and later P.K. PAGE and A.M. Klein. Culturally sophisticated, as well as socially and politically committed, the *Preview* poets saw themselves as assisting in the war effort as well as supplying 'something of the personal, the graceful and the heroic, to the atmosphere of this half-empty Dominion'—feats that were to be accomplished by blending the lyric and didactic elements in modern verse and by combining 'vivid arresting imagery' with social commentary and criticism. The amalgamation of these two magazines to form *NORTHERN REVIEW* (1945-56) suggests that too much has been made of the differences between the groups. Furthermore, in 1945 Sutherland's First Statement Press published not only Layton's vision of Jewish Montreal, *Here and now*, and Miriam WADDINGTON's *Green world*—which pictures an innocent spring and summer sensuality made more poignant by the disillusionment of a growing awareness of evil and mortality in fall and winter—but also Patrick Anderson's first Canadian collection, *A tent for April*. That book, and Anderson's *The white centre* (1946), are characterized by metaphysical and sexual images, and by a nostalgia for youth; they include pictures of wartime Montreal, and several self-conscious attempts at defining the nature of the Canadian experience.

Louis Dudek's organically structured poems in *East of the city* (1946) are written in both critical and celebratory modes, though they reflect a principally urban experience, seen from a socialist point of view. Striking imagery, and an empathy for the socially or emotionally oppressed that often ends in anger at their situation, are the defining characteristics of P.K. Page's maps of the psyche in *As ten as twenty* (1946). Anderson, who was Page's first publisher, had discovered her work in *CONTEMPORARY VERSE*, a stylistically eclectic and increasingly distinguished west-coast literary quarterly edited and published by Alan Crawley from 1941 to 1952.

A major western talent also appeared in the forties in Earle BIRNEY, whose poetry was from the first distinguished by an unsentimental yet compassionate understanding of strange or disturbing experiences, and a desire to delineate the Canadian character. *David and other poems* (1942) employs an often Prattian documentary style; in addition to the title narrative—about the way youthful innocence is ended by the need to act in the face of a mountain-climbing disaster—it contains many formally and stylistically various poems of a humorous or satirical nature. As it was in his first volume, war is a significant theme in Birney's *Now is time: poems* (1945), in which he continues to experiment with narrative. *The strait of Anian: selected poems* (1948) is a summation of Birney's first phase, and offers a critical view of Canadian life juxtaposed with an appreciative look at the power and beauty of the land.

Raymond SOUSTER's poetry is consistently simple in diction, colloquial in tone, and organic in its verse-forms. In *When we are young* (1946) he celebrates in vivid imagery the passionate sexuality of the young, and casts a cold eye on the war in Europe. *Go to sleep, world* (1947) contains many moving love poems and clearly establishes him as a poet of Toronto, revealing both the tawdrier and more vital sides of that city. Another Toronto-based poet of the period, Douglas LePAN, skilfully blends Old and New World sensibilities and subject matter, as well as a felicity of phrasing and an acuity of vision, in *The wounded prince and other poems* (1948).

Bertram WARR left Toronto for England in 1928. The years he spent observing life in London, especially in the poorer quarters, and the impact of the war on the city's people, resulted in the moving poems of *Yet a little onward* (1941). The pared, ironic diction of 'On a child with a wooden leg' is characteristic of the best of Warr's verse. His war poems were anthologized in several English books, and after his death in an air attack on Germany his promise as a poet was attested to by *In quest of beauty: selected poems* (1950). Mona Gould's *Tasting the earth* (1943) includes 'This was my brother', a bronze cast of which poem was erected at Dieppe.

5. THE CLOSE OF THE HALF-CENTURY. After the hardships of the Depression had given rise to the voice of social consciousness in Canadian poetry of the thirties, and the Second World War had led to a renewed Canadian pride in country that extended to an interest in what Canadian poets were saying about the national life, a strange lull set in at the end of the first half of the century. James REANEY's *The red heart* (1949), which won a Governor General's Award, was the only noteworthy book of that year, and it signalled a shift of the poetic centre from Montreal to Toronto. It contains some not very successful satires and humorous verses; but the poems in which Reaney looks at the world with a vivid childlike imagination, confronting fears embodied in monster and stepmother figures, and conveys that vision with often startling, fantastic, and horrific images, represent a new departure in Canadian poetry.

The achievement of Canadian poetry until mid-century was summarized in several anthologies and works of criticism published in the forties. Ralph Gustafson edited *Anthology of Canadian poetry* (1942), *A little anthology of Canadian poets* (1943), and a special Canadian issue of the American quarterly *Voices* (1943). Other magazine anthologies of Canadian verse appeared in *Poetry* (Chicago) and the British *Outposts*. A.J.M. Smith's *The book of Canadian poetry: a critical and historical anthology* (1943; rev. 1948, 1957) established the canon of Canadian poetry; it was to some extent updated by John Sutherland's *Other Canadians: an anthology of the new poetry in Canada 1940-1946* (1947). A forties' response to *New Provinces* came in Ronald Hambleton's *Unit of five* (1944), which presented a significant sample of the work of Souster, Page, Dudek, James Wreford, and Hambleton himself.

E.K. BROWN's *On Canadian poetry* (1943), the best critical book of the decade, assessed the colonial nature of Canadian poetry, delineated a three-phase developmental history, and hailed Archibald Lampman, D.C. Scott, and E.J. Pratt as three of Canada's best writers; while W.P. Percival's *Leading Canadian poets* (1948) contained essays of varying merit on twenty-nine poets. SUSAN GINGELL

1950 to 1982. In this period there was an astonishing increase not only in poetic talent but in the number of works published. The 24 books of verse published in 1959 increased to 120 in 1970. Between 1960 and 1973, 590 poets published over 1,100 books of verse, not counting anthologies, and between 1973 and 1982 a similar (undocumented) increase took place. The following survey will discuss briefly those poets who seem to have a genuine voice—not only something to say but an interesting way of saying it—and whose work has been significant in giving distinctiveness and character to Canadian poetry of the period.

1. THE FIFTIES. In this decade English-Canadian poetry consolidated and extended its seriousness and creativity, not only with mature collections but with the brilliant débuts of poets who are among the most important names in modern Canadian poetry. Much of the work of the fifties originated in the academic community, and displayed some of the effects of the continuing power of high modernism in the influence of Yeats, Auden, and Eliot. This was described in A.J.M. SMITH's preface to his *Book of Canadian poetry* (3rd edn 1957) and was revealed in his own collection *A sort of ecstasy* (1954), and in the irony, satire, and social consciousness of F.R. SCOTT's poems in his *Events and signals* (1954) and *The eye of the needle* (1957). This strain of fifties' poetry was erudite, and assumed a well-educated audience in its rich use of literary and other allusions. Another of its features, one that has been sustained, was the organization or subjection of individual short lyrics into a larger unity, and the use of a wide range of traditional forms—ballads, hymns, nursery rhymes, eclogues. Traditional forms did not necessarily support traditional values. On the contrary, those poets who used them usually did so for purposes of parody, to question accepted bourgeois values, and to suggest in the world of art and imagination alternative values.

The short poems that make up *The BOATMAN* (1957) by Jay MACPHERSON form an intricate sequence that is unified by thematic continuities and recurrent symbols. They enact a myth of creation, fall, and reconciliation in a largely comic and parodic mode—Macpherson's control of parody seizes power from the forms that are parodied. George JOHNSTON's *The cruising auk* (1959) is another collection that is integrated thematically and has many formal devices, including a single structuring symbol. These short, crisp poems are informed with wit and moral intelligence unencumbered with moralism, and a casual, almost disinterested irony. James REANEY's *A suit of nettles* (1958) is a witty imitation of Spenser's *The shepheardes calender*, structured in twelve poetic dialogues—one for each month of the year—among geese on an Ontario farm. It won Reaney his second Governor General's Award.

The display of craft, learning, wit, and allusiveness was also evident in other fifties' publications. Anne WILKINSON's *Counterpoint to sleep* (1951) and *The hangman ties the holly* (1955)—containing poems, about the sensory apprehension of the natural world, that often use word-play and traditional poetic forms like the nursery rhyme and the carol—were praised for their liveliness and their gift of parody, though they showed a strong interest in the Gothic and the macabre. The young Daryl HINE, in *The carnal and the crane* (1957), precociously revealed himself to be a highly erudite poet whose love of eloquence and verbal dignity, difficult syntax, and sometimes obscure imagery have made him less immediately popular than his strengths deserve. P.K. PAGE showed a complex sensibility, a powerful vision, and a lively wit in *The metal and the flower* (1954). Phyllis WEBB's *Even your right eye* (1956), with its eloquent diction and brilliant images, marked her as a poet worthy of notice. Another major poetic talent that appeared in the fifties—and who was part of the poetic ferment of Montreal at this time—was Leonard COHEN, whose *Let us compare mythologies* (1956), despite its grotesque imagery and its strain of black romance that was expressed in an obsession with the Crucifixion, is full of life and energy. In John GLASSCO's *The deficit made flesh* (1958), describing rural life in the Eastern Townships of Quebec, human untrustworthiness is rendered in technically skilled blank verse with an elegiac strain. Philip CHILD's *The Victorian house and other poems* (1951) contained one of the few narrative poems in a decade that was trying to find alternatives to the narrative form. Along with the title poem, however, there are lyrics that reveal a fine technical mastery. The poems in D.G. JONES' *Frost on the sun* (1957) are distanced from direct experience, which the poet subjects to a process of intensification in order to present it with verbal economy and with images that are restrained, deliberate, and powerful. R.G. EVERSON, in *Three dozen poems* (1957) and *A lattice for Momos* (1958), wrote elegant poetry that can sometimes be dense and epigrammatic and is full of imagistic comparisons, fresh humour, and a concern with myth and history.

The 1950s presented another important stream of Canadian poetry—one that would predominate in the sixties and seventies—that eschewed elegance, allusiveness, and traditional forms, adopting free verse and a colloquial, even street-wise, diction and tone. Having published two collections in the 1940s, Irving LAYTON began to hit his stride in the fifties, publishing eleven books. *A red carpet for the sun* (1959), one of the most important collections of the decade, put him squarely in the mainstream of Canadian poetry and presaged qualities that would appear more strongly in the prolific output to follow and would make him one of the most widely read of Canadian poets. In his corpus, satire and invective, occasional roughness of language, self-consciously Nietzschean and apocalyptic concerns, a Dionysian persona, and erotic verse are offset by more lyrical and self-examining poems than his somewhat raucous public image prepared us for. Layton joined Raymond SOUSTER and Louis DUDEK in founding CONTACT PRESS (1952-67), which provided a publishing outlet for them and for several other important poets of the period. Their own poems were collected in *Cerberus* (1952), and Souster's work in this volume heralded the continuities of his career. His best poems are wry but warm celebrations of Toronto urban life; some display an understated pathos. They tend to be short and tight, spoken through the voices of often unnamed characters—a device that allows him to experiment with a range of colloquial English. He published seven collections in the fifties, including *Crêpe-hanger's carnival: selected poems 1955-58* (1958), and his output has continued unabated. In this decade Louis Dudek published *24 poems* (1952), *Europe* (1955), *The transparent sea* (1956), and *En México* (1958)—books that reflected the influence of Ezra Pound's *Cantos* on his work. His strongly visual poems are at their best in the detached and distant mode of the observer. *Europe*, *En México*, and the later *Atlantis* (1967) are long, thoughtful meditations about the fate of Western civilization in the brutal twentieth century. Like Dudek, Miriam WADDINGTON began publishing in Montreal in the 1940s. Her two fifties' collections, *The second silence* (1955) and *The season's lovers* (1958), contained an intimate poetry with a lyrical bent that would become more colloquial and expressive in her later volumes.

Elizabeth BREWSTER's early poetry, *East coast* (1951) and *Lilloet* (1954), produced an unsentimental, affectionate record of isolated life in the towns and on the seacoasts of New Brunswick. In 1969 her collected poems, *Passage of summer*, appeared. The New Brunswick poet Dorothy Roberts, the daughter of Theodore Goodridge ROBERTS, showed promise in the fifties with *Dazzle* (1957) and *In star and stalk* (1959), though her later work has not become popular. Heather SPEARS wrote a powerful, disturbing chronicle of mental breakdown in *Asylum poems and others* (1958). Her poems, which relate poetry to painting and contain meditations on the creative process, include *The Danish portraits* (1967) and *From the inside* (1972).

2. THE SIXTIES AND SEVENTIES. The poets who came into prominence in the 1960s—Margaret ATWOOD, Al PURDY, Michael ONDAATJE, George BOWERING, and John NEWLOVE—changed and expanded the subject matter of Canadian poetry to include local history and documentary; family portraits and personal history conveyed in a muted, confessional mode; politics, popular culture, and surrealistic fantasy. In the sixties and early seventies the politics of Canadian poetry were nationalist, ecological, and regional, while in the later seventies they were feminist, sexual, or concerned with the growth of coercive and totalitarian régimes—as in the travel poems of Irving Layton, Eli MANDEL, Earle BIRNEY, Purdy, Patrick LANE, Atwood, and others. Another mode of the period was the series of loosely linked poems with a single concern or locale: poems unified by questions to which they are the answers, such as *Steveston* (1974) by Daphne MARLATT, or by narratives that experiment with a variety of perspectives or ways of telling a single story, such as Marlatt's *Frames of a story* (1968). We have poems whose construction is analogous to a game, such as *The circle game* (1966) by Margaret Atwood, or plotted on a specific visual field like *Baseball* (1967) by George Bowering. We have Ondaatje's collage-like biography of an artist in murder, *The collected works of Billy the Kid* (1970), and poems constructed along the lines of quite different genres, not necessarily verbal ones: *The ledger* (1975) and *Seed catalogue* (1977), both parts of *Field notes* (1981) by Robert KROETSCH. The sixties saw Amerindian legend and incantation become the source for a new mythic tradition (Susan MUSGRAVE, Kroetsch, Newlove, Purdy, Birney, Andrew SUKNASKI, bill BISSETT, Seán VIRGO, and others). A continuous feature of Canadian poetry has been interest in the land, the wilderness, and Canada's vast spaces, much of the earlier work (and Atwood's poetry) expressing these subjects in terms of terror. Some seventies' poetry, however, attempted postmodern approaches to space and time, seeing them as a continuum, a field on which the poet can compose his work—a magnetic field whose many lines of force provide not so much structure as limitations to the possibilities of structure.

What follows is a brief discussion of some of the leading poets in the two decades. The first important poetic event of the sixties was the publication of *Winter sun* (1960) by Margaret AVISON, whose metaphysical poems had been appearing in journals for almost twenty years. Though strongly religious, they did not express any easy acceptance or affirmation but rather a difficult mysticism in an idiosyncratic and compelling voice. In *The dumbfounding* (1966) Avison confronted scientific humanism and a crisis of faith with tact and insight.

The most extraordinary career of the sixties and seventies has been that of Margaret Atwood. Beginning with *The circle game*, which won a Governor General's Award—and continuing with *The animals in that country* (1968), *The JOURNALS OF SUSANNA MOODIE* (1970), and *Power politics* (1971)—she went from strength to strength in four subsequent collections, including *True stories* (1981). Hers is a poetry of statement with an epigrammatic edge, an orderly verse whose powerful images, evocations of physical disgust and Gothic consciousness, are controlled by a flat, authoritative voice and the parallel structure of her lines. Besides being the most brilliant literary accomplishment of the time, her collective poetry, fiction, and criticism from this period is phenomenally popular.

Michael Ondaatje's poetry has from the beginning struck an idiosyncratic note, displaying a sensibility that is surrealistic, yet tender, and a capacity for astonishing sensory description and physical detail. *The dainty monsters* (1967) was followed by *The man with seven toes* (1969), which tells the story of an escaped convict and his female hostage in the interior of Australia. *The collected works of Billy the Kid* (1970), which won a Governor General's Award, mixes poetry and prose, dramatic monologue, and quick shifts of narrative perspective to tell a story that is at once an adventure, a recreation of the popular culture hero, and a meditation on the relation between violence and creativity. *There's a trick with a knife I'm learning to do: poems 1973-1978* (1979) won Ondaatje a second Governor General's Award.

Eli Mandel's early poems were overtly mythological. His favourite strategy was to convey meanings in symbolic narratives, especially in the 'Minotaur poems', which confront modern experience as seen by an Icarus figure. *Fuseli poems* (1960)—which displays Mandel's learning, his syntactic complexity, and his Blakean visionary influences—speaks through a more complex persona with a powerful sense of irony and the macabre.

Black and secret man (1964) and *An idiot joy* (1967), which won a Governor General's Award—*Crusoe: poems new and selected* (1973), contains poems from both volumes—deal with place as well as the confrontation with self, and reveal a more conversational and accessible poetry, and a progress towards Mandel's very spare style of the seventies.

Earle Birney's remarkable and distinguished career as a poet, which began in 1942, continued apace in the sixties and seventies—with, notably, *Ice cod bell and stone* (1962), *Near False Creek mouth* (1964), two volumes of *Collected poems* (1966 and 1968), and the *Collected works of Earle Birney* (1975). *Rag and bone shop* (1970) experiments with typography and sound. The wonderful range of Birney's work covers several strains in Canadian poetry. His training in Anglo-Saxon poetics perhaps accounted in part for his attraction to the avant-garde sound and visual organization that influenced his concrete and sound poetry. But Birney also wrote more conventional verse, based on anecdote and light speculation, romantic lyrics, and meditations on unusual scenes or objects, often drawn from his travels, that are lightly handled philosophical poems presented in the classical manner.

Cry Ararat! poems new and selected (1967) by P.K. Page continued to exhibit her extraordinary ability to make complex visual images both accessible and ultimately mysterious. The imagery in the new poems is less glittery and crisp than in the earlier ones; in the poems set in Brazil it is intense and colourful. Characteristically, Page is witty and involved in treating the social world ('Photos of a salt mine', 'Poem in war time', 'The stenographers') and in capturing moments in the human comedy (in the section entitled 'The bands and the beautiful children').

Al Purdy, too, began to publish poetry—of a somewhat conventional nature—in the forties; but his career did not take off until the publication of *The Cariboo horses* (1965), an extremely successful volume that was enjoyed for its energy, humour, and sense of play. An engaging conversational line, enriched by quick shifts of mood and tone in dealing with travel and anecdote, characterizes his books of the sixties and seventies. His verse encompasses flat realism as well as idealism, and combines spontaneity with romance, as in *Poems for all the Annettes* (1962), *Love in a burning building* (1970), and a selected poems, *Being alive: poems 1958-1978* (1978).

In the fifties the poetry of Phyllis Webb was concerned with subtle changes in perception and understanding; her wit seemed influenced by Marianne Moore, and her carefully structured verse created a demanding and rigorous environment. The intense, very carefully crafted work that appeared after *Even your right eye* (1956) fulfilled the promise of that collection. *Naked poems* (1965) is made up of several sequences of short poems in which compression of language cuts against, and reveals, strength of feeling. This volume was very influential among younger poets, as was her *Selected poems* (1971). Miriam Waddington began to publish in the forties. In *The glass trumpet* (1966), *Say yes* (1969), and *Driving home: poems new and selected* (1972) there is a shift from angry responses to social conditions to a more personal and direct poetry that speaks of love, loss, places, aging, the gap between men and women, in attenuated short-lined poems that manage to be both tightly controlled and lyrical. This is the voice that continued to be heard in her subsequent collections.

Phyllis GOTLIEB's *Who knows one* (1961) was followed by *Within the zodiac* (1964) and *Ordinary, moving* (1969), her most interesting short collection. A learned and inventive poet, Gotlieb drew upon nursery rhymes, Petrarchan sonnets, popular songs, blues, and other familiar sound patterns, and experimented with literary typography as well as literary graffiti, in a witty and playful manner that sometimes produced *tours de force*. The spectacular long poem entitled 'Ordinary, moving'—echoing nursery rhymes, children's songs, lyrics recited for a bouncing ball, details of street life, and personal memory—is unified by witty and sometimes imperceptible transitions, and a fine ear for colloquial cadences. Though employing quintessentially ordinary fragments of language, this poem carries the reader through the energy of its voices and transitions. In 1978 Gotlieb published *The works: collected poems*.

Gwendolyn MacEWEN constructed her poetry by referring to a magical method that uses art and human love to unify a conflicted and divided world. *A breakfast for barbarians* (1966) and *The shadow-maker* (1969) are her strongest books. In the latter her language became somewhat less esoteric, and in *The armies of the moon* (1972) she linked her personal psychic journeys with the exploration of outer space. Later volumes include *Magic animals* (1975), *The fire eaters* (1976), and *The T.E. Lawrence poems* (1982).

With *The rose and the Puritan* (1958), *Bread, wine and salt* (1967), *The mysterious naked man* (1969), and *Between tears and laughter* (1971), Alden NOWLAN introduced a poetry that is humane and is centred on human experience and understanding. His poems are character sketches—clear and unemphatic compressed narratives of the thwarted lives of people in rural and small-town Nova Scotia. More personal—without being confessional—are *I'm a stranger here myself* (1974) and *I might not tell everybody this* (1982), which contain self-knowing poems that are both conversational and controlled.

Patrick ANDERSON, who was active with the *FIRST STATEMENT* group in Montreal—and whose strong volume of poems *The colour as naked* appeared in 1953—again revealed his subtle ear and talent for specificity in *A visiting distance* (1976), and in his selected poems, *Return to Canada* (1977). Fred COGSWELL, who published the work of many young poets during his more than thirty years as editor of FIDDLEHEAD PRESS, shows mastery of a wide range of both traditional and modern forms in his own books of poetry, among which are *Star-people* (1968), *Immortal ploughman* (1969), and *In praise of chastity* (1970). *A long apprenticeship: the collected poems of Fred Cogswell* appeared in 1980.

Milton ACORN started to publish in the 1960s, producing *The brain's the target* (1960), *Jaw breakers* (1963), *I've tasted my blood* (1969), and *More poems for people* (1972). His political commitment to Marxism was central to his poetry, which has an urban toughness and often focuses on political figures in relation to the common people. Full of urgency—partly owing to Acorn's use of alliteration to propel the lines forward—and radical egalitarian humanism, his poetry shows a credible and serious concern for social change. *Captain MacDougal and the naked goddess* (1982) is made up of sonnets with two voices, Acorn's and that of the goddess.

Dennis LEE's first volume was *Kingdom of absence* (1967), poems of personal and spiritual despair that experimented with sonnet variations. *Civil elegies* (1968) was a complex elegiac meditation on contemporary North American politics, the war in Vietnam and Canada's connection with it, and the country's loss of identity. It is an impressive volume, though its intended public voice is somewhat unrelieved in tone. These poems were revised for *Civil elegies and other poems* (1972), which won a Governor General's Award. *The gods* (1978) contains a previously published elegy, 'The death of Harold Ladoo' (q.v.), and a variety of short poems that experiment with typography, pace, and rhythm; several light love-lyrics; political ballads; and meditative poems of the sort we associate with Lee's earlier poetry, expressing a philosophy that is almost religious in its search for a vision of wholeness in life. In the seventies Lee published four books of children's verse—*Alligator pie* (1974), *Nicholas Knock* (1974), *Garbage delight* (1977), and *The ordinary bath* (1979)—that are much beloved for their play with language, and their celebration of the linguistic variety of Canada's place-names.

A significant impact on the progress of Canadian poetry was made in the sixties by a new movement in British Columbia that centred on the Vancouver publication *TISH: a poetry newsletter* (1961-9). The work of the *Tish* group was influenced by the theories of American poets Charles Olson, Robert Duncan, Robert Creeley, and the American West Coast school that produced the Beat poets, and by the San Francisco renaissance associated with the City Lights bookstore. The most important theorist of this movement in Canada was Frank DAVEY, whose essays in *Tish*, and in *OPEN LETTER*, First Series (1965-9), helped to define its poetic goals and ideology. The Canadian West Coast writers sought a language for poetry that valued the colloquial voice above erudition, and vitality above order; that emphasized not theme, but sound, open syntax, and the voice as an instrument of breathing. In this departure from what they saw as the academic formalism of eastern-Canadian writing, the flow and movement of the poem is the crucial poetic quality; poetry, indeed writing in general in this view, was a way of tracing the trajectories of perception, of creating a poem that is constantly happening, and in which writer and reader are fully alive. The movement was suspicious of metaphor and simile, which were seen as destroying the particularity and uniqueness of the objects of the universe in the drive to make meanings by describing things in terms of each other. Insisting that the idiosyncratic object or event, the local and the personal, were the only source of meaning in human experience, it encouraged a poetry of specific place and region, rather than a more national view of the Canadian poetic enterprise—thereby validating the locality of the West Coast as an appropriate place for poetry. These beliefs influenced not only Davey, but George Bowering (a co-founder of *Tish*), Robert Kroetsch, Daphne Marlatt, Susan Musgrave, and many others.

Frank Davey's titles include *D-Day and after* (1963), *City of the gulls and sea* (1964), *Weeds* (1970), *L'an trentième* (1972), *Arcana* (1973), and *Selected poems: the arches* (1980), edited and with an introduction by bp NICHOL. His early poetry is competent but not very interesting. *Weeds*, though modest and thoughtful, is a more energetic and lively volume. A little later in the seventies he published satisfying poems of self-discovery in which the mythic and the personal unite in the present moment of writing and reading. Able to capture colloquial language and to use repetition to ring impressive changes on it, Davey wrote a poetry of process that has substance, wit, and a personal humaneness.

George Bowering began his prolific writing career in the sixties, producing *Sticks and stones* (1963); *Points on the grid* (1964), a volume of great variety and range; *The silver wire* (1966), which seems to discover an individual tone and manner; and *Baseball: a poem in the magic number 9* (1967), a *tour de force* in which a diamond-shaped text conveys the nine innings of baseball, and each position of the game is used as a jumping-off point for words to leap across the page. The poem works out the implications of an analogy between playing baseball and writing poetry that is dependent on the notion of 'composition by field'. *Rocky Mountain foot* (1968) celebrates the landscape of Alberta, and *George Vancouver* (1970) is a poem of exploration. There are two volumes of selected poems: *Touch: selected poems 1960-1970* (1971) and *Particular accidents: selected poems* (1980). In a poetry that reflects his interest in the *process* of thinking rather than its results, Bowering combined his formal interests—in phonetic spelling, oral verse, the colloquial and conversational line, question-and-answer poems—with a wish to celebrate personal and local history and experience.

bill bissett is an experimental poet of the primitive who uses massive repetition, chant, phonetic spelling, and typographical innovation to break down the conventional restricting structures of language in order to create a new sacred vision. In *Nobody owns th earth* (1971) his topics include political protest and satiric pictures of contemporary urban values. At their best his poems are exuberant, playful, and ritualistic, with a vital and colloquial voice of their own, but by their very nature they constantly risk falling into the merely experimental and patterned, as in *northern birds in colour* (1981).

bp Nichol was the boldest and most versatile of Canada's experimental poets of this period. A member of the poetry performance group The FOUR HORSEMEN, he was a prolific writer whose titles include *Journeying & the returns* (1967), *Still water* (1970), *ABC: the aleph beth book* (1971), and *Craft dinner* (1978). His autobiographical *The martyrology* Books I & II (1972; rev. 1977) and Books III & IV (1976) is the record of a conversation with himself. Interested in exploding the habits of language-use in order to discover and liberate what remains of language after the explosion, he tries in 'Naming' and 'Probable systems 9' (which both appear in *Selected writing: as elected*, 1980) to transfer the symbol system of mathematics to language. *ABC: the aleph beth book* experiments with the graphic design of the alphabet; *Nights on prose mountain* (1970) prints very simple poems on a series of cards that can be reordered and shuffled. Nichol consistently tried to release the sound and emotion of poetry from the intellectual control of language. *Selected writing: as elected* (1980), edited by bp Nichol and Jack David, is a fine introduction to his work.

Another notable feature of this period was the explosion of poetic energy on the Prairies. The long list of prairie poets, or poets who wrote about the Prairies, included Anne MARRIOTT, John Newlove, Robert Kroetsch, George Bowering, Elizabeth Brewster, Dorothy LIVESAY, Miriam Waddington, Eli Mandel, Gary GEDDES, Peter STEVENS, Douglas BARBOUR, Ken McRobbie, Sid MARTY, Dale ZIEROTH, Andrew Suknaski, Anne SZUMIGALSKI, and Kristjana GUNNARS. One reason for this explosion was that the new experiments in colloquial, loosely conversational, anecdotal poetic language (partly launched by the *Tish* school) seemed to suit the prairie poets' interest in the local and specific. Not suffering from a lack of ghosts, prairie poets concerned themselves with such themes as space, landscape and movement, Native people, unusual characters, ancestors, and the task of making human communities within vast isolated areas. There is often a tone of restrained humour in this poetry, and a tentative, somewhat hesitant speech.

John Newlove's collections include *Grave sirs* (1962), *Mothers, and others* (1964), and *Moving in alone* (1965), an ironic volume of meditations about love. *Black night window* (1968) explores the poet's prairie origins, linking a meditation on place with a process of self-discovery and self-analysis. His later volumes, *The cave* (1970) and *Lies* (1972), which won a Governor General's Award, are harsher, more ironic and troubled. His poems of place evoke the vastness of the Canadian West, its moral history and its unacknowledged guilt. *The fat man: selected poems 1962-1972* (1977) was followed by a newer tone of celebration in *The green plain* (1981).

Originally from the Prairies, Robert Kroetsch is both a novelist and a poet. His

Stone hammer poems (1975) contains twelve versions of traditional Blackfoot stories about the trickster figure in Native mythology. In *The ledger* (1975), Kroetsch used a record of historical speculation about the shared past of the Prairies. Transforming personal experience into myth, and using lists of names, places, and objects to celebrate the past, he wrote poetry that is colloquial, sometimes racy and audacious. *The sad Phoenician* (1979) is a meditative dialogue with himself and with his past loves, about language and poetry and their power in relation to time and loss. Written under the successive unfoldings of the signs of the Phoenician alphabet, it is an elegiac celebration of their largely forgotten gift to humankind. Kroetsch was interested in the possibilities of the long poem and of creative alternatives to narrative. *Field notes: the collected poetry of Robert Kroetsch* (1981) brings together several previous volumes, including *Seed catalogue* (1977)—a meditation on the cultivation of poetry, including how to grow poetry on the prairie—into one continuing poem. The title *Field notes* puns on the postmodernist idea of 'composition by field', and suggests that these are notes taken in the field, preparatory to a larger, fuller, less-discontinuous long poem of life—which of course can never be written.

3. THE SEVENTIES AND EARLY EIGHTIES. The Canadian tradition of distinguished narrative poetry continued unabated from the fifties to the beginning of the eighties. E.J. PRATT's powerful figure stands behind this tradition, but it is authenticated through its own continuities, perhaps because there are stories still to be told for the first time. Louis Dudek wrote narratives of the fate of culture; Eli Mandel's *Life sentence* (1980) seemed to suggest the discovery of a kind of self-questioning narrative late in his poetic career. Daphne Marlatt's work created communal narrative out of oral history (*Steveston*) or thought again about the abiding power of the same old story (*Frames*). Andrew Suknaski, collecting the stories of his region and its settlement in tales and anecdotes, built a layered narrative of place that achieved monumental presence in *Wood Mountain poems*. Michael Ondaatje's *The collected works of Billy the Kid* and *Coming through slaughter* inhabit the unclear border between prose and poetry, where narrative seems to emerge from the collision of intense bits of sensory data. We even had a few traditional narratives, such as Florence McNEIL's *The overlanders* (1982), a chronicle of a remarkable woman's journey to the gold fields of British Columbia in the 1860s.

The Gothic strain in Canadian poetry continued largely in the female line, and ranged over esoteric knowledge and exotic lore in the work of Gwen MacEwen and Phyllis Gotlieb, or from within a world of incantation and wordpower in some of the Haida-inspired works of Susan Musgrave (*Songs of the sea-witch*, 1970, *The impstone*, 1976). Margaret Atwood's Gothicism, transmitted through her cool sensibility, seemed more northern European. There is a cool mysticism with a Gothic edge in the poetry of Kristjana Gunnars. At worst the Gothic falls into a kind of witch-ridden sentimentality.

If the Gothic was a largely female strain in Canadian verse of this period, surrealism seemed the purview of the men. It ranged from the outrageous and exuberant play of Joe ROSENBLATT's poetry (*Bumblebee dithyramb*, 1972), to a sense of the absurd and ironic in Ondaatje's juxtapositions, or to J. Michael YATES's grandeur. Robert PRIEST's *The visible man* (1980), which contains poetry full of flashes of insight, is sometimes surreal without appearing to know that it is. Imaginative in a strange way, Priest takes inordinate chances with logic, countering absurdity with absurdity, and expanding our sense of human emotional possibilities. His poetry, which is neither solemn nor self-mocking, is beyond irony; distanced from human sensation, it is yet not unfeeling. This surrealism seems to be partly a legacy of the earlier experimental work done in the sixties and early seventies.

Erudition returned, but in a new form: the learning in seventies' poetry was less likely to be European and high literary; the erudition ranged from a profound rethinking of biblical images and concepts in the works of Robert BRINGHURST, to a meditation based on scientific attention to the details of geology and botany in the works of Christopher DEWDNEY; from serious, organized, and detailed research into local history and oral history by Daphne Marlatt (*Steveston*) and Andrew Suknaski (*Wood Mountain poems*), to a rich and complex knowledge of the social history of foods (David DONNELL), the myths of Iceland (Kristjana Gunnars), or of the North (J. Michael Yates). The learning evinced by this poetry seems not so much a means of confirming the authors' seriousness or right to speak, as a way of suggesting that such knowledge enables a pre-existent voice or vision to express itself. While innovative and promising Canadian poetry was being written in the 1980s, there was no single, clearly superior poet whose voice and presence sprang forward as obviously and powerfully as those of

Layton in the late fifties, of Purdy in the early sixties, of Atwood and Lee and Ondaatje in the late sixties and early seventies.

The long, loose, conversational and anecdotal line was subjected to scrutiny in this period. One senses that not only the new erudition, but also a wish for more texture, animated this new verse. Sometimes this texture denotes a complex rethinking or reinventing of ways of representing consciousness (in Marlatt, for example), or an examination of personal relations that are neither sentimental nor paradox-ridden, but genuinely complex (as in Anne Szumigalski, Kristjana Gunnars, Andrew Suknaski, Bronwen WALLACE, Frank Davey's later poems, Erin MOURÉ, and Ondaatje). Poetry based merely on the contemplation of an image seemed to have exhausted much of its energy (except perhaps in the works of Roo BORSON), as had poetry about a generalized Canada, or the wilderness. Experimental poetry was less prominent in the late seventies and early eighties than it was in the sixties, though much was learned from it, and much was assimilated into something like the mainstream of Canadian poetry.

The new poets who seemed most original varied widely in both manner and subject matter. Daphne Marlatt began publishing in the late sixties, starting out with the second group of poets in the *Tish* movement. Each of her volumes represented an experiment in the use of language, narrative form, line length and construction, and in trying to represent the movement of consciousness rather than external events or objects. Her writing was informed by a high degree of theoretical awareness that nonetheless did not drown out or pre-empt her impressive poetry. *Frames of a story* (1968) retells the 'Snow Queen' from a variety of shifting perspectives, and in a variety of styles. *Steveston* (1974) is based on an oral history of the town of Steveston in British Columbia. *Vancouver poems* (1972) tries to define and recreate a sense of place and local history as forms of consciousness. Another sequence of poems, *Our lives* (1980), contains five stories in a prose-poetry long line that allowed Marlatt to explore new kinds of poetic rhythm and placement of words. *Selected writings: net work* (1980), edited by Fred WAH, is an excellent representative collection.

Dale Zieroth published his first book, *Clearing: poems from a journey* (1973), as a series of poems about the history of his ancestors on the Prairies. His second volume, *Mid-river* (1981), had a quiet authority. Though his wit was underdeveloped, his voice was careful, modest, and possessed a humorous wisdom. He wrote about family and friends, about the landscape of the mountains in British Columbia, in plain, unpretentious, rather Wordsworthian language.

Patrick Lane, after publishing several interesting small collections, established his highly respected place as one of the finest poets to have emerged in the 1970s, when Oxford published his *Poems new and selected* (1979), which won a Governor General's Award. He wrote tense and explosive poetry, headstrong but controlled, that has an energy of its own.

The work of Pier Giorgio DI CICCO is uneven in quality. Anti-intellectual, he succeeded best with foreshortened narratives about family, and though the combative stance of his poetry was occasionally appealing, it is often merely annoying and assumed. The energy in his poetry suggested both the flaws and the strengths of a writer of promise with an assertive, even aggressive voice: he is the Irving Layton of his generation—prolific, exuberant, with an interest in values. *The tough romance* (1979) is a strong and representative volume.

J. Michael Yates, in *The Great Bear Lake meditations* (1970), exploded the boundaries of philosophical musing; he displayed an intense merging of mind and sensation in his dramatization of the meeting between a human consciousness and the natural world, in a modern manifestation of the sublime.

Another poet with a feeling for the sublime, in human nature as well as in the natural world, is Robert Bringhurst, whose most achieved volume in this period was *Bergschrund* (1975). His interest in mountains and stone seems linked to an unyielding quality in the voice of his poems and in his deployment of images. There is an authority in these images, and in the way he uses his erudition. Bringhurst is a wordfinder, with a remarkably discerning though daring ear, and an acute mind. His poems on Old Testament figures, or figures from Greek thought and literature, have a genuine ease and wit; but his rather remote oratorical voice inspires respect rather than a warm identification with the poet.

Christopher Dewdney's poetry is distinctive for its use of technical terms and concepts, and for the unusual range of subjects from which it draws its analogies. The exploration of scientific systems of thought as sources of analogies for the way language functions, or the way poetry comes into being, is appealing; much of Dewdney's work, however, became an implicit 'defence of poesy', arguing that all forms of knowing are ultimately, or fundamentally, like poetry. *Alter sublime* (1980) is also interested in the semantic potential of language, drawing its analogies from the process and structure of the DNA molecule, from static electricity, and from the nerve structure of the human brain. Though this gives his work an air of wilful objectivity, of a reluctance to be personal, these poems do contain a poignant resonance. *Predators of the adoration: selected poems 1972-1982* was published in 1983.

A strong new poet to appear on the scene in the seventies was Andrew Suknaski, whose first volume, *Wood Mountain poems* (1976), collected with the help of Al Purdy and Dennis Lee, is a powerful and impressive book. It contains documentary poetry that recreates the history of southwest Saskatchewan through the voices of its people: Indians, homesteaders or various nationalities, and their survivors in the present. The presentation of this history in shifting viewpoints—the live two-way relation between past and present—gives the volume a double focus, or two sources of energy. Suknaski extended his documentary and voice-creating impulses to other groups of people in this region in *The ghosts call you poor* (1978) and *In the name of Narid* (1981), which also addresses contemporary issues in the Ukrainian community.

Another impressive poet to appear on the Prairies was Anne Szumigalski, whose *Woman reading in bath* (1974) heralded a difficult and exhilarating new voice. The poems are spoken by many different personae in a range of ages and situations in life, articulating their idiosyncratic points of view. *A game of angels* (1980) continues the power and crispness of perception of the earlier collection in a series of stunning dramatic monologues.

Mary DI MICHELE's poems were admired for their evocation of family life in an immigrant Italian urban community. *Mimosa and other poems* (1980) has three speakers from such a family, a father and two daughters—with a silent, present, mother. The volume contains poems spoken by Edvard Munch, and by a poet-painter with polio. The range, however, is less forcefully achieved than Szumilgaski's.

David Donnell's poetry is strong, intelligent, and genuinely idiosyncratic. Its humour devolves from the way it uses erudition, and from the varied tone that is never merely easily ironic in its willingness to court embarrassment and ridiculousness and come back from that edge. His weirdly lovable second collection, *Dangerous crossings* (1980), repays attention.

Roo Borson in *Rain* (1980) and *A sad device* (1982) used images and objects to delineate states of mind. Her work shows a propensity for gentle allegory; her wit and coolly personal manner allow identification with the otherness of creaturely life. The tone of her poems—somewhere between expressiveness and flatness—has a peculiar charm that comes from its being free of any sense of deliberate mystification.

The poems in *Empire, York Street* (1979), the first book by Erin Mouré, showed a relation to personal experience and consciousness that is neither self-aggrandizing nor merely cool and distant. Inhabiting the border where perception, sensation, and intellectual comprehension meet, Mouré's work has a political edge that is genuinely argumentative, and—unusual in Canadian poetry—a sense of place or historical event, conveyed together with the pressure and presence of large numbers of people who are neither ghosts nor ancestors but seem to exist in the present.

Finally, a volume by Kristjana Gunnars, *One-eyed moon maps* (1980), retells Norse myth with a modern edge and sees the Icelandic tradition as giving access to 'the other eye' of human vision, associated with the moon and with secret knowledge. The poems, with their short, crisp lines, have a slightly imagistic aura.

Nothing bears better witness to the poetry explosion of the sixties and seventies in Canada than the publication in 1982 of *The new Oxford book of Canadian verse in English*, edited by Margaret Atwood, in which 72 of its 121 poets were talents new to Canadian poetry since A.J.M. Smith's edition of 1960.

CHAVIVA HOŠEK

1983 to 1996. Since 1982 English-Canadian poetry has undergone significant changes. Regional influences are weaker than they were in the 1960s and 1970s. At the same time the canon of English-Canadian poetry has both expanded and diversified. This greater diversification has had its benefits. A much larger and less tightly knit group than in the 1970s, Canadian poets are now more likely to show the influence of international writers in their work. Moreover, contemporary Canadian poets are relying on a greater variety of formal practices than they have in the past. But this diversification also means that a relatively cohesive poetic movement, such as the West Coast *TISH* school of the 1960s, is unlikely to emerge.

At least two converging forces have contributed to the gradual disappearance of what, as recently as fifteen or twenty years ago, used to be recognizably 'Canadian' poetry. First, changing views about what defines a national literature have led many poets (though certainly not all) to turn away from distinctively Canadian themes. Second, the faded influence of the imperatives of high modernist verse, specifically T.S. Eliot's objective correlative, has meant that various permutations of the confessional mode prevail.

The thirteen-year period under consideration has seen (1) new work from several canonical poets born before 1930; (2) new and reissued work by the central poets of the 1970s; and (3) a steady growth of poets who published first books in the late 1970s and early 1980s. Though this brief survey cannot pretend to be comprehensive, it will attempt to discuss some of the more significant poetic achievements from each of these three groups.

1. Many of Canada's most distinguished poets were born within the first three decades of the twentieth century, rose to prominence in the 1950s (in some cases the 1960s), and have continued to write well into the late 1990s. The years since 1982 have witnessed a poetic resurgence in this group of modernists. Several have issued collected poems or have used selecteds to keep before us their best work, while also including new work that shows continued innovation and consolidates their place in the canon. Elegy is a keynote in the recent work of this generation; art is enlisted in bidding farewell to the many friends and colleagues who have died.

P.K. PAGE, without question one of Canada's major poets, is also one of the most admired writers of this earlier generation. *The glass air: selected poems* (1985; reissued 1991) is for many readers her most important volume; it brings together her poetry, her visual art, and her two central essays on painting and travel, allowing us to see Page as a multidimensional artist whose fine work in these many genres is closely interconnected. (Several other Canadian poets are also visual artists, among them Margaret ATWOOD, Phyllis WEBB, Anne CARSON, and Heather SPEARS. Spears' drawings appear in both her Governor General's Award-winning *The word for sand*, 1988, and *The Panum poems*, 1996.) Over the decades Page's symbology has remained largely intact—'golden', for example, continues to serve as one of her central codes for transcendence. At the same time, the formal properties of her work have increased in sophistication. 'I—Sphinx: a poem for two voices', originally written for radio in response to the music of Sibelius, exemplifies Page's ability to thread another art form, in this case music, through her carefully articulated line: 'the bullfinch double stops, sings C sharp—D'. In *Hologram* (1994) Page demonstrates her interest in experimentation with form and works with two voices once again. Weaving into her own verse lines from poets who have influenced her, Page brilliantly revives the *glosa*, a form that originated in the fourteenth-century Spanish court. Elizabeth Bishop, Rilke, Leonard COHEN, and Wallace Stevens form only a partial list of Page's sources. Page's intertextual experiment provides a new vehicle for the re-emergence of her earliest images and themes.

Since her adoption of the practices of a rigorous, Bible-based Protestantism, Margaret AVISON's poetry has assumed the burden of professing Christian faith. Like the work of her contemporaries, Avison's poetry has become increasingly elegiac, reflecting a world that, for her generation, is slowly emptying. 'The Jo Poems I – X', published in *No time* (1989), which received a Governor General's Award, are thought by many to be her best recent work, in which her faith provides a means of interpreting the death of a dear friend. But Avison never uses faith to deny her own suffering; in one of the strongest poems in this series, poem IV, the refrain, 'My friend is dead', acts as scaffolding around which Avison builds, through the complexities of her syntax, a dialectic about God and human need. Avison's *Selected poems* (1991) offers the first selection of her poetry ever published. In addition to work from each of her four volumes, it includes uncollected poems, a few translations of Hungarian poetry, and new poems, one of which, 'Birthdays', presents—in the first stanza's syntactic echoes of Dickinson, Hopkins, and Dylan Thomas—vintage Avison: 'this is the birthday-festal/star-correlated hour and place.'

The poems about the primordial world in Al PURDY's *Piling blood* (1984) hint at his millennial mood; the beginning of time suggests its end and ours. Purdy's vernacular cannot conceal in this volume—nor in any of his others—the thinking poet. The Governor General's Award given for *The collected poems of Al Purdy* (1986) acknowledged the prominent place of Purdy's *oeuvre* in Canadian literature. *Rooms for rent in the outer planets: selected poems 1962-1996* (1996), edited by Sam Solecki, reprints work from several early books and includes poems from *The woman on the shore* (1990) and *Naked with summer in your mouth* (1994). A deliberately slim volume, *Rooms for rent* allows the reader to see, by way of juxtaposition, Purdy in his various guises. Many of the more recent poems in his selected volume are elegiac in tone as Purdy confronts the deaths of family and friends and contemplates the expression of suffering in the work of other writers. In his 'The prison lines at Leningrad', Akhmatova shoulders a burden which Purdy himself increasingly feels: to speak for 'the speechless dead'.

Readers of the work of Phyllis Webb look forward to her relatively infrequent book publications with special eagerness because each volume is profoundly different from the last. Her last selected poems, *The vision tree* (1982), edited by Sharon THESEN, won a Governor General's Award. Webb's *Naked poems* (1965) secured her place as one of Canada's great love poets; it is not surprising, then, that Webb would be interested in the ghazal, an ancient Persian form whose traditional subject was idealized love. *Water and light: ghazals and anti ghazals* (1984) includes the poems of the previously published *Sunday water: thirteen anti ghazals* (1982). Like Page and Avison, Webb manipulates rhythm and syllabification in her search for new forms. In *Water and light*, she works inside the couplet of the ghazal to create variations within the ghazal's constraints. The juxtaposition of the two lines of a couplet affords Webb the opportunity to play words off one another while she treats the lines as both separate and conjoined: 'Tuned lyre (lyrebird, mynah,/parrot, parakeet, peacock) paradox—.' In *Hanging fire* (1990) clichés, advertising slogans, and famous literary quotations are forced into new syntaxes that invite associational readings, suggesting the trickery and deception of language.

In addition to publishing powerful new work—which includes *The Gucci bag* (1983), *Fortunate exile* (1987), and *Final reckoning* (1987)—Irving LAYTON has invited new readings of himself through his selected volumes. One of the most unorthodox selections to be published in Canada is his *Fornalutx: selected poems, 1928-1990* (1992), for unlike most selecteds, which aim to keep in print the best-known work of the poet, *Fornalutx* omits Layton's most famous poems, such as 'The birth of tragedy' and 'A tall man executes a jig'. Brian Trehearne, in his introduction to the book, explains that the aim of this selection was to give greater prominence to the 'less popular', 'less decorous' Layton—to the Layton who writes 'poems of damnation and disgust'. Trehearne adds that the reader will find, in addition to Layton's 'raised voice', his softer tones and is justified in claiming that Layton is one of Canada's 'most successful elegiac poets'. *Dance with desire: selected love poems* (1992) offers yet another Layton, who sets the tone in the book's dedication: 'For Miss Benjamin—the Grade Six teacher who awakened my erotic impulses and inspired my first sensual poem.'

For the late Dorothy LIVESAY, as for Layton, age presented no obstacle to the writing of erotic poetry. Her last volume of love poems, *The phases of love*, appeared in 1983. While Livesay did not leave a 'complete' poems, *The self-completing tree: selected poems* (1986), which includes such seminal pieces as 'Green rain', is clearly the selection she will be remembered by. The poems cover a span of over fifty years and are arranged according to Livesay's major themes: childhood, love, war, poverty, and racism.

Earle BIRNEY (b.1904), who died in 1995, was one of the most senior poets of the generation born before 1930. He published *Last makings*, his final book, in 1991. Introduced by Al Purdy, it collects poems of love and reminiscence, travel poems, and poems about work and childhood. And while it seems disjunctive (the selection and arrangement, with many of the poems written in the 1970s, appear arbitrary), it nevertheless reminds us that Birney was one of Canada's most accomplished poets.

The appearance of several volumes of collected poems over the last thirteen years suggests that our senior poets, many of them very productive, were reflecting on their careers. The late Ralph GUSTAFSON published his *Collected poems* (1987) in three volumes. Two books of new poems appeared in the 1990s: *Configurations at midnight* (1992) and *Visions fugitive* (1996), the latter completed shortly before his death in 1995. Even in his last volume Gustafson's strengths as a poet are apparent—his empathy and his ability to communicate music in his verse.

George JOHNSTON's *Endeared by dark: the collected poems* (1990) brings together in one gathering much of the important work of this extraordinary poet, whose metrical skills have been passed on to many attentive writers after him. Johnston's light touch, benevolent tone, and Old Norse rhythms are his trademarks. In his most recent volume, *What is to come: selected and new poems* (1996), published as part of the St Thomas Church's Poetry Series (Toronto), Johnston pays his respects to departed friends, writes of his faith, and seems to be bidding a poetic farewell to any further publication of poetry.

Poetry in English 1983 to 1996: 1

Douglas LePAN's *Weathering it: complete poems, 1948-1987* (1987) was followed by the highly charged love poems, to a young man, *Far voyages* (1990), and the haunting *Macalister; or Dying in the dark* (1995). LePan's lifetime of reading poetry is fully in evidence in the formal flexibility of poems written in couplets, tercets, quatrains, free verse, and verse drama. LePan stands out from his generation in his willingness to confront his subjects without reticence.

Other notable publications by this generation of poets include: Louis DUDEK's *Small perfect things* (1991); Douglas LOCHHEAD's *Homage to Henry Alline and other poems* (1992); Elizabeth BREWSTER's Governor General's Award-winning *Footnotes to the Book of Job* (1995), which is a selection of work published since 1985; Robin SKELTON's *Wrestling the angel: collected shorter poems 1947-1977* (1994) and *One leaf shaking: collected later poems 1977-1990* (1996); Miriam WADDINGTON's *Collected poems* (1986) and *The last landscape* (1992); and Raymond SOUSTER's *No sad songs wanted here* (1995).

2. Many of the poets who were celebrated as young writers in the mid-1970s, during an explosive and invigorating period in our literary history, rose to fame, and soon (however unwittingly) became part of what can only be described as a cult of the personality in Canada. This is particularly true of Leonard COHEN, as it is of Michael ONDAATJE, Margaret Atwood, bp NICHOL, and Gwendolyn MacEWEN. All of these writers, even those who have died, have strongly delineated public personas. The tendency on the part of critics, publishers, and readers to create legends is perhaps greater in a literary culture trying to establish itself and gain a foothold internationally. The star-making machinery does not seem to be at work for young poets in the 1990s in quite the same way it was in the 1970s.

Michael Ondaatje may be one of the few writers in English whose *fiction*, filled with poetic constructions, has had a profound influence on contemporary poetry. Echoes of his poetry and prose in the work of Canadian poets are unmistakable. His practice of metamorphosing nouns into verbs, his striking, often violent imagery, and his muted, vulnerable, semi-confessional poetic voice show themselves in much recent verse. Over approximately the last decade, Ondaatje has published two new volumes, *Secular love* (1984) and *The cinnamon peeler: selected poems* (Britain 1989; US 1991; Canada 1992, reprinted 1994). In addition, all of his early work has been reissued. 'Claude glass', in *Secular love*, is a poem of crisis, embodying 'in the half drowned room' of the speaker's pain many of the themes, images, and ideas of Ondaatje's poetry and fiction, and offers one of his most provocative versions to date of the recurring motif of submergence.

Margaret Atwood, who came to prominence as a poet in the late 1960s and early 1970s, continues to receive international recognition as Canada's best-known poet. *Murder in the dark: short fictions and prose poems* (1983) deliberately challenges the boundary between fiction and verse. Adopting the deceptively simple and highly nuanced narrative stance of the familiar Atwoodian speaker, the poet, even when referring to childhood, alludes to the danger inherent in the relationship between men and women. 'I was once the snake woman' opens *Interlunar* (1984), in Atwood's most forceful mode: lyric. Few poets in Canada have created as formidable an 'I'. Two volumes of selected poems, *Selected poems II: poems selected and new 1976-1986* (1986) and *Selected poems 1966-1984* (1990), exhibit the work of a substantial career, the more recent selection charting the growth of Atwood from a poet heavily indebted to Northrop FRYE, to a politically engaged poet ('You fit into me') who is also capable of unironic love poetry, such as she provides in 'Variation on the word *sleep*'. Some critics believe that Atwood's *Good bones* (1992) and *Morning in the burned house* (1995) are among her strongest volumes of poetry. The first returns to prose poetry: Atwood enlists myth, fairy tale, high culture, and cliché as she trains her x-ray vision on the constructedness of being female. Echoes of her earlier fiction, such as *The edible woman* (1969), can be heard in these poems and prose pieces and suggest that Atwood is revisiting central themes. The poems of *Morning in the burned house*—among them 'Manet's Olympia', 'Daphne and Laura and so forth', 'Ava Gardner reincarnated as a magnolia', and 'Helen of Troy does counter dancing'—affirm Atwood's role as the poetic authority on the manipulation of the female image. A poet of many voices, Atwood is also, in this volume, a daughter mourning the loss of her father.

Gwendolyn MacEwen's last volume, *Afterworlds* (1987)—which won a Governor General's Award, and appeared in the year of her death—is a work of apocalyptic vision. Like bp Nichol, MacEwen played an important role in our literary history, and like him, she has become part of the mythic literary landscape. Atwood and Barry CALLAGHAN have edited two volumes of MacEwen's poems: *The poetry of Gwendolyn MacEwen: volume one, the early years* (1993) and *The poetry of Gwendolyn MacEwen: volume two, the later years* (1994). Rosemary SULLIVAN's biography of MacEwen, *Shadowmaker: the life of Gwendolyn MacEwen* (1995), has done much to keep MacEwen's work and name alive.

The reissue of Dennis LEE's *Civil elegies* (1968) as *Civil elegies and other poems* (1972; 1994)—and as part of *Nightwatch: new & selected poems 1968-1996* (1996)—allows this series of contemplative poems to regain its central place. The poems of *Civil elegies* are engaged with ideas of nationhood and public space, rare subjects in contemporary Canadian poetry. In his more recent work Lee, like Atwood, uses poetry as a scalpel, but he wields it against himself. The rigour of his self-examination, however, is tempered by the rhythm of the Beat poets.

Patrick LANE's recent work, of which *Mortal remains* (1992) is a good example, is, like Lee's recent poems, a circling back to earlier themes. Poems such as 'The killer' and 'Father' feature the hauntingly real images of violence that might have been the determinants of Lane's poetics of pain.

Little bird: last letter to my father 1987-1986 (1991), by Don COLES, is, like Lane's work, a moving meditation on the lost father. Poems to the father in Canada form a kind of genre, and provide a moving account of the cultural and generational forces that reside in contemporary poetry. The recipient of a Governor General's Award, Coles' *Forests of the medieval world* (1993) is the product of a well-travelled writer with an expansive mind who is at the height of his craft. Coles' superbly wrought suite 'The Edvard Munch poems' probes the relationship between poetry, visual art, and the painter.

Leonard Cohen's *Book of mercy* (1984) was seen on its publication as a departure from his early work. It is a collection of what have been called prose poems, prayers, and psalms, all fitting descriptions of poetry that is a turning inward. Cohen's subsequent *Stranger music: selected poems and songs* (1993), while it faithfully reproduces the Cohen of 'Suzanne' in several of its selections, also offers a more meditative Cohen. 'Days of kindness', written in Hydra in 1985, is a poem of remembrance in which 'read', 'see', and 'pray' are crucial verbs.

George BOWERING's *Kerrisdale elegies* (1984) is at once a homage to, and an argument with, Rilke's *Duino elegies* and marks a turning point for Bowering. Its serious cast of mind reflects the tone of many of the poets of Bowering's generation in the 1980s. For many readers, this volume is the finest example in his *oeuvre* of what Bowering called the 'serial' poem. *George Bowering selected: poems 1961-1992* (1993) includes new poems—many of them about death—that provide a counterpoint to the public image of the playful, punning Bowering.

The evocation of place continues to be a strength in Canadian poetry. John NEWLOVE's poems in *The night the dog smiled* (1986) remind us of his important role in the development of a poetics of place. The 'I' is often subordinated to the landscape in poems that are carefully sculpted. His *Apology for absence: selected poems 1962-1992* (1993) is, in the spirit of some of Purdy's work, a celebration of Canada's physical environment.

A kind of surrealist diary in verse, Robert KROETSCH's *Excerpts from the real world* (1986) provides a splendid example of how the Canadian landscape, particularly the prairie, can find its way into love poetry. As a result of their theoretical interest in composition by field, open-endedness, and the radicalizing of form, Kroetsch, bp Nichol, and Robin BLASER were responsible, each in his own way, for the development in Canada of a form of the long poem that runs to multiple volumes. In *Completed field notes: the long poems of Robert Kroetsch* (1989), Kroetsch brought closure to what for many years looked like a lifelong experiment.

bp Nichol's death in 1988 cut short the work of a much-loved poet whose innovative poetics and diverse artistic practices set him apart. George Bowering and Michael Ondaatje selected Nichol's best work in *An H in the heart: a reader* (1994), a volume that features concrete poetry, witty word play, and also prose poems that reveal Nichol's renowned empathy.

A poetics shaped by post-structuralist theory and by the 'Language' poets in the USA has had a noticeable effect on the recent work of writers who were considered experimental in the 1970s. Like Kroetsch, Nichol, bill bissett and also Jon Whyte, Steve McCAFFERY has, through engagement with linguistic theory, challenged the meaning and role of syntax and referentiality in his poetry. The appropriately titled *The cheat of words* (1996) is an assemblage of anti-lyric poetry in which meaning is deliberately compromised.

The ground-breaking political poetry of Gary GEDDES provided, in the mid- to late 1970s, the necessary milieu in which more radical forms could thrive. His *Active trading: selected poems 1970-1995* (1996) brings together a lifetime of politically committed work. Over the last decade Robert BRINGHURST has strengthened his commitment to a socially and environmentally centred avant-garde art. In all his recent work Bringhurst reiterates the privileged position of speech over the written word. The poetry of *Pieces of map, pieces of music* (1986) endorses multiplicity rather than unity of voice. In 'The blue roofs of Japan: a score for interpenetrating voices', Bringhurst undertakes a visually breathtaking experiment with typography: where 'voices' overlap, so do lines, one voice the light-blue ink shadow of the other. *The calling: selected poems 1970-1995* (1995) further investigates the challenge of making poems through which voices sing. This time Bringhurst takes the idea to its logical conclusion by creating what he describes in his preface as 'chamber music for speaking voices . . . printed in full score'. The wide embrace of Bringhurst's work encompasses Native dialects, Chinese characters, and a multitude of meditative practices.

Like Bringhurst, the esteemed Robin Blaser writes an intertextual poetry that is open and continuous in form and eludes easy categorization. Blaser's *The holy forest* (1993) is the embodiment of many decades of achievement. This volume includes the ongoing poems of 'Image-nations' and also the admired 'Great companions', a poet-philosopher's compendium of the writers and thinkers (as various as Robert Duncan and Hannah Arendt) who have influenced Blaser's art.

E.D. Blodgett's *Apostrophes: woman at a piano* (1996), winner of a Governor General's Award, departs from *Arché/Elegies* (1983) and *Da capo: The selected poems of E.D. Blodgett* (1990) in its longer narrative lines, arranged in what resembles contemporary sonnets. This expanded form gives Blodgett the space and depth he needs to think through questions of loss, separation, and being.

3. Tremendous diversity of form, ideology, and tradition characterizes the work of the extraordinary number of poets of the mid-1980s and 1990s. 'Place' remains an important theme in this period, but its role in poetry has been altered, partly by experimental practices. Christopher DEWDNEY reinvents 'place' through the science central to his poetry. He has taken the prose poem perfected by David McFADDEN into a new dimension by incorporating the often impenetrable language of science into his diction. This work has had an important influence on young writers. In Dewdney's *Permugenesis* (1987), a book-length prose poem, the 'Unnatural grace of an Ordovician lily pond' invites the reader to reconsider the definition and role of what makes beauty in poetry. Dewdney's other publications include *The radiant inventory* (1988) and *Demon Pond* (1994), which offer much more conventional lyric poems.

Don McKAY won a Governor General's Award for his strongest book to date, *Night field* (1991). In a manner that gently echoes Dewdney, McKay integrates a scientific perspective on the natural world with the musings of an incisive consciousness. In his variety of forms, McKay demonstrates a clean exactitude.

By playing with diction and especially the line, Fred WAH in his Governor General's Award-winning *Waiting for Saskatchewan* (1985), and Douglas BARBOUR in *Story for a Saskatchewan night* (1990) ponder the relationship between the poet and the place of which he/she writes. Mia Anderson's *Château Puits '81* (1992), Kristjana GUNNARS' *Exiles among you* (1996), Anne SZUMIGALSKI's *Voice* (1995; Governor General's Award), George McWHIRTER's *A staircase for all souls: the British Columbia suite* (1993), and John STEFFLER's *The Grey Islands* (1985) examine the same problem but through more accessible verse. The place that Stephen SCOBIE attempts to inhabit in *Gospel* (1994) is the mind of Christ; in this volume the boundary between the poet and the subject is deliberately blurred.

Canadian literary culture, especially over the past ten years, has encouraged the growth of an impressive body of accessible free verse written largely, but not solely, by female poets This poetry examines, celebrates, and often mourns the experience of daily life. Lorna CROZIER is one of the best known of this group. Her *Inventing the hawk* (1992) won a Governor General's Award. More recent work includes *Everything arrives at the light* (1995) and *A saving grace: the collected poems of Mrs. Bentley* (1996). Crozier's talent lies in her ability to write verse that resonates with a diverse audience.

Some of Canada's most subtle poets produce quietly powerful poems of domestic life, much in the manner of the late Bronwen WALLACE. Rhea TREGEBOV, Dale ZIEROTH, Robyn SARAH, and Patricia Young are four very talented writers of this kind of verse. Tom WAYMAN's work poetry, including *The astonishing weight of the dead* (1994), can fruitfully be read alongside the work of this school.

Roo BORSON gained a reputation as a skilful practitioner of poetry that relies on the image as a means through which private experience can be represented. *Water memory*

(1996) will be remembered as one of her strongest collections. Marilyn BOWERING (*Autobiography*, 1996) and Susan Glickman (*Hide & seek*, 1995) also work very deftly, often ironically, with image.

Writing in the same vein are women poets who incorporate tension, ennui, often anger into the subtexts of their work. The West Coast poet Sharon THESEN is one of the finest poets of this group. *The pangs of Sunday* (1990) and *Aurora* (1995) exhibit the work of a mature poet who has emerged from the influence of the *Tish* movement with a complex understanding of the power of the ordinary voice. Although her muse is daily life, searching ideas about the significance of place and about mortality and human relationships are embedded within every poem.

Writing in a different key from Thesen, the novelist and poet Anne MICHAELS made an impressive debut with two volumes of poetry, *The weight of oranges* (1985) and *Miner's Pond* (1991) (both were reissued in one volume in 1997). Against the backdrop of a heritage darkened by the Holocaust, she creates beautiful but often disturbing images with painstaking care. Her work shows the influence of the American poet Charles Wright, who is one of the international voices figuring increasingly in the work of Canadian poets.

After Atwood, poetry by women sharpened its tone. Canada boasts many female poets who write riveting, often unsettling poems about the deep knowledge women have of their own lives. A partial list of these poets would include Susan MUSGRAVE (*Forcing the Narcissus*, 1994); Linda Rogers (*Hard candy*, 1994); Rosemary Sullivan (*Blue panic*, 1991); Evelyn Lau (*Oedipal dreams*, 1992); Judith Fitzgerald (*Rapturous chronicles*, 1991 and *River*, 1995); Paulette JILES (*Celestial navigation*, 1984; Governor General's Award); Diana Hartog (*Matinée light*, 1983); and Mary DI MICHELE (*Luminous emergencies*, 1990).

The growing feminist school of poets in Canada is notable for poetry that is politically engaged. These writers look abroad, especially to French feminist theorists such as Julia Kristeva and Luce Iriguaray. Daphne MARLATT's *Touch to my tongue* (1984) attempts to assert a so-called 'female' language through a prose-poetry that violates conventional syntax. Di BRANDT's *Mother, not mother* (1992) re-works H.D.'s couplet form to examine the conflictedness of the mother/daughter relationship. Erin MOURÉ, whose volume *Furious* (1988) won a Governor General's Award, shows in the multiple voices of *Search procedures* (1996) a distrust in the referentiality of language. Other poets writing under the influence of a similar poetics include Libby Scheier (*Sky: a poem in four pieces*, 1990); Lola Lemire Tostevin (*Gyno-Text*, 1983 and *'Sophie*, 1988); and Betsy WARLAND (*Open is broken*, 1984).

Dionne BRAND has taken the issues of feminist poetry a significant step further by writing about both gender issues and race. Brand's poetry, particularly the widely discussed volume *No language is neutral* (1990), has, along with the work of George Elliott CLARKE, helped broaden the audience for work produced by black writers, including polemical writers such as Marlene Nourbese PHILIP.

An anthology of Canadian Native literature in English (1992), edited by Daniel David Moses and Terry Goldie, has raised the profile of poets such as Jeannette C. ARMSTRONG, Daniel David MOSES, and Wayne Keon, who, like African-Canadian poets, write poems of cultural lament. These Native writers have successfully undertaken the difficult task of adapting complex historical and political issues to the forms of current poetic practice.

Several of the strongest poets writing in Canada today are better known in the USA than here. They are erudite and multilingual, and their work draws on several poetic traditions, reflecting the contemporary poet's interest in a longer narrative line. Anne CARSON, a Montreal poet and professor of classics, is a fine example of this kind of poet. Her balanced, vividly contemporary narrative poems are engaged with philosophy, literature, and ancient texts, but her erudition never overpowers the rawness of her work. The confessional/exegetical long poem 'The glass essay' in *Glass, irony and God* (1992; reissued 1995), a New Directions publication, exemplifies Carson's nimble poetics. Other titles include the collections *Short talks* (1992) and *Plainwater: essays and poetry* (1995). Carson is greatly admired in the USA and has a growing reputation in Canada.

Eric Ormsby, who was born in Atlanta, Georgia, is another Montreal writer better known in the USA. *Bavarian shrine and other poems* (1990) and *Coastlines* (1992), Ormsby's first two volumes of poetry, were published by ECW PRESS. Grove Press, New York, published *For a modest god: new and selected poems* (1997) with an introduction by John Updike. Ormsby has been praised for his 'baroque' diction and striking conceits, his powers of observation and the musicality of his verse.

The relatively new poets who are gaining an international readership exhibit an interest in experimentation with prosody, enriching free verse with their attentiveness to metre and tone and with skilful variations in stanzaic pattern. This writing is not without precedent in Canada; the work of Richard OUTRAM, for example (*Mogul recollected*, 1993), provides a Canadian connection with the work of these poets. American and British influences include James Merrill, John Hollander, Charles Tomlinson, Anthony Hecht, John Ashbery, Geoffrey Hill, and Elizabeth Bishop, to name only a few.

A.F. MORITZ, in works such as *Phantoms of the ark* (1994) and *Mahoning* (1995), can be seen as reinventing the Canadian nature poem, accommodating it to other traditions through allusions to writers as varied as Dante and William Carlos Williams, and making it a place where the life of the mind flourishes.

John Reibetanz, like Moritz a talented writer with an expanding roster of books to his credit, is remarkable for the gentle moral vision that infuses his poems. Deftly handled metaphor is only one of the formal means through which Reibetanz expresses his insights. *Morning watch* (1995), *Midland swimmer* (1996), and *Near Finisterre* (1996) have more than fulfilled the early promise of his first book, *Ashbourn* (1986).

Several very talented new writers have emerged since 1983 whose work is remarkably accomplished. Jeffery Donaldson in his formally sophisticated *Once out of nature* (1991) uses traditional forms, particularly the tercet, to meditate on high art, philosophy, and also the mundane. Elisabeth HARVOR's spirited *Fortress of chairs* (1992; 1995) reveals a writer of tremendous skill whose maturity is reflected in a highly nuanced poetic voice. Esta Spalding's *Carrying place* (1995) and *Anchoress* (1977) are the work of a flexible poet who can move between confessional lyric and empathic narrative poems with ease. Christian Bök's *Crystallography* (1994), which shows a variety of influences, including the early work of Christopher Dewdney and poststructuralist poetics, may well be one of the most innovative books of the three decades in Canada. As borders of all kinds break down, promising Canadian poets will not only expand their Canadian readership, but will no doubt tap into that wider international audience that Canadian fiction writers have already cultivated. CYNTHIA MESSENGER

Poetry in French. Canadian poetry in French has been, for a century and a half, a screen to mask the community's sense of deprivation. More often than one would imagine, poets have used the Amerindian as the analogy of precarious survival. The myth of the land, frequently using the biblical typology of the ploughman who works with God, sublimates a harsh and tedious existence. Catholic piety, occasionally vibrantly alive—as in the poetry of Roger Brien, Clément MARCHAND, and, supremely, of Rina LASNIER—sublimates the rest of life. Encouraged by Romantic melancholy or pale post-Symbolist self-effacement, the poet of the interwar years sought an elsewhere, heavenly or European, to compensate for the here and now, or indulged in a barely disguised death-wish. Death and exile are, throughout, the prevailing themes of a poetry that is the skilful transposition into art of a permanently vulnerable culture. Rebellion is muted, shamefaced. Here and there—and increasingly since the Second World War—there are traces of what has been fittingly named the walk towards the sun. The spiritual blockade of French Canada has been lifted by a handful of authentic poets who have challenged the consensus and brought the thaw—the spring that with Anne HÉBERT burst violently on the city. This evolution makes possible the Dionysiac espousal of the Sun, symbol of virile self-affirmation, of honest self-appraisal, and of the collective will to live, not merely to survive. The poets discussed below will be related to this tradition, slightly less well-known poets being given some prominence at the expense of those that have a separate entry.

1. A NECESSARY PREHISTORY. A few expatriate Frenchmen signpost the otherwise prosaic French régime. Marc Lescarbot translated his awesome apprehension of a continent, and the founding of a civilization, into the heroic stanzas of *Les muses de la Nouvelle France* (Paris, 1609). (See Writing in NEW FRANCE.) Joseph QUESNEL, who arrived from France in 1778, wrote a pastoral operetta, *Colas et Colinette* (Québec, 1808); and, in 1803, a satire on the anglophile bourgeoisie, *L'Anglomanie*, which can be read in *La BARRE DU JOUR* (juill.-déc. 1965). Joseph Mermet and Napoléon AUBIN were Europeans who contributed patriotic verse to early nineteenth-century journalism. But the important milestones in this essential prehistory are, first, the 'chants héroïques jaillis du peuple', inspired by conflict with the English or by the adventures of the fur trade, discussed by Jeanne d'Arc Lortie in *La poésie nationaliste au Canada français, 1606-1867* (1975), which includes poems like those of Pierre FALCON, or the relatively few folksongs penned in Canada that offer glimpses

of popular values and the life of the people: songs like 'Vive la Canadienne', which speaks of festivities that 'finissent par mettre tout sens dessus dessous' and point to a popular culture despised and neglected by the devotees of staid official verse. Second, tribute must be paid to the tireless efforts of Michel BIBAUD, the Montreal newspaper publisher, to create a flourishing French-language journalism in Quebec and a literary tradition with it. Bibaud's *Épitres, satires, chansons, épigrammes et autres pièces de vers* (1830; rpr. 1969), a collection of verse previously published in his papers, was the first literary work in French published in Canada. In his own satires he castigates his fellow Québécois for their illiteracy and superstition, but hails the founding of classical colleges, which he hopes will make his satire redundant. He is remembered not for his poetry but for the vision and tenacity that underlie his 'amour de rimer'.

The patriotic movement of the 1830s, which came to a head in 1837-8, inspired a number of poets—some of them publishing anonymously—to celebrate the cause of political reform and to honour those who suffered for it. Notable among them is Joseph-Guillaume Barthe (1818-93), who was extensively anthologized by James Huston.

2. THE ROMANTICS: GARNEAU TO FRÉCHETTE. Quebec literature was born in the 1840s with François-Xavier GARNEAU's vigorous response to the derogatory Durham Report in his history of Canada, which offered his compatriots 'un juste sujet d'orgueil et un motif de généreuse émulation'. Garneau's poetry, never collected in his lifetime, was anthologized by James Huston, whose four-volume *Le Répertoire national* (1848-50) saved other verse, including that of Mermet and Aubin already mentioned, from the fate of the ephemeral political newssheets in which it was printed. Garneau's patriotic and historical poems lament the passing of the 'dernier Huron' and attempt to revitalize a 'peuple submergé par la fatalité'. Huston also included numerous poems by Joseph Lenoir-Rolland (1822-61), who was too obviously inspired by Lamartine, but learned from his French model vigour and limpidity. His poetry was published posthumously in *Poèmes épars* (1916).

The hub of the Romantic revival was the bookshop of the Crémazie brothers in the 1850s. Here, the members of the MOUVEMENT LITTÉRAIRE DE QUÉBEC met to read Chateaubriand, Lamartine, Hugo, and Musset. Octave CRÉMAZIE was a national hero in his time for his 'Vieux soldat canadien' and his 'Drapeau de Carillon'. In these bookshop meetings Louis FRÉCHETTE, the other national poet of French Canada, decorated by the Académie française, was inspired to a lifelong dedication to poetry. His personal contribution was his attempt to write a large-scale work proportionate to the continent in *La légende d'un peuple* (1887), inspired by Hugo's *Légende des siècles*. Charles GILL and Robert CHOQUETTE are the only others to have taken up this challenge. Fréchette's young friend Eudore Evanturel might have been Quebec's best poet had his *Premières poésies* (1878; rpr. 1979), prefaced by Joseph MARMETTE, not been severely attacked on moral grounds by the critics. He strikes the pose of Musset's rakish heroes, Rolla or Mardoche, and over half his poems are love poems, marked by a discreet and innocent sensuality, and regret that love remains unrequited. Later private secretary to Francis Parkman, Evanturel achieved a rare personal style and a delightful conversational prosaicness that was refreshingly natural among the romantic posturings of his contemporaries. An obscure civil servant like Alfred Garneau (1836-1904; the son of François-Xavier Garneau) can occasionally surprise and delight us with his exquisite short poems, published posthumously by his son Hector as *Poésies* (1904).

Abbé H.-R. CASGRAIN, the most influential Québécois literary figure in the nineteenth century, favoured art with clear moral intentions. Poets encouraged by him wrote on themes inspired by the reigning ideology: 'le laboureur', the ploughman who 'collabore avec Dieu', or 'notre langue' from William CHAPMAN's *Les aspirations* (1904); 'faite pour chanter les gloires d'autrefois', and 'les colons' from Pamphile LE MAY's *Les gouttelettes* (1904) or some of his religious verse. The poems in these collections are typical of many others written in the second half of the nineteenth century that unite in a common theme French Canada's divine mission, the cult of the past, the cult of the soil, and the heroism of the pioneer. The finest of the 'poètes du terroir' is Nérée BEAUCHEMIN. A critical edition of his prose and poetry was prepared by Armand Guilmette (3 vols, 1973-4).

3. ÉCOLE LITTÉRAIRE DE MONTRÉAL: A CANADIAN PARNASSUS. A generation of poets was born in the late 1870s. These were the bourgeois bohemians of the ÉCOLE LITTÉRAIRE DE MONTRÉAL, which was not so much a school as a disparate crowd of friends who despised Montreal, patriotism, 'the

plough and the sword', and were dazzled by the French poetic tradition of Art for Art's sake. Jean CHARBONNEAU, poet-philosopher; Arthur de Bussières (1877-1913), infusing oriental mysticism into his elegant escapist sonnets; Abbé Joseph Melançon (1877-1956), whose pseudonym was 'Lucien Rainier', with his collected poems *Avec ma vie* (1931); Charles Gill, one of the rare Québécois to attempt narrative verse in his ambitious *Le Cap Éternité* (1919)—all take second place to the brilliant, tragic Émile NELLIGAN. The Nelligan legend tends to obscure the achievement of another tragic figure in the *École* group, Albert LOZEAU, who explored with great sensitivity his restricted existence—he was crippled with Pott's disease—in his *L'âme solitaire* (1907), for example; and of the dedicated servant of the École, Louis-Joseph Doucet (1874-1959), named 'Prince des poètes' by his fellow poets. This self-effacing regionalist poet published nearly thirty collections of verse in his lifetime and left a further thousand sonnets unpublished. He wrote as easily as he thought and as naturally as he breathed.

4. PROBLEMATIC STARS. The poets of the generations following the heyday of the École continued to adopt a very private stance. Guillaume Lahaise ('Guy Delahaye') returned from a year in Paris to work in the psychiatric clinic of Saint-Jean-de-Dieu. His subtle, highly polished poems recognize that life lies in the tiny impulses of the heart, cardiogrammed in *Les phases* (1910). Jean-Aubert LORANGER spent a year in Paris in the early 1920s and then returned to his 'pays sans amour'. His poems, influenced by Paul Éluard and the poets of the *Nouvelle Revue Française*, display the delicious restraint of Quebec poetry: 'La mer bruit au bout du jardin' (Quebec poetry is a closed garden in which the outside world is heard as a faint rustling). In his edition of Loranger's *Les atmosphères* (1970), Gilles MARCOTTE presented this little-known poet to his 'true contemporaries'. Paul MORIN's *Poèmes de cendre et d'or* (1922) prolongs the elegant, ethereal ideal of the Mediterranean world of his happiest years. *Le coeur en exil* (1913) by René Chopin (1885-1953), published in Paris, his 'patrie intellectuelle', explores all the current themes: solitude, winter, 'la splendeur du vide'. To this group of expatriates belongs Simone Routier-Drouin, an elusive poet torn between a taste for the void and a nagging sense of unrealized potential in *Tentations* (1934); but she might also be considered along with other often convent-bred sensitive feminine voices of the thirties, including Jovette-Alice BERNIER, Eva Sénécal in *La course dans l'aurore* (1929), Medjé Vézina in *Chaque heure a son visage* (1934), Cécile Chabot in *Vitrail* (1939), and Jeannine Bélanger in *Stances à l'éternel absent* (1941). Alongside this world of poetic propriety, Quebec produced a number of fiercely original voices: Émile CODERRE ('Jean Narrache'), poet of the wretched misery of the urban poor; Rodolphe DUBÉ ('François Hertel'), who escaped to Paris from the confines of his province and his religious order; Alfred DesROCHERS, whom SAINT-DENYS-GARNEAU recognized, on the publication of *À l'ombre de l'Orford* (1929), as the first to assimilate the skills of European poets while preserving intact and expressing perfectly the soul of Canada; and Rina Lasnier, who achieved an inimitable blend of sensuality and mysticism that defies critical appraisal. Gaston MIRON, in an essay of 1957, acknowledged two of these lonely voices: Alphonse Piché and Isabelle Legris. The latter's collected verse, *Le sceau de l'ellipse* (1979), contains her spirited and sensitive *Ma vie tragique* (1947). But the inter-war years belong to two poets: Hector de Saint-Denys-Garneau and Alain GRANDBOIS. Thanks to them, whereas 'you had to apologize in 1934 for being a poet, by 1944 you had almost to apologize for not being one' (Jacques Blais).

5. THE HEXAGONE YEARS: 1953 TO 1963. Gaston Miron and the other poets and film-makers who founded the Hexagone press in 1953, dedicated to 'action through publishing', acknowledged their debt to Grandbois and to the manifesto *REFUS GLOBAL* (1948), in which Paul-Émile Borduas and his group rejected the past and called for a magic release from fear and self-disgust. The first publication of the Hexagone group was a joint poetry collection, *Deux sangs* (1953), by Miron and Olivier Marchand. Among the other poets Hexagone published, Gilles HÉNAULT, Roland GIGUÈRE, and Paul-Marie LAPOINTE come first chronologically in giving Quebec poets a new vocabulary, new eyes, new rhythms. New too was their commitment to art on a wide front and the priority they gave to art in their lives. Strong links with the visual arts, and with music, were a matter of course. Jean-Guy PILON and Miron added to their writing the role of public promoter of the arts, creating an audience and stimulating publishing through broadcasts or in public meetings. Miron, fearing that publication meant automatic assimilation into the bourgeois literary establishment and alienation from a possible mass audience, refused to allow

his poems to be collected for publication until as late as 1970; his *L'homme rapaillé* (1970) won the Prix de la revue *Études françaises*, among several other prizes. Fernand OUELLETTE summed up the literary camaraderie of Hexagone and the journal *LIBERTÉ* in his poem 'Et nous aimions'.

Pierre TROTTIER in *Le combat contre Tristan* (1951) relates the French-Canadian condition to the myths and themes of universal typology. Anne Hébert in *Le tombeau des rois* (1953) continues her cousin Saint-Denys-Garneau's analysis of the Quebec sense of non-being before expressing the violent explosion of new-found life in *Mystère de la parole* (1960). Guy ROBERT's 1965 edition of the major part of the prose and poetry of Sylvain GARNEAU, *Objets retrouvés* (1951), which contains the previously unpublished poetic journal *La bleue*, is a tribute to the balance between tradition and originality achieved by this poet, who died in 1953 at the age of twenty-three. Most of the poetry of the fifties is taken up with a diagnosis of what Miron calls 'la vie agonique'—Quebec's experience of death in life. In sharp contrast, Gatien LAPOINTE marked the new beginnings of the sixties with *Le temps premier* (1962), an eloquent reconciliation with the earth that in the theme of the 'pays réinventé' became the chief preoccupation of the decade. Similarly rooted in a harsh but vividly insistent reality, the contribution of Pierre PERRAULT to the poetry of this period was acknowledged in two collected volumes of his work published in the elegant Hexagone retrospective collections *Chouennes* (1975) and *Gélivures* (1977).

6. THE 'SHOUTING SIGNPAINTERS'. Malcolm Reid gave this title to a book (1972) about Quebec in the sixties, when poetry became briefly a public act, a process culminating in the 'Night of poetry' of Feb. 1970 and the 'Poèmes et chants de la révolution' of 1971, written in protest against the application of the War Measures Act. Reid's title translates that of Paul CHAMBERLAND's *L'afficheur hurle* (1964), in which Chamberland says he passed from the *themes* of the fifties to the *problems* of the sixties—from poetry to politics. (Reid's book includes a translation of part of *Afficheur.*) Gérald GODIN, who went on to become a Parti Québécois minister, forged a virile and sturdy poetic language in his *Cantouques* (1967) and *Libertés surveillées* (1975). Paul Chamberland invented in a single title, *Terre Québec* (1964), a poem, a manifesto, and an 'art poétique'. Michèle LALONDE went even further, with *Speak white* (1974), in bending the vituperative force of racy, popular speech to the particular purposes of her anger. Over the *PARTI PRIS* years hangs the shadow of Claude GAUVREAU, a signatory of *Refus global*, who made fitful but dramatic public appearances until his much-publicized suicide in 1971. *Parti pris* published the 1300-page volume of his *Oeuvres créatrices complètes* (1971). The sixties saw two other important groups at work: women writers still absorbed in a private sensuality, and singer-poets. Monique BOSCO, poet of elegant melancholy, punctuated with racy flashes of pique, published *Jéricho* (1971). Marie LABERGE in *Reprendre souffle* (1972) mixed nostalgia with allusions to an importunate, ugly reality. Cécile CLOUTIER, in *Mains de sable* (1960), attempted the difficult art of the *haiku*. Suzanne PARADIS, novelist and poet, gradually built up her reputation with a dozen collections in twenty years, and become an able poetry critic. Of the monologuists, poet-singers, and songwriters, mention must be made of Claude PÉLOQUIN, Raoul DUGUAY, Georges Dor, Gilles VIGNEAULT, Félix LECLERC, Yvon Deschamps, Clémence Desrochers, and Raymond Lévesque, who broke the silence of the Quiet Revolution. Many saw in the prolific Gilbert LANGEVIN one of the more seriously underrated of Quebec's outstanding poet-songwriters. In *Mon refuge est un volcan* (1978) he says, 'cet enfer amical est notre domaine'.

After its founding in 1963, the bilingual campus at Moncton, New Brunswick, became a focus for the elaboration of an Acadian identity and voice, and some poets began to make names for themselves: Guy Arsenault, Raymond Leblanc, Herménégilde CHIASSON, Léonard Forest, and Ronald DESPRÉS. See ACADIAN LITERATURE.

7. DISMANTLING LYRICISM. In the late fifties and early sixties Yves PRÉFONTAINE insistently explored the myth of the inhospitable North as the symbol of the spiritual paralysis and aphasia threatening the emerging poetry of Quebec. From *Boréal* (1957; rpr. 1967) to *Débâcle* (1970) he moved from the theme of the difficulty of being to that of the land rediscovered and repossessed. The poets of the sixties rejected a too-cerebral poetry in favour of what Fernand Ouellette called 'la démence charnelle', most notably expressed in the poems of Pierre MORENCY, Michel BEAULIEU, and Alexis LEFRANÇOIS. To these should be added the Moroccan-born Juan Garcia, awarded the Prix de la revue *Études françaises* for his *Corps de gloire* (1971), which included his earlier *Alchimie du corps* (1967); Marcel Bélanger in *Prélude à la parole* (1967)

and *Plein-vent* (1971); and Pierre Mathieu in *Ressac* (1969), *Interlune* (1970), and *Mots dits québécois* (1971). Others in their wake stressed the corporeal and the phenomenological: Roger des Roches explored the latent eroticism in the act of writing (*Le corps certain*, 1975), as did Philippe Haeck in *Nattes* (1974) and *Les dents volent* (1976). Pierre Nepveu, serene and confident, typified the new maturity of Quebec culture in works such as *Couleur chair* (1980). Claude Beausoleil offered, in *Ahuntsic dream* (1975) and *Sens interdit* (1976), the acceptable face of Surrealism and a refreshing sense of humour.

8. THE SEVENTIES. This was when all the hidden assumptions with which history had loaded literary genres were challenged. The outstanding development of the Quebec cultural scene in this period was the feminist rewriting of the rules. Women writers unmasked violently, humorously, or lyrically what they considered the phallocentric conspiracy of 4,000 years of writing and the patriarchal culture of death. Central to this movement was Louky BERSIANIK's astonishing summum of anti-mysogynist theory, *L'EUGUÉLIONNE* (1976), 400 pages of fable, fact, and fantasy. Nicole BROSSARD freely interchanged poetry, essay, and fiction. A line from Yolande VILLEMAIRE's *Que du stage blood* (1977) sums up this important rewriting of a convention: 'Je est une autre.' Madeleine GAGNON sought to create a feminine consciousness and mythology, principally in *Lueur* (1979), where she blurred interestingly the boundaries between poetry, fiction, and essay. France THÉORET, in *Bloody Mary* (1977), violently recorded the bitterness of awakening to squalid and abortive womanhood and hailed Mary, the eternal feminine martyr. Josée YVON, as her title *Filles-commandos bandées* (1976) suggests, relished brutal verbal terrorism across the frontiers of sexual ambiguity. The tragically early death in 1981 of Marie UGUAY—author of *Signe et rumeur* (1976) and *L'outre vie* (1979)—robbed Quebec of another member of this vociferous sisterhood.

The proliferation of literary magazines in the seventies provided a public for an ever-increasing number of poets and a focal point for poetic creation and experiment. Sometimes this experimentation took extreme forms: Claude Gauvreau's thunder of syllables; Raoul DUGUAY's jazz poetry, accompanied by manifestos on 'le stéréo-poème audio-visuel'; Luc Racine's *Les dormeurs* (1966), inspired by serial composition in music; Lucien FRANCOEUR's typographical experiments in *Les grands spectacles* (1974); Guy ROBERT's concrete poetry; Roger Soublière's poetry in a tin can for the supermarket age; the poem-hoarding, the poem-collage, the poem-postcard, the poem-gag, and even the poem-trips and violent pornography of Denis Vanier in *Lesbiennes d'acid* (1972).

The influence on the *La* BARRE DU JOUR aesthetic of the French journal *Tel Quel*, and the French formalists, was evident in such writers as Jean-Yves Collette, Michel Gay, and André Beaudet, who saw themselves in a pre-literary phase where lyricism had to be dismantled, the language of creation exploded, and the text sabotaged in order to lay bare the unconscious mechanisms enshrined in syntax and idiom.

But this radical questioning of the act of creation was also an acknowledgement of a failure to communicate. Michel Leclerc in *La traversée du réel, précédé de Dorénavant la poésie* (1977) asked whether it was worth writing in a world hopelessly confused with violence and dust. André Beauregard adopted a similar uncertainty in *Changer la vie* (1974), a title he took from Rimbaud. For Robert Mélançon, poetry was *Peinture aveugle* (1979) because of its limited visuality. Hope was present in all these poets, but minimally—reduced to what Pierre Laberge called, in *Vue du corps précédé de Au lieu de mourir* (1979), 'le désir d'adhérer'.

The variety and extreme individuality of the poets writing since the collapse of consensus in 1970 was well illustrated by the counter-cultural movement, which spread principally from the USA. Aiming to reassert the values of personal freedom and pleasure, to release primitive impulses and save the quality of life from the consequences of rapid industrialization and urbanization, it flouted social prejudice and stereotyping by noisily espousing homosexuality and the liberalization of sex and drugs; hence the importance accorded to personal contacts, informality, and workshop-methods of literary production. A parallel reaction against materialism favoured transcendentalism and the supernatural. A bibliography compiled by Ghislaine Houle and Jacques Lafontaine, *Écrivains québécois de nouvelle culture* (1975), provides an excellent introduction to the subject. See also *Québec underground, 1962-1972* (3 vols, 1973).

Seen in perspective, Canadian poetry in French to the 1980s offered an exciting example of a culture, in search of its identity and its voice, that in many respects had found both these things. In using poetry to attempt to express the unspeakable and indefinable, Québécois poets in this period were often more linguistically adventurous and innovative than their European counterparts. Love—pursued with a single-minded faith and tenacity, but often seen as impossible—and Québécois anguish were abiding themes. Yet, while the tone was invariably sad and sombre, hope and the celebration of life broke through time and time again. This transcendence was supremely evident in Gaston Miron's 'Tête de caboche', which expresses the pure instinct for freedom; in Fernand Ouellette's unashamed eroticism and spirit of camaraderie; in Jacques BRAULT's glowing tribute to his mother in *La poésie, ce matin* (1971); in Michèle Lalonde's contribution to the collective howl of rage of the sixties; and in the work of Michel GARNEAU, who wrote in *Les petits chevals amoureux* (1977), 'un des plus beaux hymnes au plaisir' (André BROCHU).

C.R.P. MAY

1980 to 1996. THE RETURN TO INTIMACY. If in the past there was relatively clear agreement on what constituted poetry, over the course of the 1980s and 1990s the term has been extended more and more broadly, to the point where the genre itself is subject to experiments that force readers to redefine poetry on new bases. For one current of Quebec poetry, represented by poets published by Les Herbes Rouges, the notion of 'text' has replaced that of poetry, so that, under this single rubric, one finds collections of traditional rhymed verse as well as poetry that is close to narrative, or indeed reflective prose. In the work of some writers fiction subsumes the poem, wedding theory and poetry (very common with Herbes Rouges writers) or approaching the intimate or personal—drawing equally on the personal journal and the travel story, postcard, or letter. These different poetic discourses create a new way of writing about the self, whether they are limited to a dialogue between the poet and his/her own image or whether the words simply pour out as in a confession. No doubt this personal orientation comes from the attraction of autobiography. The practice of autobiography, real or fictional, can be connected to the vein of self-exploration that emerged under the influence of psychoanalysis. Poets take stock of themselves to (re)discover themselves through the fundamental urges of the self. A poet like Paul Chanel Malenfant, in *Les noms du père* (1985), combines the experienced and the imaginary. Fernand OUELLETTE published a collection (*Les heures*, 1987; Governor General's Award) in which the poet relives the last moments of his father's death. The work of such male writers followed closely behind that of women writers like Nicole BROSSARD (*Double impression (poèmes et textes 1967-1984)*, 1984; Governor General's Award), who attack patriarchically shaped words and meanings, and in Brossard's case a lesbian perspective is added. The discourse of the self, in all its forms, is a considerable part of the poetry of the 1980s and 1990s. But perhaps for some it is another way of reaffirming the hegemony of the 'subject' by inserting it in a more metaphysical perspective. In effect, even as they situate themselves within the wave of formalist writing combined with theoretic reflection on their own practice, authors who were pioneers in this orientation, like François CHARRON and Normand de Bellefeuille, turn increasingly towards writing in which the personal begins to reclaim its rights. The prolix Claude BEAUSOLEIL, through a sharp awareness of his individuality and his presence in the public arena, probes the very notion of the poem in its form and its evolution (*Dans la matière rêvant comme d'une émeute*, 1982; *S'inscrit sous le ciel gris en graphiques de feu*, 1985); while André ROY (*Action writing*, 1985; Governor General's Award; *L'accélérateur d'intensité*, 1987; Grand Prix de la Poésie de la Fondation des Forges) puts language at the service of the body and of homosexuality. Jean-Paul Daoust, in *Les cendres bleues* (1990; Governor General's Award), tells the story of a dark and tragic love between a small boy and a man of twenty. The intimate takes on a very different face with the highly refined poetry, verging on silence, of Hélène Dorion, in which the poem serves as mirror of the self and of death (*Les retouches de l'intime*, 1987; *Un visage appuyé contre monde*, 1990), or the work of Louise Cotnoir (*Plusieures*, 1984; *Les rendez-vous par correspondance*, 1984), for whom examination of the private goes hand in hand with a feminist consciousness.

Many poets in this period attempted to invent a new lyricism, less highly charged than that of the 1960s, for which the variations of the intimate constitute in the end a privileged mark of the relationship to the world and to language. For Anne-Marie ALONZO, her 'poetic fictions' combine sometimes a fragmented syntax, in constant rupture with itself, sometimes a search for the self through interpersonal exchanges, notably with other women writers (*Bleus de mine*, 1985; *L'immobile*, 1990). Film, eroticism, and pornography (Hugues Corriveau, *Forcément dans la tête*, 1985; *Apprendre à vivre*, 1988), horror (Marcel Labine, *Les papiers de l'épidémie*, 1988; Governor General's Award), and fragments from thrillers (René Lapierre, *Une encre sépia*, 1990; *Viendras-tu avec moi?*, 1996) have made their way into poetry. The fragmentation of the very idea of poetry means that anything is possible. But the dominant tendency, particularly in the 1980s, is intimism, the symptom of a turning away from the public sphere towards the private, which began in the 1960s with women's writing. Lyricism no longer feeds on the idea of collective salvation. The 1980 referendum, which marked a defeat for the 'indépendantiste' current, together with the advent around the world of neoliberalism, are among the sociopolitical and economic events that explain why poets began to explore a more individual territory. The poetry of the body celebrated by Brossard, among others, naturally led to a valorization of the self and its various strata (sexual, psychoanalytical, social). The work of France THÉORET also comes to mind; in *Nécessairement putain* (1980) and *Intérieurs* (1984) the development has tragic overtones. Linked to intimism is a heightened awareness of the everyday, even the banal, the domestic setting often serving as the emblem of the interior theatre, as in the work of Louise Warren, who succeeds in fusing story and poetry (*L'amant gris*, 1984). As for Élise Turcotte, who has twice been awarded the Prix Émile-Nelligan for her poetry (*La voix de Carla*, 1987; *La terre est ici*, 1989), her writing reveals such affinities with prose that she seems to have turned definitively towards narrative writing. For others, such as Denise DESAUTELS, poetry takes form through an encounter with a pictorial work (*Leçons de Venise*, 1991; Prix de la Fondation des Forges; *Le saut de l'ange*, 1993; Governor General's Award). Gradually the work of Michel BEAULIEU distanced itself from both formalism and lyricism. His poems, anchored in the everyday, create a dull, almost prosaic sound. Shortly before his death he published *Kaléidoscope ou Les aléas du corps grave* (1985), which won him the Grand Prix de la Fondation des Forges.

Some poets seem to want to keep their distance from intimism by shaping their writing to approach the metaphysical. François Charron is among the leading representatives of this more recent tendency. He is recognized as one of those who have deliberately rejected self-reflexive poetry in order to renew his ties to an apparently more readable language than that of the poets of the 1960s. For all that, the ascendency of meaning in his poetry gives precedence to the voice, to rhythms and phrasing that sketch rather than state what they are about (*La vie n'a pas de sens*, 1985; *Le fait de vivre et d'avoir vécu*, 1986). The individual self is more likely to be reduced to his/her essential being, without enumerating characteristics, so that what is being written about is never very far from the metaphysical. Normand de Bellefeuille, another member of the Herbes Rouges group (*Le livre du devoir*, Prix Émile-Nelligan, 1984; *Catégoriques/un, deux et trois*, 1987; Grand Prix de la Fondation des Forges), reconciles theoretic rigour with reflection based on the 'real', a term that, since Roland Barthes, has exercised a notable influence on the poetry of Roger des Roches (*L'imagination laïque*, 1982; *La réalité*, 1992). Madeleine GAGNON, through her contacts with philosophy, made an important contribution to joining thought and poem (*Pensées du poème*, 1983). And Paul CHAMBERLAND pursued work that glorifies the figure of childhood and innocence (*L'enfant doré*, 1980; *Émergence de l'adultenfant*, 1981), and his experience, from the point of view of both the senses and the mind, is expressed through the invention of a form and a term, 'géogramme', that gathers fragments of texts drawn from different fields of knowledge in order to create a planetary chart of a conception of the world that is fundamentally opposed to the established order (*Le multiple événement terrestre. Géogrammmes (1979-1985)*, 1991, and *L'assaut contre les vivants. Géogrammes 2 (1986-1991)*, 1994). Renaud Longchamps takes up some of the same preoccupations in *Légendes, suivi de Sommation sur l'histoire* (1988; Prix Émile-Nelligan) in an effort to encompass the ancient glacial origins of the Earth. Other poets echo Montaigne's maxim that to philosophize is to learn how to die. The writing of Gilles Cyr (*Andromède attendra*, 1992; Governor General's Award) is spare and takes the form of couplets, torn between the need to speak and the need to remain silent. In a way it is a worthy successor to the work of Jacques BRAULT, whose poetry, in the form of *haikus* and soliloquies, sustains a familiar conversation with death and the dead, who accompany him on his journey in writing (*Moments fragiles*, 1984; *Il n'y a plus de chemin*, 1990, Prix Alain-Grandbois; *Au petit matin*, with Robert Mélançon, 1993). Finally, among writers with a concise, lapidary style, the still undervalued Gilbert LANGEVIN played with various poetic fashions of the day; his entire output may be summed up as an ethereal desire to escape bleak reality (*Le fou solitaire*, 1980; *Comme une lexique des abîmes*, 1986; *Le dernier cercle*, 1994; Prix Alain-Grandbois). Langevin's prolific body of work came to an end with the author's death in 1995. The metaphysical temptation, which can sometimes take the form of the sacred, reveals a kind of otherworldiness in certain poets. Indeed, this phenomenon seems to have become emblematic of the 1980s and 1990s, to judge by the proliferation of 'serious' books devoted to angels, especially guardian angels. No doubt it would be rash to attribute a single meaning to this angelism, but one might suggest that it fills a need to move beyond immediate reality and the fragmentation of spiritual values to meet the invisible and touch it through childhood, its beliefs and fears.

Although marginality in poetry is increasingly difficult to identify, some poets have succeeded, regardless of the dominant currents, in destabilizing readers with their power to challenge them. Denis Vanier, a true delinquent and 'poète maudit', has written texts in which moral and physical decay vie with an aspiration towards purity (*Koréphilie*, 1981); Josée YVON, named as co-author of Vanier's collection, brings the reader face to face with abjection (*Filles-missiles*, 1986); Lucien FRANCOEUR, the rocker poet, continues to celebrate America through exaltation of psychedelics, the poets of the beat generation, and sacred Egyptian texts (*Les rockers sanctifiés*, 1982, Prix Émile-Nelligan; *Exit pour nomades*, 1985). In ACADIAN LITERATURE the young poet Serge Patrice Thibodeau is building a body of work that is beginning to gain recognition in Quebec, especially with *Le quattuor de l'errance* and *Nous, l'étranger* (both were awarded the Grand Prix de la Fondation des Forges, 1996).

But the upheavals experienced by poetry in this period were not only of a formal nature, or a matter of reaction to a political climate. They flowed as well from a phenomenon that remains relatively new for Quebec: the advent of transcultural or migrant writing, a term that applies to the emergence inside Quebec of kinds of writing inherited from other cultures, as well as to native-born francophone writers who seek in other languages the foundations of their own identity. Writing identified as 'migrant', whatever its origins—Italian, with Fulvio Caccia (*Arkos*, 1994; Governor General's Award); Egyptian, with Anne-Marie Alonzo and Mona Latif-Ghattas (*40 voix pour un exil*, 1986); or Iranian, with Bernard Antoun (*Fêlures d'un temps*, 1987), to mention only a few examples—tries to reconcile a new gaze, that of the stranger, with the irreversible condition of the exile. Nevertheless, these writers should not be defined only from this perspective; the tendency to classify them according to their origins is too strong. They themselves take part, to varying degrees, in the trend running throughout Québécois poetry in this period. This intermingling of traditions had its influence on Yolande VILLEMAIRE, who chose to move away from Western reference points (*Du côté hiéroglyphe de ce qu'on appelle le réel*, 1982; *La lune indienne*, 1994). Others, like Madeleine Gagnon in *Chant pour un Québec lointain* (1991; Governor General's Award), join the poets of exile in making Quebec a land to be rediscovered. More than ever we see in poetry what Pierre Nepveu has called 'the plurality of centres' (*L'écologie du réel*). Discourses about origins, which until recently characterized poetry in French, in Quebec and throughout the francophone world, have given way to a poetry that multiplies and relativizes the points of reference. See also MULTICULTURAL WRITING IN FRENCH. JACQUES PAQUIN

Polk, James. See NOVELS IN ENGLISH 1960 TO 1982: OTHER TALENTS, OTHER WORKS: 2.

Pollock, Sharon (b. 1936). Mary Sharon Chalmers was born in Fredericton, New Brunswick, the daughter of esteemed physician and long-time New Brunswick MLA, Everett Chalmers. She was educated in the Eastern Townships of Quebec and briefly at the University of New Brunswick, leaving in 1954 to marry Ross Pollock, a Toronto insurance broker. Separating in the early 1960s, she returned with her children to Fredericton, where she worked in various capacities, including acting, at the Playhouse Theatre (later Theatre New Brunswick). In 1966 she moved to Calgary with actor Michael Ball, performing in a semi-professional touring theatre, Prairie Players. That year Pollock won the Dominion Drama Festival best actress award for her performance in Ann Jellicoe's *The knack*. Her first stage play, *A compulsory option* (unpublished), a black comedy about paranoia, won an Alberta Culture playwriting competition in 1971 and was given its first production at Vancouver's New Play Centre the following year. Now living in Vancouver, she completed *Walsh* (1973; rev. 1974, 1983) which premièred at Theatre Calgary in November of 1973. A new production in July 1974 at the Stratford Festival's Third Stage first drew Pollock to national attention as a playwright.

Although in the years that followed Pollock increasingly built her reputation as a major Canadian dramatist, she has been equally active, artistically and administratively, in other aspects of theatre: as director, actor, dramaturge, artistic director, and theatre founder.

She was head of the Playwrights Colony at the Banff Centre School of Fine Arts (1977-80); playwright-in-residence at Alberta Theatre Projects, Calgary (1977-9) and the National Arts Centre (1980-2); briefly artistic director at Theatre Calgary (1984), and writer-in-residence at the Regina Public Library (1986). In 1988 she was appointed artistic director of Theatre New Brunswick, serving for two seasons. In reaction to the restraints of subsidized theatre, in 1992 Pollock, in partnership with her son K.C. Campbell, established an independent company at the Garry Theatre, a former movie house in the neglected Inglewood district of Calgary. She has directed in many Canadian theatres, such as the Manitoba Theatre Centre, Neptune Theatre, Magnus Theatre, and Alberta Theatre Projects—including productions of her own plays: *One tiger to a hill* (1981) at the National Arts Centre in 1981; *Doc* (1986), under the title *Family trappings*, at Theatre New Brunswick in 1986; and the première of *Saucy Jack* (1994) at the Garry Theatre in Nov. 1993. Her roles as an actor included several in her own plays: Miss Lizzie in Theatre Calgary's production of *Blood relations* (1981) in 1981; Mama George in her radio adaptation of *Getting it straight* (1992) at the International Women's Festival in Winnipeg, July 1989; and Renée in the première of *A death in the family* (unpublished), June 1993 at the Garry Theatre. Since 1977 she has maintained residence in Calgary.

Pollock's plays of the 1970s, drawn both from the past and from contemporary life, are marked by a strong commitment to political and social issues. The historical chronicle *Walsh*, structured in the episodic manner of the epic theatre, explores the treatment of Sitting Bull and his people when they fled from the USA to the Canadian Northwest after their defeat of General Custer at Little Big Horn. Major Walsh of the North-West Mounted Police is caught between personal integrity and the political expediencies of the Macdonald government of the 1870s. *Out goes you* (unpublished), a satiric comedy on contemporary British Columbia politics, followed in 1975 at the Vancouver Playhouse. Pollock returned to history with *The Komagata Maru incident* (1978), also premièred at the Vancouver Playhouse, in Jan. 1976. This is a stern indictment in presentational style of Canadian racism based on a historical event in 1914 when a shipload of Sikh immigrants was denied permission to land from Vancouver harbour. *One tiger to a hill* premièred at the Citadel Theatre, Edmonton (Feb. 1980). Inspired by the New Westminster prison hostage-taking of 1975 in which a classification officer was shot, it attacks Canadian institutional complacency and public apathy about prison reform.

In a notable shift of emphasis in the plays of the next decade, Pollock subsumes the polemics of public controversy in the personal conflicts of family life, wherein conventional value systems are challenged by the rebellious behavior of her protagonists. *Blood relations*, a study of the famous New England spinster Lizzie Borden, acquitted by the courts for the axe murder of her parents in 1892, was first produced at Theatre 3, Edmonton, in Mar. 1980. Structurally it is Pollock's most sophisticated drama to date, taking the form of a play-within-a-play: ten years after the acquittal, Lizzie's actress friend (probably the historical Nance O'Neill) acts out the crucial scenes at the time of the murders, responding to stage directions from Lizzie herself. The play explores not only the ambiguities of evidence, but also the social repressions of a middle-class spinster in the late nineteenth century. A more conventionally naturalistic work followed: *Generations* (1981), first written for radio and premièred on stage at Alberta Theatre Projects, Calgary, in Oct. 1980. It also evokes family tensions, but its conflicts inhere in contemporary prairie farm life. *One tiger to a hill, Blood relations*, and *Generations* have been published in *Blood relations and other plays* (1981); the title play won the first Governor General's Award for published drama. *Whiskey six cadenza* (1987), premièred at Theatre Calgary in Feb. 1983, is a vivid recollection of prohibition days in a southern Alberta mining community. Here the issues of an oppressive law and exploitative working conditions are expressed in the twisted relationship of parents and children. These climax in a destructive emotional triangle consisting of a flamboyant gospeller of free will who is also the local bootlegger, his adoptive daughter, and the rebellious son of a local temperance zealot. The play is published in *NeWest plays by women* (1987), edited by Diane Bessai and Don Kerr.

Pollock's next two plays, *Doc* (premièred at Theatre Calgary, Apr. 1984) and *Getting it straight*, show Pollock forging dramatic structures to accommodate an increasing interest in the subjectivity of female character. The theme of the former, partly autobiographical, is the conflict between a compulsively dedicated physician and his alcoholic wife, with particular emphasis on the impact of their discord on a growing daughter. In a further step from *Blood relations*' retrospective time frame, this play rejects linear time, directly engaging the audience in the two present-time characters' associational memory patterns. In the monodrama *Getting it straight*, Pollock explores the subjective virtually to its dramatic limits in the fragmented mind of Eme, an escaped mental patient who broods brokenly on the horrors of male aggression—in particular as manifest in the events of Hiroshima and Nagasaki. Pollock won her second Governor General's Award with *Doc* in 1986; *Getting it straight* is published in *Heroines* (1992), edited by Joyce Doolittle.

More recently Pollock has returned to historical subjects: *Fair liberty's call* (1995)—which premièred at the Stratford Festival, July 1993—and *Saucy Jack*. The former demonstrates a new complexity in the playwright's revisionary perspectives on the Canadian past, examining the moral and spiritual ravages of revolution in a Loyalist Boston family. Now living in the wilderness of early New Brunswick, the Roberts are further torn between principle and expediency in a life of hardship that is incongruously combined with the perpetuation of class privilege in the new community. In *Saucy Jack*, Pollock once more expresses her fascination with famous unsolved crimes, offering a variation on speculations concerning the identity of Jack the Ripper. Somewhat reminiscent of *Blood relations*' device of the play-within-a-play, here an actress is hired by an intimate friend of the heir presumptive to the British throne to enact the roles of the viciously slaughtered East End prostitutes. While narratively the motive is to locate and cover up possible guilt in high places, the dramatist's main purpose is to give voice to the anonymous underclass victims.

During the 1970s Pollock wrote a number of children's plays, many for production in Vancouver and Calgary theatres, such as *New Canadians* (1973), *The happy prince* (1974), *The wreck of the national line car* (1978), and *Chataqua spelt E-N-E-R-G-Y* (1979). She has also written a dozen radio scripts: her *Sweet land of liberty* won the ACTRA Nellie for Best Radio Drama of 1980. Her recent radio play, *The making of warriors*, is published in *Airborne: radio plays by women* (1991), edited by Ann Jansen. In 1981 she won a Golden Sheaf for her television play *The person's case*. Her achievement as a dramatist was acknowledged in 1987 with the Canada-Australia Literary Award. Her plays have been produced not only in Canada, but in Britain, the USA, Japan, and Australia.

Useful references to Pollock's early work can be found in *Canada's playwrights: a biographical guide* (1980), edited by Don Rubin and Alison Cranmer-Byng, and in Malcom Page, 'Sharon Pollock: committed playwright', *Canadian Drama*, 5, no. 2 (Fall 1979). See also *The work: conversations with English-Canadian playwrights* (1982), edited by Robert Wallace and Cynthia Zimmerman. For more recent overviews see Diane Bessai, 'Women dramatists: Sharon Pollock and Judith Thompson', *Post-colonial English drama* (1992), edited by Bruce King; Cynthia Zimmerman, 'Sharon Pollock: the making of warriors', in her *Playwriting women: female voices in English Canada* (1994). Pollock's papers are housed in Special Collections, University of Calgary: see the *Sharon Pollock papers: first accession* (1989), edited by Appollonia Steele and Jean F. Tener, with a biocritical essay by Denis Salter.

DIANE BESSAI

Pond, Peter. See EXPLORATION LITERATURE IN ENGLISH: 2.

Pontiac. See ABORIGINAL LITERATURE: 1.

Porcupine's Quill, The. This small publisher, which began life as the production side of PRESS PORCÉPIC, was founded in 1974 by Tim and Elke Inkster. It operates out of their combined home and printing shop in Erin, Ontario, not far north of Toronto, with the assistance of the CANADA COUNCIL and the Ontario Arts Council. Its list includes works by new writers as well as many leading Canadian authors, such as Matt COHEN, Don COLES, Steven HEIGHTON, Keath FRASER, George JOHNSTON, John METCALF, John NEWLOVE, Richard OUTRAM, Leo SIMPSON, James REANEY, and Jane URQUHART. It has reissued, in the Sherbrooke Street reprint series, books by Clark BLAISE, Hugh HOOD, Irving LAYTON, Norman LEVINE, Leon ROOKE, and Ray SMITH. In addition, its books have become known for being unusually attractive in design and production (sewn paperback bindings are standard). Editorial decisions are the responsibility of John Metcalf and Tim and Elke Inkster. Its books are distributed by General Publishing, Toronto.

WILLIAM TOYE

Potvin, Damase. See NOVELS IN FRENCH 1900 TO 1920.

Poulin, Jacques (b. 1937). Born in Saint-Gédéon, in the Beauce region of Quebec, he was educated at Université Laval, where he took a bilingual Arts degree that enabled him to earn his living for a number of years as a commercial translator.

Poulin writes with ease, grace, and humour, seeming to share none of the usual preoccupations of Quebec novelists of his generation—the Church, the land (escaping from it or rediscovering it), Quebec's political affairs. A monument explodes in *Mon cheval pour un royaume* (1967), but this first novel is less interested in terrorism than in language and communication, love and sweetness, strolls in Old Quebec City. One of the chief influences in his first three novels is J.D. Salinger: the debt is obvious, but the novels, particularly *Jimmy* (1969), are more *hommage* than imitation. *Les grandes marées* (1978) shows the influence of Kurt Vonnegut Jr and Richard Brautigan. The setting for these novels is largely the old part of Quebec City, which Poulin makes contemporary and North American, filled with light and childish delight. But one of the pervading themes is destruction—of an older order, of old buildings, old styles of life. New life springs from the old, however, and one is struck particularly by the humanity of the attitudes and characters in the novels of this very important, unjustly neglected writer. Poulin's first three novels—*Mon cheval pour un royaume*, *Jimmy*, and *Le coeur de la baleine bleue* (1979) were translated by Sheila Fischman and published as *The Jimmy trilogy* (1979).

In *Faites des beaux rêves* (1974), the most spare and subtle of Poulin's novels, the line between 'dreams' and reality is never quite clear. Camped near the Formula 1 race course at Mont Tremblant are Théo, a sportswriter; Limoilou, a girl steeped in legends; and Amadou, an accountant. Poulin focuses solely on the actions and words of these three, while they grope their way towards each other, touching only intermittently, and bask in the excitement that radiates from the racing drivers. They amuse themselves by playing games—borrowing dialogue, situations, and roles from Westerns, musical comedies, and the writings of Salinger, F. Scott Fitzgerald, and Martin Heidegger—and in the end simply go their separate ways. In *Les grandes marées* a translator of comic-strips is sent to a deserted island in the St Lawrence, where he plays tennis with a ball-machine, does battle with dictionaries (though they are his friends), and discovers—or creates—a young 'dream' girl, Marie, before being destroyed by various agents of society who invade his island. For a writer, how is it possible to live without—or with—the world? The narrative is now expanded, now interrupted, by quotations, questionnaires, flash cards, advertising clichés, bilingual announcements, recipes, instructions, equations, drawings, and comic strips. *Les grandes marées*—dream, narrative, fable, essay—is an exploration of the possibilities and the limits of narration. It was translated by Sheila Fischman as *Spring tides* (1986).

Volkswagen blues (1984) is an extensive voyage of exploration in time and space, from the northeast to the southwest of America, from the cross planted by Jacques Cartier at Gaspé in 1534 to the Californian counter-culture of the disciples of Allen Ginsberg and Lawrence Ferlinghetti. Everywhere the travellers—a writer with the *nom de plume* Jack Waterman and a young Métis woman mechanic, the Grande Sauterelle (Big Grasshopper)—encounter traces (names) and records of the French exploration of the Mississippi and the Rockies. The ostensible reason for the trip is to find Theo, brother of Jack, in San Francisco. But he is totally changed, aged, embittered, stricken by a creeping paralysis. Sheila Fischman published a translation of *Volkswagen blues*, under the same title, in 1988.

The last two novels by Poulin are rather narrative in character, concise and refined. *Le vieux chagrin* (1989) returns to the banks of the St Lawrence. The main character—who is on the trail of a cat, some fetishes, a phantom, and a little girl—enters a bungalow and a grotto reading Hemingway and *The thousand and one nights*. *La tournée d'automne* (1993) depicts the travels of a bookmobile, its driver, and a young French friend who for the last time make the rounds of villages dispersed along the Côte-Nord; it is also a farewell, and a *hommage* to books, heroes, and some typical readers.

Poulin, who lives in Paris, received the Prix David in 1995.

See also NOVELS IN FRENCH 1960 TO 1982: 3(b). LAURENT MAILHOT

Poupart, Jean-Marie. See NOVELS IN FRENCH 1960 TO 1982: 3(b).

Pour la patrie (Montréal, 1895). This separatist novel by Jules-Paul Tardivel, set in a hypothetical future, is the most enduring popular expression of Quebec's nineteenth-century religious nationalism. The federal government of 1945-6 is secretly dominated by a masonic lodge of devil-worshippers that aims to destroy the French-Canadian society of Quebec, the world's last stronghold of true religious (i.e. Catholic) life and values. The government proposes to change the Canadian constitution in a way that *seems* to perfect its federal character but will in reality destroy Quebec's autonomy and crush French Canada. A French-Canadian MP sees the danger, but is unable to convince a majority in

Parliament. Only by the strength of his piety, his submission to divine will, and acceptance of personal sacrifice does he win the miraculous intervention from heaven that defeats the Satanists and brings about the ultimate independence of Quebec.

Tardivel (1851-1905) was a Quebec City ultramontane journalist, accustomed to writing polemics, which may account for the novel's unsophisticated style, its superficial characterization, and its acceptance of Catholic faith at its simplest. He was the chief publicist in late nineteenth-century Quebec for what he called 'thorough-going Catholicism', and it was to promote that cause, rather than to portray human character or drama, that he wrote the novel. He defended the Church's important role in education and social service and held that in a Catholic society like Quebec all public life must be informed by the spirit of religion and the Church's teachings. In *Pour la patrie* he argued that this would be possible only if Quebec separated from Canada, freeing itself from non-Catholic influences.

Tardivel's representation of freemasonry as the cult of Satan was not uncommon in the 1890s. Such accusations had been made against freemasons in Europe, and Tardivel's own newspaper, *La Vérité*, republished French and Italian anti-masonic works. His novel, in turn, was reprinted in European ultramontane papers.

Called the father of Quebec separatism, Tardivel had an important influence on twentieth-century French-Canadian nationalism. Demand for his work among nationalist groups led to the republication of *Pour la patrie* in the 1930s, and it was no doubt the revival of separatism that prompted a reprint in 1974 and the English translation, *For my country: an 1895 religious and separatist vision of Québec in the mid-twentieth century* (1975), by Sheila Fischman. A.I. SILVER

Poussière sur la ville (1953). A novel by André LANGEVIN that is considered one of the classics of contemporary Quebec literature, it is about a doctor, Alain Dubois—the narrator—and his wife Madeleine, two psychologically complex characters who are convincingly portrayed. An ardent, beautiful child-woman, Madeleine is the mainspring of the plot, which concerns her infidelity with Richard Hétu and its consequences. Dubois's initial rage and humiliation culminate in his half-drunk delivery of a hydrocephalic child whom he is obliged to kill to save the mother's life—an incident that affects him profoundly: he feels crushed by an implacable fate that he can neither comprehend nor struggle against. When the curé attempts to ruin Dubois's practice and arranges to have Hétu married off to the niece of the town's leading businessman, Madeleine tries unsuccessfully to shoot her lover and then dies by turning the revolver on herself. After the funeral, Dubois resumes his medical practice—in a struggle, as he sees it, on behalf of his fellow men against God and the absurdity of the human condition: 'I shall continue my fight. God and I, we aren't even yet.' This book, which shows the influence of Albert Camus, particularly in *La peste*, is artistically one of the most successful illustrations of the existential and metaphysical ideas that flowed into Quebec from Europe after the Second World War. It remains Langevin's most popular work, both for its literary merit and for the human dilemmas it probes.

Poussière sur la ville was translated as *Dust over the city* (1955) by John Latrobe and Robert Gottlieb. A critical edition (1969) has been edited and annotated by Renald Bérubé. In 1965 it was made into a disappointing black-and-white movie, shot in Thetford Mines by Arthur Lamothe.

See Réjean Robidoux and André Renaud, *Le roman canadien-français du vingtième siècle* (1966). L.W. KEFFER

Powe, Bruce (b. 1955). Bruce William Powe was born in Toronto, Ontario, and was educated at Lawrence Park Collegiate, York University (B.A., 1977), and the University of Toronto (M.A., 1981). In this period he became deaf in one ear from being in a rock band, smoked dope, dropped acid, and tried to make sense of the hyperactive post-war baby boom. Since 1989 he has been professor of English and humanities at York University, Toronto.

Much of Powe's work explores the thesis that Canadians live in a condition of 'pluralistic' post-literacy, and thus lack any single identity. Canada is 'in process' as the first communication state, and Canadians have lost their ability to think in an electronic and technological world; thus he is the heir to Marshall MCLUHAN as a mass-age theorist.

Powe's first book was a modest series of essays on a community in transition, *Queen Street West* (1980). *The solitary outlaw* (1983) is an exploration of the lives and thoughts of Pierre Elliott Trudeau, Wyndham Lewis, Glenn Gould, Marshall McLuhan, and Elias Canetti—and concludes with his perception that literate men and women are now outlaws and exiles, with the task of maintaining language and making certain 'that human beings remain complex'. *A climate charged* (1984) is an evaluation of Canadian literature. Uneasy about the ever-increasing role of Canadian universities and the Toronto cultural establishment in shaping the idea of a national literature, Powe critiqued several major Canadian authors—finding Margaret ATWOOD limited in her appeal, Irving LAYTON overrated, and Northrop FRYE limited by his impersonal approach to literature; he was affectionate towards his mentor, Marshall McLuhan, and fond of Robertson DAVIES, with reservations.

Powe moved from his study of intellectual figures to a meditation on the fate of Canada in the global world of mechanized mass culture in *A tremendous Canada of light* (1993). This long essay (originally intended to form an addendum to a larger book, which became his novel *Outage*), on the elusive national identity of Canada, makes several thought-provoking points. Powe criticizes former Prime Minister Brian Mulroney for failing to understand his country and making economics the centre of his government policy; argues for balanced systems of electronic communication; and concludes that Canada 'is more a state in process than a nation state . . . fast forwarding into a new pattern, a model of communication linkages.'

Outage: a journey into electric city (1995), a 'novel of ideas', is almost unclassifiable. It is part critical essay, part fiction, part memoir, part therapeutic release from a broken marriage. The main character, 'Bruce', wanders through Toronto in a series of vignettes in a world that involves too much TV, too many faxes, too many cellular phones, and a variety of technocrats—radio, TV, and computer personalities. The jittery staccato style of the book tries to duplicate 'sound bytes' as 'Bruce', yearning for authentic communication in the fake world of electronic communication, moves towards a symbolic conclusion in Venice, birthplace of artistic perception and Renaissance humanism.

GEOFF HANCOCK

Prairie Fire (1978-). The oldest and most important general-interest literary magazine in Manitoba was founded by Katherine Bitney, Elizabeth Carriere, and Andris Taskans as a Winnipeg newsletter named *Writers News Manitoba*, with the intention of establishing a provincial writers' organization. By the time the Manitoba Writers' Guild was founded in 1981, the newsletter had become a literary magazine, which changed its name to *Prairie Fire* in 1983. It became a quarterly in 1984 (published with the assistance of The CANADA COUNCIL, the Manitoba Arts Council, and the City of Winnipeg). Under editor Andris Taskans, *Prairie Fire: a Canadian Magazine of New Writing* has published writers from all of Canada (including Margaret ATWOOD, Matt COHEN, Timothy FINDLEY, Robyn SARAH, Jason SHERMAN) while concentrating on writing from the Prairie Provinces, especially Manitoba. Issues have featured Patrick FRIESEN (vol. 13, no. 1), Robert KROETSCH (8, 4), Carol SHIELDS (16, 1), and Anne SZUMIGALSKI (18, 1); there have also been series featuring ethnocultural writing (2, 3), the Métis (6, 4), Franco-Manitoban writing (11,1), Mennonite writing (11, 2), Ukrainian writing (13, 3), and Jewish-Canadian writing (17.3). The magazine has sturdy and striking covers, usually in full colour.

GEOFF HANCOCK

Prairie writing. According to Edward McCOURT, author of a ground-breaking critical survey, *The Canadian West in fiction* (1949; rev. 1970), 'Prairie literature properly begins with the nineteenth-century travellers and explorers.' Henry KREISEL, on the other hand, has written in his essay 'The prairie: a state of mind' (1967) that 'All discussion of the literature produced in the Canadian West must of necessity begin with the impact of the landscape upon the mind.' Where the literature begins and where discussion begins are two separate matters, yet prairie writers and critics agree on the importance of history and geography in shaping the region's creative expressions.

In the literature of travel and exploration, several narratives stand out: Paul KANE's *Wanderings of an artist* (London, 1859; rpr. 1968), the Earl of Southesk's *Saskatchewan and the Rocky Mountains* (Edinburgh & Toronto, 1875; rpr. 1969), and Viscount Milton's and W.B. Cheadle's *Northwest passage by land* (London, 1865; rpr. 1970). The form reached its apogee in *The great lone land: a narrative of travel and adventure in the northwest of America* (London, 1872; rpr. 1968) by the Irish-born army officer William Francis Butler (1838-1910), an immensely popular book throughout the English-speaking world for more than half a century. Butler's celebrated rendition of the pre-settlement West rests on an artful combination of elegy and irony; he evokes tenantless solitudes in prose redolent of Shelley and Tennyson, Cooper and Dickens. Yet even as Butler reached an international market, 'the great lone land' of the fur-trade era was facing transformation. George Monro Grant spoke for a generation of Canadian expansionists when he marvelled at the beauty and fertility of the immense but unknown plains in *OCEAN TO OCEAN* (1873).

With the transfer of Rupert's Land to Canada in 1870, the region began to shed its mystery. Missionaries, surveyors, mounted policemen, and other 'forerunners of civilization' wrote voluminously of their experiences and predictions, but they were no match—in quantity at least—for the tourists, sportsmen, social pundits, and agricultural settlers who followed them. Touted by publicists as the 'last best west' and the 'granary of empire', the prairie frontier generated extraordinary publicity. One result was a foreshortened interval between pioneer settlement and pioneer publication. Alexander Begg's *Dot it down: a story of life in the North-west* (Toronto, 1871) was a *roman à clef* satirizing the events leading up to the 1869-70 Riel resistance; it concludes with an immigrant's guide to Manitoba. J.E. Collins scarcely waited for the shooting to stop before rushing into print with *The story of Louis Riel* (1885) and *Annette the Metis spy* (1886; rpr. 1970), sensationalized caricatures of the 1885 reprise. Meanwhile the high romance of fur-traders and Natives persisted in some early fiction: Butler's *Red Cloud, the solitary Sioux* (London, 1882), R.M. BALLANTYNE's *Red man's revenge: a tale of the Red River flood* (London, 1880), and Agnes LAUT's *Lords of the North* (New York, 1900).

The early pattern of almost simultaneous social and literary creation was sustained after the century's turn. 'Ralph Connor'—who became known world-wide for novels like *Black rock: a tale of the Selkirks* (Toronto, 1898), *The sky pilot: a tale of the foothills* (Chicago, 1899), depicting muscular Christian men and pure uplifting women on a glorious and challenging frontier—was the pen-name of the Rev. Charles W. GORDON, a central figure in Winnipeg's reformist social-gospel movement. In his later fiction—including *The foreigner* (1909) and *To him that hath* (1921)—he tried unsuccessfully to keep pace with the shocks of western Canada's willy-nilly absorption into the modern age: urbanization, the assimilation of immigrants, labour conflict, and the Great War and its aftermath. Nellie McCLUNG was another public figure from this period whose fame sprang originally from her accomplishments as a writer of popular fiction, including *Sowing seeds in Danny* (1908) and *Purple springs* (1921). R.J.C. STEAD, who earned his living as a publicist for the CPR, was the author of several volumes of Kiplingesque verse, and then published five immensely popular novels before the crowning achievement of *Grain* (1926). The notion of the artist as alienated and anti-social held scant appeal for either writers or readers in the halcyon days of the great settlement boom.

Sober second thoughts entered with the 1920s. The change in mood is evident not only in Stead's *Grain*, but in Martha OSTENSO's *Wild geese* (1925), and Frederick Philip GROVE's *Settlers of the marsh* (1925). All three novels explore the relations of men and women, parents and children, families and communities, in the context of a distinctive prairie agricultural way of life. Each has its own claims to literary autonomy and merit: it is with these three novels that genuine critical debate, rather than historical explanation, can begin. Grove has captured most of the attention, on both literary and extra-literary grounds. Certainly it is true that in his novels, essays, and autobiographical writings he explored (as none had done before, and few since) the role of the literary artist in the Canadian prairie scene, at the same time creating powerful if sombre icons of pioneer life. By comparison with Grove's *Settlers of the marsh*, *Grain* is a more innocent work of fiction, more modest in ambition, but in many ways more authentic and satisfying.

Although during the 1930s drought in the farming districts was accompanied by drought in the creative wellsprings, the combination of Depression and dustbowls has proved a fertile theme ever since. The poem by Anne MARRIOTT called 'The wind our enemy', published in a 1939 poetry collection of that name, remains one of the more notable poetic responses to that traumatic period. In fiction the short stories of Sinclair ROSS, and his novel *AS FOR ME AND MY HOUSE* (1941), constitute a significant if overrated contribution. The vicissitudes of the thirties turned the westering theme northwards, as in Ralph ALLEN's slight but enjoyable *Peace River country* (1958), and Christine VAN DER MARK's more serious and substantial *In due season* (1947; rpr. 1979).

The cultural and linguistic diversity of the prairie region is reflected to some extent in pre-Second World War writing, perhaps most vividly in the fiction and autobiographical books of Laura Goodman SALVERSON (*The Viking heart*, 1923; *Confessions of an immigrant daughter*, 1939). The novels of the 1950s on the ethnic theme included Vera Lysenko's *Yellow boots* (1954), Adele WISEMAN's *The sacrifice* (1956), and John MARLYN's *Under the ribs of death* (1957). Lacking translation into English, little of the writing done in German, Icelandic, Ukrainian, and other languages has reached the wider reading public, although Watson KIRKCONNELL's early lead in translation is attracting renewed interest. Two francophone writers, both born and educated in France, have enjoyed the advantage of translation: Maurice CONSTANTIN-WEYER—who was awarded the Prix Goncourt for *Un homme se penche sur son passé* (1928), published in English as *A man scans his past* (1929)—and Georges BUGNET, whose novel *Nipsya* (1924) also appeared in translation. Bugnet's *La forêt* (1935) was judged by E.K. BROWN to be the finest novel ever published about the Canadian West; it was translated into English as *The forest* (1976).

From 1950 on Manitoba-born French-Canadian writer Gabrielle ROY travelled in her fiction (always first published in French) with unmatched sureness and delicacy through the subtler territories of the prairie experience, whether centred on St Boniface (*The road past Altamont*, *Street of riches*), on the Interlake district (*Where nests the water hen*), or on the rural Prairies (*Garden in the wind*, *Children of my heart*). Roy's themes are joy and sadness; hope and disappointment; youth, ageing, and death; and above all, love. These universals of the human condition are contained and illumined by Roy in a prose style of classic nuance and restraint.

Fiction has been the dominant form through most of the post-war period. The short stories, radio scripts, and novels of W.O. MITCHELL, the author of *WHO HAS SEEN THE WIND* (1947), created a voice and a milieu that continue to occupy a central cell in our collective imaginative life. Henry Kreisel, whose first novel was *The rich man* (1948), showed that a career in academe need not be the death of creativity. In Manitoba W.D. VALGARDSON writes novels and short stories marked by quiet authority, and David WILLIAMS' *The river horsemen* (1981) has been well received. However, these and many other fine writers from the region must contend with the shadows thrown by greater luminaries. In 1964 Margaret LAURENCE burst on the literary scene with *The STONE ANGEL*, adding a new dimension to Canadian literature through the novel's commanding central figure and narrator, ninety-year-old Hagar Shipley. Also in the 1960s Robert KROETSCH began a fictional reclamation of his Alberta background with *The words of my roaring* (1966) and *The studhorse man* (1969); while a northern-Saskatchewan Mennonite community gave Rudy WIEBE impetus and material for *Peace shall destroy many* (1962) and *The blue mountains of China* (1970). All three writers have gone on to become dominant figures nationally, and to bring Canadian writing to the eyes of the world.

Kroetsch does not confine himself to fiction: his *The stone hammer poems* (1975) and *Seed catalogue* (1977) are long poems that explode with wit and energy. In *Twelve prairie poets* (1976) editor Laurie Ricou provides a sampling of recent poetry from the region, while Saskatchewan poets, in a co-operative venture typical of that province, have put together work from forty-one writers in *Number one northern: poetry from Saskatchewan* (1977). English departments at universities in all three Prairie Provinces—along with Saskatchewan's School for the Arts and Alberta's Banff Centre—help to generate the talent and craftsmanship that find outlets in Manitoba's Turnstone Press, Saskatchewan's Thistledown Press, and Longspoon Press of Edmonton. Throughout the region poets are busy and productive; for every poet mentioned here, there are a dozen vigorous and distinctive talents left in undeserved obscurity, but one may mention in particular the work of Joy KOGAWA, Anne SZUMIGALSKI, Dale ZIEROTH, Lorna Uher (CROZIER), Sid MARTY, and Andrew SUKNASKI—cultivators in a field first broken by figures like John NEWLOVE, Eli MANDEL, Dorothy LIVESAY, Elizabeth BREWSTER, and Miriam WADDINGTON.

In drama the community theatre movement of the 1930s and 1940s rested largely on the short plays and radio scripts of Gwen Pharis RINGWOOD, Elsie Park Gowan, and W.O. Mitchell. Their heirs included George RYGA, Ken MITCHELL—who has edited an excellent regional anthology, *Horizon: writings of the Canadian Prairies* (1977)—Joanna GLASS, Sharon POLLOCK, and John MURRELL, author of *Waiting for the parade* (1980). The theatre scene was vibrant, with a tendency towards grass-roots realism, but it did not exclude more cerebral and experimental works like Wilfred WATSON's 1969 play, *Let's murder Clytemnestra according to the principles of Marshall McLuhan*.

Critical approaches to prairie writing continue for the most part to hew to the environmentalism of Edward McCourt. In *Vertical man/horizontal world* (1973) Laurie Ricou asserted that 'the basic image of a single human figure amidst the vast flatness of the landscape serves to unify and describe Canadian prairie fiction.' Dick Harrison added something of a historical dimension to the discussion in

Unnamed country: the struggle for a Canadian prairie fiction (1977). A more eclectic source is *Writers of the Prairies* (1977), a collection of critical articles reprinted from *CANADIAN LITERATURE*; while an important debate between McCourt and Eli Mandel can be found in Richard Allen's *A region of the mind* (1973). Still missing, and sorely missed, is a lively and rigorous critical press: the *NeWest Review* stands almost alone. Thus it may be some time before any fully satisfactory critical survey of the region's writing reaches publication.

See also CRITICISM IN ENGLISH: 5(c), 5(f), 5(g), NOVELS IN ENGLISH 1960 TO 1982: OTHER TALENTS AND OTHER WORKS: 6(b), and PIONEER MEMOIRS: 3. SUSAN JACKEL

1983 to 1996. Strangely, the notion persists of 'prairie writing' as a kind of remote, fenced area best left to gophers and dust storms. One might almost imagine it hanging around the basement of Canadian literature. It could be argued that such designations manifest again the centre's desire to impose regionality on everything beyond the centre, but an informed and engaged reading of contemporary writing coming out of the Canadian West will radically alter preconceived notions of what 'prairie writing' ought to consist of.

The grassroots movement of publications and presses that sprang out of the West's growing confidence in its own voice blossomed with a vengeance in the late 1970s and the 1980s. Turnstone Press in Manitoba, Thistledown Press and Coteau in Saskatchewan, NeWest Press and Red Deer College Press, and the now-defunct Longspoon Press in Alberta, have all made available a vibrant chorus of poetry, drama, fiction, and non-fiction, and have introduced to Canadian literature a veritable orchestra of instruments. Prairie writing—which no longer figures in the tradition of the grand old men (McCOURT, KREISEL, GROVE, MITCHELL, KROETSCH, WIEBE), who were in the past credited with articulating West—is now a shifting and complex mosaic of literary style and gesture. *PRAIRIE FIRE*, *Dandelion*, *absinthe*, *blue buffalo*, *GRAIN*, and a growing number of new and innovative periodicals record the poetry and fiction of an energetic region that feels no compulsion to apologize for its location, its history, or its distance from Ontario. *Border Crossings* and *NeWest Review* contribute cultural commentary; *Prairie Bookworld* is less consistent, but provides a modicum of information on books appearing in the West. There is still tremendous need for a hard-hitting critical literary review, one that will engage with all genres of writing, both politically and textually. The senior voices of prairie writing do continue to wield considerable influence. W.O. Mitchell's remarkable novels persist in their ribald pleasure, and interest in his carnivalesque fiction and drama continued with the popular television adaptation of *Jake and the Kid*. Although Margaret LAURENCE's death in 1987 cost Canadian literature its most cherished prairie writer, her work and reputation still enjoy widespread attention, with symposia, and biographical and critical studies, appearing regularly. Her memoir *Dance on the earth* (1989) enabled a new critical appreciation of life-writing. Robert Kroetsch's anarchic influence perseveres. His publication of *The completed field notes* (1989) proclaimed the completion of his lifelong long poem, although in *A likely story* (1996) Kroetsch again embedded a variety of poems within his supposed autobiography. His *Alibi* (1983) and *The puppeteer* (1992) undress for readers narrative's self-referential conflicts. Rudy Wiebe's fiction about First Nations people has found intensified focus through his work on the North, especially in his latest novel, *A discovery of strangers* (1994), and his most brilliant book, *Playing dead: a contemplation concerning the Arctic* (1989), which takes up the perspective of a southerner looking north and seeking to discover the intricate reasons why 'Canadians have so little comprehension of our own *nordicity*'.

But these looming figures are now crowded by brilliantly innovative writers asserting an increasingly vigorous prairie presence. Carol SHIELDS, who has lived in Winnipeg since the early 1980s, won the Pulitzer Prize for her haunting genealogy *The stone diaries* (1993), after publishing eight other novels and collections of short fiction, the most striking being *Various miracles* (1985) and *The orange fish* (1989). Sandra BIRDSELL's novels *The missing child* (1989) and *The chrome suite* (1992) succeed as intense mosaics crafted from such particular moments as lightning striking a small town. Birdsell first came to attention through her Agassiz stories in *Night travellers* (1982) and *Ladies of the house* (1984).

Many other prairie writers are challenged by short fiction's intensity. Guy VANDERHAEGE's stories and novels perform subtle exhumations of conscience, particularly in *Things as they are?* (1992) and *The Englishman's boy* (1996). Greg HOLLINGSHEAD's characters in *The roaring girl* (1995) struggle to impose thoughtfulness in the midst of chaos. Sharon BUTALA's short fiction, especially the collection *Fever* (1990), transcends the strictures of realism that dog her novels. Bonnie BURNARD's collection *Women of influence* (1988) investigates the dislocation of women's ordinary lives. Armin Wiebe, in his Yasch Siemens stories, pushes the vernacular to its outrageous limit; David Arnason's Icelandic humour fractures the commonplace of fairy tales; Birk Sproxton's *The hockey fan came riding* (1990) comically ices our national sport. David Carpenter, Rosemary Nixon, Edna ALFORD, Cecelia Frey, Fred Stenson, Robert Currie, Gertrude Story, Barbara Sapergia, and Elizabeth BREWSTER all write eloquent and memorable short fiction.

In longer fiction, the West seems to provoke novels fascinated with landscape and historical idiosyncrasy. Thomas Wharton's *Icefields* (1995) waits out time on the Columbia Icefields, Peter Oliva's *Drowning in darkness* (1992) is buried under the Crowsnest Pass, Margaret Sweatman's *Fox* (1991) uses the Winnipeg strike as setting and inspiration, Nicole Markotic's *Yellow pages* (1995) amplifies the telephonic passion of Alexander Graham Bell, Geoffrey Ursell's *Perdue* (1984) witnesses the entire settlement of the West, and Darlene Barry Quaife's *Days and nights on the Amazon* (1994) speaks through the voice of that river.

Writing for the theatre has shifted from the local and historical to a broader canvas. Ken MITCHELL, Rex DEVERELL, John MURRELL, and Sharon POLLOCK continue to produce excellent work. They have been joined by brilliant mavericks like Brad FRASER (*Unidentified human remains and the true nature of love*, 1989).

Poetry from the Prairies is remarkably inexhaustible, and not simply in terms of quantity. Patrick FRIESEN, Dennis Cooley, Kristjana GUNNARS, Lorna CROZIER, Di BRANDT, Monty Reid, Robert HILLES, Anne SZUMIGALSKI, Fred WAH, Claire HARRIS, Douglas BARBOUR, Ted Blodgett, George Amabile, Chris Wiseman, Stephen Smith, Don Kerr, Tim Lilburn, Mary Howes, and Elizabeth Brewster consistently publish exciting work. Most of these writers have won major national or international awards in recognition of their distinctive poetics. Discussing in satisfactory depth how particularly each of the above poets has contributed to shaping a prairie voice would itself require a massively annotated anthology, which would be another lacuna in the pool of printed words, and an indication of how frustratingly little has been gathered for easy access and comparison. In the wake of Robert Kroetsch, the long poem enjoys particular resonance in the West; Daniel Lenoski in *Along prairie lines* (1989) anthologizes some major examples, including work by Jon Whyte, Anne MARRIOTT, and Andrew SUKNASKI.

Various anthologies have set out to articulate a critical positioning and to follow some trace of the diversity of prairie writing. *Trace: prairie writers on writing* (1986), edited by Birk Sproxton, is the most comprehensive, both historically and geographically. *Writing Saskatchewan: twenty critical essays* (1989), edited by Kenneth G. Probert, and *Contemporary Manitoba writers: new critical studies* (1990), edited by Kenneth James Hughes, both endeavour to capture the flavour of writing in those provincial settings. Various province-defined short-fiction anthologies—for example, *Made in Manitoba* (1990; Wayne Tefs, ed.), *Saskatchewan gold* (1982; Geoffrey Ursell, ed.), *Boundless Alberta* (1993; Aritha van Herk, ed.), and most recently *Due West* (1996; Wayne Tefs, Geoffrey Ursell, and Aritha van Herk, eds), have gathered samplers of contemporary short fiction, but they are inadequately comprehensive, inevitably, even if they succeed in choosing an interesting variety of established and new voices.

Accompanying the sheer energy of regional resonance is a diverse representation of the Canadian ethnic mosaic. Ven Begamudré, Hiromi Goto, Yasmin Ladha, Suzette Mayr, Caterina EDWARDS, Sarah Murphy, Claire Harris, and Fred Wah, for example, are worthy of attention for their superlative writing, but without diminishing their talent, their writing is doubly effective for the vivid difference that it adds to the community cacophony. First Nations writers are at last receiving more public exposure and recognition; their material was for too long obscured and repressed by the dominant European culture. Maria CAMPBELL's work (particularly *Halfbreed*, 1973) is influential, and she has been joined by, to name only a few, Louise Halfe, Marilyn Dumont, Richard Wagamese, Joan CLARK, Beth Cuthand, and (although he has moved east), Thomas KING. Especially notable is *Writing the circle* (1990), the first anthology to make available a selection of writing by Native women of western Canada.

Most remarkable of all is the extent to which prairie writers, arguably more than writers from any other region, are willing to push the boundaries of genre, to question expected forms, and make free with textual explorations. Kristjana Gunnars' *The prowler* (1989), for example, is posed as a novel, but by exploring time and space, history and writing, through the bifocals of fiction and criticism, it becomes a meditation on writing. Gunnars'

The rose garden (1996) pursues again the question of what literary works actually do, using Proust as a magnifying glass. Fred Wah's bio-textual *Diamond Grill* (1996) is part meditation, part Chinese café cookbook, part memoir. Monty Reid pushes poetry to another dimension, and far beyond the confinement of prose, in *Dog sleeps* (*Irritated texts*) (1993). Aritha VAN HERK's *Places far from Ellesmere* (1990) sub-titled '*a geografictione*'—a fiction mapped on the lines of geography—explores a critical reading of place as character at the same time as it incorporates an imaginative unreading of Tolstoy's *Anna Karenina*. Robert Kroetsch's *A likely story* narrates an anti-autobiography, and Beth Goobie's body-fictions, in *Could I have my body back now, please?* (1991), dissect occasions that affected a friable body. Such examples argue for a writing energy that does not simply employ the template of fiction, poetry, or drama, but seeks to find new forms to apprehend the region that it names.

Grant MacEwan's and James GRAY's popular western histories enhanced general knowledge of the Prairies; because they publicly articulated distinct regional stories, their work cannot be ignored. Nor should writers like George Melnyk and Myrna KOSTASH, who must also be recognized for their important contributions to the unfoldings of the prairie regional identity.

For all the optimism inherent in the intellectual diversity and eagerness of the Prairies, a clutch of nervous critics and writers persist in wanting the West and its writing to remain safely realist, wanting the definition of prairie writing to be determined by the writer's birthplace and genealogy, and are adamant that prairie words must enshrine a Depression-glass version of romantic insularity. In creative fact, the Prairies' ability to enfold and engage the modern and the postmodern, the realist and the transcendent, the historical and the imagined, argues that this region is greater than its geographical boundaries, far more than the pliable landscape and climate that are available for documentation. In every literary sense the Prairies are what Henry Kreisel called a visionary 'state of mind'. They are a mythic space, inspiring abundant literary effect both within and beyond their horizon.

ARITHA VAN HERK

Pratt, E.J. (1882-1964). One of the major figures in Canadian poetry, Edwin John Pratt was born in Western Bay, Newfoundland, but his father, a Methodist minister, moved the family at approximately four-year intervals among the fishing, sealing, and whaling outports of the British colony. After graduating from St John's Methodist College, Pratt served as a preacher and teacher in several remote island communities, and then attended Victoria College, University of Toronto, and majored in philosophy. Supporting his studies by doing missionary work in the West in the summers, and later serving as an assistant minister just outside Toronto, he earned his B.A. (1911), M.A. (1912) with a thesis on demonology, his B.D. (1913), and Ph.D. (1917) in theology, publishing his thesis *Studies in Pauline eschatology, and its background* (1917). In 1918 Pratt married Viola Whitney, who became a staunch United Church worker and a writer for young people. Their daughter, Mildred Claire, wrote a study of the Pratt family, *The silent ancestors: the forebears of E.J. Pratt* (1971).

In 1920 Pelham Edgar invited Pratt, who was then working as a demonstrator in the Department of Psychology, to join Victoria College's Department of English, thus re-initiating a teaching career that lasted until 1953. As a professor, Pratt published a number of articles, reviews, and introductions (including those to four Shakespeare plays), and edited Thomas Hardy's *Under the greenwood tree* (1937). Notes and commentaries by, and CBC interviews with, Pratt are available in *E.J. Pratt: On his life and poetry* (1983), and his selected prose, including texts of academic lectures, in *Pursuits amateur and academic* (1995), both edited by Susan Gingell.

As editor of *Canadian Poetry Magazine* (1936-43), Pratt fostered the growth of many younger poets. His honours included election to the Royal Society of Canada (1930), the Lorne PIERCE Medal (1940), being made Commander of the Order of St Michael and St George (1946), the Canada Council Medal (1961), and an LL.D from the University of Toronto (1961).

Pratt's first collection, *Newfoundland verse* (1923), is frequently archaic in diction, and reflects a pietistic and sometimes preciously lyrical sensibility of late-Romantic derivation, characteristics that may account for Pratt's reprinting less than half these poems in his *Collected poems* (1958). The most genuine feeling is expressed in humorous and sympathetic portraits of Newfoundland characters, and in the creation of an elegiac mood in poems concerning sea tragedies or Great War losses. The sea, which on the one hand provides 'the bread of life' and on the other represents 'the waters of death' ('Newfoundland'), is a central element as setting, subject, and creator of mood. The book contains 'A fragment from a story', the only part of Pratt's verse-drama 'Clay' to be published in his lifetime, and the conclusion to the blank-verse narrative *Rachel: a sea-story of Newfoundland in verse* (1917), which had earlier been privately printed. The section in *Newfoundland verse* picks up the story of Rachel after she has already been widowed by the sea, and relates her decline into madness and death when the sea also claims her only son. A better early indicator of Pratt's narrative skill is 'The ice-floes', a swift-paced account of a sealing disaster.

The witches' brew (1925) is a fanciful concoction of learning and nonsense, satire and celebration. Highly allusive in mythic structure and motif, it is written in the octosyllabic line that became the standard for Pratt's comedic poems. His zest for compiling humorous catalogues, his penchant for epic scale, and his interests in evolution and atavism clearly emerge for the first time. The three sea-witches' experiment to discover the effect of alcohol on fish may have been Pratt's high-spirited response to Prohibition; but the poem is really stolen by Tom, the Sea-Cat from Zanzibar, who serves as bouncer for the underwater bacchanal until Satan, scenting a way to expand his dominion into the heretofore amoral ocean, extends the experiment to Tom. Giving free rein to the primitive tendencies released by the brew, this evolutionary freak indulges in an orgy of destruction and is last seen headed for the Irish Sea, a destination no doubt chosen for Ireland's association with strong drink and pugnacious character.

In *Titans: two poems* (1926) Pratt achieves a fluid, engaging, and swiftly paced style by varying rhyme scheme, syllabic quantity, and stress patterns, and by frequently using enjambed lines. 'The cachalot' has as its epic hero a sperm whale whose dimensions are exaggerated in mock-heroic style. After a vividly described victory over a kraken, the cachalot engages in a mutually destructive battle with whalers. 'The great feud: a dream of a Pliocene Armageddon' examines the growth of racial hatred and wartime behaviour in its pictures of civil war between land and sea creatures that in the evolutionary process have only just been distinguished as species. An anachronistic *Tyrannosaurus rex* on the trailing edge of that process, and a female anthropoidal ape on the leading edge, indicate the poem's blend of the fantastic and the allegorical. The tiny-brained embattled dinosaur represents unreasoning violence that ends in self-destruction, but the ape uses her emergent intellectual powers to propagandize her forces. The poem's commentary on humanity's animal instincts is capped by the implication that the militaristic ape and her brood are the sole survivors of the volcanic eruption that ends the war.

The iron door: an ode (1927), written to commemorate Pratt's mother's death, gives voice to several positions on death and the after-life. It ends with an affirmation of faith that is nonetheless ambivalent because the narrator is left dazzled to the point of blindness outside the door between the realms of life and death when the door opens to admit the dead. The theme of *The Roosevelt and the Antinoe* (1930) is the collective self-sacrificing heroism of sailors pitting themselves against the destructive powers of nature, and facing massive odds to rescue the crew of a ship sinking in a mid-Atlantic storm. Pratt here returns to the five-beat line that became standard for his extended treatments of serious subjects. This narrative was republished, with Pratt's notes and other poems, in *Verses of the sea* (1930); this verse-and-notes format was also used in *Ten selected poems* (1947) and in the anthology *Heroic tales in verse* (1941), a book Pratt edited and prefaced.

The nature pieces in *Many moods* (1932) seem to be a thematic throwback, though some reflect a precise image-making power, and the often humorous vignettes of human character appear slight after the charting of new thematic territory in, and the stylistic vigour of, the narratives. Meditations on aging and death are numerous, but the emergence of a socially conscious voice strikes a new note. Pratt seeks antidotes to human misery in sacrifice or celebration. In a cosmic equivalent to 'The witches' brew' and a reflection of Pratt's expansive public personality, 'The depression ends' stages a banquet for all the world's unfortunates.

Irony is the structural principle on which *The Titanic* (1935) is built. The iceberg that embodies nature's Janus-faces of beauty and destructive power remains 'the master of the longitudes' when humans' hubris in thinking they have built an unsinkable ship, combined with an ironic conjunction of circumstances, results in a collision of the forces of people and nature. Sombre intimations of war and failures of communication are the focus of *The fable of the goats and other poems* (1932), which indirectly treats humans' bellicose behaviour in a number of animal allegories, the best of which are 'Silences' and 'The prize cat'. Though Pratt won a Governor General's Award for this volume, he chose to omit the title-poem from his *Collected poems* (1958), perhaps because the pacifist conclusion to the territorial disputes between warring tribes of goats proved so futile a model for human behaviour.

Of all the volumes published during the war years *Brébeuf and his brethren* (1940), for which Pratt won his second Governor General's Award, is least overtly connected to the war. Pratt's research-oriented methodology is made clear in the precise diction and detailed, documentary-style recounting of events and observation in this, his first attempt to write a national epic; but in his ethnocentrism Pratt presents the Jesuit priests as an enclave of civilization beleaguered by savages. *Dunkirk* (1941) and many of the poems of *Still life and other verse* (1943) are more immediately topical, picturing both the heroism and the atavism of which people are capable, though the propagandistic cast of many of these poems should be recognized, for heroism seems the exclusive property of the Allies, and atavism characteristic solely of the Axis forces. *They are returning* (1945) is an occasional piece that strains to give the feats of Canadian veterans classical epic stature; but *Behind the log* (1947) successfully captures the drama of individuals' wartime experiences by chronicling the hounding of an Atlantic convoy by U-boats.

Pratt's concerns with communication and bringing alive Canadian history culminated in his third Governor General's Award-winning volume, *Towards the last spike: a verse panorama of the struggle to build the first Canadian transcontinental from the time of the proposed terms of union with British Columbia [1870] to the hammering of the last spike in the Eagle Pass [1885]* (1952). Presenting an anglo/central-Canadian perspective, the poem interweaves the political battles between Sir John A. Macdonald and Edward Blake with the labourers' physical battles against mountains, mud, and the Laurentian Shield. In a metaphorical method typical of his style, Pratt characterizes the Shield as a prehistoric lizard rudely aroused from its sleep by the railroad builders' dynamite.

The collected poems of E.J. Pratt (1958) reprinted all but two poems in *Collected poems* (1944), while adding five earlier poems and a handful of previously unpublished ones. The 1958 edition serves as a map of the movement of Canadian poetry from its colonial phase towards its becoming an identifiably independent national literature. A two-part scholarly edition, *E.J. Pratt: complete poems* (1989), edited by Sandra Djwa and Gordon Moyles, includes appendices of miscellaneous poems, previously unpublished verse drama and poetry, and a descriptive bibliography by Lila Laakso.

Pratt's reputation as a major Canadian poet rests largely on his often powerfully evocative narrative poems, many of which show him as a mythologizer of the Canadian male experience; but a number of shorter philosophical works also command recognition. 'From stone to steel' asserts the necessity for redemptive suffering arising from the failure of humanity's spiritual evolution to keep pace without physical evolution and cultural achievements; 'Come away, death' is a complexly allusive account of the way the once-articulate and ceremonial human response to death was rendered inarticulate by the primitive violence of a sophisticated bomb; and 'The truant' dramatically presents a confrontation in a thoroughly patriarchal cosmos between the fiercely independent 'little genus homo' and a totalitarian mechanistic power, 'the great Panjandrum'. Pratt's choices of forms and metrics were conservative for his time; but his diction was experimental, reflecting in its specificity and its frequent technicality both his belief in the poetic power of the accurate and concrete that led him into assiduous research processes, and his view that one of the poet's tasks is to bridge the gap between the two branches of human pursuit: the scientific and artistic.

Pratt has on the whole been well served by those who have introduced collections and selections of his verse: William Rose Benét, the American edition of *Collected poems* (1945; Canadian edn, 1944); Northrop FRYE, *Collected poems* (1958); D.G. Pitt, *Here the tides flow* (1962); Peter Buitenhuis, *Selected poems of E.J. Pratt* (1968); and Djwa and Moyles, *Complete poems* (1989). Pitt's collection of early reviews and essays in *E.J. Pratt* (1969) illustrates how much the shadow of the poet's personality lay across early attempt to delineate his world view, an on-going preoccupation in Pratt criticism. This is not a flaw, however, in Sandra Djwa's *E.J. Pratt: the evolutionary vision* (1974), which fixes the intellectual background of Pratt's writing, or in Frank DAVEY's two hostile but carefully argued articles: 'E.J. Pratt: apostle of corporate man' (*CANADIAN LITERATURE*, 43) and 'E.J. Pratt: rationalist technician' (*Canadian literature*, 61). The most recent collective reappraisal of Pratt's life and work is *The E.J. Pratt symposium* (1977), edited by Glen Clever. Other monograph studies of note are Henry Wells and Carl KLINCK, *Edwin J. Pratt: the man and his poetry* (1947); John SUTHERLAND, *The poetry of E.J. Pratt: a new interpretation* (1956); Milton Wilson, *E.J. Pratt*

(1969); and Susan Gingell, *E.J. Pratt* (1982). See also David G. Pitt's *E.J. Pratt: The truant years 1882-1927* (1984) and *E.J. Pratt: The master years 1927-1964* (1987). SUSAN GINGELL

Préfontaine, Yves (b. 1937). Born in Montreal, he studied anthropology and sociology in Montreal and Paris. He was a founder of Editions de l'Hexagone in 1953; was briefly editor-in-chief of *LIBERTÉ* in 1962; and has been a radio broadcaster. In 1968 he received the Prix France-Canada and the Prix des Concours Littéraires du Québec for his poetry collection *Pays sans parole* (1961). Since 1978 he has been a senior Quebec civil servant.

His very personal poetry is composed of long, luxuriant lines that occasionally betray a surrealist imagination. Préfontaine tends to overindulge in neologisms and phonic games, but his poems try to breathe life into the elements—the vast stretches of the Far North, the cosmos, the seasons—and may be called transitive, in that they frequently involve a speaker and interlocutors. In *Boréal* (1957) and *Les temples effondrés* (1957), collections of tumultuous poems whose vigorous expression amounts almost to a desperate cry, Préfontaine speaks of tackling, mastering, and inhabiting the vast, glacial aridity of the far North, just as the poet must tackle life and the word. (A prose collection, *L'antre du poème*, 1960, calls for a new creative orientation that would give 'birth to the cry of freedom'.) The more sober tone of *À l'orée des travaux* (1970), *Débâcle* (1970), and *Pays sans parole* (1967) shows Préfontaine striving to create poetic space for Quebec, seeking through his words to free it from its former silence and give form to the 'snowy void'. In the foreword to the last collection, he affirms the North-Americanness of the Québécois, their 'francophone way of being American', and stresses the inherent danger of conformity in the nationalist theme favoured by so many Quebec poets. His poems have a strong emotional charge, stemming from the force of the words and their arrangement, the remonstrances, repetitions, and incantations addressed to a people 'shivering under a frost of words', whom he tries to warm with his speech, hoping to raise a birth-cry. *Nuaison* (1982), elegantly wrought, brings together poems written between 1964 and 1970. Slightly formalist, it marks the end of a general fervour and shows a new awareness of the limitations and fragility of disappointed hopes. Now that skepticism has replaced the passion of the Hexagone years, Préfontaine's poetic voice has become hushed.

Le désert maintenant (1987) continues to explore issues of language and political engagement and to focus on the land as a site of change. Though coloured by a sense of the linguistic and personal powerlessness evident in *Nuaison*, its lyrical poems and prose-poems express a lingering hope for social renewal among the apathetic Québécois. The speaker locates the roots of a fertile language, which could give shape to Quebec's experience, in the primitive, vital earth. The flowing rhythm of the long lines and internal rhythms underscore the potential for beauty and self-expression, even when the speaker's passionate call for awareness dissolves into bitter anger. With a piano accompaniment of his own composition and execution, Préfontaine offers a reading of the poems on audio cassette (*Le désert maintenant*, 1987). Judith Cowan's translation of the poems, *This desert now* (1993), is the first translation of Préfontaine's work in book form.

Parole tenue: poèmes 1954-1985 (1990) brings together all of Préfontaine's previously published poetry. Also included is a group of previously unpublished poems written in the 1950s: entitled 'Les épousailles', this intense poetry explores human destruction and human potential *vis-à-vis* a dynamic universe. More vehement in tone and experimental in style than *Le désert maintenant*, 'Les épousailles' reflects all the passion and the cosmic consciousness of an earlier Préfontaine. Yet the poems' especially rich vocabulary (geological terms, neologisms, archaic diction) and striking imagery impart energy and vision to *Parole tenue*, reflecting language's ongoing ability to evoke alternative realms of thought.

See Axel Maugey, 'Yves Préfontaine', in *Poésie et société au Québec 1937-1970* (1972); and Gilles MARCOTTE, 'Yves Préfontaine', in *Le temps des poètes* (1969); Susy Turcotte, 'Entre vacarme et murmure', *Nuit blanche* 44 (1991); André Marquis, 'L'épouvante ravie', *Lettres québécoises* 62 (1991); and François Dumont, 'Treading across chaos', *Ellipse* 52 (1994).

MAROUSSIA AHMED/ANNIKA HANNAN

Press Porcépic. It was founded by Dave GODFREY with Tim Inkster in 1972 in an old house in Erin, Ontario, not far from Toronto. Godfrey had left the House of ANANSI to form New Press with two partners; and then, out of a small but exceptional magazine, *Porcépic* ('porcupine' in *JOUAL*), created his third company, Press Porcépic. (In 1974 Inkster took one 'quill' from the creature that served as the company logo and renamed his company The PORCUPINE'S QUILL.)

Godfrey had seen the potential of the new small offset-printing technology that made book production fast and economical. Within five years Porcépic was publishing up to seventeen titles a year, with an emphasis on young and experimental writers; but it also published Dorothy LIVESAY's poetry and her *Right hand left hand: a true life of the thirties* (1977), as well as poetry collections by Eli MANDEL, Joe ROSENBLATT, P.K. PAGE, Jane URQUHART, and Marilyn BOWERING. Among the fiction published by Porcépic was Godfrey's *The new ancestors* (1970), which won a Governor General's Award, and *Dark must yield* (1978), a collection of fifteen stories; Kristjana GUNNARS' *The axe's edge* (1983); and the first English translation of Louky BERSIANIK's *L'EUGUÉLIONNE*.

Press Porcépic opened editorial offices in Victoria, British Columbia, when Godfrey moved there in 1976. In 1980 Porcépic formed a division called Softwoods to become the first in Canada to publish computer titles and computer-assisted learning software. By 1985 the company had 25 employees and annual software sales of over $1 million, and had developed a database for the Greater Victoria Public Library. Considered a world leader in the field of artificial intelligence, the company changed its name in 1987 to Porcépic Books, and in 1991 to Beach Holme Publishers, with a new location in Vancouver. GEOFF HANCOCK

Preview (1942-5). This Montreal-based periodical, originally intended as a literary letter in which contributors would 'preview' or try out their work, was first published in Mar. 1942. Its editorial board was made up of F.R. SCOTT, Margaret Day, Bruce Ruddick, Neufville Shaw, and Patrick ANDERSON, who was its driving spirit and most influential editor. P.K. PAGE joined the board in Issue 2 (Apr. 1942) and A.M. KLEIN in Issue 19 (Mar. 1944), his work having appeared since Issue 5 (July 1942) and Day and Shaw having already resigned as editors. Planned as a monthly, but appearing irregularly over 23 issues until early 1945, *Preview* averaged 9-to-13 mimeographed pages and had a circulation of approximately 125. It featured poetry, short stories, frequently leftist essays, and became known for the wit, technical sophistication, and cosmopolitan interests of its talented and socially concerned editors. In Dec. 1945 it merged with *FIRST STATEMENT* to form *NORTHERN REVIEW*. The legendary rivalry between *Preview* and *First Statement* has long been exaggerated. See Patrick Anderson, 'A poet past and future' (*CANADIAN LITERATURE* 56, Summer 1973), and 'Four of the Preview editors: a discussion' (*Canadian Poetry* 4, Spring/Summer 1979). See also Ken Norris, *The little magazine in Canada 1925-80* (1984).

DAVID O'ROURKE

Prewett, Frank (1893-1962). He was born on his maternal grandfather's pioneer farm at Kenilworth, near Mount Forest, Ontario, and raised in Toronto. He attended Parkdale Collegiate and University College, University of Toronto, before enlisting in 1915 in the Third Contingent of the Canadian Expeditionary Force in a unit sponsored by the T. Eaton Company of Toronto, the Eaton Machine Gun Battery. On his arrival in England he was promoted to Lieutenant in the Royal Artillery and was severely wounded and shell-shocked in 1918. During his convalescence at a Scottish hospital, Lennels, and under the care of anthropologist/psychologist W.H.R. Rivers, Prewett met Siegfried Sassoon, who was impressed by the fact that Prewett wrote poetry and claimed to have Native blood. (The claim was untrue.)

Under the tutelage and guidance of Sassoon, who appears to have been seeking a surrogate for Wilfred Owen, who had returned to action in France, Prewett was introduced to the British literati of the period and became an instant celebrity. Given his own room at Lady Ottoline Morrell's country house, Garsington, Prewett became friendly with D.H. Lawrence, T.S. Eliot, Ezra Pound, Aldous Huxley, Robert Graves, Edmund Blunden, E.M. Forster, Virginia Woolf, and the artists Dorothy Brett and Mark Gertler. Woolf, Sassoon, Morrell and others had a nickname for Prewett: 'Toronto'.

Virginia Woolf herself handset Prewett's first publication, a collection of twenty-two poems that appeared as Hogarth Pamphlet Number 17, *Poems* (1920), which included some of Prewett's finest 'trench verses', notably 'Voices of women', 'The Somme Valley, 1917', and 'The card game', interspersed with many bucolic Georgian lyrics about pastoral landscapes and pleasant nature—a reaction to the savagery of war that had left him neurasthenic. Following on the success of the pamphlet, Edward Marsh chose eight of Prewett's poems for inclusion in *Georgian poetry 1920-1922*—the only Canadian included in both the anthology and the movement. For his role in Georgianism, Prewett stands as the 'missing link' in Canadian verse between the CONFERERATION POETS and the early Modernism of the MONTREAL GROUP. Prewett was ordered home from England in 1920 by the Canadian Army after suffering from a suspected case of consumption. He hoped to establish a literary career in Canada but found the cultural environment dry and stilted. To ease his neurasthenia, he studied organ with composer Healy Willan and escorted Siegfried Sassoon around Toronto during a tour that Sassoon records in *Siegfried's journey* (1945). By 1921 Prewett had returned to England to complete his undergraduate studies at Christchurch, Oxford (the University of Toronto never having conferred his B.A., breaking the promise that servicemen would be granted their degrees upon enlistment).

Poems was followed by *The rural scene* (1922), in which Prewett continued in the tightly crafted lyrical style of the Georgian poetic. To the nature poems he added a number of tender and memorable love lyrics. By 1926 Prewett had fallen out with the Garsington circle and Georgianism was no longer fashionable. He attempted an experimental farm near Oxford with economist A.A. Carr Saunders and ecologist Charles Elton, failed at that, and took a teaching position at the Agricultural Economics Institute, Oxford, where he remained until the 1930s. In the early thirties he became a broadcaster on the BBC, devised the milk marketing system for England, edited *The Farmer's Weekly* for Lord Beaverbrook, and wrote an unsuccessful novel about a nineteenth-century peasants' rebellion in England, *The Chazzey tragedy* (1933). (Even his own brother-in-law, the Toronto journalist Gordon Sinclair, gave the book a poor review.) During the Second World War, Prewett was dismissed from the army for frail nerves (he was guarding an amunition depot), joined the Royal Air Force, and became Food Services and Supplies Advisor to Mountbatten in the South East Asian Command in Ceylon.

Prewett's later life combined poverty and obscurity. His three 1954 BBC radio broadcasts, 'Farm life in Ontario fifty years ago', recalled his early days on his grandfather's farm at Kenilworth. He died in Scotland and was buried in Inverness. Robert Graves assembled the posthumously published, *The collected poems of Frank Prewett* (1964), but the range of Prewett's talents was not revealed until the discovery by Bruce Meyer of Prewett's unpublished poems in the archives of the University of Texas, and the resulting publication of *The selected poems of Frank Prewett* (1987) edited by Meyer and Barry CALLAGHAN. See Bruce Meyer, *Frank Prewett* (1991), Profiles in Canadian Literature.

BRUCE MEYER

Priest, Robert (b. 1951). Born at Walton-on-Thames, England, he was brought to Toronto at the age of four. After briefly studying mathematics at the University of Waterloo, Priest has devoted himself to writing, composing, and performing. Seven books of his lively, amusing, and inventive poems have been published, beginning with *The visible man* (1979) and including *Scream blue living: new and selected poems* (1992). *Resurrection in the cartoon* (1997) consists of blackly humorous prose poems, ironic political poems, and mystical and transcendent meditations. An accomplished children's entertainer, he has published six books for youngsters, including *A terrible case of the stars* (1994). He performs as a rock musician, accompanied by his band Great Big Face, and has recorded LPs, CDs, and video singles. Among his familiar rock compositions are 'Congo Toronto' (1986) and 'Broken Star' (1987). COACH HOUSE PRESS released his audio tape *Rotweiller pacifist* (1990), which offers a selection of both poems and songs. For Alannah Myles he wrote the lyrics of the award-winning hit 'Song Instead of a Kiss' (1992). His CD *The Great Big Face* (1997) features 'poems, songs, sayings, chants, and iterations'. In 1992 Young People's Theatre, Toronto, produced his play *Knights of the endless day*, which was published the following year in the form of a novel. One reviewer called the work of this unique rock poet 'a truly invigorating combination of rants, raves, and reveries'.

JOHN ROBERT COLOMBO

Prochain épisode (1965). This first novel by Hubert AQUIN—written during a four-month stay in the Albert Prévost Psychiatric Institute, Montreal, where the author was being held while awaiting trial for possession of a stolen firearm—was hailed on publication as the great novel of Quebec's revolutionary period. In fact it is about paralysis, and the impossibility of revolution, as much as it is about revolution. Written in a style that alternates between a lyricism inspired by the idea of revolution and a prose corresponding to Quebec's present, it recounts the attempt of an imprisoned separatist to distract himself from reality, and to rediscover his revolutionary fervour, by writing a novel. The hero of the fictional novel—a revolutionary Quebec separatist in Switzerland—after receiving instructions about the enemy he is to kill, agrees to rejoin his lover and revolutionary comrade K. (clearly a symbol of Quebec) twenty-four hours later in Lausanne. But as the plot unfolds, contradictions emerge: the hero reveals himself as an artist rather than a man of action, and in his 'infinite hesitation' he becomes a 'fractured symbol of the revolution in Quebec'. His enemy, H. de Heutz—in his triple identity of banker, historian, and lonely aristocrat—emerges as the double or enemy-brother of the hero, the other half of the French-Canadian psyche associated with an English Canada both hated and loved. Their confrontation, in a magnificent scene in which the mythical motif of a castle suggests both an eternal embrace of opposites and the historical ambiguities of Canada's two nations, leads to stasis. In the perfection of its moving and complex structure, *Prochain épisode* transcends the historical movement that gave it birth while remaining, as the narrator writes, clearly indissociable from that moment. It speaks equally powerfully of despair, and of the unceasing hope that produces metamorphosis and revolution.

An English translation by Penny Williams, with the same title, was published in 1967 (NCL, 1973). PATRICIA SMART

Proulx, Monique (b. 1952). Born in Quebec City, she now lives in Montreal and has written for radio, television, and film. Her four books of fiction—two novels and two short-story collections—have won a number of major literary awards, including the Prix Adrienne-Choquette, the Grand Prix du *Journal de Montréal*, the Prix Québec-Paris, and the Grand Prix des libraires.

Among the hallmarks of Proulx's fiction are a taste for offbeat wordplay, particularly puns, neologisms and hyperbole, a love of irony and parody, and a wild coasting between humour and deep sadness, even despair. In fifteen short stories, each of which features either a Benoît or a Françoise at varying ages, *Sans coeur et sans reproche* (1983) takes its characters from conception (described as exploding out of a black hole in the universe) to death (a blissful return to the Milky Way), with love and friendship, work and sorrow and betrayal, in between.

Le sexe des étoiles (1987)—translated by Matt COHEN as *Sex of the stars* (1996)—is an ingenious romp of a novel that tackles, with grace and humour, the loaded question of gender identity in the late twentieth century. At the heart of the novel is Marie-Pierre Deslauriers, previously Pierre-Henri, a world-famous scientist who was a Nobel Prize candidate shortly before he underwent the first of a series of operations to turn himself into the woman he always knew he was. All the other major characters are obsessed with Marie-Pierre: her (or his?) daughter Camille, who is in love with the stars and the best-looking boy in her class; Gaby, a researcher Marie-Pierre lives with, and Dominique Larue, an impotent writer who has produced nothing for twelve years and is convinced that Marie-Pierre can cure both ailments. If having a man's body does not necessarily make one a man, as Marie-Pierre claims, what does it mean to be a man or a woman? Does sexual difference lie in the body, in the brain cells, or in the depths of the soul? Through a series of improbable coincidences, *Le sexe des étoiles* takes a long, steady look at the strange and often contradictory beliefs we cherish about masculinity and feminity. The fact that Dominique Larue's new novel ends with the same lines as Proulx's ingeniously implies that *Le sexe des étoiles* was written by both a man and a woman; the sex of the novelist is therefore also open to debate. Proulx wrote the screenplay for Paule Baillargeon's 1993 film based on the novel.

In her second novel, *Homme invisible à la fenêtre* (1993)—translated by Matt Cohen as *Invisible man at the window* (1994)—which is both more ambitious and more complex than *Le sexe des étoiles*, Proulx creates a character loosely based on a real person, the handicapped Montreal painter Yves Bussières, to whom the novel is dedicated. Since the 'Big Bang', the car accident that left him unable to move his lower limbs, Max has become obsessed with painting the infinite variety of the human body. The book is structured as a series of word portraits of the lost souls Max attracts: the actress Maggie, so beautiful she hates and envies her own smiling image on the movie screen; Julius Einhorne, a dubious—and obese—art collector in love with a very young girl; Julienne, Max's possessive mother; Lady, his lost love; and the nihilistic painter Gerald Mortimer, whose selfless devotion to Max is not accounted for until the novel's harrowing final pages. Using irony and self-mockery to keep his grief at bay, but full of clear-eyed, sometimes cruel, compassion for his fellow human beings, Max defines survival as forgetting what you once were rather than accepting what you have become.

Les aurores montréales (1996) is a series of stories and sketches about Montreal. The emphasis is on contrasts within the city—between English and French, rich and poor, beauty and ugliness—and on varying points of view: those of children, immigrants, lovers, vagrants, cleaning women, even a man who is writing a screen-play about a transsexual. This collection has been hailed by critics as one of the recent works of Québécois fiction that best sum up the 'soul' of Montreal—a world within a world in contemporary Quebec culture, deeply, viscerally French, yet increasingly open to other cultures and voices.

LORI SAINT-MARTIN

Provincial: or Halifax Monthly Magazine, The. Published in Halifax between Jan. 1852 and Dec. 1853, it was the most prominent mid-century literary journal in Maritime Canada. A monthly printed by James Barnes and Son and edited by Mary Jane KATZMANN, each of its 24 issues ran to forty or more pages. Katzmann strove to make it a vehicle for local intellectual and literary development and was successful in having the bulk of each issue locally written. There was a reasonably wide range of topics in the general articles, but her interests clearly lay in literature and history. Three series on the early history of Nova Scotia were published, as well as occasional biographies of noted Nova Scotians, such as Samuel Cunard and Herbert Huntington. She also published the first significant study of local verse in a series entitled 'Half hours with our poets', and frequently reviewed books by local authors. At the same time Katzmann tried to avoid being overly parochial. Through reviews and articles on the literary and intellectual scene in Britain and the United States, she projected a sense of cultural interchange in the North Atlantic English-speaking communities. A significant portion of each issue was filled with poetry—sentimental and moralistic, competent but not brilliant—and fiction by local writers. Mary Jane Katzmann herself contributed poetry and articles, as did Clotilda Jennings and Mary Eliza HERBERT, William T. Wishart, M.B. DesBrisay, John Sparrow THOMPSON, and Silas T. Rand. Many of the items, however, were published anonymously.

TOM VINCENT

'Psalm of Montreal, A'. See 'O God! O Montreal!'.

Pugsley, Alex. See NOVELS IN ENGLISH 1983 TO 1996: OTHER NOVELS 3.

Purdy, Al (b. 1918). Alfred Wellington Purdy (who, before settling on 'Al Purdy', signed his poems 'Alfred W. Purdy' and 'A.W. Purdy') was born in Wooler, Ontario, of what he has described as 'degenerate Loyalist stock'. He spent most of his childhood in nearby Trenton and was educated at Albert College, Belleville. During the 1930s Purdy hitched rides on freight trains to Vancouver, where he worked for several years in a mattress factory and similar establishments. In the Second World War he served in the Royal Canadian Air Force, mostly at the remote base of Woodcock on the Skeena River in northern British Columbia. Having no university training (though his wide reading eventually turned him into a remarkably erudite man), he worked at casual and manual jobs while struggling to find time to write, and he sometimes lived in poverty well into his forties. The interaction, in his writing, of literary ambitions and working-class experience has produced an anecdotal and powerfully direct poetry (visible, for example, in the title poem of *Piling blood*, 1984).

Purdy has written poems restlessly and copiously in a career that now spans more than fifty years. The publication in 1944 of his first book, *The enchanted echo*, showed the young Purdy limited by formal preoccupations, his poetry conservatively traditional and largely derivative (in part of the Canadian Romanticism of ROBERTS and CARMAN). When he published his much superior fourth volume of poems in 1959, his choice of title, *The crafte so long to lerne* (the phrase is borrowed from Chaucer), wryly celebrated his sense that he had needed to serve a long apprenticeship. By steeping himself in the poetry of writers such as D.H. Lawrence and William Carlos Williams on the one hand, and W.H. Auden and Dylan Thomas on the other—as well as by learning from the Canadian poets PRATT, BIRNEY, LAYTON, and ACORN—he had learned how to sound a distinctive contemporary note

Purdy feels he fully achieved his own voice with the publication of *Poems for all the Annettes* (1962) and *The Cariboo horses* (1965). The latter book in particular shows him writing at the top of his form, and it brought him both a Governor General's Award and a broad readership. In these and the books that followed, he developed a long-lined and colloquially free poetry that allowed him to be intellectually direct without sacrificing powerful statement and evocative poetic imagery, and made him perhaps the foremost influence on the generation of Canadian poets who came after him. Drawing freely on the miscellaneous and extensive knowledge accumulated by his generalizing and autodidactic mind, Purdy has created a poetry that is densely allusive but never obscure.

Purdy has travelled widely in Canada and abroad, gaining experiences that recognizably shaped both the content and the mood of a great deal of his poetry. Some of his strongest poems, such as 'Shoeshine boys on the

Avenida Juarez' (in *Wild grape wine*, 1968), emerge directly out of these journeys, and his most unified book of poetry, *North of summer: poems from Baffin Island* (1967), is virtually a travel-book in verse. Nevertheless, the heart of Purdy's world remains the place that is named in so many of his poems, the symbolic omphalos of his imaginative world: Roblin Lake, deep in Loyalist country near Ameliasburg, Ontario. A powerful sense of his local area informs most of the poems in *Wild grape wine*, such as 'Roblin's Mills (II)' and 'Wilderness Gothic', which have become classics in their own time. *In search of Owen Roblin* (1974) assembles a number of his poems of local history into a memorial cycle, one that powerfully evokes Canada as an old country already resonant with its own echoes. His attraction to the past has also made the elegy one of his most effective forms, whether it is a commemoration of a member of his own family ('Elegy for a grandfather'—which he first published in *Emu, remember*, 1956, and revised several times over the next thirty years), of a public figure ('For Robert Kennedy', in *Sex & death*, 1973), of his home territory ('The country north of Belleville', in *The Cariboo horses*), or of a whole race ('Lament for the Dorsets' in *Wild grape wine*—one of his most affecting poems).

Purdy has created a powerful and consistent persona in the body of his poems: while the speaker there may be capable of jokiness and broad comedy (see 'Birdwatching at the equator' in *The stone bird*, 1981; or 'Concerning Ms. Atwood' in *Naked with summer in your mouth*, 1994), he is, perhaps as a result of his pervasive self-irony, also able to express deeply felt emotion in a way that allows him to explore what might otherwise seem outworn sentimentality ('Winter at Roblin Lake') and patriotism (as in the title poem of *A handful of earth*, 1977), or to register direct and intense responses to the beauty of nature ('Late rising at Roblin Lake', in *The Cariboo horses*). If in some of his late work—he published four books of new poems in the 1980s and 1990s—he also strikes a loftier or more serious tone than in the work of his middle period, these later poems come across as shaped by a mature and hard-earned sense of perspective gained by a lifetime of poetic engagement with the world.

Over the years Purdy has published a number of books of selected poems (frequently revising earlier poems for their new appearance). *Being alive: poems 1958-78* (1978) shows his immense range and includes most of his best poems to that point. The shape of his entire career is visible in the 262 poems found in *The collected poems of Al Purdy* (1986), edited by Russell Brown—though its more than 350 pages comprise less that half Purdy's published work and about a quarter of the more than a thousand poems he estimates having written. Reading through this volume, which won a Governor-General's Award, one is impressed by the steady strengthening of quality as well as by his enormous productivity: it is a notable monument to a life dedicated to the making and reading of poems.

As one of the most peripatetic of Canadian poets, Purdy, from the 1960s forward, sometimes made several circuits a year to give readings from his poetry, which has a powerful and immediate appeal to the ear. Although his public appearances are now rare, a cassette of Purdy reading selections from *The collected poems* provides a permanent record of his engagingly idiosyncratic delivery.

From the mid-1960s Purdy was able to earn a full-time living as a freelance writer and at related tasks, such as lecturing, poetry reading, and taking positions as writer-in-residence at various universities. He worked in virtually every form of writing, and has written radio and television plays and one novel, *A splinter in the heart* (1990), about the 1918 explosion of the British Chemical plant in Trenton. A representative gathering of his critical essays, book reviews (written chiefly for *CANADIAN LITERATURE*), travel pieces, and anecdotal portraits of people and places may be found in *Starting from Ameliasburgh: the collected prose of Al Purdy* (1995), edited by Sam Solecki. Although the childhood memoir published as *Morning and it's summer* (1983) is reprinted and supplemented with other prose recollections (some previously published) in *Reaching for the Beaufort Sea: an autobiography* (1993), a stronger sense of Purdy the man comes across in his three volumes of published letters: *The Bukowski/Purdy letters 1964-1974* (1983) edited by Seamus Cooney; *The Purdy-Woodcock letters: selected correspondence 1964-1984* (1988) edited by George Galt; and, especially, *Margaret Laurence-Al Purdy: a friendship in letters* (1993) edited by John Lennox.

Purdy has edited three anthologies of verse: *Fifteen winds* (1969), *Storm warning* (1971), and *Storm warning II* (1976), which helped give a showcase to younger poets. He selected and edited the poems in *I've tasted my blood* (1969), a book by Milton ACORN, an important early influence, whose difficult friendship he dramatized in the poem 'House guest'. He also edited *Wood Mountain poems* (1976), the book that helped call attention to the talent of

Andrew SUKNASKI. A polemical anthology edited in 1968, *The new Romans*, with its critiques of the USA, is an expression of the strong cultural nationalism of that period.

Some of the best criticism of his work has come from other poets, including an important early discussion in *Al Purdy* (1970), a small book by George BOWERING; and essays by Dennis LEE, who gives a fine account of Purdy's emergence as a major figure in his Afterword to *The collected poems*. Louis K. MacKendrick's *Al Purdy* (1990), in the valuable multi-volume series Canadian Writers and Their Works (edited by Robert Lecker, Jack David, and Ellen Quigley), provides a balanced overview. George WOODCOCK's discussion, 'On the poetry of Al Purdy', can be found in his *World of Canadian writing* (1980). *Essays on Canadian Writing* no. 49 (Summer 1993), a special issue edited by MacKendrick, brings together new critical essays on Purdy by Russell Brown, Peter Stevens, Lorraine York, Sam Solecki, Rosemary SULLIVAN, and W.J. Keith, along with appreciations, an interview, and poetry and prose by Purdy himself.

RUSSELL BROWN/GEORGE WOODCOCK

Q

Quarrington, Paul (b. 1953). Born in Toronto, he attended the University of Toronto for one year in 1972. His early career was as a musician; he played bass with the rock band Joe Hall and the Continental Drift and co-produced and recorded an album, *Quarrington/Worthy* (1978), which featured a number one hit single.

Quarrington's novels are distinguished by their masterful handling of eccentric characterization and comic situations. His protagonists, fallen male figures drifting in the present but haunted by their past, must undergo trial and suffering in order to redeem their lives. His uneven first book, *The service* (1978), introduces this recurring theme in its farcical treatment of a hapless man's struggle to understand his life. The mythic quest for meaning and redemption is also evident in *Home game* (1983), which revolves around a baseball game played between circus performers and religious fundamentalists, and in *Logan in overtime* (1990), about a down-and-out former National Hockey League goaltender in an industrial hockey league who finds himself playing in the longest overtime game in the history of hockey. In *The life of hope* (1985) the narrator flees his problems in the city to Hope, Ontario, where he researches the Utopian sect that founded the town in the nineteenth century.

Much of Quarrington's writing employs a variety of postmodernist narrative techniques that self-consciously foreground the act of writing and subvert traditional assumptions about narrative coherence and unity. He dispenses with disruptive intrusions in his finest works, *King Leary* (1987), winner of the Stephen Leacock Award for Humour, and *Whale music* (1989), winner of a Governor General's Award. Both novels feature first-person interior monologues and flashbacks, an ideal narrative medium for Quarrington's linguistic dexterity and perfectly suited to his continued interest in the mind's intermingling of past and present.

In *King Leary*, an ageing hockey legend, Percival Leary (the name suggesting the fisher-king myth), recalls his life and confronts the consequences of his previous actions, and *Whale music* both examines and parodies the world of rock music through the muddled brain of its drug-dependent narrator, Des Howell. Like Leary, Howell comes to understand how his earlier lack of compassion colours his present; his musical composition for whales is a redemptive act of reconciliation with his dead brother. Quarrington satirizes the false glamour of the movie industry and its blurring of appearance and reality in *Civilization* (1994). Focused on the early days of Hollywood's first 'flickers', the book is narrated in the form of a memoir written by Thom Moss, former riding ace and cowboy-film star.

Quarrington has also written plays, including *The invention of poetry* (1990); the screenplay *Perfectly normal* (1991, Gemini Award); and two works of non-fiction: *Hometown heroes: on the road with Canada's national hockey team* (1988) and *Fishing with my old guy* (1995), a humorous reflection on the sport of angling. He edited *Original six: true stories from hockey's classic era* (1996).

COLIN BOYD

Quarry Press. It was founded in 1965 by Tom Eadie, Tom MARSHALL, and Colin Norman on the campus of Queen's University in Kingston, Ontario, with the purpose of publishing innovative poetry and fiction by new Canadian authors; the logo is a fox, an elusive yet worthwhile 'quarry'. When Bob Hilderley became publisher in 1986, the press expanded to become an enterprising and diverse publishing house located in a historic building on Kingston's waterfront. At its peak in the early 1990s, Quarry's program included up to twenty regional, national, and international titles per year, and included among its authors Mary DI MICHELE, Ken Norris, Diane SCHOEMPERLEN, Roo BORSON, Kim Maltman, Marty GERVAIS, Matt COHEN, Steven HEIGHTON, Lesley CHOYCE, W.P. KINSELLA, Gary GEDDES, George WOODCOCK, Bronwen WALLACE, and Douglas FETHERLING, Although the press now has a national scope, it still remains sensitive to the creative community of Kingston and Queen's University. (In Carol SHIELDS' novel *Swann: a mystery*, Quarry appears as Peregrine Press.)

Quarry also produced two literary magazines: *Quarry Magazine*, (1952-), *Poetry Canada Review* (1977-), and in 1996 purchased *CANADIAN FICTION MAGAZINE*.

With budgetary restraints in the 1990s Quarry scaled down its operations and reduced staff. In 1995 it became an affiliate (along with Cormorant Books and House of ANANSI) of Stoddart Publishing, Toronto.

GEOFF HANCOCK

Quebec, Writing in English in. 1. BEFORE 1870. Lower Canada and Canada East, as the area we now know as Quebec was called before Confederation, was the major centre of English-language publishing in British North America before 1870. Most of what was published then is now of interest only to specialists, but it nonetheless forms a significant part of our literary heritage and, taken in the context of its own time, repays careful reading.

Canada was a new country, and the literature written before Confederation reflects this fact. Most writers were immigrants whose literary education had taken place elsewhere, and even native-born authors were rarely more than a generation away from some other culture. Consequently there was a reliance on European literary models and a consciousness that Canadian productions fell below the highest European standards. Coexisting with this colonial diffidence, there was pride in the existence of a Canadian literature and a concern for its development as a means of demonstrating the intrinsic worth of the immigrants' chosen country to the rest of the world. In Quebec there was also the oft-stated objective of proving to the French-speaking population that British culture was superior to their own.

Most immigrants had been downwardly mobile in Britain and were seeking to repair their fortunes in the New World. Many were well-educated adults who had already published at home and found it natural to continue writing for publication in Canada. Their arrival resulted in an increase in the quantity of 'Canadian' literature; but, since all their reference points were outside the country, this also inhibited both the development of a literature rooted in the Canadian experience and the transmission from one generation to the next of what little Canadian literary tradition there was. Most of the immigrant writers were 'middle class', in the sense that they were educated and did not work with their hands; but none were well off, even by the standards of the day. They, and their readers, were located principally in Montreal and Quebec, but even outside these two cities, particularly in the English-speaking settlements in the Gaspé and the Eastern Townships, there was always someone who wrote, and a printing press nearby. In all these communities throughout the nineteenth century, amateur writers and serious readers gathered in literary clubs, debating societies, library associations, and Mechanics' Institutes, where they presented and applauded hundreds of papers on literary subjects.

The largest audience was available for works published in newspapers. Before mid-century most of these were weekly or thrice-weekly publications that, by the 1840s, had a circulation in the cities of 1,000 to 1,500 copies. By Confederation, many were dailies. The number of actual readers was much greater, since newspapers were handed round until they fell in tatters. Each edition carried at least one poem, and many devoted one of the four pages to literature—British and American, as well as Canadian. Most amateurs published anonymously in the newspaper to which they subscribed. Those with somewhat higher aspirations published in one of several dozen literary periodicals that came and went before 1870. The best known of these are the early Montreal publication *The Canadian Magazine and Literary Repository* (1823-5), *The Canadian Review and Literary and Historical Journal* (1824-6), and *The Scribbler* (1821-7); they contained the work of (among others) Oliver GOLDSMITH, Levi ADAMS, George

LONGMORE, and Adam Hood BURWELL. There was also the *MONTREAL MUSEUM* (1832-4), the first periodical edited by a woman for a female readership, which was notable for the stories of Mrs H. Bayley. In the late 1830s the Quebec *Literary Transcript* published many Quebec City writers. Beginning in the 1840s a number of didactic periodicals—devoted, on the British model, to elevating the lower classes—came and went in Montreal. Denominational periodicals, which contained 'improving' literature, were numerous and claimed a large circulation, but none lasted very long. The 1840s also saw the beginning of a tradition of short-lived satirical publications that was still thriving at Confederation. These, like *Punch in Canada* (1849-50), were based on British models but focused entirely on Canadian politics. This early evidence of the Canadian satiric bent produced at least one book, *How I came to be Governor of the island of Cacona* by William Henry Fleet (Montreal, 1852). Montreal was also the locale of *The SNOW DROP* (1847-53), one of the first children's periodicals published in Canada. The *LITERARY GARLAND* (1838-51) is well known to scholars. Immediately after Confederation *The New Dominion Monthly* (1867-79) and *The Canadian Illustrated News* (1869-83) made their appearance.

Almost all the English-language literary works published in book form in Quebec were poetry, a socially approved form of expression that carried with it none of the moral dangers of fiction. The earliest writers to publish in English were centred in the Quebec City area. The long poem *Abram's plains* (Quebec, 1789) by Thomas Cary (1751-1823) even predated the division of the colony into Upper and Lower Canada in 1791. Cary remained in Quebec as a newspaper editor and publisher, and he and his descendants played a prominent part in the life of the city. Little is known of J. Mackay, who published *Quebec hill; or Canadian scenery, a poem* (London, 1797); or of Cornwall Bayley, the author of *Canada: a descriptive poem* (Quebec, 1806).

Lower Canada was the birthplace of the poets Levi Adams and George Longmore, and of the novelist Rosanna LEPROHON—who, as young Rosanna Mullins, published her earliest poems and stories in *The Literary Garland*. James Russell, author of the second novel published in Canada, *Matilda; or the Indian's captive* (Three Rivers, 1833), also appears to have been Canadian-born. Known principally as poets, J.H. Willis (d. 1847) and W.F. HAWLEY published short fiction as well. Montreal was such an important publishing centre that Charles MAIR and Charles SANGSTER published volumes of poetry there, although they were born in Upper Canada and did not live in Montreal.

The immigrant group who settled and published in Lower Canada is dominated numerically by the Irish-born. Standish O'GRADY and Adam KIDD are best known today. Others were F.B. Ryan, Robert Sweeny (d. 1840), Walter HENRY, Mary Anne Madden (1820-1903), and Thomas D'Arcy MCGEE. Of these, only Madden, author of *Tales of the olden time* (Montreal, 1843), did not remain in Canada. She married the bookseller and publisher James Sadlier and moved to the United States. Because the Sadlier firm continued to publish in Montreal, her later works also appeared in that city. Mrs Sadlier is notable for the Roman Catholic emphasis of her many novels, and for the fact that almost her entire literary output is children's fiction. Sweeny published two volumes of poetry—*Remnants* (Montreal, 1835) and *Odds and ends* (New York, 1826)—and was a popular writer in Irish-American periodicals. Henry wrote a two-volume memoir of his career as an army surgeon; and Ryan, a Montreal doctor, a 194-page verse diatribe, *The spirit's lament; or The wrongs of Ireland* (Montreal, 1847), against the English presence in his native land. In addition to his political activities, McGee edited newspapers and wrote poetry and literary criticism. His assassination in 1868 produced a spate of books about his life and work.

Although many notable newspaper and periodical editors were Scots, there seem to be only three who published volumes of their own work in Lower Canada. David Wylie (1811-91) began his long and distinguished career in Canadian journalism as a printer in Montreal, where he republished in 1847 his *Recollections of a convict*, which had previously appeared in Scotland. John Williamson, a Scottish-born Chelsea pensioner, published a volume of his memoirs, *Narrative of a commuted pensioner* (Montreal, 1838), which is interesting for its view of the British army as seen by one of the lower ranks. He returned to Scotland on a visit in 1840 and died there. Andrew Learmont Spedon, who published five books—three works of fiction, one poetry collection, and one travel book—in Montreal in the decade between 1857 and 1866, also appears to have been born in Scotland.

Of the English-born, the most notable are Bishop G. J. Mountain and Charles HEAVYSEGE. Mountain's volume of poetry, *Songs of the wilderness* (London, 1844), was published as part of a campaign to raise funds for Bishop's College, Lennoxville. Heavysege, at the other end of the social spectrum, was a woodcarver and journalist who published a novel, two volumes of poetry, and two plays, plus miscellaneous uncollected poetry, in Montreal between 1857 and 1868. His *Saul* (Montreal, 1856), a biblical drama in blank verse, brought him fame when it was praised by Hawthorne, Emerson, and Longfellow. The Rev. Joseph Abbott's *Philip Musgrave; or Memoirs of a Church of England missionary in the North American colonies* (London, 1846) is a thinly disguised autobiographical work, so insulting to non-Anglicans that it caused a storm of protest throughout the colony and resulted in at least one pamphlet attacking Abbott's character. Mrs J. P. Grant (Emma Donoghue), author of the poetry collection *Stray leaves* (Montreal, 1865), came to Montreal from London as a young woman to join her brother, who was a newspaper proprietor. As E.J.D. she published many poems in Montreal newspapers and in *The Literary Garland*. The printer J.G. Ward, author of *The spring of life* (Montreal, 1834), a long poem about education, and theatre manager John Gaisford, author of *Theatrical thoughts* and *The minor miseries of human life* (both Montreal, 1848), appear to have been born in England.

Lower Canada was notable for the number of women writers who published there. In the early years their works appeared mostly in literary periodicals; in later years mostly in single volumes of poetry—but there are no typical female authors in this period. Margaret Blennerhassett is the generally accepted author of the anonymous *The widow of the rock* (Montreal, 1824). M. Ethelind Sawtell (*The mourner's tribute*, Montreal, 1840), 'The Widow Fleck' (*Poems on various subjects*, Montreal, 1833), and M.A. Madden all advertised their separate volumes as the work of destitute gentlewomen who needed the revenue from book sales in order to survive. Madden's stories are set in Ireland, but the poetry of Sawtell and Fleck, much of which is merely 'correct', contains a number of Canadian references of interest to students of sociological literary history. In the 1850s and 1860s in Quebec City, Mrs A. Campbell (*Rough and smooth: or, Ho! for an Australian gold field*, 1865) and Margaret Dixon McDougall (*The lady of the beacon of Araheera*, 1859) are listed as authors of single volumes; and in Montreal, Anna Louisa Walker's *Leaves from the backwoods* (1861) and Mrs Leprohon's first three novels, as well as Mrs Grant's poetry, were published.

Two American-born women who lived in Montreal for over forty years were active in periodical publishing. The sisters Harriet Cheney (1796-1889) and Elizabeth Cushing (1794-1886), widowed in 1845 and 1847 respectively, were editors and proprietors of *The Snow Drop* and edited *The Literary Garland* during its last years. They may also have edited the Unitarian periodical *The Liberal Christian* (1854-8). They published some poetry and prose in local journals, including the *Garland*, and wrote much of the content of *The Snow Drop*, but their separate volumes of literary work were issued in Boston. As young women they collaborated on one volume of children's stories. Cheney was the author of four children's books, two North American histories published in the 1820s, and two works on religious subjects, published in the 1840s. Cushing published two historical stories for children, and *Esther, a sacred drama; with Judith, a poem* (Boston, 1840). Her plays, published in *The Lady's Book* and *The Literary Garland*, are an important milestone in the development of playwriting in English Canada.

Although the better-educated writers in English could speak and read French, only two of them, because they actually lived in both cultural worlds, seem to have known, or been influenced by, contemporary writing in French. Rosanna Mullins, who married into the prominent Leprohon family, wrote novels set in Quebec that were almost immediately translated into French. She is included in most contemporary inventories of nineteenth-century French-Canadian novelists. Sir James MacPherson LeMoine (1825-1912) has been less fortunate. A prolific writer in both languages, he was accused in his own day of plagiarizing some of the Quebec legends he collected and published, and today is neglected by French critics who consider him to be English, and English critics who consider him to be French.

Early in the nineteenth century the infrastructure that supported both writer and reader—printers, literary societies, periodicals, bookstores, etc.—was in place in Quebec. Throughout the century that infrastructure continued to support a small population in the production of a surprisingly large quantity of creative works. In 1849 the seat of government for the combined Canadas moved to Toronto, and much of the publishing world (and many writers who were employed in government departments) moved with it. When the government moved to Quebec City at the beginning of the 1860s, writers and publishers moved again. Montreal, however, remained the principal English-language publishing centre in the two Canadas. As time passed, books were often published jointly in Montreal and Toronto, or in Boston or New York. For example, *Canadian homes; or, The mystery solved*, by Maple Knot (Ebenezer Clemo), was published in 1858 by John Lovell in Montreal and William Caverhill in Toronto. Lovell produced a French translation the following year. J.W.D. Moodie (*Scenes and adventures, as a soldier and settler, during half a century*, 1866), and his sister-in-law Catharine Parr TRAILL, as well as Charles Sangster and Charles MAIR, were not Montrealers—but Lovell published their books in Montreal. Similarly, Sara A. McDonald's *The Adopted Daughter; or The trials of Sabra*, first published in Ogdensburg, New York, in 1858, appeared in a second edition printed by Lovell in Montreal in 1863. Throughout the 1850s and 1860s well over a hundred literary works—as well as dozens of political, legal, scientific, historical, business, and religious monographs—were printed in that city.

As time passed, and the colony matured, more and more authors attempted to organize information. Travel guides for visitors to Montreal and Quebec, and for those touring the St Lawrence River, appeared annually; collections of songs and legends, of legal and historical documents, were also produced. There was even a *Canadian postal guide*. Henry J. Morgan's first *Sketches of celebrated Canadians* was published in 1865. The Rev. E.H. DEWART's *Selections from Canadian poets* appeared in 1864. Dewart gathered together, in a 300-page volume, the 'fugitive' poetry of Canadian writers, almost all of whom were his contemporaries. The 'Introductory Essay', in which he reflected the Canadian mood on the eve of Confederation—'A national literature is an essential element in the formation of national character'—and in which he resolutely pointed Canadian writers and readers towards the future, is generally understood to define that moment in our literary past.

MARY LU MacDONALD

2. THE MIDDLE PERIOD. Charles HEAVYSEGE springs lively out of the early soil. Born in England in 1816, he spent a lifetime trudging indomitably the indifferent streets of Montreal. His *Saul: a drama in three parts* (Montreal, 1857), a mammoth play of about 10,000 blank-verse lines, was praised by Hawthorne, Emerson, and Longfellow. Coventry Patmore declared the work to be 'indubitably one of the most remarkable English poems ever written out of Great Britain. . . . There are few things in recent poetry so praiseworthy.' The judgement runs far askew; but it is not any more wrongheaded than that of present homegrown critics who sniff at Heavysege's play. Only the most patriotic and anxious Canadian will want to read through these 436 pages, but with this book we are already a long way from the crude beginnings of poetry in Canada. *Saul* is a biblical commentary, nothing to do with Canada—a curiosity, perhaps a freak, yet a poem with passages of power, imagination, originality (this drama of 1857 suggests that God is capricious and vindictive!), and, sometimes, majesty.

In his richly comic later play, *Count Filippo; or, The unequal marriage. A drama in five acts* (Montreal, 1860), Heavysege felt compelled to be moral—he concludes in a flat field-day of penitence—but for sheer exuberance and linguistic liveliness, Canada has little to equal it. Although the suggestion was derided when it was made once before, it is repeated here: Canada's Stratford could do worse than mount a stylized production of *Count Filippo*. In Heavysege's *Jepththah's daughter* (Montreal, 1865), Northrop FRYE recognized the emergence of 'the central Canadian tragic theme'—'the indifference of nature to human values'.

From that publication to the end of the first quarter of the next century, Quebec produced no literary talent in English comparable to the gradual emergence of the CONFEDERATION POETS elsewhere in Canada. Yet this period was not entirely unproductive in the lower reaches of the province. Mrs C.M. Day's *Pioneers of the Eastern Townships: a work containing official and reliable information respecting the formation of settlements with incidents in their early history; and details of adventures, perils and deliverances* (Montreal, 1863) has an absorbing narrative, and the style is personal and sure.

In these same Eastern Townships, Bishop's University, Lennoxville, had substantial literary affiliations. Belonging to the period before Confederation that saw the birth of major Canadian poetic talent was the clergyman Frederick George SCOTT, a graduate of Bishop's, who wrote about the untamed Quebec landscape and composed impressive religious verse. William Henry DRUMMOND also studied at Bishop's, graduating in medicine. He had worked as a telegraph operator at Bord-à-Plouffe, a little village on the Rivière-des-Prairies, there making first contact with the subject of his later verse, French-Canadian lumbermen and *habitants*. Out of love for these people he portrayed them in humorous poems, cast in broken English, that made him internationally famous. (Many French Canadians enjoyed his portrayals.) His reputation has declined; but discerning readers will find in his poems warmth, affection, and self-effacement.

The tradition of the English poet writing of the French-Canadian scene is continuous. Frank Oliver Call (1878-1956), professor of English at Bishop's, wrote *Blue homespun* (1924), conventional but pleasing sonnets of the Quebec countryside, and a prose homage, *The spell of French Canada* (1926), which he extended in *The spell of Acadia* (1930). Call's *Acanthus and wild grape* (1920) points the way for later Canadian verse, developing from traditional structure (exemplified in the 'Acanthus' section) to the emerging verse form that is now called 'free' (the 'wild grape' poems). (In Ontario, W.W.E. ROSS was similarly engaged.) Imagism—Poundian and Amy Lowellian—was abroad, and Call's friend in nearby Sherbrooke, Louise Morey Bowman (b. 1882), delicately expressed the new movement in *Poetry* (Chicago), and in her collections *Moonlight and common day* (1922) and *Characters in cadence* (1938). The new poetic procedures being practised abroad were in use in English Quebec earlier than is generally realized.

A Montreal lawyer and writer, William Douw LIGHTHALL, compiled for a London publisher one of the earliest poetry anthologies of substance: *Songs of the great Dominion: voices from the forests and water, the settlements and cities of Canada* (1889; rpr. 1971). In spite of the nationalistic thrust of the selection, it still has great interest as a record of the large number of poets and versifiers who were then being published. Among the former, Lighthall had the good judgement to include all the poets of the time that we respect today; however, they are outnumbered by those whose work has sunk into a well-deserved oblivion. The anthology, considerably pruned and in smaller format, apparently for readers abroad, was published under the title *Canadian poems and lays: selections of native verse, reflecting the seasons, legends, and life of the Dominion* (London and New York, 1893).

Striding the end of this period and the beginning of the next was a professor of political science at McGill, Stephen LEACOCK, who produced almost a book a year over much of his long life. His first book was a much-reprinted textbook, *Elements of political science* (1906). But beginning with *Literary lapses* (1910), *Nonsense novels* (1911), and *SUNSHINE SKETCHES OF A LITTLE TOWN* (1912), he achieved international fame as a humorist. His many collections of comic sketches, which he produced along with numerous books of popular history, are uneven in quality, but the best of them are imperishable. His last book, *The boy I left behind me*, a fine memoir, was published in 1946, a year after his death.

3. THE LATER TWENTIETH CENTURY. The publication of the anthology *NEW PROVINCES* (1936) was a turning-point in Canadian poetry: from colonial subservience in form and, largely, content, it had by now moved towards poetic techniques that marked a coming-of-age, a spontaneous assertion of indigenous identity. A poem could no longer claim to be good because it mentioned Canada; the maple leaf was waived, the Mounties were dismounted. The inspiration and editorial judgement for *New provinces*, which was published in Toronto, issued from two Montrealers: A.J.M. SMITH and F.R. SCOTT. The book presented the work of six of Canada's 'most interesting younger poets': E.J. PRATT and Robert FINCH of Toronto and four Montreal poets, Leo KENNEDY, A.M. KLEIN, and Smith and Scott. As a student, Smith had absorbed the latest strategies of the best poets elsewhere who had rebelled against the artistic left-overs from Victorian tradition. His cogent essays in *The McGill Daily Literary Supplement* (1924-5), *The MCGILL FORTNIGHTLY REVIEW* (1925-7), and *The CANADIAN FORUM* vitalized the Canadian artistic scene. Though he moved to the United States (he summered near Magog in the Townships), Smith was a seminal force throughout his lifetime as both a critic and an anthologist. Scott, influenced by his friend Smith, was himself a vital and continuing catalyst who strengthened the literary-periodical scene with *CANADIAN MERCURY* (1928-9) and as an editor of *PREVIEW* (1942-5). Editorial meetings for Preview were held in Scott's Westmount living-room, with Bruce Ruddick, Neufville Shaw, Patrick ANDERSON, P.K. PAGE, and Klein. (Scott had already begun writing his own memorable lyrics and satiric verse: his steady productiveness and numerous collections of poetry would culminate in the publication of *The collected poems of F.R. Scott*, 1981.) This was a time when the methods of Whitman, Yeats, Eliot, Pound, and William Carlos Williams were being woven into the poetic lifeline of Canada. In 1942 John SUTHERLAND founded *FIRST STATEMENT* (1942-5); he was joined by Irving LAYTON and Louis DUDEK the next year. First Statement Press began a series of chapbooks, called New

Writers, with Layton's first collection, *Here and now* (1945). This was followed in the same year by two more first books by Montrealers: Patrick Anderson's *A tent for April* and Miriam WADDINGTON's *Green world*. When *Preview* joined strengths with John Sutherland's *First Statement*—which was of an antagonistic tendency, supporting a more proletarian and a less metaphysical and cosmopolitan stance—the amalgamation became *NORTHERN REVIEW* (1945-56).

All this Montreal activity was to prove of permanent literary worth to Canada. In New York, yet another Bishop's alumnus, Ralph GUSTAFSON, also championed the cause of Canadian poetry, contributing to John Sutherland's magazine and promoting Catherine Harmon's and Paul Arthur's *Here and Now* (Toronto, 1947-9) at the Gotham Book Mart, at which celebrated literary gathering-place the only known Canadian writer was Bliss CARMAN, who was thought to be American. In an attempt to break down the establishment of archaic anthologies then current on the bookshelves of Canada, and the indifference to Canadian literary worth abroad, Gustafson was active as an editor in this period, compiling anthologies for Pelican: *Anthology of Canadian poetry* (1942), *The Penguin book of Canadian verse* (1958; rev. 1967 and 1975), and *Canadian accent* (1944), a collection of essays, fiction, and poems.

In the decade that followed most of these Quebec writers wrote book after book—in Quebec and elsewhere. The spate of little magazines emanating from Montreal continued. Louis Dudek produced *DELTA: A Magazine of Poetry* (1957-66); induced the standard directives from Ezra Pound; and joined Irving Layton to help set *CONTACT*, the Toronto periodical of Raymond SOUSTER, on the right road. Aileen Collins launched her civilized *CIV/n* (1953-5); Michael Gnarowski and Glen Siebrasse their *Yes* (1956-70). Scott and Smith compiled their famous 'anthology of satire, invective, and disrespectful verse chiefly by Canadian writers', *The blasted pine* (1957; rev. 1967). In Montreal too Gwethalyn GRAHAM wrote her novel *Earth and high heaven* (1944), blasting anti-Semitism before anyone else on the Canadian scene. R.G. EVERSON was writing his crackling poetic imagery. Hugh MacLENNAN, in his *TWO SOLITUDES* (1945), was putting into one focus forever the two still-contentious cultures, English and French—just as A.M. Klein, with *The rocking chair and other poems* (1948), forged his own imperishable image of French-Canadian poetry. A brilliant literary career was begun by Mordecai RICHLER with his novel *The acrobats* (1954), written while he was living in Europe. Mavis GALLANT began writing her superb short fiction while she was working on the *Montreal Standard*. She left Canada in 1950 and settled in Paris, but *Home truths: selected Canadian stories* (1981) contains many stories set in Montreal, including those about Linnet Muir (an *alter ego*?). An upbringing in Montreal, marked by the publication of a book of poems, *Let us compare mythologies* (1956) by Leonard COHEN, was the foundation for another brilliant international career. Henry BEISSEL continues his activities as poet and as an inventive playwright, and Dudek remains an important critic and poet. No other city in Canada surpasses the literary heritage of English Montreal.

Passing to the Eastern Townships, Quebec's French-English southerly area, the *cantons* have been home to no less than seven winners of Governor General's Awards: Scott, Smith, MacLennan (five times), John GLASSCO, Gustafson, D.G. JONES, and Richler. At Foster, Quebec, there gathered in 1963 a formidable group of poets who were joined in important discussions by poets from Kingston and Toronto. All is summarized in the conference's *English poetry in Quebec* (1965), edited by Glassco, poet and memoirist, who lived in Foster, writing his *A point of sky* (1964), a second poetry collection of much grace, and the unsurpassed prose of *Memoirs of Montparnasse* (1970). There too he edited *The poetry of French Canada in translation* (1970), a welcome and unreciprocated gesture towards fellow poets of the French tongue. On the edges of Lake Memphramagog, which stretches into alien but sibling New England, A.J.M. Smith wrote in classic shade of his lonely land, and Mordecai Richler creates tapestries of Montreal life from the warp and woof of his upbringing. To North Hatley on Lake Massawippi came Frank Scott and Hugh MacLennan each summer to refresh their writing souls. On a single street in North Hatley lived Doug Jones, Ronald SUTHERLAND, and Gustafson: Jones critically pinning down the Canadian poetic imagination in his *Butterfly on rock* (1970) and writing his lyrics declaring *Under the thunder the flowers light up the earth* (1977); Sutherland bringing into still sharper focus Quebec's two main cultures in his interpretations, *Second image* (1971) and *The new hero* (1977), and in his novel *Snow lark* (1971); Gustafson in his books of poems bringing into juxtaposition the world he has travelled with the Canada he has known and, in his short stories, exposing the puritanism of an upbringing in the Townships. Each seventh moon in the autumn, a clutch of poets congregate in North Hatley to read their poems publicly under the organizing eye of Avrum Malus. Magazines issue from the region: *Matrix* (1977-), and *The Moosehead Review* (1977-2), which is under the editorship of the poets Robert Allen and Stephen Luxton. Doug Jones' *Ellipse*, founded in 1969 and ongoing under distinguished bilingual editorial boards and consultants, is without parallel in presenting in intertranslation the work of Québécois writers of both languages.

Novels of the 1970s from writers in Montreal presented excursions into modes of almost every category: thrillers from John BUELL, whose *Playground* (1976) is a narrative of breathless suspense about a hunter lost in the wilds of northern Quebec; a biting satire of the Péquiste attempt to legislate culture, *The underdogs* (1979), from William WEINTRAUB; and compassionate comedy, *Schmucks* (1972), from Seymour Blicker. From the Eastern Townships came a small-town *genre* painting full of Breughelian love of life in the novel *Pilgaric the death* (1967; rpr. 1980) by Bernard Epps. Among the poets of Montreal in the 1970s an amazing continuity of imaginative expression in English persisted, despite the efforts of a Péquiste government that, with its linguistic laws, attempted to stifle English-speaking talent living or yet unborn. The poets André Farkas and Ken Norris presented English-language creativity in the anthologies: *Montreal English poetry of the seventies* (1977) and *The Véhicule poets* (1979), each containing work by new poets of substantial worth: Michael Harris, David SOLWAY, Richard SOMMER, Peter Van Toorn, Marc Plourde, Tom Konyves, Stephen Morrissey, and Claudia Lapp.

The surgence and re-surgence of English creativity in Quebec in this period was extraordinary. Once officially recognized by the governmental institution of the Prix David, this was now ignored by the official bureaucracy and by French-speaking colleagues alike. Whether from the avenues of Montreal, the Appalachian lowlands of the Eastern Townships, or the accidental appearance of English-language writers in other French parishes, creativity in English persists in Quebec.

RALPH GUSTAFSON

4. RECENT WRITING. In the 1980s and 1990s English writing and literary culture in Quebec has waxed and waned in response to political pressures and individual talent. The infrastructure of literature has grown markedly, as has been demonstrated by the founding of the Quebec Society for the Promotion of English Language Literature (QSPELL, 1987), the Association des Éditeurs Anglophones du Québec (AEAQ, 1987), and the Federation of English Writers of Quebec (FEWQ, 1993). Though some writers and publishers have quit the province for personal or political reasons (Antonio D'ALFONSO and his GUERNICA EDITIONS, for example), others (Mark Abley, David HELWIG, Mary DI MICHELE, and Erin MOURÉ) have moved to Quebec from other parts of Canada and appear to thrive in the maelstrom that is literary Montreal. The poet Ann Diamond (b. 1951) has written bitterly about the marginal status of being an English writer in Quebec; others, such as the American-born novelist and translator David Homel (b. 1952), survive and flourish by working in both linguistic cultures.

English poets in Quebec can call on a long tradition, and well into the 1970s and 1980s there was a discernible historical link between the younger poets and the preceding generations of modernists. Poets like David SOLWAY and Michael Harris (b. 1944) began their careers in the 1960s, and continue to live in Montreal and to publish their work there. Now in their fifties, both poets represent a more traditional approach to poetic form, as Solway's *Selected poems* (1982) and Harris's *New & selected poems* (1992) demonstrate. Both poets teach at the college level, and have been influential mentors of younger writers. Harris, in particular, as the poetry editor of Signal Editions (an associated imprint of VÉHICULE PRESS) has brought into print the work of a host of young poets.

The Véhicule poets (Ken Norris, Endre Farkas, Stephen Morrissey, Claudia Lapp, Artie Gold, Tom Konyves, and John McAuley) represent a more experimental tradition. They were active in Montreal in the late 1970s and early 1980s, the sources of their work were as diverse as Dada and DUDEK, and they were almost bewilderingly prolific in publishing books and magazines, as well as in organizing poetry readings and other events. In recent years, Ken Norris has been editing a series of selected poetry for these writers through The Muses' Company. To date, the following collections have appeared: Gold's *The beautiful chemical waltz* (1992), Norris's *Full sun* (1993), and Konyves' *Sleepwalking among the camels: new and selected poems* (1995). Endre Farkas (b. 1948) operated The Muses' Co. for over a decade, helping to bring to notice the work of younger poets such as Ruth Taylor and Sharon H. Nelson. He was also the editor of an important anthology, *The other language* (1989), which attempted to discern a line in anglo-Quebec poetry from the generation of the 1920s to the generation of the 1980s. He also edited *Quebec suite: poems for and about Quebec* (1995). Ken Norris's *Véhicule days: an unorthodox history of Montreal's Véhicule poets* (1993) captures the spirit of unbuttoned experimentalism that the Véhicule poets stood for.

In the 1990s the English poets of Montreal have been a less obviously affiliated group of writers. With the death of Ralph GUSTAFSON in 1995, LAYTON and Dudek are now the elder statesmen, and D.G. JONES and Gary GEDDES continue to publish their work. Erin Mouré has had a noticeable success bringing a poststructuralist and feminist perspective to English poetry in Quebec, a strain more familiar in the other language. Her collection *Furious* (1988) won a Governor General's Award. There is, however, no evident cohesion in the work of the newer poets. The magazines *Zymergy* (edited by Sonja Skarstedt) and *Matrix* (edited until recently by the novelist Linda Leith, and now published out of Concordia University) published some of their poems, and an issue of *Canadian Notes & Queries* (no. 46, Spring 1992) focused on the young Montreal poets in both English and French. It remains to be seen whether English poetry in Quebec is in decline, or merely regrouping for another advance, as it has done several times in the past.

Anglo-Quebec novelists are perhaps the most visible of the writers in English in the province—not least, it must be admitted, because their work is more often published in Toronto than in Montreal. David Homel has published three novels, of which *Rat palms* (1992) is possibly the most successful. He is also well known as a translator, particularly of the work of the Haitian-born Montreal novelist Danny LaFERRIÈRE. Trevor Ferguson (b. 1947) has published several accomplished novels, including *The true life adventures of Sparrow Drinkwater* (1993). Linda Leith and Kenneth Radu worked together on *Matrix*, and both are experienced prose writers. Leith is the author of two novels, and Radu of both novels and collections of short stories. All these writers have a fairly conventional approach to storytelling and to the use of language, but within the conventions they have chosen to follow they have produced some lively work. Gail SCOTT, by contrast, is a more experimental writer, as her novel *Heroine* (1987), among others, shows; and Ann Diamond, though not writing out of the same theoretical assumptions as Scott, has published some innovative short stories and a novel, *Mona's dance* (1988). Other prose writers of some renown include George Szanto and P. Scott Lawrence.

The relations between anglophone and francophone writers in Quebec remain to some degree as disjunctive as ever. Translation from English to French has perhaps increased slightly over the last two decades, as Montreal francophone publishers have begun to discover and develop an interest among French readers in the literature of English Canada. Canonical writers—like Robertson DAVIES, Michael ONDAATJE, and Margaret ATWOOD—continue to be brought out in French by publishers in Paris rather than in Montreal; but writers at a level down are beginning to find an interested ear at home. As always, however, more works are published from English into French than vice-versa. A number of important translators work out of Quebec; among them, David Homel has already been mentioned, and one should add D.G. Jones, Sheila Fischman, and Jane Brierley. Much of even the most advanced Québécois literature is finding its way into English and has influenced English-Canadian poetry in particular, as collaborations between Daphne MARLATT and Nicole BROSSARD, for example, show. Véhicule Press has had a special interest in tracking the aesthetics of translation, and published important collections of essays on this subject, including *Mapping literature: the art and politics of translation* (1987) edited by David Homel and Sherry Simon and *Culture in transit: translating the literature of Quebec* edited by Simon (1995). Published drama in English from Quebec playwrights has been perhaps the poor cousin to poetry and fiction, though Nuage Editions in Montreal has made this area of publishing a specialty. David FENNARIO remains anglo-Quebec's most recognized playwright.

While Montreal will never regain the literary prominence in English-Canadian literature that it had in the past, English literary culture in Quebec continues to survive—and to flourish at times. Some writers clearly are stimulated by working in a predominantly French environment, and even an antagonistic political culture cannot completely repress their imaginative relation to the world. Ken Norris, in a poem entitled 'In Montreal', proposed that poets in that city 'burn out like stars'. Perhaps they do—but others seem to come along to replace them.

BRUCE WHITEMAN

Quebec, Writing in French in. See entries on writings in French in BIOGRAPHY AND MEMOIRS, CHILDREN'S DRAMA, CHILDREN'S LITERATURE, COLLECTIVE CREATIONS, CRITICISM, DRAMA, ESSAYS, FANTASTIC LITERATURE, FOLKLORE, HISTORICAL WRITING, HUMOUR AND SATIRE, *JOUAL*, MULTICULTURAL WRITING IN FRENCH, NEW FRANCE, NOVELS, POETRY, and SHORT STORIES.

Quesnel, Joseph (1746-1809). Born in Saint-Malo, France, into a prosperous family of traders and ship-chandlers, he travelled widely before his ship, transporting supplies to the Americas, was seized by the British off Nova Scotia in 1779. Through family connections with Governor Haldimand, he was allowed to settle in Lower Canada, where he remained. He soon married into a family that had enriched itself in the fur trade, to which commerce he then successfully dedicated himself, retiring after 1793 to lead the comfortable life of a landed gentleman in Boucherville. Dramatist, poet, musician, and composer, Quesnel became in his retirement the most important writer of his time in Canada.

Soon after his arrival he became involved with amateur theatricals in Montreal and was a founding member of a troupe that performed in 1790 his best-known work, *COLAS ET COLINETTE; OU LE BAILLI DUPÉ*, the first operetta written in North America. It was successful, and was revived in Quebec in 1805 and 1807 before being printed there with the date 1808, although it was apparently not published until 1812. It has continued to exert a modest influence on native dramatists to the present, having last been performed and recorded for Radio-Canada in 1968, then published (1974) in an English translation. Two other plays, neither one published or performed in Quesnel's lifetime, are *Les républicains français; ou La soirée du cabinet*, composed about 1801, and *L'Anglomanie; ou Le dîner à l'angloise*, composed two years later. He left the incomplete score for another operetta, which was to be called 'Lucas et Cécile'. He was also the author of some 34 poems, many of which appeared in newspapers of the time.

Colas et Colinette is a light comedy in three acts, with frequent musical interventions, stock characters, and a theme directly reminiscent of 'society' theatre in France of a generation or more before. The happiness of the two young lovers is menaced by a scheming village bailiff; but the heroine, Colinette, outsmarts him, and the village squire, M. Dolmont, is there to ensure that youth and virtue triumph. The music is derivative, but the recipe as a whole is not displeasing. More original is *Les républicains français* (*La BARRE DU JOUR*, été 1970), a savage satire in one act of the perceived excesses of the French Revolution. In a cabaret in Paris, five motley representatives of the New Order enthuse about the advances the Revolution has brought, while their befuddled views and progressive drunkenness depict its moral and political bankruptcy (in the eyes of the conservative Quesnel). Not published until 1970, the play had no influence in Quesnel's time—like *L'Anglomanie*, which was not published until 1932-3 in *Le Canada français*, though it is the only play by Quesnel with a Canadian setting or theme and is generally considered his best. In verse and in one act, it depicts a French-Canadian seigneur, M. Primenbourg, who is persuaded to ape English ways by his son-in-law, who is aide-de-camp to the governor. The characters are drawn from real life, the topic was current, and the lesson that one must avoid Anglomania is conveyed with an effective comic touch. *L'Anglomanie* was also published in *La Barre du jour* (juill.-déc. 1965).

Quesnel's poems comprise mainly songs, epigrams, and occasional pieces, but include references to the political situation in Lower Canada ('L'anti-Français', 'Chanson' [1807], 'Les moissonneurs'); exude a personal philosophy of life ('Le petit bonhomme vit encore!', 'À M. Panet', 'Stances marotiques à mon esprit'); reflect on his own travails as a poet in an unappreciative land ('Le rimeur dépité', 'Épître à Labadie'); and give advice to actors and writers ('Adresse aux jeunes acteurs', 'La nouvelle académie'). But they exhibit no real poetic talent. Five of the poems have been published by Michael Gnarowski in *Quelques chansons selon les manuscrits dans la collection Lande* (1970). Quesnel's plays have been analysed in depth by B. Burger in *L'activité théâtrale au Québec (1765-1825)* (1974) and by L.E. Doucette in *Theatre in French Canada* (1984), and in the entry on Quesnel in *The Oxford companion to Canadian theatre* (1989). L.E. DOUCETTE

R

Raddall, Thomas (1903-94). Thomas Head Raddall was born in the married quarters of the British Army School of Musketry at Hythe, England, where his father was an instructor. The latter's posting to Halifax in 1913 made his son a Nova Scotian and resulted in Raddall's steadfast, intimate, and rewarding bond with that province. His engrossing and candid autobiography, *In my time* (1976), tells how Raddall, too poor to attend university, served as a wireless operator on coastal stations, at sea, and on Sable Island from 1919 to 1922; he then qualified as a bookkeeper, took a job with a lumber company on the Mersey River, and soon began to write, having developed an interest in the history of his province—in Micmacs, pre-Loyalist settlers, Loyalists, privateering, and the economic diseases that befell Canada's Atlantic littoral following the age of sail. These years—which introduced him also to hunting and fishing, logging, rumrunning, business machinations, and backwoods politics—were the fullest of Raddall's life. Having published short stories in *Blackwood's Magazine* and elsewhere, Raddall chose in 1938 to become a professional writer. During the Second World War he was an officer in the West Nova Scotia Regiment, worked as a journalist and as a scriptwriter for radio, and published two collections of short stories and two novels.

Raddall's *The pied piper of Dipper Creek and other stories* (1939), with an introduction by John Buchan, won a Governor General's Award. This was followed by *Tambour and other stories* (1945); *The wedding gift and other stories* (1947); *A muster of arms and other stories* (1954); and *At the tide's turn and other stories* (1959), a selection from the earlier publications. All these collections demonstrate Raddall's knowledge of the texture of Nova Scotia life, past and present, and his facility for straightforward, entertaining storytelling.

Raddall's first historical novel, *His Majesty's Yankees* (1942), which deals with the conflicting political, economic, and emotional ties of Nova Scotians during the American Revolution, shows—in its sound use of J.B. Brebner's *The neutral Yankees of Nova Scotia* and Simeon Perkins' diaries—his enterprising, meticulous research. Its robust style also animates *Roger Sudden* (1944), a story of the Seven Years' War and the capture of Louisbourg, and *Pride's fancy* (1946), a rousing tale of a privateer in West Indies waters during the fight for Haitian independence. *The governor's lady* (1960) offers a masterful re-creation of the personality and character of Fannie Wentworth, wife of the lieutenant-governor (1792-1808) of Nova Scotia. In *Hangman's beach* (1966) the focus is twofold: Raddall evokes the 1803-12 period of the Napoleonic Wars in Halifax, with particular emphasis on French prisoners held on Melville Island; and, through his portrayal of the Peter McLeod family, delineates the boom in Nova Scotia commerce during those years.

Though best known for his historical fiction, Raddall also wrote three novels set in the twentieth century—one of which, *The nymph and the lamp* (1950), is his masterpiece. With its superbly conveyed settings (Halifax, Sable Island, and the Annapolis Valley), its astutely interwoven themes, sexual tension, and powerful characterization of the protagonist, Isabel Jardine, it is a work of enduring merit that cannot be dismissed as a romance. *Tidefall* (1953) and *Wings of the night* (1956) are mediocre by comparison: the former has to do with a seafaring villain who makes and loses a fortune, the latter with forest life and economic troubles in Nova Scotia.

That Raddall should also have published three books of history is not surprising, given his strong association with the past, his evergreen curiosity, and his investigative talents. The authoritative chronicle *Halifax, warden of the north* (1948; rev. 1965), and the discerning and spirited popular history *The path of destiny: Canada from the British Conquest to home rule, 1763-1850* (1957), both won Governor General's Awards. *Footsteps on old floors* (1968), a lighter work, contains essays on obscure but compelling 'mysteries' of Nova Scotia history, most notably that of the derelict vessel *Mary Celeste* and her missing crew. Raddall also wrote the text for *A pictorial guide to historic Nova Scotia: featuring Louisbourg, Peggy's Cove and Sable Island* (rev. 1972).

As a professional writer Raddall never asked for, nor received, money from government sources. One of the few Canadian writers in this century to achieve independence through his writing, he wrote fiction with the purpose of selling it, and succeeded in doing so without sacrificing his artistic integrity. In addition to receiving three Governor General's Awards, he was elected to the Royal

Society of Canada in 1949 and was presented with the Lorne PIERCE medal in 1956. He became a Companion of the Order of Canada in 1971.

The following titles are in the NEW CANADIAN LIBRARY: *His Majesty's Yankees*, *The nymph and the lamp*, *Pride's fancy*, *Roger Sudden*, and *At the tide's turn*.

See Alan R. Young, *Thomas Raddall and his works* (1990), and Young, ed., *Time and place: the life and works of Thomas H. Raddall* (1991).

ROBERT COCKBURN

Radin, Paul. See ABORIGINAL LEGENDS AND TALES: BIBLIOGRAPHY.

Radisson, Pierre-Esprit. See Writing in NEW FRANCE: 1.

Radu, Kenneth. See NOVELS IN ENGLISH 1983 TO 1996: OTHER NOVELS 2(b).

Rand, Silas T. See ABORIGINAL LEGENDS AND TALES: BIBLIOGRAPHY.

Randaccio, Elena. See ITALIAN-CANADIAN LITERATURE.

Rapoport, Janis (b. 1946). Born and raised in Toronto, Ontario, Rapoport received a B.A. (1967) from the University of Toronto. From 1968 to 1970 she lived in London, England, where she worked as an editor and researcher. She was an associate editor of the *TAMARACK REVIEW* from 1970 to 1982 and editor of *Ethos* from 1983 to 1987. She has been writer-in-residence at several Ontario libraries and participates regularly in readings, literary workshops, and conferences.

Rapoport has published six books of poetry: *Within the whirling moment* (1967), *Foothills* (1973), *Jeremy's dream* (1974), *Winter flowers* (1979), *Upon her fluent route* (1991), and *After paradise* (1996). From her earliest volume, Rapoport's authentic voice and poetic craft were evident. A lyric poet, she writes descriptive verse that is layered verbally and punctuated with startling, visual images. Often she strikes an intellectual pose, which can result in a poetry of cool detachment. Soon after the appearance of her first slim volume, which favoured the brief, clipped line, Rapoport began to experiment with a longer, prose-like line, now typical of her writing. In her first full-length collection, *Winter flowers*, she explores such common themes as love, human relationships, family, and children. Her later work reveals a lusher style and an interest in romanticism. Here she introduces earth mothers, goddesses, and witches whose magical powers characterize a particularly female-centred world. All of her writing asserts the value of the imagination, fantasy, faith, and change over the dullness of reason and order.

In addition to her poetry, Rapoport has written *Dreamgirls* (1979), a two-act play featuring six female characters. She has also co-edited *Landscape* (1977), a poetry anthology.

RUTH PANOFSKY

Rashid, Ian Iqbal. See GAY LITERATURE.

Ravitch, Melekh (1893-1976). One of the great Yiddish bellelettrists of the twentieth century, Melekh Ravitch—the pseudonym of Zekharye Khone Bergner—was born in Radymno, East Galicia (then an Austrian province), where he received a secular education. At age fourteen he left home to begin a restless wandering life.

Ravitch's earliest lyrics appeared in the collection *Oyf der Shvel* ('On the Threshold', 1912). His famous poem 'Spinoza' (1918) is a tribute to the philosopher, whom he ranked with Moses and Jesus. During the Great War, Ravitch was drafted into the Austrian army and wounded at the front. After the war he settled in Vienna, where he was greatly influenced by Expressionism. In *Nakete Lider* ('Naked songs', 1921) he experimented with Expressionist techniques, dispensing with rhyme, regular metric lines, and stanzas. In 1921 Ravitch moved to Warsaw, where he met Uri Zvi Greenberg and Peretz Markish. Together the three poets formed a triumvirate called 'Di Khaliastre' ('The gang'), which struggled against realism in literature. Ravitch's expressionistic poems were collected in *Di fir Zaytn fun mayn Velt* ('The four sides of my world', 1929). His subsequent retreat from Expressionism was reflected in the songs and ballads of *Kontinentn un Okeanen* ('Continents and oceans', 1937).

As secretary of the Jewish Writers Union, Ravitch was at the centre of Yiddish literary life in Warsaw until 1934, when he left Poland. After a period of wandering, he settled in Melbourne, Australia, from 1936 to 1938. Despite a lifelong fear of travelling, Ravitch proclaimed himself a citizen of the world, a poet beyond nationalism. After living briefly in Argentina, New York, and Mexico, he finally settled in Montreal in 1941. There he became a catalyst for Yiddish literary, educational, and cultural activities. He served on the board of the Jewish Public Library and founded the city's Folks University. He also published four more collections of verse, a two-volume autobiography *Dos Maysebukh fun mayn Lebn* ('The storybook of my life', 1962-4), and six volumes of an encyclopaedic work on Yiddish writers, *Mayn Leksikon* ('My lexicon', 1945-82). It was largely through his efforts that Montreal became one of the major centres of Yiddish literary activity during several decades beginning in the 1940s.

See also YIDDISH LITERATURE.

GOLDIE MORGENTALER

Reaney, James (b. 1926). 1. POETRY AND FICTION. Born in South Easthope near Stratford, Ontario, he studied English at University College, University of Toronto (M.A., 1949). He taught English at the University of Manitoba from 1949 until 1956, when he returned to Toronto to complete a doctorate, which was awarded in 1958; his thesis was 'The influence of Spenser on Yeats', supervised by Northrop FRYE. In 1951 he married Colleen Thibaudeau, also a poet, and they have a son and daughter. In 1960 he began his long career as a professor of English at the University of Western Ontario. In that year he also started the magazine *ALPHABET*, on 'the iconography of the imagination', which lasted ten years. His first book of poems, *The red heart* (1949), written when Reaney was twenty-three, received a Governor General's Award. It was followed by *A suit of nettles* (1958; 2nd edn, 1975) and *Twelve letters to a small town* (1962), both of which also won Governor General's Awards, and by *The dance of death at London, Ontario* (1963; drawings by Jack Chambers). *Poems* (1972), which includes the four previous collections, *Selected shorter poems* (1975), and *Selected longer poems* (1976) were edited by Germaine Warkentin, with extensive introductions that are among the best Reaney criticism. These books were followed by *Imprecations: the art of swearing* (1984) and *Performance poems* (1990).

The red heart, a collection of forty-two lyrics, is an intensely private, even precious book. Already the playfulness, and the somewhat child-like character of Reaney's poetic temperament—though not his technical mastery—are evident. Its central figure is a youthful artist coming to poetic terms with a provincial environment, the Perth County of Reaney's childhood. The poems are infused with a sentimental nostalgia as the poet, in the role of orphan, tries to create an imaginary play-box world of childhood as an antidote to a hostile cultural world. *A suit of nettles* is an extraordinary leap forward. Perhaps under the tutelage of Frye (see Reaney's 'The Canadian poet's predicament', *University of Toronto Quarterly*, xxvi, April 1978), Reaney draws on traditional literary structures to inform his poem, imitating Spenser's *The shepheardes calender*. A series of twelve pastoral eclogues, *A suit of nettles* focuses on a southern-Ontario town, seen from the perspective of the barnyard geese in their twelve-month cycle from birth to ritual slaughter at Christmas. An opening invocation to the Muse of Satire 'to beat fertility into a sterile land' makes Reaney's satiric purpose clear: the geese provide a repertoire of human types—lover, teacher, philosopher, poet, critic—imitating an archetypal human community struggling against victimization by time and death and the negativism in man that denies creativity. The sequence—made up of allegorical puzzles, dialogue poems, beast fables, and graphic poems—gives full play to the quirky, sardonic wit of Reaney, for whom poetry is game and mischief.

Twelve letters to a small town is a suite of lyrics—dialogue and prose poems in the form of a libretto that was set to music for chamber orchestra by John Beckwith and broadcast on CBC 'Wednesday Night' in July 1961. Reaney erects a model of Stratford, remembered from the late 1930s and early 1940s, and tries to recover the physical and spiritual environment that created him in the persona of a lively, imaginative boy, gifted with a capacity to see wonder and mystery in the simple and homely. The result is deeply attractive. Reminiscent of *Under milkwood* by Dylan Thomas, *Twelve letters* is an act of imagination by which the poet recreates his rural roots in their ideal mythological form.

The dance of death and 'Two chapters from an emblem book', published in *Poems*, derive from Reaney's enduring fascination with iconography. As Germaine Warkentin has written, 'Reaney began to think . . . one could develop a virtual iconography of the imagination, an alphabet of images which would disclose the relationship between "the verbal universe which hovers over the seed-bed of the so-called real and natural world" and the seedbed itself' ('Introduction', *Poems*). The emblem book, a combination of diagram and verbal puns, tries to identify a whole unsorted alphabet of special diagrams in the triangles, circles, and crosses that recur in art. While this interest in hieroglyph and pictograph is engaged mostly at the level of game, it is rooted in Reaney's ambition to recover a traditional interest in graphic symbols as vehicles for articulating otherwise inapprehensible metaphysical insights. (See Reaney's 'Search for an undiscovered alphabet', *Canadian Art*, vol. 22, 1965.)

In *Imprecations: the art of swearing*, Reaney rediscovers cursing, describing it as a 'lost skill'. From childhood memories of swearing to actual cursing, he reminds the reader of the delight in finding appropriate objects for one's invective, from the giant grocery chain which has destroyed the local grocer to the minister of education who has damned the world to the bad teaching of poetry. *Performance poems* collects poems and prose poems written for performance since 1960, grouping them into a calendar cycle from January to December. In his preface, Reaney suggests the poems can be read silently, aloud, or scored for many voices, and can be illustrated by 'mime, dance, musique concrete, manipulation of props and body movement'. He also includes unfinished poems, challenging the reader to fill them out with local references. With delightful exuberance, he breaks down the barriers between theatre and poetry, reminding his readers of poetry's visceral roots in nursery rhymes and street games. In his hands, poetry becomes an environment, an entire world, and reading and performing his poetry becomes a medium through which his readers discover the latent but rarely tapped energy of their own creative imaginations.

Ironically, Reaney is a poet who has been accused of bookishness and of academicism in his indebtedness to Frye. However, this is to disregard the extraordinary playfulness and the genuine understanding of myth that gives to his work what Dave GODFREY calls 'its wonderful health'. Reaney will always have his devoted readers who, like Warkentin, find his poems among the most richly satisfying written in Canada.

Reany's *The box social and other stories* (1996) presents eleven stories, written for the most part in the 1940s and 1950s, that were influential in establishing the style of writing that has since become known as 'Southern Ontario Gothic'. Margaret ATWOOD has remarked that 'without "The Bully", my fiction would have followed other paths.' As Reaney explains in 'Embro', he delights in 'the kind of story that cries out to be drawn on fresh, white snow with an icicle'. Playing sophisticated games by switching voice, he achieves a kind of 'magic realism', often through the distorted perspective and sense of disproportion of his child narrators.

Reaney is also the author of novels for young adults, such as *The boy with an R in his hand* (1965), about York (Toronto) in the 1820s, and *Take the big picture* (1986). He is a Fellow of the Royal Society, and was made an Officer of the Order of Canada in 1975.

See Alvin A. Lee, *James Reaney* (1968), Ross G. Woodman, *James Reaney* (1971), and Stan Dragland, ed., *Approaches to the work of James Reaney* (1983).

See also CRITICISM IN ENGLISH: 4 and POETRY IN ENGLISH 1950 TO 1982: 1.

ROSEMARY SULLIVAN

2. DRAMA. James Reaney turned to writing drama after he had become established as a poet. The libretto for the chamber opera *Night-blooming Cereus* by John Beckwith was completed in 1953 (though the opera was not produced until 1960), and was published in *The killdeer and other plays* (1962), which also included *The sun and the moon* and *One-man masque*. This was followed by *Colours in the dark* (1969), *Listen to the wind* (1972), and *Masks of childhood* (1972), which contains three plays: *The easter egg*, *Three desks*, and a revised version of *The killdeer*. Reaney has also written several children's plays, some of which have been published in *Apple butter and other plays for children* (1973), which includes *Geography match*, *Names and nicknames*, and *Ignoramus*. Other children's plays by Reaney are *Let's make a carol* (1965) with music by Alfred Kunz, *Don't sell Mr. Aesop* (unpublished), performed in London, Ontario, in 1968, and *At the big carwash* (unpublished), a puppet play produced in Armstrong, British Columbia, in 1979. (See CHILDREN'S DRAMA IN ENGLISH.)

Reaney's early plays brought great imagination to English-Canadian drama. Some of them, written mainly or partly in verse, treat themes also found in his poetry: the contrasting worlds of innocence and experience, the underlying evil forces in everyone, love's power to redeem, the process of growth from childhood to adolescence to maturity. Reaney prefers a non-linear, kaleidoscopic drama to one based on the assumptions of the realistic theatre. Indeed, the complexity and profusion of events in his plays often bewilder and dissatisfy audiences accustomed to realistic drama. Rich in symbolism and patterns of imagery, the plays often present a fanciful, surrealistic world; and since little attempt is made to develop plot or character, their lack of emotional depth sometimes hinders audience involvement.

The themes of the libretto for the chamber opera *Night-blooming Cereus* are loneliness and reconciliation. It was performed at Hart House Theatre, Toronto, in 1960, along with *One-man masque* (with Reaney himself as the performer)—a short poetic fantasy on birth, death, and other stages of human life. Under the title *Masque* (1974), this play was adapted by Ron Cameron for his students at Toronto's

Riverdale Collegiate, and was first runner-up in the Ontario finals of the Simpson's Collegiate Drama Festival in 1972. *The sun and the moon*, which includes elements of farce (as do most of Reaney's plays), shows the evil influences lurking in a small Ontario community and uses melodrama (a convention he is fond of) to bring these influences to the surface and to heighten the comic and redemptive dimensions of the play.

The title of one collection of Reaney's plays, *Masks of childhood*, suggests the central place of the child's world in Reaney's work—as a symbol of unspoiled innocence, a mask to hide a deeper world of evil, and a shield for those who cannot enter the adult world of risk and responsibility. *The killdeer*, in its 1972 version, emphasizes the hold of a violent or inhibiting past on the lives of children from different families; only their mutual love and forgiveness enable them to break free. (In 1991 *The killdeer* was revised again for performance at the University of Western Ontario.) *Three desks* is a macabre and farcical treatment of the childishness and hostility that can affect the life of an academic community, in this case a small liberal-arts college on the Prairies. *The Easter egg* is a symbolic exploration of Christian redemption and resurrection. *Colours in the dark*—first produced at Stratford, Ontario, in 1967 under the direction of John Hirsch—shows Reaney's surer command of the free dramatic form towards which all his plays tend. Of its forty-two scenes, which give impressions of growing up in southwestern Ontario, Reaney said: 'This one has a new play before you every two minutes.' *Listen to the wind* adds a sombre note to the optimism of some of the earlier plays: a sick boy fails to reunite his parents, though he goes to bed believing he has succeeded. The play-within-a-play technique contrasts the worlds of imagination and reality.

Reaney's ability to confront more realistic situations, while developing new forms of dramatic structure, is evident in the DONNELLY TRILOGY: *Sticks and stones: the Donnellys, part one* (1974), *The St. Nicholas hotel, Wm. Donnelly, Prop: the Donnellys, part two* (1976), and *Handcuffs: the Donnellys, part three* (1977)—about the famous Irish immigrant family that was massacred in Lucan, Ontario, in 1880. All three were published together as *The Donnellys* (1983) with scholarly apparatus by James Noonan. *The St. Nicholas hotel* won the Chalmers Award for 1974. Combining history, poetry, music, dance, marionettes, magic lanterns, liturgy, mime, and myth, the plays were written after some eight years of research on the Donnellys and their times. Reaney is clearly sympathetic to the Donnellys and rejects their reputation as 'the Black Donnellys'; he presents them as superior and heroic, even Christ-like figures, who die for their own dignity and their right to be different. The trilogy was developed in workshops with director Keith Turnbull and the NDWT Company, which presented it at Toronto's Tarragon Theatre between 1973 and 1975. In the fall of 1975 *The Donnellys* was taken on a cross-Canada tour—to nineteen communities from Vancouver to Halifax—climaxed by a final presentation of all three parts in one day at the Bathurst St Theatre in Toronto on 14 Dec. 1975. Reaney wrote a personal account of the tour, the actors' experiences, and the play's reception, in *14 barrels from sea to sea* (1977), which also contains reviews from all the cities in which it was performed. Still fascinated by his heroes, Reaney wrote a puppet play, *Sleigh without bells*—to be the first of three ghost stories about the Donnellys—which traces their influence on people after their deaths. It was performed in 1991 by the Rag and Bone Puppet Theatre in the Regional Art Gallery of London, Ontario. Reaney plans to publish a book of documents and other material he discovered while researching the Donnellys.

While *The Donnellys* is the landmark achievement of Reaney's drama to date, he has continued to write plays based on local history, at times giving them universal significance. *Baldoon* (1976), co-authored with Marty Gervais, concerns events in a small community near Wallaceburg, Ontario, in the 1830s, involving poltergeists, witchcraft, and a witch hunter, often evoked by the use of puppets and marionettes. Liberation entails the defeat of Dr McTavish's dour Presbyterianism by the exorcist Dr Troyer's joyous Shaker brand of Christianity.

Some later plays were commissioned for special groups or occasions. *The dismissal; or Twisted beards and tangled whiskers* (1978) was commissioned by Reaney's alma mater, University College, to mark the sesquicentennial of the University of Toronto in 1977. The play is above all entertainment and includes musical routines, vaudeville, and an actress playing the bearded 'President Fury' of the university in 1994-5.

In *Wacousta!* (1979) Reaney made a play from the melodramatic early Canadian novel *WACOUSTA* by John RICHARDSON. The published version of the play contains detailed descriptions of its development in workshops in London and Timmins, Ontario, before it toured Ontario in 1978. Reaney followed this with another elaborate work, *The Canadian brothers* (published in the anthology *Major Plays of the Canadian Theatre*, 1984, edited by Richard Perkyns, and performed by students at the University of Calgary in 1983) based on *The Canadian brothers; or, The prophecy fulfilled* (1840), Richardson's sequel to Wacousta.

King Whistle! (1980, in the journal *BRICK*, no. 8), written for the centenary of the Central Secondary School in Stratford, Ont., was first performed at the Avon Theatre, Stratford, in Nov. 1979. The local subject matter lacks the wide appeal of some of Reaney's other plays, as does his next play *Antler River* (unpublished), commissioned by the Urban League of London, Ontario (where Reaney lives), to celebrate the city's 125th anniversary in 1980. Reaney's commitment to London was further demonstrated by two plays (unpublished) he wrote for retired actors there—*Cloud shadows* and *Stereoscope*—which show the effects of, and the conflicts that come with, ageing. *Stereoscope*, along with his *One-man masque* and *The perfect essay*, were performed at the University of Western Ontario in 1992 during month-long celebrations paying tribute to Reaney on his retirement from teaching there.

Gyroscope (1983), performed at the Tarragon Theatre as part of the 1981 Toronto Theatre Festival, represents a return to personal vision and experience. It contains satire on sex, marriage, small-town life, and academia, and explores with humour the struggle for balance and understanding in a creative husband-wife relationship.

Much of Reaney's recent work has been librettos for Canadian composers. The first of these was the libretto for *The shivaree: opera in two acts* (1978), with music by John Beckwith, which Comus Music Theatre premièred at the St Lawrence Centre, Toronto, and on CBC radio, in 1982. The title refers to the custom—still practised in parts of southwestern Ontario—of serenading a newly wedded couple on homemade percussion instruments. In 1982 Reaney was commissioned to write a play to celebrate the city of Waterloo, Ont. The result was *I, the parade: the story of professor C.F. Thiele* (director of the Waterloo Musical Society Band for 35 years). Two successive years saw the production of two operas for which Reaney wrote the librettos: *Crazy to kill* (1988), a 'detective opera' with music by John Beckwith, heard at the Guelph Spring Festival in 1989; and *Serinette* (1990), a chamber opera with music by Harry Somers, produced as part of the Music at Sharon Festival in 1990 to mark the tenth anniversary of that festival. Both operas were popular successes. *Serinette* is the first of three librettos, on themes from Canadian history, that Reaney is writing. The second, with music by John Beckwith, is entitled *Taptoo!* He also plans to produce a music drama about the Brontë children, on which he has been working for some time.

Reaney scored another popular success with his adaptation for the stage of Lewis Carroll's *Alice through the looking-glass* (1994)—with music by Keith Thomas—which was performed at the Avon Theatre of the Stratford Festival in 1994, and repeated there in 1996. Reaney's retirement has released much creativity and flexibility in his dramatic work, which in turn have brought him widespread recognition. But none of his recent adaptations and successes has matched the originality and imagination of his earlier works such as *Colours in the dark* and *The Donnellys*.

An explanation of why Reaney began to write plays may be found in his article 'Ten years at play' in *CANADIAN LITERATURE*, 41 (Summer 1969). Some of his ideas about drama and Canadian literature may be found in the newsletter, *Halloween*, which Reaney occasionally publishes in different journals. James Stewart Reaney's *James Reaney* (1977) is a study of his father's plays in the Profiles in Canadian Drama series. Later studies of his work include Stan Dragland, ed., *Approaches to the work of James Reaney* (1983); Richard Stingle, *James Reaney and his works* (1991); and Gerald D. Parker, *How to play: the theatre of James Reaney* (1991), a detailed study of the plays.

See also DRAMA IN ENGLISH: 1953 TO 1981 and 1983 TO 1996. JAMES NOONAN

Rebel angels*, *The (1981). The first volume in the Cornish trilogy by Robertson DAVIES, it moves the novel towards 'anatomy' (one of the four categories of prose fiction Northrop FRYE defines in his 'Theory of genres', the Fourth Essay in his *Anatomy of criticism*) in its exploration of the nature of a university. Some of the characters thus appear not as fully rounded people but as mental attitudes, and ideas and theories are emphasized. The short form of the anatomy—the dialogue or colloquy—is present in the guest nights at Ploughwright College, and the exuberance of the anatomist appears in the piling up of erudite lore in catalogues, like the list of medieval terms for faeces of animals. By means of a web of allusions to Paracelsus, alchemy, medieval filth therapy, and Gypsies, Davies presents the university as an institution rooted in the Middle Ages—dedicated to the pursuit of learning and wisdom both secular and divine, but also prone to petty and gross betrayals of its professed standards.

The story is narrated alternately by Maria Magdalena Theotoky, a gifted graduate student, and Simon Darcourt, a middle-aged Anglican priest and professor of New Testament Greek. Maria is preparing to write a doctoral thesis on a Rabelais manuscript. She works in the rooms of her supervisor Clement Hollier (whose field is the thinking of medieval people and with whom she imagines herself in love), takes various graduate courses, and furthers Hollier's research. At Hollier's urging she visits Ozias Froats to see whether his research into human excrement has revealed why medieval filth therapy worked. She also introduces Hollier to her mother, a Gypsy and a restorer of stringed instruments by the medieval method of burying their wooden cases in horse manure.

In his sections Darcourt describes various academic occasions—funerals and a wedding that take place in the chapel of the College of St John and the Holy Ghost, sherry parties given by a professor, college guest nights at Ploughwright College—because he is engaged in creating a record of collegiate life. He is also one of three academics who are sorting out the estate of their old friend Francis Cornish. He thus has a chance to observe academic knowledgeability and cupidity in action. Several characters lust after (and one steals) the Rabelais manuscript that Maria has been promised and that Francis Cornish owned, and several lust after Maria herself.

A high point is the Christmas dinner to which Maria's mother Mamusia invites Clement Hollier and Simon Darcourt. One of Davies' unforgettable set pieces, this encompasses a marvellous Gypsy *crèche*, a gargantuan feast, astute fortune telling, Gypsy music, and a misdirected love-philtre. The story winds through this and other highly coloured events towards the grotesque murder of a professor, a suicide, and Maria's Gypsy wedding, and comes to rest with the final guest night of the academic year at Ploughwright College.

The novel is something of a *roman à clef.* Ploughwright is clearly based on Massey College, and the College of St John and the Holy Ghost on neighbouring Trinity, both in the University of Toronto. Several characters have antecedents that have been identified.

The rebel angels has been translated into ten languages and is available as a Penguin paperback. JUDITH SKELTON GRANT

Redbird, Duke (b. 1939). Born in Southampton, Ontario, the sixth and last child of Jack and Kathleen Richardson, he is a Status Indian. In 1978 he received his M.A. in interdisciplinary studies at York University, Toronto, and is currently a Ph.D. candidate in sociology there. In the sixties and seventies he was in the forefront of Native political organizations and was a prominent public speaker on Native issues, providing First Nations people in Canada with a new, young, and aggressive leadership. He was president of the Ontario Métis and Non-status Indian Association and director of their Land Claims Research, as well as vice-president of the Native Council of Canada, and was the subject of a biography *Red on white* (1971) by Marty Dunn. His early poems—such as 'The beaver', 'A red nation', 'I am the redman'—are fuelled with the resentment of an angry young man disgusted with the white exploitation of Canada's Native people. In contrast, the poems in his collection *Loveshine and red wine* (1981) are about the love of nature, of home and family, and are gentle and quietly domestic. In *I am a Canadian* (1978) he celebrates the people and the provinces of Canada in a stirring sixty-line prose poem. In 1989 he composed 'The Canadian Museum of Civilization' for 'Soirée Asticou', the pre-opening event of the new museum. His M.A. thesis, *We are Métis: a Métis view of the development of a Native Canadian people*, was published in 1980. Redbird has contributed significantly to film and television. For TVOntario he was writer/director for 'He Who Looks Upside Down—a Question of Justice', which won the Silver Plaque Award, Educational Category, at the Chicago International Film Festival; and he was writer/performer for a documentary film, 'Chief Dan George Reciting Duke Redbird's Poetry'. For NBC he was writer/director for a variety show, 'Strunk's Farm', and for the Canadian Broadcasting Corporation he was writer/co-director for 'Canoe for the making'.

PENNY PETRONE

Reeve, Ted. See SPORTSWRITING.

Reeves, John. See DRAMA IN ENGLISH 1953 TO 1981 and MYSERY AND CRIME.

Refus global (1948). If any single event marked the beginning of modern Quebec, it was the appearance of this manifesto, which was published privately in 400 copies as a collection of loose typewritten mimeographed pages in a portfolio designed by Jean-Paul Riopelle. The title essay was written by the painter Paul-Émile Borduas (1905-60); it also carried the signatures of fifteen members of his circle, including writers Claude GARNEAU and Thérèse RENAUD. Seven of these signatories were women: among them Françoise Sullivan, whose creative work includes choreography and dance as well as sculpture and painting, and painter Marcelle Ferron. The manifesto's attack on the role of the clergy and capitalist powers in maintaining Quebec's submission, and its description of the fear of authority, in which the majority of the population lived, provoked a *succès de scandale* in Duplessis's tightly controlled society, and brought about Borduas's dismissal from his teaching job and his subsequent exile to New York and later to Paris, where he died.

Mainly because of its description of Quebec as 'a colony trapped since 1760 within the slippery walls of fear, the usual refuge of the vanquished', *Refus global* has been viewed as the first step in the modern nationalist movement in Quebec. The manifesto, however, goes on to describe a major crisis in Western values, whose emptiness is concealed behind a veil of abstract knowledge: the only hope is in a collective refusal to submit to the utilitarian conventions of society, and in the discovery of the liberating possibilities of art. No single label seems to fit *Refus global*. The fact that it has variously been called anarchist, surrealist, nationalist, Marxist, and Freudian may explain its lasting impact. Probably its most important influence on Quebec culture derived from its clear message that art cannot isolate itself from society, and that to liberate his or her voice the artist must become allied with social revolution.

An English translation can be found in Ramsay COOK, *French-Canadian nationalism* (1969). See also Dennis Reid, *A concise history of Canadian painting* (2nd edn, 1988), and Ray Ellenwood, *The Automatiste movement in Quebec: egregore* (1992). PATRICIA SMART

Reibetanz, John. See POETRY IN ENGLISH 1983 TO 1996: 3.

Relève, La (1934-48). This monthly journal was founded in Mar. 1934 by a group of young French Canadians, among whom the prime movers were Robert CHARBONNEAU and Claude Hurtubise. Until its demise in Sept. 1948, it published 48 numbers under the name *La Relève* and 55 under the name *La Nouvelle Relève*. Among its major Quebec contributors were Robert ÉLIE, Roger Duhamel, Hector de SAINT-DENYS-GARNEAU, and Jean LE MOYNE, and it occasionally published works by such famous authors as Daniel Rops, Jacques Maritain, and Emmanuel Mounier. The magazine set out to promote the emergence of a 'national independent Catholic group' whose aim would be to 'develop an art, a literature, and a line of thought, the lack of which begins to be oppressive'. Though the founders were concerned about the state of the economy, they viewed this as a problem more related to spiritual matters and to civilization itself than to mere social and economic questions. They hoped to establish a society modelled on that of the Middle Ages, when there was harmony between the temporal and the spiritual. In accordance with these very general ideas, they considered that the problems of French-Canadian society centred on literature, Catholicism, the educational system, etc. It was against this background that the literary works of its chief contributors were produced: Robert Charbonneau and Robert Élie in the novel; Saint-Denys-Garneau in poetry; and Jean Le Moyne in the essay.

See also the entry on Robert Charbonneau and LITERARY MAGAZINES IN QUEBEC: 2.

JACQUES PELLETIER

Religion and theology. The picture of Canadian religious literature will be greatly affected by the angle from which it is approached. One may begin by considering what Canadian writers have had to say about religion, or how religion has been reflected in the national literature. Either approach would be legitimate, but the latter has been favoured here.

Faced with the immediate task of preserving faith among people who had been cut off from their roots, the pioneer clergy concentrated largely on pastoral and polemical themes. They inherited a tradition of clerical literacy that included familiarity with the Bible and other religious classics, however, and had a well-nourished professional interest in the techniques of rhetoric. Most often this expressed itself in sermons, but it occasionally found literary outlets. Thomas McCULLOCH, who flayed Roman Catholicism in his closely argued *Popery condemned by scripture and the Fathers* (1808), also set Canadian humour on its way in the *Letters of Mephibosheth Stepsure* (1821-3, reprinted in book form 1862, 1960). Bishop John Strachan, although better known for political skills than for eloquence, provided John Robert COLOMBO with material for found poems in *The Mackenzie poems, John*

Toronto: new poems by Dr. Strachan (1966). Others used homespun approaches to reach unsophisticated readers. Henry ALLINE, the author of *Two mites on some of the most important and much disputed points of divinity* (1781), could overwhelm Nova Scotian congregations with floods of highly figurative language. David Willson, founder of the Children of Peace and designer of their remarkable Sharon Temple near Toronto, showed himself a visionary of remarkable intellectual power in *The impressions of the mind* (1835). Alline and Willson were both prolific writers of hymns, of which few were of consistently high quality but many contained lines well beyond the ordinary.

Although poetry and devotional material were always ecclesiastically acceptable, the development of religious literature was long inhibited by an attitude among many Protestant denominations that virtually equated fiction with falsehood. John Carroll, a self-educated preacher, helped to undermine the taboo by publishing lively narratives drawn from Methodist experiences, such as *My boy life* (1882). Gradually the concept of wholesome fiction began to emerge, encouraged by W.H. Withrow, editor of Methodist Sunday School publications, and by James Macdonald—later editor of the *Globe*—in the unofficially Presbyterian *Westminster*. It was exploited by Ralph Connor (Charles W. GORDON), Nellie McCLUNG, R.E. KNOWLES, and Marian Keith (Mary Esther MacGREGOR) in a voluminous outpouring of novels that have largely been dismissed by critics but were immensely popular in their time.

These writers both reflected and popularized a current or theological liberalism that flowed largely from abroad but was widely influential in Canada. Queen's University, Kingston, became a notable centre of it. W.G. Jordan, in *Biblical criticism and modern thought* (1909), was one of the first of those who sought to demonstrate the compatibility of modern religious ideas with the Christian faith, while John WATSON proposed a synthesis of Kantian philosophy and an updated Christianity in *Christianity and idealism* (1893). Nathanael Burwash's neo-Baconian *Manual of Christian theology on the inductive method* (1900), once largely forgotten, has been receiving renewed attention. Biblical scholars applied the new methods to their disciplines, most fruitfully in Old Testament studies, where Canadians became especially prominent. Meanwhile, there had emerged an esoteric strain of religious thought, born of American transcendentalism and nourished by increasing familiarity with Eastern religions, that passed almost unnoticed among professional theologians but profoundly affected both the CONFEDERATION POETS and the painter Lawren Harris of the Group of Seven. The most influential publication in this genre in Canada was R.M. BUCKE's *Cosmic consciousness* (1901). That some Christian writers could be almost as heterodox in their views was indicated by the Methodist/United Church minister Salem Bland in *The new Christianity* (1920), which was claimed to represent a more radical innovation than Jesus himself had introduced.

The onset of existentialism and the impact of two world wars brought about a radical change in the Canadian theological climate. Critical methods were now almost universally accepted, at least among academics, but the problems with which they had wrestled seemed increasingly peripheral. Karl Barth, writing in the heartland of European Protestantism, challenged what he dismissed as a complacent liberalism. Most Canadians were scandalized at first by what seemed to them a step backward, but W.W. Bryden of Knox College, University of Toronto, brought Barth's ideas to scholarly attention in *The Christian's knowledge of God* (1940). Probably the most influential Canadian book reflecting the impact of Protestant neo-orthodoxy was C.N. Cochrane's *Christianity and classical culture* (1940), a sympathetic study of St Augustine's theology of history that had its provenance not in a theological college but in the history department of the University of Toronto. Meanwhile, regular visits by Étienne Gilson and Jacques Maritain had helped to establish the Pontifical Institute of Mediaeval Studies in Toronto as one of the world's most prestigious centres in its field.

Canada was beginning to achieve recognition as a minor theological centre. Then, with apparent suddenness, people began to be aware of a galaxy of Canadian theologians. The works of Bernard J.F. LONERGAN, whose *Method in theology* (1971) called attention to ways of doing theology, are being studied throughout the Catholic world. Wilfred Cantwell Smith, who first became prominent as a student of other religions with *The faith of other men* (1963), moved towards broader generalizations in *Towards a world theology* (1981). Douglas John Hall, probably the leading theologian of the United Church of Canada, has combined the customary progressivism of his denomination with a desire to recover greater theological depth for it. He has written a trilogy: *Thinking the faith* (1989), *Professing the faith*

(1993), and *Confessing the faith* (1996). Gregory Baum, who first became well known as the leading spokesperson in Canada for a newly discovered Roman Catholic ecumenism, later concentrated on Christian sociology; a number of his articles have been brought together in *Theology and society* (1987). Emil FACKENHEIM has wrestled repeatedly with the implications of the Holocaust for the understanding of Jewish existence, as in his collection of essays, *The Jewish return into history* (1978).

Although in Canada the formal examination of religion has declined markedly in recent years, religious subjects have continued to draw the attention of numerous creative and other writers. Hugh MacLENNAN's *The watch that ends the night* (1959) took its title from a well-known hymn by Isaac Watts, and Rudy WIEBE based *The blue mountains of China* (1970) on Mennonite experience. Religion furnished the theme of Margaret ATWOOD's *The HANDMAID'S TALE* (1985). It permeates the poems of Margaret AVISON, notably *The dumbfounding* (1966). Margaret LAURENCE's Manawaka novels, although subject to constant threats of banishment from school libraries, were consciously rooted in deeply held convictions. The writings of George GRANT, such as *Technology and justice* (1986), are impregnated with Christian doctrine. Even Leonard COHEN drew inspiration for *Beautiful losers* (1966) from the life of Kateri Tekakwitha, later to be recognized as a Roman Catholic saint. Literary interest in religion has been paralleled by an increasing tendency among theologians to take seriously the significance of literary expression for the understanding of faith. Examples have been Joseph C. McLelland's *The clown and the crocodile* (1970) and Alice and Kenneth Hamilton's *The elements of John Updike* (1970), while Malcolm Ross has brought the two together in *Poetry and dogma* (1954).

Religion and literature have met to great effect in Northrop FRYE's *The great code* (1982) and *Words with power* (1990). In these two books, which are regarded as the culmination of his career, Frye drew upon a lifetime of literary criticism and on the experience of many years of teaching undergraduate courses on religion and literature. His approach was that of a scholar uncommitted to a dogmatic system but deeply committed to the insights he found in the Bible. Eschewing the categories of formal theology and source criticism as largely irrelevant to his purpose, he examined the language, metaphors, and typological arrangement of this massive collection in order to draw out its essential unity of theme. Frye's importance for literary criticism, both in Canada and abroad, was impressively demonstrated shortly after his death by the calling of a conference devoted to the study of his work. The proceedings, edited by Alvin A. Lee and Robert D. Denham, were published as *The legacy of Northrop Frye* (1994). Not surprisingly, the contributors were drawn from the literary community. Not only had Frye's attitude to theologians been somewhat cavalier, but his awareness of their activities had not been kept up to date. His knowledge of the literary forms of the Bible was encyclopaedic, however, and his insights into its message were ones from which even the most knowledgeable have a great deal to learn.

JOHN WEBSTER GRANT

Remski, Matthew. See NOVELS IN ENGLISH 1983 TO 1996: OTHER NOVELS 1(a).

Renaud, Claude. See ACADIAN LITERATURE: 2(b).

Renaud, Jacques (b. 1943). Born and brought up in the Montreal working-class district of Rosemont, he attended a public secondary school. After failing his Grade XI examinations, he began a series of manual jobs, then became a clerk in the municipal film library. He has worked in advertising, as a journalist, as a researcher for a Radio-Canada TV program, and as a translator. Soon after it was founded in 1963, Renaud became associated with the *indépendantiste*/Marxist magazine *PARTI PRIS*. After a trip to India in 1970 he became attracted to yoga and Eastern mysticism. In the late 1980s he was active in the Equality Party, an extremist Anglo-rights party, only to leave it after a short time. He published a book that was critical of Quebec's language legislation, *La constellation du bouc émissaire* (1993).

Renaud's best-known novel—the first creative prose work in Quebec to use *JOUAL* for dialogue and narration—is the powerful and shocking *Le cassé* (1964), written when the author was just twenty-one and living in the squalid area of Montreal's 'Centre-Ville'. The title, a *joual* word based on the English slang expression 'broke', also conjures up images of a central figure who is beaten, crippled, and disoriented. The hero, Tit-Jean, probably the most totally alienated character in Quebec literature—the novel has been called 'le chant ultime de la dépossession'—conceives and perpetrates the brutal murder of a 'goofball' peddlar, whom he wrongfully takes to be a secret lover of his mistress. The murder assumes an escapist and ritualistic character, giving temporary feelings of liberation to the frustrated hero. Despite some weak characterization and occasional maladroit interjections by the narrator, *Le cassé* contains striking lower-depths poetry and skilful cinematic techniques. A second edition (1977) adds four short stories and the author's two-part 'Journal du *Cassé*', the first part of which consists of short texts that discuss *Le cassé* directly or indirectly; the second part includes excerpts from reviews of the first edition of *Le cassé* that document the furore caused by its inclusion in a CEGEP course in the Sorel region in 1971. The best prose work of the *parti pris* group of writers, *Le cassé* was translated by Gérald Robitaille as *Flat broke and beat* (1968). A second translation, *Broke city* (1984), was done by David Homel.

En d'autres paysages (1970) is an unsuccessful attempt to wed cosmogony and fantasy with social realism, but the book contains some fine prose-poetry and engaging character portrayals. The very short, poetic *Le fond pur de l'errance irradie* (1975) is set, one learns gradually, in Istanbul. The hero is a writer, Irradieu, who opposes ideologies and religions and sees himself as a member of a new superhuman race. In another short work, *Le cycle du scorpion* (1979), astrological symbols permeate the automatic prose-poetry of its versets. Here, as elsewhere in Renaud's work, the 'princes de tristesse' of the traditional Quebec Church are scorned in favour of a new individualistic mysticism. In the longer 'roman' *La colombe et la brisure éternité* (1979), a dove represents the female who breaks the cycle of hatred and inaugurates that of love. Creativity is the fruit of the dove's coupling with 'l'homme discursif' in an embrace marked by 'une tendresse cosmique'. *Clandestine(s) ou la tradition du couchant* (1980) owes its plural title to a group of women involved in Quebec *indépendantiste* underground activity. The hero evolves from a highly committed nationalist to a counter-culture mystic.

L'espace du diable (1989) is a collection of short stories. At the age of nineteen Renaud had published a short poetry collection, *Electrodes* (1962), full of anguish, hatred, solitude, and cold; some of the poems show the influence of the cosmic and geological themes of Alain GRANDBOIS. *Electrodes* and *Le cycle du scorpion* were reproduced in *Les cycles du scorpion. Poèmes et proses 1960-1987* (1989), more than half of the texts of which were unpublished. It has a punny, self-reflexive preface written in a mixture of *joual*, standard French, and English, and an afterword attributed to 'Long John Silver'—the author's alleged 'muse et secrétaire-trésorier'—that is clearly Renaud's more serious defence of his writing throughout his career.

For a discussion of *Le cassé* and Renaud, see Malcolm Reid's *The shouting signpainters: a literary and political account of Québec revolutionary nationalism* (1972) and B.-Z. Shek's *Social realism in the French-Canadian novel* (1977), chap. 9.

See also NOVELS IN FRENCH 1960 TO 1982: 3(d). BEN-Z. SHEK

Renaud, Thérèse (b. 1927). Born in Montreal, she was educated at the convent of the Sisters of the Holy Names in Outremont, but left school at fourteen in frustration at what she considered an outdated curriculum and began to write poetry. She was a member of the Automatiste group of artists who, along with their teacher Paul-Émile Borduas produced the manifesto *REFUS GLOBAL* in 1948. Her volume of Surrealist-inspired poems, *Les sables du rêve* (1946), illustrated by Jean-Paul Mousseau, was the group's first publication. Following her marriage to painter Fernand Leduc in 1947 in Paris (where they still live), Renaud ceased publishing until the appearance of her memoir *Une mémoire déchirée* (1978). In it she evokes her rebellious childhood and adolescence in the repressive atmosphere of Dulpessis-era Quebec, her discovery of art, and her struggle to maintain an identity and creative voice during her years as a wife and mother. Since then she has published several volumes of poetry and short stories (*Plaisirs immobiles*, 1981, *Subterfuge et sortilège*, 1988, *Jardins divers*, 1991), as well as an autobiographical fiction centred on the mother-daughter relationship, *Le choc d'un murmure* (1988).

PATRICIA SMART

***Répertoire national*, *Le*.** See ANTHOLOGIES IN FRENCH: 1 and POETRY IN FRENCH: 2.

Ricard, André (b. 1938). Born in Sainte-Anne-de-Beaupré, Quebec, he attended Université Laval and the Quebec Conservatoire d'art dramatique. He was one of the founders of the Théâtre de l'Estoc (1957-68, Quebec City), and was its artistic director from 1963 to 1968. He has written numerous scripts for television and radio, two of which, *Pour hâter la fin du monde* (1987) and *Les champs de glace* (1989), were published in *Écrits du Canada Français*. His radio play *Le Tue-Monde* was awarded the Court Métrage prize in 1976. In 1996 he was elected to the Académie des Lettres du Québec.

Though Ricard is the author of a few short stories and a poetic essay, *Les baigneurs de Tadoussac* (1993), he is known chiefly as a dramatist. He has written several one-act and eight full-length plays. Most of his characters seek to acquire power in one form or another and money is usually the means to that end. For example, *La vie exemplaire d'Alcide 1er le pharamineux et de sa proche descendance* (1973) is an epic play with fifty-four characters and twelve scenes depicting the rise and fall of a Mafia-type family. *La gloire des filles à Magloire* (1975) tells of the revenge of women driven to prostitution. *Le casino voleur* (1978) is a story of petty swindling. *Le tir-à-blanc* (1973) is about sexual domination. *Le déversoir les larmes* premièred at the Théâtre du Café de la Place in 1988 and won Montreal's Place des Arts prize.

Ricard's most ambitious undertaking is a triptych that will retrace the history of Quebec from New France to modern day. The first two parts of this teeming epic have already been completed. *La longue marche dans les Avents* (1985) is about life in New France at the time of the conquest, with parallels to Quebec of the 1970s. *Le tréteau des apatrides ou La veillée en armes* (1993), which was awarded the prize at the Concours du Théâtre du Nouveau Monde (1994), attempts to recreate the political and psychological tensions that led to the 1837 Rebellion, again with allusions to contemporary Quebec.

There is humour, often rather bitter humour, in all Ricard's plays, but his chief quality is a versatile style. He is equally at ease with the elegant, sometimes stilted language of aristocrats or refined crooks, the racy dialogue of ladies of easy virtue, and the colourful speech of the Beauce.

PAULETTE COLLET

Ricci, Nino (b. 1959). Born in Leamington, Ontario, to parents from Molise, Italy, he obtained a B.A. in English at York University, Toronto, and an M.A. in creative writing at Concordia University, Montreal; he also completed a year of study in Italian literature at the University of Florence. He has taught English at a secondary school in Nigeria, through CUSO, and creative writing and Canadian literature at Concordia University. His first novel of a projected trilogy, *Lives of the saints* (1990), received international attention and won several national and international literary awards, including a Governor General's Award; it was on the best-seller list in Canada for well over a year. This was followed by *In a glass house* (1993). Both novels deal with the protagonist's relationship with members of his Italian family, using first-person narration and a poetic and lucid prose style.

Ricci's novels make ethnicity intrinsic to the representation of contemporary realities. Many of the topics that are developed (social estrangement, intergenerational conflict, the opposition of world views, the search for identity) typify some of the concerns of other writers in Canada involved in the depiction of ethnicity, especially in the area of Italian-Canadian fiction. In *Lives of the saints* there is a constant juxtaposing of different levels of experience, rendered through myth, superstition, folklore, and modernity. In *In a glass house* the acutely introspective Victor Innocente, the protagonist-narrator, can neither be part of his social environment nor construct a stable interior world. Both novels examine the convulsions of cultural transformation, complex and conflicted family relations, the existential dimensions of daily life, and present an ambiguous, contradictory view of Canadian society from an Italian perspective. *Where she has gone*, the third volume in Ricci's trilogy, was published in the fall of 1997.

MARINO TUZI

Richard, Jean-Jules (1911-75). Born at St-Raphaël, in the Beauce region of Quebec, of farm parents (his mother was illiterate), he first left home at fourteen and began writing poetry and novels at an early age. At fifteen he attended a classical college, but was expelled after two years for protesting against a teacher's mistreatment of a fellow pupil. Independent ever since, he worked as a bookseller, freelance journalist, and construction worker. In the Depression years Richard rode the rods, took part in the 'Hunger March' of 1937, and was in a delegation that met Prime Minister R.B. Bennett to demand better pay for youth in the relief work camps.

A soldier in the Canadian army, Richard was wounded during the Normandy invasion in 1944. A short-term pension allowed him to write his first novel, *Neuf jours de haine* (1948), a grisly account of war and its dehumanization. In an ironic style, marked by breathless short sentences and sense impressions, it lashes out against Nazism, venal politicians, and militarism; but the book is wordy and repetitive. When his next novel was published, Richard was being hounded for his participation in the Left-oriented Canadian Peace Congress. *Le feu dans l'amiante* (1956) is largely journalistic fiction about the 1949 Asbestos strike, considered a turning-point in Quebec's social history. Published at the author's expense in

Toronto, it was highly critical of Premier Maurice Duplessis. It vividly conveys the dynamite blasts that regulated life in Asbestos, the all-pervading dust and silicosis, and collective attempts at social reform, but it was marred by unsubtle repetition and weak characterization. For the second edition (1971) Richard changed many characters' names to those of some twenty-five prominent politicians, writers, and artists.

During the 1950s Richard became depressed and burned a number of his manuscripts. His third novel, *Journal d'un hobo* (1965), is an overlong extension of an excellent story, 'Prélude en si mineur': the diary of a homosexual rod-runner who travels during the Depression from his native Acadia to British Columbia and relates his sexual and social adventures. Containing flashes of poetic descriptions of railway yards and hobo camps, it reflects the narrator's revolt against the social system that had caused so much grief. The sexual and social threads, however, do not fully intertwine.

In the 1970s Richard published seven books. *Faites-leur boire le fleuve* (1970), winner of the Prix Jean-Béraud, is a dramatic story of the Montreal waterfront and its conflicts between longshoremen and their anglophone bosses, and between rival groups of dockers and underworld characters. The argot and mores of the docks contrast with the genteel speech and outward manners of Westmount. *Carré Saint-Louis* (1971) is a violent, naturalistic story of young drug-pushers and users who gather in the 'square' of the title. Despite a lively style, the book is spoiled by excessive indirect narration. *Exovide Louis Riel* (1972) deals with the Saskatchewan rebellion of 1885 and the hanging of the legendary Métis leader. Here, as elsewhere, there is a tendency towards melodrama and caricature.

Comment réussir à cinquante ans (1973) is a droll novel written in the form of a TV soap opera. Satire of the media, universities, bourgeois philanthropy, and urban land speculation abounds. *Pièges* (1973) is a short novel about the psychological and sexual problems of marriage.

Le voyage en rond (1972) is a novel set in the Lower Canada of 1791. Humorous anachronisms of speech, incident, and names, and a transposition of the crisis of Oct. 1970, aim criticism at the FLQ as well as cruel, grasping, English-speaking bourgeois and francophone Catholic clergy.

Richard's last novel, *Centreville* (1973), is structured by the inadequately differentiated monologues of ten shady characters, most of whom live in a brothel, and ends with the murder of a hypocritical pimp-cum-morality-campaigner, and the suicide of the prostitute-perpetrator.

Ville rouge (1949), an early collection of short stories, filled with popular speech and vignettes of the seamier side of life—the title is an image for the blood-red brick walls of the poor areas of Montreal and Quebec City—and Richard's second novel, *Le feu dans l'amiante*, had a marked and acknowledged influence on the writers associated with *PARTI PRIS* because of their working-class subject matter and stark realism.

For an illuminating interview with Richard on his formative years and his worldview, see 'Jean-Jules Richard au présent' by Réginald Martel in *LIBERTÉ*, 81 (1972). For a discussion of Richard's early novels, see Ben-Z. Shek, *Social realism in the French-Canadian novel* (1977). An overview of Richard's work appears in Paul-André Bourque's 'De la haine à l'amour par le rire', *Livres et auteurs québécois 1973*.

See also NOVELS IN FRENCH 1940 TO 1959: 3.

BEN-Z. SHEK

Richards, David Adams (b. 1950). He grew up in Newcastle, New Brunswick, and attended St Thomas University, Fredericton, which he left to pursue a career as a writer. He now lives in Saint John with his wife and children.

The poems in *Small heroics* (1972), a New Brunswick poetry chapbook, reflect an acute awareness of rural environment and a pervading sense of disillusionment and deprivation, transformed into a sombre beauty—qualities that became the hallmark of Richards' subsequent prose. He won the Norma Epstein $1000 prize for undergraduate creative writing in Canada with a portion of his first novel, *The coming of winter* (1974, NCL), which was highly praised. In 1980 the State Publishing Agency of the USSR bought the world rights in the Russian language for this novel—appropriately, since the great Russian novelists were among Richards' strongest influences. It tells of a Miramichi Valley youth's tragicomic ineptitude and uninspired slide into marriage, counterbalanced by his love of the outdoors, and of the woods and rivers (so important to the author himself). Richards' ear for local speech patterns and his eye for the details of individual life-styles have earned him a reputation for striking realism. *Blood ties* (1976; NCL, with an Afterword by Merna SUMMERS) is a probing psychological examination of the lives of a larger number of characters from the same region. The short stories of *Dancers at night* (1978) and the novel *Lives of short duration* (1981; NCL, with an Afterword by Alistair MacLEOD), while continuing in this setting, show an increased concern with the theme of cultural and economic deprivation, and an intensified sense of human compassion. The latter, perhaps Richards' most ambitious novel, gives voice to a whole community and its history through the perceptions of three generations of characters. With *Road to the stilt house* (1985) Richards changed his style towards a more stark and compressed treatment in both subject and language. Carrying the theme of deprivation even further, it takes as its central figure a character and his family—seen by the community as mentally retarded—and discovers in this context some of the causes of social violence.

Nights below Station Street (1988) won a Governor General's Award, and began a trilogy of novels on an interrelated group of characters, completed with *Evening snow will bring such peace* (1990) and *For those who hunt the wounded down* (1993)—which was made into a powerful film by Credo Films of Winnipeg, for which Richards wrote the script. Many of Richards' characters have a comic dimension that is often missed by reviewers who feel uncomfortable in the world of his characters, but the humour is quite apparent in *Nights below Station Street*. We are intended to laugh at Adele when her nervous impatience completely derails her logical train of thought. Joe, her father, is a sort of moral hero. At the centre of the novel lies his struggle to conquer his alcoholism. His hard-won sobriety, coupled with his fine woodsmanship, empower him to save the life of a friend at the novel's end. Such 'small heroics' are at the moral centre of Richards' universe. Joe does not understand his own accomplishment, but no single character in a Richards novel ever comprehends, or is able to articulate, the whole meaning of their actions.

Perhaps this accounts for the relative weakness of Richards' collection of essays, *A lad from Brantford* (1995). Attempting to express his messages through the single, analytical voice of the essayist, Richards cannot work his magic so well, and becomes one of his own limited characters—in this case an armchair philosopher preoccupied with anti-Americanism, anti-intellectualism, and anti-materialism.

Hockey dreams (1996) is built around Richards' reminiscences of his childhood passion for the sport and his adult disillusionment over the fate of Canada's national game. The latter theme has something of the heavy-handedness of the *Brantford* essays, but is rescued by a wonderful sense of humour and by the poignant sketches of his fellow hockey-hopefuls battling it out on the frozen Miramichi. The novel *Hope in a desperate hour* (1996) expands the cast of Richards' characters into the academic world, which he came to know in Fredericton, both as a student and as writer-in-residence. The lives of two professors are entangled with those of a failed and dying hockey player, his family, and the Natives on a nearby reservation. All are stuck in varying postures of failing or failed ambition and betrayal. The orchestration of this complex plot involves the heaviest reliance on an omniscient narrator that we have seen so far in Richards' work—resulting in a new clarity, though it is acquired at some cost to the novel's subtlety and dramatic intensity.

Some reviewers have seen Richards as a very talented, but dated, modern realist. But it is possible to see his themes as participating in a timeless tragi-comic world view that, when sown upon the exotic soil of Richards' New Brunswick, yields a unique wisdom. Although Richards is not troubled by questions about the nature of reality, the challenge for post-modern criticism is to explore how Richards' fiction seems to achieve more than the sum of its parts—more, perhaps, than the author's abstract intention.

In 1996 Richards received the Best Scriptwriter award at New York's International Film Festival for the script of the Christmas film *Small gifts* (1995), produced by the Canadian Broadcasting Corporation.

The best general commentary on Richards' fiction is Sheldon Currie's 'David Adams Richards: the people on the roadway', *The Antigonish Review* 99 (Autumn 1994). See also profiles by Alden NOWLAN in *Atlantic Insight* (Apr. 1980), Phil Milner in *Books in Canada* (Oct. 1980), and Nancy Robb in *Quill and Quire* (Apr. 1988); an interview by Kathleen Scherf in *Studies in Canadian Literature*, vol.15, no.1 (1990); an article by Susan Lever, 'Against the stream: the fiction of David Adams Richards', *Australian-Canadian Studies*, vol.12, no.11 (1994); and a review article by Maria Kubacki, 'Beyond the Miramichi', *Books in Canada* (Summer 1996).

ANDREW SEAMAN

Richardson, John (1796-1852). The garrisons of Upper Canada shaped the early years of one of our earliest novelists. Born in Queenston, Upper Canada (Ontario), he grew up in Amherstburgh (Fort Malden) on the Detroit River. Richardson's father was a British medical officer and his mother the offspring of John Askin, a leading fur trader and (probably) a member of the Ottawa tribe. 1812 saw Richardson serving as a gentleman-volunteer; he and his brother were allowed to raise the British colours over the captured Fort Detroit. Captured during Tecumseh's last stand at Moraviantown in 1813, Richardson was a prisoner-of-war in Ohio and Kentucky for a year. Tecumseh remained a lifelong hero to him, and his narratives are filled with the violence and savagery that he witnessed in forest warfare. His commission in the British Army came too late for him to fight in the Napoleonic wars, so he spent 1816-18 in the garrisons of the West Indies. There he endured yellow fever and witnessed the brutalities of both the slaveholders and the army in which he served. Settling in London in 1818, then adventuring in Paris, he followed the rackety existence of a half-pay officer/adventurer on the make. In 1825 in Paris he married Jane Marsh, who died a few years later (in 1832 he wed Maria Caroline Drayson, who died in 1846).

In London again in 1826, Richardson began a productive but ill-paid career as a writer and journalist. While producing poetry, novels, memoirs, pamphlets, reports, and polemics, he also served for a while in the army and then in other occupations. As a self-educated colonial, probably of mixed white-Native ancestry, he was touchy on a number of points. Arrogant, high-spirited, obtuse, he made quarrelsomeness (and duelling) a feature of his life. David Beasley, author of a remarkable (given the scarcity of written records) reconstruction of Richardson's life, *The Canadian Don Quixote* (1977), observes that a character in the novel *Écarté* is a stand-in for his creator. That character's real-life counterpart ('endowed with a susceptibility which rendered him unable to endure even the shadow of slight or insult') suffered duelling injuries during the time in which the novel is set.

In 1826 Richardson published an anonymous account of his 1812 war experiences in the *New Monthly Magazine*, London. His first imaginative use of his North American frontier experience came with the long poem *Tecumseh; or, The warrior of the West in four cantos with notes* (London, 1828). Lurid, written in a mock-epic verse form that undermines its claims to seriousness, *Tecumseh*'s failure drove Richardson to exploit his Parisian experience in *Écarté; or, The salons of Paris* (London 1829) and *Frascati's; or scenes in Paris* (an anonymous sequel now attributed to him; London, 1830). In the same year he published the satirical, risqué poem *Kensington Gardens* (London, 1830). Also in 1830, inspired by James Fenimore Cooper's *The last of the Mohicans*, he began writing his best-known work, which used the wilderness of *Tecumseh* much more effectively. *WACOUSTA; or, The prophecy: a tale of the Canadas* (3 vols, Edinburgh, 1832) takes place during the 1763 siege of Detroit during Pontiac's uprising. Its complex Gothic plot depicts Sir Reginald Morton's monstrous revenge upon his unscrupulous rival in love, Colonel De Haldimar. Forest and garrison alike are rife with inhumanity; the narrative is also marked by surprise, disguise, bizarre coincidence, and high rhetoric. Praised by reviewers, it attained a limited popularity in Britain and the United States (not in Canada), where it was fashioned into a melodrama.

In 1835 Richardson went to Spain as a major in a mercenary force, the British Legion, fighting for the royalist side in the Carlist civil conflict of 1834-7. His *Journal of the movements of the British Legion* (London, 1836) and *Movements of the British Legion* (London, 1837) chronicle chiefly his war with his superiors—though the British Tories used both volumes to embarrass Melbourne's administration. He returned to Canada in 1838, to Montreal, as special correspondent for *The Times* of London to cover Lord Durham's efforts to re-establish Upper and Lower Canada's political structures after the 1837 rebellions. Richardson's support of Durham led to differences with his editors, who fired him. *The Canadian brothers; or, The prophecy fulfilled* (Montreal, 1840), a sequel to *Wacousta*, makes use of the author's 1812 experience as a prisoner-of-war in Kentucky. He then settled in Brockville (Ontario) and began the weekly *New Era; or The Canadian Chronicle* (1841-42). There he published his 'Recollection of the West Indies' (15 April 1842) and serialized his memoir of the War of 1812, a vivid, highly partisan account of individuals and events interspersed with long stretches of documentary reprints, published as *War of 1812* (1902).

The failure of the Brockville venture sent Richardson to nearby Kingston and a new journal, *The Canadian Loyalist and Spirit of 1812* (1843-4). In 1845 his political connections landed him a superintendency of the Welland Canal police, where the insubordination of his men led to the disbandment of the force early the next year. His beloved wife died, and he shifted to Montreal until 1849, when he tried his luck in New York. During his last, desolate years in Canada, Richardson wrote pamphlets, collected in *Eight years in Canada;*

embracing a review of the administrations of Lords Durham and Sydenham, Sir Charles Bagot, and Lord Metcalfe, and including numerous interesting letters from Lord Durham, Mr. Chas. Buller and other well-known public characters (Montreal, 1847) and *The Guards in Canada; or The point of honour; being a sequel to . . . 'Eight years in Canada'* (Montreal, 1848). Both books combine reminiscence with political and personal polemic.

Richardson's final, fatal gamble for success took place in New York. There he worked as a hack for Dewitt and Davenport, a publishing firm (devoted to pornography and anti-Catholicism) founded in 1848 by two young men. They published Richardson's *The monk knight of St. John; a tale of the Crusades* (New York, 1850) featuring the Middle Ages as background for a tale of adultery, slaughter, rape, and cannibalism. *Hardscrabble; or, The fall of Chicago. A tale of Indian warfare* (New York, 1850) and *Wau-nan-gee; or, The massacre at Chicago* (New York, [1852]) were volumes of a projected trilogy. Richardson severed his last ties with Canada in 1851 with the publication of *Matilda Montgomerie; or The prophecy fulfilled* (New York), in which he attempted to Americanize his *Canadian brothers* by expunging its anti-American passages and retitling it with the name of his American villainess. *Matilda Montgomerie* and reissues of *Écarté* and *Wacousta* were all successful American publications, though Richardson sold their rights and made little money from them. In 1851 he published anonymously *Lola Montes: or, A reply to the 'Private history and memoirs' of that celebrated lady* (New York), a defence of the notorious Irish dancer and adventuress who had arrived in New York. *Westbrook, the outlaw; or, The avenging wolf* (New York, 1853), based on a historical figure who ravaged southwestern Ontario during 1812, appeared serially in the *Sunday Mercury* and was published posthumously in book form; it sank without a trace until recovered and republished in 1973. Richardson died of a malnutrition-related illness, too poor to continue feeding his Newfoundland dog.

See Carl Ballstadt, ed., *Major John Richardson: a selection of reviews and criticism* (1972); William F.E. Morley, *A bibliographical study of Major John Richardson* (1973); David Beasley, *The Canadian Don Quixote: the life and works of Major John Richardson, Canada's first novelist* (1977); Catherine Sheldrick Ross, ed., *Recovering Canada's first novelist. Proceedings from the John Richardson conference*, (1984); Michael Hurley, *The borders of nightmare: the fiction of John Richardson* (1992); and Dennis Duffy, *A world under sentence: John Richardson and the interior* (1995). *Wacousta* appears in the NEW CANADIAN LIBRARY with an Afterword by James REANEY. Restored texts of *Wacousta* and *The Canadian brothers*, edited by D.R. Cronk (1987) and D.G. Stephens (1992) respectively, have been published by the CENTRE FOR EDITING EARLY CANADIAN TEXTS.

DENNIS DUFFY

Richardson, Keith. See CRITICISM IN ENGLISH 5(e).

Richler, Mordecai (b. 1931). Born in Montreal, Quebec, at the beginning of the Depression, Richler has depicted in his writing (particularly in the autobiographical sketches collected in *The street*, 1969), his experience of growing up in the working-class Jewish neighbourhood around St Urbain Street and of attending Baron Byng, the predominantly Jewish public high school nearby. In 1948 Richler entered Sir George Williams College (now part of Concordia University), working part-time as a reporter for the *Montreal Herald*. Never comfortable in an academic milieu, he dropped out in 1950. The following year he travelled to Europe, joining in Paris the newest generation of North American expatriate writers, which included Allen Ginsberg, Terry Southern, and Mavis GALLANT, publishing a short story there, and beginning work on his first novel. Returning to Canada in 1952, he worked briefly at the CBC before moving to England in 1954. A professional writer since that time, Richler has worked as a journalist as well as a novelist. He has also written film scripts.(His credits include *Life at the top*, 1965, and *Fun with Dick and Jane*, 1977, as well adaptations of two of his own novels: *The APPRENTICESHIP OF DUDDY KRAVITZ*, 1974, and *Joshua then and now*, 1985.) Having spent his first eighteen years as a writer abroad, Richler remarked, 'I'm a Canadian and a Jew and I write about being both. I worry about being away so long from the roots of my discontent.' He returned permanently to Quebec in 1972.

In an early interview Richler said that he wrote from a compulsion to 'say what I feel about values and about people living in a time when . . . there is no agreement on values'. In his novels, as in his essays, he is a moralist who is nevertheless capable of shocking his readers with his choice and treatment of topics. His first novel, *The acrobats* (1954), published in England and poorly received in Canada, shows him beginning his career under the influence of Hemingway, Sartre, and Malraux.

Though its cynical world-weariness seems more a product of the moment than of Richler's own vision, the novel embodies a set of interconnected concerns that recur in his later fiction: the Spanish Civil War as a testing-ground of the engaged intellectual, the place of Jews in post-Holocaust society, a preoccupation with personal responsibility, and a sense that his own generation arrived at the wrong time to take heroic action. As well, this first novel exemplifies the characteristic quality that Richler would later describe as his 'persistent attempt to make a case for the ostensibly unsympathetic man'. Though clumsy in its use of the modernist technique of fragmented narrative, *The acrobats* was successful in its day. It was reissued in an American paperback edition (as *Wicked we love*) and translated into Danish, Norse, and German. It never had a Canadian edition and Richler refuses to let it be brought back into print.

Richler's greatest strength is his debunking of the myths of his culture. His second novel, *Son of a smaller hero* (1955), was attacked by some Montreal Jews as anti-Semitic. Serving Richler in the way that *Portrait of the artist as a young man* served Joyce—as an announcement of the intellectual's need to break free from the too-binding ties of his small community—this novel depicts a young man's need both to escape the limitations of the Montreal Jewish ghetto and to leave North American society. Once he himself was abroad, however, Richler was no more inclined to spare his new community than his old. His next novel, *A choice of enemies* (1957), satirizes as poseurs the expatriate film-makers in London who saw themselves as refugees from the political persecution of the American McCarthy era.

It was not until his fourth novel, *The apprenticeship of Duddy Kravitz* (1959), that Richler fully exhibited the narrative skills and command of voice that have made him one of the foremost writers of his generation. Featuring his most morally complex character, a bumptious young hustler obsessed with acquiring land as his way out of the ghetto, this novel presents Duddy Kravitz as unreliable, a moral coward who nonetheless has moments of genuine feeling and even nobility, and with whom the reader is invited to sympathize.

One of Duddy's classmates at Fletcher's Field is Jake Hersh, later the hero of Richler's *St. Urbain's Horseman* (1971). Just as a youthful Jake can be glimpsed at several points in this 1959 novel, so a middle-aged Duddy later reappears in *St. Urbain's Horseman*. Duddy is not much changed but, with Jake at the moral centre of the novel, his stature is diminished in comparison. Together the two protagonists suggest the range of human possibility, almost two sides of the same personality—an idea implicit in the deathbed letter written to Duddy by his uncle Benjy, in which he tells him that he is 'two people' and urges him not to choose the 'brute inside you' but to be instead 'a gentleman. A *Mensch*.'

Although Richler eventually returned to writing novels of character—in *St. Urbain's Horseman* and *Joshua then and now* (1980)—during the sixties he published two surreal fables, *The incomparable Atuk* (1963) and *Cocksure* (1968), which marked him as one of the most caustic satirists of the era. Savage attacks on contemporary mores and mass society, these novels send up the poses and stereotypes of their decade. In *The incomparable Atuk* (American title: *Stick your neck out*), Richler ridiculed facile cultural nationalism by dramatizing the foolishness of an attempt to 'Canadianize' American pop culture. *Cocksure* extends his attack on the North American entertainment industry with its scabrous tale of a narcissistic Hollywood director aspiring to God-like powers, literally creating film stars tailored to the public's desires while cannibalizing his associates for their 'spare parts'. Its use of a more ribald humour than most readers then expected from serious Canadian fiction made it an object of controversy when it received (along with the collection of essays *Hunting tigers under glass*, 1968) a Governor General's Award. However disturbing it may be, *Cocksure* is a deeply conservative work, a portrait of a 'square' protagonist who clings to old values though bewildered by their inversion all around him. One of the novel's obvious influences is Evelyn Waugh, for whom Richler has expressed admiration, but *Cocksure* really belongs to the more bitterly vitriolic tradition of Jonathan Swift.

St. Urbain's Horseman, which brought Richler a second Governor General's Award, is a more humane novel, though it retains much of the comic tone and sharply satiric edge of his previous fiction. In this Kafkaesque story of Jake Hersh, a Montreal film-writer who finds himself on trial for sexual indecencies he did not commit, Richler investigates the construction of both Canadian and Jewish identity, making the book an extended reconsideration of his previous topics of exile and home. The sense of loss that pervaded his earlier fiction broadens in this work into a depiction of an existence made almost meaningless by the horrors of recent history, the lack of roots for expatriates like Jake and his friends, and the 'competing mythologies' that result in the anomie of the contemporary era. Against these forces, Jake creates a compensatory myth by synthesizing diverse elements from popular culture, his Jewish inheritance, and the raw material of his cousin Joey's life in order to create something he can believe in: a superhuman figure of authority and heroism, 'St. Urbain's Horseman'—a Jewish avenger (based on the myth of the Golem) who will right wrongs and punish evil-doers. In the novel's resolution, however, Jake finds he must also undertake the difficult but necessary task of confronting the limitations and even dangers of this myth-making, and must learn how to internalize his mythologies.

Joshua Shapiro, the protagonist of *Joshua then and now*, resembles Jake in his vulnerable humanity and in being another of Richler's misunderstood men. Where Jake was unjustly put on trial for sexual perversion, Joshua is mistakenly identified as a secret homosexual and transvestite. Where Jake wishes he could set right the wrongs of the past (his persistent fantasy is the pursuit of Joseph Mengele, then the most wanted of Nazi war criminals), Joshua avoids his present crisis by turning back to a past that haunts him because he feels he has earlier failed to show adequate moral commitment. Like Jake, Joshua must confront questions of personal responsibility and the taking of appropriate action, questions that for him are embodied in the Spanish Civil War rather than in anti-Semitism and Nazi genocide. He must eventually learn not only that the past can never be redeemed, but that to attempt to correct it may lead to a dangerous abandonment of the present. As with *St. Urbain's Horseman*, the novel ends with husband and wife clinging to one another, their affection and their bonds the best source of refuge and stability in a difficult world.

Solomon Gursky was here (1989), Richler's most ambitious work, is a complicated and sprawling novel that takes over (and sends up) the form of the multi-generational family saga. (For the second edition Richler provided a genealogical diagram to help readers with the complexities of the family line.) In this novel Richler comes to terms with the Canadian tradition he has often mocked: he writes into Canadian history and national mythology a previously overlooked Jewish dimension. Loosely based on real figures from Canadian history (such as the early fur-trader Ezekiel Solomons and, in particular, the Bronfman family), the development of the Gursky family (who, in the present, struggle over control of the giant liquor company that has emerged out of their Prohibition-era bootlegging) is shown to have been crucial to the formation of the Canadian nation and to Canada's national identity. Richler presents all of this in a long and episodic narrative that allows him to explore—and to burlesque—the myth of the Canadian North and to recast northern and Native motifs that have become well established in Canadian writing and culture: shamanism; the Franklin expedition and the failed search for the Northwest Passage; and the Trickster figure. (In *Solomon Gursky was here* Richler bases his use of Raven as Trickster on the Haida myth recreated in Bill Reid's and Robert BRINGHURST's *Raven steals the light*.) In the figure of L.B. Berger, Richler also introduces a devastating caricature of A.M. KLEIN, a poet who has sometimes been treated as an icon in the Jewish cultural community, but a figure who has troubled Richler because, as he later wrote in *Saturday Night*, Klein 'was hired to fill the humiliating office of Sam [Bronfman]'s poet laureate. Degrading himself and his sullen craft . . .' (July/August 1992). The novel is narrated by Moses Berger, L.B.'s son, who is preoccupied with understanding the truth about his father's employer, Solomon Gursky, and the nature of the mysterious and mythic figure who calls himself Sir Hyman Kaplansky. Richler's newest novel, *Barney's version*, is to be published in late 1997.

The apprenticeship of Duddy Kravitz, *A choice of enemies*, *Son of a smaller hero*, *Cocksure*, *The incomparable Atuk*, *Joshua then and now*, and *St. Urbain's Horseman* are all in the NEW CANADIAN LIBRARY, with Afterwords by David Carpenter, Neil Besner, Ray SMITH, Margaret Drabble, Peter Gzowski, Eric WRIGHT, and Guy VANDERHAEGHE.

Throughout his career Richler has also continued his journalism. Two early collections of his journalistic pieces appeared as *Hunting tigers under glass* and *Shovelling trouble* (1972). An American selection from these books was published as *Notes on an endangered species* (USA, 1974); and another selection, *The great comic book heroes* (1978), was made from them for the original New Canadian Library series. *Home sweet home: my Canadian album* (1984) draws together pieces on Canada written over a twenty-five-year span. A more recent volume of journalism, *Broadsides: reviews and opinions*, appeared in 1990. Richler has also had considerable success as author of a series of children's books, which feature a little boy who says everything twice. The first of these, *Jacob Two-Two and the Hooded Fang* (1975), has been made into a stage play and a film; it was followed by *Jacob Two-Two and the dinosaur* (1987) and *Jacob Two-Two's first spy case* (1995).

In the 1990s Richler increasingly assumed the role of public intellectual by becoming the most prominent defender of the rights of Quebec's anglophones. Richler's opening sally was in what has become a highly visible and protracted controversy over a 1991 article published in *The New Yorker*, which depicted the folly of Quebec's language laws prohibiting or limiting the use of English on signs. It provoked hostile responses and vicious personal attacks in the Quebec francophone press. Enjoying his role as gadfly, Richler expanded his polemics into a book-length diatribe, *Oh Canada! Oh Quebec! Requiem for a divided country* (1992), in which he further disturbed Québécois nationalists by also pointing to French Quebec's history of anti-Semitism. He has continued his mordant critique of separatist politics and policies in his subsequent journalism.

In 1994 Richler published his second full-length work of non-fiction, *This year in Jerusalem*. Partly a memoir (about his early experiences with the Zionist movement's efforts to establish an independent country when he was growing up in Montreal and about his later journey to Israel to see the country that eventually emerged), partly a travel book and partly a meditation on the politics of Jewish identity in the modern world, it concludes with Richler—who began his career as an expatriate—confirming Canada as his spiritual homeland.

Michael Darling's bibliography of Richler (in *The annotated bibliography of Canada's major authors*, vol. 1, 1979) remains the only guide to secondary criticism. Victor Ramraj's *Mordecai Richler* (1983) is an excellent general introduction to Richler's work up to the publication of *Joshua then and now*, and can be supplemented by *Perspectives on Mordecai Richler* (1986) edited by Darling. Ada Craniford's *Fiction and fact in Mordecai Richler's novels* (1992) is an informative study of the complicated interplay of reality and fiction in Richler's work. *The Mordecai Richler papers: first accession* (1987) is a partial guide to papers held at the University of Calgary. RUSSELL BROWN

Ricou, Laurence. See CRITICISM IN ENGLISH 5(g).

Riel trilogy. John COULTER's trilogy of plays about Louis Riel consists of *Riel* (1962), an epic stage play of Elizabethan proportions; *The crime of Louis Riel* (1976), a free adaptation of the same play for less-experienced companies to produce; and *The trial of Louis Riel* (1968), a documentary drama of Riel's trial.

Riel was first performed on 17 Feb. 1950 by the New Play Society, Toronto, at the Royal Ontario Museum Theatre, with Mavor MOORE in the title role. But not until 13 Jan. 1975 (at the height of the separatist movement in Quebec) was it given the major Canadian stage production it deserved, when it was performed at the National Arts Centre, Ottawa, directed by Jean Gascon, with French-Canadian actor Albert Millaire as Louis Riel. The large cast was drawn from both English- and French-Canadian theatre.

The action of *Riel* takes place in 1869-70 and 1885-6 in the Northwest Territories (in present-day Winnipeg, Manitoba, and Batoche, near Prince Albert, Saskatchewan). Part I is concerned with Riel's claim that the land belongs to his Métis people. In the ensuing uprising of 1869, incited both by the British attempt to take over their land and by Riel's decision to have the Ontario Orangeman Thomas Scott executed, Riel and his Métis followers are defeated. Part I ends with Riel's escape to Montana, where he marries and raises a family. Part II takes place in 1885 when the Métis send a delegation to Riel begging him to return and lead another uprising against the British. He does so and is again defeated. He is imprisoned, put on trial, and condemned to death. The play ends with his hanging.

There are echoes of the New Testament in the dialogue, with allusions to Riel as a Christ figure. Coulter imbues the 'voices' Riel hears with overtones of Joan of Arc, thus inviting comparisons between the two revolutionaries. In Part II Coulter hints at mental instability as Riel imagines himself to be an infallible religious leader, divinely inspired to lead his people to victory. The trial scene gives Coulter the opportunity to show his considerable gifts for depicting victims of injustice; as an Ulsterman, Coulter knew political unrest at first hand. The actual testimony of Riel (who insisted on defending himself) pales in contrast to that written by Coulter, which is more dramatic, though based on the substance of Riel's actual speech. Riel's subsequent hanging, accompanied by liturgical chanting, is strongly suggestive of the crucifixion and its aftermath.

Riel is a combination of epic, myth, legend, pageant, documentary, and montage. As epic it dramatizes the deeds of a historical hero in a series of events expressed in elevated language; as myth it is an allegory of a Christ-like prophet who symbolizes the larger and deeper beliefs of a nation; as legend it is the story of a Canadian hero who has assumed larger-than-life proportions; as pageant it is a procession of stylized events leading to a rich climax; as documentary it is a substantially accurate account of events and personalities; as a montage it is a composite picture of many elements produced through a rapid succession of scenes.

The crime of Louis Riel (1976) is a shortened version of *Riel* written for small-cast non-professional groups. Commissioned by the CANADA COUNCIL, it consists of a continuous flow of scenes set in motion by the 'Actor', who plays the part of the Crown Prosecutor. Functioning much like the stage manager in Thornton Wilder's *Our town*, the 'Actor' also serves the same role as a Greek chorus. The audience is invited to join the jury to determine whether Riel will live or be hanged. *The trial of Louis Riel* was commissioned by the Chamber of Commerce, Regina, Saskatchewan, in 1967 to mark Canada's Centennial and to be an annual tourist event. It is a one-act documentary of the actual court scene in which Coulter takes Riel's own words and weaves them into a lively debate featuring twenty-eight characters. The play is performed in a replica of the original courthouse, where the audience, ushered in as in a real courtroom, is scrutinized by the Constable as the Court assembles. Among the spectators are ladies of social prominence, colourfully dressed in period costume, and officers of the North West Mounted Police in scarlet uniforms. Once the counsel, witnesses, and jurymen arrive to take their seats the play begins with the usual formalities of a trial. Louis Riel, shackled with ball and chain, is placed in the dock, and the trial progresses as on the actual day. *The trial of Louis Riel* is a highly moving play, direct and shocking in its re-creation of an infamous trial.

While the *Riel* trilogy brought the plays of John Coulter to the attention of the Canadian public, it also provided the inspiration for contemporary scholars and historians to research and re-evaluate the role of Louis Riel in Canadian history. The still unresolved grievances of the Native and Métis peoples are powerfully emphasized in this trilogy. Many of the tensions plaguing Canadian society are mirrored in Riel himself, who has become a symbol for both Native-rights groups and French Canadians.

Selected criticism of *Riel* is included in *Canadian drama and the critics* (rev. ed. 1995), edited by L.W. Conolly.

GERALDINE ANTHONY

Riley, Wilma. See NOVELS IN ENGLISH 1983 TO 1996: OTHER NOVELS 4.

Ringuet. Pseudonym of Philippe PANNETON.

Ringwood, Gwen Pharis (1910-84). Born in Anatone, Washington, she was educated at the Universities of Montana, Alberta, and North Carolina. Most of her adult life was spent in Alberta and, from 1953, in Williams Lake, British Columbia. Apart from a novel, *Younger brother* (1959), and occasional short stories, drama was the focus of Ringwood's creative energies. The author of over sixty plays—dramas, musicals, children's plays, radio plays—she was a major force in the development of Canadian drama, particularly in the West. Many of her plays remain unpublished, but twenty-five of them appeared in *The collected plays of Gwen Pharis Ringwood* (1982), edited by Enid Delgatty Rutland, and some typescripts are available in the theatre section of the Metropolitan Toronto Library and the Special Collections Division of the University of Calgary Library.

In 1936 Ringwood wrote a series of ten historical plays for radio station CKUA at the University of Alberta, the scripts of which have not survived. The following year she won a Rockefeller fellowship to the University of North Carolina, where she became part of the Carolina Playmakers group. Some of her best work belongs to this period. *STILL STANDS THE HOUSE* (1938) succeeds on two levels: as a powerful evocation of the severity of prairie life during the 1930s, and as an incisive psychological portrait of a spinster's resistance to change. *Dark harvest* (1945) shows an equally sensitive response to prairie environment and character, but is marred by stilted dialogue and a contrived ending. An earlier one-act version of the same play, *Pasque flower* (1939), benefits from a tighter structure, verse dialogue, and effective symbolism.

The comic vein in Ringwood's work is revealed in a group of plays performed at the Banff School of Fine Arts in the early 1940s: *The courting of Marie Jenvrin* (1941), a flimsy piece; *The jack and the joker*; and *The rainmaker* (1975). The gentle satire of small-town Alberta folly in the later two plays works well, especially in *The rainmaker*. They were both commissioned by the Alberta Folklore and Local History Project, as was *Stampede*, performed at the University of Alberta in 1946, which, in a laboured manner, eulogizes the Alberta cowboy. Comic invention returned with *A fine coloured Easter egg; or the drowning of Wasyl Nemitchuk* (1946) and *Widger's way* (1976), both adroitly controlled comedies that rely for their effect on character idiosyncrasies and improbable—yet, within their convention, credible—plots. *Wasyl Nemitchuk* also contains a serious element—seldom totally absent from Ringwood's comedies—in its reminder of the economic and social consequences of Alberta's oil discovery.

The first of Ringwood's plays about Canada's Native people, *Lament for harmonica* (1975), is a melodramatic protest against exploitation, especially sexual exploitation, of Amerindians by white Canadians. *The stranger* has a similar theme, a slightly implausible plot, and flashes of poetry. Plot is also the weak point of *The deep has many voices*, but its expressionistic structure, imaginative use of visual and sound effects, and rich language mark this story of a young woman's search for her identity as a mature work. All the plays mentioned above were published in *The collected plays of Gwen Pharis Ringwood*.

Ringwood's musical plays include *Look behind you, neighbor* (music by Chet Lambertson), written in 1961 to celebrate the fiftieth anniversary of Edson, Alberta, and *The road runs north* (music by Art Rosoman), written for the Williams Lake Centennial Celebration in 1967 and based on the Cariboo Gold Rush.

Ringwood's plays express many themes and utilize many techniques—she was a constant explorer of dramatic structures and convention—but her main achievement was her skill in capturing a sense of place: the environment of western Canada and its people.

See Geraldine Anthony, *Gwen Pharis Ringwood* (1981). L.W. CONOLLY

Ritchie, Charles (1906-95). Charles Stewart Almon Ritchie, the elder of the two sons of William Ritchie, K.C., and Lilian Stewart, was born in Halifax, Nova Scotia. (The younger son, Roland, later became Supreme Court Justice.) The boys' education was a moveable feast, including private tutors and schools in Nova Scotia, preparatory school in England, and boarding school in Ontario. Charles Ritchie began his secondary education at the University of King's College, Halifax, and earned B.A. and M.A. degrees from Oxford University and an M.A. from Harvard. He also attended the École libre des sciences politiques in Paris. Ritchie was a Companion of the Order of Canada, a Fellow of the Royal Society of Literature, and the recipient of honorary doctorates from several Canadian universities. In 1948 he married Sylvia Smellie; they had no children.

Ritchie's public career began in 1934, when he joined Canada's fledgling Department of External Affairs. During the Second World War he was posted to London—where, despite the war, as a clever, charming bachelor he had an active social life. After the war he was a member of the group of worldly wise civil servants whose efforts built one of the most highly respected foreign services in the modern world. Over his forty-year career as a diplomat, Ritchie was Canada's Ambassador to West Germany and the United States, High Commissioner in London, permanent representative to the United Nations and the North Atlantic Treaty Organization, and a special adviser to the Privy Council.

Charles Ritchie began writing diaries in his adolescence, but did not offer them for publication until after his retirement in 1973. During his career he used them as a personal escape from the tedium of diplomatic life. However, in 1960 the British novelist Elizabeth Bowen encouraged him to publish them and by 1968 he was considering this as a retirement project. (Ritchie's close friendship with Bowen inspired her novel *The heat of the day*, which is dedicated to him.) *The siren years: a Canadian diplomat abroad, 1937-1945* (1974) excerpts the diaries written in London during the Second World War. His personal account of those years, and the occasional bits of diplomatic and political gossip, had popular appeal; but it was the diary's wit and grace, its literary distinction, that established Ritchie's reputation as a writer. *The siren years* won a Governor General's Award and was followed by *An appetite for life: the education of a young diarist, 1924-1927* (1977), *Diplomatic passport: more undiplomatic diaries, 1944-1962* (1981), and *Storm signals: more undiplomatic diaries 1962-1971* (1983). Although he spent his working life cushioned by the security of the public service, Ritchie was a frustrated novelist. Not surprisingly, the diaries read on occasion like excerpts from novels. His last published work, *My grandfather's house* (1987), richly combines autobiography and family memoir.

LEILA RYAN

Ritter, Erika (b. 1948). Born in Regina, Saskatchewan, she received a degree in English literature from McGill University before enrolling in the University of Toronto's Graduate Centre for the Study of Drama. For three years after graduation in 1970 she taught a variety of English and drama courses at Loyola College, Montreal, and then returned to Toronto to write. As well as writing for radio, television, and the stage, she has published short stories in magazines and two collections of humorous essays.

Ritter's first play was *A visitor from Charleston* (1975), produced by Loyola College in 1974, whose lead character, Eva, is addicted to the movie *Gone with the wind*. Her plan to see it for the forty-ninth time is postponed by the arrival of an earnest young salesman promoting Fantasia cosmetics. Thematically transparent and over-written, the play has little of the liveliness and wit found in *The splits* (1978), in which Megan, a writer of situation comedies for television, is as confused about her relationship to her work as she is about her relationships to men. Her estranged husband Joe—who is also a writer and reappears in her life at a most inopportune moment—serves as a model of artistic integrity. The supposition of the play is that his influence in this area will outlast their relationship. In *The splits* Ritter's specialty as a playwright comes to the fore: a skill in creating and mixing bright, snappy dialogue and zany, energetic, complex characters engaged in a battle of wit and wills.

This specialty is even more successful in her hit comedy *Automatic pilot* (1980), whose title refers to the emotional life of the central character, Charlie, a neurotic stand-up comic whose self-deprecating routine is based almost completely on autobiographical material: her husband left her for another man, and two successive lovers have failed her. Funniest when she is making jokes about her own anxieties and disappointments, we watch her transform intimate personal details into comic material. Although Charlie might be considered a sad character locked into her own limitations, it becomes apparent that her humour—which is a kind of protection, and a vulnerability as well—is also a strength. She has a resourcefulness, exuberance, and a creativity that can transform and transcend complaint—even if it is only part of her act. Because of the depth and poignancy of the characterization of Charlie, and because of the ingenuity and wit of the script, *Automatic pilot* is a wonderful play, Ritter's best. After its highly successful alternate-theatre run in Toronto, it was remounted in a more elaborate commercial production at Toronto's Bayview Playhouse in the summer of 1980. *Automatic pilot* won the Chalmers Award for 1980 and has been produced by regional theatres across the country.

Ritter's historical drama, *Winter 1671* (1979), focusing on the tragic love story of one of Louis XIV's *filles du roi* sent to New France, met a poor reception when it premièred at Toronto's St Lawrence Centre. A weighty period piece, it deals with unfamiliar terrain unsuited to Ritter's particular talents. In *The passing scene* (unpublished, 1982) the protagonist's values and confusions are characteristically close to the author's own; but the presentation of the central relationship between an investigative reporter and a lifestyle journalist extends beyond the issue of personal integrity and is given a broad public dimension. Partly because its central issues—kinds of journalism, the truth in any story—are of more interest to writers than to general audiences, the play was not consistently engaging.

Murder at McQueen (1986) is the last full-length play Ritter has had staged to date. Members of the chic McQueen Club, four successful professional single women, share the struggle to achieve some kind of substantial centre for their lives. Finding themselves out of the conventional marriage plot, they have yet to feel comfortable with a different life-script. Although hampered by the confusions of its shifting focus and the defeated tone of the text, *Murder at McQueen* is a cleverly written post-feminist comedy of manners.

During the interim between *The passing scene* and *Murder at McQueen*, Ritter won the ACTRA award for Best Radio Drama Writer (1982, for adapting *Automatic pilot*); published *Urban scrawl* (1984) and *Ritter in residence* (1987), amusing essays on city life; was writer-in-residence at Concordia University in Montreal (1984) and playwright-in-residence at Smith College (January 1985) and at the Stratford Festival (summer 1985).

See Robert Wallace and Cynthia Zimmerman, *The work: conversations with English-Canadian playwrights* (1982), and C. Zimmerman, *Playwriting women: female voices in English Canada* (1994). CYNTHIA ZIMMERMAN

Rivard, Adjutor. See ESSAYS IN FRENCH: 3.

Rivard, Jean. See *JEAN RIVARD*.

Rivard, Yvon (b. 1945). Born between Sainte-Thérèse and Hervé Junction, Quebec, he was educated at McGill University (M.A., Lettres françaises, 1968), then at the Sorbonne, Paris (1969-71); he was granted a Doctorat de troisième cycle (Lettres françaises) from the Université d'Aix-en-Provence. From 1971 to 1973 he was a professor of French and Québécois literature at the University of Vermont. Since 1973 he has been a professor of literature and creative writing at McGill University. He was one the editors of *LIBERTÉ*

(1977-95), had a regular program dealing with literature on Radio-Canada (1978-88), and wrote the scripts for three films: *Blanche est la nuit*, *L'enfant sur le lac*, and *La vie fantôme*.

Rivard's novels are notable for their poetic style, philosophical humour, and intercultural paradoxes. His narratives always deal with characters who are divided and who, in an unceasing quest for themselves, travel both mentally and physically through cultures and emotions. All his novels lead to fundamental questions often framed in single sentences that have several meanings: for example, 'The universe is a rope left in a field that a passerby in the dark takes to be a snake.' (*Les silences du corbeau*). Rivard's first novel, *Mort et naissance de Christophe Ulric* (1976), opens on a kind of magical world suffused with a poetic atmosphere that fills each instant with infinite possibilities: the deep forest is a psychological landscape for the narrator's attempt to gain a hold on his desire—symbolized by an elusive feminine figure. *L'ombre et le double* (1979) reflects on the quest itself in philosophical dialogues where humour and the deconstruction of accepted paradigms have an important place. *Les silences du corbeau* (1986), for which Rivard received a Governor General's Award, is a masterpiece built on metaphysical humour and poetic statement. It rests on dialogues among Western tourists trying to lose their ego in an ashram in India. Socratic dialogues, delicate parody, and allusive metaphysical sentences lead to the discovery of paradoxes opening on an atmosphere permeated with Zen and to parables about the abyss of nothingness at the root of meditation. *Le milieu du jour* (1995) presents in minute detail the narrator's quest for himself while caught in an eternal love triangle. His love and sincerity for both the women he is attracted to are interwoven with subtle psychological analyses based on an acute consciousness of the impossibility of grasping definite meanings, while simultaneously making enlightening discoveries: 'The only crime mankind can admit to is not having accepted being born.' With this novel Rivard can be favourably compared with such writers as Julio Cortazar, Isabel Allende, and Umberto Eco.

Rivard has also published a book of poems, *Frayère* (1976), and a book of critical essays, *Le bout cassé de tous les chemins* (1993), containing often impressionistic reflections on Robert M. Pirsig and his *Zen and the art of motorcycle maintenance*, Brecht, Rimbaud, Borgès, et al.

See Gabrielle Poulin, 'Romans, récits, contes, nouvelles', *University of Toronto Quarterly* (Summer 1977); Louise Milot, 'Savoir garder ses distances', *Lettres québécoises* (printemps 1987); Robert Viau, 'Yvon Rivard entre le rêve et l'errance', *Lettres québécoises* (hiver, 1988-89) and Patrick Imbert, 'Silences et dualisme' in *Le roman québécois depuis 1960* (1992), and 'Yvon Rivard: l'écriture paradoxale' in *Le roman contemporain au Québec (1960-1985)* (1992). PATRICK IMBERT

Robert, Guy (b. 1933). Born at Sainte-Agathe-des-Monts, Quebec, and educated at the Université de Montréal, he has taught there, at the École des Beaux-Arts, and at the Université du Québec in Montreal, where he was literary director of the university press. He has played an active part in the cultural revolution in Quebec, which he considers more important than the social and political revolution it has accompanied, and has dedicated himself to the two strategic weapons in this revolution: poetry and publishing. He founded the Éditions du Songe and was director of the important 'Poésie canadienne' series for the Librairie Déom, in which he published an excellent critical edition of the prose and verse of Sylvain GARNEAU, *Objets retrouvés* (1965). He was art critic for *Le Magazine Maclean* and wrote regularly for the periodical *Maintenant*. In the mid-1960s he was the founder and controversial director of the Musée de l'art contemporain, which he left in order to mount the much-admired international exhibition of contemporary sculpture at Expo 67, for which he wrote the catalogue, prefaced with a lengthy introduction to modern sculpture, *Sculpture* (1967).

Robert's publications began with two ambitious essays, *Vers un humanisme contemporain* (1958) and *Connaissance nouvelle de l'art* (1963), a work that attempts to explain in psychological terms man's creative activity in every branch of art—poetry, fiction, music, and the visual and plastic arts. He has written impressive essays on Quebec's major post-war artists: *Pellan, sa vie et son oeuvre* (1963), *Robert Roussil* (1965), *Jean-Paul Lemieux* (1968), *Riopelle* (1970), *Albert Dumouchel* (1971), *Borduas* (1972), and *Marc-Aurèle Fortin* (1976). His book on Lemieux won the Grand Prix littéraire de Montréal. Other works of art criticism by Robert are *L'École de Montreal* (1964), *Jérôme, un frère jazzé* (1969), *Yves Trudeau, sculpteur* (1971), and *Le grand théâtre de Québec* (1971).

As literary critic Robert has published a thematic study of the poetry of Anne HÉBERT, *La poétique du songe* (1962); *Littérature du Québec: poésie actuelle* (1970), an extended version of an anthology of contemporary poetry first published in 1964, both of which editions contain examples of his own poetry; and *Aspects de la littérature québécoise* (1970), which collects a number of Robert's essays, broadcast talks, and public lectures, including a splendid mock-serious psychoanalytical study of the 'sacre' (the blasphemous oath) in Quebec speech.

In his own verse, starting with the theme of spiritual regeneration in *Broussailles givrées* (1958) and the myths of sea and sun, memory and desire in *Et le soleil a chaviré* (1963) and *Une mémoire déjà (1959-1967)* (1968), Robert progressed through the celebration of the land, woman, and the power of the work in *Neige de mai* (1964), to the more esoteric universe of *Ailleurs se tisse* (1969), *Intrême-Orient* (1969), and *Trans-apparence* (1969)—a universe that the second of these works defines as 'orient extrême pays d'intérieur'. The poems of *Québec se meurt* (1969) express some bitterness about the constant threat to the survival of Quebec's French culture. An important and sizeable volume of poems, *Textures* (1976), contains verse from the years 1969-70, including the poems in *Intrême-Orient*.

Since 1983 Robert has continued publishing monographs celebrating the life and work of various artists: *Aux couleurs et saisons d'Armance Ricard* (1983); *Domingue* (1985) on the work of Maurice Domingue; *Pinsonnault* (1987) on the work of Suzanne Pinsonnault; *L'oeuvre de Geneviève Deslauriers* (1988); *Bellefleur, ou La ferveur à l'oeuvre* (1988) on the work of Léon Bellefleur—English translation, *Bellefleur: the fervour of the quest* (1988) by Susan Le Pan; *Petit: Gaston Petit en mission itinérante dans l'art* (1990); *Garbs: Irma Roggenkamper Garbs, sa vie et son art* (1990); *DOH: visions, dimensions, messages* (1991) on the work of Masahiko Doh); *André Michel: métamorphose* (1991); and *Dufour* (1995) on the work of Marcellin Dufour. In *Art et non finito: esthétique et dynamogénie du non finito* (1984) Robert argues that unfinished and fragmentary works of art excite our imagination and aesthetic thought in a particular way; his *Cent vingt du cercle des artistes peintres du Québec* (1989) pays tribute to the work of 120 contemporary Québécois painters.

Through his poetry and his art criticism, through his journalism and publishing, produced often in the face of bitter criticism, Robert expresses his faith in art as a social act and in the reforming power of art in society.

C.R.P. MAY/ANNIKA HANNAN

Robert, Jean-Claude. See HISTORICAL WRITING IN FRENCH 1980 TO 1996.

Roberts, Sir Charles G.D. (1860-1943). Charles George Douglas Roberts, a brother of Theodore Goodridge ROBERTS and a cousin of Bliss CARMAN, was born in Douglas, New Brunswick, and spent his childhood beside the Tantramar marshes near Sackville, N.B. His first teacher was his clergyman father, later eulogized in the poem 'Westcock hill', and another teacher was (Sir) George R. Parkin, who introduced him to the Pre-Raphaelite poets; Roberts was also educated at the University of New Brunswick. At the age of twenty he published a notable collection of poems, *Orion*, and in 1883 he became editor of the Toronto periodical *The WEEK*, but soon resigned after disagreeing with the views of its founder, Goldwin SMITH, on Canada's annexation to the United States. From 1885 to 1895 Roberts taught English literature at King's College, Windsor, Nova Scotia, and in 1896 he published his first collection of animal stories, *Earth's enigmas*. From 1897 to 1925 he supported himself by writing prose, living chiefly in New York from 1897 to 1907 and then on the Continent and finally in London, England, from 1907 to 1925. During the Great War he was a private in the British forces and was later commissioned and attached to the Canadian War Records Office in London. He returned to Canada in 1925 and spent the rest of his life in Toronto. Elected to the Royal Society of Canada in 1890, he was awarded the Lorne PIERCE Medal for distinguished service to Canadian literature in 1926 and was knighted in 1935.

Roberts was called the father of Canadian literature because the international acclaim for his early poetry inspired his generation, among them Bliss Carman and Archibald LAMPMAN, into creativity. Also the inventor of the modern animal story, a distinction that he shares with Ernest Thompson SETON, Roberts was the first writer to mythologize successfully, in both poetry and prose, the Maritime environment: its strong sense of the past, particularly the French and English struggle for 'Acadia'; its New England heritage; its farming and fishing communities beside the Tantramar marshes of the Upper Bay of Fundy; and life in the remote forests of central New Brunswick. Throughout his career he extended that capacity for mythologizing from his contemporary human and natural world to include the prehistoric world. Rarely surpassed by other writers in recreating the outdoors, he was continually fascinated by the interpenetration of civilization and the wilderness. But it is nature without the human presence that evokes in

Roberts two powerfully contrasting attitudes. In his poems he sees in nature a divine, even benevolent, spirit, finds permanence and consolation in the seasonal cycles, and emphasizes the kinship of all living things. In his animal stories, however, violence and destruction are the operative principles, and survival depends not merely on chance but on 'woodcraft'—Roberts' word for the individual creature's resourcefulness.

Roberts' long and prolific career falls into three main periods. His best-known poetry was published between 1880 and 1897. While *Orion, and other poems* (Philadelphia, 1880) shows his assimilation of classical subjects and of Tennyson and Arnold, *In divers tones* (Boston, Montreal, 1886) and *Songs of the common day* (London, Toronto, 1893) reveal the mature artist's elegiac voice, his precise yet colloquial diction, and his scrupulous realism. In 'The Tantramar revisited' the speaker refuses to inspect at close range a once-familiar landscape because in his memory it has transcended time and change. 'Canada', which was a popular patriotic piece in the 1890s, exhorts the young nation to draw its sustenance from its heroic French and British origins. The sonnet sequence of *Songs of the common day*, which describes the seasonal pattern of rural life in a detached, restrained style, contains Roberts' most satisfying poems. With his departure from King's College and the separation from his wife and family in the years 1895-7 came a change in poetic subjects: his bohemian life-style, his sojourn in large cities, and his relationships with other women are recorded in the cityscapes, the love poems, and the philosophical pieces of *New York nocturnes and other poems* (Boston, 1898) and *The book of the rose* (1903); while *New poems* (1919) has very little new material, it contains three anguished responses to the Great War. After 1925 Roberts entered his third period as a poet. His language shows new vigour and he adopts modernist techniques in *The vagrant of time* (1927). The title poem of *The iceberg, and other poems* (1934) is a successful treatment in free verse of a monstrous, non-human force; it is narrated in the first person by the iceberg itself, which in Roberts' treatment becomes a metaphor for the voyage of life. His last volume, *Canada speaks of Britain and other poems of the war* (1941), contains patriotic lyrics. Roberts made two collections of his poetry: *Poems* (1901; rev. 1907) and *Selected poems* (1936).

He published his first animal story, 'Do seek their meat from God', in *Harper's* (Dec. 1892). This and three other stories appeared in *Earth's enigmas: a book of animal and nature life* (Boston, 1896). Unlike traditional animal stories, which were frequently parables illustrating human behaviour, Roberts' stories were based on direct observation and dispensed with sentimentality and didacticism, and they freed him to deal with conduct outside the framework of Victorian morality. In the 'Introductory' to *The kindred of the wild* (1902), Roberts defined his animal story as 'a psychological romance constructed on a framework of natural science', one that 'helps us to return to nature, without requiring that we ... return to barbarism.' Alec Lucas, in his chapter 'Nature writers and the animal story' in the *Literary history of Canada* (1965), identified three kinds of Roberts' animal stories: the biography, which examines conduct or personality; the action story, which emphasizes plot and usually contains humans; and the sketch, which illustrates an elemental force governing the natural world. Accused by President Theodore Roosevelt in *Everybody's Magazine* (June 1907) of being a 'nature-fakir', Roberts argued that animals are not governed by instinct alone but by 'something directly akin to reason', an approach to animal psychology that was at odds with Darwinian determinism. Even though most of Roberts' animals are victims of the conflicting forces for survival in nature, they often evince a heroic spirit in their defeat. Occasionally, as in the full-length animal biography *Red fox* (1905), these creatures are observed by an adolescent boy much like the youthful Roberts, and here the intelligent fox eludes his animal and human enemies and finds his freedom. The highly popular animal collections, Roberts' most important contribution to prose, also include *The watchers of the trails* (1904), *The haunters of the silences* (1907), *The house in the water* (1908), *Kings in exile* (1910), *Neighbours unknown* (1911), *More kindred of the wild* (1911), *Babes of the wild* (1912), *The feet of the furtive* (1912), *Hoof and claw* (1914), *The secret trails* (1914), *The ledge on Bald Face* (1918), *Some animal stories* (1921), *Wisdom of the wilderness* (1922), *More animal stories* (1922), *They who walk in the wild* (1924), and *Further animal stories* (1936).

Always sympathetic to French Canada, Roberts translated Philippe AUBERT DE GASPÉ's *Les ANCIENS CANADIENS* (Quebec, 1863) as *The Canadians of old; an historical romance* (New York, 1890); the translation was reissued in 1905 as *Cameron of Lochiel*. In the Introduction, Roberts accepts the bilingual nature of Canadian literature, which he describes as 'a literature in two languages'.

This was followed by several boys' stories: *The raid from Beauséjour, and How the Carter boys lifted the mortgage: two stories of Acadie* (New York, 1894) and *Reube Dare's shad boat: a tale of the tide country* (New York, 1895). Roberts also wrote romances for adults, usually set in eighteenth-century Nova Scotia, in which an escape or a rescue culminates in a marriage between French and English; these stories include *The forge in the forest; being the narrative of the Acadian ranger, Jean le Mer* (New York, 1896) and *A sister to Evangeline; being the story of Yvonne de Lamourie* (Boston, 1898), both of which superficially treat the events leading up to the Expulsion of the Acadians in 1755; *By the marshes of Minas* (Boston, 1900), a group of tales; and *The prisoner of Mademoiselle* (1904). The international best-seller *Barbara Ladd* (1902) is the story of a New England girl on the eve of, and during, the American Revolution. After 1900 Roberts shifted to romances of contemporary New Brunswick, and produced two remarkable novels. *The heart of the ancient wood* (1900) tells of a young girl's kinship with the forest creatures around her; especially the she-bear Kroof, who—like Ben, the old bear in William Faulkner's novella *The bear*—is a symbol of the wilderness world that is endangered by the presence of humans. *The heart that knows* (1906), a realistic tale that is slightly marred by Roberts' deference to the expectations of his audience, deals with the cruel treatment given to an unmarried mother, and contains sympathetic portraits of Roberts' parents in the minister and his wife. The same settings are found in *In the deep of the snow* (1907), *The backwoodsmen* (1909), and *Eyes of the wilderness* (1933). *In the morning of time* (1922), a story about life in prehistoric days, opens with the supremacy of animals and closes with the ascendancy of humans; as Grôm and his tribe invent weapons and learn woodcraft, he survives not merely by chance but by reasoning.

Roberts' other writings include his chapter on New Brunswick in *Picturesque Canada* (Toronto, 1884), edited by George Monro Grant; *The Canadian guide book: the tourists' and sportsmen's guide to eastern Canada and Newfoundland* (New York, 1891); *The land of Evangeline and the gateway thither* (Kentville, N.S., 1895), a guidebook for the Dominion Atlantic Railway; *A history of Canada* (Boston, Toronto, 1897), a textbook that was rejected in a contest because it made Canadian history too interesting, and in which Roberts supports autonomous federation; *Discoveries and explorations* (1902), volume XIV of the *Nineteenth-century series: the story of human progress and events of the century*; the first volume of *The Canadian who's who* (1910); and *Canada in Flanders* (1918), the third volume of Lord Beaverbrook's history of the Canadian forces in the Great War. Roberts collaborated with Arthur L. Tunnell in editing *A standard dictionary of Canadian biography; the Canadian who was who* (2 vols, 1934 and 1938). Among the anthologies he edited were *Northland lyrics* (Boston, 1899), with poems by Roberts, Theodore Goodridge Roberts, Elizabeth Roberts Macdonald, and Bliss Carman; and *Flying colours* (1942), which is a collection of patriotic verse.

Throughout his life Roberts responded to many philosophical and literary changes. Like Carman, he began under the influence of the Romantics and Transcendentalists; and although he was often associated with the naturalistic determinism of Hamelin Garland and Jack London, he never abandoned his vision of the oneness of man and nature. Along with other writers of his generation, Roberts was dismissed by the modernists of the 1920s and 1930s, but they found it difficult to ignore his presence on the Toronto literary scene. He recognized that his life and career—as Fred COGSWELL observes in his critique of one of Roberts' last poems, 'Two rivers'—reflected a duality based on the two rivers of his youth, the Tantramar, symbolizing 'freedom and restlessness', and the St John, 'duty and roots'.

Modern editions of Roberts' writings include *The last barrier and other stories* (NCL, 1958) edited by Alec Lucas; *Poets of the Confederation* (NCL, 1960) edited by Malcolm Ross; *King of beasts* (1964) edited by Joseph Gold; *The Canadians of old* (NCL, 1974), with an introduction by Clara THOMAS; *The selected poems* (1974) edited by Desmond PACEY; *Selected poetry and critical prose* (1974), edited and with an introduction by W.J. Keith; *The heart of the ancient wood* (NCL, 1974), introduced by Joseph Gold; *By the marshes of Minas* (1977); *Earth's enigmas* (1977); *Kindred of the wild* (1977); *Seven bears* (1977); *Eyes of the wilderness and other stories* (1980); and *The lure of the wild* (1980) edited by John C. Adams; *The collected poems of Sir Charles G.D. Roberts: a critical edition* (1985) edited by Desmond Pacey; *Red Fox* (1986); and *Canadian poetry from the beginning through the First World War* (1994), selected and with an afterword by Carole Gerson and Gwendolyn Davies.

See James CAPPON, *Charles G.D. Roberts and the influences of his time* (1905), reprinted by Tecumseh Press, 1975; Elsie M. Pomeroy,

Sir Charles G.D. Roberts: a biography (1943); Desmond Pacey, *Ten Canadian poets* (1958); William H. Magee, 'The animal story: a challenge to technique', *Dalhousie Review* 44 (Summer 1964); Joseph Gold, 'The precious speck of life', *CANADIAN LITERATURE* 26 (Autumn 1965); W.J. Keith, *Charles G.D. Roberts* (1969); James Polk, 'Lives of the hunted', *Canadian Literature* 52 (Summer 1972); Robin Mathews, 'Charles G.D. Roberts and the destruction of the Canadian imagination', *Journal of Canadian Fiction* 1 (Winter 1972); Lorraine McMullen, '"The poetry of earth": a note on Roberts' sonnets', *Studies in Canadian Literature*, 1 (Summer 1972); W.J. Keith, 'A choice of worlds: God, man and nature in Charles G.D. Roberts', in *Colony and Confederation* (1974) edited by George WOODCOCK; Robert Gibbs, 'Voice and persona in Carman and Roberts', in *The Marco Polo papers: one* (1977) edited by Kenneth MacKinnon; William Strong, 'Charles G.D. Roberts' "The Tantramar revisited", *Canadian Poetry* 3 (Fall-Winter 1978); David Jackel, 'Roberts' "Tantramar Revisited": another view', *Canadian Poetry* 5 (Fall-Winter 1979); Robert H. MacDonald, 'The revolt against instinct: the animal stories of Seton and Roberts', *Canadian Literature* 84 (Spring 1980); Fred Cogswell, 'Charles G.D. Roberts', in *Canadian writers and their works: poetry series: volume two* (1983) edited by Robert Lecker, Jack David, and Ellen Quigley; Tracy Ware, 'Remembering it all well: the Tantramar revisited', *Studies in Canadian Literature* 8:2 (1983); *The proceedings of the Sir Charles G.D. Roberts symposium* (1984), edited and with an introduction by Carrie MacMillan; *The Sir Charles G.D. Roberts symposium* (1984), edited and with an introduction by Glen Clever; Barrie Davies, 'English poetry in New Brunswick 1880-1940', in *A literary and linguistic history of New Brunswick* (1985), edited and with an introduction by Reavley Gair; John Coldwell Adams, *Sir Charles god damn: the life of Sir Charles G.D. Roberts* (1986); Terry Whalen, 'Charles G.D. Roberts', in *Canadian writers and their works: poetry series: volume two* (1989), edited by Robert Lecker, Jack David, and Ellen Quigley; *The collected letters of Sir Charles G.D. Roberts* (1991) edited by Laurel Boone; and Gwendolyn Davies, 'The Song Fishermen: a regional poetry celebration', in *Studies in Maritime literary history* (1991).

GEORGE L. PARKER

Roberts, Dorothy. See POETRY IN ENGLISH 1950 TO 1982: 1.

Roberts, Paul William (b. 1955). Born in Wales, and educated at Exeter College, Oxford, where he taught until 1977, when he spent three years in India, he thereafter settled in Toronto, where he has worked in television and as a journalist. Roberts is the author of a witty, picaresque, semi-autobiographical novel, *The palace of fears* (1994), involving Oxford, high finance, film-making, and love; and the following travel books, which combine ironic views of unfamiliar locales with speculation about present-day remnants of traditions of hidden wisdom: *River in the desert: modern travels in ancient Egypt* (1993), *Empire of the soul: journeys in India* (1994), and *Journey of the Magi: in search of the birth of Jesus* (1995; American title, *The birth of Jesus: the real journey of the Magi*).

JOHN ROBERT COLOMBO

Roberts, Theodore Goodridge (1877-1953). George Edward Theodore Goodridge Roberts was born in the rectory of St Anne's Parish, Fredericton, New Brunswick. Sir Charles G.D. ROBERTS was his elder brother and Bliss CARMAN his cousin. He dropped the names George Edward of his own accord in favour of the family name Goodridge. At seventeen he left the University of New Brunswick without a degree and in 1897 acquired a position as sub-editor of *The Independent*, a New York weekly, which had published his first poem in 1888 when it was under the editorship of Carman. *The Independent* sent him as a special correspondent to cover the Spanish-American war in 1898, an experience upon which he based the novel *Hemming the adventurer* (1904). While there he caught 'Cuban fever' and returned to Fredericton to recover. During the next three years Roberts was editor of *The Newfoundland Magazine* and collected a wealth of information about outport life and history that was to form the basis of his Newfoundland novels and his tales of the Beothuks. In this period he made a journey to the Caribbean and South America on a full-rigged barkentine, an experience that he put to good use in *The wasp* (1914), and in numerous other tales and poems set in the South Seas. He returned to the Caribbean with Frances Seymour Allan on their honeymoon in 1903, and the couple remained in Barbados for two years while Theodore wrote. The first of four children—the painter Goodridge Roberts—was born there. In the next quarter-century the Roberts family travelled extensively—living in England, France, and various parts of Canada—while

Theodore published thirty-five novels and over 100 pieces in periodicals, chiefly in *The Canadian Magazine*, *The Youth's Companion*, and *The Independent*. During the Great War he served in the 12th Battalion, at one point as ADC to Max Aitken (Lord Beaverbrook), writing official accounts of the war, one of which was published as *Thirty Canadian V.C.'s* (1918). In 1930 he was awarded an honorary D.Litt. by the University of New Brunswick and in 1934 he was named a fellow of the Royal Society of Canada. In the same year he published a volume of poetry, *The leather bottle* (1934). He eventually settled in Digby, Nova Scotia.

Roberts' novels can be grouped into a half-dozen distinct categories: I. Historical romances such as *A cavalier of Virginia* (1910), or *Captain Love: the history of a most romantic event in the life of an English gentleman during the reign of George the First* (1908). II. Backwoods mysteries and adventures, such as *The golden highlander* (1910), set in the Quebec woods and billed as 'a nature and animal story', or *The master of the moosehorn and other backwoods stories* (1919). III. Wartime adventures, such as *Hemming the adventurer*, based on Roberts' Spanish-American war experience, or *The fighting Starkleys* (1922), a Great War story. IV. South Seas adventures, such as *The wasp* (1914), a pirate story, or *The islands of adventure* (1918), involving treasure and romance. V. Tales of Newfoundland and Labrador, such as his best-known novel, *The harbor master* (1913; NCL, 1968)—first published as *The toll of the tides* (1913)—or *Blessington's folly* (1914), set on the Labrador coast. VI. Native stories, namely *Flying Plover, his stories. Told him by Squat-by-the fire* (1909); *Brothers in peril. A story of old Newfoundland* (1905), an imaginative reconstruction of the life of the Beothuks in the sixteenth century; and *The red feathers* (1907; NCL, 1976), an imaginative treatment of Native myth. Several of Roberts' novels were published by L.C. Page and Company of Boston as books for young people, and virtually all of them are best viewed as juveniles. The Native stories are clearly suitable for children, particularly *The red feathers*, with its enchanting portrait of the good spirit and his magic house of pictures. All are rousing tales of adventure and romance that uphold the basic virtues of courage, honesty, fair play, and self-reliance, with a strong flavour of English gentlemanliness, but a minimum of moral cant. For a complete biography of Roberts' novels, see Reginald Eyre Watters, *A checklist of Canadian literature and background materials, 1628-1960* (2nd edn. 1972).

Roberts' serious artistic accomplishment is his poetry. Some of his earliest pieces appeared in a family connection—with poems by his older brothers William Carman and Charles G.D., his sister Elizabeth Roberts MacDonald, and Bliss Carman—entitled *Northland lyrics* (Boston, 1899). In 1926 the RYERSON PRESS published more of Theodore's poems in *The lost shipmate*—a chapbook of 150 copies—many of which were included in *The leather bottle*. Had this volume appeared forty years earlier it might have won for Theodore a reputation equal to that of his brother Charles or of Bliss Carman. Poems such as 'The sandbar' and 'Magic' are unmatched in Canadian poetry for a facility and clarity of image suggestive of high-realist painting. A collection of the remainder of Theodore Goodridge Roberts' poetry, now to be found only in scattered periodical archives, is needed, as is a collection of his short prose, which is equally inaccessible.

Aside from the introductions to the NEW CANADIAN LIBRARY editions of *The harbor master* and *The red feathers* by Desmond PACEY and Malcolm Ross, literary criticism has so far overlooked T.G. Roberts, although A.J.M. SMITH included a selection of his poetry in *The book of Canadian poetry* (3rd edn, 1957). A brief biographical sketch by Goodridge MacDonald, 'Theodore Goodridge Roberts, poet and novelist', was published in *The Canadian Author and Bookman* (Spring 1953) on the occasion of Roberts' death; and in the same year A.G. BAILEY dedicated an edition of *The FIDDLEHEAD* to Roberts (18:3,1953), with a brief appreciation of the general character of his writing. ANDREW SEAMAN

Robertson, Margaret Murray (1823-1897). Born in Stuartfield, Aberdeenshire, Scotland, she immigrated to the United States with her father, the Rev. James Robertson, and four brothers in 1832, settling first in Derby, Vermont. In 1836 they moved to Sherbrooke, Quebec, where her father served as pastor of the Congregational Church for twenty-five years. Three of her brothers—Andrew, George, and William—became prominent Montreal lawyers, while the fourth, Joseph, was a well-known businessman. Robertson taught at the Sherbrooke Academy and wrote the prize-winning *An essay on common school education* (Sherbrooke, 1864), probably her first published work. Over the next twenty-five years she wrote twelve novels that were published mainly by the Religious Tract Society and the American Sunday School Union. Set in Scotland or North America, they are all lengthy, sentimental, dialect-ridden sagas, filled with intricate relationships and 'sanctified trouble'. Her earliest works were three novels of family life in Canada. *Christie Redfern's troubles* (London, 1866) and *Shenac's work at home* (London, 1868) take place in Glengarry County, Ontario, and *The bairns; or, Janet's love and service. A story from Canada* (London, 1870) is set partly in the Eastern Townships of Quebec and partly in New England. Christie is so dedicated to nursing and consoling her motherless siblings and other people's children that her health suffers and she dies; equally selfless, Shenac helps her mother keep their fatherless family together; Janet Nasmyth is such a loving and capable housekeeper that her influence affects the eight Elliott 'bairns' well into their adult years. All three novels feature children—who grow up to be women prone to suffer through protracted love affairs—and were widely read by children and reprinted many times. So popular was *Christie Redfern* that it was offered in exchange for a kitten in the correspondence columns of *Aunt Judy's Magazine*, a British children's periodical.

In 1873, after the success of her early books, Robertson moved to Montreal and went on to write such books as *The two Miss Jean Dawsons* (New York, 1880) and *By a way she knew not; the story of Allison Bain* (New York, 1887). J.D. Borthwick, praising her 'moral and well-written books' in his article on her brother Joseph in his *History and biographical gazetteer* (Montreal, 1892), called her 'an ornament to Montreal' and 'a literary niche in Canada's monuments'.

PATRICIA DEMERS

Robin, Régine (b. 1939). Born Ryvka Ajzersztejn in Paris, France, of Polish-Jewish parents—whose Judaism, at least until the period of de-Stalinization, was subordinate to their dream of an egalitarian Communist society—Robin completed a doctorate in history at the Université de Paris (X, Nanterre) before emigrating and settling in 1977 in Montreal, where she teaches at the Université du Québec à Montréal. A member of the Royal Society of Canada, recipient of a Governor General's Award, and winner of the prestigious Prix Jacques Rousseau (1994), she is not well known to the general public.

Historian, essayist, novelist, Robin is one of Canada's most important thinkers, partly because of her interdisciplinarity and her questioning the very nature of memory and the historical process, but also because of her profound and innovative reflection on personal and collective identity in a world characterized by shifting populations and ongoing confrontations in a multiplicity of cultures. Steering a difficult path between the Scylla of the American 'melting pot' and the Charybdis of the Canadian multicultural mosaic, she explores in all her writings the question of (her) personal identity and its relation to society. Her first major text, *Le cheval blanc de Lénine; ou L'histoire autre* (Brussels, 1979; rpr. with a new introduction in 1995) bursts at the seams: achronological, skipping through historical and geographic space, braiding together fact and myth, objective details and subjective reactions, reinventing lost worlds and searching for new ones, this book, apparently about the past, is in fact the first giant step towards a future yet to be defined. Her odyssey continues in the novel *La Québécoite* (1983), a novel about a novel yet to be written. The ambiguous title, a possible play on the word *cot/coite* (silent or nonplussed), refers to the main character, unable to feel quite Québécoise as she walks the streets of Montreal, ill at ease with a language that, while resembling her native French, in fact conceals a very different reality.

In *L'amour du Yiddish: écriture juive et le sentiment de la langue, 1830-1948* (Paris, 1984), Robin retraces the history and frequently progressive nature of Yiddish writing, essentially in Eastern Europe, in an attempt to come to terms with the meaning of the language in her own life. *Le réalisme socialiste, une esthétique impossible* (Paris, 1986), for which she received a Governor General's Award, revisits the history and significance of the writing that—again in Eastern Europe, particularly in the Soviet Union—accompanied the now-dead Communist utopia. Her decision to write a biography of Kafka (*Kafka*, Paris, 1989) reflects her continued obsession with the relation of language to culture to identity. *Le roman mémoriel: de l'histoire à l'écriture du hors-lieu* (1989) explores more overtly the major theme of her first book: the need to move forward from history in order to create a new and unifying time and space. In 1989 Robin also edited a special issue of *Cahiers de recherche sociologique*, published by the Université du Québec à Montréal, entitled 'L'énigme du texte littéraire', in which her own contribution, approaching the same issue from a different angle, is concerned with the ease with which contemporary culture erases past guilt and horror, choosing either to forget, to rewrite, or to obscure under a mask of banality.

One of her most significant texts is a short article, 'Sortir de l'ethnicité', published in

Métamorphoses de l'utopie (Paris, 1992), in which, as the title indicates, she continues to reject both total assimilation and defensive ethnicity, to conclude that society must constitute some sort of 'nomadic' space, open to constant change, in which we all, with our shifting plural identities, partake in a form of universalism that recognizes both our individualness and our togetherness.

See also Maïr Verthuy, 'Qui perd sa langue . . .' in *Multi-culture, multi-écriture, la voix migrante au féminin en France et au Canada* (France, 1996), edited by Lucie Lequin and Maïr Verthuy. MAÏR VERTHUY

Robinson, Peter (b. 1950). Born in Yorkshire, England, he completed his B.A. in English literature at the University of Leeds before immigrating to Canada in 1974. He holds an M.A. from the University of Windsor and a Ph.D. from York University, Toronto, and since 1983 has taught creative writing and literature courses at Seneca, George Brown, and Humber colleges in Toronto, as well as at Ryerson Polytechnic University. He is best known for a series of seven police procedurals featuring Detective Chief Inspector Alan Banks and set in Eastvale, a fictional Yorkshire dale. These include *Gallows view* (1987), *A dedicated man* (1988), *The hanging valley* (1989), *A necessary end* (1989), *Past reason hated* (1991), which won an Arthur Ellis Award, *Wednesday's child* (1992), *Final account (*1994) and *Innocent graves* (1996). The Banks series is most successful in its presentation of the character of Banks himself, a man sensitive about his working-class origins and limited education who has (somewhat ironically) moved his family from London to Yorkshire in search of a quieter life. With his quiet, methodical ways and infinite patience in pursuing his inquiries, Banks belongs to a particular British detective-fiction tradition that features cool, ruminative, and occasionally prickly investigators (ranging from Conan Doyle's Holmes through Ruth Rendell's Wexford and Colin Dexter's Morse). It is Banks' contemplative nature, in fact, that contributes to the success of the series in terms of its perceptive social and cultural commentary. As newcomer to a rapidly disappearing ancient and venerable way of life in Yorkshire, Banks is well positioned to observe and lament its invasion by a double juggernaut consisting of egregious yuppie-style tastes migrating upward from the south of England, and of American popular culture with its proclivity toward self-absorption, instant pleasures, and gratuitous violence.

Robinson has also written two non-series crime novels: *Caedmon's song* (1990), a psychological thriller about a serial killer preying on university students in northern England, and *No cure for love* (1995), an American-set police procedural that focuses on Detective Arvo Hughes of the Los Angeles Police Department's Threat Management Unit. They are less successful than his series fiction in evoking the sense of place that characterizes his writing at its best. MARILYN ROSE

Robinson, Spider (b. 1948). Born in New York City, and educated at the State University of New York (Stonybrook), he settled in 1973 at Phinney's Cove on the Bay of Fundy, Nova Scotia; moved to Halifax, Nova Scotia; then moved again to Vancouver, British Columbia. A voluminous science-fiction writer and a 'personality', he is praised for his novels and stories and prized for his wit and talent as a speaker at SF conventions. Robinson is best known for the Star books: *Stardance* (1978; co-written with his dancer wife Jeanne Robinson), which describes a dance in zero gravity in space, and its lively successors *Starseed* (1991) and *Starmind* (1994). Puns predominate in the Callahan stories in six collections, from *Callahan's Crosstime Saloon* (1977) to *Callahan's legacy* (1996). Robinson was influenced by the bright, technological optimism of Robert A. Heinlein but also by this SF master's conception of the 'Crazy Years' of social anarchy—consequently, there is a dark, pessimistic aspect to Robinson's depiction of the uses of science and technology in such novels as *Telempath* (1976), *Mindkiller: a novel of the near future* (1982), and *Night of power* (1985). As a writer of short fiction, he also showed his range and resources to advantage in *Melancholy elephants* (1984), his sole Canadian publication, all others being published in the United States and widely translated.

JOHN ROBERT COLOMBO

Rochon, Esther. See FANTASTIC LITERATURE AND SCIENCE FICTION IN FRENCH.

Rohmer, Richard (b. 1924). Born in Hamilton, Ontario, he attended high school in Fort Erie, Ontario. After serving in the Royal Canadian Air Force as a fighter pilot in the Second World War—participating in the D-Day invasion of Normandy—he attended the University of Western Ontario (B.A., 1948) and Osgoode Hall, Toronto, to become a Toronto lawyer and businessman. A Major-General in the Militia (Air Command), he is an Officer of the Order of Canada.

Rohmer is the undisputed Canadian king of the pot-boiler, specializing in the disaster novel and the political thriller. Several of his novels deal with annexationist attempts by the USA to take over Canada: for example, *Ultimatum* (1973), in which Canada's right to its own natural resources is called into question by an energy crisis; *Exxoneration* (1974), in which Canada thwarts an American invasion; *Exodus/U.K.* (1975), in which Britain has collapsed and the flood of Anglo-Celtic immigrants to Canada leads Quebec to separate; *Separation* (1976), in which Quebec has plans to secede, but Ottawa copes—and its sequel, *Separation II* (1981); *Balls!* (1979), involving Canada's being blackmailed under threat of invasion by the USA; and some 'Cold Warrior' novels preaching against the 'Red Menace', including *Periscope Red* (1980), *Retaliation* (1982), *Triad* (1982), and *Red Arctic* (1989); science-fiction like *Starmageddon* (1986); and war novels: *Rommel and Patton; armistice in Normandy* (1986), published in the USA as *The hour of the Fox*.

All these novels are without any redeeming social importance and are equally devoid of literary values, and yet they have an urgency and vitality that overcome their inherent implausibility and improbability, and grip the reader. Rohmer is a nationalist and his novels, even at their pulp-fiction level, touch a nerve that resonates. Among Rohmer's hack-works, there is one shining nugget: *John A.'s crusade* (1995), a historical espionage novel centred on Russia's sale of Alaska to the USA, of which the hero is Canada's first Prime Minister: it is one of the best Canadian political thrillers.

Non-fiction works by Rohmer include *The green North; mid-Canada* (1970); *The Arctic imperative: an overview of the energy crisis* (1973); *E.P. Taylor; the biography of Edward Plunket Taylor* (1978); *Patton's gap; an account of the Battle of Normandy 1944* (1981); *How to write a be$t $eller* (1984); and *Massacre 747* (1984). *Death by deficit: a 2001 novel* (1995) is a portrait of a post-separation Canada on the verge of economic collapse. DAVID SKENE-MELVIN

Rolyat, Jane. Pseudonym of Jean E. McDougall. See NOVELS IN ENGLISH 1920 TO 1940: 2.

Ronfard, Jean-Pierre. See DRAMA IN FRENCH 1948 TO 1981: 4.

Rooke, Leon (b. 1934). He was born in Roanoke Rapids, North Carolina, and lived in Victoria, British Columbia, between 1969 and 1989, when he moved to Ontario. He was educated at Mars Hill College, N.C. (1953-5), and at the University of North Carolina at Chapel Hill (1955-7, 1961), where he did both undergraduate and graduate work. He served in the army in Alaska (1958-60), and edited the newspaper *Anvil* in Durham, N.C. (1967-9). He has taught English and creative writing at North Carolina, at Southwest Minnesota State University in Marshall, Minnesota, and at a number of universities in Canada. In 1981 he won the Canada-Australia Literary Prize for his work.

Rooke's collections of stories include *Last one home sleeps in the yellow bed* (1968), *The love parlour* (1977), *The broad back of the angel* (1977), *Cry evil* (1980), *Death suite* (1981), *The birth control king of the Upper Volta* (1982), *Sing me no love songs I'll say you no prayers: selected stories* (1984), *A bolt of white cloth* (1984), *How I saved the province* (1989), *The happiness of others* (1991), and *Who do you love?* (1992). Rooke has also written five novels: *Vault* (1973), *Fat woman* (1980); *The magician in love* (1981); *Shakespeare's dog* (1983), which won a Governor General's Award; and *A good baby* (1989). In continually testing the limits of fiction, he deliberately weakens traditional elements of the realistic story. Often there is little unity of action: the narrator, as in 'Brush fire', prefers frequent digression to the tale he originally set out to tell. The development of character is often minimal, with the result that many of Rooke's stories have the quality of parable or fable—skeletal dramas enacted by generic figures. Although in some stories setting can be given in such detail that it becomes the dominant element—notably in stories that chiefly evoke a mood, such as 'For love of Eleanor'—in many it is completely absent. In *The magician in love* the lack of setting creates a temporal and spatial indeterminacy essential to the universality (attaining a level of fantasy) that Rooke seeks for the magician's experiences. Other stories offer little motivation for the action: characters act out of boredom, random impulse, or some unspecified, sometimes mysterious force, as in 'When swimmers on the beach have all gone home'. Occasionally the plot is dramatic yet visibly incomplete, as if Rooke wished to posit the incompleteness of our knowledge of some events. Most of Rooke's stories are first-person narrations by characters who, caring little to explain themselves, become known to us in a fragmentary way. Other stories are related by diary entries, biographical entries, in separate interlocking narratives, or from aloof third-person perspectives. Of particular note is the wide range of voices in Rooke's work—adolescent,

American southern, West Indian, black American, even canine in his novel *Shakespeare's dog*, a *tour de force* written in pseudo-Elizabethan English. Because Rooke allows these voices to speak for themselves, without authorial mediation, they carry an intensity that more than compensates for the often fragmentary representation of action.

The female narrator of Rooke's novel *Fat woman* is the most extravagant personality among his narrators and the most vivid of his characterizations. This work, *The magician in love*, and most of the story collections focus on the difficulty of male-female relations. Characters appear isolated within themselves, essentially unknown by their mates; they connect only out of secret and bizarre desires. The stories in *Cry evil* and *Death suite* move from the desultoriness of relationships to the despair and latent violence that underlie them; appearing as routine elements in human life are murder, sadism, and pornography.

Muffins (1995) is a humorous, outrageous short story (accompanied by a 7-inch vinyl record of Rooke reading it) about a teenaged girl's relationship with her parents during and after a muffin-baking session in the kitchen. Rooke has also written several plays, including *Krokodile* (1973), *Sword/Play* (1974), *Ms America* (1984), and *The coming* (1991).

CANADIAN FICTION MAGAZINE 38 (1981) is devoted to Rooke. See also Simone Vauthier, '"Entering other skins":—or, Leon Rooke's "The end of the revolution"', in John METCALF, ed., *Writers in aspic* (1988), and Keith Garebian, *Leon Rooke and his works* (1989).

See also NOVELS IN ENGLISH 1960 TO 1982: 4. FRANK DAVEY

Roquebrune, Robert Laroque de (1889-1978). He was born at L'Assomption manor house into an aristocratic family that was deeply attached to the past. When he was four years old, his parents moved to Montreal, where he was educated. He was one of the founders of the art magazine *Le NIGOG*. In 1919 he began working for the Canadian Public Archives in Paris and became director in 1946. Throughout his life he was a contributor to many periodicals in France and Canada. He died in Cowansville, Quebec.

Roquebrune's first work, *L'invitation à la vie* (1916), a little-known collection of prose poems, is, as its title indicates, a hymn to life. All of his subsequent books but one were inspired by the past, which—because of his upbringing and his work in the Archives—was often more real to him than the present. *Les habits rouges* (Paris, 1923) takes place at the time of the 1837 rebellion. Unlike other historical novels of the period, it does not depict the English as villains. 'From the beginning, my novel was in no way nationalistic,' the author states. Though its psychology is superficial, it is well structured and received the Prix David. The unifying theme of *D'un océan à l'autre* (Paris, 1924), a second novel that is marred by an over-complicated plot, is the construction of the Canadian Pacific Railway. In collaboration with his friend Fernand Préfontaine, Roquebrune then wrote an unremarkable detective novel, *La banque en détresse* (Paris, 1926), published under the pseudonym Dick Berton. *Les dames Le Marchand* (Paris, 1927), set at the turn of the century, depicts the end of the French-Canadian aristocracy witnessed by Roquebrune in his childhood. This is a mature work, with convincing characters. *Contes du soir et de la nuit* (1942) is a collection of short stories, and *La Seigneuresse* (1960) is a novel of love and adventure set in New France.

Roquebrune's masterpiece is without question *Testament de mon enfance* (1951), translated by Felix Walter as *Testament of my childhood* (1964). In this first volume of his memoirs, he recalls the comfortable and genteel existence led by his family in l'Assomption. The book is full of humorous sketches of adventurous ancestors and colourful people. The second volume, *Quartier Saint-Louis* (1966), and especially the third, *Cherchant mes souvenirs* (1968), are less successful—perhaps because they deal with a more recent past that is less appealing to the author. Roquebrune also wrote two volumes of vivid historical essays: *Les Canadiens d'autrefois*, I (1962) and II (1966). PAULETTE COLLET

Roscoe, Patrick (b. 1962). Born of Canadian parents on the Spanish island of Formentera, he was raised in Canada and Tanzania, and left home at sixteen. He travelled widely throughout Canada, the United States, and Mexico, but feels most at home in Spain. An untrained writer, Roscoe has a natural exuberance that made him in his early twenties foremost of a new generation of fiction writers. He was winner of the 1990 CBC Radio Literary competition and took second place in 1991. He has also worked as a male prostitute.

His story collections *Beneath the western slopes* (1987) and *Love is starving for itself* (1992) are set in Mexico, and earned Roscoe a comparison with Gabriel García Marquéz for his lyrical portrayals of fantasy, mystery, and fragility in a mythical Mexican village. He took a different direction with the nineteen autobiographical pieces in *Birthmarks* (1990), powerful, often surreal accounts of how childhood experiences 'marked' the forming identity of a young male prostitute growing up in Africa and British Columbia. His novel *God's peculiar care* (1991) was even more unusual: it claims to complete the unfinished manuscript of Hollywood actress Frances Farmer, who was committed to an insane asylum in the 1940s. His novel *Lost oasis* (1995) describes an emotionally bankrupt family and their travels; as a poetic recitation of childhood grief, the book describes two decades of emotional history. GEOFF HANCOCK

Rose, Richard. See DRAMA IN ENGLISH 1953 TO 1981.

Rose-Belford's Canadian Monthly and National Review (1878-82). Hunter, Rose and Company, Toronto, which had printed *The Canadian Monthly and National Review* since its inception in 1872, in Jan. 1878 took control as publishers. Since Dec. 1876 they had also printed *Belford's Monthly Magazine: A Magazine of Literature and Art*, which combined serialized reprints of popular British and American stories with original contributions from many of the same Canadian writers appearing in *The Canadian Monthly*. In the spring of 1878 Hunter, Rose merged with Belford Brothers to form the Rose-Belford Publishing Company, and in June the two magazines were combined. The Belfords left the new company within the year, but the names of the publisher and the magazine remained unchanged until the magazine's demise in 1882.

In its first year *Rose-Belford's* was edited by George STEWART, who continued the tradition of serialized novels and social and literary comment. He introduced more American writers, as well as illustrated travel articles. After Stewart's departure Graeme Mercer ADAM, who had edited *The Canadian Monthly*, became editor of *Rose-Belford's*. The magazine grew larger, although the illustrations disappeared and a greater emphasis was placed on original material by Canadian authors, such as Ethelwyn WETHERALD, William KIRBY, Sara Jeannette DUNCAN, Charles G.D. ROBERTS, and Frederick George SCOTT. Morality, ethics, and religious issues came to the fore, along with the fiction, poetry, and reviews.

The publishers blamed 'our inchoate state as a nation' for the decision to cease publication in 1882: a greater patriotism would be required to support a magazine like *Rose-Belford's*, since the public preferred other types of literature.

See Marilyn G. Flitton, *An index to The Canadian Monthly and National Review and to Rose-Belford's Canadian Monthly and National Review 1872-1882* (1976). CAL SMILEY

Rosen, Sheldon (b.1943). Born in New York, he grew up in Rochester and received his B.A. in psychology from the University of Rochester (1965). He then took an M.A. in telecommunications and spent several years producing radio and television commercials. He moved to Toronto in 1970. His first plays include a one-act absurdist comedy, *Love mouse* (1972), *Meyer's room* (1972), a surrealist one-act play, and *The wonderful world of William Bends (who is not quite himself today)* (1972), a dark comedy featuring a humanitarian who wants to spend his life as a mohair rug, and psychiatrists who are as crazy as their patients. Meanwhile Rosen was writing a number of shows for CBC television, which he continued to do after moving to Vancouver in 1973. There he became affiliated with the writer's-workshop program of the New Play Centre, which produced a number of his one-act plays, including *The box* (1975), *Frugal repast* (1978), and *Like father, like son* (produced in 1975)—later reworked and entitled *The grand hysteric* (1978). In *The box*, which begins with an extended movement sequence, two roommates fantasize about an unopened gift; in *Frugal repast* Picasso's harlequin figures come to life; and in *Like father, like son* a seriously disturbed young man has a traumatic session with his psychiatrist. Rosen has also written a children's play, *The stag king* (produced in 1973) and the book for a musical, *Alice in Wonderland* (produced in 1974).

Although Rosen claims to prefer writing abstract and absurdist drama—his interest in movement has led to several mime theatrics including *Dwelling* (produced in 1977) and *Impact* (produced in 1980)—his most successful work to date is the naturalistic play *Ned and Jack* (1978), commissioned by the New Play Centre. Set in New York in 1922, it is about a late-night encounter between the popular American dramatist Edward Sheldon and his close friend John Barrymore, who—still in costume and full of the success of his opening night as Hamlet—climbs the fire-escape to Ned's penthouse apartment. Both artists are at a turning point in their lives: Jack is triumphant as an actor, while Ned has just learned that his paralysing illness is irreversible—he will be bedridden for the rest of his life. A sensitive and compassionate play,

Ned and Jack combines humour, intense emotion, and careful character delineation. It was well received when it opened at the New Play Centre in 1977; after considerable rewriting it ran two successive seasons at the Stratford Festival in 1978 and 1979, and in 1980 it earned for Rosen the CANADIAN AUTHORS' ASSOCIATION award for drama. After its 1980 off-Broadway run it was called one of the ten best plays of the year by Clive Barnes. A 1981 Broadway production, however, was not a commercial success.

Souvenirs (1985) was first produced off-Broadway in 1984 by the New York Theatre Workshop and was subsequently produced by Factory Theatre Lab, Toronto, and Theatre Calgary. Set on an island off Australia, it is the account of a photographer's adventures during a political insurrection.

The duck sisters, produced in 1990 by Toronto's Theatre Plus, returns to the comedic themes of Rosen's earlier writing. It is the story of two middle-aged sisters who wear duck masks as a way to advertise an out-of-the-way antique store. Even though this is their last day in business, the sisters are exuberant because a flying saucer is coming to take them away. The play was subsequently produced at the Half-Moon Theatre in Dallas, Texas. Rosen's imagistic adaptation of Ibsen's *An enemy of the people* was produced by the National Theatre School, Montreal, in 1994.

Sheldon Rosen is currently co-ordinator of the playwriting programs at the National Theatre School of Canada.

CYNTHIA ZIMMERMAN

Rosenberg, Ann. See NOVELS IN ENGLISH 1983 TO 1996: OTHER NOVELS 1(a).

Rosenblatt, Joe (b. 1933). Born in Toronto, he attended Central Technical School, which he left in grade ten. During a decade of laboring jobs, the last seven years of which he spent as a freight handler with the Canadian Pacific Railway, he became increasingly interested in socialism, poetry, and drawing. With the help of a CANADA COUNCILgrant in 1963, he was able to leave the CPR and begin a career of writing, teaching, and editing. He now lives at Qualicum Beach on Vancouver Island, British Columbia. Since his first small-press publication, *The voyage of the mood* (1960), he has accumulated a witty and eccentric body of poetry and drawings. In *The LSD Leacock* (1963) he expressed in both serious and comic terms the idea that has permeated most of his writing: the essential unity of organic forms. He declared himself here a visionary who can see beyond civilization to the interconnectedness of human, reptile, and insect life. Rosenblatt's style reiterated the paradox expressed in the book's title: conventional and visionary vocabularies collide, scientific terms are invested with unexpected poetic resonance. After the much-less-adventurous *The winter of the lunar moth* (1968), and the collection of drawings *Greenbaum* (1970), Rosenblatt returned to the language of *The LSD Leacock in Bumblebee dithyramb* (1972). The poems of this collection vigorously celebrate humanity's sharing of the fecund energy of the animal and vegetable worlds, again marrying the vocabularies of mysticism and contemporary science. In *Dream craters* (1974) and *Virgins and vampires* (1975) Rosenblatt used more conventional forms of short poetry to explore other areas of his visionary bestiary. Frogs, cats, vampires, lizards, birds, toads, and goldfish here reflect, to one another, on their common piscine heritage. *Top soil* (1976), which gathered poems from most of Rosenblatt's earlier books, won a Governor General's Award. His other books in this period included *Doctor Anaconda's solar fun club* (1978), a collection of drawings; *Loosely tied hands: an experiment in punk* (1978), a rollicking combination of his animal imagery and chant forms with the rhythms of popular music; and *The sleeping lady* (1979), a sonnet sequence exploring the 'salamander' joys of sexual love. In the 1980s Rosenblatt began writing sardonic long poems focused on ethical and political issues. *Brides of the stream* (1984) examined ecological and conservation questions; *Beds and consenting dreamers* (1994) reconsidered the history of Marxist government. Rosenblatt's writings have been collected in *Poetry Hotel: selected poems 1963-1985* (1985), *The Joe Rosenblatt reader* (1995), and *The voluptuous gardener: the collected art and writing of Joe Rosenblatt 1973-1996* (1996). Rosenblatt has also published two volumes of memoirs, *Escape from the glue factory: a memoir of a paranormal Toronto childhood* (1985) and *The kissing goldfish of Siam* (1989). From 1969 to 1983 he edited *Jewish Dialog*, an eclectic literary magazine.

See Ed Jewinski, *Joe Rosenblatt and his works* (1992).

See also POETRY IN ENGLISH 1950 TO 1982: 3.

FRANK DAVEY

Rosenfarb, Chaveh (b. 1923). Born in Lodz, Poland, she attended a Yiddish secular school and a Polish high school from which she graduated in 1941. By that time Rosenfarb and her family had been incarcerated in the Lodz ghetto, and it was there that she received her high school diploma. The Lodz ghetto was liquidated in Sept. 1994, and Rosenfarb was deported to Auschwitz. From Auschwitz she was sent to a concentration camp at Sasel, then to Bergen Belsen, where, suffering from typhus, she was liberated by the British Army in 1945. After the war she crossed the border illegally into Belgium, where she lived as a Displaced Person until her immigration to Canada. She has lived in Montreal since 1950.

Rosenfarb was profoundly affected by her experiences during the Holocaust, and her prodigious output of poetry, novels, short stories, plays, and essays deals with this topic in one way or another. She began as a poet, publishing her first collection of poetry, *Die Balade fun nekhtikn Vald* ('The ballad of yesterday's forests') in London in 1947. This was followed by the book-length poem *Dos Lied fun yidishn Kelner Abram* ('The song of the Jewish waiter Abram'; London, 1948); and the poetry collections *Geto un andere Lieder* ('Ghetto and other poems'; Montreal, 1950); and *Aroys fun gan Eiden* ('Out of Paradise'; Tel Aviv, 1965.) Rosenfarb's play *Der Foigl fun Geto* ('The bird of the ghetto'; Montreal, 1963) was translated into Hebrew and performed by the Habimah, Israeli's National Theatre, in 1966.

Finding that neither poetry nor drama could begin to express the depths of her feelings about the holocaust, Rosenfarb turned to fiction. In 1972 she published *Der Boim fun Lebn* ('The tree of life'; Tel Aviv, 1972). This monumental three-volume epic, which chronicles the destruction of the Jewish community of Lodz during the Second World War, was published in Hebrew and English. English-language excerpts appeared in *Canadian Yiddish writing* (1976) and in the American journal *Midstream* (April 1985). It was followed by the novels *Bociany* (Tel Aviv, 1983), named after a Polish village, and *Briv tsu Abrashen* ('Letters to Abrasha'; Tel Aviv, 1992).

Rosenfarb was a frequent contributor of essays to the Yiddish literary journal *Di goldene Keyt* ('The golden chain'), where in the early 1980s she also began to publish a series of short stories about the lives of Holocaust survivors in Canada. One of these stories, 'The Greenhorn', was translated by Miriam WADDINGTON for her anthology *Canadian Jewish short stories* (1990). Another, 'Edgia's revenge' (translation by Goldie Morgentaler), appeared in *Found treasures*, an anthology in English of stories by Yiddish women writers. Rosenfarb's important essay on the problems of being a Yiddish woman writer appeared in English in *Gender and text in modern Hebrew and Yiddish literature* (1992).

Rosenfarb is the winner of numerous literary awards, among them the Canadian Y.Y. SEGAL Prize, which she won twice, and the prestigious Manger Prize for Literature, awarded in Israel in 1979.

GOLDIE MORGENTALER

Ross, Alexander. See EXPLORATION LITERATURE IN ENGLISH: 2 AND HISTORICAL WRITING IN ENGLISH: 3.

Ross, Malcolm. See NEW CANADIAN LIBRARY.

Ross, Sinclair (1908-96). Born on a homestead near Prince Albert, Saskatchewan, one of three siblings, he grew up on prairie farms where his mother worked as a housekeeper after the breakdown of her marriage. Leaving high school after Grade 11, James Sinclair Ross (known as Jim) worked as a bank clerk for the Union Bank of Canada (later the Royal Bank) in a succession of small towns in Saskatchewan before being transferred to Winnipeg in 1933 and then to Montreal in 1946. Apart from four years in the Canadian army (1942-6), when he was stationed in England, he remained with the bank until his retirement in 1968. He then lived for some years in Greece and Spain, returning to Canada in 1980 and settling in Vancouver, where he died after some years of declining health related to advancing Parkinson's disease.

Ross produced a substantial body of work, and one that is more integrated than is usually acknowledged. His four novels—*As for me and my house* (1941), *The well* (1958), *Whir of gold* (1970), and *Sawbones Memorial* (1974)—and eighteen short stories published between 1934 and 1972, feature both rural and urban settings and themes, but quite consistently focus on alienated, imaginative, and often artistic characters, many of them young boys or men, who experience social pressures and strictures as oppressive and struggle to nurture a sensibility seemingly at odds with hegemonic demands, particularly for conformity to gender expectations. His short stories were collected in *The lamp at noon and other stories* (NEW CANADIAN LIBRARY, 1968), which features an introduction (now an Afterword) by Margaret LAURENCE acknowledging the influence of Ross on other western-Canadian writers such as herself, and *The race and other stories* (1982), edited and introduced by Lorraine McMullen.

Ross is best known for his early fiction, which uniquely captures the harsh, impoverished lives of prairie farmers and townspeople during the dust- and drought-ridden years of the Depression. Stories such as 'No other way' (1934), 'The lamp at noon' (1938), and 'The painted door' (1942) resonate with realistic detail reflecting the isolation, bone-wearying labour, helplessness in the face of the elements, and psychological strain, especially between husbands and wives, that Ross saw as characterizing life on the Prairies during those hard times.

Reflecting these themes as well, *AS FOR ME AND MY HOUSE* attracted little critical attention until its release in a New Canadian Library edition in 1957 (it is still in the series, with an Afterword by Robert KROETSCH), but has since become Canada's most critically contested novel. At the same time it is an amazingly complex, elusive narrative that brings all of its own assertions into question before it closes. The story of Philip Bentley, a small-town minister during the Depression who is also (apparently) a frustrated artist, is told through the diary of his pinched and equally thwarted wife. While the story does deal with the artist's struggle to survive and express himself in a narrow, claustrophobic, critical, and hypocritical environment, it simultaneously—because of the rich ambiguities that surround Mrs. Bentley's telling of the tale, and her agenda in doing so—suggests the provisionality of all truths, even those social and environmental constructions that at first seem so unassailably self-evident in this novel.

Ross's middle two novels, arising out of his own urban experience and his fascination with 'outlaws' and misfits, have been less well received. *The well*, set in Saskatchewan, is the story of a young fugitive from Montreal who is morally strengthened by spending a summer on a prairie farm. As his memories of his street gang recede and he manages to resist pressure to commit a second crime, it is clear that farm work, especially with horses, offers him a framework for spiritual renewal. *Whir of gold*, set in Montreal, portrays the near downfall of a down-and-out aspiring clarinetist from Saskatchewan, who is susceptible to the corrupting influence of a fellow roomer. His final rejection of criminal life is due less to the love of a generous woman than to the strength of his dream of becoming a musician—a dream connected to his memories of his farm family and the spirited horse he loved as a boy. Though often dismissed as melodramatic and sentimental, both novels explore Ross's most persistent themes, and invite revisionary critical thinking, particularly in the light of the now-public knowledge of Ross's homosexuality and the ways in which these novels draw together a particular constellation of elements (young men, artistic leanings, work with horses, and the ambiguities that surround prairie life and farm work for such young people) whose exploration is likely to shed new light on the rest of Ross's work.

Ross's fourth novel, *Sawbones Memorial* (1974; NCL, 1978), is in many ways a return to the territory of *As for me and my house*. Set in 'Upward', Sask., in 1948, the narrative reflects a single evening, during a retirement party for the town doctor that coincides with the opening of a long-awaited hospital named in his honour. Composed of unlinked snippets—dialogue, speeches, interior monologues, and songs—it is, like its antecedent, a profoundly disquieting story, wherein the doctor's public capitulation to Upward's norms and conventions has conferred on him a level of social power and prestige that is undercut by the evidence of secrecy, deviation, dishonesty, and sheer rebellion that are made evident through the unmediated 'bits and pieces' that make up this text, and that seem to indicate the existence of contestatory elements just below the surface of any seemingly orderly—but essentially repressive—social entity. *Sawbones Memorial* also testifies to Ross's abiding interest in narrative experiment and his debt in this regard to European writers, such as Proust and Claude Mauriac, on whose *Diner en ville* Ross's novel was modelled.

See Lorraine McMullen, *Sinclair Ross* (1980), and John Moss, ed., *From the heartland: the fiction of Sinclair Ross* (1992). A recent memoir, Keath FRASER's *As for me and my body* (1997), argues for a reconsideration of Ross's work in the light of his homosexuality and personal sexual history. MARILYN ROSE

Ross, W.W.E. (1894-1966). Born in Peterborough, Ontario, William Wrightson Eustace Ross studied geophysics at the University of Toronto, He returned from England after the First World War to begin a long career as a geophysicist at the Dominion Magnetic Observatory, Agincourt, Ontario. He contributed his first Imagist poems in 1928 to *The Dial* and *Poetry* (Chicago). He published many of these in *Laconics* (1930) and in the less-interesting *Sonnets* (1932). However, despite an admiring review by Marianne Moore (*Poetry* 35, 1931), he was not recognized as Canada's first Imagist poet until Raymond SOUSTER edited a retrospective collection, *Experiment 1923-29* (1956).

In Ross's spare, vertically narrow poems, the inquiring spirit of the New World seeks release from old sentiments, customs, and poetic conventions. Spurning the cliché of the 'old graveyards of Europe', Ross seeks 'something of the sharper tang of Canada' in the surface reflections and dark shadows of pine-surrounded lakes, where reality is recognized as profound and mysterious. The modern poet of the New World seeks illumination by objectifying the ordinary sensations of sight and sound. His explorations of the land of lake and loon thereby serve as metaphors for illumination and rejuvenation.

Shapes and sounds (1968) is a selection of Ross's poems edited by Souster and John Robert COLOMBO, with a memoir by Barry CALLAGHAN.

Ross's correspondence with A.J.M. SMITH, edited by Michael E. Darling in *Essays on Canadian writing* 16 (1979-80), reveals his virtuosity with forty-two parodies of American, British, and Canadian poets, including a self-parody. See also Bruce Whiteman's edition, *A literary friendship: the correspondence of Ralph Gustafson and W.W.E. Ross* (1984), and Don Precosky's 'W.W.E. Ross' in *Canadian writers and their works: poetry series*, vol. 3 (1987).

DAVID LATHAM

Roughing it in the bush; or, Forest life in Canada (2 vols, London, 1852). This series of autobiographical sketches by Susanna MOODIE describes her experiences, and those of her husband and their growing family, during their first seven years in Upper Canada (Ontario). The first volume (1832-4) deals with their arrival in Canada and settlement on a partially cleared farm in Hamilton Township, near Port Hope; the second (1834-9) dramatizes their struggle to wrest a living from the uncleared, largely unarable farm north of Lakefield that was part of Lt John Moodie's military land grant. Loosely chronological, the chapters are organized into subjects appropriate to the then-popular form of the sketch: studies of unusual or eccentric characters ('John Monaghan', 'Brian the still-hunter'), descriptions of local customs ('The logging bee', 'The borrowing system'), anecdotal accounts of special places or events ('Quebec' and 'The Outbreak' [of the 1837 Rebellion]), and accounts of outings or adventures ('The walk to Dummer', 'A trip to Stony Lake') are designed to provide entertainment and variety and to celebrate the genteel values, patriotism, and spirit of progressiveness that for Moodie were inherent in her English middle-class roots. She also included a good deal of her own poetry, much of which she had written in the backwoods, and added several more documentary chapters by her husband ('The land jobber', 'The village hotel', and 'Canadian sketches', the latter added to the second English edition in late 1852) and by her brother Samuel Strickland.

The importance and prominence of this work among nineteenth-century 'Canadian' books follows from Susanna Moodie's intense emotional engagement in her experiences. She sought to increase narrative interest by placing herself near the centre of all she described, much as if she were the heroine of her own autobiographical novel. In the process she offered a surprisingly candid record of her fascination with what she had encountered during what she called 'this great epoch of our lives'. Writing of her adventures nearly a decade later, and well aware of the extent to which her sister Catharine Parr TRAILL's optimism had characterized *The BACKWOODS OF CANADA*, she wished to mark not only the various kinds of alienation and discomfort she had experienced as a pioneer but also her engagement in and commitment to the future of the rising colony. The book's richness of representation owes much to her comedic ability in describing and puzzling over the curious individuals she met in the backwoods, and to her trenchant, no-nonsense examination of pioneering experience, an outlook that gives the book a strong cast of documentary authority. Its influence can be measured in part by the extent to which contemporary writers—for instance, Margaret ATWOOD in her *The JOURNALS OF SUSANNA MOODIE* (1970) and Carol SHIELDS in her novel *Small ceremonies* (1976)—have been fascinated by the complexity of Moodie's voice and vision. Moodie and her book became a part of Canada's useable past for several other writers in the twentieth century. While ostensibly written to warn members of her class not to subject themselves to conditions of wilderness and radical deculturation, Moodie's sketches suggest, finally, not so much an aversion to her experiences as a fascination with and deep involvement in them that no amount of genteel condemnation can effectively diminish. This tension is rooted in Moodie's English background and romantic temperament; it also finds force in the fact that even as Moodie lamented much of what happened to her, she recognized the psychological and emotional importance of those events in the lives of her husband and herself and sought to measure how she had been tested and how much she had grown.

Many of the sketches were composed specifically for Canadian readers and were first published in *The* LITERARY GARLAND and in *The Victoria Magazine* in 1847. Much of the book's negative cast about Canada (see the lengthy articulations of her nostalgia and the introduction of language appropriate to a highly genteel readership) was added later for the book's English audience. A sequel, *Life in the clearings versus the bush* (London, 1853), presents a more consistently positive view of the worth of settling in 'this great and rising country', while *Flora Lindsay* (London, 1854) is a superficially fictionalized account of the Moodies' preparations and emigration from England, which Moodie, in 'a freak', chose to separate from her actual Canadian experiences.

Roughing it in the bush has gone through numerous editions in England, the United States, and Canada since its initial appearance. Most notable among these are the two Richard Bentley editions of February and December 1852, George Putnam's pirated edition published in New York in July 1852, the first Canadian edition (1871), for which Moodie herself made a few deletions and textual changes, and the influential NEW CANADIAN LIBRARY edition of 1962, edited by Carl KLINCK. Crucial as it was as a text by which to introduce Canadian students to Moodie, Klinck's volume has suffered in time because of its omissions; several of Moodie's important sketches, particularly those describing her experiences in the bush north of Lakefield, were cut out. The revised NCL version (with an Afterword by Susan Glickman) provides the whole text of the Bentley second edition. However, students interested in a close study of Moodie's intentions, the book's evolution and textual history, and the historical sources of the events and people Moodie describes should consult the CENTRE FOR EDITING EARLY CANADIAN TEXTS edition of *Roughing it in the bush* (1988), edited by Carl Ballstadt. See also John Thurston, *The work of words* (1996) and Michael Peterman, *This great epoch of our lives: Susanna Moodie's 'Roughing it in the bush'* (1996). MICHAEL PETERMAN

Rouillard, Jacques. See HISTORICAL WRITING IN FRENCH 1980 TO 1996.

Rouquette, Louis-Frédéric (1884-1926). Born in Montpellier, France, he went to Paris after completing his secondary schooling but felt no love for the city and dreamed of distant lands. He became an indefatigable globetrotter, practising all trades as climate and circumstances demanded. He made several trips to Canada's Northwest and was in Alberta for a few months before his sudden death in Paris, having translated his experiences into fiction that he called 'romans vécus'.

Rouquette's books about the North-west —*Le grand silence blanc; roman vécu d'Alaska* (Paris, 1921), which is partly set in Canada; *La bête errante; roman vécu du Grand Nord canadien* (Paris, 1923); and *L'épopée blanche* (Paris, 1926), an account of the work of the Oblate Fathers, several of whom he met—depict the fight for survival in the white wilderness against soul-destroying loneliness, merciless cold, and above all the cruelty of man. Vivid description of scenery, convincing and unusual characters—such as Gregory Land, the ubiquitous postman of the Great North—and human warmth are the chief attributes of these books. PAULETTE COLLET

Roussin, Claude. See DRAMA IN FRENCH 1948 TO 1981: 3.

Routhier, A.-B. See NOVELS IN FRENCH 1900 TO 1920.

Routier-Drouin, Simone. See POETRY IN FRENCH: 4.

Roy, André (b. 1944). Born in Montreal, he edited the 'Prose du jour' series for Éditions du Jour and the 'Écrire' series for Éditions de l'Aurore; was editor-in chief of the literary magazines *SPIRALE* and *Hobo-Québec,* of which he was a founder; and has contributed numerous articles to *Cinéma-Québec* and *Le Devoir.* A position as editorial secretary with *Chroniques* ended abruptly with his rejection of the magazine's 'restrictive, totalitarian, Marxist' approach.

Roy belongs to the group of modernist poets whose works are published by Les Herbes Rouges (both the publishing house and the review of that name). His collection *L'espace de voir* (1974), followed by *En image de ça* (1974), inaugurated its series 'Lecture en Vélocipède'. In these texts, and in *N'importe quelle page* (1973), desire is seen as the originator of a succession of cinematic spectacles; the poet thus uses profusely the images of staging, make-up, visual effects, shooting angles. Roy's writings emphasize the importance of the body, whose desires and pleasures translate to the text in a 'Sextual' merging of body and text. This emphasis, as well as the place given to the relationship with the mother, unites Roy with the Quebec feminist avant-garde

(Nicole BROSSARD, for example, for whom he admits a strong affinity). The rupture of syntax, the use of blank spaces, and the unorthodox punctuation, rhythms, and words of his rather formalist writing—especially in the early work up to the publication of *Vers mauve* (1975), which constitutes a turning-point in his production—defy linear reading, but critics stress the technical brilliance and meticulous phrasing of Roy's poetry. *D'un corps à l'autre* (1976) and *Corps qui suivent* (1977) describe a series of amorous encounters in poems that articulate the pleasure of the 'sex/text', and play on intertextuality by including the theories of a host of contemporary artistic, cultural, and political figures (Bertolucci, Sollers, Schönberg, Nietzsche, Pleynet, and Mao Tse-tung, among others). The intertextual games and wordplay result in an irony that is characteristic of Roy's work, his reading of Jacques Lacan having instilled in him a passion for language and its power. *Le sentiment du lieu* (1978) was inspired by his appreciation of painting.

Roy is best known for his 'Passions' cycle, written in a filmic form: *Les passions du Samedi* (1979), a contender for the Prix Nelligan; *Petit supplément aux passions* (1980); and *Monsieur Désir* (1981), which show a new linearity that was only hinted at in the first of these collections. Dealing frankly with homosexuality in a compressed style, a sensitive and well-read narrator describes the amorous gestures and fantasies of male love in all their everyday immediacy.

A film critic, he was twice awarded Le Prix des rendez-vous du cinéma Québécois for the best published article of the year, and his film reviews appeared in *Questions de cinéma* 1 (1985) and *Questions de cinéma* 2 (1987).

La leçon des ténèbres (1983), *Les lits d'Amérique* (1983), *N'importe quelle page* (1973; republished in 1984 with *L'extrait d'elle*), and *Les sept jours de la jouissance* (1984)—where pleasure, body, and text mesh—again develop Roy's 'sex/text'. Roy won a Governor General's Award for *Action writing* (1985), and *L'accélérateur d'intensité* (1987) was awarded Le Grand Prix de Poésie de la Fondation des Forges. With *Nuits* (1984) Roy launched another cycle that included *Le spectacle de l'homme encore visible (Nuits 2)* and *De la nature des mondes animés et de ceux qui y habitent (Nuits 3)* (1994); he described these 'cycles' as an 'incessant remake', and his entire work as a 'long work in progress'. In the 1994 book he rewrites texts published in the 1970s and revisits the deconstruction, 'un-readability', and discursive subversions of the earlier writings; the focus of this 'écriture furieuse' or 'autogénèse poétique' is still set on homosexual love. *Action writing* (1985) is another retrospective of prose and verse previously published. *C'est encore le solitaire qui parle* (1986) was followed by *L'accélérateur d'intensité; suivi de, On ne sait pas si c'est écrit avant ou après la grande conflagration* (1987, 1990), which inaugurated the *Accélérateur d'intensité* tetralogy. The sombre, melancholic look at relationships and loss in *Les amoureux n'existent que sur la terre: (L'accélérateur d'intensité 2)* (1989), the menace and seven different musical forms invoked in *On sait que cela a été écrit avant at après la grand maladie: (L'accélérateur d'intensité 3)* (1992) and *Le coeur est un objet noir caché en nous: (L'accélérateur d'intensité 4)* (1995), present more variations on love, death, the process of writing, and the body's sensations, pains, and fears. *La vie parallèle: un carnet* (1994) is a book of essays consisting of a series of citations, aphorisms, and thoughts on the creative process, reading, politics, the literary establishment, and the status of the writer. Comparing his own process of writing to that employed in making a film, Roy expresses his appreciation of different art forms and their influence on his work, as well as his need to repeat and revitalize earlier works in order to create a dialogue within his writing. Taking a Barthesian pleasure in experimentation and fragmentary style, Roy creates writing that is self-reflexive, vivacious, and open to risks.

Roy is the co-editor of *Marguerite Duras à Montréal* (1984). Selections of his poems have appeared in English translation in *Ellipse* 29-30 (1982) and *Ellipse* 44 (1990), as has Daniel Sloate's translation, *The passions of Mister Desire* (1986).

See the interview by Joseph Bonenfant, Richard Giguère, and André Marquis, 'Persister et se maintenir', *Lettres québécoises* 51 (automne 1988). Studies are Philippe Haeck, 'Mon sexe bavarde' in *Naissance de l'écriture québécoise* (1979); Joseph Bonenfant and Richard Giguère, 'Les passions de l'écriture' in *Lettres québécoises* 22 (printemps 1981); André BROCHU, 'Flamboyants et profonds', *VOIX ET IMAGES* 9.3 (1984) and 'Lascaux, les limites et autres lieux', *Voix et Images* 12.1 (1986); Robert Yergeau, 'Roy, Yvon, Charlebois et Frenette: les multiples contraires de la poésie', *Lettres québécoises* 43 (automne 1986); André Marquis, 'Fantômes, dragons et cendres', *Lettres Québécoises* 52 (hiver 1989); and Sylvain Campeau, 'La BJ/NBJ: du laboratoire des signes au dandysme des sens', *Voix et Images* 17.2 (1992).

MAROUSSIA AHMED/MARIE J. CARRIÈRE

Roy, Camille. See CRITICISM IN FRENCH: 1 and NOVELS IN FRENCH 1900 TO 1920.

Roy, Fernande. See HISTORICAL WRITING IN FRENCH 1980 TO 1996.

Roy, Gabrielle (1909-83). Born in Saint-Boniface, Manitoba, she was educated there and at the Winnipeg Normal School. After teaching for some years in rural Manitoba, she travelled to England and France, where she studied drama and began to write. When war forced her return to Canada, she continued to write stories and articles in Montreal, meanwhile observing the people of Saint-Henri who were to provide the material for *BONHEUR D'OCCASION* (1945), her immensely successful first novel. She was elected to the Royal Society of Canada in 1947 and in the same year married Dr Marcel Carbotte. Made a Companion of the Order of Canada in 1967, she was also awarded the Prix David (1971) and the Molson Prize (1978) for the entire body of her work. She lived in Quebec City.

Gabrielle Roy's prairie background and passion for the Canadian Arctic gave her writing a breadth and an absence of regional pettiness not common among French-Canadian writers. Fully bilingual, she hesitated at first about whether to write in English or in her native French. She was a fine craftsman with a style that is at once simple, strong, and delicately poetic. Her characters are usually rather humble people, whom she handles without falsity or over-emotion so that they become symbols of humanity's quest for a joy that is often ephemeral, of persistent courage, and striving for an understanding with one's fellows that is seldom more than fleeting and often too late. Roy was highly adept at portraying strong women characters like the mothers in *Bonheur d'occasion* and *La petite poule d'eau*. Awarded the Prix Fémina, *Bonheur d'occasion* was the first Canadian work to win a major French literary prize. The first English version, translated by Hannah Josephson as *The tin flute* (1947), won a Governor General's Award. A new translation by Alan Brown was published in a deluxe boxed edition with two drawings of the author by Harold Town in 1980; this text was reprinted in the NEW CANADIAN LIBRARY. The central figure of *Alexandre Chenevert* (1955), Roy's other Montreal novel, is a middle-aged, emotionally inhibited bank teller who is tormented by his inability to express love in his own life and by his uselessness in face of the miseries of which he is informed daily by radio and newspapers. He dies a slow death from cancer but learns finally that love exists, even for him, and that his life has not been as valueless as he believed. The book was translated by Harry Binsse as *The cashier* (1955; NCL, with an Afterword by Marie-Claire BLAIS).

Three Manitoba books—all linked short stories rather than novels—make imaginative use of material from Roy's own past. *La petite poule d'eau* (1950), a poetic account of life in a remote settlement in northern Manitoba, was published in a deluxe edition (1971) with twenty-four original woodcuts by Jean-Paul Lemieux. The English version was translated by Harry Binsse as *Where nests the water hen* (1950; NCL, with an Afterword by Sandra BIRDSELL). The lively and varied stories in *Rue Deschambault* (1955) cover a girl's growth from childhood to adolescence in Saint-Boniface amidst people of every nation, pioneers of the West. It was translated by Harry Binsse as *Street of riches* (1957; NCL with an Afterword by Miriam WADDINGTON) and won the Prix Duvernay and a Governor General's Award. *La route d'Altamont* (1966), translated as *The road past Altamont* (1966)—by Joyce MARSHALL who wrote the Afterword to the NCL edition—provides more intense insight into the same period in this girl's life, focusing on the girl, her mother, and grandmother in four connected stories that describe a circle of time in which the generations succeed and pass one another, meeting in rare flashes of understanding, and in which journeys always lead back to their beginnings.

In *La montagne secrète* (1961), a young painter's Arctic journey and the mountain that he finds, loses, and finds again, frame a parable of the artist's lifelong quest for his subject and his efforts to express it. It was translated by Harry Binsse as *The hidden mountain* (1962; NCL 1975). The four stories of *La rivière sans repos* (1970) use the Arctic background more explicitly to depict the Inuit in a state of transition, drawn without choice into the white man's world and still uneasy with his gifts: his medicine that uselessly prolongs life, a wheelchair, the telephone. In the long title story—which was published separately in a translation by Joyce Marshall as *Windflower* (1970; NCL with an Afterword by Phyllis WEBB)—a child is born of a brief brutal meeting between an American soldier and a young Inuit girl. In her efforts to bring up and keep her son, the mother shifts between white and Inuit ways, not quite at home with either, and loses the boy finally to the white man and his wars. 'The satellites', Joyce Marshall's translation of 'Les satellites', one of the other stories, was published in *The TAMARACK REVIEW* 74

(Spring 1978). *Cet été qui chantait* (1972)—translated by Joyce Marshall as *Enchanted summer* (1976)—is a collection of nineteen stories and sketches, many very brief, each adding a dab of light or intensity to the picture of a summer in Charlevoix County in Quebec. In two later works Roy dipped again into her Manitoba past to provide new pictures and new insights. *Un jardin au bout du monde* (1975)—translated by Alan Brown as *Garden in the wind* (1977; NCL)—recaptures prairie solitude and multiculturalism in four sensitive and evocative short stories. *Ces enfants de ma vie* (1977), which won Roy a third Governor General's Award and was translated by Alan Brown as *Children of my heart* (1979), returned once more to Roy's days as a teacher in a series of narrative sketches, each centring on a single child in a lonely prairie hamlet or a Winnipeg slum.

Fragiles lumières de la terre (1978)—translated by Alan Brown as *The fragile lights of earth* (1982)—is a selection of Roy's non-fiction from 1942 to 1970: early journalistic pieces describing prairie immigrant communities (Doukhobors, Sudeten Germans, and Ukrainians, among others), and some later writing in which she expressed her debt, both literary and personal, to her prairie past. It is invaluable to students of her work. Roy also wrote three books for children: *Ma vache Bossy* (1976), translated by Alan Brown as *My cow Bossy* (1986); *Courte-Queue* (1979), translated by Alan Brown as *Cliptail* (1980); and *L'espagnole et la pékinoise*, published posthumously (1986) and translated by Patricia Claxton as *The tortoiseshell and the pekinese* (1989). Other posthumous publications were *La détresse et l'enchantement* (1984), translated by Patricia Claxton as *Enchantment and sorrow* (1987), an autobiography of her life until 1939 that was incomplete on Roy's death; and *Ma chère petite soeur, lettres à Bernadette 1943-1970* (1988), translated by Patricia Claxton as *Letters to Bernadette* (1990).

See Monique Genuist, *La création romanesque chez Gabrielle Roy* (1966); Phyllis GROSSKURTH, *Gabrielle Roy* (1969), in the Canadian Writers and Their Work series; Marc Gagné, *Visages de Gabrielle Roy* (1973); Allison Mitchan, *The literary achievement of Gabrielle Roy* (1983); and M.G. Hesse, *Gabrielle Roy* (1984). See also Paul Socken, *A concordance to 'Bonheur d'occasion' by Gabrielle Roy* (1982); and *Gabrielle Roy: creation and memory* (1996) by Linda Clemente and Bill Clemente. *Gabrielle Roy: une vie* (1996), a full-scale biography by François Ricard, is more stringent and on occasion more precise than *Enchantment and sorrow* but also affectionate and warmly appreciative of Gabrielle Roy as writer and human being.

See also NOVELS IN FRENCH 1940 TO 1959: 1.

JOYCE MARSHALL

Roy, Louise. See DRAMA IN FRENCH 1948 TO 1981: 4.

Rule, Jane (b. 1931). Born in Plainfield, New Jersey, Jane Vance Rule spent her childhood in various parts of the American mid-west and California. She received a B.A. in English (1952) from Mills College, California, and spent the following year studying seventeenth-century literature at University College, London. From 1954 to 1956 she taught English and biology at Concord Academy, Massachusetts, where she met Helen Sonthoff, with whom she has lived since 1956. In that year she moved to Vancouver and worked at the University of British Columbia—as assistant director of International House (1958-9) and periodically as lecturer in English or creative writing—until 1976, when she moved to Galiano Island, British Columbia, where she now makes her home. She was awarded an honorary D. Litt. from the University of British Columbia in 1994 and, among many other honours, the B.C. Gas Lifetime Achievement Award (1996).

Rule is perhaps best known for her unapologetic and clear-eyed writing on lesbian themes. Her first two novels focus on contrasting types of relations between women. In *Desert of the heart* (1964), set in Reno, Nevada, where the seemingly sterile but startlingly beautiful desert provides a powerful contrasting image to the Vanity Fair commercialism of the casino, two women overcome their fears and prejudices and start living together; the novel is structured on their alternating points of view. Donna Deitch's film of this novel appeared as *Desert hearts* in 1986. *This is not for you* (1970), which takes the form of a long, self-justifying letter that is not meant to be mailed, portrays a woman so trapped by her conventional attitudes and desire to conform to social norms that she withholds her love for another woman.

It would be a mistake, however, to categorize Rule as being interested in lesbian subjects that appeal to a specialized minority. She writes novels of social realism that naturally include both homosexuals and heterosexuals, but in her later novels the central focus is not on any one sort of character. She matches fictional form to the structure of society as she experiences it—not as a hierarchy but as a democratic 'concert' of characters, all of whose voices are given equal attention. In her third novel, *Against the season* (1971), the small-town setting draws characters into a group where, despite violence, pain, and a guilt imposed by the dead as well as the living, affection and love triumph. In *The young in one another's arms* (1977) residents of a Vancouver boarding-house slated for demolition form a voluntary 'family' and work together to establish a restaurant on Galiano Island. *Contract with the world* (1980) is Rule's most successful experiment in making the form of the novel reflect its egalitarian philosophy. Though the events concerning the life and work of six Vancouver artists are told almost entirely in chronological sequence, they are described from a different point of view in each chapter: the reader's view of each character is subtly changed by the perceptions of the others. This multiple voice also presents a variety of aesthetic theories and comments on the relations of art and the artist to society. In these three novels voluntary communities offer protection against stultifying isolation and such hostile outside forces as police harassment, mindless commercial exploitation, and philistinism. Tempering their serious concerns are a gentle sense of humour, a sharp ear for contemporary speech, and a careful control of image patterns, often with literary associations.

Rule's last two novels (she declared her retirement from writing in 1990, caused in part by severe arthritis) include in their study of communities a clear-eyed and sensitive focus on aging. In *Memory board* (1987), a retired doctor in her sixties is reconciled with the twin brother from whom she has been estranged for decades, to some extent because of her lesbianism. Her lover suffers from loss of memory, while the brother must reconstruct his memories of the past in order to come to terms with a new phase of his life. The new sharing of their lives is set in counterpoint to the more conventional families of his children and grandchildren. *After the fire* (1989) tells of five women, each of whom—from widowhood, divorce, or personal choice—learns to live alone, among a community of islanders who recognize the need for mutual support and for shared rituals to mark deaths and disasters.

Rule has been a prolific writer of short stories, published in various magazines and anthologies and in three collections, *Themes for diverse instruments* (1975), *Outlander* (1981) and *Inland passage* (1985). The title story of the first is a stylistic *tour de force*, outlining the branches of a family tree in patterns evocative of an orchestral piece. Several stories in each volume concern children, whose characters Rule creates convincingly and without sentimentality; this is especially apparent in a related group of family stories in *Inland passage*. The stories in *Outlander* all deal with some form of lesbian experience, whether of survivors, as in the title piece, or of the deeply damaged, as in the vivid, painful story 'In the attic of the house'. The volume ends with a selection of Rule's polemical columns from the newspaper *Body politic*, many of which are also included in the collection of essays *A hot-eyed moderate* (1985).

Rule's work consistently presents love between women as one of the many natural and acceptable forms of human expression; the question of why this viewpoint was seldom projected in the past—even by homosexual writers—is addressed in her commissioned book *Lesbian images* (1975), whose introductory essay surveys attitudes to female sexuality over the centuries and condemns the prejudices fostered by churchmen and psychologists. Its chapters on individual writers such as Radclyffe Hall, Colette, Violette Leduc, May Sarton, and Vita Sackville-West are pioneering studies of the sometimes tortured, often veiled, forms in which these women created images of their love for other women. The book was translated into German as *Bilder und Schaffen. Die lesbischer Frau in der Literatur* (1979).

CANADIAN FICTION MAGAZINE 23 (Autumn 1976) is devoted to Jane Rule; it contains a long interview by Geoff Hancock and an article by Helen Sonthoff, 'Celebration: Jane Rule's fiction'. See also Marilyn R. Schuster, 'Strategies for survival; the subtle subversion of Jane Rule', *Feminist Studies* 7, no.3 (Fall 1981), Robin Van Heck, 'The people-centred vision of Jane Rule', *Dalhousie Review* 68 (Fall 1988), and Gillian Spraggs, 'Hell and the mirror; a reading of *Desert of the heart*', in Sally Munt, ed., *New lesbian criticism* (1992). Jane Rule's account of her own life appears in the Gale autobiography series *Contemporary authors* 18 (1994) and she appears personally in the film about her life and work entitled *Fiction and other truths* (1994).

JOAN COLDWELL

Rumilly, Robert. See HISTORICAL WRITING IN FRENCH.

Russell, Ted (1904-77). Born and reared in Coley's Point, Conception Bay, Newfoundland, Edward Russell completed his high-school education at Bishop Field College in St John's, and later qualified to become a teacher at Memorial University College. He taught in a number of Newfoundland communities between 1920 and 1935, starting his career in remote Pass Island in Hermitage Bay, which was possibly the model for the imaginary outport of Pigeon Inlet in his Uncle Mose stories. In 1935 Russell joined the magistracy and eight years later became Director of Co-operation with the Newfoundland government. Part of his responsibilities in this position was to write co-operative tracts and make radio broadcasts. From 1949 to 1951 he was a member of J.R. Smallwood's administration. Subsequently he worked as an insurance salesman, broadcaster, writer, and teacher. When, late in life, he returned to teaching, he gave up what he called the 'hobby' of writing.

Russell is best known for his Uncle Mose stories, which he wrote and narrated himself on the Canadian Broadcasting Corporation in St John's, starting in 1954. Five selections from these stories have been published: *The chronicles of Uncle Mose* (1975), *Tales from Pigeon Inlet* (1977), and three titled *The best of Ted Russell* (1982-8), all edited by his daughter, Elizabeth Russell Miller. In these sketches of outport life, Russell created a gallery of intriguing local characters and summoned up a way of life that was fast changing. He was not opposed to change; he had no affection for what he once called the 'ignorance and isolation' of Newfoundland's past. But neither did he wish to rush towards some vulgar prosperity. He wanted a renovated, modern Newfoundland, with the best retained from the old values. His stories, at their best, are gentle, whimsical, and shrewd evocations of the lives of ordinary people.

Russell also wrote plays for radio. Four have been published: *The holdin' ground: a radio play* (1972); *The Hangashore* in *Baffles of wind and tide* (1973) edited by Clyde Rose; *Landwash* in *The best of Ted Russell* (1982); and *Ground swell* in *The holdin' ground and Ground swell* (1990). These are further expressions of his love for the people in the Newfoundland outports. He also wrote pamphlets promoting co-operative enterprises: *All about credit unions* (1945), *Credit committees* (1947), *Buying clubs* (1948), and *Regional credit societies* (1948).

Russell published memoirs in the St John's *Evening Telegram* in Oct. and Nov. 1966. Elizabeth Russell Miller has written his biography, *The life and times of Ted Russell* (1981).

PATRICK O'FLAHERTY

Ryerson Press, The. In 1828, when Canadian Methodists severed their formal ties with the American Methodist Episcopal Church, they determined at the same meeting to secure a press and to begin a journal and book room. Soon after its foundation in Toronto in 1829, the Methodist Book Room began to issue denominational materials, and by 1835 general trade books. In 1919 the name 'Ryerson Press' was adopted in honour of the first editor, the Methodist minister and educator Egerton Ryerson (1803-82).

For a half-century after 1829 the publication of general books was undertaken haphazardly. A coherent publishing policy emerged only with the election of William Briggs in 1879 as Book Steward; his astute business sense enabled him to amass, through agencies for British and American firms, sufficient revenue to build a Canadian list. W.H. Withrow, long-time editor of Sunday School publications, was the first editor who actively sought out writers. Since the chief market for his books was in Sunday School libraries, he depended largely on fellow clerics for wholesome narratives, such as John Carroll's *My boy life* (1882) and Egerton Ryerson YOUNG's *By canoe and dog-train among the Cree and Saulteaux Indians* (1890). Edward S. CASWELL, who joined the Press as a reader in 1881 and eventually headed the book department, made contact with a wider literary circle. His initiative brought such books as Catharine Parr TRAILL's *Pearls and pebbles* (1894), *The poems of Wilfred Campbell* (1905), and *The collected poems of Isabella Valancy Crawford* (1905), along with Canadian editions of several of Charles G.D. ROBERTS' collections of poetry.

After Caswell's departure in 1909, Briggs depended more and more on agency titles, virtually allowing his Canadian publishing program to lapse by the time of his retirement in 1918. Lorne PIERCE, who was appointed in 1920 as literary adviser and in 1922 as editor, was determined to restore the Press to its former position as the foremost publisher in Canadian writers. At first he faced determined opposition within his own organization. He was able to overcome it, in considerable measure, by building up a very profitable line of school texts. Since his publishing competitors were much more sophisticated than in Briggs' time, however, he was able to secure the lengthy lists he desired only by accepting many manuscripts of lesser quality. His great achievement, especially during his first decade and again after the Second World War under the sympathetic régime of C.H. Dickinson as Book Steward, was to start many promising authors—such as Frederick Philip GROVE, Earle BIRNEY, Dorothy LIVESAY, and Louis DUDEK—on careers that led them eventually to other publishers.

In 1970, mainly through losses incurred in connection with the purchase of an expensive but unsatisfactory colour press, The Ryerson Press was sold to the American firm McGraw-Hill.

The Ryerson imprint (1954) by W. Stewart Wallace provides a checklist of Ryerson titles from the outset, preceded by a brief but useful analysis of trends in the publishing program. JOHN WEBSTER GRANT

Ryga, George (1932-87). Born in Deep Creek, in the Athabasca region of northern Alberta, he was raised in a Ukrainian farming community there. His formal education consisted of seven years in a one-room schoolhouse and a brief period at the University of Texas in 1949, after which he worked as a farm labourer, in construction, and at a radio station in Edmonton. In 1962 he decided he could make his living as a writer, and the following year he and his wife Norma, with their children, moved to Summerland, British Columbia, where they resided until his death. His writings include plays, novels, essays, short stories, poetry, and film scripts.

Ryga's dramatic technique often blends realism, poetry, dance and song, and juxtaposes past and present, though the surrealistic devices in his plays are not always successful. Invariably he sided with the oppressed and the exploited, and spoke out against injustices in Canadian society. Three of his early plays, included in *The ecstasy of Rita Joe and other plays* (1971), edited by Brian Parker, contain heroes who are rebelling against their society or who are trapped in almost unbearable social situations. *Indian*, a one-act play, vividly portrays a Native labourer harassed by a heartless employer and an impersonal government official.

The ECSTASY OF RITA JOE (1970), in which the heroine is unable to live by the old ways of her people or adapt to the white man's ways in the city, offers a much fuller and grimmer presentation of the plight of Aboriginal people. Commissioned by the Vancouver Playhouse for Canada's centennial year, and starring Frances Hyland in the title role and Chief Dan George as her father, *Rita Joe* was the first play in English presented in the theatre of the National Arts Centre, Ottawa, in 1969; like many other of Ryga's plays, it has since been performed internationally, often in Europe, where Ryga is popular. In 1971 the Royal Winnipeg Ballet produced a ballet version at the Centre; a French translation by Gratien GÉLINAS was performed by the Comédie Canadienne in Montreal in 1970; and an authentic production with Native actors in the Amerindian roles was staged at the Prairie Theatre Exchange in Winnipeg in 1981. A less-enduring play, though very popular when first produced at the Vancouver Playhouse in 1969, is *Grass and wild strawberries* (1971), which dramatizes the conflicts between the hippie culture of the 1960s and middle-class society; but it is often a disharmonious mixture of film projection, dance, song, dialogue, and recorded vocal and musical sound.

Captives of the faceless drummer (1971), commissioned by the Vancouver Playhouse for production in Feb. 1971, centres on the kidnapping of a Canadian diplomat by a group of young revolutionaries—there are many parallels with the October Crisis of 1970. When the board of directors of the Playhouse reversed its decision to produce the play, there was a bitter controversy during which the artistic director, David Gardner, was dismissed. It was subsequently produced in Vancouver, Toronto, and Lennoxville, Quebec.

Sunrise on Sarah (1973) is the somewhat confusing story of a troubled woman and her search for liberation from the ghosts that haunt her—her parents and the men in her past. *Paracelsus* (1974), staged at the Vancouver Playhouse in 1986, has more dramatic power, though the production was not well received. It is a wide-ranging historical drama about the pioneering sixteenth-century Swiss physician and alchemist, whose relation to the present is heightened by scenes in a contemporary hospital. It was published in the volume *Two plays* (1982), along with Ryga's adaptation of Aeschylus's *Prometheus bound*, with an introduction by Mavor MOORE.

Ploughmen of the glacier (1977) and *Seven hours to sundown* (1977) show Ryga's continuing preoccupation with the quality of life in Canada. *Ploughmen* examines realistically 'the myth of the men who made the West' through an old prospector, Volcanic Brown, who represents the adventurous, exploitative spirit of the gold seekers, and a retired newspaperman, the somewhat dissolute but human Lowery. *Seven hours to sundown* is based on a confrontation in Ryga's own town between officials wanting to demolish a heritage building and a citizens' group (of which Ryga was a member) wishing to preserve it for use as a cultural centre. Though some of the characters lack sufficient motivation and the ending is inconclusive, it is a strong statement of Ryga's concern and involvement in social, political, and cultural issues.

Some of these issues are touched upon again in a one-act play, *Laddie boy*, published in *Transactions I: short plays* (1978), edited by Edward Peck. Set in a Halifax jail, it gives, in Ryga's best realistic style, a cameo picture of the gulf between rich and poor in Canada. *A letter to my son* (1982) is the story of Ukrainian immigrant Ivan Lepa's struggles to adjust to life in Canada. An earlier version of Lepa's story was presented in 1978 as one segment of *The Newcomers*, the CBC television series on immigrants to Canada. The play was a runner-up for the Governor General's Award for drama in 1984. *Portrait of Angelica* (1984), published in one volume with *A letter to my son*, and produced at the Banff School of Fine Arts in the summer of 1973, presents a picture of the people in a Mexican town seen through the eyes of a Canadian tourist, Danny Baker. Reminiscent of Dylan Thomas's *Under milk wood*, it is Ryga's most mellow play.

Other plays by Ryga that were performed but are as yet unpublished are *Nothing but a man* (in 1967), *Just an ordinary person* (in 1968), *The last of the gladiators* (in 1976, an adaptation of his novel *Night desk*), *Jeremiah's place* (1978), a children's play, and *One more for the road* (in 1985). Among the many plays he wrote for CBC radio are *The legend of Old Charlie*, aired in 1985 and published as *The Frank slide* in *Summerland* (see below), and *Brandon Willie and the great event*, heard in 1987.

Ryga published four novels: *Hungry hills* (1963; rpr. 1977), *Ballad of a stonepicker* (1966; rpr. 1976), *Night desk* (1976), and *In the shadow of the vulture* (1985). *Hungry hills* is the story of an unloved youth who makes his way as best he can, honestly and dishonestly. *Ballad of a stonepicker* depicts the struggles, physical and psychological, of a sensitive man who has sacrificed much of his life by staying with his parents on the family farm so that his younger brother can pursue studies leading to a Rhodes scholarship. *Night desk* takes the form of a rambling monologue by a vibrant, self-centred, riotous, though humane ex-wrestler and fight promoter, Romeo Kuchmir, and brings him to life as a memorable personality. *In the shadow of the vulture* is the story of indentured Mexican workers doing slave labour for Americans in subhuman conditions in a border town. The hero of this heavily symbolic action tale is Sandy Wade, a veteran of the Vietnam war who leads the Mexicans' escape to freedom from their fascist chicken-farmer owner. A translation was published in Russia in 1988. While in none of these novels was Ryga able to present more than one character in depth, all four are evocative and share an intensity of narration; all are both authentic and suspenseful. *Beyond the crimson morning: reflections from a journey through contemporary China* (1979) is a partly fictionalized, impressionistic account of Ryga's visit to China.

Two posthumous volumes have brought together many of Ryga's hitherto unpublished writings. *The Athabasca Ryga* (1990) is a collection of three essays, seven short stories, two short plays, and selections from a novel, *The bridge*—which was mostly written before the Rygas moved from Alberta to British Columbia—and a lengthy introduction on Ryga's early life and work by the editor, E. David Gregory. *Summerland* (1992), a much larger collection edited by Ann Kujundzic, includes essays and letters, screenplays and radio plays, short stories, and his final work, a five-page poem entitled appropriately 'Resurrection'. All were written during Ryga's life in Summerland, and are arranged in the book by decade.

Ryga always insisted on the rights of common people, and decried their violation by governments, bureaucracies, and oppressors of whatever origin. Even when he was shunned by the powerful and by the theatrical establishment, he continued to address these issues in eloquent speeches, in briefs to the Canadian government, in his essays, short stories, and novels, and in plays for local theatre groups that shared his concerns. Always direct and confrontational, Ryga had a large following, both of readers and of people who came to his Okanagan home for advice and encouragement.

See Peter Hay, 'George Ryga: the beginnings of a biography', *Canadian Theatre Review*, 23 (Summer 1979). The authorized biography is *The ecstasy of resistance: a biography of George Ryga* (1995) by James Hoffman. *Politics and the playwright: George Ryga* (1985), by Christopher Innes, is a detailed analysis of his development as a playwright. Ryga's many writings are housed in the archives of the University of Calgary library and listed in *The George Ryga papers* (1995).

JAMES NOONAN

S

Sadlier, Mary Anne. See FOREIGN WRITERS ON CANADA IN ENGLISH: 2.

Saga des poules mouillées, La (1981). First produced on 24 Apr. 1981 at Montreal's Théâtre du Nouveau Monde, directed by Michelle Rossignol, this powerful feminist play by Jovette MARCHESSAULT pays homage to creative works by women, especially four French-Canadian women—Laure Conan (Félicité ANGERS), Germaine GUÈVREMONT, Gabrielle ROY, and Anne HÉBERT—who meet 'in the northern regions of the Promised Land of America, in the heart of a mythical vortex'. An apparently rambling conversation on a variety of subjects, *La saga* gradually works its way towards its main objective: the revenge of women on history and literature. It is clear, however, that there is little resemblance between Marchessault's characters and their historical counterparts. From the first tableau ('The awakening'), the historically pious Laure Conan, for example, uses the coarsest language to dispel the myths she was subjected to in her time.

The first two tableaux consist of conversations—one between Conan and Guèvremont, the other between Hébert and Roy. The third tableau anachronistically unites the four women, who stay together to the end of the play. The fourth tableau establishes the idea developed in the fifth ('How forceps came to man')—that a book be written jointly by the four women to 'overcome legend, myth, and history', as Roy puts it in the sixth and final tableau, which concludes with a list of distinguished women that the book will rescue from the oblivion imposed by men.

The use of time-travel to unite the four famous authors affords the opportunity for penetrating commentary on their critics, the public response to their works, and the image of women writers. The light, comical, and iconoclastic tone of the opening tableau is quickly succeeded by a more lyrical one in which Marchessault's diction recalls the richness of the poetic imagery in her novels *Comme un enfant de la terre* (1975) and *La mère des herbes* (1980).

La saga des poules mouillées was published in an English translation by Linda Gaboriau as *The saga of the wet hens* (1982), following a 1981 première at Toronto's Tarragon Theatre.

ANNE-MARIE ALONZO

Sagard, Gabriel. See Writing in NEW FRANCE: 1.

Sagouine, La (1971). This series of sixteen monologues by Antonine MAILLET is composed of the reminiscences, grievances, anecdotes, opinions, and homilies of a seventy-two-year-old charwoman, a former prostitute, who is the wife of an Acadian fisherman. A garrulous, indomitable old woman, La Sagouine (freely translated as The Slattern), narrates a personal history that forms a mosaic in which generations, social classes, temperaments, and ideologies all find their authentic and rightful place. Expressed in a roughened, coarsened version of old domestic French, the monologues bring her world to life, from her youth to her observations on death, in tones that are sometimes pathetic—she is after all old and ailing—and sometimes laceratingly vengeful. But these qualities are offset by her irreverent humour. La Sagouine is the Acadian sister of Gratien GÉLINAS's Fridolin, and Yvon Deschamps's anonymous Montreal labourer—all three of whom speak in monologues for want of knowing how to converse or behave.

First created for radio in Moncton, New Brunswick, a selection of the monologues—brilliantly acted by Viola Léger—has been widely and successfully performed in both French and English since its presentation at the Centre d'essai des auteurs dramatiques in Montreal in Oct. 1972. *La Sagouine* brought to the theatre dramatic qualities that were due chiefly to its colourful languages. On stage La Sagouine's language, and the tone and timbre of her voice, are more compelling than her ruddy complexion, grim countenance, and props—mop, pail, clogs, and apron. Faithfully rendering the contradictions in La Sagouine's fascinating character, Léger skilfully endowed her simplicity with complexity.

An English edition of *La Sagouine*, translated by Luis de Céspedes, was published in 1979.

LAURENT MAILHOT

Saia, Louis. See DRAMA IN FRENCH 1948 TO 1981: 4.

Saint-Denys-Garneau, Hector de (1912–43). Born in Montreal, he spent his early childhood at the family's manor in Sainte-Catherine-de-Fossambault, and from 1923 lived in Montreal's middle-class Westmount district under the shadow of the Depression. His studies at Collège Sainte-Marie were interrupted by an illness that left him with a 'cardiac lesion'. With friends such as André Laurendeau, Robert ÉLIE, Paul Beaulieu, and Jean LE MOYNE, he founded a small journal, *La RELÈVE,* which sought to reconcile fearless in-depth intellectual inquiry with the demands of the Catholic faith. In 1937 Saint-Denys-Garneau underwent a spiritual crisis that filled him with self-doubt and loneliness. Reported to have once been joyous, even dynamic, he gradually withdrew from contact with others and in 1941 moved to Sainte-Catherine-de-Fossambault, where he died. (While his name has been variously given, the most recent practice is to present it as in this entry.)

Considered to be the founder of modern 'liberated' poetry in Quebec, Saint-Denys-Garneau published only one book of poems during his lifetime, *Regards et jeux dans l'espace* (1937), a highly symbolic title for a book that holds a promise of conquering space through poetic vision. Later poems were published posthumously by Robert Élie under the title 'Les solitudes'—a title he thought appropriate—as part of *Poésies complètes—Regards et jeux dans l'espace, Les solitudes* (1949). Some poems were translated by F.R. SCOTT in *Saint-Denys Garneau and Anne Hébert: translations/traductions* (1962; rev. 1978); John GLASSCO translated the *Complete poems of Hector de Saint-Denys Garneau* (1962). Saint-Denys-Garneau's diary of 1935-9, entitled *Journal* (1954), with a preface by Gilles MARCOTTE, was edited by Élie and Le Moyne. An English translation by Glassco was published in 1962. The *Journal* discusses many facets of life, art, and literature; gradually, however especially towards the end, it turns to painful self-analysis. A similar evolution can be noted in the correspondence, much of which was first presented in *Lettres à ses amis* (1961) by Robert Élie, Claude Hurtubise, and Jean Le Moyne. The letters reveal Saint-Denys-Garneau's involvement with the group of culturally and politically aware young intellectuals who were his friends, his determination to contribute to Quebec culture through poetry and painting, as well as his liveliness and sense of humour. These letters, too, end in 'complete despair' (Nov. 1938). In 1971 Benoît Lacroix and Jacques BRAULT published a major critical edition of the complete *Oeuvres*, including not only all his poetry but his autobiographical and fictional writings, as well as his correspondence.

Influenced perhaps by his experience as a painter and by the Platonic tinge of his philosophical and religious thinking, Saint-Denys-Garneau searches in his poetry for a transforming poetic vision—one that is inaccessible to the materialists who dominate society. This vision, however, is threatened from within and without and leads to progressive alienation. The poetry conveys not only the anguish of Saint-Denys-Garneau's personal experience but also his striving for a non-traditional form of expression, its themes and symbols often suggesting isolation from others, even from God, and distrust of himself. The structure of *Regards et jeux dans l'espace* traces a decline from tentative hope to despair. In the poem 'Esquisses en plein air' the poet becomes intoxicated with the light that streams from the trees, while in 'Spectacle de la danse' all movement and vision are blocked; the sequence 'Deux paysages' portrays two hills, their light and their sombre slopes marking a division between life and death, so that the water-lilies in all their splendour become funeral flowers. A series of quasi-mythical visions ensues in which the theme of death becomes all-consuming and space undergoes extreme contraction: the poet sees himself reduced to the dimensions of his rib-cage, inhabited by a bird that will devour his heart. Whether this alienation was caused by the moralizing attitudes to sex of Saint-Denys-Garneau's educators; the social, economic, and cultural dispossession experienced by young Québécois intellectuals in the thirties; the pressure of capitalistic English Canada upon Québécois nationhood; or a painful Oedipus complex—Saint-Denys-Garneau the poet has been viewed by his successors as a vanquished hero whose violence was directed towards himself rather than towards the injustices of the world. His use of deceptively simple language to create metaphors for the total adventure of the poetic self and its relations with the world ushered in the era of 'liberated verse' in Quebec. In the criticism of the 1980s and 1990s, this formal aspect of Saint-Denys-Garneau's legacy was gradually seen as meaning not only prosodic liberation, but the foreboding of a self-referential conception of poetry. The figure of Saint-Denys-Garneau appears spiritually less defeated, or at least defeated for a cause: the rise of a self-aware Quebec culture—much hoped-for in his correspondence.

See Jacques Blais, *De Saint-Denys Garneau* (1971), in the 'Dossiers de Documentation sur la Littérature canadienne-française', no. 7; Roland Bourneuf, *Saint-Denys Garneau et ses lectures européennes* (1969); Eva Kushner, *Saint-*

Denys Garneau (1967); Robert Vigneault, *Saint-Denys Garneau à travers Regards et jeux dans l'espace* (1973); Jacques Blais, *Saint-Denys Garneau et le mythe d'Icare* (1973); *Saint-Denys Garneau. Dossier de presse 1937-77* (1981); Georges Riser, *Conjonction et disjonction dans la poésie de Saint-Denys Garneau* (1984); Nicole Durand-Lutzy, *Saint-Denys Garneau. La couleur de Dieu* (1985); Jacques Roy, *L'autre Saint-Denys Garneau* (1992); Antoine Prévost, *De Saint-Denys Garneau, l'enfant piégé. Récit biographique* (1994); *Saint-Denys Garneau et la Relève* (1995), edited by Benoît Melançon and Pierre Popovic. EVA KUSHNER

St Pierre, Paul. See NOVELS IN ENGLISH 1960 TO 1982: OTHER TALENTS, OTHER WORKS: 2.

St. Ursula's Convent (Kingston, 1824). The first novel published in British North America written by a native-born author, *St. Ursula's Convent; or, The nun of Canada* was begun by Fredericton's Julia Catherine Beckwith (see HART) when she was only seventeen and was visiting relatives in Nova Scotia. Family stories and childhood journeys to Quebec probably influenced the content of the novel, but the writer's emphasis on coincidence, sentimentality, and melodrama also reflect her preoccupation with the conventions of popular romance. Focusing on the personal history of Mother St Catherine before and after she entered the Ursuline convent in Quebec, the novel eventually sees this gentlewoman reunited with her long-lost husband and children. Collateral figures add to the complexity of the plot, which introduces shipwrecks, exchanged babies, potential incest, and a nefarious priest into the drawing-room society of seigneurial Quebec and eighteenth-century Europe. Always highly moral in tone despite its melodramatic elements, the novel predictably marries off most of its titled lovers.

In her preface to *St. Ursula's Convent* Julia Beckwith expressed her wish that British America would 'cherish native genius in its humblest beginnings' and extend its 'public patronage' to those exhibiting 'real and intrinsic merit'. Published by Hugh C. Thomson of Kingston, Upper Canada (Ontario), for 9s.4d., the two-volume work received support from 147 subscribers in England, the United States, Nova Scotia, New Brunswick, and the Canadas. It was sold by booksellers in the Maritimes as well as in the Canadas and was reviewed in 1824 in *The Scribbler*, *The Canadian Magazine and Literary Repository*, and *The Canadian Review and Literary and Historical Journal*. Considered an immature work even in its own time, the novel survives today because of its historical importance. A reprint was published by the Mount Allison University library in 1978. GWENDOLYN DAVIES

Sale, Medora (b. 1943). Born in Windsor, Ontario, she was awarded a Ph.D. in medieval studies (1974) from the University of Toronto (under her birth-name, Caroline Medora Roe) and taught at Branksome Hall, Toronto, before turning to writing full time. Her six detective novels featuring Toronto police Inspector John Sanders and Harriet Jeffries, an architectural photographer, include *Murder on the run* (1985), winner of an Arthur Ellis Award, *Murder in focus* (1989), *Murder in a good cause* (1990), *Sleep of the innocent* (1991), *Pursued by shadows* (1992), and *Short cut to Santa Fe* (1994). Like Robert Barnard and Reginald Hill, whom she cites as favourite crime-fiction authors, Sale is a traditionalist whose emphasis is on complicated plotting and the solution of tangled crimes that are often interestingly and complexly connected to upper-class Toronto interests and milieux. *Murder on the run*, for example, investigates the slaying of female joggers in Toronto's parks and ravines and involves staff at one of the city's exclusive private girls' schools, while *Murder in a good cause* deals with philanthropy and poisoned herbal tea in Toronto's affluent Rosedale neighbourhood. While clever and reasonably entertaining, the series on the whole is somewhat unfocused in terms of continuity and emotional texture. The relationship between Sanders and Jeffries often seems flat and desultory; offshore settings reflecting their travels (to Martha's Vineyard in *Sleep of the innocent* and New Mexico in *Short cut to Santa Fe*) sometimes fail to resonate as felt or experienced environments; and the lead characters are at times too peripherally connected to the investigations in particular novels to permit the books to be experienced as a successful investigator-centred series.

MARILYN ROSE

Salut Galarneau! (1967). One of the funniest, happiest, and most human novels in Quebec literature, this is Jacques GODBOUT's finest work. Using a novel-within-a-novel framework, it is the story of its own genesis. Its hero, François Galarneau, a twenty-five-year-old dropout from classical college and the proprietor of a hot-dog stand on l'Île Perrot, begins to write, between customers—in a poetic, image-filled, down-to-earth Quebec French—apparently naïve observations of his society. They represent some of Godbout's best satire and record, for both himself and Quebec society, a move from alienation to identity. François dreams, as he grills hamburgers, that it is priests he is burning, he observes that Humphrey Bogart has had more influence on his contemporaries than Quebec political leaders he thinks of impaling, and he discovers that he is ineligible for most jobs in Quebec because he is neither bilingual nor from France. Despairing of his ability to be free in a society he decides is controlled by two megalomaniac generals, General Motors and General Electric, he builds a wall around his stand and resolves to live out a personal version of separatism. But inside the wall he watches American TV and realizes that the act of writing—which has led to his withdrawal—cannot survive without life. Finally deciding to rejoin the world despite its imperfections, and to use his writing to change society, François, like his creator, affirms process and change, the imperative of happiness, and (it would seem) the undesirability of radical solutions to Quebec's political and cultural dilemma. Unlike Godbout's other novels, where intellectual brilliance and irony act as protection against emotion, *Salut Galarneau!* moves beyond irony to humour. In the author's words, however, its laughter is 'tragic laughter. You laugh rather than throwing yourself into the Saint Lawrence.' It won Godbout a Governor General's Award and was translated by Alan Brown as *Hail Galarneau!* (1970). PATRICIA SMART

Salutin, Rick (b. 1942). Born in Toronto, he received a B.A. in Near Eastern and Jewish Studies from Brandeis University, Massachusetts; an M.A. in religion from Columbia University, New York; and worked on a Ph.D. in philosophy at the New School for Social Research in New York. He once considered becoming a rabbi; but, unable to find what he was looking for in religion, he was attracted by the trade-union movement on his return to Toronto in 1970, taking part in the Artistic Woodwork strike there in the early 1970s. He has written on a variety of issues for magazines such as *Harper's*, *Maclean's*, *Toronto Life*, *Weekend*, *Saturday Night*, *Quest*, *TV Times*, *Today*, and *This magazine*, of which he was an editor and is now a contributing editor. In *This Magazine* he wrote a column, 'The Culture Vulture', for many years, for which he received National Newspaper Awards for comment and criticism in 1982 and 1984. He now writes a weekly column for the *Globe and Mail*, Toronto.

Salutin's first play, *Fanshen* (unpublished), was produced by Toronto Workshop Productions in 1972 and directed by George Luscombe. Adapted from William Hinton's book about a revolution in a small Chinese village, it was Salutin's response to the 1970 October Crisis in Quebec. Other unpublished plays show his concern for the poor and oppressed in Western society: *The adventures of an immigrant*, produced at Theatre Passe Muraille, Toronto, in 1974; *I.W.A.*, about the 1959 woodworkers' strike in Newfoundland put down by Premier Smallwood—produced by the Mummers' Troupe in St John's in 1975; *Money*, a one-act musical described as 'an economic treatise concerning money as the greatest of all mystifications', produced at the Young People's Theatre in Toronto in 1976; and *Maria*, a CBC television drama, shown nationally in 1977, about a young woman fighting to unionize factory workers. Salutin demonstrated his own organizing abilities and nationalist convictions when he became chairman of the Guild of Canadian Playwrights in 1978, an organization he helped found. His continuing interest and involvement in the labour movement and social issues are evident in two books: *The organizer: Kent Rowley: a Canadian union life* (1980), a biography of a Canadian union leader, and *Good buy Canada!* (1975), written with Murray Soupcoff and Gary Dunford.

The collective approach used in several of his plays reflects Salutin's populist sentiments. *The adventures of an immigrant* and *I.W.A.* were developed with the active collaboration of the actors and director, as was his first published play, *1837: the farmers' revolt* (1976)—created in collaboration with the dynamic group of actors at Theatre Passe Muraille, Toronto, and its innovative director Paul Thompson in 1972 and 1973—about the abortive 1837-8 uprising led by William Lyon MACKENZIE. His sympathies clearly with the rebels, Salutin answered many questions raised by the drama in a lengthy introduction to another edition of the play entitled *1837: William Lyon Mackenzie and the Canadian revolution: a history/a play* (1975). The Passe Muraille production has toured many parts of Canada as well as Scotland, and was produced on CBC television in 1975. For the 150th anniversary of the 1837 rebellion, Salutin wrote a ten-part radio play for CBC 'Morningside' entitled *The reluctant patriot* (unpublished) about Samuel Chandler, a wagonmaker who spirited the fugitive Mackenzie across the border into the United States after the rebellion was suppressed.

The false Messiah: a Messianic farce (1981)—its title suggests its serio-comic nature—was produced at Passe Muraille in 1975. About a seventeenth-century Jew in a Constantinople prison who claims to be the Messiah, it shows effectively the need for hope even in the form of illusion.

Salutin's most popular and successful play is *Les Canadiens* (1977), which premièred at Montreal's Centaur Theatre in 1977. It was written with an 'assist' from goaltender Ken Dryden, who also wrote a preface to the published version. Salutin used the Montreal hockey team as a metaphor for the failures and triumphs of French Canadians from the defeat of 1759 on the Plains of Abraham to the Parti Québécois victory on 15 Nov. 1976. It received the 1977 Chalmers Award for its presentation at Toronto Workshop Productions and has been performed across Canada.

Salutin turned next to the Canadian cultural scene to portray one of its most influential figures in *Nathan Cohen: a review* (1981), based on the life and work of the drama critic (q.v.) who died in 1971. Produced at Theatre Passe Muraille in 1981, it starred the eminent Canadian actor Douglas Campbell. Although the play is well researched, it lacks character exploration and unity—weaknesses evident in other Salutin plays. This is true of *Joey* (unpublished)—presented at Toronto Workshop Productions in 1982—based on the life of Joseph Smallwood, former premier of Newfoundland, and written in collaboration with the Rising Tide Theatre company of St John's. It was warmly received in both Toronto and Newfoundland, as well as at the National Arts Centre, Ottawa, that same year.

Salutin's next two plays examined Canada's security system. *S: portrait of a spy* (1985), written with Ian Adams, on whose novel of the same name it was based, explored the character of a 'mole' who became director of counter-espionage for the Royal Candian Mounted Police before being discovered, and raised important questions about the efficiency of Canada's security service. The play premièred at the Great Canadian Theatre Company in Ottawa, directed by Patrick McDonald. In *Grierson and Gouzenko* (unpublished), a ninety-minute docudrama produced on CBC television in 1986, Salutin condemned Canada's treatment of John Grierson, founder of the National Film Board, who was forced to leave the country after allegations of espionage by Igor Gouzenko, the Russian agent turned informer.

Somewhat disillusioned by the theatre in Canada, Salutin turned his creativity to writing two novels. The first was *A man of little faith* (1988) about a director of religious education at a temple in Toronto. With humour and warmth, it explores his journey of self-discovery in a mid-twentieth-century Jewish community such as the one from which Salutin came. It received the W.H. Smith Books in Canada First Novel Award that year. Very different was his next novel, *The age of improv: a political novel of the future* (1995). More a satire and a novel of ideas, it takes place about the year 2005 when Canada's present political parties have collapsed and a disillusioned actor, Matthew Deans, becomes prime minister by using his skill at improvisation. It adroitly brings together both Salutin's experience in theatre and his experience as a political and social analyst.

Salutin has voiced his concerns in more concrete terms in several articles and columns, many of them in *This week* magazine, which became the basis of two books. The first is *Marginal notes: challenges to the mainstream* (1984), which includes pieces he had written from 1970 to 1983. Claiming marginality as a strength, he confirms his position as the most incisive left-leaning commentator in Canada. His next collection, bringing together pieces written between 1984 and 1991, is entitled *Living in a dark age* (1991), the title reflecting the more pessimistic view he took in the years immediately before and after the Free Trade Agreement between Canada and the United States. Earlier he had written the text for a cartoon booklet distributed during the 1988 federal election campaign—*What's the big deal? (Le libre-échange? Parlons-en!* (1988)—with cartoons by Terry Mosher (alias Aislin), a political cartoonist for the Montreal *Gazette*. More detailed reflections on that campaign may be found in *Waiting for democracy: a citizen's journal* (1989), a book-length memoir of Salutin's travels interviewing Canadians during the weeks leading up to election day, and his surprisingly positive comments on the results. Even more positive is his introduction to *Spadina Avenue* (1985) by Rosemary Donegan, based on a photographic history she curated at A Space Gallery in Toronto in 1984—in which Salutin comments on growing up in this Toronto area, on his father's and two uncles' work as salesmen there, and on the working people who gave him the stimulus to spend his career advocating a better life for them.

Salutin's drama is discussed in Alan Filewod's *Collective encounters: documentary theatre in English Canada* (1987); in Diane Bessai's

Playwrights of collective creation (1992), vol. 5, in the Canadian Dramatists series; and in Robert Wallace and Cynthia Zimmerman, eds, *The work: conversations with English-Canadian playwrights* (1982). James Noonan wrote an overview of Salutin's life and work in the Profiles in Canadian Literature series, vol. 8 (1991). JAMES NOONAN

Salverson, Laura Goodman (1890-1970). Laura Goodman was born in Winnipeg of Icelandic immigrant parents. Her education there and in the United States was frequently interrupted by illness and her parents' hopeful wandering throughout North America, and she was ten years old before she began to learn English. Married in 1913 to George Salverson, a railwayman, she continued to lead a transient life in Canada, supplementing her income by writing short stories for periodicals. Salverson was one of the first Canadian novelists to fictionalize the drama of immigration in the West. In her three novels that concentrate on the Scandinavian immigrant experience, she drew upon her family's failures in order to inveigh against the falsity of the Canadian dream.

In *The Viking heart* (1923; rev. 1947; NCL, 1975), considered to be her best work because of its breadth of history and almost documentary authenticity, Salverson traces the immigration of 1,400 Icelanders in 1876 to the area of Gimli, Manitoba. After chronicling their subsequent difficulties and the development of their settlement up to 1919, she concludes with the immigrants' disillusionment with Canada's participation in the war. A confirmed pacifist, Salverson presents Canada as a nation whose great potential had been betrayed and neglected by its leaders. *The dark weaver* (1937), which won a Governor General's Award, reinforces this pacifist theme. In it a composite group of Nordic immigrants settles in the West and prospers until the First World War culls their second generation and reimposes Old World chaos upon them. The title refers to the apparent indifference of a God who weaves His plots oblivious to the tragedies and prayers of the people involved. *When sparrows fall* (1925) deals with Norwegian immigrants in an American city (a thinly disguised Duluth, Minn.). Dedicated to Nellie McCLUNG, it emphasizes the feminist struggle as well as the dilemma of immigrants pressured into choosing between their ancestral traditions and the American melting pot.

After *The Viking heart*, romance increasingly weighed down Salverson's fiction, particularly her adaptations of Norse sagas: *Lord of the silver dragon: a romance of Leif the Lucky* (1927) and *The dove of El-Djezaire* (1933), which was published in England as *The dove*. In the latter book, which fictionalizes a true account of a slaving raid that took hundreds of Icelanders to the Barbary Coast, her Gothic medieval setting incongruously contrasts Icelandic and Algerian characters, speech, and customs. *Black lace* (1938), set in France under Louis XIV, is inferior to her other romances. *Immortal rock: the saga of the Kensington stone based on the Paul Knutson expedition to Greenland and America in the fourteenth century; commissioned by His Majesty King Magnus Erikson of Norway, Sweden and Skaane: his letter of authority executed at Bergen, October 28th, 1534, by Orm Ostenson, Regent* (1954) emphasizes, as do her first novels, the pre-Columbian tradition of Norse exploration in North America. It follows the Kensington Stone hypothesis to imagine the fate of the expedition at the hands of Indians in what is now Minnesota. A volume of poems, *Wayside gleams*, was published in 1924.

Salverson's autobiography, *Confessions of an immigrant's daughter* (1939), which won her a second Governor General's Award, covers her life to 1923 and describes with compassion and a sense of social injustice the struggles of immigrants in a New World that fell far short of their hopes and expectations. Salverson argued for the preservation of the Icelandic cultural identity in what she felt was a cultural vacuum in Canada. TERRENCE CRAIG

Samchuk, Ulas. See UKRAINIAN-CANADIAN LITERATURE.

Sandwell, B.K. (1876-1954). Bernard Keble Sandwell was born at Ipswich, England. He was brought to Canada as a child and educated at Upper Canada College and the University of Toronto (B.A., 1897). Editing *Saturday Night* from 1932 to 1951, he gave a long-running performance few journalists anywhere have equalled. He not only put out a thick weekly paper and made it the articulate voice of liberal Canada, but he also wrote many of its best pieces—in one issue he might contribute three or four anonymous editorials, a major book review under his own name, and a charming theatre review under a pen-name, 'Lucy Van Gogh'. He carried this off with style and integrity, becoming what Robertson DAVIES (who worked briefly for Sandwell in the 1940s) called 'unquestionably the most influential journalist in Canada'. Civil liberties were Sandwell's favourite cause, and in the 1940s he was one of a tiny minority of Canadians who vehemently criticized the expulsion of the

Japanese and Japanese-Canadians from the coastal areas of British Columbia. His clear sense of authority may have owed something to breadth of experience. He was a journalist first, then an academic, then (at *Saturday Night*) a journalist again, a career path possibly unique among prominent Canadians. In Montreal he was drama critic at the *Herald*, beginning in 1905, and later editor of the *Financial Times*. He then taught economics at McGill University for a few years and headed the department of English literature at Queen's University, Kingston. By the time he became editor of *Saturday Night*, at the age of fifty-six, he was able to discuss both the new Morley CALLAGHAN novel and the federal debt with equal confidence. His essays were collected in *The privacity agent and other modest proposals* (1928) and *The diversions of Duchesstown and other essays* (1955, posthumous). The Sandwell lines most often quoted today are those with which he greeted the appointment in 1952 of Vincent Massey as the first Canadian-born governor-general: 'Let the Old World, where rank's yet vital,/Part those who have and have not title./Toronto has no social classes—/Only the Masseys and the masses.' ROBERT FULFORD

Sanger, Peter. See Writing in the MARITIMES: 5.

Sangster, Charles (1822-93). Born at the Navy Yard, Kingston, Upper Canada (Ontario), Sangster left school to make cartridges at Fort Henry during the Rebellion of 1837 and remained there as a clerk until 1849, when he turned to a modest career in journalism: first as the editor of the *Amherstburg Courier*, then as a proofreader and bookkeeper for Kingston's *British Whig*; and finally as a reporter for Kingston's *Daily News*. He moved to Ottawa in 1868 to join the new federal post-office department, where he remained until he retired in 1886.

Demonstrating his wish to be 'Canadian in his choice of subjects', Sangster secured his reputation as the 'poet-laureate of colonial Canada' with three books of poetry: *The St. Lawrence and the Saguenay and other poems* (Kingston, 1856), *Hesperus and other poems and lyrics* (Montreal, 1860), and *Our Norland*, an undated 14-page chapbook issued by Copp Clark, Toronto. One of his best poems, the patriotic 'Brock', was commissioned for the 1859 inauguration of the monument to General Brock at Queenston Heights. It is a secular celebration of the collective self-sacrifices that passes beyond the bounds of time as all Canadians inherit the heroic tradition: 'The hero deed can not expire, / The dead still play their part.' His most ambitious work, 'The St. Lawrence and the Saguenay', presents a voyage down the St Lawrence from Kingston and up the Saguenay—a journey away from civilization towards nature and the divine creator.

Modelling his tour of Byron's *Childe Harold's pilgrimage* and Wordsworth's *The River Duddon*, and drawing on his own steamer tour recorded in 'Etchings by the Way', his series of travel letters for the Kingston *British Whig* (1853), Sangster was stirred by the picturesque scenery to muse upon its rich history (Wolfe and Montcalm and the Plains of Abraham) and rich legend (the Native maiden of the Thousand Islands who paddles nightly to care for her fugitive father). As the voyage nears the poet's source of inspiration (symbolized by the river's divine origin), he questions whether art can compete with the splendour of God's work, humbly musing that the expressive calm of silence in the northern wilderness is a 'Godlike eloquence'. But at Trinity Rock he envisions the Dream of Love achieved through the trinity of man, maiden, and God, which in turn empowers the poet to achieve the Dream of Art through the trinity of art, nature, and love. As love excites us to perceive the earth as heavenly, God inspires us to share that vision with others.

The best of Sangster's other poems are the songs and sonnets that defiantly celebrate fleeting joys in the face of death, as in 'The rapid', in which *voyageurs* gaily anticipate the euphoric danger of drowning in the shivering arrows of the rapids' spray; 'Canadian sleigh song', in which bells rings merrily despite the pursuit of time's cold, wintry shadow; and 'Sonnets written in the Orillia woods', in which a dramatic tension between reverence and defiance remains unresolved.

There is a fine introduction to the colonial laureate by E.H. DEWART in his *Essays for the times* (1898). For recent criticisms, see W.D. Hamilton, *Charles Sangster* (1971), David Latham, *Charles Sangster*, vol. 5 (1986), in Profiles in Canadian literature edited by Jeffrey M. Heath, and D.M.R. Bentley's introduction to his scholarly edition of *The St. Lawrence and the Saguenay* (1990). Frank M. Tierney edited three collections that Sangster projected but did not live to publish: *Norland echoes and other poems* (1976), *The angel guest and other poems* (1977), and the revised *Hesperus* (1979). Many weak, overly conventional poems in these books show why the young Archibald LAMPMAN took no notice of Sangster when they worked in the same postal department.

DAVID LATHAM

Sarah, Robyn (b. 1949). Born in New York City to Canadian parents, she trained as a classical musician at the Conservatoire de musique du Québec. Sarah has made Montreal—where she studied at McGill University, receiving her B.A. and M.A.—her home. Her first publication was the chapbook *Shadowplay* (1978). In 1976 she co-founded with Fred Louder Villeneuve Editions, which published her limited-edition chapbook *The space between sleep and waking* (1981). Villeneuve also published the limited edition pamphlet *Three sestinas* (1984). Until 1984 Sarah's work was known mostly by small-press, anthology, and magazine publications, though her reputation as a poet with an exquisite ear and sensibility was already established. The sestinas from the Villeneuve pamphlet were reprinted in *Anyone skating on that middle ground* (1984), Sarah's first book-length publication, in which she demonstrated the mature, accomplished style that also characterizes the poems in *Becoming light* (1987). *The touchstone: poems new & selected* (1992) focuses on the achieved work from her previous two collections to produce a volume of consistently high quality. Margaret AVISON has been quoted as saying that in Sarah's poems 'an elegant play is going on even in the most acutely painful moment of clarity, a play of pure energy.' Sarah is a formalist who moves effortlessly along a broad range of available forms, as at home with the sestina as she is with the prose-poem. This flexibility pays off for the reader in the variety and depth of voices and moods the work as a whole expresses. Sarah's training in classical music is evident in her sensitivity to sound.

A nice gazebo (1992) is a collection of stories whose restraint and depth are reminiscent of the subtle fictions of Alice MUNRO, Mavis GALLANT, and Elisabeth HARVOR. As with these writers, Sarah's main concern is with the lives of girls and women. Much of her writing appears to be autobiographical—the stories perhaps less so than the poetry, though it is only in them that any allusions are drawn from Sarah's Jewish background. Her focus in all her writing is the specificity of an individual life, the apparently insignificant surfaces, the details of things that amount, finally, to a life. The quotidian, at times overwhelming in the earlier poems, takes on a kind of visionary sanctity in the later work.

RHEA TREGEBOV

Sarah Binks (1947). Long before this book was published, its author, Paul Hiebert—then professor of chemistry at the University of Manitoba—had entertained public and private gatherings in Winnipeg with readings from the works and life of the 'Sweet Songstress of Saskatchewan'. A gentle combination of parody and burlesque (Hiebert insisted that the book is not satirical), *Sarah Binks* invites our laughter at the foibles and excesses of literary biography and criticism, and at the brilliantly bad naïve poetry of his heroine: many of Sarah's poetic effusions are masterpieces of deliberately contrived incompetence, the product of a sensibility both academic and earthy. The account of Sarah's upbringing, her family and friends, her development as a poet, her eventual success, and her untimely death is appropriately 'scholarly' in its plodding quest for facts and its ample quotations from the poet's works. Yet Hiebert treats Sarah with humorous affection, much as Stephen LEACOCK did the inhabitants of Mariposa, and many of the poems reveal a nostalgic understanding of life in the rural Canadian West before the Depression: 'Then all in fun they feed the pigs, / And plough the soil in reckless glee, / And play the quaint old-fashioned game / Of mortgagor and mortgagee' ('The farmer and the farmer's wife'); 'I sing the song of the simple chore, / Of quitting the downy bed at four, / And chipping ice from the stable door— / Of the simple chore I sing' ('The song of the chore'). Hiebert dedicated *Sarah Binks* to those 'of the West' who have seen its beauty and endured its hardships.

Additional Binksiana may be found in Hiebert's *Willows revisited* (1967) and *For the birds* (1980). Sarah is not a central figure in these books, but her shade may be said to haunt *Willows revisited*. *Sarah Binks* is in the NEW CANADIAN LIBRARY, and it has been dramatized several times. Hiebert's own views and opinions of his famous work are well presented in Reynold Siemens, '*Sarah Binks* in retrospect: a conversation with Paul Hiebert', *Journal of Canadian Fiction* 19 (1977).

DAVID JACKEL

Saul, John Ralston (b. 1947). Born in Ottawa, Ontario, he studied politics, economics, and history at McGill University (Honours B.A., 1969) and earned his doctorate at King's College, University of London (Ph.D., 1972), with a thesis on the modernization of France under Charles de Gaulle, emphasizing civil-military relations and the role of the armaments industry. From 1972 to 1975 he ran Chapel Land, a subsidiary of an English investment house in Paris; from 1976 to 1978 he was assistant to Maurice Strong, the chairman of Petro-Canada; from 1978 to 1982 he was chairman of Filmfive Inc. and Secretary of the Canada-China Trade Council. He has also been secretary, vice-president, and president of the Canadian Centre of International PEN (1987-92). He lives in Toronto.

Over twenty years Saul has created an *oeuvre* of taut, telling fiction and trenchant social criticism. His books are published in English in Toronto, London, and New York; in Paris in French; and in other languages, including Italian, Spanish, and German. While his early work was entirely fiction, in recent years he has published three books of commentary and philosophy, establishing himself as an iconoclast and polymath. In 1995 he won the Canadian Humanist of the Year Award and was named by *The Utne Reader*, an American journal, as one of '100 Visionaries Who Could Change Your Life'. The next year he won the Governor General's Award for Non-Fiction.

In his novels—which have the intrigue of Graham Greene and the social relevance of Dickens and Balzac—he strives for unity of ideas and action. They have an enduring existential quality. In *The birds of prey* (1977) he builds on the true story of the mysterious crash of a military aircraft and the death of the French Chief of Staff to expose the Machiavellian workings of the military and political hierarchy. He has denied that the book was a *roman à clef*, but its verisimilitude unnerved the French establishment and it sold two million copies. His next three novels are a thematic trilogy addressing the struggle of the individual against authority. *Baraka; or The lives, fortunes and sacred honor of Anthony Smith* (1983) describes the involvement of an international oil company in a multi-million-dollar arms deal, illuminating business in the late twentieth century. *The next best thing* (1986) follows the obsession of an art smuggler in Burma. *The paradise eater* (1988), which won the Italian Premio Litterario Internazionale, is a black comedy that deals with arms, murder, and politics in Bangkok. The novels have in common not just exotic venues and quixotic characters, but corruption, power, and morality. His fourth novel, *De si bons Américains* (1994), looks at the nouveaux riches and modern dictatorship.

Saul's growing influence in Canada and abroad flows from his social philosophy, which shows a spirited distaste for convention and an eagerness to challenge orthodoxy, and has been expressed both in books and in the popular press. His signature work is *Voltaire's bastards: the dictatorship of reason in the West* (1992), a provocative treatise that questions the failure of reason to create a rational world and takes aim at the modern power élite, Voltaire's misguided descendants. *The doubter's companion: a dictionary of aggressive common sense* (1994) is a companion volume of pointed skepticism that is less a classical dictionary than witty and biting alphabetized commentaries on Saul's affections and aversions. *The unconscious civilization* (1995), the latest of his critiques of reason and the rise of technocratic élitism, challenges the new corporatism and laments the erosion of democracy. Saul argues that the individual and democracy matter less in Western society than is widely thought: legitimacy now lies in negotiation between relevant groups based upon expertise, interest, and the ability to exercise power. The book grew out of the CBC Massey Lectures, which Saul delivered in 1995. Like the previous two critiques, it enjoyed robust sales. The Governor General's Award citation mentioned its 'courageous citizenship' and 'writerly virtuosity'.

Saul has published numerous articles in the *Spectator* (London), the *Globe and Mail* (Toronto), *Le Devoir* (Montreal), *Le Monde* (Paris), and the *New York Times*. He wrote the influential position paper, 'Culture and Foreign Policy', for the parliamentary committee's review of Canadian foreign policy, which was published as one of the position papers in 1994. ANDREW COHEN

Saunders, Marshall (1861-1947). Born in the Annapolis Valley of Nova Scotia, the daughter of an eminent Baptist minister, and educated in Halifax and for one year in Edinburgh and Orléans, France, Margaret Marshall Saunders returned to teach and write in Halifax. Holiday travels to Europe produced the shipboard atmosphere of the romantic novel *My Spanish sailor: a love story* (London, 1889), for which 'Beauty and the Beast' supplied the plot. In her late twenties she attended Dalhousie University for a year; the next year, in Ottawa, she heard the story of a gentle, homely dog, which would become the germ of *BEAUTIFUL JOE: an autobiography* (Philadelphia, 1894). Prize-winner in an American Humane Association contest, the manuscript had a six-month hunt for a publisher; but within ten years it was a phenomenal best-seller.

Saunders spent the next two years in Boston, auditing classes at Boston University and developing connections with American publishers and a sense of American reform causes. Slight stories for children, such as *Charles and his lamb* (Philadelphia, 1895) and *Daisy: a tale* (Philadelphia, 1897), kept her name alive. She then tried, more ambitiously, for an adult audience with *The house of armour* (Philadelphia, 1897) and *Rose à Charlitte: an Acadian romance* (Boston, 1898), the first set in her old Halifax home, the second in Grand Pré, N.S., where contemporary Acadians still suffer from the ancient exile and a contemporary American tries romantically to expiate his ancestral guilt. *Deficient saints: a tale of Maine* (Boston, 1899) is another contemporary adult tale of small-town duplicity; in the same year Saunders revised her first novel as *Her sailor; a love story*, changing the Nova Scotian heroine into a New England girl and developing the character of the middle-aged sailor-guardian. All these novels are fresh in style, and ingenious in plot, but none rise above the level of popular sentimental entertainment.

Saunders' forte was writing books for children. After the turn of the century she produced a long list, including the very popular *'Tilda Jane; an orphan in search of a home* (1901); *Beautiful Joe's paradise; a sequel to Beautiful Joe* (1902); *The story of the Gravelys; a tale for girls* (1903); *Alpatok; the story of an Eskimo dog* (1906); and *My pets; real happenings in my aviary* (1908), a series of essays still admired by naturalists. *Princess Sukey; the story of a pigeon and her human friends* (1905), the best of this group, is about a stiff-necked judge who, having unbent to the pigeon, finds himself adopting a raft of other pets and children.

By 1909 Marshall Saunders, who had been travelling back and forth from Halifax across the continent, to California and Rochester, N.Y., while maintaining a prodigious literary output, wound up in Orono, Maine, in enforced retirement because of a deep depression. In 1914, after adding Canadian transcontinental routes to her travels, she moved to Ontario, building in 1916 a house in Toronto with a 'toad castle' in the garden and an aviary. Her next major work, *The girl from Vermont, the story of a Vacation School teacher* (1919), is a sombre attack on children's problems: abuse, enforced labour, and lack of schooling and playgrounds. She lectured tirelessly on the animal world, which increasingly obsessed her and dominated her subsequent novels, including *Golden Dicky; the story of a canary and his friends* (1919), *Jimmy Goldcoast; or, The story of a monkey* (1924), and *Bonny Prince Fetlar; the story of a pony and his friends* (1920). Saunders' shipboard adventures, and her school experiences in Edinburgh, recollected fifty years later, give charm to her last novel, a melodramatic romance for teenaged girls, *Esther de Warren; the story of a mid-Victorian maiden* (1927).

Karen Saunders' thesis 'Margaret Marshall Saunders: children's literature as an expression of early 20th century reform' (M.A., History, Dalhousie, 1978) relates Marshall Saunders' work to the concerns of reform-minded middle-class women at the turn of the century: alcoholism, child labour, lack of play space, as well as cruelty to animals. Marshall Saunders' many novels—approaching thirty in number —can also be related to the formulaic writing for family-circle readers produced by the American writers Gene Stratton Porter and Kate Douglas Wiggin. Though Saunders' writing style was usually controlled and competent, the melodramatic plot devices she employed make her books seem contrived and facile. Her concerns, however, were central—an important indication of contemporary conscience.

Silenced sextet: six nineteenth-century Canadian women novelists, by Carrie Macmillan, Lorraine McMullen, and Elizabeth Waterston (Montreal, 1992), contains a detailed chapter on Saunders. ELIZABETH WATERSTON

Sauvageau, Yves. See DRAMA IN FRENCH 1948 TO 1981: 3.

Savard, Félix-Antoine (1896-1982). Born in Quebec City, he spent most of his youth and early manhood in Chicoutimi. He became a priest in 1922 and taught at the Chicoutimi Seminary until 1927. After serving as curate in several locations within the diocese, he established Saint-Phillipe-de-Clermont parish (Charlevoix) in 1931 and remained there until 1945, while also launching a literary career. He encouraged and recruited people in the region to reclaim land in Quebec's Northwest, and on occasion accompanied these pioneers to Abitibi. During this period also, in collaboration with Luc LACOURCIÈRE, Savard began to assemble folksongs and folktales, an initiative that led to the formation of Université Laval's folkloric archives (1944). In 1943 he began to lecture in the faculty of arts at Laval, where in 1950 he was honoured with the title of Monsignor and appointed Dean of the Faculty, a position he held until 1957. He received many distinctions, both in France and in Canada, including medals from l'Académie française (1938, 1953); the Grand Prix de la Province de Québec (1939); the Lorne PIERCE Medal (1945); the Prix Duvernay (1948); a Guggenheim Memorial Foundation grant (1957); and a Governor General's Award for *Le barachois* (1959).

Savard owes his literary fame to a prolific output of high quality. Critics have lauded the beauty of his style, the strength of his images, the judicious use of Canadianisms, and the element of poetry that imbues all his works, even the prose. His novel MENAUD, MAÎTRE-DRAVEUR (1937), a lumber-camp story set in the Charlevoix region, is now considered a classic of French-Canadian literature. (There are two English translations: *Boss of the river*, 1947, by Alan SULLIVAN and *Master of the river*, 1976, by Richard Howard.) He followed this with *L'abatis* (1943), a collection of short texts, in prose and verse, on the theme of the colonization of Quebec's Northwest. Like *Menaud, maître-draveur*, this book has been the object of revisions; there exist two other versions of the work. *La minuit* (1948) is a romance about the simple life in a small village in the Tadoussac region—the background for a defence of the traditional values of religious inspiration against the materialist ideology and the pressures of the established social order. *Le barachois*, a mixture of prose and verse, is Savard's tribute to the Acadian people, whom he came to know and love during his investigation of their folklore. In *Martin et le pauvre* (1959) he retells the legend of St Martin de Tours, who gave half his coat to a beggar. Savard also published two plays: *La folle* (1960), the pathetic story of a mother whose child is stolen from her, and *La dalle-des-morts* (1965), which recalls pioneer expeditions in British Columbia in the first half of the nineteenth century. *La symphonie du misereor* (1968), a paraphrase in verse of the Latin hymn, was reprinted in *Le bouscueil* (1972), which contains expressions of religious themes, in prose and poetry, alternating with thoughts on nature, country, and humanity. *Aux marges du silence* (1974) is a series of poems in the Japanese haiku form. Savard's memoirs were published in *Journal et souvenirs 1, 1961-1962* (1973) and *Journal et souvenirs 2, 1963-1964* (1975). His most important speeches and lectures were assembled in *Discours* (1975). The reflections begun in the two volumes of *Journal et souvenirs* were continued in the author's last publications: *Carnet du soir intérieur 1* (1978) and *Carnet du soir intérieur 2* (1979). Before the first referendum on the independence of Quebec (1980) he published in *Le Devoir*, 6 January 1978, a long text titled 'Testament politique de Félix-Antoine Savard', in which he reaffirmed his attachment to Canada, and criticized at the same time the separatist ideology. This statement set off a controversy that took the form of an avalanche of articles and letters either condemning or approving his gesture.

Sister Thérèse-du-Carmel has assembled a bibliography of all Savard's works, as well as numerous studies and commentaries on his works up to 1965, in *Bibliographie analytique de l'oeuvre de Mgr Félix-Antoine Savard* (1967). See also André MAJOR, *Félix-Antoine Savard* (1968), and Georges Straka, 'En relisant *Menaud, maître-draveur*: contribution à un inventaire du vocabulaire régional du Québec' in *Travaux de linguistique et de littérature* (Strasbourg, 1973). JULES TESSIER

Savoie, Calixte. See ACADIAN LITERATURE: 2(d).

Savoie, Jacques (b. 1951). Born in Edmunston, New Brunswick, he studied creative writing and cinema at Bathurst College, N.B., and at the University of Aix-en-Provence. A scriptwriter for cinema and television in Montreal (he received the Prix-Gémeaux in 1992 for his work on the TV series 'Bombardier'), he is also a novelist and writer of children's books.

Savoie began his literary career when he published, with Herménégilde CHIASSON and Gilles Savoie, *L'étoile maganée* (1972), an anti-book that offered—on a number of loose pages in a box—poems, designs, and photographs, and demonstrated an originality and temperament that became his trademark. In 1979 Éditions d'Acadie published Savoie's first novel, *Raconte-moi Massabielle*, which reveals a style, humour, and wit completely new in Acadian literature. This tale about an indomitable rebel, who takes refuge in a church in his abandoned village, oscillates between realism and the fantastic—Savoie sometimes cares little about credibility, but rather communicates tenderness and sentiment, bringing to life real people and real emotion. Savoie published with Boréal three novels that are more developed: *Les portes tournantes* (1984), winner of the 1984 Prix France-Acadie, which was made into a movie by Francis Mankiewicz; *Le récif du Prince* (1986); and *Une histoire de coeur* (1988). The relationships between member of a family at the time of a divorce, as well as the subject of artistic creation, especially musical creation, play an important part in these novels. Savoie rapidly conquered his public, who were drawn to his attractive characters with whom one can easily identify. But his plots have a tendency to become complicated by the competition between the narrative level and the interlocked story levels.

In 1995 Savoie returned to the novel with *Le cirque bleu*, which exploits a theme familiar to the author: the reunited family. This story of a tender, complex love—where music and poetry, realism and the fantastic, are mixed—confirms Savoie's great technical abilities, but also reveals a certain difficulty in maintaining to the end the interest aroused by the novel's beginning, which is particularly well constructed. What is obvious, however, is Savoie's lively sensitivity to the world of a child, which he expresses in a trilogy for children published with great success between 1995 and 1996: *Toute le beauté du monde*, *Une ville imaginaire*, and *Les fleurs du capitaine*.

RAOUL BOUDREAU

Sawyer, Robert J. (b. 1960). Born in Ottawa, Ontario, he was educated at Toronto's Ryerson Polytechnical Institute. Fulfilling his wish to become a professional writer of science fiction, Sawyer bonded together concerns about technology and compelling storylines in masterful ways. His stories and novels have earned him numerous distinctions, including the Canadian Science Fiction and Fantasy Award (Aurora) three times and the Science Fiction and Fantasy Writers of America's Nebula Award. In *Golden fleece* (1990, Aurora award), his first novel, the element of detection plays a critical role aboard a starship guided by a homicidal computer. The Quintaglio Trilogy chronicles life on a planet populated by sentient dinosaurs and consists of three closely written, highly detailed novels: *Far-Seer* (1992), *Fossil hunter* (1993), and *Foreigner* (1994), whose main characters are Galileo-like, Darwin-like, and Freud-like respectively. Dinosaurs and their fate figure in *End of an era* (1994), a time-travel novel set in Canada during the Cretaceous period. Toronto in the year 2011 is the setting of the Nebula-winner *The terminal experiment* (1995), a thoughtful consideration of the consequences of the discovery of proof of the existence of the human soul. Subsequent novels include *Starplex* (1996), a far-future novel that explores the origin and fate of the universe; *Frameshift* (1997), an SF thriller; and *Illegal alien* (1997), a courtroom drama with an extraterrestrial defendant. With the poet Carolyn Clink he compiled the anthology of new Canadian SF, *Tesseracts 6* (1997). One special concern of the author is succinctly expressed in the title of a public lecture he delivered in 1996: 'Science fiction as the conscience of the technological age'. Sawyer's Internet homepage is the most elaborate and interesting of any created by a Canadian writer: *http://ourworld.compuserve.com/homepages/sawyer/*.

JOHN ROBERT COLOMBO

Schermbrucker, William Gerald (b. 1938). Born in Eldoret, Kenya, of white parents of South African roots, Schermbrucker has been a teacher of English and creative writing at Capilano College, North Vancouver, since 1968, and was an editor of the *Capilano Review* from 1974 to 1983. Much of his writing has dealt with his youth in Africa. *Chameleon and other stories* (1983) depicts, with exotic colour and detail, life in Kenya during the time of the Mau Mau uprising that eventually led to independence from Britain in 1963. *Mimosa* (1988), a fictional memoir of his mother, won the B.C. Book Prize. *Motor therapy* (1993), a light and pleasant collection of stories describing trips in cars in Africa and North America, has all the exuberance of Jack Kerouac's *On the road*. Schermbrucker is also the author of a textbook, *The aims and strategies of good writing* (1976). ANTANAS SILEIKA

Schoemperlen, Diane (b. 1954). Born in Thunder Bay, Ontario, she graduated in 1976 from Lakehead University, Thunder Bay, and immediately attended a six-week writing workshop at the Banff School. She stayed for several years in Alberta, and now resides in Kingston, Ont. She has published five books of short fiction: *Double exposures* (1984); *Frogs and other stories* (1986), winner of the Writers' Guild of Alberta Award (1987); *Hockey night in Canada* (1987); *The man of my dreams* (1990), which was short-listed for the Governor General's and Trillium awards; and *Hockey night in Canada and other stories* (1991). In 1991 she won the National Magazine Award for her story 'Red plaid shirt' in *The man of my dreams. In the language of love: a novel in 100 chapters* (1994), short-listed for Smith's/*Books in Canada* First Novel Award, was published in the USA, Sweden, and Germany. Schoemperlen cites as influences Alice MUNRO, Carol SHIELDS, and Margaret ATWOOD, whose dry sense of humour she shares. Several of her stories are characterized by formal experimentalism that puts a premium on the role of the reader to fill in parentheses ('Life sentences'), to make subtle connections ('Waiting'), and to view digression in the story as the sort of natural impulse it is in real life ('A simple story'). A typical setting is the small town, where 'freedom means flirting with your best friend's husband or lover or both' ('This town'). The pitfalls of romantic relationships are common to Schoemperlen's characters, whose intimate reflections create a potent psychological realism. Also characterizing what John METCALF calls 'a recognizable Diane Schoemperlen story' is domestic realism: an attention to the furniture, food, and habits of late-1960s and 1970s Canadian families—especially those of younger women who struggle towards finding a sense of self.

See Robert R. Wilson, 'Diane Schoemperlen's fiction: the clean, well-lit worlds of dirty realism', in *Essays on Canadian Writing* 40 (1990), 80-108. SUSAN ELMSLIE

Schoolcraft, Henry Rowe. See ABORIGINAL LEGENDS AND TALES: BIBLIOGRAPHY.

Schroeder, Andreas (b. 1946). Born in Hoheneggelsen, Germany, he immigrated with his family to Canada in 1951. He studied creative writing under Michael BULLOCK and J. Michael YATES at the University of British Columbia, receiving a B.A. in 1969 and an M.A. in 1972. Schroeder has been founder and editor of *The Journal of Contemporary Literature in Translation* (1968-80), a columnist for the Vancouver *Province* (1968-73), and a lecturer on creative writing at the University of Victoria (1974-5), the University of British Columbia, (1985-7), and Simon Fraser University (1989-90). He was chair of the WRITERS' UNION OF CANADA (1976-7).

Much of Schroeder's writing in the 1970s, his most productive period, was influenced by European surrealism. His first two works were poetry collections, *The ozone minotaur* (1969) and *File of uncertainties* (1971), which focused on the violent unpredictability of twentieth-century life. He then published a collection of concrete poetry, *UNIverse* (1971), and his strongest work, a collection of short stories, *The late man* (1972). He has also written a novella, *Toccata in 'D'* (1984), and a novel, *Dustship glory* (1986). In recent years Schroeder has worked as a freelance journalist, publishing several non-fiction titles, including *The Mennonites: a pictorial history of their lives in Canada* (1990), *Carved from wood: Mission, B.C. 1891-1992* (1991), a history of the place where he lives, and *Scams, scandals and sculldu ggery* (1996). Schroeder's best-known book is *Shaking it rough* (1976), a journal of the eight-month term he spent in British Columbia prisons on a minor narcotics conviction.

FRANK DAVEY

Science fiction. See FANTASTIC LITERATURE IN FRENCH and FANTASTIC LITERATURE IN ENGLISH.

Scobie, Stephen (b. 1943). Born in Carnousie, Scotland, Scobie took an M.A. at the University of St Andrews before immigrating to Canada in 1965. After completing a doctorate in English at the University of British Columbia in 1969, he taught for ten years at the University of Alberta, then returned to the West Coast to teach at the University of Victoria. He travels widely and is very active in both the promotion of Canadian literature abroad and the examination of North American popular culture, which includes the work *Alias Bob Dylan* (1991).

Scobie wears many literary hats. He has been an editor of *Books in Canada* and *The MALAHAT REVIEW*, as well as co-founder of Longspoon Press; and as a critic he has written a full-length study, *Leonard Cohen* (1978); a critical monograph, *Sheila Watson and her works* (1984); and an exciting and provocative collection of critical essays, *Signature event Cantext* (1989). He has published numerous short stories and more than a dozen books of poetry, including *The birken tree* (1973), *McAlmon's Chinese opera* (1980), which won a Governor General's Award, *A grand memory for forgetting* (1981), *Expecting rain* (1984), *The ballad of Isabel Gunn* (1987), *Dunino* (1989), *Remains* (1990), and *Gospel* (1994).

The breadth of Scobie's poetic gifts was already apparent in *A grand memory*, which includes catchy verses that recall the songs of Cohen, some resonant and carefully modulated lyrics, such as 'The seventh wave' and 'I like to think of you asleep', and a number of intricate and finely tuned historical meditations, such as 'Darien' and the extended sequence 'Elegy'; such poems indicate clearly that Scobie ranges freely from free verse to formalism, from sound and performance poetry to tightly woven art-for-art's-sake compositions. Although he rationalizes his own lack of political engagement with the question 'Who has the right/to tell us torture?', he nevertheless feels compelled constantly to dredge up the past, lament the *temps perdus*, and 'pay/the duty of attention to the dead.'

Paying attention to the dead is what Scobie does best, in his lyrics and in his long poems. *McAlmon's Chinese Opera*, which is a subtle and moving tribute to an era and to Robert McAlmon (also portrayed in John GLASSCO's *Memoirs of Montparnasse*), the American writer who didn't make it in the Paris of the twenties and ended up selling trusses in Arizona. This poem—which owes something to the tradition that includes ATWOOD's *The JOURNALS OF SUSANNA MOODIE* and ONDAATJE's *The collected works of Billy the Kid*—has a certainty of voice and a dramatic force that derive from the blending of narrative fragments and imagistic detail.

The poetic at work here is expressed simply in 'Paris', where Scobie insists that 'those of us/who come later must learn/to love/ what is left'. In the narrative poem *The ballad of Isabel Gunn*, which has already been transformed into an opera, he lovingly reconstructs the story of a young Orkney woman who disguised herself as a man in order to accompany her lover to Canada, where she worked for the Hudson's Bay Company until the birth of her first child ended her gender-bending adventure. A similar impulse towards historical reconstruction is at work in *Gospel*, Scobie's first-person poetic rendering of the life of Christ, which plays with and exploits the slippage between poetic language—lower-case word—and the biblical reference to Christ as the Word made flesh.

While he may be seen enthusiastically announcing the death of the Author, defending the postmodernist, feminist, and deconstructionist critical barricades in Canada, and giving lively performances of his sound-poems, Scobie the poet-scribe stands well back in the shadows, observing the unfolding not only of critical theory, but also of contemporary history. From this vantage point, and with an ingrained, perhaps even Scottish, ambivalence, he composes his subtly contrived, intensely measured, and very accessible poetic fictions. GARY GEDDES

Scott, Chris (b. 1945). Born in Hull, Yorkshire, England, he was educated at the University of Hull (B.A., 1966), Manchester University (M.A., 1967), and then at the University of Pennsylvania. After a period of teaching at York University, Toronto, he moved to a small town north of Kingston.

Scott unleashed his formidable literary learning in *Bartleby* (1971), an anti-novel, in which the reader is guided by a Shandean narrator through a series of intricate, clever literary parodies. Much of the novel turns on literary puns and references. *To catch a spy* (1978) takes the delicate convolutions of the Le Carré thriller a step further—towards a world in which the doubleness of agents is both assumed and unprovable. The plot is a fictional response to the Burgess-MacLean-Philby spy scandals of the Cold War years that moves towards a meditation on the necessity of living with borrowed faiths and contingent truths in the face of an inscrutable divinity. *Antichthon* (1982), a historical novel, continues where the spy novel left off, exploring the universal suspicion in the Renaissance world of casuistry and the Inquisition in which Giordano Bruno is burnt as a heretic. Like the previous novel, it centres on a 'fictional' death, whose reality is called into question, making truth itself the subtlest corrosive in a corrupt world. Scott's concept of the suppleness of truth underlies the vitality he has brought to two otherwise hackneyed genres—the espionage novel and the historical novel.

MICHELLE GADPAILLE

Antichthon was published in Britain as *The heretic* (1985) and received high praise for the author's ability to convey the fear and humour of Bruno's interrogation, an extravagance of intellect and language fused to high and burning stakes. The transcendent word, of course, will kill the exuberant Bruno.

Hitler's bomb (1985) returns to Scott's twentieth century, which becomes increasingly more horrifying. A canny handling of spy-trade tools produces an unnerving twist of mind and motive, which the *Globe and Mail*'s reviewer called 'fresh and exciting'. (It is perhaps the nearest glimpse we have into the author's current work in progress, 'Millennium': four evolving volumes that combine the wonderful powers of human intellect and administration to describe the pathways into our confusion and pain.) *Jack* (1988) is a confession. In this mode the Ripper, Thomas Neill Cream, M.D. (McGill, 1876), uttered his claim, 'I am Jack . . .' as the trap door opened below him for the crimes of poisoning young women. Throughout the novel the first-person narrative becomes an objectifying tool that serves to mask the Ripper's identity while the body parts of crime after crime after crime are described. Blood flows rather freely between the elusive ego boundaries of the narrator/murderer. Scott won the Crime Writers of Canada Arthur Ellis Award for *Jack*.

With an inexhaustible delight in his craft, and an intellect that feeds equally on sadness and fun, comfort and terror, Scott writes about a hugely disappointing organization—his world. The razzle-dazzle of the boisterous *Bartleby* has since moved into the harder material world of late-twentieth-century monsters, which, as Scott shows us, we are just beginning to imagine. GRANT LOEWEN

Scott, Duncan Campbell (1862-1947). The son of a Methodist minister, he was born in Ottawa. His family encouraged the appreciation of music, and Scott eventually became an accomplished pianist. He attended school in Smith's Falls, Ontario, and college in Stanstead, Quebec. In 1879 his father asked Prime Minister Sir John A. Macdonald to assist him in getting his son a position in the civil service. Shortly thereafter Scott became a clerk, at $1.50 a day, in the Indian Branch (later the Department of Indian Affairs). The poet Scott's career as a civil servant brought him into contact with Native people, particularly during an extensive 1905 trip to the James Bay area as one of the commissioners to the tribes in that region, where he was called 'Da-ha-wen-non-tye', meaning 'flying or floating voice, us-ward', a reference to the poetry he wrote that sympathized with their plight. He was appointed deputy superintendent of Indian Affairs in 1923 and retired from the civil service in 1932. Elected a Fellow of the Royal Society of Canada in 1899, he became president in 1921. He was awarded an honorary doctorate by the University of Toronto in 1922; received the CMG in 1934; and an LL.D. from Queen's University in 1939.

Scott confronted an issue that, to a greater or lesser extent, troubled all the CONFEDERATION POETS: how does a writer reconcile the literary and philosophical traditions of Western civilization with the Canadian landscape and its inhabitants? Scott's earliest poems, heavily influenced by the Romantics and Victorians, demonstrate a growing facility with language and verse forms but in content reflect nothing Canadian. *The magic house and other poems* (Ottawa, 1893) contains the meditative 'In the country churchyard', a poem honouring the poet's late father and all those who struggle and toil. The belief in the dignity of labour, a crucial element of high Victorianism, is also evident in the title poem of Scott's second book, *Labor and the angel* (Boston, 1898). Though both poems could as easily have been written in London as in Ottawa, *Labor and the angel* reveals Scott's first attempts to deal with subject matter that is indigenous to the land of his birth. 'The Onondaga madonna' offers a portrait of a young Native mother whose race is dying and whose child will never know the thrill of battle. While the subject of the poem is drawn from Scott's first-hand knowledge of Native people, the poet is unable to divest himself of the weight of European sensibilities to which he is heir: the language is Romantic ('careless pose', 'forays', 'dabbled'), and the poem's central metaphor, the madonna, is imposed upon the protagonist. Scott's decision to write the poem in the form of a Petrarchan sonnet further distances form from content.

New world lyrics and ballads (1905), in which Scott struggles to bring form and content together, contains his best-known and most frequently anthologized poem, 'The forsaken', chronicling the sacrifices made by a Chippewa woman as she struggles to save her young son from starvation; when she becomes old, she is left by her son to die in the wilderness. As Lee B. Meckler has pointed out in an excellent study of this poem ('Rabbit-skin robes and mink-traps: Indian and European in "The forsaken"', *Canadian Poetry* 1, Fall/Winter 1977), the short lines and vital rhythm of Part I may be said to mime the steady enduring pulse of the woman's heart as she struggles to survive the 'great storm'. The longer lines in Part II imitate the rhythm of the older woman's ever-slowing heart. The poem's language is similarly drawn from, rather than imposed upon, its subject. The Chippewa woman's baby is wrapped in the lacings of the *tikanagan*, a Chippewa word, whereas the child in 'The Onondaga madonna' had slept in his mother's 'shawl', a European word. Scott is attempting to find a language, as well as a rhythm, that is appropriate to the life he is documenting—though he is unwilling to relinquish his Christian perspective on the world for the Amerindians' radically different view of experience. In 'The forsaken' the abandonment of the old woman is consistent with her tribe's custom (its purpose being to free the tribe of the burden of caring for the elderly), but Scott interprets the custom in the light of Christian values: the woman is forsaken. The poem contains a number of communion and resurrection metaphors and ends with the pantheistic image of the woman's being shrouded with snow before being drawn up to God's breast—the Christian imagery drawn from Scott's, and not his heroine's, culture. In 'On the way to the mission' (also in *New world lyrics*) the Christian perspective is less forced. A Native is ambushed and killed by three white men who plan to steal what they believe to be a pile of furs on his toboggan. In fact he is not transporting furs but is taking his wife's corpse to the mission for burial. The white men discover her body, with a crucifix 'under her waxen fingers', when they attempt to gather their spoils. As the Native people here are Christian, the pantheistic conclusion of the poem is appropriate: the Native and his wife are the recipients of God's beneficence as the moon goes 'on to her setting', and covers 'them with shade'.

The encroachment of European civilization on the Aboriginal way of life is Scott's most frequent theme. In 'The half-breed girl' (*Via Borealis*, 1906), the agony of being caught between the world of 'the trap and the paddle' and the world of 'loch and shieling' leads the young heroine to desperation. The elegiac

'Lines in memory of Edmund Morris', in *Lundy's Lane and other poems* (1916), is a tribute to the Canadian artist (1871-1913) who accompanied Scott on part of a 1905 expedition to James Bay. Ever present is the mingling of cultures to which the painter and poet were witnesses: both the 'wigwam' and the 'herdsmen's chalet' can be seen on the landscape.

Although his reputation rests largely on his Amerindian poems, Scott wrote poetry on other subjects. 'The piper of Arll' (*Labor and the angel*), as well as 'The sea by the wood', and its companion piece 'The wood by the sea' (*New world lyrics and ballads*), are among the most often anthologized of his non-Native poems. Keats's work is lauded in 'Ode for the Keats centenary' in *Beauty and life* (1921); a balance of Native and non-Native poems may be found in *The poems of Duncan Campbell Scott* (1926). *The green cloister: later poems* (1935) and *The circle of affection and other pieces in prose and verse* (1947) contain poems written during Scott's extensive travels in Europe. Yet even in his later years Scott published poems about the history and suffering of Native people—in 'Powassan's drum', one of the new poems included in *The poems of Duncan Campbell Scott*, and in 'At Gull Lake, 1810' in *The green cloister*, which argues that human dignity can survive the oppression and savagery by which it is so often threatened. Two selections of Scott's poetry have been published since his death: *Selected poems of Duncan Campbell Scott* (1951), with a memoir by E.K. BROWN, and *Duncan Campbell Scott: selected poetry* (1974), edited by Glenn Clever.

Scott was the author of two collections of short stories: *In the village of Viger* (Boston, 1896; NCL) and *The witching of Elspie: a book of stories* (1923). (*The circle of affection* also contains stories.) *In the village of Viger*, set in nineteenth-century Quebec, details the lives of both the villagers and those whose lives are intertwined with them. Although the characters are more appropriate to romance than to realism (a shoemaker, a pedlar, an aristocrat fallen on hard times), there is a degree of realism in these stories that is uncommon in the short fiction of the 1890s: encroaching upon the idyllic village are the forces of industrialization and urbanization. As Stan Dragland has pointed out in his introduction to the 1973 reprint of *In the village of Viger*, the village is in danger of being swallowed by the metropolis of which it is one of the 'outlying wards'. In examining a closed society being penetrated by forces that threaten to disrupt its unity, Scott was consistent with the themes he explored in his poetry about Natives. Glenn Clever has gathered a representative number of Scott's short stories in *Selected stories of Duncan Campbell Scott* (1972; rpr. 1975). It contains 'Charcoal', written some time between 1898 and 1904, based on the case of an Alberta Native who murdered both his wife's lover and a Mounted Policeman, and wounded a farm instructor. (The man was tried and executed.) Although in a letter to John Masefield, Scott said that the story was 'almost a transcript of the evidence at [Charcoal's] trial, plus facts the Indian agent gave me', it is a blend of fact and romance, as Leon Slonim has pointed out in 'The source of Duncan Campbell Scott's "Charcoal"', *Studies in Canadian Literature*, vol. 4, no. 1 (Winter 1979).

Scott wrote two biographies, *John Graves Simcoe* (1905) and *Walter J. Phillips, R.C.A.* (1947), and one play: *Pierre: a play in one act*, first performed in 1923 and published in the first volume of *Canadian plays from Hart House Theatre* (1926) edited by Vincent Massey. *The circle of affection* contains the essay 'Poetry and progress', an important document giving Scott's views on writing and music, which influenced his literary endeavours. *Untitled novel, ca. 1905* was published in 1979. Scott edited and introduced Amelia Anne Paget's *The people of the plains* (1909) and, in connection with his civil-service work, wrote *The administration of Indian affairs in Canada* (1931). Arthur S. BOURINOT has edited two selections of Scott's letters: *Some letters of Duncan Campbell Scott, Archibald Lampman, and others* (1959) and *More letters of Duncan Campbell Scott* (1960).

An important dimension of Duncan Campbell Scott's literary career concerns his relationship with his friend and fellow-poet Archibald LAMPMAN. Lampman, Scott, and Wilfred CAMPBELL collaborated on 'AT THE MERMAID INN', a column that ran in the Toronto *Globe* in 1892 and 1893. Scott sought patronage for Lampman and, after Lampman's premature death, became his literary executor. He edited *The poems of Archibald Lampman* (1900; rpr. 1974), the immediate purpose of which was to raise money for Lampman's impoverished widow and children. (Scott even shared the funeral expenses when Mrs Lampman died in 1910.) He subsequently edited Lampman's *Lyrics of earth: sonnets and ballads* (1925); joined E.K. Brown in editing *At the Long Sault and other new poems* (1943; rpr. 1974); and edited *Selected poems of Archibald Lampman* (1947). Although Scott took editorial liberties with the manuscripts, he was almost single-handedly responsible for bringing Lampman's work to the attention of twentieth-century readers.

Two journals, *Canadian Poetry: Studies, Documents, Reviews and Studies in Canadian Literature*, frequently publish articles on Scott's work, and two collections of critical essays have been published: *Duncan Campbell Scott: a book of criticism* (1974), edited by Stan Dragland, and *The Duncan Campbell Scott symposium* (1980), edited by K.P. Stich.

See the essay on Scott by Gordon Johnston in *Canadian writers and their works: poetry series: volume two* (1983) edited by Robert Lecker, Jack David, and Ellen Quigley.

GEORGE WICKEN

Scott, F. R. (1899-1985). The son of Frederick George SCOTT, Francis (Frank) Reginald Scott was born in the Rectory of St Matthew's Church, Quebec City. He was educated at Bishop's College, Lennoxville, Quebec, and at Oxford University, where he held a Rhodes scholarship, receiving a B.A. (1922) and a B.Litt. (1923) for a thesis on 'The annexation of Savoy and Nice by Napoleon III, 1860'. On his return to Canada he taught briefly at Lower Canada College and in 1924 entered the law faculty at McGill University, graduating in 1926. In 1927 he was called to the bar and in 1928 returned to McGill to teach; he was dean of law from 1961 to 1964 and retired from McGill in 1968. In 1952 he was technical-aid representative for the United Nations in Burma and from 1963 to 1971 a member of the Royal Commission on Bilingualism and Biculturalism. Scott—who has contributed equally to Canadian law, literature, and politics in both official languages—was elected to the Royal Society of Canada in 1947, awarded the Lorne PIERCE Medal for distinguished service to Canadian literature in 1962, and received a Molson Prize for outstanding achievements in the arts, the humanities, and the social sciences in 1967. His career as an interpreter of Quebec poetry culminated with a Canada Council Translation Prize for *Poems of French Canada* (1977), his work as a social philosopher with a Governor General's Award for *Essays on the constitution: aspects of Canadian law and politics* (1977), and his life as a poet with a Governor General's Award for *The collected poems of F.R. Scott* (1981).

In his career as an inspiring law teacher and social philosopher, Scott was most concerned with the nature of the constitutional and political 'forms' that must be developed to meet the needs of an emerging Canadian society. His interest in social philosophy was sparked by the Depression: he became active in left-wing political movements, and with Frank Underhill was an organizer of the League for Social Reconstruction (1932) and a contributor to its publication *Social planning for Canada* (1935). President of the League in 1935-7 and national chairman of the Co-operative Commonwealth Federation from 1942 to 1950, he was co-author with David Lewis of *Make this your Canada: a review of CCF history and policy* (1943). He edited for the Canadian Institute of International Affairs *Canada today: a study of her national interests and national policy* (1938). His study *Canada and the United States* (1941) was prepared after a year spent at Harvard on a Guggenheim Fellowship. Scott contributed to the important symposium *Evolving Canadian federalism* (1958), and with Michael Oliver co-edited *Quebec states her case* (1964), translations of excerpts from articles and speeches by French Canadians on aspects of the Quiet Revolution in that province. An authority on constitutional law and civil rights—who has been described by Walter Tarnopolsky as an 'architect of modern Canadian thought on human rights and fundamental freedoms'—Scott argued several major civil-rights cases before the Supreme Court, including Switzman v. Elbing (1957) and Roncarelli v. Duplessis (1958).

Scott is one of the most important catalysts of modern Canadian poetry, partly because of the influence of his own poetry and partly through his personality and his association with several literary groups and 'little magazines'. As a satirist in the late twenties and early thirties, he helped battle an outworn Canadian Romanticism in order to introduce the 'new poetry'; and in landscape poems such as 'Old song', 'Lakeshore', and 'Laurentian Shield' he established a northern evolutionary view of Canadian nature that later influenced such poets as Al PURDY and Margaret ATWOOD. While achieving distinction as a poet, political activist, and leading authority on constitutional law, Scott also became a figure of extraordinary importance as a commentator on both Canadian society and Canadian literature. All these activities found expression in his poetry, and all stemmed from the nationalistic concerns of Canadian intellectuals in the twenties.

Scott began to publish light verse in 1921 when he was a student at Oxford, though his knowledge of poetry had stopped with the work of the Georgians. At McGill he met A.J.M. SMITH, who introduced him to the new poets, mostly English, who were developing a 'modern' poetry. In 1925 he collaborated with Smith and Leon EDEL in founding *The McGILL FORTNIGHTLY REVIEW*, an iconoclastic journal of modernist literature and opinion. Scott's attacks on the orthodox were to range widely, but his first broadside was launched against the old poetry and its traditional forms. In 1927, in the *McGill Fortnightly*, he published a first draft of 'The Canadian authors meet', a jaunty indictment of the Canadian literary establishment, inspired by visiting a meeting of the CANADIAN AUTHORS' ASSOCIATION:

Shall we go round the mulberry bush, or shall
We gather at the river, or shall we
Appoint a Poet Laureate this fall,
Or shall we have another cup of tea?

When the *McGill Fortnightly* ceased publication in 1927, Scott became one of the editors of its successor, *The CANADIAN MERCURY* (1928-9). His association with influential literary journals and anthologies continued over succeeding decades. In 1932, in *The CANADIAN FORUM*, he published 'Anthology of Up-to-date poetry', a collection of short, blunt, sometimes satirical poetry that dealt with the social ills of the Depression (a similar collection appeared in 1935). In 1936, with Smith, he co-edited and wrote a short preface for the first anthology of modern Canadian poetry, *NEW PROVINCES: poems of several authors* (1936: rpr. 1976), which included his own verse. In 1942 he was a moving spirit in the founding of *PREVIEW*—edited by a small group that included Patrick ANDERSON, P.K. PAGE, and A.M. KLEIN. In 1945 Scott played a leading role in its merger with a rival publication, *FIRST STATEMENT*, which became *NORTHERN REVIEW* (1945-56). He was also one of the advisory editors of *The TAMARACK REVIEW* at its founding in 1956.

In May and June 1931 Scott contributed a two-part manifesto for the new poetry to *The Canadian Forum*: 'The old order of politics needs no consideration; the fact of the war was proof enough of its obsolescence. . . . Socialism and communism cast overwhelming doubt upon the value of the economic order. . . . Amid the crash of systems, was Romantic poetry to survive?' Scott's own career as a poet exemplifies the transition from a Victorian Romanticism to the modern. But, as with most moderns, there was to be a strong infusion of Romanticism in his own poetry, primarily in his use of nature as symbol, but also in his belief that poetry can change society.

Scott's poems show a progressive development: from the Imagism of late-1920s' poems like 'Old song', through the proletarian realism of the thirties, into a new, almost metaphysical richness of thought and form in the mid-forties and fifties. His first collection of poems, delayed by the Depression, was *Overture* (1945): followed by *Events and signals* (1954); *The eye of the needle* (1957), a collection of satires; *Signature* (1964); and *Selected poems* (1966). Scott's subject is often man in the generic sense, silhouetted against a natural horizon, and his characteristic metaphors develop from the exploration of man's relationships to nature and society: they involve time and infinity, world and universe, love and spirit—terms that emerge as twentieth-century humanist substitutes for the Christian vocabulary. A typical Scott poem moves from specific image (the great Asian moth of 'A grain of rice', for example), or from the natural landscape ('Hidden in wonder and snow, or sudden with summer,/This land stares at the sun in a huge silence'), to a consideration of the significance of the image in the larger pattern of human life. The human journey, in turn, is seen as a moment in time, a part of the larger cosmic flux in which matter, striving to realize itself, is thrown up briefly in waves. Scott perceives that man as a physical being comes and goes; yet he maintains that there is continuity in the human spirit and in the shared human experience.

His poetry reflects not only the wide diversity of such experience, ranging in style from the reportorial and satiric 'Summer camp' to the fine lyric 'Departure', but a strikingly flexible speaking voice that can move from the playful ('Did you ever see such asses/As the educated masses?') to the tenderly reflective, as in 'Windfall'. Scott has remarked that satire is 'inverted positive statement', and certainly the obverse of Scott the lyrical idealist is Scott the satirist. But even from the satirical inversions of poems such as 'W.L.M.K.' and 'The Canadian authors meet', we can infer both the political and poetic ideals for which Scott stands. Underlying both lyric and light verse is a central vision expressed in 'Creed':

The world is my country
The human race is my race
The spirit of man is my God
The future of man is my heaven

As a socialist poet, Scott was most concerned with the kind of social order or 'writing' that man chooses to shape his world. His fear, expressed in 'Laurentian shield' (1945), was that the language of a developing Canada—'prewords,/Cabin syllables,/Nouns of settlement'—might be reduced to the syntax of rapacious technology, 'The long sentence of its exploitation'. In 'Fort Providence' he comments ironically on the toll of the 'firetrap mental gaol'—the religious residential school that oppresses First Nations people.

Scott's poetry continues to undergo re-evaluation. His stance as a modernist has been debated by Neil Querengesser and Wanda Campbell with reference to Scott's ambiguity of perspective and vision. Moreover, Scott, who once complained, 'Where are the coolies in your poem, Ned?'—of E.J. PRATT's *Brébeuf and his brethren*—is now, in turn, criticized from the post-colonial perspective for failing to people the North in 'Laurentian Shield' with indigenous inhabitants. Gary Boire comments that Scott the political activist chooses 'a deliberately mythical form of closure for his own poem, a closure which paradoxically derives from the ancient, foreign past, while it predicts an indigenous Canadian future, which, in turn, does not accommodate indigenous Canadian peoples.'

Scott's later books of poetry include *Trouvailles: poems from prose* (1967), *The dance is one* (1973), and *Collected poems* (1981). He also collaborated with A.J.M. Smith in editing *The blasted pine: an anthology of satire, invective and disrespectful verse: chiefly by Canadian writers* (1957; rev. 1967). An early translator of poetry, he published his translations of *St-Denys Garneau and Anne Hébert* in 1962. In *Dialogue sur la traduction* (1970), an exchange of letters between Anne HÉBERT and Scott, Northrop FRYE commented in a preface that for the two poets, 'Translation here becomes a creative achievement in communication, not merely a necessary evil or a removal of barriers. One can hardly learn more in less compass about the kind of craftsmanship that goes into the making of poetry than is given in these few pages.' Scott's *Poems of French Canada* was published in 1977.

Sandra Djwa's *The politics of the imagination: a life of F.R. Scott* (1987) is a cultural biography in which she unifies the thought underlying Scott's poetry, politics, and his work as a legal activist in the context of a developing Canada. Early criticism of Scott's poetry is to be found in W.E. Collin's *The WHITE SAVANNAHS* (1936). Subsequent articles include Louis DUDEK, 'F.R. Scott and the modern poets', *Northern Review* (Dec.-Jan. 1950-1); A.J.M. Smith, 'F.R. Scott and some of his poems', *CANADIAN LITERATURE* (Winter 1967); Stephen SCOBIE, 'The road back to Eden: the poetry of F.R. Scott', *Queen's Quarterly* (Autumn 1972); Sandra Djwa, 'F.R. Scott' in a special Scott issue of *Canadian Poetry* (Winter 1975); Gary Boire, 'Canadian (tw)ink: surviving the white-outs', *Essays on Canadian Writing* (Winter 1989); Wanda Campbell, ' The ambiguous social vision of F.R. Scott', *Canadian Poetry* (Fall/Winter 1990); Neil Querengesser, '"In what the eye sees": shifting centres in the poetry of F.R. Scott', *English Studies in Canada* (Dec. 1990). See also *F.R. Scott: Canadian* (1983), papers presented at the Scott symposium sponsored by Simon Fraser University in Feb., 1981, edited by Djwa and R. St John MacDonald. SANDRA DJWA

Scott, Frederick George (1861-1944). Born in Montreal, he received a B.A. from Bishop's College, Lennoxville, Quebec, in 1881 and an M.A. in 1884. After studying theology at King's College, London, in 1882 and being refused ordination in the Anglican Church of Canada for his Anglo-Catholic beliefs, he was ordained at Coggeshall, Essex, in 1886. He served first at Drummondville, Quebec, and then in Quebec City, where he became rector of St Matthew's Church (in whose rectory his son F.R. SCOTT was born in 1899). In 1906 he was appointed a canon of the cathedral and in 1925 archdeacon. During the First World War he was chaplain to the Canadian First Division, where his courage at the front was legendary; his book *The Great War as I saw it* (1922) is a vivid war memoir. The critic M. Jeanne Yardley has shown that in spite of his book's essentially chivalric sensibility, it contains many (unconsciously) ironic elements, a feature of our modern understanding of war: as such it is atypical of other contemporary war accounts and 'suggestive of those to follow'. Scott was created CMG in 1916 and was awarded the DSO in 1918. After the war he was chaplain of the army and navy veterans and was renowned for his radical social views during the Winnipeg and Besco strikes. He was elected to the Royal Society of Canada in 1900.

F.G. Scott was popularly known as the 'poet of the Laurentians'—a lesser member of the group now known as the CONFEDERATION POETS—and was recognized in his time for his nature lyrics and for his hymns of Empire, which stressed both the new nationality and Canada's roles in the Boer and Great Wars. An epigraph from one of his poems on the North West Rebellion, celebrating Canada's western expansion, prefaced the most influential anthology of the period, W.D. LIGHTHALL's *Songs of the great Dominion* (1889). Scott's first book, *Justin and other poems*, privately printed in 1885, contains poems on religion, death, and evolution informed by Victorian pessimism; this collection was included in *The soul's quest and other poems* (Toronto, 1885; London, 1888). In 'A mood', dated Mar. 1882, Scott writes of his intense fear of death, speaking of a demon that had haunted him since childhood with 'death and dreams of death'. Several of the early narrative poems, and his later didactic novel *Elton Hazelwood* (1891), describe typically Victorian crises of faith and the recognition of 'life and death as they are'. Hazelwood links his spiritual crisis with that described in John Stuart Mill's *Autobiography* and Justin is made to ask, 'Why men should be, why pain and sin and death,/And where were hid the lineaments of God?' Scott's many religious poems and his novel offer a more explicit rendering of the Victorian pessimism underlying the poetry of his more significant contemporaries, Charles G.D. ROBERTS and Archibald LAMPMAN.

Scott's lyrics were collected in *My lattice and other poems* (Toronto, 1894). This was followed by *The unnamed lake and other poems* (Toronto, 1897), *Poems old and new* (1900), *Poems* (1910), *A hymn of empire and other poems* (1906), *In the battle silences: poems written at the front* (1916), *In sun and shade: a book of verse* (1926), *New poems* (1929), *Selected poems* (1933), and *Collected hearts* (1941). His best-known poem, 'The unnamed lake', was an important precursor of 'Old song' by F.R. Scott, and his social radicalism undoubtedly influenced his son.

Scott's poetry, with its Christian and evolutionary concerns, is nostalgically Victorian, striking an authentic and original note only in the poems of the Northland. His role as a poet of his time was discussed by the journalist Melvin O. Hammond in 'The poet of the Laurentians', *The Canadian Magazine* (Mar. 1909) and his role as a Christian radical by E.A. Palker in 'The social concern of Canon Scott', *Journal of the Canadian Church Historical Society* (Oct. 1980). His influence on more recent poetry, particularly that of F.R. Scott, is suggested by Louis DUDEK in 'F.R. Scott and the modern poets', *NORTHERN REVIEW* IV (Dec.-Jan. 1950-1). See also M. Jeanne Yardley, '"The bitterness and the greatness": reading F.G. Scott's war', *Studies in Canadian Literature* (1991). SANDRA DJWA

Scott, Gail (b. 1945?). Born in Ottawa, she grew up in a bilingual community in eastern Ontario. She was educated in English and Modern Languages at Queen's University (B.A., 1966) and in 1966-7 studied French literature at the Université de Grenoble, France. She worked as a journalist from 1967 to 1980 in Montreal, covering key political and cultural events in Quebec for an English-Canadian audience. Scott was a founding editor of the alternative political publication *The Last Post* (1970), the feminist magazine *Des luttes et des rires des femmes* (late 1970s), and the French-language cultural magazine *SPIRALE* (1979-83). From 1980 to 1991 she taught journalism at Concordia University and since 1991 has devoted her time to writing. She co-founded and worked as Quebec editor for the bilingual journal *Tessera* (1984-9), and continues to translate the writing of Quebec women, such as France THÉORET.

Scott's first book, *Spare parts* (1981), is a collection of short stories that parody journalistic style: non-sequiturs disturb the logic of cause and effect, the extraordinary clashes with the matter-of-fact, and strings of simple sentences generate emotional charges that trouble the even surface of newspaper writing. Scott's essays, collected in *Spaces like stairs* (1989), also reject the neutrality and objectivity of her former *métier*. The issue of who is writing for whom, she asserts, shapes what can and cannot be said in a given text. Scott's is a feminist project of opening spaces for women to speak, one that recognizes the variegations in the category 'women'. Her own specificity as an anglophone writing in English in Quebec who finds sustenance in French-language culture is a case in point. Traces in her writing of French rhythms and syntax, and of discussions with Nicole BROSSARD and other women in the writing group whose work is presented in *La théorie, un dimanche* (1988), are signs of the influence a minority culture (French) can have on a majority culture (English).

Scott's novels *Heroine* (1988) and *Main brides* (1993) raise questions about the novel genre, particularly its presentation of female character and her inscription in history. *Heroine* is narrated in the present tense by a woman sitting in a bathtub whose thoughts float from her struggle to write, to an old love affair set against the leftist and independence movements of 1970s Quebec, to her interest in the woman in the next room. *Main brides* is a kind of 'installation' that allows a slippage between the woman narrator sitting in a bar on Boulevard St Laurent and the women who come within her field of vision. In both novels innovation begins at the level of the sentence, with strategies of statement-making that resist fixing the subject within the field of relations. Narrative is a fleeting, incomplete structure available only indirectly through a recurring image, a glance, an encounter, or a superficial detail. The privileged centre of consciousness is abandoned in favour of making visible those subjects at the limits of the narrators' consciousness. LIANNE MOYES

Scott, Jay. See GAY LITERATURE.

Scott, Peter Dale (b. 1929). The son of F.R. SCOTT and the painter Marian Dale Scott, he was born in Montreal and educated at McGill University; University College, Oxford; and the Institute d'études politiques, Paris. Scott was a Foreign Service Officer for the Canadian Embassy in Warsaw, Poland (1959-61), a professor in the speech department at the University of California, Berkeley (1961-6), and a professor in the English department (1966-95). Scott's poetry is deeply informed by his childhood in Montreal, his time abroad and in the United States, and his close connections to his family and friends.

His first book, *Poems* (1952), was followed by *Prepositions of jet travel* (1981) and *Heart's field* (1986). But Scott established his reputation as a major poet with *Coming to Jakarta: a poem about terror* (1988). This remarkable work—with its distinctive three-line stanzas reminiscent of Ezra Pound, its spare clarity, and its seamless integration of the political and the personal—redefines the possibilities of the long poem for the twentieth century. It addresses the little-known massacre of more than a million Indonesians in 1965, and its frequent references convey Scott's familiarity with a vast array of sources, from CIA classified documents to works by politicians and anthropologists, newspaper articles, and essays. The poem's haunting drama draws the reader slowly, carefully, and above all responsibly into a world of political terror and uncertainty: the reader does not make this journey simply to witness what Scott records, but rather, like Scott, to grapple with the urgent question of personal responsibility for world events that often seem remote from everyday concerns. *Coming to Jakarta*, like Scott's other works, is also intensely personal and its force stems from Scott's adept integration of the personal with the political in a manner that illustrates how the two are interdependent. The poetic exploration of personal issues is further deepened in the long poem *Listening to the candle: a poem on impulse* (1992). Instead of focusing on a specific political situation, this book moves between different events as it records personal stories, in the three-stanza form familiar from *Coming to Jakarta*, of love and loss. The poet's voice itself is marked by an unusual rigour, honesty, and integrity. Two collections of Scott's work draw together poems that are not thematically organized: *Rumors of no law: poems from Berkeley 1968-1977* (1981) and *Murmur of the stars: selected shorter poems* (1994). These books communicate the range of Scott's poetic vision: again the poems combine a gentle, compassionate perspective with keen and incisive analysis.

In addition to his poetry, Scott is well known for several works of prose or what he calls 'parapolitics', their titles indicating Scott's interest in the covert actions and conspiracies that also inform his poetry. These works include *The war conspiracy* (1972), *The assassinations: Dallas and beyond* (1976, in collaboration with Paul L. Hoch and Russell Stetler), *Crime and cover-up: the CIA, the Mafia, and the Dallas-Watergate connection* (1977), *The Iran-Contra connection: secret teams and covert operations in the Reagan era* (1987, with Jonathan Marshall and Jane Hunter); *Cocaine politics: drugs, armies, and the CIA in Central America* (1991, with Jonathan Marshall), and *Deep politics and the death of JFK* (1993).

BARBARA LECKIE

Scouine, La (1918). This is the most important work of Albert LABERGE, both for its intrinsic merit and as a *cause célèbre* in French-Canadian literary history. Because of its attention to detail and its deterministic view of life, it has been hailed as the first realistic novel in Canada. It is set in the farming region of Beauharnois, where the author grew up, and appears to cover some fifty years from 1813. The title is a meaningless nickname made up by children for the smelly, mean, disagreeable Paulina Deschamps, the principal character. Her family is presented as typical but not ideal. Closeness to the land has a brutalizing effect, and religion has little recognizable place, apart from the ritual marking of the bread with a cross. Cross-marked loaves recur like a refrain, compressing all Laberge's feelings about traditional rural life into one haunting symbol, clearly a parody of the Communion. Family relations, while not altogether devoid of sentiment, are generally harsh and lacking in tender expression: a long-lost uncle returns, only to feel so isolated that he hangs himself. Towards the outside world the family is entirely hostile or avaricious; *La Scouine* even cheats a blind beggar.

The novel is most enjoyed for its short, finely pointed sketches, written in hard, polished prose. Many details are memorable not only for their visual and aural clarity but also for their symbolic overtones: the gelder—a sad, ugly man, the last of a family reduced to landless poverty—earns his living by suppressing reproduction. The land itself is described as leprous and cancerous, and the sound of stone on scythe is like a lament rising from the ground. The author's pity for his hapless characters emerges only from these restrained overtones. There are, however, a few moments of humour. The ending is bleak, in the manner of French Naturalism.

After an unusually long time in the writing (1899-1917), this short novel appeared in an edition of only sixty copies. Laberge was aware of the misfortunes of his friend Rodolphe GIRARD and avoided wider distribution. Extracts, published as separate stories, had already been condemned as 'pornographic'—although sexual incidents are few and unalluring. Even half a century later it would not be published in full; only extracts appeared in Gérard BESSETTE's *Anthologie d'Albert Laberge* (1962). Finally, however, the holder of the copyright relented and *La Scouine* achieved full publication in 1972.

An English translation by Conrad Dion is entitled *Bitter bread* (1977). JACK WARWICK

Scrimger, Richard. See NOVELS IN ENGLISH 1983 TO 1996: OTHER NOVELS 2(b).

Seers, Eugène (1865-1945), who used the pseudonym 'Louis Dantin', was born at Beauharnois, Canada East (Quebec), and received his early schooling at home, his secondary education at the Collège de Montréal—where he stood out, not only as an extremely brilliant student but also for being a morose and solitary youth who was remarkably sensitive, and infatuated with both beauty and literature. During a two-month trip to France and Italy he suddenly decided, in 1883, to enter the novitiate of Les Pères du Saint-Sacrement in Brussels, Belgium. Barely eighteen, he was to follow his religious vocation for twenty years. After studying philosophy for three years (1884-7) at the Gregorian University in Rome, he received his Ph.D., and the following year, at twenty-three, was ordained a priest in the Church of Saint-Sulpice in Paris. Afterwards, while he was secretary to the Father General of his congregation in Paris, he wrote frequently for the magazine *Le Très Saint-Sacrement*. At twenty-five he became superior and head of novices in Brussels and at twenty-eight was made superior and assistant-general for the congregation in Paris. On returning to Montreal, however, he underwent a profound religious crisis that resulted in his breaking with the Church. At this time he was overseeing publication of the poems of his friend Émile NELLIGAN, *Émile Nelligan et son oeuvre* (1903), which contains a thirty-four-page preface over his pseudonym, Louis Dantin. He moved to Boston, married, and practised the trade of compositor and typographer. He later moved to Cambridge, Mass., with his son, to work for the Harvard University Press (1919-38) and died there.

In the literature of French Canada, Seers is known solely by the name of Louis Dantin; from 1900 until his death he always used this pseudonym. He left a considerable *oeuvre*: some 5,000 poems were collected by his friend Gabriel Nadeau in *Poèmes d'outretombe* (1962); also worthy of mention are *Le coffret de Crusoé* (1932); three long poems published privately in small printings—*Chanson javanaise* (1930), *Chanson citadine* (1931), and *Chanson intellectuelle* (1932); and religious poems published anonymously, *Franges d'autel* (1899). Dantin also wrote short stories: *La vie en rêve* (1930), *Contes de noël* (1936), and *L'invitée* (1936). It is a pity that Dantin did not persevere in this field, for he was a born storyteller. His friend Rosaire Dion-Lévesque thought it worthwhile to publish, after Seers' death, *Les enfances de Fanny* (1951; translated by Raymond Y. Chamberlain as *Fanny*, 1974), which unfortunately added nothing to Dantin's reputation. This 286-page autobiographical novel, however, reveals some insights into a man who suffered throughout his life on behalf of the meek, the disinherited, the unwanted, and people of colour.

Dantin is most important for his literary criticism, a field in which, from 1920 to 1940, he was the undisputed master, as the following works attest: *Poètes de l'Amérique française: First series* (1928), *Second series* (1934); *Le mouvement littéraire dans les Cantons de l'Est* (1930); and *Gloses critiques: First series* (1931), *Second series* (1935). It would be worthwhile to collect—apart from the seven important prefaces to poetical works and the long preface to *Émile Nelligan*—the numerous critical essays that appeared in *La Revue moderne* in 1920-2 and 1928-33 and, between 1923 and 1942, in *L'Avenir du nord* (Saint-Jérôme), *Le Canada*, and Montreal's *Le Jour*, for which Dantin wrote 160 articles on American literature. It would also be useful to collect his voluminous correspondence (about 600 letters) and the stories 'Froment de Bethléem', 'Pauline', 'Fantôme de Pâques', 'L'aventure de Léon Millaud', and 'Le Bonhomme Noël se rachète'.

Two short posthumous works are the 21-page *Un manuscrit retrouvé à Kor-el-Fantin: la chanson nature de Saint Limond* (1963) and the 59-page *Les sentiments d'un père affectueux: lettres de Louis Dantin à son fils* (1963).

Not content merely to maintain contact with young Quebec writers and to take an active interest in French-Canadian literature,

Dantin also contributed enormously to acquainting French Canada with American literature. A devotee of beauty, the imagination, and perfection; poet, storyteller, essayist, and literary critic—he was one of the finest French-Canadian writers between the two wars.

See *Louis Dantin: sa vie et son oeuvre* (1948) by Gabriel Nadeau, who quotes extensively from Dantin's correspondence.

MAURICE LEBEL

Segal, Y.Y. (1896-1954). Yakov Yitzhak (Jacob Isaac) Segal, a major Yiddish-Canadian poet, was born in Koretz, a small village in the Ukraine. He immigrated to Canada in 1911 and settled in Montreal, where he worked first in a pants factory, later as a teacher in secular Yiddish schools, and finally as a journalist and editor for the Yiddish-language daily *Der Keneder Odler* ('The Canadian eagle'). For a time (1923-8) he lived in New York, where he came under the influence of a group of modern Yiddish poets, *Die Junge* (The Young Ones). After his return to Montreal, where he lived until his death, he became a close friend of A.M. KLEIN.

Segal, who found his own poetic voice in childhood before coming to Canada, had his first Canadian poem published in *Der Kanader Odler* in 1915. His first collection, *Vun mein Velt* ('Out of my world'; Montreal, 1918) brought him immediate recognition, not only in Canada but in New York and Poland, the two world centres of Yiddish literature before the Second World War. Although Segal was a secular Jew, he was learned in the Torah and steeped in Chassidic tradition and folklore. His lyric poetry combines religious and folk tradition, modernist American literary practice, and Canadian landscape and atmosphere. His warm, intimate style unites Jewish lament, prayer, and celebration with a modern consciousness in a highly original way.

Segal married Elke Shtaiman in 1916 and they had two daughters. One of them, Annette Segal-Zakuta, illustrated *Lieder far Yiddishe Kinder* ('Poems for Jewish children'; New York, 1964). His other books are *Bazunder* ('Apart'; Montreal, 1921), *Mein Shtub un mein Welt* ('My home and my world'; Vilnius, New York, Vienna, 1923), *Lieder* ('Poems'; New York, 1926), *Lyric* ('Lyric'; Montreal, 1930), *Mein Nigun* ('My melody'; Montreal, 1934), *Die dritte Sudeh* ('The third supper'; Montreal, 1937), *Dos Hois fun die Poshete* ('The house of the simple people'; Montreal, 1940), *Lieder un Loiben* ('Songs and praise'; Montreal, 1944), *Sefer Yiddish* ('The book of Yiddish'; Montreal, 1950), and *Letzte Lieder* ('Last poems'; Montreal, 1955).

Segal was also the author of about a hundred uncollected critical essays on Yiddish writers and writing; his manuscripts are preserved in the Jewish Public Library in Montreal. A memorial prize, the J.I. Segal Award, is given annually for the best book with Jewish content in fiction or poetry. Some of his poems have been translated into English in *A treasury of Yiddish poetry* (1969), edited by Irving Howe and E. Greenberg; *The first five years: a selection from the Tamarack Review* (1962) edited by Robert WEAVER; and in a renowned picture-book of poems for children, *The wind has wings: poems from Canada* (1969; rev. 1984), compiled by Mary Alice Downie and Barbara Robertson and illustrated by Elizabeth Cleaver.

MIRIAM WADDINGTON

Séguin, Maurice (1918-84). Born in Horse Creek, Saskatchewan, to French-Canadian parents, he was educated at Université de Montréal (B.A., 1942; M.A., 1944; Ph.D., 1948), studying under Lionel GROULX. He joined the history department of the Université de Montréal in 1948, retiring in 1984.

As a historian Séguin was instrumental in creating a neo-nationalist history in Quebec after the Second World War. Interested in the philosophy of history especially as it related to nationalism, he projected the idea of French Canadians developing as a nation striving for self-fulfilment in a state of their own. Though the author of seminal articles, Séguin did not publish his principal monograph, *La "nation Canadienne" et l'agriculture (1760-1850)*, until 1970. It broke new ground in interpretation rather than methodology as Séguin portrayed a society that had become more rural and increasingly poor with the coming of the British. Discontent with economic circumstances combined with dissatisfaction over British rule to produce the rebellions of 1837 and 1838, the first attempt to overturn the rule of imperial masters whose functions were later partially assumed by the federal government. In *L'idée d'indépendance au Québec* (1968), Séguin provided the first extended historical treatment of evolving *indépendantiste* movements in Quebec; but his portrayal of a society ever striving for, but never achieving, that goal was criticized by critics as neo-nationalist history predicated on a pessimism incapable of sustaining historiography. Séguin's work has been examined in *Maurice Séguin, historien du pays québécois vu par ses contemporains* (1987) edited by Robert Comeau, and he was portrayed in the role of the philandering professor in Denys Arcand's film, *The Decline of the American Empire.*

TERRY CROWLEY

Séguin, Normand. See HISTORICAL WRITING IN FRENCH 1980 TO 1996.

Séguin, Robert-Lionel (1920-83). Through both his parents he could trace his ancestry in Quebec to 1665. He was born in Rigaud, Vaudreuil County, where his family was the longest settled in the area. From his childhood he was filled with a sense of history and tradition. Taking doctorates in history from Laval (1961), in social sciences from the Sorbonne (1972), and in ethnology from Strasbourg (1981), Séguin (an inveterate collector, archivist, and museologist) devoted his career to the research, publication, and teaching of the historical ethnology of Quebec, his chief preoccupation being artefacts of material culture, explicated in their social and historical contexts.

Between 1958 and 1971 Séguin worked for the Musée du Québec, the National Museum of Canada, the National Film Board, Laval University (where he taught material-culture studies), the Université de Montréal (in adult education), and undertook research in France (1960, 1964-6), and in France and Quebec in 1968-70. In 1971, with Maurice Carrier, Séguin founded the Centre de documentation en civilisation traditionnelle at the then young Université du Québec à Trois-Rivières, beginning teaching in the department of history a year later. He founded and was editor of two important scholarly journals, the *Revue d'Ethnologie du Québec* (1975) and the *Archives d'Ethnologie du Québec* (1976). His published books, already numerous (see FOLKLORE IN FRENCH), were added to, as were the countless articles, papers, and talks he tirelessly produced. As a publicist of historical and folkloric research, Séguin was cut from the same cloth as Marius BARBEAU.

Elected a member of the Royal Society of Canada in 1969, Séguin was, like his illustrious peer Luc LACOURCIÈRE, a member of the Société des Dix; his honours included a Governor General's Award (1967) and the Prix Broquette-Gonin of the Académie française (1969), both of these for his *La civilisation traditionnelle de 'l'habitant aux 17ᵉ et 18ᵉ siècles* (1967); the Prix France-Québec (Paris, 1973) for his *La vie libertine en Nouvelle-France au XVIIᵉ siècle* (1972); and the Prix Duvernay (1975). Seguin's other major works include the two-volume *L'équipement oratoire et horticole du Québec ancien (XVIIᵉ, XVIIIᵉ et XIXᵉ siècles)*, published posthumously in 1989; *L'injure en Nouvelle-France* (1976); *Les ustensiles en Nouvelle-France* (1971); and *La sorcellerie au Québec du XVIIᵉ au XIXᵉ siècles* (1971), a revised and enlarged edition of the 1959 *Sorcellerie*. A posthumous volume of essays, edited by René Bouchard, *La vie quotidienne au Québec: histoire, métiers, techniques et traditions* (1983), gives a full measure of Séguin's career and accomplishments.

GERALD THOMAS

Sellar, Robert (1841-1919). Born in Glasgow, Scotland, the son of an estate factor, he was brought to Upper Canada as a boy. In 1863 he moved from a job on the Toronto *Globe* to become first editor of *The Gleaner*, a Reform paper in Huntingdon, Quebec—in that 'eastern wedge of the province between Ontario and Yankeedom'. Sellar's early editorials rejected Annexationism, deplored lavish government spending, and urged Temperance; his 'In defence of the Quebec minority', reprinted in 1894, attacked Roman Catholic encroachment into school and political systems. His editorial wrath at the 'clerical conspiracy' culminated in *The tragedy of Quebec: the expulsion of the Protestant farmers* (1907; republished, with an introduction by Robert Hill, in 1974). Independent, self-published, never part of any literary establishment, Sellar nevertheless became widely known not only for his partisan regional journalism, but also for his complex use of local materials in both historical fiction and essays.

Gleaner tales (Huntingdon, 1885) draws on interviews with Scots and Loyalist families to create vivid anecdotes of feuds, fires, and harvests; the same material is given non-fictional treatment in *History of the county of Huntingdon and of the seigniories of Beauharnois and Chateauguay* (Huntingdon, 1888), comparable as regional history to the work of James MacPherson Le Moine. *Gleaner tales: second series* (Huntingdon, 1895) adds 'Archange and Marie', a pathetic tale of Acadian exiles in Chateauguay, and 'The summer of sorrow, 1847', about Irish survivors of the cholera epidemic. Like Duncan Campbell SCOTT in *In the village of Viger* and W.E. THOMSON in *Old man Savarin and other stories* (both also 1895), Sellar suggests vanishing regional dialects and customs.

Sellar's novels illustrate three types of historical fiction: the heroic romance (*Hemlock*), the group-focused survival story (*Morven*), and the anti-romance of laborious achievement (*Gordon Sellar*). In *Hemlock: a tale of the*

War of 1812 (Montreal, 1890), a young British officer is captured by invading Americans, and a Scots settler's daughter bravely travels to the isolated mission at Oka, Quebec, to call the Native warrior Hemlock into action. Hemlock frees the captive, who then leads a force through the Chateauguay Valley and up the St Lawrence to successful battle at Crysler's Farm. *Morven: a legend of Glengarry* (1910), written in an archaic rhythm suggesting Gaelic, follows a group of Highlanders, cleared from their shielings in the 1770s, who are transported to virtual slavery in Virginia, rescued by the folk-hero Morven, and led with the help of friendly Natives through the wild Adirondacks towards the bush country north of Cornwall. *True makers of Canada: Gordon Sellar—a Scotsman of Upper Canada* (1915), covering the period 1825 to 1838, catches the naïve vigour of genuine immigrant journals and is written from the perspective of a Scottish lad, Gordon Sellar. Hard times in Scotland lead to Gordon's arduous voyage to York County, after which the narrative divides to include the story of another settler, who is a manly axeman with ideals like those of the hero of Isabella Valancy CRAWFORD's 'Malcolm's Katie'.

Sellar's early political interests are recaptured in *George Brown, the Globe, and Confederation* (Huntingdon, 1895). Careful research undertaken for *Hemlock* was reused in *The U.S. campaign of 1813 . . . to capture Montreal* (1913). Sellar's last published work was *The tragedy of Wallace* (1919), a drama of early Scotland.

There is no extended study of Sellar's work, in spite of the vigour of his narratives, the richness of his regional detail, and his unusual treatment of relations between Native people and Scots in early Quebec. Family papers, presented to the Public Archives by Sellar's son Watson (long comptroller-general for Canada), illuminate the early history of journalism in Canada.

ELIZABETH WATERSTON

Selvadurai, Shyam. See NOVELS IN ENGLISH 1983 TO 1996 and OTHER NOVELS 2(b).

Selvon, Sam. See CARIBBEAN-CANADIAN LITERATURE and Austin CLARKE.

Sernine, Daniel. See FANTASTIC LITERATURE AND SCIENCE FICTION IN FRENCH.

Service, Robert W. (1874-1958). Robert William Service was born in Preston, England, and grew up in Scotland, first in Ayrshire with his grandfather and aunts and later in Glasgow with his parents. After leaving school in 1888 he worked for the Commercial Bank of Scotland between 1889 and 1896 when, having cultivated a keen taste for a life (and literature) of adventurous, romantic experience, he left Scotland for Canada. He worked on a farm and, later, on a ranch near Duncan, Vancouver Island. In 1897-8 he wandered through the southwestern USA and Mexico, but by 1899 was again working on the Vancouver Island ranch, where he stayed until 1903, when he resumed his banking career with the Bank of Commerce, Victoria. In the summer of 1904 the bank transferred him to Kamloops; in the autumn of 1904 to Whitehorse; and in 1908 to Dawson, Yukon Territory, the setting for his best-known verse. By 1909 Service had published *Songs of a sourdough* (1907), *The spell of the Yukon* (1907), and *Ballads of a cheechako* (1909), which established his reputation as a writer of humorous, melodramatic ballads and brought him enough money to give up banking in order to write his first novel. In 1910 he visited publishers in the USA, returning overland to the Yukon in 1911, an expedition that introduced him to the land of the Mackenzie River, tales of which entered his writing. In 1912 Service left Canada, visiting the Balkans as a correspondent and eventually settling in Paris; he married in 1913. He spent 1914-16 as a war correspondent and stretcher-bearer, and was later a reporter for the Canadian government. He settled finally in Monte Carlo, where he died, although he spent the Second World War in Los Angeles, California.

Service's additional verse collections include *Rhymes of a rolling stone* (1912), *Rhymes of a Red Cross man* (1916), *Ballads of a bohemian* (1921); *Collected verse* (1930); *Complete poems* (1933); *Twenty bath-tub ballads* (1939); *Bar-room ballads* (1940); *Songs of a sun-lover* (1949); *Rhymes of a roughneck* (1950); *Lyrics of a lowbrow* (1951); *Rhymes of a rebel* (1952); *Songs for my supper* (1953); *Carols for an old codger* (1954); *Rhymes for my rags* (1956); and *Cosmic carols* (*c.* 1957). *Collected poems* (1940) contains most of the early verse and *More collected verse* (1955) contains poems published between 1949 and 1953. *Later collected verse* (1960) appeared posthumously. The best of his verse offers vivid, colourful, and often lurid tales of the Canadian North, told by either the observing or the participating 'I'. The heroes of the early work are frequently wanderers, vagabonds, or outsiders, caught between regret for what they have left behind and desire to find a new home in the cold and heartless North. In the verse of his middle period, Service seeks to wring meaning out of the carnage of the First World War, and also balances his experience with death with a close attention to details of life in post-war Europe. In his later verse he repeats frequently and rather tediously his literary commitment to the tales and the idioms of ordinary people.

Service also wrote popular fiction: *The trail of Ninety-Eight: a northland romance* (1911), *The pretender: a story of the Latin Quarter* (1914), *The poisoned paradise: a romance of Monte Carlo* (1922), *The roughneck: a tale of Tahiti* (1923), *The master of the microbe: a fantastic romance* (1926), and *The house of fear* (1927). Other books are *Why not grow young?* (1928); *Ploughman of the moon: an adventure into memory* (1945), an autobiographical account to 1912; and *Harper of heaven: a record of radiant living* (1948), about his later years. Anne Watts edited *The best of Robert Service* (1995).

See Carl F. KLINCK, *Robert Service: a biography* (1976) and James A. MacKay, *Vagabond of verse: Robert Service: a biography* (1995).

KEITH RICHARDSON

Seton, Ernest Thompson (1860-1946). Born Ernest Thompson in South Shields, England, he later adopted the name Seton, which he claimed reflected his descent from the Scottish Lord Seton, Earl of Winton. In 1866 the Thompson family immigrated to Canada, settling near Lindsay, Ontario; after 1870 they moved to Toronto, where Seton received his early education. His boyhood experiences near Lindsay and in Toronto's Don Valley, then wilderness areas, formed the basis for many of his writings. Although his talents were diverse, all his work was rooted in the single commitment, formed when he was a boy, to be a naturalist—a term that for him had a visionary as well as scientific meaning.

After graduating from the Toronto Grammar School (now Jarvis Collegiate), Seton enrolled at the Ontario College of Art. He graduated in 1879, having earned a Gold Medal and a scholarship to study at the Royal Academy in England. In 1881 he returned to Ontario, and in the following year joined his brother on a homestead near Carberry, Manitoba. His program of self-education as a naturalist then became increasingly rigorous as he made meticulous records of the behaviour of animals and birds and published *The birds of Manitoba* (Smithsonian Institution, 1891). In the meantime he travelled frequently to New York, where he was in demand as an illustrator, having been commissioned to do 1,000 illustrations of birds and animals for the twelve-volume *Century Dictionary*. Encouraged by his success as an artist, he studied in Paris for several years after 1890. In 1891 his painting 'The Sleeping Wolf' won first prize in the annual competition held at the Paris Salon. His later submissions were more controversial. The painting 'Triumph of the wolves' (1892), depicting wolves devouring the body of a man, caused an uproar that contributed to his decision to return to Canada.

In 1892 Seton was appointed official naturalist for the Government of Manitoba, a position that was largely honorary. In the same year he had made a brief visit to New Mexico and his experiences there became the basis for his most famous animal story, 'Lobo, the king of Currumpaw'. He then returned to Paris for another year, submitting another painting to the Salon competition and publishing *Studies in the art anatomy of animals* (New York, 1896). But the cool reception given in Paris to his pro-wilderness paintings led him to return in 1896 to the United States where, with the exception of various expeditions to Canada, he spent the rest of his life. In June of that year he married Grace Gallatin, who subsequently assisted him in the design of many of his books.

Seton's work as a scientist never abated. In 1908 he published the two-volume *The life histories of northern animals: an account of the mammals of Manitoba*; and, after he made a journey into the Far North, *The arctic prairies: a canoe-journey of 2,000 miles in search of the caribou* (1911). He continued to work as an illustrator, publishing *Pictures of wild animals* (1901) and *Bird portraits* (1901). But it was his animal stories that ensured his lasting fame. His first collection, containing the story of Lobo, was *WILD ANIMALS I HAVE KNOWN* (New York, 1898; NCL); it was an immediate success and was followed by numerous similar collections, often incorporating previously published stories with new ones: *Lobo, Rag, and Vixen* (1899), *The biography of a grizzly* (1900), *Lives of the hunted; containing a true account of the doings of five quadrupeds and three birds, and, in elucidation of the same, over 200 drawings* (1901), *Monarch, the big bear of Tallac* (1904), *Animal heroes* (1905), *The biography of a silver-fox* (1909), *Wild animals at home* (1913), *The slum cat* (1915), *Legend of the white reindeer* (1915), *Wild animal ways* (1916), *Woodland tales* (1921), *Old silver grizzly* (1927), *Katus, the snow child* (1927), *Chink and other stories* (1927), *Foam, the razorback* (1927), *Johnny Bear and other stories* (1927), *Krag, the Kootenay ram and other stories* (1929), *Billy, the dog that made good* (1930), *Cute coyote and other stories* (1930), and *Lobo, Bingo and the racing mustang* (1930). Although Seton tried his hand at a novel (*The preacher of Cedar Mountain*, 1917) and also wrote a drama, *The wild animal play for children* (1900), he is best known for contributing, along with Sir Charles G.D. ROBERTS, to the creation of a distinctive literary genre: the realistic animal story.

The worst of Seton's stories are maudlin. The best derive their power from his ability to synthesize his knowledge of animal behaviour, and his prophetic vision. Romantic primitivism, with its glorification of a sublime wilderness, forms a necessary context for an understanding of that vision. At the same time, later criticism has remarked that the wilderness in Seton's tales is also Darwinian. In Margaret ATWOOD's *SURVIVAL*, Seton's stories appear as a central example of a tendency to identify with the hunted victim, which Atwood views as peculiarly Canadian. Seton's strange blend of Romantic and Victorian attitudes to nature resulted from his synthesis of British, American, and Canadian influences.

In the midst of his busy writing career, Seton found time to become deeply involved in the development of a youth organization called the 'Woodcraft Indians'. His childhood interest in 'playing Indian' formed the basis for his children's story *TWO LITTLE SAVAGES; being the adventures of two boys who lived as Indians and what they learned* (1906), now considered a classic in the genre. He also wrote numerous additional books about woodcraft, including *Woodmyth and fables* (1905), *American woodcraft for boys* (1902), *The birchbark roll* (1906), *The book of woodcraft* (1911), *Rolf in the woods* (1911), *Forester's manual* (1911), and *The book of woodcraft and Indian lore* (1912).

In 1910 Seton joined Lord Baden-Powell and Daniel Beard in establishing the Boy Scouts of America. His writings formed the basis for the *Boy Scouts of America official manual* (1910). For many years he held the post of Chief Scout and enjoyed immense popularity; at the same time he began a prolonged disagreement with the administration of the association, levelling charges of militarism; they, in turn, accused Seton of pacifism. Finally, in 1915, the association expelled him on the pretext that he was not an American citizen. Until the end of his life Seton remained so bitter about this episode that he was urged by his publisher to leave all mention of it out of his autobiography. Nevertheless, the incident did nothing to stop the flow of books about woodcraft: *Manual of woodcraft Indians* (1915), *The woodcraft manual for boys* (1916), *The woodcraft manual for girls* (1916), and *Sign talk* (1918)—followed by a six-volume summary of his experience as a craftsman, *Library of pioneering and woodcraft* (1925).

There had been constant criticism, however, of Seton's animal stories from scientists who charged him with anthropomorphism. Books like *The natural history of the Ten Commandments* (1907), in which Seton attempted to demonstrate the biological source of biblical morality, added fuel to these charges. The so-called 'nature-fakir' controversy, however —the epithet was used by President Theodore Roosevelt in 1907 to dismiss the animal stories of Seton and Roberts—merely acted as a catalyst, leading Seton to redouble his scientific activity. Between 1925 and 1927 he published four volumes in a series entitled *Lives of game animals* that won him the John Burroughs and the Elliott Gold Medals, then the highest awards given for naturalist work.

The last sixteen years of Seton's life were spent near Santa Fe, New Mexico, where he settled in 1930. In 1931 he took out American citizenship. Divorced from his first wife, he married Julia Buttree, who had been his assistant, and together they set up Seton Village, a study centre for naturalists. His wife, who was many years his junior, wrote *The rhythm of the Redman in song, dance, and decoration* (1930), to which Seton provided an introduction and illustrations. His continuing admiration for Amerindian ways was reflected in *The gospel of the Redman* (1936). Over the years he enjoyed immense popularity as an oral storyteller, and as a public lecturer on conservation; but he also continued to write, publishing *Great historic animals, mainly about wolves* (1937), *The biography of an arctic fox* (1937), *Santana, the hero dog of France* (1945), and his autobiography, *Trail of an artist-naturalist* (1940).

Recent investigations of Seton's life and work have focused on his place in the Canadian tradition. Atwood's *Survival* has already been mentioned. In *Ernest Thompson Seton; man in nature and the progressive era, 1880-1915* (1978), John Henry Wadland broke new ground in defining those aspects of Seton's thought that are distinctively Canadian. The conflict with the Boy Scouts Association—omitted from the autobiography, but documented in Seton's letters and journals—promises to be an interesting case-study for future scholars. See Betty Keller, *Black Wolf: the life of Ernest Thompson Seton* (1984).

MAGDALENE REDEKOP

Sheard, Sarah. See NOVELS IN ENGLISH 1983 TO 1996: OTHER NOVELS 2(a).

Sherman, Francis Joseph (1871-1926). Born in Fredericton, New Brunswick, he attended the Collegiate School, where his teachers included George Parkin and Bliss CARMAN. He entered the University of New Brunswick at the age of fifteen, but was forced to abandon his studies for financial reasons and joined the Merchants' Bank of Halifax. Advancing quickly through the ranks while serving in Woodstock, N.B., Fredericton, Montreal, and Havana, Sherman had established the bank's influence throughout Cuba and the Caribbean by 1901, when the Merchants' Bank changed its name to the Royal Bank of Canada. He returned to the head office in Montreal in 1912 as assistant general manager. In 1919 he retired because of ill health caused by his military service in the Great War. He died in Atlantic City, USA, and is buried in Fredericton.

Although encouraged in his writing of poetry by the literary ambience of Fredericton in the post-Confederation period, Sherman was never as public or as prolific a writer as his friends Bliss Carman, Charles G.D. ROBERTS, and Theodore Goodridge ROBERTS. His collections are *Matins* (Boston, 1896), a series of romantic poems praised by both Rudyard Kipling and Carman; *In memorabilia mortis* (Cambridge, Mass., 1896), a tightly crafted sonnet series commemorating William Morris, who was much admired by Sherman and was an influence on his style; *The deserted city* (Boston, 1899), nineteen lyrical and finely disciplined sonnets on faith and love, described by Roberts as the work of a 'master sonneteer'; and *A Canadian calendar: XII lyrics* (Havana, 1900), mature and poignant lyrics on love and the seasons. *A prelude* (Boston, 1897) is a nature poem privately printed for Christmas; and the elegiac *Two songs at parting* (Fredericton, 1899) was written with John Bodkin on the occasion of Sherman's leaving the Maritimes. Lorne PIERCE edited *The complete poems of Francis Sherman* (1935), with a foreword by Sir Charles G.D. Roberts. Pierce and Roberts both acknowledge the sure craftsmanship, fastidious attention to language, and control of the sonnet form that continue to earn Sherman admiration among a sympathetic circle of poetry readers. GWENDOLYN DAVIES

Sherman, Jason (b.1962). Born in Montreal, Quebec, Sherman (the seventh of eight sons) graduated from the Creative Writing Program of York University, Toronto, in 1985. That year he founded What Publishing, which produced *what*, a literary magazine that he edited from 1985 to 1990. While Sherman is probably best known for his rapid achievement of acclaim as a dramatist, his venture with *what* marks his alternative career as a journalist whose reviews, essays, and interviews have appeared not only in the magazine he edited but in the Toronto *Globe and Mail*, *Canadian Theatre Review*, and *Theatrum*. Sherman has edited two anthologies for COACH HOUSE PRESS: *Canadian brash* (1991) and *Solo* (1993.) He has been a playwright-in-residence at Tarragon Theatre since 1992.

Sherman's first professional productions were *A place like Pamela*, produced by Walking Shadow Theatre, followed by *To cry is not so* by Theatre Smith Gilmour, both in 1990. In 1992 *The league of Nathans* (1996) was produced in a co-production by Orange Dog Theatre and Theatre Passe Muraille; it won a 1993 Chalmers Award. It tells of a reunion as adults of three boyhood friends and introduces themes that pervade Sherman's work. Principal among them is the complex problem of how an individual, in the context of histories that are both personal and social, behaves ethically. Sherman, a Canadian and a Jew, raises these issues in *The league of Nathans* against the context of the politically fraught creation of the state of Israel. In having the three boyhood friends bear the same given name, Sherman suggests that the seeming different, contradictory perspectives on being Jewish are, nevertheless, related. This history weighs on the current situation, notably in the response each of the Nathans has to the creation of the state and to the violence that Israel has levelled against Palestinians.

The complexity of the political and personal, evident in *The league of Nathans*, features strongly in *Three in the back, two in the head* (1994), for which Sherman won a Governor's General Award. The play deals with the search of Paul Jackson for answers about the murder of his father, Donald, who was working on a defence system that would create a shield against incoming missiles. The son's search for the truth about his father's death is impelled by both his personal sense of grief and his sense of his father's place in the nation's history. The father's work, like his death, is shrouded in secrecy; its true implications are suppressed for political reasons. Faced with the suppression of truth, the problem facing Paul is knowing who in the government will tell him the truth about his father, his work and his death.

Sherman returns to the impact of history on individual lives and the difficulty of being an ethical citizen in *The retreat* (1996). At a writers' retreat in the mountains (like that at Banff) two film producers, David Fine and Jeff Bloom, meet with a writer, Rachel Benjamin. While the play's conceit seems reminiscent of David Mamet's *Speed the plow*, Sherman's sense of the force of personal and social histories on the lives of individuals gives his play a complexity lacking in Mamet's. Sherman again raises the troubling question: in a web of histories, how can individuals be certain that they are making ethically correct choices?

Sherman's *Reading Hebron* was produced by Factory Theatre in 1996 and *None is too many* was produced by Winnipeg's Jewish Theatre and the Manitoba Theatre Centre in 1997. Sherman wrote the dramatic series PMO, which was heard monthly on the CBC's *Morningside*. ANN WILSON

Shields, Carol (b. 1935). Carol Warner was born in Oak Park, Illinois. In 1957 she received her B.A. from Hanover College, Indiana, and in the same year married a Canadian, Donald Hugh Shields, now a professor of civil engineering; they have five children. She became a Canadian citizen in 1971. In 1975 she received an M.A. in English from the university of Ottawa; a revision of her thesis was published as *Susanna Moodie: voice and vision* (1972). She has taught English at the universities of Ottawa, British Columbia, and Manitoba, where she is professor of English.

Shields has published three volumes of poetry—*Others* (1972), *Intersect* (1974), and *Coming to Canada* (1992)—but is best known as a novelist. *Small ceremonies* (1976) won the CANADIAN AUTHOR'S ASSOCIATION Award for best novel of 1977. This was followed by *The box garden* (1977), *Happenstance* (1980), and *A fairly conventional woman* (1982). The novels are characterized by gentle satire and careful, pleasingly accurate domestic observation. Very much concerned with the threads that connect domestic and artistic or intellectual life, Shields represents in her fiction both her experience as a wife and mother and her literary ventures: the heroine of *Small ceremonies*, for example, writes fiction and has produced a book about Susanna MOODIE. Disillusioned in early middle age, Shields' protagonists are nevertheless survivors and celebrants. They find consolation in the texture of daily life, the rush of love, and the intersection of their ordinary worlds with something really extraordinary—such as the party of deaf-mutes who dine out together so marvellously at the end of *Small ceremonies*. This sudden, lyrical blossoming in Shields' fiction is like a signature attesting to the writer's love for her own gift of observation. *Happenstance*, however, suggests that some part of perception (even when it is specifically of love) always remains stillborn: 'He loved her. But feared that something in his greeting might fall short. Some connection between perception and the moment itself would fail, would always fail.' The least successful of the novels are *The box garden*, whose plot relies on far-fetched coincidence, and *A fairly conventional woman*, which is flawed by sentimentality and spates of unconvincing dialogue. *Happenstance*, in which Shields uses a male protagonist for the first time, is an intriguing book. *Small ceremonies*, the best and most consistently believable of her novels, illustrates most clearly her special gifts of observation.

Shields' poetry is less impressive than her fiction, although marked by the same appealing sensibility. The poems are simple, domestic, generous in spirit, though often technically undistinguished. Our satisfaction typically comes in the moments of insight, but as if these moments somehow existed apart from the language and final shape of the whole. CONSTANCE ROOKE

The story collection *Various miracles* (1985) features Shields' sharp-eyed observations and odd incidents, rather than plotted stories. 'Mrs Turner cutting the grass' is about an elderly woman in shorts and halter pushing a lawn-mower in front of her Winnipeg house—a repellent sight to her neighbours. What if they knew of her youth in New York, where she gave birth to a black baby she left in a carriage in Brooklyn Heights? Or that she likes to travel and with her two sisters went to Japan, where they caught the attention of 'the Professor', a poet, who later wrote a cruel and funny poem about the three philistines that was always the most popular poem at his readings? Like Chekhov, Shields writes about ordinary people who outwardly lead unremarkable lives. In one of the stories in *The orange fish* (1989) Hazel is trying to mourn her late husband, a man who had a habit of sleeping with her best friends. On an impulse she answers a newspaper ad and gets a job, her first. To the astonishment of friends and family, she is a success. The heroine of *The republic of love* (1992) is Fay McLeod, a folklore scholar, aged thirty-five, who is ending yet another affair. Tom Avery is a radio disc jockey, thrice divorced, and forty. These two search for love, and find it, in this good-humoured urban fantasy.

Shields' novel *Swann: a mystery* (1987)—which won the Arthur Ellis Award—unfolds as a mild satire on the world of scholarship. We meet a professor, Sarah, who is a successful feminist writer; Morton, a biographer of famous poets; Rose, a librarian in a small Ontario town; and Frederic, an octogenarian journalist and publisher—each one described in a separate chapter. All four come together at a Toronto symposium in honour of a dead Canadian poet, Mary Swann. Her poems have attracted much interest because she was murdered by her husband, who dismembered her body before shooting himself. Each of the characters wants to be seen as the authority on Mary Swann. But the symposium—described in the last chapter in the form of a film script—ends in a shambles: Swann's notebooks, copies of her book, a rare photograph, and notes for a speech have vanished. These disappearances, Swann herself and her violent death, remain mysterious. We are led on a fine chase and learn very little. But Shields' characters entertain us while the hunt is on. The film *Swann*, directed by Anna Benson Gyles, was released in 1997.

Shields came to her full power in *The stone diaries* (1993), which won both a Governor General's Award and the Pulitzer Prize. It is set at first in a company mining town in Manitoba early in the twentieth century, and opens as Mercy Stone Goodwill, a stonemason's wife, is startled and bewildered by birth pangs. The novel is mainly about Daisy, the daughter she bears, and follows her through childhood, marriage, widowhood, a second marriage, motherhood, and old age in Florida. When she returns to Canada from her father's home in Indiana in search of her roots, she finds a husband, a home, and a garden. It is the last that becomes her passion. What an eye Shields has for detail! And how well she describes lonely, eccentric men: Mercy's husband the quarryman; Barker Flett, the shy botanist Daisy marries; and Barker's curmudgeon father. They are ordinary; they are unforgettable.

Shields collaborated with Blanche Howard on *A celibate season* (1991), an epistolary novel about the unavoidable ten-month separation of a married couple. She is also a published playwright. *Departures and arrivals* (1990), which takes place in an airport, was first performed in Manitoba in 1984; and she collaborated with her daughter, Catherine Shields, in writing *Fashion, power, guilt* (1995). Her most successful play is *Thirteen hands* (1993), which premièred at Winnipeg's Prairie Theatre Exchange in 1993, and in 1997 was co-produced by the National Arts Centre, Ottawa, and the Canadian Stage Company, Toronto. It presents four actors who play a group of women, most of whom were weekly bridge partners for forty-three years. These housewives and mothers form an important bond of friendship on the Tuesday evenings when they do not have to be at home and have 'a dozen eyes and thirteen hands'. They are types we recognize with pleasure, and we are moved when we hear some of their stories.

PATRICIA IRWIN

Shiels, Andrew (1793-1879). Born in rural Roxburghshire, Scotland, and largely self-educated, he immigrated to Nova Scotia in 1818 and worked as a blacksmith in Halifax. In 1828 he established himself on a farm in Dartmouth and became a leading citizen in the area, serving as a justice of the peace and in 1857 being appointed a magistrate. Perhaps the most prolific poet in nineteenth-century Nova Scotia, he wrote and published verse for over fifty years under the pseudonym 'Albyn'—frequently in local newspapers, but also in eleven books and pamphlets of verse, including *The witch of the Westcot* (Halifax, 1831), *The water lily* (Halifax, 1852), *Letter to Eliza* (Halifax, 1876), *John Walker's courtship* (Halifax, 1877), and *Dupes and demagogues* (Halifax, 1879). Although he tried his hand at a wide variety of verse forms, he was at his best writing songs and light lyrics (in the manner of Burns) and verse tales, in which he often turned to history and legend for his subjects: he was particularly interested in the history and folk stories of Nova Scotia. For Shiels, one of the main functions of verse was to dramatize and amplify human experience so that what appeared commonplace took on special meaning. He strove to express the mysterious, vital, magical spirit that lay at the heart of the world, and was able to make his readers feel the force of his love of life.

TOM VINCENT

Short stories in English. To 1982. The short story has had a long and substantial tradition in English Canada. The sketches and stories of Thomas McCULLOCH and Thomas Chandler HALIBURTON first appeared in Halifax newspapers in the 1820s and 1830s respectively. From the mid-nineteenth century on, stories by Canadian writers frequently appeared not only in Canadian newspapers but in LITERARY MAGAZINE, such as *The LITERARY GARLAND* and *The WEEK*, and in New York or Boston as well. Many writers of short fiction were women: Susanna MOODIE, May Agnes FLEMING, Rosanna LEPROHON, Sara Jeannette DUNCAN, and Susie Frances HARRISON were among the most prolific. It was only in the final two decades of the century, however, that a few significant collections made their appearance. Gilbert PARKER's romantic and melodramatic tales of the Northwest were collected in *Pierre and his people* (London, 1892), a book that became very popular. Susie Frances Harrison's *Crowded out and other sketches* (Ottawa, 1886) contains interesting stories set in both English and French Canada. The title story is about the attempts of a Canadian writer in London to achieve publication. Edward William THOMSON published the first of many stories in the Boston *Youth's Companion* in 1886; his best-known story, 'The privilege of the limits', first appeared in *Harper's Weekly* in 1891, four years before he came out with a collection, *Old man Savarin and other stories* (Toronto, 1895). The beginnings of a Canadian genre—the animal story—can be traced to Charles G.D. ROBERTS' *Earth's enigmas: a book of animal and nature life* (Boston, 1896). But in this period the most important collection, as a work of literature, was the poet Duncan Campbell SCOTT's *In the village of Viger* (Boston, 1896), a series of stories that in a quiet, superbly controlled manner create the sense of a whole community. A decade and a half later (in 1912) another enduring collection of stories appeared: Stephen LEACOCK's *SUNSHINE SKETCHES OF A LITTLE TOWN*. Like Scott's book, and like so many other Canadian collections by a single author that would come later, *Sunshine sketches* is a series of connected stories unified above all by setting, in this case the fictional Ontario town of Mariposa (Orillia).

Raymond KNISTER suggests in the introduction to his 1928 anthology *Canadian short stories* that it reflects 'a new era' in Canadian short-story writing; but in fact it can now be seen to signal the end of an era, since more than half the book was devoted to writers from an earlier period: Roberts, Scott, Thomson, Parker, Norman DUNCAN, and Leacock. In addition to their stories are two by Marjorie PICKTHALL and Mazo DE LA ROCHE, neither of whom was prolific or distinguished in this genre. The 'new era' was represented by Knister himself, Thomas Murtha, Morley CALLAGHAN, and several others who did not continue to write short fiction. The stories of Knister, who died tragically at thirty-three, did not appear in book form until the 1970s. Murtha, who vanished into school-teaching and only occasionally published in small American magazines, produced enough stories that they could be collected in *Short stories* (1980), but only after his death. Callaghan was the only 1920s writer in Knister's anthology to make a name for himself in this period: he went on to become the most influential figure in the development of the modern short story in Canada. His first collection, *A native argosy*, was published in 1929, and *Now that April's here and other stories* in 1936.

The Depression and the Second World War were dry periods in the growth of the short story in Canada. Frederick Philip GROVE, who began publishing novels in the 1920s, was also a short-story writer. His well-known 'Snow' first appeared in *Queen's Quarterly* in 1932; but it was not until 1971 that a selected stories, *Tales from the margin* edited by Desmond PACEY, was published. Though *Queen's Quarterly* also published the Manitoba and Saskatchewan stories of another novelist, Sinclair ROSS, they were not collected until 1968 in *The lamp at noon and other stories*, which appeared in the NEW CANADIAN LIBRARY. Ethel WILSON's 'Hurry, hurry' appeared in *The New Statesman and Nation* in 1937, but her first collection, *Mrs Golightly and other stories*, appeared only in 1961. The late, and sometimes posthumous, publication of short-story collections by writers who began their careers in the twenties and thirties suggests not only minimal enthusiasm for Canadian short stories but a lack of periodicals interested in publishing them. (Callaghan published mainly outside Canada.) While the work of novelists in this period received feeble though steady support through book publication, serious short fiction, on the whole, was apparently thought unworthy. However, this prejudice against story collections by a single writer was characteristic of American and British as well as Canadian publishing.

It was not until after the Second World War that the great leap forward, which Knister had thought he was witnessing, actually took place. In the 1940s Montreal provided the country with two little magazines—*PREVIEW* and *FIRST STATEMENT*—with a contemporary commitment; in 1945 they combined to form *NORTHERN REVIEW*. Poets were at the centre of this literary movement and some—notably Irving LAYTON, P.K. PAGE, and Ralph GUSTAFSON—were also writing short stories. Before her first story appeared in *The New Yorker*, Mavis GALLANT published two stories in *Preview* in 1944—'Three brick walls' and 'Good morning and goodbye'—and, in 1950, 'The flowers of spring' in *Northern Review*. The first influential anthology of the post-war period was Desmond Pacey's *A book of Canadian stories* (1947; rev. 1950, 1962), in which the youngest writers represented in the 1947 edition were P.K. Page (b. 1916) with 'The resignation', and William McConnell (b. 1917) with 'The alien'. The 'modern' stories included works by Ross ('The lamp at noon'), Leo KENNEDY ('A priest in the family'), Callaghan ('Father and son'), Mary Quayle Innis ('The bells'), and Knister ('The strawsack'). For the 1950 revision, Pacey added Ethel Wilson's 'Hurry, hurry' and W.O. MITCHELL's 'Saint Sammy'.

In the mid-fifties two writers who went on to have productive careers published their first collections: Hugh GARNER with *The yellow sweater and other stories* (1952) and Mavis Gallant with *The other Paris* (1956). At this time public broadcasting was bring two other sixties' writers, Alice MUNRO and Mordecai RICHLER (both born in 1931), to the fore. In 1954 the Canadian Broadcasting Corporation, which for some years had been broadcasting poetry and short stories in various radio series, began a regular weekly literary program, 'Anthology'. The growing interest in the short stories that were broadcast justified the publication of four books: *Canadian short stories* (1952), *Ten for Wednesday Night* (1961), *Stories with John Drainie* (1963), and *Small wonders* (1982). Hugh HOOD, whose stories have often been broadcast, once wrote that 'the CBC is far and away the most receptive and the fairest—though not the highest-paying—market for stories that I know of.' But the mid-fifties, which saw the disappearance of *Northern Review* with the death of its editor John SUTHERLAND, also saw the emergence of *The TAMARACK REVIEW* (1956-82) as a medium for short stories, publishing in its early issues work by Munro, Richler, Hood, Jack LUDWIG, and Dave GODFREY. Among older magazines, *Queen's Quarterly*, *The CANADIAN FORUM*, and *The FIDDLEHEAD* also published short fiction. (Other literary magazines that provided outlets for the writer of short fiction after the 1960s included *The MALAHAT REVIEW*, *EXILE*, *DESCANT*, and *CANADIAN FICTION MAGAZINE*.)

Through the whole of the 1950s only a handful of writers—Hugh Garner, Mavis Gallant, Morley Callaghan, Thomas RADDALL—were able to publish collections of their short stories. In Canada, as in England and the United States, it was still assumed that books of short stories wouldn't sell. This situation began to change dramatically in Canada in the 1960s, and it could be argued that in the next two decades the short story became the most interesting and varied literary genre in this country. Two major commercial publishing houses—McCLELLAND & STEWART and MACMILLAN OF CANADA—had numerous distinguished short-story writers on their lists: McClelland & Stewart with Margaret LAURENCE, Margaret ATWOOD, Rudy WIEBE, Alistair MacLEOD, among others; and Macmillan with Munro, Gallant, Jack HODGINS, Guy VANDERHAEGE, and others. But the real impetus came from the small literary publishers, and in this respect 1966 has to be seen as a momentous year in the development of the short story in Canada: the year in which OBERON PRESS was founded in Ottawa. Oberon published Leon ROOKE, John METCALF, Hugh Hood, W.P. KINSELLA, Merna SUMMERS, W.D. VALGARDSON, and a number of still younger writers, as well as short-story annuals and a variety of anthologies. The House of ANANSI and COACH HOUSE PRESS, both in Toronto, and TALONBOOKS in Vancouver were Oberon's competitors in short-story publishing. And in the early 1980s a new group of regional publishers became increasingly important. In 1981 and 1982 three well-received collections of stories by new writers were published—not in Toronto or Ottawa but by three small Western publishers: Edna ALFORD's *A sleep full of dreams* (1981) by Oolichan Books on Vancouver Island, Joan CLARK's *From a high thin wire* (1982) by NeWest Press in Edmonton, and Sandra BIRDSELL's *Night travellers* (1982) by Winnipeg's Turnstone Press. All three books are collections of connected stories: Edna Alford's take place in a nursing home for the aged, Joan Clark writes about a woman growing up in the Maritimes and then living as a wife and mother in Alberta, and Sandra Birdsell's stories are set in a small town in Alberta. Collections of linked stories, which sometimes have a weight and narrative interest lacking in books of unconnected stories, are not a Canadian discovery. Probably the seminal book of this kind is Turgenev's series of lyrical stories about the Russian countryside, *Sketches from a hunter's album* (the title used for the Penguin Classics edition), published in 1852; its North American equivalent may be Sherwood Anderson's *Winesburg, Ohio* (1919). In Canada, Scott's early *In the village of Viger* and Leacock's *Sunshine sketches* have been succeeded by, among other unified collections, Margaret Laurence's *A bird in the house* (1970), stories about growing up in small-town Manitoba; Alice Munro's *Lives of girls and women* (1971), about growing up in small-town Ontario; George ELLIOTT's *The kissing man* (1962), also about small-town Ontario; Jack Hodgins' *The Barclay family theatre* (1981) and earlier books, which bring a mythic significance to life on

Vancouver Island; and W.P. KINSELLA's stories about baseball and about life on a Native reserve in southern Alberta.

The 1970s brought a high degree of sophistication to the work of the best short-story writers in English Canada and increasing international recognition of their fiction. It may seem a paradox that at the same time, regionalism became a powerful force in the Canadian story. The critic Northrop FRYE did not see this as a paradox, however. In an interview with Robert FULFORD in the short-lived literary annual *Aurora* (1980), he said: 'I think that as a culture matures, it becomes more regional. . .'; and he added later, 'I think the country we know as Canada will, in the foreseeable future, be a federation of regions culturally, rather than a single nation.' The best regional writers are as sophisticated as any and are read in other countries partly for the insight they provide into the life of a particular locality. Alice Munro's breakthrough volume in the United States and England, *The moons of Jupiter* (1982), is a book of Ontario stories, more than half of which first appeared in *The New Yorker* and the *Atlantic Monthly*. Jack Hodgins, as we have seen, brings myth and 'magic realism' to Vancouver Island, and acknowledges the influence on his work of William Faulkner and the contemporary South American storytellers. W.D. Valgardson, in his collections beginning with *Bloodflowers* in 1973, brings a powerful dramatic sense and a great deal of literary sophistication to stories that are set in the small towns and Icelandic communities of Manitoba and other more remote places. Alistair MacLeod's sombre, reflective stories in *The lost salt gift of blood* (1976) are about Cape Breton and Newfoundland. On the urban scene, the prolific novelist and short-story writer Hugh Hood published a collection of linked stories in *Around the mountain: scenes from Montreal life* (1967). Mordecai Richler's collection, *The street* (1969), deals with Jewish ghetto life in that city. Among many other regional writers whose work is marked by literary sophistication are Howard O'HAGAN, writing chiefly about the mountain country of western Canada in *The woman who got on at Jasper Station* (1963; rpr. 1978); Rudy Wiebe, a writer of powerful, mythic stories in *Where is the voice coming from?* (1974) and *The angel of the tar sands and other stories* (NCL, 1982); and the poet Alden NOWLAN, whose stories about small-town life in New Brunswick were collected in *Miracle at Indian River* (1968).

Many ethnic strands have gone into the pattern of the contemporary short story in Canada. Margaret Laurence's first stories to achieve book publication were set in Ghana and collected in *The tomorrow-tamer and other stories* (1963). Austin CLARKE is from Barbados, and most of the stories in *When he was free and young and he used to wear silks* (1971) are about West Indians living in Toronto. Henry KREISEL, who was born in Vienna and had to flee the Nazi terror against the Jews, in *The almost meeting and other stories* (1981) wrote about both Europe and the Canadian West, bringing a cosmpolitan sensibility to his work. His 'The broken globe' is one of the most frequently anthologized of modern Canadian stories. Clarke BLAISE, born in the United States of a French-Canadian father and an English-Canadian mother, brought another kind of dual viewpoint to his stories—American and Canadian—in *A North American education* (1973). Matt COHEN in *Columbus and the fat lady* (1972) and *Night flights* (1978) wrote both regional stories set in eastern Ontario and symbolic, experimental fictions with urban backgrounds, sometimes set in Europe. Audrey THOMAS and Leon Rooke came to Canada from the United States; John Metcalf was born and brought up in England. Both Metcalf and Rooke, besides writing their own fiction, have done much for the short story in Canada as editors and anthologists. Two writers who have something in common—expatriation—are Mavis Gallant and Norman LEVINE. Gallant lives in Paris. Most of her subtle and distinguished stories take place in France and other parts of Europe. But in *Home truths* (1981) a half-dozen stories about a young woman, Linnet Muir, marvellously blend Gallant's international literary existence with a superb sense of place: Montreal during the Second World War. Levine lived for many years in Cornwall. His stories—often autobiographical, sometimes deliberately fragmentary, many of them about family life and what it is like to survive as a writer—have been widely published in England and Europe, particularly in West and East Germany. When he returned to Canada in the late 1970s for a period, his reputation as a writer of short stories blossomed. The title story of his collection *Thin ice* (1979)—about how precarious the life of a writer is—is a good, sobering note on which to end an optimistic survey of this period.

ROBERT WEAVER

1983 to 1996. The optimism over the future of the short story that became established in the 1960s and 1970s was justified by an extraordinary flowering in the 1980s and

1990s: hundreds of single-author collections and dozens of anthologies were published. Encouragement was provided by numerous summer writing schools and workshops, by degree-granting creative-writing programs in various universities across Canada, by a few small and large publishers and some three-dozen literary magazines, and by numerous literary competitions, including that of the CBC/*Saturday Night*, founded by Robert WEAVER, and the $10,000 Journey Prize (and publication in the *Journey Prize anthology*), the money coming from James Michener following the success of his Yukon-based novel *Journey*.

Many writers examined the question: What is real about living in Canada? As a result, fiction tended to follow one of two directions. The traditional or modernist story still dominated the period, with realistic characters, plots, resolutions, and attention to detail. By the 1990s the tendency was to call attention to the artifice of creating a fiction; new forms and techniques were essential for Canadians who themselves were seeking definitions. Who are we? Or as Northrop FRYE asked, where is here?

Surprisingly, though the story was the most successful genre of the last twenty years, little critical attention was paid to it. There were, however, two useful studies: W.H. New's *Forms of speech and violence* (1987) is a comparative examination of the Canadian and New Zealand short story, with a focus on Duncan Campbell SCOTT, Margaret LAURENCE, and Alice MUNRO, among the Canadian writers; and Michele Gadpaille's *The Canadian short story* (1988) is an introductory monograph that includes chapters on Mavis GALLANT, Munro, and Margaret ATWOOD.

Anthologists played an important part in articulating the nature of the Canadian short story and its changing directions. (See ANTHOLOGIES IN ENGLISH: SHORT FICTION 2, 3.) John METCALF argued that short fiction is 'language performance'; George BOWERING claimed that the postmodern story violates rules of language and form; while *CANADIAN FICTION MAGAZINE* drew attention in its editorials to the importance of images, dream, and myth in comprehending the nature of narrative. But there was never any disagreement about recognizing that achievements in the short-story form are among the triumphs of recent Canadian literature. The 1996 publication of both Mavis Gallant's *Selected stories* and Alice Munro's *Selected stories* offered a kind of climax to this period and were occasions to celebrate; indeed, both books were celebrated in international reviews. The following brief survey of titles from some 600 single-author collections published in the past fifteen years must inevitably omit many books that have contributed to the richness of the genre.

Collections of stories by gifted writers who settled in Canada relatively recently brought about the most pronounced change in our conception of the Canadian short story, in capturing our interest in India or Trinidad or Jamaica and in the suffering of the immigrant. Stories in the collections of Neil BISSOONDATH, *Digging up the mountains* (1985) and *On the eve of uncertain tomorrows* (1990), deal with the plight of the West Indian immigrant to Canada. André Alexis, also from Trinidad, in *Despair and other stories of Ottawa* (1994) uses magic realism and bizarre events to make pointed social comments about the immigrant's experience in bureaucratic Ottawa. Rohinton MISTRY's *Tales from Firozsha Baag* (1987), a superb début, is set in an apartment complex in Bombay, with the final story set in Canada. The stories in M.J. VASSANJI's *Uhuru Street* (1992) deal with characters of Asian descent in Dar es Salaam, Tanzania, who are lured by thoughts of immigrating to North America. Ven Begaumudré's stories in *A planet of eccentrics* (1990) are about isolation and misunderstanding and take place in Canada, India, and the celestial realm of Vishnu. Dionne BRAND's *Sans Souci* (1989) offers dramatic insights in the lives of Jamaican women in their homeland and in Canada, as does Makeda Silvera's *Her head a village* (1994), which looks at writing, welfare, and problems facing new immigrants.

Portrayals of contemporary life in innovative fiction were most common in short stories by dozens of female writers who emerged in the late 1980s and confronted such things as unemployment, urban violence, a fragmented society, and an uncertain future. Women's lives are depicted against a background of a corrupt or corrosive male-based patriarchal world from which women try to free themselves. Elizabeth BREWSTER's *A house full of women* (1983), Veronica Ross's *Dark secrets* (1983), Audrey THOMAS's *Goodbye Harold, good luck* (1986), Elizabeth's Hay's *Crossing the snow line* (1989), Bronwen WALLACE's *People you'd trust your life to* (1990), Diane SCHOEMPERLEN's *Frogs* (1986) and *The man of my dreams* (1990), and Margaret Atwood's *Bluebeard's egg* (1983) and *Wilderness tips* (1991) all show a preoccupation with the difficulties of communication between men and women. The infinite ways in which women develop as human beings are nearly always portrayed against the hope for changes in the condition of Canadian society itself. Many writers went beyond this to suggest that women have to make their own changes instead of waiting for society to change. Anne Cameron's *Bright's Crossing* (1990) describes the attempts of eleven women who live on Vancouver Island to have a better life.

In a post-nationalist Canada there was a strong urge to protect the community. This was very noticeable in First Nations writers such as Lee MARACLE, whose *Sojourner's truth* (1990) argues that Eurocentric literary discourse is not fully adequate to explain Native people's approach to storytelling. Thomas KING's *One good story, that one* (1993) satirizes anthropologists who attempt to collect 'creation myths', and Beth Brant's *Mohawk Trail* (1990) and *Food and spirits* (1991) are collections of Native people's stories told from a feminist perspective.

In the 1980s writers challenged traditional presentations of Canadian literature. Whether called metafiction, parody, or postmodernism, fiction moved inward and dramatized internal conflict. Many fictions involved transformations, uncertain points of view, elements of dream, meditation, or invective. Brian FAWCETT's violent and grotesque postmodern pieces in *Capital tales* (1984) and *The secret journal of Alexander Mackenzie* (1986) challenged traditional technique with authorial asides, dialogues between the narrator and a character, and quasi-autobiographical introspection. Monty Reid's *Dog speaks: irritated texts* (1993) is made up of strange, surreal pieces that draw in part on the author's experiences as a palaeontologist. Eric McCormack's *Inspecting the vaults* (1987) and Ernest Hekkanen's *Medieval hour in the author's mind* (1987) are inventive, sometimes disturbing blends of surrealism and fantasy primed by the instability of character. Ann Diamond's *Snakebite* (1989) includes one character who turns into a mermaid, and tales about forbidden companions and foreign love adventures. *Birds of a feather* (1990), a strong first collection by Montreal writer Catholyn Jansen, has stories set in a poultry-processing plant—they are seamy and violent, with a touch of the occult. Leon ROOKE is among the most inventive Canadian writers. The collections *A bolt of white cloth* (1984), *How I saved the province* (1989), and *The happiness of others* (1991) contain short stories that are darkly humorous, and quirky. The stories in Douglas GLOVER's *Dog attempts to drown man in Saskatoon* (1985) are accomplished fragments that deal with fraying relationships. Stephen Guppy's *Another sad day at the edge of the empire* (1985) is a collection of magic-realist fictions set on Vancouver Island. The experimental stories in Richard Truhlar's *Figures in paper time* (1989), which owe much to French literary theory, flow without form, drawing inspiration from mirrors and mystery movies. Geoffrey Ursell's *Way out West!* (1990) is an entertaining surreal collection that brings historical characters such as Gabriel Dumont to life.

Kristjana GUNNARS' *The axe's edge* (1983) draws upon letters, journals, folklore, and historical documents to introduce an entirely new kind of prose collage about Icelandic immigrants; this pioneering work influenced many subsequent writers describing the breakdown of tradition in a new and sometimes disrespectful land. Carol Windley's *Visible light* (1983) combines satire, magic, and fairy-tale motifs in a poetic West Coast setting. An unusual collection by Richard Taylor, *Tender only to one* (1984), deals with the final days of famous nineteenth-century painters and some imaginary isolated characters.

W.P. KINSELLA alternated between fable-like baseball fictions and tales about Native people. The stories in *The thrill of the grass* (1988), *The further adventures of Slugger McBatt* (1988), and *The Dixon Cornbelt League* (1993) combine baseball and magic realism heart-warmingly. The tales narrated by Silas Ermineskin in *The Miss Hobbema pageant* (1989) and *Brother Frank's Gospel Hour* (1994) continued Kinsella's exploration of hope, survival, and promise on the Alberta reservation of Hobbema. Keath FRASER, who made his debut with *Taking cover* (1982), published his most brilliant work in *Foreign affairs* (1986), a commanding collection of seven stories and three novellas. The title story, about a diplomat suffering a debilitating disease, is one of the masterpieces of Canadian short fiction.

The list of the PORCUPINE'S QUILL includes some of the finest stories of the 1990s. Terry Grigg's *Quickening* (1990) is a collection of rural stories set on the author's Manitoulin Island; odd characters, visionary babies, and original descriptions made her début collection memorable. Dayv James-French's *Victims of gravity* (1990) contains precisely written stories about family conflict and coping with death; Caroline Adderson's *Bad imaginings* (1993) explores the unknown in stories that include children, the aged, and the historical past. The stories in Yukon writer Patricia Robinson's *City of orphans* (1994) are vivid and wide-ranging portrayals, ranging from the bleak to the fantastic; K.D. Miller's *A litany in time of plague* (1994) examines AIDS and loneliness; Elsa Levine's stories in *Driving men mad* (1995) are versatile and detailed depictions of an odd assortment of characters.

Writers worth watching include Linda Svendsen, whose collection of eight disturbing and beautiful stories, *Marine life* (1992), was widely regarded as a triumphant début and earned comparisons with Flannery O'Conner, Carson McCullers, Barbara GOWDY, and Margaret ATWOOD. Chronicling a dysfunctional family in the 1950s, the young narrator, Adele, precisely describes her impressions of a womanizing brother and two sisters, one of whom is an emotional wreck. With witty dialogue and a positive tone, the stories deal with the potential destructiveness of love. Newfoundlander Michael Winter's *Creaking in their skins* (1994) is a collection of poetic stories, far removed from traditional Newfoundland folklore, that range from St John's to Egypt. Patricia Seaman's *The black diamond ring* (1994) contains unusual stories about women's lives and experiences, written in an elegant, impressionistic style. From central British Columbia came Holley Rubinsky's *Rapid transits* (1990), winner of the $10,000 Journey Prize; her stories deal with women caught in potentially violent events. Gayla Reid's *To be there with you* (1994)—winner of a CBC/*Saturday Night* Literary Award, the National Magazine Award for Fiction, and the Journey Prize—is a collection of stories about expatriates unable to communicate with other people in new countries, or with those they love. Robert Mullen's stories in *Americas* (1994) are exotic in style and content. Greg HOLLINGSHEAD's *White buick* (1992) and *The roaring girl* (1995; Governor General's Award) contain absurdist humour written in a direct manner that counterpoints bizarre situations and eccentric characters. Richard Teleky's *Goodnight sweetheart and other stories* (1993) presents well-crafted and poignant stories that explore life as a battle between art and reality and reveal that one needs the other. The stories in Oakland Ross's *Guerilla beach* (1994) are set primarily in war-torn El Salvador—Ross is the former *Globe and Mail* Latin American correspondent. Yann Martel, a promising new writer, wrote *The facts behind the Helsinki Roccamatios* (1993), the title story of which won the Journey Prize; it is a powerful, graphic work about dying from AIDS. Other strong and disturbing collections included Evelyn Lau's *Fresh girls* (1993), which describes the violent world of prostitution; and Kenneth J. Harvey's *The hole that must be filled* (1993), which contains violent, often repulsive subject matter, compellingly described. Other writers and collections to note include Saskatoon's J. Jill Robinson's *Saltwater trees* (1992) and *Lovely in her bones* (1993), and T.F. Rigelhof's *Je t'aime cowboy* (1993). Newfoundlander Lisa Moore's *Degrees of nakedness* (1995) offers stories that are fragmentary, disconnected, image-conscious, witty, and risk-taking.

Despite the financial uncertainties facing publishers in this period, Canadian short fiction demonstrated an enduring vitality that was manifested in an extraordinary growth in the number of publications, and in an amazing versatility in form and subject matter.

GEOFF HANCOCK

Short stories in French. Short stories have a long history in Quebec: the first short narrative text, 'Zelim', signed by 'le Canadien curieux', was published on 30 December 1778 in *La Gazette littéraire*. Strangely, though, this little tale of the Oriental type then current in France remains an isolated phenomenon, for the short narrative genre did not make its first real appearance until the 1820s, when an unsigned story entitled 'L'Iroquoise' was serialized in *La Bibliothèque canadienne* (oct.-nov. 1827), and especially the 1830s, when more than twenty stories were published. Shortly before the appearance of the first Quebec novel (*L'INFLUENCE D'UN LIVRE*, by Philippe Aubert de Gaspé, fils, 1837), which itself contained two stories that have become famous ('L'étranger' and 'L'homme de Labrador'), Pierre-Georges Boucher de Boucherville ('La tour de Trafalgar', 1835), author of the serialized novel *Une de perdue, deux de trouvées* (1849-65), and Napoléon AUBIN ('Histoire qui n'a pas de nom', 1835), the Swiss-born founder of the periodical *Le Fantasque* (August 1837), are generally considered the pioneers of the short story in Quebec.

Broadly speaking, the stories produced in the nineteenth century are marked by some features related to the literary modes of production of the time (periodicals being much more important than collections, which appeared only occasionally before 1900) and some related to aesthetic trends. From the moment that newspapers and magazines began publishing stories, we see, *mutatis mutandis*, a surge of production. Aurélien Boivin, who has researched the subject in depth, catalogued more than a thousand short stories published in the nineteenth century, which he grouped in three categories: supernatural, anecdotal, and historical. Using a slightly different method of classification, these works could also be grouped in the following generic categories: Gothic (horror stories, the macabre), traditional fantasy (folklore, legend, and especially the Christian supernatural), realistic (usually moralizing), and historical. Only a few authors stand out (for quantity, among other things, since the great majority of 'writers' did not venture to publish more than one or two texts). For the period before 1860, they include, in addition to Aubin, Eugène L'Écuyer ('Épisode de la vie d'un faux dévot', 1853) and Henri-Émile CHEVALIER, a visiting Frenchman who founded *La Ruche littéraire* in 1853 and published a number of stories (and novels) in Canada before returning to France.

Around 1860, however, as a result of the impetus given by the MOUVEMENT LITTÉRAIRE DU QUÉBEC, dominated by Octave CRÉMAZIE, Antoine GÉRIN-LAJOIE, and Abbé Henri-Raymond CASGRAIN, the short narrative genre took a distinctive direction. Not content with what had been produced until that time, the members of the group (which included Joseph-Charles TACHÉ, *Forestiers et voyageurs*, 1863) wanted to create a national literature. In 1861 they established the periodical *Les SOIRÉES CANADIENNES*, and it became the centre around which crystallized the ideology of the 'terroir', the rural homeland of the *Canadien* people, which had made its first appearance in 1846 with the publication of the short novel *La terre paternelle* by Patrice LACOMBE. Promoting an ideological discourse that was to persist until the mid-twentieth century, Casgrain in his three *Légendes canadiennes* (1860-1) illustrates—in the spirit of Charles Nodier in France—the importance of recovering the old stories that a people risks losing if they are not written down. Combining the aesthetic of the Christian supernatural with earthy realism and historical discourse, Casgrain does not hide his ambition: he proposes a model for other writers, grounded in the nationalization of French-Canadian literature. Although he did not entirely succeed (certain authors having resisted the new *diktat*), it must be admitted that—after the wave of sometimes folkloric, sometimes realistic and even humorous writing at the end of the nineteenth century represented by, among others, Louis FRÉCHETTE (*Originaux et détraqués*, 1892; *La Noël au Canada*, 1900), Pamphile LE MAY (*Contes vrais*, 1899), and Honoré BEAUGRAND (*La chasse-galerie*, 1900)—the *terroir* remained the most common subject in short narratives until the 1930s.

The reason is that at the beginning of the twentieth century an important figure made his appearance on the literary scene: Abbé Camille Roy. In a sense he took over from Casgrain as the guiding light of French-Canadian literature. Following his 1904 lecture on the nationalization of the literature and the example offered by his descriptive and nostalgic 'fiction' entitled 'Le vieux hangar' (*Le Soleil*, 28 Oct. 1905), the *terroir* school was sustained by a cohort of writers including Adjutor Rivard (*Chez nous*, 1914; *Chez nos gens*, 1918); Lionel GROULX (*Les rapaillages*, subtitled *Vieilles choses, vieilles gens*, 1916); Frère MARIE-VICTORIN (*Récits laurentiens*, 1919; *Croquis laurentiens*, 1920); and Georges Bouchard, author of the collection *Vieilles choses, vieilles gens* (1926). The latter title could serve as a generic name for this sort of writing, which differs in form from the folkloric tales of the nineteenth century and yet is close to them in its ideological orientation: attention is still directed to the past, the good old days, which it is feared will vanish forever under the pressure of modernity. In fact, this tendency was institutionalized in the themes specified for literary competitions. Thus the Société Saint-Jean-Baptiste of Montreal invited participants in its annual literary competition to write on set themes, gathering the winning texts in collections such as *La croix de chemin* (1916), *La corvée* (1917), *Fleur de lys* (1918), and *Au pays de l'érable* (1919).

This is not to say that all the twentieth-century writers of the *terroir* school working in the short narrative or descriptive genre were dragooned under the same flag, or that they celebrated the land in the same tone or fashion. Humour and irony play their part in the work of Jean-Aubert LORANGER (*À la recherche du régionalisme: le village: contes et nouvelles du terroir*, 1925) and Clément MARCHAND (*Courriers des villages*, 1937), and these elements take on a sombre tone (to say the least) in the work of the naturalist Albert LABERGE. Known and ostracized since the publication of *La SCOUINE* in 1918, he came back against the odds with several collections of short stories (including *Visages de la vie et de la mort*, 1936) published at his own expense. Others such as 'Louis Dantin', the pseudonym of Eugène SEERS (*La vie en rêve*, 1930) and Léo DESROSIERS (*Âmes et paysages*, 1922) adopted a very personal tone, and some, like Jean-Charles HARVEY, in *L'homme qui va* (1929), distanced themselves from the *terroir* and on occasion even produced a kind of science-fiction or fantastic writing, quite new for that time.

Short stories in French

Contrary to common belief, it was not in the 1960s that literary modernism first emerged—at least where the short narrative is concerned—but in the 1940s, even if the *terroir* genre kept its momentum with important works by Germaine GUÈVREMONT (*En pleine terre*, 1942) and 'Ringuet', the pseudonym of Philippe PANNETON (*L'héritage*, 1946). With innovative writers such as François 'Hertel', the pseudonym of Rodolphe DUBÉ (*Mondes chimériques*, 1940), Yves THÉRIAULT (*Contes pour un homme seul*, 1944), Alain GRANDBOIS (*Avant le chaos*, 1945), Réal Benoît (*Nézon*, 1945), and Jean-Jules RICHARD (*Ville rouge*, 1949), the genre reached an unparalleled level of invention and narrative freedom.

A revealing detail from those years: François Hertel was a Jesuit who—unlike his predecessors Casgrain, Roy, Groulx, *et al.*—demonstrated a critical mind, using the form of the philosophical dialogue (modelled on Diderot)—a sign that times were changing. He was also an acquaintance of the painter Paul-Émile Borduas, a defender of abstraction since the beginning of the 1940s, who at the end of the decade would publish the pamphlet *REFUS GLOBAL* (1948), provoking the famous scandal that drove its author into exile. Though he took a different route from Borduas, in the end Hertel himself would choose a kind of refusal and exile—inscribed between the lines of his stories, many of which are critical essays disguised as fiction.

Thériault and Grandbois, on the other hand, are among the most renowned writers of the decade. Thériault made his literary début with *Contes pour un homme seul*, a work apparently in the tradition of the *terroir* school that nevertheless subverts its rules both in subtle details and as a whole. Far from downplaying harsh realities, he presented a universe marked by madness and violence. As for Grandbois, in *Avant le chaos* he presented the existential journey of a strongly autobiographical narrator, 'Alain', as he recounts his labyrinthine travels across Europe, Africa, and Asia between the wars. Although exotic, the stories in *Avant le chaos* actually express on the level of form the exploratory urge of the French Canadian eager to know the world and to give an account of it in his work. That said, the book is not simply a collection of travel stories; rather, it is the formal expression of a complex kind of discourse, apparently free of all canonical rules. In fact, the work reveals a new trend in the short narrative genre, one that was to crystallize over the following years: the complex story that distances itself from the 'simple' form and can resemble the essay. In fact, we are beginning to see not the death of the genre but the beginning of a hybridization of discursive forms, which had the effect of liberating the imagination and creating new forms in spite of the shock produced in the field of arts and letters by the repression imposed on Borduas. But artists were shaping their texts more carefully, with a kind of self-censorship.

This was particularly evident in the 1950s—a decade that produced only about twenty-five collections, compared with more than fifty in the 1940s—with Anne HÉBERT, herself a poet, who in the title story of *Le torrent* (1950) presents a man who seeks and loses himself in the turmoil of his emotions and thoughts. But there are also female characters in *Le torrent* who cry out their anguish and search desperately, in gentleness or in violence, for ways to attain a better world ('L'ange de Dominique', 'Le printemps de Catherine'). In a sense, *Les anges dans la ville* (1959) by Wilfrid Lemoine, another poet, belongs to the same register as *Le torrent*, the narrator of the last story closely resembling that of *Le torrent*'s title story.

Realism remained the dominant trend in the 1950s, but now it was women who were producing the most distinctive collections: Gabrielle ROY (*La petite poule d'eau*, 1950; *Rue Deschambault*, 1955), Adrienne CHOQUETTE (*La nuit ne dort pas*, 1954), and Claire MARTIN (*Avec ou sans amour*, 1958). Roy would continue to produce regularly over the following decades (*La route d'Altamont*, 1966; *Un jardin au bout du monde*, 1975; *Ces enfants de ma vie*, 1977); but it is Choquette (*Laure Clouet*, 1961; *Le temps des villages*, 1975) who seems to have left the most important mark in the world of the short story, for it was her name that in the 1980s would be associated with the establishment of the Prix Adrienne-Choquette, awarded for short stories. At the beginning of what has come to be known as the Quiet Revolution (1960-8), Choquette presented in *Laure Clouet* a woman who is both the inheritor and the prisoner of a long bourgeois tradition, living in a house on Quebec's Grande Allée as if it were a tomb. A letter from a young couple who are distant relatives turns her world upside down in a painful questioning, at the end of which she seems to opt for change. While some have seen in this long story an image of Quebec society in the throes of transformation, the real importance of the work derives above all from the exceptional quality of its writing. Choquette had been creating short stories since the beginning of the 1930s, but published most of them only in periodicals; Marie Naudin has collected a number of these texts in a collection entitled *Gerbes liées* (Guérin, 1990).

As early as the 1960s, however, Québécois were beginning to acquire a taste for anthologies. Gérard BESSETTE revived the work of Laberge (*Anthologie d'Albert Laberge*, 1962) and Adrien Thério launched a series of compilations (*Conteurs canadiens français*, 1965; *L'humour au Canada français*, 1968), an undertaking that he would tirelessly pursue through both new editions and new publications (*Conteurs québécois: 1900-1940*, 1988). Beginning in the late 1950s Thério also published numerous collections of his own stories combining the *terroir*, humour, and the bizarre (*Contes de belles saisons*, 1958; *Mes beaux meurtres*, 1961; *Ceux du chemin Taché*, 1963; *La tête en fête et autres histoires étranges*, 1975).

Among other phenomena marking this decade were, on one hand, the creation of a kind of hyper-realism around the periodical *PARTI PRIS* and the publishing house of the same name, and, on the other hand the appearance of fantastic literature and science fiction. At Les Éditions parti pris there developed what might be called the *JOUAL* school, even if it was one writer in particular, Jacques RENAUD (*Le cassé*, 1964), who had his characters speak this working-class form of French. André MAJOR (*La chair de poule*, 1965) and Claude JASMIN (*Les coeurs empaillés*, 1967) seemed less inclined to use *joual*, though they were fond of representing reality through the prism of social realism: they were thus faithful to the ideology of the periodical *parti pris*, which preached leftist ideas based on socialism, secularism, and Quebec independence.

Jacques FERRON published some of his novels with parti pris, but it was primarily as a teller of tales, with *CONTES DU PAYS INCERTAIN* (1962; *Tales from the uncertain country*, 1972) and *Contes anglais* (1964) that he gained recognition, especially since these works heralded the return to a kind of fantastic literature in Quebec—athough in some hands, such as Roch CARRIER's (*Jolis deuils*, 1964), it was somewhat closer to fantasy or magic realism. It was with Claude Mathieu (*La mort exquise*, 1965) and especially Michel TREMBLAY (*Contes pour buveurs attardés*, 1966; *Stories for late night drinkers*, 1977) that fantastic literature, as such, made its first appearance, Mathieu showing more originality than Tremblay, whose imaginary world more closely resembles that of the American Howard Phillips Lovecraft or the Belgian Jean Ray.

A privileged witness of his time, Yves Thériault came to the fore in this decade with no fewer than four collections of stories combining science fiction, the fantastic, the bizarre, and realism (*Le vendeur d'étoiles*, 1961; *Si la bombe m'était contée*, 1962; *La rose de pierre*, 1964; *L'île introuvable*, 1968).

While production increased in the 1960s, with almost a hundred collections, in the 1970s that point was greatly exceeded and the pace continued to accelerate until the total for the 1980s reached some two hundred. Names that would advance the Québécois history of the genre began to emerge: André Berthiaume (*Contretemps*, 1971); *Incidents de frontières*, 1984); Louis-Philippe Hébert (*Récits des temps ordinaires*, 1972); Jacques Brossard (*Le métamorfaux*, 1974); Claudette Charbonneau-Tissot, who now signs herself Aude (*Contes pour hydrocéphales adultes*, 1974; *Banc de brume*, 1987); André Carpentier (*Rue Saint-Denis*, 1978; *Du pain des oiseaux*, 1982; *Bread of the birds*, 1993); Marie José Thériault (*La cérémonie*, 1978; *The ceremony*, 1980); Diane-Monique Daviau (*Dessins à la plume*, 1979; Jean-Pierre April (*La machine à explorer la fiction*, 1980; *TéléToTaLiTé*, 1984; *Chocs baroques*, 1990); Élisabeth Vonarburg (*L'oeil de la nuit*, 1980; Jean Éthier-Blais (*Le manteau de Ruben Dario*, 1974); *Le désert blanc*, 1986); Madeleine FERRON (*Le chemin des dames*, 1977; *Le grand théâtre*, 1989); Gérard Bessette (*La garden-party de Christophine*, 1980); Gaétan Brulotte (*Le surveillant*, 1982; *Ce qui nous tient*, 1988); Bertrand Bergeron (*Parcours improbables*, 1986), Gilles Pellerin (*Ni le lieu ni l'heure*, 1987); André Major (*L'hiver au coeur*, 1987); and Esther Rochon (*Le traversier*, 1987).

The list could go on almost indefinitely, for among the hundreds of collections published since the 1960s we find a plethora of fine writers. Québécois are not only mastering, often remarkably well, the secrets of the short narrative form with its rhetoric continually playing on ellipses, silences, and the howl of the word, but are also practising most of the major contemporary genres (magic realism, science fiction, the fantastic, not to mention all the possible varieties in the field of realism alone, whether traditional or experimental).

What is striking is that a number of writers try their hands at many of these forms at the same time. For example, André Berthiaume, André Carpentier, and Gilles Pellerin apply themselves as much to realism and the fantastic as to science fiction. On the other hand, as a specialized circle has developed around fantastic literature and science fiction, some writers have situated themselves specifically in these fields, and in the 1970s they gathered around two periodicals in particular, *Solaris* and *Imagine*. . . . Among the principal figures in this group are Jean-Pierre April, Esther Rochon, and Élisabeth Vonarburg.

The 1980s seem remarkable not only for the quantity of the writing, but above all for its growing quality. This reflects in part the fact that more and more authors, defining themselves exclusively, or almost exclusively, as short-story writers, published increasingly polished works, but also the fact that seasoned writers were favouring periodicals and publishing houses specializing in short stories. In this plethora of works, two centres are particularly important. In Montreal, *XYZ: La revue de la nouvelle*, founded in 1985 by Gaëtan Lévesque, among others, rapidly attracted a number of writers, including André Carpentier, André Berthiaume, Diane-Monique Daviau, Bertrand Bergeron, Aude, Monique PROULX, Esther Rochon, and Marie José Thériault. As is often the case in Quebec, the periodical soon acquired a publishing house, XYZ éditeur, with the same primary vocation. The second important centre, the publishing house L'Instant même, was founded in Quebec City in 1986 by Gilles Pellerin; its principal mandate was to publish the winners of the Prix Adrienne-Choquette, but it also publishes a number of other writers of the first rank, among them Bertrand Bergeron, Roland Bourneuf, Jean-Pierre Girard, and Pellerin himself.

In the 1990s the phenomenal development of the short story continued unabated. Publishers' lists include the names of authors who have come to be recognized as masters of the genre, such as André Berthiaume (*Presqu'île dans la ville*, 1991), Bertrand Bergeron (*Visa pour le réel*, 1993), André Carpentier (*De ma blessure atteint*, 1990; *Carnet sur la fin possible d'un monde*, 1992, Diane-Monique Daviau (*La vie passe comme une étoile filante*, 1993), Jean Éthier-Blais (*Le Christ de Brioude*, 1990), Daniel Gagnon (*Circumnavigatrice*, 1990), Gilles Pellerin (*Je reviens avec la nuit*, 1992), Monique Proulx (*Les aurores boréales*, 1996), Esther Rochon (*Le piège à souvenirs*, 1991), Marie José Thériault (*Portraits d'Elsa*, 1990), and Élisabeth Vonarburg (*Ailleurs et au Japon*, 1991).

Newer writers of short stories (some known as novelists or poets) are: André BROCHU (*La croix du Nord*, 1991—winner of a Governor General's Award), Hugues Corriveau (*Attention, tu dors debout*, 1996), Louise Cotnoir (*La déconvenue*, 1993), Esther Croft (*Au commencement était le froid*, 1993), Francine D'Amour (*Écrire comme un chat*, 1994), Michel Dufour (*N'arrêtez pas la musique*, 1995), Jean Pierre Girard (*Léchées, timbrées*, 1993), Louis Jolicoeur (*Saisir l'absence*, 1994), Michael Delisle (*Helen avec un secret*, 1995), and Robert Lalonde (*Où vont les sizerins flammée en été?*, 1996).

In the 1990s Franco-Ontarian authors of short stories began to be noticed for the quality of their work and were published not only in Quebec but in Ontario—in Toronto, Ottawa, and Sudbury: Marguerite Andersen (*Courts métrages et instantanés*, 1991), Michel Dallaire (*Dans ma grande maison folle*, 1995), Maurice Henrie (*La savoyane*, 1996), Pierre Léon (*Le mariage politiquement correct du petit Chaperon rouge*, 1996), Daniel Poliquin (*Le canon de Gobelines*, 1995), and Pierre Karch (*Jeux de patience*, 1991). Karch—who teaches at York University, Toronto—edits the series of short-story collections L'Ère nouvelle, published, beginning in 1988, by XYZ, Montreal; the series is a confirmation of the interprovincial exchange in the field of francophone short stories. This interchange had an interesting and successful fruition in the anthology *Voix parallèles/Parallel voices* (1993), for which the eighteen participating authors —including Margaret ATWOOD, Monique Proulx, George BOWERING, and Hélène Rioux—each translated a story by one of the other contributors.

But that is not all. The rise of the short story has attracted many more publishers and readers to anthologies and collections of previously unpublished texts. In this context more than fifty publications have appeared, the best known being the series entitled Dix Contes et Nouvelles par dix Auteurs québécois (1983-7)—five collections of short stories edited by André Carpentier. Among the most recent anthologies, besides those already mentioned, are Maurice Émond, ed., *Anthologie de la nouvelle et du conte fantastiques québécois au XXe siècle* (1987); Michel Lord, ed., *Anthologie de la science-fiction québécoise contemporaine* (1988); François Gallays, ed., *Anthologie de la nouvelle au Québec* (1993); and Gilles Pellerin, ed., *Dix ans de nouvelles* (1996); while Éditions Nuit blanche, associated with the Centre de recherche en littérature québécoise, Université Laval, has published *La nouvelle québécoise au XXe siècle* (1996), edited by Lord and André Carpentier, which grew out of a conference at the Université du Québec à Montréal. The periodical *Tangence*, linked with the Université du Québec à Chicoutimi, has published an issue entitled 'Lectures de nouvelles québécoises' edited by Lord and Carpentier (no. 50, 1996). François Gallays, Université d'Ottawa, edited *La nouvelle au Québec* (1996), a series of articles on the short story in Quebec that is volume IX of the prestigious collection 'Archives des Lettres canadiennes'. European academics, such as those at the Centre d'étude de la nouvelle contemporaine de langue française, Louvain-la-Neuve, Belgium, increasingly include short stories from Quebec in their conferences, research, and publications (for example, Vincent Engel, *Le genre de la nouvelle dans le monde francophone au tournant du XXIe siècle*, 1995). It appears that the Quebec short story is on the way to international recognition. MICHEL LORD

Shouldice, Larry. See TRANSLATIONS: FRENCH TO ENGLISH: 4.

Simard, André. See DRAMA IN FRENCH 1948 TO 1981: 3.

Simard, Jean (b. 1916). Born in Quebec City of a middle-class family, he became an avid reader at an early age. He studied at the Petit Séminaire de Québec and the École des Beaux-Arts in Montreal, where he became a professor in 1940. He won the Prix Duvernay in 1963 and is a member of the Royal Society of Canada.

Simard's first novel, *Félix* (1947; rev. 1966, paperback edition, 1986), which won the Prix Kormann de l'Académie française, was published by Éditions Variétés, for which he worked as an illustrator. It is about the upbringing of a young man of good family living in puritan, middle-class Quebec. The narrator uses satire and caricature to attack clerical education, moral prejudice, and the ignorance and stupidity of his environment. In *Hôtel de la reine* (1949) the protagonist is the same sort of anti-conformist living in a small provincial village. Simard's third novel, *Mon fils pourtant heureux* (1956; 1968), concerns an older man who reassesses his early life. Having neither turned his back on liberal values nor wholly conformed to convention, he accepts his limitations in a mature and socially responsible manner. This middle course of subdued maturity reflects Simard's attitude to literature and to reality: he describes himself as an average author and modest craftsman in the field of letters. Awarded the Prix du Cercle du Livre de France, *Mon fils pourtant heureux* is considered his best novel. In 1957, with a CANADA COUNCIL grant, Simard spent fourteen months in Europe, where he wrote *Les sentiers de la nuit* (1959), his most sombre novel, in which he depicts the solitude and moral degradation of an Anglo-Canadian from Westmount. After ten years as an essayist and translator, Simard returned to the novel with *La séparation* (1970). Taking advantage of a temporary separation, two lovers, both married—Anna, who follows her husband to Portugal, and Carl, who remains in Montreal—correspond in the hope of clarifying their relationship.

In the sixties Simard turned to essay-writing and translation. *Répertoire* (1961) and *Nouveau répertoire* (1965) comprise reflections on art, literature, writing, travel, and Quebec society. The discontinuity and variety of subjects in these books are more reminiscent of the literary journal than the essay. In *Une façon de parler* (1973), Simard reflects on language and writing: his intention is to speak of his art as an artisan would speak of his tools, his only ambition being that of a good craftsman and an honest man.

Simard has also written a play, *L'ange interdit* (1961), and short stories, *13 récits* (1964) and *Le singe et le perroquet* (1983). He has translated numerous well-known English-Canadian books: two novels by Hugh MacLENNAN (*BAROMETER RISING* and *The watch that ends the night*), three by Mordecai RICHLER (*Son of a smaller hero*, *The APPRENTICESHIP OF DUDDY KRAVITZ*, and *Jacob Two-Two meets the hooded fang*), as well as *The educated imagination* by Northrop FRYE and *The long journey: the literary themes of French Canada* by Jack Warwick.

See Jean-Charles Falardeau, 'Présentation de M. Jean Simard', *Société royale du Canada* 18 (1963-4); Pierre de Grandpré, 'La satire affûte ses traits', *Dix ans de vie littéraire au Canada français* (1966); and André Belleau, *Le romancier fictif: essai sur la représentation de l'écrivain dans le roman québécois* (1980) JACQUES MICHON

Simcoe, Elizabeth. See Writing in ONTARIO: 1.

Sime, Jessie Georgina (1868-1958). She was born in Scotland, daughter of Jessie Wilson and James Sime. At the age of eleven she moved with her parents to London, England, where, through her parents, both writers, Sime became acquainted with such notable Victorian writers as Thomas Carlyle and William Morris. Immigrating to Montreal in 1907, she soon became involved in the city's literary and intellectual community. Sime was an early modernist and realist, in her fiction and non-fiction directing attention to the social, economic, and emotional difficulties of working-class women and the urban poor. Her fiction includes *Sister woman* (1919; rpr. with an introduction by Sandra Campbell, 1992), stories mainly about working-class immigrants to Canada, and *Our little life: a novel of today* (1921; rpr. with an introduction by K. Jane Watt, 1994): set in Montreal, it is a significant early attempt at urban realism in Canadian fiction. Sime may have returned to England about 1950.

LORRAINE McMULLEN

Simonds, Merilyn. See NOVELS IN ENGLISH 1983 TO 1996: OTHER NOVELS 1(b).

Simons, Beverley (b. 1938). Born in Flin Flon, Manitoba, Simons grew up in Edmonton, Alberta, and was preparing for a career as a concert pianist when she won a creative-writing scholarship to the Banff School of Fine Arts for her one-act verse drama, *Twisted roots* (1956). After two years at McGill University, where she formed an experimental theatre group, she completed her B.A. in English and theatre at the University of British Columbia in 1959. Following two more years of working and studying in Europe, she settled in Vancouver and produced several stage, television, and film scripts while raising a young family. In 1968 she spent two months in the Far East studying theatre, and in 1972 she received a CANADA COUNCIL Senior Arts Award. Criticism over the award and continual difficulties in getting her plays produced, however, led her to abandon playwriting in the mid-seventies. While most of her plays have been published and are often studied in drama courses, her work is rarely performed.

Simons' work is highly personal, abstract, and symbolic. *Crabdance* (1969) has been aptly compared to *Waiting for Godot*: in both plays a small cast of characters, in a setting that is 'suggestive rather than detailed', performs the rituals and word-games that denote a meaningless existence and the failure of communication. While Beckett's Vladimir and Estragon wait, Sadie Golden prepares for an inevitable end. The emptiness of her life is gradually revealed as she struggles to assert her significance in a series of ritualistic relationships with three visiting salesmen. But, tragically, her efforts to use the buyer-seller, mother-son, wife-husband, mistress-lover roles for self-discovery become confused circular patterns of exploitation and victimization that can be resolved only by her death. In *Green Lawn Rest Home* (1973), a one-act play, Simons again reveals how fragile and pointless one's sense of identity is as three elderly residents of a nursing home experience the loss of their senses, passions, and memories in a series of empty social rituals that do nothing to calm their fear of the death they cannot mention. *Preparing* (1975) is a quartet of short plays—*Preparing*, *Prologue*, *Triangle*, and *The crusader*—that offer different models of the preparation for death. They employ experimental forms ranging from the naturalistic one-woman monologue of the title play, through the formalistic patterning of *Triangle*, to the stylized rituals of Japanese theatre in *The crusader*. Simons' experimentation with form, however, is most radical in *Leela means to play* (1976). Relying heavily on the symbolic devices of oriental theatre, it destroys conventional time and space with an episodic exploration of 'man's evolution through relationships, the interaction of people from his past and present'. In Simons' plays there is a progression from the personal rituals shaping *Crabdance* to the formal rituals that define *Leela means to play*, and this gradual solidification of form becomes an effective metaphor for her view of life as a preparation for death, the final meaningless ritual.

ELIZABETH HOPKINS

Simpson, Sir George. See EXPLORATION LITERATURE IN ENGLISH: 2.

Simpson, Leo (b. 1934). Leo James Pascal Simpson was born in Limerick, Ireland, and was educated in that country. He lived in England and Spain before coming to Canada in 1961. After working as publicity director and editor at MACMILLAN OF CANADA, he moved to Queensborough Township north of Belleville, Ontario, in 1966 and then settled in Madoc in 1972. He and his wife Jacqueline spent years completely and faithfully restoring the Susanna MOODIE house in Belleville, moving into the house in 1987. He was writer-in-residence at the University of Ottawa (1973-4) and the University of Western Ontario (1976-7).

Simpson is a rarity among Canadian writers, a comic novelist of ideas. His protagonists continually find themselves in absurd plights when they struggle to purge the evil influences of contemporary technology and business, and of small-town conformity. Addison Arkwright, the hero of Simpson's ambitious first novel, *Arkwright* (1971), describes himself as 'holding my ripped humanity together comically'. A violent iconoclast, he is obsessed with exposing his multi-millionaire uncle's scheme to exploit a bogus religion founded on the exaltation of failure, and is torn by contrary and ineffectual impulses throughout most of the novel. He finally attains an idyllic refuge in Crete, though he imagines that he will be forever engaged in seeking personal 'reformation'.

Two of Simpson's other novels, *The Peacock papers* (1973) and *Kowalski's last chance* (1980), are set in Bradfarrow, modelled on Belleville. Jeffrey Anchyr, the intellectual upper-class protagonist of *The Peacock papers*, and Joe Kowalski, a low-brow policeman, have in common their sense of contact with a fantasy realm scorned by their obtuse fellow-citizens. Anchyr believes himself to be guided by the nineteenth-century British novelist Thomas Love Peacock in a campaign to resist the conversion of the Bradfarrow Public Library into a computerized Data Centre, a scheme undertaken by a character based on Marshall McLUHAN. In part a loving imitation of the real Peacock's fiction, the novel upholds Peacock's preaching of traditional humanism and attacks the false faith of communications technology. The events of the book take a tragi-comic turn when Anchyr, troubled by 'much confused dying' in the modern world, proves a martyr to his sensitivity. Joe Kowalski, equally sensitive in his own sphere to human injustice, is persecuted by his chief for taking pity on an alleged bank robber who declares himself to be a leprechaun. Unlike *The Peacock papers*, *Kowalski's last chance* focuses on social rather than intellectual satire, but in both novels Simpson concocts an ingenious blend of fantasy, farce, and intellectual insight.

The lady and the travelling salesman: stories by Leo Simpson (1979) collects stories written over the previous decade and a half. Many involve the sudden reversal of stereotyped roles, as in the title story, in which an arms salesman is assaulted by a militant dogooder, or 'The savages', in which teenagers on the rampage are massacred by an earnest computer expert.

Both the themes and manner of Simpson's previous work can be found, in as lively and challenging a form as ever, in *Sailor man* (1996). Part of this novel is set in Belleville, but most of it takes place within an Ottawa commercial and residential complex that in its comprehensive range of money-making services, from a hospital maternity wing to a nursing home, is an emblem of the greed of contemporary hucksterism and a distortion of the role of a traditional community. Drawing on the stock roles of *commedia dell'arte* for his own symbolic purposes, Simpson relies on a witty narrator and farcical confrontation scenes to create a darkly comic vision of contemporary alienation: technology no longer seems to be an evil in itself so much as an easy target for commercial manipulation. Like all Simpson's fiction, *Sailor man* is playfully inventive, but also fundamentally serious in its skeptical view of contemporary life.

THOMAS E. TAUSKY

Sinclair, Lister. See DRAMA IN ENGLISH 1953 TO 1981.

Sirois, Serge. See DRAMA IN FRENCH 1948 TO 1981: 3.

Skelton, Robin (1925-97). He was born at Easington, England, emigrating after his education at Christ's College, Cambridge, and the University of Leeds (B.A., 1950, M.A., 1951). In 1963 he joined the Department of English at the University of Victoria, British Columbia, establishing a network between that university and British writers that would enrich the creative-writing department, which he founded in 1967, staying on as head until 1976. A renaissance man, who perhaps would prefer to be primarily regarded as a poet, Robin Skelton was also a scholar, editor, biographer, critic, mentor, literary angel, visual artist, and translator.

Despite the chiaroscuro of Skelton's poems—which, starting with *Patmos and other poems* (1955), extend to several baker's dozens of volumes, including a *Selected shorter poems 1947-1977* (1981) and *One leaf shaking: collected later poems* (1996)—he was, in his own words, always 'marching syntax toward a ceremony of love'. This march was measured by his understanding and devotion to form, to writing as a monastic discipline. Unlike most contemporary poets, he believed that the shape of the poem is a conscious component in the act of writing—implying discipline, while not denying sensuality, passion, or intimacy. There is always a perceptible restraint: Skelton the shaman transcends Skelton the man. The poet, dressed in black with a snow white beard like that of some Celtic Father Christmas, wearing exotic jewelry, is the persona presented in the many volumes of verse that mark his career as a writer and consummate performer. The thrilling voice that made his readings memorable can almost be heard in every poem as it explores and re-explores the exile's no-man's-land of memory and desire.

Skelton's short fiction, like his children's poems and stories, *I am me* (1994) and *Long, long ago* (1995), illuminates the dark corners inhabited by an often melancholic poet who also had lighter moments. A lover of language, he took delight in its comic arrangements, as a child does. His fiction titles, including *The parrot who could* (1987), *Hanky panky* (1990), and *Higgledy piggledy* (1992), suggest the playfulness of the stories.

Skelton, a respected scholar of Anglo-Irish literature, was the author of *The writings of J.M. Synge* (1971), *J.M. Synge and his world* (1971), *J.M. Synge* (1972), and *The world of W.B. Yeats* (1965, with Ann Saddlemyer). He also edited the work of English and North American poets for various anthologies, including *Poetry of the thirties* (1964), *Poetry of the forties* (1968), *The Cavalier poets* (1970), *Five poets of the Pacific Northwest* (1964), and *Six poets of British Columbia* (1980).

Editing and encouraging other writers were hallmarks of Skelton's career. In England he was editor of Lotus Press (1950-51). With John Peter he was a founding editor of *The MALAHAT REVIEW*, which quickly acquired an international reputation. The Thursday-night salons at the house of Robin and Sylvia Skelton were for many years a catalyst in the dialogue between Victoria's artistic communities—which the Skeltons, he as poet and visual artist and she as artist/calligrapher, were much involved in.

The Skeltons were also members of the Limners, a loose association of artists and friends, including the painters Myfanwy Pavelic and Herbert Siebner, which has been seminal to the artistic development of Victoria. Robin Skelton's writings about the visual arts included *Painters talking* (1957), *Herbert Siebner* (1979), and *House of dreams* (1983).

A practising healer, Skelton drew upon the tradition of witchcraft in his obsession for finding the language for making spells to heal a troubled world, and shapes to cut out and paste in collages of found wisdom that reveal the lost-and-found aspects of truth—an English tradition he endeavoured to impress on the New World in as many ways as he could think of. Some of his books on the occult are *Spellcraft* (1978), *Talismanic magic* (1985), and *The practice of witchcraft* (1995).

Following Skelton's retirement, he devoted himself entirely to writing, and to the joint editorship (with Charles LILLARD, Rhonda Batchelor, Sylvia Skelton, and Guy Chadsey) of Reference West, a chapbook series associated with Hawthorne Books, which hosts poetry readings encouraging indigenous writers.

Skelton's *Memoirs of a literary blockhead* (1988) tell much of his story, but does not mention the high esteem in which he was held. Like the late George WOODCOCK, he was a compulsive writer with an enormous body of published work. Some would argue that he published too much, thus obscuring his best writing. But there is no argument about his enormous contribution to literature. See Barbara E. Tuner, ed. *Skelton at 60* (1986), a tribute to Skelton from sixty writers and artists. LINDA ROGERS

Škvor, George (1916-81). George Škvor (Jiři Škvor), who wrote under the name 'Pavel Javor', was born in the South Bohemian village of Martinice, Czechoslovakia, and educated at Charles University, Prague. During and immediately following the Second World War, he worked with the Czech Cultural Council and served as deputy member of the House of Commons. When the Communists ordered his arrest, he fled to West Germany and then settled in Montreal in 1960. He took his doctoral degree in Slavic letters at the Université de Montréal in 1960. At the time of his death he was employed as a producer and broadcaster with Radio-Canada International—always a critic of the Soviet system. He died of complications following a routine medical operation in a Montreal hospital; at a time when defectors from Eastern Europe were being harassed and slain in the West, questions about his demise were raised in the House of Commons.

Javor published six books of poems in Czechoslovakia between 1938 and 1946, and another thirteen abroad from 1951 to 1980. For his achievement he was recognized by critic Petr Den as 'the official poet of Czech exile'. Ron D.K. Banerjee translated a selection of Javor's poems, titled *Far from you* (1981). It includes an essay on the poet by Marie Nemcova Banerjee and a bibliography of Javor's work in Czech, German, and French, which is complete except for the posthumous appearance of *Plamen a pisen* ('A flame and a song', 1981), issued by Sixty-Eight Publishers in Toronto.

Javor's poetry is characterized by the romantic desire to return to the comforting countryside of childhood and the reassuring values of village life. Underlying this is an awareness of the harsh blow that history dealt to the patriotic ideals of Masaryk's First Republic, which inspired the hearts and heads of an entire generation. Javor expressed regrets about the past and apprehensions about the future. Melancholy verging on sentimentality pervades much of his poetry: in Maria Bemcova Banerjee's words, Pavel Javor was 'the last poet of the Czech village.'

JOHN ROBERT COLOMBO

Škvorecký, Josef (b. 1924). Born in Nachod, Bohemia, then Czechoslovakia, he entered the faculty of medicine at Charles University, Prague, but soon transferred to philosophy, graduating in 1949 and receiving his Ph.D. in 1951. Over the next two decades he was a teacher in a girls' school, a translator of contemporary American fiction (including Faulkner's *A fable*), an editor on the Prague magazine *World Literature*, and a scriptwriter working with, among others, Miloš Forman and Jirí Menzel (Closely Watched Trains). From the early 1950s he was a central figure in the post-war Czechoslovak cultural renaissance, much of whose impetus came from the underground circle of writers and artists in Prague. In 1968, after the Soviet invasion of Czechoslovakia, Škvorecký immigrated to Canada with his wife, the writer-actress Zdena Salivarova, and became a professor of English at the University of Toronto. In 1971 he and his wife founded the Czech publishing house Sixty-Eight Publishers, which during the next 20 years published over 200 books banned in their homeland. He retired from teaching in 1990, and in the same year President Václav Havel awarded the Škvoreckýs the Order of the White Lion, Czechoslovakia's highest award for foreigners (they are Canadian citizens). Škvorecký has written and edited over 50 books, including novels, mysteries, and works of literary, music, and film criticism. The majority of his novels and short stories have been translated into English, with the best-known novels being *The cowards*, *The bass saxophone*, *Miss Silver's past*, *The miracle game*, and *The engineer of human souls*.

The publication of his first novel *Zbabelci* (1958)—later translated as *The cowards* (1970)—resulted in the banning of the book, Škvorecký's loss of his editorial post, and an extensive purge of the intellectual community. In the next ten years Škvorecký published novels, novellas, and short-story collections. Works from this period available in English translation are *The mournful demeanor of Lieutenant Boruvka* (1974), a collection of mystery stories; *The bass saxophone and Emoke* (novellas), published in one volume in 1977; and *Miss Silver's past* (1975), a mystery novel dealing with literature and censorship in a totalitarian society. In Canada during the 1970s he published in Czech two of his most ambitious and longest novels: *Mirákl* (1972)—*The miracle game* (1990)—and *Príbeh inzenýra lidských duší* (1977)—*The engineer of human souls* (1984). The latter was awarded a Governor General's Award.

The highest praise of Škvorecký's work has come from Graham Greene, for whom *The bass saxophone* and *Emoke* are 'in the same rank as James Joyce's *The dead* and the very best of Henry James's shorter novels'. The first deals with a young Czechoslovak who plays bass saxophone for a German band during the Second World War; the second is a poignant love story about a relatively cynical young man's attempt to seduce Emoke, a woman who doesn't seem to believe that love is possible in Communist Czechoslovakia. Yet Škvorecký's most substantial work seems to be in the longer novels, *The cowards*, *The miracle game*, and *The engineer of human souls*, which form part of a cycle dealing with the life and times of Daniel Smirický, a thinly disguised portrait of the author. Also in the series are *The republic of whores* (1993) and the interrelated stories of *Prima sezona*, which have been translated into English as *The swell season* (1982). The series spans forty years in Danny's life, beginning in wartime Czechoslovakia (*The cowards*) and ending in Canada of the 1970s (*Engineer of human souls*). Smirický fulfils the role of an everyman who, as an East European, has experienced some of the tragic events of the past half-century.

The concern with Czechs and history is taken in a new direction in *Dvorak in love* (1986). While the focus is on the Czech composer's life and work, especially his visit to the United States in the 1890s, the novel also deals with nearly fifty years of Czech and Slovak history and the lives of other Czechs and Slovaks who immigrated to the United States. Škvorecký's research for the novel led directly to *The bride of Texas* (1995), which is also set in the United States, but thirty years earlier during the Civil War. Like *Dvorak in love*, the novel is polyphonic and the characters and events (especially Sherman's march through the South) are described from various perspectives. Two other important narratives involve the Czech Toupelik family, especially their daughter Lida—the 'bride' of the title—and Lorraine Henderson Tracy, a writer with feminist tendencies. With *The bride of Texas*, Škvorecký's novels as a group offer a 150-year fictional social history of the Czech people.

If one of Škvorecký's dominant themes is man's fate in history, his other is the central function played by art (Smirický is a writer), which is a metaphor for freedom and free activity—a means of resisting the ideological demands of a state that insists on writing and rewriting reality and history to suit its needs. The writers and jazz musicians of Škvorecký's fiction, whether they know it or not, are what Solzhenitsyn calls a 'second government'—people who use art to celebrate the dignity and worth of human life, the necessity of certain basic human freedoms, and so on. While Škvorecký's themes are serious and weighty, there is an unsettling interweaving of the tragic and the comic in his fiction. His books are the work of a natural storyteller with a fundamentally ironic vision.

Škvorecký has also written literary criticism: essays on contemporary Czech literature, introductions to books by Czech writers, and regular Voice of America broadcasts on American, Canadian, and British literature for transmission to Czechoslovakia. His most substantial work of non-fiction is the autobiographical and historical book on the Czech cinema, *All the bright young men and women* (1972, 1975). For an autobiographical perspective on Škvorecký's years in Czechoslovakia, especially the 1950s and 1960s, the essay 'I was born in Nachod' (in *Talkin' Moscow blues*, 1988) and the memoir (with ten stories) *Headed for the blues* (1996) are particularly interesting.

An issue of the American critical journal *World Literature Today* (Autumn 1981) was devoted to the work of Škvorecký, who was awarded the prestigious Neustadt Prize for literature in 1980. Sam Solecki's *Prague blues: the fiction of Josef Škvorecký* (1990) and Paul Trensky's *The fiction of Josef Škvorecký* (1991) are book-length studies; the former has a useful bibliography; Solecki has also edited *The achievement of Josef Škvorecký* (1994), a collection of essays. There is a chapter on Škvorecký's fiction in Helena Kosková's *Hledání ztracené generace* (1987). *Danny*, a Czech journal based in Prague, is devoted to reviews, essays, and memoirs about Škvorecký's work. SAM SOLECKI

Slater, Christine. See NOVELS IN ENGLISH 1983 TO 1996: OTHER NOVELS 3.

Slater, Patrick. Pseudonym of John MITCHELL.

Slavutych, Yar. See UKRAINIAN-CANADIAN LITERATURE.

Smart, Elizabeth (1913-86). Born in Ottawa, Ontario, she was the daughter of a lawyer who was a member of the Anglo-Canadian social establishment. She attended Hatfield Hall, a private school, and at eighteen travelled to England to study piano under Katharine Goodson. When she returned to Canada in 1933, she briefly joined the staff of the *Ottawa Journal*, writing society notes. In 1937, she spent six months as the private secretary to Mrs Alfred Watts, head of the Associated Country Women of the World, on a world tour to promote the organization. With the ambition to become a writer, she submitted poems to Lawrence Durrell's Paris magazine *Booster* and, at his suggestion, began a literary correspondence with the English poet George Barker. While staying at a writers' colony in Big Sur, California, in the fall of 1940, she secured passage for Barker and his wife to the United States. A passionate love affair ensued. He became the father of her four children.

In 1941 Smart travelled alone to Pender Harbour, British Columbia, where she completed her first novel, *BY GRAND CENTRAL STATION I SAT DOWN AND WEPT* (1945), a prose poem—part incantation and part cry of pain—about passion and the loss of love. (It was reissued in England in 1966, with a Foreword by the English critic Brigid Brophy.) After giving birth in Pender Harbour to her first child, Smart took a job as a file clerk in the British Army Office in Washington, D.C., to be with Barker, who had been barred from entry into Canada on her mother's instigation. She was transferred to the Ministry of Defence in London in 1943, and supported herself and her children for the next two decades by writing copy for fashion magazines like *Vogue* and *Queen*, of which she became literary editor.

In 1977, following almost three decades of silence, Smart published a collection of poems, *A bonus*. After the poetic, incantatory style of her novel, it is surprising in its casual conversational language and clipped rhythms. The poet is less interested in metaphor and image than in theme. The book is largely about writing: the struggle to speak when silence is seductive; the battle against a sense of inadequacy; the release and elation that comes out of the pain of writing. The impulse to order and cultivate is explored in many poems about gardening. The poems in *A bonus* are not profound, but they are moving in their efforts to examine the problems of the writer who chooses to abandon the distractions of love for the necessary self-absorption of the artist: 'Growing is the strange death in life that nobody mourns.'

Smart's second novel, *The assumption of the rogues and rascals* (1978), like its predecessor, is essentially a poetic meditation without a plot structure. Set in postwar England, it explores the psychology of a woman of thirty-one, trapped in despair, who 'stops at its ardent, obstreperous source, every hopeful passion', and who cannot decide whether her hell is self-created or life's failure. The novel is structured by means of associations: snippets of conversation, dreams, memories (the fiction of Samuel Beckett provides a precedent). The rogues and rascals of the title—the misfits who at least have the courage to resist the forces of normalcy and mediocrity—are the outlawed. The novel ends with the dilemma of the writer—how and why to write—and offers an archetypal model: Philoctetes, isolated on his island with his body a running sore.

Smart lived in Canada from 1982 to 1984, and, encouraged by the poet Alice VanWart, contemplated publishing her journals. In 1984 she published an interim collection of her writings, *In the meantime*, which contains the remarkably titled story 'Dig a grave and let us bury our mother', written in 1940 while Smart stayed briefly in Mexico with the surrealist painters Wolfgang Paalen and Alice Rahon. It is the story of a love affair between two women, recorded with an erotic intensity that would have been shocking in its day. The book also contains poems and a diary from which the book draws its title: 'In the meantime: diary of a blockage'. The year before Smart died, the first volume of her journals appeared: *Necessary secrets*, edited by VanWart. Recording Smart's life from 1933 to 1941, it makes clear that the diary form was—for Smart, as it was for Virginia Woolf—less a space for confession than for rigorous experimentation as she undertook her self-imposed apprenticeship in writing. Some of the lyrical passages about landscape and love from Smart's early entries would eventually appear in her novel *By Grand Central Station I sat down and wept*.

After Smart's death, a number of new books appeared: *Autobiographies* (1987), edited by Christina Burridge, a miscellaneous collection of Smart's documents, letters, and journals dating from 1940 to 1982; *Juvenilia* (1987) edited by VanWart, a collection of early stories written between the ages of eleven and nineteen, with family letters; and *Elizabeth's garden: Elizabeth Smart on the art of gardening* (1989), which collects some of the columns she wrote for the British magazine *Harper's Bazaar*, with excerpts from her garden journals. Smart was a celebrated gardener; her garden in Suffolk was featured in an issue of *Harper's Queen* in 1975. *The collected poems*, with a forward by the British poet David Gascoyne, was published in 1992 and adds significantly to the material in *A bonus*. What Gascoyne called her 'wry', 'cheeky' truthfulness is evident in poems like 'All I know about why I write', but the most moving poem in the volume is the harrowing elegy to her daughter, Rose, who died at the age of thirty-five. *On the side of the angels* (1994), the second volume of Smart's journals dating from the 1940s to the 1980s, was also edited by VanWart. Its often exquisite lyric prose and subject—the intense confrontation with the difficulties of trying to live as mother and writer, explored with such candour as to become universal—confirmed Smart's talent for the autobiographical mode. The aphorisms she crafted to render a compassionate account of life's frustrations, particularly for women, are often brilliant, and make her journals an important contribution to women's writing.

For further reading on Smart, see the play *Memories of you* (1989) by Wendy LILL, based on Smart's life, and Rosemary SULLIVAN's biography *By heart: Elizabeth Smart/a life* (1991). ROSEMARY SULLIVAN

Smith, A.J.M. (1902-80). Arthur James Marshall Smith was born in Westmount, Montreal, the only son of English immigrant parents. He attended Westmount High School, but in his second year was taken to England, where he lived from 1918 to 1920, studied for the Cambridge Local Examinations, 'and failed everything except English and history' (he later wrote). However, in London he frequented Harold Monroe's bookshop, then the citadel of Georgian poetry, and read much in the recent war poets and the Imagists. On his return to Montreal in 1920 he completed his high-school studies, graduated in 1921, and in the same year was admitted to McGill where, yielding to parental pressure, he studied for a Bachelor of Science degree; but during his undergraduate years he edited a singularly mature *Literary Supplement* to the *McGill Daily*, in which some of his early poems appeared. On graduating in 1925, he undertook a Master's program in English and wrote a dissertation on Yeats and the Symbolist movement. At this time he met F.R. SCOTT, newly returned from Oxford. Both were in full revolt against Montreal's lingering Victorianism and conservatism, and both felt their vocation to be poetry, although Scott was studying law. The two founded *The* McGILL FORTNIGHTLY REVIEW (1925-7), which, behind its solemn title, displayed an artistic and political maturity that exerted an influence beyond the collegiate boundaries, and in effect represented the innovative spirit of the 1920s in Canada. *The McGill Fortnightly* drew to it other young writers—among them A.M. KLEIN, Leo KENNEDY, and Leon EDEL—on whom, as well as on Scott, Smith had an enduring influence. Smith in turn came under the influence of a young biology professor at

McGill, Lancelot Hogben (the future author of *Mathematics for the million* and a peripheral figure in London's Bloomsbury). Hogben, who wrote pseudonymous poems for *The McGill Fortnightly*, gave Smith the early poems of T.S. Eliot to read, and encouraged him in his revolt against philistinism and Montreal parochialism.

After receiving his M.A. in 1926, Smith taught briefly in a Montreal high school and then received a fellowship for study in Edinburgh, where he worked with H.J.C. Grierson, the pre-eminent authority on Donne, and began a doctoral dissertation on the metaphysical poets of the Anglican Church in the seventeenth century (Ph.D. 1931). Returning to Canada during the Depression, Smith was unable to find an academic post and taught in a series of small American colleges until he received an appointment at Michigan State College (later University). There he remained during the rest of his career and was, in later years, poet-in-residence. He became a naturalized American, but spent all his summers in his country place near Magog, Quebec.

In 1936 Smith, Scott, Klein, and Kennedy—the 'MONTREAL GROUP', as they now began to be called—joined with E.J. PRATT and Robert FINCH of Toronto in producing *NEW PROVINCES: poems of several authors*, (1936; rpr. 1976), a landmark in Canada's modern poetry. Smith wrote a lightly ironic and mocking preface about the concern of Canada's poets with 'pine trees, the open road, God, snowshoes or Pan', and added: 'The most popular experience is to be pained, hurt, stabbed or seared by beauty—preferably by the yellow flame of a crocus in the spring or the red flame of a maple leaf in the autumn.' The Toronto contributors felt Smith's words would produce a controversy at the expense of the volume's contents, and the preface was shelved in favour of a brief anonymous foreword (by Scott). It pointed out that the poems, appearing in the mid-thirties during an economic Depression, in reality reflected innovations of the 1920s in 'freer diction and more elastic forms'. It added that 'the search for new content was less successful than had been the search for new techniques.' Smith published his 'rejected' preface thirty-five years later in *Towards a view of Canadian letters* (1973) and in the 1976 reprint of *New provinces*, showing that he had also expressed in it his own poetic stance: a disciplining of form and emotion by which intensity is attained; a sense of the poem as 'a thing in itself'; the discarding of artificial forms (like mechanical rhyme) in favour of 'arbitrarily chosen verse patterns'. The poems in *New provinces* had an impact on Canadian verse far beyond any prefatorial pronouncements: in its implicit call for new findings and new attitudes in Canadian writing, it might be likened to the effect of the Wordsworth-Coleridge *Lyrical ballads* in 1798 on the Romantics. Smith included in this anthology at least five of his own poems that were destined for wide publication: the repeatedly anthologized 'The lonely land', 'The creek', 'News of the phoenix', 'Like an old proud king in a parable', and 'The two sides of the drum'. The effect of *New provinces* was that it established the 'Montreal Group' as the Canadian avant-garde of its time.

During his twenties and thirties Smith wrote a great deal of poetry: some of it appeared in *The CANADIAN FORUM*; the *Dial*, then edited by Marianne Moore; *Poetry* (Chicago); and in England he was published in *New Verse*. He created a kind of reservoir of his poems—some 200—which, in the ensuing years, he polished and published in his five collections. The first did not appear in book form until he was forty-one: *News of the phoenix and other poems* (1943), which won a Governor General's Award. *A sort of ecstasy: poems new and selected* (1954) reprinted one third of the *Phoenix* and added some twenty new poems. *Collected poems* (1962) contained 75 poems from the two previous collections and 25 not hitherto collected: 100 good poems, Smith argued, represented sufficient yield for any poet's lifetime. In reprinting this collection as *Poems new and collected* (1967), Smith retained 99 poems, but added another 22. In *The classic shade: selected poems* (1978) he used 60 poems from the previous collection and added some 20 occasional, satiric, and burlesque poems. In four of these collections Smith used a single epigraph from Santayana: 'Every animal has his festive and ceremonious moments, when he poses or plumes himself or thinks: sometimes he even sings and flies aloft in a sort of ecstasy.' This remained Smith's permanent view of his own poetry—that its function was decorative or ornamental—and caused critics to characterize his verse as 'lapidary'. A posthumous collected poems may reveal a more abundant Smith and reflect not simply his own judgement of his work.

Smith was master of a wide range of styles: he used pastiche, satire, burlesque, and bawdy. Yet his ribaldry could give way to simple lyricism and sensuality; he was on occasion meditative, and often colloquial. He was always authoritative, and always in quest of formal beauty, so that George WOODCOCK spoke of him as being 'among the most memorable lyric poets writing in the whole English-speaking world.' Northrop FRYE discerned the same lyrical qualities, but felt the poems betrayed a certain lack of energy. Smith defined his own tendency to the 'metaphysical' as expressing 'ideas that have entered so deeply into the blood as never to be questioned.' His poems possess an aristocratic coolness and a shrinking from common vulgarities; they also show a singular joy in life and an uneasy fear of death. The life-game of love is subsumed in his bawdy. The world's irrationalities and aggressivities are mocked and vigorously attacked, as in his poem 'News of the phoenix', or in his mordant verses on the atom bomb.

Almost entirely devoted to his worldly muse, Smith channelled much of his energy into anthologies, calling himself a 'compulsive anthologist'. In middle life he produced his *Book of Canadian poetry: a critical and historical anthology* (1943; 2nd edn 1948; 3rd edn 1957), a college anthology that became a kind of national textbook, forming the taste of younger poets and encouraging the wider reading of poetry in Canada. In this anthology one discerns Smith's insistence upon control and discipline in art. His *Oxford book of Canadian verse: in English and French* (1960), with its important introductory essay, refines his earlier selections and gains an even greater importance by including French-Canadian poetry. Smith's other Canadian anthologies are *Modern Canadian verse* (1967), again both in English and French; *The blasted pine*, with F.R. Scott (1957; rev. 1967), which bears the lengthy subtitle *An anthology of satire, invective and disrespectful verse chiefly by Canadian writers*; and *Masks of fiction: Canadian critics on Canadian prose* (1961) and *Masks of poetry: Canadian critics on Canadian verse* (1962), both edited for the NEW CANADIAN LIBRARY. For the college market he edited *The book of Canadian prose, volume 1: early beginnings to Confederation* (1965), the second volume of which was published as *The Canadian century: English-Canadian writing since Confederation* (1973); a selection from these two volumes was published in *The Canadian experience: a brief survey of English-Canadian prose* (1974). Smith also edited several non-Canadian anthologies that were published in New York. *The worldly muse* (1951) is a delightful but little-known anthology of 'serious light verse' issued by Abelard Press, which lost most of the stock in a warehouse fire shortly after publication. For the American college market Smith edited *Seven centuries of verse* (1947; 3rd edn 1966); *100 poems* (1965); *Essays for college writing* (1965); and, with M.L. Rosenthal, *Exploring poetry* (1955; 2nd edn 1973).

Smith's critical essays—written in an easy, lucid, and sometimes poetic prose—reassert his doctrines of intensity gained through discipline; the negative effects of colonialism, which Smith equated with parochialism; and his reiterated belief that a poem is 'not the description of an experience, it is in itself an experience.' His essays were collected in *Towards a view of Canadian letters: selected critical essays 1928-1971* (1973) and in *On poetry and poets: selected essays of A.J.M. Smith* (1977) in the New Canadian Library.

Smith was one of the most influential figures in Canadian poetry in the twentieth century. As a critic and anthologist he set, for the first time in Canada, high standards of poetic taste and discrimination; as a poet who combined classical Anglo-American forms with the modern temper, he infused an assured cosmopolitan strain into modern Canadian poetry—though towards the end of his life Smith felt, incorrectly, that the new generation's use of looser and less-demanding forms had shelved his own work. Whatever the vagaries of his reputation as both poet and critic, his total achievement marks Smith as a vigorous but also delicate reformer of Canadian taste through the power of his knowledge, wit, and craft. The high versatility of his considerable body of writings shapes a consistent theory and aesthetic of poetry, as Michael E. Darling's *A.J.M. Smith: an annotated bibliography* (1981) reveals.

Issue 11 (Fall/Winter 1982) of *Canadian Poetry* is entirely devoted to Smith. See also Sandra Djwa, 'A.J.M. Smith: of metaphysics and dry bones', *Studies in Canadian Literature*, vol. 3, no. 1 (Winter 1978); Issue 15 of *CANADIAN LITERATURE* (Winter 1963), which contains a 'Salute to A.J.M. Smith'; and Leon EDEL, 'The worldly muse of A.J.M. Smith', *University of Toronto Quarterly*, vol. XLVII, no. 3 (Spring 1978).

See also CRITICISM IN ENGLISH: 2, 3.

LEON EDEL

Smith, Goldwin (1823-1910). Born in Reading, England, and educated at Eton and Oxford, he established an international reputation as a journalist and controversialist. He first achieved notice in England with his advocacy of university reform and his subsequent participation in the Royal Commission examining the academic reform of Oxford University. In 1858 he was appointed Regius professor of modern history at Oxford (the future King Edward VII was one of his pupils). Writing a constant stream of letters and articles for popular journals on the religious, political, economic, and imperial issues of the day, Smith spoke from the perspective of the Manchester school of *laissez-faire* economics and frequently adopted unpopular positions, especially with his support of the Northern cause during the American Civil War. He resigned his professorship in 1866 to care for his father, following whose death Smith accepted an offer to join the staff of newly founded Cornell University in Ithaca, New York. During his tenure (1868-71), he contributed much to the young university, including his personal library, while attempting to interpret England to America and vice versa. Closer contact with party politics, however, eroded Smith's admiration for American political institutions. In 1871 he moved to Toronto, living with relatives until his marriage in 1875 to Harriet Boulton, a widow, and took up residence in her home, The Grange.

In Canada Smith lived in comfortable affluence, founded on both an inheritance from his father and his wife's money, and used his means for charitable works and to establish periodicals that commented on Canadian and international issues: *The Canadian Monthly and National Review* (1872-8), *The Evening Telegram* (1874), *The Bystander* (1880-90), *The WEEK* (1883-96), and *The Weekly Sun* (1896-1909). He wrote extensively on religious, literary, and historical subjects, concentrating on the twin issues of nationalism and imperialism, and published a collection of Latin poetry called *Bay leaves* (New York, 1890). Hostile to all forms of political oppression, Smith expressed sympathy for the Canada First movement, decried the Boer War, and ridiculed the concept of Imperial federation. He generated great public hostility with his argument for commercial union with the United States, presented most cogently in *Canada and the Canadian question* (London, 1891), which declares that geography, history, and race demand a single North American, Anglo-Saxon nation, and that attempts to frustrate these forces would lead to economic suffering for Canada. Smith's views of Canada's future—based on his idiosyncratic brand of liberalism rather than on research—reveal his underestimation of the strength of the Canadian national spirit and the influence of French Canada.

Though Smith undoubtedly enriched Canadian political discussion, his influence on events was minimal. His greatest contribution may have been his support of such publications as *The Canadian Monthly* and *The Week*, which helped to disseminate the work of the poets and authors of the time. See Elisabeth Wallace, *Goldwin Smith: Victorian liberal* (1957).

CAL SMILEY

Smith, Ray (b. 1941). Born in Inverness, Cape Breton Island, Nova Scotia, he received his B.A. (1963) from Dalhousie University, and his M.A. (1985) from Concordia University. After serving in the RCAF and working as a systems analyst, he began writing fiction in 1964. Since 1970 he has taught at Dawson College, Montreal.

A brilliant stylist, Smith has published four books of fiction: *Cape Breton is the thought control centre of Canada* (1969; rpr. 1989), *Lord Nelson Tavern* (1974; NCL, 1981) *Century* (1986), and *A night at the opera* (1992), a novel. *Cape Breton* is a collection of stories of which the most interesting are 'Colours' and 'Galoshes' (apparently influenced by J.P. Donleavy's *The ginger man*). In *Lord Nelson Tavern*—usually called a novel, but actually a collection of linked stories as is *Century*—Smith begins with a group of university students, habitués of a Halifax saloon, who weave in and out of one another's lives over the years, exchanging women, delivering monologues. The complex design is not anchored chronologically. Smith's remarkable control of voice, however, is evident throughout and is especially fine in a very funny seduction monologue delivered by a thirteen-year-old girl ('Sarah's summer holidays'). *A night at the opera* is a novel, an unconvincing satire of German culture and manners.

Smith's work is clearly within the tradition of postmodernist fiction as defined by writers like Borges and William Gass. They are elaborately crafted, playful, self-referential. In Smith's words, 'the writer says what the story is about *in the whole story*'—so that the story can equally be 'about' its linguistic components or punctuation (including an especially artful semicolon) and 'about' relations between the sexes, a prominent theme in his work, on which Smith can be peculiarly disturbing. There is something brutal in the attitude to women displayed by the men; but this nastiness, while evidently recognized as such by Smith, is not purged or contained by his awareness.

An excellent guide to what Douglas BARBOUR calls Smith's 'artful manoeuvrings' and 'linguistic shuffles' is Barbour's essay 'Ray Smith: some approaches to the entrances of *Lord Nelson Tavern*' in *OPEN LETTER* (Summer

1976). See also Lawrence Garber's essay on *Cape Breton* in J.R. (Tim) Struthers, ed., *The Montreal story tellers* (1985).

See also NOVELS IN ENGLISH 1960 TO 1982: 4. CONSTANCE ROOKE

Smith, Russell. See NOVELS IN ENGLISH 1983 TO 1996: OTHER NOVELS 3.

Smith, William, Jr. See HISTORICAL WRITING IN ENGLISH: 2.

Smucker, Barbara (b. 1915). Born in Newton, Kansas, USA, and raised as a Mennonite, she immigrated to Kitchener, Ontario, with her husband, a professor, and worked there as a librarian from 1969 to 1982. Her numerous books have dealt with political or religious oppression, racial and class discrimination, and cultural clashes. *Underground to Canada* (1977) treats the subject of American slavery; *Days of terror* (1979) chronicles the mass migration of Mennonites from Ukraine to North America; *Amish adventure* (1983) explores cultural differences between the empire-building Scots-Canadians and the Amish-Canadians who eschew modernization; and *White mist* (1985) uses time-fantasy to focus on Native-white relations in the context of environmental destruction. Smucker's carefully researched books, mostly historical fiction, give children insight into how adult power struggles have caused pain and social injustice. She has received the Ruth Schwartz Children's Book Award for *Days of terror*, the Canada Council Children's Literature Award Prize (1980), and an IODE Award for *Incredible Jumbo* (1991). In 1986 the University of Waterloo awarded her an honorary Doctor of Letters degree.

MARY HENLEY RUBIO

Smyth, Donna (b.1943). Born in Kimberley, British Columbia, she was educated at the universities of Victoria, Toronto, and London (Ph.D., 1972). She has taught English at the University of Victoria (1967-9), the University of Saskatchewan (1972-3), and, since 1973, at Acadia University.

Smyth's writing combines inquiry into philosophical questions, poetic response to the natural world, and sensitivity to the lives and thought of ordinary working people. She has published short stories in a variety of Canadian, British, and American periodicals. Her novel *Quilt* (1982) is set in rural Nova Scotia; its main characters are a young battered wife, whose husband kills himself in a rage, and an older widow who lives with the memory of having helped her invalid husband to die. Offsetting their dramatic stories are the subtle tensions in the life of a couple facing retirement and ill-health. The vicissitudes of human life are counterpointed by the cycle of the natural world. Like the quilt the women are sewing, the novel is a patchwork of different styles, suggesting an image of community and underlying purpose in apparent chaos.

Smyth used a similar patchwork technique in her scripts written for Nova Scotia's touring Mermaid Theatre. *Susanna Moodie* (1976) dramatizes the story of MOODIE's experience both as told in *ROUGHING IT IN THE BUSH* (1852) and as Margaret ATWOOD reinterpreted it in *The JOURNALS OF SUSANNA MOODIE* (1970). Atwood's poems are recited between dramatized episodes, each implicitly commenting on the other. *Giant Anna* (1978-9), winner of a CANADA COUNCIL New Play Award, is the story of Anna Swan (1846-88), the giant daughter of a Nova Scotia family, who gave up her teacher-training because of physical and social difficulties, to be exhibited as a 'freak' by the showman P.T. Barnum. Life-size giant puppets created by Tom Miller portrayed Anna and her almost equally tall husband. As they interact with smaller puppets and live actors, the contrast of physical form illustrates the need to understand those who are different. The play, which appeals to children as well as to general audiences, includes short rhymed prologues to each episode that keep the storyline clear.

Smyth's novel *Subversive elements* (1986) weaves together a supposedly fictional story of two seemingly unlikely lovers, a former monk and a much older woman, with a factual account of the writer's real-life involvement in a successful grass-roots movement to halt plans for uranium mining in Nova Scotia. Included in the text are newspaper clippings reporting the notorious libel case brought against Smyth by a prominent academic, following her opinion piece in a Halifax newspaper. The love of nature reflected in the narrator's vegetable gardening and goat farming is linked to love of the earth in general as well as to love between human beings.

Two further works demonstrate Smyth's interest in the history of Nova Scotia. She co-edited *No place like home* (1988), a collection of the diaries and letters of Nova Scotia women from 1771 to 1938. Her book for older children, *Loyalist runaway* (1991), is an adventure story set in Halifax and Boston during the American Revolution; it is based on the diaries of a Nova Scotia family.

In 1976 Smyth was one of the founders of *Atlantis*, the first interdisciplinary women's-studies journal in Canada, and was co-ordinating editor until 1981. She has contributed numerous articles of social issues to magazines and newspapers. JOAN COLDWELL

Smyth, 'Sir' John (d. 1852). By his own account a self-taught native of Canada who discovered by accident in 1837 that he could write poetry, Smyth wrote and published prolifically for the remainder of his life. In a land of many marginal native poets, 'Sir' John's work was so bad that it was safe to laugh at him. Each new poem was widely reprinted in Upper and Lower Canadian newspapers, and his two books—*Select poems* (Toronto, 1841) and *A small specimen of the genius of Canada West, and the wonders of the world* (Toronto, 1845)—were solemnly reviewed with editorial tongue-in-cheek.

Little is known of Smyth. He died in the Toronto House of Industry, but the date and place of his birth are unknown. Newspaper editors in the 1840s generally referred to him as 'old'. He was partially crippled and moved about Toronto in a small self-propelled cart. He had been a farmer, then a land agent, before conferring on himself the title of Poet Laureate. Smyth began to use the title 'Sir' after someone had shown him an entry in a British peerage register that listed a John Smyth, Baronet and Royal Engineer. His fellow Canadians humoured him by using the title.

Smyth had a simple poetic style in which the essential feature was his obvious struggle with rhyme: 'How great was the peace, good will and harmony,/That prevailed in our City of Toronto/On the celebration of the matrimony/Of our Queen, and her name will be our motto.' (*Select poems*, p. 6.) Because his poetry is so bad and so funny, some of it has found a place as comic relief in modern scholarly lectures. The content of his work, however, deserves attention. Deluded though he may have been about himself, his poems give us one of the few clues we have to lower-class Canadian attitudes of the time. An acute observer of the Upper Canadian world, he commented with an outsider's telling accuracy on the pretensions of colonial society. No admirer of the local Tories or of Americans, he was nevertheless a sentimental royalist who cheered the victories of the British army and navy. He took great pride in the progress of Upper Canada, and of Toronto in particular.

MARY LU MacDONALD

Snow Drop, The (Apr. 1847-June 1853). *The Snow Drop; or Juvenile Magazine*, one of the first Canadian periodicals for children, was edited by two sisters (née Foster) who had moved to Montreal from Boston: Mrs Eliza Lanesford Cushing (b. 1794) and Mrs Harriet Vining Cheney (b. 1796). It was published in Montreal by the firm of Lovell and Gibson, which also published *The LITERARY GARLAND*. Setting out to instruct and amuse, the magazine was directed primarily to girls, each issue providing one or two stories along with articles on historical events, famous people, natural history, and faraway places; the slight Canadian content had to do mostly with the past or with the quainter aspects of Canadian life. Most of *The Snow Drop*'s identified authors were from old or New England, like the books and periodicals from which it published selections. Although its final numbers contained an increasing proportion of original contributions, it made little impact on the Canadian literary scene. Late in its six-year existence it had a short-lived competitor, *The Maple Leaf* (June 1852-Dec. 1854), which deliberately featured Canadian content, including work by Susanna MOODIE and her sister Catharine Parr TRAILL.

See Carole Gerson, 'The *Snow Drop* and the *Maple Leaf*; Canada's first periodicals for children', *Canadian Children's Literature* 15/16 (1980). CAROLE GERSON

Soirées canadiennes, Les. A literary monthly published in Quebec City from 1861 to 1865 by members of the MOUVEMENT LITTÉRAIRE DE QUÉBEC, it was one of the first undertakings of this group of writers and historians. The formula adopted was that of Dr Joseph-Charles TACHÉ, who wanted to publish French-Canadian legends and folktales lest they be forgotten. Taché, Abbé Henri-Raymond CASGRAIN, and Dr François-Hubert-Alexandre LaRUE formed the editorial committee, with Brousseau Brothers as printers; the prospectus appeared in *Le Courrier du Canada*, 22 Feb. 1861, and the first number was published on 11 Mar. 1861.

The first year was extremely successful: more than 800 subscribers signed up. The lack of any written contract with the printers soon gave rise, however, to disagreements about the ownership and conduct of the enterprise, and to a serious split between Taché, who sided with Brousseau Brothers, and the other editors, who wanted to change printers. In Oct. 1862 eight contributors resigned. Casgrain, La Rue, and Antoine GÉRIN-LAJOIE, ignoring Taché's remonstrances, entrusted the printing for the year 1863 to another firm, Desbarats and Derbishire, and announced a change of title to *Le* FOYER *CANADIEN*. Brousseau Brothers protested and distributed a pamphlet to the subscribers (*Mémoire des Propriétaires-Editeurs*, 18 Oct. 1862), publishing the correspondence of the dispute. The *Foyer canadien* group retorted, first in their 'Prospectus' (30 Oct. 1862) and then in a satirical memorandum (*Réponse à la Mémoire de MM. Brousseau Frères*, Nov. 1862) written by LaRue. Meanwhile Taché continued to edit *Les Soirées canadiennes* single-handedly, devoting the Nov. 1862 issue to Octave CRÉMAZIE's unfinished poem 'Les trois morts' and filling 250 pages of the 1863 numbers with his own lumber-camp and backwoods tales entitled 'Forestiers et voyageurs'. The 1864 issues contained few original writings: many of them were given over to historical documents. In Aug. 1864 Taché became deputy minister in the department of agriculture and statistics and in Oct. 1865 was obliged to move to Ottawa. The numbers of the *Soirées* for the last half of 1865 were consequently delayed and appeared only in Feb. 1867. With their publication the magazine disappeared.

Like *Le Foyer canadien*, *Les Soirées canadiennes* had remarkable initial success and then slowly declined; both contributed to the literary renascence of 1860, the *Soirées* on a smaller scale and in a more limited circuit than the more prosperous *Foyer*. Each succeeding literary movement in Quebec has had its literary magazines, but almost none have achieved the prominence and the readership enjoyed by these early examples of the genre.

See Réjean Robidoux, '*Les Soirées canadiennes et Le Foyer canadien* dans le mouvement littéraire québécois de 1860', in Réjean Robidoux, *Fonder une littérature nationale: notes d'histoire littéraire* (1994), 11-133.

DAVID M. HAYNE

Solway, David (b. 1941). Born in Montreal and educated at McGill University, he has spent most of his adult life teaching English and creative writing at John Abbott College, Quebec. His first book of poems, *In my own image* (1962), appeared when he was only twenty-one, and in its rebellious romanticism suggests the influence of Leonard COHEN. After several experimental slim volumes—*The crystal theatre* (1971), *Paximalia* (1972), *The Egyptian airforce* (1973), and *Anacrusis* (1976)—Solway came to poetic maturity with *The road to Arginos* (1976).

Here the influence of Cohen is still discernible, most notably in the way the poetry rises from a fruitful tension between his Jewish background and interests and a Greek-island lifestyle that he finds creatively stimulating and attractive. But Solway and Cohen have since developed in radically different ways. Solway has shed his 'pop-culture' influences and espoused a rigorous technical discipline that has resulted in poetry that manages to combine the lyric facility and intensity of W.B. Yeats and the classical fastidiousness of Robert Graves.

Solway's subsequent volumes include *Mephistopheles and the astronaut* (1979), *Selected poems* (1982), *The Mulberry men* (children's verse, 1982), *Stones in winter* (1983), and *Bedrock* (1993), and have for the most part continued and extended the Hebraic/Hellenic debate. But his most brilliant *tour de force* is *Modern marriage* (1987), a series of fifty conversational sonnets where a human marital dispute, in the tradition of George Meredith's *Modern love* (1862), is the convenient basis for a witty and profound inquiry into life's oppositions: art/nature, soul/blood, reality/illusion, poetry/prose, movement/stasis.

Solway has also written *Education lost* (1989) and *Lying about the wolf* (1997), two independent and persuasive indictments of modern pedagogical philosophy and method; *The anatomy of Arcadia* (1992), a diary-style meditation on the all-but-forgotten distinction between tourism and genuine travel; and a number of literary essays on subjects as diverse as Shakespeare and Swift, James Joyce and Irving LAYTON. His prose is close-packed, exuberant, and intellectually challenging.

Solway's literary papers are deposited in the Thomas Fisher Rare Book Library, the University of Toronto.

W.J. KEITH

Sommer, Richard (b. 1934). Born, raised, and educated in Minnesota, USA, he attended Harvard University before coming to Canada in 1962 to teach at Concordia University, Montreal. When he retired, Sommer became increasingly interested in environmental and conservation issues. He led the fight to preserve Pinnacle Mountain, Quebec, as a natural habitat rather than as its planned use as a ski resort. This conflict and his eventual victory is documented in an NFB movie, *The Poet and the Pinnacle* (1995).

Sommer has published eight volumes of poetry, including *Blue sky notebook* (1973), *The other side of games* (1977), *Selected and new poems* (1984), *Fawn bones* (1986), and *The shadow sonnets* (1992). A constant theme of much of his poetry is one of placing himself inside reality to experience and then report any events impinging on the self that, as he states in one of his sonnets, 'is all we really have.' Irony flickers through the poems, the figure of the poet inside the poems seen in all his uncertainties and faults as well as his joys and contentments. He expresses the external world directly as he lets irony surround his responses to that reality.

Much of Sommer's concern for the life of nature and the violent inroads made on it figures in his collection *Fawn bones*. His poetic voice has remained consistent, though he has moved to a more open language, trying to merge directness, the colloquial, and the inwardly musing sides of his character. This is particularly true of *The shadow sonnets*, a collection of one hundred poems using the form to record a wide range of personal experiences, both painful and joyous. As he suggests in one of the sonnets, 'the sonnet's form is of our suffering/yet blesses, heals, accepts our offering.' He retains a firm hold on the intricacies of rhyme and rhythm, though many of the sonnets jostle and pull at the constraints as he juggles with slant rhyme and expanded rhythms. This worrying at the form creates an added tension to the poetry.

PETER STEVENS

Sono Nis Press (1968-) was founded in Victoria, British Columbia, by J. Michael YATES as a literary press to publish poetry and avant-garde fiction in quality editions. The name of the press is nonsensical, taken from a character in Yates's *The man in the glass octopus* (1968), a collection of stories and the first book published by the press.

From 1968 to 1972 the press published nearly fifty poetry or short-fiction titles. All the books were high-quality hardcover titles, printed and bound by the Morriss Company of Victoria. In 1976 Yates sold the press to them. The printer had a long-standing relationship with writers and literary publishers in B.C. ('in any typeface you want, as long as it's Baskerville'), and Richard Morriss, under the initial advisory editorship of Robin SKELTON, extended the publishing program to a dozen diversified titles a year: local histories, art books, journals, biographies, literary criticism, and scholarly books, as well as poetry collections. Its distinguished list includes Susan MUSGRAVE, Lawrence Russell, Andreas SCHROEDER, Seán VIRGO, Robert HARLOW, Robin Skelton, Robert BRINGHURST, John Robert COLOMBO, George Amabile, George JONAS, and Yates himself. Sono Nis books are never remaindered.

GEOFF HANCOCK

Soucy, Charles. See NOVELS IN FRENCH 1960 TO 1982: 3(e).

Souster, Raymond (b. 1921). Born in Toronto, he has lived there nearly all his life and rooted most of his poetry in its landscape. He grew up in the western Humberside area of the city, becoming an outstanding softball pitcher in his late teens. He joined the Bank of Commerce as a teller in 1939 and enlisted as a tradesman in the Royal Canadian Air Force in 1941. He was posted to continental defence squadrons in Nova Scotia and Newfoundland before a posting to England brought him to Europe for the final day of the war. While in Nova Scotia, Souster was inspired by John Sutherland's *FIRST STATEMENT* to publish his first little magazine, *Direction* (1943-6), mimeographed on borrowed RCAF paper. In 1944 a large selection of his poetry was included in Ronald Hambleton's *Unit of five*. On demobilization he returned to what is now the Canadian Imperial Bank of Commerce, where he worked for forty-five years until his retirement, and proceeded to write poetry steadily. He was made an Officer of the Order of Canada in 1995.

Souster's first book, *When we are young* (1946), published by John SUTHERLAND's First Statement Press, was followed by his inclusion in Sutherland's anthology *Other Canadians: an anthology of the new poetry in Canada, 1940-1946* (1947) and by the RYERSON PRESS's publication of his *Go to sleep, world* (1947). He attempted his second little magazine, *Enterprise*, in 1948 and published a pseudonymous war novel, *The winter of time*, by 'Raymond Holmes', in 1949. His third volume of poetry, *City Hall street*, appeared in 1951. The poetry of this and the preceding volumes was romantic in diction, often overstated, and opposed nature and youthful love to the ugliness of war and factory.

In 1951 Souster became a close friend of Louis DUDEK, who had just returned to Montreal from New York, and who introduced him to the work of William Carlos Williams and the poets of Cid Corman's U.S. magazine *Origin*. With Dudek's encouragement he launched his third magazine, *CONTACT* (1952-4), in which he was able to publish work by Corman and other *Origin* writers. In the spring of 1952 he joined with Dudek and Irving LAYTON to begin *CONTACT PRESS* (1952-67), the chief publisher of new poetry in Canada during the 1950s. Under the influence of Williams and Corman, Souster's style changed drastically; his line became the brief 'variable foot' of Williams, his diction became concrete and austere.

In his publications of the fifties—*Shake hands with the hangman* (1953), *A dream that is dying* (1954), *For what time slays* (1955), *Walking death* (1955), *The selected poems* (1956), *Crêpe-hanger's carnival* (1958)—Souster continued his early theme of the opposition between the 'outside' forces of love, nature, and sport and the 'inside' ones of industry and commerce. Because this was also an opposition between small and large, Souster's new poetic of understatement and economy was ideally suited to it. Late in the decade Souster began his fourth mimeographed little magazine, *Combustion* (1957-60), which reflected his continuing interest in the poetry of Corman and other American writers.

The 1960s was a period of consolidation for Souster. He published three outstanding collections: *A local pride* (1962), *The colour of the times* (1964, winner of a Governor General's Award), and *As is* (1967); and began the lengthy process of publishing or re-publishing his entire body of work with *Lost & found: uncollected poems 1945-1965* (1968) and *So far, so good* (1969). He also published the less-important books *Place of meeting* (1962), *At Split Rock Falls* (1963), *Twelve new poems* (1964), and *Ten elephants on Yonge Street* (1965); edited for Contact Press the influential anthology of young poets *New wave Canada: the new explosion in Canadian poetry* (1966); and on the demise of Contact Press in 1967 began work on another novel loosely tied to his war experiences, *On target* (1972), privately published under the pseudonym 'John Holmes'.

The re-publication of Souster's early work continued in the 1970s with *The years* (1971), *Selected poems* (1972), *Double-header* (1975), and *Rain-check* (1975); they were followed by seven volumes of *Collected poems* (1980, 1981, 1982, 1983, 1984, 1989, and 1992). The poems in *Change-up* (1974), *Extra innings* (1977), and *Hanging in* (1979) took on a retrospective tone, particularly the series 'Pictures of a long-lost world', in which Souster directed his nostalgic vision towards recapturing specific moments of twentieth-century history. Other later volumes are *Jubilee of death: the raid on Dieppe, a poem* (1984), *Flight of the roller coaster: poems for children* (1985), *It takes all kinds* (1986), *The eyes of love* (1987), *Asking for more* (1988), *Running out the clock* (1991), *Riding the long black horse* (1993), *Old bank notes* (1993), and *No sad songs wanted here* (1995). Souster's poetry is notable for its skilled use of imagism, for its vivid affirmations of the value of the commonplace object, and for its depictions of Toronto streets, parks, and suburbs. Deliberately avoiding the formally elegant poem, Souster has compiled a body of disarming lyrics in which the craft is concealed so that incidents and scenes may have all possible prominence.

During the 1970s Souster co-edited four teaching anthologies: *Generation now* (1970) and *These loved, these hated lands* (1975) with Richard Woollatt, and with Douglas LOCHHEAD *Made in Canada* (1970) and *100 Poems of nineteenth-century Canada* (1974). With Lochhead he also edited *Windflower: poems of Bliss Carman* (1986) and *Powassan's drum: poems of Duncan Campbell Scott* (1986).

Frank DAVEY's *Louis Dudek and Raymond Souster* (1981) details Souster's relationship to Dudek and Corman and offers several critical approaches to his work. See Bruce Whiteman, *Collected poems of Raymond Souster: bibliography* (1984) and Bruce Whiteman, 'Raymond Souster', in Robert Lecker, Jack David, and Ellen Quigley, eds., *Canadian writers and their works*, Poetry Series 5 (1985).

See also POETRY IN ENGLISH 1950 TO 1982: 1. FRANK DAVEY

South Asian-Canadian literature. The term South Asian writing figures so prominently in current literary criticism that it is easy to overlook the fact that it suggests a much greater unity than it actually possesses. The heterogeneity is not simply a consequence of India's accommodating a population that is divided along religious, ethnic, linguistic, and caste lines, although that in itself merits serious consideration. More importantly, the term South Asian embraces much more than the periods of diaspora that brought people directly from India to Canada. Immigrants from Sri Lanka, Pakistan, and Bangladesh, for example, also belong in this category. And there is the diaspora that began in the nineteenth century as indentured labour travelled from India to Trinidad, Guyana, Fiji, Tanzania, South Africa, Malaysia, and Singapore, and arrived in Canada after having absorbed the influences and identities of these countries as well. All these people claim a cultural link that can be traced to India, and would, if pressed, acknowledge a quality of Indianness that informs their sensibility. At the same time, they would define themselves along 'national' lines that are not exclusively Indian: Sri Lankan, Fijian, Guyanese, and so forth.

It is also not often recognized that South Asian writing does not refer only to literature written exclusively in English, although English writing, mainly because it reaches a wider audience, tends to take centre stage. Writing in Punjabi and Gujarati, for instance, has a much longer history, and is chronologically much closer to the initial migration to

Canada from India at the turn of the century. Writing in Urdu began in the 1960s and continues to enjoy a substantial readership. Although writing in Tamil did not begin until the mid-1980s, it has flourished, at least partly because it targets a readership with which it shares many cultural assumptions. Notwithstanding the vitality of these literatures, during the last two decades writing in English has been the most prominent.

In 1994 Trinidad-born Neil BISSOONDATH wrote a book entitled *Selling illusions: the cult of multiculturalism in Canada*, which was an attempt to critique the policy of multiculturalism on the basis that, regardless of its objectives, it tends to 'label' and ghettoize different groups and perpetuate hyphenated identities. Arnold Itwaru's *Closed entrances: Canadian culture and imperialism* (1994) is equally skeptical about the validity of multiculturalism, but makes the argument that multiculturalism only serves to mask the marginalization and racism that exits in Canada. One writer seeks assimilation and the other a separate identity. Between these two lies a grey area of uncertainty and ambivalence that is the subject of Uma Parameswaran's long poem *Trishanku* (1987), whose title refers to the myth of a king who lived between heaven and earth, and who is often invoked in literature to define the state of in-betweenness.

Lines of demarcation in South Asian writing are difficult to establish on the basis of attitudes or thematic preoccupations. Michael ONDAATJE, perhaps the best-known South Asian writer, hardly ever writes about the Sri Lanka he left, except in his fiction/memoir *Running in the family* (1982). His poetry and fiction are mostly about places other than Sri Lanka, and his internationalist stance has been praised by some and criticized by others. In contrast, Rohinton MISTRY, another writer who has won several awards, has been consistent in writing about Bombay, particularly about the Parsee community to which he belonged. In *Tales from Firozsha Baag* (1987) and *Such a long journey* (1991) there is very little of Canada, and these books could well be called 'Indian' literature. M.G. VASSANJI seeks a balance, although he is at his best when he portrays the Indian community that moved to East Africa at the end of the last century. His novels *The gunny sack* (1989) and *The book of secrets* (1994) are about the past, about memory and about the process of reclaiming history; *No new land* (1991) is set in Toronto and deals with the migrant community attempting to come to terms with the challenges of a new and sometimes hostile country.

In general terms, however, the various positions charted by these writers are reflected in the works of most South Asian writers. Bissoondath, with his East Indian/Caribbean background, moves easily between this world and Canada, in, for example, *A casual brutality* (1988) and his collection of short stories *On the eve of uncertain tomorrows* (1990). So does Uma Parameswaran as she locates her writing in both India and Canada. Her long poem *Trishanku* is probably her major achievement, and here she works with a multitude of voices to express the confusion of living on the cusp between worlds. Rienzi Crusz, a prolific poet, is at home in both worlds, in Sri Lanka and Canada as suggested by the titles of his poetry collections: *Elephant and ice* (1980) and *Beatitudes of ice* (1995). He and Lakshmi Gill (whose collection of poems *During rain, I plant chrysanthemums* came out in 1966) are probably among the earliest of South Asian authors writing in English.

The world that has been left behind is either recreated or transformed through memory in the work of several writers. In his novel *Shanti* (1988), Arnold Itwaru goes back to the world of colonial Guyana, and in a narrative distinguished by its poetic mode, traces the exploitation of the indentured worker on the plantations. Two collections of poems convey perceptive evocations of Sri Lanka: Asoka Weerasinghe's *Home again Lanka* (1981) and Suwanda Sugunasiri's *The faces of Galle face green* (1995).

The various impediments confronting the immigrant become the subject of Himani Bannerji's collection of poems *A separate sky* (1982) and of Surjeet Kalsey's *Footprints of silence* (1982). About the challenges that immigrants confront, Cyril Dabydeen writes poignantly in *Dark swirl* (1989). Equally evocative are Nazneen Sadiq's *Ice bangles* (1988), a realistic and powerful novel that begins in Lahore and moves to Canada, and Ven Begamudré's novel *Van de Graaf days* (1993) about middle-class immigrants and professionals and how they deal with the dichotomy between expectations and fulfilment in a new land. Krisantha Sri Bhaggiyadatta's *The 52nd state of amnesia* (1993) is a collection of experimental poems that are distinguished by their irony and depth of vision. Difficult to fit into any classification, the profound and witty Suniti Namjoshi writes fables, poems, and discontinuous narratives that explore the world of double or even triple marginalization, as in *The conversations of cow* (1985) or *The blue donkey fables* (1988). A prolific and complex writer, she demonstrates in her writing the ambivalence and richness of the phrase 'South Asian writing'.

The last few years have seen the emergence of new writers, all of whom share the sensibility of the older writers but have attempted to explore new areas of experience. Shyam Selvadurai's *Funny boy* (1994) deals with the ethnic politics of Sri Lanka and with sexual politics. Kaushalya Bannerji is an important new voice who writes with a strikingly perceptive sense of Canadian identity. Anita Rau Badami's *Tamarind Mem* (1996), the most recent addition to the repertoire of South Asian writing, remains an impressive first novel despite its conventional mode.

The importance of South Asian writing is evident in the various anthologies that have been published in recent years. *Shakti's words* (1990), edited by Diane McGifford and Judith Kearns, and *The geography of voice* (1992), edited by Diane McGifford, are both significant publications, the first devoted to women's writing. *The Toronto South Asian Review* (founded by M.G.Vassanji in 1980) has been a major outlet for South Asian writers, some of whom now have an international audience, along with *TSAR* publications.

To think of South Asian writing along binary terms of centre and margin, or in relation to nostalgia and 'home', is to simplify a body of writing that is far more complex. The difference between, say, Rienzi Crusz and Uma Parameswaran is not simply that one speaks of Sri Lanka and the other of India. Their writing is conditioned by the their ethnicity, their religious belief, their sense of identity in Sri Lanka and India, the degree to which they were influenced by the politics of colonialism, and so on. And the diversity is in turn reflected in the narrative modes they use, the traditions they draw from, and the different ways in which they contribute to Canadian writing. CHELVA KANAGANAYAKAM

Southern Ontario Gothic. Graeme GIBSON's interviews in *Eleven Canadian novelists* (1973) marked the first appearance in print of a passionate recognition by Ontario writers of the Southern Ontario Gothic. Margaret ATWOOD, Matt COHEN, Marian ENGEL, Timothy FINDLEY, Alice MUNRO, and Scott SYMONS share a sense of distinct regional, even mythological, place where horror, murder, and bodily violations are not uncommon. Rooted in the nineteenth-century romances of John RICHARDSON and the survival stories of Susanna MOODIE's pioneer experiences, the Gothic tradition extends forward to Raymond KNISTER's chronicles of the living dead in *White narcissus* (1929), Munro's *Selected stories* (1996), and Atwood's *Alias Grace* (1996). James REANEY's plays *Colours in the dark* (1969), *Baldoon* (1976), and *The Donnellys* (1974-7), as well as his short stories 'The bully' and 'The box social' (reprinted in *The box social and other stories* in 1996), also assume Gothic elements of the macabre rooted in nightmarish families and uncanny action. Carol SHIELDS' novel *Swann* (1987) makes the murder and dismemberment of poet Mary Swann by her husband, an Ontario farmer, a secret at the heart of the narrative that must be investigated and resolved, in keeping with Gothic conventions.

The best expressions of Southern Ontario Gothic celebrate life while exhuming the deadening and deforming forces beneath genteel surfaces, manifest in the merciless forces of Perfectionism, Propriety, Presbyterianism, and Prudence. Traditionally the Gothic deals with confinement, illness, madness, demonism, secrets, live burial, and fear. Usually an imperilled heroine searches for the clues to her identity in a ruin or a confining architectural space like a dungeon. In the Southern Ontario tradition, however, the threat to the female protagonist can come from the wilderness, from cabin fever, or from uncommunicative husbands. Because the Gothic often deals with the supernatural, it challenges rationality. Irrational figures like the Wild Man, the Wild Woman, fool-saints, or wendigos provide the apparition of the supernatural within the Canadian bush.

In other cases the Gothic concerns family secrets and social oppression—what might be called the irrationality of civilized institutions. This may take the form of religious difference, as in the case of 'demonic' Catholicism in *The Donnellys*. It may also take the form of finding dead or ill mothers, like the sickly Mrs Dempster in Robertson DAVIES' *FIFTH BUSINESS* (1970). Sometimes the female principle is threatening and requires elimination, as with the smart but spell-casting Zenia in Atwood's *The robber bride* (1993). In this sense the Gothic is about the impossibility of dealing with women and their bodies.

The Gothic is sometimes located in desperate domestic circumstances that produce insanity or criminal action. Novels like Joan BARFOOT's *Dancing in the dark* (1982), Tom MARSHALL's *Changelings: a double fugue* (1991), and Timothy Findley's *Headhunter* (1993) make madness in the home or in the streets an aspect of the bizarreness that underlies much of 'ordinary' Southern Ontario experience. What makes this locale so prone to Gothic tales is the failure of communication between family members or social groups. In the absence of communication, strange projections and psychological grotesqueries spring up and rapidly grow to unmanageable proportions. Malevolent fantasies are the source and sustenance of the Gothic tradition.

ALLAN HEPBURN/MICHAEL HURLEY

Spalding, Esta. See POETRY IN ENGLISH 1983 TO 1996: 3.

Spalding, Linda (b. 1943). Born Linda Dickinson in Topeka, Kansas, she received her B.A. (1965) at the University of Colorado and pursued graduate studies at the University of Hawaii at Monoa from 1970 to 1972. She has written two novels, *Daughters of Captain Cook* (1988) and *The paper wife* (1994), and lives in Toronto, Ontario, where she is the editor of *BRICK*. With Michael ONDAATJE she co-edited *The Brick reader* (1991), a collection of literary and political pieces by writers of international renown.

In *Daughters of Captain Cook* the past is a mirror that reflects and refracts the present-day life of Jesse, the female protagonist. From the narrative frame, 'Album', Jesse describes family photographs that speak of lost events, a reality past. In reminiscing about her past and contemplating her marital disappointments, Jesse wonders if her present circumstances are an inescapable fate, a legacy bequeathed to her by female ancestors, one she will pass down to her own daughter, Kit. Countering Jesse's family history is that of Paul, her husband. His is a history imbedded in ancient Hawaiian tradition and mythology and one that forces Jesse to struggle with conflicting points of view. A marked feature of *Daughters* is how Spalding acknowledges traditional Hawaiian beliefs as they are both reflected and denied by contemporary life. In *The paper wife* Colorado and Mexico provide the disparate cultural landscapes. The naïvety of a 1960s Kennedy-era American idealism confronts political issues that raise moral dilemmas for the characters. Vietnam War conscription, an illegal adoption agency operating under the guise of a beneficent orphanage in Mexico, and the inextricable links between money and power and identity provide the novel's political underpinnings.

In both novels comfortless women are common; husbands and fathers are present only in their absence. The injuries that cannot be effaced are the emotional scars left by fathers and husbands whose only meaning resides in photographs or on paper. The body is the boundary that circumscribes the geography of the nomadic lives of these women; and a sense of personal identity is rooted in the physical place they spring from and the social place they assume.

DEBORAH TORKKO

Sparshott, Francis (b. 1926). Francis Edward Sparshott was born in Chatham, England, and educated at Oxford University. He came to the University of Toronto in 1950 as a lecturer in philosophy and in 1955 joined the staff of Victoria College. A Fellow of the Royal Society of Canada since 1977, Sparshott retired as a University Professor in 1991. Philosopher by profession and poet by inclination (he was president of the LEAGUE OF CANADIAN POETS, 1977-9), Sparshott has written nine books on philosophy, ten books of poetry, and countless articles that address the relation of philosophy, literature, and the arts. He has remarked that, while poetry and philosophy are two distinct things, there is common ground, for the purpose of both is to 'discover connections that are not evident'. He has also written that poetry is 'the only thing' he takes seriously. Sparshott's philosophical concerns pervade his poetry; he is skilled at perceiving hidden relations between ideas. This is nowhere more evident than in his *The cave of Trophonius* (1983), which he describes as a 'trip of the shaman through the universe'; it won the first prize for poetry in the 1981 CBC literary competition. His first two poetry collections, *A divided voice* (1965) and *A cardboard garage* (1969), focus on poems of introspection that speak to themes of unfulfilled love, unattainable pleasures, and the sense of waste in human loneliness and isolation. Formally graceful, the poems are by turns romantic, humorous, passionate, and profound. *The naming of the beasts* and *The rainy hills* (haiku), both published in 1979, tend to feature observations and descriptions of commonplace events. All the poems in these collections have an elegant clarity of language and often give voice to a capricious irreverence, refined colloquialisms, scholarly allusions, and witty asides. Sparshott's later books of poetry, published by Childe Thursday Press of Toronto, are titled *The hanging gardens of Etobicoke* (1983), *Storms and screens* (1986), *Sculling to Byzantium* (1989), and *Views from the zucchini gazebo* (1994). His themes continue to display a wonderment at the banality of life's tiny moments. Increasingly they reveal a painful resignation to the temporality of the human condition. *Views* includes an introduction, a conclusion, and some explanatory footnotes, additions that suggest both anxiety and hope that his 'little systems of words' are carried home by the reader for whatever reason. For the most part, Sparshott's poetry is not joyous: life has engaged the mind, but seldom delighted; for all living things—be they persons, spiders, or leaves—life is fleeting. Decay as a theme creeps frequently into his work.

Sparshott's early philosophy books display the irreverence and witty asides of his early poetry, giving them a literary panache that is rare in philosophical writing. Sparshott made his reputation as a philosopher with *An enquiry into goodness and related concepts* (1958), a distinguished work that tackles the traditional concerns of ethics and explores the various meanings of 'goodness' and their relation to human satisfaction. While his journal publications cover a wide range of philosophical topics, Sparshott is perhaps best known for his work on aesthetics. In *The structure of aesthetics* (1963) he examines the concept of a work of art, the meanings of artistic language, the legitimacy and purpose of artistic criticism, and the role of art as an expression of the human condition. It concludes with a warning against scholarly theses that suggest a single function or analysis of art. *The concept of criticism* (1967) also argues for the interrelatedness of theories and functions, and urges the use of reasonable techniques, 'not just one method of criticism'. *Looking for philosophy* (1972) is a mixture of witty essays, interludes, and lively dialogues that investigate the discipline of philosophy and the philosopher's task. Sparshott accepts St Ambrose's dictum that salvation cannot be achieved by philosophy, but adds that this belief was easy for Ambrose, since he was no philosopher. This book aroused the ire of some critics, who believed that philosophers should not make jokes about philosophy. Sparshott's humour also surfaces frequently in the footnotes accompanying his philosophical works. *The theory of the arts* (1982), which Sparshott has described as his 'magnum opus', distinguishes between the classical definition of 'fine arts'—which regards art as productivity, 'a performance with respect to its design'—and the modern concept of art considered as pure creativity and expressed intuitions. Sparshott concludes that he has offered an aesthetic meta-theory—a theory about theories of art. Sparshott then turned his attention to dance as an art in *Off the ground: first steps to a philosophical consideration of the dance* (1988), a landmark work that offers historical review, hermeneutical exegesis, and ontological speculations—concluding that dance is a 'visible object of cognition' sustained by 'a system of virtual energies', representing a 'sense of achievement or wonder, a celebration of life'. But he warns the reader incessantly that these are suggestions among multiple interpretations. His most recent book of poetry contains the disclaimer that he has done 'nothing much' since his retirement. Nothing much includes the publication of two more major works of philosophy: *Taking life seriously: a study of the argument of the Nichomachean Ethics* (1994), *A measured pace: toward a philosophical understanding of the arts of dance* (1995), and many journal articles and chapters in books. For all Sparshott's interest in dance, only one of his poems directly addresses dance: 'Arabesque' (*Storms and screens*). Perhaps each book of poetry is in its own right Sparshott's choreographed metaphor for life. The reader knows that he/she is living: as in dancing, the struggle for excellence is painful, and the performance is brief.

A book (1970), published under the pseudonym 'Cromwell Kent', is a tongue-in-cheek frolic in prose, compressing into thirty-six pages the possible ingredients of the great Canadian novel: beavers, the RCMP, Russian spies, bestiality, swamps, and Bible stories.

ELIZABETH TROTT

Spears, Heather (b. 1934). Born in Vancouver, British Columbia, she received a diploma from the Vancouver School of Art and a B.A. in English (1956) from the University of British Columbia. The same year an Emily CARR Scholarship enabled her to leave for art studies in London. Marrying Lenny Goldenberg, a potter from Montreal, she settled in 1962 with her growing family on the Danish island of Bornholm, moving to Copenhagen in the 1980s. She continues to live in Copenhagen, where she teaches drawing and runs a small gallery called Upper Canada, besides making regular trips to Canada to teach, exhibit, and give readings.

As a writer Spears began with poetry, writing *Asylum pieces* (EMBLEM BOOKS, 1958) as an undergraduate after two summers working in mental hospitals. It has been followed by eight books of poetry, including *How to read faces* (1988), which won the Pat LOWTHER Memorial Award; *The word for sand* (1989), which received the same award as well as a Governor General's Award; *Human acts* (1991); *The Panum poems* (1996), which Spears wrote while making anatomical drawings at the Panum Institute, Copenhagen; and *Selected poems* (1997). She won first prize in the CBC Literary Contest in 1991. Spears has more recently turned to fiction with a post-apocalypse trilogy: *Moonfall* (1991), *The children of Atwar* (1993), and *The taming* (1996).

This is the work of someone who has scrupulously trained herself both to see and to render what she sees—scenes, activities, persons, relationships—with great candour and objectivity, and including the emotional truth of what is seen. In most of her work no added information or explanation is supplied, and the reader is required to give very full attention—to participate in the seeing. The poems are, so to speak, craggy but exhilarating. This uncompromising approach works effectively in her three novels as well: plunged into a strange world, the reader is brought close to the characters' perceptions and emotional life, while groping after the half-stated structures and connections that shape their surroundings.

JAY MACPHERSON

Spencer, Elizabeth (b. 1921). Born in Carrollton, Mississippi, she was educated at Bellhaven College and Vanderbilt University. After working as a teacher and a journalist, she set out on a 'personal road' in writing, which led her from Mississippi to Italy (on a Guggenheim Fellowship in 1956) and to Montreal, where she taught creative writing at Concordia University between 1958 and 1986. She has received three honorary doctorates—one from Concordia (1988)—and O. Henry Awards on five occasions for her short stories. She now lives in Chapel Hill, North Carolina.

Despite her success as a short-story writer, Spencer thinks of herself primarily as a novelist. She has published seven novels and two novellas. *Fire in the morning* (1948), *This crooked way* (1952), and *The voice at the back door* (1956) form a picture of the Southern world in which she grew up. *No place for an angel* (1967) and *The snare* (1972) 'bring together certain broad areas of American experience' and were not meant to be specifically 'Southern'. *The salt line* (1984), set on the Mississippi Gulf Coast, is about the rivalry of two men, and their women, and tells of the lines these people cross, which change them. *The night travellers* (1991), set in North Carolina and Montreal during the Vietnam War, is an intricate novel about the effects on a young man and his wife of his growing radicalism. The two novellas, *The light in the piazza* (1960) and *Knights and dragons* (1965), complement one another as sunny and anguished works about Americans in Italy; in 1962 the former was produced as an MGM film starring Olivia de Havilland. Spencer has published five collections of short stories, *Ship Island and other stories* (1968), *The stories of Elizabeth Spencer* (1981), with a Foreword by Eudora Welty and including *Knights and dragons, Marilee* (1981), *Jack of diamonds and other stories* (1988), and *On the Gulf* (1991). Among her most accomplished stories are 'Little brown girl', 'White angels', 'Ship Island', 'The absence', 'The Bufords', 'Judith Kane', 'The finder', 'Prelude to a parking lot', 'I, Maureen', and 'The girl who loved horses'.

Spencer does not 'seek to avoid' writing about Canada, but her Canadian stories are few in number. In the best of them, 'I, Maureen', the near-death of her affluent husband shocks the protagonist into the search for 'another world' and her other self, without which she has been psychically starved. She finds what she seeks in an unstable relationship with a poor artist-photographer in the east end of Montreal; in realizing that love and art must be transient and changing, she accepts an important truth. In 'The search', another story set in Canada, a woman is tortured by her anguish over her lost daughter and wants to be rid of the pain; suddenly her husband realizes that the hotel-owner has been right in accusing her of throwing bags of garbage from the window.

Spencer's sensibility is intuitive and non-rational; she has a sure touch when dealing with the delicate and the evanescent, with fantasy, ghosts, mysticism, miracles; with affinities, resemblances, doubles, and especially with moments of insight and self-discovery. Above all her work is about healthy escape: from the past, from other people and their expectations, from inappropriate or lingering love, from old griefs.

JEFFREY HEATH

Spirale (1979-). This monthly francophone cultural magazine is unique in Quebec and, in some ways, Canada. *Spirale* was started in September 1979 by André ROY, Laurent-Michel Vacher, and Gordon Lefebvre as an alternative to nationalistic journals such as *LIBERTÉ* and *Chroniques*, or the newspaper *Le Devoir*. In September 1981 the editorial committee expanded to include Carole David, Suzanne Lamay, and Monique LaRUE, while the review expanded to twenty-four pages and accentuated its interdisciplinary attention to cinema, theatre, and the visual arts. At a moment of financial crisis during the winter of 1982 Monique PROULX took on the directorship and a new editorial committee, including Suzanne Lamay, Ren Payant, and Gail SCOTT, replaced the original one. The editorial of December 1982 called for *Spirale* to situate culture rigorously within a global context, and over the next year the review became even more firmly committed to the historically conscious critique of the fragmentary nature of modernity without imposing epistemological norms or master narratives, a project that would demonstrate 'the necessity of the multiple, of the deconstruction of concepts which too automatically regulate our perception and our judgements'. This orientation has since been maintained by co-editors such as Jean-François Chassay (1986-92) and Sherry Simon (1986-94).

No other magazine in Quebec offers the same interdisciplinary diversity and depth of analysis on the arts, humanities, and social sciences. This is especially true of its commitment to cultural pluralism, an ideological choice that was implicit in *Spirale*'s formation and was soon after made explicit.

DAVID LEAHY

Sportswriting in English. Sportswriting in the 1990s is so much a part of modern newspaper journalism that its literary qualities can easily be ignored. Though some of this journalism is little more than an extended promotion vehicle for the sports/entertainment industry, many writers who describe sports events regularly display literary skills that have earned for this genre an overdue place in any literary history. At the same time, sport is now widely present as a theme in Canadian literature itself.

1. THE NINETEENTH CENTURY. Sportswriting in the nineteenth century was the perfect handmaiden to the development of the popular daily press. Its roots, however, are found in books describing the hunting and fishing pleasures of the New World, such as George Head's *Forest scenes and incidents in the wilds of North America; being a diary of a winter's route from Halifax to the Canadas, and during four months' residence in the woods on the borders of lakes Huron and Simcoe* (London, 1829); Frederick Tolfrey's *The sportsman in Canada* (2 vols, London, 1845), describing outdoor pleasures around Quebec City; and Campbell Hardy's *Sporting adventures in the new world; or, Days and nights of moose-hunting in the pine forests of Acadia* (London, 1855), which includes details of his tour through New Brunswick. (See also NATURE WRITING IN ENGLISH: 1.) While both Alexander Henry's *Travels and adventures in Canada and the Indian territories, between the years 1760 and 1776* (Boston, 1809), and Francis Parkman's *The conspiracy of Pontiac* (Boston, 1851), describe Native lacrosse play, and its significance in the sacking of Fort Michilimackinac in 1763, neither can be thought of as examples of the modern genre of sports writing. Not only was lacrosse at the time, in its preorganized form, not thought of as a cultural extension of everyday Native life, but the authors themselves had no conscious awareness of play as anything more than ritual.

In the early nineteenth century, sportswriting in Canada popularized sports among a largely English élite in Halifax, Montreal, and York (later Toronto). Weekly newspapers occasionally provided accounts of organized play in military garrisons and private schools. In Toronto, just prior to the 1837 Rebellion, the leading Tory newspaper, the *Patriot*, declared that 'A cricketer as a matter of course detests democracy and is staunch in allegiance to his king.' Sports coverage, though sporadic, continued through the middle of the century. The Toronto *Globe*, for instance, in 1855 published a lengthy account of a cricket match between the Darlington and Toronto clubs, attended by the Governor General's wife, Lady Head. Around the same time, annual Canadian cricket guides appeared that reflected the organized game's popularity throughout eastern Canada.

The development of indigenous sport also encouraged the treatment of games in books. The earliest, and one of the most important, was Montreal dentist W. George Beers' *Lacrosse: the national game of Canada* (Montreal, 1869). Beers was interested not only in promoting the game's virtues, but in having it declared the new country's national game. In the same vein was the work of a London, Ontario, publisher, William Bryce, whose *Bryce's Canadian baseball guide for 1876* (London, 1876), the first such publication, promoted the 'American' game of baseball—whose early history in Canada, nevertheless, was virtually contemporaneous with its growth in the United States.

When sports coverage did appear in newspapers of the day, minute-by-minute accounts of lacrosse or baseball matches dominated, with little critical analysis. One of the first consciously designated sports pages in North America, developed in the Toronto *Globe* in 1883 by W.G.H. Good, owes its origins in part to the international success of a local athlete, the rower Ned Hanlan. Montreal and Ottawa papers, and Good's Toronto rivals, did not include sports pages until the end of the century. In Montreal's case, at least part of the reason for lack of coverage was that sport was supported mainly by a small, largely upper-middle English class, who played a leading role in the development not only of lacrosse but of ice-hockey, football, and a variety of amateur sports. (It was out of their interest in sports that the Canadian Olympic Association emerged.) Organized sports were slow to take hold among most Montrealers, however, who were French-speaking.

2. THE TWENTIETH CENTURY. The earliest recognized proponents of daily sports writing included Francis Nelson, sports editor of the Toronto *Globe* prior to the First World War, and Lou Marsh (1878-1936), whose column 'Pick and Shovel' made the *Toronto Star* a leading source of objective sports reporting until his death. Canada's outstanding athlete is annually recognized by a trophy awarded in Marsh's name.

The period between the two world wars saw the flowering of a group of distinctive sports writers. Baz O'Meara of the *Montreal Star*, dubbed the dean of Canadian sportswriters, wrote a column entitled 'Passing Sport Show'. Two others, Elmer Ferguson and Ted Reeve (1902-93), were the first to be inducted into Canada's Sports Hall of Fame on the basis of their journalistic skills. Ferguson, born in Prince Edward Island, featured wry gossip in 'The Gist and Jest of It', a column he wrote in the *Montreal Herald* and later in the *Montreal Star*. Toronto-born Reeve (he led a Toronto football team, Balmy Beach, to the Grey Cup) was inspired by his voracious reading of Dickens and Thackeray. He wrote a column for the Toronto *Telegram*, featuring dramatic descriptions of such events as the 1952 rugby playoff game between Toronto and Hamilton at Toronto's Varsity Stadium: '. . . as the darkness descended on the muddy gridiron, the gaunt outline of the great, bare trees stood out against lights coming up in the buildings in the background. From the press box perch we could see the streetcars flashing by on Bloor [Street] with their bright windows, and somewhere in that grey stadium towards the close of an epic struggle between such gritty and evenly matched teams, everything new and everything old in this sport seemed to be there, everything that makes it rugby.'

As Canadian women came to sporting prominence, particularly following their gold-medal triumphs in the 1928 summer Olympics, newspapers aggressively pursued a female audience. In Toronto, where the *Star* had Alexandrine Gibb, who had managed the women's track-and-field team, the *Telegram* responded by hiring Phyllis Griffiths, women's basketball coach at the University of Toronto, while the *Globe* countered with a gold medallist in the Olympic relay team, Bobbie Rosenfeld (1905-69), who in her column combined reportorial skills with a humorous slant on games playing.

During the Depression, western Canada supported a generation of writers who command a significant place in sports journalism. Winnipeg's influence was felt in the writing of Jim Coleman, Ralph ALLEN, Trent Frayne, and Scott Young—all of whom moved to Toronto newspapers in the 1930s. As featured columnists they carried on Marsh's tradition, employing writing skills that enabled them to transform keen observation, and knowledge, into lucid, breezy, often humorous (sometimes poignant) descriptions of an event or person. (These skills have been passed on to younger columnists, such as the Toronto *Globe and Mail*'s Allen Abel, and his successor Stephen Brunt.) Jim Coleman wrote a book on Canadian horse-racing, *A hoofprint on my heart* (1971), and the other three writers have numerous books to their credit. Ralph Allen was the author of several fine novels; after his death in 1966 his newspaper and magazine articles were collected, and edited, by Christina McCALL in *The man from Oxbow: the best of Ralph Allan* (1967). Between them, Trent Frayne and Scott Young have published a great many books (some are mentioned below). Frayne's sportswriting perhaps culminated in a memoir, *The tales of an athletic supporter* (1990), on his more than forty years as a sports journalist. Scott Young's publications have included novels and collections of short stories, in addition to his books on sports and sports figures.

One of the first, and best, serious attempts to record sports history was E. King Dodds' *Canadian turf recollections* (1909), whose quirky eccentricity was spoiled by his racism ('But, oh my, how the old bigot could write!' was the later verdict of Peter Gzowski). William Perkins Bull's *From rattlesnake hunt to hockey: the story of sports in Canada and of the sportsmen of Peel, 1798 to 1934* (1934) was one of several volumes in his history of Peel County, Ontario. Works like these, however, had a sparse audience. Bull's book was limited to one thousand now very rare copies.

William A. Hewitt's *Down the stretch: recollections of a pioneer sportsman and journalist* (1958)—in which he acknowledged a debt to Dodds—combined history with personal remembrance and marked the entry of sportswriting into mainstream publishing. Hewitt—a leading organizer of the Ontario Hockey Association—is perhaps best known today as the father of Foster (1902-85), a reporter on the *Toronto Star*, who made his first hockey broadcast in March 1923 and, beginning in November 1931, became the voice of hockey for more than two decades in his broadcasts from Maple Leaf Gardens, Toronto—on radio, and then on television. The apex of Foster Hewitt's career was his calling of the 1972 Canada-Russia series. His literary efforts—such as *Hockey night in Canada* (1953)—were generally inconsequential. But in his broadcasts he popularized one of the most famous Canadian expressions, 'He shoots, he scores!', which was the title of his 1949 book.

Among William Hewitt's contemporaries was Henry Roxborough, who wrote the admirable *One hundred—not out: the story of nineteenth-century Canadian sport*, published in 1966 on the eve of Canada's Centennial celebration. More formal, historical approaches to sportswriting are seen in Nancy and Maxwell Howell's *Sports and games in Canadian life—1700 to the present* (1969), Alan Metcalfe's *Canada learns to play: the emergence of organized sport, 1807-1914* (1987), Donald Guay's *Introduction à l'histoire des sports au Québec* (1987), and *A concise history of sport in Canada* (1989) by Don Morrow and Mary Keyes, Wayne Simpson, Frank Cosentino (a notable football player in the 1960s), and Ron Lappage.

The maturing of popular sportswriting to reflect themes other than those on the field of play was influenced by incidents such as the challenge to World Figure Skating Champion Barbara Ann Scott's amateur standing in 1947. Because the City of Ottawa had given her an automobile, the International Olympic Association, under pressure from its vice-president, Avery Brundage, launched an investigation. Spurred by the new nationalism that followed Canada's participation in the Second World War, and by the often latent anti-Americanism of the Canadian public, Andy Lytle of the *Toronto Star*, Jack Park of the *London Free Press*, Montreal's Elmer Ferguson, Britt Jessup of the *North Bay Nugget*, and Alf Cottrell of the *Vancouver Sun* launched a vitriolic attack on Brundage. Their publicity led to a resolution that allowed Barbara Ann Scott to participate in—and win the gold medal at—the 1948 Winter Olympics.

Though traditionally sports writers did not take their craft very seriously—Dick Beddoes referred to their world as 'the toy universe' (an example of the metaphorical wit that frequently colours modern sports writing)—in the past fifteen years many serious books in the field of sports reporting have been published, including Peter Gzowski's hockey book *The game of our lives* (1981), an account of a year with the Edmonton Oilers, and *An unbroken line* (1983), the story of thoroughbred horse-racing in Canada; and Ken Dryden's hockey overview, *The game* (1983), and his follow-up with Roy MacGregor, *Home game* (1989).

Books about Canadian hockey, or their players, have proliferated. They include Trent Frayne's *Famous hockey players* (1973) and *The mad men of hockey* (1974); Paul QUARRINGTON's *Hometown heroes: on the road with Canada's national hockey team* (1988), a personal account of Team Canada's games in 1988 that won the LEACOCK Award for Humour; and *Dick Beddoes' greatest hockey stories* (1990). The fiction of Scott Young, who called hockey 'the language that pervades Canada', borrows freely from his sportswriting background and includes his popular series of boys' hockey stories, beginning with *Scrubs on skates* (1952). His non-fiction books on hockey include *The Leafs I knew* (1966); *100 years of dropping the puck: the history of the OHA* (1989); and *The boys of Saturday night: inside hockey night in Canada* (1990). *The best of Milt Dunnell: over 40 years of great sportswriting* (1993), edited by Robert Brehl, contains seventeen *Toronto Star* columns on hockey (and others on football, horseracing, boxing, and baseball).

On a more general level, Jack BATTEN wrote *Champions: great figures in Canadian sport* (1971); Trent Frayne's *The best of times: fifty years of Canadian sport* (1988) is an almost equal combination of text and pictures; and *Great Canadian sports stories: a century of competition* (1965), though mainly pictorial, contains alternating pieces by Frayne and Peter Gzowski on notable Canadian sports figures illustrated by many photographs, all with interesting discursive captions.

3. SPORTSWRITING IN LITERATURE. The first appearance of sporting themes in literature was in the form of versifying, such as Palmer Cox's narrative poem for children, 'The Brownies at Base Ball', which appeared in his collection *The Brownies, their book* (1887). William LIGHTHALL's *Songs of the great Dominion* (London, 1889)—an anthology of Canadian poetry intended to celebrate the country, its people, and their activities—included a section entitled 'Sports and Free Life', in which doggerel took over, as in John Lowry Stuart's 'Skating' ('And youth and beauty, love and life/Are out on the ice tonight'), Arthur Weir's 'Snowshoeing Song' ('Swiftly in single file we go/The city is soon left far below'), and the anonymous, minimalistic 'The Football Match' ('O, the kicking, stamping, punching, the gore and the glory of battle!/Kick, kick, kick, kick, kick, kick. Will you kick!'). At a somewhat higher level (though not in Lighthall's anthology) is

Charles G.D. ROBERTS' poem 'The Skater' (1901), which includes the lines, 'My glad feet shod with the glittering steel/I was the god of the winged heel'. *The sky pilot: a tale of the foothills* (1899) by Ralph Connor (Charles William GORDON) was one of the first Canadian novels to have sport, in this case baseball, as a key theme in the story. But with few exceptions the writing of fiction, poetry, and drama with a sports theme is a post-1945 phenomenon. Most Canadians' inherent attraction to sports—coupled with the media's pervasive coverage of sporting events—has been reflected in the work of creative writers such as Hugh HOOD (in his story 'Ghosts of Jarry Park'), Mordecai RICHLER (in 'Playing ball on Hampstead Heath'), George BOWERING in *Baseball: A poem in the magic number 9* (1967), Milton ACORN in 'The fights' ('In stinking dancehalls, in/the forums of small towns,/ punches are cheaper but/still pieces of death'), and James REANEY in 'The bicycle', from *Twelve letters to a small town* (1962). These were among the first modern writers to use sports—inevitably and memorably—as images and subjects.

Baseball-related fiction of literary merit includes John Craig's *Chappie and me* (1979), an autobiographical novel about a young white man from Trentville (a thin disguise for Peterborough) and his experience with a barnstorming black ball-team prior to the Second World War. The most important contemporary author who has mined baseball's rich heritage in short stories and novels is W.P. KINSELLA. The very title of one of his baseball stories (and of a 1984 short-story collection), 'The thrill of the grass', is a wonderful metaphor for baseball's appeal. His novel *Shoeless Joe* (1982) had its greatest impact in the United States, where it was developed into a major motion picture whose title, *Field of dreams*, has also become a metaphor for the American baseball fan's connection to the game. Colin Howell's *Northern sandlots: a social history of Maritime baseball* (1995), and William Humber's *Diamonds of the north: a concise history of baseball in Canada* (1995), approach the sport within the larger context of regional and Canadian culture. Stephen Brunt's *Diamond dreams: 20 years of Blue Jays baseball* (1996) is an excellent account of the career—mostly ups, with some downs—of the well-known Toronto baseball team that became one of the top teams in North America. *All I thought about was baseball: writings on a Canadian pastime* (1996), edited by William Humber and John St James, includes articles by many Canadian writers.

Not surprisingly, hockey has provided material for many Canadian creative writers. Notable are Rick SALUTIN's play *Les Canadiens* (1977), for which he received an 'assist' from Montreal goalie and future author Ken Dryden (who also wrote a Preface to the published version), and Al PURDY's poem 'Hockey players', in which hockey's role in Canada is '. . . to salve the anguish of inferiority by being good at something the Americans aren't'. The simplest, most moving, and 'classic' hockey story is Roch CARRIER's portrait of French-Canadian boyhood in *The hockey sweater* (1979, translated by Sheila Fischman)—in which he writes: 'As for church, we found there the tranquillity of God: there we forgot school and dreamed about the next hockey game. Through our daydreams it might happen that we would recite a prayer: we would ask God to help us play as well as Maurice Richard.' The gift of a Toronto Maple Leafs sweater to a young Québécois spoke volumes about Canada's two solitudes. *Hockey dreams: memories of a man who couldn't play* (1996) by David Adams RICHARDS, a lifelong hockey fan, is partly an essay on hockey but mostly a comic and vivid description of the hockey he played as a youth. Roy MacGregor—a sports columnist for the *Ottawa Citizen*—wrote *The home team: fathers, sons & hockey* (1995), which was nominated for a Governor General's Award, and followed this with *The seven a.m. practice: stories of family life* (1996), which also concentrates on the father-son relationship.

The literary magazine *DESCANT*, with a reputation for cosmopolitan themes, devoted a combined issue (56/57, Spring-Summer 1987) to 'Comedy and the Sporting Life' and included authors Paul Quarrington, George Bowering, W.P. Kinsella, and Eric WRIGHT.

The ability to weave sports seamlessly into the everyday life of one's time is magically captured in Richard WRIGHT's *The age of longing* (1995). It is only tangentially about a man who played four hockey games for the Montreal Maroons, but his sports life-style shapes the events and lives of the book's characters. Wright's book may be viewed as a response to David Whitson's critique of contemporary sports fiction. Co-author with Richard Gruneau of the critically acclaimed *Hockey Night in Canada: sport, identities and cultural politics* (1993), Whitson decried the lack of works with a sports theme in which '. . . social relations are problematized, in which the characters live in tension with the limits of their time and place, and define themselves precisely in the ways they do so.'

Such issues as high salaries, aggrieved athletes, corrupt officials, and drug abuse have demanded a much more critical viewpoint in sports journalism, and even better journalists, along with a more educated reading public. The ordinary fan, however, might sometimes wish only for the score of last night's game, and an account of the hero's role. Legend-making is more often than not left to our memories of a seemingly more innocent time—or to our imagination.

See Trent Frayne, ed., *Trent Frayne's Allstars: an anthology of Canada's best sportswriting* (1996), which includes pieces by Allen Abel, Jack Batten, Harry BRUCE, Jim Coleman, Ken Dryden, Milt Dunnell, Jim Proudfoot, and Paul Quarrington. WILLIAM HUMBER

Stacey, C.P. (1906-89). Charles Perry Stacey was born in Toronto, Ontario, and educated at the University of Toronto (B.A., 1927), Oxford University (B.A., 1929), and Princeton University (A.M., 1931; Ph.D., 1933), where he taught from 1934 to 1940. Having served in reserve units, and being interested in military history, he was commissioned into the Canadian Army in 1940 and joined the Historical Section of the General Staff, Army Headquarters, rising, with the rank of colonel, to be its director from 1945 to 1959, the year he was appointed professor of history at the University of Toronto. He was made an Officer of the Order of Canada in 1969.

The author of more than a dozen books, Stacey was a pivotal historian in depoliticizing history and ensuring its freedom from censorship. He made the official history of the Canadian Army than its ponderous predecessors in the Second World War more accessible to the intelligent general reader, but he did not foresee the battle he was forced to wage with Liberal governments to produce accounts free from censorship. Not only did Stacey succeed, but he also wrote three of the volumes: *The Canadian army, 1939-1945* (1948), winner of a Governor General's Award; *Six years of war* (1955); and *The victory campaign* (1960). His *Quebec, 1759: the seige and the battle* (1959) became the classic on the subject. The monumental *Men, arms, and governments: the military policies of Canada 1939-1945* (1970) brought together a lifetime's work. After retirement in 1975 Stacey produced a controversial study of Mackenzie King's private world in *A very double life* (1976). The two-volume *Canada and the age of conflict* (1977, 1981) examined the history of foreign policy free from the partisan biases that had previously been prominent in twentieth-century historiography. Stacey called his memoirs *A date with history: memoirs of a Canadian historian* (1983). TERRY CROWLEY

Stansbury, Joseph (1742?-1809). Born in London, England, he immigrated to Philadelphia, arriving there on 11 Oct. 1767. He opened a china shop and gradually became a prominent member of the British social set. He had the reputation of being intelligent, with an ability to write satirical and humorous political poems and songs. 'As a writer of satirical verse, free from hatred and bitterness, he was "without a rival among his brethren"' (M.C. Tyler, *The literary history of the American Revolution*, 1897). With talk of a revolution in the air, he opposed independence of the American colonies and became a British agent, acting as a go-between for Benedict Arnold and the British headquarters. He moved to New York City, where he continued to write satires directed against the Whigs. In 1783 Stansbury moved his family to the Loyalist settlement of Shelburne, Nova Scotia; but after two years of hardship and disappointment he returned to New York, where he died. His well-known poem 'To Cordelia' vividly records his feelings about pioneer life in Nova Scotia. Winthrop Sargent's *The loyal verses of Joseph Stansbury and Dr. Jonathan Odell* (Albany, 1860) is still the best collection of his verse, although he is represented in a number of Canadian anthologies.

DOUGLAS LOCHHEAD

Stead, Robert J.C. (1880-1959). Robert James Campbell Stead was born in Middleville, Ontario, and grew up in Cartwright, Manitoba. He attended Winnipeg Business College, and from 1898 to 1909 published and edited a local weekly called variously *The Rock Lake Review*, *The Rock Lake Review and Cartwright Enterprise*, and *The Southern Manitoba Review*. In 1908-9 he also edited the *Crystal City Courier*. Stead worked at other temporary occupations, including selling automobiles, and by 1912 was in Calgary, Alberta, first on the editorial staff of *The Albertan*, then from 1913 directing publicity for the colonization department of the Canadian Pacific Railway. In 1919 he moved to Ottawa to be publicity director for the Department of Immigration and Colonization, and from 1936 until his retirement in 1946 he held this position for parks-and-resources aspects of the Department of Mines and Resources. He was active in the CANADIAN AUTHORS' ASSOCIATION from its inception, and became its president in 1923.

Stead was the only writer to span the development of prairie fiction from the popular genre of romances of pioneering to realistic novels scrutinizing the values of prairie society. His five volumes of slight, patriotic verse—*The empire builders* (1908), *Prairie born* (1911), *Songs of the prairie* (1911), *Kitchener and other poems*, (1916), and *Why don't they cheer* (1918)—are of interest mainly as evidence of Stead's devotion to the imperial vision of the Prairies. Except for *The copper disc* (1931), a mystery published in the Doubleday 'Crime Club' series, Stead's novels have prairie or foothills settings. *The bail jumper* (1914), *The homesteaders* (1916), *The cow puncher* (1918), which sold 70,000 copies, *Dennison Grant* (1920), and *Neighbours* (1922) all combine romantic plots and authentic depictions of western life. They brought Stead immediate popularity rather than a lasting reputation—with the exception of *The homesteaders*, which went through five printings by 1922 and has since earned critical recognition as a central romance of pioneering. Tracing the lives of an ideal pioneer couple from their arrival in Manitoba in 1882 to the land-boom before the Great War, it develops such traditional motifs and themes of its genre as harmony with the land, the marriage of eastern refinement and western vitality, and the dangers of falling from idealism into mammonism. *The homesteaders* was reprinted in the Literature in Canada series (1973), with an introduction by Susan Wood Glicksohn.

It has been argued that Stead, the journalist and publicist, exploited a shrewd sense of the popular taste in fiction; yet even his romances show a sometimes obtrusive concern for social issues, and in his last two prairie novels he turned away from the formulas that had brought him popularity to develop his ideas and his craft. In *The smoking flax* (1925) sociological theories about rural life overpower a weak plot; but it prepared the themes and techniques that Stead developed in his next and best novel, *Grain* (1926). It portrays, from an ironic perspective, the life of Gander Stake, whose growth as a human being is stunted by the culturally impoverished environment of a prairie farm, and by an almost erotic absorption in the romance of mechanization. The technical nature and function of Stead's realism are subjects of critical debate, but Stead is credited, along with Frederick Philip GROVE and Martha OSTENSO, with initiating the sober assessment of man's spiritual alienation from the land that distinguishes prairie realism from the earlier romances of pioneering. *Grain* is in the NEW CANADIAN LIBRARY.

See Frank DAVEY, 'Rereading Stead's *Grain*', *Studies in Canadian Literature* 4 (Winter 1979), and Leslie Mundwiler, 'Robert Stead—home in the first place', *Essays on Canadian Writing* 11 (Summer, 1978).

DICK HARRISON

Steffler, John (b. 1947). He was born in Toronto, Ontario, and raised in a rural area north of the city, near Thornhill. He received a B.A. (1971) from the University of Toronto and an M.A. (1974) from the University of Guelph. He is Professor of English at Sir Wilfred Grenfell College, Memorial University of Newfoundland, in Corner Brook.

Steffler has written three volumes of poetry: *An explanation of yellow* (1981), *The Grey Islands: a journey* (1985), and *The wreckage of play* (1988). Atlantic-coast folklore reveals its influence in the storytelling nature of much of Steffler's poetry. His syntax is that of speech, and his translucent images show that the lessons taught by the Imagists have been learned well. Family, love of nature, and an often anxious contemplation of the past are some of the recurring themes in his poems. *The Grey Islands*, in which the speaker writes of a journey to islands off the east coast of northern Newfoundland, is Steffler's most important collection to date, consisting of poems and prose. As the journey progresses, the poet reveals his fascination for 'Carm', the last man to remain on the islands, a fisherman who lived an eccentric life full of deprivation and grief and was considered 'mental', but whose relationship to the island and to isolation the poet attempts to absorb. *The Grey Islands* presents both the voice of the local fisherman, who speaks only of lived experience, and the introspective voice of the poet.

Steffler's interest in multiple narratives reasserted itself in his best-known work, *The afterlife of George Cartwright* (1992), for which he won the Smithbooks/*Books in Canada* First Novel Award. It is based on the life of the eighteenth-century diarist and entrepreneur who ran a trading post in Labrador and who wrote about his experiences in a journal published in 1792. Steffler managed both to convey sympathy for Cartwright and to condemn his exploitation of the Native people with whom he lived and worked. Part history, part fiction, the novel is remarkable for its successful manipulation of a complex chronology in which the narrative ricochets through three centuries.

Steffler has also written a children's book, *Flights of magic* (1987), illustrated by his wife Shawn. CYNTHIA MESSENGER

Stegner, Wallace. See FOREIGN WRITERS ON CANADA IN ENGLISH: 2.

Stein, David Lewis (b. 1937). Born and raised in Toronto, he attended the University of Toronto, where he became interested in journalism and was features editor of the *Varsity*. After graduation he worked as a reporter for *Maclean's*, the New York *Herald Tribune* in its Paris bureau, the *Star Weekly*, and now writes a weekly column on the city for the *Toronto Star*.

Stein's journalism, often studying political activism and its social roots, stands behind his two non-fiction books—*Living the revolution: the Yippies in Chicago* (1969) and *Toronto for sale: the destruction of a city* (1972)—as well as his play *The hearing* (1978), which depicts the comic and tragic dimensions of municipal battles between real-estate developers and homeowners' associations.

Like his journalism, Stein's fiction takes the form of political protest and social commentary, with the influence of George Orwell always in evidence. In his fine first novel, *Scratch one dreamer* (1967), written while he was on a CANADA COUNCIL fellowship in London, England, Joe Fried, a middle-class Jewish liberal individualist, returns home to Toronto and his dying uncle, a former labour leader of the 1940s. Maintaining a careful and frequently comic balance between the cynical and the sentimental, the novel is a detached yet passionate study of political activism in the 1960s and of the hero's growing acceptance of individual moral choices. Stein's second novel, *My sexual and other revolutions: the memoirs of Daniel Johnson as told to David Lewis Stein* (1972), is his most vitriolic work; yet the vehemence of his social criticism—moving sometimes awkwardly among parody, satire, pornography, and blatant attack—makes the book less effective as a novel than *Scratch one dreamer*.

With Dave GODFREY and Clark BLAISE, Stein edited a collection of their short stories, *New Canadian writing* (1968); his own contributions reflect his persistent concern with the social manifestations of hatred and evil. His collection *City boys* (1978) includes both published and unpublished short fiction.

Given his reputation as an insightful and empathetic chronicler of life in Toronto, it is not surprising that Stein uses that city as both setting and character in two later novels: *The golden age hotel* (1984) and *Taking power* (1992), the latter a topical book that explores the public and private lives of a large cast of characters during the tumultuous 1970s.

DAVID STAINES

Stevens, Peter (b. 1927). Born in Manchester, England, he graduated in English and Education from the University of Nottingham (B.A., 1951). In 1957 he came to Canada and taught at both a private school and McMaster University while working on his M.A. He taught at the University of Saskatchewan (1964-8) and was the first person to receive a doctorate there in Canadian literature (1968). Stevens' thesis topic, 'The growth of modernism in Canadian poetry between the wars', led eventually to the publication of *The McGill movement* (1969), and to his editing of Raymond KNISTER's *The first day of spring and other stories* (1976). He has also written critical monographs on the poetry of Dorothy LIVESAY and Miriam WADDINGTON, whose modernist poetics profoundly influenced Stevens' sense of versification and vocalized personal presence in his poems. From 1969 to 1996 Stevens taught English and creative writing at the University of Windsor, Ontario, and served as contributing editor to *The Ontario Review* (1973-8) and as poetry editor of *The CANADIAN FORUM* (1968-73). Stevens edited with J.L. GRANATSTEIN *Forum: Canadian life and letters, 1920-1970* (1972). He founded the Sesame Press (now defunct) and has written several plays, three of which received performances in Detroit, Vancouver, and Windsor.

Stevens began writing poetry after his arrival in Canada and his first collection of poems, *Nothing but spoons* (1969), focuses on domestic events and Canadian places and landscapes. Poems such as 'Saskatchewan' from that collection represent a diary of adjustment to the new country. These subjects are expanded in *A few myths* (1971), which accommodates both conventional and experimental forms. Stevens' fascination with narrative and with individuals who observe the world from the periphery are characteristics of the books from the middle of his career, such as *Breadcrusts and glass* (1972), *Family feelings* (1974), and the chapbook *A momentary stay* (1980). *And the dying sky like blood* (1974) is a collage of poems that examine the life of Dr Norman Bethune and draws from such sources as found poetry, narrative vignettes, and lines from jazz songs of the 1930s and 1940s—material of special interest to Stevens, who contributed to CBC's Jazz Radio Canada program and who runs a Saturday-morning jazz show on a local radio station in Windsor. *The Bogman Pavese tactics* (1977) is divided into four sections, of which the first is based on P.V. Glob's discoveries of human sacrifices in northern European bogs (the same source inspired some of the best work of Irish poet Seamus Heaney), while the third continues Stevens' fascination with character-based narratives and focuses on Italian poet Cesare Pavese. *A momentary stay*, which examines the brevity and fragility of life in the context of an alienated and dispassionate world, and the chapbook *Coming back* (1981) were followed by *Revenge of the mistresses poems* (1981), which draws upon a collection of erotic photographs by fashion photographer Helmut Newton and gives voice to, and avenges, the 'used' women of the pictures. For *Out of the willow trees* (1986) Stevens returned to the material of his childhood and the important relationships in his life in a process of self-examination and re-evaluation. *Swimming in the afternoon: new and selected poems* (1992), edited by Bruce Meyer, takes its title from Kafka's off-hand diary remark about the beginning of the First World War and contains poems that confront the ways individuals are ambushed by the unexpected in life. Long attracted to the dark side of human nature and the Gothic underbelly of the contemporary psyche, Stevens in *RipRap: Yorkshire Ripper poems* (1995) takes a documentary approach to the murders and the murderer. It establishes a link between the Yorkshire of the mass murderer and that of Stevens' own past, and examines the ways in which actions become sublimated in consciousness and the process by which reality is transformed into memory—a sublimation that is both horrific and entangling.

BRUCE MEYER

Stevenson, Lionel. See CRITICISM IN ENGLISH: 2.

Stewart, George, Jr (1848-1906). Born in New York City, he came to Canada with his parents in 1851 and was educated in London, Canada West (Ontario), and in Saint John, New Brunswick. At sixteen he founded *The stamp collector's monthly gazette* (1865-7), the first periodical of its kind in Canada, and at nineteen *STEWART'S LITERARY QUARTERLY MAGAZINE* (Saint John, 1867-72). From 1872 to 1878 he was city editor of the Saint John *Daily News* and literary and dramatic editor of *The Weekly Watchman*; he went to Toronto in 1878-9 as editor of *ROSE-BELFORD'S CANADIAN MONTHLY*, but resigned after losing his court battle to get royalties from *Rose-Belford's* for his *Canada under the administration of the Earl of Dufferin* (Toronto, 1878). He next edited the Quebec *Daily Chronicle* from 1879 to 1896. He then purchased and edited the *Quebec Daily Mercury*, and when it ceased publication in 1903 he returned to the *Chronicle*. For many years he freelanced for American and Canadian magazines and contributed to reference works.

Stewart was an innovative editor whose career illustrates the hazards of professional literary journalism in nineteenth-century Canada. His *Literary Quarterly*, founded on the belief that good literature could 'elevate and refine' emotions and morals, ran out of Canadian contributors of fiction. He introduced illustrated articles into *Rose-Belford's Canadian Monthly* and expanded its fiction department to include American writers. He was a prolific reviewer of theatre productions in Saint John and Quebec City. He was also one of the first Canadian journalists to deal with contemporary events in book form. *The story of the great fire in St. John, New Brunswick* (Saint John, Toronto, Detroit, 1877) is still a reliable source book; *Canada under the administration of the Earl of Dufferin*, however, is less a history of the country than a eulogistic record of the Governor General's public duties, with long excerpts from his speeches, though Stewart narrates events like the public reaction to the Pacific Scandal (1873) in a simple and dramatic way. While he advocated higher critical standards that he had evolved under the influence of William Wordsworth and Matthew Arnold, his articles on Carlyle, Thoreau, Emerson, and Longfellow were appreciative rather than judgemental; these were collected in *Evenings in the library* (Toronto, 1878) and *Essays from reviews* (Quebec, 1st series, 1882; 2nd series, 1893). Attacking the apathy towards local writers, he pressed for a native publishing industry and for Canada's adherence to international copyright. He was a fervent interpreter of French Canada in many articles that ranged from the scholarly to the travel guide. He contributed the chapter 'Frontenac and his times' to Justin Winsor's seven-volume *Narrative and critical history of America* (Boston, 1885; see vol. IV), and his New York lecture on English- and French-Canadian literature was printed in *Canadian leaves: history, art, science, literature, commerce; a series of new papers read before the Canadian Club of New York* (New York, 1887). He was one of the first critics to argue that Canadian and American literature were distinct from British literature.

His activities and writings brought Stewart international recognition, including honorary membership in the Athenaeum Club of London; the distinction of becoming the first Canadian member (1879) of the International Literary Congress; and honorary degrees from

Laval, McGill, and Bishop's universities, and from King's College, Halifax. He was a charter member of the Royal Society of Canada (1882) and was for many years secretary of its English section and a contributor to its *Transactions*. Despite his fame and success, Stewart died in straightened circumstances; Carol Fullerton observes that 'Stewart's dream of supporting himself as a man of letters, of living by and for good literature, foundered in a society more interested in commercial enterprise than in cultural development.'

See Carol W. Fullerton, 'George Stewart, Jr., a nineteenth-century Canadian man of letters', *Papers of the Bibliographical Society of Canada*, 25 (1986), 'The theatre criticism of George Stewart, Jr.', *Theatre history in Canada* 2 (1988), and 'George Stewart, Jr.', *DICTIONARY OF CANADIAN BIOGRAPHY*, vol. 13 (1994); and George L. Parker, *The beginnings of the book trade in Canada* (1985). Stewart's essay 'Letters in Canada' is reprinted in *The search for English-Canadian literature: an anthology of critical articles from the nineteenth and early twentieth centuries* (1975) edited by Carl Ballstadt.

GEORGE L. PARKER

Stewart, Herbert. See PHILOSOPHY IN CANADA: 6.

Stewart, John. See HISTORICAL WRITING IN ENGLISH: 1.

Stewart's Literary Quarterly Magazine, Devoted to Light and Entertaining Literature (Saint John, Apr. 1867-Oct. 1872). This was the only Canadian magazine of its day to rely entirely on original contributions. The editor and publisher to Jan. 1872 was its founder George STEWART, Jr; it continued for three numbers until Oct. 1872 as *The New Brunswick Quarterly*, of which the joint editors and publishers were A.A. Stockton and G.W. Burbidge.

To counter the spread of 'trashy weeklies and immoral monthlies' from the United States, Stewart believed 'the time had come for literary development in Canada, and especially in New Brunswick. Our best writers . . . were sending their work to the British and American magazines, and I was convinced that the country could and would afford a decent support to a monthly or quarterly magazine.' Financially the *Quarterly* was not successful, even though its printer, George James Chubb, took no profit from it. Although Stewart attracted little fiction, he published poetry by James Hannay, Charles SANGSTER, Alexander McLACHLAN, and Ewan McColl; biographical sketches; and articles on history, drama, and literature. The final volumes leaned towards articles on science and religion that expounded the 'Common Sense' philosophy of Canadian intellectuals of that period. In 'Human progress—is it real?' the Rev. Moses HARVEY argued that geology proved that evolution was part of the divine plan (Oct. 1871), while 'Diana' came out against women's suffrage in '"Women's rights" and a woman's view of them' (Apr. 1870). As a critic, Stewart tried to evaluate Canadian writers by the same standards that he applied to the British and the Americans. It was now time, he maintained in a review of Charles MAIR's *Dreamland, and other poems* (January 1869), to judge a work on its artistic merits rather than merely as a phenomenon of Canadian authorship and publishing. While they were frequently cosmopolitan and lively, however, *Quarterly* writers never quite shook off a self-conscious provincialism in dealing with Canadian writing; and a spirit of parochialism infected its successor. Nevertheless, *Stewart's Quarterly* showed that Canadian journalism had the potential for higher standards.

See Carol W. Fullerton, 'George Stewart, Jr, a nineteenth-century Canadian man of letters', *Papers of the Bibliographical Society of Canada*, 25 (1986); and Fraser Sutherland, *The monthly epic: a history of Canadian magazines* (1989); two of Stewart's articles from the *Quarterly*, 'Introductory' and 'Canadian Literature', are reprinted in *Towards a Canadian literature: essays, editorials and manifestos*, 1 (1985) edited by Douglas M. Daymond and Leslie G. Monkman.

GEORGE L. PARKER

Still stands the house (1938). This one-act 'drama of the Canadian frontier' (as it is subtitled) is one of five plays Gwen Pharis RINGWOOD wrote while earning her M.A. in drama at the University of North Carolina. First produced by the Carolina Playmakers on 3 Mar. 1938, and first published in 1938 in the *Carolina Playbook*, vol. II, it is one of the most popular plays in the Canadian dramatic repertory.

The cast consists of four characters, and the action, which takes place in the Warrens' prairie farmhouse during a blizzard, is stark and simple. A real-estate salesman offers Ruth a vision of a new future near a city. Opposed to her is Hester, her sister-in-law, whose allegiance is to a house and farm as sterile as her own life. Caught between them is Hester's brother Bruce Warren, who is married to Ruth. Bruce is lost in the blizzard, and Ruth is murdered by Hester, who lapses into madness. With its claustrophobic setting in the living-room of the isolated farmhouse, presenting a powerful metaphor of Canadian life during the Depression, and its winter blizzards, offering an image of a disorder in nature that is reflected in the disorder of the Warren household, the play is a folk tragedy. Its key symbols—a broken hyacinth, a lamp not filled, a mare about to foal—reinforce Ringwood's theme of disorder and madness.

See Judith Hinchcliffe, '*Still stands the house*: the failure of the pastoral dream', *Canadian Drama* 2 (1977). ROTA HERZBERG LISTER

Stirling, Shirley. See CHILDREN'S LITERATURE IN ENGLISH 1970 TO 1996: 1(c).

Stone angel*, *The (1964). This novel by Margaret LAURENCE, which established her international reputation, is the first of her books to have a Canadian setting and the first volume of what is known as the Manawaka cycle. A draft was completed in 1962, when Laurence was living in Vancouver, and rewritten the next year in England. In 1964 it was published simultaneously in Toronto (McCLELLAND & STEWART), London (Macmillan), and New York (Knopf). It was translated into German by Herbert Schuter as *Der steinerne Engel* (Munich, 1965) and into French by Claire MARTIN as *L'ange de pierre* (Montreal, 1976).

Originally entitled *Hagar*, it is a character study of the narrator, ninety-year-old Hagar Shipley, who is fiercely battling the threat of banishment to an old people's home and the ravages of terminal disease. Friction with her son and daughter-in-law, with whom she lives, and her desperate attempt to preserve some dignity, contribute to a powerfully realized study of old age. A meeting with a stranger leads her to acquire a measure of grace before she is put into hospital where, in her last days, she is able to offer a little of the love and humility she has previously, to her cost, always withheld. Hagar's narrative, with its wit and humorous self-awareness, alternates between present action and reminiscences of the past: her Manawaka childhood; her defiant marriage to the handsome but lackadaisical Bram Shipley; life on his dusty, ramshackle farm during the Depression with her two sons; and her partial responsibility for the death of her younger son.

The interweaving of past and present is part of a larger pattern of contrasts, which are most marked in the duality of Hagar's character: she has tried to hold to the stony, puritanical pride of her Scots-Presbyterian ancestors while denying the life-loving, wild, spontaneous part of her nature that gives such vigour to her narrative. Like the stone angel marking her mother's tomb, she has been 'doubly blind' in all her human relations. Incorporating many biblical allusions, the novel offers a modern version of the archetypal quest for spiritual vision.

Early critical articles on *The stone angel* are listed in *Margaret Laurence: an annotated bibliography* (1979) by Susan J. Warwick. A collection of articles on the novel appears in *Études Canadiennes/Canadian Studies*, vol. 11 (1981). See also articles by Joan Coldwell in *Journal of Canadian Fiction*, vol. 32 (1981), William New in *Articulating West* (1972), Constance Rooke in *CANADIAN LITERATURE* 92 (1982), and Patricia Koster in *Ariel*, vol. 16 (1985).

JOAN COLDWELL

Stratford, Philip. See TRANSLATIONS: ENGLISH TO FRENCH and TRANSLATIONS: FRENCH TO ENGLISH: 3.

Stratton, Allan. See DRAMA IN ENGLISH 1953 TO 1981.

Strickland, Samuel. See Writing in ONTARIO: 1.

Stringer, Arthur (1874-1950). Arthur John Arbuthnott Stringer was born in Chatham, Ontario. He studied at the University of Toronto (1892-4) and briefly at Oxford University, before beginning a career in journalism and freelance writing, first with the Montreal *Herald* (1897-8) and then in New York, where he established himself as a capable producer of popular fiction and a minor but flamboyant figure on the fashionable literary scene. His first marriage was to actress Jobyna Howland, known as the original 'Gibson Girl'. In 1903 he bought a farm at Cedar Springs on the north shore of Lake Erie, where he lived intermittently for the next eighteen years, a period that included a brief, costly attempt at grain farming in Alberta around 1914. In 1921 he sold his Ontario farm and moved permanently to an acreage in New Jersey.

Stringer was as versatile as he was prolific. In addition to writing fifteen volumes of undistinguished verse and non-fiction prose —including *A study of King Lear* (New York, 1897)—and more than forty works of fiction, he wrote copiously for magazines and occasionally for the stage, and for the serial 'The perils of Pauline' for Hollywood. His popularity was based mainly on a series of crime adventure novels, beginning with *The wire tappers* (1906), and on a series of wilderness adventures of the North (an area unfamiliar to Stringer), beginning with *Empty hands* (1924). He occasionally attempted psychological sophistication, as in *The wine of life* (1921), and has been hailed as an early realist; but generally he worked within the conventions of sentimental romance popular around the turn of the century.

Though Stringer used Canadian settings in a few of his novels, and Canadian characters in others, the bulk of his work belongs to American literature. One of his most popular books was *Lonely O'Malley* (1905), a sentimentalization of his boyhood in Chatham and London; but he made an enduring contribution to Canadian literature with his prairie trilogy: *Prairie wife* (1915), *Prairie mother* (1920), and *Prairie child* (1921). Stringer's narrator, a New England socialite married to a dour Scots-Canadian wheat farmer, develops gradually from the optimism typical of pioneering romances, through dissillusionment as her marriage deteriorates, to mature resolve as she begins an independent life on the Prairies. Stringer's use of the diary form (though the narrative ostensibly opens as a letter to a friend) anticipates Sinclair ROSS's *AS FOR ME AND MY HOUSE* and places Stringer's trilogy in the Canadian tradition of confessions of a refined sensibility confronting the crudeness of pioneer life. Stringer attempted unsuccessfully to combine the prairie setting with a crime adventure in *The mud lark* (1932).

See Victor Lauriston, *Arthur Stringer* (1941).

See also CRITICISM IN ENGLISH: 2.

DICK HARRISON

Strube, Cordelia. See NOVELS IN ENGLISH 1983 TO 1996: OTHER NOVELS 2(a).

Such, Peter (b. 1939). Born in the east end of London, England, he immigrated to Canada in 1953 and completed his secondary schooling in Toronto before obtaining a B.A. and an M.A. in English from the University of Toronto. He has taught in high schools, colleges, and universities in Ontario and is now professor of humanities at York University, Toronto, and co-ordinator of Canadian Studies at Atkinson College. In 1971 he founded *Impulse*, a literary magazine devoted to contemporary Canadian writing, and between 1975 and 1977 was managing editor of *Books in Canada*. He was also one of the founders of the Canadian Periodical Publishers Association.

Such's first novel, *Fallout* (1969; rpr. 1977), grew out of his experience as a miner in the uranium mines near Elliot Lake while he was a student. Told in fragments, it is about the violent rape of the landscape in the search for ore—a rape that is mirrored in the violent lives of the Natives and white men caught up in the rush for precious metal—and argues that exploitation of the land demands its price in exploitation of the Native people. The novel's grimness is somewhat tempered by a lyrical love affair between one of the Natives and a young white woman. *Riverrun* (1973) is about the last days of the Beothuk people of Newfoundland, who were systematically wiped out by the white settlers, becoming extinct by 1829. Told convincingly from the point of view of the Beothuks as they make their last desperate stand for survival, having been driven from the sea's edge by the newcomers, it is a bitter epitaph for a people in tune with the riverrun, the annual migration of salmon and caribou, on which the Beothuks largely depended. *Dolphin's wake* (1979) is a thriller about an archaeologist and his wife who have spent many years in Greece. Although in this novel Such tried to escape what he calls 'the varnished-up rural past' of so much Canadian fiction, it is not as successful as his novels with a Canadian setting.

Such's other works include *Soundprints* (1972), a concise introduction to the work of six Canadian composers: John Weinzweig, Harry Somers, John Beckwith, Norma Beecroft, Walter Buczynski, and Murray Schaefer; and *Vanished peoples: the archaic Dorset and Beothuk people of Newfoundland* (1978).

PETER BUITENHUIS

Suknaski, Andrew (b. 1942). Born on a homestead near Wood Mountain, Saskatchewan, of a Polish mother and a Ukrainian father, Suknaski attended Simon Fraser University and the University of British Columbia, as well as the Kootenay School of Fine Arts and the Montreal Museum of Fine Arts School of Art and Design. He has worked at various jobs across the Prairies and in 1976 listed his occupation as 'migrant worker'. Though he has lived all over western Canada, his true home and centre remains Wood Mountain.

English was not Suknaski's first language, and the vocabulary of his poems contains a rich strain of Polish and Ukrainian, as well as many attempts to render an approximate transliteration of ethnic speech and pronunciation. Much of his early poetry, published in pamphlets by his own Elfin Plot Press, is visual in nature: concrete poems based on East Asian characters and on collage. His full emergence as an important voice in western Canadian poetry came with the publication of *Wood Mountain poems* (1976). Subsequent collections include *The ghosts call you poor* (1978), *In the name of Narid* (1981), *Montage for an interstellar cry* (1982), and *Silk Trail* (1985). In recent years, poor health has largely prevented him from writing. There is a volume of selected poems, *The land they gave away: new and selected poems* (1982), edited with an introduction by Stephen SCOBIE.

Suknaski's central subject has been the people and the heritage of Wood Mountain, and of the Prairies generally. He writes of the town's inhabitants, both present and past, of the various nationalities and generations of the settlers, and of the Native people whose land it first was. (The historical association of Wood Mountain with Sitting Bull is a recurrent topic.) Suknaski sees himself as a mythographer who honours his subjects, rather than as a historian who describes or analyses them. Like many Prairie writers, he loves the tall tale, the beer-parlour story, and the accents of the voices that recount them. Because he tries to recreate on the printed page the vividness and variety of spoken narrative, his poems tend to be long and rambling, somewhat diffuse in form, their poetic effect depending upon the choice and juxtaposition of anecdotes. The later work shows an increasing concern for those ethnic groups that have historically been relegated to the margins of society, and for a large-scale sense of world mythology.

This historically based anecdotal style, employing the rhythms of the speaking voice, became for a time a dominant influence in prairie poetry, and in the late 1970s Suknaski himself—with his beard, pipe, and coil of sweetgrass—was a presiding shaman of the region's literature. Perhaps the best view of Suknaski and his work can be found in Harvey Spak's film *Wood Mountain poems* (National Film Board, 1978). STEPHEN SCOBIE

Sullivan, Alan (1868-1947). Born in Montreal, he spent his childhood in his father's Anglican rectories in Chicago, Montreal, and Sault Ste Marie, and attended Loretto School, the most Spartan of British public schools, in Scotland. After studying civil engineering for a year at the University of Toronto (1886-7), he began a rugged career in northern Ontario that included surveying and construction for the Canadian Pacific Railway, lumbering, industrial engineering, gold mining, and prospecting. In 1904 he settled in Toronto, began to raise his large family, and, finding the sedentary life confining, turned in his free time to the literary re-creation of his past experiences. His short-story collection *The passing of Oul-i-but* (1913) marked the beginning of his full-time career as a writer at age 45. After a stint with the RAF during the First Wold War, Sullivan wrote the useful *Aviation in Canada: 1917-18* (1919). In 1920 he moved to England, where he lived—making numerous extended trips to Canada—until his death.

Of Sullivan's 43 works of fiction, some two dozen are lightweight novels of romance, mystery, and adventure set mainly in England, some published under the pseudonym 'Sinclair Murray'. Three of these—*Human clay* (1926), *In the beginning* (1926), and *A little way ahead* (1930)—deal with the paranormal. Sullivan wrote best, however, of the testing of manhood and the forging of a nation in the rugged Canadian landscape. Often his heroes discover their identity when they leave the Old Country for Canada, as in *Blantyre—alien* (1914), *The splendid silence* (1927), *Whispering lodge* (1927), and *The golden foundling* (1931). Sullivan's industrial experience, and belief in the value of labour, form the basis of *The rapids* (1920), a fictionalized account of the industrialization of Sault Ste Marie; *The inner door* (1917), on the relations between masters and men; and *The crucible* (1925). The Canadian Arctic provides a striking setting for *The magic makers* (1930) and *With love from Rachel* (1938). Sullivan's love of the North and its Native people is a major theme in his short-story collections *Under the northern lights* (1926) and *The cycle of the north* (1938), and in his four books for children. Perhaps most impressive are his historical novels, with their accurate detail and mixture of real and fictional characters. *The great divide* (1935) depicts the building of the Canadian Pacific Railway; *The fur masters* (1938) concerns the rivalry among early trading companies; *Three came to Ville Marie* (1941), winner of a Governor General's award, is set in seventeenth-century Montreal; and *Cariboo Road* (1946) is the story of prospectors who joined the Fraser Valley gold rush in 1862.

Sullivan also produced poetry, radio scripts, and magazine fiction, and in his heyday was widely read and reviewed. Several of his novels were made into films, including *The great divide*, which received a glittering première in England as *The great barrier* (1937). Workmanlike if not supremely talented, Sullivan conveyed an ethos of mainly masculine hard work, perseverance, and loyalty, which helped define Canada to itself and others.

JEAN O'GRADY

Sullivan, Rosemary (b. 1947). Born in Montreal, Quebec, she attended McGill University (B.A., 1968), the University of Connecticut (M.A., 1969), and the University of Sussex, where she earned her Ph.D. in 1972 for a thesis that was published as *The garden master: the poetry of Theodore Roethke* (1975). After teaching for a year each at the Université de Dijon and the Université de Bordeaux, she taught at the University of Victoria, British Columbia, from 1974 to 1977, when she joined the English faculty at the University of Toronto, becoming a full professor of English in 1991. Sullivan, who is widely respected as a critic, editor, poet and biographer, was a Guggenheim fellow in 1992. A founding member of the Toronto Arts group for Human Rights, she was co-ordinator of the International Congress, *The Writer and Human Rights*, for Amnesty International in 1981, and she served on the editorial boards of *DESCANT* and *This Magazine*. Her article on Elizabeth SMART in *This Magazine* won the 1986 Brascan Silver Medal for cultural journalism.

Sullivan has published two collections of poetry. *The space a name makes* (1986), which won the Gerald Lampert Award for poetry, contains evocative poems about family history, love, neighbourhood, and travel. *Blue panic* (1991) intensifies this exploration of the ordinary world and extends it to include a Chilean sequence. Both collections portray life as lived in the context of a psychological hinterland subject to both tenderness and violence. This perspective is also brought to bear in Sullivan's substantial and engrossing biographies of two writers: *By heart: Elizabeth Smart, a life* (1991) and *Shadow maker: the life of Gwendolyn MacEwen* (1995), which won both the City of Toronto Book Award and a Governor General's Award. While seeking to understand the creativity of Smart and MacEWEN, Sullivan illuminates the complexities of the interactions between life and art. In *Shadow maker* she reveals the process of writing a biography in ways that enhance our understanding not only of her subject, but of the form itself.

Sullivan has also been active as an editor: *The pool in the desert* (1984), stories by Sara Jeannette DUNCAN; *Stories by Canadian women* (1984, 1987); and *Poetry by Canadian women* (1989). She also co-edited the Canadian edition of *Elements of fiction* (1982) and *Poetry in English: an anthology* (1987). LEILA RYAN

Summers, Merna (b. 1933). Born in Mannville, Alberta, she was a reporter and free-lance writer before turning to the writing of fiction. She has written three collections of short stories: *The skating party* (1974), *Calling home* (1982), *North of the battle* (1988). Widely anthologized, her stories have won numerous literary awards.

Summers writes with insight, clarity, and in a richly textured prose about the activities and occasions of ordinary people in small-town farming communities in rural Alberta. In *The skating party* her realist stories convey the dailyness of life in the fictional but credible town of Willow Bunch during the 1930s and 1940s. They recall an era when when life was guided by old-fashioned mottoes, and social occasions united family and community. In *Calling home*, small-town values clash with city ones, and familiar ways of behaving contradict a more contemporary etiquette. Astrid in 'City wedding' makes a trip to the city to help plan her son's wedding only to learn that her hopes for a family sort of occasion are at odds with the bride's mother's fuss-and-feathers plans. As in Summers' first collection, memory is a significant underlying theme that reveals layer on layer of irony and meaning when characters probe their past to understand their present. *North of the battle* is made up of 'A time for rising' and selected stories from her first two books. In 'A time for rising' however, Glen, from Ontario, takes over the farm he inherits and finds neither a common language nor a common set of values by which to understand the locale; he is consumed by an impulse to cut down trees and pile up rocks—to change things. The story marks the beginning of the end of life as it once was in rural Alberta. Summers writes honestly about whole and imperfect characters that endure failings and triumphs, love and loss. Her stories resonate with moments of truth that speak to the condition of being alive.

Summers' *Writer's guide to grants* (1994) was published by the WRITERS' UNION OF CANADA. DEBORAH TORKKO

Sunshine sketches of a little town (1912). This has remained the most popular of Stephen LEACOCK's books. Set in Mariposa, a typical small Ontario town, it was closely based on Orillia, where Leacock had his summer home, and caused great offence to the townspeople. The 'sketches' are dominated by Josh Smith, a hotel keeper who becomes Mariposa's member of Parliament. The Mariposans believe that Smith is a hero and benefactor, but he is in fact a ruthless individualist who sees through, and plays upon, the townspeople's desire for importance and sophistication. There has been some debate over the tone of the book, with Robertson DAVIES, most notably, seeing it as particularly harsh and unforgiving. However, most readers would agree that the tone is gently ironic: there are no real villains, not even Josh Smith, whose machinations never actually do any harm; and Leacock shows genuine affection in his portrayal of the foolish but good-natured Mariposans, such as the barber-financier Jefferson Thorpe, the 'enchanted' lovers Peter Pupkin and Zena Pepperleigh, and the 'mugwump' minister Dean Drove. Underlying the book's genuine affection and sympathy is serious criticism of the Mariposans' foolish desire to become part of the big urban world of material success, and of their failure to realize that there is no place in such a world for the social continuity and genuine fellow-feeling that Mariposa, for all its limitations, fosters. *Sunshine sketches* was one of the volumes that launched the NEW CANADIAN LIBRARY, and is still in the series with an Afterword by Jack HODGINS.

See also *ARCADIAN ADVENTURES WITH THE IDLE RICH.* ZAILIG POLLOCK

Survenant, Le. See Germaine GUÈVREMONT.

Survival: a thematic guide to Canadian literature (1972). This widely read critical work by Margaret ATWOOD was written while the author was associated with the House of ANANSI. Following the tradition of popular handbooks published by the press, *Survival* was conceived as a handbook on Canadian literature for the average reader. It was written at a time when Canadians were notoriously diffident about themselves and their culture, and when Canadian literature was not considered a legitimate area of study. Based on the premise that Canadian literature was a colonial literature, imbued with implied preoccupations, the book offered an inductive study of the collective literary imagination, and of the key patterns that at that time constituted the shape of Canadian literature.

The book's thesis—that every culture has a central symbol that functions like a code of beliefs—followed the well-known theory proposed by Northrop FRYE, who suggested that 'in every culture there is a structure of ideas, images, beliefs . . . which express the view of man's situation and destiny generally held at the time' (*The modern century*, 1967). According to Atwood, the central image of Canadian culture before 1972 was that of a collective victim struggling for survival—an image that was the legacy of both a hostile natural environment and a colonial history. As a consequence, the national psychology was fatalistic, the expression of a victim mentality.

There was considerable polemical anger in Atwood's assertion that Canadians had a will to lose, and that Canadian culture was characterized by a failure of nerve (one chooses to be a victim to avoid the responsibility of self-definition). In a series of chapters exploring archetypal images in Canadian literature—nature as monster, animals as victims, Natives as persecuted, the artist as paralysed, woman as ice maiden or absent Venus—Atwood described Canadian writers as living in an unknown territory, as exiles in their own country.

Survival—which was written with intelligence, wit, and considerable audacity—was partly a political manifesto written in protest against the neglect of Canadian culture in Canada. It fell on the ears of its Canadian audience like a call to order, at a time when the realization was dawning that a Canadian literature indeed existed. Perhaps more than any other work, it helped galvanize the flurry of energy that characterized Canadian writing in the 1970s. It was reissued in 1996.

See also CRITICISM IN ENGLISH: 5(d).

ROSEMARY SULLIVAN

Sutherland, Fraser (b. 1946). Born in Pictou, Nova Scotia, he was educated at the University of King's College, Halifax, and graduated in journalism from Carleton University. He worked as a correspondent and reporter—on the *Wall Street Journal*, New York, and the *Globe & Mail*, Toronto—until 1970, when he became a freelance writer and editor. The approach Sutherland takes to his poetry is suggested by the title of his first book, *Strange ironies* (1972). Other collections of poems include *Within the wound* (1976), *Madwomen* (1978), *Whitefaces* (1986), and his most ambitious work, *Jonestown: a poem* (1996), about a religious cult leader, which combines dramatic, narrative, and epic elements. He is also the author of a novel, *In the village of Alias* (1986), and of three non-fiction works: *The style of innocence* (1972), a study of Ernest Hemingway and Morley CALLAGHAN, *John Glassco: an essay and bibliography* (1984), and *The monthly epic: a history of Canadian magazines* (1989). As an editor he published *Scotland here: a checklist of Canadian authors of Scottish ancestry* (1979), and was the founding editor of the literary magazine *Northern Journey* (1971-6).

JOHN ROBERT COLOMBO

Sutherland, John (1919-56). Born in Liverpool, Nova Scotia, he attended Queen's University, Kingston (1936-7), where he developed tuberculosis of the kidney after an athletic injury. He was confined to bed in the family home in Saint John, New Brunswick, until 1941, when, against doctor's orders, he enrolled at McGill University, Montreal, though he left several months later. In Sept. 1942, after his poems has been rejected by the Montreal magazine *PREVIEW*, he founded *FIRST STATEMENT*, with the help of Audrey Aikman (whom he married) and other McGill undergraduates. The next year Irving LAYTON and Louis DUDEK became members of the editorial board and joined Sutherland in pursuit of a Canadian realism that would express the local and particular in simple language. In 1943 Sutherland acquired a printing press and in 1945, under the imprint of First Statement Press, he made an impact with a series of important chapbooks, the first of which was Layton's *Here and now*. In late 1945 *First Statement* merged with *Preview* to form *NORTHERN REVIEW*, with Sutherland as managing editor.

In response to A.J.M. SMITH's *The book of Canadian poetry: a critical and historical anthology* (1943), Sutherland edited *Other Canadians: an anthology of the new poetry in Canada, 1940-46* (1947), in the introduction to which he vigorously attacked Smith's literary views, notably his use of the categories 'native' and 'cosmopolitan', and emphasized the need for Canadian poetry that was North American in perspective and technique. His hostile criticism (in *Northern Review*, Aug.-Sept. 1947) of Robert FINCH's *Poems*, which had won a Governor General's Award, led to the departure of the *Preview* poets from *Northern Review*'s editorial board. A year later Layton resigned. (Dudek had previously left to pursue studies in New York.) Sutherland continued to edit the magazine almost single-handedly, supporting himself by odd jobs; but his literary interests took on a conservative slant, culminating in the article 'The past decade in Canadian poetry' (Dec. 1950-Jan. 1951). Here he turned his back on many of his former literary ideals, including the importance of vitality and a kind of Nietzschean spiritual health in poetry. He continued to publish *Northern Review* until his death in Sept. 1956. Sutherland returned in his literary philosophy to the views of his early *First Statement* days, but the emphasis on spiritual health was now more religious than Nietzschean because of an earlier conversion to Roman Catholicism. *The poetry of E.J. Pratt: a new interpretation* (1956), Sutherland's study of his favourite poet, reflects his Roman Catholic beliefs to an extent that does not benefit his criticism of Pratt's poetry.

A selection of Sutherland's writings, together with a memoir by the editor, Miriam WADDINGTON, is available in *John Sutherland: essays, controversies and poems* (NCL, 1972). Waddington underlines Sutherland's strength as a textual critic and rightly argues that his frequently personal poetry has been underrated. Louis Dudek and Michael Gnarowski place Sutherland prominently in the development of Canadian modernism in their introduction to *The making of modern poetry in Canada* (1967); and Neil H. Fisher offers an informative and reliable analysis of Sutherland as editor in *First Statement 1942-1945: an assessment and an index* (1974). DAVID O'ROURKE

Sutherland, Ronald (b. 1933). Born in east-end Montreal, he was educated at McGill University (B.A., 1954; M.A., 1955) and Wayne State University (Ph.D., 1960). He has taught at the Université de Sherbrooke since 1959, heading the English department from 1962 to 1974 and founding its graduate program in comparative Canadian literature in 1963. He is the author of three books of criticism—*Frederick Philip Grove* (1969), *Second image* (1971), and *The new hero* (1977)—and two novels: *Snow lark* (1971) and *Where do the MacDonalds bury their dead?* (1976).

With the exception of his first book, Sutherland's criticism is principally concerned with themes common to novels by French- and English-speaking Canadian writers of this century. It is sustained by a theory fully expressed in 'The mainstream', a chapter in *The new hero*: Canadian literature, properly speaking, provides imaginative expression of the interaction between the French and English founding cultures of Canada. In *Second image* he groups Canadian fiction according to three interlocking themes: the land and the divine order; the breakup of the old order; and the search for vital truth. Sutherland convincingly demonstrates the affinities that link writers as diverse as GROVE, Ringuet (Philippe PANNETON), W.O. MITCHELL, Gabrielle ROY, Hubert AQUIN, Jean SIMARD, and others, showing how these authors, though writing in isolation from each other, have expressed a common sensibility informed by a shared attitude towards the land, religion, and the self.

Sutherland's theory—rooted in a generous, sensitive vision of modern Canada from a specific Quebec vantage-point—is manifested in his fiction. *Snow lark*, the story of Suzanne MacDonald, offspring of a French-English marriage who grows up in Montreal's east end, dramatizes the two cultures as they act upon an individual's search for self-knowledge and happiness. Suzanne's reconciliation of the claims of mixed ancestry is emblematic of the emergence of modern Canada. While *Snow lark* is set in Montreal, *Where do the MacDonalds bury their dead?* traces its protagonists' search for self from Quebec to Michigan, California, and Mexico. Ti-Mac, Suzanne's cousin, eventually returns home, a wiser person through his exposure to cultural diversity. The two novels are interrelated by characterization and theme, and by the world-view that frames Sutherland's two principal books of criticism: the articulation of the Canadian identity lies in the recognition of its bilingual and bicultural nature.

An indication of Sutherland's influence as a teacher, and of his scholarly and creative work, is his highly successful program in comparative Canadian literature at the Université de Sherbrooke, graduates of which are currently teaching in a number of Canadian universities and are widely published.

See also CRITICISM IN ENGLISH: 5(c).

MAX DORSINVILLE

Svendsen, Linda. See SHORT STORIES IN ENGLISH 1983 TO 1996.

Swan, Susan (b. 1945). Born in Midland, Ontario, she attended Havergal College, a private girl's school in Toronto, before studying English at McGill University, Montreal, receiving a B.A. in 1967. She then began working as a journalist with the *Toronto Telegram*. Swan eventually left the *Telegram* and began writing for magazines. Today she divides her time between writing and teaching at Glendon College, York University, Toronto.

Swan's three novels—*The biggest modern woman of the world* (1983), *The last of the golden girls* (1989), and *The wives of Bath* (1993)—display her powerful grasp of the subtleties of the social construction of gender, depicting also the sexuality of her female characters.

The biggest modern woman of the world, which was shortlisted for a Governor General's Award, tells the story of Anna Swan (1846-88), a Nova Scotian giantess. While staying true to the basic facts of Anna's biography—she worked for many years for the American showman P.T. Barnum—the novel invents and explores her inner life. Swan sets up three major themes: an exploration of the dichotomies of man/woman, 'normal'/giant, and American/Canadian, and draws explicit parallels between the subordinate or marginalized element of each pair. *The last of the golden girls* is the story of the sexual awakening of Jude and her two best friends, Bobby and Shelly. Their blossoming sexuality sparks a competition for men, which continues over ten years and poisons their friendships. A playful eroticism provides an optimistic counterpoint to a more pessimistic look at the subtleties of male control over female sexuality. *The wives of Bath* is an intriguing amalgam of genres that Swan has labeled sexual gothic. Set in the 1960s at an all-girls' school, Bath Ladies College, the novel chronicles the coming of age of Mouse Bradford, a lonely girl struggling with feelings of extreme alienation, caused in part by her misshapen body, and in part by her struggle to resist adopting any of the feminine roles she sees available. This has been Swan's most commercially successful novel.

Swan has also published two collections of short stories: *Unfit for paradise* (1982) and *Stupid boys are good to relax with* (1996).

JUSTINE WHITEHEAD

Sweatman, Margaret. See NOVELS IN ENGLISH 1983 TO 1996 and OTHER NOVELS 1(b).

Sylvestre, Guy. See ANTHOLOGIES IN FRENCH: 1.

Symons, Scott (b. 1933). Hugh Brennan Scott Symons was born in Toronto into a highly respected Rosedale family of distinguished Loyalist ancestry; he was educated at Trinity College School, Port Hope, Ontario; Trinity College, University of Toronto; King's College, Cambridge; and the Sorbonne. In 1965, when he was married with a son, curator of the Canadiana collection at the Royal Ontario Museum, and assistant professor of fine arts at the University of Toronto, he left wife, home, and job to live in Montreal and write his first novel, *Place d'Armes*. The respectable ancestry, education, and career concealed a lifelong rebellion. Bisexual from his schooldays, he was frequently at odds with parents, teachers, and institutions, and often seethed at what he believed to be the betrayal of his country by the 'Blandmen'—the Liberal politicians and business men, satellites of Mackenzie King. *Place d'Armes: a personal narrative* (1967; rpr. 1978), which takes the form of a combat journal, contains five different typefaces and two narrators, both closely modelled on Symons himself. It is by turns lyrical, bathetic, inspiring, and banal. Chiefly about the discovery of the self through the body's encounter with another man, it also concerns the discovery of French-Canadian culture through a sensuous experience of architecture and artefacts. An energetic, if confusing, work, it attacks modern advertising and what Symons sees as the accelerating destruction of both English and French traditions in Canada.

Civic Square (1969) is a huge, chaotic work that was boxed, not bound, because Symons would not reduce the 848 typewritten pages to conventional book length. Symons decorated each container—which resembles the blue box used by Birks, a fashionable Toronto store—with red feltpen pictures of birds, flowers, and phalli as his personal present to DR, the imaginary Dear Reader to whom the book is addressed. *Civic Square* is not only a blistering attack on the 'Blandmen' who run Toronto's politics, education, and finance, but also a lyrical appreciation of the natural beauty of the Ontario countryside. It is repetitive, dislocated and, once again, full of high energy.

After completing *Civic Square*, Symons went to Mexico with a young male lover. A series of flights, escapes, and hardships followed: *Place d'Armes* had been savagely reviewed; Symons' marriage was ending in divorce; his family would speak neither to him nor of him. He was awarded the Beta Sigma Phi Best First Canadian Novel Award for *Place d'Armes*, however, and Symons has claimed that this prevented his suicide. He returned to Canada and lived for a time in northern British Columbia and Newfoundland. He wrote, on commission, a coffee-table book on Canadian furniture: *Heritage—a romantic look at early Canadian furniture* (1972), with photographs by John de Visser. Filled with passion, knowledge, and taste—Symons calls it his 'furniture novel'—the book transformed the furniture and artifacts into characters who speak in a variety of authentic accents about Canada's past, and the Western tradition from which they sprang.

There followed more travel in Europe and a move to Morocco, where Symons began work on a trilogy. The first volume, *Helmet of flesh* (1986), is a riotously rich episodic account of life, love, and travels in Morocco, with a long flashback to Osprey Cove, Newfoundland. The novel is in essence an attempt to find the spiritual meaning of life through the exploration of all the senses—a poetic, dreamlike vision of life under a tropical sun.

In Symons' passion and hyperbole there are echoes of D.H. Lawrence; in his lyricism and intensity, of Malcolm LOWRY; in his elegance and opulence, of Henry James—probably his three major influences. Charles Taylor has written a fine study of his life and writings in *Six journeys: a Canadian pattern* (1977).

PETER BUITENHUIS

Szumigalski, Anne (b. 1922). Anne Davis was born in London, England, and educated privately in nearby Hampshire. During the war she worked with refugees from Belgium, and with the British Red Cross Civilian Relief as medical auxiliary, interpreter, and welfare officer. In 1946 she married Jan Szumigalski, a retired Polish Army officer. After the birth of two children she lived in Wales, then immigrated to Saskatchewan, and has lived in or near Saskatoon since 1951. Her husband worked as a surveyor and in the 1960s two more children were born. She then began a career as an arresting, complex, and experimental poet, translator, editor, and playwright. Deeply involved with the Saskatchewan and Saskatoon writing community, she was a founding member of the Saskatchewan Writers Guild, the Saskatchewan Writers and Artists colonies, the literary journal *GRAIN* (which she helped edit for nine years), and the dance-collective Saskatoon Moving; she taught at the Saskatchewan Summer School of the Arts (1967-77), and was first writer-in-residence at the Saskatoon Public Library in 1981-2. She has won dozens of awards, including two silver National Magazine Awards, the YMCA's Woman of the Year Award (1988), the Saskatchewan Order of Merit (1989), a Life Membership in The LEAGUE OF CANADIAN POETS, and two nominations for a Governor General's Award, which she won for *Voice* in 1995.

Most of Szumigalski's work shows a preoccupation with matters of the spirit, and the visionary qualities of the imagination. Many of her poems suggest a childlike appreciation of place and a mystical relationship with the encounter of landscape. She cites as her greatest influences the King James Bible, *The book of common prayer*, the writings of William Blake, and contemporary visual artists, though critics have also cited the influence of gnostic mythology, botany and herbal lore, and the occult traditions. Many of her works employ prose-poems linked to myth and fable—sources of her poetic power in poems that always surprise.

Szumigalski's publications include *BOooOm* (1973; poems for elementary schools, with Terrence Heath); the selected poems of *Woman reading in bath* (1974)—the title poem is about a woman swimming in the sea with God; *Wild man's butte: long poem for voices* (1979, with Terrence Heath); *A game of angels* (1980), which connects the poems of this world to the inspirational otherworld in comic or ironic ways; *Risks* (1983); *Litany of the Bagladies: words for dance* (1983); *Doctrine of signatures* (1983); *Instar* (1985); *Dogstones*

(1986); and *Journey/journée* (1988, with Terrence Heath). *Rapture of the deep* (1991) deals with childhood memories, which develop from those of the Christ child and the Holy Family. *Voice* (1995) is a collaboration between Szumigalski and the painter Elysa St George: full-colour reproductions, poems, and shared imagination give 'voice' to each other and create the book itself.

The word, the voice, the text: essays and memoirs (1990) looks at the sources of her imagination in childhood experience. *Z: a meditation on oppression, desire, and freedom* (1995) draws upon her war experiences as she laments the Holocaust and celebrates the regenerative capacity of the human spirit to create art.

See 'Tribute to Anne Szumigalski', a special issue of PRAIRIE FIRE (Spring 1997), edited by John Livingstone Clark.

GEOFF HANCOCK

T

Taché, Joseph-Charles (1820-94). Born in Kamouraska, Lower Canada (Quebec), he was educated at the Séminaire de Québec, where he earned his medical diploma. He practised medicine in Rimouski, which he represented in the legislative assembly from 1847 to 1857. A staunch Conservative, he remained active in politics as founding editor of *Le Courrier du Canada* and as deputy minister of agriculture; he twice represented Canada at events in Paris—in 1855, when he was made a member of the Légion d'honneur, and in 1867. His political journalism includes denunciations of anti-clericals (especially Benjamin Sulte), concern for prison reform, promotion of francophone immigration to Canada, and expansion in the Northwest. (His younger brother, Alexandre-Antonin Taché, was the first bishop of Saint-Boniface and author of *Esquisse sur le Nord-Ouest, 1869*.) Notable among Taché's non-fiction works are *Esquisse sur le Canada, considéré sous le point de vue économique* (Paris, 1855) and *Des provinces de l'Amérique du Nord et d'une union fédérale* (Québec, 1858). Writing on cultural topics, he occasionally shared with Hubert LaRUE the pseudonym 'Isidore Mesplats'.

Taché was an early collector and interpreter of French-Canadian oral legends and folk types. The fiction he created from this material, despite its clumsy didacticism, was the liveliest and most indigenous of the 1860 school. One of the founders of the École patriotique de Québec and *Les SOIRÉES CANADIENNES* (1861), which first published his major literary works, he was responsible —with LaRue, AUBERT DE GASPÉ, and H.-R. CASGRAIN—for the strong bias towards folk-tales in the new national literature. His belief that storytelling was a vital link between a people, and its land and cultural values, was well in advance of his time. *Trois légendes de mon pays* (Québec, 1861) demonstrates this principle by arranging each of three traditional tales in a narrative framework meant to recreate the atmosphere of oral storytelling. The stories—set in places now called Bic Island, Grand Sault (New Brunswick), and the Méchin Islands—demonstrate exemplary moments in the progress from barbarism to Christianity. *Forestiers et voyageurs* (Québec, 1863) is an episodic novel combining traditional and invented tales. First the author-narrator makes a journey from Rimouski to a lumber camp, with an idealized description of its social organization and the lumber industry. Then the narration is taken over by Père Michel, a roguish storyteller, who as a youth fled the law by the traditional method of becoming a *voyageur*. Thus Taché launched one of the three literary figures of his time, alongside the *seigneur* and the *défricheur* (settler). Père Michel's story has an edifying Catholic conclusion; but the taste for fun, inherent in this folk material, is not lost. Taché also supplies a striking but incomplete socio-economic portrait of the forest industry.

Les Sablons (L'Île de Sable et l'Île Saint-Barnabé) (Québec, 1885) combines Taché's last attempt to fuse topography and folklore. Sable Island (which he had considered as a possible site for a penal colony) was practically uninhabited, but memories of past expeditions and a few ghost stories (some adapted from T.C. HALIBURTON) constituted for Taché a strong Breton and French-Canadian presence on the island. Saint-Barnabé, in the Gulf of St Lawrence, is also endowed with ghostly presence owing to its fogs and notable shipwrecks. Two stories, 'Le braillard de la montagne' (1864) and 'La légende du Lac Caché' (1889), were both published in *Le Courrier du Canada*. The first is a ghost story in verse, set on the site of the present Citadel in Quebec City. The second, a fishing story that explains the name of a lake northeast of Quebec, is pleasantly free of Taché's habitual moralizing.

Although six volumes of Taché's non-fiction works have been translated, only one adaptation of his fiction appears in English: *The isle of the massacre* (1901), translated by W.C. Wood. JACK WARWICK

Talbot, Gaston. See DRAMA IN FRENCH 1981 to 1996: 2.

Tallman, Warren. See CRITICISM IN ENGLISH: 5(d).

Talon Books. One of the most important Canadian small publishers, Talon Books arose out of the small high-school poetry magazine *Talon* (1963-8), published in Vancouver. Talonbooks (as its named was styled originally) was founded by David Robinson in 1967, and had a combined imprint with Very Stone House, formed by Patrick LANE, Seymour MAYNE, and bill BISSET. David Robinson, who resigned in 1984, was succeeded by Karl Siegler, who is now president.

The important drama list of Talon Books, established by Gordon Fidler and Peter Hay, includes both English- and French-Canadian, and some American, playwrights. The first play published was James REANEY's *Colours in the dark* (1969), followed by George RYGA's *The ECSTASY OF RITA JOE* (1970). Within a decade they had plays in print by most of the major playwrights in Canada. Their best-selling author is Michel TREMBLAY.

In fiction, as in poetry, Talon Books tends to support West Coast authors, though it has published translations of novels by Marie-Claire BLAIS and Tremblay. The program began with the experimental work of bill bissett, Frank DAVEY, bp NICHOL, Daphne MARLATT, and moved on to the more established poets like Phyliss WEBB. It built a strong list of women writers, including Jane RULE, Audrey THOMAS, and Webb, whose selected poems, *The vision tree* (1982), won a Governor General's Award. An important achievement was *The Salish people* (1978), a four-volume collection of the writings of the unjustly neglected maverick anthropologist Charles Hill-Tout, edited by Ralph Maud.

The press has overcome financial difficulties through the sale of its archives, a best-selling cookbook, and emergency funding from the CANADA COUNCIL, all of which helped Talon Books continue as a major West Coast publisher. It has taken over the backlist of COACH HOUSE PRESS and its books are distributed by General Publishing.

GEOFF HANCOCK/GEORGE WOODCOCK

Tamarack Review, The (1956-82). This literary quarterly devoted to stories, poems, essays, and reviews by new and established Canadian writers was conceived by Robert WEAVER at a time when John SUTHERLAND's *NORTHERN REVIEW* was about to cease publication. Weaver enlisted as co-editors Kildare DOBBS, Millar MacLure, Ivon Owen, William Toye, and Anne WILKINSON. The editorial board was later altered by the death of Wilkinson, by resignations (Weaver and Toye remained editors to the end), and by the addition of Patricia Owen, John Robert COLOMBO, and Janis RAPOPORT as co-editors. *Tamarack* was founded in Toronto when a new generation of now-prominent writers was just beginning to publish, and before the onset of Canadian nationalism, when Canadian literature was of slight general interest. Produced in a handsome format—with covers by graphic designers that included Theo Dimson, Allan Fleming, Fred Huffman, Frank Newfeld, and Toye—it attempted to maintain a standard of literary excellence, without regional or ideological emphases, and published early, and sometimes the first, work by Timothy FINDLEY and Jay MACPHERSON (both of whom appeared in the first issue), Dave GODFREY, Hugh HOOD, Alice MUNRO, Mordecai RICHLER, and others. Dependent on volunteer editorial services and precarious financial support (much of it provided by the CANADA COUNCIL and the Ontario Arts Council), *Tamarack* did not realize its aims consistently. But for 25 years it was the most respected literary magazine in English Canada. WILLIAM TOYE

Tardivel, Jules-Paul. See ESSAYS IN FRENCH: 3 and *POUR LA PATRIE*.

Taylor, Charles M. (b. 1931). Born in Montreal, he received his BA from McGill University in 1952 and his D.Phil. from the University of Oxford in 1961. He began teaching at McGill in 1961, and was appointed Professor of Political Science and Professor of

Philosophy in 1972. From 1976 to 1981 he was the Chichele Professor of Social and Political Theory in the University of Oxford and Fellow of All Souls College. He has lectured widely throughout the world, is a Fellow of the British Academy and the Royal Society of Canada, and received the prestigious Prix Léon Gérin in 1992 for his outstanding contribution to the civic and intellectual life of Quebec. He was made a Companion of the Order of Canada in 1995.

Recognized throughout the world as one of today's outstanding moral and political philosophers, Taylor has written over a dozen books and hundreds of articles that articulate the moral and political identity of the modern age in all its complexity and density. The best introductions to his work are *Sources of the self: the making of the modern identity* (1989) and his popular Massey Lectures, *The malaise of modernity* (1991).

At the heart of Taylor's philosophy is the view that people come to discover and revise their identities in dialogues with others—dialogues that are *interpretative* in character. Almost all of Taylor's work revolves around this central and brilliant insight. We discover who we are in dialogue by interpreting what Taylor calls 'sources' that are articulated most clearly by exemplary texts in philosophy and literature. In *Sources of the self* he shows that the many and seemingly contradictory faces of modern identity can be clarified, and perhaps even reconciled, by returning to works—the 'sources'—from Plato to Nietzsche that give us their clearest articulation. Moreover, since the language we use in dialogues, from childhood on, will itself partly constitute our identity, Taylor has devoted much of his time to the philosophy of language (see the two-volume *Philosophical papers*, 1985). Of particular concern to him, given the cultural and linguistic diversity of modern societies, is the nature of cross-cultural understanding in bilingual and polylingual circumstances (*Philosophical arguments*, 1995). His political philosophy is also based on his insights regarding dialogue and interpretation. Democracy is the form of government in which citizens rule themselves by entering into deliberative public dialogues on the identity and good of their political association. He applies this theory of democracy to the problems of Canadian identity and the Canada/Quebec problem in *Multiculturalism and the 'politics of recognition'* (1992) and *Reconciling the solitudes* (1993).

For an introduction to Taylor's thought, see James Tully, ed., *Philosophy in an age of pluralism: the philosophy of Charles Taylor in question* (1994), in which scholars from a wide range of disciplines raise questions to which Taylor replies.

JAMES H. TULLY

Taylor, Drew Hayden (b. 1962). He grew up on the Curve Lake Reserve near Peterborough, Ontario, attending school on the reserve and in Lakefield, Ontario. He graduated from Seneca College, Toronto, where he studied radio and television broadcasting. An award-winning playwright, he is best known for his first play, *Toronto at Dreamer's Rock*, which won the Chalmers Award of 1992 for Best Play for Young Audiences. A one-act fantasy, it involves three Native teenagers from different time periods who meet at Dreamer's Rock, a tourist attraction that was once a sacred site. The play was published in 1990, in the same volume as another one-act play, *Education is our right*, a political satire that draws upon Dickens' *A Christmas carol*. *The bootlegger blues* (1991), a comedy, won the CANADIAN AUTHORS' ASSOCIATION Literary Award for Best Drama in 1992. In his two-act play *Someday* (1993), which has had six productions, winning a lottery allows an impoverished mother to search for Janice, her first-born daughter, who had been taken away from her by social services thirty-five years earlier. Its sequel, *Only drunks and children tell the truth*, performed at the Native Canadian Centre, Toronto, in 1996, continues the story five months later. Janice, now a successful Toronto entertainment lawyer who had been raised by adoptive parents, has discovered her birth family living on a northern Ontario reserve. But after the death of her birth mother she goes home again to reconcile herself with her Native heritage. This play won the Dora Mavor Moore Award in 1996 for the outstanding new play in the small-theatre category. Another play, *The girl who loved her horses*, was nominated for the 1996 Chalmers Award for the Best Play for Young Audiences. Taylor also writes and directs for radio and television, and is well-known for his humorous commentaries on Native issues that appear regularly in the *Globe and Mail* and the *Toronto Star*. His essay 'Pretty like a white boy' has been widely anthologized. He is co-editor of an anthology, *Voices: being Native in Canada* (1992), and is currently Artistic Director of Native Earth Performing Arts, Toronto.

PENNY PETRONE

Tecumseh. See ABORIGINAL LITERATURE: 1.

Teleky, Richard. See SHORT STORIES IN ENGLISH 1983 to 1996.

Tétreau, Jean. See FANTASTIC LITERATURE AND SCIENCE FICTION IN FRENCH.

Théoret, France (b. 1942). Born in Montreal into a working-class family, she studied at the École normale Cardinal Léger, then attended the Université de Montréal (B.A., 1968; M.A., 1977). She completed a doctorate in Études françaises at the Université de Sherbrooke in 1982. Between 1972 and 1974 she pursued studies in semiology and psychoanalysis in Paris. From 1968 to 1987 she taught literature at the CGEP level in Montreal; since then she has devoted herself full time to writing. Her articles and texts have appeared in numerous journals, in both Quebec and France, and many have been included in anthologies.

Théoret's writings, which integrate modernity with feminism, defy traditional classification. She has written prose poetry, short stories, essays, pieces for the theatre, personal and travel journals, and 'novels'. Most are texts that blur the categories as she pursues her difficult (re-)search for language to alter the stultifying and inhibiting patriarchal codes of the past. Autobiography, fiction, and theory are intertwined in her discourse, which is characterized by the presence of a female figure/voice, however designated (the narrative pronoun may change within the text), seeking to establish her identity in a language, culture, and society from which, as a woman, she feels excluded.

In 1976 Théoret wrote 'L'échantillon' as her contribution to the collective play *La nef des sorcières*, a series of feminist monologues that reached a large public. In 'L'échantillon' the worker recounts in a neutral tone the banality of her existence and her sense of alienation in the workplace and in society, but she also entertains a faint hope that the isolation may decrease. *Bloody Mary* (1977), *Vertiges* (1979), and *Nécessairement putain* (1980) are relatively brief, elliptical, and poetic texts, each illustrating differently the dialectic of revolt and alienation and seeking, with painful difficulty, the narrator's release through language, which may itself be a trap. *Bloody Mary* is the most violent and anarchical in expression, *Vertiges*, more introspective; *Nécessairement putain* centres on the figure of the prostitute, the woman most excluded from society, and develops the analogy of the prostitute and the woman writer.

Une voix pour Odile (1978), which consists of twelve brief monologues, was the first of Théoret's writings to attract broad critical attention. The inflections of the voice(s) and the swift rhythm give unity to the different texts. Her substantial 'novel' *Nous parlerons comme on écrit* (1982) is autobiography, essay, and travel diary—a juxtaposition of Mexico and Montreal. Composed of six parts, and centred in reality, it contains linear narrative as well as disconnected sketches. The author/narrator, writing of named and unnamed women, fuses details, fragments, stories, and doubts into a collective and emotional totality.

Théoret's subsequent work is varied but reinforces her principal themes. *Intérieurs* (1984) is lapidary poetry that rejects lyricism, *Entre raison et déraison* (1987) contains essays that are an intense reflection on language and on the 'inner turbulence' experienced by women. Less abstract are the short-story collection *L'homme qui peignait Staline* (1989); *Étrangeté, l'étreinte* (1992), a poetic prose reflection on women and language; and *Journal pour mémoire* (1993), which traces the author's personal and literary development. Closer to traditional form—although without dialogue or psychological description—is the novel *Laurence* (1996), which follows the life of a courageous young woman of humble origins and meagre finances who achieves a measure of emancipation and happiness through her own efforts. It is also a remarkable socio-economic portrait of Quebec from the 1920s to the 1940s.

Théoret has frequently collaborated with other women artists. Her text for the musical *Transit* (1984), written with Micheline Coulombe Saint-Marcoux (presented by the Théâtre de l'Eskabel and on television), continued the theme of interminable waiting and transformation. She contributed two texts to *La théorie, un dimanche* (1987), a collective work initiated by Nicole BROSSARD, and published *La fiction de l'ange* (1992), brief poetic texts interspersed with etchings by Francine Simonin.

Several of Théoret's works have been published in English. *L'homme qui peignait Staline* was translated as *The man who painted Stalin* (1991) by Luise von Flotow. Barbara Godard's *The tangible word, poetry and texts 1977-1983* (1991) includes her translations of *Bloody Mary*, *Une voix pour Odile*, *Vertiges*, and *Nécessairement putain*.

See 'Approprier Électre' in Patricia Smart's *Écrire dans la maison du père* (1988; *Writing in the father's house*, 1991); Louise Dupré, 'France Théoret' in *Stratégies du vertige* (1989); dossier on France Théoret, collective, edited by Patricia Smart, *VOIX ET IMAGES*, 40 (automne 1988); Karen Gould, 'France Théoret: voicing the agony of discourse' in *Writing in the feminine* (1990). BARBARA McEWEN

Thériault, Yves (1915-83). Only son of Alcide Thériault, an Acadian of partly Montagnais Indian ancestry, and Aurore Nadeau, he was born in Quebec City and from the age of seven was able, he claimed, to speak the Cree dialect taught him by his father. He received his primary and secondary education in Montreal, but quit school at fifteen to work at a host of odd jobs. After working as a radio announcer and radio script-writer in several Quebec cities, and as a tractor salesman, he published his first short story in *Le Jour* in 1941. In 1942 he married Michelle-Germaine Blanchet, the mother of his two children, and soon after became a public-relations officer and script-writer for the National Film Board.

From 1945 to 1950, while working as a script-writer for Radio-Canada, Thériault published anonymously, or under pseudonyms, an enormous quantity of 'ten-cent novels' (32 pages); at one point he was producing eleven (and his wife three) a week. In 1950 the French government awarded him a scholarship that he was obliged to refuse because of the pressure of work. In 1952, however, he travelled around the world aboard an Italian freighter, and he lived for several years in Italy. Thériault was elected to the Royal Society of Canada in 1959. In 1965 he was elected president of the Société des Écrivains Canadiens, but resigned shortly thereafter and spent two years (1965-7) as cultural director for the Department of Indian and Northern Affairs in Ottawa. A period of increasing personal difficulties, compounded by health problems, persuaded him to leave Ottawa, and in 1968 he purchased a small farm at Saint-Denis-sur-Richelieu, Quebec. In June 1970 Thériault suffered a cerebral thrombosis that left him paralysed and unable to speak, write, or talk. After a prolonged convalescence he resumed his career, becoming co-director in 1977 of a film company with his companion Lorraine Boisvenue. He received a Molson Prize in 1970, a Canada Council scholarship for established writers in 1978, and the Prix David in 1979. He lived at Rawdon, a village west of Joliette, Quebec.

Thériault was the most prolific and versatile of contemporary Quebec writers. The quantity, quality, and variety of his writing assured his popularity with the Canadian reading public; translations of *Agaguk* (1958) made him known abroad; and he is widely studied in the CEGEPs and universities of Quebec. Largely self-taught, animated by driving dynamism, bohemian restlessness, and a passion for liberty that caused him to revolt against conformism and convention, Thériault soon acquired vast experience of the seamier and more violent sides of life that are reflected in the forty books he published since *Contes pour un homme seul* (1944). These unusual, captivating, and brutal stories (twelve of which had appeared in *Le Jour*) announced the themes that he would later develop: naturalism, primitivism, exoticism, eroticism, and sublimated sexuality struggling for expression. Basic human instincts and passions, in conflict with the forces of tradition and repression, are the occasion for biting criticism of our civilization and of French-Canadian society in particular. Procreation, mutilation, and death assume special significance as his characters search desperately for individuality: Native people, Inuit, Jews, immigrants, peasants—'little people'—all battle against the forces of moral, religious, social, economic, or ethnic domination. They inhabit the forests and tundra of the Far North, or anywhere and nowhere—such as the isolated mountain village of his first novel, *La fille laide* (1950), which concerns a hired hand who commits a murder so that he and an ugly servant girl may gain possession of their employer's farm.

In 1951 Thériault published three novels: *La vengeance de la mer*, a melodrama in which a young 'prodigal son' from Gaspé escapes calamity by returning to his sick mother's bedside; *Le dompteur d'ours*, about a muscular vagabond who unleashes among the women of a remote mountain hamlet a frenzy of pent-up sexual frustrations; and *Les vendeurs du temple*, a somewhat exaggerated political and religious satire on greed in rural Quebec. *Aaron* (1954), which won the Prix de la Province de Québec, is the story of a young orthodox Jew who rejects his strict upbringing by his grandfather, Moishe, and becomes assimilated into the English-speaking business community of Montreal. The old man, his dreams shattered, awaits death in loneliness and desolation.

With the publication of *Agaguk* (winner of the Prix de la Province de Québec and the Prix France-Canada), Thériault achieved international recognition. This almost epic evocation of love and fatherhood among the Inuit of the Canadian North has been translated into numerous languages (into English by Miriam Chapin, 1967). Agaguk's evolution towards maturity is the mainspring of the action and of the various conflicts he has with the whites, his own tribe, his father, and the harsh realities of the vast and hostile tundra. The gradual civilizing of Agaguk is the work of Iriook, his wife, who twice saves her husband's life. The crux of the novel occurs when Iriook—opposing the merciless Inuit tradition—demands at gunpoint that Agaguk spare the life of the daughter she has borne him. She then convinces Agaguk to accept his daughter and the risks and responsibilities that this decision involves. *Ashini* (1960; translated by Gwendolyn Moore, 1972), which won the Prix France-Canada and a Governor General's Award, is not so much a novel as a lyric poem to the glory of the Montagnais (despite Ashini's suicide). Native myths are evoked with great beauty. Thériault ranked this book, which is a plea for justice as well as a work of art, as one of his best.

In *Amour au goût de mer* (1961) a Sicilian immigrant couple succumbs to the misery, sickness, and despair of their lonely life in Montreal. Among other themes, Thériault here criticizes French-Canadian xenophobia. *Cul-de-sac* (1961) is the story of the gradual disintegration of an engineer in his fifties, who, after a series of mishaps and suffering from ill health, decides to hasten his doom by drowning himself in drink. *Les commettants de Caridad* (1961) is set in a mountain hamlet in Andalusia—a former paradise that is altered through human pride and foolhardiness. Structurally and symbolically more complicated than many of Thériault's other novels, it was considered by him to be one of his major works.

Experimenting with new techniques, Thériault published *Si la bombe m'était contée* (1962) in which he examined the frightening subject of the atomic bomb and its effects. Another experimental novel, *Le grand roman d'un petit homme* (1963), met with relatively little success. He returned to the primitivistic vein with *Le ru d'Ikoué* (1963), a sort of prose poem that recounts how a young Algonkin lad growing up in the forest falls in love with a stream, and how this symbolic mistress tactfully guides him towards manhood. In *Les temps du carcajou* (1965) Bruno Juchereau, the surly captain of a schooner, has his unfaithful mistress gang-raped, in an orgy of sex and horror, during a fierce storm in the Gulf of St Lawrence. Filled with hatred, vengeance, and grotesque eroticism, the novel marks the antipode of *Agaguk*; its very excesses prevent the characters from coming to life. Another sadistic and violent novel, *L'appelante* (1967), also has revenge as its theme.

In 1968 Thériault accomplished the prodigious feat of publishing six books, including four novels: *La mort d'eau*, about uprooted Madelinots searching for love in Montreal; *Kesten* and *Mahigan*, two mythological tales pitting man against beast; and *N'Tsuk* (translated by Gwendolyn Moore, 1972). *N'Tsuk* has often been compared to *Ashini* because both books were written in highly poetic language, and the main characters in both are critical of modern society. The next year—as well as adapting to novel form a film by Denis Héroux, *Valérie* (1969)—Thériault published *Antoine et sa montagne* (1969), a novel set in a small village on the Richelieu River in 1835 that some critics have seen as an allegory of the contemporary French-Canadian situation; and *Tayaout, fils d'Agaguk* (1969). This novel resurrects many of the characters in *Agaguk,* although immense changes in traditional Inuit society during the eleven years separating the two novels prompted Thériault to portray a world in which no compromise between the ancient and the modern seems possible, nor any hope for the future. *Le dernier havre* (1970) concerns an eighty-year-old Gaspé fisherman, consumed with the meaninglessness of his existence, who chooses death with honour and goes down with his boat in the Gulf. More than any other of Thériault's protagonists, the old man dies reconciled with life, and, more importantly, with himself.

The characters in Thériault's next novel, *La Passe-au-Crachin* (1972)—a tale about a man's inability to communicate and the loneliness, boredom, and revolt of his wife—are not extraordinary heroes but people with human weaknesses. Through tragedy the couple learn to face the future on the basis of an imperfect, albeit workable, compromise. *Le haut pays* (1973) is a disappointing and irritating narrative that vacillates between science-fiction and pseudo-religious mysticism. In sharp contrast *Agoak, l'héritage d'Agaguk* (1975; *Agoak*, 1979) argues that a civilized man 'is something which doesn't exist'. Society's superficial veneer is constantly threatened by 'the relative proximity of primitivism' as exemplified by the assimilated Inuit, Agoak, who rapidly reverts to savagery when American tourists rape his wife. Attempting to rationalize his barbarous actions (he slashes the tourists with a hunting knife and then castrates them), Agoak cites the American massacres in Vietnam and claims that all men are descended from savages. Strikingly different is *Moi, Pierre Huneau* (1976), one of Thériault's most successful novels, in which the narrator, a former Gaspé fisherman nearly ninety years old, is compelled—like Coleridge's Ancient Mariner—to recount the tragedy that shattered his existence. Almost illiterate, but expressing a simple and sincere humanity, he relates his life story in a folksy and colourful jargon all his own.

The first novel published after Thériault's recovery in the 1970s was *La quête de l'ours* (1980). At 384 pages it is his most massive work, a diffuse narrative that nevertheless forms part of the primitivistic northern cycle begun with *Agaguk* and *Ashini* and allowed Thériault to exploit anew almost all the major themes already familiar in his earlier work. The raconteur's incantatory style is effective and the book provides a rich synthesis of the high points in Thériault's long career as a novelist. *Le partage de minuit* (1980) adds little to the author's reputation. Its social criticism—the events suggest the Duplessis era—and its denunciation of hypocrisy in dealing with homosexuality are vitiated by a simplistic psychoanalytical approach, too much reliance on eroticism to sustain interest, and structural deficiencies that suggest haste or negligence in composition.

Thériault's collections of short stories include *Le vendur d'étoiles et autres contes* (1961), for which he was awarded the Prix Mgr Camille Roy; *La rose de pierre* (1964), nine stories dealing with various aspects of love, some of which reflect a strange and explosive violence; *L'île introuvable* (1968), eighteen tales that reflect all the main themes and tendencies of Thériault's fiction; *Oeuvre de chair* (1975), which contains sixteen titillating tales, illustrated with explicit drawings by Louisa Nicol, based on the premise that sexual enjoyment is enhanced by the pleasures of the palate, and organized around recipes savoured in the course of amorous encounters; *L'étreinte de Vénus* (1981), a collection of eighteen carefully crafted detective stories that reveal another significant and previously unsuspected facet of Thériault's talent; *La femme Anna et autres contes* (1981); *Valère et le grand canot* (1981); *L'herbe de tendresse* (1983); and *Cap à l'amour!* (1990). These last four volumes—totalling over 1,000 pages—exemplify Thériault's preference for the short story. (Over a forty-year period he wrote more than a thousand stories, most of which are still unpublished.) Here the raconteur's gift of the gab, which in longer works sometimes runs away with him, is held admirably in check by the restrictions of the form.

Thériault's massive output also includes *Roi de la côte nord* (1960), the extraordinary life of Napoléon-Alexandre Comeau; *Séjour à Moscou* (1961), an essay; *Textes et documents* (1969); and, by his own count, more than 1,300 radio and television scripts. Only four of his plays are available in print: *Le samaritain* (1958; *Écrits du Canada français*, vol. 4), which won first prize in the Radio-Canada drama competition for 1952; *Le marcheur* (1968, first produced in 1950); and *Frédange* and *Les terres neuves* (1970), two-act dramas published in a single volume. Thériault was also the author of twenty-three science-fiction or adventure stories for children and adolescents (see CHILDREN'S LITERATURE IN FRENCH: 2 and 3), published between 1959 and 1969. *Cajetan et la taupe* (1979), *Les aventures d'Ori d'Or* (1979), *Popok, le petit Esquimau* (1980), *Kuanuten (Vent d'est)* (1981), and *L'or de la felouque* (1981) were written for young people.

In the decade between 1972 and 1982 fifteen re-editions of Thériault's earlier works appeared, eight of them—including *Aaron*, *Agaguk*, and *Ashini*—in 1980. Despite ill health, Thériault in this period published nine new books for adults. He was quite rightly criticized for writing hastily and carelessly, but it is perhaps premature to attempt a definitive assessment of his ultimate merit as a writer. His later short stories have added a whole new dimension to an already phenomenal career.

See Gérard BESSETTE, *Une littérature en ébullition* (1968); Maurice Émond, *Yves Thériault et le combat de l'homme* (1973); Jean-Paul Simard, *Rituel et langage chez Yves Thériault* (1979); Hélène Lafrance, *Yves Thériault et l'institution littéraire québécoise* (1984); André Carpentier, *Yves Thériault se reconte* (1985); Denis Carrier, *Bibliographie analytique d'Yves Thériault, 1940-1984* (1985); *Études littéraires*, vol. 21, n° 1 (printemps-été 1988); and Marta Hesse, *Yves Thériault: master storyteller* (1993).

See also NOVELS IN FRENCH 1940 TO 1959: 5; 1960 TO 1982: 3(c). L.W. KEFFER

Thério, Adrien. See NOVELS IN FRENCH 1960 to 1982: 3(b).

Thesen, Sharon (b. 1946). Born in Tisdale, Saskatchewan, she was raised in various parts of western Canada and educated in British Columbia. She received her B.A. (1970) and her M.A. (1974) in English literature from Simon Fraser University. In 19776 Thesen began teaching in the department of English at Capilano College, North Vancouver, from 1976 until 1992, where she also sat on the editorial board of *The Capilano Review*.

Artemis hates romance (1980), Thesen's first book of poetry, in its skillful use of the rhythms of speech, hints at the influence of Charles Olson, Robert Creeley, and the West Coast *Tish* poets. Pointed, lean, and occasionally angry, the *Artemis* poems scrutinize failed relationships and small-town life. Thesen contemplates the mundane partly by recasting it through philosophy and myth, which undergird her work. A brief stay in Montreal is one of the subjects of Thesen's chapbook *Radio New France Radio* (1981). All of the poems in this small book were republished in *Holding the pose* (1983), in which Thesen adapts the rhythms of country music, gospel, and jazz to examine loneliness, separation, torture, and ennui. The result is poems that, even when they probe the darkness, never succumb to it. *Confabulations: poems for Malcolm Lowry* (1984), which Thesen has identified as a long poem, is dedicated to Michael ONDAATJE, whose influence on this volume is evident. In LOWRY's self-destructiveness Thesen finds an Ondaatjean subject, and her verse echoes Ondaatje's in its point-blank language and slightly jagged, free-verse metre. With *The beginning of the long dash* (1987), Thesen reveals her broad reach as a poet. The ordinary is shadowed by the profound in these poems; the apparently innocent particulars of daily life reverberate with questions about the nature of being. *The pangs of Sunday* (1990), a selected volume, includes almost two dozen new poems, and is a showcase for Thesen's great skill. One detects the influence of the American poet Sharon Olds in the slightly longer lines of the new poems. In these poems narrative is carefully balanced with lyric. In *Aurora* (1995), her most accomplished work, Thesen experiments with form, using traditional stanzas (e.g., *terza rima*), free verse, and a poetic adaptation of stream-of-consciousness narrative to deepen the complexity of her response to the sensory world. Ideas are in abundance, and—as in all of Thesen's work—they live in the interstices between the lines.

Thesen is also an editor and occasional essayist. In 1982 she edited Phyllis WEBB's *The vision tree: selected poems*, and in 1991 *The new long poem anthology*. Her essays have appeared in various publications, including *A mazing space: writing Canadian women writing* (1986) and *Beyond Tish* (1991).

See the following articles in *Essays on Canadian Writing*: Bruce Whiteman, '"We talk anyway/being human": the poetry of Sharon Thesen', vol. 43 (Spring, 1991), pp. 54-66; and in the same issue, John Harris, 'In the arms of Susan', pp. 83-96.

CYNTHIA MESSENGER

Thibodeau, Serge Patrice. See ACADIAN LITERATURE: 3(a).

Thomas, Audrey (b. 1935). Audrey Grace Callahan was born in Binghamton, New York, and educated at Smith College, with a year at St Andrews University, Scotland. After teaching for a year in England, she married Ian Thomas in 1958; the couple immigrated to Canada in 1959. She received an M.A. in English (1963) from the University of British Columbia and did further work there, on Anglo-Saxon language and literature, towards a Ph.D. that was not awarded. The years 1964-6 were spent in Ghana, where her husband taught at the University of Science and Technology, Kumasi. Much of her fiction recalls her life in Africa; the foreignness of the land and its customs provide a metaphor for emotional alienation, the threat and challenge of the unknown, and exploration of the dark side of the self.

After her return to Vancouver, Thomas published her first collection of stories, *Ten green bottles* (1967), in the same year that the youngest of her three daughters was born. The lead story, 'If one green bottle', is based on the author's confinement and eventual miscarriage in a Ghanaian hospital. The sense of futility and shame accompanying this six-month-long experience haunts the narrator of *Mrs. Blood* (1970), a novel that expands the material of the story into a moving characterization of a woman so distressed by her condition that she sees herself as a nameless, fragmented being, speaking sometimes as the fearful, self-conscious, acted-upon 'Mrs. Thing', sometimes as the guilt-ridden bundle of memories and poetic visions, 'Mrs. Blood', wracked by physical and psychic forces she cannot control. *Mrs. Blood* was published in France as *Du sang* (1972).

In 1969 Thomas found the cabin on Galiano Island, British Columbia, in which, after separating from her husband in 1972, she made her home. The Gulf Island atmosphere is captured in the second of two related novellas, published in one volume: *Munchmeyer* and *Prospero on the island* (1971). This is the diary of Miranda who, in an island cabin, is writing *Munchmeyer*, a novel about a male writer who also keeps a diary. The two works can be read separately, but together they reveal subtle explorations of the nature of creativity, the interdependence of art and craft, and the emotional demands made on the artist. Such reminders of *The tempest* as Miranda's name, and the existence of a Caliban figure, provide a sometimes ironic framework for events on the 'magic' island.

Songs my mother taught me was Thomas's first novel, though it was not published until 1973. Set in the New York State of the author's childhood, it chonicles a girl's growing up, from Blakean 'innocence' in the emotionally violent world of her home and social life to 'experience', acquired through grotesque revelations of human misery in a mental hospital where she had a summer job. What appears at first to be a conventional first-person narrative is in fact a curiously constructed record of two voices, the speaker sometimes referring to herself as 'I', and sometimes as Isobel, a third person she observes from a distance, or directly addresses. *Blown figures* (1974) is Thomas's most experimental novel, where a collage method of narration and the use of space on the page reflect the schizophrenia of a woman haunted by guilt and the sense of loss from a miscarriage. She relives psychically a journey to Africa, gradually turning in her own mind into a doomed and destructive witch.

Ladies and escorts (1977) confirmed Audrey Thomas's reputation as a brilliant writer of short stories. The complex emotions and ideas explored never strain the capacities of the form, whether in stories depicting the subtle nuances of sexuality and the unfathomable depths of pain, violence, and sadness in human relations (as in 'Kill day at the government wharf' and 'Aquarius'), or in aesthetic enquiries into the mirror relationship of art to life (as in 'Rapunzel' and, powerfully, in 'Initram'). These stories show a gift for evoking place that is also one of the strengths of the epistolary novel *Latakia* (1979), which captures the atmosphere of Crete as well as of places visited on a sea-voyage to Europe. The Syrian port of Latakia, where language difficulties trigger a fierce culture-shock, provides a metaphor for the love-affair, now over, between two Canadian writers who, despite strong physical attraction, are separated by a gulf of non-comprehension, created in part by Michael's need to make Rachel his subordinate and by his resentment of her superiority as a writer. Similar doomed relationships appear in *Real mothers* (1981), which contains one of Thomas's best stories, the delicate, haunting 'Natural history'. It celebrates the love of a mother and daughter and draws together several levels of narrative into one moment of illumination. *Two in the bush and other stories* (1981) contains a selection from *Ten green bottles* and *Ladies and escorts*. The stories in *Goodbye Harold, good luck* (1986) and *The wild blue yonder* (1990) develop similarly subtle analyses of emotional life, often with a witty ironic touch that eases the pain of failed human relationships.

The mother-daughter relationship introduced in 'Natural history' is further developed in the novel *Intertidal life* (1984), where the narrator and her young daughter spend an island summer studying marine life exposed to view at low tide. This and the moon, 'shining always by reflected light', serve as metaphors for woman's place in a man's world. Gulf Island flora and fauna, stories of the Spanish explorers who navigated the coastal waters, and wry depictions of the various island communities are woven into the narrator's analysis of her failed marriage and her desperate need for love. In the novel *Graven images* (1993), two women travel to England in search of their roots (the great trees felled by the actual hurricane of 1987 offer a natural metaphor). The genealogy studied by the narrator is that of the Corbetts, Thomas's own family on her mother's side. The nuances of a grown daughter's uneasy relationship with her 90-year old mother are woven into a recreation of the past and impressions of the present. *Coming down from Wa* (1995) is another version of the return to Africa, again in search of family history, but this time with a male protagonist. The Ghanaian scene is vividly evoked, as are the traveller's discomfort, sickness, frustration, exhilaration, and joy. The eventual disclosure of the family's dark secret is, however, far less successfully handled than the epiphanic encounter with ancestors in *Graven images*.

A vigorous experimenter with narrative method and language, Thomas shows a special interest in the derivation of words, their ambiguities, and multiple connotations. She plays with literary allusions and puns (almost too flamboyantly at times) as she stretches language to catch the experience of people, mostly women, hovering on the verge of disintegration. Intertextual reference to both her own work and a multitude of literary sources serves to underscore the notion of the connectedness of experience. *Alice in wonderland* has a particular resonance for Thomas: allusion to it is woven into each of her novels.

Thomas has also written more than twenty radio plays, has won numerous awards, including the Ethel WILSON fiction award (three times) and the Marian ENGEL award, and has held many positions as writer-in-residence. She was interviewed by Elizabeth Komisar for *OPEN LETTER* III, 3 (Fall 1975) and again by George BOWERING for *Open Letter* IV, 3 (Spring 1979). A special section of the *Capilano Review* VII (Spring 1975) includes a long interview and excerpts from Thomas's African journals. An interview by Eleanor Wachtel appears in *Tessera* 5 (1988). Articles on her work appear in *CANADIAN LITERATURE*: as Robert Diotte's 'The romance of Penelope',

86 (Autumn 1980); Joan Coldwell's 'Memory organized: the novels of Audrey Thomas', 92 (Spring 1982); Pauline Bunting's 'Thomas and her rag-bag', 102 (Autumn 1984); and Frank DAVEY's 'Alternate stories: the short fiction of Audrey Thomas and Margaret Atwood', 109 (Summer 1986). A special Audrey Thomas issue of *Room of One's Own* 10 (1985) contains an interview, critical essays, and a bibliography. There are commentaries on *Intertidal life* by Linda HUTCHEON in *A mazing space: writing Canadian women writing* (1986), edited by S. Neuman and S. Kamboureli, and by Lorna Irvine in *New directions in Canadian writing* 7 (1987). See also Susan Rudy Dorscht's analysis of poststructuralism in *Blown figures* in *CANADIAN FICTION MAGAZINE* 57 (1986) and Dennis Denisoff's study of *Latakia* in *Mosaic* 26 (Fall 1993). JOAN COLDWELL

Thomas, Clara McCandless (b. 1919). Born in Strathroy, Ontario, she was educated at the University of Western Ontario (B.A. 1941; M.A. 1944) and the University of Toronto (Ph.D. 1962). She became a Fellow of the Royal Society of Canada in 1983 and is currently Professor Emerita, department of English, York University; and the York University Libraries Canadian Studies Research Fellow.

Her first book, *Canadian novelists: 1925-1945* (1946; rpr. 1970), began as an M.A. thesis and was innovative in its compilation of biographical and bibliographical listings of 122 writers. Thomas has written three biographies: *Love and work enough: the life of Anna Jameson* (1967, rpr. 1978), a ground-breaking study of the accomplished early feminist writer, art historian, and visitor to Upper Canada in 1836-7; *Ryerson of Upper Canada* (1969), on the career and times of the famous clergyman and educator Egerton Ryerson; *William Arthur Deacon: a Canadian literary life* (1982, with John Lennox), a detailed study of the life, letters, and work of the well-known literary journalist (q.v.).

Thomas is probably best known for the depth and breadth of her work on Margaret LAURENCE, which includes many articles and chapters in books, and for her perceptive *The Manawaka world of Margaret Laurence* (1975), the earliest and most influential book-length study of Laurence's writings. *Our nature—our voices* (1973), Thomas's guidebook to Canadian literature, was translated into Japanese by Professor Noburo Watanabe and published in Japan in 1981. Thomas has contributed to many literary volumes, including the chapter 'Biography' in the second edition of the *Literary history of Canada* (1976) and the chapter on Susanna MOODIE and Catharine Parr TRAILL in *The clear spirit: twenty Canadian woman and their times* (1966), edited by Mary Quayle Innis. Many of Thomas's writings have been collected in *All my sisters: essays on the work of Canadian women writers* (1994).

JOHN LENNOX

Thomas, H. Nigel. See CARIBBEAN-CANADIAN LITERATURE.

Thompson, David. See EXPLORATION LITERATURE IN ENGLISH: 2.

Thompson, John (1938-76). Born in Timperley, Cheshire, England (not Manchester as he later stated), Thompson was all but orphaned at the age of two when his father died of a heart attack and his mother sent him to live with various relatives in Manchester. He grew up parentless as a full boarder in several schools, finally attaining a scholarship to the academically excellent Manchester Grammar School. After graduation he attended the University of Sheffield, where he took his B.A. in honours psychology in 1958. After service in the British Army intelligence corps for two years, he went to the United States, where he studied comparative literature at Michigan State University and received a Ph.D.; his thesis, directed by mentor A.J.M. SMITH, was translations of poems by the French surrealist poet René Char. He moved to New Brunswick in 1966 to teach in the English department of Mount Allison University, living with his wife and daughter in a farmhouse near the Bay of Fundy shore, a locale that inspired his best poetry. His poems and translations, including sequences by Quebec poets Roland GIGUÈRE and Paul-Marie LAPOINTE, began appearing in Canadian quarterlies, and his first poetry collection from ANANSI was *At the edge of the chopping there are no secrets* (1973). The publication of his second and last collection, *Stilt Jack* (1978), was preceded by conflicts with the university, divorce, psychiatric treatment, a long struggle with alcoholism, and finally his death, apparently by suicide, at thirty-eight.

Although reviewers praised the accurate evocation of landscape in *At the edge of the chopping*, it went unnoticed that Thompson, a sophisticated student of modern poetry—Lorca, Trakl, Yeats, Neruda, and Roethke are clear influences—was working on a more ambitious level than many Canadian critics of the time could recognize. Like René Char, he sought to reveal the core truths of nature, to name the unnamable secrets, through a poetry of brief, intensely concentrated but carefully structured images. The poems in his first collection open with a series of precise metaphors: an apple tree is 'a cauldron of leaves,/ the sun a deadly furnace' that in winter bears 'a head of burnt hair/crackling faintly' against the snow. The 'plot' of *At the edge of the chopping* moves from images of fertile decay to the frozen zero of winter, when both women and the air can get thin and cold. The icy purity of stars, knives, frozen trout, and the heart's isolation are at once feared, celebrated, penetrated, embraced, abhorred. In many lines Thompson's terror seems absolute; knowledge can leave us 'cold-broken, earthed'; but the final poems in the book are restorative, offering to a grateful eye the curative power of onions and roots and redemptive words.

The indifferent reception given this astonishing book did nothing to brighten Thompson's difficult last years. His wife left him, taking their daughter; his drinking increased; he moved to Toronto for a sabbatical rest, only to hear that his house in the Tantramar Marsh had burned to the ground. *Stilt Jack* begins with the lines: 'Now you have burned your books: you'll go/with nothing but your blind, stupefied heart', and the bereft poet then enters a night-world that inverts the life-affirming natural sphere celebrated in *At the edge of the chopping*. *Stilt Jack*'s thirty-eight poems, their insistent negations and glittering cascade of images, tell of a man pushed to the limit: the title, after Yeats, can allude to a hooked fish, to a man on stilts. Yet Thompson's charity and good sense flash out in the blackness; he reminds us that after all, 'I'm still here like the sky/and the stove'. The lines shine with his scrupulous care for language and a wry Yorkshire humour. Thompson considered his form carefully; he explains in a prefatory note that his model is the ancient Persian *ghazal*, which proceeds by orderly couplets, but is a 'poem of contrasts, dreams, astonishing leaps'.

In 1995 GOOSE LANE EDITIONS, Fredericton, published *John Thompson: collected poems & translations*, a definitive edition of all of Thompson's poems, published and unpublished, including the translations, with textual notes, a bibliography, and a detailed biographical essay by the editor, Peter Sanger.

JAMES POLK

Thompson, John Sparrow (1795-1867). Thompson was born in Waterford, Ireland, and as a young man went to London. In 1827 he immigrated to Halifax, Nova Scotia. He married Charlotte Pottinger in 1829 and fathered seven children (one of whom, his namesake, was prime minister of Canada from 1892 to 1894). He was a school teacher who started a private school in Halifax; an editor of newspapers and literary magazines; and a civil servant. His government posts included that of Queen's Printer (1843-4; 1848-54). In the late 1820s and 1830s Thompson earned a limited reputation as a poet and essayist, appearing in *The Novascotian* and *The Halifax Monthly Magazine*. His poetry—competent but didactic and often ponderous—was published anonymously in *Scriptural sketches* (Halifax, 1829). His essays are reportorial rather than original in thought. Thompson made his contribution to the literary life of Nova Scotia as an editor of newspapers and magazines and as a friend and critic of young poets; in the 1830s and 1840s he was a major catalyst in stimulating literary activity, a role he shared with his friend Joseph HOWE. As editor of *The Halifax Monthly Magazine* (1830-3), *The Acadian Telegraph* (1836-7), *The Novascotian* (1838; 1840-2), *The Pearl* (1839-40), and *The Mirror* (1848), he published all the best young Nova Scotia poets of the day: Joseph Howe, Sarah and Mary Eliza HERBERT, John McPHERSON, Angus Gidney, Samuel Elder, Andrew SHIELS, and Mary Revett. He knew most of them personally, introduced them to one another, and was instrumental in getting them to think critically about their craft. Without him, literary activity would have been thinner and more diffuse. His most gifted protegé was John McPherson, whose verse he edited and published in book form in 1862.

TOM VINCENT

Thompson, Judith (b. 1954). Born in Montreal, Quebec, and raised in Connecticut, USA, and Kingston, Ontario, she graduated from Queen's University with a B.A. in English (1976) and in 1979 from the acting program of the National Theatre School, where her work in mask revealed her ability to create gripping language. Her first play, *The crackwalker* (1981), was produced by Theatre Passe Muraille in 1980 and has since been staged in major theatres world-wide. A dark, compassionate presentation of disadvantaged young people, the play explodes with unexpected violence, using language that penetrates to the viscera. As playwright-in-residence at Tarragon Theatre, Toronto, Thompson continued to create psychologically rich characters struggling to understand the secrets of their contradictory selves. *White biting dog* (1984) combines emotional intensity with a highly metaphoric theatricality, while *I am yours* (1987) reveals the subconscious desires of the characters in a more realist structure. *Lion in the streets* (1992) moves through fear and confrontation, as a young girl stalks her murderer, to a state of grace imaginatively offered through forgiveness. The prowling presence of the dead girl on the fringes of every scene tends to unite the disparate scenes, but other devices in language and structure open the play to multiple interpretations, foregrounding the constructed nature of the reality it depicts. *Sled* (1997) pursues the theme of innocence tainted or destroyed by evil, juxtaposing animal images from Native spirituality with those from Catholic sources. Thompson's plays received Chalmers Awards in 1987 and 1991 and Governor General's Awards for *White biting dog* and *The other side of the dark*, a collection of four plays: *The crackwalker*, *Pink*, *Tornado*, and *I am yours*. She received a Nelly Award (for Best Radio Drama) for *Tornado* (1988), which she later adapted for the stage and produced at the University of Guelph in 1992. The Winter 1996 issue of *Canadian Theatre Review* was entirely devoted to Thomson's work. She is professor of drama at the University of Guelph. LISBIE RAE

Thompson, Kent (b. 1936). Born in Waukegan, Illinois, he was educated at Hanover College, served in the US army from 1958 to 1961, then took an M.A. at the University of Iowa, where he was a member of the Writers' Workshop in 1962. He subsequently completed a Ph.D. in 1965 at the University of Wales. In 1966 he moved to the University of New Brunswick at Fredericton, where he was a professor of English and creative writing until retiring in 1994. Thompson was editor of *The FIDDLEHEAD* from 1967 to 1971 and from 1974 to 1975. In 1982-3 he was the Canadian Writing Exchange Fellow at the University of Edinburgh. Since his retirement Thompson has settled in Annapolis Royal, Nova Scotia, where he organized and was Artistic Director of the Annapolis Royal Theatre Company until 1996. He remains active in theatre.

Thompson is the author of five novels: *The tenants were Corrie and Tennie* (1973); *Across from the floral park* (1974); *Shacking up* (1980); *Married love: a vulgar entertainment* (1988); and *Playing in the dark* (1990). His fiction often deals with protagonists who find themselves in an unfamiliar situation with a sexually attractive stranger. For example, the fable-like *Across from the floral park* is told by a wealthy and idle narrator who discovers that a young and alluring tenant is mysteriously occupying a house he has purchased. She resists the narrator's attempts to evict her and seduces him into marriage. Although the narrator begins to learn about his new wife's past and to create a present for the two of them, in the novel's conclusion he finds himself locked out for no reason he can understand and he fatalistically begins life anew in a nearby hotel.

Thompson's concern with the way obsession and fantasies control individuals' lives is extended in his most recent novel, *Playing in the dark*, a story told in several voices about a violent, desperate love affair that runs its course without understanding, without hope. Like most of Thompson's fiction, it focuses on people barely able to cope with their lives, locked into existences of limited possibility.

Thompson's short stories have been published widely and have been collected in *Shotgun and other stories* (1979) and in *A local hanging and other stories* (1984). (In the latter collection, some of the characters from *Shacking up* reappear.) Usually quiet in tone, his short fiction has an intensity that makes it effective. Thompson has been particularly noted for his interest in what he calls 'postcard' fiction, extremely brief stories such as those collected in his *Leaping up sliding away* (1986).

Thompson has also published two books of poetry—*Hard explanations* (1968) and *A band of my ancestors* (1975), which is a sequence of twenty-four poems spoken by a Viking invading the New World—and *Biking to Blissville* (1993), a tour guide to New Brunswick. He is the editor of the anthology *Stories from Atlantic Canada* (1973), as well as of *Open windows: Canadian short short stories* (1988); and *Engaged elsewhere: short stories by Canadians abroad* (1989). His plays have been broadcast on CBC Radio and produced for the stage. One of them was produced in Nova Scotia in 1997: *A class act*, co-authored with Noel Lucas.

RUSSELL BROWN

Thomson, Edward William (1849-1924). He was born in Peel County, now part of Toronto, the son of Margaret Hamilton Foley and William Thomson. In 1864, while visiting an American relative, he briefly joined and fought with the Union Army in the American Civil War and in 1866 enlisted in the Queen's Own Rifles to fight the Fenians. Discharged the next year, he studied civil engineering for five years and from 1872 to 1878 surveyed for eastern-Ontario lumbering and railway concerns. In Dec. 1878 he became a political journalist for the Toronto *Globe*, where, except for a return to surveying in 1882 and 1883 during the Winnipeg land boom, he remained for twelve years, serving for a time as its Montreal correspondent. In 1891, disagreeing with the Liberal election platform on unrestricted reciprocity, he left the *Globe*, where he was by this time in charge of the editorial page. He became a revising editor for the Boston *Youth's Companion*—a weekly magazine that was at the height of its popularity, with the widest circulation of any American periodical—to which he had been contributing stories since winning first prize in a *Youth's Companion* short-story competition in 1886 with 'Petherick's peril'. He remained with that magazine as a revising and contributing editor until 1901, when he returned to Canada—first to Montreal, where he worked for the *Star*, and a year later to Ottawa, where he was Canadian correspondent for the Boston *Transcript*. In 1909 he was made a Fellow of the Royal Society of Literature (England) and in 1910 a Fellow of the Royal Society of Canada. He died in Boston at the home of his grandson.

A fluent writer, a politically uncompromising and independent thinker, and an entertaining conversationalist, Thomson was acquainted with major literary and political figures. He was a friend of Duncan Campbell SCOTT and Ethelwyn WETHERALD, and a close friend and admirer of Archibald LAMPMAN, whose *Lyrics of earth* (1895), after receiving several rejections, was finally published by Copeland and Day of Boston through the efforts of Thomson. (He also edited the selection and arrangement of the manuscript at Lampman's invitation.) While in Boston, Thomson remained in close touch with the Canadian literary scene, and during his tenure with the *Youth's Companion* many Canadian writers appeared in its pages. While he lived in Ottawa, he became a close friend and admirer of Henri Bourrassa and Wilfrid Laurier.

Although most of Thomson's stories were published in the *Youth's Companion*, several of his best first appeared elsewhere: 'Privilege of the limits' in *Harper's Weekly* (25 July 1891); 'Old Man Savarin' and 'Great Godfrey's lament' in the New York magazine *Two tales* (Oct. 1892); and 'Miss Minnelly's management' in *The UNIVERSITY MAGAZINE* (Oct. 1910). In the 1890s he published three collections: *Old Man Savarin and other stories* (Toronto, 1895) and two collections that seem to have been designed for a juvenile audience: *Walter Gibbs, the young boss; and other stories* (Toronto, 1896) and *Between earth and sky, and other strange stories of deliverance* (Toronto, 1897). All three were published simultaneously in Canada and the United States. *Smoky days* (New York, 1896), a long story first serialized in the *Youth's companion*, and a long poem, *This is of Aucusson and Nicolette* (Boston, 1896), brought to three the books he published in 1896. After his return to Canada in 1901 Thomson produced little fiction. In 1909 a collection of his poetry was published in Canada as *The many-mansioned house and other poems* and in the United States, slightly altered, as *When Lincoln died and other poems*. (As a boy, on a visit to Philadelphia, Thomson had an encounter with Lincoln.) This volume included a long narrative poem, 'Peter Ottawa', which had been privately printed in 1905. In 1917 Thomson reissued *Old Man Savarin* with some change in title—*Old Man Savarin stories: tales of Canada and Canadians*—and content: two stories from the 1895 collection were omitted, while two from *Between earth and sky* and three later stories were added. This collection was dedicated to Sir Arthur Quiller-Couch, who had included Thomson's poem 'Aspiration' in *The Oxford book of Victorian verse* (1912).

Thomson's fiction, though not his poetry, endures. Some of his stories are excessively sentimental; some are simply boys' stories; but the best are fine realistic stories of early Canadian life. Among the Irish, Scottish, and French-Canadian settlers and lumbermen he wrote about are some memorable characters portrayed with economy, gentle humour, liveliness of language, felicity of dialogue, and a skilful use of dialect.

See Arthur Stanley BOURINOT's edition of *The letters of Edward William Thomson to Archibald Lampman (1891-1897), with notes, a bibliography, and other material on Thomson and Lampman* (1957). The 1917 edition of Thomson's *Old Man Savarin stories* was reprinted in the Literature of Canada Series (1974), with an introduction by Linda Shesko. See also the *Selected stories of E.W. Thomson* (1973) edited by Lorraine McMullen, who wrote 'E.W. Thomson and the *Youth's Companion*', *Canadian Children's Literature* 13 (1979).

LORRAINE McMULLEN

'Threnody, A'. See 'The AKHOOND OF SWAT'.

Tin flute*, *The. See *BONHEUR D'OCCASION*.

Tippett, Maria (b. 1944). Born in Victoria, British Columbia, she began her training as a cultural historian at Simon Fraser University (Hons. B.A., 1972), and wrote with Douglas

Cole *From desolation to splendour: changing perceptions of the British Columbia landscape* (1977). This was followed by her distinguished biography, *Emily Carr* (1979, 1995), which threw a new light on the character and works of the well-known Canadian painter and writer (q.v.); it won a Governor General's Award and the John A. Macdonald Prize for Canadian History. In 1982 she received a Ph.D. from the University of London. Her *Art at the service of war: Canada, art, and the Great War* (1984) was followed by *Making culture: English-Canadian institutions and the arts before the Massey Commission* (1990). *By a lady: celebrating three centuries of Canadian women in the visual arts* (1992) is a significant and lavishly illustrated addition to the study of this branch of Canadian culture. *Between two cultures: a photographer among the Inuit* (1994), for which Tippett wrote the text, represents another direction of her research.

Becoming myself: a memoir (1996) is an engaging and frank account ofTippett's life, until the publication of *Emily Carr*, that includes her not entirely happy time as an adopted child; a period in Europe, particularly Germany; and the first phase of her university education. She has also published a collection of stories, *Breaking the cycle and other stories from a Gulf Island* (1989).

A Fellow of the Royal Society of Canada, she is also a senior research Fellow of Churchill College, Cambridge University. In 1991 she married the English historian Peter Clarke and divides her time between Cambridge, England, and her house on Bowen Island, B.C.

WILLIAM TOYE

Tish (1961-9). Founded in Vancouver in Sept. 1961, this mimeographed magazine began the writing careers of its poet-editors: Frank DAVEY, George BOWERING, Fred WAH, David Dawson, and James Reid. It was influenced by the work of both the San Francisco poet Robert Duncan and the CONTACT PRESS editors Louis DUDEK and Raymond SOUSTER. The '*Tish* group', as the five editors soon became known, argued for a poetry of spoken idiom written in lines determined by oral rhythms. Nineteen consecutive monthly issues were published by the original editors, marked by extensive discussion of poetic theory and numerous attempts at extended or series poems, notably Bowering's 'Margins' series. Writers also associated with *Tish* during this period included critic Warren Tallman, playwright Carol BOLT, and poets Daphne MARLATT (Buckle), David Cull, Red LANE, Robert Hogg, and Lionel KEARNS.

Following five issues edited between Aug. 1963 and June 1964 by a group headed by David Dawson, the general editorship of *Tish* was assumed by Dan McLeod, who later founded the counter-culture newspaper *The Georgia Straight*. Under McLeod, *Tish* directed itself mainly to the Vancouver writing community and lost the awareness of central and eastern Canada that had characterized the earlier period. The last four issues, published in 1968-9, were edited by Karen Tallman from offices shared with *The Georgia Straight* and were given over mostly to prose, particularly the diary and reflective essay. In 1969 *Tish* was unofficially replaced by *The Georgia Straight Writing Supplement*.

The founding of *Tish* marked the beginning of a distinct but inward-looking West Coast writing community that later came to publish such journals as *Iron*, *The Pacific Nation*, *BLEW OINTMENT*, *Air*, *Island*, *Pulp*, *Talon*, and *Writing*—journals rarely seen elsewhere in Canada. Paradoxically, in a national context *Tish* was also the most dramatic evidence of the emergence across the country of a new generation of poets more open to the colloquial and popular than were their forebears—a generation that included not only the *Tish* editors but such figures as John NEWLOVE and Andrew SUKNASKI in Saskatchewan and Margaret ATWOOD and David MCFADDEN in Ontario. The first nineteen issues of *Tish* were reprinted by TALONBOOKS as *Tish 1-19* (1975). Critical and historical materials concerning *Tish* have been collected by C.H. Gervais in *The writing life* (1976), and by Douglas BARBOUR in *Beyond 'Tish'* (1991).

See also LITERARY MAGAZINES IN ENGLISH: 3 and POETRY IN ENGLISH: 1950 TO 1982: 2.

FRANK DAVEY

Tit-Coq. This famous play by Gratien GÉLINAS concerns the illegitimate young soldier Arthur Saint-Jean—called Tit-Coq (little rooster) for his fighting spirit—and his search for acceptance and love. Though there is some melodrama and much comedy in its three acts with thirteen scenes, the way Tit-Coq and his fiancée Marie-Ange are caught in the cultural and religious web of Quebec in the 1940s is genuinely tragic. The play can also be read as a statement about the plight of French Canadians in a world dominated by Anglo-American culture and traditions. Tit-Coq, in his search for acceptance and identity in a hostile world, can be seen as a metaphor for Quebec in an English-speaking continent. Much of its success in Quebec can be attributed to Gélinas's use of the French spoken by working-class Québécois, who were shown in this play that their situation and language were worthy materials for the stage. Although the play may seem dated now and some of its characters stereotypes, it remains a moving presentation of Quebec society before the Quiet Revolution.

The first production of *Tit-Coq* opened at Montreal's Théâtre Monument National on 22 May 1948 and was directed by Gélinas and Fred Barry. An immediate success, it ran at that theatre until the summer recess, after which it transferred to the Théâtre du Gesù, where it played in both French and English until 1951 with basically the same cast—Gélinas played Tit-Coq in both versions—for more than 500 performances. In English it had a successful run at the Royal Alexandra Theatre, Toronto, and in Chicago. This encouraged Gélinas in 1951 to take the English version to New York, where it closed on Broadway after three performances. In 1953 it was made into a film, starring Gélinas and directed by him and René Delacroix; a subtitled English version was also made. In 1981 *Tit-Coq* had a very popular revival at the Théâtre Denise Pelletier by the Nouvelle Compagnie Théâtrale, Montreal; directed by Gélinas, this production had a dynamic young actor, Daniel Gadouas, in the title role. A televised production, starring Alain Gélinas, Gratien's son, was aired on Radio-Canada in 1984. In 1992 and 1993 it had highly popular productions at the Théâtre de la Bordée in Quebec City.

Tit-Coq was first published in French in 1950 and in English—in a too-literal English translation by Kenneth Johnstone, in co-operation with the author—in 1967; this remains its only English translation. A new edition of the French text was published in 1968 and a critical edition, edited by Laurent Mailhot, in 1980. The play was reprinted as recently as 1994. Renate Usmiani includes a careful analysis of *Tit-Coq* in her study *Gratien Gélinas* (1977). See also Jean Cléo Godin's study of *Tit-Coq*, followed by a detailed bibliography, in the *Dictionnaire des oeuvres littéraires du Québec* III (1982). Gélinas himself reveals new material concerning the play in conversations with Victor-Lévy BEAULIEU: *Gratien, Tit-Coq, Fridolin, Bousille et les autres* (1993). Finally, in Anne-Marie Sicotte's two-volume biography, *Gratien Gélinas: la ferveur et le doute* (1995-6), Gélinas's granddaughter comments at some length on the play's genesis and critical reception.

JAMES NOONAN

Tocque, Philip (1814-99). Born in Carbonear, Newfoundland, he became a clerk in the mercantile establishment of Slade, Elson and Company, where he was acquainted with the naturalist P.H. Gosse. In 1841 he became schoolmaster at Port de Grave, Conception Bay; three years later he occupied a similar position in Broad Cove (now St Philips). In 1845 he gave a series of lectures on geology in St John's and was recognized by the local press as the first Newfoundlander to lecture on scientific subjects. During the late 1840s he served as a Clerk of the Peace in Harbour Breton on Newfoundland's south coast, but in 1849 he immigrated to the United States. Although, to quote his own words, 'From my youth I have been a member of the Wesleyan Society', Tocque studied for the Episcopal ministry in the theological department of Trinity College, Hartford, Connecticut, and was admitted to Holy Orders in 1852. He subsequently served as a minister in Massachusetts; in Tusket, Nova Scotia; and in Kinmount, Waverley, and Markham, Ontario. In 1858 he was given the honorary degree of A.M. by Lawrence University of Appleton, Wisconsin. On his retirement he settled in Toronto, where he died.

Tocque's first important book was a collection of essays, entitled *Wandering thoughts; or Solitary hours* (London, 1846). These are entertaining, rambling pieces, designed to introduce young readers to the wonders of science. *A peep at Uncle Sam's farm, workshop, fisheries, &c* (Boston, 1851) describes his initial excited response to the attractions of the eastern United States. *The mighty deep* (New York, 1852), edited by Daniel P. Kidder, is a brief introduction to the subject of oceans, done with Tocque's accustomed flair. *Newfoundland: as it was, and as it is in 1877* (Toronto, 1878) combines the features of a history and a gazeteer. It amply fulfilled Tocque's patriotic intention of showing 'British and American readers that Newfoundland is something more than a mere fishing station.' *Kaleidoscope echoes: being historical, philosophical, scientific, and theological sketches, from the miscellaneous writings of the Rev. Philip Tocque, A.M.* (Toronto, 1895), edited by his daughter Annie Tocque, was his final book. It is a miscellany of personal reminiscences, devotional pieces, and 'booming' items on Newfoundland.

Tocque also published *The Newfoundland almanack*, in St John's, for the years 1848, 1849, and also 1850, the first in 1847, the other two in 1849, and *The voice of the sea: a sermon, preached on Sunday evening, Oct. 2, 1853, in St. Mary's Church, Richmond Street, Boston, to commemorate the death of the late Captain Robert Hutchings, of the British steamship 'Andes' . . .* (Boston, 1853).

Tocque was a writer of some quality whose essays have an engaging personal touch and a lucid style. His reflections on Newfoundland are occasionally penetrating and moving. See Marjorie Doyle, *A Newfoundlander in exile: the life and times of Philip Tocque* (1997).

PATRICK O'FLAHERTY

Tonge, Grizelda Elizabeth Cottnam (*c.*1803-25). Little is known of Grizelda Tonge's short life. She was born in Windsor, Nova Scotia, of a socially and politically prominent family. Both her grandmothers wrote poetry and her father was a noted orator, so that the intellectual and literary environment in which she grew up was more sophisticated than was usual at the time. Her few extant poems—notably *Lines composed at midnight* (Halifax, n.d.)—reveal a sensitive mind, but there is not enough of her writing extant to judge her talent. She died of fever in the West Indies in Demarara (now Guyana), where she had journeyed to join her father. Her literary importance lay not in her verse but in the symbolic status she achieved in the minds of a generation of young Nova Scotian writers working to create a native literature. Because she came to represent the image of the beautiful, sensitive young poet struck down just as her talent was blooming, she epitomized both the promise of native literary genius and its fragility in the harsh, stubborn soil of colonial society. Her symbolic status was enhanced by what appears to have been a premonition of her death in her last poem, 'Lines written at midnight' (1825). Joseph HOWE, in his articles 'Western rambles' (1828) and 'Nights with the muses' (1845), nostalgically refers to her as the 'highly-gifted songstress of Acadia'. TOM VINCENT

Torgov, Morley. (b. 1928). Torgov was born and raised in Sault Ste Marie, Ontario, where his family was part of the city's small Jewish community. A full-time lawyer with a practice in Toronto, he writes in his leisure time.

Torgov has published a memoir and three novels, each of which explores Jewish themes with humour and irony that are gentler than in either Mordecai RICHLER or Philip Roth, with whom he is often compared. *A good place to come from* (1974) won the LEACOCK Medal for Humour and was adapted as a mini-series for television and for the stage in Canada and the United States. A series of vignettes, it describes Torgov's experience of growing up Jewish in the predominantly Gentile world of Sault Ste Marie. *The Abramsky variations* (1977), written in three parts and set in Toronto and France, concerns three generations of the Abramsky (later Brahms) family: father Louis, son Hershel, and grandson Bart (né Kevin). Each character struggles to reconcile Jewish identity with secular ambition and all are more strongly attracted to fantasizing about people they want to emulate than to facing reality. Torgov's second novel, *The outside chance of Maximilian Glick* (1982), which also won the Leacock Medal, was first written as a children's story. It takes a comic look at twelve-year-old Maximilian, so named because his parents thought it would look impressive on the door of a law office. It is the story of a boy raised in the tiny Jewish community of Steelton, northern Ontario. Maximilian seeks to escape the overwhelming love of his parents and grandparents, who envision him making a career as a surgeon, judge, or scientist. With the help of Rabbi Kalman Teitelman, who replaces Steelton's former rabbi and with whom Maximilian forms a relationship, he eventually releases himself from the stifling expectations of others. *St. Farb's day* (1990) concerns Isadore Farb, an honest, respectable lawyer on Toronto's Bay Street. As Farb struggles with an ethical dilemma—he finds himself involved in a conflict of interest with several clients—he confronts larger moral issues linked to his Jewish identity.

RUTH PANOFSKY

Toupin, Paul. See DRAMA IN FRENCH 1948 to 1981: 1.

Traill, Catharine Parr (1802-99). Born in Kent, England, Catharine Strickland spent her first thirty years in rural Suffolk, whence her father retired after a successful docks management and importing career on the Thames. While keeping close ties to Norwich, the Strickland family lived first at Stowe House near Bungay and after 1808 at Reydon Hall on the outskirts of Southwold. At Reydon, Thomas and Elizabeth Strickland conscientiously educated their six daughters and two sons, stressing discipline, practical knowledge, and self-reliance. Though literature played little part in his curriculum, Thomas's library provided much imaginative stimulus for his daughters. Isolated for the most part, the Strickland girls were drawn to the romance of history and experimented with writing stories, plays, and poetry to pass the time. By the late 1820s all but one of them had become published writers. The eldest, Elizabeth and

Agnes, who later achieved fame and social prominence in England as co-authors of *Lives of the Queens of England* and other multi-volumed royalist biographies, began their literary careers, respectively, as editor and poet; Jane Margaret specialized in moral tales and histories; Catharine, like her younger sister Susanna (MOODIE), began as a writer of children's stories. Three members of this remarkable family—Catharine, Susanna, and their younger brother Samuel (b. 1807)—immigrated to Canada (from 1825 to 1832) and there earned recognition as recorders and interpreters of pioneer life and settlement in early-nineteenth-century Upper Canada.

Catharine was the first Strickland offspring to appear in print. Shortly after her father's death in 1818, a family friend took one of her manuscripts to London. Though she later recalled that her first book was *The tell tale*, available bibliographical evidence indicates that her first work to appear in print was either *Disobedience; or, Mind what Mama says* or *Reformation; or, The cousins*, both of which were published in 1819 by James Wodehouse. In fact, since many of her early works appeared without her name, there is considerable bibliographical confusion about the record of her pre-1832 titles, particularly in the British Library catalogue where several of her works are attributed to her sisters.

Influenced by Thomas Day, Sarah Trimmer, and other turn-of-the-century writers for children, Catharine produced virtually a book a year over the following decade. They included *Little Downy; or, The history of a field mouse* (1822—a story that was still popular fifty years later); *The tell tale; an original collection of moral and amusing stories* (1823); *The flower basket; or, Poetical blossoms: original nursery rhymes and tales* (1825); *Prejudice reproved; or, The history of the Negro toy-seller* (1826); *A sketch of the life of Linneaus, in a series of letters. Designed for young persons* (1827); *The keepsake guineas; or, The best use of money* (1828); *The step-brothers. A tale* (1828); *Sketches from nature; or, Hints to juvenile naturalists* (1830); and *Sketchbook of a young naturalist; or, Hints to the students of nature* (1831). At the same time she managed to place some of her stories in popular London 'annuals' like *Ackermann's juvenile forget me not* and *The New Year's gift*.

One pre-emigration book deserves special mention. *The young emigrants; or, Pictures of life in Canada. Calculated to amuse and instruct the minds of youth* (1826) anticipates her own removal to Canada six years later and reflects her positive approach to the challenges involved in a dramatically new life. Based on information from family friends in Canada and travel books, it is structured as a series of letters and promotes the worth of an adventurer's spirit, British resoluteness, and a Crusoe-like acceptance of untoward fate, all in the context of stable domestic life and family solidarity.

Strickland's quiet Suffolk life changed forever when, in the wake of her broken engagement to Francis Harral, she met Lt. Thomas Traill, a sensitive, sociable and well-read widower who had attended Oxford and whose social credentials included a prominent Orkney family, a decade of living on the continent, and a modest military rank. Hastily and against some Strickland family resistance, the couple married in mid-May 1832 at Reydon. Following the plans for emigration already formulated by Catharine's sister Susanna and her husband John Moodie, they set out immediately for Scotland to arrange their finances, bid farewell to Traill's family, and book summer passage for Canada.

Thomas Traill adapted to life in the Canadian backwoods far less effectively than his younger, more capable wife. Though their arrival and settlement (near present-day Lakefield, Ontario) was buffered by the kindness and resourcefulness of Catharine's brother Samuel—their neighbour, and soon the area's most successful pioneer—Thomas Traill was never happy with clearing trees, farming, or his remoteness from congenial society. Nevertheless, out of the early—and generally positive—years of pioneering experience, Catharine Traill drew the materials for her most important book, one of the few she wrote exclusively for an adult audience: *The BACKWOODS OF CANADA: being letters from the wife of an emigrant officer, illustrative of the domestic economy of British America* (London, 1836; NCL).

Thomas Traill's attempts to sell the farm on Lake Katchwanook, begun in 1835, succeeded in 1839. The family moved to Peterborough, but mounting debts, illnesses, and more mouths to feed hampered their progress in the town, despite Catharine's attempt to run a school. When in 1846 the sudden death of a young Scottish friend left them liable for his debts, they accepted the timely offer of an English friend, the Rev. George Bridges, to live rent-free in his Rice Lake home, 'Wolf Tower'. For the next thirteen years they lived in that area, particularly at 'Oaklands', where Thomas Traill, increasingly incapacitated by depressions, relied upon his wife not only to raise their seven surviving children but also to write for publication when time and opportunity allowed.

To these most difficult years of the Traills' Canadian experience belong two of Catharine's children's books, *Canadian Crusoes. A tale of the Rice Lake plains* (London, 1852) and *Lady Mary and her nurse; or, A peep into the Canadian forest* (London, 1856). The former—drawing upon the attractive landscape of the Rice Lake plains, what she knew of the history of its Native people, and the lost-child theme—dramatizes the exemplary survival of three adolescents of Scottish and French roots who, though lost in the backwoods for nearly two years, succeed in bringing their high-minded and civilized attitudes to bear on wilderness experience and bring into their midst a Native girl whom they rescue. Still popular today as an early example of writing for children in Canada, the novel is at once a testimony to British resourcefulness and a hopeful allegory of Canadian survival and unity. *Lady Mary*—which, like *Crusoes*, was reprinted under variant titles in Britain and the United States to disguise its Canadian specificity—is a stylized dialogue between teacher and child that manifests Traill's fondness for nature and her skill at close observation. Her other book of this period, *The female emigrant's guide, and hints on Canadian housekeeping* (Toronto, 1854), returns to the spirit of *The backwoods of Canada*, providing supportive counsel and practical information for women faced with the prospect of emigration and settlement in remote Britsh-American locales. Serialized in the Rev. Henry Hope's Toronto newspaper *The Old Countryman*, it was first published in four parts before it appeared as a book. Though repetitive, anecdotal, and uneven, this miscellany, published under variant titles and much edited to suit Hope's various purposes, went through ten editions in the 1850s.

Some of Traill's best writing from the late 1830s to 1860, including a sequel to *The backwoods*, did not find its way into book form. Various sketches and stories about bush life that appeared in Britain in magazines like *The Home Circle*, *Sharpe's London Journal*, *Chambers's Edinburgh Journal*, and in Canada in *The* LITERARY GARLAND and *The Anglo-American Magazine*, have been collected under the title *Forest and other gleanings: the fugitive writings of Catharine Parr Traill* (1994), edited by Michael Peterman and Carl Ballstadt.

Traill's strengths as a writer are her clarity, firm sense of identity, optimistic spirit, and above all her attention to natural detail. While her interest in flora and fauna is clearly shown in *The backwoods*, it was only after her husband's death in 1859, her subsequent removal to Lakefield, Ontario, and the maturation of her children that she had the opportunity to focus that attention. *Canadian wild flowers* (Montreal, 1868) combined her text and the paintings of Susanna Moodie's daughter Agnes Fitzgibbon. Agnes took the initiative in the project, learning lithography, organizing the material, finding a publisher, and arranging for the necessary subscribers. In the 1880s, while living in Ottawa with her second husband, Brown Chamberlain, Agnes also made possible her aunt's most significant work as a naturalist, *Studies of plant life in Canada; or, Gleanings from forest, lake and plain* (Ottawa, 1885), a fond and detailed study that earned Traill the praise of several professional botanists.

In her last decade Traill produced two more books: *Pearls and pebbles; or, Notes of an old naturalist* (Toronto, London, 1894), which includes reminiscences of her childhood and a useful biographical sketch by her grandniece, Mary Agnes Fitzgibbon, and *Cot and cradle stories* (Toronto, 1895), another children's collection. She died in Lakefield at the age of 97, still at work on book projects, her life having spanned virtually the entire nineteenth century.

See Audrey Morris, *The gentle pioneers: five nineteenth-century Canadians* (1968); David Jackel, 'Mrs. Moodie and Mrs. Traill, and the fabrication of a Canadian tradition', *The Compass*, no. 6 (1979); Carl Ballstadt, 'Catharine Parr Traill', *Canadian writers and their works*, vol. 1, Fiction series (1983); Marian Fowler, *The embroidered tent: five gentlewomen in early Canada* (1982); Michael Peterman, 'Catharine Parr Traill', *DICTIONARY OF CANADIAN BIOGRAPHY*, vol. 12 (1990); Michael Peterman, '"Splendid anachronism": The record of Catharine Parr Traill's struggles as an amateur botanist in nineteenth-century Canada', in *Re(dis)covering our foremothers: nineteenth-century Canadian women writers* (1990), edited by Lorraine McMullen; *I bless you in my heart: selected correspondence of Catharine Parr Traill* (1996), edited by Carl Ballstadt, Elizabeth Hopkins, and Michael Peterman. See also the Traill Family Collection in the National Archives of Canada. MICHAEL PETERMAN

Translations: English to French. To 1981. From nineteenth-century translations of works by Frances BROOKE (*Voyage dans le Canada; ou Histoire de Miss Montaigu*, Madame T.G.M., 1809), Rosanna LEPROHON (*Antoinette de Mirecourt; ou Mariage secret et chagrins cachés*, J.A. Genand, 1865), T.C. HALIBURTON (*Le vieux juge; ou Esquisses de la vie dans une* *colonie*, 1949), and William KIRBY (*Le chien d'or: légende canadienne*, Pamphile LEMAY, 1884), to recent translations of a biography of Terry Fox or the latest novels by Margaret ATWOOD, George BOWERING, and Alice MUNRO, more and more Canadian books are being translated from English to French. Philip Stratford remarked in his *Bibliography of Canadian books in translation* (with Maureen Newman, 1975) that four times as many works were translated between 1920 and 1960 as during the previous 350 years, and that in the sixties alone the number almost tripled, reaching 120 in 1975. Two years later the figure was 190 and in 1981 it reached 300 (240 authors translated). Even remembering that over twice as many translations are done from French to English, literary translation in Quebec—especially of novels and essays—has taken an unprecedented leap forward since the 1960s.

In the area of fiction sixty novelists and 115 titles have been translated—half of them in the past five years. Six of the best-known Canadian authors were translated and published in France: Stephen LEACOCK (*Histoires humoristiques*, 1963; *Mémoires d'une jeune fille victorienne*, 1964; *Leacock: textes choisis*, 1966); Mazo DE LA ROCHE (16 Jalna books); Malcolm LOWRY (*Écoute notre voix ô seigneur*, 1962; *Au-dessous du volcan*, 1963; *Lunar caustic*, 1963; *Ultramarine*, 1965; *Choix de lettres*, 1968; *Sombre comme la tombe où repose mon ami*, 1970; *En route vers l'île de Gabriola*, 1970); Arthur Hailey (*714, appelle Vancouver*, 1959; *Le dernier diagnostic*, 1960; *En haut lieu*, 1962; *Grand Hôtel Saint-Gregory*, 1966; *Airport*, 1969; *Detroit*, 1972); Leonard COHEN (*Le jeu favori*, 1971; *Les perdants magnifiques*, 1973); and Mordecai RICHLER (*Le choix des ennemis*, 1959; *L'apprentissage de Duddy Kravitz*, 1960; *Le cavalier de Saint-Urbain*, 1976). All these translations done in France have greatly reduced the percentage of work done in Quebec. However, half-a-dozen Montreal publishers are now actively translating novels. Two series, published by Le Cercle du Livre de France—'Deux solitudes' and 'Deux solitudes, jeunesse'—contain over thirty titles. These include two by Morley CALLAGHAN (*Telle est ma bien-aimée*, 1974, and *Cet été-là à Paris*, 1976, both translated by the director of one of the series, Michelle Tisseyre); three by Robertson DAVIES (*Cinquième emploi*, 1975; *Le lion avait un visage d'homme*, 1978; *Le monde des merveilles*, 1979—translated by Arlette Francière and Claire MARTIN); three by Margaret LAURENCE (*L'ange de pierre*, 1976; *Les oracles*, 1979; *Un dieu farceur*, 1981—translated by Claire Martin and Michelle Robinson); three by Richler (*Mon père, ce héros*. . . , 1975; *Duddy Kravitz*, 1976; *Jacob Deux-Deux et le vampire masqué*, 1977—translated by Jean SIMARD); and one each by Brian MOORE (*Le fol été de Sheila Redden*, Jean Simard, 1978), W.O. MITCHELL (*Qui a vu le vent*, Arlette Francière, 1974), Patrick Watson (*En ondes dans cinq secondes*, Laurier LaPierre, 1978), and Richard B. WRIGHT (*Un homme de week-end*, Jean Paré, 1977). Juvenile novels in translation are by Margaret Atwood (*Sur l'arbre perchés*, Michel Caillol, 1980), Jean LITTLE (*Écoute, l'oiseau chantera*, Paule DAVELUY, 1980), and Farley MOWAT (*Deux grands ducs dans la famille*, Paule Daveluy, 1980; *La malédiction du tombeau viking*, Maryse Côté, 1980).

It is notable that only four authors from the nineteenth century and ten from the period 1900-40 (Irene BAIRD, Marius BARBEAU, John GLASSCO, Angus Graham, Leacock, Lowry, L.M. MONTGOMERY, de la Roche, and Sinclair ROSS) have been translated. Even in the decades from which the most works have been translated—the forties, fifties, and sixties—many gaps remain to be filled. The selection is generally conservative, concentrating on the 'classics', such as Hugh MacLENNAN (*Deux solitudes*, Paris, 1963; *Le temps tournera au beau*, Jean Simard, 1966; and *Le matin d'une longue nuit*, Jean Simard, 1967), Callaghan, Lowry, Davies, Richler, Laurence, and including very few more recent writers. (The works of Matt COHEN, Timothy FINDLEY, Robert KROETSCH, Michael ONDAATJE, Rudy WIEBE, and others are unavailable in French translation.) The influence of feminism has prompted translations of works by such authors as Margaret Atwood (*Lady Oracle*, Marlyse Picard, 1979, and *La vie avant l'homme*, Marianne Véron, 1981), Margaret Laurence (*Un dieu farceur*, M. Robinson, 1981), and Alice Munro (*Pour qui te prends-tu?*, Colette Tonge, 1981).

English-Canadian literary circles unanimously recognize the vitality and quality of modern poetic production. However, if the number of authors translated is any indication, practically no one in Québec is acquainted with English-Canadian poetry. Three poets (Leonard Cohen, John Robert COLOMBO, and Dennis LEE) and four books have appeared in French: two by Cohen, *Poèmes et chansons* (1972) and *L'énergie des esclaves* (1974), both translated and published in Paris; Colombo's *La grande muraille de Chine* (Jacques GODBOUT, 1969); and Lee's *Élégies civiles et autres poèmes* (Marc Lebel, 1980). Fortunately in an excellent anthology, *Poèmes des quatre côtés* (1975), the poet Jacques BRAULT gives what he calls 'non-translations' of Atwood and Gwendolyn MacEWEN, and since 1969 the magazine *Ellipse* has translated some fifty Canadian poets, mainly from the forties, fifties, and sixties (including Irving LAYTON, P.K. PAGE, Raymond SOUSTER, Cohen, D.G. JONES, John NEWLOVE and Al PURDY), as well as several young poets of the seventies. *Ellipse* has certainly helped create a team of translators; but there are no experienced English-French translators of poetry in Quebec of the stamp of John Glassco, F.R. SCOTT, or D.G. Jones in English Canada.

American and British plays, translated in France and/or adapted in Quebec, are regularly produced in Montreal's French-language theatres, but English-Canadian plays are practically unknown. Those translated so far (nine authors and eleven titles) have been done for essentially selfish reasons: plays about Quebec like *Charbonneau and Le Chef* by John Thomas McDonough (*Charbonneau et Le Chef*, Paul Hébert and Pierre Morency, 1974); plays that deal with a certain Montreal milieu, like *On the job* by David FENNARIO (*À l'ouvrage*, Robert Guy Scully, 1979); or that are internationally succesful, such as *Fortune and men's eyes* by John HERBERT (*Aux yeux des hommes*, René Dionne, 1971).

Non-fiction—biography, history books, and literary criticism—is more often translated. (Surprisingly, more of such books are translated from English to French than vice versa.) The vast majority of those books that are translated—170 titles—date from the sixties and seventies. They include most English-language books on Quebec society, history, culture, and politics. The number of these translated books doubled in only five years (1977-81): presumably non-fiction will offer the most active field of translation in the future. In contrast to the poets and novelists, there are few stars here: seven titles by Marshall McLUHAN, some translated in France and some in Quebec, including *La galaxie Gutenburg* (Jean Paré, 1967), *Pour comprendre les media* (Jean Paré, 1968), and *Message et massage* (Thérèse Lauriol, 1968); three by Northrop FRYE: *Le siècle de l'innovation* (François Rinfret, 1968), *Anatomie de la critique* (Guy Durand, 1969), and *Pouvoirs de l'imagination* (Jean Simard, 1969); and two each by Peter NEWMAN, Marius Barbeau, Stanley Ryerson, and Merrill DENISON.

As Philip Stratford has stated so correctly, in the field of translation Canada is behind most other Western countries, somewhere between Iceland and Albania; yet English-Canadian and Québécois literary translators are swiftly closing the gap. Thanks to grants from the CANADA COUNCIL (since 1971), which has also instituted the Prize for Translation (1974), to the energy of certain publishers, and to the translators themselves and their Association (founded in 1975), the total number of translations published has doubled every five years for the past fifteen years. The quality of literary translation from English to French has reached a respectable level over the past few years. Jacques Brault, Jean Paré, Michelle Robinson, Jean Simard, Michelle Tisseyre, and Colette Tonge are recognized as successful translators, and a new generation—including Michel Beaulieu, Francine de Lorimier, Claire Dupond, Arlette Francière, and Yvan Steenhout—follows close on their heels.

RICHARD GIGUÈRE

1982 to 1996. Between 1982 and 1996 well-known English Canadian writers such as Matt COHEN, Robert KROETSCH, and Michael ONDAATJE were translated into French for the first time (in Quebec or in France). Works by authors already known to French-Canadian readers—Margaret ATWOOD, Robertson DAVIES, and Northrop FRYE—had already been translated. New authors like Trevor Ferguson, Steven HEIGHTON, and Brad FRASER, as well as such 'classic' authors as A.M. KLEIN —who had, until then, not been translated— were now introduced to a francophone readership. During this period support programs for the translation of Canadian writing continued to play a vital role, complemented by the GOVERNOR GENERAL'S AWARD, Translation, given for outstanding translations of various kinds of literary works. Examples of award-winning translations are: *Les âges de l'amour* (1989), poems by Dorothy LIVESAY translated by Jean Antonin Billard; A.M. Klein's novel *Le second rouleau* (1990), by Robert and Charlotte Melançon; and Jane Jacobs' *Systèmes de survie* (1996), translated by Christiane Teasdale.

A number of novels by Atwood have been published in French, some translated in Quebec by Hélène Filion (*Marquée au corps*, 1983; *La femme comestible*, 1984; *L'oeil-de-chat*, 1990; etc.), others in France (*La servante écarlate*, 1987; *La voleuse d'hommes*, 1994, among others). The French version of *Coming through slaughter*, by Ondaatje, was published by Boréal, Montreal, as *Le blues de Buddy Bolden*, translated by Robert Paquin. However, Ondaatje's other novels in translation (*La peau d'un lion*, 1989; *Un air de famille*, 1991; *Le patient anglais*, 1993) were published by French publishing houses. The Deptford trilogy by

Robertson Davies, published in the 1970s by the Cercle du Livre de France, was republished in 1989 by Éditions Payot. Other works by the same author (*Un homme remarquable*, 1992; *La lyre d'Orphée*, 1993) have also been published in France by Éditions de l'Olivier. Some novels by Timothy FINDLEY were Franco-Quebec co-editions (*Le chasseur de têtes*, 1996, for example), while other of his works were published only in France (*Grand Elysium Hotel*, 1986; *Le dernier des fous*, 1996). The 1996 French literary festival Les Belles Étrangères, held in Paris, was dedicated to English-Canadian literature. On this occasion the Literary Translators Association of Canada (LTAC) pointed out that often it was Canadians who first translated those English-Canadian authors into French who were now being acclaimed by Paris.

Two novels by Robert Kroetsch are now available in translation: *Badlands* (1985) and *L'étalon* (1990). The former was translated by Georges-André Vachon, himself a novelist and essayist; the latter by Marie José Thériault, daughter of novelist Yves THÉRIAULT, and also a writer. Daniel Poliquin, author of *L'écureuil noir* (1994) and *Canon des Gobelins* (1995), has translated Jack Kerouac (*Avant la route*, 1990), Matt Cohen (*Monsieur Vogel*, 1990), and Douglas GLOVER (*Le récit de voyage en Nouvelle-France de l'abbé peintre Hugues Pommier*, 1994). Ivan Steenhout, who has published poetry under the pseudonym Alexis LeFRANÇOIS (*Comme tournant la page*, 1978), has translated Trevor Ferguson (*Onyx John*, 1990).

Further translations include stories by Guy VANDERHAEGHE (*Une histoire de mon temps*, 1990; *En chute libre*, 1991); by Steven Heighton (*Théâtre de revenants*, 1994); and by Alistair MacLEOD (*Cet héritage au goût de sel*, 1994). To mark its twentieth birthday LTAC published a collection of seven stories by Joyce MARSHALL, *Blood and bone/En chair et en os* (1995), in their original version and in translation; Marshall is the translator of Gabrielle ROY and a founding member of LTAC. Some feminist novelists have been translated.For example, *Héroïne* (1988)by Gail SCOTT appeared in French one year after first publication in English, and *Ana historique* (1992) by Daphne MARLATT brought its translators, Paul Gagné and Lori Saint-Martin, the Prix John-GLASSCO awarded annually by LTAC to a literary translator for a first publication. Controversy broke out in 1993 when the Governor General's Award, in the category 'novels and short prose' in French, was awarded to Nancy HUSTON for her *Cantique des plaines*, a version based on her *Plainsong*, which was first published in English. Quebec editors such as Jacques Lanctôt of the VLB publishing house were incensed that a 'simple translation' of a work already in print should receive the award. Numerous works by Lucy Maud MONTGOMERY were published in French in the 1980s by Éditions Pierre Tisseyre (translated by Henri-Dominique Paratte and Paule Daveluy) and by Québec/Amérique (translated by Hélène Rioux).

English-Canadian poets are still little translated into French. Dorothy Livesay has been translated and translations exist, among others, of Margaret Atwood (*Politique de pouvoir*, 1995) by Louise Desjardins; Miriam WADDINGTON (*En guise d'amants*, 1994) by Christine Klein-Lataud; D.G. JONES (*Le soleil cogne*, 1995) by Camille Fournier; and Mary DI MICHELE (*Pain et chocolat*, 1996) by Frank Caucci, the three last works being published by Les Éditions du Noroît. *Contre-taille. Poèmes choisis de vingt-cinq auteurs canadiens-anglais* (1996), translated by Pierre DesRuisseaux, is a bilingual edition with a foreword by Louis DUDEK. The journal *Ellipse* continues to present in translation anglophone poets such as Margaret AVISON, Lorna CROZIER, Ralph GUSTAFSON, A.M. Klein, Patrick LANE, E.J. PRATT, Robyn SARAH, and John THOMPSON. Certain thematic numbers have been devoted to contemporary love poetry (no. 39, 1988), to the Symposium 'Aux Canadas' in honour of Philip Stratford (no. 51, 1994), and to the poetry of Montreal (no. 56, 1996).

There have been few translations of English-Canadian drama in this period. Plays by Brad Fraser (*Des restes humains non identifiés et la vraie nature de l'amour*, 1993; *L'homme laid*, 1993; *Pauvre superman*, 1995) are well known in Quebec; works by Sharon POLLOCK (*Liens de sang* and *Doc*) and Tomson HIGHWAY (*Les reines de la réserve*) have also been translated. Other dramatists whose plays have been translated are Anne CHISLETT, John GRAY, John MURRELL, and George F. WALKER.

Margaret Atwood became known to francophone readers as an essayist with the publication in 1987 of her *Essai sur la littérature canadienne*. Northrop Frye has been translated in France (*Le grand code: la Bible et la littérature*, 1984; *La parole souveraine: la Bible et la littérature II*, 1994), and in Quebec (*Shakespeare et son théâtre*, 1988, translated by Charlotte Melançon, winner of the 1988 Prix John-Glassco). She also translated Charles TAYLOR into French (*Grandeur et misère de la modernité*, 1992). Mordecai RICHLER's essay, *Oh Canada! Oh Québec! Requiem pour un pays divisé*, appeared in 1992, in a translation by Daniel

Poliquin, and Neil BISSOONDATH's *Le marché aux illusions: la méprise du multiculturalisme* (1995) was translated by Jean Papineau. The impressive works of the historian Bruce Trigger have also appeared in translation: *Les Indiens, la fourrure et les Blancs* (1990), done by Georges Khal, and *Les enfants d'Aataensic: l'histoire du peuple huron* (1991), by Jean-Paul Sainte-Marie and Brigitte Chabert Hacikyan (Governor General's Award). Before *Systèmes de survie* (1996), Jane Jacobs had published in French *Les villes et la richesse des nations* (1992). In the anthology *Montréal en prose 1892-1992*, edited by Nathalie Fredette, texts about Montreal by writers such as Clark BLAISE, Louis Dudek, Hugh HOOD, Norman LEVINE, and Hugh MacLENNAN appear in French.

In a series of conversations between Margaret Atwood and Victor-Lévy BEAULIEU, first broadcast by Radio-Canada, the two authors talked about childhood, mythology, and their work. These conversations were published as *Deux sollicitudes* (1996); the blurb on the cover of the book read in part: 'this work, instead of confirming the Canadian and Québécois archetype of the two solitudes, is that of a lovely complicity, if not of a pronounced solicitude.'

See Paul Morisset, 'La face cachée de la culture québéçoise', *L'actualité* 10, no. 11 (nov. 1985), and Suzanne Martin, 'Traduire ou not translate, that is the question', *Possibles* 17.2 (printemps 1993). PATRICIA GODBOUT

Translations: French to English. Approximately ninety per cent of all French-to-English literary translations in Canada have appeared in the quarter-century since the CANADA COUNCIL inaugurated its program of financial support for literary translation in 1972. Readers now have access in English to approximately 300 works of fiction, 100 books of poetry, and more than 50 plays, as well as numerous other works: anthologies in various genres; journals and travel accounts; autobiography and literary criticism; folklore and folksongs; and children's books. This survey will examine some of these publications in four historical periods, the dividing dates being 1960, 1972, and 1982.

1. TO 1960. The first French-Canadian novel to be translated into English was Philippe-Joseph AUBERT DE GASPÉ's *Les ANCIENS CANADIENS* (1863), which appeared in two translations: first, by Georgiana Pennée as *The Canadians of old* (1864), and then by Charles G. D. ROBERTS as *The Canadians of old: an historical romance* (1890); after the turn of the century both were reissued under different titles. From 1900 to the start of the Quiet Revolution, 67 literary translations were published—an average of little more than one book per year. Almost two-thirds of these were novels, half of them written by just four authors (Louis HÉMON, Maurice CONSTANTIN-WEYER, Roger LEMELIN, and Gabrielle ROY). The relatively prompt translation of their works into English indicates the popularity of the originals, though the quality of the translated version was often inferior. One notorious example is Hannah Josephson's 1947 translation of Roy's *BONHEUR D'OCCASION* (1945) as *The tin flute*, which has become probably the most widely read Quebec novel in translation, despite grave errors in interpretation throughout. Roy's major revisions to her novel in the 1947 French edition immediately made the Josephson translation as obsolete as it was unreliable. Comparable weaknesses can also be found in Lukin Barette's *Sackcloth for banner* (1938), a bowdlerized version of Jean-Charles HARVEY's *Les demi-civilisés* (1934); and *Boss of the river* (1947), Alan SULLIVAN's translation of Félix-Antoine SAVARD's *MENAUD, MAÎTRE-DRAVEUR* (1937). New translations of these novels appeared after 1975; the best of the three is the excellent English version of Harvey's work as *Fear's folly* (1982), John GLASSCO's last translation. Other important texts rendered into English in this period include Ringuet's (Philippe PANNETON's) *TRENTE ARPENTS* (1938), translated by Felix and Dorothea Walter as *Thirty acres* (1940), and Germaine GUÈVREMONT's *Le survenant* (1945), translated by Eric Sutton as *The outlander* (1950). In other genres the sixty-year period preceding the Quiet Revolution was quiet almost to the point of silence: translations of five slim books of poetry (by Louis FRÉCHETTE, Hector de SAINT-DENYS-GARNEAU, and three Hexagone poets), two obscure plays, eight travel accounts, one children's book, two anthologies (one of poetry, one of prose and poetry), and seventeen collections of folklore and folksongs (especially works by Marius BARBEAU and Edith FOWKE).

2. 1960 TO 1971. During the 1960s the rate of literary translation into English increased dramatically in Canada, from an average of one title to six per year, including twenty-seven novels, five volumes of poetry, three plays, and nine works of literary history and criticism. Although funds to support the translation of Canadian literature were scanty during this period, Centennial pride produced an upsurge of cultural activity; and political and social change in Quebec

prompted translators and publishers alike to make quickly available in English several texts documenting the progress of the Quiet Revolution. Thus Claude JASMIN's *Ethel et le terroriste* (1964) soon appeared in English as *Ethel and the terrorist* (1965), translated by David Walker; Hubert AQUIN's *PROCHAIN ÉPISODE* (1965) appeared two years later under the same title; and Jacques GODBOUT's *Le couteau sur la table* (1965) was published in English as *Knife on the table* (1968)—the last two titles translated by Penny Williams. Throughout the decade publishers turned their attention to works of fiction from the 1940s and 1950s (only occasionally considering earlier texts). Works by such major writers as Yves THÉRIAULT, Marie-Claire BLAIS, Gérard BESSETTE, and Roch CARRIER appeared in English, along with translations of three additional works of fiction by Gabrielle Roy, and the first English versions of novels by Réjean DUCHARME, Gilles MARCOTTE, and Jacques RENAUD.

In poetry the important anthology *French-Canadian poetry in translation* (1970), of which John Glassco was editor and chief translator, was something of a milestone. It was supplemented by two collections edited by Fred COGSWELL, *One hundred poems of modern Quebec* (1970) and *A second hundred poems of modern Quebec* (1971); three individual translations of Anne HÉBERT's poetry; English editions of Alain GRANDBOIS and Émile NELLIGAN; and especially the emergence in 1969 of the bilingual periodical *Ellipse* at the Université de Sherbrooke. It would be difficult to exaggerate the importance of this journal, which in its first two years introduced to anglophone readers eight new Quebec poets as well as the prose of Roch Carrier, and presented a special issue called 'Octobre/October'. Translators also turned their attention to modern Quebec drama, appropriately beginning with English versions of three works by Gratien GÉLINAS (the first modern Quebec dramatist), and there were several literary autobiographies and works of criticism translated into English. Of particular merit in these categories were excellent translations by John Glassco of Saint-Denys-Garneau's diary of 1935-9 as *Journals of Saint-Denys Garneau* (1962), and by Philip Stratford of both Claire MARTIN's *DANS UN GANT DE FER* (1965) and *La joue droite* (1966) as *In an iron glove* (1968), and Jean LE MOYNE's *Convergences* (1961) as *Convergence: essays from Quebec* (1966). In the areas of literary history and biography, Gérard Tougas's *Histoire de la littérature canadienne-française* (1964) and the first two volumes of the *DICTIONARY OF CANADIAN BIOGRAPHY/ DICTIONNAIRE BIOGRAPHIQUE DU CANADA* (with all French material translated for the English edition) also made a welcome appearance. Among the translations of important historical journals, letters, and early travel accounts could be found Michael Macklem's two new English versions of Samuel de Champlain's voyages (*Works*, 1970) and Joyce MARSHALL's *Word from New France: the selected letters of Marie de l'Incarnation* (1967).

3. 1972 TO 1981. In a December 1971 memorandum to the federal cabinet, Secretary of State Gérard Pelletier outlined his plan to establish the Canada Council's Translation Grants Programme with the objective of encouraging the translation of approximately 60 works annually—an initiative that was very likely prompted, in part at least, by the events of October 1970 in Quebec. In the decade that followed, the federal program funded the French-to-English translation of almost 250 books, more than half of them literary texts. English translations published in this period once again included a predominance of fiction (83), with 20 volumes of poetry, 27 of drama, and 28 anthologies and works of literary criticism, as well as travel accounts, children's books, and folklore.

While translators were very active in the 1970s, some of their work was inaccurate and unreliable, and few could depend on knowledgeable editors to give their translations the requisite scrutiny. Examples include David Lobdell's many translations of fiction for OBERON PRESS, and some of the translations of Alan Brown, especially the highly unsatisfactory retranslation of Roy's *Bonheur d'occasion* (*The tin flute*, 1980), in which some very competent work was undermined by many oversights, much imprecision and awkward phrasing, and several mistranslations. While the general content of the French text was transcribed into English, most of the original's colour and style was lost. The weaknesses of these and other literary translations published between 1976 and 1981—Irène Currie's unwitting 1976 translation of an expurgated edition of Rodolphe GIRARD's *MARIE CALUMET* is another case in point—are fully described in the 'Letters in Canada' section of the *University of Toronto Quarterly*'s summer issues (1977-82).

Much excellent work, however, was also completed in this decade, in particular by Sheila Fischman (who began her work as the translator of Roch Carrier, and is the only translator in Canada to have twice won the Canada Council Translation Prize), as well as by Carol Dunlop, Ray Ellenwood, and Philip Stratford. Of considerable merit are Fischman's *The 'Jimmy' trilogy* (Jacques POULIN) and *The fat woman next door is pregnant* (Michel Tremblay); Dunlop's *Deaf to the city* (Marie-Claire Blais); all of Ellenwood's work, especially *Vanishing spaces* (Guillaume Charette), *Entrails* (Claude GAUVREAU), and *The cart* (Jacques FERRON); and everything by Stratford, notably the two anthologies *Stories from Quebec* and *Voices from Quebec*, and *The madman, the kite and the island* (Félix LECLERC). At the same time there were many distinguished individual achievements that were cause for celebration: Larry Shouldice's *Daydream mechanics* (Nicole BROSSARD); the collaborative effort of nine translators in *Les strategies du réel/The story so far 6* (1980), an anthology of Quebec prose and poetry of the 1970s edited by Nicole Brossard; D.G. JONES's *The terror of the snows* (Paul-Marie LAPOINTE); Barry CALLAGHAN's *Treatise on white and tincture* (Robert Marteau); Fred Cogswell's anthology *The poetry of modern Quebec*; and Betty Bednarski's selection from Jacques Ferron's work in *Tales from the uncertain country*.

There can also be added the translations by winners of the newly created Canada Council Translation Prizes: 1973—Alan Brown, *The antiphonary* (Hubert Aquin, *L'antiphonaire*); 1974—Sheila Fischman, *They won't demolish me!* (Roch Carrier, *Le deux-millième étage*) and *The wolf* (Marie-Claire Blais, *Le loup*); 1975—John Glassco, *Complete poems of Saint-Denys Garneau*; 1976—Joyce Marshall, *Enchanted summer* (Gabrielle Roy, *Cet été qui chantait*); 1977—F.R. SCOTT, *Poems of French Canada*; 1978—Michael Bullock, *Stories for late-night drinkers* (Michel Tremblay, *Contes pour buveurs attardes*); 1979—Allan Van Meer, *Greta the divine* (Renald Tremblay, *La céleste Gréta*; *Looking for a job* (Claude Roussin, *Une job*); and *A little bit left* (Serge Mercier, *Encore un peu*; 1980—Larry Shouldice, *Contemporary Quebec criticism*; and 1981—Ray Ellenwood, *Entrails* (Claude Gauvreau, 'Les Entrailles').

Smaller presses in particular played a key role in the surge of translation activity in the 1970s, notably House of ANANSI, New Press, TALONBOOKS, PRESS PORCÉPIC, EXILE EDITIONS, COACH HOUSE PRESS, Harvest House, Tundra, and NC Press—often setting high standards of excellence for the larger houses. This wide-ranging interest in translating French-Canadian literary texts accounted for the healthy state of the art in the mid-1970s. In 1976 alone, for example, literary works in translation were completed by 33 translators and published by two dozen different houses.

The outburst of translation activity between 1976 and 1978 can be explained to some extent by the election of René Lévesque's Parti Québécois in November 1976, since political upheaval in Quebec almost invariably activates in anglophone publishers and readers a renewed interest in translations of Quebec writing. In the years following the setting up of the Canada Council Translation Grants Programme (clearly, in part at least, a response to the October Crisis), many significant initiatives emerged: the establishment in 1973 of two annual $2500 Translation Prizes (increased to $5000 in 1976); the founding of the Association for Canadian and Quebec Literatures (1972), which organized a 1977 conference called 'Traduire notre poésie/The Translation of Poetry' (substantially recorded in *Ellipse* 21); the founding of the Association des traducteurs littéraires/Literary Translators' Association (ATL/LTA) in May 1975; the publication of Philip Stratford's bilingual *Bibliography of Canadian books in translation: French to English and English to French/Bibliographie de livres canadiens traduits de l'anglais au français et du français à l'anglais* (1975; 2nd ed., 1977); and the appearance in the *University of Toronto Quarterly*, beginning in the Summer 1977 issue, of an annual detailed review of French-Canadian literature in translation in 'Letters in Canada'.

In the early 1980s, economic challenges notwithstanding, many translators and publishing houses strongly asserted the cultural and social importance of translation, and explored the possibilities and limitations of translation as an art form: see especially *Ellipse* 21. Its bilingual format continued to reflect the central role of translation as one permitting a dialogue between two interested, if isolated, parties. Just such a conversation, delighting in the close encounter of two languages, took place between Anne Hébert and her translator, F.R. Scott, in *Dialogue sur la traduction à propos du 'Tombeau des rois'* (1970). Similar affection and grateful exchange were suggested elsewhere—for example, in Jacques Ferron's dedication of *Les confitures de coings* (1972) to Betty Bednarski, who had just completed her translation of his tales. Louise MAHEUX-FORCIER demonstrated that Canada's two solitudes might indeed meet through the translation of its literary texts by using as the epigraph for her short-story collecetion *En toutes lettres* (1980) a text from Robertson DAVIES' *World of wonders*, as translated by Arlette Francière and Claire Martin. Such developments were encouraging, as was the possibility of renewed commitment to the practice of translation in Canada in the light of the Applebaum-Hébert report on Canadian culture. This optimism at the beginning of the 1980s was perhaps given a fillip by the defeat of the first PQ referendum on sovereignty-association.

4. 1982 TO 1996. Throughout this period the Canada Council continued to fund literary translation, supporting an almost equal number of projects from French to English and English to French, though the former constituted only ten per cent of all Canadian translations. In the 1980s and 1990s English-language literary translators produced an annual average of ten works of fiction, two books of poetry, and six plays (at times translated for production but not subsequently published). As a rule, each year a few non-fiction texts (including works on critical theory) were translated; and small magazines often devoted some space to the translation of literary texts. Major figures such as Roy, Blais, Hébert, Brossard, Tremblay, Carrier, and Antonine MAILLET—along with finalists and winners of Quebec prizes—were the most likely candidates for rapid translation into English; and some important works were retranslated. Throughout the 1980s there was a steady increase in quantity, prompted in part by a healthy economy and political uncertainty surrounding the future of Quebec within Canada. And translators, in the quality of their work, demonstrated an increasing mastery of craft, displayed in many excellent translations that are far too numerous to list.

By the end of the decade the practice of translation in Canada was said to be flourishing and revitalized; and the evidence suggests that there was indeed solid ground for optimism. With the single exception of 1990, the *University of Toronto Quarterly* produced an annual survey of French-to-English translation activity in Canada in informative and discerning articles by Kathy Mezei, Barbara Godard, Sherry Simon, and Jane Koustas. The bilingual journal *Ellipse*, after somewhat slower activity in the early 1980s, in 1986 settled into the steady production of two issues per year, and published 26 issues in this period. Three of them are of particular interest to students of translation theory and practice: nos. 29/30 (1982), no. 50 (1993), and no. 51 (1994). The significant work of *Ellipse* was accompanied throughout the 1980s by many encouraging developments and important publications in the field of literary translation. In 1982 ATL/LTA established an annual John Glassco Translation Prize for the best book-length translation by a new translator published in the preceding year. In April 1982 the University of Ottawa hosted a symposium on 'Translation in Canadian Literature', and published the papers in *Reappraisals: symposium on translations* (1983) edited by Camille La Bossière. From 1985 to 1988 the LEAGUE OF CANADIAN POETS presented an annual F. R. Scott Translation Award to highlight significant work in the translation of poetry. (There were five winners of this award: 1985—Robin SKELTON, *George Faludy: selected poems 1933-1980* and Roger Greenwald, *The silence afterward: the selected poems of Rolf Jacobsen*; 1986—Gertrude Sanderson, *Within the mystery* by Jacques BRAULT; 1987—George MCWHIRTER, who edited *Selected poems of José Emilio Pacheo*; and 1988—Arlette Francière, *Kaleidoscope* by Michel BEAULIEU.) Soon after the October 1986 meeting of the ATL/LTA in Montreal (proceedings published in 1987 by VÉHICULE PRESS as *Mapping literature: the art and politics of translation*, edited by David Homel and Sherry Simon), Canadian translators had a new forum to discuss translation theory and practice: in the annual publication *Traduction, terminologie, rédaction: études sur le texte et ses transformations* (Université du Québec à Trois-Rivières). In its second issue it published the proceedings of the May 1988 conference—in Windsor, Ontario—of the newly formed Canadian Association for Translation Studies. In 1987 Michel Tremblay's celebrated play *Les BELLES-SOEURS* was successfully translated into modern Scots dialect (*The guid sisters*) for the Edinburgh Festival. The following year Kathy Mezei published the bilingual *Bibliography of criticism on English and French literary translations in Canada, 1950-1986: annotated*; the journal *CANADIAN LITERATURE* (no. 117) produced a 'Translation' issue, incorporating papers from the Learned Societies meeting in Saint-Boniface in 1986 and additional articles and reviews on the subject; and Columbia University's *Translation: the journal of literary translation* published a special Canadian issue. By the end of this decade Coach House Press had revived its distinguished translation series; and new reflections on the practice and problems of translation were published by Sherry Simon (*L'inscription sociale de la traduction au Québec*, 1989) and Betty Bednarski (*Autour de Ferron: littérature, traduction, altérité*, 1990).

Since 1982 nearly 100 literary translators have published their work in Canada, much of it distinguished. Although half published only a single work, two (David Lobdell and Sheila Fischman) published more than 20 works each, and were able to sustain careers as full-time literary translators. When Lobdell died in the early 1990s, his work-in-progress (Blais's *Pierre*) was completed by Philip Stratford. The untimely death of Larry Shouldice, the prize-winning translator and distinguished editor for many years of *Ellipse*, deprived Canada of one of its most accomplished and gifted practitioners of the art of literary translation. Among the most active and successful literary translators since 1982 have been David Homel, Luise von Flotow, Ray Chamberlain, Philip Stratford, and Linda Gaboriau.

Philip Stratford's nearly simultaneous translation in 1986 of René Lévesque's memoirs is a memorable example of his abilities. The subject of translation appeared in novels by two Quebec writers: Nicole Brossard's *Le désert mauve* (1987), in which many aspects of translation figure prominently, and Yves Préfontaine's *This desert now* (1993), translated by Judith Cowan, about the relationship of poet and translator. The subject was investigated by Kathy Mezei in 'The scales of translation', *University of Ottawa Quarterly* (1984), about the work of D.G. Jones as poet and translator. (See also Ann Wall's article on Sheila Fischman in *Quill and Quire*, Apr. 1988; and Sherry Simon's interview with Fischman in *Culture in transit*, 1995.) David Homel's paper 'The translator translated', presented at the 'Aux Canadas' conference in 1992, provided unique insights into matters of translation, as do a number of translators' notes added to published work. The interest of these translators remains firmly fixed on the contemporary scene. In the 1980s only nine of the significant literary works translated originally appeared before 1960 (among them, *A man of sentiment: the memoirs of Philippe-Joseph Aubert de Gaspé 1788-1871*, 1988; translated by Jane Brierley), and only eleven in the 1960s; whereas nearly 100 of the works translated during the 1980s originally appeared after 1970. Since 1990 only about a dozen of the significant literary works published in French before 1980 have appeared in translation, two of which pre-date 1970. With rare exceptions, the usual practice for publishers of translations is to present contemporary and very recent work; most such publishers are represented by a single work. Only six publishing houses have produced ten or more French-to-English literary translations in this period: GUERNICA EDITIONS, Oberon, EXILE EDITIONS, Coach House, Talonbooks, and McCLELLAND & STEWART. In translated works produced since 1982, there is an overwhelming bias in favour of fiction: approximately 100 novels, 20 works of short fiction, 39 of poetry, 22 of drama, and 29 works of non-fiction.

The works published since 1982 include many distinguished translations, in particular the winners of the Canada Council Translation Prize (known after 1986 as the Governor General's Literary Award, Translation) and the John Glassco Prize, first awarded in 1982, which honours the work of first-time translators. (For winners of the Translation Prize between 1986 and 1996, see GOVERNOR GENERAL'S LITERARY AWARDS.) In addition to the accomplishments of new and seasoned translators, there are many other distinguished works, of which only a few can be mentioned: the many translations of poetry by D.G. Jones, including *The fifth season* and *The march to love* (Lapointe) and *Embers and earth* (MIRON); Fischman's *In the shadow of a wind* (Hébert), *Volkswagen Blues* (Poulin), and *Juliette Pomerleau* (BEAUCHEMIN); Stratford's *Pélagie: the return to a homeland* (Maillet) and *Blind painting* (Melançon); Godard's *These our mothers* and *Picture theory* (Brossard); Shouldice's *Champagne and opium* (Grandbois) and *Voices of deliverance*; Homel's *Ha! ha!* (Ducharme) and *Vanishing villages* (Marchand); and Judith Cowan's translations of Gérald Godin, especially *Exterminated angel*, which Godin himself said was superior to the original.

Translation activity in the 1990s continued to be encouraging in some ways. In 1991 Women's Press published Susanne de Lotbinière-Harwood's searching analysis of the translation process in *Re-belle et infidèle/ The body bilingual*, an investigation advanced the following year by the many distinguished panelists who attended the 'Aux Canadas' conference in Montreal. One of these translators, David Homel, subsequently published his paper 'Dans les deux sens (la traduction littéraire au Canada)' in the 'Traduire' issue of *LIBERTÉ* 35, 1 (Feb. 1993), which also included 'L'écrivain clandestin', a translation of a 1978 article, 'Translation as creation', by the conference's guest of honour, Philip Stratford. In 1994 Sherry Simon added two significant works to the ongoing discussion of literary translation in Canada: *Le trafic des langues: traduction et culture dans la littérature québécoise* (Boréal) and *Culture in transit: translating the literature of Quebec* (Véhicule). Other encouraging signs in the early 1990s included the 'Pédagogie de la traduction' series from the University of Ottawa Press under the direction of Jean Delisle; the Canada Council's funding of Canadian literature translated into languages other than French and English; the wide variety of Quebec writing available to unilingual anglophone readers;

and the energetic activity of many small Canadian presses in the field of literary translation, including Véhicule, Guernica, and Coach House.

Unfortunately these positive signs were accompanied by less-encouraging ones. In January 1990 the Toronto *Globe and Mail* noting the marginalized status of literary translation in Canadian publishing; and by the middle of the decade literary translation activity from French to English was only half that from English to French. The tariff for translation (ten cents a word) had not changed since 1984. Federal and provincial governments steadily reduced arts funding, the recession in the early years of the decade slowed the pace of translation, and many publishers abandoned the practice of publishing translations, citing as their reasons the lack of public interest and profitability. In 1993, when Nancy HUSTON's *Cantique des plaines* (her own 'translation' of her novel *Plainsong*) won the Governor General's Award for French fiction, the ensuing outcry occasioned not only some lingering questions about what constituted a true translation and what an original work, but also some very real tensions between the literary 'solitudes'. (Some disputants seemed to forget that, in the 1940s, Ringuet and Gabrielle Roy won the same award for their novels *Thirty acres* and *The tin flute* translated into English.) Most disturbing of all was the closing of Coach House Press in the summer of 1996, after the withdrawal of provincial-funding guarantees—especially distressing and ironic, since works published by this press had won the Governor General's Award for English translation in two of the preceding three years, and again a few months after the shutdown. (This was sadly reminiscent of Lester & Orpen Dennys, a Toronto publisher of distinguished translations in the late 1980s, only a few years before its untimely demise.)

Facing the new millennium, Canadian readers of literary translations might well be torn between hope and anxiety. *Ellipse* endures, but Coach House Press is gone. Canada has never had so many skilled translators, but where are they to find adequate funding and supportive readers? A wide range of excellent works is available to unilingual anglophone readers, but many important Quebec works have not yet been translated. In an article in the Toronto *Globe and Mail*, 16 Nov. 1996, about the Governor General's Awards, Ray Conlogue wrote: 'The relatively few titles translated from French mean that new books that have a major impact in Quebec don't necessarily get translated into English'; as examples, he mentioned André Laurendeau's journals about the Bilingualism and Biculturalism Commission meetings, and Fernand DUMONT's *La génèse de la société québécoise*. At a time when Canadian citizens and readers face not only the millennium but also the prospect of a third Quebec referendum on separation from Canada, translation emphatically remains a compelling necessity for cultural and political encounter and dialogue—the indispensable bridge where we can meet, touch, and greet each other.

JOHN J. O'CONNOR

Travel literature in English. The title of this entry (which excludes EXPLORATION LITERATURE) refers primarily to books organized around personal travel experiences in Canada that created important images of the country, penned mostly by visitors such as Dickens, Trollope, Butler, and Cram—and then, after the Second World War, by Canadian writers. A second kind of travel literature includes works in which Canadians effectively described foreign places and their experiences there.

There are many English-language books that throw light on early perceptions of the northern portion of North America. The first were Richard Hakluyt's *Divers voyages touching the discovery of America . . .* (London, 1582; rpr. 1969) and *The principal navigations, voyages and discoveries of the English nation* (London, 1589; rpr. 1969); and a work by Samuel Purchas, who had assisted Hakluyt and come into possession of his unpublished manuscripts, publishing them with his own collection of exploration voyages in *Purchase his pilgrimes . . .* (London, 1625; rpr. 1905). Enabling British readers to follow the first passages to and into northern New World territories, these books were supplemented by translations from the French: Louis Hennepin's *A new discovery of a vast country in America* (London, 1699), Baron Lahontan's *New voyages to North-America* (London, 1703; rpr. 1940), and Pierre-François-Xavier Charlevoix's *Journal of a voyage to North-America* (London, 1761; rpr. 1966). The Swedish botanist Peter Kalm, who visited North America in 1749-50, published a journal of his travels in Swedish (3 vols, 1753-61). An English translation was made by J.R. Forster, *Travels into North America . . .* (London, 1770-1), of which a modern edition was edited by Adolph B. Benson: *The America of 1750: Peter Kalm's travels in North America* (2 vols, 1937); it was reprinted by Dover Publications as *Peter Kalm's travels in North America* (2 vols, 1966). Volume II contains Kalm's detailed and historically valuable account of his visits to Montreal and Quebec (where he found the most cultivated people in North America), of the villages between the two towns, and of his journey west to Lake Ontario and Niagara Falls. The American Jonathan Carver set a basic itinerary through inland territory in *Travels through the interior parts of North America* (London, 1778; rpr. 1974), but Canada as a destination for self-conscious tourists seeking the picturesque in scenery appears first in Isaac Weld's *Travels through the State of North America and the Provinces of Upper and Lower Canada during the years 1795, 1796, and 1797* (London, 1799; rpr. 1970), which publicizes 'romantic' Quebec, 'sublime' Niagara Falls, the 'charming' Thousand Islands, and the excitement of movement in canoe and bateau. John Lambert's two-volume *Travels through Lower Canada, and the United States of North America in the years 1806, 1807, and 1808* (London, 1810; rpr. 1959) provides in Volume 1 probably the most vivid description, illustrated with aquatints, of Quebec City and environs, and of Montreal, in the early nineteenth century. A third intention—to analyse immigration possibilities—animated the American John Ogden's *A tour, through Upper and Lower Canada. By a citizen of the United States. Containing a view of the present state of religion, learning, commerce, agriculture, colonization, customs and manners, among the English, French, and Indian settlements* (Litchfield, 1799; rpr. 1917). George Heriot provided the picturesque and the practical in *Travels through the Canadas, containing a description of the picturesque scenery on some of the rivers and lakes; with an account of the productions, commerce, and inhabitants of these provinces* (2 vols, London, 1807; rpr. 1971). Meanwhile readers were reminded of a savage hinterland in Alexander Henry's *Travels and adventures in Canada and the Indian territories between the years 1760 and 1776* (New York, 1809; rpr. 1921).

After the War of 1812 several Americans made peaceful trips into Canada by the Lake Champlain route and produced friendly reports, such as Benjamin Silliman's *Remarks made on a short tour between Hartford and Quebec in the autumn of 1819* (New Haven, 1820?). With comparable urbanity Lt Francis Hall sketched his *Travels in Canada and the United States in 1816 and 1817* (London, 1818) with emphasis on the friendly *habitants* and the 'inoffensive' Indians—and the 'Yankeefied' Upper Canadians. Scots accustomed to the sharp humour of *Blackwood's Magazine* made witty copy even of the comfortless backwoods, as in John Howison's youthful *Sketches of Upper Canada, domestic, local, and characteristic* (Edinburgh, 1821; rpr. 1966), Basil Hall's more judicious Canadian chapters in his *Travels in North America in the years 1827, 1828* (Edinburgh 1829; rpr. 1974), and William 'Tiger' Dunlop's *Statistical sketches of Upper Canada, for the use of emigrants* (London, 1832; rpr. 1967). Other books of the period, like the Tiger's, reflect involvement longer than a visitor's tour: Edward Talbot's engaging *Five years' residence in the Canadas* (London, 1824); John MacTaggart's rollicking account of bush-whacking and canal-building, *Three years in Canada* (London, 1829); and George Head's *Forest scenes and incidents in the wilds of North America; being a diary of a winter's route from Halifax to the Canadas, and during four month's residence in the woods on the borders of Lakes Huron and Simcoe* (London, 1829; rpr. 1970).

Soldiers wrote well on tours of duty—and furloughs—during tense times leading to the Rebellion of 1837 in what is now Ontario. A clergyman, Isaac Fidler, reflects Family Compact interests in *Observations on professions, literature, manners, and emigration in the United States and Canada made during a residence there in 1832* (London, 1833; rpr. 1974). But the best picture of those days, and deservedly the best-known of all Canadian travel books, was Anna Jameson's *Winter studies and summer rambles in Canada* (London, 1838; rpr. 1965)—the inward journeyings of her studies counterbalancing her rambles towards Lake Huron in search of fellow-intellectuals like Colonel Talbot, and of Natives beyond the sphere of Toronto, during her eight-month stay in Upper Canada.

Politics preponderated after the Act of Union of 1841, in books like James Silk Buckingham's *Canada, Nova Scotia, New Brunswick, and the other British provinces in North America* (London, 1843). Garrison life in Sir Richard Bonnycastle's *The Canadas in 1841* (London, 1841) and *Canada and the Canadians in 1846* (London, 1846; rpr. 1969), in J.E. Alexander's *L'Acadie; or seven years' exploration in British America* (London, 1849), and in George Warburton's charming *Hochelaga; or England in the New World* (London, 1846) brought tales of drills, sports, and dashing sleigh-rides with pretty French-Canadian girls. The writing style of these officers shows a contemporary response to the ebullience of Charles Dickens, whose own fancy was caught by the humour and energy of military barracks in the entertaining Canadian scenes of his *American notes* (London, 1842). The Dickens touch is also seen in Francis Bond Head's *The emigrant* (London, 1846), a lively report of his tours as governor. The scientist Charles Lyell on his tour observed fossils, flood-tracings, and rifts as he rode from Niagara northwards. His *Travels in North America; with geological observations on the United States, Canada, and Nova Scotia* (London, 1845; rpr. 1909) might be read in conjunction with John Bigsby's *The shoe and canoe; or Pictures of travel in the Canadas, illustrative of their scenery and of colonial life* (London, 1850; rpr. 1969), a surgeon-geologist's narrative that dramatically traces boundary-commission surveys as far west as Lake of the Woods.

At mid-century many churchmen wrote about religious zeal in remote regions. Most interesting of the missionary travels is Peter JACOBS' *Journal . . . from Rice Lake to the Hudson's Bay Territory and returning* (Toronto, 1853), an insider's view of frontier missions by a Christianized Native. The Indian Territory is featured in a work by the famous governor of the Hudson's Bay Company, Sir George Simpson: *Narrative of a journey around the world in the years 1841 and 1842* (London, 1847). John Palliser's *Solitary rambles and adventures of a hunter in the Prairies* (London, 1853) and Alexander Ross's *Fur hunters of the Far West: a narrative of adventure in the Oregon and Rocky Mountains* (London, 1855; rpr. 1961) are retrospective to earlier days in Indian lands. Paul KANE's *Wanderings of an artist among the Indians of North America from Canada to Vancouver's Island and Oregon through the Hudson's Bay Company Territory and back again* (London, 1859) vividly describes the western Native at mid-century. Kane's revision from journal entries and rough sketches into carefully crafted narratives and paintings can be traced in Russell Harper's *Paul Kane's frontier* (1971). The popularity of Longfellow's *The song of Hiawatha* (1855) and *EVANGELINE* (1847) created reader demand for accounts of Native life and for 'Evangeline' visits, such as Fred Cozzens' *Acadia; or, A month with the Bluenoses* (New York, 1859), and Campbell Hardy's *Sporting adventures in the New World; or, Days and nights of moose-hunting in the pine forests of Acadia* (London, 1855).

To tamer regions the 1850s brought lady travel-writers, via the newly built railways. Their bright, self-assured reports are best exemplified in Isabella Bird Bishop's *An Englishwoman in America* (London, 1856; rpr. 1966) and the Hon. Amelia Murray's *Letters from the United States, Cuba, and Canada* (London, 1856). Other observers contrasted peaceful Canada and the schismatic States, as in Capt. Henry Murray's *Lands of the slave and the free* (London, 1855) and the German J.G. Kohl's *Travels in Canada, and through the States of New York and Pennsylvania* (London, 1861). Anthony Trollope turned the contrast to brilliant use in *North America* (London, 1862), using Niagara Falls as a focus for his uncertainties about power, freedom, and perspective. A subtle American response to the contrast is Henry David Thoreau's little book *A Yankee in Canada*, written in 1850 (Boston, 1866; rpr. 1961). Thoreau sneers at British pomp and military ceremony, but does not resist the attractions of old Quebec. Military manoeuvres in preparation for Fenian raids produced a vigorous book in Lt Francis Duncan's *Our garrisons in the West* (London, 1864).

Three books of the 1860s show how personality can flow through travel accounts. In *The English cricketers' trip to Canada and the United States* (London, 1860) Fred Lillywhite tells how rollicking spirits, even in the face of sea-sickness, were a match for defeats, bad weather, and overpowering celebratory banquets. The two-man trip of Dr Walter Butler Cheadle, playing Man Friday to Viscount Milton's Crusoe, was doubly recorded: in Milton's *The North-West Passage by land* (London, 1865; rpr. 1970) and in Dr Cheadle's revealing private journal, *Cheadle's journal of trip across Canada, 1862-1863*, which was not published until 1931.

That northwest world became the setting for two classic books by William Francis Butler. *The great lone land: a narrative of travel and adventure in the northwest of America* (London, 1872; rpr. 1968) created unforgettable images of the voyage westward, of the Red River atmosphere in Riel's time, and of the wild-rose plains beyond. Butler's *The wild north land* (London, 1873; rpr. 1910) described Plains Natives with accuracy and panache. Several fine books followed, reporting the push westward by the railroad: George Monro Grant's *OCEAN TO OCEAN* (Toronto, 1873; rpr. 1970), Charles Horetzky's *Canada on the Pacific* (Montreal, 1874), and the Earl of Southesk's *Saskatchewan and the Rocky Mountains* (Edinburgh, 1875), based on his diary of 1825.

Fraser Rae, a responsible journalist, followed the railway builders with *Columbia and Canada* and *Newfoundland to Manitoba* (London, 1877 and 1881). A more ambitious style appears in *England and Canada: a summer tour between old and New Westminster* (London, 1884) by Sandford Fleming, who had been chief engineer of the Canadian Pacific Railway. Fleming, as grand old railway magnate, sets his trip against constant memories of the tumultuous days of construction. *B.C. 1887* (London, 1888) is by two young Englishmen, J.A. Lees and W.J. Clutterbuck, who as 'innocents abroad' enjoyed immensely the splendours and absurdities of transcontinental travel and northward forging. The height of self-conscious styling appears in Rudyard Kipling's *Letters of Marque* (London, 1889; rpr. in *American notes* 1974), with its brilliant vignettes of Victoria as the western terminus of empire, and in his later *From sea to sea* (New York, 1899) and *Letters to the family: notes on a recent trip to Canada* (1908). Another sprightly narrative recounts a west-to-east trip by the Australian Stuart Cumberland: *The Queen's Highway* (London, 1887). Yet the easiest-to-read cross-country account is the unassuming, naïve report of two English lads who describe their adventures as farmhands working their way from Ontario to British Columbia and back to Calgary; their letters home were published by their father, A.J. Church, as *Making a start in Canada* (London, 1889).

Pullman cars set the elegant stage for books of the 1890s: Edward Roper's *By track and trail: a journey through Canada* (London, 1891), Lady Aberdeen's *Through Canada with a Kodak* (Edinburgh, 1893), and Douglas Sladen's *On the cars and off* (London, 1895). Roper and Sladen deserve a place among the most entertaining of all travel writers, but Lady Dufferin's *My Canadian journal, 1872-78* (London, 1891; rpr. 1971), gaily describing earlier vice-regal travel, rivals these more carefully crafted books in tone and drama.

Although Klondike news revived popularity of stark stories of the manly North, as in Warburton Pike's *The Barren Ground of northern Canada* (London, 1892), turn-of-the-century attention focused mostly on immigrant opportunities. An imperialist optimism—sounded officially in *Canadian pictures drawn with pen and pencil* (London, 1885) by the Marquis of Lorne, governor general of Canada from 1878 to 1883—was echoed in James Lumsden's thoughtful *Through Canada in harvest time* (1903), and in a group of lighter, brighter illustrated books, such as R.E. Vernède's *The fair Dominion; a record of Canadian impressions* (1911). But W.H.P. Jarvis, in *Letters of a remittance man* (1907), and N.P.R. Noel, in *Blanket-stiff* (1912), wryly noted that the imperial welcome was not always firmly woven in the West. The American writer Anson Gard hailed the Canadian drift from imperialism in his highly readable *The last West* (1904) and in other volumes. The publication of *Walt Whitman's diary in Canada* (edited by W.S. Kennedy, 1903)—about a trip Whitman made from London, Ont., to the Saguenay in 1880—presented a memorable picture of harvest days in the older provinces of Ontario and Quebec, and reminded turn-of-the-century readers that Americans had long assumed that Canada would inevitably drift into affiliation with the USA.

Several books of this pre-war period fuse discussions of farming with feminism, notably Marian Cran's *A woman in Canada* (1911) and *Wheat and woman* (1914). The war blocked this spate of books; but all pre-war themes appear, finely handled, in Rupert Brooke's *Letters from America* (1916).

The aftermath of war brought new conditions and a new tone. Motor travel gave a plot-line for many brash books, such as Percy Gomery's *A motor-scamper cross Canada: a human-interest narrative of a pathfinding journey from Montreal to Vancouver* (1922). Sophisticated memoirs of pre-war trips include V.H. Rikki's *Ups and downs in Canada* (1922). But most travel books now ruefully reported 'downs': bleak journeys through a world of cabooses and rooming-houses, as in G.M. Westbury's *Misadventures of a working hobo in Canada* (1930). Many well-educated young Englishmen, drifting westward, faced and described a 'land of bull and bale-wire', to quote E.F.G. Fripp's *The outcasts of Canada* (1932). Few pleasure-travellers chose Canada when Europe was inexpensive and fashionable.

After the Second World War more and more Canadians wrote travel books about their country. There was a brief revival of old-style coast-to-coast travelogues, as in Dorothy Duncan's *Here's to Canada* (1943). Early hardships, artificially recreated, provided the main interest of Mary Bosanquet's *Saddlebags for suitcases* (1942) and *Canada ride* (1944). Bruce HUTCHISON tried for a more ambitious portrait—one that had a great popular success—in the seasonal sequence of *The unknown country* (1942) in which the motif of journeying recurs, though it is not strictly a travel book.

Air travel brought the Far North into easier reach and facilitated reports like P.G. Downes' *Sleeping island* (1946) and Peter Scott's *Wild geese and Eskimos* (1951). The hardships of wilderness travel continued to receive major emphasis in modern travel accounts, as presented by Canadians such as Farley MOWAT and Pierre BERTON.

In the 1950s two authentic and substantial books reported a search for origins. In *Ravens and prophets: an account of journeys in British Columbia, Alberta, and Southern Alaska* (1952) George WOODCOCK is particularly interesting in his account of a quiet trip through remote British Columbia settlements. In *Canada made me* (1958) Norman LEVINE, as an 'angry young man', travels from Halifax to

Ottawa to the Cariboo and finds a land of sleaziness, slush, and social emptiness. A long-familiar note—the old resentment against anti-British sentiment in Canada—sounds in Dennis Godfrey's *No Englishman need apply* (1965). In the same year the Canadian novelist Edward MCCOURT described a modest coast-to-coast journey in *The road across Canada*. The newly important Québécois perspective added poignance to a travel book by the Montreal journalist Eugène Cloutier, whose *Le Canada sans passeport* (2 vols, 1967) was abridged and translated by Joyce MARSHALL as *No passport: a discovery of Canada* (1968; rpr. 1973). An interesting idea for a Canadian travel book—exploring 'the Line', the Canada/USA border from the Bay of Fundy to Yukon/Alaska—was brought to life by Marian Botsford Fraser in her entertaining *Walking the Line: travels along the Canadian/American border* (1989). *Ribbon of highway* (1992) by Kildare DOBBS is his account of a transcontinental journey across Canada by Greyhound bus.

A selection of books on travel abroad written by Canadians would include such early reports as Emily Murphy's *The impressions of Janey Canuck abroad* (1902), Dean Harris's *Days and nights in the Tropics* (1905), and Cora Hind's *My travels and findings* (1939). The publication of Canadian writers' serious impressions of foreign places really began with George Woodcock's books on Mexico (*To the city of the dead*, 1957) and Peru (*Incas and other men*, 1959); his books on India, Asia, the Malabar Coast, and the South Seas were to follow. Travel books of particular interest because of the eminence of the authors (politician, novelist, poet) are Jacques Hébert's and Pierre Trudeau's *Two innocents in Red China* (tr. by Ivon Owen, 1968); Margaret LAURENCE's *The prophet's camel bell* (1983), about Somaliland; Gwendolyn MacEWEN's *Mermaids and ikons: a Greek summer* (1978); and P.K. PAGE's *Brazilian journey* (1987). About Greece, George Galt wrote *Trailing Pythagoras* (1982) and *A journey through the Aegean Islands* (1988). Two other notable travel writers are Ronald WRIGHT, author of *Cut stones and crossroads: a journey in the two worlds of Peru* (1984), *On Fiji islands* (1986), and *Time among the Maya: travels in Belize, Guatemala, and Mexico* (1989); and Paul William ROBERTS, who wrote *River in the desert: modern travels in ancient Egypt* (1993) and *Empire of the soul: journeys in India* (1994).

See also Kildare DOBBS, *Away from home: Canadian writers in exotic places* (1985); Eve-Marie Kröller, *Canadian travellers in Europe, 1851-1900* (1987); *Saturday Night traveller* (1990), a collection of travel pieces that had appeared in *Saturday Night* magazine about faraway places (by Dobbs, M.T. KELLY, Alberto MANGUEL, Audrey THOMAS, Ronald Wright, and others) edited by George Galt; and the bibliography *The travellers: Canada to 1900* (1989), edited by Elizabeth Waterston *et al.*

Most early travel books are available on microfilm. Excellent bibliographies appear in Norah Story, *The Oxford companion to Canadian history and literature* (1967) after entries on British North America, Canada, individual provinces, and territories or regions (e.g. Barren Grounds). Surveys of travel books are included in the *Literary history of Canada* (vol. II, 2nd edn, 1975). Useful introductions appear in selective anthologies, such as Gerald Craig, *Early travellers in the Canadas* (1955); Mary Quayle Innis, *Travellers west* (1956); and James Doyle, *Yankees in Canada* (1980).

ELIZABETH WATERSON

Tregebov, Rhea (b. 1953). Born Rhea Block in Saskatoon, Saskatchewan, she was raised in Winnipeg, Manitoba, and attended the University of Manitoba for her B.A. and then did graduate work at Cornell and Boston Universities (M.A., 1978). Since 1978 she has lived in Toronto, Ontario, and has been freelance editor, translator, poetry-workshop instructor, and business writer. She has served as co-editor of *Fireweed*, a feminist quarterly.

A lyric poet, Tregebov has published four books of poetry: *Remembering history* (1982), which won the Pat LOWTHER Award for the best book of poetry by a woman; *No one we know* (1986); *The proving grounds* (1991); and *Mapping the chaos* (1995). Tregebov's work explores the impact of history and memory on personal lives. Stylistically she prefers the long, punctuated line and often uses the striking details of daily life to evoke sensual images. In her first volume, Tregebov sees history as fixed and permanent, a view she reconsiders in the collections that follow. Increasingly she comes to recognize and celebrate the mutable 'chaos' of life in poems that treat such varied themes as the legacy of the Holocaust, the destructiveness of nuclear power, her son's near-death from severe asthma, the death of loved ones, urban life, and gardening, a favourite subject. Always aware of the potential tragedy that looms beneath the surface of life, she seeks to integrate darkness and light in verse that finally rejects pessimism.

Tregebov has also written three books for children—*The extraordinary ordinary everything room* (1991); *The big storm* (1992); and *Sasha and the wiggly tooth* (1993)—and has edited *Work in progress: building feminist culture* (1987); *Sudden miracles: eight women poets* (1991); *Frictions: stories by women* (1989); and *Frictions II: stories by women* (1993).

Tregebov's series of poems, 'Whoever you think you are', won the *MALAHAT REVIEW* Long Poem Competition in 1994; she has also received *Prairie Schooner*'s Readers' Choice Award. RUTH PANOFSKY

Tremblay, Michel (b. 1942). Born and raised on rue Fabre in the Plateau Mont-Royal section of Montreal (where most of his plays and novels are set), he studied graphic arts after high school and became a linotype operator, like his father and brother. His first play, *Le train*, was written in 1959, won first prize in the 1964 'Jeunes auteurs' contest of Radio-Canada, and was produced on television. But *Les BELLES-SOEURS* (1968), written in 1965 and produced in 1968, is regarded as the true beginning of a career that rapidly brought fame to Tremblay, enabling him to devote himself entirely to his writing. (A translation by Bill Glassco and John Van Burek was published in 1974; rev. 1992.) A full cycle of plays followed, describing other facets and characters of the same universe; it ended with *Damnée Manon, sacrée Sandra* (1977), translated by Van Burek in 1981, with the same title. He later wrote *L'impromptu d'Outremont* (1980, translated by Glassco and Van Burek as *The impromptu of Outremont*, 1981), which reflects the preoccupations of the more bourgeois neighbourhood he moved to in 1974 and, at the same time, sets the scene for major changes in Tremblay's writing: in tune with the new post-referendum dramaturgy of the eighties, the time had come to tone down 'kitchen-sink realism' and nationalist symbolism. Two major plays—they both got Chalmers Awards—exemplify this new trend: *Albertine, en cinq temps* (1984, translated as *Albertine in five times* in 1986 by Glassco and Van Burek), a fascinating and innovative depiction of Albertine between the ages of 30 and 70, and *Le vrai monde?* (1987, translated in 1988 by Glassco and Van Burek as *The real world?*), a self-reflexive Pirandellian play about the playwright—describing his own family life. *La maison suspendue* (1990, translated with the same title by Van Burek in 1991) and *Marcel poursuivi par les chiens* (1992, translated by Van Burek in 1992 as *Marcel pursued by hounds*) link up characters on stage with those described in the novels about the Plateau Mont-Royal and in two autobiographical novels, *Le coeur découvert* (1986, translated by Sheila Fischman in 1989 as *The heart laid bare*) and *Le coeur éclaté* (1993), which draw on his love affair with a young actor.

The Plateau Mont-Royal setting must be seen as a true microcosm of alienated Quebec: most characters are doomed, from birth to death, to a dead-end. The most powerfully tragic play in this regard is *À TOI, POUR TOUJOURS, TA MARIE-LOU* (1971)—translated by Glassco and Van Burek as *Forever yours, Marie-Lou* (1975)—in which two sisters, Carmen and Manon, confront their parents, Leopold and Marie-Lou, who have been dead ten years. (It was imagined as a musical quartet.) Manon sits in a rocking chair trying to resemble her mother, whose destiny she perpetuates in a masochistic acceptance of a frustrated and dull life, while Carmen, dressed as a cow-girl, has become a country-and-western singer in a cheap nightclub. Carmen reappears in *Sainte Carmen de la Main* (1976, translated by Glassco and Van Burek in 1981) in which she is killed for having tried to liberate (or 'redeem') her transvestite and prostitute friends. Carmen is a central figure in Tremblay's plays, for she exemplifies the full meaning of transvestism—in the sense of *le travestissement*, which means not only cross-dressing but misrepresentation—a major theme in his plays dealing mainly with show-business or homosexuality, such as the musical-comedy *Demain matin, Montréal m'attend* (1972); *La Duchesse de Langeais* (1970, translated, with other plays, by Van Burek in 1976), *Hosanna* (1973, translated by Glassco and Van Burek in 1974), *Les héros de mon enfance* (1976), and *Damnée Manon, sacrée Sandra*. All these plays present an interesting and basically realistic depiction of a marginal milieu, where the struggle for social recognition and true human love is often dramatic. However, one must also consider these characters as symbolic figures for a whole collectivity—Quebec—in which borrowing someone else's identity always seems the only way to success and respectability. Hence Carmen's decision to drop the lyrics and tunes learned in Tennessee, and to sing her own songs describing the real problems of her friends, can lead only to her death. Hence also (but more positively) the final scene of *Hosanna*, in which the two male lovers—one of them, 'Hosanna', garbed as Elizabeth Taylor in *Cleopatra*—undress, shedding all pretences and make-believe to accept their true selves and affirm their identities.

Other aspects of the metaphorical use of transvestism are shown in *Damnée Manon, sacrée Sandra*. Manon, Marie-Louise's daughter, is still rocking her life away in the kitchen chair, but her mysticism now verges on fetishism and madness. 'Sandra' is a male transvestite whose sole concern in life seems to be with sex. He is opposed to Manon as sharply as his white costume is opposed to her black dress, his 'avocado sea-green' lipstick to the burgundy colour of her rosary. But as Sandra describes the black 'god' from Martinique whom he loves, and Manon tells about her love for Christ, the true meaning of the play becomes clear: 'religion and sex stem from the same craving for an absolute', as the playwright explained to Martial Dassylva in *La Presse* (26 Feb. 1977).

Remembering Tremblay's repeated statement that there are no 'real men in Quebec', most critics have noted that Tremblay's world is dominated by women—just as Quebec society, and particularly its French and religious characteristics, owe much to the obstinacy of women. *Bonjour, là, bonjour* (1974)—translated by Glassco and Van Burek in 1975—seems to shed new light on this matter. It deals with the love between a brother and sister, Serge and Nicole, a social taboo seldom treated so openly; such a relationship meets social and family attitudes head on—but these are shown to be hypocritical, for the whole family is unknowingly entangled in incestuous desires. Very strikingly, however, the characters who stand out in this mostly feminine universe are two men, father and son; all the women are trying to seduce or possess Serge, who craves only for the love of his deaf father. The play climaxes in Serge's long-contained cry: 'I love you, Papa!' Thus his love for his sister—and this might apply to some homosexual relationships depicted by Tremblay—seems a perverse manifestation of his quest for his father's love. More generally, this might allow us to see the portrayal of ineffectual men in other plays from the same perspective. The weak and sometimes despicable male characters in *Les belles-soeurs*, *Forever yours, Marie-Lou*, and *En pièces détachées* (1970)—translated by Allan Van Meer as *Like death warmed over* (1973)—are the hidden face of this obsessive quest, the importance of which is again shown in *Les anciennes odeurs* (first produced and published in 1981), in which the older lover is clearly identified as a father-image by the younger one, who talks incessantly about his dying father. It was translated by John Stowe as *Remember me* (1984).

Trois petits tours (1971) contains three short plays, which appear in English as *Berthe*, *Johnny Mangano and his astonishing dogs*, and *Gloria Star*, along with *Surprise! Surprise!*—translated by Van Burek in *La Duchesse de Langeais and other plays* (1976).

Most of Tremblay's plays have been performed in English outside Quebec. Toronto's Tarragon Theatre has produced *Forever yours, Marie-Lou* (1972), *Hosanna* (1974), *Bonjour, là, bonjour* (1975), *Sainte Carmen de la Main* (1978), and *Damnée Manon, sacrée Sandra* (1979). The St Lawrence Centre for the Arts, Toronto, produced *Les belles-soeurs* (1973) and *Surprise! Surprise!* (1975), while *La Duchesse de Langeais* was performed in English at New College, University of Toronto, in 1978. *Like death warmed over* has been produced at the Manitoba Theatre Centre in Winnipeg (1973); *Johnny Mangano and his astonishing dogs* in Edmonton (1980); and *The impromptu of Outremont* at the Vancouver Arts Centre (1980).

Outside Canada *Hosanna* has been produced twice in New York, without much success. *Bonjour, là, bonjour*, however, has been produced widely in the USA, and had a production in Japan in 1981. *À toi, pour toujours, ta Marie-Lou* was performed widely in France, Belgium, Switzerland, and Great Britain; *Les belles-soeurs* in Paris; *Hosanna* in Paris, Antwerp, and The Netherlands; and *La Duchesse de Langeais* in France and Belgium. Finally, *Hosanna* and *Damnée Manon, sacrée Sandra* have been performed in New Zealand; and *Forever yours, Marie-Lou* was given its Italian première in Rome in 1979. In Scotland, William Findlay and Martin Bowman translated *Les belles-soeurs* into Scottish dialect as *The guid sisters* (1988) and *La maison suspendue* as *House among the trees*: the production of these plays were enormously successful and gave a significant impulse to the cultural life of Scotland.

Tremblay has also translated and adapted into French Aristophanes' *Lysistrata* (1969), Paul Zindel's *The effect of gamma rays on man-in-the-moon marigolds* (1970) and *And Miss Reardon drinks a little* (1971); four short plays by Tennessee Williams collected in *Le pays du dragon* (produced in 1971); Dario Fo's *Mistero Buffo* (produced in 1973); Roberto Athayde's *Aparaceu a Margarida* (produced in 1976); Gretchen Cryer's *I'm getting my act together and taking it on the road* (1981); Anton Chekhov's *Uncle Vanya* (1983); Gogol's *Inspector-General* (1985); and Albee's *Who's afraid of Virginia Woolf?* (1988). He wrote the scenarios and dialogues for three films directed by André Brassard: *Françoise Durocher, waitress* (1972), *Il était une fois dans l'Est* (1974), and *Le soleil se lève en retard* (1977). He also wrote the scenario for *Parlez-nous d'amour* (1976) by Jean-Claude Lord and a television adaptation of Gabrielle ROY's *BONHEUR D'OCCASION* in 1977.

In the field of fiction, Tremblay published as early as 1966 *Contes pour buveurs attardés* (translated by Michael BULLOCK as *Stories for late-night drinkers*, 1977); this was followed by *La cité dans l'oeuf* (1969) and *C't'à ton tour, Laura Cadieux* (1973). None of these seemed a major work, whereas the Plateau Mont-Royal chronicles—*La grosse femme d'à-coté est enceinte* (1978), *Thérèse et Pierrette à l'école des saints-anges* (1980), *La Duchesse et le roturier* (1982), *Des nouvelles d'Édouard* (1984), and *Le premier quartier de la lune* (1989) have been generally hailed by readers and critics as very important. Unlike his plays, which were often written out of anger, these novels are imbued with love, tenderness, and a generosity of spirit; they made Tremblay a major novelist of the 1980s. Sheila Fischman has translated three of them: *The fat woman next door is pregnant* (1981), *Thérèse and Pierrette and the little hanging angels* (1984), and *The first quarter of the moon* (1994). In 1995 Tremblay published *La nuit des princes charmants*. He has also published three books of memoirs in which he tells which works most influenced his life and writing in the fields of cinema (*Les vues animées, suivi de Les loups se mangent entre eux*, 1990), theatre (*Douze coups de théâtre*, 1992), and literature (*Un ange cornu avec des ailes de tôle*, 1994).

Tremblay was honoured with the title of Chevalier de l'Ordre des Arts et des Lettres de France in 1984; was awarded the Prix David in 1988 for his entire work; and has received many honorary doctorates from Canadian universities.

See the Fall 1979 issue of *The Canadian Theatre Review*; the tenth chapter of Jean Cléo Godin and Laurent Mailhot's *Théâtre québécois II* (1980); John Ripley's 'From alienation to transcendence, the quest for selfhood in Michel Tremblay's plays', in *CANADIAN LITERATURE* 85 (Summer 1980); and Renate Usmiani, *Michel Tremblay* (1982). The winter 1982 issue of *VOIX ET IMAGES*, devoted entirely to Michel Tremblay, contains a long critical bibliography prepared by Lorraine Camerlain and Pierre Lavoie. *Le monde de Michel Tremblay* (1993), edited by Gilbert David and Pierre Lavoie, presents a series of studies covering the entire work, from *Les belles-soeurs* to *Marcel poursuivi par les chiens*.

See also DRAMA IN FRENCH 1948 TO 1981: 3, 4; 1981 TO 1996:3; and NOVELS IN FRENCH 1960 TO 1982:3(a). JEAN CLÉO GODIN

Tremblay, Rénald. See DRAMA IN FRENCH 1948 to 1981: 3.

Trente arpents (1938). This classic of French-Canadian literature by Philippe PANNETON (pseud. 'Ringuet') was warmly received by critics both in France, where it first appeared, and in Canada. It won the Prix David and the Prix des Vikings of the French Academy; was translated into English under the title *Thirty acres* (1940; NCL 1960) by Felix and Dorothea Walter, and into German and Dutch; and has been reprinted several times—in Canada with an introduction by Jacques Cotnam (1971) and in France in the collection 'J'ai lu' (1981). The English translation won a Governor General's Award.

Trente arpents is the tragic story of the rise and fall of Euchariste Moisan, who is entirely devoted to his land. After years of success—the envy of his neighbours—the sale of a piece of his land and the failure of a law-suit against one of his neighbours bring Euchariste humiliations and ruin. His son Étienne, who persuades Euchariste to cede his land to him and to visit his favourite son Ephrem in the USA, refuses to send his father the money for a return ticket to his village, and the old man will likely end his life as a nightwatchman in an American industrial town, unable to communicate with anyone but his son—not even with his own grandchildren and his son's wife, since he speaks no English and they speak no French. Set in the Trois-Rivières area between 1887 and 1932, *Trente arpents* reveals a society on the verge of radical change. It opposes progress to traditions, city life to rural life, younger to older generations, and life to death. Above all, it denounces the farmer's subservience to his land. As shown by the title as well as by several critics—for example, Jacques Viens in *La terre de Zola et Trente arpents de Ringuet* (1970)—the main character of *Trente arpents* is the land itself, and that is what gives the novel its universality.

Panneton, who took nine years to write *Trente arpents*, did not want the term 'regionalist' to be applied to his novel; he was anxious to achieve realism by avoiding the extremes of both naturalism and idealism. He moved away from the traditional French-Canadian *roman de la terre*, which, since *La terre paternelle* (1846) by Patrice LACOMBE, had offered a romantic and idealistic vision of the farmer's life in order to promote agriculturist ideologies. Panneton refused to use literature as an excuse for reviving the past, or to put it to the service of a political cause. JACQUES COTNAM

Trottier, Pierre (b. 1925). Born in Montreal, he studied law at the Université de Montréal and joined the Department of External Affairs in 1949. He has held diplomatic posts in Moscow, Djakarta, London, Lima, and Paris, and was Canadian Ambassador to UNESCO, a post he held from 1979 to 1983. He first became known as a poet with *Le combat contre Tristan* (1951)—reprinted in *Sainte-Mémoire*—which presents the excitement of foreign travel experienced by a French Canadian working abroad. His poetry is laden with memory, culture, and thought. *Poèmes de Russie* (1957) stresses the inner life and suggests an obsession with origins. Hence the theme of androgyny arises: 'I made the first Eve part of my own being.' The beautiful poem 'Ce bois de mystère' celebrates the mother loved for her voice, her hands, her eyes, her form, her fear, her words, her death. The next collection, *Les belles au bois dormant* (1960)—dedicated to the memory of his mother, who died in 1958—is a quest for self that travels 'between my daughter who has just been born / And my mother who has just died.' This is rich, highly descriptive poetry. Trottier's major poetic work was appropriately called *Sainte-Mémoire* (1972). It reprints the 'retours' that had first appeared in *Écrits du Canada français* (no. 13, 1962; no. 29, 1970): the return of Oedipus, a man's return to his homeland; the return of Don Quixote, who drove out fear; the return of the androgyne, man reunited with himself—'I discovered Eve within me. The same soul within two bodies.' Playing on the term for seasonal migration ('transhumance'), Trottier created a beautiful new word: 'transâmance' (migration of souls) 'to denote the unity or transfer of souls between two bodies', the formula for a new kind of love. 'Your life and mine are one! Such is the language of the *transâmance* when one finds his equal.'

Mon Babel (1963) is a collection of 17 short essays on the French-Canadian identity. Trottier examines the Quebec milieu, its myths, culture, and place in the world, presenting a universe populated with familiar characters: Laius and Danaus, Tristan, Hamlet, Shakespeare, Corneille, Racine. Filled with their voices, their watchful eyes, this is both descriptive and poetic writing in which Trottier adapts his Canadian heritage, his American culture, his religion and myths to a patient reworking of history and memory. Referring to *Mon Babel*, Trottier later wrote: 'We must push hard against death . . . to exorcize it. It is a matter of getting rid of the heritage of SAINT-DENYS-GARNEAU before moving on to other things.' *Un pays baroque* (1979), a collection of 13 assorted essays centring on the culture and history of Canada as an English-French-American world entity, is Trottier's most lively and impressive book. Often witty and intentionally insolent, and with many autobiographical references, these essays are of great literary and historical value. Trottier defines the baroque as the 'reconsideration of fixed forms, and the quest, whether exuberant or tortured, for a new form.' The 'baroque land' is 'Kanada'—or 'Carien', because 'nada' in Spanish means 'rien' in French, or 'nothing'. Situated in 'Amerika', whose destiny is 'Americainfinitive', its capital is Ottawa, or the 'Anglo-French cultural ambiguity'.

The two suites of poems in *La chevelure de Bérénice* (1986) evoke original aspects of love, relating to both the mother and the female lover. 'Lilith', 'Mères', and 'Coma Bérénices' are major poems of Québécois literature, both for their polished technique and for their broad thematic range. *En vallées closes: poèmes, 1951-1986* (1989) presents the total *oeuvre* of an author who is obsessed with such themes as love, death, time, space, and modern and ancient culture. The poems are a celebration of the encounter between man and woman, East and West, modern times and the origins of mythical time. The erotic hymn of Apollinaire comes to mind here, as much as the enquiring, broad-ranging intellect of Alain GRANDBOIS.

Ma dame à la licorne (1988) is a lively essay, in seventeen chapters, that displays the knowledge of the world gained by an author who has travelled widely. Also a spiritual autobiography of an intellectual journey, it is in fact the best critical presentation of Trottier as both poet and prose-writer. Trottier's work represents a major body of Québécois thought, as significant as that of Father Ernest Gagnon in *L'homme d'ici* (1963) and Jean LE MOYNE in *Convergences* (1961).

Trottier received the Prix David in 1960 and the Prize of the Société des gens de lettres in 1964. He has been a member of the Royal Society of Canada since 1978.

For a discussion of *Le combat contre Tristan*, *Poèmes de Russie*, and *Mon Babel*, see Pierre de Grandpré, *Dix ans de vie littéraire au Canada français* (1966). See also Gilles Marcotte, 'Diplomate, essayiste et poète, Pierre Trottier', in *Québec 64* (1964). JOSEPH BONENFANT

Trudel, Marcel (b. 1917). Born at St-Narcisse-de-Champlain, Quebec, he was educated at Université Laval (B.A., 1938; L.ès L., 1941; D. ès L., 1945) and did research at Harvard University (1945-7). He was professor of history at Laval from 1947 to 1965, director of the Institute of Canadian Studies at Carleton

University, Ottawa (1965-6), and head of the history department at the Université d'Ottawa (1966-8). In 1971 he was made an Officer of the Order of Canada, and he was awarded the Molson Prize in 1980.

The author of more than two dozen titles—some of them in two volumes—and specializing in the history of New France, Trudel became an essential figure in transforming Quebec's history from wishful romanticism to rigorous intellectual pursuit, in putting an end to the rhetorical indulgence that had turned Quebec historical writing into religious and ideological manifesto. He emphasized extensive work on contemporary historical sources, turning some of his graduate seminars into extended examinations of just one historical text. The three volumes of his *Histoire de la Nouvelle-France—Les vaines tentatives, 1524-1603* (1963), *Le comptoir, 1604-1627* (1966), which won a Governor General's Award, and *La seigneurie des Cent-Associés, 1627-1663* (1973)—were condensed and translated by Patricia Claxton for The Canadian Centenary Series to create *The beginnings of New France, 1524-1663* (1973), of which Chapter 18 was based on Trudel's *Le terrier du Saint-Laurent en 1663* (1972) and *La population du Canada en 1663* (1973). All these books explored vast unplumbed areas of Quebec's past. Writing also on slavery in New France, demographic and settlement history, and the beginnings of Montreal, among other subjects, Trudel revealed his skill in meticulous reconstruction.

He served as directeur général adjoint of the *DICTIONARY OF CANADIAN BIOGRAPHY/ DICTIONNAIRE BIOGRAPHIQUE DU CANADA* in its founding years (1961-5). His autobiography was entitled *Mémoires d'un autre siècle* (1987). TERRY CROWLEY

Trudel, Sylvain. See NOVELS IN FRENCH 1983 to 1996: 6, 7.

Tulchinsky, Karen. See LESBIAN LITERATURE.

Turcotte, Élise. See NOVELS IN FRENCH 1983 to 1996: 6, 7.

Turgeon, Pierre. See NOVELS IN FRENCH 1960 to 1982: 3(a), 1983 to 1996: 7.

Two little savages (1906). This classic of children's literature by Ernest Thompson SETON (now translated into many languages) grew out of his work with youth groups in the United States. By 1903 fifty 'tribes' had formed, calling themselves 'Seton's Indians' or 'Woodcraft Indians'. During that year Seton published, in *Ladies Home Journal*, a serialized story for boys, an expanded version of which later became *Two little savages: being the adventures of two boys who lived as Indians and what they learned*. Although written in the third person, the story is semi-autobiographical and records Seton's adventures in the summer of 1876, when he holidayed with the Blackwell family near Lindsay, Ontario. In the woods near the farm, Seton and the son of Blackwell 'played Indian' and developed games that were later incorporated in Boy Scout rituals still used in many parts of the world.

Two little savages, en episodic adventure story, provided Seton with a framework into which he could interpolate instructions on woodcraft (generously illustrated with his own detailed drawings). The story describes an initiation rite in which the testing of a boy's knowledge of birds and trees merges with an archetypal pattern. Yan (as the young Seton) confronts a sequence of trials, demonstrates his courage, and is finally pronounced a hero. Since the story ends with Yan's resolve to 'strive and struggle as a naturalist', the book could be viewed as an autobiographical *Bildungsroman*. Variations of many of the same episodes appear in Seton's autobiography, *Trail of an artist-naturalist* (1940).

MAGDALENE REDEKOP

Two solitudes (1945). This novel by Hugh MacLENNAN, for which he won his first Governor General's Award, aroused more public interest than critical attention because of its theme of Canadian unity, which had been strained in the 1942 plebiscite on conscription, and its apposite title, drawn from Rilke. Although Rilke and MacLennan both had individuals in mind as the solitudes that touch and protect each other, the application to the dominant cultural groups in Canada has since become a cliché.

Two solitudes is structured in four parts: the first two treat the period 1917 to 1921 and the second two the years 1934 and 1939. Part I, set in the rural Quebec parish of Saint-Marie-des-Érables, has two interests. One is the struggle between the proud, anti-clerical, progressive Athanase Tallard and the Anglophobe parish priest, Father Beaubien, who opposes change. The second interest is the attempt of Yardley, a retired sea-captain, to settle in the parish where, ironically, he is more acceptable than Tallard, whose political loyalties, affiliation with English-speaking capitalists, estrangement from his Anglophobe son Marius, and second marriage to an Irish girl threaten the status quo. Part II ends in utter defeat for Tallard: a failed marriage, a broken family, financial ruin, the loss of his family home, and death, which is preceded by a return to the Church. MacLennan's treatment in the first half of Tallard, Yardley, and the younger generation is deft and sympathetic; the story moves with almost tragic inevitability. But as George WOODCOCK and others have noted, the second half of the book—centring on Paul Tallard, the son of Athanase by his second marriage, and on Paul's courtship of Heather Methuen against the backdrop of the English community of Montreal and the business career of Huntley McQueen—is neither sympathetic nor dramatic. McQueen is treated satirically (he has overtones of Mackenzie King); and Paul's and Heather's marriage, intended to suggest a French-English détente, is unconvincing. Paul is more like a spokesman for the author's beliefs and hopes than a fully realized character. It is typical of MacLennan's early optimistic writing about national problems that the realities of the situation should be rendered more persuasively than their resolution.

The novel, then, is not an unqualified success. With its abrupt period divisions, its point of view that changes from the objective to the personal and didactic, leading characters who in the beginning are lively and realistic (Tallard *père*, Yardley) and then become mere symbols (Paul, Heather, and the other *Anglais*) or shadows (Marius), it lacks cohesiveness. If the sense that the components are ill-yoked does not suit the theme, however, it suits the title. For all its faults *Two solitudes* is a sensitive and creditable attempt to portray the tensions and differences in Quebec that culminated in the Quiet Revolution (a decade and a half before that event took place) and the possibility of reconciliation. It is a landmark in Canadian nationalistic fiction.

D.O. SPETTIGUE

Tynes, Maxine. See Writing in the MARITIMES: 5.

U

Uguay, Marie (1955-81). Born in Montreal, she studied at the Collège Marguerite Bourgeoys and at the Université du Québec à Montréal. In 1976 she published her first collection of poems, *Signe et rumeur*, which was followed in 1979 by *L'outre-vie*, and in 1982 by the posthumous collection *Autoportraits*. In 1986 these three collections were reissued in one volume under the title *Poèmes* by Les Éditions du Noroît, with some previously unpublished work and a preface by Jacques BRAULT.

The first collection immediately revealed a poetry that is personal, intimate, and concise, and that stood apart from the formalist tendencies of the 1970s. As its title suggests, *Signe et rumeur* attempts to reconcile art and life through exploration of (as Hélène Dorion has said) the possibilities of aphorism and analogy. With *L'outre-vie* Uguay emerged as one of the outstanding voices of her generation. In this collection—illustrated, as was *Autoportraits*, with photographs by Stéphan Kovacs—Uguay pursued her search for a poetic language intimately connected with life, though she knew she had cancer. Illness gave a tragic depth to her introspection, but Uguay did not abandon the idea of reconnecting with the world, beyond the cruel experience she was living through. *L'outre-vie* received an enthusiastic reception from critics, especially Michel BEAULIEU and Jean Royer, who have often paid tribute to Uguay's solemn authenticity.

The posthumous texts gathered in *Autoportraits* and *Poèmes* clearly reveal the rapid maturation of Uguay's writing, as well as her persistent quest for the 'other', beyond the individual fate; in them her unfinished work finds an undeniable fulfilment. In their anthology of Quebec poetry, *La poésie québécoise des origines à nos jours* (1986), Laurent Mailhot and Pierre Nepveu note a 'rare limpidité d'évocation' in these last poems. A 1981 film about Uguay, in which she touches on her conception of life and poetry, was directed by Jean-Claude Labrecque.

See Marie Uguay, *La vie, la poésie. Entretiens avec Jean Royer* (1983); Hélène Dorion, '*Signe et rumeur* et *L'outre-vie*, recueils de poésies de Marie Uguay', *Dictionnaire des oeuvres littéraires du Québec*, vol. IV (1984), pp. 742-6; and Suzanne PARADIS, 'Marie Uguay. *Autoportraits*', *Livres et auteurs québécois* (1982), pp. 144-6. FRANÇOIS DUMONT

Uher, Lorna. See Lorna CROZIER.

Ukrainian-Canadian literature. Ukrainian immigration to Canada began in the 1890s, when large numbers of peasants resolved to quit their oppressed and impoverished homeland in Western Ukraine (then under Austro-Hungarian rule) for a fresh start in the New World. Attracted by the promise of free land, the first immigrants took up homesteads on the Prairies, or worked as labourers in frontier and urban enterprises. By the outbreak of the First World War an estimated 170,000 Ukrainians had settled in Canada, although they were then often confusingly identified as Ruthenians, Russians, Galicians, Romanians, Austrians, and Poles. Today more than a million Canadians claim whole or partial Ukrainian ancestry, most tracing their roots back to one of three major periods of immigration: 1891-1914, 1923-1939, or 1947-1955. A small influx of Ukrainians from Poland and Yugoslavia in the 1980s, and in recent years from Ukraine itself, has not had a noticeable impact on Ukrainian-Canadian literature. Significantly, eighty-five per cent of Ukrainian Canadians are now Canadian-born, the vast majority residing in the large cities of central and western Canada. (See Jars Balan, *Salt and braided bread: Ukrainian life in Canada*, 1984).

West Ukrainian literature contains a number of fascinating works inspired by the initial exodus of Ukrainians to the New World. The best known is a short story by the renowned Expressionist writer Vasyl Stefanyk, 'Kaminnyi khrest' (Lviv, 1899), which was included in a collection of his stories translated by Joseph Wizwuk with C.H. Andrusyshen and published as *The stone cross* (1971). The story's moving depiction of a peasant family's traumatic departure from a Galician village 'almost exactly recorded', as the author later acknowledged, the real-life experience of Stefan Didukh (d. 1911), who homesteaded in rural east-central Alberta, near the present-day town of Chipman. Before leaving his native land, Didukh erected a stone cross atop a hill on his property, where it remains to this day as a monument to Canada's Ukrainian pioneers. A planned visit to Canada by Vasyl Stefanyk never materialized, but his youngest son, Yuri (1909-85), settled in Edmonton in 1948, where he played an active role in the development of Ukrainian-Canadian letters. Besides serving for more than a decade as the head of the emigré writers' association, 'Slovo' (The Word), Yuri Stefanyk produced a collection of essays under the pen-name Yuri Klynovy, and edited several collections of stories and other works by single West Ukrainian and immigrant authors.

Most first-wave Ukrainian emigrants were hard-working and thrifty *muzhiks* (peasants) with little or no formal education. A survey conducted in 1916 showed that 48 per cent of male and 70 per cent of female immigrants were illiterate in any language—statistics that remained high among Ukrainian Canadians until the 1940s. Nevertheless members of the pioneer generation were often multilingual, and they came from a part of Ukraine where the level of culture had been steadily rising since the mid-nineteenth century, thanks to an expanding network of institutions that promoted self-reliance. Similar bodies were transplanted to Canada, including enlightenment and 'reading' societies (*chytalnias*) where the literate would read books and periodicals aloud for the benefit of those who were unlettered. Furthermore, the newcomers shared a rich oral tradition that served as the fertile soil from which Ukrainian-Canadian literature sprang less than seven years after the onset of immigration.

Ukrainian literature in Canada originated in the songs, stories, and sayings of the first colonists, who spontaneously created nostalgic or bitter laments about their lives, or hopeful panegyrics celebrating their new land. The first published Ukrainian poem written in Canada was a song composed by Ivan Zbura (1860-1940), a farmer in the Beaver Creek colony northeast of Edmonton. Titled 'Kanadiiski emigranty' ('Canadian emigrants') and dated 30 December 1898, it compares life in the old country with that in the new, finding the latter much to be preferred. Sincere and vibrant, like a lot of immigrant writing, it is of greater historical and sociological than literary value; but many similar folk-poems from the early period show considerable flair and a natural grasp of technique.

The founding in 1903, in Winnipeg, of the first Ukrainian newspaper in Canada, *Kanadiiskii Farmer* ('Canadian Farmer'), was a signal event because it provided authors with easy access to a Cyrillic press, as well as a reading public. *Farmer* was soon followed by numerous other periodicals, in which we find the earliest attempts at Ukrainian *belles-lettres* in Canada. Winnipeg became the leading centre of Ukrainian publishing, and within a few years titles by immigrant authors started to appear, alongside translations and reprints of Old World classics. One of the first anthologies of indigenous folk poetry, *Pisni pro Kanadu i Avstriiu* ('Songs about Canada and Austria', 1908), went through six editions and a name change ('Songs about the Old and New Countries') necessitated by wartime tensions, selling over 50,000 copies. The final edition of 1927 contained thirty songs, mostly in the traditional *kolomyika* form, by fifteen authors.

Probably the most prominent writer of the pioneer era was Paul Crath (also spelled Krat, 1882-1952), who emigrated in 1907 from central Ukraine. A student revolutionary forced to flee both Russian and Austro-Hungarian authorities, Crath immediately joined the leading ranks of the nascent Ukrainian-Canadian intelligentsia and soon after his arrival helped to launch the Winnipeg-based socialist newspaper *Chervonyi prapor* ('The red flag', 1907-09). Crath's first book, *Sotsialistychni pisni* ('Socialist songs', 1909), was a best-selling collection of verse issued under the pseudonym, P. Ternenko. It contained his left-wing adaptation of Ivan Franko's patriotic hymn *Ne pora* ('It is not time yet', 1880), as well as the first Ukrainian translation of 'The Internationale'—which was used without acknowledgement by the Soviet government until it was replaced by a new version in the 1920s. Crath also produced a number of ideologically oriented prose works during these years, such as the short story 'Vizyta "Chervonoi Druzhyny"' ('The visit of the "Red Legion"', 1912). It presented a reminiscence of political unrest in Ukraine as related by a newly fired CPR striker to fellow labourers sitting around a campfire by Lake Winnipeg. Other fiction in a similar vein were *Koly lekshe bude?* ('When will it be better?' 1912) and the humorous *Poslidnne khodzhennie Boha po zemli* ('The last day God walked the earth', 1915). On the eve of the Great War, Krat began publishing a scathingly anti-clerical monthly called *Kadylo* ('Incensory', 1913), which mercilessly lampooned both Ukrainian Catholic and Russian Orthodox ecclesiastics. However, in 1914 he experienced a spiritual transformation that led to his enrolment in a Presbyterian seminary and subsequent ordination into the ministry in 1917. Around this time Crath collaborated with Florence Randal Livesay on the first translation of Ukrainian songs into English, *Songs of Ukraina* (1916), and worked on both the Presbyterian Church's Ukrainian-language organ, *Ranok* ('Dawn', est. 1905), and the left-wing newspaper *Robochyi narod* ('The working people'). He also wrote the first work of Utopian literature in the Ukrainian language, *Koly ziishlo sontse: opovidannia z 2000 roku* ('When the sun rose: a tale from the year 2000'), issued in Toronto in 1918. Responding in part to previous novels in this genre by Edward Bellamy (*Looking backward: 2000-1887*, 1888), William Morris (*News from nowhere*, 1890), and H.G. Wells (*When the sleeper wakes*, 1899), Crath created a story set in Vancouver that elaborated a strongly ecological and uniquely multicultural vision of future society. Thus, his novella presciently depicts the extensive use of solar technology, and has as its hero a medical student named Petro Ivanchuk —who is engaged to a Canadian woman fluent in his native tongue after having lived for three years in independent Ukraine! Passionately committed to the cause of Ukraine's political and spiritual liberation, Crath worked for more than a decade as a missionary in Western Ukraine (1924-36) before returning to Canada to become a pastor in the United Church. In 1940 he assisted Florence Randal Livesay in rendering Hryhorii Kvitka-Osnovianenko's novel *Marusia* into English, and later, with Watson KIRKCONNELL, translated an excerpt from the twelfth-century *Tale of Ihor's campaign: Prince Ihor's raid against the Polovtsi* (1947). His final posthumous work was a somewhat eccentric account of Ukraine's history, *Ukrains'ka starodavnist'* ('Ukrainian antiquity', 1958).

In a lighter vein is the *oeuvre* of Jacob Maydanek (1891-1984), the author of an early theatrical hit, *Manigrula* (1915), whose title is a corruption of the Ukrainian word for 'immigrant'. Chiefly known for his cartoon strip about the misadventures of a Falstaffian Ukrainian-Canadian labourer named Vuiko Shtif Tabachniuk (Uncle Steve Tobacco), Maydanek edited and published a humorous magazine called *Vuiko* ('Uncle', 1924-5), and eventually issued two compilations of his drawings and writings (in 1931 and 1959). He is the subject of a 1983 film documentary, *Laughter in my soul*, produced by the National Film Board. Besides Crath and Maydanek, Honore Ewach (1900-64) stands out among other authors of the pioneer generation. Active as a poet, he produced in 1932 a novella about life in a Manitoba Ukrainian settlement that was translated by Ray Serwylo as *Call of the land* (1986).

The internment of thousands of Ukrainians as 'enemy aliens' during the First World War, accompanied by censorship of the immigrant press, understandably put a damper on intellectual activity for several years. However, with the resumption of large-scale Ukrainian immigration in the 1920s, Ukrainian-Canadian literature entered an exciting new phase that found its most vital expression in the theatre. Beginning shortly after the turn of the century, performances of Ukrainian-language dramas were soon being regularly staged in immigrant settlements large and small from Sydney, Nova Scotia, to Vancouver, British Columbia. The huge audience for theatrical entertainments encouraged many aspiring authors to try playwriting. The first indigenously written stage work was a melodrama by the Protestant Ukrainian minister and pioneer activist John Bodrug (1874-1952). Called *Ubiinyky* ('The murderers', 1909), it had its Canadian première in Winnipeg in 1910 and was produced widely and frequently until the mid-1950s. Besides compiling a Ukrainian grammar and a Ukrainian-English dictionary, Bodrug translated John Bunyan's *Pilgrim's progress* and some 200 hymns into Ukrainian. Another early stage work was *V starim i novim kraiu* ('In the Old and the New Country', 1910), written by Bodrug's fellow Protestant cleric Sigmund Bychinsky (1880-1947). Regarded as the first Ukrainian-Canadian literary critic, Bychinsky went on to write book-length biographical studies of Martin Luther and Jan Hus, and a 1928 history of Canada that was introduced by the Rev. Charles GORDON of Winnipeg (the novelist Ralph Connor). Besides translating *Ben Hur* into Ukrainian, Bychinsky and his wife Anna helped to render a selection of Taras Shevchenko's poems into English, published by the medical missionary A.J. Hunter as *The Kobzar of Ukraine* (1922). His novel about immigrant life in Saskatchewan, *Kliuch zhuravli* ('A flight of cranes'), was published in Ukraine in 1997.

Indicating the special allure that the stage held for would-be Ukrainian authors in Canada, between 1909 and 1942 over 120 plays are known to have been written by more than two dozen different dramatists. The leading playwrights of this era were Semen Kowbel (1877-1966); Myroslav Irchan (the *nom de plume* of Andrii Babiuk, 1897-1937); Dmytro Hunkiewich (1893-1953); Alexander Luhowy (the pseudonym of Oleksander Ovrutskyi-Schvabe, 1904-62); Michael Petrowsky (1897-1982); and P. Pylypenko (the pen name of Philip Ostapchuk, 1898-1967). Collectively they wrote 107 plays, all but thirteen of them in Canada. Some plays, like Kowbel's *Divochi mrii* ('Girlish dreams', 1920), and Hunkiewich's *Krovavi perly* ('Bloody pearls', 1926-7), even entered the repertoires of theatre companies in Ukraine.

Of the above dramatists, Myroslav Irchan stands out for the quality and range of his writing. Coming to Canada in 1923 on the invitation of Ukrainian communists, Irchan was employed for six-and-a-half years as a cultural and political agitator in Winnipeg, the most productive period in his tragically curtailed life. In addition to serving as the founding editor of *Robitnytsia* ('The woman worker') and contributing to various periodicals in North America and Soviet Ukraine, while in Canada Irchan produced an impressive body of short and long fiction, two volumes of memoirs (dealing with his experiences in the Civil War), poetry, ten plays, and a manual of stagecraft. His most successful drama, *Rodyna shchitkariv* ('Family of brushmakers'), received more than seventy Canadian productions between 1924 and 1959, and was also performed widely in Soviet Ukraine during his lifetime and afterwards. Ten other plays by Irchan were staged no fewer than 127 times in Ukrainian Canadian centres big and small, while four of his theatrical translations and adaptations were mounted at least sixty-three times in communities that included Coalhurst, Alberta, and Steveston, British Columbia.

Quick to embrace Canadian themes, Irchan laid bare the exploitation of immigrant labourers in a 1924 novella, *Karpats'ka nich* ('Carpathian nights'). He also took up the cause of Aboriginal people in a poignant sketch, 'Vudzhena ryba' ('Smoked fish', 1924), and a short story, 'Smert Asuara' ('The death of Asuara', 1927). However, feeling cut off from the momentous changes taking place in Communist Ukraine, and confined by the limited perspectives available to him in Canada, Irchan determined to contribute to the building of a new society in his homeland. In 1929 he decided to move with his family to the Ukrainian Socialist Republic, where he felt his literary and political aspirations could be fully realized. Ironically, shortly before his departure he was hailed by Charles Roslin in a *Saturday Night* article (9 February 1929) as possibly 'the most popular and influential author in the country'.

Overseas again, Irchan threw himself into agitational, cultural, and literary endeavours. While in Canada he had given public lectures and written about the Revolution, in Ukraine he similarly publicized his experiences living abroad in the Ukrainian emigration. He also spent several months at a commune established by Ukrainian-Canadian Communists north of Odessa, documenting their achievements in a 134-page account entitled *Z prerii*

Kanady v stepy Ukrainy ('From the Prairies of Canada to the Steppes of Ukraine', 1930). He then began work on an ambitious novel set in Canada whose working title was 'The Prairies', but his efforts were cut short by his arrest in the Stalinist purges of 1933. Denounced as an 'enemy of the people' along with thousands of other patriotically minded Ukrainian Communists, Irchan was exiled to Siberia and died there in unknown circumstances in 1937. Subsequently rehabilitated during the Khrushchev thaw of the late 1950s, when selected literary works by him were first reissued in Ukraine, Irchan's home in his native village of Piadyky was later made into a museum that carefully skirted the details of his premature death.

The ranks of the interwar Ukrainian literary community were similarly reinforced by the writer and nationalist diplomat Mykyta Mandryka (1886-1979), dispatched to Canada in 1928 by the Ukrainian Party of Socialist Revolutionaries. The author of ten Canadian collections of verse and epic poetry, Mandryka also edited a 1941 anthology of immigrant writing, and wrote (in English) the comprehensive *History of Ukrainian literature in Canada* (1969).

However, a special place in Ukrainian-Canadian letters of the first half of the twentieth century belongs to the writer Illia Kiriak (1889-1955)—the name is sometimes spelled Kyriiak. Arriving in Winnipeg from Western Ukraine in 1907, Kiriak worked for several years as an itinerant labourer in frontier industries before finding employment as a typesetter on two short-lived Edmonton Ukrainian newspapers. Eventually obtaining a Canadian education in Vegreville and Camrose, Kiriak went on to teach for seventeen years in a variety of one- and two-room schools in the large Ukrainian bloc settlement of rural east-central Alberta. Unable to continue his career because of a nervous condition, he spent the latter part of his life working for the Northern Alberta Railway, and for the Ukrainian Self-Reliance League of Canada. Kiriak made his début in print with an apocalyptic short story entitled 'Hirkyi son' ('Bitter dream', 1912), after which he became a longtime contributor of literary works and articles to the newspaper *Ukrains'kyi holos* ('Ukrainian voice'). However, he is chiefly remembered for his epic trilogy *Syny zemli* ('Sons of the soil', 1939-45), which he wrote in 1927-8 but was only issued in book form over the course of the Second World War. This 1,110-page saga, a Ukrainian-Canadian classic, provides a panoramic overview of three generations of an immigrant family. Although conventional in form and style, it entertainingly chronicles many of the important stages in the development of Ukrainian-Canadian life. A fictionalized synthesis of the individual stories of Kiriak's friends and neighbours in the bloc settlement—depicting such landmark occasions as the erection of the church and the pioneer schoolhouse, and the first awkward intermarriage—*Syny zemli* pays tribute to the Ukrainian pioneers and their successful integration into Canadian society. A clumsily abridged translation, *Sons of the soil*, was published by the RYERSON PRESS in 1959.

With the end of hostilities in Europe in 1945 and the influx of 35,000 'displaced persons' from war-torn Ukraine via German refugee camps, all aspects of Ukrainian-Canadian community life were transformed and revitalized. The new immigrants were much better educated than their predecessors, and typically preferred to settle in the cities of central Canada. Having witnessed the horrors of Stalinism and Nazism, and survived the hardships of famine and strife, they brought with them a passionate Ukrainian nationalism that often dominated their world view. It is generally acknowledged that the foremost author among the post-war immigrants was Ulas Samchuk (1905-87), a professional writer who emigrated with a number of books already published in Ukraine and abroad. Eight titles by him were published in Canada, including a novel about the immigrant experience, *Na tverdi zemli* ('On the hard earth', 1967). However, critics suggest that his Canadian attempts at fiction were less successful than the works he had produced in Europe. A selection of his prose has been reissued in Ukraine since the change of political climate brought about by independence.

Other noteworthy writers in the generation of the 'displaced persons' are the poet and humorist Borys Oleksandriv (a.k.a. Swyryd Lomachka, the pseudonyms of Borys Hrybinsky, 1921-79), and the poets Volodymyr Skorupsky (1912-85) and Oleh Zujewsky (1920-96). Similarly distinguished figures are Nicholas Prychodko (1904-80), Ivan Bodnarchuk (1914-90), Alexander Smotrych (the pen-name of Alexander Floruk, b. 1922), and Oleksa Hay-Holowko (b. 1910). The latter published a steady stream of poetry, short stories, and novels, as well as an autobiographical narrative about his youth in Ukraine and Russia and the early days of the Nazi invasion of Ukraine that was published in English as *Duel with the devil* (1986). He has also edited three anthologies of Ukrainian-Canadian poetry. But the chief popularizer and promoter of immigrant writing in this prolific group is the poet and literary historian Yar Slavutych (b. 1918), who has had two books of verse issued in English translation: *Oasis* (1959), and *Conquerors of the Prairies* (1974, 1984), along with *Three narratives and six poems* (1992). Besides being active an an editor and publisher, Slavutych has written extensively on various aspects of Ukrainian-Canadian literature and culture. The only playwright of note is Wasyl Sofroniw Levytsky (1899-1975), whose impact was somewhat limited because of the overall decline of Ukrainian theatre in the post-war years. An English sampling of the work of these third-wave authors can be found in the anthology *Yarmarok: Ukrainian writing in Canada since the Second World War* (1987), edited by Yuri Klynovy and Jars Balan.

Because until recently political circumstances did not permit a new injection of immigrant talent from Ukraine, the creation of Ukrainian-language literature appears to be rapidly coming to an end in Canada. Although a handful of Canadian-born authors occasionally write in their ancestral tongue, almost all now write in English. The first to cross linguistic lines was Anna Kuryla-Bychinsky (1883-1970), the wife of the aforementioned Sigmund, who placed a couple of short stories drawn from the lives of immigrant women in *Maclean's* in 1924 and 1926. Sporadic efforts were made by others in her wake, but breakthrough success was only achieved by Vera Lysenko (1910-75) with *Men in sheepskin coats: a study in assimilation* (1947), and the novels *Yellow boots* (1954) and *Westerly wild* (1956)—the second of which is now available in a 1992 reprint. Her accomplishments have since been eclipsed by such distinctive women writers as Maara Haas (née Lazechko, b. 1920), best known for her novel *The street where I live* (1976); Gloria Kupchenko Frolick (1927-93), the late-blooming author of the *The chicken man* (1990) and *Anna Veryha* (1992); Helen Potrebenko (b. 1940), a West Coast poet and prose writer; and Myrna KOSTASH, whose four works of creative non-fiction include the oft-reprinted *All of Baba's children* (1977) and an East European travelogue, *Bloodlines* (1993). A multi-talented freelancer with a translation from Ukrainian to her credit—Solomea Pavlychko's *Letters from Kiev* (1992)—Kostash wrote the script for the popular NFB drama *Teach me to dance* (1977), directed by Ann Wheeler. Some males who have achieved recognition as writers in English are playwright Ted Galay (b. 1941), poet Andrew SUKNASKI (b. 1942), essayist George Melnyk (b. 1946), and investigative journalist Victor Malarek (b. 1948). But the most celebrated figure in this literary group is George RYGA, the subject of a 1995 biography by James Hoffman. Ryga's voluminous output embraces several works that draw directly on his Ukrainian roots, such as his television dramas 'Ninth Summer' (1972) and '1927' (The 'Visit from the Pension Lady' segment in *The Newcomers* series, 1979), and his play *A letter to my son* (1982), written in commemoration of ninety years of Ukrainian settlement in Canada.

A new talent to emerge in the last decade is the novelist, poet, and critic Janice KULYK KEEFER, whose work in all three genres has garnered widespread praise. Her novel *The green library* (1996) explores both the post-war immigrant experience and the relationship of the Ukrainian diaspora to the homeland. Several other Ukrainian Canadian writers show similar promise, though they are still in the process of establishing their reputations. Some of them are represented in a special number of the journal *PRAIRIE FIRE*, 'Echoes from Ukrainian Canada' (Autumn 1992), issued in celebration of the Ukrainian-Canadian centennial.

Because of its long history, richness, scope, and diversity, Ukrainian writing in Canada offers much that is of interest to the scholar. It provides a brightly contrasting thread within the broad fabric of Canadian literature, and forms one of the most dynamic and expansive literary sub-cultures outside of English and French writing. Besides the writers mentioned above, three researchers who have made extensive contributions to the study of Ukrainian Canadian writing are Peter Krawchuk (b. 1911), Michael Marunchak (b. 1914), and the visual poet Jars Balan (b. 1952). The latter also belongs to a cadre of literary translators in Canada who have helped to make Ukrainian-language writing accessible in English and French. Michael Luchkowich (1892-1973), Borys Oleksandriv, and Marco Carynnyk (b. 1943) are other members of this specialized fraternity, providing bridges of understanding and multicultural awareness.

JARS BALAN

Umfreville, Edward. See EXPLORATION LITERATURE IN ENGLISH: 2.

Underhill, Frank. See HISTORICAL WRITING IN ENGLISH: 5.

University Magazine, The (1907-20). A Montreal quarterly edited by Andrew MacPHAIL, it succeeded the semi-annual *McGill University*

Magazine (1901-6), edited by Charles Moyse, which had appeared ten times. The new periodical took over its subscription list of under 1,000 and numbered its volumes consecutively, beginning with vol. VI. Although theoretically directed by an editorial committee drawn from McGill, the University of Toronto, and Dalhousie College, Halifax, *The University Magazine* was under Macphail's control from the beginning. Notable for paying its contributors—the average fee of $25 was more than many a weekly wage—the magazine was financially guaranteed by Macphail himself, although McGill University and the University of Toronto and various benefactors made occasional contributions. It drew upon the best contributors from English-speaking Canada, along with some from outside the country, and under Macphail's rigorous editorial direction set a standard of excellence, while attaining a circulation of nearly 6,000, a level that no comparable Canadian quarterly subsequently matched. Macphail himself contributed 43 pieces of political comment and social criticism (for which he took no payment). Although welcoming purely literary contributions—for example, 'Addison as a literary critic' by E.K. Broadus (Feb. 1909)—the magazine, for Macphail, was a vehicle to advance what he described as 'correct thought', which had to do with a Canada that was rural, traditional, imperial in sentiment, and, aside from Quebec, overwhelmingly British in ethnic composition. When his ideals had seemed to become things of the past—and for various other reasons, including failing eyesight and financial pressures—Macphail discontinued the magazine. IAN ROSS ROBERTSON

University of British Columbia Press. The third largest university press in Canada, UBC Press was founded in 1971 to replace the University of British Columbia's Publication Centre, which had been in operation since 1961. From 1971 to 1980, under its first director Anthony Blicq and editor Jane Fredeman, it published an average of ten books a year within four areas of concentration: western North America, English and French-Canadian literary criticism, Asia and the Pacific Rim, and international law. By 1988 the yearly average of books produced grew to fifteen, and included such notable works as Robin Fisher's *Contact and conflict* (1977), *The Canadian yearbook of international law*, The *BC historical atlas*, and George MacDonald's *Haida monumental art* (1983; rpr. 1994). Despite these and other achievements, with the departure of Blicq in 1980 the Press struggled throughout the decade not only to find an able replacement but also to establish a fresh mandate and editorial direction. Michael Goldberg and Basil Stuart-Stubbs took over for an interim period; followed by James Anderson, and, in 1990, by Peter Milroy, its current director. Among the new policies adopted in 1990 by Milroy, editor Jean Wilson, and the Press's publication's committee was the exclusion of literary criticism from the areas of publication and the broadening of other regional and international undertakings, such as Native Studies, the Canadian North, forestry, and fisheries. To date the Press's list of monographs, collections, and textbooks in print approaches 400 titles. BURKE CULLEN

University of Toronto Press. Founded in 1901, the first university press to be established in Canada and the tenth to be established in North America, the University of Toronto Press Incorporated is one of the largest university presses on the continent. It began as a small printing department of the University, producing examination papers and calendars. It now comprises, along with its publishing activities, a book-manufacturing plant and seven bookstores on three Toronto campuses, and distributes books for about thirty other publishers, most of them Canadian. It was incorporated in 1992 as an independent, not-for-profit corporation maintained outside the University budget. It issues between 120 and 135 new books annually and has a backlist of about 1,500 titles. It also publishes some twenty academic journals, most of them quarterlies. General policies are determined by a board appointed by the University, and publications are approved by an academic editorial board appointed by the president of the university. Its net income, after all operating and capital expenses have been met, is devoted to the publication of scholarly research, reference works, and general books of culture and social significance. Its publications—which have won many international and national awards for their contributions to knowledge and for their design and production—are sold worldwide through a network of exclusive agents and representatives, and, in the United States, through its own office and warehouse in Buffalo.

Publishing mainly in the humanities and social sciences, the Press draws its authors from across Canada and from many other countries. Major multi-volume publications include the *Collected works of John Stuart Mill*, the *Collected works of Erasmus* (translated into

English), the DICTIONARY OF CANADIAN BIOGRAPHY, the *Collected works of Northrop Frye*, the *Letters of Bernard Shaw*, and the David Milne Project. Although most of its works are intended for an academic readership, it also publishes general books of mainly Canadian interest, including the *Literary history of Canada* (1965; rev. 1976), Russell Harper's *Painting in Canada; a history* (1966; 2nd edn 1977), the *Encyclopaedia of music in Canada* (1982; 2nd edn 1992), the three-volume *Historical atlas of Canada* (1987-93), and the annual *Canadian books in print* and *Canadian who's who*. Long-term best-sellers have included John Porter's *Vertical mosaic* (1965), Marshall McLUHAN's *Gutenberg galaxy* (1962), and R. MacGregor Dawson's *Government of Canada* (1947; 5th edn 1970). About 500 of its titles are available in paperback.

IAN MONTAGNES

Urquhart, Jane (b. 1949). Born Jane Carter in Little Long Lac, Ontario, she moved with her family to Toronto at the age of five and was educated at Havergal College. She graduated from the University of Guelph with a B.A. in English (1971) and art history (1976). She married the painter Tony Urquhart in 1976. She has been writer-in-residence at several Canadian universities and has also led creative-writing workshops.

Urquhart's first publications were books of poetry: *I'm walking in the garden of his imaginary palace* (1982; a collaborative effort with her husband); *False shuffles* (1982); and *The little flowers of Madame de Montespan* (1984). Her delicately worded verse explores, among other things, illusion, memory, and transformation in different areas of human experience.

Similar themes are found in her fiction, beginning with *The whirlpool* (1986), three separate stories of nineteenth-century Canadians whose lives are interconnected by different events and symbols, notably that of the whirlpool—to which Canadian history is also linked: a character reflects that the whirlpool is like 'history . . . moving nowhere and endlessly repeating itself'. (In 1992 *The whirlpool*—in French translation—was the first Canadian book to win France's prestigious Prix du Meilleur Livre Étranger.) *Storm glass* (1978) is a collection of stories related to perception, memory, and transformation; it includes an unusual five-story sequence about wheelchairs. *Changing heaven* (1990) is a modern-day *Wuthering Heights*: Ann, a Canadian scholar, travels to England to research Emily Brontë, while two ghosts—the spirits of Brontë herself and of another nineteenth-century woman killed in a balloon crash—haunt the same territory. Urquhart, always intrigued by nineteenth-century culture, was influenced by some 'creative and passionate' contemporary criticism, including Gilbert and Gubar's *The madwoman in the attic* (1979) and Fanny Ratchford's *The Brontës' web of childhood* (1941). The passion that suffused Brontë's fiction is woven throughout this strange, evocative novel as Ann encounters a latter-day Heathcliff. In *Away* (1993) a new series of transatlantic and historical connections are found in her exploration of the Irish influence in Canada. Urquhart, herself of Irish extraction, grew up listening to a wealth of Celtic tales. In the novel, oral tales about the O'Malley family, passed down through four generations of women, encompass aspects of both Irish and Canadian history. In 1994 Urquhart was co-winner of the (Ontario) Trillium Award for *Away*; in the same year she won the Marian ENGEL Award for Outstanding Prose (Fiction) Written by a Canadian Woman.

JENNIE RUBIO

V

Vac, Bertrand. Pseudonym of Aimé PELLETIER.

Vadeboncoeur, Pierre (b. 1920). Born in Montreal's Outremont district, he attended Collège Brébeuf and is a retired lawyer and economist. Vadeboncoeur might have become a judge or cabinet minister, but after working as technical adviser to the Confédération des syndicats nationaux, he became a full-time writer in 1975. He first wrote for *Cité libre* and then for *indépendantiste* and reformist publications and political parties. His first collection of essays, *La ligne du risque* (1963), is comparable to Jean LE MOYNE's *Convergences* (1961). Though he writes about trade-unionism, his true topics are joyfulness, freedom, and creativity. His guiding spirit is the painter Paul-Émile Borduas. 'Art', he writes, 'has been a far more important and less dubious leader for us than history.'

An outspoken polemicist and letter-writer, Vadeboncoeur has not given the bulk of his time to the practice of these 'martial arts'. *Lettres et colères* (1969), *Un génocide en douce* (1976), and other such occasional works pale beside the substantial essay *La dernière heure et la première* (1970), about French Canada's absence from history, which he sees as a delay that may be turned to advantage, a marginal position filled with potential. *Un amour libre* (1970), a story of childhood, is a tale of strength-in-weakness and fresh beginnings, in which Vadeboncoeur plays freely with the fates, and works as much with images as with ideas. The moralist has not, however, disappeared; he re-emerges in *Indépendances* (1972), a eulogy for opposition, for counterstrokes, for youth.

The most controversial of Vadeboncoeur's essays has been *Les deux royaumes* (1978). The magazine *LIBERTÉ* devoted an entire issue (no. 26) to commentary on this book, running the gamut from unqualified praise to utter refutation. Had Vadeboncoeur abandoned his social and political conscience for religious evasiveness? Had he gone from realism to idealism, from audacious writing to sermonizing and commentary in the style of Rousseau, Proust, and André MAJOR? Between the two kingdoms—this world and the other, whatever that might be—Vadeboncoeur maintained a precarious balance. Teetering on the edge of an abstract ideal, he was rescued by what is perceptible in his art, the imprint of his work on the language.

Trois essais sur l'insignifiance (1983), attacking American cultural imperialism and conformity, followed in the Paris edition by a glowing *Lettre à la France*, has been widely discussed. *Essais inactuels* (1987) also contains 'Célébration de la France'—where France is represented as eternal, creative, and revolutionary. *L'absence* (1985), an essay in the second person, is a lyrical reflection and an intimate discourse on art, death, and love. In the same vein, in *Essai sur une pensée heureuse* (1989) and *Le bonheur excessif* (1992) the aesthetic, the ethical, and the metaphysical are called on, and mutually reinforce each other. *Dix-sept tableaux d'enfant* (1991) is at the same time the work of a father, an art critic, and a semiotician. LAURENT MAILHOT

Valgardson, W.D. (b. 1939). William Dempsey Valgardson was born in Winnipeg, but spent most of his childhood in Gimli, Manitoba. He received a B.A. (1961) from United College, a B.Ed. (1965) from the University of Manitoba, and an M.F.A. (1969) in creative writing from the University of Iowa. He served as chair of the English department of Cottey College in Nevada, Missouri, from 1970 to 1974, before returning to Canada to join the creative-writing faculty of the University of Victoria, British Columbia.

Valgardson is the author of two novels, *Gentle sinners* (1980) and *The girl with the Botticelli face* (1992); two collections of poetry, *In the gutting shed* (1976) and *The carpenter of dreams* (1986); and four collections of short stories: *Bloodflowers* (1973), *God is not a fish inspector* (1975), *Red dust* (1978), and *What can't be changed shouldn't be mourned* (1990)—all of which draw on his knowledge of the Icelandic communities near Gimli. In the short stories Valgardson's spare and rigorously concrete style mirrors both the cold, brittle landscape in which the stories are set and the harsh fates that befall most of the central characters. Occasionally, however, they are marred by endings that strain for subtlety. *Gentle sinners*, which won the *Books in Canada* First Novel Award, departs from the realism of the stories to give mythological complexity to the familiar theme of a country boy's struggle against the corruption of town life. In contrast, *The girl with the Botticelli face* is a rather disagreeable novel about a troubled, misogynistic, recently divorced man whose hatred of women, particularly his ex-wife, is at odds with his claimed belief in love and acceptance.

Valgardson has also written several radio plays and is the author of two highly praised children's books: *Thor* (1994) and *Sarah and the people of Sand River* (1996). FRANK DAVEY

Vallières, Pierre. See ESSAYS IN FRENCH: 6.

Vanderhaeghe, Guy (b. 1951). Born and raised in Esterhazy, Saskatchewan, he majored in history at the University of Saskatchewan (B.A., 1971; M.A., 1975) and pursued further studies at the University of Regina (B.Ed., 1978). Though he has worked as a teacher, an archivist, and a researcher, he now devotes his time chiefly to writing. He lives in Saskatoon.

Influenced by such prairie novelists as Margaret LAURENCE, Sinclair ROSS, and Robert KROETSCH, Vanderhaeghe began writing short stories in the late 1970s. 'What I learned from Caesar' was included in *80: best*

Canadian stories; and 'The watcher' was the 1980 winner of *CANADIAN FICTION MAGAZINE*'s annual contributors' prize for short fiction. The twelve stories in *Man descending* (1982), which won a Governor General's Award—ranging in setting from the drought and economic depression of the Prairies in the 1930s to Jubilee year in London—follow in a roughly chronological pattern, from childhood to old age, the pain and disillusionment of various male protagonists as they struggle to transcend their fear and loneliness. Suffused with compassion and subtle humour, Vanderhaeghe's compelling fiction belongs in the prairie tradition to which its author is indebted.

Having established himself as an important new voice in Canadian literature with the success of *Man descending*, Vanderhaeghe collected a number of his earlier short fictions in *The trouble with heroes* (1983), a title that signals his preoccupation here with heroes and notions of heroism in both the classical and the contemporary worlds. What unites these complex forays through time and space is Vanderhaeghe's uniformly affirmative vision of the stubbornness of the human spirit; each story can be read as a brief testament to the determination of individuals to survive physically, emotionally, and spiritually even when circumstances prove bleak and unforgiving. Indeed, in his stories some truer heroism proves to lie in the survival of life, rather than just in the survival of death, in 'the stubborn refusal of men and women to submit to circumstances', as Vanderhaeghe observes.

Vanderhaeghe then turned to writing novels. *My present age* (1984) centres on Ed, a 'man descending', who was already developed in the final two stories of the first collection. Abandoned by his wife Victoria, Ed, an existential anti-hero of the 1980s, embarks on a quixotic quest to find her, the quest becoming his journey back into his own past and his comic and painful confrontations with his own self-deceptions. In *Homesick* (1989), which won the City of Toronto Book Award, Vanderhaeghe returned to the deeply troubled and troubling setting of eastern Saskatchewan. At the novel's centre is the strongwilled Vera Monkman, a widow and the mother of a young boy. A complex and compelling story of her fitful reunion with both her father, an aging widower, and the prairie community in which she lives, *Homesick* probes the often exhausting emotional dynamics of individuals and communities whose sense of 'home' is marked by equal parts longing and claustrophobic terror.

The 1990s saw Vanderhaeghe expand and test his literary and social visions in a number of genres. He returned to the story form with the polished *Things as they are?* (1992), ten pieces that reflect on what one character describes as 'the pitiless refusal to delude oneself' and to see clearly in order to struggle towards the 'acceptance of things as they are'.

Awarded the Governor General's Award and the Saskatchewan Book Awards, and shortlisted for the Giller Prize, Vanderhaeghe's third novel, *The Englishman's boy* (1996), comprises two causally linked and masterfully entwined stories: the cold-blooded massacre of an encampment of Assiniboine at Cypress Hills in 1873 (based on an actual though little-known incident from Canadian history) and the wholly fictional recounting of a 1920s Hollywood mogul's obsessive drive to manipulate this tale in support of his own morally degraded social vision. Serving this mogul is Harry Vincent, a relocated Saskatchewan native whose own moral passivity and stalled writing career render him the stereotypical Canadian foil to the American's powerful revisionist impulse. Hired to track down the elusive Shorty McAdoo, a cowboy extra and reputed 'Indian fighter' who may (or may not) know the 'true' story of the sadistic massacre, Vincent remains woefully unwilling or unable to scrutinize his own complicity as the increasingly sinister chain of events unfolds around him. Vanderhaeghe eschews his usual comic overtones in *The Englishman's boy* in order to foreground the intense though characteristically understated ironies permeating the lives and stories of his main characters. The novel marks a kind of watershed in Vanderhaeghe's fiction and is his most accomplished work to date, accentuating his ear for well-tuned dialogue, his sensitivity to language and sparse rhythms, and his apparently effortless evocation of time, place, and character.

Vanderhaeghe has also published two plays that garnered critical and public attention: *I had a job I liked. Once.* (1992), which won the CANADIAN AUTHORS' ASSOCIATION Award for Drama, and *Dancock's dance* (1996). In the former, which was first performed at Saskatoon's Persephone Theatre in 1991, a police station serves as the setting for a young man's confrontation with the law; his interrogation by a rule-conscious sergeant leads the officer to the painful discovery of the impossibility of passing judgement. In the latter, which was first performed at the Persephone in 1995, the setting is the Saskatchewan Hospital for the Insane during the great flu epidemic of 1918. The inmates, led by the shell-shocked

Lieutenant John Dancock, take over the hospital's nursing and administrative duties and teach a rigid superintendent the relative impossibility of strict codes of conduct and the need for human and humane compassion.

Since 1993 Vanderhaeghe has been Visiting Professor of English at St Thomas More College, University of Saskatchewan. In 1987 he won the British Geoffrey Faber Memorial Prize, and in 1997 he received an honorary D.Litt. from the University of Saskatchewan.

Vanderhaeghe was interviewed by Morris Wolfe for *Books in Canada* 13 (Feb. 1984) and by Andrew Garrod for *Speaking for myself: Canadian writers in interview* (1986). See also Nicholas von Maltzahn, *Guy Vanderhaeghe*, Profiles in Canadian Literature, series 8 (1991). DAVID STAINES

van der Mark, Christine (1917-69). Born in Calgary, Alberta, she attended Normal School and taught for five years in rural Alberta schools. She then completed a B.A. and M.A. at the University of Alberta, studying creative writing under F.M. Salter; in 1946 she submitted her first novel, *In due season*, as her thesis. During three years of writing and teaching at the university she married, and from 1953 to 1964 her husband's work led the family to Montreal, Pakistan, the USA, England, and the Sudan, before they settled in Ottawa. Despite her many travels she continued writing stories, articles, and a short novel with a Pakistani setting, *Hassan*. In 1960 she began *Honey in the rock* (1966), to be completed in Ottawa and followed by three unpublished works: *Where the long river flows*, a novel of the Mackenzie; *Paul Goss*, about a rural teacher succumbing to the isolation of northern Alberta; and *No longer bound*, an autobiographical piece.

In due season (1947) explores, from a distinctive female point of view, the human costs of pioneering. Its protagonist develops a farm in the northern-Alberta bush and raises a family through the 1930s with no help from her amiably shiftless husband. In the process she becomes hard and unscrupulous, alienating her neighbours and losing her daughter to a Métis sweetheart. A vivid and convincing evocation of northern life, the novel won the Oxford-Crowell prize for Canadian fiction. *Honey in the rock* is less elemental and more social in its emphasis. Interweaving the romantic awakenings and frustrations of a tightly knit community of 'Brethren in Christ' in southern Alberta in 1936-7, it has moments of dramatic intensity; but the plot dissipates its force in complications, and the setting lacks the compelling quality of *In due season*.

See 'Afterword' by van der Mark's daughter, Dorothy Wise, in the 1966 reprint of *In due season*. DICK HARRISON

van Herk, Aritha (b. 1954). Born in Wetaskiwin, Alberta, to Dutch immigrant parents, she studied at the University of Alberta (B.A., 1977; M.A., 1978). Van Herk's first published short story won the Miss Chatelaine Short Fiction Award in 1976; her first novel, *Judith* (1978), won the $50,000 Seal Books First Novel Award; and in 1978 she received the Alberta Achievement Award in Literature. The editor and co-editor of several anthologies of fiction, her own short fiction widely published, and her novels available in multiple editions, van Herk is a professor of literature and creative writing at the University of Calgary.

Judith, the story of a young woman's awakening into feminist consciousness as a secretary/mistress-turned-pig-farmer (a re-visioned Circe), launched van Herk's career as a bawdy/body images-of-women novelist whose work merges mythic and historical women with contemporary feminist heroines. Judith struggles with a gendered inheritance that would insist she remain 'Judy', as she comes to terms with her eroticized relationships with her father, her boss, her neighbours' son, and herself. The novel reduces formal experiment to a disturbing narrative slippage between the present and past selves of the protagonist, Judith/Judy, to illustrate her struggle with the stereotypes of Daddy's girl, boss's mistress, spinster farmer, and potential wife.

van Herk's second novel, *The tent peg* (1981) fuses the biblical Jael with J.L., a young woman who disguises herself as a man in order to be hired as cook for a geological survey team working in the far North. There, once her gender identity is known, the story seems less about her search for independence (it comes remarkably easily) and more about how her presence mythically transforms the lives of the men with whom she works. van Herk's own experience in the North, as well as her love/hate affair with the masculine penchant for naming, mapping, and mining the land, receives its first fictional treatment in this novel.

van Herk returns to these matters in her most bawdy novel, *No fixed address: an amorous journey* (1986; nominated for a Governor General's Award), a picaresque journey that reverses the usual gender dynamics of the genre with its sexually aggressive, multi-talented heroine Archne Manteia, pantyless regional sales rep for Ladies' Comfort Limited, specializing in women's underwear. This job supplies the material reason for Arachne's travels, but the psychic reason is that Arachne loves motion for its illusion of escape from her constricted possibilities as a woman, and the opportunity it affords for mapless intercourse with the land and actual intercourse with as many different types of men as possible. Arachne eventually disappears off the map into the far North, leaving only a trail of coloured panties behind her.

Places far from Ellesmere: a geografictione: explorations on site (1990) continues van Herk's work on genre bending, rebellious women, and the North, in its fusion of autobiography, travel book, fiction, and criticism, the latter in the form of an extended essay on *Anna Karenina*. Taking herself and Anna (in the form of Tolstoy's book) to Ellesmere Island offers revisionist opportunities similar to her earlier work, but in both more theorized and more personalized forms. This blend of the theoretical, personal, fictional, and critical is also the hallmark of van Herk's two collections of essays, *In visible ink: crypto-frictions* (1991) and *A frozen tongue* (1992), where the writer-as-critic engages in dialogue and debate with her multiple and conflicting predecessors and contemporaries, particularly writers from the Canadian West. These essays are stylistic and self-consciously gendered rivals to Robert KROETSCH's essays on similar themes.

DONNA PALMATEER PENNEE

Van Schendel, Michel (b. 1929). Born in France, he immigrated to Canada in 1952, settling in Montreal. Since 1969 he has taught at the Université du Québec à Montréal. He quickly became known as a journalist, critic, essayist, and translator, and also wrote scripts for documentary films—but he is best known as a poet. *Poèmes de l'Amérique étrangère* (1958) and *Variations sur la pierre* (1964) are examples of a tendency to determine and to know himself and his physical environment by means of his poetry, a tendency that has been seen as a poetic analogy to the fictional worlds of Jacques GODBOUT and Hubert AQUIN. Van Schendel won a Governor General's Award for *De l'oeil et de l'écoute* (1980). *L'impression du souci; ou L'étendue de la parole* (1993) combines two extended prose poems. The first, 'N gatifs: poème critique', envisions a number of photographs that are not displayed but come to life through Schendel's charged prose. The second, 'Sentiers pour un oeillet: critique du poème', sets up a journal about the writing of poetry. Together these two poems merge critical and poetic idioms into a highly expressive language that pays testimony to specific events but does not lose sight of historical contexts.

From 1968 to 1971 Van Schendel edited the journal *Socialisme québécois*. His collected essays are published in *Rebonds critiques: questions de littérature*, of which two of three projected volumes appeared in 1992 and 1993.

STEFAN HAAG

Van Vogt, A.E. (b. 1912). Alfred Elton Van Vogt was born to parents of Dutch ancestry in Winnipeg, Manitoba, and raised in Neville and Swift Current, Saskatchewan, and then in Morden and Winnipeg, Man. He wrote his earliest science-fiction and fantasy stories in the Winnipeg Public Library before moving to Ottawa, where he was employed by the Department of National Defence. He then lived for two years in Toronto. Van Vogt's first story, 'Black destroyer', appeared in the July 1939 issue of *Astounding Science*, along with fiction by Robert A. Heinlein and Isaac Asimov, and this conjunction of talents marked the beginning of SF's so-called Golden Age. With this story, subsequently included in *The voyage of the Space Beagle* (1950), Van Vogt found his *métier*: incident-packed prose, concepts galore, superhuman conflict, heroic action to save civilization if not entire solar-systems, and dream-like logic. He wrote some 600,000 words of fantastic fiction during the Canadian years, including much of his most imaginative prose. Between 1940 and 1942 he published in magazines the original versions of *The weapon shops of Isher* (1951), an epic of libertarianism, and *Slan* (1946; rev. 1951), a classic novel of the persecution of a mutant whose telepathic powers hold the key to the survival of individualism.

In 1944 Van Vogt immigrated to the United States and since then has resided in Hollywood, California, where he was briefly associated with Dianetics and Scientology. One of the leading contributors to SF's Golden Age, he has written more than fifty novels and collections of stories, including *The world of Null-A* (1948), *The war against the Rull* (1959), *The Silkie* (1969), and *The battle of forever* (1971). As he once explained, 'Science fiction, as I personally try to write it, glorifies man and his future.'

JOHN ROBERT COLOMBO

Vassanji, M.G. (b. 1950). Moyez G. Vassanji was born in Nairobi, Kenya, and grew up in Dar es Salaam, Tanzania. After his high-school education he moved to the United States, where he studied physics at the Massachusetts Institute of Technology (B.Sc., 1974) and at the University of Pennsylvania (Ph.D., 1978). This was also a period when he was actively involved in the study of Sanskrit and ancient Indian literature. He then moved to Toronto, Canada, and taught physics at the University of Toronto before becoming a full-time writer. He lives in Toronto with his wife and two children.

Vassanji began his literary career with the publication of *The gunny sack* in 1989, a novel that won the Regional Commonwealth Prize. *No new land* (1991), set in Toronto, deals with the immigrant community in the suburb of Don Mills, and recalls the Indians from East Africa whose mistreatment in Uganda inspired a mass exodus. A witty and poignant collection of short stories entitled *Uhuru Street*, set in Dar es Salaam, came out in 1992. His novel *The book of secrets* (1994) won the first Giller Prize. Vassanji is also the founder of the journal *The Toronto Review of Contemporary Writing Abroad* (known earlier as *The Toronto South Asian Review*).

At the end of the first chapter of *No new land*, the narrator claims that 'we are but creatures of our origins, and however stalwartly we march forward ... the ghosts from our past stand not far behind and are not easily shaken off.' These ghosts have been Vassanji's constant preoccupation as he attempts in his fiction to reclaim the past and give expression to the experiences of his community, which migrated from India to East Africa at the turn of the century. The need to portray the complexity of the Indian community gives to his writing a sense of urgency, commitment, and a strong referential surface. At the same time, his awareness of the constructedness of history lends a metafictional and experimental quality to his work. The combination of realism and artifice is at its best in *The book of secrets*.

See Charles Sarvan, 'M.G. Vassanji's *The gunny sack*: a reflection on history and the novel', *Modern Fiction Studies* (Autumn 1991); Amin Malak, 'Ambivalent affiliations and the postcolonial condition: the fiction of M.G. Vassanji', *World Literature Today* (Spring 1993); Michael Bucknor, 'Postcolonial enquiries in Vassanji's *The gunny sack*', *The Toronto Review of Contemporary Writing Abroad* (Summer 1995).

CHELVA KANAGANAYAKAM

Véhicule Press. It began in November 1972 as a literary co-op and small printing company in the back room of the Véhicule Art Gallery in Montreal—with the aid of LIP (Local Initiatives Program) money. Simon Dardick joined the co-op in the fall of 1973 and eventually became chief publisher. In 1979 Véhicule was accepted into the block-grant program of the CANADA COUNCIL. The printing company was dissolved in 1980 and Véhicule's publishing became primarily (not entirely) dedicated to English writing in Montreal.

GEOFF HANCOCK

Vézina, **France**. See DRAMA IN FRENCH 1948 to 1981: 4.

Victims of tyranny*, *The (2 vols, Buffalo, 1847). This early Canadian novel by Charles E. Beardsley is a republican's version of the political and personal conflicts in the brief public career of a young Irish immigrant to York (Toronto), Upper Canada. The hero, Joseph Wilcox, is a thinly disguised representation of the actual Joseph Willcocks, a member of the legislative assembly and critic of government who was killed fighting with the Americans in the War of 1812. Wilcox is presented as a romantic paragon, a champion of truth and justice and tragic victim of the forces of self-serving oligarchy—the 'Family Compact', epitomized by the Rev. Whifler, the principal antagonist, and Mr Carleton (caricatures of the Rev. John Strachan and Provincial Secretary William Jarvis). These power-obsessed villains eventually provoke Wilcox's enlistment with the invading American forces and he is ultimately killed while championing republican ideas. The compression of events covering more than a decade into the space of several months heightens the drama of the novel. One of its more engaging characters, ironically, is Sam Johnson—to his unresourceful creator a resourceful and witty model American, clearly patterned on the stereotyped Sam Slick of Thomas Chandler HALIBURTON. Though characterization tends towards caricature, and dialogue towards diatribe, and though the novel's concluding section is too diffuse, *The victims of tyranny* is nonetheless an impassioned and provocative narrative of actual characters and events from early Canadian history.

The author, about whom nothing is known, was apparently a member of the republican branch of an American family divided by the American Revolution. The Loyalist branches of the Beardsleys settled in New Brunswick and Upper Canada, where the men became prominent lawyers, and maintained contact with the American branches. The knowledge of the internal affairs of York and Upper Canada displayed in the novel suggests that Beardsley must have lived, for a while at least, in Toronto. He very likely had his novel published in Buffalo because he could not find a Toronto publisher.

CHARLES R. STEELE

Vie en prose*, *La (1980). This novel by Yolande VILLEMAIRE caused something of a sensation because of its exuberance and formal experimentation. Its self-consciousness begins with the very title, playing on the popular Edith Piaf song (*La vie en rose*). The book interweaves a novel-in-the-making; a journal; a collections of letters; fragments of conversation; reflections on writing, literature, and the counter-culture; and a heterogeneity of places and people.

A certain Vava (Eva Vera Indianapolis!) has the first and almost last (nearly identical, equally vague) word during a meeting of a women's collective that is considering a manuscript for publication, submitted by one 'Noémie Artaud'. A report on this is being prepared by a central 'character', Nane Yelle, whose 'real' name is Noé Vladimira Yelle, also known as Danielle Yelle. It is never clear whether Nane is a character in a novel being written by Solange Tellier or Thériault, or one of the other 'characters' of *La vie en prose*, or is a character of the aforementioned novel itself. Perhaps she is all three. Many of the members of the collective bear anagrammatic names (Nane-Anne, Alice-Celia, Laure-Aurel), indicating an identity that is always provisional, ephemeral, substitutive, according to the critic Pierre Nepveu. He sees Villemaire as a product of an environment where reality is elusive, the territory of culture fragmented, and feelings of collective solidarity are breaking down. In *La vie en prose* this is evident in the higgledy-piggledy juxtaposition of events in California, New York, Provence, Rome, Arizona, Britain, Mexico, Egypt, with various locations in Quebec, and in the eccentric linking of Rosa Luxembourg and Marilyn Monroe. Real events—the 1976 Montreal Olympics, the assassination of Italian premier Aldo Moro, the death of John Diefenbaker—are inserted into the trials and tribulations of the fictional women mentioned above.

Conversations are reported in direct and indirect style, most often in hyper-*JOUAL*, with some humorous turns of phrase that play on the ambiguity of unassimilated borrowings from English. This self-deprecating look at popular Québécois speech is coupled with grave quotations from Émile NELLIGAN and, more often, parodic puns on lines from Réjean DUCHARME, Claude GAUVREAU, Hubert AQUIN, and others. References to literature range through Quebec writing to European and American authors, and to feminists (Sylvia Plath, Virginia Woolf, Kate Millett, Gertrude Stein, and Anaïs Nin). Feminism, however, is just one minor component in a heterogeneous framework of cultural and socio-political references of great variety. The stress is on the counter-cultural, the writing celebrating energy more than meaning.

BEN-Z. SHEK

Viets, Roger (1738-1811). Born in Simsbury, Connecticut, he prepared himself for Church of England orders at Yale College, graduating in 1758. After several years as a lay reader, he was ordained in London in 1763 and returned to Simsbury, where he was parish priest until he immigrated to Nova Scotia as a Loyalist refugee in late 1785. During the American Revolution, Viets had remained loyal to the monarchy and was jailed in 1777 on suspicion of aiding British fugitives. Upon immigrating to Nova Scotia he was assigned to the parish of Digby, a new Loyalist town, and served there as rector of Trinity Church until his death. He published six sermons between 1787 and 1800, and left a large collection in manuscript form. His theology was orthodox and not particularly challenging intellectually, but in their logical clarity and persuasive rhetoric his sermons reveal a strong, active, passionate mind as they project a vision of an ordered, cohesive society bound together by unanimity and mutual respect. The implication is that all the fundamental elements of human happiness lie within the reach of the Loyalist refugees. Viets' *Annapolis Royal; a poem* (Halifax, 1788), written in the same vein, is of historical interest as the first separate imprint of verse written and published in what is now Canada. The author's emphasis falls on harmony—in nature, in man, and in the universe—and the image that emerges is therefore idyllic; but the poem explicitly integrates life in Loyalist Nova Scotia into the vision of emotional, moral, and spiritual contentment that was central to prevailing eighteenth-century views of human experience and social purpose. The poem is inspirational, not because it is idyllic, but because it asserts that the recently dispossessed refugees are not isolated from the mainstream of human civilization. T.B. Vincent has edited a modern edition of this poem (1979).

TOM VINCENT

Vigneault, Gilles (1928-96). Born in Natashquan, Quebec, on the north shore of the St Lawrence, he was educated at Université Laval, where he was influenced and encouraged by Félix-Antoine SAVARD. He then taught at various high schools and at Laval, during which time he founded *Émourie* (in 1959), a poetry magazine that ran for thirteen issues, and the publishing firm Éditions de l'Arc. In 1960 he made his début as a *chansonnier*; his first triumphant Montreal concert was held later that year. The universal quality of his *chansons* and his individual and versatile performing style—his voice, sometimes almost raucous in exultation, at other times tender; his jigs and step-dances; and the wild semaphoring of his long arms—made him equally popular in English Canada and in Europe. His most famous *chanson*, 'Mon pays'—which he claimed was not separatist or even nationalist in intent, as is generally believed, but a personal lament for coldness and the inability to share love or experience—won an international award when sung by Monique Leyrac in Poland in 1965. He was awarded the Molson Prize in 1982.

Vigneault's poems and *chansons* alike are carefully structured, the work of a highly disciplined writer. Some vividly describe his native region of Natashquan, its violent seasons and life lived precariously between the forest and the sea, and such characters as Jack Monoloy and Jos Monferrand, real persons from his youth whom he raised to mythic proportions. Woman often appears in these poems as nature or explicitly as a river or some other aspect of the region for which he felt tenderness. More personal poems concern love and the difficulty of loving, solitude and the passage of time, and what man has done with his world. His collections are *Étraves* (1959); *Balises* (1964); *Avec les vieux mots* (1964); *Pour une soirée de chansons* (1965); *Quand les bateaux s'en vont* (1965), winner of a Governor General's Award; *Les gens de mon pays* (1967); *Tam ti delam* (1967); *Paroles de chanson* (1969); *Ce que je dis c'est en passant* (1970); *Les dicts du voyageur sédentaire* (1970); *Exergues* (1971); *Les neufs couplets* (1973); *Je vous entends rêver* (1974); *Natashquan, le voyage immobile* (1976); *À l'encre blanche* (1977); *Silences, poèmes 1957-1977* (1978); *Autant de fois que feuille tremble au vent* (1982), which includes as well as brief lyric poems a short story and photographs of Vigneault; and *Assonnances* (1984). In *Le printemps: quatre saisons vues par un peintre et un poète* (1996) the painter Fernand Labele has illustrated a number of Vigneault's poems and songs of the last half-century. Vigneault also published *Contes sur la pointe des pieds* (1960), *Contes du coin de l'oeil* (1966), and *La petite heure* (1979)—collections of brief prose pieces, more fables than stories, that make some comment on man's frailty or his alienation from nature and himself. The first two books were published together as *Les dicts du voyageur sédentaire: contes poétiques* (1970). *Contes sur la pointe des pieds* is also available in a bilingual edition, with translation by Paul Allard, as *Tales (sur la pointe des pieds)* (1972). Vigneault wrote the text for *Où la lumière chante* (1966), a book about Quebec City with photographs by François Lafortune. *Gilles Vigneault* (Paris, 1977) is a collection of his songs, with music.

Vigneault's poetry is discussed in *An outline of contemporary French-Canadian literature* (1972) by J. Raymond Brazeau. Studies in French are by Aline Robitaille (1968) and by Lucien Rioux (Paris, 1969) in the Chansonniers d'aujourd'hui series. See also Donald Smith, *Gilles Vigneault, conteur et poète* (1984). *Fernand Seguin rencontre Gilles Vigneault* (1969), which is based largely on the transcript of a television interview, presents Vigneault's own thoughts about his life and work. English translations of some of his poems are in *The poetry of French Canada in translation* (1970) edited by John GLASSCO.

JOYCE MARSHALL

Vigneault, Robert. See ESSAYS IN FRENCH: 5.

Villemaire, Yolande (b. 1949). Born in Saint-Augustin, Comté des Deux-Montagnes, near Montreal, she holds a B.A. in dramatic art (1970) and an M.A. in literary studies (1974) from the Université du Québec à Montréal, and writes on theatre and literature for many French-language periodicals. A poet, novelist, and playwright, she has taught literature at the Rosemont CEGEP since 1974. Her varied, ever-changing writing reflects her travels (in Egypt, France, Morocco, Mexico, Spain, India), and her spiritual exploration. Villemaire's first book, *Meurtres à blanc* (1974), is a comic thriller, packed with action and corpses, in which Marie Dubreuil, a Québécoise spy and whodunit fan, sets out to find another woman who is on the run in Morocco. The exuberance of the writing and the originality of the form of this novel heralded a remarkable writer.

Following two collections of poetry, *Machine-t-elle* (1974) and *Terre de mue* (1978), and a story, *Que du stage blood* (1977), Villemaire published *La* VIE EN PROSE (1980), a fragmented work of celebratory writing. At once a novel, poem, and essay, it presents several female characters—members of a women's editorial collective—in a chronicle in which lives lived and written collide. Transgressing the borders of fiction, drawing on esoteric beliefs, and making full use of intertextuality, Villemaire was awarded the *Journal de Montréal*'s prize for young authors. She also won Radio-Canada's prize for radio scripts (1980) for her play *Belles de nuit*, published in 1983 with two other plays, *Les égoûts de New York* and *Un jour de printemps l'hiver*. Pursuing the exploration of writing that began with *La vie en prose*, in 1982 Villemaire published three works: *Adrénaline* (poetry and prose), *Ange amazone* (a novel), and *Du côté hiéroglyphe de ce qu'on appelle le réel* (prose). She founded the women's writing group Rrose Sélavy, which produced collective publications and performance events between 1983 and 1988. Two collections of poetry are related: *Les coïncidences terrestres* (1983) and *Jeunes femmes rouges toujours plus belles* (1984). A more focused novel, less fragmented than Villemaire's other fiction, and steeped in passion and sensuality, is *La constellation du cygne* (1985; *Journal de Montréal* literary prize). It tells the story of Celia Rosenberg, a young Jewish prostitute whose lover is a Nazi officer; the novel's settings are the Paris of 1940, Germany, and Poland. A collection of poems also appeared in 1985 under the title *Quartz et mica*. *Vava* (1989) is a 700-hundred-page minutely detailed chronicle of eighteen years in the life of Vava Lacleur, a passionate young woman who is twenty in 1968 (and a character in *La vie en prose*). From 1989 to 1991 Villemaire lived in an ashram in Maharashtra, India, returning to Quebec with a novel, *Le dieu dansant* (1995), and a collection of poetry, *La lune indienne* (1994).

RAYMOND BERTIN

Virgo, Seán (b. 1940). Born in Mtarfa, Malta, to an Anglo-Irish family, Virgo has experienced the picaresque lifestyle of Ireland's Travelling People (Gypsies). He has lived in England (B.A., University of Nottingham), Greece, Ireland, and, finally, Canada—always looking for a possible state of grace. He has earned his living from writing, and from teaching at various Canadian universities, including that of Victoria, British Columbia, and Waterloo, Ontario—where he was a significant mentor to younger writers.

Virgo's collections of poetry—*Pieces for the old earth man* (1973); *Island* (1975), with Paul and Lutia Lauzon; *Kiskatinaw songs* (1977), with Susan MUSGRAVE; *Deathwatch on Skidegate Narrows* (1979); and *Selected poems* (1992)—resonate with the influences of Native culture and spirit religion from time spent in the Queen Charlotte Islands of British Columbia. In these books Virgo is the medium for a fusion of Celtic and Aboriginal voices. His style—clean, cryptic, and allusive—is almost liturgical in its artful simplicity.

In Virgo's fiction—*White lies and other fictions* (1979), *Through the eyes of a cat: Irish stories* (1983), *Selakhi* (1987), *Wormwood* (1989), *White lies . . . plus two* (1990), *Waking in Eden* (1990), and the chapbook story *The scream of the butterfly* (1996), an account of a metaphysical experience on the west coast of Vancouver Island—the poetic dialectic of innocence and experience is his machinery for confabulation. The novel *Selakhi* is a re-creation of the life of the artist Paul Rimbaud. Central to every story is lost or potential salvation and apocalyptic intimations that the human and natural order are ever threatened by the outburst of so-called civilization.

LINDA ROGERS

Vizinczey, Stephen (b. 1933). Born in Káloz, Hungary, he had three youthful plays banned by Communist censors, but graduated with honours from Budapest's Academy of Theatre and Film Arts in the spring of the fateful year 1956. A few months later he was fighting in the revolution; not long after, with the revolutionaries defeated by the Soviets, he was on his way to the West. In retrospect, this early life presages his development as a romantic intellectual who injects contemporary ideas into works of wide popular appeal. By 1957 he was in Montreal, learning English while writing scripts for the National Film Board. In 1961 he founded and edited a short-lived but much-admired magazine, *Exchange*. In the mid-1960s he wrote his first novel while working on CBC radio documentaries in Toronto. Discouraged by the tepid response of Canadian publishers, he created a one-book publishing company, Contemporary Canada Press, and brought out *In praise of older women: the amorous recollections of András Vajda* (1965), a crisply written account of a young man's sexual awakening, narrated by a Hungarian-born philosophy professor at the University of Saskatchewan. A celebrated best-seller in Canada, it eventually appeared in many successful translations, and was twice the basis for feature films, in 1977 and 1997. Vizinczey shortly after moved to England and began writing for, among others, *The Times* and the *Sunday Telegraph*; his essays have appeared as two impressive collections, *The rules of chaos* (1969) and *Truth and lies in literature* (1986). His long-awaited second novel, *An innocent millionaire* (1983), turned out to be a sweeping, Balzacian view of modern American society, examining the Mafia, corporate polluters, and a corrupt justice system through the eyes of a young man who finds sunken treasure in the Caribbean. *The man with the magic touch*, a novel of social criticism influenced by magic realism, has been successfully published in Spanish but has yet to find an English-language publisher the author regards as adequate. Vizinczey translated and introduced *Be faithful unto death* (1995), a Hungarian classic by Zsigmond Moricz, originally published in 1921.

ROBERT FULFORD

Voaden, Herman (1903-91). Born in London, Ontario, he graduated from Queen's University in 1923 and then embarked on a long teaching career that included positions at Toronto's Central High School of Commerce (head of English, 1928-64), Queen's University, and the University of Toronto. In the 1920s Voaden was also active as a director and actor at Hart House Theatre, University of Toronto; the Detroit Repertory Theatre; and the Sarnia Little Theatre. In 1930-1 he studied drama at Yale University with George Pierce Baker, and later held several key administrative positions in Canadian arts organizations. He was president of the Canadian Arts Council (1945-8) and national director of the Canadian Conference of the Arts (1966-8). He was a Fellow of the Royal Society of Arts and a Member of the Order of Canada.

The promotion of a Canadian artistic culture and identity, together with teaching, consumed a good deal of Voaden's time and energy; but he also managed to make notable contributions to Canadian experimental theatre and to edit several valuable drama anthologies. His career as a playwright began with the expressionist *Symphony: a drama of motion and light for a new theatre*, co-written with the painter Lowrie Warrener in 1930; it was published in the journal *Canadian Drama* in 1982. Rejecting what he saw as the mediocrity and stifling uniformity of contemporary theatre, he created in *Symphony* what he termed 'symphonic theatre', consisting of a striking coalescence of light, music, dance, and rythmic speech. At Yale, Voaden wrote a realistic drama of the north called *Wilderness*—in *Canada's last plays: the developing mosaic*, vol.3 (1980) edited by Anton Wagner—but a revised version, *Rocks*, first produced in 1932, again revealed Voaden's interest in dramatic innovation. The experiment continued with *Earth song* (1976; prod. 1932), *Hill-land* (prod. 1934), and *Murder pattern* (1980; prod. 1936). *Murder pattern* (based on an actual Ontario murder case) is Voaden's best play, and combines a clear narrative line with drum-beats, chorus, and an expressionistic set and lighting. Adaptations and more original work followed. *MARIA CHAPDELAINE*, an adaptation of Louis HÉMON's novel, was performed in 1938 and needed a large complement of choir, orchestra, dancers, narrators, and actors. *Ascend as the sun* was produced in Toronto in 1942; *Esther*, a dramatic symphony with music by Godfrey Ridout, was performed, also in Toronto, in 1952; and *Emily Carr*, a stage biography, was produced in Kingston in 1960.

Among the anthologies Voaden edited were *Six Canadian plays* (1930), *On stage: plays for school and community* (1945; rev. in 1966 as *'Nobody waved good-bye' and other plays*), *Four plays of our time* (1960), and *Look both ways: theatre experiences* (1975). Of these, *Six Canadian plays* remains the most important, representing as it does the first attempt to bring together a collection of Canadian dramatic literature. The six plays, all with northern settings, were written for a competition organized by Voaden at the Central High School of Commerce in 1929. The collection, said Voaden in his preface, 'attempts to strike the note of Canadianism which some of our painters have asserted with such courage in their own medium of expression.'

As a playwright Voaden remained isolated from predominant fashions and conventions; much of his work was too complex (and too expensive) for regular production. As theatrical administrator and theorist, however, he had a vital and positive effect on the shape of twentieth-century Canadian theatre.

A vision of Canada: Herman Voaden's dramatic works 1928-1945 (1993), edited by Anton Wagner, contains a wide selection of Voaden's plays, together with a comprehensive and sympathetic introduction and several useful appendices. Typescripts of several of Voaden's plays are in the Metropolitan Toronto Library, and a 1976 taped interview with the playwright is in the Public Archives of Ontario. The Voaden Papers are in the York University Archives, Toronto.

L.W. CONOLLY

Voix et Images. This magazine was first conceived in Oct. 1968 as 'Cahiers de Sainte-Marie', but on publication appeared as *Littérature canadienne*. The following year the name was changed to *Voix et Images du pays*. It was published under the auspices of the literary studies department of the Université du Québec à Montréal, directed by Renald Bérubé. Its nine numbers, irregularly produced, were chiefly devoted to literary and cultural works having to do with Quebec. In Sept. 1975 the magazine changed its name again to *Voix et Images*, but later appended as a subtitle a new version of one of its former titles, 'Littérature québécoise'. Appearing three times a year, it was directed by Jacques Allard and an editorial board consisting of Renald Bérubé, Joseph Bonenfant, André BROCHU, and various academics from Quebec and Canadian universities. From then on the magazine contained an interview with a notable author, studies of that author's work, and a bibliography, along with studies of other authors' works, literary articles, and bibliographical notes. In 1981 André Vanasse replaced Allard as editor—the members of the 1982 editorial board included Allard, Bernard Andrès, André Brochu, Jacques Michon, and Lucie Robert—but the format remained the same. Having undergone a period when a semiotic orientation was dominant, the magazine returned to a more eclectic approach and to its original concern for literary history and related subjects, and textual analysis.

After 1983, while continuing as the only scholarly journal devoted solely to Québécois literature, *Voix et Images* strengthened its reputation under the successive direction of Bernard Andrès, Jacques Pelletier, Lucie Robert, and Louise Dupré. Published three times a year, it strove to maintain a balance, covering both established and promising new authors, and specific themes. The year 1994 was typical, with issues on SAINT-DENYS-GARNEAU, Anne-Marie ALONZO, and 'Science et fiction au Québec'. Moreover, following the demise of the *Revue d'histoire littéraire du Québec et du Canada français*, *Voix et Images* welcomed more contributions on literary history, and in the areas of the eighteenth and nineteenth centuries—as in numbers 50 ('L'âge de la critique'), 59 ('Archéologie du littéraire au Québec'), and 65 (Henri-Raymond CASGRAIN). The magazine published indexes in 1988 and 1992.

JACQUES PELLETIER/PIERRE HÉBERT

Vonarburg, Élisabeth. See FANTASTIC LITERATURE AND SCIENCE FICTION IN FRENCH.

Wacousta; or, The Prophecy (3 vols, Edinburgh, 1832). The complex plot of this forest Gothic romance by John RICHARDSON unfolds through surprise and flashback: each chapter opens with an astonishment that is followed by an explanation. Set in Fort Detroit during Pontiac's 1763 rollback of British power, the story is the culmination of a grievance that originated during the savaging of the Scottish Highlands following the defeat of the Jacobites in 1745. We learn at the novel's end that Sir Reginald Morton fell in love with the sequestered Clara Beverley while on occupation duty, only to lose her to the treachery of his friend, Charles De Haldimar. Through a frame-up, Morton also lost his commission. Two decades later, having fled to France and served as an officer in the famous battle on the Plains of Abraham in 1759, Morton has become the dreaded Wacousta, Pontiac's chief adviser during the siege of the fort commanded by De Haldimar. Wacousta's scheme of revenge, ultimately fatal, also ends in the deaths of De Haldimar, his younger son Charles, and his daughter Clara.

The epigraph comes from an eighteenth-century imitation of Elizabethan revenge tragedy, and the novel depicts a noble spirit maddened by injustice, whose scheme of vengeance exceeds in horror the original wrong. The violence and suspense that mark the narrative—the surefire formula of hushed expectancy broken by shock—coexist with tedious exposition and courtship scenes. The dialogue often demonstrates why the novel was quickly adapted into a melodrama: '"Almighty Providence", aspirated the sinking Clara . . . "can it be that the human heart can undergo such change?" "Ha! ha! such cold pompous insolence amuses me," vociferated Wacousta.' Nevertheless *Wacousta*'s intensity and energy, its moments of passion and high feeling, its depiction of nature as both comforting and monstrous, its sexually perverse undertones—and its development of the potential of Canadian space and time to include all this—have bestowed upon it a continuing critical interest.

In addition, its garrison-versus-wilderness theme, and its ultimate moral equation of the two, have influenced much subsequent Canadian writing; its preoccupation with violence and terror and its retailing of sexual perversity interest a contemporary public; and the sheer exuberance of its plotting appeals to a postmodern sensibility. Rather than sober speculation and representation, *Wacousta* resembles a nightmare: it embodies an aspect of the Canadian imagination in search of the fantastic and surreal.

Every edition since the first has been significantly shortened, the most reduced being the 1967 NEW CANADIAN LIBRARY edition; the present NCL edition, with an Afterword by James REANEY, is complete and unabridged. In 1987 the CENTRE FOR THE EDITING OF EARLY CANADIAN TEXTS published a scholarly edition, edited by D.R. Cronk. James Reaney's dramatization was staged in 1978.

See Dennis Duffy, *'A tale of sad reality:' John Richardson's 'Wacousta'* (1993), in the ECW PRESS Canadian Fiction Studies series (1993).

DENNIS DUFFY

Waddington, Miriam (b. 1917). Miriam Dworkin was born into an intellectual Jewish family in Winnipeg, Manitoba, where she lived for fourteen years. She attended high school in Ottawa, the University of Toronto (B.A., 1939), and studied social work in Toronto and Philadelphia. Married to Patrick Waddington (from whom she was later divorced), she has two sons. In 1945 she moved to Montreal, where she was active in social work and the literary life there, contributing to John SUTHERLAND's *FIRST STATEMENT*. In 1960 she moved back to Toronto, where she worked for the North York Family Services. She joined the English faculty at York University in 1964 and retired as a professor in 1983. She now lives in Vancouver, British Columbia.

Waddington's first collection of poems, *Green world* (1945), was published by First Statement Press. In it and *The second silence* (1955), both of which celebrate childhood, greenness, and sun, her experiences are transmuted through traditions of fairy tale and of a pastoralism that includes Blake, Wordsworth, and Archibald LAMPMAN. Her imagery is intense and visual. The more abstract social poems present a green world as an antidote to broken lives; in a world of lost vision she would have us move into suspended moments from the past, put on 'bandages of light'. Doors and windows offer thresholds to 'other selves' that we are invited to recover, and memory emerges in metaphors of water, presenting the need for descent and flow. In *The season's lovers* (1958), which uses set forms and a public voice to convey important truths, some messages snap aphoristically into place, while others trail off in irresolute language. The last, more metaphysical part works well with playful, intimate language. There is, however, a falling off from her earlier lyricism, which critics generally believe informs her best mode.

The glass trumpet (1966) represents a great leap forward. Content to live with uncertainties and small topics, Waddington here presents life in touchingly simple words and finds an oral style that is whimsical and clever, The poems shove forward with gusto, becoming expressively staccato through a shift to very short, lightly punctuated lines, a departure she assigns in part to the influence of Gertrude Stein. She frees up sounds and meanings by breaking syllables across lines, and by using the line itself as a unit of meaning. *Say yes* (1969), affected by Apollinaire's experiments with the page, shows further formal departures: punctuation and capitalization virtually disappear, and the left margin begins to crumble; words disintegrate even more into new units and meanings; and the voice begins to imitate sounds for which we have no words, and to speak in flexible interpolation. The facetious poems in *Say yes*, like those in *The glass trumpet*, are less determined by phonetic echoes than were the early poems. The modest claims and understatements in the love poems show Waddington's skill in finding symbolic weight in ordinary things. *Say yes* also laments the erosion of her powers: 'I had such words . . . I knew a certain/leaf language from somewhere but now/it is all used up.' *Call them Canadians* (1968) includes humane poems (all untitled) in response to a set of photographs. *Dream telescope* (1972) lacks the charge of her best work, while *Driving home: poems new and selected* (1972) contains only five or six outstanding new pieces. *The price of gold* (1972), *Mister Never* (1978), and *The visitants* (1981) contain excellent work and continue to articulate the centres of Waddington's poetry, though few poems reach the level of her writing in the 1960s. Several concerns that emerged in the 1970s—prophecy, feminism, and ageing—occasionally turn into coyness or didacticism; but in these collections Waddington's lifelong outrage at injustice (which in her essays she attributes to her Jewish upbringing) takes on new life. In *Collected poems* (1986), which adds 40 pages of 'uncollected poems', Waddington, out of respect for history, chose to forgo 'both omissions and revisions' to her published material.

The 'Afterword' is a brief but illuminating literary biography. This was followed by the collection *The last landscape* (1992).

The short fiction in *Summer at Lonely Beach* (1982)—stories about initiation that are mainly anecdotal and meditative, with little dialogue—is close to poetry, making use of rapid summary and tenuous closures. Like many of Waddington's poems, it draws on her early childhood in southern Manitoba.

Waddington has written valuable criticism in numerous reviews and essays, seeking to bring to our appreciation writing that addresses our cultural and political lives. She wrote a pioneering work, *A.M. Klein* (1970), for the Copp Clark series Studies in Canadian Literature, and edited *The collected poems of A.M. Klein* (1974) and *John Sutherland: essays, controversies and poems* (1972). Much of her own prose has been gathered in *Apartment Seven: selected essays* (1989), in which she articulates her political idealism, her romantic aesthetics, and her abiding sense of what it is to be positioned as the outsider.

Among the few long pieces on Waddington, the most valuable are: Cathy Matyas, 'Miriam Waddington', in Jeffrey M. Heath, ed., *Profiles in Canadian literature*, vol. 4 (1982); Albert MORITZ, 'For a far stare: the sweet sanity of Miriam Waddington', in *Books in Canada* (May 1982); and L.R. Ricou, 'Into my green world: the poetry of Miriam Waddington', in *Essays on Canadian Writing* 12 (1978), which also contains a useful bibliography compiled by Ricou. The National Archives, Ottawa, have a Waddington collection.

See also POETRY IN ENGLISH 1950 TO 1982: 1 and 2. DENNIS COOLEY

Wade, Bryan (b.1950). Born in Sarnia, Ontario, he studied creative writing at the University of Victoria before taking an M.F.A. in Motion Picture and Television at the University of California in Los Angeles. He has written and directed for television and worked as a screenwriter. As a playwright he was especially prolific in the 1970s, writing surrealist fantasies typical of the period. *Alias* (1974, prod. 1975) is characteristic: its cast includes the Lone Ranger (who is having an identity crisis), Tonto, and a mobile six-foot penis. The dialogue of *Blitzkreig* (1974), featuring Hitler and Eva Braun, alternates between lurid fantasies of sex and violence that seem merely self-indulgent and a banality that is quite chilling. The latter vein is more effectively explored in *Underground* (1975), a three-character play of sex and power games, conventional in its subject matter and technical formality, but full of enigmatic menace.

This side of the Rockies (1977) is split between the surrealist style and a new realism; it also introduces a sense of the uncanny in the characters' relationship to nature that resurfaces occasionally in later plays despite their generally realistic manner. *Tanned* (1976), set in British Columbia's cottage country, creates a languid, erotic atmosphere with frustration and violence beneath the surface. *Breakthrough* (1986, prod. 1978) concerns the relations between the painter Tom Thomson and a woman from England; it explores a number of promising themes but fails to relate them convincingly. There is a stronger sense of direction in *Polderland* (1984, prod. 1985): set in a Dutch farmhouse during the Second World War, it shows a group of Canadian soldiers who have taken a German prisoner; some human contact develops among the characters, but in the end the imperatives of war take over. *The right one* (1989) is an engaging if surprisingly conventional romantic comedy about a disaster-plagued wedding in which the occasional touches of Wade's earlier non-realistic manner seem out of place. It is as though he had lost touch with the impulses of his earlier work but still felt an obligation to them. ALEXANDER LEGGATT

Wagamese, Richard. See NOVELS IN ENGLISH 1983 TO 1996.

Wah, Fred (b. 1939). Born in Swift Current, Saskatchewan, Wah grew up in the Kootenay region of British Columbia, in Trail and Nelson. Although he studied music at the University of British Columbia, his primary interest has been poetry. While in Vancouver in the sixties he was part of the *TISH* movement, helping to found the group's poetry newsletter. As a graduate student he went to the University of New Mexico to study with Black Mountain poet Robert Creeley and to the State University of New York in Buffalo to work with Creeley and Charles Olson, the founder and major theorist of the Black Mountain school. During this period, Wah edited or co-edited three magazines: *Sum*, the *Niagara Frontier Review*, and *The Magazine of Further Studies*. After completing his M.A. at Buffalo, Wah returned to the Kootenays, where he taught at Selkirk College and then became founding co-ordinator of the writing program at David Thompson University Centre during its brief existence. In this period he edited the little magazine *Scree*. He has also been a contributing editor with *OPEN LETTER* since its inception and was the managing editor of its sister periodical *Swift Current*,

Canada's first electronic literary magazine. Wah has edited Daphne MARLATT's *Selected writing: net work* (1980) and, with Frank DAVEY, *The Swift Current anthology* (1986). In 1989 he joined the English faculty of the University of Calgary.

Wah has published fifteen books of poetry. *Selected poems: Loki is buried at Smoky Creek* (1980) collects poems from his early books: *Lardeau: selected first poems* (1965), *Mountain* (1967), *Tree* (1972), *Among* (1972), *Earth* (1974), and *Pictograms from the interior of B.C.* (1975)—along with newer poems (some of which reappear in *Breathin' my name with a sigh*, 1981). One can see in *Loki is buried at Smoky Creek* a style characteristic of most of Wah's writing: following the tenets of Black Mountain and the *Tish* group, it is spare, imagistic poetry largely concerned with nature and the events of daily life. In *Breathin' my name with a sigh*, Wah's playful connection of the sound of his name to the sounds of air being exhaled is partly grounded in the Black Mountain concern for breath; it also reveals his fascination with the interplay of language and pure sound. Wah's playfulness is also evident in his next book, *Owners manual* (1981), in which the poems take the form of a set of instructions about how to live.

Waiting for Saskatchewan (1985), for which Wah won a Governor General's Award, picks up poems from *Breathin' my name with a sigh* and *Grasp the sparrow's tail* (1982), and, adding new poetry, transforms the selections into a unified book-length work. In this book Wah continues his exploration of the auditory aspects of his poetry, in the context both of Black Mountain ideas about breath and of concepts connected to Asian practices of concentration. As well, believing that in order to understand who we are we must be conscious not only of our physical existence but also of part of our heritage, Wah begins, through an imagined exploration of his father's experience, what has become an ongoing exploration of his own inheritance. His mother was a Swedish-born Canadian while his father, born in Canada but raised in China, was a mixture of Chinese, Scots, and Irish, and Wah inherited not only his father's Chinese surname but also a sense of not belonging to a specific ethnic group. Wah's later collections—such as *Rooftops* (1987), *Limestone lakes utaniki* (1989), and *So far* (1991)—have made this exploration not so much into ethnic identity as into the experience of being of mixed heritage. Wah's message in these collections is not that of one forever displaced, but is about the complexity of inheritance and the consequent need to explore it without attempting to create a clear definition of its nature. As well, Wah shows that there is another dimension of belonging: one's physical reality. The present reality of the Kootenays, his family, his friends, and his own experience are shown to constitute identity as much as his complicated past.

The linked books *Music at the heart of thinking* (1987) and *Alley alley home free* (1992) make evident Wah's continuing interest in sound. In both, Wah seeks to escape the way in which articulation limits meaning by introducing the principles of jazz improvisation into his writing. Although the attempt to escape the fixed nature of the word may be foredoomed, one can see in these books Wah's increasing control over the musicality of his language.

Diamond Grill (1996), Wah's first work of prose, is a return to the world of his parents and his childhood and is his most ambitious book. This partly invented memoir (he calls it a 'biotext') moves towards the prose poem and blurs the line between fiction and fact. In its invocation of both the intensely localized and Canadian experience of a small-town Chinese diner in 1951, and in its investigation of the complicated international history that surrounds it, *Diamond Grill* attempts to deal with the nature of hybridity in a country in which identity has traditionally been seen in terms of belonging to well-defined ethnic groups.

George BOWERING's Introduction to Wah's 1980 *Selected poems* remains a good critical starting-point. Pamela Banting has several times written on Wah's work; see her discussions in *Body Inc.: a theory of translation poetics* (1995). *Beyond 'Tish'* (1991), a collection of essays, interviews, and poetry edited by Douglas BARBOUR, has essays on Wah by Jeff Derksen and Ed Dyck, and provides a valuable context for his writing.

RUSSELL BROWN/DONNA BENNETT

Walker, David (b. 1911). David Harry Walker was born in Dundee, Scotland, and attended the Royal Military College, Sandhurst (1929-30). He pursued a military career in the Black Watch (1931-47), serving in India (1932) and the Sudan (1936). His first connection with Canada occurred in 1938 when he was aide-de-camp to the Governor General, Lord Tweedsmuir. Walker was captured in France in 1940 and held prisoner-of-war until 1945, an experience on which he based his novel *The pillar* (1952). In 1945-6 he served as an instructor at Staff College, Camberly, England, before taking up his last official military post as comptroller to the Viceroy of India. In 1947 he retired, with the rank of major, to take up a new career as professional writer, ultimately settling in St Andrews, New Brunswick. From 1957 to 1961 he was a member of the Canada Council. Walker has been awarded a D. Litt by the University of New Brunswick (1955), and won two Governor General's Awards, for *The pillar* and *Digby* (1953).

A prolific writer of fast-paced adventure stories, Walker has tried his hand at everything from international espionage (*Cab-Intersec*, 1968; published in England as *Devil's plunge*), to children's stories (*Dragon Hill*, 1962). Few of his works are related directly to Canada, though *Mallabec* (1965), *Where the high winds blow* (1960), *Pirate Rock* (1969), and some of the short stories in *Storms of our journey and other stories* (1964), are set in Canada. Two of his novels—*Geordie* (1950) and *Harry Black* (1956)—were made into films. Walker's other books are: *The storm and the silence* (1949), *Sandy was a soldier's boy* (1957), *Winter madness* (1964), *Come back, Geordie* (1966), *Big Ben* (1970), *The Lord's pink ocean* (1972), *Black Dougal* (1973), *Ash* (1976), and *Pot of gold* (1977). In 1984 he published his memoirs, *Lean, wind, lean*. A brief discussion of Walker's books for young people, particularly *Dragon Hill* and *Pirate Rocke*, may be found in sheila Egoff's *The republic of childhood* (2nd edn, 1975), where his insight into character is praised. ANDREW SEAMAN

Walker, George F. (b. 1947). The youngest of four children of working-class parents, he was born and raised in Toronto's East End. In 1970 he responded to a call for scripts from Toronto's newly founded Factory Theatre Lab by writing *The Prince of Naples* (1972), a two-character farce in which a young and ostensibly liberated student challenges the rational thinking of his older and more conventional mentor. Produced by the Factory in 1971, it marked the beginning of a long association in which Walker served as the theatre's playwright-in-residence from 1971 to 1976 and as its artistic director in 1978-9. In 1977 he began a three-year association with Toronto Free Theatre, which produced a number of his plays. In 1981 he was playwright-in-residence at the New York Shakespeare Festival, which produced in 1982 the American première of his first critically acclaimed work, *Zastrozzi: the master of discipline* (1977). Despite his ongoing association with the Factory Theatre, Walker's plays have also premièred in Toronto at the Tarragon (*Science and madness*, 1982) and the Canadian Stage (*Better living*, 1986); at the Mark Taper Forum, Los Angeles (*Nothing sacred*, 1988); at Vassar College in a production by the New York Film and Stage Co. (*Escape from happiness*, 1991); and at the Green Thumb Theatre for Young People, Vancouver (*Tough!*, 1994).

Walker's career has been unprecedented in English Canada. He has won two Governor General's Awards (for *Criminals in love* and *Nothing sacred*) as well as the Toronto Arts Award for Drama in 1994. Productions of his plays have won numerous Chalmers and Dora Mavor Moore Awards. He is also a noted director of his own productions, most recently the remount in 1995 of *Nothing sacred*—an adaptation of Turgenev's *Fathers and sons*—at the restored Winter Garden Theatre, Toronto. Walker has produced a body of work that, by 1997, includes twenty stage plays and numerous radio and television scripts, making him the most published and produced playwright in English Canada. His plays have been mounted in hundreds of productions around the world, have been translated into several languages, and have developed a critical and popular respect that led to Walker's being named in 1993 one of the hundred most powerful people in American theatre and to the publication of a critical anthology of his work, *Shared anxiety* (1994).

If Walker's plays have been a rich source of material for actors and directors, they have posed something more of an enigma for critics, who have not always known quite what to make of the seemingly pastiched concoctions of cinematic forms and techniques, cartoon characters, serious political and philosophical issues, and bizarre, even grotesque, theatrical flourishes. Early critics, for example, mistook Walker for an absurdist or surrealist because of the very early plays' evocation of patterns from those theatrical traditions. *The Prince of Naples* and *Ambush at Tether's End* (1972), for example, use stock absurdist devices to reach decidedly non-absurdist conclusions.

Critic Gregory Sinclair has described Walker's dramatic technique as 'scouring artistic graveyards for dead stereotypes and mouldy subgenres, stitching them all together and watching them career madly across the stage.' The Frankensteinean metaphor is, perhaps, apt for a playwright who delights in revivifying traditional theatrical conventions by inserting pop-cultural and B-movie references into them. At first Walker's unorthodox technique and periodic stylistic changes suggested a playwright who was himself careering madly across the theatrical landscape.

However, as Walker's craft has matured, a consistent theatrical technique has emerged, one that Richard Knowles has described as 'per-version', a persistent warping and reconfiguration of received forms into new, independent ones in order to disrupt dominant discourses. If there are any threads running through all Walker's plays, they can be located in his understanding of language, style, even structural forms as the building blocks out of which not only art but human subjectivity and culture are constructed, and through which power is constituted and wielded. By twisting, or perverting, these forms and processes, Walker's plays both foreground the forms' role in cultural constructions and suggest new ways of constituting such power.

Much has been written about Walker's use of cinematic forms, a stylistic preference that continues even in the more recent plays' use of 'gangster' and 'tough' movie plots and characters. Walker himself has remarked that 'I tend to like to frame the world, and use various genres to do that. "B" movies are a generic frame that gives me freedom to jump off in any direction that I want to or that the characters will take me.' Thus, for example, the cartoon exaggerations and comic grotesques that pervade his early plays shift to stereotypical characters and structural clichés of Hollywood B-movies in the plays anthologized in *Three plays by George F. Walker* (1978). But in all these plays Walker perverts the conventions and thus exposes their ideological blindness. A play such as *Beyond Mozambique* (1975), for example, uses the B-movie conventions to express what the B-movies themselves did not: the desperation and ugliness of a decaying imperialist centre endlessly regurgitating its own cultural debris.

In the middle group of plays the comic structure becomes somewhat more conventional, but the emphasis on manipulating these conventional forms to raise questions about their attendant political and philosophical ideologies continues. *Gossip* (1984) and *Filthy rich* (1984), two 'detective movies', expose the bankrupt morality and decadent mores of the rich and famous that Walker locates at the centre of media-warped society. In *Gossip* the crime-drama convention of the revelation scene is exaggerated out of all proportion, and in *Filthy rich* the crime-drama conventions themselves break down when their basic requirement of clear and distinguishable good and evil proves to be naïve.

In *Theatre of the film noir* (1981) and *The art of war* (1984) Walker again draws on the formats of cinematic suspense to spin the webs of sexual and political intrigue that are his metaphors for contemporary confusion and decay. Using the characters and conventions of horror films in *Science and madness* (1982), he expands upon this technique, developing a Gothic collage whose portrayal of the classic struggle between good and evil revives the conflict of *Zastrozzi*, in which Zastrozzi, the arch-villain of Western Europe—derived from Shelley's play of the same name—confronts Verezzi, his idealistic opposite. *Zastrozzi* demonstrates the playwright's ability to merge philosophical issues with powerful characterizations, urbane dialogue, and intricate plot in a fast-paced series of visually striking scenes that are as intellectually sophisticated as they are theatrically exciting.

Walker's most recent group of plays—often called the East End plays, after the title of the 1988 anthology that collects three of them (*Criminals in love*, *Better living*, and *Beautiful city*) as well as for their evocation of the working-class neighbourhoods of Walker's own East End Toronto upbringing—are his most mature plays to date. Though in them Walker turns to the conventions of realist drama, he does not abandon the cartoonish characters or the interest in cultural forms and relations of power that characterized his earlier works. The first of the East End plays, *Criminals in love* (1984), introduces a set of characters that reappear over several later plays. They include several matriarchal figures who battle the forces of corruption in their neighbourhoods in order to carve out a safe place for their families to flourish. The heroes in these plays are typically 'ordinary folk' who have been pushed too far and are finally standing up for themselves, and the villains typically represent the organized forms of power, whether the Mafia, politicians, or the police, who have taken them for granted. The women in these families are almost all strong, and the men either weak or violently controlling. The development of more overt political, particularly class, issues, begun already in *Gossip* and *Filthy rich*, becomes predominant in these plays.

Walker's plays are all highly metatheatrical, and the East End plays are no exception, with characters often resolving conflicts through ruses, disguises, and performances. In *Love and anger* (1990), for example, the characters win a victory over the corrupt newspaper boss, Conner, by fabricating evidence against him and by 'trying' him in a mock courtroom. Performance, itself a form of power, thus offers one resolution of the fascination all Walker's plays have with the various forms power can take, from the ruthless cruelty of

Zastrozzi and Hackman (*The art of war*), to the homespun wisdom and dangerous stubbornness of Nora Quinn (*Better living* and *Escape from happiness*, 1992) and Gina Mae Sabatini (*Beautiful city*), to the creative and unorthodox performances of numerous characters, such as Petie Maxwell (*Love and anger*) and William (*Criminals in love*). What is perhaps especially obvious, because of its subtlety in the East End plays, is Walker's unusual ability to hold up the quotidian and reveal the magical, the sublime, and the ridiculous, harnessing them all to the service of a theatricality that is at once politically, aesthetically, culturally, and philosophically astute.

See Robert Wallace, 'Looking for the light: a conversation with George F. Walker', *Canadian Drama* 14 (1988).

ROBERT WALLACE/ED NYMAN

Wallace, Bronwen (1945-89). She was born in Kingston, Ontario, and educated at Queen's University (B.A., 1967; M.A., 1979). Her mother was of United Empire Loyalist stock, and her father's family lived on the same farm for over 200 years. A political activist, she worked in Windsor, Ontario, in the 1970s with auto-workers, and co-founded a women's bookstore; in Kingston in the 1980s she worked in a battered women's shelter. All these experiences appear in her poetry. In the late 1980s she was a teacher of creative writing and women's studies at Queen's. She also wrote a highly personal and feminist column for two years on the Monday op-ed page of the Kingston *Whig-Standard*. A late starter, she published her first book at thirty-five. (In her memory, the WRITERS' DEVELOPMENT TRUST established an annual award for the best writer under thirty-five with achievements in fiction or poetry.) A literary pioneer, she had a vital and humane voice, free of rhetoric. 'That spark in a synapse . . ./saying look, you have time, even yet,/to come to love this too.'

Wallace was heavily influenced by Al PURDY, whose example taught her to structure poems as narratives instead of lyrics. Her intention was to organize poems the way women get together to tell stories. Story, for Wallace, was never complete but achieved its meaning through cumulative effect. Her poems were often two or three pages long, with exact details of ordinary lives shining from within. Her first collection was *Marrying in the family*, which was published in one volume with *Bread & chocolate* by Mary DI MICHELE (1980). She followed this with *Signs of the former tenant* (1983), *Common magic* (1985), and the dazzling collection *The stubborn particulars of grace* (1987). Magic and love were found in the most common things: a kitchen or livingroom; the places people live in, even the poet's hands, became 'wings'. *Common magic* also included poems of marital strife and male anger; *Stubborn particulars* included poems about working in a battered women's shelter, the importance of conversation over the dinner table, and planting daffodils as an act of faith in the future.

Wallace's posthumous publications, edited by Carolyn Smart, include *People you'd trust your life to* (1990), short stories about nurturing female relationships, love and its obstacles, and finding the divine in the commonplace; *Keep that candle burning bright and other poems* (1991); *Against the world: essays* (1992), her newspaper columns, 1992; and *Two women talking: correspondence 1985-1987* (1993) with Erin MOURÉ. Wallace made two films: *All You Have to Do* (1982) about living with cancer, made seven years before she was diagnosed with the disease; and *That's Why I'm Talking* (1985), which celebrated four poet-friends: Robert PRIEST, Mary di Michele, Pier Giorgio DI CICCO, and Carolyn Smart.

See Donna Bennett, 'Bronwen Wallace and the meditative poem', *Queen's Quarterly*, vol. 98, no. 1 (Spring 1992); and *Open Letter 9: special issue on Bronwen Wallace*, Susan Rudy Dorscht and Eric Savoy, eds, 7th Series (Winter 1991).

GEOFF HANCOCK

Wallace, Frederick William (1886-1958). The son of a ship captain, Wallace was born in the seafaring dockland community of Govan, then on the outskirts of Glasgow, Scotland, where he was educated in local schools and briefly at Allen Glen Academy. Here he was naturally drawn to the masculine world of the sea, idealizing the courage, skill, and strength of such men as his father. To his immense frustration, however, he came of age just as the world he admired was coming to a close, as iron and steam replaced sail and wood. Instead of apprentice seaman, his first job was as a shipping clerk, initially at Glasgow, and then—following his family's move to Hudson, Quebec, in 1904—at Montreal. Wallace continued to dream of life at sea from behind his desk, and began to write short stories based on events in his father's career. These were sufficiently popular with his friends that in 1908 he became a freelance writer, specializing in adventure stories for various magazines directed at men such as himself, office-bound and bored. But it was a vicarious existence, to which he could bring no experience of his own.

The turning-point in Wallace's life came in August 1911, when he was sent by *Canadian Century* magazine to cover a fishermen's regatta in Digby, Nova Scotia. Here he was introduced to the Banks fishermen, who still made their living on the water and under sail. Insinuating himself aboard a working trip, he quickly gained the respect of the fishermen for his skill, knowledge, and fortitude, and was accepted as a working member of the crew. Six more such trips with the Banks fishermen of Digby were the grist from which he milled his publications: three novels, *Blue water* (1914), *The Viking blood* (1920), and *Captain Salvation* (1925); three collections of short stories, *The shack locker* (1916), *Salt seas and sailormen* (1922), and *Tea from China* (1926); as well as innumerable magazine and newspaper articles, both fiction and non-fiction. In 1914 Wallace was hired as the founding editor of the industrial journal *Canadian Fisherman*, a position he held almost continuously until shortly before his death. He then began to compile records relating to the deep-sea wooden sailing vessels built in the Maritime region, which led to the publication of his *Wooden ships and iron men* (1924); *In the wake of the windships* (1926); and *The record of Canadian shipping* (1929). He also wrote an account of a voyage he made aboard one such vessel in 1920, *Under sail in the last of the clippers* (1936).

Wallace's reputation as a writer rested for a long period on his historical compilations, which helped to establish an image of a nineteenth-century golden age of economic activity in the Maritime region. Recent scholarship, however, has superseded, and in large measure discredited, this work. As for his fiction, it was quickly dated by its stock characters and romantic plots—boy wins girl after much adventure. It nevertheless retains a historical interest for those exploring issues of gender and the development of urban middle-class masculinity. Wallace's fiction, for all its romanticism, also provides detailed and realistic accounts of the working life of the Banks fishermen on the eve of mechanization. Indeed, his work was praised by fishermen, in marked contrast to the reception they gave to Frank Parker DAY's near-contemporary novel *Rockbound* (1928). Wallace returned to the description of the world of the Banks fishing schooner at length in his autobiography, *Roving fisherman* (1955), which, shorn of the romanticism of his fiction, offers a unique picture of men at work on the water. It is likely to emerge as his lasting contribution to Canadian literature and history.

M. BROOK TAYLOR

Wallace, J.S. (Joe) (1890-1975). Toronto-born, raised in Truro and North Sydney, Nova Scotia, he attended St Francis Xavier University and worked in advertising, running as a candidate in provincial and federal elections before joining the Communist Party of Canada the year following its formation in 1921. He wrote for the labour press, attended the Conference for the Unemployed in Ottawa in 1933, and when the Party was outlawed was interned at Petawawa, Ontario, in 1941-2. Imprisonment inspired his early verse. Five collections of lyric and satiric poems appeared, beginning with *Night is ended* (1942) and ending with *A radiant sphere* (1964). The latter volume was issued in Moscow in three editions of 10,000 copies each—in Russian, English, and Chinese. With Wilson MacDONALD, he toured Russia and China in 1956-7. Both a committed Communist and a devout Roman Catholic, he died in a Catholic convalescent home in Vancouver. *Joe Wallace: poems* (1981) brings together 300 poems and verses that show his ability to write socially committed light verse ('The American way of life: / You can get away with murder / If you use a golden knife') and, on occasion, lyric poems of intensity, notably his elegy for Norman Bethune and his poem on tolerance, which begins 'All my brothers are beautiful.'

JOHN ROBERT COLOMBO

Wallen, James. See NOVELS IN ENGLISH 1983 TO 1996: OTHER NOVELS 3.

Walmsley, Tom (b.1948). Born in Liverpool, England, he came to Canada early in life and was raised in Oshawa, Ontario, dropping out of high school in grade ten. His published work includes two books of poetry—*Rabies* (1975), and *Lexington hero* (1976)—and a novel, *Doctor Tin* (1979). He is also the author of a number of plays: *The working man* (1976), *The Jones boy* (1978), *Something red* (1980), *White boys* (produced in 1982), *Getting wrecked* (produced in 1985), and *Mr. Nice Guy* (produced in 1986), written with Dolly Reisman. The plays are by far the best part of his work.

The only conventional facet of Walmsley's drama is its formal realism. Sex and violence pervade his stage: obscenities riddle his dialogue. But his plays are never simply exercises in sensationalism. Even *The working man*, for all its graphic violence, focuses on the psychological drama. Although the principal characters in *The Jones boy* are drug addicts, the play is not 'about' heroin but about the quest for self-knowledge and the meaning of courage and honour in a criminal subculture that offers only unreflective barbarism as an ideal. The full-length *Something red*, Walmsley's most ambitious play, moves through scenes of extreme physical and psychological brutality to climactic moments in which a character stands revealed to others and himself. The protagonist, Bobby, is a memorable creation. Dishonourable and self-seeking in all his relationships, revolting in his sexual obsessions, he also bears traces of tragic grandeur. He is faithful only to his most wayward impulses—the 'monstrous forms of being', in Ionesco's words, that inhabit the human psyche; yet when he makes his last appearance, having committed an appalling sex murder, our responses are pity and fear. In *White boys* the playwright presents his familiar character types within the framework of farce. The full-length play works well at the level of a revue skit; but the idiom obstructs the necessary development of the theme, which is, once again, infantile impulse baffled by the demands of adult experience. *Getting wrecked* is a musical treatment of the theme of teenage abuse of alcohol, and *Mr. Nice Guy* treats the theme of wife battering.

The most serious limitation of Walmsley's theatre is its narrow focus. The characters and milieu offer only a remote relation to society at large. His work, although increasingly expert, tends to turn in on itself as the playwright delves ever deeper into extreme, anarchic states of being. But within their restricted compass, Walmsley's plays—*The Jones boy* and *Something red* in particular—generate a power that is rare in contemporary Canadian drama.

MICHAEL TAIT

Warland, Betsy (b. 1946). Since emigrating from the United States to Canada in 1972, she has become a significant figure in feminist and lesbian writing. She helped conceive and co-ordinate in 1983 the landmark conference 'Women and Words/Les femmes et les mots' at the University of British Columbia, and she has edited extensively, helping to bring to publication the work of many feminist writers in such vehicles as '(f.)Lip: a newsletter of feminist innovative writing', *Telling it: women and language across cultures* (1990), and, as sole editor, *InVersions: writing by dykes, queers & lesbians* (1991).

Warland's poetry is intensely personal, and in *A gathering instinct* (1981) she records sequences of pain and loss in relationships. She highlights the difficulties of constructing a self in language, using a lower case 'i' to identify her first-person voice. In the wake of the 'Women and Words' conference, the 1980s in Canada became a period of intense feminist experimentation with language, and Warland participated energetically in this collective investigation. In *open is broken* (1984) she explores etymological and homonymic webs of meaning, and breaks the bounds of conventional discourse. Increasing syntactical fracture characterizes her contribution to a feminist poetics, a process she continues in *serpent (w)rite: (a reader's gloss)* (1987) and *Proper deafinitions: collected theorograms* (1990). *The bat had blue eyes* (1993) examines memories of childhood sexual abuse and the mechanisms by which language paralyses and erases experiences whose articulation is taboo. For instance, in the phrase 'I clings', Warland syntactically relegates the first-person pronoun to the third-person, objectifying her own voice and thus illustrating its erasure.

Warland has also written collaboratively with Daphne MARLATT in *Double negative, Daphne Marlatt* (1988) and *Two women in a birth* (1994).

ANNE RAYNER

Warr, Bertram (1917-43). Born in Toronto, Ontario, Warr was educated there. After working in Muskoka and Halifax during the late 1930s, his poverty made him decide to leave Canada to pursue his literary ambitions in England. He arrived in England after stowing away on a passenger liner, worked as a clerk for a London oyster company, and joined the Fire Service at the start of the Second World War. Though a pacifist, he was 'called up' and joined the Royal Air Force in 1941. He perished on a raid over Essen, Germany, in April 1943.

Warr's poetry appeared in various British literary magazines and anthologies. Shortly before joining the RAF he published a small pamphlet, *Yet a little onwards* (1941), in the Resurgam Younger Poets Series. That collection of fourteen poems reflects Warr's early response to the war in 'War widow' and his socialist leanings in 'Working class' and 'To a passionate socialist'. Warr shared with his British contemporaries of this period a desire to blend both politics and realism in a controlled free-verse style that is metaphorically sensual; but unlike English poets of the Apocalyptic or Personalist movements (e.g., Henry Treece, Nicholas Moore, and G.S. Fraser), Warr maintained a conscious and open-eyed attitude, and an imagistic system of realism that locates his work closer to that of Dorothy LIVESAY and Earle BIRNEY. Warr's sense of uneasy pessimism, declared in the introduction to *Yet a little onwards*, 'ours is an age of renunciation . . . of probing and reflection', lends his work a contemplative aspect that goes beyond mere agitprop or manifesto poetry, hallmarks of other verse from the Second World War.

His poetry was revived by Earle Birney (who had discovered Warr's work in England during his own service) and Len Gasparini and published in *Acknowledgement to life: the collected poems of Bertram Warr* (1970). In his Preface, Birney asserts that had Warr survived the hostilities, he would likely have become an important voice in Canadian poetry.

BRUCE MEYER

Wars, The (1977). This novel brought Timothy FINDLEY to prominence in Canadian literary circles, though he had published his first novel a full decade before. His third novel, it won a Governor General's Award and became a film (directed by Robin Phillips, 1983); its popularity continues unabated today, and it is regularly taught in literature courses.

The wars expresses a general trend in Canadian fiction of the 1970s: the self-conscious exploration of history as text—what the critic Linda HUTCHEON has called 'historiographic metafiction'. For his tale of a nineteen-year-old Canadian soldier in the First World War, as told through the eyes of a researcher and various witnesses, Findley drew much of the documentary material from letters written by his uncle (Thomas Irving Findley), who served with the artillery in France, and he supplemented them with readings in the published texts of the period—from the poetry of Wilfrid Owen and Siegfried Sassoon to E.M. Remarque's *All quiet on the Western Front* (1929). Far from decrying the indebtedness of Findley's novel to powerful fictional and poetic predecessors, reviewers tended to praise his use of such material as a means of validation.

In the literary nationalism that dominated the early 1970s there was an imperative to locate *The wars* either in cosmopolitan literary company or in a newly reconceptualized Canadian 'tradition'. For this reason, *The wars* is a pivotal text for students of Canadian literary canonization in the years following the Centennial celebrations of 1967.

Of the many features of *The wars* that have attracted critical inquiry, the spare, cinematic style is prominent. Noteworthy too is Findley's division of the novel into five sections, themselves subdivided into numbered sections and punctuated by transcripts of witnesses' memories, which suggests a concern with history's construction and the very status of knowledge. Documented fact is radically destabilized; Robert, trapped in the barn at the end of the novel, cries out, 'We shall not be taken.' To the male-centred mindset that Findley would continue to critique in later novels such as *Not wanted on the voyage* (1984), 'we' can only be constructed as Robert plus other human beings—he is part of a conspiracy against authority and is therefore punished by fire.

For further consideration of *The wars* as a novel crucially concerned with issues of language and knowledge, see Diana Brydon, '"It could not be told": making meaning in Timothy Findley's *The wars*', *Journal of Commonwealth Literature* 21:2 (1986). For a fresh reading of *The wars* in relation to its First World War intertexts—that discloses not only its indebtedness to those works but how it crucially reconfigures their narrative devices—see Evelyn Cobley, 'Postmodernist war fiction: Findley's *The wars*', *CANADIAN LITERATURE* 147 (Winter 1995). Carol Roberts' and Lynne Macdonald's *Timothy Findley: an annotated bibliography* (1990) provides useful information about contemporary reviews of *The wars* as well as articles on the novel.

The wars was made into a film (1983), directed by Robin Phillips.

LORRAINE YORK

Watmough, David (b. 1926). Born in Epping Forest, near London, England, Watmough spent most of his childhood in Cornwall, where he learned the idiosyncratic rhythm of his prose. Forced by the Depression to leave his boyhood home, he has forever after employed the voice of the exile in stories that describe the outsider looking homeward, back to the disintegrating family and now unfamiliar landscape. He was educated at Coopers' School, London, served in the Royal Navy during wartime, then attended King's College, University of London, where he studied theology, the subject of his first book, *A church renascent* (1951).

After a few years in the United States, where he worked as a freelance writer, Watmough immigrated to Vancouver, British Columbia, in 1960 (he became a Canadian citizen in 1969), where he has worked as a print, radio, and television/radio critic, and has produced a cycle of plays, stories, and novels—all with an autobiographical impulse. Watmough's novels are *No more into the garden: chronicles of Davey Bryant* (1978)—for which he was given the Best Novel of the Year Award by Giovanni's Room, a leading gay bookstore in Philadelphia. *Unruly skeletons* (1982), *The year of fears* (1987), *Thy mother's glass* (1992),

The time of the kingfishers (1994), and *Hunting with Diana* (1996). His collections of stories are *Ashes for Easter* (1972), *From a Cornish landscape* (1975), *Love and the waiting game* (1975), *The Connecticut countess* (1984), *Fury* (1984), and *Vibrations in time* (1986). *Collected shorter fiction of David Watmough: 1972-82* was published in 1982.

Davey Bryant is the persona we encounter in most of Watmough's fiction. In fact, every story would appear to belong to a composite Davey, his life in transparent layers, as if by telling and reading variations on the story the writer and the listener/reader will finally come to an understanding of what it means to be a man alienated from his own culture by the accident of his homosexuality and the progress of history. Irony is Watmough's way of dealing with inevitable cruelties—it distances him from a sentimental childhood, which is also the paradise he seeks in each new fiction and every human relationship.

Watmough has also written monodramas—solo performance pieces—in which he takes the role of writer/performer. These have been published in *Ashes for Easter and other monodramas* (1972). LINDA ROGERS

Watson, John (1847-1939). Born in Glasgow, Scotland, and educated at Glasgow University, he came to Queen's University, Kingston, Ontario, in 1872 to be a professor of logic, metaphysics, and ethics, replacing John Clark MURRAY, who had accepted a chair at McGill. Watson was the central figure in the Hegelian movement that dominated Canadian philosophy from the 1870s until after the First World War, and did much to shape religious, political, and cultural ideas in Canada in this period. His rational version of Christianity formed a significant part of the intellectual basis of the union that resulted in the formation of the United Church of Canada in 1925. Religion was central to Watson's work. His religious views were first expounded in *Christianity and idealism: the Christian life in relation to the Greek and Jewish ideals and to modern philosophy* (New York, 1896). Believing that all reality formed a rational unity within which the highest values could be realized, Watson sought a rational religion that could unite all people around demonstrable truths, and render intelligible both human history and the life of the individual. Though a decade separates *The philosophical basis of religion: a series of lectures* (1907) from *Christianity and idealism*, his fundamental position remained the same. Watson's books attracted international recognition and this culminated in the invitation to give the Gifford Lectures in Scotland in 1910-12, which led to his monumental *Interpretation of religious experience* (2 vols, 1912). Much of Watson's reputation rests on his *Philosophy of Kant explained* (1908) and *Kant and his English critics: a comparison of critical and empirical philosophy* (Glasgow, 1881), both of which have been frequently reprinted and continue to be read. His *Philosophy of Kant as contained in extracts from his own writings* (Glasgow, 1888) was widely used by undergraduates. His introductory texts, *Comte, Mill & Spencer, an outline of philosophy* (Glasgow, 1895), later adapted as *An outline of philosophy* (1908), helped shape the minds of two generations of Canadian students. These books also contain a good deal of original philosophy, as does Watson's *Hedonistic theories from Aristippus to Spencer* (Glasgow, 1895). The First World War gave rise to *The state in peace and war* (1919), a treatise devoted to the ideal of a world government based on the principles of tolerance and the integral development of national cultures, which Watson thought characteristic of the emerging British Commonwealth and of the established pluralist tradition in Canada. He advocated widespread land reform and an economic system that, while rewarding hard work, would guarantee fairness and decent living conditions to everyone. Watson's lucid prose style made his books accessible and helps to account for their wide readership. His purely literary works, however, had only a modest success. He wrote several plays, which remain unpublished, though they were performed and generally well received at Queen's. He also wrote some poetry. His influence generally stemmed from the generations of Presbyterian clergymen who were educated by him, and from the frequency with which his students attained senior posts in the civil service in Ottawa.

LESLIE ARMOUR, ELIZABETH TROTT

Watson, Sheila (b. 1909). Born in New Westminster, British Columbia, she lived during her early years on the grounds of the Provincial Mental Hospital, in New Westminster, where her father, Dr Charles Edward Doherty, was superintendent until his death in 1922. She attended primary and secondary schools at the convent of the Sisters of Sainte Anne, New Westminster, and took her first two years of university at the Convent of the Sacred Heart, Vancouver. She received a B.A. (1931) in Honours English from the University of British Columbia; earned her academic teaching certificate in 1932; and completed an M.A. (1933) at UBC.

During the next few years Watson taught elementary school in a succession of British Columbia classrooms. In 1941 she married the poet Wilfred WATSON. In the post-war years Sheila Watson undertook another series of short-term teaching posts—at Moulton College, Toronto (1946-8), a sessional lectureship at UBC (1948-50), and at a high school in Powell River, B.C. (1950-51)—before spending two years in Calgary, during which she wrote her celebrated novel *The double hook* (1959). After short periods in Edmonton and France, she entered upon doctoral studies at the University of Toronto in 1957, completing a dissertation on Wyndham Lewis, under the direction of Marshall McLUHAN, in 1965. She was appointed to the faculty of the University of Alberta in 1961, and retired as full professor in 1975. Her uncollected prose was published as a special number of the journal *OPEN LETTER* (1975). *Four stories* (1979) was followed by *Five stories* (1984), which added a fifth story, 'and the four animals', to the original four. A second novel, *Deep Hollow Creek*—written in the 1930s, but not published until 1992—has a semi-autobiographical basis in Watson's experiences as a teacher at Dog Creek in the interior of British Columbia in 1935-7, and can be read as an early writing of various aspects of *The double hook*.

The double hook is considered by many to be the first truly modern Canadian novel. Concerned to avoid both regionalism and realistic reportage, Watson created in this text a highly poetic and elliptical narrative written in biblical rhythms, in chapters that resemble stanzas, and in images that dwarf plot and action. The novel depicts the struggle of members of a small village to move from despair to hope, from apathy to action, in a world where pagan and Christian symbolisms have blurred, and silence proves more eloquent than language. The discontinuous and highly imagistic style of the work reiterates the distrust of discursive language that it embodies. The novel is in the NEW CANADIAN LIBRARY and appeared in Swedish as *Dubbelkrocken* (1963; translated by Artur Lundkvist) and in French as *Sous l'oeil de coyote* (1976; translated by Arlette Francière).

Watson's stories, written in the same period as *The double hook*, reflect a similarly austere and precise use of language and image. Most focus on spiritual paralysis, and give mythological names to the characters to avoid the semblance of realism. The characters thus appear oppressed by myth, and struggle against its authority as personified in parent, priest, or nun.

With Douglas BARBOUR, Stephen SCOBIE, Wilfred Watson, and Norman Yates, Sheila Watson co-edited the little magazine *White Pelican* (1971-8). She has been honoured by the publication of *Figures in a ground: Canadian essays on modern literature collected in honor of Sheila Watson* (1978), edited by Diane Bessai and David Jackel. See also Stephen Scobie, *Sheila Watson and her works* (1984), George BOWERING, ed., *Sheila Watson and The double hook* (1985), and F.T. Flahiff, 'Afterword', *The double hook* (NCL, 1989). FRANK DAVEY

Watson, Wilfred (b. 1911). Born in Rochester, England, and educated at Maldon Grammar School, Maldon, Essex, he immigrated with his family in 1926 to Duncan, British Columbia. After a year at Duncan High School he began thirteen years of work in a tidewater sawmill, meanwhile reading, writing poetry, and exploring the coasts and mountains of Vancouver Island. In 1940 he enrolled in English at the University of British Columbia, graduating in 1943, whereupon he joined the Canadian navy for the remainder of the war. He received an M.A. from the University of Toronto in 1946 and a Ph.D. in 1951. After teaching English briefly at the University of British Columbia, he taught at the University of Alberta, first in Calgary and later in Edmonton, where he served as a distinguished teacher and scholar until his retirement in 1976. With his wife Sheila WATSON he co-founded the little magazine *White Pelican* (1971-8). He lives in Nanaimo, B.C.

As both experimental poet and dramatist, Watson explores contemporary media-conditioned sensibilities. His first collection of poems, *Friday's child* (1955), which won a Governor General's Award, contained apparently conventional verse that nevertheless bore the seeds of the radical writing to follow. The poems of his second collection, *The sorrowful Canadians and other poems* (1972), are curiously analogous to his drama in their use of space, for which Watson uses the term *mise en page*. Unlike most concrete poetry, Watson's offers both context and content: the size or positioning of various typefaces modulates verbal intensity, so that the eye is bombarded by a typographical 'voice' speaking with the insistence of choral utterance in the plays. His number/grid poems—in which each stanza or grid provides for 17 words juxtaposed typographically to the numbers one to nine—were published in *I begin with counting* (1978) and *Mass on cowback* (1982). The discipline of the grid method of ordering his poems is also reflected in the finely honed short verse-play

Woman taken in adultery (published in Diane Bessai, ed., *Prairie performance*, 1980; Edmonton Fringe, 1987), which concisely illustrates Watson's facility for drawing satiric portraits within rapidly shifting time-space environments. A comprehensive gathering of the poetry is found in *Poems collected unpublished new* (1986), with an introduction by Thomas Peacocke.

Watson's work as a playwright has been influenced by the Theatre of the Absurd and by his interest in the theories of Marshall McLUHAN, with whom he collaborated in *From cliché to archetype* (1970). An argument between Watson and McLuhan emerges in the play *Let's murder Clytemnestra according to the principles of Marshall McLuhan*, produced at the Studio Theatre, University of Alberta, in Nov. 1969. *O holy ghost, dip your finger in the blood of Canada, and write, I love you*, which premièred at the Studio Theatre in Dec. 1967, exploits sound, movement, visuals, and scenic inter-cuts in dealing with the flower-power trendiness of the 1960s; it combines satiric sketch, chorus, music, and projections in order to focus on big business, the Vietnam war, and the modern dehumanization occurring in professional life.

Watson's habit of wrenching the language of biblical and literary tradition into contemporary contexts marks for him the first step towards theatrical expression. Thus, in such plays as *Cockrow and the gulls* (Studio Theatre, Mar. 1962), *Trial of Corporal Adam* (Coach House Theatre, Toronto, May 1964), and *Wail for two pedestals* (Yardbird Suite, Edmonton, Nov. 1964; published in the *Humanities Association Bulletin*, Autumn 1965), various versions of the Day of Judgement are comically thrust into surrealistic contemporary settings; traditionally sacred questions are filtered through the distorting lens of modern-day secularity. Higgins in *Cockrow* is an armchair socialist from Nanaimo who represents the failure of the common man to fulfil his social and spiritual potential. *Wail for two pedestals* presents two famously absent characters of modern drama—Godot and Lefty—in order to satirize the Theatre of the Absurd itself.

In *The young man from Cagliari*, the first play of a trilogy based on the life and political times of Italian Marxist martyr, Antonio Gramsci, Watson applies number/grid structures to extended dramatic form. In the trilogy as a whole (*Gramsci x 3*, 1983; Studio Theatre, Mar. 1980), he variously converts the traditions of Greek tragedy, the medieval morality play, and modern political drama into iconoclastic statements on the dehumanizing consequences of the intellectual failure of contemporary mass man. Watson's full-length plays are gathered in *Plays at the iron bridge; or, The autobiography of Tom Horror* (1989), edited by Shirley Neuman with an introduction by Gordon Peacock. His *The Baie-Comeau angel and other stories* (1993) contains the same mordant prisms of irony, fantasy, and humour through which Watson eyes the world in all his writing.

Critical recognition of Watson's work is limited. His reputation as a poet still rests primarily on *Friday's child*, which was cited with particular interest by Northrop FRYE in his resumé of new poetry in 1955 (*The bush garden*, 1972). See Stephen SCOBIE, 'Love in the burning city: the poetry of Wilfred Watson', *Essays on Canadian Writing* 18-19 (Summer/Fall 1980); and Diane Bessai, 'Wilfred Watson', *Dictionary of literary biography 60* (1987).

DIANE BESSAI

Watters, R.E.. See CRITICISM IN ENGLISH: 5(c).

Wayman, Tom (b. 1945). Born in Hawkesbury, Ontario, he was raised in Prince Rupert and Vancouver, British Columbia. He attended the University of British Columbia, where he edited the student newspaper, *The Ubyssey*, and did graduate work at the University of California. He has worked at a wide variety of jobs in the United States and Canada, including teaching at the Kootenay School of Writing. In 1976 he won the A.J.M. SMITH Prize for 'distinguished achievement in Canadian poetry'.

His first poetry collection was *Waiting for Wayman* (1973); his many subsequent volumes include *For and against the rain: blues, yells, and chuckles* (1974); *Free time: industrial poems* (1977); *A planet mostly sea* (1979); *Living on the ground: Tom Wayman country* (1980); *The face of Jack Munro* (1986); and *The astonishing weight of the dead* (1994). There is one major volume of selected poems: *Did I miss anything?: selected poems* (1993). Wayman has also edited several anthologies of work-related poetry, notably *Going for coffee* (1981), and has published two collections of critical essays on the same topic: *Inside job: essays on the new work writing* (1983) and *A country not considered: Canada, culture, work* (1993).

Wayman's poetry is about what he describes as 'the central experience of everyday life—which is what people do for a living, their work.' He writes of the various jobs he has held; tells the stories of people he has worked with; and speculates on the social, political, and even metaphysical implications of the work experience. While his point of view is clearly pro-labour, Wayman seldom makes dogmatic political statements, though he can be aroused to passionate indignation (as in the powerful title poem of *The face of Jack Munro*). His analyses of the effects of people's jobs on their lives are clear, sensible, often humorous, and convincingly argued.

Much of this poetry is necessarily narrative, conveyed in a straightforward, realist tone, with very little reliance on metaphor or self-consciously 'poetic' figures of speech. Often the poetic effect depends upon the witty deployment of an ironic persona—the third-person 'Wayman' who acts as a self-deprecatory character and narrator. The rhythms are prosaic and sometimes flat, and, while this effect works well in the ironic narrative mode, it is less successful in more conventionally 'lyric' poems.

Wayman's major concern and achievement have been to rescue realism in poetry from its position, as he sees it, 'somewhere at the bottom of the heap', and to assert the worth, dignity, and complexity of daily work as a poetic subject. STEPHEN SCOBIE

Weaver, Robert (b. 1921). Born in Niagara Falls, Ontario, he was educated there and in Toronto. From 1942 to 1945 he served first in the RCAF, and then in the Canadian army. After his discharge he enrolled at the University of Toronto and took his degree in Philosophy and English (1948). In the same year he was hired by the Canadian Broadcasting Corporation as a program organizer in the Talks and Public Affairs Department, and in this role he was associated with a number of the most important cultural programs on Canadian radio. These included 'Critically Speaking', which he began shortly after joining the CBC; 'Stories with John Drainie', which ran from 1959 to 1965; and 'Anthology', which he launched in 1953 and produced until 1985. Weaver was also closely involved in the cultural flagship program 'CBC Wednesday Night', which began in 1948, and with its successors. He retired from the CBC in 1985. In 1979 he founded, and is organizer of, the CBC Literary Competition, which is now in assocation with *Saturday Night*; he is fiction editor of that magazine.

As a program organizer and producer for radio, Weaver played an important role as a kind of impresario in the Canadian literary world, encouraging writers, producing their works, and giving them employment as critics and commentators. At a time when publishers and magazine editors lost interest in short stories, Weaver produced them on his radio programs, and in the process virtually discovered Mordecai RICHLER, Alice MUNRO, and other writers. His editing activities soon extended beyond radio: when the cessation of *NORTHERN REVIEW* and *CONTEMPORARY VERSE* in the early 1950s left Canada without a literary magazine of any consequence, he and a group of Toronto writers and editors established *The TAMARACK REVIEW* (1956-82), of which he was the inspiring force. Weaver's interest in the short story led him into the preparation of anthologies. These include the five Oxford volumes *Canadian short stories: First series* (1960), *Second series* (1968), *Third series* (1978), *Fourth series* (1985), and *Fifth series* (1991); and *Ten for Wednesday Night* (1961). Another of his anthologies, *The first five years* (1962), consists of writings selected from the early issues of *Tamarack*. Weaver also edited a collection of stories by Mavis GALLANT, *The end of the world and other stories* (1973); with William Toye, *The Oxford anthology of Canadian literature* (1973; 2nd edn, 1981); *The Anthology anthology: a selection from 30 years of CBC Radio's 'Anthology'* (1984); and with Margaret ATWOOD, *The Oxford book of Canadian short stories in English* (1986; 2nd edn, 1995).

GEORGE WOODCOCK

Webb, Phyllis (b. 1927). Born in Victoria, British Columbia, and educated at the University of British Columbia, she ran as a CCF candidate for the provincial legislature at the age of twenty-two. In 1950 she travelled to Montreal, where she did a year of graduate studies at McGill University. Webb lived in England, Paris, San Francisco, and Toronto, then taught at UBC for four years. In Toronto she conceived the CBC radio program 'Ideas' and was its executive producer from 1966 to 1969, after which she returned to the West Coast to settle on Saltspring Island.

Webb's early poetry—published with poems by Gael Turnbull and Eli MANDEL in *Trio* (1954), and separately in *Even your right eye* (1956)—is both formal and rhetorical, with considerable clarity of statement and elegance of diction. With the publication of *Naked poems* (1965), language and sentiment are pared to the bone in a series of interconnected minimalist poems, whose narrator claims to be 'only remotely/human' and determined to ensure that 'the area of attack/is diminished'. In *Selected poems* (1971), Webb's work becomes steadily more expansive, taking greater risks with content and form while not forgetting the hard-won lessons of economy and control.

Webb's subsequent collections include *Wilson's bowl* (1980), *Sunday water: thirteen anti ghazals* (1982), *The vision tree: selected poems* (1982), which won a Governor General's Award, *Water and light: ghazals and anti ghazals* (1984), and *Hanging fire* (1990). Her poetry is unique for its musicality and intellectual play, achieving a wonderful synchronicity of sound and idea. Her readers are invited to participate in the choreography of a nimble and discriminating mind as it selects, examines, and shapes its poetic materials. From this privileged position the reader can, to use Webb's own phrase, respond to 'the dance of the intellect in the syllables'.

As well as being a poet's poet, Webb has written a number of important and finely spun essays on poetry and poetics. Her essays, reviews, and radio talks were first collected in *Talking* (1982); a second volume, *Nothing but brush strokes: selected prose*, appeared in 1995, and included a photo-collage of the visual art that has been her chief focus in recent years. Of particular interest are her comments on the poetic line, and the process by which many of her poems have come into being. In 'Message machine' (which first appeared in *Language in her eye* (1990), edited by Libby Scheier, Sarah Sheard, and Eleanor Wachtel), Webb characterizes herself as an ambivalent minimalist with a hyper-sensitive inner ear, so preoccupied with picking up subtle messages and fine-tuning them that she sometimes appears out of touch with her earlier political self; and yet, she argues, the poems deal with 'Marxian class struggle, animals rights, violent revolution, if only by means of glancing blows. The dialectic goes deep in my nature.'

Although she is a perceptive and acute critic, Webb, in a note written for *The second Macmillan anthology* (1989), puts her own critical activities into perspective: 'The proper response to a poem is a poem. We burrow into the paper to court in secret the life of plants, the shifting moon's space-walks, the bliss, the roses, the glamorous national debt. Someone to talk to, for God's sake, something to love that will never hit back.'

See Helen W. Sonthoff, 'Structure of loss', *CANADIAN LITERATURE* 9 (Summer 1961); John Hulcoop, 'Phyllis Webb and the priestess of motion', *Canadian Literature* 32 (Spring 1967), and Janice Williamson, ed., *Sounding differences: conversations with seventeen Canadian women writers* (1993). GARY GEDDES

Week, The (1883-96). This 'Canadian Journal of Politics, Society, and Literature' was founded by Goldwin SMITH and published in Toronto by F. Blackett Robinson for the purpose of 'stimulating our national sentiment, guarding our national morality, and strengthening our national growth'. It appeared between 6 Dec. 1883 and 20 Nov. 1896. (Charles G.D. ROBERTS was editor for the first three months.) *The Week* conveys an accurate impression of the intellectual currents and cultural taste of its day. Leading writers and intellectuals contributed stories, poems, essays, commentary on current issues, and reviews of literature, drama, and music. Topics frequently debated include realism and naturalism in literature, the problem of reconciling religion with Darwinism, and the Canadian copyright situation. Awareness of international trends in fiction is indicated in the reviews, while the publication of villanelles, rondeaux, and triolets demonstrates Canadian interest in the revival of French fixed forms that was currently underway in England. Frequent poetry contributors include Archibald LAMPMAN, 'Fidelis' (Agnes Maule MACHAR), 'Seranus' (Susie Frances HARRISON), 'Sarepta' (Edward Burroughs Brownlow), Ethelwyn WETHERALD, and Frederick George SCOTT. The livelist columnist and essayist was Sara Jeannette DUNCAN.

See Claude T. Bissell, 'Literary taste in central Canada during the late nineteenth century', *Canadian Historical Review* 31, no. 2 (Sept. 1950), and D.M.R. Bentley, *A checklist of literary materials in The Week* (1978).

LORRAINE McMULLEN

Weintraub, William (b. 1926). Born in Montreal and educated at McGill University (B.A., 1947), Weintraub began his career at the *Montreal Gazette*, where he worked as a reporter for two years. He subsequently freelanced as a journalist and broadcaster and held a staff position at *Weekend Magazine* before launching a successful and prolific career as a script writer, film producer, and director, primarily with the National Film Board, writing scripts and commentaries for more than 100 documentary NFB films. In 1985 he was program producer of sixteen half-hour dramatic films (a co-production of the NFB and Atlantis films) based on short stories by, among other Canadian authors, Alice MUNRO, Brian MOORE, Margaret LAURENCE, Timothy FINDLEY, and Mordecai RICHLER.

Weintraub is the author of three critically acclaimed books: the satirical novels *Why rock the boat?* (1962, winner of a Province of Quebec Literary Award) and *The underdogs* (1979), and a lively history of Montreal in one of its most exciting periods, *City unique: Montreal days and nights in the 1940s and '50s* (1996). Both his novels lampoon the more lunatic aspects of life in Quebec. *Why rock the boat?* parodied the workings of a fictional Montreal English-language newspaper, delighting critics everywhere but in Montreal, where the local papers were frosty in their reception. Published three years after the first electoral success of the Parti Québécois, *The underdogs* was set in the future, twenty years after the purported creation of the Republic of Quebec. This time the main butt of Weintraub's biting humour was the nationalist policy of the separatists, in particular their restrictive linguistic and cultural legislation.

Weintraub adapted both his novels to other dramatic forms. He wrote and directed the film version of *Why rock the boat?* (1974), which became one of the most widely viewed Canadian features (his screenplay won a First Prize at the Canadian Film Awards), and he turned *The underdogs* into a play. Rejected as being unfair to francophones by Montreal's Centaur Theatre, which had initially rented space to the production in 1989, it was not performed until 1996, and then not in Montreal but in Cobourg, Ontario.

Weintraub took early retirement from the NFB in 1986 to devote himself to writing.

ELAINE KALMAN NAVES

Weinzweig, Helen (b. 1915). Helen Tenenbaum was born in Poland and came to Toronto at the age of nine. Her formal education ended abruptly after high school when the Depression impelled her to go to work—successively as a stenographer, receptionist, and salesperson. She married the composer John Weinzweig in 1940 and has two sons.

Weinzweig, who has read widely—especially the work of Conrad, Jerzy Kosinsky, John Barth, Borges, and Ivy Compton Burnett—published her first novel, *Passing ceremony* (1973), when she was fifty-seven. Its 117 pages display the ellipsis and compression of good poetry. About a weird wedding between a homosexual and a promiscuous woman, the story is recounted by the principals and wedding guests through bits of internal monologue. Everyone is bored with the ceremony and trapped in various isolations of ennui, hatred, sickness, fantasy, or self-disgust. Composed of reverie, memory, quick perceptions, and fantasy, this novel is *a tour de force* on an unattractive subject. Weinzweig's second novel, *Basic black with pearls* (1980), as technically assured as *Passing ceremony*, is a more unified work; also short—only 135 pages—it consists of the internal monologue of one person, Shirley Kazenbowski, née Silverberg, alias Lola Montez. Shirley is in pursuit of her lover, Coenrad, a secret agent, who has apparently given her a coded message for an assignation in Toronto. Written totally subjectively, the novel never discloses whether the adventure is madness or sanity. It is both comic and pathetic: high romance and sordid reality collide and collude in a slow waltz through a labyrinth that is also the familiar cityscape of Toronto. The novel won the City of Toronto Book Award in 1981. *A view from the roof* (1989) is a collection of thirteen of Weinzweig's short stories—including 'Causation', 'A view from the roof', 'What happened to Ravel's Bolero?', and 'The man without memories'—that have many of the qualities of her longer fiction.

See also NOVELS IN ENGLISH 1960 TO 1982: 3.

PETER BUITENHUIS

Welch, Lilianne. See Writing in the MARITIMES: 5.

Wells, Kenneth McNeill (1905-88). Born in Mitchell, Ontario, he grew up in Orillia and attended the University of Western Ontario. After two years in Europe (1926-8), where he published *Absit omen* (1927), a collection of lyric poems, he returned to Canada to become a journalist with the *London Advertiser*, the *Orillia Newsletter*, and finally the *Toronto Evening Telegram*. From the 1930s to the 1960s (except for a stint in the Canadian Army), he lived on his farm, 'The Owl Pen', in Medonte Township, Simcoe County, where he kept an apiary and wrote the articles for the *Telegram* that later became his country books. In the 1950s Wells abandoned journalism and farming for the pleasure of cruising Georgian Bay. He later lived for five years on his yacht, *The Sea Owl*, having at last discovered—strangely, in the light of his Owl Pen books—a 'magical world ... after long years of yearning' (*Cruising the North Channel*, p. xv).

Wells' country books—*The Owl Pen* (1947; reprinted 1995), *By Moonstone Creek* (1949), *Up Medonte way* (1951), and *By Jumping Cat Bridge* (1956)—all autobiographical, all arranged by seasons, are a mixture of anecdote, farce, and local pioneer history. Wells generally avoids purple-passage descriptions of nature and depicts his farm neighbours realistically; but his books seem superficial. Wells was no dirt farmer, and his farm world is a setting for the farcical misadventures of a greenhorn and the cute pet-like pranks of farm animals. Except for his wife Lucille Oille's woodcuts, the farming books are largely inconsequential treatments of the rural tradition. His cruising books—*Cruising the Georgian Bay* (1958), *Cruising the Trent-Severn waterway* (1959), *Cruising the North Channel: trailer boating where the North begins* (1961), and *Cruising the Rideau waterway* (1965)—are guides that neatly blend local history and navigational information and are preferable to *The moonstruck two* (1964), a narrative in the Owl-Pen style about a voyage to New Orleans in an outboard skiff.

ALEC LUCAS

Wetherald, Agnes Ethelwyn (1857-1940). The daughter of English Quaker parents, she was born in Rockwood, Ontario, received her early education at home, and later studied at a Quaker school in New York State and at Pickering College in Ontario. She became a journalist and contributed to many Canadian and American periodicals; for a time she was the editor of the women's department of the Toronto *Globe*, using the pseudonym 'Bel Thistlewaite'. Although Wetherald's poems had begun appearing in the late 1870s, her first collection, *The house of the trees and other poems* (Boston), was not published until 1895. Later volumes were *Tangled in stars* (1902), *The radiant road* (1909), *The last robin: lyrics and sonnets* (1907), *Tree-top mornings* (1921), and her collected *Lyrics and sonnets* (1931). Her early work was favourably received by reviewers on both sides of the Atlantic, and praised by influential contemporaries, including Archibald LAMPMAN. Major anthologies of the time, including Wilfred CAMPBELL's *Oxford book of Canadian verse* (1913) and John Garvin's *Canadian poets* (1916), gave her extensive representation. Her treatment of nature, the main subject of many of her poems, has been described as shallow and sentimental, and much of her other work is judged to be conventional in style and thought. This criticism, however, is too dismissive: Wetherald's presentation of nature is often sensual and occasionally erotic; her technical skill, particularly in the sonnet form, is at times of a very high order. Some poems, in their gravity and restraint, recall the work of Emily Dickinson, a resemblance that Wetherald's as-yet unexamined Quaker background and New England connections (most of her books were published in Boston) would clarify.

Wetherald also wrote *An Algonquin maiden: a romance of the early days of Upper Canada* (Montreal, 1887) in collaboration with G. Mercer ADAM, a novel that—as Pauline JOHNSON noted—failed to avoid the usual inaccuracies and sentimental stereotypes; and the introduction to J.W. Garvin's *Collected poems of Isabella Valancy Crawford* (1905).

DAVID JACKEL

Wevill, David (b. 1935). Born in Yokohama, Japan, of Canadian parents, he left Japan shortly before the Second World War and was educated in Toronto, Ontario, and at Trinity College School, Port Hope, before taking his B.A. (1957) at Caius College, Cambridge, England. During his Cambridge years he became a member of Philip Hobsbaum's 'The Group' (a workshop of poets that included Peter Redgrove, Peter Porter, George MacBeth, and Zulfikar Ghose). During this period, Wevill won England's Eric Gregory Award for Poetry, the only Canadian to do so. He was also the only Canadian to appear in A. Alvarez's landmark anthology *The new poetry* (1965). He was a runner-up for a Governor General's Award for *A Christ of the ice-floes* (1966). His friendship with Sylvia Plath and Ted Hughes led to the break-up of his first marriage, events that have been chronicled in various biographies of Plath. Following a period in Burma, where he taught at the University of Mandalay, and a sojourn in Spain, Wevill moved to Austin, Texas, where he is Professor of English at the University of Texas.

Wevill's poetry weaves an intricate mixture of cultural legend and autobiographical reflection in which he sets the understanding of his own life, its joys and various personal difficulties, against the suffering of other artists (Ezra Pound, Robert Schumann, Yasunari Kawabata) as if they are conduits to the solace that he seems to crave. The early works, which portray an uncertain, often lonely individual, the middle works which offer a modern man in search of a dependable though oblique personal mythology, and the later works which present an understanding of a man's position within the experience of his own life, form an opus of self-exploration where the only answer is the Faulknerian edict of endurance and perseverance. His poems often depict the women in his life—his dying mother, his three daughters, and his lost lovers—and they become more than recurring characters or motifs, muse-like in their presence, both troubling and inspiring him.

His poetry—especially in his most recent works in *Other names for the heart: new and selected poems, 1964-1984* (1985), *Figure of eight: new poems and selected translations* (1987), and *Child eating snow* (1994)—shows the marked influence of those poets whose works he has translated, namely Lorca, Neruda, Machado, Paz, and the Hungarian Ferenc Juhász. Wevill has noted their influence, particularly in reference to his use of landscape, which he views not as 'nature, but as "something out there"'. Into this landscape Wevill often interjects a solitary, contemplative figure who is more at home in his own mind than in his physical environment, as in the early poems 'At Rideau Falls' from *Birth of a shark* (1964), or in the title poem from *A Christ of the ice-floes*. Wevill's is a poetry of the searcher, a recurring theme that signals both his personal restlessness and the need to 'create complete poems, not just passing observations'. One of his most complete poems is the title piece from *Birth of a shark*, in which the world is seen from the obtuse perspective of a young shark who finds himself among a threatening hoard of swimmers.

Wevill's next three volumes of poetry—*Firebreak* (1971), *Where the arrow falls* (1974), and the prose poems in *Casual ties* (1983)—mark an experimental phase in his work where he appears to be looking for direction and foundation in both poetry and life. *Casual ties* concludes with a vision of a man, like Shakespeare's Prospero, casting his book into the sea. However, in *Other names for the heart*, a poetic rebirth at the urging of publisher Barry CALLAGHAN, Wevill rediscovers his poetic and personal roots in Japan in 'Snow country', a reflection on Japanese novelist Yasunari Kawabata's tragic story of a geisha and a wealthy businessman. The title poem—in which the persona sees human passion as a form of obsession that must be endured in the name of life and art—examines the isolated passions of Robert Schumann during that composer's final days. In 'Summer morning', which concludes *Child eating snow*, Wevill re-examines his personal life from the perspective of a survivor: 'You see the world/you saw fifty years ago but had/no words for. Having the words/now makes the light hold still a moment/and the moment resembles your life.'

See Bruce Meyer and Brian O'Riordan, 'Where the arrow falls: an interview with David Wevill', *Lives and works: interviews with Canadian authors* (1992). BRUCE MEYER

Whalley, George. See BIOGRAPHY AND MEMOIRS IN ENGLISH: 3.

Wharton, Thomas. See NOVELS IN ENGLISH 1983 TO 1996: OTHER NOVELS 1(a).

White Savannahs, The (1936). This was the first book-length work on English-Canadian literature written from a purely critical standpoint, that of the modernist movement of the years after the First World War. Its author, William Edwin Collin (1893-1984), an English-born academic trained in France, taught Romance Languages at the University of Western Ontario from 1923 to 1959. To his study of eight English-speaking poets and one French prose-writer, he brought (i) the inwardness and subjectivity of late nineteenth-century French critical writing; (ii) the 'neoclassical' critical theories of T.E. Hulme; and (iii) the influence of myth criticism, which was then being felt by such poets as T.S. Eliot. Collin was attracted to the first English-Canadian writers able to assimilate and learn from the modernist movement whose writing directly challenged the genteel tradition then dominant in Canadian literature. He first explored these new green shoots of creativity, struggling to emerge beneath the frozen 'white savannahs' of Canadian culture, in several essays produced between 1931 and 1934 for *The CANADIAN FORUM* and *The University of Toronto Quarterly*.

In Archibald LAMPMAN and Marjorie PICKTHALL Collin saw a retreat from the search for cosmic order into a repressed fiction of 'nature'. An essay—somewhat unrelated to the others—on the novelist Marie LE FRANC hints at how Collin connected myth criticism with both a theory of style and a general view of civilization. But the core of the book was his attentive and enthusiastic reading of the 'Montreal poets'—F.R. SCOTT, A.M. KLEIN, A.J.M. SMITH, Leo KENNEDY—and their contemporaries E.J. PRATT and Dorothy LIVESAY. For Collin most of these poets, like their 'metaphysical' forebears in the seventeenth century, redefined the word 'natural' in terms that would preserve the human in 'a real world of living and mechanical forces'. Though Collin recognized their common ground, his critical method richly elicited the independent virtues of each writer: the link between Imagist and socialist in Livesay, the stern ethical centre in Scott, the fruitful confrontation of heritages in Klein, a certain austerity and reserve in Smith. His deepest rapport was with Kennedy, whom he saw—not very persuasively—as providing at last the redemptive pattern linking man with the natural order that Lampman could not envision.

Though *The white savannahs*—which was reprinted in 1975 with an introduction by Germaine Warkentin—did not sell well in 1936, its influence on Canadian poetry and critical writing was considerable, both in its contribution to what A.J.M. Smith called 'a new climate of opinion among readers and publishers of poetry in Canada' and in the exemplary wit, enthusiasm, and elegance of its critical prose. Though Collin produced no later book, his annual essay on 'French-Canadian Letters'—which he wrote for *The University of Toronto Quarterly*'s 'Letters in Canada', from 1941 to 1956—was of equal distinction and influence.

See also CRITICISM IN ENGLISH: 3.

GERMAINE WARKENTIN

Whitman, Walt. See Richard Maurice BUCKE, FOREIGN WRITERS ON CANADA IN ENGLISH: 2, and TRAVEL LITERATURE IN ENGLISH.

Whittaker, Herbert (b. 1910). Born in Montreal, he studied design at the École des Beaux-Arts. He began designing for Montreal amateur theatres in 1933 and reviewing film, ballet, and theatre for the Montreal *Gazette* in 1934, serving as the paper's lead critic from 1937 to 1949. In 1949 he joined the Toronto *Globe and Mail* as theatre and film critic. He became its theatre and ballet critic in 1952, and reviewed theatre until his retirement in 1975, when he was named the *Globe*'s critic emeritus. Whittaker was a strong supporter of Canadian actors, playwrights, and directors in his theatre criticism. As chairman of the Toronto Drama Bench (1972-5) and founding chair of the Canadian Theatre Critics Association since 1980, Whittaker has also sought to strengthen the field of theatre criticism itself. Besides designing and directing several prize-winning productions for over twenty amateur companies in Montreal and Toronto from 1933 to 1982, Whittaker directed and designed for the Jupiter Theatre in Toronto in 1951; directed for the Crest Theatre in 1954 and 1956; and designed sets and costumes for the 1961-2 tour of the Canadian Players. He served as a governor of the Dominion Drama Festival from 1949 to 1968; was a member of the Board of Trustees of the National Arts Centre from 1976 to 1982; and has been an advisory board member of Theatre Canada and the Shaw Festival. Unlike Nathan COHEN, who kept aloof from the theatre community, Whittaker maintained an involvement in live theatre that made him aware of the economic and artistic difficulties of Canadian productions. His criticism (unlike Cohen's) generally accented positive aspects. He has said: 'Appreciation has always been more important than fault-finding in the theatre critic's lexicon. I think I make my points quite clear without a hammer.'

Besides numerous articles, Whittaker has written about the theatre in 'Whittaker's Montreal: a theatrical autobiography 1910-1949', *Canadian Drama* 12.2 (1986) and in *Whittaker's theatricals* (1993). His career is surveyed in John Rittenhouse's 'Herbert Whittaker: a theatre life', *Theatre History in Canada* (Spring 1982). A collection of Whittaker's theatre criticism appears in *Whittaker's theatre* (1985), edited by Ronald Bryden with Boyd Neil. See also Richard Russell Hanson, 'Principal witness: Herbert Whittaker and Canadian drama, 1949-1975', Ph.D. thesis, University of Toronto, 1997. ANTON WAGNER

Who has seen the wind (1947), by W.O. MITCHELL, is one of Canada's most beloved novels. Structured in four parts and set in a Saskatchewan town, it dramatizes Brian O'Connal's growth from age four to twelve, and his youthful struggle to comprehend 'the ultimate meaning of the cycle of life' in the face of loss and death. Prairie, family, and town all contribute to his awakening sense of perspective and social responsibility. By the novel's end young Brian, originally self-centred in his innocence, has matured to the point that he imagines his future as a 'dirt doctor', pledged to minister to the land and the difficult environmental conditions affecting the lives of the people he loves. But Brian's growth has an inverse quality, as Mitchell's allusions to Wordsworth suggest. In childhood Brian is closest to nature and the divine; he experiences intimations of immortality particular to a prairie boyhood. As he ages his social identity begins to take shape; 'the feeling' he often experienced occurs far less frequently.

In Brian's growth the prairie is a vast romantic stage, its vitality symbolized by characters like the Bens and Saint Sammy. In contrast, the town seems ruled by the restrictions and cruelties of a life-denying puritanism. Brian's most effective teachers are associated with the prairie or the peripheries of town, where waspish élitism, racial prejudice, unfairness, and hypocrisy have less place. Though melodramatically schematized, *Who has seen the wind* has a freshness of perspective, a cogency of theme, a vividness of voice and event, and a vitality of presentation that contribute to its continuing popularity and prominence—its status as a 'classic'—in Canadian letters. First published in Canada by MACMILLAN, and in the United States by Little, Brown, the shorter and edited American version was the basis for reprints for over thirty years. A coffee-table edition with illustrations by William Kurelek appeared in 1976. It was not until 1991, however, that McCLELLAND & STEWART published an edition that restored the text as Mitchell had intended it. A film based on the novel, directed by Alan King, was released in 1977. See Dick Harrison, *Intimations of mortality: W.O. Mitchell's 'Who has seen the wind'* (1993). MICHAEL PETERMAN

Wiebe, Rudy (b. 1934). Born on the family farm in a small Mennonite community near Fairholme, Saskatchewan, of parents who came to Canada from the Soviet Union in 1930, he began writing seriously as an undergraduate at the University of Alberta (1953-6), from which he received an M.A. (1960) in creative writing. Wiebe then studied abroad (1957-8) at the University of Tübingen, Germany. He returned to Canada in 1958, taught at the Mennonite Brethren Bible College, edited the *Mennonite Brethren Herald* (1962-3), and then became assistant professor of English at Goshen College, Indiana (1964). In 1967 he joined the English Department of the University of Alberta, Edmonton, and since 1992 has been Professor Emeritus.

Wiebe has written eight novels: *Peace shall destroy many* (1962), *First and vital candle* (1966), *The blue mountains of China* (1970; NCL), *The temptations of Big Bear* (1973; NCL, with an Afterword by Robert KROETSCH), *The scorched-wood people* (1977), *The mad trapper* (1980), *My lovely enemy* (1983), and *A discovery of strangers* (1994). (*The temptations of Big Bear* and *A discovery of strangers* received Governor General's Awards.) He has also produced three collections of short stories—*Where is the voice coming from?* (1974), and *Alberta / a celebration* (1979), which contains photographs by Tom Radford and commentary by Harry Savage; selections from these books were reprinted in *The angel of the tar sands and other stories* (NCL, 1982)—and a play, *Far as the eye can see* (1977). In addition he has edited several anthologies of short stories: *The story makers* (1970); *Stories from western Canada* (1972); *Stories from Pacific and Arctic Canada* (1974), co-edited with Andreas SCHROEDER; *Double vision: twentieth century stories in English* (1976); *Getting here: Edmonton story anthology* (1977); and *More stories from western Canada* (1980), co-edited with Aritha VAN HERK.

The two aspects of Wiebe's life that are most important to his art are that he is a Westerner and that he was born, and continues to be, a Mennonite whose first language was Low German. His fiction, though experimental in style and form (his major novels are among our most successful experimental works), is resolutely committed to a radical and ecumenical Christian vision. *Peace shall destroy many*, *First and vital candle*, and *The blue mountains of China* are essentially about man's struggle to live a moral and spiritual life in a world where such terms and assumptions are increasingly considered archaic and even obsolete. The first dramatizes—in a realistic style and within a relatively conventional four-part seasonal structure—the conflicts that arise during the Second World War in a Mennonite community in Wapiti, Sask. Most of the action is seen through the eyes of the protagonist, Thom Wiens, an earnest and inquiring young man who is torn between the old ways (represented by the dogmatic and bullying Deacon Block) and the new (embodied in, and articulated by, the reforming Joseph Duecke). The novel's central question—how does one live a truly Christian life in a fundamentally non-Christian world?—is raised again in *First and vital candle*, which depicts the life of Abe Ross, who has lost his faith. An ambitious, closely organized work, containing many powerful scenes of Native and Inuit life, the novel is finally too portentous and didactic. In *The blue mountains of China* Wiebe turned to the historical and epic mode characteristic of his major novels. It offers both a criticism of the materialism and one-dimensionality (Marcuse's term) of modern life, and an affirmative alternative. At the centre of this episodic novel, covering almost a century of Mennonite history—including the heroic 1920s emigration from Soviet Russia to Canada and later to Paraguay—is a vision of various forms of Christian action and commitment: from the passive but firm belief of Frieda Friessen to the active witnessing of the cross-carrying John Reimer, who is walking through western Canada in search of the scattered Mennonite communities that still cling to the original revelation.

Wiebe has written extensively about Native people, in part because they resemble the Mennonites in their concern for a community embodying spiritual values, and because they exist on the periphery of, and in opposition to, modern society. Wiebe's commitment to this body of western experience—which is traditionally ignored, or misinterpreted, in Canadian history and fiction—is reflected in minor works, such as some of the stories in *Alberta/a celebration* and *Where is the voice coming from?* and the adventure novel *The mad trapper*, as well as in *The temptations of Big Bear*, *The scorched-wood people*, and *A discovery of strangers*.

By means of a complex polyphonic, multiple-viewpoint narrative structure, incorporating much documentary material, Wiebe tries in *The temptations of Big Bear* to present the Native point of view, especially Big Bear's struggle to understand the changes taking place in the West in the last decades of the nineteenth century. This often brilliant, often difficult novel covers twelve years—from Big Bear's refusal to sign a treaty in 1876, through his inadvertent involvement in the killings at Frog Lake in 1884, to his imprisonment and death. A massive attempt at fictive translation, it attempts to give one culture (ours) an imaginative sense of another (the Cree's). Wiebe most effectively conveys the Native way of life in several panoramic set scenes: the Cree attack on a Blood village, Big Bear's last thirst dance, and the last Buffalo hunt in which his people search for the remnants of the once-great herds. To emphasize the conflict between the two cultures Wiebe uses opposed sets of images: the whites, described predominantly in images drawn from civilization, are all angles and straight lines; the Natives are represented in images drawn from nature, with the result that Big Bear is a curve, a wave of life, a bird, a tree, and finally, in the novel's resonant closing image, a rock. More significantly, however, he is associated with the wind, with spirit, and—like most of Wiebe's fictional heroes—with speech and vision.

Big Bear—in this novel, and in the tragic nature of his life—anticipates another visionary and revolutionary, Louis Riel, the central, heroic figure in *The scorched-wood people*. (Riel appears on the periphery of *The temptations of Big Bear*, is mentioned in *Peace shall destroy many*, and his grave is visited by Abe Ross in *First and vital candle*.) Like Big Bear, Riel articulates and embodies a vision of western community. Wiebe's complex portrait of him (both in form and content), and of the Métis, is historical revisionism with a vengeance: Wiebe refuses to accept the traditional interpretations of the man and his era offered by such historians as A.R.M. Lower, Donald CREIGHTON, and George Stanley. Instead of presenting Riel as mad (and the Métis as a marginal group impeding progress), Wiebe describes him in Christological terms as a visionary and a millenarian, the prophet of a vision of community that stands in direct opposition to the expansionist capitalist 'vision' of Macdonald. Wiebe has argued that the border between fiction and history has been called into doubt in our era. In *The scorched-wood people* he holds our interest by filling in the lacunae of history, providing details that no one person could have known by means of an omniscient posthumous narrator, Pierre FALCON, the poet of the Métis, who had seen Riel. *My lovely enemy* (1983), uses the story of a love affair between a professor of history at the University of Alberta and a graduate student as the basis for an exploration of Wiebe's traditional concerns: man's relationship to God, the relevance of Christianity, and the nature and scope of human and divine love. The challenging narrative technique, combining realism and fantasy, is the perfect medium for Wiebe's central theme that love, erotic or spiritual, transcends time. However, this ambitious novel, which includes a rewriting of Dostoevsky's 'Grand Inquisitor' episode, has a major weakness: the author's slightly sentimental attitude towards his three central characters.

The mad trapper is a novel that fleshes out Wiebe's essay and short story about Albert Johnson, the 'mad trapper' who shot a Mountie and became the object of a lengthy and widely publicized chase through the North. (The essay can be found in *Figures in a ground: Canadian essays on modern literature collected in honour of Sheila Watson*, 1978, edited by Diane Bessai and David Jackel.) Wiebe's least ambitious work, it is in essence a well-told adventure story.

Focusing on the 1820-21 expedition of John Franklin (1786-1847) to the Arctic coast of what is today Canada, *Playing dead: a contemplation concerning the Arctic* (1989) is a series of interrelated essays in which Wiebe interweaves his impressions of the North, Inuit narratives, and discussions of various explorers from Franklin to Vilhjalmur Stefansson. Like the novel it anticipates, the book is notable both for its sensitive and informed treatment of Native and Inuit ways of life and for its refusal to simplify or sentimentalize them. Describing the pre-European past, for instance, Wiebe comments that 'no more before than after Europeans arrived was there a great deal of "noble savage" paradise discernible here.' In retrospect the book seems like a set of preparatory sketches for *A discovery of strangers*, which recasts the sections dealing with Franklin's first expedition in the form of a historical novel that shows the English explorers and their misconceived expedition from several viewpoints, including that of the Tetsot'ine or Yellowstone people who helped them survive. Thoroughly researched and often drawing on period materials, the novel interweaves excerpts from journals kept by Robert Hood and John Richardson, Native narratives, myths and songs—and the story of the expedition, which provides it with a unifying narrative drive. At the heart of the novel are Franklin's obsession with the journey and the love affair between Robert Hood and Greenstocking, a historical figure named in Franklin's narrative and perhaps Wiebe's most fully realized female portrait. This relationship serves, ironically, to emphasize the irreconcilable disparity between Europeans and Native people when, at the novel's end, Greenstocking refuses to acknowledge to the English that her child is Hood's.

Wiebe's novels and stories stress that the 'signs' of God's presence are, and will always be, visible and available: man need only be receptive to the various incarnations taking place around him. The writings are filled with homely figures who, shadowed by biblical originals, function as Christ-like scapegoats, reminding others of a fully Christian life. No other Canadian writer, French or English, has made as concerted an attempt to give the peoples of the First Nations a voice in fiction. Critical debate about Wiebe's novels, however, has often focused less on his themes than on his style, which some readers have found ponderous in rhythm and tortuous in syntax. For his admirers, Wiebe's so-called 'difficult' style is the necessary expression of the fiction's complex attitude to life and its ambitious attempt to render non-European modes of thought, being, and expression.

Most of the best criticism on Wiebe has been collected in *A voice in the land: essays by and about Rudy Wiebe* (1981) edited by W.J. Keith; it includes interesting interviews with Wiebe. Keith is also the author of *Epic fiction: the art of Rudy Wiebe* (1981). More recent, and more theoretical in orientation, is Penny van Toorn's *Rudy Wiebe and the historicity of the word* (1995). Also of value are an interview with Donald Cameron in his *Conversations with Canadian novelists*, volume two (1973); Magadalene Redekop's 'Rudy Wiebe', *Profiles in Canadian Literature*, vol. 2 (1981) edited by Jeffrey Heath; and the following essays: Keith's introduction to the 1975 NCL edition of *The blue mountains of China*; R.P. Bilan's 'Wiebe and the religious struggle', *CANADIAN LITERATURE* 77 (Summer 1978); Sam Solecki's 'Giant fictions and large meanings: the novels of Rudy Wiebe,' *CANADIAN FORUM*, vol. 60, no. 707 (March 1981); and Pierre Spriet's 'Les formes du refus dans les nouvelles de Rudy Wiebe', *Recherches Anglaises et Américaines* 16 (1983).

See also NOVELS IN ENGLISH 1960 TO 1982: 2. SAM SOLECKI

Wild animals I have known (New York, 1898; NCL). The first and most famous of many collections of animal stories by Ernest Thompson SETON, it includes the perennially popular 'Lobo, the King of Currumpaw' and seven other stories. Since publication it has never been out of print, and it exists in numerous translations. Along with Charles G.D. ROBERTS' *The kindred of the wild* (1902), it marked the beginning of a new genre: the realistic animal story. Seton's innovation was to make an animal, rather than a human, the central character. His goal was to make a moral point about man's relation to animals and to the wilderness they inhabit, emphasizing the need for man to live in harmony with nature. His work as a naturalist supplied the raw material for his stories. He insisted that his animal biographies were all fact, but admitted that they were often composite portraits, based on his observations of many animals of a species.

The story of the wolf Lobo was first published in *Scribner's Magazine* (Nov. 1894). Based on a real episode that took place in 1892 when Seton visited New Mexico, it describes the killing of Blanca, the capture of her mate Lobo, and his mysterious death during captivity. Seton's fellow scientists, arguing that a wolf cannot die of a broken heart, challenged his assertion that his stories were factual. Repeated charges of anthropomorphism—the 'nature-fakir controversy'—acted as a catalyst to increase Seton's productivity in scientific publications; but they did not keep him from writing numerous collections of stories following his popular formula.

MAGDALENE REDEKOP

Wilkinson, Anne (1910-61). Born in Toronto, Ontario, Anne Gibbons spent her early years there and in London, Ontario; she was educated privately by tutors, and at progressive schools in the USA and France. She married F.R. Wilkinson, a surgeon, in 1932 (they were divorced twenty-two years later) and brought up a family of three children in Toronto.

Anne Wilkinson's reputation as a writer was made with two books of poetry, *Counterpoint to sleep* (1951) and *The hangman ties the holly* (1955), but she was equally accomplished in prose. In *Lions in the way* (1956) she traced the story of her distinguished family, the Oslers, who originally settled in the backwoods of Ontario, in Tecumseth Township. Her great-grandmother, Ellen Osler, raised nine children, four of whom developed outstandingly successful careers: Featherston and

Britton Bath Osler as eminent lawyers; Sir William Bath Osler as Regius Professor of Medicine at Oxford; and her grandfather Sir Edmund Osler as a financier and member of Parliament. The figure who emerges most clearly, however, is Ellen, to whose courage and strong personality these men owed their success. The book provides a lively social history of Upper Canada. An epilogue brings the tale up to Wilkinson's own childhood, when she spent long periods in her grandfather's Toronto mansion, Craigleigh. This luxurious house is also described in the beautifully written autobiographical piece, 'Four corners of my world', originally published in *The TAMARACK REVIEW* 20 (Summer 1961), of which she was a founding editor and generous patron. A.J.M. SMITH included this memoir in *The collected poems of Anne Wilkinson* (1968), where poems and fragments from periodicals and manuscripts are added to the two volumes of poetry published in her lifetime. Smith's edition was re-issued, with a new introduction by Joan Coldwell, as *The poetry of Anne Wilkinson and a prose memoir* (1990). 'Four corners of my world' is a much-abridged version of the full-length autobiography Wilkinson submitted for publication late in her life. It remained unpublished until it was included in *The tightrope walker: autobiographical writings of Anne Wilkinson* (1992), edited by Joan Coldwell. This volume also contains the journals Wilkinson wrote between 1947 and 1956, the years of her productivity as a poet as well as of the disintegration of her marriage. The journals create an intimate portrait of a woman balancing the demands of motherhood and poetry; they also provide a valuable record of social and literary history, relating to both Toronto and Canada. The autobiography and the journals testify to Wilkinson's love for, and close bond with, her mother, Mary Osler Gibbons Boyd.

The 'four corners' of Wilkinson's world are seen as archetypes: the Gothic family home in London; the classical Craigleigh; the romantic summer home on Lake Simcoe; and the mysteriously evocative oceanside house in Santa Barbara, California, where her mother spent winters. A similar shaping of material into a quaternity characterizes Wilkinson's poetry, where this method of seeing unity in multiplicity, especially in imagery of the four elements, emphasizes her own sense of identity and her oneness with nature. Her poetry is both highly sensuous and wittily intellectual; even in the most passionate of her love poems she plays with puns and with references to her eclectic reading. Her subjects range from the landscapes of her family's 'summer acres', where she insists on the spirituality of the senses, to philosophical enquiries based on Kafka, Empedocles, and medieval texts. A.J.M. Smith's prefatory essay to *The collected poems* gives a fine analysis of these aspects of her work, as also of her poems of love and death. Smith points to the celebration of metamorphosis in her poetry—a motif found, too, in her story for children, *Swann and Daphne* (1960). Delightfully illustrated by Leo Rampen, it tells of two mysterious children: instead of hair the boy has feathers and the girl has leaves. In an ironic comment on the relation of the sexes, the girl sacrifices her own plans and turns into a birch tree in order to free the boy for a life of adventure with the wild swans.

Robert Lecker analyses the polar oppositions in Wilkinson's imagery in 'Better quick than dead: Anne Wilkinson's poetry', *Studies in Canadian Literature*, III, no. 1 (Winter, 1978). Douglas BARBOUR emphasises Wilkinson's passionate celebration of life in 'Day thoughts on Anne Wilkinson's poetry', *A mazing space* (1986), edited by S. Neuman and S. Kamboureli. Katherine Acheson studies the use made of Wilkinson's journals by a later novelist in 'Anne Wilkinson in Michael Ondaatje's "In the skin of a lion": writing and reading class', *CANADIAN LITERATURE* 145 (Summer 1992). Joan Coldwell's feminist analysis of the editorial process in relation to Wilkinson appears in *Editing women*, the published proceedings of the 1995 editorial conference, University of Toronto, as 'Walking the tightrope with Anne Wilkinson'. See also Christopher Armitage, *Anne Wilkinson and her works* (1989).

See also POETRY IN ENGLISH 1950 TO 1982: 1.

JOAN COLDWELL

Williams, David (b. 1945). Born in Souris, Manitoba, he grew up in a number of Saskatchewan towns, most importantly in Lac Vert. His parents and paternal grandfather, strong fundamentalists, tried to block his entry into journalism at University of Western Ontario, and succeeded in sending him to Briercrest Bible Institute (near Moose Jaw), from which he graduated with a pastor's diploma in 1965. He nevertheless attended the University of Saskatchewan (B.A. Hons., 1968) and the University of Massachusetts (M.A., 1970; Ph.D., 1973). He teaches Canadian literature and Milton at the University of Manitoba.

Brilliantly evoking prairie landscapes, language, and social conflict, Williams' first three novels—the 'Lacjardin' trilogy—show the influence of Milton's and Melville's searching for myths that would make sense of suffering. *The burning wood* (1975), built on his haunting memory of sitting in his grandfather's Stony Lake Bible Camp and hearing the drums of the Chagoness Indian Reserve, follows Williams' *alter ego*, Joshua Cardiff, as he runs away from Bible Camp with his Cree friend Thomas. Joshua's sense of personal damnation, and of a Christian society that has betrayed its ideals, results in his wish to 'go Indian', but the hilarious attempt to resurrect the buffalo hunt—with stolen Clydesdales and reluctant cattle—ends in tragedy.

The river horsemen (1981) even more convulsively mixes Cree culture with prairie fundamentalism by calling up personal and collective pasts in an effective use of Faulkner's interior monologues. Having lost parents, women, and God in the Depression, the four horsemen paddle up the South Saskatchewan River from Lacjardin to Saskatoon. The river's monstrous underworld of corpses and inexplicable drownings matches the dissolving world on shore, where not only dust, but also the Regina riots and Edward VIII's abdication oppress. As funny as it is apocalyptic, the novel expands in a series of layered parodies: of the gospels and revivalism in the faith-healer Jack Cann; of the Cree trickster Wisahkecahk in Many Birds and Billy O'Jibway; of the shaman in Fine Day; and of a republican Huck Finn in the profane Ukrainian boy, Nick. Jack, believing that he must die as God, and Many Birds, believing that his ex-lover Agnes ought to feel his sexual prowess one more time, bring the novel to its explosive conclusion, while more humane possibilities are imagined in Fine Day's hesitant remembering of the spirit world and Nick's location of his abused mother.

Struck by the parallels between his own familial history and the Brynhild cycle, Williams next fictionalized his maternal grandfather in *Eye of the father* (1985) as the scapegrace Magnus Vangdal, whose flight from his father's house in Hardangerfjorden (Norway) lands him in Lacjardin. His alias, Magnus Sigurdson, proves prophetic as he goes through fire to rescue Hilda and later abandons her. Finally a lost soul in a new country, Magnus becomes one of the Old Ones from whom he fled, who can bequeath only a full ostomy pouch to his daughters, his democratic self-invention as 'Cabin John' having proved in all other ways empty. Hilda, however, refuses a Wagnerian immolation. Under the rune, which signifies necessity or constraint, she and her descendants struggle to accept Magnus's legacy without repeating his life.

Williams has published two books of literary criticism, *Faulkner's women: the myth and the muse* (1977) and *Confessional fictions: a portrait of the artist in the Canadian novel* (1991), as well as numerous papers on Canadian literature.

See Dave Jenkinson, 'David Williams', *Connections two: writers and the land* (1983); David Williams, 'After post-modernism', *Trace: prairie writers on writing* (1986), edited by Birk Sproxton; and Reinhold Kramer, 'Canada, then scatology, then the novels of David Williams', *Studies in Canadian Literature* 15:2 (1990).

REINHOLD KRAMER

Williamson, Janice. See LESBIAN LITERATURE.

Willis, John H. See ESSAYS IN ENGLISH: 1.

Wilson, Ethel (1888-1980). Born Ethel Davis Bryant at Port Elizabeth, South Africa, where her father was a Methodist missionary, she was taken to England in 1890 on the death of her mother and brought up by relatives. In 1898, after her father died, she came to Canada and lived with her grandmother in Vancouver in circumstances drawn upon later for *The innocent traveller* (1949; NCL, with an Afterword by P.K. PAGE). Like Frankie Burnaby in *Hetty Dorval* (1947; NCL, with an Afterword by Northrop FRYE), she attended boarding schools, first in Vancouver and then in England. After receiving a teacher's certificate from the Vancouver Normal School in 1907, she taught at various local schools until 1920. In 1921 she married Dr Wallace Wilson, then at the beginning of a distinguished medical career (he was president of the Canadian Medical Association in 1946-7).

Wilson's writing career began late. She started to publish short stories in the *New Statesman and Nation* in the late 1930s, and her first novel did not appear until 1947. *Hetty Dorval* is an accomplished work, remarkable for the way in which the story of the 'experienced' *Hetty Dorval* is told through the 'innocent' Frankie Burnaby, a girl growing up in the British Columbia hinterland. The plot is a trifle forced, but Wilson demonstrates an ability to combine stylistic clarity and technical sophistication with the authorial poise, humour, and good sense that characterize all her fiction. Her next novel, *The innocent traveller*, employs elements from her own family history in tracing the life of Topaz Edgeworth from precocious three-year-old in the English Midlands to still irrepressible centenarian in Vancouver. Besides offering a wholly credible portrait of a character rarely encountered in fiction—the unconventional, unfrustrated middle-class spinster who lives a passive, unremarkable yet full and happy life—the novel offers a convincing presentation of social developments in England and Canada over a long period (the 1840s to the 1940s).

Wilson's later fiction reveals an increasing interest in portraying various kinds of women at times of personal crisis, and in exploring spiritual and religious values. *The equations of love* (1952; NCL, with an Afterword by Alice MUNRO) is made up of two novellas. 'Tuesday and Wednesday' follows the life of an ordinary couple for two days, on the second of which the husband dies; 'Lilly's Story' traces an unmarried mother's determination to bring up her child independently and decently. Both involve people who never penetrate below the surface of life, but they are portrayed with understanding and sympathy. *Swamp angel* (1954; NCL, with an Afterword by George BOWERING), perhaps Wilson's finest artistic success, divides its attention between a woman escaping a disastrous marriage to start a new life on a remote lake in northern British Columbia, and a retired circus-performer whose memories of her past threaten to spoil her present. It is a touching, sensitively written, wise novel that delicately raises profound questions about human responsibility and the meaning of life.

Wilson's final novel, *Love and salt water* (1956; NCL, with an Afterword by Anne MARRIOTT), is darker in tone. Most of the characters are wounded, physically or emotionally, by the Second World War. The central figure, Ellen Cuppy, has a painful childhood (she discovers her mother dead; her father soon remarries), and her initiation into the adult world is deftly presented in all its clumsiness and uncertainty. Here, as elsewhere in Wilson's novels, the focus is not so much on what happens as on personal responses to what happens. Human relationships, especially love, are invariably Wilson's main subject; and in this novel the pain and danger implicit in emotional commitments, symbolized by the salt water of the title, are given particular emphasis.

Unfortunately Wilson published little after 1961. Her later years, after her husband died in 1966, were spent in seclusion and often ill health until her death. Her novels, then, are about everyday topics—love, the failure to love, hope and despair, all-too-human fear and courageous determination. Her characters are not immediately memorable, but Wilson shows that they are more remarkable than they seem. She approaches them with compassion balanced by firmness; she is not afraid to discuss her characters with her readers in Victorian fashion, but her attitudes belong solidly to her own time. George WOODCOCK has caught the curious tensions in her work by describing Wilson as an Edwardian sensibility who acquired a contemporary ironic intelligence. She writes with wit and grace but does not ignore human triviality or evil. Her novels demonstrate that it is possible to combine serenity, good humour, and intelligence in twentieth-century fiction without seeming incongruous.

The majority of Wilson's short stories, many of them predating the novels, were collected and published as *Mrs Golightly and other stories* (1961; NCL). They range in tone from the warm comedy of 'Mrs Golightly and the first convention' to the bleak presentation of gratuitous violence in 'Fog' and 'Hurry, hurry'; from garrulous monologue in 'I just love dogs' to sophisticated experiments with narrative viewpoint in 'A drink with Adolphus'. The last story in the collection, 'The window', is an effective moral parable that draws together many strands from her work as a whole. Despite this variety in her short stories, the collection is unified by Wilson's mature perception and unostentatious artistic control.

David Stouck has collected other writings in *Ethel Wilson: stories, essays, letters* (1987). See also Mary McAlpine's biography *The other side of silence* (1988), Desmond PACEY's critical study *Ethel Wilson* (1968), and the proceedings of the University of Ottawa 'Ethel Wilson Symposium' (1981). A bibliography by Bonnie Martyn McComb appears in *The annotated bibliography of Canada's major authors* 5 (1984).

W.J. KEITH

Wilson, Milton. See CRITICISM IN ENGLISH: 4.

Wilson, Robert Charles. See FANTASTIC LITERATURE IN ENGLISH: 1.

Wiseman, Adele (1928-92). Born in Winnipeg, Manitoba, to Jewish parents who emigrated from the Ukraine, she received a B.A. in English and psychology (1949) from the University of Manitoba and then, to support her early intention to be a writer, took a variety of jobs as executive secretary, teacher, and social worker in Canada and abroad. She and her husband, Dmitry Stone, made their home in Toronto; they had one daughter, Tamara.

Wiseman's imagination was shaped by her Eastern European Jewish heritage. Her first novel, *The sacrifice* (1956; rpr. 1968), received a Governor General's Award; it was followed by

Crackpot (1974; NCL, with an Afterword by Margaret LAURENCE). In both novels Wiseman interprets modern Jewish experience as reflected in the lives of people who immigrated to the Canadian Prairies between the two world wars. *The sacrifice* uses the biblical story of the patriarch's willingness to sacrifice his son as the metaphorical base for the tragic story of a new Abraham who repeatedly suffers the blows of a hostile fate and, though he is dedicated to the search for moral and spiritual perfection, is eventually driven to murder. Like the heroes of Greek tragedy, Abraham is over-proud; only at the end does he recognize the need to love, to accept weakness in himself and others, and to acknowledge the mysterious co-existence of creativity and destruction. The novel depicts the hardships of immigrant experience, with sharp criticism of exploitation in the garment trade, ruthless business practices, and social snobbery. *Crackpot* is also set in a Jewish ghetto, now recognizably the north end of Winnipeg during the Depression. Unlike the former novel, which used a traditional pattern and an omniscient narrator, *Crackpot* experiments with unconventional sentence structures and language appropriate to the uneducated perceptions of Hoda, a fat prostitute who never loses her child-like trust and clear-sightedness. Through this seemingly unprepossessing character, Wiseman celebrates life in all its richness and complexity and, at the moment when Hoda must choose to commit incest, demonstrates the paradoxical knotting of good and evil within one action. *Crackpot* is full of laughter as well as pathos and is given poetic richness by an intricate symbolism, especially to do with light, based on the Kabbalah. Like its predecessor, this novel contains much social criticism, particularly of the educational and welfare systems, but the method is more satirical and, in the tradition of Jewish humour, much of the laughter is self-directed. Rachel WYATT's dramatized version of *Crackpot* was staged in Calgary and Victoria in 1996.

Wiseman wrote the short text that accompanies Joe ROSENTHAL's sketches in *Old markets, new worlds* (1964), stressing the importance of the old-style markets to an immigrant community. This piece is reprinted in *Memoirs of a book-molesting childhood* (1987), a collection of personal and often witty essays, of which the final one reflects on her parents' death. Much of their life story is told episodically in *Old woman at play* (1978), an illustrated book whose main concern is the formation of an aesthetic theory from her mother's primitive art of doll-making. Wiseman spent many years on two plays of social criticism: *Testimonial dinner* (1978), a study of three generations of a Canadian Jewish family, was published privately; a portion of *The Lovebound*, set on a Jewish refugee ship in 1939, appears in *Journal of Canadian Fiction* 31/32 (1981), which also contains Wiseman's story 'The country of the hungry bird' and Roslyn Belkin's interview with Wiseman, 'The consciousness of a Jewish artist'. A final short story about physically handicapped youth was published in *The MALAHAT REVIEW* (Spring 1992).

See Michael Greenstein, 'Vision and movement in *The sacrifice*', *CANADIAN LITERATURE* 80 (Spring 1979); Marco LoVerso, 'Language private and public: a study of Wiseman's *Crackpot*', *Studies in Canadian Literature* 9 (1984); and J.M. Kertzer, 'Wiseman's *Old woman at play* and the structure of enigma', *Canadian Poetry* 24 (1989). The 1993 biographical guide published in ECW PRESS was written by Michael Greenstein.

See also NOVELS IN ENGLISH 1960 TO 1982: 1. JOAN COLDWELL

Wiseman, Christopher (b. 1936). Born, raised, and educated in England, he taught there and in Scotland and settled in Canada in 1969 after completing graduate studies in creative writing at the University of Iowa. He was a professor of English at the University of Calgary, where he founded the creative-writing division of the English department in 1973. He retired from the university in 1997.

His first two books of poetry published in Canada were *Waiting for the barbarian* (1971) and *The barbarian file* (1974). The persona of the titles, developed from a poem by the Greek poet Cavafy, is a questioning and at times gullible man striving to be decent in an increasingly uncivilized world. He speaks in a satirical voice that comments, sometimes sardonically, sometimes with honest doubt or inquisitive ignorance, on the foibles, immoralities, mischiefs, and betrayals of contemporary society. The direct honesty of approach is part of the poet's continuing quest for sensible and serious values that are often undermined by loss and insensitivity. The poems are included in *Postcards home: poems new and selected* (1988) and *Missing persons* (1989), both volumes winning the Alberta Poetry Award. In 1988 Wiseman was given the Alberta Achievement Award for Excellence in the literary arts.

He has also published a book of criticism, *Beyond the labyrinth: a study of Edwin Muir's poetry* (1978). A more recent volume of poems, *Remembering Mr. Fox* (1995), has a dedication to another poet 'who hears the old voices', an apt comment on Wiseman's own poetry.

PETER STEVENS

Withrow, William Henry (1839-1908). Born in Toronto, he attended the University of Toronto (B.A., 1863; M.A., 1864). He was admitted to the Methodist ministry in 1866, and became the editor of its major cultural organ, the *Canadian Methodist Magazine*, in 1874. He remained its editor, and one of its major contributors, for more than a quarter of a century. Many of his articles—especially his biographical sketches, travel accounts, and serialized fiction—were published in book form. Moral didacticism pervades all of his writing, appropriately and inevitably in his sketches of religious figures: works such as *Worthies of early Methodism* (Toronto, 1878), *The romance of missions* (Toronto, 1879), *Men worth knowing; or Heroes of Christian chivalry* (Toronto, 1881), and *Missionary heroes* (Toronto, 1883). This persistent, unrelieved tone is less acceptable, however, in his fiction, which is further diminished, especially in dramatic effect, by too much use of history-writing paraphernalia. These traits undermine *The king's messenger; or, Lawrence Temple's probation: a story of Canadian life* (Toronto, 1879); *Neville Trueman: the pioneer preacher. A tale of the War of 1812* (Toronto, 1880); *Valeria: the martyr of the catacombs. A tale of early Christian life in Rome* (Toronto, 1882); *Life in a parsonage; or, Lights and shadows of the itineracy* (London, 1885); and *Barbara Heck. A tale of early Methodism in America* (Toronto, 1895). Some of these novels were popular enough to be reprinted in subsequent editions, and in England and the United States, but Withrow was better known in his own time as the author of the historical study *The catacombs of Rome and their testimony relative to primitive Christianity* (New York, 1874), and for his *History of Canada* (Toronto, 1876), which was subsequently reprinted in several different editions. His travel books, *A Canadian in Europe; being sketches of travel in France, Italy, Switzerland, Germany, Holland and Belgium, Great Britain, and Ireland* (Toronto, 1881), and *Our own country: Canada scenic and descriptive*... (2 vols, Toronto, 1889), were successfully characterized by lively, light, informative narrative. *The native races of North America* (Toronto, 1895) is simply a compilation of selections from the work of other writers.

Withrow's stature in his own day was recognized by the award of a D.D. from Victoria University in 1880, and by his election to the Royal Society of Canada in 1884.

CHARLES R. STEELE

Wood, Joanna E. (d. 1919). Born in Lanarkshire, Scotland, she lived for a short time with her family in the southern United States, then moved to Queenston Heights, Ontario. During her writing career she did much travelling in Britain and Europe, and lived for periods in the USA, particularly Boston. She died in Detroit.

Wood was the author of several novels, the strongest of which are *The untempered wind* (New York, 1894; Toronto, 1898), in which an unmarried woman, betrayed in love, raises her child in a moralistic and censorious small Ontario town with the fictional name of Jamestown; *Judith Moore; or, Fashioning a pipe* (Toronto, 1898), in which a singer leaves the pressures and exploitation of the European and American musical worlds for a simple, pastoral life in rural Ontario; and *A daughter of witches* (Toronto, 1900), in which an idealistic Boston Transcendentalist is almost ruined by the venom of his wife's thwarted love. Wood's other novels include *Farden Ha'* (London, 1901) and *A martyr to love* (New York, 1903). H.J. Morgan in *Canadian men and women* (1912) lists three other titles: *The lynchpin sensation*, *Unto the third generation*, and *Where waters beckon*. Wood also wrote short fiction for the New York weeklies, often using the pen-name 'Jean d'Arc', and competed successfully in American short-story contests, in which she made several thousand dollars.

For the most part Wood is a sentimental novelist whose central theme is love. Her characters are often two-dimensional, her plots melodramatic, her language ornate and artificial. However, her work is transitional, at its best containing passages of penetrating social analysis and statement, with a clear indebtedness to the school of realism, particularly to Thomas Hardy, which was noted by contemporary critics. She shows remarkable insight into the Canadian small town, whose cultural character, folkways, and speech she depicts with a skill that goes well beyond much of the local-colour fiction of her day. Her most successful novel in this respect is *The untempered wind*, in which the strict moral codes, hypocrisy, and parochialism of the small town are clearly delineated. The first novelist to express what E.K. BROWN would later define as the central impediments to creativity in Canada—puritanism, colonialism, and the frontier spirit—Wood stands at the beginning of a tradition of fiction that examines the Canadian small town critically. In *Judith Moore* and *A daughter of witches* a more humorous tone emerges as she captures the colour and vitality of rural life through the speech of her minor characters. Wood is also significant as a member of the important post-Confederation group of writers who sought a native literature in local settings and characters. While not blind to the limitations of the small town, she does subscribe to a myth of Canada, shared by many of her generation, as an unspoiled place of innocence and potential, a refuge from the corruption and pressures of Europe and the United States. This myth is expressed in powerful, mystical terms in the image of the North in *Judith Moore*.

Wood enjoyed a favourable reputation in literary circles in the late 1890s, largely based on *The untempered wind*. *Current literature* (vol. XVI, 1894, p. 378) called this novel 'the strongest and best American novel of the year.' Canadian critics were slower to respond, but *The Canadian Magazine* (vol. X, 1898, p. 460) assessed Wood as one of the three leading Canadian novelists of the day, in the ranks of Gilbert PARKER and Charles G.D. ROBERTS. Her novels were reviewed in Britain in such journals as *The Bookman*, *The Outlook*, *The Spectator*, *The Westminster Gazette*, and *The Athenaeum*, where she was discussed as a writer who had an individual style, the particular strengths of which were a quiet humour and strong character portraits.

CARRIE MacMILLAN

Wood, Ted (b. 1931). Born Edward John Wood in Shoreham, Sussex, England, he lived in London until the outbreak of the Second World War. Enforced relocation to rural Worcestershire, which left him with a lifelong love of the countryside, was followed by service in RAF Coastal Command. In 1954 he immigrated to Canada, where he was a policeman in Toronto for three years. In 1957 he joined MacLaren Advertising as a copywriter, eventually becoming a creative director. He now lives in Whitby, Ontario.

While employment in law enforcement and advertising provided food and shelter for his growing family, Wood found time to write and sell short stories to Canadian and American magazines and to write television plays; he also collaborated on the musical comedy *Mister Scrooge*, which was produced in Toronto and on CBC television. In 1974 he published a collection of Chekhovian short stories, *Somebody else's summer*.

His *Dead in the water* (1984) won the Scribner's Crime Novel Award, and publication in the USA and Canada. The book featured a small-town policeman, Reid Bennett, and his dog Sam—the entire law enforcement needs of Murphy's Harbour, a fictional resort community in the Kawartha region of Ontario. Bennett's and Sam's popularity was enough to extend the series though *Murder on ice* (1984) to its current tenth title, *A clean kill* (1995), and to have the books also published in England and in many translations. A second series featuring a peripatetic Toronto-based bodyguard, John Locke, has thus far extended to three titles: *Hammerlocke* (1986), *Lockestep* (1987) and *Timelocke* (1991). JOHN NORTH

Woodcock, George (1912-95). Born in Winnipeg, Manitoba, to British parents, he was raised and educated in England. In the late 1930s, while mixing in the London literary world that included Dylan Thomas, Roy Campbell, Herbert Read, and George Orwell, Woodcock emerged as a poet and radical pamphleteer, part of a socially committed literary underground whose pacifism only intensified as a world war approached. During the war he performed non-military duties as a conscientious objector, edited the anarchist publication *War Commentary* (later *Freedom*), and founded the radical literary magazine *Now*, which he edited until 1947. In retrospect the pamphlets he wrote in this period fathered his later more lasting works, such as *Anarchism: a history of libertarian ideas and movements* (1962) and *Gandhi* (1971), though the young Woodcock gave little indication of the important and prolific literary figure he would later become. His early work ran from collections of verse, such as *The white island* (1940) and *The centre cannot hold* (1943), to *The incomparable Aphra: a life of Mrs. Aphra Behn* and *The writer and politics: essays* (both 1948). They all reflect the fluent writing style and the precise mixture of literary and political curiosity that seemed peculiar to him alone. The nature of the recipe is tied to Woodcock's belief in literary anarchism, the anti-doctrine whose most popular historian he became.

Within the general view that society is best served by individuals who are not organized under the yoke of government, Woodcock found room for himself as an independent journalist, historian, and literary commentator equally unconstrained by the academy or by slavish devotion to only one or two disciplines. As an anarchist, his antecedents were the notable libertarian thinkers of the nineteenth century whose biographer he became in such books as *William Godwin: a biographical study* (1946) and *Pierre-Joseph Proudhon: a biography* (1956). In the same vein is *The anarchist prince: a biographical study of Peter Kropotkin* (1950), written in collaboration with Ivan Avakumovic, as was *The Doukhobors* (1968).

Woodcock's literary ancestors, however, would stretch from Defoe and William Cobbett to any of the late-Victorian generalists to whom nothing humanly interesting could be totally foreign.

In 1949 Woodcock returned to Canada, settling in British Columbia, eventually in Vancouver, and carrying on his profession as a writer with even greater vigour. All his Canadian writings, even the most personal, tended to be informed by his interest in the role of the arts in a free society and the way many past eras and more primitive cultures point up weaknesses in our own. While one should be wary of seeing his career as compartmentalized, it is possible to break down his work into several convenient, if maddeningly overlapping, categories.

As a prolific travel writer Woodcock produced personal narratives rather than guidebooks, though such stylized works as *To the city of the dead: an account of travels in Mexico* (1957) and *Incas and other men: travels in the Andes* (1959) are full of observations on the history, geography, economy, and culture of the regions being examined. Other travel books are *Faces of India: a travel narrative* (1964), *Asia, gods and cities: Aden to Tokyo* (1966), *Kerala: a portrait of the Malabar coast* (1967), and *South Sea journey* (1976). It is no coincidence that all the above deal with areas once part of either the Spanish or the British empires, for in Woodcock colonialism is often seen as government writ large, and the lowly native as a metaphor for the individual within the dreaded state. These ideas are still more apparent in related works of history, such as *The Greeks in India* (1966), *The British in the Far East* (1969), *Into Tibet: the early British explorers* (1971), and *Who killed the British Empire?* (1974).

Woodcock's travel books, all of them examples of a type more common in Britain than in North America—informal and objective in approach, wide-ranging in subject-matter—were thus the fountainhead for other of his works, including his many publications on Canada. After *Ravens and prophets: an account of journeys in British Columbia, Alberta and southern Alaska* (1952), in which he saw the region as deliciously untamed yet foreign, Woodcock gradually became a Canadian nationalist whose nationalism was rooted in the cause of regionalism and decentralization. Such is the viewpoint conveyed to foreign audiences in *Canada and the Canadians* (1970; rev. 1973) and *The Canadians* (1979), and expressed more stridently for domestic consumption in *Confederation betrayed!* (1981), whose format harks back to his numerous early pamphlets. The underlying concern with local cultural history surfaced fully in such biographical studies as *Amor De Cosmos, journalist and reformer and Gabriel Dumont: the Métis chief and his lost world* (both 1975). The subtitle of the latter is significant for, as in *Peoples of the coast: the Indians of the Pacific Northwest* (1977), Woodcock often laments or tries to evoke a lost world—one in which anarchism was the natural state of man. Also in this vein are *The walls of India* (1985) and *Caves in the desert: travels in China* (1988).

In his literary criticism, too, one can see Woodcock constantly refining certain tenets that came early to him. In its search for the perfect marriage of imaginative and political activity (somewhat akin to Tolstoy's idealized balance of the intellectual and the physical), *The paradox of Oscar Wilde* (1950) is virtually a blueprint for later bio-critical studies, such as *The crystal spirit: a study of George Orwell* (1966)—for which he won a Governor General's Award; *Dawn and the darkest hour: a study of Aldous Huxley* (1972); and *Herbert Read: the stream and the source* (1972). These books also showed his preference for the radical and his inclination towards sociological over textual criticism (which he nevertheless did not disregard), as did *Odysseus ever returning: essays on Canadian writers and writing* (NCL, 1970), *The world of Canadian writing: critiques and recollections* (1980), and *Northern spring: the flowering of Canadian literature* (1987). All are important collections, showing to best advantage the style and disposition that are also obvious in two monographs, *Hugh MacLennan* (1969) and *Mordecai Richler* (1971), which present Woodcock as a questioner and leveller rather than as an explainer and champion, which he tended to be when discussing younger regionalist authors.

As regards influences, Woodcock was both a transmitter and a receiver—the latter particularly in his verse. In poetry collections from *Imagine the South* (1947) to *Selected poems* (1967), he was essentially a British poet from between the wars in outlook and style. In his newer verse—collected in *Notes on visitations: poems, 1936-1975* (1975) and *The kestrel and other poems* (1978)—Auden had been supplanted as an influence by Margaret ATWOOD, and the writer had been virtually redefined and rejuvenated. His most finely crafted collection of poetry was likewise his last: *The cherry tree on Cherry Street* (1994).

Among Woodcock's many other books—each expressing strains in his previous writings—are *Civil disobedience* (1966), *Henry Walter Bates: naturalist of the Amazon* (1969), *Thomas*

Merton, monk and poet: a critical study (1978), and *Two plays* (1978). He also edited several anthologies drawn from CANADIAN LITERATURE, which he founded in Vancouver in 1959 and edited until 1977. *The rejection of politics and other essays on Canada, Canadians, anarchism and the world* (1972) suggests the enormous volume of his journalism, while *A George Woodcock reader* (1980), edited by Douglas FETHERLING, gives a broader hint of its scope. *Taking it to the letter* (1982) is a selection of his correspondence with other Canadian writers. *Letter to the past* (1983) is the first volume of his autobiography, covering the years before his return to Canada. He completed the story of his life in *Beyond the blue mountains* (1987) and *Walking through the valley* (1994).

In his last few years, Woodcock turned to history with renewed vigour, and with as much concern for historiographical ideas as for mere historical information. Three such works were *A social history of Canada* (1988); the unjustly overlooked distillation of his ideas, *The marvellous century: archaic man and the awakening of reason* (1988); and *The century that made us: Canada 1814-1914* (1989).

Woodcock was a vital force in Canadian writing, and a constant link between the Canadian tradition and those of other English-language cultures.

See Peter Hughes, *George Woodcock* (NCL, 1974), and Dennis Duffy, 'George Woodcock: voyager of liberty', *Canadian Literature* 83 (Winter 1979).

See also CRITICISM IN ENGLISH: 5(f).

DOUGLAS FETHERLING

Wright, Eric (b. 1929). Born in South London, England, he immigrated to Canada at the age of twenty-one, completed his B.A.(1957) at the University of Manitoba and an M.A.(1963) at the University of Toronto, then taught English at Ryerson Polytechnical Institute, Toronto (1958-89). He is best known for his series of ten police procedurals featuring Metropolitan Toronto Police Inspector Charlie Salter, including *The night the gods smiled* (1983), which won an Arthur Ellis Award, a City of Toronto Book Award, and Britain's John Creasy Memorial Award for a best first crime novel, followed by *Smoke detector* (1984), *Death in the old country* (1985), which also won an Arthur Ellis Award, *A single death* (1986), *A body surrounded by water* (1987), *A question of murder* (1988), *A sensitive case* (1990), *Final cut* (1991), *A fine Italian hand* (1992), and *Death by degrees* (1993).

While officially assigned to Special Duties rather than Homicide, Salter tends to stumble across or inherit stubborn investigations, and the chief interest in the series lies less in the solving of recalcitrant murders (which tend to be ordinary and fairly easily unravelled in any case) than in the character, peregrinations, and observations of Salter himself, a husband and father whose life revolves around his twenty-year marriage, a comfortable if occasionally patchy union between the Cabbagetown-born Salter and his middle-class wife whose family is prominent in Prince Edward Island. Indeed it is the life of the city of Toronto itself, as Salter observes its landmarks and moves through its neighbourhoods, that most distinguishes the series, along with Salter's wry comments about class and power in a society that imagines itself to be classless. The novels are noteworthy too for Wright's lucid and agreeably laconic style.

Wright has also written two non-Salter books, *Moodie's tale* (1994), a satirical account of post-secondary education in Ontario in general and academic posturing in particular, as told through the precocious rise of British immigrant William Moodie through the ranks at the 'W.C. Van Horne Institute' in Toronto—an ascent that is followed by an equally precipitous descent into a second career as a backwoods fishing guide, a job that proves the need for remarkably similar survival skills. *Buried in stone* (1996) features Mel Pickett, a retired Toronto detective who first appeared in *A sensitive case* and who finds himself investigating a murder at 'Larch River', a small town on the edge of the Canadian Shield. *Death of a Sunday writer* (1996), set in Ottawa and Toronto, introduces Lucy Trimble, a middle-aged bed-and-breakfast owner who takes over her nephew's detective agency, and the search for his murderer.

MARILYN ROSE

Wright, L.R. (b. 1939). Laurali Ruth (Bunny) Wright was born in Saskatoon, Saskatchewan, received an M.A. from Simon Fraser University, Burnaby, British Columbia, and worked for the *Fraser Valley Record*, the Calgary *Albertan*, and the Calgary *Herald* (1968-77), before retiring from newspaper work. Although she has written four mainstream novels—including *Neighbours* (1979), which won the Search-for-a-New-Alberta-Novelist Award, *The favorite* (1982), *Among friends* (1984), and *Love in the temperate zone* (1988)—Wright is best known for her eight-novel crime-fiction series featuring Staff Sergeant Karl Alberg of the Sechelt detachment of the Royal Canadian Mounted Police. Located on the 'Sunshine Coast', a peninsula just north of Vancouver, British Columbia, accessible only by ferry, the Alberg series includes *The suspect* (1985), which was the first Canadian novel to win an Edgar Award from the Mystery Writers of America in the best-novel category; *Sleep while I sing* (1986); *A chill rain in January* (1990), which won an Arthur Ellis Award; *Fall from grace* (1991); *Prized possessions* (1993); *A touch of panic* (1994); *Mother love* (1995), which also won an Arthur Ellis Award; and *Strangers among us* (1996). Wright's interest in this series is less in the actual detection of crime or criminals (indeed, the criminal is often known or easily suspected from the outset) than in the question of criminal or psychological motivation. Often compared to Ruth Rendell, P.D. James, and Patricia Highsmith, Wright is superb in the creation of atmosphere and suspense as crimes appear to unfold with a certain chilling inevitability within the boundaries of an otherwise normal, indeed pristine and picturesque, island community. The series is animated by the continually developing relationship between the divorced Alberg, who is forty-four at the start of the series, and Cassandra Mitchell, the town's librarian, who is several years younger; in *Strangers among us* they are in their fifties, poised to marry.

Among the best of Canadian crime fiction, Wright's novels attest to the unexpected (often bizarre) levels of emotional complexity that may characterize even apparently ordinary human lives. Her interleaved narratives—in which several parallel stories typically impact smoothly upon one another within the framework of the novel—testify to the ways (in Wright's view) in which individuals, however independent they may imagine themselves to be, ultimately share the fate of the community at large. MARILYN ROSE

Wright, Richard (b. 1937). Born in Midland, Ontario, Richard Bruce Wright attended Ryerson Polytechnical Institute, Toronto, and then worked briefy in journalism before embarking on a decade of work for two Toronto publishers, Macmillan and Oxford University Press. He left publishing in 1970 and for many years has taught English at Ridley College.

Wright's first work of fiction, *Andrew Tolliver* (1965), was a children's book. His first novel for adults, *The weekend man* (1970), was widely praised, and like his subsequent fiction was published in the United States and England as well as Canada; it has also been translated into French, Italian, Japanese, Spanish, and Swedish. Wes Wakeham is the first example of a type found throughout Wright's fiction: a man of gentle instincts out of sympathy with the common ambitions of his society and embittered by separation from a rich and domineering wife. Having drifted from one inconsequential job to another, Wakeham is an outsider by temperament and conviction; he defines a weekend man as 'a person who has abandoned the present in favour of the past or the future', and has an air of amused detachment in common with the hero of Walker Percy's *The moviegoer*, a novel Wright says has influenced his work. Fred Landon, the protagonist of *In the middle of a life* (1973), approaches life with middle-aged wariness and resignation rather than with youthful cynicism. His efforts to find harmony with his existing family and to establish a new romantic bond are related in a style that reflects the wistful melancholy of his character. This novel won the Faber fiction award in England.

Wright abandoned sober realism for exuberant comedy in *Farthing's fortunes* (1976). Presented as the artless tape-recorded memoirs of an ancient wandering Canadian, the novel incorporates graphic vignettes of the social history of half a century, including Toronto low and high life in the 1890s, the Yukon gold rush, the Battle of the Somme, and the Depression. The book cleverly manipulates storytelling conventions and deliberately evokes well-worn stereotypes—the good-hearted whore, the loud-mouthed American entrepreneur, the love-starved poet—in imitation of the picaresque novel. In *Final things* (1980) Wright returned to the novel of character with a memorable portrait of a burnt-out sportswriter who is consumed by thoughts of revenge when his teenage son is brutally murdered. As a study of a decent middle-aged man tortured by feelings of failure, the novel has much in common with *In the middle of a life*; but it attains a shattering emotional intensity beyond the range of the earlier book as the protagonist closes in on his son's killer. An astute observer of social realities, Wright explores in *The teacher's daughter* (1982) the relationship of a lonely teacher and a young ex-convict.

Tourists (1984) has as its middle-aged protagonist a private-school teacher who, with his perpetually unfaithful wife, becomes immersed in a series of increasingly violent encounters with an American couple while on holiday in Mexico. The novel is a dark comedy that draws on the irritations founded on trans-border 'cultural stereotypes': the narrator thinks of the appropriately named Ted

Hacker as 'just another vulgar, loud-mouthed know-it-all American', while Hacker regards him, with some justice, as 'a stuffy, uptight little Canadian shit'.

In Richard Wright's portrait gallery of lonely, wistful people, no character is more appealing than Kay Ormsby, the idealistic, literary former teacher who is a central figure in *Sunset Manor* (1990). As the title suggests, a retirement home (or 'facility' as its formidable administrator calls it) is at the heart of the novel, and old age, seen in an unsentimental, often unsparingly comic way, is its underlying subject. All the characters are, as Wright says of an imaginary novelist in another book, 'psychologically cornered by the prospect of finitude'. Only Miss Ormsby, though urged by her cheerful young doctor to 'forget all this nonsense about death', realizes that 'only by thinking of death can one come to value and enjoy life.'

The age of longing (1995) was very favourably reviewed and nominated for both a Governor General's Award and the Giller Prize. It returns to Wright's familiar territory of middle-age, and to some of the settings of Wright's own life in a Georgian Bay town (pictured in the mid-1930s, shortly before Wright was born) and the publishing business. At the same time, the novel has a more unvaried gravity than most of its predecessors, a tone that is imparted to the novel by its intelligent but melancholy narrator, an editor who returns to his home-town to cope with his mother's death and his own heart attack. The class divisions of Huron Falls, mirrored in Howard Wheeler's own puritanical mother and fun-loving father, are searchingly explored. Two characters who never meet embody much of the book's pathos in their doomed attempts to convert talent and early promise into lasting success: Buddy Wheeler seeks the prize most valued by Huron Falls—success in the National Hockey League—but returns home defeated 'like thousands of young men in small towns everywhere'; Charles Pettinger is an embittered, isolated novelist who, after a fictional debut much like Wright's own, and many years of silence, produces a failed magnum opus.

Particularly in his latest novels, Wright shows his characters stumbling as they seek through various expedients to 'forget for a while the muddle and death that await us all'. There is much art as well as sad truth in his images of Ontario life.

See also NOVELS IN ENGLISH 1960 TO 1982: OTHER TALENTS, OTHER WORKS: 6(a).

THOMAS E. TAUSKY

Wright, Ronald (b. 1948). Born in England, he studied at Cambridge University, where he received a B.A. and M.A. in archaeology. He immigrated to Canada in 1970 and began doctoral studies at the University of Calgary, dropped out after two years, supported himself as a truck driver, failed at farming, and began a series of long trips to South America. His first book, *Cut stones and crossroads: a journey in the two worlds of Peru* (1984), deftly evokes the complex world of contemporary Andean Peru, leading the reader on a bracing overland journey to the major sites of the Incas, and offering an acutely perceptive cultural commentary on the world of their descendants. Wright acquired a working knowledge of the Quechua language and produced two records of traditional Inca music, *The Inca harp* and *Music of the Incas: Aylla Sulca*.

On Fiji Islands (1986), the least erudite of Wright's non-fiction books, is an exploration of Fijian society leavened by the low comedy of serendipitous, on-the-road encounters. *Time among the Maya: travels in Belize, Guatemala, and Mexico* (1989) offers a *tour d'horizon* of early and contemporary Mayan culture. Like Wright's book on Peru, this one takes the form of a literary travel narrative yet delves deeply into ethnology and pre-Columbian history. These intellectual concerns are again pursued in *Stolen continents: the New World through Indian eyes since 1492* (1992), published to coincide with the quincentenary of Columbus's first voyage to America. A chronicle of the post-Columbian period from the point of view of five native-American peoples (the Aztecs, Mayas, Incas, Cherokees, and Iroquois), *Stolen continents* gives a dramatic account of the European invasions experienced by these five nations, their centuries-long resistance to annihilation, and their reaffirmation of themselves in recent decades. *Home and away* (1993) is a collection of Wright's journalism.

Wright is a talented literary craftsman; his travel writing is distinguished by its wit, learning, and supple prose. Unlike many literary sojourners from the industrialized world, he exhibits a deep sympathy for less materially advanced cultures and accepts them on their own terms. His mocking eye is reserved for hypocrisy and self-delusion wherever he finds them.

Wright's first novel, *A scientific romance* (1997), is a brilliant dystopian satire. Set in Britain five centuries in the future when industrial civilization is but a faint archaeological memory, the book hands down a wry judgement on contemporary avarice and on late industrial society's ravaging of the natural world. GEORGE GALT

Writers' Development Trust, The. Founded in 1976 by Margaret ATWOOD, Graeme GIBSON, Margaret LAURENCE, and Pierre BERTON, it is a registered charitable organization, incorporated under federal charter, whose primary goal is the advancement of Canadian literature and the support, including financial support, of Canadian writers. Its specific objectives are to increase recognition of the contribution writers make to the cultural richness of Canada; use the knowledge and insights of established writers to inspire gifted young students; recognize and reward excellence in the craft of writing and the creation of literature; provide financial aid to Canadian writers; engage in educational programs for Canadian schools; and accept and administer funds obtained through wills, bequests, endowments, and donations. The Trust is perhaps best known for its annual Great Literary Dinner Party, which began in 1986 and by 1987 had raised more than one million dollars towards its goal of a permanent endowment fund of two million dollars. The Dinner Party is actually a series of dinner parties held in private homes across Canada, each one featuring a celebrated Canadian writer.

The Writers' Development Trust also provides generous financial support annually to the Canadian Writers' Foundation, which assists indigent writers of recognized merit; and administers the Woodcock Foundation, endowed initially by George and Inge WOODCOCK in 1989, in its aim to raise a two-hundred-thousand-dollar endowment. The Trust has established a permanent fund of $125,000 to maintain the Marian ENGEL Award, valued at $10,000, given annually for oustanding prose writing by a Canadian woman in mid-career. It also administers the Bronwen WALLACE Memorial Award of one thousand dollars annually to help young poets or short-fiction writers at the beginning of their career; the Gordon Montador Award—named after the late publisher of Summerhill Press—given annually since 1993 to the best Canadian non-fiction book on social issues (past winners were Ronald WRIGHT, 1993; Michael IGNATIEFF, 1994; Neil BISSOONDATH, 1995; and John Ralston SAUL, 1996); and the annual Thomas RADDALL Atlantic Fiction Award of $14,000 (past winners were Wayne Johnston, 1991; Herb Curtis, 1992; John STEFFLER, 1993; David Adams RICHARDS, 1994; Bernice MORGAN, 1995; and M.T. Dohaney, 1996). The Trust also sponsors the annual Margaret Laurence Memorial Lecture (by a distinguished Canadian writer on the subject of writing) and the Merle Shain Memorial Lecture, on the subject of human relationships.

The Trust's most recent project has been its promotion of Canada Book Day, which it began in 1996 with a slogan—'Give someone a book, See what happens'—that epitomizes the triple objective of promoting reading, literacy, and Canadian literature. It is held on 23 April to coincide with International Book Day. EUGENE BENSON

Writers' Union of Canada, The. Following initial planning in 1972 when Margaret LAURENCE was the interim Chair of a group of writers interested in forming a professional association, the Union held its first meeting in Ottawa on 3 November 1973, when its Constitution was formally accepted. A preamble to the Constitution sets forth the Union's objectives: 'to unite writers for the advancement of their common interests; to foster writing in Canada; to maintain relations with publishers; to exchange information among members; to safeguard the freedom to write and publish; and to advance good relations with other writers and their organizations in Canada and all parts of the world'. In its first five years the Union was chaired by Marian ENGEL (1973-4), Graeme GIBSON (1974-5), David Lewis STEIN (1975-6), Andreas SCHROEDER (1976-7), and Timothy FINDLEY (1977-8). Many of Canada's most distinguished writers have led the Union in the following years. Executive directors have included Alma Lee, Mary Jacquest, and Penny Dickens. There were 43 members in the first year; in 1997-8 there were more than 1000. Membership is open to fiction and non-fiction writers and poets (Canadian citizens or landed immigrants) who have published one trade book in the previous seven years. The secretariat is located in Toronto.

Major achievements by The Writers' Union include the adoption, in 1976, of a model trade-book contract; the implementation, in 1978, of legislation (Schedule 'C') that prohibits Canadian bookstores from importing remaindered foreign editions of Canadian books; the institution by the CANADA COUNCIL, in 1984, of a program of grants (valued at $400,000) for non-fiction writers; the implementation, in 1986, of a Public Lending Right, funded by the federal government at three million dollars in the first year, to compensate writers for the use of their books in public and university libraries; and the establishment, in 1991, of a Racial Minorities Committee. 'Agenda Renewal', a document setting out the Union's goals for the next decade, was approved in 1992.

Services offered by the Union include contract advice, help with reading tours, manuscript evaluation for beginning writers, and assistance from its Grievance Committee. A directory of members is published from time to time, the most recent being that of 1993. EUGENE BENSON

Wrong, George. See HISTORICAL WRITING IN ENGLISH: 7.

Wyatt, Rachel (b. 1929). Born in Bradford, Engand, she was educated in Yorkshire and studied nursing in London before immigrating to Canada with her husband and children in 1957. She began writing radio drama in the early 1970s; over seventy-five of her deftly constructed radio plays have been produced by the CBC, thirty by the BBC. She has published stories in a wide range of magazines, from *Punch* to *Chatelaine* to *Quarry*, as well as four novels with House of ANANSI: *The string box* (1970), *The Rosedale hoax* (1977), *Foreign bodies* (1982), and *Time in the air* (1985). Wyatt's longer fiction suggests British comedy-of-manners in the vein of Evelyn Waugh or Nancy Mitford, but the merriment is tempered by the melancholy of the characters, often expatriates who seem dislocated, lost in the surreal cityscapes of North America. Thus *The string box* follows a British journalist, pining for pubs and greensward, through the carnival world of Toronto broadcasting. *Foreign bodies*, perhaps her best novel, revisits the classic Canadian theme of genteel British immigrants making do, as Yorkshire academics on an exchange program, in a Toronto of vile weather, folkways, and high prices, while also finding their lives wrenched askew by an equally displaced Pakistani.

Two stage plays presented at Tarragon Theatre, Toronto, *Geometry* (1983) and *Chairs and tables* (1984), are also nominally comedies, but a painful unease lurks beneath the witty verbal surfaces and marital chess-games of Canada's upper-middle classes. Wyatt's 1995 stage adaptation of Adele WISEMAN's novel *Crackpot* for Theatre Calgary, about an earthy Winnipeg prostitute, may be seen as a distinctively uncharacteristic departure. However, a book-length sequence of short stories, *The day Marlene Dietrich died* (1995), brings us back to more familiar Wyatt territory, as middle-edged retirees are shadowed by memories of the sex goddess of the 1930s and 1940s, as well as by a sense of roads not taken, opportunities missed.

As an instructor in, then director of, the Writing Program at the Banff Centre for the Arts in Alberta since 1986, Wyatt is active in the Canadian literary scene. She has taught writing courses in Toronto and Victoria, and for eight years managed a series of radio drama workshops at Arctic College, Iqaluit, Baffin Island. As well travelled as her characters, she has lived in many places in Ontario, and in the early 1990s moved with her family to Victoria, British Columbia. Her substantial body of work reflects this geographical catholicity, and all of her writing displays an assured technique, well-tuned irony, solid craftsmanship, and a keen sense of the dislocation that can undermine characters who may seem, at first, very much at home.

JAMES POLK

Wynand, Derk (b. 1944). Born in Bad Suderode, Germany, he came to Canada in 1952 and was educated at the University of British Columbia (B.A., 1966; M.A., 1969). In 1969 he joined the Creative Writing Department of the University ofVictoria, where he is now full professor and chair. He has had a long association with *The MALAHAT REVIEW*, as assistant editor (1973-5) and editor since 1992.

Wynand's poetry and fiction are strongly influenced by the surrealists, fabulists, and absurdists, including the Austrian H.C. Artmann (whom Wynand has translated), Karl Krolow, Franz Kafka, and Friederike Mayröcker. Because Wynand's writings originate from such esoteric sources, his work has not received much critical attention in Canada. However, his sparse and laconic poems, stories, and translations have appeared in over 300 periodicals in the USA, Canada, and Europe and have been widely broadcast on various CBC radio programs. His chapbooks *Locus* (1971) and *Pointwise* (1979) are filled with metaphors about the double standards of contemporary living. His style is precise, but his disturbing imagery often relies on symbolist or fabulist devices to create jarring images of alientation. *Locus* is vaguely surreal and *Pointwise* is at once bleak and wittily ironic about nebulous human relationships. In *Snowscapes* (1974) Wynand counterpoints prose-poems and poetic styles about snow, in which he finds searching metaphors for the dilemma of modern humanity. Human experience becomes a white void. Love, children, poetry, and the barest acts of survival are only muffled communications that leave no trace.

One cook, once dreaming (1980) is an admirable series of vignettes in stripped-down prose about an anonymous cook and his wife some place in Central Europe. Dreams, scenes, fantasies, and role reversals accumulate to form a single powerful metaphor about the search for a meaningful relationship. *Airborne* (1994) is a chapbook written as a 3000-word sentence about loneliness using the metaphor of a solo pilot; *Door slowly closing* (1995) is another chapbook. Other poetry titles include *Second person* (1983), *Heat waves* (1988), and *Closer to home* (1997).

Wynand has also translated three volumes of H.C. Artmann's work—*Under the cover of a hat/Green-sealed message* (1985), *Sweat and industry* (1992), and *The quest for Dr. U* (1993)—and Erich Wolfgang Skwara's *Black sails* (1996). GEOFF HANCOCK

Wynne-Jones, Tim (b. 1948). He was born in Bromborough, Cheshire, England, and brought to Canada at the age of three. He graduated from the University of Waterloo (B.A.) and York University (M.F.A.), Toronto. His fiction, whether for adults or for children, engages and entertains, provides exotic atmosphere or exotic characterization, and combines both gothic and comic elements. *Odd's end* (1980), a thriller about a psychotic intruder, was followed by *The knot* (1982), a murder mystery set in Toronto. His best-known adult work is *Fastyngange* (1988), a novel imaginatively narrated by an oubliette (a small dungeon), which follows the novel's heroine from Somerset, England, to Toronto. Among Wynne-Jones's popular children's books, all written with great verve, are the picture-book trilogy—*Zoom at sea* (1983), *Zoom away* (1985), *Zoom upstream* (1992), illustrated by Eric Beddows; two collections of stories, *Some of the kinder planets* (1993), winner of a Governor General's Award, and *The book of changes* (1994); and a novel, *Maestro* (1995), which also won a Governor General's Award. He has written a version for children of Victor Hugo's *The hunchback of Notre Dame* (1996). A British-French film adaptation of *Odd's end*, set in Brittany, was released in 1995.

JOHN ROBERT COLOMBO

Yates, J. Michael (b. 1938). Born in Fulton, Missouri, he was educated at the University of Kansas City (B.A., 1960, M.A., 1961), then studied comparative literature at the University of Michigan. He taught comparative literature at Ohio University and the University of Alaska from 1963 to 1966. In 1967 he moved to Vancouver, where he served until 1971 as an influential and highly regarded professor of creative writing and as writer-in-residence at the University of British Columbia. While at UBC Yates encouraged the beginnings of Andreas SCHROEDER's magazine *Contemporary Literature in Translation* and *CANADIAN FICTION MAGAZINE*. He also founded the SONO NIS PRESS. Yates's poems and stories have been anthologized widely, and have appeared in dozens of little magazines in Canada and abroad.

Yates was a key figure in the early 1970s in the development of a distinctive style of fiction and poetry that he called 'West Coast surrealism'. Widely read in European and Latin American literatures, he writes in a 'non-realist' or abstract style; his subject is consciousness itself, not the description of the external details of everyday life. Much of his work centres on 'the polarities between absolute wilderness and absolute technology'. Dismantling accepted views of reality and discourse, his poetry is innovative, moody, intellectual, metaphysical, and occasionally puzzling. Critics have called him self-indulgent, referring not only to his work but to his lavish self-published collections, which often reprint existing volumes. His early collections—*Spiral of mirrors* (1967), *Hunt in an unmapped interior* (1967), and selections from *The Great Bear Lake meditations* (1970)—were reprinted in *Nothing speaks for the blue moraines* (1973).

Canticle for electronic music (1967), which made Yates's reputation as a poet, is an intriguing, enigmatic volume in which the mind is seen as a vast library consumed by the fire of consciousness, which cannot be located; our knowledge is left behind as scorched paper. The poems are twenty-four canticles, each with eight stanzas, three lines long.

The Great Bear Lake meditations—in which a kind of nightmarish surrealism is grafted onto the experience of the North, with death seen as the ultimate desire—is a remarkable sequence of prose-poems. Yates meditates on madness, travelling north to escape from civilization, fear, isolation, and death. 'Great Bear' becomes a place, a legend, the edge of the mind, a totem power rising from darkness, as the poetic voice, on the verge of suicide, searches for the elusive nothing of the Self.

Parallax (1971) is a collection of prose-poems that form a sequence about the bleakness of existence both within and without. *The abstract beast* (1971), Yates's most successful and accessible book, includes several stories and eight one-act stage and radio plays, including 'The broadcaster' and 'Night freight'. *Quarks* (1975) includes three one-act plays: *The net*, *Search for the tse tse fly*, and *The calling*.

Breath of the snow leopard (1974), new and selected poems, is a difficult but compelling collection in which Yates further explores the illusory quality of human existence. He also explores the 'fiction' of personality that the mind creates to make life comprehensible, and suggests that language may be inadequate to express poetic experience. *The Qualicum physics* (1975) is a long, difficult poem based on two-line aphorisms. Yates's next highly cerebral collection, *Esox nobilior non esox lucius* (1978), contains a metaphysical vision that is obscured by abstract and opaque metaphors, word-plays, word coinages, and surreal imagery using birds, the sea, fish, and fishing. *Fugue Brancusi* (1983) is a challenging philosophical exploration using fugal arrangements of statement, variation, and coda, with repetitions of certain words and phrases, and suggestions that a poem can be as pure as music, or as abstract as sculpture.

At his best with prose-poems and aphorisms on the notion of being, Yates wrote one of his most profound poems as a result of a trip to the Queen Charlotte Islands, on B.C.'s northwest coast. Sensitive to the conflicting concerns of loggers, the environmentalists, and the plight of the Haida, Yates meditates in free verse on life and death, consciousness, and eternity in *INSEL: the Queen Charlotte Islands meditations* (1983), which explores the idea of an island of the self surrounded by a sea so dark it cannot properly be expressed even by poetry.

A selection from seven volumes of Yates's poetry up to 1986 appears in two volumes: *The completely collapsible portable man: selected shorter lyrics* (1984) and *Schedule of silence: the collected longer poems, 1960-1986* (1986).

Fazes in elsewhen: new and selected fiction (1977) includes work previously published in *Man in the glass octopus* (1968). Yates calls his Borges-inspired stories 'fictions' to emphasize their parabolic or allegoric nature. Often plotless, and with characters unnamed, they are set in technological worlds where cameras, radios, telephones, and libraries are seen as threats to individuality.

On the way to work as a Vancouver CBC-radio public-relations employee in 1978, Yates was injured in a car accident that resulted in memory loss. He stopped writing. He took a job as a prison guard and for twelve years worked in three different prisons. His 'unrepentant memoir', *Line screw: my twelve riotous years working behind bars in some of Canada's toughest jails* (1993), is a fast-paced, upbeat debunking of prison myths; he sees guards and convicts as allies, at the mercy of both an obsessive and badly managed bureaucracy.

Charles LILLARD discusses Yates's impact on B.C. writing in Issue 45 of *The MALAHAT REVIEW* (January 1978). See also Ronald B. Hatch, 'Beyond permanence: the poetry of J. Michael Yates and Robin BLASER', *West Coast Review* 20 (1986), and Peter Buitenhuis, 'J. Michael Yates', *Dictionary of literary biography* 60 (1987). GEOFF HANCOCK

Yee, Paul (b. 1956). Born in Spalding, Saskatchewan, orphaned when very young, and raised by an aunt in Vancouver's Chinatown, Paul Yee received a B.A. and M.A. in history at the University of British Columbia and worked as an archivist in Vancouver before turning his hand to writing fiction for young people. *Roses sing on new snow: a delicious tale* (1991), a folktale about an artist, and *Tales from Gold Mountain: stories of the Chinese in the New World* (1989), a collection of original tales, use many of the conventions of European folktales but adapt them to the pioneer Chinese-Canadian setting and to the demands of Yee's persistent themes: the inability of an Old World culture to survive on New World soil; the wrongheadedness of attempts at such transplantation; and the power of food and art to assuage the sense of cultural and geographical displacement immigrants feel. *The curses of third uncle* (1986) and *Breakaway* (1994) are both historical novels. Distilled into clean, concrete prose and naturally paced dialogue are the dramas of young adults struggling with identity and assimilation—struggles that are partly worked out through the paradoxical achievement of individualism through community.

Ghost train (1996), winner of a Governor General's Award, is set, like Yee's other fiction, in pioneer British Columbia and records the historical segregation, dislocation, and loneliness of Chinese immigrants in Canada. The protagonist is a painter whose art performs the dual function Yee, as historian and storyteller, envisions for his own art: it provides a conduit into the past from which it records the sufferings and triumphs of a pioneer Chinese-Canadian community; and it thereby works as an instrument of spiritual consolation and liberation.

Yee has also written *Saltwater city: an illustrated history of the Chinese in Vancouver* (1988) and *Struggle and hope: Chinese in Canada* (1995).

MARIE C. DAVIS

Yiddish literature. Yiddish literature in Canada began in the first decades of the twentieth century, when East European Jews, seeking refuge from the poverty and persecution of their native countries, began arriving in large numbers. They settled mainly in Montreal, Toronto, and Winnipeg. Unlike earlier Jewish immigrants to Canada, who had come from Britain or the United States, these new arrivals were Yiddish-speaking. Yiddish, a Germanic language with a large admixture of Hebrew, as well as Slavic and Romance elements, was, until the Second World War, the most widely used of Jewish languages. It originated in the tenth century, although modern Yiddish literature is generally dated from the mid-nineteenth century.

That literature slowly took root in Canada, primarily in Montreal. From 1900 to the Second World War, Jews made up Montreal's largest immigrant community and Yiddish was, after French and English, the city's most widely spoken language. This resulted in a culture of remarkable self-sufficiency and vitality, which earned for Montreal a reputation among Jews as 'the Jerusalem of North America'. Yiddish literary activity in the city can be divided into two overlapping periods: the time up to the First World War, and the post-Holocaust years. The first immigrants established schools, newspapers, libraries, literary journals, synagogues, hospitals, and social services, all of which conducted their business in Yiddish. Among the most important of these for the development of Yiddish literature was the Yiddish-language daily *Der keneder Odler* ('The Canadian Eagle') founded in 1907 by H. Wolofsky. This newspaper—which ceased publication in the 1980s—served as a literary forum for Yiddish writers. The renowned Hebrew-Yiddish author Reuben Brainin (1862-1939) was editor of the *Odler* for a number of years, as was the eminent poet Y.Y. SEGAL and the respected essayist Israel Rabinovitch (1894-1964). The newspaper also published the work of such major literary figures as Moishe Shaffir (1909-88), Ida Maze (1893-1962), Yaacov Zipper (1900-83), Sholem Shtern (1906-92), the historian Shimshon Dunsky (1899-1981), and the pedagogue Shloyme Wiseman (1899-85).

The Yiddish writers of Montreal took an active part in community life and were often respected public figures. Their literary activity was supported and encouraged by such institutions as the Jewish Public Library, which ran lecture series, often featuring invited literary luminaries from the USA and Europe, as well as local writers. The result was that Montreal became a favourite stop for some of the greatest names in modern Yiddish literature—Itsik Manger and I.B. Singer among them. Enhancing the literary life of Yiddish Montreal, and augmenting its international reputation, were the literary salons, where writers congregated regularly. The most important of these took place in the homes of Ida Maze, Arthur and Manya Lermer, and Yehuda and Sheindel Elberg.

After the Second World War, Canadian Yiddish literature was given another boost by the arrival of survivors of the conflagration in Europe. Among the major writers who settled in Montreal during and immediately following the war were Melekh RAVITCH in 1941, and Rokhl H. KORN in 1948, both established poets with international reputations by the time of their arrival in Canada. The younger poet and novelist Chava ROSENFARB, a Holocaust survivor, arrived in 1950 and did most of her writing in Canada. So too did the novelist Yehuda Elberg (b. 1912), who arrived in 1956.

Stylistically the first period of Yiddish literature in Canada was dominated by the literary movements of Europe and the United States. The poet Y.Y. Segal, for instance, was greatly influenced by the modernist school, and especially by its New York exponents, the poets Mani Leib and Moishe Leib Halperin. In general, Yiddish writers in Canada tended to look outside the country for their inspiration, settings, and subjects. This was especially true of the post-Holocaust generation of writers, for whom the Holocaust and Israel were major topics. Nevertheless, there were exceptions to this international focus: Montrealer Sholem Shtern wrote a two-volume epic called *In Kanada* (1960, 1963), and Y.Y. Segal devoted a large number of his poems to descriptions of Montreal. Ravitch and Korn extolled the beauty of the Canadian countryside.

The post-Second World War period also saw the arrival in Montreal of Dora Wasserman (b. 1919), founder of the Yiddish Theatre (1956), one of the city's most successful and enduring cultural institutions, which is still performing plays in Yiddish under the directorship of Wasserman's daughter Bryna.

Montreal was also home to a number of world-renowned scholars, including the Talmudist Simkhe-Bunim Pietruszhka (1893-1950). The Roskies family produced two internationally respected scholars of Yiddish literature, Ruth R. Wisse (b. 1936) and David Roskies (b. 1948). Wisse was instrumental in establishing the Jewish Studies department at McGill University, one of the largest independent Jewish Studies departments in North America.

The decline of Yiddish as a spoken language has meant that much of the work that goes on in the 1990s consists of an attempt to reclaim the literature through translation into English and French. One project of this kind is under way in Toronto, where the co-operative effort of a group of women translators resulted in *Found treasures* (1994), an anthology of translated stories by Yiddish women writers. While Toronto never developed into as strong a centre of Yiddish culture as Montreal, it did attract the writers Isaac Goldkorn (1911-82), Peretz Miransky (1908-93), Simcha Simchovitch (b. 1921), and the scholar Nachman Shemen (1912-93). Gershon Pomerantz (1900-68), the editor of the literary journal *Di Feder*, which had an international circulation, also made his home in Toronto.

Separatist agitation and the resulting political turmoil in Quebec, starting in the mid-1970s, caused the migration of many Montreal Jews, mostly to Toronto, where they have swelled the ranks of the already existing Yiddish-speaking community. Thus, in the 1990s the centre of Yiddish cultural activity has shifted from Montreal to Toronto, where Yiddish has also gone into the universities, being taught at the University of Toronto and in private Jewish day schools.

Winnipeg supported a flourishing Yiddish community for much of this century and was the site of the first secular Yiddish day schools to be established in North America. It attracted the great Yiddish writer and educator Avrom Golomb (1888-1982) to teach in its schools. Other local Yiddish writers were Falik Zolf (1896-1961) and Samson Heilik (b. 1917).

See P. Anctil and G. Caldwell, eds, *Juifs et réalités juives au Québec* (1984), published by the Institut québécois de recherche sur la culture; H.L. Fuchs, *Hundert Yor yidishe un hebraishe Literature in Kanada* ('A hundred years of Yiddish and Hebrew literature in Canada', 1980); I. Robinson, P. Anctil, M. Butovsky, eds, *An everyday miracle: Yiddish culture in Montreal* (1990); and S. Rojansky, ed, *Kanadish* (Buenos Aires, 1974).

GOLDIE MORGENTALER

Young, David. See NOVELS IN ENGLISH 1983 TO 1996: OTHER NOVELS 1(a).

Young, Egerton Ryerson (1840-1909). Born at Crosby, Upper Canada (Ontario), he was educated at the Normal School, Toronto, and was ordained a Methodist minister in 1867 following several years of schoolteaching. After successful months in a Hamilton pastorate, he accepted a call to the mission at Norway House on Lake Winnipeg in the spring of 1868. There, and at Berens House, he gathered the experiences of travel and mission work among northern Natives that formed the basis for his later career. Having discovered and developed his gifts as a publicist during a mission fundraising tour in 1873-4, he was in great demand as a speaker upon his return to Ontario pastorates in 1876 and after. In 1888 he exchanged the pulpit for the lecture platform, spending several years in the USA and England, where he gave highly acclaimed talks, complete with illuminated hand-tinted lantern slides, on Native lore and the adventurous life of Methodist missionaries in the wilds of northern Canada. When these materials began to appear in book form in England, the USA, and Canada, the popular lecturer was guaranteed a large and loyal readership because he had toured in all three countries.

Young's *By canoe and dog train among the Cree and Salteaux Indians* (London, 1890) is a somewhat rambling narrative of missionary trials and triumphs, enlivened by dramatic and humorous anecdotes and a vigorous prose style. *Stories from Indian wigwams and northern campfires* (London, 1893; facsimile reprint 1970) is an expansion and reworking of these experiences, with entertainment and Christian uplift kept in fairly even balance. A foray into fiction—'a nosegay of facts tied with the ribbon of romance', as the title page has it—is less successful: in *Oowikapun; or, How the Gospel reached the Nelson River Indians* (London, 1894) the sentimental and didactic plot and characters work at cross-purposes to

Young's natural gift for anecdote and campfire tales. *The apostle of the North, Rev. James Evans* (New York, 1899) is a biographical defence of the controversial founder of the Norway House mission and the inventor of a Cree syllabic alphabet. Other books by Young are *On the Indian trail: stories of missionary work among the Cree and Saulteaux Indians* (New York, 1897); *Indian life in the great North-west* (1900); *Algonquin Indian tales* (1903); and several books of adventure for juveniles: *Three boys in the Wild North Land, summer* (London, 1896); *Winter adventures of three boys in the Great Lone Land* (London, 1899); *My dogs of the Northland* (1902); *The children of the forest; a story of Indian lore* (1904); *Hector, my dog: his autobiography* (1905); and *Battle of the bears* (1907). According to H.J. Morgan, Young was at the century's turn 'one of the most successful writers, especially of books for boys, in the Dominion'.

Ryerson had a son and namesake, E. Ryerson Young (1869-1962), who also wrote books for young people, including *Duck Lake* (1905), *Just dogs* (1926), and *Three arrows: the young buffalo hunter* (1932). SUSAN JACKEL

Young, Ian. See GAY LITERATURE.

Yvon, Josée (1950-94). She was born in Montreal in the working-class district of rue Ontario, where she was still living at the time of her death. After taking the *cours classique* at Collège Ste-Marie, she studied literature and then theatre at Université du Québec à Montréal. In 1971 she obtained a B.A., specializing in theatre studies, and began a master's degree on Brecht at the Dusseldorf Schauspielhaus, Germany, that she did not complete. She worked as a stage manager, touring with the Théâtre Sans Fil and the Grand Cirque Ordinaire, as a scriptwriter at Radio-Québec, and as a barmaid, teacher at the Rosemont CEGEP, and lecturer at the Bois-de-Boulogne and Édouard-Montpetit CEGEPs. She contributed to many periodicals not only in Montreal but in Paris, elsewhere in Europe, and in the USA. In she 1977 received a CANADA COUNCIL grant for an exchange with feminist-lesbian writers in California.

Yvon's work, like her life, was a true descent into hell. A radical writer of marginality, in poetic stories fraught with violence, madness, and death she brought to life 'girls without names' and the 'living dead': drug addicts, prostitutes, transsexuals, homosexuals, transvestites, women used as guinea-pigs, and women warriors. The titles of her published works, usually compound names, speak for themselves: *Filles-commandos bandées* (1976), *La chienne de l'Hôtel Tropicana* (1977), *Travesties-kamikazes* (1980), *Gogo-boy* (1983), *Danseuses-mamelouks* (1982), *Filles-missiles* (1980), *Maîtresses-cherokees* (1986), *Les laides otages* (1990), and *La cobaye* (1993). She also wrote several works with Denis Vanier, who was her companion for eighteen years and called himself 'her lesbian brother'. These essays are *Koréphilie* (1981), *Phases critiques* (1981), *L'âme défigurée* (1984), and *Travaux pratiques* (1987). Yvon sublimated the reality of her marginality through writing in which prose and poetry combine, and in which murder, torture, rape, and drugs are symbols of social oppression. Stricken with AIDS and nearly blind, she died in June 1994, leaving an unfinished manuscript entitled *Manon la nuit*, whose subject was blindness.

RAYMOND BERTIN

Z

Zaremba, Eva. See LESBIAN LITERATURE and MYSTERY AND CRIME: 1980 TO 1996.

Zeller, Ludwig (b. 1927). Born in Río Loa, Chile, and educated at the University of Chile, he worked in Santiago for the ministry of education (1953-68), exhibiting and publishing collages and surrealist texts. With his wife, the artist Susana Wald, he settled in Toronto in 1971, where he attracted a following as artist and poet and issued texts in English, French, and Spanish under the Oasis imprint. In 1979 the Hamilton Art Gallery held a major retrospective of the couple's work titled 'By Four Hands'.

In the country of the antipodes: poems 1964-1979 (1979), edited and largely translated by A.F. MORITZ and Susana Wald, collects more than sixty poems from ten publications and includes a concise bibliography of Zeller's verbal and visual work. In his introduction Moritz found four characteristics of the poetry: it questions, it presents man as pilgrim, it displays distrust of rationality, and it offers an 'examination of reality'. Intensely surreal, Zeller's work consists of dream imagery replete with audacious references and rhetorical flourishes that are entirely out of keeping with the hitherto realistic mode and anecdotal idiom of English-Canadian poetry.

Since 1994 Wald and Zeller have maintained a second residence in Oaxaca, Mexico, where their art and poetry have found enthusiastic acceptance. Zeller selected the texts included in *The invisible presence: sixteen poets of Spanish America, 1925-1995* (1996), which were translated into English by his daughter, Toronto-based translator Beatriz Zeller. A.F. Moritz and Theresa Mortiz translated the poems in *Body of insomnia* (1996). Zeller's *Los engranajes del encantamiento* ('The Gears of Enchantment') (Mexico City, 1996) offers 400 pages of poetry and collage along with detailed listings of publications and exhibits.

JOHN ROBERT COLOMBO

Zend, Robert (1929-85). Born in Budapest, Hungary, he graduated from Péter Pázmány University in 1953 and worked for the Budapest press as cartoonist and columnist. Following the revolution in 1956, he left Hungary and settled in Toronto. In 1969 he received an M.A. in Italian Studies from the University of Toronto. He held staff and then contract positions with the Canadian Broadcasting Corporation, first as shipper, film librarian, and film editor, then as radio producer, writing and producing over 100 programs for CBC Radio's 'Ideas'.

Zend wrote prose and poetry in both Hungarian and English; after 1964, he favoured English. His earliest substantial collections of poems are *From zero to one* (1973) and *Beyond labels* (1982), both in English versions undertaken with John Robert COLOMBO. Zend's poems display a ready wit and a willingness to take flights of fancy. Imaginative, almost surreal fugues are characteristic of the longer poems in *From zero to one*: an automatic record player begins to play records for its own enjoyment; the ghost of a dead wife continues to haunt the family home; office-workers take refuge in a secret room that seems to exist in another dimension; and a message from outer space proves to be either nonsense or higher sense. The poems in *Beyond labels* are similar, except that here the poet shows more formal ingenuity and invention, especially with his 'Ditto poems' and 'Drop poems', which are reminiscent of concrete poetry. This book also includes the poet's address to Amnesty International, which examines the destructive compulsion some people feel to label other people.

Zend explored the visual elements in poetry in the post-Concrete experiments that make up *Oab* (vol. I, 1983; vol. 2, 1985), a curious yet characteristic composition that is difficult to describe because its effects are predominantly graphic. He explored the verbal elements in public readings, having formed with Robert PRIEST and Robert Sward the poetry-performance group known as The Three Roberts. The texts they performed have appeared in *Premiere performance* (1984), *On love* (1984), and *On childhood* (1985).

Since Zend's death five books have appeared, their publication arranged by the poet's wife, Janine Zend. Three are collections of Hungarian poetry—*Versek, képversek* (1988), *Hazám törve kettővel* (1991), and *Fából vaskarikatúrák* (1993)—and there are two books of prose written in English. *Daymares: selected fictions on dreams and time* (1991), with a foreword by Colombo and an afterword by Northrop FRYE, collects Zend's shorter prose and some free-ranging poems that display a decision to be light-hearted in dealing with the darker aspects of life. *Nicolette* (1993) is a novel, written in short 'takes', ranging over two continents, with vivacity and charm that are more French than Hungarian or English. Frye wrote: 'Zend was a notably free spirit who was among us for a while and, who, now that he has gone, is irreplaceable. All we can do is read and admire what he has left us.'

JOHN ROBERT COLOMBO

Zieroth Dale (David) (b. 1946). Born in Neepawa, Manitoba, a farming community north of Winnipeg, where his German grandfather settled, he attended local schools and moved to Toronto in the mid-sixties, where his strongly felt, plain-spoken poems of prairie life began appearing in such anthologies as ANANSI's *Mindscapes* and *Storm warning*, edited by Al PURDY. Zieroth's first collection with Anansi, *Clearings: poems from a journey* (1973) contains his most widely anthologized work, poems drawing on Prairie memories (e.g., 'Father', 'Hunters of the deer'), set forth in a soberly reflective, unadorned style. A move to Invermere, British Columbia, where he worked as a park ranger, inspired *Mid-river* (1981), which uses Banff-Kootenay landscapes for meditations on the vulnerability and redemptive strengths of the natural world. After another move to

Vancouver came *When the stones fly up* (1985), poems that reach back in time to the poet's Manitoba roots, and back yet further to European ancestors preparing their voyage to the New World. *The weight of my raggedy skin* (1991) wryly focuses on fatherhood, family, and scenes from domestic life as lived in North Vancouver, where much of Zieroth's energies have gone into his teaching at Douglas College and his long-time editorship of *Event*, a West Coast magazine concentrating on new talent in Canadian poetry and prose.

JAMES POLK

The Canadian Oxford Dictionary

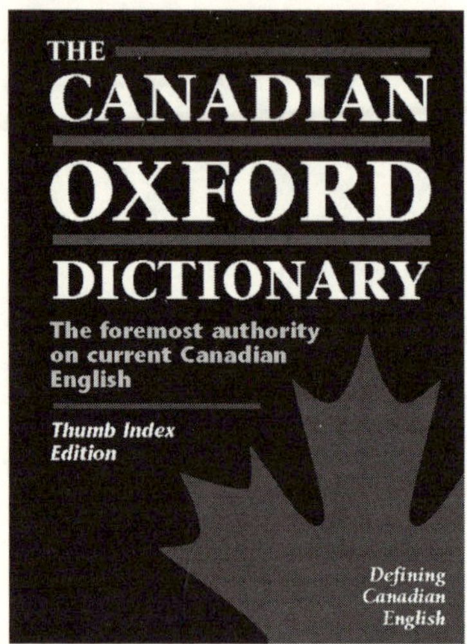

The *Canadian Oxford Dictionary* establishes a new authoritative standard for dictionaries in Canada. This book serves Canadians like no other dictionary, answering their basic questions about the language by giving them advice on Canadian spelling and usage, and defining more Canadian words and senses (almost 2000) than any other dictionary. With about 140,000 words, it combines in one reference book information on English as it is used worldwide and as it is used particularly in Canada. Definitions, worded for ease of comprehension, are presented within entries in order of their familiarity or frequency in Canadian usage, making the dictionary easy to consult.

The dictionary is exceptionally reliable in its description of Canadian English because it is based on thorough research into the language. It represents five years of work by five professionally trained Canadian lexicographers examining almost 20 million words of Canadian text, and another 20 million words of American, British, Australian, and other international English sources. These databases represent over 8000 different Canadian sources. Favoured Canadian pronunciations have been determined by surveying a nationwide group of respondents.

An added feature of this dictionary is its encyclopedic element. It includes short biographies of over 1000 Canadians and 4000 individuals and mythical figures of international significance, and over 5000 place names, more than 1200 of them Canadian.

With the publication of the *Canadian Oxford Dictionary*, Oxford University Press adds another work to its highly respected range of dictionaries.

Publication date: June 1998

ISBN: 0-19-541120-X